LONGMAN
NEW GENERATION
DICTIONARY

LONGMAN
NEW GENERATION
DICTIONARY

Longman

Longman Group Limited
Burnt Mill
Harlow
Essex
England

First published 1981

ISBN 0 582 55626 0

Printed in Great Britain by
Richard Clay Limited (The Chaucer Press)
Bungay, Suffolk

Contents

The Dictionary

Using your Dictionary

This dictionary tells you many things about English words, in a small space. To make full use of it, you should read this section first:

Finding a word

Alphabetical order   The words are arranged in alphabetical order, from A to Z. This means that if you want to look up **tortoise**, you look among the words beginning with **t**. But there are a great many **t** words, so look next at the second letter of **tortoise**, which is **o**. Words beginning **to** come after the **ti** words like **tissue**, and before the **tr** words like **tracksuit**. But there are still quite a lot of **to** words, so look next at the third letter, which is **r**. Words beginning **tor** come after the **top** words like **topknot** and before **tos** words like **toss**. Then look at the fourth letter, and so on.

Guide letters   The "guide letters" at the top of each page will help you to find a word quickly: for the page that has **tortoise** on it, the guide letters are **tou**. This comes after **tortoise**: **tou** after **tor**. But the guide letters for the page before are **too**, which comes before **tortoise**: **too** before **tor**. You will find **tortoise** on the pages that have the words between **too** and **tou**.

Spelling   One important reason for looking up a word in the dictionary is to find out how to spell it. This is a problem, because when one cannot spell a word, how is one to find it in alphabetical order? If you were writing an essay about prehistoric animals, you might want to mention the **pterodactyl**. This word sounds as if it began **ter** like **terrible**, but you will not find it among the **ter** words. To get over this difficulty, we have included a Spelling Table on page 787, at the back of the book. This tells you that one of the possible ways of spelling the **t** sound is **pt**. You will find **pterodactyl** among the **p** words, on the page beginning with the guide letters **psa**.

Sound-alikes   Sometimes two or more words have the same sound but different spellings, like **night** and **knight** or **rain, rein**, and **reign**. Here, again, the spelling table will suggest different possible spellings, so that if you want to write about *the* **reign** *of Henry VIII* you will find the word among the **rei** words, and if you want to write *It began to* **rain** you will find that one among the **rai** words. Notice that you can use the Table to spell the middles and endings of words as well as the beginnings: here it tells you that **ai, ei**, and **eig** are all possible ways to spell the vowel sound that is spelt with **a** in **make**.

The main entry

The words printed in alphabetical order in **black** letters, down the left of each column, are the "main entries" in the dictionary. A main entry is usually a single word, like **house** or **go**; but it may also be

a two or more parts joined with a hyphen: **house-trained; go-kart**
b two or more words printed with spaces between them: **house agent; go on**
c letters that stand for a group of words: **GCE**

All these kinds of main entry are arranged in alphabetical order. That means that you will find **go on** among the **goo** words, after **goof** and **googly**.

Look-alikes   Sometimes two or more words have the same spelling, but are still different words. Perhaps one is a noun and the other a verb:

lead[1] *v* to show somebody the way...
lead[2] *n* a guiding example...

Or perhaps they are pronounced differently, or have different word-histories and quite unrelated meanings:

lead[3] *n* a soft heavy metal that is an element, used...

(Notice that **lead**[1] and **lead**[2] rhyme with "seed", but **lead**[3] rhymes with "bed".)
   These look-alike words are shown separately in the dictionary, with raised numbers after them.
   If two words are different because one of them is always written with a capital letter, they are shown separately:

reformation *n* improvement...
Reformation *n* the religious movement in Europe...

If two words are different because one of them is always used in the plural, they are shown separately:

green[1] *adj* **1** of a colour between yellow and blue...
greens *n* green leafy vegetables...

Part of speech

The dictionary tells you how each main entry is used in a sentence; what its "part of speech" is. Here are the short forms used:

abbrev. for abbreviation for: **GCE**	*pron* pronoun: **it, them**
adj adjective: **tall**	*v* verb: **make, sew**
adv adverb: **partly**	*v adv* verb + adverb: **go on**
conj conjunction: **and, but**	*v adv prep* verb + adverb + preposition:
interj interjection (used as a	**put up with**
sudden remark): **ouch!**	*v adv; prep* verb + adverb *or* verb +
n noun: **dog, wine**	preposition: **lay off**
prep preposition: **in, of**	*v prep* verb + preposition: **fall for**

Combined parts of speech   Sometimes when a word can be used in two ways in a sentence, the two parts of speech are combined:

miaow *n, v* (to make) the crying sound a cat makes

When **miaow** is a noun, it means "the crying sound a cat makes", as in *I heard a loud miaow*. When it is a verb, it means "to make the crying sound a cat makes", as in *The cat began to miaow*.

Word forms

After the part of speech, the dictionary will often tell you how the form of the main entry word can change. It may tell you the plural of a noun:

man *n* **men**
or the past tense, past participle, and present participle of a verb:
sing *v* **sang, sung, singing**
or the comparative and superlative forms of an adjective:
bad[1] *adj* **worse, worst**
These word forms are shown only where they may cause difficulty. The plural of
car *n* is **cars**, but **cars** is not shown in the dictionary because it is formed in the
ordinary way, by adding -s. (See **Word parts**, page 784).
    When only the end part of a word changes, only part of the word is written out:
dirty *adj* **-ier, -iest**
Here, we show **dirtier**, which means "more dirty", and **dirtiest**, which means
"most dirty".
    When a letter is doubled, or a *k* added to a final *c*, it is shown like this:
beg *v* **-gg-**
picnic[2] *v* **-ck-**
The full spelling is **begged, begging; picnicked, picnicking**

Choosing the right sense

Often one main entry word may have two or more different meanings. Each
meaning is clearly numbered, and usually the meaning that is used most often
comes first:

canker[1] *n* **1** a sore caused by a disease which attacks wood and the flesh of
animals and people **2** (a) spreading evil:
Violence is the canker in our society

Some words have many different meanings, so it is important to find the right
one. If you hear the word **canker** in a sentence like "Our cat has a canker in its
ear" you will want to look at sense **1**. If you read it in a piece of writing about
politics, you will look at sense **2**. The example sentences will often help you to
choose the right meaning: "Violence" may be a spreading evil, but it can't be a
"sore".

Punctuation of meanings

To understand the meanings properly, you will need to know the special ways in
which certain punctuation marks are used.
Round brackets (   ) are used ⸱
a to show the kind of subject or object used with a verb, or the kind of noun used
with an adjective:
lay[1] *v* **4** (of birds, insects, etc.) to produce (an egg or eggs)
This means that *birds* and *insects* are the usual subjects of the verb **lay** in this
meaning, and **eggs** are the usual objects, as in *The hen laid an egg.*
gnarled, *adj* **1** (of a tree, its trunk or branches) rough and twisted, with hard
lumps, esp. as a result of age **2** (of hands and fingers) twisted, with swollen joints,
and rough skin. . .
The first meaning usually applies to trees, the second to hands.
b to give various other kinds of information about a word:
offside *adj, adv* **1** (in certain sports). . .
c to show that something can be either included or left out:
magenta *n, adj* (of) a dark purplish red. . .

This means that the word *of* is needed in the explanation of **magenta** when it is used as an adjective: *a magenta dress* (= a dress of a dark purplish red) but not when it is used as a noun: *Magenta is her favourite colour* (= A dark purplish red is her favourite colour.)

The slash / means that either of two choices is possible:

occupy *v* **3**. . . *occupy a bed/a taxi*

The straight line | is used to separate examples of a single meaning:

on [1] *prep* **5a** during; at the time of: *on Tuesday|on June 1st*

Related words

At the end of a word's explanation, you will sometimes find words that can be built up by adding an ending to the main entry word being explained. These built-up words are not explained, because if you understand the main entry word and you understand the ending, you will know what the two of them mean when added together. (For a list of endings, see **Word parts** on page 784).

Punctuation of related words There are three ways of showing these words:

a dark [1] *adj*. . . ~**ness** *n*
This means that -**ness** is added onto **dark** to make a noun **darkness** (see **Word parts**).

b violate *v*. . . -**lation** *n*
Sometimes the main word changes its spelling slightly before the ending is added. Only part of the new word **violation** is written out; just enough to show the spelling clearly.

c curly *adj*. . . **curliness** *n*
Here the main word is a short one with a slight change in spelling before the ending, and so the new word is written out in full.

Special expressions

Sometimes a phrase has a special meaning, which cannot be guessed even if you know the meanings of all the words in it. For example, **split hairs** is nothing to do with the hair on your head; it means "to concern oneself with unimportant differences". Many of these phrases are shown, not as main entries (which would mean looking for this particular phrase under **s**) but at the main entry for the most important or unusual word in the phrase, after the ordinary meanings. You will find **split hairs** in black letters as part of the explanation of **hair**.

Sometimes a word or meaning is most often used in some particular expression. Such expressions are shown like this:

glazing *n* **2** the piece of glass used to fill a window (esp. in the phrase **double glazing**)

Variants

Sometimes there is more than one way to spell a main entry word:

caftan, kaftan *n* a long loose garment. . .

Either spelling is correct, but the commonest one comes first. This is the spelling that you will want to use yourself. For long words, only the part which is spelt differently is shown:

generalize, -ise *v*. . .

Sometimes there is another word with the same meaning as the main entry word:

lapwing also **pewit, peewit**—*n* a type of bird. . .

This means that **lapwing** is the usual word, but **pewit** or **peewit** can be used instead.

A word may have the same meaning as the main entry word, but be used in special circumstances:

collarbone also (*medical*) **clavicle**—*n* either of a pair of bones. . .

Here, **clavicle** is the special word for **collarbone** that doctors use.

For many kinds of animal and person there is a general word that is used for both sexes, and a more particular word that is used for only one sex. In such cases, we show the general word first:

fox *n* 1 (*fem.* **vixen**)—**a** any of several types of small doglike flesh-eating wild animal. . .

duck *n* 1 (*masc.* **drake**)—any of various common swimming birds. . .

Special words

Most of the words in the dictionary would be used and understood, both in speaking and writing, anywhere in the world where English is used. But some words, or meanings of words, are used particularly in one country or area:

checkers *n US* draughts

This tells you that the game we call "draughts" is called **checkers** in America.

Other words are no longer used, but may be found in old books, or in the Bible:

thee *old use* (object form of THOU) you

A word may belong particularly to literature or poetry:

slay *v* **slew, slain, slaying** *literature* to kill. . .

Words used by specialists are marked *law, medicine,* or *technical*:

quark *n technical* the smallest possible piece of the material. . .

Words that belong particularly to serious writing are marked *esp. written*; you would be unlikely to use these words in everyday talk with your friends. On the other hand, words that belong more to friendly conversation are marked *esp. spoken*; you may prefer not to use these when writing a composition. Words marked *sl* (slang) would not often be used at all in writing or for serious purposes, though everyone uses slang words and meanings sometimes in talking:

fatigue [2] *v esp. written* to make tired

telly *n esp. spoken* television

fag [3] *n sl* a cigarette

Unpleasant words connected with the body are marked *vulgar*, and should be avoided when talking to strangers or at a polite party. Words showing that the speaker dislikes the person or thing he is talking about are marked *offensive*. On the other hand, polite words for things felt to be sad, dirty, or unpleasant are marked *polite*. Words used in a joking way are marked *humour*, and those that sound foolishly overimportant are marked *pompous*.

senior citizen *n polite* an old person

Words or phrases marked *not standard* may be in common use, but are considered by many people to be incorrect. They should be avoided in writing:

ain't *not standard* a shortened form of *am not, is not*. . .

Words or phrases that are borrowed from foreign languages and still felt to be foreign are marked *French, German, Latin,* etc.:
ad hoc *adj, Latin* made, arranged, etc. for a particular purpose...
The official names under which products are sold are marked *trademark:*
biro *n trademark* a ballpoint.

Cross-references

There are several ways of drawing your attention to related words in other parts of the dictionary. These related words are usually shown in SMALL CAPITALS:

a A more exact or specialized word is needed in an explanation:
salt [1] *n* **1** a very common colourless or white solid substance (SODIUM CHLORIDE) used to preserve...

b A word is used only in combination with another word:
laureate *adj* see POET LAUREATE
(At **poet laureate** you will find out how **laureate** is used.)

c Two words have an important likeness or difference:
legato *adj, adv* (of music) played with the notes sliding...
—compare STACCATO

d Some additional information can be found by looking up another word:
lama *n* a type of Buddhist priest—see also DALAI LAMA
rain [2] *v*...—see also RAIN OFF

e A word has the same meaning as another main entry of two or more words:
divining rod *n* DOWSING ROD
This tells you that **dowsing rod** is itself a main entry.

f Two words are often confused with each other:
decided *adj*... ⚠ DECISIVE
This sign means "Be careful!"

g Several words are compared in a Usage Note:
adorn *v* **1**...—see DECORATE (USAGE)
(If you turn to **decorate**, you will find a Usage Note explaining the difference between **adorn, decorate, garnish,** etc.)

h The main entry word is illustrated in a picture:
drill [2] *n* **1**...   ☞ OIL
electricity *n* **1**...   ◎
(There is a picture of a **drill** on the **oil** page. There is a picture of electrical processes and equipment on the same page as the word **electricity**.)

i There is another word with the opposite meaning:
offside *adj, adv* **2** being on the right-hand side, esp. of an animal or of a car, road, etc.—opposite **nearside**
(Here, **nearside** is not printed in CAPITALS, because you do not need to look it up in order to understand its difference from **offside**.)

Usage notes

Sometimes you will find a Usage Note after all the meanings of a main entry word. The Usage Notes explain small differences between the meanings of words. They also give useful advice about the best use of words, and how to avoid common mistakes in your writing.

Janet Whitcut

Preface

Our main intention in compiling this dictionary has been to provide a work for older children and young adults from which they will obtain the real satisfaction that a competent user of traditional reference books enjoys; thus the dictionary concentrates on developing the skills of consulting and understanding the main components of the monoligual dictionary entry, that is headword (or entry word) and definitions (meanings or senses).

Once a person has gained the experience (and resultant confidence) of finding what he or she requires in a dictionary, a habit is established which goes well beyond satisfying the immediate need. Dictionaries, too often for many people the representatives of a forbidding (and perhaps even frightening) linguistic authority, have traditionally lagged behind the real needs of their purchasers. We wished to change this at a seminal stage, so that enjoyment of our text will lead on to the facility to get the most out of dictionaries in future years. Being able to make real use of the great scholarly English dictionaries available in libraries (whether of British or American origin), is almost a prerequisite in many areas of further education, formal or informal. And yet for many people there are seemingly insuperable barriers to be overcome. We have tackled the problem of removing these in the following ways:

1 Finding the entry one wants

Research has shown us that certain methods of presenting dictionary entries on the page are very much easier to use than others. It happens that the majority of British dictionaries (with some notable exceptions) use a system that is inherently (and quite unnecessarily) difficult. Even for a skilled user this is a source of frustration. But for a beginner to dictionaries it can be permanently demotivating.

The logical smallest unit of vocabulary is not, as one might at first expect, the word but might be several words. Orthographic practice suggests for quite separate reasons that *toothbrush* is written as one word, whereas *top hat* is not. And this practice is inconsistent even between publishers and printers in one English-speaking area. Similarly a verb like to *make up* and a noun like *make-up* clearly belong close together in any sensible dictionary sequencing. The technique used in this dictionary is to provide separate main entries for compounds, whether spelt as one word, hyphenated, or as more than one word (with spaces). This makes for a page with a much larger number of short entries rather than fewer long entries. An overwhelming preference for this approach has been demonstrated to us in market research.

2 Providing the right vocabulary

Now that the reader has found the right page and position, we must try to ensure that the word or meaning that he or she is looking for is there. We cannot of course guarantee, in a small dictionary, that this will be the case. But if we make sure that *every word is entered for good reason*, then our chances of success are much higher. Most dictionaries contain entries that nobody ever looks up. This can only be avoided by adopting a scientific approach to what is entered. Dictionaries like this one are compiled by large teams selected for their breadth of knowledge and writing skills. Through the use of the computer as a highly efficient filing system, we can extract and analyse a special area of vocabulary, at the touch of a button.

Mathematics, earth sciences, and all the other subjects (whether major school disciplines or not) can be listed separately, edited separately, and submitted to the inspection of those few individuals who have spent a lifetime studying their vocabulary (and the chief needs of a person tackling a subject in the first years). An analysis of textbooks up to those used in preparation for fifth-form examinations is one technique that we have used. The result should be a vocabulary that accurately reflects everyday needs – not biased towards the literary or scholarly – but covering the whole spectrum from pure science through technology and crafts to history, literature, and the arts, with special attention paid to new and important ideas and concepts.

3   Clear definitions by the use of formal controls
Now that the word has been found, how can we ensure that the user understands the definition? Too often dictionaries claim simple and clear explanations but fail to provide them – because the writing teams are so familiar with the specialist terminology in their own fields that they fail to realise when they are using it. We all of us fall into this trap when talking to those outside our own discipline or specialist area. Only by adopting a degree of formal control on the vocabulary permitted in definition – made possible again by the vast resources of the computer – can we justify our claim. This is that *the definitions are always written using simpler terms than the words they describe.* The stylishness and elegance of the definitions written within this vocabulary are a tribute to the writing team who have shown so much ability in writing within these constraints.

4   The illustrations and pictures
Our major break with dictionary tradition in this work has been to supplement the text with information which we hope will stimulate and interest our readers and make the book fun to use. Pictures are much better than words in conveying certain kinds of information – and they enable us to operate outside the limitations of alphabetical order.

We are able to give an overview to a subject (or subdivision of a subject) and provide extra vocabulary; to show how named parts relate to a whole; how grouped items relate and compare. We make no excuses for introducing this feature. Tests in schools and with parents and children have shown us that when exposed to the material, the vast majority are enthusiastic. We believe that the grey and tedious connotations that the word *dictionary* conjures up for most people are not an essential part of the book's nature. Dictionaries can be both useful and enjoyable.

Paul Procter
Editor-in-Chief

Subject consultants

Drama and film
D. Adland, Teacher and Author
Art
N. Billington, Head of Art and Technology Department, Pocklington School
Religion, philosophy, and ethics
Dr. N. Bull, Author
Life sciences
J. Bushell, Senior Lecturer in Science, Newman College of Education
Music
M. Callaghan, Head of Music, De La Salle College of Higher Education
Manchester
Environmental sciences
S. McB. Carson, Environmental Education Consultant
Technical studies
T. Dodd, Staff Inspector, Inner London Education Authority
Literature and mythology
I. Forsyth, ILEA Centre for Language in Primary Education
Home economics and crafts
K. E. Johnson, Advisory Teacher, Inner London Education Authority,
Westminster College SW11
Crafts
M. Jordan, Head of Design & Technology, Richard Hale School, Hertford
Technical studies
J. L. Leeks, Head of Design and Technology, Sedgehill School, ILEA
Mathematics
P. Nunn, Head of Mathematics, Watford Grammar School
History and politics
John Robottom, Author
Sports
D. W. Smith, Headmaster, Padgate Church of England Primary School,
Warrington
Language
C. B. Wightwick, Headmaster, King's College School, Wimbledon

Editor-in-Chief
Paul Procter

Clerical administration
Linda O'Donnell

Clerical
Melanie Ashurst
Ursula Lawrence
Elaine Roberts

Computer systems
Ken Moore
Christine Barnes
Computaprint Ltd.
Computer Data
Processing Ltd.

Managing editor
Janet Whitcut

Senior editor
Peter Adams

Lexicographers
Joyce Andrews
Christine Bauly
Jacqueline Billington
Barbara Burge
Valerie Dudley
Anne Evans
Bonnie Hearn
Veronica Sarson
Susan Saxby
Michael Scherk
Alma Sutherland
Elizabeth Webster

Design and production
Arthur Lockwood
Clive McKeough
Ruth Swan

Illustrations
Ray Burrows
Diagram Visual
Information Ltd.
Illustra Design Ltd.
Kathleen King
Oxford Illustrators Ltd.

Organisation and Methods
Pat Hill

Acknowledgments

The publishers and the editorial team of this dictionary wish to express their thanks to all those who have contributed advice and suggestions, particularly:

Professor Randolph Quirk, University College London

B. T. Bellis, Headmaster, The Leys School, Cambridge

Christopher Candlin, Director, Institute for English Language Education, University of Lancaster

Tudor David, Managing Editor of *Education*

Dr. Dennis Hamley, County English Adviser, Hertfordshire

Maura Healy, Second Mistress, Quintin Kynaston School, London

R. Howes, Assistant County Librarian (Reference & Information), Buckinghamshire County Council

Dr. Harry Judge, Director, Department of Educational Studies, University of Oxford

Akram Khan, Inspector of Schools with special responsibility for Multicultural Education, City of Birmingham Education Department

Michael Marland CBE, Headmaster, North Westminster Community School, London; Honorary Professor of Education, Warwick University

Dame Margaret Miles, DBE, formerly Headmistress of Mayfield School

Kim Taylor, Head of Educational Programme Services, IBA

John Tomlinson, Director of Education for Cheshire

David Walker, Head of Science, Simon Balle School, Hertford

The members of the Longman Dictionary & Reference Book Department, and the authors of the *Longman Dictionary of Contemporary English*

A

A, a A's, a's *or* As, as 1 the first letter of the English alphabet 2 **from A to Z** from beginning to end

A¹ the 6th note in the musical scale of C major or the musical key based on this note

A² *abbrev. for:* ampere

A³ *n, adj* (a film) that may be unsuitable for children under 14 —compare AA, U, X

a also (*before a vowel sound*) **an**— *indefinite article* 1 one: *I gave him a pound/an egg* 2 one member of a class or group: *a cat spits* 3 each; every: *6 times a day*

A-1 *adj* 1 of the best quality; very good 2 in good health: *Today I am feeling A-1*

AA¹ *n, adj* (a film) that children under 14 are not admitted to see in a cinema —compare A, U, X

AA² *abbrev. for:* Automobile Association

abacus *n* a frame holding wires on which small balls can be moved, used for teaching children how to count, or, esp. in eastern countries, for calculating

abandon¹ *v* 1 to leave completely and for ever: *They abandoned the burning ship* 2 to give up, esp. without finishing: *The search was abandoned* 3 to give (oneself) up completely to a feeling, desire, etc. — **-donment** *n*

abandon² *n* the state when one's feelings and actions are uncontrolled: *They shouted in gay abandon*

abase *v* **abased, abasing** to make (esp. oneself) humble — ~**ment** *n*

abash *v* to cause to feel uncomfortable or ashamed: *He stood abashed as his mistakes were pointed out*

abate *v* **abated, abating** 1 to become less strong: *The ship waited till the storm abated* 2 *literature* to make less: *His pride was not abated by his mistakes* — ~**ment** *n*

abattoir *n* a slaughterhouse

abbess *n* a woman who is the head of a convent for women —compare ABBOT

abbey *n* **abbeys** (esp. formerly) a building in which Christian monks or nuns live apart from other people and work as a group for God; monastery or convent

abbot *n* a man who is the head of a monastery for men —compare ABBESS

abbreviate *v* **-ated, -ating** to make shorter

abbreviation *n* 1 the act of making shorter 2 a shortened form of a word (such as *Mr*)

ABC *n* 1 the alphabet, as taught to children 2 the simplest facts about something: *classes in the ABC of cooking*

abdicate *v* **-cated, -cating** to give up (officially): *to abdicate (from) the throne* | *He abdi-*

cated all responsibility for the child — **-cation** *n*

abdomen *n* *medical* a main part of the body in animals, being in man the part between the chest and legs and in insects the end part of the body joined to the thorax ⟶RESPIRATION — **-dominal** *adj*

abduct *v* to take away (a person) unlawfully, often by force: *She has been abducted* — **abduction** *n*

aberrant *adj* changed from what is usual: *aberrant behaviour under the influence of drugs*

aberration *n* a usu. sudden change away from habitual behaviour ; sudden forgetfulness: *She hit him in a moment of aberration*

abet *v* **-tt-** to encourage or give help to (a crime or criminal): *The police claim he aided and abetted the thief* — ~**tor** *n*

abeyance *n* *esp. written* the condition of not being in force or in use: *The custom has fallen into abeyance*

abhor *v* **-rr-** to feel very great hatred and dislike for: *Most people abhor cruelty to children*

abhorrent *adj* hateful; detestable: *Cruelty is abhorrent to him* — **-rence** *n*

abide¹ *v* to bear; tolerate: *I can't abide rude people*

abide² *v* **abode, abided, abiding** *literature and old use* 1 to stay: '*Abide with Me*' 2 to live (in or at a place)

abide by *v prep* **abided, abiding by** 1 to be faithful to; obey: *abide by the club rules* 2 to wait for or accept: *You must abide by the judgment* — **abidance by** *n esp. written*

abiding *adj* without end; lasting: *an abiding friendship*

ability *n* **-ties** power and skill: *great musical ability* —see GENIUS (USAGE)

abject *adj* 1 as low as possible; deserving great pity: *abject slavery* 2 not deserving respect; showing lack of self-respect: *an abject slave* — ~**ly** *adv* — **abjection** *n*

abjure *v* **-jured, -juring** *esp. written* to swear a solemn promise, esp. publicly, to give up — **abjuration** *n*

ablative *adj, n* (of or concerning) a particular form of a Latin noun with the meaning of *by, with,* or *from* the noun

ablaze *adj* 1 on fire: *The house was quickly ablaze* 2 shining brightly: *The ladies were ablaze with jewels*

able *adj* 1 having the power, skill, knowledge, time, etc., necessary to do something: *I was able to help her* —opposite **unable** 2 skilled: *an able rider*

able-bodied *adj* strong and active

ablutions *n* *pompous or humour* the act of washing oneself

ably *adv* in an able manner: *He could play the horn very ably*

abnormal *adj* different (usu. in a bad sense) from what is ordinary or expected: *Is the child*

abnormal *in any way?* -see NATURAL (USAGE)
— ~ly *adv* — ~ity *n*

aboard *adv, prep* on or into (a train, aircraft, bus, etc.): *They went aboard the ship*

abode[1] *n literature, old use, or esp. written* place where one lives; home

abode[2] *past tense of* ABIDE

abolish *v* to stop: *Bad laws ought to be abolished*

abolition *n* the act of putting an end to something: *the abolition of slavery* — ~ist *n*

A-bomb *n* ATOM BOMB

abominable *adj* detestable: *Their treatment of prisoners was abominable* — -bly *adv*

abominate *v* -nated, -nating *esp. written* to have great hatred and dislike for

abomination *n* 1 great hatred; disgust 2 a very hateful or nasty thing or act

aboriginal *adj* of or about people or living things existing in a place from the earliest times or since the place was first described

aborigine *n* a member of a group, tribe, etc., that has lived in a place from the earliest times or since the place was first described, esp. in Australia

abort *v* 1 to give birth too early to —compare MISCARRY 2 to cause to be born too soon so that the child cannot live: *The doctor had to abort the baby* 3 *technical* to end before the expected time because of some trouble

abortion *n* 1 the act or an example of giving birth or causing to give birth early, esp. within the first 20 weeks of the baby's existence inside a woman, so that the child cannot live 2 a badly-formed creature produced by such a birth 3 a plan or arrangement which breaks down before it can develop properly —compare MISCARRIAGE, STILLBIRTH

abortionist *n* a person who intentionally causes an abortion

abortive *adj* coming to nothing; unsuccessful: *an abortive attempt to build a railway* — ~ly *adv*

abound *v* to exist in large numbers: *Animals abound here*

about[1] *adv* 1 also **around**— here and/or there: *I've left my purse somewhere about* 2 *esp. spoken* almost: *I'm about ready* —see also COME ABOUT

about[2] *prep* 1 also **around**— here and there in: *They walked about the streets* 2 also **around**— surrounding: *the wall about the prison* 3 concerning: *What about father?* 4 concerned with: *Do the shopping and don't be long about it* —see also SET ABOUT

about[3] *adj* 1 moving; active: *He was up and about very early* 2 just ready: *We're about to start*

above[1] *adv* 1 in or to a higher place: *the clouds above* 2 on an earlier page or higher on the same page: *See above for the address* 3 higher; more: *20 and above*

above[2] *prep* 1 higher than: *We flew above the clouds.* | *An admiral is above a captain.* | *He's above stealing* —compare **above someone's** HEAD 2 **over and above** in addition (to) 3 **above oneself** a self-satisfied b excited

aboveboard *adj* without any attempt to deceive: *He was quite open and aboveboard*

abracadabra *n, interj* (a word spoken to encourage the working of magic)

abrade *v* **abraded, abrading** *technical* to wear or cause to wear away by rubbing

abrasion *n technical* 1 loss of surface by rubbing 2 a place where the surface, esp. of the skin, has been worn away

abrasive[1] *adj* 1 causing the wearing away of a surface 2 tending to annoy; rough: *an abrasive voice* — ~ly *adv*

abrasive[2] *n* a substance, such as sand, used for polishing or removing a surface

abreast *adv* 1 side by side: *cycling 2 abreast* 2 **keep/be abreast of** to have the latest information on

abridge *v* **abridged, abridging** to make shorter by using fewer words

abridgment, abridgement *n* 1 the act of making shorter 2 something, such as a book, that has been made shorter

abroad *adv* 1 to or in another country: *living abroad* 2 over a wide area: *The news spread abroad that the results were out* 3 *old use* out of doors: *He was abroad early*

abrogate *v* **-gated, -gating** *esp. written* to put an end to the force or effect of: *to abrogate a law* ⚠ ARROGATE — **-gation** *n*

abrupt *adj* 1 sudden and unexpected: *an abrupt stop* 2 rough and impolite — ~ly *adv* — ~ness *n*

abscess *n* a pus-filled swelling on or in the body

abscond *v esp. written* to go away suddenly and secretly because one has done something wrong

absence *n* 1 the state or a period of being away: *Behave yourself during my absence* 2 non-existence; lack: *absence of information*

absence of mind *n* a state in which one forgets one's surroundings or what one is doing

absent[1] *adj* 1 not present: *How many are absent today?* 2 showing lack of attention: *an absent look* — ~ly *adv*

absent[2] *v esp. written* to keep away: *He absented himself from the meeting*

absentee *n* a person who stays away: *There were many absentees*

absenteeism *n* regular absence without good cause, esp. from work

absent-minded *adj* so concerned with one's thoughts as not to notice what is going on — ~ly *adv* — ~ness *n*

absinth, absinthe *n* a bitter green very strong alcoholic drink

absolute *adj* 1 complete; perfect: *absolute honesty* 2 having complete power: *An absolute ruler can do just as he pleases* 3 not allowing any doubt: *absolute proof of his guilt* 4 without any conditions: *an absolute promise* **5** not depending on or measured by comparison with other things —opposite **relative** — ~ **ness** *n*

absolutely *adv* **1** completely: *You are absolutely wrong* **2** without conditions: *You must agree absolutely* **3** *esp. spoken* certainly: *'Do you think so?' 'Absolutely!'*

absolute zero *n* the lowest temperature that is thought to be possible

absolution *n* forgiveness for wrongdoing

absolutism *n* the principle that complete power should be held by one or a limited number of rulers

absolve *v* **1** (of a priest) to give forgiveness for wrongdoing **2** to free from fulfilling a promise or a duty

absorb *v* **1** to take or suck in (liquids) **2** to take in (knowledge, ideas, etc.) **3** to take up all the attention, time, etc., of: *absorbed in a book* **4** (of a big country, business, etc.) to make into a part of itself; take over

absorbent *n, adj* (something) that is able to absorb

absorbing *adj* taking all one's attention; very interesting

absorption *n* **1** the act or action of absorbing or of being absorbed **2** the taking up of all one's attention, time, etc. **3** the taking over of little countries, businesses, etc. by big ones

abstain *v* to keep oneself from — ~ **er** *n*

abstemious *adj* having, being, or allowing (oneself) only a little food, drink, or pleasure: *an abstemious meal* — ~ **ly** *adv* — ~ **ness** *n*

abstention *n* the act or an example of keeping oneself from doing something, esp. from voting

abstinence *n* the act of keeping away from pleasant things — **-nent** *adj*

abstract¹ *adj* **1** *technical* thought of as a quality rather than as an object or fact: *'Hunger' is an* **abstract noun** **2** general as opposed to particular: *Your ideas seem a little abstract* **3** (in art) connected with or producing abstracts —compare REPRESENTATIONAL

abstract² *n* **1** a shortened form of a statement, speech, etc. **2** a painting, drawing, etc., that does not try to represent an object realistically

abstract³ *v* *technical* to remove by drawing out gently

abstracted *adj* inattentive to what is happening; deep in thought — ~ **ly** *adv*

abstraction *n* the state of not attending to what is going on

abstruse *adj* *esp. written or humour* difficult to understand — ~ **ly** *adv* — ~ **ness** *n*

absurd *adj* **1** against reason or common sense: *Even sensible men do absurd things* **2** funny because clearly unsuitable, false, foolish, or impossible: *You look absurd in your wife's hat!* — ~ **ly** *adv* — ~ **ity** *n*

abundance *n* a great quantity: *an abundance of food and drink*

abundant *adj* more than enough: *abundant supplies of firewood* — ~ **ly** *adv*

abuse¹ *v* **abused, abusing** **1** to say unkind or rude things to or about **2** to put to wrong use: *to abuse one's power*

abuse² *n* **1** unkind or rude words: *He shouted a stream of abuse* **2** wrong use: *the use and abuse of figures to prove things* **3** an unjust or harmful custom

abusive *adj* using or containing unkind or rude language: *an abusive letter* — ~ **ly** *adv* — ~ **ness** *n*

abut on *v prep* **-tt-** *esp. written* (of land or buildings) to lie next to or touch on one side

abysmal *adj* very bad: *The food was abysmal*

abyss *n* a great hole which appears bottomless

A/C *abbrev. for:* account

academic¹ *adj* **1** concerning teaching or studying **2** concerning those subjects taught to provide skills for the mind —compare TECHNICAL **3** of a college or university: *academic dress* **4** *offensive* not concerned with practical examples: *The question of how many souls exist in heaven is academic*

academic² *n* a member of a college or university, esp. one who teaches

academician *n* a member of an academy

academy *n* **-mies** **1** a society of people interested in the advancement of art, science, or literature, to which members are usu. elected as an honour **2** a school for training in a special art or skill: *a military academy*

accede *v* **acceded, acceding** *esp. written* **1** to agree: *He acceded to our request* **2** to take a high post or position after someone has left it

accelerate *v* **-rated, -rating** **1** to move faster **2** *esp. written* to cause to happen earlier —compare DECELERATE

acceleration *n* **1** the act of increasing speed **2** the rate at which speed is increased in a certain time: *The new car has good acceleration*

accelerator *n* **1** the apparatus used to increase the speed of a machine (esp. a car) **2** *technical* a machine for making very small pieces of matter (PARTICLES) move very quickly

accent¹ *n* **1** importance given to a word, a vowel, or syllable by saying it with more force or on a different musical note: *The accent in the word 'important' is on the 2nd syllable* **2** the mark used, esp. above a word or part of a word, in writing or printing to show how to say it **3** a particular way of speaking, usu. connected with a country, area, or class: *a thick German accent*

accent² *v* **1** to pronounce with added force or on a different musical note **2** to mark with an accent **3** to accentuate

accentuate *v* **-ated, -ating** **1** to pronounce with great force **2** to give more importance to: *The dark frame accentuates the brightness of the picture* — **-ation** *n*

accept *v* **1** to take or receive, esp. willingly; *I cannot accept your gift* **2** to believe; admit; agree to: *I accept your reasons for being late* **3** to take responsibility for: *I'll accept the blame*

acceptable *adj* good enough to be received

Your work is not acceptable. | *an acceptable gift*
— **-ability** *n* — **-bly** *adv*
acceptance *n* 1 the act of accepting or of being accepted 2 favour; approval
access *n* 1 entrance: *Access to that building is restricted* 2 means or right of using, reaching, or entering: *Students need easy access to books*
accessible *adj* 1 easy to get or get into, to, or at: *The books are easily accessible* 2 easily persuaded or influenced — **-ibility** *n*
accession *n esp. written* 1 the act of coming to a position 2 agreement, as to a demand
accessory *n* **-ries** 1 something which is not a necessary part of something larger but which makes it more beautiful, useful, effective, etc.: *The car's accessories include a radio* 2 the hat, shoes, etc., that complete a woman's clothes: *a black dress with matching accessories* 3 also *(law)* **accessary**— a person who is not present at a crime but who helps another in doing something criminal, either before or after the act
acciaccatura *n* (the instruction for) an unsatisfactory-sounding note played at the same time as the main note or chord and then quickly released
accidence *n technical* the rules in language which are concerned with the inflectional changes in the form of words according to their work (as in *sing, sang, sung* or in *body, bodies*)
accident *n* 1 something, esp. something unpleasant or damaging, that happens unexpectedly or by chance: *I had an accident and broke all the glasses* 2 **by accident of** by the chance or fortune of: *By accident of birth he was rich*
accidental *adj* happening by chance — ~**ly** *adv*
accident-prone *adj* more likely to have accidents than usual
acclaim *v* 1 to greet with loud shouts of approval 2 to declare to be, esp. with loud shouts of approval: *acclaimed as the best writer of the year* — **acclaim** *n*
acclamation *n* loud approval or shouts of welcome
acclimatize *v* **-tized, -tizing** 1 to cause to become accustomed to the conditions of weather, in a new part of the world 2 to cause to become accustomed to new conditions and places — **-tization** *n*
accolade *n* strong praise and approval: *His new book received many accolades*
accommodate *v* **-dated, -dating** *esp. written* 1 to provide with a room in which to live or stay 2 to have enough space for 3 to bring (something) into agreement with something else: *a chair which accommodates its shape to a person's position* 4 to change (oneself or one's habits, way of life, etc.) to fit new conditions
accommodating *adj* 1 ready to change to suit new conditions 2 willing to help — ~**ly** *adv*
accommodation *n* 1 a place to live: *Accommodation is expensive in this city* 2 the act of

changing something so that it suits new conditions 3 the act of settling a (business) disagreement 4 something that helps
accompaniment *n* 1 something which is usually found with something else 2 music played on a musical instrument to support singing or another instrument
accompanist *n* a person who plays a musical accompaniment
accompany *v* **-nied, -nying** 1 to go with, as on a journey 2 to happen or exist at the same time as: *Lightning usually accompanies thunder* 3 to make supporting music for
accomplice *n* a person who helps one to do wrong
accomplish *v* to succeed in doing; perform: *We accomplished nothing*
accomplished *adj* skilled: *an accomplished singer*
accomplishment *n* 1 the act of finishing work successfully 2 something successfully done: *her accomplishment in improving hospital conditions*
accord¹ *v* 1 to be of the same nature or quality: *Peaceful words do not accord with violence* 2 *esp. written* to give: *He was accorded permission to use the library*
accord² *n* 1 agreement (esp. in the phrase **in/out of accord (with)**) 2 **of one's own accord** without being asked
accordance *n* agreement: *in accordance with your orders*
according as *conj* depending on whether
accordingly *adv* 1 in a way suitable to what has been said or what has happened: *You told me to lock the door and I acted accordingly* 2 therefore; so
according to *prep* 1 as stated or shown by: *According to my watch it is 4 o'clock* 2 in a way that agrees with: *Pay is according to ability*
accordion *n* a portable musical instrument played by pressing the middle part together and so causing air to pass through holes opened and closed by keys worked by the fingers —compare CONCERTINA
accost *v* 1 to go up to and speak to 2 to go up to and ask for money or suggest sex
account¹ *n* 1 a written or spoken report; story: *Give us an account of what happened* 2 consideration: *Take into account the boy's illness* 3 advantage; profit: *He put his knowledge to good account* 4 a statement of money received and paid out, as by a bank or business: *The accounts show we have spent more than we received* 5 a statement of money owed: *Add the cost of this to my account* 6 a sum of money kept in a bank which may be added to and taken from: *My account is empty* —see also CURRENT ACCOUNT, DEPOSIT ACCOUNT, SAVINGS ACCOUNT, CREDIT ACCOUNT 7 **bring/call (someone) to account (for)** a to cause or force (someone) to give an explanation (of) b to punish (someone) (for) 8 **on account of** because of. 9 **on no account** also **not on**

any account— not for any reason **10 on one's own account a** so as to advance one's own interests **b** at one's own risk **c** by oneself

account² *v* to consider: *He was accounted a wise man*

accountable *adj* with the duty of having to give an explanation; responsible: *You will be held accountable for it*

accountancy *n* the work or job of an accountant

accountant *n* a person whose job is to keep and examine the money accounts of businesses or people

account for *v prep* to give an explanation for: *He could not account for his mistake*

accredit *v* **1** to send abroad as an official representing the government **2** to give the power to act for an organization: *an accredited representative of the firm* **3** to recognize or state that (something) is of a certain standard

accretion *n esp. written* **1** increase by natural growth or by the gradual addition of matter on the outside **2** something added or the result of something having been added: *The layer of dirt was the accretion of ages*

accrue *v* **accrued, accruing** *esp. written* to become bigger or more by addition: *The interest on my bank account accrued over the years*

accumulate *v* **-lated, -lating** to make or become greater in quantity or size: *He quickly accumulated a large fortune*

accumulation *n* **1** the act of accumulating **2** matter, material, etc., that has come together or grown

accumulative *adj* **1** cumulative **2** tending or trying to accumulate (esp. money or goods) — ~ly *adv*

accumulator *n* **1** a battery that can be recharged **2** a part of a computer where numbers are stored **3** a set of bets on 4 or more horse races. The money won on each race is added to the money put on the next race

accurate *adj* careful and exact: *an accurate statement* — -acy *n* — ~ly *adv*

accursed also **accurst—** *adj* **1** under a curse; suffering very bad fortune **2** hateful because causing bad fortune, suffering, etc. — ~ly

accusative *n, adj* (the case in the grammar of Latin, Greek, German, etc.) showing that the word is the direct object of a verb

accuse *v* **accused, accusing** to charge with doing wrong or breaking the law: *The police accused him of murder* — ~r, -sation *n* — accusingly *adv*

accused *n, adj* (the person) charged with a crime: *The accused was found guilty*

accustom *v* to make used to: *He accustomed himself to the cold*

accustomed *adj* **1** usual: *her accustomed smile* **2** in the habit of; used to: *He is accustomed to working hard*

ace *n* **1** a playing card or other object, used in games, that has a single mark or spot and which

usu. has the highest or the lowest value **2** *esp. spoken* a person of the highest skill in something: *an ace at cards* **3** (in tennis) a service that the opponent cannot hit back **4 within an ace of** *esp. spoken* very close to

acerbity *n esp. written* bitterness

acetate *n* a chemical made from acetic acid

acetic acid *n* the acid that gives vinegar its taste

acetylene *n* a colourless gas which burns brightly and is used in certain types of lamp and in cutting and joining pieces of metal

ache¹ *v* **ached, aching** **1** to have or suffer a continuous dull pain: *I ache all over* **2** to have a strong desire: *He was aching to go*

ache² *n* a continuous pain

achieve *v* **achieved, achieving** **1** to finish successfully: *He will never achieve anything* **2** to get as the result of action: *He hopes to achieve all his aims soon* — **achievable** *adj*

achievement *n* **1** the successful finishing or gaining of something **2** something successfully finished or gained esp. through skill and hard work

Achilles' heel *n* a weak point, esp. in a person's character

acid¹ *adj* **1** having a bitter taste like that of vinegar **2** bad-tempered **3** of or concerning a chemical acid

acid² *n* **1** a chemical substance containing hydrogen the place of which may be taken by a metal to form a salt —compare ALKALI **2** *sl* LSD

acidify *v* **-fied, -fying** to make into or become an acid

acidity *n* the quality of being acid

acid test *n* a test to prove whether something is as valuable as stated or will do what it is supposed to do

ack-ack *n esp. spoken now rare* an antiaircraft gun or fire from such a gun

acknowledge *v* **-edged, -edging** **1** to recognize the existence (of): *I acknowledge the truth of your statement* **2** to admit (as): *He was acknowledged to be the best player* **3** to show that one is grateful for: *His long service was acknowledged with a present* **4** to state that one has received: *We must acknowledge his letter*

acknowledgment, -edgement *n* **1** the act of acknowledging **2** something given, done, or said as a way of thanking **3** a statement, letter, etc., saying that something has been received

acme *n* the highest point of development, success, etc.: *the acme of perfection*

acne *n* a disease (common among young people) in which small raised spots appear on the face and neck

acorn *n* the fruit or nut of the oak tree, which grows in a cuplike holder

acoustic *adj* **1** of or concerning sound or the sense of hearing **2** (esp. of a musical instrument) making its natural sound, not helped by electrical apparatus — ~ally *adv*

acoustics *n* 1 the study of sound 2 the qualities which make a place good, bad, etc., for hearing: *The hall has good accoustics*

acquaintance *n* 1 information or knowledge, as obtained through personal experience: *I have some acquaintance with the language* 2 a person whom one knows, esp. through work, but who may not be a friend

acquaintanceship *n* 1 the state of being socially acquainted 2 the number of people with whom one is socially acquainted: *He has a wide acquaintanceship*

acquaint with *v prep* 1 to make (oneself or someone) familiar with 2 **be acquainted (with) a** to have knowledge (of) **b** to have met socially

acquiesce *v* **-esced, -escing** *esp. written* to agree, often unwillingly, without argument: *He acquiesced in his parents' plans* — **-escence** *n*

acquiescent *adj* ready to agree without argument — ~**ly** *adv*

acquire *v* **acquired, acquiring** 1 to get for oneself by one's own work, skill, action, etc.: *He acquired a knowledge of the language by careful study* 2 to come into possession of: *He acquired some property*

acquisition *n* 1 the act of acquiring 2 something or someone acquired: *This car is my latest acquisition*

acquisitive *adj* in the habit of acquiring or collecting things — ~**ly** *adv* — ~**ness** *n*

acquit *v* **-tt-** 1 to give a decision that (someone) is not guilty, esp. in a court of law: *They acquitted him of murder* 2 *literature* to cause to act in the stated way: *He acquitted himself rather badly*

acquittal *n* the act of declaring or condition of being found not guilty —opposite **conviction**

acre *n* a measure of land; 4, 840 square yards or about 4, 047 square metres: *The area of a football field is a little over 2 acres*

acreage *n* the area of a piece of land measured in acres

acrid *adj* 1 bitter 2 bitter in manner: *an acrid speech*

acrimony *n* bitterness, as of manner or language — **-nious** *adj* — **-niously** *adv*

acrobat *n* a person skilled in walking on ropes or wires, balancing, walking on hands, etc., esp. at a circus — ~**ic** *adj* — ~**ically** *adv*

acrobatics *n* the art and tricks of an acrobat

acronym *n* a word made up from the first letters of the name of something, esp. an organization (such as *NATO* from North Atlantic Treaty Organization)

across *adv, prep* 1 from one side to the other (of): *a bridge across the river* 2 to or on the opposite side (of): *We swam across* —see also COME ACROSS, CUT ACROSS, GET ACROSS, PUT ACROSS, RUN ACROSS

acrostic *n* a set or group of words or lines (as of a poem), written one below the other, in which all the first, last, or other particular letters form a word or phrase

acrylic fibre *n* a type of threadlike material made by man, used for clothes ◁ REFINERY

act¹ *v* 1 to represent, esp. on the stage: *Olivier is acting ('Othello') tonight* 2 *offensive* to play the part of, as in a play: *He is always acting the experienced man* 3 *offensive* to behave as if performing on the stage: *She always seems to be acting* 4 to take action: *Think before you act!* 5 to behave as stated: *to act bravely* 6 to produce an effect: *Does the drug take long to act?* —see also ACT UP

act² *n* 1 *esp. written* a deed (of the stated type): *an act of cruelty* 2 a law: *Parliament has passed an Act forbidding the killing of animals for pleasure* 3 one of the main divisions of a stage play: *Hamlet kills the king in Act 5 Scene 2* 4 one of a number of short events in a theatre or circus performance 5 *offensive, esp. spoken* an example of insincere behaviour used for effect (often in the phrase **put on an act)** 6 **get in on the/someone's act** *esp. spoken* to get a share of an/someone's activity, and esp. any advantages that may come as a result —see also ACT UP

acting¹ *adj* who is taking the place of: *the acting President*

acting² *n* the art of representing a character, esp. on a stage or for a film

action *n* 1 movement using force or power for some purpose: *Take action before it is too late* 2 something done: *Actions are more important than words* 3 the way in which a body moves: *The horse has a fine action* 4 the way in which a part of the body or a machine works: *the action of the heart* 5 the moving parts of a machine or instrument: *The action of this piano is stiff* 6 effect: *the action of light on photographic film* 7 a charge in a court of law: *to bring an action against someone* 8 a fight between armies or navies: *The action lasted 5 hours* 9 the chain of events in a play or book rather than the characters in it: *The action took place in a village* 10 *sl* the most productive, interesting, or exciting activity in a particular field, area, or group: *London is where the action is!* 11 **out of action** out of operation; no longer able to do a typical activity

action painting *n* abstract painting where the paint is put on in various unusual ways, as by throwing or pouring

activate *v* **-ated, -ating** 1 to cause to be active; bring into use 2 to make radioactive — **-ation** *n*

active¹ *adj* 1 doing things or always ready to do things: *He is very active* 2 able to produce the typical effects or act in the typical way: *Be careful! That dangerous chemical is still active!* 3 (of a verb or sentence) having as the subject the person or thing doing the action (as in *The boy kicked the ball*) —compare PASSIVE — ~**ly** *adv*

active² *n* also **active voice**— the active part or form of a verb

active service *n* on active service (in the armed forces) actually fighting

activist *n* a person taking an active part, esp. in a political movement

activity *n* **-ties** **1** the condition of being active **2** something that is done or is being done, esp. for interest or education **3** action

actor *n* a man who acts a part in a play or film

act out *v adv* to express (thoughts, unconcious fears, etc.) in actions rather than words

actress *n* a female actor

Acts also the Acts of the Apostles— *n* one of the books in the Bible. It describes the deeds of the first followers of Christ

actual *adj* existing as a real fact: *The actual amount was not large*

actuality *n* **-ties** *esp. written* **1** the state of being real; existence **2** something that is real; fact

actually *adv* **1** in actual fact; really **2** strange as it may seem: *The vicar actually offered me a drink!*

actuary *n* **-ries** a person who advises insurance companies on how much to charge for insurance, after considering the risks of fire, death, etc. — **-arial** *adj*

act up *v adv* *esp. spoken* to behave or perform badly: *The car's engine is acting up*

acuity *n* *esp. written* fineness or sharpness, esp. of the mind or the senses of sight or hearing

acumen *n* *esp. written* ability to judge quickly and well: *business acumen*

acupuncture *n* the method of stopping pain and curing diseases by pricking parts of the body with needles, used esp. in China

acute *adj* **1** able to notice small differences, as of meaning or sound; sharp: *an acute sense of smell* **2** severe; strong; deep: *in acute pain* **3** important enough to cause anxiety: *an acute lack of food* **4** (of a disease) coming quickly to a dangerous condition —compare CHRONIC **5** (of an angle) being less than 90 degrees; narrow ⟶MATHEMATICS **6** (of an accent put above a letter to show pronunciation) being the mark over é (as in *élite, café*) —compare GRAVE, CIRCUMFLEX — ~**ly** *adv* — ~**ness** *n*

AD *abbrev. for:* (in the year) since the birth of Christ —compare BC

ad *n* *esp. spoken* advertisement

adage *n* an old wise phrase; proverb

adagio *adv, adj, n* **-gios** (a piece of music) played slowly

adamant *adj* *esp. written* hard, immovable, and unyielding: *I am adamant about it* — **-mancy** *n* — ~**ly** *adv*

Adam's apple *n* that part at the front of the throat that is seen to move when a person talks or swallows

adapt *v* to change so as to be or make suitable for new needs, different conditions, etc.: *He adapted an old car engine to drive his boat* △ ADOPT

adaptable *adj* able to change or be changed so

as to be suitable for new needs, different conditions, etc. — **-ability** *n*

adaptation *n* **1** the art of adapting or the state of being adapted: *an adaptation of a play for radio* **2** something that has been adapted

adapter, -or *n* a person or thing that makes something suitable for a new purpose, esp. a plug that makes it possible to use more than one piece of electrical machinery from a single socket

ADC *abbrev. for:* aide-de-camp

add¹ *v* **1** to put together with something else so as to increase the number, size, importance, etc.: *The fire is going out; will you add some wood?* **2** to join so as to find the sum: *If you add 5 and/to 3 you get 8* **3** to say also: *I should add that we are very pleased* **4** add fuel to the fire *esp. spoken* to make someone feel even more strongly about something —see also ADD UP, ADD UP TO

addendum *n* **-da** something that is added or is to be added, as at the end of a book

adder *n* a small poisonous snake found in northern Europe and northern Asia

addict¹ *v* to cause to need or be in the habit of having, taking, etc.: *He became addicted to the drug* —compare DEVOTED, HOOKED

addict² *n* a person who is unable to free himself from a harmful habit, esp. of taking drugs — ~**ive** *adj*

addiction *n* **1** the state of being addicted **2** an example of this

addition *n* **1** the act of adding, esp. of adding two or more numbers together **2** something added: *A new baby is often called an addition to the family*

additional *adj* added — ~**ly** *adv*

additive *n* a substance added in small quantities to something else, as to improve the quality, or add colour, taste, etc.

addle *v* **addled, addling** **1 a** to cause (an egg) to go bad **b** (of an egg) to go bad **2** *esp. spoken* **a** to confuse **b** to become confused

address¹ *v* **1** to write (on an envelope, parcel, etc.) the name of the person meant to be the receiver, usu. with the place where that person lives or works **2** to direct speech or writing to **3** *esp. written* to cause (oneself) to begin to speak to a person or group **4** *esp. written* to put (oneself) to work at: *He addressed himself to the problem* **5** to speak or write to, using a particular title of rank: *Don't address me as 'officer'* **6** (in golf and other games) to bring one's club, cue, etc., into the correct position before hitting (the ball)

address² *n* **1 a** the number of the building, name of the street and town, etc. where a person lives or works **b** such information written down **2** a speech, esp. one that has been formally prepared, made to a group of people **3** *esp. written* manner of expression; behaviour **4** skill and readiness, esp. in conversation **5** also **form of address**—the correct title to be used to someone in speech or writing

addressee *n* the person to whom a letter, parcel, etc., is addressed

add

8

add up v adv esp. spoken to make sense: The various facts in the case just don't add up
add up to v adv prep. spoken to amount to: Your answer adds up to a refusal
adenoids n 1 the growth between the back of the nose and the throat —compare TONSIL 2 esp. spoken the condition in which this is swollen and sore — -noidal adj — -noidally adv
adept[1] n a person who is highly skilled in something: An adept in the art of stealing
adept[2] adj highly skilled — ~ly adv
adequate adj 1 enough for the purpose: We took adequate food for the holiday 2 having the necessary ability or qualities: I hope you will prove adequate to the job 3 only just good enough: The performance was adequate — ~ly adv — -quacy n
adhere v adhered, adhering to stick firmly: The 2 surfaces adhered (to each other)
adherence n 1 the act or condition of sticking to something firmly 2 the act or condition of remaining in favour of something in spite of difficulties
adherent n a person who favours and remains with a particular idea, opinion, or political party
adhere to v prep esp. written to follow steadily; be faithful to (an idea, opinion, belief, etc.): You must adhere to the plan
adhesion n the state of being stuck together or the action of sticking together
adhesive[1] adj that can stick or cause sticking
adhesive[2] n an adhesive substance
ad hoc adj Latin made, arranged, etc., for a paticular purpose: An ad hoc committee is one specially established to deal with a particular subject
adieu interj, n adieus or adieux French goodbye
ad infinitum adv Latin without end
adipose adj technical of or containing animal fat; fatty
adjacent adj esp. written very close; either touching or almost touching; next: They live in adjacent streets
adjacent angles n technical two angles which are next to each other and have one arm in common
adjacent side n technical the side of a right-angled triangle which joins the vertex containing a given angle to the vertex containing the right angle
adjective n a word which describes the thing for which a noun stands (such as black in the sentence She wore a black hat) — -tival adj — -tivally adv
adjoin v to be next to, very close to, or touching: Our house adjoins theirs
adjourn v 1 to bring (a meeting, trial, etc.) to a stop, esp. for a particular period or until a later time; to come to such a stop 2 to go to another place, esp. for a rest: We adjourned to the garden — ~ment n

adjudicate v -cated, -cating esp. written or technical 1 to act as a judge (esp. in competitions) 2 to make a decision about — -cation n
adjunct n something that is added or joined to something else but is not a necessary part of it
adjure v adjured, adjuring esp. written to urge solemnly: She adjured him to tell the truth
adjust v 1 to change slightly, esp. in order to make suitable for a particular job or new conditions: I must adjust my watch, it's slow 2 to put into order: Your collar needs adjusting — ~able adj — ~ment n
adjutant n an army officer responsible for the office work in a battalion
ad lib adv Latin, esp. spoken spoken, played, performed, etc., without preparation
ad-lib v -bb- esp. spoken to invent and deliver (music, words, notes, etc.) without preparation — ad-lib adj
administer v 1 to control (esp. the business or affairs of a person or group) 2 to put into operation: The courts administer the law — -tration n
administrative adj of or concerning the control of affairs, as of a country or business: administrative responsibilities — ~ly adv
administrator n 1 a person who directs the affairs, as of a country or business 2 a person who is good at arranging and directing 3 a person who is officially appointed to look after the business or property of another
admirable adj worthy of admiration: an admirable meal — -bly adv
admiral n (a man who holds) a very high rank or the highest rank in the navy
Admiralty n the group appointed by the government to control the navy
admiration n 1 a feeling of pleasure and respect: She was filled with admiration for his courage 2 a person or thing that causes such feelings: His skill made him the admiration of his friends
admire v admired, admiring 1 to regard with pleasure and respect; have a good opinion of: I admire her for her bravery 2 to look at with pleasure
admirer n a person who admires, esp. a man who is attracted to a particular woman: She has many admirers
admissible adj that can be allowed or considered: an admissible excuse — -bility n
admission n 1 allowing or being allowed to enter or join a school, club, building, etc. 2 an act of allowing someone to enter or join 3 the cost of entrance: Admission £1 4 a statement saying or agreeing that something is true (usu. something bad): He made an admission of guilt USAGE Admission is used for entrance price and/or 'permission to go in'. Admittance is sometimes used for the latter. Admittance cannot be used for 'admission of guilt'.
admit v -tt- 1 to permit to enter: I cannot

admit you yet **2** to have space or room for: *The church admits only 200 people* **3** to confess: *The thief admitted his crime*

admittance *n* allowing or being allowed to enter: *I was unable to gain admittance* —see ADMISSION (USAGE)

admittedly *adv* it must be admitted (that)

admixture *n* a substance that is added to another in a mixture

admonish *v esp. written* to scold or warn gently — ~ing *adj* — ~ingly *adv*

admonition *n* gentle scolding or warning — -tory *adj*

ad nauseam *adv Latin* to an annoying degree, esp. through being repeated for a long time: *We have heard your complaints ad nauseam*

ado *n* anxious activity; trouble; excitement: *Without more ado he jumped into the water and swam off*

adobe *n* a building brick made of earth and straw dried in the sun, used esp. in hot countries

adolescent *adj, n* (of) a boy or girl in the period between being a child and being a grown person; young teenager of about 13–16 — -cence *n*

adopt *v* **1** to take (someone, esp. a child) into one's family to look after as one's own, taking on the full responsibilities in law of the parent — compare FOSTER **2** to take and use as one's own: *I adopted their methods* **3** to approve formally: *The committee adopted his suggestions* **4** to choose, esp. as a representative △ ADAPT

adoption *n* the act or a case of adopting

adoptive *adj esp. written* having adopted: *Those are Susan's adoptive parents*

adorable *adj* worthy of being loved deeply

adoration *n* **1** religious worship and praise **2** deep love and respect

adore *v* **adored, adoring** **1** to worship as God **2** to love deeply and respect highly: *an adoring look* **3** *esp. spoken* to like very much: *She adores the cinema*

adorn *v* **1** to add beauty or ornament to —see DECORATE (USAGE) **2** to add importance or attractiveness to: *He adorned his story with improbable adventures*

adornment *n* **1** the act of adorning **2** an ornament

adrenalin *n* a hormone made by the body during anger, fear, anxiety, etc., causing quick or violent action

adrift *adv, adj* (esp. of boats) not fastened, and driven about by the sea or wind

adroit *adj* having or showing ability to use the skills of mind or hand, esp. quickly — ~ly *adv* — ~ness *n*

adsorb *v technical* to hold (molecules of a gas or liquid) in a layer on the surface — **adsorption** *n*

adulation *n* praise that is more than is necessary or deserved, esp. to win favour — -lator *n* — -latory *adj*

adult *adj, n* (of) a fully grown person or animal,

esp. a person over an age stated by law, usu. 18 or 21

adulterate *v* **-ated, -ating** to make impure or of poorer quality by the addition of something: *milk adulterated with water* — **-ation** *n*

adulterer *fem.* **adulteress**— *n* a married person who has had sexual relations with someone outside the marriage — **adultery** *n* — **-terous** *adj*

advance[1] *v* **advanced, advancing** **1** to move or come forward: *The soldiers advanced* **2** to improve or move forward: *His employer advanced him (to a higher position)* **3** to bring forward to an earlier date or time —opposite **postpone** **4** to move forward: *The work is not advancing*

advance[2] *n* **1** forward movement: *Our advance was slow* **2** a development: *advances in space travel* **3** money that is paid before the proper time or lent: *an advance of a month's pay* **4** **in advance (of) a** before in time **b** in front (of)

advanced *adj* **1** far on in development: *advanced studies* **2** modern (in ideas, way of living, etc.): *Her advanced ideas are difficult to accept*

advanced level *n* A LEVEL

advancement *n* **1** the act of advancing **2** the obtaining of a higher position

advances *n* efforts made to become friends with or to gain favourable attention from; offers of love: *She refused his advances*

advantage[1] *n* **1** something that may help one to be successful or to gain a desired result: *He had the advantage of wealth* **2** profit; gain **3** **Advantage X** (in tennis) (said when X has won the point after deuce) **4** **take advantage of a** to make use of; profit from **b** to make use of somebody, as by deceiving them

advantage[2] *v* **-taged, -taging** *esp. written* to be of profit to; benefit

advantageous *adj* helpful; bringing a good profit — ~ly *adv*

advent *n* arrival

Advent *n* **1** the coming of Christ to the world **2** the period of the 4 weeks before Christmas

adventitious *adj esp. written* not expected or planned: *the adventitious birth of their 5th child* — ~ly *adv*

adventure *n* **1** a journey, activity, etc., that is exciting and often dangerous: *an adventure in the mountains* **2** excitement, as in a journey or activity; risk: *He lived for adventure*

adventurer *n* **1** a person who has or looks for adventures **2** a person who hopes to get a high place in society by dishonest, dangerous, or sexually immoral means

adventuress *n* a female adventurer

adventurous *adj* **1** eager for adventure; bold **2** full of danger — ~ly *adv*

adverb *n* a word which adds to the meaning of a verb, an adjective, another adverb, or a sentence, and which answers such questions as *how? when?* or *where?* (as in 'He ran *slowly*.') — ~ial *n, adj* — ~ially *adv*

adversary n -aries a person or group to whom one is opposed

adverse adj esp. written not in favour of: an adverse decision △ AVERSE — ~ly adv

adversity n -ties bad fortune; trouble: a time of adversity

advert n esp. spoken an advertisement

advertise v -tised, -tising 1 to make known to the public, as in a newspaper, or on film or television: They advertised a used car for sale 2 to ask by placing an advertisement in a newspaper, shop window, etc.: We should advertise for a gardener — ~r n

advertisement n 1 also ad— a notice of something for sale, services offered, etc., as in a newspaper, painted on a wall, or made as a film 2 the action of advertising

advertising n the business which concerns itself with making known to the public what is for sale and encouraging them to buy, esp. by means of pictures in magazines, notices in newspapers, and commercials on television

advice n 1 opinion given by one person to another on how that other should act: I asked the doctor for his advice 2 a letter or report, esp. from a distant place giving information about delivery of goods

advisable adj that is advised or thought best to do; sensible: It is advisable to leave now — -sability n

advise v advised, advising 1 to tell (somebody) what one thinks should be done 2 esp. written to inform: I have advised her that we are coming

advisedly adv after careful thought; purposely

adviser n a person who gives advice, esp. to a government or business

advisory adj 1 having the power or duty to advise 2 containing advice

advocacy n the act or action of supporting an idea, way of life, person, etc.

advocate[1] n 1 law a person, esp. a lawyer, who speaks in defence of or in favour of another person 2 a person who speaks for or supports an idea, way of life, etc. —see also DEVIL'S ADVOCATE

advocate[2] v -cated, -cating to speak in favour of: I do not advocate building large factories

adze n an axe with the blade set at a right angle to the handle, used for shaping large pieces of wood

aegis n under the aegis of literature with the protection or support of

aeon, eon n a period of time too long to be measured

aerate v -ated, -ating 1 to put air or gas into (a liquid, esp. a drink) as by pressure 2 to allow air to act upon: Blood is aerated in the lungs — -ation n

aerial[1] adj 1 of, in, from, or concerning the air 2 moving or happening in the air — ~ly adv

aerial[2] n a wire, rod, or framework put up, often on top of a house, to receive radio or television broadcasts ⊃ ELECTRICITY

aerobatics n 1 the art of doing tricks in an aircraft, such as rolling over sideways or flying upside down 2 a group of such tricks — aerobatic adj

aerobic adj technical using or needing oxygen: an aerobic organism —compare ANAEROBIC — ~ally adv

aerodrome n a small airport

aerodynamics n 1 the science that studies the forces of moving air and other gases and the forces that act on bodies moving through the air 2 the qualities necessary for movement through the air — aerodynamic adj — -ically adv

aeronautics n the science of the operation and flight of aircraft — aeronautic, -ical adj

aeroplane n a flying vehicle that is heavier than air, that has wings, and has at least one engine ⊚

aerosol n a small container from which liquid can be sprayed in a fine mist

aerospace adj of the air around the earth and the space beyond it: an aerospace vehicle

aertex n trademark a loosely woven material used for shirts and underclothes

aesthete n a person who has a carefully developed sense of beauty, esp. beauty in art

aesthetic adj 1 of or concerning the sense of beauty 2 having a developed sense of beauty △ ASCETIC ~ally adj

aesthetics n the study, science, or philosophy of beauty, esp. beauty in art

afar adv literature far off

affable adj easy to talk to; pleasant — -bility n — -bly adv

affair n 1 something that has been done or is to be done; business: affairs of state 2 a happening: The meeting was a noisy affair 3 a sexual relationship between 2 people not married to each other, esp. one that lasts for some time

affect v 1 to cause some result or change in: Smoking affects health 2 to cause feelings in: She was deeply affected by his death 3 (of a disease) to attack △ EFFECT

affectation n offensive 1 unnatural behaviour: She is without affectation 2 a feeling or manner that is pretended

affected adj 1 offensive not real or natural; pretended: an affected interest in art 2 moved to sorrow, anger, etc. 3 attacked by a disease — ~ly adv — ~ness n

affecting adj causing deep feeling

affection n gentle, lasting love, as of a parent for its child

affectionate adj showing gentle love — ~ly adv

affidavit n a written statement made after an oath to tell the truth, for use as proof in a court of law

affiliate v -ated, -ating (esp. of a society or

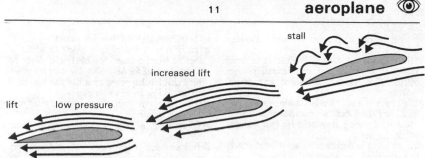

Airflow over the wing creates an area of low pressure above and high pressure below. This is lift, an upward force. As the angle at which the wing meets the air increases, so does lift. At too great an angle airflow becomes turbulent, lift is lost, and the wing stalls.

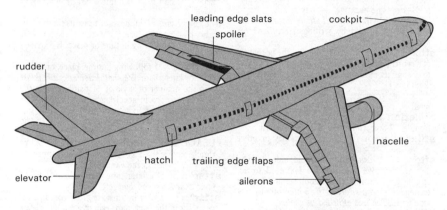

A modern aircraft needs several aerodynamic aids, such as the spoilers and flaps, which give it added lift, as well as the conventional control surfaces (ailerons, elevator, and rudder) to direct it. On a light aircraft, driven by propeller, the engine cover is called the cowling, rather than the nacelle.

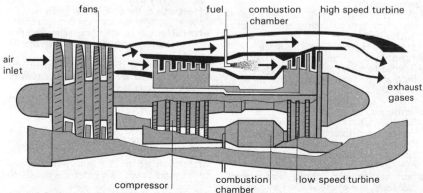

The turbofan engine gets its thrust not only from the ejection of the products of burning fuel with the air drawn in, but also from the fan blades spinning in the airstream with a propeller-like effect.

group) to join or connect: *affiliated organizations*

affiliation *n* 1 the act of affiliating or being affiliated 2 a connection or relationship, often official: *This club has affiliations with several societies*

affinity *n* -ties 1 relationship or close likeness: *The French and Italian languages have many affinities* 2 strong attraction: *He feels a strong affinity for her*

affirm *v* 1 to declare (usu. again, or in answer to a question): *He affirmed his love for her* — compare DENY 2 to promise to tell the truth in a court of law, but without mentioning God or the Bible in the promise — ~**ation** *n*

affirmative *n, adj often written* (a word) declaring 'yes': *The answer was a strong affirmative* —opposite **negative** — ~**ly** *adv*

affix¹ *v* 1 to fix or stick: *I affixed a stamp to the envelope* 2 to add by writing: *He affixed his name to the letter*

affix² *n* a group of letters added to the beginning of a word (prefix) or the end of a word (suffix) to change its meaning or its use (as in '*untie*' and '*kindness*')

afflict *v* to cause to suffer in the body or mind

affliction *n esp. written* 1 suffering; grief; trouble 2 something which causes suffering

affluent *adj* having plenty of money or other possessions — -**ence** *n*

afford *v* 1 (*usu. with* can, could, able to) to be able to buy: *We can afford a house* 2 to do, spend, give, bear, etc., without serious loss or damage: *Can you afford £5?* 3 *literature* to provide with: *The tree afforded us shelter*

afforest *v* to plant with trees in order to make a forest — ~**ation** *n*

affray *n* affrays *esp. written* a fight in a public place, esp. between small groups

affront¹ *v* to be rude to or hurt the feelings of, esp. in public

affront² *n* an act, remark, etc., that is rude to someone or hurts his feelings, esp. when intentional or in public

Afghan¹ *n* a person from Afghanistan

Afghan² *adj* of, from, or about Afghanistan

aficionado *n* -dos *Spanish* a keen follower

afield *adv* far away, esp. from home: *Do not go too far afield*

afire *adv, adj* on fire: *He set the house afire*

aflame *adv, adj* on fire

afloat *adv, adj* 1 on or as if on water; floating: *Help me get my boat afloat* 2 on ship; at sea: *How long did you spend afloat?* 3 covered with water; flooded 4 out of debt: *Lend me some money to keep me afloat*

afoot *adv, adj often offensive* being prepared, made ready, or in operation: *There is a plan afoot to destroy this building*

aforesaid also **aforementioned**— *adj esp. written* said or named before or above: *The aforesaid person was present*

aforethought *adj law* see MALICE

afraid *adj* 1 full of fear: *Don't be afraid of dogs* 2 worried about possible results: *Don't be afraid of asking for help* 3 *polite* sorry for something that has happened or is likely to happen: *I am afraid I've broken your pen*

afresh *adv esp. written* once more: *I must start this painting afresh*

African *adj, n* (a person) belonging to Africa ⌐꒒ MAP

Afrikaans *n* a language of South Africa very much like Dutch ⌐꒒ LANGUAGE

Afrikaner *n* a South African whose native language is Afrikaans, esp. a descendant of the Dutch settlers of the 17th century

Afro *n* **Afros** a hairstyle for men and women in which the hair is shaped into a large round bushy mass

aft *adv technical* in, near, or towards the stern of a boat —opposite **fore** ⌐꒒ SAIL

after¹ *adv* following in time or place: *We arrived soon after*

after² *prep* 1 following in time, place, or order; behind; later than: *We shall leave after breakfast* 2 in the manner or style of: *A painting after the great master* 3 in accordance with: *a man after my own heart* 4 in search of; with a desire for: *The policeman ran after the thief* 5 with the name of: *The boy was named after his uncle* USAGE Do NOT say: *We went home after.* After should not be used as an adverb in an expression like this. —see AFTERWARDS

after³ *conj* at a later time than (when): *I found your coat after you had left*

after⁴ *adj* 1 later in time: *He grew weak in after years* 2 in the back part, esp. of a boat: *the after deck*

after all *conj, adv* 1 in spite of everything: *So you see I was right after all!* 2 it must be remembered (that): *I know he hasn't finished, but, after all, he is very busy*

afterbirth *n* the material that comes out of a woman just after she has given birth to a child

aftereffect *n* an effect (usu. unpleasant) that follows some time after the cause or after the main effect

afterglow *n* 1 the light that remains in the western sky after the sun has set 2 a pleasant feeling that remains after the main feeling

afterlife *n* -lives 1 the life believed by some people to follow death 2 the later part of one's life, esp. after a particular event

aftermath *n* the result or period following a bad event such as an accident, storm, etc.: *the aftermath of the war*

afternoon *adj, n* 1 (of) the period between midday and sunset 2 a rather late period: *the afternoon of her life*

afters *n esp. spoken* the part of a meal that comes after the main dish, usu. something sweet —see also DESSERT

aftershave also (*esp. written*) **aftershave**

lotion— *n* a liquid with a pleasant smell for use on the face after shaving

aftertaste *n* a taste that stays after the cause is no longer there

afterthought *n* 1 an idea that comes later 2 something added later

afterwards *adv* later; after that —see AFTER (USAGE)

again *adv* 1 once more: *Please say that again* 2 in addition 3 **now and again** sometimes (but not very often)

against *prep* 1 in an opposite direction to: *We sailed against the wind* 2 in opposition to: *He was against the new motorway* 3 next to; touching: *She leant against the wall*

agape *adv, adj* 1 wide open 2 in a state of wonder: *The children were agape (with excitement)*

agate *n* a hard stone with bands of colour, used in jewellery

age[1] *n* 1 the period of time a person has lived or a thing has existed: *What is your age?* 2 one of the periods of life: *At 40 a man has reached middle age* 3 an advanced or old period of life: *bent with age* 4 the particular time of life at which a person becomes able or not able to do something: *under age drinking is illegal* 5 all the people living at a particular time: *This age doesn't know what poverty is* 6 *esp. spoken* a long time: *It's been ages/an age since we met* 7 **(be/come) of age** (to be or reach) the particular age, usu. 18 or 21, when a person becomes responsible in law for his own actions, and is allowed to vote, get married, etc.

age[2] *v* **aged, aging** *or* **ageing** 1 to make or become old 2 to make or become fitter for use with the passage of time: *The wine aged well*

aged[1] *adj* 1 being of the stated number of years: *My son is aged 10 years* 2 (of wine, cheese, meat, etc.) having a fully-developed taste by having been left untouched in the proper conditions for some time

aged[2] *adj* very old

age group also **age bracket**— *n* the people between 2 particular ages considered as a group

ageing, aging *n* 1 the action of growing old 2 the changes that happen, as to wine, cheese, or a person's body, as time passes 3 the action of allowing or causing these changes

ageless *adj* 1 never growing old or never showing signs of it 2 never changing: *ageless truth* — ~ness *n*

agency *n* **-cies** 1 a business that makes its money esp. by bringing people into touch with others or the products of others: *an employment agency* 2 the place of business of a person who represents a business: *The large firm has agencies everywhere* 3 the power or force which causes a result: *the agency of heat*

agenda *n* **-das** *or* **-da** a list of the subjects to be considered at a meeting

agent *n* 1 a person who acts for another, esp. one who looks after or represents the business affairs of a person or firm 2 a person who makes money by bringing people into touch with others or the products of others 3 a person or thing that works to produce a result: *Rain and sun are the agents which help plants to grow*

agent provocateur *n* **agents provocateurs** *French* a person employed, esp. by the government or police, to encourage criminals or those working against the state to take open action so that they can be caught

age of consent *n* the age at which a person is considered to be old enough to marry or have sexual relations without breaking the law

agglomerate[1] *v* **-ated, -ating** to collect or gather into a mass or heap without organization — **-ation** *n*

agglomerate[2] *n* a mass or heap, esp. of pieces of rock from a volcano melted and united by heat

agglutination *n* the action of sticking things together, or of becoming stuck together, esp. in a jelly-like form: *agglutination of red blood cells*

aggrandizement, -isement *n* *often offensive* increase or improvement in size, power, or rank: *personal aggrandizement*

aggravate *v* **-vated, -vating** 1 to make more serious or dangerous: *The lack of rain aggravated the already serious lack of food* 2 *esp. spoken* to annoy —see ANGRY (USAGE) — **-tion** *n*

aggregate[1] *adj* *esp. written* collected into one group, total, or mass: *What were your aggregate wages last year?*

aggregate[2] *v* **-gated, -gating** *esp. written or technical* to come or bring together into a group or mass

aggregate[3] *n* 1 *esp. written* a mass or total made up of small parts 2 *technical* the materials, such as sand and small stones, that are added to cement to form concrete

aggregation *n* 1 the collecting together into a mass or of a number of different things 2 a group or mass formed by this

aggression *n* 1 the starting of a quarrel, fight, or war, esp. without just cause 2 an attacking action made without just cause

aggressive *adj* 1 *offensive* always ready to quarrel or attack: *He is very aggressive* 2 not afraid of opposition: *A successful businessman must be aggressive* — ~ly *adv* — ~ness *n*

aggressor *n* *offensive* a person or country that begins a quarrel, fight, war, etc., with another, esp. without just cause

aggrieved *adj* *esp. written* suffering from a personal offence, showing hurt feelings, etc.

aggro *n* *sl* trouble, esp. fighting, as between groups of young people

aghast *adj* shocked

agile *adj* able to move quickly and easily — ~ly *adv* — **-ility** *n*

aging *n* ageing

agitate *v* **-tated, -tating** 1 to shake (a liquid) or move (the surface of a liquid) about 2 to cause anxiety to 3 to argue strongly in public or to act for or against some political or social change — **-tation** n

agitator n a person who excites and influences other people's feelings esp. toward political or social change

aglow adj bright with colour or excitement: *The sky was aglow with the setting sun*

agnostic n, adj **1** (a person) who believes that one can only have knowledge of material things and that nothing is or can be known about God or life after death —compare ATHEIST **2** (a person) who claims that something can neither be proved nor disproved — ~**ism** n

ago adj back in time from now; in the past: *He left 10 minutes ago*

agog adj esp. *spoken* excited and expecting something to happen: *The children were all agog as the actor drew his gun*

agonize, -ise v **-nized, -nizing** esp. *spoken* to suffer great pain or anxiety: *To agonize over a decision*

agonized, -ised adj expressing great pain: *an agonized cry*

agonizing, -ising adj causing great pain — ~**ly** adv

agony n **-nies** very great pain: *He lay in agony until the doctor arrived*

agony column n *humour* PERSONAL COLUMN

agoraphobia n an unhealthy fear of open spaces —opposite **claustrophobia** — **-bic** n, adj

agrarian adj of land, esp. farmland or its ownership

agree v **agreed, agreeing 1** to accept an idea, opinion, etc., esp. after argument; approve: *He agreed to my idea* **2** to have or share the same opinion, feeling, or purpose

agreeable adj **1** to one's liking: *agreeable weather* **2** ready to agree: *Are you agreeable?*

agreeably adv pleasantly: *I was agreeably surprised*

agreement n **1** the state of having the same opinion, feeling, or purpose: *We are in agreement* **2** an arrangement or promise of action, as made between people, groups, businesses, or countries: *You have broken our agreement by not doing the work* **3** the use of matching forms (e.g. in number, gender, person, or case) of noun, adjective, verb, etc., in a sentence —compare CONCORD

agree with v prep **1** to be in accordance with: *Your story agrees with his* **2** esp. *spoken* to suit the health of: *The soup did not agree with me* —see also DISAGREE WITH **3** (of nouns, adjectives, verbs, etc.) to have the same number, gender, person, or case as: *A pronoun must agree in number and gender with the noun it refers to*

agriculture n the art or practice of farming, esp. of growing crops — **-tural** adv — **-tur(al)ist** n

aground adv, adj (of a ship) in, into, on, or onto the shore or bottom of a sea, lake, etc. (often in the phrase **run aground**)

ah interj a cry of surprise, pity, pain, joy, dislike, etc.: *Ah, there you are!*

aha interj a cry of surprise, satisfaction, amused discovery, etc.: *Aha, so it's you hiding there*

ahead adv, adj **1** in or into a forward position; in or into the future: *One man went ahead to clear the road.* | *The days ahead will be busy* **2 ahead of a** in advance of **b** better than **3 get ahead** to do well

ahem interj a cough used to attract attention, give a slight warning, express doubts, etc.

aid¹ v to give support to —see also **aid and** ABET

aid² n **1** support; help: *He went to the aid of the hurt man* **2** a person or thing that helps: *A dictionary is an important aid in learning a new language* —see also DEAF AID, HEARING AID, VISUAL AID

aide n a person who helps, esp. a person employed to help a government minister

aide-de-camp n **aides-de-camp** *French* a military or naval officer who helps an officer of higher rank in his duties

ail v esp. *spoken* to be ill and grow weak

aileron n the movable back edge of the wing of an aircraft, used esp. to keep the aircraft level or help it turn —compare ELEVATOR ⇒ AEROPLANE

ailment n an illness, usu. not serious

aim¹ v **1** to point or direct (a weapon, remark, etc.) towards some object, esp. with the intention of hitting it: *He aimed the gun carefully* **2** to direct one's efforts: *I aim to be a writer*

aim² n **1** the act of directing a weapon, remark, etc.: *The hunter took aim* **2** the desired result of one's efforts; purpose: *What is your aim in working so hard?*

aimless adj without any purpose — ~**ly** adv — ~**ness** n

ain't *not standard* shortened form of am not, is not, are not, has not, and have not

air¹ n **1** the mixture of gases which surrounds the earth and which we breathe: *The fresh air made him feel hungry* **2** the sky or the space above the ground: *He jumped into the air* **3** the sky as something through which to fly **4** the general character or appearance of something; appearance of, or feeling caused by, a person or place: *an air of excitement at the meeting* **5** that part of a piece of music that is easily recognized and remembered; tune **6 clear the air a** to make the air in a place fresh again, as by opening the windows **b** to get rid of misunderstanding, doubt, etc., by stating the facts clearly **7 in the air** esp. *spoken* **a** (of stories, rumours, etc.) being passed on from one person to another **b** not fully planned or settled **8 into thin air** esp. *spoken* completely out of sight or reach —see also AIRS

air² v **1** (of clothes, sheets, beds, etc.)to dry or become dry by putting in a place that is warm or dry **2** to make or become fresh by letting in air: *We aired the room by opening the windows* **3** to make known to others, esp. in a noisy manner: *They tired of him airing his knowledge*

airbase *n* a place where military aircraft land and take off

airbed *n* a rubber or plastic bed filled with air

airbladder *n* (in some animals, esp. fishes and plants) a small fleshy bag containing air

airborne *adj* **1** (esp. of seeds) carried about by the air **2** (esp. of aircraft) in the air **3** (of soldiers) trained to fight in an area after being dropped by parachute

airbrick *n* a brick with holes through it to allow air into and out of a room or building

airbus *n* an aircraft for carrying large numbers of passengers on short or middle-distance flights at regular times

air chief marshal *n* (a man who holds) the 2nd highest rank in the R.A.F.

air commodore *n* (a man who holds) the 5th highest rank in the R.A.F.

air-conditioning *n* the system that uses one or more machines (**air-conditioners**) to keep air in a building cool and usu. dry in the summer — -tioned *adj*

aircraft *n* -craft a flying machine of any type, with or without an engine

aircraft carrier *n* a warship which can carry naval aircraft and which has a large flat surface where they can take off and land

aircraftman also **aircraftsman**— *n* (a man who holds) the lowest rank in the R.A.F.

aircushion *n* air forced out from under a hovercraft to support it

Airedale *n* a type of large terrier with a rough coat

airfield *n* a place where aircraft may land and take off but which need not have any large buildings for storage or repairs

airforce *n* that part of the military organization of a country that is concerned with attack and defence from the air

airgun *n* a gun which uses strong air pressure to fire a bullet

airhostess *n* a woman who looks after the comfort of the passengers on an aircraft

airily *adv* **1** in a gay manner **2** delicately

airing *n* **1** the leaving of clothes, sheets, etc., in the open air or in a warm place to get dry **2** the act of allowing fresh air into a room **3** the making public of one's opinions, knowledge, etc. **4** the act of going for a walk, ride, etc., in the fresh air

airing cupboard *n* a cupboard that is heated and used to air clothes, sheets, etc.

airlane *n* a path through the air regularly used by aircraft in flight

airless *adj* lacking fresh air; stuffy

airletter *n* **1** a sheet of very thin paper (already stamped for posting) on which a letter can be written and which is then folded and stuck at the edges and sent by air without an envelope **2** any letter that is sent by air

airlift *v* to carry large numbers of people or amounts of supplies by aircraft, esp. to or from a place that is difficult to get to — **airlift** *n*

airline *n* a business that runs a regular service for carrying passengers and goods by air

airliner *n* a large passenger aircraft

airlock *n* **1** a bubble in a tube or pipe that prevents the passage of a liquid **2** an enclosed space into which or from which air cannot accidentally pass, as in a spacecraft or apparatus for working under water

airmail *n* letters, parcels, etc., sent by air

airplane *n US* an aeroplane

airpocket *n* a downward flow of air in the sky which can cause an aircraft to lose height suddenly

airport *n* a place where aircraft can land and take off, which has several buildings, and which is regularly used by paying passengers

air raid *n* an attack by military aircraft

airs also **airs and graces**— *n* *offensive* (esp. of a woman) unnatural manners or actions that are intended to make people think one is more important than one really is (esp. in the phrases **give oneself airs, put on airs**)

air-sea rescue *n* the work of saving people from aircraft that have crashed into the sea

airship *n* *now rare* an aircraft that uses gas to make it lighter than air and an engine to make it move forward

airsick *adj* sick or ill through the effects of flying in an aircraft — ~ness *n*

airspace *n* the sky above a country and regarded its property

airstrip *n* a stretch of land that may be used by aircraft to take off and land, as in war, but not as a regular arrangement

air terminal *n* the building in which passengers come together before getting on board an aircraft or from which they leave at the end of a flight

airtight *adj* not allowing air to pass in or out

air vice-marshal *n* (a man who holds) the 4th highest rank in the R.A.F.

airway *n* an airline (used only in proper names): *Imperial Airways*

airworthy *adj* (of aircraft) in proper and safe working condition — -thiness *n*

airy *adj* airier, airiest **1** open to the fresh air **2** *offensive* affected **3** *offensive* having little substance **4** light-hearted; careless **5** of, like, or in the air

aisle *n* **1** a passage, usu. one of two, leading through the length of a church and divided from the nave by a row of pillars ⊂⊐ CATHEDRAL **2** a narrow passage between rows of seats, shelves, etc., as in a theatre or large shop

aitch *n* a way of spelling the name of the letter *H, h*

ajar *adv, adj* (of a door) not quite closed

akimbo *adj, adv* with arms bent at the elbows and hands on the hips (esp. in the phrase **with arms akimbo**)

akin *adj* having the same appearance, character, etc.; like: *His writing is akin to mine*

alabaster *n* a transparent soft mainly white stone used for making ornaments

à

à la carte adj, adv French (of cooked food sold in a restaurant) according to a menu where each dish has its own separate price —compare TABLE D'HOTE

alack interj old use a cry expressing sorrow

alacrity n esp. written quick and willing readiness

à la mode adv according to the latest fashion or style

alarm¹ n 1 a warning of danger, as by ringing a bell or shouting: Raise the alarm! 2 any apparatus, such as a bell, noise, flag, by which a warning is given 3 (the apparatus that makes the noise in) an alarm clock 4 sudden fear and anxiety as caused by the possibility of danger

alarm² v 1 to excite with sudden fear and anxiety 2 to make conscious of danger

alarm clock also **alarm**— n a clock that can be set to make a noise at any particular time to wake up sleepers

alarmist n offensive a person who raises unnecessary alarm

alas interj literature a cry expressing grief or fear

albatross n any of various large strong mostly white seabirds famous for their ability to fly long distances

albeit conj esp. written even though: It was a small albeit important mistake

albino n -nos 1 a person with a pale milky skin, very light hair, and eyes that are pink because of a lack of colouring matter 2 an animal that lacks the typical colouring and is usu. white with pink eyes

album n 1 a book whose pages have little or no writing and which is used for collecting photographs, stamps, etc. 2 LONG-PLAYING RECORD

albumen n any of various substances (PROTEINS) contained in much animal and vegetable matter (such as the white or colourless part of a bird's egg)

alchemy n the early form of chemistry concerned with trying to turn all metals into gold — -ist n

alcohol n 1 the pure colourless liquid present in wine, beer, spirits, etc. that can make one drunk 2 the drinks containing this 3 any of a class of chemical substances of which the alcohol in wine is one

alcoholic¹ adj 1 containing alcohol 2 suffering from alcoholism — ~ally adv

alcoholic² n a person unable to break the habit of drinking alcoholic drinks too much, esp. one whose health is damaged because of this — compare DRUNKARD

alcoholism n 1 the habitual drinking of a lot of alcohol 2 the diseased condition caused by this

alcove n a small partly enclosed space in a room or set into a wall or hedge

alder n a type of birch tree which grows in wet places

alderman n -men a member of a town, city, or

county council who is of high rank and is chosen by the elected members

ale n beer, esp. one that is pale in colour

alert¹ adj watchful and ready (to meet danger): He is an alert boy — ~ly adv — ~ness n

alert² n 1 a warning to be ready for danger —opposite all clear 2 the period in which people remain especially watchful for danger

alert³ v to warn: The doctor alerted me to the dangers of smoking

A level also **advanced level**— n 1 the higher of the 2 standards of GCE examinations, necessary for entrance to a university 2 an examination of this standard in a particular subject —compare O LEVEL

alfalfa n US lucerne

algae n simple plants that live in or near water and are usu. very small ☞PLANT, EVOLUTION

algebra n a branch of mathematics in which symbols and letters are used instead of numbers — ~ic(al) adj — ~ically adv

algorithm n technical a list of instructions which are carried out in a fixed order to calculate a number — ~ic adj

alias¹ adv (esp. of a criminal) also called

alias² n a name other than the officially recognized name used by a person (esp. a criminal) on certain occasions

alibi n -s an argument that a person charged with a crime was in another place at that time and that he therefore could not have done it: Have you an alibi? —see EXCUSE (USAGE)

alien¹ adj 1 belonging to another country or race 2 different in nature or character: an alien concept

alien² n a foreigner who has not become a citizen of the country where he or she is living —compare CITIZEN, NATIONAL

alienate v -ated, -ating to make unfriendly

alienation n 1 separation from a person with whom one was formerly friendly 2 a feeling of not belonging to one's surroundings: The dull nature of many jobs leads to alienation

alight¹ v alighted or alit esp. written to get off at the end of a journey; come down from the air —see DISMOUNT (USAGE)

alight² adj 1 on fire; in flames 2 having the lights on

align, aline v to come, bring, form, make, or arrange into a line; to join and agree: We must align ourselves with the workers

alignment, aline- n 1 the act of forming or arranging into a line 2 the line or lines formed in this way 3 (of people or countries) the act of forming into groups with the same ideas, aims, etc. or such a group

alike¹ adj being (almost) the same: The 2 brothers are very alike

alike² adv in (almost) the same way; equally

alimentary canal n the tubelike passage leading from the mouth to the stomach and onwards

alimony n money that a man has been ordered

to pay regularly to his wife after they have been separated or divorced in a court of law

alive *adj* **1** having life **2** active: *Although old he is still very much alive* **3** still in existence: *The argument was kept alive by the politicians* **4 alive with** covered with or full of (living things)

alkali *n* **-lis** or **-lies** *technical* any of various substances that form chemical salts when combined with acids —compare ACID — ~**ne** *adj*

all¹ *adj* the complete amount, quantity, or number of; the whole of

all² *adv* **1** completely: *The table was all covered with papers* **2** to a very great degree; much: *With help we will finish all the sooner* **3** for each side: *The score is 3 all* **4 all along** *esp. spoken* all the time **5 all but** almost **6 (not) all there** *esp. spoken* (not) having a good quick mind **7 all the same** *esp. spoken* even so **8 all the same to** *esp. spoken* not making any difference or causing any worry to **9 all told** counting everyone or everything **10 all up (with)** *esp. spoken* at an end; ruined

all³ *pron* **1** everybody or everything: *He gave all he had* **2 all in all** *esp. spoken* everything **3 all of** fully: *It'll cost all of £5* **4 all that** *esp. spoken* so very: *Things aren't all that good* **5 (not) at all** (not) in any way: *I do not agree at all* —see also NOT at all **6 for all** in spite of **7 for all one knows, cares, etc.** *esp. spoken* as far as one knows, cares, etc. **8 it was all one could do (not) to** *esp. spoken* it was very difficult to **9 once and for all** for the last time

Allah *n* (the Muslim name for) God

allay *v* allayed, allaying *esp. written* to make (fear, anger, doubt, etc.) less

all clear *n* a signal that danger is past

allege *v* alleged, alleging *esp. written* to state or declare without proof or before finding proof — **-gation** *n*

allegedly *adv* according to charges made without proof

allegiance *n* loyalty and support to a king, country, idea, etc.

allegory *n* **-ries** a story, poem, painting, etc., in which the characters and actions represent good and bad qualities, or the style in which this is done — **-ical** *adj* — **-ically** *adv*

allegretto *adv, adj, n* **-tos** (a piece of music) played fairly fast but not very fast

allegro *adv, adj, n* **-gros** (a piece of music) played in a rapid manner and full of life

alleluia *n, interj* halleluja

allergy *n* **-gies** **1** a condition of being unusually sensitive to something eaten, breathed in, or touched, in a way that causes pain or suffering **2** *esp. spoken* a strong dislike (for) — **-ic** *adj*

alleviate *v* **-ated, -ating** to make (pain, suffering, anger, etc.) less —compare AMELIORATE — **-ation** *n*

alley *n* alleys **1** a narrow street or path between buildings in a town **2** a path in a garden or park, esp. one bordered by trees or bushes **3**

a long narrow piece of ground, or floor, along which heavy balls are rolled in order to knock over skittles —see also BLIND ALLEY

all fours *n* **on all fours** down on one's hands and knees

alliance *n* **1** the act of allying or the state of being allied **2** a close agreement or connection between countries, groups, families, etc.

allied *adj* related, esp. by common qualities: *painting and other allied arts*

alligator *n* **1** a large cold-blooded fierce animal (like the crocodile) that lives on land and in lakes and rivers in the hot wet parts of America and China **2** its skin turned into leather —compare CROCODILE

all in *adj* *esp. spoken* worn out: *I am all in at the end of the day*

all-in *adj* with everything included: *an all-in price*

alliteration *n* the appearance of the same sound or sounds at the beginning of 2 or more words that are next to or close to each other (as in "Round the rocks runs the river") — **-tive** *adj* — **-tively** *adv*

all-night *adj* lasting or open all through the night

allocate also allot— *v* **-cated, -cating** **1** to divide and give: *We must allocate the money* **2** to set apart for somebody or some purpose: *That space has been allocated for a new hospital* — **-tion** *n*

allot *v* **-tt-** to allocate

allotment *n* **1** allocation **2** a small piece of land rented out to people who will grow vegetables on it

all-out *adj* *esp. spoken* using all possible effort: *an all-out attempt to climb the mountain* — **all out** *adv*

all over *adv* **1** everywhere: *He looked all over for the book* **2** at an end **3** *esp. spoken* in every part or quality: *That sounds like my father all over*

allow *v* **1** to permit **2** to make possible (for): *Your gift allows me to buy a car* **3** to give, esp. money or time

allowable *adj* that may be allowed — **-bly** *adv*

allowance *n* **1** something, esp. money, provided regularly or for a special purpose: *an allowance of £5, 000 a year* **2** money taken off the cost of something, usu. for a special reason —compare DISCOUNT **3** the taking into consideration of facts that may change something, esp. an opinion **4** share

allow for *v prep* to take into consideration

alloy¹ *n* alloys a metal made by mixing together 2 or more different metals

alloy² *v* alloyed, alloying to mix (one metal) with another

all-purpose *adj* able to be used in all conditions or for all purposes: *an all-purpose cleansing fluid*

all right *adv, adj* **1** safe or healthy: *Is the driver*

all

all right? **2** *esp. spoken* (in a way that is) acceptable, satisfactory, or unobjectionable: *He mended my radio all right* **3** Yes; I/we agree **4** beyond doubt: *He's ill all right*

all round *adv esp. spoken* in regard to everything: *All round it's not a bad car*

all-round *adj* having ability in many things — ~**er** *n*

allspice *n* a strong-tasting powder obtained from the berry of a West Indian tree and used in cooking

all-time *adj* greatest, biggest, most, etc., ever known: *Sales have reached an all-time high*

allude to *v prep* **alluded, alluding to** *esp. written* to speak of but not directly: *It was clear she was alluding to Jones*

allure¹ *v* **allured, alluring** to attract by the offer of something pleasant

allure² *n* attraction: *Her face has a certain allure*

allurement *n* **1** something that attracts **2** the act of attracting

allusion *n esp written* the act of speaking but not directly, or something spoken of without directness, esp. while speaking about something else — **-sive** *adj* — **-sively** *adv*

alluvium *n* **-viums** *or* **-via** soil put down by rivers, lakes, floods, etc. — **-vial** *adj*

ally¹ *v* **allied, allying** to join or unite, as by political agreement or marriage: *The small country allied itself to the stronger power*

ally² *n* **allies 1** a country that is joined to one's own by political agreement, esp. one that will provide support in war **2** a person who helps or supports one

alma mater *n Latin, esp. written & humour* the school or university where a person was taught

almanac *n* a book giving a list of the days of a year, together with the times of sunrise and sunset, changes in the moon, the rise and fall of the sea and other information of interest

almighty *adj* **1** having the power to do anything: *God Almighty* **2** *esp. spoken* very big, strong, great, etc.: *an almighty crash*

almond *n* a kind of fruit tree or its edible nuts

almond-eyed *adj esp. spoken* having long narrow eyes, like those of people from the East

almoner *n* a medical social worker who looks after the needs of the sick in a hospital

almost *adv* very nearly

alms *n* money, food, clothes, etc., given to poor people

alms-house *n* a house, usu. one of a group, provided in former times by a rich person, in which old or poor people could live without paying rent

aloft *adv* at or to a great height: *The smoke rose aloft*

alone¹ *adj* only: *He alone knows the secret*

alone² *adv* without others: *He lived alone* USAGE Alone is neither good nor bad: *She prefers to live alone.* Solitary and lone may be neutral, but

may also imply loneliness. Forlorn and desolate mean great sadness because of being left alone.

along¹ *prep* in the direction of the length of; following the course of: *We walked along the road*

along² *adv* **1** forward; on: *My roses are coming along nicely* **2** with others or oneself: *I took my sister along* **3** all along all the time **4** along with together with

alongside¹ *adv* close to and in line with the edge (of something); along the side: *We brought our boat alongside*

alongside² *prep* side by side with

aloof *adj, adv* **1** at a distance; not joining in (with): *He kept himself aloof from the others* **2** distant in feeling or interest; reserved — ~**ly** *adv* — ~**ness** *n*

aloud *adv* **1** in a voice that may be heard: *He read the poem aloud* **2** in a loud voice: *to cry aloud*

alpaca *n* **1** a sheeplike animal of Peru, related to the llama **2** cloth made from the wool of this animal

alpenhorn *n* a very long wooden horn formerly used in Switzerland, esp. to call sheep and cows

alpha *n* **1** the first letter of the greek alphabet (A, α) **2** a mark for excellent work by students

alphabet *n* the set of letters used in writing any language, esp. when arranged in order — ~**ical** *adj* — ~**ically** *adv*

alpha particle *n* a very small piece of matter (that has a positive charge) that is thrown out by some radioactive substances

alpine *adj* **1** of or concerning any high mountain **2** very high **3** growing on parts of mountains that are too high for trees to grow on

already *adv* by or before a stated, suggested, or expected time: *When we got there he had arrived already* —see JUST (USAGE)

alright *adv* all right USAGE Alright is very common now, but some people think **all right** is better English.

Alsatian also **German Shepherd dog**— *n* a large wolflike dog often used by police or to guard property

also *adv* as well; too: *I also bought a present*

also-ran *n* a horse that ran in a race but was not one of the first 3 at the end

altar *n* **1** a table or raised level surface on which things are offered to a god **2** (in the Christian service of communion) the table on which the bread and wine are blessed

altarpiece *n* a painting or other work of art behind an altar

alter *v* **1** to make or become different: *This shirt must be altered* **2** *polite* to castrate — ~**able** *adj*

alteration *n* **1** the act of making or becoming different **2** a change; something changed

altercation *n esp. written* **1** noisy disagreement **2** a noisy disagreement

alter ego *n* **alter egos** *Latin, literature* a very close and trusted friend

alternate¹ adj **1** (of 2 things) happening by turns: *a week of alternate rain and sunshine* **2** one of every 2; every second: *He works on alternate days* **3** (esp. of leaves on a stem) growing first on one side of the stem and then on the other △ ALTERNATIVE — ~ly adv

alternate² v **-nated, -nating** to follow or cause to follow by turns — **-nation** n

alternate³ technical (of an angle) occuring on opposite sides of a line at its intersections with two other lines

alternating current n flow or supply of electricity that changes direction with regularity, esp. at a rapid rate —compare DIRECT CURRENT

alternative¹ adj (of 2 things) that may be used, had, done, etc., instead of another; other △ ALTERNATE — ~ly adv

alternative² n something that may be taken or chosen instead of one or several others: *There are several alternatives to your plan* USAGE Some writers do not like such sentences as *We have several alternatives to choose from* because they think there should be only 2 **alternatives**; but the word is quite often used like this.

alternator n a dynamo for producing alternating current

although conj in spite of the fact that; though

altimeter n an aneroid barometer used, esp. in an aircraft, for recording height

altitude n **1** height **2** a high place or area **3** the distance of the sun, the moon, a star, etc., above the horizon, measured as an angle — compare ELEVATION

alto¹ n **-tos** **1** also **countertenor**— (a man with or a musical part for a man with) a high singing voice, between soprano and tenor **2** also **contralto**— (a woman with or a musical part for a woman with) a low singing voice, between soprano and tenor **3** (of a family of instruments) the instrument which plays notes in the area between soprano and tenor

alto² adj of, for, concerning, or having the range or part of an alto

altogether¹ adv **1** completely: *not altogether bad* **2** considering all things

altogether² n **in the altogether** humour nude

altruism n unselfish consideration of the needs of others before one's own —compare EGOISM — **altruist** n — **-istic** adj — **-istically** adv

alum n a chemical substance used in medicine and preparing leather

aluminium n a light, easily shaped, silver-white metal that is an element

always adv **1** at all times; at each time: *She always looks cheerful* **2** for ever

am — short form' **m** -1st person sing. pres. tense of BE

AM amplitude modulation; a system of broadcasting in which the amplitude of the radio wave varies in accordance with the signal being transmitted: *an AM radio* —compare FM

a.m. adv ante meridiem; before midday: *8 a.m. (train) from London* —opposite **p.m.**

amalgam n technical a mixture of metals, one of which is mercury

amalgamate v **-ated, -ating** **1** (of businesses, groups, etc.) to join or unite **2** to mix; combine — **-ation** n

amass v to gather or collect (money, goods, power, etc.) in great amounts

amateur¹ n **1** a person who paints pictures, performs plays, takes part in sports, etc., for enjoyment and without being paid for it —compare PROFESSIONAL, DILETTANTE **2** a person without experience or skill in a particular art, sport, etc.

amateur² adj **1** of, by, or with amateurs: *amateur football* **2** being an amateur or amateurs: *an amateur actor* **3** lacking skill: *His performance was amateur*

amateurish adj offensive lacking skill; not good — ~ly adv — ~ness n

amatory adj literature & poetic concerning or expressing love, esp. sexual love: *an amatory look*

amaze v **amazed, amazing** to fill with great surprise: *Your knowledge amazes me* — ~ment n

amazing adj causing great surprise or wonder because of quantity or quality — ~ly adv

amazon n a strong powerful woman, esp. one who is tall and likes sports — ~ian adj

ambassador fem. **ambassadress**— n a minister of high rank representing his country in another country — ~ship n — ~ial adj

amber n **1** a yellowish brown hard clear substance used for jewels, ornaments, etc. **2** its colour

ambergris n a waxy substance produced in the intestines of a whale, used in the production of perfumes

ambidextrous adj able to use either hand with equal skill — ~ly adv

ambience n literature the character, quality, etc., of a place: *The restaurant has a pleasant ambience*

ambiguous adj **1** able to be understood in more than one way; of unclear meaning: *an ambiguous reply* **2** uncertain; unclear △ AMBIVALENT — **-guity** n — ~ly adv — ~ness n

ambition n **1** strong desire for success, power, riches, etc.: *That politician is full of ambition* **2** that which is desired in this way: *A big house is my ambition*

ambitious adj **1** having a strong desire for success, power, riches, etc. **2** showing or demanding a strong desire for success, great effort, great skill, etc.: *an ambitious attempt* — ~ly adv — ~ness n

ambivalent adj having opposing feelings towards, or opinions about △ AMBIGUOUS — **-lence** n — ~ly adv

amble¹ v **ambled, ambling** to walk at an easy gentle rate

amble² *n esp. spoken* a walk at an easy gentle rate

ambrosia *n* (in Ancient Greek and Roman literature) the food of gods —compare NECTAR

ambulance *n* a motor vehicle for carrying sick or wounded people, esp. to hospital

ambush¹ *v* to attack from a place where one has hidden and waited

ambush² *n* **1** a surprise attack from a place of hiding **2** the place where the attackers hide

ameliorate *v* **-rated, -rating** *esp. written* to cause to become better or less bad —compare ALLEVIATE — **-ration** *n*

amen *interj* (used at the end of a prayer or hymn) may this become true; so be it

amenable *adj* able to be guided or influenced (by): *amenable to reason*

amend *v* to make changes in the words of (a rule or law) △ EMEND

amendment *n* **1** the act of improving or changing: *Your plan needs some amendment* **2** a change made in or suggested for a law, statement, etc.

amends *n* something done to repair or pay for some unkindness, damage, etc.: *Make amends for your rudeness*

amenity *n* **-ties** **1** a thing or condition in a hotel, place, etc., that one can enjoy and which makes life pleasant **2** pleasantness

American *adj, n* (a person) belonging to America, esp. the United States of America ☞ MAP

American football *n* an American game like rugby played by 2 teams of 11 players each

American Indian also **Amerindian**— *n* one of the original people of America

Americanism *n* a word, phrase, speech sound, etc., of English as spoken in America

amethyst *n* a type of purple quartz, used in jewellery

amiable *adj* of a pleasant nature; friendly △ AMIABLE — **-bility** *n* — **-bly** *adv*

amicable *adj* as suitable between friends; peaceful: *We reached an amicable agreement* — △AMIABLE **-bility** *n* — **-bly** *adv*

amid also **amidst**— *prep literature* in the middle of; among

amidships *adv* technical in the middle of the ship

amino acid *n* any of several substances that are elementary building blocks of proteins

amiss¹ *adv* in a bad way; wrongly: *You judge his character amiss*

amiss² *adj* **1** wrong; imperfect: *Is something amiss?* **2** out of place; (a) bad (idea)

amity *n esp. written* friendship

ammeter *n* an instrument for measuring electric current in amperes ☞ ELECTRICITY

ammonia *n* a strong gas with a sharp smell, used in explosives, refrigerators, and fertilizers

ammonite *n* the fossil of a type of sea animal that no longer exists

ammunition *n* bullets, bombs, explosives, etc., esp. things fired from a weapon

amnesia *n* loss of memory, either in part or completely

amnesty *n* **-ties** a general act of forgiveness, esp. by a state to those guilty of political crimes against it

amoeba *n* **-bas** or **-bae** a very small living creature consisting of only one cell — **-bic** *adj*

amok also **amuck**— *adv* **run amok** to go or run wild, esp. with a desire to kill

among also **amongst**— *prep* **1** in the middle of; surrounded by: *I live among the mountains* —see BETWEEN (USAGE) **2** in a group consisting of: *She is among my most welcome visitors*

amoral *adj* having no understanding of right and wrong: *Young children are amoral* —compare IMMORAL — **~ity** *n*

amorous *adj* of, concerning, expressing, or easily moved to love, esp. sexual love — **~ly** *adv* — **~ness** *n*

amorphous *adj* having no fixed form or shape — **~ly** *adv* — **~ness** *n*

amount *n* a quantity or sum: *Large amounts of money* USAGE With plural nouns it is better to use number: *the number of mistakes | the amount of money.*

amount to *v prep* to be equal to: *Your words amount to a refusal*

amour *n becoming rare* a sexual relationship, esp. one that is secret

amp *n technical or esp. spoken* **1** an ampere **2** an amplifier

ampere, ampère *n* (a standard measure of the flow of electric current past a point, equal to) the current which flows when a voltage of one volt is applied to a resistance of one ohm —compare VOLT

ampersand *n* the sign & for the word 'and'

amphibian *n* **1** an animal (such as a frog) that is able to live both on land and in water ☞ EVOLUTION **2** a motor vehicle that can travel both on land and in water

amphibious *adj* able to live or move both on land and in water

amphitheatre *n* a building with rows of seats on a slope surrounding a lower central usu. circular area, esp. one built in ancient Rome used for competitions and theatre performances

amphora *n* **-ras** or **-rae** a narrow clay pot with 2 handles used, esp. in ancient Rome and Greece, for storing wine, oil, etc.

ample *adj* **1** enough or more than is necessary: *We have ample money* **2** with plenty of space; large: *an ample garden* — **-ply** *adv*

amplifier *n* an instrument, as used in radios and record players, that makes electrical current or power stronger

amplify *v* **-fied, -fying** **1** to explain in greater detail **2** to increase the power of (something, esp. sound coming through electrical instruments) **3** to make larger or greater — **-fication** *n*

amplitude *n* **1** largeness of space **2** large

amount; fullness **3** *technical* the distance between the middle and the top (or bottom) of a wave (such as a sound wave)

ampoule also **ampule**— *n* a small usu. glass container for medicine that is to be injected

amputate *v* **-tated, -tating** to remove (part of the body) by cutting off, esp. for medical reasons: *to amputate a leg* —compare EXCISE — **-tation** *n*

amputee *n* a person who has had an arm or leg amputated

amuck *adv* amok

amulet *n* an object worn in the belief that it will protect one against evil, disease, etc.

amuse *v* **amused, amusing** **1** to satisfy or excite the sense of humour: *Your story amuses me* **2** to cause to spend time in a pleasant manner: *She amused the child for hours*

amusement *n* **1** the state of being amused; enjoyment **2** something that causes one's time to pass in an enjoyable way: *Big cities have many amusements*

amusement arcade *n* a room full of machines which spin numbers or with which one can play games after putting coins into them

amylase *n* *technical* a chemical substance (ENZYME) (as in saliva) that breaks down starch

an *indef article* (the form of the indefinite article used before a word that starts with a vowel sound) : *an apple | an hour*

anachronism *n* **1** the mistake of placing something in the wrong period of time: *It is an anachronism to say 'Julius Caesar looked at his watch'* **2** a person or thing that is or appears to be in the wrong period of time — **-nistic** *adj* — **-nistically** *adv*

anaconda *n* a large non-poisonous South American snake that kills creatures for food by crushing them

anaemia *n* the unhealthy condition of not having the proper number of red cells in the blood

anaemic *adj* suffering from anaemia

anaerobic *adj* *technical* not using or needing oxygen: *Many bacteria are anaerobic* —compare AEROBIC — **~ally** *adv*

anaesthesia *n* **1** the state of being unable to feel pain, heat, etc., esp. as produced by doctors, so that treatment can be given painlessly **2** the act or action of producing this state

anaesthetic *n* a substance that produces an inability to feel pain, heat, etc., either in a limited area (**local anaesthetic**) or in the whole body, together with unconsciousness (**general anaesthetic**) — **anaesthetic** *adj*

anaesthetist *n* a doctor who gives an anaesthetic to a patient before he is treated by another doctor

anaesthetize, -ise *v* **-ized, -izing** to make unable to feel pain, with or without producing unconsciousness

anagram *n* a word or phrase made into another

by changing the order of the letters: *'Silent' is an anagram of 'listen'*

anal *adj* of, concerning, or near the anus

analgesia *n* *technical* the condition of being unable to feel pain even though conscious

analgesic *n, adj* a substance causing analgesia

analogue *n* *esp. written* something that is like or that may be compared with something else

analogue computer *n* a computer that works by measuring rather than by counting — compare DIGITAL COMPUTER

analogy *n* **-gies** **1** a degree of likeness or sameness: *There is an analogy between the way water moves in waves and the way light travels* **2** the act of explaining by comparing with another thing that has a certain likeness — **-gous** *adj*

analyse *v* **-lysed, -lysing** **1** to examine carefully (esp. by dividing into parts) in order to find out about —compare SYNTHESIZE **2** *esp. US* to psychoanalyse

analysis *n* **-ses** **1** a separation of a substance into parts: *The analysis of the food showed the presence of poison* —compare SYNTHESIS **2** an examination of something together with thoughts and judgments about it **3** *esp. US* psychoanalysis — **-lytic, -lytical** *adj* — **-lytically** *adv*

analyst *n* **1** a person who makes an analysis, esp. of chemical materials **2** *esp. US* a psychoanalyst

anarchism *n* the political belief that society should have no government, laws, police, etc., but should be a free association of all its members — **-chist** *n* — **-chistic** *adj* — **-chistically** *adv*

anarchy *n* **1** absence of government or control **2** lawlessness and social and political disorder caused by this **3** absence of order — **-chic, -chical** *adj* — **-chically** *adv*

anatomy *n* **-mies** **1** the scientific study of the bodies and parts of animals **2** the body or parts of a person or animal **3** the dissection of a body or part of an animal to study the way it is built ⊚ — **-ist** *n* — **-ical** *adj* — **-ically** *adv*

ancestor *fem.* **ancestress**— *n* a person, esp. one living a long time ago, from whom another is descended — **-tral** *adj*

ancestry *n* **-tries** the ancestors of a person's family considered as a group or as a continuous line

anchor[1] *n* **1** a piece of heavy metal, usu. a hook with 2 arms, for lowering into the water to keep a ship from moving **2** a person or thing that provides strong support and a feeling of safety **3** **weigh anchor** to pull up the anchor and move off

anchor[2] *v* **1** to stop sailing and lower an anchor to keep a ship from moving **2** to fix or be fixed firmly

anchorage *n* **1** a place where ships may anchor **2** something to (or the means by) which something else is fixed

anchorite *fem.* **anchoress**— *n* a hermit

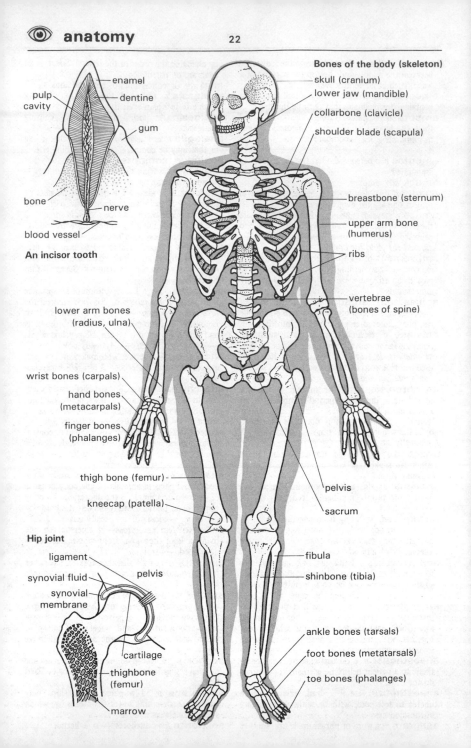

Muscles

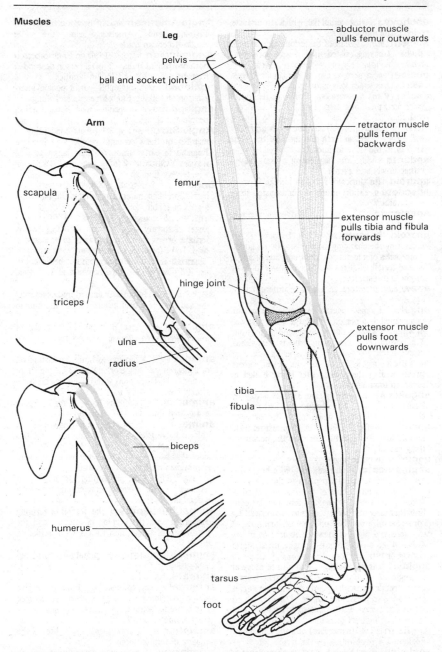

Leg

abductor muscle
pulls femur outwards

pelvis

ball and socket joint

retractor muscle
pulls femur
backwards

Arm

femur

scapula

extensor muscle
pulls tibia and fibula
forwards

triceps

hinge joint

extensor muscle
pulls foot
downwards

ulna

radius

biceps

tibia

fibula

humerus

tarsus

foot

Muscles in the limbs often work in pairs - for example the triceps
contracts to straighten the arm and the biceps contracts to bend (flex) it.

anchovy n -vies a small fish with a strong taste, often made into a paste

ancient¹ adj 1 in or of times long ago: *ancient Rome* 2 having existed since a very early time 3 *often humour* very old —see OLD (USAGE)

ancient² n a person, esp. a Roman or Greek, who lived in times long ago

ancillary adj, n -ries *esp. written or technical* (a person) providing help or additional service

and conj 1 as well as; too 2 (used to express result or explanation): *Water the seeds and they will grow* 3 **and so forth** and more of the same kind or in the same manner

andante n, adj, adv (a piece of music) played rather slowly and evenly

android (in stories) a robot in human form

anecdote n a short interesting or amusing story — -dotal adj

anemone n 1 a plant that produces white, red, or blue flowers 2 SEA ANEMONE

aneroid barometer n a barometer for measuring the changing air pressure by its action on the sides of a metal container emptied of air. It is used to tell what the weather is going to be or height above sea level

anew adv *literature* in a new or different way; again

angel n 1 a messenger and servant of God, usu. represented as a person with large wings dressed in white 2 a spirit that watches and guards one 3 a person, esp. a woman, who is very kind, beautiful, etc. — ~ic adj — ~ically adv

angelica n a plant or its clear green sweet-smelling stem used, after being boiled in sugar, to ornament cakes

angelus n 1 a prayer said 3 times a day by Roman Catholics 2 the sound of a bell rung in churches to tell people when to say this prayer

anger¹ n a fierce feeling of displeasure, usu. leading to a desire to hurt or stop the person or thing causing it

anger² v to make angry

angina pectoris also **angina**— n a heart disease causing sudden sharp pains in the chest

angle¹ n 1 an amount of turning, measured in degrees, and shown in diagrams by two straight lines that meet at a point ☞ TRIGONOMETRY 2 a corner, as of a building or piece of furniture 3 esp. *spoken* a point of view: *Look at it from my angle* 4 **at an angle** not upright or straight; sloping or turning away

angle² v angled, angling 1 to turn or move at an angle 2 *often offensive* to represent (something) from a particular point of view: *She angles her reports to please her editor*

angle for v prep *often offensive* to try to get esp. by tricks or indirect questions

Anglican n, adj (a member) of a the Church of England ☞ WORSHIP — ~ism n

anglicism n an English word or phrase that is in common use in another language

angling n the sport of catching fish with a hook and line — -gler n

Anglo-American adj of or concerning both England and America, esp. the US: *Anglo-American trade*

Anglo-Indian adj, n 1 (of) an English person born or living in India 2 (of) a person descended from both English and Indian families

anglophile also **anglophil**— n a person interested in and liking English people and things

anglophobe n a person who hates English people and things

Anglo-Saxon adj, n 1 (of or concerning) a member of the Germanic people who lived in England in early times, or their language ☞ HISTORY, LANGUAGE 2 (of or concerning) a person who is very English

angora n 1 a goat, rabbit, or cat with long hair 2 woollen material made from this hair from a goat or rabbit

angry adj **angrier, angriest** 1 filled with anger 2 stormy — **angrily** adv USAGE **Annoy, irritate,** or **vex** are not as strong as **to be angry** or **mad.** To be **furious** or in a **rage** are even stronger. **Aggravate** is used like **annoy,** but it is better not to use it if possible —compa PROVOKE, RILE, BOTHER, IRK

angst n *German* anxiety caused by considering the sad state of world affairs and/or the human condition

anguish n very great pain and suffering, esp. of mind: *She was in anguish over her missing child* — ~ed adj

angular adj 1 having, forming, consisting of, or concerning an angle or angles 2 having sharp corners 3 (of a person) with the bones able to be clearly seen — ~ity n

animadvert v *pompous* to speak about, esp. in a way that finds fault — -version n

animal¹ n 1 a living creature having senses and able to move itself when it wants to 2 all this group except human beings 3 a person considered as lacking a mind and behaving like a wild non-human creature 4 a mammal

animal² adj 1 of, concerning, or made from animals 2 usu. *offensive* concerning the body: *animal desires*

animal husbandry n the branch of farming concerned with the keeping of animals and the production of animal materials, such as milk and meat

animal kingdom n all animal life considered as a group

animate¹ adj alive

animate² v -mated, -mating 1 to bring or give life or excitement to: *Laughter animated his face* 2 to cause to become active; interest: *His excitement animated us all*

animation n 1 excitement; spirit; life 2 the making of film cartoons

animism n 1 a religion according to which natural objects and all living things have souls 2 the belief that the soul exists apart from the body — animist n, adj

animosity n -ties powerful, often active, hatred

aniseed n the strong-tasting seeds of the anise plant, used esp. in alcoholic drinks such as anis

ankle n 1 the joint between the foot and the leg 2 the thin part of the leg just above the foot

annals n 1 a record of events, discoveries, etc., produced every year, esp. by learned societies 2 historical records in general

anneal v to make (metal, glass, etc.) hard by cooling slowly after heating until soft

annex v 1 to join or add to a greater thing 2 to take control and possession of (land, a small country, etc.) esp. by force — ~ation n

annexe, annex n a building joined or added to a larger one

annihilate v -lated, -lating to destroy completely: We annihilated the enemy — -lation n

anniversary n -ries 1 a day which is an exact year or number of years after something has happened: the anniversary of the day I met you —compare BIRTHDAY 2 a ceremony, feast, etc., held on this day

Anno Domini esp. written AD

annotate v -tated, -tating to add short notes to (a book) to explain certain parts — -tation n

announce v announced, announcing 1 to make known publicly or clearly: They announced the date of their wedding 2 to state in a loud voice (the name of a person or thing on arrival, as of people at a party or aircraft at an airport) 3 to read (news) or introduce (a person or act) on the radio, television, etc. — ~r n

announcement n a statement saying what has happened or what will happen

annoy v annoyed, annoying to cause trouble; make a little angry, esp. by repeated acts: These flies are annoying me — ~ance n

annual¹ adj (happening, appearing, etc.) every year or once a year, esp. about the same date — ~ly adv

annual² n 1 a plant that lives for only one year or season 2 a publication produced once a year having the same title but containing different items

annuity n -ties 1 a fixed sum of money paid each year to a person for a stated period or until death 2 a type of insurance which provides a yearly income from a certain age until death

annul v -ll- technical to cause (a marriage, agreement, law, etc.) to cease to exist — annulment n

annular adj esp. written shaped like a ring

annunciation n the angel Gabriel's words to the Virgin Mary telling her that she was to give birth to Christ

anode n technical the part of a battery which collects electrons, often a rod or wire shown as (+) —compare CATHODE

anoint v to put oil on (a person), esp. in a religious ceremony — ~ment n

anomalous adj esp. written or technical different from what is the usual type: in an anomalous position — ~ly adv

anomaly n -lies esp. written 1 unusual irregularity 2 a person or thing that is different from the usual type

anon¹ adv old use or poetic soon

anon² abbrev. for: anonymous

anonymous adj 1 with name unknown 2 without the writer's name: an anonymous letter — -mity n — ~ly adv

anorak n a short coat which has a hood to keep out wind and rain —compare PARKA

anorexia also anorexia nervosa— n technical a dangerous condition in which there no desire to eat

another¹ adj 1 a second: another piece of cake 2 different from the first or other

another² pron 1 one more of the same sort: She has taken another of my books 2 a person other than oneself: Is it brave to die for another? —see EACH OTHER (USAGE)

answer¹ n 1 a reply, as to a question or polite greeting 2 a reply in the form of action: In answer to my shouts people ran to help 3 a reply to an argument or charge 4 something which is discovered as a result esp. of thinking, using figures, etc.: Having all the figures she found the answer quickly: it was 279 5 a piece of usu. written work to show knowledge or ability, as in an examination

answer² v 1 to give an answer (to) 2 to do something as a reply (to): I answered with a smile 3 to attend or act in reply to (a sign, such as a telephone ringing, a whistle, etc.): I telephoned this afternoon, but nobody answered 4 to act or move in reply; obey: The dog answers to his name 5 to be satisfactory for: This tool will answer our needs 6 to be as described in; to fit: He answers the description you gave 7 to reply to (a charge or argument) USAGE Answer and reply are the usual verbs for answering questions; respond is rarer but has the same meaning. Retort or (rare) rejoin are angrier: 'Why should I?' she retorted.

answerable adj 1 able to be answered 2 responsible: I shall be answerable for what he does 3 having to explain or defend one's actions: I am answerable to the government for my actions — -bly adv

answer for v prep 1 to be or become responsible for: to answer to for his safety 2 to promise that (something) is good: I will answer for the truth of what he has said 3 to act, pay, or suffer as a result of: You will have to answer for your behaviour

ant n a small insect living on the ground in well-ordered groups and famous for hard work ☞ INSECT

antacid n, adj (a medicine) preventing an acid condition, esp. in the stomach

antagonism n (an example of) active opposition or hatred between people or groups

antagonist n a person or thing opposed to

ant

another, esp. actively △ PROTAGONIST — ~ic adj — ~ically adv

antagonize v **-nized, -nizing** to cause to become an enemy

antarctic adj, n (of or concerning) the most southern part of the world —compare ARCTIC

Antarctic Circle n an imaginary line of latitude at a certain distance from the south pole, below which line there is no darkness for half the year and little light for the other half —compare ARCTIC CIRCLE, ☞ GLOBE

anteater n any of several animals that eat ants, esp. one with a long sticky tongue ☞ MAMMAL

antecedence n esp. written the act or state of going or being before, esp. in time — **-dent** adj

antecedent n technical the word, phrase, or sentence that comes before, and is represented by, a pronoun

antechamber also **anteroom**— n a small room leading to a larger one

antedate v **-dated, -dating** 1 to write too early a date on (a letter, paper, etc.) 2 to be earlier in history than —opposite **postdate**

antediluvian adj humour old-fashioned; very old

antelope n any of various types of graceful grass-eating animals like deer, having horns and able to run very fast

ante meridiem adv Latin, rare A.M.

antenatal adj technical existing or happening before birth: An **antenatal** clinic is a place where pregnant women go for medical examinations

antenna n **-nae** a long thin sensitive hairlike organ existing, esp. in pairs, on the heads of some insects and animals that live in shells, and used for feeling ☞ INSECT

anterior adj 1 earlier in time 2 usu. technical nearer the front —opposite **posterior**

anthem n 1 a religious song to be sung in a church, esp. by a choir 2 literature any ceremonial song of praise —see also NATIONAL ANTHEM

anther n the male part of a flower which contains the pollen that makes the female part of a flower bear fruit or seeds ☞ FLOWER

anthill n a raised mass of earth, pieces of wood, etc., in which ants live

anthology n **-gies** a collection of poems, or of other writings, often on the same subject, chosen from different books or writers

anthracite n a very hard kind of coal that burns slowly and without smoke —opposite **bituminous coal**

anthrax n a serious disease which attacks cattle, sheep, etc., and is sometimes caught from them by human beings

anthropoid adj technical or offensive (of an animal) like a man or (of a person) like an ape ☞ PRIMATE

anthropology n the scientific study of the nature of man, including the development of his body, mind, and society —compare ETHNOLOGY — **-gist** n — **-gical** adj — **-gically** adv

anthropomorphism n the idea that gods, animals, or objects have human forms or qualities — **-phic** adj

antiaircraft n, adj (gunfire) against enemy aircraft

antibiotic n, adj (a medical substance, such as penicillin) produced by living things and able to stop the growth of, or destroy, harmful bacteria that have entered the body — ~ally adv

antibody n **-ies** a substance which is produced by the body in response to a specific harmful substance (ANTIGEN) associated with a disease and which helps to fight against the disease

antic adj literature (of behaviour or movement of the body) strange, awkward, or amusing —see also ANTICS

anticipate v **-pated, -pating** 1 sometimes considered bad usage to expect: We are not anticipating trouble 2 to do something before: We anticipated our competitors by buying the land 3 to see (what will happen) and act as necessary, often to stop someone doing something: We anticipated where they would try to cross 4 to provide for the probability of (something) happening 5 to make use of, deal with, or consider before the right or proper time: Do not anticipate your earnings by spending too much — **-pation** n

anticipatory adj 1 that anticipates 2 done or happening in advance or too soon

anticlimax n 1 something unexciting coming after something exciting: To be back in the office after a holiday is an anticlimax 2 often humour a sudden change from something noble, serious, exciting, etc., to something foolish, unimportant, or uninteresting

anticlockwise adj, adv in the opposite direction to the hands of a clock -opposite **clockwise**

antics n strange or unusual behaviour, esp. with odd, amusing, or foolish movements of the body

anticyclone n technical a mass of air that is heavy, causing settled weather, either hot or cold, in the area over which it moves

antidote n a substance to stop a poison working, or to prevent the effects of a disease

antifreeze n a chemical substance put in water to stop it from freezing in very cold weather, esp. in a car radiator

antigen n a substance which, when introduced into the body, causes the formation in the blood of another substance (ANTIBODY) that fights against disease

antihero n **-es** the most important character, esp. in modern literature, when represented as no braver, stronger, or cleverer than ordinary people —compare HERO, VILLAIN

antiknock n any of several chemical substances added to petrol to make car engines run smoothly

antilogarithm also (esp. spoken) **antilog**— n the number represented by a logarithm ☞ MATHEMATICS

antimacassar n a piece of ornamental cloth

put on the back of a chair to protect it from marks left by hair oil

antimatter *n* technical matter made of elementary particles opposite to the ordinary ones

antimony *n* a silver-white metal that is an element, used esp. in the production of other metals

antipathy *n* -thies a fixed unconquerable dislike or hatred — -thetic *adj*

antipersonnel *adj* (of bombs) intended to hurt people, not destroy property, by exploding into small pieces

antiperspirant *n* a man-made chemical substance that helps to stop the skin sweating — compare DEODORANT

Antipodes *n* literature or humour Australia (and New Zealand)

antiquarian *adj* of or concerning things that are very old or people who study, collect, or sell such things — **antiquarian** *n*

antiquary *n* -ries an antiquarian

antiquated *adj* old and not suited to present needs or conditions —see OLD (USAGE)

antique[1] *adj* esp. written or literature old and therefore valuable —see OLD (USAGE)

antique[2] *n* a piece of old furniture, jewellery, etc., that is becoming rare and valuable

antiquity *n* -ties 1 great age: *The nobleman was proud of his family's antiquity* 2 the ancient world, esp. of Rome or Greece 3 a building, work of art, etc., remaining from ancient times

antirrhinum *n* a snapdragon

anti-Semitism *n* hatred of Jews — **-Semitic** *adj* — **-Semite** *n*

antiseptic *n, adj* (a chemical substance) able to prevent flesh, blood, etc., from developing disease, esp. by killing bacteria

antisocial *adj* 1 that causes damage to public property or the way in which people live together peacefully: *Playing music too loudly is antisocial* 2 opposed to an orderly society or way of life 3 selfish 4 not liking to mix with other people

antithesis *n* -ses 1 complete difference; contrast 2 the direct opposite: *The antithesis of death is life* 3 the putting together in speech or writing, of 2 opposite ideas

antler *n* either of the pair of branched horns of a stag

antonym *n* a word opposite in meaning to another word: *'Pain' is the antonym of 'pleasure'* —opposite **synonym**

anus *n* technical the hole through which solid food waste leaves the bowels —compare COLON, RECTUM

anvil *n* 1 a shaped iron block on which hot metals are hammered to the shape wanted 2 a small bone inside the ear

anxiety *n* -ties 1 fear or an example of this, esp. as caused by uncertainty 2 a cause of this 3 *esp. spoken* a strong wish to do something: *anxiety to please*

anxious *adj* 1 feeling anxiety; fearful: *He was anxious for his safety* 2 causing anxiety or worry

3 having a strong wish to do something; eager — **~ly** *adv*

any[1] *adj, pron* 1 one or some of whatever kind: *Choose any you like* 2 one, some, or all, of whatever quantity; an unstated number or amount: *Have you got any money?* 3 none at all: *I haven't any money* 4 of the usual or stated kind: *This isn't any ordinary fish* 5 the smallest or least possible amount or degree of: *It isn't any use* 6 no matter which, what, where, how, etc.: *Any room will do* 7 esp. spoken a, an, or one: *This car hasn't any engine!* 8 as much as possible: *He will need any help he can get* 9 **in any case** also **at any rate**— whatever may happen 10 unlimited or unmeasured in amount, number, etc.: *I have any number of things I must do today* —see EITHER (USAGE)

any[2] *adv* in any degree; at all: *Do you feel any better?*

anybody also **anyone**— *pron* 1 any person 2 a person of importance: *If you want to be anybody you must work hard* 3 **anybody's guess** esp. spoken a matter of uncertainty —see EVERYBODY (USAGE)

anyhow *adv* esp. spoken 1 without any regular order; in a careless manner: *His clothes were thrown down just anyhow* 2 in any case 3 (used to show a change of subject): *John's a good friend of mine. Well anyhow, I left the next morning*

anyroad *adv* bad usage anyway

anything[1] *pron* 1 any one thing; something: *Is there anything in that box?* 2 no matter what: *Anything will do to keep the door open* 3 a thing of any kind, esp. something important or serious: *I was cut but it wasn't anything* 4 anything but not at all; far from 5 **as easy/fast/strong, etc., as anything** sl very easy/fast/strong, etc. 6 **if anything** if there is any difference 7 **like anything** sl (used to add force to a verb): *We ran like anything* 8 **or anything** (suggests that there are other possibilities): *If he wants to call me or anything, I'll be here*

anything[2] *adv* at all: *Is this box anything like what you need?*

anyway *adv* esp. spoken in any case: *I shall go and see him anyway*

anywhere *adv* 1 (in, at, or to) any place: *Did you go anywhere yesterday?* 2 in, at, or to no matter what place: *Sit anywhere*

aorta *n* the largest artery in the body, taking blood from the heart

apace *adv* literature & old use at a great speed; quickly

apart *adv* 1 separate; away: *The buildings are miles apart* 2 to pieces: *He tore the chicken apart and began to eat* 3 in or into a state of separation, independence, disconnection: *If I see the 2 boys apart I don't know which is which* 4 **apart from** without considering

apartheid *n* the keeping separate of races of different colours, esp. in South Africa

apartment *n* 1 a room, esp. a large or splendid one, or one used by a particular person or group **2** a flat

apathetic *adj* without feeling or interest; lacking desire to act — ~**ally** *adv*

apathy *n* lack of feeling or interest in something or everything; lack of desire or ability to act in any way

ape¹ *n* **1** a large monkey without a tail or with a very short tail (such as a gorilla or chimpanzee) ⎯⇒ PRIMATE, MAMMAL **2** *usu. offensive* a person who copies the behaviour of others

ape² *v* **aped, aping** to copy

aperitif *n* a small alcoholic drink taken before a meal

aperture *n* **1** a hole, crack, or other narrow opening **2** the opening in a camera, telescope, etc., that admits light ⎯⇒ OPTICS

apex *n* **-es** *or* **apices** **1** *technical or esp. written* the top or highest part of anything (e.g. the vertex opposite the base of a triangle) **2** the highest point of power or success

aphelion *n* *technical* the point where the orbit of an object through space is farthest from the sun

aphid also **aphis**— *n* any of various small insects (such as the greenfly) that live on the juices of plants

aphorism *n* a true or wise short saying or principle

aphrodisiac *n, adj* (a medicine, drug, etc.) causing sexual excitement

apiary *n* **-ries** *technical* a place where bees are kept, esp. a place in which there are several hives — **-rist** *n*

apiece *adv* to, for, or from each person or thing; each

apish *adj* *usu. offensive* like an ape, esp. in trying foolishly to behave like others — ~**ly** *adv* — ~**ness** *n*

aplomb *n* power to remain calmly bold in appearance and behaviour in moments of difficulty

apocalypse *n* the showing of hidden things, esp. the telling of what will happen when the world ends

apocalyptic *adj* **1** *often offensive* telling of great misfortunes in the future: *apocalyptic predictions* **2** of or like the end of the world: *apocalyptic scenes of death and destruction* — ~**ally** *adv*

Apocrypha *n* a collection of Jewish and/or early Christian books sometimes, but usu. not, included in the Bible

apocryphal *adj* not regarded as true, certain, or real: *an apocryphal story*

apogee *n* **1** the point at which a body, such as the moon, a planet, or a spacecraft, is farthest from the larger body round which it is revolving — compare PERIGEE **2** the highest point of success

apologetic *adj* **1** expressing sorrow for some fault or wrong **2** as if unwilling to cause trouble: *He spoke in an apologetic voice* — ~**ally** *adv*

apologize, -ise *v* **-gized, -gizing** to express

sorrow, as for a fault or causing pain: *I apologized to her for stepping on her foot*

apology *n* **-gies** **1** a statement expressing sorrow for a fault, causing trouble or pain, etc. **2** a defence or explanation of a belief, idea, etc.: *Shelley's 'Apology for Poetry'* **3** *esp. spoken* a very poor example of something: *This is an apology for a meal* —see EXCUSE (USAGE)

apoplectic *adj* **1** of, concerning, or having apoplexy **2** having a red face and easily made angry — ~**ally** *adv*

apoplexy *n* the loss of the ability to move, feel, think, etc., usu. caused by a blockage or bursting of one of the blood vessels in the brain; stroke

apostle *n* **1** any of the 12 followers of Christ chosen by Him to spread His message to the world **2** any of the early Christians who introduced Christianity to a country, area, etc.

apostolic *adj* **1** of or concerning an apostle, esp. one of the 12 **2** of or concerning the Pope — ~**ally** *adv*

apostrophe *n* the sign (') used in writing **a** to show that one or more letters or figures have been left out of a word or figure (as in *don't* and *'47* for *do not* and *1947*) **b** before or after *s* to show possession (as in *John's hat, ladies' hats, children's hats*)

apothecary *n* **-ries** *old use* a person with a knowledge of chemistry who mixed and sold medicines; pharmacist

appal *v* **-ll-** to shock deeply; fill with fear, hatred, etc.

appalling *adj* **1** causing fear; shocking, terrible **2** *esp. spoken* of very bad quality: *appalling food* — ~**ly** *adv*

apparatus *n* **-tuses** *or* **-tus** **1** a set of instruments, machines, tools, materials, etc., that work together or are needed for a particular purpose **2** a group of parts that work together inside a body: *The breathing apparatus includes the nose, throat, and lungs*

apparel *n* *literature & old use* clothes, esp. of a fine or special sort

apparent *adj* **1** easily seen or understood **2** not necessarily true or real; seeming: *Their apparent grief turned to laughter*

apparently *adv* it seems (that); as it appears

apparition *n* the spirit of a dead person moving in bodily form; ghost

appeal¹ *n* **1** a strong request for help, support, mercy, etc.: *an appeal for forgiveness* **2** power to move the feelings; attraction; interest **3** a call to a higher court to change the decision of a lower court **4** (esp. in sports) a call from a player for a decision from the referee or umpire

appeal² *v* **1** to make a strong request for help, support, etc.; beg: *He appealed for mercy* **2** to please, attract, or interest: *She appeals to me* **3** to call on a higher court to change the decision of a lower court **4** (esp. in sports) to call for a decision, as from the referee

appealing *adj* **1** able to move the feelings:

appealing eyes 2 attractive or interesting — ~**ly** *adv*

appeal to *v prep* 1 to look for support in: *We appealed to his better nature* 2 to point to or show as reason or proof

appear *v* 1 to come into sight: *A car appeared over the hill* 2 to seem; look: *He appears to want to leave* 3 to come to a certain place, esp. in view of the public, as for attention or sale: *His book will be appearing in the shops soon* 4 to be present officially as in a court of law: *He had to appear before the committee* 5 to be found; exist

appearance *n* 1 the act of appearing, as to the eye, mind, or public 2 that which can be seen; look: *He had an unhealthy appearance* 3 **put in/make an appearance (at)** to attend, esp. for a short time only

appearances *n* that which can be seen but which may be false; looks: *Don't judge by appearances*

appease *v* **appeased, appeasing** to make calm or satisfy, esp. by yielding to demands or by giving or doing something: *They appeased him by saying sorry*

appeasement *n* 1 the act of appeasing 2 the political idea that peace can be obtained by giving an enemy what he demands

appellation *n* esp. written a name or title, esp. one that is formal or descriptive

append *v* esp. written to add or join

appendage *n* something added, joined to, or hanging from something, esp. something larger

appendicitis *n* a diseased state of the appendix, usu. causing it to be medically removed

appendix *n* **-dixes** or **dices** 1 also **vermiform appendix**— a short wormlike organ leading off the bowel, and having little or no use ☞ DIGESTION 2 something added, esp. information at the end of a book

appertain to *v prep* esp. written to belong to by right: *the responsibilities appertaining to the chairmanship*

appetite *n* 1 a desire or wish, esp. for food: *Don't spoil your appetite* 2 a desire to satisfy any bodily want: *sexual appetites* 3 **whet someone's appetite** to make someone eager for more of something —see DESIRE (USAGE)

appetizer *n* something small and attractive eaten at the beginning of a meal to increase the desire for food —see also HORS D'OEUVRE

appetizing *adj* causing desire, esp. for food — ~**ly** *adv*

applaud *v* 1 to praise (a play, actor, etc.) esp. by clapping 2 to express strong agreement with

applause *n* loud praise, esp. by clapping

apple *n* 1 a hard round fruit with white juicy flesh and usu. a red, green, or yellow skin that grows on a tree of the rose family 2 **the apple of someone's eye.** *esp spoken* the person or thing most liked

applejack *n* US very strong alcoholic drink made from apples

apple pie *n* **in apple-pie order** *esp.spoken* in perfect arrangement or order

appliance *n* an apparatus, or tool for a particular purpose, often one on a larger machine

applicable *adj* 1 able to have an effect 2 directed towards: *This rule is not applicable to foreigners* 3 suitable for; correct

applicant *n* a person who makes a request, esp. officially and in writing, for something such as a job

application *n* 1 the putting to use 2 the quality of being useful or suitable: *That rule has no application to this case* 3 a request or act of requesting, esp. officially and in writing 4 the putting of one thing onto another, esp. medicine onto the skin 5 careful and continuous attention or effort: *He worked with great application*

applied *adj* (esp. of a science) put to practical use

appliqué¹ *n* (esp. in dress-making) ornamental work of one material sewn or stuck on to a larger surface of another material

appliqué² *v* **-quéd, -quéing** to put (ornamental work) on a larger surface

apply *v* **applied, applying** 1 to request something, esp. officially and in writing 2 to bring or put into use: *Apply as much force as is necessary* 3 to put on or next to: *Apply medicine to his wound* 4 to have an effect; be directly related: *This rule does not apply* 5 to cause to work hard or with careful attention

appoint *v* 1 to put in or choose for a position, job, or purpose: *to appoint a new teacher* 2 to set up or make by choosing: *to appoint a committee* 3 esp. written to arrange; decide: *Let's appoint a day to meet*

appointed *adj* 1 arranged; decided: *an appointed meeting place* 2 chosen for a position or job

appointment *n* 1 the agreement of a time and place for meeting or such a meeting: *He will only see you by appointment* 2 (the choosing of someone for) a position, job, or office: *the appointment of a chairman*

apportion *v* to divide into and give as shares: *apportion the money fairly* — ~**ment** *n*

apposite *adj* esp. written exactly suitable to the present moment, conditions, etc.

apposition *n* a state of affairs in grammar in which one noun phrase is put immediately after a noun phrase which describes the same person or thing

appraisal *n* 1 the act of working out the value, quality, or condition of something 2 a statement of value, quality, or condition

appraise *v* **appraised, appraising** to judge the worth, quality, or condition of — **appraiser** *n*

appreciable *adj* enough to be felt or considered important — **-bly** *adv*

appreciate *v* **-ated, -ating** 1 to be thankful for: *I appreciate your help* 2 to understand and enjoy the good qualities of: *Do you appreciate good wine?* 3 to understand fully (the worth or amount of) **4** to increase in value: *This house has appreciated (in value)*

appreciation *n* **1** judgment, as of the quality, worth, or facts of something **2** a written account of the worth of something **3** grateful feelings: *He showed no appreciation of my advice* **4** rise in value, esp. of land or possessions

appreciative *adj* **1** grateful **2** feeling or showing understanding or admiration — ~ly *adv*

apprehend *v esp. written* to seize (a person who breaks the law); arrest

apprehension *n* **1** anxiety, esp. about the future; fear: *She felt apprehension for her safety* **2** *esp. written* ability to understand

apprehensive *adj* fearful, esp. about the future; worried — ~ly *adv*

apprentice¹ *n* a person who is under an agreement to serve, usu. for low wages, a person skilled in a trade, in order to learn that person's skill

apprentice² *v* **-ticed, -ticing** to make or send as an apprentice: *apprenticed to an electrician*

apprenticeship *n* the condition or period of being an apprentice

apprise *v* **apprised, apprising** *esp. written, becoming rare* to inform: *He was apprised of our arrival*

approach¹ *v* **1** to come near or nearer (to): *We approached the camp* **2** to speak to, esp. about something for the first time: *Did he approach you about a loan?* **3** to begin to consider or deal with (something non-material): *He approached the idea with caution*

approach² *n* **1** the act of approaching: *the approach of winter* **2** a means or way of entering: *All approaches were blocked* **3** a speaking to someone for the first time, esp. in order to begin close personal relations: *making approaches to strangers* **4** a method of doing something: *That player's approach to music is quite new*

approachable *adj* **1** able to be reached **2** *esp. spoken* easy to speak to or deal with

approbation *n esp. written* praise

appropriate¹ *v* **-ated, -ating** **1** to set aside for some purpose: *The government appropriated a large sum for building works* **2** to take for oneself; steal: *The minister appropriated government funds*

appropriate² *adj* correct or suitable: *His bright clothes were not appropriate for a funeral* — ~ly *adv* — ~ness *n*

appropriation *n* **1** the act of setting aside something for a special purpose **2** something, esp. money, set aside for a particular purpose **3** the act of taking something for oneself; theft

approval *n* **1** the act of approving **2** official permission **3 on approval** also *esp. spoken* **on appro**—(of goods) to be returned without payment if not found satisfactory

approve *v* **approved, approving** to agree officially to — **approvingly** *adv*

approved school *n esp. written* COMMUNITY HOME

approve of *v prep* to consider good, right, wise, etc.: *I don't approve of wasting time*

approx *abbrev. for:* approximate(ly)

approximate *adj* nearly correct but not exact — ~ly *adv*

approximate to *v prep esp. spoken* to come near in amount, quality, condition, character, etc.: *What was said approximated to the facts*

approximation *n* **1** a result, calculation, description, drawing, etc., that is not exact but is good enough **2** the state of being or getting near, as to a position, quality, or number

Apr. *abbrev. for:* April

apricot *n* **1** a round soft pleasant-tasting but slightly sour fruit with a furry outside like a peach and a single large stone. It is orange or yellow and red in colour **2** yellowish orange

April *n* the 4th month of the year

April fool *n* a person who has been made fun of by a trick on the morning of April 1st

apron *n* **1** a simple garment worn over the front part of one's clothes to keep them clean while working or doing something dirty or esp. while cooking **2** also **apron stage** — that part of a stage in a theatre in front of the proscenium arch **3** (in an airport) the hard surface on which planes are turned round, loaded, unloaded, etc.

apron strings *n esp. spoken* the strings of an apron regarded as a sign of control, as of a boy or man by his mother or wife (esp. in the phrase **tied to his mother's/wife's apron strings**)

apropos¹ *adv French* **1** very suitably for the time, place, or state of affairs: *He spoke very apropos* **2** by the way

apropos² *adj French* very suitable for the time or conditions

apse *n* the curved or many-sided arched end of a building, esp. the east end of a church ⟳CATHEDRAL

apt *adj* **1** having a tendency to do something; likely: *This shoe is apt to slip* **2** clever and quick to learn and understand: *an apt student* **3** exactly suitable: *an apt remark* — ~ly *adv* — ~ness *n*

aptitude *n* natural ability or skill, esp. in learning —see GENIUS (USAGE)

aqualung *n* an apparatus used under water to provide a diver with air, esp. a container of compressed air carried on the back with a tube to take the air to a mouthpiece or watertight mask

aquamarine *n* **1** a type of clear blue-green precious stone, used in jewellery **2** the colour of this

aquaplane *v* **-planed, -planing** (of cars and car tyres) to slide forwards without control on a wet road, not touching the real road surface at all

aquarium *n* **-iums** *or* **-ia** **1** a glass container for fish and other water animals **2** a building (esp. in a zoo) containing many of these

Aquarius *n* **1 a** the 11th division of the belt of stars, (zodiac) represented by a man pouring water **b** the group of stars (constellation) formerly in this division **2** a person born under this sign ⫸ZODIAC

aquatic *adj* **1** living in or on water: *aquatic plants* **2** happening in or on water: *aquatic sports* — ~**ally** *adv*

aqueduct *n* a pipe, bridge, or canal, that carries a water supply, esp. one higher than the land around it ⫸BRIDGE

aqueous *adj technical* of, like, containing, or in water — ~**ly** *adv*

aquiline *adj* of or like an eagle: *An aquiline nose is thin and curves like an eagle's beak*

Arab *n* **1** a person from a country where Arabic is spoken, esp. North Africa or the Arabian Peninsula **2** a type of fast graceful horse — ~**ian** *adj*

arabesque *n* **1** a fancy ornamental pattern of twisted shapes of flowers, leaves, fruits, etc. **2** a flowing ornamental line, as in writing **3** a position in ballet

Arabic *adj, n* (of or concerning) the Semitic language or writing of the Arabs

Arabic numeral *n* any of the signs commonly used for numbers (such as 1, 2, 3, 4, etc.) — compare ROMAN NUMERAL

arable *adj* (of land) suitable or used for growing crops — **arable** *n*

arachnid *n* **-nids** *or* **-nidae** the class of insect-like animals with 8 legs that includes spiders and scorpions

arbiter *n* a person or group that has complete control or great influence over actions, decisions, etc.: *Beau Brummel was once the arbiter of fashion* ⚠ ARBITRATOR

arbitrary *adj* **1** of power that is uncontrolled and used without considering the wishes of others: *The arbitrary decisions of the factory owners angered the workers* **2** *often offensive* decided by or based on personal opinion or chance rather than reason: *My choice was quite arbitrary* — **-rily** *adv* — **-riness** *n*

arbitrate *v* **-trated, -trating** to act as a judge in (an argument), esp. at the request of both sides — **-trator** *n* — **-tration** *n*

arboreal *adj technical* of, concerned with, or living in trees

arboretum *n* **-tums** *or* **-ta** a garden of trees, esp. one for show or scientific study

arbour *n* a sheltered place, esp. with a seat, in a garden, usu. made by training trees or bushes into an arch

arc¹ *n* **1** part of a curve: *An arc of 110° is the part of a circle subtended by an angle of 110° at the centre* ⫸MATHEMATICS **2** a very powerful flow of electricity through the air or gas between 2 points, as in an **arc lamp** or arc welding

arc² *v* **arced** *or* **arcked; arcing** *or* **arcking** **1** to make or follow a curved course **2** (of electricity) to make an arc or flash, as at a bad connection

arcade *n* a covered passage, esp. one with an arched roof or with a row of shops on one or both sides

Arcadia *n* an area or scene of simple pleasant country life

arch¹ *n* **1** a curved top sometimes with a central point resting on 2 supports **2** something with this shape, esp. the middle of the bottom of the foot

arch² *v* to make into or form the shape of an arch

arch³ *adj* amused, gay, or intended to attract; coy: *an arch smile* — ~**ly** *adv*

archaeology *n* the study of the buried remains of ancient times, such as houses, pots, tools, and weapons — **-gical** *adj* — **-gically** *adv* — **-gist** *n*

archaic *adj* belonging to the past —see OLD (USAGE) — ~**ally** *adv*

archaism *n* a word or phrase no longer in general use

archangel *n* a chief angel in the Jewish, Christian, and Muslim religions

archbishop *n* a Christian priest in charge of the churches and bishops in a very large area

archdeacon *n* an Anglican priest of high rank who directly serves under a bishop

archduke *n* a prince esp. of the royal family of Austria esp. in former times

archer *n* a person who shoots arrows from a bow, esp. as a sport or (formerly) in war

archery *n* the sport of shooting arrows

archetype *n* a perfectly typical example of something — **-typal** *adj* — **-typical** *adj* — **-typically** *adv*

archipelago *n* **-goes** *or* **-gos** **1** a number of small islands making a group **2** an area of sea containing such a group

architect *n* a person who plans new buildings and sees that they are built properly

architecture *n* **1** the art and science of building, including its planning, making, and ornamentation **2** the style or manner of building, esp. as belonging to a particular country or period of history ⫸PAINTING — **-tural** *adj* — **-turally** *adv*

architrave *n* the part of a classical building that rests just on top of the columns

archives *n* **1** old papers, such as records, reports, lists, and letters of a particular group, family, country, etc., kept esp. for historical interest **2** the place where such papers are stored — **-vist** *n*

archway *n* **-ways** **1** a passage with a roof, esp. one supported on arches **2** an entrance through an arch

arctic *adj* **1** of or concerning the most northern part of the world **2** very cold —compare ANTARCTIC

Arctic *n* the most northern part of the world —opposite Antarctic

Arctic Circle *n* a line of latitude at a certain distance from the North Pole, north of which line there is no darkness for half the year and little light for the other half —compare ANTARCTIC CIRCLE ⫸GLOBE

arc welding n the joining together of pieces of metal by means of an arc of electricity

ardent adj strongly felt; eager — ~ly adv

ardour n strength of feeling

arduous adj needing much effort; difficult — ~ly adv — ~ness n

are¹ short form 're pres. tense of BE a (2nd person sing.): You are my cousin b (1st, 2nd, and 3rd person pl.): We/you/they are friends

are² n a measure of area, equal to 100 square metres

area n 1 a particular space or surface 2 a part of the world 3 the measure of a surface: the area of a rectangle 4 a subject or specialist field of ideas or work

arena n 1 an enclosed area for public shows, sports, etc. 2 a scene or place of activity, esp. of competition

argon n a chemically inactive gas that is an element

argot n French speech spoken and understood by only a small class of people, esp. thieves

arguable adj 1 doubtful in some degree 2 able to be supported with reasons: It is arguable that the criminal is a necessary member of society — -bly adv

argue v argued, arguing 1 to reason strongly in defence of one's opinions 2 literature to show; suggest: The way he spends money argues him to be a rich man 3 to give reasons to prove or try to prove 4 to disagree in words; quarrel

argument n 1 a reason given to support or disprove something: There are many arguments against smoking 2 the use of reason to persuade someone: We must settle this by argument not by fighting 3 a disagreement; quarrel

argumentative adj liking to argue — ~ly adv

aria n a solo in an opera or oratorio

arid adj 1 dry and barren 2 unproductive — ~ity n — ~ly adv

Aries n 1 a the first division of the belt of stars, (ZODIAC) represented by a ram b the group of stars (CONSTELLATION) formerly in this division 2 a person born under this sign ☞ ZODIAC

aright adv literature correctly; properly

arise v arose, arisen 1 to come into being; happen 2 old use to get up; stand up

aristocracy n -cies 1 the people of the highest social class, esp. from noble families 2 the best or most powerful members of any group or class, in any activity 3 government by people of the highest social rank

aristocrat n 1 a member of an aristocracy 2 the finest example of a group or type — ~ic adj — ~ically adv

arithmetic n 1 the science of numbers — compare MATHEMATICS 2 the adding, subtracting, multiplying, etc., of numbers — ~al adj — ~ally adv

arithmetical progression n a sequence of numbers, each number being obtained from the one before by the addition of a fixed number (as in 2, 4, 6, 8, 10)

ark n (in the Bible) a large ship, esp. the one built by Noah to escape the flood

Ark of the Covenant n a chest that represented to the Jews the presence of God and which contained the laws of their religion

arm¹ n 1 either of the 2 upper limbs of a human being or other 2 legged animal 2 something that is shaped like or moves like an arm 3 the part of a garment that covers the arm 4 the part of a chair on which the arm rests 5 **at arm's length** at a safe distance away 6 **with open arms** gladly and eagerly — ~less adj

arm² v 1 to supply with or have weapons or armour 2 to supply what is needed for a purpose

armada n literature a fleet of armed ships

armadillo n -los a small animal of tropical America, covered in bands of bonelike shell

armament n 1 the weapons of an armed force 2 the act of arming a country for war

armature n 1 the moving part of a dynamo in which the electricity is made 2 the part of an electric motor in which the movement is produced 3 an iron bar in an instrument (such as an electric bell) moved by a magnet

armband n a band worn round the arm

armchair n a chair with arms

armed adj 1 carrying or supplied with weapons 2 having what is necessary

armed forces also **armed services, services**— n the military forces of a country

armful n all that a person can hold in one or both arms

armhole n an opening in a garment through which the arm is put

armistice n an agreement made during a war to stop fighting, usu. for a limited period

armour n 1 protective metal covering on fighting vehicles, ships, and aircraft, and as worn by fighting men in former times ◉ 2 vehicles with such covering 3 a protective covering of plants or animals

armoured adj 1 protected by armour 2 having fighting vehicles protected by armour

armoured car n a military vehicle with light armour and usu. with a powerful gun

armourer n 1 a person who makes and repairs weapons and armour 2 a person in charge of weapons

armour plate n specially hardened metal used as armour — **armour-plated** adj

armoury n -ies a place where weapons are stored

armpit n the hollow place under the arm at the shoulder

arms n 1 weapons 2 COAT OF ARMS 3 **bear arms** literature to serve as a soldier 4 **lay down one's arms** to surrender 5 **take up arms** literature a to get ready to use weapons b to become a soldier 6 **under arms** (of soldiers) armed 7 **up in arms** very angry and ready to argue or fight

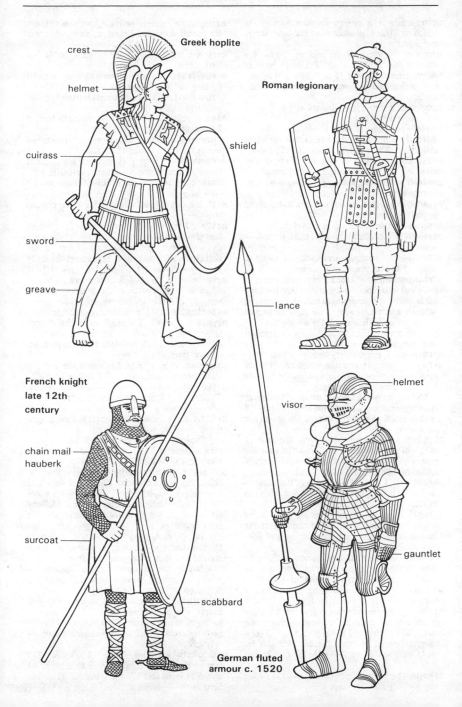

crest

Greek hoplite

helmet

Roman legionary

cuirass

shield

sword

greave

lance

**French knight
late 12th
century**

helmet

visor

chain mail
hauberk

surcoat

gauntlet

scabbard

**German fluted
armour c. 1520**

arms race *n* a struggle between countries in which each tries to produce more and better weapons than the other

army *n* **armies** **1** the military forces of a country that fight on land **2** a large body of people trained for war **3** any large group, esp. one with some purpose: *an army of workers/ants*

aroma *n* a strong usu. pleasant smell — ~**tic** *adj* — ~**tically** *adv*

arose *past tense of* ARISE

around[1] *adv* **1** on all sides; about; in every direction **2** near in time, number, etc.; about

around[2] *prep* **1** on all sides of; all round: surrounding **2** round: *driving around Yorkshire*

arouse *v* **aroused, arousing** to cause to wake or become active

arpeggio *n* **-gios** the notes of a musical chord played one after the other

arr. *abbrev. for:* **a** arrive **b** arrival

arraign *v* to charge or attack in words — ~**ment** *n*

arrange *v* **arranged, arranging** **1** to set in order **2** to plan in advance; prepare

arrangement *n* **1** the act of putting into or of being put into order **2** something that has been put in order: **3** something arranged, planned, or agreed in a particular way **4** the act of making an agreement or settlement **5** the setting out of a piece of music **6** the result of this: *an arrangement for piano*

arrant *adj literature* very bad: *an arrant thief*

array[1] *v* **arrayed, arraying** *literature* **1** to set in order: *The soldiers were arrayed on the opposite hill* **2** to dress, esp. splendidly

array[2] *n* **-rays** **1** a fine show or collection, as in a shop window **2** an ordered force or army **3** clothes, esp. for a special occasion: *She put on her finest array*

arrears *n* **1** money owed from the past **2** work still waiting to be done **3 in arrears a** in the state of owing money that should be paid regularly **b** (esp. of money) being owed

arrest[1] *v* **1** to seize (someone) in the name of the law **2** to bring to an end; stop **3** to catch and fix (esp. somebody's attention)

arrest[2] *n* **1** the act of arresting or of being arrested **2** *technical* the act of stopping or the state of being stopped **3 under arrest** held prisoner by the police

arrester wires *n* an arrangement of wires for reducing the speed of naval aircraft landing on an aircraft carrier — compare CATAPULT

arrival *n* **1** the act of arriving **2** a person or thing that arrives or has arrived

arrive *v* **arrived, arriving** **1** to reach a place or position, esp. the end of a journey: *arrive home | arrive at a decision* **2** to happen; come **3** (of a baby) to be born **4** to win success: *Now that his books were sold in every shop he felt that he had arrived*

arrogant *adj* proud and self-important in a rude way — ~**ly** *adv* — **-ance** *n*

arrogate *v* **-gated, -gating** *esp. written* to claim for oneself without the right of law △ ABROGATE

arrow *n* a thin straight pointed stick that is shot from a bow

arrowhead *n* a pointed piece of stone or metal forming the tip of an arrow

arrowroot *n* a kind of flour made from a certain root, and used to thicken sauces

arse *n vulgar* **1** a person's or animal's bottom **2** the anus

arsenal *n* a building where weapons and explosives are made or stored

arsenic *n* **1** a grey element **2** a poisonous chemical form of this — **arsenic, arsenical** *adj*

arson *n* the criminal act of setting fire to property — ~**ist** *n*

art[1] **thou art** *old use* (when talking to one person) you are

art[2] *n* **1** the making or expression of something beautiful, such as painting **2** things produced in this way (esp. in the phrase **work of art**) **3** fine skill esp. in such making or expression: *the art of painting well | the art of making friends*

arterial *adj* **1 a** of or like an artery **b** (of blood) which is being sent from the heart —compare VENOUS **2** (of a road, railway, etc.) main

arteriosclerosis *n* hardening of the arteries

artery *n* **-ries** **1** a blood vessel that carries blood from the heart to the rest of the body —compare VEIN ⟹RESPIRATION **2** a main road, railway, river, etc.

artesian well *n* a well in which the water is under pressure and rises to the surface by itself

artful *adj* **1** clever; crafty —compare ARTLESS **2** skilfully put together —compare ARTY — ~**ly** *adv* — ~**ness** *n*

arthritis *n* a disease causing pain and swelling in the joints of the body — **-tic** *adj*, *n*

artichoke *n* **1** also **globe artichoke** — a plant with a globe of leaves, eaten as a vegetable **2** JERUSALEM ARTICHOKE

article[1] *n* **1** a particular or separate thing or object, esp. one of a group **2** a piece of writing in a newspaper, magazine, etc. **3** the English words "a" or "an" (**indefinite article**) and "the" (**definite article**) or the words that do the same work in other languages

article[2] *v* **-cled, -cling** to place under agreement to train under someone in a profession: *I am articled to a firm of lawyers*

articles *n* also **articles of apprenticeship**— a written agreement between someone learning a profession or job and the employer

articulate[1] *adj* **1** able to express thoughts clearly —opposite **inarticulate** **2** (of speech) having clear separate sounds or words **3** having parts connected by joints: *an articulate insect* — ~**ly** *adv* — ~**ness** *n*

articulate[2] *v* **-lated, -lating** **1** to speak **2** to express clearly and effectively **3** to unite or be united by joints that allow movements: *an articulated lorry* — **-lation** *n*

artifact, arte- n anything made by man

artifice n 1 a skilful device, esp. one intended to deceive 2 inventive skill, esp. in deceiving

artificer n literature a skilled workman

artificial adj 1 made by man; not natural 2 insincere; unreal — ~ly adv — ~ity n

artificial insemination n the putting of male seed (SPERM) into a female by means of an instrument, used esp. to improve the quality of cows and horses

artificial respiration n any method of making a person start breathing again —see also KISS OF LIFE

artillery n 1 large guns 2 the part of the army using such weapons

artisan n a skilled workman

artist n 1 a painter; someone who practises one of the other arts 2 a person who shows inventive skill in his work 3 an actor, singer, or other performer

artiste n a professional singer, actor, dancer, etc.

artistic adj 1 of, concerning, or typical of art or artists 2 made with skill and imagination; beautiful 3 liking what is well done in art — ~ally adv

artistry n -ries artistic skill

artless adj simple; natural —compare ARTFUL, ARTY — ~ly adv — ~ness n

art nouveau n French a late 19th century style of art and ornament using flowing plant like shapes

arts n those subjects that are not part of science, esp. as taught at a university: History is an arts subject —see also BA, MA ☞ PAINTING

arty adj often offensive making a show of being interested in art —compare ARTFUL, ARTLESS — **artiness** n

as[1] adv 1 to the same degree or amount; equally: Paul runs fast, but I run just as fast 2 when considered in the stated way: Britain as seen by a foreigner

as[2] conj 1 (used to link parts of a comparison) He can run as fast as I can. | She likes him as much as Paul (= as much as Paul does or as much as she likes Paul) | He works in the same office as my brother 2 (used to introduce a reason, result, purpose, or example) I can't come tonight as I'm going to a concert. | He was so careless as to leave his coat in Geneva. | Jane brought her camera so as to photograph the procession. | Such animals as lions and tigers/Animals such as lions and tigers are kept in the zoo 3 while: She dropped her programme as she stood up 4 **as it were** in a manner of speaking: He is my best friend, my second self, as it were 5 **as of right** by right: All the money is yours as of right 6 **as yet** up to now; so far

as[3] pron 1 in accordance with what: David, as you know, is a scientist. | It is just as you like 2 in accordance with the way in which: He is quite good, as boys go

as[4] prep 1 like 2 in the state, character, condi-

tion, job, etc. of being: The kitten uses that box as a bed. | I saw Oliver as Romeo —see LIKE (USAGE)

asbestos n a soft grey fireproof mineral like a mass of threads that is used for protection against heat

ascend v esp. written 1 to move upwards; rise 2 to climb 3 **ascend the throne** to become king or queen —compare DESCEND

ascendancy, -dency n governing or controlling influence; power

ascendant, -dent[1] n **in the ascendant** having a controlling power or strong influence

ascendant, -dent[2] adj 1 moving upwards; rising 2 greater in control or influence

ascension n the act of moving upwards

Ascension Day n the Thursday 40 days after Easter

ascent n 1 the act of going or climbing up; act of rising · 2 a way up; upward slope, path, etc.

ascertain v esp. written to discover; get to know — ~able adj

ascetic adj not allowing oneself bodily pleasures; living very simply △ AESTHETIC — **ascetic** n — ~ally adv — ~ism n

ascorbic acid n vitamin C

ascribe to v prep ascribed, ascribing ATTRIBUTE TO: No one knows who wrote the tune 'Greensleeves' but it is often ascribed to Henry VIII — **ascribable to** adj prep

asexual adj without sex or sexual organs — ~ly adv — ~ity n

as for prep with regard to; concerning (esp something less important)

ash[1] n a common forest tree that produces black buds, or its hard wood

ash[2] n the powdery remains left after something has burnt

ashamed adj 1 feeling shame, guilt, or sorrow 2 unwilling to do something through fear of feeling shame or of being laughed at: He was ashamed to ask such a simple question — ~ly adv

ashen adj ash-coloured; pale grey

ashore adv on, onto, or to the shore or land

ashtray n -trays a small dish for cigarette ash

Ash Wednesday n the Wednesday which is the first day of Lent

ashy adj -ier, -iest 1 like, consisting of, or covered with ash 2 grey; ashen

Asian also **Asiatic**— n, adj (a native) of Asia ☞ MAP

aside[1] adv to or towards the side; out of the way: She stepped aside to let him pass. | Joking aside, we really must do something —compare put on/to one SIDE

aside[2] n 1 words spoken by an actor to the audience, not to the other characters 2 a remark not intended to be heard by everyone present

as if also **as though**— conj 1 as it would be if: It was as hot as if we were on the sun 2 as one would do if: He gobbled up his food as if he were starving

asinine *adj* stupid; like an ass

ask *v* **1** to request (information) **2** to make a request for or to **3** to demand; expect **4** to invite

ask after *also* (*esp. written*) **enquire after, inquire after**— *v prep esp. spoken* to enquire about the health or well-being of

askance *adv* with distrust (only in the phrase **look askance**)

askew *adv* crookedly

asking price *n* the price a seller states he wants for his goods

aslant *adv, adj* not straight or level; sloping

asleep *adj* **1** sleeping **2** (of an arm or leg) unable to feel; numb **3 fall asleep a** to go to sleep **b** *polite* to die

as long as *conj* **1** *also* **so long as**— if and only if: *You may borrow this book as long as you promise to give it back*

as of *also* **as from**— *prep* from (the time stated): *As of today you are in charge*

as opposed to *prep* as completely different from; in contrast to

asparagus *n* **asparagus** a plant whose young green stems are eaten as a vegetable

aspect *n* **1** *literature* appearance, esp. an expression of the face **2** a particular side of a many-sided state of affairs, idea, plan, etc. **3** the direction in which a window, room, building, etc., faces —see VIEW (USAGE) **4** the form a verb takes to mark the difference in time, as between a continuing action (as in *is singing*) and a completed action (as in *sang*)

aspen *n* a tall tree whose leaves move in the slightest wind

asperity *n* **-ties** *esp. written* **1** roughness; harshness, esp. of manner **2** a bitter unkind word or remark

aspersion *n* *esp. written, often pompous or humour* an unkind or harmful remark (esp. in the phrase **cast aspersions**)

asphalt[1] *n* a black sticky material used for the surface of roads

asphalt[2] *v* to cover with asphalt

asphyxia *n* *rare or technical* asphyxiation

asphyxiate *v* **-ated, -ating** to make or become unable to breathe air; suffocate — **-ation** *n*

aspic *n* a clear jelly made from bones

aspidistra *n* a type of plant with broad green pointed leaves

aspirant *n* a person who hopes for and tries to get something important

aspirate[1] *v* **-rated, -rating** to pronounce (a word or letter) with the sound of the letter H or to treat it as though it were so pronounced (as in French *(le) héros* but not in *(l') homme*)

aspirate[2] *n* the sound of the letter H or the letter itself

aspiration *n* **1** strong desire to do something important **2** an object of such desire **3** the pronunciation of the letter H

aspire *v* **aspired, aspiring** to direct one's hopes and efforts to some important aim

aspirin *n* **-rin** *or* **-rins** (a tablet of) a medicine that lessens pain and fever

as regards *prep* **1** with regard to; as for **2** according to; by: *correctly placed as regards size and colour*

ass *n* **1** any of a family of animals including the donkey, which are like horses but smaller and with longer ears **2** *esp. spoken* a stupid foolish person

assail *v* *esp. written* to attack violently

assailant *n* *esp. written* an attacker

assassin *n* a person who murders (a ruler or politician)

assassinate *v* **-ated, -ating** to murder (a ruler, politician, etc.) — **-ation** *n*

assault[1] *n* **1** a sudden violent attack **2** *law* (the threat of) an unlawful attack with blows against another person

assault[2] *v* to attack suddenly and violently

assault and battery *law* an attack which includes actual blows

assault craft *n* a small fast boat used to get an attacking army from a large ship to the shore

assay[1] *n* **assays** a test to discover the quality of or material in something, esp. something made of or containing metal

assay[2] *v* **assayed, assaying** **1** to test for quality or to discover what materials are present **2** *literature* to attempt (something difficult) — **~er** *n*

assegai *n* a wooden spear with an iron point, used in southern Africa

assemblage *n* **1** a group or collection **2** the act of bringing, coming, or putting together

assemble *v* **-bled, -bling** **1** to gather or collect together **2** to put together

assembler *n* a computer program that automatically converts instructions written in a symbolic code into the equivalent machine code

assembly *n* **-blies** **1** a group of people esp. for a special purpose **2** a meeting together of people **3** a law-making body

assembly line *n* an arrangement of workers and machines in which each person does a particular job and the work is passed on down the line until the product is complete

assent[1] *v* to agree to a suggestion, idea, etc.

assent[2] *n* **1** agreement **2 by common assent** by general agreement

assert *v* **1** to state or declare forcefully **2** to make a claim to; defend in words **3** to show, esp. forcefully **4 assert oneself a** to act in a way that shows one's power, control, etc. **b** to behave in a way that attracts notice

assertion *n* **1** the act of asserting **2** a forceful statement or claim

assertive *adj* marked by or expressing forceful statements or claims — **~ly** *adv* — **~ness** *n*

assess *v* **1** to decide the amount or value of **2** to judge the quality or worth of — **~ment** *n*

assessor *n* **1** a person who calculates the value of property or the amount of income or taxes **2**

a person who advises a judge on specialist matters

asset n a valuable possession, quality, or skill —opposite liability

asseverate v -rated, -rating esp. written to declare solemnly and forcefully — -ation n

assiduous adj having or showing careful and continual attention — ~ly adv — -duity n

assign v 1 to give as a share or for use or as a task 2 to fix or give as a time, place, or reason — ~able adj

assignation n a meeting, esp. a secret meeting with a lover

assignment n 1 a job which one is given or to which one is being sent 2 the act of assigning

assimilate v -lated, -lating 1 to become or allow to become part of (a group, country, etc.) 2 a to take (food) into the body through the digestive system b (of food) to be digested 3 to understand or use properly — -lation n

assist v to help or support — ~ance n

assistant n a person who helps another, as in a job

assizes n assizes (in Britain until 1971) a meeting of a court held by a judge travelling from one country town to another

associate[1] v -ated, -ating 1 to join as friends or as partners in business 2 to connect in one's mind

associate[2] n 1 a person connected with another, esp. in work 2 associate member a member of a society with only limited rights

association n 1 a society of people joined together for a particular purpose 2 the act of joining or the state of being joined with somebody or something 3 the act of connecting things, esp. in the mind

Association Football n soccer

associative operation n technical an operation in which the position of the brackets does not affect the answer when 3 numbers are combined: Multiplication and addition are associative operations, but division and subtraction are nonassociative

assonance n the sounding alike of words, esp. the vowels of words (as in born and warm)

assorted adj of various types mixed together

assortment n a group of mixed things; mixture

assuage v assuaged, assuaging esp. written to relieve; soothe

assume v assumed, assuming 1 to take as a fact without proof; suppose 2 to take upon oneself: to assume new duties

assumption n something that is taken as a fact without proof

assurance n 1 also self-assurance— strong belief in one's own ability 2 a trustworthy statement; promise 3 insurance: life assurance

assure v assured, assuring 1 to promise; try to persuade 2 to make (oneself) certain 3 to

insure, esp. against death —see INSURE (USAGE)

assured[1] adj 1 also self-assured— having or showing certainty of one's own abilities 2 having or showing certainty: an assured demand for such goods — ~ly adv

assured[2] n -sured or (rare) -sureds a person whose life has been insured

aster n a garden flower with a bright yellow centre

asterisk also star— n a starlike mark (*) used a to call attention to a note at the bottom of a page b to mark that certain letters are missing from a word

astern adv 1 in or at the back part (STERN) of a ship 2 (of a ship) backwards

asteroid also minor planet— n one of many small planets revolving round the sun in orbits mostly between Mars and Jupiter

asthma n a disease which makes breathing very difficult at times — ~tic adj, n — ~tically adv

as though conj AS IF

astir adj 1 awake and out of bed 2 in a state of excitement

as to prep with regard to: As to my holiday, I'll decide what to do later

astonish v to produce surprise or wonder in (someone)

astonishment n great surprise or wonder

astound v to shock with surprise

astrakhan n lamb's skin with the wool fixed in tight little curls

astray adj, adv 1 off the right path or way 2 into bad or wrong ways

astride adv, prep with a leg on each side (of): astride a horse

astringent[1] adj 1 able to tighten up the skin or stop bleeding 2 severe; bitter — -gency n — ~ly adv

astringent[2] n technical a substance that tightens up the skin or the blood vessels and so stops bleeding

astrolabe n an instrument used formerly for measuring the positions of heavenly bodies — compare SEXTANT

astrology n the art of understanding the supposed influence that the heavenly bodies have on our lives — -ger n — -gical adj — -gically adv

astronaut n a space traveller ☞ SPACE

astronomical adj 1 of or concerning the stars or their scientific study 2 esp. spoken (of an amount or number) very large — ~ly adv

astronomy n the scientific study of the sun, moon, stars, etc. ☞ SPACE — -er n

astrophysics n the scientific study of the physical and chemical nature of the stars — -ical adj — -icist n

astute adj clever; sharp-witted — ~ly adv — ~ness n

asunder adv esp. in literature 1 apart from each other in position 2 into pieces

asylum n   1 a place of safety   2 shelter, esp. as given by one country to people who have left another for political reasons   3 *becoming rare* MENTAL HOSPITAL

asymmetric also **-ical—** adj having sides that are not alike —opposite **symmetrical** — ~ally adv

at prep   1 **a** in a certain place in time or space: *at home* | *at Christmas* **b** on a point on a scale: *It melts at 90°.* | *at 60 pence each*   2 towards, intending, or intended to hit: *Those remarks were aimed at me*   3 as a sign or result of feelings caused by: *I laughed at his silliness*   4 in the field or area of: *good at French*

at all adv   1 in any degree: *I don't like him at all*   2 ever: *She doesn't smoke at all*

ate   past tense of EAT

atheist n a person who disbelieves in the existence of God —compare AGNOSTIC — ~ic(al) adj — ~ically adv — **atheism** n

athlete n a person skilled at games needing strength and speed

athlete's foot n a disease caused by a fungus between the toes

athletic adj   1 of or concerning athletes or athletics   2 strong in body: *an athletic girl*

athletics n a branch of sport involving running, jumping, and throwing

athwart prep *rare* across

atishoo interj the sound of a sneeze

atlas n a book of maps

atmosphere n   1 the mixture of gases that surrounds any heavenly body, esp. the earth   2 the air   3 the feeling produced by the surroundings

atmospheric adj   1 of or concerning the earth's atmosphere   2 producing feelings of mysterious beauty, strangeness, etc.: *That music's very atmospheric*

atmospheric diving suit n a suit that allows a diver to work at great depths without the need to reduce the pressure afterwards

atmospherics n a continuous crackling noise in a radio caused by electrical forces in the atmosphere

atoll n a ring-shaped island made of coral

atom n   1 the smallest piece of an element that still has the same qualities and can combine with other substances ⊚   2 *esp. spoken* a very small bit

atom bomb also **atomic bomb—** n a bomb whose very powerful explosion is caused by splitting an atom and setting free its force

atomic adj   1 of or concerning an atom or atoms   2 working by atomic energy — ~ally adv

atomic energy n also **nuclear energy—** the powerful force that is given out when the middle part (NUCLEUS) of an atom is changed, as by being split

atomic mass unit n *technical* a unit of mass equal to 1/12th of the mass of an atom of carbon

atomic number n the number of electrically charged particles (PROTONS) in the middle part (NUCLEUS) of an atom of a particular element

atomic pile n NUCLEAR REACTOR

atomic weight n the weight of an atom of an element expressed in atomic mass units

atomize, -ise v   -mized, -mizing to turn (a liquid) into a fine spray

atonal adj (of music) not based on any ordered scale of notes — ~ly adv — ~ity n

atone v atoned, atoning to make repayment (for harm done, failure to act, etc.) — ~ment n

atop prep *esp. in literature or pompous* on, to, or at the top of

atrium n atria   1 the central main room of an ancient Roman house   2 *technical* either of the 2 spaces in the top of the heart that receive blood from the main veins of the body and push it through into the 2 lower spaces (VENTRICLES) ☞ RESPIRATION

atrocity n -ties   1 great evil, esp. cruelty   2 a very evil, esp. cruel, act   3 *esp. spoken* something that is very displeasing or ugly — -cious adj — -ciously adv

atrophy v -phied, -phying   1 to waste away   2 to weaken; come to an end — **atrophy** n

attach v to fix; fasten; join

attaché n *French* a person who is employed to help an ambassador

attaché case n a thin hard case with a handle, for carrying papers

attachment n   1 the act of attaching or of being attached   2 something that is fixed to something else   3 something that fixes or fastens   4 fondness or friendship

attach to v prep   1 to join as a member of   2 *esp. written* to come to; be connected with: *No blame attaches to him for the accident*   3 **be attached to** to be fond of

attack¹ v   1 to bring violence (on), esp. with weapons   2 to speak or write strongly against   3 to harm, esp. by a continuing action: *The disease attacked his bones*   4 to begin with eagerness: *He attacked the food as if he had not eaten for a week* — ~er n

attack² n   1 violence intended to harm   2 writing or words intended to hurt or damage   3 a sudden period of illness, usu. serious: *a heart attack*

attain v to succeed in arriving at; reach — ~able adj

attainment n   1 the act of attaining   2 something successfully reached or learnt, esp. a skill

attar n a pleasant-smelling oil obtained from flowers

attempt¹ v to make an effort at; try

attempt² n   1 an effort made to do something   2 **attempt on someone's life** an effort to murder someone

attend v   1 to pay attention   2 to be present at   3 to look after; give help; serve

attendance n   1 the act of attending: *a doctor in attendance on the sick man*   2 the act of being present, esp. regularly: *attendance at school* 3 the number of people present

attendant[1] *adj* 1 connected with: *One of the attendant difficulties during the war was lack of food* 2 serving; on duty to help and look after: *several attendant helpers*

attendant[2] *n* 1 a person who looks after another 2 a person employed to look after and help visitors to a public place: *a museum attendant*

attention[1] *n* 1 the act of fixing the mind, esp. by watching or listening 2 particular care, notice, or action 3 a military position in which a person stands straight and still: *to stand at attention*

attention[2] *also* 'shun— *interj* a military order to stand at attention

attentive *adj* 1 taking careful notice; listening carefully 2 careful to fulfil the wishes of another — ~ly *adv* — ~ness *n*

attenuate *v* -ated, -ating *esp. written or technical* to make or become thin, weak, less valuable, etc. — -ation *n*

attest *v* to be or give proof of

attic *n* a part of a building just below the roof

attire[1] *v* attired, attiring *esp. written* to put on clothes; dress

attire[2] *n* *esp. written* dress; clothes

attitude *n* 1 the position or manner of standing of the body 2 a manner of feeling and behaving 3 judgment; opinion

attorney *n* -neys a lawyer

attorney general *n* attorneys general *or* attorney generals the chief law officer of a state or nation

attract *v* 1 to cause to like, admire, notice, or turn towards 2 to draw towards one 3 to draw by unseen forces

attraction *n* 1 the act of attracting 2 something which attracts 3 *technical* (in science) the force by which bodies tend to approach each other —opposite repulsion

attractive *adj* 1 having the power to attract 2 having good looks — ~ly *adv* — ~ness *n*

attribute *n* a quality belonging to or forming part of the nature of a person or thing

attribute to *v prep* -buted, -buting to 1 to believe (something) to be the result of 2 *also* ascribe to— to consider (something) to have been written by (someone): *This tune is usually attributed to J.S. Bach* — -table *adj* — -tion *n*

attrition *n* 1 wearing away 2 tiring and weakening (esp. in the phrase war of attrition)

attune to *v prep* attuned, attuning to to cause to become used to or ready for

atypical *adj* unusual; not typical — ~ly *adv*

aubergine *also* eggplant— *n* a plant whose large purple fruit is eaten as a vegetable

auburn *adj, n* (esp. of hair) reddish-brown

auction[1] *n* 1 public sale of goods to the person who offers the most money —see also DUTCH AUCTION 2 (in some card games) the time when players compete to fix the contract

auction[2] *v* to sell by auction — ~eer *n*

audacious *adj* 1 daring; brave 2 daringly impolite or disrespectful — audacity *n* — ~ly *adv*

audible *adj* able to be heard — -bility *n* — -bly *adv*

audience *n* 1 the people listening to or watching a performance, speech, show, etc. 2 a formal meeting between somebody powerful and somebody less important: *The queen allowed him an audience of 20 minutes*

audio *adj* *technical* connected with or used in the broadcasting or receiving of sound radio signals —compare VIDEO

audio-visual *adj* 1 of, for, or concerning both sight and hearing 2 made to help learning and teaching by using both sight and hearing

audit *v* to examine (money accounts) officially — audit *n* — auditor *n*

audition[1] *n* 1 a test performance requested of a singer, actor, etc. 2 *technical* the act or power of hearing

audition[2] *v* to test or be tested by an audition

auditorium *n* the space in a theatre, hall, etc., where the audience sits

auditory *adj* *technical* of, by, or for hearing

au fait *adj French* fully informed; familiar: *I was new at the school and not yet au fait with its customs*

Aug. *abbrev. for:* August

auger *n* an instrument for making large holes in wood or in the ground

aught *pron* for aught I know *literature* for all I know

augment *v* *esp. written* to increase in size, amount, quality, etc. — ~ation *n*

augemented *adj* (of a musical interval) made half a step greater than the interval in a major scale

au gratin *adj French* gratinée

augur *v* *literature* to be a sign of; foretell

augury *n* -ries a declaration or sign which foretells the future

august *adj literature* noble and grand — ~ly *adv*

August *n* the 8th month of the year

auk *n* a short-winged northern seabird which dives for fish

aunt *also* (*esp. spoken*) auntie, aunty— *n* 1 the sister of one's father or mother, the wife of one's uncle, or a woman whose brother or sister has a child ☞ FAMILY 2 a woman who is a friend of a small child or its parents

Aunt Sally *n* Aunt Sallies 1 a wooden figure of a woman at fairs, at which people throw things 2 a person or thing that is the object of complaints, funny remarks, etc.

au pair *n French* a young foreigner who lives with a family in return for doing light housework

aura *n* a feeling that seems to surround and come from a person or place △ AURORA

An atom is made up of electrons orbiting a central nucleus, composed of protons and neutrons. The numbers of each component vary according to the element – an 'atomic number' indicates the number of protons in the nucleus. Protons have a positive electric charge, electrons a negative charge, and neutrons no charge at all. When an atom loses or gains an electron it gains an electric charge and is then called an ion. Isotopes are formed by the addition of neutrons to the nucleus.

electron orbit

nucleus

⊕ proton

◎ neutron

● electron

A water molecule is formed by the combination of two hydrogen atoms and an oxygen atom. Unstable by themselves, these atoms find stability by sharing their electrons.

hydrogen atoms

oxygen atom

water molecule

Periodic table

Period	Group IA	IIA	IIIA	IVA	VA	VIA	VIIA	VIII			IB	IIB	IIIB	IVB	VB	VIB	VIIB	
1	1 H																	2 He
2	3 Li	4 Be											5 B	6 C	7 N	8 O	9 F	10 Ne
3	11 Na	12 Mg											13 Al	14 Si	15 P	16 S	17 Cl	18 Ar
4	19 K	20 Ca	21 Sc	22 Ti	23 V	24 Cr	25 Mn	26 Fe	27 Co	28 Ni	29 Cu	30 Zn	31 Ga	32 Ge	33 As	34 Se	35 Br	36 Kr
5	37 Rb	38 Sr	39 Y	40 Zr	41 Nb	42 Mo	43 Tc	44 Ru	45 Rh	46 Pd	47 Ag	48 Cd	49 In	50 Sn	51 Sb	52 Te	53 I	54 Xe
6	55 Cs	56 Ba	57* La	72 Hf	73 Ta	74 W	75 Re	76 Os	77 Ir	78 Pt	79 Au	80 Hg	81 Tl	82 Pb	83 Bi	84 Po	85 At	86 Rn
7	87 Fr	88 Ra	89‡ Ac	104 –														

* Lanthanides
‡ Actinides

*58 Ce	59 Pr	60 Nd	61 Pm	62 Sm	63 Eu	64 Gd	65 Tb	66 Dy	67 Ho	68 Er	69 Tm	70 Yb	71 Lu
‡90 Th	91 Pa	92 U	93 Np	94 Pu	95 Am	96 Cm	97 Bk	98 Cf	99 Es	100 Fm	101 Md	102 No	103 Lr

Table of chemical elements

element	symbol	atomic weight	element	symbol	atomic weight	element	symbol	atomic weight
Actinium	Ac	227	Hafnium	Hf	178.4	Promethium	Pm	147
Aluminium	Al	26.982	Helium	He	4.003	Protactinium	Pa	231.036
Americium	Am	243	Holmium	Ho	164.930	Radium	Ra	226.025
Antimony	Sb	121.7	Hydrogen	H	1.008	Radon	Rn	222
Argon	Ar	39.94	Indium	In	114.82	Rhenium	Re	186.2
Arsenic	As	74.922	Iodine	I	126.905	Rhodium	Rh	102.906
Astatine	At	210	Iridium	Ir	192.2	Rubidium	Rb	85.467
Barium	Ba	137.34	Iron	Fe	55.84	Ruthenium	Ru	101.0
Berkelium	Bk	247	Krypton	Kr	83.80	Samarium	Sm	150.4
Beryllium	Be	9.012	Lanthanum	La	138.905	Scandium	Sc	44.956
Bismuth	Bi	208.980	Lawrencium	Lr	256	Selenium	Se	78.9
Boron	B	10.81	Lead	Pb	207.2	Silicon	Si	28.08
Bromine	Br	79.904	Lithium	Li	6.94	Silver	Ag	107.868
Cadmium	Cd	112.40	Lutetium	Lu	174.97	Sodium	Na	22.990
Caesium	Cs	132.905	Magnesium	Mg	24.305	Strontium	Sr	87.62
Calcium	Ca	40.08	Manganese	Mn	54.938	Sulphur	S	32.06
Californium	Cf	251	Mendelevium	Md	257	Tantalum	Ta	180.947
Carbon	C	12.011	Mercury	Hg	200.5	Technetium	Tc	97
Cerium	Ce	140.12	Molybdenum	Mo	95.9	Tellurium	Te	127.6
Chlorine	Cl	35.453	Neodymium	Nd	144.2	Terbium	Tb	158.925
Chromium	Cr	51.996	Neon	Ne	20.17	Thallium	Tl	204.3
Cobalt	Co	58.933	Neptunium	Np	237.048	Thorium	Th	232.038
Copper	Cu	63.54	Nickel	Ni	58.7	Thulium	Tm	168.934
Curium	Cm	247	Niobium	Nb	92.906	Tin	Sn	118.6
Dysprosium	Dy	162.5	Nitrogen	N	14.007	Titanium	Ti	47.9
Einsteinium	Es	254	Nobelium	No	255	Tungsten	W	183.8
Erbium	Er	167.2	Osmium	Os	190.2	Uranium	U	238.029
Europium	Eu	151.96	Oxygen	O	15.999	Vanadium	V	50.941
Fermium	Fm	257	Palladium	Pd	106.4	Xenon	Xe	131.30
Fluorine	F	18.998	Phosphorus	P	30.974	Ytterbium	Yb	173.0
Francium	Fr	223	Platinum	Pt	195.0	Yttrium	Y	88.906
Gadolinium	Gd	157.2	Plutonium	Pu	244	Zinc	Zn	65.38
Gallium	Ga	69.72	Polonium	Po	209	Zirconium	Zr	91.22
Germanium	Ge	72.5	Potassium	K	39.09			
Gold	Au	196.967	Praseodymium	Pr	140.908			

aural *adj technical* of or received through hearing — ~**ly** *adv*

au revoir *interj French* till we meet again; goodbye

auricle *n* 1 the part of the ear that is on the outside of the head 2 an atrium in the heart

aurora *n* -**ras** *or* -**rae** bands of coloured light in the night sky seen either in the most northern parts of the world (**aurora borealis** or **northern lights**) or in the most southern parts (**aurora australis** or **southern lights**) △ AURA

auspices *n* **under the auspices of** with the help, support, and favour of

auspicious *adj esp. written* 1 giving signs of future success 2 lucky — ~**ly** *adv*

Aussie *n sl* an Australian

austere *adj* 1 lacking comfort; hard 2 serious; severe; self-controlled 3 without ornament; plain — ~**ly** *adv* — -**ity** *n* : *a time of austerity*

Australasian *n, adj* (a person, language, or thing) of Australia, New Zealand, or the surrounding islands

Australian *n, adj* (a person, language, or thing) of Australia ☞ MAP

Australian Rules football *n* an Australian game rather like rugby, which is played between 2 teams of 18 players

australopithecus *n* a type of early man of southern Africa

authentic *adj* known to be what it is claimed to be; real; genuine — ~**ally** *adv* — ~**ity** *n*

authenticate *v* -**ated,** -**ating** to prove (something) to be authentic — -**ation** *n*

author *n* 1 the writer of a book, newspaper article, play, poem, etc. 2 the originator or maker of anything, esp. an idea or plan

authoritarian[1] *adj* favouring or demanding obedience to rules and laws whether or not they are right △ AUTHORITATIVE — ~**ism** *n*

authoritarian[2] *n* 1 a person who believes that rules and laws should always be obeyed whether or not they are right 2 a person who is continually giving orders to others

authoritative *adj* 1 behaving as if giving orders 2 possessing the power to give orders 3 that may be used or trusted as having a respected store of knowledge or information: *We want a dictionary that will be an authoritative record of modern English* —compare DEFINITIVE △ AUTHORITARIAN — ~**ly** *adv*

authority *n* -**ties** 1 the ability, power, or right to control and command 2 a person or group with this power or right, esp. in public affairs 3 right or official power, esp. for some stated purpose 4 a person, book, etc., whose knowledge or information is dependable, good, and respected

authorization, -**isation** *n* 1 right or official power to do something 2 a paper giving this right

authorize, -**ise** *v* -**ized,** -**izing** 1 to give power to 2 to give permission for

authorship *n* the identity of the author of a book, play, poem, etc.

autism *n* a mental illness in which the imagination becomes too important and good personal relationships cannot be formed — -**tic** *adj* : *autistic children* — -**tically** *adv*

autobiographical *also* **autobiographic**— *adj* of or concerning the facts of one's own life, esp. as written in a book — ~**ly** *adv*

autobiography *n* -**phies** 1 a book written by oneself about one's own life 2 such books or the writing of such books —compare BIOGRAPHY

autocracy *n* -**cies** 1 rule by one person with unlimited power 2 a country ruled in this way

autocrat *n* 1 a ruler with unlimited power 2 a person who orders things to be done without considering the wishes of others — ~**ic** *adj* — ~**ically** *adv*

Autocue *n trademark* a machine that enables a person being televised (e.g. a newsreader) to read a script while keeping his eyes on the camera

autograph[1] *n* a person's handwriting, esp. his signature

autograph[2] *v* to write one's signature on (a book, letter, etc. that one has written)

autograph book *also* **autograph album**— *n* a book of empty pages which friends and famous people can sign

automate *v* -**mated,** -**mating** to control and operate by machinery, without human help

automatic[1] *adj* 1 (of a machine) able to work without human help 2 done without thought, esp. as a habit 3 certain to happen — ~**ally** *adv*

automatic[2] *n* something, such as certain weapons, cars, etc., in which some parts work automatically

automation *n* the act or practice of using machines that need little or no human control

automaton *n* -**ta** *or* -**tons** 1 a machine that moves or works by itself 2 a person who acts like a robot

automobile *n* a car

Automobile Association *n* a British club for motorists, providing help with repairs on the road

autonomy *n* the condition of self-government, esp. of a group within a country — -**mous** *adj* — -**mously** *adv*

autopsy *n* -**sies** an examination of a dead body to discover the cause of death

autumn *n* the season between summer and winter — ~**al** *adj* — ~**ally** *adv*

auxiliary[1] *adj* giving help, esp. of less importance

auxiliary[2] *n* -**ries** 1 a person or thing that gives help 2 a foreign soldier or army in the service of a country at war

auxiliary verb *n* a verb that goes with another verb to show person, tense, etc. (such as *am, was,* and *have* in *"I am running"*, *"He was run over"*, *"they have heard"*)

auxin *n technical* a plant hormone

av. *abbrev. for:* average

avail[1] *v literature* to be of use

avail[2] *n* advantage; use (esp. in the phrases **of no/little avail, without avail, to no avail**)

available *adj* **1** able to be got, obtained, used, etc. **2** able to be visited or seen — **-ability** *n* — **-ably** *adv*

avail of *v prep* to give (oneself) the advantage of: *avail oneself of every opportunity*

avalanche *n* **1** a large mass of snow, ice, rocks, etc. crashing down the side of a mountain **2** a large quantity that has arrived suddenly

avant-garde *n, adj French* (of) the people who produce the newest ideas, esp. in the arts

avarice *n esp. written* greed for money — **-cious** *adj* — **-ciously** *adv*

avaunt *interj old use* go away

Ave. *abbrev. for:* avenue

avenge *v* avenged, avenging **1** to get satisfaction for (a wrong) by punishing the wrongdoer **2** to punish somebody for a wrong done to (oneself or somebody else) —see REVENGE (USAGE) — ~**r** *n*

avenue *n* **1** a road between 2 rows of trees **2** a wide street in a town **3** the way to a result (often in the phrase **explore every avenue**) — compare BOULEVARD

aver *v* **-rr-** *esp. written* to state forcefully; declare

average[1] *n* **1** the amount found by adding together several quantities and then dividing by the number of quantities: *The average of 3, 8, and 10 is 7* **2** a level or standard regarded as usual or ordinary — **average** *adj*

average[2] *v* **-raged, -raging** **1** to be or come to an average **2** to do, get, or have as a usual quantity **3** to calculate the average of

averse *adj* not liking; opposed △ ADVERSE

aversion *n* **1** strong dislike; hatred (often in the phrase **take an aversion to**) **2** a person or thing disliked (esp. in the phrase **someone's pet aversion**)

aversive *adj technical* tending or causing to avoid something that is unpleasant or painful

avert *v* **1** to prevent happening; avoid **2** to turn away (one's eyes, thoughts, etc.)

aviary *n* **-ries** a large cage or enclosure for keeping birds in

aviation *n* **1** the art or science of flying aircraft **2** the aircraft industry

aviator *n old use* the pilot of an aircraft

avid *adj* eager; keen — ~**ity** *n* — ~**ly** *adv*

avocado also **avocado pear**— *n* **-dos** *or* **-does** an eatable green pear-shaped tropical fruit with a large seed and smooth oily flesh

avocation *n* work that is done for pleasure; hobby

avocet *n* any of various wading birds with a long beak

avoid *v* **1** to escape: *I avoided being punished* **2** to keep away from, esp. on purpose — ~**able** *adj* — ~**ance** *n*

avoirdupois *n, adj French* the system of

weights used, esp. formerly, in Britain, the standard measures being the ounce, pound, and ton —compare METRIC SYSTEM

avow *v esp. written* to state openly; admit — ~**al** *n*

avowed *adj* openly declared or admitted — ~**ly** *adv*

avuncular *adj* of, like, or concerning an uncle — ~**ly** *adv*

await *v* **1** to wait for **2** to be in store for; be ready for

awake[1] also **awaken**— *v* **awoke** *or* **awaked, awaked** *or* **a woken** **1** to wake **2** to make or become conscious or active

awake[2] *adj* **1** having woken; not asleep **2** conscious (of) **3 wide awake a** not at all sleepy **b** not easily deceived

awakening *n* **1** the act of waking from sleep **2** the act of becoming conscious or concerned

award[1] *v* **1** to give officially as a prize **2** to give by a decision in a court of law

award[2] *n* **1** something given officially, esp. a prize **2** a decision, or that which is given by a decision, in a court of law **3** a sum of money given to a student so that he can afford to study

aware *adj* having knowledge or consciousness — ~**ness** *n*

awash *adj* **1** washed over by waves **2** floating about in the waves

away *adv* **1** from this or that place; to, at, or in another place **2** to an end; to nothing: *The water boiled away* **3** continuously: *He sawed away at the thick branch till at last it was cut through*

awe[1] *n* a feeling of respect mixed with fear and wonder

awe[2] *v* **awed, aweing** *or* **awing** to fill with awe

awe-inspiring also **awesome**— *adj* causing feelings of awe — ~**ly** *adv*

awestruck also **awestricken**— *adj* filled with awe

awful *adj* **1** terrible; shocking **2** *esp. spoken* very bad: *awful weather* **3** *literature & old use* causing feelings of awe — ~**ness** *n*

awfully *adv esp. spoken* (used to give more force to an expression) very: *awfully cold*

awhile *adv esp. in literature* for a short time

awkward *adj* **1** clumsy **2** not well made for use; difficult to use; causing difficulty **3** (of a person) difficult to deal with **4** embarrassing — ~**ly** *adv* — ~**ness** *n*

awl *n* a small pointed tool for making holes in leather —compare BRADAWL, GIMLET

awning *n* a canvas covering used to protect shop windows, ships' decks, etc., from sun or rain

awoke *past tense of* AWAKE

awoken *past part. of* AWAKE

awry *adv, adj* **1** crooked; out of shape **2** not as planned or intended

axe[1] *n* **axes** **1** a tool with a heavy metal blade on the end of a long handle used to cut wood **2** *esp. spoken* (in the phrases **give/get the axe**) sudden ending, esp. because of lack of money, of a one's employment **b** a plan **3 have an axe to grind** *esp. spoken* to have private and often selfish reasons for one's actions

axe² *v* **axed, axing** to remove suddenly from a job, a list of plans for completion, etc.

axiom *n* a basic assumption that is generally accepted as true; postulate — ~**atic** *adj* — ~**atically** *adv*

axis *n* **axes** 1 the imaginary line round which a spinning body turns ⊒ GLOBE 2 **a** LINE OF SYMMETRY **b** a line around which similar parts of a body are regularly arranged ⊒ MATHEMATICS

axis of rotation *n* the line about which a body rotates

axle *n* the rod which passes through the centre of a wheel ⊒ CAR

axon *n* *technical* a long thin part of a nerve cell that carries messages away from the main body of the cell

aye, ay¹ *adv Scots* always; continually

aye² *adv dialect, poetic, or sailing* yes

aye³ *n* a vote or voter in favour of something —opposite **nay**; compare YEA

azalea *n* a type of rhododendron bush with bright flowers

azimuth *n* the angle on the earth's surface between a north-south line and the position or direction of something, esp. a star, seen from a place on the earth

azure *adj, n* bright blue, as of the sky

B

B, b **B's, b's** or **Bs, bs** the second letter of the English alphabet

b *abbrev. for:* born: *b 1885*

B **a** the 7th note in the musical scale of C major **b** the musical key based on this note

BA *abbrev. for:* Bachelor of Arts

baa *n, v* **baaed, baaing** (to make) the sound made by a sheep or lamb

babble¹ *v* **-bled, -bling** 1 to talk quickly, foolishly, or in a way that is hard to understand —compare BABEL 2 to express by babbling 3 to repeat foolishly; tell (secrets) 4 to make continuous speechlike sounds: *a babbling baby | a babbling stream* —compare BURBLE

babble² *n* 1 talk that is childish, foolish, or hard to understand —compare BABEL 2 a confused sound of many voices 3 a sound like that of water running over stones —compare BURBLE

babbler *n* a person who babbles

babe *n* 1 *literature & poetic* a baby 2 *sl esp. us* a girl: *Hi there, babe!*

babel *n* a scene of confusion, noise of many voices, or disorder (as in the Bible story of the tower of Babel) —compare BABBLE

baboon *n* any of several types of large doglike monkeys of Africa or S. Asia ⊒ MAMMAL

baby¹ *n* **babies** 1 a very young child, esp. one who has not learnt to speak 2 a very young animal or bird 3 **a** the youngest of a group **b** a small member of a group 4 a person who behaves like a baby 5 *sl esp. US* a person, esp. a girl or woman: *I've got a gun here, baby, so hand over your money*

baby² *v* **babied, babying** *esp. spoken* to treat like a baby; give a great deal of care or attention to

babyhood *n* the period of time when one is a baby

babyish *adj* like a baby

baby-minder *n* a person who takes care of babies while their mothers are working

baby-sit *v* **-sat, -tt-** to take care of children while their parents are out — ~**ter** *n*

baby tooth *n* MILK TOOTH

baccarat, -ra *n French* a card game played for money

bacchanal *n* *esp. in literature* a wild, disorderly, and drunken party — ~**ian** *adj*

baccy *n* *sl* tobacco

bachelor *n* an unmarried man — ~**hood** *n*

bachelor girl *n* an unmarried woman, esp. a young independent one —compare SPINSTER

bachelor's degree *n* a first university degree

back¹ *n* 1 the part of the body of a human or animal down the middle of which runs the backbone 2 the less important side or surface (of an object) 3 (of a building) the side opposite to the main entrance 4 (of a vehicle) **a** the inside part behind the driver **b** the outside surface opposite to the usual direction of movement 5 the furthest part (from the point towards which a group of people are facing or moving) 6 (of a chair) the part that one leans against when sitting 7 (of a book or newspaper) the last part; end 8 (in games like football) a player or position that defends the area near the team's own goal —compare FORWARD, CENTRE 9 **at the back (of)** behind 10 **back to back** with the backs facing each other 11 **break the back of** to do most of; do the worst part of (something that must be done) 12 **be glad to see the back of someone** *esp. spoken* to be glad when someone goes away 13 **have/with one's back to the wall** (to be) in a bad state of affairs, that is hard to get out of 14 **put one's back into** to work very hard at 15 **put someone's back up** *esp. spoken* to annoy someone 16 **turn one's back on** to avoid; go away from (esp. when one should stay) — ~**less** *adj*

back² *adv* 1 towards or at the back: *to tie one's hair back* 2 to or at a place or time where something or someone was before: *Put the book back on the shelf* 3 (of a clock) so as to show an earlier time

back³ *adj* 1 long past 2 (of money) owed from an earlier time: *back pay/rent* 3 at the back: *back door*

back⁴ *v* 1 to go or cause to go backwards: *The car backed through the gate* 2 to support and encourage, often with money 3 to bet money on 4 to be or make the back of: *curtains backed with a plastic material* 5 *technical* (of the wind) to change direction anti-clockwise —compare VEER —see also BACK DOWN, BACK OUT, BACK UP

backache *n* (a) pain in the back

backbench *n* members of Parliament who do not hold official positions —compare FRONTBENCH — ~er *n*

backbite *v* -bit, -bitten, -biting to speak unkindly of an absent person — ~r *n* — -biting *n*

backbone *n* 1 the main support of a group, association, plan, etc. 2 the spine 3 strength of character 4 to the backbone completely; in all ways

backchat *n* rude talk in reply to someone

backcloth *n* a backdrop

backcomb *v* to comb (hair) against the direction of growth, to produce a bouffant effect

backdate *v* -dated, -dating to agree to give (something) a starting date earlier than the date of the agreement: *The increase in pay agreed in June will be backdated to January*

back down *v adv* to admit that one was wrong

backdrop *n* a painted cloth hung at the back of a stage

backer *n* 1 someone who supports a plan with money 2 someone who backs a horse

backfire¹ *n* an explosion in a petrol engine which makes a loud noise but does not drive the car forward

backfire² *v* -fired, -firing 1 to produce a backfire 2 to have an effect opposite to that intended

backgammon *n* a board game for 2 players, using round pieces and dice

background *n* 1 the scenery or ground behind something, e.g. in a printing or photograph 2 a position as unnoticeable as possible: *to remain in the background* 3 the conditions existing when something happens or happened: *The election took place against a background of widespread unemployment* 4 a person's family, experience, and education

backhand¹ *n* also **backhand stroke**— a stroke (as in tennis) made with the back of the hand turned in the direction of movement —compare FOREHAND

backhand² *adv, adj* backhanded

backhanded *adj, adv* 1 using or made with a backhand 2 using or made with the back of the hand 3 a backhanded compliment a remark that might cause either pleasure or displeasure

backhander *n esp. spoken* a bribe

backing *n* 1 material or moral help 2 something that is used to make the back of an object 3 (esp. in popular music) the music that is played by those other than the main performer or performers

backlash *n* 1 a sudden violent backward movement after a forward one 2 a movement

against a growing belief or practice, esp. against a political or social development

backlog *n* a group of things to be done that were not done at the proper time

backmost *adj* farthest back

back number *n* also **back issue** — a newspaper, magazine, etc., earlier then the most recent one

back out *v adv* to fail to fulfil a promise, contract, etc.

backpedal *v* -ll- 1 to pedal backwards, as on a bicycle 2 *esp. spoken* to take back a statement; draw back from some promised action

backside *n sl* a person's or animal's bottom

backslide *v* -slid, -sliding to fall back into wrong-doing — -slider *n*

backspace *n* the part that one presses to make a typewriter move back towards the beginning of the line

backstage *adv* 1 behind the stage in a theatre 2 in secret

back street *n* a street away from the main streets, esp. in a poor area

backstroke *n* a swimming stroke done on one's back

backtrack *v* to go back over the same path

backup *n* a thing or person ready to be used in place of another or to help another

back up *v adv* to support

backward *adj* 1 directed towards the back, the beginning, or the past 2 returning: *the backward journey* 3 behind in development 4 unsure of oneself; shy — ~ly *adv* — ~ness *n*

backwards *adv* 1 away from one's front; towards the back 2 with the back first: *walking backwards* 3 with the back where the front should be; back to front 4 bend/fall over backwards to try as hard as possible or almost too hard

backwash *n* 1 a backward movement (as of water or air) produced by a force pushing forward (like a boat engine) 2 *esp. spoken* the (usu. unpleasant) indirect result of an action

backwater *n* 1 a pool which is part of a river but out of the main stream 2 a place (or state of mind) not influenced by outside events or new ideas

backwoods *n* (esp. in N. America) uncleared land far away from towns

bacon *n* 1 salted or smoked meat from the back or sides of a pig, often sold in thin slices 2 **bring home the bacon** *sl* to succeed, esp. in providing for one's family 3 **save one's bacon** *esp. spoken* to have a narrow escape

bacteria *n sing.* -rium very small living things, each consisting of a single cell, and some of which cause disease —compare ⏞GERM, MICROBE, PLANT, ECOLOGY, FOOD, EVOLUTION — -rial *adj*

bacteriology *n* the scientific study of bacteria — -ologist *n*

Bactrian *adj* see CAMEL

bad¹ *adj* worse, worst 1 not of acceptable quality; poor **2** unfavourable **3** decayed: *bad fish-* **4** morally wrong **5** not suitable for a purpose: *very bad light in this room* **6** unpleasant: *bad news* **7** harmful: *Smoking is bad for your health-* **8** not healthy: *bad teeth* **9** not feeling healthy or happy **10** serious; severe: *a bad cold | a bad defeat* **11** incorrect: *bad grammar* **12** (of language or a word) not used in polite society **13 in bad faith** dishonestly; without intending to carry out a promise **14 feel bad about** *esp. spoken* to be sorry or ashamed about **15 go bad** to become unfit to eat **16 have/get a bad name** to lose or have lost people's respect **17 (It's/That's) too bad** *esp. spoken* I'm sorry: *Too bad you couldn't come last night* — ~**ness** *n*

bad² *n* **1** that which is bad **2 go to the bad** to begin living in an immoral or evil way

bad blood also **bad feeling**— *n* angry feeling

bad debt *n* a debt that is unlikely to be paid

bade *past tense & part. of* BID

bad form *n* unacceptable behaviour

badge *n* a sign worn to show a person's employment, rank, membership of a group, etc.

badger¹ *n* a grey burrowing animal that has a white face with 2 black stripes, and is active at night

badger² *v* to ask again and again

badinage *n* playful language making fun of somebody; banter

badly *adv* **worse, worst** **1** in a bad manner **2** by a great deal: *badly beaten in the race* **3** a great deal; very much

badly-off *adj* **worse-off, worst-off** **1** poor **2** lacking desirable possessions: *badly-off for friends*

badminton *n* a tennis-like game in which a small feathered object (SHUTTLECOCK) is hit over a high net

baffle¹ *v* **-fled, -fling** to bring to a halt by confusing: *The examination question baffled me completely and I couldn't answer it* — -**ing** *adj* — -**ingly** *adv* — ~**ment** *n*

baffle² *n* *technical* a board or other means of controlling the flow of air, water, or sound passing through an enclosed space

bag¹ *n* **1** a container made of soft material, opening at the top **2** the quantity of usu. small birds or animals shot or caught on any one occasion —compare KILL **3** a bagful **4 in the bag** *sl* as desired: *Don't worry. We've got the match in the bag*

bag² *v* **-gg-** **1** to put into a bag or bags **2** *esp. spoken* to kill or catch (animals or birds): *We bagged a rabbit* **3** *sl* to take or keep : *Try to bag seats at the back for us* **4** *esp. spoken* to hang loosely, like a bag: *His trousers bagged at the knees*

bag and baggage *adv* with all one's belongings

bagatelle *n* something considered to be small and unimportant; a trifle

bagful *n* **bagfuls** *or* **bagsful** the quantity in a bag

baggage *n* **1** luggage **2** army equipment such as tents, beds, etc. **3** *humour* a good-for-nothing young woman

baggy *adj* **-gier, -giest** *esp. spoken* hanging in loose folds

bagpipes also (*esp. spoken*) **pipes**— *n* any of several types of musical instrument played in Scotland and elsewhere, in which air stored in a bag is forced out through pipes to produce the sound

bags¹ *n sl* lots: *He has bags of money!*

bags² *n* wide trousers

bail¹ *n* money left with a court of law so that a prisoner may be set free until he is tried

bail² *n* either of 2 small pieces of wood laid on top of the stumps in cricket

bailey *n* **-leys** **1** the outer wall of a castle **2** a courtyard inside these walls ⇨ CASTLE

Bailey bridge *n* a bridge made up of sections that can be put together quickly

bailiff *n* **1** *law* an official, esp. one who takes possession of property when money is owed **2** a man who looks after a farm for the owner

bail out *v adv* **1** to pay bail for **2** to remove water from (a boat) **3** to pay money to save from failure

bairn *n* *Scots & N English* a child

bait¹ *v* **1** to provide (a hook or trap) with bait **2** to make (an animal or a person) angry intentionally: *bear baiting*

bait² *n* **1** food used to catch fish or animals **2** something that attracts attention or causes desire **3 rise to the bait a** (of a fish) to take bait near the surface of the water **b** (of a person) to respond to something offered as bait, either by being attracted or by becoming angry

baize *n* thick woollen cloth

bake *v* **baked, baking** **1** to cook in an oven **2** to harden by heating

Bakelite *n* *trademark* any of several kinds of plastics or things related to plastics

baker *n* a person who bakes bread and cakes, esp. professionally

baker's dozen *n* 13

bakery *n* **-ries** a place where bread is baked and/or sold

baking powder *n* a powder put into bread and cakes to make them rise

baksheesh *n* (in the Middle East) money given as a tip or to the poor

balaclava *n* a woollen helmet that leaves the face free but covers the head, ears, and neck

balalaika *n* a Russian guitar with a triangular body

balance¹ *n* **1** an instrument for weighing things by making the amounts in 2 hanging pans equal **2** a weight or influence on one side equalling that on the other **3** a state where all parts have their proper weight **4** money or something else remaining or left over: *a bank balance* **5 in the balance** uncertain(ly) **6 off balance** unsteady or unsteadily **7 on balance** all things considered

balance² *v* **-anced, -ancing** **1** to consider or

compare **2** to be or cause to be steady, esp. in a difficult position **3** to be or cause to be of equal weight, importance, or influence to (something/each other) **4** to have no more money going out than coming in: *My accounts balance for the first time this year!*

balanced *adj* having a calm firm mind

balanced diet *n* the right quantities and kinds of food for health

balance of payments also **balance of trade**— *n* the money coming into a country in comparison with that going out

balance of power *n* **1** a position in which all sides are equally strong, esp. in political or military power **2** the power of one group in comparison with that of another

balance wheel *n* a wheel that keeps a machine moving steadily

balcony *n* **-nies** **1** a platform built out from an upper window of a building **2** the seats upstairs in a theatre or cinema

bald *adj* **1** with little or no hair **2** plain; without ornament — ~**ness** *n*

balderdash *n* nonsense

balding *adj* becoming bald

baldly *adv* spoken plainly

bale *n* a large bundle of goods or material

baleful *adj* full of hate and desire to do harm — -**fully** *adv*

bale out *v adv* **baled, baling out** to escape from an aircraft by parachute

balk, baulk *v* **1** to stop or get in the way of on purpose **2** to be unwilling to face or agree to something

ball[1] *n* **1** a round object used in play; anything of a round shape **2** a ball as thrown or kicked in cricket, football, etc. **3** a rounded part of the body: *the ball of the foot* **4 on the ball** *esp. spoken* showing up-to-date knowledge

ball[2] *n* **1** a large formal occasion for dancing **2** *sl* a very good time

ballad *n* **1** a song or poem which tells a story **2** a popular usu. sentimental song

ballast[1] *n* heavy material carried by a ship to keep it steady, or by a balloon to stop it going too high

ballast[2] *v* to fill with ballast

ball bearing *n* one of a number of small metal balls in a machine, helping it to run more easily

ballcock *n* a kind of tap, worked by a floating ball which rises and falls

ballerina *n* a female ballet dancer

ballet *n* **1** a dance in which a story is told without speech or singing **2** the music for such a dance **3** the art of a ballet dancer

ballistics *n* the study of the movement of objects thrown or fired through the air — **ballistic** *adj*

balloon[1] *n* **1** a bag of light material filled with hot air or a light gas **2** a small rubber bag that can be blown up, used as a toy **3** anything shaped like this, esp. the space round the words spoken by cartoon figures **4 the balloon goes up** the action starts

balloon[2] *v* to get bigger or rounder like a balloon being blown up

ballooning *n* the sport of flying in a balloon — -**ist** *n*

ballot[1] *n* **1** a paper used to vote **2** the number of votes recorded

ballot[2] *v* to decide by secret voting

ballpoint also **biro, ballpoint pen**— *n* a pen having a small steel ball that rolls ink onto the paper

balls up *v adv* *vulgar sl* to spoil — **balls-up** *n*

ballyhoo *n* noisy publicity

balm *n* a pleasant-smelling oily liquid used to relieve pain

balmy *adj* -**ier, -iest** (of air) soft and warm

balsa *n* the very light strong wood of a tropical American tree, used esp. to make models

balsam *n* **1** a tree that yields balm **2** balm

balustrade *n* a handrail with supporting posts

bamboo *n* **1** a tall plant of the grass family **2** the hard hollow jointed stems of this plant

bamboo curtain *n* (a name for) the border between China and the rest of the world — compare IRON CURTAIN

bamboozle *v* -**zled, -zling** *sl* to deceive

ban *v* -**nn-** to forbid, esp. by law — **ban** *n*

banal *adj* *offensive* uninteresting because very common — ~**ity** *n*

banana *n* a long curved yellow-skinned tropical fruit

banana republic *n* a Central or South American country that is industrially undeveloped and politically unsteady

band[1] *n* **1** a thin flat narrow piece of material, esp. for fastening things together or forming part of a garment: *hatband* **2** a stripe **3** any of several areas of like shape into which a larger whole can be divided, such as a band of radio waves

band[2] *v* to put a band or bands on —see also BAND TOGETHER

band[3] *n* **1** a group of people formed for some common purpose **2** a group of musicians, esp. one that plays "popular" music —compare ORCHESTRA

bandage[1] *n* a strip of material for binding round a wound

bandage[2] *v* -**daged, -daging** to bind with a bandage

bandanna, -dana *n* a large coloured handkerchief worn round the neck or head

b and b *abbrev. for* BED AND BREAKFAST

bandit *n* an armed robber — ~**ry** *n*

bandoleer, bandolier *n* a shoulder-belt for carrying bullets

bandsman *n* -**men** a musician in a band

bandstand *n* a platform with a roof where a band can play music in the open air

band together *v adv* to unite, usu. with some special purpose

bandwagon *n* **jump on the bandwagon** to do or say something just because it is popular

bandy¹ *v* **-died, -dying** to exchange (words or blows)

bandy² *adj* **-dier, -diest** 1 (of legs) curved outwards at the knees 2 also **bandy-legged**— having such legs

bandy about *v adv* to spread (rumours) about by talking

bane *n* a cause of bad things (esp. in the phrase **the bane of one's existence/life**) — ~**ful** *adj* — ~**fully** *adv*

bang¹ *v* 1 to strike sharply 2 to thump or slam noisily 3 to make a sharp loud noise

bang² *n* 1 a sharp blow 2 a sudden loud noise

bang³ *adv esp. spoken* right; directly; exactly: *We came bang up against more trouble*

bang⁴ *n esp. US* a fringe cut straight across the forehead

banger *n* 1 a sausage 2 a noisy firework 3 an old unreliable car

bangle *n* a circular bracelet

bang-on *interj esp. spoken* exactly correct; just right

banish *v* 1 to send away, usu. out of the country, as a punishment 2 to stop thinking about: *Banish that thought from your mind* — ~**ment** *n*

banister *n* a handrail guarding the edge of stairs or a landing

banjo *n* **-jos** *or* **-joes** a stringed musical instrument with a long neck and a drum-like body ☞ MUSIC

bank¹ *n* 1 land along the side of a river, lake, etc. 2 a mound of earth, sand, snow, etc. 3 a mass of clouds

bank² *v* (of a car or aircraft) to move with one side higher than the other, esp. when making a turn —see also BANK ON, BANK UP

bank³ *n* a row, esp. of oars, in an ancient boat

bank⁴ *n* 1 a place in which money is kept and paid out on demand, and where related activities go on 2 a place where something is held ready for use 3 a supply of money in a game of chance or the person in charge of it

bank⁵ *v* to put or keep in a bank

bankbook also **passbook**— *n* a book showing the money one puts into and takes out of a bank

banker *n* 1 a person who controls a bank 2 the player who keeps the bank in various games of chance

banker's card *n* CHEQUE CARD

banker's order *n* STANDING ORDER

bank holiday *n* an official public holiday

banking *n* the business of a bank or a banker

bank note *n* a piece of paper money issued for public use

bank on also **bank upon**— *v prep* to depend on

bank rate *n* the rate of interest fixed by a central bank, such as the Bank of England

bankrupt¹ *n* a person who is unable to pay his debts

bankrupt² *v* to make bankrupt or very poor

bankrupt³ *adj* 1 unable to pay one's debts 2 no longer able to produce anything good 3 completely without (good things) — ~**cy** *n*

bank up *v adv* to form into a mass

banner *n* 1 a flag 2 a long piece of cloth on which a sign is painted, usu. carried between 2 poles

banner headline *n* a large headline in a newspaper

bannock *n* a kind of flat bread made of oatmeal

banns *n* a public declaration, esp. in church, of an intended marriage

banquet¹ *n* a dinner in honour of a special person or occasion, esp. one at which speeches are made

banquet² *v* to take part in a banquet

banshee *n* (esp. in Ireland) a spirit whose cry is believed to foretell a death in the house

bantam *n* a small kind of chicken

bantamweight *n* a boxer weighing between 112 and 118 pounds

banter *v* to speak playfully or jokingly —**banter** *n* — ~**ing** *adj* — ~**ingly** *adv*

baptism *n* 1 a Christian ceremony in which a person is touched or covered with water to show that he has joined the Church 2 **baptism of fire a** a soldier's first battle **b** any unpleasant first experience of something — ~**al** *adj*

Baptist *n* a Christian who believes that people should not to be baptised until old enough to understand its meaning

baptize, -ise *v* **-tized, -tizing** 1 to perform the ceremony of baptism on 2 to give a name to at baptism

bar¹ *n* 1 a long piece of wood or metal used as a fastening or barrier 2 something that blocks things off or makes them difficult or impossible to do 3 a slab of solid material: *a bar of soap* 4 an underwater bank across the mouth of a river, entrance to a harbour, etc. ☞ SAIL 5 a narrow band of colour or light 6 (in music) **a** a group of notes **b** the downward lines marking these off in writing MUSIC 7 a counter or a room with a counter where alcoholic drinks are sold 8 **behind bars** in prison 9 **the prisoner at the bar** the person being tried in a court of law

bar² *v* **-rr-** 1 to close with a bar 2 to keep in or out by barring a door, gate, etc. 3 to block (movement or action): *to bar the way* 4 not to allow: *Guns are barred in Alice's restaurant* 5 to mark with a band or broad line

bar³ *prep* 1 except 2 **bar none** without any exceptions —see also BARRING

Bar *n* the profession of barrister

barb *n* the sharp curved point of a fish hook, arrow, etc.

barbarian *n* an uncivilized person

barbaric *adj* 1 of, like, or like that of a barbarian 2 very cruel — **-barism** *n* — ~**ally** *adv*

barbarity *n* **-ties** cruelty of the worst kind

barbarize, -ise v -ized, -izing to make cruel or savage

barbarous adj 1 uncivilized 2 very cruel 3 showing many mistakes in the use of language — ~**ly** adv

barbecue¹ n 1 a large framework on which to cook over an open fire 2 food, esp. meat, cooked in this way 3 an outdoor party at which food is cooked in this way

barbecue² v -cued, -cuing to cook on a barbecue

barbed adj 1 having one or more barbs 2 sharply and unkindly funny: a barbed remark

barbed wire n wire with short sharp points in it

barbel n a type of large fresh-water fish

barber n a person who cuts men's hair and shaves them —compare HAIRDRESSER

barber's pole n a pole with a red and white spiral pattern outside a barber's shop

barbiturate n medical any of various chemical substances that calm the nerves and put people to sleep

barcarole -olle— n a piece of music like the rowing songs of Venetian boatmen

bard n literature 1 a poet 2 **the Bard (of Avon)** Shakespeare

bare¹ adj 1 naked; uncovered 2 empty: a bare room 3 not more than; only: A bare word would be enough — ~**ness** n

bare² v bared, baring to take off a covering; bring to view

bareback adj, adv (riding) without a saddle

barefaced adj shameless: a barefaced trick — ~**ly** adv

barely adv 1 in a bare way 2 only just; hardly: —see HARDLY (USAGE)

bargain¹ n 1 an agreement, esp. one to do something in return for something else 2 something bought cheaply

bargain² v to talk about the conditions of a sale, agreement, or contract

bargain for also **bargain on—** v prep be prepared for

barge¹ n 1 a large flat-bottomed boat for carrying heavy goods on a canal or river 2 a large rowing boat used on ceremonial occasions

barge² v barged, barging to move about quickly but clumsily

bargee n a man who works on a barge

barge in v adv to rush in rudely; interrupt

barge into v prep 1 to interrupt 2 BUMP INTO

baritone n (a man with) the male singing voice lower than tenor and higher than bass

barium n a soft silver-white metal that is an element and is found only in combination with other substances

bark¹ v 1 to make the sound that dogs make 2 (of a gun) to sound when fired 3 to speak in a sharp loud voice: The officer barked out an order

bark² n 1 the sound made by a dog 2 a sound like this 3 a voice like this, or words spoken in such a voice

bark³ n the strong outer covering of a tree

bark⁴ v 1 to take the bark off 2 to knock the skin off (esp. in the phrase **bark one's shin**)

bark, barque⁵ n a sailing ship with 3 masts

barker n a person who stands outside a place of public amusement shouting to people to come in

barley n a plant grown for food and making beer and spirits

barley sugar n a kind of boiled sweet

barley water n a drink made from barley

barley wine n a very strong beer

barman fem. **-maid—** n -men a person who serves drinks in a bar

bar mitzvah n 1 a Jewish boy who at 13 has reached the age of religious responsibility 2 the ceremony to celebrate this

barmy adj -ier, -iest sl foolish or a little mad ⚠ BALMY

barn n a farm building for storing crops

barnacle n a small shellfish which clings in large numbers on rocks, ships' bottoms, etc.

barn dance n a social gathering for country dancing

barnyard n a yard on a farm with barns and other buildings round it

barometer n an instrument for measuring air pressure, esp. in order to forecast changes in the weather — **-metric** adj — **-metrically** adv

baron n 1 a nobleman with the lowest rank in the British House of Lords 2 esp. US a very powerful businessman —see also BARONESS — ~**ial** adj

baroness n a woman who **a** is the wife of a baron, or **b** is of noble rank in her own right

baronet n a knight, or his title which passes on to his son when he dies — ~**cy** n

barony n -ies the rank or lands of a baron

baroque adj, n 1 (of, like, or about) a highly ornamental style common in all the arts in Europe around the 17th century 2 (of works of art) greatly, or too greatly, ornamented

barque n a bark, ship

barrack v to interrupt a meeting by shouting

barracks n **barracks** buildings that soldiers live in

barracuda n -da or -das any of several types of flesh-eating tropical fish

barrage¹ n 1 the firing of a number of heavy guns at once to protect advancing soldiers 2 (of speech or writing) a large number of things put forward very quickly: a barrage of questions

barrage² v -raged, -raging to deliver a barrage against

barred adj 1 having bars 2 having bands of different colours

barrel n 1 a round wooden container with curved sides and a flat top and bottom 2 a tube-shaped part of something: a gun barrel

barrel organ n a musical instrument which is

played by turning a handle, producing a sound like that of an organ

barren adj **1** (of female animals) unable to bear young **2** (of trees or plants) bearing no fruit **3** (of land) having poor soil **4** useless; empty: *a barren argument* — ~**ness** n

barricade¹ v **-caded, -cading 1** to block or close off with a barricade **2** to keep in by means of a barricade

barricade² n a wall built quickly to block the advance of an enemy

barricades n a field or subject where there are sharp disagreements: *She fought on the barricades for women's rights*

barrier n something placed in the way in order to control people or things moving forward

barring prep **1** excepting **2** if there is/are not: *We shall return at midnight, barring accidents* —see also BAR

barrister n a lawyer who has the right of speaking in the higher courts of law —compare SOLICITOR

barrow¹ n a tumulus

barrow² n **1** a small handcart **2** a market stall with wheels **3** a wheelbarrow

Bart abbrev. for baronet

barter v to exchange goods for other goods — **barter** n

basalt n a type of dark greenish-black igneous rock

base¹ n **1** the bottom of something, on which it stands **2** the starting point of something: *The base of the thumb is where it joins the hand* **3** a centre from which a start is made in an activity, often one where supplies are kept **4** a military camp **5** a line on which a geometrical figure stands **6** *technical* the number in relation to which others are built up: *Ordinary numbers use base 10, but many computers work to base 2* —see BINARY, DENARY **7** the number around which logarithms are built -see LOGARITHM **8** the main part of a mixture **9** (in chemistry) a substance which combines with an acid to form a salt **10** (in the game of baseball) any (esp. the first 3) of the 4 points which a player must touch in order make a run

base² adj esp. in literature dishonourable — ~**ly** adv — ~**ness** n

baseball n a game played with a bat and ball between 2 teams of 9 players each, on a large field of which the centre is 4 bases that a player must touch in order to score a run

base-born adj old use of humble birth

baseless adj without a good reason

baseline n a line serving as a base , esp the back line at each end of a tennis court

basement n rooms in a house below street level —compare CELLAR

base metal n a metal which is not precious —compare NOBLE

base on also **base upon**— v prep **based, basing** to give (something) a reason or starting point in: *One should always base one's opinions on facts*

bases pl. of BASIS

bash¹ v esp. spoken to hit hard

bash² n esp. spoken **1** a hard blow **2** have a **bash** sl to make an attempt

bashful adj shy — -**fully** adv — -**fulness** n

basic adj more necessary than anything else, and on which everything else rests or is built

Basic n a simple language for programming a computer

basically adv with regard to what is most important

Basic English n an international form of English which uses a small number of words to express a large number of ideas

basics n the simplest but most important parts of something

basil n a type of sweet-smelling plant used in cooking

basilica n **1** an ancient Roman courtroom round at one end with pillars supporting the roof **2** a building of this type used as a Roman Catholic church

basin n **1** a shallow container for water **2** a round container for food **3** the area of country from which a river collects its water **4** the deep part of a harbour **5** a wide part of a canal with moorings

basis n **bases 1** that from which something is started or developed **2** the most necessary or important part of something: *The basis of this drink is orange juice*

bask v **1** to sit or lie in the sunshine **2** to enjoy (someone's favour)

basket n **1** a container made of woven sticks or other such material **2** an open net fixed to a metal ring high up off the ground, through which the ball mush be thrown in basketball

basketball n a game in which each team of 5 players tries to throw a large ball through the other team's basket

basketry n **1** the art of making baskets and other such things **2** also **basketwork**— objects produced by this art

bas-relief n French **1** a form of art in which the background is cut away slightly so that the main figures stand out **2** an example of this kind of art

bass¹ n **bass** or **basses** a kind of edible fish

bass² adj (of a voice or musical instrument) deep or low in sound ☞ MUSIC

bass³ n **1** (a man with) the lowest male singing voice **2** also **bass line**— the lowest part in written music —compare TREBLE

bass clef n (in music) a sign, 𝄢 showing that the following notes are lower than middle C — compare TREBLE CLEF

basset also **basset hound**— n a type of dog with a long body, short legs, and large ears

bassinet n a baby's bed or pram made of basketwork

bassoon n a low-sounding double reed woodwind instrument

bastard n **1** a child of unmarried parents **2** sl

a person (usu. a man) that one strongly dislikes **3** *sl* a man; fellow

bastardize, -ise *v* **-ized, -izing** to reduce from a better to a worse state or condition — **-ization** *n*

baste¹ *v* **basted, basting** to join together in long loose stitches; tack

baste² *v* (in cookery) to pour melted fat over

baste³ *v sl* to hit hard, usu. with a stick

bastion *n* **1** a part of the wall of a castle that stands out from the main part ☞ CASTLE **2** an especially strong point in defence

bat¹ *n* **1** any of several types of wooden stick used for hitting a ball in various games **2** a sharp blow **3** a batsman

bat² *v* **-tt-** **1** to hit with or as if with a bat **2** (in cricket and baseball) to hit a ball or have a turn to bat — **batter** *n*

bat³ *n* any of several kinds of flying mouselike animals that are active at night ☞ MAMMAL —see also BATS, BATTY

bat⁴ *v* **1** to blink quickly **2** **not bat an eyelid** to show no sign of one's feelings

batch *n* a set; group; quantity: *a batch of orders*

bated *adj* **with bated breath** hardly breathing in anxious anticipation

bath¹ *n* **1** an act of washing one's whole body **2** water for a bath **3** also **bathtub**— a container in which one sits to bath **4** *technical* liquid in a container, used for a special purpose —see also BATHS

bath² *v* **1** to give a bath to **2** to have a bath

bath chair *n* a kind of covered wheelchair

bathe *v* **bathed, bathing** **1** to go swimming **2** to pour water or other liquid over, usu. for medical reasons **3** to spread over with (or as if with) light, water, etc.: *bathed in sunlight* — **bathe** *n* — **~r** *n*

bathing *n* the act or practice of going into water to swim

bathing suit *n* a swimming costume

bath mat *n* a usu. washable mat used in a bathroom

bathos *n* a sudden change from very beautiful or noble ideas, words, etc., to very common or foolish ones △ PATHOS

bathrobe *n* a loose garment worn before and after bathing

bathroom *n* a room containing a bath (and possibly a toilet)

baths *n* **baths** a public building used for bathing or swimming

bathyscaphe *n* a ship for going very deep into the sea

batik *n* a way of printing patterns on cloth by putting wax on the part not to be coloured, and melting it off afterwards

batman *n* **-men** (in the armed services) an officer's personal servant

baton *n* **1** a short thin stick used by a conductor to show the beat of the music **2** a short stick carried as a badge of office or rank **3** a police-

man's truncheon **4** a short tube passed from one runner to the next during a race **5** a hollow metal rod usu. with a ball at one end, used for show by the leader of a ceremonial march

bats *adj sl* mad

batsman *n* **-men** the player in cricket who tries to hit the ball with a bat

battalion *n* a group of usu. 500–1,000 soldiers

batten *n* a long board used for fastening other pieces of wood

batten down *v adv* (on ships) to fasten with boards of wood

batten on also **batten upon**— *v prep* to live well by using (someone) for one's own purposes

batter¹ *v* **1** to beat hard and repeatedly **2** to cause to lose shape or be badly damaged by continual hard beating or by continual use

batter² *n* a mixture of flour, eggs, and milk, beaten together and used in cooking

battering ram also **ram**— *n* a large heavy log formerly used in war for breaking through gates

battery *n* **-ies** **1** a number of big guns together with the men who serve them **2** a group of connected electric cells ☞ ELECTRICITY **3** a line of boxes in which hens are kept so that they will lay eggs frequently —compare FREE RANGE **4** a large group or set of things: *He faced a battery of cameras* **5** *law* striking another person (esp. in the phrase **assault and battery**)

batting crease also **crease**— *n* POPPING CREASE

battle¹ *n* a fight between enemies or opposing groups; a struggle

battle² *v* **-tled, -tling** to fight or struggle

battleaxe *n* **1** a kind of heavy axe, formerly used as a weapon **2** a fierce and forceful, often unpleasant woman

battle cruiser *n* a type of large fast warship with heavy guns, but with lighter armour than a battleship

battlefield also **battleground**— *n* a place at which a battle is or has been fought

battlements *n* a low wall round the flat roof of a castle, with spaces to shoot through ☞ CASTLE

battle royal *n* **battle royals** *or* **battles royal** a fierce battle or struggle

battleship *n* the largest and most heavily armed kind of warship

batty *adj* **-tier, -tiest** *sl* mad — **battiness** *n*

bauble *n* something ornamental, but of little real value

baulk *v* to balk

bauxite *n* the ore from which aluminium is obtained

bawdy *adj* **-ier, -iest** (of talk, jokes, etc.) about sex — **-dily** *adv* — **-diness** *n*

bawl *v* to shout in a loud, rough voice

bay¹ *adj, n* **bays** (a horse whose colour is) reddish-brown

bay² *n* any of several trees like the laurel, with leaves used in cooking

bay³ n a part or division of a building or room which may stand out from the rest and is often between 2 pillars —see also SICKBAY

bay⁴ v **bayed, baying** to make repeatedly the deep cry of a hound N — **bay**

bay⁵ n **hold/keep at bay** to keep someone or something some distance away

bay⁶ n part of the sea or of a large lake enclosed in a curve of the land

bay leaf n a leaf of the bay tree, used for adding taste in cooking

bayonet¹ n a long knife fixed to the end of a rifle

bayonet² v to drive a bayonet into

bay window n a window built outwards from the wall —compare BOW WINDOW

bazaar n 1 an Eastern marketplace 2 a sale to get money for some good purpose

bazooka n a light anti-tank gun that rests on the shoulder when fired

BBC abbrev. for: British Broadcasting Corporation —compare ITA, ITV

BC abbrev. for: Before (the birth of) Christ —compare AD

be v pres. tense I am, you are, he is, we are, you are, they are, (short forms I'm, you're, he's, we're, you're, they're,) (negative short forms I'm not, isn't, aren't) past tense I was, you were, he was, we were, you were, they were (past negative short forms wasn't, weren't), past part. been, pres. part. being 1 (a helping verb, forming various tenses); We're going now. | He was bitten by a dog 2 (a verb which connects the subject of a sentence with another word or other words to give information about the subject): Horses are animals. | This book is mine. | He will be happy. | The old lady was upstairs 3 to exist

beach¹ n the shore of the sea or a lake or the bank of a river, esp. one used for swimming and sunbathing

beach² v to run onto the shore: to beach a boat

beach buggy also **dune buggy**— n **-gies** a motor vehicle with very large tyres for use on sand beaches

beachcomber n 1 a person who makes a living from what he finds on the beach 2 a long rolling wave

beachhead n a strong position (usu. on a beach) seized by an invading army —compare BRIDGEHEAD

beacon n 1 a signal fire, commonly on a hill 2 a tall object or a light which acts as a guide or warning 3 BELISHA BEACON

bead¹ n 1 a small object which can be threaded onto a string or wire and worn with others esp. round the neck, for ornament 2 a small drop of liquid 3 **draw a bead (on)** to take aim (at)

bead² v 1 to ornament with beads 2 to cover with small drops

beading n a long narrow piece of wood used for ornamenting walls, furniture, etc.

beadle n a uniformed officer in some universities

beady adj **-ier, -iest** (esp. of an eye) small, round, and shining, like a bead

beagle n a small, smooth-haired dog used in the hunting of hares (**beagling**) on foot

beak n 1 the hard horny mouth of a bird, a turtle, etc. ☞ BIRD 2 anything shaped like this

beaker n 1 a drinking cup 2 a small glass cup as used in a laboratory

be-all and end-all n 1 the most important thing 2 the one thing that does the whole job

beam¹ n 1 a large long heavy piece of wood, steel, or concrete, esp. one used to support a building 2 **broad in the beam** sl wide across the hips

beam² n 1 a ray of light 2 radio waves sent out along a narrow path 3 a bright look or smile

beam³ v 1 to send out light; shine 2 to smile brightly and happily 3 (of the radio) to send out in a certain direction

beam-ends n **on one's beam-ends** sl almost without any money

bean n 1 any of various climbing plants or the seed or pod it bears, esp. one that can be used as food 2 a seed of certain other plants, from which food or drink can be made: coffee beans 3 esp. spoken a valueless thing: not worth a bean 4 sl the smallest possible coin: I haven't a bean 5 **full of beans** esp. spoken active and eager 6 **spill the beans** sl to tell a secret, usu. unintentionally

bear¹ n **bears** or **bear** 1 any of various kinds of usu. large and heavy animals with thick rough fur ☞ MAMMAL 2 a rough, bad-mannered, bad-tempered man —see also GREAT BEAR

bear² v **bore, borne, bearing** 1 esp. written to carry from one place to another; carry away 2 to support 3 to have or show 4 to keep (a feeling) in one's mind (in relation to someone) 5 to be suitable for 6 to give birth to 7 to produce (a crop or fruit) 8 to suffer: to bear pain —see USAGE 9 to carry (oneself) in a certain way 10 to behave in a certain way 11 to turn in the stated direction 12 to have: x bears no relation to y 13 **bear in mind** to keep in one's memory —see also BEAR DOWN, BEAR DOWN ON, BEAR ON, BEAR OUT, BEAR UP, BEAR WITH USAGE Compare **bear, endure, stand, tolerate. Bear, stand,** and **endure** have almost the same meaning: I can't bear/stand/endure the new teacher; but **bear** and **stand** are commoner, **endure** is stronger. They are also used, particularly **endure**, for great bodily hardship: He endured/bore/stood the pain as long as he could. **Tolerate** is used of people or behaviour, but not of suffering.

bearable adj that can be borne or suffered — **-bly** adv

beard¹ n 1 hair on the face below the mouth 2 long hairs on a plant, as on barley — **~less** adj

beard² v to face or deal with (someone) boldly

bearded *adj* having a beard

bear down *v adv* 1 to defeat 2 to use effort; push

bear down on also **bear down upon**— *v adv prep* 1 to come near threateningly 2 to weigh heavily on

bearer *n* 1 a person who bears or carries 2 a person who helps to carry the body at a funeral 3 a fruit-producing tree or plant 4 *esp. Indian* a male servant

bear hug *n* a rough tight hug

bearing *n* 1 manner of holding one's body or way of behaving 2 connection with or influence on something 3 *technical* the part of a machine in which a rotating rod is held, or which turns on a fixed rod —compare BALL BEARING 4 *technical* a direction or angle as shown by a compass 5 giving birth

bearings *n* understanding of one's position or the state of affairs

bear on also **bear upon**— *v prep* to show some connection with

bear out *v adv* to support the truth of

bearskin *n* a tall fur cap worn by certain British soldiers

bear up *v adv* 1 to continue (in spite of difficulties) 2 to support something without becoming broken 3 CHEER UP

bear with *v prep* to show patience towards

beast *n* 1 an animal, esp. a large farm animal 2 an unpleasant, cruel person or thing

beastly[1] *adj* **-lier, -liest** strongly dislikeable: *a beastly person/habit* —compare BESTIAL — **-liness** *n*

beastly[2] *adv esp. spoken* very (esp. unpleasantly or badly)

beast of burden *n* an animal which carries things

beat[1] *v* **beat, beaten** or **beat, beating** 1 to hit repeatedly 2 to shape by hitting 3 to hit, move, or cause to move regularly: *to beat a drum* | *The heart beats* 4 to mix rapidly: *to beat eggs* —see also BEAT UP 5 to defeat; do better than 6 **Beat it!** *sl* Go away at once! 7 **beat time** to make movements in time with music —see also BEAT DOWN, BEAT IN, BEAT UP

beat[2] *n* 1 a single stroke or blow, esp. as part of a series 2 a regular sound produced by or as if by repeated beating 3 time in music or poetry 4 the usual path followed by a policeman duty

beat[3] *adj sl* very tired

beat down *v adv* to persuade (someone) to reduce a price

beaten *adj* 1 (of metal) made to take a certain shape by hammering. 2 defeated 3 **off the beaten track** far from places where people often go
2 a person who drives wild birds or animals towards the guns of those waiting to shoot them

beatific *adj* giving or showing great joy or peaceful happiness — ~**ally** *adv*

beat in *v adv* to break open by hitting repeatedly

beating *n* the act of giving repeated blows, usu. for punishment

Beatitudes *n* the statements about those who are blessed made by Jesus in the Bible (Matthew 5: 3-12)

beatnik *n* (in the late 1950's and early 1960's) a hippie

beat up *v adv* to hurt severely by hitting

beau *n* **beaux** or **beaus** 1 *old use or literature* a man of fashion 2 *old use* a boyfriend

Beaujolais *n* a type of French red wine

beauteous *adj poetic* beautiful — ~**ly** *adv*

beautician *n* a person who gives beauty treatments

beautiful *adj* 1 having beauty —compare HANDSOME, PRETTY 2 *esp. spoken* very good — ~**ly** *adv*

beautify *v* **-fied, -fying** to make beautiful

beauty *n* **-ties** 1 qualities that give pleasure to the senses or lift up the mind 2 someone (usu. female) or something beautiful 3 *esp. spoken* someone or something very good (or bad): *Your black eye is a real beauty!*

beauty parlour also **beauty salon**— *n* a place where women are given beauty treatments, esp. of the face, hair, skin, and nails

beauty spot *n* a dark-coloured spot on a woman's face, formerly considered attractive

beaver *n* 1 a broad-tailed animal of the rat family which builds dams across streams ☞ MAMMAL 2 its valuable fur 3 **eager beaver** a person who is almost too keen on working hard

beaver away *v adv sl* to work hard, but rather ploddingly

becalmed *adj* (of a sailing ship) unable to move because of the lack of wind

because *conj* for the reason that: *I do it because I like it* —see REASON (USAGE)

beck *n* **at someone's beck and call** ready to do everything someone asks

beckon *v* to make a sign to call (someone)

become *v* **became, become, becoming** 1 to come to be: *He became king* 2 to suit be suitable to or to be fitting for: *That dress becomes you*

become of *v prep* to happen to

becoming *adj* 1 looking very well on the wearer 2 proper; suitable: *His laughter was not becoming on that solemn occasion* — ~**ly** *adv*

bed[1] *n* 1 an article of furniture to sleep on 2 a piece of ground prepared for plants 3 a level surface on which something rests; base 4 the bottom of a river, lake, or sea 5 a stretch of rock stratum 6 **go to bed with** *esp. spoken* to have sexual relations with

bed[2] *v* **-dd-** 1 to fix on a base (or beneath the surface); embed 2 to plant in a bed or beds —see also BED OUT

bed and board *n* lodging and food

bed and breakfast *n* a night's lodging and breakfast the following morning

bedaub *v* to smear

bedbug *n* a type of wingless blood-sucking insect that lives esp. in beds

bed

bedclothes *n* the sheets, covers, etc. put on a bed

bedding *n* 1 materials on which a person or animal can sleep 2 bedclothes

bedeck *v* to hang ornaments, jewels, flowers, etc. on

bedevil *v* -ll- to trouble greatly — ~ment *n*

bedfellow *n* a companion

bedimmed *adj literature* made less able to see or understand clearly: *eyes bedimmed with tears*

bedlam *n* 1 a wild noisy place or activity 2 *old use* a hospital for mad people

bed linen *n* the sheets and pillowcases for a bed

bedouin *n* **bedouin** *or* **bedouins** a wandering desert Arab

bed out *v adv* to plant in enough space for growth

bedpan *n* a low wide vessel used for emptying the bowels without getting out of bed —compare CHAMBER POT

bedpost *n* one of the posts at the 4 corners of an old-fashioned bed

bedraggled *adj* with dirty, untidy clothes and hair

bedridden *adj* confined to bed (eg. because of illness)

bedrock *n* 1 the solid rock supporting the soil 2 the facts on which a belief rests

bedroom *n* a room for sleeping in

bedside *n* the side of a bed

bedside manner *n* a doctor's behaviour when visiting a sick person

bed-sitter also (*esp. written*) **bed-sitting room** (*esp. spoken*) **bed-sit**— *n* a single room for living and sleeping in

bedsore *n* a sore on the skin, caused by lying in bed for too long

bedspread *n* a cover spread over a bed

bedstead *n* the main framework of a bed

bee *n* 1 a type of insect that makes honey, often lives in groups, and can sting painfully ☞ INSECT 2 **a bee in one's bonnet** an unreasonably fixed idea

beech *n* a type of tree with smooth grey trunk, spreading branches, and dark green or copper-coloured leaves

beech mast *n* beech nuts

beef¹ *n* 1 the meat of farm cattle 2 *esp. spoken* (power of) the muscles

beef² *v sl* to complain

Beefeater *n* a soldier of the ceremonial guard in the Tower of London

beefsteak *n* a thick piece of the best part of beef

beefy *adj* -ier, -iest *esp. spoken* (of a person) big, strong, and perhaps fat

beeline *n* **make a beeline for** to go quickly and directly towards

been 1 *past part. of* BE 2 **a** gone and come back from: *They have been to India* **b** arrived and left: *Has the postman been?* —compare GO

beer *n* 1 a type of alcoholic drink made from grain 2 a separate drink or container of this 3 any of several kinds of drink made from plants: *ginger beer*

beeswax *n* wax made by bees, used esp. for making furniture polish

beet *n* SUGAR BEET

beetle¹ *n* any of several types of insect with hard wing coverings ☞ INSECT

beetle² *v* -tled, -tling *sl* (of people) to move off quickly

beetroot *n* a plant with a large round red root, cooked and eaten as a vegetable

befall *v* -fell, -fallen *esp. written* to happen (to), esp. as if by fate

befit *v* -tt- to be proper or suitable to — ~ting *adj* — ~tingly *adv*

before¹ *adv* 1 in advance; ahead 2 at an earlier time; already

before² *prep* 1 in front of: *He stood before her* 2 earlier in time than: *the day before yesterday* 3 **before the mast** *literature* on a sailing ship 4 **before one's time** too soon to be accepted by people: *Darwin was before his time with his ideas*

before³ *conj* 1 earlier than the time when 2 more willingly than: *He'd die of hunger before he would steal*

beforehand *adv* 1 in advance 2 too early; hasty —compare BEHINDHAND

befriend *v* to act as a friend to; help

befuddle *v* -dled, -dling to confuse

beg *v* -gg- 1 to ask for (food, money, etc.) 2 to ask humbly for 3 to allow oneself: *I beg to point out that you are wrong* 4 (of a dog) to sit up with the front legs held against the chest 5 to avoid: *Your answer seems to beg the real question*

beget *v* **begot, begotten** *or* **begot, begetting** 1 *Bible & old use* to become the father of 2 to produce: *Hunger begets crime*

beggar¹ *n* 1 a person who lives by begging 2 *sl* a fellow

beggar² *v* 1 to make very poor 2 **beggar description** to be beyond the powers of language to describe

beggarly *adj* 1 of or like a beggar 2 much too little for the purpose — **-liness** *n*

beggary *n* the state of being very poor

begin *v* **began, begun, beginning** 1 to start 2 **to begin with** as the first reason: *We can't go. To begin with, it's too cold*

beginner *n* a person who begins some activity, esp. one that is new to them

beginning *n* the start; starting point; origin

beg off *v adv* to excuse (oneself or others)

begone *v poetic usu. imperative* to go away at once

begonia *n* any of a related group of showy flowering plants

begot *past tense of* BEGET

begotten *past part. of* BEGET

begrudge *v* **begrudged, begrudging** to grudge

beguile v **beguiled, beguiling** 1 to deceive; cheat 2 to cause (time) to pass without being noticed 3 to charm — **-ling** adj — **-lingly** adv — ~**ment** n

begum n (in India and Pakistan) a Muslim lady of high rank

begun past part. of BEGIN

behalf n **on behalf of someone/someone's behalf** (acting, speaking, etc.) for someone

behave v **behaved, behaving** 1 to act; bear oneself 2 to act in an acceptable or polite way 3 (of things) to act in a particular way

behaviour n way of behaving

behaviourism n the idea that the scientific study of the mind should be based on measurable facts about behaviour rather than on people's reports of their thoughts and feelings — **-rist** n

behead v to cut off the head of as a punishment

behest n esp. written a command (esp. in the phrase **at the behest of**)

behind[1] adv 1 to the back; at the back; where something or someone was earlier 2 late: I've got behind with my homework

behind[2] prep 1 to or at the back or farther side of 2 in support of: Don't be afraid - we're all behind you! 3 **behind the times** out of date

behind[3] n sl the buttocks —see also BOTTOM

behindhand adv late; slow —compare BEFORE-HAND

behold v **beheld** literature & old use 1 to see 2 imperative look at! — ~**er** n

beholden adj having to feel grateful (to)

behove v **behoved** esp. written to be necessary, proper, or advantageous for

beige n, adj a very pale brown

being[1] n 1 existence; life 2 the qualities or nature of a thing, esp. a living thing 3 a living thing, esp. a person

being[2] adj **for the time being** for a limited period

belabour v 1 to talk about at unnecessary length 2 to attack with words 3 to beat heavily, as with a stick

belated adj arriving too late — ~**ly** adv

belay v **belayed, belaying** technical to make fast (a ship's rope)

belch[1] v 1 to pass wind noisily out through the mouth 2 to throw out with force or in large quantities: Chimneys belch smoke

belch[2] n the act or sound of belching

belfry n **-fries** 1 a space where bells are hung, as in a church tower ☞ CATHEDRAL 2 **be/have bats in the belfry** sl to be rather mad —see also BATS, BATTY

belie v **belied, belying** 1 to give a false idea of 2 to show to be false

belief n 1 trust 2 the feeling that something is true or real 3 something believed; an idea which is considered true 4 **beyond belief** too strange to be believed —see UNBELIEF (USAGE)

believe v **believed, believing** 1 to have a firm religious faith 2 to consider to be true or honest: to believe someone 3 to hold as an opinion; suppose — **believable** adj — **believably** adv

believe in v prep 1 to have faith or trust in (someone) 2 to consider to be true; consider to exist 3 to consider (something) to be of worth

believer n 1 a person who has religious faith 2 a person who believes in (something or perhaps someone)

Belisha beacon also **beacon**— n a flashing orange light on a post that marks a zebra crossing

belittle v **-tled, -tling** to cause to seem small or unimportant

bell n 1 a round hollow metal vessel, which makes a ringing sound when struck 2 the sounding or stroke of a bell 3 something with the form of a typical bell 4 **as sound as a bell** esp. spoken **a** healthy **b** in perfect condition

bell-bottoms n trousers that are very wide at the bottom

bellboy n **-boys** a boy or man employed by a hotel or club to take guests to their rooms, give them messages, etc.

belle n a popular and attractive girl or woman

bellicose adj warlike; ready to quarrel or fight — **-cosity** n

belligerency also **belligerence**— n the state of being angry and ready to fight — **-erent** adj

bellow v 1 to make the loud deep sound typical of a bull 2 to shout (something) in a deep voice — **bellow** n

bellows n **bellows** an instrument used to blow air into a fire or an organ

bell push n a button that when pressed rings a bell

belly n **-lies** 1 esp. spoken the part of the human body which contains the stomach and bowels 2 something curved or round like this

bellyache[1] n an ache in the stomach

bellyache[2] v **-ached, -aching** sl to complain, perhaps unjustly

belly button n sl the navel

bellyful n sl too much: I've had a bellyful of your silly advice

belly-land v esp. spoken to land (a plane) on the undersurface without use of the landing apparatus — **belly landing** n

belly laugh n esp. spoken a deep full laugh

belong v 1 to be suitable: A telephone belongs in every home 2 to be in the right place: That chair belongs in the other room

belongings n those things which belong to one

belong to v prep 1 to be the property of 2 to be a member of 3 to be connected with

beloved adj, n (a person) that one loves very much

below[1] adv 1 in or to a lower place; on a lower level 2 on or to a deck lower than the main deck of a ship 3 lower on the same page or on the following page: See p.85 below

below[2] prep in a lower place than; on a lower level than

belt¹ *n* **1** a band worn around the waist **2** a continous band of flexible material used for driving a machine or for carrying materials —compare FAN BELT **3** an area that has some special quality: *the Corn Belt*

belt² *v* **1** to fasten with a belt **2** to fasten (to something) with a belt: *He belted on his sword* **3** to hit with a belt **4** *esp. spoken* to hit very hard: *I belted him in the eye* **5** *sl* to travel fast

belt out *v adv esp. spoken* to sing loudly

belt up *v adv sl not polite* to be quiet —see also SHUT UP

bemoan *v* to be very sorry because of

bemused *adj* completely puzzled and confused

bench *n* **1** a long seat for 2 or more people **2** the seat where a judge sits in court **3** the judge himself or judges as a group **4** a long worktable

bench mark *n* a mark made on something fixed at a point of known height, from which heights and distances can be measured in map-making

bend¹ *v* **bent, bending** **1** to force or be forced into or out of a curve or angle **2** to lean away or cause to lean away from an upright position **3** to direct (one's efforts) to: *He bent his mind to the job* —see also BENT, BENT ON, **bend over** BACKWARDS

bend² *n* **1** the act or action of bending or the state of being bent **2** something that is bent, such as a curved part of a road or stream **3 round the bend** *sl* mad

bend before *v prep* to yield to

bended *adj* **on bended knee(s)** *literature* kneeling, esp. to ask a favour

bends *n* a painful disease caused by gas in the blood suffered by deep-sea divers who come to the surface too quickly

beneath¹ *adv esp. written* in a lower position; below

beneath² *prep* **1** in or to a lower position than; below; under and often close or touching **2** not suitable to or worthy of

Benedictine *n* a member of a Christian religious order founded by Saint Benedict

benediction *n* a blessing —compare MALEDICTION

benefactor *fem.* **benefactress**—*n* a person who does good or who gives money for a good purpose —compare MALEFACTOR — **-tion** *n*

beneficent *adj esp. written* doing good; kind —compare MALEFICENT — **-cence** *n* — ~**ly** *adv*

beneficial *adj* (of non-living things) helpful; useful — ~**ly** *adv*

beneficiary *n* **-ries** the receiver of a benefit, esp. a person who receives property left by someone who has died

benefit¹ *n* **1** advantage; profit **2** money provided by the government as a right, esp. in sickness or unemployment

benefit² *v* (of non-living things) to be useful, profitable, or helpful to

benefit from also **benefit by**— *v prep* to gain by

benefit of the doubt *n* the right to favourable consideration in the absence of complete proof of wrongness or guilt

benevolence *n* the desire to do good — **-ent** *adj*

benighted *adj literature* lost in moral darkness — ~**ly** *adv*

benign *adj* **1** having or showing a kind or gentle nature **2** *medical* (of a disease) not dangerous to life — ~**ly** *adv*

benignity *n esp. written* kindness; gentleness

bent¹ *adj sl* **1** dishonest —opposite **straight** **2** homosexual

bent² *past tense & part.* of BEND

bent on also **bent upon**— *adj* with one's mind set on

benumbed *adj* having all sense of feeling taken away

benzene also **benzol**— *n* a colourless liquid that burns quickly and is obtained from coal

bequeath *v esp. written* to give or pass on to others after death — **bequest** *n*

berate *v* **berated, berating** *esp. written* to scold

bereave *v* **bereaved** *or* **bereft, bereaving** to take away, esp. by death — ~**ment** *n*   USAGE **Bereaved** is a much stronger and sadder word than **bereft**, although both words mean that one has lost something: *to be bereft of one's senses | a bereaved mother* (= one whose child has died).

bereaved *adj esp. written* whose close relative or friend has just died

bereft *adj* completely without

beret *n* a round soft flat hat

berk *n sl* a fool

berry *n* **-ries** a small soft fruit

berserk *adj* mad with violent anger

berth¹ *n* **1** a place where a ship can be tied up, as in a harbour **2** a sleeping place in a ship or train

berth² *v* **1** (of a ship) to come into port to be tied up **2** to bring (a ship) into port to be tied up

beryl *n* a type of precious stone, usu. green

beseech *v* **besought** *or* **beseeched, beseeching** *literature* to ask anxiously; plead

besetting *adj* (of something bad) continuously present

beside *prep* **1** at or close to the side of **2** in comparison with **3 beside the point** having nothing to do with the main point or question **4 beside oneself (with)** almost mad (with trouble or strong emotion) —see BESIDES (USAGE)

besides *adv, prep* in addition (to); as well(as) USAGE Compare **beside, besides, except:** 1 **Beside** can be used at the end of a sentence: *That's the girl you were sitting beside.* **Besides** cannot. 2 **Besides** means "as well as"; **except** means "but not; leaving out", and follows **all, none,** etc.: *All of us passed besides John* means that John passed too, but *All of us passed* **except** *John* means that John did not pass.

besiege *v* **besieged, besieging** **1** to surround with armed forces **2** to press with questions, requests, letters, etc. **3** to cause worry or trouble to: *doubts that besieged him*

besmirch *v* to damage (a person or his character) in the opinion of others

besotted *adj* made stupid or foolish by strong drink or powerful feeling

besought *past tense & part. of* BESEECH

bespeak *v* **bespoke, bespoken** *esp. written* to show; be a sign of

bespoke *adj* (of clothes) specially made to someone's measurements

best¹ *adj* (*superlative of* GOOD) **1** of the highest quality, moral values, skill, usefulness, etc. **2 the best part of** most of: *I stayed the best part of a week*

best² *adv* (*superlative of* WELL) **1** in the best way **2** most **3 as best one can** in the best way one is able

best³ *n* **1** the best state or part **2** something that is best **3** the greatest degree of good or quality **4** one's greatest, highest, or finest effort, state or performance **5 get the best of (someone)** to defeat (someone) **6 make the best of** to do as much or as well as one can with: *to make the best of a bad state of affairs*

best⁴ *v* to defeat (someone)

bestial *adj* (of human beings and their behaviour) like an animal in being nasty, cruel, or shameful —compare BEASTLY — **~ly** *adv* — **~ity** *n*

bestir *v* **-rr-** to cause (oneself) to move quickly or become active

best man *n* the friend and attendant of the bridegroom at a wedding

bestow *v* to give — **~al** *n*

bestrew *v* **bestrewed, bestrewn** *or* **bestrewed** *esp. written* **1** to lie scattered over **2** to strew

bestride *v* **bestrode, bestridden, bestriding** *esp. written* to sit or stand on or over with legs apart

best-seller *n* something (esp. a book) that sells in very large numbers

bet¹ *n* **1** an agreement to risk money on the result of a future event **2** a sum of money so risked

bet² *v* **bet** *or* **betted, betting** to risk (money) on the result of a future event

beta *n* **1** the 2nd letter of the Greek alphabet (B, β) **2** also **B-** a mark for between average and good work by students

beta particle *n* an electron thrown out by some radioactive substances

betel nut *n* a hard nut with a bitter taste chewed in Asia

bête-noire *n* **bêtes-noires** *French* a person or thing one dislikes most

betide *v* **Woe betide (you, him, etc.)** you, he, etc., will be in trouble

betray *v* **betrayed, betraying** **1** to be disloyal or unfaithful to **2** to give away or make known: *Her face betrayed her nervousness* — **~er** *n* — **~al** *n*

betroth *v* *becoming rare* to promise to give (oneself or another) in marriage **~al** *n* : *her betrothal* —compare ENGAGEMENT

better¹ *adj, n* (*comparative of* GOOD) **1** of higher quality, moral value, usefulness, etc.: *You're a better man than I am* **2 be better than one's word** to do more than one has promised **3 the better part of** more than half

better² *adj* (*comparative of* WELL) completely well; improved in health: *She'll be much better soon*

better³ *adv* (*comparative of* WELL) **1** in a more excellent, thorough, admirable, etc., way: *She knows the story better than I.* | *You look better in blue* **2 had better** ought to; should: *You'd better be there*

better⁴ *v* **1** to improve or cause to improve: *try to better last year's record* **2 better oneself** to educate oneself or earn more money — **~ment** *n*

better, bettor⁵ *n* a person who bets

betters *n* people of higher rank or greater worth: *one's elders and betters*

between¹ *prep* **1** in the space or at the time separating: *I sat between them.* | *He arrived between 6 and 7 last night* **2** as a connection of: *a train service between Leeds and Liverpool* **3** with a part for each of: *Between us we managed to finish the job* USAGE Compare **among** and **between. Between** must be followed by 2 things. It is better not to say: **between** *each house.* It is usually considered correct to follow **between** by 2 things only, and **among** by 3 or more: *Divide it* **between** *the 2/***among** *the 3 children.* But always use **between** when speaking of the exact position of something or a place, even if more than 2 things follow: *Switzerland lies* **between** *France, Germany, Austria, and Italy.*

betwixt and between *adv* neither one thing nor the other

beurre manié *n* *French* a mixture of flour and butter, used to thicken a stew, sauce, etc., to which it is added in small pieces —compare ROUX

bevel¹ *n* **1** the slope of a surface at an angle other than a right angle **2** a tool for making such a sloping edge or surface

bevel² *v* **-ll-** to make a bevel on

beverage *n* a liquid for drinking, esp. tea, coffee, milk, etc.

bevy *n* **-ies** a large group or collection

beware *v* to be careful: *Beware of the dog*

bewilder *v* to confuse, esp. by the presence of lots of different things — **~ment** *n*

bewitch *v* **1** to have a magic effect, often harmful, on **2** to charm as if by magic: *a bewitching smile* —compare ENCHANT

Bey *n* **1** (the title of) a governor or officer esp. in the Middle East **2** (the Turkish word for) Mr

beyond[1] *adv* on or to the further side; further: *Men can travel to the moon and beyond*

beyond[2] *prep* **1** on or to the further side of: *What lies beyond the mountains?* **2** later than: *Don't stay there beyond midnight* **3** out of reach of; much more than: *The fruit is beyond my reach.* | *His bad behaviour is beyond a joke*

bias[1] *n* **1** (that which causes) the rolling of a ball in the game of bowls in a curve **2** an influence for or against; prejudice **3** a tendency of mind: *a scientific bias* **4** cut (cloth) on the bias to cut diagonally across the line of the threads

bias[2] *v* **-s-** *or* **-ss-** to cause to form settled favourable or unfavourable opinions without enough information to judge fairly

bias binding *n* a narrow band of material cut on the bias, for use when sewing curved edges or corners of cloth

bib *n* **1** a cloth or plastic shield tied under a child's chin to protect its clothes **2** the top of an apron or overalls

bible *n* (a copy of) a holy book: *This dictionary should be your bible when studying English*

Bible *n* **1** (a copy of) the holy book of the Christians, consisting of the Old Testament and the New Testament **2** (a copy of) the holy book of the Jews; the Old Testament — **-lical** *adj* — **-lically** *adv*

bibliography *n* **-phies** **1** the history or description of books or writings **2** a list of all writings used in the preparation of a book or article — **-pher** *n*

bibulous *adj* *usu. humour* too fond of drink

bicarbonate also **bicarbonate of soda**— and *esp. spoken* **bicarb**— *n* a chemical substance used esp. in baking or taken with water to settle the stomach

bicentenary *n* **-ries** the day or year exactly 200 years after a particular event

biceps *n* **biceps** the large muscle on the front of the upper arm ☞ ANATOMY

bicker *v* to quarrel, esp. about small matters

bicycle also **cycle**, (*esp. spoken*) **bike**— *n, v* **-cled, -cling** (to ride) a 2-wheeled vehicle which one pedals with the feet — **bicyclist** *n*

bid[1] *v* **bade** *or* **bid, bidden** *or* **bid, bidding** **1** to say (a greeting or goodbye) **2** to tell (someone to do something): *Do as you're bidden* — **~der** *n*

bid[2] *v* **bid, bidding** **1** to offer (a price): *He bid $5 for an old book* **2** (in playing cards) to declare one's intention of winning (a certain number of tricks): *I bid 2 spades* — **~der** *n*

bid[3] *n* **1** an offer to pay a certain price at a sale or auction **2** an offer to do some work at a certain price; tender: *Bids for building the bridge were invited* **3** (a turn to make) a declaration of the number of tricks a cardplayer says he intends to win

biddable *adj* easily led or controlled

bidding *n* **1** order; command (esp. in the phrases **at one's bidding, do someone's bidding**) **2** the act or action of making bids

bide *v* **bided, biding bide one's time** to wait until the right moment

bidet *n* a kind of small bath for sitting across to wash the lower parts of the body

biennial *adj* **1** (of events) happening once every 2 years **2** (of plants) living for 2 years and producing flowers in the second year — **~ly** *adv*

bier *n* a movable stand for taking the dead to the grave

biff *n, v sl* (to give) a quick hard blow

bifocals *n* glasses having an upper part for looking at distant objects, and a lower part for reading — **bifocal** *adj*

big[1] *adj* **-gg-** **1** of more than average size, weight, importance, etc. **2** doing a great deal of some activity: *a big spender* **3** *literature* (of a woman) pregnant: *big with child* **4** have big ideas to want to do something important — **~ness** *n*

big[2] *adv sl* **1 talk big** to talk as if one were more important than one really is **2 think big** to plan to do a great deal

bigamy *n* the state of being married to 2 people at the same time — **-mist** *n* — **-mous** *adj* — **-mously** *adv*

big bang theory *n* the idea that everything began with the explosion of a single mass of material so that the pieces are still flying apart —compare STEADY STATE THEORY

big deal *interj sl* (showing that one considers something unimportant): *'So they live in a mansion. Big deal!'*

big end *n technical* the part of a connecting rod in a car engine which joins onto the crank

big game *n* the largest wild animals hunted for sport

bighead *n esp. spoken* a person who thinks too highly of his own importance

bigot *n* a person who thinks strongly and unreasonably that his own opinion is correct — **~ed** *adj* — **~edly** *adv* — **~ry** *n*

big top *n* a very large tent used by a circus

bigwig *n sl* an important person

bike *n, v* **biked, biking** *esp. spoken* bicycle

bikini *n* a 2-piece bathing suit for women

bilateral *adj* of, on, or with 2 sides; between or concerning 2 parties: *a bilateral agreement* — compare MULTILATERAL — **~ly** *adv*

bilateral symmetry *n technical* the quality possessed by an object (e.g. the human body) whose 2 halves are mirror images of each other

bilberry *n* **-ries** a low bushy plant growing on hillsides or its edible bluish fruit

bile *n* **1** a bitter green-brown liquid formed in the liver which breaks up fat in order to digest it **2** bad temper — **bilious** *adj* — **biliousness** *n*

bilge *n* **1** the broad bottom of a ship **2** also **bilge water**— dirty water in the bottom of a ship

bilingual *adj* of, containing, or expressed in 2

languages: *a bilingual French-English dictionary*
2 able to speak 2 languages equally well

bill[1] *n* the beak of a bird ☞ BIRD

bill[2] *v* **bill and coo** (of lovers) to kiss and speak softly to each other

bill[3] *n* **1** a plan for a law, written down for a parliament to consider **2** a list of things bought and their price **3** a printed notice **4** *US* a piece of paper money; note: *a 5-dollar bill* **5 fill the bill** to be suitable **6 foot the bill** to pay and take responsibility

bill[4] *v* to advertise in printed notices: *billed (to appear) as Hamlet*

billboard *n* *US* a hoarding

billet *v, n* (to provide with) a lodging-house for a soldier

billhook *n* a tool with a hooked blade and a handle, used esp. for cutting branches off trees

billiards *n* a game played on a cloth-covered table with balls knocked against each other or into pockets at the corners and sides using cues — **billiard** *adj*

billion *adj, n, pron* **billion** *or* **billions** **1** the number 1, 000, 000, 000; 10^9 **2** the number 1, 000, 000, 000, 000; 10^{12} — **~th** *adj, n, pron, adv*

bill of fare *n* **bills of fare** a menu

bill of health *n* **a clean bill of health** a favourable report (on someone's health)

billow[1] *n* **1** a wave, esp. a very large one **2** a rolling mass like this — **~y** *adj*

billow[2] *v* **1** to rise and roll in waves **2** to swell out, as a sail

billy *also* **billycan**— *n* **-lies** a vessel used for cooking or boiling water

billy goat *n* a male goat —compare NANNY GOAT

billy-o *also* **billy-oh**— *n* **like billy-o** *sl* a lot; very fast or fiercely: *to run like billy-o*

bimonthly *adv, adj* **1** appearing or happening every 2 months: *a bimonthly magazine* **2** *bad usage* appearing or happening twice a month

bin *n* a large wide-mouthed container with a lid for bread, flour, etc., or for waste —see also DUSTBIN

binary *adj technical* **1** consisting of 2 things or parts; double: *2 stars turning round each other form a binary star* **2** using the digits 0 and 1 only: *The binary system of numbers is used in digital computers* ☞ CALCULATOR

binary operation *n technical* an operation combining 2 similar terms to give a third: *Addition, subtraction, multiplication, and division are binary operations*

bind[1] *v* **bound, binding** **1** to tie; tie together: *Bind the prisoner's hands together.* | *She bound (up) her hair* **2** to bandage **3** to fasten together and enclose in a cover: *to bind a book* **4** to strengthen or ornament with a band of material: *The dress is bound with ribbon* **5** to stick together: *This dough isn't wet enough to bind properly* **6** to cause to obey esp. by a law or a promise: *I am bound by this agreement* **7** to

make or declare it necessary for (someone) to do something: *They bound me to remain silent* **8** to unite: *Many things bind us (together)* —see also BOUND

bind[2] *n sl* an annoying state of affairs

binder *n* **1** a person who binds, esp. books **2** a machine that binds things together, esp. one that binds corn when it is cut **3** a substance that causes things to stick together **4** a usu. removable cover, esp. for holding sheets of paper, magazines, etc.

binding[1] *n* **1** the action of a person or machine that binds **2** a book cover **3** material sewn or stuck along an edge for strength or ornament

binding[2] *adj* that must be obeyed

bind over *v adv law* to declare it necessary for (someone) to cause no more trouble: *He was bound over to keep the peace*

bindweed *n* a twining garden weed, esp. wild convolvulus

binge *n sl* a spree: *They went on a binge last night*

bingo *n, interj* **1** a game played by covering numbered squares on a card **2** an expression of joy at a sudden successful result

binnacle *n* a box with a lamp in which a ship's compass is kept

binocular *adj* **1** of, related to, or made for the use of both eyes: *binocular vision* **2** of or for binoculars: *a binocular case*

binoculars *n* a pair of glasses used for looking at distant objects with both eyes ☞ OPTICS

binomial *n, adj technical* (an expression) consisting of 2 terms connected by the sign $+$ or the sign $-$ (like $a + b$ or $x - 7$): *the binomial theorem*

biochemistry *n* (the scientific study of) the chemistry of living things

biodegradable *n* able to be broken down esp. into harmless products by the action of living things (such as microorganisms)

biographer *n* a writer of biography: *Boswell was the biographer of Dr Johnson*

biography *n* **-phies** (the type of literature concerned with) an account of a person's life —compare AUTOBIOGRAPHY — **-phic, -phical** *adj* — **-phically** *adv*

biological warfare *also* **germ warfare**— *n* the use of living things such as bacteria for harming the enemy in a war

biology *n* **1** the scientific study of living things: *to study biology* **2** the scientific facts about the life of a living thing: *the biology of bacteria* — **-gical** *adj* : *biological studies* — **-gically** *adv* — **-gist** *n*

biomass *n* the amount of living matter in an area or volume

bionic *adj* having greater speed, strength, etc. than an ordinary animal: *a bionic dog*

biosphere *n technical* the part of the Earth in which life can exist

bipartisan *adj* representing 2 political parties: *a bipartisan committee*

bipartite *adj* **1** being in 2 parts **2** shared by 2 parties

biped *n* a 2-footed creature

biplane *n* an aircraft with 2 sets of wings, one above the other —compare MONOPLANE

birch¹ *n* **1** any of several kinds of tree, with smooth wood and thin branches **2** a rod or bunch of sticks made from its wood, used for caning people

birch² *v* to whip or cane as a punishment

bird *n* **1** a creature with wings and feathers 👁
☞ EVOLUTION **2** *sl* a person, usually a young woman **3** *sl* a rude noise made as a sign of disapproval: *They gave the actor the bird* **4 birds of a feather** people of the same kind **5 early bird** a person who gets up or arrives early **6 kill 2 birds with one stone** to get 2 results with one action

bird-brained *adj sl* stupid; silly

birdie *n* **1** (used to or by children) a bird; little bird **2** (in golf) the hitting of the ball into the hole in one stroke fewer than average —compare EAGLE, PAR

bird of passage *n* **birds of passage** a bird that flies regularly, according to the season, from one area to another

bird of prey *n* **birds of prey** a bird (e.g. a hawk, owl, or falcon) that kills other animals for food

bird's-eye view *n* **1** a view seen from high up, as if by a flying bird **2** a general view

biro *n* **biros** *trademark* a ballpoint: *written in biro*

birth *n* **1** the act or time of being born: *She weighed 8 pounds at birth* **2** the act or fact of producing young (often in the phrase **give birth to**) **3** family origin: *French by birth* **4** beginning; start; origin: *the birth of a new political party*

birth control *n* various methods of limiting the number of children born —see also CONTRACEPTIVE

birthday *n* **-days** the date on which someone was born

birthmark *n* an unusual mark on the body at birth

birthrate *n* the number of births during a given time: *The birthrate is down this year*

birthright *n* that which belongs to a person because of his/her birth esp, as a member of a certain nation

biscuit *n* **1** any of many types of flat thin dry sweetened or unsweetened cake **2** pottery, china, etc., after its first heating in the kiln but before the glaze is put on **3 take the biscuit** *sl* to be the best/worst thing one has ever seen or heard of

bisect *v technical* to divide into 2 equal parts — ~ion *n*

bisexual *adj, n* **1** (a person) possessing qualities of both sexes **2** (a person) sexually attracted to people of both sexes — ~ity *n* — ~ly *adv*

bishop *n* **1** a priest in charge of the other priests in a large area **2** a chess-piece that can be moved any number of squares diagonally

bishopric *n* a diocese

bismuth *n* a grey-white metal that is an element

bison *n* any of several large wild cowlike animals formerly common in Europe and North America

bisque *n* a thick cream soup, usu. made with fish

bistro *n* **-tros** a small or simple restaurant

bit¹ *n* **1** a metal bar put in the mouth of a horse as part of a bridle and used for controlling its movements ☞ HORSE **2** a part of a tool for making holes **3 take the bit between its/one's teeth** (of a person) to begin with determination

bit² *n* **1** a small piece, quantity, or amount: *He ate every bit of the pudding.* | *an interesting bit of news* | *There's a little bit of time left* **2** a short time: *Wait a bit!* **3 a bit (of)** *esp. spoken* **a** to some degree; rather: *I'm a bit tired tonight* | *Don't believe all he says - he's a bit of a boaster* **b** at all: *I'm not a bit tired now*

bit³ *n* the standard measure of stored computer information

bitch¹ *n* **1** a female dog **2** *rude* a woman —see also SON OF A BITCH

bitch² *v sl* to complain: *Don't bitch about the heat*

bitchy *adj* **-ier, -iest** tending to make nasty remarks about other people — **bitchily** *adv* — **bitchiness** *n*

bite¹ *v* **bit, bitten, biting** **1** to cut, seize, or attack with the teeth: *My monkey doesn't bite.* | *The boy bit into the apple* **2** to make or put into the stated condition in this way: *The dog has bitten a hole in my trousers* **3** (of insects) to prick the skin (of) and draw blood: *The mosquitoes are biting me* **4** (of fish) to accept food on a fisherman's hook **5** to take hold of something firmly: *The car's tyres would not bite on the snow* **6 bite one's lips** to try to hide one's anger or displeasure **7 bite someone's head off** to speak to or answer someone angrily **8 bite the dust** *sl* **a** to be killed **b** to be completely defeated

bite² *n* **1** an act of biting **2** a piece bitten off **3** *esp. spoken* something to eat: *He hasn't had a bite (to eat) all day* **4** a wound made by biting, esp. by an animal **5** sharpness; bitterness: *There's a bite in this cold wind*

biting *adj* painful; cruel: *a biting wind* — ~ly *adv*

bitter¹ *adj* **1** having a sharp biting taste like beer or black coffee —opposite **sweet** **2** (of cold, wind, etc.) very sharp, biting, etc. **3** causing pain or grief: *a bitter disappointment* **4** filled with, showing, or caused by unpleasant feelings: *bitter enemies* **5 to the bitter end** *esp. spoken* to the very end — ~ly *adv* — ~ness *n*

bitter² *n* bitter beer

bittern *n* **bitterns** *or* **bittern** any of several kinds of brown long-legged waterbirds which make a deep hollow sound

number of living species

perching/songbirds swallows, wrens, thrushes	5,110
toucans, woodpeckers	377
kingfishers, hoopoes, hornbills, bee-eaters	192
trogons	35
mouse-birds	6
swifts, hummingbirds	388
frogmouths, nightjars	92
owls	132
cuckoos	143
parrots, parakeets, cockatoos, macaws	317
doves, pigeons	301
plovers, sandpipers, gulls, terns, auks	293
cranes, rails, coots, bustards	185
grouse, quail, turkeys, pheasants	250
vultures, hawks, eagles, falcons	274
screamers, swans, geese, ducks	149
herons, storks, flamingos	117
pelicans, gannets, cormorants	50
albatrosses, fulmars, petrels	81
grebes	17
divers	4
tinamous	42
rheas	2
kiwis	3
cassowaries, emus	4
ostriches	1
penguins	15

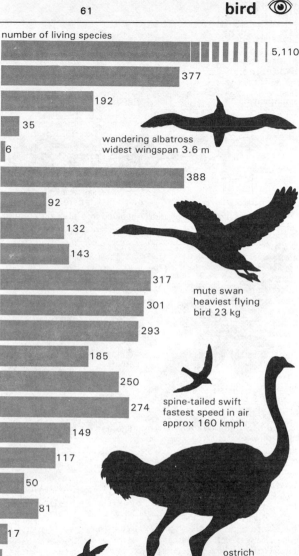

wandering albatross
widest wingspan 3.6 m

mute swan
heaviest flying
bird 23 kg

spine-tailed swift
fastest speed in air
approx 160 kmph

ostrich
largest living
bird 2.7 m tall

hummingbird
smallest bird
57 mm long

Scientists now think that birds developed from the extinct reptiles we call dinosaurs. Birds have evolved by natural selection so that there are 27 major groups, as shown on the chart. The groups near the top are more highly evolved and intelligent than those lower down.

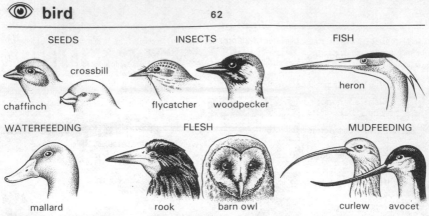

SEEDS INSECTS FISH

crossbill

chaffinch

flycatcher woodpecker

heron

WATERFEEDING FLESH MUDFEEDING

mallard rook barn owl curlew avocet

The beaks of birds have gradually evolved into their different shapes according to the type of food the bird lives on.

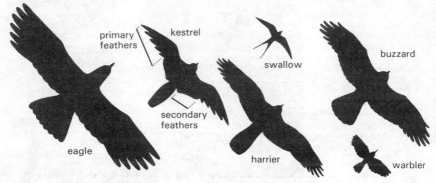

primary feathers kestrel

swallow buzzard

secondary feathers

eagle harrier warbler

A bird can often be identified by its wing shape, particularly if it hovers and glides, like a bird of prey.

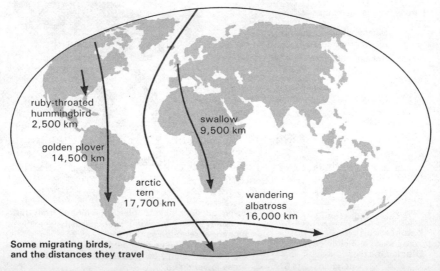

ruby-throated hummingbird 2,500 km

swallow 9,500 km

golden plover 14,500 km

arctic tern 17,700 km

wandering albatross 16,000 km

Some migrating birds, and the distances they travel

bittersweet *adj* pleasant, but mixed with sadness: *bittersweet memories*

bitty *adj* **-tier, -tiest** consisting of little bits — **-tiness** *n*

bitumen *n* a sticky substance such as asphalt or tar, esp. as used in road-making ☞ REFINERY — **-minous** *adj*

bituminous coal also **soft coal**— *n* a type of coal that gives off a lot of smoke when burning —compare ANTHRACITE

bivalve *n* *technical* a shellfish, such as an oyster, with 2 shells joined together ☞ EVOLUTION

biweekly *adv, adj* appearing or happening every 2 weeks: *a biweekly magazine*

bizarre *adj* strange; peculiar; odd — ~**ly** *adv*

blab *v* **-bb-** *sl* to tell a secret: *Someone must have blabbed!*

blabber *v* to talk foolishly or too much

black *adj* **1** of the colour of coal; of the darkest colour; without light: *a black cat* —opposite **white 2** (of coffee) without milk or cream **3** (of a person) of a black-skinned race: *a black scientist* **4** very dirty: *Your hands are black!* **5** (of feelings, news, etc.) very bad: *It's a black day for us* **6** very angry or annoyed: *a black look* **7** *literature* evil: *black-hearted* **8** funny about unpleasant or dangerous people or states of affairs (in the phrases **black humour, black comedy**) — ~**ness** *n*

black² *n* **1** the colour that is black: *dressed in black* **2** a person of a black-skinned race **3** in **the black** having money in a bank account — opposite **in the red**

black³ *v* **1** to make black: *to black someone's eye* —see also BLACK OUT **2** (esp. of a trade union) to declare it wrong to work with (goods, a business firm, etc.)

blackamoor *n* *old use or humour* a black person, esp. a man

black and blue *adj* (of a person) badly bruised: *He punched me until I was black and blue*

black and tan *n* **black and tans** a British soldier who fought against Irish independence in 1920–21

black and white *n* writing: *I want this agreement in black and white*

blackball *v* to vote against a person who wants to join a group

black belt *n* (a person who holds) a high rank in the practice of Judo, Karate, etc

blackberry *n* **-ries** (the edible berry of) various types of bramble — ~**ing** *n*: *go blackberrying*

blackbird *n* any of various types of bird of which the male is black

blackboard *n* a dark smooth surface for writing or drawing on with chalk

black box *n* an apparatus for controlling a machine or recording information: *The black box showed why the plane had crashed*

blackcurrant *n* (a bush that bears) a type of small round blue-black garden fruit

Black Death *n* the illness (probably BUBONIC PLAGUE) that killed large numbers of people in the 14th century

blacken *v* **1** to make or become black or dark **2** to speak or write bad things about (esp. someone's character)

black eye *n* bad bruising round a person's eye

blackguard *n* a scoundrel

blackhead *n* a kind of spot on the skin

black hole *n* a portion of outer space containing a body of such high density that everything near it, including light itself, is pulled inside

black ice *n* an invisible layer of hard slippery ice on a road

blacking *n* a substance that is put on an object to make it black

black lead *n* plumbago

blackleg *n, v* **-gg-** (to act as) a person who continues to work when others are on strike

blacklist *n, v* (to put on) a list of people, groups, countries, etc. about whom something unfavourable is known and against whom action may be taken

blackly *adv* **1** angrily **2** sadly or unfavourably

black magic *n* magic used for evil purposes

blackmail *v* to make (someone) give money by threatening to reveal a secret unles money is paid — **blackmail** *n* — ~**er** *n*

Black Maria *n* *sl* a vehicle used by the police to carry prisoners

black market *n* the unlawful buying and selling of goods, foreign money, etc. — ~**eer** *n*

blackout *n* **1** a period of darkness caused by a failure of the electric power supply or enforced during wartime as a protection from air attack **2** a loss of consciousness for a short time

black out *v* **1** to cover (esp. writing) so as to hide completely: *The date on the letter had been blacked out* **2** to faint

black pepper *n* pepper made from crushed pepper seeds with the dark outer covering still on

black power *n* the belief that in any country black people should have a share of power which is in accordance with the number of black people in that country

black pudding *n* a kind of sausage made of blood, fat, and grain

black sheep *n* **black sheep** a worthless member of a respectable group

Blackshirt *n* a member of the former Italian Fascist party

blacksmith also **smith**— *n* a metalworker who makes and repairs things made of iron, esp. one who makes horseshoes

black spot *n* a stretch of road where an unusually large number of accidents have happened

blackthorn *n* a bush with sharp prickles, white flowers, and small plum-like fruit —see SLOE

black tie *adj* (of parties and other social occasions) requring those attending to wear formal clothes

bladder n 1 a bag of skin inside the body in which waste liquid (URINE) collects before it is passed out 2 a bag of skin, leather, or rubber which can be filled with air or liquid

blade n 1 the flat cutting part of a knife, sword, razor, or other cutting tool 2 the flat wide part of an oar, a propeller, a cricket bat, etc. 3 a long flat plant leaf, esp of grass

blame v, n **blamed, blaming** 1 (to give) the responsibility for (something bad): *They blamed the failure on George.* | *George took the blame* 2 **be to blame** to be guilty: *The children were not to blame* — ~**less** adj — ~**lessness** n — ~**worthy** adj — ~**worthiness** n

blanch v 1 to make (a plant or plant product) colourless, white, or less strong-tasting: *blanched almonds* 2 to become white with fear, cold, etc. ⚠ BLENCH

blancmange n a jelly-like pudding made mainly from milk, cornflour, and sugar

bland adj 1 not giving offence; gentle 2 mild; tasteless: *bland food* — ~**ly** adv — ~**ness** n

blandishments n acts of pleasing used to make a person agree, usu. to a wrong act

blank¹ adj 1 without writing, print, or other marks: *a blank page* 2 expressionles; without interest: *a blank look* — ~**ly** adv — ~**ness** n

blank² n 1 an empty space: *My mind was a complete blank.* | *Please fill in this blank* 2 **draw a blank** to be unsuccessful

blank cartridge also **blank—** n a cartridge that contains an explosive but no bullet

blank cheque n 1 a cheque signed and given to someone else to write in the amount of money 2 CARTE BLANCHE

blanket n 1 a thick covering used esp. on beds to protect from cold 2 a thick covering: *a blanket of mist*

blank verse n unrhymed poetry: *Most of Shakespeare's plays are written in blank verse*

blare v, n **blared, blaring** (to make) a sharp, loud, and unpleasant sound: *the blare of car horns*

blarney n esp. *spoken* soft pleasant persuasive speech

blasé adj French tired of pleasure: *I've been abroad so often that I've got blasé about it*

blaspheme v **-phemed, -pheming** to speak or write without respect for (God or religious matters) — ~**r**, **-my** n — **-mous** adj — **-mously** adv

blast¹ n 1 a quick strong movement of air: *an icy blast of wind* 2 (the powerful rush of air caused by) an explosion: *The blast from the bomb blew out all the windows in the area* 3 **(at) full blast** (of work, activity, etc.) fully: *He was working (at) full blast in order to complete the order before the holidays*

blast² v 1 to break up (esp. rock) by explosions 2 to strike with explosives 3 to cause to dry up

and die by heat, cold, lightning, etc: *The icy wind had blasted the new spring growth* 4 to damn — **-ed** adj

blast³ interj (used for expressing great annoyance)

blast furnace n a container for smelting iron

blast off v adv (of a spacecraft) to take off — **blast-off** n

blatant adj shameless; offensively noticeable: *blatant disregard for the law* — ~**ly** adv

blaze¹ n 1 the sudden sharp shooting up of a flame; a big dangerous fire: *The roadside grass became a blaze* 2 brightly shining light or bright colour: *The flowers made a blaze of red* 3 an explosion of angry feeling: *In a blaze of anger he shouted at them* —see also ABLAZE, BLAZES — **-zing** adj

blaze² v **blazed, blazing** 1 to (begin to) burn with a bright flame 2 to show very bright colour; shine brightly or warmly

blaze³ n a white mark, esp. on the front of a horse's head

blaze away v adv to fire guns rapidly

blazer n a jacket, sometimes with the badge of a school, club, etc., on it

blazes n sl hell: *Go to blazes!*

bleach v to make or become white

bleak adj cold and cheerless: *bleak winter weather* | *Two weeks in hospital seems a bleak prospect* — ~**ly** adv

bleary adj **-ier, -iest** (of eyes) red and clouded by tiredness, tears, etc. — **blearily** adv — **bleariness** n

bleat v, n 1 (to make) the sound of a sheep, goat, or calf 2 (to make) a weak complaint: *He's always bleating about something*

bleed v **bled, bleeding** 1 to lose blood 2 (of the heart) to feel as if wounded by sorrow: *My heart bleeds for the starving children* 3 to draw blood from (esp. as was done by doctors in former times) 4 to make (someone) pay too much money: *The landlord bled them dry for their flat*

bleeding adj sl bloody

bleep n, v (to send out, or call by means of) a high sound sent out by a machine to attract someone's attention: *The nurse bleeped the doctor*

blemish v, n (to spoil by) a mark that spoils beauty or perfection: *a face blemished by a scar* | *a character without blemish*

blench v to make a sudden movement in fear; recoil ⚠ BLANCH

blend¹ v 1 to mix: *Blend the sugar and flour* 2 to produce (tea, coffee, whisky, etc.) from a mixture of several varieties 3 to go well together; harmonize; combine: *The countryside and the houses seem to blend (into each other)*

blend² n a product of blending: *a blend of coffee*

blender n 1 a person or machine that blends 2 a liquidizer

bless v **blessed** or **blest, blessing** 1 to ask God's favour for (sometimes used humorously): *Bless* *this house* | *Well, bless my soul!* **2** to make holy: *The priest blessed the bread and wine* **3** to praise or call holy: *Bless the name of the Lord!* — compare DAMN

blessed *adj* **1** holy; favoured by God; fortunate: *blessed with good health* **2** happy; desirable: *a few moments of blessed silence* **3** *sl* (used to give force to expressions of displeasure): *They've sold the whole blessed lot* — ~ly *adv* — ~ness *n*

Blessed Sacrament also **Sacrament**— *n* (used in the Roman Catholic and Anglican churches) (the holy bread eaten at) the Christian ceremony of the Eucharist

blessing *n* **1** an act of asking or receiving God's help, or protection: *the blessing of the Lord* **2** something one is glad of: *Count your blessings* **3** approval; encouragement: *Father gave his blessing to our holiday plans* **4 a blessing in disguise** something not very pleasant, which turns out to be a good thing after all

blew *past tense of* BLOW

blight[1] *n* **1** any of several diseases of plants **2** a condition of disorder and ugliness: *the blight of litter on the beach*

blight[2] *v* to spoil or attack with blight

blighter *n sl* a man; fellow; boy: *You lucky blighter!*

blimey *interj sl* (used for expressing surprise)

blind[1] *adj* **1** unable to see: *He is blind in one eye* **2** intended for those who cannot see: *a blind school* **3** not understanding or caring: *He is blind to the effect of his actions* **4** careless; thoughtless; uncontrolled: *blind rage* **5** without reason or purpose: *the blind forces of nature* **6** navigating with instruments only, inside an aircraft without looking outside: *a blind landing* **7** in or into which it is difficult to see: *a blind corner* **8** *sl* slightest (esp. in the phrase **not take a blind bit of notice**) **9 bake blind** to cook (pastry) by itself, a filling being added later **10 turn a blind eye (to)** to take no notice of **11 the blind leading the blind** people with little information advising people with even less — ~ly *adv* — ~ness *n*

blind[2] *v* **1** to make unable to see: *He was blinded by the smoke* **2** to make unable to notice or understand: *His desire to do it blinded him to all the difficulties*

blind[3] *n* **1** a covering made of cloth or other material that is fastened above a window and pulled down to cover it —see also ROLLER BLIND, VENETIAN BLIND **2** a way of hiding the truth by giving a false idea

blind alley *n* a street with no way out at the other end

blind date *n* **1** a date between a man and a woman who have not met before **2** either of the 2 people who take part in such a meeting

blindfold *n, v* (to cover with) something, such as a piece of material, that covers the eyes to prevent seeing

blind man's buff *n* a game in which a blindfolded person tries to catch the others

blind spot *n* **1** the point in the eye where the nerve enters, which is not sensitive to light **2** a part of an area that cannot be seen easily

blink[1] *v* **1** to shut and open (the eyes) quickly **2** (of distant lights) (to seem) to go rapidly on and off

blink[2] *n* **1** an act of blinking **2 on the blink** *esp. spoken* (of machinery) not working properly

blink at *v* to show surprise at

blinkers *n* a pair of flat pieces of leather fixed beside a horse's eyes to prevent it seeing objects at its sides — **-ered** *adj*

blinking *adj sl* bloody: *You blinking fool!*

blip *n* an image produced on a radar screen

bliss *n* complete happiness: *What bliss to be going on holiday* — ~ful *adj* — ~fully *adv* — ~fulness *n*

blister *n, v* **1** (to form) a water-filled swelling under the skin, caused by rubbing, burning, etc.: *blisters on my feet* | *My feet blister easily* **2** (to cause) a swelling on the surface of things such as painted wood: *The heat blistered the paint* — ~ing *adj* : *the blistering sun* — ~ingly *adv*

blithe *adj* free from care: *a blithe spirit* — ~ly *adv*

blitz[1] *n* **1** a sudden heavy attack, esp. from the air, or a period of such attacks **2** *sl* a period of great activity for some special purpose: *I must have a blitz to get my room tidy*

blitz[2] *v* to make blitz attacks on: *London was blitzed during the war*

blizzard *n* a long severe snowstorm

bloated *adj* unpleasantly swollen: *bloated with too much food*

bloater *n* a fish (esp. a herring) that has been salted and smoked

blob *n* a drop or small round mass

bloc *n French* **1** a group of people, political parties, or nations that act together **2 en bloc** all together; all at once

block[1] *n* **1** a solid mass or piece of wood, stone, etc. **2** a quantity of things considered as a single whole: *a block of seats in a theatre* **3** a piece of wood or metal with words or drawings cut into its surface, for printing **4** a large building divided into separate parts (esp. flats or offices) **5** a building or group of buildings between 2 streets: *Turn left after 2 blocks* **6** something that gets in the way or that stops activity: *a road block* | *a block in the pipes* **7** the large piece of wood on which people were beheaded **8 knock someone's block off** *sl* to knock someone's head off

block[2] *v* to prevent (movement, activity, or success): *to block the enemy's advance*

blockade *v* **-aded, -ading** to shut off a place by warships or soldiers to prevent any people or goods from coming or going — **blockade** *n*

blockage *n* a state of being blocked or something that causes a block: *a blockage in the pipe*

block and tackle *n* an arrangement of wheels and ropes for lifting heavy things

blockbuster *n* something that is very effective

or popular: *our new film will be a real block-buster*

blockhouse *n* a small strong building used as a shelter (as from enemy gunfire)

block in also **block out**— *v adv* to make a rough drawing of

block letters also **block capitals**— *n* CAPITAL LETTERS

bloke *n esp. spoken* a man; fellow

blond *adj, n* **1** (*fem.* **blonde**) (a person) with fair skin and hair **2** (of hair) light-coloured (usu. yellowish)

blood¹ *n* **1** red liquid which carries oxygen to all parts of the body and is pumped round by the heart **2** family relationship: *of noble blood* **3** **bad blood** strong unpleasant feeling: *There is bad blood between them* **4** **Blood is thicker than water** Relatives are really more important than friends **5** **fresh/new blood** a new person or new people (in a firm, group, etc.): *We need an injection of new blood with fresh ideas* **6** **in cold blood** cruelly and on purpose: *I couldn't kill the mouse in cold blood* **7** **make someone's blood boil** to make someone very angry **8** **make someone's blood run cold** to make someone very frightened

blood² *v* to give (someone) a first experience: *He's just being blooded at the game*

blood bank *n* a store of human blood for use in hospital treatment

bloodbath *n* the killing at one time of a great many people

bloodcurdling *adj* causing strong feelings of fear

blood feud *n* a long-lasting quarrel between people or families, with murders on both sides

blood group also **blood type**— *n* any of the 4 classes into which human blood can be divided according to the presence or absence of certain substances

blood heat *n* a temperature about that of the human body

bloodhound *n* a kind of large dog with long floppy ears and a good sense of smell

bloodless *adj* **1** without blood **2** without killing or violence: *a bloodless victory* **3** lacking in spirit or human feeling — ~ly *adv* — ~ness *n*

bloodletting *n* **1** the former medical practice of bleeding people **2** bloodshed

blood poisoning also (*technical*) **septicaemia**— *n* a dangerous condition in which an infection spreads from a small area of the body through the bloodstream

blood pressure *n* the force with which blood travels through the blood vessels

blood relation *n* a relative by direct family connections rather than by marriage

bloodshed *n* killing, usu. in fighting

bloodshot *adj* (of the eyes) having the white part coloured red

blood sport *n* a sport (as fox-hunting) in which an animal is hunted and killed

bloodstain *n* a mark or spot of blood — **bloodstained** *adj*

bloodstream *n* the blood as it flows through the blood vessels of the body

bloodsucker *n* an insect that sucks blood from animals

bloodthirsty *adj* having or showing eagerness to kill or too much interest in violence — **-ily** *adv* — **-iness** *n*

blood vessel *n* any of the tubes through which blood flows in the body -see VEIN, ARTERY, CAPILLARY

bloody¹ *adj* **-ier, -iest** **1** covered with blood **2** connected with wounding and killing — **bloodily** *adv* — **bloodiness** *n*

bloody² *adj, adv sl not polite* (used for giving force to a judgment): *It's bloody wonderful!* | *'Lend you $5? Not bloody likely!'*

bloody mary *n* **bloody marys** a drink made by mixing vodka and tomato juice

bloody-minded *adj offensive* opposing the reasonable wishes of others: *Our bloody minded foreman wouldn't give us a tea break* — ~ness *n*

bloom¹ *n* **1** a flower **2** a covering of fine powder on ripe grapes, plums, etc. **3** **in the bloom of** at the best time of/for: *in the bloom of youth/beauty*

bloom² *v* **1** to produce flowers, come into flower, or be in flower **2** to be or become rich in plant life **3** to be or look healthy: *blooming with health* **4** to develop: *Their friendship bloomed* —compare BLOSSOM

bloomer *n humour sl* a big mistake

bloomers *n* a woman's loose undergarment, similar to knickers

blooming *adj, adv sl* bloody

blossom¹ *n* **1** (a mass of) the flowers of a flowering tree or bush: *apple blossom* | *the blossom on the trees* **2** **in blossom a** (esp. of a tree or bush) bearing flowers **b** at a high stage of development: *a friendship in full blossom*

blossom² *v* **1** (esp. of a flowering tree or bush) to produce or yield flowers; bloom **2** to develop; grow: *Jane is blossoming out into a beautiful girl* —compare BLOOM

blot¹ *n* **1** a mark that spoils or makes dirty: *a blot of ink on the paper* **2** a fault or shameful act: *a blot on one's character* **3** **blot on the landscape** something ugly that spoils the look of its surroundings

blot² *v* **-tt-** **1** to make blots (on): *This pen blots easily* **2** to dry or remove with or as if with blotting paper

blotch *n* **1** a reddened mark on the skin **2** a large spot of colour: *a blotch of ink* — ~y *adj*

blotter *n* **1** a large piece of blotting paper **2** a curved piece of wood to hold blotting paper

blotting paper *n* special thick soft paper which can take up liquids, used to dry wet ink after wrting

blotto *adj sl* very drunk

blouse n a usu. loose garment for women, reaching from the neck to the waist

blow¹ v **blew, blown, blowing** 1 to move by a current of air: *The wind has blown my hat off* 2 to send out a strong current of air (esp. from the lungs) 3 to make or give shape to by forcing air into or through: *to blow glass* 4 to sound by forcing air into or through: *The horn blew* 5 (of an electrical fuse) to break or be broken suddenly 6 *sl* to lose or spend: *I blew $10 at cards* 7 *sl* to leave suddenly and quickly: *Let's blow now* 8 *sl* damn: *Well, I'll be blowed!* 9 **blow hot and cold (about)** to be for and against in turns 10 **blow one's own trumpet/horn** to say good things about oneself 11 **blow one's top/stack** *sl* to become violently angry 12 **blow someone's mind** *sl* to fill someone with strong feelings of wonder or confusion —see also MIND-BLOWING 13 **There she blows!** said on a ship by the first person who sees a whale —see also BLOW IN, BLOW OUT, BLOW UP

blow² n an act or example of blowing

blow³ v *literature* to bloom: *a full-blown rose*

blow⁴ n 1 a hard stroke with the hand, a weapon, etc.: *a blow on the head* 2 a shock or misfortune: *It was a great blow when he failed to pass the exam* 3 **come to blows** also **exchange blows**— to start fighting 4 **strike a blow for** to do something important for: *Strike a blow for freedom*

blow-by-blow adj describing events in detail in the order in which they happened (esp, in the phrase **blow-by-blow account)**

blower n 1 a person who blows 2 an apparatus for producing a current of air or gas 3 *sl* the telephone: *Get him on the blower at once!*

blowfly n **-flies** any of various flies that lay their eggs on meat

blowhole n a whale's nostril, at the top of its head

blow in v adv *sl* to arrive unexpectedly: *Jim has just blown in*

blowlamp also **blowtorch**— n a device from which a mixture of gas or a liquid and air is blown out so as to give a very hot flame

blowout n 1 *sl* an occasion with a lot of eating and drinking 2 the bursting of a tyre, container, etc. by pressure of the contents on a weak spot 3 a case of uncontrolled oil or gas leakage in an oil or gas well

blow out v adv 1 to stop or cause to stop burning: *Jane blew the flame out* 2 to drive or be driven out by the force of a gas or liquid: *The explosion blew the windows out*

blowpipe a tube used for blowing small stones or poisoned arrows, used as a weapon

blow-up n 1 an explosion 2 a sudden moment of anger 3 a photographic enlargement

blow up v adv 1 to explode or be destroyed by exploding: *blow up the bridge* 2 to make or be made firm by filling with air: *blow up a bal-*

loon/tyres 3 to enlarge: *blow up a photograph* 4 to become suddenly angry

blowy adj **-ier, -iest** esp. spoken windy: *a blowy day*

blowzy, blowsy adj **-zier, -ziest** (of a woman or her appearance) fat, dirty, and untidily dressed

blubber¹ n the fat of whales, seals, etc from which oil is obtained

blubber² v to weep noisily

bludgeon n, v (to hit repeatedly with) a heavy-headed stick: *bludgeon to death*

blue¹ adj 1 of the colour of the clear sky on a fine day: *a blue dress | Your hands are blue with cold* 2 sad, depressed: *I'm feeling rather blue today* 3 **scream/shout blue murder** to complain loudly 4 **till one is blue in the face** unsuccessfully for ever — ~ness n — **bluish** adj

blue² n (a) blue colour: *dressed in blue*

blue baby n a baby whose skin is bluish at birth because there's something wrong with its heart

bluebell n any of various plants with blue bell-shaped flowers

blueberry n **-ries** US a bilberry

bluebird n a small blue singing bird in North America

blue blood n the quality of being a nobleman by birth

bluebottle n a large blue fly; the blowfly

blue cheese n cheese with lines of blue mould made to grow in it to give it a special flavour

blue chip n, adj (an industrial share) that is costly and of good quality

blue-collar adj esp. US of, relating to, or being workers who work with their hands —compare WHITE-COLLAR

blue film n a cinema film about sex

blue moon n a very long time: *I haven't seen you in a blue moon*

blueprint n a plan for a machine or a building, esp. in white on blue paper

blues n 1 a piece or type of slow, sad music from the Southern US: *a well-known blues singer* 2 the state of being sad: *a sudden attack of the blues*

bluestocking n a woman who is thought to be too highly educated

bluff¹ adj (of a person or his manner) rough, plain, and cheerful: *He had a bluff way of speaking* — ~ly adv — ~ness n

bluff² n a high steep bank or cliff

bluff³ v 1 to deceive by pretending to be stronger, cleverer, surer of the truth, etc., than one is: *He's only bluffing* 2 to find or make (one's way) by doing this: *He could bluff his way through any difficulty*

bluff⁴ n 1 the action of bluffing 2 **call someone's bluff** to tell someone who is bluffing to do what he threatens to do, guessing that he will not be able to: *When he threatened to dismiss me I called his bluff*

blunder¹ v 1 to make a blunder 2 to move awkwardly or unsteadily, as if blind: *He blundered through the dark forest* — ~er n

blunder n a stupid or unnecessary mistake: *to make a blunder*

blunderbuss n an old kind of gun with a wide-mouthed barrel

blunt¹ adj **1** (of a knife, pencil, etc.) not sharp **2** rough and plain, without trying to be polite or kind: *a few blunt words* — ~**ness** n — ~**ly** adv

blunt² v to make blunt

blur v -rr- to make difficult to see or see with: *Tears blur my eyes* — **blur** n : *My memory of the accident is only a blur*

blurb n a short description of the contents of a book

blurt out v adv to say suddenly and without thinking

blush¹ v **1** to become red in the face, from shame or embarrassment: *She blushed as red as a rose* **2** to be ashamed: *I blush to admit it* — ~**ingly** adv

blush² n **1** a case of blushing **2 spare someone's blushes** to avoid making someone blush

bluster v **1** to speak loudly and threateningly, often to hide lack of real power **2** (of wind) to blow roughly — **bluster**, ~—**er** n

blustery adj (of weather) windy: *a blustery winter day*

b o abbrev. for: body odour

boa¹ also **boa constrictor**— n a tropical snake that kills creatures for food by crushing them

boa² n FEATHER BOA

boar n a male pig —compare HOG, SOW

board¹ n **1** a thin flat piece of cut wood; plank **2** a stiff flat surface used for a special purpose: *drawing board | chessboard | darts board | bread board | noticeboard* **3** the cost of meals: *board and lodging* —compare LODGING **4** a committee or association with a special responsibility: *Our company has 3 women on its board of directors* **5 above board** completely open and honest **6 across the board** including all groups or members: *a wage rise of 10 pounds a week across the board* **7 go by the board** (of plans, arrangements, etc.) to come to no result; fail completely **8 on board** in or on a ship or public vehicle **9 sweep the board** to win (nearly) everything

board² v **1** to cover with boards or boarding **2** to go on board a ship or public vehicle **3** to get or supply meals and usu. lodging for payment: *She arranged to board some students from the university*

boarder n **1** a person who pays to sleep and eat at another person's house; lodger **2** a schoolchild who lives at the school —opposite **dayboy, daygirl**

boarding n boards laid side by side: *The windows were covered with boarding*

boardinghouse n a private lodging house that supplies meals

boarding school n a school at which children live instead of going there daily from home

boardroom n a room in which the directors of a company hold meetings

boards n old use and pompous the theatre; the stage: *He has been on the boards* (=been an actor)*all his life*

boast v **1** to talk or say proudly or to praise oneself: *He's just boasting* **2** to have cause to be proud of: *This village boasts three shops* — **boast** n : *His boast is that he's the best* — **boaster** n

boastful adj full of self-praise — ~**ly** adv — ~**ness** n

boat¹ n **1** a small vessel for travelling on water: *a fishing/sailing/rowing boat* **2** any ship: *Are you going by boat or by air?* **3 in the same boat** facing the same dangers **4 rock the boat** to make matters worse —see VESSEL (USAGE)

boat² v to use a small boat for pleasure (often in the phrase **go boating**)

boater n a type of straw hat

boat hook n a long pole with a hook on the end, to pull or push a small boat

boathouse n a small building by the water in which boats are kept

boatswain, bosun n (the rank of) a chief seamen on a ship, who calls the men to work and looks after the boats, ropes, etc. —compare COX

bob¹ v -bb- **1** to move quickly and repeatedly up and down, as on water: *The small boat was bobbing on the sea* **2** to curtsy quickly: *She bobbed politely at me*

bob² n a bobbing movement, esp. a curtsy

bob³ v -bb- to cut (a woman's hair) so as to leave hanging loosely, esp. to the shoulders — **bob** n

bob⁴ n bob esp. spoken a former British coin, the shilling (=5p)

bobbin n a small roller on which thread is wound, as in a sewing machine —compare REEL

bobsleigh also **bobsled**— v, n (to ride in) a small vehicle for sliding down snowy slopes (tobogganing)

bod n esp. spoken a person

bode¹ v **boded, boding** literature to be a sign of; foretell

bode² past tense of BIDE

bodice n the usu. close-fitting upper part of a woman's dress or undergarment above the waist

bodily¹ adj of the human body: *bodily comforts* —see also PHYSICAL

bodily² adv (esp. of movement) in a body or as a whole; completely: *He picked the child up bodily*

bodkin n a long thick blunt needle with a large eye

body n -ies **1** the whole of a person or animal as opposed to the mind: *You can imprison my body but not my mind* **2** this without the head or limbs: *a wound on his leg and another on his body* **3** this when it is dead: *Where did you bury his body?* **4** a large amount: *The oceans are large bodies of water* **5** a number of people who do something together: *The House of Commons is an elected body* **6** a person: *Mrs Jones was a dear old body* **7** technical an object; piece of matter: *The sun, moon, and stars are heavenly bodies* **8**

full strong quality: *I like a wine with plenty of body* **9** the main part; *The audience sat in the body of the hall*

bodyguard *n* someone who guards an important person

body politic *n* **bodies politic** citizens as forming a state under a government

body snatcher *n* a person who removes dead bodies from their graves

body stocking *n* a closely-fitting garment in one piece that covers the body and often the arms and legs

bodywork *n* the body of a motor vehicle, as opposed to the engine, wheels, etc.

Boer *adj* of or related to the white people of South Africa who came there from Holland —see also AFFRIKAANS

boffin *n* a scientist

bog *n* **1** (an area of) soft wet ground **2** *sl* lavatory

bog down *v adv* -gg- to sink or cause to sink as if into a bog: *I got bogged down by the difficult homework*

bogey, bogy, bogie *n* **bogeys, bogies 1** also **bogey man**— an imaginary evil spirit used for threatening children **2** an imaginary fear **3** *esp. spoken* a bit of dirty mucus in the nose

boggle *v* -gled, -gling to throw or be thrown into state of confusion: *What an impossible job! The mind boggles* (=I can't imagine doing it) —see also MIND-BOGGLING

boggy *adj* -gier, -giest (of ground) soft and wet —see BOG

bogie, bogey, bogy *n* either of 2 frames containing 4 or 6 wheels under each end of a railway engine or carriage, that make it able to go round curves

bogus *adj* pretended; false

bohemian *adj, n* (a person) that does not follow the usual rules of social life: *When he was a student he led a bohemian life*

boil¹ *n* a swelling under the skin, that is full of pus and eventually bursts

boil² *v* **1** to (make the contents of a vessel) reach or continue to be at the temperature at which liquid changes into a gas: *Peter boiled the kettle* **2** to cook in water at 100°C: *Boil the potatoes for 20 minutes* **3** to cause to reach the stated condition by cooking in water: *soft-boiled eggs* **4 make someone's blood boil** to make someone very angry —see also HARD-BOILED

boil³ *n* **1** an act or period of boiling: *Give the clothes a good boil* **2** boiling point

boil down *v adv* to make or become less by boiling

boil down to *v adv prep esp. spoken* to be or mean (something), leaving out the unnecessary parts: *The whole matter boils down to the fact that you two don't like each other*

boiler *n* a container for making hot water, as in a house, or for boiling water, as in a steam engine

boiler suit *n* a garment made in one piece, worn for dirty work; overalls

boiling point *n* **1** the temperature at which a liquid boils ☞ PHYSICS **2** the point at which high excitement, anger, etc., breaks into action

boil over *v adv* **1** (of a liquid) to flow over the sides of a container as it boils: *The milk is boiling over* **2** to get out of control: *The argument boiled over into open war*

boisterous *adj* **1** (of a person or his behaviour) noisily cheerful and rough **2** (of weather) wild and rough — ~ly *adv* — ~ness *n*

bold *adj* **1** daring; courageous; adventurous: *a very bold action* **2** (of the appearance of something) strongly marked; clearly formed: *a drawing done in a few bold lines* **3 as bold as brass** rude(ly); without respect — ~ly *adv* — ~ness *n*

boldface *n* (in printing) thick black letters

bole *n* the trunk of a tree

bolero *n* -ros **1** (the music for) a type of Spanish dance **2** a short jacket open at the front

boll *n* the seed case of the cotton plant

bollard *n* a short thick post either for tying ships' ropes to or to restrict the movement of traffic in a street

boll weevil *n* a small grey insect that attacks the cotton plant

boloney *n* *sl* talk that is mostly lies

Bolshevik *n, adj* (a supporter) of the system of government introduced in the USSR in 1917 or of any system like this; (a) Marxist — -vism *n*

bolshy *adj* -shier, -shiest causing trouble, esp by being too stubborn

bolster *n* a long round pillow that stretches right across the bed

bolster up *v adv* to give support and encouragement: *bolster up someone's pride*

bolt¹ *n* **1** a round bar with a spiral thread which can fit into a nut or threaded hole to fasten things together **2** a metal bar that slides across to fasten a door or window **3** a quantity of cloth rolled up **4** a short heavy arrow to be fired from a crossbow **5** a thunderbolt

bolt² *v* **1** to run away suddenly, as in fear: *The horse bolted* **2** to swallow hastily: *He bolted (down) his breakfast* **3** to stay or keep in a given state with a bolt: *These 2 parts are bolted together* **4** to fasten with a bolt: *Bolt the door*

bolt³ *adv* straight and stiffly: *He made the children sit bolt upright*

bolt⁴ *n* **1** an act of running away **2 make a bolt for** to try to escape quickly by way of

bolthole *n* a place to which one can bolt for safety

bomb¹ *n* **1** a hollow container filled with explosive, or with other chemicals of a stated effect: *a time bomb | a smoke bomb* **2** the atomic bomb, or the means of making and using it: *Has that country got the bomb now?* **3 (go) like a bomb** *esp. spoken* (to go) **a** (of a vehicle) very fast b very successfully **4 spend/cost a bomb** *esp. spoken* to spend/cost a lot of money

bomb² *v* to attack with bombs, esp. by dropping them from aircraft

bombard *v* **1** to keep attacking heavily (as if) with gunfire: *bombarded with questions* **2** (in science) to direct a stream of fast-moving particles at (an atom)

bombardier *n* **1** the man on a bomber aircraft who drops the bombs **2** (a member of) a low rank in the part of the army using artillery

bombardment *n* (an) attack with big guns: *a noise of heavy bombardment*

bombast *n* high-sounding insincere words with little meaning — ~ic *adj* — ~ically *adv*

bomber *n* **1** an aircraft that carries and drops bombs —compare FIGHTER **2** a person who plants bombs in order to kill people, cause damage, etc.

bombshell *n* *esp. spoken* a great and often unpleasant surprise

bona fide *adj, adv Latin law* real(ly); sincere(ly); in good faith

bona fides *n Latin law* sincerity; honest intentions: *His bona fides are unquestionable*

bonanza *n* *esp.* US **1** a lucky find in digging for gold, silver, or oil **2** something very profitable

bonbon *n* *French* a sweet made of sugar in a fancy shape, or of chocolate with a soft filling

bond¹ *n* **1** a paper in which a government or company promises to pay back with interest money that has been invested: *4½% National Savings bonds* **2** a written agreement with the force of law: *enter into a bond* **3** a feeling, likeness, etc., that unites 2 or more people or groups: *bonds of friendship* **4** a state of being stuck together: *This new glue makes a firmer bond* **5 one's word is (as good as) one's bond** one's spoken promise can be completely trusted

bond² *v* to stick together (as if) with glue: *These 2 substances won't bond together*

bondage *n* the condition of being a slave

bonded *adj* made of 2 or more thicknesses of material stuck together: *bonded wood*

bonds *n* chains, ropes, etc., for tying up a prisoner

bone¹ *n* **1** (one of) the hard parts of the body, round which are the flesh and skin —see also SKELETON ⇒ ANATOMY **2 all skin and bone** very thin **3 cut to the bone** to reduce (costs, services, etc.) as much as possible: *The bus service has been cut to the bone* **4 feel in one's bones** to believe strongly though without proof **5 make no bones about** to feel no doubt or shame about — ~less *adj*

bone² *v* **boned, boning** to take the bones out of: *Will you bone this joint of meat for me?* — ~d *adj*

bone china *n* (cups, plates, etc., made of) fine white clay mixed with crushed animal's bones

bone-dry *adj esp. spoken* perfectly dry

bonehead *n sl* a stupid person — ~ed *adj*

bone-idle *adj* completely lazy

bone meal *n* crushed bones, used for improving the soil

bone up on also **mug up**— *v adv prep esp. spoken* to study hard, esp. for a special purpose

bonfire *n* a large fire built in the open air

bongo also **bongo drum**— *n* **-gos** or **-goes** either of a pair of small drums played with the hands

bonhomie *n French* cheerfulness; easy friendliness

bonkers *adj sl* mad

bonnet *n* **1** a round head-covering tied under the chin, worn by babies and in former times by women **2** a soft flat hat worn by men, esp. soldiers, in Scotland **3** a metal lid over the front of a car —see also **a** BEE **in one's bonnet**

bonny *adj* **-nier, -niest** *esp. Scots* **1** pretty and healthy: *a bonny baby* **2** satisfactory; skilful: *a bonny fighter* — **bonnily** *adv*

bonus *n* **1** an additional payment beyond what is usual, or expected: *The workers got a Christmas bonus* **2** anything pleasant in addition to what is expected: *The win on the pools was a real bonus*

bony *adj* **-ier, -iest** **1** very thin so that the bones can be seen: *her bony hand* **2** (of food) full of bones: *bony fish*

boo *interj, n, v* **boos; booed, booing** (to express) a shout of disapproval or strong disagreement

boob *n, v sl* (to make) a foolish mistake

boobs *n sl* a woman's breasts

booby *n esp. spoken* a silly person

booby prize *n* a prize given for coming last

booby-trap *v* **-pp-** to provide with a booby trap

booby trap *n* **1** a hidden bomb which explodes when some harmless-looking object is touched **2** any harmless trap used for surprising someone

boohoo *v, n, interj* **-hooed, -hooing** (to make) the sound of childish weeping

book¹ *n* **1** a collection of sheets of paper fastened or bound together as a thing to be read, or to be written in **2** one of the main divisions or parts of a larger written work (as of a long poem or the Bible) **3** any collection of things fastened together in a cover: *a book of stamps* **4 make (a) book on** to offer to take bets on the results of **5 throw the book at** to make all possible charges against —see also BOOKS

book² *v* **1** to arrange in advance to have (something): *You'll have to book up early* **2** to enter charges against, esp. in the police records: *booked on a charge of speeding* — ~able *adj* — ~ing *n*

bookcase *n* a piece of furniture consisting of shelves to hold books

bookend *n* one of a pair of supports to hold up a row of books

book in *v adv* to have a place kept for one at a hotel **2** to report one's arrival as, at a hotel desk, an airport, etc.

booking office *n* an office where tickets are sold, esp. at a railway station

bookish *adj* having or showing more interest in ideas from books than in practicalities — ~**ly** *adv* — ~**ness** *n*

bookkeeping *n* the act of keeping accounts — **bookkeeper** *n*

booklet *n* a small book; pamphlet

bookmaker also (*esp. spoken*) **bookie, turf accountant**— *n* a person who takes bets, esp. on horse races

bookmark also **bookmarker**— *n* something to mark one's place in a book

books *n* written records of money, names, etc.: *How many names are there on your books?* —see also BOOK

bookstall *n* a stall selling books, magazines, etc.

book token *n* a card that can be exchanged for books at a bookshop

bookwork *n* the study of books as opposed to practical work

bookworm *n* 1 an insect that eats the binding and paste of a book 2 *often offensive* a person who is very fond of reading

boom¹ *n* 1 a long pole on a boat, to which a sail is fastened ⎯☞SAIL 2 a long pole used on a derrick 3 a long pole on the end of which a camera or microphone can be moved about 4 a heavy chain fixed across a river to stop things (such as logs) floating down or prevent ships sailing up

boom² *v* 1 to make a deep hollow sound 2 to grow rapidly, esp. in value, importance, etc.: *Business is booming* — **boom** *n*

boomerang *n* a curved stick which flies in a circle and comes back when thrown, used for hunting by Australian Aborigines

boon *n* something favourable; a comfort: *Radio is a boon to the blind*

boon companion *n* a good friend

boor *n offensive* a rude ungraceful person — ~**ish** *adj* — ~**ishly** *adv* — ~**ishness** *n*

boost¹ *v* 1 to push up from below 2 to increase: *to boost prices* 3 to help to improve: *We need to boost our spirits* 4 *technical* to increase (esp. the supply of electricity or water) in force, pressure, or amount

boost² *n* 1 a push upwards 2 an increase in amount 3 an act that brings encouragement: *a boost to our spirits*

booster *n* 1 a person who boosts 2 *technical* an apparatus for boosting

boot¹ *n* **to boot** besides: *He is dishonest, and a coward to boot*

boot² *n* 1 a covering of leather, rubber, or canvas for the foot with a part for supporting the ankle 2 an enclosed space at the back of a car for luggage 3 a blow given by or as if by a foot wearing a boot: *The thief gave me a boot in my stomach* 4 *sl* the act of sending someone away rudely, esp. from a job: *He got the boot*

boot³ *v* 1 to kick 2 also **boot out** —to send away rudely

bootee *n* a boot or sock with a short leg, esp. a baby's woollen boot

booth *n* 1 a movable covered shelter used at a market or fairground 2 a small enclosed place: *a telephone booth*

bootleg¹ *adj* (of or about alcoholic drink) unlawful

bootleg² *v* **-gg-** to make, carry, or sell bootleg drink — **-legger** *n*

bootstraps *n* one's own efforts (in the phrase **by one's own bootstraps**)

booty *n* goods stolen by thieves or taken by a victorious army

booze *v, n* **boozed, boozing** *sl* (to drink) an alcoholic drink — **boozy** *adj* — **boozily** *adv* — **booziness** *n*

boozer *n sl* a pub

bop *n* 1 *sl* a blow that strikes a person 2 also **bebop**— a type of jazz

borage *n* a type of blue-flowered European herb whose leaves are used to flavour food

Bordeaux *n* white or red wine from Bordeaux, in France —compare CLARET

border¹ *n* 1 an edge 2 (land near) the dividing line between 2 countries

border² *v* 1 to put a border on 2 to be a border to; come close to: *fields bordered by woods* 3 to have a common border with: *France borders Germany*

borderland *n* 1 land at or near the border 2 a condition between 2 other conditions and like each of them in certain ways: *the borderland between sleeping and waking*

borderline¹ *n* (a line marking) a border

borderline² *adj* close to the border between one type or standard and another: *a borderline case*

bore¹ *v* **bored, boring** to make a round hole or passage in or through something: *bore through solid rock* — ~**r** *n*

bore² also **borehole**— *n* a hole made by boring esp. for oil, water, etc.

bore³ *past tense of* BEAR

bore⁴ *n* a very large wave caused by a tide running up a narrow river

bore⁵ *n* 1 *offensive* a person who causes others to lose interest, esp. by continual dull talk 2 something which is rather unpleasant: *It's a bore having to go out again*

bore⁶ *v* to make uninterested — ~**dom** *n*

born¹ *adj* 1 brought into existence by or as if by birth: *The baby was born at 8 o'clock* 2 at birth; originally: *born French | nobly born*

born² *past part. of* BEAR

borne *past part. of* BEAR

borough *n* a town, or a division of a large town, with certain rights and powers of government

borrow *v* 1 to take for a certain time and with intention to return: *to borrow £5 from a friend* 2 to take or copy: *English has borrowed (words) from many languages* — ~**er** *n* — ~**ing** *n*

borscht, borshcht also **borsch**— *n* an East European soup, made either of beetroot or cabbage

borstal *n* a prison school for young offenders

borzoi *n* a type of large long-haired swift dog developed in Russia to hunt wolves

bosh *n, interj sl* nonsense

bosom¹ *n* the front of the human chest, esp. the female breasts; the part close to the heart: *She held the child to her bosom* —compare BREAST, HEART

bosom² *adj* very close (esp. in the phrase **bosom friend**)

bosomy *adj* having well-developed breasts

boss¹ *n* a round usu. metal ornament which stands out from the surface of something

boss² *n* employer; person having control over others

boss³ *v* to behave like a boss

boss-eyed *adj sl* cross-eyed

bossy *adj* **-ier, -iest** *offensive esp. spoken* fond of giving orders — **bossiness** *n*

bosun also **bos'n, b's'n**— *n* a boatswain

botanical *adj* of, related to, or obtained from plants: *a botanical garden*

botanize, -ise *v* **-nized, -nizing** to study plant life and collect examples of plants

botany *n* the scientific study of plants — **-nist** *n*

botch *v, n esp. spoken* (to do) a bad piece of work: *I've made a botch of it*

both¹ *adj* being the 2; having to do with the one and the other: *both shoes*

both² *pron* the one as well as the other: *Both of us thought so* —see EACH (USAGE)

both³ *conj* **both . . . and . . .** not only . . . but also . . .: *both New York and London have traffic problems*

bother¹ *v* **1** to cause to be nervous; annoy or trouble, esp. in little ways: *I'm busy: don't bother me* —compare ANGRY (USAGE) **2** to cause inconvenience to oneself: *Don't bother about it* **3** *sl* (used for adding force to expressions of displeasure): *Bother the lot of you!*

bother² *n* **1** (a cause of) trouble or anxiety: *We had a lot of bother finding our way* **2** also *sl* **bovver**— violence or threatening behaviour — ~**some** *adj*

bottle¹ *n* **1** a container, typically of glass or plastic, with a narrow neck and usu. no handle **2** alcoholic drink: *John's on the bottle again!*

bottle² *v* **-tled, -tling** to put into or preserve in bottles: *bottling wine*

bottle-feed *v* **-fed, -feeding** to feed (as a baby) with a bottle, rather than with the breast

bottle green *n, adj* dark green

bottleneck *n* **1** a place where a road narrows **2** a condition that slows down advance

bottle up *v adv* to control in an unhealthy way: *bottling up your feelings*

bottom *n* **1** the base on which something stands; the lowest part, inside or outside: *the bottom of the stairs* **2** the ground under an area of water: *the bottom of the sea* **3** the lowest position or situation: *at the bottom of the class* **4** the far end: *at the bottom of our garden* **5** the part of the body on which one sits **6** the cause:

Who is at the bottom of all this trouble? **7** **Bottoms up!** *esp. spoken* Finish your drinks! **8** **knock the bottom out of** to take away the necessary support on which something rests: *The bad news knocked the bottom out of market prices* **9** **the top and bottom of it** the truth; the whole of it

bottom drawer *n old use* (the place for) the clothes, sheets, etc., which a girl collects before getting married

bottomless *adj* with no bottom or limit; very deep: *a bottomless pit*

botulism *n* a serious form of food poisoning

boudoir *n* a woman's dressing room, bedroom, or private sitting room

bouffant *adj* (of hair or a dress) puffed out

bough *n* a branch of a tree

bought *past tense and part. of* BUY

bouillabaise *n French* a strong-tasting dish made from fish

bouillon *n French* a clear soup

boulder *n* a large stone or a mass of rock

boulevard *n* a broad street, usu. having trees on each side —compare AVENUE

bounce¹ *v* **bounced, bouncing** **1 a** (of a ball) to spring back or up again from the ground **b** to cause (a ball) to do this **2** to jump or cause to jump or spring up and down or move with a springing movement: *She bounced the baby* **3** *sl* (of a cheque) to be returned by a bank as worthless

bounce² *n* **1** the act or action of bouncing: *The ball has plenty of bounce* **2** lively, often noisy behaviour: *She has a lot of bounce* — **bouncy** *adj* — **-ily** *adv* — **-iness**

bounce back *v adv* to recover after a setback

bouncer *n* **1** a person or thing that bounces **2** a strong man employed to throw out unwelcome visitors **3** also **bumper**— (in cricket) a fast ball that springs up sharply

bouncing *adj* (esp. of babies) full of health

bound¹ *adj* going (to): *bound for home*

bound² *v* to mark the edges of; keep within a certain space: *London is bounded by the Home Counties*

bound³ *adj* **1** fastened by or as if by a band; kept close to: *bound to one's job* **2 a** certain: *It's bound to rain soon* **b** compelled: *I'm bound to blame him* **c** determined: *He's bound to go, and nothing will stop him* **3** (of a book) fastened within covers: *bound in leather*

bound⁴ *n* a jump or bounce

bound⁵ *v* to jump or bounce

boundary *n* **-ries** **1** the limiting or dividing line of surfaces or spaces: *the boundaries of the country* **2** the outer limit of anything: *the boundaries of knowledge* **3** (in cricket) **a** the line which marks the limit of the field of play **b** a hit to or over this line, that is worth 4 (or 6) runs

bounder *n old sl* a cad

boundless *adj* without limits: *boundless imagination* — ~**ly** *adv* — ~**ness** *n*

bounds *n* **1** the furthest limits; the limits beyond which one may not go: *beyond the bounds of reason* **2 out of bounds** forbidden to be visited

bounteous *adj literature* willing to give or given freely — ~**ly** *adv* — ~**ness** *n*

bountiful *adj literature* freely given; plentiful: *bountiful gifts* — ~**ly** *adv*

bounty *n* **-ties 1** generosity **2** something that is given generously **3** money given by a government for some special act or service

bouquet[1] *n* flowers picked and fastened together in a bunch

bouquet[2] *n* the smell of wine, etc.: *a rich bouquet*

bouquet garni *n French* a small bunch of herbs used to flavour soups, stews, etc.

bourbon *n* a type of American whisky

bourgeois *n, adj* bourgeois *French* **1** (of, related to, or typical of) a member of the middle class **2** *offensive* (a person) very concerned with possessions and good manners

bourgeoisie *n French* the middle class — compare PROLETARIAT

bout *n* **1** a short period of activity **2** an attack of illness: *bouts of fever* **3** a boxing match

boutique *n French* a shop or department in a store selling modern clothes

bouzouki *n* a Greek musical instrument like a mandolin

bovine *adj technical* of or like a cow or ox

bow[1] *v* **1** to bend forward the head or upper part of the body to show respect or yielding: *Bow to the Queen* **2** to express in this way: *He bowed his thanks* — ~**ed** *adj*

bow[2] *n* **1** a movement of bowing —compare CURTSY **2 take a bow** to come on stage to receive praise at the end of a performance

bow[3] *n* **1** a piece of wood held in a curve by a tight string and used for shooting arrows —see also CROSSBOW, LONGBOW **2** a long thin piece of wood with stretched horsehairs fastened along it, used for playing stringed instruments **3** an ornamental looped knot

bow[4] *v* **1** *technical* to bend or curve **2** to play on a musical instrument with a bow

bow[5] *n* the forward part of a ship —compare STERN

bowdlerize, -ise *v* **-ized, -izing** to remove from (a book, play, etc.) those parts considered unfit for children or ladies: *This dictionary has been bowdlerized*

bowels *n* **1** also **bowel**— a long pipe from the stomach by which waste matter leaves the body —compare INTESTINE **2** the inner, lower part

bower *n literature* a pleasant shaded enclosed place in a garden

bowl[1] *n* **1** a deep round container for holding liquids, flowers, sugar, etc. **2** anything in the shape of a bowl: *the bowl of a pipe* — ~**ful** *n*

bowl[2] *n* **1** a ball for rolling in the game of

bowls **2** an act of rolling the ball in the games of bowls or bowling

bowl[3] *v* **1** to roll (a ball) in the games of bowls or bowling **2** to play the games of bowls or bowling **3** (in cricket or rounders) to throw (the ball) towards the batsman **4** (in cricket) to force (a batsman) to leave the field by bowling a ball which hits the wicket **5** to cause to roll: *The wind bowled his hat down the street*

bow-legged *adj* having the legs curving outwards at the knee

bowler[1] *n* a person who bowls, esp. in cricket

bowler[2] also **bowler hat**— *n* a man's round hard hat, usu. black

bowline also **bowline knot**— *n* a special sort of knot which does not slip, used esp. by sailors

bowling *n* any of various games in which balls are rolled at an object or a group of objects: *tenpin bowling*

bowl over *v adv* **1** to knock down by running **2** to give a great surprise to: *I'm quite bowled over*

bowls *n* an outdoor game in which one tries to roll a big ball as near as possible to a small ball called ' the jack '

bowman *n* **-men** an archer

bow out *v adv* to leave, or stop doing something

bowsprit *n* a pole sticking out from the bow of a ship to which ropes from the sails are fastened

bow tie *n* a tie fastened with a knot in the shape of a bow

bow window *n* a window built outwards from the wall in a curve —compare BAY WINDOW

box[1] *n* **boxes** *or* **box** a type of small evergreen tree, often used in hedges

box[2] *n* **1** a container for solids, usu. with stiff sides and a lid: *a shoebox* **2** a small room or enclosed space: *a box at the theatre* **3** (in cricket) a rounded piece of metal or plastic worn by the batsman to protect his testicles **4** *sl* television: *What's on the box tonight?*

box[3] *v* to put in one or more boxes

box[4] *v* to fight (someone) or hit with the fists: *They boxed (with) each other* — ~**er** *n*

Box and Cox *v* to take turns in doing something

boxer *n* a type of largish short-haired dog of German origin

boxing *n* the sport of fighting with the fists

Boxing Day *n* a public holiday on the first weekday after Christmas

box kite *n* a kite shaped like 2 or more open-ended connected boxes

box number *n* a number used as a mailing address

box-office *adj* of or about the ability of a play, film, etc., to make a profit: *a box-office success*

box office *n* a place in a theatre, cinema, concert hall, etc., where tickets are sold

boy[1] *n* **boys 1** a young male person **2** a son, esp. young **3** a person of any age who acts like a

boy 4 a male person, of any age, from a given place: *He's a local boy* **5** (now considered offensive) a male servant of a different race **6** *becoming rare* (used in forming phrases for addressing men): *Thank you, dear boy* — ~**hood** *n* — ~**ish** *adj* — ~**ishly** *adv* — ~**ishness** *n*

boy² *interj sl* (expressing excitement): *Boy, what a game!*

boycott *v* **1** to refuse to do business with: *They're boycotting the shop* **2** to refuse to attend or take part in: *to boycott a meeting* — **boycott** *n*

boyfriend *n* a male companion to a woman

boys *n* men who are thought of as young and as forming a group in some way: *to spend a night with the boys*

boy scout also **scout**— *n* a member of an association (the **(boy) scouts**) for training boys in character and self-help —compare GIRL GUIDE

Br also **Brit**— *abbrev. for:* British

bra also **brassiere**— *n* a woman's close-fitting undergarment worn to support the breasts

brace¹ *n* **1** something used for supporting, stiffening, or fastening **2** a rope used to tighten a sail **3** a wire worn inside the mouth, to straighten the growth of teeth —see also SPLICE **the main brace**

brace² *v* **braced, bracing** **1** to make stronger **2** to provide or support with a brace: *His back was heavily braced* **3** to set firmly: *He braced his foot against the wall* **4** to prepare (oneself), usu. for something unpleasant: *Brace yourself for the shock!*

brace³ *n* brace (usu. in hunting or shooting) a pair: *several brace of wild birds* —compare PAIR, COUPLE

bracelet *n* a band or ring worn round the wrist or arm as an ornament

braces *n* elastic cloth bands worn over the shoulders to hold up trousers: *a pair of braces*

bracing *adj* fresh and health-giving

bracken *n* a kind of fern common on heaths, hillsides, etc.

bracket¹ *n* **1** a piece of metal or wood put in or on a wall to support something: *a lamp bracket* **2** either of a pair of signs ((-), < - >, or { -}) used for enclosing a piece of information

bracket² *v* **1** to enclose in brackets **2** to regard as belonging together: *Don't bracket them (together)*

brackish *adj* (of water) not pure; a little salty — ~**ness** *n*

bract *n* a leaflike part of a plant, often brightly coloured and growing in groups of a flowerlike appearance

bradawl *n* a small tool with a sharp point for making holes —compare AWL, GIMLET

brag¹ *v* **-gg-** to speak in praise of oneself

brag² *n* a type of card game

braggart *n* *offensive* a person who brags too much

Brahman also **Brahmin**— *n* a Hindu of the highest caste

braid¹ *v* **1** *esp. US* to plait **2** to ornament with braid

braid² *n* **1** *esp. US* a plait **2** a woven band of threads to put on material: *gold braid for a uniform*

braille *n* (a way of) printing with raised round marks which blind people can read by touch ☞ CODE

brain¹ *n* **1** *medical* the organ in the upper part of the head, which controls thought and feeling **2** the mind **3** a person with a good mind: *the best brains in the country* **4 have something on the brain** to think about something continually

brain² *v* **1** to kill by knocking out the brains of **2** to hit hard on the head

brainchild *n* somebody's idea or invention

brain drain *n* the movement of large numbers of highly-skilled people to countries where they can earn more money

brainless *adj* *offensive* foolish — ~**ly** *adv*

brains *n* **1** the material of which the brain consists **2** the ability to think: *He's got brains*

brainstorm *n* a sudden great disorder of the mind

brainwash *v* *esp. spoken, offensive* to cause to change beliefs by means not limited to reason or force: *Don't let advertisements brainwash you* — ~**ing** *n*

brainwave *n* *esp. spoken* a sudden clever idea

brainy *adj* **-ier, -iest** *esp. spoken* clever — **braininess** *n*

braise *v* **braised, braising** to cook slowly in a covered dish

brake¹ *n* an apparatus for slowing and bringing to a stop (as of a wheel or car) ☞ CAR

brake² *v* **braked, braking** **1** to cause to slow or stop: *to brake a car* **2** to use a brake

bramble *n* the wild prickly bushes of the rose family; the wild form of blackberry

bran *n* the crushed skin of wheat and other grain separated from the flour

branch¹ *n* **1** an armlike stem growing from the trunk of a tree or from another stem **2** an armlike part or division of some material thing: *a branch of a river* **3** a division of a non-material thing: *a branch of knowledge*

branch² *v* **1** to become divided into branches: *Follow the road until it branches* **2** to form such a division: *the road branches to the right*

brand¹ *n* **1** a class of goods which is the product of a particular producer **2** a special kind: *his own brand of humour* **3** a piece of burnt or burning wood **4** a mark made (as by burning) usu. to show ownership: *These cattle have my brand on them*

brand² *v* **1** to mark with a brand **2** (of bad experiences) to leave a mark on: *Prison has branded him for life* **3** to give a lasting bad name to: *branded as a thief*

brandish *v* to wave about

brand-new *adj* completely new

brandy *n* **-dies** a strong alcoholic drink usu. made from wine

brandy snap *n* a thin sticky kind of biscuit tasting of ginger

brash *adj* **1** *offensive* rudely disrespectful and proud **2** hasty and too bold — ~ly *adv* — ~ness *n*

brass *n* **1** a very hard bright yellow alloy of copper and zinc **2** an object made of this metal, esp. a musical wind instrument **3** (the players of) the set of brass instruments in an orchestra —see also STRINGS, WOODWIND, PERCUSSION **4** *sl* money **5** *sl* shameless daring: *How did she have the brass?*

brass band *n* a band consisting of brass musical instruments

brassed off *adj sl* tired and annoyed; fed up

brassiere *n* a bra

brass tacks *n* **get down to brass tacks** to come to the real business

brassy *adj* **-ier, -iest** **1** like brass in colour **2** like brass or brass musical instruments in sound **3** (esp. of a woman) shameless and loud in manner

brat *n offensive* a child, esp. a bad-mannered one

bravado *n* the showing of courage or boldness

brave¹ *adj* courageous and ready to suffer danger or pain — ~ly *adv* — ~ry *n*

brave² *v* **braved, braving** to meet (danger, pain, or trouble) without showing fear: *St George braved the dragon*

brave³ *n* a young North American Indian warrior

bravo *interj, n* **-vos** a cheer for someone

brawl *n, v* (to take part in) a noisy quarrel which usu. includes fighting — ~er *n*

brawn *n* **1** human muscle; muscular strength **2** (pieces of) pork boiled and pressed in a pot with jelly

brawny *adj* **-ier, -iest** strong; muscular — -iness *n*

bray *v* **brayed, braying** to make the sound that a donkey makes — **bray** *n*

brazen *adj* **1** *literature* like brass, esp. in producing a loud unmusical sound **2** shameless — ~ly *adv*

brazier *n* a container for burning coals

breach¹ *n* **1** an act of breaking, not obeying, or not fulfilling a law, promise, custom, etc.: *in breach of contract* **2** an opening, esp. one made in a wall by attackers

breach² *v* to break an opening in

breach of promise *n law* a failure to fulfil a promise, esp. a promise to marry someone

breach of the peace *n law* unlawful fighting in a public place

bread *n* **1** a common food made of baked flour: *a loaf of bread* **2** food generally: *our daily bread* **3** means of staying alive: *to earn one's bread* **4** *sl* money **5** **break bread with** *pompous* to eat with

breadcrumb *n* a small bit of bread

breaded *adj* covered with breadcrumbs and cooked

breadline *n* **1** a queue of poor people waiting for free food **2** **on the breadline** very poor

breadth *n* **1** (the) distance from side to side; width **2** a wide stretch **3** the quality of taking everything or many things into consideration: *breadth of mind* **4** **the length and breadth of** every part of —see also HAIR'S BREADTH

breadwinner *n* the person who works to supply a family with food, money, etc.

break¹ *v* **broke, broken, breaking** **1** to separate into parts suddenly or violently, but not by cutting or tearing **2** to separate or become separated from the main part in this way **3** to make or become unusable by damage: *He broke his wristwatch* **4** to make or become, suddenly or violently: *The prisoner broke loose* **5** to open the surface of: *to break the skin* **6** to disobey; not keep: *to break the law* **7** to force a way (into, out of, or through): *He broke into the shop* **8** to bring under control: *to break a horse* **9** to do better than: *to break a record in sports* **10** to make known: *to break the news* **11** to interrupt (an activity): *Let's break for a meal* **12** to bring or come to an end: *to break the silence* **13** to come esp. suddenly into being or notice: *as day breaks* **14** to fail as a result of pressure: *His health broke* **15** to change suddenly in direction, level, loudness, etc.: *His voice broke when he was 15* **16** to discover the secret of: *She broke their code* **17** (in tennis) to win a game against the server **18** **break the back of** to finish the main or the worst part of **19** **break camp** to pack up everything and leave a camping place **20** **break cover** to run out from a hiding place **21** **break the ice** to get through the first difficulties in starting a conversation **22** **break new/fresh ground** to make new discoveries **23** **break step** to march irregularly **24** **break wind** to let out gases from the stomach and bowels —see also BREAK AWAY, BREAK DOWN, BREAK EVEN, BREAK IN, BREAK INTO, BREAK OF, BREAK OUT, BREAK THROUGH, BREAK UP

break² *n* **1** an opening made by breaking or being broken: *a break in the clouds* **2** a pause for rest: *a coffee break* **3** a change from the usual pattern: *a break from the past* **4** the time of day before sunrise when daylight first appears: *at daybreak* **5** (in cricket) a change of direction of the ball **6** (in snooker and billiards) the number of points made by one player during one continuous period of play **7** (in tennis) a case of winning a game from the server **8** a chance; piece of luck: *Give him a break*

breakage *n* **1** the action of breaking **2** a broken place or part **3** the articles or value of the articles broken: *breakages of £37*

break away *v adv* **1** to escape **2** to cease (often political or religious) connection with, or loyalty to

breakdown *n* **1** a sudden failure in operation **2** a sudden weakening of the body or mind: *a nervous breakdown*

break down v adv 1 to destroy; reduce to pieces 2 to defeat or be defeated 3 (of machinery) to fail to work 4 to fail 5 to lose control of one's feelings: *He broke down and wept* —compare CRACK 6 to change chemically: *Food is broken down by chemicals* 7 to separate into different kinds —compare BREAK UP

breaker n a large wave that rolls onto the shore

break even v adv to do business without making either a profit or a loss

breakfast n, v (to eat) the first meal of the day

break-in n the unlawful entering of a building, using force

break in v adv 1 to enter a building by force 2 to interrupt 3 to bring under control; help (someone) to become accustomed to work

breaking and entering n the crime of housebreaking

break into v prep 1 also **burst into**— to enter by force 2 to interrupt 3 to begin suddenly: *to break into song* 4 to use part of, unwillingly: *to break into one's savings*

breakneck adj very fast or dangerous: *breakneck speed*

break of v prep to cure of (a habit): *They broke him of his addiction*

break out v adv to escape (from): *to break out of prison*

breakthrough n 1 the action of forcing a way through the enemy: *a military breakthrough* 2 a discovery, or the action of making a discovery, that will lead to other discoveries: *a scientific breakthrough*

break through v adv to advance in spite of opposition

breakup n (esp. of a relationship) a coming to an end

break up v adv 1 to divide into small pieces 2 to bring or come to an end or cease to be together: *Their marriage broke up* 3 (of a school or pupil) to begin the holidays 4 to amuse or distress greatly: *That joke really broke me up* —compare BREAK DOWN

breakwater n a thick wall built to lessen the force of the sea near a harbour

bream n **bream** a kind of freshwater fish with a thick flat body

breast¹ n 1 either of the 2 parts of a woman's body that produce milk, or the smaller similar parts on a man 2 the upper front part of the body between the neck and the stomach 3 literature the part of the body where the feelings are supposed to be: *a troubled breast* —compare HEART, BOSOM

breast² v 1 literature to stand up fearlessly against 2 to meet and push aside with one's chest

breastbone n the upright bone in the front of the chest, to which the top 7 pairs of ribs are connected ☞ ANATOMY

breast-feed v -fed, -feeding to feed (a baby) from the breast —compare SUCKLE

breastplate n a piece of armour to protect the chest

breaststroke n a way of swimming with one's chest downwards, making circular motions with the arms and legs

breath n 1 air taken into and breathed out of the lungs: *Let me get my breath back* 2 an act of breathing air in and out once: *a deep breath* 3 a movement of air: *hardly a breath of air* 4 a word about or slight sign of: *a breath of spring in the air* 5 a moment (in the phrases **in one breath, in the same breath, in the next breath**) 6 **catch one's breath a** to stop breathing for a moment because of strong feeling **b** to get one's breath 7 **draw/take breath** to have a rest 8 **hold one's breath** to stop breathing for a time 9 **take one's breath away** to make one unable to speak from surprise, pleasure, etc. 10 **waste one's breath** to talk uselessly, without effect

breathalyse v -lysed, -lysing to test (a driver) with a breathalyser

breathalyser n an apparatus used by the police to measure the amount of alcohol that the driver of a car has drunk

breathe v **breathed, breathing** 1 to take into (and send out of) the lungs (air, gas, etc.) 2 literature to live: *the greatest man who ever breathed* 3 to whisper 4 to give or send out (a smell, a feeling, etc.): *He'll breathe new life into the team* 5 (of flowers, wine, cloth, etc.) to take in air 6 **breathe down someone's neck** to keep too close a watch on what someone is doing 7 **breathe one's last** to die

breather n a short pause for a rest

breathing n the act or action of breathing: *heavy breathing*

breathing space n a pause for rest to get ready for further efforts

breathless adj 1 not breathing; dead 2 needing to breathe rapidly: *breathless from effort* 3 causing one to breathe with difficulty: *breathless haste* 4 causing one to hold one's breath: *a breathless silence* — ~ly adv — ~ness n

breathtaking adj very exciting or unusual — ~ly adv

breathy adj -ier, -iest (esp. of the voice) not clear or strong; with noticeable noise of breath — **breathily** adv — **breathiness** n

breech n the back end of a gun barrel

breeches n short trousers fastened at or below the knee —see also RIDING BREECHES

breeches buoy n a means of saving lives at sea, by which the person is held in a sling like a pair of breeches and pulled along a rope to shore

breed¹ v **bred, breeding** 1 (of animals) to produce young 2 to keep for the purpose of producing young: *He breeds cattle* 3 to train; educate; bring up 4 to cause or be the beginning of — ~er n

breed² n a kind or class of animal (or plant) usu. developed by man: *a breed of dog*

breeding n 1 the producing of young 2 the business of keeping for the purpose of producing young 3 (training in) polite social behaviour: *a person of fine breeding*

breeze¹ n a light gentle wind

breeze² v breezed, breezing *esp. spoken* 1 to move swiftly and unceremoniously: *He breezed in and demanded tea* 2 to pass easily: *She breezed through her exams*

breezeblock n a light-weight building-block made of cement and cinders

breezy adj -ier, -iest 1 of or having fairly strong breezes: *a breezy day* 2 cheerful and bright in manner: *She called a breezy good morning* — breezily adv — breeziness n

brethren n (usu. in solemn address) brothers: *dearly beloved brethren*

breve n a long musical note equal to 2 semibreves ☞ MUSIC

brevity n shortness: *the brevity of his life*

brew¹ v 1 to make (beer) 2 to make tea or coffee ready for drinking 3 (esp. of something bad) to prepare or be in preparation or ready to happen: *A storm was brewing*

brew² n the result of brewing: *Do you like this brew?*

brewer n a person who makes beer

brewery n -ies a place where beer is made

brew-up n *esp. spoken* the act or action of making tea or coffee

briar n a tobacco pipe made from the root of a brier

bribe¹ v bribed, bribing to influence unfairly by favours or gifts: *He bribed the policeman* — ~ry n

bribe² n something offered or given in bribing

bric-a-brac n small ornaments in a house

brick n 1 (a hard piece of) baked clay used for building 2 something in the shape of a brick: *a brick of ice cream* 3 sl a very nice trustworthy person 4 **drop a brick** sl to make a blunder

brickbat n a piece of something hard (like a brick), esp. when thrown in anger

bricklayer n a workman who lays bricks — -laying n

brick up v adv 1 also **brick in**— to fill completely with bricks 2 to enclose behind a wall of bricks: *He bricked the body up*

brickwork n any piece of building work using bricks

bride n a girl or woman about to be married, or just married — -dal adj

bridegroom also **groom**— n a man about to be married, or just married

bridesmaid n an unmarried girl or woman who attends the bride on the day of the marriage ceremony

bridge¹ n 1 something that carries a road over a valley, river, etc., and is usu. built of wood, stone, iron, etc. ◉ 2 the raised part of a ship on which the officers stand when on duty 3 the bony upper part of the nose 4 the part of a pair of spectacles that rests on or above the nose

bridge² v bridged, bridging to build a bridge across

bridge³ n a card game for 4 players, usu. played as contract bridge

bridgehead n a strong position far forward in enemy land —compare BEACHHEAD

bridle¹ n leather bands on a horse's head for controlling it ☞ HORSE

bridle² v -dled, -dling 1 to put a bridle on 2 bring under control: *Bridle your tongue* 3 to show anger or displeasure, esp. by an upward movement of the head and body

bridle path n a path for horseback riding

Brie n a type of soft French cheese

brief¹ adj 1 short, esp. in time: *a brief letter* 2 **in brief** in as few words as possible — ~ly adv

brief² n 1 a short statement, esp. one giving facts about a law case 2 a set of instructions setting limits to someone's powers or duties: *It's my brief to instruct him*

brief³ v to give last instructions or necessary information to: *Let me brief you before the meeting* — ~ing n

briefcase n a flat case for carrying papers or books, which opens at the top

briefs n very short close-fitting underpants or panties

brier, briar n a wild bush covered with thorns, esp. the wild rose bush

brig n a ship with 2 masts and large square sails

brigade n 1 a part of an army, of about 5, 000 soldiers 2 a group of people who have certain duties: *the Fire Brigade*

brigadier n an officer in the British army, commanding a brigade

brigadier-general n an officer of middle rank in the American armed forces

brigand n a bandit — ~age n

brigantine n a ship like a brig, but with fewer sails

bright adj 1 giving out or throwing back light very strongly 2 strong, clear, and easily seen: *bright red* 3 famous 4 full of life; cheerful: *bright eyes* 5 clever; quick at learning: *a bright child* 6 showing signs of future success: *a bright future* — ~ly adv — ~ness n

brighten v to make or become bright: *She brightened (up) my life*

brilliant adj 1 very bright, splendid, or showy 2 very clever; causing great admiration: *a brilliant speaker* 3 having or showing great skill (esp. in playing a musical instrument): *a brilliant artist* — -liance n — -liancy n — ~ly adv

brim¹ n 1 the top edge of a cup, bowl, etc., esp. with regard to the contents: *full to the brim* 2 the bottom part of a hat which turns outwards to give shade or protection against rain —compare CROWN

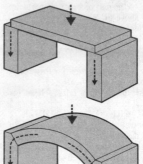

beam bridge

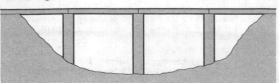

arch bridge

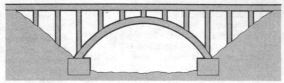

suspension bridge

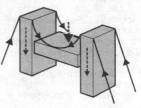

cantilever bridge
the weight of the centre span
is counterbalanced by weight
on the other side of the piers

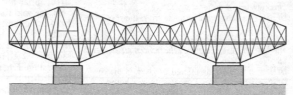

stayed girder
works on the same principle
as the cantilever,
but employs cables

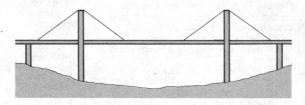

aqueduct
the Romans used layers
of arches to carry water
over shallow valleys.
When a road or railway
line is carried in this
way, the structure is
called a viaduct.

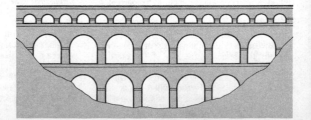

brim² v **-mm-** to be brimful: *brimming over with joy*

brimful, -full adj overflowing

brimstone n **fire and brimstone** the fires of hell

brindled adj having brownish fur or hair with marks of another colour

brine n **1** water containing salt, used for preserving food **2** *literature* seawater — **briny** adj

bring v **brought, bringing 1** to come with or lead: *Bring me the book* **2** to cause or lead to: *Spring rains bring summer flowers* **3** to sell or be sold for: *This old car will bring about £10* **4** *law* to make officially: *bring a charge against* **5** to cause to come: *Her cries brought the neighbours* **6** to cause to reach a certain state: *Bring them together* **7 bring to book** to force to give an explanation, or to be punished —see also BRING DOWN, BRING FORTH, BRING FORWARD, BRING IN, BRING OFF, BRING ON, BRING OUT, BRING ROUND, BRING UNDER, BRING UP

bring down v adv to move (a figure) from one list to another, when dividing

bring forth v adv old use to produce, esp. give birth to

bring forward v adv **1** (in bookkeeping) to move to the top of the next page (the total at the bottom of an earlier page) **2** also **put forward**— to bring nearer the time of: *We'll bring the party forward* **3** to introduce: *A plan was brought forward*

bring in v adv **1** to produce as profit or earnings: *The boys bring in £60 a week* **2** to ask to come to one's help: *to bring in advisers*

bring off v adv to succeed in (something difficult)

bring on v adv **1** to cause **2** to cause to advance: *This warm weather should bring on the crops* **3** to help or improve: *Study should bring on your Maths*

bring out v adv **1** to produce: *to bring out a new kind of soap* **2** also **draw out**— to cause to develop: *to bring out the worst in someone* **3** also **draw out**— to encourage, esp. to talk: *Company should bring her out a bit* **4** to cause to strike: *bring the workers out*

bring round v adv **1** also **bring around, bring to**— to cause to regain consciousness **2** to persuade into a change of opinion: *Bring him round to our point of view*

bring under v adv to control and defeat, usu. by political force: *Those who oppose us will be brought under*

bring up v adv **1** to educate and care for until grown-up **2** to raise or introduce (a subject): *to bring up the question* **3** to vomit (one's food) **4** to cause to stop suddenly: *He was brought up short* **5 bring up the rear** to be the last in a line

brink n **1** an edge at the top of a cliff or other steep high point **2** a state of dangerous nearness (esp. in the phrases **on/to the brink of**)

brisk adj **1** quick and active: *a brisk walker* **2** pleasantly cold and strong: *a brisk wind* ⚠ BRUSQUE — ~**ly** adv — ~**ness** n

brisket n the breast of an animal esp. a joint of beef

bristle n, v **-tled, -tling** (to stand up like) short stiff coarse hair: *a face covered with bristles* | *His hair bristled with anger*

bristly adj **-tlier, -tliest 1** like or full of bristles **2** difficult to deal with

bristols n sl a woman's breasts

Brit abbrev. for: British

British adj, n (the people) of Britain ☞ MAP — ~**er** n

British thermal unit n the quantity of heat needed to raise one pound of water one degree fahrenheit

Briton n a native of Britain

brittle adj **1** hard but easily broken: *Glass is brittle* **2** easily damaged, hurt, or destroyed: *a brittle friendship* **3** lacking warmth or depth of feeling: *brittle gayness*

broach v **1** to open (an unopened bottle) **2** to introduce in conversation (esp. in the phrase **broach the subject**)

broad¹ adj **1** wide: *broad shoulders* **2** not limited; general: *broad opinions* | *a broad general idea* **3** easy to see or understand: *a broad suggestion* **4** full and clear (esp. in the phrase **broad daylight**) **5** (of a local accent or way of speaking) strong: *He spoke broad Scots* **6** (esp. of subjects for laughter) bold and rude: *broad jokes* — ~**ly** adv — ~**ness** n

broad² n sl a woman

broad bean n a large flat kind of bean eaten as a fresh vegetable

broadcast¹ adj of, related to, or made public by radio (or television) broadcasting

broadcast² n a single radio (or television) presentation

broadcast³ v **broadcast, broadcasting 1** to spread around; make widely known: *to broadcast the gossip* **2** to send out or give (as) a radio or television presentation: *The BBC broadcasts every day* — ~**er** n — ~**ing** n

broadcloth n thick woollen cloth of good quality

broaden v to make or become broad or broader

broadloom adj, n technical (a carpet) which is woven on a wide loom

broadminded adj showing willingness to respect the opinions and actions of others — ~**ly** adv — ~**ness** n

broadsheet n something (as a poem or an advertisement) printed on one side of a large sheet of paper

broadside n **1** the side of a ship above the waterline **2** the firing of all the guns on one side of a ship at the same time **3** a forceful attack in words

broadsword n old use or literature a sword

with a broad flat blade, esp. one held with both hands ☞ WEAPON

brocade n ornamental cloth usu. of silk with a raised pattern

broccoli n a type of open cauliflower whose young flower heads are eaten as a vegetable

brochure n a small thin book, esp. one giving instructions or details of a service offered: *a holiday brochure*

brogue¹ n a strong thick shoe, esp. one with a pattern made in the leather

brogue² n the way in which the Irish speak English

broil v to make or be very hot or too hot: *It's broiling today!*

broke¹ adj sl completely without money (often in the phrases **flat/ stony broke**)

broke² past tense of BREAK

broken¹ adj 1 violently separated into smaller pieces 2 damaged or spoilt by breaking: *a broken clock/leg* 3 disobeyed or not fulfilled: *a broken law/promise* 4 brought to an end; crushed: *a broken marriage | a broken spirit* 5 imperfectly spoken or written: *broken English* — ~ly adv — ~ness n

broken² past part. of BREAK

broker n a person who does business for another

brolly n -lies sl an umbrella

bromine n an element that is usu. in the form of a red poisonous liquid, used in photography and medicine

bronchial adj of or about the bronchial tubes: *bronchial disease*

bronchial tube n either of the 2 branches connecting the windpipe with the lungs

bronchitis n an inflammation of the bronchial tubes — -tic adj

bronco n -cos a wild or half-wild horse of the western US

brontosaurus n -ri any of various types of very large 4-footed and probably plant-eating dinosaurs

bronze¹ v bronzed, bronzing to give the appearance or colour of bronze to: *bronzed by the sun*

bronze² n 1 an alloy mainly of copper and tin 2 the dark reddish-brown colour of this 3 a work of art made of bronze

Bronze Age n the time when men used tools made of bronze before iron-working was known, about 4–6, 000 years ago

brooch n an ornament worn on women's clothes, fastened by a pin

brood¹ n a family of young birds or other young creatures all produced at the same time

brood² v 1 to sit on eggs as a hen does 2 to continue to think, usu. angrily or sadly (about): *Don't brood about it* — ~er n

brood³ adj kept for giving birth to young: *a brood hen*

brood over v prep to hang closely over: *A cloud brooding over the hills*

broody adj -ier, -iest 1 like a mother bird

wanting to sit on her eggs 2 having or showing sadness and silence — -dily adv — -diness n

brook¹ v to allow or accept without complaining: *He would brook no interruptions*

brook² n a small stream

broom n 1 a type of large bushy plant with yellow flowers that grows on sandy or waste land 2 a large sweeping brush, usu. with a long handle

broomstick n the long thin handle of a broom

Bros. abbrev. for: Brothers

broth n soup in which meat, fish, or vegetables have been cooked

brothel n a house of prostitutes

brother¹ n 1 a male relative with the same parents ☞ FAMILY 2 a male member of the same group: *We must all stand together, brothers!* 3 (a title for) a male member of a religious group, esp. a monk — ~ly adj — ~liness n

brother² interj (an expression of slight annoyance and/or surprise)

brotherhood n 1 a group of men, usu. monks, living a religious life together 2 an association for a particular purpose

brother-in-law n brothers-in-law 1 the brother of one's husband or wife 2 the husband of one's sister 3 the husband of the sister of one's husband or wife ☞ FAMILY

brought past tense and part. of BRING

brow n 1 a forehead 2 the upper part of a slope or a hill

browbeat v -beat, -beaten, -beating to frighten into obedience by fierceness

brown¹ adj, n (of) a colour like black mixed with orange which is that of coffee — ~ish adj

brown² v to make or become brown or browner: *browned by the sun*

brownie n a fairy believed to perform helpful services at night

Brownie n a member of the Girl Guides from 8 to 11 years old

brown off v adv sl to cause to lose interest and/or become angry: *I'm really browned off* —compare CHEESE OFF

brown rice n unpolished rice in its outer covering

brown study n in a brown study deep in thought

browse¹ n a period of time spent in browsing

browse² v browsed, browsing 1 to feed on young plants, grass, etc.: *goats browsing on shrubs* 2 to read here and there in books, esp. for enjoyment: *to browse through some books*

brucellosis n a disease of farm animals and man

bruise¹ v bruised, bruising 1 to cause one or more bruises on: *She bruised her knee* 2 to show one or more bruises: *Soft fruit bruises easily*

bruise² n a discoloured place where the skin of a human, animal, or fruit has been injured by a blow but not broken

bruiser n esp. spoken a big rough strong man

brunch *n esp. spoken* a combination of breakfast and lunch

brunette *n* a white person (usu. a woman) with dark hair

brunt *n* **bear the brunt of** to suffer the worst part of

brush¹ *n* **1** also **brushwood**— small branches broken off from trees or bushes **2** (land covered by) small trees and bushes — compare SCRUB

brush² *n* **1** an instrument for cleaning, smoothing, or painting, made of sticks, stiff hair, nylon, etc.: *a clothesbrush* **2** the tail of a fox **3** an act of brushing: *Give my coat a brush* **4** a light touch in passing: *He felt the brush of her dress*

brush³ *v* **1** to clean or smooth with a brush: *to brush the floor* **2** to remove with or as if with a brush: *to brush dirt off*

brush⁴ *v* **1** to pass lightly over or across; touch lightly in passing: *The breeze brushed his cheek* **2** to move lightly or carelessly: *She just brushed past*

brush⁵ *n* a short and unimportant involvement: *a brush with the police*

brush-off *n* **brush-offs** *sl* a clear refusal to be friendly or to listen: *She gave me the brush-off*

brush off *v adv* to disappear or come off with brushing: *The dirt will brush off easily*

brush up also **polish up**— *v adv* to improve one's knowledge of (something partly forgotten) by study: *I must brush up my French* — **brush-up** *n*

brusque *adj* quick and rather impolite: *brusque behaviour* ⚠ BRISK — ~**ly** *adv* — ~**ness** *n*

brussels sprout also *sprout*—— *n* a small tight bunch of leaves, used as a vegetable, which grows in groups on the sides of a tall stem

brutal *adj* **1** having or showing no fine or tender human feeling: *a brutal attack* **2** severe: *the brutal truth* — **-tality** *n* — **-tally** *adv*

brutalize, -ise *v* **-ized, -izing** to make brutal or unfeeling — **-ization** *n*

brute¹ *adj* like an animal in being cruel or very strong: *brute strength*

brute² *n* **1** an animal, esp. a large one: *a brute of a hound* **2** an unfortunate animal: *The horse broke its leg, the poor brute* **3** a rough, cruel, or bad-mannered person, esp. a man — **brutish** *adj* — **brutishly** *adv*

B.Sc. *abbrev. for:* Bachelor of Science; (a title for someone who has) a first university degree in a science subject

bubble¹ *v* **-bled, -bling** **1** to form, produce, or rise as bubbles **2** to make the sound of bubbles rising in liquid: *The pot bubbled quietly* **3** (usu. of women) to express a lot of a good feeling: *Mary was bubbling with joy*

bubble² *n* **1** a ball of air or gas usu. contained in a liquid shell: *to blow soap bubbles* **2** the sound or appearance of a boiling mixture: *the bubble of the cooking pot* **3** something empty or not lasting — **bubbly** *adj*

bubble and squeak *n* a dish consisting of fried potatoes and vegetables (esp. cabbage)

bubble gum *n* chewing gum that can be blown into bubbles

bubbly *n sl* champagne

bubonic plague *n* a disease (common in former times) that spreads from rats to man, and usu. causes death

buccaneer *n* a sea-robber; pirate

buck¹ *n* **bucks** *or* **buck** **1** (*fem.* **doe**)—the male of certain animals, esp. the deer, the rat, the rabbit, and the antelope **2** *sl, esp. US* an American dollar

buck² *v* (esp. of a horse) to jump up with all 4 feet off the ground —see also BUCK UP

bucked *adj esp. spoken* made more cheerful; pleased: *We were bucked by the good news*

bucket¹ *n* a usu. round open metal or plastic container with a handle, for carrying liquids; pail

bucket² *v* **1** *esp. spoken* to pour very hard: *rain bucketing down* **2** to move roughly and irregularly: *The car bucketed down the road*

buckle¹ *n* a fastener for joining the ends of 2 straps, or for ornament

buckle² *v* **-led, -ling** **1** to fasten with a buckle **2** to make or become bent or wavy: *The shock buckled the wheel of my bicycle*

buckle down *v adv* to begin to work seriously

buckshee *adj, adv sl* without payment

buckshot *n* coarse lead shot

buckskin *n* strong soft yellowish leather from the skin of a deer or goat

bucktooth *n* **-teeth** a large front tooth that sticks out

buck up *v adv* **1** to hurry up **2** to cheer up

buckwheat *n* small black grain much used as hen food

bucolic *adj literature* having to do with country life — ~**ally** *adv*

bud¹ *n* a flower (or leaf) before it opens —see also NIP **in the bud**

bud² *v* **-dd-** to produce buds

bud³ *n sl* buddy

Buddhism *n* an Asiatic religion growing out of the teaching of Gautama Buddha ☞ WORSHIP — **Buddhist** *n*

budding *adj* beginning to develop: *a budding poet*

buddy *n* **-ies** *esp. spoken* a companion to; partner: *He's my buddy*

budge *v* **budged, budging** to move a little: *I can't budge this rock*

budgerigar also *esp. spoken* **budgie**— *n* a small bright-coloured Australian bird, often kept in a cage

budget¹ *n* **1** a plan of how to spend or take in money: *a family / government budget* **2** the quantity of money stated in either type of plan — ~**ary** *adj*

budget² *v* to plan spending: *save money by budgeting*

buff¹ *n, adj* a faded yellow colour

buff² *v* to polish with something soft

buff³ *n esp. spoken* a person who is very interested in a subject: *a film buff*

buffalo *n* **-loes** *or* **-lo** 1 any of several very large black Asian and African cattle with long curved horns 2 a bison

buffer *n* 1 a spring on the front and back of a railway engine or carriage to take the shock when it runs into anything 2 a person or thing that lessens a shock

buffer state *n* a smaller peaceful country between 2 larger ones, serving to lessen the chance of war between them

buffet¹ *n* a blow or sudden shock

buffet² *v* to strike sharply or repeatedly

buffet³ *n* a meal laid out for guests who serve themselves

buffoon *n* a rough noisy fool — ~ery *n*

bug¹ 1 *US* any small insect —compare BEETLE 2 *esp. spoken* a germ 3 *sl* an apparatus for listening secretly to conversations 4 a bedbug

bug² *v* **-gg-** *sl* to fit with a secret listening apparatus: *The police have bugged my office*

bugbear *n* a cause of concern, perhaps without reason: *the bugbear of rising prices*

buggery *n vulgar or law* sodomy

buggy *n* **-gies** 1 a light one-horse carriage 2 *US* a pram

bugle *n* a brass wind instrument, like a trumpet but shorter — ~r *n*

build¹ *v* **built, building** to make by putting pieces together: *He built a model ship out of wood* —see also BUILD IN, BUILD ON, BUILD UP — ~er *n*

build² *n* shape and size, esp. of the human body: *We are of the same build*

build in *v adv* to make a fixed part of usu. a room: *built-in cupboards*

building *n* 1 something usu. with a roof and walls that is intended to stay in one place 2 the business of making objects of this sort

building society *n* **building societies** an association into which people put money which is then lent to those who want to buy or build houses

build on¹ *v adv* to make as an additional building: *This part of the hospital was built on later*

build on² *v prep* to base (something) on: *His argument is built on facts*

build up *v adv* 1 to increase; develop: *to build up one's strength* — **buildup** *n*

bulb *n* 1 a round root of certain plants 2 any object of this shape, esp. the glass part of an electric lamp that gives out light — ~ous *adj*

bulge¹ *n* a swelling of a surface — **bulgy** *adj* — **bulgily** *adv* — **bulginess** *n*

bulge² *v* **bulged, bulging** to swell out

bulk *n* 1 great size or quantity 2 the main part: *The bulk of the work has been done* 3 roughage

bulkhead *n* any of several walls which divide a ship into separate parts

bulky *adj* **-ier, -iest** 1 big 2 having great size in comparison with weight: *a bulky sweater* — **-ily** *adv* — **-iness** *n*

bull¹ *n* 1 the male form of cattle 2 the male of the elephant, the whale, and other animals 3 **take the bull by the horns** *esp. spoken* to face difficulties without fear

bull² *n* a solemn official letter from the Pope

bull³ *n, interj sl* foolish rude talk; nonsense

bulldog *n* any of several types of English dog with a short neck and front legs far apart

bulldoze *v* **-dozed, -dozing** 1 to clear with a bulldozer 2 to cause to obey by force or threat: *They bulldozed him into agreeing*

bulldozer *n* a powerful machine used for pushing heavy objects, earth, etc., out of the way

bullet *n* a type of shot fired from a gun, usu. long and with a rounded or pointed end —compare SHOT, SHELL

bulletin *n* 1 a short public notice: *the latest bulletin about the President's health* 2 a short news report or printed news sheet

bulletproof *adj* that stops bullets

bullfight *n* a ceremonial fight between men and a bull — ~ing *n* — ~er *n*

bullfinch *n* a type of small songbird with a bright reddish breast and a strong beak

bullfrog *n* a type of large American frog with a loud croak

bullion *n* bars of gold or silver

bullock *n* a young bull which cannot breed —compare STEER

bullring *n* an arena for bullfights

bull's-eye *n* 1 the circular centre of a target that people try to hit when shooting 2 a kind of large hard round sweet 3 a circular window

bully *v* **-lied, -lying** to use one's strength to hurt or frighten (weaker people) — **bully** *n*

bully off *v adv* to start a game of hockey — **bully-off** *n*

bulrush *n* any of several kinds of tall grasslike waterside plants

bulwark *n* a strong wall for defence or protection

bum¹ *n sl* a person's bottom

bum² *v* **-mm-** *sl* to beg

bum³ *n US* a wandering beggar

bum⁴ *adj sl* very bad: *some bum advice*

bum around *v adv sl* to spend time lazily or travelling for enjoyment

bumble *v* **-bled, -bling** *sl* to speak without making much sense

bumblebee *n* a type of large hairy bee which hums loudly

bumf, bumph *n sl* dull material that must be read

bummer *n sl* something bad, esp. a drug experience

bump¹ *v* 1 to strike or knock with force or violence 2 to move with much jolting, as of a wheeled vehicle over uneven ground —see also BUMP INTO, BUMP OFF

bump² *n* 1 a sudden forceful blow or shock 2 a raised round swelling

bumper¹ *adj* plentiful or large: *a bumper crop*

bumper² *n* 1 a bar fixed on the front or back

of a car for protection **2** (in cricket) a bouncer **3** *US* a railway buffer

bump into *v prep esp. spoken* to meet by chance

bumpkin *n esp. spoken* an awkward foolish fellow

bump off *v adv sl* to murder

bumptious *adj* putting forward one's own opinions or interests noisily and with little regard for others — ~ly *adv* — ~ness *n*

bumpy *adj* -ier, -iest with many bumps — -ily *adv* — -iness *n*

bun *n* **1** a small round sweet cake **2** a mass of hair fastened into a tight round shape, usu. at the back of the head

bunch¹ *n* **1** a number of things fastened, held, or growing together: *a bunch of flowers/keys* **2** *esp. spoken* a group

bunch² *v* **1** to form into one or more bunches **2** (of cloth) to gather into folds

bundle¹ *n* **1** a number of articles tied, fastened, or held together **2** a number of fine threadlike parts lying closely together, esp. nerves, muscles, etc.

bundle² *v* -dled, -dling **1** to move or hurry roughly: *They bundled the children off to school* **2** to   store in a disordered way

bung¹ *n* a round stopper to close the hole in a container

bung² *v esp. spoken* to throw

bungalow *n* a house all on one level

bungle *v* -gled, -gling to do (something) badly: *to bungle a job* — ~r *n*

bung up *v adv esp. spoken* to block up: *My nose is bunged up with a cold*

bunion *n* a painful lump on the first joint of the big toe

bunk¹ *n* **1** a bed fixed to the wall that is often one of 2 or more one above the other **2** BUNK BED

bunk² *n sl* nonsense

bunk³ *n* **do a bunk** *sl* to run away

bunk bed also **bunk**— *n* either of usu. 2 beds fixed one above the other

bunker *n* **1** a place to store coal **2** (in golf) a sandy hole, from which it is hard to hit the ball **3** a strongly-built shelter for soldiers, esp. underground

bunkum *n sl* nonsense

bunny *n* -nies (*used esp. by or to children*) a rabbit

Bunsen burner *n* a burner for scientific work, in which gas is mixed with air before burning

bunting¹ *n* any of several small birds related to the finches

bunting² *n* flags and ornamental hangings for special occasions

buoy¹ *n* **buoys** a floating object fastened to the bed of the sea to show ships where there are rocks

buoy² *v* **buoyed, buoying** to keep (someone or something) floating — ~ancy *n* — ~ant *adj* — ~antly *adv*

Burberry *n trademark* -rys a type of raincoat

burble *v* -bled, -bling **1** to make a sound like a stream flowing over stones **2** to talk quickly but foolishly or not clearly —compare BABBLE

burden¹ *n esp. written* **1** a heavy load **2** a duty hard to do properly

burden² *v* to load or trouble

burden³ *n* the main point: *the burden of the story*

burden of proof *n law* the responsibility of proving something

burdensome *adj* causing a burden — ~ness *n*

burdock *n* a type of plant with hooked seed clusters

bureau *n* **bureaux** **1** a large desk or writing-table with a wooden cover to close it **2** a government department or business office: *a travel bureau*

bureaucracy *n* -cies **1** government officers **2** a group of people like this in a business **3** government by such officers rather than by those who are elected, often supposed to have excessive rules

bureaucrat *n* a member of a bureaucracy — ~ic *adj* — ~ically *adv*

burette *n* a glass tube marked off with degrees of measurement, used for measuring liquid or gas

burgeon *v esp. written* to grow; develop: *burgeoning cities*

burgess *n old use or pompous* a free man of a city, having the right to elect representatives

burgh *n Scots* a borough — ~er *n*

burglar *n* a thief who breaks into houses, shops, etc. —compare HOUSEBREAKER — ~y *n*

burgle *v* -gled, -gling to break into a building and steal

Burgundy *n* a type of French wine

burial *n* the putting of a dead body into a grave

burlesque *n* speech, acting, or writing in which a serious thing is made to seem foolish or a foolish thing is treated solemnly

burly *adj* (of a person) strongly and heavily built — -liness *n*

burn¹ *v* **burnt** *or* **burned, burning** **1** to be on fire **2** to shine: *a light burning* **3** to be unpleasantly hot: *the burning sand* **4** to experience a very strong feeling: *She is burning to tell you the news* **5** to hurt, damage, or destroy by fire: *He burnt all his papers* **6** to use for power, heating, or lighting: *ships that burn coal*

burn² *n* **1** a hurt place produced by burning: *burns on her hand* **2** an act of firing the motors on a spacecraft

burner *n* the part of a cooker, heater, etc., that produces flames —see also CHARCOAL BURNER

burning *adj* **1** on fire or producing great heat: *a burning house | a burning fever* **2** (of feelings) very strong: *a burning interest in science*

burnish v to polish (esp. metal), usu. with something hard and smooth

burnous, burnouse n a long one-piece hooded loose outer garment worn esp. by Arabs

burnt *past tense & part. of* BURN

burnt-out also **burned-out**— *adj* worn out by too much use or improper use: *burnt-out machines*

burn up v adv **1** to be destroyed by great heat **2** sl to travel at high speed along: *to burn up the road*

burp¹ n sl a belch

burp² v **1** esp. spoken to help (a baby) to belch- **2** sl to belch

burr¹ n **1** a long loud hum **2** a way of pronouncing English with a strong "r"-sound

burr, bur² n a prickly seed-container of certain plants

burrow¹ n a hole in the ground made by an animal, esp. a rabbit, in which it lives or hides

burrow² v to make by digging: *to burrow a hole*

bursar n a person in a college or school who has charge of money, property, etc.

bursary n -aries a scholarship

burst¹ v burst, bursting **1** to break suddenly, esp. by pressure from within **2** to come suddenly, often with force: *She burst through the door* **3** (in the -ing form) to be filled to the breaking point: *I am bursting with joy*

burst² n a sudden outbreak: *a burst of laughter*

burst out v adv to begin suddenly: *They burst out laughing*

burton n gone for a Burton sl a missing b broken c killed

bury v -ied, -ying **1** to put into the grave **2** to hide away: *The dog has buried a bone*

bus¹ n a large passenger-carrying motor vehicle, esp. a public one

bus² v -ss- to carry (or travel) by bus

busby n -bies **1** a type of small fur hat worn by certain soldiers **2** esp. spoken a bearskin

bush n **1** a small low tree **2** wild country in Australia or Africa

bushbaby n -bies a type of small monkey-like African animal

bushed adj esp. spoken very tired

bushel n a measure, esp. of grain; about 36.5 litres

bush telegraph n the sending of messages by smoke signals, beating drums, etc.

bushwhack v **1** to live out in the bush **2** to ambush — ~er n

bushy adj -ier, -iest (of hair) growing thickly — bushiness n

business n **1** one's work **2** trade and the getting of money **3** a particular money-earning activity such as a shop **4** a duty: *It's a teacher's business to make children learn* **5** an affair; event; matter; thing: *a strange business* — ~man, — ~woman n

businesslike adj practical and thorough

business hours n the time during which business is done

busk v esp. spoken to play music in the street for money — ~er n

busman n -men a bus driver

busman's holiday n a holiday spent doing one's usual work

bus stop n a fixed place where buses stop for passengers

bust¹ n **1** the human head, shoulders, and chest, esp. as shown in sculpture **2** a woman's breasts

bust² v busted or bust, busting esp. spoken to break, esp. with force

bust³ v busted, busting sl (of the police) a to arrest b to raid

bust⁴ n sl a complete failure

bust⁵ adj esp. spoken **1** broken **2** go bust (of a business) to fail

bustle¹ v -tled, -tling to be busy, often with much noise

bustle² n noisy activity: *the bustle of the big city*

bustle³ n a frame formerly used for holding out the back of a woman's dress

bust-up n sl a noisy quarrel, sometimes with fighting

busy¹ adj -ier, -iest **1** working; not free **2** full of work: *a busy day* — busily adv — busyness n

busy² v -ied, -ying to keep (oneself) busy: *He busied himself with answering letters*

busybody n -ies a person who takes too much interest in the affairs of others

but¹ conj **1** rather; instead: *not one, but 2!* **2** in spite of this: *tired but happy* **3** except for the fact that: *I was going to write, but I lost your address*

but² prep except: *no one but me* —see also BUT FOR

but³ adv all but almost: *The job is all but finished!*

but⁴ n ifs and buts unnecessary doubts: *I'm tired of your ifs and buts*

butane n a natural gas used for cooking, heating, and lighting

butch adj sl showing a lot of male tendencies: *a butch woman* — butch n

butcher¹ n a person who kills animals for food or sells meat

butcher² v **1** to kill (animals) and prepare for sale as food **2** to kill bloodily or unnecessarily — ~y n

but for prep if not for: *But for my brother's help, I would not have finished* —compare EXCEPT FOR, SAVE

butler n the chief male servant of a house

butt¹ v to strike or push with the head or horns: *He butted his head against the wall* —see also BUTT IN — butt n

butt² n a person or thing that people make fun of

butt³ _n_ 1 a large, thick, or bottom end of something 2 a cigarette end

butt⁴ _n_ a large barrel for liquids

butter¹ _n_ 1 yellow fat made from milk 2 a substance like butter: _peanut butter_ — ~y _adj_

butter² _v_ to spread with butter

butter bean _n_ any of several types of large broad bean often sold dried

buttercup _n_ any of several yellow wild flowers

butterfingers _n_ butterfingers _esp. spoken_ a person who is likely to drop things

butterfly¹ _n_ -flies any of several insects with 4 often beautifully-coloured wings ☞ INSECT

butterfly² _n_ a way of swimming chest downwards, moving both arms together in a circular motion while kicking the legs up and down

buttermilk _n_ the liquid that remains after butter is made from milk

butterscotch _n_ hard toffee made from sugar and butter

butter up _v adv sl_ to flatter (someone)

buttery _n_ -ies a room from which food and drink are served

butt in _v adv sl_ to interrupt, usu. by speaking

buttock _n_ either of the 2 fleshy parts on which a person sits

button¹ _n_ 1 a small usu. round or flat thing fixed to a garment and passed through a buttonhole to act as a fastener 2 a button-like object for starting, stopping, or controlling a machine

button² _v_ to fasten with buttons

buttoned up _adj_ 1 not talking much 2 (of a piece of work) successfully completed

buttonhole¹ _n_ 1 a hole for a button 2 a flower to wear on one's coat or dress

buttonhole² _v_ -holed, -holing to stop and force to listen: _She buttonholed me outside the door_

buttress¹ _n_ a support for a wall ☞ CASTLE

buttress² _v_ to support : _She buttressed her argument with solid facts_

buxom _adj_ (of a woman) attractively fat and healthy-looking

buy¹ _v_ bought, buying 1 to obtain (something) by giving money (or something else of value) 2 to be exchangeable for: _Our money buys less than it used to_

buy² _n esp. spoken_ an act of buying

buyer _n_ a person who buys, esp. the head of a department in a department store

buyer's market _n_ a state of affairs in which goods are plentiful, causing prices to be low — compare SELLER'S MARKET

buy off also buy over— _v adv_ to bribe

buy out _v adv_ to gain control of by buying: _to buy out a business_

buy up _v adv_ to buy all the supplies of: _to buy up all the sugar in London_

buzz¹ _v_ 1 to make a low hum, as bees do 2 to make a low confused whisper: _The crowd buzzed with excitement_ 3 to call with a buzzer 4 to fly low and fast over: _Planes buzzed the crowd_

buzz² _n_ 1 a noise of buzzing 2 a signal by a buzzer 3 _sl_ a telephone call: _give him a buzz_

buzzard _n_ a type of heavy slow-flying bird of prey ☞ BIRD

buzzer _n_ an electric signalling apparatus

buzz off _v adv sl_ to go away

by¹ _prep_ 1 near; beside: _standing by the window_ 2 by way of; through: _to enter by the door_ 3 past: _He walked by me_ 4 not later than: _By tomorrow he'll be here_ 5 as a result of action on the part of: _written by Shakespeare_ 6 in accordance with: _to play by the rules_ 7 to the amount of: _His horse won by a nose_ 8 using; by means of: _She earned money by writing._ | _We went by air_ 9 (in measurements and operations with numbers); _a room 15 feet by 20 feet_ | _to divide X by Y_ 10 (showing the size of groups that follow each other): _The animals went in 2 by 2_ 11 _technical_ having (the stated male animal, esp. a horse) as a father: _Golden Trumpet, by Golden Rain out of Silver Trumpet_

by² _adv_ 1 past: _Please let me by_ 2 near: _Do it when nobody is by_

by and by _adv_ before long; soon

by and large _adv_ on the whole; in general

bye¹ _n_ (in cricket) a run made off a ball that the batsman did not touch —see also LEG BYE

bye² _interj_ goodbye

by-election _n_ an election held between regular elections to fill a vacant position

bygone _adj_ past: _in bygone days_

bygones _n_ let bygones be bygones to forget and forgive bad things in the past

bylaw, byelaw _n_ a law made not by the central government but by a local council, a railway, etc.

by-line _n_ a line at the beginning of a newspaper or magazine article giving the writer's name

bypass¹ _n_ a passage or road to one side, esp. a way round a town

bypass² _v_ to avoid: _Let's bypass the town_

by-product _n_ 1 something formed in the process of making something else 2 an additional unexpected result —compare END PRODUCT

byre _n_ _dialect_ a farm building for cattle

bystander _n_ a person standing near; onlooker

byte _n_ _technical_ a unit of information capacity equal to 8 bits

by the way _adv_ (introducing a new subject): _By the way, what happened to the money?_

byway also bypath— _n_ -ways a small road or path not much used

byword _n_ a name taken as representing some quality: _The general's name had become a byword for cruelty in war_

C

C, c 1 the third letter of the English alphabet 2 the Roman numeral for 100

c *abbrev. for:* circa (about)

C¹ the note beginning the row of notes which form the musical scale of C major

C² *abbrev. for:* centigrade

cab *n* 1 a taxi 2 (in former times) a horse-drawn carriage for hire 3 the driver's part of a bus, railway engine, etc.

cabal *n* a small group of people who make secret plans

cabaret *n* a performance of popular music and dancing in a restaurant

cabbage *n* a type of large round vegetable with thick green leaves used as food

cabby, cabbie *n* -bies *esp.spoken* a taxi driver

caber *n* a long heavy wooden pole used in Scotland in games: *to toss the caber*

cabin *n* 1 a small room on a ship usu. for sleeping 2 a small roughly built house

cabin boy *n* a servant-boy on a ship

cabin cruiser *n* a large motor boat with cabins

cabinet *n* 1 a piece of furniture with drawers and shelves 2 the most important government ministers, who meet as a group

cable¹ *n* 1 a thick heavy strong rope, wire, or chain 2 a set of telegraph or telephone wires underground or under the sea 3 a telegraphed message

cable² *v* -bled, -bling to send by telegraph

cable car *n* a car supported in the air and pulled by a continuous cable

cable railway *n* a railway along which vehicles are pulled by a continuous cable fastened to a motor

cable's length *also* **cable length**— *n sailing* 600ft; 100 fathoms; 1/10 of a nautical mile

cable stitch *n* a twisted and knotted pattern in knitting

caboodle *n* **the whole caboodle** *sl* the lot; everything

cache¹ *n* (a secret place for keeping) provisions or valuable things

cache² *v*, **cached, caching** to store in a cache

cachet *n* 1 a mark to show high quality 2 high social position

cackle *v* -led, -ling 1 to make the noise made by a hen after laying an egg 2 to laugh or talk with henlike sounds — **cackle** *n* — **cackler** *n*

cacophony *n* a mixture of unpleasant sounds —opposite **euphony** — **-onous** *adj*

cactus *n* -tuses *or* -ti any of a number of prickly fleshy desert plants

cad *n* a man who behaves dishonourably — ~**dish** *adj*

cadaver *n esp. medical* a dead human body

cadaverous *n* very pale; thin and unhealthy

caddie, caddy *v, n* -died, -dying (to act as) a person who carries golf clubs for someone else

cadence *n* 1 a a rhythm b a set of chords which complete a phrase of music 2 the rise and fall of the voice

cadenza *n* (in a concerto) an ornamental part, played by a single musician

cadet *n* 1 a student in a military college 2 a member of a cadet corps

cadet corps *n* **cadet corps** an organization which gives simple military training to schoolboys

cadge *v* **cadged, cadging** to get by begging: *He cadged 20p* — **cadger** *n*

cadmium *n* a bluish-white metal that is an element, used esp. for coating metal objects

cadre *n* an inner group of highly trained people in a political party or military force

Caerphilly *n* creamy-white mild Welsh cheese

caesarean section *also* **caesarean**— *n* (in a difficult birth) an operation in which the abdomen and uterus are cut to take the baby out

caesura *n* a pause in a line of poetry or piece of music

cafe, café *n* a small restaurant serving light meals —compare RESTAURANT

cafeteria *n* a restaurant where people collect their own food and drink

caffeine *n* a stimulant found in coffee and tea

caftan, kaftan *n* a long loose Eastern garment usu. of cotton or silk

cage¹ *n* **caged, caging** 1 a framework of wires or bars in which animals or birds may be kept 2 an enclosed area for prisoners 3 (in a mine) the framework in which men and apparatus are raised to or lowered from the surface

cage² *v* to put into a cage

cagey *adj* -ier, -iest *esp.spoken* careful; secretive — **cagily** *adv* — **caginess** *n*

cagoule *n* a long waterproof coat with a hood, like an anorak

cairn *n* a heap of stones piled up, esp. on mountains

caisson *n* 1 a large watertight box, which allows men to work under water 2 a floating box for raising sunken ships

cajole *v* -joled, -joling to persuade by praise or deceit

cake¹ *n* 1 a food made by baking flour, eggs, sugar, etc. 2 a round flat piece of food: *a potato cake* 3 a solid block: *a cake of soap*

cake² *v* **caked, caking** to cover thickly

calamine lotion *n* a liquid for soothing skin irritations

calamitous *adj* being or causing a calamity — ~**ly** *adv*

calamity *n* -ties a terrible event

calcify *v* -fied, -fying to make or become hard by adding lime

calcium *n* a silver-white metal that is an element, found in bones, teeth, and chalk

calculable *adj* that can be worked out or measured — **-bly** *adv*

calculate *v* **-lated, -lating** 1 to work out by using numbers 2 to estimate 3 to plan; intend

calculating *adj* coldly planning future actions; crafty

calculating machine also **calculator**— *n* a simple machine which can carry out number operations —compare COMPUTER

calculation *n* 1 the act of calculating 2 the result of calculating: *His calculation was correct*

calculator *n* 1 a person who calculates 2 a calculating machine 👁

calculus *n* **-li** or **-luses** 1 *medical* a chalky stone which sometimes forms in the body 2 (in mathematics) a way of making calculations about variable quantities —see also DIFFERENTIAL, INTEGRAL ☞ MATHEMATICS

caldron *n* a cauldron

calendar *n* 1 a system which names, arranges, and numbers each day of each month of the year 2 a set of tables or sheets showing this system

calendar month *n* a month according to the calendar —compare LUNAR MONTH

calendar year *n* a period of time from a date in one year to the same date in the next year, esp. from January 1st

calender *n* a machine for rolling, pressing, and smoothing paper, cloth, etc.

calends *n* the first of the month in the ancient Roman calendar —compare IDES

calf¹ *n* **calves** 1 the young of the cow or of some other large animals 2 calfskin

calf² *n* **calves** the fleshy back part of the human leg below the knee

calf love *n* PUPPY LOVE

calfskin *n* leather from the skin of a young cow

calibrate *v* **-brated, -brating** 1 to measure the diameter of (a tube) 2 to check the graduations on (the scale of a measuring instrument) — **-ation** *n*

calibre *n* 1 the diameter of a tube or gun 2 the size of a bullet 3 the quality of something or someone: *This work's of high calibre*

calico *n* a type of cotton cloth

caliph, khalif *n* (a title formerly given to) a Muslim ruler — ~**ate** *n*

call¹ *v* 1 to shout; cry out: *He called for help* 2 to make a short visit: *The milkman calls once a day* 3 to telephone or radio to 4 to (try to) cause to come or happen by speaking loudly or by sending an order: *Mother is calling me.* | *The president called an election* 5 to waken (someone) 6 to name: *We'll call the baby Jean* 7 to say that (someone) is: *She called me fat* 8 (in card games) **a** to bid **b** to say what will be trumps —see also **call someone's** BLUFF; **call it a** DAY; **call to** MIND; **call the** TUNE

call² *n* 1 a shout; cry 2 a short usu. formal or business visit 3 a command; summons: *The min-ister waited for a call to the palace* 4 (in card games) a bid 5 (in sports and games) the decision of the umpire 6 an attempt to telephone someone; telephone conversation 7 **at/on call** ready to work at a command: *The nurse is on call tonight* —see also PORT OF CALL; **call of** NATURE

call box also **telephone kiosk, phone box, telephone box**— *n* a small enclosed shelter containing a public telephone

caller *n* 1 a person who makes a short visit 2 a person making a telephone call 3 a person who calls out numbers in a game or instructions in a dance

call for *v prep* to need; deserve: *Your remark was not called for*

call girl *n* a prostitute who contacts her clients by telephone

calligraphy *n* beautiful hand writing — **-pher, -phist** *n*

calling *n* a feeling of duty to do a particular job: *He had a calling to become a priest*

callipers *n* 1 an instrument with 2 legs used for measuring 2 fixed metal supports for weak legs

call off *v adv* to cause not to take place

call on also **call upon**— *v prep* 1 to visit 2 to ask to do something: *I will now call on Jean for an answer*

callous *adj* unkind; without feelings — ~**ly** *adv* — ~**ness** *n*

call out *v adv* to bring out on strike: *The miners' leader called out his men*

callow *adj* 1 (of a bird) without feathers; young 2 (of a person or behaviour) without experience; immature

call sign *n* 1 a ship's signal to attract attention 2 a sound sent out by a radio station to show which station it is

call-up *n* an order to serve in the armed forces

call up *v adv* 1 to bring back to memory 2 to order to join the armed forces

callus also **callosity**— *n* an area of thick hard skin

calm¹ *n* 1 an absence of wind or rough weather 2 a time of peace and quiet — **calm** *adj*

calm² *v* to make calm: *The mother calmed her child*

calor gas *n* *trademark* a type of butane usu. sold in metal containers for use where there is no gas supply

calorie *n* 1 a measure of heat 2 a measure of the energy that a food will produce

calorific *adj* *technical* heat-producing

calorimeter *n* an apparatus in which heat is measured

calumniate *v* **-ated, -ating** to speak calumnies about

calumny *n* **-nies** an incorrect and unjust thing said about a person

calvary *n* **-ries** a model of the Crucifixion

calve *v* **calved, calving** to give birth to a calf

calves *pl. of* CALF

Pocket electronic calculator

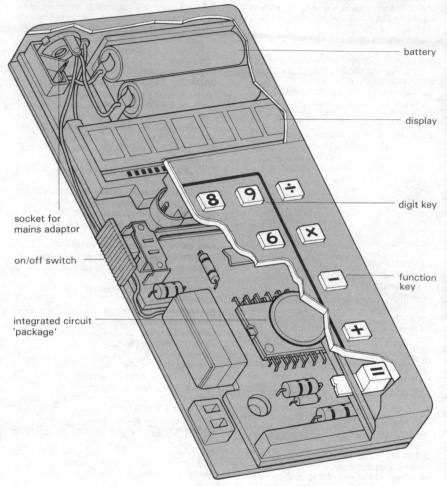

- battery
- display
- digit key
- function key
- socket for mains adaptor
- on/off switch
- integrated circuit 'package'

The usual decimal system of numbers is based on groups of ten. Thus 700 could be expressed as seven groups of ten tens. The binary system, used in computers, is based on groups of two. It has only two symbols--0 and 1; the first tells the machine 'electric current off', and the second means 'electric current on'. The symbol 1 in the right-hand column of a binary number stands for 1; in the next column to the left it stands for 2; in the third for 4; in the fourth for 8; and so on. Counting the total in this way of all the 1s, and ignoring the 0s, will give you the number as a decimal.

$$6749 \equiv 6 \times 10^3 + 7 \times 10^2 + 4 \times 10^1 + 9 \times 10^0$$
$$\equiv 6 \times 1000 + 7 \times 100 + 4 \times 10 + 9 \times 1$$
$$1101 \equiv 1 \times 2^3 + 1 \times 2^2 + 0 \times 2^1 + 1 \times 2^0$$
$$\equiv 1 \times 8 + 1 \times 4 + 0 \times 2 + 1 \times 1$$
$$\equiv 13 \text{ as a decimal number}$$

Calvinism *n* the Christian teachings of John Calvin (1509–64) — **-ist** *adj*, *n*

calypso *n* **-sos** or **-soes** a type of West Indian song based on a subject of interest

calyx *n* **calyces** or **calyxes** *technical* a ring of sepals round a flower ⇨ FLOWER

cam *n* a wheel or part of a wheel shaped to change circular movement into vertical or horizontal movement ⇨ CAR

camaraderie *n* the fellowship and good will of comrades

camber *n*, *v* (to give or have) a slight upward curve in a surface which causes water to run off

cambric *n* a fine white linen or cotton cloth

came *past tense of* COME

camel *n* **1** either of 2 large long-necked animals used for riding or carrying goods in desert countries—**a** the Arabian dromedary with one hump **b** the Asian Bactrian camel with 2 humps **2** a light yellow-brown colour

camelhair also **camel's hair**— *n* a thick yellowish brown woollen cloth

camellia *n* a type of East Asian bush or its roselike flower

Camembert *n* *French* soft rich French cheese with a greyish-white outside and a yellowish inside

cameo *n* **-eos** **1** a piece of jewellery consisting of a raised design on a small fine flat stone of a different colour **2** a short piece of writing or acting

camera *n* **1** an apparatus for taking photographs or filming ⇨ OPTICS **2** the part of the television system which changes images into electrical signals **3 in camera** *esp. written* privately

cameraman *n* **-men** a person who works a camera

cami-knickers also **cami-knicks**— *n* a woman's garment combining camisole and knickers

camisole *n* (esp. in former times) a woman's short undergarment for the top half of the body

camomile, **chamomile** *n* a type of plant with sweet-smelling white and yellow flowers — compare DAISY

camouflage¹ *n* a way of using colouring or shape which makes it difficult to see something: *Many animals have a natural camouflage which hides them from their enemies*

camouflage² *v* **-flaged, -flaging** to hide by using camouflage: *The military vehicles were camouflaged*

camp¹ *n* a place where people live **a** in tents or huts for a short time usu. for pleasure or **b** unwillingly: *a labour camp*

camp² *v* **1** to pitch a camp **2** to sleep in a tent — **~er** *n*

campaign¹ *n* **1** a set of military actions with a purpose **2** a set of actions to obtain a result in politics or business

campaign² *v* to take part in a campaign — **~er** *n*

campanology *n* the making or esp. ringing of bells — **-gist** *n*

camp bed *n* a narrow portable folding bed

camphor *n* a strong-smelling white substance obtained from trees, used in medicine and to keep insects away — **~ated** *adj*

campion *n* any of several types of small common plant with small white or red flowers

campus *n* the grounds of a university, college, or school

camshaft *n* a rod to which a cam is fastened

can¹ *v* **could**, *negative short form* **can't** **1** to know how to: *I can swim* **2** to be able to: *Can you get home in time?* **3** to be allowed to: *In rugby any player can pick up the ball* **4** may; might: *Can this be for me?* **5** will: *Can you hold on, please?*

can² *n* a tin in which foods are preserved without air

can³ *v* **-nn-** to preserve (food) by putting in a can

Canadian *n*, *adj* (a person, language, or thing) of Canada

canal *n* **1** a watercourse dug in the ground **a** to allow ships or boats to travel along it **b** to bring water to or remove water from an area **2** *medical* a narrow passage in the body

canalize, **-ise** *v* **-lized, -lizing** to deepen, straighten, or widen (a river) — **-lization** *n*

canapé *n* a small piece of bread with a savoury spread

canary¹ *n* **-ies** a type of small yellow bird usu. kept as a pet

canary² *n*, *adj* (having) a bright yellow colour

canasta *n* a card game using 2 packs of cards

cancan *n* (esp. in France in the 19th century) a stage dance in which women kick their legs high

cancel *v* **-ll-** **1** to give up (a planned activity) **2** to declare that (something) is to be without effect: *She cancelled her order* **3** to mark (a postage stamp) officially to prevent re-use **4** to balance; equal **5** to cross out (writing) **6** *technical* (of both sides of an equation or both numbers of a fraction) to permit division by the same number or quantity: *Will 2xy=4xp cancel by anything?*

cancellation *n* **1** cancelling or having been cancelled **2** an example of this: *Because there have been cancellations you can come on the trip*

cancer *n* **1** (an) abnormal growth in the body that often spreads to other parts **2** (a) spreading evil: *Violence is the cancer of our society* — **~ous** *adj* — **~ously** *adv*

Cancer *n* **1 a** the 4th division of the ZODIAC belt of stars, represented by a crab **b** the group of stars (CONSTELLATION) formerly in this division **2** a person born under this sign —see also TROPIC OF CANCER ⇨ ZODIAC

candela *n* **-las** *technical* a measure of the strength of light

candelabrum also **candelabra**— *n* **-brums** or

-bra an ornamental holder for several candles or lamps —compare CANDLESTICK

candid *adj* **1** directly truthful, even when the truth is unwelcome **2** (of a camera) used for photographing people without their knowledge — **~ly** *adv*

candidate *n* **1** a person taking an examination **2** a person who wants, or whom others want, to be chosen for a position

candidature *n* being a candidate: *his candidature for the next election*

candied *adj* cooked in sugar until shiny: *candied fruit*

candle *n* a wax stick with a wick which gives light when it burns

candlelight *n* the light produced by candles

Candlemas *n* a Christian feast on February 2nd

candlepower *n* the amount of light coming from an object

candlestick *n* a holder for one or more candles —compare CANDLELABRUM

candlewick *n* **1** the wick of a candle **2** (material having) an ornamental pattern made of rows of tufts separated by bare material

candour *n* being sincerely honest and truthful

candy *n* **-dies** *esp. US* a sweet; sweets

candyfloss *n* a fluffy mass of fine sugar threads eaten as a sweet

cane¹ *n* **1 a** the hard smooth often hollow stem of certain tall grasses such as bamboo **b** the straight stem of certain fruit-producing plants such as the blackberry **2** the punishment of beating with a cane

cane² *v* **caned, caning** to beat with a cane

canine *adj, n technical* (of or like) a dog or related animal

canine tooth *n* one of 4 sharp pointed teeth in the mouth

canister *n* a usu. metal container for a dry substance

canker¹ *n* **1** a sore caused by a disease which attacks wood and the flesh of animals and people **2** (a) spreading evil: *Violence is the canker in our society* — **~ous** *adj* ⚠ CANCER

canker² *v* to destroy by canker

cannabis *n* the parts of the Indian hemp plant which can be made into hashish and marijuana

cannelloni *n* large hollow tubes of pasta filled with meat or cheese

cannibal *n* **1** a person who eats human flesh **2** an animal which eats the flesh of its own kind — **~ism** *n* — **~istic** *adj*

cannibalize, -ise *v* **-ized, -izing** to use (a broken machine) to provide spare parts for another

cannon¹ *n* **cannons** *or* **cannon** a powerful gun fixed to the ground or onto a carriage or to be fired from an aircraft ☞ CASTLE

cannon² *v* to strike forcefully; knock

cannon³ *n* (in billiards) a shot in which the ball is aimed to strike both the other balls

cannonade *n* a continuous heavy firing by large guns

cannonball *n* (used in former times) a heavy iron ball fired from a cannon

cannot can not

canny *adj* **-nier, -niest 1** clever; not easily deceived **2** *N English* nice; good **3** *Scots* careful — **cannily** *adv*

canoe¹ *n, v* **canoed, canoeing** (to travel by) a long light narrow boat, pointed at both ends, and moved by a paddle — **-ist** *n*

canon¹ *n* **1** an established law of the Christian Church **2** the central and holiest part of the Mass **3** an official list of the writings of a certain author or forming part of a collection

canon² *n* a Christian priest with special duties in a cathedral

canonize, -ise *v* **-ized, -izing** to declare (a dead person) a saint

canopy *n* **-pies 1** a cover fixed above a bed or seat or carried on posts above a person on ceremonial occasions **2** the enclosure over the cockpit of a plane

canst thou canst *old use* (when talking to one person) you can

cant¹ *n* **1** a sloping surface **2** a movement which causes sloping

cant² *v* to slope; tilt

cant³ *n* **1** special words used by a particular group of people esp. to keep the meaning secret **2** talk meant to deceive people

cantab *abbrev.* of Cambridge University

cantaloup, -loupe *n* a type of large round green melon with juicy orange flesh

cantankerous *adj* bad-tempered; quarrelsome — **~ly** *adv* — **~ness** *n*

cantata *n* a musical work for singers, shorter than an oratorio

canteen *n* **1** a restaurant in a factory, office-building, etc. **2** a set of cutlery **3** a small usu. leather container in which drink is carried

canter¹ *n* **1** a horse's movement which is fast but slower than a gallop **2** a ride on a cantering horse: *I'm going for a canter*

canter² *v* to move at a canter

cantilever *n* a beam standing out from an upright and used for supporting a balcony, one end of a bridge, etc. ☞ BRIDGE

canto *n* **-tos** one of the divisions of a long poem

cantor *n* the man who sings and leads the people in prayer in a Jewish religious service

canvas *n* **1** strong rough cloth used for tents, sails, bags, etc. **2** a piece of this used for an oil painting **3 under canvas a** in tents **b** (of a ship) with sails spread

canvass, -vas *v* to go about asking for political support, orders for one's goods, or opinions

canyon *n* a deep narrow steep-sided valley usu. with a river —see VALLEY (USAGE)

cap¹ *n* **1** a soft flat head-covering **2** this given as a sign of honour: *He has 2 caps for cricket* **3** an often white head-covering sometimes worn by women servants **4** a protective covering for the end of an object: *the cap on the bottle* **5** a small paper container of explosive, usu. used in toy guns **6** also **Dutch cap, diaphragm**— a small round cap-shaped object fitted inside a woman's vagina to allow her to have sex without having children (= as a CONTRACEPTIVE)

cap² v **-pp- 1** to put a cap on **2** to give a cap as a sign of honour **3** to improve on (what someone has said or done)

cap. caps. *abbrev. for:* capital letter

capability n -ties **1** being capable **2** having the skills and apparatus necessary for war: *nuclear capability*

capable *adj* **1** having the power to do **2** clever — **-bly** *adv*

capacious *adj* able to hold a lot — ~ly *adv* — ~ness *n*

capacitance n (a measure of) the ability of a set of electrical conductors to store an electric charge

capacitor n an electrical component providing capacitance ☞ ELECTRICITY

capacity n -ties **1** the amount that something can hold **2** ability; power: *He has a big capacity for enjoying himself* —see GENIUS (USAGE) **3** character; position: *speaking in my capacity as minister*

cape¹ n a piece of land joined to the coast and standing out into the sea

cape² n a long loose outer garment hanging from the shoulders

cape coloured also **coloured**— n a person of Cape Province, South Africa, who has white and non-white ancestors

caper¹ n a small dark-coloured flower-bud used for giving a sourish taste to food or the bush on which these grow

caper² v to jump about joyfully

caper³ n **1** a gay jumping movement **2** a childish trick

capillary n -ries a very fine hairlike tube such as the smaller bloodvessels in the body ☞ SKIN

capillary attraction n the force which causes a liquid to rise up a narrow tube

capital¹ *adj* **1** punishable by death **2** excellent **3** (of a letter) written in its large form (such as A, B, C) rather than its usual form (such as a, b, c)

capital² n **1** a town which serves as the centre of government ☞ MAP **2** wealth, esp. when used to produce more wealth **3** a capital letter

capital assets n *technical* everything that has money value in a business, such as machines, buildings, etc.

capital gains n profits made by selling possessions

capitalism n production and trade based on the private ownership of wealth

capitalist¹ n a person who owns or controls much wealth (capital) and esp. who lends it at interest

capitalist² also **capitalistic**— *adj* practising or supporting capitalism

capitalize on v prep to use (something) to one's advantage

capital punishment n the death penalty

Capitol n (in the United States) the building in Washington where Congress meets

capitulate v -lated, -lating to yield to the enemy; surrender — **-tion** n

capon n a male chicken with its sex organs removed, to fatten it for eating

caprice n a sudden change of mind or behaviour; whim

capricious *adj* likely to change suddenly; untrustworthy; governed by caprice: *The weather is so capricious* — ~ly *adv* — ~ness *n*

Capricorn n **1 a** the 10th division of the zodiac belt of stars, represented by a goat **b** the group of stars (CONSTELLATION) formerly in this division **2** a person born under this sign —see also TROPIC OF CAPRICORN ☞ ZODIAC

capsicum n *technical* a rounded red or green fruit used as a vegetable with a distinctive, sometimes hot, taste

capsize v -sized, -sizing (esp. of a boat or ship) to turn or be turned over

capstan n a round drumlike machine turned to wind up a rope that pulls, or raises heavy objects

capsule n **1** an amount of medicine in an outer covering, the whole of which is swallowed **2** the part of a spaceship occupied by the pilots and which can be separated after take-off

captain¹ n **1** the leader of a team or group **2** the person in command of a ship or aircraft **3** a military or naval officer

captain² v to be captain of; command; lead

caption n **1** a written explanation with a picture **2** a heading; title

captivate v -vated, -vating to charm, excite, and attract (someone or something)

captive *adj, n* **1** (a person) taken prisoner esp. in war **2** (one who is) imprisoned: *captive animals* — **-vity** n

captive audience n a group of people who are not able or not allowed to stop listening or watching: *Television provides a captive audience for advertisers*

captor n *usu. written* a person or animal who has captured someone or something

capture¹ n taking or being taken by force

capture² v -tured, -turing **1** to take prisoner **2** to take control of by force from an enemy; win; gain **3** to preserve in an unchanging form on film, in words, etc.

car n **1** also **motor car**— a vehicle with 3 or usu. 4 wheels and driven by a motor, esp. one for carrying people ⊙ **2** a carriage or vehicle on a railway or cable **3** any small vehicle as part of a lift, balloon, airship, etc.

carafe n an ornamental bottle for serving wine or water

caramel n **1** burnt sugar used for giving food

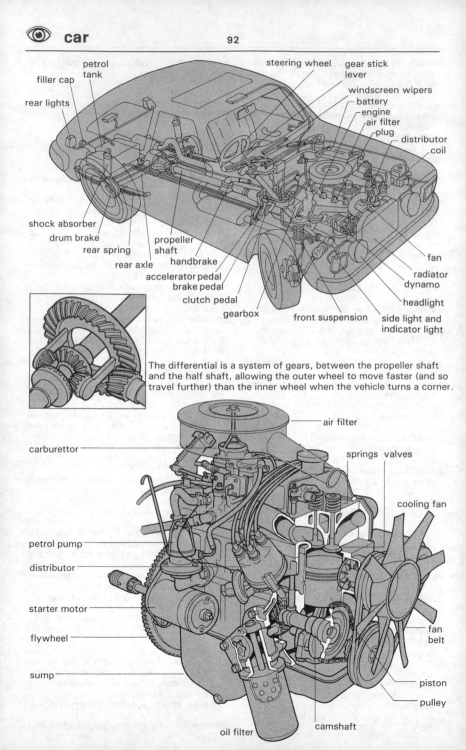

petrol tank
filler cap
rear lights
steering wheel
gear stick lever
windscreen wipers
battery
engine
air filter
plug
distributor
coil
shock absorber
drum brake
rear spring
rear axle
propeller shaft
handbrake
accelerator pedal
brake pedal
clutch pedal
gearbox
fan
radiator
dynamo
headlight
front suspension
side light and indicator light

The differential is a system of gears, between the propeller shaft and the half shaft, allowing the outer wheel to move faster (and so travel further) than the inner wheel when the vehicle turns a corner.

air filter
carburettor
springs valves
cooling fan
petrol pump
distributor
starter motor
flywheel
sump
fan belt
piston
pulley
oil filter
camshaft

Car engine cylinder

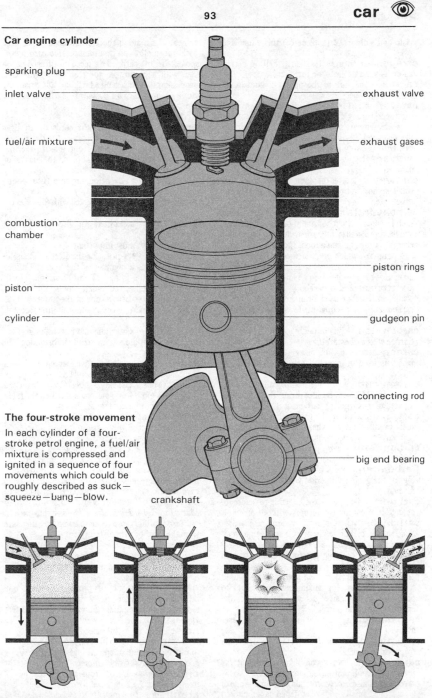

sparking plug

inlet valve

fuel/air mixture

exhaust valve

exhaust gases

combustion chamber

piston rings

piston

cylinder

gudgeon pin

connecting rod

The four-stroke movement

In each cylinder of a four-stroke petrol engine, a fuel/air mixture is compressed and ignited in a sequence of four movements which could be roughly described as suck—squeeze—bang—blow.

big end bearing

crankshaft

induction stroke compression stroke power stroke exhaust stroke

car

taste and colour 2 (a piece of) this eaten as a sweet

carapace *n* a protective hard shell on certain animals, such as crabs or tortoises

carat *n* a measure of the purity of gold or the weight of jewels

caravan *n* 1 a group of people travelling together through desert areas 2 a covered horse-drawn cart in which people such as gipsies live or travel 3 a vehicle which can be pulled by car, with cooking and sleeping facilities

caravanning *n* the taking of holidays in a caravan

caraway *n* a type of plant grown for its very small strong-tasting seeds which flavour bread, cakes, etc.

carbohydrate *n* 1 any of various substances, such as sugar, which consist of oxygen, hydrogen, and carbon, and which provide the body with energy 2 *esp. spoken* a food, such as cake, bread, and potatoes, which contain these substances

carbon *n* 1 an element found in a pure form as diamonds or graphite, or in an impure form as coal ⊸ ECOLOGY 2 also **carbon paper**— thin paper coated with carbon used for making copies 3 also **carbon copy**— a copy made using this paper; duplicate

carbonated *adj* containing carbon dioxide: *Carbonated drinks are fizzy* — -**tion** *n*

carbon black *n* fine black powder of carbon which is used in inks and in paints and in making rubber

carbon dating *n* a method of calculating the age of an old object by measuring the amount of a particular ISOTOPE of carbon in it

carbon dioxide *n* the gas produced when animals breathe out or when carbon is burned — compare CARBON MONOXIDE ⊸ ECOLOGY

carboniferous *adj* producing or containing carbon or coal

Carboniferous *adj, n technical* (of or belonging to) the geological period when much coal was formed

carbonize, -ise *v* -**ized,** -**izing** to (cause to) change into carbon by burning without air

carbon monoxide *n* a poisonous gas produced when carbon (as in petrol) burns in a small amount of air —compare CARBON DIOXIDE

carbuncle *n* a large painful swelling (type of boil) under the skin

carburettor, -retter *n* an apparatus, esp. used with car engines, for mixing air and petrol to produce the explosive gas which burns in the engine to provide power ⊸ CAR

carcass, -case *n* the body of a dead animal, esp. as meat

carcinogen *n medical* a substance which tends to produce cancer

card[1] *n, v* (to use) a comblike instrument for preparing wool, cotton, etc., for spinning

card[2] *n* 1 also *esp. written* **playing card**— one of a pack of 52 small sheets of stiffened paper marked to show number and suit and used for various

games 2 **a** a small sheet of stiffened paper usu. with information on it: *a membership card* **b** *esp. spoken* visiting card 3 **a** a piece of stiffened paper usu. with a picture on the front and a message inside sent to a person on a birthday, at Christmas, etc.: *a get-well card* **b** a postcard 4 a list of events, esp. at a sports meeting —see also CARDS

card[3] *n* stiffened paper

cardamom *n* (one of) the seeds of an East Indian fruit used in medicine and for flavouring

cardboard *n, adj* (made from) a stiff paperlike material used for making boxes, the backs of books, etc.

card-carrying *adj* belonging to a (usu. political) organization

cardiac *adj medical* connected with (diseases of) the heart

cardigan *n* a knitted woollen jacket with sleeves

cardinal[1] *adj* most important

cardinal[2] *n* 1 a priest of the Roman Catholic church, who is a member of the **Sacred College** which elects the Pope 2 any of various North American finches, the male being bright red

cardinal number *n* one of the numbers 1, 2, 3, etc. —compare ORDINAL number (first, second, third, etc.)

cardpunch *n* a machine that puts holes in cards so that computers can read information on them

cards *n* 1 also *esp. written* **playing cards**— a pack of 52 cards 2 games played with such a set 3 **get one's cards** *esp. spoken* to be dismissed from one's job 4 **lay/put one's cards on the table** *esp. spoken* to be completely honest

cardsharp also **cardsharper**— *n* a person who plays cards deceitfully, esp. to make money

care[1] *n* 1 worry; anxiety; sorrow; grief 2 charge; keeping; protection; responsibility: *under the doctor's care* 3 serious attention; effort: *Do your work with care!* 4 carefulness in avoiding harm, damage, etc.: *Cross the road with care* 5 **care of** also **c/o** (used when addressing letters to mean) living at the address of: *John Smith, care of Mary Jones, 14, High Street* 6 **take into care** to put (esp. a child) into a home owned by the state to make sure of proper treatment

care[2] *v* **cared, caring** 1 to like; want: *I don't care to play football* 2 to mind; be worried, anxious, or concerned (about): *She didn't care where her son went*

career[1] *n* 1 a job or profession which one intends to follow for life 2 the general course of a person's working life: *Churchill's career* 3 fast violent speed: *The horse went at full career*

career[2] *v* to go at full speed; rush wildly

care for *v prep* 1 to like: *I don't care for tea* 2 to nurse (someone or something); look after: *He's good at caring for sick animals*

carefree *adj* 1 free from anxiety; happy 2 irresponsible: *He's carefree with his money*

careful *adj* 1 taking care to avoid danger: *You must be careful crossing the road* 2 showing attention to details: *He's a careful worker* 3 done with care; showing care: *Doctors made a careful examination* 4 *esp. spoken* not wanting to spend money; ungenerous — ~ly *adv* — ~ness *n*

careless *adj* 1 not taking care; inattentive: *A careless driver is a danger* 2 not showing care or thought; done without care 3 free from care; untroubled 4 thoughtless; not worried: *He's careless about money* — ~ly *adv* — ~ness *n*

caress *n, v* (to give) a light tender touch or kiss showing one's love for someone

caretaker *n* also (*esp. Scots*) **janitor**— a person who looks after a school or other public building and does small repairs, cleaning, etc. —compare JANITOR, PORTER

caretaker government *n* a government which holds office between the end of one government and the appointment of the next

careworn *n* *literature* showing the effect of grief, worry, or anxiety: *the careworn face of the mother of a large poor family*

cargo *n* -goes (one load of) freight carried by a ship, plane, or vehicle

caribou *n* -bous *or* -bou a type of North American reindeer

caricature[1] *n* 1 a representation of a person made so that parts of his character appear more noticeable, odd, or amusing than they really are 2 an amusing representation by one person of another's voice, manners, character 3 the art of doing this

caricature[2] *v* -tured, -turing to represent in caricature — -turist *n*

caries *n* *medical* decay of the bones and esp. teeth — -ious *adj*

carillon *n* (tune played on) a set of bells sounded by hammers

Carmelite *n* a member of the Roman Catholic religious order of **Our Lady of Mount Carmel**

carmine *n, adj* (having) a deep purplish red colour

carnage *n* the killing of many animals or esp. people

carnal *adj* of the flesh, bodily, or esp. sexual: *carnal desires*

carnation *n* a type of plant or its sweet-smelling white, pink, or red flowers

carnelian *n* a cornelian

carnival *n* public rejoicing often with processions and shows

carnivore *n* a flesh-eating animal —compare HERBIVORE ⟶ MAMMAL — -rous *adj*

carol[1] *n* 1 a religious song sung esp. at Christmas 2 *literature or poetic* a joyful song

carol[2] *v* -ll- 1 to sing joyfully 2 to sing carols (esp. from house to house)

carotid *adj* of or being the main artery or arteries that supply the head

carouse *v* -roused, -rousing *literature* to make merry, esp. by drinking — -sal *n*

carp[1] *v* *esp. spoken* to find fault continuously and unnecessarily

carp[2] *n* **carp** *or* **carps** a type of large edible freshwater fish

carpal *adj* *medical* belonging to or connected with (the bones in) the wrist

car park *n* 1 an open place or building where cars and other vehicles may be parked, often for a small payment

carpel *n* *technical* the female seed-producing part of a flower

carpenter *n* a person who makes and repairs wooden objects —compare JOINER — -try *n*

carpet[1] *n* 1 heavy woven material for covering floors 2 a shaped piece of this material, usu. fitted to the size of a particular room

carpet[2] *v* 1 to cover (as if) with a carpet 2 *esp. spoken* to reprimand (someone): *He was carpeted for bad work*

carpet bag *n* a bag made from carpet and used in former times by travellers

carpet bagger *n* *offensive* a person who travels to a place to interfere in its political life, esp., in the United States, a Northerner active in the South in the 1860's and '70's

carport *n* an open shelter, often built against a side of a house, in which a car is kept

carriage *n* 1 a wheeled vehicle, esp. horse-drawn 2 a railway passenger vehicle 3 (the cost of) moving goods from one place to another 4 a wheeled support for moving a heavy object, esp. a gun 5 a movable part of a machine: *This printing machine has a carriage which holds and moves the paper* 6 the manner of holding one's head and body; deportment 7 **carriage forward** *technical* the cost of carrying (the goods) is to be paid by the receiver 8 **carriage paid/free** *technical* the cost of carrying (the goods) has been paid by the sender

carriageway *n* -ways the part of a road on which vehicles travel —see also DUAL CARRIAGEWAY

carrier *n* 1 a person or business that carries goods or passengers from one place to another 2 *medical* a person or animal that passes diseases to others without suffering from the disease 3 a military vehicle or ship which carries soldiers, planes, weapons, etc. 4 a framework fixed to a vehicle to hold bags, goods, etc.

carrier bag *n* a cheap strong paper or plastic bag for carrying shopping

carrier pigeon also **homing pigeon**— *n* a pigeon trained to carry small messages from one place to another

carrion *n* dead and decaying flesh

carrot *n* a type of vegetable with a fairly long orange-red root

carroty *adj* (esp. of the hair) having an orange-red colour

carry *v* -ried, -rying 1 to bear (someone or something) in one's arms, on one's back, etc., while moving 2 to act as the means by which (a person or thing) is moved from one place to another; transport; convey: *Pipes carry oil across the desert* 3 to bear the weight of (something) without moving: *This pillar carries the whole roof* **4** to keep or hold (something) with one; wear: *In Britain police do not carry guns* **5** to move or hold (oneself) in a certain way **6** to pass from one person to another; spread: *Many serious diseases are carried by insects* **7** to be able to reach a certain distance; transmit; cover space: *Her voice does not carry far* **8** (of a shop) to have (goods) for sale **9** to put (a number) into the next column to the left as when doing addition **10** to contain: *The report carried a serious warning of future trouble* **11** to have as a usual or necessary result: *Such a crime carries a serious punishment* **12** to win the sympathy, support, or agreement of: *The government carried the country and won the election* **13** (esp. of a law or plan) to be approved **14** **carry all/everything before one** to be completely successful **15 carry the can** *esp. spoken* to take the blame **16 carry weight (with)** to have influence (with)

carrycot *n* a small easily carried cot with handles, in which a baby can sleep

carry forward also **carry over**— *v adv* (when adding up accounts) to make a total at the bottom of a column of figures, ready to be moved to the top of the next page for further addition

carry off *v adv* **1** to perform or do (a part, action, duty, etc.) easily and successfully **2** to win (the prize, honour, etc.)

carry-on *n esp. spoken* a piece of silly usu. annoying behaviour

carry on *v adv* **1** to continue, esp. in spite of an interruption or difficulties **2** *esp. spoken* to behave in a very excited and anxious manner

carry on with *v adv prep esp. spoken* to have a love affair with (someone)

carryout *adj, n US & Scots* takeaway

carry out *v adv* to fulfil; complete: *to carry out a plan, order, etc.*

carry-over 1 the total of one page of an account carried forward to the top of the next page **2** (a piece of) business left from an earlier date

carry through *v adv; prep* to help (someone) to continue during (an illness, difficult period, etc.): *His courage carried him through (his illness)*

cart¹ *n* **1** a usu. 2-wheeled vehicle drawn by an animal and used for carrying goods **2** any of various types of small light wooden vehicle with 2 or 4 wheels and moved by hand

cart² *v* **1** to carry in a cart **2** *esp. spoken* to carry as if in a cart, usu. in a disrespectful manner: *The police carted the prisoners off to prison* **3** *esp. spoken* to carry by hand: *Must you cart that bag round all day?*

cartage *n* the cost of having goods carted from one place to another

cartel *n* **1** independent companies combined together to limit competition **2** political groups combined for common action

carter *n* a person whose job is driving carts

carthorse *n* a big powerful horse used for heavy work

cartilage *n* (a piece of) strong elastic substance found instead of bone in young animals and round the joints of older animals —compare GRISTLE — **-ginous** *adj*

cartography *n* the science or art of making maps — **-pher** *n*

carton *n* a box made from cardboard for holding goods

cartoon *n* **1** a humorous drawing, often dealing satirically with something in the news **2** also (*esp. written*) **animated cartoon**— a cinema film made by photographing a set of drawings —see also STRIP CARTOON — **~ist** *n*

cartridge *n* **1** a metal or paper tube containing explosive and a bullet for use in a gun **2** (in a record player) a small case containing the stylus that changes needle movement into electrical power **3** a container holding magnetic tape used with a tape recorder —compare CASSETTE

cartwheel *n, v* (to make) a circular movement in which a person stretches his arms above himself then moves sideways off his feet, onto one hand, then onto the other hand (so that his feet are above and his head below), and then back onto his feet —compare SOMERSAULT

carve *v* **carved, carving 1** to cut (usu. wood or stone) in order to make a special shape **2** to cut (cooked meat) into pieces or slices **3** to make or get by hard work: *He carved out a name for himself* — **~r** *n*

carving *n* something shaped or made by carving

caryatid *n technical* a pillar shaped like a clothed female figure

cascade¹ *n* anything that seems to pour or flow downward

cascade² *v* **-caded, -cading** to (cause to) pour in quantity

case¹ *n* **1** an example: *a case of stupidity* **2** a particular occasion or state of affairs: *Pauline's stupid, but it's different in the case of Mary; she's just lazy* **3 a** (of diseases) a single example: *This is a case of fever* **b** a person suffering from an illness **4 a** a set of events needing police inquiry **b** a person being dealt with by the police, a social worker, etc. **5** a question to be decided in a court of law **6** the facts and arguments supporting one side in a disagreement or in a question brought before a court: *The police have a clear case against the prisoner* **7** (in grammar) (changes in) the form of a word (esp. of a noun, adjective, or pronoun) showing its relationship with other words in a sentence **8 in case** for fear that; lest; because it may happen that **9 in case of a** for fear that (that stated event) should happen: *We insured the house in case of fire* **b** if (the stated event) should happen: *Break the glass in case of fire*

case² *n* **1** a container in which goods can be stored or moved **2** a suitcase **3** an outer covering for holding a filling: *a pastry case*

case³ *v* **cased, casing** to enclose or cover with a case

casein *n* a protein found in milk and cheese — **caseous** *adj*

casement window also **casement**— *n* a window that opens like a door —compare SASH WINDOW

casework *n* social work concerned with the difficulties of a particular person, family, etc. — ~**er** *n*

cash[1] *n* 1 money in coins and notes 2 **cash on delivery** C.O.D.

cash[2] *v* to exchange (a cheque or other order to pay) for cash

cash and carry *n, adj* (a usu. large shop where goods are) sold cheaply if paid for at once and taken away by the buyer

cash crop *n* a crop produced for sale, not for the grower's use —compare SUBSISTENCE CROP

cash desk *n* (in a shop) the desk where payments are made

cashew *n* a type of tropical American tree or its small curved nut

cash flow *n* the flow of money payments to, from, or within a business

cashier *n* a person in charge of money receipts and payments in a bank, hotel, shop, etc.

cash in *v adv* to take advantage or profit (from): *Let's cash in on the fine weather and go out for the day*

cashmere *n* fine soft wool from a type of goat which lives in Kashmir

cash register *n* a machine in shops for calculating and recording the amount of each sale and the money received

casing *n* 1 a protective covering, esp. the outer rubber covering of a car tyre 2 the frame of a door or window

casino *n* -**nos** 1 a building used for gambling 2 a type of card game for 2 or 4 players

cask *n* a barrel-shaped container for holding liquids

casket *n* an ornamental box for holding small valuable things

casserole *n* a deep covered dish in which food may be cooked and served

cassette *n* 1 a container for photographic film which can be fitted into a camera 2 a container holding magnetic tape which can be fitted into a tape recorder —compare CARTRIDGE

cassock *n* a long garment worn by priests and by people helping at religious services

cast[1] *v* cast, casting 1 to throw or drop 2 to throw off; remove: *Every year the snake casts (off) its skin* 3 to give (a vote) 4 to give an acting part to (a person) 5 to make (an object) by pouring hot metal (or plastic) into a mould 6 to make and put into effect (a spell)

cast[2] *n* 1 an act of throwing 2 the actors in a play, moving picture, etc. 3 a stiff protective covering of cloth and cement, for holding a broken bone in place while it gets better —see also PLASTER CAST 4 an object cast in a mould 5 general shape or quality: *the noble cast of his head* 6

becoming rare a slight squint 7 a small pile of earth left by worms when they make a hole

castanets *n* a musical instrument made from 2 shells of hard wood fastened to the thumb by a string and played by being knocked together by the fingers

castaway *n* -**ways** 1 a person surviving shipwreck by reaching the shore of a strange country 2 a person made to leave a ship by force and left on land

cast away *v adv* to leave (someone) somewhere as the result of a shipwreck

cast down *v adv* to lower in spirit; upset

caste *n* 1 division of society based on differences of wealth, rank, rights, profession, or job 2 any of the groups resulting from this division, in which a person usu. finds himself at birth, esp. one of the social classes of Hindu society

castellated *adj technical* (of a building) having defences like a castle

caster, -or *n* 1 a small wheel fixed to the base of a piece of furniture so that it can be easily moved 2 a container with small holes in the top so that sugar, salt, etc., may be evenly spread over foods —compare SALTCELLAR

caster sugar *n* very fine white sugar

castigate *v* -**gated, -gating** *esp. written* 1 to punish severely in order to correct 2 to express strong disapproval of (a person, behaviour, or someone's ideas) — -**gation** *n*

casting *n* 1 an object shaped by having been cast 2 the act of choosing actors for a play or film 3 (in fishing) the act of throwing the hook, fastened to the line, into the water

cast-iron *adj* 1 made of cast iron 2 hard; unbreakable; unyielding

cast iron *n* a hard but brittle type of iron, made by pouring molten iron into a mould

castle[1] *n* 1 a strongly-built building made in former times to be defended against attack ⊚ 2 also **rook**— (in the game of chess) one of the powerful pieces placed on the corner squares of the board at the beginning of each game

castle[2] *v* -**tled, -tling** (in the game of chess) to move the king 2 squares towards either of his own castles and put the castle on the square that the king has moved across

cast-off *adj* (esp. of clothes) unwanted by someone else — **castoff** *n*

cast off *v adv* 1 (of a boat or ship) to set free or be set free on the water by untying a rope 2 to give or throw away (clothes no longer wanted) 3 (in knitting) to remove (stitches) from the needle in such a way that the finished garment does not come undone

cast on *v adv* (in knitting) to put (the first stitches) onto a needle

castor *n* a caster

castor oil *n* a thick fatty oil made from the seeds of the **castor-oil plant** and used esp. as a laxative

castor sugar *n* CASTER SUGAR

castrate *v* -**trated, -trating** to remove the sex

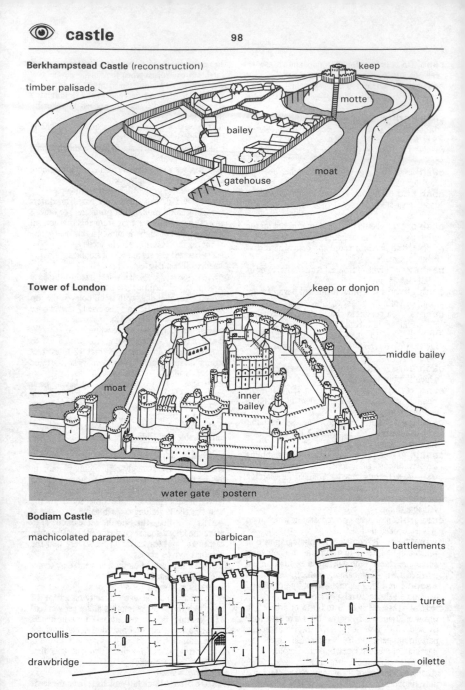

Berkhampstead Castle (reconstruction)

timber palisade

keep

motte

bailey

gatehouse

moat

Tower of London

keep or donjon

middle bailey

moat

inner bailey

water gate   postern

Bodiam Castle

machicolated parapet

barbican

battlements

portcullis

turret

drawbridge

oilette

Straight, narrow loopholes were used for shooting arrows through.
An *oilette* is a gunport with a rounded hole for a cannon.
An *oubliette* is a cell where prisoners were put and forgotten about.

organs of (an animal or person) —compare EMAS-CULATE, NEUTER, SPAY — **-tration** n

casual[1] adj **1** resulting from chance **2** not serious or thorough **3** informal; not for special use **4** not close: a casual friendship **5** (of workers) employed for a short period of time — ~ly adv — ~ness n

casual[2] n a person employed for a short period of time

casualty n **-ties 1** a person hurt or killed in an accident or war **2** a person or thing defeated or destroyed **3** also **casualty ward, department**— a place in a hospital where people hurt in accidents are treated

cat n **1** a small animal with soft fur and sharp teeth and claws, often kept as a pet or in buildings to catch mice and rats **2** any of various types of animals related to this, such as the lion or tiger **3** **let the cat out of the bag** esp. spoken to tell a secret (often unintentionally) **4 rain cats and dogs** esp. spoken to rain very heavily

cataclysm n a violent and sudden change or event, esp. a serious flood or earthquake — ~ic adj

catacomb n an underground burial place with many passages and rooms △ HECATOMB

catalogue n, v **-logued, -loguing** (to make) a list of places, names, goods, etc. in a special order so that they can be found easily

catalyst n a substance which, without itself changing, causes chemical activity to quicken — **-lytic** adj — **-lysis** n

catamaran n a type of boat with 2 narrow parallel hulls

cat-and-mouse adj esp. spoken consisting of continuous chasing, near-seizures and waiting for the right moment to attack

catapult n, v **1** (to use) a small Y-shaped stick with a rubber band fastened between the forks to shoot small stones at objects **2** (to use) a powerful apparatus for helping planes take off from a ship —compare ARRESTER WIRES **3** (to use) a machine for throwing heavy stones into the air, used, in former times, as a weapon for breaking down walls

cataract n **1** a large waterfall or steep swiftly flowing stretch of river **2** medical a growth on the eye causing a slow loss of sight

catarrh n (a disease causing) a flow of thick liquid (MUCUS) in the nose and throat, as when one has a cold — ~al adj

catastrophe n a sudden and terrible event that causes suffering, misfortune, or ruin — **-phic** adj — **-phically** adv

cat burglar n a thief who enters buildings by climbing up walls, pipes, etc.

catcall v, n (to make) a loud whistle expressing disapproval or displeasure

catch[1] v caught, catching **1** to get hold of; seize **2** to trap (esp. an animal) after chasing or hunting; take **3** to find unexpectedly; come upon suddenly; discover by surprise: Mother caught me stealing **4** to be in time for: to catch the train **5** to get (an illness) **6** to cause to become hooked, held, fastened, or stuck, accidentally or on purpose **7** to hit (a person or animal); strike: The blow caught him on the head **8** to attract (esp. interest or attention) **9** to get or notice for a moment: I caught sight of my friend in town **10** to start to burn, work, operate: The fire caught quickly **11** to hear; understand: I didn't catch what you said **12** (in cricket) to send (a player) off the field by taking and holding a ball knocked off the bat before it touches the ground **13 catch one's breath** to draw in one's breath for a moment from surprise, fear, shock, etc. — **-er** n

catch[2] n **1** an act of seizing and holding a ball **2** esp. spoken (the amount of) something caught: Her husband was a good catch. They say he's very rich **3** a hook or other device for fastening something or holding it shut **4** esp. spoken a hidden or awkward difficulty: That question looks easy, but there's a catch in it

catching adj esp. spoken (of a disease) infectious

catchment area n **1** also **catchment basin, catchment**— the area from which a lake or river gets its water **2** also **catchment**— the area from which people are sent to a central school, hospital, etc.

catch on v adv to become popular

catch out v adv to show (someone) to be at fault

catchpenny adj worthless, but made to appear attractive through cheapness or showiness

catchphrase n a phrase which becomes popular for a time, so that everyone uses it

catch up v adv **1** to come up from behind; draw level with **2** to bring or come up to date

catchword n a word or phrase repeated so often that it becomes representative of a political party, newspaper, etc.; slogan

catchy adj **-ier, -iest** tending to catch the interest or attention — **catchily** adv

catechism n **1** a small book holding a set of questions and answers used esp. for Christian religious instruction **2** instruction, esp. about religion, taught by the question-and-answer method — **catechist** n

categorical adj unconditional; wholly fixed; absolute — ~ly adv

categorize, -ise v **-rized, -rizing** to put in a category

category n **-ries** a division or class in a system for dividing objects into groups according to their nature

cater v to provide food and drink, usu. for payment, at a public or private party — ~er n

caterpillar n the larva of the butterfly and other insects

caterpillar tractor n a large heavy vehicle which moves along on an endless chain of metal plates fastened over the wheels (**caterpillar**)

cater to v prep to provide with what is necessary; specialize in satisfying

caterwaul v, n (to make) a loud unpleasant catlike sound

catfish n -fish or fishes any of various types of large-headed fish with long whisker-like feelers around the mouth

catgut n strong cord made from the bowel skin of animals and used for the strings of musical instruments

catharsis n -ses written or technical the action of getting rid of troublesome feelings by expressing them as **a** under the influence of tragic art, which is said to purge the emotions by pity and terror **b** under the influence of drugs, psychoanalysis, or emotional relationships — **-tic** adj

cathedral n the chief church of a diocese, typically a large building of beautiful design ◉

catherine wheel n a type of circular firework that is pinned to an upright surface and spins when set on fire

catheter n a thin tube that is put into blood vessels or other passages in the body to put in or take out liquids

cathode also **negative pole**— n the part of a battery from which electrons leave, often a rod or wire represented by the sign [-] —compare ANODE

cathode ray tube n a glass instrument in which streams of electrons from the cathode (**cathode rays**) are directed onto a flat suface, where they give out light, as in a television receiver

catholic adj esp.written (esp. of likings and interests) general; widespread; broad

Catholic¹ adj of, being, or connected with a church which claims to be the descendant of the early Christian church ⫐ WORSHIP — **-ism** n

Catholic² n ROMAN CATHOLIC: Is he a Catholic or a Protestant?

catkin n a stringlike bunch of soft small furry flowers that grows on certain trees (such as the willow or birch)

catnap n esp.spoken a very short light sleep

cat-o'-nine tails n -tails a whip of 9 knotted cords formerly used for punishing people

cat's cradle n a game played with string wound round the fingers and passed from one finger to another to make various shapes

cat's eye n a small reflecting stud fixed in the road to help drivers at night

cat's paw n esp. spoken a person who is used by another to do difficult or dangerous things

cat suit n esp.spoken a close-fitting garment for the whole body —compare LEOTARD, WET SUIT

cattle n large 4-legged farm animals, esp. cows

cattle grid n a set of poles put over a hole in the road, which cars can cross but cattle cannot

catty also **cattish**— adj **-tier, -tiest** esp. spoken spiteful — **cattiness** n — **cattily** adv

catwalk n 1 a narrow raised way esp. along a bridge or round a large machine 2 a narrow stage down the middle of a room, on which fashion shows are held

caucus n 1 a meeting of a committee of a political party 2 a group of people in a political party strong enough to control the party's policy

caught past tense & part. of CATCH

caul n a skin covering a baby before birth, part of which often covers the baby's head when it is born

cauldron, cal- n old use a large open metal pot for boiling liquids over a fire

cauliflower n a type of vegetable with green leaves around a large white head of undeveloped flowers

caulk v to stop (usu. a ship) from letting in water by pressing waterproof material into cracks in the wood

causal adj 1 of or showing the relationship of cause and effect 2 being a cause — **~ly** adv

cause¹ n 1 something which produces an effect; a person, thing, or event that makes something happen 2 reason: Don't complain without (good) cause— compare REASON 3 a principle or movement strongly supported

cause² v **caused, causing** to lead to; be the cause of

cause célèbre n **causes célèbres** French an action in a court of law that receives a great deal of public interest

causeway n **-ways** a raised road or path, often across water

caustic¹ n (any of various types of) chemical substance able to destroy by chemical action

caustic² adj 1 able to burn or destroy by chemical action; corrosive 2 bitter; unpleasant; sour; nasty: caustic remarks — **~ally** adv

cauterize, -ise v **-ized, -izing** medical to burn (a wound, snake bite, etc.) with a very hot iron to destroy infection

caution¹ n 1 a spoken warning 2 great care; the act of paying attention or of taking care 3 old sl a person or thing whose behaviour causes amusement

caution² v 1 to warn against possible danger 2 to warn about doing something often with the threat of punishment for repeating it

cautionary adj esp. written or humour giving advice or a warning

cautious adj careful; paying attention — **~ly** adv — **~ness** n

cavalcade n a ceremonial procession of riders, carriages, etc.

cavalier¹ n 1 old use a gentleman trained in arms and horsemanship 2 (in mid 17th century England) a supporter of Charles I in the war against Parliament —compare ROUNDHEAD

cavalier² adj 1 proud; selfish; thoughtless 2 informal and easy in manners, esp. towards ladies

cavalry n soldiers who fight on horseback — **~man** n

cave n a deep natural hollow place **a** underground **b** in the side of a cliff or hill

caveat emptor Latin (a warning in buying and selling) let the buyer take the risk of buying something of bad quality

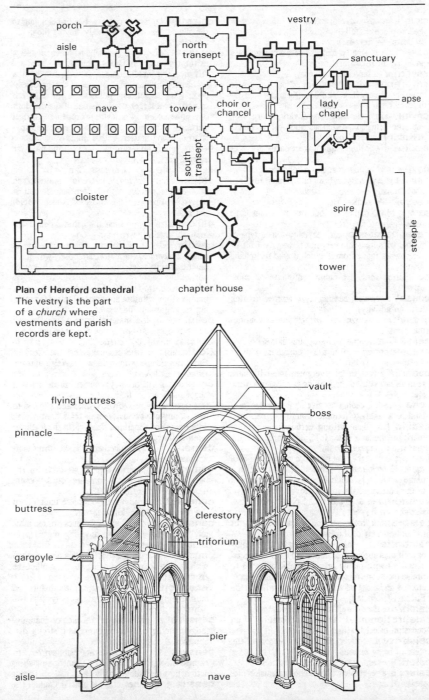

Plan of Hereford cathedral
The vestry is the part
of a *church* where
vestments and parish
records are kept.

cave in v adv **caved, caving in** (of a roof or hollow place) to fall in or down or cause to fall in or down — **cave-in** n

caveman n **-men** a manlike creature who lived in a cave in prehistoric times

cavern n a large deep cave

cavernous adj 1 containing many caves or caverns 2 very large and deep; being or suggesting a cavern — ~**ly** adv

caviar, -are n the salted roe of various large fish, esp. the sturgeon, eaten as food. It is highly regarded and very costly

cavil v **-ll-** to find fault unnecessarily — ~**er** n

cavity n a hollow space in a solid mass

cavort v esp. spoken (esp. of a person) to dance about noisily —compare CAPER

cavy n **-ies** GUINEA PIG

caw v, n (to make) the loud cry of various large birds (such as crows)

cayenne pepper also **cayenne**— n a type of pepper with long thin very hot-tasting red fruit, or the powder made from it which is used for spicing food

cc abbrev. for: 1 cubic centimetre 2 cubic capacity

cease[1] v **ceased, ceasing** esp. written to stop (esp. an activity)

cease[2] n esp. written **without cease** continuously

cease-fire n an act of stopping fighting

ceaseless adj esp. written unending; without ceasing — ~**ly** adv

cedar n a type of tall evergreen tree with hard reddish wood used for making pencils, furniture, etc.

cede v **ceded, ceding** to give up; surrender (usu. land or a right) to (another country or person)

cedilla n (when writing certain languages) a mark put under a letter (as ç in French) to show that it has a special sound

ceiling n 1 the inner surface of the top of a room 2 technical the greatest height at which a plane can fly 3 technical the height above ground of the bottom of the lowest clouds

celandine n a type of small plant with yellow star-shaped flowers

celebrant n technical the priest who performs the holiest part of the Eucharist

celebrate v **-brated, -brating** 1 to enjoy oneself on a special occasion 2 to mark (a special occasion) with public or private rejoicings 3 to praise (someone or something) in writing, speech, etc. 4 technical (of a priest) to perform (esp. the Eucharist) officially

celebrated adj well-known; famous

celebration n 1 the act of celebrating 2 an occasion of celebrating

celebrity n **-ties** 1 a famous person 2 the state of being famous

celerity n esp. written speed; quickness

celery n a vegetable with bunched greenish-white stems

celestial adj esp. written 1 of or belonging to the sky or heaven 2 heavenly; having the qualities of a god

celibate adj, n (a person who is) unmarried, esp. as the result of a religious promise — **-bacy** n

cell n 1 a small room **a** in a prison **b** in a monastery or convent 2 one of the groups of people in a secret, esp. political, organization 3 one part of a larger whole, as one of the divisions of a honeycomb 4 a device for making electrical current by chemical action 5 a very small division of living matter, with a nucleus

cellar n an underground room, usu. used for storing goods—compare BASEMENT

cell division n 1 meiosis 2 mitosis

cello also (esp. written) **violoncello**— n **-los** a type of 4-stringed violin with a deep sound, that is played held between the knees ☞ MUSIC — **cellist** n

cellophane n trademark thin transparent material used for wrapping goods

cellular adj 1 of, containing, or consisting of cells 2 technical (of materials) loosely woven 3 having many holes; able to hold much liquid; porous

celluloid n trademark a plastic substance made mainly from cellulose and formerly used for making photographic film

cellulose n the material from which the cell walls of plants are made, used for making paper

Celsius n, adj centigrade

Celtic adj of (the languages of) the Celts, a European people who include the Welsh and the Bretons ☞ LANGUAGE

cement[1] n 1 a grey powder, made from a burned mixture of lime and clay, which becomes like stone when mixed with water and allowed to dry 2 any of various types of thick hard-drying adhesives used for filling holes, as in the teeth, or joining things

cement[2] v to join together or make firm (as if) with cement

cemetery n **-teries** a place set aside for the burial of the dead —compare CHURCHYARD, GRAVEYARD

cenotaph n a monument built as a reminder of the dead, esp. those killed in war

censor[1] n an official who examines printed matter, films, etc. to remove anything regarded as harmful — ~**ship** n

censor[2] v to examine (books, films, letters, etc.) with the intention of removing anything offensive △ CENSURE

censorious adj having the habit of fault-finding; severely critical — ~**ly** adv ~**ness** n

censure[1] n esp. written the act of blaming, judging unfavourably, or expressing strong disapproval △ CENSOR

censure[2] v **-sured, -suring** esp. written to express strong disapproval of (someone or their actions); judge unfavourably

census n **censuses** 1 an official count of a

country's total population   **2** an official count of anything of importance for governmental planning

cent *n* (a coin worth) 0.01 of any of certain money standards, such as the dollar ☞ MONEY

centaur *n* (in Greek and Roman mythology) one of a race of animals said to be half man and half horse

centenarian *n* a person who is at least 100 years old

centenary *n* -ries the day or year exactly 100 years after a particular event

centennial *adj* 100th

centigrade also **Celsius**— *adj, n* (of, in, or related to) the scale of temperature in which water freezes at 0° and boils at 100° —compare FAHRENHEIT

centigram *n* a weight equal to a 100th part of a gram

centime *n French* (a coin worth) 0.01 of any certain money standards, such as the franc

centimetre *n* a measure of length equal to 0.01 metres or 0.4 inches

centipede *n* a type of insect-like creature with a long many-jointed body and a pair of legs on each joint ☞ EVOLUTION

central *adj* **1** being the centre **2** being at, in, or near the centre **3** chief; main; of greatest importance **4** convenient; easily reached: *Our house is very central for the shops* **5** *medical* of or related to the central nervous system — ~ly *adv*

central heating *n* a system of heating buildings in which heat is produced at a single point and carried by pipes or ducts to the various parts of the building

centralize, -ise *v* -ized, -izing (esp. of the controlling power of government) to gather or cause to gather under central control — -ization *n* — -ism *n*

central nervous system *n* the part of the nervous system consisting of the brain and the spinal cord

central processor *n* the main processor that controls other devices and performs operations on data in a computer

centre[1] *n* **1** a middle part or point; the exact middle, esp. the point around which a circle is drawn ☞ MATHEMATICS **2** a point, area, person, or thing that is the most important in relation to an interest, activity, or condition **3** having a moderate position esp. in politics **4** (in sport) a player in a team who plays in or near the middle of the field —compare BACK, FORWARD

centre[2] *v* centred, centring **1** to (cause to) have a centre **2** to (cause to) have as a main subject **3** to place in or at the centre **4** (in sports) to pass (a ball) to the centre of a field

centreboard *n* a keel which can be raised or lowered through the bottom of a small sailing boat

centre forward also **striker**— *n* (in football)

the player from each team who plays in the centre of the field

centre of gravity *n* that point in any object on which it will balance

centrifugal *adj* tending to move in a direction away from the centre —opposite **centripetal**

centrifuge *n* a machine for spinning a container round very quickly so that **centrifugal force** forces any solids to the bottom of the container

centripetal *adj* tending to move in a direction towards the centre —opposite **centrifugal**

centurion *n* (in the army of ancient Rome) an officer commanding a company of about 100 men

century *n* -ries **1** a period of 100 years **2** one of the 100-year periods counted from the supposed year of Christ's birth **3** (in cricket) 100 runs made by one player in one innings

Cepheid variable *n* a type of star whose variation of brightness is used by astronomers to find the distances of remote galaxies

ceramics *n* **1** the art or practice of making bricks, pots, etc., by shaping clay and baking until hard **2** articles produced in this way — **ceramic** *adj*

cereal *n* **1** any kind of grain **2** a plant which is grown to produce grain **3** (any of various types of) food made from grain, esp. eaten at breakfast

cerebellum *n* -lums or -la *medical* a small part of the back of the brain, concerned with the movement of muscles

cerebral *adj* **1** *medical* of or connected with the brain **2** *esp. written or humour* tending to or showing (too much) serious thinking — ~ly *adv*

ceremonial *n* **1** the special order and formal rules of ceremony, esp. in religious life **2** a ceremony — **ceremonial** *adj*

ceremonious *adj* fond of ceremony and formal behaviour; done according to ceremony — ~ly *adv* — ~ness *n*

ceremony *n* -nies **1** a special formal and well-established set of actions used for marking an important private or public, social or religious event **2** the special order and formal behaviour demanded on particular occasions **3** **stand on/upon ceremony** to follow formal rules of behaviour

cerise *adj, n* (having) a clear red colour

cert *n sl* a certainty

certain[1] *adj* **1** sure; established beyond doubt or question **2** sure; having no doubt: *I'm certain she saw me*

certain[2] *adj* **1** not named or described but taken as known; some particular: *Certain laws exist to protect customers* **2** some but not a lot of

certainly *adv* **1** without doubt; surely **2** (as a polite or strong way of answering a question) yes; of course

certainty *n* -ties **1** the state of being certain;

freedom from doubt **2** a clearly established fact

certifiable *adj* **1** that can be certified **2** *spoken* mad

certificate *n* an official document stating that a certain fact or facts are true: *a birth certificate*

certificated *adj* having successfully completed training for a profession: *a certificated nurse*

certify *v* **-fied, -fying** **1** to declare that (something) is correct **2** to declare, esp. after some kind of test **3** to give a certificate to (someone) declaring successful completion of training for a profession **4** *esp. spoken* to officially declare (someone) mad

certitude *n* the state of being or feeling certain

cerulean *adj* deep blue, like a clear sky

cervix *n* **-vices** *or* **-vixes** *medical* a narrow neck-like opening into an organ, esp. into the womb ☞REPRODUCTION, EMBRYO — **-ical** *adj*

cessation *n* a short pause or a stop

cesspit also **cesspool**— *n* an underground container or hole, in which a house's sewage is gathered

cetacean *adj, n technical* (of or connected with) a mammal which lives in water, such as a whale

cha-cha also **cha-cha-cha**— *n* **-chas** a spirited dance of Latin American origin

chafe¹ *v* **chafed, chafing** **1** to (cause to) become sore, or uncomfortable by rubbing **2** to rub (part of the body) to get warm **3** to become or be impatient, or annoyed

chafe² *n* a sore caused by rubbing

chaff¹ *n* **1** the outer husks of wheat, barley, etc. **2** dried plant stems used as food for farm animals

chaff² *v esp. spoken* to make fun of (someone) good-humouredly

chaffinch *n* a type of small bird, with a cheerful song, common in Europe ☞ BIRD

chagrin *n, v* (to cause someone to feel) sorrow, anger, or disappointment, caused by unfulfilled hopes or failure

chain¹ *n* **1** (a length of) usu. metal rings, connected to one another, used for fastening, supporting, ornamenting, etc. **2** a number of connected things, such as events, shops, mountains, etc.

chain² *v* to limit the freedom of (someone or something) as if with a chain

chain gang *n* a group of prisoners chained together for work

chain letter *n* a letter sent to several people who are asked to send copies to several more people

chain mail also **chain armour**— *n* armour made of small metal rings joined together ☞ ARMOUR

chain reaction *n* **1** a number of events so related to each other that each causes the next **2** a related set of chemical changes in which action in some atoms causes changes in others

chain saw *n* a saw made up of an endless chain fitted with teeth and driven by a motor

chain store also **multiple store**— *n* (one of) a number of usu. large shops of the same kind under one ownership

chair¹ *n* **1** a piece of furniture to sit on, which has typically a back, seat, 4 legs, and sometimes arms **2** the office or official seat of someone, such as a chairman, in charge of a meeting **3** the position of professor: *the chair of chemistry*

chair² *v* **1** to be chairman of (a meeting) **2** to lift up and carry (someone), usu. as a sign of admiration

chair lift *n* an apparatus which carries people, esp. skiers, up and down slopes by means of chairs hung from a moving wire

chairman also **chairperson** (*fem.* **chairwoman**)— *n* **-men** a person **a** in charge of a meeting **b** who directs the work of a committee, department, etc. — ~**ship** *n*

chaise *n* any of several types of small light usu. 2-wheeled carriages, for 2 people, drawn by 1 horse

chaise longue *n* **chaises longues** *or* **chaise longues** *French* a couch, with an arm at only one end, on which one can sit and stretch out one's legs

chalet *n* **1** a wooden house with a steep roof, esp. common in Switzerland **2** a hut used by shepherds in the Alps during the summer **3** a small bungalow or hut, esp. in a holiday camp

chalice *n* a gold or silver cup, used to hold wine in Christian services such as the Mass

chalk¹ *n* **1** a type of limestone formed from the shells of very small sea animals, used for making lime and various writing materials **2** (a piece of) this material, white or coloured, used for writing or drawing — ~**y** *adj*

chalk² *v* to write, mark, or draw with chalk

chalk up *v adv esp. spoken* **1** to succeed in getting (esp. points in a game) **2** to charge to someone's or one's own account

challenge¹ *v* **-lenged, -lenging** **1** to call (someone) to compete against one, esp. in a fight, match, etc. **2** to demand official proof of the name and aims of (someone) **3** to question the lawfulness or rightness of (someone or something) **4** to call (a person or thing) to competitive action or effort; test the abilities of (a person or thing) — ~**r** *n*

challenge² *n* **1** an invitation to compete in a fight, match, etc. **2** a demand usu. by a soldier, to stop and prove who and what one is **3** the quality of demanding competitive action, interest, or thought **4** an expression of doubt about the lawfulness of something

challenging *adj* **1** causing competitive interest, esp. because new, unusual, or difficult **2** causing great interest; fascinating — ~**ly** *adv*

chamber *n* **1** *old use* a room, esp. a bedroom **2** an elected or appointed law-making body: *In Britain the upper chamber is the House of Lords, the lower the House of Commons* **3** an enclosed space, esp. in a body or machine—see also CHAM-BERS

chamberlain *n* an official appointed to direct the housekeeping affairs of noblemen

chambermaid *n* a female servant employed to clean and tidy bedrooms, as in a hotel

chamber music *n* music written for a small group of instruments for performance in a private home

chamber pot *n* a vessel for liquid and solid body waste, usu. used in the bedroom by an old or sick person and kept under the bed —compare BEDPAN

chambers *n law* a set of rooms where a judge deals with minor matters

chameleon *n* 1 any of various types of small lizards able to change their colour to match their surroundings 2 a person who changes his behaviour, ideas, etc., to suit his own purposes

chamois also **chammy, shammy**— *n* **chamois** 1 also **chamois leather**— a type of soft leather from the skin of a kind of mountain goat (the **chamois**) 2 a piece of this used as a cloth for washing and polishing objects

champ¹ *v* 1 also **chomp**— (of a horse) to bite (food, the bit, etc.), noisily 2 *esp. spoken* to be impatient; be eager

champ² *n esp. spoken* a champion

champagne *n* a type of costly French white wine containing a lot of bubbles, usu. drunk on special occasions

champion¹ *n* 1 a person who fights for, or defends a principle, movement, person, etc. 2 a person or animal unbeaten in competition

champion² *v* to fight for, support strongly, or defend (a principle, movement, person, etc.)

champion³ *adj esp. spoken* very good; better than most

championship *n* 1 the act of championing 2 a competition held to find the champion

chance¹ *n* 1 the force that seems to make things happen without cause; luck; good or bad fortune 2 (a) possibility; likelihood that something will happen 3 a favourable occasion; opportunity 4 a risk —see also RUN the chance/danger of, STAND a chance USAGE Compare **chance, opportunity** and **occasion**: **Chance** or **opportunity** imply that something is luckily possible for one at a favourable time: *I had the chance/opportunity to see him.* An **occasion** is either the moment when something happens or a reason: *on the occasion of her wedding* | *I had occasion to visit Paris*

chance² *v* **chanced, chancing** 1 to take place by chance; happen by accident 2 to take a chance with; risk

chance³ *adj* accidental; unplanned

chancel *n* the eastern part of a church, where the priests and choir usu. sit ☞ CATHEDRAL

chancellery *n* **-ies** 1 the position, rank, or office of a chancellor 2 the building holding a chancellor's offices

chancellor *n* 1 (in various countries) the chief

minister of state 2 a state or law official of high rank: *The most important judge in Britain is the* **Lord Chancellor** 3 the official head of various universities —compare VICE-CHANCELLOR

chance on also **chance upon**— *v prep* to meet by chance; find by chance

chancery *n* **-ries** an office for the safe-keeping of official papers

chancy *adj* **-ier, -iest** *esp. spoken* risky; uncertain as to the result — **-iness** *n*

chandelier *n* a branched ornamental holder for electric lights or candles, usu. hanging from the ceiling

change¹ *v* **changed, changing** 1 to (cause to) become different 2 to give, take, or put something in place of (something else, usu. of the same kind) 3 to put (different clothes) on oneself 4 to put (fresh clothes or coverings) on a baby, child, bed, etc. 5 to give (money) in exchange for money of a different type 6 to leave and enter (different vehicles) in order to continue or complete a journey 7 to cause the engine of a vehicle to be in a different (higher or lower) gear: *Change into a lower gear when you go up the hill* 8 **change gear(s)** to make a change in speed by causing the engine of a vehicle to be in a different gear 9 **change hands** to go from the ownership of one person to another —compare EXCHANGE

change² *n* 1 (an example of) the act or result of changing 2 something different done for variety, excitement, etc. 3 a a fresh set of clothes b something fresh used in place of something old 4 the money returned when the amount given is more than the cost 5 money in small units

changeable *adj* 1 (esp. of the weather) likely to change 2 often changing; variable — **-bly** *adv* — **-ness** *n*

change into *v prep* to become or cause to become (something different)

changeless *adj* marked by the absence of change — **~ly** *adv*

changeling *n* a child left in place of another, esp. one supposedly left by fairies

change of life *n esp. spoken* the menopause

change of state *n technical* the change that occurs when a solid melts to become a liquid, a liquid boils to become a gas, or the reverse processes take place

changeover *n* a change from one activity to another; an important change

change over *v adv* to make a complete change

channel¹ *n* 1 the bed of a stream of water 2 the deepest part of a river, harbour, or sea passage 3 a narrow sea passage connecting 2 seas 4 a passage for liquids 5 any course or way along which information travels 6 a particular band of radio waves used for broadcasting television; television station or the programmes broadcast by it 7 a way, course, or direction of thought or action

channel² v **-ll-** 1 to direct 2 to form a channel in 3 to take or go in a channel

chant¹ v 1 to sing (words) to a chant 2 to repeat (words) continuously in time: *The crowd chanted "Down with the government"*

chant² n 1 an often-repeated tune, in which the time is controlled by the words, esp. used in religious services 2 words continuously repeated in time

Chanticleer n *literature* (the name of a) cock

chaos n 1 a state of complete disorder and confusion 2 *poetic* the state of the universe before there was any order

chaotic adj in a state of complete disorder and confusion; confused — ~**ally** adv

chap¹ n esp. spoken a man or boy; fellow

chap² v **-pp-** (of human skin) to become or cause to become sore and cracked

chap³ n a small crack or sore in the skin or lip

chap⁴ also **chop—** n the fleshy covering of a jaw

chapel n 1 a place, such as a small church, a room in a hospital, prison, etc., but not a parish church, used for Christian worship 2 a part of a church with its own altar used esp. for private prayer —compare CHURCH 3 (esp. in England and Wales) a place of Christian worship used by non-conformists 4 the religious services held in such places 5 (in Scotland) a Roman Catholic church

chaperon, -one¹ n 1 an older person (usu. a woman) who accompanies a young unmarried woman in public 2 an older person present at a young people's party to be responsible for good behaviour

chaperon, -one² v **-oned, -oning** to act as a chaperon to (a person or people)

chaplain n a priest responsible for the religious needs of a school, a club, a part of the armed forces, an important person, etc. —see also PADRE — ~**cy** n

chaplet n 1 a string of small beads 2 a band of flowers worn on the head

chaps n protective leather covers worn over trousers, esp. when riding a horse

chapter n 1 one of the main divisions of a book, usu. having a number or title 2 a special period in history; number of connected happenings

char¹ v **-rr-** to (cause to) become black by burning

char² n a charwoman

char³ n sl tea

character¹ n 1 (in writing or printing systems) a sign, letter, or mark: *Chinese is written in characters* 2 the combination of qualities which makes one thing different from another 3 moral strength; honesty; integrity 4 esp. spoken a person 5 a person in a book, play, etc. 6 esp. spoken an odd or humorous person —compare CHARACTERISTIC, REPUTATION

character² adj 1 (of a person) able to play an

unusual, odd, or difficult part in a play 2 (of a part in a play) needing the qualities of such a person

characteristic¹ adj typical; representing a person's or thing's usual character — ~**ally** adv

characteristic² n a special easily recognized quality of someone or something —compare CHARACTER, REPUTATION

characterization n (an example of) the act or practice of characterizing

characterize, -ise v **-ized, -izing** 1 to describe the character of (someone or something) 2 to be typical of (someone or something)

characterless adj without character; ordinary

charades n a game in which words are acted by players, often part (SYLLABLE) by part, until guessed by other players

charcoal n (pieces of) the black substance made by burning wood in a closed container, used for fuel or in sticks for drawing with

charcoal burner n a person whose job is making charcoal

charge¹ v **charged, charging** 1 to ask in payment 2 to record (something) to someone's debt 3 to rush in or as if in an attack 4 to declare officially and openly (that something is wrong) 5 to command; give as a responsibility: *He charged me to look after his daughter* 6 **a** to load (a gun) **b** *literature* to fill (a glass) 7 (cause to) take in the correct amount of electricity

charge² n 1 the price asked or paid for an article or service —see COST (USAGE) 2 care; control; responsibility 3 **a** a person or thing for which one is responsible **b** a duty; responsibility 4 an order; command 5 a spoken or written statement blaming a person for breaking the law, or doing something morally wrong: *The charge was murder* 6 a rushing forceful attack 7 the amount of explosive to be fired at one time 8 (a quantity of) electricity put into a battery or other electrical apparatus 9 **in charge of** responsible for

chargeable adj 1 that can be charged, blamed, held responsible, or accused 2 (of money costs) that can be added to an account or paid by someone

charged adj 1 having strong feelings or purpose: *emotionally-charged* 2 tending to cause strong feelings or much argument

chargé d'affaires n **chargés d'affaires** *technical & French* an official who acts as a deputy ambassador or represents his government in a country to which no ambassador has been appointed

charger n old use or literature a horse for battle

charge with v prep to give (someone) the duty of

chariot n a 2-wheeled horse-drawn vehicle used in ancient times in battles, races, etc. — ~**eer** n

charisma n -mas or -mata great personal charm which gives the power to influence others — ~**tic** adj — ~**tically** adv

charitable adj full of goodness; forgiving; generous; concerned with the poor: a charitable club — -**bly** adv

charity n -ties 1 the giving of help to the poor 2 an organization that gives this help 3 **charity begins at home** one's first duty is to one's family 4 (**as**) **cold as charity** unfeeling; unfriendly

charlatan n offensive a person who falsely claims to have (usu. medical) knowledge or skill —compare QUACK

Charleston n a lively dance, esp. popular in the 1920's

charlotte n a dish made of layers of (usu.) apple and of breadcrumbs

charm[1] n 1 a magic word or act 2 an object worn to keep away evil or bring luck 3 the power or ability to please or win over 4 **work like a charm** esp. spoken to be a complete success

charm[2] v 1 to please; win over; delight 2 to control or protect (something) as if by magic — ~**er** n — ~**ing** adj — ~**ingly** adv

chart[1] n 1 a map, esp. a detailed map of a sea area 2 (a sheet of paper with) information in written or illustrated form: weather chart

chart[2] v 1 to make a map or chart of 2 esp. spoken to make a rough plan, in writing

charter[1] n 1 an official document giving rights, freedoms, etc. 2 the practice of hiring or renting buses, planes, etc.: charter flights

charter[2] v to hire or rent (a plane, bus, etc.)

chartered accountant n an accountant who has full professional recognition

charwoman also **charlady**, **char**— n **charwomen** a woman who works as a cleaner

chary adj -ier, -iest careful; cautious — **charily** adv

Charybdis n see SCYLLA

chase[1] v **chased**, **chasing** to run after; to hunt; to drive away

chase[2] n 1 an act of chasing 2 **give chase** to chase

chase[3] v technical to engrave wood or metal — ~**r** n

chaser n a weaker alcoholic drink drunk after a stronger one

chasm n a very deep crack or opening in the earth or ice

chassis n chassis 1 the framework on which the body and working parts of a vehicle, radio, etc. are fastened or built 2 the frame and working parts of a car, radio, etc. as opposed to its body 3 the landing apparatus of a plane

chaste adj 1 pure in word, thought, and deed, esp. sexually pure 2 simple: He wrote in a chaste style — ~**ly** adv

chasten v to correct by punishment; purify; cause (a person or behaviour) to improve

chastise v -tised, -tising esp. written to punish severely, usu. by beating — ~**ment** n

chastity n the state of being sexually pure — compare CELIBACY

chat[1] v esp. spoken to talk in a friendly manner

chat[2] n esp. spoken a gossipy conversation

château, chat- n -teaus or -teaux French a castle or large country house in France

chattel n law an article of movable property (esp. in the phrase **goods and chattels**)

chatter[1] v 1 to talk rapidly and idly at length 2 (of certain animals and birds) to make rapid speechlike sounds 3 to knock together, esp. through cold or fear — ~**er** n

chatter[2] n 1 rapid small talk 2 a rapid knocking sound made by teeth, machines, etc.

chatterbox n esp. spoken a talkative person, esp. a child

chatty adj -tier, tiest esp. spoken talkative

chat up v adv esp. spoken (esp. of men) to make friends with by talking to (esp. a woman)

chauffeur[1] n a person employed to drive someone's car

chauffeur[2] v to act as driver for (a person)

chauvinism n unreasoned belief in the superiority of one's own nation, group, or sex to any other: male chauvinism — -**ist** n, adj — -**istic** adj — -**istically** adv

cheap[1] n **on the cheap** esp. spoken without paying the full cost

cheap[2] adj 1 low in price; good value 2 charging low prices —opposite expensive 3 needing little effort: The army won a cheap victory 4 worth little 5 a of poor quality; shoddy b vulgar 6 **dirt cheap** esp. spoken at a very low price 7 **feel cheap** esp. spoken to feel ashamed — ~**ly** adv — ~**ness** n

cheapen v to make or become cheaper in price or value

cheap-jack adj of bad quality

cheat[1] n 1 a dishonest person 2 an example of cheating; deceitful trick 3 a card game in which 2 or more players try to win by cheating

cheat[2] v 1 to trick (someone) 2 to act dishonestly or deceitfully to win an advantage, esp. in a game 3 to escape as if by deception: The swimmers cheated death in spite of the storm

check[1] n 1 a stop; control: We've kept the disease in check for a year now 2 something which stops, controls, etc. 3 an examination to make certain that something is correct 4 a standard against which something can be examined 5 a receipt; ticket or object for claiming something 6 a pattern of squares 7 the position of the king in chess when under direct attack

check[2] v 1 to stop; control; hold back 2 to test, examine, or mark to see if correct

checked adj having a pattern of squares

checkers n US draughts

check in v adv to report one's arrival, as at an airport

checkmate[1] v -mated, -mating 1 to win a game of chess by preventing the opponent's king from being moved 2 to stop; completely defeat

checkmate² *n* **1** (in chess) the position of a king when under direct attack from which escape is impossible **2** (a) complete defeat

checkout *n* **1** a desk in a self-service shop where one pays **2** the time at which a guest must leave a hotel room

check out *v adv* **1** to leave a hotel after paying the bill **2** *esp. spoken* to prove true after inquiries

checkup *n* a general medical examination

cheddar *n* a type of firm smooth cheese

cheek¹ *n* **1** a fleshy part on either side of the face **2** *esp. spoken* a buttock **3** *esp. spoken* insolence **4 cheek by jowl (with)** in close association or very close together

cheek² *v esp. spoken* to behave disrespectfully towards (someone)

cheeky *adj* **-ier, -iest** *esp. spoken* disrespectful; rude — **cheekily** *adv* — **cheekiness** *n*

cheep *v, n* (to make) the weak high noise made by young birds

cheer¹ *n* **1** a shout of praise, encouragement, etc. **2** happiness; gaiety: *He's always full of cheer at Christmas*

cheer² *v* **1** to shout in praise, approval, or support **2** to give encouragement, hope, help, or support to

cheerful *adj* happy; in good spirits; causing happiness; willing — ~**ly** *adv* — ~**ness** *n*

cheering *adj* encouraging; gladdening

cheerio *interj esp. spoken* goodbye

cheerless *adj* dull; without comfort; saddening — ~**ly** *adv* — ~**ness** *n*

cheers *interj esp. spoken* **1** (when drinking someone's health) good health **2** goodbye

cheery *adj* **-ier, -iest** bright; cheerful: *a cheery greeting* — **cheerily** *adv* — **cheeriness** *n*

cheese *n* **1** food made from pressed milk curds **2** a usu. large shaped and wrapped quantity of this

cheesecake *n* a pastry or biscuit case filled with soft cheese, sugar, etc.

cheesecloth *n* **1** a thin cotton cloth used for wrapping cheeses **2** a heavier cotton cloth used for making garments

cheese off *v adv* **cheesed, cheesing** *sl* to tire (someone) thoroughly; annoy: *You look cheesed off with life*

cheeseparing *adj, n offensive* (marked by) great meanness over money

cheetah *n* a swift spotted animal of the cat family, like a small leopard

chef *n* a male head cook in a hotel or restaurant

chemical¹ *adj* of, connected with, used in, or made by chemistry — ~**ly** *adv*

chemical² *n* any substance used in or produced by chemistry

chemise *n* a woman's shirtlike undergarment

chemist *n* **1** a scientist who specializes in chemistry **2** also *esp. written* **pharmacist** a person skilled in making medicine or who owns or runs a pharmacy

chemistry *n* **1** the science which studies elements and compounds **2** the chemical make-up and behaviour of a substance: *the chemistry of lead*

chemotherapy *n* the use of chemical substances to treat diseases

cheque *n* **1** a specially printed order form to a bank to pay money **2 crossed cheque** a cheque which must be put into a bank account before being paid **3 blank cheque** a signed cheque given to the person to whom it is payable who writes on it the amount to be paid later

cheque card *n* a card which promises that the bank will pay out the money written on a person's cheques up to a certain amount

chequer *v* **1** to cover with a pattern of differently coloured squares **2** to mark by changes of good and bad luck; vary: *He'd had a chequered past in the government*

cherish *v* **1** to care for tenderly; love **2** to keep (hope, feelings, love, etc.) in mind

cheroot *n technical* a cigar with both ends cut square

cherry *n* **-ries** a small usu. red round fruit with a stonelike seed, or the tree on which this grows

cherub *n* **-ubs** *or* **-ubim** *Bible & literature* an angel, usu. shown in paintings as a beautiful fat child; a pretty, innocent child — ~**ic** *adj* — ~**ically** *adv*

chess *n* a game for 2 players, with 16 pieces (**chessmen**) each, which are moved across a square board with 64 black and white squares (**chessboard**), in an attempt to trap the opponent's king

chessman *n* **-men** any of the 32 pieces used in chess

chest *n* **1** the upper front part of the body **2** a large strong box for valuables or goods **3 get (something) off one's chest** to confess

chesterfield *n* a thickly padded sofa with a back and sides

chestnut¹ *n* **1** an edible reddish-brown nut or the tree upon which this grows —compare HORSE CHESTNUT **2** a reddish-brown horse **3** *esp. spoken* a stale joke or story

chestnut² *adj, n* (having) a deep reddish-brown colour

chest of drawers *n* **chests of drawers** a piece of furniture with several drawers

chesty *adj* **-ier, -iest** *esp. spoken* **1** (esp. of women) having a well-developed chest **2** as if from the chest (esp. in the phrase **chesty cough**) — **chestily** *adv*

chevalier *n rare* **1** a member of certain honourable groups or orders **2** a knight

chevron *n* a V-shaped piece of cloth, one (or more) of which, on a uniform sleeve, shows the wearer's rank

chew¹ *v* **1** to crush (food or tobacco) with the teeth **2 bite off more than one can chew** *esp. spoken* to attempt more than one can deal with **3 chew the fat** *esp. spoken* to chat **4 chew over** to think over (a question, difficulty, etc.)

chew² *n* the act of chewing

Chianti *n* a dry still red Italian table wine

chiaroscuro *n* -ros *Italian* **1** representation in art, using light and shadow to give a feeling of depth **2** the treatment of light and dark parts in a picture

chic *adj, n* (showing) good style: *I like your chic hat* — ~**ly** *adv*

chicanery *n* **1** deception by false reasoning —see also SOPHISTRY **2** (a piece of) deceitful practice, esp. in law

chichi *adj French* pretending to be fashionable but appearing showy

chick *n* **1** the young of a bird, esp. a chicken **2** *sl* a young woman

chicken¹ *n* **1** the domestic hen kept to give eggs and meat **2** the cooked meat of the young hen or cock **3** *sl* (*used esp. by children*) a coward **4 count one's chickens before they're hatched** to base plans on something which has not yet happened

chicken² *adj sl* lacking courage

chickenfeed *n* *sl* a small unimportant amount of money

chickenhearted also **chicken-livered—** *adj* cowardly — ~**ness** *n*

chicken out *v adv* *offensive sl* to fail to do something through fear

chicken pox *n* a disease, caught esp. by children, marked by a slight fever and spots

chickpea *n* an edible pealike seed

chickweed *n* a low-growing small-leaved usu. white-flowered plant, eaten by birds

chicory *n* **1** a plant grown for its roots and leaves which can be eaten raw as a vegetable **2** a powder made from its dried crushed roots used to flavour coffee

chide *v* chided *or* chid , chided *or* chid *or* chidden, chiding *literature* to scold

chief¹ *n* **1** a leader; ruler; person with highest rank; head of a party, organization, etc.: *a Red Indian chief | the chief of police* **2** *sl* a boss **3** (used as a humorous but polite form of address by one man to another): *'Where to, Chief?' the taxi driver asked me*

chief² *adj* highest in rank; most important: *the chief constable/inspector/justice/crop*

chiefly *adv* **1** mainly; mostly but not wholly: *Bread is chiefly made of flour* **2** above all

chief of staff *n* **chiefs of staff** a high ranking officer in the armed forces who serves as main adviser to a commander

chieftain *n* the leader of a tribe, clan, etc.

chiffchaff *n* a small greyish songbird

chiffon *n* a transparent silky material used for scarves, dresses, etc.

chiffonier, -fonnier *n* a narrow ornamental chest of drawers, often with a movable mirror fixed on top

chignon *n* *French* a knot of hair worn by a woman at the back of the head

chihuahua *n* a type of very small dog

chilblain *n* an itching swelling usu. on the toes, ears, or fingers, caused by coldness and poor circulation

child *n* **children** **1** a baby; boy or girl; son or daughter; descendant ⟶FAMILY **2** *offensive* **a** an adult who behaves childishly **b** an inexperienced person: *a child in money matters* **3** a product; result **4 get someone/be with child** *literature* to make someone/be pregnant

childbearing *n* the act of giving birth — **childbearing** *adj*

childbirth *n* the act of giving birth

childhood *n* **1** the condition or period of time of being a child **2 second childhood** weakness of mind caused by old age; dotage

childish *adj* **1** of, or like a child **2** *offensive* having a manner unsuitable for an adult; immature —compare CHILDLIKE — ~**ly** *adv* — ~**ness** *n*

childlike *adj* of or typical of a child, esp. having an innocent quality —compare CHILDISH

child's play *n* something easy to do: *Driving a car isn't child's play*

chill¹ *v* **1** to make or become cold, esp. without freezing **2** to (cause to) feel cold as from fear

chill² *adj* **1** cold: *a chill wind* **2** unfriendly; discouraging: *a chill meeting*

chill³ *n* **1** an illness marked by shivering **2** an unpleasant coldness: *a chill in the air* **3** a discouraging feeling, often of fear

chilli *n* **chillies** the very hot-tasting seed case of the pepper plant or a hot red powder made from this, used for flavouring food —compare PEPPER

chilly *adj* -ier, -iest **1** disagreeably cold **2** unfriendly; discouraging: *He was given a chilly welcome* — **chilliness** *n*

chime¹ *n* **1** the sound made by a set of bells **2** a musical sound like this: *The chime of the clock woke him* **3** a set of bells rung to produce a tune **4** a musical instrument which makes a bell-like sound when struck

chime² *v* **chimed, chiming** **1** to (cause to) make bell-like sounds **2** to show (the time) by making a bell-like sound: *The clock chimed one o'clock*

chime in *v adv* *esp. spoken* **1** to interrupt or join in a conversation: *He's always ready to chime in with his opinion*

chimera, -maera *n* **1** an imaginary monster made up of parts of different animals **2** an impossible dream; unreal fancy

chimerical also **chimeric—** *adj* imaginary; fanciful — ~**ly** *adv*

chimney *n* -neys a hollow passage often rising above a roof for smoke to be carried off ⟶GEOGRAPHY

chimneybreast *n* the wall in a room with the fire at its centre —compare MANTELPIECE

chimneypot *n* a short pipe at the top of a chimney

chimneystack *n* the part of a chimney which rises above the roof of a building

chimneysweep also **chimneysweeper** , (*esp.*

spoken) **sweep**— *n* a person who cleans the insides of chimneys

chimpanzee also (*esp. spoken*) **chimp**— *n* a large African ape

chin *n* 1 the front part of the face below the mouth 2 (**Keep your**) **chin up!** *esp. spoken* Don't give up

china *n* 1 a hard white substance made by baking fine clay at high temperatures —compare PORCELAIN 2 plates, cups, etc., made from this

china clay *n* a very fine clay used in making china; kaolin

chinchilla *n* 1 a small South American rodent with soft pale grey fur 2 its fur

Chinese *adj* of or related to China, its people, or their language

Chinese chequers *n* a game for 2–6 players in which small balls are moved from hole to hole on a board shaped like a 6-pointed star

Chinese lantern also **Japanese lantern**— *n* a folding lantern of coloured paper

chink¹ *n* 1 a narrow crack or opening 2 a narrow beam of light shining through such a crack

chink² *n, v* clink

chinless *adj* 1 having a receding chin 2 *esp. spoken* weak and cowardly 3 **chinless wonder** a foolish person, often upper class

chintz *n* a cotton cloth printed with patterns, used for curtains, furniture covers, etc.

chinwag *n sl* an informal conversation; chat

chip¹ *n* 1 a small piece of brick, wood, paint, etc., broken off 2 a crack or mark left when a small piece is broken off 3 a flat plastic counter representing money in games of chance 4 a long thin piece of potato cooked in deep fat 5 a tiny set of electronic components and their connections, produced as a single unit in or on a small slice of material such as silicon, that can replace a larger conventional circuit ◉ 6 **chip off the old block** *esp. spoken*(usu. said by and about males) a person very like his father

chip² *v* 1 to (cause to) lose a small piece from the surface or edge: *This rock chips easily* 2 to cut (potatoes) into small pieces to cook as chips

chipboard *n* board made from waste pieces of wood, used as a building material

chip in *v adv esp. spoken* 1 to break into a conversation 2 to add (one's share of money or activity): *I could only afford to chip in a few pounds*

chipmunk *n* a small American black and white striped squirrel-like animal

Chippendale *adj, n* (of, being, or related to) an 18th-century English furniture style

chipping *n* a small rough piece of stone used when putting new surfaces on roads, railway tracks, etc.

chippy *n* -**pies** *sl* a shop which sells cooked fish and chips

chiropody *n* the professional care and treatment of the human foot — -**dist** *n*

chirp also **chirrup**— *v* 1 to make the short

sharp sound(s) of small birds or some insects 2 to speak gaily in a way that sounds like this — **chirp** *n*

chirpy *adj* -**ier**, -**iest** *esp. spoken* (of people) in good spirits; cheerful — **chirpily** *adv* — **chirpiness** *n*

chisel¹ *n* a metal tool with a sharp edge at the end of a blade, used for cutting into or shaping wood, stone, etc.

chisel² *v* -**ll**- 1 to cut or shape with a chisel 2 *sl* to get (something) by deceitful or unfair practices — ~**ler** *n*

chit¹ *n esp. spoken* 1 a young child 2 *offensive* a pert young woman: *a chit of a girl*

chit² *n* a written note; a voucher; a pass

chitchat *n esp. spoken* gossip

chivalrous *adj* 1 of or relating to chivalry 2 (esp. of men) marked by bravery, generosity, etc. — ~**ly** *adv*

chivalry *n* 1 (in the Middle Ages) the beliefs or practices of knights as a group 2 the qualities of a knight 3 (when speaking of a man) good manners, esp. towards women

chive *n* a grasslike herb related to the onion, used to flavour food

chivy, chivvy also **chevy, chevvy**— *v* -**ied**, -**ying** *esp. spoken* to annoy (someone) by continually arguing, scolding, etc.

chloride *n* a compound of chlorine

chlorinate *v* -**nated**, -**nating** to disinfect by putting chlorine into (a substance, esp. water) — -**nation** *n*

chlorine *n* a greenish-yellow, strong-smelling gas that is an element , used to make cloth white and water pure

chloroform¹ *n* a colourless strong-smelling chemical liquid, used as an anaesthetic and in industry as a solvent

chloroform² *v* to treat with chloroform in order to make unconscious

chlorophyll *n* the green-coloured substance in the stems and leaves of plants that changes chemicals into the substances necessary for growth when sunlight is present —see PHOTOSYNTHESIS 🔊ECOLOGY

chock *n* a wedge of wood under something, such as a door or wheel to prevent movement

chock-a-block *adj, adv esp. spoken* very crowded; packed tightly: *chock-a-block with cars*

chock-full *adj esp. spoken* completely full

chocolate¹ *n* 1 a solid sweet usu. brown substance made from the crushed seeds of the cacao tree 2 a small sweet made with this substance 3 a sweet brown powder from this substance, used for flavouring foods and drinks 4 a drink made from hot milk and this powder

chocolate² *adj, n* (having) a usu. dark brown colour

choice¹ *n* 1 the act of choosing 2 the power, right, or chance of choosing 3 someone or something chosen 4 a variety from which to choose

choice² *adj* 1 (esp. of food) of high quality:

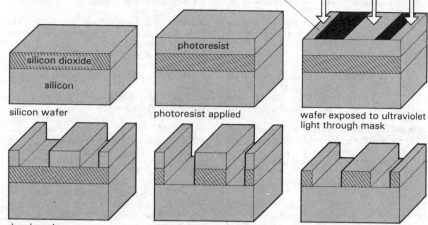

silicon dioxide
silicon

silicon wafer

photoresist

photoresist applied

mask

wafer exposed to ultraviolet light through mask

developed

silicon dioxide etched

photoresist removed

The chip

Silicon chips are made from wafers of pure silicon crystal, treated so that complete electrical circuits are formed within the solid material (solid-state). The wafer is first etched (see above) then 'doped' with phosphorus and boron to produce n and p type silicon. Finally aluminium interconnections are laid down with more silicon dioxide. Chips may be made for data storage (memory), as processors (microprocessors), or as a combination of both (the microcomputer shown below is the kind of chip to be found in a pocket calculator).

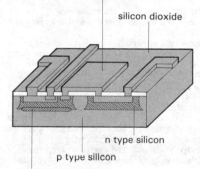

aluminium interconnections

silicon dioxide

n type silicon

p type silicon

n + type silicon

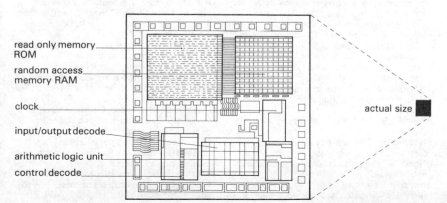

read only memory ROM

random access memory RAM

clock

input/output decode

arithmetic logic unit

control decode

actual size

choice apples 2 *literature* well chosen: *He told the story in choice phrases* — ~**ly** *adv* — ~**ness** *n*

choir *n* a group of people who sing together or the part of a church where such a group sits: *a church/school choir* ☞CATHEDRAL

choirboy *n* a boy who sings in a church choir

choke¹ *v* **choked, choking** 1 to (cause to) struggle to breathe or (cause to) stop breathing because of blocking of or damage to the windpipe 2 to fill (a space or passage) completely: *The roads were choked with traffic.* | *choked up with anger*

choke² *n* 1 the act of choking 2 an apparatus that reduces the amount of air going into a car engine to make starting easier

choke back *v adv* to control (esp. violent or very sad feelings)

choker *n* a narrow band of material, worn tightly round a woman's neck

cholera *n* an infectious often fatal tropical disease which attacks esp. the stomach and bowels

choleric *adj* easily made angry; bad-tempered — ~**ally** *adv*

cholesterol *n* a substance (STEROID) found in most cells of the body from which some fats and body-controlling substances (HORMONES) are made

choose *v* **chose , chosen, choosing** 1 to pick out from a number; select 2 to decide: *He chose not to go home*

choosy, choosey *adj* -**ier, -iest** careful in choosing; hard to please: *Jean's very choosy about food*

chop¹ *v* -**pp-** 1 to cut by repeatedly striking with or as if with an axe 2 to cut into small pieces 3 to strike (a ball) with a quick downward stroke

chop² *n* 1 a quick short cutting blow 2 a short quick downward stroke or blow 3 a slice of meat usu. containing a bone: *lamb chops* 4 **get the chop** *sl* to be dismissed from work

chop³ *v* 1 **chop and change** to keep changing (direction, one's opinion, plans, etc.) 2 **chop logic** to use false arguments which seem reasonable

chopper *n* 1 a heavy sharp-ended tool for cutting meat or wood; axe 2 *sl* a helicopter 3 *sl* a motorcycle or type of bicycle

choppy *adj* -**pier, -piest** 1 (of water) covered with short rough waves 2 (of wind) variable — **choppiness** *n*

chopstick *n* either of a pair of narrow sticks used for eating Chinese food

chop suey *n* a Chinese-style dish made of bits of vegetables, meat or fish, with rice —compare CHOW MEIN

choral *adj* of, related to, or sung by a choir or chorus

chorale *n* 1 (a tune for) a hymn 2 a choir; chorus

chord¹ *n* a combination of 2 or more musical notes sounded together ⚠ CORD

chord² *n* 1 a straight line joining 2 points on a curve ☞MATHEMATICS 2 see VOCAL CORDS 3

strike a chord to call up memory or feelings 4 **touch the right chord** to make clever use of someone's feelings

chore *n* 1 a daily job, esp. in a house 2 a difficult or disliked task: *It's such a chore to do the shopping every day!*

choreography *n* the art of dancing or of arranging dances for the stage — -**er** *n*

chorister *n* a member of a choir, esp. in a church

chortle¹ *v, n* -**tled, -tling** (to give) a laugh of satisfaction; chuckle

chorus¹ *n* 1 a group of people who sing together 2 a piece of music for such a group 3 a group of dancers, singers, or actors who play a supporting part in a film or show 4 a piece of music played or sung after each verse of a song 5 something said by many people at one time: *a chorus of shouts* 6 *technical* **a** (esp. in ancient Greek drama) a group of actors who used poetry and music to explain the action **b** (in Elizabethan plays) a person who makes speeches throughout explaining the action

chorus² *v* to sing or speak at the same time

chose *past tense of* CHOOSE

chosen *past part. of* CHOOSE

chowder *n* a thick soup of fish or shellfish

chow mein *n* a Chinese-style dish made of bits of meat and cooked vegetables and noodles — compare CHOP SUEY

Christ¹ *n* also **Jesus Christ**— the founder of Christianity believed by Christians to be the son of God and to live forever in heaven

Christ² *interj* also **Jesus Christ, Jesus**— (used to show unwelcome surprise): *Christ! I've forgotten the keys!*

christen *v* 1 to baptise and give a name to (someone esp. a child) 2 to name (esp. a ship) at an official ceremony — ~**ing** *n*

Christendom *n* 1 all Christian people 2 *old use* the Christian countries of the world

Christian¹ *n* 1 a person who believes in Jesus Christ and his teachings, usu. a member of a Christian church ☞WORSHIP 2 a good person

Christian² *adj* 1 believing in Christianity 2 of or related to Christ, Christianity, or Christians 3 having qualities such as kindness, generosity, etc.

Christianity *n* the religion based on the life and teachings of Christ ☞WORSHIP

Christian name *n* FIRST NAME

Christian Science *n* a branch of Christianity including belief in curing illness by means of faith

Christmas *n* 1 also **Christmas Day** — a Christian festival held annually on December 25th in honour of Christ's birth 2 the period just before, and the 12 days just after, this

Christmas Eve *n* the day, and esp. the evening, before Christmas

chromatic *adj* of or related to the musical scale which consists completely of semitones — ~**ally** *adv*

chrome *n* 1 a hard alloy of chromium with other metals, esp. used for plating objects 2 a yellow pigment: *chrome yellow*

chromium *n* a blue–white metal that is an element, used for plating objects

chromosome *n* *technical* a threadlike body found in the nucleus of all living cells, which controls the character of a young plant, animal, or cell

chronic *adj* 1 (of diseases) continual; lasting a long time: *a chronic cough* 2 (of a sufferer from a disease or illness) seriously suffering from a long-lasting disease or illness: *a chronic alcoholic* —compare ACUTE 3 *sl* very bad; terrible: *a chronic sense of humour* — ~ally *adv*

chronicle¹ *n* a record of historical events, arranged in order of time

chronicle² *v* -cled, -cling to record as in a chronicle — ~r *n*

chronology *n* -gies 1 the science which measures time and gives dates to events 2 a list or table arranged according to the order of time

chronometer *n* *technical* an instrument for measuring time exactly

chrysalis *n* chrysalises a pupa in a hard case-like shell —compare COCOON

chrysanthemum *n* a garden plant with large showy flowers; its flower

chubby *adj* -bier, -biest having a round usu. pleasing form; plump — **chubbiness** *n*

chuck¹ *v* 1 *esp. spoken* to throw (something) carelessly; fling 2 *sl* to give up; leave: *He's decided to chuck his old job (in)* 3 **chuck it (in)** *sl* to stop it: *Chuck it or I'll hit you* 4 **chuck (someone) under the chin** to tap gently under the chin

chuck² *n* a gentle stroke under the chin

chuck³ *n* 1 meat, esp. beef, taken from the side of an animal just above the top of the front legs 2 an apparatus for holding a tool or a piece of work in a machine

chuckle *v* -led, -ling to laugh quietly — **chuckle** *n*

chuck out *v adv esp. spoken* 1 to force (a person) to leave 2 to throw away; get rid of

chug *v, n* (to move while making) a knocking sound of or as if of an engine running slowly

chum *n* *esp. spoken* a good friend, esp. among boys — ~my *adj*

chump *n* *sl* a fool

chunk *n* *esp. spoken* a short thick piece or lump; a fairly large amount

chunky *adj* -ier, -iest short and rather fat: *a chunky little man* 2 having a thick knotted pattern: *a chunky sweater* 3 (esp. of food) containing thick solid pieces: *chunky marmalade*

church¹ *n* 1 a building for public Christian worship 2 public Christian worship 3 the profession of the clergy 4 religious power (as compared with state power) 5 Christians everywhere considered as one body

Church of England *n* the state church which is established by law in England, has married priests and bishops, and whose head is the King or Queen

Church of Scotland *n* the official established Presbyterian church in Scotland

churchwarden *n* (in the Church of England) either of 2 officers elected by the congregation, to be responsible for the church's property and money

churchyard *n* an open space around a church, used as a burial ground —compare CEMETERY, GRAVEYARD

churl *n* 1 a rude person with bad manners 2 *old use* a person of low birth, esp. a peasant

churlish *adj* *literature* bad-tempered — ~ly *adv* — ~ness *n*

churn *n* 1 a container in which milk is stirred violently until it becomes butter 2 a large metal container for milk

churn² *v* 1 to make butter by beating (milk) 2 to (cause to) move about violently

churn out *v adv esp. spoken* to produce a large quantity of (something), like a machine: *She churns out poetry day and night*

chute *n* 1 a slide down which something may be passed 2 *esp.spoken* a parachute

chutney *n* -neys a hot-tasting pickle of various fruits, peppers, and sugar

CIA *abbrev. for:* the Central Intelligence Agency of the US

cicada also **cicala**— *n* a winged tropical insect which makes a shrill chirping sound

CID *abbrev. for:* the Criminal Investigation Department in the UK —see also SCOTLAND YARD

cider, cyder *n* an alcoholic drink made from apple juice

cigar *n* a roll of uncut tobacco leaves for smoking

cigarette *n* a narrow tube of finely cut tobacco rolled in thin paper for smoking

cilia *n* *technical* the many long hairlike often movable parts on the surface of some cells

C-in-C *abbrev. for:* commander in chief

cinch *n* *sl* something easy; a certainty

cinder *n* 1 a small piece of partly burned wood, coal, etc. 2 the waste left after metal has been melted from ore; slag

cinders *n* ashes

cine *n* *esp. spoken* cinematography

cinema *n* 1 a theatre in which films are shown 2 also (*esp. US*) movies — the art or industry of making moving pictures

cinematography *n* *technical* the art or science of making moving films — **-phic** *adj*

cinnamon *n* sweet-smelling spice from the bark of a tropical Asian tree

cinquefoil *n* any of various plants with leaves divided into 5 parts

cipher, cypher¹ *n* 1 the number 0; zero 2 a person of little importance 3 (a system of) secret writing; code

cipher, cypher² *v* to encipher

circa *prep esp. written* (used esp. with dates) about: *He was born circa 1060 and died in 1118*

circadian *adj technical* (esp. of body changes) of or related to a period of about 24 hours

circle[1] *n* **1** a curved line which passes through a set of points which are all the same distance from a centre ⟶MATHEMATICS **2** something having the general shape of this line; ring: *a circle of trees* **3** an upper floor in a theatre, usu. with seats set in curved lines **4** a group of people with common interests: *He has a large circle of friends* —see also VICIOUS CIRCLE, FULL CIRCLE

circle[2] *v* **-cled, -cling** **1** to draw or form a circle around (something) **2** to move or travel in a circle

circlet *n* a narrow ornamental band worn round the head, arms, or neck

circuit *n* **1** a complete route: *the circuit of the old city walls* **2** the complete circular path of an electric current ⟶ELECTRICITY **3** a set of electrical parts for some special purpose: *a television circuit* **4** a regular journey from place to place made by a judge to hear law cases **5** a group of establishments offering the same films, plays, etc. —see also CLOSED CIRCUIT TELEVISION, SHORT CIRCUIT

circuitous *adj esp. written* going indirectly, round about: *the river's circuitous course* — ~ly *adv*

circular[1] *adj* **1** round; shaped like a circle **2** forming or moving in a circle: *circular saw | circular railway* **3** indirect; roundabout

circular[2] *n* a printed advertisement, paper, or notice for a large number of people

circulate *v* **-lated, -lating** **1** to (cause to) move or flow along a closed path: *Blood circulates round the body* **2** to (cause to) spread widely: *The news of defeat quickly circulated* **3** to move about freely: *The prince circulated from group to group at the party*

circulation *n* **1** the flow of gas or liquid around a closed system, esp. of blood through the body **2** the movement of something such as news or money from place to place or from person to person: *His book has been taken out of circulation* —compare TRAFFIC **3** the average number of copies of a newspaper, magazine, etc., sold

circulatory system *n* the system of blood vessels and heart, concerned with the circulation of blood round the body

circumcise *v* **-cised, -cising** to cut off the foreskin at the end of the penis of (a man) or part of the clitoris of (a woman) — **-ion** *n*

circumference *n* **1** the perimeter of a circle; distance round ⟶MATHEMATICS **2** the line round the outside edge of a figure, object, or place; periphery — **-ential** *adj*

circumflex *n, adj* (of) an accent mark put above a letter to show pronunciation (as in the ê and ô in French *tête* and *hôtel*) —compare GRAVE, ACUTE

circumlocution *n esp. written* a roundabout way of saying something — **-tory** *adj*

circumnavigate *v* **-gated, -gating** *esp. written* to sail completely round (esp. the earth) — **-gation** *n*

circumscribe *v* **-scribed, -scribing** **1** *esp. written* to keep within limits **2** *technical* to draw or form a circle passing through all the outside corner points (VERTICES) of (a geometrical figure)

circumspect *adj esp. written* careful; cautious — ~ly *adv* — ~ion *n*

circumstance *n* **1** a fact, detail, condition, or event which influences what happens: *The police want to consider each circumstance* **2** formal usu. official ceremony (esp. in the phrase **pomp and circumstance**)

circumstances *n* **1** the state of a person's financial affairs: *easy / reduced circumstances* **2** the state of affairs, esp. those beyond one's control: *The circumstances forced me to accept* **3** **in/under no circumstances** never; regardless of events

circumstantial *adj* **1** *esp. written* of or dependent on circumstances **2** *esp. written* (esp. of a description) containing all the details **3** *law* (of proof concerning a crime) worth knowing but not directly important (esp. in the phrase **circumstantial evidence**) — **-ly** *adv*

circumvent *v* **1** to defeat; outwit; frustrate: *The king tried to circumvent his enemies* **2** to avoid: *to circumvent the laws* — ~ion *n*

circus *n* **1** a company of skilled performers and trained animals who give public performances, often in a large tent (the BIG TOP) **2** a public performance by such a group **3** an open space where streets join together: *Oxford Circus* **4** *offensive* a noisy badly behaved group of people **5** (in Ancient Rome) an open space surrounded by seats in which sports, races, etc., took place

cirque *n technical* a corrie ⟶GEOGRAPHY

cirrhosis *n medical* a serious disease of esp. the liver

cirrus *n* a type of feathery cloud usu. at a height of 20–40, 000 feet ⟶CLOUD

cissy *n* **-sies** a sissy

cistern *n* a container for storing rainwater or as part of the system which flushes a toilet

citadel *n* a fortress usu. commanding a city; a place of safety and defence in war

citation *n* **1** the act of citing **2** *technical* a quotation

cite *v* **-cited, -citing** to quote or mention: *It's no use citing the Bible to a non-Christian*

citizen *n* **1** a person who lives in a particular city or town, esp. one who has voting or other rights **2** a member of a particular country by birth or naturalization who may expect protection from it —compare NATIONAL, ALIEN — ~ship *n*

citizenry *n* the whole body of citizens

citric acid *n* a weak acid found in the juice of oranges, lemons, etc.

citron *n* **1** a lemon-like fruit or the small tree on which it grows **2** the skin of this preserved in sugar and used for flavouring cakes

citrus, -trous adj being a fruit, like orange or lemon, with a sour taste and from an evergreen tree

city n **cities** **1** a large and important town usu. with a centre for business and amusements, and often having a cathedral **2** the people who live in such a place

City n the influential British centre for money and business, which is a part of London —compare WALL STREET

city-state n (esp. in former times) a city which, with the surrounding country area, forms an independent state ⊏₣GREEK

civic adj of a city or town; of a citizen: a civic event/civic duties

civics n a study of the rights and duties of citizens, the way government works, etc.

civil adj **1** of the general population; not military or religious: civil government | civil marriage **2** of all citizens: civil rights | civil liberty **3** (of law) dealing with the rights of private citizens - see CIVIL LAW **4** polite enough to be acceptable: Keep a civil tongue in your head! —see also CIVILLY

civil defence n the protection of a country against military attack, by an official organization of civilians (**civil defence corps**)

civil engineering n the planning, building, and repair of public works, such as roads, bridges, buildings, etc.

civilian n, adj (a person) not of the armed forces

civility n **-ties** (an act or expression of) politeness, courtesy, etc.

civilization, -sation n **1** an advanced stage of human social development **2** the type of advanced society of a particular time or place: the civilizations of ancient China and Japan **3** modern society with all its comforts **4** the act of civilizing or of being civilized

civilize, -lise v **-lized, -lizing** **1** to (cause to) bring from a lower to a highly developed stage of social organization: The Romans hoped to civilize the barbarians **2** esp. spoken to (cause to) improve in education and manners: We should civilize that boy

civil law n **1** the body of law concerned with judging private quarrels between people and dealing with the rights of private citizens, rather than with military or criminal cases **2** the body of law of Ancient Rome and the modern systems of law based upon it **3** the law of a particular state as opposed to international law —compare COMMON LAW

civil liberty n **-ties** freedom of thought, speech, action, etc., so long as this does not harm others

civilly adv politely

civil rights n rights, such as freedom, equality, etc., which belong to a citizen whatever his race, religion, colour, sex, etc.

civil servant n a person in the civil service

civil service n **1** all the national government departments except the armed forces, law courts, and religious organizations **2** all the people employed in this: The civil service ought to obey the elected government

civil war n (a) war between opposing groups of people from the same country fought within that country

civvies, civies n sl clothes worn by ordinary people as opposed to a military uniform

clack v to (cause to) make one or more sudden quick sounds: Stop clacking your pencils! — **clack** n

clad adj literature covered; clothed: The old lady was clad in a fur coat. | ill-/poorly-clad | an armour-clad ship

claim¹ v **1** to ask for or demand (a title, property, money, etc.) as the rightful owner or as one's right: Did you claim on the insurance after your car accident? **2** to declare to be true; maintain

claim² n **1** a demand for something as one's own by right: a claim for money **2** a right to something: The poor have a claim to our sympathy **3** a statement of something as fact: The government's claim that war was necessary was mistaken **4** something claimed, esp. an area of land or a sum of money **5** jump a claim to take land that another person has claimed —see also STAKE a claim — ~ant n

clairvoyance n the power of seeing things not normally present to the senses — **-ant** n, adj

clam n **1** a soft-bodied edible shell-fish (BIVALVE), that lives in sand or mud **2** sl a quiet secretive person

clamber v to climb using both feet and hands and with difficulty — **clamber** n

clammy adj **-mier, -miest** unpleasantly sticky, damp, and usu. cold: clammy hands/weather — **-mily** adv — **-miness** n

clamorous adj marked by confused noise and shouting — ~**ly** adv

clamour n, v (to make) a loud continuous usu. confused noise or complaint

clamp n, v (to fasten with) an apparatus for holding things firmly together by turning a screw

clampdown n esp. spoken a sudden usu. official limitation or prohibition: a clampdown on the sale of foreign cars

clamp down v adv esp. spoken to become more firm; make limits: to clamp down on criminal activity

clam up v adv **-mm-** sl to become silent: She clammed up whenever I mentioned her husband

clan n **1** (esp. in the Scottish Highlands) a group of families, all originally descended from one family; tribe **2** humour a large family

clandestine adj done secretly often for an unlawful reason — ~**ly** adv — ~**ness** n

clang v to (cause to) make a loud ringing sound, as when metal is struck — **clang** n

clanger n sl a very noticeable mistake or unfortunate remark (esp. in the phrase **drop a clanger**)

clangor, -gour *n* a loud long sound — ~**ous** *adj* — ~**ously** *adv*

clank[1] *v* to (cause to) make a short loud sound, as of a heavy metal chain — **clank** *n*

clannish *adj often offensive* (of a group of people) supporting each other against outsiders — ~**ly** *adv* — ~**ness** *n*

clansman *n* **-men** a member of a clan

clap[1] *v* **-pp-** **1** to strike (one's palms) loudly together **2** to show approval by doing this; applaud **3** to strike lightly with the open hand: *He clapped his son on the back* **4** *esp. spoken* to put, place, or send quickly: *The judge clapped the criminal in prison* **5 clap eyes on** *esp. spoken* to see (someone or something): *It's many years since I clapped eyes on him*

clap[2] *n* **1** a loud explosive sound: *a clap of thunder* **2** the sounds of hands being clapped **3** a light friendly hit

clap on *v adv esp. spoken* to put (something) on quickly: *He clapped his hat on*

clapped-out *adj esp. spoken* very tired, old, or worn-out

clapper *n* **1** a bell's striker **2** *sl* a talkative person's tongue **3** a person or thing that claps

clapperboard *n* a board on which the details of a scene about to be filmed are written, held up in front of the camera

clappers *n* **like the clappers** *esp. spoken* very fast

claptrap *n esp. spoken* worthless speech or writing to win applause

claret *n* red wine, esp. from Bordeaux in France —compare BORDEAUX

clarify *v* **-fied, -fying** **1** to make or become clearer and more easily understood: *When will the government clarify its position on equal pay for women?* **2** to make (a liquid, butter, etc.) clear or pure — **-ification** *n*

clarinet *n* a long tubelike single-reed woodwind instrument, often made of wood and played by blowing through — ~**(t)ist** *n*

clarion *n* **1** a small trumpet used in former times **2** the sound made by this

clarity *n* clearness: *clarity of thinking*

clash[1] *v* **1** to come into opposition: *The enemy armies clashed.* | *Those colours she's wearing clash* **2** (of events) to be inconveniently at the same time : *Her wedding clashed with my examination* **3** to (cause to) make a loud confused noise

clash[2] *n* **1** a loud confused noise **2** an example of opposition or disagreement: *clash of interests* **3** a fight; battle: *a border clash*

clasp[1] *n* **1** a fastener for holding 2 things together **2** a firm handgrip or an embrace

clasp[2] *v* **1** to seize firmly; embrace **2** to fasten with a clasp

class[1] *n* **1** the division of a society into groups of different social and political status: *The nation is divided by the question of class* **2** a social

group: *the ruling classes | the upper class* —see also MIDDLE CLASS, WORKING CLASS **3** a division of people or things according to rank, behaviour, achievement, quality, etc.: *a first class degree* **4** a grouping of plants or animals **5** a level of quality of travelling conditions on a train, plane, boat, etc.: *(a) first class (ticket) to Birmingham, please* **6** a group of pupils or students taught together or the time during which they are taught **7** *technical* (in statistics) a set of values which are grouped together **8** *esp. spoken* high quality (of people and things)

class[2] *v* **1** to put into a class; classify **2** to consider: *I class that as wickedness*

class-conscious *adj* actively aware of belonging to a particular social class — ~**ness** *n*

classic[1] *adj* **1** having the highest quality; of the first class **2** serving as a standard, model, or guide; well known, esp. as the best example **3** of or belonging to an established set of artistic or scientific standards

classic[2] *n* **1** a piece of literature or art, a writer, or an artist of lasting importance: *Shakespeare's plays were classics* **2** a famous event usu. with a long history, esp. (in horse races) one of the 5 chief English flat races

classical *adj* **1** following ancient Greek or Roman models in literature or art or in their style; simple but good; influenced by classicism **2** (of music) composed with serious artistic intentions (as opposed to popular music) **3** (of music, esp. that before 1800) following established rules of style and rhythm —compare ROMANTIC **4** traditional: *Classical scientific ideas about light were changed by Einstein* **5** concerned with the study of the humanities (esp. Greek and Latin) and general sciences as opposed to technical subjects: *a classical education* **6** classic

classicism also **classicalism**— *n* **1** the principles underlying the art or literature of ancient Greece or Rome **2** (in art and literature) the quality of simplicity and restraint following ancient models **3** the use of such principles in art or literature —compare ROMANTICISM, REALISM

classics *n* the languages and literature of ancient Greece and Rome

classification *n* **1** the act or result of classifying **2** a class or category into which something is placed **3** (esp. in libraries) a system for arranging titles

classified *adj* **1** divided or arranged in classes: *the classified advertisements in the newspaper* **2** (of government, esp. military, information) officially secret

classify *v* **-fied, -fying** **1** to arrange or place (animals, plants, books, etc.) into classes **2** to mark or declare (information) secret

classless *adj* **1** (of societies) not divided into social classes **2** belonging to no particular social class — ~**ness** *n*

classmate *n* a member of the same class in a school, college, etc.

classroom n a room in which lessons are taught

classy adj -ier, -iest esp. spoken stylish; fashionable; of high class

clatter¹ v to (cause to) move with a number of rapid knocking sounds

clatter² n 1 a number of rapid short knocks; rattle 2 noise; busy activity: the busy clatter of the city

clause n 1 (in grammar) a group of words containing a subject and finite verb, forming a sentence or part of a sentence, and often doing the work of a noun, adjective, or adverb —compare PHRASE, SENTENCE 2 a separate part or division of a document

claustrophobia n medical an unhealthy fear of being enclosed in a confined space —opposite agoraphobia — -phobic n, adj

clavichord n an early type of piano

clavicle n medical (esp. in human beings) the bone forming the front part of the shoulder; collar-bone

claw¹ n 1 a sharp usu. curved nail on the toe of an animal or bird 2 something shaped like this (such as a crab's pincers or the forklike end of a **claw hammer)**

claw² v to tear, seize, pull, etc., with claws or nails

clay n heavy earth, used for making bricks, pots, earthenware, etc., when baked — ~ey adj

claymore n an ancient Scottish 2-edged sword

clay pigeon n a plate-shaped piece of baked clay thrown up into the air to be shot at

clean¹ adj 1 not dirty; disease-free; fresh; pure 2 without mistakes; readable: a clean copy of the report 3 morally or sexually pure; honourable; free from guilt; fair, sportsmanlike: a clean life | (esp. spoken) a clean joke | a clean fighter 4 (of animals) that can lawfully be eaten by Jews according to their religion 5 well-formed; streamlined; even; regular; clear; precise: the clean shape of the railway engine | a clean cut | a clean style 6 **clean sweep** a complete change or victory 7 **come clean** esp. spoken to confess — ~ness n

clean² adv 1 all the way: The bullet went clean through (his arm) 2 esp. spoken completely: I'm clean out (of food) 3 esp. spoken in a fair way: Play the game clean

clean³ v 1 to make or become clean: Metal ornaments clean easily 2 to cut out the bowels and inside parts of the body from (birds, fish, and animals that are to be eaten) —see also CLEAN OUT, CLEAN UP

clean-cut adj 1 well shaped; having a smooth surface; regular; neat: a clean-cut hair style | a clean-cut boy 2 clear in meaning; definite: a clean-cut explanation

cleaner n 1 a person whose job is cleaning offices, houses, etc. 2 a machine, apparatus, or substance used in cleaning

cleaner's n 1 a place where clothes, material,

etc., can be taken to be cleaned, usu. with chemicals, for payment —see also DRY CLEANER'S 2 **take (someone) to the cleaner's** esp. spoken to cause (someone's) ruin

clean-limbed adj (esp. of a young man) tall, well-made, and active-looking

cleanliness n habitual cleanness

cleanly¹ adj -ier -iest personally neat and clean

cleanly² adv in a clean manner

clean out v adv 1 to make (the inside of something) clean and tidy 2 a to take all the money of (someone) by stealing or by winning b to steal everything from (a place)

cleanse v cleansed, cleansing 1 to make (usu. a cut, wound, etc.) clean 2 to remove (an illness or sin) from (a person) by or as if by cleaning

cleanser n a substance, such as a chemical liquid or powder, used for cleaning

clean-shaven adj with all hair on the face shaved off

clean up v adv 1 to clean thoroughly: It's your turn to clean (the bedroom) up 2 to remove by cleaning 3 esp. spoken to gain (money) as profit

clear¹ adj 1 bright; transparent: a clear sky | clear eyes 2 easily heard, seen, read, or understood 3 thinking without difficulty: a clear thinker 4 certain; confident: She is quite clear about her plans 5 untroubled: a clear conscience 6 free from obstructions: a clear road 7 of a pure and even colour: a clear skin 8 obvious: a clear case of murder 9 complete: a clear victory — ~ness n

clear² adv 1 in a clear manner 2 out of the way: She jumped clear 3 esp. spoken completely: He got clear away —see also STEER **clear of**

clear³ v 1 to make or become clear 2 to remove from; take away: Clear the plates away. | We must clear the area of enemy soldiers 3 to free from blame: The prisoner was cleared 4 to pass by or over without touching: The horse cleared the fence 5 esp. spoken to satisfy the official conditions of: The car cleared customs 6 to give official permission to: The building plans have been cleared 7 to pass (a cheque) through a clearing house 8 esp. spoken to earn (a large amount of money) 9 to repay (a debt) in full 10 **clear the air** to remove doubt and bad feeling —see also CLEAR OFF, CLEAR OUT, CLEAR UP

clear n esp. spoken **in the clear** free from danger, blame, or debt

clearance n 1 the act or result of clearing 2 the distance between one object and another passing close to it: The clearance between the bridge and the top of the car was 10 feet 3 official acceptance that one is not a traitor

clearance sale n a time when a shop sells surplus goods cheaply

clear-cut adj 1 having a regular outline 2 clear in meaning: clear-cut plans

clear-headed adj sensible — ~ly adv — ~ness n

clearing *n* an open area of land in a forest

clearinghouse *n* an establishment where banks exchange cheques and settle accounts

clearly *adv* 1 in a clear manner 2 obviously: *clearly a mistake*

clear off *v sl* to leave a place

clear out *v adv* 1 *esp. spoken* to leave esp. a building or enclosed space 2 to collect and throw away 3 to clean thoroughly

clearout *n esp.spoken* the act of clearing out

clear-sighted *adj* 1 able to see clearly 2 able to make judgments about the future — ~ly *adv* — ~ness *n*

clear up *v adv* 1 to explain: *to clear up the mystery* 2 to tidy up; finish: *lots of work to clear up* 3 to come to an end: *I hope your troubles clear up soon*

clearway *n* -ways a stretch of road on which cars may stop only when in difficulties

cleavage *n* 1 the act of splitting 2 the quality of certain minerals to split usu. along straight lines 3 *esp.spoken* the space between a woman's breasts

cleave *v* **cleaved** *or* **cleft** *or* **clove** , **cleaved** *or* **cleft** *or* **cloven, cleaving** 1 to divide with a blow 2 to make by cutting: *to cleave a path through the forest* 3 to split esp. along natural lines

cleaver *n* a butcher's chopping knife

cleave to *v prep* **cleaved to** *or* **clove to** *old use* to remain faithful to

clef *n* a symbol in music at the beginning of a stave to show the pitch ⟁MUSIC

cleft *n* a crack or opening

cleft palate *n* an unnatural crack in the palate, with which people are sometimes born

clematis *n* any of various types of flowering climbing plants

clemency *n* 1 mercy 2 (esp. of the weather) mildness

clement *adj* 1 *literature* merciful 2 (esp. of the weather) gentle — ~ly *adv*

clench *v* 1 to close tightly 2 to hold firmly

clerestory *n* -ries the upper part of the wall of a building, esp. a church, rising above the roof of a lower part of the same building and usu. containing windows ⟁CATHEDRAL

clergy *n* the members of esp. the Christian priesthood, who are permitted to perform religious services

clergyman also (*old use*) **cleric**— *n* -men a Christian priest or minister

clerical *adj* 1 of or concerning the clergy 2 of or concerning a clerk — ~ly *adv*

clerk *n* a person employed in an office, shop, etc., to keep records, accounts, etc.

clever *adj* 1 quick at learning and understanding 2 skilful, esp. at using the hands or body: *a clever worker* 3 being the result of a quick able mind: *a clever idea* 4 *esp.spoken* (often of an insincere person) appearing able or skilful — ~ly *adv* — ~ness *n*

clever dick *n sl* a show-off

cliché *n* an unchanging idea or expression used so commonly that it has lost its force — ~d *adj*

click¹ *n* a slight short sound, as when a key turns in a lock

click² *v* 1 to make or cause to make a slight short sound 2 *esp.spoken* to be understood: *Her joke suddenly clicked* 3 *esp.spoken* to be a success: *That film's really clicked* 4 *esp.spoken* to be a quick success, esp. with members of the opposite sex: *They clicked with each other*

client *n* 1 a person who pays esp. a lawyer for advice, or who gets help from the social services 2 a customer

clientele *n* those who use the services of a business, shop, professional man, etc.

cliff *n* a high very steep face of rock, ice, earth, etc., esp. on a coast

cliffhanger *n esp.spoken* 1 a competition or fight of which the result is in doubt until the very end 2 (esp. on the radio and on television) an event or episode which ends in suspense

climacteric *n literature* an important turning point; period in life when important changes take place in the human body

climactic *adj* of or forming a climax ⚠ CLIMATIC

climate *n* 1 the average weather conditions at a particular place 2 the general temper or opinions of a group of people or period of history: *the moral climate*

climatic *adj* of or related to climate ⚠ CLIMACTIC — ~ally *adv*

climatology *n* the science that studies climate

climax¹ *n* 1 that part in a related set of events, ideas, expressions, etc., which is most powerful, interesting, and effective, and which usu. comes near the end 2 (of a play, book, film, etc.) the most important part, usu. near the end 3 an orgasm

climax² *v* to (cause to) reach a climax

climax community also **climax**— *n* -ties *technical* all the plant life which will grow in an undisturbed area

climb¹ *v* 1 to go esp. up, over, or through, esp. by using the hands and feet 2 to go up (esp. mountains) as a sport 3 to rise to a higher point 4 to slope upwards 5 (esp. of a plant) to grow upwards, esp. along a supporting surface 6 *esp. spoken* to get into or out of clothing usu. quickly

climb² *n* 1 a journey upwards made by climbing 2 a very steep slope

climb down *v adv* to admit that one has been wrong

climb-down *n* an act of admitting that one has made a mistake

climber *n* 1 a person or thing that climbs 2 *esp.spoken* a person trying to reach a higher social position (esp. in the phrase **social climber**)

clinch¹ *v* 1 to fix (a nail) firmly in place by bending the point over 2 to fasten (esp. pieces of

wood) tightly together by or as if by doing this **3**
esp.spoken to settle (a business agreement) (esp. in
the phrase **clinch a deal**) **4** (of 2 boxers) to hold
each other tightly with the arms

clinch² *n*   **1** (in boxing) the position of the 2
fighters when holding each other tightly   **2** *sl* the
position of 2 lovers embracing

clincher *n* *esp.spoken* a last point which ends an
argument

cling *v* **clung, clinging** to hold tightly; stick
firmly

clinging *adj*   **1** (esp. of clothes) tight-fitting   **2**
too dependent upon another person

clinic *n*   **1** a building or part of a hospital where
a group of people, esp. doctors, give treatment   **2**
an occasion in a hospital when medical students
are taught by looking at ill people

clinical *adj*   **1** (of medical teaching) given in a
hospital and using ill people as examples   **2** of or
connected with a clinic or hospital   **3** cold;
appearing more interested in the scientific than the
personal details of a case   — ~**ly** *adv*

clinical thermometer *n* *technical* a thermometer for measuring the temperature of the
human body

clink¹ *v* to make or cause to make a slight
knocking sound like that of pieces of metal lightly
hitting each other   — **clink** *n*

clink² *n* *sl* a prison

clinker *n* (a lump of) the partly burnt matter left
after coal or other minerals have been burned

clip¹ *v* **-pp-** to fasten with a clip

clip² *n*   **1** a small plastic or usu. metal object for
holding things tightly together or in place   **2** a
magazine in or fastened to a gun, from which
bullets and explosive can be rapidly passed into the
gun for firing

clip³ *v* **-pp-**   **1** to cut with scissors or another
sharp instrument   **2** to leave out (parts of a word
or sentence) when speaking or to shorten in this
way   **3** to put a hole in (a ticket)   **4** *esp.spoken*
to strike with a short quick blow

clip⁴ 1 the act of clipping   **2** *technical* the quantity
of wool cut from a flock of sheep at one time   **3**
esp.spoken a short quick blow   **4** *esp.spoken* a
fast speed   **5** a usu. short excerpt from a cinema
film

clipboard *n* a small hard board with a usu. metal
clip at the top to hold sheets of paper in place

clipper *n*   **1** a fast sailing ship built in former
times to travel long distances   **2** a person who
clips or cuts

clippers *n* a usu. scissor-like tool for clipping

clippie *n* *sl* a bus conductress

clipping *n* a piece cut off or out of something

clique *n* a closely united usu. small group of
people who do not allow others easily to join their
group   — ~**y, -ish** *adj*   — **-ishness** *n*

clitoris *n* a small part of the female sex organ
which enlarges when sexually excited

cloaca *n* **-cae** the last part of the bowels of some
animals, such as birds, from which body wastes
and eggs leave the body

cloak¹ *n*   **1** a loose outer garment, usu. sleeveless
2 something which covers or hides: *His behaviour
was a cloak for his evil intentions*

cloak² *v* to hide or cover (ideas, thoughts, beliefs,
etc.)

cloak-and-dagger *adj* (esp. of plays, films,
stories, etc.) dealing with adventure, mystery,
and/or espionage

cloakroom *n*   **1** a room, as in a theatre, where
coats, bags, etc., may be left for a short time, usu.
under guard   **2** *polite* a lavatory

clobber¹ *v* *sl*   **1** to attack or strike repeatedly
2 to defeat

clobber² *n* *sl*   **1** the belongings that one carries
around with one   **2** clothes

cloche *n*   **1** an often glass or transparent cover
to protect young plants   **2** a close-fitting
bell-shaped woman's hat

clock¹ *n*   **1** an instrument for measuring and
showing time   **2** *esp.spoken* a mileometer; speedometer   **3** *sl* someone's face   **4 around/round
the clock** all day and night without stopping   **5
put the clock back a** (in countries which change
the time at the beginning of winter and summer)
to move the hands of a clock back one or 2 hours
b to set aside modern laws, ideas, etc., and stay
with old-fashioned ones —see also O'CLOCK

clock² *v*   **1** to time: *I clocked him while he ran
a mile*   **2** *sl* to strike

clock in also **clock on**— *v adv*   **1** to start work
2 to record the time when one arrives at work, usu.
on a special card —compare CLOCK OUT

clock out also **clock off**— *v adv*   **1** to finish
work   **2** to record the time when one leaves work,
usu. on a special card —compare CLOCK IN

clock tower *n* a usu. 4-sided tower, often part
of a church, with a clock face on each of the sides
near the top

clock up *v adv* *esp. spoken*   **1** to record (a
distance travelled, points won, etc.)   **2** to reach (a
certain speed)   **3** to accumulate: *He clocked up
large debts*

clock-watcher *n* *offensive esp. spoken* one
who thinks only of how soon his work will end —
-watching *n*

clockwise *adj, adv* in the direction in which the
hands of a clock move when looked at from the
front —opposite **anticlockwise**

clockwork *n*   **1** the machinery that works a
clock, or machinery like this that runs from energy
stored in a coiled spring, wound up with a
key   **2 like clockwork** without trouble

clod *n*   **1** a lump or mass, esp. of clay or earth   **2**
esp. spoken a stupid person

cloddish *adj* stupid   — ~**ly** *adv*   — ~**ness**
n

clodhopper *n* *esp. spoken* an awkward countryman

clog¹ *n* a kind of wooden shoe or one with a thick
usu. wooden sole

clog² *v* **-gg-** to make or become blocked

cloister¹ *n* a covered passage enclosing an open
square garden or courtyard, with archways facing

inwards, usu. part of a religious building ⊂͞℈CATH-
EDRAL

cloister² v to shut away from the world in or as
if in a convent or monastery

clone¹ n technical the nonsexually-produced
descendants of a single plant or animal

clone² v **cloned, cloning** to form or cause to form
a clone

clop v, n **-pp-** (to make) a sound like horses'
hoofs

close¹ v **closed, closing** 1 to shut 2 to make
or be not open to the public 3 to stop or cause to
stop operation: This factory is closing (down) 4
to bring to an end: She closed her speech 5 to
bring or come together: His arms closed tightly
round her —opposite **open** —see also CLOSE DOWN,
CLOSE IN, CLOSE UP, CLOSE WITH

close² n an end (often in the phrases
bring/come/draw to a close)

close³ n 1 an enclosed area or space, esp.
around a cathedral; courtyard 2 a narrow
entrance or passage usu. leading into a courtyard

close⁴ adj 1 near 2 **a** near in relationship **b**
with deep feeling: close friends 3 **a** tight **b** narrow; limited 4 thorough: a close watch 5 lacking fresh or freely moving air: close weather 6 in
which the competitors are almost equal; decided
by a very narrow margin 7 secretive 8 not
generous: close with money see also **close** SHAVE
— ~ly adv — ~ness n

close⁵ adv 1 near: Don't come so close! 2
close to home esp. spoken near the (often unpleasant) truth: What she said was very close to home
—see also **close to the** WIND

close call n esp. spoken a narrow escape

close-cropped adj also **close-cut**— (of the
hair) short

closed adj 1 (esp. of a shop or public building)
not open to the public 2 open only to a special
few: a closed membership

closed book n 1 something of which one
knows nothing 2 something completed

closed circuit n 1 an uninterrupted path
round which electricity can flow 2 (in television)
a system which sends signals by wire to a limited
number of receivers

close down v adv (of a radio or television
station) to stop broadcasting for the night

closed shop n an establishment in which members of a particular trade union are the only ones
hired

closefisted adj sl not generous

close-grained adj having a fine natural grain

close-hauled adj technical (of a sailing ship)
having the sails arranged for sailing as nearly
against the wind as possible to gain the best advantage from it

close in v adv 1 to have fewer hours of daylight
2 to surround gradually: The enemy began to
close in

close-knit adj tightly bound together by beliefs
and activities

close-lipped adj silent or saying little

close season also **closed season**— n the period
of each year when certain animals, birds, or fish
may not by law be killed for sport

closet¹ n a cupboard, esp. for a special purpose
—compare CUPBOARD

closet² v to enclose (esp. oneself) in a private
room

close thing n something bad that nearly happened

close-up n a usu. large-scale photograph taken
from very near

close up v adv 1 to close completely —see also
close up SHOP 2 to bring or come nearer each
other: Close up the ranks!

close with v prep 1 to come to an agreement
with 2 literature to begin to fight: The 2 armies
closed with each other

closing price n the price of business shares at
the end of the day's business on the stock
exchange

closing time n the time, usu. fixed by law, at
which a business establishment stops work, esp.
the time at which a pub stops serving drinks

closure n (an example of) the act of closing

clot¹ n 1 a thickened or half-solid mass, usu.
formed from a liquid, esp. blood 2 sl a stupid
person

clot² v **-tt-** to form into clots

cloth n 1 material made from wool, hair, cotton, etc., by weaving, and used for making garments, coverings, etc. 2 a piece of this used for a
special purpose: a tablecloth

clothe v **clothed, clothing** 1 to provide clothes
for 2 literature to cover as if with clothing: Mist
clothed the hills

clothes n garments

clotheshorse n a framework on which clothes
are hung to dry, usu. indoors

clothing n often written & technical garments
worn together on different parts of the body

clotted cream n thick cream made from
heated milk

cloud¹ n 1 (a variously-shaped mass of) very
small drops of water in the air ◉ 2 a mass of
dust, smoke, etc., which floats in the air 3 (an
area of) darkness in something otherwise transparent: There was some cloud in the beer 4 something that causes unhappiness or fear: Her death
was a cloud on an otherwise happy year

cloud² v 1 to cover or become covered with or
as if with clouds 2 to make uncertain, confused,
etc.: Age clouded his memory 3 to make or
become less transparent or darker

cloudbank n a thick mass of low cloud

cloudburst n a sudden heavy fall of rain

cloud-capped adj literature (of mountains,
hills, etc.) having the top surrounded by clouds

cloud chamber n technical a vessel full of
dust-free air and steam in which a scientist can
observe the behaviour of ions of gas

cloud-cuckoo-land n an imaginary place of
unreal dreams

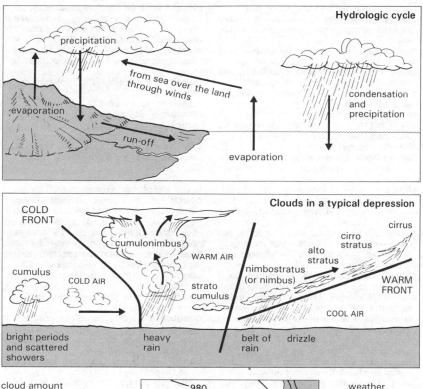

Hydrologic cycle

precipitation

from sea over the land through winds

condensation and precipitation

evaporation

run-off

evaporation

Clouds in a typical depression

COLD FRONT

cumulonimbus

WARM AIR

cirrus

cirro stratus

alto stratus

cumulus

COLD AIR

strato cumulus

nimbostratus (or nimbus)

WARM FRONT

COOL AIR

bright periods and scattered showers

heavy rain

belt of rain

drizzle

cloud amount

◑ 1/8
◕ 2/8
◑ 3/8
◐ 4/8
◕ 5/8
◕ 6/8
◑ 7/8
● 8/8
⊗ sky obscured

wind

◎ calm

○ 1-2 knots

○ 3-7 knots

add 5 knots for each extra half feather

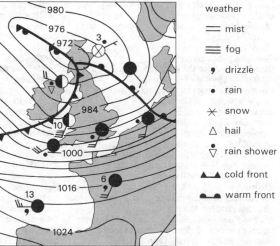

weather

≡ mist
≡ fog
, drizzle
• rain
✳ snow
△ hail
▽ rain shower
▲▲ cold front
●● warm front

A weather map like this shows temperature, speed, and direction of winds, atmospheric pressure (the whirly lines, called isobars, link areas of equal pressure), fronts (areas where warm and cold air meet, usually producing rain), and local conditions.

cloud nine *n* **on cloud nine** *sl* very happy

cloudy *adj* **-ier, -iest** **1** full of clouds; overcast **2** not clear or transparent **3** uncertain — **cloudiness** *n*

clout *v sl* to strike, esp. with the hand — **clout** *n*

clove¹ *n* the dried bud of an Asian flower, used whole or as a powder for flavouring food

clove² *n* any of the small pieces into which a garlic bulb can be divided

clove³ *past tense of* CLEAVE

clove hitch *n* a knot used esp. at sea for fastening a rope around a bar of wood

cloven *past part. of* CLEAVE

cloven hoof also **cloven foot**— *n* a foot, such as that of a cow, sheep, goat, etc., divided into 2 parts

clover *n* **1** any of various types of small usu. 3-leafed flowering plants often used as cattle food **2 in clover** *esp. spoken* living in comfort —see also FOUR-LEAF CLOVER

clown¹ *n* **1** a performer, esp. in the circus, who makes people laugh **2** a person who acts stupidly — ~**ish** *adj* — ~**ishly** *adv* — ~**ishness** *n*

clown² *v* to behave like a clown

cloy *v* **cloyed, cloying** (esp. of sweet sticky food) to become unpleasant by too much being eaten

club¹ *n* **1** a society of people who join together for sport, amusement, etc. **2** also **clubhouse**— a building where such a society meets **3** a heavy wooden stick, thicker at one end than the other, used as a weapon **4** a specially shaped stick for striking a ball in certain sports, esp. golf **5** a playing card with one or more 3-leafed figures printed on it in black —compare DIAMOND, HEART, SPADE **6 in the club** *sl* expecting a baby

club² *v* **-bb-** to beat with a club

clubfoot *n* (the condition of having) a badly shaped foot twisted from birth — ~**ed** *adj*

club together *v adv* **-bb-** to share the cost of something with others

cluck *v* to make the low short noise that a hen makes — **cluck** *n*

clue *n* something that helps to find an answer to a question, difficulty, etc.

clueless *adj sl* helpless; stupid

clue up *v adv* **clued, cluing** up *esp. spoken* well-informed

clump¹ *n* **1** a group of trees, bushes, plants, etc. **2 a** a heavy solid lump or mass **b** *technical* a mass of bacteria or other cells **3** a heavy sound, such as that of slow footsteps

clump² *v* **1** to walk with slow heavy footsteps **2** *technical* to gather into or form a clump: *The bacteria clumped together*

clumsy *adj* **-sier, -siest** **1** awkward in movement or action **2** done or made awkwardly — **clumsily** *adv* — **clumsiness** *n*

clung *past tense and past part. of* CLING

cluster¹ *n* a group of things of the same kind growing or being close together

cluster² *v* to gather or grow in clusters

clutch¹ *v* to hold tightly

clutch² *n* **1** the fingers or hands in the act of clutching **2** the act of clutching **3** an apparatus, as in a car, which allows working parts to be connected or disconnected ☞CAR

clutch³ *n* a number of eggs laid by a bird, esp. a hen, at one time, or the group of chickens born from these

clutches *n* control: *in the clutches of the enemy*

clutter¹ *v* to make untidy

clutter² *n* (a collection of) things scattered untidily

cm *abbrev. for:* centimetre(s)

c/o *abbrev. for:* care of (esp. used when writing addresses): *John Smith c/o Dorothy Smith*

Co.¹ *abbrev. for:* county

Co.² *n* **and Co.** and Company

C.O. *abbrev. for:* Commanding Officer

coach¹ *n* **1** a large enclosed 4-wheeled horse-drawn carriage, used esp. in former times or in official ceremonies **2** a bus used for long-distance travel or touring **3** a railway carriage **4** a person who trains sportsmen for games, competitions, etc. or someone employed privately to train a student for an examination

coach² *v* **1** to train or teach (a person or group) **2** to act as a coach

coachman *n* a person employed to drive a horse-drawn coach

coagulate *v* **-lated, -lating** (esp. of an organic liquid) to change from a liquid into a solid or nearly solid mass, esp. by chemical action — **-lation** *n* — **-lant** *adj*

coal *n* **1** a black or dark brown mineral mined from the earth, which can be burned to give heat, and from which gas, coal tar, etc., can be made **2** a flaming, burning, or already burnt piece of this mineral

coalbunker *n* a small low structure for storing coal

coalesce *v* **-lesced, -lescing** to grow together or unite — **coalescence** *n*

coalface *n* the part of a seam from which coal is cut

coalfield *n* a coalmining area

coal gas *n* gas from coal, used esp. for lighting and heating

coalhole *n* **1** a small room, usu. a cellar, where coal is stored **2** a hole through which coal is poured into this room

coalition *n* **1** the act of uniting into one body **2** a union of political parties, usu. to form a government

coalmine also **coal pit** , **pit**— *n* a mine from which coal is obtained

coalscuttle also **scuttle**— *n* a bucket for carrying coal

coal seam also **coal measure**— *n* a thick bed of coal in a mine

coal tar *n* a thick black sticky liquid made by heating coal without air, from which many drugs and chemical products may be obtained

coarse *adj* **1** not fine **2** having a rough surface: *coarse cloth* 3 rough in manner: *coarse behaviour* — ~ly *adv* — ~ness *n*

coarse fish *n* coarse fish *or* coarse fishes (the meat of) any freshwater fish except salmon and trout

coarsen *v* to make or become coarse

coast[1] *n* 1 the land next to the sea 2 an area bordering the sea — ~al *adj*

coast[2] *v* to keep moving after effort has ceased, esp. to travel down a hill without using any power

coaster *n* 1 a ship which sails from port to port 2 a small round mat placed under a bottle, glass, etc., to protect a surface

coastguard *n* a person serving in the coast guard

coast guard *n* an organization whose officers watch for ships in danger and prevent unlawful activity at sea

coastline *n* the outline of a coast, esp. as seen from sea

coat[1] *n* 1 an outer garment with long sleeves, usu. worn for warmth 2 an animal's fur, wool, hair, etc. 3 a covering spread over a surface: *a coat of paint*

coat[2] *v* to cover with a coat: *coated in dust*

coating *n* a covering of any substance spread over a surface

coat of arms *n* a group of patterns or pictures, usu. painted on a shield or shield-like shape, used by a noble family, town council, etc., as their special sign

coat of mail *n* armour made from metal rings or plates

coat tails *n* the long divided piece of material which hangs down from the back of a man's dress coat

coax *v* 1 to persuade by kindness 2 to obtain by persuading gently — ~ingly *adv*

cob *n* 1 also **corncob**— the long hard central part of an ear of corn 2 a male swan 3 a strong short-legged horse 4 a type of nut, esp. one from the hazel tree

cobalt *n* a strong silver-white magnetic metallic element, used in blue colouring materials and in making metals

cobber *n* *Australian & New Zealand, esp. spoken* a friend

cobble *v* -bled, -bling to pave the surface of (a road) with cobblestones

cobbler *n* 1 a shoemender 2 a careless workman

cobblestone also **cobble**—— *n* a naturally rounded or specially shaped stone, formerly used for surfacing roads

Cobol *n* a language for programming a computer, used esp. for business

cobra *n* a type of African or Asian poisonous hooded snake

cobweb *n* a very fine network of sticky threads made by a spider to catch insects

cocaine *n* a drug sometimes used for preventing

pain or taken first for pleasure and then from habit by addicts

cochineal *n* (bright red colouring matter for food made from) the dried body of a tropical American insect

cochlea *n* -leas *or* -leae *medical* a spiral-shaped tube-like part of the inner ear where the hearing nerves are

cock[1] *n* 1 a fully-grown male bird, esp. a chicken 2 a tap, valve, etc., for controlling flow in a pipe 3 the hammer of a gun 4 the position of a gun's hammer when drawn back for firing 5 *sl* (used by men to men): *Excuse me, cock*

cock[2] *v* 1 to set (the hammer of a gun) in position for firing 2 to cause (parts of the body) to stand up: *The horse cocked its ears* 3 to tilt

cock[3] *n* 1 the act of cocking 2 a slight slope

cockade *n* an ornamental rosette worn on the hat as a sign of rank, membership of a society, etc.

cock-a-doodle-doo *n* -doos the loud long cry made by a cock

cock-a-hoop *adj esp. spoken* very happy

cock-a-leekie, cocka- also cocky-leeky— *n esp. Scots* a soup made from boiled chicken and vegetables, esp. leeks

cock-and-bull story *n* -stories *esp. spoken* an improbable story told as if true

cockatoo *n* -toos a type of Australian crested parrot

cockchafer *n* a European beetle which destroys vegetation

cockcrow *n* early morning; sunrise

cocked hat *n* a 3-cornered hat with turned-up edges, worn in former times or with special uniforms

cockerel *n* a young cock

cocker spaniel also cocker— *n* a type of dog with long ears and silky coat

cockeyed *adj sl* 1 foolish 2 crooked

cockfight *n* a fight between 2 fully-grown spurred cocks, watched as a sport — ~ing *n*

cockle *n* a type of edible soft-bodied sea animal that lives in a pair of heart-shaped shells

cockleshell *n* a type of heart-shaped shell

Cockney *n* -neys a Londoner, esp. one from the East End

cockpit *n* the part of a plane or racing car in which the pilot and copilot sit ⊂ℲAEROPLANE

cockroach *n* any of several types of large black insect, often living in dirty houses ⊂ℲINSECT

cockscomb *n* 1 also coxcomb— *literature* a jester's cap 2 the red fleshy growth on a cock's head

cocksure *adj esp. spoken* too sure of oneself

cocktail *n* 1 a mixed alcoholic drink 2 a small quantity of specially prepared seafood eaten at the start of a meal —see also FRUIT COCKTAIL

cocktail dress *n* a short dress worn on formal occasions

cocky *adj* -ier, iest *esp. spoken* too sure of oneself — cockiness *n*

cocoa *n* 1 a dark brown powder made by crushing the cooked seeds of the cacao tree, used for giving foods and drinks a sweet chocolate flavour **2** a drink made from hot milk or water mixed with this powder

coconut *n* **1** a large brown hard-shelled nut with hard white flesh and a hollow centre filled with a milky juice **2** the flesh of this eaten raw as food

coconut shy *n* **-shies** a game in which people pay to throw balls at coconuts in order to win a prize by knocking them off posts

cocoon *n* a protective case of silky threads in which a pupa is enclosed —compare CHRYSALIS

cod¹ also **codfish—** *n* **cod** *or* **cods** a type of large edible North Atlantic sea fish

cod² *v* **-dd-** *sl* to make a fool of

C.O.D. *abbrev. for:* Cash on Delivery; payment to be made at the time and place of delivery

coda *n* a usu. independent passage that ends a piece of music

coddle *v* **-dled, -dling** **1** to cook (eggs, fruit, etc.) slowly in water just below boiling point **2** *esp. spoken* also **mollycoddle—** to treat too tenderly

code¹ *n* **1** a system of using words, letters, numbers, etc., to keep messages secret ⊚ **2** a system of signals used instead of letters and numbers in a message that is to be broadcast, telegraphed, etc. —see also MORSE CODE **3** a body of established social customs: *a code of behaviour* **4** a collection of laws

code² also **encode—** *v* **coded, coding** to translate into a code

codeine *n* a drug made from opium, used as a pain-killer, esp. for headaches and colds

codger *n* *esp. spoken* a peculiar old man

codicil *n* *law* an addition to a will

codify *v* **-fied, -fying** to arrange (esp. laws) into a code — **-fication** *n*

cod-liver oil *n* oil obtained from the liver of the cod and related fishes and containing important vitamins

codpiece *n* an often ornamented piece of material used esp. in the 15th and 16th centuries to cover the front opening of men's tight trousers

codswallop *n* *sl* nonsense

coed *adj* *esp. spoken* coeducational

coeducation *n* the system of educating boys and girls together — ~**al** *adj*

coefficient *n* *technical* **1** a number written before and multiplying a variable: *In 8pz=4 the coefficient of pz is 8* **2** a measure of the quality possessed by a substance under fixed conditions

coelacanth *n* a sea fish thought to have died out 70, 000, 000 years ago until one was caught near South Africa in 1938

coelenterate *n* any of a group of sea creatures without backbones, such as corals and jelly fishes

coerce *v* **coerced, coercing** **1** to make (an unwilling person or group) do something, by force, threats, etc. **2** to keep under control by using

force; repress — **-ion** *n* — **-ive** *adj* — **-ively** *adv*

coexist *v* **1** to exist together at the same time **2** (of countries with opposed political systems) to live together in peace — ~**ence** *n* — ~**ent** *adj*

C of E *abbrev. for:* Church of England

coffee *n* **1** a brown powder made by crushing the dark beans of the coffee tree, used for making drinks or flavouring food **2** a drink made by adding hot water and/or milk to this powder

coffee bar *n* a place where light meals, sweets, and nonalcoholic drinks are served

coffeepot *n* a container in which coffee is made or served

coffee table *n* a small long low table on which coffee may be served, magazines arranged, etc.

coffee-table book *n* a large costly book, usu. with many pictures, placed so that visitors can see and admire it

coffer *n* a large strong chest for valuables

coffers *n* *esp. spoken* money ready for use, imagined as in coffers

coffin *n* the box in which a dead person is buried

cog *n* any of the teeth round the edge of a wheel that cause it to move or be moved by another wheel

cogent *adj* convincing: *cogent reasons* — **-ency** *n* — ~**ly** *adv*

cogitate *v* **-tated, -tating** *esp. written* to think seriously — **-ion** *n*

cognac *n* a type of brandy made in Southwestern France

cognate *adj* *technical* related in origin: *Italian and Spanish are cognate languages*

cognition *n* *technical* the power or action of knowing, including consciousness of things and judgment about them — **-ive** *adj* — **-ively** *adv*

cognizant *adj* *written or law* aware: *The judge was not cognizant of the case*

cognoscenti *n* *Italian* connoisseurs

cogwheel *n* a toothed wheel (esp.a gearwheel) that can move or be moved by another wheel of the same type

cohabit *v* *esp. written* (of one or more unmarried people) to live as if married — ~**ation** *n*

cohere *v* **cohered, cohering** to stick together

coherence also **coherency—** *n* natural or reasonable connection, esp. in thoughts or words

coherent *adj* easily understood; consistent — ~**ly** *adv*

cohesion *n* **1** sticking together tightly **2** the force which holds parts of a solid or liquid together — **-ive** *adj* — **-ively** *adv*

cohort *n* **1** (in the ancient Roman army) a group of between 300 and 600 soldiers under one commander, being a 10th part of a legion **2** any group or company of people, esp. soldiers joined together **3** *often offensive* a companion

Code This is a very simple code. More complicated codes can be formed using whole words or numbers.

```
a b c d e f g h i j k l m n o p q r s t u v w x y z
        ↑
        a b c d e f g h i j k l m n o p q r s t u v w x y z
```

Braille

A	B	C	D	E	F	G	H	I	J	K	L	M	N	O

P	Q	R	S	T	U	V	W	X	Y	Z	and	for	of	the

Morse

A	B	C	D	E	F	G	H	I	J

K	L	M	N	O	P	Q	R	S	T

U	V	W	X	Y	Z

Semaphore

A & 1   B & 2   C & 3   D & 4   E & 5   F & 6   G & 7   H & 8   I & 9

J & direction   K   L   M   N   O   P   Q   R

S   T   U & attention   V   W   X   Y   Z   numeral sign

Hieroglyphs

eye   dove   flower   angle   to find   old age   heaven, sky   god

coiffure n a style of arranging a woman's hair — -**fured** adj

coil[1] v to wind into a ring or spiral: *Coil the rope up*

coil[2] n 1 a connected set of rings into which a rope, wire, etc., can be wound ⟶MATHEMATICS 2 a single one of these rings 3 *technical* a an electrical component made by winding a continuous piece of wire into some shape, used for carrying an electric current b 2 parts like this in a car that use induction to produce a high-voltage spark ⟶ ELECTRICITY 4 a type of intrauterine device fitted inside a woman as a contraceptive

coin[1] n a piece of metal, usu. flat and round, made by a government for use as money

coin[2] v 1 to make (coins) from metal 2 to invent (a word or phrase) — ~**er** n

coinage n 1 the making of coins: *The government has the right of coinage* 2 metal coins in large numbers 3 an invented word or phrase

coincide v -**cided**, -**ciding** 1 to happen at the same time 2 to be in agreement: *My beliefs and yours don't coincide*

coincidence n 1 a combination of chance events that seem planned 2 the condition or fact of coinciding — -**tal** adj — -**tally** adv

coincident adj 1 *esp. written* existing or happening in the same position and time 2 being in complete agreement

coir n a thick hard-wearing material made from the coarse hairy covering of the coconut, used for making ropes, mats, etc.

coitus also **coition**— n *medical* sexual intercourse — **coital** adj

coitus interruptus n *Latin* the practice of taking the man's sex organ out of the woman's sex organ before the sex act is completed, to prevent the woman having a baby

coke n the solid substance that remains after gas has been removed from coal by heating

col n a low place between 2 high points in a mountain range, esp. where easily crossed ⟶GEOGRAPHY

cola n any of several types of non-alcoholic drink

colander also **cullender**— n a bowl-shaped pan with many small holes, for separating liquid from food

cold[1] adj 1 having a low temperature 2 not feeling warm 3 *esp. spoken* (in games) still a long way from finding an object, the answer, etc. 4 *esp. spoken* unconscious, esp. as the result of a blow (esp. in the phrase **out cold**) 5 unkind 6 (esp. of a woman) frigid 7 cooked but not eaten hot —see also **have cold feet** (FOOT), **in cold** BLOOD, **to make someone's** BLOOD **run cold** — ~**ly** adv — ~**ness** n

cold[2] n 1 the absence of heat; low temperature; cold weather 2 an illness, esp. of the nose and/or throat, common in winter 3 (out) **in the cold** *esp. spoken* seemingly unwanted

cold-blooded adj 1 having a body temperature that changes according to the surrounding temperature 2 cruel: *a cold-blooded murder* 3 *esp. spoken* very sensitive to cold

cold chisel n a chisel for cutting metal

cold comfort n something that gives little consolation

cold cream n a thick white sweet-smelling cream for cleaning and smoothing the skin of the face, neck, and hands

cold feet n *esp. spoken* loss of courage (in the phrases **get/have cold feet**)

cold fish n an unfeeling person

cold frame n a small glass-covered frame and the soil it encloses, used for protecting young plants

cold-hearted adj unkind — ~**ly** adv — ~**ness** n

cold shoulder n *esp. spoken* intentionally unsympathetic treatment (esp. in the phrase **give/get the cold shoulder**)

cold-shoulder v *esp. spoken* to give the cold shoulder to

cold snap n a sudden short period of very cold weather

cold sore also **fever blister**— n a sore (a type of HERPES) on or near the lips, or within the mouth, that often comes with a cold or fever

cold storage n storage (as of food or furs) in a cold place

cold sweat n a state in which one sweats and feels cold from fear

cold war n a severe political struggle between states with opposed political systems, without actual fighting

coleslaw n finely cut cabbage in a dressing eaten as a salad

coley n coley or coleys any of several types of edible sea fish

colic n a severe pain in the stomach and bowels — ~**ky** adj

collaborate v -**rated**, -**rating** 1 to work with someone else 2 to help an invader — -**ration** n — -**rator** n

collage n a picture made by sticking various materials or objects onto a surface

collapse[1] v -**lapsed**, -**lapsing** 1 to fall or drop down or inwards suddenly 2 to fold into a shape that takes up less space 3 to fall helpless or unconscious 4 to fail completely 5 *medical* (of a lung or blood vessel) to fall into a flattened mass

collapse[2] n 1 (an example of) falling down or inwards 2 (an example of) completely breaking down: *the collapse of the pound* 3 (an example of) completely losing strength and/or will: *a nervous collapse*

collapsible adj that can be collapsed for easy storing

collar[1] n 1 the part of a shirt, dress, or coat that stands up or folds down round the neck 2 a close-fitting ornamental neck band 3 a leather or metal band round an animal's neck 4 a round leather object put round the shoulders of a horse to help it pull a vehicle or other object 5 techni-

cal a band or coloured marking round the neck **6** any of various ring-like machine parts —see also BLUE-COLLAR, WHITE-COLLAR

collar² *v* **1** *esp. spoken* to seize **2** *sl* to take without permission

collarbone also (*medical*) **clavicle**— *n* either of a pair of bones joining the ribs to the shoulders of humans ⟶ANATOMY

collate *v* **-lated, -lating** *technical* to arrange (the sheets) of in the correct order

collateral¹ *adj* *written or technical* **1** side by side; parallel **2** additional, but with less importance; supporting **3** descended from the same person but through a different line: *Cousins are collateral relatives* **4** of, related to, based on, or being collateral

collateral² *n* *technical* property or something valuable promised to a person if one is unable to repay money borrowed from that person — compare SECURITY

colleague *n* a fellow worker, esp. in a profession

collect¹ *n* a short prayer, varying from day to day, read near the beginning of some religious services

collect² *v* **1** to gather together **2** to gather (objects) as a hobby, for study, etc. **3** to call for and take away **4** to regain control of (oneself, one's thoughts, senses, etc.) **5** to obtain payment of (money): *The government collects taxes*

collected *adj* controlled; calm — ~ly *adv*

collection *n* **1** the act of collecting **2** the emptying of a post-box by a postman **3** a group of objects collected as a hobby, for study, etc. **4** a sum of money collected, esp. at a religious service **5** a pile of material, dirt, etc., often unwanted

collective¹ *adj* **1** formed by collection; considered as a whole: *our collective mistakes* **2** of or related to a number of people or groups considered as one **3** shared by a group: *collective ownership* — ~ly *adv*

collective² *n* a group: *a workers' collective*

collective bargaining *n* talks between unions and employers about working conditions, wages, etc.

collective farm *n* a large state farm, usu. in socialist countries, made by joining a number of small farms together, and controlled by the farm workers

collective leadership *n* (esp. in communist countries) control of a government by a group of leaders

collective noun *n* *technical* a noun singular in form but naming a collection of people, animals, or things as a group

collectivism *n* *technical* the system under which the means of production are owned and controlled by the state

collectivize , -ise *v* **-ized, -izing** to bring (industry, farms, etc.) under the control of the state or people

collector *n* **1** a person employed to collect taxes, tickets, etc. **2** a person who collects stamps, coins, etc., for interest

collector's item also **collector's piece** —— *n* an object of interest to collectors because of its beauty or rarity

colleen *n* *Irish* a girl

college *n* **1** a school for higher education **2** a body of teachers and students forming a separate part of certain universities **3** any of certain large public or private schools **4** *technical* a body of people with a common profession, purpose, etc.: *the Royal College of Nurses*

collegiate *adj* **1** of or related to a college or students **2** having colleges: *a collegiate university*

collide *v* **-lided, -liding** **1** to meet and strike (together) violently **2** to disagree strongly

collie *n* a type of dog used for tending sheep or kept as a pet

collier *n* **1** a person employed to cut coal in a mine **2** a ship for carrying coal

colliery *n* **-ries** a coal mine and its buildings, machinery, etc.

collision *n* (an example of) colliding

colloquial *adj* of, suitable for, or related to ordinary conversation — ~ism *n* — ~ly *adv*

collude *v* **-luded, -luding** *esp. written or law* to act together with the secret intention of cheating — **-lusion** *n*

collywobbles *n* *esp. spoken* a slight stomach-ache usu. caused by nervousness

cologne also **eau de cologne**— *n* a refreshing perfume

colon¹ *n* the lower part of the large intestine in which food changes into solid waste matter and passes into the rectum ⟶DIGESTION

colon² *n* a mark (:) used in writing and printing to introduce a statement, example, etc.

colonel *n* an officer of middle rank in the army or American air force

Colonel Blimp also **Blimp**— *n* a self-important old man with old-fashioned political ideas

colonial¹ *adj* **1** of or related to colonies or to a colonist **2** of or related to the 13 British colonies which formed the United States **3** *technical* living in, consisting of, or forming a colony: *colonial plants*

colonial² *n* a person living in a colony, who is not a native of the place —compare COLONIST

colonialism *n* the principles or practice of having colonies abroad —compare IMPERIALISM, NEOCOLONIALISM — **-ist** *n, adj*

colonist *n* a person who settled in a new colony soon after it was established — compare COLONIAL

colonize, -ise *v* **-nized, -nizing** to make into a colony — **-nization** *n* — ~r *n*

colony *n* **-nies** **1** a country or area under the control of a distant country and often settled by people from that country **2** a group of people of the same nationality, profession, etc., living together: *the French colony in Saigon* **3** a group of the same kind of plants or animals growing or living together in close association **4** all the bacteria growing together as the descendants of a single cell

Colorado beetle *n* -beetle *or* -beetles a black-and-yellow insect that damages potatoes

coloration *n* arrangement of colours; colouring

coloratura *n* **1** rapid difficult musical passages to ornament sung music **2** music with much of this ornamentation **3** a female singer, esp. a soprano, who specializes in singing such music

colossal *adj* very large in size or quantity — ~ly *adv*

colossus *n* -suses *or* -si a person or thing of very great size, importance, or ability

colostrum *n* the liquid produced by a woman's breasts for the first few days after a baby is born

colour¹ *n* **1** the quality which allows the eyes to see the difference between (for example) a red and a blue flower of the same size and shape **2** red, blue, green, black, brown, yellow, white, etc. **3** (a) substance used for giving one of these special qualities to something: *The artist painted in water-colours* **4** the complexion **5** details or behaviour of a place, thing, or person, that excite: *the life, noise, and colour of the market* **6** **give/lend colour to** to make appear likely or true **7** **off colour** *esp. spoken* rather ill

colour² *v* **1** to cause to have colour or a different colour esp. with a crayon or pencil **2** to take on or change colour **3** to give a special effect or feeling to: *Personal feelings coloured his judgment* **4** to become red in the face

colour bar *n* the set of customs, laws, or other differences which prevent people of different colours from mixing freely

colour-blind *adj* unable to see the difference between certain colours — **colour blindness** *n*

coloured¹ *adj* **1** the stated colour: *a cream-coloured dress* **2** belonging to a race that does not have a white skin

coloured² *n* **1** any person belonging to a race that does not have a white skin **2** CAPE COLOURED

colourfast *adj* having colour which will not fade or run — ~ness *n*

colourful *adj* **1** full of colour or colours; bright **2** likely to excite the senses or imagination: *a colourful event*

colouring *n* **1** a substance for giving a special colour to another substance; dye **2** healthy or ill appearance as expressed by skin colour

colourless *adj* **1** without colour **2** pale **3** dull: *a colourless existence* — ~ly *adv* — ~ness *n*

colours *n* **1** the official flag of a country, ship, part of the army, etc. **2** a dress, cap, piece of material, etc., worn as a sign of one's club, school, etc. **3** **in its true colours** as it really is **4** **show one's true colours** to show one's real character, esp. for the first time **5** **with flying colours** with great success

colour scheme *n* the arrangement of various colours in a room, painting, etc., to produce a desired effect

colt *n* a young male horse

Colt *n* *trademark* a type of pistol

coltish *adj* playful in an awkward manner; high-spirited — ~ly *adv* — ~ness *n*

columbine *n* any of several types of plants with colourful 5-pointed downward-hanging flowers

Columbine *n* a young girl in English pantomime, the daughter of Pantaloon and in love with Harlequin —see also COMMEDIA DELL'ARTE

column *n* **1** a pillar used in a building as a support or ornament or standing alone as a monument **2** anything looking like a pillar: *a column of smoke* **3** one of 2 or more divisions of a page, lying side by side and separated by a narrow space, in which lines of print are arranged **4** an article by a particular writer, that regularly appears in a newspaper or magazine **5** many rows of people, vehicles, etc., following behind the other **6** a list of numbers arranged one under the other —see also FIFTH COLUMN

columnist *n* a person who writes a regular article for a newspaper or magazine

coma *n* a state of deep unconsciousness, caused by disease, poisoning, a blow, etc.

comatose *adj* **1** *technical* in a coma **2** *esp. written* of or like a coma

comb¹ *n* **1** a toothed piece of bone, metal, plastic, etc., used for cleaning, tidying, and straightening the hair or worn in a woman's hair for ornament **2** a thing like this in shape or use, such as an object used for carding wool, cotton, etc. **3** an act of combing **4** the red growth of flesh on a cock's head

comb² *v* **1** to clean or arrange (esp. the hair) with a comb **2** to search thoroughly

combat¹ *v* -tt- to fight

combat² *n* (a) struggle between 2 men, armies, ideas, etc.

combatant *n* a person playing or ready to play a direct part in fighting

combative *adj* eager to fight — ~ly *adv*

combination *n* **1** combining or being combined **2** a number of people or things united in a common purpose **3** the list of special numbers or letters needed to open a combination lock **4** something that results from 2 or more things, esp. chemicals, being combined **5** *technical* one of the sets into which a list of numbers, letters, etc., can be arranged

combinations also (*esp. spoken*) **coms** —— *n* any of various types of undergarments to cover the upper and lower parts of the body and legs

combine¹ *v* -bined, -bining to come, bring, or act together

combine² also **combine havester**— *n* a machine that reaps, threshes, and cleans grain

combined operations also **combined exercises**— *n* war operations in which air, land, and sea forces work together

combo *n* **-bos** a small band that usu. plays jazz or dance music

combustible *adj, n* (a substance) that burns easily

combustion *n* catching fire and burning

come *v* **came** , **come, coming** **1** to move towards the speaker or a particular place **2** to arrive in the course of time: *Uncle's birthday is coming soon* **3** to reach: *The water came to my neck* **4** to be (in a place in a set): *Monday comes after Sunday* **5** to happen or begin: *In time I came to love her* **6** to happen as a result of the stated cause **7** to become: *The buttons came unfastened* **8** to be offered, produced, etc.: *Milk comes from cows* **9 come full circle** to end at the place where one started **10 come home to** *esp. spoken* to be fully understood by **11 come and go** to change **12 come unstuck** to meet with failure —see also **come** CLEAN, **come a** CROPPER **13 how come** *esp. spoken* how did it happen (that) **14 to come** in the future —see also COME ABOUT, COME ACROSS, COME AGAIN, COME ALONG, COME AWAY, COME BY, COME DOWN, COME DOWN ON, COME DOWN TO, COME DOWN WITH, COME FORWARD, COME IN, COME IN FOR, COME INTO, COME OF, COME ON, COME OUT, COME OUT IN, COME ROUND, COME THROUGH, COME TO, COME UNDER, COME UP, COME UP AGAINST

come about *v adv* **1** to happen **2** (of a ship or the wind) to change direction

come across[1] also **come upon**— *v prep* to meet or discover, esp. by chance

come across[2] *v adv* to be effective and well received: *Your speech came across very well*

come again *v adv* **1** to return **2 Come again?** *esp. spoken* What did you say?

come along *v adv* **1** also **come on**— to advance: *How's your work coming along?* **2** also **come on**— to improve in health: *Mother's coming along nicely* **3** to happen: *Take every chance that comes along* **4** also **come on**— to follow **5 Come along!** *esp. spoken* Try harder!

come-at-able *adj sl* accessible

come away *v adv* **1** to leave **2** to become disconnected without being forced: *The handle came away in my hands*

comeback *n* **1** a return to a former position of strength or importance after a period of absence **2** a clever quick reply

come by *v prep* to obtain: *Jobs are hard to come by*

Comecon *n* Council for Mutual Economic Aid; an organization to encourage trade and friendly relations among 9 communist countries, including the Soviet Union —compare COMMON MARKET

comedian *n* **1** an actor who **a** tells jokes or does amusing things **b** acts in funny plays or films **2** *esp. spoken* a person who amuses others **3** a person who cannot be taken seriously

comedienne *n* a female comedian

comedown *n* *esp.spoken* **1** a fall in importance, rank, or respect **2** a disappointment

come down *v adv* **1** to be passed on from one period of history to another: *This song comes down to us from the 10th century* **2** to be reduced in price **3** to lose position, respect, or rank **4** to fall **5** to leave a big city for the country **6** to leave university (esp. Oxford or Cambridge) **7 come down to earth** to return to reality

come down on *v adv prep* **1** to ask forcefully **2** to punish or scold

come down to *v adv prep* to be able to be reduced to: *What do our choices in this come down to?*

come down with *v adv prep* esp. spoken to catch (an illness)

comedy *n* **-dies** **1** an amusing play, film, or other work which ends happily **2** an event, activity, or type of behaviour in real life that is amusing **3** the amusing quality of a play, film, book, person's behaviour, etc.

come forward *v adv* to offer oneself to fill a position, give help, etc.

come- hither *adj* esp. spoken purposefully attractive in a sexual way

come in *v adv* **1** to become fashionable, seasonal, etc. **2** to start to take part in a game **3** to take place in a race: *to come in third* **4** to be elected **5** to arrive as expected: *Has the train come in yet?* **6** (of the sea) to rise **7** to be received as income **8** to be (esp. in the phrases **come in handy, come in useful**) **9** to gain advantage: *Where do I come in?* —see also **when one's** SHIP **comes in**

come in for *v adv prep* **1** to receive as a share or as a right: *She came in for a fortune* **2** to receive (esp. blame)

come into *v prep* **1** to gain (a sum of money), esp. by inheritance **2** to begin to be in: *to come into fashion* **3 come into one's own** to gain respect, power, praise, etc., by showing one's true worth

comely *adj* **-lier, -liest** *literature* attractive — **comeliness** *n*

come of *v prep* **1** to be descended from: *She comes of a good family* **2** to result from: *Will good come of your actions?* **3 come of age** to reach an age (usu. 18 or 21) when one is considered by law to be responsible for oneself

come on[1] *v adv* **1** to appear at the appointed time: *The player came on late* **2** *esp. spoken* to start: *I can feel a cold coming on*

come on[2] *v prep* COME ACROSS

come out *v adv* **1** to be seen, as in a photograph: *Mary comes out well in pictures* **2** to be published: *When does John's book come out?* **3** (of a young lady of the upper classes) to be officially introduced in upper-class society **4** to be removed; disappear: *This ink blot hasn't come out* **5** to refuse to work: *The workers are coming out*

come out in *v adv prep* esp. spoken to be partly covered by (marks caused by disease)

come round *v adv* **1** also **come to**— to regain consciousness **2** to change sides or opinions: *to come round to our way of thinking* **3** to happen regularly: *Birthdays come round too quickly when one is older* **4** to become calmer after being angry: *Leave him alone and he'll soon come round*

comet *n* a heavenly body with a bright head and a long less bright tail that moves round the sun

come through[1] *v adv* **1** to arrive as expected: *Have your results come through yet?* **2** to do what is needed or expected: *John has come through with the money*

come through[2] *v adv; prep* to survive (a dangerous crisis): *John was so ill he was lucky to come through*

come to[1] *v prep* **1** to concern: *When it comes to politics I know nothing* **2** to reach all the way to: *The water came to my waist* **3** to amount to: *The bill came to $5.50* **4** to enter the mind of: *Suddenly the words came to me* **5 come to heel a** (of a dog) to follow closely just behind the owner **b** (of a person) to obey **6 come to oneself a** to regain self-control **b** *literature* to regain consciousness **7 come to pass** *usu. written* to happen

come to[2] *v adv* COME ROUND

come under *v prep* **1** to be governed or controlled by: *This committee will come under the Education Department* **2 come under the hammer** to be sold at an auction

come up *v adv* to become, esp. after cleaning: *The silk dress came up beautifully*

come up against *v adv prep* to meet (usu. opposition): *The workers came up against their employer's meanness*

come-uppance *n esp. spoken* a well-deserved punishment or misfortune

come up with *v adv prep esp. spoken* to think of (a plan, reply, etc.); produce: *He couldn't come up with an answer*

comfort[1] *n* **1** the state of being free from suffering **2** help, kindness, etc., given to a person who is suffering: *a word of comfort to a dying man* **3** a person or thing that gives strength or hope, or that makes grief or pain easier: *He was a great comfort to me when I was ill* — ~**less** *adj*

comfort[2] *v* to give comfort to — ~**er** *n*

comfortable *adj* **1** giving comfort: *a comfortable chair* **2** not experiencing too much pain, grief, anxiety, etc.: *My mother is comfortable after her operation* — **-bly** *adv*

comfortably off *adj* fairly rich

comfrey *n* -**freys** a tall wild plant with rough hairy leaves and purple or white flowers

comic[1] *adj* intended to amuse

comic[2] *n* **1** *esp. spoken* a person who is amusing, esp. a professional comedian **2** a magazine for children containing comic strips

comical *adj* amusing in an odd way: *That's a comical hat you're wearing* — ~**ly** *adv*

comic strip also **strip cartoon**— *n* a set of drawings telling a short story, often with words to show what the characters are saying

coming[1] *n* arrival

coming[2] *adj* arriving: *the coming joyful season*

comma *n* the mark (,) used in writing and printing, for showing a short pause

command[1] *v* **1** to direct with the right to be obeyed; order: *Our leader is not fit to command us* —see ORDER (USAGE) **2** to deserve and get: *This man is able to command respect* **3** *esp. written* to be in a position to use: *to command great wealth* **4** to be in a position to control: *This fort commands the valley*

command[2] *n* **1** an order: *All his commands were obeyed* **2** control: *The army is under the king's command* **3** a division of the army, air force, etc., under separate control: *pilots of the Southern Air Command* **4** a group of officers with the power to give orders: *the German High Command* **5** the ability to use: *a good command of French*

commandant *n* the chief officer in charge of a military organization

commandeer *v* to seize for public, esp. military use: *The soldiers commandeered the house to use as offices*

commander *n* **1** an officer of middle rank in the navy **2** the officer of any rank who is in charge of a group of soldiers: *The commander of our group is 25*

commander in chief *n* an officer in control of all the armed forces of a country, area, etc.

commanding *adj* **1** having command: *Who's your commanding officer?* **2** controlling, because of a strong position: *a commanding position on a hill* **3** deserving or expecting respect and obedience: *a commanding manner*

commandment *n* **1** *literature* a command **2** any of the 10 laws (**Ten Commandments**) which according to the Bible were given by God to Moses on Mount Sinai

commando *n* -**dos** *or* -**does** a member of a small fighting force trained to make quick attacks into enemy areas

commedia dell'arte *n Italian* a form of Italian comedy of the 16th and 17th centuries, with characters such as Harlequin, Pantaloon, Columbine, and Pierrot. It influenced English pantomime and Punch and Judy

commemorate *v* -**rated**, -**rating** **1** to give honour to the memory of **2** to be in memory of: *The Monument was built to commemorate the Fire of London* — -**ration** *n* — -**rative** *adj*

commence *v* -**menced**, -**mencing** *esp. written* to begin — ~**ment** *n*

commend *v esp. written* **1** to recognize officially as worthy of praise, notice, etc.; speak favourably of — ~**able** *adj* — ~**ably** *adv*

commendation *n* **1** *esp. written* praise **2** an official honour

commensurate *adj esp. written* equal in size, quality, or length of time

comment[1] *n* an opinion, explanation, or judgment: *What comments have you about my son's behaviour?*

comment[2] *v* to make a remark; give an opinion: *The king does not comment on election results*

commentary n -ries 1 a written collection of opinions, explanations, judgments, etc., on a book, event, person, etc. 2 a description spoken during an event, match, etc.

commentate v -tated, -tating to give a commentary

commentator n a broadcaster who gives a commentary

commerce n the buying and selling of goods, esp. between different countries

commercial¹ adj 1 of, related to, or used in commerce 2 a likely to produce profit: Oil has been found in commercial quantities b desiring to make a big profit without regard for other considerations: This musician only makes commercial records 3 (of television or radio) paid for by charges made for advertising — ~ly adv

commercial² n an advertisement on television or radio

commercialize, -ise v -ized, -izing to make (something) a matter of profit: Christmas is very commercialized — -cialism n

commercial traveller n a person who travels from place to place to get orders for his firm's goods

commie n sl usu. offensive a communist

commiserate with v prep -rated, -rating with to feel or express sympathy or pity for — -ration n

commissar n 1 the official name of a minister in the Soviet government until 1946 2 (in the Soviet Union) an official of the Communist Party who works in the armed forces to teach its principles and make sure of loyalty

commissariat n technical 1 a department in the army dealing with the supply of provisions 2 the supply of provisions to the army

commission¹ n 1 a job, duty, or power 2 a group of people appointed to perform certain duties 3 the act of doing something wrong or unlawful 4 an amount of money paid to a salesman, usu. related to the value of the goods he sells: He gets 10% commission on his sales 5 (an official paper appointing someone to) any of several high ranks in the armed forces 6 out of commission (esp. of a ship) waiting for repair

commission² v 1 to give a commission to: I was commissioned a general in 1939 2 to place a special order for: The king commissioned a new piece of music 3 to bring (a ship) into active service

commissionaire n a uniformed attendant at the entrance to a theatre, hotel, etc. △ COMMISSIONER

commissioned officer n a middle-or high-ranking officer in the armed forces appointed by a commission signed by the head of state —compare NON-COMMISSIONED OFFICER

commissioner n 1 a member of a commission 2 an official in charge of a Government department △ COMMISSIONAIRE

commit v -tt- 1 to do (something bad or unlawful) 2 to order to be placed under the control of another, esp. in prison or in a mental hospital: He was found guilty and committed 3 to promise to a certain cause, position, opinion, or course of action: The government can't commit any more money to the Health Service 4 commit oneself to make one's opinions known 5 commit to memory esp. written to memorize

commitment n 1 a promise to follow a certain course of action 2 a responsibility: I don't want any commitments

committal n esp. US the act of sending a person to prison or to a mental hospital

committed adj 1 having given one's whole loyalty to a particular aim, job, or way of life: a committed nurse 2 in a state of having promised

committee n a group chosen to do a particular job or for special duties

committee stage n law the stage between the second and third reading of a bill, when it is examined by a small committee in either House of Parliament

commode n a movable lavatory

commodious adj esp. written having plenty of space: a commodious drawer — ~ly adv

commodity n -ties 1 a thing of use, esp. something sold for profit: Commodities are exchanged for money 2 an article of trade or commerce, esp. a farm or mineral product

commodore n an officer of middle rank in the navy

common¹ adj 1 belonging to or shared equally by 2 or more; united: a common desire to defeat the enemy 2 found or happening often and in many places: Rabbits and foxes are common in Britain 3 ordinary: the common man 4 coarse in manner — ~ness n

common² n an area of open grassland which people are free to use: the village common

common denominator n technical a denominator that can be divided without remainder by all the denominators of a given number of fractions

commoner n a person not of a noble family

common factor n technical a quantity by which a number of other quantities may be divided without remainder: 5 is a common factor of 10 and 20

common land n land that may be used by everyone

common-law adj according to common law: She's his common-law wife, having lived with him for 20 years

common law n technical 1 the body of law originating in England and the modern law based upon it —compare CIVIL LAW 2 the unwritten law, esp. of England, based on custom and court decisions rather than on laws made by Parliament

commonly adv usually

Common Market also (technical & usu. written) **European Community**— a West European political and economic organization to encourage trade and friendly relations between its 9 member states —compare COMECON

common multiple *n technical* a number which contains 2 or more smaller numbers an exact number of times: *12 is the lowest common multiple of 3 and 4*—see also LCM

common noun *n technical* a noun that is not the name of a particular person, place, or thing: *"Book" and "sugar" are common nouns* — opposite **proper noun**

common-or-garden *adj esp. spoken* ordinary: *a common-or-garden house*

commonplace¹ *n* a well-known remark worn out by too much use: *Her speeches are full of commonplaces* —compare CLICHÉ, PLATITUDE, TRUISM

commonplace² *adj* 1 ordinary 2 (of remarks) well-known and worn out by too much use

common room *n* (in schools, colleges, etc.) a room for the use of teachers or students when they are not teaching or studying

Commons *n* HOUSE OF COMMONS

common sense *n* practical good sense and judgment

commonwealth *n esp. written* 1 all the people of a country or state 2 a state

Commonwealth *n* 1 an organization of independent states formerly part of the British Empire, to encourage trade and friendly relations among its members 2 the official title of some countries or states: *The Commonwealth of Puerto Rico* 3 England from 1649 to 1660, esp. under Cromwell

commotion *n* noisy confusion or excitement; violent and noisy movement

communal *adj* 1 of or shared by a community or group 2 of, related to, or based on racial, religious, or language groups

commune¹ *v* **-muned, -muning** *esp. poetic* to exchange thoughts or feelings: *The friends communed together*

commune² *n* 1 (a house for) a group of people who live together, though not of the same family, and share their lives and possessions 2 a group of people who work as a team for the general good, esp. in farming. They usually own and control the means of production 3 (in some countries, such as France and Belgium) the smallest division of local government

communicable *adj* (of illnesses, ideas, etc.) that can be passed from one person to another — **-bly** *adv*

communicate *v* **-cated, -cating** 1 *esp. written* to make known 2 *esp. written* to pass on (a disease, heat, movement, etc.) 3 *esp. written* to share or exchange opinions, news, information, etc.: *Has the Minister communicated with the President?*

communication *n* 1 the exchange of information, news, or ideas 2 something communicated —see also COMMUNICATIONS

communication cord *n* a chain running the length of a train which a passenger may pull to stop the train in an emergency

communications *n* the ways of travelling, moving goods, and sending information, between 2 places; roads, railways, radio, telephone, television, etc.

communicative *adj* readily willing to talk or give information

communion *n* 1 a group of people having the same religious beliefs 2 *literature* the sharing or exchange of thoughts, ideas, feelings, etc.: *Wordsworth was in communion with the hills and lakes*

Communion *n* HOLY COMMUNION —compare MASS

communiqué *n French* an official report or declaration, usu. to the public or newspapers

communism *n* a classless social and political system in which the means of production are owned and controlled by the state or the people as a whole, and the goods and wealth produced shared according to the principle 'from each according to his ability, to each according to his needs' —compare SOCIALISM — **-ist** *n* — **-istic** *adj*

Communism *n* 1 the belief in communism as the best possible form of society, which will one day be established generally 2 the international political movement aimed at establishing communism 3 the present political and economic system of any country ruled by the Communist party — **-ist** *n* — **-istic** *adj*

community *n* **-ties** 1 a group of people living together and/or united by shared interests, religion, nationality, etc. 2 *technical* a group of plants or animals living together in the same surroundings, usu. dependent on each other 3 *technical* a group of men and/or women who lead a shared life of prayer and work according to a set of religious rules 4 the public: *A politician serves the community*

community centre *n* a building where people can meet for social, educational, or other purposes

community home *n* a special home for boys and girls who have broken the law, where they live and receive training

commutation *n* a reduction in a punishment

commutative *adj technical* independent of the order in which an operation is performed: *Addition is commutative, but subtraction is not*

commutator *n technical* an apparatus in electric motors, machines, etc., for changing the direction of flow of an electric current

commute *v* **-muted, -muting** 1 to make (a punishment) less severe: *His punishment was commuted from death to life imprisonment* 2 *esp. written* to exchange (one thing, esp. one kind of payment) for another 3 to travel regularly between one's home and work (esp. by train)

commuter *n* a person who makes a regular journey between home and work, esp. by train

compact¹ *adj* firmly and closely packed

together; solid — ~ly *adv* — ~ness *n* — ~ed
adj

compact² *n* a small flat usu. round container for
face powder, a powder puff, and a mirror

compact³ *n technical* an agreement between 2
or more parties, countries, etc.

companion *n* 1 a person who spends time
with another 2 a person hired to help, live with,
or travel with another esp. older or ill person 3
either of a matching pair of things 4 *technical*
(used in some British titles of honour): *Benjamin
Britten C.H. (Companion of Honour)*

companionable *adj* friendly

companionship *n* the relationship of companions

companionway *n* the steps from the deck of
a ship to the area below —compare GANGWAY

company *n* 1 **-nies** companionship: *I was
grateful for Jean's company* 2 companions 3 a
body of (usu. about 120) soldiers, usu. part of a
regiment or battalion 4 the officers and men of a
ship 5 a group of people combined together for
business or trade; firm: *a bus company* 6 the
members of such a group whose names do not
appear in a firm's official name (in the phrase **and
Company**): *Robinson and Company*

comparable *adj esp. written* 1 that can be
compared 2 worthy of comparison: *Our house is
not comparable with yours* — **-bly** *adv*

comparative¹ *adj* 1 measured or judged by
comparison: *the comparative wealth of families*
2 of or related to the form of adjectives or adverbs
expressing increase in quality, quantity, or degree:
'Bigger' is the comparative form of 'big'—compare
POSITIVE, SUPERLATIVE"4 4 — ~ly *adv*

comparative² *n technical* also **comparative
degree** — the form of an adjective or adverb that
shows increase in quality, quantity, or degree:
'More suitable' is the comparative of 'suitable'

comparatively *adv* to a certain degree

compare *v* **-pared, -paring** 1 to examine or
judge (one thing) against another: *If you compare
the handwritings you'll find many similarities* 2
to show the likeness of (one thing) with another:
*It's impossible to compare Buckingham Palace
and my house*

compare with *v prep* to be worthy of comparison with: *Walking can't compare with flying*

comparison *n* 1 comparing 2 a statement of
the points of likeness and difference between 2
things 3 likeness: *There is no comparison
between frozen and fresh food* 4 (in grammar)
the changing of the form of an adverb or adjective
to show the 3 degrees of positive, comparative, and
superlative

compartment *n* one of the parts into which an
enclosed space is divided: *His maps are in a small
compartment in the front of his car*

compartmentalize, -ise *v* **-ized, -izing** to
divide into compartments

compass *n* 1 an instrument for showing direction, usu. with a freely-moving magnetic needle
which always points to the north ☞ GLOBE 2

any of several other instruments used for this
purpose 3 a V-shaped instrument for drawing
circles, measuring distances on maps, etc.

compassion *n* sympathy for the misfortunes of
others, with a desire to help or show mercy ~ate
adj — ~ately *adv*

compatible *adj* that can exist or work in agreement — **-bility** *n* — **-bly** *adv*

compatriot *n* a person of the same country as
another: *John and Jean are Compatriots*

compel *v* **-ll-** to make do something by or as if
by force: *The rain compelled us to stay indoors* —
compelling *adj* — **compellingly** *adv*

compendious *adj esp. written* giving the main
information about a subject in a short but complete
form — ~ly *adv*

compendium *n technical* a short but detailed
account of facts, information, a subject, etc.

compensate *v* **-sated, -sating** to provide with
a balancing effect for some loss or something
lacking; make a suitable payment for loss: *Many
firms compensate their workers if they are hurt at
work* — **-sation** *n* — **-satory** *adj* —compare
CONSOLATION, RECOMPENSE

compere¹ *n* a person who introduces the acts in
a show

compere² *v* **-pered, -pering** to act as a com-
pere in

compete *v* **-peted, -peting** to try to win something in competition: *John competed for a place in
the final*

competence *n* 1 ability to do what is needed;
skill —see GENIUS (USAGE) 2 *law* **a** ability to
act: *within a court's competence* **b** the state of
having the necessary age, citizenship, etc. to enter
and speak in a court of law

competent *adj* 1 able to do what is needed 2
esp. law having the power to deal with something:
*This court is not competent to deal with your
case* 3 very satisfactory: *a competent job* — ~ly
adv

competition *n* 1 the act of competing: *He
was in competition with 10 others for the job* 2
a test of strength, skill, etc.: *a horticultural competition* 3 the struggle to gain advantage, profit, or
success: *keen competition for first place* 4 the
person or people against whom one competes —
-itive *adj* — **-itively** *adv* — **-itiveness** *n*

competitor *n* a person, team, firm, etc., competing with another or others

compilation *n* 1 compiling 2 something
compiled, such as a report, collection of writings,
etc.

compile *v* **-piled, -piling** to put (facts, information, etc.) together in a collection: *He compiled
enough information to write a book on heraldry*

compiler *n* 1 someone who compiles information, reports, etc. 2 a computer program that
translates instructions in a high-level programming language into machine code

complacency also **complacence**— *n often
offensive* a feeling of quiet pleasure, or content-

ment with oneself — **complacent** *adj* ⚠ COM-PLAISANT — **complacently** *adv*

complain *v* to express feelings of annoyance, pain, unhappiness, grief, etc. — ~**er** *n* — ~**ing** *adj* — ~**ingly** *adv*

complaint *n* 1 a statement expressing annoyance, dissatisfaction, grief, etc. 2 a cause or reason for complaining 3 something, such as an illness, causing pain or discomfort: *a chest complaint*

complaisance *n* esp. written willingness to do what pleases others

complaisant *adj* esp. written ready and willing to please others; ready to agree ⚠ COMPLACENT — ~**ly** *adv*

complement¹ *n* 1 something that completes: *A fine wine is a complement to a good meal* 2 technical the number or quantity needed to make something complete, esp. the full number of officers and men needed for a ship 3 (in grammar) **a** a word or phrase (esp. a noun or adjective) that follows a verb and describes esp. a noun or pronoun that comes before it **b** a similar word or phrase that comes immediately after the object of a verb and describes it: *The word 'cold' is a complement in the sentence 'John is cold'* ⚠COM-PLIMENT

complement² *v* to make complete ⚠ COMPLI-MENT

complementary *adj* 1 supplying what is lacking or needed by another or each other for completion: *Supermarkets and their customers are complementary* 2 making up 90° together, or with another angle: *complementary angles* ⚠COM-PLIMENTARY

complementary colours *n* colours which when mixed make white or grey

complement of a set *n* technical the set of all elements which do not belong to a stated set

complete¹ *adj* 1 whole and in order: *John's birthday did not seem complete without his father* 2 finished: *When will work on the railway be complete?* — ~**ness** *n*

complete² *v* -pleted, -pleting to make whole or perfect: *I need one more stamp to complete my collection* — ~**ly** *adv* — -**tion** *n*

complex¹ *adj* 1 consisting of many closely related or connected parts: *A complex network of roads connects Glasgow and Edinburgh* 2 difficult to understand or explain: *His ideas were too complex* 3 (of a word or sentence) consisting of a main part and one or more other parts: *'If it rains, I won't go' is a complex sentence. 'I won't go,' is the main part* —compare COMPOUND — ~**ity** *n*

complex² *n* 1 a system consisting of a large number of closely related parts 2 technical a closely connected group of unconscious images, wishes, fears, etc., which influence a person's behaviour —see INFERIORITY COMPLEX 3 esp. spoken a fixed, often confused, feeling about something: *You've got a complex about spiders*

complexion *n* the natural colour and appearance of the skin, esp. of the face

compliance *n* 1 obedience 2 the tendency to yield too willingly to the wishes of others

compliant *adj* readily acting in accordance with a rule, order, demand, etc. — ~**ly** *adv*

complicate *v* -cated, -cating 1 to make difficult to understand or deal with 2 to make (esp. an illness) worse: *bronchitis complicated by pleurisy*

complicated *adj* 1 consisting of many connected parts: *a complicated machine* 2 difficult to understand or deal with — ~**ly** *adv* — ~**ness** *n*

complication *n* 1 the act of complicating 2 something that adds new difficulties: *The union's demand was a complication they had not expected* 3 a confused relationship of parts: *The complications of this machine make it difficult to handle* 4 a new illness that arises during the course of another illness, thus making treatment more difficult

complicity *n* -ties the act of taking part with another person in some wrongful action —see also ACCOMPLICE

compliment¹ *n* an expression of praise or respect: *to pay compliments to the girls* ⚠ COMP-LEMENT

compliment² *v* to praise someone with a compliment ⚠ COMPLEMENT

complimentary *adj* 1 expressing praise, respect, etc. 2 given free, out of kindness or respect: *complimentary tickets* ⚠ COMPLEMEN-TARY

compliments *n* good wishes: *My compliments to the chef!*

comply *v* -plied, -plying to act in accordance with a demand, rule, etc.

component *n* any of the parts that make up a whole (esp. a machine or system)

compose *v* -posed, -posing 1 to make up; form: *The teacher asked what water was composed of* —compare COMPRISE 2 to write (music, poetry, etc.) 3 to make calm, quiet, etc.: *Jean soon composed herself*

composer *n* a person who writes music

composite *adj, n* (something) made up of a number of different parts or materials

composition *n* 1 the act of putting together parts to form something 2 a result of this, such as a piece of music or art or a poem 3 a short piece of writing done as an educational exercise 4 something consisting of a mixture of various substances

compositor *n* Technical a person who arranges words, sentences, pages, etc., for printing

compost¹ *n* a mixture of decayed plant or animal matter, such as cut grass or leaves, used for making the soil richer

compost² *v* 1 to cover with compost 2 to make compost from

composure n complete control over one's feelings; calmness

compote n fruit cooked in sweetened water, usu. served as a sweet

compound[1] v 1 to put together to form a whole: *He compounded various substances into an effective medicine* 2 to add to or increase (something bad): *Our mistakes were compounded by those of others*

compound[2] adj 1 (of a single whole) consisting of 2 or more separable parts, substances, etc. 2 (of a word or sentence) consisting of 2 or more main parts: *'Childcare' is a compound word consisting of 'child' and 'care'* compare COMPLEX

compound[3] n 1 a combination of 2 or more parts, substances, etc., esp. a chemical consisting of at least 2 different elements combined in such a way that it usu. has qualities different from those of the substances from which it is made —compare ELEMENT, MIXTURE 2 a compound word or sentence

compound[4] n a group of buildings enclosed by a wall, fence, etc.

compound eye n an eye, as in an insect, made up of very many small parts each of which sees part of the whole

compound fracture n *medical* a broken or cracked bone which cuts through the surrounding flesh, making an open wound

compound interest n interest calculated on the original sum of money lent or borrowed and on all the unpaid interest already earned —compare SIMPLE INTEREST

compound leaf n *technical* a leaf consisting of several small leaves joined to a single stem

comprehend v *esp. written* to understand — **-hensible** adj — **-hensibility** n

comprehension n 1 understanding 2 the ability of the mind to understand 3 an exercise to test and improve a pupil's ability to understand language

comprehensive[1] adj 1 thorough; broad 2 of or related to education in a comprehensive — ~ly adv

comprehensive[2] n a school where pupils of all abilities and from all social classes are taught from the age of 11

compress[1] v to force (a substance) into less space; press together — ~ible adj — ~ibility n — ion n

compress[2] n a small thick pad of soft material pressed to part of the body to stop bleeding, reduce fever, etc.

compressor n an apparatus for compressing gas or air

comprise v -prised, -prising 1 to consist of; include: *The United Kingdom comprises England, Wales, Scotland, and Northern Ireland* 2 to make up: *15 separate republics comprise the Soviet Union* —compare COMPOSE

compromise[1] n 1 the act of settling a difference of opinion by each side yielding some of its demands and agreeing to some of the demands of the other 2 an agreement reached in this way: *a compromise between comfort and economy*

compromise[2] v -mised, -mising 1 to settle a difference of opinion by taking a middle course 2 to make open to dishonour, danger, etc.: *John felt compromised by his friendship with the criminal*

compulsion n 1 force or influence that makes a person do something 2 a strong usu. unreasonable desire that is difficult to control

compulsive adj resulting from a compulsion: *compulsive smoking* — ~ly adv — ~ness n

compulsory adj put into force by the law, orders, etc.: *Education is compulsory in Britain* — **-rily** adv —opposites optional, voluntary

compunction n an awkward feeling of guilt: *That woman had no compunction about lying*

computation n (the result of) the act of calculating

compute v -puted, -puting to calculate (a result, answer, etc.)

computer n an electric calculating machine that can store and recall information and make calculations at very high speeds —compare CALCULATING MACHINE.

computerize v -ized, - izing 1 to store (information) in a computer 2 to use a computer to control (an operation, system, etc.): *The firm has computerized its wages department*

comrade n 1 a close companion, esp. one who shares difficult work or troubles 2 (esp. used as a title in Communist countries) a citizen; fellow member of a union, political party, etc.

comradeship n companionship

con[1] adv against

con[2] n 1 an argument or reason against (esp. in the phrase **pros and cons**) 2 a person or vote against: *There are more pros than cons*

con[3] n *sl* CONFIDENCE TRICK

con[4] v -nn- *sl* to trick in order to make money: *They've conned me out of all my money!*

concave adj curved inward, like the inside surface of a hollow ball: *a concave mirror* —opposite convex — **concavity** n

conceal v to hide; keep from being known — ~ment n

concede v -ceded, -ceding 1 to admit as true, just, or proper, often unwillingly 2 to give as a right; yield: *The champion conceded 10 points* 3 to end a game or match by admitting defeat

conceit n also **conceitedness**— too high an opinion of one's own abilities, value, etc. — ~ed adj — ~edly adv

conceivable adj that can be thought of or believed — **-bly** adv

conceive v -ceived, - ceiving 1 *technical* to become pregnant with: *Our first child was conceived in March* 2 to think of; consider: *Scientists first conceived the idea of the atomic bomb in the 1930s*

concentrate[1] v -trated, -trating 1 to keep or direct (all one's thoughts, efforts, attention, etc.):

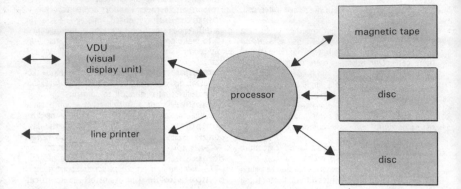

The diagram above shows how information (data) flows within a computer system. The VDU (visual display unit) looks like a television screen attached to a typewriter keyboard. Information or instructions can be displayed on the screen and put into the computer (input) by typing on the keyboard. The processor takes information from the VDU and either stores it on magnetic disc or tape, or carries out any processing on it as directed by a set of instructions in the computer, called the program. The processor can also retrieve stored information and show it on the VDU screen or print it on paper through the line printer (printout).

The diagram below shows what the computer components look like. There may be many VDU's linked to one computer by cable, in fact police stations around Britain have VDU's (terminals) linked to a central computer. This helps the police to obtain information about stolen cars much more quickly.

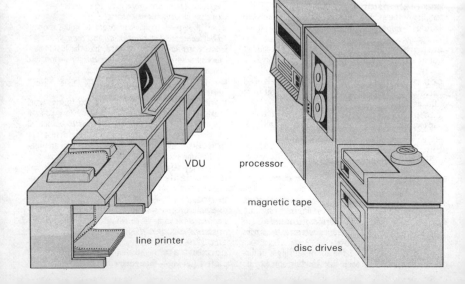

Concentrate on your work **2** to come or bring together in or around one place: *The crowds concentrated in the centre of the town* **3** technical to strengthen by reducing the per cent of water in a solution

concentrate² n a concentrated form of something: *orange juice concentrate*

concentrated adj increased in strength by the removal of liquid or the addition of more of a substance

concentration n technical **1** the act of concentrating; close or complete attention **2** the measure of the amount of a substance contained in a liquid: *What is the concentration of salt in sea water?*

concentration camp n a large enclosed area where political prisoners or people considered as threats to the state are imprisoned

concentric adj technical having the same centre: *concentric circles* —compare ECCENTRIC ⟋MATHEMATICS

concept n a general idea, thought, or understanding

conception n **1** the act of forming an idea, plan, etc. **2** a general understanding; *I have some conception life in the Middle Ages* **3** technical the starting of a new life by the union of a male and a female cell

conceptualize, -ise v **-ized, -izing** to form a concept of

concern¹ v **1** to be about: *This story concerns a good girl and a wicked fairy* **2** to be of importance or interest to; have an effect on **3** to make unhappy or troubled **4** to worry; interest: *A doctor should concern himself with your health*

concern² n **1** a matter of interest or importance to someone: *Your homework isn't my concern* **2** serious care or interest: *a nurse's concern for a sick man* **3** worry **4** a business — ~ed adj — ~edly adv

concerning prep about

concert n **1** a musical performance by a number of singers or musicians or both —compare RECITAL **2** in concert working together; in agreement

concerted adj planned or done together by agreement; combined: *a concerted effort* — ~ly adv

concert grand n a piano of the largest size, played esp. at concerts

concertina¹ n a small accordion, held and played in the hands by pressing in from both ends

concertina² V **-naed, -naing** esp. spoken to become pressed together as the result of a crash: *The heavy lorry concertinaed when it hit the wall*

concerto n **-tos** a piece of music for one or more solo instruments and orchestra, usu. consisting of more than one movement and lasting about an hour

concert pitch n technical the degree of high-

ness or lowness of music, used as the standard for all instruments

concession n **1** the act of yielding **2** a point or thing yielded, esp. after a disagreement **3** a right given by a government, owner of land, etc., to do something: *oil concessions in the North Sea*

concessive clause n a clause, often introduced by 'although', which shows willingness to concede a point that goes against the main argument of a sentence: *A concessive clause begins the sentence 'Although you are right about that, you are wrong about everything else'*

conch n a snail-like tropical sea animal or its large twisted often brightly coloured shell

conciliate v **-ated, -ating** to remove the anger or distrust of; win the support or friendly feelings of — **-tion** n — **-tory** adj

concise adj short and clear; expressing much in few words — ~ly adv

conclude v **-cluded, -cluding** **1** esp. written to come or bring to an end: *We concluded the meeting* **2** to arrange or settle **3** to come to believe after consideration of known facts — **-clusion** n

conclusive adj putting an end to doubt: *conclusive proof* — ~ly adv

concoct v to make by mixing or combining parts; make up: *Jean concocted a splendid meal out of scraps* — ~ion n

concord n **1** complete peace and agreement: *The 2 tribes lived in concord* **2** technical an agreement, esp. a treaty, establishing peace and friendly relations **3** agreement between words, esp. with regard to their number, gender, person, or case: *In the sentence 'We really have enjoyed ourselves', 'we' and 'have' show concord of number, 'we' and 'ourselves' show concord of number and person* —compare AGREEMENT

concordance n esp. written technical an alphabetical list of the words used in a book or collection of books by one writer, with information about where they can be found and usu. about how they are used

concordat n technical an agreement between the church and state on matters of religion

concrete¹ adj **1** technical existing as something real or solid: *Beauty is not concrete but a window is* **2** particular; definite: *a concrete proposal* — ~ly adv

concrete² n a building material made by mixing sand, small stones, cement, and water

concrete³ v **-creted, -creting** to cover with concrete

concubine n a woman who lives with a man as his wife

concur v **-rr-** esp. written **1** to agree **2** to happen at the same time: *Everything concurred to produce the desired effect* — ~rence n

concurrent adj **1** existing or happening at the same time **2** technical having only one common point **3** being in agreement — ~ly adv

concuss v to damage (the brain) with a heavy blow, shock, or violent shaking — ~ion n

condemn v 1 to express strong disapproval of 2 to state the punishment for, esp. one of death or long imprisonment: *The prisoner was condemned to death* 3 to declare officially unfit for use: *This house is condemned* — ~ation n

condemned cell n a room where prisoners are kept who are to be punished by death

condensation n 1 change from a gas to a liquid or, sometimes, to a solid: *condensation of steam to water* 2 small drops of a liquid or solid substance formed in this way; drops formed when steam becomes cool 3 (an example or result of) the act of making a book, speech, etc., shorter

condense v -densed, -densing 1 (of a gas) to become liquid, or sometimes solid, esp. by cooling ☞ CLOUD 2 to put into a smaller form: *a condensed report*

condensed milk n milk thickened by taking away some of its water, sweetened and sold in tins

condenser n 1 an apparatus that makes a gas change into a liquid 2 *old use* a capacitor

condescend v 1 to agree to do something beneath one's social rank: *The general condescended to eat with the soldiers* —compare DEIGN 2 to act in a manner that makes one appear of a higher social rank than others: *She condescends to all her neighbours* — -cension n

condiment n *esp. written* a powder or liquid used to flavour food: *Pepper and salt are condiments*

condition[1] n 1 a state of being or existence: *the condition of weightlessness* 2 general health or fitness: *to improve your condition by running* 3 a disease 4 something stated as necessary for something else: *She will join us on one condition: that we divide the profits*

condition[2] v *esp. technical* to train: *conditioned by upbringing*

conditional[1] adj 1 depending on a certain condition or conditions 2 expressing a condition or supposition: *A conditional sentence often begins with the words 'if' or 'unless'* — ~ly adv

conditional[2] n a form of a verb used to state what would happen in certain conditions

conditioned reflex also **conditioned response**— n *technical* a reflex developed as the result of repeated treatment or training

conditions n terms, esp. of payment: *You have it on very favourable conditions*

condolence n sympathy for someone who has experienced sadness, misfortune, etc.: *My condolences on your mother's death*

condole with v prep -doled, -doling with to express sympathy to

condom n a usu. rubber covering worn over the male sex organ during sexual relations, used as a means of birth control (CONTRACEPTIVE) and/or a protection against disease

condone v -doned, -doning to forgive (wrong behaviour); treat (a wrong action) as harmless

condor n a very large American vulture

conducive adj *esp. written* likely to produce: *Exercise is conducive to health* — ~ness n

conduct[1] n 1 *esp. written* behaviour 2 direction of the course of (a business, activity, etc.)

conduct[2] v 1 *esp. written* to behave (oneself): *Your children conduct themselves well* 2 to direct the course of (a business, activity, etc.) 3 to lead or guide (a person, tour, etc.) 4 to stand before and direct the playing of (musicians or a musical work) 5 to act as the path for (electricity, heat, etc.): *Plastic won't conduct electricity*

conduction n the passage of electricity or heat along wires, water through pipes, etc.

conductive adj *technical* able to conduct electricity, heat, etc.: *Copper is a highly conductive metal* — -tivity n

conductor n 1 a person who directs the playing of a group of musicians 2 a person employed to collect fares on a public vehicle 3 a substance that conducts electricity, heat, etc.: *Wood is a poor conductor of heat*

conduit n a pipe or passage for carrying water, gas, electric wires, etc.

cone n 1 a solid object with a circular base and a point at the top ☞ MATHEMATICS 2 a hollow or solid object shaped like this: *ice cream cones* 3 the fruit of a pine or fir, consisting of a number of seed - containing pieces, shaped like this 4 a type of cell in the area at the back of the eye (RETINA) that is sensitive esp. to the different colours in light —compare ROD

confection n *esp. written* a sweet-tasting dish

confectioner n a person who makes or sells sweets, ice cream, etc.

confectionery n -ries cakes, sweets, etc.

confederacy also **confederation**— n -cies *technical* a political union of several peoples or states — -ate n, adj

confer v -rr- *esp. written* 1 to give (a gift, title, honour, etc.) 2 to talk together; compare opinions — ~ment n

conference n a meeting held so that opinions on a subject, or subjects, can be exchanged: *A conference of states was held today* —see also PRESS CONFERENCE

confess v 1 to admit (a fault, crime, etc.) 2 *technical* to make (one's faults) known to a priest or God

confessed adj not secretive; open; by one's own admission — ~ly adv

confession n an example of admitting one's crimes, faults, etc. or a religious service at which this is done

confessional n a usu. enclosed place in a church where the priest hears people make their confession

confetti n small pieces of coloured paper thrown about, esp. at weddings

confide *v* -fided, -fiding to tell secretly to a person one trusts

confidence *n* 1 faith 2 belief in one's own or another's ability 3 some personal matter told secretly to a person

confidence trick also *sl* **con**— *n* a trick to cheat a person of money

confident *adj* feeling or showing confidence —opposite **diffident** — ~ly *adv*

confidential *adj* 1 to be kept secret: *confidential information* 2 trusted with private matters: *a confidential secretary* — ~ity *n* — ~ly *adv*

confiding *adj* trustful — ~ly *adv*

configuration *n* the arrangement or shape of something: *the configuration of the moon's surface*

confine *v* -fined, -fining 1 to enclose within limits 2 *medical* to keep (a woman about to give birth to a baby) in bed: *She was confined on the 20th and gave birth on the 21st*

confinement *n* 1 also **lying-in**— the time during which a woman about to give birth is kept in bed 2 confining or being confined: *confinement to a small room*

confines *n* limits

confirm *v* 1 to support; make certain; give proof of 2 *technical* to admit to full membership of a church — ~ation *n*

confirmed *adj* firmly settled in a particular way of life: *a confirmed bachelor*

confiscate *v* -cated, -cating to seize without payment in order to keep, destroy, give to others, etc.: *The teacher confiscated my radio* — **-cation** *n* — **-catory** *adj*

conflagration *n* *esp. written* a very large fire that destroys much property

conflict¹ *n* 1 a war; struggle 2 the meeting of opposing ideas or beliefs: *conflict between religion and science* 3 a disagreement

conflict² *v* to be in opposition

confluence *n* *esp. written* the flowing together of 2 or more streams

conform *v* to be obedient to, be in agreement with, or act in accordance with established patterns, rules, etc.: *Most people conform to the customs of society* — ~ist *adj*, *n*

conformity also **conformance**— *n* action or behaviour in agreement with established rules, customs, etc.

confound *v* to confuse and surprise

confounded *adj* damned

confront *v* to face boldly or threateningly: *They were confronted by terrorists* — ~ation *n*

confront with *v prep* to cause to meet: *A teacher should not confront his pupils with too much information in one lesson*

Confucius *n* an important Chinese thinker, alive about 2, 500 years ago, who taught that one should be loyal to one's family, friends, and rulers, and treat others as one would like to be treated — **-cian** *adj* — **-cianism** *n*

confuse *v* -fused, -fusing 1 to make more difficult to understand 2 to mix up; mislead: *We tried to confuse the enemy* 3 to fail to tell the difference between: *I'm always confusing salt and sugar* — ~d *adj* — ~-dly *adv* — **-fusing** *adj* — **-fusingly** *adv*

confusion *n* 1 disorder: *The room was in complete confusion* 2 the state of being confused

conga *n* a dance of Latin American origin, in which the dancers form a long winding chain

congeal *v* (of a liquid) to become thick or solid: *The blood congealed*

congenial *adj* *esp. written* pleasant — ~ly *adv*

congenital *adj* *medical* (of diseases) existing at or from one's birth — ~ly *adv*

conger eel *n* a type of large edible eel

congest *v* 1 *medical* (of a blood vessel or part of the body) to become full of liquid 2 to make or become full or blocked — ~ion *n*

conglomerate *n* 1 a rounded mass of various materials gathered together 2 *technical* a rock consisting of small rounded stones held in a rocky mass 3 a large firm that controls the production of goods of varying kinds

conglomeration *n* a collection of many different things

congratulate *v* -lated, -lating 1 to speak to with praise and admiration for a happy event or something successfully done: *We congratulated him on passing the examination* 2 to have pleasure or pride in for something successfully done: *You can congratulate yourself on your performance* — **-lation** *n* — **-latory** *adj*

congregate *v* -gated, -gating to gather together

congregation *n* 1 a group of people gathered together 2 a group of people worshipping in a church — ~al *adj*

congress *n* 1 the elected law-making body of certain countries 2 a formal meeting of representatives of societies, countries, etc., to exchange information and opinions: *a medical congress*

Congress *n* the highest law-making body of the US — ~ional *adj*

congressman (-*fem.* **-woman**)— *n* **-men** a member of a congress, of Congress, or of the House of Representatives

congruent *adj* (of figures in geometry) having the same size and shape: *congruent triangles*

conical *adj* shaped like a cone — ~ally *adv*

conic section *n* *technical* a figure made on the surface of a cone by an imaginary flat surface (PLANE) passing through it

conifer *n* any of various types of mostly evergreen tree which bear cones ☞ PLANT, EVOLUTION — ~ous *adj*

conjecture¹ *n* (the formation of) an idea, opinion, etc., from incomplete information **-tural** *adj*

conjecture² *v* -tured, -turing *esp. written* to form (an opinion) from incomplete information

conjugal also **connubial**— *adj* *esp. written* concerning the relationship between husband and wife

conjugate v -gated, -gating technical 1 to give the various forms of (a verb) that show number, person, tense, etc.: Can you conjugate 'to have'? —compare DECLINE, INFLECT 2 (of a verb) to have various forms to show number, person, tense, etc.: 'To have' conjugates irregularly 3 (of single-celled simple forms of life) to join together with another in conjugation

conjugation n technical 1 a class of verbs which conjugate in the same way —compare DECLENSION, INFLECTION 2 the exchange of nuclear material between 2 single-celled simple forms of life (BACTERIA) just before each cell divides

conjunction n 1 a word such as 'but', 'if', 'because', 'and' that connects parts of sentences, phrases, etc. 2 esp. written a combination 3 technical a situation when the earth, Mercury or Venus, and the Sun, or the earth, the Sun and any planet, are in a straight line —compare OPPOSITION

conjunctiva n -vas or -vae medical a very fine transparent skin that covers and helps to protect the inside surface of the eyelid and the surface of the eye

conjunctivitis n medical a painful disease of the conjunctiva of the eye, with redness and swelling

conjure v -jured, -juring 1 to cause to appear by or as if by magic 2 to do clever tricks which seem magical, esp. by very quick movement of the hands — -er, -or n

conjure up v adv 1 to imagine (something) or to cause to be imagined or remembered 2 to produce as if by magic

conk v sl to strike, esp. on the head, with a heavy blow

conker n esp.spoken the shiny brown nut-like seed of the horse chestnut

conkers n a children's game in which one person swings a conker on a string to try and break his opponent's conker

connect v 1 to join; unite 2 (of trains, buses, etc.) to be so planned that passengers can change to another or from one to the other: This flight connects with the New York one — ~ed adj — ~ion n

connecting rod n a rod that joins 2 moving parts, esp. one connecting the piston to the crankshaft in an internal-combustion engine

conning tower n technical a raised enclosed place on a submarine, which is used as an entrance and to keep watch

connive v -nived, -niving to work together secretly for some wrong or unlawful purpose -vance n

connive at v prep to avoid noticing or reporting (that which one ought to oppose): The policeman connived at the escape

connoisseur n a person with a good understanding of a complex subject: a connoisseur of fine wines

connote v -noted, -noting (of a word) to suggest in addition to the formal meaning —compare DENOTE — -ation n

connubial adj esp. written conjugal

conquer v 1 to take (land) by force 2 to defeat 3 to gain control over (something unfriendly or difficult): Man has yet to conquer the stars — ~or n

conquest n 1 the act of conquering: This land is ours by right of conquest 2 something conquered

conquistador n -dores or -dors Spanish a Spanish conqueror of Mexico and Peru in the 16th century

consanguinity n esp. written relationship by birth

conscience n an inner sense that judges one's actions, and makes one feel guilty, good, evil, etc.

conscientious adj showing or done with great care, attention, or seriousness of purpose: a conscientious worker — ~ly adv — ~ness n

conscientious objector n a person who refuses to serve in the armed forces because of moral or religious beliefs — conscientious objection n

conscious adj 1 able to understand what is happening: He is hurt but still conscious 2 knowing; understanding: John isn't conscious of his bad manners — ~ly adv — ~ness n USAGE In psychology, **conscious** is compared with **subconscious** or **unconscious**: the conscious/subconscious/unconscious mind

conscript¹ n a person made to serve in one of the armed forces by law

conscript² v to make (someone) serve in one of the armed forces by law — ~ion n

consecrate v -crated, -crating to declare or set apart as holy, often in a special ceremony: When was this church consecrated? — -ration n

consecutive adj following in regular or unbroken order: The numbers 4, 5, 6 are consecutive —compare SUCCESSIVE — ~ly adv

consensus n a general agreement; collective opinion

consent¹ v to agree

consent² n agreement

consequence n 1 something that follows from an action or condition 2 esp. written importance: Is it of any consequence to you?

consequent adj esp. written following as a result: The flooding was consequent upon the heavy rain

consequential adj esp. written 1 important: a consequential decision 2 consequent

consequently adv as a result

conservancy n -cies a body of officials appointed to control and protect esp. a river or other watercourse

conservation n 1 the act of conserving; preservation 2 the controlled use of a limited supply

of natural things, to prevent waste or loss — ~ist
n

conservation of energy n technical the principle that the total amount of energy within the universe can never vary

conservation of mass also **conservation of matter**— n technical the principle that the total mass within the universe can never vary

conservatism n 1 the belief that the established order of society should be kept as it is for as long as possible and then changed only slowly 2 dislike of change, esp. sudden change: conservatism in matters of language — -tive adj, n — -tively adv

Conservative adj, n (of, concerning, or being) a member or supporter of a Conservative Party

Conservative Party n any of several political parties, such as one in Britain, that tend to be opposed to great or sudden changes in the established order of society and favour competition as the way to bring industrial wealth

conservatory n -ries 1 a glass enclosed room where delicate plants are grown 2 a school teaching music or acting

conserve¹ v -served, -serving to use carefully without waste; preserve

conserve² n fruit preserved by being cooked in sugar

consider v 1 to think about: I'm considering changing my job 2 to regard as: I consider it a great honour

considerable adj fairly large or great in amount, size, or degree — -bly adv

considerate adj thoughtful of the rights or feelings of others — ~ly adv — ~ness n

consideration n 1 careful thought: We shall give your request careful consideration 2 thoughtful attention to the wishes and feelings of others 3 a reason: A number of considerations led me to refuse

considered adj 1 reached after careful thought: a considered opinion 2 highly regarded: a highly considered general

considering prep, conj, adv when one considers, or takes everything into account: He did poorly considering his age | Her speed was good, considering

consign v 1 to send to a person or place for sale 2 esp. written to give (something or someone) into the care of another: He consigned his soul to the devil

consignee n esp. written the person to whom something is delivered

consignment n 1 the act of consigning 2 a number of goods consigned together 3 **on consignment** sent to a person or shop that pays only for what is sold and returns what is unsold: We usually order goods on consignment

consistency also **consistence**— n -cies 1 the state of always keeping to the same principles: The government's actions lack consistency 2 the degree of firmness or thickness: Mix the butter and sugar to the consistency of thick cream

consistent adj continually keeping to the same principles or course of action; having a regular pattern — ~ly adv

consist of v prep to be made up of: The United Kingdom consists of Great Britain and Northern Ireland

console¹ v -soled, -soling to give comfort or sympathy to in times of disappointment or sadness — -lation n — -latory adj

console² n a radio or television set made to stand on the floor

consolidate v -dated, -dating 1 to make or become strong or firm: to consolidate one's position 2 to combine into fewer or one: Several small businesses consolidated into one large company — -dation n

consols also (esp. written) **consolidated annuities**— n technical interest-bearing British government bonds repayable on demand

consommé n French clear soup made from meat and/or vegetables

consonance n technical a pleasant sounding combination of musical notes —opposite **dissonance**

consonant n 1 any of the speech sounds made by partly or completely stopping the flow of air through the mouth 2 any of the letters of the English alphabet except a, e, i, o, u —compare DIPTHONG, VOWEL

consort n the wife or husband, esp. of a ruler —compare PRINCE CONSORT

consortium n -tiums or -tia technical a combination of a number of companies, banks, etc., for a common purpose

consort with v prep to spend time in the company of (esp. bad people)

conspicuous adj attracting attention: She's very conspicuous in that hat — ~ly adv — ~ness n

conspiracy n -cies a secret plan, or the act of secretly planning, to do something unlawful

conspire v -spired, -spiring 1 to plan together secretly: The criminals conspired to rob a bank 2 (of events) to combine — -rator n — -ratorial adj — -ratorially adv

constable n 1 a policeman of the lowest rank 2 technical (esp. in former times) an important official in a royal or noble household

constabulary n -ries the police force of a particular area or country

constancy n 1 firmness of mind; freedom from change 2 faithfulness: constancy between husband and wife

constant¹ adj 1 unchanging: a constant speed 2 happening all the time: constant argument 3 literature faithful: a constant friend — ~ly adv

constant² n technical something, esp. a number or quantity, that never varies ⟹ PHYSICS

constellation n an apparent group of stars as seen from the Earth, often having a name

consternation n great surprise, shock, and fear

constipate v -pated, -pating to get or cause constipation

constipation n the condition of being unable to empty the bowels frequently enough and/or effectively

constituency n -cies a parliamentary division whose people elect one or a number of people to represent them in a law-making body

constituent[1] n a voter in a constituency

constituent[2] adj being one of the parts that make a whole: *the constituent parts of an atom*

constitute v -tuted, -tuting esp. written to make up: *7 days constitute a week*

constitution n 1 the body of laws and principles which govern a country 2 the general condition of a person's body or mind: *He has a weak constitution* 3 the way in which something is made up 4 constituting

constitutional[1] adj 1 established, limited, or allowed by a constitution 2 of or related to the constitution of a person's body or mind: *a constitutional weakness* — ~ly adv

constitutional[2] n a walk taken for one's health

constrain v to make (someone) do something by force or by strongly persuading: *I felt constrained to do what he told me* — ~t n

constrained adj awkward: *a constrained manner* — ~ly adv

constrict v to make (esp. a blood vessel) narrower or tighter — ~ion n — ~ive adj

construct v 1 to make by putting together or combining parts: *to construct a bridge | a difficult sentence to construct* 2 to draw (a geometrical figure) using suitable instruments — ~ion n ~or n — ~ional adj

constructive adj helping to improve or develop something — ~ly adv — ~ness n

construe v -strued, -struing 1 to place a certain meaning on (a sentence, statement, action, etc.); understand 2 to explain the relationship of (words in a sentence)

consubstantiation n technical the belief that the body and blood of Christ exist together with the bread and wine offered by the priest during the Mass —compare TRANSUBSTANTIATION

consul n 1 a person appointed by a government to protect and help its citizens in a foreign country 2 a chief public official in ancient Rome — ~ar adj — ~ship n

consulate n the official building in which a consul lives or works

consult v to go to for information, advice, etc. — ~ation n — ~ative adj

consultant n 1 a high ranking hospital doctor who has responsibility for the treatment given to many hospital patients and also gives specialist advice to outpatients 2 a person who gives specialist professional advice — -ancy n

consulting adj of or related to advice or a consultant: *a doctor's consulting room*

consume v -sumed, -suming 1 to eat or drink ☞ FOOD 2 to use up 3 (of a fire) to destroy

consumer n a person who buys and uses goods and services ☞FOOD

consummate adj esp. written perfect; skilled: *a consummate musician* — ~ly adv

consummate v -mated, -mating esp. written 1 to make perfect 2 to make (a marriage) complete by having sex — -tion n

consumption n 1 consuming or the amount consumed 2 old use tuberculosis of the lungs

consumptive adj old use of, related to, or suffering from tuberculosis of the lungs — consumptive n

cont. abbrev. for: continued

contact[1] n 1 the condition of meeting, touching or coming together with 2 relationship 3 an electrical part that can be moved to touch or not touch a like part, thus completing or interrupting an electrical circuit

contact[2] v to get in touch with by message, telephone, etc.

contact lens n a very small thin lens which fits closely over the eye to improve sight

contagion n 1 the spreading of a disease by touch 2 a disease spread in such a way

contagious adj 1 (of a disease) that can be spread by touch 2 having a contagious disease 3 tending to spread easily from person to person: *Her laughter's contagious!* —compare INFECTIOUS — ~ly adv — ~ness n

contain v 1 to have within itself: *Beer contains alcohol* 2 to enclose: *How big is the angle contained by these 2 sides?*

container n 1 a box, barrel, bottle, etc., for holding something 2 a very large usu. metal box in which goods are packed for easy transport

containerize, -ise v -ized, -izing technical to use containers for the movement of (goods) — -ization n

contaminate v -nated, -nating to make impure by mixing with dirty or poisonous matter: *The river was contaminated with waste* — -nation n

contd. abbrev. for: continued

contemplate v -plated, -plating 1 to look at quietly and solemnly 2 to think deeply about — -lation n — -lative adj

contemporaneous adj esp. written originating or happening during the same period of time as another — ~ly adv

contemporary[1] adj 1 of or belonging to the same time 2 of or belonging to the present: *contemporary furniture* —compare MODERN

contemporary[2] n -ries a person born or living at the same time as another

contempt n the feeling that someone or something is of a lower rank and undesirable: *I feel contempt for dishonest behaviour* —compare DISDAIN, SCORN — ~ible adj — ~ibly adv

contempt of court n the offence of behaving badly in a court of law, esp. by disobeying a judge's order

contemptuous *adj* feeling or expressing contempt: *She's contemptuous of my humble home* —compare DISDAINFUL, SCORNFUL △ CONTEMPTIBLE — ~ly *adv*

contend *v* 1 to compete; fight 2 to claim: *The man contended that it was not his fault* — -tention *n*

contender *n* (esp. in sports) a person who takes part in a competition, often to win a title or prize

content¹ *adj* satisfied; happy — ~ment *n* — ~ed *adj*

content² *v* to make (a person or oneself) happy or satisfied

content³ *n* happiness; satisfaction

content⁴ *n* 1 the subject matter of a book, paper, etc. 2 the amount of a substance contained in something: *a high food content*

contentious *adj esp. written* 1 tending to argue 2 likely to cause argument — ~ly *adv* — ~ness *n*

contents *n* 1 a table at the front of a book with details of what the book contains 2 that which is contained in an object or book

contest¹ *v esp. written* to compete for; fight (for) — ~ant *n*

contest² *n* 1 a struggle or fight 2 a competition: *a beauty contest*

context *n* 1 the setting of a word, phrase, etc., among the surrounding words, phrases, etc., often to explain its meaning: *Can you tell the meaning of this word from its context?* — ~ual *adj* — ~ually *adv*

contiguous *adj* touching; next (to); having a common border: *England is contiguous to/with Wales* — -guity *n* — ~ly *adv*

continence *n esp. written* the ability to control oneself, esp. one's desires and feelings — -ent *adj*

continent *n* any of the 7 main masses of land on the earth: *Africa is a continent* — ~al *adj*

Continent *n* Europe without the British Isles — ~al *adj*

continental breakfast *n* a light breakfast usu. of bread, butter, jam, and coffee

continental drift *n technical* the very slow movement of the continents across the surface of the earth

continental quilt *n* a duvet

continental shelf *n* a plain under the sea forming the border to a continent, typically ending in a very steep slope to the ocean's depths

contingency *n* -cies a possibility; an unlikely event

contingent¹ *adj* 1 dependent on something uncertain 2 accidental — ~ly *adv*

contingent² *n* a representative group forming part of a large gathering: *Have the Scottish contingent arrived yet?*

continual *adj* repeated; frequent: *He hates these continual arguments* — ~ly *adv*   USAGE Continual is often used of bad things: **continual** *hammering* | *these* **continual** *interruptions.* Continuous is used of things or events that are connected without a break, but may have a beginning and end: *3 days'* **continuous** *flight* | *2 rivers connected to form one* **continuous** *waterway.*

continue *v* -ued, -uing to go or cause to go on: *The fighting continued for a week.* | *The road continues for 5 miles* — -uation *n*

continuity *n* 1 the state of being continuous: *There's no continuity between the parts of his book* 2 the arrangement of the parts of a film, broadcast, etc., in correct uninterrupted order

continuous *adj* continuing without interruption —see CONTINUAL (USAGE) — ~ly *adv*

continuum *n* -uums *or* -ua 1 something which is without parts and the same from beginning to end: *the continuum of time* 2 anything that changes only by regular degrees and keeps a common character from beginning to end: *a continuum from the lowest to the highest forms of life*

contort *v* to twist violently out of shape — ~ion *n*

contortionist *n* a person who twists his body into unnatural positions to amuse

contour¹ *n* 1 the shape of an area: *the contour of the British coast* 2 also **contour line** — an imaginary line drawn on a map to show the areas at or above a certain height above sea level

contour² *adj* related to or following the contours of the land: *contour farming*

contraband *adj, n* (of, concerning, or being) goods which it is unlawful to bring into or send out of a country or to own

contrabass *n* DOUBLE BASS

contraception *n* birth control; the act or practice of preventing sex from resulting in the birth of a child, and/or the methods for so doing

contraceptive *adj, n* (of, concerning, or being) a drug or any object or material used inside or outside the sex organs as a means of preventing an act of sex from resulting in the birth of a child: *contraceptive advice* —see also CAP; CONDOM; INTRAUTERINE DEVICE; PILL; SHEATH

contract¹ *n* 1 a formal agreement, having the force of law, between 2 or more people or groups 2 a signed paper on which the conditions of such an agreement are written 3 *technical* (in the card game bridge) an agreement between partners to try and win a stated number of tricks

contract² *v* 1 to arrange by formal agreement 2 to get (something unwanted): *He contracted a fever* 3 to make or become smaller in size: *Metal contracts as it cools* —opposite **expand**

contract bridge *n* —see BRIDGE

contractile also **contractible** — *adj technical* that can contract or be contracted

contraction *n* 1 contracting 2 the shortened form of a word or words: '*Won't*' *is a contraction of* '*will not*' 3 *technical* a very strong movement of a muscle, esp. of the muscles around the baby inside a woman who is about to give birth

contractor *n* a person or firm that provides materials or labour for building jobs

contract out *v adv* to promise, esp. officially, not to take part

contractual *adj* of, related to, or agreed in a contract: *a contractual duty* — ~**ly** *adv*

contradict *v* 1 to declare to be wrong or untruthful 2 (of a statement, fact, etc.) to be opposite in nature or character to: *Your actions contradict your principles* — ~**ion** *n* — ~**ory** *adj*

contralto *n* -tos a woman alto

contraption *n esp. spoken* a strange-looking machine or apparatus: *Does this contraption work?*

contrapuntal *adj* of, using, or related to musical counterpoint — ~**ly** *adv*

contrariwise *adv* in the opposite manner or direction; conversely: *I like the sun, and, contrariwise, I hate the rain*

contrary[1] *n* -ries the opposite

contrary[2] *adj* difficult to handle or work with; unreasonably keeping to one's own opinions or plans: *Mrs Smith is too contrary to make friends easily* — -**ily** *adv* — -**iness** *n*

contrary[3] *adj* completely different; wholly opposed: *contrary opinions*

contrast[1] *n* 1 the act of contrasting 2 (a) difference or unlikeness, esp. of colour or brightness —compare HARMONY

contrast[2] *v* 1 to compare so that differences are made clear: *The writer contrasts good with evil* 2 to show a difference when compared: *Your actions contrast with your principles*

contravene *V* -vened, -vening to break (a law, rule, custom, etc.) — -**vention** *n*

contribute *v* -uted, -uting 1 to join with others in giving or supplying: *Allan didn't contribute to Jane's present when she left the office* 2 to supply (a written article) to a newspaper, magazine, etc. — -**bution** *n*

contributor *n* a person who contributes

contributory *n* 1 helping to bring about a result: *Your stupidity was a contributory cause of the fire* 2 (of a pension or insurance plan) paid for by workers as well as by their employers

contrite *adj* caused by, feeling, or showing guilt and sorrow — ~**ly** *adv*

contrition *n* sincere sorrow for one's wrong actions and thoughts

contrive *v* -trived, -triving 1 to plan, usu. with skill and deceit 2 to form or make in a clever way: *to contrive a dress from bits and pieces* 3 to cause (something) to happen as planned or in spite of difficulty: *He contrived to escape* — -**vance** *n*

contrived *adj* unnatural and forced: *contrived gaiety*

control[1] *v* -ll- 1 to have power over 2 to have directing influence over; direct; fix the time, amount, degree, or rate of: *The pressure of steam is controlled by this button* 3 to test by compari-

son with a chosen standard: *a controlled experiment* — ~**ler** *n*

control[2] *n* 1 the power to control or influence 2 guidance; the fixing of the time, amount, degree, or rate of an activity; act of controlling 3 *technical* a standard against which a scientific study can be judged

control tower *n* a building at an airport, or construction on an aircraft carrier, which instructs planes when to land and take off

controversy *n* -sies (an) argument about something over which there is much disagreement — -**sial** *adj* — -**sially** *adv*

contuse *v* -tused, -tusing *medical* to bruise — -**sion** *n*

conundrum *n* a question which can only be answered by guessing; riddle

conurbation *n* a number of cities and towns that have spread and joined together to form one network

convalesce *v* -lesced, -lescing to spend time getting well after an illness — ~**nce** *n* — ~**nt** *adj, n*

convection *n* the movement caused by warm gas or liquid rising, and cold gas or liquid sinking: *Warm air rises by convection*

convector *n* a heating apparatus in which air becomes hot by passing over hot surfaces and then moves about an enclosed space by convection

convene *v* -vened, -vening to meet or gather, or call to meet or gather — ~**r, -or** *n*

convenience *n* 1 fitness; suitableness: *We bought this house for its convenience* 2 a suitable time: *Please come at your convenience* 3 an apparatus, machine, service, etc., which gives comfort or advantage to its user 4 personal comfort or advantage 5 PUBLIC CONVENIENCE

convenient *adj* 1 suited to one's needs: *a convenient time* 2 near: *Our house is convenient for the shops* — ~**ly** *adv*

convent *n* a house or set of buildings in which nuns live

convention *n* 1 a formal agreement: *The countries agreed to sign the convention* 2 (an example of) accepted practice, esp. with regard to social behaviour: *It is a convention that men should open doors for ladies* 3 a meeting of a group of people with a shared purpose: *a teachers' convention*

conventional *adj* 1 following accepted practices and customs sometimes too closely 2 (of a weapon) not atomic — ~**ly** *adv*

converge *v* -verged, -verging to come together towards a common point: *The lines seemed to converge* — -**nt** *adj* — -**nce** *n*

conversant *adj* familiar (with someone or something)

conversation *n* (an) informal talk in which people exchange news, feelings, etc. — ~**al** *adj* — ~**ally** *adv* — ~**alist** *n*

converse[1] *v* -versed, -versing to talk informally

converse² *adj* opposite: *I hold the converse opinion* — ~**ly** *adv* — **converse** *n*

convert¹ *v* **1** to persuade a person to accept a religion, political belief, etc. **2** to change to or into another substance or state, or from one use or purpose to another: *Coal can be converted to gas by burning* **3** (in rugby and American football) to kick (a ball) over the bar of the goalposts — **-version** *n*

convert² *n* a person who has been persuaded to accept a religion, political belief, etc.

converter *n* *technical* **1** a furnace in which steel is made according to the **Bessemer process** **2** also **convertor** — an apparatus that changes the form in which information is written so that it can be accepted by a computer

convertible¹ *adj* **1** (of a type of money) that can be freely exchanged for other types of money: *The dollar is convertible* **2** that can be converted: *a convertible bed that changes into a seat* — **-bility** *n*

convertible² *n* a car with a roof that can be folded back

convex *adj* *technical* curved outward, like the outside edge of a circle: *a convex mirror* — opposite **concave** — ~**ity** *n* — ~**ly** *adv*

convey *v* **-veyed, -veying** **1** to take or carry from one place to another: *Wires convey electricity* **2** to make known: *Words convey meaning* — ~**er**, ~**or** *n*

conveyance *n* **1** conveying **2** *law* an official paper by which the right of ownership of a property is given by one person to another **3** *esp. written* a carriage or other vehicle

conveyancing *n* *law* the branch of law concerned with preparing conveyances

convict¹ *v* to give a decision that (someone) is guilty of a crime, esp. in a court of law: *He was convicted of murder*

convict² *n* a person who has been found guilty of a crime and sent to prison, esp. for a long time

conviction *n* **1** the act of convicting **2** an occasion on which one has been convicted — opposite **acquittal** **3** (a) very firm and sincere belief

convince *v* **-vinced, -vincing** to cause to believe or feel certain — compare PERSUADE — **-d** *adj*

convincing *adj* serving to convince: *a convincing speech* — ~**ly** *adv*

convivial *adj* **1** fond of eating, drinking, and company **2** merry: *a convivial party* — ~**ly** *adv* — ~**ity** *n*

Convocation *n* (in certain universities) an organization of graduates that holds regular formal meetings

convoke *v* **-voked, -voking** *esp. written* to call together for a meeting

convolution *n* *esp. written* a fold; twist — **-ted** *adj*

convolvulus *n* any of various types of climbing plants like the bindweed

convoy¹ *v* **-voyed, -voying** (of an armed ship, vehicle, soldiers, etc.) to go with and protect (a group of ships, vehicles, etc.)

convoy² *n* **1** a group of ships or vehicles, esp. if protected by an armed ship, vehicle, etc. **2** a protecting force of armed ships, vehicles, soldiers, etc.

convulse *v* **-vulsed, -vulsing** to shake violently — **-sion** *n* — **-sive** *adj* — **sively** *adv*

cony, coney *n* rabbit fur, esp. when made to look like the fur of some other animal

coo¹ *v* **cooed, cooing** **1** to make the low soft cry of a dove or pigeon, or a sound like this **2** to speak softly and lovingly: *The parents cooed to their baby*

coo² *n* **coos** the low soft cry of a dove or pigeon

cook¹ *n* a person who prepares and cooks food — compare CHEF

cook² *v* to prepare (food) for eating by using heat

cooker *n* **1** an apparatus on or in which food is cooked **2** a fruit intended to be cooked: *These apples are cookers* — compare EATER

cookery *n* the preparation of food

cookie also **cooky** — *n* a biscuit

cool¹ *adj* **1** neither warm nor cold; pleasantly cold **2** calm; unexcited **3** lacking warm feelings; not as friendly as usual — ~**ish** *adj* — ~**ly** *adv* — ~**ness** *n*

cool² *v* to make or become cool — ~**er** *n*

cool³ *n* **1** something neither warm nor cold: *the cool of the evening* **2** *sl* calmness of temper: *Try and keep your cool*

coolant *n* *technical* (a type of) liquid used for cooling

coolie *n* (esp. in Asia) an unskilled worker

coop *n* a cage for small creatures, esp. hens

cooper *n* a person who makes or repairs barrels

cooperate, co-operate *v* **-rated, -rating** to work or act together for a purpose — **-rator** *n*

cooperation, co-op- *n* **1** the act of working together for a purpose **2** willingness to help — **-tive** *adj* — **-tively** *adv*

cooperative, co-op- also **co-op** — *n* a firm, farm, shop, etc., owned and controlled by the people who work in it or use its services

Cooperative, Co-op- also **Co-op** — *n* any of a large chain of British shops (**Cooperative Wholesale Society**) originally intended to provide goods cheaply and share the profits among the people who bought there

co-opt *v* (of the members of an elected group) to choose (someone not elected) as a fellow member

coop up *v adv* to enclose; limit the freedom of

coordinate¹ *adj* **1** equal in importance: *coordinate clauses in a sentence* **2** of or based on coordinates — ~**ly** *adv*

coordinate² *n* *technical* any of an ordered set of numbers and/or letters that give the exact position of a point, as on a map: *These coordinates should show you your position*

coordinate³ v **-nated, -nating** to work or cause to work together, esp. to increase effectiveness: *Let us coordinate our efforts*

coordinates n separate women's garments that can be worn together, esp. in matching colours, such as a shirt and skirt

coordination n **1** coordinating **2** the way in which muscles work together when performing a movement

coot n a water bird with dark grey feathers and a short beak

cop¹ n esp. spoken a policeman

cop² n sl **1 a fair cop** a fair arrest **2 not much cop** worthless

cope v **coped, coping** to deal successfully with something

Copernican system n the idea, put forward by Copernicus (1473–1543), that all the planets travel round the sun —compare PTOLEMAIC SYSTEM

copier n a person or machine that copies

copilot n a pilot who shares in the control of a plane

coping n a protective covering of stone or brick on top of a wall or roof

copious adj plentiful: *copious tears* — ~ly adv

cop-out n sl a failure to take the responsibility of making a difficult decision or of doing what one thinks right

copper¹ n **1** a soft reddish metal that is an element, is easily shaped, and allows heat and electricity to pass through it easily **2** esp. spoken a coin of low value made of this or of bronze **3** a metal vessel, esp. one in which clothes are boiled — ~y adj

copper² n, adj (having) a reddish-brown colour

copper³ n esp. spoken a policeman

copperplate n neat regular curving handwriting, usu. with all the letters of a word joined together

coppersmith n a person skilled at working in copper

coppice also **copse**— n a wood of small trees or bushes

copra n the dried flesh of the coconut, from which oil is pressed for making soap

Coptic Church n a branch of the Christian Church based in Ethiopia and Egypt

copula n technical a verb which joins the subject of a sentence with the complement which describes or defines the subject: *In the sentence 'The house seems big', 'seems' is a copula*

copulate v **-lated, -lating** esp. written to have sexual intercourse — **-lation** n

copy¹ n **1** a thing made to be exactly like another **2** a single example of a magazine, book etc.: *a copy of 'The Times'* **3** technical material ready to be printed

copy² v **-ied, -ying 1** to make a copy of **2** to follow as a pattern: *Jean always copies the way I dress*

copybook n a book containing examples of good handwriting, formerly used in schools

copyboy fem. **copygirl**— n **-boys** a young person who does unskilled jobs in a newspaper office

copycat n esp. spoken a person who regularly and without thought copies other people

copyright n the right in law to be the only producer, seller, or broadcaster of a book, play, film, record, etc., for a fixed period of time

copywriter n a person who writes the words for advertisements

coquetry n **-tries** flirtatious behaviour by a woman

coquette n a flirtatious woman — **coquettish** adj

cor interj sl (an expression showing surprise)

coracle n a small light round boat, built like a wicker basket and covered with animal skins

coral¹ n a white, pink, or reddish substance formed from the bones of sea polyps. It is often used for making jewellery ⊸ EVOLUTION

coral² adj, n (having) a pink or reddish orange colour

cor anglais n **cors anglais** French a double reed woodwind instrument like the oboe, but with a lower note

corbel n technical a piece of stone or wood built out from a wall as a support for a beam or other heavy object

cord n **1** (a length of) thick string or thin rope **2** also **chord**— a part of the body, such as a nerve or number of bones joined together, that is like a length of this in appearance: *the vocal cords* **3** cloth, such as corduroy, with raised lines on the surface △ CHORD

cordial¹ adj warmly friendly — ~ity n — ~ly adv

cordial² n fruit juice which is added to water

cordillera n Spanish a system of mountain ranges

cordon n a line of police, soldiers, military vehicles, ships, etc., placed around an area to protect or enclose it

cordon bleu n **cordon bleus** or **cordons bleus** French a prize given for high quality cooking

cordon off v adv to enclose (an area) with a cordon

cords also **corduroys**— n esp. spoken corduroy trousers

corduroy n thick strong cotton cloth with thin raised lines on it, used esp. for making outer clothing

core¹ n **1** the most important or central part of anything: *an apple core* **2 a** a bar of magnetic metal used in an electric motor **b** a tiny ring-shaped piece of magnetic metal (e.g.ferrite) used in computer memories

core² v **cored, coring** to remove the core from (a fruit) — ~r n

corespondent n law a person charged with adultery with the wife or husband of a person wanting a divorce △ CORRESPONDENT

corgi n **corgis** a small dog with short legs, a long back, and a foxlike head

coriander n a small plant or its dried hot-tasting seeds used to flavour food

Corinthian adj of the most richly ornamented style of ancient Greek architecture —compare DORIC; IONIC

cork[1] n **1** the bark of the cork oak found in Southern Europe and North Africa **2** a round piece of this material (or a substitute) used to seal a bottle

cork[2] v to close (the neck of a bottle or other object) tightly with a cork

corkscrew n a pointed twisted piece of metal with a handle, for drawing corks out of bottles

corm n the thick round underground stem of certain plants, from which the flowers and leaves grow: *a crocus corm*

cormorant n a large black fish-eating seabird with a long neck and a hooked beak

corn[1] n **1** (the seed of) any of various types of grain plants, esp. wheat **2** also **maize, Indian corn** — *esp US & Australian* (the seed of) a type of tall plant grown for its ears of yellow seeds: *sweet corn*

corn[2] v to preserve (meat) in salt or salty water: *corned beef*

corn[3] n a painful area of thick hard skin on the foot, usu. on or near a toe

corncob n the woody central part of an ear of corn

cornea n a strong transparent protective covering on the front outer surface of the eye — ~l adj

cornelian also **carnelian**— n a reddish, reddish-brown, or white stone used in jewellery or ornaments

corner[1] n **1** (the inside or outside of) the point at which 2 lines, surfaces, or edges meet: *the corners of the page* **2** the place where 2 roads or paths meet: *the corner of Smith Street and Beach Road* **3** (in football) a kick taken from the corner of the field: *He scored from a corner*

corner[2] v **1** to force into a difficult or threatening position: *The dog cornered the rat* **2** to gain control of (the buying, selling, or production of goods) **3** to turn a corner: *My car corners well*

cornerstone n **1** a stone set at one of the bottom corners of a building, often put in place at a special ceremony **2** something of first importance

cornet n **1** a small brass musical instrument, played by blowing, like a trumpet but softer sounding **2** also (*esp. US*) **cone**— a thin wafer container, round at one end and pointed at the other, for ice-cream, eaten together with its contents

cornflakes n small flakes of coarsely crushed corn, usu. eaten at breakfast

corn flour n fine white flour made from crushed corn, rice, or other grain, used in cooking to thicken liquids

cornflower n a small wild European plant sometimes grown in gardens for its showy blue, white, or pink flowers

cornice n an ornamental border at the top edge of the front of a building or pillar or round the top inside edges of the walls in a room

Cornish adj of Cornwall or its language ☞ LANGUAGE

cornucopia n a horn-shaped ornamental container overflowing with fruit, flowers, grain, etc., used in art as a sign of plenty

corny adj **-ier, -iest** esp. spoken old-fashioned; said or repeated too often

corolla n technical the part of a flower formed by the petals, usu. brightly coloured to attract insects ☞ FLOWER

corollary n **-ries** esp. written **1** a result **2** a statement that follows from another statement for which proof exists

corona n **-nas** or **-nae** the light seen round the sun when the moon passes directly in front of it

coronary adj medical of or related to either of the blood vessels that supply blood directly to the heart

coronary thrombosis also esp. spoken **coronary**— n **-ses** a medical condition in which there is a blood clot in either blood vessel (ARTERY) of the 2 supplying blood directly to the heart; heart attack

coronation n the ceremony at which a ruler is crowned

coroner n a public official who inquires into a person's death when it is not clearly the result of natural causes

coronet n a small crown worn by princes or noblemen

corporal[1] adj esp. written of, on, or related to the body: *corporal punishment*

corporal[2] n a noncommissioned officer of low rank in the army or British air force

corporate adj **1** of, belonging to, or shared by all the members of a group **2** of, belonging to, or related to a corporation — ~ly adv

corporation n **1** a group of people elected to govern a town **2** a body of people permitted by law to act as a single person, esp. for purposes of business: *John works for a large American chemical corporation*

corporation tax n technical a tax on a firm's profits

corps n **corps 1** a trained army group with special duties: *the medical corps* **2** a branch of the army equal to 2 divisions **3** a group of people united in the same activity: *the diplomatic corps*

corps de ballet n **corps de ballet** French a group of ballet dancers

corpse n a dead body

corpulent adj very fat — **-lence, -lency** n

corpuscle n any of the red or white cells in the blood

corral[1] n **1** (esp. in Western America) an enclosed area where cattle, horses, etc., are kept **2** an enclosed area within a ring of carts for protection against attack

corral² v -ll- 1 to drive (animals) into a corral 2 to arrange (carts) into a corral

correct¹ v 1 to make right; mark the mistakes in 2 to cure of a fault, esp. by punishing: *Mary hates to correct her children* — ~ion *n* — ~ive *adj, n*

correct² *adj* right: *a correct answer* — ~ly *adv* — ~ness *n*

correlate, corelate v -lated, -lating to (show to) have a close shared relationship or causal connection — -tion *n* — -tive *adj*

correspond v 1 to match: *These goods don't correspond with my order* 2 to exchange letters regularly — ~ence *n* — ~ent *adj*

correspondence course *n* an educational course in which information and work are exchanged between the teacher and student by post

correspondent *n* 1 a person with whom another exchanges letters regularly 2 someone employed by a newspaper, radio station, etc., to report news from a distant area: *a war correspondent* △ CORESPONDENT

corresponding *adj* matching: *Rights carry with them corresponding responsibilities* — ~ly *adv*

corridor *n* a passage, esp. enclosed

corrie *n Scots* a steep-sided semicircular hollow, formed by glacial action in the side of a mountain

corrigendum *n* -da *technical* something to be made correct, esp. in a printed book

corroborate v -rated, -rating to support or strengthen (an opinion, belief, etc.) by fresh information — -rator *n* — -rative *adj*

corroboration *n* 1 corroborating 2 information which corroborates an opinion, belief, etc.

corrode v -roded, -roding to make or become worn or destroyed slowly, esp. by chemical action — -rosion *n* — -rosive *adj* — -rosively *adv*

corrugate v -gated, -gating to give or have wavelike folds: *corrugated iron* — -tion *n*

corrupt¹ v to change from good to bad — ~ible *adj* — ~ibility *n*

corrupt² *adj* 1 immoral; wicked 2 dishonest; open to bribery: *a corrupt judge* — ~ly *adv* — ~ness *n*

corruption *n* 1 corrupting 2 dishonesty; immoral behaviour 3 decay; impurity

corsair *n* 1 a pirate from North Africa who robbed ships at sea in former times 2 the ship sailed by a group of such pirates

corset *n* a very tight-fitting undergarment worn, esp. by women, to give shape to the waist and hips — ~ed *adj*

cortege, -tège *n esp. written* a procession of attendants, esp. at a funeral

cortex *n* -tices *technical* 1 the outer covering of an organ, esp. the grey matter covering the brain 2 the part of a plant between the outer skin and the vascular middle

coruscate -cated, -cating v *esp. written* to flash: *a coruscating jewel*

corvette *n technical* a small fast warship which protects other ships from attack, esp. by submarines

cos¹ *conj esp. spoken* because

cos² *abbrev. for:* cosine

cosh *n, v esp. spoken* (to strike with) a short metal pipe or rubber tube, usu. filled with a heavy material

cosignatory -ries— *n esp. written* a person signing together with others: *Britain and Germany were cosignatories of the agreement*

cosine *n technical* a measure of the size of an angle calculated by dividing the length of the side adjacent to it in a right-angled triangle by the length of the hypotenuse ☞ TRIGONOMETRY

cos lettuce also **cos**— *n* a type of lettuce with long leaves

cosmetic¹ *n* a beauty preparation such as a face-cream, body-powder, etc.

cosmetic² *adj* of, related to, or causing increased beauty — ~ian *n*

cosmic *adj* of or related to the whole universe — ~ally *adv*

cosmic dust *n* very small pieces of free matter in space

cosmic ray *n* rays a stream of radiation reaching the earth from outer space

cosmology *n* -gies 1 the study of the origin and arrangement of the universe 2 an explanation of this origin and development

cosmonaut *n* a Soviet astronaut

cosmopolitan¹ *adj* 1 consisting of people from many different parts of the world: *a cosmopolitan crowd* 2 not narrow-minded; showing wide experience 3 *technical* (of an animal or plant) existing in most parts of the world

cosmopolitan² *n* 1 a person who has gained wide experience of the world by travelling 2 a person with wide interests and international opinions, who might feel at home anywhere or nowhere

cosmos *n* the universe considered as an ordered system

cosset v -tt- to pay a great deal of attention to making (a person) comfortable and contented

cost¹ *n* 1 the price of making or producing something 2 the amount paid or asked for goods or services 3 something needed, given, or lost, to obtain something: *He saved his daughters at the cost of his own life*

cost² v cost, costing 1 to have (an amount of money) as a price 2 to cause (loss or disadvantage) to: *Your crime will cost you your life*

cost³ v to calculate the price to be charged for: *The job was costed by the builder at about $150*

co-star¹ *n* a famous actor or actress who appears together with another in a film or television play

co-star² v -rr- to appear as a co-star

costermonger also **coster**— *n* a person who

sells fruit and vegetables from a cart in the street, esp. in London

costly *adj* **-lier, -liest** **1** expensive **2** won at a great loss: *the costliest war in history* — **-liness** *n*

cost of living *n* the cost of buying the goods and services thought necessary to provide the average accepted standard of living: *The cost of living is going up*

cost price *n* the price a shopkeeper pays for an article, as opposed to his selling price

costume *n* **1** the clothes typical of a certain period, country, rank, etc. esp. as worn by an actor or actress **2** *becoming rare* a woman's suit consisting of a matching skirt and short coat — **-mier** *n*

costume jewellery *n* precious-looking jewellery made from cheap materials

cosy¹ *adj* **cosier, cosiest** warm and comfortable: *a cosy little house* — **cosily** *adv* — **cosiness** *n*

cosy² *n* **cosies** a covering for a boiled egg or teapot to keep the contents warm

cot *n* a small bed for a young child, usu. with movable sides so that the child cannot fall out

cotangent *n* *technical* the fraction calculated for an angle by dividing the length of the sides next and opposite to it in a right angled triangle

cottage *n* a small house, esp. in the country

cottage cheese *n* soft white cheese made from sour milk

cottage industry *n* **-tries** an industry in which people work at home with their own tools or machinery

cottage loaf *n* a loaf of bread made of a small round piece stuck on top of a larger one

cottage pie *n* SHEPHERD'S PIE

cotton *n* **1** a tall plant grown in warm areas for the soft white hair that surrounds its seeds **2** this soft white hair used to make thread, cloth, cotton wool, etc. **3** thread or cloth made from this: *a cotton dress*

cotton wool *n* a soft mass of cotton used to clean parts of the body or apply medical liquids

cotyledon *n* *technical* a leaflike part within a seed. It contains food for the growing plant and may protect the stem when it first appears

couch¹ *v* to express in a certain way: *The refusal was couched in friendly language*

couch² *n* **1** a long piece of furniture, usu. with a back and arms, on which more than one person may sit **2** a bed-like piece of furniture on which a person lies to be examined by a doctor

couchette *n* a narrow shelf-like bed on a train which folds up to the wall when not in use

couch grass also **couch**— *n* any of several types of coarse grass that spread by long creeping roots

cougar also **mountain lion, puma**— *n* **-gars** or **-gar** a large powerful brown wild cat from the mountainous areas of North America and South America

cough¹ *v* **1** to push air out from the throat suddenly, with a rough explosive noise, esp.

because of discomfort in the lungs or throat during a cold or other infection **2** to clear from the throat by doing this: *She coughed up the bone* **3** to make a sound like a cough

cough² *n* **1** a condition marked by repeated coughing **2** an act or sound of coughing: *She gave a nervous cough*

cough up *v adv sl* to produce (esp. money or information) unwillingly

could *v* *negative short form* **couldn't** **1** *past tense of* can: *I could run faster then* **2** (used to say that something would or might be possible): *I could come tomorrow if you like* **3** (in requests) would: *Could you tell me the time, please?* **4** should: *You could at least have met me at the station!* **5** might: *I wrote down the number so that I could remember it*

council¹ *n* a group of people appointed or elected to make laws, rules, or decisions or to give advice

council² *adj* of, owned by, or related to a district, borough, or county council

councillor *n* a member of a council △COUNSELLOR — ~**ship** *n*

counsel¹ *n* **1** advice: *Listen to an old man's counsel* **2** *law* a barrister or barristers

counsel² *v* **-ll-** *esp. written* to advise

counsellor *n* an adviser △COUNCILLOR

count¹ *v* **1** to say the numbers in order **2** to name one by one in order to find the whole number in a collection; add up: *Count these apples* **3** to consider: *Count yourself lucky to be alive* **4** to have value or importance: *Skill counts for a lot in this game* — ~**able** *adj*

count² *n* **1** an act of counting; total reached by counting **2** one of a number of crimes of which a person is accused: *found guilty on all counts*

count³ *n* (the title of) a European nobleman with the rank of earl

count down *v adv* to count backwards in seconds to zero, esp. before sending a spacecraft into space — **countdown** *n*

countenance¹ *n* *esp. written* **1** the expression of the face: *a sad countenance* **2** approval: *Father refuses to give countenance to your plans*

countenance² *v* **-nanced, -nancing** to give support or approval to; allow

counter¹ *n* **1** a narrow table or flat surface on which goods are shown or at which people in a shop, bank, etc., are served **2** **under the counter** privately, secretly, and often unlawfully

counter² *n* **1** a person or machine that counts, esp. an electrical apparatus that records the number of times an event happens **2** a small flat object used in games instead of money

counter³ *v* to move or act in opposition to

counter⁴ *adv, adj* (in a manner or direction that is) opposite: *He acted counter to all advice*

counter⁵ *n* **1** something that is opposed **2** (in boxing or fencing) a blow or movement intended to stop and return an attack

counteract *v* to lessen or oppose the effect of by

opposite action: *This drug should counteract the poison* — ~ion *n*

counterattack¹ *n* an attack made to oppose or return an enemy attack

counterattack² *v* to make a counterattack (on) — ~er *n*

counterclockwise *adj, adv* anticlockwise

counterespionage *n* spying to uncover and oppose enemy espionage

counterfeit¹ *v* to copy closely in order to deceive — ~er *n*

counterfeit² *adj* made exactly like something real in order to deceive: *a counterfeit coin*

counterfoil *n* a part of a cheque, money order, etc., kept by the sender as a record

counterintelligence *n* activity intended to keep valuable information from the enemy, to deceive the enemy, to prevent sabotage, or to gather political and military information

countermand *v* to declare ineffective, often by giving a different order

countermeasure also **countermove**— *n* an action to oppose another action or state of affairs: *Government countermeasures against rising prices*

counteroffensive *n* a large-scale attack made to oppose or return an enemy attack

counterpane *n* a bedspread

counterpart *n* a person or thing that serves the same purpose as another

counterpoint *n* **1** the combining of 2 or more tunes to be played together as a single whole **2** a tune added to another in this way

counter-revolution *n* a movement arising from opposition to a revolution or a revolutionary government — ~ary *adj, n*

countersign *v* to sign (a paper already signed by someone else)

countersink¹ *v* **-sank, -sunk, -sinking** *technical* **1** to enlarge (the top of a hole) so that the head of a screw will fit level with the surface **2** to fit (a screw) into such an enlarged hole

countersink² *n* *technical* a tool for countersinking the tops of holes

countertenor *n* a male alto

countess *n* **1** (the title of) the wife of an earl or count **2** a noblewoman who holds the rank of earl or count

countinghouse *n* (esp. in former times) a business office where accounts and money are kept

countless *adj* too many to be counted

count on also **count upon**— *v prep* **1** to depend on; trust **2** to expect; take into account —see RELY ON (USAGE)

count out *v adv* to declare (a boxer who fails to rise from the floor after 10 seconds) to be loser of a fight

countrified *adj* of, like, or belonging to the country or country people; unsophisticated

country *n* **-tries** **1** a nation or state with its land or population ⇨MAP **2** the people of a nation or state: *The country is opposed to war* **3**

land with a special nature: *mining country* **4** the land outside cities or towns; land used for farming or left unused: *a day in the country | a country house* —see FOLK (USAGE)

country dance *n* any of several native English dances for several pairs of dancers arranged in rows or circles

countryman *fem.* **countrywoman**— *n* **-men** **1** a person from one's own country; compatriot **2** a person living in the country

country music also **country and western**— *n* popular music in the style of the southern and western US

country seat *n* the country house of a wealthy landowner

countryside *n* land outside the cities and towns, used for farming or left unused

county *n* **-ties** a large area divided from others for purposes of local government

county borough *n* (until 1973) a large town with the same local government powers as a county

county council *n* a body of people elected to govern a county

county court *n* a local court of law that deals with non-criminal cases —compare CROWN COURT

county town *n* the chief town of a county, where the main local government offices are

coup *n* **1** a clever move or action that obtains the desired result **2** also **coup d'état** —a sudden or violent seizure of state power by a small group

coupé also **coupe**— *n* an enclosed motor vehicle usu. with 2 seats

couple¹ *v* **-pled, -pling** **1** to join together **2** (of animals) to mate

couple² *n* **1** 2 things of the same kind: *a couple of socks* **2** a man and a woman together, esp. a husband and wife **3** *esp. spoken* a few; several: *I'll have a couple of drinks* —compare BRACE, PAIR

couplet *n* 2 lines of poetry, one following the other, that are of equal length and end in the same sound

coupling *n* something that connects 2 things, esp. 2 railway carriages

coupon *n* **1** a ticket that shows the right of the holder to receive some payment, service, etc. **2** a printed form on which goods can be ordered, an enquiry made, a competition entered, etc.

courage *n* **1** the ability to control fear in the face of danger, hardship, pain, misfortune, etc.; bravery **2 have the courage of one's convictions** to be brave enough to do or say what one thinks is right **3 take one's courage in both hands** to gather enough courage to do something one is afraid of

courageous *adj* brave; fearless: *It was courageous of you to save the drowning man* — ~ly *adv* — ~ness *n*

courgette *n* a small green marrow eaten cooked as a vegetable

courier n 1 a messenger, esp. one on urgent or official business 2 someone who goes with and looks after travellers on a tour

course¹ n 1 movement from one point to another; continuous movement in space or time: *During the course of the flight drinks will be served* 2 the path over which something moves: *The ship was blown off course* 3 an area of land or water on which a race is held or certain types of sport played 4 a plan of action 5 a set of lessons on one subject or a group of subjects 6 a set of events of a planned or fixed number, as of medical treatment 7 any of the several parts of a meal 8 **a matter of course** that which one expects to happen 9 **in due course** without too much delay 10 **of course** certainly; naturally; as everyone knows or must agree 11 **run/take its/their course** (of an illness, state of affairs, number of events, etc.) to continue to its natural end 12 **stay the course** to continue something through to the end in spite of difficulties

course² v **coursed, coursing** to flow or move rapidly: *Tears coursed down his cheeks*

coursing n the sport of chasing hares or rabbits with dogs

court¹ n 1 a room or building in which law cases can be heard and judged 2 the judge, law officials, and people attending, gathered together to hear and judge a law case 3 the officials, noblemen, servants, etc., who attend a king or queen 4 an area, or part of an area, specially prepared and marked for various ball games, such as tennis 5 also **courtyard** —an open space wholly or partly enclosed by buildings

court² v 1 to pay attention to a an influential person whose favour one seeks b a woman a man hopes to marry 2 to try to obtain (a desired state): *The teacher courted popularity by giving his pupils very little work* 3 to risk (something bad), often foolishly or without enough thought: *to court danger/defeat*

courteous adj polite and kind — ~ly adv — ~ness n

courtesan n (esp. in former times) a woman who takes payment for sex from noble and socially important people —compare PROSTITUTE

courtesy n -sies 1 polite behaviour; good manners 2 a polite or kind action or expression 3 **by courtesy of** because of the kindness of or permission given by (someone) usu. without payment

courtier n (esp. in former times) a noble who attended at the court of a king or other ruler

courtly adj -lier, -liest suitable for a royal court; worthy of respect: *courtly behaviour* — -liness n

court-martial¹ n **courts-martial** or **court martials** 1 a military court of officers appointed to try people for offences against military law 2 a trial before such a court

court-martial² v -ll- to try in a military court

courtship n 1 the act of courting 2 special behaviour, dancing, or activity, used by animals to attract each other before mating

courtyard n a space enclosed by walls or buildings, next to or within a castle, large house, etc.

cousin n 1 the child of one's uncle or aunt ⟹ FAMILY 2 a person or thing of a closely related type

couture n the business of making and selling fashionable women's clothes — **couturier** n

cove n a small sheltered opening in the coastline; small bay

coven n a gathering of usu. 13 witches

covenant n 1 a formal solemn agreement between 2 or more people or groups 2 a written promise to pay a regular sum of money to a church, charity, etc.

Coventry n **send (someone) to Coventry** (of a group of workers, people, etc.) to refuse to speak to (someone) as a sign of disapproval or as a punishment

cover¹ v 1 to place or spread something upon, over, or in front of (something) 2 to hide; conceal 3 to be or lie on the surface of; spread over: *Dust covered the furniture* 4 to have as a size: *The town covers 5 square miles* 5 to travel (a distance): *I want to cover 100 miles by dark* 6 to watch for possible trouble: *The police are covering all roads out of town* 7 to report the details of as for a newspaper: *I want a reporter to cover the trial* 8 to be enough money for: *Will $10 cover the cost of a new skirt?* 9 to protect as from loss; insure 10 to protect (a person) by aiming a gun at an enemy: *You run out the back while I cover you from the window* 11 to keep a gun aimed at (someone): *The police had the criminal covered* 12 (of a gun, castle, etc.) to command; control: *This fort covers the harbour entrance* 13 to act in place of (someone who is absent): *Will you cover for John today, Jean?* 14 to include; consist of; take into account: *The talk covered the history of medicine*

cover² n 1 anything that protects by covering, esp. a piece of material 2 a lid; top 3 the outer front or back page of a magazine or book 4 a cloth used on a bed to make it warmer: *Do you need some more covers on your bed?* 5 shelter or protection: *The flat land gave the soldiers no cover* 6 insurance against loss, damage, etc. 7 something that hides or keeps something secret: *This business is a cover for unlawful activity* 8 **under separate cover** in a separate envelope

coverage n 1 the amount of protection given by insurance 2 the amount of time and space given by a reporter to a piece of news or event 3 the way in which a piece of news or event is reported

cover charge n a charge for service made by a restaurant

covered wagon n a large horse-drawn vehicle with an arch-shaped cloth-covered top in which settlers crossed North America in the 19th century

cover girl *n* a pretty girl whose picture appears on the cover of a magazine

covering *n* something that covers or hides

covering letter *n* a letter sent with a parcel or another letter

coverlet *n* a bedspread

cover note *n* a receipt for the payment of insurance money which protects one until the policy is ready

cover point *n* *technical* a fielding position or fielder, facing and slightly in front of the batsman in cricket, and just over ⅓ of the way to the edge of the playing area

covert¹ *adj* secret; hidden — ~ly *adv*

covert² *n* a shelter of bushes for animals

covet *v Bible* to envy

covetous *adj* envious — ~ly *adv* — ~ness *n*

cow¹ *n* 1 the fully-grown female form of cattle, elephants, and certain other large animals 2 *offensive sl* a woman —see also SACRED COW

cow² *v* to conquer or bring under control by violence or threats: *The natives were cowed by the army*

coward *n* a person unable to face danger, pain, or hardship because he lacks courage — ~ly *adj* — ~ice *n* — ~liness *n*

cowbell *n* a bell hung from the neck of a cow

cowboy *n* 1 a man, usu. working on horseback, employed to look after cattle, esp. in the western US and Canada 2 *sl* a wild irresponsible fellow

cower *v* to bend low and draw back as from fear, pain, shame, cold etc.: *The dog cowered when its master beat it*

cowhand *n* 1 a person hired to tend cows 2 a cowboy

cowl *n* 1 a loose hood, esp. worn by monks 2 a metal chimney-top covering moved by the wind to point in the direction that allows smoke to escape most easily

cowling *n* a removable metal cover for an aircraft engine ⟶ AEROPLANE

cowpat *n* *polite* a lump of cow dung

cowpox *n* a disease of the cow, which is not serious, but, when given to man, as by vaccination, protects against smallpox

cowrie, cowry *n* -ries a shiny brightly-marked tropical shell

cowshed also **cowhouse**— *n* a building in which cows are milked or sheltered

cowslip *n* a small yellow wild flower of the primrose family

cox¹ also *(esp. written)* **coxswain**— *n* 1 a person who guides a rowing boat, esp. in races 2 the sailor in charge of a ship's boat —compare BOAT-SWAIN

cox² also *(esp. written)* **coxswain**— *v* to guide (a rowing boat), esp. in races

coxcomb *n* 1 a foolish showy man 2 a cockscomb

coy *adj* **coyer, coyest** (esp. of a woman or her behaviour) playfully modest in the presence of others — ~ly *adv* — ~ness *n*

coyote *n* -otes *or* -ote a type of small wolf native to western North America and Mexico

coypu *n* -pus *or* -pu a large South American water rat whose fur is valuable —compare NUTRIA

CP *n* *esp. spoken* Communist Party

crab¹ *n* a type of edible sea animal with a broad roundish flattened shell-covered body and 5 pairs of legs

crab² *v* -bb- *esp. spoken* to complain in a bad-tempered way

crab apple also **crab**— *n* a small sour apple or the wild tree that bears it

crabbed *adj* 1 bad-tempered; sour 2 (of writing) difficult to read because the letters are too close together — ~ly *adv* — ~ness *n*

crab louse also **crab** *n* a type of louse that lives in the hair around the human sexual organs

crabwise also **crabways**— *adv* sideways, esp. awkwardly

crack¹ *v* 1 to make or cause to make a sudden explosive sound: *The whip cracked* 2 to break or cause to break, esp. after a blow, without dividing into separate parts: *The vase cracked when dropped* 3 to break or cause to break open 4 to change or cause to change suddenly or sharply in direction, level, loudness, etc.: *His voice cracked with grief* 5 *esp. spoken* to tell (a joke) in a clever or amusing way 6 to lose control or effectiveness: *Is John about to crack up?* 7 to strike or cause to strike with a sudden blow 8 to discover the secret of: *to crack a code* 9 *esp. spoken* to open for drinking 10 *technical* to separate into simpler compounds: *Oil is cracked by heating under pressure* 11 **cracked up to be** *esp. spoken* believed to be 12 **get cracking** also **get weaving** —*esp. spoken* to get down to work without delay

crack² *n* 1 a loud explosive sound: *a crack of thunder* 2 a narrow space: *The door opened just a crack* 3 a split caused by a sharp blow 4 a sudden sharp blow 5 *esp. spoken* an attempt: *He made a crack at writing* 6 a clever quick forceful joke, reply, or remark 7 a sudden change in the level or loudness of the voice 8 **at the crack of dawn** at the first light of day

crack³ *adj* skilful: *a crack shot*

crack down *v adv* to become more severe: *The government is about to crack down on guerrillas*

cracked *adj* *esp. spoken* (of a person) foolish

cracker *n* 1 a small thin unsweetened biscuit 2 a paper toy which bangs when its ends are pulled, used esp. at Christmas

crackers *adj* *esp. spoken* (of a person) mad

crackle¹ *v* -led, -ling to make or cause to make small sharp sudden repeated sounds: *The fire crackled*

crackle² *n* the noise of repeated small sharp sounds

crackling *n* 1 the hard skin on baked pork 2 crackle

crackpot *adj, n esp. spoken & often humour* (of, belonging to, or being) a person with very strange, foolish, or mad ideas

cradle¹ *n* **1** a small (rocking) bed for a baby **2** the place where something begins: *Greece was the cradle of democracy* **3** any of various frameworks used for supporting or holding something

cradle² *v* -**dled, -dling** to hold gently

craft¹ *n* **1** a job or trade needing skill, esp. with one's hands **2** all the members of a particular trade or profession as a group

craft² *n* **craft** a small boat, aircraft, or spacecraft

craftsman *n* -**men** a highly skilled worker — ~**ship** *n*

crafty *adj* -**ier, -iest** cleverly deceitful — **craftily** *adv* — **craftiness** *n*

crag *n* a high steep rough rock or mass of rocks

craggy *adj* -**gier, -giest** **1** steep and rough; having many crags **2** (esp. of a man's face) rough in appearance; strongly marked

cram *v* -**mm-** **1** to force or press into too small a space: *to cram people into a railway carriage* **2** to prepare hastily for an examination — ~**mer** *n*

cramp¹ *n* severe pain from the sudden tightening of a muscle

cramp² *n* a frame or tool with a movable part which can be screwed tightly in place, used for holding things together

cramp³ *v* **1** to fasten tightly with a cramp **2** to prevent the natural growth or development of

cramped *adj* **1** limited in space **2** (of writing) having badly-formed letters written too closely together

crampon *n* also **climbing iron**— a metal framework with spikes underneath, fastened to the bottom of boots to make climbing easier

cramps also **stomach cramps**— *n* sharp pains in the stomach

cranberry *n* -**ries** a bush or its small red sour-tasting berry

crane¹ *n* **1** a machine for lifting and moving heavy objects ⟹ OIL **2** a type of large tall fish-eating bird with very long legs, beak, and neck

crane² *v* **craned, craning** to stretch out (one's neck) esp. to get a better view

crane fly *n* -**flies** *esp. written* DADDY LONGLEGS

cranium *n* -**niums** or -**nia** *medical* the part of the skull that covers the brain — -**ial** *adj* — -**ially** *adv*

crank¹ *n* **1** an apparatus for changing movement in a straight line into circular movement consisting, in its simplest form, of a handle fixed at right-angles to a rod ⟹ STEAM, CAR **2** *sometimes humour & esp. spoken* a person with very strange, odd, or peculiar ideas

crank² *v* **1** to use a crank to turn (a rod) **2** to use a crank to start (a car)

crankshaft *n* a rod turning, or driven by, a crank ⟹ STEAM, CAR

cranky *adj* -**ier, -iest** *esp. spoken* **1** very strange; peculiar **2** (of a machine or apparatus) in need of repair

cranny *n* -**nies** *esp. humour or literature* a small narrow opening: *a cranny in the wall* —see also NOOKS **and crannies** — -**nied** *adj*

crap¹ *n* *vulgar sl* **1** solid waste matter passed from the bowels or the act of passing this **2** nonsense

crap² *v* -**pp-** *vulgar sl* to pass waste matter from the bowels

crash¹ *v* **1** to have or cause to have a sudden, violent, and noisy accident **2** to move violently and noisily: *The elephant crashed through the forest* **3** to make or cause to make a sudden loud noise **4** (in the world of business and money matters) to fail suddenly **5** *sl* to spend the night in a particular place; sleep — **crash** *adv*

crash² *n* **1** a sudden loud noise **2** a violent vehicle accident **3** a sudden severe business failure

crash³ *adj* marked by a very great effort to reach quickly the desired results: *a crash diet*

crash barrier *n* a strong fence or wall built to keep vehicles and/or people apart where there is a possibility of danger or accident

crash helmet *n* a strong protective head covering for racing car drivers, motorcyclists, etc.

crashing *adj esp. spoken* very great: *a crashing fool*

crash-land *v* (of a plane) to land quickly because of an emergency — **crash landing** *n*

crass *adj* **1** stupid; coarse **2** very great: *crass ignorance* — ~**ly** *adv* — ~**ness** *n*

crate¹ *n* **1** a box or framework for holding fruit, bottles, furniture, etc. **2** *esp. spoken* an old car or plane in great need of repair

crate *v* **crated, crating** to pack into a crate

crater *n* **1** the round bowl-shaped mouth of a volcano **2** a round hole in the ground formed by an explosion **3** a flat-bottomed steep-sided round hole on the surface of the moon and some other heavenly bodies, sometimes with a mountain in the centre

cravat *n* a piece of material loosely folded and worn round the neck by men

crave *v* **craved, craving** to have a very strong desire for — -**ing** *n*

craven *n, adj offensive* (a person) completely lacking courage — **cravenness** *n* — **cravenly** *adv*

crawl¹ *v* **1** to move slowly with the body close to the ground, or on the hands and knees **2** to go very slowly: *The traffic crawled along* **3** to be completely covered by worms, insects, or other such animals or to have a sensation of being covered by them: *That apple is crawling with worms* **4** *esp. spoken* to try to win the favour of someone of higher rank by being too nice to them

crawl² *n* **1** a very slow movement **2** also **Aus-**

tralian crawl — a rapid way of swimming while lying on one's stomach, moving first one arm and then the other over one's head, and kicking the feet up and down

crayfish also **crawfish**— *n* **-fish** *or* **-fishes** a type of small edible shellfish with 4 pairs of walking limbs and a pair of powerful pincers used for seizing food

crayon *n, v* (to draw with) a stick of coloured wax or chalk

craze¹ *v* **crazed, crazing** **1** to make very excited, angry, or mad **2** *technical* to make small fine cracks on the surface of (a cup, plate, etc.)

craze² *n* a very popular fashion, usu. for a very short time

crazy *adj esp. spoken* **-zier, -ziest** **1** mad; foolish **2** very fond (of) or interested (in): *She's crazy about dancing* — **-zily** *adv* — **-ziness** *n*

crazy paving *n* irregular pieces of stone fitted together to make a path

creak *v, n* (to make) the sound of a badly-oiled door when it opens — **creaky** *adj* — **creakily** *adv* — **creakiness** *n*

cream¹ *n* **1** the edible thick fatty slightly yellowish liquid that separates from and rises to the top of milk when left to stand **2** food made of or containing a sweet soft smooth substance, like this **3** a preparation made thick and soft like cream, esp. used for softening and improving the skin or as a medicine: *face cream* **4** the best part of anything: *the cream of society* — **creamy** *adj* — **creaminess** *n*

cream² *adj, n* (having) the yellowish-white colour of cream

cream³ *v* **1** to beat (food) until creamy **2** to prepare (a vegetable, meat, etc.) with cream or a creamy liquid: *creamed potatoes*

cream cheese *n* a soft white smooth cheese made from milk and sometimes cream

cream horn *n* a hollow horn-shaped pipe of sweet pastry baked and filled with cream

cream off *v adv* to remove (the best)

cream of tartar *n* see TARTAR

cream soda *n* a sweet gassy vanilla-flavoured drink

crease¹ *n* **1** a line made on cloth, paper, etc., by crushing, folding, or pressing **2** a line marked on the ground to show special areas or positions in certain games

crease² *v* **creased, creasing** to make a line or lines appear on (a garment, paper, cloth, etc.) by folding, crushing, or pressing: *Don't sit for too long or you'll crease your new dress*

create *v* **1** **-ated, -ating** to cause (something new) to exist; produce (something new): *We've created a beautiful new house from an old ruin* **2** to appoint to a special rank or position: *He was created Prince of Wales* **3** *esp. spoken* to be noisily angry: *Will you stop creating and go to sleep?*

creation *n* **1** the act of creating **2** something produced by man's invention or imagination: *an*

artist's creation **3** the universe, world, and all living things

Creation *n* the story of the earth's origin as told esp. in the Bible

creative *adj* having the ability to produce, or producing, new and original ideas and things: *creative thinking* — ~**ly** *adv* — -**vity**, -~**ness** *n*

creator *n* a person who creates

Creator *n* God

creature *n* **1** an animal of any kind **2** (*used in expressions of feeling*) a person: *She was a poor creature* **3** a strange or terrible being: *creatures from outer space*

creature comforts *n* food, clothes, etc., that increase bodily comfort

crèche *n* *French* a place where babies and young children are cared for by specially-trained people while their mothers work —compare PLAYGROUP, NURSERY

credence *n* acceptance as true; belief

credentials *n* a letter or other written proof of a person's position, trustworthiness, etc.

credibility gap *n* the difference between what someone, esp. a politician, says and what he means or does

credible *adj* deserving or worthy of belief; trustworthy: *He is hardly credible as a politician* △ CREDITABLE — **-ibility** *n* — **-bly** *adv*

credit¹ *n* **1** belief; trust; faith: *This story is gaining credit* **2** public attention; approval: *i got no credit for my work* **3** a cause of honour: *You're a credit to your team* **4** a system of buying goods or services when they are wanted and paying for them later —compare HIRE PURCHASE **5** a period of time during which the full price of an article bought under this system must be paid: *six months' credit* **6** the quality of being likely to repay debts and be honest with money: *His credit is good* **7** (the amount of) money in a person's account, as at a bank —compare DEBIT **8** (esp. in the US) a measure of a student's work, esp. at a university, often equal to one hour of class time a week

credit² *v* to believe

creditable *adj* deserving praise, honour, approval, etc.: *a creditable effort* △ CREDIBLE — **-bly** *adv*

credit account *n* an account with a shop which allows one to take goods at once and pay for them later

credit card *n* a card provided by a business firm allowing the holder to obtain goods and services without payment of cash

credit note *n* a note given by a shop when goods have been returned as faulty, allowing one to buy other goods of the same value

creditor *n* a person or firm to whom money is owed

credit squeeze *n* a period during which the government makes it very difficult to buy or borrow on credit, usu. in an effort to reduce spending and increase saving

credit with v prep **1** to give credit to (someone) for (something) **2** to increase (an account) by (the stated amount of money): *Please credit my account with $10*

credo n **-dos** a statement of beliefs and principles

credulity n too great a willingness to believe, esp. without proof — **-lous** adj — **-lously** adv — **-lousness** n

creed n **1** a short statement of religious belief, esp. the formal statement said at certain church services **2** a system of beliefs or principles

creek n **1** a long narrow body of water reaching from the sea, a lake, etc., into the land **2** US a small narrow stream

creep[1] v **crept, creeping** **1** to move slowly and quietly (with the body close to the ground) **2** to grow along the ground or a surface: *a creeping plant* **3** to have an unpleasant sensation, as of worms, insects, etc., moving over the skin: *His ghost story made my flesh creep*

creep[2] n **1** sl an unpleasant person who tries to win the favour of a person of higher rank, esp. by praising insincerely **2** the slow movement of loose soil, rocks, etc.

creeper n any of various types of plant which climb up trees and walls or grow along the ground

creepers n shoes with thick rubber soles

creep into v prep to begin to happen in: *Mistakes are creeping into your work*

creepy adj **-ier, -iest** esp. spoken causing or feeling an unpleasant sensation of fear — **creepily** adv — **creepiness** n

creepy-crawly n **creepy-crawlies** esp. spoken a creeping insect

cremate v **-mated, -mating** to burn (a dead person) at a special funeral ceremony — **cremation** n

crematorium also **crematory**— n **-iums** or **-ia** a building, usu. surrounded by a pleasant garden, in which dead people are cremated

crème de menthe n French a thick sweet green peppermint-flavoured alcoholic drink

creole adj, n **1** (of, being, or related to) a language which is formed by the combination of a European language with one or more others, and which has become the native language of its speakers —compare PIDGIN **2** (of, being, or related to) a person of mixed European and African blood

creosote n, v **-soted, -soting** (to paint something with) a thick brown oily liquid used for preserving wood and as a disinfectant

crepe, crêpe n French **1** light soft thin cloth, with a finely lined and folded surface **2** also **crepe rubber**— rubber tightly pressed to have a finely lined and folded surface, used esp. for the soles of shoes **3** a small very thin pancake

crepe paper also **crepe**— n thin brightly coloured paper with a finely lined and folded surface, esp. used for making paper chains, streamers, etc.

crept past tense and past part. of CREEP

crepuscular adj literature of, like, or related to the time when day is changing into night or night into day; faint

crescendo[1] n **-dos** **1** a gradual increase of force or loudness, esp. of music —opposite **diminuendo** **2** esp. spoken the point of greatest excitement

crescendo[2] adj, adv gradually increasing in force or loudness

crescent n **1** the curved shape of the moon during its first and last quarters, when it forms less than ½ a circle ☞ MATHEMATICS **2** something shaped like this, esp. a curved row of houses **3** this shape as a sign of the faith and religion of Muslims —compare CROSS

cress n any of several types of very small plants whose leaves are eaten raw

crest n **1** a showy growth of feathers on top of a bird's head **2** the top of something, esp. of a mountain, hill, or wave **3** a special ornamental picture used as a personal mark on letters or envelopes — ~**ed** adj

crestfallen adj disappointed; sad

Cretaceous adj technical of the period of time about 140, 000, 000 to 170, 000, 000 years ago, when chalk-rocks were formed

cretin n **1** medical a person whose development of mind and body has been stopped in early childhood because of a weakness in the thyroid **2** sl a stupid foolish person

crevasse n a deep open crack, esp. in thick ice ☞ GEOGRAPHY

crevice n a narrow crack, esp. in rock

crew[1] n **1** all the people working on a ship, plane, etc. (except the officers) **2** a group of people working together: *a stage crew*

crew[2] v to act as the crew

crew cut n a very closely cut style of hair for men

crib[1] n **1** an open box or wooden framework holding food for animals **2** esp. spoken something copied dishonestly from another's work

crib[2] v **-bb-** esp. spoken to copy dishonestly from someone else

cribbage also (esp. spoken) **crib**— n a card game in which the number of points made by each player is shown by placing very small pieces of wood in holes arranged in rows on a small board

crick n, v (to cause) a painful stiffening of the muscles, esp. in the back or the neck, making movement difficult

cricket[1] n a type of small brown insect, the male of which makes loud short noises by rubbing its leathery wings together ☞ INSECT

cricket[2] n an outdoor game played with a ball, bat, and wickets, by 2 teams of 11 players each — ~**er** n

cried past tense and past part. of CRY

cries 3rd person sing. pres. tense of CRY

crime n **1** an offence which is punishable by law; unlawful activity in general **2** esp. spoken a shame: *It's a crime the way he treats her* —compare SIN

criminal n a person who carries out a crime or crimes — **criminal** adj — ~ly adv

criminology n the scientific study of crime and criminals — **-gist** n

crimp v 1 to press into small regular folds 2 to curl (hair), esp. by using a rod of hot iron

crimplene n trademark a type of man-made material that tends not to become creased when crushed, folded, or pressed

crimson¹ adj, n (having) a deep slightly purplish red colour

crimson² v to become or make crimson

cringe v **cringed, cringing** 1 to bend and move back, esp. from fear or dislike: The slaves cringed from the whip 2 to behave towards a person of higher rank with humbleness and lack of self-respect

crinkle v **-kled, -kling** to make or become creased by crushing or pressing — **crinkle** n — **crinkly** adj

crinoline n a petticoat of stiff material worn in former times usu. containing a light bell-shaped frame

cripple¹ n a person partly or wholly unable to use one or more of his limbs, esp. the legs

cripple² v **-pled, -pling** 1 to hurt or wound in such a way that use of one or more of the limbs is made difficult or impossible 2 esp. spoken to make useless; weaken seriously

crisis n **-ses** 1 the turning point in a serious illness, at which there is a sudden change for better or worse 2 a turning point in the course of anything: a political crisis

crisp¹ adj 1 hard; dry; easily broken 2 firm; fresh: a crisp apple 3 (of style, manners, etc.) quick; clear 4 (of the air, weather, etc.) cold; dry; fresh — ~ly adv — ~ness n

crisp² v to make or become crisp, esp. by cooking or heating — ~y adj — ~iness n

crisp³ also **potato crisp**— n a thin piece of potato cooked in very hot fat, dried, and usu. sold in packets

crisscross n, v (to mark with or form) a pattern of crossing lines — **crisscross** adj, adv

criterion n **-ria** or **-rions** an established rule, standard, or principle, on which a judgment is based

critic n 1 a person skilled in forming and expressing judgments about the good and bad qualities of something, esp. art, music, etc. 2 a person who finds fault with someone or something

critical adj 1 finding fault; judging severely 2 marked by careful attention and judgment: a critical thinker 3 very serious: a critical illness 4 of or related to the work of a critic 5 technical (in science) of, being, or related to a fixed value as of pressure, temperature, etc. at which a substance changes suddenly — ~ly adv

criticism n 1 the act of forming and expressing judgments about the good or bad qualities of anything, esp. artistic work 2 such a judgment

3 unfavourable judgment or opinions; disapproval

criticize, -ise v **-cized, -cizing** 1 to find fault with; judge severely: The teacher criticized my answer 2 to make judgments about the good and bad points of: Would you like to read and criticize my new book?

critique n an article, book, set of remarks, etc., criticizing esp. an idea or a person's philosophy

croak v, n 1 (to make) a deep low noise such as a frog makes 2 (to speak with) a rough voice as if one has a sore throat

crochet v to make, using a **crochet-hook** which forms new stitches by drawing thread through other stitches — **crochet** n

crock n a vessel made from baked clay

crockery n cups, plates, pots, etc., esp. made from baked clay

crocodile n **-diles** or **-dile** 1 any of several types of large reptile that live on land and in lakes and rivers in the hot wet parts of the world, the skin of which is used as leather —compare ALLIGATOR 2 a line of people, esp. schoolchildren, walking in pairs

crocodile tears n tears or other signs of sorrow that are insincere

crocus n a type of small low-growing garden plant with a single purple, yellow, or white flower

croft n (esp. in Scotland) a very small farm

crofter n a person who rents (or sometimes owns) a croft

croissant n French a piece of buttery breadlike pastry, shaped like a crescent

crone n a bent old woman

crony n **-nies** esp. spoken a friend

crook¹ n 1 a long stick or tool with a bent or curved end: a shepherd's crook 2 a bend or curve 3 esp. spoken a thief

crook² v to bend: She crooked her arm to carry the parcel

crooked adj 1 not straight; bent 2 esp. spoken dishonest — ~ly adv — ~ness n

croon v 1 to sing with (too) much feeling 2 to sing gently in a low soft voice

crop¹ n 1 a plant or plant product such as grain, fruit, or vegetables grown or produced by a farmer 2 the amount of such a product produced and gathered in a single season or place: a good crop 3 a baglike part of a bird's throat where food is stored and partly digested 4 also **hunting crop, riding crop**— a short riding whip consisting of a short fold of leather fastened to a handle 5 the handle of a whip 6 a very short haircut

crop² v **-pp-** 1 (of an animal) to bite off and eat the tops of (grass, plants, etc.) 2 to cut (a person's hair or a horse's tail) short 3 to plant with a crop 4 to bear a crop: The beans have cropped well this year

cropper¹ n a plant bearing a crop

cropper² n sl **come a cropper a** to fall heavily **b** to fail completely

crop up v adv esp. spoken to arise, happen, or

appear, unexpectedly: *A difficulty has cropped up at work*

croquet *n* an outdoor game played on grass in which players knock wooden balls through a number of small metal hoops with a long-handled wooden mallet

croquette *n* a small ball of crushed meat, fish, vegetables, etc., covered with beaten egg and/or breadcrumbs, cooked in deep fat

cross¹ *n* **1** an upright post with a shorter bar crossing it near the top **a** on which Christ and others were nailed by their hands and feet and left to die in ancient times **b** which is worn round the neck as a sign of Christian faith **c** which is built on graves or public places to remind people of the dead **2** any of various representations of this, used for ornament, in art, heraldry, etc. **3** an ornament of this shape worn as an honour; a medal, esp. for military bravery **4** this shape as the sign of the Christian faith or religion — compare CRESCENT **5** an example of sorrow or suffering as a test of one's patience or goodness: *Everyone has his own cross to bear* **6** a figure or mark formed by one straight line crossing another, as X **7** an animal or plant that is a mixture of breeds: *a tiglon is a cross between a lion and a tiger* — see also HYBRID **8** a combination of 2 different things **9** an act of crossing the ball in soccer **10 on the cross** diagonally; from corner to corner

cross² *v* **1** to go, pass, or reach across **2** to lie or pass across each other: *Our letters crossed in the post* **3** to place or fold across each other: *Jean sat with her legs crossed* **4** to oppose (someone or his plans, wishes, etc.) **5** to draw a line across **6** to draw 2 lines across (a cheque) to show that it must be paid into a bank account **7** to make a movement of the hand forming a cross on (oneself) as a religious act **8** to cause (an animal or plant) to breed with one of another kind **9** (in soccer) to kick (the ball) across the field towards the centre, esp. towards the goal

cross³ *adj* angry; bad-tempered — ~ly *adv* — ~ness *n*

Cross *n* the cross on which Christ died

crossbar *n* a bar joining 2 upright posts, esp. the bar joining 2 goalposts

crossbenches *n* seats in both houses of Parliament on which members sit who do not belong to the official government or opposition parties — -bencher *n*

crossbow *n* a powerful ancient weapon consisting of a bow fixed crosswise on a grooved stock down which arrows are fired mechanically — compare LONGBOW

crossbreed *v* -bred, -breeding (of an animal or plant) to breed with one of another breed — compare INBREEDING, INTERBREED — **crossbreed** *n* -bred *adj*

crosscheck *v* to find out the correctness of by using a different method

cross-country *n* -tries a race run not on a track but across open country and fields — **cross-country** *adj, adv*

crosscurrent *n* a current as in the sea, a river, etc., moving across the general direction of the main current

cross-examine also **cross-question** — *v* d, ining to question (a witness already questioned by the opposing side in a court of law) to test the answers and information given — **cross-examination** *n* — **cross-examiner** *n*

cross-eyed *adj* having one or both eyes turned in towards the nose

cross-fertilize, -ise *v* -lized, -lizing **1** to cause male sex cells from one plant to unite with those of a female plant **2** to influence with ideas from different areas or fields of study — -lization *n*

crossfire *n* one or more lines of gunfire firing across the direction of movement

cross-grained *adj* **1** (of wood) having the grain running across rather than along; having an irregular grain **2** *esp. spoken* difficult to please; argumentative

cross-hatching *n* lines drawn across part of a diagram to show that it is made of different material, or to produce the effect of shade in a drawing

crossing *n* **1** a journey across the sea **2** a place where 2 lines, tracks, etc., cross **3** a place at which a road, river, etc., may be crossed

crossover *n* an arrangement of lines by which a train may move from one track to another

crossply *adj* (of a motor tyre) made stronger by cords pulled tightly across each other inside the rubber

cross-pollinate *v* -nated, -nating to cross-fertilize — **cross-pollination** *n*

cross-purposes *n* **at cross purposes** with different and opposing purposes in mind

cross-question *v* to cross-examine — ~er *n*

cross-refer *v* to direct from one place in a book to another place in the same book

cross-reference *n* a note directing the reader from one place in a book to another place in the same book: *In this dictionary cross-references are shown in capital letters*

crossroads *n* **crossroads** **1** a place where 2 or more roads cross **2** a point at which an important decision must be taken

cross-section *n* **1** (a drawing of) a surface made by cutting across something, esp. at right angles to its length **2** a typical or representative example of the whole: *a cross-section of British society*

cross-stitch *n* a stitch shaped like an X made by crossing one stitch over another at right angles

cross talk *n* rapid exchange of clever remarks, esp. between 2 comedians

crosswind *n* a wind blowing (nearly) at right angles to the line of flight of a plane, direction of movement of traffic on a road, etc.

crossword also **crossword puzzle**— *n* a game in which words are fitted into a pattern of numbered squares in answer to numbered clues in such a way that words can be read across as well as down when the game is completed

crotch n 1 also **crutch**— the place between the tops of the legs of the human body 2 also **crutch**— the place where the legs of a pair of trousers, undergarment, etc., join

crotchet n technical a musical note, having a quarter of the value of a semibreve ☞ MUSIC

crotchety adj esp. spoken (esp. of someone old) bad-tempered; liking to argue or complain

croton n any of a group of mostly tropical plants. Some of them have beautiful leaves and are grown as house plants

crouch v to lower the body close to the ground by bending the knees and back — **crouch** n

croup[1] n the fleshy part above the back legs of certain animals, esp. the horse ☞ HORSE

croup[2] n medical a disease of the throat, esp. in children, that makes breathing difficult and noisy and causes coughing — **croupy** adj

croupier n a person who collects and pays out money lost and won at a gambling table

crouton n French a small square piece of toasted bread eaten in soup

crow[1] n 1 any of various types of large shiny black birds with a loud hoarse cry 2 **as the crow flies** in a straight line

crow[2] v, n 1 (to make) the loud high cry of a cock 2 (to make) wordless sounds of happiness or pleasure (esp. of a baby)

crowbar n an iron bar with a bent V-shaped end used as a lever

crowd[1] v to fill or come together in large numbers: Shoppers crowded into the store

crowd[2] n 1 a large number of people gathered together 2 a particular social group 3 people in general

crowded adj 1 completely full of people 2 uncomfortably close together — **~ness** n

crown[1] n 1 an ornamental head covering made of gold with jewels in it, worn by a king or queen as a sign of royal power 2 a circle of flowers or leaves worn on the head as a sign of victory, honour, or rank 3 a decoration of this shape used in art, ornaments, heraldry, etc. 4 the governing power of a kingdom that has limited the personal political power of its king or queen: Crown land actually belongs to the state 5 the rank of king or queen 6 the top or highest part of anything, as of the head, hat, mountain, etc. —compare BRIM 7 a British coin worth 25 pence, used in former times as money but now made only on ceremonial occasions to be kept not spent 8 the part of the tooth which can be seen 9 the most perfect point of anything

crown[2] v 1 to give royal power to by solemnly placing a crown on the head of 2 to place a circle of flowers or leaves on someone's head as a sign victory 3 to complete worthily: Success crowned his efforts 4 esp. spoken to hit (someone) on the head

crown colony n -nies a British colony ruled

by a governor appointed by the British government, not elected by the people

crown court n a British law court for judging criminal cases

crown prince n the man who has the lawful right to be king after the death of the present king or ruling queen

crown princess n 1 the woman who has the lawful right to be ruling queen after the death of the present king or ruling queen 2 the wife of a crown prince

crow over v prep to delight in (the defeat or misfortune of someone)

crow's nest n a small box or shelter near the top of a ship's mast from which a man can watch for danger, land, etc.

crucial adj of deciding importance — **~ly** adv

crucible n 1 a vessel in which substances are heated to very high temperatures 2 the hollow part at the bottom of a furnace in which melted metal collects

crucifix n a cross with a figure of Christ on it

crucifixion n the act of crucifying

Crucifixion n the death of Christ on the Cross

crucify v -fied, -fying 1 to kill (someone) by nailing or binding to a cross and leaving to die 2 to be very cruel or unpleasant to esp. by unfair public attack

crude adj 1 in a raw or natural state; untreated: crude oil 2 lacking grace, education, or sensitive feeling: crude behaviour 3 not skilfully made, done, or finished — **~ly** adv

crudity n -ties also **crudeness** — the state or quality of being crude

cruel adj 1 liking to cause pain or suffering; unkind; merciless 2 painful; causing suffering: a cruel wind — **~ly** adv — **~ness** n

cruelty n -ties also **cruelness** — the state or quality of being cruel

cruet n 1 a set of containers for pepper, salt, oil, mustard, vinegar, etc., standing on a specially shaped holder 2 any one of these containers

cruise[1] v cruised, cruising 1 to sail in an unhurried way searching for enemy ships or for pleasure 2 (of a car, plane, etc.) to move at a practical rather than high speed

cruise[2] n a sea voyage for pleasure

cruiser n 1 a large fast warship 2 a cabin cruiser

crumb n 1 a very small piece of dry food, esp. bread or cake 2 a small amount: crumbs of knowledge

crumble[1] v -bled, -bling 1 to break into very small pieces 2 to decay; come to ruin: Her hopes crumbled to nothing

crumble[2] n 1 a cooked dish of sweetened fruit covered with a mixture of flour, fat, and sugar 2 the mixture of flour, fat, and sugar cooked in this dish

crumbly adj -blier, -bliest easily crumbled

crummy adj -mier, -miest sl of poor quality; worthless; unpleasant

crumpet n a small thick round breadlike cake with holes in one side, usu. eaten hot with butter —compare MUFFIN

crumple v -pled, -pling 1 to make or become full of creases by pressing, crushing, etc. 2 esp. spoken to fall down; lose strength: The enemy crumpled under our attacks

crunch¹ v 1 to crush (food) noisily with the teeth 2 to make a crushing noise: The stones crunched under the car tyres — **crunchy** adj

crunch² n 1 a crushing sound 2 esp. spoken a difficult moment at which an important decision must be made: If it comes to the crunch they'll support us

crusade¹ n 1 any of the Christian wars to win back the Holy Land (Palestine) from the Muslims in the 11th, 12th, and 13th centuries 2 a struggle or movement for the defence or advancement of an idea, principle, etc.: a crusade against crime

crusade² v -saded, -sading to take part in a crusade — ~r n

crush¹ v 1 to press with great force so as to break, hurt, or destroy the natural shape or condition 2 to press tightly: The people crushed through the gates 3 to destroy completely, esp. by using force: to crush all opposition 4 to crumple

crush² n 1 uncomfortable pressure caused by a great crowd of people 2 a drink made by crushing the juice from fruit 3 esp. spoken a strong foolish and short-lived liking or love for someone

crust n 1 the hard usu. brown outer surface of baked bread 2 a piece of bread with this on one side 3 the baked pastry on a pie 4 a hard outer covering (as of earth or snow)

crustacean adj, n (of, belonging to, or being) any of a group of animals with a hard outer shell that are closely related to the spiders: Lobsters and crabs are crustaceans ☞ EVOLUTION

crusty adj -ier, -iest 1 having a hard well-baked crust 2 bad-tempered; bad-mannered — **crustily** adv — **crustiness** n

crutch n 1 a stick of wood, metal, or other material, with a piece that fits under the arm, for supporting a person who has difficulty in walking 2 a support like this in shape or use: Religion was her crutch 3 the crotch

crux n the part of a matter that is the most difficult to understand or deal with satisfactorily

cry¹ v cried, crying, 3rd person sing. pres. tense cries 1 to produce tears from the eyes with or without sounds expressing grief, sorrow, sadness, etc. 2 to make loud sounds expressing fear, sadness, or some other feeling: The boy cried out with pain 3 (of certain animals and birds) to make one's natural sound 4 to make known by shouting out —see also **cry** WOLF; CRY OFF; CRY OUT FOR

cry² n cries 1 any loud sound, sometimes expressing fear, pain, etc. 2 a loud call; shout 3 a period of crying 4 a general public demand or complaint: a cry for lower taxes 5 a call to action: a battle cry 6 the natural cry of certain animals or birds 7 **in full cry a** (of a group of dogs) making loud noises as they hunt an animal **b** (of a person) eagerly demanding or attacking

crying adj esp. spoken (esp. of something bad) that demands attention

cry off v adv to fail to fulfil a promise or agreement

cry out for v adv prep to be in great need of (something); demand (something)

crypt n an underground room, esp. under a church

cryptic adj hidden; secret; mysterious: a cryptic message —compare ELLIPTIC — ~**ally** adv

cryptogram n a message or writing in secret letters

cryptography n the study of secret writing and codes — **-pher** n — **-phic** adj — **-phically** adv

crystal n 1 also **rock crystal** —a transparent kind of quartz that looks like ice 2 a shaped piece of this used as an ornament or jewel 3 transparent colourless glass of very high quality 4 a very small regular shape with surfaces in even arrangement, formed naturally by a substance on becoming solid

crystal gazing n the practice of looking steadily into a crystal ball in an attempt to see what is going to happen in the future — **crystal gazer** n

crystalline adj 1 of or like crystal; very clear; transparent 2 made of crystals

crystallize, -ise v -lized, -lizing 1 to form or cause to form crystals: At what temperature does sugar crystallize? 2 to make or become clear, settled, or fixed in form: to crystallize one's ideas 3 to preserve (fruit) by covering the surface with sugar and leaving to harden — **-lization** n

CSE n Certificate of Secondary Education

cu. abbrev. for: cubic

cub n 1 the young of various types of meat-eating wild animals, such as the lion, bear, etc. 2 a member of the cubs 3 a young and inexperienced person, esp. male

cubbyhole n a small enclosed space

cube¹ n 1 a solid object with 6 equal square faces ☞ MATHEMATICS 2 the number made by multiplying a number by its square; a product in which the same number is repeated 3 times: The cube of 3 is 27 $(3 \times 3 \times 3 = 27)$

cube² v cubed, cubing 1 to form a product in which the same number appears 3 times 2 to cut into cubes

cube root n the number which when cubed equals the given number

cubic adj 1 being a measurement of the space that would fit into a cube with edges of the stated length: a cubic inch 2 having the form of a cube

cubicle n a very small enclosed division of a

cub

larger room, as for dressing or undressing at a swimming pool

cubism *n* a 20th century art style in which the subject matter is represented by geometric shapes — **cubist** *n*

cubit *n Bible* an ancient measurement of length equal to the length of the arm between the wrist and the elbow, usu. between 18 and 22 inches (=between 45 & 56 centimetres)

cuboid *n technical* a solid object with 6 faces, of which the opposite faces are parallel congruent rectangles, and the adjacent faces are perpendicular

cub reporter *n* a young inexperienced newspaper reporter

cubs *n* a division of the boy scouts for younger boys

cuckoo¹ *n* **-oos** 1 a type of grey European bird that lays its eggs in other birds' nests 2 the call of this bird

cuckoo² *adj sl* stupid; mad; foolish

cuckoo clock *n* a small wall clock with a wooden bird inside that comes out to tell each hour with the call of a cuckoo

cuckoo-spit *n* the whitish liquid produced on the stems and leaves of plants by a certain insect

cucumber *n* a type of long round vegetable with a dark green skin and very light green watery flesh, usu. eaten raw with cold food or pickled

cud *n* food that has been swallowed and brought up again to the mouth from the first stomach of certain animals, such as the cow, sheep, etc., for further chewing (esp. in the phrase **chew the cud**)

cuddle *v* **-dled, -dling** to hold lovingly and closely in the arms — **cuddle** *n* — **cuddlesome, cuddly** *adj*

cudgel *n, v* **-ll-** (to strike or beat with) a short thick heavy stick or other such object

cue¹ *n* 1 (esp. in a play) a word, phrase, or action serving as a signal for the next person to speak or act: *to miss one's cue* 2 an example of how to behave, what to do, etc.: *Follow my cue*

cue² *n* a long straight wooden rod, slightly thicker at one end than the other, used for pushing the ball in billiards, snooker, etc.

cuff¹ *n* 1 the end of a sleeve 2 **off the cuff** without preparation

cuff² *v* to strike lightly with the open hand — **cuff** *n*

cuff link *n* a buttonlike object that passes through 2 small buttonholes on a shirt cuff to fasten it

cuirass *n* a piece of armour covering the upper half of the body but not the arms

cuisine *n French* a style of cooking

cul-de-sac *n* **cul-de-sacs** *or* **culs-de-sac** a street with only one way in or out

culinary *adj* of, related to, or suitable for the kitchen or cooking

cull¹ *v* 1 to choose from among others: *to cull the prettiest flowers* 2 to take from a group and

kill (a weak or unproductive animal) 3 to search through (a group of animals) and kill the weakest and least productive: *Every year seals are culled because it is said that they eat too much fish*

cull² *n* 1 an act of culling 2 an animal killed because it is weak or unproductive

culminate in *v prep* **-nated, -nating in** to reach the highest point, degree, or development in

culmination *n* the highest point

culottes *n* trousers shaped to look like a skirt

culpable *adj* deserving blame; guilty: *culpable behaviour* — **-bility** *n* — **-bly** *adv*

culprit *n* the person guilty or believed to be guilty of a crime or offence

cult *n* 1 (the group of people believing in) a particular system of religious worship, with its special customs and ceremonies 2 worship of or loyalty to a person, principle, etc.: *a cult of leadership* 3 (the group of people following) a popular fashion or a particular interest

cultivable *adj* that can be cultivated

cultivate *v* **-vated, -vating** 1 to prepare (land) for the growing of crops 2 to plant, grow, and raise (a crop) 3 to improve or develop by careful attention, training, or study: *to cultivate a love of art* 4 to encourage the growth of friendship with or the good will of

cultivated *adj* 1 having or showing good education and manners, sensitivity, etc. 2 (of land) used for growing crops

cultivation *n* 1 the act of cultivating 2 the state or quality of being cultivated

cultivator *n* 1 a person who cultivates 2 a tool or machine for loosening the earth around growing plants, destroying unwanted plants, etc.

culture *n* 1 artistic and other activity of the mind and the works produced by this 2 a state of high development in art and thought existing in a society and represented at various levels in its members: *a man of little culture* 3 the arts, customs, beliefs, and all the other products of human thought made by a people at a particular time 4 development and improvement of the mind or body by education or training 5 the practice of raising animals and growing plants or crops 6 (a group of bacteria produced by) the practice of growing bacteria for scientific or medical use — **-al** *adj* — **-ally** *adv*

cultured *adj* 1 grown or produced by man: *a cultured pearl* 2 having or showing good education, good manners, sensitivity, etc.

culvert *n* a pipe for waste water that passes under a road, railway line, bank of earth, etc.

cumbersome *adj* heavy and awkward to carry, wear, etc.

cumin *n* 1 a type of small plant or it s pleasant-smelling seedlike fruit used for cooking and medicine

cummerbund *n* a broad belt of cloth worn round a man's waist, esp. as part of formal evening dress

cumulative *adj* increasing steadily in amount

by one addition after another: *cumulative interest* — ~ly *adv*

cumulonimbus *n* a type of very thick dark cloud towering as high as 4 miles, that is often accompanied by lightning and heavy rain ☞ CLOUD

cumulus *n* a type of thick white feathery cloud ☞ CLOUD

cuneiform *adj, n* (of, related to, or written in) wedge-shaped letters used in writing by the Babylonians, Assyrians, and other peoples of ancient Mesopotamia

cunning *adj, n* (showing or having) cleverness in deceiving —compare GUILE — ~ly *adv*

cup¹ *n* **1** a small round container, usu. with a handle, from which liquids are drunk **2** also **cupful** — the amount held by one cup **3** a specially shaped ornamental vessel, usu. made of gold or silver, given as a prize in a competition **4** a specially prepared drink of wine or other alcoholic drink: *cider cup*

cup² *v* **-pp-** to form (esp. the hands) into the shape of a cup

cupboard *n* a set of shelves enclosed by doors, where articles may be stored

cupboard love *n* love shown with the intention of gaining something by it

cup cake *n* a small round cake, often covered with chocolate, baked and/or served in a cup-shaped container

cup final *n* (esp. in football) the last match to decide the winning team in a competition — compare CUP-TIE

cupid *n* a beautiful winged boy carrying a bow and arrows, used in art for representing love

cupidity *n* very great desire, esp. for money and property

cupola *n* a small dome forming (part of) a roof

cuppa *n* esp. spoken a cup of tea

cup-tie *n* (esp. in football) a match between 2 teams competing in a competition —compare CUP FINAL

cur *n* a nasty person who likes to quarrel

curate *n* a priest of the lowest rank who helps a parish priest — **-acy** *n*

curator *n* the person in charge of a museum, library, etc. — ~**ship** *n*

curb¹ *n* **1** a length of chain or leather passing under a horse's jaw and fastened to the bit **2** a controlling influence

curb² *v* **1** to control (one's feelings, temper, spending, etc.) **2** *technical* to control (a horse) by pulling the curb

curd *n* the thick soft almost solid substance that separates from milk when it becomes sour, eaten as food or used for making cheese —see also LEMON CURD, WHEY

curdle *v* **-dled, -dling** to form or make into curds —see also BLOODCURDLING

cure¹ *v* **cured, curing** **1** to bring health to (a person) in place of disease or illness, esp. by medical treatment: *This medicine should cure you*

2 to make (a disease, illness, etc.) go away, esp. by medical treatment **3** to remove (something bad): *Government action to cure unemployment* **4** to preserve (food, skin, tobacco, etc.) by drying, hanging in smoke, covering with salt, etc.

cure² *n* **1** a course of medical treatment **2** a drug or medicine that cures an illness, disease, etc.: *a cure for the common cold* **3** something that cures something bad — **-rable** *adj*

curé *n* French a parish priest in France

cure-all *n* something that makes all bad things better

curfew *n* **1** a rule that all people should be indoors by a stated time **2** the time during which people must be indoors according to this rule **3** (in former times) the ringing of a bell to mark the time of night at which lights and fires had to be put out

curia *n* **-iae** **1** (in former times) the king's court of justice **2** the Pope and the officials assisting him, responsible for the organization of the church

curio *n* **-ios** an object, valuable because of its age, rarity, or beauty

curiosity *n* **-ties** **1** the desire to know or learn **2** a strange, interesting, or rare object, custom, etc.

curious *adj* **1** eager to know or learn **2** having or showing too much interest in other people's affairs **3** odd; strange; peculiar: *a curious state of affairs* **4** interesting because rare; unusual — ~ly *adv*

curl¹ *v* **1** to twist into or form a curl or curls: *I'm going to have my hair curled* **2** to move in a curve or spiral: *Smoke curled above the fire*

curl² *n* **1** a small lock of twisted hair **2** something with the shape of the lines on a screw **3** the state of having this shape or being in masses of this type

curler *n* a specially-made round object round which hair is twisted to make it curl

curlew *n* a type of bird with brownish feathers and a long curved beak ☞ BIRD

curling *n* a Scottish winter sport played by sliding flat heavy stones (**curling stones**) over ice towards a mark called the **tee**

curling iron also **curling tong** — *n* a heated instrument used for curling or straightening the hair

curl up *v adv* to lie or lay comfortably with the limbs drawn close

curly *adj* **-ier, -iest** having curls — **curliness** *n*

curmudgeon *n* esp. spoken a bad tempered man, esp. old

currant *n* **1** a small dried seedless grape **2** any of various types of small bushes or the small fruits in bunches on them: *a blackcurrant bush*

currency *n* **-cies** **1** common use; general acceptance **2** the particular type of money in use in a country: *German currency*

current¹ *adj* **1** belonging to the present time:

current fashions **2** commonly accepted: *This word is no longer in current use* — ~ly *adv*

current² *n* **1** a continuously moving mass of liquid or gas, esp. flowing through slower-moving liquid or gas **2** flow of electricity —see also ALTERNATING CURRENT, DIRECT CURRENT ⏃ ELECTRICITY **3** *technical* the rate of flow measured in ampéres **4** a general tendency: *the current of public opinion*

current account *n* a bank account from which money can be taken out at any time by cheque —compare DEPOSIT ACCOUNT, SAVINGS ACCOUNT

curriculum *n* **-la** *or* **-lums** a course of study in a school, college, etc. —see also EXTRACURRICULAR

curriculum vitae also **résumé**— *n* **curricula vitae** *Latin, esp. written* a short written account of one's education and past employment, used esp. when looking for a new job

curry¹ *v* **-ried, -rying** **1** to cook (meat, vegetables, eggs, etc.) in a thick hot-tasting liquid **2** **curry favour** to try and win attention, often by insincere means

curry² *n* **-ries** (a dish of) meat, vegetables, etc., cooked in a thick hot-tasting liquid, usu. eaten with rice

curry powder *n* a mixture of spices crushed into a fine powder, used for making curry

curse¹ *n* **1** a word or sentence asking God, heaven, a spirit, etc., to bring down evil on someone or something **2** the evil called down in this way: *Our tribe is under a curse* **3** a cause of misfortune, evil, etc.: *Foxes can be a curse to farmers* **4** a word or words used in swearing **5** *sl* (a period of) menstruation: *to have the curse*

curse² *v* **cursed, cursing** **1** to call down God's anger, evil, etc., upon (someone) **2** to swear (at)

cursed also **curst**— *adj* **1** hateful: *I hate the cursed fool!* **2** *esp. spoken* annoying: *I wish that cursed dog would be quiet* — ~ly *adv*

cursive *adj* written in a flowing, rounded style with joined letters; in handwriting rather than printing — **ly** *adv*

cursory *adj* (of work, reading, etc.) not thorough; done without attention to details — **-rily** *adv*

curt *adj* rudely short in speech, manner, etc. — ~ly *adv* — ~ness *n*

curtail *v* to cut short; reduce: *to curtail public spending* — ~ment *n*

curtain¹ *n* **1** a piece of hanging cloth that can be drawn to cover a window or door or to divide a room **2** a sheet of heavy material drawn across or lowered in order to conceal or reveal a stage **3** something that covers, hides, etc.: *a curtain of smoke* —see also BAMBOO CURTAIN; IRON CURTAIN

curtain² *v* to provide (a window, house, etc.) with a curtain

curtain call *n* the appearance of actors and actresses at the end of a performance

curtains *n sl* the end: *If your work doesn't improve it will be curtains for you*

curtsy, curtsey *v* **-sied, -sying; -seyed, -seying** (of a woman or girl) to bend the knees and lower the head and shoulders as an act of respect — compare BOW — **curtsy, curtsey** *n*

curvaceous, -cious *adj sl* (of a woman) having a pleasingly well-developed figure — ~ly *adv*

curvature *n* the degree to which something is curved

curve *v* **curved, curving** to bend round with no sharp angles — **curve** *n*

cushion¹ *n* **1** a bag filled with a soft substance on which a person can lie, sit, etc. **2** something like this in shape or purpose: *Hovercrafts ride on a cushion of air*

cushion² *v* **1** to lessen the force of: *Nothing can cushion the blow* **2** to protect from hardship or sudden change: *The princess led a cushioned life* **3** to provide with a cushion or cushions

cushy *adj* **-ier, -iest** *esp. spoken* (of a job, style of life, work, etc.) needing little effort — **cushiness** *n*

cusp *n technical* **1** a pointed end, esp. of a tooth **2** the point formed by 2 curves meeting: *the cusp of a crescent* ⏃ MATHEMATICS

cuss¹ *n sl* **1** a man: *a peculiar old cuss* **2** a curse

cuss² *v sl* to curse

cussed *adj sl* **1** obstinate **2** cursed — ~ly *adv* — ~ness *n*

custard *n* **1** a thick sweet yellow sauce made by mixing custard powder with boiling milk **2** EGG CUSTARD

custard powder *n* a powder of fine flour, colouring, and flavourings

custodian *n* **1** a person in charge of a public building **2** *esp. written* a person with custody — ~ship *n*

custody *n* **1** the act or right of caring for someone, esp. when given by law: *The father was given custody of the children* **2** the state of being cared for or guarded: *The stolen car is now in police custody* **3** detention: *The criminal was taken into custody by the police* — **-dial** *adj*

custom *n* **1** an established social practice **2** regular support given to a shop by its customers **3** the habitual practice of a person: *His custom was to get up early and have a cold bath*

customary *adj* usual: *It is customary to give people gifts on their birthday* — **-rily** *adv*

customer *n* **1** a person who buys from a shop or trader **2** *sl* a person one has to deal with: *an odd customer*

customs *n* **1** taxes paid on goods entering or (less often) leaving a country **2** the government organization to collect these taxes **3** a place where travellers' belongings are searched when leaving or entering a country —compare EXCISE

customs duty *n* **-ties** tax paid on goods entering or (less often) leaving a country

customs union *n* an arrangement between independent states to remove taxes on goods moving between them and to charge broadly equal taxes on goods entering them from elsewhere

cut¹ v cut, cutting 1 to make an opening in, separate, or remove (something) with a sharp edge or instrument: *to cut a cake* 2 to make with a sharp instrument: *to cut a hole* 3 to shorten with a sharp instrument: *Your nails need cutting* 4 to grow (a tooth) 5 to interrupt (a supply of gas, electricity, etc.): *The water was cut for 2 hours yesterday* 6 to make (esp. a public service) smaller, less frequent, etc.: *cutting train services* 7 to remove, so as to improve: *All sex and violence were cut from the picture before it was shown* 8 to hurt the feelings of: *His cruel remark cut me deeply* 9 to be absent on purpose from: *to cut school* 10 to bring down a tree with an axe, saw, etc. 11 to gather in (corn, wheat, etc.) 12 to divide (a pile of playing cards) in 2 before dealing 13 to cross: *The line AC is cut by line PQ at point Z* 14 to make (a ball) spin by striking: *cut the ball to the right* 15 to stop filming: *'Cut!' shouted the director* 16 to walk across rather than round (a corner) 17 to make (a record) 18 **cut and run** *sl* to escape by running —see also CUT ACROSS, CUT BACK, CUT DOWN, CUT IN, CUT OUT, CUT UP

cut² n 1 the result of or something obtained by cutting 2 a reduction: *cuts in government spending* 3 the style in which clothes are made: *I don't like the cut of his new suit* 4 a stroke with a sword, knife, etc. 5 an act of removing a part: *Before this play is broadcast several cuts must be made* 6 a share: *The government takes a 50% cut of oil profits* 7 a quick sharp stroke in cricket, tennis, etc. 8 **a cut above** of higher quality or rank than

cut across v prep 1 to take a shorter way across (a field, corner, etc.) 2 to go beyond or across the limits of: *a new group of members of parliament that cuts across party lines*

cut-and-dried adj 1 settled in advance 2 done according to a standard method

cutback n a planned decrease; reduction

cut back v adv 1 to prune (a plant) close to the stem 2 to reduce in amount: *to cut back on industrial production*

cut down v adv 1 to bring down by cutting 2 to reduce in amount: *to cut down (on) smoking* 3 (of a disease) to kill or make unable to walk

cute adj cuter, cutest delightfully pretty and often small — ~ly adv — ~ness n

cut glass n glass ornamented or shaped by having patterns cut on it

cuticle n an outer hard covering (as of an insect or round the lower edges of the toenails and fingernails)

cut in v adv 1 to interrupt: *Don't cut in while I'm talking* 2 to drive into a space between cars in a dangerous way likely to cause an accident

cutlass n a short slightly curved sword

cutler n a person who makes, sells, or repairs knives or other cutting instruments

cutlery n knives and other cutting instruments, esp. those used when eating

cutlet n 1 a small slice of meat or fish 2 a flat croquette : *a nut cutlet*

cutoff n 1 a fixed limit or stopping point 2 an apparatus for stopping or controlling the flow in a pipe

cutout n 1 a figure cut out of wood or paper 2 something that interrupts or disconnects an electric circuit

cut out v adv 1 to remove, reduce, or make by cutting: *to cut out a dress* 2 to stop: *to cut out smoking* | *Every time I got the car started, the engine cut out*

cut-price adj cheap; reduced

cut-rate adj sold at a price below the standard charge

cutter n 1 a small fast boat belonging to a larger ship, esp. used for moving supplies or passengers 2 an instrument for cutting 3 a worker whose job is cutting cloth, metal, etc.

cutthroat n a murderer; fierce criminal

cutting¹ n 1 a stem, leaf, etc., cut from a plant and put in soil or water to grow into a new plant 2 a piece cut out from a newspaper, magazine, etc. 3 a passage cut through higher land so that a road, railway, etc., can pass

cutting² adj 1 bitter; severe: *the teacher's cutting remarks* 2 (esp. of the wind) uncomfortably strong and cold 3 sharp-edged: *Where's your cutting knife?* — ~ly adv

cutting room n a room where cinema films, tapes, etc. are edited

cuttlefish n cuttlefish— a type of squidlike sea animal with long tentacles that puts out a black inky liquid when attacked

cut up v adv 1 to cut into pieces 2 to cause suffering to: *Jean was really cut up when her husband left her*

cwm n a corrie - see VALLEY (USAGE)

cwt abbrev. for: hundredweight

cyanide n a type of very strong poison

cybernetics n the scientific study of the way in which information is moved about and controlled in machines, the brain, and the nervous system — **-ic** adj — **-ically** adv

cyclamate n any of various man-made sweeteners, used (esp. formerly) instead of sugar

cycle¹ n 1 a number of related events happening in a regularly repeated order: *the cycle of the seasons* ECOLOGY 2 the time needed for this to be completed: *a 50-second cycle* 3 a bicycle or motorcycle

cycle² cycled, cycling to bicycle — **-ist** n

cyclic also **cyclical**— adj happening in cycles — ~ally adv

cyclone n a very violent wind moving very rapidly in a circle round a calm centre —see TYPHOON (USAGE)

cyclopedia n an encyclopedia

cyclops n (in ancient Greek stories) a one-eyed giant

cyclorama n a wall or screen at the back of a stage on which lighting effects, such as moving clouds, may be projected

cygnet *n* a young swan

cylinder *n* 1 a solid figure with parallel sides (a PRISM)and circular ends ◁☞MATHEMATICS 2 an object or container shaped like this, esp. a hollow tube 3 the vessel within which a piston moves in an engine STEAM

cylindrical *adj* shaped like a cylinder — ~ly *adv*

cymbal *n* either of a pair of round thin metal plates struck together to make a loud ringing noise, used in music — ~ist *n*

cynic *n* sometimes offensive a person who thinks that all men act in their own interests, who sees little good in anything, and who shows this by making unkind remarks — ~al *adj* — ~ism *n* — ~ally *adv*

cynosure *n* ESP. WRITTEN a centre of attention △ SINECURE

cypher *n, v* cipher

cypress *n* a type of coniferous tree with dark green leaves, or its hard wood

Cyrillic *adj, n* (of) the alphabet used for Russian, Bulgarian, Mongolian, etc.

cyst *n* an enclosed often liquid-filled growth in or on the body

cystitis *n* a disease of the bladder

cytology *n* the scientific study of cells — -gist *n*

cytoplasm *n* technical the jellylike material inside a living cell but outside its centre (NUCLEUS) — ~ic *adj*

czar *n* (*fem.* **czarina**) a tsar

Czech *adj* of Czechoslovakia

D

D, d D's, d's *or* Ds, ds 1 the 4th letter of the English alphabet 2 the Roman numeral for 500

D (in Western music) a the second note in the row of notes which form the musical scale of C major b the musical key based on this note

d *abbrev. for* (old) penny/pence —see PENNY

dab[1] *v* -bb- 1 to touch lightly or gently: *dab the wound with a wet cloth* 2 to spread with light quick strokes: *dab paint on the fence* — dab *n*

dab[2] *n* dab *or* dabs any of several kinds of flat fish

dab[3] *n sl* a person who is very clever or good at something: *She's a dab at sailing*

dabble *v* -bled , -bling to work at something without serious intentions ~r *n: sometimes offensive*

dabchick *n* a type of small waterbird of the grebe family - compare GREBE

da capo *adj, adv* (in music) (to be played) once again, starting from the beginning

dachshund *n* a type of small dog with short legs, a long body, and long hanging ears

dad also **daddy**— *n* esp.spoken a father

daddy longlegs also (*esp. written*) **crane fly**— *n* daddy longlegs a type of flying insect with long legs

dado *n* -dos a band of different coloured paint round the lower part of a wall of a room

daemon *n* literature (in ancient Greek stories) a being like a spirit, halfway between gods and men △ DEMON — ~ic *adj* — ~ically *adv*

daffodil *n* a type of yellow flower of early spring

daft *adj* esp.spoken silly — ~ly *adv* — ~ness *n*

dagger *n* 1 a short pointed knife used as a weapon 2 also **obelisk**— a sign (+) used in printing to draw attention to something

dahlia *n* any of several types of brightly-coloured big garden flowers

Dail Eireann also (*esp.spoken*) **Dail**—— *n* the lower house of the Irish parliament

daily[1] *adj, adv* (happening, appearing, etc.) once every day

daily[2] *n* -lies 1 a newspaper sold every day except Sunday and perhaps Saturday 2 also **daily help**— esp. spoken a woman servant who comes in to clean a house daily

dainty[1] *n* -ties an especially nice piece of food, usu. small and sweet, like a little cake

dainty[2] *adj* -tier, -tiest 1 small and delicate 2 not easy to please, esp. about food: *a dainty eater* — -tily *adv* — -tiness *n*

daiquiri *n* a type of sweet alcoholic mixed drink (COCKTAIL)

dairy *n* -ies 1 (on a farm) a place where milk is kept and butter and cheese are made 2 a farm where milk, butter, and cheese are produced 3 a shop where milk, butter, etc. are sold — ~ing *n*

dairyman *fem.* **dairymaid**— *n* a person who works in a dairy

dais *n* a raised part of the floor at one end of a room, for important people

daisy *n* -sies a very common type of small wild or garden flower, yellow in the centre and white round it

Dalai Lama also **Grand Lama**— *n* the head of Tibetan Buddhism

dally *v* -lied, -lying to waste time: *Don't dally or we'll be late* — **dalliance** *n*

dally with *v prep* 1 to play with (an idea) 2 to play at a love relationship with (someone)

dalmatian *n* a type of large white dog with black spots

dam[1] *n* the mother of a 4-legged animal — compare SIRE

dam[2] *n* a wall or bank built to keep back water

dam[3] *v* -mm- 1 to build a dam across: *to dam the river* 2 to keep back by means of a dam: *to dam up the water*

damage[1] *n* 1 harm; loss: *The storm caused great damage* 2 sl the price (esp. in the phrase **What's the damage?**)

damage² v -aged, -aging to cause damage to

damages n law money that must be paid for causing damage

damask n, adj 1 (a kind of cloth) ornamented with a special pattern 2 poetic the pink colour of the large sweet-smelling **damask rose**

Dame n (the title of) a woman who has been given a rank of honour equal to that of knight

dame school n old use a small private school for young children, often kept by an old woman

damn¹ v 1 (esp. of God) to send to punishment without end after death 2 to declare to be very bad: The newspapers all damned the play — compare BLESS

damn² also **damnation**— interj sl (an expression of anger)

damnation n damning or being damned: to fear damnation

damning adj that is very strongly against: damning information against them

Damocles n **sword of Damocles** something bad that may happen at any time

damp¹ also **dampness**— n wetness

damp² v to dampen

damp³ adj rather wet: a damp room — ~ly adv

damp course n a layer of material in a wall to prevent wetness from coming up through the bricks

damp down v adv to make (a fire) burn more slowly

dampen v 1 to make or become damp 2 to make (feelings) less happy: Nothing can dampen my spirits on this glorious morning

damper n 1 a metal plate, door, etc., that can be moved to control the amount of air that reaches a fire 2 an influence that makes dull or sad: His sad face put a damper on our party

damsel n 1 old use a young unmarried woman of noble birth 2 pompous a girl

damson n a type of plum tree or its purple fruit

dance¹ v **danced, dancing** 1 to move to music 2 to move quickly up and down: The waves danced in the sunlight — **dancer** n

dance² n 1 an act of dancing 2 (the name of) a set of movements performed to music, usu. including leg movements: The waltz is a beautiful dance 3 a party for dancing: to go to a dance 4 a piece of music for dancing: The band played a slow dance

dandelion n a type of small wild bright-yellow flower

dandle v to move (esp. a baby) up and down in play

dandruff n a common disease in which bits of dead skin form among the hair

dandy n -dies a man who spends too much time and money on his clothing and appearance — **dandified** adj

danger n 1 the possibility of harm: The sign says 'Danger! Falling rocks' 2 a cause of danger:

danger: the dangers of smoking — ~ous adj — ~ously adv

danger money n additional pay for dangerous work

dangle v -gled, - gling to hang or swing loosely: He dangled the keys on his chain

Danish adj of Denmark, its people, or their language ⟶ LANGUAGE

Danish pastry n -tries (a) pastry made from a rich light dough

dank adj unpleasantly wet and usu. cold — ~ness n

dapper adj (esp. of small men) neat in appearance and quick in movements

dappled adj 1 marked with many cloudy roundish spots of a different colour from their background: a dappled horse 2 marked with many spots of sun and shadow: the dappled shade of a tree

dapple-grey n, adj (a horse that is) grey with spots of darker grey

Darby and Joan n any happily married elderly husband and wife

dare¹ v **dared, daring** pres. tense negative short form **daren't** 1 to be brave or rude enough (to): I don't know how you dare to say such things! 2 to be brave enough to face: He dared many dangers 3 to challenge: He dared me to jump

dare² n a statement that someone is not brave enough to do something

daredevil n, adj (a person) who is very brave but not properly careful

daring adj 1 very brave 2 unusual; new: a daring idea 3 shocking: a daring film — ~ly adv — **daring** n

dark¹ adj 1 without light 2 tending towards black 3 evil 4 sad; unfavourable: look on the dark side 5 secret; hidden: He kept his plans dark — ~ly adv — ~ness n

dark² n 1 the absence of light: to see in the dark 2 a dark colour

Dark Ages n the period in European history from about AD 476 (the fall of Rome) to about AD 1000

darken v to make or become dark

dark horse n a competitor who may be successful although not much is known about him

darkroom n a dark room in which photographs can be developed

darling n, adj (a person) who is very much loved

darn¹ v to repair (a hole in cloth or a garment with a hole) by passing threads through and across — **darn** n

darn² n, adj, adv, interj damn

darning n 1 making darns 2 clothes that need to be darned

dart¹ n 1 a small sharp-pointed object to be thrown, shot, etc., as a weapon or in games 2 a quick movement in a direction: He made a dart for the door 3 a fold made to make a garment fit better, and held together by sewing

dart² v 1 to move suddenly and quickly 2 to

throw out suddenly: *He darted an angry look at his enemy*

dartboard *n* a circular board at which darts are thrown

darts *n* any of several games in which darts are thrown at a dartboard

dash¹ *v* 1 to run quickly: *I must dash to catch a train* 2 to strike with great force: *The waves dashed the boat against the rocks* 3 to break by throwing with great force 4 to destroy or ruin (hopes, spirits, etc.): *The angry letter dashed my hopes* 5 damn: *Dash it all*

dash² *n* 1 a sudden quick run 2 (the sound of) liquid striking: *the dash of the waves against the ship* 3 a small amount of something mixed or added: *a dash of pepper* 4 a mark (—) used in writing and printing —compare HYPHEN 5 a long sound used in sending messages by telegraph: *The message consisted of dots and dashes* —compare DOT 6 **cut a dash** to have a strong effect that makes people remember your appearance and style

dashboard *n* an instrument board in a car, where many of the controls are

dashing *adj* having a lot of bravery and style: *a dashing young officer* — ~**ly** *adv*

data *n* facts; information   USAGE This is now coming to be used as a singular noun: *This data is very interesting.* Many people do not like this use of the word.

data bank *n* a collection of data, esp. for a computer

data processing *n* the use of data by computers

date¹ *n* a small brown sweet fruit with a long stone or the palm tree which produces this fruit

date² *n* 1 time shown by the number of the day, the month, and the year 2 a period in history: *This Greek dish is of very early date* 3 an arrangement to meet at a particular time and place 4 **out of date** old fashioned —see also BLIND DATE

date³ *v* **dated, dating** 1 to know the date of: *I can't date that old house exactly* 2 to write the date on: *Please date your letters* 3 to seem no longer in fashion: *This music is beginning to date* — **datable, dateable** *adj*

dated *adj* out of date

dateline *n* a line in a newspaper article that gives its date and place of origin

dative *adj, n* (of or being) the indirect object

daub *v* to cover with something soft and sticky: *to daub the wall with paint*

daughter *n* 1 someone's female child ☞ FAMILY 2 something thought of as a daughter: *French is a daughter language of Latin* — ~**ly** *adj*

daughter-in-law *n* **-s-in-law** the wife of one's son ☞ FAMILY

daunt *v* to cause to lose courage: *The examination questions were rather daunting*

dauphin *n French* the eldest son of the king of France

davit *n* a long curved pole (usu. one of a pair) that hangs or swings out over the side of a ship and is used for lowering and raising boats, goods, etc.

dawdle *v* **-dled, -dling** *esp. spoken* to spend time doing nothing; move very slowly — ~**r** *n*

dawn¹ *v* (of the day, morning, etc.) to begin to grow light

dawn² *n* 1 the time of day when light first appears before the sun rises —compare DUSK, TWILIGHT 2 the beginning or first appearance: *the dawn of civilization*

dawn on *v prep* to become gradually known by (someone): *It dawned on me where I'd seen him before*

day *n* **days** 1 a period of light: *I can see by day, but not by night* 2 a period of 24 hours 3 a period of time: *In my day things were different* 4 a struggle or competition: *We've won the day* 5 **call it a day** to finish working for the day 6 **pass the time of day** to have a short conversation

dayboy *fem.* **daygirl**— *n* **-boys** a pupil who lives at home but goes to a school where some children live —opposite **boarder**

daybreak *n* dawn

daydream *n, v* (to have) a pleasant dreamlike set of thoughts during waking hours — ~**er** *n*

daylight *n* 1 the light of day 2 the 'light' of public knowledge

day nursery *n* **-ries** a place where small children can be left during the day while their parents are working

day of reckoning *n* **days-** a time when the results of mistakes or misdeeds are felt

day release course *n* an educational course attended by workers during the working day

day return *n* a ticket to go and come back again on the same day

dayroom *n* a room for reading, writing, and amusement, used only during the day, esp. in schools, hospitals, etc. —compare COMMON ROOM

day school *n* a school whose pupils attend only during the day on weekdays

day-to-day *adj* 1 taking place during several days one after the other: *life's day-to-day difficulties* 2 planning with little thought for the future: *They lived an aimless day-to-day existence*

daze *v* **dazed, dazing** to make unable to think or feel clearly: *After the accident John was dazed* — **daze** *n* — ~**dly** *adv*

dazzle *v* **-zled, -zling** 1 to make unable to see by throwing a strong light in the eyes 2 to cause wonder to: *She was dazzled by her success* — **dazzle** *n*

DC *abbrev. for:* direct current

D-day *n* 1 6 June 1944, the day on which the Allied forces landed in northern France during World War 2 2 a day on which a planned action is to begin

DDT *n* a type of chemical that kills insects

deacon *fem.* **deaconess**— *n* an officer of various Christian churches, below a priest

dead¹ *adj* 1 no longer alive or without life 2

unable to feel: *It's so cold that my fingers feel dead* **3** not in use: *a dead language* **4** without the necessary power, movement, or activity: *The television's been dead since the storm* **5** very tired **6 a** (of a ball) out of play **b** (of a ball) unable to bounce **c** (of ground where ball games are played) on which the ball does not roll fast **7** (of sounds or colours) dull **8** complete: *a dead stop* — ~**ness** *n*

dead² *n* **in the dead of** in the quietest period of

dead³ *adv* **1** completely: *She stopped dead.* | *dead certain* **2** directly: *dead ahead*

deaden *v* to cause to lose strength: *to deaden the pain*

dead heat *n* a race in which there is no single winner

dead letter *n* a letter that cannot be delivered or returned to the sender: *the dead-letter office*

deadline *n* a date or time before which something must be done

deadlock *n* a disagreement which cannot be settled

deadly¹ *adj* **-lier, -liest** **1** likely to cause death: *a deadly disease* **2** aiming to destroy: *a deadly enemy* **3** highly effective: *a deadly argument against his plan* **4** very great; total: *deadly seriousness* **6** like death in dullness: *a deadly conversation* **7** making it impossible for the spirit or soul to advance further (esp. in the phrase **the seven deadly sins**) —compare VENIAL **sin** — **-liness** *n*

deadly² *adv* **1** suggesting death: *deadly pale* **2** very: *deadly serious*

deadly nightshade *n* a type of poisonous European plant of the potato family with dark purple flowers and black berries

dead man's handle *n* a handle which will bring a vehicle to a stop if not held continually by the driver

deadpan *adj esp. spoken* with no show of feeling, esp. when telling jokes as if they were serious

dead reckoning *n* the mapping of the position of a ship or aircraft without looking at the sun, moon, or stars

dead shot *n* **1** a shot that hits exactly **2** a person who can fire such shots

deadweight *n* the whole weight of something that does not move at all

deaf *adj* **1** unable to hear **2** unwilling to listen: *deaf to all my prayers* — ~**ness** *n*

deaf-aid *n* HEARING AID

deafen *v* to make deaf

deaf mute *n, adj* (a person) who is deaf and cannot speak

deal¹ *n* **1** a quantity or degree: *a great deal of support* **2** the giving out of cards to players in a game

deal² *v* **dealt, dealing** **1** to give as one's share of something: *It's my turn to deal the cards* **2** to strike (in the phrase **deal someone a blow**) —see also DEAL IN, DEAL WITH

deal³ *n* **1** an act of dealing **2** *esp. spoken* treat-

ment received: *a raw deal* **3** an arrangement to the advantage of both sides: *to do a deal*

deal⁴ *n* fir or pine wood

dealer *n* **1** a person who deals cards **2** a person in a business: *a used-car dealer*

deal in *v prep* to buy and sell: *This shop deals in woollen goods*

dealing *n* method of business; manner of behaving: *plain honest dealing*

deal with *v prep* **1** to do business with: *I've dealt with this shop for 20 years* **2** to take action about: *Children are tiring to deal with* **3** to be concerned with: *This book deals with the troubles in Ireland*

dean *n* **1** (in several Christian churches) an officer in charge of several priests or church divisions **2** (in some universities) a person in charge of a division of study or of students

deanery *n* **-ries** **1** the area controlled by a dean **2** the official home of a dean

dear¹ *adj* **1** much loved **2** (used at the beginning of a letter) **3** precious: *Life is dear to him* **4** costly — ~**ness** *n*

dear² *n* a person who is loved

dear³ *interj* (used for expressing surprise, sorrow, etc.): *Oh dear! I've lost my pen*

dearest *n* a much-loved person

dearly *adv* **1** with much good feeling: *I should dearly love to go to Scotland* **2** at a high price: *He paid dearly for his experience*

dearth *n esp. written* a lack

death *n* **1** the end of life **2** the cause of loss of life or destruction: *If you go out you'll catch your death of cold*

deathbed *n* the bed on which someone dies

deathblow *n* **1** a killing blow or shock **2** something that destroys or ends: *His refusal to help us dealt a deathblow to our plans*

death duty *n* **-ties** money that must be paid to a government on land, money, goods, etc., left on the death of the owner

deathless *adj* unforgettable: *deathless fame* — ~**ly** *adv*

death mask *n* a copy of a dead person's face made by pressing soft wax down over the face

death rate *n* the number of people per 1, 000 who die in a particular year in a particular place

death rattle *n* an unusual sound sometimes made by a person near death

death's-head *n* a human skull representing death

death toll *n* the number of people who died in a particular way: *a large death toll from that railway accident*

death trap *n* something that may be very dangerous to life: *a boat that was a death trap*

deathwatch *n* **1** any of various small insects that make a sound like the tick of a clock, esp. in old buildings **2** a period of watching beside a dying person

death wish *n* a conscious or unconscious desire for death

débâcle n French 1 a sudden and disorderly rush of people 2 a sudden failure

debar from v prep -rr- to prevent (someone) from: Until recently, women were debarred from owning land here

debase v **debased, debasing** to lower in value or in the opinion of others: Such unkind action debases you — ~ment n

debate[1] n a meeting in which a question is talked over by people or groups, each expressing a different point of view: a debate in Parliament

debate[2] v **debated, debating** 1 to argue about 2 to consider the arguments for and against: I debated the idea in my mind — -table adj — ~r n

debauch v to lead away from socially approved behaviour — **debauch/debauchery** n

debenture n a written promise by a government or a company to pay a debt and a fixed rate of interest on the debt

debilitate v **-tated, -tating** to make weak: a debilitating disease — **debility** n

debit[1] n a record of money spent or owed — compare CREDIT

debit[2] v to charge in an account: Debit $10 against Mr. Smith

debonair adj charming and well-dressed

debouch v to come out from a narrow place into a broader place

debris n French the remains of something broken or destroyed

debt n 1 something owed: a debt of $10 2 the state of owing: in debt 3 debt of honour a debt that a gentleman will pay although the law does not force him to

debtor n a person who owes money

debut n French 1 a first public appearance: The singer made his debut as Mozart's Don Giovanni 2 a formal entrance into society by a young woman

debutante also (esp. spoken) **deb**— n a woman making her debut

Dec. abbrev. for: December

decade n a period of 10 years

decadence n a fall to a lower or worse level — **-ent** adj — **-ently** adv

decamp v 1 to leave a place where one has camped 2 to leave any place quickly

decant v to pour (liquid) from one container into another — ~er n

decapitate v **-tated, -tating** to cut off the head of — **-tation** n

decathlon n a competition in athletics consisting of 10 separate events

decay v **decayed, decaying** 1 to go or cause to go bad: Sugar can decay the teeth 2 to lose health, power, etc. — **decay** n

decease n esp. written & law death: Upon your decease the house will pass to your wife — ~d adj, n

deceit n 1 dishonesty 2 a deception

deceitful adj dishonest — ~ly adv — ~ness n

deceive v **deceived, deceiving** to cause (someone) to accept as true or good what is false or bad — **deceiver** n

decelerate v **-rated, -rating** to go or cause to go slower —compare ACCELERATE

December n the 12th and last month of the year

decent adj 1 fitting; proper: decent behaviour 2 rather good: quite a decent meal — **decency** n — ~ly adv

decentralize, -ise v **-ized, -izing** to move from one big place to several smaller places — **-ization** n

deception n 1 deceiving or being deceived 2 something that deceives; a trick

deceptive adj misleading — ~ly adv — ~ness n

decibel n technical a measure of the loudness of sound

decide v **decided, deciding** 1 to arrive at an answer or make a choice about: to decide where to go | They decided to fly 2 to bring to a clear end: One blow decided the fight

decided adj 1 very easily seen or understood: a decided turn to the left 2 sure of oneself: a man of very decided opinions △ DECISIVE — ~ly adv

deciduous adj technical of or being a tree whose leaves fall off in winter —opposite **evergreen**; compare CONIFEROUS

decimal[1] adj having to do with the number 10 — ~ly adv

decimal[2] also **decimal fraction**— n a number like .5, .375, .06, etc. —see also DECIMAL NOTATION

decimalize, -ise v **-ized, -izing** to change to a decimal system — **-ization** n

decimal notation n technical a method of representing numbers with a fractional part, and a whole number part: 25.17 in decimal notation = 25+1/10+7/100

decimal place n technical the position of a figure in a row to the right of a decimal point: If you divide 11 by 9 and calculate the division to 4 decimal places, the answer is 1.2222

decimal point n the point dividing the whole number from the fraction part in decimal notation

decimate v **-mated, -mating** to destroy a large part of — **-mation** n USAGE **Decimate** used to mean ' to kill at least 1/10 of'. It now often means ' to kill at least 9/10 of', but many people feel that this use is bad English.

decipher v to discover the meaning of (esp. a code) —compare ENCIPHER

decision n 1 a choice or choosing: Whose decision was it? 2 the quality of being able to make choices with firmness —opposite **indecision**

decisive adj 1 having the quality of deciding: a decisive influence 2 having determination or firmness: a decisive person 3 unquestionable: a *decisive advantage* ⚠ DECIDED — ~ly *adv* — ~ness *n*

deck *n* 1 a floor built across a ship 2 a surface like this, such as the floor of a bus 3 *esp US* a pack of cards

deckchair *n* a folding chair with a long seat of cloth (usu. canvas)

deckhand *n* a man or boy hired to do unskilled work on a ship

deck out *v adv* to make more beautiful or gay: *The street was decked out in flags*

declaim *v* to say loud and clear, with pauses and usu. hand movements to increase the effect — **declamation** *n* — **declamatory** *adj*

declaration *n* 1 the act of declaring: *a declaration of war* 2 something declared: *a written declaration of all the goods you bought abroad*

declare *v* **declared, declaring** 1 to make known publicly or officially: *Jones was declared the winner* 2 to state with great force 3 to make a full statement of (property for which money may be owed to the government): *Have you anything to declare?* 4 (of the captain of a cricket team) to end the innings before all the team are out 5 (in the game of bridge) to say which type of card will be trumps — **declarable** *adj* — **declaratory** *adj*

declared *adj* openly admitted: *a declared enemy of mine* — **declaredly** *adv*

declension *n* (*in grammar*) a class of nouns and/or adjectives which have the same forms —compare CONJUGATION, INFLECTION

declination *n technical* the angle of a compass needle, east or west, from true north: *a declination of 15 degrees*

decline¹ *v* **declined, declining** 1 to slope downwards 2 to move from a better to a worse position: *The old man's health declined rapidly* 3 to refuse, usu. politely 4 (in grammar) to give the different forms of (a noun, pronoun, or adjective) —compare CONJUGATION, INFLECT

decline² *n* a period of deterioration

declutch *v* to step on the clutch of a car

decode *v* **decoded, decoding** to discover the meaning of (a code) —compare ENCODE

decolonize, -ise *v* **-nized, -nizing** to give freedom from colonial rule to — **-nization** *n*

decompose *v* **-posed, -posing** to decay or break up — **-position** *n*

decompress *v* to reduce the pressure of or on — ~ion *n*

decompression chamber *n* a room in which a diver can be brought back gradually to normal atmospheric pressure

decontaminate *v* **-nated, -nating** to remove dangerous impure substances from — **-nation** *n*

décor *n French* the ornamental furnishing and arranging of a place

decorate *v* **-rated, -rating** 1 to provide with something ornamental: *streets decorated with flags* 2 to paint the walls or outside of a house 3 to give (someone) an official mark of honour, such

as a medal — **-ation** *n* USAGE **Decorate** is used of rooms, houses, etc. It is not used of people. **Adorn** is particularly used of people. **Ornament**, **embellish**, and **garnish** cannot be used of people. **Garnish** is used particularly of cooking.

decorative *adj* ornamental — ~ly *adv*

decorator *n* 1 a house painter 2 INTERIOR DECORATOR

decorous *adj* (of appearance or behaviour) correct — ~ly *adv*

decorum *n* decorous behaviour or appearance

decoy¹ *n* **decoys** 1 a figure of a bird used for attracting wild birds within range of guns 2 a trick for getting a person into a dangerous position

decoy² *v* **decoyed, decoying** to deceive (a person) into danger

decrease¹ *v* **decreased, decreasing** to make or become less: *Our sales are decreasing* —opposite **increase**

decrease² *n* 1 decreasing or being decreased 2 the amount by which something decreases

decree¹ *n* 1 an official command or decision (by a king, government, etc.) 2 *esp US* a judgment in a court of law

decree² *v* **decreed, decreeing** to order or bring into being by decree: *They have decreed an end to this fighting*

decree nisi *n* **decrees nisi** *law* (in former times) an order by a court that a divorce should have effect at a certain future time unless a cause is shown why not

decrepit *adj* weak or in bad condition from age or use — ~ude *n*

decry *v* **decried, decrying** to speak ill of

dedicate *v* **-cated, -cating** to set apart for a holy purpose

dedicated *adj* (esp. of people) very interested in or working hard for an idea, purpose, etc. — ~ly *adv*

dedicate to *v prep* 1 to give to a cause, purpose, or action: *The doctor dedicated his life to finding a cure* 2 to declare (a book, performance, etc.) to be in honour of (esp. a person): *He dedicated his first book to his mother*

dedication *n* 1 dedicating or being dedicated 2 the words used in dedicating

deduce *v* **deduced, deducing** 1 to decide (a particular fact) from general principles 2 *bad usage* to infer — **-ducible** *adj* — **-duction** *n* — **-ductive** *adj*

deduct *v* to take away (a part) from a total — ~ible *adj* — ~ion *n*

deed *n* 1 something done on purpose: *good deeds* 2 *law* a paper that proves and records an agreement

deem *v esp. written* to consider: *He would deem it an honour if the minister came to see him*

deep¹ *adj* 1 going far down or in 2 not near the surface 3 wide: *a deep border* 4 going a stated amount in an understood direction: *cars parked 3 deep* 5 difficult to understand or get to know: *deep scientific principles* | *a deep person* 6 mysterious and strange: *a deep dark secret* **7** able to understand things thoroughly: *a deep mind* **8** strong; difficult to change: *deep feelings* **9** (of a colour) strong and full but not bright **10** (of a sound) low — ~**ly** *adv* — ~**ness** *n*

deep² *adv* **1** to a great depth **2** late: *deep into the night*

deepen *v* to make or become deeper: *to deepen the well*

deep freeze *n* a freezer

deep fry *v* **-fried, -frying** to fry (food) totally covered in oil or fat

deep-laid *adj* planned in secret: *deep-laid plans*

deep-rooted also **deeply rooted**— *adj* strongly fixed in one's nature: *a deep-rooted habit*

deep-seated *adj* **1** far below the surface: *a deep-seated illness* **2** deep-rooted

deer *n* **deer** any of several types of grass-eating fast 4-footed animal, of which the males often have wide branching antlers ⇨ MAMMAL

deerstalker *n* a kind of soft hat pointed in front and at the back, with ear-flaps

deface *v* **defaced, defacing** to spoil by writing or making marks on — ~**ment** *n*

de facto *adj, adv Latin* in actual fact, though not perhaps justly —compare DE JURE

defame *v* **defamed, defaming** to damage the good name of (a person or group) — **defamatory** *adj* — **defamation** *n*

default *v* to fail to fulfil a contract, agreement, or duty — **default,** ~**er** *n*

defeat¹ *v* **1** to beat; win a victory over **2** to cause to fail: *It was lack of money that defeated their plan*

defeat² *n* defeating or being defeated —opposite **victory**

defeatism *n* thinking, acting, or talking in a way that shows one expects to be defeated — **-ist** *n*

defecate *v* **-cated, -cating** *esp. written* to pass waste matter from the bowels — **-cation** *n*

defect¹ *n* a fault: *defects in a machine* — ~**ive** *n*

defect² *v* to desert a political party, group, or movement, esp. in order to join an opposing one — ~**or** *n* — ~**ion** *n*

defence *n* **1** defending: *the defence of one's country* **2** means used in defending: *Mountains are a defence against the wind* **3** a speech or arguments defending oneself, esp. in a court of law **4** the lawyers who defend someone in court —compare PROSECUTION **5** the part of a team that tries to defend its own goal — ~**less** *adj*

defend *v* **1** to protect against attack **2** to play at (a position) so as to keep an opponent from winning **3** to show the rightness of, by argument **4** to act as a lawyer for **5** to oppose attack: *He's better at defending than attacking*

defendant *n* a person against whom a charge is brought in court —compare PLAINTIFF

defensible *adj* that can be defended — **-bly** *adv*

defensive *adj* **1** that defends: *defensive weapons* —opposite **offensive** **2** seeming to expect attack: *I wonder why he's so defensive about his wife?* — ~**ly** *adv* — ~**ness** *n*

defer *v* **-rr-** to put off until later — ~**ment** *n*

deference *n* regard for another's wishes, opinions, etc. — **-ential** *adj* — **-entially** *adv*

defer to *v prep* **-rr-** to yield to, esp. in opinion: *defer to more experienced people*

defiance *n* **1** defiant behaviour **2** **in defiance of** in open disregard for

defiant *adj* fearlessly refusing to obey — ~**ly** *adv*

deficiency *n* **-cies** **1** being deficient **2** a lack: *deficiencies in this plan*

deficient *adj* lacking: *food deficient in iron* — ~**ly** *adv*

deficit *n* **1** an amount which is too small: *a deficit of rain* **2** the amount by which money that goes out is more than money that comes in

defile *v* **defiled, defiling** to destroy the pureness of — ~**r** *n* — ~**ment** *n*

define *v* **defined, defining** **1** to give the meaning(s) of (a word or idea) **2** to explain the qualities, nature, etc., of: *to define the position of the government* **3** to show the limits of: *a clearly defined shape outside the window*

definite *adj* **1** having clear limits **2** undoubted: *a definite success* **3** firm and willing to act: *definite behaviour* —compare DEFINITIVE

definite article *n* (*in grammar*) **1** (in English) the word 'the' **2** (in other languages) a word or form with uses or meanings like 'the' —compare INDEFINITE ARTICLE

definitely *adv* **1** in a definite way **2** without doubt: *He is definitely coming*

definition *n* **1** defining **2** an exact statement of the nature of something **3** clearness: *This photograph lacks definition*

definitive *adj* **1** that provides a final decision: *a definitive victory* **2** that cannot be improved: *the definitive life of Byron* —compare DEFINITE, AUTHORITATIVE — ~**ly** *adv*

deflate *v* **deflated, deflating** **1** to make or become smaller by losing air or gas — opposite **inflate** **2** to cause (someone) to feel less important or good: *a deflating remark*

deflation also **disinflation**— *n* **1** deflating or being deflated **2** a decrease in the amount of money, which is meant to produce lower prices —compare INFLATION, REFLATION

deflationary also **disinflationary**— *adj* producing deflation of money

deflect *v* to turn from a straight course: *Mary threw a stone at John but it was deflected away from him by a tree*

deflection *n* **1** a turning aside or off course **2** a movement away from 0 (or the base position) by a measuring pointer or needle

deflower *v* *esp. in literature* to have sex with (someone who has not had sex before)

defoliate *v* **-ated, -ating** to use (a) chemical

substance on plants in order to make their leaves drop off — -**iant** n — -**iation** n

deform v to spoil the form or appearance of — ~**ation** n

deformity n -**ties** **1** being deformed **2** an obvious imperfection or fault

defraud v to deceive so as to get something wrongly

defray v **defrayed, defraying** esp. written to pay: to defray the cost

defrost v **1** to make or become unfrozen **2** to remove ice from — ~**er** n

deft adj effortlessly skilful — ~**ly** adv — ~**ness** n

defunct adj esp. written or law dead

defuse v **defused, defusing** **1** to remove the fuse from **2** to make less dangerous: to defuse a dangerous situation

defy v **defied, defying**, 3rd person sing. pres. tens **defies** **1** to show no fear of nor respect for: to defy the law **2** to dare; challenge: I defy you to give me one good reason **3** to remain unreachable by: It defies description

degenerate[1] adj worse in comparison with a former acceptable state — **degeneracy** n

degenerate[2] n a person of anti-social actions or serious sexual misbehaviour

degenerate[3] v -**rated, -rating** **1** to pass from a higher to a lower type or condition: The road degenerated into a path **2** to fall below a proper condition or standard — -**ration** n — -**rative** adj

degrade v **degraded, degrading** **1** to lower in the opinion of oneself or others: A dishonest action like that will degrade you **2** technical to change from a higher to a lower kind of living matter, or from a compound chemical to a simpler one — **degradation** n

degree n **1** a step or stage in a set rising in order from lowest to highest: getting better by degrees **2** technical any of various measures: Water freezes at 32 degrees Fahrenheit (32°F) or 0 degrees Centigrade (0°C). | an angle of 90 degrees (90°) **3** a title given by a university **4** esp. old usc a rank in society: a lady of high degree

dehorn also **dishorn**— v to remove the horns from (cattle)

dehumanize, -ise v -**ized, -izing** to remove human qualities from — -**ization** n

dehydrate v -**drated, -drating** **1** to remove all the water from **2** to lose water from the body — ~**d** adj — -**dration** n

deice also **de-ice**— v **deiced, deicing** technical to make or stay free of ice

deify v -**fied, -fying** **1** to make a god of **2** to treat as of the highest value: to deify money — **deification** v

deign v sometimes offensive to lower oneself to: Now that she is married to a rich man, she no longer deigns to visit us — compare CONDE-SCEND

deity n -**ties** **1** the rank or real nature of a god **2** a god or goddess **3** a person considered and treated as very good and/or powerful

Deity n God

déjà vu n French the feeling of remembering something when experienced for the first time

dejected adj low-spirited — ~**ly** adv

dejection n lowness of spirits

de jure adj, adv Latin by right; of right — compare DE FACTO

delay[1] n **1** delaying or being delayed **2** an example of being delayed: delays on roads because of heavy traffic

delay[2] v **delayed, delaying** **1** to put off until later **2** to make late **3** to act slowly

delectable adj delightful — -**bly** adv

delectation n delight; pleasure; amusement

delegate[1] n a person acting for others

delegate[2] v -**gated, -gating** **1** to give (part of one's power, rights, etc.) for a certain time: I have delegated my command to Captain Roberts **2** to appoint as one's representative

delegation n **1** delegating or being delegated **2** a group of delegates

delete v **deleted, deleting** to cut out (esp. something written): Delete his name from the list — -**tion** n

deleterious adj esp. written harmful — ~**ly** adv

delft also **delf** , **delftware**— n a kind of pottery with bright, often blue, ornamentation, first made in Delft, Holland

deliberate[1] adj **1** carefully planned: taking deliberate action **2** on purpose: That shooting was not accidental, but deliberate **3** (of speech, thought, or movement) slow; careful — ~**ly** adv — ~**ness** n

deliberate[2] v -**rated, -rating** to consider (difficult questions) carefully, often in meetings with other people — -**ative** adj

deliberation n **1** deliberating **2** being careful and unhurried in speech, thought, or movement

delicacy n -**cies** **1** being delicate **2** something good to eat but rare or costly

delicate adj **1** needing careful handling: a delicate piece of china **2** needing tact: a delicate subject **3** easily yielding to illness: a delicate child **4** very pleasing but not strong: delicate colours —see THIN (USAGE) — ~**ly** adv

delicatessen n a shop that sells delicacies, esp. those ready to eat when sold

delicious adj pleasing; delightful — ~**ly** adv — ~**ness** n

delight[1] n **1** a high degree of pleasure **2** something that gives great pleasure

delight[2] v **1** to give great pleasure **2** to take great pleasure in doing something: She delights in cooking lovely meals

delightful adj highly pleasing — ~**ly** adv

delineate v -**ated, -ating** **1** to draw **2** to describe in detail — -**ation** n

delinquency n -**cies** **1** being delinquent **2** behaviour not in accordance with social standards

or with the law —see also JUVENILE DELIN-
QUENCY

delinquent¹ *n* a person who is delinquent

delinquent² *adj* having a tendency to break the law or to do socially unacceptable things

delirium *n* 1 an excited dreamy state in serious illness 2 a very excited state: *a delirium of joy* — **-rious** *adj* — **-riously** *adv*

delirium tremens *n esp. written* d t's

deliver *v* 1 to set free 2 to hand over 3 to help in the birth of 4 to say; read aloud 5 to send (something aimed or guided) to the intended place: *deliver a blow*

deliverance *n* freeing or being freed from danger or bad conditions — **-er** *n*

delivery *n* **-ies** 1 *esp. written* deliverance 2 handing over or being handed over: *The next postal delivery is at 2 o'clock* 3 the birth of a child 4 the act of speaking in public or throwing a ball in a game: *a good delivery*

delivery man *n* **-men** *esp. US* a man who delivers goods to customers, usu. locally

dell *n* a small wooded grassy valley

delouse *v* **deloused, delousing** to remove lice from

Delphic also **Delphian**— *adj* of the ancient Greek city of Delphi or its famous oracle

delphinium also **larkspur**— *n* any of a large group of upright branching plants related to the buttercup or the flower of this plant

delta *n* 1 the 4th letter of the Greek alphabet (Δ δ) 2 a piece of low land shaped like a Δ where a river joins the sea ⟲ GEOGRAPHY

delta wing *n* an aircraft wing or pair of wings with a shape like a Δ

delude *v* **deluded, deluding** to mislead or trick

deluge¹ *n* 1 a great flood 2 very heavy rain

deluge² *v* **deluged, deluging** 1 to cover with a great flood 2 to pour out a great flood of things over (someone): *The minister was deluged with questions*

delusion *n* 1 deluding or being deluded 2 a false belief —see ILLUSION (USAGE) — **-sive** *adj*

de luxe *adj French* of especially good quality

delve *v* **delved, delving** to search deeply

demagogue *n offensive* a leader who tries to gain power by appealing to feelings rather than by argument — ~**ry** *n* — **-gogic** *adj* — **-ically** *adv*

demand¹ *n* 1 a claim 2 the desire for goods or services: *Oil is in great demand these days*

demand² *v* 1 to claim as if by right: *I demand my money!* 2 to need urgently: *This work demands your attention*

demanding *adj* needing a lot of attention: *A new baby can be very demanding*

demarcate *v* **-cated, cating** 1 to mark the limits of 2 to set apart; separate — **-tion** *n*

demean *v esp. written* to lower in the opinion of oneself or others: *Such behaviour demeans you*

demeanour *n esp. written* outward manner: *his gentle demeanour*

demented *adj* mad — ~**ly** *adv*

demerara sugar *n* brown sugar, usu. from the West Indies

demerit *n* a fault or failing

demesne *n* land round a great house for the use of a lord or king: *the royal demesne*

demigod *fem.* **demigoddess**— *n* 1 (in ancient stories) someone greater than a man but less than a god 2 a person more like a god than a man

demijohn *n* a narrow-necked bottle enclosed in basketwork and holding from about 5 to 45 litres

demise *n esp. law* death or end

demist *v* to clean steam from (car windows) — ~**er** *n*

demo *n* **demos** *esp. spoken* a demonstration

demobilize, -lise also **demob**— *v* **-lized, -lizing** to send back from the army to peacetime life — **-lization** *n*

democracy *n* **-cies** 1 government by the people or their representatives 2 a country governed by its people or their representatives 3 social equality

democrat *n* a person who believes in democracy

Democrat *adj, n* (a member or supporter) of the **Democratic party**, one of the 2 largest US political parties —compare REPUBLICAN

democratic *adj* 1 of, related to, or favouring democracy 2 favouring and practising social equality — ~**ally** *adv* — **-ratization** *n*

demography *n* the study of population statistics — **-pher** *n* — **-phic** *adj*

demolish *v* to destroy; tear down — **-ition** *n*

demon *n* 1 a spirit, person, or emotion that is evil 2 a person of unusual concentration or energy: *a demon for work* △ DAEMON — ~**ic** *adj* — ~**ically** *adv*

demoniacal also **demoniac**— *adj* 1 possessed by a demon 2 of or like a demon: *demoniacal cruelty* — **demoniacally** *adv*

demonstrable *adj* that can be easily shown — **-bly** *adv* — **-bility** *n*

demonstrate *v* **-strated, -strating** 1 to show clearly 2 to prove or make clear, esp. by reasoning 3 to show the value or use of, esp. to a possible buyer 4 to arrange or take part in a public march or show of strong feeling — **-tion** *n*

demonstrative *adj* 1 that demonstrates 2 that shows feelings openly: *a demonstrative action* — ~**ly** *adv*

demonstrative pronoun also **demonstrative**— *n* a pronoun that points out the one meant and separates it from others of the same class: '*This*' and '*that*' can be demonstrative pronouns

demonstrator *n* 1 a person who demonstrates 2 a person who helps a lecturer by doing practical work with students

demoralize, -ise *v* **-ized, -izing** to reduce the

courage or spirit of: *Defeat demoralized our army* — **-ization** *n*

demote *v* **demoted, demoting** to lower in rank or position — **demotion** *n*

demur *v* **-rr-** *esp. written* to show signs of being against something; raise objections: *They demurred at paying*

demure *adj* (esp. of women and children) quiet, serious, and modest, or pretending to be so — ~**ly** *adv* — ~**ness** *n*

den *n* **1** the home of a wild animal **2** a centre of secret or unlawful activity

denary *adj technical* using the digits 0, 1, 2, 3, 4, 5, 6, 7, 8, 9: *the denary system*

denial *n* **1** the act or a case of denying **2** a statement denying something

denied *past tense and past part. of* DENY

denier a measure of the fineness of ... 'reads of silk, cotton, etc.: *15-denier stockings*

denies *3rd person sing. pres. tense of* DENY

denigrate *v* **-grated, -grating** *esp. written* to declare to be not very good — **-gration** *n*

denim *n* a strong cotton cloth used esp. for jeans

denims *n* jeans

denizen *n esp. written* an animal, plant, or person that lives in a particular place

denomination *n* **1** a religious group with special beliefs **2** a standard of value or quantity: *coins of many denominations*

denominator *n* the number below the line in a fraction

denote *v* **denoted, denoting** **1** to be a name of **2** to be a mark of, or a mark that: *A smile may denote pleasure* —compare CONNOTE — **denotation** *n*

denouement *n French* the end of a story when everything is worked out

denounce *v* **denounced, denouncing** to speak or write against

dense *adj* **1** closely packed together: *a dense crowd* **2** stupid — ~**ly** *adv* — ~**ness** *n*

donsity *n* **-ties** **1** the quality of being dense **2** *technical* the relation of the mass to its volume

dent¹ *n* a hollow place on a surface made by a blow or pressure: *a dent in one's car*

dent² *v* to show or cause to show one or more dents

dental *adj* of or related to teeth

dentifrice *n esp. written* toothpaste or tooth powder

dentine *n technical* the hard substance forming the main part of a tooth under the enamel

dentist also (*esp. written*) **dental surgeon** — *n* a person professionally trained to treat teeth — ~**ry** *n*

denture *n* also **plate**— a set of false teeth

dentures also (*esp. spoken*) **false teeth**— *n* a pair of dental plates fitted with man-made teeth

denude *v* **denuded, denuding** to strip or make bare: *Rain denuded the hill of soil*

denunciation *n* an example of denouncing

deny *v* **denied, denying, 3rd person sing. pres. tense** **denies** **1** to declare untrue; refuse to believe —compare AFFIRM **2** to disclaim connection with: *He denied his country* **3** to refuse to give or allow: *He denied his children love* **4 deny oneself** to go without pleasure —see REFUTE (USAGE)

deodorant *n* a substance that destroys or hides unpleasant smells, esp. body smells

deodorize, -rise *v* **-rized, -rizing** to remove the unpleasant smell of

depart *v* **1** *esp. written* to leave; go away **2** *polite* also **depart this life**— to die — ~**ed** *adj* — ~**ure** *n*

department *n* **1** any important division of a government, business, school, etc. **2** (in various countries) a political division rather like a British county **3** *esp. spoken* an area of activity or responsibility: *Advertising is my department* — ~**al** *adj*

department store *n* a large shop divided into separate departments, in which different goods are sold

depend *v* **That depends** I have certain doubts about that —see also DEPEND ON

dependable *adj* that can be trusted — **-bly** *adv* — **-bility** *n*

dependant also **dependent**— *n* a person who depends on another, esp. for money

dependence *n* **1** the quality or state of being dependent, esp. being influenced or supported by a person or thing **2** trust **3** a need; reliance: *dependence on sleeping pills*

dependency *n* **-ies** a country controlled by another

dependent *adj* that depends on

dependent clause also **subordinate clause**— *n* a clause which cannot stand by itself, but can help to make a sentence when joined to a main clause: '*When I arrived*' *is a dependent clause in* '*When I arrived, she had left* '

depend on also **depend upon**— *v prep* **1** to trust; rely on: *My children depend on me* **2** to vary according to: *Our picnic depends on the weather*

depict *v esp. written* to represent by a picture, words, etc. — **depiction** *n*

depilatory *adj, n* **-ries** (a substance) that gets rid of unwanted hair, esp. on the human body

deplete *v* **depleted, depleting** to reduce in quantity, value, etc. — **depletion** *n*

deplore *v* **deplored, deploring** to be very sorry about; regret strongly — **-rable** *adj* — **-rably** *adv*

deploy *v* **deployed, deploying** to spread out or arrange for action: *The armies deployed before the battle* — ~**ment** *n*

depopulate *v* **-lated, -lating** to reduce greatly the population of — **-lation** *n*

deport¹ *v* to send (an undesirable person) out of the country — **deportation** *n*

deport² *v esp. written* to behave (oneself)

deportee *n* a person who has been deported or who is to be deported

deportment n esp. written the way a person, esp. a young lady, stands and walks

depose v **deposed, deposing** to remove from a high office, esp. the throne — **deposition** n

deposit[1] v 1 to put down or let fall: *Deposit the sand here* 2 to place in a bank, safe, or building society

deposit[2] n 1 something deposited: *gold deposits* 2 a part payment of money, made so that the seller will not sell the goods to anyone else 3 an act of depositing

deposit account n a bank or building society account which earns interest —compare SAVINGS ACCOUNT, CURRENT ACCOUNT

deposition n a usu. written statement, which is solemnly declared to be true, made to a court of law

depositor n a person who deposits money in a bank account or building society

depository n **-ries** a person or place that stores things safely

depot n 1 a storehouse 2 a place where new soldiers are trained

deprave v **depraved, depraving** to make bad in character — **depravation** n

depravity n **-ties** 1 the quality of being depraved 2 a depraved act, habit, etc.

deprecate v **-cated, -cating** esp. written to express disapproval of; deplore △ DEPRECIATE — **-catingly** adv — **-cation** n

deprecatory adj 1 apologetic 2 disapproving

depreciate v **-ated, -ating** 1 to reduce the value of: *War depreciates money* 2 (esp. of money) to fall in value △ DEPREC ATE — **-atory** adj — **depreciation** n

depredation n esp. written an act of ruining or taking by force: *the depredations of war*

depress v 1 to push down; lower 2 to cause to sink to a lower level or position: *Does mass unemployment depress wages?* 3 to lessen the activity or strength of 4 to sadden; discourage — **depressing** adj — **depressingly** adv — **depressed** adj

depression n 1 an act of pressing down or the state of being pressed down 2 a part of a surface lower than the other parts 3 an area where the air pressure is low in the centre and higher towards the outside: *A depression usually brings bad weather* ☞ CLOUD 4 sadness and hopelessness 5 a period of reduced business activity and high unemployment

deprivation n 1 the act of depriving or the state of being deprived 2 a lack or loss: *the deprivations of the poor*

deprived adj lacking sufficient education, food, money, etc: *deprived children*

deprive of v prep **deprived, depriving of** to take away from or prevent from using

dept. abbrev. for: department

depth n 1 deepness: *The lake's depth is 30 feet* 2 out of/beyond one's depth beyond one's ability to understand 3 in depth done with great thoroughness

depth charge also **depth bomb**— n a bomb that explodes under water —compare MINE

depths n 1 the deepest parts 2 the middle: *the depths of winter*

deputation n a group of representatives

depute v **deputed, deputing** esp. written 1 to appoint as one's representative 2 to give (part of one's power) to someone else: *I have deputed the accounts to John*

deputize, -tise v **-tized, -tizing** to act as deputy

deputy n **-ties** 1 a person appointed to act for another 2 a member of parliament in certain countries, such as France 3 (in the US) a person appointed to help a sheriff

derail v to force or run off the railway line — ~**ment** n

derange v **deranged, deranging** to disorder or disturb (the mind) — ~**ment** n

Derby n a famous English horse race

derelict adj left to decay

dereliction n failure to do as one ought (esp. in the phrase **dereliction of duty**)

deride v **derided, deriding** to laugh at; make fun of — **derision** n — **derisive** adj — **derisively** adv

derisory adj deserving being laughed at because useless or not enough — **-rily** adv

derivative n 1 something coming from something else: *French is a derivative of Latin* 2 the limit of the ratio of the change in a continuously changing function to the change in its independent variable as the latter change comes closer to O; the gradient of a curve at a particular point

derive from v prep **derived, deriving from** 1 to obtain from 2 to come from — **derivable** adj — **derivation** n

dermatitis n a disease of the skin, marked by redness, hotness, swelling, and pain

dermatology n the study of the skin, esp. of its diseases — **-ogist** n

derogatory adj esp. written showing lack of respect: *derogatory remarks* — **-rily** adv

derrick n 1 a machine for lifting heavy objects 2 a tower over an oil well for lifting the drill and other apparatus ☞ OIL

derring-do n old use or humour daring

derv n trademark an oil product used in diesel engines

dervish n a member of certain Muslim religious groups famous for dancing, shouting, etc.

desalinize, -nise also **desalinate , desalt** — v **-nized, -nizing** to remove salt from — **-nization** n — **-nation** n

descant n 1 music sung or sometimes played at the same time as other music and usu. higher, meant to ornament the main music and increase its effect 2 (that which can produce) high music; soprano; treble 3 poetic a song

descend v to come, fall, or sink from a higher

to a lower level; go down: *in descending order of importance* —compare ASCEND

descendant *n* a person or other living thing that has another as grandfather or grandmother, great-grandfather, etc.

descended *adj* being a descendant

descend on also **descend upon**— *v prep* to arrive at or attack suddenly: *Guests/thieves descended on us*

descent *n* **1** a downward movement; going down **2** family origins: *She is of German descent* **3** a sudden attack or visit

describe *v* **described, describing** **1** to give a picture of in words **2** to draw or move in the shape of: *to describe a circle*

description *n* **1** the act of describing **2** something that describes: *a good description of life* **3** a sort or kind (esp. in the phrases **of that description; of every description; of all descriptions**) — **-tive** *adj* — **-tively** *adv* — **-tiveness** *n*

descry *v* **descried, descrying** *literature* to notice something far off

desecrate *v* **-crated, -crating** **1** to use (something holy) for worldly purposes **2** to put to an improper use — **-cration** *n*

desegregate *v* **-gated, -gating** to end racial segregation (in) — **-ation** *n*

desensitize, -tise *v* **-tized, -tizing** to make less sensitive to light, feelings, etc. — **-tization** *n*

desert¹ *n* a large, sometimes sandy, piece of land where there is very little rain and less plant life than elsewhere

desert² *v* **1** to leave empty or leave completely **2** to leave in a difficult position: *My friends have deserted me!* **3** to leave (military service) without permission — **deserter** *n* — **desertion** *n*

deserts *n* that which is deserved, esp. if bad (esp. in the phrase **just deserts**)

deserve *v* **deserved, deserving** to be worthy of; be fit for: *The best player deserved to win* — **deservedly** *adv* — **deserving** *adj*

déshabillé *n* French dishabille

desiccant *n* *technical* a chemical substance that makes things dry

desiccate *v* **-cated, -cating** to dry (esp. food for later use) thoroughly

design¹ *v* **1** to draw or plan out **2** to intend; mean: *a book designed for colleges* — **~er** *n*

design² *n* **1** a plan, drawing, or pattern of how to do or make something **2** the arrangement of parts of a product: *This machine is of bad design* **3** purpose; intention; plot —see also DESIGNS, DESIGNEDLY

designate¹ *adj esp. written* chosen for an office but not yet placed in it

designate² *v* **-nated, -nating** **1** *esp. written* to point out or call by a special name: *These lines designate roads* **2** to appoint: *I am designating you to act for me* — **-nation** *n*

designedly *adv* on purpose

designing *adj offensive* intending to deceive: *a designing criminal*

designs *n* evil plans: *They have designs on your money*

desirable *adj* **1** worth having, doing, or desiring: *For doctors it is desirable to know about medicine* **2** causing desire, esp. sexual desire — **-bility** *n* — **-bly** *adv*

desire¹ *v* **desired, desiring** **1** *esp. written* to wish or want very much **2** to wish to have sexual relations with — **desirous** *adj*

desire² *n* **1** a strong wish, often for sexual relations: *his desire for Cleopatra* | *my desire to return* **2** something or someone desired USAGE One can feel **desire** for anything. **Appetite** is only for things of the body, esp. food, and **lust** (*offensive*) is a very strong word, particularly for sex.

desist *v* *esp. written* to not do any more; stop: *He desisted from smoking*

desk *n* a table, often with drawers, at which one reads, writes, etc.

desolate¹ *adj* sad and deserted by people — ~**ly** *adv* — **-lation** *n*

desolate² *v* **-lated, -lating** to make very sad: *She was desolated by his death*

despair¹ *v* to lose all hope

despair² *n* **1** complete lack or loss of hope **2** the cause of this feeling (esp. in the phrase **the despair of**)

despairing *adj* showing or causing despair — ~**ly** *adv*

despatch *n*, *v* dispatch

despatches *n* dispatches

desperado *n* **-does** or **-dos** a bold, merciless criminal

desperate *adj* **1** ready for any wild act: *a desperate criminal* **2** wild or dangerous; done as a last attempt **3** (of a state of affairs) very difficult and dangerous — ~**ly** *adv* — **-ation** *n*

despicable *adj* that should be despised: *It is despicable to desert your children* — **-bly** *adv*

despise *v* **despised, despising** to regard as worthless, bad, etc. —compare DISDAIN

despite *prep esp. written* in spite of

despondent *adj* feeling a complete loss of hope; discouraged: — ~**ly** *adv* — **-dency** *n*

despot *n* a ruler with total power — ~**ic** *adj* — ~**ically** *adv* — ~**ism** *n*

dessert *n* the sweet dish in a meal served after the main dish

dessertspoon *n* a spoon between a teaspoon and a tablespoon in size, used for eating dessert

dessertspoonful also **dessertspoon**— *n* **-s** or **-spoonful** the amount held by one dessertspoon

dessert wine *n* a usu. sweet wine often served with dessert or between meals

destination *n* a place to which someone or something is going; end of a journey

destined *adj* intended for some special purpose: *He was destined for the army*

destiny *n* **-nies** **1** fate; that which must happen **2** that which seems to decide man's fate, thought of as a person or a force

destitute *adj* **1** lacking the simplest necessary

things of life (food, clothing, shelter, money) **2** lacking; completely without — **-tution** *n*

destroy *v*   **destroyed, destroying**   **1** to tear down or apart; ruin; wreck   **2** to kill (esp. a tame animal)

destroyer *n* a small fast warship

destruction *n*   **1** the act of destroying or state of being destroyed   **2** that which destroys: *Pride was her destruction*

destructive *adj* causing or tending to destruction — ~**ly** *adv* — ~**ness** *n*

desultory *adj esp. written* passing from one thing to another without purpose: *a desultory life* — **-rily** *adv*

detach *v* to separate and remove — ~**able** *adj*

detached *adj*   **1** not connected   **2** (of a house) not connected to any other building   **3** not influenced by feelings or other people's opinions — ~**ly** *adv*

detachment *n*   **1** the act of detaching or state of being detached   **2** a military force sent from the main group on special duty

detail¹ *n* a small point or fact or group of such points: *an eye for detail*

detail² *v*   **1** to appoint to some special duty: *He detailed them to look for water*   **2** to give a lot of facts about

detain *v*   **1** to keep (a person) from leaving   **2** to delay

detainee *n* a person detained officially, esp. for political reasons

detect *v* to find out; notice: *I detected anger in his voice* — **detector** *n*

detection *n*   **1** the act of detecting   **2** the work of a detective

detective *n* a policeman who hunts out information on crimes

détente *n French* (a state of) easier and calmer political relations, esp. between countries

detention *n*   **1** the act of detaining or state of being detained   **2** being kept in school after school hours as a punishment

deter *v* **-rr-** to discourage or prevent from acting (as by threats)

detergent *n* a chemical cleaner, esp. for clothing or dishes —compare SOAP

deteriorate *v*   **-rated, -rating** to make or become worse — **-ration** *n*

determinant *n technical* a number associated with square matrices: *For the (2X2) matrix M=* $\binom{a\,b}{c\,d}$ *the determinant of M = ad - bc*

determination *n*   **1** firm intention   **2** strong will; firmness   **3** the act of determining

determine *v*   **-mined, -mining**   **1** to form a firm intention in the mind: *He determined to go*   **2** to decide   **3** to limit; control   **4** to find out and fix exactly: *to determine the moon's position*

determined *adj* firm; decided

determinism *n* the belief that acts of the will, natural events, or social changes are settled and decided by earlier causes —compare FREE WILL

deterrent *n, adj* (something) that deters — **-rence** *n*

detest *v* to dislike strongly — ~**able** *adj* — ~**ably** *adv* — ~**ation** *n*

detonate *v*   **-nated, -nating** to explode suddenly — **-nation** *n*

detonator *n* an apparatus used to detonate a strong explosive

detour¹ *n* a way round something: *a detour around the town*

detour² *v* to make a detour

detract from *v prep*   **1** to take something away from; make less the value of   **2** to say evil things about: *He always tries to detract from the work of his competitors* — **detraction** *n* — **detractor** *n*

detriment *n*   **1** harm; damage (esp. in the phrases **without detriment to** and **to the detriment of**)   **2** a cause of harm or damage — ~**al** *adj* — ~**ally** *adv*

detritus *n technical* substances, such as sand, rubbed away from rocks by the wind or by water

deuce *n*   **1** (in tennis) 40–40; 40 points to each player   **2** *old sl* (used for adding force to an expression) the devil: *Deuce take it!*

Deuteronomy *n* the 5th book of the Old Testament of the Bible

devalue *v*   **-ued, -uing** to reduce the value of (money, work, etc.) —compare REVALUE — **-uation** *n*

devastate *v*   **-stated, -stating** to destroy completely; lay waste — **-station** *n*

devastating *adj*   **1** destroying completely   **2** *esp.spoken* very good; able to obtain the desired result: *You look devastating* — ~**ly** *adv*

develop *v*   **1** to make or become larger, more complete, more active, etc.: *to develop a business/one's mind/an illness*   **2** to think out or present fully: *to develop an idea*   **3** (in photography) to make or become visible on a film or photographic paper   **4** to bring out the economic possibilities of (land, water, etc.)

developer *n*   **1** (in photography) a substance that brings out the image on a photographic plate or film after a picture has been taken   **2** a person who develops land or buildings (esp. by improving them)

developing country also **developing nation**— *n*   **-tries** a poor country that is trying to become richer and to improve the living conditions of its people

development *n*   **1** the act of developing or the state of being developed   **2** the amount or result of such developing: *the great development of his chest muscles*   **3** a developed piece of land, esp. one with houses   **4** a new event or piece of news

developmental *adj esp. written* of or about the development of the mind or body — ~**ly** *adv*

deviant *adj, n* (a person or thing) that differs from the normal — **-ance** *n*

deviate v -ated, -ating to be different or move away (from normal behaviour)

deviation n 1 a noticeable difference from what is normal 2 the difference between the north as shown by a magnetic compass and true north: *a deviation of 5°*

device n 1 an instrument; invention; tool 2 something (such as a special phrase) which is intended to produce a particular artistic effect in a work of literature 3 a drawing, esp. one used by a noble family as its special sign 4 a plan or trick 5 **leave someone to his own devices** to leave (someone) alone, without help

Devil n the strongest evil spirit; Satan

devil n 1 an evil spirit or person 2 a high-spirited person, ready for adventure 3 *esp. spoken* (in expressions of strong feeling) fellow; man; boy: *You lucky devil!* 4 *sl* (used to give force to various expressions): *What the devil happened?* —compare DICKENS, DEUCE 5 go to the **devil** to be ruined 6 **Go to the devil!** *sl* Go away at once! 7 **the very devil** very difficult or painful — ~ish adj — ~ishness n

devil² v -ll- to cook in a hot-tasting thick liquid: *devilled eggs*

devilment also **devilry**— n 1 evil behaviour 2 wildly merry behaviour

devil's advocate n a person who argues against his beliefs in order to test ideas

devious adj not direct; tricky: *a devious person/route* — ~ly adv — ~ness n

devise v devised, devising to plan or invent (esp. cleverly)

devoid adj esp. written empty (of); lacking (in): *devoid of feeling*

devolution n the giving of part of government or personal power, work, duties, etc. to another person or group

devolve on also **devolve upon**— v prep devolved, devolving on (of power, work. etc.) to go to (another person or group); be passed to

devolve to v prep law (of land, goods, etc.) to become the property of, on the death of the owner

devoted adj loyal, loving, or fond (of)—compare ADDICT — ~ly adv

devotee n French a person devoted to someone or something, esp. religion

devote to v prep devoted, devoting to to give completely to: *He has devoted his life to helping the blind*

devotion n the act of devoting or the condition of being devoted, esp. to religion

devour v 1 to eat up quickly and hungrily 2 (of a feeling) to possess (a person) completely

devout adj 1 seriously concerned with religion 2 serious; felt deeply: *a devout hope* — ~ly adv — ~ness n

dew n water droplets which form on cold surfaces overnight — **dewy** adj — **dewily** adv — **dewiness** n

dewlap n a hanging fold of loose skin under the throat of a cow, dog, etc.

dexterous also **dextrous**— adj clever and skilful, esp. with the hands — ~ly adv — -rity n

dextrose n a form of sugar found in many fruits

dhoti n a cloth worn between the legs and round the lower part of the body by some Hindu men

dhow n a coastal ship with one large sail, used esp. by Arabs

diabetes n a disease in which there is a lack of insulin or the body becomes insensitive to insulin, causing there to be too much sugar in the blood — -betic adj

diabolic also **diabolical**— adj of or coming from the devil; wicked or cruel — ~ally adv

diadem n literature a crown

diaeresis n -ses a sign (¨) placed over the 2nd of 2 vowels to show that it is pronounced separately from the 1st

diagnose v -nosed, -nosing to discover the nature of (a disease)

diagnosis n -ses (the result of) diagnosing — compare PROGNOSIS — -nostic adj

diagonal n, adj 1 (in the direction of) a straight line joining 2 opposite corners of a 4-sided flat figure ☞ MATHEMATICS 2 (any straight line) which runs in a sloping direction — ~ly adv

diagram n a plan, figure, or drawing, often showing an arrangement of parts — ~matic adj

dial¹ n 1 the face of an instrument such as a clock showing time, speed, etc., by a pointer and figures—see also SUNDIAL 2 the plate on the front of a radio, with a pointer and numbers, used to find a particular station 3 the wheel on a telephone with holes for the fingers, which is moved round when one makes a telephone call

dial² v -ll- to call (a number, person, or place) on a telephone with a dial

dialect n a separate form of a language, spoken in one part of a country — ~al adj

dialogue n a conversation, usu. in a book or between people with different views

diameter n a straight line going from side to side through the centre of a circle; a chord which passes through the centre of a circle ☞ MATHEMATICS

diametrically adv completely; directly (in the phrases **diametrically opposite, diametrically opposed**)

diamond¹ n 1 a very hard, valuable jewel, usually colourless 2 an ornament set with one or more of these jewels: *Shall I wear my diamonds tonight?* 3 a figure with 4 straight sides of equal length that stands on one of its points 4 a playing card with such figures in red —compare SPADE, CLUB, HEART 4 (in baseball) a the area of the field inside the 4 bases b the whole playing field 5 **rough diamond** a kind person with rough manners

diamond² adj indicating the 60th yearly return of some important date: *diamond jubilee*

diaper n US a nappy

diaphanous *adj* (esp. of cloth) so fine and thin that it can be seen through

diaphragm *n* **1** the muscle that separates the lungs from the stomach **2** any thin partition of metal or skin, esp. one which is moved by sound **3** the group of small plates controlling the amount of light entering a camera ☞ OPTICS **4** a contraceptive cap

diarist *n* the writer of a diary

diarrhoea, -rhea *n* an illness in which the bowels are emptied too often and in too liquid a form

diary *n* **-ries** **1** (a book containing) a daily record of a person's life **2** a book with separate spaces for each day of the year, in which one writes down things to be done

Diaspora *n* the scattering of the Jews in various countries outside Palestine, after they were sent out of Babylon

diatom *n* any of several types of very small water plants (ALGAE)

diatonic scale *n* (in music) a set of 8 notes with a fixed pattern of spaces between the notes

diatribe *n* a long violent attack in speech or writing

dibble *n, v* **-bled, -bling** (to plant or make holes in the earth by means of) a small pointed garden tool

dice¹ *n* **dice** **1** a small 6-sided block, with a different number of spots from 1–6 on the various sides **2** any game of chance played with these USAGE The old singular form **die** is not used now except in the old saying **The die is cast** = The decision has been made and cannot now be changed.

dice² *v* **diced, dicing** **1** to play dice (with someone, for money, etc.) **2** to cut (food) into small square pieces: *diced carrots* **3 dice with death** to take great risks

dicey *adj* **-ier, -iest** *esp.spoken* risky and uncertain

dichotomy *n* **-mies** a division into 2 parts, esp. 2 that are opposites

dickens *n* *esp. spoken* (used for giving force to an expression): *What the dickens is that?* — compare DEUCE, DEVIL

dicker *v* to argue about the price; haggle

dicky *adj* **-ier, -iest** *esp.spoken* weak; unsound: *a dicky heart*

dickybird *n* any small bird

dictate¹ *v* **-tated, -tating** **1** to say (words) for someone else to write down: *She dictated a letter* **2** to state (demands, conditions, etc.) with the power to enforce — **-tation** *n* *The teacher gave us a French dictation*

dictate² *n* an order which should be obeyed

dictator *n* a ruler who has complete power — ~**ial** *adj*

dictatorship *n* **1 a** the position or government of a dictator **b** the period of a dictator's rule **2** a country ruled by a dictator

diction *n* **1** choice of words and phrases **2** the way in which a person pronounces words — compare ENUNCIATION

dictionary *n* **-ries** **1** a book that lists words in alphabetical order, with their meanings **2** a book like this that gives, for each word, one or more words in another language with approximately the same meaning: *a German-English dictionary* **3** a book like this with words from a special subject

dictum *n* **-ta** *or* **-tums** a formal statement of opinion; wise saying

did *1st, 2nd, and 3rd person sing. and pl. past tense of* DO

didactic *adj* **1** meant to teach **2** *offensive* too eager to teach: *a didactic fool* — ~**ally** *adv*

diddle *v* **-dled, -dling** *sl* to get something from (someone) dishonestly; cheat

didst **thou didst** *old use* (when talking to one person) you did

die¹ *v* **died, dying** **1** to stop living **2** to cease: *The day is dying in the west* **3** (of knowledge, ideas, etc.) to become lost and forgotten

die² *n* **1** a metal block used for pressing or cutting metal, plastic, etc., into shape **2** an instrument used for making a screw or bolt **3** *old or US sing. of* dice

die-casting *n* the making of metal objects by forcing the liquid metal under pressure into a mould — compare INJECTION MOULDING

diehard *n* a person who stubbornly opposes change

diesel engine also **diesel**— *n* an engine in which heavy oil is exploded by hot air

diet¹ *n* **1** a person's usual food and drink **2** a limited list of food, eaten for one's health, to lose weight, etc. (often in the phrases **be/go on a diet**) — **dietary** *adj*

diet² *v* to live on a diet

diet³ *n* (in certain countries) a parliament

dietetics *n* the science of food diets — **-tetic** *adj* — **dietician, -titian** *n*

differ *v* **1** to be unlike **2** (of people) to disagree

difference *n* **1** a way of being unlike **2** an amount of unlikeness: *The difference between 5 and 11 is 6* **3** a disagreement **4 split the difference** to agree on an amount halfway between

different *adj* **1** unlike; not of the same kind **2** separate; other: *They go to different schools* **3** *esp. spoken* unusual — ~**ly** *adv* USAGE **Different, or differently, from** is correct. Some people say **different to**: *He is different to me*, and some Americans say **different than**. It is better to use neither of these. **Indifferent** can only be followed by to: *I am indifferent to maths.*

differential¹ *adj* of or depending on a difference

differential² *n* **1** the amount of difference between things, esp. between wages for different jobs **2** a mathematical derivative

differential calculus *n* the inverse of integral calculus; one of the 2 ways of making calculations about quantities which are constantly changing

differential gear n an arrangement of gears on a car's back axle allowing one back wheel to turn faster than the other when the car goes round a corner ☞ CAR

differentiate v -ated, -ating 1 to see a difference or make different; distinguish 2 to find the mathematical derivative of (a function) — compare INTEGRATE — -ation n

difficult adj 1 not easy; hard to do, understand, etc. 2 (of people) hard to get along with; not easily pleased

difficulty n -ties 1 the quality of being difficult; trouble 2 something difficult; a trouble: money difficulties

diffident adj not believing in one's own powers; too humble —opposite confident — ~ly adv — -dence n

diffract v to break up (light), forming dark and light or coloured bands (SPECTRUM) — ~ion n

diffuse[1] adj 1 diffused: diffuse light 2 using too many words — ~ly adv — ~ness n

diffuse[2] v -fused, -fusing to spread out in all directions: to diffuse knowledge — -fusion n

dig[1] v dug , digging 1 to break up and move (earth): dig a garden 2 to make (a hole) by taking away earth 3 to bring to light; uncover 4 sl to like or understand: Do you dig jazz? 5 dig someone in the ribs to touch someone with one's elbow, as to share a joke —see also DIG AT, DIG UP — ~ger n

dig[2] n esp. spoken 1 a quick push: Give him a dig! 2 a an ancient place being uncovered by archaeologists b the digging up of such a place

dig at v prep to speak to in an unpleasant way

digest[1] n a greatly shortened written account; summary

digest[2] v 1 to change into a form that the body can use: Sugar digests easily 2 to think over and understand — ~ible adj — ~ibility n

digestion n power to digest food: a weak digestion

digestive[1] adj connected with or helping in the digesting of food

digestive[2] n trademark a type of plain usu. unsweetened biscuit

digestive system n the whole length of the tube (ALIMENTARY CANAL) in the body down which food travels while it is being digested ⊚

digit n 1 any numeral from 0 to 9 2 a finger or toe — ~al adj

digital computer n a computer that performs operations by counting rather than by measuring —compare ANALOGUE COMPUTER

dignify v -fied, -fying to give dignity to — -fied adj

dignitary n -ries a person with a high position, esp. in the church

dignity n -ties 1 true nobleness of character 2 calm and formal behaviour 3 a high rank, office, or title 4 beneath one's dignity below

one's moral or social standard 5 stand on one's dignity to demand proper respect

digress v (of a writer or speaker) to turn aside (from the subject) — ~ion n

digs n ESP. spoken lodgings

dig up v adv 1 to find, esp. by digging 2 ESP. spoken to collect by searching: Can you dig up any money?

dike, dyke n 1 a thick bank or wall, esp. to prevent flooding —compare DAM 2 a narrow passage dug to carry water away; ditch

dilapidated adj broken and old; falling to pieces — -dation n

dilate v dilated, dilating to make or become wider or further open by stretching: The cat dilated its eyes — -lation n

dilatory adj causing delay; slow

dilemma n a situation in which one must choose between 2 evils USAGE Many people feel that dilemma should mean a choice between only 2 possibilities: I am in a dilemma whether to do maths or English. They do not like sentences like: I am in a dilemma whether to do maths, English, or biology.

dilettante n, adj -tes or -ti usu. offensive (typical·of) a person who amuses himself with an art, science, etc., without taking it seriously — compare AMATEUR

diligent adj hardworking; steady; careful — ~ly adv — -gence n

dill n a plant, related to the carrot plant, whose seeds are used to give a special taste to food

dillydally v -lied, -lying esp. spoken to waste time, usu. by being unable to make up one's mind

dilute v diluted, diluting to make (a liquid) weaker or thinner: He diluted the paint with oil — dilution n — ~d adj

dim[1] adj -mm- 1 (of a light) not bright 2 not easy to see 3 (of eyes) not able to see clearly 4 esp. spoken (of people) stupid 5 take a dim view of esp. spoken to think badly of — ~ly adv — ~ness n

dim[2] v -mm- to make or become dim

dime n a coin of the US and Canada, worth 10 cents or 1/10 of a dollar

dimension n a measurement in any one direction: A line has one dimension and a square has 2

dimensions n size

diminish v to make or become smaller — -nution n

diminished adj (of a musical interval) made half a note less than the interval in a minor scale

diminuendo n -dos Italian (in music) a decrease in loudness —opposite crescendo

diminutive[1] n a word formed by adding an ending expressing smallness to another word: 'Duckling' is a diminutive of 'duck'

diminutive[2] adj very small

dimple n a little hollow place on the skin, esp. in the cheek

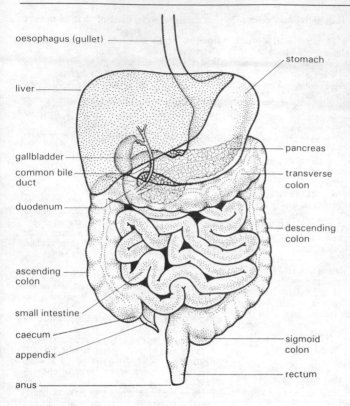

oesophagus (gullet)

stomach

liver

gallbladder

pancreas

common bile duct

transverse colon

duodenum

descending colon

ascending colon

small intestine

caecum

appendix

sigmoid colon

anus

rectum

The digestive system

Digestion is a process by which food is broken down into simple substances which can be absorbed into the bloodstream. In the mouth, food is partly broken down by chewing and the action of enzymes in saliva before it passes down the gullet and into the stomach. Acid and enzymes in the stomach break the food down further before it enters the duodenum, the beginning of the small intestine, into which also flow bile (produced by the liver) from the gallbladder and enzymes from the pancreas. Digestion is almost completed in the small intestine; any remaining material passes through into the colon (large intestine), where waste products are formed into faeces.

Sources of nutrients in food

Carbo-hydrates

sugars

milk
fruit
jam
honey
cakes

starch

bread
potatoes
peas

Proteins

lean meat
egg white
beans
fish
milk
cheese

Fats

milk
butter
cheese
egg yolk
margarine

Minerals

iron
liver
oatmeal
eggs

calcium
cheese
skim milk
sardines

Vitamins

A liver, kidney, eggs, dairy products, fish, liver oils, fresh green vegetables

B$_1$ yeast, wheat germ, most meats

B$_2$ milk, offal, lean meat, fish

C oranges, lemons, blackcurrant, dark green leafy vegetables

D fish liver, eggs

E whole grain cereal, vegetable oils, wheat germ

K leafy vegetables, eg cabbage, spinach

dimwit *n esp. spoken* a stupid person — **dim-witted** *adj*

din *n* a loud, continuous, and unpleasant noise

dine *v*
dined, dining 1 *esp. written* to eat dinner 2 to give a dinner for (often in the phrase **wine and dine**) — **diner** *n*

dingdong *adj, n esp. spoken* (of a fight or argument) with each side taking the lead, time after time

dinghy *n* **-ghies** a small open boat ☞ SAIL

dingo *n* **-goes** an Australian wild dog

dingy *adj* **-gier, -giest** dirty and faded — **dingily** *adv* — **dinginess** *n*

dining car also **restaurant car**— *n* a carriage on a train where meals are served

dining table *n* a table esp. for having meals on

dinner *n* 1 a day's main meal, eaten either at midday or in the evening 2 a formal evening meal, for a special occasion

dinner jacket *n* a man's black coat for rather formal evening occasions

dinner service also **dinner set**— *n* a complete set of plates and dishes for dinner

dinner table *n* a table on which dinner is being served

dinosaur *n* any of several types of large long-tailed reptiles that lived in prehistoric times ☞ PREHISTORIC

dint *n* 1 a hollow on a hard surface, made by a blow; dent 2 **by dint of** by means of

diocese *n* the area under the government of a bishop — **-cesan** *adj*

diode *n* an electrical apparatus that allows current to pass through it in one direction only

dip¹ *v* **-pp-** 1 to put into a liquid for a moment and then take out 2 to put (an animal) quickly into a chemical liquid that kills insects 3 to drop or lower slightly, often just for a moment: *to dip a car's headlights*

dip² *n* 1 *esp. spoken* a quick swim 2 a slope down; slight drop in height 3 the act of dipping: *Give the sheep a dip* 4 any liquid used for dipping: *a savoury dip*

diphtheria *n* a serious infectious disease of the throat which makes breathing difficult

diphthong *n* a compound vowel sound made by pronouncing 2 vowels quickly one after the other: *The vowel in 'my' is a diphthong* —compare CONSONANT, VOWEL

diploma *n* an official paper showing that a person has successfully finished a course of study or passed an examination

diplomacy *n* 1 the art and practice of conducting relations between nations 2 skill at dealing with people — **-mat** *n* **-matic** *adj* — **-matically** *adv*

dipper *n* a long-handled cup for taking liquid out of a container

dipsomania *n* an uncontrollable desire for alcoholic drinks; alcoholism — **~c** *n*

dipstick *n* a stick used to measure the depth of a liquid, esp. the oil in a car engine

dipswitch *n* an instrument in a car for lowering the beam of the headlights

dire *adj* 1 (of needs and dangers) very great 2 causing great fear: *a dire warning*

direct¹ *v* 1 to tell (someone) the way (to a place) 2 to control and manage (the way something is done) 3 to order: *The policeman directed the crowd to leave* —see ORDER (USAGE) 4 to write the address on (a letter) 5 to aim (attention, remarks, etc.)

direct² *adj* 1 straight 2 leading from one point to another without stopping and without anything coming between: *a direct flight | a direct result* 3 honest and easily understood 4 exact: *He's the direct opposite of his brother* — **~ness** *n*

direct³ *adv* in a straight line; without stopping or turning aside

direct current *n* a flow of electricity that moves in one direction only —compare ALTERNATING CURRENT

direction *n* 1 control: *under my direction* 2 the course on which or point to which a person or thing moves or is aimed

directional *adj* connected with direction in space

directions *n* instructions; commands

directive¹ *adj* meant to instruct and direct

directive² *n* an official order

directly¹ *adv* 1 in a direct manner: *directly opposite the church* —opposite **indirectly** 2 at once 3 *esp. spoken* soon

directly² *conj esp. spoken* as soon as

direct object *n* the noun or noun phrase needed to complete a statement using a transitive verb: *In 'I have lost the money', 'the money' is the direct object*

director *n* 1 a person who directs an organization 2 a member of the board of directors who run a company 3 a person who directs a play or esp. a film, instructing the actors, cameramen, etc. —compare PRODUCER — **~ship** *n*

directorate *n* a board of directors

Director of Public Prosecutions *n* (in Britain) the government lawyer who decides in important cases whether a person shall be tried by a court

directory *n* **-ries** a list of names, facts, etc.

direct speech *n technical* the actual words of a speaker, repeated without changes in the grammar —opposite **indirect/reported speech**

direct tax *n* (a) tax such as income tax which is actually collected from the person who pays it, rather than on the sale of goods or services (as with VAT) — **~ation** *n*

dirge *n* a slow sad song or piece of music, esp. one for a dead person

dirigible *n* a huge guided balloon that carries people; airship

dirk *n* a short sword; dagger

dirndl *n* a wide skirt with a tight waist, or with a close-fitting bodice

dirt n 1 unclean matter, esp. in the wrong place 2 soil; loose earth 3 nasty talk or writing about sex; smut; pornography 4 *esp. spoken* nasty talk about people 5 **dirt cheap** *esp. spoken* very cheap

dirt farmer n *US* a farmer who earns his living by farming his own land, esp. without hired help

dirty[1] *adj* **-ier, -iest** 1 not clean or making not clean: *a dirty job* 2 *esp. spoken* unpleasantly concerned with sex: *dirty stories* 3 *esp. spoken* (of the weather) rough and unpleasant 4 **do the dirty on someone** *sl* to treat someone in a mean way 5 **give someone a dirty look** *esp. spoken* to look at someone in a nasty way — **dirtily** *adv*

dirty[2] *v* **-ied, -ying** to make or become dirty

dirty[3] *adv sl* very: *a dirty big house*

disability n **-ties** the state of being disabled or something that disables

disable v **-bled, -bling** to make (a person) unable to use his body properly — ~**ment** n

disadvantage n 1 an unfavourable condition or position: *His bad health is a disadvantage* 2 loss; damage; harm — ~**ous** *adj* — ~**ously** *adv*

disaffected *adj* lacking loyalty (esp. to a government) — **-tion** n

disafforest v to cut down the forests of — ~**ation** n

disagree v **-greed, -greeing** to have different opinions or meanings; differ — ~**ment** n

disagreeable *adj* 1 unpleasant 2 bad-tempered and unfriendly: *Don't be so disagreeable* — ~**ness** n — **-ably** *adv*

disagree with *v prep* (of food or weather) to have a bad effect on

disappear v 1 to go out of sight 2 to cease to exist; become lost — ~**ance** n

disappoint v 1 to fail to fulfil the hopes of: *I'm sorry to disappoint you* 2 to defeat (a plan or hope) — ~**ed** *adj* — ~**edly** *adv* — ~**ing** *adj* — ~**ingly** *adv* — ~**ment** n

disapprobation n *esp. written* disapproval

disapprove v **-proved, -proving** to have a bad opinion (of): *He disapproves of my going out to work* — **-proval** n — **-provingly** *adv*

disarm v 1 to give up or take away weapons; reduce the size and strength of armed forces — opposite **arm** 2 to drive away anger from or win over: *His friendliness disarmed all opposition* — **-ament** n

disarray n a state of disorder: *with her clothes in disarray*

disassociate v **-ated, -ating** to dissociate

disaster n a sudden great misfortune — **-trous** *adj* — **-trously** *adv*

disavow v *esp. written* to refuse to admit (knowledge, a connection, etc.); deny — ~**al** n

disband v to break up and separate: *The club has disbanded* — ~**ment** n

disbar v **-rr-** to make (a barrister) leave the profession (the BAR) — ~**ment** n

disbelief n lack of belief —see UNBELIEF (USAGE)

disbelieve v **-lieved, -lieving** to refuse to believe — **-liever** n

disburse v **-bursed, -bursing** *esp. written* to pay out (money) — ~**ment** n

disc n 1 something round and flat 2 a gramophone record ⊃ COMPUTER 3 a flat piece of cartilage between the bones (VERTEBRAE) of one's back

discard v to get rid of as useless

disc brakes n brakes which work by the pressure of a pad against a disc in the centre of a wheel

discern v to see or understand, esp. with difficulty: *It was difficult to discern the truth* — ~**ible** *adj* — ~**ibly** *adv*

discerning *adj* able to decide and judge; having good taste: *a discerning man/mind* — **-ment** n

discharge[1] *v* **-charged, -charging** 1 to send or let out: *The chimney discharges smoke.* | *The judge discharged the prisoner* 2 to dismiss (a person) from a job 3 to pay (a debt) 4 to perform (a duty) or promise 5 to shoot (a gun, arrow, etc.) 6 a (of a ship) to unload b to unload (a ship) 7 a (of an electrical apparatus) to send out electricity b to remove electricity from (an electrical apparatus) 8 *law* to put an end to (a court order)

discharge[2] n 1 the action of discharging or state of being discharged 2 an order that discharges 3 that which is discharged: *a discharge of electricity*

disciple n 1 a follower of a great teacher (esp. religious) 2 any of the 12 first followers of Christ; apostle — ~**ship** n

disciplinarian n a person who is good at making people obey orders

discipline[1] n 1 training of the mind and body, usu. according to rules 2 control, order, or obedience: *discipline in the classroom* 3 punishment 4 a branch of learning, such as history or mathematics — **-plinary** *adj*

discipline[2] *v* **-plined, -plining** 1 to train, esp. in order to control 2 to punish

disc jockey n **-eys** a person who introduces pop records (e.g. at a discotheque or on radio or television)

disclaim v to say that one does not own or does not claim; deny

disclaimer n a statement which disclaims

disclose v **-closed, -closing** to make known; uncover: *to disclose the truth*

disclosure n 1 the act of disclosing 2 a secret which is disclosed

disco n **-cos** *esp. spoken* a discotheque

discolour v to change colour for the worse — **discoloration** n

discomfit v *esp. written* to upset (a plan or person) ⚠ DISCOMFORT — ~**ure** n

discomfort n 1 lack of comfort or anything that causes such a lack 2 slight anxiety or shame ⚠ DISCOMFIT

discommode v -moded, -moding *literature* to incommode

discompose v -posed, -posing *esp. written* to disturb or upset (a person) — **-posure** n

disconcert v to cause to feel doubt and anxiety — ~**ingly** adv

disconnect v 1 to undo the connection of 2 to break the telephone connection between (2 people)

disconnected adj (of ideas) badly connected; not well planned — ~**ly** adv — **-nection** n

disconsolate adj hopelessly sad and unwilling to be comforted — ~**ly** adv

discontent[1] v to make dissatisfied and unhappy — ~**ed** adj — ~**edly** adv

discontent[2] also **discontentment**— n lack of contentment; dissatisfaction

discontinue v -ued, -uing *esp. written* to stop or end — **-tinuance** n

discontinuous adj not continuous in space or time; with gaps or breaks — ~**ly** adv — **-tinuity** n

discord n 1 disagreement between people, usu. causing argument or conflict 2 a musical chord which sounds unpleasant or unsatisfying because it needs another chord to complete it — compare HARMONY — ~**ant** adj — ~**antly** adv — ~**ance** n

discotheque also (*esp. spoken*) **disco**— n a club where people dance to pop records

discount[1] n 1 a reduction made in the cost of buying something 2 **at a discount a** below the usual price **b** *esp. written* not valuable or wanted

discount[2] v to pay little attention to

discountenance v -nanced, -nancing *esp. written* to disapprove of (behaviour or actions)

discount store also **discount house**— n a shop where goods are sold below the normal price

discourage v -aged, -aging 1 to take away courage from: *Defeat discourages me* 2 to try to prevent, esp. by showing disfavour — **-agingly** adv — ~**ment** n

discourse n *esp. written* a serious conversation, speech, or piece of writing

discourse upon also **discourse on**— v prep -coursed, -coursing upon *esp. written* to make a long formal speech about

discourteous adj *esp. written* not polite — ~**ly** adv — ~**ness** n

discourtesy n -sies *esp. written* (an act of) discourteousness

discover v to find out or find, esp. for the first time: *Columbus discovered America in 1492* —see INVENT (USAGE) — ~**able** adj — ~**er** n — ~**y** n

discredit[1] v 1 to cause people to lose faith in 2 to refuse to believe in (ideas)

discredit[2] n 1 loss of belief and trust 2 someone or something that is harmful to a person's good name 3 doubt and disbelief

discreditable adj (of behaviour) shameful; bringing discredit — **-bly** adv

discreet adj (of people or behaviour) careful in what one says; showing good sense — ~**ly** adv

discrepancy n -cies lack of agreement (between stories, amounts, etc.)

discrete adj *esp. technical* separate; discontinuous — ~**ly** adv — ~**ness** n

discretion n 1 the quality of being discreet 2 the ability to decide what to do: *You must use your own discretion* 3 **at someone's discretion** according to someone's decision — ~**ary** adj

discriminate v -nated, -nating to see or make a difference: *to discriminate against white people*

discrimination n 1 ability to choose the best by seeing small differences 2 *often offensive* treating different things or people in different ways — **-nating** adj

discriminatory adj *often offensive* making distinctions, often unfairly

discursive adj passing from one subject or idea to another without plan: *a discursive report* — ~**ly** adv — ~**ness** n

discus n a heavy plate which is thrown as far as possible, as a sport

discuss v to talk about or over; consider — ~**ion** n

disdain[1] n lack of respect (for) —compare CONTEMPT, SCORN

disdain[2] v to regard as below notice: *She disdained to answer* —compare DESPISE

disdainful adj showing disdain —compare CONTEMPTUOUS, SCORNFUL — ~**ly** adv

disease n an illness caused by infection or unnatural growth — ~**d** adj

disembark also **debark**— v 1 (of people) to go on shore from a ship 2 to put on shore (people or goods) — ~**ation** n

disembodied adj existing without a body

disembowel v -ll- to take out the bowels of

disembroil v *esp. written* to set free (from confusion and difficulty)

disenchant v to set free from illusions or being charmed — ~**ment** n

disencumber v *esp. written* to free (someone) from something heavy or inconvenient

disengage v -gaged, -gaging 1 to make or become loose, free, or separate: *Disengage the gears* 2 (of soldiers, ships, etc.) to stop fighting and go or take (oneself) away — ~**ment** n

disentangle v -gled, -gling to free or become free from confusion or a tangle — ~**ment** n

disestablish v to take away the official position (from the Church of England) — ~**ment** n

disfavour n *esp. written* 1 dislike; disapproval 2 the state of being disliked: *fallen into disfavour*

disfigure v -ured, -uring to spoil the beauty of — ~**ment** n

disfranchise also **disenfranchise**— v -chised, -chising to take a citizen's rights, esp. the right to vote, away from —opposite **enfranchise** — ~**ment** n

disgorge v -gorged, -gorging 1 to throw out of the stomach through the mouth 2 (of a river) to pour out

disgrace¹ v -graced, -gracing to bring shame or disgrace on

disgrace² n 1 shame; loss of respect 2 a cause of shame and loss of respect: *Your shirt is a disgrace!* 3 **be in disgrace** *esp. spoken* (esp. of a child) to be regarded with disapproval because of something one has done

disgraceful adj causing disgrace — ~ly adv

disgruntled adj annoyed and disappointed

disguise¹ v -guised, -guising 1 to change the appearance of, so as to hide the truth: *She disguised herself as a man* 2 to hide (the real state of things)

disguise² n 1 something worn to hide who one really is 2 **in disguise a** disguised **b** hidden but real: *His illness became a blessing in disguise, when he married his nurse*

disgust¹ n a strong dislike caused by an unpleasant sight, sound, etc.

disgust² v to cause a feeling of disgust in

dish¹ n 1 a large, flat, and often round plate from which food is served 2 prepared food of one kind: *Cake is his favourite dish* 3 any object shaped like a dish, esp. the large reflector of a radio telescope 4 *esp. spoken (said by men)* a pretty girl 5 a dishful

dish² v *esp. spoken* to ruin (a person or his hopes) —see also DISH OUT, DISH UP

dishabille also **déshabillé**— n *French* the state of being only partly dressed (usu. said of a woman)

disharmony n -nies disagreement; lack of harmony — -monious adj

dishcloth n a cloth for washing or drying dishes

dishearten n to cause to lose hope — ~ment n

dishes n all the plates, cups, knives, forks, etc., used for a meal

dishevelled adj (of a person, his appearance, etc.) untidy

dishful n the amount that a dish will hold

dishonest adj not honest — ~ly adv — ~y n

dishonour¹ n loss of honour or a cause of lost honour — ~able adj — ~ably adv

dishonour² v to bring dishonour to

dish out v adv *esp. spoken* to hand out

dish up v adv 1 to put (food) into dishes, ready to be eaten 2 *esp. spoken* to produce (facts or arguments)

dishwasher n a person or machine that washes dishes

dishy adj -ier, -iest *esp. spoken* having sexual charm

disillusion v to show the unpleasant truth to: *Don't disillusion her* — ~ed adj — ~ment n

disincentive n something that discourages action or effort

disinclined adj not feeling like; unwilling — -clination n

disinfect v to clean so as to destroy bacteria — ~ion n

disinfectant n a disinfecting substance

disingenuous adj (of a person or behaviour) not open or sincere —compare INGENUOUS — ~ly adv — ~ness n

disinherit v to take away from (one's child) the right to inherit one's goods after one's death — ~ance n

disintegrate v -grated, -grating to break up into small pieces — -gration n

disinter v -rr- *esp. written* to dig up (esp. a body from a grave) — ~ment n

disinterested adj 1 acting fairly because not influenced by personal advantage: *a disinterested judgement* 2 usu. considered bad usage not caring; uninterested — ~ly adv — ~ness n

disjointed adj (of words or ideas) not well connected — ~ly adv — ~ness n

dislike¹ v -liked, -liking not to like

dislike² n 1 a feeling of not liking 2 **take a dislike to** to begin to dislike

dislocate v -cated, -cating 1 to put the bones of (a joint) out of place 2 to put (plans, business, etc.) out of order; disrupt — -cation n

dislodge v -lodged, -lodging to force out of a position — ~ment n

disloyal adj not loyal — ~ly adv — ~ty n

dismal adj showing or causing sadness: *dismal weather* — ~ly adv

dismantle v -tled, -tling 1 to take (a machine or article) apart 2 to take away the furniture, machines, etc., from (a building or ship) — ~ment n

dismay v, n -mayed, -maying (to fill with) a feeling of fear and hopelessness

dismember v to cut or take (a body, country, etc.) apart — ~ment n

dismiss v 1 *esp. written* to send away (from employment)—compare SACK 2 to allow to go: *to dismiss a class* 3 to put away (a subject) from one's mind 4 (of a judge) to stop (a court case) 5 (in cricket) to end the innings of (a player or team) — ~al n

dismount v 1 to get down (as from a horse or bicycle) 2 to take down (esp. a gun) from its base USAGE One **dismounts** from anything that one **rides** with one's legs hanging down on each side, such as horses, bicycles, motorcycles, and scooters; one **gets off** or *esp. written* **alights** from a bus or train, and **gets out of** a car or taxi.

disobedient adj not obeying — ~ly adv — -ence n

disobey v -beyed, -beying to fail to obey

disorder¹ v to put into disorder; confuse

disorder² n 1 lack of order; confusion 2 a riot 3 a slight disease or illness: *a stomach disorder*

disorderly adj 1 untidy; confused 2 violent

in public: *a disorderly meeting*—see DRUNK — -**liness** *n*

disorganize, -ise *v* -ized, -izing to throw into disorder (arrangements, a system, etc.) — -**ization** *n*

disorientate also disorient— *v* -tated, -tating to cause (someone) to lose the sense of direction — -**tation** *n*

disown *v* to refuse to accept as one's own; reject

disparage *v* -aged, -aging to make sound of little value — -**agingly** *adv* — ~**ment** *n*

disparate *adj* of different character — ~**ly** *adv*

disparity *n* -ties difference or inequality: *a great disparity in age*

dispassionate *adj* (of a person or his behaviour) calm and fair — ~**ly** *adv* — ~**ness** *n*

dispatch, despatch[1] *v* 1 to send off: *dispatch letters* 2 to finish quickly: *We soon dispatched the cake* 3 to kill

dispatch, despatch[2] *n* 1 sending off 2 a government message, or one sent to a newspaper by one of its writers 3 speed and effectiveness: *with great dispatch*

dispatch box *n* a box for official papers

dispatches, despatches *n* messages sent to a government to describe a battle: *He was mentioned in dispatches*

dispel *v* -ll- to drive away; scatter

dispensable *adj* not necessary

dispensary *n* -ries a place where medicines are dispensed and where medical attention is given

dispensation *n* 1 *esp. written* the act of dispensing 2 an event that seems specially arranged by God or Nature

dispense *v* dispensed, dispensing 1 to deal out; give out 2 to mix and give out (medicines) according to a doctor's prescription — **dispenser** *n*

dispense with *v prep* 1 to do without 2 to make unnecessary

dispensing chemist *n* a person who mixes and sells medicines

disperse *v* dispersed, dispersing 1 to scatter in different directions: *A prism disperses light* 2 to place at different points — **dispersal** *n* — **dispersion** *n*

dispirit *v* to discourage; dishearten

displace *v* -placed, -placing 1 to force out of the usual place 2 to take the place of

displaced person *n* displaced persons a person forced to leave his/her own country

displacement *n* technical the weight of water pushed aside by a ship floating in the water

display[1] *v* displayed, displaying to show

display[2] *n* displays 1 the act or action of displaying 2 a collection of things displayed 3 on display being shown publicly

displease *v* -pleased, -pleasing to cause displeasure to

displeasure *n* angry dislike and disapproval

disposable *adj* that can be freely used or thrown away: *disposable cups*

disposal *n* 1 arrangement 2 the act or action of getting rid of 3 use or control (esp. in the phrase at someone's disposal)

dispose *v* -posed, -posing to put in place: *to dispose soldiers for battle*

disposed *adj* willing

dispose of *v prep* to get rid of; finish with

dispose to *v prep* to give a certain feeling or tendency to: *He is disposed to anger*

disposition *n* 1 a general tendency of character 2 a general feeling: *We felt a disposition to leave*

dispossess *v* esp. written to take the possession or use away from: *They've dispossessed me of my house!* — ~**ed** *adj* — ~**ion** *n*

disproportion *n* a lack of proportion; lack of proper relation between the parts

disproportionate *adj* lacking proportion; unequal: *His pain was disproportionate to the injury* — ~**ly** *adv*

disprove *v* -proved, -proving to prove to be false

disputable *adj* not necessarily true — -**tably** *adv*

disputant *n* esp. written or law a person who disputes, esp. one who is arguing or quarrelling

dispute[1] *v* disputed, disputing 1 to argue about or contest (something) 2 to disagree about; doubt 3 to resist: *Our soldiers disputed the enemy advance* — **disputation** *n* — **disputatious** *adj* — **disputatiously** *adv*

dispute[2] *n* 1 an argument or quarrel 2 in dispute (with) in disagreement (with) 3 in/under dispute being argued about

disqualification *n* 1 the act of disqualifying or state of being disqualified 2 something that disqualifies

disqualify *v* -fied, -fying to make or declare unfit or unable: *Her youth disqualifies her from office*

disquiet[1] *v* to make anxious

disquiet[2] *n* anxiety and/or dissatisfaction

disregard[1] *v* to ignore

disregard[2] *n* 1 the act of disregarding or the state of being disregarded 2 lack of proper attention; neglect

disrelish *n* esp. written a feeling of dislike

disrepair *n* the state of needing repair

disreputable *adj* having a bad character or name — ~**ness** *n* — -**tably** *adv*

disrepute *n* lack of people's good opinion

disrespect *n* lack of respect — ~**ful** *adj* — ~**fully** *adv*

disrobe *v* -robed, robing esp. written to take off (esp. ceremonial outer) clothing: *The judge disrobed*

disrupt *v* to bring or throw into disorder: *An accident disrupted the railway* — ~**ion** *n* — ~**ive** *adj* — ~**ively** *adv*

dissatisfy *v* -fied, fying to fail to satisfy; displease — -**faction** *n*

dissect v 1 to cut (an animal, plant, etc.) into parts in order to study it 2 to study carefully, part by part (esp. to find faults) — ~ion n

dissemble also (esp. written) **dissimulate**— v -bled, -bling to hide (one's feelings, intentions, etc.) — ~r n

disseminate v -nated, -nating esp. written to spread (news, ideas, etc.) widely — -nation n

dissension n a disagreement

dissent v to disagree — **dissent** n

dissenter n a person who dissents — -ing adj

dissertation n a long usu. written discussion of a subject, esp. one written for a higher university degree

disservice n a harmful action

dissident adj, n (a person) openly disagreeing with a group: political dissidents — -dence n

dissimilar adj unlike — ~ly adv — ~ity n

dissimulate v -lated, -lating esp. written to dissemble — -lation n

dissipate v -pated, -pating 1 to cause to disappear or scatter; lose: He dissipated the gloom with his smile 2 to spread out and disappear: The crowd dissipated 3 to waste or use up foolishly: He dissipated his large fortune — -pation n

dissipated adj spending his/her life or energy in search of foolish pleasure

dissociate also **disassociate**— v -ated, -ating to separate from union with; disconnect: I've dissociated myself from your crime — -ation n

dissolute adj leading a bad life; dissipated — ~ly adv — ~ness n

dissolution n 1 the separation of a thing into its parts 2 decay or death 3 the breaking up of an association, group, etc.: the dissolution of Parliament

dissolve v -solved, -solving 1 to make or become liquid by putting into liquid: Dissolve the salt in water 2 to break up or end: He dissolved the meeting 3 to waste away, fade away, or disappear: His strength dissolved 4 to lose one's self-control because of strong feeling: to dissolve in/into tears — -soluble adj

dissonance n 1 a sounding together or combination of musical notes which do not sound pleasant —opposite **consonance** 2 a lack of agreement among beliefs, or between beliefs and actions — -nant adj — -nantly adv

dissuade v -suaded, -suading to advise successfully against: I dissuaded her from joining — -suasion n

distaff n now rare 1 the stick from which the wool is pulled in spinning 2 **on the distaff side** on the woman's side of the family

distal adj medical far from the point of joining or origin —opposite **proximal** — ~-ly adv

distance n 1 separation in space or time: What is the distance to London? 2 a distant point or place 3 **go the distance** (in sports, esp. boxing) to keep running, fighting, etc., till the end of the match

distant adj 1 separate in space or time; far off; away 2 coming from or going to a distance: a distant journey 3 not closely related: distant relations 4 not friendly — ~ly adv

distaste n dislike; displeasure

distasteful adj causing distaste — ~ly adv — ~ness n

distemper¹ n a disease of animals, esp. dogs and rabbits, causing fever, disordered breathing, and general weakness

distemper² n a paint that can be thinned by mixing with water

distend v esp. written to swell or make swollen — -tension n

distil v -ll- 1 to make (a liquid) into gas and then make the gas into liquid, as when separating alcohol from water 2 to separate in this way: to distil alcohol from potatoes — ~lation n

distiller n a person who distils, esp. alcohol

distillery n -ries a factory that distils whisky, gin, etc.

distinct adj 1 different: a distinct political party 2 clearly seen, heard, smelt etc.: a distinct smell — ~ly adv — ~ness n USAGE Anything clearly noticed is **distinct**: There's a distinct smell of beer in this room. A thing or quality that is clearly different from others of its kind is **distinctive**, or **distinct** from: Beer has a very **distinctive** smell; it's quite **distinct** from the smell of wine.

distinction n 1 difference 2 the quality of being unusual, esp. unusually good : a writer of distinction 3 a special mark of honour

distinctive adj clearly marking a difference: Each rank has a distinctive sign —see DISTINCT (USAGE) — ~ly adv — ~ness n

distinguish v 1 to recognize, see, hear, etc.: I can distinguish them at a distance 2 to make or recognize differences 3 to set apart as different: Elephants are distinguished by their trunks 4 to win (oneself) honour

distinguishable adj 1 that can be clearly seen, heard, etc. 2 that can be clearly recognized as different: Those objects are not easily distinguishable

distinguished adj marked by excellence or fame

distort v 1 to twist out of the true meaning: Stop distorting what I've said 2 to twist out of shape, normal condition, etc. — ~ion n

distract v 1 to take (a person, mind etc.) off something: Don't distract me 2 to confuse or trouble

distraction n 1 the act of distracting or the state of being distracted: driven to distraction 2 something or someone that distracts; amusement

distraught adj anxious and troubled almost to madness

distress¹ n 1 great suffering, sorrow, or

embarrassment; pain or great discomfort **2** a
state of danger: *sailors in distress*

distress² *v* to cause distress to

distressed area *n* now rare an area of continuing high unemployment

distribute *v* **-uted, -uting** **1** to divide among
several: *to distribute books to students* **2** to
spread out; scatter **3** to give out or deliver **4** to
supply (goods), esp. to shops — **-tribution** *n* —
-tributional *adj*

distributive *adj* distributing: *the distributive
trades* — ~ly *adv*

distributor *n* **1** a person or thing that distributes **2** an instrument which sends electric current in the right order to each sparking plug in a
car engine ⌐CAR

district *n* a part of a country, city, etc.; area: *a
postal district*

distrust¹ *v* to lack trust in

distrust² *n* lack of trust: *a distrust of banks* —
~ful *adj* — ~fully *adv*

disturb *v* **1** to change the usual condition of:
Wind disturbed the water **2** to break in upon or
interrupt (an activity, person, etc.) **3** to cause to
become anxious **4 disturb the peace** *law* to cause
public disorder

disturbance *n* **1** an act of disturbing or the
state of being disturbed: *The police charged 5 men
with causing a disturbance* **2** something that disturbs

disturbed *adj* having an illness of the mind or
feelings: *emotionally disturbed*

disunite *v* **-nited, -niting** to divide

disunity *n* lack of unity; disagreement

disuse *n* the state of no longer being used: *That
law has fallen into disuse* — ~d *adj*

ditch¹ *n* a long narrow not very deep V- or
U-shaped trench

ditch² *v sl* to get rid of; leave suddenly: *He
ditched the hat in the lake*

dither¹ *v esp. spoken* to be in a dither

dither² also **dithers**— *n esp. spoken* nervous
excitement and inability to decide

ditto *n* **-tos** **1** *esp. spoken* the same: ' *He said
we should do it.* ' *I say ditto* ' **2** a mark (·)
meaning the same: *one black pencil at 12p¨ blue
¨15p* (=one black pencil at 12p, one blue pencil at
15p)

ditty *n* **-ties** a short simple song

diuretic *n, adj* (a medicine) that causes a flow of
urine

diurnal *adj technical* of, related to, or active in
daytime rather than nighttime —opposite **nocturnal** — ~ly *adv*

div. *abbrev. for:* **1** divided **2** *esp. spoken*
division

divan *n* **1** a long soft seat on a wooden base,
usu. without back or arms, placed against a wall
2 also **divan bed** — the same used for sleeping

dive¹ *v* **dived, diving** **1** to jump down or go
down swiftly, esp. into water: *He dived off the
cliff* **2** to move quickly and suddenly into some
place, activity, etc.: *to dive into a doorway* **3** to

put one's hand quickly into something, esp. in
order to get something out

dive² *n* **1** an act of diving **2** *esp. spoken* a not
very respectable pub, meeting place, etc.

diver *n* a person who dives, esp. one who works
at the sea bottom in special dress with a supply of
air ⌐OIL

diverge *v* **-verged, -verging** to go out in different directions: *Our opinions diverge* — **divergence, -gency** *n* — **divergent** *adj*

divers *adj old use* many different

diverse *adj* different: *diverse interests* — ~ly
adv

diversify *v* **-fied, -fying** to make different or
various: *That factory has diversified its products*

diversity *n* **-ties** variety or difference: *a diversity of interests*

divert *v* **1** to turn aside or away from something: *They diverted the river* **2** to amuse; entertain — **diversion** *n* — **diversionary** *adj*

divertimento *n* **-tos** *or* **-ti** a usu. light musical
work for a few instruments, with several movements

divest of *v prep esp. written* to take off or away
from: *They divested the king of his robes/power*

divide¹ *v* **divided, dividing** **1** to separate into
parts, groups, shares, different directions, etc.: *to
divide a cake* | *The road divides at the river* **2** to
find out how many times one number contains or
is contained in another number: *15 divided by 3 is
5* **3** to be an important cause of disagreement
between: *I hope this will not divide us* **4** to vote
by separating into groups for and against: *Parliament divided on the question*

divide² *n technical* a line of high land that comes
between 2 different river systems; watershed

dividend *n* **1** that part of the money made by
a business which is divided among those who own
shares in the business, or the amount going to each
shareholder **2** a number divided by another:
When 15 is divided by 3, 15 is the dividend
—compare DIVISOR

dividers *n* an instrument for measuring or marking off lines, angles, etc.

divination *n* the act of discovering the
unknown, esp. the future

divine¹ *adj* **1** of, related to, or being God or a
god **2** *esp. spoken* very very good — ~ly
adv

divine² *v* **divined, divining** **1** to discover or
guess (the unknown, esp. the future) by or as if by
magic **2** to find or look for (water or minerals)
under ground —compare DOWSE — **diviner** *n*

divine right *n* a king's right to rule seen as a gift
from God

divingboard *n* a board fixed at one end, esp.
high off the ground, off which people dive into the
water

divining rod *n* DOWSING ROD

divinity *n* **-ties** **1** the quality or state of being
divine **2** a god or goddess **3** theology

Divinity *n* God

divisible *adj* that can be divided without leaving a remainder: *15 is divisible by 3*

division *n* **1** separation or dividing **2** one of the parts or groups into which a whole is divided **3** a large military or naval group, esp. one able to fight on its own **4** something that divides or separates **5** disagreement **6** the act of finding out how many times one number is contained in another: *the division of 15 by 3* **7** a vote in Parliament in which all those in favour go to one place and all those against go to another

division of labour *n* a system in which members of a group specialize in different jobs in order to increase total production

divisive *adj* tending to divide people — ~ly *adv* — ~ness *n*

divisor *n* the number by which another number is divided: *When 15 is divided by 3, 3 is the divisor* —compare DIVIDEND

divorce[1] *n* **1** a complete end of a marriage declared by a court of law —compare SEPARATION **2** a separation

divorce[2] *v* **divorced, divorcing** **1** to end a marriage between (a husband and wife) or to (a husband or a wife): *The court divorced them* **2** to separate: *It is hard to divorce love and duty*

divorcée *n* French a divorced woman

divot *n* a piece of turf removed in playing a golf stroke

divulge *v* **divulged, divulging** *esp. written* to tell (a secret) — ~nce *n*

divvy *v* **-vied, -vying** *sl* to divide: *Divvy it up between us*

dixieland also **dixieland jazz**— *n* old-style (traditional) jazz

dizzy *adj* **-zier, -ziest** **1** having an unpleasant feeling that things are going round and round **2** causing this feeling (esp. in the phrase **a dizzy height**) **3** having a pleasant feeling of excitement and lightness **4** *esp. spoken* silly — **dizzily** *adv* — **dizziness** *n*

DJ *abbrev. for:* DISC JOCKEY

djellaba also **djellabah, jellaba**— *n* a long loose garment with wide sleeves and a hood, worn esp. by Arabs in hot countries

DNA *technical abbrev. for:* deoxyribonucleic acid; the acid which carries genetic information in a cell

do[1] *v* **did, done, doing**, *3rd person sing. pres. tense* **does**, *pres. tense negative* **don't, doesn't**, *past tense negative* **didn't** **1** (a helping verb, used to make negative statements and orders): *He didn't come.* | *Don't go yet* **2** (a helping verb, used to form questions): *Did he arrive in time?* **3** (a helping verb used to give extra force, and often said with emphasis): *He did come, after all!* | *Not only did he come, but he brought his sister, too* **4** (a helping verb which takes the place of a verb already just used, or about to be used as an answer): *'What are you doing?' 'I'm cooking.'* | *He likes skating and so does she*

do[2] *v* **1** (with actions and nonmaterial things): *to do woodwork/a lesson* | *to do 80 miles an hour* **2**

(with action nouns ending in *-ing*): *He does the cooking* **3** (with certain nonmaterial expressions): *I did my best to help him.* | *I used to do business with him.* | *Those who do good will find peace* **4** (with people and nonmaterial things) to give or provide with: *That picture doesn't do her justice* **5** (with people) to be enough for: *"Will $5 do you?" "It will do me nicely"* **6** to cheat: *You've been done!* **7** *esp. spoken* to punish; hurt **8** to serve: *The barber will do you next* **9** to perform as or copy the manner of: *Olivier did "Othello" last night* **10** to arrange: *to do one's hair* **11** to clean: *to do one's teeth* **12** to cook: *I do fish very well* **13** to prepare: *Do us a report* **14** to behave; act: *Do as you're told!* **15** to be suitable: *Will $5 do?* **16** (in the *-ing*-form) happening: *What's doing tonight?* **17 That will do!** That's enough! **18 do one's own thing** *sl* to do what is personally satisfying **19 How do you do?** *polite* (a form of words used when introduced to someone: in later meetings, say "How are you?") **20 make do (with something)** also **make (something) do**— *esp.spoken* to use (something) even though it may not be perfect or enough **21 That does it!** (an expression showing that enough, or too much has been done) **22 What do you do?** What is your work? —see also DO FOR, DO IN, DO UP

do[3] *n* **dos** or **do's** *esp. spoken* **1** a big party **2 dos and don'ts** rules of behaviour

do, doh[4] *n* **1** the first or lowest note in the (sol-fa) musical scale **2** the 8th or highest note in the same scale

dobbin *n* a name for a working horse (not a race horse)

docile *adj* easily taught or led — **docility** *n*

dock[1] *n* a common broad-leafed plant that grows by the roadside

dock[2] *v* to take away a part of: *to dock a man's wages*

dock[3] *n* a place where ships are loaded or repaired

dock[4] *v* to bring to, come to, or remain in a dock

dock[5] *n* the place in a law court where the prisoner stands

docker *n* a person who loads and unloads ships

docket *n* *esp. written or technical* **1** a copy of a receipt, showing the details written on it **2** a label tied to a parcel showing where it is to be taken to

dockyard *n* a place where ships are built or repaired

doctor[1] *n* **1** a person holding one of the highest degrees given by a university **2** a person whose profession is to attend to sick people

doctor[2] *v* *esp. spoken* **1** to give medical treatment to **2** to repair **3** to change for some purpose, often dishonestly: *doctoring the election results* **4** to make (an animal) unable to breed

Doctor of Philosophy also (*esp. spoken*) D

Phil, PhD —— *n* (a person having) an advanced university degree

doctrinaire *adj offensive* typical of a person who tries to put ideas into action without considering the real world

doctrine *n* something taught, esp. a principle or system of principles: *Christian doctrine* — **-trinal** *adj*

document *v, n* (to prove with one or more of) a paper that gives information or support for an argument: *Can you document your claim?* — ~**ary** *adj*

documentary *n, adj* **-ries** (relating to) a presentation of facts through the arts, esp. on the radio or in the cinema: *a documentary about coal miners* —compare FEATURE

dodder *v esp. spoken* **1** (of a person) to become weak and shaky, usu. from age **2** (of a person) to walk slowly and shakily, usu. from age — ~**er** *n* — ~**ing** *adj*

doddle *n esp. spoken* something very easy to do: *That test was a doddle*

dodge¹ *v* **dodged, dodging** **1** to move suddenly aside, esp. to avoid **2** *esp.spoken* to avoid by a trick or dishonesty — ~**r** *n* : *a tax dodger*

dodge² *n* **1** an act of avoiding by a sudden movement **2** *esp. spoken* a clever way of avoiding something or of tricking someone

dodgems also **dodgem cars**— *n* (at fairs) small electric cars that people drive around in an enclosed space

dodgy *adj* **-ier, -iest** *esp. spoken* **1** risky and possibly dangerous: *a dodgy plan* **2** cleverly and perhaps dishonestly tricky: *a dodgy person* **3** not safe to use: *a dodgy chair*

dodo *n* **dodoes** or **dodos** a large flightless bird that no longer exists

doe *n* the female of any animal of which the male is called a buck, esp. a deer or rabbit

doer *n esp. spoken* (esp. in comparisons) an active person

does *3rd person sing. pres. tense of* DO

doff *v old use or pompous* to take off (esp. outer garments and hats) —opposite **don**

do for *v prep* **1** *sl* to murder **2** **done for** *esp. spoken* worn out or about to die

dog¹ *n* **1** a common 4-legged flesh-eating animal, esp. any of the many varieties used by man as a companion or for hunting, working, etc. **2** the male of this animal and of certain animals like it, esp. the fox and the wolf **3** *esp. spoken* a fellow: *a gay dog* **4 lead a dog's life** *esp. spoken* to have a life with many troubles **5 Let sleeping dogs lie** Leave alone things which may cause trouble **6 not have a dog's chance** *esp. spoken* to have no chance at all **7 top dog** *esp. spoken* the person on top, who has power —compare UNDERDOG **8 treat someone like a dog** *esp. spoken* to treat someone very badly —see also DOGS, **dog in the MANGER**

dog² *v* **-gg-** to follow closely (like a dog); pursue

dogcart *n* **1** a 2-wheeled vehicle, pulled by a horse, with seats back to back **2** a small cart to be pulled by a large dog

dog collar *n humour* a priest's collar

dog days *n* the hottest days of the year

doge *n* the highest government official in Venice and in Genoa, in former times

dog-eared *adj* (esp. of papers) having the corners of the pages bent down with use

dog-eat-dog *adj* marked by cruel merciless self-interest

dogfight *n* a fight between armed aircraft

dogfish *n* any of several kinds of small sharks

dogged *adj* refusing to give up in the face of difficulty: *By dogged effort she did well in the exam* — ~**ly** *adv* — ~**ness** *n*

doggerel *n* poetry that is silly or badly written

doggo *adv* **lie doggo** *sl* to hide quietly until the fear of being discovered is past

doghouse *n* **in the doghouse** *esp. spoken* in disfavour or shame

dogie *n US* a motherless calf in a group of cattle

dogleg *n* a sharp bend in a golf course, road, racetrack, etc.

dogma *n* an important belief or set of beliefs that people are often expected to accept without reasoning: *Church dogma* — ~**tic** *adj* — ~**tically** *adv* — ~**tism** *n*

do-gooder *n* **do-gooders** *offensive* a person who tries ineffectively to do good things for others

dog paddle *n* a simple swimming stroke in which one kicks the legs and makes small quick circles with the arms

dogs *n* **1** a sports event at which dogs (esp. greyhounds) race and bets are made **2 go to the dogs** to lead a wasteful life or to become ruined

dogsbody *n* **-ies** *esp. spoken* a person in a low position with the least interesting work

dog-tired *adj esp. spoken* very tired

doh *n* (in music) do

doily, doyley, doyly *n* **-lies** a small ornamented piece of cloth or paper placed on or underneath a plate, bowl, dish, etc.

do in *v adv* **1** *sl* to murder **2** *esp. spoken* to tire completely: *I'm done in after that walk!*

doing *pres. part. of* DO

doings *n* **doings** *esp. spoken* **1** things that are done or happen, esp. social activities **2** any small thing, esp. the name of which one forgets: *Put the doings on the table*

doldrums *n* **1** a place on the ocean where there is no wind **2 in the doldrums** *esp. spoken* **a** in a low and sad state of mind **b** inactive

dole *n* **1** something doled out **2 go/be on the dole** *esp. spoken* to start to receive/to receive money from the government because one is unemployed

doleful *adj* sad in a self-pitying way — ~**ly** *adv* — ~**ness** *n*

dole out *v adv* **doled, doling out** to give small amounts of (money, food, etc.) (to people in need)

doll *n* 1 a small figure of a person, esp. for a child to play with 2 *sl* a young woman or girl, esp. one with charm or one who dresses too finely

dollar *n* 1 any of various standards of money, used in the US, Canada, Australia, New Zealand, Hong Kong, etc. It is worth 100 cents and its sign is $ ☞ MONEY 2 a piece of paper, coin, etc., of this value

dollop *n esp. spoken* 1 a shapeless mass, esp. of food 2 a small unmeasured amount

doll's house *n* a child's toy house which can hold small dolls , toy furniture, etc.

doll up *v adv esp. spoken* to dress prettily

dolly *n* -lies 1 (used esp. by and to children) a doll 2 *technical* a flat surface on wheels for moving heavy objects, such as a television camera

dolly bird also **dolly—** *n sl* a pretty young woman, esp. one wearing fashionable clothes

dolmen also **cromlech—** *n* a group of upright stones supporting a large flat stone, built in ancient times in Britain and France

dolorous *adj poetic* sorrowful — ~**ly** *adv*

dolphin *n* a type of toothed sea-animal 2-3 metres long, which swims in groups and is very intelligent ☞ MAMMAL

dolt *n offensive* a slow-thinking foolish fellow — ~**ish** *adj* — ~**ishly** *adv*

domain *n* 1 land controlled by one person, a government, etc. 2 a subject of activity or knowledge: *History is my domain* 3 (in set theory) a set of items which are linked (MAPPED) to another set (the RANGE)

dome *n* a rounded top, esp. on a building or room — ~**d** *adj*

Domesday Book *n* a record of all the lands of England, showing their size, value, ownership, etc., made in 1086 on the orders of William the Conqueror

domestic¹ *adj* 1 of the house or family 2 liking home life 3 of one's own country — ~**ally** *adv*

domestic² *n* a domestic servant, usu. female

domestic animal *n* an animal that is not wild, esp. one kept on a farm

domesticate *v* -cated, -cating 1 to make (an animal) able to serve man, esp. on a farm — compare TAME 2 to cause to enjoy home life and duties — -cation *n*

domesticity *n* -ties 1 home and family affairs or life 2 a liking for such life

domestic science *n* (in some schools) the study of housekeeping, cooking, etc. —see also HOME ECONOMICS

domestic service *n* the work of a servant in a house

domicile¹ *n* 1 *esp. written* the place where one lives 2 *law* the place where for official purposes one is considered to live, whether or not one really spends much time there

domicile² *v* -ciled, -ciling *esp. written* to estab-

lish or settle in a place: *He is domiciled in London*

domiciliary *adj esp. written or law* of, like, to, or at a home; as in a home: *a domiciliary visit*

dominance *adj* the fact or state of dominating; importance, power, or control

dominant¹ *adj* 1 dominating: *a dominant nature* 2 (of one of a pair of body parts) being stronger than the other: *The right hand is dominant in most people* 3 *technical* (of groups of qualities passed on from parent to child (GENES)) being the quality that actually appears in the child when more than one are passed on: *Brown eyes are dominant and blue eyes are recessive*

dominant² *n* the 5th note of a musical scale of 8 notes —compare TONIC,

dominate *v* -nated, -nating 1 to have power (over), control (over), or the most important place (in): *She dominates her sisters. | Sports dominate in that school* 2 to be higher than: *The mountain dominated the town*

domination *n* the act of dominating or state of being dominated

domineer *v usu. offensive* to desire to control others, usu. without consideration of their feelings

Dominican *n* a member of a ROMAN CATHOLIC religious order established by St. Dominic in 1215 and esp. interested in preaching

dominion *n* 1 *esp. literature* power or control: *to hold dominion over a large area* 2 land under the control of one person or government 3 any self-governing nation of the Commonwealth other than Britain: *Canada is a dominion*

domino *n* -noes one of a set of flat pieces of wood, bone, etc., with a different number of spots on each, used for playing games

dominoes *n* any of several games played with a set of usu. 28 dominoes

don¹ *n* a university teacher, esp. at Oxford or Cambridge

don² *v* -nn- *old use or pompous* to put on (clothing and hats) — opposite **doff**

Don *n* (in Spanish-speaking countries) a polite title used before a man's first name

donate *v* donated , donating to make a gift of, esp. for a good purpose —see also DONOR — -ion *n*

done 1 finished: *Have you done with the scissors?* 2 past part. of DO

donjon *n* a massive inner tower of a castle as built in former times ☞ CASTLE

Don Juan *n esp. spoken* a man who is a great lover

donkey *n* -keys 1 a type of animal of the horse family, but smaller and with longer ears; ass 2 a stupid or stubborn person

donkey jacket *n* a thick jacket reaching down to the top of the legs, and usu. with leather or plastic across the shoulders

donkey's years *n sl* a very long time

donkeywork *n esp. spoken* the hard uninteresting part of some job (esp. in the phrase **do the donkeywork**)

donnish adj related to or typical of a university teacher, esp. in being more interested in ideas than life — ~**ly** adv

donor n a person who gives or donates: a kidney donor

doodle v **dled** , **dling** to draw irregular lines, figures, etc., aimlessly while thinking about something else — **doodle** n

doom[1] n a terrible fate, such as unavoidable destruction: to meet one's doom

doom[2] v to cause to experience something unavoidable and unpleasant, such as death or failure

Doomsday n (in Christianity) the last day of the world's existence, when God will judge all men

door n **1** a movable flat surface that opens and closes the entrance to a building, room, or piece of furniture: the kitchen/cupboard door **2** a doorway **3** any entrance: This agreement opens the door to peace **4** (in certain fixed phrases) house; building: My sister lives only 2 doors away. | The salesman went from door to door **5 answer the door** to go and open the door to see who has knocked or rung **6 at death's door** literature near death **7 by the back door** secretly or by a trick **8 out of doors** outdoors **9 show someone the door** to make it clear that someone is not welcome and should leave **10 show someone to the door** to go politely to the door with someone who is leaving

doorbell n a bell provided for visitors to a house to ring for attention

doorkeeper n a person who guards a building's door and lets people in and out

doorman n **-men** a man in a hotel, theatre, etc., who watches the door, helps people to find taxis, and usu. wears a uniform

doormat n a mat placed by a door for cleaning dirt from the bottom of shoes

doornail n **dead as a doornail** sl dead

doorstep n **1** a step before an outer door **2** sl a very thick slice of bread

doorstopper also **doorstop**— n an apparatus for holding a door open or preventing it bumping against the wall

doorway n **-ways** an opening for a door

dope[1] n **1** esp. spoken a drug forbidden by law except on the orders of a doctor, usu. taken to improve a sports performance or give a pleasant effect **2** sl information **3** sl a stupid person

dope[2] v **doped** , **doping** esp. spoken to give a drug to or put a drug in

dopey, dopy adj **-ier** , **-iest 1** esp. spoken having a dulled mind, as if because of alcohol or a drug **2** sl stupid

Doppler effect n the change in the pitch of sound according to whether its source is approaching the listener or going away

Doric adj related to, like, or typical of the oldest and simplest style of ancient Greek building — compare IONIC, CORINTHIAN

dormant adj inactive, esp. not actually growing: dormant animals asleep for the winter

dormer also **dormer window**— n an upright window in a sloping roof

dormitory[1] also (esp. spoken) **dorm**— n **-ries** a large room with many beds

dormitory[2] adj being a place where people live but do not work: a dormitory town

dormouse n **-mice** a type of very small European forest animal with a long furry tail, rather like a squirrel

dorsal adj of, on, or near the back, esp. of an animal — compare VENTRAL

dose[1] also **dosage**—— n **1** a measured amount (esp. of medicine) given or to be taken at one time **2** anything (usu. unpleasant) that has to be taken or borne: a dose of hard work

dose[2] v **dosed** , **dosing** often offensive to give a dose, esp. of medicine, to

doss n sl a short sleep

doss down v adv sl to find a place to sleep

dosser n sl a person who sleeps in a doss-house

dosshouse n sl a cheap lodging house

dossier n a set of papers containing a detailed report

dost thou dost old use (when talking to one person) you do

dot[1] n **1** a small usu. round spot: a dot on the letter i **2** a short sound or flash forming part of a letter when sending messages, esp. by telegraph —compare DASH **3 on the dot** esp. spoken at the exact time **4 the year dot** sl, often offensive a very long time ago

dot[2] v **-tt- 1** to mark with a dot **2** to cover with or as if with dots: a lake dotted with boats **3** to hit sharply

dotage n weakness of the mind caused by old age (esp. in the phrase **in one's dotage**)

dote on also **dote upon**— v prep **doted** , **doting on** to show too much fondness for

doth old use does

dotty adj **-tier** , **tiest** esp. spoken foolish or insane

double[1] adj **1** having or made up of 2 parts that are alike: double doors **2** for 2 people, animals, etc.: a double bed **3** having 2 different qualities: a double purpose

double[2] n **1** something that is twice another in quantity, strength, speed, or value: I paid $2 for this and Mr. Smith offered me double (= $4) for it **2** an alcoholic drink of spirits, with twice the amount usu. sold **3** a person who looks like another: He is my double **4** an actor or actress of similar build or appearance who takes the place of another in a film for some special, esp. dangerous, purpose **5 at the double** (esp. of soldiers) at a rate between walking and running **6 double or quits** the decision (in a game where money is risked) to risk winning twice the amount one has already won, or losing it all **7 on the double** esp. spoken very quickly —see also DOUBLES

double³ *adv* **1** twice (the amount, size, or quality): *10 is double 5* **2** 2 together

double⁴ *v* **-led**, **-ling** **1** to multiply (a number or amount) by 2: *Sales doubled in 5 years* **2** to make a sudden sharp turn: *He doubled (back) on his route* **3** to sail round by changing direction quickly **4** to fold or bend sharply or tightly over —see also DOUBLE AS

double as *v prep* to be or act as in addition to being or acting as something else: *In the play, Mary is playing the part of the dancer and doubling as the mother*

double-barrelled *adj* **1** (of a gun) having 2 barrels fixed side by side **2** *esp. spoken* (of family names) connected by a hyphen (as in *Smith-Fortescue*)

double bass also **bass**— *n* the largest and deepest instrument of the violin family

double bed *n* a bed for 2 people — **double-bedded** *adj*

double-breasted *adj* (of a coat) with one side of the front across the other and usu. with a double row of buttons and a single row of buttonholes

double-check *v* **1** to examine (something) twice carefully **2** (in the game of chess) to check with 2 pieces at the same time

double chin *n* a fold of loose skin between the face and neck

double cream *n* specially thick cream

double-cross *v sl* to cheat by pretended friendship — **double cross** *n* — **double-crosser** *n*

double-dealer *n* a deceiver — **-dealing** *n*

double-decker *n* a bus with 2 floors

double-dutch *n humour* speech or writing that one cannot understand

double-edged *adj* **1** having 2 useful edges **2** having 2 purposes, usu. quite different

double-entry book-keeping *n* a way of keeping accounts in which everything is written twice, as an outgoing and as an incoming amount

double first *n* **1** a bachelor's degree with results at the highest level in 2 subjects **2** the holder of such a degree

double-glaze *v* **-glazed**, **glazing** to provide (a window) of (a room) with an additional sheet of glass — **-zing** *n*

double Gloucester *n* an orange cheese rather like cheddar

double-jointed *adj* having joints that allow unusual movement backwards as well as forwards

double-park *v* to park (a vehicle) beside a vehicle already parked

double-quick *adj, adv esp. spoken* very quick(ly)

doubles *n* **doubles** a match (esp. of tennis) between 2 pairs of players —see also MIXED DOUBLES

doublet *n* a man's tight-fitting garment for the upper body, worn in Europe from about 1400 to the middle 1600s

double take *n esp. spoken* a quick but delayed movement of surprise (esp. in the phrase **do a double take**)

double-talk *v* to use rapid or difficult language, often a mixture of sense and nonsense, in order to confuse, amuse, etc. (someone), or get (something) — **double-talk** *n* — **double-talker** *n*

double time *n* double wages paid to people who work at weekends or on public holidays

doubloon *n* a former gold coin of Spain and Spanish America

doubly *adv* **1** to twice the degree **2** in 2 ways: *He is doubly troubled, by illness and poverty*

doubt¹ *v* **1** to be uncertain (about) **2** to mistrust: *I doubt his honesty* **3** to consider unlikely: *I doubt that he'll come* — **~er** *n* USAGE Some people think *I* **doubt** *whether he'll come* is better than *I* **doubt** *if he'll come*. In the negative form this verb must be followed by *that*: *I don't* **doubt** *that he'll come*.

doubt² *n* **1** a feeling of uncertainty of opinion **2** a feeling of mistrust or disbelief: *I have doubts about him* **3 without doubt** it is certain —see also NO DOUBT USAGE **1 Doubt** is followed by *that* after *no* or *not*: *There is some* **doubt** *(as to) whether he is guilty.* | *There is no* **doubt** *that he is guilty.* **2** *Without* **doubt** and **undoubtedly** express a stronger sense of knowing the real truth than **no doubt** or **doubtless**, which can be used as an adverb meaning not much more than 'I think' or 'I agree.'

doubtful *adj* **1** full of doubt; not trusting **2** uncertain **3** not probable **4** of questionable honesty, value, etc.: *a doubtful fellow* — **~ly** *adv*

doubtless *adv* **1** without doubt **2** probably —see DOUBT (USAGE)

douche *n* (an instrument for forcing) a stream of water into or onto any part of the body to wash it

dough *n* **1** flour mixed with other dry materials and water for baking **2** *sl, esp. US* money

doughnut *n* a small round cake fried in fat and usu. covered with sugar

doughty *adj* **-tier**, **-tiest** *old use or humour* able; strong; brave

doughy *adj* **-ier**, **-iest** like dough, often because not cooked enough

do up *v adv* **1** to fasten: *Do up your buttons* **2** to repair: *to do up the house* **3** to wrap **4** to make (oneself) more beautiful

dour *adj* hard and cold in one's nature; unsmiling — **~ly** *adv*

douse, dowse *v* **doused, dousing** to put into water or throw water over

dove *n* **1** any of various types of pigeon; soft-voiced bird often used as a sign of peace **2** *esp. US* a politician in favour of peace —opposite **hawk**

dovecote, **-cot**— *n* a box or house built for doves

dovetail¹ *n* **1** a way of joining 2 pieces esp. of wood with a shaped piece sticking out at the end of one piece fitting closely into a cut-out place in the other piece **2** a joint formed in this way

dovetail² v **1** to join by means of dovetails **2** to fit skilfully together

dowager n **1** a woman who has a noble title received from her husband who is dead **2** a grand-looking rich old lady

dowdy adj **-dier, -diest 1** (esp. of a woman) badly, dully dressed **2** (esp. of dresses) uninteresting; old-fashioned — **-dily** adv — **-diness** n

dowel n a pin (often of wood) in one part which fits into a hole in the other part

down¹ adv **1** towards or into a lower position: *Lift that box down from the shelf* **2** to or into a sitting or lying position **3** in or towards the south: *down in London* **4** to or towards a point away from the speaker, though not always a point at a lower level: *Walk down to the shop with me* **5** (with verbs of fixing or fastening) firmly; safely: *Stick down the envelope* **6** on paper; in writing: *'Did you write down the number?' 'I have it down somewhere.'* **7** (of money to be paid at once) in cash: *You can buy this car for $30 down and $5 a week for 3 years* **8** to the moment of catching, getting, or discovering: *The men hunted the lion down* **9** into silence: *The speaker was shouted down* **10** to a state of less activity, force, power, etc.: *Please turn the radio down* **11** from an earlier or past time: *These jewels have been passed down in our family for 300 years* **12** **down under** esp. spoken in or to Australia or New Zealand

down² adj **1** in a low position, esp. lying on the ground: *The telephone wires are down!* **2** directed or going down **3** being at a lower level: *Sales are down* **4** being in a state of reduced or low activity or spirits **5** esp. spoken US finished: *8 down and 2 to go* **6** **down for** entered on the list for (a race, school, etc.) **7** **down on** esp. spoken having a low opinion of or dislike for

down³ prep **1** to or in a lower or descending position; along; to the far end of: *He ran down the hill* **2** to or in the direction of the current of: *to go down the river*

down⁴ n **have a down on someone** esp. spoken to have a low opinion of, or feel dislike for, someone

down⁵ v **1** to knock to the ground or defeat **2** to swallow quickly (esp. a liquid) **3** **down tools** (of workers) to stop working, esp. to strike

down⁶ n fine soft feathers, hair, etc.

down-and-out adj, n **down-and-outs** (a person) suffering from bad fortune, lack of work, etc. — ~**er** n

down at heel adj **1** (of shoes) worn away underneath the heels **2** wearing shoes with worn-down heels and well-worn clothes

downbeat n the downward stroke of the conductor of a group of musicians, showing the first note of a bar of music —compare UPBEAT

downcast adj **1** having low spirits **2** directed downwards: *downcast eyes*

downer n esp. spoken a drug that makes feelings dull

downfall n **1** a sudden fall, esp. from high rank, or anything causing such a fall: *Drink was his downfall* **2** a fall of rain, esp. when sudden or heavy

downgrade v **-graded, -grading** to lower in rank, importance, etc.

downhearted adj having low spirits — ~**ly** adv

downhill¹ adv **1** towards the bottom of a hill **2** towards a worse state (esp. in the phrase **go downhill**)

downhill² adj **1** sloping towards the bottom of a hill **2** esp. spoken easy: *The hardest part is over; the rest is downhill*

Downing Street n **1** the London street in which the Prime Minister lives **2** the government of Great Britain

down payment n a part of the price paid at the time of buying or delivery, with the rest to be paid later, usu. in instalments

downpour n a heavy fall of rain

downright¹ adv esp. spoken thoroughly: *It makes me downright angry*

downright² adj esp. spoken **1** plain; direct; honest **2** thorough: *a downright shame*

downs n low rounded usu. chalk hills covered with grass

Down's syndrome also **mongolism**— n an abnormal weakness of mind and body with which some people are born. They usually have broad flattened heads and faces and sloping eyes

downstage adv, adj towards or at the front of a theatrical stage

downstairs adj, adv on or to a lower floor and esp. the main or ground floor of a building: *to come downstairs* — **downstairs** n

downstream adv, adj (moving) towards the mouth of a river

down-to-earth adj practical

downtrodden adj treated badly by those in power

downward adj towards or in a lower place or condition: *a downward glance*

downwards adv **1** in a downward direction **2** from an earlier time: *downwards through the years*

downwind adj, adv (going or being) in the direction that the wind is moving

downy adj **-ier, -iest** like or covered with down

dowry n **-ries** the property that a woman brings to her husband in marriage

dowse¹ v **dowsed, dowsing** to douse

dowse² v to try to find underground streams or minerals with a dowsing rod —compare DIVINE — —**dowser** n — —**dowsing** n

dowsing rod also **divining rod**— n a Y-shaped stick which points towards a place with underground water or minerals when held by a person with special ability

doyen (fem. **doyenne**)— *n* the oldest, longest-serving, or most experienced member of a group

doyley, doyly *n* **-lies** a doily

doze *v* **dozed, dozing** to sleep lightly — **doze** *n*

dozen *abbrev.* **doz.**— *adj, n* **dozen** *or* **dozens** 1 a group of 12 2 **dozens of** *esp. spoken* lots of —see also BAKER'S DOZEN

dozy *adj* **-ier, -iest** 1 sleepy 2 *esp. spoken* stupid — **-ily** *adv* — **-iness** *n*

D Phil *n abbrev. for:* Doctor of Philosophy

Dr *abbrev. for:* Doctor

drab *adj* **-bb-** uninteresting; cheerless: *drab lives* — ~ly *adv* — ~ness *n*

drabs *n* see DRIBS

drachma, drachm *n* **-mas** *or* **-mae** the standard of money of modern Greece ☞ MONEY

draconian *adj* very severe or cruel: *draconian laws*

draft¹ *n* a rough written form of anything or a rough plan

draft² *v* to make a draft of

draftsman *n* **-men** also **draughtsman**— a person who makes drawings or plans of new buildings, machines, etc.

drag¹ *n* 1 the action or an act of dragging 2 something that is dragged along over a surface 3 something or someone that makes it harder to go forwards 4 the force of the air that acts against the movement of an aircraft 5 *sl* something dull and uninteresting: *Your party was a drag* 6 *sl* an act of breathing in cigarette smoke 7 *sl* woman's clothing worn by a man

drag² *v* **-gg-** 1 to pull (a heavy thing) along: *dragging a tree along* 2 to cause to come or go unwillingly 3 to move along too slowly: *He dragged behind the others* 4 to look for something by pulling a heavy net along the bottom of (a body of water): *to drag the lake for a body* —see also DRAG DOWN, DRAG OUT, DRAG UP

drag down *v adv* to cause to feel weak after an illness

dragnet *n* 1 a net pulled along a river or lake bottom to bring up anything that may lie there 2 a network of actions and methods for catching criminals

dragon *n* an imaginary fire-breathing animal in children's stories

dragonfly *n* **-flies** any of a group of large brightly-coloured insects, with a long body and 2 pairs of large thin wings ☞ INSECT

dragoon *n* (in former times) a heavily armed soldier on horseback

dragoon into *v prep* to force into (doing something) by violent measures

drag out *v adv* 1 to last or draw out a very long time 2 to force to be told: *They dragged the secret out of me*

drag up *v adv esp. spoken* 1 to bring up (a child) in a poor way, esp. without good manners 2 to raise (a subject) unnecessarily

drain¹ *v* 1 to flow or cause to flow off gradually or completely 2 to make or become gradually dry or empty of fluid, energy, etc.: *Let the glasses drain* 3 to carry away the surface water of: *They want to drain the land* 4 to empty by drinking the contents of 5 to make weak and tired by using up the forces of body, mind, or feelings

drain² *n* 1 a pipe, tube, etc., that drains matter away 2 something that empties or uses up

drainage *n* 1 the act or action of draining 2 something that is drained off, such as liquid 3 a means for draining, such as a pipe or tube 4 also **drainage basin** — an area drained

draining board *n* a sloping board with a wavy surface, on which wet dishes are placed to dry

drainpipe *n* a pipe for drainage, esp. of water and waste from buildings

drainpipe trousers *n esp. spoken* tight narrow pipelike trousers

drake *n* a male duck

dram also **drachm**— *n* 1 a small measure of weight 2 a small measure of liquid 3 *esp. spoken* a small alcoholic drink

drama *n* 1 a play 2 plays as a form of literature ☞ LITERATURE 3 an exciting or dangerous group of events: *the drama of international politics*

dramatic *adj* 1 of or related to drama 2 exciting 3 catching the imagination by unusual appearance or effects: *a dramatic woman* — ~ally *adv*

dramatics *n* 1 the study or practice of theatrical arts such as acting 2 *offensive* striking or excited behaviour or expression

dramatis personae *n Latin* 1 the characters or actors in a play 2 a list of these people

dramatist *n* a writer of plays ☞ LITERATURE

dramatize, -ise *v* **-tized, -tizing** 1 to change (a book, report, etc.) into a play 2 to present in a striking or exciting manner — **-tization** *n*

drank *past tense of* DRINK

drape¹ *v* **draped, draping** 1 to cover with (folds, usu. of cloth) 2 to cause to stretch out loosely or carelessly: *He draped his legs over the chair*

drape² *n* an arrangement in or of folds

draper *n* a person who sells women's clothes, cloth, curtains, etc.

drapery *n* **-ies** 1 (*US* dry goods)— the trade of or goods sold by a draper 2 cloth arranged in folds, or such an arrangement

drastic *adj* strong, sudden, and often violent or severe: *drastic changes* — ~ally *adv*

drat *v* **-tt-** *sl* damn

draught¹ *n* 1 a current or flow of air 2 an act of swallowing liquid or the amount of liquid swallowed at one time 3 the depth of water needed by a ship to float 4 **on draught** (esp. of beer) from a barrel 5 a small round piece used in playing draughts

draught² *adj* 1 (of animals) used to pull loads: *a draught horse* 2 from a barrel: *draught beer*

draughtboard *n* a board on which draughts is played

draughts *n* a game for 2, each with 12 round pieces, on a board of 64 squares

draughtsman *n* a draftsman

draughty *adj* **-tier, tiest** with cold draughts blowing through

draw¹ *v* **drew, drawn, drawing** 1 to pull a cart: *drawn by a horse* 2 to cause to go in a stated direction: *to draw someone aside* 3 to attract: *drawn towards him* 4 to cause to come 5 (of people) to take (a breath) in 6 to cause (blood) to flow 7 to bring or pull out, esp. with effort: *to draw a tooth* 8 to remove the bowels from: *to draw a chicken* 9 to collect (liquid) in a container: *to draw water from the well* 10 (of a ship) to need (a stated depth of water) in order to float 11 to get, receive, or take: *to draw money from a bank* 12 to bend (a bow) ready to shoot an arrow 13 to pull out (a weapon) for use 14 to end a game, battle, etc. without either side winning 15 to make pictures with a pencil, pen, etc. 16 a to make with a pencil, pen, etc. b to make a picture of in this way 17 to prepare (esp. a cheque) properly: *to draw a cheque on one's bank* 18 to produce or allow an air current: *The chimney draws well* 19 **draw the/a line** to fix a border against some activity or between 2 areas: *to draw the line at stealing* 20 **draw the curtain** to close or open the curtain —see also DRAW FOR, DRAW IN, DRAW ON, DRAW OUT, DRAW UP

draw² *n* 1 an act or example of drawing: *He picked a winning number on the first draw* 2 a state of affairs in which neither side wins: *The game was a draw* 3 a person or thing that attracts

drawback *n* a difficulty or disadvantage

drawbridge *n* a bridge that can be pulled up to let ships pass, to protect a castle from attack, etc. ☞ CASTLE

drawer *n* a sliding boxlike container with an open top (as in a desk)

drawers *n* an undergarment for the lower body, no longer commonly worn

draw for *v prep* to draw lots for

draw in *v adv* 1 (of a day) to become dark 2 to arrive 3 to move to one side of the road: *The bus drew in* 4 (of people) to take in (a breath) 5 CLOSE IN

drawing *n* 1 the art of making pictures with a pen, pencil, etc. 2 a picture made by drawing

drawing board *n* 1 a flat piece of wood on which paper is laid to draw on 2 **go back to the drawing board** *esp. spoken* to start again after one's first attempt has failed

drawing pin *n* a short nail with a broad head for pressing in with a thumb

drawing room *n* *esp. written* LIVING ROOM

drawl *v* to speak slowly, with vowels greatly lengthened — **drawl** *n*

drawn¹ *adj* 1 twisted: *a face drawn with sorrow* 2 (of games, battles, etc.) ended with neither side winning

drawn² *past part.* of DRAW

draw on *v prep* also **draw upon**— to make use

of: *I shall have to draw on my money/imagination*

draw out *v adv* 1 to stretch: *to draw out the wire* 2 to have more hours of daylight 3 to leave: *The train drew out* 4 to take (money) from a bank 5 to show the general idea of: *I drew out a quick plan of my idea* 6 BRING OUT

drawstring *n* a string that can be made tighter or looser, used for fastening clothes, bags, etc.

draw up *v adv* 1 to form and usu. write: *to draw up a plan* 2 to place in prepared order: *The soldiers were drawn up* 3 (of a vehicle) to stop at a certain point 4 to make (oneself) stand straight, often proudly

dray *n* **drays** a low strong 4-wheeled cart without sides

dread¹ *v* to fear greatly

dread² *n* a great fear or cause of such fear: *a dread of heights*

dreadful *adj* 1 causing great fear; terrible: *dreadful pain* 2 unpleasant — ~**ness** *n*

dreadfully also (*bad usage*) **dreadful**— *adv* 1 in a dreadful manner 2 *esp. spoken polite* very: *I'm dreadfully sorry*

dream¹ *n* 1 a group of thoughts, images, or feelings experienced during sleep 2 a similar experience when awake 3 a state of mind in which one has such an experience and does not pay much attention to the real world 4 something not real but hoped for: *Her dream is a new bicycle* 5 *esp. spoken* a thing or person notable for beauty or excellence: *Their new house is a dream*

dream² *v* **dreamed** or **dreamt, dreaming** 1 to have (a dream) about something 2 to imagine

dreamboat *n* *sl* a very attractive person of the opposite sex

dreamer *n* 1 a person who dreams 2 a person who has impractical ideas

dreamless *adj* (of sleep) without dreams; peaceful — ~**ly** *adv*

dreamlike *adj* as in a dream; unreal

dream up *v adv* *sl often offensive* to think of or imagine

dream world *n* a world of false and unreal ideas

dreamy *adj* **-ier, -iest** 1 (of a person) not practical 2 peaceful and beautiful: *dreamy eyes* 3 not clear, sharp, or exact: *dreamy music* 4 *young girls' sl* wonderful; beautiful: *a dreamy dress* — **-ily** *adv* — **-iness** *n*

dreary *adj* **-ier, -iest** 1 sad or saddening 2 *esp. spoken* dull — **-ily** *adv* — **-iness** *n*

dredge¹ *v* **dredged, dredging** to use a dredger (in, on, or for something)

dredge² *v* to cover (food) lightly by scattering (something powdery) over it: *She dredged a little sugar over the cake*

dredger *n* also **dredge**— a machine or ship used for digging up soil from below water

dregs *n* 1 bitter bits in a liquid that sink to the bottom 2 the most worthless part of anything: *the dregs of society*

drench *v* to make thoroughly wet

dress[1] v 1 to put clothes on 2 to provide with clothes 3 to make or choose clothes for: *The princess is dressed by a famous dressmaker* 4 to put on special formal clothes for the evening 5 to arrange, finish, clean, or otherwise prepare: *to dress stone* 6 to clean and put medicine and a protective covering on (a wound) 7 to decorate: *to dress a Christmas tree* 8 to arrange goods interestingly in (esp. a shop window) 9 **dressed to kill** *esp. spoken* wearing very showy clothes —see also DRESS DOWN, DRESS UP

dress[2] n 1 clothing, esp. outer clothing or that worn on special occasions 2 a woman's or girl's outer garment that covers the body from shoulder to knee or below

dress[3] adj 1 related to or used for a dress 2 (of clothing) suitable for a formal occasion: *a dress shirt* 3 requiring or permitting formal dress

dressage n the performance by a horse of various actions as a result of the rider's guidance

dress circle n the first row of raised seats in a theatre

dress down v adv to scold — **dressing-down** n

dresser[1] n a piece of furniture for holding dishes, cutlery, etc., with open shelves above and cupboards below

dresser[2] n a person who dresses, esp. in the stated way: *a fashionable dresser*

dressing n 1 a usu. liquid mixture for adding to a dish, esp. a salad 2 material used to cover a wound

dressing gown n a long loose coat, worn before or after sleeping or bathing

dressing table n a low table with a mirror, usu. in a bedroom, at which a woman sits while arranging her hair, making up her face, etc.

dress rehearsal n the last rehearsal of a play before its public performance, usu. in costume

dress up v adv 1 to make more attractive or interesting, esp. with clothing 2 (usu. of children) to wear someone else's clothes for fun

dressy adj -ier, -iest 1 showy in dress 2 (of clothes) showy or ornamental

drew past tense of DRAW

dribble[1] v -bled, -bling 1 to flow or let flow little by little: *Saliva dribbled from his lip.* | *The baby is dribbling* 2 to move (esp. a ball) by a number of short kicks or strokes with foot, hand, or stick

dribble[2] n 1 a small slowly-moving stream or flow 2 a very small or unimportant quantity

driblet n 1 a very small or unimportant bit 2 a drop of liquid

dribs n **dribs and drabs** *esp. spoken* small and unimportant amounts

dried past tense and past part. of DRY

dried fruit n raw fruit preserved by drying

dried milk n MILK POWDER

drier n a dryer

drift[1] n 1 a movement or tendency without visible purpose and usu. slow: *the government's aimless drift* 2 a mass of matter blown up by

wind: *snow drifts* 3 earth, sand, stones, and rock left by running water or a glacier 4 the general meaning of a conversation, book, etc.

drift[2] v 1 to float or be driven along as if by wind, waves, etc.: *They drifted out to sea* 2 to pile up under the force of wind or water

drifter n *often offensive* a person who drifts, esp. one who travels or moves about aimlessly

driftwood n wood blown onto the shore by wind

drill[1] v 1 to make (holes) with a drill 2 to make holes in: *to drill someone's teeth* 3 **a** to train (soldiers) in military movements **b** to practise military movements under instruction 4 to instruct by repeating: *Drill them in sums*

drill[2] n 1 a tool or machine for making holes ☞ OIL 2 training and instruction, esp. by means of repetition 3 *esp. spoken* the correct way of doing something effectively: *What's the drill here?*

drill[3] n 1 a machine used for planting seeds in rows 2 a row of seeds planted in this way

drill[4] v to plant (seeds) in rows

drill[5] n a type of strong cotton cloth: *drill trousers*

drily adv see DRY

drink[1] v drank, drunk, drinking 1 to swallow (liquid) 2 to take in: *drinking air into his lungs* 3 to give or join in (a toast) 4 to use alcohol, esp. too much 5 to bring to a stated condition by taking alcohol: *He drank himself to death*

drink[2] n 1 a liquid suitable for swallowing 2 the habit or an act of drinking alcohol: *Have another drink!*

drinkable adj suitable for drinking

drinker n 1 a person who drinks 2 a person who drinks alcohol, esp. too much

drink to v prep to wish success by drinking a toast

drip[1] v -pp- 1 to fall or let fall in drops: *Water is dripping from the roof* 2 to overflow: *a voice dripping with sweetness*

drip[2] n 1 the action of falling in drops 2 (an apparatus for holding) liquid put into a blood vessel at a slow rate 3 *sl* a dull and unattractive person

drip-dry[1] v -dried, -drying to dry smoothly after hanging when wet

drip-dry[2] adj that will dry smooth and needs no ironing if hung wet: *a drip-dry shirt*

dripping[1] n fat and juices that have come from meat during cooking

dripping[2] adv **dripping wet** very wet

drive[1] v drove, driven, driving 1 to force, usu. to go or do something: *to drive trade away* | *Steam drives the engine* 2 to guide and control (a vehicle): *She drives well* —compare RIDE 3 to take in a vehicle as stated: *Can you drive me to the station?* 4 (of a vehicle) to perform in the stated way: *This car drives well* 5 to produce by opening a way: *to drive a tunnel* 6 (esp. of rain) to move along with great force 7 to collect (esp. snow) into large heaps

drive[2] n 1 a journey in a vehicle 2 an act of

hitting a ball, the distance a ball is hit, or the force with which it is hit **3** a driveway **4** a strong well-planned effort by a group for a particular purpose: *a membership drive* **5** a competition of the stated type, esp. a card game: *a whist drive* **6** an important need which causes a person to act: *the sex drive* **7** a forceful quality of character that gets things done **8** the apparatus by which a machine is set or kept in movement: *This car has front-wheel drive*

drive at *v prep esp. spoken* (*in* -*ing form*) to mean: *What are you driving at?*

drive-in *n, adj* (a place) that people can use while staying in their cars: *a drive-in cinema*

drivel¹ *v* -**ll**- to talk stupidly — ~**ler** *n*

drivel² *n* nonsense

driver *n* **1** a person who drives **2** a golf club with a wooden head, for hitting the ball long distances at the beginning of play —see also SCREWDRIVER

driveway *n* -**ways** a usu. private road through a park or to a house

driving *adj* **1** passing on force: *a driving wheel* **2** having a great effect or force: *driving rain / influence* **3** of or about guiding and controlling vehicles, esp. cars: *a driving school*

driving licence *n* a licence to drive a motor vehicle

drizzle *v* -**zled**, -**zling** to rain lightly — **drizzle** *n* — **drizzly** *adj*

drogue *n* **1** something pulled behind an aircraft for other aircraft to shoot at **2** also **drogue parachute** — a small arachute that pulls out a larger one or slows down a falling object

droll *adj* humorously odd or unusual — **drolly** *adv* — ~**ness** *n*

drollery *n* -**ries** **1** droll humour **2** an example of this

dromedary *n* -**ries** a type of camel with one hump

drone¹ *n* **1** a male bee **2** *offensive* a person who lives off the work of others **3** a pilotless aircraft or ship controlled by radio

drone² *v* **droned, droning** **1** to make a continuous low dull sound **2** to say in a low dull voice without variation

drone³ *n* **1** a continuous dull low sound **2** a fixed deep note sounded continuously in some music

drool *v offensive* **1** to let saliva flow from the mouth, as at the sight of food **2** to talk foolishly **3** to show pleasure in a foolish way

droop¹ *v* **1** to hang or bend downwards **2** to weaken: *His spirits drooped* — **droop** *n*

drop¹ *n* **1** the amount of liquid that falls in one small mass **2** the smallest possible amount of liquid **3** a small round sweet **4** a fall: *a long drop into the hole* **5** that which is dropped: *a drop of food from an aircraft* **6 get the drop on someone** *sl* to get quickly into a more favourable position than someone —see also DROPS

drop² *v* -**pp**- **1** to fall or let fall suddenly or in drops **2** to let fall or lower: *to drop a handker-*

chief| *to drop one's voice* **3** to go lower; become less: *Prices dropped* **4** *esp. spoken* to let (someone) get out of a vehicle: *Drop me at the corner* **5** to leave out, esp. from a team: *I've been dropped for Saturday's match* **6** to give up: *He's dropped his old friends* **7** *drug-users' sl* to take (drugs) **8** to come or go informally: *Drop in and see us* **9** to get further away from a moving object by moving more slowly than it: *Our car dropped behind* **10 drop someone a line/note** to write a short letter to someone

dropkick¹ *n* (in rugby) a kick made by dropping the ball onto the ground and kicking it as it rises —compare PLACEKICK, PUNT

dropkick² *v* to kick (a ball or goal) by making a dropkick

droplet *n* a very small drop (as of a liquid)

drop off *v adv esp. spoken* to fall asleep

dropout *n* **1** a person who leaves school or college without completing the course **2** a person who leaves ordinary society and tries to live differently

dropper *n* a short glass tube often with a rubber bulb at one end for pressing, used for measuring out liquid by drops

droppings *n* waste matter from the bowels of animals

drops *n* liquid medicine to be taken drop by drop

drop shot *n* (in tennis, badminton, and such games) a shot played so that the ball just clears the net and immediately drops to the ground

dropsy *n* a gathering of liquid under the skin or in the organs because of any of various diseases — -**sical** *adj*

dross *n* **1** useless material which comes to the surface of melted metal **2** waste or impure matter

drought *n* a long period of very dry weather

drove¹ *n* a group of esp. farm animals moving in a body

drove² *past tense of* DRIVE

drover *n* a person who drives cattle or sheep, esp. to market

drown *v* **1** to die by being under water too long **2** to kill by holding under water too long **3** to cover completely or make thoroughly wet, usu. with water **4** to cause (oneself) to become very active in something: *He drowned himself in work* **5** to cover up (a sound) by making a loud noise

drowse¹ *v* **drowsed, drowsing** **1** to sleep lightly **2** to be inactive — **drowse** *n*

drowsy *adj* -**sier**, -**siest** **1** ready to fall asleep **2** making one sleepy — -**sily** *adv* — -**siness** *n*

drub *v* -**bb**- *esp. spoken* **1** to beat severely (with a stick) **2** to defeat thoroughly

drudge¹ *v* **drudged, drudging** to do hard or uninteresting work

drudge² *n* a person who drudges

drudgery *n* hard dull work

drug¹ *n* **1** a medicine or material used for making medicines **2** a habit-forming substance

drug² *v* -**gg**- to add drugs to, or give drugs to, esp.

so as to produce unconsciousness: *to drug a sick man*

drugstore *n* *esp. US* a pharmacy which sells medicines, beauty products, films, and simple meals

druid *n* a member of the ancient Celtic priesthood

drum¹ *n* 1 a circular musical instrument whose tight skinlike surface is struck by hand or with a stick 2 a sound like that of such an instrument 3 a piece of machinery or a large container shaped like a drum

drum² *v* -**mm**- 1 to beat or play a drum 2 to make drum-like noises: *He drummed on the table with his fingers* —see also DRUM INTO, DRUM OUT, DRUM UP

drumhead *n* the material (such as skin or plastic) stretched over each end of a drum

drum into *v prep esp. spoken* to put firmly into someone's mind by continuous repeating

drum majorette *n* (esp. in the US) a showily-dressed girl who marches in front of a musical band

drummer *n* a person who plays a drum

drum out *v adv* to dismiss or send away formally

drumstick *n* 1 a stick for beating a drum 2 (of food) the lower part of the leg of a bird

drum up *v adv* 1 to call together by or as if by beating a drum 2 to obtain by continuous effort and esp. by advertising: *to drum up business*

drunk¹ *adj* 1 under the influence of alcohol: *drunk and disorderly* 2 overcome with success or joy

drunk² *n* *offensive* a person who is drunk

drunk³ *past part. of* DRINK

drunkard *n* *offensive* a person who is drunk often —compare ALCOHOLIC

drunken *adj* 1 drunk 2 resulting from or marked by too much drinking of alcohol: *a drunken sleep* — ~ly *adv* — ~ness *n*

dry¹ *adj* **drier, driest** 1 not wet 2 (of parts of the earth) emptied of water: *a dry lake* 3 no longer giving milk 4 without tears or other liquid substances from the body: *dry sobs* 5 having or producing thirst: *I am feeling very dry* 6 (esp. of bread) without butter or not fresh 7 (of alcoholic drinks, esp. wine) not sweet 8 without rain or wetness 9 not allowing the sale of alcoholic drink: *a dry state* 10 dull and uninteresting: *The book was as dry as dust* 11 amusing without appearing to be so; quietly ironic: *dry humour* — **dryly, drily** *adv* — **dryness** *n*

dry² *v* **dried, drying** 1 to make or become dry: *Dry your hands* 2 to preserve (food) by removing liquid: *dried fruit* —see also DRY OUT, DRY UP

dryad *n* (in ancient Greek stories) a spirit who lived in a tree; wood nymph

dry battery also **dry cell**— *n* -**ries** an electric battery containing chemicals made into a paste rather than a liquid

dry-clean *v* to clean (clothes, material, etc.), without using water — **dry-cleaning** *n*

dry cleaner's *n* a shop where clothes, materials, etc. are dry-cleaned

dry dock *n* a basin enclosing a ship, which can be drained to repair the ship

dryer, drier *n* 1 a person who dries 2 a machine that dries

dry ice *n* carbon dioxide in a solid state, used mainly to keep food cold

dry out *v adv* 1 to give up or cause to give up dependence on alcoholic drink 2 to make or become completely dry

dry rot *n* disease in wood which turns it into powder

dry-shod *adj* without wetting the shoes or feet

dry up *v adv* 1 to make or become completely dry 2 *sl* SHUT UP 3 to forget one's lines while acting in a play

dry wall also **dry walling, dry-stone wall**— *n* a wall made of stones put together without the aid of any mortar, set up esp. to separate fields

d t's also (*esp. written*) **delirium tremens**— *n* an excited state in which unreal things are seen, caused by much drinking of alcohol

dual *adj* 1 consisting of 2 parts or having two parts like each other 2 having a double character

dual carriageway *n* a main road with a dividing strip between traffic going in opposite directions

dub¹ *v* -**bb**- 1 to make a knight by a ceremonial touch on the shoulder with a sword 2 *humour* to name humorously or descriptively

dub² *v* to give different sound effects to, or change the original spoken language of (a film, radio show, or television show)

dubbin¹ also **dubbing**— *n* a grease for making leather softer

dubbin² *v* to treat with dubbin

dubious *adj* 1 causing doubt; of uncertain value or meaning 2 feeling doubt 3 possibly dishonest: *a dubious character* — ~ly *adv* — ~ness *n*

ducal *adj* of, like, or fit for a duke

ducat *n* a kind of gold coin

duchess *n* (the title of) a the wife of a duke b a woman of ducal rank in her own right

duchy *n* -**ies** (used esp. in names) the lands of a duke or duchess

duck¹ *n* **ducks** *or* **duck** 1 (*masc.* **drake**)— a swimming bird with short legs and short neck, some wild, some kept for food 2 the meat of this bird 3 *esp. spoken* a person one likes: *She's a sweet old duck* 4 (in cricket) the failure to make any runs —see also LAME DUCK

duck² *v* 1 to lower (one's head or body) quickly, esp. so as to avoid being hit 2 to push under water: *He ducked his head in the stream* 3 *esp. spoken* to try to avoid (a difficulty or something unpleasant): *He tried to duck out of going* — **duck** — **ness** *n*

duck³ *n* a strong cotton cloth

duckboards *n* narrow boards with spaces between, for walking over wet or muddy ground

ducking stool n a seat on one end of a long pole, formerly used for ducking unpleasant people as a punishment

duckling n a young duck or its meat as food

ducks and drakes n a game in which one makes flat stones jump along the surface of water

duckweed n any of various plants that grow on the surface of water

duct n 1 a thin narrow tube in the body which carries liquids, esp. from glands 2 any kind of pipe for carrying a liquid or gas or an electric power line —see also AQUEDUCT, VIADUCT

ductile n that can be pressed, pulled into shape, or changed easily — -tility n

ductless gland n ENDOCRINE GLAND

dud n sl a person or thing that is worthless, or unable to serve a desired purpose: a dud cheque

dude ranch n a cattle ranch that offers holiday activities for tourists

dudgeon n **in high dudgeon** in a state of bad temper

due[1] adj 1 owed or owing as a debt or right —see DUE TO (USAGE) 2 proper: drive with due care 3 payable 4 expected; supposed (to): The next train is due at 4 o'clock —see also DULY

due[2] n something that rightfully belongs to someone (esp. in the phrase **give someone his due**)

due[3] adv (before north, south, east, and west) directly; exactly

duel[1] n 1 a fight with guns or swords, between 2 people 2 a struggle or argument between any 2 opposed people, groups, or animals

duel[2] v -ll- to fight a duel with (another person or each other)

duenna n (esp. in Spanish- and Portuguese-speaking countries) an older woman who watches over the daughters of a family; a chaperon

dues n official payments: harbour dues

duet n a piece of music for 2 performers

due to prep because of; caused by: His illness was due to bad food USAGE Compare **due to** and **owing to**. **due** is an adjective and should really be used only with nouns: His absence was **due to** the storm. Many people are now beginning to use **due to** with verbs, treating it like **owing to** or **because of**: He arrived late **due to/owing to** the storm.

duffel bag, duffle bag n a round bag made of strong cloth, for carrying belongings

duffel coat, duffle coat n a loose coat of heavy woollen cloth with a furry surface (**duffel**), usu. fastened with toggles

duffer n esp. spoken a foolish person or slow learner

dug past tense and past part. of DIG

dugong n a large mostly tropical breast-feeding sea animal with flippers and a forked tail ☞ MAMMAL

dugout n 1 a small light boat made by cutting out a deep hollow in a log 2 a (usu. military) shelter dug in the ground —compare TRENCH

duke n (the title of) a nobleman of the highest rank —see also DUCHESS

dukedom n 1 the rank of a duke 2 a duchy

dulcimer n a small European musical stringed instrument of former times, played with light hammers

dull[1] adj 1 (of colour or surfaces) not bright, strong, or sharp 2 (of sound) not clear; low 3 (of weather, the sky, etc.) cloudy; grey 4 (of the senses) not of good quality 5 (of pain) not clearly felt 6 slow in understanding: dull children 7 uninteresting; unexciting: The company was very dull — ~y adv — ~ness n

dull[2] v to make or become dull: This will dull the pain

dullard n a dull slow-thinking person

duly adv in a due manner; properly: Your suggestion has been duly noted

dumb adj 1 unable to speak: We were struck dumb 2 unwilling to speak: to remain dumb despite torture 3 esp. spoken stupid — ~ly adv — ~ness n

dumbfound, dumfound v to make unable to speak because of surprise or lack of understanding

dumbwaiter n 1 a small table that turns round on a fixed base, put on a larger table and used for serving food 2 a small lift used esp. in restaurants for moving food, plates, etc.

dum-dum n a soft-nosed bullet that spreads out upon hitting an object

dummy n -mies 1 an object made to look like and take the place of a real thing 2 something like a human figure made of wood or wax and used to make or show off clothes 3 a rubber thing for sucking, put in a baby's mouth to keep it quiet

dummy run n a trial run

dump[1] v 1 to drop or unload in a heap or carelessly 2 sl to get rid of suddenly 3 to sell (goods) in a foreign country at a very low price

dump[2] n 1 a place for dumping something (such as waste material) 2 (a place for) a stored supply of military materials 3 offensive a dirty and untidy place: This town's a real dump

dumper also **dumper truck**— n a vehicle with a large movable container on the front, that is used for carrying and emptying heavy loads

dumpling n 1 a lump of boiled dough, served with meat 2 a sweet food made of pastry with fruit inside it

dumps n (**down**) **in the dumps** esp. spoken sad and in low spirits

dumpy adj -ier, -iest (esp. of a person) short and thick — -iness n

dun adj, n 1 (of) a brownish-grey colour that lacks brightness 2 a horse of this colour

dunce n a slow learner; stupid person

dunderhead n a stupid person

dune also **sand dune**— n a sandhill (often long and low) piled up by the wind on the seashore or in a desert

dung n solid waste material passed from the bowels of animals (esp. cows and horses), often mixed with soil to make manure

dungarees *n* trousers made of heavy cotton cloth, usu. blue

dungeon *n* a close dark prison, usu. underground, beneath a castle

dunk *v* to dip food into liquid while eating

duo *n* **duos** **1** 2 musicians who play duets **2** *esp. spoken* a pair

duodecimal *adj technical* of 12 or 12's; concerning calculation by 12's

duodenum *n* **-na** *or* **-nums** *technical* the first part of the bowel below the stomach — **-nal** *adj*

dupe¹ *n* a person who is deceived (by someone else)

dupe² *v* **duped, duping** to trick or deceive

duplicate¹ *adj* consisting of 2 that are exactly alike: *a duplicate key*

duplicate² *n* something that is exactly like another; copy

duplicate³ *v* **-cated, cating** **1** to copy exactly **2** to make again; make double — **-cation** *n*

duplicator *n* a machine that makes copies of written, printed, or drawn material

duplicity *n* deceit; deception

durable *adj* long-lasting: *durable clothing* — **-bly** *adv* — **-bility** *n*

duration *n* **1** continuance in time: *an illness of short duration* **2** the time during which something lasts

durbar *n* ₄ *Indian & Pakistani* a court or ceremonial gathering held by Indian princes in former times

duress *n* unlawful force or threats: *The promise was made under duress*

Durex *n trademark* a condom

during *prep* all through, or at some point in the course of: *Let us go on a picnic one day during the holidays*

durst *old use past tense of* DARE

dusk *n* the time when daylight is fading; darker part of twilight, esp. at night —compare DAWN, TWILIGHT

dusky *adj* **-ier, -iest** **1** darkish in colour **2** shadowy: *the dusky light of the forest* — **-iness** *n*

dust¹ *n* **1** powder made up of very small pieces of waste matter **2** finely powdered earth: *In the summer we have a great deal of dust* **3** powder made up of small pieces of some substance: *gold dust* **4** *literature* the earthly remains of bodies once alive **5 throw dust in someone's eyes** *esp. spoken* to deceive someone —see also BITE **the dust** — ~**less** *adj*

dust² *v* **1** to clean the dust from; remove dust **2** to cover with dust or fine powder: *to dust a cake with sugar*

dustbin *n* a container with a lid, for holding refuse

dustbowl *n* an area that suffers from dust storms and long periods without rain

dustcart *n* a lorry which goes from house to house in a town to collect the contents of dustbins

duster *n* a cloth or tool for dusting furniture

dust jacket *also* **dust cover, jacket**— *n* a paper cover put as a protection round a book, often having writing and pictures describing the book

dustman *n* **-men** a man employed to remove refuse from dustbins

dustpan *n* a flat pan with a handle into which dust can be brushed

dustsheet *n* a large sheet used for throwing over furniture, shop goods, etc., in order to keep the dust off

dustup *n sl* a quarrel or esp. a fight

dusty *adj* **-ier, -iest** covered with dust

Dutch *adj* **1** of the people, country, or language of the Netherlands (Holland) **2 go Dutch (with someone)** to share expenses —see also DOUBLE-DUTCH

Dutch auction *n* a public sale at which the price is gradually reduced until somebody will pay it

Dutch barn *n* a wall-less building with a curved roof supported on a frame, used for storing crops

Dutch cap *n* a contraceptive cap

Dutch courage *n esp. spoken* the courage that comes from being drunk

Dutch elm disease *n* a disease caused by a type of fungus that attacks and kills elm trees

Dutch uncle *n* a person who scolds firmly, but with kindness

dutiable *adj* (of goods) on which one must pay duty

dutiful *also* (*esp. written*) **duteous**— *adj* having or showing a sense of duty; with respect and obedience — ~**ly** *adv* — ~**ness** *n*

duty *n* **duties** **1** what one must do either because of one's job or because one thinks it right: *It's my duty to help you* **2** a type of tax: *customs duties*

duty-free *adj, adv* allowed to be sold in a country without tax: *a duty-free shop*

duvet *also* **continental quilt**— *n French* a large bag filled with soft warm material, such as feathers, used on a bed to take the place of all other coverings

dwarf¹ *n* **1** a person, animal, or plant of much less than the usual size **2** a small imaginary manlike creature in fairy stories

dwarf² *v* **1** to prevent the proper growth of **2** to cause to appear small by comparison: *The new building dwarfs all the shops*

dwell *v* **dwelt** *or* **dwelled, dwelling** *esp. written* to live —see LIVE (USAGE)

dwelling *n esp. written & humour* a house, flat, etc., where people live

dwell on *also* **dwell upon**— *v prep* to think, speak, or write a lot about: *Don't dwell so much on your past*

dwindle *v* **-dled, -dling** to become gradually fewer or smaller

dye¹ *n* a vegetable or chemical substance, usu. liquid, used to colour things —compare PAINT

dye² *v* **dyed, dyeing** to give or take (a stated)

colour by means of dye: *She dyed the dress (red)* — **dyer** *n* USAGE Compare **die** (verb): **dies, died, dying.**

dyed-in-the-wool *adj often offensive* impossible to change: *a dyed-in-the-wool Republican*

dying *pres. part. of* DIE

dyke *n, v* dike

dynamic *adj* **1** *technical* of force or power that causes movement —opposite **static 2** (of people) full of power and activity — ~**ally** *adv*

dynamics *n* **1** the science that deals with matter in movement **2** (in music) changes of loudness

dynamite¹ *n* **1** a powerful explosive used in mining **2** *esp. spoken* something or someone that will cause great shock, surprise, admiration, etc.: *That news story is dynamite*

dynamite² *v* **-mited, -miting** to blow up with dynamite

dynamo *n* **-mos** a machine (esp. small) which turns some other kind of power into electricity —compare GENERATOR, MAGNETO ELECTRICITY CAR

dynasty *n* **-sties 1** a line of kings all of the same family **2** the time during which the same family of kings rules a country — **dynastic** *adj*

dysentery *n* a painful disease of the bowels that causes them to produce diarrhoea, blood, and mucus

dyslexia also (*esp. written*) **word blindness**— *n technical* inability to read, not resulting from lack of intelligence but caused by difficulty in seeing letters — **dyslexic** *adj*

dyspepsia *n* difficulty in digesting food; indigestion — **-peptic** *adj, n*

E

E, e E's, e's *or* Es, es the 5th letter of the English alphabet

E¹ *(in Western music)* the third note in the musical scale of C major or the musical key based on this note

E² *abbrev. for:* east(ern)

e *technical* the sign used in mathematics for the base of the system of natural logarithms, having a value of about 2.71828

each¹ *adj* every one separately: *Give a piece to each child* USAGE Compare **both** and **each: Both** is used for 2 things taken together; **each** for any number of things taken separately: *Both of us won a prize.* | *Each of us won a prize.* In the first example there may be one shared prize , or two prizes. In the second there are two prizes. **Both** always takes a plural verb. **Each** is usually singular except when following a plural subject, or to avoid saying *his or her:* *Each member of the party must do their best.* —see EVERY (USAGE)

each² *pron* every one separately

each³ *adv* for or to every one

each other also **one another**— *pron* (means that each of 2 or more does something to the other or others): *The kittens were chasing each other* USAGE Some people like to say **each other** about 2 people or things, and **one another** about more than 2, but this is not a fixed rule.

each way *adv technical* (in gambling) to win if the horse or dog backed comes first, second, or third in a race

eager *adj* keen; full of interest or desire: *He listened with eager attention* —see also **eager** BEAVER — ~**ly** *adv* — ~**ness** *n*

eagle *n* **1** any of various types of very large strong birds of prey with hooked beaks and very good eyesight BIRD **2** (in golf) an act of hitting the ball into the hole, taking 2 strokes fewer than is average for that particular hole

eagle-eyed *adj* **1** having very good eyesight **2** looking very keenly (at something): *Peter watched eagle-eyed*

ear¹ *n* **1** the organ of hearing in man and animals **2** attention or notice: *She has the minister's ear* **3** keen recognition of sounds, esp. in music and languages: *an ear for music* **4 all ears** *esp. spoken* listening attentively **5 by ear** to play (music) from memory of the sound alone **6 out on (one's) ear** *sl* suddenly thrown out of a place or dismissed from a job **7 up to (one's) ears in** *esp. spoken* deep in or busy with **8 wet behind the ears** *sl* immature and without experience

ear² *n* the head of a grain-producing plant such as corn or wheat, used for food

earache *n* a pain in the ear

eardrum *n* a tight thin skin inside the ear, which makes one hear the sound waves that beat against it

earful *n* as much talk, esp. angry, as one can bear: *He's going to get an earful from me!*

earl *n* a British nobleman of high rank —see also COUNTESS — ~**dom** *n*

earliest *n* **at the earliest** and no earlier

earlobe *n* the round fleshy piece at the bottom of the ear

early¹ *adv* **-lier, -liest 1** before the usual, arranged, or expected time **2** towards the beginning of a period

early² *adj* **1** arriving, developing, happening, etc., before the usual, arranged, or expected time —compare LATE **2** happening towards the beginning of the day, life, a period of time, etc. — compare LATE **3** happening in the near future: *I hope for an early answer* —see also **early** BIRD — **-liness** *n*

early closing *n* a day in the week on which shops are shut in the afternoon

early on *adv* near the beginning or at an early period

early warning system *n* a network of radar stations which give information in advance when an enemy air attack comes near

earmark¹ *n* **1** a mark on the ear of a farm

animal to show to whom it belongs   2 sign(s) that tell(s) you what something is

earmark² v to set aside (something, esp. money) for a particular purpose

earmuff n one of a pair of ear coverings, worn to protect a person's ears from cold

earn v 1 to get (money) by working 2 to get (something that one deserves) because of one's qualities: He earned the title of 'The Great' — ~er n

earnest¹ n seriousness: It is snowing in real earnest (=very hard)

earnest² adj determined and serious: an earnest attempt — ~ly adv — ~ness n

earnings n 1 money which is earned by working 2 money made by a company: profit

earphone n a piece of apparatus that turns electrical signals into sounds and is held over the ear

earpiece n 1 one of 2 pieces, as of a hat or cap, which cover the ears to keep them warm 2 one of the 2 pieces of a pair of glasses which hold the glasses on to the ears 3 an earphone

earring n an ornament worn on the ear

earshot n within/out of earshot within/beyond the distance up to which a sound can be heard

earth¹ n 1 the world on which we live 2 the earth's surface as opposed to the sky 3 soil in which plants grow 4 also (abbrev.) E— the wire which connects a piece of electrical apparatus to the ground ☞ ELECTRICITY 5 the hole where certain wild animals live, such as foxes 6 down to earth direct and practical 7 on earth esp. spoken (used for giving force to an expression): What on earth is it?

earth² v to connect a piece of electrical apparatus to the ground

Earth n the name of our world

earthbound adj unable to leave the surface of the earth

earthen adj 1 made of earth 2 made of baked clay

earthenware n cups, dishes, pots, etc., that are earthen

earthly adj 1 of this world as opposed to heaven; material 2 possible: There's no earthly reason for me to go

earthquake n a sudden shaking of the earth's surface, which may cause great damage ☞ GEOGRAPHY

earthshaking adj of the greatest importance to the whole world — ~ly adv

earth up v adv to cover (the roots and part of the stems of a plant) with earth

earthwork n a bank of earth used (esp. formerly) as a protection against enemy attack

earthworm n a common kind of long thin worm which lives in the soil

earthy adj -ier, -iest more concerned with things of the body than with things of the mind — earthiness n

earwax n yellow wax which is formed inside the ear

earwig n a type of insect with 2 curved toothlike parts on its tail ☞ INSECT

ease¹ n 1 the state of being comfortable and without worry: a life of ease 2 the ability to do something without difficulty: to jump over with ease 3 ill at ease uncomfortable and nervous 4 (stand) at ease (used esp. as a military command) (to stand) with feet apart —compare stand EASY, at ATTENTION

ease² v eased, easing 1 to take away (pain or worry) 2 to make more comfortable 3 to make looser 4 to become less difficult: Their relationship has eased 5 to cause (something) to move as stated, by using care: I eased the drawer open with a knife

easel n a wooden frame to hold a blackboard or a picture while it is being painted

ease up also ease off— v adv to work less hard

easily adv 1 without difficulty 2 without doubt: She is easily the prettiest here

east¹ adv towards the east

east² n 1 (to, facing, or in) the direction in which the sun rises ☞ GLOBE 2 one of the 4 main points of the compass, which is on the right of a person facing north 3 (of wind) (coming from) this direction: The wind is in the east —compare EASTERLY

East n the eastern part of world, esp. Asia —compare ORIENT

eastbound adj travelling towards the east

Easter n the yearly feast-day when Christians remember the death of Christ and his rising from the grave

Easter egg n 1 an egg to be eaten at Easter, made of chocolate, sugar, etc. 2 a hen's egg, painted in bright colours, to be eaten at Easter

easterly adj towards or coming from the east

eastern adj of or belonging to the east part of the world or of a country —see NORTH (USAGE)

easternmost adj esp. written farthest east

eastward adj going towards the east —compare EASTERLY

eastwards adv towards the east

easy¹ adj -ier, -iest 1 not difficult 2 comfortable and without worry: He leads a very easy life —compare EASE 3 (of) easy virtue old use (of) low sexual morals 4 I'm easy esp. spoken I'll willingly accept what you decide 5 on easy terms (when buying a car, furniture, etc.) (to pay) a little at a time instead of all at once — easiness n

easy² adv 1 easier said than done harder to do than to talk about 2 easy does it Do it less quickly and/or with less effort!; relax! 3 go easy work less hard 4 go easy on (someone) to be less severe with (someone) 5 go easy on (something) not to use too much of it 6 stand easy (used esp. as a military command) stand more comfortably than when at ease

easy chair n a big comfortable chair usu. with arms

easygoing adj taking life easily

eat v ate, eaten, eating 1 to take into the mouth

and swallow 2 to use regularly as food: *Tigers eat meat* 3 to have a meal: *What time do we eat?* 4 **be eaten up with** (jealousy, desire, etc.) to be completely and violently full of 5 **eat one's words** to take back what one has said; say that one is sorry for having said something

eatable *adj* in a fit condition to be eaten USAGE A food is **eatable** if it is fresh, and satisfactorily prepared: *The bread was so old that it was hardly eatable/was* **uneatable**. A substance is **edible** if it is possible to treat it as food: *Are these berries* **edible**, *or are they poisonous?*

eater *n* 1 a person who eats in the particular stated way: *a heavy eater* (=he eats a lot) 2 a fruit of the kind that one eats raw —compare COOKER

eat into *v prep* to use part of (something): *Our holiday has eaten into our savings*

eats *n esp. spoken* cooked or prepared food, ready for eating

eau de cologne *n French* cologne

eaves *n* the edges of a usu. sloping roof which come out beyond the walls

eavesdrop *v* -pp- to listen secretly (to a conversation) — **-dropper** *n*

ebb¹ *n* the flow of the sea away from the shore: *The tide is on the ebb* —see also FLOOD TIDE; compare FLOW 2 decay; low state

ebb² *v* 1 (of the sea) to flow away from the shore 2 to grow less; become slowly lower and lower

ebb tide *n* the flow of the sea away from the shore —opposite **flood tide**

ebony¹ *n* a kind of hard black wood

ebony² *n, adj* (having) the colour of ebony

ebullience *n* the quality of being full of happiness and excitement —see also EXUBERANCE — **-ient** *adj* — **-iently** *adv*

EC *abbrev. for:* European Community

eccentric¹ *adj* 1 (of a person or his behaviour) peculiar; rather strange 2 (of 2 or more circles) not drawn round the same centre —compare CONCENTRIC ☞ MATHEMATICS 3 (of movement) not (moving) in a regular circle: *Mars, Venus, and the other planets move in eccentric orbits* — ~**ally** *adv* — ~**ity** *n*

eccentric² *n* an eccentric person

ECG *abbrev. for:* 1 electrocardiogram 2 electrocardiograph

echelon *n* (in a group of people) a level: *the lower echelons of the civil service*

echinoderm *n* any of a group of sea creatures, some with spiny skins, such as starfish and sea urchins

echo¹ *n* -oes a sound sent back or repeated, as from a wall of rock or inside a cave

echo² *v* echoed, echoing 1 to come back or cause to come back as an echo 2 to copy or repeat

éclair also **chocolate éclair**— *n French* a small finger-shaped cake made of pastry, with cream inside and chocolate on top

eclectic *adj esp. written* not following any one system or set of ideas, but using parts of many different ones △ ESOTERIC — ~**ism** *n* — ~**ally** *adv*

eclipse¹ *n* 1 the disappearance, complete or in part, of the sun's light when the moon passes between it and the earth, or of the moon's light when the earth passes between it and the sun 2 the loss of fame, success, etc.: *Once a famous actress, she is now in eclipse*

eclipse² *v* eclipsed, eclipsing 1 (of the moon or earth) to cause an eclipse (of sun or moon) 2 to do or be much better than; to make (someone or something) lose fame and appear dull by comparison 3 make dark or troubled: *Our happiness was eclipsed by the news*

ecliptic *n technical* the path along which the sun seems to move

ecology *n* -gies (the study of) the pattern of relations of plants, animals, and people to each other and to their surroundings ◉ — **-gist** *n* — **-gical** *adj*

economic *adj* 1 connected with trade, industry, and wealth; of or concerning economics: *The country is in a bad economic state* 2 profitable: *She let her house at an economic rent*

economical *adj* not wasteful; using money, time, goods, etc., carefully — ~**ly** *adv*

economics *n* 1 the science of the way in which industry and trade produce and use wealth 2 the principles of making profit, saving money, and producing wealth — **-mist** *n*

economic sanctions *n* the non-military means by which one or more nations compel another nation to obey them by refusing to buy from or sell to that nation

economize, -mise *v* -mized, -mizing to save (money, time, goods, etc.) instead of being wasteful

economy¹ *n* -mies 1 (an example of) the careful use of money, time, strength, etc. 2 an economic system

economy² *adj* 1 cheap or big (and good value): *economy prices/size* 2 intended to save money: *In our school we had an economy drive to save energy*

ecosystem *n* an ecological system which relates all the plants, animals, and people in an area to their surroundings, considered as a whole

écru *adj, n French* beige

ecstasy *n* -sies a state of very strong feeling, esp. of joy and happiness

ecstatic *adj* causing or experiencing ecstasy — ~**ally** *adv*

ecumenical, oecu- *adj* favouring, or tending towards, Christian unity all over the world — **-cally** *adv* — ~**ism** *n*

eczema *n* a red swollen condition of the skin, esp. of babies

Edam *n* a yellow pressed cheese from the Netherlands, made in balls and coated in red wax

eddy¹ *n* eddies a circular movement of water, wind, dust, smoke, etc.

eddy² *v* eddied, eddying to move round and

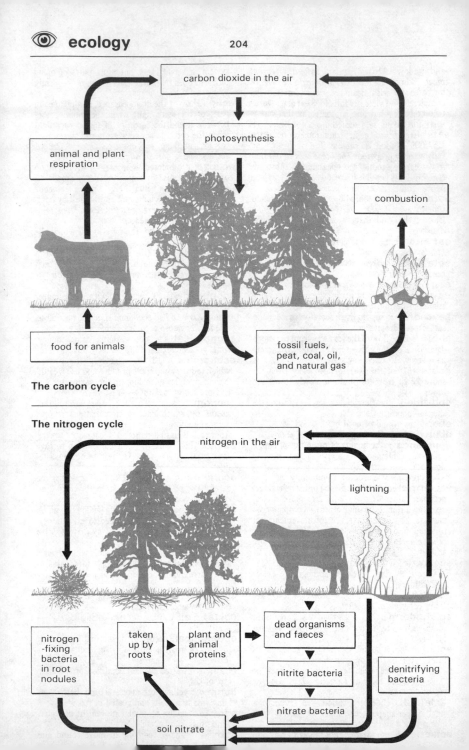

The carbon cycle

The nitrogen cycle

round: *The crowd eddied about in the market-place*

Eden *n* **1** (in the Bible) the garden where Adam and Eve lived before their disobedience to God **2** a beautiful place which gives joy

edge¹ *n* **1** the thin sharp cutting part of a blade, a tool, etc.; cutting line where 2 sides meet **2** the narrowest part along the outside of a solid **3** a border: *the edge of the cliff* **4** **have the edge on** be better than **5** **on edge** nervous **6** **set some-one's teeth on edge** to give an unpleasant feeling to someone

edge² *v* **edged, edging** **1** to place an edge or border on **2** to move little by little **3** (in cricket) to hit (the ball) off the edge of the bat

edgeways also **edgewise**— *adv* **1** sideways **2** **get a word in edgeways** to get a chance to speak (when someone else is speaking)

edging *n* something that forms an edge or border

edgy *adj* **-ier, -iest** nervous — **edgily** *adv*

edible *adj* fit to be eaten; eatable —see EATABLE (USAGE) — **edibility** *n* — ~**-s** *n*

edict *n* **1** (in former times) an official public order proclaimed by authority **2** an order or command

edification *n* the improvement of character or the mind

edifice *n* *esp. written or pompous* a large build-ing, such as a palace or church

edify *v* **-fied** , -fying *esp. written* to improve (the character or mind of): *edifying books*

edit *v* **1** to prepare for printing (usu. the writing of another person) **2** to prepare from collected material (a film, radio performance, or record-ing)

edition *n* **1** one printing of a book, newspaper, magazine, etc. **2** the form in which a book is printed: *a paper-back/hard-back edition of a book* —compare REPRINT

editor *n* a person who edits — ~**ship** *n*

editorial¹ *adj* of or related to an editor: *editorial control* — ~**ly** *adv*

editorial² also **leader, leading article**—— *n* a part of a newspaper (usu. written by the editor) giving an opinion on some question of the day

educate *v* **-cated, -cating** to teach; train the character or mind of: *He was educated at a very good school* — ~**or** *n*

educated guess *n* a guess based on a certain amount of information

education *n* **1** (the results of) teaching or the training of mind and character **2** a field of knowledge dealing with how to teach effectively: *a college of education*

educational *adj* of, about, or providing educa-tion — ~**ly** *adv*

educationist also **educationalist**— *n* a special-ist in how to make education effective

educe *v* **educed, educing** to arrive at usu. through reasoning from known facts —compare DEDUCE

EEC *abbrev. for:* European Economic Com-munity; Common Market

EEG *abbrev. for: (medical)* **1** electroencephalo-gram **2** electroencephalograph

eel *n* a type of fish that is shaped like a snake and is hard to hold

e'en *adv* short form of (poetic) even

e'er *adv* short form of (poetic) ever

eerie *adj* **eerier, eeriest** causing fear because weird: *It's eerie in a wood at night* — **eerily** *adv* — **eeriness** *n*

efface *v* **effaced, effacing** **1** to rub out; destroy the surface of **2** to forget (esp. in the phrase **efface the memory of**) **3** to behave (one-self) so as not to be noticed by other people: *a very quiet self-effacing person* — ~**ment** *n*

effect¹ *n* **1** a result **2** a result produced on the mind or feelings **3** **in effect a** in operation: *The old system will remain in effect until May* **b** for all practical purposes: *She is, in effect, the real ruler* **4** **take effect a** to come into operation **b** to begin to produce results: *The medicine quickly took effect* **5** **to . . . effect** with . . . general meaning: *He called me a fool, or words to that effect*

effect² *v* *esp. written* to cause, produce, or have as a result: *I will effect my purpose* △ AFFECT

effective *adj* **1** having a desired effect; pro-ducing the desired result: *an effective method* **2** actual; real —compare EFFICACIOUS, EFFICIENT — ~**ly** *adv*

effectiveness *n* the ability or power to have a desired effect

effectives *n* *esp. US* armed men ready to serve

effector *n* *technical* a part of the body (such as a muscle) that acts in response to messages it receives from the brain passed down the nerves —compare RECEPTOR

effects *n* *esp. written or law* belongings; per-sonal property

effectual *adj* (of actions but not of the people who do them) effective: *effectual action against unemployment* — ~**ness** *n* — ~**ly** *adv*

effectuate *v* **-ated, -ating** *esp. written* to carry out successfully

effeminate *adj* offensive (of a man or his behaviour) like a woman; unmanly — ~**ly** *adv* — **-acy** *n*

effervesce *v* **-vesced, -vescing** (of a liquid) to have bubbles of gas forming inside, usu. by chemi-cal action — **-vescence** *n* — **-vescent** *adj* — **-vescently** *adv*

effete *adj* weak; exhausted — ~**ness** *n*

efficacious *adj* (esp. of medicines and medical treatment) producing the desired effect; effective —compare EFFECTIVE, EFFICIENT — ~**ly** *adv*

efficacy also **efficacity**— *n* *esp. written* the state or quality of being efficacious

efficient *adj* working well and without waste —compare EFFECTIVE, EFFICACIOUS — ~**ly** *adv* — **-ency** *n*

effigy *n* **-gies** the figure or picture of a person: *an effigy of Guy Fawkes*

effluent n technical **1** liquid waste that flows out esp. from a factory and may be harmful **2** the liquid that comes out from a chemical treatment plant for sewage

effort n **1** the use of strength; trying hard with mind or body: *He can lift the box without effort* **2** a show of strength: *At least make an effort* **3** the result of trying: *Finishing the work in one day was an effort*

effortless adj making and needing no effort when doing something — ~**ly** adv — ~**ness** n

effrontery n **-ries** bold rudeness and insolence without any sensation of shame

effusion n **1** offensive an example of the expression of strong feelings in words, often in the form of bad poetry **2** esp. written a strong outward flow of liquid or gas

effusive adj pouring out feelings without control: *an effusive welcome* — ~**ly** adv — ~**ness** n

e.g. abbrev. for: (Latin) exempli gratia; for example

egalitarian adj holding the belief that all men are equal and should have equal rights — ~**ism** n

egg n **1** a rounded object containing new life, which comes out of the body of a female bird, snake, etc. ⟹ REPRODUCTION, EMBRYO **2** (the contents of) this when used for food **3** the seed of life in a woman or female animal, which joins with the male sperm to make a baby —see also FERTILIZE, OVUM ⟹ REPRODUCTION **4 a bad egg** a worthless and dishonest person

eggcup n a small container to hold an egg that has been boiled in its shell

egg custard n a boiled or baked mixture of eggs and sweetened milk

egghead n usu. offensive a highly educated person; highbrow

eggnog n an alcoholic drink to which egg, sugar, and spices have been added

egg on v adv to encourage strongly: *Mary egged her husband on to steal the money*

eggplant n an aubergine

eggshell n **1** the shell, or hard outside part, of a bird's egg **2** very thin and delicate (esp. in the phrase **eggshell china**)

egg timer n a container, working like a small hourglass, used to time the boiling of eggs — compare HOURGLASS

ego n egos the self, esp. as seen in relation to other selves or to the outside world

egocentric adj offensive selfish — ~**ally** adv — ~**ity** n

egoism n usu. offensive the quality or state of always thinking about what will be the best for oneself — **-ist** n — **-istic** adj — **-istical** adj — **-istically** adv

egotism n offensive the quality or state of talking too much about oneself and believing that one is very important —compare EGOISM — **-ist** n — **-istic** adj — **-istical** adj — **-istically** adv

ego trip n sl an act that gives selfish pleasure to the ego

egregious adj offensive noticeably bad: *an egregious mistake* — ~**ly** adv

egress n esp. written exit —opposite ingress

Egyptian adj that belongs to, or is a native of, Egypt

eh interj esp. spoken (used for showing surprise or doubt, or when asking someone to agree)

eiderdown n a thick covering for a bed filled with down or other soft material

eight adj, n, pron **1** the number 8 **2** a rowing-boat for racing that holds 8 men — **eighth** adj, n, pron

eighteen adj, n, pron the number 18 — ~**th** adj, n, pron, adv

eighty adj, n, pron **-ties** the number 80 — **eightieth** adj, n, pron, adv

eisteddfod n a meeting in Wales at which poets, singers, and musicians compete

either¹ adj **1** one or the other of 2 **2** one and the other of 2; each: *He had a policeman on either side of him*

either² pron one or the other of USAGE **Either** and **neither** pronouns are usually singular when written, although many people use them as plural when they are followed by plural: **neither** *of the books is very interesting*, is correct but: **neither** *of the books are very interesting*, is acceptable when spoken. **None** is usually plural in such sentences, and **any** is always plural before a plural.

either³ conj (used before the first of 2 or more choices separated by or) USAGE Either . . . **or** and **neither** . . . **nor** are plural when the word next to the verb is plural. **Either** *my father or my brothers are coming*; but: **either** *my brothers or my father is coming*. The plural is also used in speech to avoid saying *he or she: if either David or Janet come, they will want a drink*.

either⁴ adv (used with negative expressions) also: *I haven't read it and my brother hasn't either*

ejaculate v **-lated, -lating 1** to cry out or say suddenly **2** medical to throw out suddenly and with force from the body (esp. the male sperm) — **-tion** n

eject v to throw out with force: *The police ejected them* — ~**ion**, ~**or** n

ejector seat n a type of seat which throws out the pilot from a plane, when he can no longer control it and must reach the ground by parachute

eke out v adv eked, eking out to cause to last longer, by being careful or by adding something else: *to eke out a small income by taking in washing*

elaborate¹ adj full of detail; carefully worked out: *an elaborate machine* — ~**ly** adv — ~**ness** n

elaborate² v **-rated, -rating** to add more detail to (something) — **-tion** n

elapse v elapsed, elapsing (of time) to pass away

elastic *adj* **1** which springs back into the original shape after being stretched: *an elastic band* **2** not stiff or fixed; able to be changed to fit all cases: *elastic rules* — **elastic** *n* — ~**ity** *n*

elastic band *n* RUBBER BAND

elate *v* **elated, elating** to fill with pride and joy: *elated by success* — **elated** *adj*

elation *n* the state or quality of being filled with pride and joy

elbow[1] *n* **1** the joint where the arm bends, esp. the outer point of this **2** the part of a garment which covers this arm joint **3** an L-shaped joint shaped like this arm joint, in a pipe, chimney, etc. **4 out at elbow(s) a** a badly dressed and poor-looking **b** (of a garment) worn out and with holes in it

elbow[2] *v* to push with the elbows: *He elbowed me out of the way*

elbow grease *n esp. spoken* hard work with the hands, esp. polishing and cleaning

elbowroom *n* space in which to move freely

elder[1] *n* also **elder tree**— a type of small tree, with white flowers and red or black berries (**elderberry**)

elder[2] *adj* **1** (esp. in a family) the older of 2 people: *my elder brother* —compare OLDER **2** older than another person (esp. a son) of the same name —compare YOUNGER

elder[3] *n* **1** the older of 2 people **2** a man who holds an official position in some Christian churches

elderly *adj* (of a person) getting near old age: *My father is getting elderly now*

eldest *adj, n* (a person, esp. in a family, who is) oldest of 3 or more

elect[1] *adj* elected to or chosen for an office but not yet officially placed in it

elect[2] *v* **1** to choose (someone) by voting **2** to decide (to do something), esp. about the future: *He elected to become a doctor*

election *n* (an example of) the choosing of representatives to fill a position, esp. a political office, by vote

electioneer *v* to work at persuading people to vote for a political party —see also CANVASS — ~**ing** *n*

elective *adj* (of a position) filled by election

elector *n* a person who votes or has the right to vote in an election

electoral *adj* connected with **a** an election **b** the electors: *the electoral system*

electoral roll also **electoral register**— *n* the list of people in an area who have the right to vote in elections

electorate *n* all the people in the country who vote or have the right to vote, seen as a group

electric *adj* **1** being, using, or producing electricity: *an electric spark* —compare ELECTRICAL, ELECTRONIC **2** produced by electricity **3** very exciting: *His speech had an electric effect upon the listeners* — ~**ally** *adv*

electrical *adj* **1** concerned with electricity **2** using electricity in some way: *electrical apparatus* —compare ELECTRIC, ELECTRONIC — ~**ly** *adv*

electric blanket *n* a blanket with electric wires passing through, used for making a bed warm

electric chair *n* a machine used for killing murderers in some states of the US, or the punishment itself

electric fence *n* a wire fence through which electricity is passed

electrician *n* a person whose job is to fit and repair electrical apparatus

electricity *n* **1** the power which is produced by friction, by a battery, or by a generator, and which gives us heat, light, and sound, and drives machines ◉ **2** electric current

electric shock *n* a shock caused by electricity

electric shock therapy also **electroconvulsive therapy**— *n medical* the treatment of diseases of the mind by giving electric shocks

electrify *v* -**fied, -fying 1** to pass an electric current through **2** to change (something) to a system using electric power **3** to excite greatly — -**fication** *n*

electrocardiogram *n medical* the drawing that is made by an electrocardiograph —compare ELECTROENCEPHALOGRAM

electrocardiograph *n medical* a piece of apparatus that records in the form of a drawing the electrical changes that take place in the heart as it beats —compare ELECTROENCEPHALOGRAPH

electrocute *v* -**cuted, -cuting** to kill by passing electricity through the body — -**cution** *n*

electrode *n* either of the terminals at which the current enters and leaves a battery or other electrical apparatus —see also ANODE, CATHODE

electroencephalogram *n medical* the drawing that is made by an electroencephalograph —compare ELECTROCARDIOGRAM

electroencephalograph *n medical* a piece of apparatus that records in the form of a drawing the electrical activity of the brain —compare ELECTROCARDIOGRAPH

electrolysis *n* **1** the separation of a liquid into its chemical parts by passing electricity through it (from an anode to a cathode) **2** the destruction of hair roots by means of an electric current

electrolyte *n* any of various liquids, such as copper sulphate, which can be broken down into their chemical parts by passing electricity through them

electromagnet *n* a magnet that consists of a wire carrying electric current wrapped round a piece of material, such as iron

electron *n* a 'bit' of negative electricity moving round one 'bit' of positive electricity (PROTON) inside an atom —see also NEUTRON ⭢ ATOM

electronic *adj* **1** connected with electrons **2** connected with any apparatus that works by electronics —compare ELECTRIC, ELECTRICAL

electronics *n* **1** the branch of science that deals with electrons **2** the branch of industry that

A standard domestic 3-pin plug

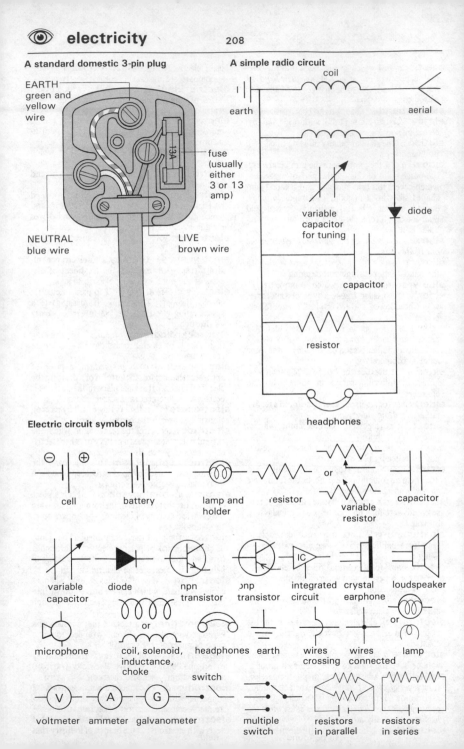

EARTH
green and
yellow
wire

13A

fuse
(usually
either
3 or 13
amp)

NEUTRAL
blue wire

LIVE
brown wire

A simple radio circuit

coil

earth

aerial

variable
capacitor
for tuning

diode

capacitor

resistor

headphones

Electric circuit symbols

⊖ ⊕

cell

battery

lamp and
holder

resistor

or

variable
resistor

capacitor

variable
capacitor

diode

npn
transistor

pnp
transistor

IC

integrated
circuit

crystal
earphone

loudspeaker

microphone

or

coil, solenoid,
inductance,
choke

headphones

earth

wires
crossing

wires
connected

or

lamp

switch

V

A

G

voltmeter

ammeter

galvanometer

multiple
switch

resistors
in parallel

resistors
in series

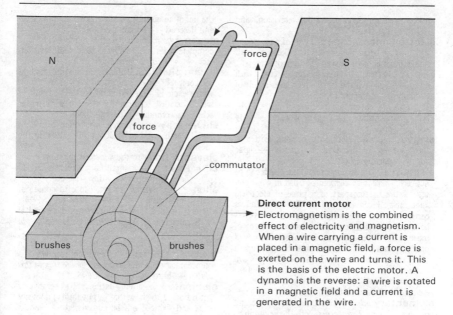

Direct current motor
Electromagnetism is the combined
effect of electricity and magnetism.
When a wire carrying a current is
placed in a magnetic field, a force is
exerted on the wire and turns it. This
is the basis of the electric motor. A
dynamo is the reverse: a wire is rotated
in a magnetic field and a current is
generated in the wire.

A transformer is two
coils of wire linked by a
soft iron core. An
alternating voltage is
applied to one coil
which sets up a
changing magnetic field
in the iron, which in turn
sets up an electric
current in the second
coil. The voltage
obtained depends on the
ratio of the turns in the
two coils and on the
voltage applied.

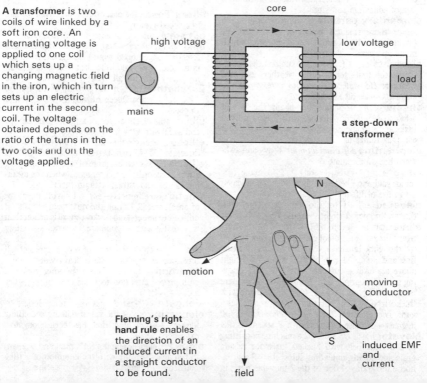

a step-down
transformer

**Fleming's right
hand rule** enables
the direction of an
induced current in
a straight conductor
to be found.

makes such products as radio, television, and recording apparatus

electron microscope *n* a type of microscope which uses a beam of electrons to make very small things large enough to see ☞ MICROSCOPE

electroplate *v* -plated, -plating to cover with a thin surface of metal, usu. silver, as a result of electrolysis —compare GALVANIZE

elegant *adj* having the qualities of grace, style, beauty, and fashion: *an elegant woman* — ~ly *adv* — -ance *n*

elegy *n* -gies a type of poem or song written to show sorrow for the dead △ EULOGY — -giac *adj* — -giacally *adv*

element *n* 1 a quality or amount which can be noticed: *There is an element of truth in what you say* 2 the heating part of a piece of electrical apparatus 3 *old use* any of the 4 substances earth, air, fire, and water, from which (it was believed) everything material was made 4 any of more than 100 substances that consist of atoms of only one kind and that in combination make up all other substances: *Both hydrogen and oxygen are elements, but water is not* —compare COMPOUND

elemental *adj* of the powers of nature: *the elemental violence of the storm*

elementary *adj* 1 (of a question) simple and easy to answer 2 concerned with the beginnings, esp. of education and study

elementary particle *n technical* any of the 20 or more smallest pieces of any substance (including electrons, protons, and neutrons) which make up atoms ☞ ATOM

elements *n* 1 (of a school subject) the beginnings; the first steps 2 the weather, esp. bad weather: *He walked on, quite careless of the elements* —see also ELEMENTAL

elephant *n* -phants *or* -phant the largest 4-footed animal now living, with 2 long curved tusks and a long nose called a trunk with which it can pick things up ☞ MAMMAL

elephantine *adj often humour* heavy and awkward like an elephant

elevate *v* -vated, -vating 1 to make (the mind, soul, etc.) better, higher, or more educated 2 to raise or lift up

elevated *adj* 1 (of thoughts, language, etc.) fine and noble 2 slightly drunk; tipsy

elevation *n* 1 *esp. written* (the state resulting from) the act or action of elevating 2 *esp. written* (of thoughts, language, etc.) the quality of being fine and noble 3 *esp. written* a hill 4 height above sea-level —compare ALTITUDE 5 (a drawing of) a flat upright side of a building —compare PLAN, PERSPECTIVE, FACADE 6 the angle made with the horizon by some pointing apparatus, such as a gun: *The gun was fired at an elevation of 60 degrees* —see also TRAJECTORY ☞ MATHEMATICS

elevator *n* 1 *US* a lift 2 a machine consisting of a moving belt with buckets, used for raising grain and liquids, unloading ships, etc. 3 a storehouse for grain 4 one of the 2 movable parts in the tail of an aircraft which make it able to climb and descend —compare AILERON

eleven *adj, n, pron* 1 the number 11 2 a complete team of 11 players in football, cricket, etc. — ~th *adj, n, pron, adv*

eleven-plus *n* (in Britain until the introduction of comprehensive education) an examination which each 11 year old child took, the result of which decided whether he went to a grammar school or secondary modern school

elevenses *n esp. spoken* tea, coffee, or a light meal, which is taken at about 11 o'clock in the morning

eleventh hour *n* the very last moment

elf *n* elves a type of small fairy which is said to play tricks on people — ~in, ~ish *adj*

elicit *v esp. written* to get, cause to come out (facts, information, etc.) — ~ation *n*

elide *v* elided, eliding to leave out the sound of in pronunciation: *Most people elide the 'd' in 'Wednesday'*

eligible *adj* 1 suitable to be chosen, esp. as a husband 2 belonging to the group from which a choice must be made: *Are you eligible to join this club?* — -bility *n* — -bly *adv*

eliminate *v* -nated, -nating 1 to remove or get rid of 2 to show that (a possibility) does not exist and so need not be considered — -nation *n*

elite *n French* the best or most important people in a social group

elitism *n* rule by an elite — elitist *adj, n*

elixir *n literature* 1 an imaginary liquid which scientists once hoped would change other metals into gold, or make life last for ever 2 an imaginary cure for all evils

Elizabethan *adj, n* (a person) of the period 1558–1603, when Queen Elizabeth I was queen of England

elk *n* elks *or* elk a type of large deer of Europe and Asia with very big flat antlers

ellipse *n* a circle that has been stretched in one direction ☞ MATHEMATICS

ellipsis *n* -ses (an example of) the leaving out of a word or words from a sentence when the meaning can be understood without them

elliptic also **elliptical**— *adj* 1 having the shape of an ellipse 2 having the quality of ellipsis 3 difficult to understand because more is meant than is actually said —compare CRYPTIC — ~ally *adv*

elm *n* also **elm tree**— any of several types of tall broad-leaved tree or its hard heavy wood

elocution *n* the art of clear speaking in public, with proper attention to voice control — ~ary *adj* — ~ist *n*

elongate *v* -gated, -gating to make longer

elongation *n* 1 the act of making something longer 2 something that has been elongated; extension

elope *v* eloped, eloping (of a man and woman) to run away secretly with the intention of getting married — ~ment *n*

eloquent adj 1 able to make good, clear speeches 2 (of a speech) fluent and clear — **-quence** n — ~**ly** adv

else adv 1 besides; in addition: *Who else did you see?* 2 in or at a different place, time, or way; apart from that mentioned: *When else can we meet?* 3 **or else** or otherwise: *He must pay $100 or else go to prison*

elsewhere adv at, in, or to another place: *We must look elsewhere*

elucidate v **-dated, -dating** esp. written to explain or make clear: *Please elucidate the reasons for your action* — **-dation** n

elude v **eluded, eluding** 1 to escape from, esp. by means of a trick: *The fox succeeded in eluding the hunters* 2 to escape from the memory of: *Your name eludes me*

elusive also **elusory**— adj difficult to catch or remember: *He's such an elusive person; you never know where he is* — ~**ly** adv — ~**ness** n

elver n a young eel

elves pl. of ELF

elvish adj elfish

Elysium n **-siums, -sia** 1 (according to the ancient Greeks) the home of the happy dead 2 literature any place or state of great happiness — **-sian** adj

'em pron esp. spoken or dialect them

emaciate v **-ated, -ating** to cause to become very thin: *The prisoners were terribly emaciated* — **-ation** n

emanate from v prep **-nated, -nating from** 1 (of ideas, orders, etc.) to come originally from: *The suggestion emanated from the committee* 2 (of gas, light, etc.) to come out from: *A bad smell emanated from the dead dog* — **emanation** n

emancipate v **-pated, -pating** to make free socially, politically, and in law — **-pator** n

emancipation n 1 the act of emancipating 2 the condition of being emancipated: *She showed her emancipation by piloting an aircraft*

emasculate v **-lated, -lating** medical 1 to take away the power of becoming a father from; castrate —compare NEUTER, SPAY 2 take away all the life and strength from — **-lation** n

embalm v to prevent (a dead body) from decaying by treating it with chemicals — ~**er** n — **embalmment** n

embankment n a wide wall of stones or earth, which is built to keep a river from overflowing its banks, or to carry a road or railway over low ground

embargo[1] n **-goes** an official order forbidding an action, esp. the movement of ships, or trade

embargo[2] v **-goed, -going** to lay an embargo on

embark v to go, put, or take on a ship: *We embarked at Liverpool for New York* — ~**ation** n

embark on also **embark upon**— v prep to start (something new or difficult)

embarrass v 1 to cause to feel ashamed or socially uncomfortable 2 to cause to feel anxious about money: *He was embarrassed by debts* — ~**ingly** adv

embarrassment n 1 a the act of embarrassing b the state of being embarrassed 2 a difficulty about money 3 a person or thing that embarrasses

embassy n **-sies** 1 a group of officials, usu. led by an ambassador, who are sent by a government to do its business with the government of another country 2 the official building where an ambassador and those assisting him work in a foreign country

embattled adj surrounded by enemies

embed v **-dd-** to fix firmly in: *a crown embedded with jewels*

embellish v 1 to make more beautiful, esp. by adding ornaments 2 to add details, perhaps untrue, to (a statement or story): *I asked him not to embellish the truth with ideas of his own* —see DECORATE (USAGE) — ~**ment** n

ember n a red-hot piece of wood or coal, esp. in a fire that has died down

embezzle v **-zled, -zling** to take and use for oneself in a wrong way (money that is placed in one's care) — ~**ment** n — **-zler** n

embitter v to fill with painful or bitter feelings: *He was embittered by his experiences* — ~**ment** n

emblazon v to ornament (a shield or flag) with a coat of arms

emblem n an object which is the sign of something —compare SYMBOL — ~**atic** adj — ~**atically** adv

embodiment n someone or something in which something is embodied

embody v **-ied, -ying** 1 (of works, writings, etc.) to express 2 to give a body to (a spirit): *the embodied spirits of the dead* 3 (of things) to contain or include: *The new car embodies many improvements*

embolden v to help (somebody to do something) by giving the necessary courage

embolism n medical a blocking of a blood vessel, or whatever causes such a blockage

emboss v to cause (an ornamental raised pattern) to appear on (metal, paper, etc.) by pressing; ornament (metal, paper, etc.) with a raised pattern

embowered adj poetic enclosed or surrounded, esp. by plants and trees

embrace[1] v **embraced, embracing** 1 to take and hold (another or each other) in the arms as a sign of love 2 (of things) to contain or include: *This book embraces many subjects* 3 esp. written to make use or take willingly: *He embraced my offer to employ him* 4 to become a believer in: *He embraced the Muslim religion*

embrace[2] n the act of embracing

embrocation n esp. written a liquid medicine used for rubbing any part of the body that is stiff or aching from exercise —compare LINIMENT

embroider v 1 to do ornamental needlework

on (cloth) **2** to improve (a story) by adding imaginary details

embroidery n **-ies** the act or result of embroidering

embroil v to cause to join in (a quarrel): *John and Peter embroiled Mary in their quarrel*

embryo n **-os** **1** the young of any creature before birth, or before coming out of an egg 👁 —compare FOETUS **2 in embryo** still undeveloped — ~**nic** adj

emend v to take the mistakes out of (written matter) before printing ⚠ AMEND — ~**ation** n

emerald[1] n a bright green precious stone

emerald[2] adj, n (of) the colour of an emerald; clear bright green

emerge v **emerged, emerging** **1** to come or appear (from/out of somewhere): *The sun emerged from behind the clouds* **2** to become known as a result of inquiry — **-gence** n

emergency n **-cies** an unexpected and dangerous happening which must be dealt with at once

emergent adj emerging, esp. from a poor and dependent state into a richer independent state

emery n the powdered form of a very hard metal, which is used for polishing things and making them smooth —see also CARBORUNDUM

emetic n, adj (something, esp. medicine) eaten or drunk to cause a person to bring up food from the stomach through the mouth (VOMIT)

emigrant n a person who emigrates —compare IMMIGRANT

emigrate v **-grated, -grating** to leave one's own country in order to go and live in another — **-tion** n   USAGE Some birds **migrate** twice a year between hot and cold countries. The word can also be used of people who travel regularly to and fro. The people or birds are called **migrants**, and the practice is called **migration**. A person **emigrates** (goes permanently) from one country, and **immigrates** or becomes an **immigrant** into another. Thus **emigration** is the process of leaving a country permanently, and **immigration** is the process of entering and settling in a new country.

émigré n *French* a person who leaves his own country, usu. for political reasons

eminence n the quality of being famous and of a high rank, esp. in learning, science, the arts, etc.

eminent adj (of people) famous and admired; having eminence

eminently (of qualities or abilities) unusually

emir n a Muslim ruler, esp. in Asia and parts of Africa

emirate n the position, state, power, lands, etc., of an emir

emissary n **-ries** a person who is sent with an official message or task, often secret

emission n **1** an act or the action of emitting **2** something which is emitted **3** the passing out of male sexual liquid (SEMEN) from the male organ (PENIS), or the liquid itself

emit v **-tt-** to send out (esp. heat, light, smell, sound)

Emmentaler, -thaler also **Swiss cheese**— n a type of cheese of Swiss origin with a mild taste and large holes

emollient n, adj (something, esp. a medicine) which softens the skin and cures it when it is sore

emolument n esp. written money or other form of profit received for work; wage —compare SALARY; see PAY (USAGE)

emotion n **1** a strong instinctive feeling: *Love, hatred, and grief are emotions* **2** strength of feeling: *His voice shook with emotion* — ~**less** adj — ~**lessly** adv — ~**lessness** n

emotional adj **1** having feelings which are strong or easily moved **2** (of words, literature, music, etc.) **a** showing strong feeling **b** able to cause strong feeling; emotive **3** with regard to the emotions: *emotional difficulties* — ~**ly** adv

emotive adj which causes strong feeling; emotional: *'Home' is a more emotive word than 'house'* — ~**ly** adv

empathy n **1** the state of imagining oneself to be another person, and of understanding him/her: *She feels empathy with her son* —compare SYMPATHY **2** the state of imagining that a work of art or an object of nature shares one's own feelings, and therefore of understanding and enjoying it

emperor n (fem. **empress**) the head of an empire

emphasis n **-ses** special force given to certain words or details, in speaking, writing, etc., to show their importance — **-atic** adj — **-atically** adv

emphasize, -ise v **-sized, -sizing** to place emphasis on

emphysema n medical a diseased condition in which the lungs become swollen with air, causing difficulty in breathing

empire n a group of countries under one government, usu. ruled by an emperor 🔏 ROMAN

Empire adj, n (esp. of dress and furniture) (belonging to, fashionable in) the period of Napoleon I of France, 1804-1815

empirical adj guided only by practical experience rather than by scientific ideas out of books — ~**ly** adv — **-cism** n

emplane v **emplaned, emplaning** esp. written to get or put onto an aircraft

employ v **employed, employing** **1** to use or take on as a paid worker: *The firm employs about 100 men* **2** to use: *The police sometimes have to employ force* **3** to spend time: *She employs her free time in sewing*

employable adj suitable to be employed

employee n a person who is employed

employer n a person who employs others

employment n **1** the state of being employed **2** the act of employing

employment agency n **-cies** a private business which makes a profit by helping people to find work or workers

employment exchange also **labour**

Fertilization

When an egg (ovum) is released from the ovary, it travels down the
fallopian tube and may be fertilized by a spermatozoon. If fertilization
takes place the egg usually implants in the lining of the womb. An egg
takes several days to travel from the ovary to the womb.

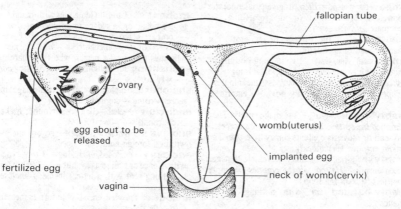

fallopian tube

ovary

egg about to be
released

fertilized egg

vagina

womb(uterus)

implanted egg

neck of womb(cervix)

A nine month old foetus

When the fertilized egg starts to grow and develop, it is known as an
embryo. After 3 months the embryo looks like a human and it is then
usually called a foetus. Throughout the 9 months of pregnancy, the embryo
takes in food and oxygen from its mother through the placenta and
umbilical cord.

placenta

amniotic fluid

umbilical cord

foetus or embryo

womb(uterus)

neck of womb(cervix)

vagina

exchange— n a Government office which helps those who want work or workers

emporium n -riums or -ria esp. written 1 a market; large shop or (esp. US) store 2 a centre for trade: Singapore, emporium of the East

empower v esp. written to give (someone) the power or lawful right (to do something) — compare ENABLE, ENTITLE

empress n 1 the wife of an emperor 2 a female head of an empire

empty¹ adj -ier, -iest 1 containing nothing or nobody: an empty cup 2 esp. spoken hungry 3 offensive without sense or purpose; meaningless: empty promises — **emptily** adv — **emptiness** n

empty² v -tied, -tying 1 to make empty: They emptied the bottle 2 (of a place, a container, etc.) to send or move its contents somewhere else: The room emptied very quickly

empty³ n -ties a container or vehicle that has been emptied: He took all the empties (=empty bottles) back to the shop

empty-handed adj with nothing in the hands

empty-headed adj esp. spoken (of people) foolish and silly

empty set n technical a set with no members, usu. written 0 or { }

emu n emus or emu a large Australian bird, smaller than the ostrich, which runs well but cannot fly

emulate v -lated, -lating to try to do as well as or better than (another person) — **-tion** n

emulsify v -fied, -fying technical to make into an emulsion

emulsion n 1 a creamy mixture of liquids (esp. used as a medicine) 2 the substance on the surface of a photographic film which makes it sensitive to light 3 EMULSION PAINT — **-sive** adj

emulsion paint n a type of paint in which the colour is mixed into an emulsion, and which is not shiny when dry —compare GLOSS PAINT

enable v -bled, -bling 1 to make (a creature) able (to do something): a bird's wings enable it to fly 2 to give (someone) the power or right (to do something) —compare EMPOWER, ENTITLE

enact v 1 (of the Government) to make or pass (a law) 2 to perform or represent (a part of a play) — **~ment** n

enamel¹ v -ll- to cover or ornament with enamel

enamel² n 1 a glassy substance which is put as an ornament or protection onto objects made of metal or clay 2 the hard smooth outer surface of the teeth

enamelware n metal pots and pans for the kitchen which are covered with enamel

enamoured adj very fond of; liking very much

encamp v to make or be in a camp: to encamp for the night — **~ment** n

encapsulate v -lated, -lating 1 to enclose in

or as if in a capsule 2 to shorten (facts, information, etc.)

encase v encased, encasing to cover completely (as) with a case

enchain v to put or hold in chains — **~ment** n

enchant v 1 to fill (someone) with delight 2 to use magic on: a palace in an enchanted wood —compare BEWITCH — **~ment** n

enchanter fem. **enchantress**— n 1 a person who uses magic 2 a person who is enchanting

enchanting adj delightful: an enchanting child — **~ly** adv

encipher also **cipher**— v to put (a message) into secret writing —compare DECIPHER

encircle v -cled, -cling to surround; make a circle round — **~ment** n

enclave n French a piece of territory enclosed within a foreign land

enclose v enclosed, enclosing 1 to surround with a fence or wall so as to shut in 2 to put (esp. something sent with a letter) inside: I enclose a cheque for £50.00 — **-sure** n

encode v encoded, encoding to turn (a message) into code —compare DECODE

encomium n -miums or -mia esp. written an expression of very high praise

encompass v esp. written 1 to surround on all sides 2 also **compass**— to succeed in causing (usu. a bad result): He encompassed the ruin of his enemies

encore¹ n French 1 a call (=Please do it again!) made by an audience 2 a song or other performance which is given again because it is asked for — **encore** interj

encore² v encored, encoring to express approval of (a performer or a performance) by shouting ' encore! '

encounter¹ v 1 to meet or be faced by (something bad, esp. a danger or a difficulty) 2 to meet unexpectedly

encounter² n a sudden meeting (usu. either unexpected or dangerous)

encounter group n a group of people who meet together for training in greater sensitivity to their own and one another's feelings

encourage v -aged, -aging to give courage or hope to (someone); urge (someone) on to fresh efforts — **-agingly** adv — **~ment** n

encroach v to go beyond what is right; intrude — **~ment** n

encrust v to cover with a thin hard outer covering, sometimes for ornament: a crown encrusted with jewels

encumber v to make free action or movement difficult for (someone): He is encumbered with debts — **-brance** n

encyclical also **encyclical letter**— n a letter sent round by the Pope to all his churches

encyclopaedia, -pedia n a book or set of books dealing with every branch of knowledge, or with one particular branch, in alphabetical order

encyclopaedic, -pedic adj (of knowledge,

memory, etc.) wide and full, like the contents of an encyclopaedia — ~**ally** adj

end¹ n **1** the point(s) where something stops **2** the furthest point from here: *He's down at the end of the garden* **3** the latest point in time: *the end of the year* **4** a little piece that is left over: *cigarette ends* —see also ODDS AND ENDS **5** an aim or purpose: *saving money to a particular end* **6** death: *a peaceful end* **7** a particular part of a business **8** at a loose end having nothing to do **9** at an end finished **10** end on with the narrow sides hitting each other **11** end to end with the narrow sides touching each other **12** go off the deep end to lose control of oneself; become angry **13** keep one's end up to go on facing difficulties bravely and successfully **14** make (both) ends meet to get just enough money for one's needs **15** no end of *esp. spoken* an endless amount of **16** on end a (of time) continuously b upright

end² v to finish

endanger v to cause danger to

endearing adj that endears one to someone: *an endearing smile* — ~**ly** adv

endearment n (an expression of) love

endear to v prep to cause (someone, esp. oneself) to be loved (by someone)

endeavour¹ v to try

endeavour² n an effort; attempt

endemic adj (esp. of diseases) found regularly in a particular place: *an endemic disease of the chest among miners* —compare EPIDEMIC, PANDEMIC

ending n the end, esp. of a story, film, play, or word: *a happy ending*

endless adj **1** never finishing: *The journey seemed endless* **2** technical (of a belt, chain, etc.) circular; with the ends joined — ~**ly** adv

endocrine adj medical making substances (HORMONES) *which are poured directly into the bloodstream of the body*

endocrine gland also **ductless gland**— n medical any of several organs of the body (the PITUITARY, THYROID, etc.) which pour hormones into the bloodstream of the body

endorse v endorsed, endorsing **1** to write, esp. one's name, on the back of (esp. a cheque) **2** to write a note on (a driving licence) to say that the driver has broken the law **3** *esp. written* to express approval of; confirm: *I fully endorse your opinions* — ~**ment** n

endow v to give a large amount of money which brings in a yearly amount for use: *to endow a hospital* — ~**ment** n

endowment policy n -cies technical an arrangement by which a person pays money regularly over a number of years so that an agreed amount will be paid to him at the end of that time, or to his family if he dies first; type of insurance

endow with v prep to make rich from birth with (any good quality or ability): *endowed with beauty*

end product n technical something which is produced as the result of a number of operations: *Our raw materal is oil, and our end product is nylon stockings* —compare BY-PRODUCT

endurance n the state or power of enduring: *Long-distance runners need great endurance*

endure v endured, enduring **1** to bear (pain, suffering, etc.) —see BEAR (USAGE) **2** *esp. written* to last: *His books will endure for ever* **3** to remain alive: *They can not endure much longer* — -**durable** adj — -**ring** adj — **ring**ly adv

endways also **endwise**— adv **1** with the end forward; not sideways **2** end to end

enema n (an instrument used for) the action of introducing liquid (such as medicine) into the bowels, through the anus

enemy n -mies **1** a person who hates or dislikes another person; one of 2 or more people who hate or dislike each other: *His behaviour made him many enemies* **2** someone or something that wants to harm, or is against (someone or something): *The army advanced to meet the enemy*

energetic adj full of energy — ~**ally** adv

energy n -gies **1** (of people) the quality of being full of life: *Young people usually have more energy than the old* **2** the power one can use in working: *to devote all one's energies to a job* **3** the power which does work and drives machines: *atomic/electrical energy*

enervate v -vated, -vating to make weak: *He was enervated by his long illness*

en famille adv French among the family

enfeeble v -bled, -bling to make (someone) weak — ~**ment** n

enfold v to enclose; wrap: *She enfolded the child in her arms*

enforce v enforced, enforcing **1** to cause (a rule or law) to be carried out: *The police enforce the law* **2** to make (something) happen, esp. by force **3** to give greater force to (an argument, a piece of advice, etc.) — ~**able** adj — ~**ment** n

enfranchise v -chised, -chising **1** to give the right to vote —opposite **disfranchise** —see also SUFFRAGE **2** to free (slaves) — ~**ment** n

engage v engaged, engaging **1** to arrange to employ: *engage a new secretary* **2 a** (of machine parts) to lock together: *This wheel engages with that wheel and turns it* **b** to cause (machine parts) to do this **3** to take up (time, attention, etc.) **4** to attack: *They engaged the enemy (in battle)*

engaged adj **1** (of people) busy **2** (of a telephone line) in use **3** (of seats, tables, etc.) reserved **4** having agreed to marry: *Edward and I have got engaged*

engagement n **1** an agreement to marry — compare BETROTHAL **2 a** a promise to meet a person, or to do something: *I can't come because I have an engagement* **3** a battle

engaging adj charming: *an engaging smile* — ~**ly** adv

engender v esp. written to cause (a state, condition, etc.): *Dirt engenders disease*

engine *n* 1 a piece of machinery with moving parts which changes power (from steam, electricity, oil, etc.) into movement ☞ CAR 2 also **locomotive**— a machine which pulls a railway train 3 FIRE ENGINE

engineer¹ *n* 1 a person who designs machines, roads, bridges, harbours, etc.: *an electrical/a civil/mining engineer* 2 a skilled person who controls an engine or works with machines

engineer² *v* 1 to plan and make as an engineer does: *The road is very well engineered* 2 to cause by planning: *His enemies engineered his ruin*

engineering *n* 1 the science of an engineer 2 the result of engineering: *The Queen admired the engineering of the new railway*

English¹ *adj* belonging to England ☞ KING

English² *n* 1 the people of England 2 the language of England ☞ LANGUAGE 3 **the Queen's/King's English** good correct English

English breakfast *n* cooked bacon and eggs followed by toast and marmalade —compare CONTINENTAL BREAKFAST

English horn *n* *US* COR ANGLAIS

engraft *v* to graft

engrave *v* **engraved, engraving** 1 to cut (words, pictures, etc.) on wood, stone, or metal 2 to prepare (metal plates) in this way, for printing — **engraver** *n*

engraving *n* 1 the art of an engraver 2 a picture printed from an engraved plate: *an old engraving of London Bridge*

engross *v* to fill completely the attention of: *Engrossed in his book he forgot the time*

engrossing *adj* very interesting: *an engrossing book* — ~ly *adv*

engulf *v* to destroy by swallowing up: *The stormy sea engulfed the small boat*

enhance *v* **enhanced, enhancing** to increase (good things) — ~ment *n*

enigmatic *adj* (of things, events, or behaviour) mysterious — ~ally *adv*

enjoin *v* *esp. written* to order: *He enjoined obedience on the soldiers* —see ORDER (USAGE)

enjoy *v* **enjoyed, enjoying** 1 to get happiness from 2 to possess or use (something good): *He has always enjoyed   very good health* 3 **enjoy oneself** to experience pleasure — ~ment *n*

enjoyable *adj* pleasant — **-bly** *adv*

enlarge *v* **enlarged, enlarging** to make or grow larger: *This photograph should enlarge well*

enlargement *n* 1 enlarging 2 a photograph printed in a larger size than the original —opposite **reduction** 3 *technical* the transformation of an object into a similar one

enlarge on also **enlarge upon**— *v prep* to add length and detail to what has been said

enlighten *v* to cause to understand: *Peter thought the world was flat until I enlightened him!*

enlightened *adj* having true understanding

enlightenment *n* the act of enlightening: *This is difficult and I need enlightenment*

Enlightenment *n* the period in the 18th century in Europe, when certain thinkers taught that science and reason would improve the human condition

enlist *v* 1 to enter or cause to enter the armed forces 2 to obtain (help, sympathy, etc.): *Can I enlist your help?* — ~ment *n*

enlisted man *n* *US* a member of the armed forces below an officer

enliven *v* to make more active or cheerful

en masse *adv* French all together

enmesh *v* to catch as if in a net

enmity *n* the feeling of being an enemy: *He felt great enmity towards his brother*

ennoble *v* **-bled, -bling** 1 to make (someone) a nobleman 2 to make better and more honourable: *ennobled by suffering* — ~ment *n*

ennui *n* French tiredness caused esp. by having nothing to do —compare BOREDOM

enormity *n* **-ties** 1 great evil 2 enormousness, esp. of difficulty: *the enormity of the job of feeding the whole world*

enormous *adj* very large indeed — ~ness *n*

enormously *adv* very much indeed: *It interests me enormously*

enough¹ *adj* as much or as many as may be necessary: *enough seats | enough money*

enough² *adv* 1 to the necessary degree: *warm enough to swim* 2 **fair enough** all right; satisfactory 5 **sure enough** as expected: *He said he would come, and sure enough he came*

enough³ *pron* a quantity or number which satisfies need: *I have enough to do*

en passant *adv* French by the way

enquire *v* **enquired, enquiring** to inquire

enquiry *n* **-ries** an inquiry

enrage *v* **enraged, enraging** to make very angry — **enraged** *adj*

enrapture *v* **-tured, -turing** to fill (someone) with great joy — **enraptured** *adj*

enrich *v* to make rich — ~ment *n*

enrol, enroll *v* **-ll-** to make (oneself or another person) officially a member of a group

enrolment, enroll- *n* 1 (an example of) enrolling 2 the number enrolled: *The school has an enrolment of 2, 000 pupils*

en route *adv* French on the way: *en route from London to Rome*

ensanguined *adj* literature covered with blood

ensconce *v* **ensconced, ensconcing** *esp. written or humour* to place or seat (esp. oneself) comfortably: *He ensconced himself in a chair* — **ensconced** *adj*

ensemble *n* French 1 also **tout ensemble**— a set of things that combine to make a whole 2 a small group of musicians who regularly play together 3 **a** a piece of music written for a small number of different instruments **b** (in opera) a piece of combined singing by all the performers 4 a matching set of women's clothes, such as a dress, coat, and shoes

enshrine *v* **enshrined, enshrining** to put or keep in a holy place — **enshrined** *adj*

ent

enshroud v to cover and hide, as with a shroud — **enshrouded** adj

ensign n 1 a flag on a ship that shows what nation the ship belongs to 2 (in Britain before 1871) an officer of the lowest rank in the army

enslave v **enslaved, enslaving** to make into a slave — ~**ment** n

ensnare v **ensnared, ensnaring** to catch in or as if in a snare

ensue v **ensued, ensuing** esp. written to happen afterwards (often as a result)

ensure v **ensured, ensuring** to make (something) certain (to happen) —see INSURE (USAGE)

entail v 1 to make (an event or action) necessary: Writing a history book entails a lot of work 2 law (esp. in former times) to leave (land) allowing passage at death only from father to son (or as arranged) but not sale: The land is entailed on the eldest son

entangle v **-gled, -gling** to cause (string, hair, etc.) to become twisted or mixed (with something else): The sailor's legs got entangled with the ropes

entanglement n 1 entangling or being entangled 2 something which involves one in difficulties

entente n French a friendly relationship between countries: the entente between Britain and France

enter v 1 to come or go into: to enter a room 2 to come in: Please do not enter without knocking 3 to become a member of: to enter the army 4 to write down (names, amounts, etc.) in a book

enter for v prep to put (a name) on a list for: John entered (himself) for the examination

enter into v prep 1 to begin: to enter into a contract 2 to take part in: He entered into the spirit of the game 3 to be a part of

enteritis n a painful infection of the bowels causing diarrhoea

enterprise n 1 a plan to do something daring or difficult 2 the courage that is needed for this 3 the way of carrying on business: private enterprise 4 an organization, esp. a business firm

enterprising adj having or showing enterprise — ~**ly** adv

entertain v 1 to give a party (for): He does his entertaining in restaurants 2 to amuse: A teacher should entertain as well as teach 3 to be willing to think about (an idea, doubt, etc.)

entertainer n a person who entertains professionally

entertaining adj amusing: an entertaining story — ~**ly** adv

entertainment n 1 the act of entertaining 2 (a) public amusement: A cinema is a place of entertainment

enthral, enthrall v **-ll-** to hold the complete attention of (someone): The boy was enthralled by the soldier's stories — **enthralled** adj — **enthralling** adj — ~**ingly** adv

enthrone v **enthroned, enthroning** to place (a king, queen, or bishop) on a throne — ~**ment** n

enthroned adj seated on or as if on a throne

enthuse v **enthused, enthusing** to show enthusiasm

enthusiasm n a strong feeling of interest and admiration: his enthusiasm for Eastern music — **-ast** n — **-astic** adj — **-astically** adv

entice v **enticed, enticing** to persuade by offering something pleasant — ~**ment** n — **-ticing** adj — **-ticingly** adv

entire adj with nothing left out; complete: an entire set of Shakespeare's plays — ~**ly** adv

entirety n completeness (esp. in the phrase **in its entirety**)

entitle v **-tled, -tling** 1 to give (to a book, play, etc.) a title 2 to give (someone) a right: Officers are entitled to travel first class —compare EMPOWER, ENABLE — ~**ment** n

entity n **-ties** a single separate and independent existence

entomb v esp. written & literature to put or contain in or as if in a grave — ~**ment** n

entomology n the scientific study of insects ⚠ ETYMOLOGY — **-gist** n — **-gical** adj

entourage n French all the people who surround and follow an important person

entr'acte, entracte n French (a performance given during) the time between acts in a play

entrails n the inside parts of an animal, esp. the bowels

entrance¹ n 1 an opening by which one enters —compare ENTRY 2 the act of entering: The actor made only 2 entrances

entrance² v **entranced, entrancing** to delight greatly — **entranced** adj

entrant n 1 a person who enters a profession 2 a person or animal that enters for a race or competition

entrap v **-pp-** esp. written to catch as if in a trap — ~**ment** n

entreat v to beg earnestly: I entreat your help — ~**ingly** adv

entreaty n **-ties** esp. written an earnest request

entrée n French 1 the freedom to enter 2 a small meat dish, served before the main dish at a formal dinner

entrench, intrench v 1 to dig a trench in the ground 2 to place (oneself) in a safe position: He entrenched himself behind his newspaper

entrenched adj (of customs, beliefs, etc.) firmly established

entrepreneur n French 1 a person who plans and starts a business 2 a person who arranges for the performance of shows —compare IMPRESARIO

entropy n 1 a measure of the difference between the temperatures of something which heats and something which is being heated 2 the state which the universe will reach when all the heat is spread out evenly **3** the tendency of heat and other forms of energy to spread out and gradually disappear

entrust, intrust *v* to give (someone) the charge of (something): *I entrusted the child to your care*

entry *n* **entries 1** the act of coming or going in **2** the right to enter: *a street with a 'No Entry' sign* △ ENTRÉ **3** the act or result of writing something down on a list **4** a person, thing, or group entered in a race or competition

entwine *v* **entwined, entwining** to twist together —compare ENTANGLE

enumerate *v* **-rated, -rating** to list one by one: *He enumerated all his reasons* — **-ration** *n*

enunciate *v* **-ated, -ating** to pronounce (a word, opinion etc.): *An actor must enunciate clearly.* | *He enunciated his views* — **-tion** *n*

envelop *v* to wrap up or cover completely: *He enveloped himself in blankets* — ~**ment** *n*

envelope *n* a covering which contains something, esp. the cover of a letter

enviable *adj* **1** (of a person) causing envy: *an enviable young man* **2** very desirable: *an enviable job* — **-bly** *adv*

envious *adj* feeling or showing envy: *She was envious of her sister's beauty* —see JEALOUS (USAGE) — ~**ly** *adv*

environment *n* **1** the conditions which influence development: *Children need a happy home environment* **2** the air, water, and land in which man lives: *new laws to prevent the pollution of the environment* — ~**al** *adj* — ~**ally** *adv*

environmentalist *n* a person who tries to prevent the environment from being spoilt — **-ism** *n*

environs *n* the neighbourhood surrounding a town

envisage *v* **-aged, -aging** to see in the mind as a future possibility: *Henry Ford envisaged an important future for the motor car*

envoy *n* **envoys** a messenger, esp. one sent by one government to do business with another

envy¹ *n* a feeling one has towards someone when one wishes that one had his qualities or possessions —compare JEALOUSY

envy² *v* **envied, envying** to feel envy for or of

enzyme *n* a catalyst produced by certain living cells, which can cause chemical change in plants or animals without itself being changed

eon *n* an aeon

epaulet, -lette *n* a shoulder ornament, esp. on a uniform

épée *n* a sharp-pointed stiff narrow sword, used in fencing —compare FOIL, SABRE

ephemeral *adj* having a very short life — **-rally** *adv*

epic¹ *adj* (of stories, events, etc.) full of brave action and excitement: *the epic fight of one small ship against 6 enemy ships* — ~**ally** *adv*

epic² *n* a long poem telling the story of the deeds of gods and great men

epicentre *n* *technical* the place on the Earth's

surface just over the part where an earthquake begins

epicure *n* a person who takes great interest in food and drink — ~**an** *adj, n*

epidemic¹ *adj* very common in one place for a time: *Violence is reaching epidemic levels* — compare ENDEMIC, PANDEMIC

epidemic² *n* a large number of cases of the same infectious disease at the same time

epidermis *n* *medical* the outside layer of an animal or plant ⊃ SKIN

epigram *n* a short amusing poem or saying — ~**matic** *adj* — ~**matically** *adv*

epilepsy *n* a nervous disorder which causes sudden uncontrolled movement and loss of consciousness — **-ptic** *adj, n*

epilogue *n* the last part of a play or piece of literature —opposite **prologue**

Epiphany *n* the feast of the Christian church, on January 6th, in memory of the coming of the 3 kings

episcopal *adj* **1** of or concerning bishops **2** (of a church) governed by bishops

episcopalian *adj, n* (a member) of an episcopal church

episode *n* one separate event: *one of the funniest episodes in my life*

epistle *n* *esp. written or humour* a letter

Epistle *n* any of the letters written by the first followers of Christ

epitaph *n* a short description of a dead person, often written on his gravestone

epithet *n* an adjective expressing praise or blame: *He insulted me, using rude epithets*

epitome *n* a thing or person that shows a quality to a very great degree: *My cat is the epitome of laziness*

epitomize, -mise *v* **-mized, -mizing** to be an epitome of

epoch *n* **1** a period of historical time — compare ERA ⊃ ERA **2** an important event

epsilon *n* the 5th letter of the Greek alphabet (Ε, ε)

equable *adj* **1** (of temperature or character) even and regular **2** (of a person) of even temper △ EQUITABLE — **-bly** *adv*

equal¹ *adj* **1** (of 2 or more) the same in number, value, etc.: *Cut the cake into 6 equal pieces* **2** (of a person) having enough strength, ability, etc.: *Bill is quite equal to running the office* **3 on equal terms** (meeting or speaking) as equals

equal² *n* a person that is equal (to another or to oneself)

equal³ *v* **-ll- 1** (of sizes or numbers) to be the same (as): *'x=y' means that x equals y* **2** to be as good, clever, etc. (as): *None of us can equal her*

equalitarian *adj* egalitarian

equality *n* being equal

equalize, -ise *v* **-ized, -izing** to make equal — **-ization** *n*

equally *adv* **1** to an equal degree: *both equally*

pretty **2** in equal shares: *They shared the work equally*

equanimity *n* calmness of mind

equate *v* **equated, equating** to make equal: *You can't equate his poems with his plays*

equation *n* **1** a statement that 2 expressions are equal: $x+2y=7$ *is an equation* **2** equating

equator *n* an imaginary line drawn round the world halfway between its north and south poles ⟹ GLOBE — ~ial *adj* — ~ially *adv*

equerry *n* **-ries** a male attendant on the royal family

equestrian *adj, n* (a person) riding on a horse

equidistant *adj* equally distant: *Rome is about equidistant from Cairo and Oslo*

equilateral *adj* (of a triangle) having all 3 sides equal ⟹ MATHEMATICS

equilibrium *n* a state of balance

equine *adj* of or like a horse

equinox *n* one of the 2 times in the year (about March 21 and September 22) when day and night are of equal length: *the vernal* (=spring) *and autumnal equinoxes* — **-noctial** *adj*

equip *v* **-pp-** to provide with what is necessary: *He equipped himself to go sailing*

equipage *n* (in former times) a carriage, with its horses and attendants

equipment *n* **1** the things needed: *office equipment* **2** equipping

equipoise *n* technical a state of balance

equitable *adj* fair and just —opposite **inequitable** △ EQUABLE — **-bly** *adv*

equities *n* a company's ordinary shares

equity *n* the principle of justice which may be used to correct a law

equivalent[1] *adj* same; equal: *He changed his pounds for the equivalent amount of dollars* — **-ence** *n* — ~ly *adv*

equivalent[2] *n* that which is equivalent

equivocal *adj* having a doubtful meaning; questionable —opposite **unequivocal** — ~ly *adv*

equivocate *v* **-cated, -cating** to speak in an equivocal way on purpose to deceive — **-tion** *n*

er *interj* (a hesitation noise)

era *n* a period of time named after or starting from an important event: *The era of space travel has begun.* | *The Christian era starts with the birth of Christ* — compare EPOCH ◉

eradicate *v* **-cated, -cating** to put an end to (something bad) — **-cation** *n*

erase *v* **erased, erasing** to rub out or remove (esp. a pencil mark) — ~r *n*

erasure *n* **1** erasing **2** a place marked by erasing

ere *prep, conj* poetic before: *ere morning*

erect[1] *adj* **1** upright; not stooping **2** medical (of the penis) in a state of erection — ~ly *adv* — ~ness *n*

erect[2] *v* to build or set up: *to erect a tent*

erectile *adj* medical (esp. of the penis) that can fill with blood, which makes the part stand upright

erection *n* **1** the building of something: *the erection of the new hospital* **2** the state of the penis when upright

erg *n* a measure of work: *It takes about 350 ergs to lift a pin one inch*

ergo *adv* Latin therefore

ergonomics *n* the study of the conditions in which people work most effectively with machines

ermine *n* **ermines** or **ermine** a stoat or its white winter fur often worn by kings and judges

erode *v* **eroded, eroding** (of acids, water, etc.) to eat into; wear away: *The sea erodes the rocks* **2** to become worn away

erogenous *adj* technical (of parts of the body) sexually sensitive

erosion *n* eroding: *soil erosion by wind* — **-sive** *adj* — **-siveness** *n*

erotic *adj* of sexual desire: *an erotic picture* — ~ism *n* — ~ally *adv*

err *v* to do something wrong: *To err is human* (old saying)

errand *n* a short journey made to get something or to carry a message —see also FOOL'S ERRAND

errant *adj* **1** mistaken; erring **2** wandering away and doing bad things: *She went to London to bring back her errant daughter*

erratic *adj* changeable without reason; irregular — ~ally *adv*

erratum *n* **-ta** Latin a mistake in printing or writing

erroneous *adj* esp. written (of a statement, a belief, etc.) incorrect — ~ly *adv*

error *n* **1** a mistake; something done wrongly **2** being wrong in behaviour or beliefs

ersatz *adj* German used instead of the real thing

Erse *n* Irish Gaelic

erudite *adj* esp. written (of a person or a book) full of learning — ~ly *adv* — **-dition** *n*

erupt *v* (of a volcano) to explode and pour out fire

eruption *n* **1** erupting **2** an unhealthy spot or area on the skin △ IRRUPTION

escalate *v* **-lated, -lating** **1** (of war) to increase by stages **2** (of prices) to rise — **-lation** *n*

escalator also **moving staircase**— *n* a set of moving stairs

escalope *n* a boneless slice of pork, beef, or veal usu. fried in egg and breadcrumbs

escapade *n* an exciting, and sometimes dangerous and mischievous act usu. carried out for fun

escape[1] *v* **escaped, escaping** **1** to reach freedom: *The prisoners have escaped* **2** (of liquids or gases) to find a way out: *gas escaping from the pipe* **3** to avoid (an evil): *escaped death* **4** to be unnoticed by: *Nothing escaped his attention*

escape[2] *n* **1** the act of escaping: *The thief made his escape* **2** a case of escaping by a liquid or gas: *an escape of gas* **3** something that frees one from dull reality: *She reads love stories as an escape* —see also ESCAPISM

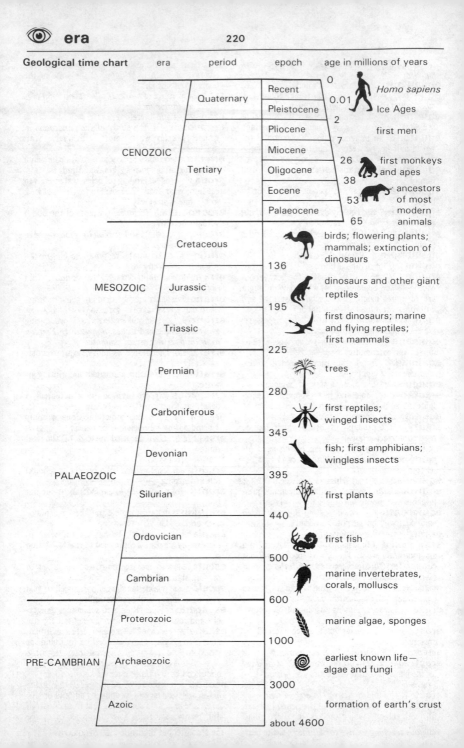

Geological time chart

era	period	epoch	age in millions of years	
CENOZOIC	Quaternary	Recent	0	*Homo sapiens*
		Pleistocene	0.01	Ice Ages
		Pliocene	2	first men
	Tertiary	Miocene	7	
		Oligocene	26	first monkeys and apes
		Eocene	38	ancestors of most modern animals
		Palaeocene	53	
			65	
MESOZOIC	Cretaceous			birds; flowering plants; mammals; extinction of dinosaurs
			136	
	Jurassic			dinosaurs and other giant reptiles
			195	
	Triassic			first dinosaurs; marine and flying reptiles; first mammals
			225	
PALAEOZOIC	Permian			trees
			280	
	Carboniferous			first reptiles; winged insects
			345	
	Devonian			fish; first amphibians; wingless insects
			395	
	Silurian			first plants
			440	
	Ordovician			first fish
			500	
	Cambrian			marine invertebrates, corals, molluscs
			600	
PRE-CAMBRIAN	Proterozoic			marine algae, sponges
			1000	
	Archaeozoic			earliest known life— algae and fungi
			3000	
	Azoic			formation of earth's crust
			about 4600	

escapement n the part of a clock or a watch which controls the moving parts inside △ ESCARP-MENT

escape velocity n -ties the speed at which an object moves fast enough to get free from the pull of a planet, and not fall back

escape wheel n a revolving toothed wheel in a clock or watch which makes a fork vibrate

escapism n activity intended to provide escape from reality — **escapist** adj, n

escarpment n a long hill with one short steep face and one long gently sloping side △ ESCAPE-MENT

eschew v esp. written to avoid on purpose: eschew bad company

escort¹ n 1 a person or people who go with another: The prisoner travelled under police escort 2 a man who takes a woman out for the evening

escort² v to go with (someone) as an escort

escutcheon also **scutcheon**— n a shield with a coat of arms on it

Eskimo adj of a people living in the far north of North America and Siberia

esoteric adj secret and mysterious △ ECLECTIC — ~ally adv

ESP abbrev. for: EXTRASENSORY PERCEPTION

espadrille n Spanish a light canvas shoe with a rope sole

especial adj special

especially adv 1 to a particularly great degree: I love Italy, especially in summer 2 specially: This crown was made especially for the King

Esperanto n an invented language, intended for international use

espionage n French spying; the work of finding out political secrets

esplanade n a level open space for walking; seafront promenade

espouse v espoused, espousing esp. written to support an aim, idea, etc.: He espoused the cause of equal rights for women

espresso n -sos Italian coffee made by forcing steam through ground coffee

esprit de corps n French loyalty among the members of a group

espy v espied, espying esp. written to see suddenly: One day Robinson Crusoe espied a footprint in the sand

Esq., also **Esquire** n (used as a title of politeness usu. written after a man's name): Peter Jones, Esq.

essay¹ essayed, essaying v to try (to do something): to essay a task

essay² n essays a piece of writing, usu. short and on one subject — ~ist n

essay³ n an attempt or effort: She made her first essays at cooking

essence n 1 the most important quality of a thing, which makes it what it is: The essence of his religious teaching is love for all men 2 the best

part of a substance, reduced to a jelly, liquid, etc.: essence of roses —compare EXTRACT

essential¹ adj 1 a necessary: Food and drink are essential to life b forming the central part of: Her most essential quality is kindness 2 technical of an essence: essential oils

essential² n 1 something that is necessary 2 something that forms the essence (of something): the essentials of grammar

essentially adv basically: She's essentially kind

establish v 1 to set up (an organization) 2 to place in a position: He established his son in business 3 to make certain of: to establish the truth of a story 4 to make (a rule) 5 to cause people to believe in (a claim, fact, etc.): She established her fame as an actress

establishment n 1 establishing 2 a business organization: These 2 hotels are both excellent establishments

Establishment n often offensive the organizations and people who are said to control public life and resist changes

estate n 1 a piece of land in the country, usu. with a large house on it 2 a piece of land on which buildings have all been built together in a planned way 3 the whole of a person's property, according to the law 4 old use (esp. of France before the Revolution) social or political class: The 3 estates of the realm (=country) were the lords, the priests, and the common people

estate agent n a person whose business is to sell and buy houses and land —compare HOUSE AGENT — **estate agency** n

estate car also **shooting brake,** US **station wagon**— n a private car which carries both people and goods, usu. with a door at the back

esteem¹ n respect; good opinion: All David's friends held him in high esteem —compare ESTIMATION

esteem² v 1 to respect greatly 2 to believe to be (esp. something good): I did not esteem him to be worthy —compare ESTIMATE

estimable adj worthy of esteem

estimate¹ v -mated, -mating 1 to calculate the value of something: I estimate her age at 35 —see also UNDER/OVERESTIMATE —compare ESTEEM, ESTIMATION 2 to calculate the cost of doing a job —compare QUOTE — **-tor** n

estimate² n 1 a calculation (of the value, degree, or quality of something): My estimate of her character was wrong 2 an offer to do a job for a certain price: We got 2 or 3 estimates before having the roof repaired —compare QUOTATION

estimation n judgment or opinion: He has lowered himself in my estimation —compare ESTEEM

estrange v estranged, estranging to make unfriendly: His behaviour estranged him from his brother — ~ment n

estuary n -ries the mouth of a river, into which the sea enters at high tide ☞ GEOGRAPHY

et al. *Latin* and the others: *Are George, Peter, et al. coming to the party?*

etc., also **et cetera** *adv Latin* and the rest; and so on

etch *v* to draw (a picture) by cutting lines on a metal plate with a needle and acids — ~**er** *n*

etching *n* **1** the art of etching **2** a picture printed from an etched metal plate

eternal *adj* going on for ever: *Rome has been called the Eternal City* — ~**ly** *adv*

eternal triangle *n* the troubled state of affairs resulting from the love of two people for another person

eternity *n* **-ties 1** time without end; state of time after death **2** a very long time

ether *n* a light colourless liquid made from alcohol . It is used in industry and as an anaesthetic

ethereal, aethereal *adj* of unearthly lightness; like a spirit — **-ally** *adv*

ethic *n* a system of moral behaviour: *the Christian ethic*

ethical *adj* **1** of ethics **2** morally good: *I oughtn't to do that; it's not ethical* — ~**ly** *adv*

ethics *n* **1** the science of morals **2** moral rules

ethnic also **ethnical**— *adj* of a racial, national, or tribal group — ~**ally** *adv*

ethnography *n* the scientific description of the different races of man — **-pher** *n* — **-phic** *adj* — **-phically** *adv*

ethnology *n* the science of the different races of man —compare ANTHROPOLOGY — **-gist** *n* — **-gical** *adj* — **-gically** *adv*

ethyl *n* a liquid which is added to petrol to reduce engine noise (ANTI-KNOCK)

ethyl alcohol *n technical* ordinary alcohol which can be drunk —compare METHYL ALCOHOL

etiolate *v* **-lated, -lating** to make (a plant) grow long stems and small pale leaves by keeping in the dark — **-lation** *n*

etiquette *n* the formal rules of proper behaviour

etymology *n* **-ies 1** the scientific study of the history and changing meanings of words △ ENTOMOLOGY **2** the history of a particular word △ ENTOMOLOGY — **-gical** *adj* — **-gically** *adv* — **-gist** *n*

eucalyptus *n* a type of tall tree, such as the Australian gum tree, which produces an oil used for treating colds

Eucharist *n* (the bread and wine taken at) the Christian ceremony based on Christ's last supper on Earth —see also MASS, COMMUNION — ~**ic** *adj*

Euclidean *adj* of the discoveries of Euclid about geometry

eugenics *n* the study of ways of breeding stronger and cleverer people — **eugenic** *adj* — **-ically** *adv*

eulogize, -gise *v* **-gized, -gizing** *esp. written* to make a eulogy about

eulogy *n* **-gies** *esp. written* (a speech containing) high praise usu. of a person △ ELEGY — **-gistic** *adj* — **-gistically** *adv*

eunuch *n* a man who has been castrated

euphemism *n* (the use of) a pleasanter name for something unpleasant: *'Fall asleep' is a euphemism for 'die'* △ EUPHUISM — **-istic** *adj* — **-istically** *adv*

euphonious *adj* (of language) pleasant in sound

euphonium *n* the highest of the tuba group of brass wind instruments, with valves

euphony *n* pleasantness of sound, esp. in language —opposite **cacophony**

euphoria *n* a feeling of happy excitement — **euphoric** *adj* — **-cally** *adv*

euphuism *n* a peculiar, difficult, and rather insincere style of literature fashionable in England in the 16th and early 17th centuries △ EUPHEMISM

Eurasian *adj* **1** of Europe and Asia **2** of mixed European and Asian birth

eureka *interj Greek* (used as a cry of victory at making a discovery) I have found it!

Eurocrat *n* an official of the EUROPEAN Community

Eurodollar *n* a US dollar which has been put into European banks

European *adj* **1** of or related to Europe ☞ MAP HISTORY **2** (of people) white: *He looks European*

European Community *n esp. written* COMMON MARKET

eustachian tube *n medical* either of the 2 tubes which join the ears to the throat

euthanasia *n* the painless killing of very ill or old people

EVA *abbrev. for:* (in space travel) extra-vehicular activity

evacuate *v* **-ated, -ating 1** to take (people) away from (a place) **2** to empty (the bowels) — **-ation** *n*

evacuee *n* a person who has been evacuated

evade *v* **evaded, evading 1** to escape from: *evaded an enemy* **2** to avoid, or avoid doing (something one should do)

evaluate *v* **-ated, -ating** to calculate the value of — **-ation** *n*

evanescent *adj* soon fading away, disappearing — **-cence** *n*

evangelical *adj, n* (a member) of certain Protestant Christian churches who give special importance to the Bible rather than to rituals and sacraments — ~**ism** *n*

evangelist *n* a person who travels from place to place and holds religious meetings — **-lism** *n* — **-listic** *adj*

Evangelist *n* any of the 4 writers (Matthew, Mark, Luke, and John) of the 4 gospels

evaporate *v* **-rated, -rating** to change into

steam and disappear: *The sun will evaporate the mist* ⟶ CLOUD — -ration *n*

evaporated milk *n* tinned milk, from which part of the water has been evaporated

evasion *n* evading: *the fox's clever evasion of the dogs*

evasive *adj* which evades or tries to evade: *an evasive answer* — ~ly *adv* — ~ness *n*

eve *n* 1 the night or the day before a religious feast or holiday: *New Year's Eve* 2 the time just before an important event: *on the eve of our examination* 3 poetic evening

even[1] *adj* 1 flat, level: *Cut the bushes even with the fence* 2 unchanging: *an even temperature* 3 equal: *He won the first game and I won the second, so now we're even* 4 (of a number) that can be divided exactly by 2: *2, 4, 6, 8, etc.* are even numbers —opposite **odd** — ~ly *adv* — **evenness** *n*

even[2] *adv* 1 (*used before the surprising part of a statement*) which is more than might be expected: *Even John doesn't go out in the summer* (so certainly nobody else does). | *John doesn't go out even in the summer* (so certainly not in the winter) 2 indeed; and one might almost say: *He looked pleased, even delighted* 3 still; yet: *It's even colder than yesterday*

even-handed *adj* fair and equal; equally balanced

evening *n* 1 the end of the day and early part of the night 2 a party, performance, etc., happening in the evening: *a musical evening*

evening dress *n* the clothes worn by women, and special black clothes worn by men, for formal evening occasions

evening star *n* a planet, esp. Venus, when it appears in the western sky in the evening — compare MORNING STAR

even out *v adv* to become level: *Prices should even out*

evens also **even odds**— *n* chances that are the same for and against (as when one bets £1 on a race to win £1)

evensong *n* the evening service in the Church of England

event *n* 1 a happening: *the chief events of 1977* 2 a race, competition, etc., arranged as part of a day's sports: *The next event will be the 100 yards race* 3 **at all events** in spite of everything: *She had a terrible accident, but at all events she wasn't killed* 4 **in any event** whatever may happen: *I'll probably see you but in any event I'll telephone* 5 **in the event of (something)** if (something) happens: *He asked his sister to look after his children in the event of his death*

even-tempered *adj* having a calm good temper

eventful *adj* full of important events: *an eventful life* — ~ly *adv* — ~ness *n*

eventual *adj* happening at last: *the eventual success of his efforts*

eventuality *n* -ties a possible event: *prepared for any eventuality*

eventually *adv* in the end: *He worked so hard that eventually he made himself ill*

eventuate in *v prep* -ated, -ating in *esp. written or pompous* to result in; have as a result

even up *v adv* to make equal: *I'll pay for the taxi, to even things up*

ever *adv* 1 at any time: *Have you ever been to Paris?* 2 at any time before: *faster than ever* 3 (used for giving force to an expression): *I pulled as hard as ever I could* 4 always: *the ever-increasing population* 5 **ever so/such** esp. spoken very 6 **for ever** forever   USAGE **what ever? how ever?** etc., are sometimes written **whatever? however?** but this is not thought to be good English. — compare WHATEVER, HOWEVER, WHENEVER, WHEREVER, WHOEVER, WHICHEVER

evergreen *adj, n* (a tree or bush) that does not lose its leaves in winter —opposite **deciduous** (*adj* only)

everlasting *adj* 1 lasting for ever: *everlasting life* 2 lasting for a long time or too long

everlastingly *adv* in an everlasting manner: *He's everlastingly giving me advice*

evermore *adv* literature always: *He swore to love her for evermore*

every *adj* 1 each, counted one by one (of more than 2): *I enjoyed every minute of it* 2 once in each: *He comes every day* 3 as much as possible: *She made every attempt* 4 **every other a** the 1st, 3rd, 5th or the 2nd, 4th, 6th **b** all the others: *Every other girl but me got a prize!*   USAGE Use **every** with a singular verb, when thinking of a whole group: **Every** *child knows it.* Use **each** when thinking of one at a time. Compare **everyone** and **every one: every one** means "each person or thing" and can be followed by of: **every one** *of the children* —see EVERYBODY (USAGE)

everybody also **everyone**— *pron* every person   USAGE **Anybody, every,** and **everybody** are followed by a singular verb. They are sometimes followed by a plural pronoun to avoid saying *he or she:* **Everybody** *started waving their flags.* In written English one would say: **Everybody** *started waving his or her flag* —see EVERY (USAGE)

everyday *adj* ordinary and usual: *my everyday shoes, not my best ones*

everything *pron* all; the whole, made up of a number of things: *Everything is ready for the party*

everywhere *adv* in, at, or to every place: *I've looked everywhere*

evict *v* to take (a person) away (from a house or land) by law — ~ion *n*

evidence *n* 1 (esp. in science or law) words or things which prove a statement or make a matter more clear: *Can you show me any evidence for your statement?* 2 **in evidence** able to be seen and noticed: *Mrs Jones was much in evidence at the party* 3 **turn Queen's/King's evidence** (of a criminal) to speak against another criminal in a lawcourt

evident adj clear because of evidence: *It's evident that you are tired* — ~ly adv

evil¹ adj -ll- very bad; wicked; harmful: *evil thoughts* — evilly adv

evil² n (a) great wickedness or misfortune: *'Deliver us from evil'* (prayer)

evil eye n the supposed power to harm people by looking at them

evil-minded adj having bad thoughts and desires — evil-mindedly adv — evil-mindedness n

evince v evinced, evincing esp. written to show clearly (a feeling, quality, etc.): *He evinced great sorrow*

eviscerate v -rated, -rating esp. written to cut out the bowels and other inside parts of the body from

evocative adj that produces memories and feelings

evoke v evoked, evoking to produce or call up (a feeling): *Her singing evoked public admiration* — evocation n

evolution n 1 the development of the various types of plants, animals, etc., from fewer and simpler forms ☞ 2 a gradual development: *the evolution of the modern car* — ~ary adj

evolve v evolved, evolving to develop gradually

ewe n a female sheep —compare RAM

ewer n a large, wide-mouthed jug, used for water

exacerbate v -bated, -bating to make worse (pain, diseases, etc.) — -bation n

exact¹ v esp. written to demand and obtain by force, threats, etc.: *He exacted obedience from the children* — ~ion n

exact² adj correct and without mistakes: *the exact time* — ~ness, ~itude n

exacting adj demanding much care, effort, and attention: *exacting and tiring work* — ~ly adv

exactly adv 1 with complete correctness: *The train arrived at exactly 8 o'clock* 2 just; quite: *The doctor told him not to smoke, but he did exactly the opposite* 3 I agree!: *'We need a drink.' 'Exactly! Let's have one'*

exaggerate v -rated, -rating to make (something) seem larger, better, worse, etc., than in reality: *It was a rabbit, not a lion; you're exaggerating as usual!* — ~d adj — ~dly adv

exaggeration n (an example of) exaggerating

exalt v 1 to praise highly 2 to raise (a person) to a high rank △ EXULT

exaltation n the joy of success: *The news filled them with exaltation*

exalted adj 1 of high rank 2 full of the joy of sucess: *an exalted state of excitement* — ~ly adv

examination n 1 also (esp. spoken) exam a test of knowled 2 (an act of) examining: *a medical examination | the examination of the witnesses*

examine v -ined, -ining 1 to look at closely, in order to find out something: *The doctor examined her carefully* 2 to ask (a person) questions, in order to measure knowledge or find out something —compare CROSS-EXAMINE — -iner n

example n 1 something taken from a number of things of the same kind, which shows a general rule: *Her rudeness was a typical example of her usual bad manners* 2 a person, or behaviour, that is worthy of being copied: *Mary's courage is an example to us all* 3 make an example of someone to punish someone so that others will be afraid to behave as he did

exasperate v -rated, -rating to annoy or make angry — -ration n — -ratedly adv — -ratingly adv

excavate v -vated, -vating 1 to make (a hole) by digging 2 to uncover by digging — -vation n

excavator n 1 a person who excavates 2 a large machine that digs and moves earth in a bucket at the end of a 2-part arm

exceed v 1 to be greater than: *The cost will not exceed £50* 2 to do more than: *exceeding the speed limit*

exceedingly adv very: *exceedingly kind*

excel v -ll- to be very good; be better than: *She excels as a teacher*

Excellency n -cies (the word used when speaking to or of certain persons of high rank): *His Excellency the Spanish ambassador*

excellent adj very good; of very high quality — -ence n — ~ly adv

except¹ v to leave out: *You will all be punished; I can except no one* — ~ed adj : *Everyone enjoyed walking home, John excepted; he grumbled all the way* — ~ing prep

except² also excepting— prep but not; leaving out: *all the questions except for the last one | I like her except when she's angry* —see BESIDES (USAGE) —compare BUT FOR, SAVE

except³ conj apart from: *She can do everything except cook*

exception n 1 (a case of) excepting or being excepted: *You will all be punished. I can make no exceptions* 2 take exception (to) to be made angry (by) 3 with the exception of except; apart from

exceptionable adj esp. written that can cause someone to take exception —opposite unexceptionable

exceptional adj unusual, often in a good sense — ~ly adv

excerpt n a piece taken from a book, speech, or musical work

excess¹ n 1 the fact of exceeding, or an amount by which something exceeds 2 something more than is reasonable: *an excess of anger* 3 in excess of more than: *to spend in excess of one's income*

excess² adj additional; more than usual: *excess postal charges*

excesses n actions so bad that they pass the limits expected of human behaviour

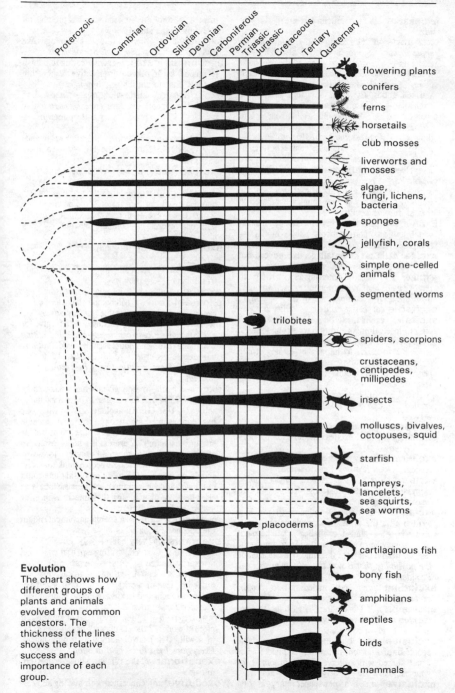

flowering plants

conifers

ferns

horsetails

club mosses

liverworts and mosses

algae, fungi, lichens, bacteria

sponges

jellyfish, corals

simple one-celled animals

segmented worms

trilobites

spiders, scorpions

crustaceans, centipedes, millipedes

insects

molluscs, bivalves, octopuses, squid

starfish

lampreys, lancelets, sea squirts, sea worms

placoderms

cartilaginous fish

bony fish

amphibians

reptiles

birds

mammals

Proterozoic · Cambrian · Ordovician · Silurian · Devonian · Carboniferous · Permian · Triassic · Jurassic · Cretaceous · Tertiary · Quaternary

Evolution
The chart shows how different groups of plants and animals evolved from common ancestors. The thickness of the lines shows the relative success and importance of each group.

excessive adj too much; too great — ~**ly** adv

exchange¹ n 1 exchanging: *He gave me an apple in exchange for a cake* 2 also **telephone exchange**— a central place where all the telephone wires are joined so that people may speak to each other 3 a place where business men meet to buy and sell goods: *the Corn Exchange | the Stock Exchange* —see also EMPLOYMENT EXCHANGE

exchange² v **exchanged, exchanging** 1 to give and receive (something in return for something else): *John exchanged hats with Peter* — compare CHANGE 2 **exchange contracts** to complete the first stages in buying or selling a house 3 **exchange words/blows** to quarrel/fight — ~**able** adj

exchange rate also **rate of exchange**— n the value of the money of one country compared to that of another country

Exchequer n the Government department which collects and controls public money — compare TREASURY

excise¹ n the tax on certain goods produced and used inside a country —compare CUSTOMS

excise² v **excised, excising** esp. written to remove by or as if by cutting out: *excised an organ from the body* —compare AMPUTATE — **-sion** n

excitable adj easily excited — **-bility** n

excite v **excited, exciting** 1 to cause (someone) to lose calmness and to have strong feelings, often pleasant: *The story excited the little boy very much* 2 to cause to happen by raising strong feelings: *The king's cruelty excited a rising of the people* 3 to make active: *Strong coffee excites your nerves*

excited adj full of strong, pleasant feelings: *The excited children were opening their presents* — ~**ly** adv

excitement n being excited

exciting adj that excites one: *an exciting story* — ~**ly** adv

exclaim v to say suddenly, because of strong feeling: *'Good heavens!' he exclaimed*

exclamation n 1 exclaiming 2 the word(s) expressing a sudden strong feeling: *'Good heavens!' is an exclamation*

exclamation mark n a mark (!) which is written after the words of an exclamation

exclude v **excluded, excluding** 1 to keep out (from somewhere) 2 to leave out from among the rest 3 to shut out from the mind: *We can exclude the possibility that it was the baby who shot the President*

excluding prep not including: *30 people, excluding me*

exclusion n 1 excluding: *His exclusion from the club hurt him very much* 2 **to the exclusion of** so as to leave out

exclusive¹ adj 1 a that excludes unsuitable people b (of a person) not willing to make friends 2 not shared with others: *This bathroom is for your exclusive use* — ~**ly** adv — ~**ness** n

exclusive² n 1 a newspaper story at first printed by only one newspaper 2 a product on sale only in the stated shop

exclusive of prep without; excluding: *The hotel charges £6 a day, exclusive of meals*

excommunicate v **-cated, -cating** to punish (someone) by driving out from active membership in the Christian church — **-tion** n

excoriate v **-ated, -ating** esp. written 1 to rub the skin from: *His legs were excoriated by the prickles* 2 to express a very bad opinion of — **-ation** n

excrement n esp. written the solid waste matter passed out through the bowels —compare EXCRETA

excrescence n esp. written an ugly growth on an animal or plant

excreta n esp. written the solid and liquid waste matter passed out esp. through the bowels

excrete v **excreted, excreting** esp. written to pass out (excreta) —compare SECRETE — **-tion** n

excruciating adj (of pain) very bad — ~**ly** adv

exculpate v **-pated, -pating** to free (someone) from blame — **-pation** n

excursion n a short journey for pleasure

excusable adj (of behaviour) that can be forgiven —opposite inexcusable — **-bly** adv

excuse¹ v **excused, excusing** 1 to forgive for a small fault: *Please excuse my bad handwriting* 2 to make (bad behaviour) seem less bad: *Nothing will excuse his cruelty to his children* 3 to free (someone) from a duty: *Can I be excused from football practice*

excuse² n the reason given when asking to be forgiven: *Have you any excuse to offer for coming so late?* USAGE An **apology** is given when one has done something wrong, and may include **reasons**. An **excuse** is a reason that seems untrue and unsatisfactory. A **pretext** is a fake reason. An **alibi** is often used to mean an excuse to escape blame or punishment. Some people think that **alibi** should only be used to mean proof that one could not have done a criminal act because one was elsewhere. A **plea** means that one is asking for understanding and mercy.

ex-directory adj (of a telephone number) not in the telephone book

execrable adj very bad — **-bly** adv

execrate v **-crated, -crating** esp. written to feel or express hatred of; curse — **-cration** n

execute v **-cuted, -cuting** 1 to carry out (an order or piece of work) 2 law to carry out the orders in (a will) 3 to kill as a lawful punishment: *executed for murder*

execution n 1 the carrying out of an order or piece of work 2 the act of carrying out the orders in a will 3 (a) lawful killing as a punishment: *Executions used to be held in public*

executioner n the official who executes criminals

executive¹ adj concerned with making and carrying out decisions: *a man of great executive ability*

executive² *n* a person or group in an executive position

executor *fem.* **executrix—** *n* the person or bank that carries out the orders in a will

exemplary *adj* 1 suitable to be copied as an example: *exemplary behaviour* 2 which should serve as a warning: *an exemplary punishment*

exemplify *v* -fied, -fying to give an example of — -fication *n*

exempt¹ *adj* freed (from a duty, payment, etc.): *exempt from military service* — ~ion *n*

exempt² *v* to make exempt

exercise¹ *n* 1 (a) use of any part of the body or mind so as to strengthen and improve it: *get more exercise* 2 a question or set of questions to be answered by a pupil for practice 3 the use of a power or right (esp. in the phrase **the exercise of**) 4 a movement made by soldiers, naval ships, etc., to practise fighting

exercise² *v* -cised, -cising 1 to give or take exercise 2 to use (a power or right): *exercise patience*

exert *v* to use (strength, skill, etc.) — ~ion *n*

exeunt *v pl. of* EXIT

ex gratia *adj, adv Latin* (of a payment) (made) as a favour

exhale *v* exhaled, exhaling to breathe out (air, gas, etc.) — -lation *n*

exhaust¹ *v* 1 to tire out 2 to use up completely: *My patience is exhausted*

exhaust² *n* 1 also **exhaust pipe**— the pipe which allows unwanted gas, steam, etc., to escape from an engine or machine ☞ CAR 2 the gas or steam which escapes through this pipe

exhaustion *n* 1 being tired out 2 exhausting or being exhausted: *the exhaustion of our food supplies*

exhaustive *adj* thorough: *to make an exhaustive study* — ~ly *adv* — ~ness *n*

exhibit¹ *v* 1 to show in public 2 to show other people that one possesses (a feeling, quality, etc.) — ~or *n*

exhibit² *n* something exhibited

exhibition *n* 1 a public show of objects 2 an act of exhibiting 3 money given by a school or university to a specially deserving student — compare SCHOLARSHIP 4 **make an exhibition of oneself** to behave foolishly in public

exhibitionism *n* 1 the behaviour of a person who wants to be looked at and admired: *He jumped into the lake, out of pure exhibitionism* 2 INDECENT EXPOSURE — -ist *n* — -istic *adj*

exhilarate *v* -rated, -rating to make (someone) cheerful and excited — -ration *n*

exhilarating *adj* that exhilarates people: *exhilarating air* — ~ly *adv*

exhort *v* to urge or advise strongly: *The general exhorted his men to fight well* — ~ation *n*

exhume *v* exhumed, exhuming *esp. written* to take (a dead body) out of the grave — **exhumation** *n*

exigency *n* -cies an urgent need; an emergency — **exigent** *adj* — **exigently** *adv*

exiguous *adj esp. written* too small in amount; not enough — ~ly *adv* — ~ness *n*

exile¹ *n* 1 unwanted absence from one's country, often for political reasons 2 a person who has been forced to leave his country

exile² *v* exiled, exiling to send into exile

exist *v* 1 to live or be real: *The Roman Empire existed for several centuries* 2 (of a person) to continue to live, esp. with difficulty: *so poor they can hardly exist*

existence *n* 1 existing: *the existence of God* 2 life; way of living

existent *adj* existing now: *the only existent copy*

existential *adj* related to existence: *'There is no God' is an existential statement*

existentialism *n* the belief that man is free to choose his actions and that these determine his nature — -list *adj, n*

exit¹ *v pl.* exeunt *Latin* (*used as a stage direction*) goes out; goes off stage USAGE In stage directions, **exit** comes before its subject, does not take 's' in the 3rd person singular, and has only one tense.

exit² *n* 1 a way out 2 an act of leaving, esp. of an actor: *Make your exit through the door at the back of the stage*

exodus *n* a going out or leaving by many people

Exodus *n* the 2nd book of the Bible, which tells how the Israelites left Egypt

exonerate *v* -rated, -rating to free from blame: *The officer was exonerated from the charge* — -ration *n*

exorbitant *adj* (of cost, demands, etc.) unreasonably great: *exorbitant prices* — -tance *n* — ~ly *adv*

exorcize, -cise *v* -cized, -cizing 1 to drive out (an evil spirit) from a person or place 2 to free (a person or place) from an evil spirit — -cism *n* — -cist *n*

exoskeleton *n* an outside supporting structure of an animal without a backbone (such as an insect)

exotic *adj* unusual; from or as if from a far country: *an exotic purple bird* — ~ally *adv*

expand *v* to make or grow larger —opposite contract — ~able *adj* — **expansion** *n*

expand on *v prep* to make (a story, argument, etc.) more detailed by addition

expanse *n* a wide space

expansive *adj* 1 able to expand or causing expansion 2 friendly and willing to talk ⚠ EXPENSIVE — ~ly *adv* — ~ness *n*

expatriate¹ *v* -ated, -ating 1 to cause to leave the native country by force or law — compare REPATRIATE 2 to remove (oneself) from one's own country

expatriate² *n* a person living abroad

expect v 1 to think (that something will happen or that one will receive something): *I expect he'll pass the examination* 2 to wait for 3 to believe and hope: *The officer expected his men to do their duty* 4 to suppose; think: *'Who broke that cup?' I expect it was the cat.'* 5 **be expecting** to be pregnant

expectancy n hope; the state of expecting

expectant adj 1 hopeful: *The expectant crowds waited for the queen* 2 **expectant mother** a pregnant woman — ~ly adv

expectation n 1 the condition of expecting 2 **against all expectation(s)** in spite of what was expected 3 **beyond expectation** more or better than was hoped 4 **in expectation of** expecting

expectorate v -rated, -rating to spit

expedient adj (of a course of action) useful or helpful for a purpose: *She thought it expedient not to tell her mother* —opposite **inexpedient** — **expedient, -ency** n — ~ly adv

expedite v -dited, -diting esp. written to make (a plan or arrangement) go faster: *The builders promised to expedite the repairs*

expedition n (the persons, vehicles, etc., going on) a journey

expeditionary adj of an expedition of war (esp. in the phrase **expeditionary force**)

expeditious adj esp. written (of people and their actions) quick — ~ly adv

expel v -ll- 1 to force out: *to expel air from one's lungs* 2 to dismiss officially (from a school, club, etc.)

expend v to spend or use up (esp. time, care, etc.)

expendable adj that may be used up for a purpose

expenditure n using up: *the expenditure of time, effort, and money*

expense n 1 cost 2 **at someone's expense a** with someone paying the cost **b** (esp. of a joke or trick) against someone: *He tried to be clever at my expense* 3 **spare no expense** to try hard without considering cost

expense account n the record of money spent in the course of one's work, which will be paid by one's employer

expensive adj costing a lot of money ⚠ EXPANSIVE — ~ly adv

experience¹ n 1 knowledge or skill which comes from practice rather than from books 2 something that happens to one and has an effect on the mind: *Our journey by camel was quite an experience*

experience² v -enced, -encing to undergo as an experience

experienced adj having the right kind of experience: *an experienced doctor*

experiment¹ n (a) trial made in order to learn or prove something — ~al adj — ~ally adv

experiment² v to make an experiment — ~ation n

expert adj, n (a person) with special knowledge or training — ~ly adv — ~ness n

expertise n skill in a particular field; know-how

expiate v -ated, -ating to pay for or make up for (a wicked action): *He tried to expiate his crimes by giving money to the church* — **-ation** n

expiration also **expiry**— n the end of a period of time

expire v expired, expiring 1 to come to an end: *My season ticket will expire this week* 2 literature to die

explain v 1 to give the meaning (of something): *Explain what this word means* 2 to be the reason for; account for — ~er n

explanation n 1 explaining 2 something that explains: *The only explanation for his behaviour is that he's mad*

explanatory adj that explains: *a few explanatory words* —see also SELF-EXPLANATORY ⚠ EXCLAMATORY

expletive n a word used for swearing; oath or curse

explicable adj esp. written (of behaviour or events) that can be explained —opposite **inexplicable** — **-bly** adv

explicate v -cated, -cating esp. written to explain in detail

explicit adj (of statements, rules, etc.) clear and fully expressed: *explicit directions* —opposite **inexplicit** —compare IMPLICIT — ~ly adv — ~ness n

explode v exploded, exploding 1 to blow up or burst 2 to show sudden violent feeling: *to explode with anger*

exploded adj technical (of a drawing, model, etc.) showing the parts of something separated but in correct relationship to each other

exploit¹ n a brave, bold, and successful deed

exploit² v 1 to use (a person) unfairly for one's own profit: *to exploit the poor* 2 to use or develop (a thing) fully so as to get profit: *to exploit the oil under the sea* — ~ation n — ~er n

exploratory adj done in order to learn something: *The doctors carried out an exploratory operation*

explore v explored, exploring 1 to travel into or through (a place) for the purpose of discovery 2 to examine carefully in order to learn more: *explored the possibilities* — **explorer** n — **-ration** n

explosion n 1 (a loud noise caused by) an act of exploding —compare IMPLOSION 2 a sudden bursting out: *explosions of laughter* 3 a sudden increase

explosive¹ adj 1 that can explode 2 that can cause people to explode: *The question of race today is an explosive one* — ~ly adv — ~ness n

explosive² n an explosive substance

Expo n Expos a world exposition

exponent n 1 a person who expresses a belief

or idea: *an exponent of the opinions of Freud* **2** technical also **index**— - a sign written above and to the right of a number or letter in mathematics to show how many times that quantity is to be multiplied by itself: *In 12³ the number 3 is the exponent*

exponential *adj* (in mathematics) containing an exponent: *yˣ is an exponential expression*

export¹ *v* to send (goods) out of a country for sale —compare IMPORT — ~**able** *adj* · — ~**ation** *n* — ~**er** *n*

export² *n* **1** exporting **2** something that is exported: *the chief exports of Australia* —compare IMPORT **3 invisible exports** money brought into a country in other ways than by the sale of goods

expose *v* exposed, exposing **1** to uncover: *to expose one's skin to the sun* **2** to leave (a baby) to die of cold and hunger out of doors **3** to make known (a secretly guilty person or action): *I threatened to expose him* **3** to uncover (a film) to the light, when taking a photograph

exposition *n* **1** explaining and making clear: *a full exposition of his beliefs* **2** an international exhibition of the products of industry

expostulate *v* -lated, -lating *esp. written* to complain loudly — -**lation** *n*

exposure *n* **1** being exposed to the weather: *He nearly died of exposure* **2** exposing, or the experience of being exposed: *I threatened him with public exposure* **3** the amount of film that must be exposed to take one photograph **4** the length of time that a film must be exposed: *These 2 pictures were taken with different exposures* ☞ OPTICS

expound *v* to give an exposition of: *The priest expounded his religion*

express¹ *adj* **1** (of a command, wish, etc.) clearly stated; explicit **2** (of an intention or purpose) special: *I came with the express purpose of seeing you* **3** going or sent quickly: *an express letter*

express² *n* **1** also **express train** — a fast train: *the 9.30 express to London* **2** a service given by the post office, railways, etc., for carrying things faster

express³ *v* **1** to show (a feeling, opinion, or fact) in words or in some other way: *She expressed her thanks* **2** to press (oil, juice, etc.) out: *juice expressed from oranges*

express⁴ *adv* by express: *sent the parcel express*

expression *n* **1** expressing: *They greeted him with many expressions of pleasure* **2** the showing of feeling: *She sings with much expression* **3** a word or phrase: *'To kick the bucket' is a slang expression meaning 'to die'* **4** a look on a person's face **5** (in mathematics) a collection of terms separated from each other by + and -: *x² + 4 is an expression*

expressionism *n* a movement in art to express the artist's feelings —compare IMPRESSIONISM — **expressionist** *n, adj*

expressionless *adj* (esp. of a voice or face) without expression — ~**ly** *adv*

expressive *adj* full of feeling and meaning — ~**ly** *adv* — ~**ness** *n*

expressly *adv* **1** clearly: *I told you expressly to do it* **2** on purpose

expropriate *v* -ated, -ating to take away, often for public use: *The State expropriated his palace* — -**ation** *n* — -**ator** *n*

expulsion *n* expelling or being expelled

expunge *v* expunged, expunging to rub out or remove from a list, book, etc.

expurgate *v* -gated, -gating to make (a book, play, etc.) pure by taking out anything improper — -**gation** *n*

exquisite *adj* **1** very finely made or done: *an exquisite white fur coat* **2** (of pain, pleasure, or sensation) very great — ~**ly** *adv* — ~**ness** *n*

ex-serviceman *fem.* **ex-servicewoman**— *n* a person formerly in the armed forces

extant *adj* (esp. of anything written, painted, etc.) still existing

extemporaneous *adj* extempore — ~**ly** *adv* — ~**ness** *n*

extempore *adj, adv* in haste, without preparation: *an extempore speech*

extemporize, -rise *v* -rized, -rizing to perform extempore — -**rization** *n*

extend *v* **1** (of space, land, or time) to reach, stretch, or continue **2** to make longer or greater: *to extend one's garden* **3** to stretch out (a part of one's body) **4** to give or offer (help, friendship, etc.): *to extend a warm welcome to him*

extended family *n* -lies a family that contains not only a father, mother, and children but also other relatives

extension *n* **1** extending or of being extended **2** a part which is added to make anything longer, wider, or greater **3** any of many telephone lines which connect the switchboard to various rooms or offices **4 University Extension** teaching and examining students who cannot attend a university all the time

extensive *adj* **1** covering a large surface **2** large in amount: *extensive damage* — ~**ly** *adv* — ~**ness** *n*

extent *n* **1** the length or area to which something extends: *the full extent of the Sahara desert* **2** (a) degree: *I agree with you to some extent*

extenuate *v* -ated, -ating to lessen the seriousness of, by finding excuses: *He stole the money, but there are extenuating circumstances* — -**tion** *n*

exterior *n* the outside: *the exterior of the house* — **exterior** *adj*

exterminate *n* to kill (all the creatures or people in a place, or all of a kind) — -**nation** *n*

external *adj* **1** on, of, or for the outside **2** foreign: *external affairs* — ~**ly** *adv*

external evidence *n* proof that comes from outside and not from what is being examined —compare INTERNAL EVIDENCE

exterritorial *adj* extraterritorial

extinct adj 1 no longer existing: *The mammoth is extinct* 2 (of fire) no longer burning: *an extinct volcano*

extinction n 1 extinguishing or making extinct 2 being or becoming extinct

extinguish v to put out (a light or fire)

extinguisher n an instrument for putting out small fires by spraying liquid chemicals on them

extirpate v -pated, -pating to destroy completely by or as if by pulling up the roots — -pation n

extol v -ll- to praise very highly

extort v to obtain by force or threats: *to extort a promise from him*

extortion n extorting: *a promise obtained by extortion* — ~er, ~ist n

extortionate adj (of a demand, price, etc.) too high — ~ly adv

extra¹ adj, adv beyond what is usual

extra² n 1 something added, for which an extra charge is made 2 a film actor who has a small part in a crowd scene: *We need 1000 extras for the big scene when they cross the Red Sea* 3 a special edition of a newspaper 4 a run in cricket not made off the bat

extract¹ v 1 to pull out: *to extract a tooth* 2 to take out with a machine, or by chemical means: *oil extracted from cottonseed* 3 to choose and usu. copy (examples from a book)

extract² n 1 a product obtained by extracting: *meat extract* —compare ESSENCE 2 a passage that has been extracted: *a few extracts from his letter*

extraction 1 extracting 2 the origin (of a person's family): *an American of Russian extraction*

extracurricular adj outside the regular course of work (CURRICULUM) in a school

extradite v -dited, -diting to send (someone accused of a crime who has escaped abroad) back for trial: *The English murderer was caught by the French police and extradited to Britain* — -dition n

extramural adj 1 outside a town or an organization 2 (of students, courses, etc.) connected with but outside a university: *the university extramural department* —compare INTRAMURAL

extraneous adj 1 coming from outside: *not part of the tree, but an extraneous growth* 2 not belonging: *extraneous events in a story* — ~ly adv

extraordinary adj 1 very strange 2 more than ordinary: *a girl of extraordinary beauty* 3 as well as the ordinary one(s): *There will be an extraordinary meeting next Wednesday* — -rily adv

extrapolate v -lated, -lating 1 (in mathematics) to estimate the value of a function at a given point from its known values at previous points 2 a to guess (the future) from facts already known b to use (facts already known) so as to guess the future

extrasensory perception also E S P— adj

knowledge obtained without the use of the ordinary 5 senses

extraterrestrial adj (coming from) outside the earth

extravagant adj excessive; uncontrolled; wasteful esp. of money — -ance n — ~ly adv

extravaganza n 1 a play or musical work in which usually foolish things are treated solemnly 2 a very grand and costly show

extravert n an extrovert

extreme¹ adj 1 at the very beginning or very end 2 the greatest possible: *extreme heat* 3 going beyond the usual limits: *extreme opinions*

extreme² n 1 an extreme degree: *Sometimes he eats too much and sometimes nothing. He goes from one extreme to the other* —compare EXTREMITY 2 go/be driven to extremes to act too violently

extremely adv very

extremism n (esp. in politics) being extreme — **extremist** n

extremities n the human hands and feet: *His extremities were frozen*

extremity n -ties 1 the highest degree of suffering or misfortune: *an extremity of pain* 2 the last extremity the greatest possible danger or misfortune —compare EXTREME

extricate v -cated, -cating to set free from something that it is difficult to escape from: *to extricate a driver from a wrecked car* — -cable adj — -cation n

extrinsic adj esp. written ˙ not forming a part; not really belonging —opposite intrinsic

extrovert, extravert n a sociable person who likes to spend time with other people rather than in thinking —opposite introvert — -version n

extrude v extruded, extruding 1 to push or force out by pressure: *to extrude toothpaste from the tube* 2 technical to shape (plastic or metal) in this way, by forcing through an instrument with a screw inside a tube (a DIE) — extrusion n

exuberant adj overflowing with life and high spirits — -ance n — ~ly adv

exude v exuded, exuding to flow out slowly

exult v to rejoice; to show delight: *The people exulted at the victory* △ EXALT — ~ant adj — ~antly adv — ~ation n

eye¹ n 1 the organ of sight, of which there are 2 at the front of the human head 2 the front part of this organ, with the coloured parts which can be seen: *Her children have blue eyes* 3 the power of seeing: *To the painter's eye, this would be a beautiful scene* 4 the hole in a needle through which the thread passes 5 the dark spot on a potato, from which a new plant can grow 6 the calm centre of a storm, esp. of a hurricane 7 a small link of metal into which a hook fits for fastening: *Her dress fastens with hooks and eyes* 8 catch someone's eye a (of things) to be noticed b to draw someone's attention to oneself 9 get/keep one's eye in (esp. in cricket and other ball games) to get/keep, through practice, the ability to judge the speed and direction of a ball **10 have an eye for** to have the ability to see, judge, and understand clearly **11 in the eye/eyes of the law** according to the law; as the law sees it **12 more than meets the eye** more than actually appears or is seen **13 one in the eye for** *esp. spoken* a disappointment or defeat for **14 see eye to eye** to agree completely —see also EYES — **~less** *adj*

eye² *v* **eyed, eyeing** *or* **eying** to look at closely or with desire: *She eyed me jealously*

eyeball *n* the whole of the eye, including the part hidden inside the head, which forms a more or less round ball

eyebrow *n* **1** the line of hairs above each of the 2 human eyes **2 raise one's eyebrows** to express surprise, doubt, displeasure, or disapproval

eyebrow pencil *n* a stick of coloured material in a holder, used for darkening the eyebrows

eyecup also **eyebath**— *n* a small cup for holding liquid used for bathing the eyes

eyelash *n* any of the small hairs of which a number grow from the edge of each eyelid in humans and most hairy animals

eyelet *n* a metal-edged hole in material such as leather or cloth for a rope or cord to be passed through

eyelid *n* either of the pieces of covering skin which can move down to close each eye

eyeliner *n* (a) paint used around the eyes to give a usu. dark outline

eye-opener *n* something surprising, which makes a person see a truth he did not formerly believe

eyepiece *n* the lens at the eye end of an instrument such as a microscope or telescope ⮕ TELESCOPE, MICROSCOPE

eyes *n* **1** *pl. of* EYE **2 all eyes** watching closely and attentively **3 close/shut one's eyes** to refuse or decide not to notice **4 keep one's eyes open/skinned/peeled** *esp. spoken* to keep a sharp look-out **5 make (sheep's) eyes at (someone)** to look at (someone) with sexual love **6 make someone open his eyes** to surprise someone **7 open someone's eyes to** to make someone know or understand **8 throw dust in someone's eyes** to deceive someone on purpose **9 with one's eyes open** *esp. spoken* knowing what may possibly happen

eye shadow *n* coloured paint used on the eyelids to give the eyes more importance

eyesight *n* the power of seeing

eyesore *n* something ugly to look at (esp. when many people can see it)

eyestrain *n* a painful and tired condition of the eyes, as caused by reading very small print

eyetooth *n* -teeth either of the 2 long pointed canine teeth at the 2 upper corners of the mouth

eyewash *n* **1** liquid for bathing the eyes **2** *esp. spoken* something said or done to deceive: *He pretends to be busy, but it's all eyewash*

eyewitness *n* a person who himself sees an event happen, and so is able to describe it, for example in a law court

eyrie, eyry, aery, eyry *n* -ries the nest of a bird of prey (esp. an eagle) built high in rocks or cliffs

F

F, f **F's, f's** *or* **Fs, fs** the 6th letter of the English alphabet

F¹ the 4th note in the musical scale of C major or the musical key based on this note

F² *abbrev. for:* fahrenheit

fa *n* the 4th note in the sol-fa musical scale

Fabian *n, adj* (of) a member of a socialist political group, the **Fabian society**

fable *n* **1** a short story that teaches a moral or truth, esp. a story in which animals or objects speak **2** a story about great people who never actually lived; legend; myth **3** a false story or account

fabric *n* **1** cloth made by threads woven together in any of various ways **2** framework, base, or system: *the fabric of society* **3** the walls, roof, etc., of a building

fabricate *v* **-cated, -cating 1** to make or invent in order to deceive: *to fabricated a story* **2** to make, esp. by putting parts together — **-tion** *n*

fabulous also *(esp. spoken)* **fab**— *adj* **1** (nearly) unbelievable: *a fabulous amount* **2** *esp. spoken* very good or pleasant; excellent **3** existing or told about in fables: *fabulous creatures*

fabulously *adv* very (rich, great, etc.)

facade *n* **1** the front of a building —compare ELEVATION **2** an appearance, esp. one that is false: *a facade of honesty*

face¹ *n* **1** the front part of the head from the chin to the hair **2** a look or expression **3** a position of respect (esp. in the phrases **lose** *or* **save one's face**) —see also FACE-SAVER **4** part of the surface of a solid, contained between edges **5** the front, upper, outer, or most important surface of something **6** the surface of a rock, either on or below the ground, from which coal, gold, diamonds, etc., are dug: *The miners work at the face for 7 hours each day* ⮕ GEOGRAPHY **7** the style or size of a letter as used by a printer **8 fly in the face of** to act in opposition to, on purpose **9 have the face** to be bold or rude enough to **10 in the face of** against (something which opposes) **11 on the face of it** judging by what one can see; apparently **12 put a good/bold face on something** to behave or make it appear as if things are better than they are **13 set one's face against** to oppose strongly

face² *v* **faced, facing 1** to have or turn the face or front towards or in a certain direction **2** to meet or oppose firmly and not try to avoid: *He* *faced up to his difficulties* **3** to need consideration or action by: *The difficulty that faces us is the number of those in need* **4** to cover or partly cover (esp. the front part of) with a different material

facecloth also **face flannel**— *n* a small cloth used to wash the face, hands, etc.

faceless *adj* without any clear character: *crowds of faceless people*

face-lift *n* a medical operation to make the face look younger by tightening the skin

face out *v adv* to oppose or deal with bravely

face-pack *n* a cream spread over the face to clean and improve the skin, and removed after a short time

face powder *n* a sweet-smelling powder spread on the face to make one look nice

face-saver *n* something that saves someone's self-respect — **face-saving** *adj*

facet *n* **1** any of the many flat sides of a cut jewel or precious stone **2** any of the many parts of a subject to be considered

facetious *adj* using or tending to use unsuitable jokes — ~ly *adv* — ~ness *n*

face value *n* the value, cost, or importance of something, as it appears on the surface

facial[1] *adj* of or concerning the face — ~ly *adv*

facial[2] *n* a beauty treatment in which the skin of the face is treated with various substances and may also be massaged

facile *adj* **1** easily done or obtained: *facile success* **2** too easy; not deep; meaningless: *facile remarks* — ~ly *adv* — ~ness *n*

facilitate *v* **-tated, -tating** to make easy or easier; help: *The broken lock facilitated my entry* — **-tation** *n*

facilities *n* means to do things; that which can be used: *One of the facilities is a large library*

facility *n* **-ties** **1** (an) ability to do or perform something easily: *His facility in languages is surprising* **2** easiness **3** an advantage; convenience

facing *n* **1** an outer covering or surface, as of a wall, for protection, ornament, etc. **2** (a piece of) additional material put into parts near the edges of a garment when it is being made, to improve it in strength and thickness

facings *n* (of a garment, esp. a uniform) the collar and cuffs made in a different colour from the rest

facsimile *n* an exact copy, as of a picture or piece of writing

fact *n* **1** something that has actual existence or an event that has actually happened or is happening; something true; information regarded as true: *The detective asked for for facts, not opinions* **2** law deed; crime: *an accessory after the fact* **3 as a matter of fact, in fact** really the truth is that

faction *n* **1** a group or party within a larger group, esp. one that makes itself noticed **2** argument, disagreement, fighting, etc., within a group or party

fact of life *n* **facts of life** something that exists and that must be considered —see also FACTS OF LIFE

factor *n* **1** any of the forces, conditions, influences, etc., that act with others to bring about a result: *His manner is a factor in his success* **2 a** (in arithmetic) a whole number which, when multiplied by one or more whole numbers, produces a given number: *2, 3, 4, and 6 are all factors of 12* **b** (in algebra) an expression which will divide into a given expression

factorize, -ise also **factor**— *v* **-ized, -izing** to divide into factors

factory *n* **-ries** a building or group of buildings where goods are made, esp. in great quantities by machines

factory farm *n* an animal farm in which the animals are kept in small cages inside large buildings and made to grow or produce eggs, milk, etc., very quickly — **factory farming** *n*

factotum *n* a servant who has to perform all kinds of work

facts of life *n* *polite* the details of sex and how babies are born

factual *adj* of, concerning, or based on facts: *a factual account* — ~ly *adv*

faculty *n* **-ties** **1** the power or ability to do something particular: *He has the faculty to learn languages easily* —see GENIUS (USAGE) **2** a natural power or ability, esp. of the mind **3 a** a branch of learning, esp. in a university: *law/science faculty* **b** all the teachers, and sometimes all the students of such a branch

fad *n* a short-lived but keenly followed interest or practice — ~**dish** *adj* — ~**dishly** *adv*

fade *v* **faded, fading** **1** to lose or cause to lose strength, colour, freshness, etc.: *Cut flowers soon fade* **2** to disappear or die gradually: *The shapes faded (away) into the night* **3** (in film or sound mixing, as in cinema or broadcasting) to change the strength of (sound or vision) slowly

faeces *n* *esp. written & technical* the solid waste material passed from the bowels — **faecal** *adj*

faery, faerie *n* **-ries** *literature* the world or power of fairies; the imaginary world of stories

fag[1] *v* **-gg-** **1** to work hard **2** (of a student in certain English public schools) to have to do jobs for another student

fag[2] *n* **1** an unpleasant and tiring piece of work **2** a young student who fags for an older student

fag[3] *n* *sl* a cigarette

fag end *n* **1** the last, end, or remaining part of something: *the fag end of the day* **2** the last bit of a smoked cigarette

fagged also **fagged out**— *sl* very tired

faggot *n* **1** a bunch of small sticks for burning **2** a ball of cut-up meat mixed with bread, which is cooked and eaten

Fahrenheit[1] *adj* of, in, or related to the fahrenheit scale of temperature

Fahrenheit[2] *n* a scale of temperature in which water freezes at 32° and boils at 212° —compare CENTIGRADE

faience n a special type of clay, made into cups, dishes, etc., ornamented with bright colours, and baked hard

fail v 1 to be (judged in a test to be) unsuccessful (in) 2 to decide that (somebody) has not passed an examination 3 to not produce the desired result; not perform or do: *Last year the crops failed* 4 to be of little or no use when needed: *His friends failed him when he needed money* 5 to lose strength; become weak 6 (of a business) to be unable to continue

failing¹ n a fault, imperfection, or weakness

failing² prep in the absence of; without

fail-safe adj made so that a failure in any part causes the whole machine, plan, etc., to come to a stop

failure n 1 lack of success; failing 2 a person, attempt, or thing that fails 3 (an example of) the state of being unable to perform: *(a) heart failure* 4 inability of a business to continue

faint¹ adj 1 weak and about to lose consciousness: *He felt faint* 2 performed in a weak manner; lacking strength, courage, or spirit: *faint praise* 4 lacking clearness, brightness, strength, etc.: *faint sound* — ~ly adv — ~ness n

faint² v to lose consciousness, as because of loss of blood, heat, or great pain

faint³ n an act or condition of fainting

fair¹ adj 1 free from dishonesty or injustice: *a fair businessman* 2 that is allowed to be done, given, etc., as under the rules of a game: *It is not fair to kick another player in football* 3 fairly good, large, fine, etc. 4 not stormy; fine; clear 5 having a good clear clean appearance or quality: *a fair copy of a report* 6 (esp. of a person's skin or hair) light in colour; not dark 7 (of women) *esp. old use* beautiful; attractive — ~ness n

fair² adv in a just or honest manner or according to the rules; fairly: *to play fair*

fair³ n 1 a funfair 2 a market, esp. one held at a particular place at regular periods 3 a very large show of goods, advertising, etc.: *a book fair*

fair game n someone or something that it is easy but not unfair to attack

fairground n an open space on which a funfair is held

fairly adv 1 in a manner that is free from dishonesty, injustice, etc.: *He told the facts fairly* 2 in a manner that is allowed or according to certain rules 3 for the most part; rather; quite: *He paints fairly well* 4 completely; plainly

fair play n 1 (in sport) play that is according to the rules 2 action, treatment, punishment, etc., that is fair and just, esp. in being equal to all concerned

fair sex n GENTLE SEX

fairway n -ways that part of a golf course in which the grass is cut short but not so short as around the holes

fair-weather adj present in times of success, absent in times of trouble (esp. in the phrase **fair-weather friend**)

fairy n -ries a small imaginary figure with magical powers and shaped like a human

fairy light n a small coloured light, esp. one of a number used to ornament a Christmas tree

fairy tale also **fairy story**— n 1 a story about fairies and other magical people 2 a story or account that is hard to believe, esp. one intended to deceive — **fairy-tale** adj

fait accompli n **faits accomplis** something that has already been done and that cannot be changed

faith n 1 strong belief; trust, which may go beyond reason or proof: *He has faith in my ability* 2 word of honour; promise: *I kept/broke faith with them* 3 the condition of being sincere; loyalty: *to act in good faith* 4 belief and trust in and loyalty to God 5 something that is believed in strongly, esp. a system of religious belief; religion

faithful adj 1 full of or showing loyalty: *a faithful friend* 2 believing strongly in religion 3 sure to do what has been promised or what is expected: *faithful worker* 4 true to the facts or to an original: *faithful account* 5 loyal to one's (marriage) partner by having no sexual relationship with anyone else —compare UNFAITHFUL — see also FIDELITY — ~ness n

faithfully adv 1 with faith 2 exactly: *I copied the letter faithfully* 3 **yours faithfully** the usual polite way of introducing one's name at the end of a letter

faith healing n a method of treating diseases by prayer and religious faith — **faith healer** n

faithless adj 1 not acting according to promises or duty; disloyal; false 2 without belief or trust, esp. in God — ~ly adv — ~ness n

fake¹ v **faked, faking** 1 to make or change (esp. a work of art) so that it appears better, more valuable, etc. 2 to pretend: *She faked illness* — **faker** n

fake² n a person or thing that is not what he or it looks like: *The painting looked old but was a recent fake*

fake³ adj made and intended to deceive

fakir n a Hindu or Muslim beggar who is regarded as a holy man

falcon n a bird of prey, esp. one that has been trained by man to hunt ☞ BIRD

falconer n a person who keeps, trains, or hunts with falcons — **falconry** n

fall¹ v **fell, fallen, falling** 1 to descend or go down freely, as by weight or loss of balance; drop: *The clock fell off the shelf* 2 to come down from a standing position, esp. suddenly: *He fell to his knees* 3 to become lower in level, degree, or quantity: *Their voices fell* 4 to come or happen, as if by descending: *Night fell quickly* 5 to pass into a new state or condition; become: *fall asleep* 6 to hang loosely: *His hair falls over his shoulders* 7 to drop down wounded or dead, esp. to die in battle 8 to be defeated or conquered: *The city fell (to the enemy)* 9 to lose power or a high position 10 to slope in a downward direction: *The land falls* towards the river **11** (of the face) to take on a look of sadness, disappointment, shame, etc., esp. suddenly **12 fall over backwards/oneself to do something** to be very eager or too eager to do something —see also FALL FOR, FALL IN, FALL IN WITH, FALL ON, FALL OUT, FALL THROUGH, FALL TO

fall² *n* **1** the act of falling: *He suffered a fall* **2** (the quantity of) something that has fallen: *a fall of rocks* **3** a decrease in quantity, price, demand, degree, etc. **4** the distance through which anything falls **5** the defeat of a city, state, etc.; surrender or capture —see also FALLS

fallacious *adj* **1** likely or intended to deceive **2** containing or based on false reasoning — ~ly *adv*

fallacy *n* **-cies** **1** a false idea or belief **2** false reasoning, as in an argument

fallen *past part. of* FALL

fall for *v prep* **1** to accept and be cheated by: *Don't fall for his tricks* **2** *esp. spoken* to fall in love with, esp. suddenly

fallible *adj* able or likely to make a mistake or be wrong — **-bility** *n*

fall in *v adv* to form or cause to form proper lines or order: *Fall in, men!*

fall in with *v adv prep* **1** to meet by chance **2** to agree to (an idea, suggestion, etc.)

fall on also **fall upon**— *v prep* to attack eagerly

fallopian tube *n* one of the 2 tubes in a (human) female through which eggs pass to the womb —see also OVIDUCT ⫷ REPRODUCTION EMBRYO

fallout *n* the radioactive dust that is left floating in and descending through the air after an atomic (or nuclear) explosion

fall out *v adv* **1** to leave proper lines or order: *Fall out, men!* **2** to quarrel

fallow *n, adj* (land) dug or ploughed but left unplanted to improve its quality

fallow deer *n* **-deer** a small deer of Europe and Asia with a light brownish-yellow coat

falls also **fall**— *n* a place where the river makes a sudden drop, as over a cliff; waterfall: *Niagara Falls*

fall through *v adv* to fail to be completed: *The plan fell through*

fall to *v adv* to begin to eat or attack

false *adj* **1** not true or correct **2** declaring what is untrue; deceitful **3** not faithful or loyal **4** not real: *false teeth* **5** made or changed so as to deceive — ~ly *adv* — ~ness *n* — **falsity** *n*

false alarm *n* a warning of something bad, which does not happen

falsehood *n* **1** an untrue statement **2** the telling of lies

false pretences *n* acts or appearances intended to deceive: *He obtained money from her under false pretences*

false start *n* **1** an occasion in a race when a runner leaves the starting line too soon **2** a start in some activity which fails and has to be given up

false teeth *n* dentures

falsetto *n* **-tos** **1** (the use of) an unnaturally high voice by a man, esp. in singing **2** a man with such a singing voice

falsify *v* **-fied, -fying** to make false as by changing or telling lies about something — **-fication** *n*

falter *v* **1** to walk or move unsteadily, as through weakness and fear **2** to speak or say in a weak and broken manner **3** to lose strength; hesitate; slow down: *His business is faltering* — ~ingly *adv*

fame *n* the condition of being well known and talked about — ~d *adj*

familial *adj* of, concerning, or typical of a family —see also HEREDITARY

familiar¹ *n* a close friend

familiar² *adj* **1** generally known, seen, or experienced; common: *a familiar sight* **2** having a thorough knowledge (of): *I am familiar with that book* **3** informal; easy: *He wrote in a familiar style* **4** too friendly for the occasion

familiarity *n* **-ties** **1** thorough knowledge (of) **2** freedom of behaviour usu. only expected in the most friendly relations; informality

familiarize, -ise *v* **-ized, -izing** to make well known

family¹ *n* **-lies** **1** any group of people related by blood or marriage, esp. a group of 2 grown-ups and their children - ⊙ **2** children: *Have you any family?* **3** all those people descended from a common ancestor **4** a group of things related by common characteristics, esp. a group of plants, animals, or languages **5 in the family way** *esp. spoken* pregnant

family² *adj* suitable for children as well as older people: *a family film*

family allowance *n* a sum of money paid weekly to every family for each child

family circle *n* the closely related members of a family

family doctor *n esp. spoken* GENERAL PRACTITIONER

family planning *n* the controlling of the number of children born in a family and the time of their birth

family tree *n* a map or plan of the relationship of the members of a family, esp. over a long period

famine *n* (a case of) very serious lack of food: *Many people die of famine every year*

famish *v* to suffer or cause to suffer from very great hunger — ~ed *adj*

famous *adj* very well known USAGE **Famous** is stronger than **well-known**. **Notorious** means 'famous for something bad'. **Infamous** is a strong word meaning 'wicked', but not necessarily 'widely known'.

famously *adv* very well

fan¹ *n* any of various instruments meant to make a flow of air, esp. cool air ⫷CAR

fan² *v* **-nn-** **1** to cause air, esp. cool air, to blow on (something) with or as if with a fan **2** to excite

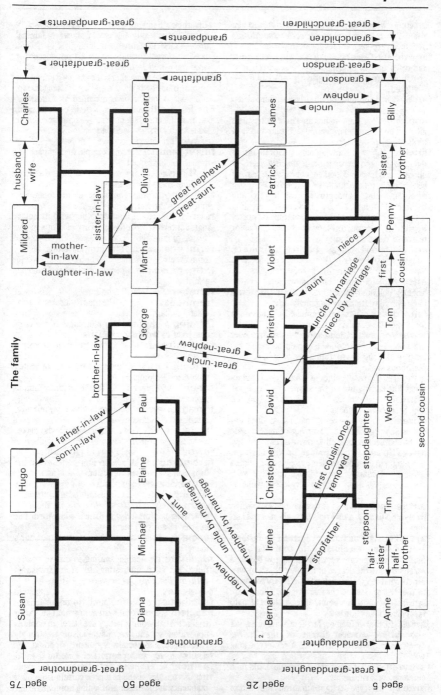

The family

aged 75   aged 50   aged 25   aged 5

to activity with or as if with a fan **3** to spread like a fan: *The soldiers fanned out across the hillside*

fan³ *n* a very keen follower or supporter

fanatic also **fanatical**— *adj* showing very great and often unreasoning keenness, esp. in religious or political matters — **fanatic** *n* — ~**ism** *n* — ~**ally** *adv*

fan belt *n* a continuous belt driving a fan to keep an engine cool

fancier *n* a person who has an active or business interest in breeding or training certain types of birds, dogs, plants, etc.

fanciful *adj* **1** showing imagination rather than reason and experience: *a fanciful poet* **2** unreal; imaginary **3** odd in appearance, esp. in being highly ornamented — ~**ly** *adv*

fancy¹ *n* **-cies** **1** imagination, esp. in a free and undirected form **2** the power of creating imaginative ideas and expressions, esp. in poetry **3** an image, opinion, or liking not based on fact or reason: *I've taken a fancy to that silly hat*

fancy² *v* **-cied, -cying** **1** to form a picture of; imagine **2** to believe without being certain **3** to have a liking for; wish for: *I fancy that girl*

fancy³ *adj* **-cier, -ciest** more ornamental, brightly coloured, expensive, or finer than ordinary everyday (things) — **fancily** *adv*

fancy dress *n* unusual or amusing clothes worn for a special occasion: *a fancy dress ball*

fanfare *n* a short loud piece of usu. trumpet music played to introduce a person or event

fang *n* a long sharp tooth, as of a dog or a poisonous snake

fanlight *n* a small window over a door, sometimes but usually not in the shape of a fan

fanny *n* **-nies** *esp. US sl* the part of the body on which one sits; buttocks

fantasia *n* **1** a piece of music that does not follow any regular style **2** a piece of music made up of a collection of well-known tunes

fantastic *adj* **1** odd, strange, or wild in shape, meaning, etc.; not controlled by reason or related to reality: *fantastic dream/story/fears* **2** very great or large **3** *esp. spoken* very good; wonderful — ~**ally** *adv*

fantasy *n* **-sies** **1** imagination, esp. when freely creative **2** a creation of such an imagination

far¹ *adv* **farther** *or* **further** , **farthest** *or* **furthest** **1** at or to a great distance: *to travel far from home* **2** a long way; very much: *far too busy* **3** **as/so far as** to the degree or distance that **4** **how far** to what degree or distance **5** **in as/so far as** to the degree that **6** **So far, so good** Things are satisfactory up to this point, at least —see also GO far, FAR-OUT, FARSIGHTED

far² *adj* **farther** *or* **further, farthest** *or* **furthest** **1** also **farther**— more distant of the 2: *the far/farther side of the street* **2 a far cry** a long way

faraway *adj* **1** distant **2** (of the look in a person's eyes) dreaming

farce *n* **1** a (type of) light humorous play full of

silly things happening **2** an occasion or set of events that is a silly and empty show — **farcical** *adj* — **farcically** *adv*

fare¹ *v* **fared, faring** *rare* to get on; succeed: *I fared quite well in the exam*

fare² *n* **1** the price charged to carry a person, as by bus, train, or taxi **2** a paying passenger, esp. in a taxi **3** food, esp. as provided at a meal

Far East *n* the countries in Asia east of India, such as China, Japan, etc. —compare MIDDLE EAST, NEAR EAST — ~**ern** *adj*

farewell *n, interj* goodbye

farfetched *adj* (of an example or comparison) improbable or forced

far-flung *adj* at or spread over a great distance: *far-flung trade connections*

farinaceous *adj* consisting of or containing much flour or starch

farm¹ *n* an area of land, together with its buildings, concerned with the growing of crops or the raising of animals

farm² *v* to use (land) for growing crops, raising animals, etc.

farmer *n* a man who owns or plans the work on a farm

farmhand *n* a farm labourer

farmhouse *n* the main house on a farm, where the farmer lives

farming *n* the practice or business of being in charge of or working on a farm

farm out *v adv* to send (work) for other people to do

farmyard *n* a yard surrounded by or connected with farm buildings

far-out *adj* *sl* very different or uncommon; strange: *far-out ideas*

farrago *n* **-goes** a confused collection; mixture: *a farrago of useless information*

farrier *n* a person (usu. a blacksmith) who makes and fits shoes for horses

farrow *v* (of a female pig) to give birth

farsighted *adj* also **farseeing**— able to see the future effects of present actions — ~**ness** *n*

farther *adv, adj* (comparative of FAR) at or to a greater distance or more distant point; further

farthest *adv, adj* (superlative of FAR) most far

farthing *n* (formerly) a British coin worth one quarter of an (old) penny

fascia *n* a board over a shop bearing the shop's name

fascinate *v* **-nated, -nating** to charm powerfully; be very interesting to: *I'm fascinated with/by Buddhist ceremonies* — **-ting** *adj* — **-tingly** *adv*

fascination *n* charm; power to fascinate

Fascism *n* a political system in which all industrial activity is controlled by the state, no political opposition is allowed, nationalism is strongly encouraged, and socialism violently opposed

fascist *n, adj* (a supporter) of Fascism

fashion¹ *n* **1** the way of dressing or behaving that is considered the best at a certain time **2** a manner; way of making or doing something: *He* behaves *in a very strange fashion* **3 after a fashion** not very well

fashion² *v* to shape or make (something into or out of something else) usu. with one's hands or with only a few tools

fashionable *adj* (made, dressed, etc.) according to the latest fashion —compare OLD-FASHIONED — **-ably** *adv*

fashion designer *n* someone whose job is to design new styles in clothes

fast¹ *adj* **1** quick; moving quickly **2** firm; firmly fixed: *The colours aren't fast and may wash out* **3** (of a photographic film) suitable for being exposed for a very short time **4** (of a clock) showing a time that is later than the true time **5** allowing quick movement: the fast lane of the motorway —see also HARD-AND-FAST **6 make fast** to tie firmly: *Make the boat fast*

fast² *adv* **1** quickly **2** firmly; tightly: *to stick fast*

fast³ *v* to eat no food, esp. for religious reasons

fast⁴ *n* an act or period of fasting: *He broke his fast by drinking some milk*

fasten *v* to make or become firmly fixed or closed: *He fastened (up) his coat*

fastener *n* something that fastens things together —see also ZIP

fastening *n* something that holds things shut, esp. doors and windows

fastidious *adj* difficult to please, and disliking anything at all dirty, nasty, or rough — ~**ly** *adv* — ~**ness** *n*

fastness *n* the quality of being firm and fixed: *the fastness of a colour*

fat¹ *adj* **-tt-** **1** (of creatures and their bodies) having (too) much fat **2** (of meat) containing a lot of fat —compare LEAN **3** thick and well-filled **4** (esp. of land) producing plentiful crops **5 a fat lot of** *sl* no; not any: *A fat lot of good/of use that is!* — ~**ness** *n*

fat² *n* **1** the material under the skins of animals and human beings which helps to keep them warm **2 a** this substance considered as food **b** vegetable oil in a solid form used in the same way

fatal *adj* **1** causing or resulting in death **2** very dangerous and unfortunate —compare FATEFUL

fatalism *n* the belief that events are decided by fate and are outside human control — **-ist** *n* — **-istic** *adj*

fatality *n* **-ties** *esp. written* **1** a violent accidental death **2** the quality of being fatal

fatally *adv* **1** so as to cause death **2** as was very unfortunate

fate *n* **1** the imaginary cause beyond human control that is believed to decide events **2** an end or result, esp. death: *They met with a terrible fate*

fated *adj* caused or fixed by fate: *We were fated to meet*

fateful *adj* (of a day, event, or decision) important (esp. in a bad way) for the future —compare FATAL — ~**ly** *adv*

Fates *n* the 3 goddesses who, according to the ancient Greeks, decided the course of human life

fathead *n* *esp. spoken* a fool; stupid person

father *n* a male parent ☞ FAMILY — ~**less** *adj*

Father 1 (a title of respect for) a priest, esp. in the Roman Catholic Church **2** God; the 1st member of the Christian Trinity (=3 Gods in 1)

Father Christmas also (*esp. US*) **Santa Claus**— *n* an imaginary old man in red clothes with a long white beard who is said to bring children their presents at Christmas

father figure *n* an older man on whom one depends for advice and help

fatherhood *n* the state of being a father

father-in-law *n* **fathers-in-law** the father of a person's wife or husband ☞ FAMILY

fatherly *adj* like or typical of a father — **-liness** *n*

fathom¹ *n* a measure (6 feet or 18 metres) of the depth of water

fathom² *v* to get at the true meaning of; come to understand: *I can't fathom your meaning* —compare UNFATHOMABLE

fathomless *adj* too deep to be measured or understood

fatigue¹ *n* **1** great tiredness: *pale with fatigue* **2** *technical* the tendency of a metal to break as the result of repeated bending (often in the phrase **metal fatigue**)

fatigue² *v* **fatigued, fatiguing** *esp. written* to make tired

fatten *v* to make (a creature) fat: *You need fattening up a bit*

fatty¹ *adj* **-tier, -tiest** (of food) containing a lot of fat — **-tiness** *n*

fatty² *n* **-ties** *esp. spoken offensive* a fat person

fatuous *adj* very silly: *a fatuous remark* — **-tuity** *n* — ~**ly** *adv* — ~**ness** *n*

fault¹ *n* **1** a mistake or imperfection **2** a bad point, but not of a serious moral kind, in someone's character: *Your only fault is carelessness* **3** *technical* (in geology) a crack in the earth's surface, where one band of rock has slid against another **4** (in games like tennis) a mistake in a service, which may lose a point **5 at fault** in the wrong

fault² *v* **1** to find a fault in **2** (of rocks) to break and form a fault

faulty *adj* **-ier, -iest** (esp. of machines, apparatus, etc.) having faults — **faultily** *adv*

faun *n* a type of ancient Roman god of the fields and woods. They were like a man with a goat's horns and legs

fauna *n* (a list of) all the animals living wild in a particular place, or belonging to a particular age in history: *the fauna of the forest* —compare FLORA

faux pas *n* **faux pas** *French* a social mistake, in words or behaviour

favour¹ *n* **1** encouragement and approval; willingness to be kind **2** unfairly generous treatment; (too much) sympathy for one person as compared to others: *She always favours her son* **3** a kind act that is not forced or necessary: *Will you do me a favour and phone for me?* **4** a badge or coloured ribbon worn to show that one belongs to a political party, supports a football team, etc. **5 in favour of a** believing in or choosing; on the side of **b** (of a cheque) payable to —see also CURRY **favour**, RETURN **a favour, without** FEAR **or favour**

favour² *v* **1** to regard or treat with favour **2** (of conditions) to make pleasant and easy **3** (of a child) to look like (a parent): *He favours his father with his brown eyes*

favourable *adj* **1** (of a message, answer, etc.) saying what one wants to hear **2** (of conditions) advantageous; favouring — **-rably** *adv*

favoured *adj* having special advantages; favourite: *a favoured corner*

favourite¹ *n* **1** something or someone that is loved above all others **2** someone who receives too much favour: *A teacher shouldn't have favourites* **3** (in horseracing) the horse in each race that is expected to win

favourite² *adj* being a favourite: *his favourite son*

favouritism *n offensive* the practice of showing favour

fawn *n* **1** a young deer less than a year old **2** a light yellowish-brown colour

fawn on *v adv* **1** (of dogs) to jump on, rub against (someone) etc., as an expression of love **2** to try to gain the favour of by over-praising and being insincerely attentive: *fawning on their rich uncle*

FBI *n abbrev for*: (in the US) Federal Bureau of Investigation; the department of the police that is controlled by the central government, and is particularly concerned with national security

fealty *n* **-ties** *old use* loyalty: *He swore fealty to the king*

fear¹ *n* **1** the feeling that one has when danger is near: *to be without fear* **2** danger **3** *old use* great respect (in the phrase **the fear of God**) **4 No fear!** *esp. spoken* (in answer to a suggestion that one should do something) Certainly not! **5 without fear or favour** with justice

fear² *v esp. written* **1** to be afraid of **2** to be afraid (for the safety of someone or something) **3 I fear** (*used when telling bad news*) I'm sorry that I must now say

fearful *adj* **1** (making someone) afraid: *a fearful storm* **2** very great; frightful: *a fearful waste of time!* — ~**ly** *adv* — ~**ness** *n*

fearless *adj* without fear — ~**ly** *adv* — ~**ness** *n*

fearsome *adj humour* causing fear; horrible: *a fearsome sight*

feasible *adj* able to be carried out or done; possible —compare PLAUSIBLE — **-sibility** *n* — **-sibly** *adv*

feast¹ *n* **1** a splendid esp. public meal; a specially good or grand meal: *The king gave/held*

a feast **2** a day kept in memory of some happy religious event

feast² *v* to provide for someone, or have, a specially good or grand meal: *We feasted on chicken and coconuts*

feat *n* a clever esp. bodily action, showing strength, skill, or courage: *His leap was quite a feat*

feather¹ *n* **1** one of the many parts of the covering which grows on a bird's body **2 feather in one's cap** a deserved honour that one is proud of

feather² *v* **1** to put feathers on: *to feather arrows* **2** to cover with feathers (esp. in the phrase TAR **and feather**) **3** to make the blade of an oar lie flat on the surface of the water **4 feather one's nest** to make oneself rich, esp. dishonestly, through a job in which one is trusted

featherbed¹ *n* a mattress filled with feathers

featherbed² *v* **-dd-** to give (a group of people) generous help and special advantages

feather boa *n* a stole made of feathers, worn by women about the neck, esp. in former times

featherbrained *adj* very silly and thoughtless

featherweight *n* a boxer weighing between 118 and 126 pounds (535 to 57 kilos)

feathery *adj* **1** covered with feathers **2** soft and light

feature¹ *n* **1** a (typical or noticeable) part or quality **2** any of the noticeable parts of the face **3** a special long article in a newspaper: *a front-page feature on coalmining* **4** a full-length cinema film with an invented story portrayed by actors — compare DOCUMENTARY

feature² *v* **-tured, -turing** **1** to include as a special feature: *a new film featuring Dustin Hoffman* **2** to be present as a feature: *Fish features largely in their diet*

featureless *adj* uninteresting, because of having no noticeable features

features *n* the face, considered as a group of parts

febrile *adj medical* of or caused by fever

February *n* **-ries** the 2nd month of the year

feckless *adj* without purpose or plans for the future ⚠ RECKLESS — ~**ly** *adv* — ~**ness** *n*

fecund *adj* very fertile; very productive — ~**ity** *n*

federal *adj* **1** of or formed into a political federation: *Switzerland is a federal republic* **2** (in the US) of or relating to the central government of the federation as compared with those of the States that form it

Federal Bureau of Investigation *n* FBI

federalism *n* **1** the belief in political federation **2** the federal system of government — **-ist** *n*

federation *n* a group of states, clubs, trade unions, etc., that have come together to act as one organization on important matters while still managing their own internal affairs

fed up *adj esp. spoken* unhappy, tired, and discontented, esp. about something dull one has had too much of

fee *n* a sum of money paid for professional services to a doctor, lawyer, private school, etc.

feeble *adj* -bler, -blest weak; with little force — **feebly** *adv* — ~ness *n*

feed¹ *v* **fed, feeding** 1 to give food to 2 (of animals or babies) to eat: *The horses fed quietly* 3 to put, supply, or provide, esp. continually: *to feed the wire into the hole*

feed² *n* 1 a meal taken by an animal or baby 2 food for animals: *hen feed* 3 the part of a machine through which the machine is supplied: *a blockage in the petrol feed*

feedback *u* information passed back to a person, machine, or organization about the results of a set of actions

feeder *n* 1 (*humour*, except of animals or plants) one that eats (in the stated way) 2 a branch road, airline, railway line, etc., that joins into a main one

feeding bottle *n* a bottle with a rubber teat from which a baby can suck liquids

feed up *v adv* to make (a creature) fat and healthy by giving it lots of good food: *He needs feeding up*

feel¹ *v* **felt, feeling** 1 to get knowledge of by touching with the fingers: *Feel the quality of the cloth* 2 to experience (the touch or movement of something) 3 to experience (a condition of the mind or body); be consciously: *Do you feel hungry yet?* 4 to believe, esp. for the moment (something that cannot be proved): *She felt that he no longer loved her* 5 to (be able to) experience or suffer from sensations 6 **feel free to do something** to be welcome to do something —see also **feel** CHEAP, **feel** UP TO

feel² *n* 1 the sensation caused by feeling something: *This cloth has a warm woolly feel* 2 an act of feeling 3 **get the feel of** to become used to and skilled at

feeler *n* 1 an insect's antenna 2 **put out feelers** to make a suggestion as a test of what others will think or do

feel for *v prep* to be sorry for; be unhappy about the suffering of

feeling¹ *n* 1 a consciousness of (something felt in the mind or body): *a feeling of shame/thirst* 2 a belief or opinion, not based on reason 3 the power to feel sensation: *He lost all feeling in his toes* 4 excitement of mind; emotion; understanding: *He played the piano with feeling*

feeling² *adj* showing strong feelings: *a feeling look* — ~ly *adv*

feel out *v adv* SOUND OUT

feign *v* to pretend to have or be; put on a false air of: *a feigned illness*

feint¹ *n* an action performed to draw the enemy's attention away from the real danger

feint² *v* to make a feint

feldspar also **felspar**— *n* any of several types of pink or white silicate found in many kinds of rock

felicitate *v* -tated, -tating *esp. written* to congratulate — -tations *n*

felicitous *adj esp. written* (of words or remarks) suitable and well-chosen — ~ly *adv*

felicity *n* -ties *esp. written* happiness: *a lifetime of perfect felicity*

feline *adj, n* (of or like) a cat or related animal

fell¹ *v* 1 to cut down (a tree) 2 *esp. written* to knock down (a person)

fell² *adj literature* evil, dangerous, and terrible: *a fell disease* —see also **at one fell** SWOOP

fell³ *n N English* high wild rocky country where no crops can grow

fell⁴ *past tense of* FALL

fellow *n* 1 *esp. spoken* a man 2 a member of a society connected with some branch of learning 3 a high-ranking member of an Oxford or Cambridge college 4 someone with whom one shares a (stated) activity or spends time in a (stated) place: *We were schoolfellows*

fellow feeling *n* (a) feeling in common; sympathy for someone like oneself

fellowship *n* 1 a group or society 2 the position of **a** a fellow of a college **b** a paid research worker at a university 3 the condition of being friends through sharing or doing something together; companionship

fellow traveller *n* 1 someone with whom one is travelling 2 someone who is sympathetic to the aims of the communist party though not a member

felon *n* a criminal guilty of felony

felony *n* -nies *law* any of a group of serious crimes, such as murder or armed robbery — compare MISDEMEANOUR — -nious *adj*

felspar *n* feldspar

felt¹ *n* thick firm cloth made of wool, hair, or fur, pressed flat: *a felt hat*

felt² *past tense and past part. of* FEEL

female¹ *n* a female person or animal

female² *adj* 1 of the sex that gives birth to young 2 (of plants or flowers) producing fruit 3 *technical* having a hole made to receive a p art that fits into it: *a female plug*

feminine¹ *adj* 1 of or having the qualities suitable for a woman 2 (in grammar) in a class of words that are not masculine or neuter: *'She' is a feminine pronoun* — -nity *n*

feminine² *n* the class of feminine words

feminism *n* the principle that women should have the same rights and chances as men — -ist *n*

femme fatale *n* **femmes fatales** *French* a woman who attracts men into danger by her mysterious charm

femur *n* **femurs** or **femora** *medical* the long bone in the upper part of the leg — **femoral** *adj*

fen *n* an area of low wet land, esp. in the east of England

fence¹ *n* 1 a wall made of wood or wire, dividing 2 areas of land   2 someone who buys and sells stolen goods   3 **sit on the fence** *usu. offensive* to avoid taking sides in an argument, in order to see where one's own advantage lies

fence² *v* **fenced, fencing**   1 to fight with a sword as a sport   2 to avoid giving an honest answer to a question —compare HEDGE   3 to put a fence round

fencer *n* someone who fences as a sport

fencing *n*   1 the sport of fencing   2 **a** material for making fences **b** all the fences in an area

fend *v* **fend for oneself** to look after oneself

fender *n*   1 a low metal wall round an open fireplace, to stop the coal from falling out   2 any object that hangs over the side of a boat to protect it from damage by other boats or when coming to land

fend off *v adv* to push away; act to avoid

fennel *n* a plant with yellow flowers whose leaves and seeds are used for flavouring food

feral *adj esp. written* (of an animal) wild, esp. after living with people and escaping

ferment¹ *v*   1 to work up to a state of fermentation   2 to work up to a state of political trouble and excitement △ FOMENT

ferment² *n* (the condition of) political trouble and excitement: *The whole country was in a state of ferment*

fermentation *n* the period or event of increasing in size and becoming filled with gas by chemical change, caused by the action of certain living substances such as yeast

fern *n* a type of green flowerless plant with feathery shaped leaves ⊂⟆ EVOLUTION PLANT — **ferny** *adj*

ferocious *adj* fierce, cruel, and violent — ~**ly** *adv* — ~**ness** *n*

ferocity *n* the quality or state of being ferocious

ferret¹ *n* a small fierce European animal of the weasel family, which catches rats and rabbits by going into their holes

ferret² *v*   1 to hunt rats and rabbits with ferrets   2 to search: *to ferret out the truth*

ferrite *n* any of several substances that consist mainly of iron and are used in computer memories

ferrous *adj technical* related to or containing iron

ferrule *n* a metal band or cap that is put on the end of a thin stick or tube to stop it from splitting

ferry¹ *v* **-ried, -rying** to carry on or as if on a ferryboat

ferry² also **ferryboat**— *n* **-ries** a boat that goes across a river or any other narrow stretch of water, carrying people and things

fertile *adj*   1 producing many young, fruits, or seeds: *Some fish are very fertile: they lay 1000's of eggs* —see also FRUITFUL   2 (of land) which produces or can produce good crops   3 (of living things) able to produce young   4 inventive; full of suggestions, ideas, etc.: *a fertile imagination*

fertility *n*   1 the condition or state of being fertile   2 the rate of reproducing children in a given group at a given time

fertilize, -ise *v* **-lized, -lizing**   1 to start the development of young in (a female creature or plant): *Bees fertilize flowers*   2 to put fertilizer on (land) — **-lization** *n*

fertilizer *n* (any type of) chemical or natural substance that is put on the land to make crops grow better —compare MANURE

ferule *n* a flat ruler used for hitting schoolchildren on the hand as a punishment

fervent *adj* that is, feels, or shows strong and warm feelings: *a fervent desire to win* — **-vency** *n* — ~**ly** *adv*

fervid *adj* that shows strong and serious feeling — ~**ly** *adv*

fervour *n* the quality of being fervent or fervid

fester *v* (of a cut or wound) to become infected and diseased

festival *n*   1 also **festivity**— public gaiety and feasting   2 a time regularly marked out for this; a (religious) feast: *Christmas is one of the Christian festivals*   3 a time of the stated entertainment or at the stated place: *a pop festival*

festive *adj* of or suitable for a festival

festivity *n* **-ties** a festival

festoon *v, n* (to hang) a chain of flowers, leaves, ribbons, etc., between 2 points as an ornament

fetch *v*   1 to go and get and bring back: *Fetch the doctor!*   2 *esp. spoken* to be sold for   3 to attract; bring: *a story that fetched the tears to one's eyes*

fetch up *v adv esp. spoken* to arrive; end up, esp. without planning

fete¹ *n French* a day of festival held usu. out of doors and often to collect money for a special purpose

fete² *v* **feted, feting** to show honour to with public parties and ceremonies

fetid *adj* smelling bad: *the fetid breath of a lion*

fetish *n*   1 an object that is worshipped as a god and thought to have magic power   2 (in psychology) **a** a practice, material, or object whose presence is necessary for sexual satisfaction **b** a strong unhealthy desire or need   3 **make a fetish of** to take too seriously; admire to a foolish degree

fetishism *n*   1 the religion of fetish worshipping   2 the practice of having a fetish — **-ist** *n*

fetlock *n* the back part of a horse's leg near the foot, that has longer hairs on it than the upper part ⊂⟆ HORSE

fetter¹ *n* a chain for the foot of a prisoner

fetter² *v* to bind with or as if with fetters: *fettered by responsibility* —compare UNFETTERED

fettle *n* condition; state of body and mind (in the phrase **in fine/good fettle**)

feud¹ *v* to keep up a feud

feud² *n* a state of strong dislike and/or violence

which continues over some time as a result of a quarrel, usu. between 2 people, families, or clans

feudal *adj law* of or relating to the system by which people held land, and received protection, in return for giving work or military help as practised in Western Europe from about the 9th to the 15th century —see also FIEF — ~ism *n*

fever *n* 1 a medical condition caused by many illnesses, in which the sufferer suddenly develops a very high temperature 2 any of a group of (stated) diseases that cause this: *yellow fever* 3 an excited state: *in a fever of impatience*

fevered *adj* 1 (as if) suffering from fever: *fevered cheeks* 2 too excited (often in the phrase **a fevered imagination**)

feverish *adj* 1 having or showing a slight fever 2 caused by fever

feverishly *adv* very fast and in a state of high excitement: *working feverishly to finish the job*

few *adj, pron, n* 1 (of plurals; used without a, to show the smallness of the number) not many; not enough: *who has fewest mistakes?* 2 (of plurals; used with a) a small number, but at least some: *Can you stay a few days longer?* 3 **few and far between** rare; not happening often 4 **quite a few** also **a good few** a fair number (of) —see LESS (USAGE)

fey *adj offensive* silly in a sensitive artistic way; not practical

fez *n* **fezzes** or **fezes** a kind of round red hat with a flat top and no brim, worn by some Muslim men

ff. *abbrev. for:* and the following (pages, verses, etc.)

fiancé (*fem* **fiancée**)— *n French* a man to whom a woman is engaged —compare BETROTHED

fiasco *n* **-cos** the complete failure of something planned

fiat *n Latin, esp. written* an order by a ruler

fib *v, n* **-bb-** *esp. spoken* (to tell) a small unimportant lie — ~**ber** *n*

fibre *n* 1 one of the thin thread-like parts that form many animal and plant growths such as wool, wood, or muscle. Some plant fibres are spun and woven into cloth 2 a mass of these, used for making cloth, rope, etc. 3 a (type of) thread made chemically for weaving: *man-made fibre* 4 roughage in food 5 (of mind or morals) **a** quality **b** strength

fibreglass *n* material made from glass fibres. It is used esp. for building light boats and for keeping out the cold, and its most modern use is for furnishing materials

fibrous *adj* like or made of fibres

fibula *n medical* the outer of the 2 bones in the lower leg

fickle *adj* not loyal in love or friendship; often changing — ~**ness** *n*

fiction *n* 1 stories or novels about things that did not really happen, or imagined accounts of real events, as compared to other sorts of literature like history or poetry —compare NONFICTION 2 an invention of the mind; an untrue story

fictional *adj* belonging to fiction; told as a story —compare FICTITIOUS — ~**ly** *adv*

fictionalization, -isation *n* the turning of an account of true events into a story

fictitious *adj* untrue; invented; not real — compare FICTIONAL — ~**ly** *adv*

fiddle[1] *n* 1 *esp. spoken* a violin, or any musical instrument of that family 2 *sl* a dishonest practice 3 (**as**) **fit as a fiddle** perfectly healthy

fiddle[2] *v* **-dled, -dling** *esp. spoken* 1 to play the fiddle 2 to play about (with something): *Stop fiddling with that pen!* 3 to prepare (accounts) dishonestly to one's own advantage — ~**r** *n*

fiddle-faddle *n esp. spoken* silly unimportant nonsense

fiddlesticks *interj* Nonsense!; How silly!

fiddling *adj* unimportant and silly; too small: *a fiddling little key*

fidelity *n* 1 faithfulness; loyalty —see also FAITHFUL —compare INFIDELIT Y 2 (of something copied or reported) truthfulness; closeness in sound, facts, colour, etc. to the original —see also HI-FI

fidget[1] *n esp. spoken* someone, esp. a child, who fidgets

fidget[2] *v* 1 to move one's body around restlessly, so as to annoy people: *children fidgeting in church* 2 to make nervous and restless

fidgety *adj esp. spoken* restless

fie *interj old use or humour* (expressing disapproval or shock) Shame!: *Fie upon you!*

fief *n* a piece of land held under the feudal system

field[1] *n* 1 a stretch of land on a farm marked off in some way or surrounded by a fence or wall, and used for animals or crops 2 any open area where **a** the stated game is played **b** the stated substance is mined: *an oilfield* **c** the stated activity is practised: *an airfield* **d** the surface is of the stated kind: *a field of snow* 3 a branch of knowledge or activity: *the field of art* 4 the place where practical operations happen, as compared to places where they are planned or studied, such as offices, factories, and universities —see also FIELD-TEST, FIELDWORK 5 (in physics) the area in which the (stated) force is felt: *a gravitational field* ☞ ELECTRICITY 6 (in horseracing) all the horses in the race except the favourite

field[2] *v* 1 (in cricket and baseball) to catch or stop (a ball that has been hit) 2 to be (a member of) the team whose turn it is to do this because they are not batting 3 to put into operation; produce (an army, team, etc.)

field day *n* **-days** 1 a day of army training 2 a time of unusually pleasant and exciting action: *The newspapers will have a field day with this story!*

fielder also **fieldsman**— *n* (in cricket or baseball) any of the players whose business it is to field the ball

field event *n* a competitive sports event, such as jumping, that is not a race

field glasses *n* large binoculars, esp. for use out of doors

field gun *n* a light gun with wheels

field hockey also **hockey**— *n esp. US* a game played by 2 teams of 11 players each, on a field, with sticks and a ball —compare ICE HOCKEY

Field Marshal *n* the officer of highest rank in the British army

field of vision *n* **fields of vision** the whole space within seeing distance; all that can be seen

field-test *v* to try out in normal use, conditions, etc. — **field test** *n*

fieldwork *n* study done in the field

fiend *n* **1** a devil or evil spirit **2** a very wicked person **3** someone very keen on (the stated object of desire, or way of spending time)

fiendish *adj* **1** fierce and cruel: *a fiendish temper* **2 a** (of behaviour) very clever; not plain or simple **b** (of difficulty or cleverness) very great — ~ness *n*

fierce *adj* **1** angry, violent, and cruel **2** (of heat, strong feelings, etc.) very great — ~ly *adv* — ~ness *n*

fiery *adj* **-ier, -iest** **1** flaming and violent; looking like fire: *fiery red hair* **2** quickly moved to anger or violent action

fiesta *n Spanish* (esp. in the Roman Catholic countries of Southern Europe and South America) a religious holiday with public pleasure-making

fife *n* a small musical pipe of the flute family, with high notes. It is played in bands with drums

fifteen *adj, n, pron* **1** the number 15 **2** a complete team of 15 players in rugby union football — ~th *adj, n, pron, adv*

fifth *adj, n, pron, adv* 5th

fifth column *n* a group of people who are secretly sympathetic to the enemies of the country they live in, and work to help them during a war — ~ist *n*

fifty *adj, n, pron* **-ties** the number 50 — **-tieth** *adj, n, pron, adv*

fifty-fifty *adj, adv* (of shares or chances) equal(ly)

fig¹ *n* **1** a soft sweet fruit with many small seeds, growing chiefly in warm countries. It is often eaten dried **2** the broad-leaved tree that bears this fruit

fig. *abbrev. for:* figure

fight¹ *v* **fought, fighting** **1** to use violence against (another or others) as in a battle **2** to use argument against (someone, or each other): *He and his wife are always fighting* **3** to take part in (a war, battle, etc.) **4** to try to prevent; stand against: *to fight a fire*

fight² *n* **1** a battle; an occasion of fighting **2** also **fighting spirit** — the power or desire to fight: *There's no fight left in him*

fighter *n* **1** someone who fights, in battle or for sport; a soldier or boxer **2** also **fighter plane**— an aircraft, usu. heavily armed, used in offensive and defensive operations to destroy enemy aircraft in the air —compare BOMBER

fighting chance *n* a small but real chance if great effort is made

figment *n* something believed but not real (in the phrase **a figment of one's imagination**)

figurative *adj* (of words) used in some way other than the ordinary meaning, to make a word picture or comparison: *'A sweet temper' is a figurative expression* —compare LITERAL — ~ly *adv*

figure¹ *n* **1** (the shape of) a whole human body, as shown in art or seen in reality **2** the human shape, considered from the point of view of being attractive: *exercises to improve one's figure* **3** an important person (of the stated kind): *a political figure* **4** any of the number signs from 0 to 9: *Write the number in words and in figures* **5** (used before the number of a map, drawing, etc. in a book) **6** a line drawing such as a square, circle, or diagram, used in study or for explaining something

figure² *v* **-ured, -uring** **1** to take part: *Roger figured as chief guest* **2** *US esp. spoken* to consider; believe: *I figured you'd want tea* **3** *That figures!* That seems reasonable and what I expected

figured *adj* ornamented with a small pattern: *figured silk*

figurehead *n* **1** an ornament formerly placed at the front of a ship, often in the shape of a person **2** someone who is the head or chief in name only

figure of eight *n* **figures of eight** anything of the shape of an 8, such as a knot or stitch, or a pattern made by a moving skater on the ice

figure of speech *n* **figures of speech** an example of the figurative use of words

figure on *v adv esp. US* to plan on; include in one's plans

figure out *v adv esp. US* to work out; understand by thinking

figures *n* **1** an amount with the stated number of digits (esp. in the phrases **3/4/5/6 figures**) **2** sums: *I'm no good at figures*

figurine *n* a small ornamental human figure made of baked clay, cut stone, etc.

filament *n* a thin thread, such as that inside an electric light bulb

filch *v* to steal secretly (something of small value)

file¹ *v, n* **filed, filing** (to rub or cut with) a steel tool with a rough face, used for rubbing down, smoothing, or cutting through hard surfaces: *a nail file*

file² *v* **1** to put (papers or letters) in a file **2** *law* to send in or record officially: *to file an application*

file³ *n* **1** any of various arrangements of drawers, shelves, boxes, or cases, for storing papers in an office —see FILING CABINET **2** a collection of papers on one subject, stored in this way **3** a collection of related data treated as a unit in a computer

file⁴ v, n (to move in) a line of people one behind the other (often in the phrase **in single file**)

filial adj of or suitable to a son or daughter

filibuster¹ n US (a case of) filibustering

filibuster² v US to try to delay or prevent action in a parliament or other lawmaking body, by being very slow and making long speeches

filigree n delicate ornamental wire work

filing cabinet n a piece of office furniture with drawers, for storing papers in

filing clerk n someone whose work is to file papers

filings n very small sharp bits that have been rubbed off a metal surface with a file

fill¹ v 1 to make or become full 2 to enter or cause to enter (a position) 3 to put a filling into (a tooth) 4 to fulfil; meet the needs or demands of: *to fill a prescription* —see also FILL IN, FILL OUT, FILL UP

fill² n a full supply; the quantity needed to fill something; as much as one can or wants to take

fillet¹ n a piece of fish or meat for eating, with the bones removed

fillet² v to make meat or fish into fillets

fill-in n esp. spoken someone or something that fills in

fill in v adv 1 a to put in (whatever is needed to complete something): *Fill in your name on this cheque* b to complete (something) by putting in whatever is needed: *to fill in one's income tax form* 2 esp. spoken to supply the most recent information to: *Please fill me in on what happened* 3 to take someone's place: *Can you fill in for Steve tonight;*

filling n 1 (in dentistry) a an act of putting material into a hole to preserve a tooth b (the material in) a hole in a tooth that is filled in this way 2 a food mixture folded inside pastry, sandwiches, etc.

filling station also **service station**, (US) **gas station**— n a garage that sells petrol and oil and repairs motor vehicles

fillip n 1 (a light blow given by) bending one's finger against one's thumb and letting it go suddenly 2 an encouragement; something that increases attraction and interest

fill out v adv to get fatter

fill up v adv to make or become completely full

filly n -lies a young female horse —compare COLT

film¹ n 1 a thin skin of any material: *plastic film* 2 (a roll of) the prepared substance on which one takes photographs or makes cinema pictures ⏞ OPTICS 3 a story or subject which is photographed and projected onto a screen to give the effect of movement

film² v to make a cinema picture (of)

film over v adv to become dull, as if covered with a film

filmstrip n (a length of) photographic film by

means of which photographs, drawings, etc., can be shown separately one after the other as still pictures

filmy adj -ier, -iest (esp. of cloth) so fine and thin that one can see through it — **filminess** n

filter¹ n 1 an apparatus containing paper, sand, etc., through which liquids can be passed so as to make them clean 2 a (coloured) glass that reduces the quantity or changes the quality of the light admitted into a camera or telescope

filter² v 1 to send through a filter 2 a (of a group) to move slowly b (of an idea) to become gradually known 3 (of traffic in Britain) to turn left, when traffic going right or straight ahead must wait until a red light changes to green

filter out v adv to remove (solids or light) by means of a filter

filter tip n 1 a filter on the end of a cigarette 2 a cigarette with a filter — **filter-tipped** adj

filth n 1 very nasty dirt 2 words, curses, etc., that are very rude or vulgar — ~y adj — ~ily adv — ~iness n

filthy lucre n pompous money

fin n 1 any of the winglike parts that a fish uses in swimming 2 a part shaped like this, on a man-made object such as a car, aircraft, or bomb

final¹ adj 1 last; coming at the end 2 that cannot be changed: *I won't go, and that's final!*

final² n 1 the last and most important in a set of matches 2 the last edition of a daily newspaper 3 the last and most important examination in a college course

finalist n one of the people left in the final, after the others have been defeated

finality n the quality of being or seeming final: *'No!' he said with finality*

finalize, -ise v -ized, -izing to finish (plans, arrangements, etc.); make final

finally adv 1 at last 2 so as not to allow further change: *It's not finally settled yet*

finance¹ n (the science of) the control of (esp. public) money — **-cial** adj — **-cially** adv

finance² v financed, financing to provide money for

finances n the amount of money owned by esp. a government or business

financial year n the yearly period over which accounts are calculated: *to pay one's taxes at the end of the financial year*

financier n someone who controls or lends large sums of money

finch n any of many kinds of small singing birds with strong beaks, such as the chaffinch, that eat seeds

find¹ v found, finding 1 to discover, esp. by searching; get (someone or something that was hidden or lost) 2 to learn or discover (a fact that was not known) 3 to discover (someone or something) to be, by chance or experience: *When we arrived, we found him in bed* 4 (of things) to reach; arrive at: *The bullet found its mark* 5 to know that (something) exists or happens 6 law to decide (someone) to be: *'How do you find him?'* *'We find him not guilty, my lord'* **7** to provide: *The cook gets $30 a week and all found* (=food, shelter, etc. all provided) —see also **find** WANTING

find² *n* something good or valuable that is found

finder *n* someone who finds something

fin de siècle *adj French* of, relating to, or typical of, the end of the 19th century

finding *n* **1** *law* a decision made by a judge or jury **2** something learnt as the result of an official enquiry

find out *v adv* **1** to learn or discover (a fact that was hidden) **2** to discover (someone) in a dishonest act: *I've found you out at last, you cheat!*

fine¹ *n* an amount of money paid as a punishment

fine² *v* **fined, fining** to take money from as a punishment — **finable, fineable** *adj*

fine³ *adj* **1** beautiful and of high quality; better than most of its kind **2 a** very thin: *fine hair* **b** in very small grains or bits: *fine sugar* —opposite **coarse** —see THIN (USAGE) **3** (of weather) bright and sunny; not wet **4** (of a person or conditions) healthy and comfortable: *This flat's fine for 2 people* **5** delicate; to be understood only with an effort: *fine points of an argument* **6** (of work) delicate and careful; on a small scale: *fine sewing* **7** (of words) too grand and perhaps not true: *That's all very fine, but what about me?* **8** terrible: *Your shoes are in a fine muddy state* —**ness** *n*

fine⁴ *adv* **1** so as to be very thin or in very small bits **2** very well: *It suits me fine* **3 cut/run it fine** *esp. spoken* to allow only just enough time and no more

fine arts *n* those arts such as painting, music, and sculpture, that are chiefly concerned with producing beautiful rather than useful things ⇨ PAINTING

fine print *n* **1** very small printing **2** something that is on purpose made difficult to understand, such as part of an agreement or contract

finery *n* gay, beautiful clothes and ornaments, perhaps too grand for the occasion

fines herbes *French* a mixture of herbs added to flavour food during cooking

finesse *n* *French* delicate skill in guiding relations between people

fine-tooth comb also **toothcomb**— *n* a comb with the teeth very close together, used esp. for getting insects out of one's hair

finger¹ *n* **1** one of the 5 movable parts with joints at the end of each human hand **2** one of 8 such parts (as opposed to the thumbs) **3** the part of a glove that is made to fit one of these parts **4 keep one's fingers crossed** to hope for the best **5 pull one's finger out** *sl* to start working hard

finger² *v* to feel or handle with one's fingers

fingerboard *n* the part of a stringed instrument against which the fingers press the strings so as to vary the note

finger bowl *n* a small basin in which one person can wash his sticky fingers while sitting at a meal

fingering *n* the method of using particular fingers when playing a musical instrument

fingernail *n* one of the hard flat pieces at the ends of the fingers

fingerplate *n* a metal or glass plate that is fastened to a door near the handle or keyhole, to keep off dirty fingermarks —compare PLATE

fingerprint *n* the mark of a finger, as used in the discovery of crime ⇨ SKIN

fingerstall also **stall**— *n* a cover for a hurt finger

fingertip *n* **1** the end of a finger **2 have something at one's fingertips** to have a ready knowledge of something

finicky also **finical, finickity**— *adj* too delicate and fussy about details; disliking many things, esp. kinds of food: *He's finicky about his food*

finis *n* *Latin* (written at the end of a book or cinema film) The End

finish¹ *v* **1** to reach or bring to an end; reach the end of (an activity): *What time does the concert finish?* | *We finished up in Paris* **2** to put the last touches or polish to (something that one has made): *to finish off a dress*

finish² *n* **1** the end or last part, esp. of a race **2** the appearance or condition of having been properly finished, with paint, polish, etc.: *the beautiful finish of old French furniture*

finished *adj* **1** ended **2** properly made and complete: *the finished product* **3** at the end of one's powers, without hope: *He's finished as an actor*

finishing school *n* a private school where rich young girls learn how to behave in social life

finish with *v prep* **1** to have no more use for **2** to have no further relationship with (someone): *I've finished with Mary*

finite *adj* **1** having an end or limit: *a finite number of possibilities* —opposite **infinite** **2** (in grammar) referring to the forms of a verb which indicate tense and subject: *'Am', 'was', and 'are' are finite forms of the verb 'to be', and 'being' and 'been' are* **non-finite** — ~**ly** *adv*

finnan haddock also **finnan haddie**— *n* a haddock preserved and made yellow by treating with smoke

Finnish *adj* of or related to the language, people, or country of Finland

fiord *n* a fjord

fir *n* also **firtree**— a straight coniferous tree with needleshaped leaves that bears seeds in cones

fire¹ *n* **1** the condition of burning; flames and great heat **2** a heap of burning material, lit on purpose for cooking, heat, etc.: *to sit round the fire* **3** a piece of gas, or electrical, apparatus for warming a room, with the flames or red-hot wires able to be seen **4** shooting by guns; firing: *Hold your fire* (=don't shoot) **5** strong feeling and excitement: *The boy is full of fire* **6 catch fire** to begin to burn **7 fire and sword** burning and killing in war   **8 hang fire** (of events) to develop too slowly   **9 open/cease fire** to start/stop shooting   **10 play with fire** to take great risks   **11 set on fire** also **fire, set fire to**— to light (something not really meant to burn)   **12 under fire** being shot at: *to show courage under fire*   **13 would go through fire and water** would face great hardship and danger

fire² *v*   **fired, firing**   **1** (of a person or a gun) to shoot off bullets: *She fired her gun at them*   **2** to send off with speed and force: *A rocket was fired at the moon.* | *He fired questions at the boys*   **3** to set on fire   **4** to bake (clay pots, dishes, etc.) in a kiln   **5** *esp. spoken* to dismiss from a job; sack: *Get out! You're fired!*   **6** to excite: *He was fired with the desire to visit China*

fire alarm *n* a signal, such as a bell, to warn people of fire

firearm *n* a gun

fireball *n* a ball of fire, such as a cloud of burning dust and gases, a meteor, a ball-shaped flash of lightning, etc.

firebrand *n*   **1** a flaming piece of wood   **2** a person who regularly causes anger and excitement among others

firebreak *n* a narrow piece of land cleared of trees, to prevent forest fires from spreading

firebrick *n* a fireproof brick used in fireplaces, chimneys, etc.

fire brigade *n* an organization for preventing and putting out fires

firebug *n* a person who purposely starts fires to destroy property; arsonist

fireclay *n* the kind of clay used in making firebricks

firecracker *n* a small firework that explodes loudly several times and jumps each time it explodes

firedamp *n* a mixture of gases that forms in mines and can explode when mixed with air

firedog *n* an andiron

fire drill *n* the set of things to be done to leave a burning building safely, which should be practised regularly

fire engine *n* a special vehicle that carries firemen and fire-fighting apparatus to a fire

fire escape *n* a set of metal stairs leading down outside a building to the ground, by which people can escape in case of fire

fire extinguisher *n* a smallish metal container with water or chemicals inside for putting out a fire

firefly *n*   **-flies** a type of insect with a tail that shines in the dark —compare GLOW-WORM

fireguard *n* a protective metal framework put round a fireplace

fire hydrant *n* a hydrant used as a water supply for fighting fires

fire irons *n* the metal tools, such as a poker, tongs, and shovel, used for looking after a coal fire

firelight *n* the soft light thrown from a fire in the fireplace

firelighter *n* a piece of a substance which flames easily and helps to light a coal fire

fireman *n*   **-men**   **1** a person whose job is putting out fires   **2** a person who looks after the fire in a steam engine or furnace

fireplace *n* the opening for a fire in the wall of a room, with a chimney above it

fireproof *v, adj* (to make) unable to be damaged by heat

fire-raising *n* the crime of starting fires on purpose; arson

fire risk *n* a possible cause of fire

fireside *n* the area around the fireplace, often thought of as representing the pleasures of home life

fire station *n* a building for firemen and their fire-fighting apparatus

firestorm *n* a storm caused when a large fire draws in wind and rain to take the place of the hot rising air

firetrap *n* a building which is dangerous because it may easily catch fire and be difficult to get out of

firewalking *n* the act of walking over hot stones, ashes, etc., esp. as an act of faith in some religions — **-walker** *n*

firewatcher *n* a person who watches for fires, esp. those caused by enemy bombing in war — **-watching** *n*

firewater *n* *esp. spoken* strong alcoholic drink, such as whisky

firework *n* a small container filled with an explosive chemical powder that burns to produce a show of light and noise, or explodes with a loud noise

firing line *n*   **1** the position nearest to the enemy   **2 be in the firing line** to be the object of attack, blame, etc.

firing squad *n* a group of soldiers with the duty of putting an offender to death by shooting

firkin *n* a small cask holding about 9 gallons

firm¹ *adj*   **1** strong; solid; hard   **2** (in business, esp. of money) not tending to become lower in value: *The pound stayed firm against the dollar*   **3** steady: *Is that chair firm enough?*   **4** staying strong; not changing or yielding: *a firm belief/believer* | *a firm hold* — **~ly** *adv* — **~ness** *n*

firm² *v* to make or become firm: *The jelly firmed quickly*

firm³ *n* a business company

firm⁴ *adv* firmly

firmament *n* *literature* the sky; heavens

first¹ *adj, n, pron*   **1** the person, thing, or group to do or be something before any others: *Ann was the first to arrive*   **2** a British university examination result of the highest quality: *He got a first*   **3 at first** at the beginning   **4 the first** the slightest

first² *adv*   **1** before anything else   **2** for the first time: *when we first met*

first aid *n* treatment to be given by an ordinary

person to a person hurt in an accident or suddenly taken ill

firstborn *n, adj* **firstborn** (the) eldest among the children in a family: *the firstborn child*

first-class *adj* of the highest or best quality: *first-class work*

first class *n* **1** a class of mail in which letters and parcels are delivered as quickly as possible **2** the best and costliest type of seating, esp. on a train: *to travel first class* **3** a university degree of the highest quality

first cousin *n* the child of one's uncle or aunt ☞ FAMILY

first-degree *adj* of the lowest level of seriousness: *first-degree burns*

first floor *n* the 1st floor of a building above ground level —compare GROUND FLOOR

firstfruits *n* **1** the first of the   harvest, esp. as offered to God at a service **2** the earliest results

firsthand *adj, adv* (learnt) directly from the point of origin: *firsthand information*

firstly *adv* first (in a list of reasons, arguments, etc.); in the first place   USAGE Some people do not like this word, and would rather use *first* in sentences like this: *There are 3 reasons against it: First . . .*

first name *n* **1** the name that stands first in one's full name: *Smith's first name is Peter* **2** any of the names before one's surname: *Smith's first names are Peter George*

first night *n* the evening on which the first public performance of a show, play, etc., is given

first offender *n* a person found guilty of breaking the law for the first time

first person *n technical* **1** a form of verb or pronoun used to show the speaker: *'I', 'me', 'we', and 'us' are first person pronouns* **2** a way of telling a story in which, esp. by frequent use of the first person, the teller shows that he took part in the story

first-rate *adj* of the best or highest quality: *first-rate materials*

first thing *adv* at the first moment, esp. in the morning: *I'll phone you first thing*

firtree *n* a fir

fiscal *adj esp. written* of or related to public money, taxes, debts, etc. — ~ly *adv*

fish¹ *n* **fish** *or* **fishes** **1** a creature whose blood changes temperature according to the temperature around it, which lives in water and uses its fins and tail to swim ☞ EVOLUTION **2** part of one of these, when used as food **3** any fairly large creature that lives in water, such as a whale **4 drink like a fish** to drink too much alcohol **5 like a fish out of water** uncomfortable because one is in a strange place, among strangers, etc.

fish² *v* **1** to try to catch fish; to search (for something under water) as with a hook: *to fish for trout | Why are you fishing around in your pockets?* **2** to catch fish in (a piece of water): *This river has been fished too much* **3** *a esp. spoken* to

try to attract admiring words **b** to enquire indirectly: *fishing for information*

fishcake *n* a small round flat cake made of cooked fish and potato

fisherman *n* **-men** a man who catches fish, for sport or for his living —compare ANGLER

fishery *n* **-ries** a part of the sea where the industry of catching sea fish is practised

fish finger *n* a small finger-shaped piece of fish, covered with breadcrumbs

fishing *n* the sport or job of catching fish

fishing tackle *n* the things needed in order to catch fish for sport, such as **fishhooks**, **fishing-line**, and a **fishing-rod**

fishmonger *n* someone who sells fish in a shop

fish slice *n* a kitchen tool with a broad blade for lifting and serving pieces of food

fishwife *n* **-wives** a woman who works in a fish market: *scolding like a fishwife*

fishy *adj* **-ier, -iest** **1** tasting or smelling of fish **2** seeming false; making one doubtful: *a fishy story*

fission *n* the splitting into parts of certain atoms to free their powerful forces ☞ ATOM

fissure *n* a deep crack in rock or earth

fist *n* the hand with the fingers closed in tightly

fisticuffs *n humour* fighting with the fists

fistula *n* a long pipelike ulcer

fit¹ *n* **1** the appearance of the signs of slight illness in a sudden way, for a short time: *a fit of coughing* **2** a period of loss of consciousness with strange, uncontrolled movements of the body: *to have fits* **3** a sudden violent feeling: *in a fit of anger* **4 by/in fits and starts** continually starting and stopping; not regularly

fit² *adj* **-tt-** **1** right and suitable: *a meal fit for a king* **2** in good health; strong in bodily condition: *He runs to keep fit* **3 fit to burst** *esp. spoken* (as if) about to explode: *laughing fit to burst* **4 fit to drop** *esp. spoken* (as if) about to fall on the ground **5 see/think fit to do** to decide to do (esp. something foolish) —see also **(as) fit as a FIDDLE**

fit³ *v* **-tt-** **1** to be the right size or shape (for): *The lid fits badly* **2** to make clothes the right size and shape for: *It's difficult to fit him—he's so fat* **3** to provide, and put correctly into place: *to fit new locks on the doors* **4** to be suitable (for): *His behaviour doesn't fit his new position* **5** to make suitable: *Her height fitted her for netball* **6 fit the bill** to be just what one wants —see also FIT OUT, FIT UP

fit⁴ *n* the way in which something fits: *This coat's a beautiful fit*

fitful *adj* restless: *to spend a fitful night* — ~ly *adv*

fitment *n* a piece of fitted furniture: *bathroom fitments*

fitness *n* **1** the quality of being suitable **2** the state of being fit in body

fit out *v adv* to supply with necessary things: *to fit out a ship*

fitted *adj* **1** including (a part, piece of apparatus, etc.) **2** fixed in place: *a fitted carpet*

fitter *n* someone whose work is either **a** putting together machines or electrical parts or **b** cutting out and fitting clothes

fitting¹ *adj* right for the purpose or occasion: *It is fitting that we should remember him on his birthday*

fitting² *n* **1** an occasion of putting on clothes that are being made for one, to see if they fit: *to go for a fitting* **2** something necessary that is fixed into a building but able to be moved: *electric light fittings* —compare FIXTURE **USAGE** Note this fixed phrase: *fittings and fixtures/fixtures and fittings*

fit up *v adv* to arrange (esp. a place); provide (as or with): *to fit up one of the bedrooms as an office*

five *adj, n, pron* the number 5

five-day week *n* a working week that leaves Saturday free as well as Sunday

five o'clock shadow *n* a darkness on the lower part of a man's face caused by hair growing during the day after his morning shave

fiver *n esp. spoken* £5 or a 5 pound note

fives *n* a ball game in which the ball is hit with the hand or a bat against 3 walls

fix¹ *v* **1** to fasten firmly (into the stated position): *Fix the door open* **2** to agree on; arrange: *We've fixed the date for the wedding* **3** to protect (colours or photographic film) from the effects of light, by chemical treatment **4** to cook, prepare, or put in order: *Let me fix you a drink!* **5** to use unfair or illegal influence on (someone or something) so as to make sure of a desired result: *Can they fix the judge?* **6** *sl* to deal with; get even with (someone): *I'll fix George* —see also FIX ON, FIX UP

fix² *n* **1** *esp. spoken* an awkward or difficult position **2** *drug-users' sl* an injection (of the stated drug) **3** a decision on one's position in space (as when on a ship) reached by looking at the stars, taking measurements, etc.

fixation *n* **1** (in psychology) a strong unhealthy feeling (about) or love (for): *a mother fixation* **2** the act of fixing (esp. a photographic film)

fixative *n* a chemical used for sticking things together, holding things in position, or fixing colours

fixed *adj* **1** fastened; not movable **2** arranged; decided on: *The date's not fixed yet*

fixedly *adv* unchangingly; with great attention (in phrases like **to stare fixedly**)

fixed star *n* a star so distant that its movement can be measured only by very exact calculations over long periods, unlike that of the planets

fixity *n* the quality of being fixed: *fixity of purpose*

fix on *v adv* **1** to settle one's choice on; decide to have: *We've fixed on the 14th of April for the wedding* **2** to direct (one's eyes, attention, etc.) steadily at **3** **fix the blame/the crime on (someone)** to decide that someone is guilty

fixture *n* **1** something necessary, such as a bath, that is fixed into a building and sold with it —compare FITTING **2** a match or sports competition taking place on an agreed date

fix up *v adv* to provide (someone) with; make the arrangements for (someone): *We must fix him up with a job*

fizz¹ *v* (of a liquid, usu. a drink) to produce gas bubbles, making the sound typical of this — ~y *adj*

fizz² *n* the sound of fizzing

fizzle *v* -zled, -zling to fizz weakly

fizzle out *v adv* to come to nothing after a good start; end disappointingly: *The plan fizzled out*

fjord, fiord *n* a deep narrow arm of the sea between cliffs or steep slopes, esp. in Norway

flabbergast *v esp. spoken* to surprise very much; shock

flabby *adj* -bier, -biest **1** having too soft flesh; (of muscles) too soft **2** morally weak — -bily *adv* — -biness *n*

flaccid *adj* not firm enough; weak and soft: *flaccid stems* — ~ity *n*

flag¹ *n* any of various types of plant with blade-like leaves, such as the wild iris. They grow in wet places

flag² *also* **flagstone** — *n* a flat square of stone for a floor or path

flag³ *n* **1** a square or oblong piece of cloth, usu. with a pattern or picture on it and fastened by one edge to a flagpole or rope: *to fly the flag of Norway* **2** **show the white flag** to yield; show that one is cowardly or afraid **3** **under the flag (of)** serving or protected (by)

flag⁴ *v* -gg- to cause (a car or train) to stop by waving one's arm or a flag at the driver

flag⁵ *v* to be or become weak and less alive or active: *his flagging interest in the subject* — compare UNFLAGGING

flagellate *v* -lated, -lating *esp. written* to whip, esp. as a religious punishment — -lation *n*

flagellum *n* -la a long thin part of a tiny creature (MICROORGANISM) that it whips around to move through the liquid it lives in

flageolet *n* a small wind-instrument like a recorder, with 6 holes for the fingers

flag of convenience *n* **flags of convenience** a flag, belonging to a nation not really their own, that is flown by some ships to avoid taxation because nobody knows what country they really belong to

flagon *n* **1** a large container, like a jug, for liquids, usu. with a lid **2** a large bottle in which esp. wine is sold, containing about twice as much as an ordinary bottle

flagpole *n* a long pole to raise a flag on, too large to hold in the hand

flagrant *adj* open and shameless: *flagrant cheating* △ FRAGRANT — -ancy *n* — ~ly *adv*

flagship *n* the ship on which the commander of a group of naval warships sails

flagstaff *n* a flagpole, or stick to which a flag is fastened for waving in the hand

flagstone *n* a flag for flooring

flag-waving *n* *offensive* the noisy expression of national military feeling

flail¹ *n* a wooden stick swinging from the end of a long handle, used esp. in former times for threshing grain

flail² *v* to wave violently but aimlessly about

flair *n* a natural ability to do some special thing: *a flair for writing* △ FLARE

flak *n* *German* anti-aircraft guns and their bursting explosive shells

flake¹ *n* 1 a light leaflike little bit of something soft: *flakes of snow* 2 a thin flat broken-off piece of something hard: *a flake of rock*

flake² *v* **flaked, flaking** to fall off in flakes: *The paint's beginning to flake off*

flake out *v adv esp. spoken* to faint or collapse

flaky *adj* **-ier, -iest** made up of, tending to break into, flakes — **flakiness** *n*

flamboyant *adj* 1 brightly coloured and noticeable: *a flamboyant shirt* 2 (of a person or his behaviour) showy, gay, and bold — ~**ly** *adv* — **-boyance** *n*

flame¹ *n* 1 (a tongue of) red or yellow burning gas: *The sticks burst into flames* 2 **in flames** burning: *a city in flames* 3 **old flame** someone with whom one used to be in love

flame² *v* **flamed, flaming** to become red, bright, etc. by or as if by burning: *The candles flamed brighter*

flamenco a kind of Spanish dancing and music, very fast and exciting

flame-thrower *n* a gun-like instrument that throws out flames or burning liquid under pressure, used as a weapon of war or in clearing wild land

flaming *adj* 1 burning brightly; bright: *a flaming red sunset* 2 *sl* (used for adding force to a rude word): *You flaming fool!* —compare BLOODY

flamingo *n* **-gos** *or* **-goes** a tall tropical water bird with long thin legs, pink and red feathers, and a broad beak curved downwards

flammable *adj US & technical* inflammable —opposite **non-flammable** USAGE **Flammable** and **inflammable** are not opposite in meaning. They have the same meaning, but **flammable** is used in the US and is also the *technical* word in Britain, while everyone uses **inflammable** when it means 'easily excited'.

flan *n* a round flat open pie made of pastry or cake, with a filling of fruit, cheese, etc.

flange *n* the flat edge that stands out from the main surface of an object such as a railway wheel, to keep it in position

flank¹ *n* 1 the side of a person or esp. of an animal, between the ribs and the hip 2 the side

of a mountain or building 3 the side of a moving army: *The enemy attacked us on the left flank*

flank² *v* to be placed beside: *a road flanked with tall trees*

flannel¹ *n* 1 a kind of smooth loosely-woven woollen cloth with a slightly furry surface 2 a piece of cloth used for washing oneself; facecloth 3 *esp. spoken* meaningless though attractive words

flannel² *v esp. spoken* to save (oneself), find (one's way) by using meaningless though impressive words

flannelette *n* cotton cloth with a furry surface that looks like flannel

flannels *n* men's flannel trousers, esp. as worn for summer games like cricket

flap¹ 1 the sound of flapping 2 a light blow given by flapping 3 a wide flat thin part of anything that hangs down, esp. so as to cover an opening: *the flap of a tent* 4 *esp. spoken* a state of excited anxiety: *Don't get in a flap* —see also UNFLAP-PABLE

flap² *v* **-pp-** 1 to wave slowly up and down or to and fro, making a noise: *The bird flapped its wings.* | *The sail flapped in the wind* 2 *esp. spoken* to be excited and anxious

flapjack *n* a mixture of oats and other things baked into a sweet cake

flare¹ *v* **flared, flaring** to burn with a bright flame, but uncertainly or for a short time

flare² *n* 1 a flaring light: *a sudden flare as she lit the gas* 2 something that provides a bright light out of doors, as a signal at an airfield 3 the quality of being flared △ FLAIR

flared *adj* (of trousers or a skirt) shaped so as to get wider by degrees towards the bottom

flare up *v adv* to show sudden increased heat, anger, or violence: *Trouble may flare up in the city* — **flare-up** *n*

flash¹ *v* 1 (of a light) to appear or exist for a moment: *The lightning flashed* 2 to make a flash with; shine for a moment (at): *She flashed a smile at him* 3 to move very fast: *The days flashed by* 4 to show for a moment: *to flash a message on the screen* 5 (of an idea) to come suddenly: *It flashed through his mind that she might be a spy* 6 *sl* to show the sexual parts, esp. on purpose to shock others —see also FLASHER

flash² *n* 1 a sudden quick bright light: *flashes of lightning* 2 one movement of a light or flag in signalling 3 a first short news report, received by telegraph, radio, etc. 4 (in photography) **a** the method or apparatus for taking photographs in the dark **b** a flashgun 5 **flash in the pan** a sudden success that offers no promise for the future, because it will not be repeated 6 **in a/like a flash** very quickly, suddenly, or soon

flash³ *adj* 1 sudden, violent, and short (in phrases like **flash flood, flash fire**) 2 *esp. spoken* modern, attractive, and costly-looking: *a flash car* —compare FLASHY

flashback *n* part of a cinema film that goes

back in time to show what happened earlier in the story

flashbulb n an electric lamp in which metal wire or foil burns brightly for a moment, for taking a flash photograph

flasher n 1 something that flashes, such as a traffic signal or a light on a car 2 sl a man who habitually shows his sexual parts unexpectedly to strangers

flashgun n a device for providing a flash for flash photography

flashlight n 1 an electric torch 2 a light used for signals, as in a lighthouse

flash point n the temperature at which the gas from oil will make a small flash, but not catch fire, if a flame is put near it

flashy adj -ier, -iest over-ornamented; unpleasantly big, bright, etc., and perhaps not of good quality —compare FLASH — **flashily** adv: flashily dressed — **flashiness** n

flask n 1 a narrow-necked bottle, as used by scientists in the laboratory 2 a flat bottle for carrying alcohol or other drinks in the pocket or fastened to one's belt, saddle, etc. 3 also **thermos, thermos flask, vacuum flask**— a bottle having 2 thin glass walls between which a vacuum is kept, used for keeping the contents either hot or cold 4 the amount of liquid that a flask contains

flat[1] adj -tt- 1 parallel with the ground; smooth and level: The earth is round, not flat 2 having a broad smooth surface and little thickness: flat cakes 3 (of beer and other gassy drinks, or their taste) having lost the gas 4 dull; uninteresting: Everything seems so flat since Robert left 5 (in music) lower than the true note —compare SHARP 6 (in music) half a note lower than (in the phrases A flat, B flat, C flat, etc.) ☞ MUSIC 7 complete; firm; with no more argument: She gave me a flat refusal 8 (of a tyre) without enough air in it 9 (of the feet) not having proper arches 10 (of a battery) needing to be connected with a supply of electric current and charged 11 esp. spoken (after an expression of time, showing surprise at its shortness) exactly; and not more: I got dressed in 3 minutes flat! 12 **fall flat** (of an idea or plan) to fail; have no effect — ~**ness** n

flat[2] n 1 a low level plain, esp. near water: mud flats 2 the flat part or side: I hit him with the flat of my hand 3 a movable upright piece of wooden or canvas stage scenery, representing esp. the wall of a room 4 (the sign,♭, for) a flat note in music —compare SHARP ☞ MUSIC 5 **on the flat** on level ground

flat[3] adv 1 esp. spoken completely: He's flat broke 2 (in music) lower than the true note —compare SHARP

flat[4] also **apartment**— n a set of rooms esp. on one floor, including a kitchen and bathroom, usu. one of many such sets in a building or block

flatfish n any of several kinds of flat bony sea fish such as sole or plaice

flatlet n a very small flat

flatly adv 1 in a dull level way: It's hopeless, he

said flatly 2 completely; firmly (in phrases like flatly refuse)

flat out[1] adv esp. spoken 1 at full speed: working flat out 2 (of speech) directly; plainly

flat out[2] adj esp. spoken completely tired out

flat racing n the sport of horseracing on flat ground with nothing to be jumped over —compare STEEPLECHASE

flat rate n one charge including everything, to which nothing will be added

flat spin n esp. spoken a state of excited confusion

flatten v to make or become flat: The hills flatten out here

flatter v 1 to praise too much or insincerely in order to please 2 to make feel important, beautiful, clever, etc.: She was flattered at the invitation 3 to make (someone) look too beautiful: a flattering photograph 4 **flatter oneself** to have the pleasant though perhaps mistaken opinion — ~**er** n

flattery n -ries 1 the action of flattering 2 a flattering remark

flatulence n the feeling of discomfort caused by too much gas in the stomach

flaunt v offensive to show for public admiration (something one is proud of): to flaunt one's new fur coat ⚠ FLOUT

flautist n someone who plays the flute, esp. as a profession

flavour[1] n 1 a taste; quality that only the tongue can experience: a strong flavour of cheese 2 the quality of tasting good or pleasantly strong — ~**less** adj

flavour[2] v to give flavour to: to flavour with chocolate

flavouring n something added to food to give or improve the flavour

flaw[1] n a small sign of damage, such as a mark or crack, that makes an object not perfect: a flaw in a plate — ~**less** adj — ~**lessly** adv

flaw[2] v to make a flaw in

flax n 1 a plant with blue flowers, that is grown for its stem and oily seeds 2 the thread made from the stems of this plant; linen

flaxen adj (of hair) pale yellow

flay v flayed, flaying 1 to remove the skin from (a creature) 2 to scold violently; attack severely in words

flea n 1 any of a group of small jumping insects without wings, that live on blood ☞ INSECT 2 **send someone off with a flea in his/her ear** to drive someone away feeling foolish because of a short severe scolding

fleabite n 1 the bite of a flea 2 something small and not very troublesome, though unpleasant

fleapit n sl a cheap dirty cinema or theatre

fleck[1] v to mark or cover with flecks: The grass was flecked with sunlight

fleck[2] n 1 a small mark or spot 2 a grain or drop: flecks of dust

fledged adj (of a bird) having developed wing feathers for flying —compare FULLY-FLEDGED

fledgling n a young bird that is learning to fly

flee v **fled, fleeing** 1 to escape (from) by hurrying away 2 **flee the country** to go abroad for safety

fleece¹ n a sheep's woolly coat; the amount of wool cut from one sheep at one time —compare SHEEPSKIN

fleece² v **fleeced, fleecing** to rob (of a lot of money) by a trick or by charging too much money: *They fleeced us at that hotel!*

fleecy adj **-ier, -iest** woolly like a fleece

fleet¹ n 1 a number of ships, such as warships in the navy 2 a group of buses, aircraft, etc., under one control

fleet² adj literature fast; quick: *a fleet-footed runner* — ~**ly** adv — ~**ness** n

fleeting adj (of time or periods) short; passing quickly — ~**ly** adv

Fleet Street n 1 the area in London where most of the important newspaper offices are 2 the influence of newspaper writing: *Fleet Street can make or break a politician*

flesh n 1 the soft substance, including fat and muscle, that covers the bones and lies under the skin 2 the meat of animals used as food 3 the soft edible part of a fruit or vegetable 4 man's body as opposed to his mind or soul: *The spirit is willing but the flesh is weak* 5 **flesh and blood a** human beings: *sorrows more than flesh and blood can bear* **b** relatives 6 **go the way of all flesh** to die 7 **one's pound of flesh** the exact amount of what is owed to one, esp. when this will cause the person who owes it great pain or trouble 8 **in the flesh** in real life

flesh wound n a wound which does not reach the bones or the important organs of the body

fleur-de-lis, fleur-de-lys fleurs-de-lis or fleurs-de-lys— n a stylized drawing of a lily flower, formerly used on the coat of arms of the French royal family

flew past tense of FLY

flex¹ v to bend and move (one of one's limbs, muscles, etc.) so as to stretch and loosen, esp. in preparation for work

flex² n (a length of) bendable insulated electric wire used for connecting an electrical apparatus to a supply

flexible n 1 that can bend or be bent easily 2 that can change or be changed to be suitable for new needs, changed conditions, etc. — **-ibly** adv — **-ibility** n

flibbertigibbet n a silly person, usu. a woman —see also FLIGHTY

flick¹ n a short light blow or movement as with a whip, duster, finger, etc.

flick² v 1 to strike with a flick: *She flicked the dust away* 2 to move with a light quick blow: *to flick the switch*

flicker v 1 to burn unsteadily; shine with an unsteady light: *The candle flickered out* 2 to move backwards and forwards quickly and unsteadily: *Shadows flickered on the wall* — flicker n

flick knife n a knife with a blade inside the handle that springs into position when a button is pressed

flicks n esp. spoken the cinema

flier, flyer n someone or something that flies, esp. a pilot

flies n 1 the front opening of a pair of trousers 2 the large space above a stage from which staff control and move the scenes used in a play

flight¹ n 1 the act of flying: *a bird's first flight from the nest* ☞ AEROPLANE 2 the distance covered or course followed by a flying object 3 a trip by plane: *Did you have a good flight?* 4 the aircraft making a journey: *flight Number 447 to Geneva* 5 a group of birds or aircraft flying together: *a flight of pigeons* 6 a set (of stairs, as between floors)

flight² n the act of running away or fleeing

flight deck n 1 (on a ship built to carry military aircraft) the surface for taking off or landing 2 (in a plane) the room at the front from which the pilot and his helpers control the plane

flightless adj unable to fly

flight lieutenant n a commissioned officer of low rank in the Royal Air Force

flight sergeant n a noncommissioned officer of high rank in the Royal Air Force

flighty adj **-ier, -iest** (esp. of a woman or her behaviour) too influenced by sudden desires or ideas; often changing — **flightiness** n

flimsy¹ adj **-sier, -siest** 1 (of material) light and thin 2 (of an object) easily broken or destroyed; lacking strength — **-sily** adv — **-siness** n

flimsy² n **-sies** a very thin sheet of typing paper, used esp. when several copies of something are made

flinch v to move back when shocked by pain, or in fear of something unpleasant: *John didn't flinch once while his wound was cleaned*

fling¹ v **flung, flinging** 1 to throw violently 2 to move (part of oneself) quickly or violently: *She flung back her head proudly* 3 **fling oneself into** to begin (an activity) with great interest or force

fling² n 1 an act of flinging; throw 2 a short wild time of satisfying one's own desires (in the phrase **have one's/a fling**)

flint n 1 very hard fine-textured grey stone that makes very small flashes of flame when struck with steel 2 a piece of this used in former times for striking fire —see also TINDERBOX 3 a small piece of iron or other metal used like a chip of flintstone to light the petrol or gas in cigarette lighters

flintlock n a gun used in former times, in which the explosive powder was lit by striking flint ☞ WEAPON

flinty adj **-ier, -iest** 1 very hard; like flint 2 cruel; unmerciful: *a flinty heart*

flip¹ *v* **-pp-** **1** to send (something) spinning, often into the air, by striking with a light quick blow **2** to turn over: *to flip an egg over in the pan* **3** *sl* to become highly excited or mad: *My brother has really flipped*

flip² *n* **1** a quick light blow, esp. one that sends something spinning into the air **2** a drink made by mixing wine or a stronger alcoholic drink with sugar and egg

flip³ *adj* **-pp-** *esp. spoken* flippant

flip-flop *n* **1** a type of sandal held on by the toes and loose at the back **2** the sound of something flapping loosely

flippant *adj* disrespectful about serious subjects, esp. when trying to be amusing: *flippant remarks* — **-pancy** *n* — ~**ly** *adv*

flipper *n* a limb of certain larger sea animals that are not fish (esp. seals), with a flat edge used for swimming

flipping *adj, adv sl* bloody

flip side *n* the side of a record that has the song or piece of music on that is of less interest or less popular than that on the other side

flirt¹ *v* (esp. of a woman) to behave with a member of the opposite sex in a way that attracts interest and attention

flirt² *n* a person, esp. a woman, who likes flirting

flirtation *n* **1** the act of flirting **2** a short love affair which is not serious

flirtatious *adj* **1** that likes to flirt: *a flirtatious young girl* **2** of or related to flirting — ~**ly** *adv* — ~**ness** *n*

flirt with *v prep* **1** to think about but not very seriously **2** to deal lightly with: *to flirt with danger*

flit *v* **-tt-** **1** to fly or move lightly or quickly: *The birds flitted from branch to branch* **2** *Scots & NEnglish* to move house

float¹ *n* **1** a piece of wood or other light object that floats, used on a fishing line or to support the edge of a fishing net **2** an air-filled container used instead of wheels by planes that land on water **3** a large flat vehicle on which special shows, ornamental scenes, etc., are drawn in processions —see also MILK FLOAT **4** a sum of money collected in advance and kept for use if an unexpected need arises —compare KITTY

float² *v* **1** to stay or cause to stay at the top of liquid or be held up in air without sinking: *Wood floats on water* **2** to move easily and lightly as on moving liquid or air: *The logs float down the river* **3** to establish (a business, company, etc.) by selling shares **4** to suggest: *The idea was first floated before the war* **5** to vary freely in exchange value from day to day: *the floating pound* — ~**er** *n*

floating *adj* **1** not fixed or settled in a particular place: *a floating population* **2** **floating voters/vote** the people who do not vote for a fixed political party but change their loyalty

floating dock *n* a dock that can be lowered in the water to allow a ship to enter and then raised

to bring the ship out of the water for repairs, painting, etc.

flock¹ *n* **1** a group of sheep, goats, or birds **2** a crowd; large number of people **3** the group of people who regularly attend a church

flock² *v* to gather or move in large crowds

flock³ *n* **1** small pieces of wool, hair, etc. used for filling cushions, mattresses, etc. **2** soft material (on the surface of another) esp. forming ornamental patterns: *flock curtains*

floe *n* a large mass of ice floating on the sea

flog *v* **-gg-** **1** to beat severely with a whip or stick, esp. as a punishment **2** *sl* to sell or try to sell **3 flog a dead horse a** to waste one's time with useless efforts **b** to keep repeating something already understood or accepted

flogging *n* a severe beating with a whip or stick, esp. as punishment

flood¹ *n* **1** the covering with water of a place that is usu. dry **2** a large flow: *a flood of complaints*

flood² *v* **1** to fill or become covered with water: *The river flooded the valley* **2** to overflow **3** to arrive or go in such large numbers as to be difficult to deal with: *Requests flooded in after the advert* **4** to cover or spread into completely: *The room was flooded with light*

floodgate *n* a gate used for controlling the flow from a large body of water

floodlight *n, v* **-lighted** *or* **-lit, -lighting** (to light with) a large electric light that produces a very powerful and bright beam of light

flood tide *n* the flow of the tide inwards; rising tide —opposite **ebb tide**

floor¹ *n* **1** the surface on which one stands indoors; surface nearest the ground **2** (of the sea, a cave, etc.) the bottom **3** a level of a building; storey **4** a level area specially prepared for a particular purpose: *a dance floor* **5** the part of a parliament or council building where members sit and speak **6 take the floor** to start dancing, as at a party or in a dance hall **7 wipe the floor with** to defeat totally

floor² *v* **1** to provide with a floor: *floored with boards* **2** to knock down: *He floored his attacker* **3** *esp. spoken* to beat; defeat or make helpless with surprise or confusion: *I was floored by his argument*

floorboard *n* a board in a wooden floor

flooring *n* material used for making floors

floor show *n* an entertainment performed in a restaurant, nightclub, etc.

flop¹ *v* **-pp-** **1** to move or fall heavily or awkwardly: *All he does is flop about the house all day* **2** *esp. spoken* (of a plan, a performance, etc.) to fail badly; be unsuccessful

flop² *n* **1** the movement or noise of flopping **2** *esp. spoken* a failure

floppy *adj* **-pier, -piest** soft and falling loosely: *floppy material* — **floppily** *adv* — **floppiness** *n*

floppy disk *n* a disc made of soft magnetized

plastic, on which computer instructions may be stored

flora *n* **1** all the plants growing wild in a particular place, or belonging to a particular age in history: *the flora of chalk areas* —compare FAUNA **2** a list or description of such plants

floral *adj* of flowers: *floral patterns*

florid *adj* **1** (too) richly ornamented **2** (of a person's face) red — ~**ly** *adv*

florin *n* (until 1971) a silver-coloured British coin worth 2 shillings

florist *n* a person who keeps a flower shop

floss *n* **1** a mass of waste rough silk threads from the outer covering spun by a silkworm **2** fine silk, spun but not twisted, used for cleaning between one's teeth and for sewing —see also CANDYFLOSS

flotilla *n* a group of small warships, usu. destroyers

flotsam and jetsam *n* **1** waste material floating about in the sea, or washed up onto the shore **2** broken unwanted things lying about **3** people without homes or work, who move helplessly through life

flounce[1] *v* **flounced, flouncing** to move violently in a temper: *She flounced out of the house*

flounce[2] *n* a deep frill with loose folds sewn onto a garment for ornament — ~**d** *adj*

flounder *v* **1** to move with great difficulty, esp. making violent efforts not to sink: *He floundered through the deep snow* **2** to struggle or lose control when speaking or doing something ☞ FOUNDER

flour *n, v* (to cover with) powder made from grain, esp. wheat, used for making bread, pastry, cakes, etc. —see also PLAIN FLOUR, SELF-RAISING FLOUR — ~**y** *adj*

flourish[1] *v* **1** to wave in the hand and so draw attention to (something): *He flourished his letter in his mother's face* **2** to grow healthily; be successful; be well: *a flourishing business* **3** to be alive or producing results at a certain time in history: *Chaucer flourished at the end of the 14th century* — ~**ingly** *adv*

flourish[2] *n* **1** a showy fancy movement or manner that draws people's attention to one: *He opened the door with a flourish* **2** a curve or ornament in writing

flout *v* to treat without respect or consideration; go against: *You've flouted my orders* ⚠ FLAUNT

flow[1] *v* **1** (of liquid) to run or spread smoothly; pour: *The stream flowed rapidly* **2** to move along smoothly without pause: *The cars flowed in a steady stream* **3** (of hair, cloth, etc.) to fall loosely and gracefully **4** (of the tide) to rise; come in —compare EBB —see also FLOWING

flow[2] *n* **1** a pouring out: *a flow of oil* **2** the movement or rate of flowing **3** a supply of gas, electricity, etc. **4** the rise of the tide —compare EBB

flow diagram also **flowchart**— *n* a drawing in which particular shapes and connecting lines are used for showing how each particular action in a

system is connected with or depends on the next or another

flower[1] *n* **1** the part of a plant, often beautiful and coloured, that produces seeds or fruit 👁 **2** a plant that is grown for the beauty of this part **3** *in literature* the best part: *the flower of youth* — ~**less** *adj*

flower[2] *v* **1** (of a plant) to produce flowers **2** to develop; come to be in its best state: *His genius flowered*

flowerbed *n* a piece of ground, esp. in a garden, in which flowers are grown for ornament

flowering *n* a high point of development, esp. when reached for the first time

flowerpot *n* a pot to hold earth for growing a plant

flowery *adj* **-ier, -iest** **1** full of or ornamented with flowers **2** (too) much ornamented; full of fanciful words

flowing *adj* moving, curving, or hanging gracefully: *flowing handwriting* — ~**ly** *adv*

flown *past part. of* FLY

flu *n esp. spoken* influenza

fluctuate *v* **-ated, -ating** **1** to rise and fall: *fluctuating prices* **2** to change from one state to the opposite: *His feelings fluctuated between excitement and fear* — **-ation** *n*

flue *n* a narrow passage up which smoke or heat passes; the inside part of a chimney

fluent *adj* **1** speaking, writing, or playing music in an easy smooth manner: *He is fluent in 5 languages* **2** (of speech, writing, etc.) expressed readily and without pause — **-ency** *n* — ~**ly** *adv*

fluff[1] *n* **1** soft light loose waste from woollen or other materials **2 a** very soft fur or hair on a young animal **b** the first very fine feathers on a bird — ~**y** *adj* — ~**iness** *n*

fluff[2] *v* **1** to make (something soft) appear larger by shaking or by brushing or pushing upwards: *She fluffed up her hair* **2** *esp. spoken* to do (something) badly or unsuccessfully: *The cricketer fluffed the catch*

fluid[1] *adj* **1** having the quality of flowing, like liquids, air, gas, etc.; not solid **2** unsettled; not fixed: *fluid ideas* — ~**ity** *n*

fluid[2] *n* **1** a liquid **2** *technical* a fluid substance

fluid ounce *n* (a measure of liquid equal to) one 20th of a pint or 0.0284 of a litre

fluke[1] *n* a type of flat worm that attacks and eats a sheep's liver

fluke[2] *n esp. spoken* a piece of accidental good fortune; accidentally skilful action: *The shot was a fluke*

fluky, -ey *adj* **-ier, -iest** *esp. spoken* happening by a fluke

flummery *n* **-ries** unnecessarily unclear and showy language or intentionally confusing activity

flummox *v esp. spoken* to confuse and make uncertain what to write, say, or do: *She was flummoxed by the question*

Parts of a flower

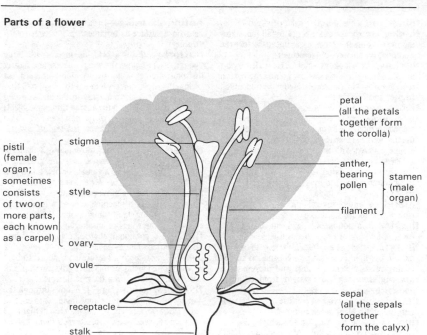

pistil
(female
organ;
sometimes
consists
of two or
more parts,
each known
as a carpel)

stigma

style

ovary

ovule

receptacle

stalk

petal
(all the petals
together form
the corolla)

anther,
bearing
pollen

filament

stamen
(male
organ)

sepal
(all the sepals
together
form the calyx)

Cross-section of a leaf

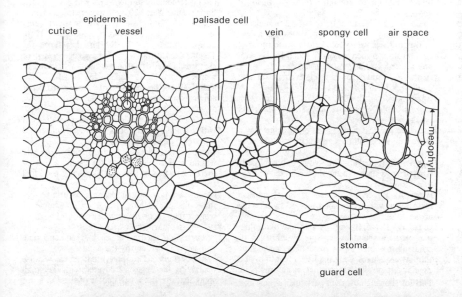

cuticle

epidermis
vessel

palisade cell

vein

spongy cell

air space

mesophyll

stoma

guard cell

flung *past tense and past part. of* FLING

flunk *v esp. spoken esp. US* **1** to fail (an examination or course) **2** to mark as unsatisfactory the examination answers of (someone)

flunkey, -ky *n* **-keys, -kies** **1** a male servant in ceremonial dress in a wealthy house **2** a person who tries to win someone's favour by too much respect and obedience

fluorescent *adj* **1** (of a substance) giving out bright white light when electric or other waves are passed through **2** (of lighting, a lamp, etc.) producing light by means of electricity passed through a tube covered with material having this quality — **-cence** *n*

fluoridate *v* **-dated, -dating** to add a fluoride to (a water supply) to make people's teeth grow stronger

fluoride *n* any of several combinations of fluorine with another substance

fluorine *n* a non-metallic element, usu. in the form of a poisonous pale greenish-yellow gas

flurry¹ *n* **-ries** **1 a** a sudden sharp rush of wind or rain **b** a light fall of snow **2** a sudden shared feeling causing confused noise and movement: *a flurry of excitement* **3** a state of troubled hurry and excitement

flurry² *v* **-ried, -rying** to confuse; make nervous and uncertain about what to do

flush¹ *v* (of birds) to fly up suddenly

flush² *n* **1** a sudden flow (of liquid, esp. water) **2** an act of cleaning with a sudden flow of water **3** a flow of water for washing out a toilet **4** a flow of blood to the face, giving a red appearance **5** a sudden increase in depth or area esp. of colour: *The rain brought a flush of green to the land* **6** a sudden feeling of success, joy, rage, etc. **7** a high condition of strength: *the first flush of youth*

flush³ *v* **1** to clean or drive out **2** to make or become empty of waste matter by means of a flow of water: *The lavatory won't flush* **3** to turn red as a result of a sudden flow of blood to the skin: *She flushed with anger* **4** to make red

flush⁴ *adj* exactly on a level; even in surface: *cupboards flush with the wall*

flush⁵ *adv* **1** in a flush way: *The door fits flush into its frame* **2** exactly; fully: *He hit him flush on the jaw*

flush⁶ *n* (in card games) a set of cards held by a person, in which the cards belong to the same suit

fluster¹ *v* to make hot, nervous, and confused

fluster² *n* a state of being flustered: *She was put in a fluster by the unexpected guests*

flute¹ *n* a pipelike wooden or metal musical instrument with finger holes, played by blowing across a hole in the side

flute² *v* **fluted, fluting** **1 a** to play on a flute **b** to make a sound like a flute by whistling or speaking in a high sweet voice **2** to make long thin inward curves along the whole length of at a regular distance from each other, as an ornament: *fluted pillars*

fluting *also* **flutings—** *n* a set of hollow curves cut on a surface as ornament: *plates edged with fluting*

flutter¹ *v* **1** (of a bird, an insect with large wings, etc.) to move the wings quickly and lightly without flying **2** to fly by doing this **3** (of wings) to move quickly and lightly **4 a** (of a thin light object) to move quickly in the air: *The flag fluttered in the wind* **b** to cause (a thin light object) to do this: *She fluttered her handkerchief* **5** to move in a quick irregular way: *She fluttered her eyelids*

flutter² *n* **1** a fluttering movement **2** a state of excited interest: *His arrival put the girls in a flutter* **3** *esp. spoken* a gamble or bet, taken in a light way: *to have a flutter on the horses* **4** *technical* a shaking movement that causes a fault in the action of a machine, esp. as **a** in a record player, causing faulty high sounds —compare wow **b** in the wings of an aircraft

flux *n* **1** continual change; condition of not being settled: *Things have been in a state of flux since father's death* **2** a substance added to help clean molten metal, or to help in soldering 2 pieces of metal together **3** a flow or flowing

fly¹ *v* **flew, flown, flying** **1** to move through the air by means of wings or a machine **2** to control and guide (an aircraft, helicopter, etc.) in flight **3** to carry or send in an aircraft: *He's flying his car to Europe* **4** to use (a particular airline) for travelling by **5** to cross (a stretch of water) by flying: *to fly the English Channel* **6** to be carried along in the air: *Clouds were flying across the sky* **7** (of something fixed at one end) to wave or float in the air **8 a** to raise in the air on the end of a thread, rope, etc.: *to fly a kite* **b** to show (a flag) ceremonially in this way **9** to pass rapidly; hurry: *Time flies* **10** *esp. spoken* to leave in a hurry: *I'm late; I must fly* **11** to move suddenly and with force: *The window flew open* **12** to escape (from); flee **13 the bird has flown** the person needed or wanted has gone away or escaped **14 let fly (at) a** to attack with blows or words **b** to shoot **15 make the dust/feathers/fur/sparks fly** to cause a quarrel or a fight —see also **as the** CROW **flies, fly in the** FACE **of,** FLYING, **fly off the** HANDLE

fly² *n* **flies** **1** any of several types of small insect with 2 wings (esp. the housefly) **2** any of several types of flying insect: *a butterfly* **3** a copy of a winged insect made of thread, feather, or silk wound round a hook used for catching fish **4 there are no flies on someone** someone is not a fool and cannot be tricked

fly³ *n* **1** a type of light carriage used in former times for public hire, drawn by one horse **2** trouser flies: *Your fly's undone*

fly⁴ *adj sl* sharp and clever

flyaway *adj* (of dress or esp. hair) soft and loose and easily blown out by the wind

flyblown *adj* **1** (of meat) unfit to eat because containing flies' eggs **2** covered with the small spots that are the waste matter of flies **3 a** not pure or bright and new; in a bad condition **b** worthless because used many times before

fly-by-night *n, adj* **fly-by-nights** *offensive* **1** (a person or business) that is not firmly established, but is interested only in making quick profits, esp. by slightly dishonest methods **2** (a debtor) who runs away

flyer *n* a flier

fly-fishing *n* the practice of fishing in a river or lake with a fly

fly half also **standoff half**— *n* (in rugby) a fast-running player whose job is to pass the ball out to the line of players who will try to gain points with it

flying[1] *adj* **1** (of a jump) made after running for a short distance **2** very short: *a flying visit*

flying[2] *n* the action of travelling by aircraft, as a means of getting from one place to another or as a sport

flying buttress *n* a half arch joined at the top to the outside wall of a large building, used for supporting the weight of the wall ⟶ CATHEDRAL

flying colours *n* **1** flags shown as a sign of victory **2 with flying colours** in a splendid and worthy manner

flying doctor *n* (in Australia and other countries) a doctor who goes by aircraft to visit the sick in distant lonely places, in answer to radio messages

flying saucer *n* any of several types of usu. plateshaped spaceships which many people claim to have seen flying across the sky and believe to be piloted by creatures from another world

flying squad *n* a group of special police cars and men who are always ready for quick action when a serious crime takes place

flying start *n* **1** a start to a race in which one or more competitors begin to move the moment the starting signal is given (or just before it), and so gain an advantage over the others **2** a very good beginning

flyover *n* a place where roads or railways cross each other and where one passes high over the other by way of a kind of bridge

flypaper *n* a length of paper covered with a sticky or poisonous substance to trap flies in a room

flypast *n* a display by aircraft flying in a special formation on a ceremonial occasion, esp. at a low level in front of a crowd

flysheet *n* an additional sheet that is put over a tent for protection in rainy weather

flyswatter *n* an instrument for killing flies, usu. made of a flat square piece of plastic or wire net fixed to a handle

flyweight *n* a boxer who weighs 112 pounds or less

flywheel *n* a wheel which, because of its heavy weight, keeps a machine working at an even speed

FM *abbrev. for:* frequency modulation; a system of broadcasting, usu. on VHF, in which the elec-

tric signal that carries the sound waves has a wave that is always of the same strength but comes at a varying number of times per second, and provides very clear words and music for the listener — compare AM

FO *abbrev. for:* FOREIGN OFFICE

foal *v, n* **1** (to give birth to) a young horse **2 in/with foal** (of a female horse) having a young horse developing inside the body

foam[1] *n* **1** a whitish mass of bubbles on the surface of a liquid or on skin **2** a chemical substance in this form, such as one used in controlling dangerous fires **3** FOAM RUBBER — **foamy** *adj*

foam[2] *v* to produce foam: *The mad dog was foaming at the mouth*

foam rubber *n* soft rubber full of small bubbles, used for making chair seats, mattresses, etc.

fob *n* a short chain or band of cloth to which a watch is fastened

fob off *v adv* **-bb-** **1** to gain acceptance for (something) by deceit: *The salesman fobbed off the faulty machine on the lady* **2** to deceive (someone) into accepting something

focal length *n* the distance from the middle of a lens to its focus

focal point *n* a focus

fo'c'sle also **forecastle**— *n* the front part of a ship, where the sailors live

focus[1] *n* **-cuses** or **-ci** **1** (in mathematics) a point from which lines are drawn to any points on a conic section in such a way that the lengths of these lines are related to each other by some law **2** the point at which beams of light or heat, or waves of sound meet after their direction has been changed ⟶ OPTICS **3** the central point; centre of interest: *to be a focus of attention* **4 in (to)/out of focus** (not) having or giving a clear picture because the lens is (is not) correctly placed — **focal** *adj*

focus[2] *v* **-s-** or **-ss-** **1** to bring into a focus: *to focus one's mind on work* **2 a** to arrange the lens in (an instrument) so as to obtain a clear picture **b** to make (a picture) clear by doing this

fodder *n* **1** rough food for cattle or horses, gathered from the fields and stored **2** things or people used for supplying a continuous demand

foe *n* *esp. written* an enemy

foetus *n* **1** *technical* a young creature inside the mother, esp. at a later stage when all its parts have been developed for use at birth —compare EMBRYO ⟶ EMBRYO **2** a young human in the early stages of development inside the mother, esp. before it is recognizable as a baby or able to live separately — **foetal** *adj*

fog[1] *n* **1** very thick mist **2** mistiness on a photographic plate or film, or on a print from such a film **3 in a fog** *esp. spoken* in a state of mind in which something cannot be understood

fog[2] *v* **-gg-** **1** to make or become difficult to see through because of a misty covering: *Steam has fogged my glasses* **2** to make or become unclear owing to fog: *Light has fogged this film*

fog

fogbank *n* a heavy mass of fog on the surface of the sea

fogbound *adj* prevented by fog from working or travelling as usual

foggy *adj* **-gier, -giest** **1** not clear because of fog; very misty **2** unclear: *I've only a foggy idea what it was all about* — **foggily** *adv* — **fogginess** *n*

foghorn *n* a loud horn used as a warning of fog by and to ships

fog lamp *n* a lamp on the front of a vehicle that gives a strong beam of light during fog

fogy, fogey *n* **fogies, fogeys** a slow uninteresting old person who dislikes changes and does not understand modern ideas

foible *n* a small rather foolish personal habit or weakness of character, which the person who has it finds rather pleasing

foil¹ *v* to prevent from succeeding: *We foiled his attempt to escape*

foil² *n* a type of light narrow sword with a covered point, used in fencing —compare EPEE, SABRE ☞ WEAPON

foil³ *n* **1** metal beaten or rolled into very thin paperlike sheets **2** paper covered with this; silver paper **3** a person or thing of a kind that makes more noticeable the better or different quality of another: *The wicked uncle acts as a foil to the noble prince*

foist *v* **1** to cause (someone or something unwanted) to be borne or suffered for a time: *He foisted himself on them for the weekend* **2** FOB OFF

fold¹ *n* **1** a sheltered corner of a field where farm animals, esp. sheep, are kept for protection, surrounded by a fence or wall **2 return to the fold** to come back home or to return to one's religion

fold² *v* **1** to turn or press back one part of (something, esp. paper or cloth) and lay on the remaining part; bend into 2 or more parts: *She folded the tablecloth* **2** to bend (a limb) close to the body: *The cat folded its tail round its front feet* **3** to press (a pair of limbs) together: *He folded his arms* **4** to wrap: *Fold a piece of paper round the flowers* **5** to be able to be bent back; close up: *Does this table fold?* **6** *esp. spoken* to fail: *The business has folded (up)*

fold³ *n* **1** a part of a thin flat material laid over another part: *The curtain hung in heavy folds* **2** a mark made by folding; a crease: *to iron folds out of a dress* **3** a hollow part inside something folded **4 a** a bend in a valley **b** a hollow in a hill **5** *technical* a bend in the bands of rock and other material that lie one under the other beneath the surface of the earth

foldaway *adj* that can be folded up out of the way or out of sight: *a foldaway bed*

folder *n* a folded piece of cardboard used for holding loose papers

fold in *v adv* to mix into a mixture that is to be cooked, by turning over gently with a spoon

foliage *n* **1** leaves, esp. growing leaves **2** gathered or arranged leaves, branches, and flowers

folk¹ *n* **1** people **2** people of one race or nation, or sharing a particular kind of life   USAGE A **state** is either a **country**, or one of the **States** making up a **country** such as the US. A **nation** is a group of people, usually sharing a language and history, and usually but not always living in the same area. A **race** is a group of people of similar colour and physical type: *the European races*. A **tribe** is a fairly small closely-knit community and often non-industrialized. The word **people** is often now preferred for such a group. The population of a country are the **people** or, sometimes, the **folk**. **Folk** usually denotes a shared culture; one does not use the term in political speeches: **folk** *dancing*

folk² *adj* of, connected with, or being music or any other art that has grown up among working or country people as an important part of their way of living and belongs to a particular area, trade, etc., or that has been made in modern times as a copy of this

folklore *n* all the knowledge, beliefs, habits, etc., of a racial or national group, still preserved by memory, or in use from earlier times — **-lorist** *n*

folks *n* *esp. spoken* **1 a** family; relations **b** parents: *I'd like you to meet my folks* **2** people: *Well, folks, shall we go?*

folktale *n* a popular story passed on by speech over a long period of time

follicle *n* any of the small holes in a person's or animal's skin, from which hairs grow ☞ SKIN

follow *v* **1** to come, arrive, go, or leave after; move behind in the same direction **2** to go in the same direction as: *Follow the river* **3** to come next in order or on a list: *May follows April* **4** to carry on (a certain kind of work): *He follows the trade of baker* **5** to keep in sight or pay attention to: *He followed the speaker's words closely* **6** to understand clearly: *I can't follow his line of reasoning* **7** to take a keen interest in: *He follows all the cricket news* **8** to accept and act according to: *Will you follow my advice?* **9** to be or happen as a necessary effect or result (of): *Disease often follows war* **10 as follows** as now to be told: *The results are as follows.....* **11 to follow** as the next dish; as the next thing to eat —see also FOLLOW ON, FOLLOW THROUGH, FOLLOW UP, **follow in the** FOOTSTEPS of

follower *n* an admirer or supporter of some person, belief, or cause

following¹ *adj* **1** next **2** that is/are to be mentioned now: *Please send the following goods: one bag of rice and one of flour* **3** (of wind or sea) moving in the same direction as a ship; helping

following² *n* **1** the one or ones about to be mentioned **2** a group of supporters or admirers: *He has a large following*

following³ *prep* after

follow on *v adv* (of a cricket team) to take a second innings straight after the first as a penalty for scoring less than the opponent's first total by an amount fixed in the rules — **follow-on** *n*

follow-through *n* (in sports) the part of a stroke made after hitting the ball

follow through *v adv* **1** also **follow out**— to complete; carry out exactly to the end: *to follow through a line of inquiry* **2** (in tennis, golf, etc.) to complete a stroke by continuing to move the arm after hitting the ball

follow-up *adj, n* (of or being) a thing done or action taken to continue or add to the effect of something done before: *follow-up visits*

follow up *v adv* **1** to act further on: *to follow up a suggestion* **2** to take further action after

folly *n* **-lies** **1** foolishness **2** an unwise act, habit, etc.: *the follies of youth* **3** a building of strange or fanciful shape, that has no particular purpose, esp. as built only to be looked at

foment *v* to help (something evil or unpleasant) to develop △ FERMENT — **~ation** *n*

fond *adj* **1** loving in a kind, gentle, or tender way: *He signed the letter, 'With fondest love, Cyril'* **2** foolishly loving: *A fond mother may spoil her child* **3** foolishly trusting or hopeful: *He has a fond belief in his own cleverness* **4** having a great liking or love (for) — **~ly** *adv* — **~ness** *n*

fondant *n* a type of sweet made of fine sugar, that melts in the mouth

fondle *v* **-dled, -dling** to touch gently and lovingly; stroke softly

fondue, fondu *n French* **1** a dish made with melted cheese, into which pieces of bread are dipped **2** a dish consisting of small pieces of food, such as meat or fruit, that are cooked in or dipped into a hot liquid

font *n* a large vessel in a church, usu. made of stone, that contains the water used for baptizing people

food *n* **1 a** something that living creatures or plants take into their bodies to give them strength and help them to develop and to live **b** something solid for eating: *We get food there, but never anything to drink* **2** an edible substance **3** subject matter (for an argument or careful thought) ◉

food chain *n* a series of living things each of which eats a living thing lower down in the series ☞ FOOD

food poisoning *n* a painful stomach disorder caused by eating poisonous or decaying food

foodstuff *n* a substance used as food, esp. a simple food material that is to be cooked or mixed with other foods for eating

fool¹ *n* **1** a person whom one considers to be silly; person lacking in judgment or good sense **2** (in former times) a manservant at the court of a king or noble, whose duty was to amuse his master; jester **3** a dish of cooked soft fruit, pressed into a liquid and beaten up with cream **4** (the) **more fool you** I think you were a fool —see also APRIL FOOL

fool² *v* **1** to deceive; trick **2** to speak or behave in a silly way: *Can't you stop fooling?*

fool about also **fool around**— *v adv* to spend the time doing nothing useful: *He just fools about all day long*

foolery *n* **-ries** **1** silly behaviour **2** a silly action, speech, thing, etc.

foolhardy *adj* too bold; taking or needing useless or unwise risks — **-diness** *n*

foolish *adj* unwise; without good sense — **~ly** *adv* — **~ness** *n*

foolproof *adj* **1** that cannot go wrong: *a foolproof plan* **2** very simple to understand, use, work, etc.: *a foolproof machine*

foolscap *n* (in Britain) a size of writing paper about 17×13½ inches

fool's errand *n* an effort that is seen in the end to be useless (esp. in the phrases **go on/send someone on a fool's errand**)

fool's paradise *n* a carelessly happy state, in spite of a threat of change (esp. in the phrases **be/live in a fool's paradise**)

foot¹ *n* **feet** **1** the movable part of the body at the end of the leg, below the ankle, on which a man or an animal stands **2** (*pl. sometimes* **foot**) (a measure of length equal to) 12 inches or about ·305 metres **3** the bottom part; base: *the foot of the page* **4** the lower end (of anything) where feet lie: *the foot of the bed* **5** manner of walking; step: *fleet of foot* **6** the part of a stocking or sock that covers the foot **7** a division of a line in poetry, in which there is usu. a strong beat and one or 2 weaker ones: *In the line 'The way/was long/the wind/was cold', the words between each pair of upright lines make up a foot* **8** soldiers who march and fight on foot; infantry **9 a foot in both camps** a position not completely favouring one side or the other, so that each thinks it has one's support **10 a foot in the door** a beginning of influence, favour, etc. **11 fall on one's feet** *esp. spoken* to come out of a difficult state of affairs without harm; have good luck **12 find one's feet** to become used to new or strange surroundings; settle in **13 get a foot in** *esp. spoken* to get a chance to be in **14 get/have cold feet** to be too nervous to do something, esp. losing courage just before something **15 keep one's feet** to be able to remain standing; not fall **16 my foot** *esp. spoken* I don't believe it **17 put a foot wrong** to say or do anything wrong **18 put one's best foot forward a** to walk as fast as possible **b** to make one's best effort **19 put one's feet up** *esp. spoken* to rest by lying down or sitting with one's feet supported on something **20 put one's foot down a** *esp. spoken* to speak and act firmly on a particular matter **b** *sl* to drive very fast **21 put one's foot in it** *esp. spoken* to say the wrong thing or make an awkward mistake **22 set foot in/on** to enter; visit —see also SWEEP **someone off his feet,** UNDER-FOOT

foot² *v esp. spoken* to pay (a bill)

footage *n* **1** measurement or payment by the

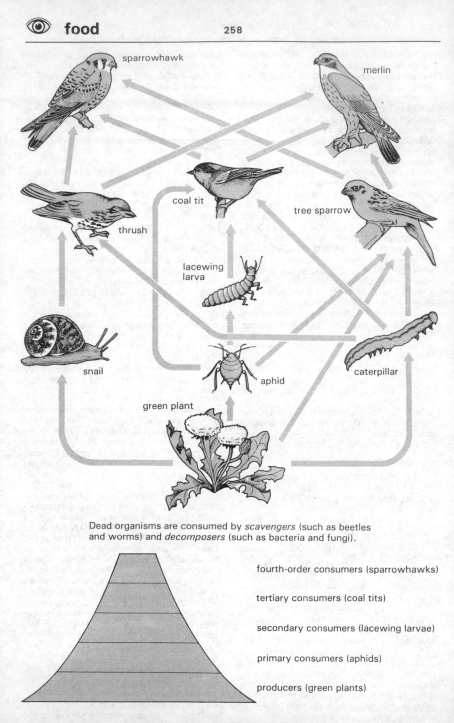

Dead organisms are consumed by *scavengers* (such as beetles and worms) and *decomposers* (such as bacteria and fungi).

fourth-order consumers (sparrowhawks)

tertiary consumers (coal tits)

secondary consumers (lacewing larvae)

primary consumers (aphids)

producers (green plants)

In the sea, plankton are the producers in the food web.

foot **2** length of cinema film used: *some old footage of the early fliers*

foot-and-mouth disease *n* a disease of cattle, sheep, and goats, in which spots appear in the mouth and on the feet, and which often causes death

football *n* **1** any of several games for 2 teams in which a ball is kicked and/or thrown about a field in an attempt to get goals, esp. **a** soccer **b** rugby **2** any of several types of large ball filled with air, usu. made of leather, used in these games — ~**er** *n*

football pools *n* see POOLS

footboard *n* **1** a narrow board running along the outside of a railway carriage **2** a sloping board against which the driver of a carriage or car can rest his feet

footbridge *n* a narrow bridge to be used only by people on foot

footfall *n* a sound made by setting the foot on the ground; the sound of a footstep

foothill *n* a low hill at the bottom of a mountain or chain of mountains

foothold *n* **1** a space (as on a rock) where a foot can be placed to help one to continue to climb up or down **2** a first introduction or entrance that may lead to success: *It isn't easy to get a foothold as an actor*

footing *n* **1** a firm placing of the feet; room or a surface for the feet to stand on: *She lost her footing and fell* **2** a sure position; base: *Is this business on a firm footing?* **3** a special condition or quality of relationship suited to a certain state of affairs: *The army is now on a peacetime footing* **4** an accepted place in some group

footle *v* **-tled, -tling** *esp. spoken* to behave or waste in a careless way: *footling her time away*

footlights *n* a row of lights along the front edge of the floor of a stage at the theatre, to show up the actors

footling *adj* worthless; unimportant

footloose *adj* free to go wherever one pleases and do what one likes; without family or business ties

footman *n* **-men** a manservant who opens the front door, introduces visitors, waits at table, etc., and often is dressed in special livery

footnote *n* a note at the bottom of a page in a book, that explains some word or sentence, adds some special remark or information, etc.

footpath *n* a narrow path or track for people to walk on

footplate *n* a metal plate covering the floor of a railway steam engine, where the men driving the train stand

footprint *n* a footshaped mark left lying on, or pressed into, a surface that has been trodden on

footslog *v* **-gg-** *esp. spoken* to march or walk a long way in tiring conditions — ~**ger** *n* — ~**ging** *n*

footsore *adj* having tender, painful, or swollen feet, esp. as a result of much walking: *They came in hungry and footsore*

footstep *n* **1** a mark or sound of a person's step **2** the distance covered by one step **3 follow in the footsteps of** to follow an example set by (someone else in the past)

footstool also **stool**— *n* a low support on which a seated person can rest his feet

footsure also **surefooted**— *adj* able to walk firmly without slipping or falling in difficult places

footwear *n* *technical* shoes and boots

footwork *n* the use of the feet, esp. skilfully in dancing, sports, etc.

fop *n* *offensive* a man who takes a womanish interest in fine clothes and graceful manners — ~**pish** *adj*

for¹ *prep* **1** that is/are intended to belong to, be given to, or be used in connection with: *a present for Mary* **2** in order to reach, get, or have: *We set off for London* **3** at/on/in (the time of): *She's coming for Christmas* **4** representing; taking the place of; instead of; corresponding to: *Red is for danger.* | *I'll do it for you* **5** in favour of; in support of: *They work hard for charity* **6** as regards; in regard to: *an ear for music* **7** because of: *You look better for your holiday* **8** in spite of: *For all his efforts, he didn't succeed* —compare DESPITE, NOTWITHSTANDING **9** considering how little: *For all the good we've done we might as well have left it as it was* **10** at the price of: *a pen for 50 pence* **11** as the price of: *50 pence for a pen* | *a bad mark for every mistake* **12** (of time or distance) the space of; over the space of; during: *We ran for 2 miles.* | *He stayed for a week* —compare SINCE **13** *used with a noun/pronoun in the object form and a verb in the infinitive to make a phrase which could be expressed as a clause: The bell rang for the lesson to begin* (=in order that it should begin) **14** *usu. offensive* **that's . . . for you!** as you must agree, that's what ... is like **15 there's . . . for you!** that's the complete opposite of . . .: *He just grabbed the money and left — there's gratitude for you!*

for² *conj* *esp. written* because: *We must start early, for we have a long way to go*

for. *abbrev. for:* foreign

forage¹ *n* **1** food supplies for horses and cattle **2** an act or the action of foraging

forage² *v* **-aged, -aging** *esp. spoken* to hunt about or search: *The campers went foraging for wood to make a fire*

forasmuch as *conj* *esp. Bible or law* because; as it is a fact that

foray *n, v* **-ays; -ayed, -aying** (to make) a sudden rush into enemy country, usu. by a small number of soldiers, in order to damage or seize arms, food, etc.

forbear¹ *v* **-bore, -borne, -bearing** *esp. written* **1** to make no attempt to do something that one has the right to do, esp. in a generous and merciful way: *He forbore claiming the reward* **2** to use self-control to avoid a wished-for but inconvenient action: *The wounded man could not forbear to cry out*

forbear² n a forebear

forbearance n control of one's feelings so as to show patient forgiveness

forbearing adj long-suffering; gentle and merciful

forbid v -bade or -bad, -bidden, -bidding 1 to command not to do something: I forbid you to use my car 2 to command that (something) must not be done: Smoking is forbidden in the concert hall 3 God forbid (that) I very much hope it will not happen (that)

forbidden adj 1 not allowed; against the teachings of religion 2 that may not be used, entered, or visited by ordinary people: the forbidden city

forbidding adj having a fierce, unfriendly, or dangerous look: She has a forbidding manner — ~ly adv

force¹ n 1 natural or bodily power; active strength: the force of the explosion 2 fierce or uncontrolled use of strength; violence: The thief took the money from the old man by force 3 technical (measurement of) a power that changes or may produce change of movement in a body on which it acts or presses: The force of gravity makes things fall to earth 4 a person, thing, belief, action, etc., that has a strong enough influence to cause widespread changes in a way of living, or that has uncontrollable power over living things: the forces of evil | the forces of nature 5 strong influence on the mind: I was persuaded by the force of his argument. | force of habit 6 a group of people banded together or trained for some kind of action, esp. military action: land and sea forces | the police force 7 in force in large numbers: The police were there in force 8 in(to) force (of a rule, order, law, etc.) in(to) effect, use, or operation 9 join forces (with) to unite (with) for a purpose

force² v forced, forcing 1 to make (an unwilling person or animal) do something; drive: The rider forced his horse on through the storm 2 to push using force: We had to force the window open 3 to produce by unwilling effort; produce with difficulty or against nature: forced laughter 4 to hasten the growth of (a plant) by the use of heat 5 force one's/someone's/the pace to take or cause to take faster or too fast action

forced adj done or made because of a sudden happening which makes it necessary to act without delay: a forced landing

force-feed v -fed, -feeding to feed (a person or animal) by forcing food or esp. liquid down the throat

forceful adj (of a person, words, ideas, etc.) strong; powerful —compare FORCIBLE — ~ly adv — ~ness n

force majeure n French force or power that cannot be acted or fought against

forcemeat n meat cut up very small and mixed with herbs, used esp. for stuffing a chicken, joint of meat, etc., that is to be cooked

forceps n a medical instrument with 2 long thin blades joined at one end or in the middle, used for holding objects firmly: When a baby is being born forceps may be used to assist it

forces n the army, navy, and fighting airmen of a country

forcible adj 1 using bodily force: The police made a forcible entry into the house 2 (of a person, manner of speaking, etc.) having power to influence the mind —compare FORCEFUL

forcibly adv 1 in a forcible manner 2 strongly: His manner reminded me forcibly of his father's

forcing bag n a triangular-shaped bag of folded paper in which icing, cream, etc. is placed and then forced out through a specially-shaped tube to form a decorative pattern, as on a cake

ford n, v (to cross at) a place in a river where the water can be crossed on foot, in a car, etc., without using a bridge — ~able adj

fore¹ adv towards, in, or near the front part, esp. of a boat —opposite aft ⟶ SAIL

fore² adj front: the fore part of an aircraft

fore³ n come to the fore to become well-known; come to have a leading position

fore and aft adv 1 from the bow to the stern of a boat; lengthwise 2 in, at, or towards both the front and back of a boat: The captain ordered 2 flags to be placed fore and aft

forearm¹ v to prepare for an attack before the time of need

forearm² n the lower part of the arm between the hand and the elbow

forebear, for- n a person from whom the stated person is descended; ancestor

forebode v -boded, -boding to be a warning of (something unpleasant)

foreboding n a feeling of coming evil: She had a foreboding that she'd never see him again

forecast n, v -cast or -casted, -casting (to make) a statement of future events, based on some kind of knowledge or judgment: The weather forecast

forecastle n a fo'c'sle

foreclose v -closed, -closing to repossess property because of someone's failure to repay a mortgage: The building society will be forced to foreclose — -closure n

forecourt n 1 a courtyard in front of a large building 2 (in tennis) the part of the court between service line and net

foredoomed adj intended by or as if by fate to reach a usu. bad state or condition: foredoomed to failure

forefather n 1 a relative in the far past; (male) ancestor 2 a person of an earlier period in the stated place or condition: the forefathers of the village

forefinger also index finger— n the finger next to the thumb, with which one points

forefront n the most forward place; leading position: in the forefront of the fighting

forego v -went, -gone, -going to forgo

foregoing adj esp. written having just been mentioned

foregone conclusion *n* a result that is or was certain

foreground *n* 1 the nearest part of a scene in a view, a picture, or a photograph 2 the most important or noticeable position: *She likes to keep herself in the foreground*

forehand *n, adj* (in games such as tennis) (a stroke) played with the inner part of the hand and arm facing forward —compare BACKHAND

forehead *n* the part of the face above the eyes and below the hair

foreign *adj* 1 to, from, of, in, being, or concerning a country or nation that is not one's own or not the one being talked about: *foreign travel | I can't understand him; he must be foreign* 2 having no place (in); having no relation (to): *Love is foreign to his nature* 3 coming or brought in from outside; not belonging; harmful

foreign aid *n* help in the form of money, goods, etc., given to poorer countries by a richer country

Foreign and Commonwealth Office also **Foreign Office**— *n* the British government department which deals with foreign affairs —compare HOME OFFICE

foreigner *n* a person belonging to a country other than one's own

foreknowledge *n* knowledge about something before it happens

forelock *n* a piece of hair growing just above and falling over a person's forehead

foreman *n* -men 1 (fem. **forewoman**)— a skilled and experienced workman who is put in charge of other workers 2 the leader of the jury who speaks for the rest and reports to the court what they have decided

foremost *adj* 1 most important; leading 2 furthest forward; first

forename *n* *esp. written* FIRST NAME

forenoon *n* *esp. written* the time before midday; morning

forensic *adj* *technical* related to or used in the law and the tracking of criminals: **forensic science**

foreordain *v* *esp. written* to arrange or decide from the very beginning that, or how, (something) shall happen or be done: *Some people believe that their lives are foreordained*

forepart *n* the front or first part

forerunner *n* 1 a sign or warning that something is going to happen 2 a person who prepares the way for, or is a sign of the coming of, a more important person: *The alchemists were the forerunners of the scientists of today*

foresail *n* the chief and lowest square sail on the front mast of a ship ⇨ SHIP

foresee *v* -saw, -seen, seeing to form an idea or judgment about (the future); expect: *We should have foreseen this trouble* — ~able *adj*

foreshadow *v* *esp. literature* to be a sign of (what is coming); represent or be like (something that is going to happen)

foreshore *n* the part of the seashore which **a** is left dry when the tide goes down **b** is between the edge of the sea and the part of the land that has grass, buildings, etc.

foreshorten *v* to draw with the lines and shapes in the distance smaller, shorter, and closer together, as they appear to the human eye

foresight *n* the ability to imagine what will probably happen; care or wise planning for the future —compare HINDSIGHT

foreskin *n* a loose fold of skin covering the end of the male sex organ (PENIS)

forest *n* 1 (a large area of land thickly covered with) trees and bushes, either growing wild or planted for some purpose 2 a large number of upright objects close together: *a forest of hands*

forestall *v* 1 to prevent (someone) from doing (something) by doing the action first oneself 2 to spoil (the arrangements) of (someone) by doing something earlier than expected: *She forestalled my attempt to meet her off the train by coming to the house*

forester *n* 1 an officer who is in charge of a forest and looks after trees and animals, guards against fires, etc. 2 a man who works in a forest, cuts down trees, etc.

forestry *n* the science and practice of planting and caring for large areas of trees

foreswear *v* -swore, -sworn, -swearing to forswear

foretaste *n* a small early experience (of something that will come later)

foretell *v* -told, -telling to tell (what will happen in the future)

forethought *n* wise planning or consideration of future needs

forever, for ever *adv* 1 for all time: *We left our old home forever* 2 continually: *He's forever mending his motorbike*

forewarn *v* to warn (someone) of coming danger, unpleasantness, etc.

foreword *n* a short introduction at the beginning of a book, usu. about the writer and his work —see PREFACE (USAGE)

forfeit¹ *n* . what must be lost or forfeited for something

forfeit² *v* to have (something) taken away from one because some agreement or rule has been broken, or as a punishment, or as the result of some action: *You have forfeited your chance of getting your money back* — ~ure *n*

forfeit³ *adj* taken from one, by law, as a punishment: *The traitor's life was forfeit to the crown*

forgave *past tense of* FORGIVE

forge¹ *n* 1 (a building or room containing) a large apparatus with a fire inside, used for heating and shaping metal objects 2 a large apparatus that produces great heat inside itself, used for melting metal, making iron, etc.

forge² *v* forged, forging 1 to form by heating and hammering 2 to make a copy of (something) in order to deceive: *a forged passport*

forge³ *v* to move with a sudden increase of speed and power: *The racehorse forged ahead*

forger n a person who forges in order to deceive

forgery n -ries 1 the act or an action of deceitful forging: *He was sent to prison for forgery* 2 something that has been forged

forget v -got, -gotten, -getting 1 to fail to remember: *I forget where to go* 2 to fail to remember to bring, buy, etc., (something): *Don't forget the cases* 3 to stop thinking about (something): *'I'm sorry I broke your teapot.' 'Forget it.'* 4 to fail to give attention to: *He forgot his old friends when he became rich* 5 **forget oneself** to lose one's temper or self-control

forgetful adj having the habit of forgetting: *forgetful of one's duties* — ~ly adv — ~ness n

forget-me-not n a type of low-growing plant with small usu. pale blue flowers

forging n a piece of forged metal

forgivable, -give- adj that can be forgiven: *a forgivable mistake* — **-bly** adv

forgive v -gave, -given, -giving to say or feel that one is no longer angry about and/or wishing to give punishment to (someone) for (something): *I'll never forgive you*

forgiveness n 1 the act of forgiving or state of being forgiven 2 willingness to forgive

forgiving adj willing or able to forgive: *a forgiving nature* — ~ly adv

forgo, fore- v -went, -gone, -going *often humour* to give up (esp. something pleasant): *to forgo all company*

fork¹ n 1 a metal or plastic instrument for holding or carrying food to the mouth, having a handle at one end with 2 or more points at the other 2 a wooden-handled farm or gardening tool with 2 or more metal points at one end used for breaking up the soil 3 a place where something long and narrow divides, or one of the divided parts: *a fork in the road* 4 one of the 2 parallel metal points at the front of a bicycle, motorcycle, etc., between which the wheel is fixed

fork² v 1 to lift, carry, move, etc., with a fork 2 (of something long and narrow) to divide, esp. into 2 parts 3 to take the (left or right) fork of a road

forked adj 1 having one end divided into 2 or more points: *a forked tongue* 2 that divides into 2 or more parts at a point

forked lightning n lightning in the form of a line of wavy angles, usu. dividing into 2 or more parts near the bottom —compare SHEET LIGHTNING

forkful n an amount that is or can be picked up on a fork

forklift also **forklift truck**— n a small vehicle with a movable apparatus on the front, used for lifting and lowering heavy goods

fork out v adv esp. spoken to pay (money) unwillingly

forlorn adj esp. literature or written deserted and miserable: *The lost dog had a forlorn look*

—see ALONE (USAGE) — ~ly adv — ~ness n

form¹ n 1 shape; appearance; body: *She has a tall graceful form* 2 a general plan or arrangement; kind or sort: *Different countries have different forms of government* 3 the way in which a work of art is put together: *a master of form* 4 ceremony; rule or custom: *a form of marriage* 5 esp. spoken behaviour of the stated type in relation to what is expected: *Schoolboys often think it bad form to tell a teacher of another boy's wrong-doing* 6 (esp. in sport) condition of skill, fitness, and standard of performance: *The footballer's been out of form* 7 spirits: *Tom is in fine form* 8 a way in which a word may be written or spoken as a result of variations in spelling or pronunciation, according to some rule: *There are 2 forms of the past of 'to dream': 'dreamed' and 'dreamt'* 9 a printed paper divided by lines into separate parts, in each of which answers to questions must be written down 10 a long wooden seat, usu. without a back 11 a class in a British school, and in some American schools

form² v 1 to take shape; appear; develop: *Steam forms when water boils* 2 to take the shape of: *The buildings formed a hollow square* 3 to make: *Eskimoes form igloos out of blocks of ice* 4 to develop as a result of thought, effort, experience, or training: *form a friendship* 5 to make according to rule: *to form a correct sentence* 6 to make up; gather together; arrange: *forming a club* 7 to be; be the substance of 8 to stand or cause to stand or move in a certain order: *The soldiers formed into a line*

formal adj 1 ceremonial; according to custom: *a formal dinner party* 2 stiff in manner and careful about correctness of behaviour: *He's very formal with everybody* 3 having a set or regular shape: *a formal garden* 4 unreal; belonging to appearance only: *There's only a formal likeness between the 2 brothers* —compare CONVENTIONAL, TYPICAL — ~ly adv

formaldehyde n a type of colourless gas

formalin n a liquid made by mixing formaldehyde with water, used for disinfecting, hardening leather, preserving, making plastic, etc.

formality n -ties 1 careful attention to rules and accepted forms of behaviour: *There's no time for formality in everyday life* 2 an act in accordance with law or custom: *There are a few formalities to be gone through before you enter a foreign country* 3 an act which has lost its real meaning

format n the size, shape, etc., in which something is produced or arranged: *The dictionary was reprinted in a new format*

formation n 1 the shaping or developing of something: *Her front teeth were irregular in formation* 2 an arrangement of people, ships, aircraft, etc.; order: *drawn up in battle formation* 3 a thing which is formed; way in which a thing is formed: *cloud formations*

formative adj having influence in forming or

developing: *a child's formative years* — ∼**ly** *adv*

former *adj esp. written* **1** of an earlier period: *a former judo champion* **2** the first of 2 people or things just spoken about: *Of swimming and football he much preferred the former* —opposite **latter**

formerly *adv* in earlier times: *This painting was formerly owned privately, but now it belongs to the nation* —opposite **latterly**

Formica *n trademark* a type of strong plastic made in thin sheets, used esp. for surfacing tables

formidable *adj* **1** very great and frightening; causing fear, doubt, anxiety, etc.: *a formidable voice* **2** difficult; hard to defeat: *a formidable question* — -**bly** *adv*

formless *adj* **1** without shape **2** *usu. offensive* lacking order or arrangement — ∼**ly** *adv* — ∼**ness** *n*

formula[1] *n* -**las** *or* -**lae** **1** *technical* a general law, fact, etc., expressed shortly by means of a group of letters, numbers, etc.: *The chemical formula for water is* H_2O **2** a list of the substances used in making something, such as a medicine, a fuel, a drink, etc., sometimes with description of how they are to be mixed: *the secret formula for a new rocket fuel* **3** a combination of things, events, etc., which will lead almost unavoidably to the stated result: *Drinking and driving is a formula for trouble* **4** a combination of suggestions, plans, etc., that can be agreed on by both sides: *The employers and the union leaders have agreed an acceptable formula for wages*

formula[2] *adj* of, related to the use of, or being a racing car that has a size, weight, engine, etc., that is expressed, according to a set of rules, by the stated number or word: *Formula one cars are the most powerful*

formulate *v* -**lated**, -**lating** **1** to express in a short clear form **2** to invent and prepare (a plan, suggestion, etc.) — -**ation** *n*

fornicate *v* -**cated**, -**cating** *esp. law or Bible* to have sexual relations with someone outside marriage — -**tion** *n*

forsake *v* -**sook**, -**saken**, -**saking** *esp. written* to desert; give up completely: *She forsook the religion of her family* —see also GODFORSAKEN

forswear, fore- *v* -**swore**, -**sworn**, -**swearing** *esp. written* to make a solemn promise to give up or to stop doing (something): *Some priests have to forswear marriage*

forsythia *n* a type of bush that bears bright yellow flowers in spring, before its leaves appear

fort *n* **1** a strongly made building used for defence at some important place **2 hold the fort** to look after everything while someone is away

forte[1] *n* a strong point in a person's character or abilities: *Games are his forte*

forte[2] *n, adj, adv* (a piece of music) played in a loud and forceful manner —see also FORTISSIMO —compare PIANO

forth *adv esp. Bible or literature* forward: *from this day forth*

forthcoming *adj* **1** happening or appearing in the near future: *a list of forthcoming events* **2** ready; offered when needed: *No answer was forthcoming* **3** *esp. spoken* ready to be helpful and friendly: *None of them were very forthcoming*

forthright *adj* direct in manner and speech: *His forthright behaviour offends some people* — ∼**ness** *n*

forthwith *adv esp. literature* at once

fortieth *adj, n, pron, adv* 40th

fortification *n* **1** the act or science of fortifying **2** towers, walls, gun positions, etc., set up as a defence

fortified wine *n* (any of several types of) alcoholic drink made by adding a small amount of strong alcohol (such as brandy) to wine: *Sherry is a fortified wine*

fortify *v* -**fied**, -**fying** **1** to build forts on; strengthen against possible attack: *a fortified city* **2** to strengthen: *After praying he faced his difficulties with a fortified spirit* — -**fiable** *adj* — -**fier** *n*

fortissimo *n, adj, adv* -**mos** (a piece of music) played in a very loud and forceful manner —see also FORTE

fortitude *n* courage in bearing trouble, pain, etc., without complaining

fortnight *n* 2 weeks

fortnightly *adj, adv* (happening, appearing, etc.) every fortnight or once a fortnight

Fortran *n* a language for programming a computer used esp. for mathematical operations and machine control

fortress *n* a large fort; place strengthened for defence

fortuitous *adj* happening by chance — ∼**ly** *adv* — ∼**ness** *n*

fortunate *adj* having or bringing good fortune; lucky

fortunately *adv* by good chance; luckily. *Fortunately the train was on time for once*

fortune *n* **1** fate; chance, esp. as an important influence on one's life; luck: *She had the good fortune to be free from illness* **2** whatever happens in the future to a person by chance, good or bad: *Through all his changing fortunes, he never lost courage* **3** success; good luck: *Fortune smiled on him* **4** wealth; a great amount of money, possessions, etc.

fortune hunter *n usu. offensive* a person who tries to marry for money

fortune-teller *n* a person, usu. a woman, who claims to be able to tell fortunes

forty *adj, n, pron* -**ties** the number 40

forty-five *n esp. spoken* **1** also **.45**— a small pistol, having a barrel that is 0·45 of an inch across on the inside **2** also **45**— a record that is played by causing it to turn round 45 times every minute

forum *n* **1** an open place in ancient Rome used

for public business **2** any place or meeting where public matters may be discussed

forward¹ *adj* **1** directed towards the front; advancing: *a forward movement* **2** near, at, or belonging to the front: *the forward part of the train* **3** particularly or unusually advanced or early in development: *a forward child* **4** (esp. of a young person) unpleasantly sure of oneself, too bold, often in sexual matters **5** ready and eager: *He's always forward with help* **6** getting on fast (with work, study, plans, etc.): *How far forward are your plans?* **7** advanced; modern: *very forward in one's thinking* — ~ly *adv* — ~ness *n*

forward² also **forwards**— *adv* **1** towards the front in the direction one is facing: *Take 2 steps forward* **2** towards the future: *We look forward and try to plan wisely* **3** to an earlier time: *They moved the meeting forward from the 20th to the 18th* **4** into a noticeable position: *The lawyer brought forward some new reasons* **5** also **on**— (of a clock) so as to show a later time

forward³ *n* one of the attacking players in teams of various sports (such as soccer, rugby, and hockey) —compare CENTRE, BACK

forward⁴ *v* **1** to send forward or pass on (letters, parcels, etc.) to a new address **2** *esp. written* to send: *We are forwarding you our catalogue* **3** to help advance the development of — ~ing *n*

forward⁵ *adv sailing* in or towards the front part of a ship —compare AFT

forward-looking *adj* planning for or concerned with the future

forward pass *n (esp. in rugby)* an act of throwing the ball in the direction of one's opponents' goal (which is against the rules)

forwent, fore- *past tense of* FORGO

fossil¹ *n* **1** a hardened part or print of an animal or plant of long ago, that has been preserved in rock, ice, etc. **2** *offensive* an old person with unchanging ideas or habits

fossil² *adj* **1** being or in the condition of a fossil **2** being made of substances that were living things in the distant past: *Coal is a fossil fuel*

fossilize, -ise *v* **-ized, -izing** to make or become a fossil — **-ization** *n*

foster *v* **1** to help (something) to grow or develop; encourage: *to foster an interest in music* **2** to take (someone, esp. a child) into one's family to look after and bring up as one's own, usu. for a certain period and without taking on the full responsibilities in law of the parent: *We fostered the young girl while her mother was in hospital* —compare ADOPT

fought *past tense and past part. of* FIGHT

foul¹ *adj* **1** evil-smelling or evil-tasting; unclean; impure: *a foul-tasting medicine* **2** (of a pipe, chimney, etc.) blocked with dirt or waste matter, so that liquid, smoke, etc., cannot pass freely **3** *technical, esp. sailing* (of a rope, chain, etc.) twisted; knotted; mixed up in disorder **4** (of weather) rough; stormy **5** evil; cruel; shameful: *Murder is a foul deed* **6** (of language) full of

curses **7** *esp. spoken* very bad; unpleasant: *I've had a foul morning* **8** (in sport) against the rules: *He struck his opponent a foul blow* — ~ly *adv* — ~ness *n*

foul² *n* (in sport) an act that is against the rules

foul³ *v* **1** to make or become dirty, impure, or blocked with waste matter: *The dog's fouled the path* **2** (in sports, esp. football) to be guilty of a foul: *Smith ran into Jones and fouled him* **3** *sailing* (of a boat) to run against (another) **4** (of a rope, chain, etc.) to get mixed up or twisted with (something)

foul play *n technical* criminal violence in association with a person's death; murder: *The police suspect foul play*

found¹ *v* **1** to build or start building (something large): *The castle is founded on solid rock* **2** to begin the development of; establish: *This company was founded in 1724* **3** to start and support by supplying money: *The rich man founded a hospital* —see also FOUND ON

found² *v* **1** to melt (metal) and pour into a hollow mould —see also FOUNDRY **2** to make (something) of metal in this way

found³ *past tense and past part. of* FIND

foundation *n* **1** the act of starting the building or planning of something large, or starting some kind of organization **2** a building and the organization connected with it, planned for a good purpose and supported in some special way **3** **a** an organization that gives out money for certain special purposes **b** the money held by such an organization **4** that on which a belief, custom, way of life, etc., is based; basis: *Slavery provided the foundation for many ancient types of society* **5** FOUNDATION CREAM

foundation cream *n* a mixture of oils and other substances that women rub into their faces before putting on powder

foundation garment *n* an undergarment worn by women, shaped so as to support and control the body

foundations also **foundation**— *n* **1** the solid stonework, brickwork, etc., first set in holes dug deep in the earth, to support the walls of a building: *to lay the foundations of a new hospital* **2** the base; that by which things are supported, or on which they are based: *He laid the foundations of his success by study and hard work*

foundation stone *n* a large block of stone, on which words are usually cut, which is laid at a public ceremony by some important person, when an important building is begun

founder¹ *n* a person who founds something: *Mohammed was the founder of the Muslim religion*

founder² *v* **1** (of a ship) to fill with water and sink **2** to come to nothing; fail: *The plan foundered for lack of support* △ FLOUNDER

founding father *n literature or esp. written* a founder

found on also **found upon**— v prep to base on: a story founded on fact

foundry n **-dries** a place where metals are melted down and poured into shapes to make separate articles or parts of machinery, such as bars, wheels, etc.

fountain n 1 (an apparatus of pipes, sometimes hidden inside beautiful stone figures or bowls set in an ornamental lake or smaller piece of water in a garden, or other open space, producing) a stream of water that shoots straight up into the air 2 a flow, esp. rising straight into the air: *A fountain of water shot from the pipe* 3 the place where something begins or is supplied: *The ruler was respected as the fountain of honour*

fountainhead n literature a source

fountain pen n a pen with a container (BARREL) giving a continuous supply of ink as one writes with it

four adj, n, pron 1 the number 4 2 (esp. in games of cards) a set or group of 4: *to make up a four for cards* 3 (in cricket) 4 runs, usu. gained by hitting the ball to the edge of the field 4 a 4 man rowing-boat for racing 5 . . . **and four** . . . pulled by 4 horses: *a coach and four*

foureyes n esp. spoken, usu. humour a person who wears glasses

four-leaved clover also **four-leafed clover**, **four-leaf clover**— n a clover plant having a set of 4 leaves instead of the usual 3, said to bring good luck

four-letter word n any of several words made up of usu. 4 letters, that are not considered to be polite

four-poster also **four-poster bed**— n a large old kind of bed, with posts at the 4 corners to support a frame for curtains

fours n **on all fours** (of a person) on the hands and knees

foursquare adj brave and unyielding

fourteen adj, n, pron the number 14 — ~**th** adj, n, pron

fourth adj, n, pron adv 4th

fourth dimension n time

Fourth of July n the national Independence Day of the US

fowl n **fowls** or **fowl** 1 a farmyard bird, esp. a hen 2 old use & poetic a bird —see also WILDFOWL

fowling piece n a gun for firing small shot, used for shooting certain types of bird, esp. ducks

fox[1] n 1 (fem. **vixen**)— **a** any of several types of small doglike flesh-eating wild animal with a bushy tail, esp. **b** a type of European animal with reddish fur, preserved in Britain to be hunted and often said to be clever and deceiving 2 the skin of this animal, used as fur on clothing 3 esp. spoken, usu. offensive a person who deceives others by means of clever tricks: *He's a sly old fox*

fox[2] v esp. spoken 1 **a** to deceive cleverly; trick **b** to be too difficult for someone to understand:

The question foxed me completely 2 to pretend

foxglove n a type of tall straight plant bearing pink or white bellshaped flowers all the way up its stem

foxhole n a hole in the ground from which soldiers fire at the enemy

foxhound n a type of dog with a keen sense of smell, trained to track down and kill foxes

foxhunt n a hunt of foxes by foxhounds and people riding on horses — ~**er** n — ~**ing** n

foxtrot n, v (to dance) a type of formal dance with short quick steps

foxy adj **-ier, -iest** offensive like a fox, in appearance or nature; not to be trusted

foyer n an entrance hall to a theatre or hotel, where people gather and talk

Fr abbrev. for: Father (as a religious title)

fracas n **fracas** or **fracases** a noisy quarrel, usu. between a number of people, which often ends in a fight

fraction n 1 a very small piece or amount: *She spends only a fraction of her earnings* 2 (in mathematics) a division or part of a whole number: $\frac{1}{3}$ and $\frac{5}{8}$ are fractions —see also IMPROPER FRACTION, PROPER FRACTION, VULGAR FRACTION

fractional adj 1 so small as to be unimportant 2 (in mathematics) of, related to, or being a fraction

fractionally adv to a very small degree

fractious adj 1 (esp. of a child or an old or sick person) restless and complaining; bad-tempered about small things and ready to quarrel 2 (of an animal) difficult to control — ~**ly** adv — ~**ness** n

fracture[1] n technical, esp. medical or written the act or result of breaking or cracking something, esp. a bone

fracture[2] v **-tured, -turing** technical esp. medical or written to break or crack: *He fell and fractured his upper arm*

fragile adj 1 easily broken, damaged, or destroyed: *This vase is fragile* 2 **a** slight in body or weak in health: *The old lady looks very fragile* **b** usu. humour not in a good condition of health and spirits; weak: *'I'm feeling rather fragile after all that beer last night,' he said* — -**gility** n

fragment[1] n 1 a small piece broken off: *She dropped the bowl and it broke into fragments* 2 an incomplete part, esp. of a work of art

fragment[2] v 1 to break into fragments 2 to cause to be made up of incomplete parts, esp. not understandable: *The interruption fragmented his argument*

fragmentary also **fragmental**— adj 1 made up of pieces; not complete: *His knowledge of the subject is fragmentary* 2 being a fragment or fragments

fragmentation n separation into small pieces: *A* **fragmentation bomb** *is one that explodes into small pieces*

fragrant adj having a sweet or pleasant smell

fra

(esp. of flowers) ⚠ FLAGRANT — ~ly *adv* — -ance *n*

frail *adj* 1 not strongly made or built: *That bridge is too frail to take a man's weight* 2 weak or slight: *Her frail hands could hardly hold a cup*

frailty *n* -ties 1 the quality of being frail 2 a weakness of character or behaviour: *One of the frailties of human nature is laziness*

frame¹ *v* **framed, framing** 1 to surround with a solid protecting edge or border: *to frame a picture in wood* 2 to act as a setting or background to: *A hat framed her pretty face* 3 to build; make: *Forts are framed for defence* 4 to give shape to (words, sentences, ideas, etc.); express: *An examiner must frame his question clearly* 5 *esp. spoken* to cause to seem guilty of a crime by means of carefully planned but untrue statements or proofs: *He was framed by the real criminals*

frame² *n* 1 the main supports over and around which something is stretched or built: *Some small boats are made of skins stretched over a wooden frame* 2 the hard solid parts which are fitted together to make something: *a bicycle frame* 3 the form or shape of a human or animal body: *a man with a powerful frame* 4 a firm border or case into which something is fitted or set, or which holds something in place: *a window frame* 5 a setting; background; surroundings: *The trees make a pleasant frame to the house* 6 also **cold frame** — a large wooden box set in the ground and having a sloping glass roof that can be raised or lowered, used for protecting and growing young plants 7 one of a number of small photographs making up a cinema film 8 a complete stage of play in games such as snooker and bowling

frame of mind *n* **frames of mind** the state or condition of one's mind or feelings

frame of reference *n* **frames of reference** a set or system of facts, ideas, etc., that give a particular meaning or show how a thing is placed in relation to another thing

frame-up *n* *esp. spoken* a carefully prepared plan to make someone appear guilty of a crime; invented charge against someone

framework *n* 1 a supporting frame; structure 2 a plan or system: *the framework of modern government* 3 FRAME OF REFERENCE

franc *n* the standard coin in the money system of France, Switzerland, Belgium, and many countries that formerly belonged to France ☞ MONEY

franchise *n* 1 the right to vote in a public election, esp. a parliamentary one 2 a special right or freedom given by the government or by a producer of goods to one person or one group of people, esp. to carry on a type of business in a particular place or to sell the goods produced by a particular factory

Franciscan *adj, n* a (friar) belonging to the Christian religious group called the **Order of Friars Minor**, started by St Francis in 1209

frangipani *n* a small tropical American tree with scented flowers

frank¹ *adj* free and direct in speech; open in manner; plain and honest — ~ness *n* — ~ly *adv*

frank² *v* to print a sign on a letter to show that the charge for posting has been paid

frankfurter *n* a type of small reddish smoked pork and beef sausage

frankincense *n* a type of sticky substance obtained from certain trees which is burnt to give a sweet smell, used esp. at religious ceremonies

franklin *n* a man in medieval Britain who owned a small area of land and did not have any duties to do or services to give to a lord in return for it

frantic *adj* 1 in an uncontrolled state of feeling; wildly anxious, afraid, happy, etc.: *That noise is driving me frantic* 2 *esp. spoken* marked by hurried and disordered activity — ~ally *adv*

fraternal *adj* 1 of, belonging to, or like brothers: *There's a fraternal likeness between the 2 boys* 2 friendly; brotherly: *fraternal greetings* — ~ly *adv*

fraternity *n* -ties 1 a group of men belonging to a religious organization, living together under a certain set of rules 2 any association of people having work, interests, etc., in common: *a member of the medical fraternity* 3 *esp. written* the state of being brothers; brotherly feeling

fraternize, -ise *v* -nized, -nizing 1 to meet and be friendly with someone as equals: *Army officers may not fraternize with their men* 2 to have friendly relations (with members of an enemy nation): *The soldiers were forbidden to fraternize* — -nization *n*

fratricide *n* the murder or murderer of a brother or sister — -cidal *adj*

Frau *n* (of a German woman) Mrs

fraud *n* 1 (an act of) deceitful behaviour for the purpose of gain, which may be punishable by law 2 *offensive* a person who pretends or claims to be what he is not: *People who tell your future by means of a pack of cards are frauds* 3 *offensive* a thing which is not, or does not do, what is claimed for it

fraudulence *n* behaviour or actions intended to deceive — -ent *adj* — -ently *adv*

fraught *adj* 1 full of (something that has or gives warning of a probable unpleasant result): *The journey was fraught with difficulties* 2 *esp. spoken* troubled by small anxieties **USAGE** Careful writers say that **fraught** must be followed by *with*: *fraught with danger*. However, the word is used in rather informal speech to mean that someone is worried or conditions are difficult: *You're looking very fraught, Mildred! Is there anything the matter?*

Fraulein *n* (of a German woman) Miss

fray¹ *n* **frays** *literature* (the state of activity or action of a person who joins in) a fight, game, argument, quarrel, etc.: *Are you ready for the fray?*

fray² v **frayed, fraying** 1 to make (rope, cloth, etc.) thin or worn by rubbing, so that loose threads develop 2 (of rope, cloth, etc.) to develop loose threads 3 (of a person's temper, nerves, etc.) to become worn out: *Tempers began to fray in the hot weather*

freak¹ n 1 a living creature of unnatural form 2 *esp. spoken* a person with rather strange habits or ideas 3 a peculiar happening: *By some strange freak, snow fell in Egypt a few years ago* 4 a sudden strange wish or change of mind 5 *sl* a fan: *a film freak*

freak² adj unnatural in degree or type; very unusual: *a freak storm*

freakish adj unusual; unreasonable — ~ly adv — ~ness n

freak out v adv *esp. spoken* to make or become greatly excited or anxious, esp. because of drugs — **freak-out** n

freckle n a small flat brown spot on the skin — **-led** adj

free¹ adj 1 moving about at will; not tied up, bound, or held in prison: *The prisoner wished to be free again* 2 owing no service or duty to anyone; not in the power of anyone; independent 3 self-governing; not controlled by the state; having a form of government that respects the rights of private people: *Britain is a free country* 4 without payment of any kind; given away: *a free gift* 5 not controlled or limited in any way or not accepting any control, esp. by rule or custom: *He gave me free access to his library* 6 (esp. of bodily action) natural; graceful: *free movement to music* 7 not fixed onto anything; not set in position; loose: *the free end of a flag* 8 not busy: *The doctor will be free soon* 9 not being used; not kept for anybody: *Can you find a free space to park the car?* 10 (of a way or passage) open; not blocked 11 generous; full in quantity: *She's free with her money* 12 *offensive* too friendly; lacking in respect: *The boy's manner is rather free to his teachers* 13 without (someone or something unwanted); safe from : *The old lady is never free from pain* 14 a without making or asking payment of: *free of charge* b clear of; no longer troubled by: *You'll be glad when you're free of her* 15 not prevented in any way; allowed: *She'll be free to enjoy herself soon* 16 (in chemistry) not combined with any element; pure

free² adv 1 in a free manner: *Don't let the dog run free* 2 without payment: *Babies travel free on buses* 3 in a loose position; so as to be no longer joined: *He pushed the window until it swung free*

free³ v **freed, freeing** 1 to set free 2 to make (a slave) free 3 to move or loosen (a person or thing when prevented from moving): *It took half an hour to free the trapped man* 4 to take away from (a person or animal) anything uncomfortable, inconvenient, difficult, unwelcome, etc.: *Can you free me from duty for an hour?*

freeboard n the distance between the level of

the water and **a** the upper edge of the side of a boat or **b** the top of a structure that is in water

freebooter n a person who makes war in order to seize all he can; pirate

freeborn adj not born as a slave

Free Church n a Nonconformist church

freedman *fem.* **freedwoman**— n **-men** (esp. in Roman times) a former slave freed by his master or by the law

freedom n 1 the state of being free: *The master gave the slave his freedom* 2 certain rights, often given as an honour: *They gave her the freedom of their house* 3 the power to do, say, think, or write as one pleases 4 the condition of being without something harmful or unpleasant: *freedom from pain* —compare LIBERTY

free enterprise n the carrying on of trade, business, etc., without much government control

free-fall n 1 the condition of falling freely through air or space without being held back by anything 2 the part of a jump or fall from an aircraft which is made before the jumper opens a parachute

free-for-all n *esp. spoken* an argument, quarrel, etc., in which many people join and express their opinions, esp. noisily

freehand adj (of drawing or a drawing) done by hand, without the use of a ruler or other instrument — **freehand** adv

free hand n unlimited freedom of action: *He's given his brother a free hand to direct the business*

freehanded adj generous in giving

freehold n, adj (with) ownership of land or buildings for an unlimited time and without any conditions: *They bought it freehold* —compare LEASEHOLD — ~**er** n

free house n an inn not controlled by a particular beer-making firm, but getting and selling whatever kind of beer it chooses

free kick n (in football) an unopposed kick given to one team when a rule of the game is broken by the other team

freelance¹ n, adj (done by) a writer or other trained worker, esp. a newspaper writer, who earns his money without being in the regular employment of any particular organization

freelance² v **-lanced, -lancing** to work as a freelance — **-lancer** n

free-living adj living for pleasure, esp. for food and drink — **free-liver** n

freely adv 1 willingly; readily: *I freely admit I was wrong* 2 openly; plainly: *You may speak freely* 3 without any limitation on movement or action: *Oil the wheel; then it will turn more freely* 4 generously: *He gives freely to charity* 5 in great amounts: *to bleed freely*

freeman n **-men** a person who, as an honour, has been given certain special rights in a city: *The famous politician was made a freeman of the City of London* —see also FREEDOM

Freemason also **mason**— n a man belonging to an ancient and widespread society (the **Free and**

Accepted Masons), the members of which give help to each other and to other people, treat each other like brothers, and have certain signs and words by which they are known to each other

freemasonry *n*   **1** also **masonry**— the system and practices of the Freemasons   **2** the natural unspoken understanding and friendly feeling between people of the same kind, or with the same interests, beliefs, etc.: *There's a sort of free-masonry among people who race in cars*

freepost *n* an arrangement by which a business firm pays the cost of letters sent to it by post

free-range *adj* being, concerning, or produced by hens that are kept under natural conditions in a farmyard or field —compare BATTERY

free rein *n* complete freedom of action: *Give free rein to your imagination*

free speech *n* the right to express one's ideas in public, without being prevented by the government

freestanding *adj* standing alone without being fixed to a wall, frame, or other support

freestone *n* any kind of building stone (such as sandstone or limestone) that is easily cut

freestyle *n, adj*   **1** (of) a competition or method of swimming using the crawl stroke   **2** (in wrestling) the use of movements according to choice, not set rules

freethinker *n* a person who forms his religious opinions on reason and not on Christian teaching — **-thinking** *adj*

free verse *n* poetry in a form that does not follow any regular pattern

freeway *n* **-ways** a wide high-speed road which either has no roads crossing it or has closely controlled points of entering and leaving

free will *n* the belief that every person has the power to decide freely what he will do, and that his actions are not fixed in advance by God — compare PREDESTINATION, DETERMINISM

freeze[1] *v* froze, frozen, freezing   **1** to harden into ice as a result of great cold   **2** to make or become solid at a very low temperature: *She slipped on the frozen mud*   **3** to be unable or to make unable to work properly as a result of ice or low temperatures: *The engine has frozen up*   **4** (of land, a solid surface, etc.) to become coveredwith ice and snow   **5** (of weather) to be at or below the temperature at which water becomes ice: *It froze hard last night*   **6** *esp. spoken* to be, feel, or become very cold: *It's freezing in this room*   **7** to make very cold, stiff, or without feeling: *He looks half frozen*   **8** to stop suddenly or make or become quite still   : *The teacher froze the noisy class with a single look*   **9** to become unfriendly in manner: *They sat in frozen silence*   **10** to preserve (food) by means of very low temperatures   **11** to fix prices or wages officially at a given level for a certain length of time   **12** to prevent (business shares, bank accounts, etc.) from being used, by government order

freeze[2] *n*   **1** a period of very cold icy weather   **2** a fixing of prices or wages at a certain level

freeze-dry *v* **-dried, -drying** to preserve (esp. food) by drying in a frozen state

freezer *n*   **1** also **deep freeze** — a type of large refrigerator in which frozen food can be stored for a long time   **2** also **freezing compartment** — an enclosed specially cold part of a refrigerator for making small ice blocks, storing frozen foods, etc.

freezing point *n*   **1** also **freezing** — the temperature (0 degrees Centigrade) at which water becomes ice   **2** the temperature at which any particular liquid freezes: *The freezing point of alcohol is below that of water* ⇨PHYSICS

freight[1] *n*   **1** (money paid for) the carrying of goods by some means of transport   **2** the goods carried in this way

freight[2] *v*   **1** to send (something) as freight   **2** to load (esp. a ship) with goods: *The boat is freighted with coal*

freighter *n* a ship or aircraft for carrying goods

freightliner *n* a train that carries large amounts of goods in special containers

French[1] *adj* belonging to France, its people, etc.: *French wine*

French[2] *n*   **1** the people of France   **2** the language of France ⇨ LANGUAGE

French bean *n* a type of bean having a narrow green pod, used as a vegetable of which both the bean and the pod are eaten

French dressing *n* a liquid made of oil and vinegar, used for putting on salads

French fry *n* **-fries** *esp. US* a potato chip

French horn *n* a type of brass wind instrument made of thin pipe wound round and round into a circular form, with a wide bell-shaped mouth

French kiss *n* a kiss made with the mouth open, and usu. with the tongues touching

French leave *n* absence from work or duty taken without permission (esp. in the phrase **take French leave**)

French letter *n* *esp. spoken* a (rubber) sheath —see CONDOM

French loaf *n* a type of long thin round loaf

French polish *n, v* (to treat wooden furniture with) a liquid mixture of shellac and alcohol which gives a hard and lasting shine

French windows *n* a pair of light outer doors made up of squares of glass in a frame, usu. opening out onto the garden of a house

frenetic *adj* showing frantic activity; overexcited — ~**ally** *adv*

frenzy *n* **-zies** a state of wild uncontrolled feeling; sudden, but not lasting, attack of madness: *In a frenzy of hate he killed his enemy* — **-zied** *adj* — **-ziedly** *adv*

frequency *n* **-cies**   **1** the repeated or infrequent happening of something: *The frequency of accidents on that road gives the doctors a lot of work*   **2** *technical* a rate at which something happens or is repeated: *a frequency of 200 000 cycles* *per second* 3 a particular number of radio waves per second at which a radio signal is broadcast: *This radio station broadcasts on 3 different frequencies*

frequent¹ *adj* common; found or happening often; repeated many times; habitual — ~ly *adv*

frequent² *v esp. written* to be often in (a place, someone's company, etc.)

fresco *n* -coes *or* -cos a picture or the art of painting such a picture in water colour on a plaster surface

fresh *adj* 1 in good condition because not long gathered, caught, produced, etc.; not spoilt in taste, appearance, etc., by being kept too long; new 2 (of water) not salt; drinkable 3 (of food) not preserved by added salt, tinning, bottling, freezing, or other means 4 newly prepared; newly cooked: *Let me make you a fresh pot of tea* 5 lately arrived, happened, found, grown, or supplied: *Fresh goods appear in our shops every week* 6 clean: *He put on fresh clothes* 7 (an) other and additional; renewed: *He's making a fresh attempt to pass his examination* 8 (an) other and different: *It's time to take a fresh look at this affair* 9 not tired; young, healthy, and active; strengthened: *The plants look fresh after the rain* 10 (of colour) pure; bright; clear 11 (of skin) clear and healthy 12 (of paint) newly put on; not dry 13 (of air) pure; cool 14 *often technical* (of wind) rather strong; gaining in force 15 *esp. spoken* (of weather) cool and windy 16 (of a person) inexperienced (in): *She's quite fresh to office work* 17 *esp. spoken* (too) bold with someone of the opposite sex: *She's trying to get fresh with my brother* —see also AFRESH — ~ness *n*

freshen up *v adv* to cause (someone) to feel more comfortable by washing

freshly *adv* (*before a past part.*) just lately; recently

freshwater *adj* 1 of or living in rivers or inland lakes: *freshwater fish* 2 containing water that is not sea water

fret¹ *v* -tt- 1 to be or make continually worried and anxious, dissatisfied, or bad-tempered about small or unnecessary things: *The child's fretting for his absent mother* 2 to wear away, damage, or make a pattern on by continual rubbing or biting: *Wind fretted the surface of the water*

fret² *n esp. spoken* an anxious complaining state of mind

fret³ *v* -tt- to ornament with wood cut out in patterns

fret⁴ *n* one of the raised lines on the neck of a guitar or like stringed instrument which show where to place the fingers to obtain the note one wants

fretful *adj* complaining and anxious, esp. because of dissatisfaction or discomfort — ~ly *adv* — ~ness *n*

fretsaw *n* a type of metal saw having a thin blade fixed at each end to a frame, used for cutting out patterns in thin sheets of wood

fretwork *n* 1 the art of making ornamentally cut wooden patterns 2 thin wood cut in a pattern 3 a pattern of lines and spaces: *a fretwork of sunlight and shadow*

Freudian *adj* 1 of, related to, or in accordance with the ideas and practices developed by Sigmund Freud concerning the way in which the mind works, and how it can be studied 2 *esp. spoken* concerned with or arising from ideas of sex in the mind that are not openly expressed

Freudian slip *n esp. spoken* an act of accidentally saying something different from what was intended, by which one seems to show one's true thoughts

Fri. *abbrev. for:* Friday

friar *n* a man belonging to any of several Christian religious groups who, esp. in former times, lived only by begging and had no possessions or fixed place in which to live, and who travelled around the country teaching the Christian religion and doing good works —compare MONK, NUN

friary *n* -ies a building in which friars lived, after their rules of living were changed

fricassee *v, n* -seed, -seeing (to cook) a dish of pieces of bird or other meat in a thick sauce

friction *n* 1 the force which tries to stop one surface sliding over another: *Friction gradually caused the sliding box to slow down and stop* 2 the rubbing, often repeated, of 2 surfaces together, or of one against another 3 unfriendliness and disagreement caused by 2 opposing wills or different sets of opinion, ideas, or natures: *If they have to share a room there'll probably be friction*

Friday *n* -days the 6th day of the week —see also GIRL FRIDAY, GOOD FRIDAY, MAN FRIDAY

fridge *n esp. spoken* a refrigerator, esp. in the home

friend *n* 1 a person who shares the same feelings of natural liking and understanding, the same interests, etc., but is not closely related 2 a helper; supporter; adviser; person showing kindness and understanding: *Our doctor's been a good friend to us* 3 a person from whom there is nothing to fear 4 a companion: *The dog is a faithful friend of man* —see also BOYFRIEND, GIRLFRIEND 5 *esp. written* a useful quality, condition, or thing: *Bright light is the painter's best friend* 6 a person who is being addressed or spoken of in public: *Friends, we have met here tonight ......* 7 a a person whose name one does not know, esp. one who is seen regularly or often: *What can I do for you, my friend?* b a stranger noticed for some reason, usu. with amusement or displeasure: *Our friend with the loud voice is here again*

Friend *n* a member of the Christian group called the **Society of Friends**; Quaker

friendless *adj* without friends or help — ~ness *n*

friendly *adj* -lier, -liest 1 acting or ready to act as a friend: *A friendly dog came to meet us* 2 sharing the relationship of friends (with): *Bill is* very friendly with Ben **3** favouring; ready to accept ideas: *This company has never been friendly to change* **4** kind; generous; supporting or protecting; ready to help: *You're sure of a friendly welcome here* **5** not an enemy **6** not causing or containing unpleasant feelings when in competitions, arguments, etc. — **-liness** *n*

friendly society *n* an association, usu. of workmen, to which the members pay small weekly sums, and which provides money when they are ill and/or in their old age

friendship *n* the condition of sharing a friendly relationship

frieze *n* **1** an ornamental border along the top of the wall of a building, sometimes above pillars **2** a patterned border along the top of wallpaper in a room

frigate *n* a type of small fast-moving armed naval ship, used for travelling with and protecting other ships

fright *n* **1** the feeling or experience of fear **2** an experience that causes sudden fear; shock: *You gave me a fright by knocking so loudly* **3** *esp. spoken* a person who or thing that looks silly, unattractive, or shocking

frighten also (*literature*) **fright—** *v* **1** to fill with fear **2** to influence or drive by fear: *He frightened off his attacker by calling for the police* — ~**ingly** *adv*

frightened *adj* **1** in a state of fear **2** habitually afraid: *Some people are frightened of thunder* —see also AFRAID

frightful *adj* **1** fearful; terrible; shocking: *The battlefield was a frightful scene* **2** *esp. spoken* very bad; unpleasant; difficult: *frightful weather* — ~**ness** *n* — ~**ly** *adv*

frigid *adj* **1** very cold; having a continuously low temperature **2** cold in manner; unfriendly; lacking in warmth and life: *a frigid smile* **3** (of a woman) having an unnatural dislike for sexual activity — ~**ly** *adv* — ~**ness** *n*

frigidity *n* **1** coldness of temperature **2** coldness of personal or sexual feeling

frill *n* **1** an ornamental edge to a dress, curtain, etc., made of a band of cloth of which one edge is gathered together and sewn down in tight folds, and the other edge is left free **2** an ornamental band of cut paper, put around something — ~**ed** *adj* — ~**y** *adj* — ~**iness** *n*

frills *n* **1** things that may be thought ornamental or pleasant, but are not necessary **2** behaviour that is not natural, or that is intended to make one seem different from or better than others: *There are no frills about him*

fringe¹ *n* **1** an ornamental edge of hanging threads, sometimes twisted or knotted, on a curtain, tablecloth, garment, etc. **2** a line of things which borders something: *A fringe of trees stood round the pool* **3** a short border of hair, with the lower edge usu. cut in a straight line, hanging over a person's forehead **4** a border of long hair on part of an animal, or of hairlike parts on a plant **5** the part farthest from the centre; edge: *It was*

easier to move about on the fringe of the crowd **6** a group which is only loosely connected with a political or other movement, and may not agree with it on all points —see also LUNATIC FRINGE

fringe² *v* **fringed, fringing** to act as a fringe to

fringe benefit *n* added favours or services given with a job, besides wages: *One of the fringe benefits is free meals*

frippery *n* **-ries** **1** foolish unnecessary useless ornamentation, esp. on a garment **2** a cheap useless small ornament

Frisbee *n* *trademark* a platelike piece of plastic that people throw to each other as a game

Frisian *n* a black-and-white cow of a breed that give a large quantity of milk

frisk *v* **1** to run and jump about playfully **2** *esp. spoken* to search (someone) for hidden weapons, goods, etc., by passing the hands over the body — **frisk** *n*

frisky *adj* **-ier, -iest** overflowing with life and activity; joyfully alive — **-ily** *adv* — **-iness** *n*

fritter *n* a thin piece of fruit, meat, or vegetable, covered with batter and cooked in hot fat: *apple fritters*

fritter away *v adv* to waste (time, money, etc.)

frivolity *n* **-ties** **1** the condition of being frivolous: *frivolity of mind* **2 a** a frivolous act or remark **b** any form of light pleasure or amusement: *People enjoy a few frivolities during their holidays*

frivolous *adj* unable to take important matters seriously; silly; enjoying useless pleasures: *He has a frivolous nature; he cares for nothing but amusement* — ~**ly** *adv* — ~**ness** *n*

frizz *v, n* *esp. spoken* (to force hair into) tight short wiry curls

frizzle *v* *esp. spoken* (of very hot fat, or something being cooked in hot fat) to make small exploding noises: *The sausages were frizzling in the pan*

frizzy *adj* **-ier, -iest** *esp. spoken* (of hair) very tightly and crisply curled

fro *adv* away —see TO AND FRO

frock *n* *becoming rare* a woman's or girl's dress

frock coat *n* a type of long coat for men, worn in the 19th century

frog *n* **1** any of several types of small hairless tailless animal, usu. brownish-green, that live in water and on land, have long back legs for swimming and jumping, and croak —compare TOAD **2** a fastening to a coat or other garment, often ornamental, consisting of a long button and a circular band for putting it through **3** a 3-sided horny part in the middle of the bottom of a horse's foot

frogman *n* a skilled underwater swimmer who wears an aqualung for breathing, and flippers to increase the strength of his leg movements, esp. one who works under water in this way —compare SKIN DIVER

frogmarch v **1** to force (a person) to move forward with the arms held together firmly from behind: *They frogmarched him into the yard* **2** to carry (a person) face downwards with 4 people holding the arms and legs

frogspawn n a nearly transparent mass of frog's eggs

frolic¹ v **-ck-** to play and jump about gaily

frolic² n an active and enjoyable game of amusement; playful expression of high spirits: *The children had a frolic before bedtime*

frolicsome adj playful; merry

from prep **1** (*showing a starting point in time*) beginning at: *From the moment he saw her, he loved her* **2** (*showing a starting point in place*) having left; beginning at: *a letter from Mary* **3** (*showing a starting point in rank, order, price, number, amount, etc.*): *He rose from office boy to managing director* **4** out of: *Bread is made from flour*

frond n **1** a leaf of a fern or of a palm **2** a delicate feathery leaf or leaflike part

front¹ n **1** the position directly before someone or something: *The teacher called the boy to the front* **2** the surface or part facing forwards, outwards, or upwards **3** the most forward or important position: *the front of the train* **4** **a** the most important side of a building, containing the main entrance or facing the street **b** a side of a large important building: *The west front of the church contains some fine old windows* **5** a road, often built up and having a protecting wall, by the edge of the sea, esp. at a resort —see also PROMENADE **6** the manner and appearance of a person: *He always presents a smiling front to the world* **7** a line along which fighting takes place in time of war, together with the part behind it concerned with supplies **8** a combined effort or appearance against opposing forces: *The members of the government formed a united front against the party in opposition* **9** often humour a group of people making a combined effort for some purpose: *She worked on the home front* (= in her own country), *helping to produce weapons for the army* **10** a widespread and active political movement: *The People's Front is seeking to gain supporters* **11** a line of separation between 2 masses of air of different temperature: *a cold/warm front* ☞ CLOUD **12** esp. spoken a person, group, or thing used for hiding the real nature of a secret or unlawful activity: *The import firm was a front for drug smuggling* **13 in front of a** in the position directly before **b** in the presence of

front² v (of a building) to have the front towards; face to: *The head post office fronts the railway station*

front³ adj **1** being at, related to, or coming from the front **2** being at the front: *the front row at a concert* **3** at or connected with the front of a building: *the front garden* **4** esp. spoken being a front: *They used a front organization to hide their trade in forbidden goods*

frontage n a part of a building or of land that stretches along a road, river, etc.

frontal adj **1** of, at, or to the front: *full frontal nudity* **2** (of an attack) direct; (as if) from the front **3** of or related to a weather front: *A frontal system is moving in from the west* — **-ally** adv

frontbench n government ministers or leading members of the opposition party, who sit on one of the front seats in Parliament —compare BACKBENCH — **~er** n

frontier n **1** the limit or edge of the land of one country, where it meets the land of another country **2** the border between settled and wild country, esp. that in the US in the past: *The frontier in America was rough and lawless in the old days* **3** a border between the known and the unknown: *The frontiers of medical knowledge are being pushed farther back*

frontispiece n a picture or photograph at the beginning of a book, on the left-hand page opposite the title page

front line n **1** the most advanced or responsible position: *in the front line of the fight against disease* **2** a line along which fighting takes place in time of war or the part behind it concerned with supplies — **front-line** adj

front-page adj esp. spoken very interesting, important, or exciting; worthy of being printed on the front page of a newspaper

front rank n the highest position of importance or quality: *This painter is not in the front rank* — **front-rank** adj

front-runner n a person who has the best chance of success in competing for something

frost¹ n **1** weather at a temperature below the freezing point of water; frozen condition of the ground and/or air: *Frost can kill off a young plant* **2** a period or state of this **3** a white powdery substance formed on outside surfaces from very small drops of water when the temperature of the air is below freezing point: *The grass was covered with frost* **4** **of frost** technical below the freezing point of water: *There was 5 degrees of frost last night*

frost² v **1** to make or become covered with frost: *The cold has frosted the windows* **2** to roughen the surface of a sheet of glass so that it is not possible to see through

frostbite n swelling, discoloration, and sometimes poisoning of a person's limbs, caused by a great cold

frostbitten adj **1** suffering from frostbite: *frostbitten toes* **2** (of a plant) damaged or killed by frost

frostbound adj (of the ground) hardened by frost

frosting n esp. US icing

frosty adj **-ier, -iest 1** a stingingly cold; cold with frost: *a frosty day* **b** covered or seeming to be covered with frost **2** unfriendly; cold: *a frosty greeting* — **-ily** adv — **-iness** n

froth¹ n **1** a white mass of bubbles formed on top of or in a liquid, or in the mouth; foam **2**

offensive a light empty show of talk or ideas: *The play was nothing but froth* — ~**y** *adj* — ~**ily** *adv* — ~**iness** *n*

froth² *v* **1** to make or throw up froth: *The beer frothed as it was poured out* **2** to produce froth on or in: *Froth up the soap mixture*

frown¹ *v* **1** to draw the brows together in anger or effort, so as to show disapproval or to protect the eyes against strong light, causing lines to appear on the forehead **2** (of a thing) to have a dangerous or unfriendly appearance when seen from below: *The mountains frown down on the plain* — ~**ingly** *adv*

frown² *n* **1** a serious or displeased look, causing lines on the forehead; act of frowning **2** the lines left on the forehead by this act

frowzy, -sy *adj* **-zier, -ziest** *offensive* (of a person, clothes, etc.) not neat or clean for a long time, esp. when in an enclosed space

froze *past tense of* FREEZE

frozen *past part. of* FREEZE

frugal *adj* **1** not wasteful; careful in the use of money, food, etc.: *frugal habits* **2** small in quantity and cost: *a frugal supper of bread and cheese* — ~**ly** *adv* — ~**ity** *n*

fruit¹ *n* **1** an object that grows on a tree or bush, contains seeds, is used for food, but is not usu. eaten with meat or with salt **2** these objects in general, esp. considered as food **3** a type of this object: *Apples, oranges, and bananas are fruit* **4** *technical* a seed-containing part of any plant **5** a result, good or bad: *His failure is the fruit of laziness*

fruit² *v* (of a tree, bush, etc.) to bear fruit

fruitcake *n* a cake containing small dried fruits, nuts, etc.

fruit cocktail *n esp. US* a mixture of small pieces of fruit eaten at the beginning or end of a meal

fruiterer *n* a person who sells fruit, esp. in a shop

fruit fly *n* **-flies** any of several types of small fly that feed on fruit or decaying vegetable matter

fruitful *adj* **1** successful; useful; producing good results: *a fruitful meeting* **2** *old use* (of living things) bearing many young or much fruit — ~**ly** *adv* — ~**ness** *n*

fruition *n* fulfilment (of plans, aims, desired results, etc.): *The plan was finally brought to fruition*

fruitless *adj* (of an effort) useless; unsuccessful; not bringing the desired result: *The search proved fruitless* — ~**ly** *adv* — ~**ness** *n*

fruit machine *n* ONE-ARMED BANDIT

fruits *n* **1** plants used for food or from which food can be produced, such as vegetables, corn, etc.: *the fruits of the earth* **2** rewards: *to enjoy the fruits of one's work*

fruit salad *n* a dish made of several types of fruit cut up and served at the end of a meal

fruity *adj* **-ier, -iest** **1** like fruit; tasting or smelling of fruit **2** *sl* amusing in an improper direct way, esp. about matters of sex: *a rather fruity story* **3** *esp. spoken* (of voice) too rich and deep

frump *n offensive* a dull old-fashioned woman (or man), esp. one who wears old-fashioned clothes — ~**ish** *adj* — ~**y** *adj*

frustrate *v* **-trated, -trating** **1** to prevent the fulfilment of; defeat (someone or someone's effort): *The weather frustrated our plans* **2** to cause to have feelings of annoyed disappointment: *2 hours' frustrating delay* — **-ation** *n*

fry¹ *v* **fried, frying** **1** to cook in hot fat or oil **2** *esp. spoken* to have the skin burnt: *We shall fry in this hot sun*

fry² *n* **fry** a small fish that has just come out of its egg —see also SMALL FRY

frying pan *n* **1** a flat long-handled pan, used for frying food esp. in the home **2** **out of the frying pan into the fire** out of a bad position into a worse one

fry-up *n esp. spoken* a frying of various foods, such as eggs, sausages, potatoes, etc., in order to make a quick meal

ft *abbrev. for:* **1** foot **2** feet

fuchsia¹ *n* any of several types of graceful garden bush with hanging bell-like flowers in 2 colours of red, pink, bluish-red, or white

fuchsia² *adj, n* (of) a bright reddish-purple colour

fuddle *v* **-dled, -dling** to make (a person, the mind, etc.) slow and unable to work clearly, esp. as a result of drinking too much alcohol — **fuddle** *n*

fuddy-duddy *n* **-duddies** *offensive* a person who does not understand or approve of modern ideas

fudge¹ *v* **fudged, fudging** **1** to put together roughly or dishonestly: *This writer has fudged up a lot of old ideas* **2** to avoid taking firm determined action on (something): *The government have fudged the issue of equal rights*

fudge² *n* a type of soft creamy light brown sweet made of sugar, milk, butter, etc.

fuel¹ *n* **1 a** (a type of) material that is used for producing heat or power by burning: *Wood, coal, oil, gas, and petrol are different kinds of fuel* **b** material that can be made to produce atomic power **2** something that increases anger or any other strong feeling: *Being asked to work longer hours added fuel to the flames of their discontent*

fuel² *v* **-ll-** to provide with   fuel

fug *n* a heavy unpleasant airless condition of a room or other enclosed space caused by heat, smoke, or the presence of many people: *There's a fug in here; please open the window* — ~**gy** *adj*

fugitive¹ *adj* **1** escaping; running away **2** *esp. literature or written* **a** hard to keep present in the mind: *a fugitive thought* **b** passing rapidly; not lasting, esp. in interest or importance: *The value of most newspaper writing is only fugitive*

fugitive² *n* a person escaping from the law, the police, danger, etc.: *a fugitive from justice*

fugue *n* 1 a piece of music in which one or 2 tunes are repeated or copied by voices or instrumental parts which begin one after the other, and continue to repeat and combine the tunes with small variations so as to make a pattern 2 musical writing in this form

führer, fueh- *n* German a leader or guide; ruler who has unlimited power

fulcrum *n* **-crums** *or* **-cra** the point on which a lever turns or is supported in lifting or moving something

fulfil *v* **-ll-** 1 to do or perform: *A nurse has many duties to fulfil* 2 to carry out (an order, conditions, etc.); obey 3 to keep or carry out faithfully (a promise, agreement, etc.) 4 to supply or satisfy (a need, demand, or purpose) 5 to make or prove to be true; cause to happen as appointed or predicted: *His belief that the world would end was not fulfilled* 6 to make true; carry out (something wished for or planned, such as hopes, prayers, desires, etc.) 7 to develop and express the abilities, character, etc., of (oneself) fully: *She fulfilled herself as a mother*

fulfilment *n* 1 the act of fulfilling or condition of being fulfilled: *His plans have come to fulfilment* 2 satisfaction after successful effort: *a sense of fulfilment*

full[1] *adj* 1 (of a container) filled with liquid, powder, etc., as near to the top as is convenient in practice 2 (of a container) filled to the top 3 (of a space) containing as many people, objects, etc., as possible; crowded: *a full train* 4 containing or having plenty (of): *Her eyes were full of tears* 5 *esp. spoken* well fed, often to the point of discomfort; satisfied: *I can't eat any more; I'm full up* 6 complete; whole: *the full truth of the matter* 7 the highest or greatest possible: *He drove at full speed* 8 possessing all the rights or qualities of the stated position: *Only full members are allowed to vote* 9 a having the mind and attention fixed only (on): *full of her own importance* b overflowing (with a feeling, quality, etc.): *full of excitement* 10 (of a part of a garment) wide; flowing; fitting loosely 11 (of a shape, a body, or its parts) a round; rounded; fleshy: *full breasts* b *polite* fat: *This shop sells dresses for the fuller figure* 12 (of colour, smell, sound, taste, or substance) deep, rich, and powerful: *wine with a full body* 13 *literature* having had one's share and more: *He died full of years and honours* —see also (at) full PELT, in full SWING, (at) full TILT

full[2] *adv* 1 straight; directly: *The sun shone full on her face* 2 very; quite: *They knew full well that he had lied*

full[3] *n* 1 the greatest height, degree, point, etc.: *The tide's at the full* 2 **in full** completely: *The debt must be paid in full*

fullback *n* (esp. in football) a defending player whose position is at the end of his own half of the field, or the farthest from the centre

full-blooded *adj* 1 of unmixed race: *a full-blooded Indian* 2 forceful: *a full-blooded*

argument 3 having all typical qualities to a great degree: *a full-blooded socialist* — ~**ness** *n*

full-blown *adj* fully developed: *The fighting may develop into a full-blown war*

full board *n* (in lodgings, hotels, etc.) the providing of all meals

full circle *adv* through a set of developments that lead back to the starting point: *It's January 1st; the year has come full circle*

fuller *n* a person whose work is to clean and thicken newly made cloth

fuller's earth *n* a type of dried clay sometimes made into a powder, used in former times for removing oil from cloth, but now used esp. in treating impure oils

full house *n* 1 (at a theatre, cinema, sports ground, etc.) as large an attendance of people as possible 2 (in the card game of poker) 3 cards of one kind, and a pair of another kind

full-length *adj* 1 (of a photograph, painting, etc.) showing a person from head to foot 2 (of a garment) reaching to the ground 3 (of a play, book, etc.) not short; not shorter than is usual

full moon *n* the moon when seen as a circle

fullness, fulness *n* 1 *esp. written* completeness: *In the fullness of her joy, she could hardly speak* 2 the condition of being full

full-scale *adj* 1 large; making use of all known facts, information, etc.: *He's writing a full-scale history of 19th century France* 2 (of an activity) of not less than the usual kind; not shortened, lessened, etc., in any way; total: *a full-scale war* 3 using all one's powers, forces, etc.: *a full-scale attack*

full stop[1] *also* **period, point**— *n* a point (.) marking the end of a sentence or a shortened form of a word

full stop[2] *adv* see PERIOD (*adv*)

full-throated *adj* using the voice freely; loud

full-time *adj, adv* 1 working or giving regularly the proper number of hours or days in an employment, course of study, etc. —compare PART-TIME 2 **a full-time job** *esp. spoken* an activity or duty that leaves one no free time

full toss *also* **full pitch**— *n technical* (esp. in cricket) a throw in which the ball has not bounced when it arrives at the place it was aimed at — **full toss** *adv*

fully *adv* 1 quite; at least: *It's fully an hour since he left* 2 completely; altogether: *fully trained*

fully-fashioned *adj* (of a knitted garment) made to fit the body exactly

fully-fledged *adj* 1 (of a young bird) having grown all the feathers, and now able to fly 2 completely trained: *a fully-fledged nurse*

fulminate *v* **-nated, -nating** to declare one's opposition very strongly and angrily: *My grandfather fulminates against the youth of today* — **-ation** *n*

fulness *n* fullness

fulsome *adj* giving an unnecessarily and unpleasantly large amount of praise: *He was too fulsome in his praise* — ~**ly** *adv* — ~**ness** *n*

fumble v **-bled, -bling** 1 to move the fingers or hands awkwardly in search of something, or in an attempt to do something 2 to handle (something) without neatness or skill; mishandle: *The cricketer fumbled the catch* — **-bler** n

fume v **fumed, fuming** 1 to show signs of great anger and restlessness (often in the phrase **fume and fret**) 2 to give off fumes

fumes n heavy strong-smelling air given off from smoke, gas, fresh paint, etc., that causes a pricking sensation when breathed in

fumigate v **-gated, -gating** to clear of disease, bacteria, or harmful insects by means of chemical smoke or gas: *The man was declared infectious and his clothes and bed had to be fumigated* — **-gation** n

fun n 1 playfulness: *The little dog's full of fun* 2 amusement; enjoyment; pleasure or its cause: *Have fun at the party tonight* 3 amusement caused by laughing at someone else: *He's become a figure of fun* 4 **for fun** also **for the fun of it** | **the thing**— for pleasure; without serious purpose

function[1] n 1 a special duty (of a person) or purpose (of a thing): *The function of a chairman is to lead and control meetings* 2 **a** a public ceremony: *The Queen attends many official functions* **b** *esp. spoken* a large or important gathering of people for pleasure or on some special occasion 3 **a** a quality or fact which depends on and varies with another: *The size of the crop is a function of the quality of the soil and the amount of rainfall* **b** *technical* (in mathematics) a relationship in which every member of one set (the DOMAIN) is linked with exactly one member (the IMAGE) of another set (the RANGE) **c** a variable which depends on another variable according to such a function: *In X = 5y, X is a function of y* ☞ MATHEMATICS

function[2] v (esp. of a thing) to be in action; work: *The machine doesn't function properly*

functional adj 1 made for or concerned with practical use without ornamentation: *functional furniture* 2 made for or having a special purpose 3 *medical* (of a disease or disorder) having an effect only on the working of an organ, not on the organ itself —compare ORGANIC — ~ly adv

functionary n **-ries** usu. offensive a person who has unimportant or unnecessary official duties

fund[1] n 1 a store or supply (of non-material things) ready for use as needed: *The speaker had a fund of examples to prove his points* 2 a supply or sum of money set apart for a special purpose: *the school sports fund*

fund[2] v esp. technical to provide money for (an activity, organization, etc.): *The work is funded by the government*

fundamental[1] adj 1 (of a non-material thing) deep; being at the base, from which all else develops: *a fundamental difference between their aims* 2 (of a non-material thing) of the greatest importance; having a greater effect than all others: *a fundamental cause of his success* 3 (of a non-material thing) very necessary: *Fresh air is fundamental to good health* 4 (of a quality) belonging to a person's or thing's deep true character

fundamental[2] n a rule, law, etc., on which a system is based; necessary or important part: *A fundamental of good behaviour is consideration for others*

fundamentalism n the belief in and support of the older teachings of the Christian Church, esp. concerning the exact truth of the words of the Bible — **-ist** n, adj

fundamentally adv in every way that matters, is important, or is related to the true deep character of someone or something: *She is fundamentally unsuited to office work*

funds n money in one's possession, ready for use: *My funds are a bit low*

funeral n 1 a ceremony, usu. religious, of burying or burning a dead person 2 a procession taking a dead person to be buried or burned 3 *esp. spoken* a difficulty or unpleasantness that concerns or will concern someone alone: *If you choose to do it, it's your funeral*

funerary adj technical suited or used for a funeral: *a funerary urn*

funereal adj heavy and sad; suitable to a funeral: *We all sat in funereal silence* — ~ly adv

funfair n 1 a noisy brightly lit show which for small charges offers big machines to ride on, games of skill, and other amusements, esp. one that moves from town to town 2 also **amusement park**— an outdoor area where such a show is held

fungicide n a chemical substance used for preventing or destroying fungus

fungous adj technical of, like, or related to fungus

fungus n **-gi** or **-guses** 1 any of several types of simple fast-spreading plant without flowers, leaves, or green colouring matter, which may be in a large form, (mushrooms, toadstools, etc.), or in a very small form, (mildew, mould, etc.) ☞ PLANT, EVOLUTION 2 **a** these plants in general, esp. considered as a disease **b** these plants in a large group 3 a disagreeable thing of sudden growth or appearance: *A fungus of ugly little houses sprang up* — **-goid** adj — **-gal** adj

funicular also **funicular railway**— n a small railway up a slope or a mountain, worked by a thick metal rope, often with one carriage going up as another comes down

funk[1] n esp. spoken a state of great fear; inability to face a difficulty or an unpleasant duty

funk[2] v to avoid or try to avoid because of fear or lack of will: *We funked telling her the truth*

funky adj **-ier, -iest** (of jazz or like music) having a simple coarse style and feeling, like the blues

funnel[1] n 1 a metal chimney for letting out smoke from a steam engine or steamship 2 a tubelike vessel that is large and round at the top and small at the bottom, used in pouring liquids or powders into a vessel with a narrow neck

funnel² v -ll- 1 to pass through or as if through a funnel 2 (esp. of something large or made up of many parts) to pass through a narrow space: *The large crowd funnelled through the gates* 3 to form into the shape of a funnel: *He funnelled his hands*

funnily adv 1 a in a strange or unusual way b in an amusing way 2 **funnily enough** strange to say

funny adj -nier, -niest 1 amusing; causing laughter 2 strange; hard to explain; unusual: *What can that funny noise be?* 3 esp. spoken out of order; not quite correct; rather dishonest: *There's something funny about the telephone; it won't work* 4 esp. spoken a slightly ill: *She felt a bit funny* b slightly mad: *He went rather funny after his wife died* 5 esp. spoken deceiving; using tricks; too clever: *Don't get funny with me* — -niness n

funny bone n esp. spoken the tender part of the elbow, which hurts very much if it is knocked sharply

fur¹ v -rr- to make or become covered with fur

fur² n 1 the soft thick fine hair that covers the body of some types of animal, such as bears, rabbits, cats, etc. —compare HAIR 2 a hair-covered skin of certain types of animal, such as foxes, rabbits, mink, etc., which has been or will be treated and used for clothing 3 (a garment) made of one or more of these 4 a greyish covering on the tongue 5 a hard covering on the inside of pots, hot-water pipes, etc., caused by lime in heated water —see also SCALE

furbish v 1 to make (something of metal that has not been used for a long time) bright and shining 2 to improve the appearance of (something old and worn): *We're furbishing up our house with a fresh coat of paint* 3 to put (something out of use) back into working condition: *You'll need to furbish up your French* —see also REFURBISH

furious adj 1 very angry in an uncontrolled way —see ANGRY (USAGE) 2 powerful: *a furious blow* 3 wild; uncontrolled: *a furious temper* — ~ness n — ~ly adv

furl v 1 to roll or fold up and bind (a sail, flag, fan, umbrella, etc.) 2 to be able to be rolled or folded up

furlong n (a measure of length equal to) 220 yards or 201 metres

furlough n absence from duty, usu. for a length of time, esp. as permitted to government officers, soldiers, and others serving outside their own country; holiday —see HOLIDAY (USAGE)

furnace n 1 an apparatus in a factory, in which metals and other substances are heated to very high temperatures in an enclosed space 2 a large enclosed fire used for producing hot water or steam

furnish v 1 to put furniture in (a room or building); supply with furniture 2 esp. written to supply (what is necessary for a special purpose)

furnishings n articles of furniture or other articles fixed in a room, such as a bath, curtains, etc.

furniture n all large or quite large movable articles that are placed in a house, room, or other area, in order to make it convenient, comfortable, and/or pleasant to live in such as beds, chairs, tables, etc.

furore n a sudden burst of angry or excited interest among a large group of people

furrier n a person who prepares furs for use as clothing, makes fur garments, and/or sells them

furrow¹ n 1 a long narrow track cut by a plough in farming land when the earth is being turned over in preparation for planting 2 any long deep cut or narrow hollow between raised edges, esp. in the earth 3 a deep line or fold in the skin of the face, esp. the forehead

furrow² v to make furrows in

furry adj -rier, -riest of, like, or covered with fur

further¹ adv, adj (comparative of FAR) 1 more: *Don't try my patience any further* 2 farther: *too tired to walk any further* 3 later: *There'll be a further performance*

further² v to help (something); advance; help to succeed: *to further the cause of peace*

furtherance n esp. written helping forward; continuation: *He's gone to the university for the furtherance of his studies*

further education also (esp. US) **adult education**— n education after leaving school, but not at a university

furthermore adv also; in addition

furthermost adj most distant; farthest away

further to prep esp. written (used esp. in business letters) in order to give additional information on the same subject as: *Further to our letter of February 5th....*

furthest adv, adj (superlative of FAR) farthest

furtive adj quiet, secret, and/or not direct, as expressing guilty feelings; trying or hoping to escape notice: *The thief was furtive in his movements* — ~ly adv — ~ness n

fury n furies 1 very great anger 2 a state of very great anger: *fly into a fury for the slightest reason* 3 a wildly excited state (of feeling): *a fury of impatience* 4 wild force or activity: *the fury of the storm* 5 esp. spoken a fierce angry woman or girl: *Jane's a little fury if she can't get what she wants*

Fury n Furies one of 3 snake-haired goddesses in ancient Greek beliefs, who punished crimes

furze n gorse

fuse¹ n 1 a long string treated with an explosive powder, or a narrow pipe filled with this powder, used for carrying fire to an explosive article and so causing it to blow up: *He lit the fuse and ran for shelter* 2 an apparatus screwed into a bomb, shell, or other weapon, which causes it to explode when touched, thrown, etc.

fuse² *n* **1** a (small container with a) short thin piece of wire, placed in an electric apparatus or system, which melts if too much electric power passes through it, and thus breaks the connection and prevents fires or other damage: *A fuse has blown* ⇨ ELECTRICITY **2** *esp. spoken* a failure of electric power, owing to the melting of one of these

fuse³ *v* **fused, fusing** **1** (of metal) to melt or cause to melt in great heat: *Lead fuses at a low temperature* **2** to join or become joined by melting: *Copper and zinc are fused to make brass* **3** to stop or cause to stop working owing to a fuse: *The lights have fused* **4** to unite

fused *adj* (of a piece of electric apparatus) fitted with a fuse

fuselage *n* the main body of an aircraft, in which travellers and goods are carried ⇨ AEROPLANE

fusillade *n* a rapid continuous firing of shots

fusion *n* **1** (a) melting or joining together by melting: *This metal is formed by the fusion of 2 other types of metal* ⇨ ATOM **2** (a) uniting or mixing: *The British nation is the result of the fusion of several races*

fuss¹ *n* **1** unnecessary, useless, or unwelcome expression of excitement, anger, impatience, etc.: *What a fuss about nothing!* **2** an anxious nervous condition: *to get into a fuss* **3** a show of annoyance probably resulting in punishment: *There's sure to be a fuss when they find the window's broken* **4** unwanted or unnecessary activity; hurry: *What's all this fuss about?*

fuss² *v* **1** to act or behave in a nervous, restless, and anxious way over small matters **2** to make nervous

fusspot also **fussbudget**— *n esp. spoken* a very fussy person

fussy *adj* **-ier, -iest** **1** *usu. offensive* nervous and excitable about small matters **2** *usu. offensive* too much concerned about details: *He's fussy about his food* **3** *esp. spoken* concerned; caring: *Are you fussy what time we have dinner?* **4** *offensive* (of dress, furniture, etc.) having too much ornament — **fussily** *adv* — **fussiness** *n*

fustian *n* *becoming rare* (made from) a type of rough heavy cotton material

fusty *adj* **-tier, -tiest** *offensive* **1** (of a room, box, clothes, etc.) having an unpleasant smell as a result of having been shut up for a long time, esp. when damp **2** not modern — **-tiness** *n*

futile *adj* **1** *often offensive* (of an action) having no effect; unsuccessful; useless **2** *offensive* (of a person) worthless; of no importance; lacking ability to succeed — **-lity** *n*

future *adj, n* **1** (belonging to or happening in) the time after the present: *The future is unknown to us* **2** (expected, planned, arranged, etc., for) the life in front of a person; that which will happen to someone or something: *I wish you a happy future* **3** (in grammar) (being) the tense of a verb that expresses what will happen at a later time: *The future (tense) of English verbs is formed with the help of "shall" and "will"* **4** *esp. spoken* likelihood of success: *There's no future in this job*

futureless *adj* having nothing to expect or hope for

futures *n* *technical* (agreements or contracts for) goods bought and sold in large quantities at the present price, but not produced or sent till a later time: *Cotton futures (=cotton crops not yet grown) are selling at high prices*

futuristic *adj* of strange modern appearance; having no connection with known forms of art — ~**ally** *adv*

futurity *n* **-ties** **1** future time **2** what will happen or exist in the future

fuzz¹ *n* *esp. spoken* **1** fluff **2** a mass or light fine growth of short hair that stands up

fuzz² *n* *sl* the police

fuzzy *adj* **-ier, -iest** *esp. spoken* **1** (of hair) standing up in a light short mass **2** not clear in shape, esp. at the edges; misty: *The television picture is fuzzy tonight* **3** (of cloth, a garment, etc.) having a raised soft hairy surface **4** (of a substance) like a fine soft mass of hair — **fuzzily** *adv* — **fuzziness** *n*

G

G, g **G's, g's** *or* **Gs, gs** the 7th letter of the English alphabet

G¹ the 5th note in the musical scale of C major or the musical key based on this note

G² *abbrev. for:* *technical* the gravitational constant

G, g *abbrev. for:* the force on a given object due to gravity at the earth's surface

g *abbrev. for:* *technical* acceleration due to gravity

gabardine, -erdine *n* a strong material often used for making coats

gabble *v, n* **-bled, -bling** (to say) words or word-like sounds spoken so quickly that they cannot be heard clearly

gable *n* the 3-cornered upper end of a wall where it meets the roof — ~**d** *adj*

gad about also **gad around**— *v prep; adv* **-dd-** *esp. spoken* to travel round for enjoyment — **gadabout** *n*

gadget *n esp. spoken* a small machine or useful apparatus

gadgetry *n esp. spoken* gadgets generally

Gaelic *adj* of one of the Celtic languages, esp. that of Scotland, or those of Ireland and the Isle of Man

gaff *n* **1** a stick with a strong hook, used to pull big fish out of the water **2** **blow the gaff** *sl* to let a secret become known

gaffe *n* a remark or act which means something

unpleasant to other people, though the person who makes or does it does not think so at the time

gaffer n **1** (a name for) an old man, esp. in the country **2** sl a boss

gag¹ v **-gg- 1** to put a gag into the mouth of **2** to prevent from speaking or expressing something **3** esp. US to be unable to swallow and start to vomit

gag² n **1** something put over or into the mouth to keep it still or esp. to prevent the person from talking or shouting **2** esp. spoken a joke or funny story

gaggle n **1** a number of geese together **2** a group of noisy talkative people, esp. women

gaiety n **-ties 1** also **gayness**— the state of being gay **2** joyful events and activities

gain¹ n **1** the act of making a profit; increase in wealth **2** a profit; increase in amount

gain² v **1** to obtain (something useful, necessary, wanted, etc.): to gain experience **2** to make (a profit or increase in amount): The car gained speed **3** (of a watch or clock) to move too fast and show a time later than the correct time **4** esp. written to reach, esp. with effort or difficulty: We finally gained the summit

gainful adj esp. written for which one is paid: gainful employment — ~**ly** adv

gain on also **gain upon**— v prep to reduce the distance between oneself and (a competitor)

gait n a way or manner of walking: a rolling gait

gaiter n either of a pair of cloth or leather coverings used formerly to cover the leg from knee to ankle, or just the ankle, and still sometimes worn formally by priests

gala adj, n (of) a feast-time or special public amusement

galactic adj of or concerning a galaxy

galantine n a dish made of meat cut into small pieces, shaped into a loaf, cooked with spices and eaten cold

galaxy n **-ies 1** any of the large groups of stars which make up the universe **2** a splendid gathering of people, esp. those famous, beautiful, or clever

Galaxy n the large group of stars in which our own sun lies —see also MILKY WAY

gale n **1** a weather condition in which a strong wind blows **2** a sudden noise, esp. laughter: A gale of laughter came from inside

gall¹ n **1** old use bile **2 a** a feeling of bitterness or hatred **b** sl rudeness

gall² n **1** a painful place on an animal's skin, esp. on that of a horse **2** a swollen place on a tree or plant

gall³ v to hurt or be painful to: Her unkind remarks galled me

gallant n literature a man, usu. young, who is very well-dressed and/or attentive to women

gallantry n **-tries** literature **1** (an act of) polite attention paid by a man to a woman **2** (an act of) bravery, esp. in battle — **gallant** adj

gall bladder n an organ of the body, like a small bag, in which bile or gall is stored ☞ DIGESTION

galleon n a large sailing ship, formerly used esp. by the Spaniards

gallery n **-ries 1** a private room, hall, or building where works of art are shown and usu. offered for sale **2** a public building where paintings (and perhaps other works of art) are shown **3** an upper floor built out from an inner wall of a hall or theatre, from which activities below may be watched, esp. the highest one with the cheapest seats **4** a covered passage, open on one side **5** a long narrow room, such as one used for shooting practice **6** a level underground passage in a mine or joining natural caves

galley n **-leys 1** a ship which was rowed by slaves, esp. an ancient Greek or Roman warship **2** a ship's kitchen

galley proof also **galley**— n any of the long sheets of paper on which a printer prints a book so that mistakes can be corrected before it is divided into pages

Gallic adj **1** of the ancient country of Gaul, or race of Gauls **2** French

gallicism n a French word or expression, used in English or another language

gallivant v esp. spoken to go around amusing oneself

gallon n a measure for liquids, 8 pints or 4 quarts (in Britain 4·54, in America 3·78 litres)

gallop¹ n **1** the fastest movement of a horse, when all 4 feet come off the ground together **2** a ride at this speed **3** a rush

gallop² v **1** to go, or cause to go, at a gallop **2** (of a person or animal) to go very fast

gallows n **gallows** the wooden frame on which murderers used to be killed by hanging from a rope

gallows humour n literature a type of humour which makes unpleasant or dangerous people or things seem funny —compare BLACK humour

gallstone n a hard stone in the gall bladder

Gallup poll n trademark a special count of opinions in a country, esp. so as to guess the result of a political election, by questioning a number of people chosen to represent the whole population

galore adj (in) plenty: money galore

galosh n an overshoe

galvanism n the production of electricity by chemical means, esp. as in a battery

galvanize, -ise v **-nized, -nizing 1** to put a covering of metal, esp. zinc, over (a sheet of another metal, esp. iron), by using electricity — compare ELECTROPLATE **2** to shock into action: Fear galvanized him into action

galvanometer n an instrument for measuring small electric currents

gambit n **1** (in chess) a set of moves in which a piece is risked for later advantage **2** an action or esp. use of language which is used to produce a future effect, esp. as part of a trick or clever plan —compare PLOY

gamble¹ v -bled, -bling 1 a to play cards or other games for money; risk money on horse races b to risk one's money in business 2 to take the risk that something will go well, or as one wishes, after doing something that depends on it — **-bler** n

gamble² n a risky matter or act

gamboge n a deep yellow colour

gambol v -ll- to jump about in play, as lambs do — **gambol** n

game¹ n 1 a form of play or sport, or one example or type of this —see also GAMES 2 a set of things, usu. a board and counters which are used to play such a game indoors 3 a single part of a set into which a match is divided, as in tennis 4 wild animals, some birds and some fish, which are hunted or fished for food, esp. at certain seasons as a sport —see also BIG GAME 5 a trick or secret plan: *What's your game?* 6 **fair game** a troublesome animals which can fairly be shot b a person who can justly be attacked in words 7 **Two can play at that game** You are not the only one that can get advantages by behaving in such a way, I can too!

game² v gamed, gaming to gamble

game³ adj 1 brave and ready for action: *a game fighter* 2 willing: *Who's game for a swim?* — **~ly** adv

game⁴ also (*esp. spoken*) gammy— adj (of a limb, esp. a human leg) unable to be used properly because of something wrong

gamekeeper n a man employed to raise and protect game, esp. birds, on private land

games n games 1 a school subject, including the playing of team games and other forms of bodily exercise out of doors 2 (in names) a particular set of games and sports competitions: *the Olympic Games*

gamesmanship n the art of winning by using the rules to one's own advantage without actually cheating

gamete n either of 2 cells, one male and one female, that join together to form a compound cell (ZYGOTE) in fertilization

gamma n 1 the 3rd letter of the Greek alphabet(Γ, γ) 2 a mark for between average and only fair work by students

gamma ray n -rays a beam of short wave radiation, which goes through solid objects

gammon n the meat from the back part and leg of a pig when it has been preserved by smoke or salt

gammy adj esp. spoken (of a limb)game

gamp n esp. spoken & humour an umbrella, esp. a large one

gamut n the whole range of a subject, including the smallest details and the most general ideas

gamy, gamey adj -ier, -iest (of meat) having the strong taste of game which has been kept for some time before cooking — **gaminess** n

gander n 1 a male goose 2 esp. spoken a look

gang n 1 a group of people working together,

such as prisoners or building workers 2 a group of criminals 3 *often offensive* a group of friends who are against other groups

gangling adj unusually tall, thin, and awkward

ganglion n a mass of nerve cells

gangplank n a wooden board used to make a bridge to get into or out of a ship or to pass from one ship to another

gangrene n a disease which is the decay of the flesh of part of the body because blood has stopped flowing there, usu. after a wound — **-grenous** adj

gangster n a member of a gang of criminals, esp. those who use guns to threaten and kill

gangway¹ n -ways 1 an opening in the side of a ship and the gangplank connecting it to the land —compare COMPANIONWAY 2 a clear space between 2 rows of seats in a cinema, theatre, bus, or train; aisle

gangway² interj Make room!; Get out of the way!

gannet n -nets or -net a type of fish-eating seabird

gantry n -tries a metal frame which is used to support movable heavy machinery or railway signals

gaol n, v jail — **~er** n

gaolbird n esp. spoken a jailbird

gap n 1 an empty space between 2 objects or 2 parts of an object: *a gap in the fence* 2 an amount of distance or difference 3 a lack (of something): *There are gaps in my knowledge*

gape v gaped, gaping 1 to look hard in surprise, esp. with the mouth open △ GAWP 2 to come apart or open: *His shirt gaped open*

garage¹ n 1 a building in which motor vehicles can be kept 2 a place where petrol can be bought and cars repaired

garage² v -aged, -aging to put in a garage

garb¹ n literature or humour clothing of a particular style, esp. that which shows one's type of work or appears unusual

garb² v to dress

garbage n esp. US rubbish

garble v -bled, -bling to repeat in a confused way which falsifies the facts: *a garbled account*

garden¹ n 1 a piece of land, often near a house, on which flowers and vegetables may be grown 2 a public park with flowers, grass, paths, and seats

garden² v to work in a garden, making plants grow — **~er** n — **~ing** n

garden city n -cities a town or suburb planned and built to have plenty of grass, trees, and open spaces —compare NEW TOWN

gargantuan adj very big

gargle¹ v -gled, -gling to wash the throat with liquid by blowing through it at the back of the mouth

gargle² n 1 an act of gargling 2 liquid with which one gargles

gargoyle n a hollow figure of a man or animal

on a roof or wall, esp. of a church, through whose mouth rain water is carried away ⇒ CATHEDRAL

garish adj unpleasantly bright: *garish colours* — ~**ly** adv — ~**ness** n

garland v, n (to place) a circle of flowers, leaves, or both, round the neck for ornament or as a sign of victory

garlic n an onion-like plant whose strong-tasting root (CLOVE) is used in cooking

garment n esp. written (the name used, esp. by the makers, for) an article of clothing

garnet n a type of jewel or its deep red colour

garnish¹ v to add to (something) as an ornament and, in the case of food, as an improvement to its taste —see DECORATE (USAGE)

garnish² n a sauce, pieces of fruit, or any of the things which are used to make food look and taste better

garret n a usu. small unpleasant room at the top of a house; attic

garrison¹ n 1 a group of soldiers living in a town or fort and defending it 2 a fort or camp where such soldiers live

garrison² v to guard in a garrison: *The soldiers garrisoned the town*

garrotte¹ n 1 a metal collar or wire which may be tightened round the neck to strangle a person 2 an act of putting to death by this means

garrotte² v -rotted, -rotting to put to death by tightening a garrotte

garrulous adj habitually talking too much, esp. about unimportant things — ~**ly** adv — **-lity** n — ~**ness** n

garter n 1 a band of elastic material worn round the leg to keep a stocking up 2 (**the Order of**) **the Garter** the highest title given in the English honours system

gas¹ n gases 1 (a type of) substance like air, which is not solid or liquid ⇒ PHYSICS 2 a substance of this type which is burnt in the home to supply heat for the rooms and cooking and formerly for light 3 also **laughing gas**— such a substance, called **nitrous oxide**, used as a general anaesthetic by a dentist while he pulls a tooth out 4 US esp. spoken petrol ⇒ REFINERY 5 esp. spoken unimportant talk 6 **step on the gas** to increase the speed (of the car) — ~**eous** adj

gas² v -ss- 1 to poison with gas 2 to talk a long time about unimportant things

gas chamber n a room which can be filled with gas to put animals or people to death

gash n, v (to make) a large deep cut or wound

gasholder also **gasometer**— n a very large round metal container from which gas is piped to houses and buildings

gasify v -fied, -fying to make or become gas — **-fication** n

gasket n a flat piece of soft material which is placed between two surfaces so that oil, gas, etc., cannot escape ⇒ CAR

gasoline, -lene also (esp. spoken) **gas**— n US petrol

gasp v 1 to catch the breath suddenly and audibly esp. because of surprise, shock, lack of air, etc. 2 to say while breathing in this way: *He gasped out the message* — **gasp** n

gas ring n a small round metal gas pipe with holes to release gas. It is used for cooking

gassy adj -sier, -siest 1 full of (a) gas 2 having the qualities of (a) gas — **gassiness** n

gastric adj of or belonging to the stomach

gastroenteritis n a painful illness in which the stomach, intestines, etc., are swollen causing diarrhoea

gastronomy n the art and science of cooking and eating good food — **-nomic** adj — **-nomically** adv

gasworks n gasworks a place where gas for use in the home is made from coal

gate n 1 a movable frame, often barred, which closes an opening in a fence, wall, etc. 2 either of a pair of large frames as used to control the water level at locks, or to close the road at a level crossing 3 a gateway

gateau n -teaux French a specially attractive type of large cream cake from which slices are cut

gatecrash v to join a party uninvited — ~**er** n

gatepost n a post to support or fasten a gate

gateway n -ways 1 an opening in a fence, wall, etc., across which a gate may be put 2 a way of finding: *Hard work is the gateway to success*

gather¹ v 1 to come or bring together: *Gather round, and I'll tell you a story* 2 to obtain (information or qualities) bit by bit: *He gathers facts about UFOs* 3 to collect or pick: *Gather your toys up* 4 to understand from something said or done: *I didn't gather much from the confused story* 5 to draw (material) into small folds

gather² n something produced by gathering: *She made gathers in the skirt*

gathering n a meeting

gauche adj French awkward (in social behaviour); doing and saying the wrong things — ~**rie** n

gaudy adj -dier, -diest too bright in colour and/or with too many ornamental details — **-dily** adv — **-diness** n

gauge¹ n 1 a standard measure of weight, size, etc., to which objects can be compared 2 the thickness of wire or certain metal objects, or the width of the barrel of a gun 3 the distance between the rails of a railway or between the wheels of a train 4 an instrument for measuring size, amount, etc., such as the width of wire, the amount of rain

gauge² v gauged, gauging 1 to measure by means of a gauge 2 to judge the worth, meaning, etc., of

gaunt adj 1 thin, as if ill or hungry —compare HAGGARD 2 (of a place) bare and unattractive — ~**ness** n

gauntlet¹ n 1 (in former times) a soldier's

metal-covered glove ☞ ARMOUR **2** a long protective glove covering the wrist

gauntlet² n (esp. in former times) a punishment, in which 2 rows of men beat a man running between them (only in the phrase **run the gauntlet** = to experience violent attack)

gauze n fine net-like material which can be seen through, sometimes used in medicine to cover wounds, or as a curtain — **gauzy** adj

gave past tense of GIVE

gavel n a small hammer used by a chairman, a judge in America, or an auctioneer selling things in public, who strikes a table with it to get attention

gavotte n a merry, fast dance from France, danced esp. in former times, or the music for this

gawk v to look at something foolishly

gawky adj **-kier, -kiest** (of a person) awkward in movement — **-kiness** n

gawp v to look at something foolishly, esp. with the mouth open △ GAPE

gay adj **gayer, gayest 1** cheerful **2** bright or attractive, so that one feels happy to see it, hear it, etc.: *gay colours/music* **3** only concerned with pleasure: *the gay life* **4** *esp. spoken* homosexual — ~**ness** n

gaze¹ v **gazed, gazing** to look steadily — **gazer** n

gaze² n a steady fixed look

gazebo n **-bos** a place where one can sit in the sun, such as a summerhouse

gazelle n **-zelles** or **-zelle** any of a number of types of antelope, which jump in graceful movements and have beautiful large eyes

gazette n, v **gazetted, gazetting** (to print in) a newspaper, esp. one from the government giving lists of people who have been employed by them, important notices, etc.

gazetteer n an alphabetical list of names of places, as at the end of a book of maps

gazump v *sl* to refuse to sell a house to (someone who thinks he has bought it) and sell instead to someone who has offered more money

GCE *abbrev. for:* General Certificate of Education; an examination in one of many subjects set by various universities and taken in schools by pupils aged 15 or over

gear¹ n **1** a set of things collected together, esp. when used for a particular purpose: *climbing gear* **2** an apparatus or part of a machine which has a special use in controlling a vehicle: *steering gear* **3 a** any of several arrangements, esp. of toothed wheels in a machine, which allows power to be passed from one part to another so as to control the power, speed, or direction of movement ☞ MACHINERY **b** a gearwheel **4** *sl* clothes

gear² to supply with gears

gearbox n a metal case containing the gears of a vehicle

geared up adj in a state of esp. anxious excitement and expectation about an activity

gear lever also **gear stick**— n the apparatus which controls the gears of a vehicle

gear to v prep to connect (something) closely to (something else): *Education should be geared to children's needs*

gearwheel n a toothed wheel that can move or be moved by another wheel of the same sort

gecko n **-os** or **-oes** a type of lizard esp. of tropical countries

gee-gee n (used esp. by or to children or humour sl) a horse

geese pl. of GOOSE

geezer n *sl* a man, often one who is thought to be a little peculiar

Geiger counter n an instrument for finding and measuring radioactivity

geisha also **geisha girl**— n a Japanese girl who is trained to dance, sing, and perform the various arts which amuse men

gel¹ n *technical* a substance in a state between solid and liquid; jelly

gel² v **-ll-** to jell

gelatine also (*esp. technical*) **gelatin**— n a clear substance which comes out of boiled animal bones, used for making jellies — **-nous** adj

geld v to remove the testicles of (certain male animals)

gelding n an animal, usu. a horse, that has been gelded

gelignite n a very powerful explosive

gem n **1** a precious stone, esp. when cut into a regular shape **2** a thing or esp. person of especial value

Gemini n **1 a** the third division of the belt of stars (ZODIAC) represented by twins **b** the group of stars (CONSTELLATION) formerly in this division **2** a person born under this sign ☞ ZODIAC

gen n *sl* the information —see also GENNED-UP

gendarme n *French* a French soldier who acts as a policeman

gender n **1** (in grammar) the state of being masculine, feminine, or neuter **2** *esp. spoken* the division into male or female; sex

gene n any of several small parts of the threadlike parts (CHROMOSOMES) in the centre (NUCLEUS) of cells. Each of these parts controls the development of the qualities in a living thing which have been passed on (INHERITED) from its parents

genealogy n **-gies** (the study of) the history of the members of a family up to the present, or a description or representation of this — **-gist** n — **-logical** adj — **-logically** adv

genera pl. of GENUS

general¹ adj **1** concerning or felt by everybody or most people: *general anxiety* **2** not limited to one thing, place, etc.: *general education* **3** not detailed; describing the main things only: *Give me a general idea* **4** chief: *Major-General* **5 general practice** the part of the medical service in which one doctor treats all illnesses; job of a family doctor —see also GENERAL PRACTITIONER **6 in general a** also **as a general rule**— usually **b** (*after* *a pl. noun*) most: *People in general like her* — compare GENERALLY

general² *n* an officer of very high rank in the army or in command of an army

general election *n* an election in which all the voters in the country take part at the same time to choose the members of parliament

generality *n* **-ties** **1** the quality of being general **2** *literature* the greater part **3** a general statement; point for consideration which is not at all detailed

generalize, -ise *v* **-ized, -izing** **1** to make a general statement (about) **2** to form or state an opinion after considering a small number of the facts **3** to put into a more general form that covers a larger number of cases — **-ization, -isation** *n*

generally *adv* **1** usually **2** by most people: *The plan has been generally accepted* **3** without considering details, but only the main points

general practitioner *n* a doctor who is trained in general medicine and who treats people in a certain local area

general staff *n* the officers in an army who work for the commanding officers

general strike *n* the stopping of work by most of the workmen in the country at the same time

generate *v* **-rated, -rating** **1** *esp. written* to cause to exist **2** *technical* to produce (heat or electricity): *a generating station*

generation *n* **1** the act or action of generating: *Falling water may be used for the generation of electricity* **2** a period of time in which a human being can grow up and have a family, perhaps 25 or 30 years **3** a those who are the same number of steps from an ancestor: *We belong to the same generation* **b** people of roughly the same age group **4** all the members of any developing class of things at a certain stage: *second generation computers*

generative *adj* having the power to produce or generate

generator *n* a machine which generates, usu. electricity —compare DYNAMO, MAGNETO

generic *adj* **1** of or concerning a genus **2** shared by or typical of a whole class of things — ~**ally** *adv*

generosity *n* **-ties** **1** the quality of being generous **2** a generous act

generous *adj* **1** showing readiness to give money, help, kindness, etc. **2** in large amounts: *a generous meal* — ~**ly** *adv*

genesis *n* **-ses** *esp. written* the beginning or origin: *the genesis of space travel*

genetic *adj* of or concerning genes or genetics — ~**ally** *adv*

genetics *n* the study of how living things develop according to the effects of those substances passed on in the cells from the parents —see also GENE, HEREDITY — **-icist** *n*

genial *adj* cheerful and kind; good-tempered — **-ally** *adv* — ~**ity** *n*

genie also **djinn**— *n* **-nies** *or* **-nii** a magical spirit in Arab fairy stories

genitals also **genitalia**— *n* the outer sex organs — **genital** *adj* — **genitally** *adv*

genitive *adj, n* (in grammar) (a form or a word) showing esp. possession or origin —compare POSSESSIVE

genius *n* **1** great ability, esp. in producing works of art **2** a person of such ability or of very high intelligence **3** a special ability, sometimes unpleasant in effect: *a genius for mathematics* USAGE **Genius** is a very strong word: *Einstein was a genius.* **Talent** is a less strong word. **Skill** and **ability** can be learnt, unlike **talent** and **genius** which are inborn. One born with a **capacity** or **aptitude** for something may develop **skill** if taught. **Competence** is a satisfactory but not unusual degree of **skill.** A **faculty** is a **skill** or **talent** in one area: *the faculty of learning by heart.*

genned-up *adj* *sl* well-informed —see also GEN

genocide *n* the act of killing a whole group of people, esp. a whole race

genre *n* *French* a class of works of art or literature according to their type of subject

genteel *adj* **1** unnaturally polite, esp. so as to appear socially important **2** *old use* very polite, and thus known to be of a high social class — **-teelly** *adv* — **-tility** *n*

gentian *n* (the blue flower of) any of various plants that grow in mountainous areas

gentile *adj, n* (a person who is) not Jewish

gentle *adj* **1** kind and ready to help others **2** soft in movement: *a gentle wind* **3** *old use* high-born — ~**ness** *n* — **-ly** *adv*

gentlefolk also **gentlefolks**— *n* people of high social class; gentry

gentleman *n* **-men** **1** a man who behaves well and can be trusted to act honourably **2** *polite* a man **3** (in former times) a man who had a private income and did not need to work —compare LADY — ~**ly** *adj*

gentleman's agreement *n* an unwritten agreement made between people who trust each other

gentleman's gentleman *n* a valet

gentle sex also **fair sex**— *n* women considered as a group

gentry *n* people of high social class

Gents, Gents' *n* *esp. spoken* a public lavatory for men

genuflect *v* to bend the knee as a sign of religious respect — ~**tion** *n*

genuine *adj* (of an object or feelings) real — ~**ly** *adv* — ~**ness** *n*

gen up *v adv* **-nn-** *sl* to learn, or inform of the facts thoroughly: *We genned him up*

genus *n* **genera** a division of a family of living things, which usu. includes several closely related species —see also GENERIC

geocentric *adj* having, or measured from, the earth (world) as the central point

geography *n* the study of the world and its countries, seas, rivers, towns, etc. ⊚ — **-pher** *n* — **-phical** *adj* — **-phically** *adv*

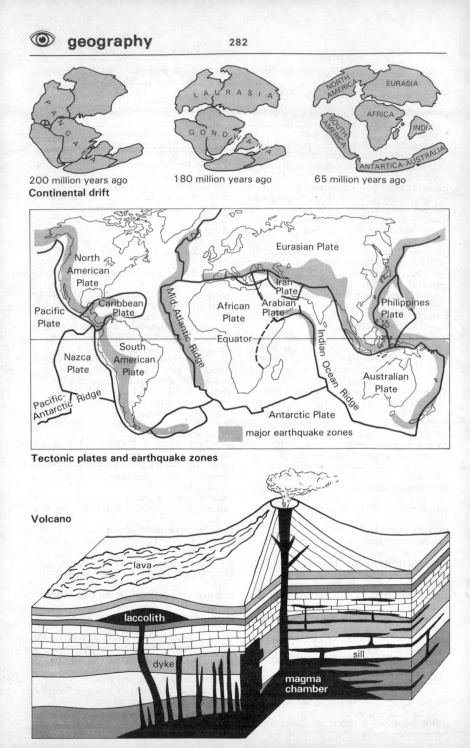

200 million years ago · 180 million years ago · 65 million years ago
Continental drift

North American Plate · Pacific Plate · Caribbean Plate · Nazca Plate · South American Plate · Pacific-Antarctic Ridge · Mid-Atlantic Ridge · African Plate · Equator · Iran Plate · Arabian Plate · Eurasian Plate · Indian Ocean Ridge · Philippines Plate · Australian Plate · Antarctic Plate

major earthquake zones

Tectonic plates and earthquake zones

Volcano

lava · laccolith · dyke · sill · magma chamber

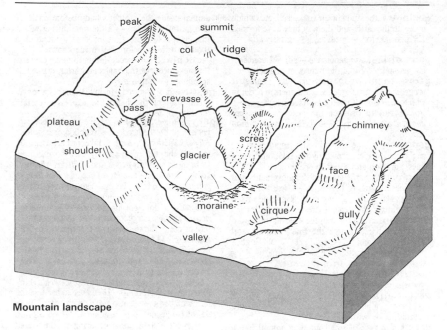

Mountain landscape

Features of the coastline

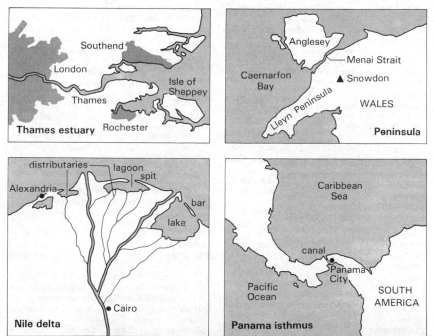

Thames estuary

Peninsula

Nile delta

Panama isthmus

geology *n* the study of the rocks, soil, etc. which make up the earth, and the way they have formed ⏤ GEOGRAPHY — **-gical** *adj* — **-gically** *adv* — **-gist** *n*

geometrical also **geometric**— *adj* **1** concerning geometry **2** like the figures in geometry

geometrical progression also **geometric progression**— *n* a sequence of numbers in order in which each is multiplied by a fixed number (COMMON RATIO) to produce the next: *In the geometrical progression 1, 2, 4, 8, 16, ... the common ratio is 2*

geometry *n* the study in mathematics of the angles and shapes formed by the relationships of lines, surfaces, and solids in space

geophysics *n* the study of the movements and activities of parts of the earth — **-ical** *adj*

georgette *n* thin strong cloth, esp. made from silk, from which women's dresses may be made

Georgian *adj* **1** of, or in the style of, the period of rule of King George the First, Second, and Third, esp. from 1714 to 1811 **2** of English poetry and other literature of the time of King George the 5th, esp. from 1912 to 1922

geotropism *n* (a) movement of a plant part towards or away from the pull of gravity

geranium *n* any of many closely-related types of garden or pot plant with red or white flowers, and scented leaves with rounded lobes

gerbil *n* a type of small jumping animal like a mouse, found in the deserts of Africa and Asia and often kept as a pet

geriatrics *n* the medical treatment and care of old people — **-ic** *adj* — **-trician** *n*

germ *n* **1** a very small invisible creature living on food or dirt or in the body, so causing disease —compare BACTERIA, MICROBE **2** a beginning point, esp. of an idea **3** also **germ cell**— a small part or cell of a living thing which can grow into a new plant, animal, etc.

German *adj* **1** of or from Germany **2** of the language of Germany, Austria, and large parts of Switzerland ⏤ LANGUAGE — **~ic** *adj*

germane *adj* relevant: *a germane idea*

German measles *n* an infectious disease in which red spots appear briefly on the body. It may damage unborn children if caught by their mothers

germicide *n* a substance which kills germs

germinal *adj* in the earliest stage of development —see GERM

germinate *v* **-nated, -nating** **1** to start growing or cause to start growing **2** to develop or cause to develop — **-nation** *n*

germ warfare *n* BIOLOGICAL WARFARE

gerrymander *n* to divide (an area) for election purposes so as to give an unfair advantage to one side

gerund *n* a verbal noun

gestapo *n* *German* secret police using cruel methods, esp. the secret police of the Nazi period in Germany in the 1930's-1940's

gestation *n* **1** the carrying of a child or young animal inside the mother's body before birth **2** also **gestation period** — **a** the time during which this happens **b** the time of development of a thought or idea, before it is made known

gesticulate *v* **-lated, -lating** to make expressive movements of the hands and arms, esp. while speaking — **-lation** *n*

gesture *n, v* **-tured, -turing** (to make) a movement, usu. of the hands, to express a certain meaning or feeling

get *v* **got, getting** **1** to receive or experience: *I got a blow on the head* **2 a** to obtain or acquire: *I'll get something to eat* **b** to take, or deal with **3** to reach the start of an activity: *Get moving!* **4** to bring (something) to a start: *I'll get the car going* **5** (to cause oneself to) become: *The food's getting cold* **6** to be; become : *to get trapped* **7** to bring (into a certain state): *I'll get them dressed* **8** to cause to do: *I got him to help* **9** to move to or arrive at: *We got there early* **10** to put or move into or out of the stated place: *Get that cat out of the house* **11** to succeed in (doing): *If I get to get him I'll ask* **12** to catch (an illness) **13** *esp. spoken* to understand: *He never gets the message* **14** *esp. spoken* to annoy or cause strong feeling to: *That gets me where it hurts* **15** *esp. spoken* to hit: *I got him with a potato* **16** *old use* to become the father of; beget —see also **get/be with** CHILD **17** to defeat (someone) in an argument: *I'll get him on that point* **18** to come or bring to the stated degree of success: *My son is really getting somewhere* **19 get (something) done** **a** to cause (something) to be done; have **b** *esp. spoken* to experience (something being done to one) **c** *esp. spoken* to do (something necessary): *I'll just get these dishes washed* **20 get above oneself** to have too good an opinion of oneself **21 get (something or someone) right/wrong** *esp. spoken* to understand (something or someone) correctly/wrongly USAGE In writing it is better to avoid **get**, and to use **become, receive, obtain, move,** etc., according to the meaning. —see also GET ACROSS, GET AROUND, GET AWAY WITH, GET BY, GET DOWN, GET DOWN TO, GET HOME, GET OFF WITH, GET ON, GET ON FOR, GET ONTO, GET OUT OF, GET OVER, GET ROUND, GET ROUND TO, GET THROUGH, GET TOGETHER, GET UP, GET UP TO

get across also **get over**— *v adv* to be or cause to be understood or accepted: *Did your speech get across to the crowd?*

get around also **get round**— *v prep* to avoid or find a way to deal with (something) to one's advantage: *To get around the tax laws*

get-at-able *adj* accessible

getaway *n* **-ways** *esp. spoken* an escape: *They made a clean getaway*

get away with *v adv prep* to succeed in (a deceit)

get by *v adv* **1** to continue one's way of life: *To get by on a small income* **2** to be good enough but not very good: *Your work will just get by*

get down *v adv* **1** (of children) to leave the table after a meal **2** to swallow with difficulty: *Get the medicine down* **3** to record in writing **4**

to make (someone) feel nervous, ill, or sad: *The bad weather is getting me down*

get down to *v adv prep* to begin to give serious attention to: *to get down to work*

get home also **go home**— *v adv* (usu. of an unpleasant truth about the person spoken to) to be understood as intended

get off with *v adv prep esp. spoken* to start a relationship with (someone of the other sex)

get on *v adv* 1 to be friends 2 to become later or older: *Time is getting on* 3 to continue, often after interruption or despite difficulty: *Get on with your work!* 4 to hurry 5 to succeed: *To get on in one's job*

get on for *v adv prep* to be almost reaching, in time, age, or distance : *Grandfather is getting on for 80*

get onto *v prep* 1 to get in touch with (someone) 2 to learn of deceit by (someone): *The police finally got onto him* 3 to be elected or appointed to 4 to begin to talk about or work at: *How did we get onto that subject?* 5 to enter esp. as a passenger: *They got onto the plane at Cairo*

get out of *v adv prep* 1 to escape or cause to escape responsibility for: *He tried to get out of helping his mother* 2 to be able to stop or leave: *to get out of a bad habit* 3 to force (something) from (someone): *The police got the truth out of him* 4 to gain from: *What does he get out of gambling?*

get over¹ *v adv* 1 to reach the end of (something): *You'll be glad to get your operation over* 2 GET ACROSS

get over² *v prep* 1 to return to one's usual state of health, happiness, etc., after a bad experience of or with: *to get over an illness* 2 to find a way to deal with: *Can we get over this difficulty?* 3 I **can't/couldn't get over** I am/was very much surprised at

get round¹ *v adv esp. spoken* to travel

get round² *v prep* 1 GET AROUND 2 to persuade (someone) to accept one's own way of thinking

get round to *v adv prep* to do (a task) at last, after a long interval

get through¹ *v adv* 1 to reach someone, esp. by telephone 2 to be or cause to be understood by (someone): *Get it through to him that he must rest* 3 to finish 4 to pass or be passed through a parliament

get together *v adv* to have a meeting or party: *When can we get together?*

get-together *n* a friendly informal meeting for enjoyment

getup *n esp. spoken* 1 a set of clothes, esp. unusual clothes 2 the outer appearance

get up *v adv* 1 to rise or cause to rise from bed in the morning 2 to leave or cause to leave one's bed after illness 3 (of a wind, fire, etc.) to arise and increase 4 to arrange or perform: *to get up a play* 5 to study: *to get up one's notes* 6 to ornament or change the appearance of: *She got*

herself up in a new dress 7 to increase the amount of: *get up steam/speed*

get up to *v adv prep* to reach: *What page have you got up to?*

gewgaw *n* a bright attractive valueless ornament or toy

geyser *n* 1 a natural hot water spring which from time to time rises suddenly into the air 2 an apparatus which is used in kitchens, bathrooms, etc., for heating water by gas

ghastly *adj* -lier, -liest 1 (of a person) very pale and ill-looking 2 causing great fear: *ghastly news* 3 *esp. spoken* very bad: *We had a ghastly time at the party* — **-liness** *n*

ghee, ghi *n Indian & Pakistani* melted butter, as used in India, often made from buffalo milk

gherkin *n* a small green cucumber which is usually eaten after being pickled in vinegar

ghetto *n* -tos a part of a city in which a group of poor people live who are usu. not accepted as full citizens

ghost¹ *n* 1 (the spirit of) a dead person who appears again 2 **the ghost of a** the slightest — **~ly** *adj* — **~liness** *n*

ghost² *v* to write in someone else's name for money

ghoul *n* 1 a spirit which (in Eastern stories) takes bodies from graves to eat them 2 a person who delights in (thoughts of) dead bodies and other nasty things — **~ish** *adj* — **~ishness** *n*

GHQ *abbrev. for:* General headquarters

GI *n* **GI's** or **GIs** a soldier in the US army, esp. during World War 2

giant *n* 1 a man who is much bigger than is usual 2 a very big, strong creature in fairy stories in the form of a man, but often unfriendly to human beings and very cruel and stupid 3 a person of great ability: *a giant among writers* 4 something very large: *That packet is a giant* — **giant** *adj*

giant panda also **panda**— *n* a large bearlike animal that has black and white fur, eats bamboo shoots, and lives in China

gibber *v* (of monkeys and men) to talk or appear to talk very fast (sometimes because of fear) in a way that is meaningless to the hearer — **~ish** *n*

gibbet *n* (in former times) the gallows or wooden post with another piece at right angles at the top, used to hang criminals

gibbon *n* any of several types of small ape with no tail and long arms, which lives in trees

gibe, jibe *n* a remark which makes someone look foolish, or points out someone's faults: *Don't make gibes about her behaviour*

gibe at, jibe at *v prep* **gibed, gibing at** to make a gibe about

giblets *n* the parts, such as the heart and liver, of a bird which are taken out before the bird is cooked, but are edible when cooked

giddy¹ *adj* -dier, -diest 1 feeling unsteady, as though everything is moving round oneself and/or as though one is falling **2** causing a feeling of unsteady movement and/or falling: *a giddy height* **3** not serious; too interested in amusement: *She's a giddy thing* — **giddily** *adv* — **giddiness** *n*

gift *n* **1** something which is given freely; present **2** a natural ability to do something: *a gift for music* **3** *sl* something obtained easily, or cheap at the price

gifted *adj* **1** having one or more special abilities; talented **2** more intelligent than most

gig¹ *n* a small 2-wheeled one horse carriage used esp. in former times

gig² *n* *sl* a job, esp. a musician's job for a certain period

gigantic *adj* unusually large in amount or size — ~ally *adv*

giggle¹ *v* -gled, -gling to make giggles

giggle² *n* a form of uncontrollable laughter esp. by young girls

gigolo *n* -los **1** a man who is paid to dance with a woman as her partner **2** *offensive* a man who is paid to be a woman's lover and companion

gild *v* **1** to cover thinly in gold or gold paint **2** to make bright as if with gold — ~er *n* — ~ing *n*

gilded *adj* fortunate and rich

gill¹ *n* a measure equal to ¼ pint or 0·142 litres

gill² *n* **1** one of the organs through which a fish breathes by taking in water to pass over them **2** *esp. spoken & humour* the area of skin around the neck and under the ears

gillie, gilly *n* -lies (in Scotland) a man who serves a sportsman while he is shooting or fishing

gilt *n* shiny material, esp. gold, used as a thin covering

gilt-edged *adj* **gilt-edged shares/stock/securities** shares, esp. those offered for public sale by the Government, paying a small rate of interest but unlikely to fail

gimlet *n* a tool which is used to make holes in wood so that screws may enter easily —compare AWL, BRADAWL

gimmick *n* *esp. spoken* **1** a trick object or part of an object which is used to draw attention **2** a special way of acting or point of appearance which is noticeable: *an advertising gimmick* — ~y *adj*

gin¹ *n* a machine, esp. one for separating cotton from its seeds

gin² *n* a colourless alcoholic drink made from grain and certain berries

ginger¹ *n* **1** a plant with a hot strong root which is used in cooking **2** the quality of being active

ginger² *adj, n* (of) an orange-brown colour, esp. the least usual colour of human hair

ginger ale also **ginger beer**— *n* a gassy drink made with ginger

gingerbread *n* a cake or biscuit with ginger in it

gingerly *adj, adv* (in a way that is) careful and controlled in movement so as not to cause harm: *He gingerly picked it up*

ginger nut also **ginger snap**— *n* a hard biscuit with ginger in it

ginger up *v adv* to make more effective, exciting, or active: *Ginger up your ideas*

gingham *n* a type of woven checked cotton used for girl's dresses and tablecloths

gipsy *n* -sies **1** a member of a dark-haired race which may be of Indian origin and now travels about in carts, motor vehicles, and caravans, earning money as horse dealers, musicians, fortune tellers, etc. **2** *esp. spoken & sometimes offensive* a person who habitually wanders

giraffe *n* **giraffes** *or* **giraffe** a type of African leaf-eating animal with a very long neck and legs and orangeish skin with dark spots ⊰ MAMMAL

gird *v* **girded** *or* **girt, girding** *esp. written & literature* to fasten round/with: *The climber girded himself with a rope*

girder *n* a strong beam, usu. of iron or steel, which supports the smaller beams in a floor or roof or forms the support of one part of a bridge

girdle¹ *n* **1** an undergarment for women meant to hold the flesh firm; sort of light corset **2** a cord tied round the waist to hold loose clothes in **3** *literature* something which encircles something else

girdle² *v* -dled, -dling to enclose or surround

gird on *v adv* *esp. literature* to fasten on, usu. a belt: *He girded his sword on*

gird up *v adv* *esp. literature* to roll (clothes) up to the waist

girl *n* **1 a** a young female person **b** a daughter: *My little girl is ill* **2** *esp. spoken* a woman: *the girls' football team* **3 a** a woman worker: *shop girls* **b** (esp. formerly) a female servant **4** a girlfriend **5** **old girl a** *old use* a friendly way of speaking to a woman **b** a female former pupil of a school

girl Friday *n* -days a female secretary or helper in an office who does all the useful and important jobs that the man in charge wants done

girlfriend *n* a girl companion, esp. one with whom a boy or man spends time and shares amusements

girl guide *n* a member of an association for girls, the **Girl Guides**, who take part in activities like camping, and learn useful skills —compare BOY SCOUT

girlhood *n* the state or time of being a young girl

girlie, girly *adj* *esp. spoken* showing young women with (almost) bare bodies in sexy and exciting poses: *a girlie magazine*

girlish *adj* like or suitable to a girl — ~ly *adv* — ~ness *n*

giro *n* **giros** a system of British banking in which a central organization runs the accounts which are held at different branches, esp. that used by the Post Office (**National Giro**)

girt *past tense and past part.* of GIRD

girth *n* a band which is passed tightly round the

middle of a horse, donkey, etc., to keep a load or saddle firm

gist *n* the general meaning, esp. of a long statement; main points (as of an argument)

give¹ *v* **gave, given, giving** **1** to pass into someone's hands or care: *Give me the baby* **2** to hand (something) over as a present **3** to pay in exchange: *She gave him a pound for his help* **4** to cause to experience: *The news gave us a shock* **5** to produce: *Cows give milk* **6** to allow to have: *Give me a chance* **7** to be the cause of (someone's illness): *He's given me flu* **8** to set aside (time, thought, strength, etc.) for a purpose **9** to tell in words: *Give me more information* **10** to show: *That clock gives the right time* **11** to offer (a performance or amusement): *We are giving a party* **12** to admit the truth of: *It's too late now. I give you that* **13** to allow (part of one's body) to be used by another person: *She gave him her hand to shake* **14** to do an action: *She gave a shout* **15** to cause to believe because of information given: *I was given to understand that he was ill* **16** to bend or stretch under pressure: *The leather will give with wearing* **17** **give it to someone straight** *sl* to scold someone in an angry or direct way **18** **give (someone) what for** *sl* to scold severely, or perhaps beat, (someone) **19** **give way (to) a** to yield, as in an argument or when driving a car **b** to break **c** to become less useful or important than: *Steam trains gave way to electric trains* **d** to allow oneself to show (esp. a feeling) **20** **What gives?** *sl* (showing surprise) What's going on? —see also GIVE OFF, GIVE ONTO, GIVE OUT, GIVE OVER, GIVE OVER TO, GIVE UP ON — **giver** *n*

give² *n* the quality of moving (esp. bending, stretching, or loosening) under pressure: *There is give in leather*

give-and-take *n* willingness of each person to yield to (some of) the other's wishes

giveaway *n* **-ways** **1** something unintentional that makes a secret known: *Her tears were a dead giveaway of her real feelings* **2** **at giveaway prices** very cheap

given¹ *adj* **1** fixed for a purpose and stated as such: *Do it within the given time* **2** if allowed or provided with: *I'd come and see you in Austria, given the chance* **3** (at the end of official papers) written, signed, and marked with the date: *given on the 15th day of April, in the year 1543* **4** **be given to** to be in the habit of: *He's given to taking long walks*

given² *prep* if one takes into account

give off *v adv* to send out (esp. a liquid, gas, or smell)

give onto also **give on—** *v prep* to have a view of, or lead straight to: *The window/door gives onto the garden*

give out *v adv* **1** to give to each of several people: *Give out the examination papers* **2** also **run out—** *esp. spoken* to come to an end: *Our food has given out* **3** *esp. spoken* to stop working: *The engine gave out* **4** to make known publicly: *The news was given out* **5** to send out (esp. a noise): *The radio is giving out a signal*

give over *v adv* **1** *esp. spoken* to stop (doing something): *Give over hitting your little brother* **2** to deliver to someone's care: *We gave him over to the police*

give over to *v adv prep* **1** to set (a time or place) apart for **2** also **give up to—** to give (oneself or something) completely to (something): *to give oneself over to one's work*

give up on *v adv prep* *esp. spoken* to have no further hope for

gizzard *n* the second stomach of a bird where food is broken into powder with the help of small stones it has swallowed

glacé *adj French* **1** (of fruits) covered with sugar or sugar syrup **2** (of leather, silk, etc.) smooth and shiny

glacial *adj* **1** of or concerning ice or glaciers **2** of or concerning an ice age **3** *esp. spoken* very cold

glacier *n* a mass of ice which moves very slowly down a mountain valley ☞ GEOGRAPHY

glad *adj* **-dd-** **1** (of people) pleased and happy about something **2** causing happiness: *glad news* **3** *polite* very willing: *I'll be glad to help you* — ~**ness** *n* — ~**ly** *adv*

gladden *v* to make glad or happy: *The sight gladdened his father's heart*

glade *n* *literature* an open space in a wood or forest

gladiator *n* an armed man in ancient Rome who fought against men or wild animals in the arena — ~**ial** *adj*

gladiolus *n* **-li** *or* **-luses** a type of garden plant with sword-shaped leaves and tall, brightly-coloured flowers

glad rags *n* *esp. spoken* fine clothes; (one's) best clothes

glamorize, -ise *v* **-rized, -rizing** to make (something) appear better, more attractive, etc., than in reality — **-rization** *n*

glamorous, -ourous *adj* having or causing glamour: *a glamorous job/girl* — ~**ly** *adv*

glamour *n* **1** charm and beauty with a romantic power of attraction: *the glamour of foreign countries* **2** personal charm which excites admiration and esp. attracts men to women

glance¹ *v* **glanced, glancing** **1** to give a rapid look: *He glanced at his watch* **2** to flash with reflected light: *The glasses glanced in the firelight* **3** **glance one's eye down/over/through, etc.** to give a hurried reading or look

glance² *n* **1 a** a rapid look: *One glance told me he was ill* **b** a rapid movement of the eyes **2** a flash of light, usu. from a bright object **3** a blow which slips to the side: *A sudden glance of the sword cut his shoulder* **4** **at a glance** with one look; at once

glance off *v adv; prep* to touch with a light blow and move off at once

glancing *adj* (of a blow) which slips to one side — ~**ly** *adv*

gland _n_ an organ of the body which produces a liquid substance, either to be poured out of the body or into the blood stream — ~**ular** _adj_

glare¹ _v_ **glared, glaring** **1** to shine with a strong light and/or unpleasantly: _The sun glared out of the blue sky_ **2** to look in an angry way

glare² _n_ **1** a hard, unpleasant effect given by a strong light: _a red glare over the burning city_ **2** an angry look or stare **3** a state which continually draws the attention of the public: _the glare of publicity_

glaring _adj_ **1 a** (of light) hard and too bright **b** (of colours) too bright **2** (of mistakes) very noticeable **3** fierce-looking: _glaring eyes_ — ~**ly** _adv_

glass _n_ **1** a hard transparent solid material made from sand melted under great heat **2** a collection of objects made of this: _glass and china_ **3** an object made of or containing this, and shaped to make things seem larger, esp. a telescope **4** a drinking vessel **5** an apparatus with a pointer which indicates when bad weather is coming; barometer **6** _esp. spoken_ a mirror

glassblower _n_ a person who blows into hot liquid glass in order to shape it, and who can make bottles, glass animals, etc.

glasses also **eyeglasses**— _n_ **2** pieces of specially-cut glass usu. in a frame and worn in front of the eyes for improving a person's ability to see —see also SUN GLASSES

glass fibre _n_ fibreglass

glasshouse _n_ _sl_ a military prison

glasspaper _n_ paper with fine particles of glass stuck on one side, used to rub things smooth

glassware _n_ glass objects generally, esp. dishes, drinking glasses, etc.

glass wool _n_ a material made of a mass of very thin glass threads **a** for use esp. as insulation to prevent the loss of heat (as from buildings) **b** which can be used for cleaning because it is so hard, and for packing objects inside parcels

glassy _adj_ **-ier, -iest** **1** like glass, esp. (of water) smooth and shining **2** (of eyes) of a fixed expression, as if without sight or life

glaze¹ _v_ **glazed, glazing** **1** to put a shiny surface on (pots and bricks) **2** to cover (esp. window frames) with glass **3** (of eyes) to become dull and lifeless **4** to cover (food) with a substance giving a shiny surface

glaze² _n_ **1** a shiny surface, esp. one fixed on pots by heat **2** a transparent covering of oil paint spread over solid paint, esp. to change the effect of the colours **3** a jelly-like substance which may be spread over cold cooked meats or, if sweet, over a flan

glazier _n_ a workman who fits glass into window frames

glazing _n_ **1** the action or job of a glazier **2** the piece of glass used to fill a window (esp. in the phrase **double glazing**)

GLC _abbrev. for:_ Greater London Council

gleam¹ _n_ **1** a shining light, esp. one making objects bright: _the red gleam of the firelight_ **2** a

sudden flash of light **3** a sudden showing of a feeling or quality for a short time: _A gleam of interest came into his eye_

gleam² _v_ **1** to give out a bright light **2** (of a feeling) to be expressed with a sudden light: _Amusement gleamed in his eyes_

glean _v_ **1** to collect grain left behind after the harvest **2** to collect (various unwanted objects) **3** to gather (facts or information) in small amounts and often with difficulty — ~**er** _n_

gleanings _n_ **1** the grain gathered in the fields after the harvest **2** small amounts of information or news, perhaps gathered with difficulty

glee _n_ **1** a feeling of joyful satisfaction at something which pleases one: _She danced with glee when she saw the new toys_ **2** a song for 3 or 4 voices together — ~**ful** _adj_

glen _n_ a narrow mountain valley, esp. in Scotland or Ireland

glib _adj_ **-bb-** **1** able to speak well and easily, whether speaking the truth or not **2** spoken too easily to be true: _a glib excuse_ — ~**ly** _adv_ — ~**ness** _n_

glide¹ _v_ **glided, gliding** **1** to move (noiselessly) in a smooth, continuous manner, which seems effortless: _The boat glided over the river_ **2** to use a glider

glide² _n_ a gliding movement

glider _n_ a plane without an engine, or its pilot

gliding _n_ the sport of flying gliders

glimmer¹ _v_ to give a very faint, unsteady light

glimmer² _n_ **1** a faint unsteady light **2** a small sign: _a glimmer of hope_

glimmerings _n_ a glimmer : _glimmerings of interest_

glimpse¹ _v_ **glimpsed, glimpsing** to have a passing view of: _I glimpsed her among the crowd_

glimpse² _n_ **1** a quick look at or incomplete view of: _I caught a glimpse of our new neighbour_ **2** a moment of understanding: _His worried face gave me a glimpse of his true feelings_

glint¹ _v_ to give out small flashes of light, as the eyes of an eager person are supposed to do: _His eyes glinted when he saw the money_

glint² _n_ a flash of light, as from a shiny metal surface or a light colour against a dark background

glissando _n, adj, adv_ **-di** or **dos** (a piece of music) played by sliding the finger along the notes

glisten _v_ to shine from or as if from a wet surface — ~**ing** _adj_ — ~**ingly** _adv_

glitter¹ _v_ to shine brightly with flashing points of light

glitter² _n_ **1** a brightness, as of flashing points of lights: _the glitter of broken glass_ **2** attractiveness; glamour — ~**ing** _adj_

gloat _v_ to look at something or think about it with satisfaction, often in an unpleasant way — ~**ingly** _adv_

global _adj_ of or concerning the whole earth: _global travel_ — **globally** _adv_

globe _n_ **1** an object in the shape of a round

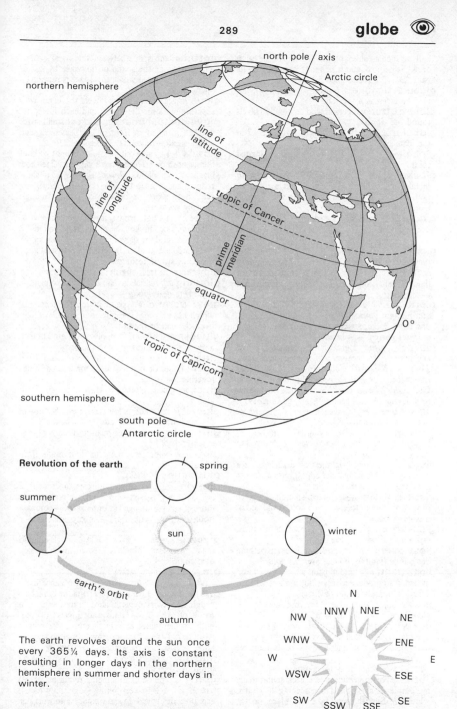

north pole / axis

Arctic circle

northern hemisphere

line of latitude

line of longitude

tropic of Cancer

prime meridian

equator

0°

tropic of Capricorn

southern hemisphere

south pole

Antarctic circle

Revolution of the earth

spring

summer

sun

winter

earth's orbit

autumn

The earth revolves around the sun once every 365¼ days. Its axis is constant resulting in longer days in the northern hemisphere in summer and shorter days in winter.

N

NNW NNE

NW   NE

WNW   ENE

W   E

WSW   ESE

SW   SE

SSW SSE

S

Points of the compass

ball   2 such an object on which a map of the earth or sky is painted, and which may be turned on its base ◉   3 a round glass fish bowl

globe artichoke *n* a plant whose leafy flower may be eaten as a vegetable

globetrotter *n* a person who habitually travels round the world

globular *adj*   1 in the form of a globule   2 in the form of a globe

globule *n* a small drop of a liquid or melted solid

glockenspiel *n* a musical instrument with metal bars, each of which gives out a different musical note, and played by striking with 2 small hammers

gloom *n* -ier, -iest   1 darkness   2 a feeling of deep sadness — ~y *adj* — ~ily *adv* — iness *n*

glorify *v* -fied, -fying   1 to give praise and thanks to (God); worship (God)   2 to give glory or fame to   3 to cause to appear more important than in reality: *It's not a house but a glorified hut* — -fication *n*

glorious *adj*   1 having, or worthy of, great fame and honour: *glorious deeds*   2 beautiful: *a glorious day*   3 *esp. spoken* very enjoyable: *What a glorious party!* — ~ly *adv*

glory *n* -ries   1 great fame or success; praise and honour: *The general was crowned with glory*   2 beauty   3 special beauty or cause for pride: *That tree is the glory of the garden*   4 praise offered to God: *Glory be to God*   5 happiness in heaven (esp. in the phrases **send to glory, go to glory**)

glory hole *n* *esp. spoken* a room, cupboard, or drawer for unwanted articles

glory in *v prep* -ried, -rying in   1 to be very happy about: *He gloried in his new freedom*   2 to enjoy in a selfish way

gloss¹ *n*   1 shiny brightness on a surface   2 a pleasant but deceiving outer appearance: *a gloss of good manners*   3 GLOSS PAINT

gloss² *n, v* (to provide) an explanation of a piece of writing, esp. in the form of a note at the end of a page or book

glossary *n* -ries a list of explanations of words, esp. unusual ones, at the end of a book

gloss over *v adv* to speak kindly of (something bad); hide (faults): *to gloss over his failure*

gloss paint *n* a kind of paint which is used esp. on wood to produce a very shiny surface when it dries -compare EMULSION PAINT

glossy *adj* -ier, -iest shiny and smooth — glossily *adv* — glossiness *n*

glossy magazine also (*esp. spoken*) **glossy-** *n* a magazine printed on good quality shiny paper with (usu.) lots of pictures, as of fashionable clothes

glottal *adj* concerning the glottis

glottal stop *n* *technical* a speech sound made by completely closing and then opening the glottis, which in English may take the place of /t/ between vowel sounds or may be used before a vowel sound

glottis *n* the space between the vocal cords , which produce the sound of the voice by fast or slow movements in which this space is repeatedly opened and closed

glove *n* a garment which covers the hand, with separate parts for the thumb and each finger

glove compartment *n* a sort of small space or shelf in a car in front of the passenger seat, where small articles may be kept

glow¹ *v*   1 to give out heat and/or light without flames or smoke: *The hot coals glowed*   2 to show bright strong colours: *glowing flowers*   3 to show redness and heat in the face (and the body), esp. after hard work or because of strong feelings: *glowing with pride*

glow² *n*   1 a light from something burning without flames or smoke   2 brightness of colour   3 the feeling and/or signs of heat and colour in the body and face, as after exercise or because of good health or strong feelings

glower *v* to look angrily — ~ingly *adv*

glowing *adj* which give(s) a favourable picture: *a glowing description* — ~ly *adv*

glow-worm *n* a type of insect, the female of which has no wings and gives out a greenish light from the end of the tail

glucose *n* a natural form of sugar found in fruit and vegetables and used   in the body

glue¹ *n* a sticky substance which is obtained from animal bones or fish and used for joining things together — ~y *adj*

glue² *v* glued, gluing or glueing to join with glue

glum *adj* -mm- sad; in low spirits, esp. because of disappointment — ~ly *adv* — ~ness *n*

glut *n* a larger supply or quantity than is necessary: *a glut of eggs*

gluten *n* a protein found in flour made from wheat

glutinous *adj* sticky

glutton *n*   1 a person who eats too much   2 *esp. spoken* a person who is always ready to do more of something hard or unpleasant —compare GOURMAND — ~ous *adj* — ously *adv* — ~y *n*

glycerine, -rin *n* a sweet sticky colourless liquid made from fats, which is used in making soap, medicines, and explosives

gm. *abbrev. for:* gram

G.M.T. *abbrev. for:* Greenwich Mean Time

gnarled *adj*   1 (of a tree, its trunk or branches) rough and twisted, with hard lumps, esp. as a result of age   2 (of hands and fingers) twisted, with swollen joints, and rough skin, as from hard work or old age   3 (of a person) rough in appearance, as if beaten by wind and weather

gnash *v* to make a noise with (one's teeth) by biting hard in anger or worry

gnat *n* a type of small stinging flying insect

gnaw *v*   1 a to keep biting (something hard), esp. until destroyed: *to gnaw a bone* b to worry or give pain to: *Grief gnaws my heart*   2 to make (a way) or destroy by doing this

gnawing *adj* painful and/or worrying: *gnawing hunger*

gneiss *n* a type of hard rock with light and dark bands formed from earlier rocks which were pressed together under heat

gnome *n* **1** (in fairy stories) a little (old) man who lives under the ground and guards stores of gold **2** a (stone) figure representing this **3 the gnomes of Zurich** *esp. spoken* powerful bankers said to control supplies of money to foreign governments

gnu also **wildebeest**— *n* **gnu** *or* **gnus** a type of large South African antelope with a tail and curved horns

go[1] *v* **went, gone, going** **1** to leave the place where the speaker is (so as to reach another): *I must go/be going* **2** to travel or move: *We went by bus* **3** to reach (as far as stated): *The roots go deep* **4** to start an action: *Get going on the work* **5** a to do (an activity) **b** *esp. spoken* to do (something undesirable): *Don't go saying that!* **6** to be placed, esp. usually placed: *The boxes go there* **7** (of machines) to work (properly) **8** to become (by a natural change, or by changing on purpose): *She's going grey* **9** to remain (in a certain state): *Her complaints went unnoticed* **10** to be sold: *going cheap* **11** to be spent or used: *Half our money goes on food* **12** to cease or disappear: *Summer's going* **13** to be got rid of: *This car must go* **14** a to die or (sometimes) to become unconscious: *He went out like a light* **b** to be damaged; to weaken or wear out: *My voice has gone* **15** to be or have to be accepted or acceptable: *Anything goes* **16** to happen (in a certain way): *The hours went slowly* **17** a to be stated, said, or sung in a certain way **b** to have or suit a certain tune: *The tune goes like this* **18** to divide a certain sum so as to give an exact figure: *3 into 2 won't go* **19** to make the stated sound: *The guns went 'boom'* **20** to match or fit: *This paint doesn't go* **21** to make a movement: *When he waved, he went like this* **22** to be sent for consideration: *Your suggestion will go before the committee* **23** to be about to, or be planning to, travel (to a place): *We are going to France* **24** to lose one's usual powers of control as in illness, when confused or mad: *He's really let himself go* **25** (of people) to work or move, esp. with unusual effort or result: *Her tongue goes 19 to the dozen* **26** to be on average or in general (in cost, quality, etc.): *She was a good cook, as cooks go* **27** to state or do up to or beyond a limit: *It's quite good, as far as it goes* **28 be going** to be present for use, sale, or enjoyment: *Is there any food going?* **29 be going to (do or happen)** (showing a future action or happening as certain, decided on, or impossible to avoid): *It's going to rain* **30 from the word go** from the beginning **31 go a long way** also **go far**— **a** (of money) to buy a lot **b** (of a person) to succeed **32 go and** *esp. spoken* to go in order to **b** *esp. spoken* (expresses surprise): *She went and won first prize!* **33 go it alone** to act independently **34 3, 6, etc., months gone** *esp.*

spoken having been pregnant for 3, 6 months, etc. —see also GO ABOUT, GO ALONG, GO-AS-YOU-PLEASE, GO AT, GO BACK ON, GO BY, GO DOWN, GO FAR, GO FOR, GO IN FOR, GOING, GOING-OVER, GOINGS-ON, GO OFF, GO ON, GO OUT, GO OVER, GO ROUND, GO SLOW, GO THROUGH, GO UNDER, GO UP, GO WITH

go[2] *n* **goes** **1** the quality of being full of activity: *The children are full of go* **2** *esp. spoken* an attempt to do something: *He had a go at the exam* **3** one's turn (esp. in a game): *It's my go* **4 all systems go** we're ready for take-off **5 from the word go** from the beginning **6 it's all go** it's very busy **7 it's no go** it hasn't/won't happen **8 on the go** working all the time

go about[1] *v adv* **1** to be often out in public (with someone) **2** *esp. spoken* to travel **3** (of a ship) to turn round to face in the opposite direction

go about[2] *v prep* **1** to perform or do: *to go about one's business* **2** also **set about**— to begin working at

goad *n* **1** a sharp-pointed stick for driving cattle by pricking them **2** something which urges a person to action

goad into *v prep* to cause (someone) to (do something) by strong or continued annoyance

goad on *v adv* to keep (someone) active by strong or continual annoyance: *He was goaded on to work harder*

go-ahead[1] *n* permission to act: *to get the go-ahead*

go-ahead[2] *adj* (of people) active in using new methods

goal *n* **1** one's aim or purpose; a place or object one wishes to obtain or reach: *His goal is a place at University* **2** (in games like football) the place where the ball, puck, etc. must go for a point to be gained, or the point thus gained

goalkeeper also (*esp. spoken*) **goalie**— *n* the player in a football team who is responsible for preventing the ball from getting into his team's goal

goal line *n* a line at either end and usu. running the width of a playing area, on which a goal or goalpost is placed

goalmouth *n* the area immediately in front of the goal

go along *v adv* **1** to continue (acting, moving to a place, using a plan, etc.) **2** to agree with; support: *to go along with a suggestion* **3** also **get on, go on** (of people and activities) to advance; go well

goalpost *n* either of the 2 wooden posts, sometimes with a bar between them at a certain height, which mark the goal in various games

go-as-you-please *adj esp. spoken* cheerful, lazy, and not asking for much

goat *n* **1** a type of 4-legged animal related to the sheep, which also gives milk and a hairy sort of wool, which can climb steep hills and rocks and eat almost anything **2** *sl* a man who is very active sexually —see also BILLY GOAT, NANNY GOAT, KID

go at *v prep* **1** also (*esp. when the object is a*

person) **go for**— to attack: *Our dog went at the postman* **2** to work hard at: *to go at one's studies* **3** also **go for**— to be sold at (a cheap price): *coats going at £5*

goatee *n* a little pointed beard (like the hair on a male goat's chin)

gob¹ *n sl* a mass of something sticky, as of liquid from the mouth

gob² *n sl* the mouth: *Shut your gob!*

go back on *v adv prep* **1** to break (a promise, agreement, etc.) **2** to be disloyal to (someone)

gobble¹ *v* **-bled, -bling** to eat very quickly, and sometimes noisily

gobble² *v, n* (to make) the sound a turkey makes

gobbledygook, -degook *n sl* meaningless but important-sounding official language

go-between *n* a person who takes messages from one person or side to another, because they themselves cannot meet

goblet *n* a drinking vessel, usu. of glass or metal, with a base and stem but no handles, and used esp. for wine

goblin *n* a usu. unkind or evil spirit which plays tricks on people —compare HOBGOBLIN

go by *v prep* **1** to be guided by: *Don't go by that old map* **2** to judge by: *Going by her clothes, she must be very rich* **3** go by the name of to be called, probably in addition to one's real name

god *n* **1** (*fem.* **goddess**) a being (one of many) which is worshipped, as one who made or rules over (a part of) the life of the world ◉ **2** a person or thing to which too great an importance is given

God *n* **1** the being who in the Christian, Jewish, and Muslim religions is worshipped as maker and ruler of the world **2** God forbid/grant that May it not happen/happen that **3** God (alone) knows *esp. spoken* It's impossible to say

godchild *n* **-children** (in the Christian religion) the child for whom one takes responsibility by making promises at a baptism —compare GODPARENT

godforsaken *adj* (of a place) empty, containing nothing useful or interesting, etc.

godless *adj* wicked; not showing respect to or belief in God — **~ly** *adv* — **~ness** *n*

godly *adj* **-lier, -liest** *esp. written* showing obedience to God by leading a good life

godown *n* (in parts of Asia) a warehouse esp. at ports

go down *v adv* **1** to become lower **2** (of a wind, fire, etc.) to lessen in force **3** to become less swollen: *This tyre is going down* **4** to become less valuable, or reach a lower social level: *The neighbourhood is going down* **5** to be accepted: *His speech went down well* **6** to be recorded: *This day will go down in history* **7** also **go up**— to reach as far as **8** to leave a university after a period of study or a city for a less important place **9** to be defeated or destroyed: *The city went down before the enemy*

godparent *n* the person (**godfather** or **god-**

mother) who makes promises to help a Christian newly received into the church at a baptismal ceremony —compare GODCHILD

gods *n esp. spoken* the seats high up at the back of a theatre

godsend *n* an unexpected lucky chance or thing: *It was a godsend that he was there*

go far *v adv* **1** to be successful; succeed: *He will go far (in his job)* **2** to satisfy many needs

go for *v prep esp. spoken* **1** GO AT **2** to attack with words: *My wife went for me* **3** to try to obtain or win (something or someone): *to go for a job/a prize* **4** to attempt (to get or do) **5** to like or be attracted by **6** to concern or be true for (someone or something) in the same manner as for others

go-getter *n* a forceful and determined person who is likely to get what he wants

goggle *v* **-gled, -gling** to look hard with the eyes wide open or moving around, as in surprise

goggle box *n sl* a television

goggles *n* (a pair of) large round glasses with an edge which fits against the skin to keep dust, water, etc. from the eyes

go-go *adj* of or concerned in a form of fast exciting dancing, usu. performed by one or more girls in front of watchers

go in for *v adv prep* **1** to take part in (a test of skill or knowledge) **2** to (start to) make a habit of (doing), esp. for enjoyment

going¹ *n* **1** the act of leaving: *Our going was delayed* **2** the act or speed of travel: *slow going* **3** the condition or possibility of travel: *The mud made it heavy going*

going² *adj* **1** in existence: *He's the biggest fool going* **2** as charged at present: *the going rate* **3** working; in operation: *The store is a going concern*

going-over *n* **goings-over** *esp. spoken* **1** a (thorough) examination and/or treatment: *The car needs a proper going-over* **2** a scolding

goings-on *n esp. spoken* activities, usu. of an undesirable kind

go-kart *n* a small 4 wheeled racing vehicle made of an open framework, with an engine

gold *n* **1** a valuable soft yellow metal that is an element used for making coins, jewellery, etc. **2** coins or objects made of this metal generally **3** the colour of this metal **4** kindness, gentleness in behaviour, etc. (esp. in the phrases **heart of gold, as good as gold**)

golden *adj* **1** made of gold **2** of the colour of gold **3** very fortunate or favourable: *a golden opportunity*

Golden Age *n* a period of time, either real or imaginary, when art and literature were at their best

golden handshake *n* a large amount of money given to someone when he leaves a firm, esp. when he retires

golden jubilee *n* the 50th yearly return of the date of some important personal event, esp. of becoming a king and queen

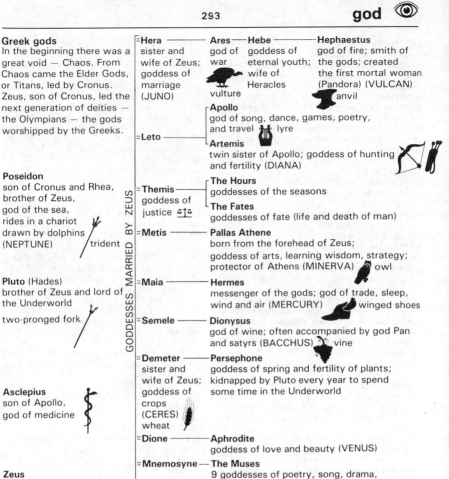

Greek gods

In the beginning there was a great void — Chaos. From Chaos came the Elder Gods, or Titans, led by Cronus. Zeus, son of Cronus, led the next generation of deities — the Olympians — the gods worshipped by the Greeks.

GODDESSES MARRIED BY ZEUS

= Hera
sister and wife of Zeus; goddess of marriage (JUNO)
vulture

    Ares — god of war

    Hebe — goddess of eternal youth; wife of Heracles

    Hephaestus — god of fire; smith of the gods; created the first mortal woman (Pandora) (VULCAN) anvil

= Leto

    Apollo
god of song, dance, games, poetry, and travel   lyre

    Artemis
twin sister of Apollo; goddess of hunting and fertility (DIANA)

= Themis
goddess of justice

    The Hours
goddesses of the seasons

    The Fates
goddesses of fate (life and death of man)

= Metis

    Pallas Athene
born from the forehead of Zeus; goddess of arts, learning wisdom, strategy; protector of Athens (MINERVA)   owl

= Maia

    Hermes
messenger of the gods; god of trade, sleep, wind and air (MERCURY)   winged shoes

= Semele

    Dionysus
god of wine; often accompanied by god Pan and satyrs (BACCHUS)   vine

= Demeter
sister and wife of Zeus; goddess of crops (CERES)
wheat

    Persephone
goddess of spring and fertility of plants; kidnapped by Pluto every year to spend some time in the Underworld

= Dione

    Aphrodite
goddess of love and beauty (VENUS)

= Mnemosyne

    The Muses
9 goddesses of poetry, song, drama, dancing,

= Eurynome

    The Graces
3 goddesses of beauty and joy

MORTALS MARRIED BY ZEUS

= Alcmene

    Heracles
mortal hero noted for his strength; accepted as a god into Olympus

= Danaë

    Perseus
hero who beheaded the Gorgon Medusa and saved Andromeda

= Electra

    Dardanos

= Europa

    Minos
king of Crete

= Leda

Helen
wife of Menelaus; abducted by Paris, son of king of Troy —this caused the Trojan War

The Dioscuri
Castor and Pollux, famous for brotherly affection

Poseidon
son of Cronus and Rhea, brother of Zeus, god of the sea, rides in a chariot drawn by dolphins (NEPTUNE) / trident

Pluto (Hades)
brother of Zeus and lord of the Underworld

two-pronged fork

Asclepius
son of Apollo, god of medicine

Zeus
son of Cronus; father of gods and men; god of thunder and lightning

Roman gods
Some of the Roman gods were adopted from the Greek pantheon and given new names (shown in brackets eg. **Zeus** = JUPITER)

golden syrup *n* a sweet thick liquid made from sugar, used in cooking and as a spread

golden wedding also **golden wedding anniversary** — the 50th yearly return of the date of a wedding

goldfield n a place where gold can be found

goldfinch *n* a type of small singing bird with red, yellow, and black feathers

goldfish *n* goldfish a small fish which is kept as a pet in glass bowls, and in ornamental pools

goldmine *n* 1 a place where gold is mined from the rock 2 a very successful profit-making business or activity

gold plate *n* 1 articles such as dishes, made of gold 2 a covering of gold on top of another metal — **-plated** *adj*

gold rush *n* the state of affairs when gold is found somwhere and many people go there hoping to find a lot of gold

goldsmith *n* a person who makes objects out of gold

gold standard *n* the practice of using the value of gold as a standard on which to base the value of money

golf *n, v* (to play) a game in which people drive small, hard balls into holes with special clubs, trying to do so with as few strokes as possible — ~**er** *n*

golliwog, golly- also **golly—** *n* a child's doll made of soft material, dressed like a little man, and with a black face with big white eyes and black hair standing out round his head

gonad *n* a male or female organ in which the cells are produced from which young may be formed

gondola *n* 1 a long narrow flat-bottomed boat with high points at each end, used only on the canals in Venice 2 a hanging framework for workmen to stand in when they are painting or repairing high walls and windows 3 any of several types of vehicles, containers, or seats which are fixed to a framework but can swing backwards and forwards or from side to side

gondolier *n* a man who guides and drives a gondola forward by moving a long-handled oar at the back

gone *past part. of* GO

goner *n esp. spoken* someone who will soon die

gong *n* 1 a round piece of metal hanging from a frame, which when struck with a stick gives a deep ringing sound, as used in Eastern music or to call people to meals 2 *sl* a medal

gonorrhea, -rhoea *n* a disease of the sex organs, passed on during sexual activity —compare SYPHILIS

goo *n esp. spoken* 1 sticky material 2 (words which seem to express) unnaturally sweet feelings; sentimentalism

good¹ *adj* **better, best** 1 having the right qualities: *a good play* 2 suitable; favourable: *The weather's good* 3 morally right: *to do a good deed* 4 (of people) kind; helpful 5 (esp. of children) well-behaved 6 suitable for its purpose: *a good idea* 7 enjoyable: *a good story* 8 useful to the health or character: *Milk is good for you* 9 (of food) fresh 10 strong; in good condition; working well: *You need good shoes for hill-walking* 11 having the ability to do something: *good at languages* 12 worthy of respect: *my good man* 13 of a higher standard or quality than average 14 effective in use (usu. over a period of time): *The ticket is good for one month* 15 safe from loss of money: *a good risk* 16 large in size, amount, etc: *a good distance* 17 at least or more than: *a good mile away* 18 (in expressions of feeling): *Good gracious!* 19 (in greetings): *Good morning/afternoon/evening/day* 20 a **good deal/few** quite a lot 21 complete; thorough: *Have a good look* 22 **All in good time** (it will happen) at a suitable later time; be patient 23 **as good as** almost (the same thing as) 24 **good and .....** *esp. spoken esp. US* very; completely 25 **good for** likely to produce (an effect or money) 26 **in good time** early 27 **It's a good thing** It's fortunate 28 **make good** to be successful, esp. wealthy 29 **make something good a** to pay for; make up; repair b to put into effect: *make good a promise*

good² *n* 1 that which is right and useful in accordance with religious moral standards: *an influence for good* 2 that which causes gain or improvement: *I work for the good of my family* 3 good people generally: *Christians believe the good go to heaven when they die* 4 **do someone good** to improve someone, esp. in health or behaviour 5 **for good (and all)** for ever 6 **no good/not much good (doing something/to someone)** useless 7 (an amount) **to the good** with a profit of (an amount)

good book *n esp. spoken* the Bible

good-for-nothing *adj, n* (a person who is) worthless, who does no work, etc.

Good Friday *n* **-days** the Friday before Easter

good-humoured *n* having or showing a cheerful, friendly state of mind —see also HUMOUR — ~**ly** *adv*

goodish *adj* 1 quite good, but not very good in quality 2 rather large, long, far, etc.: *a goodish distance*

good-looking *adj* attractive

good-natured *adj* naturally kind; ready to help, to forgive, not to be angry, etc. — ~**ly** *adv*

goodness *n* 1 the quality of being good 2 the best part, esp. (of food) the health-giving part 3 (used in expressions of surprise and annoyance): *My goodness!*

good offices *n* power or behaviour which helps someone out of a difficulty: *He got some money through the good offices of his bank manager*

goods *n* 1 possessions which can be moved, not houses, land, etc. 2 heavy articles which can be carried by road, train, etc. 3 articles for sale 4 **deliver the goods** to produce in full what is expected

goods and chattels n law personal possessions

good sense n the ability to judge and act wisely

goodwill n 1 kind feelings towards or between people and/or willingness to act to increase the good fortune of the others: *There is goodwill between the former enemies* 2 the value of the popularity, the regular customers, etc., of a business as part of its worth when being sold

goody n -ies 1 a sweet; pleasant thing to eat 2 something particularly attractive, pleasant, good, or desirable

goody-goody n goody-goodies a person who likes to appear good so as to please others, not because he or she is really good

gooey adj gooier, gooiest 1 sticky and (usu.) sweet: *gooey cakes* 2 over-sweet; sentimental — see also GOO

goof n sl a foolish person

go off¹ v adv 1 a to explode b to ring or sound loudly: *The alarm went off at 7a.m.* 2 (of food) to go bad 3 esp. spoken to lose skill, quality, etc.: *The book goes off after 50 pages* 4 to cease to be felt: *The pain went off* 5 to succeed or fail: *How did your plan go off?* 6 to fall asleep or lose consciousness: *Has the baby gone off yet?* 7 to cease operation 8 go off with to take away without permission

goofy adj -ier, -iest silly; slightly mad — **goofiness** n

googly n -glies (in cricket) a ball bowled as if to go in one direction which in fact goes in the other direction

goon n sl a silly person

go on¹ v adv 1 to take place or happen: *What's going on here?* 2 also go along— (of people and activities) to advance; go well 3 to keep complaining or scolding 4 also run on— to keep talking 5 to continue without stopping, or after a stop: *Go on, I'm listening* 6 to behave continually in a certain way: *If he goes on like this he'll lose his job* 7 (of time) to pass 8 esp. spoken to support oneself (at the stated level); manage: *How did you go on for money while you were out of work?* 9 to be put into operation: *The heating goes on later* 10 go on (with you)! I don't believe you! 11 to be going/go on with esp. spoken (to use) for the moment

go on² v prep to use as a reason or base for further action: *We were just going on what you had said*

goose n geese 1 (male gander) any of a family of large web-footed birds 2 the white bird of this family that is kept on farms 3 the meat of this bird 4 a silly person, esp. female

gooseberry n -ries 1 the small round green edible fruit of a bush 2 play gooseberry to be present with a man and woman who would rather be alone

gooseflesh also goose pimples— n a condition in which the skin is raised up in small points where the hairs grow out, due to cold or fear

goosestep n a stiff-legged high-stepping march

go out v adv 1 to leave the house 2 to travel (to a distant place): *My friends went out to Africa* 3 to be made public: *Have the notices gone out?* 4 (of time) to end: *March went out with high winds* 5 to stop burning or shining 6 (of the tide) to go back to its low level 7 to cease to be fashionable or customary: *Short skirts went out some time ago* 8 to be in sympathy (with): *Our thoughts go out to absent friends*

go over¹ v prep 1 to visit and examine: *to go over the factory* 2 to look at or examine for a purpose: *We went over the list and chose 2* 3 to repeat: *I'll go over the explanation*

go over² v adv (of a performance) to be received: *His jokes went over well*

gopher n a ratlike American burrowing animal

gore¹ n literature blood

gore² v gored, goring to wound with the horns or tusks

gore³ n a part of a garment, usu. of a skirt, which is a piece of material widening towards the bottom — **gored** adj

gorge n a narrow steep-sided valley usu. made by a stream —see VALLEY (USAGE)

gorge on also gorge with— v prep gorged, gorging on to fill (oneself) with (food)

gorgeous adj esp. spoken 1 delightful: *This cake is gorgeous* 2 very beautiful — ~ly adv — ~ness n

gorgon n 1 a fierce and ugly woman 2 any of 3 imaginary sisters in ancient Greek stories who had snakes for hair, and the sight of whom turned people to stone

Gorgonzola n a type of strong-tasting Italian cheese

gorilla n a tailless animal which is the largest of the manlike apes, is very strong, and lives in Africa

gormless adj esp. spoken stupid and thoughtless — ~ly adv

go round v adv, prep 1 to travel about 2 also go around— to be enough for everyone: *Is there food to go round?*

gorse also furze— n a type of wild bush with prickles and bright yellow flowers

gory adj -ier, -iest 1 literature covered in blood —see GORE 2 full of bloodshed: *a gory film*

gosling n a young goose

go slow v adv to put the least effort into work, as a form of strike — go-slow n

gospel n a set of instructions or teachings

Gospel n any of the 4 accounts of Christ's life and teaching in the Bible

gossamer n light silky thread made by spiders

gossip¹ n 1 talk or writing, not necessarily correct, about other people's actions and private lives —compare RUMOUR 2 a person who likes to gossip

gossip² v to talk or write gossip

got *past tense and past part. of* GET

Gothic *adj* **1** of or concerning an ancient Germanic people called **Goths** **2** of a style of building common in Western Europe between the 12th and 16th centuries, with pointed arches, tall thin pillars, and coloured glass in the windows **3** of a type of printing with thick, pointed letters

go through¹ v adv to be approved officially: *Their plans went through*

go through² v prep **1** to experience: *to go through a war* **2** to finish **3** to be accepted by: *The law has gone through Parliament* **4** to perform one's part in (a ceremony) **5** to examine

gouache *n French* **1** a sort of paint which contains gum to make it thicker, and is mixed with water **2** a picture using this paint

Gouda *n* a type of mild yellowish Dutch cheese, usu. round

gouge *n* a tool for hollowing out wood

gouge out v adv **gouged, gouging out** to press or dig out with force

goulash *n* meat and vegetables cooked with paprika

go under v adv **1** (of a floating object) to sink **2** to fail or get into difficulties: *With her worries, she's sure to go under*

go up v adv **1** to rise: *Prices have gone up* **2** to be built: *How many houses have gone up?* **3** to blow up or be destroyed in fire: *The whole house went up in flames*

gourmand *n French* a person who eats too much —compare GLUTTON △ GOURMET

gourmet *n French* a person who knows a lot about food and drink and what goes well together △ GOURMAND

gout *n* a disease which makes the smaller joints swell painfully — ~y *adj*

govern v **1** to rule: *We have a queen, but it is Parliament that governs* **2** to control or guide (actions and feelings): *Don't let fear govern your decision* **3** to determine the nature of: *The tides are governed by the movements of the moon*

governess *n* a female teacher who lives in a family and educates their children at home

government *n* **1** governing: *The king was not suited to government, and ruled badly* **2** the people who rule — ~al *adj*

governor *n* **1** a person or one of a group controlling certain types of organization: *a prison governor* **2** (esp. in former times) a person who rules over a state or province on behalf of the central government **3** the elected head of an American state — ~ship *n*

Governor-General *n* **Governors-General** or **Governor-Generals** a person who represents the King or Queen in some Commonwealth countries

go with v prep **1** also **go along with**— to be in agreement with **2** to be often found with, esp. as a result of: *Happiness doesn't always go with money* **3** to match: *Mary's blue dress goes with her eyes*

gown¹ *n* **1** *old use or US* a long dress: *an evening gown* **2** a loose outer garment, usu. black, worn for special ceremonies by judges, teachers, etc. **3** a loose garment worn for some special purpose: *a dressing gown*

GP *abbrev. for:* GENERAL PRACTITIONER

GPO *abbrev. for:* General POST OFFICE

grab¹ v **-bb-** to seize with a sudden, rough movement, esp. for a selfish reason: *He grabbed the coin and ran off*

grab² *n* a sudden attempt to seize something

grace¹ *n* **1** fineness in movement, form, or behaviour, esp. that which seems effortless and attractive **2** kindness: *She had the grace to say that he was right* **3** a delay allowed as a favour, as for payment, work, etc.: *I'll give you a week's grace to finish the work* **4** a prayer before or after meals, giving thanks to God **5** the mercy (of God): *By the grace of God the ship survived the storm* **6** a way of speaking to or of a duke, duchess, or archbishop: *Your/His/Her Grace* **7** **in someone's good graces** in someone's favour

grace² v **graced, gracing** to ornament; give pleasure, by one's/its presence: *Fine furniture graced the rooms*

graceful *adj* **1** (of shape or movement) attractive to see **2** suitably and pleasantly expressed —see GRACIOUS (USAGE) — **-fully** *adv*

grace note also **ornament**— *n* a note added to the main tune that makes it sound more attractive

graceless *adj* **1** awkward in movement or form **2** lacking in good manners — ~ly *adv* — ~ness *n*

Graces *n* the 3 Greek goddesses who represented various forms of beauty

gracious *adj* **1** polite, kind and pleasant, esp. to those who have no claim on one's attention: *She was gracious enough to show us round her home* **2** used in speaking of royal persons: *Her Gracious Majesty* **3** having those qualities made possible by wealth: *gracious living* — ~ly *adv* — ~ness *n* USAGE A person or animal is **graceful** in bodily movements: *a graceful young girl*. The word is also used when one apologizes, or thanks people, in a whole-hearted way: *She thanked the Headmistress gracefully for the prize*. When **gracious** is used of people or their behaviour, it suggests a very grand person being polite to someone less important: *The Queen thanked them graciously*.

gradation *n* a stage in a set of changes: *A good actor can express every gradation of feeling from joy to grief*

grade¹ *n* **1** a degree of rank or quality **2** a mark for the standard of a piece of schoolwork

grade² v **graded, grading** to separate into levels: *potatoes graded according to size*

gradient *n* the degree of slope, as on a road: *A gradient of 1 in 4 is a rise of one metre for every 4 metres forward* ☞ MATHEMATICS

gradual *adj* happening slowly and by degrees — **-ually** *adv* — ~ness *n*

graduate¹ *adj, n* **1** (of) a person who has completed a university degree course **2** (a) postgraduate: *a graduate student*

graduate² *v* **-ated, -ating** **1** to obtain a degree at a university, esp. a first degree **2** to arrange in order of degree or quality **3** *technical* to make marks showing degrees of measurement (on)

graduation *n* **1** graduating **2** a mark showing a measure of degree, as on a scale **3** a ceremony at which one receives proof of having gained a university degree

graffiti *n* drawings or writing on a wall, esp. of a rude or political nature

graft¹ *v* **1** to make a graft on a tree or body **2** to join

graft² *n* **1** a branch cut from one plant and bound inside a cut in another usu. stronger related plant, so that it produces further growth **2** a piece of healthy skin or bone used to replace that in a damaged part of the body: *a skin graft on the burnt leg* **3** *esp. US* the practice of obtaining money unlawfully or unfairly, esp. by using political influence

grain *n* **1** a seed of rice, wheat, etc. **2** crops from plants which produce such seeds **3** a piece of a substance which is made up of small hard pieces: *a grain of sand* **4** the arrangement of the threads or fibres in wood, flesh, rock, and cloth, or the pattern these make **5** a small measure of weight, used for medicines (1/7000 of a pound or ·0648 gram)

gram, gramme *n* a measure of weight, 1/1000 of a kilogram

grammar *n* **1** (the study and practice of) the rules by which words change their forms and are combined into sentences **2** a book which teaches these rules

grammarian *n* a person who studies and often writes books about grammar

grammar school *n* (the educational activity of) a school for children over the age of 11, where they study for examinations which may lead to higher education

grammatical *adj* **1** concerning grammar **2** correct according to the rules of grammar: *a grammatical sentence* — ~**ly** *adv*

gramophone *n* *becoming rare* RECORD PLAYER

gran *n* *esp. spoken* a grandmother

granary *n* **-ries** a storehouse for grain

grand¹ *adj* **1** splendid in appearance: *a grand view* **2** important, or thinking oneself so: *a very grand lady* **3** *esp. spoken* very pleasant: *a grand party* **4** complete (esp. in the phrase **the grand total**) — ~**ly** *adv* — ~**ness** *n*

grand² *n* *esp. spoken* GRAND PIANO

grandad, granddad *n* *esp. spoken* **1** a grandfather **2** (a name for an old man)

grandchild *n* **-children** the child (**grandson** or **granddaughter**) of someone's son or daughter ☞ FAMILY

granddaughter *n* the daughter of someone's son or daughter ☞ FAMILY

grandeur *n* great beauty or power, often combined with great size: *the grandeur of nature*

grandfather *n* the father of someone's father or mother ☞ FAMILY

grandfather clock *n* a tall clock which stands on the floor

grandiloquent *adj* using long, important-sounding words — **-quence** *n*

grandiose *adj* intended to seem important, splendid, etc.

grand master *n* the top rank of chess player

Grand Master *n* the head of certain organizations, such as freemasons

grandmother *n* the mother of someone's father or mother ☞ FAMILY

Grand National *n* a horse race with jumps (STEEPLECHASE) held yearly

grandparent *n* the parent (**grandfather** or **grandmother**) of someone's father or mother

grand piano *n* **-os** a large piano with strings set across, not upright

grand slam *n* **1** the winning of all of a set of sports competitions **2** the winning of all the card tricks possible at one time, esp. of 13 in the game of bridge

grandson *n* the son of someone's son or daughter ☞ FAMILY

grandstand *n* a large group of raised seats, sometimes roofed, from which to watch sports matches, races, etc.

grand tour *n* (in former times) a tour of Europe, esp. as part of the education of a young English gentleman

grange *n* a country house with farm buildings

granite *n* a hard type of grey rock, used for building and making roads

granny, grannie *n* **-nies** *esp. spoken* a grandmother

grant¹ *v* **1** to give, esp. what is requested: *He granted them leave to go* **2** to admit to (the truth of): *I grant you that she's a good player*

grant² *n* a sum of money given by the state to a person or an organization, for a special purpose: *Students often have to live on a small grant*

granulate *v* **-lated, -lating** to make or form into granules

granule *n* a small bit like a fine grain — **-lar** *adj*

grape *n* a small round juicy fruit, usu. green or dark purple, which grows in bunches and is used for making wine

grapefruit *n* **grapefruit** *or* **grapefruits** a large round yellow fruit, with a thick skin like an orange but a more acid taste

grapevine *n* **1** a vine **2** a secret way of spreading news: *I heard it on the grapevine*

graph *n* a drawing showing the relationship between 2 variables ☞ MATHEMATICS

graphic *adj* **1** concerned with written signs, usu. letters or drawings **2** which gives a clear account: *a graphic description* **3** also **graphical**— by a graph — ~**ally** *adv*

graphite *n* a black substance (a kind of CARBON)

which is used in paints, oil for machines, electrical apparatus and for the writing material in the middle of pencils (usu. called "lead")

grapnel n an iron instrument with several hooks, used as an anchor, for searching for an object on the bottom of a river or lake, or (formerly) for pulling an enemy's boat close to one's own

grapple with v prep **-pled, -pling with** to seize and struggle with

grasp¹ v **1** to take or keep a firm hold of, esp. with the hands **2** to succeed in understanding: *I grasped the main points*

grasp² n **1** a firm hold: *I kept her hand in my grasp* **2** reach: *Success is within his grasp* **3** control; power: *in the grasp of a wicked man* **4** understanding: *work beyond my grasp*

grasping adj offensive eager for more, esp. money — ~ly adv

grass¹ n **1** various kinds of common low-growing green plants with blade-like leaves **2** land covered by grass **3** any of various types of green plant with tall straight stems and flat blades **4** sl a person (often a criminal) who informs the police about criminals **5** sl cannabis

grass² v **1** to cover (land) with grass **2** sl (esp. of a criminal) to inform the police about the action of criminals

grasshopper n a type of jumping insect which makes a sharp noise by rubbing parts of its body together ⟨→ INSECT

grassland n a stretch of land covered mainly with grass, often used for grazing

grass roots n **1** the ordinary people: *grass roots opinion* **2** the basic facts: *to go back to grass roots*

grassy adj **-sier, -siest** covered with growing grass

grate¹ n the bars and frame which hold the fuel in a fireplace

grate² v **grated, grating** **1** to rub (usu. food) on a hard rough surface so as to break into small pieces: *grated cheese* **2** to make a sharp unpleasant sound: *The key grated in the lock*

grateful adj feeling or showing thanks to another person — ~ly adv — ~ness n

grater n an instrument for grating things, often one of metal with sharp rough points

gratify v **-fied, -fying** **1** to give pleasure and satisfaction to: *She was gratified by their praise* **2** to satisfy (a desire): *Now she can gratify her wish to see Europe* — -fication n — ~ing adj — ~ingly adv

gratinée also **au gratin**— adj French (of cooked food, usu. vegetables) having a rough, crumbly surface, browned in the oven or under the grill

grating¹ n a frame or network of bars, usu. metal, to protect a hole or window

grating² adj (of a sound) sharp, hard, and unpleasant — ~ly adv

gratis adv, adj free

gratitude n gratefulness

gratuitous adj **1** not deserved or necessary

2 done freely, without reward or payment — ~ly adv — ~ness n

gratuity n **-ties** a gift of money **a** for a service done **b** to a worker or member of the armed forces leaving employment

grave¹ n the place in the ground where a dead person is buried

grave² adj **1** serious in manner: *His face was grave* **2** important and needing attention and (often) worrying: *The sick man's condition is grave* — ~ly adv

grave³ adj (of a mark (ACCENT) put above a letter to show pronunciation on or to differentiate between two words) being the mark over è — compare ACUTE, CIRCUMFLEX

gravel¹ n a mixture of small stones with sand, used on the surface of roads or paths

gravel² v **-ll-** to cover with gravel

gravelly adj **1** of or covered with gravel **2** having a low sharp hard sound: *a gravelly voice*

gravestone n a stone put up over a grave bearing the name, dates of birth and death, etc., of the dead person

graveyard n a piece of ground, sometimes near a church, where people are buried -compare CHURCHYARD, CEMETERY

gravitate towards also **gravitate to**— v prep **-tated, -tating towards** to be drawn towards: *Everyone gravitated towards the kitchen*

gravitation n **1** gravitating **2** the force of gravity — ~al adj

gravity n **1 a** seriousness of manner: *to behave with gravity* **b** worrying importance —see GRAVE **2** the natural force by which objects are attracted to each other, esp. that by which a large mass pulls a smaller one to it: *Anything that is dropped is pulled by gravity towards the centre of the earth*

gravy n **-vies** **1** the juice which comes out of meat as it cooks **2** this juice thickened to serve with meat and vegetables

gravy boat n a small long-shaped jug for gravy

graze¹ v **grazed, grazing** **1** (of animals) to feed on grass **2** to cause (animals) to feed on grass: *We can't graze the cattle till summer* **3** to use (land) for grazing

graze² v **1** to touch lightly while passing: *The plane's wing seemed to graze the treetops* **2** to break the surface of (esp. the skin) by rubbing against something: *She grazed her knee*

graze³ n a surface wound

grease¹ n **1** animal fat when soft after being melted **2** a thick oily substance

grease² v **greased, greasing** to put grease on —see also **grease someone's** PALM

grease gun n a hand instrument for forcing grease into machinery

greasepaint n the make-up used by actors and actresses on their faces

greaseproof adj (of paper) which does not let grease pass through it

greasy adj **-ier, -iest** **1** covered with grease or

containing it: *greasy food/hair* **2** slippery: *The roads are greasy* — **greasily** *adv* — **greasiness** *n*

great¹ *adj* **1** of excellent quality or ability: *the great men of the past* **2** important: *a great occasion* **3** large in amount or degree: *a great many* **4** (of people) unusually active in the stated way: *He's a great talker* **5** (*usu. before another adj. of size*) big **6 great with child** *Bible* pregnant — ~ness *n*

great² *n* important people: *He has connections with the great*

Great Bear *n* the Plough

greatcoat *n* a heavy overcoat, esp. military

Great Dane *n* a type of very large smooth-haired dog

Greater *adj* (in names) of a kind which is considered large, or larger than a closely-related type: *Is that bird a Greater Yellowlegs?* opposite **lesser**

greatly *adv* to a large degree: *greatly to be feared*

Great Seal *n* an official mark put on important state papers —compare PRIVY SEAL

grebe *n* any of several types of short-tailed waterbird which can swim under water and are found esp. in lakes —compare DABCHICK

Grecian *adj* (of style or appearance) Greek, esp. like that of ancient Greece

greed *n* strong desire to obtain a lot or more than is fair, esp. of food, money, or power: *greed for gold* — ~y *adj* — ~ily *adv* — ~iness *n*

Greek *adj* of or concerning the people, language, art, etc., of Greece ☞ HISTORY ◉

green¹ *adj* **1** of a colour between yellow and blue, which is that of leaves and grass **2** young or unripe: *Green apples are sour* **3** young and/or inexperienced and therefore easily tricked **4** pale in the face, as from sickness, fear, etc. **5** (esp. of memories) fresh, in spite of the passing of time **6** also **green with envy**— very jealous — **greenness** *n* — ~ish *adj*

green² *n* **1** (a) green colour **2** a smooth stretch of grass, for a special purpose, as for playing a game or for the general use of the people of a town: *a village green | a bowling / putting green*

green belt *n* a stretch of land, round a town, where building is not allowed

greenery *n* green leaves

green fingers *n* natural skill in making plants grow

greenfly *n* **greenfly** *or* **greenflies** a very small green insect which feeds on the juice from young plants

greengage *n* a kind of greenish-yellow plum

greengrocer *n* a shopkeeper who sells vegetables and fruit —compare GROCER

greenhorn *n* **1** a young inexperienced person who is easily cheated **2** a beginner at some kind of work or skill

greenhouse *n* a building with glass roof and sides and often heated, used to protect growing plants

green light *n* the sign, or permission, to begin an action: *Our plan's been given the green light*

green pepper also **sweet pepper**— *n* the green fruit of the capsicum plant, used as a vegetable

greenroom *n* a room in a theatre or concert hall where performers can rest

greens *n* green leafy vegetables that are cooked and eaten —compare GREENERY

green tea *n* tea made from leaves which have been heated with steam, rather than dried

Greenwich Mean Time (*abbrev.* **G.M.T.**) also **Greenwich time**— *n* the time at a place near London (Greenwich) where there is a certain point which represents the line dividing east from west. Times in the rest of the world are compared to this and said to be a number of hours earlier or later

greet *v* **1** to welcome with words, actions, or an expression of feeling: *She greeted him with a loving kiss* **2** to come suddenly to the eyes, ears, etc.: *Complete disorder greeted us*

greeting *n* **1** a form of words or an action used on meeting someone: *She didn't return my greeting* **2** a good wish: *Christmas greetings*

gregarious *adj* **1** living in groups **2** (of people) liking the companionship of others — ~ly *adv* — ~ness *n*

Gregorian calendar *n* the system of arranging the days and months of the year which has been generally used since 1582, when Pope Gregory the 13th introduced it

Gregorian chant *n* a kind of church music for voices alone, according to rules laid down by Pope Gregory the 1st —see also PLAINSONG

gremlin *n* a wicked little spirit, said to cause damage to aircraft engines

grenade *n* a small bomb which can be thrown by hand or fired from a gun

grenadier *n* **1** a soldier, formerly one who threw grenades **2** a member of a special part of the British army, the **Grenadiers** or **Grenadier Guards**

grenadine *n* a sweet liquid made from pomegranates and used in drinks

grew *past tense of* GROW

grey¹ *adj* **1** of a colour like black mixed with white which is that of ashes and rain clouds **2** having grey hair: *She's going grey* **3** (of the face) pale because of sudden fear or illness **4** dull, colourless — ~ness *n* — ~ish *adj*

grey² *n* (a) grey colour

grey³ *v* **greyed, greying** (esp. of hair) to become grey

greyhound *n* a type of thin long-legged dog which can run swiftly in hunting and racing

Greyhound *n trademark* (in the US) a type of long-distance bus

grey matter *n* **1** the substance of the brain and nervous system which contains cell bodies, esp. the central part of the brain **2** *esp. spoken* the power of thought

grid *n* **1** a set of bars set across each other in a frame **2** the network of electricity supply wires

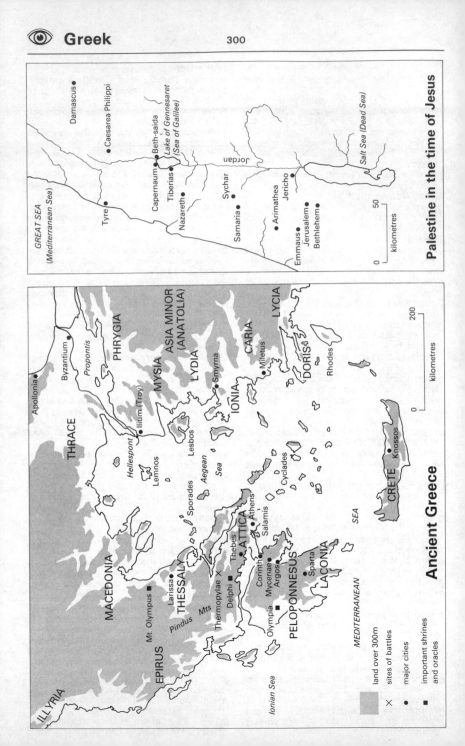

Palestine in the time of Jesus

Ancient Greece

connecting power stations **3** a system of numbered squares printed on a map so that the exact position of any place on it may be stated or found

griddle *n* a round iron plate for baking over a fire

grief *n* **1** great sorrow, esp. at the death of a loved person **2** a cause of sorrow or anxiety: *His behaviour was a grief to his mother*

grievance *n* a report of or cause for complaint, esp. of unjust treatment: *The workers met to discuss their grievances*

grieve *v* **grieved, grieving 1** to suffer from grief, esp. over a loss: *grieving for her dead husband* **2** to cause grief to

grievous *adj* **1** very seriously harmful: *a grievous mistake* **2** (of wounds, pain, etc.) severe **3 grievous bodily harm** *less law* hurt done to a person's body in an attack, for which the attacker may be charged in a court of law — ~**ly** *adv* — ~**ness** *n*

griffin, griffon, gryphon *n* an imaginary animal with a lion's body and the wings and head of an eagle

grill¹ *v* **1** to cook (something) under or over direct heat **2** *sl* to question severely and continuously: *He was grilled for hours by the police*

grill² *n* **1** the cooking apparatus used for grilling food **2** meat cooked this way **3** a restaurant which serves mainly grilled foods

grille *n* a framework of metal bars filling a space in a door or window or separating a bank or post office clerk from the public

grim *adj* **-mm- 1** cruel, hard, or causing fear: *a grim expression* **2** determined in spite of fear: *a grim smile* **3** *esp. spoken* unpleasant; not cheerful: *I've had a grim day* — ~**ly** *adv* — ~**ness** *n*

grimace *v* **-maced, -macing** to make an expression of pain, annoyance, etc., which twists the face: *She grimaced at the sight of all the work* — **grimace** *n*

grime¹ *n* a surface of thick black dirt: *He was covered with grime* — **-my** *adj* — **-miness** *n*

grime² *v* **grimed, griming** to begrime

grin¹ *v* **-nn-** to make a grin: *to grin with pleasure* —compare SMILE

grin² *n* a wide smile which shows the teeth

grind¹ *v* **ground, grinding 1** to crush into small pieces or a powder by pressing between hard surfaces: *She grinds her coffee beans* **2** to rub (esp. the teeth) together or against something, so as to make a noise **3** to make smooth or sharp by rubbing on a hard surface: *to grind the knives and scissors* **4** to press upon with a strong twisting movement: *He ground his knee into the man's stomach* — ~**er** *n*

grind² *n* **1** hard uninteresting work: *He finds study a real grind* **2** a long steady tiring effort of movement, such as a race

grind down *v adv* to oppress

grindstone *n* a round stone which is turned to sharpen tools, knives, etc.

grip¹ *v* **-pp- 1** to take a very tight hold (of): *She gripped my hand* **2** to attract and hold (someone's attention): *The strange stories gripped the hearers*

grip² *n* **1** a very tight forceful hold **2** control: *He kept a firm grip on his children* **3** power of understanding or doing: *I played badly; I seem to be losing my grip* **4 a** something which grips: *a hair grip* **b** a handle to be gripped **5 come/get to grips with** to deal seriously with (something difficult)

gripe¹ *v* **griped, griping** to cause or feel pain, esp. in the stomach: *a griping pain*

gripe² *v* **griped, griping** *sl* to complain continually: *Mother gripes at me when I'm late* — ~**r** *n*

gripe³ *n* *sl* a complaint

gripes *n* *sl* sudden and severe stomach pains

gripping *adj* that holds the attention: *a gripping film* — ~**ly** *adv*

grisly *adj* **-lier, -liest** unpleasant because of destruction, decay, or death shown or described: *the grisly remains of the bodies* —compare GRUESOME

grist *n* **1** *old use* grain ready for grinding **2 (all) grist to someone's/the mill** used for someone's profit

gristle *n* a smooth clear substance in meat found near the bones —compare CARTILAGE — **-tly** *adj*

grit¹ *n* **1** small pieces of a hard material, usu. stone: *Grit is spread on icy roads to make them less slippery* **2** *sl* determination; lasting courage — **gritty** *adj*

grit² *v* **-tt- grit one's teeth** to become more determined

grizzle *v* **-zled, -zling** *esp. spoken* (esp. of young children) to cry quietly and continually

grizzled *adj* greyish (-haired)

grizzly bear also **grizzly**— *n* a large fierce brownish-grey bear of the Rocky Mountains of North America

groan¹ *v* **1** to make a groan or talk in a groaning way **2** to suffer: *The people groaned under the taxes*

groan² *n* **1** a rather deep loud sound of suffering, worry, or disapproval **2** a sound caused by the movement of wood or metal parts heavily loaded: *The chair gave a groan when the fat woman sat down*

groat *n* (in England up to the middle of the 17th century) a silver coin worth 4 (old) pence

grocer *n* a shopkeeper who sells dry and preserved foods, like flour, sugar, rice, and other things for the home, such as matches and soap —compare GREENGROCER

groceries *n* the goods sold by a grocer

grocery *n* **-ies** the shop or trade of a grocer

grog *n* a mixture of strong drink (esp. rum) and water

groggy *adj* **-gier, -giest** *esp. spoken* weak because of illness, shock, etc., esp. when not able to walk steadily: *The boxer was looking groggy* — **groggily** *adv*

groin *n* 1 the hollow place where the tops of the legs meet the front of the body 2 a groyne

groom¹ *n* 1 a person who is in charge of horses 2 a bridegroom

groom² *v* 1 to take care of (horses), esp. by rubbing, brushing, and cleaning 2 to take care of the appearance of (oneself), by dressing neatly, keeping the hair tidy, etc. 3 (of animals) to clean the fur and skin of: *Monkeys groom each other* 4 to prepare (someone) for a special position or occasion: *grooming her for stardom*

groove¹ *n* a long narrow path or track made in a surface, esp. to guide the movement of something: *The cupboard door slides along a groove*

groove² *v* **grooved, grooving** to make grooves in

groovy *adj* **-ier, -iest** *sl* attractive or interesting in the fashion of the time

grope *v* **groped, groping** 1 to try to find something, or to make one's way, by feeling with the hands without being able to see : *He groped in his pocket for his ticket* 2 to search with uncertainty of success: *groping after the truth* 3 *sl* to feel over the body of (a person) so as to get sexual pleasure — **grope** *n* — **-ingly** *adv*

gross¹ *adj* 1 unpleasantly fat 2 (of people's speech & habits) rough, impolite, and offensive: *shocked by his gross words* 3 *law* clearly wrong in law; inexcusable 4 total: *The gross weight of the box of chocolates is more than the weight of the chocolates alone* —compare NET — ~**ly** *adv* — ~**ness** *n*

gross² *n* the whole; the greater part

gross³ *v* to gain as total profit or earn as a total amount: *The company grossed £2, 000, 000 last year*

gross⁴ *n* **gross** *or* **grosses** a group of 144; 12 dozen

grotesque *adj* 1 strange and unnatural so as to cause fear or be laughable: *a grotesque monster* 2 concerning the strange and unnatural, esp. in art — ~**ly** *adv* — ~**ness** *n*

grotto *n* **-toes** *or* **-tos** a natural or man-made cave

grotty *adj* **-tier, -tiest** *sl* bad, unpleasant, etc.: *a grotty little room* — **grottiness** *n*

grouch¹ *n* *esp. spoken* a bad-tempered complaint: *She's always got a grouch about something* —compare GROUSE — ~**y** *adj* — ~**iness** *n*

grouch² *v* *esp. spoken* to complain; grumble

ground¹ *n* 1 the surface of the earth: *The branch fell to the ground* —compare FLOOR 2 soil; earth: *The ground is dry* 3 a piece of land used for a particular purpose: *a football ground* 4 a background: *The curtains have white flowers on a blue ground* 5 a base for argument, study, etc. 6 **get off the ground** to make a successful start 7 **give ground** to yield; retreat 8 **go to ground** (esp. of a fox or criminal) to go into hiding

ground² *v* 1 a (of a boat) to strike against the

bottom or the ground b to cause (a boat) to do this 2 to cause (a pilot or plane) to come to or stay on the ground: *aircraft grounded because of thick mist* 3 to base: *I ground my argument on experience*

ground³ *past tense and past part. of* GRIND

ground bait *n* food dropped in a river, lake, etc., to attract fish to where one is fishing

ground bass *n* a tune repeated in the bass while the notes or tunes for the higher parts change

ground crew also **ground staff**— *n* the team of men at an airport who take care of aircraft between flights

ground floor *n* the part of a building at ground level —compare FIRST FLOOR

grounding *n* a complete training in the main points which will enable thorough study or work on some subject: *a good grounding in mathematics*

groundless *adj* (of feelings, ideas, etc.) without base or good reason — ~**ly** *adv* — ~**ness** *n*

groundnut also **peanut, monkey nut**— *n* a kind of edible nut which grows in a shell under the ground

ground plan *n* a drawn plan of a building at ground level

ground rent *n* rent paid to the owner of land which is let for building on

grounds *n* 1 small bits of solid matter which sink to the bottom of a liquid, esp. coffee 2 a reason (esp. in the phrase **on (the) grounds**) 3 land surrounding a large building, such as a country house or hospital 4 a large area used for a particular purpose: *fishing grounds*

groundsel *n* a wild plant with yellow flowers

groundsheet *n* a sheet of waterproof material used by campers who sleep on the ground

groundsman *n* **-men** a man employed to take care of a sports field

groundwork *n* the work which forms the base for some kind of study or skill

group¹ *n* 1 a number of people or things placed together 2 a number of people of the same interests, beliefs, age, race, etc. 3 a set of things or organizations connected in a particular way: *blood group A*

group² *v* to form into groups: *We can group animals into several types*

group captain *n* an officer of middle rank in the Royal Air Force, equal to a captain in the Navy or colonel in the Army

grouping *n* a (way of) arrangement into a group: *The new grouping of classes means larger numbers in each class*

group practice *n* a working partnership of doctors

grouse¹ *n* **grouse** any of several kinds of smallish fat birds which are shot for food and sport

grouse² *v* **groused, grousing** *esp. spoken* to complain —compare GROUCH — **grouse** *n*

grove *n* a group of trees

grovel *v* **-ll-** 1 to lie or move flat on the ground, esp. in fear or obedience: *The dog grovelled at his* *feet* **2** to be shamefully humble and eager to please: *He grovels to anyone important* — ~**ler** *n*

grow *v* **grew, grown, growing** **1** (of living things or parts of them) to increase in size by natural development: *Grass grows after rain* **2** (of plants) to exist and be able to develop: *Cotton grows wild here* **3** to cause to or allow to grow: *He grows vegetables* **4** to increase in numbers, amount, etc.: *The village is growing into a town* **5** to become (gradually): *The noise grew louder* —see also GROW INTO, GROW ON, GROW UP

grower *n* a person who grows plants, fruit, etc., for sale

growing pains *n* difficulties at the beginning of an activity, which will not last

grow into *v prep* **1** to become: *He's grown into a fine young man* **2** to become big enough for (clothes): *She'll grow into this coat*

growl *v* **1** (usu. of animals) to make a deep rough sound in the throat to show anger or give warning **2** to make a sound like this: *growling thunder* — **growl** *n* — **growler** *n*

grown *adj* **1** (of a person) of full size or development **2** (of living things) developed in a certain way: *well-grown*

grown-up¹ *adj* fully developed: *She has a grown-up daughter*

grown-up² *n esp. spoken* a fully grown and developed person —compare ADULT

grow on *v prep* to become gradually more pleasing or more of a habit to (someone): *Modern music is starting to grow on me*

growth *n* **1** the act or rate of growing and developing: *Trees take many years to reach their full growth* **2** increase in numbers or amount: *a sudden growth in membership of the club* **3** something which has grown **4** a lump produced by an unnatural and unhealthy increase in the number of cells in a part of the body —compare TUMOUR

grow up *v adv* **1** to develop from child to man or woman **2** to arise: *The custom grew up of dividing the father's land between the sons*

groyne, groin *n* a low wall built out into the sea, to prevent it from washing away the shore

grub¹ *v* **-bb-** to dig: *grubbing for worms*

grub² *n* **1** an insect in the wormlike form it has when just out of the egg **2** *esp. spoken* food

grubby *adj* **-bier, -biest** dirty

grudge¹ also **begrudge**— *v* **grudged, grudging** to give or allow unwillingly

grudge² *n* a cause for dislike, esp. of another person, real or imagined: *She has a grudge against me*

grudging *adj* ungenerous: *She was very grudging in her thanks* — ~**ly** *adv*

gruel *n* a kind of thin porridge

gruelling *adj* very hard and tiring — ~**ly** *adv*

gruesome *n* (esp. of something connected with death or decay) shocking and sickening — compare GRISLY — ~**ly** *adv* — ~**ness** *n*

gruff *adj* **1** (of the human voice) deep and rough **2** (of behaviour) rough; unfriendly or impatient, esp. in one's manner of speaking — ~**ly** *adv* — ~**ness** *n*

grumble¹ *v* **-bled, -bling** to express discontent: *He has nothing to grumble about* — **-bler** *n*

grumble² *n* a complaint

grumbling *adj* (of the human appendix) unwell; causing pain

grumpy *adj* **-ier, -iest** bad-tempered, esp. because of low spirits: *She's very grumpy when her tooth aches* — **grumpily** *adv* — **grumpiness** *n*

grunt¹ *v* **1** to make short deep rough sounds in the throat, as if the nose were closed: *a grunting pig* **2** (of human beings) to make such sounds, esp. when dissatisfied, in pain, or tired

grunt² *n* a sound like that of a pig

Gruyère *n* a kind of hard cheese with holes in it, from Switzerland

gryphon *n* a griffin

G-string *n* a narrow piece of cloth worn on the lower part of the body by striptease dancers

guano *n* the waste droppings of seabirds, used as manure

guarantee¹ *n* **1** a written statement by the maker of an article agreeing to repair or replace it within a certain time if it is faulty **2** an agreement to be responsible for the fulfilment of someone else's promise, esp. for paying a debt **3** something of value given to someone to keep until the owner has fulfilled a promise, esp. to pay **4** something that happens which makes something else certain

guarantee² *v* **-teed, -teeing** **1** to give a guarantee **2** to promise: *I guarantee you'll enjoy yourself*

guarantor *n technical or law* a person who agrees to be responsible for another person's fulfilling a promise, esp. paying a debt

guaranty *n* **-ties** *technical or law* a guarantee, esp. of payment

guard¹ *n* **1** a state of watchful readiness to protect or defend (esp. in the phrase **on guard**) **2** a position for defence, esp. in a fight: *He got in under his opponent's guard* **3** a person or group whose duty is to guard: *a prison guard* **4** a member of a group of special soldiers, originally those who guarded the king or queen: *a Horse Guard* —see also GRENADIER **5** a railway official in charge of a train **6** an apparatus which covers and protects: *a mudguard*

guard² *v* **1** to defend; keep safe, esp. by watching for danger: *The dog guarded the house* **2** to watch (a prisoner) in order to prevent escape **3** to control

guarded *adj* (of speech) careful; not saying too much — ~**ly** *adv*

guardian *n* **1** someone that guards **2** *law* a person who looks after another's child esp. after the parents' death —see also WARD — ~**ship** *n*

guardrail *n* **1** a bar of wood or metal placed to protect people, esp. from falling from a bridge or stairs **2** also **check rail** — an additional railway line, on curves, to prevent the train running off the lines

guardsman n -men a soldier or officer in the Guards

guard's van n the part of a train where the guard travels

guava n a type of small tropical tree or its round fruit with pink or white flesh and seeds in the centre

gudgeon n gudgeons or gudgeon **1** a type of small fish which fishermen use as bait **2** a person who is easily cheated

guerrilla, guerilla n a member of an unofficial fighting group which attacks the enemy in small groups unexpectedly

guess¹ v **1** to form (a judgment) or risk giving (an opinion) without knowing or considering all the facts: *Guess how much it cost* **2** to get to know by guessing: *She guessed my thoughts*

guess² n **1** an attempt to guess **2** an opinion formed by guessing

guesswork n the act of guessing, or the judgment which results

guest n **1** a person who is in someone's home by invitation **2** a person who is invited out and paid for at a theatre, restaurant, etc.: *Come to the concert as my guests* **3** a person who is lodging in a hotel, or as a **paying guest** in someone's home **4** a person who is invited to perform: *a guest singer*

guesthouse n a private house where visitors may stay and have meals for payment

guffaw v to laugh loudly, and perhaps rudely — **guffaw** n

guidance n help; advice

guide¹ n **1** something or somebody that shows the way, esp. someone whose job is to show a place to tourists **2** something which influences or controls a person's actions or behaviour: *Don't take your friend's experience as a guide* **3** also **guide book**— a book which gives a description of a place, for the use of visitors **4** an instruction book **5** GIRL GUIDE **6** a part of a machine which holds the moving parts in the right places

guide² v guided, guiding **1** to show the way: *He guided the man home* **2** to control (the movements of) **3** to influence strongly: *Be guided by your feelings*

guided missile n a missile guided by electrical means to its target

guild n **1** an association for businessmen or skilled workers in former times **2** an association of people with like interests: *the Townswomen's Guild*

guilder n a Dutch coin (GULDEN) or (in former times) a gold or silver coin of the same value

guildhall n a building in which members of a guild used to meet, sometimes now the **town hall**

guile n deceit, esp. of a clever, indirect kind: *Don't trust her: she's full of guile* —compare

CUNNING — ~**ful** adj — ~**fully** adv — ~**fulness** n

guileless adj (apparently) lacking in any deceit — ~**ly** adv — ~**ness** n

guillemot n any of several kinds of northern web-footed seabird

guillotine¹ n **1** a French machine for beheading criminals, having a heavy blade sliding down between 2 posts **2** a machine for cutting paper **3** the act of fixing a time to vote on a law in Parliament, so that argument about it will not go on too long

guillotine² v -tined, -tining **1** to use a guillotine as punishment on: *Many nobles were guillotined during the French Revolution* **2** to limit (argument) in Parliament

guilt n **1** the fact of having broken a law: *His guilt is proved* **2** responsibility for something wrong; blame **3** the knowledge or belief that one has done wrong: *His face showed guilt* — ~**less** adj — ~**lessly** adv — ~**lessness** n

guilty adj -ier, -iest **1** having broken a law or disobeyed a moral or social rule: *guilty of murder* **2** feeling or showing guilt: *I have a guilty conscience about losing your letter* — **guiltily** adv — **guiltiness** n

guinea n a former British gold coin, worth one pound one shilling (£1.05)

guinea fowl n guinea fowl a type of large grey bird with white spots which may be kept for its eggs and for food

guinea pig n **1** also **cavy**— a small furry tailless ratlike animal, often kept as a pet **2** a person who is the subject of some kind of test: *He was used as a guinea pig for the new drug*

guise n esp. written **1** an outer appearance: *the same old ideas in a different/new guise* **2** a style of dress (only in the phrase **in the guise of**): *He appeared in the guise of a woodcutter*

guitar n **1** a 6-stringed musical instrument played by plucking, having a long neck, and a wooden body like a violin but larger **2** any of a number of other musical instruments like this, such as one (an **electric guitar**) with a solid body and a sound that is increased electrically ☞ MUSIC

gulden also **guilder**— guldens or gulden the standard coin of the Netherlands ☞ MONEY

gulf n **1** a large deep stretch of sea partly enclosed by land: *the Persian Gulf* **2** a deep hollow place in the earth's surface: *A great gulf opened before us* **3** a great area of division, esp. between opinions

Gulf Stream n a current of warm water which flows north eastward in the Atlantic Ocean from the Gulf of Mexico towards Europe

gull¹ also **seagull**— n any of several kinds of largish flying seabirds

gull² v to trick or cheat: *We were gulled into buying what we didn't need*

gullet n the inner part of the throat ☞ DIGESTION

gullible *adj* easily tricked — **-bility** *n* — **-bly** *adv*

gully, -ley *n* **-lies** 1 a small narrow valley cut esp. into a hillside by heavy rain —see VALLEY (USAGE) ☞ GEOGRAPHY 2 a deep ditch 3 (in cricket) a fielding position just behind and at right angles to the batsman

gulp¹ *v* 1 to swallow hastily: *Don't gulp your food* 2 to make a sudden swallowing movement as if surprised or nervous

gulp² *n* 1 the action of gulping 2 a large mouthful

gum¹ *n* either of the 2 areas of flesh in which the upper and lower sets of teeth are fixed

gum² *n* 1 any of several kinds of sticky substance obtained from the stems of some plants 2 a substance used to stick things together 3 a hard transparent jelly-like sweet 4 a sweet plastic substance to be chewed but not swallowed

gum³ *v* **-mm-** to stick with gum

gumboil *n* *esp. spoken* a painful swelling on the gum

gumboot *n* a wellington

gummy *adj* **-mier, -miest** sticky — **gumminess** *n*

gumption *n* *esp. spoken* common sense and ability to act bravely

gun *n* 1 a weapon from which bullets or shells are fired through a barrel 2 a tool which forces out and spreads a substance by pressure: *a grease gun* 3 **jump the gun a** to start running in a race before the signal to start has been given **b** to start before getting permission —see also CANNON

gunboat *n* a small heavily armed naval warship for use in coastal waters

gunboat diplomacy *n* the use of a threat or show of armed force by a country to support a claim, demand, complaint, etc., against another

gundog *n* a type of dog trained to help in the shooting of birds for sport

gun down *v adv* to shoot, causing to fall dead or wounded

gunfire *n* the sound or act of firing guns

gun for *v prep* **gunning for** searching for in order to attack

gunge *n sl* any unpleasant, dirty, and/or sticky substance

gunman *n* **-men** a criminal armed with a gun

gunmetal *n* 1 a metal which is a mixture of copper, tin, lead, and zinc from which chains, belt fasteners, etc., are made 2 also **gunmetal grey**— a dark blue grey colour

gunner *n* 1 a member of a part of an armed force which uses artillery 2 a crew member of a large bomber who protects the aircraft from attacks by enemy aircraft with gunfire

gunpoint *n* **at gunpoint** under a threat of shooting

gunpowder *n* an explosive material in powder form

gunrunner *n* a person who unlawfully and secretly brings guns into a country — **-running** *n*

gunshot *n* 1 the distance reached by a shot from a gun 2 the act or sound of firing a gun 3 a bullet fired from a gun

gunsmith *n* a person who makes and repairs small guns

gunwale, gunnel *n* *technical* the upper edge of the side of a boat ☞ SAIL

guppy *n* **-pies** a type of small fish which bears its young alive

gurgle *v* **-gled, -gling** 1 (esp. of babies) to make a sound like water flowing unevenly 2 to flow with such a sound — **gurgle** *n*

guru *n* **-s** an Indian religious teacher

gush¹ *v* 1 to flow out in large quantities, as from a hole or cut: *Oil gushed from the broken pipe* 2 to express admiration, pleasure, etc., in a great flow of words, foolishly or without true feeling — **~ing** *adj* — **~ingly** *adv*

gush² *n* 1 a (sudden) flow: *The wound re-opened in a gush of blood* 2 a sudden rush (of words) 3 a sudden show (of strong feeling): *a gush of enthusiasm*

gusset *n* a piece of cloth sewn into a garment to strengthen and/or widen it

gust *n* a sudden strong rush of air, or of rain, smoke, etc., carried by wind

gusto *n* eager enjoyment: *He started painting with great gusto*

gusty *adj* **-ier, -iest** (of weather) with wind blowing in gusts

gut¹ *n* 1 the foodpipe which passes through the body 2 strong thread made from this part of animals

gut² *v* **-tt-** 1 to take out the inner organs of (a dead animal) 2 to destroy completely the inside of (a building), esp. by fire

gut³ *adj* *esp. spoken* arising from one's strongest feelings and needs: *a gut reaction*

gutless *adj* *esp. spoken* cowardly — **~ness** *n*

guts *n* *esp. spoken* 1 the bowels or intestines 2 bravery; determination: *He has a lot of guts*

gutta-percha *n* a soft rubber-like material obtained from the sap of certain Malayan trees

gutter¹ *n* 1 a small ditch between a road and the pavement to carry away rainwater 2 an open pipe fixed at the lower edge of a roof to carry away rainwater 3 the lowest poorest social conditions

gutter² *v* (of a candle) to burn unevenly

gutter press *n* *offensive* the kind of newspapers which tend to be full of shocking stories about people's personal lives

guttersnipe *n* a child of the poorest part of a town, living in the worst conditions

guttural *adj* (of speech) produced harshly and deep in the throat

guvnor, guv'nor also **guv**— *n sl* one's employer

guy¹ also **guy rope**— *n* **guys** 1 a rope, wire, or chain used to steady a load while it is being raised 2 a rope stretched from the top or side of a pole or from the side of a tent to the ground, to hold it in place

guy² n **1** *esp. spoken, esp. US* a man **2** any of the stuffed figures representing Guy Fawkes that are burnt on November 5th **3** *esp. spoken* a person wearing strange and comical clothes

guy³ v **guyed, guying** to copy in a funny way so as to make others laugh: *The politician was guyed by the comedian*

Guy Fawkes Night n November 5th, when guys are burnt and fireworks are lit

guzzle v **-zled, -zling** to eat or drink greedily — **guzzler** n

gym n **1** a gymnasium **2** gymnastics

gymkhana n a local sports meeting, esp. horse racing, jumping, etc.

gymnasium n **-ums** or **-a** a hall with wall bars, ropes, etc., for climbing, jumping, etc.

gymnast n a person who trains and is skilled in bodily exercises — ~**ic** adj — ~**ically** adv

gymnastics n the training of the body by exercises

gymslip n a sleeveless dress formerly often worn by girls as part of a school uniform

gynaecology n the study in medicine of pregnancy and childbirth, and of women's diseases — **-logical** adj — **-logist** n

gyp n sl sharp pain or punishment (in the phrase **give someone gyp**)

gypsum n a soft white chalklike substance

gyrate v **-rated, -rating** to swing round and round a fixed point: *The dancers gyrated to the beat of the music* — **-tion** n

gyroscope also **gyro**— n a heavy wheel which spins inside a frame, used for keeping ships and aircraft steady, and also as a toy — **-scopic** adj

H, h H's, h's or Hs, hs the 8th letter of the English alphabet

habeas corpus n *law Latin* (the right to demand) a written order for a prisoner to appear in court, as a protection against unlimited imprisonment without charges (esp. in the phrase **a writ of habeas corpus**)

haberdasher n a shopkeeper who sells dressmaking materials

haberdashery n **-ies** a haberdasher's shop or department in a store or the goods sold there

habit n **1** customary behaviour: *It's my habit to get up early* **2** a special kind of clothing, esp. that worn by monks and nuns

habitable adj which can be inhabited

habitat n the natural home of a plant or animal

habitation n **1** the act of inhabiting: *a house too old for human habitation* **2** a place to live in

habitual adj **1** usual: *his habitual greeting* **2** by habit: *a habitual thief* — ~**ly** adv

habituate to v prep **-ated, -ating** to accustom (oneself) to

hacienda n a large South American house, usu. with farming land

hack¹ v to cut, esp. roughly or in uneven pieces: *They hacked their way through the trees*

hack² n a rough cutting movement or blow

hack³ n **1** an old or worn-out horse **2** a light horse for riding **3** a person who does a lot of poor quality work, esp. writing stories

hack⁴ v to ride through the country on horseback, for pleasure — **hack** n

hacking cough n a noisy painful cough

hackles n the long feathers or hairs on the back of the neck of certain birds and animals, which stand up straight in times of danger

hackney n **-neys 1** a horse for driving or riding **2** a high-stepping breed of horse

hackney carriage n *esp. written or technical* **1** a taxi **2** a horse-drawn carriage for hire, esp. formerly

hackneyed adj repeated too often

hacksaw n a tool with a fine-toothed replaceable blade, often used for cutting metal

had short form **'d**— **1** past tense of HAVE **2** past part. of HAVE

haddock n **haddock** or **haddocks** a common edible sea-fish

Hades n the Greek land of the dead

haemoglobin n a red colouring matter, found in red blood cells, which contains iron and carries oxygen

haemophilia n a disease which affects only males, but may be passed on by the mother or father to the children, and which makes the sufferer bleed for a long time after a cut or bruise **-philiac** n, adj

haemorrhage n a flow of blood, esp. a long or large and unexpected one

haemorrhoid n a swollen blood vessel at the opening (ANUS) at the lower end of the bowel —see also PILES

haft n the handle of an axe or of some long-handled weapons

hag n an ugly or unpleasant old woman, esp. a witch

haggard adj having hollow places around the eyes, as from great tiredness —compare GAUNT

haggis n **-gises** or **-gis** a Scottish food made from the inner organs of a sheep cut up and boiled inside a skin made from the stomach

haggle v **-gled, -gling** to argue over fixing a price

ha-ha¹ interj (a shout of laughter)

ha-ha² n **ha-has** a ditch used to divide property

hail¹ n **1** water frozen into little hard balls **2** a number of things which strike suddenly with violence: *a hail of bullets*

hail² v (of hail) to fall

hail³ v **1** to call out to by name or in greeting:

An old friend hailed me **2** to recognize as important by calling out (a title): *They hailed him king*

hail as *v prep* to recognize as: *They hailed it as a work of art*

hail from *v prep* to come from

hailstone *n* a small ball of hail

hair *n* **1** a fine threadlike growth from the skin of a person or animal ☞ SKIN **2** a mass of such growths, such as that on the human head — compare FUR **3 get in (someone's) hair** *esp. spoken* to annoy (someone) **4 split hairs** to concern oneself with unimportant differences — ~**less** *adj*

hairbrush *n* a brush used to smooth the hair and get out dirt

haircut *n* **1** an occasion of having the hair cut **2** the style the hair is cut in

hairdo *n* **-dos** the style a woman's hair is shaped into

hairdresser *n* a person who cuts, sets, or changes the colour of hair (esp. women's) — compare BARBER — **-sing** *n*

hairgrip *n* a small often ornamented clip that a woman fixes or slides into her hair to keep it in place

hairline *n* **1** a very thin line **2** a narrow crack **3** the place on the forehead where the hair starts growing

hairnet *n* a net worn over the hair to keep it in place

hairpiece *n* a piece of false hair used to make one's own hair seem thicker

hairpin *n* a U-shaped wire pin to hold the hair in position

hairpin bend *n* a narrow U-shaped curve where a road turns back, as when going up a steep hill

hair-raising *adj* very frightening

hair-restorer *n* (a) substance or liquid that is supposed to make hair grow again

hair's breadth also **hairbreadth**— *n* a very short distance: *We missed by a hair's breadth*

hair slide also **slide**— *n* a small fastener to keep a girl's hair in place

hair-splitting *n* too much interest in unimportant differences and points of detail, esp. in argument

hairspring *n* a delicate spring which controls the even running of a watch

hairy *adj* **-ier, -iest** **1 a** (not usu. describing the hair on the head) having a lot of hair: *a hairy chest* **b** having a rough surface like hair **2** *sl* exciting in a frightening way: *a hairy drive* — **-iness** *n*

hake *n* **hake** or **hakes** any of several kinds of edible sea fish

halberd *n* a weapon used formerly, with a blade on a long handle ☞ WEAPON

halcyon *adj literature* calm or peaceful (esp. in the phrase **halcyon days**)

hale *adj literature* healthy

half¹ *n* **halves** **1** either of the 2 equal parts into which something is or could be divided; ½; 50%

2 either of 2 parts or periods of time into which something is divided: *Neither side scored in the first half* **3 by halves** incompletely: *Better not do it at all than do it by halves* **4 go halves (in/on something)** *esp. spoken* to share (the cost of something)

half² *n* **halfs** or **halves** **1** something which has ½ the value or quantity of something, such as a coin, ticket, weight, or measure: *Give me a penny for 2 halfs* **2** a halfback

half³ *pron* either of the 2 parts of a thing or group: *Half of them are here*

half⁴ *adj* being ½ in amount: *half a minute*

half⁵ *adv* **1** partly: *half cooked* **2** half 7, 8, 9, etc. (of time) 7.30, 8.30, 9.30, etc. —see PAST

half a crown also **half crown**— *n* **half crowns** (in Britain before 1971) a large silver-coloured coin worth 2 shillings and 6 old pence (12½p)

half a dozen also **half dozen**— *adj, n* **half dozens** 6: *half a dozen eggs*

halfback also **half**— *n* (in games like football) a player or position between the forwards and the backs

half-baked *adj* lacking planned judgment

half-breed also **half-caste**— *n, adj sometimes rude* (a person) with parents of different races

half-brother *n* a brother related through one parent only ☞ FAMILY

half cock **go off (at) half cock** to fail esp. because of poor preparation

half-hearted *adj* showing little effort and no real interest —compare WHOLE-HEARTED — ~**ly** *adv* — ~**ness** *n*

half-holiday *n* **-days** half a day free from school, studies, etc.

half line *n technical* part of a line, with one definite end, that extends indefinitely in one direction

half-mast *n* a position of the flag near the middle of the mast or flagpole, to show sorrow as at the death of an important person

half moon *n* **1** the shape of the moon seen when half the side facing the earth is showing **2** something of this shape

halfpenny *n* **halfpennies** or **halfpence** **1** (in Britain, before 1971) a coin, 2 of which made an old penny; ½d **2** also **half p-** (in Britain, after 1971) a very small coin, 2 of which make a new penny; ½p USAGE **halfpennies** is used for numbers of coins, **halfpence** for amounts of money —see PENNY (USAGE)

half-sister *n* a sister related through one parent only ☞ FAMILY

half term *n* a short holiday, usu. 2 or 3 days, in the middle of a school term

half-timbered *adj* of an old style of house building with the wood of the frame showing in the walls

half time *n* the period of time between 2 parts of a game

halftone also **half step**— *n US* a semitone

half volley *n* **-leys** (esp. in tennis and cricket)

a stroke in which the ball is hit the moment it bounces

halfway *adj, adv* at the midpoint between 2 things

half-wit *n* a person of weak mind — ~**ted** *adj* — ~**tedly** *adv*

halibut *n* -**but** *or* -**buts** a kind of very large edible fish

halitosis *n* *medical* bad breath

hall *n* 1 a large room in which meetings, dances, etc., can be held 2 the passage just inside the entrance of a house, from which the rooms open

halleluja also **alleluia**— *interj, n* (a song, cry, etc., expressing) praise, joy, and thanks to God

hallmark¹ *n* 1 the mark made on objects of precious metal to prove that they are silver or gold 2 a typical piece of behaviour or an object which shows the nature of a person or thing: *Clear expression is the hallmark of good writing*

hallmark² *v* to make a hallmark on

hall of residence also **hall**— *n* **halls of residence** a building where several students live and sleep

hallow *v* to make holy: *a hallowed place*

Hallowe'en *n* the night of October 31, when it was once believed that witches rode and ghosts appeared

hallstand *n* a piece of furniture with hooks for hats and coats

hallucinate *v* -**nated**, -**nating** to see things which are not there

hallucination *n* something apparently seen which is not really there, often as the result of a drug or a mental illness — -**atory** *adj*

hallucinogenic *adj* causing hallucination

halo *n* -**loes** *or* -**los** 1 a golden circle around the heads of holy persons in religious paintings 2 a bright circle of light, as around the sun or moon in misty weather

halt¹ *v* to stop: *The train was halted by the signal*

halt² *n* 1 a stop or pause (esp. in the phrase **come to a halt**) 2 a small railway station: *a country halt*

halter *n* 1 a rope or leather band fastened round a horse's head, esp. to lead it 2 a rope for hanging criminals

halterneck *adj* (of a garment, esp. a dress) that leaves the wearer's back uncovered and is held in place by a band of material around the neck

halting *adj* stopping and starting as if uncertain: *a halting voice* — ~**ly** *adv*

halve *v* **halved, halving** 1 to divide into halves 2 to reduce to half

halves *pl. of* HALF

halyard *n* *technical* a rope used to raise or lower a flag or sail ☞ SAIL

ham¹ *n* 1 preserved meat from a pig's leg 2 an actor whose acting is unnatural, with extreme gestures and a booming way of speaking 3 a person who receives and/or sends radio messages using his own apparatus

ham² *v* -**mm**- to act (a part on stage) unnaturally or wildly

hamburger *n* a flat circular cake of minced meat, esp. as eaten in a bread roll

ham-fisted also **ham-handed**— *adj* clumsy

hamlet *n* a small village

hammer¹ *n* 1 a tool with a heavy head for driving nails into wood, or for striking things to break or move them 2 something made to hit something else, as in a piano, or part of a gun 3 a small bone in the ear 4 **come under the hammer** to be sold by auction 5 **throwing the hammer** a sport in which competitors throw a metal ball on the end of a wire as far as possible

hammer² *v* 1 to strike with a hammer 2 to hit repeatedly

hammer and sickle *n* the sign of a hammer crossing a sickle, representing communism

hammer out *v adv* to come to a decision about by detailed discussion: *to hammer out a plan*

hammock *n* a long piece of cloth or net which can be hung up by the ends to form a bed

hamper¹ *v* to cause difficulty in activity: *The snow hampered my movements*

hamper² *n* a large basket with a lid

hamster *n* a type of small animal with pouches in its cheeks for storing food, kept as a pet

hamstring¹ *n* a cordlike tendon at the back of the leg, joining a muscle to a bone

hamstring² *v* -**strung**, -**stringing** to cut the hamstring, destroying the ability to walk

hand¹ *n* 1 the movable parts at the end of the arm, including the fingers 2 a pointer or needle on a clock or machine 3 handwriting: *He writes a clear hand* 4 a set of playing cards held by one person in a game 5 (in squash and badminton) the period of play from the time a player becomes server until he becomes receiver 6 a measure equal to 0.1 metres, used in measuring a horse's height at the shoulder 7 a sailor on a ship 8 a workman 9 encouragement given by clapping the hands (in the phrases **give a (good, big) hand to**, **get a (big, good) hand**) 10 quality of touch (esp. in the phrases **have a light/heavy hand**) 11 help (esp. in the phrases **give/lend a hand to**) 12 control (esp. in the phrases **get/become out of hand**) 13 **at first hand** when known through direct experience 14 **at hand** near in time or place 15 **bring up by hand** to feed (an animal that has no mother) so that it can live and grow 16 **get/keep one's hand in** to get used to an activity by practising 17 **get the upper hand** to get control or power 18 **have one's hands full** to be very busy 19 **on every hand** in all directions 20 **on the one/other hand** as one point in the argument/as an opposite point: *I want to go to the party, but on the other hand I ought to be studying* 21 **out of hand** (esp. of decisions not to do something) at once and without further thought 22 **throw in one's hand** to accept defeat 23 **turn one's hand to** to begin to practise (a skill) —see also SHAKE **hands**, HOLD **hands**

hand² *v* 1 to give from one's own hand into

someone else's: *Hand me that book* **2 hand it to (someone)** to admit (someone's) success, esp. in something mentioned next —see also HAND DOWN, HAND ON, HAND OVER

handbag *n* a small bag for a woman's money and personal things

handball *n* an American game in which a ball is hit against a wall by the hand

handbarrow *n* a handcart

handbill *n* a small printed notice or advertisement to be given out by hand

handbook *n* a short book giving information about a subject —compare MANUAL

handbrake *n* a brake that prevents a vehicle from moving when parked

handcart *n* a small cart which can be pushed or pulled by hand

handcuff *v* to put handcuffs on

handcuffs *n* metal rings joined together, for fastening the wrists of a criminal

hand down also **hand on, pass down**— *v adv* to give or leave to people who are younger or come later

handful *n* **1** an amount which is as much as can be held in the hand **2** a small number: *a handful of people* **3** a living thing that is difficult to control: *That child is quite a handful*

handicap¹ *n* **1 a** a disability: *Blindness is a great handicap* **b** disadvantage: *Being small is a handicap in this crowd* **2** a race, sport, or game in which the stronger competitors are disadvantaged by weights, running further than others, etc.

handicap² *v* **-pp-** **1** to cause to have a disadvantage **2** (of a disability) to prevent (someone) from acting and living in the usual way: *physically handicapped*

handicraft *n* a skill needing use of the hands, such as sewing, weaving, etc.

handiwork *n* **1** work demanding the skilful use of the hands **2** something that someone has made: *God's handiwork*

handkerchief *n* **-chiefs** *or* **chieves** a piece of cloth or thin soft paper for drying the nose, eyes, etc.

handle¹ *n* **1** a part of an object for holding it or for opening it **2 fly off the handle** *esp. spokcn* to lose one's temper

handle² *v* **-dled, -dling** **1** to feel or move with the hands **2** to deal with; control **3** to treat: *Handle children kindly* **4** to use (goods) in business, esp. for sale —see also CARRY **5** (of a car, boat, etc.) to obey controlling movements in the stated way — **handleable** *adj*

handlebars *n* the steering bar of a bicycle or motorcycle

handler *n* a person who controls an animal

handloom *n* a small machine for weaving by hand

hand luggage *n* a traveller's small bags, cases, etc.,

handmade *adj* made by hand

handmaiden also **handmaid**— *n old use* a female servant

hand on *v adv* **1** to give from one person to another: *Please read this and hand it on* **2** HAND DOWN

handout *n* **1** something given free, such as food, clothes, etc., esp. to someone poor **2** information given out, esp. a printed sheet

hand over *v adv* to give control of: *to hand over command of a ship*

handpick *v* to choose (the best ones) out of a group

handrail *n* a bar of wood or metal fixed beside a place where one walks for holding onto, esp. near stairs

handshake *n* an act of shaking each other's right hand as a greeting or farewell between 2 people

handsome *adj* **1 a** (esp. of men) good-looking **b** (esp. of women) attractive with a firm, large appearance —compare BEAUTIFUL, PRETTY **2** generous: *a handsome present* — ~**ly** *adv*

hand-to-hand *adj* very close (esp. in the phrase **hand-to-hand fighting**) — **hand to hand** *adv*

hand-to-mouth *adj* (of a way of life) with just enough money, food, etc., to live — **hand to mouth** *adv*

handwork *n* work done by hand —compare HANDIWORK

handwriting *n* writing done by hand

handy *adj* **-ier, -iest** **1** useful and simple to use **2** clever in using the hands: *handy with her needle* **3** near: *The shops are handy* — **-ily** *adv* — **-iness** *n*

handyman *n* **-men** a person who does repairs and practical jobs, esp. in the house

hang¹ *v* **hung, hanging** **1** to fix at the top so that the lower part is free: *to hang curtains* **2** to be in such a position: *The curtains hang well* **3** to keep (certain types of meat) in this position until ready to be eaten **4** to show (a set of paintings) publicly **5 a** to fix (wallpapcr) on a wall **b** to fix (a door) in position on its hinges **6** *esp. spoken* damn (esp. in the phrases **I'll be hanged, Hang it!**) **7 hang fire** to stop happening or continuing: *Our plans must hang fire for a time* —see also HANG ABOUT, HANG BACK, HANG ON, HANG OUT, HANG UP

hang² *v* **hanged, hanging** to kill or die, as in punishment for a crime, by dropping with a rope around the neck

hang³ *n* **1** the shape or way something hangs: *I don't like the hang of this coat* **2 get/have the hang of** *esp. spoken* to be able to understand, use, or work

hang about *v adv* *esp. spoken* **1** to wait without purpose or activity **2** to delay or move slowly

hangar *n* a big shed where planes are kept

hang back *v adv* to be unwilling to act or move: *We hung back in fear*

hangdog *adj* (of an expression) ashamed

hanger *n* a hook and crosspiece to fit inside the

shoulders of a dress, coat, etc., to keep its shape when hung up

hanger-on n **hangers-on** a person who tries to be friendly, esp. for his own advantage

hang gliding n the sport of gliding using a large kite

hanging n the punishment for crime in which death is caused by hanging from a rope round the neck

hangings n curtains and other materials hanging over the walls, windows, doors, etc., of a house

hangman n **-men** a person who hangs criminals

hangnail n a piece of torn skin near the bottom of the fingernail

hang on¹ v adv esp. spoken **1** to keep hold of something **2** to wait, as on the telephone

hang on² also **hang upon—** v prep **1** to pay close attention to: The boy hangs on her every word **2** to depend on

hang out v adv esp. spoken to live or spend much time: He hangs out in an old house

hangover n the feeling of headache, sickness, etc., the day after drinking too much alcohol △ OVERHANG

hangup n sl something which a person gets unusually worried about, finds very difficult, etc.

hang up v adv **1** to put on a hook: Hang your coat up **2** to finish a telephone conversation by putting the receiver back: 'I must hang up now' **3** to delay

hank n a length or loose ring of hair, wool, etc.

hanker v to have a strong wish (usu. for something one cannot have): He hankers for friendship

hankering n a strong wish; longing

hankie, -ky n **-kies** esp. spoken a handkerchief

hanky-panky n improper behaviour of a not very serious kind

Hansard n the printed report of what is said in Parliament

hansom also **hansom cab—** n a 2-wheeled horse-drawn carriage

hap n old use luck

haphazard adj happening in a disorderly manner — ~ly adv

hapless adj poetic unlucky: a hapless fate

haply adv old use perhaps

happen v **1** to take place **2** to have the good or bad luck (to) **3** to be true by or as if by chance: It so happened that I saw him yesterday

happening n an event

happen on also **happen upon, chance (up)on—** v prep to find by chance: I happened on an old country inn

happen to v prep to take place and have an effect on: A bad accident happened to that family

happy adj **-pier, -piest 1** feeling or giving pleasure **2** suitable: not a very happy remark **3** polite pleased: I'll be happy to meet him **4** (of wishes) joyful (esp. in phrases like **Happy New Year, Happy Birthday**) — **-pily** adv — **-piness** n

happy-go-lucky adj showing a lack of careful thought or planning; easy-going

happy medium n the middle way of doing (something) when opposite ways are suggested

hara-kiri n a Japanese way of ceremoniously killing oneself by cutting open the stomach

harangue¹ n a loud or long speech, esp. one which blames those listening to it

harangue² v **harangued, haranguing** to attack or try to persuade with a harangue

harass v **1** to trouble continually **2** to make repeated attacks against: They harassed the enemy

harassment n being harassed

harbinger n literature a person or thing that lets one know that something is to happen or is on its way —compare HERALD

harbour¹ n an area of sheltered water where ships are safe from rough seas

harbour² v **1** to give protection to, esp. by giving food and shelter to (someone bad): Harbouring criminals is an offence in law **2** to keep in the mind: to harbour a secret wish — ~er n

hard¹ adj **1** which cannot easily be broken, pressed down, bent, etc. **2** difficult (to do or understand): hard questions **3 a** forceful: a hard push **b** needing or using force of body or mind: hard work **4** full of difficulty: a hard life **5** (of people, punishments, etc.) not gentle: a hard woman **6** (in English pronunciation) **a** (of the letter c) pronounced as k rather than s **b** (of the letter g) pronounced as in get rather than as in rage **7** (of water) which contains lime, preventing soap from mixing properly with the water **8** (of a drug) being one on which a user can become dependent so that he will be ill if he does not take it **9** unpleasant to the senses, esp. because too bright or too loud: her hard voice —see also HARD UP

hard² adv **1** with great effort: Think hard and work hard **2** heavily: It's raining hard **3 be hard done by** to be unfairly treated **4 be hard put to it** to have great difficulty **5 die hard** (of habits) to be lost with difficulty —compare DIEHARD **6 hard at it** working with all one's force in some activity —see also HARD UPON

hard-and-fast adj (of rules) fixed and unchangeable

hardback n a book with a strong stiff binding —compare PAPERBACK

hard-bitten adj very firm in argument and decision, esp. when made so by hard experience

hardboard n a material made out of fine pieces of wood pressed into sheets and used as a light wood

hard-boiled adj **1** (of eggs) boiled until the

yellow part is hard **2** not showing feeling, esp. when made bitter through long experience

hard by *adj, adv* very near

hard-core *adj often offensive* which refuses to change, yield, or improve: *hard-core opposition*

hard core *n* **1** the broken brick, stone, etc., used as a base when a road is built **2** *often offensive* the people most concerned at the centre of an activity, esp. when opposed to some other group

harden *v* **1** to make or become hard or firm **2** to make or become hard or unkind: *I hardened my heart against him*

harden to *v prep* to make less sensitive to: *Dennis is becoming hardened to failure*

hardheaded *adj* practical and thorough, esp. in business

hard-hearted *adj* having no kind feelings — ~ly *adv* — ~ness *n*

hardihood *n* boldness

hardiness *n* see HARDY

hard labour *n* a punishment which consists of hard bodily work such as digging

hard liquor *n* strong drink which contains a lot of alcohol

hard luck also **tough luck, hard lines**— *interj, n* (sorry about your) bad luck

hardly *adv* **1** almost not: *I could hardly wait* **2** not reasonably: *I can hardly ask him for more money* USAGE **Hardly, scarcely**, and **barely** are correctly followed by *when* in such sentences as: **Hardly** *had he arrived when she started complaining.* Do not use *than* in such sentences except after *no sooner*: *No sooner had he arrived than she started complaining.* **Hardly** and **scarcely** (but not **barely** or *no sooner*) can be followed by *any, ever,* and *at all*, to mean "almost no", "almost never", and "almost not": *hardly any money | I scarcely ever see her*

hardness *n* the state of being hard

hard of hearing *adj* **harder of hearing** unable to hear properly

hardship *n* something that causes suffering, such as lack of money, hard work, etc.

hard shoulder *n* an area that has been given a hard surface, beside a motorway, where cars may stop if in difficulty

hard up *adj* not having enough esp. money

hard upon also **hard on**— *prep* **1** soon after **2** close behind

hardware *n* **1** goods for the home and garden, such as pans, tools, etc. —compare IRONMONGERY **2** machinery used in war **3** machinery which makes up a computer —compare SOFTWARE

hardwearing that can be used for a long time without wearing out

hardwood *n* strong heavy wood like oak, used to make good furniture —opposite **softwood**

hardy *adj* **-dier, -diest** **1** strong; able to bear cold, hard work, etc. **2** (of plants) able to live through the winter above ground — **-diness** *n*

hare¹ *n* **hares** or **hare** an animal with long ears, a divided upper lip, a short tail and long back legs which make it able to run fast. It is larger than a rabbit, and does not live in a hole ☞ MAMMAL

hare, hair² *v* **hared, haring** *esp. spoken* to run very fast: *He hared off down the road*

harebell *n* a wild plant with one bell-shaped blue flower; the bluebell of Scotland

harebrained *adj* very impractical; quite foolish

harelip *n* (the condition of having) the top lip divided into 2 parts, because of its not developing properly — **-lipped** *adj*

harem *n* **1** the place in a Muslim house where the women live **2** the women who live in this

haricot also **haricot bean**— *n* any of several types of small white bean

hark *v literature* to listen: *Hark! I can hear their voices*

hark at *v prep esp. spoken* to listen to (someone or something disapproved of)

hark back *v adv esp. spoken* to mention or think over things which happened in the past

harlequin *n* a character in English pantomime, in love with the beautiful Columbine and dressed in a costume boldly patterned with diamonds —see also COMMEDIA DELL'ARTE

Harley Street *n* (a street which gives its name to) an area of London where important private doctors work

harlot *n old use* a prostitute — ~ry *n*

harm¹ *n* damage; wrong: *He means no harm* — ~ful *adj* — ~fully *adv* — ~fulness *n*

harm² *v* to hurt; damage: *Getting up early won't harm you!*

harmless *adj* that cannot cause harm — ~ly *adv* — ~ness *n*

harmonic *n technical* any of a set of higher notes produced when a musical note is played; overtone

harmonica *n* a mouthorgan

harmonium *n* a kind of organ worked by pumped air

harmonize, -ise *v* **-nized, -nizing** **1** to add another set of notes to, either in writing or while performing: *The singers began to harmonize the new song* **2** to be or bring into agreement: *The colours don't harmonize*

harmony *n* **-nies** **1** notes of music combined together in a pleasant sounding way —compare DISCORD, UNISON **2** peacefulness: *My cat and dog live in perfect harmony* —compare DISCORD — **-nious** *adj* — **-niously** *adv* — **-niousness** *n*

harness¹ *n* **1** the leather bands used to control a horse or fasten it to a cart **2** something of this type, such as the straps fastened round a baby's body to support or confine it

harness² *v* **1** to put a harness on or fasten with a harness **2** to use (a natural force) to produce useful power: *harness a river to make electricity*

harp *n* a large musical instrument with strings running from top to bottom of an open 3-cornered frame, played by stroking or plucking the strings with the hands — ~ist *n*

harp on *v prep* to talk a lot about sorrows or worries: *Don't keep harping on like that*

harpoon¹ *n* a spear with a long rope, used for hunting large fish or whales

harpoon² *v* to catch with a harpoon

harpsichord *n* an early musical instrument, like a piano except that the strings are plucked

harpy *n* -**pies** 1 a creature in Greek stories, half woman, half bird, very cruel and greedy 2 a cruel greedy person

harquebus *n* an arquebus

harridan *n* a bad-tempered unpleasant woman

harrier *n* 1 a kind of falcon ☞ BIRD 2 a cross-country runner

Harris Tweed *n* *trademark* woollen cloth woven by hand on the island of Harris

harrow *n* a farming machine with sharp metal teeth on a frame, used to break up the surface of the earth after ploughing

harrowing *adj* which causes feelings of pain and worry: *a harrowing experience*

harry *v* -**ried**, -**rying** 1 to attack repeatedly 2 to trouble continually: *They harry him for money*

harsh *adj* 1 unpleasant to the senses: *a harsh light* 2 showing cruelty or lack of kindness — ~**ly** *adv* — ~**ness** *n*

hart *n* a full-grown male deer, esp. a red deer, over 5 years old; stag —compare HIND

harum-scarum *adj, adv* (acting) wildly and thoughtlessly

harvest¹ *n* 1 the gathering of the crops 2 the time of year when crops are picked

harvest² *v* to gather (a crop) —compare REAP

harvester *n* 1 a person who gathers the crops 2 a machine which cuts grain and gathers it in

has *short form* '**s**— 3rd person sing. pres. tense of HAVE

has-been *n* *esp. spoken* a person or thing no longer important, useful, etc.

hash *n* 1 a main dish containing meat cut up in small pieces, esp. when re-cooked 2 a mess or muddle (esp. in the phrase **make a hash of it**)

hashish also (*sl*) **hash**— *n* the most powerful form of cannabis. It is the hardened juice from the plant

hasp *n* a metal fastener for a box, door, etc., which usu. fits over a hook and is fixed by a padlock

hassle¹ *n* *esp. spoken* a difficult argument or struggle

hassle² *v* -**sled**, -**sling** *esp. spoken* to argue

hast **thou hast** *old use* (when talking to one person) you have

haste *n* quick urgent movement or action: *Make haste!* (=hurry!)

hasten *v* 1 to move or happen faster: *He hastened home* 2 to be quick to say, because the hearer may imagine something else has happened: *I hasten to say that he is not hurt*

hasty *adj* -**ier**, -**iest** 1 done in a hurry: *a hasty meal* 2 too quick in acting or deciding, esp. with a bad result: *a hasty temper* — -**ily** *adv* — -**iness** *n*

hat *n* 1 a covering placed on top of the head 2 **keep under one's hat** to keep secret 3 **old hat** old-fashioned 4 **pass the hat round** to collect money, esp. for someone

hatch¹ *n* 1 (on a ship or aircraft) **a** also **hatchway**— an opening through which people and things can pass **b** the cover used to close this ☞ AEROPLANE 2 an opening in a wall, esp. to pass food through

hatch² *v* 1 (of an egg) to break, letting the young bird out 2 to come or bring out of an egg —compare INCUBATE 3 to make up (a plan or idea)

hatchback *n* a car having a door at the back which opens upwards

hatchery *n* -**ies** a place for hatching eggs

hatchet *n* 1 a small axe with a short handle 2 **bury the hatchet** to become friends again after a bad quarrel

hatching *n* fine lines drawn on or cut into a surface —see CROSS-HATCHING

hate¹ *n* a strong feeling of dislike

hate² *v* **hated**, **hating** 1 to have a great dislike of: *I hate cruelty* 2 to dislike: *She hates fish*

hateful *adj* very unpleasant to experience — ~**ly** *adv* — ~**ness** *n*

hath *old use* has

hatless *adj* not wearing a hat

hatpin *n* a long pin used, esp. formerly, to fasten a lady's hat to her hair

hatred *n* the state or feeling of hating

hatter *n* a maker or seller of hats

hat trick *n* 3 successes of the same type coming one after the other, esp. in sports

hauberk *n* a coat of armour made up of several metal rings (CHAIN MAIL) ☞ ARMOUR

haughty *adj* -**tier**, -**tiest** proud — -**tily** *adv* — -**tiness** *n*

haul¹ *v* 1 to pull hard 2 to force to appear before an official body; summons: *hauled up before the court* —see also HAVE UP

haul² *n* 1 the act of hauling 2 **a** the amount of fish caught in a net **b** the amount of something gained, esp. stolen goods

haulage *n* 1 **a** the business of carrying goods by road **b** the charge for this 2 the act of hauling

haulier *n* a person who runs a haulage business

haulm *n* the stems of crops like peas, beans, potatoes, etc., left after gathering

haunch *n* 1 the fleshy part of the human body between the waist and knee —compare HINDQUARTERS 2 the back leg of an animal

haunt¹ *v* 1 to visit (a place) regularly 2 to appear in as a ghost: *A headless man haunts the castle* 3 to be always in the thoughts of: *haunted by his words*

haunt² *n* a place to go to regularly: *a favourite haunt*

haunting *adj* which remains in the thoughts — ~ly *adv*

hauteur *n* French *esp. written* haughtiness

Havana *n* a cigar made in Cuba or from Cuban tobacco

have¹ *short form* **'ve**— *v* **had, having 1** (a helping verb, forming the perfect tense): *I've been reading.* | *Have you finished?* **2** also **have got**— to possess, or contain as a part: *She has blue eyes.* | *This coat has no pockets* **3** to receive or take: *I had a letter today.* | *He had a hot bath* **4** to enjoy or experience: *We're having a party* **5** to allow: *I can't have you running up and down all day* **6 a** to cause to be done: *I had my hair cut* **b** to experience: *I had my car stolen* **7 had better** ought to **8 have to** also **have got to**— must: *I have to go now*

have² *n esp. spoken* a trick —see also HAVES

haven *n* a place of calm and safety

have-nots *n* the poor

have on¹ *v adv* **1** also **have**— to trick, usu. by pretending something not true: *I've been had!* **2** also **have got on**— to be wearing: *He had a beautiful new suit on* **3** also **have got on**— have arranged to do: *I have nothing on for tonight*

have on² also **have got on**— *v prep* **1** to have recorded against: *You've got nothing on me* **2 have nothing on** to be not nearly as good as

haver *v* Scots to talk foolishly

haversack *n now rare* a bag carried usu. over one shoulder when walking —compare RUCK-SACK

haves *n* the rich

have up *v adv* to take to court: *He was had up for dangerous driving*

havoc *n* widespread damage or confusion: *His ideas are causing havoc in the office*

haw¹ *n* the red berry of the hawthorn tree

haw² *v* see HUM **and haw**

haw³ *interj* (the sound made in a loud laugh)

hawk¹ *n* **1** any of many types of bird, often large, which catch other birds and small animals with their claws for food, and are active during the day **2** a person who believes in using force — opposite **dove** — ~ish *adj* — ~ishness *n*

hawk² *v* to sell (goods) in the street or at the doors of houses — ~er *n*

hawk-eyed *adj* able to see well or watch closely

hawser *n* a thick rope, or steel cable as used on a ship

hawthorn also **may**— *n* a tree with white or red flowers which has red berries in autumn

hay *n* **1** grass which has been cut and dried, esp. for cattle food **2 make hay a** to dry grass in the sun **b** to make use of chances: *'Make hay while the sun shines'* (=while conditions are favourable) — **haymaker** *n* — **haymaking** *n*

hay fever *n* an illness rather like a bad cold, but caused by breathing in pollen from the air

haystack also **hayrick**— *n* a large pile of hay built for storing

haywire *adj sl* disorganized and confused (esp. in the phrase **to go haywire**)

hazard¹ *n* a danger: *a health hazard*

hazard² *v* to risk: *I hazarded a guess*

hazardous *adj* containing risks or danger — ~ly *adv* — ~ness *n*

haze *n* **1** light mist or smoke: *a haze of cigarette smoke* **2** a feeling of confusion or uncertainty: *a haze of tiredness*

hazel¹ *n* a type of tree which bears edible nuts

hazel² *n, adj* (of) a light or greenish brown colour

hazy *adj* **-ier, -iest 1** misty; rather cloudy **2** unclear: *I'm rather hazy about the details* — **-ily** *adv* — **-iness** *n*

H-bomb *n* HYDROGEN BOMB

H.C.F. *abbrev. for:* highest common factor: *The H.C.F of 12 and 30 is 6*

he¹ *pron* (used as the subject of a sentence) **1** that male person or animal: *Be careful of that dog—he sometimes bites* **2** (with general meaning): *Everyone should do what he considers best* —compare THEY

he² *n* a male animal: *Is your dog a he?*

he³ *n* the game of tag

head¹ *n* **1 a** the part of the body which contains the eyes, ears, nose and mouth, and the brain—in man on top of the body, in other animals in front **b** (in man) the part of the head above and behind the eyes: *My head aches* **2** the end where this part rests: *at the head of the bed* **3** the mind or brain: *a good head for figures* **4** a ruler or leader, esp. a headmaster: *the head of a firm* **5** the front side of a coin which often bears a picture of the ruler's head (esp. in the phrase **heads or tails?**) — see also OBVERSE **6** a person or creature: *3 head of cattle* **7** a part at the top of an object which is different or separate from the body: *the head of the nail* **8** the white centre of a boil or pimple on the skin when it is about to burst **9** the top or front: *the head of the queue* **10** a headland: *Beachy Head* **11** the top part of some plants, when several leaves or flowers grow together there: *heads of lettuce* **12** the white froth on the top of drinks such as beer **13 a** a body of water at a certain height, from which it may fall to produce power to work machinery **b** the pressure or force produced by falling water or by a quantity of steam **14 above/over someone's head** beyond someone's understanding **15 bite someone's head off** *esp. spoken* to answer severely **16 bang one's head against a brick wall** to keep making an effort without getting any result **17 a bring something to a head** to cause to reach a point where something must be done **b come to a head** to reach this point **18 bury one's head in the sand** to avoid facing some difficulty **19 give someone his head** to allow someone freedom to do as he likes **20 go to someone's head a** to intoxicate someone **b** to make someone too proud, or conceited **21 head over heels a** turning over in the air head first **b** completely: *head over heels in love* **22 keep one's head above water** to be able to live on one's income **23 not be able to make head or tail of** to be unable to understand —see also **head and** SHOULDERS **above**

head² *adj* chief: *the head cook*

head³ *v* **1** to be at the front or in charge of **2** to strike (a ball) with the head **3** to move in a certain direction: *heading home* —see HEAD OFF, HEAD FOR

headache *n* **1** a pain in the head **2** *esp. spoken* a great difficulty — **-achy** *adj*

headband *n* a band worn on the forehead, usu. to keep the hair back from the face

headboard *n* a board at the head of a bed

headdress *n* an ornamental covering for the head

header *n* **1** a jump, as into water, headfirst; dive **2** (in football) **a** a striking of the ball with the head **b** the person who strikes it

headfirst also **headlong**— *adj, adv* **1** with the rest of the body following the head **2** in foolish haste

head for *v prep* **1** to go to: *'Where are you heading for?'* **2** to act in such a manner as to cause or fail to avoid: *You're heading for an accident if you drink and drive*

headhunter *n* **1** a person who cuts off his enemies' heads and keeps them **2** a person who tries to attract specially able people to other jobs by offering them better pay and more responsibility

heading *n* a title at the top of a piece of writing

headland *n* an area of land running out into the sea

headless *adj* without a head

headlight also **headlamp**— *n* a powerful light on the front of a vehicle

headline¹ *n* **1** the heading in large letters above a newspaper report **2** a main point of the news, as read on radio or television

headline² *v* **-lined, -lining** to give a headline to

headman *n* **-men** a chief, esp. of a tribal village

headmaster *fem.* **headmistress**— *n* the teacher in charge of a school

head off *v adv* **1** to cause to move in a different direction: *We headed them off by calling from the field* **2** to prevent

head-on *adv, adj* with the head or front parts meeting, usu. violently: *a head-on car crash*

headphone *n* either of the 2 parts of metal, plastic, etc. made to fit over the ears to receive radio messages and suchlike, and which join over the top of the head

headpiece *n* something which fits closely over the head, such as the helmet of a suit of armour

headquarters *n* **-ters** the office or place where the people work who control a large organization

headrest *n* something which supports the head

headroom *n* space to move considered as height

above a vehicle passing under a bridge, through a tunnel, etc.

headship *n* the position or period in office of a headmaster or leader

headstrong *adj* determined to do what one wants against all other advice

headway *n* forward movement against a difficulty: *making headway*

headwind *n* a wind blowing directly against one

heady *adj* **-ier, -iest** **1** (of ideas and actions) done or formed in a foolish hurry **2** (of alcohol and its effects) tending to make people drunk, giddy, etc. **3** with a feeling of lightness and excitement: *heady with success*

heal *v* to make or become healthy, esp. to grow new skin — **~er** *n*

health *n* **1** the state of being well, without disease **2** the condition of the body: *in poor health* **3** (before drinking) (a wish for a toast to) someone's success and continued freeeedom from illness (esp. in the phrases **drink a health, your health!**)

healthful *adj* likely to produce good health: *healthful activity*

healthy *adj* **-ier, -iest** **1** strong, not often ill **2 a** healthful **b** good for the mind or character: *That book is not healthy reading for a child* **3** showing good health: *a clear healthy skin* — **healthily** *adv* — **healthiness** *n*

heap¹ *n* **1** a pile or mass of things one on top of the other **2** *esp. spoken* a lot: *a heap of trouble*

heap² *v* **1** to pile up **2** to collect or gain in large amounts: *He heaped up great wealth*

hear *v* **heard, hearing** **1** to receive and understand by using the ears: *I can hear knocking* **2** to be told: *I heard that he was ill* **3** to give a hearing (esp. to a case in court): *The judge heard the case* **4 won't/wouldn't hear of** to refuse to allow **5 Hear! Hear!** (a shout of agreement)

hearer *n* a person who hears

hear from *v prep* to receive news from, usu. by letter: *I heard from him last week*

hearing *n* **1** the sense by which one hears sound: *Her hearing is getting worse* **2** the distance at which one can hear; earshot: *Don't talk about it in his hearing* **3** listening: *At first hearing I didn't like the music* **4** a chance to be heard explaining one's position: *Try to get a hearing* **5** *law* a trial of a case before a judge

hearing aid *esp. spoken* also **deaf-aid**— *n* a small electronic device fitted near the ear which makes sounds seem louder

hearken *v literature* to listen

hear of *v prep* to know of: *I've never heard of anyone doing that*

hearsay *n* things which are said rather than proved

hearse *n* a car which is used to carry a body in its coffin to the funeral

heart *n* **1** the organ inside the chest which forces the blood through the blood vessels and round the body ☞ RESPIRATION **2** the same organ thought of as the centre of the feelings: *He has a kind heart* —compare BREAST, BOSOM **3** something shaped like this organ **4** a playing-card with one or more figures of this shape printed on it in red: *the Queen of Hearts* —compare DIAMOND, CLUB, SPADE **5** the centre (of something large, and of certain leafy vegetables): *Let's get to the heart of the matter* **6** courage, strength of mind (esp. in the phrases **take heart, lose heart**) **7 after one's own heart** just of the type one likes **8 at heart** a in reality: *He's dishonest at heart* b in one's care: *I have your health at heart* **9 by heart** by memory: *to learn by heart* **10 eat one's heart out** to be very troubled **11 from the bottom of one's heart** with real feeling **12 have one's heart in** to be interested in: *I tried to learn music but I didn't have my heart in it* **13 heart and soul** with all one's feelings or agreement **14 have one's heart in one's mouth** to feel very afraid or worried **15 in one's heart of hearts** in one's most secret feelings: *In my heart of hearts I knew it wasn't true* **16 take (something) to heart** to feel the effect of something deeply and take suitable action **17 wear one's heart on one's sleeve** to show one's feelings **18 with all one's heart** with deep feeling

heartache *n* deep feelings of sorrow and pain

heart attack *n* a sudden medical condition often causing death, in which the heart beats irregularly and painfully, as because of a coronary thrombosis

heartbeat *n* **1** the action of the heart as it pushes the blood **2** the sound this action makes

heartbreak *n* deep sorrow; terrible disappointment

heart breaker *n* a person who hurts others' feelings deeply

heartbreaking *n* **1** which causes great sorrow **2** (of work or activity) very tiring and producing no good result — ~ly *adv*

heartbroken also **broken hearted**— *adj* deeply hurt in the feelings

heartburn *n* an unpleasant burning in the chest, caused by too much acid in the stomach and throat; sign of indigestion

hearten *v* to encourage: *He was heartened by her kindness*

heartening *adj* strengthening; encouraging — ~ly *adv*

heart failure *n* the stopping of the movement of the heart, esp. at death

heartfelt *adj* deeply felt; true

hearth *n* **1** the area round the fire in one's home, esp. the floor of the fireplace **2** the home: *hearth and home*

heartless *adj* cruel; unkind — ~ly *adv* — ~ness *n*

heartrending *adj* which causes a feeling of deep sorrow or pity — ~ly *adv*

heartsick *adj* low-spirited; very unhappy

heartstrings *n* deep feelings of love and pity: *The child's cries tugged at my heartstrings*

heartthrob *n* *sl* a very attractive man with whom girls fall in love

heart-to-heart *adj, n* (a talk) done freely, mentioning personal details, without hiding anything

heartwarming *adj* giving a feeling of pleasure, esp. because of a kindness done — ~ly *adv*

heartwood *n* the older harder wood at the centre of a tree —compare SAPWOOD

hearty *adj* **-ier, -iest** **1** warm-hearted: *a hearty greeting* **2** strong and healthy (esp. in the phrase **hale and hearty**) **3** (of meals) large **4** too cheerful, esp. when trying to appear friendly — **-tily** *adv* — **-tiness** *n*

heat¹ *v* to make or become warm or hot: *Heat some milk*

heat² *n* **1** the quality or quantity of being warm or cold: *Measure the heat of the water* **2** a hotness; warmth: *heat from the fire* b hot weather: *I can't think in this heat* **3** a state of excitement: *in the heat of the argument* **4** a state of sexual excitement happening regularly to certain female animals: *Our dog is on heat* **5** *technical* the force produced by the movement of groups of atoms **6** a part of a race or competition whose winners compete against other winners until there is a small enough number for a final —see also DEAD HEAT

heated *adj* angry — ~ly

heater *n* a machine for heating air or water, by burning gas, oil, electricity, etc.

heath *n* an open piece of wild unfarmed land; moor or common

heathen *n* a person who does not belong to one of the large established religions: *He converted the heathens to Christianity* —compare PAGAN — ~ish *adj* — ~dom *n*

heather *n* a plant which grows as a small bush on open windy moors and has pink, purple, or sometimes white flowers

heating *n* a system for keeping rooms and buildings warm

heat rash *n* **1** PRICKLY HEAT **2** also **heat spot**— a raised red swelling on the skin during hot weather

heat wave *n* a period of unusually hot weather

heave¹ *v* **heaved, heaving** **1** to pull and lift **2** to rise and fall regularly: *His chest heaved after the race* **3** *esp. spoken* to throw: *Heave a brick through the window* **4** to give out (a sad sound): *He heaved a loud groan*

heave² *v* **hove, heaving** (of a ship) to move in the stated direction or manner: *Another ship hove alongside*

heave³ *n* **1** a pull or throw **2** an upward movement or set of such movements at regular times: *the heave of waves*

heaven *n* **1** the place where God or the gods are believed to live; place of complete happiness where the souls of good people supposedly go after death 2 the sky 3 great happiness or a very happy place: *I was in heaven at the news*

heavenly *adj* 1 of, from, or like heaven; in or belonging to the sky: *The sun, moon, and stars are heavenly bodies* 2 *esp. spoken* wonderful: *What heavenly weather!*

heaven-sent *adj* happening at just the right moment

heavenwards *adv* towards the sky or heaven

heave to *v adv* **hove, heaving to** *technical* (of a ship) to stop moving

heavy[1] *adj* **-ier, -iest** 1 of a certain weight, esp. of a weight that makes moving or lifting difficult 2 of unusual force or amount: *heavy rain* 3 serious; full of hard work: *This book is heavy reading.* | *I've had a heavy day* 4 sad: *heavy news* 5 a feeling or showing difficulty or slowness in moving: *a heavy sleeper* b difficult to do or move in: *The soil makes heavy walking* 6 (of food) rather solid 7 (of weather) a still, without wind, dark, etc. b (at sea) stormy, with big waves 8 *esp. spoken* a severe (towards): *a teacher who is heavy on his pupils* b using in large quantities: *This car is heavy on oil* 9 **make heavy weather of something** to make something more difficult than it really is — **-ily** *adv* — **-iness** *n*

heavy[2] *n* **-ies** a serious usu. male part in a play, esp. a bad character

heavy-duty *adj* (of clothes, tyres, machines, oil, etc.) made to be used a lot, or to take rough treatment

heavy-handed *adj* 1 awkward; tending to break and spoil things 2 rather unkind or unfair in one's treatment of others — **~ly** *adv* — **~ness** *n*

heavyhearted *adj* sad

heavy hydrogen *n* a type of hydrogen heavier than the more common isotope

heavy industry *n* **-tries** organizations that produce goods (such as coal, steel, or chemicals) which are used in the production of other goods

heavy petting *n* sexual play up to but not including sexual intercourse

heavy water *n* water containing heavy hydrogen

heavyweight *n, adj* 1 (a person or thing) a of more than average weight b having great importance or influence 2 (a boxer) of the heaviest class, weighing 175 pounds or more

Hebraic *adj* of or concerning the Hebrew people, language, or civilization

Hebrew *adj* 1 of the Jews 2 of the language used by the Jews

hecatomb *n* 1 *literature* the killing of great numbers of people 2 (in ancient times) the public killing of 100 oxen △ CATACOMB

heck *interj, n sl* hell: *a heck of a lot*

heckle *v* **-led, -ling** to interrupt (a speaker or speech) with confusing or unfriendly remarks, esp. at a political meeting — **heckler** *n*

hectare *n* (a measure of land which equals) 10,000 square metres

hectic *adj* full of excitement and hurried movement: *a hectic day* — **~ally** *adv*

he'd *short form of* 1 he would: *He'd go* 2 he had: *He'd gone*

hedge[1] *n* 1 a row of bushes or small trees acting as a fence 2 a protection: *a hedge against inflation*

hedge[2] *v* **hedged, hedging** 1 to make a hedge round (a field) 2 to refuse to answer directly —compare FENCE 3 **hedge one's bets** to protect oneself against loss by supporting more than one side in a competition or struggle

hedge about with *v adv prep* to surround with: *Building a house is hedged about with laws*

hedgehog *n* a small insect-eating animal which comes out only at night. It rolls itself into a ball and erects sharp spines when made afraid — compare PORCUPINE ⨂ MAMMAL

hedgehop *v* **-pp-** to fly a plane low, rising over trees, bushes, etc. — **-hopper** *n*

hedge in *v adv* HEM IN

hedgerow *n* a row of bushes, esp. along country roads, or separating fields

hedge sparrow *n* a type of common small bird of Europe and America

hedonism *n* 1 the idea that pleasure is the most important thing 2 the living of a life of pleasure — **-ist** *n* — **-istic** *adj*

heebie-jeebies *n esp. spoken* 1 nervous anxiety 2 a feeling of strong dislike or annoyance

heed[1] *v* to give attention to: *to heed my warning*

heed[2] *n* attention: *Take heed of what I say* — **~ful(ly)** *adj (adv)* — **~fulness** *n* — **~less(ly)** *adj (adv)*

heel[1] *n* 1 the back part of the foot 2 the part of a shoe, sock, etc., which covers this, esp. the raised part of a shoe underneath the foot: *to wear high heels* 3 **at/on one's heels** very closely behind 4 **bring to heel** to force to obey one 5 **cool one's heels** also **kick one's heels**— to be made to wait for some time unwillingly 6 **turn on one's heel** to turn round suddenly 7 **under someone's heel** in someone's power

heel[2] *v* 1 to put a heel on (a shoe) 2 (esp. of a dog) to move along at someone's heels 3 (in rugby) to send (the ball) back with the heel to another player of one's own team, esp. from the scrum

heelball *n* a type of black or brown wax used by shoemakers

heel over *v adv* to lean over at an angle, ready to fall: *The ship heeled over*

hefty *adj* **-tier, -tiest** 1 big and strong: *a hefty man* —compare HUSKY 2 (of objects) big and difficult to move — **heftily** *adv*

hegemony *n* leadership of one state over a group of others

Hegira, Hejira *n* the escape of Muhammad from Mecca to Medina in the year 622 A.D.

heifer *n* a young cow which has not borne a calf

heigh-ho *interj* (the sound of a sigh, expressing tiredness, worry, etc.)

height *n* **1** the quality or degree of being tall or high: *to measure the height of the tower* **2** (a point at) a fixed or measured distance above another point: *at a height of 10 feet above the ground* **3** a high position or place: *from a great height* **4** the main point; highest degree: *the height of the summer*

heighten *v* to make or become greater in degree: *As she waited, her fears heightened*

heinous *adj literature* very shameful; very bad — ~**ly** *adj* — ~**ness** *n*

heir *n fem.* **heiress**— the person who has the lawful right to receive the property or title of an older member of the family who dies

heir apparent *n* **heirs apparent** the heir whose right to receive the family property or title cannot be taken away until he dies

heirloom *n* a valuable object handed down in a family over many years

heir presumptive also **presumptive heir**— *n* **heirs presumptive** a person who is an heir (esp. to a position as a ruler) only until someone else with a stronger right is born

held *past tense and past part. of* HOLD

helicopter *n* a type of aircraft which is made to fly by a set of large fast-turning metal blades, and which can land in a small space, take off vertically, and stay still in the air

heliograph *n* an instrument which sends messages by reflecting flashes of sunlight

heliotrope *n* a purplish colour

heliport *n* a helicopter airport

helium *n* a gas that is an element, is lighter than air, will not burn, and is used in airships and some kinds of lights

helix *n* -**ices** a spiral curve, either corkscrew-shaped or on one plane

hell¹ *n* **1** (esp. in the Christian and Muslim religions) a place where the souls of the wicked are said to be punished after death **2** a place or state of great suffering **3** *sl* (a swear word, used in anger or to strengthen an expression) devil: *a hell of a good car* **4** **for the hell of it** *esp. spoken* for fun **5** **hell for leather** *esp. spoken* very fast **6** **like hell a** *esp. spoken* very much: *He worked like hell to get it built* **b** *sl* not at all: *Like hell he paid! I did!* **7** **play hell with** *esp. spoken* **a** to cause damage to (something) **b** to be very angry with

hell² *interj sl* (an expression of strong anger or disappointment)

hell-bent *adj esp. spoken* determined (to do something) and careless of danger

Hellene *n* a Greek, esp. an ancient Greek

Hellenic *adj* of or concerning the Greeks, their works of art, etc., esp. before Alexander the Great ☞ LANGUAGE

Hellenistic *adj* of or concerning the history, civilization, or art of ancient Greece and other nations conquered or influenced by Alexander the Great

hellish *adj* **1** like or suitable for hell **2** *esp. spoken* terrible: *a hellish problem*

hellishly *adv* very badly; devilishly

hello also **hallo, hullo**— *interj, n* -**los** **1 a** (the usual word of greeting) **b** (the word used for starting a telephone conversation): *Hello, is Mrs. Brown there?* **2** (an expression of surprise): *Hello! What's happening now?* **3** (a call for attention to a distant person): *Hello! Is anybody there?*

helm *n* **1 a** the tiller which guides a ship **b** the position from which things are controlled: *our new leader at the helm* **2** *old use* a helmet

helmet *n* a covering to protect the head, as formerly used by men wearing armour, and now as worn for protection by soldiers, motorcyclists, policemen, firemen, etc. ☞ ARMOUR

helmsman *n* -**men** a person who guides and controls, esp. when steering at the helm of a boat

helot *n* **1** a slave in ancient Sparta in Greece **2** a member of any social group which is not respected

help¹ *v* **1** to do part of the work for; be of use to **2** to encourage or produce favourable conditions for : *Trade helps industry to develop* **3** to avoid; prevent; change: *I couldn't help crying* **4** to serve food or drink to: *"Can I have a drink?" "Help yourself!"* **5** **more than one can help** as little as is possible or necessary

help² *n* **1** the act of helping; aid **2** something or somebody that helps: *You're a good help to me* **3** a person, esp. female, employed to do housework: *The new help left after a week*

helpful *adj* willing to help; useful — ~**ly** *adv* — ~**ness** *n*

helping *n* a serving of food

helpless *adj* unable to look after oneself or to act without help: *a helpless child* — ~**ly** *adv* — ~**ness** *n*

helpmate also **helpmeet**— *n esp. Bible* a useful partner, usu. a wife

help out *v adv* to give help at a time of need

helter-skelter¹ *adv, adj* in a great hurry; disordered/disorderly: *She went helter-skelter down the stairs*

helter-skelter² *n* an amusement in a fairground where one sits down and slides round and round from the top of a tower to the bottom

hem¹ *n* **1** the edge of a piece of cloth when turned under and sewn down, esp. the lower edge of a skirt or dress

hem² *v* -**mm**- to make a hem on

he-man *n* -**men** a strong manly man

hem in also **hedge in, hem about, hem around**— *v adv* to surround tightly: *hemmed in by the enemy*

hemisphere *n* **1** half a sphere **2** a half of the earth, esp. the northern or southern above or below the equator ☞ GLOBE

hemline *n* the position of the hem; length of a

dress, skirt, etc.: *When fashion changes hemlines are raised or lowered*

hemlock *n* 1 a poisonous plant with white flowers and finely divided leaves 2 the poison made from this

hemp *n* any of a family of plants used for making rope and rough cloth, and also a drug called cannabis —see also MANILA **hemp**

hen *n* 1 the female chicken often kept for its eggs on farms 2 a female bird of which the male is the cock: *a hen pheasant*

henbane *n* 1 a type of poisonous wild plant with yellow flowers 2 the poison taken from this

hence *adv* 1 for this reason or from this origin: *The town was built on the side of a hill: hence the name Hillside* 2 *esp. written or old use* from here or from now: *2 miles hence*

henceforth also **henceforward**— *adv* (esp. of promises, decisions, and results) from this time on: *I promise never to lie to you henceforth* — compare HEREAFTER

henchman *n* **-men** *usu. offensive* a faithful supporter, esp. of a political leader, who obeys without question and may use violent or dishonest methods

henna *n* 1 a type of bush grown in some Asian countries which produces a reddish-brown dye 2 the dye from this, which may be used to colour the hair

hennaed *adj* coloured with henna

hen party *n* **-ties** *esp. spoken & humour* a party for women only —compare STAG **party**

henpecked *adj* scolded by one's wife and obedient to her

hepatic *adj technical* of, relating to, or produced by the liver

hepatitis *n* a disease of the liver

Hepplewhite *adj, n* (of, being, or related to) a late 18th-century English furniture style known for its graceful curves and elegance

her¹ (*possessive form of* SHE) belonging to her: *her dress*

her² *pron* (*object form of* SHE): *Can you see her?* —see ME (USAGE)

herald¹ *n* 1 (in former times) a person who carried messages from a ruler and gave important news to the people 2 an official who keeps records of the coats of arms of noble families 3 a messenger or sign of something about to come, happen, etc. —compare HARBINGER

herald² *v* to be a sign of something coming: *The singing of the birds heralded the day*

heraldry *n* the study and use of coats of arms — **-dic** *adj*

herb *n* any of several plants whose leaves, stems, or seeds are used to flavour food or to make medicine

herbaceous *adj* (of a plant) soft-stemmed, not woody: *a herbaceous border round our garden*

herbal *adj* (made) of herbs

herbalist *n* a person who grows or sells herbs, esp. for making medicine

herbivore *n* an animal that eats only plants —compare CARNIVORE — **-vorous** *adj*

Herculean *adj* of or showing great strength: *Herculean effort*

herd¹ *n* 1 a group of animals of one kind which live and feed together: *a herd of elephants* 2 *offensive* people generally, thought of as acting all alike with no person having his own opinions: *the herd instinct*

herd² *v* 1 to group together: *They herded into the corner* 2 to look after or drive in a herd: *The farmer herded the cows into the field*

herdsman *n* **-men** a man who looks after a herd of animals

here *adv* 1 at, in, or to this place: *Come here!* 2 at this point of time: *I came to a difficulty— here I stopped* 3 (used for introducing something or somebody): *Here is the news....* 4 here and there scattered about 5 here goes! now I'm going to have a try (to do something difficult) 6 here, there, and everywhere in every place 7 Here you are Here's what you want 8 neither here nor there not connected with the matter being talked about

hereabouts *adv* somewhere near here

hereafter¹ *adv esp. written* after this time: *Hereafter please address all communications to our factory* —compare HENCEFORTH, THEREAFTER

hereafter² *n* the life after death: *Her religion promises happiness in the hereafter*

hereby *adv esp. written or law* by this means: *I hereby declare her elected* —compare THEREBY

hereditary *adj* 1 a (of a position, right, etc.) which can be passed down from an older to a younger person, esp. in the same family b who can receive by law such a position, right, etc. 2 passed down from parent to child in the cells of the body: *a hereditary disease* — **-rily** *adv*

heredity *n* the fact that living things have the ability to pass on their own qualities from parent to child in the cells of the body

heresy *n* **-sies** 1 the fact of holding a contrary belief, esp. in official religion 2 such a belief, or an act or statement which shows it

heretic *n* a person who favours heresy or is guilty of a heresy — ~al *adj* — ~ally *adv*

herewith *adv* (in business) with this letter or written material

heritable *adj* (of qualities, diseases, etc.) which could be inherited by one's descendants

heritage *n* 1 something which one receives by right from an older member of the family 2 a condition of life, such as that of one's family or social group, into which one is born

hermaphrodite *n, adj* (a living thing) with the organs or appearance of both male and female — **-ditic** *adj*

hermetic also **hermetical**— *adj* very tightly closed; airtight: *A hermetic seal is used on this glass bottle* — ~ally *adv*

hermit *n* 1 (esp. in former times) a holy man who lived alone, thinking and praying 2 a person who avoids other people

hermitage n a place where a hermit lives or has lived

hernia also **rupture**— n **1** an unhealthy condition in which an organ of the body pushes through the body wall, usu. when the intestine pushes throuh the wall of the abdomen **2** this stretched part of the body wall

hero fem. **heroine**— n **-roes 1** a person remembered for bravery, strength, or goodness, esp. for an act of courage under difficult conditions **2** the most important character in a play, poem, story, etc.

heroic adj **1** showing the qualities of a hero **2** large or grand: a heroic manner — ~**ally** adv

heroics n speech or actions which are meant to appear grand, though they mean nothing

heroin n a drug made from morphine, which is used for lessening pain, and which one can become addicted to

heroism n **1** the quality of being a hero **2** great courage: an act of heroism

heron n **herons** or **heron** a type of bird which has long legs and lives near water, where it catches small animals to eat

herpes n a skin disease in which red spots spread around various parts of the body —compare SHINGLES, COLD SORE

Herr n (the German word for) Mr

herring n **-ring** or **-rings 1** an edible fish which swims in large shoals in the sea **2 red herring** a fact or point which draws attention away from the main point

herringbone n (used esp. of an ornamental arrangement of bricks or of a sewing stitch) a pattern where 2 sides slope in opposite directions, forming a continuous line of V's

hers pron (possessive form of SHE) that/those belonging to her: The sheep are hers

herself pron **1** (reflexive form of SHE): She cut herself **2** (strong form of SHE): She herself said so **3** esp. spoken (in) her usual state of mind or body: She's more herself today

hortz n **hertz** (a measure meaning) one time each second: These radio waves are coming at 15, 000 hertz

he's short form of **1** he is: He's a writer **2** he has: He's got 2 cars

hesitancy also **hesitance**— n the state or quality of being hesitant

hesitant adj showing uncertainty or slowness about deciding to act: She's hesitant about making friends — ~**ly** adv

hesitate v **-tated, -tating** to pause in doubt during or before an action — **-tating** adj — **-tatingly** adv — **-tion** n

Hesperus n poetic EVENING STAR

hessian n a thick rough type of hemp cloth

heterogeneous adj of many different kinds: a heterogeneous mass of papers — ~**ly** adv — **-neity** n

heterosexual adj, n (of or being) a person attracted in the usual way by people of the other sex — ~**ly** adv — ~**ity** n

het up adj esp. spoken excited; anxious: all het up about going

hew v **hewed, hewed** or **hewn, hewing 1** to cut by striking blows with an axe or weapon **2** to cut and shape out from a larger mass by blows: Miners hew coal

hewer n a person who hews wood, or coal in the mines

hexagon n a plane figure with 6 sides — ~**al** adj

hexagram n a 6-pointed star made up from 2 triangles ☞ MATHEMATICS

hey interj (a shout used to call attention or to express surprise, interest, etc.): Hey! Where are you going?

heyday n **1** the highest point of strength or prosperity: In the heyday of the British Empire **2** the best time of one's youth, when one is strong and cheerful

hey presto interj esp. spoken **1** suddenly **2** (used by someone performing a magic trick) Here is the result of my trick!

hi interj **1** hey **2** esp. spoken hello

hiatus n a space ɛ where something is missing

hibernate v **-nated, -nating** (of animals) to be or go into a state like a long sleep during the winter — **-nation** n

hibiscus n a tropical plant with large bright flowers

hiccup, hiccough n, v (to make) a movement in the chest which stops the breath and causes one to make a sudden sharp sound

hickory n **-ries** a type of tree of North America which bears nuts, or its hard wood

hide¹ v **hid, hidden, hiding 1** to put or keep out of sight; make or keep secret: You're hiding some important facts **2** to place oneself so as to be unseen: I'll hide behind the door

hide² n an animal's skin, esp. when used for leather

hide³ n a place from where a person may watch animals, esp. birds, without being seen by them

hide-and-seek n a children's game in which some hide and others search for them

hideaway n **-ways** a place where one can go to avoid people

hidebound adj having fixed unchangeable opinions

hideous adj having a terrible effect on the senses: a hideous face — ~**ly** adv — ~**ness** n

hiding¹ n esp. spoken a beating: You deserve a good hiding!

hiding² n the state of being hidden: He went into hiding

hie v **hied, hying** or **hieing** old use or humour to go quickly

hierarchy n **-chies** the organization of a system into higher and lower ranks: a hierarchy of moral values — **-chical** adj — **-chically** adv

hieroglyph n a picture-like sign which represents a word, esp. in the writing system of ancient Egypt — ~**ic** adj — **-ics** n

hi-fi *n* **hi-fis** high fidelity apparatus for reproducing recorded sound

higgledy-piggledy *adj, adv* in disorder

high¹ *adj* **1 a** (not usu. of living things) reaching some distance above ground: *a high wall* **b** at a point well above the ground: *high in the sky* **2** important; chief: *high office in the government* **3** showing goodness: *high principles* **4** near the top of the set of sounds which the ear can hear: *a very high voice* **5** above the usual level, rate of movement, etc.: *the high cost of food* **6** (of time) at the most important or mid-point of: *It's high time we went* **7** (of food) not fresh **8** *esp. spoken* **a** drunk **b** under the effects of drugs **9 hold one's head high** to show pride and courage, esp. in difficulty —see also HIGHER

high² *adv* **1** to or at a high level in position, movements or sound: *They climbed high* **2** to or at a high or important degree esp. of social movement: *He's risen high in the world* **3 high and dry** without help: *He left me high and dry* **4 high and low** everywhere

high³ *n* **1** a high point: *The price reached a new high* **2** *esp. spoken* a state of great excitement and often happiness produced by or as if by a drug **3** an anticyclone

high-and-mighty *adj esp. spoken* too proud

highboard *n* a divingboard placed 5, 7.5, or 10 metres above the water

highborn *adj* of noble birth

highbrow *n sometimes offensive* a person thought to show more than average knowledge of art and intellectual interests —compare LOWBROW, MIDDLEBROW

high chair *n* a chair with long legs at which a baby or small child can sit, esp. to eat at table or from a   tray joined to the chair

high-class *adj* **1** of good quality **2** of high social position

high commission *n* the office of a high commissioner and the people who work there

high commissioner *n* a person like an ambassador who represents one Commonwealth country in another

high court *n* the court which is above all the rest and can reverse the decision of a lower court

higher *adj* **1** see HIGH **2** more advanced, esp. in development, organization, or knowledge needed: *higher mathematics*

higher education *n* education at a university or college

high explosive *n* powerful explosives

highfalutin *adj esp. spoken* foolishly trying to appear grand: *a highfalutin manner*

high fidelity also **hi-fi**— *adj* (of tape recorders, record players, etc.) able to give out sound which represents very closely the details of the original sound before recording

high-flier, -flyer *n* a clever person who has high aims

high-handed *adj* using one's power too force-fully: *It was high-handed to punish the child* — ~**ly** *adv* — ~**ness** *n*

high horse *n* **on one's high horse** behaving, esp. talking, as if one knows best

high jump *n* a sport in which people jump over a bar which is raised higher and higher

high-keyed *adj* at a high level of sound or excitement —compare KEYED-UP

highland *adj, n* (of) a mountainous area

highlander *n* a person from a mountainous land, esp. in Scotland

Highland fling *n* a Scottish dance

high-level *adj* **1** at a high level **2** in or at a position of high importance: *high-level peace talks* **3** of or relating to a computer language in which one instruction orders the computer to do several things

high-life *n* the enjoyable life of the rich and fashionable, full of amusement, good food, etc.

highlight¹ *n* **1** *technical* the area on a picture or photograph where most light appears to fall **2** an important detail which stands out from the rest: *the highlights of the competition*

highlight² *v* to pick out as an important part

highly *adv* **1** to a high degree; very: *highly pleased* **2 a** very well: *highly paid* **b** very much: *highly salted*

highly-strung *adj* nervous; excitable

high-minded *adj* (of people) having high principles, perhaps too high — ~**ly** *adv* — ~**ness** *n*

Highness *n* (a title used of or to certain royal persons): *Your Highness*

high-powered *adj* showing great force: *a high-powered car*

high-pressure *adj* **1** (of a machine or substance) which uses or is at high pressure **2** (of an action, job, or person) carried out or working with great speed and force

high priest *n* the chief priest, as in a temple

high-principled *adj* honourable

high-rise *adj* higher or taller than usual

highroad *n* a main road; broad high street —compare HIGHWAY

high school *n esp. US* a secondary school esp. for children over 14

high seas *n* the oceans of the world which do not belong to any particular country

high season *n* the time of year when business is greatest and prices are highest

High Sheriff also **Sheriff**— *n* the royally-appointed chief officer in a county of Britain with various duties in courts and in ceremonies

high-spirited *adj* **1** full of fun; adventure-loving **2** (of an animal or its behaviour) active, esp. nervously active, and hard to control

high street *n* the main street of a town: *Camden High Street*

high table *n* the raised table at which the teachers (DONS) at a college eat

high tea *n* an early-evening meal taken instead of afternoon tea and late dinner

high-tension *adj* which carries a powerful electrical current: *high-tension wires*

high tide *n* **1** the moment when the water is highest up the sea shore because the tide has come in **2** the point on the shore which the water reaches at this moment

high treason *n* the crime of putting one's country or its ruler in danger by giving help to their enemies

high water *n* **1** the moment when the water in a river is at its highest point because of the tide **2** the point on the river bank which the water reaches at this moment

high water mark *n* **1** a mark showing the highest point reached by a body of water, such as a river **2** the highest point of success

highway *n* -ways *esp. US* a broad main road used esp. by traffic going in 2 directions

Highway Code *n* the official list of rules for the behaviour of drivers on British roads

highwayman *n* -men (in former times) a man who used to stop horsemen and carriages on the road and rob them of their money —compare FOOTPAD

hijack *v* to take control of (a vehicle or aircraft) by force of arms, to obtain money or political objectives — **hijack** *n* — ~**er** *n* — ~**ing** *n*

hike¹ *v* **hiked, hiking** to go on a hike — **hiker** *n* — **hiking** *n*

hike² *n* a long walk in the country, such as one taken by a group of people for a whole day

hilarious *adj* full of or causing laughter — ~**ly** *adv* — ~**ness** *n*

hilarity *n* cheerfulness, expressed in laughter

hill *n* **1** a raised part of the earth's surface, not so high as a mountain, and not usu. so bare **2** the slope of a road or path

hillbilly *n* -lies *U.S. often offensive* a farmer or someone from a small country place

hillock *n* **1** a little hill **2** a heap of earth shaped like a hill

hilly *adj* -ier, -iest full of hills

hilt *n* **1** the handle of a sword, or of a knife used as a weapon **2** up to the hilt completely: *She's up to the hilt in trouble*

him *pron* (*object form of* HE): *I met him yesterday* USAGE After some verbs, the object pronouns **him, it, me, them, us, you** are always used when another verb follows: *I heard him singing. After some verbs, and after prepositions, there is a choice, and usually the forms **his, its, my, their, our, your** are considered better English: I remember you/your telling me that. | Are you in favour of us/our joining the group?* This rule also applies to nouns: *This led to the country/the country's losing a lot of trade.* —see ME (USAGE)

himself *pron* **1** (*reflexive form of* HE): *He hurt himself* **2** (*strong form of* HE): *He told me so himself* **3** *esp. spoken* (in) his usual state of mind or body: *He doesn't seem himself today*

hind¹ *n* **hinds** or **hind** a female deer, esp. of the red deer family —compare HART

hind² *adj* (usu. of animals' legs) belonging to the back part

hinder *v* **1** to stop (someone from doing something): *You're hindering me in my work* **2** to prevent: *You're hindering my work*

hindmost *adj* old use furthest behind

hindquarters also **quarters**— *n* the back part of an animal including the legs —compare HAUNCHES

hindrance *n* **1** the act of hindering **2** something or somebody that hinders

hindsight *n* the ability to see how and why something happened, esp. to know that it could have been prevented —compare FORESIGHT

Hindu *adj* of Hinduism

Hinduism *n* the Hindu religion esp. as practised in India and its customs, such as its caste system, the belief that one returns after death in another form, etc. ☞ WORSHIP

hinge¹ *n* **1** a metal part which joins 2 objects together and allows the first to swing around the usu. fixed second, such as one joining a door to a post **2** the point on which something else depends: *The home is the hinge on which family life turns*

hinge² *v* **hinged, hinging** to fix on hinges: *The cupboard door is hinged so it opens on the left*

hinge on also **hinge upon**— *v prep* to depend on: *Everything hinges on what we do next*

hint¹ *n* **1** a small or indirect suggestion **2** a small sign: *a hint of summer in the air* **3** useful advice: *helpful hints*

hint² *v* to suggest indirectly: *I hinted that I was dissatisfied*

hinterland *n* the inner part of a country, beyond the coast or the banks of an important river

hip¹ also **rose hip**— *n* the red fruit of the rose

hip² *n* the fleshy part of either side of the human body above the legs

hip³ *interj* **hip, hip, hooray!** (a cry or cheer)

hip⁴ *adj* -pp- *sl* of or favouring the latest fashions in behaviour, amusements, etc.

hipbath *n* a bath in which one can sit but not lie

hip flask *n* a small usu metal bottle for carrying spirits, . made to fit into a hip pocket

hippie, hippy *n* a person who is against the standards of ordinary society, esp. when he shows this by dressing in unusual clothes, living in groups together, and sometimes taking drugs for pleasure

Hippocratic oath *n* the promise made by medical students to try to save life and to follow the standards set for the medical profession

hippodrome *n* **1** an open place for horse-shows and shows with animals (esp. circuses) **2** a theatre

hippopotamus also (*esp. spoken*) **hippo**— *n* -muses or -mi, hippos a large African animal with a thick hairless skin, which lives near water ☞ MAMMAL

hipster *n* a person who is hip

hire¹ *n* hiring or being hired

hire² *v* **hired, hiring** 1 to get the use of for a special occasion by payment 2 to employ for a time for payment

hireling *n offensive* 1 a person whose services may be hired 2 a person who cares only for the money he earns, not the type of work —compare MERCENARY

hire out *v adv* to give the use of for payment

hire purchase also (*esp. spoken*) **the never never** — *n* a system of payment for goods by which one pays small sums of money with interest regularly after receiving the goods —compare CREDIT

hirsute *adj* 1 hairy 2 with hair on the face; with the beard and hair of the head uncut

his *adj, pron* 1 that/those belonging to him: *That's not mine, it's his* 2 (with general meaning): *Everyone must do his best* —compare THEIR, THEIRS

hiss¹ *v* 1 to make a sound like a continuous "s" 2 to say in a sharp whisper: *to hiss a warning* 3 also **hiss at**— to show disapproval and dislike of

hiss² *n* a hissing sound

histogram *n technical* a diagram on which the area of each column represents the frequency of the corresponding value or class

histology *n* the study of the cells of the body

historian *n* a person who studies history and/or writes about it

historic *adj* 1 important in history 2 of recorded history —compare PREHISTORIC

historic present also **historical present**— *n* the present tense, as used to tell a story which happened in the past, when the teller wants to make it sound more real

history *n* **-ries** 1 (the chronological study of) past events 2 (the study of) the development of anything in time: *the history of the English Language* 3 a (written) account of history 4 a long story including details of many events: *She told me her life history* 5 **make history** to do or be concerned in something important which will be remembered ⊚ — **-rical** *adj* — **-rically** *adv*

histrionic *adj* 1 concerning the theatre or acting 2 done or performed in a theatrical way; not showing real feelings — **-ics** *n* — **~ally** *adv*

hit¹ *v* **hit, hitting** 1 to give a blow to; strike 2 **a** to come against with force **b** to cause to do this by accident or on purpose 3 *esp. spoken* to reach: *We hit the main road here* 4 to have a bad effect on: *Inflation hits the housewife's pocket* (=money) 5 (in cricket) to score: *He hit 3 runs* 6 **hit the nail on the head** to be exactly right (in saying something) 7 **hit the sack** *sl* to go to bed 8 **hit (someone) for six** to defeat or surprise (someone) completely by quick action

hit² *n* 1 a blow; stroke 2 a move which brings something against another with force: *The arrow scored a hit* 3 a successful musical or theatrical performance 4 a remark which causes the desired effect, esp. if unpleasant: *That joke was a nasty hit at me*

hit-and-run *adj* 1 (of a road accident) of a type in which the guilty driver does not stop to help 2 (of a person) who behaves in this way

hitch¹ *v* 1 to fasten by hooking a rope or metal part over another object 2 *esp. spoken* to travel by getting (rides in a car) 3 **get/be hitched** *sl* to get/be married

hitch² *n* 1 a short, sudden push or pull (up): *He gave his sock a hitch* 2 a type of knot used by sailors 3 a difficulty which delays something for a while

hitchhike *v* **-hiked, -hiking** to go on a (long) journey by getting rides in other people's cars — **-hiker** *n*

hither *adv* 1 *old use* to here 2 **come-hither look** *esp. spoken* a look which attracts, esp. sexually

hitherto *adv esp. written* until this/that time

hit off *v adv* 1 to act or draw a good likeness of (someone) 2 **hit it off (with)** *esp. spoken* to have a good relationship (with)

hit on also **hit upon**— *v prep* to find by lucky chance or have a good idea about

hit-or-miss *adj* which depends on chance

hit out at *v adv prep* 1 also **hit out against**— to disagree violently with and attack in words 2 to hit

hit parade *n now rare* a list of popular records (of songs) in order of the number which are sold of each

hive *n* 1 a also **beehive**— a place where bees live, like a small hut or box **b** the group of bees who live together 2 a crowded busy place (esp. in the phrase **a hive of industry**)

hive off *v adv* **hived, hiving off** to separate: *to hive off parts of a firm*

HMS *abbrev. for:* 1 His/Her Majesty's Service 2 His/Her Majesty's Ship

hoard¹ *n* 1 a (secret) store, esp. of something valuable 2 a large amount ⚠ HORDE

hoard² *v* to store secretly — **~er** *n*

hoarding *n* 1 a fence round a piece of land, esp. when building is going on 2 a high fence or board on which large advertisements are stuck

hoarfrost *n* white frost

hoarse *adj* 1 (of a voice) harsh-sounding, as though the surface of the throat is rough 2 having a voice of this type —compare HUSKY — **~ly** *adv* — **~ness** *n*

hoary also (*literature*) **hoar**— *adj* **-ier, -iest** 1 (of hair) grey or white 2 having grey or white hair in old age — **hoariness** *n*

hoax¹ *n* a trick, esp. one which makes someone believe something which is not true

hoax² *v* to play a trick on — **~er** *n*

hob *n* 1 a metal shelf beside an open fire where food and water could be heated 2 a flat surface, such as the top of a cooker, having several usu. round heating devices on top of which food may be cooked

hobble *v* **-bled, -bling** 1 to walk in an awkward

way, with difficulty **2** to fasten together 2 legs (esp. of a horse)

hobby *n* **-bies** an enjoyable free time activity

hobbyhorse *n* **1** a child's toy like a horse's head on a stick **2** a fixed idea to which a person keeps returning in conversation

hobgoblin *n* a goblin

hobnail *n* a big-headed nail used for strengthening the soles of heavy shoes and boots — ~**ed** *adj*

hobnob *v* **-bb-** *sometimes offensive* to have a (pleasant) social relationship

hobo *n* **hoboes** or **hobos** *US sl* a tramp

Hobson's choice *n* lack of choice

hock¹ *n* **1** a joint of meat from an animal's leg, above the foot **2** (in animals) the middle joint of the back leg ⫸ HORSE

hock² *n* (any of) several kinds of German white wine

hock³ *n* **in hock** *sl* pawned

hockey *n* FIELD HOCKEY

hocus-pocus *n* **1** trickery **2** pointless activity or words, esp. when they distract from a real event

hod *n* **1** a boxlike container with a long handle, for carrying bricks **2** a coalscuttle

hoe¹ *n* a long-handled garden tool used for breaking up the soil and removing weeds

hoe² *v* **hoed, hoeing** **1** to use a hoe **2** to remove or break with a hoe

hog¹ *n* **hogs** or **hog** **1** a castrated male pig kept for meat —compare BOAR, SOW **2** a dirty person who eats too much

hog² *v* **-gg-** *sl* to take and keep (all of something) for oneself

Hogmanay *n* (in Scotland) New Year's Eve and its festivities

hogshead *n* a barrel, esp. one which holds 52½ gallons (=238·5 litres)

hogwash *n* esp. US nonsense

hoi polloi *n* offensive Greek the common people

hoist¹ *v* to raise up by force, esp. when using ropes on board ship

hoist² *n* **1** an upward push **2** an apparatus for lifting heavy goods

hoity-toity *adj* offensive behaving in a proud way

hold¹ *v* **held, holding** **1** to keep or support with a part of the body, esp. with the hands **2** to put or keep (a part of the body) in a certain position: *Hold (yourself) still* **3** to keep back or control: *We held our breath in fear* **4** to be able to contain: *How much does the pan hold?* **5** (esp. of an army) to keep in control or in one's possession: *The city is held by the enemy* **6** to possess (money, land, or position) **7** to keep (someone) in (an interested state of mind) **8** to keep in the stated position or condition: *She held them at arm's length* **9** to express one's belief (that); consider **10** to continue: *Can the good weather hold?* **11** (of a ship or aircraft) to follow correctly **12** (of objects) to keep in position and/or support:

The roof was held up by pillars **13** to make (something) happen: *We were holding a meeting* **14 hold court** to receive admirers in a group **16 hold good** to be true **17 hold hands (with)** to hold the hand (of another) or the hands (of each other), esp. as a sign of love **18 Hold it!** Don't move! **19 hold one's own** to keep one's (strong) position, even when attacked —see also HOLD AGAINST, HOLD BACK, HOLD DOWN, HOLD FORTH, HOLD OFF, HOLD ON, **hold one's** GROUND, hold out, HOLD OVER, **hold the** FORT, HOLD TO, HOLD UP, **hold** WATER, HOLD WITH

hold² *n* **1** the act of holding; grip (esp. in the phrases **take/get/catch/lay hold of, keep hold of, lose hold of**) **2** something which can be held, esp. in climbing: *Can you find a hold for your hands?* —compare FOOTHOLD **3** grip; influence; control: *He's got a good hold of his subject*

hold³ *n* the part of a ship (below deck) where goods are stored

hold against *v prep* to put the blame for (something) on (someone)

holdall *n* a large travelling bag or small case

hold back *v adv* **1** also **keep back**— to make (something) stay in place; control **2** also **hold in, keep back**— to control, esp. feelings **3** also **keep back**— to prevent the development of **4** also **hang back, hang behind**— to be slow or unwilling to act **5** to keep (something) secret

hold down *v adv* **1** to keep (esp. a job) **2** to keep at a low level: *to hold prices down*

holder *n* **1** a person who has control of or possesses land, money, or titles **2** something that holds

hold forth *v adv* to speak at length

holding *n* something which is in one's possession, esp. land or shares —see also SMALLHOLDING

holding company *n* **-nies** a firm or company whose main business is to hold a controlling number of the shares of other companies

hold off *v adv* **1** also **keep off**— to keep or remain at a distance: *Mary tends to hold off from people* **2** also **put off**— to delay **3** also **keep off**— to be delayed; stay away

hold on *v adv* **1** to wait (often on the telephone) **2** to continue in spite of difficulties **3** HOLD OUT

hold out *v adv* **1** to offer **2** to last: *Will the car hold out till we reach London?* **3** also **hang on, hold on**— to last in spite of difficulties **4** to extend: *He held out his hand*

hold out for also **stick out for**— *v adv prep* to demand firmly and wait in order to get

hold out on *v adv prep esp. spoken* **1** to keep a secret from **2** to refuse to support or reply to

hold over¹ *v adv* **1** to move to a later date **2** to continue (a show) longer than originally planned

hold over² *v prep* to use (usu. knowledge of something) as a threat against (someone)

hold to also **hold by, keep to**— *v prep* to follow

European history and civilization

Neolithic (New Stone Age) culture		c6500 start of farming in Europe
c2500 B.C. start of Bronze Age in Europe	5000 B.C.	c3500 invention of wheel, plough, and sail in Near East 1
c2000 B.C. building of Stonehenge		c3000-1400 Minoan civilization, based in Crete 2
		c1400-1200 Mycenaean civilization in Greece and Crete
c1100 B.C. development of the alphabet		c1200 siege of Troy by the Greeks
c1000 B.C. start of Iron Age in Europe	1000 B.C.	776 first Olympic Games held in Greece 3
		753 supposed date of foundation of city of Rome 4
c800-500 B.C. Archaic Age of Greek culture		510 last Etruscan king of Rome expelled – start of Roman Republic
c500-338 B.C. Classical Age of Greek culture	500 B.C.	490 Battle of Marathon – Greeks defeat Persians
		431-404 Peloponnesian War between Sparta and Athens
		338 Greece conquered by Philip II of Macedon, father of Alexander the Great
323-31 B.C Hellenistic Age of Greek culture	300 B.C.	290 Rome completes conquest of central Italy 5
		202 Hannibal finally defeated by Rome
	200 B.C.	146 Rome conquers Greece
	100 B.C.	49 Julius Caesar conquers Gaul (France)
		44 assassination of Caesar – civil war in Rome 6
rise of Rome		27 end of Roman Republic, start of Roman Empire
c27 B.C.-200 A.D. height of Roman culture	1 A.D.	c4 B.C.-30 A.D. life of Jesus Christ 7
		43 Romans invade and conquer Britain
c45-312 early growth of Christianity	100	117 Roman Empire reaches its greatest extent
c250 decline of Roman Empire begins	200	238 attacks on Roman Empire by Goths (Germanic tribes) begin
	300	312 Constantine, Roman emperor, converted to Christianity 8
		330 capital of Roman Empire transferred to Constantinople
		c370 Asian tribes, the Huns, attack Europe 9
		395 Roman Empire divided into two parts, Eastern and Western
c450-1000 "Dark Ages" (period of decline of culture in most of Europe)	400	410 Visigoths sack Rome; final withdrawal of Romans from Britain
		449 first invasion of Britain by Angles, Saxons, and Jutes
		451-2 Attila the Hun invades Gaul and Italy
		455 Vandals sack Rome 10
		476 fall of the Western Roman Empire 11
		486 foundation of Frankish kingdom, to become a major power until c843
	500	c500 "King" Arthur was probably a British chieftain fighting Anglo-Saxons at this time
age of monastic culture and early Christian missions		c530 revival of Eastern Roman Empire – rise of Byzantine civilization
		590 Gregory I becomes Pope – rise of papacy as political power
	600	597 first Christian missionaries arrive in England
	700	711 Islam army from North Africa conquers most of Spain
start of Arab influence in southern Europe		c790-1050 Vikings from Scandinavia attack England, Ireland, and other parts of Europe 12
start of Viking Age	800	800 Charlemagne, king of the Franks, is crowned Holy Roman Emperor 13
		865 Danish Vikings invade England
		871 Alfred, king of Wessex, drives the Danes back to East Anglia 14
	900	959 Edgar becomes first king of all England
c1000-1500 Middle Ages (Medieval period)	1000	1013 Canute (Cnut) of Denmark invades England, becomes king in 1016
		1054 split of Christian Church into Roman (Western) and Greek (Eastern) branches
c1100 first universities founded		1066 Norman invasion of England – Battle of Hastings – William becomes king
c1100-1300 great cathedrals built		1096 First Crusade, aiming to capture the Holy Land from Saracens 15
	1100	1154 civil wars in England end with accession of Henry II, first Plantagenet king

1271 Marco Polo travels to China	**1200**	1215 Magna Carta signed **1**
		1270 Eighth (and last) crusade
c1300 cultural revival in Italy – Dante, Giotto	**1300**	1314 Battle of Bannockburn – Scots defeat English **2**
		1337 Hundred Years War (England v France) begins
		1348 Black Death (plague) kills about half the population **3**
		1381 Peasants' Revolt in England
	1400	1415 Battle of Agincourt – English defeat French
		1431 Joan of Arc tried and burnt
		1453 end of Hundred Years War – England loses all possessions in Europe
1455 first printed book, in Germany		1453 fall of Byzantine Empire
		1455-85 Wars of Roses (Yorkists v Lancastrians) in England
c1485 Age of Exploration		1492 Columbus sails to America **4**
c1500 Renaissance period (rebirth of art and learning) spreads from Italy through Western Europe	**1500**	1494-1516 wars in Italy, involving France and the Habsburgs
		1521 Martin Luther excommunicated – start of Protestant Reformation
		1524-6 Peasants' War in Germany and Austria
		1534 Henry VIII breaks with Rome **5**
		1545 Council of Trent – start of Counter-Reformation
		1562-98 religious wars in France
Spanish dominance		1571 Battle of Lepanto – Turkish fleet defeated
		1572 St Bartholomew's Day Massacre of Huguenots (French Protestants)
Elizabethan age in England – Shakespeare, Drake, Raleigh		1582 Netherlands declare independence from Spain
		1588 Spanish Armada defeated by England **6**
c1610 start of modern science – Galileo, Kepler	**1600**	1618-48 Thirty Years War in Germany
		1642-9 Civil Wars in England – Parliamentarians (Roundheads)
Dutch dominance		defeat Royalists (Cavaliers)
		1660 restoration of monarchy in England
French dominance		1661-1715 rule of Louis XIV in France **7**
		1688 "Glorious Revolution" in England limits king's power
c1700-1800 "Age of enlightenment"	**1700**	1702-13 War of Spanish Succession
British dominance		1707 Union of England and Scotland **8**
c1720 main Baroque period of music – Bach, Handel		c1720 rise of Austria and Prussia as major powers
		1740-8 War of Austrian Succession
c1770 start of Industrial Revolution		1756-63 Seven Years War
		1772 partition of Poland
c1780-1825 main Classical period of music – Mozart, Beethoven		1775-83 War of American Independence
		1789 French Revolution **9**
c1800 start of Romantic period in literature, art, music	**1800**	1803-15 Napoleonic Wars **10**
		1812 Napoleon invades Russia
		1815 Napoleon is defeated at Waterloo and exiled
c1820 rise of democracy and nationalism begins		1821 War of Greek Independence
		1848 revolutions in many countries of Europe **11**
1837-1900 Victorian Age in Britain		1854-6 Crimean War
		1857-8 Indian Mutiny **12**
c1850-1912 age of European imperialism in Africa		1861 unification of Italy
		1870 Franco-Prussian War
1896 first modern Olympics		1871 unification of Germany
1903 powered aircraft flight	**1900**	1914-18 World War I **13**
c1920 rise of modern art, music, literature – Picasso, Stravinsky, James Joyce		1917 Russian Revolution
		1920 League of Nations founded
		1924 first Labour government in Britain
1920-38 development of radio, cinema, television		1926 General Strike in Britain
		1933 Hitler becomes Chancellor of Germany – Nazi period begins
		1936-8 Spanish Civil War
1945 first atom bomb		1939-45 World War II **14**
		1945-7 Communist takeover in Eastern Europe **15**
"Cold War"		1957 foundation of European Economic Community
1956-80 independence of most European colonies in Africa		("Common Market")
		1973 Britain, Eire, Denmark, join "Common Market"
1969 first man on moon		

or cause to follow exactly or keep to: *I shall hold to my decision*

holdup *n* 1 a delay, as of traffic 2 also (*esp. spoken*) **stickup**— an attempt at robbery by threatening people with a gun

hold up *v adv* 1 to delay 2 to stop in order to rob 3 to show as an example: *His son was held up as a model of hard work* 4 HOLD OUT 5 KEEP UP 6 to raise

hold with *v prep* to approve of

hole¹ *n* 1 an empty space within something solid 2 a the home of a small animal b *esp. spoken* a small unpleasant living-place 3 *esp. spoken* a position of difficulty: *I am in rather a hole* 4 (in golf) a hollow place on the green into which the ball must be hit 5 **pick holes in something** to criticize something, esp. when it is not really faulty

hole² *v* **holed, holing** 1 to make a hole in 2 to put (a ball) in a hole in golf: *to hole in one*

hole up *v adv sl esp. US* to hide, as a means of escape: *The criminals holed up in a factory*

holiday¹ *n* **-days** 1 a time of rest from work, a day (often originally of religious importance) or longer 2 **on holiday/on one's holidays** having a holiday, esp. over a period of time USAGE **Holiday** is the usual British word for a break from work; **vacation** is the American word. **Vacation** is also used by British universities and lawyers: *The college is closed during the vacation.* Soldiers and civil servants go on **leave**, and the word is also used in such expressions as **sick leave, leave** *of absence.* **Furlough** is an uncommon word for military holidays, used when someone stationed abroad goes home to his own country on holiday.

holiday² *v* **-dayed, -daying** to have a period of holiday

holidaymaker *n* a person on holiday

holiness *n* the state or quality of being holy

Holiness *n* (a title of the Pope): *His/Your Holiness*

holler *v esp. US spoken* 1 to shout out 2 to cry out, as to scold, to attract attention, or in pain — **holler** *n*

hollow¹ *adj* 1 having an empty space inside; not solid 2 (of parts of the body) lacking flesh: *hollow cheeks* 3 having a ringing sound like the note when an empty container is struck 4 (of feelings, words, etc.) not real; empty of meaning 5 **beat (someone) hollow** *esp. spoken* to defeat (someone) completely — **~ly** *adv* — **~ness** *n*

hollow² *n* a space sunk into something, esp. into the ground

hollow out *v adv* to make a hollow place in

holly *n* **-lies** a type of small tree with dark green shiny prickly leaves and red berries

hollyhock *n* a tall garden flower

Hollywood *n* an area in Los Angeles, California, where films have been made from the early days of silent cinema until present times

holocaust *n* the loss of many lives, esp. by burning

holster *n* a leather pistol holder, esp. one that hangs on a belt around the waist

holy¹ *adj* **holier, holiest** 1 of God and religion: *the Holy Bible* 2 (of a person or life) in the service of God and religion, esp. when leading a pure life 3 *sl* very bad: *He's a holy terror*

holy² *n* **holies** a most holy place (only in the phrase **holy of holies**)

Holy Communion *n* the religious service in Protestant churches in which bread and wine are shared, in solemn ceremony, as a sign of Christ's body and blood in remembrance of his death; the Eucharist —compare MASS

Holy Spirit also **Holy Ghost**— *n* the 3rd member of the Christian Trinity

Holy Week also **Passion Week**— *n* (in the Christian Church) the week between Palm Sunday and Easter

homage *n* 1 signs of great respect (esp. in the phrases **pay/do homage to someone**) 2 a ceremony of former times in which a man recognized the power of another, esp. a king, over him

homburg *n* a soft felt hat for men, with a wide brim

home¹ *n* 1 a the house where one lives b the place where one was born or habitually lives 2 the house and family one belongs to 3 a place where a living thing can be found living and growing wild: *India is the home of elephants* 4 a place for the care of a group of people or animals of the same type, but not a family: *a children's home* 5 (in some games and sports) a place which a player must aim to reach, such as the goal or the finishing line of a race (esp. in the phrase **the home stretch/straight** (=the last part)) 6 **at home a** in the house or family **b** ready to receive visitors 7 **leave home** to leave one's family to live independently, esp. after an argument —see HOUSE (USAGE) — **~less** *adj* — **~lessness** *n*

home² *adv* 1 to or at one's home 2 as far as possible and/or to the right place: *He drove the nail home* —see also **if/when one's** SHIP **comes home**

home³ *adj* 1 of, related to, or being a home, place of origin, or base of operations: *the home office of an international firm* 2 domestic: *the home country* 3 prepared, done, or intended for use in a home: *home cooking* 4 working, playing, or happening in a home area: *the home team*

home⁴ *v* **homed, homing** (of birds such as pigeons) to find one's way back to the starting place —see also HOME IN ON, HOMING

home brew *n* beer made at home — **~ed** *adj*

homecoming *n* an arrival home, esp. after long absence

home economics *n* (the modern name for) the study of the home, family, and household affairs —see also DOMESTIC SCIENCE

home from home *n* a place as welcoming and comfortable, etc., as one's own house

homegrown *adj* (of plants for food) grown in the home country

Home Guard *n* (in the Second World War) (a member of) the citizen army formed at home to help to defend Britain —compare TERRITORIAL ARMY

home help *n* a woman who is sent in by the medical and social services to do housework for someone who is ill or very old

home in on *v adv prep* to aim exactly towards

homeland *n* one's native country

homely *adj* **-lier, -liest 1** simple **2** not good-looking — **-liness** *n*

homemade *adj* *sometimes offensive* made at home, not bought from a shop

Home Office *n* the British government department which deals with home affairs —compare FOREIGN AND COMMONWEALTH OFFICE

Homeric *adj* of the poet Homer, or the style of his poetry; epic

home rule *n* self-government by one part of a larger state or empire

homesick *adj* feeling a great wish to be at home, when away — **~ness** *n*

homespun *adj, n* **1** (cloth from thread) spun at home, esp. in former times **2** (something) simple and ordinary

homestead *n* a house and land; a farm with its buildings

hometown *n* the town where one was born and/or passed one's childhood

home truth *n* a fact about someone which is unpleasant for him to know, but true

homeward *adj* going towards home

homewards *adv* towards home

homework *n* **1** studies which must be done at home so as to learn and prepare for what is studied at school **2** preparation done before taking part in an important activity —compare HOUSEWORK

homicidal *adj* likely to murder

homicide *n* *esp. written or law* (an act of) murder

homing *adj, n* **1** (of) the ability to find one's way home, as used by pigeons and in animal behaviour **2** (of) the ability of some machines, esp. modern weapons of war, to guide themselves onto the place they are aimed at

homing pigeon *n* **1** a pigeon trained to return to a particular place, esp. as used in races **2** CARRIER PIGEON

homoeopath, homeo- *n* a person, usu. a doctor, who treats a disease by giving very small amounts of a drug which in larger amounts would usually produce an illness like that disease — **~ic** *adj* — **~ically** *adv*

homoeopathy, homeo- *n* the practice of medicine in the manner of homoeopaths

homogeneous *adj* formed of parts of the same kind — **-neity** *n* — **~ly** *adv*

homogenize, -ise *v* **-nized, -nizing** to make (the parts of a whole, esp. a mixture) become evenly spread: *homogenized milk*

Homo sapiens *n* Latin the form of man today; people generally

homosexual *adj, n* (of or being) a person sexually attracted to members of the same sex

hon. *abbrev. for:* honorary

Hon. *abbrev. for:* Honourable

hone *v* **honed, honing** to sharpen (knives, swords, etc.) with a whetstone

honest *adj* **1** trustworthy **2** showing such qualities: *an honest face* **3** direct; not hiding facts — **~y** *n*

honestly *adv* **1** in an honest way **2 a** really; speaking truthfully **b** (used for expressing strong feeling usu. mixed with disapproval): *Honestly! What a thing to do!*

honest-to-goodness *adj esp. spoken* pure and simple

honey *n* **1** the sweet sticky material produced by bees, eaten on bread **2** *esp. US* darling **3** *esp. US spoken* something excellent

honeybee *n* the bee which makes honey

honeycomb *n* **1** a container of beeswax consisting of 6-sided cells in which honey is stored by the bees **2** something like this in shape

honeycombed *adj* filled with holes, passages, etc.

honeydew *n* *poetic* ambrosia

honeyed *adj* (of words) flattering

honeymoon[1] *n* **1** the holiday taken by newly-weds **2** a pleasant period of time

honeymoon[2] *v* to have one's honeymoon — **~er** *n*

honeysuckle *n* a climbing plant, growing both wild and in gardens, with sweet-smelling flowers

honk[1] *n* **1** the sound a wild goose makes **2** the sound made by a car horn

honk[2] *v* to make or cause to make a honk

honorary *adj* **1** (of a rank, a university degree, etc.) given as an honour, not according to the usual rules **2** (of an office or position held) without payment for one's services ⚠ HONOURABLE

honour[1] *n* **1** great respect, often publicly expressed **2** high standards of character or reputation: *to fight for the honour of one's country* **3** a person who brings respect (to): *He's an honour to his parents* **4** (a title of respect for a judge): *Your/His Honour* **5** (a polite word): *Would you do me the honour of dancing with me?* **6** *often humour* the chastity of a woman (esp. in the phrase **lose one's honour**)

honour[2] *v* **1** to respect by feelings or by an action which shows feelings: *I'm honoured by your presence* **2** to keep (an agreement), often by making a payment, as in giving money for a cheque or bill

honourable *adj* **1** worthy of honour or respect **2** showing good character ⚠ HONORARY — **-bly** *adv*

Honourable (*abbrev.* **Hon.**)— *adj* (a title given to the children of certain British noblemen, to judges, and various officials, including Members of Parliament when talking to one another in the House of Commons)

honourable mention *n* a special mark of

honour in a competition or show, given for work of high quality that has not won prizes

honours *n* **1** marks of respect, such as titles given in Britain to important people on the Queen's birthday and at New Year in the **honours list** **2** a specialized university undergraduate degree, or a level gained in it **3 do the honours** *esp. spoken* to act as the host or hostess, as by offering drink

hooch *n US sl* alcoholic drink, esp. whisky

hood *n* **1 a** a covering for the head and neck usu. fastened on at the back, as to a coat **b** a covering for the head of a hunting bird **2** something like a hood which fits over the top of something else, as over a chimney to keep the wind out **3** a folding cover over a car, pram, etc. **4** *US* the bonnet covering the engine of a car **5** *sl* a hoodlum

hooded *adj* hidden by a covering

hoodlum *n sl* a violent and/or criminal person

hoodoo¹ *n* **-doos** *esp. US spoken* **1** a person or thing which brings bad luck **2** voodoo

hoodoo² *v* **-dooed, -dooing** *esp. US spoken* to bring bad luck on (someone)

hoodwink *v* to deceive

hooey *n US sl* nonsense

hoof *n* **hoofs** *or* **hooves** **1** the hard foot of certain animals, as of the horse —compare PAW ☞ HORSE **2 on the hoof** (of a meat animal) before being killed for meat

hoo-ha *n esp. spoken* a fuss

hook¹ *n* **1** a curved piece of metal, plastic, etc., for catching something on or hanging things on **2** something curved or bent like this: *Hook of Holland* **3 a** (in cricket, golf, etc.) a flight of a ball away from a course straight ahead **b** (in boxing) a blow given with the elbow bent **4 be/get off the hook** to be/get out of one's difficulties

hook² *v* **1** to catch with or as if with a hook: *to hook a fish* **2** to hang on or fasten with or as if with a hook **3** to make into the shape of a hook: *He hooked his arm* **4 a** (of a ball) to travel in a hook **b** to hit (a ball) in a hook

hookah *also* **water pipe**— *n* a tobacco pipe whose smoke is drawn through water by a long tube

hooked *adj* **1** shaped like a hook **2** having one or more hooks **3** caught on or as if on a hook **4** *esp. spoken* **a** dependent (on drugs) **b** having a great liking for and very frequently using, doing, eating, etc. —compare ADDICTED

hooker *n* **1** *US sl* a prostitute **2** (in rugby) a player whose job it is to kick the ball backwards to his own team after it has been thrown into the scrum

hook up *v adv* to connect to a power supply or central system

hooky, hookey *n sl* truant (only in the phrase **play hooky**)

hooligan *n* a noisy rough person who fights, breaks things, etc. — ~ **ism** *n*

hoop¹ *n* **1 a** a circular band of wood or metal, esp. round a barrel **b** such a band used as a child's toy **2** a circular frame, as formerly used to hold women's skirts out, or for animals to jump through at the circus **3** a metal arch through which the ball is driven in croquet

hoop² *v* to put a hoop on (a barrel) —see also COOPER

hoop-la *n* a game in which prizes are won when a ring is thrown right over them

hooray *interj, n* hurray

hoot¹ *v* **1** to make or cause to make a hoot **2** *esp. spoken* to laugh very much

hoot² *n* **1** the sound an owl makes **2** the sound made by a car or ship's horn **3** a shout of dislike, unpleasant laughter, etc. **4 not care a hoot/2 hoots** *esp. spoken* not to care at all

hooter *n* **1** a siren or whistle, esp. which signals the beginning or end of work **2** *sl* the nose

hoover¹ *n* *trademark* VACUUM CLEANER

hoover² *v* *esp. spoken* to vacuum

hooves *pl.* of HOOF

hop¹ *v* **-pp-** **1 a** (of people) to jump on one leg **b** (of small creatures) to jump **2** to cross by hopping **3 Hop it!** *sl* Go away! **4 hopping mad** very angry —see also HEDGEHOP

hop² *n* **1** an act of hopping; jump **2** *esp. spoken* an informal dance **3** *esp. spoken* a distance travelled by a plane before landing: *It's a short hop from London to Paris* **4 catch someone on the hop** *esp. spoken* to meet someone when he is unprepared —see also HOP, STEP, AND JUMP

hop³ *n* a tall climbing plant with flowers or its seed-cases which when dried are used for flavouring beer

hope¹ *v* **hoped, hoping** **1** to wish and expect; desire in spite of doubts **2 hope against hope** to continue to hope when there is little chance of success

hope² *n* **1** the expectation of something happening as one wishes **2** a person or thing that seems likely to bring success: *You're my only hope/last hope*

hopeful¹ *adj* **1** (of people) feeling hope **2** giving cause for hope of success — ~ **ness** *n*

hopeful² *n* a person who seems likely to succeed, or who desires to succeed: *a young hopeful*

hopefully *adv* **1** in a hopeful way **2** *esp. spoken* if our hopes succeed: *Hopefully we'll be there by dinnertime* USAGE Many teachers and writers of British English consider it incorrect to use **hopefully** to mean 'If our hopes succeed'; 'It is to be hoped that---'. This use is, however, becoming very common.

hopeless *adj* **1** (not usu. of people) showing lack of hope: *hopeless tears* **2** giving no cause for hope **3** *esp. spoken* useless: *Your work is hopeless* — ~ **ly** *adv* — ~ **ness** *n*

hopper *n* a funnel through which grain or coal is passed

hop-picker *n* a person or machine that gathers hops

hopscotch *n* a children's game in which a stone

is thrown onto numbered squares and each child hops and jumps from one to another

hop, step, and jump n TRIPLE JUMP

horde n 1 a large number or crowd: *a horde of children* 2 (in history) a large wandering group of people of a certain nationality, esp. a fighting one ⚠ HOARD

horizon n 1 the limit of one's view, where the sky seems to meet the earth or sea 2 the limit of one's thoughts

horizontal adj, n (in) the flat position, along or parallel to the ground —compare VERTICAL — ~ly adv

hormone n any of several substances produced by organs of the body of a plant or animal (esp. ENDOCRINE GLANDS)and directed into the bloodstream or sap so as to influence growth, development, etc. in other parts of the body

horn n 1 a hard pointed growth found in a pair on the top of the heads of cattle, sheep, and goats 2 something like these growths, as on a snail 3 the material that these growths are made of 4 any of a number of musical wind instruments: *the French horn* 5 a warning apparatus, as in a car 6 **take the bull by the horns** to face a difficult thing or person — ~like, ~ed adj — ~less adj

hornet n a large wasp-like insect which can sting

hornet's nest n a lot of trouble and anger between people (esp. in the phrase **stir up a hornet's nest**)

horn in v adv sl to interrupt or join uninvited

hornpipe n 1 a type of dance, esp. performed by sailors 2 the music for this dance

horn-rimmed adj (of glasses) surrounded by an edge made of horn or a material like it

horny adj -ier, -iest hard and rough

horology n the art of making clocks and watches and of measuring time

horoscope n a set of ideas about someone's character and future, gained by knowing the positions of the stars or planets at the time of his birth

horrendous adj really terrible; causing great fear — ~ly adv

horrible adj 1 causing horror 2 esp. spoken very unkind, unpleasant, or ugly — -bly adv

horrid adj horrible — ~ly adv — ~ness n

horrify v -fied, -fying to shock; fill with horror — ~ingly, -fically adv — -fic adj

horror n 1 a feeling of great shock, fear, and dislike 2 the quality of causing this feeling: *the horror of war* 3 an unpleasant person: *He is a little horror* 4 **Chamber of Horrors** (in a waxworks display) the room where murderers, torturers, etc., are represented 5 **horror film** a film of a popular type in which fearful things happen which could not happen in reality

horrors n 1 a state of great fear: *have the horrors* 2 things, events, or actions that cause horror: *the horrors of war*

horror-stricken also **horror-struck**— adj filled with horror

hors de combat adj, adv French unable to fight, because wounded

hors d'oeuvre n -d'oeuvres or -d'oeuvre French savoury food offered in small amounts at the beginning of the meal

horse n 1 a type of large strong animal with mane, tail, and hooves which men ride and use for pulling and carrying heavy things ☞ MAMMAL ◉ 2 VAULTING HORSE 3 **dark horse** a person whose abilities are hidden 4 **eat like a horse** to eat a lot 5 **Hold your horses!** Don't rush hastily into anything 6 **put the cart before the horse** to do or put things in the wrong order

horse around also **horse about**— v adv **horsed , horsing around** esp. spoken to play roughly

horseback n **on horseback** (riding) on a horse

horsebox n a large vehicle for transporting a horse

horse chestnut n 1 a large flowering tree 2 an inedible nut from this tree; a conker — compare CHESTNUT

horsefly n -flies a large fly that stings horses and cattle

horselaugh n a loud (impolite) laugh

horseman (fem. **horsewoman**)— n -men a person who rides a horse, esp. one who rides well — ~ship n

horseplay n rough noisy behaviour

horsepower (abbrev. HP)— n **horsepower** a measure of the power of an engine, representing the force needed to pull 550 pounds one foot a second

horseracing n the practice of racing horses ridden by jockeys, for money

horseradish n a plant whose root is used to make a strong-tasting sauce for meat

horse sense n COMMON SENSE

horseshoe n 1 also **shoe**— a curved piece of iron nailed under a horse's foot ☞ HORSE 2 something made in this shape

horse-trading n argument about prices or about who should do what — **horse trader** n

horsewhip v -pp- to beat (someone) hard

horsy adj -ier, -iest 1 interested in horses, fond of riding, etc. 2 of a horselike appearance — **horsiness** n

hortative also **hortatory**— adj esp. written (of advice, speech, etc.) encouraging

horticulture n the science of growing fruit, flowers, and vegetables — -tural adj — -turalist n

hosanna n, interj Bible a shout of praise to God

hose[1] n (used esp. in shops) stockings or socks

hose[2] also **hosepipe**— n (a piece of) rubber or plastic tube which can direct water onto fires, a garden, etc.

Points of the horse

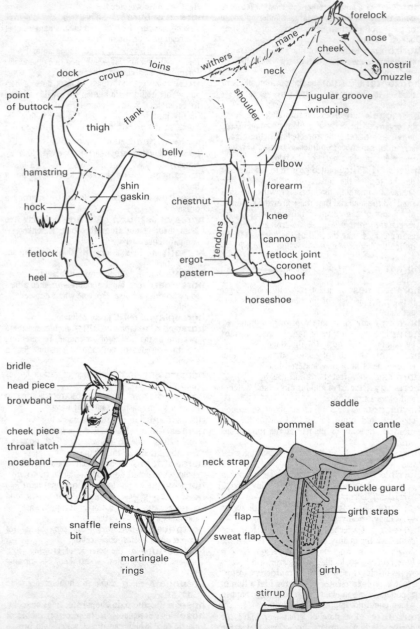

forelock
nose
cheek
mane
withers
neck
nostril
muzzle
loins
dock
croup
point of buttock
thigh
flank
hamstring
shin
gaskin
hock
fetlock
heel
belly
shoulder
jugular groove
windpipe
elbow
forearm
chestnut
tendons
ergot
pastern
knee
cannon
fetlock joint
coronet
hoof
horseshoe

bridle
head piece
browband
cheek piece
throat latch
noseband
snaffle bit
reins
martingale rings
neck strap
saddle
pommel
seat
cantle
buckle guard
girth straps
flap
sweat flap
girth
stirrup

Harness of the horse

hose³ v **hosed, hosing** to use a hose on, esp. for washing

hosier n a shopkeeper who sells socks and men's underclothes

hosiery n socks, stockings, underclothes, etc.

hospice n 1 a house made for travellers to stay in, esp. when kept by a religious group 2 a usu. small hospital for patients who will not recover

hospitable adj showing the wish to attend to the needs of others, esp. by feeding them, asking them into one's home, etc. — **-bly** adv

hospital n a place where ill people stay and have treatment

hospitality n 1 the quality of being hospitable 2 food, a place to sleep, etc., when given to a guest (esp. in the phrase **partake of someone's hospitality**)

hospitalize, -ise v **-ized, -izing** to put (a person) into hospital — **-ization** n

host¹ n a large number

host² n 1 a man who receives guests 2 old use or humour an innkeeper (note the phrase **mine host**) 3 an animal or plant on which some lower form of life is living as a parasite

host³ v to act as host at (a party, friendly meeting, etc.)

host⁴ n the holy bread eaten at Holy Communion

hostage n a person kept by an enemy so that the other side will do what the enemy wants

hostel n 1 a building in which certain types of person can live and eat, such as students, young people working away from home, etc. 2 YOUTH HOSTEL

hostelry n **-ries** old use an inn

hostess n 1 a female host 2 a young woman who acts as companion, dancing partner, etc., in a social club 3 an airhostess

hostile adj 1 belonging to an enemy 2 unfriendly; showing dislike

hostilities n acts of fighting in war

hostility n the state of being unfriendly

hot adj **-tt-** 1 having a certain degree of heat, esp. a high degree 2 causing a burning taste: *Pepper makes food hot* 3 (of news) very recent 4 excitable: *a hot temper* —compare HEATED 5 a esp. spoken (of people) (tending to be) sexually excited b esp. spoken sexually exciting 6 sl (of stolen goods) difficult to pass on, esp. soon after the crime has taken place 7 esp. spoken clever, well-informed, and usu. very interested 8 **get hot** (in a guessing game) to get near something hidden or to guess nearly right 9 **get hot under the collar** to get angry 10 **not so hot** esp. spoken not very good

hot air n meaningless talk

hotbed n a place or condition where growth of some undesirable state or activity goes on: *The city is a hotbed of crime*

hot-blooded adj showing strong feelings; passionate

hotchpotch n a number of things mixed up without any order

hot cross bun n a type of spicy bun with a cross-shaped mark on top, eaten on Good Friday

hot dog n a long red sausage in a bread roll

hotel n a building where people can stay for payment

hotelier n a man who keeps a hotel

hot flush n a sudden feeling of heat in the skin, esp. as experienced by women at the menopause

hotfoot v **hotfoot it** esp. spoken to move fast — **hotfoot** adv

hothead n a person who does things in haste, without thinking — ~**ed** adj — ~**edly** adv

hothouse n a warm building where delicate plants can grow; greenhouse

hot line n a direct, usu. telephone, line between heads of government, to be used at times of crisis

hotly adv 1 in anger and with force 2 closely and eagerly (often in the phrase **hotly pursued**)

hotplate n a metal surface, usu. on an electric stove, for cooking food

hotpot n a mixture of meat and vegetables (esp. potatoes and onions), cooked slowly in a pot

hot rod n an old car rebuilt for high speed rather than appearance —compare STOCK CAR

hot seat n esp. spoken a position of difficulty from which one must make important decisions

hot spot n a place where there is much unrest

hot stuff n esp. spoken 1 something of very good quality 2 something or someone exciting or dangerous, esp. sexually

hot-tempered adj quick-tempered

Hottentot adj 1 (of a person) of a race of Southern Africa 2 of the language of this race

hot water n trouble (in the phrases **get into/be in hot water**)

hot-water bottle n a usu. rubber container filled with hot water for warming a bed

hound¹ n 1 a hunting dog, esp. a foxhound 2 a person who is disliked

hound² v to chase or worry continually: *Tell him to stop hounding me*

hound's-tooth also **hound's-tooth check**— n a pattern of broken checks used esp. on cloth and clothes

hour n 1 the period of time, 60 minutes, of which 24 make a day 2 a time of day when such a new period starts: *He arrived on the hour* 3 a distance which one can travel in this period of time: *It's only an hour away* 4 a fixed point or period of time: *The hour has come for a serious talk* 5 a certain period of time: *spent happy hours together* 6 a time, esp. an important one like the present 7 **after hours** later than the usual times of work or business 8 **(at) the eleventh hour** (at) the last moment 9 **the small hours** also (humour) **the wee hours**— the hours soon after midnight (1, 2, 3 o'clock) 10 **zero hour** the time when something happens, after a certain period of waiting has passed

hourglass n a glass container made narrow in

the middle like a figure 8 so that the sand inside can run slowly from the top half to the bottom, taking just one hour —compare EGGTIMER

hour hand *n* the small pointer on a clock which shows the hour nearest in time

hourly *adj, adv* (happening, appearing, etc.) every hour or once an hour

house¹ *n* 1 a a building for people to live in b the people in such a building 2 a building for animals or goods 3 an important family, esp. noble or royal: *the House of Windsor* 4 a a building in which children live at school, with its own name b a division of a school, esp. for sports competitions 5 a a business firm, esp. one controlled by a family and/or one in the business of publishing b a large building used for business —compare BUILDING 6 the people voting after a debate: *The house divided* 7 a theatre, or the people in it 8 a place where people meet for a certain purpose: *a public house* 9 **keep house** to do or control the cleaning, cooking and other things usu. done in a house 10 **on the house** (usu. of drinks) being paid for by the people in charge, as by the owner of a public house, by a firm, etc. 11 **(as) safe as houses** very safe USAGE Americans often use **home** to mean **house**: *She has a beautiful* **home**. British people distinguish between **home** and **house**. **Home** is the place to which one feels one belongs, and where one feels comfortable. A **house** is simply a building in which one lives.

house² *v* **housed, housing** 1 to provide with a place to live 2 to provide space for storing

House *n* 1 House of Commons 2 House of Representatives

house agent *n* a person who arranges for houses to be rented or sold —compare ESTATE AGENT

house arrest *n* **under house arrest** forbidden to leave one's house by a government

houseboat *n* a boat fitted with everything necessary for living there

housebound *adj* not able to move out of the house, or to spend much time outside it

housebreaker *n* a thief who enters a house by force, esp. during the day —compare BURGLAR

housecoat *n* a woman's dressing gown

housecraft *n* DOMESTIC SCIENCE

housefather (*fem.* **housemother**)— *n* a person who acts as parent to children with no families, who live in a special home together

housefly *n* **-flies** the most common type of fly

household¹ *n* all the people living together in a house

household² *adj* having the special responsibility of guarding the king or queen, or the royal palace: *household cavalry*

householder *n* a person who owns or is in charge of a house

household name also **household word**— *n* a thing or person known and spoken of by almost everybody

housekeeper *n* a person who has charge of the running of a house —see also HOUSE

housekeeping *n* 1 the care, cleaning, cooking, etc., of and for a house and the people who live in it 2 also **housekeeping money** — an amount of money set aside each week or month by the husband and/or wife to pay for things needed in the home

housemaid *n* a female servant who cleans the house

housemaid's knee *n* a painful swelling of the knee

houseman *n* **-men** a junior doctor completing hospital training, and often living in the hospital

house martin *n* a bird, related to the swallow, which sometimes makes a nest under the roof of a house

housemaster *fem.* **housemistress**— *n* a teacher who is in charge of one house of a school

housemother *n* a woman doing the work of a housefather

house of cards *n* **houses of cards** a plan which is too badly arranged to succeed

House of Commons also **Commons**— *n* the lower but more powerful of the 2 parts of the British or Canadian parliament, the members of which are elected by anybody over 18 years of age who is not a member of the House of Lords

house of correction *n* **houses of correction** *old use* a prison

House of Lords also **Lords**— *n* the upper but less powerful of the 2 parts of the British parliament, the members of which have positions because of their rank or titles of honour —compare HOUSE OF COMMONS

House of Representatives also **House**— *n* the lower of the 2 parts of the central law-making body in such countries as New Zealand, Australia, the US, etc. —compare SENATE

house party *n* **-ties** a party lasting for several days, esp. in a large country house

house-proud *adj* liking perfect order in the house and often spending too much time on keeping it so

houseroom *n* **not give (something) houseroom** not to accept (something) which one finds very unpleasant

Houses of Parliament *n* the buildings in which the British parliament sits

house sparrow *n* a very common small brown bird of the sparrow family

house-to-house also **door-to-door**— *adj* (done by) visiting each house in turn

house-trained *adj* 1 (of house pets) trained to go out of the house to empty the bowels or bladder 2 *humour* (of people) taught to be tidy at home

housewarming *n* a party given on moving into a new house

housewife *n* **-wives** a woman who works at home for her family, cleaning, cooking, etc. — ~ly *adj*

housework *n* work done in taking care of a house, esp. cleaning —compare HOMEWORK

housing *n* 1 the act or action of providing a place to live 2 the places provided 3 protective covering, as for machinery: *the engine housing*

hove *technical or humour past tense and sometimes past part. of* HEAVE

hovel *n* a small dirty dwelling

hover *v* 1 (of birds, certain aircraft, etc.) to stay in the air in one place 2 (of people) to wait around one place — **hoverer** *n*

hovercraft *n* (*trademark*) a sort of boat which moves over land or water by means of a strong force of air underneath

how¹ *adv* 1 (*in questions*) **a** in what way or by what means: *How can I get to Cambridge?* **b** in what condition, of health or mind: *How is mother?* **c** by what amount; to what degree: *How much does this cost?* 2 (in exclamations): *How they cheered!* 3 **How come?** *esp. spoken (in/or as an expression of surprise)* Why is it? How can it be that . . . ? 4 **How do you do?** also **How d'ye do?** (the phrase used to someone just met or introduced to the speaker) 5 **How's that?** (in cricket) (a call suggesting that the batsman is out)

how² *conj* the fact that: *Do you remember how he arrived almost at the end of the party?*

howdah *n* a covered and ornamented seat on an elephant's back

how do you do also **how d'ye do**— *n* **a fine how do you do** *esp. spoken* a mixed-up or difficult state of affairs

however¹ *conj* in whatever way

however² *adv* 1 to whatever degree 2 in spite of this: *It's raining. However, I think we should go* —see EVER (USAGE)

howitzer *n* a short heavy gun which fires shells high over a short distance

howl¹ *v* 1 to make howls 2 to say or express with a howl: *He howled (out) my name* 3 to weep loudly

howl² *n* a long loud cry, as in pain, anger, etc., esp. that made by wolves and dogs

howl down *v adv* to make a loud disapproving noise to prevent (someone) from being heard

howler *n* esp. spoken a silly mistake, esp. when the wrong word is used in writing

howling *adj* esp. spoken very great: *a howling success*

hoyden *n* a noisy rude girl — ~**ish** *adj*

hp *abbrev. for:* 1 horsepower 2 hire purchase

HQ *abbrev. for:* Headquarters

hr hrs *abbrev. for:* hour

HRH *abbrev. for:* His/Her Royal Highness

ht *abbrev. for:* height

hub *n* 1 the central part of a wheel, to which the rim is connected 2 the centre of activity or importance

hubbub *n* a mixture of loud noises

hubby *n* -**bies** *esp. spoken* a husband

hubcap *n* a metal covering over the centre of the wheel of a motor vehicle

hubris *n* Greek a pride in oneself, sometimes bringing ruin

huddle¹ *v* -**dled, -dling** to crowd together

huddle² *n* a crowd of people, or a number of things, close together and not in any order

hue *n* 1 a colour 2 a degree of brightness in colour

hue and cry *n* noisy behaviour either when searching for something or showing opposition to something: *They raised a hue and cry against the new rule*

huff¹ *v* to breathe noisily

huff² *n* a state of bad temper (esp. in the phrase **go into a huff**) — ~**ish**, ~**y** *adj* — ~**ily** *adv* ~**iness** *n*

hug¹ *v* -**gg-** 1 to hold tightly in the arms 2 to hold on to (an idea) with a feeling of pleasure or safety 3 to go along while staying near: *The boat hugged the coast*

hug² *n* the act of hugging —compare BEAR HUG

huge *adj* very big — ~**ness** *n*

hugely *adv esp. spoken* very much

hugger-mugger *n, adj, adv* 1 (in) secrecy 2 (in) disorder

Huguenot *n* a French Protestant in the 16th and 17th centuries

huh *interj* (used for asking a question or for expressing surprise or disapproval)

hulk *n* 1 the body of an old unseaworthy ship 2 a heavy, awkward person or creature

hulking *adj* big, heavy, and awkward

hull¹ *n* the main body of a ship ☞ SAIL

hull² *n* the outer covering of some grain, fruit, and seeds —compare HUSK

hull³ *v* to take the hull off; shell (peas and beans)

hullabaloo *n* -**loos** a lot of noise, esp. of voices

hullo *interj, n* -**los** hello

hum¹ *v* -**mm-** 1 (of bees and certain animals) to make a continuous buzz 2 (of people) to make a buzzing sound esp. as a way of singing 3 (of work being carried out) to be active: *Things are starting to hum* — **hum** *n*

hum² *v* -**mm-** **hum and haw** to express uncertainty

human¹ *adj* 1 of or concerning man 2 showing the feelings, esp. those of kindness, which people are supposed to have: *He seems quite human now* —opposite **inhuman**—compare HUMANE

human² also **human being**— *n* a man, woman, or child, not an animal

humane *adj* 1 showing human kindness — opposite **inhumane**—compare HUMAN 2 **humane killer** something which can be used to kill animals painlessly

humanism *n* 1 a system of thought concerned with the needs of man, and not with religion 2 the study in the Renaissance of ancient Greek and Roman ideas — -**ist** *n, adj* — -**istic** *adj*

humanitarian *n, adj* (a person) concerned

with trying to improve the living standards of human beings

humanitarianism *n* the beliefs and practices of a humanitarian

humanities *n* studies such as literature, the languages of ancient Greece and Rome, history, etc.; the arts

humanity *n* 1 the quality of being humane or human 2 human beings generally

humanize, -ise *v* -ized, -izing 1 to cause to be or seem human 2 to make humane

humankind *n literature* mankind

humanly *adv* according to human powers: *It's not humanly possible*

humble¹ *adj* 1 a (of people) low in rank or position b (of positions) unimportant 2 having a low opinion of oneself and a high opinion of others 3 **your humble servant** a way of ending a letter before signing it, used esp. formerly — — **-bly** *adv*

humble² *v* -bled, -bling to make (someone or oneself) humble or lower in position

humbug¹ *n* 1 a hard boiled sweet usu. tasting of mint 2 deceiving acts or talk 3 nonsense 4 a person who pretends to be something he is not

humbug² *v* -gg- to trick

humdinger *n esp. spoken US* a wonderful person or thing

humdrum *adj* too ordinary; without change

humerus *n* the bone in the top half of the arm

humid *adj* (of air and weather) containing water

humidity *n* the (amount of) water contained in the air

humiliate *v* -ated, -ating to cause to feel humble or to lose the respect of others — **-ation** *n*

humility *n* the quality of being humble

hummingbird *n* any of many kinds of very small birds whose fast-beating wings hum

humorist *n* a person who makes jokes

humorous *adj* funny — ~**ly** *adv*

humour¹ *n* 1 the ability to be amused: *a sense of humour* 2 the quality of causing amusement 3 *becoming rare* a state of mind; mood (only in certain phrases): *in a bad humour* 4 *old use* any of 4 liquids thought in the Middle Ages to be present in the body in varying degrees, and to influence the character

humour² *v* to keep (someone) happy by acceptance of (esp.) foolish wishes, behaviour, etc.

hump¹ *n* 1 a lump or round part which stands out noticeably 2 a lump on the back, as on a camel 3 *esp. spoken* a feeling of bad temper or dislike of life in general: *It's giving me the hump* 4 **over the hump** past the worst part

hump² *v* 1 to curve into a hump 2 *esp. spoken* to carry on the back

humpback *n* a hunchback — ~**ed** *adj*

humph, h'm *interj* (a sound made mostly with the lips closed to express doubt or dissatisfaction)

humus *n* rich soil made of decayed plants, leaves, etc. —compare MULCH

Hun *n* a member of a race who ravaged many parts of Europe in the 4th and 5th centuries

hunch¹ *n esp. spoken* an idea based on feeling rather than on reason

hunch² *v* to pull into a rounded shape: *She hunched her shoulders*

hunchback *n* (a person with) a back mis-shaped by a round lump —see also HUMP — ~**ed** *adj*

hundred *adj, n, pron* -dred *or* -dreds the number 100 — ~**th** *adj, n, pron, adv*

hundredweight (*abbrev.* cwt)— *n* -weight 112 pounds

hung *past tense and past part. of* HANG

hunger¹ *n* 1 the wish or need for food 2 a strong wish: *hunger for excitement* 3 lack of food

hunger for *also* **hunger after**— *v prep* to want very much

hunger march *n* a procession by people, esp. when unemployed, to make known the difficulties of those who cannot afford to eat — ~**er** *n*

hunger strike *n* a refusal to eat as a sign of protest — ~**er** *n*

hungry *adj* -grier, -griest 1 feeling or showing hunger 2 causing hunger (esp. in the phrase **hungry work**) 3 with a strong wish: *We're hungry for news* 4 **go hungry** to remain without food — **-grily** *adv*

hunk *n* a thick piece, esp. of food, broken or cut off

hunkers *n esp. spoken* the haunches

hunt¹ *v* 1 to chase in order to kill (animals and birds) either for food or sport 2 to chase foxes on horseback with hounds 3 to search (for) USAGE In Britain one goes **shooting** with a gun, on foot. **Hunting** means using hounds to chase the animal. The **hunters** usually follow on horses. In America the word **hunting** is used for both these sports.

hunt² *n* 1 an act of hunting 2 a the act of hunting foxes b the people who regularly hunt foxes together 3 a search

hunt down *also* **hunt out**— *v adv* to succeed in finding after much effort

hunter *n* 1 a person or animal that hunts, usu. wild animals 2 a strong horse used in foxhunting 3 someone who searches too eagerly (esp. for something of advantage to himself): *a fortune hunter*

hunting *n* the action of hunting, esp. (in Britain) foxhunting

hunting ground *n* a place where one may hope to find what one is searching for

hunting pink *n, adj* (of) the red colour of the coats worn by fox hunters

hunt out *v adv* 1 HUNT DOWN 2 *also* **hunt up**— to search for with much effort

huntress *n* a female hunter

huntsman n -men 1 a hunter 2 the person in charge of the hounds during a fox hunt

hurdle¹ n 1 a wooden frame used with others for making fences 2 a frame for jumping over in a race 3 a difficulty to be overcome

hurdle² v -dled, -dling to run a hurdle race — -dler n

hurdy-gurdy n -gurdies a sort of small barrel organ

hurl v 1 to throw with force 2 to shout out violently: He hurled curses

hurly-burly n noisy activity

hurray, hooray also (becoming rare) hurrah— interj, n -ays a shout of joy or approval (note the phrase hip, hip, hurray)

hurricane n a violent wind storm, esp. in the West Indies —see TYPHOON (USAGE)

hurricane lamp n a lamp which has a cover to protect the flame from wind

hurried adj done in haste — ~ly adv

hurry¹ v -ried, -rying 1 to be or make quick in action, sometimes too quick 2 to send or bring quickly: A doctor hurried to the accident

hurry² n 1 haste; quick activity 2 need for haste

hurt¹ v hurt, hurting 1 to cause pain and/or injury to (esp. a part of the body) 2 to cause to feel pain 3 to cause pain to (a person's feelings) 4 esp. spoken to have a bad effect (on): It won't hurt to wait a bit USAGE When hurt means bodily damage, one may be slightly/badly/seriously hurt. Do not use badly or seriously when speaking of unhappiness caused by someone's behaviour: I was very hurt at his words. —see WOUND (USAGE)

hurt² n 1 harm; damage, esp. to feelings 2 injury to the body

hurtful adj harmful; painful to the feelings — ~ly adv — ~ness n

hurtle v -tled, -tling to rush with great speed

husband¹ n the man to whom a woman is married ⟶ FAMILY

husband² v esp. written to save carefully and/or make the best use of: to husband one's strength

husbandry n esp. written farming

hush¹ v to be or make silent and/or calm — compare SHUSH

hush² n (a) silence, esp. a peaceful one

hush-hush adj esp. spoken (of plans, arrangements, etc.) secret

hush money n money paid secretly to prevent some shameful fact from being known publicly

hush up v adv to keep secret by forcing silence about — hush-up n

husk¹ n 1 the dry outer covering of some fruits and seeds —compare HULL 2 the useless outside part of something

husk² v to take the husks off

husky¹ adj -kier, -kiest 1 (of a person or voice) difficult to hear and breathy —compare HOARSE 2 (of a person) big and strong —compare HEFTY — -kily adv — -kiness n

husky² n -kies a type of large working dog used by Eskimoes

hussar n a soldier in the   cavalry

hussy n -sies a badly behaved girl or woman (note the phrases brazen/shameless hussy)

hustings n the speeches, attempts to win votes, etc., before an election

hustle¹ v -tled, -tling to move fast

hustle² n hurried activity (esp. in the phrase hustle and bustle)

hut n a small building, often made of wood, esp. one used for living in or for shelter

hutch n a small box or cage with one side made of wire netting, esp. one for keeping rabbits in

hyacinth n a plant with bell-shaped flowers, which grows from a bulb

hyaena n a hyena

hybrid n a living thing produced from parents of different breeds: The hybrid from a donkey and a horse is called a mule

hybridize, -ise v -ized, -izing to produce or cause to produce a hybrid — -ization n

hydra n 1 a (in ancient Greek stories) a snake with many heads which grew again when cut off b an evil thing which is difficult to destroy 2 a small freshwater animal with tentacles

hydrangea n a shrub with clusters of large brightly-coloured flowers

hydrant n a street water pipe for public use

hydrate n technical a combination of a chemical substance with water

hydraulic adj concerning or moved by the pressure of water or other liquids: Hydraulic cement hardens under water pressure — ~ally adv

hydraulics n the science which studies the use of water to produce power

hydrocarbon n technical any of several chemical compounds of hydrogen and carbon, such as gas or petrol

hydrochloric acid n an acid containing hydrogen and chlorine

hydroelectric adj concerning or producing electricity by the power of falling water — ~ally adv

hydrofoil n a type of large motor-boat which raises itself out of the water as it moves

hydrogen n a gas that is an element, without colour or smell, is lighter than air, and burns very easily

hydrogen bomb also H-bomb, fusion bomb— n a bomb which explodes when the central parts of hydrogen atoms join together

hydrogen peroxide n technical peroxide

hydrolysis n -lyses tehnical the breaking up of a chemical compound to which water is added

hydrophobia n 1 rabies 2 fear of water

hydroplane n a flat-bottomed motor-boat which can move very fast over the surface of the water

hydroponics n the science of growing plants in water with chemical substances added, rather than in soil — hydroponic adj

hyena, hyaena *n* a carnivorous dog-like animal of Africa and Asia with a cry like a laugh

hygiene *n* 1 the study and practice of health, esp. by paying attention to cleanliness 2 cleanliness generally

hygienic *adj* 1 causing or keeping good health- 2 clean — ~**ally** *adv*

hygroscopic *adj technical* tending to absorb water from the atmosphere

hymen *n* a fold of skin partly closing the vagina of a virgin

hymn *n* a song of praise, esp. to God

hyperbola *n* a curve which never reaches the axes that it curves towards ☞ MATHEMATICS

hyperbole *n* exaggeration

hyperbolic also **-ical** — *adj* 1 of, marked by, or tending to use hyperbole 2 of, related to, or being like a hyperbola

hypercritical *adj* too ready to see faults — ~**ly** *adv*

hypermarket *n* a very large supermarket

hypersensitive *adj* unusually sensitive — **-tivity** *n*

hypha *n* **-ae** a tiny cylindrical thread, many of which make up the body (MYCELIUM) of fungus

hyphen *n* a short line (-) which can join words or syllables —compare DASH

hypnosis *n* (the production of) a sleep-like state in which a person can be controlled by the person who produced it — **-notic** *adj* — **-notically** *adv*

hypnotic suggestion *n* (a) suggestion made to someone under hypnosis

hypnotism *n* the practice of hypnosis — **-tist** *n*

hypnotize, -ise *v* **-tized, -tizing** to produce hypnosis in

hypochondria *n* a state of unnecessary anxiety about one's health — **-driac** *n, adj*

hypocrisy *n* **-sies** the practice of pretending to be something very different from, and usu. better than, what one actually is

hypocrite *n* one who practises hypocrisy — **-critical** *adj* — **-critically** *adv*

hypodermic¹ *adj* (of an instrument) which is injected beneath the skin — ~**ally** *adv*

hypodermic² *n* a needle for injecting drugs into the body; hypodermic syringe or needle

hypotenuse *n* the longest side of a right-angled triangle , which is opposite the right angle ☞ TRIGONOMETRY, MATHEMATICS

hypothermia *n* a medical condition in which the body temperature falls below the usual level

hypothesis *n* **-ses** an idea which is thought suitable to explain the facts about something

hypothetical *adj* supposed to be so; not yet proved to be true — ~**ly** *adv*

hyrax *n* any of several kinds of small mammal, similar to a marmot ☞ MAMMAL

hysterectomy *n* **-mies** the medical operation for removing the womb

hysteria *n* 1 a condition of nervous excitement in which the sufferer laughs and cries uncontrol-

lably and/or shows strange changes in behaviour or bodily state 2 wild excitement, as of a crowd of people — **-ric** *n*

hysterical *adj* 1 in a state of hysteria 2 (of feelings) expressed wildly — ~**ly** *adv*

hysterics *n* attack(s) of hysteria

Hz *abbrev. for:* hertz

I

I, i **I's, i's** *or* **Is, is** 1 the 9th letter of the English alphabet —see also CROSS **one's "t's" and dot one's "i's"** 2 the Roman numeral for 1

I *pron* (used as the subject of a sentence) the person speaking: *I'm your mother, aren't I?/am I not?* USAGE In speech, people often use **I** as the 2nd of 2 objects after a verb or preposition, although this is not considered good English. DO NOT SAY: *He knows you and I.* | *People like George and I* | *between you and* **I**. If one removes the first of the objects one can easily see that the phrase is wrong: *He knows* **I**. | *People like* **I** | *between* **I** *(and you) see* ME (USAGE)

iamb also **iambus** — *n* a measure of poetry consisting of one weak beat followed by a strong one (as in the word "alive") — ~**ic** *adj, n*

Iberian *adj* of Spain and Portugal

ibidem also **ibid** — *adv Latin* in the same place, usu. in a (part of a) book already mentioned

ibis *n* **ibises** *or* **ibis** a type of bird living in warm wet areas

ICBM *abbrev for:* INTERCONTINENTAL BALLISTIC MISSILE

ice¹ *n* 1 water which has frozen to a solid 2 a serving of ice cream 3 **break the ice** to begin to be friendly with strangers, or to begin something difficult 4 **cut no ice (with someone)** to have little effect (on someone) 6 **keep (something) on ice** to keep for later use

ice² *v* **iced, icing** 1 to make very cold by using ice 2 to cover (a cake) with icing

ice age *n* any of several periods when ice covered many northern countries

iceberg *n* a large piece of ice floating in the sea, mostly below the surface

icebound *adj* that cannot be reached because of the presence of ice

ice cap also **ice sheet** — *n* a lasting covering of ice, such as that on the north and south Poles

ice cream *n* a sweet frozen mixture, usu. containing milk products and eggs

ice-cream soda also **soda** — *n* a dish made from ice cream, syrup, and soda water, usu. served in a tall glass

ice field *n* a very large area of ice, esp. on the sea

ice hockey *n* a team game like field hockey played on ice

idl

Icelandic _adj_ of Iceland, its people, or their language ☞ LANGUAGE

ice-lolly _n_ **-lies** a sweet-flavoured piece of ice on a stick

ice skate _n_ a skate for use on ice

ice-skate _v_ **-skated, -skating** to skate on ice — **ice-skater** _n_ — **ice-skating** _n_

ice water _n_ water made very cold, esp. for drinking

ichneumon fly _n_ **-flies** a type of insect which lays eggs inside the larva of other insects

icicle _n_ a pointed stick of ice formed when running water freezes

icing also **frosting**— _n_ a mixture of sugar with liquid, used to cover cakes

icon, ikon _n_ an image of a holy person

iconoclast _n_ a person who attacks widely-held beliefs or customs — ~**ic** _adj_

icy _adj_ **icier, iciest** 1 very cold 2 covered with ice — **icily** _adv_ — **iciness** _n_

I'd _short form of_ 1 I had 2 I would

ID card _n esp. spoken_ IDENTITY CARD

idea _n_ 1 a picture in the mind 2 a plan 3 an opinion 4 a guess; feeling of probability 5 understanding (esp. in the phrase **no idea**) 6 a suggestion or sudden thought: _What a good idea!_ 7 **one's idea of** (used for expressing what one likes a lot) 8 **The idea!** also **What an idea!**— (an expression of surprise at something strange or silly)

ideal¹ _adj_ 1 perfect 2 expressing perfection unlikely to exist in reality: _the ideal system of government_ —opposite **real** ⚠ IDYLL — ~**ly** _adv_

ideal² _n_ 1 a perfect example 2 (a belief in) high or perfect standards

idealism _n_ 1 the system of living according to one's ideals, or the belief that such a system is possible: _youthful idealism_ 2 (in philosophy) the belief that ideas are the only real things —compare REALISM

idealist _n_ a person who has ideals or who believes in or practises idealism — ~**ic** _adj_ — ~**ically** _adv_

idealize, -ise _v_ **-ized, -izing** to imagine or represent as perfect or as better than in reality — **-ization** _n_

idem _pron Latin_ (of a book, writer, etc., already mentioned) the same

identical _adj_ the same; exactly alike — **-cally** _adv_ USAGE It is always correct to say **identical** _with_: _This chair is_ **identical** _with mine._ Although many people now say **identical** _to_, this is not thought to be such good English.

identical twin _n_ either of a pair of children or animals born from one egg of the mother and usu. looking alike

identification _n_ 1 the act of identifying or state of being identified 2 means (such as an official paper) of proving who one is

identification parade _n_ a row of people, including one or more police suspects, whom a witness to the crime tries to recognize

identify _v_ **-fied, -fying** 1 to prove or show the identity of 2 to show or feel to be identical: _I'd identify the 2 tastes_

identify with _v prep_ 1 to cause or consider (someone) to be connected with (something): _He is closely identified with the scandal_ 2 to consider (something) equal to (something): _Never identify opinions with facts_ 3 to feel sympathy for (someone), or feel that one shares (something): _We can identify with your fears_ USAGE It is rather modern and American to use this verb in sentences like _She_ **identified with** _foreign workers_ rather than saying _She_ **identified** _herself with_ . . . Some people do not like it.

identikit _n_ a collection of parts which can be fitted together to produce pictures of different faces, so that witnesses may choose the face most like the criminal's

identity _n_ **-ties** 1 who or what a particular person or thing is: _Please prove your identity_ 2 sameness; exact likeness 3 _esp. spoken_ identification

identity card also **ID card, identity certificate** — _n_ a card with one's name, photograph, signature, etc., which proves who one is

identity element _n technical_ a quantity that leaves unaltered any set in which it is included: _The identity element when ordinary numbers are added is 0_

identity transformation _n technical_ a mathematical transformation that leaves unaltered a figure being transformed

ideogram _n_ a written sign for word that shows meaning rather than sound, as in Chinese

ideology _n_ **-ogies** _sometimes offensive_ a set of ideas, esp. if typical of a social or political movement: _Marxist ideology_ — **-ogical** _adj_ — **-ogically** _adv_ — **-ogist** _n_

ides _n literature_ (in the ancient Roman calendar) a date or period of time around the middle of the month (esp. in the phrase **the Ides of March**, meaning March 15th, when Julius Caesar was killed) —compare CALENDS

idiocy _n_ **-cies** 1 the state of being very foolish 2 _technical_ the state of being an idiot 3 an act of stupidity

idiom _n_ 1 a phrase which means something different from the meanings of the separate words: _To be "hard up" is an idiom meaning to lack money_ 2 the way of expression typical of a person or a people in their use of language

idiomatic _adj_ typical of a native speaker of the language: _idiomatic English_ — ~**ally** _adv_

idiosyncrasy _n_ **-sies** 1 a peculiarity of one person 2 _esp. spoken_ a peculiar act

idiot _n_ 1 a foolish person 2 _old use or technical_ a person of very weak mind usu. from birth — compare IMBECILE — ~**ic** _adj_ — ~**ically** _adv_

idle¹ _adj_ 1 **a** not working **b** (of time) not used for doing anything 2 lazy 3 of no use; not producing anything good (note the phrase **idle gossip**) — ~**ness** _n_ — **idly** _adv_

idle² _v_ **idled, idling** 1 to waste time doing

nothing 2 (of an engine) to run slowly because it is disconnected and not being used for useful work — **idler** n

idol n 1 an image worshipped as a god 2 someone or something admired or loved too much

idolater (fem **idolatress**)— n a worshipper or admirer of idols — **-trous** adj — **-trously** adv — **-try** n

idolize, -ise v **-ized, -izing** to treat as an idol

idyll, idyl n 1 a simple, happy period of life, often in the country, or a scene from such a time 2 a description of this, esp. a poem about country life △ IDEAL — ~ic adj — ~ically adv

i.e. abbrev. for: (Latin) id est; that is to say: females, i.e. girls and women —compare NAMELY, VIZ

if¹ conj 1 supposing that; on condition that: We'll go only if it rains 2 although: a pleasant if noisy child 3 whether: Did she say if she was coming? USAGE It is more correct to say If only I were rich! | If he were older we could take him than If only I was . . . If he was . . . . But when if means whether it must be followed by was: I don't know if he was there.

if² n **ifs and buts** reasons given for delay

igloo n **-loos** an Eskimo house made of hard icy blocks of snow

igneous adj technical formed from molten rock (MAGMA)

ignite v **ignited, igniting** to start or cause to start to burn

ignition n 1 the act or action of igniting 2 the means, or apparatus for, starting an engine by electrically firing the gases from the petrol

ignoble adj dishonourable — **-bly** adv

ignominious adj of a type which brings strong public disapproval; shameful to one's pride — ~ly adv

ignominy n **-nies** 1 a state of shame or dishonour 2 an act of shameful behaviour

ignoramus n an ignorant person

ignorance n lack of knowledge

ignorant adj 1 lacking knowledge —see IGNORE (USAGE) 2 esp. spoken rude, impolite

ignore v **ignored, ignoring** not to take notice of USAGE To be **ignorant** of something is not to know it: He is quite **ignorant** of Latin. To **ignore** something is to pretend not to know or see it: She saw him coming but she **ignored** him.

iguana n a type of large tropical American lizard

ikon n an icon

ilk n kind, type, etc., or (originally) place or family (usu. in the phrase **of that ilk**)

ill¹ adj **worse, worst** 1 not well in health 2 hurt 3 bad: ill luck —see SICK (USAGE)

ill² adv 1 badly, poorly, cruelly, or unpleasantly: The child has been ill-treated 2 scarcely: I can ill afford it

ill³ n a bad thing: the ills of life

ill-advised adj unwise

ill-assorted adj that do not go well together

ill at ease adj not comfortable because of lack of understanding or skill

ill-bred adj badly behaved or rude

illegal adj against the law —compare LEGAL, ILLEGITIMATE — ~ly adv — ~ity n

illegible also **unreadable**— adj which cannot be read —compare UNREADABLE — **-bility** n — **-bly** adv

illegitimate adj 1 not allowed by the rules —compare ILLEGAL 2 born to an unmarried mother — ~ly adv — **-macy** n

ill-fated adj unlucky

ill-favoured adj ugly, esp. in the face

ill-gotten adj obtained by dishonest means (usu. in the phrase **ill-gotten gains**)

illiberal adj 1 not in favour of allowing people to do as they like: illiberal opinions 2 ungenerous — ~ity n — **-rally** adv

illicit adj (done) against a law or a rule — ~ly adv

illimitable adj which cannot be measured: illimitable spaces

illiterate adj, n unable to read and write — ~ly adv — **-racy** n

ill-natured adj of a bad-tempered character: an ill-natured remark

illness n (a) disease; unhealthy state of the body

illogical adj without or going against logic — ~ly adv

ill-timed adj (done) at the wrong time: an ill-timed remark

ill-treat v to be cruel to — ~ment n

illuminate v **-nated , -nating** 1 to give light to or to ornament with lights 2 (esp. in former times) to paint with gold and bright colours — **-ation** n

illuminating adj that helps to explain: an illuminating remark

illuminations n a show of ornamental lights in a town

illusion n 1 the condition of seeing things wrongly 2 a false appearance or idea: His confidence was an illusion —see also OPTICAL ILLUSION USAGE An **illusion** is usually something that seems true to the senses, but is known to be false: the **illusion** that the sun goes round the earth. A **delusion** is something really believed by a person who is **deluded** or even mad: his **delusion** that he is Napoleon the first.

illusionist n a person who plays tricks on the eyes in a stage performance

illusory also **illusive**— adj deceiving and unreal; based on an illusion

illustrate v 1 **-trated, -trating** to add pictures to (something written) 2 to show the meaning of by giving related examples: The gift illustrates her generosity — **-ive** adj — **-ively** adv

illustration n 1 the act of illustrating 2 a picture to go with the words of a book, speaker, etc. 3 an example which explains the meaning of something

illustrator n a person who draws pictures

illustrious adj famous for great works: an illustrious name — ~ly adv

ill will n bad feeling

image n 1 a picture esp. in the mind 2 a copy: He's the image of his father 3 a metaphor or simile; a vivid phrase which suggests a picture to the reader 4 someone's appearance as seen by other people: Her image was poor 5 technical a a picture formed of an object in front of a mirror or lens b (in set theory) an item in a set (the RANGE) to which a member of another set (the DOMAIN) is linked (MAPped)

imagery n images generally, esp. as used in literature

imaginable adj that can be imagined

imaginary adj 1 not real, but produced from pictures in one's mind 2 (of a number) having a square less than 0

imagination n 1 the act of imagining or the ability to imagine 2 the mind: It's all in your imagination 3 esp.spoken something only imagined and not real

imaginative adj 1 that shows use of the imagination 2 good at inventing imaginary things or new ideas: an imaginative child △ IMAGINARY — ~ly adv

imagine v -gined, -gining 1 to form in the mind: I can imagine the scene clearly 2 to suppose or have an idea about, esp. mistakenly or without proof: He imagines that people don't like him

imam n a Muslim priest and/or prince, or someone who studies Muslim law

imbalance n a lack of balance: population imbalance, in which more males are born than females

imbecile n a fool or stupid person —compare IDIOT — -ility n

imbibe v imbibed, imbibing to drink or take in

imbroglio n -glios an occasion or state of affairs filled with confused action

imbue with v prep imbued, imbuing with to fill (someone) with (usu. feeling or opinion)

imitate v -tated, -tating 1 to take as an example: You should imitate his way of doing things 2 to copy the behaviour, appearance, speech, etc., typical of -compare IMPERSONATE 3 to appear like something else — -ation, -ativeness n — -ative adj — -atively adv

imitator n someone who imitates

immaculate adj pure; unspoilt; unmarked; without fault: immaculate behaviour/shoes — ~ly adv

immaterial adj 1 unimportant: It's immaterial whose fault it was 2 without substance: The soul is immaterial

immature adj 1 not fully formed or developed 2 showing a lack of control and good sense in one's behaviour — ~ly adv — -turity n

immeasurable adj that cannot be measured — -bly adv

immediacy also **immediateness**— n nearness or urgent presence

immediate adj 1 done or needed at once: an immediate reply 2 nearest; next: in the immediate future

immediately adv, conj at once; as soon as: immediately I'd eaten

immemorial adj going back to ancient times (note the phrase from/since time immemorial)

immense adj very large — -ensity n

immensely adv very much

immerse v immersed, immersing 1 to put deep under water: immersed in a bath 2 to cause to enter deeply into an activity: immersed in work — -sion n

immersion heater n an electric water heater for use in a house

immigrate v -grated, -grating to come into a country to make one's life and home there —see EMIGRATE (USAGE) — -gration n — -grant n

imminent adj which is going to happen very soon: A storm is imminent —compare IMPENDING — ~ly adv — -ence, -ency n

immobile adj unmoving — -bility n

immobilize, **-lise** v -lized, -lizing to make unable to move: The car is immobilized

immoderate adj beyond sensible limits: immoderate eating — ~ly adv — -racy n

immodest adj offensive 1 telling the good things about oneself 2 (usu. concerning women) showing private parts of the body or behaving too freely with men —compare INDECENT — ~ly adv — ~y n

immolate v -lated, -lating to kill as a sacrifice — -lation n

immoral adj 1 not considered good or right: Stealing is immoral 2 offensive to society's ideas of what is good or right, esp. in sexual matters; obscene —compare AMORAL —SEE MORAL (USAGE) — ~ally adv — ~ity n

immortal adj that will not die; that continues for ever — ~ity n

immortalize, -ise v -ized, -izing to give endless life or fame to

immovable adj which cannot be moved or changed — -bly adv

immune adj 1 unable to be harmed because of special powers in oneself: immune to disease 2 protected — immunity n △ IMPUNITY

immunize, **-nise** v -nized, -nizing to make immune against a particular disease by putting certain substances into the body —see also INOCULATE — -nization n

immure v immured, immuring to imprison

immutable adj unchangeable: immutable laws of nature — -bly adv — -bility n

imp n 1 a little devil 2 a naughty child —see also IMPISH

impact n 1 the force of one object hitting another 2 the force of an idea, invention, system, etc.

impacted adj (usu. of a WISDOM TOOTH) growing in the wrong direction

impair v to spoil or weaken — ~**ment** n

impala n **-las** or **la** a type of large brownish African antelope

impale v **impaled, impaling** to run a sharp stick or weapon through — ~**ment** n

impalpable adj **1** which cannot be felt by touch **2** not easily understood

impart v to give (qualities, knowledge, etc.)

impartial adj fair — ~**ly** adv — ~**ity** n

impassable adj which cannot be travelled over △ IMPOSSIBLE

impasse n a point where further movement is blocked

impassioned adj moved by deep feelings

impassive adj showing no feelings — ~**ly** adv — **-sivity** n

impatient adj **1** not patient **2** eager: *impatient to see his wife* — ~**ly** adv — **-ience** n

impeach v law to accuse of or charge with a serious crime, esp. against the state

impeccable adj faultless — **-bly** adv

impecunious adj having little or no money — ~**ly** adv — ~**ness** n

impedance n technical (a measure of) the power of a piece of electrical apparatus to stop the flow of an alternating current

impede v **impeded, impeding** to get in the way of; make (something) difficult to do — **-iment** n : *He has a speech impediment*

impel v **-ll-** to push or drive forward: *Hunger impelled the cat to go hunting*

impending adj (usu. of something unpleasant) about to happen —compare IMMINENT

impenetrable adj **1** which cannot be gone into or through **2** not able to be understood or helped: *an impenetrable difficulty*

impenitent adj not sorry — **-tence** n — ~**ly** adv

imperative[1] adj **1** urgent **2** showing proud power: *an imperative manner* **3** of, about, or using the imperative — ~**ly** adv

imperative[2] n (an example of) the use of the verb to express a command: *In "Come here!" the verb "come" is in the imperative*

imperceptible adj unable to be noticed — **-bility** n — **-bly** adv

imperfect[1] adj **1** not perfect **2** of or about the imperfect — ~**ion** n — ~**ly** adv

imperfect[2] n (an example of) the tense of the verb which shows a continuing action in the past

imperfective adj, n (an example) of a verb (esp. in Russian) which shows continuing action in the past, present, or future —compare PERFECTIVE

imperial adj **1** concerning an empire or its ruler .**2** (of a measure) British standard △ IMPERIOUS — ~**ly** adv

imperialism n **1** the making of empires **2** the belief in the good of empires **3** *offensive* the gaining of political and trade advantages over poorer nations by a powerful country —compare COLONIALISM, NEOCOLONIALISM —

-ist adj, n — **-istic** adj — **-istically** adv

imperil v **-ll-** to put in danger

imperious adj **1** (too) commanding or as if commanding **2** urgent: *imperious need* △ IMPERIAL — ~**ly** adv — ~**ness** n

imperishable adj which will not wear out: *imperishable fame*

impermanent adj which will change or be lost — **-nence** n

impermeable adj which substances (esp. liquids) cannot get through

impersonal adj **1** not showing feelings in one's behaviour **2** not human **3** (in grammar) having no subject, or a subject represented by meaningless or empty "it" (such as *rained* in *it rained*) — ~**ly** adv

impersonate v **-nated, -nating** to pretend to be by copying the appearance, behaviour, etc., of (another person) —compare IMITATE — **-nation** n — **-nator** n

impertinent adj rude or not respectful — **-nence** n — ~**ly** adv

imperturbable adj that cannot be worried — **-bility** n — **-bly** adv

impervious adj **1** not allowing anything to pass through: *impervious to liquids* **2** too certain in one's opinions to be changed

impetuous adj acting too hastily and thoughtlessly — **-osity** n — ~**ly** adv

impetus n **1** the force of something moving **2** a push forward: *adding impetus to my ideas*

impiety n **-ies** (an act showing) lack of respect, esp. for religion — **impious** adj — **impiously** adv

impinge on also **impinge upon**— v prep **impinged, impinging on** to have an effect on: *Television is impinging on your homework* △ IMPUGN

impish adj like an imp — ~**ly** adv — ~**ness** n

implacable adj which cannot be satisfied or reduced: *implacable dislike*

implant v to fix in deeply

implement[1] n a tool or instrument

implement[2] v to carry out or put into practice: *to implement one's ideas*

implicate v **-cated, -cating** to show that (someone else) is also to blame —compare INVOLVE

implication n **1** the act of implicating **2** the act of implying —compare INFERENCE, INSINUATION

implicit adj **1** meant though not plainly expressed: *an implicit threat* —compare EXPLICIT **2** unquestioning and complete — ~**ly** adv

implore v **implored, imploring** to ask earnestly for

implosion n bursting inwards —compare EXPLOSION

imply v **implied, implying** **1** to express indirectly: *Refusal to answer implies guilt* —see INFER (USAGE) **2** to cause to be necessary

impolite adj not polite — ~**ly** adv — ~**ness** n

impolitic *adj* not wise

imponderable *adj, n* (something) of which the importance cannot be measured

import[1] *v* to bring in (something) esp. from abroad: *imported silk*— compare EXPORT — ~ **er** *n*

import[2] *n* something brought into a country from abroad or the act of so doing —compare EXPORT

important *adj* **1** which matters a lot **2** powerful — **-ance** *n* — ~**ly** *adv*

importation *n* **1** the act of importing **2** something new brought in from an outside area, esp. an object or way of behaviour typical of another place —compare EXPORTATION

importunate *adj* **1** always demanding things **2** urgent — ~**ly** *adv* — **-nity** *n*

importune *v* **-tuned, -tuning** *esp. written* to beg (someone) repeatedly for

impose *v* **imposed, imposing** **1** to establish (an additional payment) officially: *impose taxes* **2** to force the acceptance of **3** to force unwelcome presence on **4** to take unfair advantage, in a way that causes additional work and trouble — **-sition** *n*

imposing *adj* powerful in appearance; strong or large in size: *an imposing building* — ~**ly** *adv*

impossible *adj* **1** not possible **2** hard to bear; very unpleasant: *He makes life impossible for us* △ IMPASSABLE — **-bility** *n* — **-bly** *adv*

impostor *n* someone who deceives by pretending to be someone else

impotent *adj* **1** lacking power to do things **2** (of a man) generally unable to perform the sex act — **-tence** *n* — ~**ly** *adv*

impound *v* *esp. written or law* to take and shut up officially until claimed

impoverish *v* **1** to make poor **2** to make worse or incomplete by the removal of something important

impracticable *adj* that cannot be used in practice △ IMPRACTICAL — **-bility** *n* — **-bly** *adv*

impractical *adj* not sensible or reasonable; not practical △ IMPRACTICABLE — ~**ly** *adv* — ~**ity** *n*

impregnable *adj* which cannot be entered or conquered by attack — **-bility** *n* — **-bly** *adv*

impregnate *v* **-nated, -nating** **1** esp. *written* to make pregnant **2** (of a substance) to enter and spread completely through (another substance)

impresario *n* **-os** the business manager of a theatre or concert company, or of a single famous performer —compare ENTREPRENEUR

impress *v* **1** to press (something) into something else, or to mark as a result of this pressure: *a pattern impressed on clay* **2** to fill (someone) with admiration: *I was impressed by his performance* **3** to make the importance of (something) clear to: *Impress on him the value of hard work*

impression *n* **1** the act of impressing or state of being impressed **2** a mark left by pressure **3** the image a person or thing gives to someone's mind: *What's your impression of him?* **4** a feeling

about the nature of something **5** an attempt to copy, usu. in a funny way, the most interesting points of

impressionable *adj* easy to influence — **-bly** *adv* — **-bility** *n*

impressionism *n* a style of painting (esp. in France, 1870–1900) which produces effects by light and colour rather than by details of form —compare EXPRESSIONISM — **-ist** *adj*

impressionist *n* **1** a person who practises or favours impressionism in painting **2** a person who does impressions, esp. as a theatrical performance

impressionistic *adj* **1** based on impressions rather than on knowledge, fact, or detailed study **2** impressionist — ~**ally** *adv*

impressive *adj* causing admiration by giving one a feeling of size and/or importance — ~**ly** *adv* — ~**ness** *n*

imprint *v, n* (to print or press) a mark on something

imprison *v* to put in prison or withhold freedom from — ~**ment** *n*

improbable *adj* not likely to have happened or to be going to happen: *Snow is improbable in the summer* — **-bility** *n* — **-bly** *adv*

impromptu[1] *adj, adv* (said or done) at once without preparation

impromptu[2] *n* **-tus** (in music) a short piece which may have been made up without preparation, or seems so

improper *adj* **1** not suitable: *an improper remark* **2** not correct **3** showing thoughts which are not socially acceptable, esp. about sex (esp. in the phrase **an improper suggestion**) — ~**ly** *adv* — **-priety** *n*

improper fraction *n* a fraction in which the number above the line is greater than the one below it

improve *v* **improved, improving** **1** to make better **2** to get better: *His health's improving* — ~**ment** *n*

improvident *adj* not preparing for the future — **-dence** *n* — ~**ly** *adv*

improvise *v* **-vised, -vising** to do or make (something) unprepared, usu. because a sudden need has arisen: *He improvised a tune on the piano* — **-visation** *n*

imprudent *adj* unwise and thoughtless (in one's actions) — **-dence** *n* — ~**ly** *adv*

impudent *adj* shamelessly bold; disrespectful — **-dence** *n* — ~**ly** *adv*

impugn *v* to raise doubts about △ IMPINGE ON

impulse *n* **1** a single push, or a force acting for a short time in one direction along a wire, nerve, etc.: *an electrical impulse* **2** a sudden wish to do something: *She acted on impulse*

impulse buying *n* the sudden urge to buy goods one does not really want. It is encouraged by shopkeepers who put suitable objects where they can easily be reached

impulsion *n* **1** the act of impelling or state of being impelled **2** a push forward; impulse

impulsive *adj* having or showing a tendency to act on impulse — ~**ly** *adv* — ~**ness** *n*

impunity *n* certainty of not being punished (usu. in the phrase **with impunity**) △ IMMUNITY

impure *adj* **impurer, impurest** 1 not pure, but mixed with something else 2 morally bad; of bad sexual habits: *impure thoughts* — **-rity** *n*

imputation *n* 1 the act of imputing something to someone 2 a charge of crime or suggestion of something bad: *an imputation of guilt*

impute to *v prep* **imputed, imputing to** to blame on: *Doctors impute the spread of disease to poor hygiene*

in¹ *prep* 1 (so as to be) contained by (something with depth, length, and height); within: *to live in the house* 2 surrounded by (an area); within and not beyond: *cows in a field* 3 shown or described as the subject of: *a character in a story* 4 (showing employment): *She's in business/in politics* 5 wearing: *dressed in silk* 6 towards (a direction): *in the wrong direction* 7 using to express oneself; with or by means of: *Write it in French* 8 at some time during; at the time of: *in the afternoon* 9 (with lengths of time) **a** during not more than the space of: *He learnt English in 3 weeks* **b** after: *I'll come in an hour* **c** during; for: *My first good meal in a week* 10 (showing the way something is done or happens): *in fun* 11 (showing a relation or proportion) per: *a tax of 40p in the $* 12 (showing quantity or number): *in part* (=partly) 13 as to; as regards: *lacking in courage* 14 having or so as to have (a condition): *in danger* 15 as a/an; by way of: *in reply* 16 **in all** together; as the total 17 **in that** because

in² *adv* 1 (so as to be) contained or surrounded; away from the open air, the outside, etc.: *Let's go in there where it's warm* 2 (so as to be) present (esp. at home): *The train isn't in yet* 3 from a number of people, or from all directions to a central point: *Letters have been pouring in* 4 **a** (of one side in a game such as cricket) batting: *Our side went in first* **b** (of the ball in a game such as tennis) inside the line 5 (so as to be) fashionable: *Long skirts came in last year*

in³ *adj* 1 *sl* fashionable: *This is the in place to go now* 2 burning: *Is the fire still in?*

in⁴ *n* **the ins and outs (of something)** the various parts and difficulties to be seen when something is looked at in detail

inability *n* **-ties** lack of power or skill

inaccessible *adj* which cannot be reached — **-bility** *n* — **-bly** *adv*

inaccurate *adj* not accurate — ~**ly** *adv* — **-racy** *n*

inaction *n* lack of action or activity — **-tive** *adj* — **-tively** *adv* — **-tivity** *n*

inadequate *adj* 1 not good enough in quality, ability, size, etc.: *I feel inadequate to the occasion* 2 (of a person) not good at looking after oneself, esp. in social life — ~**ly** *adv* — **-acy** *n*

inadmissible *adj* which cannot be allowed — **-bility** *n* — **-bly** *adv*

inadvertent *adj* (done) without paying attention or by accident — ~**ly** *adv* — **-tence** *n*

inalienable *adj* which cannot be taken away (often in the phrase **inalienable rights**)

inane *adj* empty of meaning; really stupid — **-ity** *n* — ~**ly** *adv*

inanimate *adj* not living — ~**ly** *adv* — ~**ness** *n*

inapplicable *adj* which cannot be used or is unrelated to the subject — **-bility** *n* — **-bly** *adv*

inappropriate *adj* not suitable — ~**ly** *adv* — ~**ness** *n*

inapt *adj* unsuitable — ~**ly** *adv* — ~**ness** *n*

inaptitude *n* lack of ability

inarticulate *adj* 1 (of speech) not well-formed 2 not able to express oneself clearly — ~**ly** *adv* — ~**ness** *n*

inasmuch as *conj* owing to the fact that: *Forgive them, inasmuch as they are young*

inattention *n* lack of attention — **-tive** *adj* — **-tively** *adv* — ~**tiveness** *n*

inaudible *adj* that is too quiet to be heard — **-bility** *n* — **-bly** *adv*

inaugurate *v* **-rated, -rating** 1 to introduce into a new place or job by holding a special ceremony 2 to start (a public affair) with a ceremony 3 to be the beginning of — **-tion** *n* — **-ral** *adj*

inauspicious *adj* not giving good hopes for the future —compare AUSPICIOUS — ~**ly** *adv* — ~**ness** *n*

inboard *adj* inside a boat—compare OUTBOARD MOTOR

inborn *adj* part of one's nature: *an inborn ability*

inbound *adj* *US* (when travelling) coming home

inbred *adj* 1 having become part of one's nature as a result of early training 2 resulting from inbreeding

inbreeding *n* breeding from (closely) related members of a family —compare INTERBREED, CROSSBREED

Inc *abbrev. for:* (in the US) Incorporated: *General Motors, Inc* —compare LTD

incalculable *adj* which cannot be counted or measured — **-bly** *adv*

incandescent *adj* giving a bright light when heated — **-cence** *n* — ~**ly** *adv*

incantation *n* words, or the saying of words, used in magic

incapable *adj* not able to do something — **-bility** *n* — **-bly** *adv*

incapacitate *v* **-tated, -tating** to make (someone) not able to do something — **-pacity** *n*

incarcerate *v* **-rated, -rating** *esp. written* to imprison — **-ration** *n*

incarnate¹ *adj* in the form of a body (not a spirit or idea): *the devil incarnate*

incarnate² *v* **-nated, -nating** 1 to put (an idea, spirit, etc.) into bodily form 2 to embody — **-nation** *n*

Incarnation *n* (in Christianity) the coming of God to earth in the body of Jesus Christ

incendiary¹ *n* **-ries** also **incendiary bomb** — a bomb which causes fires

incendiary² *adj* which causes fires

incense¹ *n* any of several substances that give off a sweet smell when burnt

incense² *v* **incensed, incensing** to make very angry

incentive *n* **1** an encouragement to greater activity **2** the urge and ability to get things done

inception *n* the beginning

incessant *adj* never stopping — ~**ly** *adv*

incest *n* a sexual relationship between close relatives in a family — ~**uous** *adj* — ~**uously** *adv*

inch¹ *n* **1** a measure of length; 1/12 of a foot (about 0.025 metres) **2 within an inch of** very near **3 not give/budge an inch** not to change one's opinions at all

inch² *v* to move slowly and with difficulty: *I inched (my way) through the hole*

inchoate *adj* not fully formed

incidence *n* the rate of happening: *a high incidence of disease* △ INCIDENT

incident *n* **1** an event **2** an event that includes violence: *In a recent incident 2 bombs exploded* △ INCIDENCE

incidental *adj, n* **1** (something) happening or appearing irregularly or as a less important part of something important **2** (something, esp. a fact or detail which is) unimportant

incidentally *adv* BY THE WAY

incinerate *v* **-rated, -rating** to destroy by burning — **-ration** *n*

incinerator *n* a machine for burning unwanted things

incipient *adj* at an early stage: *incipient disease* — **-ience, -iency** *n*

incise *v* **incised, incising** *technical* to make a cut into (something) with a special tool — **-cision** *n*

incisive *adj* going directly to the main point of the matter — ~**ly** *adv*

incisor *n* any of the teeth at the front of the mouth, which have one cutting edge

incite *v* **incited, inciting** to cause or encourage to a strong feeling or action: *He incited them to anger* — ~**ment** *n*

incline¹ *v* **inclined, inclining** **1** to slope **2** to cause to move downwards: *to incline one's head (in greeting)* **3** to encourage to feel, think, etc. **4** to tend (to); feel drawn (to): *I incline to another point of view* **5** to tend (to); be likely (to show a quality): *I incline to fatness* — **-nation** *n*

incline² *n* a slope

inclined *adj* **1** encouraged; feeling a wish (to) **2** likely; tending (to)

inclined plane *n* *technical* a flat sloping surface that meets the horizontal at an angle which is less than a right angle

inclose *v* **inclosed, inclosing** to enclose

inclosure *n* an enclosure

include *v* **included, including** to have or put in as a part; contain in addition to other parts: *The price includes postage* — **-ding** *prep* — ~**d** *adj* — **-usion** *n*

inclusive *adj* **1** containing or including everything (or many things): *an inclusive charge* **2** including all the numbers or dates — ~**ly** *adv* USAGE Americans say *Monday* **through** *Friday* to mean *Monday to Friday* **inclusive**. When British people say *Monday* **to/till** *Friday*, it is not clear whether Friday is included. The American phrase is now coming into use in Britain, but is still thought to be American.

incognito¹ *adj, adv* hiding one's identity, esp. by taking another name

incognito² *n* **-tos** a false identity or name

incoherent *adj* showing lack of suitable connections between ideas or words — **-ence** *n* — ~**ly** *adv*

incombustible *adj* which cannot be burnt

income *n* money which one receives regularly, usu. payment for one's work, or interest from investments

income tax *n* tax on one's income

incoming *adj* coming towards one; about to enter or start (to be)

incommensurable *adj* which cannot be compared in size with

incommensurate *adj* too small in comparison to what is needed

incommode *v* **-moded, -moding** *pompous* to trouble (someone) — **-dious** *adj* — **-diously** *adv*

incommunicable *adj* which cannot be said or made known

incommunicado *adv, adj* kept out of communication

incommunicative *adj* uncommunicative

incomparable *adj* too great to be compared with other examples: *incomparable wealth* — **-bility** *n* — **-bly** *adv*

incompatible *adj* not suitable to be together: *incompatible parts* — **-bility** *n* — **-bly** *adv*

incompetent *adj, n* (someone) completely unskilful: *an incompetent teacher* — **-ence, -ency** *n* — ~**ly** *adv*

incomplete *adj* not complete; not perfect — ~**ly** *adv* — ~**ness** *n*

incomprehensible *adj* which cannot be understood and/or accepted — **-bility** *n* — **-bly** *adv*

incomprehension *n* the state of not understanding

inconceivable *adj* **1** which is too strange to be thought real: *It once seemed inconceivable that men should travel to the moon* **2** impossible; which can't happen — **-bility** *n* — **-bly** *adv*

inconclusive *adj* which has not led to a decision or result — ~**ly** *adv* — ~**ness** *n*

incongruous *adj* comparing strangely with what surrounds it — ~**ly** *adv* — ~**ness** *n* — **-uity** *n*

inconsequential *adj* unimportant: *an inconsequential idea* — ~ity *n* — ~ly *adv*
inconsiderable *adj* of small size or worth
inconsiderate *adj offensive* not thinking of other people's feelings — ~ly *adv* — ~ness *n*
inconsistent *adj* not agreeing with something else/one another; changeable: *Those two remarks are inconsistent* — ~ly *adv* — -ency *n*
inconsolable *adj* who cannot be comforted — -bly *adv*
inconspicuous *adj* not easily seen; not attracting attention — ~ly *adv* — ~ness *n*
inconstant *adj esp. written* tending to change; unfaithful in feeling: *an inconstant lover* — -stancy *n*
incontestable *adj* which cannot be changed by argument; incontrovertible: *incontestable proof* — -bility *n* — -bly *adv*
incontinent *adj* unable to control the urine in the bladder or the faeces in the intestines so that either is passed from the body when one does not wish to pass it — -nence *n*
incontrovertible *adj* which cannot be disproved — -bly *adv*
inconvenience *v* -enced, -encing to make things difficult for
inconvenient *adj* causing difficulty; not what suits one: *an inconvenient time* — ~ly — *adv* — -ence *n*
incorporate *v* -rated, -rating 1 to include as a part of a group: *The new plan incorporates the old one* 2 to join with one another/someone else in making a company or corporation — -ration *n*
incorporated (abbrev **Inc**)—— *adj esp. written & US* formed into a corporation according to law —compare LIMITED
incorrect *adj* not correct — ~ly *adv* — ~ness *n*
incorrigible *adj* (of people or behaviour) very bad and unable to be improved — -bility *n* — -bly *adv*
incorruptible *adj* 1 which cannot decay or be destroyed 2 who is too honest to be persuaded or bribed from his or her judgment — -bility *n* — -bly *adv*
increase¹ *v* increased, increasing to make or become larger in amount or number —opposite decrease
increase² *n* 1 a rise in amount, numbers, etc. 2 on the increase increasing — -singly *adv*
incredible *adj* too strange or good to be believed; unbelievable: *an incredible excuse* — -bility *n* — -bly *adv*
incredulous *adj* showing disbelief — -ulity *n* — ~ly *adv*
increment *n* (an) increase in money or value — ~al *adj* — ~ally *adv*
incriminate *v* -nated, -nating to cause to seem guilty of a crime or fault — -nation *n*
incrustation *n* dirt or material laid down on top of something —compare ENCRUST

incubate *v* -bated, -bating 1 to hatch (eggs) by sitting on them, or otherwise keeping them warm —compare HATCH 2 to plan or think over 3 *medical* to be holding an infection in one's body until it appears as a disease
incubation *n* 1 the act of incubating 2 a the time taken for incubating eggs b the time taken for a disease to develop
incubator *n* a machine for a keeping eggs warm until they hatch b keeping alive babies that are born early
incubus *n* -buses *or* -bi a male devil supposed to have sex with a sleeping woman —compare SUCCUBUS
incumbency *n* -cies 1 something that is incumbent; duty 2 the field of activity or the period in office of an incumbent
incumbent¹ *n* 1 a priest in the Church of England who is in charge of a church and its parish 2 *esp. US* the holder of a usu. political office
incumbent² *adj* being the moral duty of (someone): *It's incumbent on you.....*
incur *v* -rr- to receive (some unpleasant thing) as a result of certain actions: *to incur a debt*
incurable *adj* that cannot be cured — -bility *n* — -bly *adv*
incursion *n* a sudden attack on or entrance into a place which belongs to other people
indebted *adj* very grateful to (someone) for help given — ~ness *n*
indecent *adj* 1 not decent: *an indecent joke* —compare IMMODEST 2 not reasonable (in amount or quality): *indecent wages* (=too little) — ~ly *adv* — -cency *n*
indecent assault *n law* an assault involving sexual violence
indecent exposure *n* the intentional showing of part of one's body (esp. the male sex organ) in public
indecipherable *adj* which cannot be deciphered or understood — -bility *n* — -bly *adv*
indecision *n* uncertainty
indecisive *adj* 1 giving an uncertain result: *an indecisive victory* 2 unable to make decisions — ~ly *adv* — ~ness *n*
indecorous *adj* showing bad manners — ~ly *adv* — ~ness *n*
indeed *adv* 1 (*said in answer to a speaker who has suggested the answer*) certainly: *'Did you hear the explosion?' 'Indeed I did!'* 2 on the contrary: *'I won't do it!' 'Indeed you will!'* 3 (*used after* very + *adjective or adverb to make the meaning even stronger*): *very large indeed*
indefatigable *adj* that shows no sign of tiring
indefensible *adj* 1 which cannot be excused: *indefensible behaviour* 2 which cannot be defended
indefinite *adj* 1 not clear: *indefinite responsibilities* 2 not fixed, esp. as to time: *at an indefinite date* — ~ness *n* — ~ly *adv*

indefinite article *n* a or an — compare DEFI-NITE ARTICLE

indelible *adj* which cannot be rubbed out — **-bly** *adv*

indelicate *adj* not polite or modest — ~ **ly** *adv* — **-cacy** *n*

indemnify *v* **-fied, fying** 1 to pay or promise to pay (someone) in case of loss, hurt, or damage 2 to repay — **-fication** *n*

indemnity *n* **-ties** 1 protection against loss, esp. in the form of a promise to pay 2 also **indemnification**— payment for loss of money, goods, etc.

indent *v* to start (a line of writing) further into the page than the others

indentation *n* 1 a space pointing inwards: *the indentations in a coastline* 2 a space at the beginning of a line of writing

indenture *n* a written agreement between an apprentice and his master

independent¹ *adj* 1 not needing other things or people 2 (of money) belonging to one privately, so that one can live without working 3 **a** habitually taking decisions alone **b** the result of taking one's own decisions: *independent work* 4 not governed by another country — **-ence** *n* — ~ **ly** *adv*

independent² *n* a person who does not belong to a political party

independent clause also **main clause**— *n* a clause which can make a sentence by itself. It may have one or more dependent clauses as parts of it or joined to it: *"I spoke to him" is the independent clause in the sentence "When he came in, I spoke to him"*

indescribable *adj* which cannot be described — **-bly** *adv*

indestructible *adj* which is too strong to be destroyed — **-bility** *n* — **-bly** *adv*

indeterminable *adj* which cannot be decided or fixed — **-bly** *adv*

indeterminate *adj* not clearly seen as, or not fixed as, one thing or another — **-nacy** *n*

index¹ *n* **-dexes** or **-dices** 1 an alphabetical list at the back of a book, of names, subjects, etc., mentioned in it and the pages where they can be found 2 a sign—compare INDICATION 3 *technical* also **exponent**— a number which shows how many times to multiply a number by itself, such as the number 4 in the expression $2^4 = 2 \times 2 \times 2 \times 2 = 16$ 4 the system of numbers by which prices, costs, etc., can be compared to a former level (esp. in the phrase **cost of living index**)

index² *v* 1 to provide with an index 2 to include in an index 3 to prepare an index — ~ **er** *n*

index finger *n* a forefinger

Indian *n, adj* 1 belonging to or connected with India 2 also **American Indian**— belonging to or connected with any of the original peoples of America except the Eskimos

Indian file *n, adv* SINGLE FILE

Indian hemp *n* a type of hemp used for ropes and mats, which produces a drug

Indian ink *n* a type of dark black ink

Indian summer *n* 1 a period of warm weather in the autumn 2 a time in old age when one feels as well as in one's youth

india rubber *n* *technical* rubber, esp. as used for making toys or rubbing out pencil marks

indicate *v* **-cated, -cating** 1 to point out: *He indicated the shop* 2 to make a sign (for): *He indicated that I could leave* 3 to make clear 4 to show the direction in which one is turning in a vehicle 5 to suggest: *The car's failure to start indicates a flat battery* — **-ation** *n*

indicative¹ *adj* 1 showing; suggesting: *His presence is indicative of his wish to help* 2 of the indicative — ~ **ly** *adv*

indicative² *n* a verb form or set of verb forms (MOOD) that shows an act or state as a fact

indicator *n* 1 a needle or pointer on a machine showing the measure of some quality, or a substance which shows what is happening in a chemical mixture 2 any of the lights on a car which flash to show which way it is turning 3 something that gives an idea of the presence, absence, nature, quantity, or degree of something else

indices *pl. of* INDEX

indict *v* to charge formally with an offence in law — ~ **ment** *n* — ~ **able** *adj*

indifferent *adj* 1 not interested in; not caring about or noticing: *I was indifferent to the cold* 2 not very good—see DIFFERENT (USAGE) — ~ **ly** *adv* — **-ence** *n*

indigenous *adj* native; belonging (to a place) — ~ **ly** *adv*

indigent *adj* *esp. written* poor — **-gence** *n*

indigestible *adj* 1 (of food) which cannot be easily broken down in the stomach into substances to be used by the body 2 (of facts) which cannot be taken into the mind easily — **-bility** *n* — **-bly** *adv*

indigestion *n* illness or pain caused by the stomach being unable to deal with the food which has been eaten

indignant *adj* expressing or feeling surprised anger — **-ation** *n* — ~ **ly** *adv*

indignity *n* **-ties** 1 a state which makes one feel undignified or that one is on public show 2 an act which makes one feel loss of dignity, self-control, etc.: *the indignity of being treated as if one were a child*

indigo *n* a colour or dye of a dark blue-purple

indirect *adj* 1 not straight; not directly connected 2 not paid directly but through price rises (esp. in the phrase **indirect taxation**) 3 a meaning something which is not directly mentioned: *an indirect remark/answer* **b** happening in addition to, or instead of, what is directly meant: *the indirect result* — ~ **ly** *adv* — ~ **ness** *n*

indirect object *n* the person (or sometimes the thing) that the direct object is given to, made for, etc.: *"Him" is the indirect object in "I asked him a question"*

indirect speech also **reported speech**— n the style used to tell what somebody said without repeating the actual words: 'She said, 'I don't want to go'' becomes in indirect speech "she said (that) she didn't want to go" —opposite **direct speech**

indiscernible adj which cannot be seen

indiscipline n lack of discipline

indiscreet adj not acting carefully and politely — -**cretion** n — ~ **ly** adv

indiscriminate adj not choosing or chosen carefully — ~ **ly** adv

indispensable adj that is too important to live without — -**bility** n — -**bly** adv

indisposed adj 1 not very well (in health) 2 not very willing — -**position** n

indisputable adj which is too certain to be questioned — -**bly** adv

indistinct adj not clear — ~ **ly** adv — ~ **ness** n

indistinguishable adj which cannot be seen or known to be different — -**bly** adv

individual[1] adj 1 (often with each) single; particular; separate 2 suitable for each person or thing only: Individual attention must be given to every one 3 (of a manner, style, way of doing things) particular to the person, thing, etc., concerned (and different from others) — ~ **ly** adv

individual[2] n 1 a single being or member of a group, treated separately 2 a person—see PEOPLE (USAGE)

individualism n the idea that the rights and freedom of the individual are the most important rights in a society — -**ist** n, adj — -**istic** adj

individuality n the character and qualities which make someone or something different from all others

individualize, -ise v -**ized, -izing** to cause to change according to the special needs or character of a person or thing: an individualized T-shirt with your name on — -**ization** n

indivisible adj which cannot be divided — -**bility** n — -**bly** adv

indoctrinate v -**nated, -nating** usu. offensive to put ideas into (someone's) mind — -**nation** n

Indo-European adj of or concerning a group of languages that includes most of those spoken in Europe (and now spread to America and parts of Africa), Persia, and India ☞LANGUAGE

indolent adj lazy — ~ **ly** adv — -**lence** n

indomitable adj that is too strong to be discouraged: his indomitable spirit — -**bly** adv

indoor adj which is (done, used, etc.) indoors

indoors adv to, in, or into the inside of a building

indrawn adj drawn into the body: an indrawn breath

indubitable adj unquestionable — -**bly** adv

induce v **induced, inducing** 1 to lead (someone) (into an act) often by persuading 2 to cause or produce

inducement n (something, esp. money, which provides) encouragement to do something

inductance n technical (a measure of) the ability of one electric current in one circuit to cause a current in another or the same circuit by induction

induction n 1 the act or action of inducting 2 the action of inducing 3 also **induction course** — introduction into a new job, organisation, etc. 4 technical the production of electricity in one object by another which already has electrical (or magnetic) power 5 (the act, action, or result, or an example of) a way of reasoning using known facts to produce general laws

inductive adj 1 technical using electrical or magnetic induction 2 using or showing induction: inductive reasoning — ~ **ly** adv

inductor n an electrical component used to provide induction

indulge v **indulged, indulging** 1 to yield, perhaps too much, to the desires of (someone), esp. habitually 2 to let oneself have (one's wish to do or have something, etc.) — ~ **nt** adj — ~ **ntly** adv

indulgence also **pardon**— n 1 the habit or an act of indulging 2 (in the Roman Catholic Church) (an act or example of) freedom from the punishment for wrongdoing, given by a priest

industrial adj 1 of industry and the people who work in it: industrial unrest 2 having highly developed industries ⚠ INDUSTRIOUS — ~ **ly** adv

industrial archaeology n a study of the factories, machinery, and products of earlier stages of the industrial revolution

industrial estate also **trading estate**— n a special area of land where factories are built

industrialism n the system by which a society gains its wealth esp. through industries and machinery

industrialist n a person who is closely concerned in the system of earning profits in industry

industrialize, -ise v -**ized, -izing** to develop or cause to become developed industrially — -**ization** n

industrial revolution n a period of time when society becomes industrialized through the introduction of new machines (as in Britain around 1750–1850)

industrious adj hard-working ⚠ INDUSTRIAL — ~ **ly** adv — ~ **ness** n

industry n -**tries** 1 (the work of) factories and large organizations generally 2 the private owners and shareholders of such factories and organizations 3 a particular sort of work, usu. employing lots of people and using machinery 4 continual hard work

inebriate[1] v -**ated, -ating** esp. written to make drunk — -**ation** n

inebriate[2] adj, n esp. written (someone who is) habitually drunk

inedible adj not suitable for eating — -**bility** n — -**bly** adv

ineducable *adj* who cannot be educated — **-bility** *n* — **-bly** *adv*

ineffable *adj* **1** which is too wonderful to be described in words **2** (esp. of the name of God in some religions) not to be spoken aloud: *the ineffable name* — **-bility** *n* — **-bly** *adv*

ineffective *adj* which does not produce any result or who cannot do anything well — **-ly** *adv* — ~**ness** *n*

ineffectual *adj* which does not give a good enough effect, or who is not able to get things done: *an ineffectual plan* — ~**ly** *adv*

inefficient *adj* that does not work well so as to produce good results quickly — ~**ly** *adv* — **-ciency** *n*

inelegant *adj* **1** not showing good manners **2** awkward — ~**ly** *adv* — **-gance** *n*

ineligible *adj* not eligible — **-bility** *n*

inept *adj* **1** foolishly unsuitable: *an inept remark* **2** totally unable to do things — ~**ly** *adv* — ~**itude**, ~**ness** *n*

inequality *n* **-ties** **1** lack of equality **2** a difference in size, amount, etc., esp. in justice **3** *technical* the fact or statement that two quantities are not equal

inequitable *adj* unjust — **-bly** *adv*

inequity *n* **-ties** injustice; unfairness

ineradicable *adj* which cannot be completely removed

inert *adj* **1** lacking the power to move: *inert matter* **2** not acting chemically with other substances: *inert gases* **3** (of people) slow to activity; lazy — ~**ly** *adv* — ~**ness** *n*

inertia *n* **1** the force which prevents a thing from being moved when it is standing still, and keeps it moving when it is moving **2** the state of being powerless to move or too lazy to move

inescapable *adj* which cannot be escaped from or avoided

inessential *adj, n* (something) not at all necessary

inestimable *adj* too great to be calculated — **-bly** *adv*

inevitable *adj* which cannot be prevented from happening; which always happens: *An argument was inevitable* — **-bility** *n* — **-bly** *adv*

inexact *adj* not exact — ~**itude**, ~**ness** *n*

inexcusable *adj* which is too bad to be excused — **-bly** *adv*

inexhaustible *adj* which will never run out — **-bly** *adv*

inexorable *adj* whose actions or effects cannot be changed or prevented by one's efforts — **-bly** *adv* — **-bility** *n*

inexpedient *adj* (of acts) not expedient; not suitable or advisable — **-iency, -ience** *n*

inexpensive *adj* not expensive — ~**ly** *adv*

inexperience *n* lack of experience — ~**d** *adj*

inexpert *adj* not good at doing something — ~**ly** *adv*

inexpiable *adj* which cannot be expiated — **-bly** *adv*

inexplicable *adj* which cannot be explained or understood — **-bility** *n* — **-bly** *adv*

inexpressible *adj* (of feelings) too great to be expressed in words — **-bly** *adv*

inextinguishable *adj* (of fire and feelings) which cannot be put out or destroyed

inextricable *adj* **1** which cannot be escaped from **2** which cannot be untied or separated — **-bly** *adv*

infallible *adj* never making mistakes; always having the right effect: *an infallible cure* — **-bility** *n*

infallibly *adv* **1** in an infallible way **2** always; without fail

infamy *n* **-mies** **1** the quality of being known for wicked behaviour **2** an act which is evil or wicked — **-mous** *adj*

infancy *n* **1** early childhood **2** a beginning or early period of existence

infant *n* a very young child — **infant** *adj*

infanticide *n* the crime of killing a child, or a person guilty of this crime

infantile *adj* **1** *often offensive* like (that of) a small child **2** concerning, or happening to, small children

infantry *n* soldiers who fight on foot — ~**man** *n*

infant school *n* a school for children from about 5 to 7 years of age

infatuated *adj* filled with a strong unreasonable feeling of love for — **-ation** *n*

infect *v* **1** to put disease into the body of (someone): *The disease infected her eyes* **2** to make impure by spreading into **3** to make (someone else) have feelings of the same type: *She infected them with her laughter*

infection *n* **1** the state or result of being infected, or the action of infecting **2** an illness brought by infection: *suffering from a lung infection*

infectious *adj* **1** (of a disease) which can be spread by infection, esp. in the air **2** *esp. spoken* contagious — ~**ly** *adj* — ~**ness** *n*

infelicitous *adj* not suitable: *an infelicitous remark* — **-licity** *n*

infer *v* **-rr-** to draw the meaning from (something): *What can I infer from your letter?* — compare IMPLY — ~**ence** *n* — ~**ential** *adj* — ~**entially** *adv* USAGE Correctly, it is the listener or reader who **infers** things: *I looked at his boots and inferred that he must be a policeman.* The speaker or writer **implies** things: *He said it was late,* **implying** *that we ought to go home.* People now often say **infer** for **imply**, but this is not thought to be good English.

inferior[1] *adj* **1** *technical* lower in position: *an inferior court of law* **2** (of people and things) not good or less good in quality or value — ~**ity** *n*

inferior[2] *n* *often offensive* a person of lower rank, esp. in a job —compare SUPERIOR, SUBORDINATE

inferiority complex *n* a state of mind when one feels oneself of less value than others

infernal *adj* **1** of hell: *the infernal powers* **2** *esp. spoken* bad; terrible — ~**ly** *adv*

inferno *n* **-nos** a place or state that is like hell

infertile *adj* **1** not fertile; not able to produce young **2** (of land) not able to grow plants — **-tility** *n*

infest *v* to cause trouble to or in, by being present in large numbers: *Mice infested the old house* — ~**ation** *n*

infidel *n old use & offensive* (used esp. in former times by Christians and Muslims of each other) someone who does not follow one's own religion; unbeliever

infidelity *n* **-ties** **1** (an example or act of) disloyalty **2** (an act of) sex with someone other than one's marriage partner; unfaithfulness—compare FIDELITY

infighting *n* competition and disagreement which goes on between close members of a group

infiltrate *v* **-trated, -trating** to go or send into and among (the parts or members of something): *The enemy infiltrated our land* — **-trator** *n* — **-tion** *n*

infinite *adj* **1** without limits or end — opposite **finite** **2** very large; as much as there is — ~**ly** *adv*

infinitesimal *adj* very small — ~**ly** *adv*

infinitive *n, adj* (of) the form of the verb that expresses its meaning without saying who or what did the action or when it was done. It is commonly used after other verbs and with *to* before it (such as *go* in *I can go, I want to go,* and *It is important to go*)—see also SPLIT **an infinitive**

infinity *n* **-ties** a limitless or very large amount of time or space

infirm *adj* weak in body or mind, esp. from age — ~**ity** **n**

infirmary *n* **-ries** a hospital or sickroom

inflame *v* **inflamed, inflaming** to make angry

inflamed *adj* red and swollen because hurt or diseased: *an inflamed eye* — **inflammation** *n*

inflammable *adj* **1** also **flammable**— which can be set on fire —opposite **nonflammable** **2** easily excited or made angry —compare INFLAMMATORY; SEE FLAMMABLE (USAGE)

inflammatory *adj* likely to cause anger or violence —see also INFLAME; compare INFLAMMABLE

inflate *v* **inflated, inflating** to fill until swelled with air, gas, etc. —opposite **deflate** — **-atable** *adj*

inflated *adj* **1** blown up (as with air) **2** (of prices) risen to a high level **3** giving a false appearance of importance: *inflated ideas*

inflation *n* **1** the act of inflating or state of being inflated **2** the rise in prices thought to be caused by increases in the costs of production or an increase in the money supply —compare DEFLATION, REFLATION

inflationary *adj* of or likely to cause price inflation

inflect *v* **1 a** (of a word) to change in form at its end according to use **b** to cause (a word) to change in form according to use: *a highly inflected language* —compare CONJUGATE, DECLINE **2** (esp. of the voice) to change or cause to change, esp. in level, according to the needs of expression

inflection, also **inflexion** *n* **1** the act or result of inflecting —compare CONJUGATION, DECLENSION **2 a** the part of a word which can be changed: *In 'largest', -est is the inflection meaning 'most'* **b** a movement up or down of the voice: *A question usually ends on a rising inflection* —see also INTONATION

inflexible *adj* **1** which cannot be bent — compare FLEX, FLEXIBLE **2** not changeable; unbending: *an inflexible decision* — **-bility** *n* — **-bly** *adv*

inflict on also **inflict upon**— *v prep* to force (something unwanted or unpleasant) on (someone): *Don't inflict your ideas on me* — **-tion** *n*

influence[1] *n* **1** power, or a person with the power, to gain an effect on the mind of: *He's a good/bad influence* **2** the power to get things done by use of wealth, position, etc. — **-ential** — *adj* — **-entially** *adv*

influence[2] *v* **-enced, -encing** to have an effect on; affect

influenza also **flu**— *n* a disease which is like a bad cold but more serious

influx *n* the arrival, or movement inside, of large numbers/quantities: *an influx of ants* —compare FLUX

info *n esp. spoken* information

inform *v* to tell; give information to — ~**ant** *n* — ~**ative** *adj* — ~**atively** *adv*

informal *adj* not formal; casual: *informal clothes* — ~**ity** *n* — ~**ly** *adv*

information *n* (something which gives) knowledge in the form of facts

informed *adj* **1** knowing things; having all the information: *He is well-informed* **2** having and using suitable knowledge: *an informed guess*

informer *n sometimes offensive* a person who informs against another, esp. to the police ⚠ INFORMANT

infraction *n esp. written* the act or an example of breaking a rule

infra dig *abbrev. for: Latin & humour* **infra dignitatem** beneath one's dignity

infrared *adj* of the heat-giving rays of light of longer wave-length than the red light which can be seen —compare ULTRAVIOLET

infrastructure *n* the system which supports the operation of an organization

infrequent *adj* not happening often — ~**ly** *adv* — **-quency** *n*

infringe *v* **infringed, infringing** to go against or take over (the right of another) — ~**ment** *n*

infuriate *v* **-ated, -ating** to make very angry

infuse *v* **infused, infusing** **1** to steep (a substance such as tea) in hot water so as to make a liquid of a certain taste **2** to fill (someone) with (a quality): *He infused eagerness into the men*

infusion *n* **1** the act of infusing **2** a liquid made in this way, often for medical use **3** (an example of) the act of mixing or filling (with something new): *an infusion of new ideas*

ingenious *adj* having or showing cleverness at making or inventing things: *an ingenious idea* △ INGENUOUS — ~ly *adv* — **ingenuity** *n*

ingenuous *adj* simple, open, innocent, and inexperienced —compare DISINGENUOUS △ INGENIOUS — ~ly *adv* — ~ness *n*

ingest *v technical* to take (food) into the body — ~ion *n*

inglenook *n* (a seat in) a partly enclosed space near a large open fireplace

inglorious *adj literature* shameful; bringing dishonour — ~ly *adv*

ingot *n* a lump of metal in a regular shape; bar (of gold or silver)

ingrained *adj* fixed deep (inside): *ingrained dirt/habits*

ingratiate *v* **-ated, -ating** to make (oneself) very pleasant to someone in order to gain favour — **-ing** *adj* : *an ingratiating smile* — **-ingly** *adv*

ingratitude *n* ungratefulness

ingredient *n* a particular one of a mixture of things, esp. in cooking

ingrown also **ingrowing**— *adj* growing inwards, esp. into the flesh

inhabit *v* to live in —see LIVE (USAGE) — ~able *adj*

inhabitant *n* a person (or sometimes an animal) that lives in a particular place

inhale *v* **inhaled, inhaling** to breathe (something) in

inhaler *n* an apparatus which is used for inhaling medicine in the form of vapour

inharmonious *adj* not suitable to something else/each other: *inharmonious colours* — ~ly *adv* — ~ness *n*

inherent *adj* forming a natural part

inherently *adv* in itself or oneself; by its or one's nature; as such

inherit *v* **1** to receive (property, a title, etc.) left by someone who has died; to take possession of what one has the right to as heir **2** to receive (qualities of mind or body) from one's parents, grandmother or grandfather, etc. — ~ance *n*

inhibit *v* to hold back from, or make (someone) hold back: *Thirst inhibited the desire to eat* — ~ion *n*

inhibited *adj* unable to express what one really feels or do what one really wants: *too inhibited to laugh freely* —compare UNINHIBITED — ~ly *adv*

inhospitable *adj* **1** not showing kindness; unwelcoming **2** not forming a shelter; not suitable to stay in — **-bly** *adv*

inhuman *adj* very cruel, lacking in feelings, etc.

inhumane *adj* not showing human kindness — ~ly *adv*

inhumanity *n* **-ties** cruelty; an act harmful to other human beings

inimical *adj esp. written* very unfavourable (to)

inimitable *adj* too good for anyone else to copy —see IMITATE — **-bly** *adv*

iniquity *n* **-ties** (an act of) injustice or wickedness — **-ous** *adj* — **-ously** *adv*

initial[1] *adj* which is (at) the beginning of a set: *initial talks* — ~ly *adv*

initial[2] *n* a large letter at the beginning of a name, esp. when used alone to represent a person's first name(s) and last name

initial[3] *v* **-ll-** to sign one's name by writing one's initials

initiate[1] *v* **-ated, -ating** **1** to start (something) working **2** to introduce esp. with a special ceremony **3** to introduce to (someone) some secret or mysterious knowledge

initiate[2] *n* a person who is instructed or skilled in some special field

initiation *n* a ceremony of initiating, esp. one through which a young man or woman is officially recognized as an adult in a particular society

initiative *n* **1** the first movement or act which starts something happening (esp. in the phrase **take the initiative**) **2** the ability to do things in a way one has worked out for oneself: *I did it on my own initiative*

inject *v* to put (liquid) into with a syringe

injection *n* **1** the act or occasion of injecting **2** the liquid used for this: *a large/small injection*

injection moulding *n* the method or result of making rubber or plastic objects by forcing the liquid material under pressure into a mould — compare DIE-CASTING

injudicious *adj* not wise or sensible — ~ly *adv* ~ness — **n**

injunction *n law* a command or official order to do or not to do something—compare ENJOIN

injure *v* **injured, injuring** **1** to hurt (a living thing) **2** to offend: *Did I injure her (feelings)?* — **-rious** *adj* — **-riously** *adv* USAGE One can be *slightly/badly/seriously* **injured**. —see WOUND (USAGE)

injury *n* **-ries** **1** harm; damage to a living thing **2** an act that damages or hurts

injustice *n* not being just; unfairness

ink *n* coloured liquid used for writing (or drawing)

ink in *v adv* to complete with ink (something drawn in pencil or left unfilled)

inkling *n* a possible idea or a suggestion (only in the phrases **to have an/no/some/any inkling, to give someone an inkling**)

inkstand *n* a flat piece of hard material shaped to hold ink-bottles, pens, etc.

inkwell *n* an inkpot which fits into a hole in a desk

inky *adj* **-ier, -iest** **1** marked with ink **2**

inklike; very dark black — **inkiness** n — **inkily** adv

inlaid adj **1** set ornamentally into another substance **2** having another substance set in

inland¹ adj inside a country, not near the coast or other countries: *inland trade*

inland² adv towards or in the heart of the country

Inland Revenue n the office which collects, or the money collected as, national taxes

in-laws n the father and mother, and sometimes other relatives, of the person someone has married

inlay n **inlays 1** an inlaid pattern, surface, or substance **2** a filling of metal or another substance used in the inside of a decayed or damaged tooth

inlet n **1** a narrow stretch of water reaching from a sea, lake, etc., into the land or between islands **2** a way in (for water, liquid, etc.)

in loco parentis adv Latin having the responsibilities of a parent towards someone else's children

inmate n a person sharing a room or building with others, esp. unwillingly as in a hospital or prison

in memoriam prep Latin in memory of

inmost also **innermost**— adj **1** farthest inside **2** most well hidden: *inmost desires*

inn n a small hotel or place where one can stay and/or drink alcohol, eat meals, etc.

innards n esp. spoken the inner parts, usu. of the stomach

innate adj (of qualities) which someone was born with — **~ly** adv

inner adj **1** inside; closest to the centre: *the inner ear* **2** secret, esp. if of the spirit: *an inner meaning* —opposite **outer**

inner tube n the tube inside a tyre which is filled with air

innings n **innings** the period of time during which a cricket team or player bats

innocent¹ adj guiltless; harmless; simple — **~ly** adv — **-cence** n

innocent² n a simple person with no knowledge of evil —compare IDIOT

innocuous adj harmless; not offensive — **~ly** adv — **~ness** n

innovate v **-vated, -vating** to make changes — **-vator** n

innovation n **1** the introduction of something new **2** a new idea, method, or invention

Inns of Court n the college-like law societies in London, to one of which an English barrister must belong

innuendo n **-does** or **-dos** a suggestion of something unpleasant which is not stated

innumerable adj too many to be counted

inoculate v **-lated, -lating** to introduce a weak form of a disease into (a living body) as a protection against the disease —compare VACCINATE, INJECT — **-lation** n

inoffensive adj not causing any harm or dislike — **~ly** adv — **~ness** n

inoperable adj **1** that cannot be cured by operation **2** which cannot be put into practice or made to continue: *an inoperable plan*

inoperative adj not able to work or take effect

inopportune adj **1** unsuitable in time: *an inopportune moment* — **~ly** adv — **~ness** n

inordinate adj beyond reasonable limits: *inordinate demands* — **~ly** adv

inorganic adj **1** not of living material; not organic **2** not showing the pattern typical of natural growth — **~ally** adv

inorganic chemistry n the scientific study of inorganic material

in-patient n someone staying in a hospital for treatment —compare OUTPATIENT

input n something put in for use, esp. by a machine, such as electrical current or information for a computer ☞ COMPUTER

inquest n an official inquiry usu. to find out the cause of someone's death

inquietude n anxiety

inquire, en- v **inquired, inquiring** to ask; to seek information: *She inquired after your health* — **~r** n

inquiring, en- adj that shows an interest in knowing about things (esp. in the phrase **an inquiring (turn of) mind**) — **~ly** adv

inquiry, en- n **-ies 1** an act of inquiring; a question **2** investigations to find out the reason for something or how something happened USAGE **Enquiry** and **inquiry** are almost exactly the same. **Enquiry** is more often used, especially in the plural, about requesting information (*your kind enquiries about my health*) and **inquiry** for a long serious study: *an inquiry into the diseases caused by smoking.*

inquisition n usu. offensive an inquiry, esp. one that is carried out with little regard for the rights of the people being questioned — **-tor** n — **-torial** adj — **-torially** adv

Inquisition n (in former times) the official Roman Catholic organization for the discovery and punishment of heresy

inquisitive adj of an inquiring nature — **~ly** adv — **~ness** n

inroad n an effort or activity that lessens the quantity or difficulty of what remains afterwards: *Teaching makes inroads on my time* —compare INCURSION

insalubrious adj not healthy —see HEALTHY

insane adj mad — **~ly** adv — **-anity** n

insanitary adj not clean

insatiable adj that cannot be satisfied: *insatiable curiosity* — **-bly** adv

inscribe v **inscribed, inscribing 1** to mark with writing; engrave **2** to write a name in (a book, esp. one given as a present on a special occasion) —compare INSCRIPTION

inscription n something inscribed -compare INSCRIBE, LEGEND

inscrutable *adj* (of people and their acts) whose meaning is hidden or hard to find out; mysterious: *an inscrutable smile* — **-bility** *n* — **-bly** *adv*

insect *n* a small creature with no bones and a hard outer covering, 6 legs, and a body divided into 3 parts, such as an ant or fly ⟳EVOLUTION ◎

insecticide *n* (any of various types of) chemical substance made to kill insects — **-cidal** *adj*

insectivorous *adj* eating insects as food ⟳PRIMATE, MAMMAL — **insectivore** *n* : *An anteater is an insectivore*

insecure *adj* **1** not safe; likely to give way or fall **2** (feeling) afraid; (feeling) unsupported — **-curity** *n* — ~**ly** *adv*

inseminate *v* **-nated, -nating** to put or introduce male seed into (a female) — **-ation** *n* —see also ARTIFICIAL INSEMINATION

insensibility *n* **1** *old use* lack of ability to feel or to be moved by feelings **2** unconsciousness

insensible *adj* **1** *old use* unable to have feelings (of) —see INSENSITIVE **2** not conscious — compare SENSELESS **3** unaware (of); lacking knowledge of **4** too small to be noticed: *an insensible change* USAGE NOT the opposite of **sensible**.

insensitive *adj* **1** lacking feeling: *insensitive to pain* **2** not kind to others because one does not understand how they feel; tactless — **-tivity** *n* — ~**ly** *adv*

inseparable *adj* that cannot be separated — **-bility** *n* — **-bly** *adv*

insert *v* to put something inside (something else): *to insert a key in a lock* — **insert**, ~**ion** *n*

in-service *adj* (taking place) during one's work (esp. in the phrase **in-service training**)

inset *n* something put as an addition into something else, esp. a picture or map set inside the frame of a larger one, or additional pages in a book

inshore *adv* near, towards, or to the shore — **inshore** *adj*

inside[1] *n* the area within something else; the part that is nearest to the centre, or that faces away from other people or from the open air

inside[2] *adj* **1** to or on the area within (something else), esp. in a house; facing the inside **2** at or from the heart or centre of the action: *the inside story*

inside[3] *prep* on or to the inside of; within USAGE **Inside** and **within** can both mean 'surrounded by', although **inside** is used in spoken rather than written English and more often refers to small things: *inside the box | within the castle.* **Within** is more often used than **inside** to mean "not beyond": *within a mile | within 3 weeks.*

inside[4] *adv* **1** to or in the inside **2** *sl* in prison

insidious *adj* unnoticed in action but harmful in the end: *the insidious growth of decay* ⚠ INVIDIOUS — ~**ly** *adv* — ~**ness** *n*

insight *n* **1** the power of using one's mind to understand something deeply **2** an example of this, or the understanding which results (esp. in the phrase **have an insight**)

insignia *n* badges or objects which represent the power of an official or important person

insignificant *adj* not (seeming or looking) of value and/or importance — **-cance** *n* — ~**ly** *adv*

insincere *adj* not sincere — ~**ly** *adv* — **-cerity** *n*

insinuate *v* **-ated, -ating** to suggest (something unpleasant) by one's behaviour or questions — **-ation** *n*

insinuate into *v prep* to cause (oneself or something) to become part of (something): *to insinuate oneself into someone's favour*

insipid *adj* lacking a strong effect, esp. a taste: *an insipid character* — ~**ly** *adv* — ~**ness** *n* — ~**ity** *n*

insist *v* **1** to declare firmly **2** to order (something to happen): *I insisted on him going* — ~**ence**, ~**ency** *n*

insistent *adj* **1** repeatedly insisting or making demands **2** needing to be done, answered, etc.; urgent: *an insistent message* — ~**ly** *adv*

in situ *adv Latin* in its original place

in so far as also **insomuch as** —— *conj* to the degree that

insolent *adj* showing disrespectful rudeness — ~**ly** *adv* — **-solence** *n*

insoluble *adj* **1** which cannot be made right, brought to a good result, or solved **2** which cannot be dissolved

insolvent *adj* not having money to pay what one owes — **-vency** *n*

insomnia *n* habitual inability to sleep — ~**c** *n, adj*

insouciance *n* the state of not caring about anything — **-ant** *adj*

inspect *v* **1** to examine (the details of something) **2** to make an official visit to judge the quality of — ~**ion** *n*

inspector *n* **1** an official who inspects **2** a police officer of middle rank — ~**ate,** ~**ship** *n*

inspiration *n* **1** the act of inspiring or state of being inspired **2** something or someone which causes one to feel inspired **3** a good idea — ~**al** *adj*

inspire *v* **inspired, inspiring 1** to encourage ability or feeling in (someone): *You inspire me with admiration* **2** to give unusual power to do good, esp. as from God **3** to be the force which produces (usu. a good result): *His music was inspired by love*

inspired *adj* so good as to seem to show inspiration, esp. from God: *an inspired guess*

inst. *abbrev. for:* (in business letters) of this present month: *on the 24th inst.*

instability *n* **1** lack of stability; unsteadiness **2** a tendency to act in changeable ways

install *v* **1** to settle in an official position, esp. with ceremony **2** to set (an apparatus) up, ready

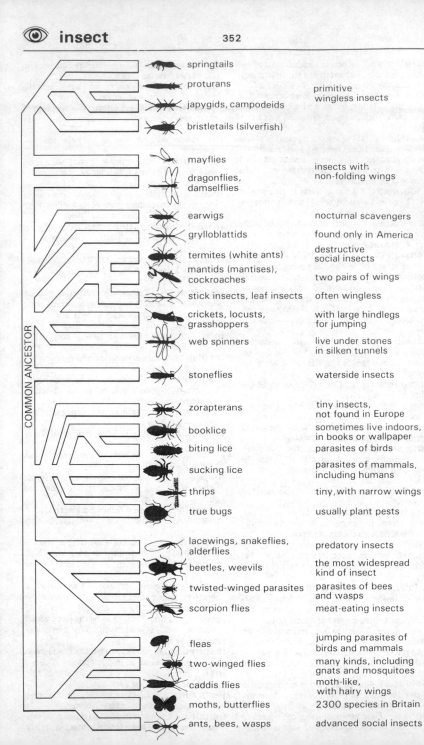

springtails

proturans

japygids, campodeids

bristletails (silverfish)

primitive
wingless insects

APTERYGOTA

mayflies

dragonflies,
damselflies

insects with
non-folding wings

earwigs — nocturnal scavengers

grylloblattids — found only in America

termites (white ants) — destructive
social insects

mantids (mantises),
cockroaches — two pairs of wings

stick insects, leaf insects — often wingless

crickets, locusts,
grasshoppers — with large hindlegs
for jumping

web spinners — live under stones
in silken tunnels

stoneflies — waterside insects

EXOPTERYGOTA

zorapterans — tiny insects,
not found in Europe

booklice — sometimes live indoors,
in books or wallpaper

biting lice — parasites of birds

sucking lice — parasites of mammals,
including humans

thrips — tiny, with narrow wings

true bugs — usually plant pests

lacewings, snakeflies,
alderflies — predatory insects

beetles, weevils — the most widespread
kind of insect

twisted-winged parasites — parasites of bees
and wasps

scorpion flies — meat-eating insects

fleas — jumping parasites of
birds and mammals

two-winged flies — many kinds, including
gnats and mosquitoes

caddis flies — moth-like,
with hairy wings

moths, butterflies — 2300 species in Britain

ants, bees, wasps — advanced social insects

ENDOPTERYGOTA

COMMON ANCESTOR

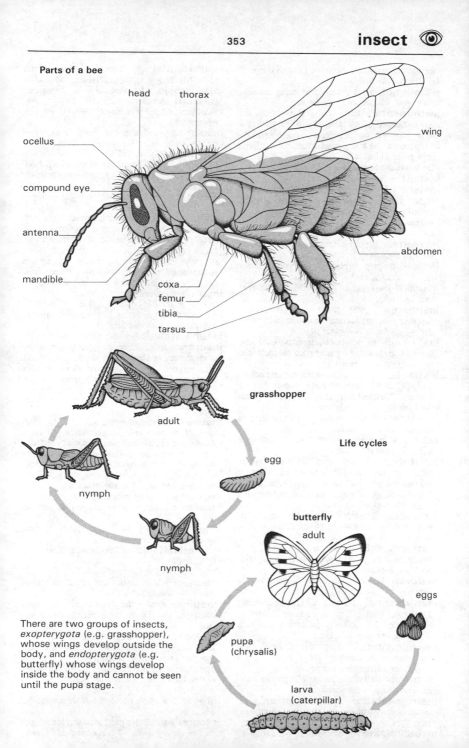

Parts of a bee

ocellus
head
thorax
compound eye
antenna
mandible
wing
coxa
femur
tibia
tarsus
abdomen

grasshopper

adult

Life cycles

egg

nymph

nymph

butterfly

adult

eggs

pupa
(chrysalis)

larva
(caterpillar)

There are two groups of insects, *exopterygota* (e.g. grasshopper), whose wings develop outside the body, and *endopterygota* (e.g. butterfly) whose wings develop inside the body and cannot be seen until the pupa stage.

for use **3** to settle somewhere: *I installed myself in front of the fire*

installation *n* **1** installing or being installed **2** an apparatus set up ready for use

instalment *n* **1** one of several payments: *the last instalment of my debt* **2** a single part of a book, play, etc. which appears in regular parts

instance *n* **1** a single fact, event, etc., expressing a general idea: *an instance of bad behaviour* **2 for instance** for example

instant[1] *n* a moment of time

instant[2] *adj* **1** happening at once **2** urgent: *in instant need* **3** which can be prepared quickly: *instant coffee* — ~**ly** *adv* : *Come instantly!* — ~**aneous** *adj* — ~**aneously** *adv* — ~**aneousness** *n*

instead *adv* in place of that: *It's too wet to walk, we'll go swimming instead*

instead of *prep* in place of: *Will you go to the party instead of me?*

instep *n* the upper surface of the foot between toes and ankle

instigate *v* **-gated, -gating** to start (something happening) by one's action: *He instigated the murder* — **-gation** *n* — **-gator** *n*

instil *v* **-ll-** to put (ideas, feelings, etc.) into someone gradually: *I instilled good manners into my children* — ~**lation** *n*

instinct *n* **1** a force in animals causing behaviour not based on learning: *Some animals hunt by instinct* **2** natural feelings: *Trust your instincts* — ~**ive** *adj* — ~**ively** *adv*

institute[1] *v* **-tuted, -tuting** to set up for the first time (a society, rules, etc.)

institute[2] *n* a society formed for a purpose: *a scientific institute*

institution *n* **1** instituting **2** a habit, custom, etc., which has existed for a long time: *Marriage is an institution* **3** a large society or organization **4** the building in which such an organization works — ~**al** *adj*

instruct *v* **1** to teach **2** to order: *I instructed him to come early* —see ORDER (USAGE) — ~**or** *n*

instruction *n* **1** instructing; teaching **2** advice on how to do something: *an instruction book* — ~**al** *adj*

instructive *adj* giving useful information — ~**ly** *adv*

instrument *n* **1** a tool: *medical instruments* **2** an object such as a piano, horn, etc. played to give music **3** someone or something used as a tool: *an instrument of fate*

instrumental *adj* **1** part of the cause of: *I was instrumental in catching the criminal* **2** (of music) for instruments, not voices

instrumentalist *n* a person who plays a musical instrument —compare VOCALIST

instrumentation *n* writing or arranging music for instruments —compare ORCHESTRATION

insubordinate *adj* disobedient — **-nation** *n*

insubstantial *adj* **1** lacking substance; not real **2** lacking solidity: *an insubstantial meal*

insufferable *adj* unbearable in behaviour: *insufferable rudeness* — **-bly** *adv*

insufficient *adj* not enough — ~**ly** *adv* — **-ciency** *n*

insular *adj* **1** of or like an island **2** narrow in mind —compare PAROCHIAL — ~**ity** *n*

insulate *v* **-lated, -lating** **1** to cover (something) to prevent the passing of electricity, heat, sound, etc. **2** to protect (a person) from ordinary experiences

insulation *n* **1** insulating or being insulated **2** material which insulates

insulator *n* something which prevents the passing esp. of electricity —compare NONCONDUCTOR

insulin *n* a hormone produced naturally by an organ in the body (the PANCREAS) which allows sugar to be used to give energy, esp. such a substance given to sufferers from a disease (DIABETES) which makes them lack this substance

insult[1] *v* to offend

insult[2] *n* something which insults

insuperable *adj* not to be conquered: *insuperable problems* — **-bly** *adv*

insupportable *adj* unbearable

insurance *n* **1** agreement to pay money in case of misfortune (such as illness, death, or accident): *life insurance* **2** money paid to or by an **insurance company** as a result of such an agreement **3** protection: *Buy a lock as insurance against thieves*

insurance policy *n* **-cies** a contract of insurance

insure *v* **insured, insuring** to protect by insurance: *My house is insured against fire* USAGE **Assure** and **ensure** both mean "to make certain": *You may rest assured.* **Assurance** means that one is sure of oneself. **Insurance** and sometimes **assurance** are used for protection through money. **Reassure** does *not* mean "to **assure** again".

insured *adj* having insurance

insurer *n* a person or company that provides insurance

insurgent *n, adj* (a person) ready to fight against those with power

insurmountable *adj* too large, difficult, etc., to be dealt with

insurrection *n* (a) rebellion — ~**ist** *n*

intact *adj* whole; untouched: *The clock arrived intact* — ~**ness** *n*

intaglio *n* **-glios** the art of making a picture, ornament, etc., by cutting a pattern into a surface

intake *n* **1** the amount or number taken in: *a large intake of students* **2** the place in a tube, pipe, etc., where fluid is taken in

intangible *adj* which cannot be known by the senses, but exists: *an intangible quality* — **-bility** *n* — **-bly** *adv*

integer *n* a whole number: *6 is an integer, but 6⅔ is not*

integral[1] *adj* **1** (of a part) necessary: *an integral part of the argument* **2** concerning an integer

integral² n the sum of the values that a function has taken; the area under a curve

integral calculus n technical the inverse of differential calculus; one of the 2 ways of making calculations about quantities which are constantly changing

integrate v **-grated, -grating** 1 to join to something else to form a whole: I integrated your suggestion with my plan 2 to cause (people) to join: to integrate a criminal into society 3 to find the mathematical integral of (a function) — compare DIFFERENTIATE — **-gration** n — ~**d** adj

integrity n 1 strength and firmness of character 2 wholeness; completeness

intellect n the ability to reason —see INTELLIGENCE (USAGE)

intellectual¹ adj 1 concerning the intellect 2 having reasoning powers —see INTELLIGENCE (USAGE); compare SPIRITUAL — ~**ly** adv

intellectual² n a person who lives by using his mind and is interested in thinking

intelligence n 1 ability to reason and understand 2 information: intelligence about enemy planes — **-gent** adj — **-gently** adv USAGE An **intellectual**, or **intellectual** person, is one who has developed his brain and **intellect**, is highly educated, and is interested in subjects that exercise the mind. One can be very **intelligent**/have great **intelligence**, without knowing much. A small child with a clever quick mind is **intelligent** but he can hardly be an **intellectual**.

intelligence quotient (abbrev. **IQ**)— n a measure of intelligence, with 100 representing the average

intelligible adj which can be understood — opposite **unintelligible**; compare ARTICULATE — **-bility** n — **-bly** adv

intemperate adj immoderate esp. in eating and drinking — **-ance** n — ~**ly** adv

intend v to plan; mean: I intend to go. | It was intended as a joke

intense adj strong, esp in quality: intense cold — ~**ly** adv — **-sity** n

intensifier n a word which makes an adjective stronger: "Very" is an intensifier, as in "very good"

intensify v **-fied, -fying** to make or become more intense — **-fication** n

intensive adj 1 giving attention to detail; thorough: Intensive care is given to the seriously ill 2 intense — ~**ly** adv

intent¹ n 1 law intending to do something bad: with intent to steal 2 purpose: with good intent 3 to all intents and purposes very nearly

intent² adj with attention: an intent look — ~**ly** adv — ~**ness** n

intention n a plan; purpose: It wasn't my intention to hurt

intentional adj on purpose —opposite **unintentional** — ~**ly** adv

interact v to have an effect on each other: The 2 ideas interact — ~**ion** n

interbreed v **-bred** (of parents of different kinds) to produce young: Can lions and tigers interbreed? —compare CROSSBREED, INBREEDING

intercalate v **-lated, -lating** to put (esp. a day) into a calendar

intercede v **-ceded, -ceding** to speak in favour of another — **-cession** n

intercept v to stop and usu. seize (a moving person or thing) — ~**ion** n

interceptor n 1 someone who intercepts 2 a fast, short-range fighter aircraft, used in defensive operations —compare FIGHTER

interchange¹ v **-changed, -changing** to put each of (2 things) in the place of the other

interchange² n 1 an exchange 2 a place where one leaves one form of public transport to get on another

interchangeable adj usable in place of each other — **-bility** n — **-bly** adv

intercollegiate adj among members of different colleges: intercollegiate sports

intercom n a system for talking through a machine to people at other desks, offices, etc.

intercommunicate v **-cated, -cating** to communicate with each other — **-cation** n

intercontinental adj between different continents: intercontinental trade

intercontinental ballistic missile (abbrev. **ICBM**)— n a missile that can be fired a very great distance

intercourse n 1 an exchange of feelings, actions, etc., between people 2 SEXUAL INTERCOURSE

interdependent adj depending on each other — **-dence** n — ~**ly** adv

interdict n an order not to do something

interest¹ n 1 a readiness to give attention: I have no interest in politics 2 a subject which one gives attention to: Eating is his only interest 3 advantage or favour: It's in your interest to speak out —compare ADVANTAGE 4 a share (in a company, business, etc.) 5 money paid for the use of money: money lent at 6% interest

interest² v to cause (someone) to have interest, desire, etc. — ~**ing** adj — ~**ingly** adv

interested adj 1 concerned; having interest 2 personally concerned; on whom there will be an effect: the interested party

interests n people concerned in an activity: business interests

interfacing n fabric fixed inside a garment (between the outer surface and the facing) to strengthen it and help it to keep its shape

interfere v **-fered, -fering** 1 to get in the way 2 to push oneself into someone else's affairs

interference n 1 interfering 2 the noises and activities which spoil the working of electrical apparatus, esp. a radio

interim¹ n the time between 2 events

interim² adj temporary: an interim report

interior adj, n (the part which is) inside: interior furnishings

interior decorator *n* a person who plans the colours, furnishings, etc., for the inside of a room

interject *v* to make a sudden remark between others

interjection *n* 1 an exclamation 2 interjecting

interlace *v* **-laced, -lacing** to join by twisting over and under: *interlaced branches*

interleave also **interleaf**— *v* **-leaved, -leaving** to put (sets of pages) together, one page from one set following one from another

interlink *v* to join together: *interlinked fates*

interlock *v* to fasten or be fastened together, esp. so that movement of one part causes movement in others

interloper *n* a person or creature found among others, with no right to be there —compare INTRUDER

interlude *n* free time between activities or parts of a play, film, etc.

intermarry *v* **-ried, - rying** to become connected by marriage: *The 2 families have been intermarrying for 100 years* — **-riage** *n*

intermediary *n, adj* **-ries** (a person) coming between 2 other things, groups, people, often to bring them into agreement

intermediate *adj* between 2 others; halfway

intermezzo *n* **-zos** *or* **-zi** a short piece of music played alone, or connecting longer pieces

interminable *adj* endless — **-bly** *adv*

intermingle also **intermix**— *v* **-gled, -gling** to mix together: *The rivers met and intermingled*

intermission *n* esp. US (in a concert, play, etc.) an interval

intermittent *adj* happening, then stopping, then happening again — ~**ly** *adv*

intern *v* to put in prison esp. in wartime for political reasons — ~**ment** *n*

internal *adj* 1 of or in the inside, esp. of the body 2 not foreign: *internal trade* — ~**ly** *adv*

internal-combustion engine *n* an engine which produces power by burning something (such as petrol) inside

internal evidence *n* proof that comes from what is under consideration rather than other pieces of writing, witnesses, etc. —compare EXTERNAL EVIDENCE

internalize, -ise *v* **-ized, -izing** to make (a principle or pattern of behaviour) part of the self as the result of learning — **-ization** *n*

international[1] *adj* concerned with more than one nation — ~**ly** *adv*

international[2] *n* 1 an international sports match 2 a player in such a match

International *n* any of 4 international left-wing political associations

internationalism *n* the principle that nations should work together, because their differences are less important than their common needs — **-ist** *n*

internationalize, -ise *v* **-ized, -izing** to make

international, esp. to bring under international control — **-ization** *n*

internecine *adj* 1 concerned with conflict within a group 2 (of war) destroying both sides

internee *n* someone interned

interpersonal *adj* concerning relations between people

interplanetary *adj* between planets: *interplanetary travel*

interplay *n* interaction: *the interplay of coloured lights*

Interpol *n* the International Police

interpolate *v* **-lated, -lating** to put in (additional words) — **-lation** *n*

interpose *v* **-posed, -posing** 1 to put or come between 2 to say between parts of a conversation — **-position** *n*

interpret *v* 1 to understand or show the meaning of 2 to put (spoken words) into another language —compare TRANSLATE — ~**er** *n* — ~**ative**, ~**ive** *adj*

interpretation *n* 1 interpreting 2 the performance of the intentions of a musician, writer, etc., by a performer

interracial *adj* between races — ~**ly** *adv*

interregnum *n* **-nums** *or* **-na** 1 a period when a country has no ruler, because the new ruler has not yet started to rule 2 a break between events

interrelate *v* **-lated, -lating** to bring together in close connection: *Wages and prices are interrelated* — **-lation, -lationship** *n* : *the interrelation between wages and prices*

interrogate *v* **-gated, -gating** to question formally — **-gation** *n* — **-gator** *n*

interrogative[1] *adj* which asks a question — ~**ly** *adv*

interrogative[2] *n* 1 an interrogative sentence, phrase, or form 2 a word (such as *who, what, which*) used in a question

interrogatory *adj* questioning

interrupt *v* 1 to break the flow of (something continuous) 2 to break the flow of speech of (someone) — ~**ion** *n*

intersect *v* to cut across

intersection *n* 1 intersecting 2 a point where roads, lines, etc., intersect 3 *technical* (in mathematics) the set of members that occur in both of 2 sets —compare UNION ☞MATHEMATICS

intersperse *v* **-spersed, -spersing** to set here and there among other things

interstellar *adj* between stars: *interstellar space*

interstice *n* a small space between things

intertwine *v* **-twined, -twining** to twist together

interval *n* 1 a period between events 2 such a period between the parts of a play, concert, etc. 3 (in music) the difference in pitch between 2 notes 4 **at intervals** happening after equal periods or appearing at equal distances: *at 20-minute intervals*

intervene *v* -vened, -vening **1** to interrupt so as to prevent or cause something: *I intervened and stopped the fight* **2** to come between: *in the intervening years* — -vention *n*

interview¹ *n* **1** a meeting where a person is asked questions, esp. to decide whether to offer him a job or college place **2** such a meeting to discover an important person's actions, points of view, etc.

interview² *v* to question in an interview — ~er *n*

interweave *v* -wove, -woven, -weaving to weave together

intestate *adj esp. law* not having made a will: *to die intestate*

intestine *n* the tube carrying food away from the stomach —see also SMALL INTESTINE, LARGE INTESTINE; compare BOWELS ⫷DIGESTION — -tinal *adj*

intimate¹ *v* -mated, -mating to make known indirectly; suggest — -mation *n*

intimate² *adj* **1** close in relationship: *intimate friends* **2** personal; private: *intimate beliefs* **3** in a sexual relationship: *They were intimate* **4** resulting from close connection: *intimate knowledge of Spain* — ~ly *adv* — -macy *n*

intimate³ *n* a person closely connected with another

intimidate *v* -dated, -dating to frighten (someone) into doing what one wants — -dation *n*

into *prep* **1** to the inside of: *They broke into his store* **2** so as to be in: *to fall into the water | to get into a temper* **3** so as to be: *to translate it into French* **4** (used when dividing one number by another): *3 into 6 goes twice* **5** *sl* keen on; interested in: *He's into modern music*

intolerable *adj* too difficult, painful, etc., to be borne — -bly *adv*

intolerant *adj* not able to accept beliefs, behaviour, etc., different from one's own — ~ly *adv* — -rance *n*

intonation *n* rise and fall in the pitch of the voice

intone *v* intoned, intoning to say (a poem, prayer) in a level voice

in toto *adv Latin* totally

intoxicate *v* -cated, -cating **1** to make drunk **2** to cause wild excitement in: *Success intoxicated him* — -cant *adj, n* — -cation *n*

intractable *adj* difficult to control — -bility *n* — -bly *adv*

intramural *adj* within an organization, such as a single school: *intramural sports* compare EXTRAMURAL

intransigent *adj* refusing to change one's mind — -gence *n* — -gently *adv*

intransitive *n, adj* (a verb) which does not have a direct object —compare TRANSITIVE — ~ly *adv*

intrauterine device (*abbrev.* IUD)— *n* the loop or coil; an object (CONTRACEPTIVE) **placed in** a woman's womb to prevent her from having children

intravenous *adj* within a vein: *an intravenous injection* — ~ly *adv*

intrench *v* to entrench

intrepid *adj* fearless — ~ly *adv* — ~ity *n*

intricate *adj* containing much detail and difficult to understand — ~ly *adv* — -cacy *n*

intrigue¹ *v* intrigued, intriguing **1** to interest greatly **2** to make a secret plot

intrigue² *n* **1** plotting **2** a plot

intrinsic *adj* part of the nature or character of someone or something —opposite **extrinsic** — ~ally *adv*

intro *n* -s *sl* an introduction

introduce *v* -duced, -ducing **1** to make known for the first time to each other or someone else **2** to bring in for the first time: *They introduced the idea that children should learn to drive* **3** to bring or put in: *The first notes introduce a new type of music. | to introduce the pipe into the hole* — -ductory *adj*

introduction *n* **1** introducing or being introduced **2** an occasion of telling people each others' names **3** an explanation at the beginning of a book or speech —see PREFACE (USAGE) **4** the beginning part: *the story's introduction*

introspection *n* the habit of examining one's own thoughts and feelings

introspective *adj* tending to think deeply about oneself

introvert *n, adj* (a person) of an introverted type —opposite **extrovert**

introverted *adj* concerned with one's own thoughts, acts, life, etc., rather than with activities with others — introversion *n*

intrude *v* intruded, intruding **1** to bring in unnecessarily: *He intruded his own ideas into the argument* **2** to come in when not wanted — ~r, -usion *n*

intrusive *adj* tending to intrude

intuition *n* **1** the power to know without reasoning **2** a piece of knowledge that results: *an intuition that her friend was ill* — -tive *adj* — -tively *adv*

inundate *v* -dated, -dating to flood — -dation *n*

inure *v* inured, inuring to accustom by experience: *The soldier was inured to danger*

invade *v* invaded, invading **1** to attack and take control of (a country, city, etc.) **2** to enter in large numbers: *Holiday makers invaded the seaside* **3** to enter into and spoil: *to invade someone's privacy* — ~r *n*

invalid¹ *adj* not correct, esp. in law — ~ly *adv* — ~ity *n*

invalid² *n* a person made weak by illness: *my invalid mother* — ~ism *n*

invalidate *v* -dated, -dating to make incorrect — -dation *n*

invaluable *adj* valuable beyond measure: *invaluable help* —see WORTHLESS (USAGE)

invariable adj which cannot vary — **-bly** adv — **-bility** n

invariant adj technical fixed; unchanged

invasion n an act of invading

invective n violent attacking speech

inveigh against v prep to attack bitterly with words

inveigle into v prep **-gled, -gling into** to trick (someone) into (doing something)

invent v **1** to make up or produce (something new): Bell invented the telephone in 1876 **2** to make up (something untrue): The whole story was invented — **-or** n USAGE One **discovers** something that existed before but was not known, such as a place or a fact. One **invents** something that did not exist before, such as a machine or a method.

invention n **1** inventing **2** something invented

inventive adj able to invent or think in new ways — ~**ly** adv — ~**ness** n

inventory n **-ries** a list, esp. of all the goods in a place

inverse¹ n **1** that which is opposite in order or position **2** technical a member of a set which combines with another member to give the identity element

inverse² adj **1** opposite in order or position **2** technical having the opposite effect **3** in **inverse relation/proportion to** one getting bigger as the other gets smaller — ~**ly** adv

invert v to put in the opposite position, esp. upside down — **inversion** n

invertebrate adj, n (a creature) with no backbone —compare VERTEBRATE

inverted comma n QUOTATION MARK

invest v to put (money) into something in order to make more money: invest £100 in the business

investigate v **-gated, -gating** to examine thoroughly — **-gator** n — **-gation** n

investiture n a ceremony to accept someone into office

investment n **1** investing **2** something invested or in which one invests: an investment of £100 in a business

inveterate adj habitual: an inveterate liar

invidious adj which will make people unjustly offended or jealous of one another ⚠ INSIDIOUS — ~**ly** adv — ~**ness** n

invigilate v **-lated, -lating** to watch over (an examination) to prevent dishonesty — **-lator** n — **-lation** n

invigorate v **-rated, -rating** to give strength to

invincible adj too strong to be conquered — **-bility** n — **-bly** adj

inviolable adj not to be attacked, changed, etc.: inviolable rights — **-bility** n

invisible adj **1** that cannot be seen **2** not usually recorded in statements of profit: invisible earnings/exports — **-bility** n — **-bly** adv

invitation n **1** inviting **2** a request to be present or take part **3** an encouragement

invite v **invited, inviting** **1** to ask (somebody) to a social occasion **2** to ask for, esp. politely: Questions were invited after the meeting **3** to encourage: Some shops invite crime by making it easy to steal

inviting adj tempting: inviting goods in the shop window — ~**ly** adv

invoice¹ n a bill for goods received

invoice² v **invoiced, invoicing** **1** to make an invoice for (goods) **2** to send an invoice to (someone)

invoke v **invoked, invoking** **1** to call out for: I invoked his kindness **2** to call into use: to invoke the powers of the law — **-vocation** n

involuntary adj not done from choice — **-tarily** adv — **-tariness** n

involve v **involved, involving** **1** to cause (someone) to become connected: Don't involve me in your mistakes —compare IMPLICATE **2** to include: This job involves living abroad — ~**ment** n

involved adj **1** complicated **2** (of a person) closely connected in relationships and activities

invulnerable adj that cannot be harmed — **-bility** n — **-bly** adv

inward adj **1** on or towards the inside **2** of the mind or spirit — ~**ly** adv

inwards adv towards the inside

iodine, -din n an element used in photography and medicine

ion n an atom which has been given (+) positive or (-) negative force by taking away or adding an electron ⎯→ ATOM

Ionic adj related to a style of ancient Greek building: an Ionic pillar —compare CORINTHIAN; DORIC

ionize, -ise v **ionized, ionizing** to turn into or form ions — **-ization** n

ionosphere n a part of the earth's atmosphere which directs radio waves around the earth

iota n **1** the 9th letter of the Greek alphabet (I, i) **2** a very small amount

IOU abbrev. for: "I owe you"; a piece of paper admitting a debt

IPA abbrev. for: International Phonetic Alphabet

IQ abbrev. for: INTELLIGENCE QUOTIENT

IRA abbrev. for: Irish Republican Army

irascible adj tending to get angry — **-bility** n — **-bly** adv

irate adj esp. written angry — ~**ly** adv — ~**ness** n

iridescent adj showing changing colours as light falls on it — **-cence** n

iridium n a hard metal which is an element

iris n **1** a tall yellow or purple flower with large leaves **2** the coloured part of the eye round the pupil

Irish adj of Ireland

Irish stew n meat, potatoes, and onions boiled together

irk v to annoy —compare ANGER

irksome adj troublesome

iron[1] n 1 a useful silver-white metal that is an element 2 a heavy metal object with a handle, pointed at the front and flat underneath, used for making cloth smooth 3 any of the set of 9 golf clubs with metal heads, used for driving a ball short distances —compare WOOD

iron[2] adj of great strength; unyielding: *an iron will*

iron[3] v to make smooth with an iron: *I've ironed your shirt*

Iron Age n the historical period when iron was first used . It came after the Bronze Age, which used a softer metal

Iron Curtain n (in Europe) the border between the Communist countries and the others, which cannot be easily crossed

ironic also **ironical**— adj expressing irony; bitterly funny: *an ironic saying* — ~**ally** adv

ironing board n a long narrow table on which clothes are ironed

iron lung n a machine which helps one breathe by putting repeated pressures on the chest

ironmonger n a shopkeeper who sells hardware, esp. metal goods — ~**y** n

iron out v adv 1 to remove or find an answer to: *to iron out the difficulties* 2 to remove with an iron: *iron out the creases in her dress*

iron rations n small amounts of nourishing foods, such as chocolate, carried by soldiers, climbers, etc.

irons n chains to keep a prisoner from moving

ironwork n shaped objects made of iron — compare WROUGHT IRON

ironworks n **ironworks** a factory for preparing iron and making iron objects

irony n -ies 1 use of words in which there is a contrast between what is said and what is meant 2 an event which has the opposite result from what is expected: *life's little ironies*

irradiate v -ated, -ating 1 to throw light on 2 to treat as with X-rays

irrational adj 1 without power to reason 2 against reasonable behaviour — ~ity n — ~ly adv

irrational number n a number (e.g. e, π √2) which when expressed as a decimal does not stop or recur —compare RATIONAL NUMBER

irreconcilable adj which cannot be brought into agreement — -**bly** adv

irrecoverable adj which cannot be recovered — -**bly** adv

irredeemable adj that cannot be redeemed — -**bly** adv

irreducible adj which cannot be made smaller or simpler — -**bly** adv

irrefutable adj too strong to be disproved: *an irrefutable argument* — -**bly** adv

irregular[1] adj 1 (of shape) uneven; not level 2 (of time) at unevenly separated points 3 not according to the rules 4 (in grammar) not following the usual pattern: *an irregular verb* — ~ly adv

irregular[2] n a soldier in a non-regular army

irregularity n -ties 1 being irregular 2 something irregular, such as crime or unevenness

irrelevant adj not having any connection with something: *Age is irrelevant for this job* — ~ly adv — -**vance**, -**vancy** n

irreligious adj against or without religion

irremediable adj not able to be put right — -**bly** adv

irreparable adj not able to be repaired — -**bly** adv

irreplaceable adj too special to be replaced

irrepressible adj too forceful to be held back: *an irrepressible talker* — -**bly** adv

irreproachable adj faultless — -**bly** adv

irresistible adj too desirable or strong to be resisted: *an irresistible child | an irresistible force* — -**bly** adv

irresolute adj unable to take decisive action — -**lution** n

irrespective of prep without regard to

irresponsible adj not thinking of the effect of one's actions — -**bility** n — -**bly** adv

irretrievable adj that cannot be recovered — -**bly** adv

irreverent adj lacking respect, esp. for religion — -**rence** n — ~ly adv

irreversible adj which cannot be turned back to a former state — -**bly** adv

irrevocable adj that cannot be undone: *an irrevocable decision* — -**bly** adv

irrigate v -gated, -gating to supply water to (dry land) with canals or pipes — -**gable** adj — -**gation** n

irritable adj tending to get angry at small things — -**bility** n — -**bly** adv

irritate v -tated, -tating 1 to annoy 2 technical to cause (something living, esp. part of a body) to act when influenced by a force 3 to make sore: *Wool irritates my skin* — -**tant** n

irritation n 1 irritating or being irritated 2 a sore place

irruption n esp. written a sudden rush: *an irruption of love* △ ERUPTION

is short form 's— 3rd person sing. pres. tense of BE: *He/she/it is welcome. | Father's here. | What is/what's that?*

Islam n 1 the Muslim religion, started by Mohammed —see also PROPHET 2 the people and countries that practise this religion ⇒ WORSHIP — ~ic adj

island n 1 a piece of land surrounded by water 2 something standing alone or apart: *an island of pleasure in a dull evening* 3 a raised place in the middle of the road, where people crossing can wait

islander n a person who lives on an island

isle n poetic an island

islet n a small island

isobar *n* a line on a map joining places where the air pressure is the same

isolate *v* **-lated, -lating** **1** to separate from others: *Floods isolated our village* **2** to separate from others for examination: *They have isolated the virus* — **-lation** *n*

isolationism *n* the principle that a country should not concern itself with the affairs of other countries — **-ist** *n, adj*

isomer *n* a chemical compound with the same atoms as another, but differently arranged

isometry *n* *technical* a transformation of a figure into another with identical lengths and angles: *Translations, rotations, and reflections are isometries*

isosceles triangle *n* a triangle having 2 equal sides ☞MATHEMATICS

isotherm *n* a line on a map joining points where the temperature is the same

isotope *n* any of the forms of the same element having different atomic weights ☞ATOM

Israeli *adj* of the modern state of Israel

Israelite *adj* of the ancient kingdom of Israel

issue¹ *n* **1** coming or bringing out **2** something given out: *a daily issue of milk* **3** something published again: *today's issue of 'The Times'* **4** an important point: *The real issue is . . .* **5** *old use and law* children (esp. in the phrase **die without issue**)

issue² *v* **issued, issuing** **1** to bring out (esp. something printed) for public attention **2** to provide officially: *issued the soldiers with guns*

issue from *v prep* to come from: *smoke issuing from the chimneys*

isthmus *n* a narrow area of land with sea on each side, joining 2 large land masses ☞GEOGRAPHY

it¹ *pron* **1 a** that thing: *'Where's my dinner?' 'The cat ate it'* **b** that person or animal whose sex is unknown or not thought important: *What a beautiful baby—is it a boy?* **2** (used as a subject in various verb patterns): *It's raining. | It's Thursday. | It felt funny being called Grandmother. | As it happens, I'm French. | It was Jean who shot the President* **3 if it weren't/hadn't been for** without the help or influence of **4 That's it a** That's complete **b** That's right **5 catch it** *esp. spoken* to get into trouble **6 have had it** *esp. spoken* to have no further hope of success: *We've had it: the bus left 5 minutes ago* —see HIM (USAGE)

it² *n* **1** the most important person in a game **2** *sl* **a** a very important person: *He thinks he's it* **b** the important point: *This is it—I have to make my mind up*

i.t.a. *abbrev. for*: initial teaching alphabet

ITA *abbrev. for*: Independent Television Authority —compare BBC

Italian *adj* of Italy ☞LANGUAGE

italics *n* writing or printing with small sloping letters: *This sentence is in italics* —compare ROMAN   — **italic** *n*

itch¹ *v* **1** to feel a soreness which one wants to scratch **2** to cause this soreness: *The wound itches* **3** *esp. spoken* to desire to do something: *I'm itching to go*

itch² *n* **1** an itching feeling **2** a strong desire

itchy *adj* **-ier, -iest** **1** feeling or causing an itch **2** **itchy feet** *esp. spoken* a desire to wander — **-iness** *n*

it'd *short form of* **1** it would: *It'd be all right* **2** it had: *It'd rained*

item *n* a single thing among a set

itemize, -ise *v* **-ized, -izing** to set out the details of

itinerary *n* **-ries** a plan of a journey

ITN *abbrev. for*: Independent Television News

its *adj* (*possessive form of* IT) belonging to it: *The cat washed its ears*

it's *short form of* **1** it is: *It's raining* **2** it has: *It's rained*

itself *pron* **1** (*reflexive form of* IT): *The cat's washing itself* **2** (*strong form of* IT): *We won't buy new tyres when the car itself is so old* **3 in itself** without considering the rest

ITV *abbrev. for*: Independent Television — compare BBC

IUD *abbrev for*: INTRAUTERINE DEVICE

ivory *n* **-ries** **1** a hard white substance, of which elephants' tusks are made **2** the creamy colour of ivory

ivory tower *n* a place where one avoids the reality of ordinary life

ivy *n* **ivies** a plant which climbs up walls and has shiny 3- or 5-pointed leaves

J

J, j **J's, j's** *or* **Js, js** the 10th letter of the English alphabet

jab¹ *v* **-bb-** to push (something pointed): *He jabbed his stick into my face*

jab² *n* **1** a push with something pointed **2** a quick straight blow **3** *sl* an injection

jabber¹ *v* to talk or say quickly and not clearly — **~er** *n*

jabber² *n* quick unclear speech

jack *n* **1** an apparatus for lifting something heavy, such as a car, off the ground —see also JACK UP **2** also **knave**— any of the 4 playing cards with a picture of a man and usu. a rank between the 10 and the queen **3** the small white ball at which players aim in bowls

jackal *n* any of several types of wild animal of the dog family

jackass *n* a fool

jackboot *n* a large high boot

jackdaw *n* a noisy bird of the crow family

jacket *n* **1** a short coat with sleeves **2** any outer cover: *potatoes in their jackets* **3** DUST JACKET

Jack Frost *n* frost considered as a person

jack-in-the-box *n* a children's toy which is a box from which an amusing figure jumps when the top is opened

jack knife¹ *n* **jack knives** a usu. large folding pocket knife

jack knife² *n* **jack knifes** a dive in which the body is folded and then straightened before entering the water

jack-knife *v* **-knifed, -knifing** to bend sharply in the middle: *The train jack-knifed*

jack-of-all-trades *n*   **jacks-of-all-trades** a person who can do many kinds of work (but may not be good at any of them)

jack-o'-lantern *n* a lamp made by sticking a lighted candle into a hollow pumpkin with a face cut in the outside

jackpot *n* the biggest amount of money to be won in a game of chance

Jack Robinson *n* **before you could/can say Jack Robinson** *esp. spoken* quickly and unexpectedly

jack up *v adv* to lift with a jack

Jacobean *adj, n* (a person) of the period 1603 to 1625, when James I was king of England

Jacobite *adj, n* (a person) that wanted a descendant of King James II to be king of England

jade *n* a precious usu. green stone used in jewellery

jaded *adj* tired from too much of something

jag¹ *v* **-gg-** to tear unevenly

jag² *n* **1** a sharp point or edge **2** an uneven hole

jag³ *n* *esp. spoken* a period of excitement and wild activity

jagged also **jaggy**— *adj* having a sharp uneven edge — ~**ly** *adv*

jaguar *n* a large spotted wild cat of Central and South America and Mexico

jail¹ also **gaol**— *n* a prison

jail² also **gaol**— *v* to put in jail

jailbird also **gaolbird**— *n* *esp. spoken* a person who has spent a lot of time in prison

jailbreak *n* an escape from prison

jailer also **gaoler**— *n* a person in charge of a prison

jalopy *n* **-ies** *humour* a worn-out old car

jam¹ *v* **-mm-** **1** to pack tightly into a small space: *I can't jam another thing into this bag* **2** to push forcefully: *She jammed the lid down on my finger.* | *He jammed the brakes on* **3** (of parts of machines) to get stuck **4** to block (radio messages) by broadcasting noise

jam² *n* **1** a mass of people or things jammed together: *a traffic jam* **2 in a jam** *esp. spoken* in trouble

jam³ *n* fruit boiled and preserved in sugar, for spreading on bread

jamb *n* a side post of a door or window

jamboree *n* **1** a noisy happy party **2** a large gathering of boy scouts

jammy *adj* **-mier, -miest** *sl* **1** easy: *a jammy exam* **2** lucky

jam session *n* an unrehearsed jazz performance

jangle *v* **-gled, -gling** to make or cause to make the sound of metal striking against metal

janissary also **janizary**— *n* **-ries** (until 1962) a member of a special group of soldiers in Turkey

janitor *n* **1** *esp. US* a caretaker **2** a person who guards a door —compare PORTER

January *n* **-ries** the first month of the year

japan *v* **-nn-** to cover (wood, metal, or pottery) with a hard shiny black paint

japonica *n* an ornamental bush from Japan with bright red flowers

jar¹ *v* **-rr-** **1** to make an unpleasant sound **2** to give an unpleasant shock to **3** to go badly together: *jarring opinions/colours*

jar² *n* an unpleasant shock

jar³ *n* a container like a bottle with a short neck and wide mouth: *2 jars of jam*

jargon *n* language that is hard to understand, esp. because it is full of special words

jasmine *n* any of several climbing plants with sweet-smelling white or yellow flowers

jaundice *n* a disease of the liver that makes the skin yellow

jaundiced *adj* **1** suffering from jaundice **2** mistrustful or jealous

jaunt *n* a short journey, usu. for pleasure

jaunty *adj* **-tier, -tiest** satisfied with life: *a jaunty wave of the hand* — **-tily** *adv* — **-tiness** *n*

javelin *n* a light throwing spear, now used mostly in sport

jaw¹ *n* **1** also **jawbone**— either of the 2 face bones which hold the teeth **2** the appearance of the lower jaw: *a square jaw*

jaw² *v* *esp. spoken* to talk

jaws *n* **2** parts of a tool which can grip or crush something

jay *n* **jays** any of several noisy brightly-coloured birds of the crow family

jaywalk *v* to cross streets carelessly — ~**er** *n*

jazz *n* **1** any of several types of music originated by black Americans, usu. with a strong beat and some free playing by each musician ⟶MUSIC **2** *sl* nonsense

jazz up *v adv sl* to make more active, bright, or enjoyable

jazzy *adj* **-ier, -iest** *sl* attracting attention, as with bright colours: *a jazzy car* — **-ily** *adv*

jealous *adj* **1** fearing to lose what one has; possessive **2** wanting to get what another has: *He is jealous of their success* — ~**ly** *adv* — ~**y** *n* USAGE If one is **envious** or feels **envy** of a person, one wishes one had their luck, possessions, or qualities. If one is **jealous** or feels **jealousy,** one hates the lucky person who has something one should have received oneself. It is a stronger and more unpleasant feeling.

jeans *n* strong cotton trousers, worn for work and informally

jeep n a type of car for travelling over rough ground

jeer v to laugh rudely (at): *The crowd jeered the prisoners* — **jeer** n

Jehovah n a name given to God in the Old Testament

Jehovah's Witness n a member of a Christian group that believes every word of the Bible

jell also **gel**— v **1** to set like jelly **2** (of ideas, thoughts, etc.) to take a clear shape

jellied adj prepared in jelly

jelly n **-lies 1** soft food that shakes when moved, made with gelatine: *orange jelly* **2** fruit juice boiled with sugar and cooled to become a spread for bread: *apple jelly* **3** any material between a liquid and solid state

jellyfish n *-fish or -fishes* a sea creature with a body like jelly 🖝EVOLUTION

jemmy n **-mies** an iron bar used by burglars to break open doors, windows, etc.

jeopardize, -dise v **-dized, -dizing** to endanger

jeopardy n danger: *in jeopardy*

jerk¹ v to move with a jerk: *He jerked his head back*

jerk² n a short quick strong pull or movement

jerkin n a short coat, usu. sleeveless

jerky adj **-ier, -iest** with jerks — **-ily** adv — **-iness** n

jeroboam n a large wine bottle that holds 4 times the amount of an ordinary wine bottle

Jerry n **-ries** *sl now rare* (a soldiers' name for) a German

jersey n **-seys 1** a sweater **2** fine usu. woollen cloth used esp. for dresses

Jersey n **-seys** a light brown cow that produces high-quality milk

Jerusalem artichoke n a potato-like vegetable

jess n a short strap on the leg of a hawk, to which a leash can be fastened

jest¹ n a joke: *in jest*

jest² v *esp. written* to joke: *a jesting remark* — **jestingly** adv

jester n a man who in former times amused rulers by telling jokes, singing, etc.

Jesuit n **1** a member of the Society of Jesus, a Roman Catholic religious group **2** an untrustworthy crafty person

jesuitical also **jesuitic**— adj untrustworthy or crafty — **-cally** adv

jet¹ n a hard black mineral that can be polished, used in ornaments

jet² v **-tt-** to come or send out in a jet or jets: *The water jetted out*

jet³ n **1** a narrow stream of liquid, gas, etc., forced through a small hole: *jets of water* **2** a narrow opening from which this is forced out **3** an aircraft powered by a jet engine

jet⁴ v **-tt-** to travel by jet aeroplane

jet-black adj very dark shiny black

jet engine n an engine that pushes out hot gases behind it, and is used to make aircraft fly 🖝AEROPLANE

jet lag n tiredness after a long fast journey across time zones: *On arriving from New York, he could not tackle the problem because of jet lag*

jet propulsion n powering a plane by jet engines — **jet-propelled** adj

jetsam n see FLOTSAM AND JETSAM

jet set n the rich and successful people who go everywhere by jet

jettison v to throw away

jetty n **-ties** a wall built out into water, for getting on ships or as a protection against the waves

Jew n a person descended from the inhabitants of ancient Israel, or practising their religion —see also HEBREW 🖝WORSHIP — ~ **ish** adj

jewel n **1** a precious stone, often fitted in an ornament or in the machinery of a watch **2** a person or thing of great value

jewelled adj ornamented with jewels

jeweller n a person who deals in jewels

jewellery, -elry n ornaments with jewels

jib¹ n a small sail 🖝SAIL

jib² n the long arm standing out at an angle from a crane or derrick

jib at v prep **-bb-** to be unwilling to do or face (something)

jibe n a gibe

jiffy n *esp. spoken* a moment: *I won't be a jiffy*

jig¹ n **1** a quick gay dance **2** a quick short movement, esp. up and down

jig² v **-gg- 1** to dance a jig **2** to move with quick up-and-down movements

jiggered adj *sl* **1** very surprised: *I'll be jiggered!* **2** very tired

jiggery-pokery n *esp. spoken* dishonest tricks

jiggle v **-gled, -gling** *esp. spoken* to move from side to side with quick light jerks — **jiggle** n — **-gly** adj

jigsaw n **1** a fretsaw **2** JIGSAW PUZZLE

jigsaw puzzle n a picture made up of irregular pieces to be fitted together

jihad n a holy war fought by Muslims

jilt v to get rid of or desert (a lover or somebody one has promised to marry)

jingle¹ v **-gled, -gling** to sound with a jingle

jingle² n **1** a sound as of small bells **2** a simple poem with a very regular beat

jingo n **by jingo!** (an expression of eagerness): *You're right, by jingo!*

jingoism n *offensive* blind love of one's country, esp. that which has a military tendency — **-ist(ic)** adj

jinx n a person or thing that brings bad luck

jitters n *esp. spoken* anxiety before an event: *I get the jitters before exams* — **jittery** adj

jive¹ n (a dance to) popular music with a strong regular beat

jive² v **jived, jiving** to dance a jive

Jnr abbrev. for: Junior

job *n* **1** a piece of work: *Do a better job next time* **2** something hard to do: *It was a job to talk with all that noise* **3** *sl* a crime, esp. robbery or a beating **4** regular paid employment: *He has a job in a bank* **5 a good/bad job** *esp. spoken* a good/bad thing: *He's gone, and a good job too!* USAGE One is **appointed** to a **post** or **position**. These are grander words for a **job**. An **appointment** is not a **job**, but it can mean the act of **appointing** someone: *Recent government* **appointments** *include* .... **Vocation** is used of certain professions such as teaching or nursing, which people enter for serious moral reasons. People **work** in all these **jobs**, but *out of* **work**, *the* **workers**, *looking for* **work**, are used particularly of people who work with their hands —see WORK (USAGE)

Job *n* a man in the Bible who was patient through many sufferings: *the patience of Job*

jobber *n* a person who buys and sells on the Stock Exchange

job lot *n* a group of different things sold together

jockey[1] *n* **-eys** a person who rides in horse races, esp. professionally

jockey[2] *v* **-eyed, -eying 1** to get (someone to do something or into a position) by tricks **2 jockey for position** to try skilfully to get into a good position

jockstrap *n* *esp. spoken* a tight-fitting support for the male sex organs during sports

jocular *adj* *esp. written* causing laughter; merry — ~**ly** *adv* — ~**ity** *n*

jodhpurs *n* trousers for horse riding that are tight below the knee and loose above

jog[1] *v* **-gg- 1** to shake or push slightly **2** to move slowly and unsteadily: *The carriage jogged along the track* **3** to move along steadily and uneventfully **4** to run slowly and steadily **5 jog someone's memory** to make someone remember — ~**ger** *n*

jog[2] *n* **1** a slight shake, push, or knock **2** also **jog trot**— a slow steady run

John Bull *n* **1** England **2** a typical Englishman

johnny *n* **-nies** *esp. spoken* a fellow

join[1] *v* **1** to fasten; connect: *to join the ends of a rope* **2** to bring together: *to join people in marriage* **3** to take part in: *Will you join me in a drink?* **4** to become a member of: *to join the army* **5** to run into; meet: *Where does the path join the road?*

join[2] *n* a place where 2 things are joined

joiner *n* a woodworker who makes doors, windowframes, etc., inside a building —compare CARPENTER

joinery *n* woodwork in buildings

joint[1] *n* **1** a way of making a join **2** a thing used for making a join **3** a place where things join ⟶ANATOMY **4** a large piece of meat **5** *sl* a public place, esp. one of amusement **6** *sl* a cigarette containing cannabis **7 out of joint** (of an arm, leg, etc.) out of the proper position

joint[2] *adj* shared by 2 or more people: *a joint account with the bank* — ~**ly** *adv*

joint[3] *v* to divide (meat) at the joints

join up *v adv* to join the army, navy, etc.

joist *n* one of the beams on which a floor rests

joke[1] *n* **1** anything said or done to cause amusement **2** a person, thing, or event that is not taken seriously —see also PRACTICAL JOKE

joke[2] *v* **joked, joking** to tell or make jokes — **jokingly** *adv*

joker *n* **1** a person who jokes **2** *esp. spoken* a person not to be taken seriously **3** an additional playing card, which in some games may have any value

jolly[1] *adj* **-lier, -liest 1** merry; happy **2** *esp. spoken* slightly drunk **3** nice; pleasant — **jollily** *adv* — **jollity, jolliness** *n*

jolly[2] *adv* *esp. spoken* very: *a jolly good thing*

jolly[3] *v* **-lied, -lying** *esp. spoken* to urge gently: *They jollied her into going*

Jolly Roger *n* the pirate flag of former times, showing a skull and crossbones

jolt[1] *v* to shake or shock

jolt[2] *n* a sudden shake or shock

Jonah *n* a person who brings bad luck

joss stick *n* a stick of incense

jostle *v* **-tled, -tling** to knock or push against (someone)

jot[1] *n* a very small amount: *not a jot of truth*

jot[2] *v* **-tt-** to write quickly

jotting *n* a rough note

joule *n* *technical* a measure of energy or work equal to 10^7 ergs

journal *n* **1** a diary **2** a periodical

journalism *n* the profession of producing, esp. writing for newspapers — **-ist** *n* — **-istic** *adj*

journey[1] *n* **-neys** a trip of some distance —see TRAVEL (USAGE)

journey[2] *v* **-neyed, -neying** to travel

journeyman *n* **-men** a trained workman who works for another: *a journeyman printer*

joust *v* (in former times) to fight on horseback with spears, as sport

jovial *adj* (esp. of fat old men) friendly or jolly — ~**ly** *adv* — ~**ity** *n*

jowl *n* the side of the lower face —see also CHEEK **by jowl**

joy *n* **joys 1** great happiness **2** a person or thing that causes joy **3** *esp. spoken* success: *I tried to phone her, but I didn't have any joy*

joyful *adj* full of joy — ~**ly** *adv* — ~**ness** *n*

joyless *adj* without joy; unhappy — ~**ly** *adv* — ~**ness** *n*

joyous *adj* *esp. in literature* full of or causing joy — ~**ly** *adv* — ~**ness** *n*

joyride *n* *esp. spoken* a ride for pleasure in a vehicle, esp. a stolen vehicle

joystick *n* a stick that controls an aircraft

JP also **justice of the peace**— *n* the judge in small law courts; magistrate

Jr *abbrev. for:* Junior

jubilant *adj* joyful — ~**ly** *adv*

jubilation n great joy; rejoicing

jubilee n a period of great rejoicing, esp. to mark or remember some event

Judaism n the religion and civilization of the Jews

Judas n a traitor

judder v to shake violently

judge¹ v **judged, judging** 1 to act as a judge in (a law case) 2 to give a decision about (someone or something), esp. in a competition: *to judge horses* 3 to give an opinion about: *A man should be judged by his deeds*

judge² n 1 an official who has the power to decide questions brought before a law court 2 a person with the knowledge, experience, or right to make decisions or give opinions: *I'm no judge of music*

judgment, judgement n 1 an official decision given by a law court 2 an opinion: *to form a judgment* 3 the ability to judge: *a man of weak judgment*

judgment day also **last judgment, day of judgment**— n the day when God will judge all men

judicature n 1 the power to judge in a law court 2 the judiciary

judicial adj of, by, or connected with a law court, judge, etc.: *a judicial decision* △ JUDICIOUS — ~ly adv

judiciary n **-ries** the judges in law considered as one group

judicious adj having good judgment, the ability to form sensible opinions, etc. △ JUDICIAL — ~ly adv — ~ness n

judo n a type of Japanese fighting developed from jujitsu

jug¹ n 1 a pot for liquids with a handle and a lip for pouring 2 sl prison

jug² v **-gg-** to boil in a closed pot: *jugged hare*

juggernaut n 1 a great force that destroys everything it meets 2 esp. spoken a large long-distance lorry that may be a danger to other vehicles

juggle v **-gled, -gling** 1 to keep (several objects) in the air at the same time, throwing them up and catching them 2 to play with (something): *to juggle ideas* 3 to do something dishonest: *Don't juggle with your accounts* — ~r n

jugular vein n either of 2 large blood vessels in the neck that return blood from the head

juice n 1 the liquid part of fruit, vegetables, and meat 2 sl anything that produces power, such as electricity, petrol, etc.

juicy adj **-ier, -iest** 1 full of juice: *a juicy orange* 2 interesting, esp. because providing information: *all the juicy details* — -iness n

jujitsu, jiujitsu n a type of Japanese fighting in which you hold and throw your opponent

jukebox n a machine which plays records when a coin is put in

julep n an American drink in which alcohol and sugar are poured over ice, and mint is added

Julian calendar n the calendar brought in by Julius Caesar in 46 B.C. and used until the Gregorian Calendar was introduced

July n **Julies** the 7th month of the year

jumble¹ v **-bled, -bling** to mix in disorder

jumble² n a disorderly mixture

jumble sale n a sale of used clothes, toys, etc., to get money for some good work

jumbo adj very large: *a jumbo jet*

jump¹ v 1 to spring suddenly and quickly: *jump out of the water* 2 to spring over: *He jumped the stream* 3 to make a quick sudden movement, usu. upwards: *His heart jumped for joy.* | *Oil prices jumped sharply* 4 esp. spoken to travel on (a train) without paying 5 to attack suddenly 6 **jump to it** esp. spoken to hurry 7 **jump the gun** to start something too soon

jump² n an act of jumping —see also HIGH JUMP, LONG JUMP

jumped-up adj conceited because of having risen quickly

jumper¹ n a person or horse that jumps

jumper² n a knitted garment for the upper body, pulled on over the head; sweater

jumpy adj **-ier, -iest** nervously excited — **-pily** adv — **-piness** n

junction n a place of joining or uniting: *a railway junction*

juncture n esp. written a point in time (esp. in the phrase **at this juncture**)

June n the 6th month of the year

jungle n 1 a thick tropical forest 2 a disorderly mass: *the jungle of tax laws*

junior adj 1 younger 2 of lower rank: *a junior minister* —compare MINOR — **junior** n

Junior n esp. US the younger: *John Smith Junior is the son of John Smith*

juniper n a low evergreen bush with a pleasant-smelling oil

junk¹ n 1 esp. spoken old useless things 2 esp. spoken poor material: *This book is junk* 3 sl the dangerous drug heroin

junk² v esp. spoken to get rid of as worthless

junk³ n a Chinese sailing ship with a flat bottom and rather square sails

junket n 1 milk made solid by adding an acid (RENNET) 2 esp. spoken, esp. US a trip, esp. one made on public money

junkie, junky n **-ies** sl a person who takes heroin as a habit

Junoesque adj (of a woman) tall and queenly

junta n Spanish a government come to power by armed force

Jupiter n the largest planet of the group that includes the Earth, 5th in order from the sun

juridical adj esp. written of or related to law or judges — ~ly adv

jurisdiction n 1 the power held by an official body, esp. a court of law 2 the right to use such power: *to accept the court's jurisdiction* 3 the limits of this right (esp. in the phrases **within/outside someone's jurisdiction**)

jurisprudence *n* *esp. written* the science or knowledge of law

jurist *n* *esp. written* a person with a thorough knowledge of law

juror *n* a member of a jury

jury *n*   **juries** 1 a group of people chosen to decide questions in a law court 2 a group chosen to judge a competition: *the jury of the Miss World competition*

juryman (*fem.* **jurywoman**)— *n* **-men** a juror

just[1] *adj* 1 fair and honest 2 well-deserved: *a just reward* 3 exact: *a just balance* — ~**ly** *adv* — ~**ness** *n*

just[2] *adv* 1 exactly: *He was sitting just here.* | *He came just as I was leaving* 2 very near the present or stated time: *They've just arrived.* | *just after Christmas* 3 almost not: *You only just caught the train* 4 (*esp. spoken*) completely: *That's just perfect!* 5 merely: *just the door squeaking, not a ghost* USAGE **Already**, **yet**, and **just** (when it is used of time) were formerly not used with the past tense. Expressions like the following are now common in spoken *US* English: *I already saw him.* | *The bell just rang.* | *Did you eat yet?* These are coming into British English, but some people do not like them.

just about *adv* very nearly: *just about here*

justice *n* 1 being just; fairness 2 correctness: *the justice of his remarks* 3 the power of the law: *to bring a criminal to justice*

Justice *n* a part of the title of a judge: *Mr Justice Smith*

Justice of the Peace *n*   **Justices of the Peace** *esp. written* a JP

justify *v* **-fied, -fying** to give or be a good reason for — **-fiable** *adj* — **-fiably** *adv* — **-fication** *n*

jute *n* a substance used for making rope and rough cloth, from either of 2 plants grown esp. in E India and Bangladesh

jut out *v adv* **-tt-** to stick out: *The wall juts out into the road*

juvenile[1] *adj* 1 of or for young people: *juvenile books* 2 young and foolish

juvenile[2] *n* *esp. written* a young person

juvenile delinquency *n* crimes or antisocial behaviour by juveniles — **-quent** *n*

juxtapose *v* **-posed, -posing** to place side by side — **-position** *n*

K

K, k K's, k's *or* Ks, ks the 11th letter of the English alphabet

kaftan *n* a caftan

Kaiser *n* *German* (the title of) the king of Germany (1871–1918)

kaleidoscope *n* 1 a tube fitted with mirrors and pieces of coloured glass which shows coloured patterns when turned 2 anything with changing colours, patterns, etc.: *The sunset was a kaleidoscope of colours* — **-scopic** *adj* — **-scopically** *adv*

kangaroo *n* **-roos** an Australian animal (MAR-SUPIAL) which jumps along on large back legs and carries its young in a special pocket ⇒ MAM-MAL

kaolin *n* fine white clay used for making cups, plates, etc., and in medicine

kapok *n* light soft cotton-like material used for stuffing

kappa *n* the 10th letter of the Greek alphabet (K, κ)

kaput *adj* *sl, German* broken; finished

karat *n* a carat

karate *n* a Japanese fighting style without weapons, using blows with the hands and feet

karma *n* (in Hinduism and Buddhism) the force produced by a person's actions which influences the rest of his life and future lives

kayak *n* a narrow covered boat used by Eskimos, or any similar boat

K.C. also (*esp. written*) **King's Counsel** — (the title given, when a king reigns, to) a British barrister of high rank —compare Q.C.

kebab, -bob *n* cut up meat and vegetables cooked on a stick

kedgeree *n* a dish of rice and fish mixed, with eggs and sometimes cream

keel *n* 1 a long bar along a boat's bottom from which the frame of the boat is built up ⇒ SAIL 2 **on an even keel** without any sudden changes; without trouble

keelhaul *v* (in former times) to drag (someone) under a ship's keel

keel over *v adv* to fall over sideways

keen[1] *adj* 1 sharp; cutting 2 (of the mind, feelings, senses, etc.) strong, quick at understanding, etc.: *a keen mind* | *keen sorrow* | *keen sight* 3 with eagerness and activity: *a keen struggle for power* | *She is not keen to come* 4 *esp. spoken* having a strong liking for: *keen on politics* — ~**ly** *adv* — **keenness** *n*

keen[2] *v* to express sorrow loudly, often by a song or cry — **keen** *n*

keep[1] *v* **kept, keeping** 1 to fulfil: *She kept her promise* 2 to guard; protect: *May God keep you!* | *to keep a secret* 3 to take care of: *She kept her sister's children* 4 to own, employ, or have the use of: *to keep a house* 5 to own and take care of, usu. in order to make money: *to keep cows* | *They keep a shop* 6 to have or hold for some time: *Please keep this until I come back.* | *The shop keeps all writing needs* 7 to have without the need of returning: *Keep the change* 8 to cause to continue to be: *That kept her warm.* | *Her illness kept her in hospital.* | *The tyrant kept the people down* 9 to continue to be: *She kept warm/ studying* 10 to remain fit to eat: *This fish won't keep* 11 to delay: *What kept you?* see also KEEP ON, **keep** TIME, KEEP UP

keep[2] *n* 1 a great tower of a castle 2 necessary

goods and services (esp. in the phrase **earn one's keep**)

keeper *n* a person who guards, protects, or looks after: *zoo keeper* | *shopkeeper* | *doorkeeper* | *wicket keeper*

keeping *n* 1 care or charge: *She left her jewellery in her sister's keeping* 2 **out of/in keeping (with something)** not in/in agreement (with something)

keep on *v adv* 1 to continue: *Prices keep on increasing* 2 to continue to have or employ: *I've kept both gardeners on* 3 to talk continuously: *He keeps on about his operation.* | *Don't keep on at me about it!*

keeps *n* **for keeps** *sl* for ever

keepsake *n* something given to be kept in memory of the giver

keep up *v adv* 1 to cause to remain high: *She kept up her spirits by singing* 2 to keep in good condition: *keep up a house* 3 to continue: *keep up the good work* 4 to remain the same: *Will the fine weather keep up?* 5 to keep out of bed 6 to remain level: *I had to run to keep up with you* 7 **keep up with the Joneses** to stay level with one's neighbours socially

keg *n* a small barrel

kelvin *n* a degree in a scale of temperature according to which absolute zero=0°

ken¹ *v* **-nn-** Scots to know

ken² *n* the limits of knowledge (esp. in the phrases **beyond/outside/not within one's ken**)

kennel¹ *n* a small house for a dog

kennel² *v* to keep or put in a kennel

kennels *n* **kennels** a place where small animals are looked after while their owners are away

kept *past tense and past part. of* KEEP

kerb *n* a line of raised stones separating the footpath from the road

kerchief *n* **-chiefs** *or* **-chieves** a cloth to cover the head

kerfuffle *n* esp. spoken unnecessary noisy excitement

kernel *n* 1 the part inside the shell of a nut 2 the part of a seed inside its hard covering: *the kernel of a grain of corn* 3 the important or main part of something

kerosene *n* US paraffin ☞REFINERY

kestrel *n* a red-brown falcon which feeds on small animals and insects and is often seen hovering ☞BIRD

ketch *n* a small sailing-ship with 2 masts

ketchup also **catsup**— *n* a thick sour liquid made usu. from tomatoes, used for flavouring

kettle *n* a usu. metal pot with a lid, handle, and spout for heating water

kettledrum *n* a large metal drum with a curved bottom

key¹ *n* **keys** 1 a usu. metal instrument for locking or unlocking, winding (a clock), tightening or loosening (a spring), etc. 2 any part in an apparatus that is pressed with the finger: *the keys of a piano/a typewriter* 3 something that explains or helps you to understand: *a key to the* grammar exercises 4 someone or something very important: *a key man* 5 a set of musical notes with a certain starting note: *in the key of C* 6 a winglike seed of certain types of tree (such as the sycamore)

key² *v* **keyed, keying** to make ready or suitable for: *factories keyed to the needs of the army* —see also KEY UP

keyboard¹ *n* a row of keys on an apparatus: *the keyboard of a piano or typewriter*

keyboard² *v* 1 to work the keyboard of (a machine, esp. a computer) 2 to provide a machine with (information) by working a keyboard — ~er *n*

key money *n* money demanded before a person is allowed to begin living in a flat or house

keynote *n* 1 the note on which a musical key is based 2 the central idea: *The keynote of his speech was that we need higher wages*

key ring *n* a ring on which keys are kept

key signature *n* a sign, consisting of one or more sharps and flats, at the beginning of a section of music to show what key it is in ☞ MUSIC

keystone *n* 1 the middle stone in the top of an arch 2 something on which everything else depends

key up *v adv* to make excited or nervous: *I was keyed up about the exam* —compare HIGH-KEYED

kg. abbrev. for: kilogram

khaki adj, *n* 1 a yellow-brown colour 2 cloth of this colour, esp. as worn by soldiers

khalifate *n* a caliphate — **khalif** *n*

khan *n* (a title of) a ruler or official in Asia

kibbutz *n* **-zim** *or* **-zes** a settlement in Israel where many people live and work

kibosh *n* **put the kibosh on** *sl* to put an end to (a hope, plan, etc.)

kick¹ *v* 1 to hit with the foot 2 (esp. in rugby) to score by doing this: *kick a goal* 3 to move the feet backwards and forwards 4 esp. spoken to make by complaining: *kick up a fuss* —see also KICK ABOUT, KICK OFF — ~er *n*

kick² *n* 1 an act of kicking 2 *sl* a sharp feeling of excitement: *She drives fast for kicks* 3 esp. spoken power to produce an effect: *This wine has a lot of kick*

kick about¹ also **kick around**— *v prep* esp. spoken 1 to travel in (a place): *He's been kicking about Africa* 2 KNOCK ABOUT

kick about² *v adv* esp. spoken 1 to lie unnoticed: *My cap's kicking about somewhere* 2 to treat roughly

kickback *n* *sl* money for services that have helped you to make money

kick off *v adv* to start a football match — **kickoff** *n*

kick-start *n* 1 a way of starting a machine, esp. a motorcycle, by pushing down a special part 2 the part that is pushed down to start a machine

kid¹ n 1 a young goat 2 leather made from its skin 3 *esp. spoken* a child

kid² v *-dd- esp. spoken* 1 to pretend or deceive: *He's not really hurt: he's only kidding* 2 **You're kidding!** I don't believe you — **kidder** n

kiddie, -dy n **-dies** *sl* a child

kid gloves n gentle methods of dealing with people: *Don't treat those young criminals with kid gloves*

kidnap v *-pp-* to take (someone) away unlawfully in order to demand money or something else for his safe return — **kidnapper** n

kidney n **-neys** one of 2 organs in the lower back, shaped like a bent oval, which separate waste liquid (URINE) from the blood

kidney bean n a type of edible bean shaped like a kidney

kidney machine n a machine that can do the work of damaged human kidneys

kill¹ v 1 to cause to die 2 to destroy: *That mistake killed his chances* 3 **kill time** to make time pass by finding something to do — **~er** n

kill² n 1 the animal(s) killed in hunting — compare BAG 2 the act of killing 3 **in at the kill** present at the end of a struggle, competition, etc.

killer whale n a fierce meat-eating whale 20 to 30 feet long

killing n **make a killing** to make a lot of money suddenly

killjoy n **-joys** a person who spoils people's pleasure

kiln n an oven for baking pots, bricks, etc.

kilner jar n *trademark* a large glass vessel with a tight lid, for preserving fruit and vegetables

kilogram also **kilo** — n 1, 000 grams

kilohertz also **kilocycle** — n **-hertz** 1, 000 hertz

kilometre n 1, 000 metres

kilowatt n 1, 000 watts

kilt n a short pleated skirt worn by Scotsmen

kimono n **-nos** a long coatlike Japanese garment

kin n *old use* **next of kin** a person's closest relative or relatives —see also KITH AND KIN; —compare KINDRED

kind¹ n 1 a group that are alike; type; sort: *people of many kinds | the only one of its kind* 2 nature or type: *different in size but not in kind* 3 **in kind** (of payment) using goods rather than money 4 **of a kind** a of the same kind b of poor quality: *coffee of a kind* —see also KIND OF USAGE Do not write: *Those kind / sort of questions are very difficult.* You should use this form: *That kind/sort of question is very difficult.* **Kind** and **sort** are singular nouns.

kind² adj helpful; gentle and well-wishing: *Be kind to animals*

kindergarten n NURSERY SCHOOL

kindle v **-dled, -dling** 1 to set fire to or catch fire 2 to cause to start: *His cruelty kindled hatred*

in my heart 3 to show excitement: *When she saw him her eyes kindled*

kindling n materials for lighting a fire, esp. dry wood, leaves, etc.

kindly¹ adj **-lier, -liest** friendly; sympathetic — **-liness** n

kindly² adv 1 in a kind manner 2 please: *Kindly put it back* 3 **take kindly to** to accept easily: *He didn't take kindly to your remarks*

kindness n 1 being kind 2 a kind action

kind of adv *esp. spoken, esp. US* in a certain way: *She kind of hoped to be invited*

kindred¹ n 1 family relationship 2 one's relatives —compare KIN

kindred² adj related: *Italian and Spanish are kindred languages*

kinetic adj *technical* of or about movement — **~ally** adv

kinetic art n art that includes the use of moving objects

kinetic energy n the power of something moving, such as running water

kinetics n the science that studies the action of force in producing movement

king n 1 (the title of) the male ruler of a country, usu. the son of a former ruler 2 a very powerful or outstanding member of a group: *a king among men* 3 (in certain games) **a** a very important piece **b** any of the 4 playing cards with a picture of a king and a rank above the queen — **~ly** adj **— ~ship** n ⊚

kingcup n a marsh plant with big yellow flowers related to the buttercup

kingdom n 1 a country under a king or queen 2 an area over which someone has control: *The cook's kitchen is her kingdom* 3 any of the 3 great divisions of natural objects: *the animal/plant/mineral kingdom* 4 **the Kingdom of God** the rule of God USAGE A **kingdom** may be ruled over by a **queen**, like Britain at present.

kingfisher n a small bird with bright feathers that feeds on fish

kingmaker n a person who can influence appointments to high office

kingpin n the most important person in a group

Kings n either of 2 books of the Old Testament

King's English n see ENGLISH

kink n 1 a twist in hair, a pipe, etc. 2 a peculiarity of the mind or character — **~y** adj

kinsfolk n members of one's family

kinship n 1 family relationship 2 likeness (in character, understanding, etc.)

kiosk n 1 a small open hut, often used to sell newspapers 2 a public telephone box

kip¹ n *sl* 1 sleep 2 a place to sleep: *to find a kip*

kip² v *-pp- sl* to sleep or go to bed

kipper n a smoked salted herring cut open

kirk n *Scots* a church

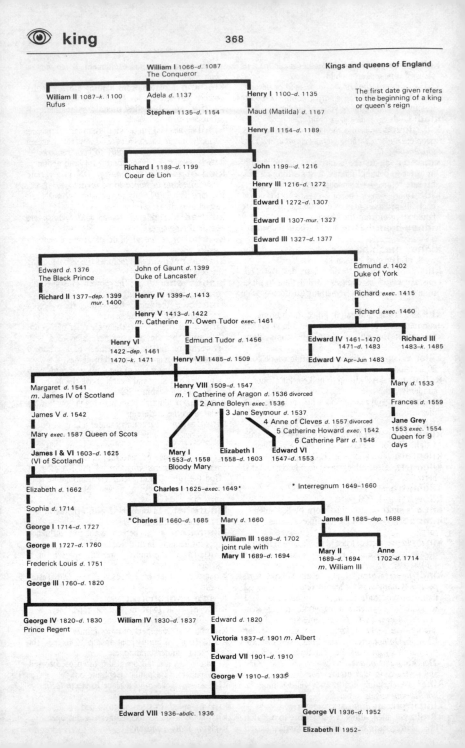

Kings and queens of England

The first date given refers to the beginning of a king or queen's reign

kirtle *n* *old use* a woman's loose outer garment or skirt

kiss¹ *v* 1 to touch with the lips as a greeting or sign of love 2 to express by kissing: *He kissed them goodbye* 3 to touch gently: *The wind kissed her hair* 4 **kiss the dust/ground** to show acceptance of defeat — ~**able** *adj*

kiss² *n* 1 an act of kissing 2 **kiss of life** a method of reviving a drowning person by breathing into his mouth

kisser *n* 1 a person who kisses 2 *sl* the mouth

kit *n* 1 the clothes and other articles of a soldier, sailor, traveller, etc. 2 a set of articles needed for a purpose: *a toy aircraft kit* —see also KIT OUT

kitchen *n* a room used for cooking

kitchenette *n* a very small kitchen

kitchen garden *n* a garden for one's own fruit and vegetables

kitchen-sink drama *n* serious plays about working-class home life

kite *n* 1 a type of large hawk that kills small animals 2 a very light frame covered with paper or cloth for flying at the end of a long string 3 *technical* a quadrilateral with one line of symmetry ☞ MATHEMATICS

kith and kin *n* relatives and usu. friends

kit out also **kit up**— *v adv* -tt- to supply with necessary things: *all kitted out for the holiday*

kitsch *n* silly worthless popular ornamental objects, poems, etc., which pretend to be art — ~**y** *adj*

kitten *n* a young cat — ~**ish** *adj* — ~**ishly** *adv*

kittiwake *n* any of several kinds of gull with long wings

kitty¹ *n* -ties a cat or kitten

kitty² *n* -ties 1 (in some card games) money put out by all the players at the beginning and taken by the winner —compare POT 2 *esp. spoken* money collected by a group for an agreed purpose

kiwi *n* -s 1 a New Zealand bird with very short wings that cannot fly 2 *sl* a New Zealander

klaxon *n* a very loud horn or its noise

Kleenex *n* *trademark* thin soft paper, used as a handkerchief

kleptomania *n* a disease of the mind causing an uncontrollable desire to steal — ~**c** *n*

km *abbrev. for:* kilometre(s)

knack *n* a skill or ability: *He has a knack of making friends*

knacker *n* 1 a person who buys and kills old horses 2 a person who buys and breaks up old buildings, ships, etc.

knackered *adj* *sl* very tired

knave *n* 1 *old use* a dishonest man 2 a jack in cards — **knavish** *adj* — **knavishly** *adv* — **knavishness, knavery** *n*

knead *v* 1 to mix (flour and water for bread) together by pressing with the hands 2 to press in a similar way on (something, such as a muscle)

knee¹ *n* 1 the middle joint of the leg 2 the part of a garment that covers the knee

knee² *v* **kneed, kneeing** to hit with the knee

kneecap *n* the bone in front of the knee ☞ ANATOMY

kneel *v* **knelt, kneeling** to go down on the knee(s): *She knelt to pray*

knell *n* 1 the sound of a bell on a sad occasion 2 anything warning of something sad

knew *past tense of* KNOW

knickerbockers *n* loose breeches that fit tightly just below the knees, worn esp. in former times —compare PLUS FOURS

knickers *n* women's underpants

knick-knack, nicknack *n* a small ornamental object

knife¹ *n* **knives** a blade fixed in a handle for cutting

knife² *v* **knifed, knifing** to strike with a knife used as a weapon

knife-edge *n* on a knife-edge **a** very anxious about some future result **b** with the results extremely uncertain: *The plan's success was balanced on a knife-edge*

knight¹ *n* 1 (in former times) a noble soldier on horseback serving a ruler 2 a man given the title 'Sir' by the king or queen of England 3 (in chess) a piece, usu. with a horse's head, that moves 2 squares forward and one to the side — ~**hood** *n* — ~**ly** *adj*

knight² *v* to make (someone) a knight

knit *v* **knitted** *or (rare)* **knit, knitting** 1 to make (clothing) by joining threads into a network by means of long needles: *knit a sock* 2 *technical* to use the commonest stitch in this activity: *Knit one, purl one* —see also PLAIN 3 to unite closely: *The 2 edges of that broken bone will knit together smoothly* — ~**ter** *n*

knitting *n* that which is being knitted

knitwear *n* knitted clothing

knives *pl. of* KNIFE

knob *n* 1 a round handle or control button 2 any round lump: *a knob of butter* — ~**bly** *adj*

knock¹ *v* 1 to strike a blow, usu. making a noise: *Please knock on the door* 2 to hit hard 3 *sl* to express unfavourable opinions about 4 (of an engine) to make a noise because something is mechanically wrong 5 *sl* to surprise greatly; shock —see also KNOCK ABOUT, KNOCK BACK, KNOCK DOWN, KNOCK OFF, KNOCK ON, KNOCK OUT, KNOCK UP

knock² *n* 1 a sound caused by knocking 2 a piece of bad luck or trouble 3 *esp. spoken* (in cricket) a player's innings

knockabout *adj* 1 causing laughter by rough noisy acting; slapstick 2 (of clothes, cars, etc.) suitable for rough use

knock about¹ also **knock around**— *v prep esp. spoken* to lie unnoticed in (a place): *That's been knocking about the house for years*

knock about² also **knock around**— *v adv esp. spoken* 1 to be present or active: *He's been knocking about here for years* 2 to travel continuously: *He's knocked about in Africa* **3** to be seen in public (with someone) **4** to treat roughly: *He knocks his wife about*

knock back *v adv esp. spoken* **1** to drink (something) quickly **2** to cost: *That car knocked her back $5000* **3** to surprise: *The news knocked him back*

knockdown *adj* the lowest possible (esp. in the phrase **knockdown price**)

knock down *v adv* **1** to destroy (a building, bridge, etc.) by blows **2** to strike to the ground with a vehicle **3** to sell at an unusually low price

knocker *n* **1** a person who knocks **2** a metal instrument for knocking on a door

knockers *n sl* a woman's breasts

knock-kneed *adj* having knees that turn inwards

knock off *v adv* **1** *esp. spoken* to stop work **2** *sl* to steal **3** to reduce a total payment by: *I'll knock $2 off* **4** *esp. spoken* to do or finish quickly

knock on also **knock forward—** *v adv* (in rugby) to break the rules by causing (the ball) to fall in front of one by dropping a catch — **knock-on** *n*

knockout *n* **1** also (*sl*) **KO—** a knocking out of one boxer by another **2** *esp spoken* someone or something causing admiration

knock out *v adv* **1** (in boxing) to make (one's opponent) unable to rise for 10 seconds **2** *esp. spoken* to surprise **3** (of a drug) to put to sleep **4** to force out of a competition: *Our team was knocked out early* —see also **knock the** BOTTOM **out of**

knock up *v adv* **1** *esp. spoken* to make in a hurry: *to knock up a meal* **2** *esp. spoken* to make (money, a score, etc.): *He knocked up 45 runs* **3** *esp. spoken* to awaken by knocking **4** (esp. in tennis) to practise before beginning a game **5** *esp. spoken* to tire (someone)

knot¹ *n* **1** a lumplike fastening formed by tying **2** a hard mass in wood where a branch has come off a tree **3** a hard mass: *His muscles stood out in knots* **4** a small close group of people **5** a measure of the speed of a ship, about 1,853 metres (about 6,080 feet) per hour

knot² *v* **-tt-** to make a knot in or join with knots: *to knot the rope tightly*

knotty *adj* **-tier, -tiest** **1** (of wood) containing knots **2** full of difficulties: *a knotty question*

know¹ *v* **knew** , **known, knowing** **1** to have (information): *I know that is true* **2** to have learnt: *I know how to swim* **3** to have seen, heard, etc.: *I've known him to run faster than that* **4** to experience: *He has known both grief and happiness* **5** to be familiar with (someone): *I've known him for years* **6** to recognize: *She knows good food* **7** **know all the answers** to behave as if one knew everything **8** **you know** (used for adding force to a statement): *You'll have to try harder, you know* —see also **know** APART

know² *n* **in the know** well-informed

know-all also **know-it-all—** *n* a person who behaves as if he knew everything

know-how *n esp. spoken* practical skill

knowing *adj* showing secret understanding: *a knowing smile*

knowingly *adv* **1** in a knowing manner **2** intentionally: *She would never knowingly hurt anyone*

knowledge *n* **1** that which is known; understanding: *a knowledge of French* **2** familiarity with: *a good knowledge of London* —compare LEARNING

knowledgeable *adj* having knowledge; well-informed — **-bly** *adv*

known¹ *adj* generally recognized (as being something): *a known criminal*

known² *past part. of* KNOW

knuckle *n* **1** a finger joint **2** **rap over the knuckles a** (to give) a blow on the knuckles **b** (to make) an attack with words

knuckle down *v adv* **-led, -ling down** to start working hard

knuckle-duster *n* a metal covering for the knuckles, to make punches harder

knuckle under *v adv* to yield

KO¹ *n esp. spoken* a knockout

KO² *v* **ko'd, ko'ing** *esp. spoken* KNOCK OUT

koala also **koala bear—** *n* a type of Australian animal (MARSUPIAL) like a small furry bear with no tail, which climbs trees ⇒MAMMAL

kohl *n* a powder used in the East as eye makeup

kookaburra *n* an Australian bird with a cry like laughter

kopeck, -pek also **copeck** —— *n* (a coin worth) 0.01 of a rouble ⇒MONEY

Koran *n* the holy book of the Muslims — ~**ic** *adj*

kosher *adj* **1** of or about food which is lawful for Jews to eat **2** *esp. spoken* proper: *Things were all kosher*

kowtow¹ also **kotow—** *n* a former Chinese ceremony of touching the ground with the head as a sign of respect

kowtow² also **kotow—** *v* **1** to perform a kowtow **2** to be too humble: *Don't kowtow to him*

kraal *n S African* an enclosed area for cows, sheep, etc. at night

Kremlin *n* **1** the buildings in Moscow from which the Soviet Union is ruled **2** the government of the Soviet Union

krona *n* **-nor** the standard coin in the money system of Sweden ⇒MONEY

krone *n* **-ner** the standard coin in the money system of Denmark and Norway ⇒MONEY

kudos *n* praise, thanks, etc., (for something done): *He got a lot of kudos for his work*

Ku Klux Klan *n* (in the US) a secret organization whose members must be Protestant white men born in the United States

kung fu *n* a Chinese style of fighting related to karate

kw *abbrev. for:* kilowatt(s)

kwashiorkor *n* a tropical children's disease caused by protein deficiency

L, I L's, I's *or* Ls, Is **1** the 12th letter of the English alphabet **2** the Roman numeral for 50
L *abbrev. for:* (on an L-plate) learner; a driver who has not yet passed his test
la *n* the 6th note in the sol-fa musical scale
Lab *abbrev. for:* LABOUR PARTY
label¹ *n* **1** a piece of material fixed to something, on which is written what it is, where it is to go, etc. **2** a word or phrase describing a group or class
label² *v* **-ll-** **1** to fix a label on **2** to describe as: *His enemies labelled the boy a thief*
laboratory *also* lab— *n* **-ies** a place where a scientist works, with apparatus for examining and testing materials
laborious *adj* needing or showing great effort or difficulty — ~ly *adv* — ~ness *n*
labour¹ *n* **1** work or effort —see WORK (USAGE) **2** workers, esp. those who use their hands **3** giving birth **4** a piece of work —see also HARD LABOUR
labour² *v* **1** to work, esp. hard **2** to move with difficulty; struggle: *She laboured up the hill*
Labour *n, adj* (of or supporting) the Labour party — ~ite *n*
Labour Day *n* Labour Days a day when workers make a public show with marches, meetings, etc.
labourer *n* a worker whose job needs strength rather than skill
labour exchange *n* EMPLOYMENT EXCHANGE
labour of love *n* labours of love a piece of work done gladly
Labour party *n* Labour parties a political party trying to improve the conditions of the less wealthy
labour under *v prep* to suffer from: *He laboured under a misunderstanding*
Labrador *n* a kind of large dog
laburnum *n* a small ornamental tree with long hanging stems of yellow flowers
labyrinth *n* **1** a network of twisting and crossing passages; a maze **2** something complicated or difficult to understand — ~ine *adj*
lace¹ *n* **1** a string pulled through holes in neighbouring edges to draw them together: *shoelaces* **2** a netlike ornamental cloth
lace² *v* laced, lacing **1** to draw together with a lace **2** to pass (a string, thread, etc.) through holes in (something) **3** to add a little alcohol to (weaker drink)
lace into *v prep esp. spoken* to attack (someone) with words or blows
lacerate *v* **-rated, -rating** *technical* to tear

(flesh) roughly: *He lacerated his face* — **-ration** *n*
lachrymal *adj* of or concerning tears or the organ (**lachrymal gland**) that produces them
lack¹ *v* **1** to be without; not have **2** to have less than enough of; need USAGE To **lack** something is to be without it, but one may be quite happy about this: *He lacks conscience.* If one is **short** of something one has less than enough, and to be *in* **want** of anything is to need it badly.
lack² *n* absence or need: *The plants died for lack of water*
lackadaisical *adj* lazy and not interested — ~ly *adv*
lackey *n* **-eys** *offensive* a person who obeys another without question
lacking *adj* **1** not present; missing: *Help was lacking* **2** *esp. spoken* with low powers of thought
lacklustre *adj* (esp. of eyes) lacking brightness
laconic *adj* using few words — ~ally *adv*
lacquer *n, v* (to cover with) a transparent, sometimes coloured, substance used to form a hard shiny surface on metal or wood, or for making hair stay in place
lacrosse *n* a field game played by 2 teams, each player having a long stick with a net at the end to throw, catch, and carry the small hard ball
lactic acid *n* an acid found in sour milk
lactose *n* a sugar found in milk
lacy *adj* **-ier, -iest** of or like lace
lad *n* **1** a boy; youth **2** *esp. N English* a fellow **3** *esp. spoken* a rather bold man
ladder¹ *n* **1** a frame of 2 bars or ropes of equal length joined by shorter bars that form steps for climbing **2** a fault in a stocking caused by stitches coming undone **3** (in sports such as table tennis) a list of players who play each other regularly to decide who is best
ladder² *v* to cause to develop a ladder in a stocking
laddie, -dy *n* **-dies** *esp. Scots* a boy; lad
laden *adj* **1** heavily loaded: *bushes laden with fruit* **2** deeply troubled: *laden with sorrow*
la-di-da, lah-di-dah *adj esp. spoken* pretending to be of high social position by using unnaturally fancy manners
Ladies, -dies' *n* Ladies(') a women's public lavatory
ladies' man, lady's man *n* a man who enjoys women's company
ladle¹ *n* a large deep long-handled spoon for lifting liquids out of a container
ladle² *v* ladled, ladling to serve (food) with or as if with a ladle
lady *n* ladies **1 a** a woman of good social position or good manners —compare GENTLEMAN **b** a woman in control: *the lady of the house* **2** *polite* a woman
Lady *n* a title put before the name of **a** a woman of noble rank **b** the wife of a knight or the wife or

daughter of a nobleman of certain ranks: *Lady Wilson* **c** another title: *Lady President*

ladybird *n* a small round beetle, often red with black dots

lady-in-waiting *n* **ladies-in-waiting** a lady who attends a queen or princess

lady-killer *n* *esp. spoken* a man who charms women

ladylike *adj* looking or behaving like a lady

ladyship *n* the word used to or of a Lady (in the phrases **her ladyship; your ladyship**)

lag¹ *v* **-gg-** to move more slowly: *He lagged behind us*

lag² *v* **-gg-** to cover (water pipes and containers) to prevent heat loss

lag³ *n* *sl* a man sent to prison

lager *n* light beer

lagging *n* material used to lag a water pipe or container

lagoon *n* a lake of sea water, partly or completely separated from the sea

lah-di-dah *adj* la-di-da

laid *past tense and past part. of* LAY

lain *past part. of* LIE

lair *n* a wild animal's home

laird *n* a Scottish landowner —compare SQUIRE

laissez-faire, laisser-faire *n* *French* (the principle of) allowing people's activities to develop without control

laity *n* **1** people who are not priests, ministers, etc. **2** people without a particular professional training, as compared with those who have it

lake¹ *n* a large mass of water surrounded by land

lake² also **crimson lake——** *n* a deep bluish-red colouring matter

lama *n* a type of Buddhist priest of Tibet and Mongolia —see also DALAI LAMA

lamb¹ *n* **1** a young sheep **2** its meat **3** *esp. spoken* a young gentle person

lamb² *v* (of sheep) to give birth

lambaste also **lambast—** *v* **-basted, -basting** *esp. spoken* to attack fiercely

lambda *n* the 11th letter of the Greek alphabet (Λ, λ)

lambskin *n* **1** the skin of a lamb, esp. with its wool **2** leather made from lambskin

lame¹ *adj* **1** not able to walk easily or properly as a result of weakness or accident **2** not easily believed: *a lame excuse* — ~**ly** *adv* — ~**ness** *n*

lame² *v* **lamed, laming** to make lame

lamé *n* cloth containing gold or silver threads

lame duck *n* a helpless person or business

lament¹ *v* to feel or express sorrow — ~**ation** *n*

lament² *n* **1** a strong expression of sorrow **2** a piece of music expressing sorrow, esp. for a death

lamentable *adj* **1** sad **2** bad in quality — **-bly** *adv*

laminate¹ *v* **-nated, -nating** **1** to split into thin layers **2** to make (a strong material) by

uniting many layers **3** to cover with thin metal or plastic sheets

laminate² *n* material made by laminating

lam into *v prep* **-mm-** *sl* to attack with words or blows

lamp *n* an apparatus for giving light —see also BLOWLAMP

lamp-black *n* a black colouring material made from soot

lampoon *n, v* (to attack by means of) a piece of fierce writing making a person, government, etc. look foolish — ~**ist** *n*

lamppost *n* a pillar supporting a lamp which lights a public area

lamprey *n* **-preys** a snakelike fish with a sucking mouth ⟶EVOLUTION

lampshade *n* a cover for a lamp

lance¹ *n* a long spear used by mounted soldiers in former times

lance² *v* **lanced, lancing** to cut (flesh) with a medical instrument usu. to let pus escape

lancer *n* a soldier in a regiment formerly armed with lances

land¹ *n* **1** the solid dry part of the earth's surface **2** part of the earth's surface all of the same natural type: *forest land | lowland* **3** a country or nation: *war between lands* **4** earth; soil **5** ground owned as property: *You are on my land* **6** ground used for farming **7 see how the land lies** to try to discover the present state of affairs

land² *v* **1** to come to, bring to, or put on land or water: *The ship landed the goods at Dover. | Our plane landed on the sea* **2** to come, put, arrive, or cause to arrive in a condition or place: *That will land him in prison* **3** to catch (a fish) **4** *esp. spoken* to obtain; gain **5** *esp. spoken* to strike: *I landed a blow on his nose*

landau *n* a 4-wheeled carriage with 2 seats and a top that folds back in 2 parts

land breeze *n* a light wind blowing from the land to the sea

landed *adj* owning or made up of land: *a landed family | landed property*

landfall *n* the first sight of land after a journey by sea or air

landing *n* **1** the level space or passage at the top of stairs **2** arriving or bringing to land **3** a place where people and goods are landed

landing stage *n* a level surface, floating or over water, onto which passengers and goods are landed

landlady *n* **-dies** **1** a woman who owns and runs a small hotel **2** a female landlord

landlocked *adj* enclosed or almost enclosed by land

landlord *n* **1** a person, esp. a man, from whom someone rents property **2** a person, esp. a man, who owns or runs a hotel, pub, etc. —compare LANDLADY

landlubber *n* *esp. spoken* a person not used to ships — ~**ly** *adj*

landmark *n* **1** a tall tree, building, etc., by which one can tell one's position **2** something that marks an important point in history or a person's life **3** something marking the limits of a piece of land

landmine n a bomb in or on the ground, which blows up when a person or vehicle passes over it

land rover n trademark a type of car for driving over rough ground

landscape[1] n **1** a wide view of scenery **2** a picture of such a scene

landscape[2] v **-scaped, -scaping** to improve or arrange (land) with gardens, trees, etc.

landscape gardening n the art of arranging trees, paths, etc.

landslide n **1** a sudden fall of earth or rocks **2** a very large, often unexpected, success in an election

landward adj, adv towards the land — ~s adv

lane n **1** a narrow, often winding, road **2** a fixed route used by ships, aircraft, etc. **3** any of the parallel parts into which wide roads are divided

language n **1** the system of human expression by words **2** a particular system of words: the Russian language **3** any system of signs, movements, etc., used to express meanings: The movement of a cat's tail is part of its language **4** words, phrases, style, etc., peculiar to a group or individual: the poet's/chemist's language **5** impolite or shocking words (esp. in the phrases **bad language, strong language**) ⊚

language laboratory n **-tories** a room in which people can learn foreign languages using tape recorders

languid adj lacking strength or will ⚠ LIMPID — ~ly adv

languish v **1** to lack strength or will **2** to experience long suffering: to languish in prison **3** to become unhappy through desire: She languished for his love

languor n esp. literature **1** an often pleasant lack of strength or will **2** a feeling of tender sadness and desire — ~ous adj — ~ously adv

lank adj **1** very thin **2** (of hair) straight and lifeless — ~ly adv — ~ness n

lanky adj **-ier, -iest** (esp. of a person) very thin and tall — **lankily** adv — **lankiness** n

lanolin n a fatty substance obtained from wool, used in skin creams

lantern n **1** a container that protects a light **2** technical the top of a building (such as a lighthouse), with windows on all sides

lantern-jawed adj having long narrow jaws and hollow cheeks

lanyard n a cord on which a knife or whistle is hung round the neck

lap[1] n **1** the front part of a seated person between waist and knees **2** the clothes covering this

lap[2] v **-pp-** **1** (in racing, swimming, etc.) to be at least one lap ahead of (a competitor) **2** to race

completely round the track: He lapped in 2 minutes

lap[3] n **1** (in racing, swimming, etc.) a single journey round the track **2** one part of a plan or action

lap[4] v **-pp-** **1** to drink by taking up with quick tongue movements **2** to hit with little waves and soft sounds —see also LAP UP

lap[5] n **1** an act of lapping a liquid **2** the sound of lapping, as of waves

lapdog n a small pet dog

lapel n the part of a coat front below the neck that is folded back on each side

lapidary n **-ries** a person skilled in cutting and polishing precious stones

lapis lazuli n a type of bright blue stone

lapse[1] n **1** a small fault or mistake of memory, behaviour, etc. **2** a gradual passing away: after a lapse of several years

lapse[2] v **lapsed, lapsing** **1** to pass gradually: to lapse into silence **2** to fail in correct behaviour, duty, etc. **3** (of business agreements, rights, etc.) to come to an end

lapsed adj no longer following the practices, esp. of one's religion

lap up v adv **-pp-** to accept (esp. something heard) without thought

lapwing also **pewit, peewit**— n a type of bird with raised feathers on its head

larceny n **-nies** law stealing

larch n **1** a type of tall coniferous tree with bright green needle-like leaves **2** its strong hard wood

lard[1] n purified pig fat, used in cookery

lard[2] v **1** to put lard or bacon into or on (meat) before cooking **2** to ornament (speech or writing) with noticeable phrases

larder n a room or cupboard for food —see also PANTRY

large adj **1** more than usual in size, number, or amount; big **2** **at large a** (esp. of dangerous people or animals) free; uncontrolled **b** as a whole: The country at large is hoping for changes —see also BY AND LARGE — ~ness n

large-hearted adj generous, kind, or forgiving — ~ness n

large intestine n the lower bowel, where food becomes solid waste —compare SMALL INTESTINE

largely adv **1** to a great degree; chiefly: largely desert land **2** in great quantity

largesse n French generosity to those in need

largo adv, adj, n **-gos** (a piece of music) played slowly or solemnly

lark[1] n esp. spoken something done for a joke

lark[2] n any of several small light brown birds with long pointed wings, esp. the skylark

lark about also **lark around**— v adv esp. spoken to play around

larrup v esp. spoken to hit; beat

larva n **-vae** the wormlike young of an insect between leaving the egg and changing into a winged form — ~l adj

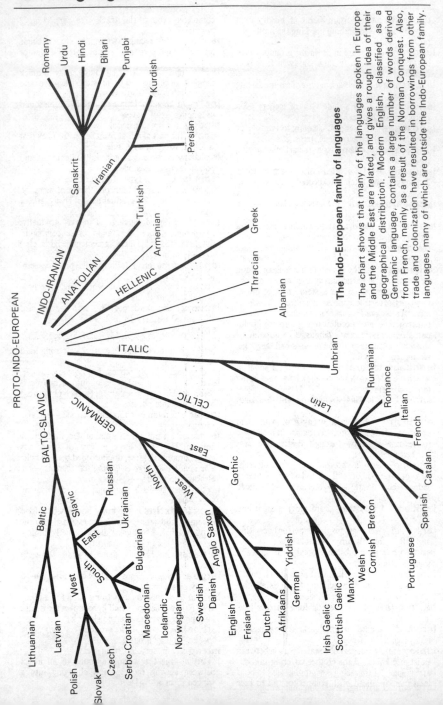

The Indo-European family of languages

The chart shows that many of the languages spoken in Europe and the Middle East are related, and gives a rough idea of their geographical distribution. Modern English, classified as a Germanic language, contains a large number of words derived from French, mainly as a result of the Norman Conquest. Also, trade and colonization have resulted in borrowings from other languages, many of which are outside the Indo-European family.

PROTO-INDO-EUROPEAN

INDO-IRANIAN
- Sanskrit
  - Romany
  - Urdu
  - Hindi
  - Bihari
  - Punjabi
- Iranian
  - Kurdish
  - Persian

ANATOLIAN
- Turkish

- Armenian

HELLENIC
- Greek
- Thracian

- Albanian

ITALIC
- Umbrian
- Latin
  - Rumanian
  - Romance
  - Italian
  - French
  - Catalan
  - Spanish
  - Portuguese

CELTIC
- Irish Gaelic
- Scottish Gaelic
- Manx
- Welsh
- Cornish
- Breton

GERMANIC
- East
  - Gothic
- North
  - Icelandic
  - Norwegian
  - Swedish
  - Danish
- West
  - English
  - Frisian
  - Dutch
  - Afrikaans
  - German
  - Yiddish
  - Anglo Saxon

BALTO-SLAVIC
- Baltic
  - Lithuanian
  - Latvian
- Slavic
  - East
    - Russian
    - Ukrainian
  - South
    - Bulgarian
    - Macedonian
    - Serbo-Croatian
  - West
    - Polish
    - Slovak
    - Czech

laryngitis *n* a painful swollen condition of the larynx

larynx *n* the hollow boxlike part at the upper end of the windpipe in which sounds are produced — **laryngeal** *adj*

lasagna *n* long flat pieces of pasta wider than spaghetti

lascivious *adj* causing or feeling uncontrolled sexual desire — ~**ly** *adv* — ~**ness** *n*

laser *n* an apparatus that produces a very powerful beam of light that has various uses including cutting materials, sending messages, and making fine measurements —compare MASER

lash¹ *v* 1 to strike with or as if with a whip 2 to move violently or suddenly: *The cat's tail lashed about* 3 to attack violently with words 4 to tie firmly

lash² *n* 1 the thin striking part of a whip 2 a stroke with a whip 3 a sudden movement 4 violent beating: *the lash of the waves* 5 *old use* an official whipping 6 an eyelash

lashing *n* 1 a beating 2 a rope for binding

lashings *n* *esp. spoken* plenty, esp. of food and drink

lash out *v adv* 1 to attack someone with violence or violent words 2 *esp. spoken* to give out (esp. money) in large quantities

lass also **lassie**— *n* *Scots & N English* 1 a young girl or woman 2 a girlfriend

lasso¹ also **lariat**— *n* **-sos** a rope with one end that can be tightened in a noose for catching horses and cattle

lasso² *v* **-soed, -soing** to catch with a lasso

last¹ *adj, pron* 1 (the one or ones) after all others: *He was the last to arrive.* | *the last post* 2 the one before now; most recent: *the last election* | *last Thursday*

last² *adv* 1 after all others 2 at the time in the past nearest to now: *When did we last meet?*

last³ *v* 1 to continue: *Our holiday lasts 10 days.* | *a lasting sorrow* 2 to be enough for: *This food will last them 3 days*

last⁴ *n* a model of a human foot, used by shoemakers

last judgment *n* JUDGMENT DAY

lastly *adv* in the end: . . . *Lastly, let me mention my wife*

last straw *n* the trouble that makes the total unbearable when added to one's present troubles

last word *n* 1 the word or phrase that ends an argument 2 *esp. spoken* the most modern example: *the last word in cars*

latch *n* 1 a simple fastening for a door, gate, etc., worked by dropping a bar into a slot 2 a spring lock for a house door

latch on *v adv* *esp. spoken* to understand; CATCH ON

latch onto *v prep* *esp. spoken* 1 to understand 2 a to forbid (someone) to go b to refuse to leave (someone)

late¹ *adv* 1 after the expected time 2 towards the end of a period 3 of late recently

late² *adj* 1 arriving, developing, happening, etc., after the expected time 2 happening towards the end of a period 3 happening or existing recently: *the late government* 4 recently died: *her late husband* 5 just arrived; fresh: *some late news* — ~**ness** *n*

latecomer *n* someone who arrives late

lately *adv* recently

latent *adj* existing but not yet noticeable, active, etc.: *a latent infection* — **-tency** *n*

latent heat *n* the additional heat necessary to change a solid (at its melting point) into a liquid, or a liquid (at its boiling point) into a gas

lateral *adj* of, at, from, or towards the side — **-rally** *adv*

latest *n* 1 the most recent news, fashion, or example: *Have you heard the latest?* 2 **at the latest** and no later: *tomorrow at the latest*

latex *n* a thick whitish liquid produced by certain plants, esp. the rubber tree

lath *n* a long flat narrow piece esp. of wood used to support plaster, tiles, or slates

lathe *n* a machine that turns a piece of wood or metal round and round against a sharp tool that shapes it

lather¹ *n* 1 a a white mass of soap and water bubbles b the sweat of a hard-ridden horse, which looks like this 2 **in a lather** worried because hurried — ~**y** *adj*

lather² *v* 1 to produce a lather 2 to cover with lather 3 *esp. spoken* to attack with blows

Latin *n, adj* 1 (of) the language of ancient Rome ⌐ LANGUAGE 2 (a member) of any nation that speaks a language that comes from Latin

Latin American *adj* of the Spanish- or Portuguese-speaking countries of America

latitude *n* 1 the distance north or south of the equator measured in degrees —compare LONGITUDE ⌐ GLOBE 2 freedom in action, expression, etc.

latitudinal *adj* of latitude

latrine *n* (esp. in camps) a toilet, often just a hole in the ground

latter *adj* *esp. written* 1 nearer to the end; later: *the latter years of his life* 2 the second of 2 people or things just spoken of: *Did he walk or swim? The latter seems unlikely* —opposite **former**

latterly *adv* lately —opposite **formerly**

lattice *n* 1 an open framework of flat wooden or metal lengths crossed over 2 a window with many small pieces of glass held together by bands of lead

laudable *adj* deserving praise —compare LAUDATORY — **-bility** *n* — **-bly** *adv*

laudatory *adj* expressing praise —compare LAUDABLE

laugh¹ *v* to express amusement, happiness, disrespect, etc., by making explosive sounds, usu. while smiling

laugh² *n* 1 the act or sound of laughing 2 *esp. spoken* something done for a joke

laughable *adj* 1 funny 2 foolish or silly — **-bly** *adv*

laughing gas *n* a gas used to produce unconsciousness, esp. for short dental operations

laughingstock *n* somebody or something very foolish

laughter *n* the act or sound of laughing

launch¹ *v* 1 to set (a boat) into the water 2 to send (a modern weapon or instrument) into the sky or space 3 to throw with great force 4 to begin (an activity, plan, etc.)

launch² *n* a large usu. motor-driven boat for use on rivers, harbours, etc.

launching pad also **launching site**— *n* a base from which rockets are launched ⊂⊃SPACE

launch out *v adv* to begin something new

launder *v* to wash and usu. iron (clothes, sheets, etc.)

launderette also (*esp .US*) **laundromat**— *n* a place where the public may wash clothes in coin-operated machines

laundress *n* a woman who washes and irons clothes

laundry *n* **-dries** 1 a place where clothes are washed and ironed 2 clothes, sheets, etc., needing washing or just washed

laureate *adj* see POET LAUREATE

laurel *n* 1 a kind of small tree with smooth shiny evergreen leaves 2 a circle of these leaves, given as a sign of honour

laurels *n* 1 honour or fame 2 **rest on one's laurels** to be satisfied with what one has done already

lava *n* 1 molten rock flowing from a volcano 2 rock formed by the cooling of molten lava — compare MAGMA

lavatory also (*esp. spoken*) **lav**— *n* **-ries** 1 a large seatlike bowl connected to a drain, used for getting rid of the body's waste matter 2 a room or building containing this

lavender *n* 1 a plant with small sweet-smelling pale purple flowers 2 the dried flowers and stems of this plant used for giving stored clothes, sheets, etc., a pleasant smell 3 pale purple

lavish *adj* 1 very generous or wasteful: *a lavish spender* 2 produced in great quantity: *lavish praise* — ~ly *adv* — ~ness *n*

lavish on *v prep* to give generously or wastefully: *He lavished kindness on his friends*

law *n* 1 a rule supported by government power that members of society must follow 2 the whole body of such rules in a country: *The law forbids stealing* 3 the whole body of these rules and the way they work: *to study law* 4 an accepted rule of behaviour: *the laws of cricket* 5 a statement of what always seems to happen in certain conditions: *Boyle's law is a scientific principle* 7 *esp. spoken* the police or a policeman 8 **be a law unto oneself** to do what one wishes, regardless of laws 9 **go to law** to begin a law case 10 **lay down the law** to give an opinion or order firmly

law-abiding *adj* obeying the law

lawbreaker *n* a criminal

lawful *adj* 1 recognized or allowed by law: *a lawful marriage* 2 obeying the law — ~ly *adv* — ~ness *n*

lawless *adj* 1 (of a place) not governed by laws or where laws are ignored 2 uncontrolled; wild — ~ly *adv* — ~ness *n*

lawn¹ *n* a stretch of smooth ground covered with closely cut grass

lawn² *n* fine smooth material, as used in summer dresses, handkerchiefs, etc.

lawn tennis *n* tennis, esp. when played on grass

lawsuit also **suit**— *n* a noncriminal case in a law court

lawyer *n* a person (esp. a solicitor) whose business is the law

lax *adj* 1 careless or lazy; not strict 2 lacking in control; loose: *lax muscles* — ~ly *adv* — ~ness, ~ity *n*

laxative *n, adj* (a substance that is) mildly purgative

lay¹ *v* **laid, laying** 1 to place, put, or set: *Lay it on the table.* | *to lay bricks* 2 to place knives, forks, etc., on, ready for a meal (esp. in the phrase **lay the table**) 3 to cause to settle: *The rain laid the dust* 4 (of birds, insects, etc.) to produce (an egg or eggs): *The hens aren't laying* 5 to bet (esp. money) on the result of some happening 6 to put into a particular condition, esp. of weakness, helplessness, etc.: *The country was laid in ruins* —see also LAY LOW 7 to make (a claim, charge, etc.) in an official way: *to lay claim to a title* 8 to cover or spread over: *He laid mats on the floor* 9 **lay hold of** to catch and hold firmly —see also LAY ABOUT, LAY IN, LAY INTO, LAY OFF, LAY ON, LAY OUT, LAY UP   USAGE Do not confuse **lay** (laid) with **lie** (lay, lain). A person, or creature, always **lays** something: *The hen lays an egg.* | *She laid the table.* BUT the verb **lie** does not take an object: *She went to lie down.* | *The book lay on the table.* A third verb, **lie** (lied) means 'to tell a lie'.

lay² *n* **lays** the manner or position in which something lies

lay³ *adj* 1 (in a religion) of or by people who are not priests, ministers, etc. 2 (in a profession) not trained

lay⁴ *n* **lays** a short poem or song, esp. one that tells a story

lay⁵ *past tense of* LIE

layabout *n esp. spoken* a lazy person

lay about *v prep* to attack wildly

lay-by *n* **-bys** a space by a road where vehicles may pull over safely

layer¹ *n* 1 a thickness of some material laid over a surface: *Cover them with a layer of earth* 2 a bird that lays eggs 3 a plant stem that has been fastened partly under the ground, to root and become a separate plant

layer² *v* 1 to make a layer of; put down in layers 2 to fasten (a stem) down and cover with earth

lay in *v adv* to store a supply of

lay into *v prep* to attack

lay low v adv 1 to bring down 2 to make ill

layman n -men 1 a person who is not a priest 2 a person not trained in a particular subject, as compared with those who are

lay off v adv; prep 1 to stop employing (a worker) 2 esp. spoken to stop: Lay off hitting me!

lay on v adv 1 to provide 2 also **lay upon**— to put (some serious responsibility) upon (someone) 3 **lay it on a** to go beyond the truth in telling something **b** to praise too greatly

layout n 1 the planned arrangement of a town, building, etc. 2 the way in which printed matter is set out on paper

lay out v adv 1 to spread out 2 to plan (a building, town, etc.) 3 to knock (a person) down 4 esp. spoken to spend

lay up v adv 1 to store for future use 2 (of an illness) to keep indoors or in bed 3 to put (a boat) out of service

laze v lazed, lazing to rest lazily

lazy adj lazier, laziest 1 disliking activity 2 encouraging inactivity: a lazy afternoon — **-zily** adv — **-ziness** n

lb abbrev. for: pound (weight)

lbw abbrev. for: leg before wicket

LCM abbrev. for: least/lowest common multiple: 20 is the LCM of 4 and 5

lea n poetic an open piece of grassy land

leach v technical 1 to separate substances from (a material, such as soil) by passing water through- 2 (of substances in a material) to disappear by the action of water

lead¹ v led, leading 1 to show (somebody) the way; guide 2 to be the means of reaching a place: The path leads to the village 3 to direct, control, or govern (an army, people, etc.) 4 (esp. in sports) to be ahead 5 to start or open a game, esp. of cards, with: She led her highest card 6 to experience; pass: He led a hard life —see also LEAD ON

lead² n 1 a guiding example 2 a clue; hint 3 the front place in a race, competition, etc. 4 the distance by which a person or thing is in front: Our product has a good lead over our competitor's 5 (in card games) the right to play the first card 6 the chief acting part in a play or film 7 the opening part of a newspaper article 8 also **leash**— a length of leather, chain, etc., tied to a dog to control it 9 a wire that carries electrical power 10 **take the lead** to start an action or take control

lead³ n 1 a soft heavy metal that is an element, used for waterpipes, to cover roofs, etc. 2 a thin rope with a weight on one end lowered from a ship to measure the water's depth 3 graphite, esp. used in pencils —see also WHITE LEAD

leaden adj 1 made of lead 2 dull grey: a leaden sky 3 sad: a leaden heart

leader n 1 a person or thing that leads, esp. one that directs a group, movement, etc. 2 the first violin player of an orchestra 3 an editorial: the leaders in 'The Times'

leadership n 1 the position of leader 2 the qualities necessary in a leader 3 a group of people who lead

leading adj 1 most important; chief 2 guiding or controlling

leading question n a question formed so that it suggests the answer

lead on v adv to cause (someone) to believe something false or do something foolish

leaf n leaves 1 one of the usu. flat green parts of a plant that grow from a stem or branch 2 any thin flat object, such as a book page, a sheet of gold, a removable part of a tabletop, etc. 3 **turn over a new leaf** to start again, with better behaviour

leafed adj leaved

leaflet n 1 a small sheet of printed matter 2 one part of a leaf made up of several parts

leaf mould n dead decaying leaves which form a rich top surface to soil

leaf through v prep, adv to turn the pages of (a book, magazine, etc.) quickly

leafy adj -ier, -iest covered with leaves

league¹ n old use about 3 miles or 5 kilometres

league² n 1 a group of people, countries, etc., joined together for protection or for some aim 2 a group of sports clubs or players that play matches amongst themselves 3 **in league (with)** working together, often for a bad purpose

league³ v leagued, leaguing to unite in a league

leak¹ v 1 to let through or pass through a leak 2 to make known (secret information)

leak² n 1 a small accidental hole through which something flows 2 the liquid, gas, etc., that escapes through such a hole 3 an accidental spreading of secret information 4 sl an act of passing water from the body

leakage n the act or amount of leaking or that which leaks through

leaky adj -ier, -iest letting liquid leak in or out: a leaky bucket — **-ily** adv — **-iness** n

lean¹ v leant or leaned, leaning 1 to rest in a sloping position: She leaned against his shoulder 2 to rest (something) in a sloping position: Lean it against the wall 3 **lean over backwards** to make every possible effort

lean² adj 1 without much fat: lean meat | a lean man 2 producing or having little value — ~**ness** n

lean³ n the lean part of meat

leaning n a feeling or opinion

lean-to n -tos a small roofed building that rests on the side of a larger one

leap¹ v leapt or leaped, leaping 1 to spring; jump 2 to pass, rise, etc., rapidly: The idea leaped into his mind

leap² n 1 a sudden jump 2 a sudden increase in number, quantity, etc.

leap at v prep to accept (a chance, offer, etc.) eagerly

leapfrog n a game in which one person bends down and another jumps over him

leap year n a year, every 4th year, in which February has 29 days instead of 28

learn v learned or learnt, learning 1 to gain knowledge (of) or skill (in): *I'm learning French.* | *to learn quickly* 2 to memorize: *Learn this list of words* 3 to become informed: *She'll learn of my success* 4 **learn one's lesson** to suffer so much from doing something that one will not do it again — ~er n   USAGE In British English **learnt** is as common as **learned** in the past, although Americans usually say **learned**. **Learnt** may be preferred to avoid confusion with **learned**, the adjective.

learned adj having or passing on much knowledge gained by study: *a learned professor/book* — ~ly adv

learning n deep knowledge gained by study —compare KNOWLEDGE

lease¹ n a written agreement by which an owner gives the use of a property to somebody for a period in return for rent

lease² v leased, leasing to give or take (property) on a lease

leasehold n, adj (property) held on a lease —compare FREEHOLD — ~er n

leash n a dog's lead

least¹ adj (superlative of LITTLE) 1 smallest in size, amount, etc. 2 slightest: *I haven't the least idea*

least² n 1 the smallest thing, amount, etc.: *Giving him food was the least we could do* 2 **at least** if nothing else 3 **at the least** not less than

least³ adv 1 in the smallest amount, degree, etc.: *when we least expected it* 2 **least of all** especially not 3 **not least** partly; quite importantly: *Trade has been bad, not least because of increased costs*

leather n animal skin treated to preserve it

leatherette n cheap material that looks like leather

leathery adj hard and stiff: *leathery meat*

leave¹ v left, leaving 1 to go away or go away from: *The car left the road.* | *We must leave early* 2 to cease to remain in or with: *I am leaving England/my wife* 3 to allow to remain: *The window was left open* 4 to allow to remain undone, untaken, etc.: *Leave that work for now* 5 to give into the care of someone: *I'll leave buying the tickets to you* 6 to give (through a will) after the death of the giver 7 to have left over: *2 from 8 leaves 6*

leave² n 1 permission 2 permission to be absent, esp. from army service 3 time spent in such an absence 4 a holiday —see HOLIDAY (USAGE) 5 **take leave of** to say goodbye to —see also FRENCH LEAVE, SICK LEAVE

leaved also **leafed**— adj having leaves

leaven v 1 to add a substance such as yeast to (flour and water) to make it rise 2 to influence; change

leaves pl. of LEAF

leave taking n esp. written the act of saying goodbye and going away

lecher n a man continually looking for sexual pleasure — ~ous adj — ~ously adv — ~y, ~ousness n

lectern n a sloping table for holding a book, esp. the Bible in a church

lecture¹ n 1 a talk in front of people, esp. as a method of teaching 2 a long solemn scolding

lecture² v -tured, -turing to give a lecture (to)

lecturer n 1 a person who gives lectures 2 a university teacher

lecture theatre n a room with seats in rows for talks, lectures, etc.

led past tense & past part. of LEAD

ledge n a narrow flat shelf

ledger n 1 an account book of a business 2 also **leger**— a short line added above or below the usu. 5 lines on which music is written, for high and low notes

lee n 1 shelter, esp. from rough weather 2 the side away from the wind —see also LEE SHORE, LEE TIDE

leech n 1 any of several types of small wormlike creatures that prick the skin of animals and drink their blood 2 a person who profits from another

leek n an onion-like vegetable with a long white fleshy stem

leer¹ v to look with a leer — ~ingly adv

leer² n an unpleasant smile showing cruel pleasure, sexual thoughts, etc.

lees n the bitter undrinkable sediment of wine

lee shore n a shore onto which the wind blows from the sea

lee tide n a tide moving in the same direction as the wind, and so higher than the usual tide

leeward¹ adj, adv with or in the direction of the wind; away from the wind —compare WINDWARD

leeward² n the direction in which the wind blows

leeway n -ways 1 the amount a ship or aircraft is blown off its course 2 additional time, space, money, etc., that allows a chance to succeed in doing something

left¹ adj 1 on or belonging to the side of the body that usu. contains the heart 2 on, by, or in the direction of one's left side 3 belonging to or favouring the left in politics

left² n 1 the left side or direction 2 the left hand 3 political parties that favour the equal division of wealth and property and generally support the workers rather than the employers

left³ adv towards the left

left⁴ past tense and past part. of LEAVE

left-hand adj 1 on or to the left side 2 on, for, with or done by the left hand

left-handed adj 1 using the left hand rather

than the right **2** made for use by a person who does this — ~**ly** adv — ~**ness** n

leftist n, adj (a supporter) of the left in politics

left overs n food remaining uneaten after a meal (served at a later meal)

left wing adj, n **1** (of) a group of a political party favouring more socialist measures than the rest of the party **2** (of) the player in certain sports, such as football, whose position is on the left of the field — **left-winger** n

leg n **1** a limb on which an animal walks and which supports its body **2** that part of this limb above the foot **3** the part of a garment that covers the leg **4** one of the supports on which a piece of furniture stands **5** that part of a cricket field behind and to the left of a right-handed batsman facing the bowler **6 leg before wicket** a way in which a batsman can be out, by (usu. accidentally) stopping a ball that would have hit the wicket with his leg

legacy n -**cies 1** money or personal possessions that pass to someone on the death of the owner according to his will **2** a lasting result

legal adj **1** allowed or made by law; lawful —compare ILLEGAL **2** of, concerning, or using the law — ~**ly** adv — ~**ity** n

legal aid n the services of a lawyer provided free to people too poor to pay for them

legalize, -ise v -**ized, -izing** to make lawful — -**ization** n

legal tender n money which must be accepted when offered in payment

legate n technical a member of a legation

legation n **1** a group of government servants, working under a minister below the rank of ambassador, who represent their government abroad **2** the official home or offices of the minister in charge of the group

legato adj, adv (of music) played with the notes sliding smoothly into each other —compare STACCATO

leg bye n a run in cricket made after the ball has touched the batsman's leg or any other part of his body except his hands —see also BYE

legend n **1** an old story about great deeds of ancient times, sometimes a true tale to which marvellous events have been added later **2** the words or phrase on a coin **3** a famous person or act, esp. in a particular area of activity — ~**ary** adj

leger also **leger line**— n a musical ledger

leggings n pieces of strong cloth, or leather, worn to protect the legs, esp. from foot to knee

legible adj (of handwriting or print) that can be read, esp. easily —opposite illegible — -**bility** n — -**bly** adv

legion n **1** a division of the ancient Roman army containing between 3000 and 6000 foot soldiers **2** a group of present or former soldiers or other armed men — ~**ary** n

legislate v -**lated, -lating** to make laws — -**tor** n

legislation n **1** the act of making laws **2** a body of laws

legislative[1] adj **1** of or concerning the making of laws **2** having the power to make laws **3** ordered by or in accordance with a body of laws — ~**ly** adv

legislative[2] n the body of people who have the power to make laws

legitimate adj **1** according to law or another body of rules or standards **2** born of parents who are married to each other —opposite illegitimate — ~**ly** adv — -**macy** n

legitimatize, -tise also **legitimize, -mise**— v -**tized, -tizing 1** to make lawful **2** to make (a child) legitimate, esp. by the marriage of the parents

legume n **1** any plant of the bean family that bears seeds in a thin pod which breaks in two along its length **2** the pod of such a plant — -**minous** adj

leisure n time when one is free from employment or other duties; free time — ~**d** adj

leisure centre n a group of buildings designed for free time activities

leisurely adj, adv without haste — -**liness** n

leitmotive, -tif n German a musical phrase that is played at various times during an opera (or like musical work) to suggest particular characters or ideas

lemming n a small ratlike animal living esp. in northern Europe, which sometimes travels long distances in large groups without regard to possible danger

lemon n **1** a type of fruit like an orange but with a light yellow skin and sour juice **2** light bright yellow

lemonade also **fizzy lemonade**— a yellow drink tasting of lemons and containing bubbles of gas

lemon curd also **lemon cheese**— n a cooked mixture of eggs, butter, and lemon juice, eaten on bread

lemon squash n a drink made from lemon juice and sugar, to which water is added before it is drunk

lemur n any of several kinds of monkey-like forest animals that are active at night, found in Madagascar ⌐PRIMATE

lend v lent, lending **1** to give (someone) the use of (something, such as money or a car) for a limited time **2** to give out (money) for profit, esp. as a business —see LOAN (USAGE) — ~**er** n

length n **1** the measurement from one end to the other or of the longest side of something **2** the measure from one end to the other of a horse, boat, etc., used in stating distances in races **3** a piece of something, esp. of a certain length or for a particular purpose **4** the amount of time from the beginning to the present or to the end **5 at length a** after a long time; at last **b** for a long time; in many words

lengthen v to make or become longer

lengthy adj -**ier, -iest 1** very long **2** (esp. of

speeches and writings) of too great a length — **-ily** *adv* — **-iness** *n*

lenient *adj* **1** merciful in judgment; gentle **2** allowing less than the highest standards of work, behaviour, etc. — **-ience** *n* — ~ **ly** *adv*

lens *n* **1** a piece of transparent material, curved on one or both sides, which makes a beam of light passing through it bend, spread out, become narrower, etc., used in glasses for the eyes, cameras, microscopes, etc. ☞ OPTICS, TELESCOPE **2** a similar structure found behind the black opening (PUPIL) in front of the eye, which helps the eye to form a picture (IMAGE) on its light-sensitive area (RETINA)

lent *past tense and past part. of* LEND

Lent *n* the 40 days before Easter, during which many Christians give up some of their usual pleasures

lentil *n* the small round seed of a beanlike plant, dried and used for food

lento *adj, adv* (of music) played slowly

Leo *n* **Leos** **1 a** the 5th division in the zodiac belt of stars, represented by a lion **b** the group of stars (CONSTELLATION) formerly in this division **2** a person born under this sign ☞ ZODIAC

leopard (*fem.* **leopardess**)— *n* **leopards** *or* **leopard** a type of large meat-eating catlike animal, yellowish with black spots, found in Africa and Southern Asia ☞ MAMMAL

leotard *n* a single close-fitting garment, worn esp. by dancers —compare CAT SUIT, WET SUIT

leper *n* a person who has leprosy

leprechaun *n* (in old Irish stories) a kind of fairy in the form of a little man

leprosy *n* a serious disease which makes the skin hard and scaly, and attacks the nerves. It used to be much feared because it was infectious, and no cure was known until recently

lesbian *adj, n* (of or concerning) a woman who is sexually attracted to other women — ~ **ism** *n*

lese-majesty also **lèse-majesté**— *n* French criminal action against a king or government

lesion *n* a wound or disease of the skin

less[1] *adj, pron* (comparative of LITTLE) **1** a smaller amount (than); not so much (of): *I was given less cake and fewer biscuits than she had.* | *Can we have a bit less noise/less of that noise?* **2** **none the less** but all the same; in spite of everything; nevertheless **USAGE** It is considered better English to use **fewer** rather than **less** with plural nouns, as in the first example.

less[2] *adv* **1** not so; to a smaller degree (than): *Jane's less beautiful than Susan* **2** not so much: *Try to shout less*

less[3] *prep* not counting; minus: *Now I owe you 90p; that's $1 for the concert ticket less the 10p I lent you yesterday*

lessee *n* a person who by written agreement is given the use of a house, building, or land for a certain time in return for payment to the owner (the LESSOR)

lessen *v* to make or become less

lesser *adj, adv esp. written* not so great or so much as the other in worth, degree, size, etc.

lesson *n* **1** the period of time a pupil or class studies a subject, esp. as one of many such periods **2** something taught to or learned by a pupil, esp. in school **3** the part of a subject taught or studied at one time **4** something from which one should learn **5** a short piece read from the Bible during religious services

lessor *n* a person who lets a house, building, or land by a written agreement (LEASE) to someone else (the LESSEE) for a certain time, in return for payment

lest *conj esp. written* **1** in order that .... not; in case: *I obeyed her lest she should be angry* **2** for fear that

let[1] *n* **1** *esp. law* anything that prevents something from being done (in the phrase **without let or hindrance**) **2** (in games such as tennis) a stroke that must be played again, esp., in tennis, when a service hits the top of the net on its way over

let[2] *v* **let, letting** **1** to allow (to do or happen) **2** (the named person) must, should, may: *Let each man decide for himself* **3** to give the use of (a room, a building, land, etc.) in return for regular payments **4** **let alone** even less: *The baby can't walk, let alone run* **5** **let blood** *medical* to purposely draw blood, so as to cure someone **6 let's** *esp. spoken* I suggest that we should; why not ....: *Let's go swimming on Saturday* —see also LET DOWN, LET OFF, LET ON, LET OUT

let[3] *n* **1** an act of renting a house or flat to (or from) someone **2** a house or flat that is (to be) rented

letdown *n esp. spoken* a disappointment

let down *v adv* **1** to make (a garment) longer **2** to cause (someone) to be disappointed; fail to keep a promise to (someone) **3** **let one's hair down** *esp. spoken* to behave informally; enjoy oneself freely

lethal *adj* able or certain to kill

lethargy *n* the state of being sleepy or unnaturally tired; lazy state of mind — **-gic** *adj*

let off *v adv* **1** to cause (something) to explode or be fired **2** to excuse (someone) from punishment

let on *v adv esp. spoken* to tell a secret

let out *v adv* **1** to make (a garment) wider —compare TAKE IN **2** to allow people to use (vehicles, horses, etc.) for a certain period, in return for payment

letter *n* **1** a written or printed message sent usu. in an envelope **2** one of the signs in writing that represents a speech sound

letterbox *n* **1** a box in which letters may be posted **2** a hole or box in the front of a building for receiving letters

letterhead *n* the name and address of a person or business printed on their writing paper

lettering *n* **1** the act of writing, drawing, etc., letters or words **2** the letters or words written or drawn, esp. with regard to their style

lettuce *n* **1** a type of garden plant with large

closely packed pale green leaves **2** these leaves, used in salads

leucocyte *n* WHITE BLOOD CELL

leukaemia *n* a disease (a type of cancer) in which the blood contains too many white blood cells and which often causes death

level¹ *n* **1** a smooth flat surface, esp. a wide area of flat ground **2** a position of height: *The garden is arranged on 2 levels* **3** general standard, quality, or degree **4** an instrument used by surveyors to measure differences in height

level² *v* **-ll-** **1** to make or become flat and even **2** to raise or lower to the same height everywhere or to the height of something else **3** to knock or pull down to the ground **4** to make or become equal in position, rank, strength, etc.

level³ *adj* **1** having a surface which is the same height above the ground all over **2** flat; smooth **3** equal in position or standard **4** steady and unvarying

level⁴ *adv* so as to be level

level at *v prep* to aim (a weapon) at

level crossing *n* a place where a road crosses a railway, usu. protected by gates that shut off the road while a train passes

level with *v prep esp. spoken* to speak freely and truthfully to

lever¹ *n* **1** a bar used for lifting or moving something heavy . One end is placed under or against the object, the other end is pushed down hard, and the bar turns on a fixed point (FULCRUM) ⟹MACHINERY . **2** any part of a machine working in the same way

lever² *v* to move (something) with a lever — ~**age** *n*

leveret *n* a young hare

leviathan *n* something very large and strong

levity *n esp. written or pompous* lack of respect for serious matters

levy¹ *n* **-ies** a payment asked for for a special purpose

levy² *v* **-ied, -ying** to demand and collect officially

lewd *adj* **1** wanting or thinking about sex, esp. in a manner not socially acceptable **2** impure; rude; dirty; obscene — ~**ly** *adv* — ~**ness** *n*

lexical *adj technical* of or concerning words — ~**ly** *adv*

lexicography *n* the writing and making of dictionaries

lexicon *n* a dictionary, esp. of an ancient language

liable *adj* **1** likely to, esp. from habit or tendency **2** responsible, esp. in law, for paying for something **3** likely to suffer in law — **-bility** *n* : *His liability to lose his temper lost him many friends.* | *The business failed because its assets were not so great as its liabilities*

liar *n* a person who tells lies

lib *n esp. spoken* liberation (esp. in the phrases **women's lib, gay lib**) — ~**ber** *n*: *The women's libbers are trying to get into this men's club*

Lib *abbrev. for* : LIBERAL PARTY

libation *n* an offering of wine to a god, esp. in ancient Greece and Rome

libel¹ *n* **1** *law* a printed or written statement, picture, etc., that unfairly damages the reputation of a person **2** the printing of such a statement, picture, etc. —compare SLANDER

libel² *v* **-ll-** to print a libel against — ~**lous** *adj* — ~**lously** *adv*

liberal¹ *adj* **1** willing to understand and respect the ideas and feelings of others **2** favouring some change, as in political or religious affairs **3** favouring a wide general knowledge, the broadening of the mind, and wide possibilities for self-expression **4** giving or given freely and generously

liberal² *n* a person with wide understanding, who is in favour of change — ~**ism** *n*

Liberal *n, adj* (a person) supporting or connected with the Liberal party — ~**ism** *n*

liberal arts *n techical* all university subjects except science and mathematics

liberality *n* **-ties** also **liberalness**— **1** generosity **2** broadness of mind

liberalize, -ise *v* **-ized, -izing** to make or become liberal — **-ization** *n*

liberally *adv* **1** generously; freely **2** in great amount; in large quantities

Liberal party *n* a British political party whose aims are social and industrial improvement without too much power being passed to the government or any one group (such as trade unions or manufacturers) in society

liberate *v* **-rated, -rating** **1** to set free; allow to escape **2** *technical* to cause or allow (gas) to escape from a chemical substance — **-rator** *n*

liberated *adv* having or showing freedom of action in social or sexual matters

liberation *n* setting free or being set free

liberties *n* rights given by a king or any powerful ruling body

liberty *n* **-ties** **1** freedom from oppressive government or foreign rule **2** freedom from control, service, being shut up, etc. **3** freedom of speech or behaviour which is taken without permission and is sometimes regarded as rude: *'I allowed myself the liberty of reading your letters.'* *'What a liberty!'* —compare FREEDOM

libido *n* the sexual urge

Libra *n* **1 a** the 7th division in the zodiac belt of stars, represented by a pair of scales **b** the group of stars (CONSTELLATION) formerly in this division **2** a person born under this sign ⟹ZODIAC

librarian *n* a person who is in charge of or helps to run a library — ~**ship** *n*

library *n* **-ies** **1 a** (part of a) building which contains books that may be looked at or borrowed, by the public (**public library**) or by members of a special group **2** a collection of books

librettist *n* the writer of a libretto

libretto *n* **-tos** the words of a musical play (such as an opera)

lice *pl. of* LOUSE

licence *n* **1** an official paper giving permission

to do something, usu. in return for a fixed payment: *a dog licence* **2** permission given, esp. officially, to do something **3** freedom of action, speech, thought, etc. **4** misuse of freedom, esp. in causing harm; uncontrolled behaviour **5** the freedom claimed by an artist to disobey the rules of his art or to change the facts in order to improve a work of art —see also POETIC LICENCE

license, -cence *v* to give official permission to or for

licensed, -cenced *adj* having official permission, esp. to sell alcoholic drinks

licensed victualler *n* *technical* a keeper of a shop or inn who is permitted to sell alcoholic drinks

licensee *n* a person to whom official permission is given, esp. to sell alcoholic drinks or tobacco

licensing laws *n* the laws in Britain that limit the sales of alcoholic drinks to certain times and places

licentiate *n* **1** a person given official permission, esp. by a university, to practise a special art or profession **2** a (written) declaration that this permission has been given

lichen *n* a dry-looking greyish, greenish, or yellowish flat spreading plant that grows on stones and trees ⇾EVOLUTION, PLANT

lick¹ *v* **1** to move the tongue across (a surface) in order to taste, clean, make wet, etc. **2** (esp. of flames or waves) to pass lightly or rapidly over or against (a surface) **3** *esp. spoken* to beat or defeat — ~ing *n*

lick² *n* **1** the act of licking **2** a small amount of cleaning, paint, etc.) **3** *esp. spoken* speed: *running down the hill at a great lick*

licorice *n* liquorice

lid *n* **1** the removable top of a box or other hollow container **2** an eyelid

lido *n* **-dos 1** a public swimming bath open to the air **2** a special place on the water's edge used for swimming and sunbathing

lie¹ *v* **lay, lain, lying 1** to be in a flat resting position on a surface, as on the ground or a bed **2** to be in a described place, position, or direction: *The town lies to the east* **3 lie in state** (of a dead body) to be placed in a public place so that people may honour it **4 lie low** to be in hiding —see LAY (USAGE)

lie² *v* **lied, lying** to tell a lie

lie³ *n* an untrue statement purposely made to deceive —see also WHITE LIE

lieder *n* *German* German songs, esp. those which are part of serious 19th-century music

liege *n* *old use* **1** also **liege lord**— a lord to whom others must give loyalty and service **2** also **liege man**— a man who must give loyalty and service to his lord

lieutenant *n* **1** a person who acts for, or in place of, someone in a higher position; deputy **2** an officer of low rank in the navy, British army, etc.

life *n* **lives 1** the active force that makes those forms of matter (animals and plants) that grow

through feeding and produce new young forms like themselves, different from all other matter (stones, machines, objects, etc.) **2** matter having this active force **3** the state or period in which animals and plants are alive **4** the condition of existence, esp. of a human being **5** the period between birth and death, between birth and a certain point in somebody's life, or between a certain point in somebody's life and their death: *I had been a coward all my life.* | *a life member* **6** the period for which a machine, organization, etc., will work or last **7** living things in general: *plant life* **8** existence as a collection of widely different experiences **9** spirit; strength; force; cheerfulness **10** also **life imprisonment** — the punishment of being put in prison for a length of time which is not fixed **11** also **life story** — a biography **12** using a living person as the subject of painting, drawing, etc.: *life classes*

life assurance also **life insurance**— *n* an agreement between a company and a person, by which, in return for regular payments, either that person will receive a sum of money on reaching a certain age or, if he dies, another (named) person will receive it

life belt *n* a belt made of a material that will float, used for preventing a person from sinking after falling into water

lifeboat *n* **1** a strong boat kept on shore and used for saving people in danger at sea **2** one of the small boats carried by a ship for escape in case of wreck, fire, etc.

life buoy also **buoy**— *n* **-buoys** a circle, usu. made of cork, thrown to somebody who has fallen into water to prevent them from sinking

life cycle *n* the regular changes in form of a species of living matter in the course of its life, such as that of insects from egg to wormlike form and then to winged form

lifeguard *n* a swimmer employed, as at a swimming bath, to help swimmers in danger

life history *n* **-ries** the regular development of a particular animal or plant in the course of its life

life jacket *n* an air-filled garment that is worn round the chest to support a person in water

lifeless *adj* **1** having no life **2** lacking strength, spirit, interest, or activity — ~ly *adv* — ~ness *n*

lifelike *adj* very much like real life or a real person

lifeline *n* a rope used for saving life, esp. at sea

lifelong *adj* lasting all one's life

life peer *n* a person who has been made a peer but who cannot pass the title on to his eldest son when he dies — compare PEER OF THE REALM

lifer *n* *sl* a person who has been sent to prison for life

lifetime *n* the time during which a person is alive

lift¹ *v* **1** to raise or rise from one level and hold or move to another level **2** (esp. of clouds, mist, etc.) to move upwards, melt, or disappear **3** to take and use; steal

lift² *n* **1** the act of lifting, rising, or raising **2** a lifting force, such as an upward pressure of air on the wings of an aircraft ⟶AEROPLANE **3** (*US* **elevator**)— an apparatus in a building for taking people and goods from one floor to another **4** a free ride in a vehicle

lift-off also **blast-off**— *n* the start of the flight of a spacecraft

ligament *n* one of the strong bands that join bones or hold some part of the body in position

light¹ *n* **1** the natural force that is produced by or redirected from objects and other things, so that we see them **2** something that produces such force and causes other things to be seen, such as a lamp or torch **3** something that will set something else, esp. a cigarette, burning: *Can you give me a light, please?* **4** brightness, as in the eyes, showing happiness or excitement **5** the bright part of a painting **6** the condition of being publicly seen or known (in the phrases **come/bring to light**) **7** the way in which something is regarded: *look at the matter in a new light*

light² *adj* **1** having light; not dark; bright **2** not deep or dark in colour; pale

light³ *v* **lit** or **lighted**, **lighting** **1** to start or cause to start to burn **2** to cause to give light; give light to: *We lit the candle and the candle lit the room* **3** to make or become bright with pleasure or excitement

light⁴ *adj* **1** of little weight; not heavy **2** small in amount **3** easy to bear or do; not difficult or tiring: *light punishment* **4** (of sleep) from which one wakes easily; not deep **5** (of food) easily digested **6** (of wine and other alcoholic drinks) not very strong **7** (of books, music, plays, actors, etc.) having the intention of amusing only; not deep in meaning **8** (of soil) easily broken up; loose; sandy **9** (of cake, bread, etc.) full of air; well risen; not heavy — ~**ness** *n*

light⁵ *adv* without much luggage: *I travel light*

light bulb *n* a bulb that produces electric light

lighten¹ *v* to make or become brighter or less dark

lighten² *v* **1** to make or become less heavy, forceful, etc. **2** to make or become more cheerful or less troubled

lighter¹ *n* a large flat-bottomed boat used for loading and unloading ships

lighter² *n* **1** something that lights or sets on fire **2** also **cigarette lighter**— an instrument that produces a flame for lighting cigarettes

light-hearted *adj* cheerful; happy

light heavyweight *n, adj* (a boxer) weighing between 160 and 170 pounds

lighthouse *n* a tower with a powerful flashing light that guides ships or warns them of dangerous rocks

lighting *n* **1** the act of making something give light or start burning **2** the system, arrangement,

or apparatus that lights a room, building, street, etc., or the quality of the light produced

lightly *adv* **1** with little weight or force; gently **2** to a slight or small degree: *lightly cooked*

lightning¹ *n* a powerful flash of light in the sky usu. followed by thunder —see also FORKED LIGHTNING, SHEET LIGHTNING

lightning² *adj* very quick, short, or sudden: *a lightning visit*

lightning conductor *n* a metal wire leading from the highest point of a building to the ground to protect the building from lightning

lightning strike *n* a sudden stopping of work by dissatisfied workers, usu. without warning

lights *n* the lungs of sheep, pigs, etc., used as food

lightship *n* a small ship with a powerful flashing light anchored near a dangerous place to warn other ships

lightweight *n, adj* **1** (a person or thing) **a** of less than average weight **b** lacking in strength of character or in ability to think deeply **2** (a boxer) weighing between 126 and 135 pounds

light year *n* (a measure of length equal to) the distance that light travels in one year (about 95,000,000,000,000 kilometres or 6,000,000,000,000 miles), used for measuring distances between stars

lignite *n* a soft material like coal, used for burning

likable, likeable *adj* (of a person) pleasant; attractive

like¹ *v* **liked, liking** **1** to be fond of; find pleasant **2** to wish: *I'd like to see you* — **-king** *n* : *to have a liking for sweets*

like² *adj* the same in many ways; alike

like³ *prep* **1** in the same way as; having the same qualities as; typical of **2** for example: *There are several people interested, like Mr Jones and Dr Simpson* **3** **feel like** to wish to have **4** **look like** to seem probably USAGE Note the difference between these uses of **like** and **as**: *Let me speak to you* **as** *a father* (=I am your father and I am speaking in that character). | *Let me speak to you like a father* (=I am not your father but I am speaking in the way your father might).

like⁴ *n* something of the same kind, quality, or value: *I've never seen its like anywhere else*

like⁵ *conj* *esp. spoken* in the same way as: *Do you make bread like you make cakes?*

likelihood *n* the fact or degree of being likely

likely¹ *adj* **-lier, -liest** **1** probable; expected **2** suitable to give results: *a likely plan*

likely² *adv* probably

likeness *n* sameness in form: *a family likeness*

likewise *adv esp. written* in the same way; the same also

lilac *n* **1** a type of tree with pinkish purple or white flowers giving a sweet smell **2** a purple colour like these flowers

lilt¹ *v* to have a regular pattern of usu. pleasant sound

lilt² *n* **1** a regular pattern of rising and falling

sound **2** this quality in a song **3** a song with this quality

lily *n* **-ies** any of several types of plant with large flowers of various colours, but esp. the one with clear white flowers

lily of the valley *n* lilies of the valley a type of plant with 2 green leaves and several small bell-shaped flowers with a sweet smell

limb *n* **1** a leg, arm, or wing of an animal **2** a large branch of a tree — ~less *adj*

limber up *v adv* to make the muscles stretch easily by exercise, esp. before a race

limbo *n* -bos a state of uncertainty

lime¹ *n* **1** also **quicklime**— a white substance obtained by burning limestone, used in making cement **2** the substance (**slaked lime**) made by adding water to this

lime² *v* **limed, liming** to add lime to (fields, land, etc.) to control acid substances

lime³ also **lime tree** , **linden**— *n* a type of tree with yellow sweet-smelling flowers

lime⁴ *n* **1** a type of tree which bears a fruit like a small green lemon **2** the fruit of this tree **3** also **limejuice** — a drink made from this fruit, which is often used to flavour other drinks

limelight *n* a lot of attention from the public

limerick *n* a type of short poem with 5 lines, usu. humorous

limestone *n* a type of rock containing mainly calcium (the material in bones) —see also LIME

limey *n* limeys *esp. spoken, esp. US* an Englishman

limit¹ *n* the farthest point or edge of something

limit² *v* to keep below or at a certain point or amount — -~ation *n*

limited *adj* **1** small in amount, power, etc. **2** (of a company) having to pay back debts only up to a fixed limit

limited liability *n* **-ties** *technical* the necessity of paying back debts only up to a limit: *a limited liability company*

limitless *adj* without limit or end — ~ ly *adv* — ~ ness *n*

limousine *n* **1** a car with the driver's seat separated from the back by a sheet of glass **2** a luxurious car

limp¹ *v* to walk with an uneven step, one leg moving less well than the other — **limp** *n* : *The operation cured his limp*

limp² *adj* lacking strength or stiffness — ~ ly *adv* — ~ ness *n*

limpet *n* a type of very small sea animal with a shell, which clings tightly to rocks

limpid *adj* *esp. in literature* (esp. of liquid) clear; transparent △ LANGUID — ~ly *adv* — ~ity *n*

Lincoln green *n* a bright green colour, esp. of a cloth

linctus *n* liquid medicine to cure coughing

linden *n* a lime tree

line¹ *v* **lined, lining** to make or be an inner covering for

line² *n* **1** a piece of string, wire, or thin cord **2** a thin mark with length but no width, which can be drawn on a surface **3** a cord with a hook at the end, used for fishing **4** a limit or edge marked by a drawn line **5** a row **6** a queue **7** a set of people following one another in time, esp. a family —see also LINEAGE **8** a row of words in a poem **9** a railway track **10** a system for travelling by or moving goods by road, railway, sea, or air: *an airline | a shipping line* **11** *technical* the equator **12** a business, profession, trade, etc. **13** an area of interest (esp. in the phrase **in one's line**) **14** a type of goods: *a new line in hats* —see also **line of least** RESISTANCE, STEP **out of line**

line³ *v* **1** to mark with lines or wrinkles **2** to form rows along —see also LINE UP

lineage *n* the line of descent from one person to another in a family — **lineal** *adj* — **lineally** *adv*

linear *adj* **1** of or in lines **2** (in art) using outlines to show form **3** of length: *linear measurements*

line drawing *n* a drawing done with a pen or pencil

lineman also **linesman**— *n* a man who takes care of railway lines or telephone wires

linen *n* **1** a type of cloth made from flax **2** sheets and bedclothes, tablecloths, etc.

line of symmetry *n* *technical* a line that divides a flat shape into 2 congruent shapes: *A kite is a quadrilateral with one line of symmetry*

lineout *n* (in rugby) 2 parallel lines of players to whom the ball is thrown after it has gone off the field of play

liner *n* a large passenger ship

lines *n* **1** a set of written lines to be copied by a pupil as a punishment **2** the words learnt by an actor to be said in a play **3** *literature* a poem: *'Lines on the death of Nelson'* — see also MARRIAGE LINES

line segment *n* *technical* the part of a line between 2 points on the line

linesman *n* **-men** (in sport) an official who stays at the side of the playing area and decides when the ball has gone out of the playing area

line up *v adv* to move into a row, side by side or one behind the other

ling *n* a type of plant very like heather, with bell-shaped pink flowers

linger *v* to delay going; be slow to disappear — ~ er *n* — ~ ing *adj* — ~ ingly *adv*

lingerie *n* *esp. written & technical* underclothes for women, esp. for sale in shops

lingo *n* **-goes** *sl* **1** a language, usu. foreign **2** a type of speech full of expressions one cannot understand —compare JARGON

lingua franca *n* **-cas** a language used between people whose native languages are different. It may originally have been made up of parts of several languages

linguist *n* **1** a person who studies and is good at foreign languages **2** a person who studies linguistics

linguistic *adj* concerning words, languages, or linguistics — ~ **ally** *adv*

linguistics *n* the study of language in general and of particular languages, of the patterns of their grammar, sounds, etc., their history, origins, and use

liniment *n* a liquid to be rubbed on the skin, esp. to help stiffness of the joints —compare EMBROCATION

lining *n* material covering or for covering the inner surface of a garment, box, etc.

link¹ *n* **1** something which connects 2 other parts **2** one ring of a chain —see also MISSING LINK

link² *v* **1** to join or connect **2** to be joined — ~ **age** *n*

links *n* **links** a piece of ground on which golf is played

linnet *n* a type of small brown singing bird

linoleum also **lino** , **oilcloth**— *n* a material used esp. as a floor-covering, made up of strong cloth coated with a mixture of linseed oil and other substances

linseed *n* the seed of flax

linseed oil *n* the oil from linseed, used in linoleum, in some paints, inks, etc.

lint *n* soft material used for protecting wounds

lintel *n* a piece of stone or wood forming the top part of the frame of a door or window

lion (*fem.* **lioness**)— *n* **lions** *or* **lion** a type of large animal of the cat family which lives mainly in Africa. The male has a thick growth of hair (MANE) over the head and shoulders

lion-hearted *adj* very brave

lionize *v* **-ized, -izing** to treat (a person) as important; cause to be famous

lip *n* **1** one of the 2 edges of the mouth **2** this area with the ordinary skin around there, esp. round the top below the nose **3** the edge (of a hollow vessel or opening) **4 a stiff upper lip** a lack of expression of feeling

lip gloss *n* creamy material for making the lips look glossy

lipid *n* any of a class of fatty substances in living things, such as fat, oil, or wax

lip-read *v* to watch people's lip movements so as to understand what they are saying

lip service *n* **pay lip service to** to support in words, but not in fact

lipstick *n* (a stick-shaped mass of) material for brightening the colour of the lips

liquefy *v* **-fied, -fying** to make or become liquid

liqueur *n* any of several types of very strong alcoholic drink usu. drunk in small quantities after a meal

liquid¹ *adj* **1** (esp. of something which is usu. solid or gas) in the form of a liquid **2** (of money in banks, not coin) which can be obtained as coin (esp. in the phrase **liquid assets**) **3** (of sounds) clear and flowing, with pure notes

liquid² *n* (a type of) substance not solid or gas, which flows and has no fixed shape: *Water is a liquid* ⟲PHYSICS

liquidate *v* **-dated, -dating 1** to get rid of; destroy or kill **2** to arrange the end of business for (a company), esp. when it has too many debts **3** (of a company) to bring business to an end in this way, esp. becoming bankrupt **4** *technical* to pay (a debt) — **-ation** *n*

liquidator *n* an official who ends the trade of a particular business, esp. to pay its debts

liquidity *n* the state of having money, or goods that can easily be sold for money

liquidize *v* **-ized, -izing** to crush (esp. fruit or vegetables) into a liquid-like form

liquidizer also **blender**— *n* a small kitchen machine that makes solid foods into liquid forms such as soups

liquor *n* **1** *written or technical* alcoholic drink **2** the liquid produced from a boiled food, such as the juice from meat

liquorice, licorice *n* a sweet black substance produced from a plant, as used in medicine and sweets

lira *n* **-e** *or* **-as** a standard coin in the money system of Italy ⟲MONEY

lisp¹ *v* to pronounce sounds which are not clear, esp. when the tongue is placed on the teeth, making the 's' seem like ·'th' — ~ **ingly** *adv*

lisp² *n* the fault in speech of lisping

list¹ *n* a set of names of things written one after the other, so as to remember them

list² *v* esp. *written* to write in a list

list³ *v* (esp. of a ship) to lean or slope to one side

list⁴ *n* a leaning position, esp. of a ship

listen *v* to give attention in hearing — ~ **er** *n*

listen in *v adv* **1** to listen to the radio —see also TUNE IN **2** to listen to the conversation of other people, esp. when one should not

listless *adj* lacking power of movement, activity, etc. — ~ **ly** *adv* — ~ **ness** *n*

list price *n* the manufacturers' suggested price for an article

lists *n* **1** (in former times) a piece of ground for fighting on horseback —see JOUST **2 enter the lists** to take part in a competition, argument, etc.

lit *past tense and past part. of* LIGHT

literacy *n* the state or condition of being able to read and/or write

literal *adj* **1** exact: *a literal account of a conversation* **2** giving one word for each word (as in a foreign language) **3** following the usual meaning of the words —compare FIGURATIVE — ~ **ly** *adv* : *to translate literally* — ~ **ness** *n*

literary *adj* **1** of or concerning literature **2** producing or studying literature **3** more typical of literature, esp. that of former times, than of ordinary speech or writing

literate *adj* able to read and write —opposite **illiterate** — ~ **ly** *adv*

literature *n* **1** written works which are of

literature

Development of western literature

Historical events		Date	Development
	2000	c2300BC	Earliest known literary writings: Egyptian prayers 1
	1500	c1500–1200BC	the *Vedas*, Sanskrit (Indian) poems
1200 Siege of Troy	1000	c850BC	Homer's *Iliad* and *Odyssey*, Greek epic poems 2
500–300 Golden age of		580BC	Aesop's *Fables* (in Greek)
Greece	500	c480BC	Tragic drama in Greece: chief writers Aeschylus,
323 Alexander the Great			Sophocles, Euripides
dies		c420–350BC	Greek philosophers and historians: Plato, Thucydides 3
146 Romans conquer		c250BC	Beginning of Latin literature
Greece	1	60BC–20AD	Great age of Latin poetry: chief writers Virgil,
Birth of Christ			Catullus, Horace, Ovid 2
117 Height of Roman	100		
Empire			
238 Barbarians begin to	200	up to 200	Later Latin poets and historians: Juvenal, Tacitus 3
attack Rome	300		
476 Fall of western Roman	400	400	rise of Christian literature: St Augustine's *Confessions;*
Empire; 'Dark Ages' in			St Jerome translates Bible from Hebrew to Latin.
western Europe	500	c550	Welsh poets (bards) write poems about heroic warriors 4
530 Rise of monasteries	600	670	Caedmon, first known English poet, writes religious verse
789 First Viking attack on	700	c700	*Beowulf,* greatest Anglo-Saxon epic
England		c730	Venerable Bede's *History* of England (in Latin)
871 King Alfred fights	800	c850	the *Edda,* collection of Norse poems written in Iceland 4
Danes	900		
1066 Norman conquest of	1000	c1050	the *Mabinogion,* collection of Welsh tales
England	1100	c1100	the *Song of Roland,* greatest French medieval epic
			The Old English language develops into Middle English
		c1110	Development of the Miracle Play, chief type of medieval drama
	1200	c1200	Period of Icelandic sagas, prose epics about Viking history
1348 Black Death	1300	1310	Dante's *Divine Comedy,* greatest Italian poem
		1360	*Piers Plowman,* long allegorical English poem
		1395	Geoffrey Chaucer's *Canterbury Tales* 5
1474 First printed book in	1400	1470	Sir Thomas Malory's *Morte d'Arthur,* stories about King Arthur
English	1500	c1500	The Middle English language develops into Modern English
1521 Protestant			The Renaissance (rebirth of art and learning)
Reformation			spreads from Italy to other countries 5
1588 Spanish Armada		c1580–1620	Great Elizabethan period of English poetry and drama:
	1600		Edmund Spenser, William Shakespeare, Ben Jonson
		1605–15	Cervantes' *Don Quixote* (in Spanish), satirizing heroic stories 6
		1611	Authorized Version of the Bible made in England
1642–9 English Civil Wars		1634	First Passion Play performed at Oberammergau
1661–1715 rule of Louis		1660–70	Great age of French drama: Corneille, Racine, Molière
XIV in France		1674	John Milton's *Paradise Lost,* a religious epic
		1678	John Bunyan's *Pilgrim's Progress* 6
1756–63 Seven Years War	1700	c1680–1740	Classical ('Augustan') period of English writing: satirical verse
1770 Start of Industrial			(Alexander Pope), criticism and biography (Samuel Johnson)
Revolution		1719	Daniel Defoe's *Robinson Crusoe*
1775–83 War of American		1726	Jonathan Swift's *Gulliver's Travels* 7
Independence		c1745	development of the novel in England:
1789 French Revolution			Henry Fielding's *Tom Jones*
		1755	Samuel Johnson's *Dictionary of the English Language*
1803–15 Napoleonic Wars	1800	c1780–1820	The Romantic period in English literature:
1837 Reign of Queen			William Wordsworth, Lord Byron, Sir Walter Scott
Victoria begins		1832	Death of Goethe, Germany's greatest poet and dramatist
1848 Revolutionary		c1840–1900	classical period of the novel: Thackeray *(Vanity Fair)*
movements in Europe			and Dickens *(David Copperfield)* in England, Flaubert
1861–5 American Civil War			*(Madame Bovary)* and Zola *(Germinal)* in France, Tolstoy
			(War and Peace) and Gogol *(Dead Souls)* in Russia
		1840–50	development of major American literature:
			Edgar Allan Poe, Herman Melville *(Moby-Dick)*
		1850	Tennyson's *In Memoriam,* his most profound work 8
		1868–9	Browning's *The Ring and the Book,* a long narrative poem
1914–18 World War I	1900	1880–1905	Major tragic dramatists: Henrik Ibsen (Norwegian), Anton
1920–38 Rise of cinema,			Chekhov (Russian), August Strindberg (Swedish)
radio, television		after 1915	Modern English literature: poets W. B. Yeats
1939–45 World War II			and T. S. Eliot, novelists James Joyce
			and D. H. Lawrence, playwright G. B. Shaw
		after 1945	Post-war literature: Dylan Thomas (Welsh), 9
			Samuel Beckett (Irish), Alexander Solzhenitsyn (Russian)

artistic value **2** printed material, esp. giving information ⊙

lithe *adj* able to bend and move easily — ~**ly** *adv*

lithium *n* a soft silver-white element that is the lightest known metal

lithograph *n* a picture, pattern, etc. made by printing from a piece of stone or metal — ~**ic** *adj* — ~**y** *n*

litigate *v* **-gated, -gating** *technical* to bring a case in a court of law — **-gant** *n* — **-gation** *n* : *Litigation is often expensive for the litigants*

litmus *n* a colouring material, often put in paper (**litmus paper**), which turns red when touched by acid and blue when touched by alkali

litre *n* a measure of liquid equal to about 1¾ pints

litter[1] *n* **1** things thrown away, esp. paper scattered untidily **2** straw used as an animal's bed **3** a bed with handles for carrying a person **4** a group of young animals born at the same time to one mother

litter[2] *v* to cover or scatter untidily

little[1] *adj* **1** small **2** short **3** young

little[2] *adv* **less, least 1** to only a small degree: *a little known fact* **2** not at all: *They little thought that they were being watched*

little[3] *adj, pron, n* **less, least 1** not much; not enough **2** a small amount, but at least some: *She speaks a little French* **3 make little of a** to treat as unimportant **b** to understand little

little finger *n* the finger on the hand furthest from the thumb

little people also **little folk**— *n* *esp. Irish* fairies

littoral *n, adj esp. written & technical* (land) on or along the (sea) shore — ~**ly** *adv*

liturgy *n* **-gies** a fixed form of worship in the Christian church — **-gical** *adj* — **-gically** *adv*

livable, liveable *adj* **1** worth living **2** suitable to live in **3 livable with** acceptable to live with

live[1] *v* **lived, living 1** to be alive; have life **2** to continue to be alive **3** to have one's home; dwell **4** to keep oneself alive: *live on fruit* —see also LIVE UP TO   USAGE **Dwell** and **reside** (both *written*) are used like **live** when speaking of a place: *to* **live/dwell/reside** *in China*. **Inhabit** means "to live in": *They* **inhabit** *the tropical forests.*

live[2] *adj* **1** alive; living **2** (of lighted coal or wood) still burning **3** having power which can be used in an explosion and flames when it hits something hard: *a live bomb* **4** carrying free electricity which can shock anyone who touches it ☞ELECTRICITY **5** (of broadcasting) seen and/or heard as it happens

live birth *n* *technical* (a birth resulting in) a baby born alive

livelihood *n* the way by which one earns enough to pay for what is necessary

livelong *adj esp. poetic* (of the day or night) whole: *the livelong day*

lively *adj* **-lier, -liest** full of quick movement, thought, etc. — **-liness** *n*

liven up *v adv* to make or become lively

liver[1] *n* a large organ in the body which produces bile and cleans the blood ☞DIGESTION

liver[2] *n* a person who lives in the stated way: *an evil liver*

liverish *adj esp. spoken* suffering from sickness, esp. after eating and/or drinking too much

livery *n* **-ries** uniform of a special type for servants — **-ried** *adj*

livery stable *n* a place where owners may pay to have horses kept, or where horses may be hired

lives *pl. of* LIFE

livestock *n* animals kept on a farm

live up to *v adv prep* to keep to the high standards of

livid *adj* **1** blue-grey, as of bruises **2** (of the face) very pale **3** *esp. spoken* very angry — ~**ly** *adv*

living[1] *adj* alive now

living[2] *n* earnings used to buy what is necessary to life: *to make a living in industry*

living room also **sitting room**— *n* the main room in a house where people can do things together, usu. apart from eating

lizard *n* any of several types of reptile, with a rough skin, 4 legs, and a long tail

llama *n* a type of animal of South America with thick woolly hair

load[1] *n* **1** an amount being carried, or to be carried, esp. heavy **2** the amount which a certain vehicle can carry **3** the power of an electricity supply

load[2] *v* **1** to put a full load on or in (something) **2** to put a charge or film into (a gun or camera)

loaded *adj* **1** containing a hidden trap: *a loaded question* **2** *esp. spoken* having lots of money

loadstone *n* a lodestone

loaf[1] *n* **loaves 1** bread shaped and baked in one large piece **2** *sl* one's head and mind **3** food moulded in a solid piece: *meat loaf*

loaf[2] *v esp. spoken* to waste time, esp. by not working — ~**er** *n*

loam *n* good soil made of sand, clay, and decayed plant material — ~**y** *adj*

loan[1] *n* **1** something which is lent **2** an amount of money lent **3** the act of lending

loan[2] *v esp. US* to give (someone) the use of; lend   USAGE The Americans use **loan** to mean **lend**: *He* **loaned** *me $10.* The word is often used in British English to mean "to lend for a long period": *He* **loaned** *his collection to the gallery* but many people do not like the word to be used simply for **lend**.

loanword *n* a word originally from a foreign language

loath, loth *adj* unwilling

loathe *v* **loathed, loathing** to feel hatred or great dislike for — **-thing** *n*

loathsome *adj* which causes great dislike; very unpleasant — ~**ly** *adv* — ~**ness** *n*

loaves *pl. of* LOAF

lob¹ *v* **-bb-** to send (a ball) in a high gentle curve

lob² *n* **1** (in cricket) a ball thrown underarm (= by the hand coming up towards the level of the shoulder) **2** (in tennis) a ball hit high into the air

lobby¹ *n* **-bies** **1** a hall or passage, which leads from the entrance to the rooms inside a building **2** (in the House of Commons) one of 2 passages where members go to vote for or against something **3** a group of people who unite for or against an action, so that those in power will change their minds: *the clean air lobby*

lobby² *v* **-bied, -bying** **1** to meet (a member of parliament) in order to persuade him/her to support one's actions and needs **2** to be active in bringing about a change in the law in this way

lobe *n* **1** also **earlobe**— the round fleshy piece at the bottom of the ear **2** *technical* any rounded division of an organ, esp. the brain and lungs — ~**d** *adj*

lobster *n* **1** a type of 8-legged shellfish with a pair of powerful pincers the flesh of which can be eaten **2** the flesh of this as food

lobsterpot *n* a trap shaped like a basket, in which lobsters are caught

local¹ *adj* **1** of or in a certain place, esp. the place one lives in **2** *technical* concerning only a particular part, esp. of the body: *a local infection*

local² *n esp. spoken* **1** a person who lives in the place he is in **2** a pub near where one lives, esp. which one often drinks at

local colour *n* details in a story or picture which are true to the time or place being represented

locality *n* **-ties** a place or area, esp. in which something happens or has happened

localize, -ise *v* **-ized, -izing** **1** to set in a particular place, time, etc. **2** to keep within a small area: *to localize the pain* — **-ization** *n*

locally *adv* **1** in a local area **2** near by

locate *v* **located, locating** **1** to find or learn the position of **2** to fix or set in a certain place — ~**d** *adj*

location *n* **1** a place or position **2** an appropriate place away from a film studio, where one or more scenes are made

loch *n Scots* a lake, or a part of the sea almost surrounded by land

loci *pl. of* LOCUS

lock¹ *n* a small piece of hair

lock² *n* **1** an apparatus for closing and fastening something by means of a key **2** the part of a gun which fires it **3** a stretch of water closed off by gates so that the level can be raised or lowered to move boats up or down a slope **4** a hold which wrestlers may use to prevent the opponent from moving **5** (in a machine) the state of being stopped: *in the lock position* **6** the degree to which a steering wheel can be turned **7 lock, stock, and barrel** completely

lock³ *v* **1** to fasten with a lock **2** to put in a place and lock the entrance: *lock the car in the garage* **3** to become fixed or blocked: *I can't control the car; the wheels have locked* —see also LOCK OUT — ~**able** *adj*

locker *n* **1** a small cupboard for keeping things in, esp. at a school where there is one for each pupil **2 Davy Jones's locker** *humour* the bottom of the sea, meaning death by drowning

locket *n* a metal case usu. on a chain and worn around the neck in which small pictures can be kept

lockjaw *n* tetanus

locknut *n* a nut which keeps another one from unscrewing

lockout *n* the employers' action of not allowing men to go back to work until they accept an agreement

lock out *v adv* **1** to prevent (workmen) from entering a place of work until a disagreement is settled as the employers want it **2** to keep out of a place by locking the entrance

locks *n poetic* the hair of the head

locksmith *n* a person who makes and repairs locks

lockstitch *n* the usual type of sewing machine stitch, in which a thread from above the material and one from below fasten together at small distances apart

lockup *n* a small prison or prison-like room where a wrongdoer may be kept for a short time

locomotion *n technical* movement; ability to move

locomotive¹ *adj technical* concerning or causing movement

locomotive² *n esp. written* a railway engine

locum also *esp. written* **locum tenens**— *n* a doctor or priest doing the work of another who is away

locus *n* **loci** *technical* a set of points which may consist of lines, curves, planes, regions, or a single point or isolated points: *The locus of points in a plane which are the same distance from a fixed point is a circle*

locust *n* a type of insect of Asia and Africa like a grasshopper, which flies from place to place in large groups, often destroying crops ⟜INSECT

lode *n technical* an amount of metal in its natural form as ore

lodestar *n* **1** *esp. in literature* the pole star, used as a guide by sailors **2** a guide or example to follow

lodestone, loadstone *n* a piece of iron which acts as a magnet

lodge¹ *v* **lodged, lodging** **1** to stay, usu. for a short time and paying rent **2** to settle firmly in a position **3** to make (a statement) officially: *to lodge a complaint*

lodge² *n* **1** a small house near the entrance to a large house **2** a small house for hunters, sportsmen, etc., to stay in while crossing wild country **3** a room for a porter, as in a block of flats or a college **4** (the meeting place of) a local branch of freemasons **5** *technical* a beaver's home

lodger *n* a person who pays rent to stay in somebody's house

lodging *n* a place to stay —compare BOARD

loess *n* a type of yellowish powdery soil common in China

loft¹ *n* **1** a room under the roof of a building; attic **2** a room over a stable, where hay is kept

loft² *v* (esp. in cricket and golf) to hit (a ball) high — ~ed *adj*

lofty *adj* -ier, -iest **1 a** of unusually high quality of thinking, feeling, desires, etc. **b** showing belief of being better than other people **2** *poetic* high — -ily *adv* — -iness *n*

log¹ *n* **1** a thick piece of wood from a tree **2** an official written record of a journey, as in a ship, plane, or car **3** an apparatus which measures the speed of a ship

log² *v* -gg- to record in a log

loganberry *n* -ries a type of red fruit grown from a plant which is half blackberry and half raspberry

logarithm also *esp. spoken* **log**— *n* the power to which a given base, such as 10, must be raised to give a stated number: *The logarithm of 100 is 2 because 10² = 100* ⟶MATHEMATICS — ~ic *adj* — ~ically *adv*

logbook *n* *esp. spoken* REGISTRATION DOCUMENT

logger *n* a person whose job is to cut down trees

loggerheads *n* **at loggerheads** always disagreeing

logic *n* **1** the science of reasoning by formal methods **2** a way of reasoning — ~al *adj* — ~ally *adv* USAGE Both **logical** and **reasonable** can mean "in accordance with reason"; but **logical** is used when we speak of the rules of **logic**, and **reasonable** when we mean ordinary common sense: *a logical argument* | *no reasonable doubt*. A person may be said to have *a logical mind*, but we do not usually call him *a logical person*.

logistics *n* **1** the study or skill of moving soldiers, supplying them with food, etc. **2** the ways in which the details of a military operation are handled — **logistic** *adj* — **-cally adv**

loin *n* (a piece of) meat from the lower part of an animal —see also SIRLOIN

loincloth *n* a covering for the lower part of the body above the legs, usu. for men, worn in hot countries esp. by poor people

loins *n* **1** the lower part of the body below the waist and above the legs **2 gird up one's loins** to prepare for action

loiter *v* to move about with frequent stops — ~er *n*

loll *v* **1** to be in a lazy loose position: *lolling in a chair* **2** to hang down loosely: *The dog's tongue lolled out*

lollipop *n* **1** a type of hard sweet made of boiled sugar, to be eaten from a stick **2** anything like this, esp. frozen juice on a stick

lollipop man *fem.* **lollipop woman**— *n* **-men, -women** a person whose job is to stop traffic (so that school children can cross)

lollop *v* *esp. spoken* to move with long ungraceful steps

lolly *n* **-lies 1** *sl* money **2** *esp. spoken* a lollipop

lone *adj* without (other) people —see ALONE (USAGE)

lonely *adj* -lier, -liest **1** alone: *a lonely life in the country* **2** unhappy because of being alone or without friends **3** (of places) without people —see ALONE (USAGE) — **-liness** *n*

loner *n* a person who spends a lot of time alone

lonesome *adj* *esp. spoken* **1** feeling lonely **2** which makes one feel lonely: *a lonesome place*

long¹ *adj* **1 a** measuring a good deal from one end to the other **b** covering a great distance or time **2** covering a certain distance or time **3** which seems to last more than is wished —see also **in the long** RUN, **in the long** TERM

long² *adv* (for) a long time

long³ *n* **1** before long after a short period of time; soon **2 for long** for a long time

long⁴ *v* to want very much — ~ing *n, adj* — ~ingly *adv*

longboat *n* the largest type of boat carried by a sailing vessel

longbow *n* a powerful bow made of a single piece of wood, for use with arrows —compare CROSSBOW

long-distance call *n* US TRUNK CALL

long division *n* the method of dividing numbers with many digits by others, in which each stage is written out

long drink *n* a large drink of something which does not contain a lot of alcohol such as beer

longevity *n* great length of life

longhand *n* full writing by hand, not in any shortened or machine-produced form —compare SHORTHAND

longhop *n* (in cricket) a ball that bounces a long way in front of the batsman, so that it can easily be hit

longish *adj* quite long

longitude *n* the position on the earth east or west of a meridian, usu. measured, from Greenwich —compare LATITUDE ⟶GLOBE

longitudinal *adj* **1** of or concerning longitude **2** in length; going from end to end, not across — ~ly *adv*

long johns *n* *esp. spoken* underclothes with long legs for men

long jump *n* a sport in which people jump as far as possible along the ground

long odds *n* the probability in betting in which one of 2 results is very likely or unlikely; a far from even chance

long-playing record also **album, LP**— *n* a larger type of record which turns fairly slowly and plays for a long time (perhaps ½ an hour each side)

long-range *adj* concerning or covering a long distance or time

longship *n* a type of long narrow open warship once used by the Vikings

longshoreman *n* -men *esp. US* a man employed to unload goods from ships

long shot *n* an attempt which one makes with little real hope of success

longsighted also (*esp. US*) **farsighted**— *adj* able to see objects clearly only when they are far from the eyes —opposite **shortsighted**

longstanding *adj* which has existed in the same form for some time

longsuffering *adj* patient under continued difficulty

long-term *adj* for or in the distant future

long ton *n technical* a measure of weight equal to 2, 240 pounds

long wave *n* radio broadcasting on waves of 1,000 metres or more in length

longwinded *adj* (of a person or a way of speaking) saying too much esp. slowly and dully — ~ **ly** *adv* — ~ **ness** *n*

loo *n* **loos** *esp. spoken* a lavatory

loofah, loofa *n* the dried framework of a plant, used in washing the body

look¹ *v* **1** to give attention in seeing; use the eyes **2** to seem by expression or appearance —see also LOOK AFTER, LOOK BACK, LOOK DOWN ON, LOOK FORWARD TO, LOOK IN, LOOK INTO, LOOK ON, LOOK OUT, LOOK THROUGH, LOOK TO, LOOK UP LOOK UP TO, look LIKE

look² *n* **1** an act of looking **2** an expression, esp. in the eyes **3** an appearance —see also LOOKS

look after *v prep* to take care of (someone or something)

look back *v adv* **1** to remember **2** to fail to advance (in the phrase **never look back**): *After he got the advantage at the beginning of the competition he never looked back* (= he won)

look down on *v adv prep* to have or show a low opinion of (esp. someone thought less important)

look forward to *v adv prep* to expect to feel pleasure in (something about to happen)

look-in *n esp. spoken* **1** the chance to take part or succeed **2** a quick look or visit

look in *v adv esp. spoken* to pay a short visit

looking glass also *esp.spoken* **glass**— *n becoming rare* a mirror

look into *v prep* to examine the meaning or causes of

look on¹ *v adv* to watch while others take part —see also ONLOOKER

look on² also **look upon**— *v prep* to consider; regard

lookout *n* **1** a future possibility **2** the act of keeping watch **3** a place to watch from **4** a person who keeps watch **5 one's own lookout** a state of affairs one must take care of for oneself, without others' help **6 on the lookout for** searching for

look out *v adv* **1** to take care **2** to keep watching (for) **3** to choose from one's possessions: *to look out a party dress*

looks also **good looks**— *n* an attractive appearance

look through *v prep* to look at without seeming to notice (a person), on purpose or because of deep thought

look to *v prep* **1** *esp. written* to be careful about (esp.) improving (something): *We must each look to our own work* **2** to depend on the action of: *We look to you for help*

look up *v adv* **1** to get better, esp. after being bad **2** to find (information) in a book **3** to find and visit (someone) when in the same place

look up to *v adv prep* to respect (someone)

loom¹ *n* a frame or machine for weaving thread into cloth

loom² *v* **1** to come into sight without a clear form, esp. in a fearsome and unfriendly way **2** to appear great and very worrying in the mind

loony *n, adj* -ies; -ier, -iest *sl* (a person who is) mad or foolish; a lunatic

loony bin *n sl* MENTAL HOSPITAL

loop¹ *n* **1** the shape made by a piece of string, wire, rope, etc., when curved back on itself **2** something having this shape, esp. one used as a handle or fastening: *Carry the parcel by this loop of string* **3** a piece of loop- shaped metal or plastic fitted inside a woman to prevent her from having children —see also INTRAUTERINE DEVICE **4** a circular path made by an aircraft in flight **5** a set of commands in a computer program that are repeated until a certain condition is met

loop² *v* **1** to make, make into, or form a loop or loops **2** to pass through a loop, esp. in order to fasten: *Loop that end of the rope through this and knot it* **3** to fasten with a loop of string, rope, etc.

loophole *n* **1** a way of escaping or avoiding something, esp. one provided by a rule or agreement written without enough care **2** a small opening in a castle wall, esp. for shooting arrows through ⟶CASTLE

loose¹ *adj* **1** not tied up, shut up, etc.; free from control **2** not bound together, as with string or in a box **3** not firmly fixed; not tight **4** (of clothes) not fitting tightly, esp. because too big **5** made of parts that are not tight together **6** not exact **7** having many sexual adventures: *a loose woman* **8** not well controlled: *She has a loose tongue and will tell everybody* **9** careless, awkward, or not exact: *Loose play lost them the match* **10** (of the bowels) allowing waste matter to flow naturally, or more than is natural **11** not given a fixed purpose **12 at a loose end** having nothing to do — ~ **ly** *adv* — ~ **ness** *n*

loose² *v* **loosed, loosing** **1** to let loose; untie; make free **2 a** to cause (an arrow) to fly **b** to fire (a gun, weapon, etc.) **3** to free from control

loose³ *adv* in a loose manner; loosely

loose⁴ *n* **on the loose** free, esp. having freedom

from the control of the law or freedom to enjoy oneself

loosebox *n* a space inside a horse's stable where it need not be tied up

loose-leaf *adj* (of a book) able to have pages put in and taken out

loosen *v* **1** to make or become less firm, fixed, tight, etc. **2** to make or become less controlled or more easy and free in movement **3** to set free; unfasten

loosen up *v adv* to make ready for action by exercising the muscles

loot[1] *n* goods taken away unlawfully, as by invading soldiers or by thieves

loot[2] *v* to take loot (from) — ~er *n*

lop[1] *v* **-pp-** to cut branches off from a tree

lop[2] *v* **-pp-** (esp. of an animal's ears) to hang downwards loosely

lope *v* **loped, loping** (esp. of animals) to move easily and fairly fast with springing steps — **lope** *n*

lop-sided *adj* having one side heavier or lower than the other; not balanced

loquacious *adj esp. written* liking to talk a great deal — **~ly** *adv* — **-city** *n*

lord[1] *n* **1** a man who rules people; ruler; master **2** a nobleman of high rank **3** a powerful person in a particular industry **4 as drunk as a lord** very drunk

lord[2] *v* **lord it (over someone)** to behave like a lord (to someone), esp. in giving orders

Lord *n* **1** God **2** (part of the title of certain official people) **3 Lord (only) knows** no one knows

lordly *adj* **-lier, -liest** **1** suitable for a lord; grand **2** behaving like a lord, esp. in giving orders — **-liness** *n*

Lords *n* **1** the members of the House of Lords as a group **2** HOUSE OF LORDS

lordship *n* **1** the power or rule of a lord **2** (the title used when speaking to or of) a judge or certain noblemen

Lord's Prayer also **Our Father—** the most important Christian prayer, beginning 'Our Father, which art in heaven, '

lore *n* knowledge or wisdom, esp. unscientific, about a certain subject or possessed by a certain group of people: *a countryman's weather lore*

lorgnette *n* a pair of glasses held in front of the eyes by a long handle

lorry also **truck—** *n* **-ries** a large motor vehicle for carrying goods

lose *v* **lost, losing** **1** to come to be without, as through carelessness; fail to find **2** to fail to win, gain, or obtain **3** to cause the loss of **4** to come or cause to come to be without (money) **5** to have less of **6** to have taken away or cease to possess, as through death, destruction, ruin, or time: *She lost her parents recently* **7** to free oneself from: *to lose one's fear of water* **8** to fail to hear, see, or understand: *His voice was soft and I lost some of his words* **9** to fail to use; waste: *The doctor lost no time in getting the sick man to hospital* **10**

to fail to keep: *I've lost interest in that subject* **11** to be too late for; miss: *We just lost the train* **12** to give all one's attention to something so as not to notice anything else: *He lost himself in the book* **13** (of a watch or clock) to work too slowly by (an amount of time) **14** to cause (oneself) to miss the way —see also LOST

lose out *v adv* **1** to make a loss (often large) (from something) **2** to be defeated, esp. in an unlucky way

loser *n* a person who has been defeated

loss *n* **1** the act or fact of losing possession **2** the harm, pain, damage, etc., caused by losing something **3** a failure to keep or use **4** a failure to win or obtain **5** a person, thing, or amount that is destroyed or taken away **6** a failure to make a profit **8 at a loss a** at a price lower than the original cost **b** unable or uncertain what to do, think, or say; confused

loss leader *n* an article sold at a low price in order to attract people into a shop

lost *adj* **1** no longer possessed **2** that cannot be found **3** unable to find the way **4** not used, obtained, or won **5** destroyed, ruined, killed, drowned, etc.: *Sailors lost at sea* **6 a** no longer belonging to: *My son was lost to me when he married* **b** no longer possible for (somebody) **c** not noticing: *He was lost to the world in this task* **7** having no influence on

lost cause *n* an effort or action which has been or will now certainly be defeated

lost property *n* articles found in public places which are kept in a special office for people to reclaim

lot[1] *n* **1** a great quantity, number, or amount **2** the whole quantity, number, or amount: *Give me the lot* **3** a group of people or things of the same type; amount of a substance or material **4 a lot/lots** much; a great deal

lot[2] *n* **1** an article or a number of articles sold together, as in an auction sale **2** a building (and its grounds) where films are made **3** *sl* person; character: *He was always a bad lot* **4** one of several objects used for coming to a decision by chance **5** the use of such objects to make a choice or decision: *decide by drawing lots* **6** the decision or choice made in this way: *The lot fell to/on me* **7** share **8** one's way of life; fortune; fate

loth *adj* loath

lotion *n* a liquid mixture, used on the skin or hair to make it clean and healthy

lottery *n* **-ries** **1** an arrangement in which people buy tickets, a few of which are picked by chance to win prizes —compare RAFFLE **2** something whose result or worth is uncertain or risky

lotus *n* **1** a white or pink flower found, esp. in Asia, on the surface of shallow lakes **2** (in ancient Greek stories) a fruit which caused the eater to feel contented, dreamy, and unwilling to be active

lotus-eater *n* a person who leads a contented

dreamy life unconcerned with the business of the world

loud[1] *adj* 1 being or producing much sound; not quiet; noisy 2 attracting attention by being unpleasantly noisy or colourful — ~ly *adv* — ~ness *n*

loud[2] *adv* loudly; in a loud way

loudhailer *n* a megaphone

loudmouth *n* a person who talks too much and in an offensive manner — ~ed *adj*

loudspeaker also **speaker**— *n* an apparatus that turns electrical current into sound ⟹ELECTRICITY

lough *n* (in Ireland) a lake or a part of the sea almost surrounded by land

lounge[1] *v* **lounged, lounging** 1 to stand or sit in a leaning lazy manner 2 to pass time in a lazy manner, doing nothing — ~r *n*

lounge[2] *n* 1 an act or period of lounging 2 a comfortable sitting room in a house or hotel

lounge bar *n* SALOON BAR

lounge suit *n* a man's informal daytime suit

lour also **lower**— *v* 1 to look in a dissatisfied bad-tempered manner; to frown 2 (of the sky or weather) to be dark and threatening

louse *n* **lice** 1 any of several types of small insect that live on the skin and in the hair of people and animals ⟹INSECT 2 *sl* a worthless person deserving no respect

lousy *adj* **-ier, -iest** 1 covered with lice 2 *esp. spoken* very bad, unpleasant, useless, etc.

lout *n* a man or boy with bad manners — ~ish *adj*

louvre *n* an arrangement of sloping bands of wood, metal, etc., fixed in a frame across a window to allow some light in but keep strong sun out

lovable, loveable *adj* 1 deserving, causing, or worthy of love 2 pleasant; attractive

love[1] *n* 1 a strong feeling of fondness for another person 2 warm interest and enjoyment and attraction (to): *love of music* 3 the object of such interest and attraction 4 a person who is loved 5 also (*bad usage or humour*) **luv**— (a friendly word of address) 6 *esp. spoken* a person or thing that one loves or likes very much: *Isn't that puppy a love!* 7 (in tennis) the state of having no points 8 **no love lost between** no friendship between —see also MAKE **love (to)**

love[2] *v* **loved, loving** 1 to feel love, desire, or strong friendship (for) 2 to have a strong liking for; take pleasure in 3 to have sex with

love affair *n* 1 an experience of love between 2 people, esp. between a man and a woman 2 a sexual relationship

lovechild *n* **-children** *old use or polite* a bastard

loveless *adj* 1 not giving or able to give love; cold 2 not receiving love 3 without love

lovelorn *adj* sad because one's love is not returned

lovely[1] *adj* **-lier, -liest** 1 beautiful, attractive, etc., esp. to both the heart and the eye 2 *esp.*

spoken very pleasant: *a lovely meal* — **-liness** *n*

lovely[2] *n* **-lies** *esp. spoken* a beautiful woman: *Come here, my lovely!*

lovemaking *n* 1 words or actions expressing love or sexual desire 2 the act of having sex

lover *n* 1 a man in love with or having a sexual relationship with a woman outside of marriage 2 a person who is very keen on something

lovesick *adj* sad or sick because of unreturned love

loving *adj* showing or expressing love; fond — ~ly *adv*

loving cup *n* a large drinking vessel, usu. with handles, that is sometimes passed round at a ceremonial feast

low[1] *v* *esp. in literature* to moo

low[2] *adj* 1 not measuring much from the base to the top; not high 2 being not far above the ground, floor, base, or bottom 3 being or lying below the general level of height 4 being near or at the bottom of a supply or measure 5 on the ground, as after a blow, or dead: *I laid him low with my gun* 6 lacking in strength; weak: *He is low with flu* 7 lacking spirit; unhappy 8 small in size, degree, amount, worth, etc. 9 regarding something as of little worth; unfavourable: *I have a low opinion of that book* 10 near the bottom in position or rank 11 not worthy, respectable, good, etc. 12 cheap: *a low price* 13 for a slow or slowest speed: *Use a low gear when driving slowly* 14 hidden; unnoticed: *The escaped prisoner lay low* 15 not greatly developed; simple: *low plant life* 16 not loud; soft — ~ness *n*

low[3] *adv* 1 in or to a low position, point, degree, manner, etc. 2 near the ground, floor, base, etc.; not high 3 (in music) in or with deep notes 4 quietly; softly 5 **run low** to become less than enough

low[4] *n* 1 a point, price, degree, etc., that is low 2 an area of low pressure in the air

lowborn *adj* *literature* born to parents of low social rank

lowbrow *n* usu. *offensive* a person who is satisfied with simple music, painting, poetry, etc. —compare HIGHBROW, MIDDLEBROW

lowdown *n* *sl* the plain facts or truth, esp. when not generally known

low-down *adj* worthless; dishonourable

lower[1] *v* to lour

lower[2] *adj* in or being the bottom part

lower[3] *v* 1 to make or become smaller in amount, price, degree, strength, etc. 2 to move or let down in height 3 to bring (someone, esp. oneself) down in rank, worth, or opinion, as by doing something not worthy or wrong; to disgrace

lower case *n, adj* (a type of letter) written in its usual small form (such as *a, b, c,*) rather than in its capital form (such as A, B, C,)—compare UPPER CASE

lower class *n* a social class generally regarded as being of the lowest rank; the working class

Lower House also **Lower Chamber**— *n* one of the 2 branches of a law-making body, esp. the one that is larger, more representative, and more powerful

low-key also **low-keyed**— *adj* 1 controlled in style or quality; not loud or bright 2 *esp. spoken* not important; weak

lowland *n, adj* (an area of land) that is lower than the land surrounding it — ~er *n*

low-level *adj* 1 at a low level 2 of or relating to computer language in which one instruction orders the computer to do one thing

lowly[1] *adv* 1 in a low position, manner, or degree 2 in a manner that is not proud

lowly[2] *adj* **-lier, -liest** 1 low in rank, position, or degree 2 not grand or proud; simple; humble — **-liness** *n*

low profile *n* the state of not drawing attention to oneself or one's actions

low season *n* the time of year when business is least and prices are lowest

low tide *n* 1 the moment when the tide is at its lowest point on the shore 2 this point on the shore

low water *n* 1 the moment when a river is at its lowest point because of the tide 2 this point on the river bank

loyal *adj* true to one's friends, group, country, etc.; faithful — ~ly *adv*

loyalist *n* a person who remains faithful to an existing government, esp. during fighting with those who want to change it

loyalty *n* **-ties** 1 the quality of being loyal 2 a connection which binds a person to someone or something to which he is loyal

lozenge *n* 1 a small flat sweet, esp. one containing medicine 2 a figure having 4 straight and equal sides and 2 sharp angles 3 something made in this shape, such as a piece of a window

LP *n* LONG-PLAYING RECORD

L-plate *n* one of 2 flat squares, marked with a letter L, that must be fixed to the front and back of a vehicle when the driver is a learner

LSD also (*sl*) **acid**— *n* a tasteless drug causing one to see the world in a strange way and to see things that do not exist

Lsd, £sd *n esp. spoken* (a word used, esp. before decimal money was introduced, for) money

Ltd *abbrev.* (*used after the name of a limited liability company*) for: limited: *M.Y. Dixon and Son, Ltd, Booksellers*

lubricant *n* a substance, esp. oil, able to make parts of a machine move more easily

lubricate *v* **-cated, -cating** 1 to put oil or an oily substance into (the moving parts of a machine) to make them work more easily 2 to make smooth and able to move or be moved easily — **-cation** *n* — **-cator** *n*

lucerne *n* a type of plant used for feeding farm animals

lucid *adj* 1 easy to understand; clear 2 when able to understand: *The madman does have occasional lucid moments* — ~ly *adv* — ~ity *n*

luck *n* 1 that which happens, either good or bad, to a person in the course of events by, or as if by, chance; fate; fortune 2 success as a result of chance; good fortune 3 **be down on one's luck** to have bad luck, esp. to be without money 4 **worse luck** unfortunately

luckless *adj* 1 without good fortune 2 ending in failure

lucky *adj* **-ier, -iest** having, resulting from, or bringing good luck — **-ily** *adv* — **-iness** *n*

lucky dip *n* 1 a barrel filled with wrapped objects of various values, into which a person may put his hand and pick out one, for a payment 2 something whose result depends on chance; a lottery

lucrative *adj* bringing in plenty of money; profitable — ~ly *adv*

lucre *n* money; profit (esp. in the phrase **filthy lucre**)

ludicrous *adj* causing disrespectful laughter; very foolish; ridiculous — ~ly *adv* — ~ness *n*

ludo *n* a children's board game played with counters

luff *v sailing* to bring the front of a sailing boat closer to or directly facing the wind

lug[1] *v* **-gg-** *esp. spoken* to pull or carry with great effort and difficulty

lug[2] *n esp. spoken* a heavy or difficult pull

lug[3] *n* a little piece that sticks out from something, such as a handle of a cooking pot

luggage *n* the cases and bags of a traveller

lugger *n* a type of small sailing boat

lugubrious *adj* doing and feeling little because unhappy; too sorrowful — ~ly *adv* — ~ness *n*

lugworm also **lug**— *n* a type of small worm found by the sea, used by fishermen for bait

lukewarm *adj* 1 (esp. of liquid) not much hotter than cold 2 showing hardly any interest; not eager

lull[1] *v* 1 to cause to sleep or rest 2 to come or bring to an end; make or become less active

lull[2] *n* a period in which activity is less

lullaby *n* **-bies** a song to help children go to sleep

lumbago *n* pain in the lower back

lumbar *adj medical* of or belonging to the lower part of the back

lumber[1] *v* to move awkwardly

lumber[2] *n* 1 useless or unwanted articles, such as furniture, stored away somewhere 2 *esp. US* timber

lumber[3] *v esp. spoken* to cause difficulty to (someone), esp. by giving unwanted responsibility: *I'm lumbered with Mary's puppy for the weekend*

lumberjack *n* (esp. in the US and Canada) a man who cuts down trees

lumber-room *n* a room in which useless furniture, broken machines, etc., are stored

luminous *adj* 1 giving light; bright 2 easily understood; clear — ~ly *adv* — **-nosity** *n*

lump¹ *n* **1** a mass of something solid without a special size or shape **2** a hard swelling on the body **3** *esp. spoken* a heavy awkward person **4** a small square-sided block (of sugar) **5** *esp. spoken* the group of workers in the building industry who are not employed on a continuous contract, but only as and when needed **6 lump in the throat** a tight sensation in the throat caused by unexpressed pity, sorrow, etc.

lump² *v* to form into lumps

lump³ *adj* **1** not divided into parts; all together **2** being in the form of lumps

lump⁴ *v* **lump it** *esp. spoken* to accept bad conditions without complaint (often in the phrase **like it or lump it**)

lump together *v adv* to consider as a unity

lumpy *adj* -ier, -iest filled or covered with lumps

lunacy *n* -cies **1** madness **2** (an act of) foolish or wild behaviour

lunar *adj* **1** of or concerning the moon **2** made for use on or around the moon

lunar month *n* a period of 28 days, being the time the moon takes to circle the earth —compare CALENDAR MONTH

lunatic¹ *n* **1** *old use or offensive* a person suffering from an illness of the mind **2** a wildly foolish person

lunatic² *adj* wildly foolish

lunatic asylum *n* rare MENTAL HOSPITAL

lunatic fringe *n* the wildest or least sensible people in a group

lunch¹ also (*esp. written*) **luncheon**— *n* a meal eaten at midday

lunch² *v* to eat lunch

luncheon meat *n* meat (usu. pork), pressed into a loaflike form

lung *n* either of the 2 breathing organs in the chest of man or certain other creatures (mammals, birds, reptiles, and some amphibians) ⫐RESPIRATION — see also IRON LUNG

lunge *v, n* lunged, lunging (to make) a sudden forceful forward movement, with the body or a knife

lungfish *n* -fish or -fishes any of several types of fish that breathe partly by means of a lunglike organ

lupin *n* a type of tall garden plant with many flowers

lurch¹ *n* **leave someone in the lurch** *esp. spoken* to leave someone alone and helpless; desert someone

lurch² *n, v* (to make) a sudden irregular movement forward or sideways

lure¹ *n* **lured, luring 1** something that attracts by promising pleasure **2** attraction; promise **3** an apparatus, such as a plastic bird or fish, to attract animals into a place where they can be caught **4** a group of bright feathers fastened together, used for attracting a hunting bird back to its master while it is being trained

lure² *v* to attract or tempt, esp. away from what one should do

lurgy *n* -gies *humour* an illness or disease

lurid *adj* **1** unnaturally bright; strongly coloured **2** shocking, esp. because violent; unpleasant — ~ly *adv* — ~ness *n*

lurk *v* **1** to wait in hiding, esp. for an evil purpose **2** to move quietly as if having done wrong and not wanting to be seen **3** to exist unseen

luscious *adj* **1** having a very pleasant taste or smell; sweet **2** very attractive; beautiful **3** ripe and healthy — ~ly *adv* — ~ness *n*

lush *adj* **1** (of plants, esp. grass) growing very well, thickly, and healthily **2** *esp. spoken* comfortable, esp. as provided by wealth

lust *n* **1** strong sexual desire, esp. when uncontrolled or considered wrong **2** strong usu. evil desire; eagerness to possess: *lust for power* —see DESIRE (USAGE)

lust for also **lust after**— *v prep* to desire eagerly, esp. sexually

lustful *adj* full of strong, esp. sexual, desire — ~ly *adv* — ~ness *n*

lustre *n* **1** brightness as of light reflected from a shiny surface **2** glory; fame

lustrous *adj* *esp. in literature* shining; brilliant — ~ly *adv*

lusty *adj* -ier, -iest **1** full of strength, power, health, etc. **2** full of sexual desire — -ily *adv* — -iness *n*

lute *n* a type of stringed musical instrument, having a long neck and a pear shaped body, played with the fingers and used esp. in former times — -anist, -enist *n*

luv *n* *bad usage or humour* love

luxuriant *adj* **1** growing well, esp. in health and number **2** very productive **3** very highly ornamented **4** having or showing the comforts of wealth —compare LUXURIOUS — ~ly *adv* — -ance *n*

luxuriate in *v prep* -ated, ating in *esp. written* to enjoy oneself lazily in

luxurious *adj* **1** very fine and costly **2** providing the greatest comfort **3** fond of comfort and of satisfying the senses: *He had luxurious habits* —compare LUXURIANT — ~ly *adv*

luxury *n* -ries **1** great comfort, as provided without worry about the cost **2** something that is not necessary and not often had or done but which is very pleasant

lycée *n* a French school for older pupils, either in France or for (esp.) French children abroad

lychee *n* a South East Asian tree or its fruit, with a hard rough nutlike shell and a sweet white flesh that contains a single seed

lychgate *n* a gate with a roof, leading into a churchyard ⫐CATHEDRAL

lying *pres. part. of* LIE

lymph *n* a clear watery liquid formed in the body of animals which passes into the blood system — ~atic *adj*

lynch *v* (esp. of a crowd of people) to attack and put to death, esp. by hanging, (a person thought to be guilty of a crime), without a lawful trial

lynx *n* **lynxes** or **lynx** a type of large strong wild cat with long legs and a short tail

lyre a type of ancient Greek U-shaped, stringed musical instrument

lyric[1] *adj* **1** of or intended for singing **2** expressing strong personal feelings, usu. in song-like form: *lyric poet/poetry* **3** joyful: *a lyric passage of music*

lyric[2] *n* **1** a short poem suitable for singing **2** a poem or other form of expression about strong personal feelings

lyrical *adj* full of admiration, pleasure, eagerness, etc. — ~**ly** *adv*

lyricism *n* **1** lyric style or quality, esp. in poetry **2** an expression of strong personal feeling

lyrics *n* the words of a modern popular song

M

M, m **M's, m's** or **Ms, ms** **1** the 13th letter of the English alphabet **2** the Roman numeral for 1000

m *abbrev. for:* metre

ma *n esp. spoken* **1** (a name for mother, not considered polite) **2** (a name for an (old) woman, not considered polite)

MA *abbrev. for:* Master of Arts; (a title for someone who has) a university degree which can be taken one or 2 years after a BA (=first degree)

ma'am *n polite* (a short form for madam, now used for addressing the Queen)

mac *n esp. spoken* a mackintosh

macabre *adj* causing fear, esp. because connected with death —compare GRUESOME

macadam *n* a material made of small broken stones mixed with tar which is rolled on roads to make a smooth hard surface

macadamize, -ise *v* **-ized, -izing** to cover (a road surface) with macadam

macaroni *n* a food made of thin tubes of pasta —compare SPAGHETTI

macaroon *n* a small flat cake made mainly of sugar, egg, and almonds △ MAROON

macaw *n* a brightly-coloured parrot of Central and South America

mace[1] *n* **1** an ornamental rod which is carried or placed before an official in certain ceremonies as a sign of power **2** a short heavy club with sharp points around the head, used as a weapon in former times ☞WEAPON

mace[2] *n* a cooking spice made from the dried shell of a nutmeg

mace-bearer *n* a person who carries a mace before an official in a ceremony

macerate *v* **-ated, -ating** to make or become soft by putting or being left in water — **-ation** *n*

Mach *n* the speed of an aircraft in relation to the speed of sound: *A plane flying at Mach 2 is flying at twice the speed of sound*

machete also **machet**— *n* a broad heavy bladed knife used in South America and elsewhere

Machiavellian *adj* (of people and actions) using cunning to gain one's own aims, esp. in politics; scheming

machination *n* a plan for doing harm

machine[1] *n* **1** a man-made instrument or apparatus which uses power (such as electricity) to perform work **2** a group of people that controls the activities of a political party

machine[2] *v* **machined, machining** **1** to make or produce by machine, esp. in sewing and printing **2** to produce according to exact measurements by use of a cutting machine: *The edge must be machined down to 0.3 millimetres*

machine code *n* a language in which a computer operates, and into which other languages have to be translated

machinegun *n* a gun which fires rapidly as long as the trigger is pressed ☞WEAPON

machinery *n* **1** machines in general **2** the working parts of an apparatus **3** a system or organization by which action is controlled

machine tool *n* a power-driven tool for cutting and shaping

machinist *n* a person who uses a machine at work, esp. for sewing

mackerel *n* **-rel** or **rels** **1** a type of sea fish with blue-green bands across its body and oily strong-tasting flesh **2 a mackerel sky** a sky with bands of high white cloud

mackintosh also (*esp. spoken*) **mack, mac**— *n* a raincoat

macramé *n* the art or practice of knotting string together in ornamental patterns

macrobiotic *adj* concerning a type of food which is thought health giving, because of the presence of whole grains in flour products and the use of vegetables grown without chemicals

macrocosm *n* **1** the world as a whole; universe **2** any large system containing smaller systems —compare MICROCOSM

mad *adj* **-dd-** **1** suffering from a disorder of the mind **2** (of a dog) suffering from a disease (RABIES) which causes wild and dangerous behaviour; rabid **3** very foolish and careless of danger **4** filled with strong feeling, interest, etc. **5** *esp. spoken* angry **6** like **mad** *esp. spoken* very hard, fast, loud, etc. —see ANGRY (USAGE)

madam *n* **1** (a respectful way of addressing a woman) **2** (a young) female who likes to give orders: *She's a little madam, she won't do anything I suggest* **3** a woman who is in charge of a house of prostitutes

Madam *n* **Mesdames** *French* **1** (a word of address used to begin a business letter to a woman, after the word *Dear*) **2** (a word for addressing a woman official, followed by the name of her office)

Madame *n* **Mesdames** *French* (the French

Pulley

Gears

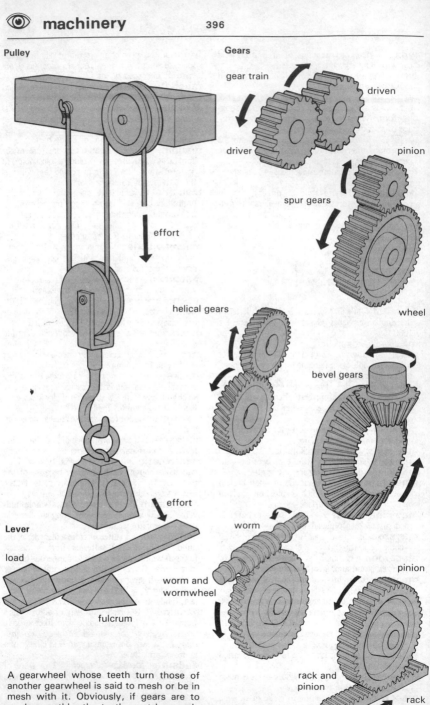

gear train

driven

driver

pinion

spur gears

wheel

effort

helical gears

bevel gears

effort

Lever

load

worm

fulcrum

worm and
wormwheel

pinion

rack and
pinion

rack

A gearwheel whose teeth turn those of
another gearwheel is said to mesh or be in
mesh with it. Obviously, if gears are to
work smoothly, the teeth must be evenly
spaced.

word for Mrs., used as a title for certain married women, usu. French ones)

madcap *adj* wild and thoughtless — **madcap** *n*

madden *v* to make wild or angry

maddening *adj* 1 causing much pain or worry 2 *esp. spoken* very annoying — ~**ly** *adv*

madder *n* a plant from whose roots a red dye is obtained

made[1] *past tense and past part. of* MAKE

made[2] *adj* 1 sure of success: *When you find gold you're made for life* 2 completely suited: *a night made for love*

Madeira *n* a strong wine produced in the island of Madeira

Madeira cake *n* a type of heavy yellow sponge cake

Mademoiselle *n* mesdemoiselles *French* (the French word for Miss, used as a title for a young unmarried French girl)

made-to-measure *adj* bespoke

madhouse *n* 1 (in former times) a mental hospital 2 *esp. spoken* a place where there is a noisy and/or disorderly crowd of people

madly *adv* 1 in a wild way as if mad 2 *esp. spoken* very (much)

madman (*fem.* **madwoman**)— *n* -men a person who is mad

madness *n* 1 the state of being mad 2 behaviour that appears mad

Madonna *n* 1 Mary, the mother of Christ in the Christian religion 2 a picture or figure of Mary

madrigal *n* a non-religious song for several singers without instrumental accompaniment. It was popular in England in the 16th century

maelstrom *n esp. in literature* 1 a violent whirlpool 2 the violent and possibly destructive force of events

maestro *n* -tros *or* -tri a great or famous musician, esp. conductor

mafia *n* an organization of criminals who control many activities by threats of violence, esp. in the west of Sicily and more recently in the US

magazine *n* 1 a sort of book with a paper cover and usu. large-sized pages, which contains writing, photographs, and advertisements, and which is sold every week or month 2 a storehouse or room for arms, explosives, bullets, etc. 3 the part of a gun, or similar weapon, in which cartridges are placed before firing 4 the place where the film is kept away from the light in a camera

magenta *n, adj* (of) a dark purplish red colour or colouring matter

maggot *n* a small wormlike creature, which hatches from the eggs of a fly, found on flesh and food — ~**y** *adj*

magi *pl. of* MAGUS

Magi *n* (in the Christian religion) the three wise men who visited and brought gifts for the baby Jesus

magic[1] *n* 1 the system of trying to control

events by calling on spirits, secret forces, etc. 2 *technical* the system of thought which imagines that images or parts of objects have a power over the objects themselves 3 the art employed by a conjurer who produces unexpected results by tricks 4 a a strange influence or power b a charming and/or mysterious quality

magic[2] *adj* caused by or used in magic

magical *adj* of strange power, mystery, or charm — ~**ly** *adv*

magic eye *n esp. spoken* a photoelectric cell

magician *n* 1 (in stories) a person who can make strange things happen by magic 2 a person who does magic tricks; conjurer

magisterial *adj* having or showing the power of a master; like (that of) someone who is in complete control of an action, subject, etc. — ~**ly** *adv*

magistrate *n* an official who has the power to judge cases in the lowest courts of law; justice of the peace — -**acy** *n*

magma *n* hot melted rock found below the solid surface of the earth

magnanimity *n* the quality of being generous, esp. by helping others — -**mous** *adj* — -**mously** *adv*

magnate *n* a man who has a leading position in business or industry, or who owns land

magnesium *n* a silver-white metal that is a simple element, burns with a bright white light, and is used in making fireworks and light alloys

magnet *n* 1 any object which can draw iron towards it either naturally or because of an electric current being passed through it ⟶ ELECTRICITY 2 a person or thing which draws or attracts (people) — ~**ic** *adj* — ~**ically** *adv* — ~**ism** *n*

magnetic pole *n* one of 2 points near the north pole or the south pole towards which the compass needle points

magnetic tape *n* a tape on which sound or other information can be recorded

magnetize, -ise *v* -ized, -izing 1 to give the qualities of a magnet to 2 to attract or draw by magnetism

magneto *n* -tos an apparatus containing several magnets, able to produce electricity esp. in a car —compare GENERATOR, DYNAMO

Magnificat *n* the song of Mary, the mother of Jesus Christ, which praises God for his favour to her, which is sung as a prayer in the Church of England

magnification *n* 1 the act of magnifying 2 the power of magnifying a stated number of times: *The lens has a magnification of 8*

magnificent *adj* great, grand, generous, etc. — -**cence** *n* — ~**ly** *adv*

magnify *v* -fied, -fying to make (something) appear larger than in reality — -**fier** *n*

magnifying glass *n* a glass lens, with a frame and handle, which makes what is seen through it look bigger

magnitude *n* 1 greatness of size or importance 2 the degree of absolute or apparent brightness of a star

magnolia *n* a type of tree with large sweet-smelling flowers

magnum *n* (a large bottle containing) a measure of about 1·5 litres, esp. for wine

magpie *n* a type of noisy black and white bird of the crow family which often takes small bright objects

magus *n* **magi** *esp. written* a magician

maharaja, -jah *n* (the title of) an Indian prince

maharani, -ee *n* (the title of) the wife of a maharaja

mah-jong, -jongg *n* a Chinese game, for 4 players, played with small painted pieces of wood, bone, etc.

mahogany *n* **-nies** 1 a type of tree or its dark reddish wood, used for furniture 2 a reddish-brown colour

maid also **maidservant**— *n* 1 a female servant —see also MILKMAID, OLD MAID 2 *literature & old use* an unmarried girl

maiden[1] *n* 1 *literature* an unmarried girl 2 also **maiden over**— (in cricket) an over in which no runs are made

maiden[2] *adj* 1 fresh; not used before 2 first; not done before: *the maiden flight of an aircraft* 3 (of a woman) unmarried: *a maiden aunt*

maidenhead *n* *old use* 1 (for a woman) the state of being a virgin 2 the hymen

maidenhood *n* *literature* the condition or time of being a young unmarried girl

maidenly *adj* *literature* like or suitable to a maiden; sweet, gentle, etc.

maiden name *n* the family name a woman has before marriage

maid of honour *n* an unmarried lady who serves a queen or princess

mail[1] *n* 1 the postal system directed and worked by the government 2 letters and anything else sent or received by post, esp. those travelling or arriving together 3 also **mail train**— (esp. in names) a train which carries mail: *the Irish Mail*

mail[2] *v* *esp. US* to.post

mail[3] *n* armour made of metal plates or rings —compare CHAIN MAIL

mailbag *n* a bag made of strong cloth for carrying mail in trains, ships, etc.

mailing list *n* a list of names and addresses kept by an organization, to which it posts information

mail order *n* a method of selling goods in which the buyer chooses them from a catalogue at home and his order is posted to him

maim *v* to harm bodily so as to cripple

main[1] *n* 1 a a chief pipe supplying water or gas, or a chief wire carrying electricity into a building: *a gas main* —see also MAINS b a chief sewer pipe taking waste, water, etc., out from a building 2 *poetic* the sea 3 **in the main** on the whole; usually; mostly

main[2] *adj* 1 chief; first in importance or size 2 **by main force** *esp. literature* by all the strength of the body

main clause *n* INDEPENDENT CLAUSE

mainland *n* a land mass, considered without its islands

mainline *v* *sl* to inject (a drug) into one of the veins (e.g. for pleasure)

main line *n* one of the chief railway lines

mainly *adv* chiefly

mainmast *n* the chief mast on a ship

mains *adj* supplied from a main: *mains electricity*

mainsail *n* the chief sail on a ship, usu. that on the mainmast ⌐SAIL

mainspring *n* 1 the chief spring in a watch 2 the chief force or reason that makes something happen

mainstay *n* **-stays** 1 someone or something which provides the chief means of support 2 a rope stretching from the top of the mainmast in a ship to the bottom of a shorter pole in front

mainstream *n* the usual way of thinking or acting in a subject

maintain *v* 1 to continue to have, do, etc., as before 2 to support with money 3 to keep in existence 4 to keep in good condition, by repairing and taking care of 5 to state as true; argue for (an opinion) — ~**able** *adj*

maintenance *n* 1 the act of maintaining 2 money given to wives and/or children by a husband who does not live with them

maintenance order *n* an order made by a law court for a person to pay maintenance

maisonette, maisonnette *n* a small flat or house arranged as a separate living place and usu. on more than one floor

maize *n* American corn

majesty *n* greatness; a show of power, as of a king or queen — **-tic** *adj* — **-tically** *adv*

Majesty *n* **-ties** (a title for addressing or speaking of a king or queen)

major[1] *adj* 1 greater in degree, size, etc. 2 *old public school* being the elder of 2 brothers of the stated name in the same school: *Brown major* —opposite **minor** 3 (in music) based on or being a scale with 4 semitones between the first and third notes 4 (of an operation) more than usually risky

major[2] *n* 1 a middle ranking officer in the army or American airforce 2 *esp. written & law* a person who has reached the age (now 18 in Britain) at which he is fully responsible in law for his actions —compare MINOR

major general *n* a high ranking officer in the army or American airforce

majority *n* **-ties** 1 the greater number or part; a number or part that is more than half 2 the difference in number between a large and smaller group (e.g. of votes) 3 *law* the state or time when one has, in law, reached the grown-up state 4 **in the majority** (one of) the greater number of people or things -compare MINORITY

majority² adj reached by agreement of most, but not all, of the members of a group

make¹ v **made, making** 1 to produce by work or action 2 to tidy (a bed that has just been slept in) 3 to put into a certain state, position, etc.: *Too much food made him ill* 4 to earn, gain, or win: *He makes a lot of money in his job* 5 to force or cause (a person to do something/a thing to happen): *The pain made him cry out* 6 to represent as being, doing, happening, etc.; cause to appear as: *This photograph makes her look very young* 7 to calculate (and get as a result): *What time do you make it?* 8 to add up to; come to (an amount) as a result: *2 and 2 make 4* 9 to be counted as (first, second, etc.) 10 to have the qualities of: *This story makes good reading* 11 to travel (a distance) or at (a speed): *The train was making 70 miles an hour* 12 to arrive at or on: *We just made the train* 13 to form (into or from): *The navy has made a man of him* —see also **make a** FOOL **of** 14 to put forward for consideration or acceptance (a suggestion of payment or a gift): *Let me make you a present of it* 15 *esp. written* to be about (to): *He made to speak, but I stopped him* 16 *esp. spoken* to give the particular qualities of; complete: *It's the bright paint which really makes the room* —see also **make** GOOD 17 **make as if to** to be about to: *He made as if to speak* 18 **make believe** to pretend 19 **make it a** to arrive in time*b**esp. spoken* to succeed 20 **make love (to) a** to have sex (with) **b** *esp. old use* to show that one is in love (with) 21 **make one's way** to go 22 **make or mar/break** which will cause success or complete failure: *a make or break decision/plan* —see also MADE, **make** DO, MAKE FOR, MAKE OF, MAKE OFF, MAKE OUT, MAKE OVER, MAKE UP, MAKE UP FOR, MAKE UP TO

make² n 1 the type to which a set of (man-made) objects belongs, esp. the name of the makers 2 **on the make** *sl* **a** searching for personal profit or gain **b** trying to obtain a sexual experience with someone

make-believe n a state of pretending or the things which are pretended

make for v prep 1 to move in the direction of (usu. quickly or purposefully) 2 also **make at**— to move to attack 3 to result in: *Large print makes for easier reading*

make of v prep to understand (partly or at all) by: *I don't know what to make of his behaviour*

make off v adv to escape in a hurry

make out v adv 1 to see or understand with difficulty 2 to write in complete form: *to make out a list* 3 *esp. spoken* to succeed (in business or life generally) 4 to have a (esp. friendly) relationship: *How did you make out with your new employer?* 5 *esp. spoken* to claim or pretend (that someone or something is so), usu. falsely: *He makes out he's younger than me* 6 to argue as proof: *I'm sure we can make out a case for allowing you another holiday*

make over v adv 1 to change: *The garage has been made over into a play room* 2 to pass over

possession of, esp. in law: *His wealth was made over to his children*

maker n 1 one of the people (esp. a firm) who make something 2 God: *The old man died and went to meet his Maker*

makeshift adj used at the time because there is nothing better —see also **make** SHIFT

make-up n 1 the combination of qualities (in a person's character) 2 **a** powder, paint, etc., worn on the face **b** an appearance produced by the use of this **c** the art of using this to prepare the face for working under bright lights on stage

make up v adv 1 to become friends again after (a quarrel) 2 to use special paint and powder on the face of (someone or oneself) so as to change or improve the appearance 3 to invent (a story, poem, etc.), esp. in order to deceive 4 to prepare (a drug), esp. according to a doctor's note 5 to make (an amount or number) complete 6 to produce (something) from (material) by cutting and sewing 7 to arrange ready for use: *make up a bed*

make up for v adv prep 1 to repay for (what was bad before) with something good: *This beautiful autumn is making up for the wet summer* 2 **make up for lost time** to work fast, because of time lost earlier

make up to v adv prep 1 to try to gain the favour of (someone) by appearing friendly or by flattering them 2 **make it up to someone/make (it) up to someone for something** to repay someone with good things in return for something good done or something bad experienced by him

making n 1 the cause of great improvement: *Hard work will be the making of him* 2 **in the making a** while being made **b** ready to be produced: *There's a fortune in the making for anyone willing to work hard*

makings n the possibility of developing (into)

maladjusted adj (of a person) of a character which has developed unsuitably, so that the person cannot be happy or behave well in his surroundings — **-justment** n

maladministration n carelessness and lack of ability in carrying out duties, usu. by someone official

maladroit n *esp. written* not skilful in action or behaviour; awkward — ~**ly** adv — ~**ness** n

malady n **-dies** *esp. written* 1 something that is wrong with a system or organization 2 *old use* an illness

malaise n 1 a feeling of illness without any particular appearance of disease 2 a lack of wellbeing, esp. shown in lack of activity

malapropism n a wrong use of a word, in which a word is used which sounds like the correct word, but means something quite different (as in *'Poor Uncle Ted! He went on a trip up the river and was eaten by an allegory'*)

malapropos adj, adv *esp. written & pompous* unsuitable or unsuitably for the occasion

malaria n a disease of hot countries, caused by a small living thing which enters the blood when the person is bitten by certain types of mosquito — ~l *adj* : *malarial fever* | *malarial swamps*

Malay also **Malayan** — *adj* of the people or language of Malaysia

malcontent *n* a person dissatisfied with a state of affairs, esp. with politics — ~ed *adj*

male¹ *adj* 1 of the sex that does not give birth to young 2 suitable to or typical of this sex, rather than the female sex 3 (of a part of a machine) made to fit into a hollow part

male² *n* a male person or animal

malediction *n* *esp. written or literature* a curse —compare BENEDICTION

malefactor *n* *esp. written or literature* a person who does evil; criminal —compare BENEFACTOR

maleficent *adj* *esp. written or literature* able to do, or doing, evil —compare BENEFICENT — -cence *n*

malevolent *adj* *esp. literature* having or expressing a wish to do evil to others — -lence *n* — ~ly *adv*

malformed *adj* made or shaped badly — compare DEFORM — -mation *n*

malfunction *n* *esp. written* a fault in operation

malice *n* 1 the wish, desire, or intention to hurt 2 **with malice aforethought** *law* (of a criminal act) planned before it was done

malicious *adj* feeling or expressing malice — ~ly *adv*

malign¹ *adj* *often literature* (of things) harmful; causing evil — ~ity *n*

malign² *v* to express evil of, esp. wrongly

malignant *adj* 1 full of hate and a strong wish to hurt 2 (of a disease or condition) serious enough to cause death —compare BENIGN — -nancy *n* — ~ly *adv*

malinger *v* to avoid work by pretending to be ill — ~er *n*

mall *n* *US* a shopping precinct

mallard *n* **mallards** or **mallard** a type of wild duck ⟶ BIRD

malleable *adj* 1 (of metals) able to be beaten, pressed, rolled, etc., into a new shape 2 (of people, character, nature, etc.) easily formed or changed — -bility *n*

mallet *n* 1 a wooden hammer 2 a wooden club with a long handle, used in croquet and polo

mallow *n* a type of plant with pink or purple flowers and fine hairs on its stem and leaves

malmsey *n* a sweet dark type of Madeira

malnutrition *n* feeding with too little or poor food

malodorous *adj* *esp. written or pompous* having a bad smell

malpractice *n* unlawful activity, usu. for personal advantage, by a person in a responsible or trusted position

malt¹ *n* grain, usu. barley, which has been kept in water for a while, then dried, and is used for preparing drinks, like beer

malt² *v* 1 to make into malt 2 to make or treat with malt

Maltese *adj* of the people or language of the island of Malta

Maltese cross *n* a cross with 2 points at the end of each of the 4 arms

Malthusian *adj* connected with, esp. supporting, the writings of Thomas Malthus (1776–1834), which say that the world population will grow faster than its food supply if not controlled

maltreat *v* to treat roughly and/or cruelly — compare ILL-TREAT — ~ment *n*

mama, mamma *n* *now rare* (a name for) mother

mamba *n* a type of large very poisonous African tree snake

mammal *n* an animal which is fed when young on milk from the mother's body ⟶ EVOLUTION ⟲

mammary *adj* *technical* of or concerned with the breast

mammoth¹ *n* a kind of hairy elephant, larger than the modern one, which lived on earth during the early stages of human development —compare MASTODON

mammoth² *adj* very big

man¹ *n* **men** 1 a fully-grown human male ⟶ PRIMATE MAMMAL 2 a human being 3 a **men** in general: *Man is taller than woman* b the human race: *Man lives in a changing world* 4 a a husband: *They had been man and wife for 50 years* b esp. spoken a husband or lover : *waiting for her man to come out of prison* 5 a fully-grown working male or a soldier of low rank: *He is in charge of several men at work* 6 a male person with courage, firmness, etc.: *The army will make a man of you* 7 the right male person: *Here's the man for the job* 8 any of the objects moved in a board game 9 **as one man** with the agreement of everyone 10 **man about town** a (rich) man who spends all his time at social gatherings, in clubs etc. 11 **the man in the street** the average person, who represents general opinion 12 **man of God** a priest 13 **man of my/your/his word** a keeper of promises 14 **man of the world** a man of wide experience — ~like *adj* — ~ly *adj* : *The boy walked with a manly stride* — ~ liness *n* —see PEOPLE (USAGE)

man² *v* **-nn-** to provide with people for operation: *Man the guns*

manacle¹ *n* one of a pair of iron rings for fastening the hands or feet of a prisoner

manacle² *v* **-cled, -cling** to put manacles on

manage *v* **-aged, -aging** 1 a to control (esp. a business) b to deal with or guide, esp. skilfully 2 to succeed in dealing with (a difficult movement or action) 3 to succeed in living, esp. on a small amount of money 4 *esp. spoken* to succeed in taking or using: *I can't manage another mouthful*

manageable *adj* easy to control or deal with — -bility *n*

management *n* 1 the act of managing esp. a

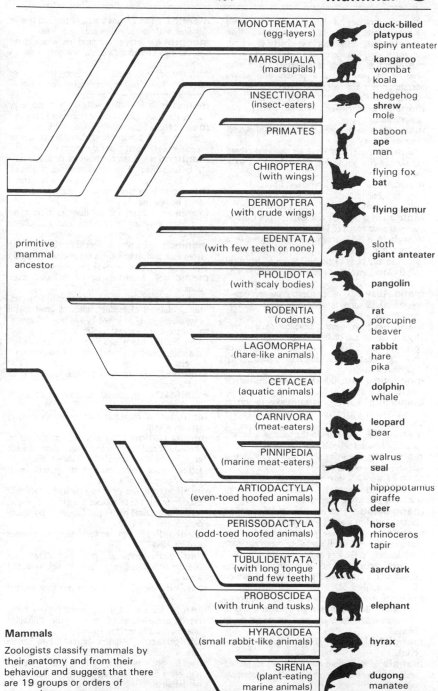

MONOTREMATA
(egg-layers)
duck-billed platypus spiny anteater

MARSUPIALIA
(marsupials)
kangaroo wombat koala

INSECTIVORA
(insect-eaters)
hedgehog **shrew** mole

PRIMATES
baboon **ape** man

CHIROPTERA
(with wings)
flying fox **bat**

DERMOPTERA
(with crude wings)
flying lemur

EDENTATA
(with few teeth or none)
sloth **giant anteater**

PHOLIDOTA
(with scaly bodies)
pangolin

RODENTIA
(rodents)
rat porcupine beaver

LAGOMORPHA
(hare-like animals)
rabbit hare pika

CETACEA
(aquatic animals)
dolphin whale

CARNIVORA
(meat-eaters)
leopard bear

PINNIPEDIA
(marine meat-eaters)
walrus **seal**

ARTIODACTYLA
(even-toed hoofed animals)
hippopotamus giraffe **deer**

PERISSODACTYLA
(odd-toed hoofed animals)
horse rhinoceros tapir

TUBULIDENTATA
(with long tongue and few teeth)
aardvark

PROBOSCIDEA
(with trunk and tusks)
elephant

HYRACOIDEA
(small rabbit-like animals)
hyrax

SIRENIA
(plant-eating marine animals)
dugong manatee

primitive mammal ancestor

Mammals

Zoologists classify mammals by their anatomy and from their behaviour and suggest that there are 19 groups or orders of mammals

business or money **2** skill in dealing with (usu.) a person (esp. in the phrase **more by luck than management**) **3** the people in charge of a firm, industry, etc., considered as one body

manager n **1** (*fem.* **manageress**) a man who controls a business **2** a person who makes arrangements: *She had to be a good manager to live on so little money*

managerial adj of or concerning a manager or management

man-at-arms n a soldier of former times, esp. one with heavy armour

manatee n a type of large sea mammal related to the sea cow but with a rounded tail ⫗MAMMAL

mandarin n **1** a high official in China's former empire **2** an important official **3** also **mandarin orange**— a small kind of easily peeled orange

Mandarin n the official form of the Chinese language; language of Peking and the north

mandate n **1** a command to act, given by a higher to a lower official **2** the right and power given to any body of people chosen to represent others to act according to the wishes of those who voted for it

mandatory adj **1** containing or carrying a command **2** which must be done/so: *It's mandatory to pay a debt*

mandible n technical **1** the lower jaw or jawbone of an animal or fish **2** the upper or lower part of a bird's beak **3** one of the 2 biting or holding mouth parts in insects and crabs ⫗INSECT

mandolin n a round-backed musical instrument rather like a lute

mandrill n a kind of large baboon (a sort of monkey) with bright colours on its face and lower parts behind

mane n the long hair on the back of a horse's neck, or around a lion's face ⫗HORSE

man-eater n a living thing which eats human flesh — **man-eating** adj

man Friday n **-days** a trustworthy male helper —compare GIRL FRIDAY

manful adj brave; determined — ∼ly adv

manganese n a greyish white metal that is an element used in making glass, steel, etc.

mange n a skin disease of animals, esp. dogs and cats, caused by a small insect-like creature (MITE) and leading to the loss of hair and poor health

mangel-wurzel n one of certain kinds of vegetable with a large round root which is grown on farms as cattle food

manger n **1** a long food container for horses and cattle **2 dog in the manger** a person who does not wish others to enjoy what he cannot enjoy himself

mangle[1] v **-gled, -gling** to tear to pieces; crush

mangle[2] n a machine with rollers which presses water from clothes, sheets, etc. —compare WRINGER

mango n **-goes** or **-gos** a type of tropical tree or its fruit with sweet yellow-coloured flesh

mangrove n a type of tropical tree which grows on swampland and puts down new roots from its branches

mangy adj **-ier, -iest 1** suffering from mange **2** esp. spoken of bad appearance because of loss of hair, as in mange — **-gily** adv

manhandle v **-dled, -dling 1** to move by using the body **2** to handle (a person) roughly

manhole n an opening, usu. with a cover through which a man can go down to examine or repair underground pipes and wires

manhood n **1** the condition or period of time of being a man **2** the good qualities of a man, such as courage **3** the sexual powers of a man

manhour n (a measure of) the amount of work done by one man in one hour

mania n **1** a very forceful disorder of the mind **2** a desire so strong that it seems mad: *a mania for fast cars* **3** a strong unreasonable desire

maniac n **1** a person (thought to be) suffering from mania of some kind: *a sex maniac* **2** a wild thoughtless person — ∼al adj — ∼ally adv

manic adj technical of or suffering from mania

manic-depressive n, adj (a person) with continual changes of feeling, states of great joyful excitement being followed by sad hopelessness

manicure v **-cured, -curing** to give (a) treatment for the hands and (esp.) the fingernails, including cleaning, cutting, etc. — **manicure** n — **-rist** n

manifest[1] adj esp. written plain to see or clear to the mind — ∼ly adv

manifest[2] v esp. written to show (something or itself) plainly

manifest[3] n technical a list of goods carried, esp. on a ship

manifestation n **1** esp. written the act of showing or making clear and plain **2** esp. written anything said or done which shows clearly (a feeling, belief, truth, etc.) **3** an appearance or sign of presence of a spirit

manifesto n **-tos** or **-toes** a (written) statement making public the intentions of a group of people, esp. of a political party: *the Labour party manifesto*

manifold[1] adj esp. written many in number and/or kind

manifold[2] n technical a pipe which allows gases to enter or escape from an engine, such as that of a car ⫗CAR

manikin, manni- n a man of less than normal size; dwarf

manila, -nilla n **1** strong brown paper **2** also **manila hemp**— a plant grown in the Philippine Islands, used in making rope

manipulate v **-lated, -lating 1** to handle (esp. a machine), usu. skilfully **2** to use (someone) for one's own purpose by skilfully influencing, often unfairly or dishonestly — **-lative** adj — **-lation** n

man jack n a man, considered as a single person (in the phrase **every man jack**)

mankind n the human race, both men and women

man-made adj 1 produced by the work of men; not found in nature 2 (of materials) not made from natural substances but from combinations of chemicals; synthetic

manna n 1 the food which in the Bible was provided by God for the Israelites in the desert 2 anything which comes unexpectedly to help one, when one is in need

manned adj (of machines, esp. in space) having men on board

mannequin n 1 becoming rare a person, usu. a woman, employed to model new clothes 2 a figure used for showing clothes in shop windows; tailor's dummy

manner n 1 esp. written the way in which anything is done or happens 2 a personal way of behaving towards other people: a very rude manner 3 a way or style of writing, painting, building, etc., typical of one or more persons, of a country, or of a time in history 4 **all manner of** every sort of 5 **in a manner of speaking** if one may express it this way 6 **not by any manner of means** not at all

mannered adj having or showing an unnatural way of acting

mannerism n 1 a peculiar habit of behaving, speaking, etc. 2 the repeated use of a trick of style in the arts, such as writing or painting

manners n 1 (polite) social practices or habits: table manners 2 social behaviour; ways of living (esp. of a nation): the manners and customs of the ancient Egyptians

mannish adj offensive (of a woman) like a man in behaviour, appearance, etc. — ~ly adv — ~ness n

manoeuvrable adj that can be moved easily, esp. turned: a very manoeuvrable car — -bility n

manoeuvre[1] n 1 the planned moving of (part of) an army or of warships; a set of such moves for training purposes 2 a skilful move or clever trick, intended to deceive, to gain something, etc.

manoeuvre[2] v -vred, -vring 1 a to cause (a soldier or ship) to perform one or more manoeuvres b (of a soldier or ship) to perform one or more manoeuvres 2 to move (to a position) esp. skilfully: It was difficult to manoeuvre the table into the room — ~-vrer n

man-of-war also **man-o'-war**— n **men-of-war** old use a naval warship

manor n 1 the land administered by its lord (a nobleman, or church organization) under the feudal system, some of which was kept by the lord, the rest being rented to farmers who paid by giving services, esp. labour, and part of their crops 2 a large house with land 3 sl a police district — ~ial adj

manpower n 1 the number of people needed for a certain type of work, as in industry or police 2 the workpower of people rather than machines

manse n the house of a minister, esp. in the Church of Scotland

manservant n **menservants** a male servant

mansion n a large house

manslaughter n law the crime of killing a person, unlawfully but not intentionally

mantelpiece n a frame around a fireplace, esp. the part on top (**mantelshelf**) where one can put ornaments —compare CHIMNEYBREAST

mantilla n a piece of thin material worn by Spanish women, covering the head; sort of veil or shawl

mantis n PRAYING MANTIS

mantle[1] n 1 old use a cloak 2 a cover made of netlike material, which is put over a gas flame in a lamp and becomes very bright

mantle[2] v -tled, -tling literature to cover: Snow mantled the trees

man-to-man adj esp. spoken open; without unnecessary politeness

manual[1] adj of or using the hands — ~ly adv

manual[2] n a (small) book giving information about something —compare HANDBOOK

manufacture[1] n the act of manufacturing

manufacture[2] v -tured, -turing 1 to make by machinery, esp. in large quantities 2 to invent (an untrue story, reason, etc.) — ~r n

manure[1] n animal waste which is put on the land to improve the crops —compare FERTILIZER

manure[2] v **manured, manuring** to put manure on

manuscript n 1 the first or only copy of a book or piece of writing, esp. written by hand 2 a handwritten book, of the time before printing was invented

Manx adj of the Isle of Man, its people, or the language once spoken there

Manx cat n a kind of cat which has no tail

many adj, pron, n —see MORE, MOST 1 a great number (of): Were there many people at the play? 2 **in so many words** in exactly those words 3 **many's the time, day, etc., (that)** there have been many times, days, etc., (that) 4 **one too many for** (someone) clever enough to beat (someone)

many-sided adj 1 with many sides 2 with many meanings 3 having many different qualities — ~ness n

Maoism n belief in and practice of the principles of Mao Tse Tung, the first leader of modern China — -ist adj, n

Maori adj of the language or customs of the original peoples of New Zealand

map[1] n 1 a representation of the earth's surface, showing the shape of countries, the position of towns, the height of land, etc. ⊙ 2 a plan of the stars in the sky or of the surface of the moon or a planet 3 a representation showing the position or state of anything 4 (**put something**) **on the map** esp. spoken (to cause something to be) considered important

The British Isles — physical

land over 500m
land over 100m

▲ peaks over 900m

0   100km

NORTHERN IRELAND

Am ARMAGH
At ANTRIM
D DOWN
F FERMANAGH
L LONDONDERRY
T TYRONE

REPUBLIC OF IRELAND

Cl CLARE
Co CORK
Cv CAVAN
Cw CARLOW
Do DONEGAL
Du DUBLIN
G GALWAY
Kd KILDARE
Ke KERRY
Kk KILKENNY
La LAOIS
Le LEITRIM
Lf LONGFORD
Li LIMERICK
Lo LOUTH
Ma MAYO
Me MEATH
Mo MONAGHAN
O OFFALY
R ROSCOMMON
S SLIGO
T TIPPERARY
Wa WATERFORD
We WEXFORD
Wi WICKLOW
WM WEST MEATH

SCOTLAND

B BORDERS
C CENTRAL
D DUMFRIES AND GALLOWAY
F FIFE
G GRAMPIAN
H HIGHLAND
L LOTHIAN
S STRATHCLYDE
T TAYSIDE

0   100km

ENGLAND

A AVON
Bd BEDFORDSHIRE
Bk BERKSHIRE
Bu BUCKINGHAMSHIRE
Ca CAMBRIDGESHIRE
Ch CHESHIRE
Cl CLEVELAND
Co CORNWALL
Cu CUMBRIA
Db DERBYSHIRE
Do DORSET
Du DURHAM
Dv DEVON
E ESSEX
ES EAST SUSSEX
G GLOUCESTERSHIRE
GL GREATER LONDON
GM GREATER MANCHESTER
Ha HAMPSHIRE
He HERTFORDSHIRE
Hu HUMBERSIDE
HW HEREFORD AND WORCESTER
IW ISLE OF WIGHT
K KENT
La LANCASHIRE
Le LEICESTERSHIRE
Li LINCOLNSHIRE
M MERSEYSIDE
Nd NORTHUMBERLAND
Nf NORFOLK
Nh NORTHAMPTONSHIRE
Nt NOTTINGHAMSHIRE
NY NORTH YORKSHIRE
O OXFORDSHIRE
Sf SUFFOLK
Sh SHROPSHIRE
So SOMERSET
St STAFFORDSHIRE
Sy SURREY
SY SOUTH YORKSHIRE
TW TYNE AND WEAR
Wa WARWICKSHIRE
Wi WILTSHIRE
WM WEST MIDLANDS
WS WEST SUSSEX
WY WEST YORKSHIRE

WALES

C CLWYD
D DYFED
Gd GWYNEDD
Gt GWENT
MG MID GLAMORGAN
P POWYS
SG SOUTH GLAMORGAN
WG WEST GLAMORGAN

The British Isles — political

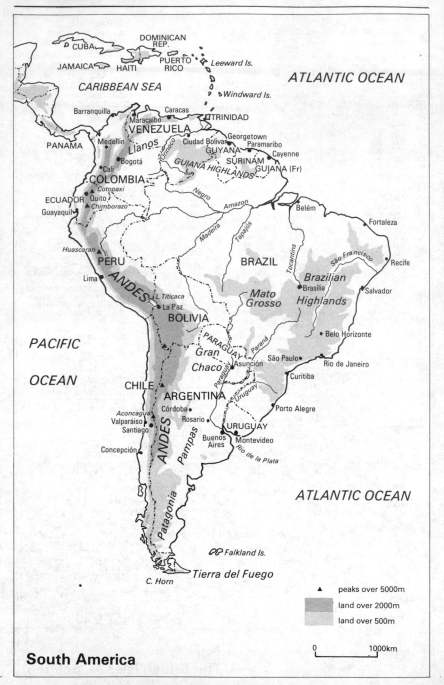

South America

CUBA
JAMAICA
HAITI
DOMINICAN REP.
PUERTO RICO
Leeward Is.
CARIBBEAN SEA
Windward Is.
ATLANTIC OCEAN

Barranquilla
Maracaibo
Caracas
TRINIDAD
VENEZUELA
Georgetown
Paramaribo
PANAMA
Medellín
Llanos
Ciudad Bolívar
GUYANA
Cayenne
Cali
Orinoco
SURINAM
GUIANA (Fr)
Bogotá
COLOMBIA
GUIANA HIGHLANDS
Cotopaxi
Negro
ECUADOR
Quito
Amazon
Belém
Chimborazo
Guayaquil
Fortaleza
Madeira
Tapajós
Huascarán
Tocantins
São Francisco
PERU
BRAZIL
Recife
ANDES
Brazilian
Lima
Salvador
L.Titicaca
Mato
Brasília
La Paz
Grosso
Highlands
BOLIVIA
Belo Horizonte
PARAGUAY
Paraná
PACIFIC
Gran
São Paulo
OCEAN
Chaco
Asunción
Rio de Janeiro
Paraguay
Curitiba
CHILE
ARGENTINA
Uruguay
Porto Alegre
Aconcagua
Córdoba
Valparaíso
Rosario
URUGUAY
Santiago
Buenos
Montevideo
Aires
Rio de la Plata
Concepción
ANDES
Pampas
Patagonia
ATLANTIC OCEAN
Falkland Is.
Tierra del Fuego
C. Horn

▲ peaks over 5000m

land over 2000m

land over 500m

0   1000km

Europe

0   500km

land over 1000m

European Economic Community

<u>FRANCE</u>   founder member of the EEC, 1957

<u>DENMARK</u>   member of the EEC, 1973

<u>GREECE</u>   member of the EEC, 1981

Reykjavik
ICELAND

Narvik

Trondheim
SWEDEN
FINLAND
Bergen
Oslo
NORWAY
Tampere
Turku
Helsinki

L. Vänern   Stockholm
Göteborg
L. Vättern

North Sea

Riga

REPUBLIC OF IRELAND
Dublin

UNITED KINGDOM

Copenhagen
DENMARK
Malmö
Baltic Sea

Hamburg
U.S.S.R.

ATLANTIC OCEAN

London
Amsterdam
Rotterdam
Antwerp
Brussels
Lille
Bonn
Essen
Weser
Rhine
Elbe
EAST
BERLIN
GERMANY
Leipzig
Dresden
Oder
Warsaw
Vistula
Lodz
POLAND
Prague
Cracow
Lvov
CZECHOSLOVAKIA

Paris
Loire
Oise
Seine
Strasbourg
WEST GERMANY
Danube

Bay of Biscay

FRANCE

Bordeaux
Massif
Central
Dordogne
Garonne
Pyrenees

Saône
Rhône
Berne
S
Zurich
Munich
Vienna
AUSTRIA
THE ALPS
Trieste
Budapest
HUNGARY
RUMANIA

Turin
Milan
Po
Genoa
ITALY
Zagreb
Sava
Belgrade
Bucharest

PORTUGAL
Douro
Tagus
Madrid
Ebro
Barcelona
Corsica
YUGOSLAVIA
Danube

Lisbon
SPAIN
Guadalquivir
Valencia
Balearic Is.
Sardinia
Rome
Apennines
Naples
Adriatic Sea
Tirane
Sofia
BULGARIA
A

Straits of
Gibraltar

Mediterranean
Sicily
Malta
Sea

GREECE
Aegean
Athens
Sea

A   ALBANIA
B   <u>BELGIUM</u>
L   <u>LUXEMBOURG</u>
N   <u>NETHERLANDS</u>
S   SWITZERLAND

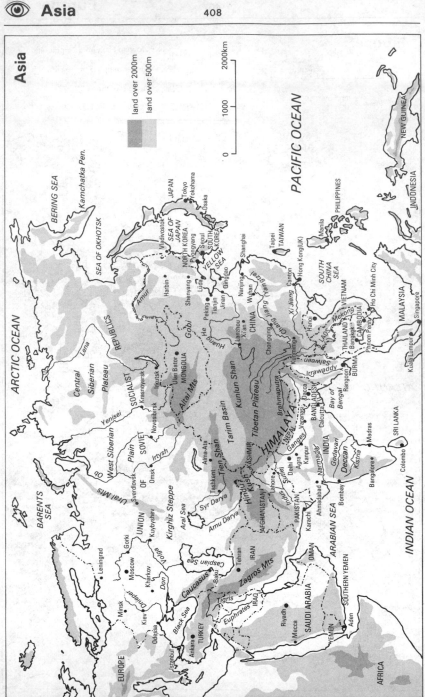

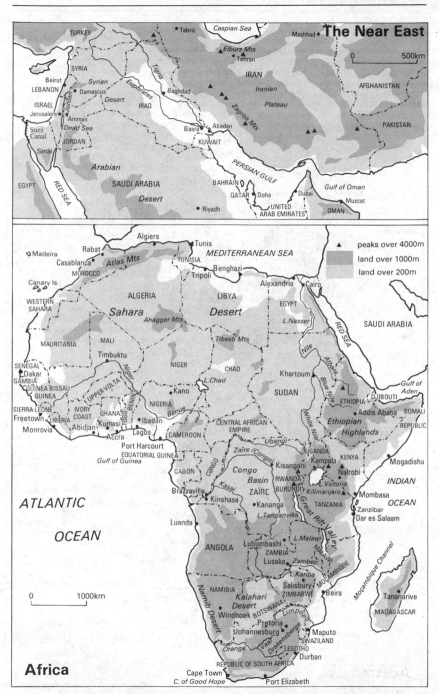

The Near East

0   500km

TURKEY
Tabriz
Caspian Sea
Mashhad

Elburz Mts
Tehran

SYRIA
Beirut
LEBANON
Damascus
Syrian
Euphrates
Tigris
IRAN
Iranian
Plateau
AFGHANISTAN

ISRAEL
Jerusalem
Amman
Desert
Baghdad
IRAQ
Zagros Mts
PAKISTAN

Suez
Canal
Dead Sea
JORDAN
Basra
Abadan

Sinai
KUWAIT

EGYPT
RED SEA
Arabian
SAUDI ARABIA
Desert
BAHRAIN
QATAR
Doha
Riyadh
UNITED
ARAB EMIRATES
Dubai
PERSIAN GULF
Gulf of Oman
Muscat
OMAN

Algiers
Tunis
MEDITERRANEAN SEA

Madeira
Rabat
Casablanca
MOROCCO
Atlas Mts
TUNISIA
Tripoli
Benghazi
Alexandria
Cairo

peaks over 4000m

land over 1000m

land over 200m

Canary Is
WESTERN
SAHARA
ALGERIA
Sahara
Ahagger Mts
LIBYA
Desert
EGYPT
L.Nasser
SAUDI ARABIA

MAURITANIA
MALI
Timbuktu
NIGER
Tibesti Mts
CHAD
L.Chad
Khartoum
SUDAN
RED SEA
Nile
Atbara

SENEGAL
Dakar
GAMBIA
GUINEA BISSAU
GUINEA
Niger
UPPER VOLTA
Kano
NIGERIA
Benue
CENTRAL AFRICAN
EMPIRE
Blue Nile
White Nile
ETHIOPIA
Addis Ababa
DJIBOUTI
SOMALI
REPUBLIC
Gulf of
Aden

SIERRA LEONE
Freetown
LIBERIA
Monrovia
IVORY
COAST
GHANA
TOGO
BENIN
Ibadan
Lagos
CAMEROON
Ethiopian
Highlands
Kumasi
Abidjan
Accra
Port Harcourt
EQUATORIAL GUINEA
Gulf of Guinea
GABON
Ubangi
Zaïre (Congo)
Kisangani
UGANDA
Kampala
KENYA
Nairobi
Mogadishu

Congo
Basin
ZAÏRE
Kasai
CONGO
Brazzaville
Kinshasa
Kananga
RWANDA
BURUNDI
L.Victoria
Kilimanjaro
TANZANIA
Mombasa
Zanzibar
Dar es Salaam
INDIAN
OCEAN

ATLANTIC

OCEAN

Luanda
L.Tanganyika
Great Rift Valley

ANGOLA
Lubumbashi
L.Malawi
ZAMBIA
Lusaka
Zambezi
MALAWI
MOÇAMBIQUE

0   1000km
NAMIBIA
L.Kariba
Salisbury
ZIMBABWE
Beira
Moçambique Channel
Tananarive
MADAGASCAR

Namib Desert
Kalahari
Desert
BOTSWANA
Windhoek
Pretoria
Johannesburg
Orange
Vaal
Limpopo
Drakensberge
SWAZILAND
Maputo
LESOTHO
REPUBLIC OF SOUTH AFRICA
Durban

Africa
Cape Town
C. of Good Hope
Port Elizabeth

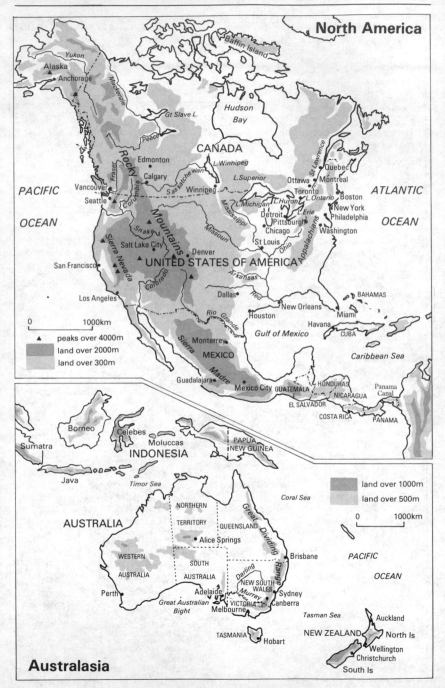

North America

Baffin Island

Alaska
Anchorage

Yukon

Mackenzie

Gt Slave L.

Hudson Bay

Peace

CANADA

Edmonton

L.Winnipeg

Calgary

Saskatchewan

Winnipeg

L.Superior

St Lawrence

Quebec

Ottawa Montreal

Toronto

L.Michigan L.Huron L.Ontario Boston

PACIFIC

Vancouver

Seattle

Columbia

Fraser

Rocky

ATLANTIC

New York

Detroit L.Erie

Philadelphia

Pittsburgh

OCEAN

Mountains

Snake

Salt Lake City

Missouri

Mississippi

Chicago

St Louis

Ohio

Washington

Appalachians

OCEAN

Sierra Nevada

San Francisco

Denver

UNITED STATES OF AMERICA

Colorado

Arkansas

Los Angeles

Dallas

Red

BAHAMAS

0   1000km

▲ peaks over 4000m

land over 2000m

land over 300m

Rio Grande

Houston

New Orleans

Miami

Havana

CUBA

Gulf of Mexico

Caribbean Sea

Sierra

Monterrey

MEXICO

Madre

Guadalajara

Mexico City GUATEMALA HONDURAS

Panama

EL SALVADOR

NICARAGUA

Canal

COSTA RICA

PANAMA

Sumatra

Borneo

Celebes

Moluccas

PAPUA
NEW GUINEA

Java

INDONESIA

Timor Sea

Coral Sea

land over 1000m

land over 500m

AUSTRALIA

NORTHERN

TERRITORY

QUEENSLAND

Great Dividing Range

0   1000km

WESTERN

AUSTRALIA

Alice Springs

SOUTH

AUSTRALIA

Brisbane

PACIFIC

Perth

Darling

NEW SOUTH
WALES

Murray

Adelaide

Sydney

OCEAN

Great Australian
Bight

VICTORIA

Canberra

Melbourne

Auckland

TASMANIA

Hobart

Tasman Sea

NEW ZEALAND

North Is

Wellington

Christchurch

South Is

Australasia

map² v -pp- 1 to make a map of 2 *technical* to represent the pattern of (something) on something else

maple n (the wood of) a type of tree with many-pointed leaves found in the northern half of the world, one kind of which yields a sugary liquid (**maple syrup**)

map out v adv to plan (time, an event, etc., esp. in the future)

mapping n *technical* (in set theory) a mathematical operation which associates each element of one set (the DOMAIN) with one or more items in another set (the RANGE)

mar v -rr- esp. *literature* to spoil —see also MAKE or mar

maraca n a hollow fruit shell filled with beans, beads, etc. and used as a musical instrument

maraschino n -nos a type of cherry which has been kept in a liqueur, used for ornamenting cakes and sweets

marathon n 1 a running race of about 26 miles, esp. at the Olympic Games 2 any prolonged activity that tests one's power

maraud v (of people or animals) to move around in search of something to steal, burn, or destroy — ~er n

marble n 1 a hard limestone used for building, sculpture, gravestones, etc. and usu. showing an irregular colouring 2 *literature* **a** a smooth and white quality **b** a hard and cold quality 3 a small hard ball of glass used by children in the game of marbles

marbled adj marked with irregular colours and lines

marbles n 1 a game in which small hard glass balls are rolled at each other 2 **lose one's marbles** *humour sl* to become mad

march¹ v 1 to walk with a regular step like a soldier 2 to force to walk (away): *The mother marched her child up to bed* —see also FROG-MARCH — ~er n

march² n 1 the act of marching 2 the distance covered while marching: *It was a day's march from the city to the camp* 3 regular movement forward 4 a piece of music played in regular time that can be marched to 5 marching by a large number of people to make ideas or dissatisfactions public: *a hunger march* 6 **on the march a** moving forward **b** moving ahead and improving: *Science is on the march* 7 **steal a march on (someone)** to gain advantage over (someone) by acting quickly

March n the third month of the year

marching orders n 1 orders given to soldiers to move from one place to another 2 *esp. spoken* official notice that one's services are no longer needed

marchioness n the wife of a marquis, or the title of a noblewoman of the same rank

Mardi gras n *French* (a feast held in some countries on) the last day before the beginning of LENT; Shrove Tuesday

mare n a female horse

margarine also esp. spoken **marge**— n a food prepared from animal and/or vegetable fats used instead of butter

margin n 1 one or both sides of a page near the edge, where there is no writing or printing 2 the area on the outside edge of a larger area: *the margin of the stream* 3 an amount above what is necessary, esp. for success 4 (in business) the difference between the buying and selling price —compare PROFIT MARGIN

marginal adj 1 (printed or written) on or in a margin 2 of small importance or amount 3 (of a seat in parliament) which may be lost or won by a small number of votes so that it may pass into the control of a new political party 4 (of land) too poor to produce many crops, and farmed only when more crops are specially needed — ~ly adv

marigold n any of several types of flower with a golden-yellow head

marijuana, -huana n the common form of the drug cannabis; dried flowers, stems, and leaves of the Indian hemp plant

marimba n a kind of musical instrument like a xylophone

marina n an area near the sea where small boats can come into harbour, people can stay in hotels, etc.

marinade n a mixture of wine and/or vinegar, oil, spices, etc., in which meat or fish can be soaked before cooking to give it a special taste and soften it

marinate also **marinade**— v -nated, -nating to keep (meat or fish) in a marinade before cooking

marine¹ adj 1 of, near, living in, found in, or obtained from the sea 2 of ships and their goods and trade at sea, esp. concerning the navy

marine² n 1 the ships of a country which carry goods or travellers (only in the phrases **merchant/mercantile marine**) 2 a soldier who serves on a naval ship or in the navy

mariner n *technical* or *poetic* a sailor or seaman

marionette n a small figure moved by strings or wires at a theatre performance; sort of puppet

marital adj of or concerning (the duties of) marriage — ~ly adv

maritime adj 1 concerning ships or the sea 2 living or existing near the sea

marjoram n a herb with sweet-smelling leaves and flowers, used in cooking to give a special taste

mark¹ n 1 a spot, line, or cut that spoils the natural colour or appearance of something 2 an object or sign serving as a guide —see also BOOK-MARK, LANDMARK 3 an action or sign showing a feeling, quality, or condition: *a mark of respect* 4 a spot on the face or body by which a person or animal can be recognized —see also BIRTHMARK 5 a figure or printed or written sign which shows something —see also POSTMARK, TRADEMARK 6 a figure, letter, or sign which represents a judgment of quality in another's piece of work, behaviour, performance in a competition, etc. **7** the object or place one aims at **8** the suitable level of quality (in the phrases **up to/below the mark**) **9** the starting place, esp. for a race: *The runners were all quick off the mark* **10** a sign, usu. a cross, made by a person who cannot write his name **11** (esp. with numbers) a particular type of a machine: *The Mark 4 gun is stronger than the old Mark 3* **12** (**give someone**) **full marks** (**for** (**doing**) **something**) to admire (an action or quality) **13** (**fall**) **wide of the mark a** (to be) far from the subject **b** (to be) far from being correct **14 make one's mark** (**on**) to gain success, fame, etc., (in) by showing one's best qualities **15 not** (**quite**) **up to the mark** not (very) well (in health) **16 On your marks, get set, go!** (used for starting a race)

mark² *v* **1** to make a mark on, esp. one that spoils the appearance **2** to receive an unwanted mark, causing a spoiled appearance **3** to show (by position) **4** to cover with marks, esp. on the body **5 a** to give a mark of quality: *He marked the work 10 out of 10* **b** to record the presence, absence, etc., of **6** to show (the qualities of): *She has the qualities that mark a good nurse* —see also MARKED **7** (in football, hockey and such games) to stay in close attention on (an opponent) **8** to pay attention to **9** to be a sign of **10 mark time a** to make the movements of marching while remaining in the same place **b** to spend time on work, business, etc., without advancing —see also MARK DOWN, MARK OFF, MARK OUT, MARK UP

mark³ *n* the standard coin in the money system of Germany ⊋MONEY

markdown *n* the amount by which a price is made lower

mark down *v adv* **1** to note in writing **2** to reduce (goods) in price **3** to give a lower mark to

marked *adj* **1** having marks by which to be recognized **2** noticeable **3** (typically) having: *This writer's plays are marked by a gentle humour* **4 a marked man** a man who is being watched by an enemy, and therefore likely to come to harm — ~**ly** *adv*

marker *n* an object which marks a place

market¹ *n* **1** a building, square, or open place for buying and selling goods **2** a gathering of people to buy and sell on certain days at such a place: *market day* **3** an area, country, or countries, where there is a demand for goods: *a world market* **4** demand for goods: *There's no market for hot ice cream* **5** (the state of) trade in certain goods, esp. the rate of buying and selling: *There's great activity in the tea market* **6 in the market** (**for**) ready to buy **7 on the market** (of goods) for sale **8 play the market** to buy and sell business shares to try to make a profit

market² *v* to offer for sale — ~**able** *adj* — ~**ability** *n* — ~**er** *n*

market garden *n* a large area for growing vegetables and fruit for sale — ~**er** *n* — ~**ing** *n*

marketing *n* the various activities by which goods are supplied, advertised, and sold — compare MARKET RESEARCH

market place *n* **1** an open area where a market is held **2** the place where goods are sold to the public (as apposed to where they are made, sent out, etc.)

market price *n* the price which buyers will pay for something

market research *n* the study of what people buy and why, usu. done by firms to try to increase sales —compare MARKETING

market town *n* a town where a market is held, esp. one for selling sheep, cattle, etc.

marking *n* (one of a set of) coloured marks on an animal's skin, fur, or feathers

marking ink *n* special washable ink for marking names on cloth

mark off *v adv* **1** to make into a separate area by drawing lines **2** to note (something) as being done, esp. on a list

mark out *v adv* **1** to draw (an area) with lines **2** to show or choose (someone) as suitable to have, get, etc. (usu. future advance, esp. in work)

marksman (*fem.* **markswoman**)— *n* -**men** a person who can hit the right mark easily, usu. with a gun — ~**ship** *n*

markup *n* the amount by which a price is raised

mark up *v adv* to raise (goods) in price

marl *n* a type of soil formed of clay and lime

marlinespike *n* a pointed iron rod which seamen use for separating the twisted threads of a rope so that it can be joined to another

marmalade *n* a type of jam usu. made from oranges

marmoreal *adj literature* of or like marble, esp. as being white and/or cool

marmoset *n* any of several types of very small monkey from Central and South America

maroon¹ *n* (in former times) a slave of black West Indian origin, who has run away from his master △ MACAROON

maroon² *v* **1** to put (someone) off a ship in a deserted place **2** to leave (one or more people) alone, with no means of getting away

maroon³ *n, adj* (of) a very dark red-brown colour

maroon⁴ *n* a small rocket used as a signal, esp. at sea

marquee *n* a large tent, esp. for public events

marquetry *n* (the art of making) a type of pattern in wood, in which different coloured pieces are fitted together, esp. on the surface of furniture

marquis, marquess *n* (the title of) a nobleman of high rank —see also MARCHIONESS

marriage *n* **1** the union of a man and woman by a ceremony in law **2** the state of being so united

marriageable *adj esp. written* (esp. of girls)

suitable (in age, character, appearance, etc.) for marriage — **-bility** *n*

marriage lines *n* the official certificate which proves that a marriage has taken place

married *adj* 1 having a husband or wife 2 having as or like a husband/wife: *He's married to his work* 3 of the state of marriage

marrow *n* 1 the soft fatty substance in the centre of bones ⏤ANATOMY 2 the most important and necessary part 3 also **vegetable marrow**— a type of dark green vegetable which can grow very big

marry *v* **-ried, -rying** 1 to take (a person) in marriage 2 (of a priest or official) to perform the ceremony of marriage for (2 people) 3 to cause to take in marriage

Mars *n* the planet 4th in order from the sun, and next to the earth

marsh *n* (a piece of) land that is all or partly soft and wet, because of its low position

marshal¹ *n* 1 an officer of the highest rank in certain armies and airforces 2 an official who is in charge of making arrangements for an important public ceremony 3 (in the US) an official who carries out the judgments given in a court of law; one who has the duties of a sheriff

marshal² *v* **-ll-** 1 to arrange (esp. facts) in good or correct order 2 to lead (a person) to the correct place, esp. on a ceremonial or important occasion

marshalling yard *n* a railway yard in which trains are put together

marsh gas *n* gas formed by dead vegetable matter in a marsh; methane

marshmallow *n* a type of soft round sweet

marshy *adj* **-ier, -iest** 1 of or like a marsh 2 (of a place) having a lot of marsh

marsupial *adj, n* (one) of the type of animal (a kind of MAMMAL) which is born only partly developed and is carried until grown in a pouch on the mother's body ⏤ MAMMAL

mart *n* a market

marten *n* 1 any of several types of small animal, kept or hunted for their fur 2 the fur of this animal

martial *adj* of or concerning war, soldiers, etc. — ~**ly** *adv*

martial law *n* government under special laws by the army

Martian *adj, n* (a person) of the planet Mars, usu. in imaginary stories

martin *n* any of several types of bird (including the **house martin** and **sand martin**) of the swallow family

martinet *n* a person who demands total obedience to rules and orders

martini *n* a cocktail made by mixing gin, vermouth, and bitters

martyr¹ *n* 1 a person who dies or suffers for his beliefs 2 *esp. spoken* a person who gives up his own wishes or chance of gain or who accepts something unpleasant in order to please others: *John likes to make a martyr of himself*

martyr² *v* to put to death, or cause to suffer greatly, for a belief

martyrdom *n* 1 the state of being a martyr 2 the death or suffering of a martyr

marvel¹ *n* 1 a wonder; wonderful thing or example 2 *esp. spoken* a person or thing that causes surprise: *You're a marvel to work so hard at your age*

marvel² *v* **-ll-** to wonder; feel great surprise

marvellous *adj* wonderful, esp. because surprisingly good — ~**ly** *adv*

Marxism *n* the teaching of Karl Marx on which communism is based, which explains the changes in history according to the struggle between social classes — **-ist** *n, adj*

Marxism-Leninism *n* Marxism as explained, added to, and practised by Lenin — **Marxist-Leninist** *n, adj*

marzipan *n* a sweet almond-flavoured paste, used for making some sweets and for putting on top of cakes

mascara *n* a dark coloured make-up for the eyelashes

mascot *n* an object, animal, or person thought to bring good fortune

masculine¹ *adj* 1 of or having the qualities suitable for a man 2 (in grammar) in a class of words that are not feminine or neuter: *'He' is a masculine pronoun*

masculine² *n* the class of masculine words

masculinity *n* the quality or state of being masculine

maser *n* an apparatus for producing a very powerful beam of microwave radiation —compare LASER

mash¹ *n* 1 a mixture of grain, bran, etc., and water used as food for animals 2 *esp. spoken* mashed potatoes

mash² *v* to crush into a soft substance: *mashed potatoes*

mask¹ *n* 1 a covering for (part of) the face which hides or protects it 2 a covering like a face, often of paper, as worn by some actors and in some tribal religious and magical ceremonies —see also DEATH MASK 3 an appearance which hides the truth or reality; any form of pretending: *a mask of loyalty* — ~**ed** *adj*

mask² *v* 1 to cover with a mask 2 to hide (esp. feelings)

masking tape *n* sticky material in a long narrow strip, which can be used for covering the edge of an area one wishes to leave unpainted when one is painting

masochism *n* the wish to be hurt so as to gain (sexual) pleasure —compare SADISM — **-chist** *n* — **-chistic** *adj*

mason *n* 1 a stonemason 2 a Freemason

masonic *adj* or of connected with Freemasons, their beliefs, practices, etc.

masonry *n* 1 the skill of preparing and fixing stones in building 2 Freemasonry

masque *n* a form of theatrical play often performed in the 16th & 17th centuries, written in poetry and with music, dancing, and songs

masquerade¹ *n* **1** a masked ball **2** something pretended; hiding of the truth

masquerade² *v* **-raded, -rading** to pretend (to be) — **-rader** *n*

mass¹ *n* a piece of music written specially for all the main parts of the Mass

mass² *n* **1** a quantity or heap (of matter) **2** *esp. spoken* a large number (of people or things) **3** (in science) the amount of matter in a body, measured by the power used in changing its movement

mass³ *v* to gather together in large numbers

mass⁴ *adj* of or for a mass, esp. of people: *a mass murderer*

Mass *n* (used in the Catholic and Orthodox churches) the Eucharist —compare COMMUNION

massacre *v* **-cred, -cring** **1** to kill (a number of people) without mercy **2** *esp. spoken* to defeat severely — **massacre** *n*

massage *v* **-saged, -saging** to treat (a person's body) by pressing and rubbing to take away pain or stiffness — **massage** *n*

masses *n* the lower classes of society

masseur (*fem.* **masseuse**)— *n* a man who gives massages

massive *adj* **1** of great size; strong and heavy **2** (of qualities and actions) great; powerful — ~ly *adv* — ~ness *n*

mass media *n* the modern means of giving news and opinions to large numbers of people, esp. radio and television —see MEDIA (USAGE)

mass-produce *v* **-duced, -ducing** to produce (goods) in large numbers to the same pattern — **-duction** *n*

mast *n* **1** a long upright pole for carrying flags or sails on a ship SAIL **2** a flagpole —see also HALF-MAST **3** an upright metal framework for radio and television aerials

mastectomy *n* **-mies** an operation for the removal of a breast

master¹ *n* **1** a man in control of people, animals, or things —compare RINGMASTER **2** (*fem.* **mistress**)— a man who is the head of a house and family **3** also **master mariner**— a man who commands a ship carrying goods or people, or a large fishing boat **4** (*fem.* **mistress**)— *esp. written and old use* a male teacher **5** a man who employs workmen or servants **6** a skilled workman with his own business: *a master builder* **7** a man of great skill in art or work with the hands —see also OLD MASTER, GRAND MASTER

master² *adj* chief; most important: *the master bedroom*

master³ *v* **1** to gain control over **2** to gain as a skill

Master *n* *becoming rare* (a title for addressing) a young boy

master-at-arms *n* **masters-at-arms** an officer with police duties in a naval or passenger ship

masterful *adj* having or showing an ability or

wish to control others— compare MASTERLY — ~ly *adv*

master key *n* **-keys** a key that will open several different locks

masterly *adj* showing great skill—compare MASTERFUL — **-liness** *n*

mastermind *v* *esp. spoken* to plan (a course of action), usu. in detail and cleverly

master of ceremonies *n* **masters of ceremonies** a person whose duty is to see that ceremonies are carried out properly at a public social occasion

Master of Hounds *n* **Masters of Hounds** a man in charge of a foxhunt

masterpiece also **masterwork**— *n* a piece of work, esp. art, which is the best of its type or the best a person has done

master's degree also (*esp. spoken esp. US*) **master's**— *n* a second university degree in any of several subjects, such as **Master of Science** (M.S c)

mastership *n* the state of having command or control

masterstroke *n* an action done with great skill which results in complete success

masthead *n* the top of a (ship's) mast

mastic *n* **1** a substance from the resin of a tree which is used to make varnish **2** a substance used for preventing liquid from entering or escaping, esp. from joints in pipes

masticate *v* **-cated, -cating** *esp. written* to chew — **-cation** *n*

mastiff *n* a type of large powerful dog

mastitis *n* inflammation of the breast

mastodon *n* a type of large animal like an elephant, which lived 1, 000s of years ago — compare MAMMOTH

mastoid also **mastoid bone**— *n* a small round point of bone behind the ear

masturbate *v* **-bated, -bating** to excite the sex organs (of) by handling, rubbing, etc. — **-bation** *n* — **-batory** *adj*

mat¹ *n* **1** a piece of rough strong material used for covering part of a floor —see also DOORMAT **2** a very small rug or piece of carpet **3** a small piece of material used for putting under objects on furniture —see also TABLEMAT **4** a knotted mass, esp. of hair

mat² *v* **-tt-** to (cause to) become knotted in a thick mass: *matted hair*

mat³ **matt** *adj* of a dull, not shiny, surface: *mat paint*

matador *n* the man who kills the bull in bullfighting

match¹ *n* **1** a person who is equal in strength, ability, etc., (to another) **2 a** something like or suitable to something else: *We can't find a match for this ornament* **b** a number of things suitable together: *The hat and shoes are a perfect match* **3** *esp. old use* **a** a person considered as a possible husband or wife **b** a marriage **4** a game or sports event where teams or people compete

match² *v* **1 a** to be equal to (a person) (in a

quality): *You can't match him in good looks* **b** to find an equal for: *This hotel can't be matched for friendliness* **2** to be like or suitable for use with (something else) **3** to find something like or suitable for use with **4** to cause to compete (with)

match³ *n* a short thin stick with a head covered by chemicals which catch fire when rubbed or struck against a rough surface

matching *adj* (esp. of colours and appearance) which are the same or suited

matchless *adj* which has no equal in quality — ~**ly** *adv*

matchmaker *n* a person who tries to encourage people to marry each other — **making** *n*

match point *n* the position in a game, esp. tennis, when the player who is leading wins the match if he gains the next point

matchwood *n* **1** wood suitable for making matches **2** wood split into small thin pieces

mate¹ *n, v* **mated, mating** checkmate

mate² *n* **1** a fellow workman or friend **2** (not in the navy) a ship's officer in command after the captain **3** a helper to a skilled workman: *a builder's mate* **4** one of a male–female pair, usu. of animals

mate³ *v* **mated, mating** to form (into) a pair, esp. of animals, for sexual union: *Birds mate in the spring*

material¹ *adj* **1 a** of or concerning matter or substance, not spirit: *The storm did a great deal of material damage* **b** of the body, rather than the mind or soul: *She's too poor to satisfy her family's material needs* **2** important and necessary: *We must make a material change in our plans* **3** *law* concerning information necessary for a just decision: *material evidence* — ~**ly** *adv*

material² *n* **1** anything from which something is or may be made **2** woven cloth from which clothes may be made **3** knowledge of facts from which action may be taken or a (written) work may be produced: *collecting material for a book* **4** people considered for what they may become after training or development: *no officer material among these recruits* —see also RAW MATERIAL

materialism *n* **1** the belief that only matter exists, and that there is no world of the spirit **2** a state of mind or way of life which enjoys the material pleasures of the world rather than activities of the mind or spirit — **ist** *n, adj* — **istic** *adj* — **istically** *adv*

materialize, -ise *v* **-ized, -izing 1** to take on, or cause to take on, bodily form **2** to become real — **ization** *n*

maternal *adj* **1** of, like, or natural to a mother **2** related through the mother's side of the family —compare PATERNAL — ~**ly** *adv*

maternity *n* **1** motherhood **2** the bodily condition of becoming a mother; pregnancy and giving birth: *a maternity dress*

matey *adj* **-ier, -iest** *esp. spoken* friendly

mathematics also (*esp. spoken*) **maths**— *n* the study or science of numbers —compare ARITH-

METIC — **ical** *adj* — **ically** *adv* — **ician** *n*

matinée *n* a performance of a play, music, etc., given in the afternoon

matinée coat *n* a small, usu. woollen, coat for a young baby

matins *n* a morning service in the Church of England

matriarchy *n* **-chies** (an example of) a social system in which the (oldest) woman is head of the family — **matriarch** *n* — **matriarchal** *adj*

matricide *n* (a person who commits) the crime of killing one's mother

matriculate *v* **-lated, -lating** to (allow to) become a member of a university, esp. after an examination or test — **lation** *n*

matrilineal *adj* of or being a system in which property passes through the female side of the family

matrimony *n* *esp. written* the state of marriage (esp. in the phrase **holy matrimony**) — **monial** *adj*

matrix *n* **matrices** *or* **matrixes 1** a mould into which melted metal or other suitable material is poured to form the right shape **2** (in mathematics, science, etc.) an arrangement of numbers or terms in a rectangle made up of rows and columns ☞ MATHEMATICS

matron *n* **1** (the title of) a woman in charge of a hospital who has control over the work of all the nurses and other staff, but not over doctors (now officially called a **senior nursing officer**) **2** (the title of) a woman who is in charge of domestic and medical arrangements for children to live in a school **3** *esp. literature or old use* an older married woman, esp. one of quiet careful behaviour

matronly *adj* **1** fatter than a young girl should be **2** (of a woman) dignified like a matron

matt *adj* mat; dull

matter¹ *n* **1** the material which makes up the world and everything in space which can be seen or touched, as opposed to thought or mind **2** a subject itself as opposed to the form in which it is spoken or written about: *subject matter* **3** a (business) affair; subject to which one gives attention **4** a trouble or cause of pain, illness, etc. **5** written material: *reading matter* **6** pus **7** a **matter** of an amount (of time, distance, money, etc.) which is: *It's only a matter of hours till the doctor arrives*

matter² *v* **1** to be important: *It doesn't matter if I miss my train* **2** *technical* to form and give out pus

matter of course *n* a natural or usual event: *I lock the door as a matter of course* — **matter-of-course** *adj*

matter-of-fact *adj* concerned with facts, not imagination; practical, not fanciful

matting *n* rough material for mats and for packing goods

mattock *n* a tool for breaking up hard soil, with a metal head at right angles to the long handle

mattress *n* a large bag, usu. filled with wool,

👁 **mathematics** 416

Symbols

+	add	$\not<$	not less than	$\subset$	is a subset of
−	subtract	$\propto$	is proportional to	A'	the complement of A;
×	multiply	$\equiv$	is identical or congruent to		the set of all the
÷	divide	$\perp$	is perpendicular to		elements of ε which are
=	equal to	$\parallel$	is parallel to		not elements of A
$\neq \div$	not equal to	$\sqrt{x}$	square root of x	$\therefore$	therefore
$\simeq \approx$	approximately equal to	%	per cent	$f(x)$	function of x: if $f(x) \equiv x^2$
>	greater than	$x\%$	$\dfrac{x}{100}$		then $f(2) = 4$, $f(-1) = 1$
$\geq$	greater than or equal to			π pi	the ratio of the length of
<	less than	$\overrightarrow{AB}$	vector AB		the circumference of a
$\leq$	less than or equal to	$\cup$	union of 2 sets		circle to the diameter of
$\gg$	much greater than	$\cap$	intersection of 2 sets		the circle: approximately
$\ll$	much less than	ε	the entity or universal set		3.1416 or $\frac{22}{7}$
$\not>$	not greater than	ϕ	the empty set		

Areas of geometrical figures

Triangle area $= \frac{1}{2} \times a \times h$ or

$$\sqrt{s(s-a)(s-b)(s-c)},$$

where $s = \frac{1}{2}(a+b+c)$

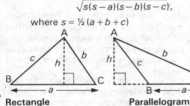

Rectangle
area $= a \times b$

Parallelogram
area $= b \times h$

Trapezium
area $= \frac{1}{2}(a+b) \times h$

Circle
area $= \pi r^2$
length of
circumference $= 2\pi r$

Algebraic formulae

General formula for the solution of a quadratic equation:

If the general form of a quadratic equation is taken to be $ax^2 + bx + c = 0$, then the roots are given by the formula

$$x = \frac{-b \pm \sqrt{b^2 - 4ac}}{2a}$$

Sum of the roots of a quadratic equation $= \dfrac{-b}{a}$

Product of the roots of a quadratic equation $= \dfrac{c}{a}$

Volumes and surface areas of geometrical solids

Cuboid volume $= a \times b \times h$
surface area $= 2 \times (a \times b + a \times h + b \times h)$

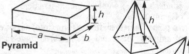

Pyramid
volume $= \frac{1}{3} \times$ base area $\times$ perpendicular height (h)

Cone
volume $= \frac{1}{3} \times \pi \times r^2 \times h$
curved surface area $= \pi \times r \times l$

Cylinder
volume $= \pi \times r^2 \times h$
curved surface area $= 2 \times \pi \times r \times h$
total surface area $= 2 \times \pi \times r \times (h+r)$

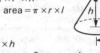

Sphere
volume $= \frac{4}{3} \times \pi \times r^3$
surface area $= 4 \times \pi \times r^2$

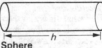

Other formulae

Interest

If P is the principal, T is the number of years, R is the rate per cent and I is the interest, with simple interest

$$I = \frac{PTR}{100}$$

Speed, distance, and time

If a body moves at a constant speed then:
distance travelled = speed × time.

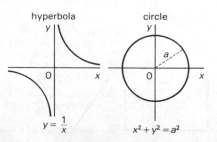

Graphs and calculus

The 30 pupils in a class vote for their favourite record out of the 5 records A, B, C, D, and E as follows: 30% for A, 5% for B, 10% for C, 40% for D, and 15% for E. These figures can be represented in a histogram or bar graph as below.

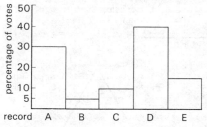

The same information can be illustrated in a pie chart as below.

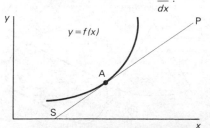

The slope AB goes *up 1* unit for *d* units *horizontally*; the gradient is *1* in *d* or *1/d*. The gradient can also be expressed as the percentage *1/d × 100%*. Thus if *d = 4* units, the gradient is *1 in 4* or *25%*.

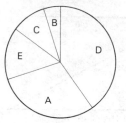

The gradient of the point A on the curve $y = f(x)$ is the gradient of the tangent at point A; SP. Using calculus, the gradient is found by differentiating to obtain $\dfrac{dy}{dx}$.

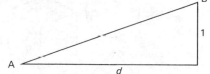

Distance, time, and velocity

If a particle moves a distance of x metres along a straight line in t seconds then the velocity of the particle is given by

$\dfrac{dx}{dt}$ metres per second.

If the velocity is v then the acceleration at any time is given by

$\dfrac{dv}{dt}$ metres per second per second.

In a graph of velocity, v, against time, t, the shaded area between the curve and the time axis gives the distance that has been travelled up to the time T. Using calculus, this area is found by integrating to obtain

$x = \int v \, dt$

(x equals the integral of v with respect to t).

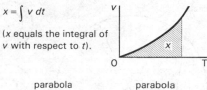

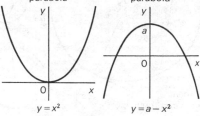

parabola   parabola

$y = x^2$ $y = a - x^2$

parabola   cubic

$y^2 = x$ $y = x^3$

hyperbola   circle

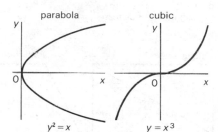

$y = \dfrac{1}{x}$ $x^2 + y^2 = a^2$

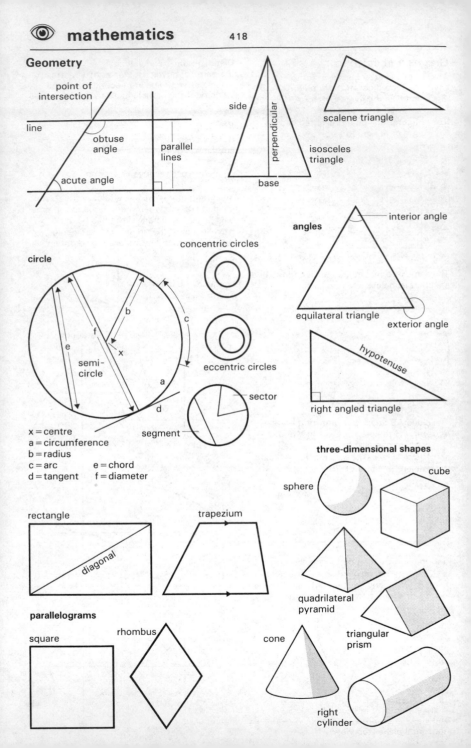

Geometry

point of intersection

line

obtuse angle

acute angle

parallel lines

side

perpendicular

base

isosceles triangle

scalene triangle

angles

interior angle

equilateral triangle

exterior angle

hypotenuse

right angled triangle

circle

concentric circles

eccentric circles

semi-circle

sector

segment

x = centre
a = circumference
b = radius
c = arc   e = chord
d = tangent   f = diameter

three-dimensional shapes

sphere

cube

rectangle

diagonal

trapezium

quadrilateral pyramid

triangular prism

parallelograms

square

rhombus

cone

right cylinder

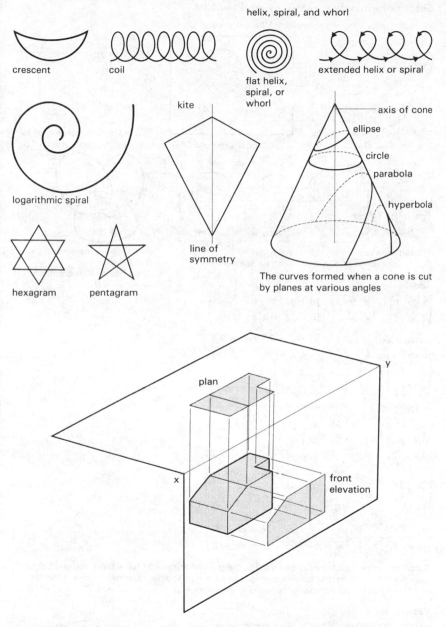

helix, spiral, and whorl

crescent

coil

flat helix,
spiral, or
whorl

extended helix or spiral

logarithmic spiral

kite

line of
symmetry

axis of cone

ellipse

circle

parabola

hyperbola

The curves formed when a cone is cut
by planes at various angles

hexagram

pentagram

plan

y

x

front
elevation

plans and elevations

A projection of a solid object onto a vertical plane (side or
end view) is called an elevation. A plan is a projection onto a
horizontal plane (top view).

Sets, determinants, matrices, and vectors

Venn diagrams showing the relations between sets.

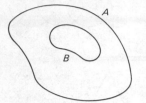

B is a subset of A

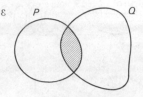

A' is the complement of A

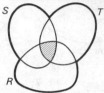

Shaded area represents $P \cap Q$ – the intersection of P and Q

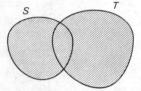

Shaded area represents $S \cup T$ – the union of S and T

$D \cap F = \phi$
D and F are disjoint

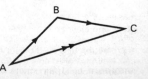

Shaded area represents $R \cap S \cap T$
Area inside outer boundary represents $R \cup S \cup T$

Addition

$$\begin{pmatrix} a & b & c \\ d & e & f \end{pmatrix} + \begin{pmatrix} g & h & i \\ j & k & l \end{pmatrix} = \begin{pmatrix} a+g & b+h & c+i \\ d+j & e+k & f+l \end{pmatrix}$$

Subtraction

$$\begin{pmatrix} a & b \\ c & d \\ e & f \end{pmatrix} - \begin{pmatrix} g & h \\ i & j \\ k & l \end{pmatrix} = \begin{pmatrix} a-g & b-h \\ c-i & d-j \\ e-k & f-l \end{pmatrix}$$

Multiplication

$$3\begin{pmatrix} a & b & c \\ d & e & f \\ g & h & i \end{pmatrix} = \begin{pmatrix} 3a & 3b & 3c \\ 3d & 3e & 3f \\ 3g & 3h & 3i \end{pmatrix}$$

$$\begin{pmatrix} a & b \\ c & d \\ e & f \end{pmatrix}\begin{pmatrix} g & h & i \\ j & k & l \end{pmatrix} = \begin{pmatrix} ag+bj & ah+bk & ai+bl \\ cg+dj & ch+dk & ci+dl \\ eg+fj & eh+fk & ei+fl \end{pmatrix}$$

$$\begin{pmatrix} g & h & i \\ j & k & l \end{pmatrix}\begin{pmatrix} a & b \\ c & d \\ e & f \end{pmatrix} = \begin{pmatrix} ag+ch+ei & bg+dh+fi \\ aj+ck+el & bj+dk+fl \end{pmatrix}$$

Note that for two matrices to be added or subtracted they must have the same number of rows and of columns and for two matrices to be multiplied the number of rows in the first must be equal to the number of columns in the second.

Vectors

A vector describes a quantity like a displacement, velocity, acceleration, or force.

The displacement $\overrightarrow{AC}$ is the vector sum of the displacements $\overrightarrow{AB}$ and $\overrightarrow{BC}$, i.e. $\overrightarrow{AC} = \overrightarrow{AB} + \overrightarrow{BC}$.

hair, feathers, rubber, or metal springs, on which one sleeps

mature¹ *adj* **1 a** a fully grown and developed **b** typical of a fully developed mind, controlled feelings, etc.; sensible **2** (of cheese, wine, etc.) ready to be eaten or drunk; ripe **3** carefully decided — ~**ly** *adv*

mature² *v* **matured, maturing** to become or cause to become mature — -**ration** *n*

maturity *n* the state or time of being mature

maudlin *adj* showing foolish sadness in a pitiful way

maul *v* **1** (esp. of animals) to hurt by tearing the flesh: *mauled by a lion* **2** to handle roughly or in an unwelcome way

maunder *v* **1** to talk in an unclear and usu. complaining way **2** to walk or act in a tired slow unhappy way

Maundy Thursday *n* -**days** the Thursday before Easter when in England by an old custom the King or Queen gives **Maundy money** to certain poor people

mausoleum *n* a large tomb raised over a grave of a famous or important person

mauve *adj, n* (of) a pale purple colour

maverick *n* **1** a young cow or horse without its owner's mark **2** a person who acts independently, esp. among politicians

mawkish *adj* having or expressing feelings, of love, admiration, etc., in a silly way — ~**ly** *adv* — ~**ness** *n*

maxi *n, adj* *esp. spoken* (any woman's garment) of full length reaching to the feet

maxim *n* a rule for good and sensible behaviour, esp. when expressed in a short well-known saying

maximal *adj* as great as possible: *to make maximal use of something* —compare MINIMAL — ~**ly** *adv*

maximize, -mise *v* -**mized, -mizing** to increase to the greatest possible size — **mization** *n*

maximum *n, adj* -**ma** *or* -**mums** (being) the largest number, amount, etc.: *He smokes a maximum of 10 cigarettes a day* —compare MINIMUM

may¹ *v* *negative short form* **mayn't** **1** to be in some degree likely to: *He may come or he may not* **2** to have permission to: *May I come in?* **3** I/we hope very much that: *May there never be another world war!* **4** (*expressing purpose*) can: *Sit here, so that I may see your face more clearly* **5 may as well** to have no strong reason not to: *There's nothing on TV, so you may as well switch it off* — compare MIGHT

may² *n* hawthorn flowers

May *n* **Mays** the 5th month of the year

maybe *adv* perhaps: *'Will they come?' 'Maybe not'*

mayday *n* -**days** a radio signal used as a call for help

May Day *n* —**Days** the 1st of May

mayfly *n* -**flies** a type of small fly which has a short life ☞ INSECT

mayhem *n* **1** *law* serious bodily wounding,

esp. that which causes a limb to be useless **2** *esp. spoken* disorder and confusion

mayonnaise *n* a thick cold yellowish sauce made from eggs, oil, etc.

mayor *n* the chief person of a city or town — ~**al** *adj*

mayoress *n* the wife or chosen companion of a male mayor, or a lady who is a companion to a woman mayor and is present with her at ceremonial occasions

maypole *n* a pole which can be ornamented with flowers and round which people dance on May 1st

maze *n* an arrangement in lines with a central point reached by twists and turns, some of them blocked, so that it is difficult to get into the centre and out again —compare LABYRINTH ☞ PUZZLE

mazurka *n* **1** a quick gay Polish dance **2** a piece of music for this

MC *abbrev. for:* master of ceremonies

MD *abbrev. for:* Doctor of Medicine

me *pron* (*object form of* I): *He bought me a drink.* | *That's me on the left of the photograph* USAGE After *as, than*, and *be*, the object pronouns **him, her, me, us, them** are used in speech. The subject pronouns **he, she, I, we, they** should be used in writing: *I'm fatter than him.* BUT, in writing: *I am fatter than he* —see I, HIM (USAGE)

mead *n* an alcoholic drink made from honey and water

meadow *n* **1** grassland on which cattle, sheep, etc., may feed **2** a field of grass for animals to eat, esp. grass which is cut and dried to make hay

meadowsweet *n* a common type of wild flower with large heads of many little white flowers and a strong sweet smell

meagre *adj* **1** (of the body or a part of the body) too thin **2** not enough in quantity, quality, strength, etc.: *a meagre income* — ~**ly** *adv* — ~**ness** *n*

meal¹ *n* **1** an amount of food eaten at one time **2** the occasion of eating a meal

meal² *n* grain which has been crushed into a powder

mealy *adj* -**ier, -iest** **1** like or containing meal **2** pale in colour and/or powdery in form: *mealy potatoes* —see also FLOURY

mealy-mouthed *adj* of a type of person who tends to express things not freely or directly, using words which are not plain in meaning, esp. when something unpleasant must be said

mean¹ *adj* **1** ungenerous; unwilling to share or help **2** unkind; unpleasant **3** (esp. of abilities) poor; bad: *He's no mean cook* — ~**ly** *adv* — ~**ness** *n*

mean² *v* **meant, meaning** **1** to represent (a meaning): *What does this word mean?* **2** to intend (to say): *She said Tuesday, but meant Thursday* **3** to be determined about/to act on: *I mean what I say* **4** to intend (to be) because of abilities, fate, etc.: *He is meant to be a great man* **5** to be a sign of: *The dark clouds mean* *rain* **6** to be of importance by (a stated amount): *His work means everything to him* **7 be meant to** to have to; be supposed to: *You're meant to leave a tip*

mean³ *n* **1 a** *technical* the value found when the numbers of a set are added together and then divided by the number in the set: *The mean of 7, 9, 14* $= \dfrac{7+9+14}{3} = 10$ **b** the average **2** a state or way of behaviour or course of action which is not extreme —see also HAPPY MEDIUM

meander *v* **1** (of rivers and streams) to flow slowly, turning here and there **2** (of people or talk) to speak or move in a slow aimless way — ~**ingly** *adv*

meanderings *n* a wandering course or movement

meaning *n* **1** the idea which is intended to be understood: *Explain the meanings of these foreign words* **2** importance or value: *the meaning of life*

meaningful *adj* of important meaning or purpose — ~**ly** *adv* — ~**ness** *n*

meaningless *adj* without meaning or purpose — ~**ly** *adv* — ~**ness** *n*

means *n* **means** **1** a method or way (of doing): *The quickest means of travel is by plane* **2** money, income, or wealth, esp. large enough for comfort **3 by all means** certainly; please do —see also WAYS AND MEANS USAGE This word is used with either a sing. or a pl. verb when it means 'a way to an end': *This is a dangerous means.* | *Such means are unpleasant.* When it means 'money or material possessions', **means** is always pl.: *Her means are small.*

means test *n often offensive* an inquiry into the amount of money a person has, when he needs money from the state

meant *past tense and past part. of* MEAN

meantime *n* the time between 2 events: *They go to town on Saturdays, and in the meantime shop in the village*

meanwhile also *esp. spoken* **meantime**— *adv* **1** in the meantime: *They'll be here soon. Meanwhile, we'll have some coffee* **2** during the same period of time: *Eve was cutting the grass, and Adam was meanwhile planting roses*

measles *n* an infectious disease in which the sufferer has a fever and small red spots on the face and body

measly *adj* **-lier, -liest** *esp. spoken* of small value, size, etc. — **-liness** *n*

measurable *adj* which is large enough or not too large to be reasonably measured — **-bly** *adv*

measure¹ *n* **1** a system for calculating amount, size, weight, etc. **2** an amount in such a system **3** an instrument or apparatus used for calculating amount, length, weight, etc., esp. a stick or container —see also TAPE MEASURE **4** a certain amount **5** true amount or quality: *There are no words to express the full measure of my gratitude* **6** an action taken to gain a certain end: *If he refuses to pay I shall take measures against him* **7**

a musical bar or poetic pattern of sounds which are repeated (METRE) —see also MADE-TO-MEASURE

measure² *v* **-sured, -suring** **1** to find the size, length, amount, degree, etc., (of) in standard measurements **2** to consider carefully (the effect of) **3** to be of a certain size

measure against *v prep* to see if the size of (something) is right by comparing with (something else): *I measured the coat against her and found it was too long*

measured *adj* careful; exact; steady: *He spoke in measured words*

measureless *adj esp. literature* too great to be measured

measurement *n* **1** the act of measuring **2** a length, height, etc., found by measuring

measure up *v adv* to show good enough qualities (for): *He didn't measure up to the job*

meat *n* **1** the flesh of animals, apart from fish and birds, which is eaten **2** the flesh of animals, including birds but not fish, as opposed to their bones **3** *old use* food (esp. in the phrase **meat and drink**) **4** valuable matter, ideas, etc.: *There was no real meat in his speech*

meatball *n* a small round ball made out of minced meat

meaty *adj* **-ier, -iest** **1** full of meat **2** full of valuable ideas — **meatiness** *n*

mecca *n* a place that many people wish to reach

mechanic *n* a person who is skilled in using, repairing, etc., machinery

mechanical *adj* **1** of, connected with, moved, worked, or produced by machinery **2** (of people or their acts) as if moved by machinery — ~**ly** *adv*

mechanics *n* **1** the science of the action of forces on objects **2** the science of making machines **3** the ways of producing or doing: *the mechanics of printing* —compare TECHNIQUE

mechanism *n* **1** the different parts of a machine arranged together, and the action they have **2** the arrangement and action which parts have in a whole: *the mechanism of the brain* — **-istic** *adj* — **-istically** *adv*

mechanize, -nise *v* **-nized, -nizing** to supply machines to, instead of using the effort of human beings or animals for work on — **-nization** *n*

medal *n* a round flat piece of metal, or a cross, with a picture and/or words on it, which is usu. given as an honour for a special achievement, in memory of an important event, etc.

medallion *n* a round medal like a large coin, or a pattern like this, used for ornament

medallist *n* a person who has won a medal, esp. in sport

meddle *v* **-dled, -dling** to interest oneself in what is not one's concern; interfere — ~**r** *n* — ~**some** *adj*

media *n* the newspapers, television, and radio; mass media USAGE **Media** and **mass media** are now beginning to be used with a sing. verb, but many people still think this is bad English.

medial adj 1 in the middle position 2 average — ~ly adv

median n technical 1 (in a triangle) the line joining a vertex to the mid-point of the opposite side 2 the middle value in a set of numbers arranged in order of size

mediate v -ated, -ating to act as a peacemaker, coming between opposing sides to bring about peace, agreement, etc. — -ation n

mediator n 1 a person who mediates 2 technical (in mathematics) a line that cuts another at its midpoint and is perpendicular to it

medic n esp. spoken a medical student or doctor

medical[1] adj 1 of or concerning medicine and treating the sick 2 of the treatment of disease by methods other than operation —compare SURGICAL — ~ly adv

medical[2] n esp. spoken a medical examination (of the body)

medicament n esp. written or technical a substance used on or in the body to treat a disease

medicate v -cated, -cating to cover, fill, or mix with a medical substance: medicated shampoo

medication n 1 the act of medicating 2 esp. written a medical substance, esp. a drug

medicinal adj 1 used for medicine 2 having the effect of curing, like medicine — ~ly adv

medicine n 1 a substance used for treating disease 2 the science of treating and understanding disease

medicine ball n a large heavy ball used in exercise for strengthening the muscles

medicine man n -men (in societies that still believe in magic, because they have not developed modern ways of thinking) a man believed to have magical powers over people and nature —see also WITCHDOCTOR

medieval adj of the period in history between about 500 and 1500 (the Middle Ages)

mediocre adj of medium quality or ability but usu. not good enough — -crity n

meditate v 1 -tated, -tating to think seriously or deeply 2 to fix the attention on one matter, having cleared the mind of thoughts, esp. for religious reasons and/or to gain peace of mind 3 to plan or consider carefully — -ion n — -ive adj — -ively adv

Mediterranean adj of or near the Mediterranean sea or the countries around it ☞ MAP

medium[1] n -dia or -diums 1 a method for giving information; form of art: The theatre is his favourite medium —see also MASS MEDIA, MEDIA 2 a substance in which objects or living things exist, or through which a force travels: A fish in water is in its natural medium 3 a middle position: a happy medium

medium[2] n -diums a person who claims to have power to receive messages from the spirits of the dead

medium[3] adj of middle size, amount, quality, value, etc.

medium wave n radio broadcasting or receiving on waves of medium length (between about 150 and 550 metres)

medley n -ley 1 a mass or crowd (of different types) mixed together: a medley of ideas 2 a piece of music made up of parts of other musical works △ MELODY

meek adj gentle in nature; yielding to others' actions and opinions — ~ly adv — ~ness n

meet[1] v met, meeting 1 to come together (with), by chance or arrangement 2 to find or experience 3 to come together or close: The cars met head-on 4 to get to know or be introduced (to) for the first time: Come to the party and meet some interesting people 5 to join at a fastening point: My skirt won't meet round my middle 6 to gather together 7 to touch, (as if) naturally: Their lips met 8 to answer, esp. in opposition 9 to be there at the arrival of: The taxi will meet the train 10 to pay 11 to satisfy

meet[2] n a gathering of men on horses with hounds to hunt foxes

meet[3] adj old use & Bible suitable; right

meeting n 1 the coming together of people, by chance or arrangement 2 a gathering of people, esp. for a purpose

meet with v prep to experience or find by chance: They met with an accident

megahertz also **megacycle**— n -hertz 1, 000, 000 hertz

megalith n a large stone which has usu. been standing since before historical times, perhaps raised as a religious or other type of sign

megalithic adj 1 made of or using megaliths 2 of times when megaliths were raised, before the time of recorded history

megalomania n the belief that one is more important, powerful, etc., than one really is — ~c n

megaphone also **loudhailer**— n an instrument shaped like a horn which makes the voice louder, so that it can be heard over a distance

megaton n (a measure of force of an explosion equal to that of) 1, 000, 000 tons (about 1, 016, 000, 000 kilograms) of a type of powerful explosive called TNT: a 5-megaton bomb

meiosis n the division of a cell into 2 new cells, in such a way that each of the resulting cells has only a half set of character-bearing parts (CHROMOSOMES) —compare MITOSIS

melancholy[1] n sadness, esp. over a period of time and not for any particular reason — -ic adj

melancholy[2] adj 1 sad 2 causing sadness: melancholy news

mélange n French a mixture of many types

melee n a struggling or disorderly crowd

mellifluous adj having a sweet smooth flowing sound

mellow[1] adj 1 (of fruit and wine) sweet and ripe or mature, esp. after being kept for a long time 2 (of colours and surfaces) soft, warm, and smooth, esp. worn so by time 3 wise and gentle through age or experience **4** *esp. spoken* pleasant to be with, esp. because rather drunk — ~**ly** *adv* — ~**ness** *n*

mellow² *v* to make or become (more) mellow

melodious *adj* sweet-sounding; tuneful — ~**ly** *adv* — ~**ness** *n*

melodrama *n* **1** a form of exciting play of the Victorian theatre, often with suffering heroines, daring heroes, etc. **2** a very exciting event which causes strong feelings or interest

melodramatic *adj* exciting in effect, often too much so to be thought real — ~**ally** *adv*

melody *n* **-dies 1** the arrangement of music in a pleasant way **2** a song or tune ⚠ MEDLEY **3** the part which forms a clearly recognizable tune in a larger arrangement of notes — **-ic** *adj*

melon *n* any of a few kinds of fruit which are large and rounded, with very juicy edible flesh inside a firm skin

melt *v* **1** to become or cause (a solid) to become liquid **2** to make or become gentle, sympathetic, etc. **3** to disappear or cause to disappear **4** (of a colour, sound, or sensation) to become lost (in another) by moving gently into or across **5 melt in the mouth** (of solid food) to be soft or tender when eaten USAGE The adjective **molten** means **melted** but it is only used of things that melt at a very high temperature: **molten** *rock/metal* | **melted** *chocolate/ice*

melt down *v adv* to make (a metal object) liquid by heating, esp. so as to use the metal again

melting *adj* (esp. of a voice) gentle, soft, and pleasant — ~**ly** *adv*

melting point *n* the temperature at which a solid melts ☞ PHYSICS

member *n* **1** a person belonging to a club, group, etc. **2 a** a part of the body, such as an organ or limb **b** the male sexual organ

Member of Parliament *n* Members of Parliament an MP

membership *n* **1** the state of being a member of a club, society, etc. **2** all the members of a club, society, etc.

membrane *n* **1** soft thin skin in the body, covering or connecting parts of it **2** a very thin sheet that forms the outer layer of all living cells — **-ous** *adj*

memento *n* **-tos** *or* **toes** a small object which reminds one, esp. of a holiday, a friend, etc.

memo *n* **-os 1** a note of something to be remembered **2** a note from one person or office to another within a firm or organization

memoir *n esp. written* **1** a story of someone's life, esp. a personal one **2** a short piece of writing on a subject the writer has studied

memoirs *n* the story of one's own life

memorable *adj* **1** which is worth remembering **2** noticeable; special — **-bly** *adv*

memorandum *n* **-da** *or* **-dums 1** a short agreement in writing, to sell, to form a company, etc. **2** *esp. written* a memo

memorial *n* **1 a** an object, such as a stone monument, in a public place in memory of a

person, event, etc. **b** a custom which serves the same purpose: *a memorial service* **2** a historical record: *memorials of a past age*

memorize, -rise *v* **-rized, -rizing** to learn and remember, on purpose

memory *n* **-ries 1** the ability to remember events and experience **2** an example of remembering **3** the time during which things happened which can be remembered

men *pl. of* MAN

menace¹ *n* **1** something which suggests a threat or brings danger **2** *esp. spoken* a troublesome person or thing

menace² *v* **-aced, -acing** *esp. written* to threaten — **-acingly** *adv*

ménage à trois *n French* a relationship in which 3 people, such as a married pair and a lover of one of the pair, live together

menagerie *n* a collection of wild animals; zoo

mend¹ *v* **1** to repair (a hole, break, fault, etc.) in (something) **2** to improve: *mend one's ways* **3** *esp. spoken* to regain one's health — ~**er** *n*

mend² *n* **1** a part mended after breaking or wearing **2** a patch or darn in material **3 on the mend** *esp. spoken* getting better after illness

mendacious *adj esp. written* (esp. of a statement) not truthful; lying — **-city** *n* — ~**ly** *adv*

Mendelian *adj* of the ideas of G. Mendel (1822–1884), who showed that qualities are passed on from parent to young according to rules

mendicant *adj, n* (a person) living as a beggar

mending *n* clothes to be mended

menfolk *n* **1** *esp. spoken* men **2** male relatives

menial¹ *adj* **1** not interesting or important **2** *old use* of or suitable for a servant — ~**ly** *adv*

menial² *n often offensive* a servant in a house, esp. one who must do all the hardest work

meningitis *n* an illness in which the outer part of the brain may be inflamed

meniscus *n technical* the curved surface of liquid in a tube

menopause also **change of life**— *n* the time when a woman's periods stop, usu. in middle age

menses *n esp. written or technical* the material mixed with blood that is lost from a woman's womb about once a month; menstrual flow —see also PERIOD

menstrual *adj* concerning a woman's periods

menstrual period *n esp. written* a monthly flow of blood from a woman's body ☞ REPRODUCTION

menstruate *v* **-ated, -ating** to have a natural flow of blood from the womb; lose the menses — **-ation** *n*

mensurable *adj esp. written* which can be measured

mensuration *n technical* the study and practice of measuring length, area, and volume

mental *adj* 1 of the mind 2 done only in or with the mind 3 concerning disorders or illness of the mind: *a mental hospital* 4 *bad usage* mad — ~**ly** *adv*

mental age *n* a measure of a person's ability and development of mind, according to the usual age at which such ability would be found

mental hospital also **mental home**— *n* a hospital or other building where people suffering from illness of the mind are treated

mental illness *n* illness of the mind

mentality *n* -**ties** 1 the abilities and powers of the mind 2 character; habits of thought

menthol *n* a white minty substance — ~**ated** *adj*

mention¹ *n* 1 the act of mentioning: *He made no mention of her wishes* 2 a short remark about something 3 *esp. spoken* a naming of someone, esp. to honour them: *He was given a mention in the list of helpers*

mention² *v* 1 to tell about in a few words, spoken or written 2 to say the name of: *He mentioned a useful book*

mentor *n* a person who habitually advises and helps another who knows less than him

menu *n* a list of dishes, esp. in a restaurant

Mephistopheles *n* (a name for) the devil, in his most wicked form — ~**lean** *adj*

mercantile *adj* 1 of or concerning merchants 2 of trade and commerce

Mercator's projection also **Mercator projection**— *n* a way of drawing a map so that it can be divided into regular squares

mercenary¹ *n* -**ries** a soldier who fights for the country that pays him, not for his own country —compare HIRELING

mercenary² *adj* influenced by the wish to gain money or other reward

mercerize, -ise *v* -**ized, -izing** to make (cotton thread) smooth by special treatment

merchandise¹ *n* things for sale; goods for trade

merchandise² *v* -**dised, -dising** to try to persuade people to buy (goods)

merchant *n* a person who buys and sells goods

merchantman also **merchant ship**— *n* -**men** a ship carrying goods

merchant navy also **mercantile marine**— *n* -**navies** those ships of a nation which are used in trade

merciful *adj* 1 showing mercy 2 by the kindness of God or fortune — ~**ly** *adv* — ~**ness** *n*

merciless *adj* showing no mercy — ~**ly** *adv* — ~**ness** *n*

mercury also **quicksilver**— *n* a heavy silver-white metal that is an element, which is liquid at ordinary temperatures and is used esp. in scientific instruments such as thermometers and barometers

Mercury *n* the planet nearest to the sun

mercy *n* -**cies** 1 willingness to forgive, not to punish 2 kindness or pity towards those who suffer or are weak 3 *esp. spoken* a fortunate event 4 **at the mercy of** powerless against

mercy killing *n* euthanasia

mere¹ *n* 1 *poetic* a small lake 2 (*as part of a name*) a lake: *Lake Windermere in Cumbria*

mere² *adj* nothing more than

merely *adv* only and nothing else

meretricious *adj* *esp. written* attractive on the surface, but of no value or importance — ~**ly** *adv* — ~**ness** *n*

merge *v* **merged, merging** 1 to become lost in or part of something else/each other 2 (of firms or companies) to combine

merger *n* a joining of 2 or more companies or firms

meridian *n* 1 an imaginary line drawn on maps from the north pole to the south over the surface of the earth 2 *technical* midday, when the sun reaches its highest point

meringue *n* 1 a sort of light cake made of sugar and the white part of eggs, beaten together 2 the same mixture, sometimes used as part of a sweet dish

merino *n* material made from the soft wool of a type of sheep

merit¹ *n* the quality of deserving praise, reward, etc.; personal worth

merit² *v* *usu. written* to deserve; have a right to

meritocracy *n* -**cies** 1 a social system which gives the highest positions to those with the most ability 2 the people who rule in such a system

meritorious *adj* *esp. written* deserving reward or praise — ~**ly** *adv*

mermaid — *masc.* **merman** *n* (in stories) a young and usu. attractive woman with the bottom half of her body like a fish's tail

merriment *n* laughter and sounds of enjoyment

merry *adj* -**rier, -riest** 1 cheerful, esp. laughing 2 causing laughter and fun: *a merry joke* 3 *esp. spoken* rather drunk — -**rily** *adv* — -**riness** *n*

merry-go-round *n* a roundabout

merrymaking *n* fun and enjoyment, esp. eating, drinking, and games — -**er** *n*

mescalin, -line *n* a drug which is obtained from a type of cactus

mesh¹ *n* 1 (a piece of) material woven with small holes between the threads 2 the threads in such material: *The fish were caught in the meshes of the net* 3 a trap: *a mesh of lies*

mesh² *v* 1 to connect; be held (together): *The wheels meshed* ☞ MACHINERY 2 (of qualities, ideas, etc.) to fit together suitably

mesmerize, -ise *v* -**ized, -izing** 1 to surprise very much, esp. so as to make speechless and unable to move 2 *esp. old use* to hypnotize

mess *n* 1 a state of disorder or untidiness 2 *esp. spoken* a person whose appearance, behaviour, or thinking is in a disordered state 3 dirty material, esp. passed from an animal's body 4 *esp. spoken* trouble **5** a place to eat, esp. for soldiers or other members of the armed forces —see also MESS UP

mess about also **mess around**— *v adv* **1** to act or speak stupidly **2** to move or work without speed or plan **3** to treat badly or carelessly

message *n* **1** a spoken or written piece of information passed from one to another **2** the important or central idea: *the message of this book*

messenger *n* a person who brings a message

messiah *n* **1** a new leader in a (new) religion, esp. one whom prophets told of, and esp. Christ in the Christian religion or the man still expected by the Jews **2** *esp. spoken* a person who brings new ways and saves people from difficulty — **-ianic** *adj*

Messrs *n* (used chiefly in writing as the *pl.* of Mr., esp. in the names of firms): *Messrs Ford and Dobson, piano repairers*

mess up *v adv esp. spoken* to disorder, spoil, etc. — **mess-up** *n*

mess with *v prep esp. spoken* to cause trouble to

messy *adj* **-ier, -iest** **1** untidy **2** dirty — **messily** *adv* — **messiness** *n*

met *past tense and past part. of* MEET

metabolism *n* the chemical activities in a living thing by which it gains energy, esp. from food — **-ic** *adj*

metabolize, -lise *v* **-lized, -lizing** to use for the metabolism

metacarpal *adj, n* (of) one of the small bones in the hand

metal¹ *n* any usu. solid shiny mineral substance of a group which can all be shaped by pressure and used for passing an electric current, and which share other properties: *Copper and silver are both metals*

metal² *v* **-ll-** to cover (a road) with a surface of broken stones

metallic *adj* **1** of, like, or containing metal **2** with a ringing quality (of sound): *a sharp metallic note*

metallurgy *n* the study and practice of removing metals from rocks, melting them, and using them — **-gical** *adj* — **-gist** *n*

metalwork *n* **1** objects shaped in metal **2** the study and practice of making metal objects — ~**er** *n*

metamorphosis *n* **-ses** (a) complete change from one form to another, esp. in the life of an insect

metaphor *n* (the use of) a phrase which describes one thing by stating another thing with which it can be compared (as in *the roses in her cheeks*) without using the words 'as' or 'like' —compare SIMILE — ~**ical** *adj* : *We didn't really mean he had green fingers, it was a metaphorical phrase*

metaphysical *adj* **1** of or concerning metaphysics **2** (of poetry) concerning a 17th century style of poetry which combined strong feelings with clever arrangements of words — ~**ly** *adv*

metaphysics *n* a branch of philosophy concerned with the science of being and knowing

metatarsal *adj, n* (of) one of the small bones in the foot

meteor *n* any of various small pieces of matter in space that form a short-lived line of light if they fall into the earth's atmosphere

meteoric *adj* **1** of or concerning a meteor **2** like a meteor, esp. in being very fast or in being bright and short-lived: *a meteoric rise to fame* — ~**ally** *adv*

meteorite *n* a meteor that has landed on the earth

meteoroid *n* a piece of matter in space smaller than an asteroid

meteorology *n* the study of weather conditions and their causes — **-gical** *adj* — **-gist** *n*

mete out *v adv* **meted, meting out** *esp. written & literature* to give carefully as if in measured amounts

meter *n* a machine which measures the amount used: *a gas meter*

methane *n* a natural gas which is formed from decaying matter and burns easily, sometimes causing explosions in mines —see also WILL-O'-THE-WISP

method *n* **1** a way or manner (of doing) **2** (the use of) an orderly system or arrangement: *to use method rather than luck*

method acting also **the Method**— *n technical* a way of acting in which the actor tries to imagine that he really is the character he is portraying

methodical *adj* careful; using an ordered system — ~**ly** *adv*

Methodism *n* a Christian group which follows the teachings of John Wesley — **-dist** *adj, n*

methodology *n* **-gies** *technical* the set of methods used for study or action in a particular subject — **-gical** *adj* — **-gically** *adv*

meths *n esp. spoken* methylated spirits

Methuselah *n often humour* a very old or very old-fashioned person, named after the man in the Bible who was said to have lived for 969 years

methyl alcohol also **methanol** *technical*, **wood alcohol**— *n* a type of poisonous alcohol found in some natural substances, such as wood —compare ETHYL ALCOHOL

methylated spirits *n* alcohol for burning, in lamps, heaters, etc.

meticulous *adj* very careful — ~**ly** *adv* — ~**ness** *n*

métier *n* one's trade, profession, or type of work

metre¹ *n* (any type of) regular arrangement of notes or esp. words (as in poetry) into strong and weak beats —see also RHYTHM

metre² *n* (a measure of length equal to) 39·37 inches

metric *adj* concerning the system of measurement based on the metre

metrical also **metric**— *adj* (of poetry) arranged in regular beats — ~**ly** *adv*

metricize, -cise *v* **-cized, -cizing** to change to the metric system — **-cation** *n*

metric system *n* a system of weights and measures, in which the standard measures are the kilogram for weight and the metre for length —compare AVOIRDUPOIS

metric ton *n* 1, 000 kilos

metro *n* **-ros** an underground railway system —compare UNDERGROUND

metronome *n* an instrument that indicates the speed at which a piece of music should be played

metropolis *n* *esp. written* a very large city — **-tan** *adj*

mettle *n* *esp. written* **1** the quality of courage **2** the will to continue struggling

mettlesome *adj* *esp. in literature* high-spirited

mews *n* **mews** a street formerly used as stables, that has been partly rebuilt so that people can live there

mezzanine *n* a floor that comes between the ground floor and the next floor up

mezzo[1] *adv technical* (in music) quite; not too

mezzo[2] *n* **-zos** *esp. spoken* a mezzo-soprano

mezzo-soprano *n* **-nos** **1** (a part in singing for) a woman's voice that is not so high as a soprano's nor so low as a contralto's **2** a woman singer with this voice

mezzotint *n* **1** a way of printing pictures from a metal plate which has a rough surface that is polished in places to produce areas of light and shade **2** a picture printed in this way

mg *abbrev. for:* milligram

mi *n* the third note in the sol-fa musical scale

miaow also **mew, meow**— *n, v* (to make) the crying sound a cat makes

miasma *n* a thick poisonous mist — ~**l** *adj*

mica *n* a glasslike substance that is much used in making electrical instruments

mice *pl. of* MOUSE

Michaelmas *n* 29th September, the feast day in honour of Saint Michael

Michaelmas daisy *n* **-sies** a type of tall garden plant that bears flat bluish-red or pink flowers

mickey *n* **-eys** also **mickey finn** **1** *sl* an alcoholic drink to which a drug has been secretly added **2 take the mickey (out of someone)** *esp. spoken* to tease someone

microbe *n* a living creature that is so small that it cannot be seen without a microscope; bacterium —compare BACTERIA, GERM

microbiology *n* the scientific study of very small living creatures, such as bacteria — **-gical** *adj* — **-gist** *n*

microcosm *n* a small system or group of people that represents all the qualities, activities, etc., of something larger —compare MACROCOSM

microelectronics *n* the making of electrical devices using very small components, esp. semiconductors ⇒ CHIP

microfilm[1] *n* (a length of) film for photographing something in a very small size

microfilm[2] *v* to photograph (something) using microfilm

micromesh *n* a very fine net material used esp. for making stockings

micrometer *n* an instrument for measuring very small objects

micron *n* one 1, 000, 000th of a metre

microorganism *n* a living creature (such as a BACTERIUM or PROTOZOON) too small to be seen without a microscope

microphone also *esp. spoken* **mike**— *n* an instrument for carrying or recording sound (as in radio, telephones, etc.) or in making sounds louder

microprocessor *n* a small computer in or on a chip

micropyle *n* *technical* a small hole in the seed case of many plants

microscope *n* an instrument that makes very small near objects seem larger ◎

microscopic *adj* **1** of or by means of a microscope **2** *often spoken* very small — ~**ally** *adv*

microwave *n* an electric wave of very short length, used esp. in sending messages by radio, in radar, and in cooking food

mid *prep poetic* among; in the middle of

midday *n* the middle of the day; 12 o'clock noon

midden *n* a large heap of waste matter, esp. from animals

middle[1] *adj* in or nearly in the centre; at the same distance from 2 or more points, or from the beginning and end of something

middle[2] *n* **1** the central part, point, or position **2** *esp. spoken* the waist or the part below the waist

middle[3] *v* **-dled, -dling** (esp. in cricket) to succeed in hitting (a ball, stroke, etc.) with the middle of a bat

middle age *n* the years between youth and old age

Middle *adj* (of a language) of a form that developed from an earlier stage, and into a later stage: *Middle English was spoken from about AD 1100 to 1450* —compare OLD

Middle Ages *n* the period in European history between about AD 500 and 1500

middlebrow *n* *sometimes offensive* a person who likes and is satisfied with music, painting, poetry, etc., that is of average good quality but is not very difficult to understand —compare HIGH-BROW, LOWBROW

middle class *adj, n* (of) the social class to which people belong who are neither noble, very wealthy, etc., nor manual workers

middle ear *n* the middle of the 3 parts of the ear

Middle East *n* the countries in Asia west of

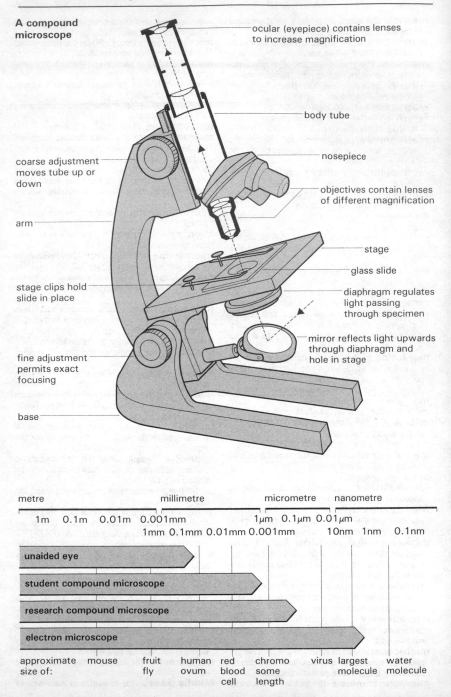

A compound microscope

ocular (eyepiece) contains lenses to increase magnification

body tube

coarse adjustment moves tube up or down

nosepiece

objectives contain lenses of different magnification

arm

stage

glass slide

stage clips hold slide in place

diaphragm regulates light passing through specimen

mirror reflects light upwards through diaphragm and hole in stage

fine adjustment permits exact focusing

base

metre			millimetre			micrometre		nanometre
1m	0.1m	0.01m	0.001mm			1μm 0.1μm 0.01μm		
			1mm 0.1mm 0.01mm 0.001mm				10nm 1nm	0.1nm

unaided eye

student compound microscope

research compound microscope

electron microscope

| approximate size of: | mouse | fruit fly | human ovum | red blood cell | chromo some length | virus | largest molecule | water molecule |

India, such as Iran, Iraq, Syria, etc., —compare FAR EAST, NEAR EAST, EAST — **Middle Eastern** adj

middle finger n the longest finger

middleman n -**men** a person who buys goods from a producer, and sells to a shopkeeper or directly to a user

middle school n **1** a school for children between the ages of 9 and 13 **2** a part of a secondary school for children of about 14 and 15

middleweight adj, n **1** (a person or thing) of average weight **2** (a boxer) who weighs more than 147 but not more than 160 pounds

middling adj esp. spoken **1** that is neither good nor bad in quality, kind, etc.; average **2** esp. dialect neither very well nor ill

midfield n the players who play in front of the defenders in soccer and whose main job is to send the ball forward to the attackers

midge n a type of very small flying insect, like a mosquito

midget n **1** a very, or unusually, small person **2** very small, compared with others of the same kind

midi n, adj esp. spoken (any woman's garment) reaching down to about halfway between knee and ankle

midland adj of the middle or central part of a country

Midlands n the central parts of England

midnight n 12 o'clock at night

midnight sun n the sun that can be seen at midnight in the very far north or south of the world

mid-off n (a person fielding at) the position on the cricket field behind and just to the left of the bowler

mid-on n (a person fielding at) the position on the cricket field behind and just to the right of the bowler

midriff n esp. spoken the part of the human body between the chest and the waist

midshipman n -**men** a boy or young man who is being trained to become a naval officer

midst n literature or old use the middle part or position

midsummer n **1** the middle of summer **2** the summer solstice (22nd June)

Midsummer Day n -**Days** 24th June

midway adj, adv (that is) halfway or in a middle position

midweek n, adj (happening during) the middle days of the week

midwicket n (a person who fields or is fielding in) the position on the cricket field in front and to the right of the bowler, and about halfway to the edge of the field

midwife n -**wives** a woman trained to help other women when they are giving birth — ~**ry** n

mien n esp. in literature a person's appearance, manner, or expression of face, as showing a feeling

miffed n esp. spoken slightly angry

might¹ v negative short form **mightn't** **1** to be or have been in some small degree likely to: He might come or he might not | Did you see that car nearly hit me? I might have been killed **2** polite (in questions) to have permission to; be allowed to: 'Might I come in?' 'Yes, you may' **3 a** (expressing purpose) could: I wrote down his telephone number, so that I might remember it **b** (with words expressing hope, wish, or fear) would: The prisoner had hopes that he might be set free **4** ought to; should: You might at least say 'thank you' when someone helps you **5** (in reported speech) may: He told us that he might come, but he might not. | He asked whether he might leave it with her. | He said he feared she might not live much longer. | He said I might go if I wished **6 might as well** may as well —compare MAY, COULD

might² n power; strength; force

mightily adv **1** with power or strength; greatly **2** esp. spoken, becoming rare very

mighty¹ adj -**ier**, -**iest** **1** often literature or Bible having great power or strength; very great **2** literature appearing strong and powerful because of great size **3 high and mighty** a offensive considering oneself important **b** of high rank and great power

mighty² adv esp. spoken very

migraine n a severe and repeated headache, typically with disorder of the eyesight

migrant n a person or animal, esp. a bird, that migrates

migrate v **migrated**, **migrating** **1** to move from one place to another, esp. for a limited period **2** (of birds and fish) to travel regularly from one part of the world to another, according to the seasons of the year —see EMIGRATE (USAGE) — -**ory** adj

migration n **1** the act of migrating **2** a movement of many people, birds, etc., in a body from one part of the world to another ☞ BIRD

mikado n -**dos** (a title given by foreigners in former times to) the ruler of Japan

mike n esp. spoken a microphone

mild¹ adj **1** (of a person, his nature, temper, etc.) gentle; soft —see also MEEK **and mild** **2** not hard or causing much discomfort or suffering; slight: a mild fever **3** (of food, drink, etc.) not strong or bitter in taste: a mild cheese — ~**ness** n

mild² n a type of beer that has a mild taste

mildew¹ n **1** a plant disease in which plants become covered with a soft usu. whitish growth **2** a soft usu. whitish growth that forms on food, leather, etc., in warm damp conditions — ~**y** adj

mildew² v to become or cause to become attacked by or covered with mildew

mildly adv **1** in a mild manner **2** slightly

mile n **1** (a measure of length or distance equal to) 1, 609 metres or 1, 760 yards **2** esp. spoken a very long way; a great deal: There's no one within miles of him as a cricketer —see also NAUTICAL MILE

mileage *n* 1 the distance that is travelled, measured in miles 2 also **mileage allowance**— a fixed amount of money paid for each mile that is travelled

mileometer *n* an instrument fitted in a car or other vehicle to record the number of miles it travels

miler *n* *esp. spoken* a person/horse that runs in one-mile races

milestone *n* 1 a stone at the side of a road, on which is marked the number of miles to the next town 2 an (important) date, time, or event in a person's life, or in history: *The invention of the wheel was a milestone in the history of man*

milieu *n* -s *or* -x surroundings, esp. a person's social surroundings

militant[1] *adj* having or expressing a readiness to fight or use force; taking an active part in a war, fight, or struggle: *A few militant members of the crowd started throwing stones at the police* △ MILITARY — **-cy** *n* — **~ly** *adv*

militant[2] *n* a militant person

militarism *n* *usu. offensive* belief in war or the use of armed force in the directing of a nation's affairs at home and abroad — **-rist** *n* — **-ristic** *adj* — **-ristically** *adv*

militarize, -rise *v* -rized, -rizing 1 to supply (a country, area, etc.) with military forces and defences 2 to give a military character to (something) 3 to change (something) for military use

military *adj* of, for, by, or connected with soldiers, armies, or war △ MILITANT — **military** *n*

militate against *v prep* -tated, -tating against to act, serve, or have importance as a reason against △ MITIGATE

militia *n* a body of men not belonging to a regular army, but trained as soldiers to serve in time of need or war —compare HOME GUARD

milk[1] *n* 1 a white liquid produced by human or animal females for the feeding of their young, and (of certain animals, such as the cow and goat) drunk by human beings or made into butter and cheese 2 a whitish liquid or juice obtained from certain plants and trees: *coconut milk* 3 **in milk** (esp. of a cow) in a condition to produce milk —see also CONDENSED MILK

milk[2] *v* 1 to take milk from (a cow, goat, or other animal) 2 to get money, knowledge of a secret, etc., from (someone or something) by clever or dishonest means

milk chocolate *n* chocolate made with the addition of milk and sugar

milker *n* 1 a person who milks 2 a cow that gives milk in a stated way or amount

milk float *n* a vehicle used by a milkman for delivering milk

milkmaid *n* (esp. in former times) a woman who milks cows; dairymaid

milkman *n* -men a man who goes from house to house each day to deliver milk

milk powder also **dried milk**— *n* a powder made by taking away all the water from milk

milk pudding *n* a sweet food made with rice or a like substance, baked with milk

milk run *n* *esp. spoken* a familiar and frequently travelled journey or course

milk shake *n* a drink of milk and flavouring of fruit, chocolate, etc., whisked together

milk tooth *n* -teeth a tooth belonging to the first set of teeth of young children and animals

milky *adj* -ier, -iest 1 made of, containing, or like milk 2 (of water or other liquids) not clear; cloudy — **milkiness** *n*

Milky Way *n* the pale white band of stars and clouds of gas that can be seen across the sky at night

mill[1] *n* 1 also **flourmill**— (a building containing) a machine for crushing corn or grain into flour —see also WATERMILL, WINDMILL 2 a factory or workshop, esp. in the cotton industry 3 a small machine in which a stated material can be crushed into powder: *a coffee mill* —see also RUN-OF-THE-MILL

mill[2] *v* 1 a to crush (grain) in a mill b to produce (flour) by this means 2 to press or roll (a metal) in a machine 3 to mark (the edge of something made of metal, esp. a coin) with regularly placed lines

mill about also **mill around**— *v adv* *esp. spoken* to move without purpose in large numbers

millenium *n* -nia 1 a period of 1,000 years 2 a future age in which all people will be happy, contented, and living in good conditions

miller *n* a man who owns or works a mill that produces flour

millet *n* 1 the small seeds of certain grasslike plants used as food 2 a plant producing such seeds

millibar *n* a standard amount used in measuring the pressure of the atmosphere

milligram *n* 1,000th of a gram

millilitre *n* 1,000th of a litre

millimetre *n* 1,000th of a metre

milliner *n* a person who makes and/or sells women's hats — **~y** *n*

million *adj, n, pron* **million** *or* **millions** the number 1,000,000; 10^6 — **~th** *adj, n, pron, adv*

millionaire *n* a person who has 1,000,000 pounds or dollars; very wealthy man

millipede, millepede *n* a type of small creature rather like a long centipede ⇨ EVOLUTION

millpond *n* a stretch of water kept in place by a bank built across a stream, used for driving the wheel of a watermill

millrace *n* the fast-flowing current of water that turns the wheel of a watermill

millstone *n* 1 one of the 2 circular stones between which corn is crushed into flour in a mill 2 a person or thing that gives someone great trouble, anxiety, etc.: *His lazy son is a millstone round his neck*

millwright *n* a skilled workman who makes and repairs windmills and watermills

milt *n* (the organ of a male fish containing) seeds that cause the eggs of female fish to grow

mime¹ *n* **1** an act or the practice of using actions to show meaning, as for amusement **2** acting without speech, as in ballet **3** an actor who performs without using words

mime² *v* **mimed, miming** **1** to act in mime **2** to copy the appearance, behaviour, manners, etc., of (someone) in an amusing way

mimetic *adj usu. technical* having or showing the ability, habit, or quality of copying

mimic¹ *n* **1** a person who copies, or who is good at copying another's manners, speech, etc., esp. in a way that causes laughter **2** **a** an animal that copies the actions of people **b** a bird that can copy the human voice

mimic² *adj* **1** not real; pretended **2** giving protection by being like something else: *the mimic colouring of zebras*

mimic³ *v* **-ck-** **1** to copy (someone or something), esp. in order to make people laugh **2** to appear so like (something else) as to deceive people into thinking it is the real thing

mimicry *n* **1** the act of mimicking **2** (of animals, insects, birds, etc.) a likeness, in colour, patterns, etc., to a more dangerous species, that gives protection against enemies

min *abbrev. for:* **1** minimum **2** minute(s)

minaret *n* a tall thin tower, one or more of which form part of a mosque

mince¹ *v* **minced, mincing** **1** to cut (esp. meat) into very small pieces **2** *offensive* to walk taking unnaturally short steps, esp. (of a man) in a womanlike way **3** **mince matters/one's words** to speak of something bad or unpleasant using soft language, and avoiding plain direct words

mince² *n* minced meat

mincemeat *n* **1** a mixture of currants, dried fruit, dried orange skin, and other things, but no meat, that is used as a sweet filling to put inside pastry **2** **make mincemeat of** *esp. spoken* to defeat completely; destroy

mince pie *n* a small round covered piece of pastry filled with mincemeat

mincer also **mincing machine**— *n* a machine that cuts food, esp. meat, into very small pieces

mind¹ *n* **1** thoughts; a person's way of thinking or feeling **2** the quality which gives the ability to think or feel; intellect: *He has a very sharp mind* **3** a person who thinks, esp. one with a good brain and the ability to lead, to control, etc. **4** intentions: *Nothing was further from my mind* **5** **call/bring to mind** to remember **6** **have a good mind to** *esp. spoken* to have a strong wish to; be very near a decision to **7** **in one's right mind** not mad; able to think rightly **8** **make up one's mind** to reach a decision **9** **put someone in mind of someone or something** to cause someone to remember, esp. because of a likeness in appearance, character, manners, etc. **10** **speak one's mind** to express plainly one's thoughts and opinions, even if unpleasant to hear **11** **to one's mind** in one's opinion; according to the way in which one thinks

mind² *v* **1** to be careful (of); pay close attention (to): *Mind the holes in the road.* | *Mind you read the questions carefully before you begin* **2** to have a reason against or be opposed to (a particular thing); be troubled by or dislike: *I don't mind if you go home early* **3** to take care or charge of; look after: *He stayed at home and minded the baby* **4** *dialect esp. Scots* to remember: *I mind the time when we were in Edinburgh together* **5** **never mind a** do not feel sorry, sad, or troubled **b** it does not matter (about); it is not important **6** **never you mind** *esp. spoken* it is not your business, and you are not to be told **7** **would you mind** *polite* please: *Would you mind making a little less noise?*

mind-blowing *adj esp. spoken* **1** very exciting; very shocking **2** (of a drug) causing one to see strange things in the mind, have strange feelings, etc.

minded *adj* having in some degree the will or desire: *He has enough money to travel all over the world, if he were so minded*

mind-expanding *adj esp. spoken* (of a drug) causing all one's senses and feelings to become stronger and deeper than usual

mindful *adj esp. written* giving thought or careful attention (to); not forgetful (of): *mindful of his promises* — ~ness *n*

mindless *adj* **1** *offensive* not having, needing, or using the power of thinking; stupid: *It's tiring and mindless work* **2** not giving thought or attention (to); regardless or forgetful (of): *mindless of danger* **3** *esp. in literature* having no mind; not controlled by the mind of man: *the mindless forces of nature* — ~ly *adv* — ~ness *n*

mind reader *n often humour* a person who is thought to, or claims to, be able to know what another person is thinking without being told — **mind reading** *n*

mind's eye *n* the imagination; the memory: *The old lady can still see in her mind's eye the house where she lived as a child*

mine¹ *adj old use, poetic* (before a vowel sound or *h*, or often a noun) my: *Mine eyes have seen the glory of the coming of the Lord.* | *Mine host* | *mother mine*

mine² *pron* (*Possessive form of* I) that/those belonging to me: *That bag's mine; it has my name on it*

mine³ *n* **1** a hole, usu. under the ground, from which coal, gold, tin, and other mineral substances are dug: *a tinmine* —see also COALMINE, GOLDMINE, and compare QUARRY **2** a person from whom or thing from which one can obtain a great deal (of something, esp. information or knowledge): *a mine of information about the history of the village* **3** a metal case containing explosives, that is placed just below the ground or on or below the surface of the sea and is exploded from far away or when something strikes it —compare DEPTH CHARGE **4** (a passage dug underground beneath an enemy position, containing) an explosive

mine⁴ *v* **mined, mining** **1** to dig or work a mine

in (the earth) **2** to obtain by digging from a mine **3** to lay mines in or under **4** to destroy by mines **5** to dig a mine under: *to mine the castle walls* —compare UNDERMINE

minefield *n* **1** a stretch of land or water in which mines have been placed **2** something that is full of hidden dangers

minelayer *n* a ship or aircraft used for putting mines into the sea — **-laying** *n*

miner *n* a worker in a mine △ MINOR

mineral¹ *n* any of various esp. solid substances that are formed naturally in the earth (such as stone, coal, salt, etc.)

mineral² *adj* of, connected with, containing, or having the nature of minerals; belonging to the class of minerals: *Salt is a mineral substance*

mineral kingdom *n* one of the 3 divisions into which the world is generally divided; all matter except animals and plants

mineralogy *n* the scientific study of minerals — **-gist** *n*

mineral oil *n* any type of oil that is obtained from the ground

mineral water *n* **1** water that comes from a natural spring and contains minerals, often drunk for health reasons **2** water to which gas has been added as a drink **3** a nonalcoholic drink containing gas, sweetened and given a particular taste (as of orange)

minestrone *n* a type of soup (of Italian origin) containing vegetables, small pieces of pasta, and meat juices

minesweeper *n* a ship fitted with special apparatus for taking mines from the sea — **-sweeping** *n*

mingle *v* **-gled, -gling** *esp. in literature* **1** to mix (with another thing or with people) **2** to mix (different things) together

mingy *adj* **-gier, -giest** *esp. spoken* not generous, with money or in quantity; stingy

mini *n* *esp. spoken* anything that is smaller than others of its kind usually are, esp. **a** (*trademark*) a type of small car **b** a miniskirt

miniature *n* **1** a very small painting of a person **2** a very small copy or representation of anything: *The child has a collection of miniature farm animals*

miniaturist *n* an artist who paints miniatures

minibus *n* a large van fitted with seats so that between 6 and 12 people can travel in it

minim *n* a musical note that is sounded only half as long as a whole note (SEMIBREVE) ☞ MUSIC

minimal *adj* of the smallest possible amount, degree, or size: *Her clothing was minimal* — compare MAXIMAL — **~ly** *adv*

minimize, -mise *v* **-mized, -mizing** to put the value, importance, effect, etc., of (something) at the lowest possible amount; consider, judge, or treat (something) not seriously: *He'd made a serious mistake, and it was no use trying to minimize its seriousness*

minimum *n* **-ma** or **-mums** the least, or the smallest possible, quantity, number, or degree — compare MAXIMUM

mining *n* the action or industry of getting minerals out of the earth by digging

minion *n* *offensive esp. literature* a person who, in order to please, is full of praise for his master, behaves towards him like a slave, and receives special favours from him

minister¹ *n* **1** a person in charge of a particular department of the government **2** a person of lower rank than an ambassador, who represents his government in a foreign country **3** a clergyman usu. belonging to the Presbyterian or Nonconformist Church — **~ial** *adj* — **~ially** *adv*

minister to *v prep esp. in literature* to serve; perform duties to help

ministration *n* (a) giving of help and service, esp. by a priest — **-trant** *n*

ministry *n* **-tries** **1** a government department led by a minister or the building in which the department works: *the Ministry of Defence* **2** the office, position or period of office of a minister **3** the group of ministers forming a government **4** priests, considered as a body **5** the priests' profession: *Our son wants to enter the ministry*

mink *n* a type of small weasel-like animal or its valuable brown fur

minnow *n* any of several types of very small freshwater fish

minor¹ *adj* **1** lesser or smaller in degree, size, etc. **2** *medical* not dangerous to life: *a minor illness* **3** *old public school* being the younger of 2 boys (usu. brothers) of the stated name (esp. at the same school): *Simkins minor* —opposite **major**, compare JUNIOR **4** (in music) based on a minor key: *a symphony in F minor* —compare MAJOR

minor² *n law* a person who has not yet reached the age at which he is fully responsible in law for his actions △ MINER

minority *n* **-ties** **1** the smaller number or part; a number or part that is less than half: *Only a minority want an election now* **2** a small part of a population which is different from the rest in race, religion, etc. **3** of or supported by a small, or the smaller, number of people **4** *law* the state or time when one has not yet, in law, reached the age of full responsibility —compare MAJORITY

minority government *n* a government which has fewer seats in parliament than the combined opposition parties

minor key *n* **-keys** **1** a musical key which gives the music a sad sound **2 in a minor key** (of speech or writing) quietly; not causing excitement; sadly

minor planet *n* an asteroid

minor third *n* (in music) an interval of 3 semitones between 2 notes

Minotaur *n* a legendary creature which had the body of a man and the head of a bull, and which lived in the underground maze (LABYRINTH) of Crete

minster n (now usu. part of a name) a great or important church: *York Minster*

minstrel n 1 (in the Middle Ages) a musician who travelled about the country singing songs and poems 2 one of a company of performers who travel about and give amusing shows to people on holiday by the sea, at fairs, etc.

mint sauce n a sauce made of finely-chopped mint leaves mixed with vinegar and sugar, served with lamb
perfect condition

mint² v to make (a coin)

mint³ n 1 any of several types of small plant, which have leaves with a particular smell and taste, used in preparing drinks and food 2 peppermint

mint sauce n a sauce made of finely-chopped mint leaves mixed with vinegar and sugar, seved with lamb

minuet n (a piece of music for) a type of slow graceful dance first performed in France about 300 years ago

minus¹ prep 1 made less by (the stated figure or quantity): *17 minus 5 leaves 12* 2 being the stated number of degrees below the freezing point of water: *The temperature was minus 10 degrees* 3 *esp. spoken* without: *He was minus 2 front teeth after the fight* —*opposite* **plus**

minus² n also **minus sign** — a sign (-) used for showing **a** that the stated number is less than zero **b** that the second number is to be taken away from the first

minuscule adj very small

minute¹ n 1 one of the 60 parts into which an hour is divided 2 *esp. spoken* a very short space of time: *I'll be ready in a minute* 3 one of the 60 parts into which a degree of angle is divided: *The exact measurement of this angle is 80 degrees 30 minutes*

minute² v **minuted, minuting** to make a note of (something) in the minutes of a meeting

minute³ adj 1 very small, in size or degree 2 giving attention to the smallest points; very careful and exact — ~**ness** n

minute hand n the longer of the 2 hands on a watch or clock, that shows the minutes

minutely adv 1 to a very small degree 2 very carefully and exactly 3 into very small pieces

minuteman n **-men** an American citizen who was ready, if given a minute's warning, to serve as a soldier in the war of independence against Great Britain

minutes n a written record of business done, decisions taken, etc., at a meeting

minutia n **-tiae** a very small point, that often does not seem worth considering; small exact detail

minx n *offensive, often humour* a young girl who does not behave with proper respect towards those older than her

miocene adj of the period in the world's history which started about 22, 000, 000 years ago and lasted until the pliocene period

miracle n 1 an act or happening (usu. having a good result), that cannot be explained by the laws of nature 2 a wonderful surprising unexpected event 3 a wonderful example (of a quality, ability, etc.)

miracle play also **mystery play**— n **-plays** a type of theatrical play, often performed in the Middle Ages, based on stories from the Bible or of Saints —*compare* MORALITY PLAY

miraculous adj very wonderful; caused, or seeming to be caused, by powers beyond those of nature — ~**ly** adv

mirage n 1 a strange effect in a desert, in which distant objects seem near, or in which objects appear which are not really there 2 a wish, dream, etc., that cannot come true

mire n *esp. in literature* deep mud — **miry** adj

mirror¹ n 1 a shiny or polished surface that reflects images that fall on it 2 a true faithful representation (of something): *the mirror of public opinion*

mirror² v to show, as in a mirror

mirth n *esp. in literature* merriness and gaiety expressed by laughter — ~**ful** adj — ~**fully** adv — ~**less** adj

misadventure n 1 *esp. in literature* (an accident; event caused by) bad luck 2 **death by misadventure** *law* the death or killing of a person by accident

misadvise v **-vised, -vising** to give (a person) wrong advice

misalliance n a uniting of people that is wrong or unsuitable, esp. a marriage with a person of a different social class

misanthrope also **misanthropist**— n a person who hates everybody, trusts no one, and avoids being in the company of others —*compare* MISOGYNIST, PHILANTHROPIST — **-thropy** n — **-thropic** adj — **-thropically** adv

misapply v **-plied, -plying** to use wrongly or for a wrong purpose — **-lication** n

misapprehend v *esp. written* to understand (something) in a mistaken way

misapprehension n a mistaken understanding

misappropriate v **-ated, -ating** *esp. written or technical* to take dishonestly and put to a wrong use — **-ation** n

misbegotten n 1 *offensive or humour* (of a person) worthless; contemptible 2 *offensive or humour* (of an idea, plan, opinion, etc.) badly produced or formed

misbehave v **-haved, -having** to behave (oneself) badly or improperly — ~**d** adj — **-iour** n

miscalculate v **-lated, -lating** to calculate wrongly — **-lation** n

miscall v to call (someone or something) by a name that is wrong, untrue, or not deserved

miscarriage n an act or case of producing lifeless young before the proper time of birth —*compare* ABORTION, STILLBIRTH

miscarriage of justice n law (a) failure by the law courts to do justice

miscarry v **-ried, -rying** 1 (of a woman) to have a miscarriage 2 (of an intention, plan, etc.) to be unsuccessful

miscast v **-cast, -casting** to give (an actor or actress) an unsuitable part

miscellaneous adj of several kinds or different kinds; having a variety of sorts, qualities, etc. — ~ly adv — ~ness n

miscellany n **-nies** 1 a mixture of various kinds 2 a collection of writings on different subjects, often by different writers

mischance n esp. written (an example of) bad luck

mischief n 1 bad, but not seriously bad, behaviour or actions, as of children, probably causing trouble, and possibly damage or harm 2 troublesome playfulness 3 esp. spoken a person, esp. a child, who is often troublesomely playful 4 damage, harm, or hurt done by a person, animal, or thing

mischievous adj 1 having or showing a liking for mischief 2 offensive causing harm, often with intention — ~ly adv — ~ness n

misconceive v **-ceived, -ceiving** 1 to think (something) out badly and without proper consideration 2 esp. written to be mistaken in one's understanding of (something); misconstrue: He completely misconceived my meaning — **misconception** n

misconduct[1] n esp. written 1 bad behaviour, esp. improper sexual behaviour 2 bad control, as of a business company

misconduct[2] v esp. written 1 to behave (oneself) badly or improperly, esp. with a person of the opposite sex 2 to control (something, such as a business or business affairs) badly

misconstruction n 1 mistaken understanding 2 open to misconstruction that may be understood wrongly

misconstrue v **-strued, -struing** to place a wrong meaning on (something said or done)

miscount v to count wrongly — **miscount** n

miscreant n old use a person of evil character and deeds, deserving to be hated

misdate v **-dated, -dating** 1 to put a wrong date on (a letter, cheque, etc.) 2 to give a wrong date to (something, such as an historical event)

misdeal v **-dealt, -dealing** to deal wrongly, as when giving cards to players — **misdeal** n

misdeed n esp. written or literature a wrong or wicked deed

misdemeanour n 1 a bad or improper act that is not very serious 2 law a crime that is less serious than, for example, stealing or murder — compare FELONY

misdirect v 1 to direct (someone) wrongly 2 to address (a letter, parcel, etc.) wrongly 3 to use (one's strength, abilities, etc.) for a wrong purpose — ~ion n

misdoing n esp. literature or esp. written a bad act; misdeed

miser n offensive a person who loves money and hates spending it — ~ly adj — ~liness n

miserable adj 1 very unhappy 2 causing unhappiness, discomfort, etc.: miserable conditions 3 very poor (in quality) or very small or low (in degree or amount): a miserable failure

miserably adv 1 in a way that causes great discomfort, unhappiness, etc.: a miserably cold morning 2 in or to a very bad or low degree: She failed miserably

misery n **-ries** 1 great unhappiness or pain and suffering (of body or of mind) 2 offensive esp. spoken a person who is always unhappy and complaining, esp. one who does not like others to enjoy themselves

misfire v **-fired, -firing** 1 (of a gun) to fail to send out the bullet when fired 2 (of a car engine) to produce irregularly, or to fail to produce, the flash that explodes the petrol mixture 3 (of a plan, joke, etc.) to fail to have the desired or intended result — **misfire** n

misfit n a person who does not fit well and happily into his social surroundings or the position he holds

misfortune n 1 bad luck, often of a serious nature 2 a very unfortunate condition, accident, or event

misgiving n a feeling or feelings of doubt, fear (of the future), and/or distrust

misgovern v to govern badly or unjustly — ~ment n

misguide v **-guided, -guiding** to lead or influence (someone) into a wrong or foolish course of action — ~d adj — ~dly adv

mishandle v **-dled, -dling** to handle or treat (something or someone) roughly, without skill, or insensitively

mishap n an unfortunate or unwanted happening usu. not of a serious nature

mishear v **-heard, -hearing** to hear (someone or something) mistakenly

mishmash n esp. spoken an untidy, disorderly mixture

misinform v to tell (someone) something that is incorrect or untrue, either on purpose or by accident

misinterpret v to put a wrong meaning on (something said, done, etc.) — ~ation n

misjudge v **-judged, -judging** to judge (a person, action, time, distance, etc.) wrongly — ~ment n

mislay v **-laid, -laying** to lose by putting (something) in a place and forgetting where

mislead v **-led, -leading** to cause (someone) to think or act wrongly or mistakenly; guide wrongly, sometimes with the intention to deceive: Her appearance misled him — ~ingly adv

mismanage v **-aged, -aging** to control or deal with badly or wrongly — ~ment n

mismatch v to match wrongly or unsuitably — **mismatch** n

misnomer n a wrong or unsuitable name given to someone or something

misogynist *n* a person who hates women — compare MISANTHROPE, PHILANTHROPIST — **-gyny** *n*

misplace *v* **-placed, -placing** **1** to put in an unsuitable or wrong place or position **2** to have (good feelings) for an undeserving person or thing: *misplaced admiration for a silly book* **3** to mislay — ~**ment** *n*

misprint[1] *v* to make a mistake in printing (a word, letter, etc.)

misprint[2] *n* a mistake in printing

mispronounce *v* **-nounced, -nouncing** to pronounce incorrectly — **-nunciation** *n*

misquote *v* **-quoted, -quoting** to make a mistake in reporting (words) spoken or written by (a person) — **-quotation** *n*

misread *v* **-read, —reading** **1** to read (something) wrongly **2** to make a mistake in understanding (something read or thought about): *The general misread the enemy's intentions*

misreport *v* to give an incorrect account of (something), such as (words) spoken by (someone), often on purpose

misrepresent *v* to give an incorrect account, explanation, or description of (someone, or someone's words or actions), in such a way that unfavourable ideas may be spread — ~**ation** *n*

misrule[1] *v* **-ruled, -ruling** to misgovern

misrule[2] *n* **1** government that is bad, or that lacks order **2** *esp. in literature* disorder; lawlessness

miss[1] *v* **1** to fail to hit, catch, find, meet, touch, hear, see, etc. (something or someone): *The falling rock just missed my head.* | *He arrived too late and missed the train* **2** to avoid or escape from (something unpleasant) by such a failure: *I was lucky to miss the traffic accident* **3** to discover the absence or loss of (someone or something): *She didn't miss her bag till she got home* **4** to feel or suffer from the lack of (something): *Give the beggar a coin; you won't miss it* **5** to feel sorry or unhappy at the absence or loss of (someone or something): *He missed his dog which had died* —see also HIT-OR-MISS, MISSING, MISS OUT

miss[2] *n* a failure to hit, catch, hold, etc., that which is aimed at

miss[3] *n* **1** (a form of address used) **a** (by pupils to) a woman teacher **b** (esp. by shopkeepers, servants, etc., to) an unmarried woman **c** (by anyone to) a waitress, girl working in a shop, etc. **2** technical a girl whose dress size is between that of a child and a woman

Miss *n* **1** (a title placed before the name of) an unmarried woman or a girl: *Miss Brown* **2** (a title placed before) the name of a place or a type of activity which a young unmarried woman has been chosen to represent, usu. for reasons of beauty: *Miss England 1982*

missal *n* a book containing the complete religious service during the year for Mass in the Roman Catholic church

misshapen *adj* (esp. of the body or a part of it) badly or wrongly shaped or formed

missile *n* **1** a rocket which can be aimed at a distant object —see also GUIDED MISSILE, INTERCONTINENTAL BALLISTIC MISSILE **2** *esp. written* an object or weapon thrown by hand or shot from a gun or other instrument: *The angry crowd threw bottles and other missiles at the players*

missing *adj* not to be found; not in the proper or expected place; lost

missing link *n* a form of creature, supposed but not proved to have existed, mid-way in the development of man from monkey-like creatures

mission *n* **1** a group of people, esp. a country's delegates, who are sent abroad for a special reason: *a British trade mission to Russia* **2** the duty or purpose for which these people are sent: *The mission was to sell more cars* **3 a** a building or offices where the work of these people is planned or carried out **b** a building or group of buildings in which a particular form of religion is taught, medical services are given, poor people are helped, etc. **4** the particular work for which one believes oneself to have been sent into the world: *Nursing is her mission in life*

missionary *n* **-ries** a person sent usu. to a foreign country, to teach and spread his religion

missive *n* *esp. humour or pompous* a letter, esp. one of great, or too great length

miss out *v adv* **1** to leave out **2** to lose a chance to gain advantage or enjoyment: *She always misses out, because she's never there*

misspell *v* **-spelt** *or* **-spelled, -spelling** to spell wrongly — ~**ing** *n*

misspend *v* **-spent, -spending** to spend (time, money, etc.) wrongly or unwisely; waste

misstate *v* **-stated, -stating** to state (a fact, argument, etc.) wrongly or falsely — ~**ment** *n*

missus, missis *n* *esp. spoken* **1** *bad usage* the wife of the man speaking, spoken to, or spoken about: *How's the missus?* **2** *now rare* (used esp. among servants) the woman who is the head, or wife of the head, of a house or family

mist[1] *n* **1** thin fog —see also SCOTCH MIST **2** a film, esp. one formed of small drops of water, through which it is hard to see clearly: *the mist of her tears* **3** something that makes understanding or good judgment difficult

mist[2] *v* to cover with mist

mistake[1] *v* **-took , -taken , -taking** **1** to have a wrong idea about (someone or something); understand wrongly **2** not to recognize (someone or something)

mistake[2] *n* a wrong thought, act, etc.; something done, said, believed, etc., as a result of wrong thinking or understanding, lack of knowledge or skill, etc.: *a spelling mistake*

mistake for *v prep* to think wrongly that (someone or something) is (someone or something else): *They mistook him for his brother*

mistaken *adj* **1** (of a person) wrong; having understood incorrectly **2** (of a statement, idea, etc.) misunderstood **3** (of an action, idea, etc.) incorrect; not well-judged; based on wrong thinking, lack of knowledge, etc.: *She trusted him, in the mistaken belief that he was honest* — ~**ly** *adv*

mister *n*   **1** *bad usage* sir   **2** *esp. spoken* a man who has not got a title of rank or profession that he can add to his name

Mister *n* (*sometimes used in writing*) Mr

mistime *v*   -**timed**, -**timing** to do or say (something) at a wrong or unsuitable time: *a mistimed remark about the cooking*

mistletoe *n* a type of plant (a PARASITE) that grows on trees, has pale green leaves, and small white berries, and is often hung in rooms at Christmas time

mistress *n*   **1** a female master: *a new English mistress*   **2** a woman with whom a man has a sexual relationship, usu. not a socially acceptable one

Mistress *n old use or Scots* (a title placed before the name of) any woman or girl

mistrust *v* not to trust; distrust — **mistrust** *n*

mistrustful *adj* having or showing mistrust; distrustful — ~**ly** *adv* — ~**ness** *n*

misty *adj*   -**ier**, -**iest**   **1** full of, covered with, or hidden by mist   **2** not clear to the mind; vague: *misty memories of his childhood* — -**ily** *adv* — -**iness** *n*

misunderstand *v* -**stood**   **1** to understand wrongly; put a wrong meaning on (something said, done, etc.) or on something said by (someone)   **2** to fail to see or understand the true character or qualities of (someone): *His wife misunderstands him*

misunderstanding *n*   **1** the act of misunderstanding   **2** an example of this: *Her poor French often leads to misunderstandings when she visits France*   **3** a disagreement less serious than a quarrel

misuse *v*   -**used**, -**using** to use in a wrong way or for a wrong purpose; treat badly — **misuse** *n*

mite *n*   **1** a small child, esp. for whom one feels sorry   **2** any of several types of very small insect-like creature   **3** *esp. literature or Bible* a very small offering, esp. of money, from someone who cannot afford more

mitigate *v*   -**gated**, -**gating** *esp. written*   **1** to lessen the seriousness of (wrong or harmful action): *Nothing could mitigate the cruelty with which she had treated him*   **2** to lessen (the evil, harm, etc., caused by some action)   **3** to make (suffering of any kind) easier to bear: *to mitigate the sufferings of the dying woman* △ MILITATE AGAINST — -**gation** *n*

mitigating circumstances *n often law* conditions that make a crime, mistake, etc., less serious, and that may lessen the punishment

mitosis *n technical* the division of a cell into 2 new cells, in such a way that each of the resulting cells has a complete set of chromosomes — compare MEIOSIS

mitre *n*   **1** a tall pointed hat worn by bishops and archbishops   **2** also **mitre joint** — a joint between

2 pieces of wood, in which each is cut at an angle of 45 degrees forming a right angle between the pieces, as in the corners of a picture frame

mitt *n*   **1** a special type of glove for protection: *an oven mitt* | *a baseball mitt*   **2** *sl, often humour* a hand   **3** a mitten

mitten *n*   **1** a glove in which all 4 fingers are covered by one baglike part   **2** a covering for the hand and wrist, but not for the fingers

mix¹ *v*   **1** to combine so as to form a whole, of which the parts have no longer a separate shape, appearance, etc., or cannot easily be separated: *You can't mix oil and water*   **2** to prepare (such a combination): *His wife mixed him a hot drink*   **3** to be or enjoy being in the company of others: *He mixes well in any company*   **4** **mix it** *esp. spoken* to fight roughly —see also MIX UP

mix² *n*   **1** a combination of different substances: *cake mix*   **2** a group of different things, people, etc.

mixed *adj*   **1** of different kinds   **2** of or for both sexes: *a mixed school*   **3** combining people of 2 or more races or religions: *a mixed marriage*

mixed bag *n esp. spoken* a collection of things of many kinds and qualities

mixed doubles *n* **mixed doubles** a match or competition in which a man and a woman play against another man and woman

mixed farming *n* work on a farm which includes different kinds of farming, such as cattle raising and corn growing

mixed metaphor *n* a use of 2 different metaphors together, producing a foolish effect: '*The ship of state is going off the rails*' *is a mixed metaphor*

mixed up *adj*   **1** connected (with something or someone bad): *Don't get mixed up in the quarrels of other people*   **2** troubled in mind, and unable to think clearly

mixer *n*   **1** an apparatus by or in which substances are mixed   **2** a person who mixes well or badly with other people   **3** *technical* a person who balances and controls the words, music, and sounds recorded for a film

mixture *n*   **1** a set of substances mixed together, which keep their separate qualities while combined: *cough mixture* —compare COMPOUND   **2** a combination: *a mixture of sadness and humour*

mix up *v adv*   **1** to confuse (someone) or mistake (something)   **2** to put into disorder: *Don't mix up those papers* — **mix-up** *n*

mizzen, mizen *n* the lowest square sail on a mizzenmast

mizzenmast *n* the tall mast nearest the stern of a ship with 3 masts

mm *abbrev. for:* millimetres

mnemonic *adj, n* (something, esp. a verse) used to help one remember: *The spelling guide* 'i before e except after c' *is a mnemonic* — ~**ally** *adv*

mo *n esp. spoken* a very short time: *Wait a mo*

moan¹ *n*   **1** a low sound of pain, grief, or suffering   **2** sounds that give the idea of sadness: *the moan of the wind*   **3** a complaint, expressed in a discontented voice: *She always has some moan or another*

moan² *v* **1** to make a moan **2** to express with moans: *The prisoner moaned out a prayer for mercy* **3** to complain — ~**er** *n*

moat *n* a long deep hole dug for defence round a castle, fort, etc., and usu. filled with water ☞ CASTLE

mob¹ *n* **1** a large noisy esp. violent crowd **2** the common people **3** a group of lawbreakers — **mob** *adj*

mob² *v* **-bb-** **1** (of a group) to attack: *The large bird was mobbed by all the smaller birds* **2** (of a group of people) to crowd around from interest or admiration: *When he left the hall the party leader was mobbed by his supporters*

mobile¹ *adj* **1** movable; not fixed **2** driven from place to place in a vehicle: *a mobile library* **3** changing quickly, as of a person's face — **-ility** *n*

mobile² *n* an ornament or work of art made of small models, cards, etc., and hung up on wires or string so that they are moved by currents of air

mobilize, -ise *v* **-ized, -izing** **1** to gather together (people or things) for a particular use: *to mobilize one's resources* **2** (of armed forces) to become ready for war — **-zation, -sation** *n*

mobster *n* a gangster

moccasin *n* a simple soft leather shoe, as first worn by North American Indians

mocha *n* coffee of fine quality, first brought from the Red Sea port of Mocha

mock¹ *v* **1** to laugh at (someone or something) when it is wrong to do so; speak or act as if one is not serious, esp. when one should be: *He went to church only to mock* **2** to copy in such a way that the person or thing copied is laughed at: *He made the boys laugh by mocking the way the teacher spoke* — ~**er** *n* — ~**ingly** *adv*

mock² *n* **make a mock of** make a mockery of

mock³ *adj* not real or true; like something real: *a mock battle*

mockery *n* **-ries** **1** laughing at something that should not be laughed at **2** a person or thing deserving to be laughed at **3** something not worthy of respect or consideration: *The medical examination was a mockery; the doctor hardly looked at the child*

mockingbird *n* an American bird that copies the songs of other birds

mock-up *n* a representation or model of something planned to be made

modal *adj* *technical* **1** of or concerning the mood of a verb **2** of or concerning musical modes **3** (of music) written in one or more of the modes — ~**ly** *adv*

modal auxiliary *n* **-ries** a verb which goes with the infinitive of another verb, for example, *can, shall, must*

mod con *n* a modern convenience; something that makes living easier, such as central heating

mode¹ *n* **1** a way of behaving, speaking, etc.: *His new wealth changed his whole mode of life* **2** technical a way in which something happens: *This fever will return from time to time, if it follows its usual mode* **3** technical either the major or the minor scale in modern western music **4** technical any of the 8 scales (such as **Dorian** and **Phrygian**) in ancient music, much used also esp. in folk music since then **5** the number that occurs most often in a large collection of numbers; the value occurring with greatest frequency in a set

mode² *n* the fashion —see also A LA MODE

model¹ *n* **1** a small representation or copy **2** a person or thing almost exactly like another: *She's a perfect model of her aunt* **3** a person or thing worthy to be copied: *This pupil's work is a model of neatness* **4** a person employed to wear clothes and to show them to possible buyers **5** a person employed to be painted by an artist **6** an article which is one of a number of articles of a standard pattern: *The car industry's always producing new models*

model² *v* **-ll-** **1 a** to make in a soft substance: *to model pots in clay* **b** to make a model of **2** to act as a model **3** to show (an article of clothing) as a model: *A girl was chosen to model the silk dress*

model³ *adj* **1** being a small copy: *model cars* **2** deserving to be copied: *a model mother*

model on also **model upon**— *v prep* to form as a copy of: *She modelled herself on her mother*

moderate¹ *adj* **1** of middle degree, power, or rate **2** within sensible limits **3** of only average quality: *This pupil has only moderate ability* **4** not favouring extreme political or social ideas — ~**ly** *adv*

moderate² *v* **-rated, -rating** to make or become less

moderate³ *n* a person with moderate opinions —compare EXTREMIST

moderation *n* **1** reduction in force, degree, rate, etc. **2** the ability of keeping one's desires within reasonable limits; self-control **3 in moderation** within sensible limits

moderato *n, adj, adv* **-tos** (a piece of music) played at an average even speed

moderator *n* **1** a person who tries to help people or sides to reach an agreement **2** a chairman of a church court **3** technical a substance (such as graphite or water) used for slowing down the action of neutrons in an atomic reactor **4** an examiner who makes sure that an examination paper is fair, and that the marks are of the right standard

modern¹ *adj* **1** of the present time; not ancient **2** new and different from the past **3** (of a language) in use today —compare CONTEMPORARY —see also SECONDARY MODERN — ~**ity** *n*

modern² *n* a person living in modern times or with modern ideas

modernism *n* the spirit, thought, or character of modern times — **-ist** *adj, n*

modernistic *adj* favouring modern ideas, systems, etc. — ~**ally** *adv*

modernize, -ise *v* **-ized, -izing** **1** to make

suitable for modern use **2** to become modern —
-ization n

modest adj **1** having a lower opinion than is
probably deserved, of one's own ability, successes,
etc.; hiding one's good qualities **2** not large in
quantity, size, value, etc. **3** avoiding anything
improper or impure — ~**ly** adv — ~**y** n

modicum n a small amount

modify v **-fied, -fying 1** to change, esp.
slightly **2** to make less hard to accept or bear: to
modify one's demands **3** (in grammar) (of a
word) to describe or limit the meaning of (another
word): The adverb 'quietly' modifies the verb 'talk'
in the phrase ' to talk quietly ' — **fication** n

modish adj fashionable — ~**ly** adv

modulate v **-lated, -lating 1** to vary the
strength, nature, etc., of (a sound) **2** to pass from
one musical key to another: The music modulates
from G to D **3** technical to vary the size or rate
of (a radio wave or signal) — **-ation** n

module n technical **1** a standard part used in
building, making furniture, etc. **2** a part of a
space vehicle that can be used independently —
modular adj

mogul n a person of very great power, wealth, or
importance: the moguls of the film industry

MOH abbrev. for: Medical Officer of Health;
a doctor responsible for public health in an area

mohair n (cloth made from) the long fine silky
hair of the Angora goat

Mohammedan also **Muhammadan**— adj, n
(a) Muslim — ~**ism** n

moiré also **watered silk**— n French silk
material, with a shiny surface like waves on
water

moist adj **1** slightly wet **2** (esp. of food) not
unpleasantly dry — ~**ly** adv — ~**ness** n

moisten v to make or become slightly wet

moisture n water, or other liquids, in small
quantities or as steam or mist

moisturize, -ise v **-ized, -izing** to remove
dryness: moisturizing cream

molar n, adj (any) of the large back teeth with
rounded or flattened surfaces for breaking up
food

molasses n a thick dark sweet liquid from
sugarcane

mole[1] n a small dark brown slightly raised mark
on a person's skin, usu. there since birth

mole[2] n a small insect-eating animal with very
small eyes and soft dark fur, which digs passages
underground and lives in them ☞ MAMMAL

mole[3] n a strong stone wall built out into the sea
as a defence against the waves, or to act as a road
(as from the shore to an island)

molecule n the smallest part of any substance
that can be separated from the substance without
losing its own chemical form and qualities, and
consists of one or more atoms ☞ ATOM — **-ar**
adj

molehill n a small heap of earth thrown up by a
mole digging

molest v **1** to trouble or annoy (a person or

animal) intentionally **2** to attack or annoy sexually — ~**ation** n

moll n sl a criminal's woman companion

mollify v **-fied, -fying** to make (a person or his
feelings) calmer, less angry, etc. — **-fication** n

mollusc n any of a class of animals with soft
bodies without a backbone or limbs and usu. a
shell: Limpets, snails, and octopuses are molluscs
☞ EVOLUTION

mollycoddle v **-dled, -dling** to treat too softly,
paying too much attention to health, comfort, etc.
— **mollycoddle** n : She made her son a mollycoddle

Molotov cocktail n a simple bomb for throwing, made from a bottle filled with petrol

molten adj (of metal or rock) melted by great
heat —see MELT (USAGE)

molto adv (in music) very: molto allegro (=very
quickly)

molybdenum n a silver-white metal that is an
element used in strengthening and hardening
steel

moment n **1** a period of time too short to
measure **2** the time for doing something: Choose
your moment to ask him **3** esp. written importance: a matter of great moment **4** technical (a
measure of) the turning power of a force —see also
on the SPUR of the moment

momentary adj lasting for a very short time ⚠
MOMENTOUS — **-rily** adv

moment of truth moments of truth n a
moment when something very important, dangerous, etc., will happen or be done

momentous adj of very great importance or
seriousness: the momentous news that war had
begun ⚠ MOMENTARY

momentum n **-ta** or **-tums 1** technical the
quantity of movement in a body, measured by
multiplying its mass by the speed at which it
moves: As the rock rolled down, it gathered
momentum **2** the force gained by the development of events: The struggle is gaining momentum
every day

Mon. abbrev. for: Monday

monarch n a king, queen, etc. ☞ KING —
~**ic**, ~**ical** adj

monarchism n monarchic government or principles — **-chist** n, adj

monarchy n **-chies 1** rule by a king or
queen **2** a state ruled by a king or queen

monastery n **-teries** a building in which
monks live according to religious rules —compare
NUNNERY

monastic adj of monasteries or monks —
~**ism** n — ~**ally** adv

Monday n **-days** the second day of the week

monetary adj esp. technical of or connected
with money

money n **1** metal coins, or paper notes with
their value printed on them, used in buying and
selling ⊚ **2** wealth: Money doesn't always bring
happiness —see also PIN MONEY, POCKET MONEY —
~**less** adj

Old and new forms of money

credit card

sharks teeth

luncheon voucher

Maria Theresa silver thaler – all dated 1780 but minted until recently. It is the only coinage that Middle Eastern tribes trust, and is used for trade.

first paper money – issued in China c1350

Currency

Country	basic unit	subdivision	Country	basic unit	subdivision
Albania	lek	quintars	Japan	yen	sen
Argentina	new peso	centavos			
Australia	Australian dollar	cents	Kenya	Kenyan shilling	cents
Austria	schilling	groschen	Lebanon	Lebanese pound	piasters
			Liechtenstein	Swiss franc	centimes
Belgium	Belgian franc	centimes	Luxemburg	Luxemburg franc	centimes
Brazil	new cruzeiro	centavos			
Bulgaria	lev	stotinki	Malta	Maltese pound	20 shillings 240 pence
Canada	Canadian dollar	cents	Mexico	peso	centavos
Chile	escudo	centesimos	Monaco	French franc	centimes
China	yuan	fen	Morocco	dirham	francs
Cyprus	Cyprus pound	mils			
Czechoslovakia	koruna	halers	Netherlands	gulden/guilder	cents
			New Zealand	N.Z. dollar	cents
Denmark	krone	öre	Nigeria	naira	kobo
			Norway	krone	öre
Egypt	Egyptian pound	piastres			
			Pakistan	rupee	paisas
Finland	markka	pennis	Poland	zloty	groszy
France	franc	centimes	Portugal	escudo	centavos
Germany (West)	deutschmark	pfennigs	Saudi Arabia	riyal	qurush
Germany (East)	ostmark	pfennigs	South Africa	S.A. rand	cents
Greece	drachma	lepta	Soviet Union	rouble	kopecks
Guatemala	quetzal	centavos	Spain	peseta	centimos
			Sweden	krona	öre
Hong Kong	H.K. dollar	cents	Switzerland	Swiss franc	centimes
Hungary	forint	fillér			
			Turkey	Turkish lira	kuruṣ
Iceland	króna	aurar			
India	rupee	paise	United Kingdom	pound sterling	pence
Iran	rial	dinars	United States of		
Iraq	Iraqi dinar	fils	America	dollar	cents
Irish Republic	Irish pound	20 shillings 240 pence	Yugoslavia	dinar	paras
Israel	shekel	new agorot			
Italy	lira	centesimi	Zimbabwe	Zimbabwe dollar	cents

moneychanger *n* a person whose business is exchanging the money of the country for that of another

money-grubber *n* a person so eager to become rich that he will do even the lowest kind of work to reach his purpose — **money-grubbing** *adj*

moneylender *n* 1 a person who lends money for interest 2 a usurer

moneymaker *n* 1 a person who can always earn money 2 something that brings in money — **moneymaking** *adj, n*

money order *n* an official paper of a certain value (higher than that of a postal order), which can be bought by one person for payment to another

money-spinner *n esp. spoken* something that brings in a lot of money

mongol *n* a person suffering from Down's syndrome

mongolism *n* DOWN'S SYNDROME

mongoose *n* **-gooses** a type of small furry eastern animal that kills snakes and rats

mongrel *n* an animal, esp. a dog, whose parents were of mixed or different breeds

monitor[1] *n* 1 a pupil chosen to help the teacher: *Jimmy has been made dinner money monitor* 2 a television set used in a television studio, to make sure that the picture and sound are clear, and to choose the best to be broadcast 3 an apparatus for finding whether there is a fault in the broadcasting of news, messages, etc. 4 any of several types of large lizard in Africa, Asia, and Australia

monitor[2] *v* to listen to (a radio broadcast, esp. from abroad) in order to gain information

monk *n* a member of an all-male group united by a promise to give their lives to a religion and living together in a monastery —compare FRIAR, NUN — ~**ish** *adj*

monkey *n* **-keys** 1 any of several types of long-tailed active tree-climbing animals, belonging to that class most like man ⟶ PRIMATE 2 *esp. spoken* a child who plays annoying tricks

monkey about also **monkey around**— *v adv* **-keyed, -keying about** *esp. spoken* to play in a foolish way

monkey business *n esp. spoken* troublesome or deceptive behaviour

monkey nut *n* a peanut

monkey wrench *n* a tool that can be adjusted for holding or turning things of different widths

mono[1] also (*esp. written*) **monophonic**— *adj* using a system of sound recording, broadcasting, or receiving in which the sound appears to come from one direction only when played back: *a mono record* —compare STEREO

mono[2] *n* **-os** *esp. spoken* mono sound production

monochrome *n* (the use of) only one colour in painting, photography, etc. — **monochrome** *adj*

monocle *n* an apparatus like glasses, but for one eye only

monogamy *n* the custom of having only one

wife or husband at one time — **-mous** *adj* — **-mously** *adv*

monogram *n* a figure formed of 2 or more letters, esp. a person's initials, joined together and often printed, sewn on handkerchiefs, etc. — ~**med** *adj*

monograph *n* an article or short book on one particular subject (scientific, medical, etc.)

monolith *n* a large pillar made from one mass of stone

monolithic *adj* 1 of or related to a monolith 2 forming a very large tall whole: *the monolitic buildings* 3 forming a large unchanging whole, in which very little freedom is allowed: *People aren't free to express opinions in a monolithic state* — ~**ally** *adv*

monologue *n* 1 a spoken part in a play or film, for a single performer 2 a poem or other piece of writing intended to be spoken by one person only 3 *esp. spoken* a rather long speech by one person

monomania *n* a condition of the mind in which a person is interested in only one particular subject — ~**c** *n*

monophonic *adj esp. written* mono

monoplane *n* an aircraft with a single wing each side —compare BIPLANE

monopolize, -lise *v* **-lized, -lizing** 1 to have or get complete unshared control of 2 to take wholly for oneself, not allowing others to share — **-list** *n* — **-lization** *n*

monopoly *n* **-lies** 1 a right or power of only one person or one group to provide a service, trade in anything, produce something, etc. 2 possession or control not shared by others 3 *trademark* a game in which the winner obtains all the pretended money, property, etc.

monorail *n* (a vehicle travelling on) a railway with a single rail

monosodium glutamate *n* a man-made substance often added to factory-prepared foods to improve their flavour

monosyllabic *adj* 1 (of a word) having one syllable 2 (of speech) formed of words with one syllable: *monosyllabic replies, such as 'yes' and 'no'* — ~**ally** *adv*

monosyllable *n* a word of one syllable

monotheism *n* the belief that there is only one God —compare POLYTHEISM — **-ist** *n*

monotone *n* a manner of speaking or singing in which the voice continues on the same note

monotonous *adj* dull; lacking variety — **-ny**, ~**ness** *n* — ~**ly** *adv*

Monsieur *n* **Messieurs** *French* (the title of a French man): *Monsieur Legrand*

monsignor *n* (a title given to) any of various Roman Catholic priests of high rank

monsoon *n* 1 (the season of) heavy rains which fall in India and nearby countries from about April to October 2 *technical* the wind that brings these rains

monster *n* 1 an unusually large animal, plant, or thing: *a monster aircraft* 2 a creature that is unnatural in shape, size, or qualities, and usu. frighteningly ugly: *a sea monster* **3** a person so evil as to cause strong hatred, fear, etc.: *The judge told the murderer that he was a monster*

monstrosity *n* **-ties** **1** a creature or thing of unnatural shape or unusual size **2** something very ugly: *The palace is a monstrosity*

monstrous *adj* **1** of unnaturally large size, strange shape, etc. **2** so bad as to cause strong hatred: *monstrous cruelty* — ~**ly** *adv*

montage *n French* a picture made by combining several separate pictures

month *n* one of the 12 named divisions of the year —see also LUNAR MONTH, CALENDAR MONTH

monthly[1] *adj, adv* (happening, appearing, etc.) once a month

monthly[2] *n* **-lies** a magazine appearing once a month

monthly period *n* MENSTRUAL PERIOD

monument *n* **1** a building, gravestone, statue, etc. that preserves the memory of a person or event **2** a building or place considered worthy of preservation for its historic interest or beauty **3** an outstanding example (of): *His actions are a monument to foolishness*

monumental *adj* **1** of or intended for a monument **2** very large and of lasting worth **3** very great in degree: *monumental efforts*

monumentally *adv* to a very great degree: *monumentally stupid*

moo *v, n* **mooed, mooing; moos** (to make) the noise a cow makes —see also LOW

mooch about *v adv esp. spoken* to wander about slowly and aimlessly

mood[1] *n* **1** a state of the feelings: *a happy mood* **2** a bad-tempered state of feeling: *He's in one of his moods*

mood[2] *n technical* any of various groups of verb forms, esp. expressing **a** a fact (INDICATIVE) **b** a command or request (IMPERATIVE) **c** a condition, doubt, etc. (SUBJUNCTIVE)

moody *adj* **-ier, -iest** **1** having changeable moods **2** bad-tempered, or unhappy, esp. without reasons — **moodily** *adv* — **moodiness** *n*

Moog synthesizer *n trademark* a musical synthesizer

moon *n* **1** the body which moves round the earth once every 28 days, and can be seen in the sky at night ⌁SPACE **2** a body that moves round a planet other than the earth **3** *esp. poetic* a month: *many moons ago* — ~**less** *adj*

moon about also **moon around**— *v adv esp. spoken* to behave in an aimless unhappy way

moonbeam *n* a beam of moonlight

moonlight[1] *n* the light from the moon

moonlight[2] *v* **-lighted, -lighting** *esp. spoken* to have a second job besides a regular one — ~**er** *n*

moonshine *n esp. spoken* **1** nonsense **2** *esp. US* alcoholic drink produced unlawfully

moonstone *n* a milky-white stone used in making cheap jewels

moonstruck *adj esp. spoken* suffering from slight madness, supposed to be caused by the influence of the moon

moor[1] *n* a wide, open, often raised area covered with rough grass or bushes, that is not farmed because of its bad soil

moor[2] *v* to fasten (a boat) to land, the sea bed, etc. by means of ropes, an anchor, etc.

moorhen also **water hen**— *n* **-hens** *or* **-hen** a water bird with black feathers and a bright red or orange mark above its beak

moorings *n* **1** a place where a boat is moored **2** the ropes used for mooring

Moorish *adj* of or related to the Muslim Arab peoples (**Moors**) who ruled in Spain from 711 to 1492

moose *n* **moose** a large deer, with very large flat horns, that lives in north America (and in Europe, where it is called an elk)

moot *v* to state (a question, matter, etc.) for consideration and argument

moot point also **moot question**— *n* an undecided point

mop[1] *n* **1** a tool for washing floors, made of a long stick with either threads of thick string, or a sponge, on one end **2** a tool like this for washing dishes **3** *esp. spoken* a thick mass (of unbrushed hair), standing up from the head

mop[2] *v* **-pp-** to clean or wipe with a mop

mope *v* **moped, moping** to be in low spirits

moped *n* a bicycle with a small engine

moppet *n esp. spoken* a child, esp. a girl

moraine *n* a mass of earth, rocks, etc., carried down by a glacier and left in a line at its edge or end ⌁GEOGRAPHY

moral[1] *adj* **1** concerning good or evil, right or wrong; ethical **2** based on the idea of what is right (compared with what is lawful): *moral courage* **3** pure in matters of sex —opposite **immoral** **4** able to recognize the difference between right and wrong —compare AMORAL **5** teaching that which is right in behaviour: *a moral lesson* USAGE Although **immoral** means 'morally bad', it is not always the opposite of **moral**, which often means 'in connection with good or bad': **moral** *principles* | **moral** *standards*. The same difference applies to **immorality**, a strong word for bad behaviour, and **morality**: *He led a life of* **immorality**.∥*an act of doubtful* **morality**. **Morals** *are* **moral** principles, which can be either good or bad.

moral[2] *n* a good lesson in behaviour that can be learnt from a story or happening

moral certainty *n esp. written* a probability so great that one feels sure, without proof

morale *n* one's state of mind with regard to confidence, strength of spirit, etc.: *The trapped men kept up their morale by singing* △ MORALS

moralist *n* a person who teaches or studies moral principles

moralistic *adj* having very firm unyielding narrow ideas about behaviour — ~**ally** *adv*

morality *n* **-ties** rightness of behaviour

morality play *n* **-plays** an old form of play (often performed in the years 1400–1600), in which good and bad qualities were represented as people —compare MIRACLE PLAY

moralize, -ise v -ized, -izing to express one's thoughts (often not welcome) on the rightness or, more usually, the wrongness of behaviour — ~r n

morally adv **1** in a moral manner **2** with regard to good behaviour **3** esp. written almost completely: morally certain

Moral Re-Armament n OXFORD GROUP

morals n rules of behaviour, esp. in matters of sex —see MORAL (USAGE) △ MORALE

morass n **1** a stretch of soft wet ground, dangerous for walking **2** a difficult or evil position from which it is almost impossible to free oneself

moratorium n -ria a declaration that a particular activity will be stopped or delayed for a period

morbid adj **1** having an unhealthy interest in unpleasant matters, esp. death **2** medical diseased — ~ity n — ~ly adv

mordant adj (esp. of the manner of expressing thoughts) hurtfully biting or cutting — ~ly adv

mordent n (in music) (the instruction for) an extra group of notes, of which the main note and either the note immediately above or that immediately below it are played alternately a set number of times

more[1] adj, pron, n (comparative of MANY, MUCH) **1** a greater number, quantity, or part (of): There are more cars on the roads in summer than in winter. | 50 is more than 40 **2** an additional or further number, amount, or quantity (of): I've given you all you asked for; what more d'you want? | I have to write 2 more letters **3 more or less a** nearly: The work's more or less finished **b** about: The repairs will cost $50, more or less

more[2] adv **1** to a greater degree: His illness was more serious than we thought. | He seems to care more for his dogs than for his children **2** oftener or longer: You ought to practise more **3** again (in the phrases **any more, once more, no more**): The old man doesn't travel any more. | The teacher said he'd repeat the question once more **4 no more** neither: He can't afford it, and no more can I **5 the more . . ., the more/less . . .** to the degree that . . ., to an equal/less degree . . .: The more angry he became, the more she laughed at him

moreover adv in addition; besides: The price is too high, and moreover, the house isn't in a suitable position

mores n written or technical fixed moral customs and standards

morgue n US a building in which dead bodies are kept until it is discovered who they were —compare MORTUARY

moribund adj **1** (of a thing) near to the end of existence **2** near to death

Mormon n a member of a religious body, formed in 1830 by Joseph Smith in the US, and calling itself The Church of Jesus Christ of Latter-Day Saints — ~ism n

morn n poetic morning

morning n **1** the first part of the day, from sunrise usu. until the midday meal **2** the part of the day from midnight until midday: 2 o'clock in the morning

morning coat n a coat that comes down to the waist in front, and slopes down to the knees at the back, worn as part of morning dress

morning dress n formal clothes worn by a man at daytime ceremonies

morning sickness n (a feeling of) sickness in the early morning, suffered by pregnant women

morning star n a planet, esp. Venus, when it appears in the eastern sky in the morning — compare EVENING STAR

morocco n fine soft leather made esp. from the skin of goats, used esp. for covering books

moron n a very foolish person

moronic adj very stupid — ~ally adv

morose adj not cheerful; looking angry or unhappy — ~ly adv — ~ness n

morphine n a substance having a strong effect on the nerves and used for stopping pain

morris dance n an old English country dance for a group of men, who wear special clothes to which small bells are often fixed

morrow n literature the following day

Morse code also (esp. spoken) **Morse**— n a system of sending messages in which each letter is represented by one or more short signals (DOTS) and long signals (DASHES) in sound or light ☞CODE

morsel n a very small piece or quantity

mortal[1] adj **1** that must die; not living for ever —opposite immortal **2** human; of human beings **3** causing death: a mortal wound **4** (of an enemy) having a lasting hatred **5** (of a fight) continuing until death or complete defeat: mortal combat **6** (of danger, fear, etc.) so great as to fill the mind with thoughts of death **7** esp. spoken very great: It's a mortal shame

mortal[2] n esp. in literature a human being (as compared with a god, a spirit, etc.)

mortality n **1** the number or rate of deaths from a certain cause: a high mortality from this disease **2** being mortal —opposite immortality

mortally adv **1** in a manner that causes death: mortally wounded **2** very greatly: mortally afraid

mortar[1] n **1** a heavy gun with a short barrel, firing an explosive that falls from a great height **2** a bowl in which substances are crushed with a pestle

mortar[2] n a mixture of lime, sand, and water, used in building

mortarboard n a flat square usu. black cap worn by teachers, university lecturers, etc.

mortgage[1] n **1** an agreement to have money lent, esp. so as to buy a house, with the house or land belonging to the lender until the money is repaid **2** the amount lent on a mortgage

mortgage² v -gaged, -gaging to give the right to the ownership of (a house, land, etc.) in return for money lent

mortify v -fied, -fying 1 to hurt (a person's) feelings, causing loss of self-respect 2 to conquer natural human desires of (oneself or the body) by self-punishment (esp. in the phrase **mortify the flesh**) — **-ication** n

mortise¹ -tice n technical a hole cut in wood or stone to receive the tenon of another piece, and thus form a joint

mortise² -tice v -tised, -tising technical 1 to join by means of a mortise and tenon 2 to make a mortise in (wood, stone, etc.)

mortise lock n a lock that fits into a hole in the edge of a door

mortuary n -ries a special room or building where a dead body is kept until the funeral — compare MORGUE

mosaic n 1 (a piece of ornamental work produced by) the fitting together of small pieces of coloured stone, glass, etc. so as to form a pattern or picture 2 something made by putting together a number of different things: *The sky this morning is a mosaic of blue and white*

moselle n white wine produced esp. in the valley of the River Mosel in Germany

Moslem n, adj a Muslim

mosque n a building in which Muslims worship

mosquito n -toes any of several types of small flying insect that prick the skin and then drink blood, one of which can cause malaria

mosquito net n a net placed over a bed as a protection against mosquitoes

moss n (any of several types of) a small flat green or yellow flowerless plant that grows in a thick furry mass on a wet surface ⟹PLANT, EVOLUTION — ~y adj

most¹ adj, pron (superlative of MANY, MUCH) 1 greatest in number, quantity, or degree: *The money should be shared among those who have the most need of it.* | *Which is most—10, 20, or 30?* 2 nearly all: *Most of his time is spent travelling* 3 **for the most part** nearly completely; in almost all cases

most² adv 1 to the greatest degree: *the most comfortable hotel* | *You can help me most by peeling the potatoes* 2 very; quite: *It's most annoying* USAGE **Most** can mean 'very' only before adjectives and adverbs that express personal feeling or opinion: *most beautiful* | *most certainly.* | You cannot say *most tall* | *most quickly.*

most³ n 1 the greatest amount: *the most we could afford* 2 **at (the) most** not more than: *She's at most 25 years old* 3 **make the most of** to get the greatest gain from

mostly adv mainly

M.o.T. n esp. spoken a regular official examination of cars more than 3 years old, to make sure they are fit to be driven

mote n a very small piece or grain, esp. of dust

motel n a hotel for travelling motorists, made up of separate small houses, each with space for a car

motet n a piece of church music, usu. for voices only

moth n 1 any of several types of quite large winged insects, related to the butterfly but not so brightly coloured, which fly mainly at night and are attracted by lights ⟹ INSECT 2 an infection of clothes by young moths which eat wool, fur, etc.

mothball n a small ball of a strong-smelling substance (esp. NAPHTHALENE), used for keeping away the moth —compare CAMPHOR BALL

mothballs n the state of being stored but not used: *He keeps his car in mothballs during the winter*

moth-eaten adj 1 destroyed by the moth 2 very worn out and scruffy: *moth-eaten old chairs*

mother¹ n 1 a female parent ⟹FAMILY 2 one's own female parent 3 a female head of a group of nuns —see also MOTHER SUPERIOR 4 a cause: *Hunger is often the mother of crime* — ~less adj

mother² v 1 to care for (someone) like a mother 2 to give birth to

Mother n 1 a title of respect for a mother: *Mother Teresa* —see also MOTHER SUPERIOR 2 esp. spoken a title given to an old woman: *Old Mother Williams*

mother country n -tries the country of one's birth; one's native land

motherhood n being a mother

mother-in-law n -s-in-law the mother of a person's husband or wife ⟹ FAMILY

motherly adj like a mother — **-liness** n

Mother Nature n nature

mother-of-pearl n a hard smooth shiny substance inside the shell of certain shellfish, used for making ornamental articles

Mother Superior n Mothers Superior or Mother Superiors the female head of a convent

mother-to-be n mothers-to-be a pregnant woman

mother tongue n a person's native language

motif also motive— n 1 a subject, pattern, idea, etc., forming the main base on which a work of art is made 2 a single or repeated pattern or colour 3 an arrangement of notes, forming a main part of a musical work

motion¹ n 1 the state of moving: *The train was in motion* 2 a single movement 3 a suggestion formally put before a meeting, which is the subject of arguments for and against 4 an act of emptying the bowels

motion² v to signal by means of a movement: *She motioned to the waiter*

motionless adj quite still — ~ly adv — ~ness n

motion picture US a film

motivate v -vated, -vating to provide (someone) with a reason for doing something: *He was* *motivated only by his wish to help me* — **-ion** *n*

motive[1] *n* a reason for action — **~less** *adj*

motive[2] *adj technical* (of power, force, etc.) causing movement: *the motive power that turns this wheel*

motley *adj* 1 of different kinds, esp. good and bad: *a motley collection of books* 2 (esp. of a garment) of mixed unconnected colours

motocross *n* a motorcycle race over a rough track including steep hills, streams, etc.

motor[1] *n* 1 a machine that changes power, esp. electrical power, into movement ☞ ELECTRICITY 2 a car

motor[2] *adj* 1 driven by an engine: *a motor mower* 2 of, for, or concerning vehicles driven by an engine: *the motor industry* 3 *technical* of, related to, or being a nerve that causes a muscle to move

motor[3] *v becoming rare* to travel by car — **~ist** *n*

motorbike *n* a motorcycle

motorboat *n* a small ship driven by an engine or electric motor

motorcade *n* a procession of cars

motorcar *n* a car

motorcycle *n* a large heavy bicycle with an engine — **-clist** *n*

motoring *n* travelling in a car

motor scooter *n* a low bicycle-like vehicle with an engine, 2 small wheels, and usu. a wide curved front to protect the legs

motorway *n* **-ways** a very wide road esp. for fast long-distance vehicles

mottled *adj* marked irregularly with variously coloured spots

motto *n* **-tos** 1 a few words taken as the guiding principle of a person, a school, etc. —compare SLOGAN 2 an amusing or clever short saying

mould[1] *n* loose earth, esp. good soft soil rich in decayed vegetable substances

mould[2] *n* 1 a hollow vessel having a particular shape, into which a melted substance is poured, so that when the substance hardens, it takes this shape 2 *esp. in literature* (a person's) nature considered as having been shaped by family type, education, etc.: *He's made in his father's mould*

mould[3] *v* 1 to shape or form (something solid) 2 to shape or form (character, behaviour, etc.)

mould[4] *n* a soft woolly growth on substances which have been left a long time in warm wet air

moulder *v* to decay slowly: *mouldering walls*

moulding *n* 1 the giving of shape to a soft substance 2 an ornamental edge that stands out from a surface 3 an object produced from a mould

mouldy *adj* **-ier, -iest** 1 covered with or smelling of mould 2 *sl* bad in quality 3 stingy: *a mouldy 5 pence for all the work we've done* — **mouldiness** *n*

moult[1] *v* 1 (of a bird) to lose feathers 2 (of an animal) to lose hair or fur

moult[2] *n* **in moult** moulting

mound *n* 1 a small hill 2 a large pile: *a mound of letters*

mount[1] *v* 1 to get on (a horse, a bicycle, etc.) 2 to go up; climb 3 to provide (someone) with a horse or other animal, a bicycle, etc., to ride on 4 to rise in level: *The temperature mounted into the 90s* 5 to fix on a support or in a surrounding substance : *He mounted the photograph on paper* 6 to prepare or begin (an attack) 7 to prepare and produce (a play) for the stage 8 *technical* (of a male animal) to get up on (a female animal) for sex 9 **mount guard** to be on guard duty

mount[2] *n* 1 an animal on which one rides 2 something on which or in which a thing is fixed

mountain *n* 1 a very high hill 2 a very large amount: *a mountain of dirty clothes to wash* — **~ous** *adj*

mountain ash *n* a rowan tree

mountaineer *n* a person who climbs mountains

mountaineering *n* the climbing of mountains

mountainous *adj* 1 full of mountains: *mountainous country* 2 very large or high: *mountainous waves*

mountain range *n* a group of mountains, esp. in a row

mountebank *n literature & now rare* a man who, by clever talk, deceives people into buying something of no use or into believing worthless promises

Mountie *n esp. spoken* a member of the **Royal Canadian Mounted Police** who often worked on horseback

mourn *v* to grieve; be sorrowful

mourner *n* a person who attends a funeral

mournful *adj* sad; causing, feeling, or seeming to express sorrow — **~ly** *adv* — **~ness** *n*

mourning *n* 1 grief, esp. for a death 2 the clothes worn to show grief at a death

mouse *n* **mice** 1 any of several types of small furry animal with a long tail, rather like a small rat 2 a quiet person who is easily frightened

mouser *n* a cat that catches mice

mousetrap *n* a trap for mice, worked by a spring

moussaka *n* a Greek dish made from meat and aubergines, often with cheese on top

mousse *n* a dish made from cream, eggs, usu. gelatine, and flavourings, mixed and then chilled

moustache *n* hair on the upper lip

mousy *adj* **-ier, -iest** 1 of or like mice 2 (of hair) dull brownish-grey 3 (of a person) unattractively plain and drab — **mousiness** *n*

mouth[1] *n* 1 the opening on the face through which an animal or human being eats and makes sounds 2 an opening: *the mouth of the cave* 3 **keep one's mouth shut** *esp. spoken* to avoid speaking; keep silent

mouth[2] *v* to say, esp. repeatedly without understanding or sincerity: *He crept into the corner, mouthing curses*

mouthful *n* as much (food or drink) as fills the mouth

mouthorgan *n* a small musical instrument, played by being held to the mouth and blown into or sucked through; harmonica

mouthpiece *n* **1** the part of a musical instrument, a telephone, etc. that is held in or near the mouth **2** a person, newspaper, etc. that expresses the opinions of others: *This newspaper is the mouthpiece of the government*

mouth-to-mouth *adj* of, related to, or being a method of resuscitation in which one places one's mouth tightly against the mouth of the person who is not breathing and blows air into his lungs

mouthwash *n* any of several liquids used in the mouth, to freshen it, cure infection, etc.

mouth-watering *adj* (of food) very good

movable, **moveable** *adj* that can be moved; not fixed

move¹ *v* **moved, moving** **1** to change or cause to change place or position **2** to change or cause to change: *The government's opinions on this matter haven't moved* **3** *esp. spoken* to travel, run, etc., very fast: *That car was really moving* **4** (in games such as chess) to change the position of (a piece) **5** to change (one's place of living or working): *to move house* **6** to cause (a person) to have feelings —see also MOVING **7** to cause to act: *I felt moved to speak* **8** (of work, events, etc.) to go forward: *Work on the new building is moving quickly* **9** to lead one's life (esp. among people of a certain class): *She moves in the highest circles of society* **10** to put forward (a suggestion) **11** to empty (the bowels) —see also MOVE ON — ~ **r** *n* —see also PRIME MOVER

move² *n* **1** a movement **2** an act of going to a new home, office, etc. **3** (in games such as chess) an act of moving a piece from one square to another **4** a step in a course of action: *a move to stop the war* **5 get a move on** *esp. spoken* to hurry up

movement *n* **1** moving; activity **2** a particular act of moving ☞ NERVE **3** a group of people united for a particular purpose: *the trade union movement* **4** a general feeling directed towards something new: *the movement towards greater freedom for women* **5** a main division of a musical work, esp. of a symphony **6** the moving parts of a machine, esp. a clock or watch

movements *n* the whole of a person's activities

move on *v adv* **1** to change to something new: *I think we've talked enough about that; let's move on* **2** to go or send away: *'Come on, sir, move on,' said the policeman*

movie *n* *esp. US* a film

movies *n* *esp. US* the pictures: *going to the movies*

moving *adj* **1** causing strong feelings, esp. of pity: *a moving story* **2** that moves; not fixed — ~**ly** *adv*

moving staircase *n* an escalator

mow *v* **mowed, mown** *or* **mowed, mowing** to cut (grass, corn, etc.), or cut that which grows in (a field or other area), with a mower or scythe

mow down *v adv* to kill in great numbers: *The soldiers were mown down by the enemy*

mower *n* **1** a machine for mowing, esp. (a **lawnmower**) one for cutting grass in gardens **2** a person who mows

MP *abbrev. for:* **1** Member of Parliament, esp. a person who has been elected to the House of Commons **2** (*esp. spoken*) a military policeman

mpg *abbrev. for:* miles per gallon

mph *abbrev. for:* miles per hour

Mr, also (*rare*) **Mister** *n* **1** a title for a man who has no other —compare MESSRS **2** a title for certain people in official positions: *Mr Chairman* **3** used before the name of a place, sport, etc., to form a title for a man representing that thing: *Mr Baseball*

MRA *abbrev. for: (esp. US)* Moral Re-Armament

Mrs *n* **1** a title for a married woman who has no other **2** used before the name of a place, sport, etc., to form a title for a married woman representing that thing: *Mrs 1982 in her modern kitchen*

Ms *n* a title for a woman who does not wish to call herself either "Mrs" or "Miss"

MSc *abbrev. for:* Master of Science; a university science degree at the first level above the BSc

mu *n* the 12th letter of the Greek alphabet (M, μ), representing a micron

much¹ *adj, pron, n* —see MORE, MOST **1** a large quantity, amount, or part (of): *far too much work | I haven't read much of it* **2 I thought as much** I expected that **3 make much of a** to treat as important **b** to understand a lot: *I couldn't make much of that book* **c** to treat with a show of fondness **4 not much of a** not a very good: *not much of a day (=bad weather)*

much² *adv* **1 a** frequently: *Do you go there much?* **b** to a great degree: *I don't like that idea much* **2** by a large degree: *much worse* **3 much more/less** and even **more/less**: *I can hardly walk, much less run*

muchness *n* **much of a muchness** the same in most ways

muck *n* *esp. spoken & dialect* **1** dirt **2** manure **3** useless material **4 make a muck of a** to dirty **b** to spoil

muck about also **muck around**— *v adv esp. spoken* to behave in a silly way for fun

muck in *v adv esp. spoken* to join in work or activity: *If we all muck in we'll soon finish the work*

muck out *v adv* to clean (stables or other places where animals live)

muckrake *v* **-raked, -raking** to search out and tell unpleasant stories about well-known people — ~**r** *n* — **-raking** *n*

muck up *v adv esp. spoken* **1** to dirty **2 a** to

spoil (an arrangement) **b** to do wrong: *to muck up an examination*

mucky *adj* **-ier, -iest** *esp. spoken & dialect* **1** dirty **2** (of weather) bad; stormy

mucous *adj technical* of or producing mucus

mucous membrane *n* the skin on delicate parts of the body which is kept wet and smooth by mucus

mucus *n* a slippery liquid produced in certain parts of the body (such as the mouth and nose), and by snails to help them move

mud *n* very wet sticky earth

mud bath *n* a beauty or health treatment in which mud is put on the skin

muddle *v* **-dled, -dling 1** to put into disorder **2** to confuse in the mind: *I get muddled when they give orders so quickly* — **muddle** *n* — ~**r** *n*

muddle along *v adv* to continue in a confused manner, without a plan

muddle-headed *adj* having a muddled mind — ~**ness** *n*

muddle through *v adv* to have successful results without the best methods of reaching them

muddy *adj* **-dier, -diest 1** covered with mud **2** (of colours) like mud: *a muddy brown* **3** not clear: *muddy thinking* — **-diness** *n*

mudflat *n* a stretch of muddy land, covered by the sea at high tide

mudguard *n* a metal cover over the wheel of a vehicle to keep the mud from flying up

mudpack *n* a mud bath for the face

muesli *n* grain, nuts, dried fruits, etc., mixed with milk and eaten for breakfast

muezzin *n* a man who calls Muslims to prayer from the minaret of a mosque

muff¹ *n* a short tube of thick soft cloth or fur, in which one can keep one's hands warm

muff² *v* **1** to miss: *to muff a catch* **2** to do (a bit of work) less well than one might: *I hate making speeches —I'm always afraid of muffing it*

muffin *n* a thick round breadlike cake usu. eaten hot with butter —compare CRUMPET

muffle *v* **-fled, -fling 1** to make (a sound) less easily heard: *The sound of the bell was muffled by the curtains* **2** to cover thickly and warmly

muffler *n esp. old use* a scarf

mufti *n* ordinary clothes, not a uniform which one has been wearing

mug¹ *n* **1** a round drinking vessel with straight sides and a handle, not usu. with a saucer **2** *sl* the face **3** *esp. spoken* a foolish person easily deceived —see also MUG'S GAME

mug² *v* **-gg-** to rob with violence, as in a dark street — **mugger** *n* — **mugging** *n*

muggins *n sl* a fool

muggy *adj* **-gier, -giest** (of weather) unpleasantly warm but not dry — **-giness** *n*

mug's game *n esp. spoken* an action that is unlikely to be rewarding or profitable

mug up *v adv esp. spoken* to study closely: *to mug up the law*

mulatto *n* **-tos** a person with one black parent and one white one

mulberry *n* **-ries 1** a tree whose leaves are the food of silkworms **2** the dark purple edible fruit of this tree

mulch¹ *n* a covering of material, often decaying plants, which is put over the roots of plants to protect and improve them —compare HUMUS

mulch² *v* to cover with a mulch

mule¹ *n* **1** the animal which is the young of a donkey and a horse **2** a sort of spinning-machine

mule² *n* a shoe or slipper with no back, but only a piece of material across the toes to hold it on

muleteer *n* a man who drives mules

mulish *adj* stubborn — ~**ly** *adv* — ~**ness** *n*

mull *v* to heat (wine or beer) with sugar, spices, etc.

mullah *n* a Muslim teacher of law and religion

mullet *n* any of several types of edible sea fish

mulligatawny *n* a strong hot spiced soup

mullion *n* the esp. stone part running up and down between the glass parts of a window — ~**ed** *adj*

mull over *v adv; prep* to think over

multifarious *adj* of many types — ~**ly** *adv* — ~**ness** *n*

multiform *adj* having several different shapes or ways of seeming

multilateral *adj* concerning or including more than 2 (usu. political) groups of people: *a multilateral agreement* —compare BILATERAL — ~**ly** *adv*

multilingual *adj* **1** containing or expressed in many languages **2** able to speak many languages

multimillionaire *n* a person who has several million pounds or dollars

multiple¹ *adj* including many different parts, types, etc.

multiple² *n* a number which contains a smaller number an exact number of times: $3 \times 4 = 12$; *so 12 is a multiple of 3*

multiple sclerosis *n* a disease in which an important covering around the nerves is gradually reduced, causing more and more difficulties in movement and physical control

multiple store *n* CHAIN STORE

multiplex *adj technical* having many parts

multiplication *n* **1** the combining of 2 numbers by adding one of them to itself as many times as the other states; the process of forming the product of 2 numbers by repeated addition: $2 \times 4 = 8$ *is an example of multiplication* **2** increasing in number

multiplicity *n* **1** a large number **2** a great variety

multiply¹ *v* **-plied, -plying 1** to combine by multiplication: *to multiply 2 numbers together* **2** to increase: *to multiply one's chances of success*

3 to breed: *When animals have more food, they generally multiply faster*

multiply² *adv* in a multiple way

multiracial *adj* of several races of people

multistorey *adj* (of a building) having several floors

multitude *n* **1** a large number: *a multitude of thoughts* **2** *old use & Bible* a large crowd **3** ordinary people, not well educated: *The multitude may laugh at his music, but we know better*

multitudinous *adj* very large in number — ~ly *adv* — ~ness *n*

mum¹ *adj* not saying anything

mum² *interj* **Mum's the word** Silence must be kept about this

mum³ *n esp. spoken* mother

mumble *v* **-bled, -bling** to speak unclearly

mumbo jumbo *n esp. spoken* mysterious meaningless talk or activity

mummify *v* **-fied, -fying** to preserve as a mummy — **-fication** *n*

mumming *n* **go mumming** (esp. in former times) to visit people at Christmas and give a traditional performance in a group — **mummer** *n*

mummy¹ *n* **-mies** a dead body preserved from decay by special treatment

mummy² *n* **-mies** mother

mumps *n* an infectious illness in which swellings appear esp. round the neck and face

munch *v* to eat with a strong movement of the jaw

mundane *adj* ordinary and dull — ~ly *adv*

municipal *adj* concerning a town under its own government: *municipal affairs* — ~ly *adv*

municipality *n* **-ties** a town or area having its own local government

munificence *n esp. written* generosity — **-cent** *adj* — **cently** *adv*

munitions *n* arms such as bombs, guns, etc. — **munition** *adj*

mural¹ *adj* of, like, or on a wall

mural² *n* a painting painted on a wall —see also FRESCO

murder¹ *n* **1** the crime of killing a person unlawfully **2** *esp. spoken* a very difficult or tiring experience

murder² *v* **1** to kill unlawfully, esp. on purpose **2** to ruin (language, music, etc.) by a bad performance — ~er *n* — ~ess *n*

murderous *adj* **1** likely to cause death **2** violent **3** of or like murder — ~ly *adv* — ~ness *n*

murk *n literature* darkness

murky *adj* **-ier, -iest** *literature* **1** dark and unpleasant: *a murky night* **2** shameful: *a murky secret* — **murkily** *adv*

murmur¹ *n* **1** (speech with) a soft low sound: *a murmur of voices | the murmur of the stream* **2** a complaint: *He obeyed without a murmur*

murmur² *v* **1** to make a soft sound, esp. to speak in a quiet voice **2** to complain in private — ~ing *n*

muscle *n* (one of) the pieces of elastic material in the body which can tighten to produce movement ⟶ ANATOMY — ~d *adj*

muscle-bound *adj* having over-developed muscles after too much exercise

muscle in *v adv* **-cled, -cling in** *sl* to force one's way into an activity

muscular *adj* **1** of muscles: *the muscular system* **2** having big muscles: *a muscular body* — ~ly *adv*

muscular dystrophy *n* a disease in which the muscles become gradually weaker

muse¹ *v* **mused, musing** to think deeply — **musingly** *adv*

muse² *n* **1** an ancient Greek goddess, one of 9, who each represented an art or science **2** the force which seems to help someone to write, paint, etc. —compare INSPIRATION, INSPIRE

museum *n* a building where interesting objects are kept and usu. shown to the public

mush¹ *n* **1** a soft mass of material, esp. food **2** *esp. spoken* sentimentality

mush² *n sl* **1** a face **2** a fellow

mushroom¹ *n* **1** any of several types of fungus, some of which are edible **2** anything which develops fast

mushroom² *v* **1** to spread in the shape of a mushroom: *The smoke mushroomed into the sky* **2** to develop fast **3** to gather mushrooms: *mushrooming in the woods*

mushy *adj* **-ier, -iest** **1** like mush: *mushy potatoes* **2** (of writing, plays, etc.) too sentimental

music *n* **1** the arrangement of sounds in pleasant patterns and tunes **2** a written set of notes: *a sheet of music* ◉ **3 face the music** to admit to blame and accept the punishment

musical¹ *adj* **1** of music **2** skilled in music: *a musical child* **3** pleasant to hear — **-ly** *adv*

musical² *n* a musical play or film with spoken words, songs, and often dances

musical box *n* a box which plays music by clockwork when the lid is lifted

musical chairs *n* a party game in which, when the music stops, each person tries to sit on a chair, although there is one chair too few

music centre *n* a piece of electronic apparatus which contains a radio and can play records and play and record cassettes

music hall *n* a theatre show combining the sale of drinks with short variety performances by singers, conjurers, etc. —compare VARIETY

musician *n* a performer, writer, or student of music —compare COMPOSER

musk *n* a strong smelling material produced by a male deer (the **musk deer**), used in making perfumes — ~y *adj*

musket *n* an early gun used before the invention of the rifle ⟶ WEAPON

musketeer *n* a soldier with a musket

muskrat *n* a North American water rat, or its valuable fur

Muslim also **Moslem**— *n, adj* (a person) of the

Development of western music

birth of Christ	**1 A.D.**	
476 fall of Western Roman Empire	**500**	c400 Ambrosian system of plainsong (church music)
590 Gregory I becomes Pope	**600**	c600 Gregorian system of plainsong
	700	c750 lute introduced to Europe by Arabs **1**
789 first Viking attack on England	**800**	855 earliest known attempts at polyphony (two or more melodies played together)
	900	c900 organs in use – earliest keyboard instruments **2**
	1000	c950 beginning of modern system of music notation
1066 Norman Conquest	**1100**	c1100 troubadours (minstrels) active in France **3**
1215 Magna Carta	**1200**	c1225 *Sumer is icumen in*, the earliest known canon
	1300	
1492 Columbus crosses Atlantic	**1400**	c1440 through John Dunstable, English music has major influence 1465 first printed music
1521 Protestant Reformation 1588 Spanish Armada c1600-1750 Baroque period	**1500**	c1550 lutes, viols, and recorders in common use **4** 1580 *Greensleeves* first mentioned (probably written earlier)
1611 Authorized Version of Bible	**1600**	c1600 development of modern system of scales and keys 1607 Monteverdi's *Orpheus*, one of the first operas **5** 1666 first Stradivarius violin made by Antonio Stradivari
1704 Battle of Blenheim c1750-1825 Classical period	**1700**	1709 early type of piano invented in Italy 1721 J. S. Bach's *Brandenburg Concertos;* 1722, Bach's *The Well-Tempered Clavier*, Part I **6** 1741 Handel's oratorio *The Messiah* 1744 *God Save the King* first published c1750 development of modern form of sonata and symphony
1789 French Revolution		1791 Mozart's opera *The Magic Flute* **7** 1792 Haydn's *Surprise Symphony*
1807 Wordsworth's *Intimations of Immortality* 1812 Napoleon retreats from Moscow 1815 Battle of Waterloo c1825-1900 Romantic period 1837 reign of Queen Victoria begins	**1800**	c1800 development of modern orchestra 1807 Beethoven's *Fifth Symphony* **8** 1819 Schubert's *Trout Quintet* 1830 Berlioz's *Fantastic Symphony* 1832 Mendelssohn's overture *Fingal's Cave* c1835 modern type of piano developed **9** 1838 Schumann's piano pieces *Scenes of Childhood* 1839 Chopin's *Preludes* c1840 tonic sol-fa system of sight-reading invented
1848 Communist Manifesto by Marx and Engels 1854-6 Crimean War 1859 Charles Darwin's *Origin of Species* 1870 Franco-Prussian War 1877 phonograph invented 1889 Eiffel Tower completed	**1850**	1859 Wagner's opera *Tristan and Isolde* 1867 Johann Strauss's waltz *Blue Danube* **10** 1870 Delibes's ballet *Coppélia* **11** 1876 Wagner's four-part opera *The Ring of the Nibelungs* 1880 Gilbert and Sullivan's operetta *The Pirates of Penzance* 1882 Tchaikovsky's *1812 Overture* 1887 Verdi's opera *Othello* **12** 1888 Brahms's *Second Cello Sonata* 1889 Richard Strauss's symphonic poem *Don Juan* 1893 Dvôrák's *New World Symphony* 1895 first 'Prom' (Henry Wood Promenade Concert) in London **13** 1899 Elgar's *Enigma Variations,* Schoenberg's string sextet *Verklärte Nacht* **14**
1899-1902 Boer War	**1900**	

Twentieth-century music

	1900	Scott Joplin, composer and founder of ragtime music
		Marie Lloyd and Sir Harry Lauder, leading music-hall singers
1904 first radio broadcast of music		1904 Giacomo Puccini's opera *Madame Butterfly* **1**
		1905 Claude Debussy's *La Mer*
	1910	1911 Gustav Mahler's *Das Lied von der Erde* ('Song of the Earth')
1914-18 World War I		1913 Igor Stravinsky's ballet *The Rite of Spring*
1917 Russian Revolution		c1915 rise of jazz in New Orleans
		1917 first jazz records made, by Original Dixieland Jass Band **2**
		Irving Berlin, composer of songs and musical comedies
1920 first general radio broadcasts	**1920**	1920 Gustav Holst's orchestral suite *The Planets* **3**
		King Oliver, cornettist and New Orleans bandleader (best recordings 1923-4)
		Louis Armstrong ("Satchmo"), cornet/trumpet-player, first great jazz soloist (best recordings 1923-8) **4**
		1921 Arnold Schoenberg invents 12-note system of music composition
		Jelly Roll Morton, pianist/New Orleans bandleader/first jazz composer (best recordings 1926-8) **5**
		Bessie Smith, classic Blues singer (best recordings 1923-8)
		George Gershwin, composer of jazz-based symphonic music, songs, musicals
		Bix Beiderbecke, trumpet-player in Chicago style (best recordings 1927-8)
		Earl "Fatha" Hines, jazz pianist (best recordings 1928-postwar)
		Fats Waller, jazz pianist, singer, composer (best recordings 1928-39) **6**
		1928 Maurice Ravel's ballet *Bolero* **7**
		Sir Noel Coward, composer and performer of cabaret songs
		Bing Crosby, founder of "crooning" singing style
1929 beginning of economic slump (Depression)		Cole Porter, composer of songs and Broadway musicals
		Paul Robeson, singer of Negro spirituals
	1930	Jerome Kern, composer of Broadway musicals
		Edith Piaf, French singer of *chansons*
1933 Hitler comes to power in Germany		Richard Rodgers, Lorenz Hart, and Oscar Hammerstein, composers of Broadway musicals
c1935 development of electric instruments (organs, guitars, etc.)		Robert Johnson, leading exponent of Country Blues (best recordings 1936-7)
		Count Basie, pianist/bandleader in Kansas City/Swing style (best recordings 1936-40)
		Billie Holiday, Swing jazz singer (best recordings 1937-9) **8**
		Lester Young ("Pres"), Kansas City/Swing tenor saxophonist (best recordings 1936-40)
		Duke Ellington, pianist/composer/bandleader in New York Swing style (best recordings 1939-41) **9**
		Glen Miller, trombonist/Swing bandleader **10**
		Frank Sinatra, crooner
1939-45 World War II	**1940**	1941 Dmitri Shostakovitch's *Leningrad Symphony*
1942 magnetic recording tape invented		Charlie "Bird" Parker, originator (with Dizzy Gillespie) of Bop style of jazz (best recordings 1945-8)
		1945 Benjamin Britten's opera *Peter Grimes* **11**
		Nat "King" Cole, crooner/pianist
1948 LP record invented	**1950**	Chuck Berry, City Blues/pop guitarist and singer
		B. B. King, Urban Blues guitarist/singer
		Elvis Presley, rock'n'roll singer, founder of modern pop music **12**
		Johnny Cash, country music guitarist/singer
		Buddy Holly, rock'n'roll guitarist/singer
1958 introduction of stereo records	**1960**	1960 Karlheinz Stockhausen's *Kontakte* (electronic music)
		Bob Dylan, folk-based composer/singer/guitarist/rock band leader **13**
		The Beatles, rock songwriters/performers **14**
		The Rolling Stones, rock band
		Jimi Hendrix, flamboyant electric guitarist/singer **15**
1969 first man on moon		Pink Floyd, electronic rock band

Clefs

G or treble clef   F or bass clef

C clef

alto clef   tenor clef

C clef is called tenor clef or alto clef, depending on where it is placed on the staff.

Key signatures

C   G   D   A   E   B   F#   C#
A minor   E minor   B minor   F# minor   C# minor   G# minor   D# minor   A# minor

F   Bb   Eb   Ab   Db   Gb   Cb
D minor   G minor   C minor   F minor   Bb minor   Eb minor   Ab minor

Time signatures

$\frac{2}{2}$ = 2 minims in a bar = ♩♩ $\frac{4}{4}$ or 𝄴 = 4 crotchets in a bar = ♩♩♩♩

The top number tells you how many beats in a bar, and the bottom one tells you the value of the beat.

Notes and their values

breve | semibreve | minim | crotchet | quaver | semiquaver   notes

rests

Each note is played or sung exactly half as long as the one in the row above.

semibreve
minims
crotchets
quavers
semiquavers

When a note has a dot after it, it is held for exactly half as long again. In the second bar of 'God Save the Queen' (below), the first note is the same length as 3 quavers.

Names of notes

E F G A B C D E F G — A – B — D E F G A B C D E F G
middle C

ledger lines are needed for notes above or below the pitch of those on the staff ⟶

First bars of 'God Save the Queen'

clef   slur

brace

God save our   gra-cious Queen   Long live our

staff

key signature   repeat sign   time signature   bar   bar line

Instructions how to play

staccato   pause

accent mark

crescendo (getting louder)   decrescendo (getting softer)

religion started by Mohammed —see also ISLAM, MOHAMMEDAN ☞ WORSHIP

muslin *n* a very fine thin cotton material

musquash *n* the fur of the muskrat

mussel *n* a small edible sea mollusc with a black shell in 2 parts

must¹ *v* *3rd person sing.* **must** *negative short form* **mustn't** 1 to have to because it is necessary: *I must leave at 6* 2 to be, do, etc., very probably: *I must look funny in this hat!*

must² *n* *esp. spoken* something necessary: *Warm clothes are a must in the mountains*

mustang *n* a small wild American horse; bronco

mustard *n* 1 a yellow-flowered plant with seeds from which a hot-tasting powder can be made 2 a thick mixture of this powder with water, eaten with food

muster¹ *v* 1 to gather or collect: *to muster one's courage* 2 to come together: *The troops mustered on the hill*

muster² *n* 1 a gathering of people to march or be inspected 2 **pass muster** to be satisfactory

musty *adj* -ier, -iest smelling unpleasantly old: *musty old books* — **mustiness** *n*

mutable *adj* able or likely to change — **-bility** *n*

mutant *n* a living thing which has a quality produced by a change in all its cells (a MUTATION)

mutation *n* 1 change in the cells of a living thing producing a new quality in the material or parts of the body, sometimes causing illness 2 an animal or plant showing such a change

mute¹ *adj* silent; without speech — ~ly *adv* — ~ness *n*

mute² *n* 1 a person who cannot speak 2 technical an object which softens the sound of a musical instrument

mute³ *v* muted, muting to reduce the sound of: *to mute a violin* — **muted** *adj*

mutilate *v* -lated, -lating 1 to damage; maim: *Her arm was mutilated in the accident* 2 to spoil: *You've mutilated the story by making such big changes* — **-tion** *n*

mutiny¹ *n* -nies the taking of power from the person in charge, esp. from a ship's captain — **-ous** *adj*

mutiny² *v* -nied, -nying to take part in a mutiny — **-eer** *n*

mutt *n* *esp. spoken* a fool

mutter¹ *v* to speak (usu. angry or complaining words) in a low voice — ~er *n*

mutter² *n* a sound of muttering

mutton *n* the meat from a sheep

mutual *adj* 1 equally shared by each one: *mutual interests* 2 equally so, one towards the other: *mutual enemies* — ~ity *n* — ~ly *adv* USAGE People often use **mutual** of things shared between 2 or more: *a mutual friend*. Others believe strongly that the right word here is **common**, and that **mutual** should be kept only for what each feels or does towards the other: *our mutual admiration* (=I admire you and you admire me).

muzak *n* *trademark* recorded music played continuously in some restaurants, places of work, etc.

muzzle¹ *n* 1 the front part of an animal's face, with the nose and mouth ☞ HORSE 2 the front end of a gun barrel 3 a covering round an animal's mouth, to prevent it from biting

muzzle² *v* -zled, -zling 1 to put a muzzle on 2 to prevent from telling something

muzzy *adj* -zier, -ziest 1 not clear: *The television picture's muzzy* 2 not thinking clearly, as because of illness or alcohol — **-zily** *adv* — **-ziness** *n*

my *adj* (*possessive form of* I) 1 belonging to me: *my car | my mother* 2 a cry of surprise, pleasure, etc.: *My! What a clever boy you are*

mycelium *n* -lia the mesh of tiny threads (HYPHAE) which makes up the body of a fungus

mycology *n* the study of fungi

mynah, myna also **mynah bird**— *n* any of several large dark Asian birds which can learn to talk

myopia *n* *esp. written* inability to see distant objects clearly; short-sightedness — **-pic** *adj* — **-pically** *adv*

myriad *adj, n, pron* *literature* (of) a great number: *A myriad of thoughts passed through her mind*

myrrh *n* a sticky gum from trees used in making perfume, incense, etc.

myself *pron* 1 (*reflexive form of* I): *I cut myself in the kitchen* 2 (*strong form of* I): *I had to do the shopping myself* 3 *esp. spoken* (in) my usual state of mind or body: *I feel more myself today*

mysterious *adj* 1 not easily understood 2 secret 3 suggesting mystery — ~ly *adv* — ~ness *n*

mystery *n* -ries 1 something which cannot be easily explained 2 a strange secret quality: *stories full of mystery* 3 a religious teaching that is beyond human understanding

mystery play *n* -plays MIRACLE PLAY

mystic¹ *adj* 1 of or like a religious mystery: *a mystic symbol* 2 magic: *mystic words* 3 mysterious

mystic² *n* a person who practises mysticism

mysticism *n* the gaining of real knowledge of God by prayer and meditation — **-tical** *adj* — **-tically** *adv*

mystify *v* -fied, -fying to bewilder: *I'm quite mystified about what happened* — **-fication** *n*

mystique *n* *French* an air of mystery which something has, esp. because it is admired: *the mystique of the fashion industry*

myth *n* 1 an ancient usu. religious or magical story, which explains natural or historical events 2 a false story or idea: *the myth that elephants never forget* ~ **ical** *adj*

mythological *adj* concerning myths or the study of them

mythologist *n* a person who studies and knows a lot about myths

mythology n -gies a system of beliefs contained in myths: *Greek and Roman mythology*
myxomatosis n a serious disease of rabbits

N, n N's, n's *or* Ns, ns— the 14th letter of the English alphabet
N *abbrev. for*: North(ern)
Naafi n -s the organization which runs shops and eating places in British military establishments
nab v -bb- *esp. spoken* **1** to seize as a thief; arrest **2** to get for oneself, seize, or catch quickly
nabob n **1** (in the 18th and 19th centuries) a man who became rich in the East and returned to Europe **2** a governor of any of the parts of India during the Mogul Empire
nacelle n *technical* an enclosure containing one of the engines on an aircraft ☞ AEROPLANE
nadir n **1** the point in the heavens directly below a person looking from earth —opposite **zenith 2** the lowest point, as of hope or fortune
nag¹ n a horse
nag² v -gg- **1** to try to persuade by continuous complaining **2** to worry or annoy continuously: *a nagging headache* — ~ger n
nag³ n *esp. spoken* a person who has the habit of nagging
naiad n -ads *or* -ades (in ancient Greek literature) a young female water nymph
nail¹ n **1** a thin piece of metal with a point at one end and a flat head at the other for hammering into a piece of wood or other material **2** a fingernail or toenail **3 hard as nails** *esp. spoken* **a** without any tender feelings **b** physically tough **4 hit the nail on the head** *esp. spoken* to do or say something exactly right
nail² v to fasten with a nail or nails
nailbrush n a small stiff brush for cleaning hands and fingernails
nail file n a small instrument with a rough surface for shaping fingernails
nail varnish n coloured or transparent liquid which dries to give a hard shiny surface on fingernails and toenails
naive, naïve adj **1** having or showing no experience (as of social behaviour), esp. because one is young **2** believing too readily what anyone says or what is most favourable — ~ly adv
naivety, naïvety, -eté n -ties **1** the state of being naive **2** a naive action or statement
naked adj **1** (of a person's body) not covered by clothes: *He was naked to the waist* **2** not covered by the usual covering: *a naked hillside* (=without trees) **3** not hidden; plain to see: *the naked truth-* **4** (of the eye) without any instrument to help one

see: *too small to see with the naked eye* — ~ly adv — ~ness n
name¹ n **1** the word or words that someone or something is called by **2** a usu. offensive title for someone: *to call someone (nasty) names* **3** fame; reputation **4 in name only** in appearance or by title but not in fact **5 in the name of** by the right or power of
name² v **named, naming 1** to give a name to: *They named the baby John* **2** to identify: *Can you name all the plants in the garden?* **3** to choose or appoint; specify: *We've named August 23rd for our wedding day* USAGE In *British English* one **names** a baby *after* its father, but Americans may also say *We* **named** *him for his father*, or *The college is* **named** *for George Washington.*
nameless adj **1 a** not known by name; anonymous: *a nameless town in ancient Britain* **b** not to be known by name: *a certain person who shall be nameless* **2** never given a name: *nameless plants* **3** (esp. of feelings) not clear enough to describe: *nameless fears* **4** too terrible to name: *nameless crimes*
namely adv that is to say: *Only one person can do the job, namely you* —compare I.E.; VIZ.
namesake n one of 2 or more people with the same name
nanny n -nies a woman employed to take care of children
nanny goat n a female goat —compare BILLY GOAT
nap¹ v -pp- **1** to have a nap **2 catch someone napping** *esp. spoken* to find, or take advantage of, someone off guard or not doing his duty
nap² n *esp. spoken* a short sleep, esp. during the day
nap³ n the soft surface on some cloth and leather, made by brushing the short fine threads or hairs usu. in one direction —compare PILE
nap⁴ n a type of card game
nap⁵ v (esp. of a newspaper writer) to say that one thinks (a certain horse) will win a race
napalm n a jelly made from petrol, which burns fiercely and is used in bombs
nape n the back (of the neck), near the head
naphtha n any of the various liquid chemicals used esp. for starting fires, removing dirt from clothes, and as a solvent
naphthalene n a white strong-smelling solid substance used esp. in mothballs
napkin n a usu. square piece of cloth or paper used esp. for protecting one's clothes during a meal
nappy n -pies *esp. spoken* a piece of soft cloth or paper worn between the legs of a baby to absorb its excreta
narcissism n too great love for one's own abilities or esp. appearance — -sist n — -sistic adj — -sistically adv
narcissus n -suses *or* -si any of several types of white or yellow flowers of early spring, such as the daffodil

narcotic¹ *n* a drug which in small amounts causes sleep or takes away pain, and in large amounts is harmful and habit-forming

narcotic² *adj* **1** taking away pain or causing sleep: *a narcotic drink* **2** of or related to narcotics

nark *v sl* to annoy: *He was narked by her words*

narky *adj* **-ier, -iest** *sl* bad-tempered

narrate *v* **-rated, -rating** *esp. written* to tell (a story); describe (an event or events) in order

narration *n* **1** the act of narrating **2** a narrative

narrative¹ *n* **1** that which is narrated: *a narrative of last week's events* **2** the act of narrating

narrative² *adj* **1** telling a story or having the form of a story: *a narrative poem* **2** of or concerning storytelling: *the narrative art*

narrator *n* **1** a person in some books, plays, etc., who tells the story or explains what is happening **2** a person who narrates a story

narrow¹ *adj* **1** small from one side to the other, esp. in comparison with length or with what is usual **2** limited; restricted **3** almost not enough or only just successful: *a narrow escape* —opposite **wide, broad** — ~**ness** *n*

narrow² *v* **1** to decrease in width: *to narrow her eyes* **2** to limit; restrict

narrow boat *n* a long narrow canal boat

narrow gauge *n* a size of railway track which is less than 4 feet 8½ inches wide: *a narrow-gauge railway* —see also GAUGE

narrowly *adv* **1** hardly; only just: *One car narrowly missed hitting the other one* **2** in a narrow way or form or within narrow limits **3** in a thorough and usu. doubting way

narrow-minded *adj offensive* considering only part of a question or favouring only one opinion —opposite **broadminded** — ~**ness** *n*

narwhal *n* **-whals, -whal** a type of whale of the northern ocean, hunted for its oil and the long tusk of the male

nasal *adj* **1** of or related to the nose: *breathe through the nasal passage* **2** sounding through the nose: *a nasal voice* — ~**ly** *adv*

nascent *adj esp. written* beginning to grow or develop: *nascent ability*

nasturtium *n* a type of garden plant with orange, yellow, or red flowers and circular leaves

nasty *adj* **-tier, -tiest** *esp. spoken* **1** ugly; unpleasant **2** harmful; dangerous — **-tily** *adv* — **-tiness** *n*

natal *adj* of or connected with someone's birth

nation *n* **1** a large group of people living in one area and usu. having an independent government —compare COUNTRY **2** a large group of people with the same language and culture: *the Indian nations in the western United States* —see FOLK (USAGE) — ~**al** *adj* — **ally** *adv*

national *n* a person, esp. someone abroad, who belongs to another, usu. stated, country: *American nationals in England* —compare CITIZEN, ALIEN

national anthem *n* the official song of a nation

national debt *n* the total amount of money owed by the government of a country

National Front *n* a minor British political party that is hostile to nonwhite immigration

National Health Service *n* (in Britain) the system of medical treatment for everyone paid for by taxes

National Insurance *n* (in Britain) a system of insurance run by the government, into which workers and employers make regular payments, and which provides money for the unemployed, old, or ill

nationalism *n* **1** (too great) love of and pride in one's country **2** desire by a people or nation to form an independent country — **-list** *n, adj* — **-listic** *adj* — **-listically** *adv*

nationality *n* **-ties** **1** membership of a country by a person —compare CITIZENSHIP **2** a large group of people with the same race, origin, language, etc.: *the different nationalities of the USSR*

nationalize, -ise *v* **-ized, -izing** (of a central government) to buy or take control of (a business, industry, etc.) — **-ization** *n*

national park *n* a usu. large area of land which is kept in its natural state by the government for people to visit and for plants and animals to live in

national service *n* the system of making all men serve in the armed forces for a limited period; conscription

National Socialism *n* technical Nazism

National Trust *n* a British organization which takes care of beautiful places and buildings

nation state *n* a people (a nation) living together as one politically independent state

native¹ *adj* **1** belonging to or being the place of one's birth: *her native language* **2** (of a person) belonging to a country from birth: *a native Englishman* **3** growing, found, etc., in a place; not brought in from another place: *a house built of native stone* **4** often offensive and becoming rare of or concerning the original people, esp. the non-Europeans, of a place: *a native village*

native² *n* **1** someone who was born (in a place) **2** someone who lives in a place all the time or has lived there a long time **3** often offensive and becoming rare someone who belongs to an earlier or original people, esp. the non-Europeans, living in a place: *The government of the island treated the natives badly* **4** a plant or animal living naturally in a place

nativity *n* pompous birth: *I have just visited the place of my nativity*

Nativity *n* **-ties** the birth of Christ

NATO *n* the North Atlantic Treaty Organization; a group of countries including Britain, the US, etc., agreeing to give military help to each other

natter *v esp. spoken* to talk continuously about unimportant things; chatter — **natter** *n*

natty *adj* -tier, – tiest *esp. spoken* neat in appearance; smart — -tily *adv*

natural¹ *adj* 1 of, concerning, or being what is or happens ordinarily in the world, esp. a not caused, made, or controlled by people: *the natural mineral wealth of a country* —compare MAN-MADE, ARTIFICIAL **b** of or concerning forces which can be explained: *a natural explanation for the strange event* 2 expected from experience; usual: *It's natural to shake hands with someone you've just met* 3 not looking or sounding different from usual: *Try to look natural for your photograph* 4 belonging to someone from birth; not learned: *natural charm* 5 (of a person) not needing to be taught; having a skill or quality already in oneself: *a natural musician* 6 (of a family member) actually having the stated relation even if not in law: *John was adopted as a baby: he never knew his natural parents* 7 (of a note in music) not sharp or flat: *Don't sing C sharp, sing C natural!* — ~ness *n* USAGE When **natural** means 'ordinary', or 'what is to be expected', the opposite is **unnatural** or **abnormal: Supernatural** is the opposite of **natural** when one is thinking of gods, fairies, or spirits.

natural² *n* 1 *esp. spoken* someone or something well suited or certain to succeed: *The horse is a natural to win the next race* 2 (in music) **a** a note which is not raised or lowered by a sharp or flat; a white note on the piano: *a piece of music played only on the naturals* **b** also **natural sign** — the sign ♮ showing that a note is not raised or lowered

natural gas *n* gas which is taken from under the earth or the sea

natural history *n* the study of plants, animals, and rocks

naturalist *n* a person who studies plants or animals

naturalize, -ise *v* -ized, -izing 1 to make (a person born elsewhere) a citizen of a country: *He was naturalized after living in Britain for 10 years* 2 to bring (a plant or animal) into a new place to live like a native: *Some European birds have become naturalized in America* — -ization *n*

natural law *n* (a) scientific law about the behaviour of objects: *the natural law that gases become hot under pressure*

naturally *adv* 1 by nature 2 without trying to look or sound different from usual 3 of course; as one could have expected: *'Did you win the game?' 'Naturally.'*

natural resources *n* land, forests, mineral wealth, etc.

natural science *n* biology, chemistry, and physics

natural selection also **survival of the fittest**— *n technical* the course of events by which plants and animals best suited to the conditions around them live while those not suited to these conditions die

nature *n* 1 the qualities which make someone or something different from others; character 2 type; kind; sort: *ceremonies of a solemn nature* 3 the whole world, esp. as something lasting and not changed by people: *the beauties of nature* | *a struggle against nature* —see also SECOND NATURE

naturism *n* nudism — -ist *n*

naught *n* 1 nought 2 *old use & poetic* nothing: *to care naught for it*

naughty *adj* -tier, -tiest bad in behaviour; not obeying a parent, teacher, set of rules, etc. **a** (of children or their actions): *It's naughty to pull your sister's hair* **b** *humour* (of grown-up people): *It was naughty of Father to stay out so late* —see WICKED (USAGE) — -tily *adv* — -tiness *n*

nausea *n* a feeling of sickness and desire to vomit

nauseate *v* -ated, -ating 1 to cause to feel sick: *a nauseating smell* 2 to be hateful to (someone); sicken

nauseous *adj* causing nausea: *a nauseous smell* — ~ly *adv* — ~ness *n*

nautical *adj* of or concerning sailors, ships, or the practice of sailing — ~ly *adv*

nautical mile *n* a measure of distance, used at sea, equal to 1, 852 metres

nautilus also **chambered nautilus**— *n* -luses or -li a type of small animal (MOLLUSC) of the South Pacific and Indian Oceans which lives in a spiral-shaped shell

naval *adj* of, concerning, or belonging to a navy or ships of war

nave *n* the long central part of a church ☞ CATHEDRAL

navel *n* a small mark or sunken place in the middle of the stomach, left when the umbilical cord was cut at birth

navigable *adj* (of a river or other body of water) deep and wide enough to allow ships to travel — -gability *n*

navigate *v* -gated, -gating 1 to direct the course of (a ship, plane, vehicle, etc.) 2 to go by sea, air, etc. from one side or end to the other of (a place) — -ion *n*

navigator *n* the officer on a ship or aircraft who has the job of recording and controlling its course

navvy *n* -vies a labourer doing a heavy unskilled job in digging or building

navy *n* -vies the organization, including ships, people, buildings, etc., which makes up the power of a country for war at sea

navy blue also **navy**— *adj, n* very dark blue (colour)

nay¹ *adv* 1 *old use* no —opposite **yea** or **aye** 2 *literature* not only that but also (used for adding something stronger or more exact to what has been said): *a bright, nay a blinding light*

nay² *n* nays a vote or voter against an idea, law, etc.: *to count the nays* —opposite **aye**

Nazi *n* Nazis a person belonging to the National Socialist political party of Adolf Hitler which controlled Germany from 1933 to 1945 — **Nazi** *adj* — **Nazism** *n*

N B, n b (*used esp. in writing, to begin a note*) nota bene; take notice; note well

NCO *n esp. spoken* NONCOMMISSIONED OFFICER

NE *abbrev. for:* northeast(ern)

Neanderthal man *n* a type of early human creature who lived in Europe during the early stone age —compare CAVEMAN

neapolitan *adj* (of ice cream) in the shape of a brick with 3 or 4 bands of different colours and tastes

neap tide also **neap**— *n* a very small rise and fall of the tide at or soon following the time of the first and third quarters of the moon —compare SPRING TIDE

near¹ *adj, adv, prep* not far from in distance, time, degree, quality, etc.; close (to): *the near future | a house near the river | It's not exactly right, but it's near enough*

near² *adj* **1** closely related: *Only near relatives were invited to the wedding* **2** (of one of 2 things) a left-hand: *the near front wheel of a car | the pony's near foreleg* —opposite **off b** closer: *the near bank of the river* — ~ness *n*

near³ *v* to come closer (to)

nearby *adj, adv, prep* near; within a short distance (from): *a football match being played nearby | in a nearby field*

Near East *n* the countries round the eastern Mediterranean Sea, esp. Turkey —compare FAR EAST, MIDDLE EAST, EAST — ~ern *adj*

nearly *adv* almost; not quite or not yet completely: *The job's nearly finished. | I nearly beat him at chess last night*

nearside *adj* on the left-hand side, esp. of a car, road, etc.: *the nearside back light of a car* — opposite offside

neat *adj* **1** showing care in appearance; tidy: *neat handwriting* **2** liking order and good arrangement: *Cats are neat animals* **3** simple and exact; elegant: *a neat description* **4** clever and effective: *a neat trick* **5** *esp. spoken* (of alcoholic drinks) without ice or water or other liquid: *I like my whisky neat* — ~ly *adv* — ~ness *n*

nebula *n* **-lae** or **-las** **1** a mass of gas and dust in space, often seen as a bright cloud at night **2** a galaxy which has this appearance — ~r *adj*

nebulous *adj* **1** not clear, esp. in meaning or expression; vague **2** cloudy: *a nebulous liquid* — **-losity** *n* — ~ly *adv* — ~ness *n*

necessaries *n* things which are needed USAGE One needs **necessaries**; one would die if one did not have **necessities**, a much stronger word: *a few necessaries for the journey | Water is a necessity of life.*

necessarily *adv* in a way that must be so; unavoidably: *Good-looking food doesn't necessarily taste good*

necessary *adj* **1** that must be had or obtained; needed: *Food is necessary for life* **2** that must be; determined or fixed by the nature of things: *Death is the necessary end of life*

necessitate *v* **-tated, -tating** *esp. written* to make necessary

necessitous *adj pompous* poor; needy — ~ly *adv*

necessity *n* **-ties** **1** the condition of being necessary, needed, or unavoidable; need **2** something that is necessary: *Food and clothing are necessities of life* **3** the condition of being poor or in need: *He was forced by necessity to steal a loaf of bread* —see NECESSARIES (USAGE)

neck¹ *n* **1** the part of the body between the head and shoulders **2** this part of the body of an animal, used as food **3** the part of a garment for this part of the body **4** the part of something which is shaped like this part of the body: *the neck of a bottle* **5 get it in the neck** *esp. spoken* to be severely scolded or punished **6 neck and neck** *esp. spoken* (of 2 horses, people, etc., in competition) equal in position **7 risk one's neck** to endanger one's life **8 up to one's neck in** also **up to one's ears in** — *esp. spoken* deeply concerned in: *up to my neck in debt*

neck² *v esp. spoken* to kiss, caress, etc.

neckerchief *n* **-chiefs** or **-chieves** a square of cloth which is folded and worn around the neck

necklace *n* a string of jewels, beads, pearls, etc., on a chain of gold, silver, etc., worn round the neck as an ornament

neckline *n* the line made by the neck opening of a piece of women's clothing

necromancy *n literature* **1** the practice which claims to learn about the future by talking with the dead **2** magic, esp. evil magic — **-er** *n*

nectar *n* **1** (in ancient Greek and Roman literature) the drink of the gods —compare AMBROSIA **2** a sweet and good-tasting drink: *taste the nectar of success* **3** the sweet liquid collected by bees from flowers

nectarine *n* a kind of small hard peach with a smooth skin

née *adv* French (*used after a married woman's name and before her original family name*) formerly named; born with the name: *Mrs. Carol Cook née Williams*

need¹ *n* **1** the condition of lacking or wanting something necessary or very useful: *children's need for milk* **2** what must be done; obligation: *No need to go yet: it's still early* **3** *esp. written* something necessary to have: *supply all our needs* **4** *esp. written* the state of not having enough food or money; poverty: *illness, need, and other troubles of the world* **5 if need be** if it's necessary: *I must finish this job! I'll work all night if need be*

need² *v* *negative short form* needn't **1** to have a need for; want for some useful purpose; lack; require: *Children need milk. | My shirt needs a button. | This job needs a lot of care, attention, and time. | You didn't need to tell him the news; it just made him sad* **2** to have to: *We needn't go yet; the show doesn't start for an hour. | Need you go so soon? | You needn't have told him the news; he knew it already*

needful *adj now rare* necessary; needed: *the instruments needful for his work* — ~**ly** *adv*

needle¹ *n* 1 a long metal pin used in sewing for pulling thread, with a sharp point at one end and a hole in the other end for the thread 2 a thin pointed object that seems to look like this: *a pine needle* 3 any of various thin rods with points or hooks used in working with wool or other cloth: *knitting needles* 4 (in a record player) the very small pointed jewel or piece of metal which touches a record as it turns and picks up the sound recorded on it; stylus 5 a very thin hollow pointed tube at the end of a hypodermic syringe which is pushed into someone's skin to put a liquid (esp. medicine) into the body 6 a long thin pointer fixed to the centre of a usu. circular surface, as in a compass 7 **needle in a haystack** something very small which is hard to find in a big place

needle² *v* -**dled, -dling** *esp. spoken* to annoy by repeated unkind remarks; tease

needless *adj* not needed; unnecessary — ~**ly** *adv*

needlewoman *n* -**women** a woman who sews

needlework *n* 1 sewing and embroidery; work, esp. fancy work, done with needle and thread 2 examples of this work: *chairs covered with needlework*

needs *adv old use or humour* necessarily: *Your fool of a brother must needs telephone just as we were going out!*

needy *adj* -**ier, -iest** poor; not having enough to live on: *those who are poor and needy* — **neediness** *n*

ne'er-do-well *n* -**wells** a useless or lazy person who never does any good work

nefarious *adj esp. written* against laws or moral principles; wicked — ~**ly** *adv* — ~**ness** *n*

negate *v* **negated, negating** 1 to cause to have no effect; neutralize 2 to disprove the truth or fact of; deny — **-gation** *n*

negative¹ *adj* 1 declaring 'no ': *a negative answer* | *negative expressions like 'not at all'* — opposite **affirmative** 2 without any active, useful, or helpful qualities: *negative advice that only tells you what not to do* 3 showing the lack of what was looked for, hoped for, or expected: *The test for bacteria was negative* (=none were found) 4 (of or in electricity) of the type that is based on electrons and is produced by rubbing resin with wool 5 (of a photograph or film) showing dark places in nature as light and light places as dark 6 a (of a number or quantity) less than zero: *a negative profit* (=a loss) b of or concerning such a quantity: *the negative sign* (=the sign -) — ~**ly** *adv*

negative² *n* 1 a statement saying or meaning ' no'; a refusal or denial: *The answer to my request was a strong negative* —opposite **affirmative** 2 one of the words and expressions ' no ',

' not ', ' nothing ', ' never ', ' not at all ', etc. 3 a negative photograph or film

negative pole *n* (of a magnet) the end which naturally turns away from the earth

neglect¹ *v* 1 to give no or too little attention or care to 2 to fail (to do something), esp. because of carelessness or forgetfulness: *Don't neglect to lock the door*

neglect² *n* 1 the action of neglecting 2 the condition or fact of being neglected: *an old person living in unhappy neglect*

neglectful *adj* in the habit of neglecting things: *a mother who is neglectful of her children* — ~**ly** *adv* — ~**ness** *n*

negligee *n* a woman's light and usu. fancy nightdress

negligent *adj* 1 not taking or showing enough care 2 showing little effort; careless in a usu. pleasant way: *to dress with negligent grace* — ~**ly** *adv* — **-gence** *n*

negligible *adj* too slight or unimportant to make any difference or to be worth any attention — **-bly** *adv*

negotiable *adj* 1 open to being settled or changed by being negotiated 2 that can be passed through, along, etc., or dealt with 3 (of a cheque or money order) that can be exchanged for money

negotiate *v* -**ated, -ating** 1 to talk with another person or group in order to settle a question; try to come to an agreement 2 to produce (an agreement) or settle (a piece of business) in this way: *The trade union negotiated a new contract* 3 to deal with: *a player negotiating a hard piece of music* — **-ation** *n* — **-ator** *n*

Negress *n technical or not polite* a Negro woman

Negro *n* -**es** *technical or not polite* 1 a person belonging to a division of mankind, with black or dark skin, living in Africa south of the Sahara 2 a descendant of such people, living in the US or elsewhere

neigh *v, n* (to make) the long loud cry that a horse makes

neighbour *n* one of 2 or more people that live near one another

neighbourhood *n* 1 a group of people and their homes forming a small area within a larger place such as a town: *a quiet neighbourhood* 2 the area around a point, place, or amount (esp. in the phrase **in the neighbourhood (of)**): *He paid in the neighbourhood of $500 for the car*

neighbouring *adj* (as of places) near or close by

neighbourly *adj* friendly; like a good neighbour — **-liness** *n*

neither¹ *adj, pron* not one and not the other of 2: *'Which of the books did you like?' 'Neither (of them)! They were both dull.'* | *Neither book was exciting; they were both dull* —compare EITHER, NONE

neither² *conj* (used before the first of 2 or more choices separated by 'nor') not either: *He neither* ate, drank, nor smoked; he liked neither the meal nor the cigarettes —compare EITHER . . . OR

neither³ adv also not: "I can't swim!" "Neither can I!" —see EITHER (USAGE)

nelson n (in wrestling) a way of holding an opponent by putting one arm (a **half nelson**) or both arms (a **full nelson**) under the opponent's arms and pressing the back of his neck with the hands

nemesis n -ses literature just and esp. unavoidable punishment, often considered as a goddess or an active force

neocolonialism n the trading and political practices by which a powerful country indirectly exercises control over esp. recently independent countries —compare COLONIALISM, IMPERIALISM

neolithic adj technical of, being, or concerning the latest period of the stone age, when people began to settle in villages, grow crops, keep animals, polish stone for tools, and use the wheel: neolithic villages — compare PALEOLITHIC

neologism n 1 (the use of) a new word or expression 2 (the use of) a new meaning for a word

neon n a chemically inactive gas that is an element found in small amounts in the air

neon light also **neon lamp**— n a glass tube filled with neon which lights when an electric current goes through it

neophyte n a student of an art, skill, trade, etc., with no experience; beginner

nephew n 1 the son of one's brother or sister ⫞FAMILY 2 the son of one's wife's or husband's brother or sister —compare NIECE

ne plus ultra n Latin & literature the point of highest quality that can be reached: the ne plus ultra of church music

nepotism n the practice of favouring one's relatives when one has power or a high office ·

Neptune n the planet 8th in order from the sun

nereid n (in ancient Greek literature) a young nymph living in the sea

nerve¹ n 1 any of the threadlike parts of the body which form a system to carry feelings and messages to and from the brain ⊕ 2 strength or control of mind: a man of nerve 3 rude or disrespectful boldness 4 any of the stiff lines on a leaf or an insect's wing 5 **strain every nerve** to try as hard as possible

nerve² v **nerved, nerving** to give courage to

nerve cell n any of the cells that form part of the nervous system

nerveless adj esp. spoken 1 weak or without courage or power 2 not nervous; cool — ~ly adv — ~ness n

nerve-racking, -wracking adj esp. spoken difficult to do or bear calmly because annoying and tiring to the mind, or dangerous

nerves n esp. spoken 1 a condition of great nervousness: She gets nerves before every examination 2 **get on someone's nerves** to make someone annoyed or bad-tempered

nervous adj 1 a excited and anxious; worried b of or resulting from this kind of condition: a nervous smile c (of a person) easily excited and worried 2 of or related to the nervous system of the body, or to the feelings: a nervous disease 3 slightly afraid; timid: nervous of going too near the wild animals — ~ly adv — ~ness n

nervous breakdown n an unnatural condition of deep worrying, anxiety, weeping, and tiredness

nervous system n the system in animals (=the brain, spinal cord, and nerves) which receives and passes on feelings, messages, and other such information from inside and outside the body

nervy adj -ier, -iest esp. spoken nervous and anxious

ness n (usu. in names of places) a point of land stretching out into a body of water: Dungeness in Kent

nest¹ n 1 a hollow place built or found by a bird for a home and a place to hold its eggs 2 the settled and protected home of any of certain other animals or insects: an ants' nest 3 a protected place for hiding or evil activity: a nest of crime 4 a group of like objects which fit closely into or inside one another: a nest of tables

nest² v 1 to build or use a nest 2 to fit closely inside another thing or each other: nested cooking pots

nest egg n an amount of money saved for future use

nestle v -tled, -tling 1 to settle into a warm, close, or comfortable position 2 to lie or rest warmly, closely, or comfortably: villages nestling among the mountains

nestling n a young bird who has not left the nest

Nestor n literature a wise old adviser

net¹ n 1 a material of strings, wires, threads, etc. twisted, tied, or woven together with regular equal spaces between them —compare MESH 2 any of various objects made from this, such as a a large piece spread out under water to catch fish b a carrier for goods c a length dividing the 2 sides of the court in tennis, badminton, etc. d the goal in football, hockey, etc. 3 a trap made from this: a butterfly net 4 technical a flat drawing which, when folded, forms a solid 5 a piece of material in a frame, used (as by firemen) for catching someone falling or jumping

net² v -tt- 1 to catch in or as if in a net: netted no fish large enough to keep 2 to cover with a net: Net the fruit trees to protect them from birds

net³ adj 1 (of an amount) when nothing further is to be subtracted: net profit (=after tax, rent, etc. are paid) —compare **gross** 2 when everything has been considered; final: The net result of the tax changes was to make the rich even richer 3 (of a price) not allowed to be made lower: The price of the book is $3 net

net⁴ v -tt- to gain as a profit

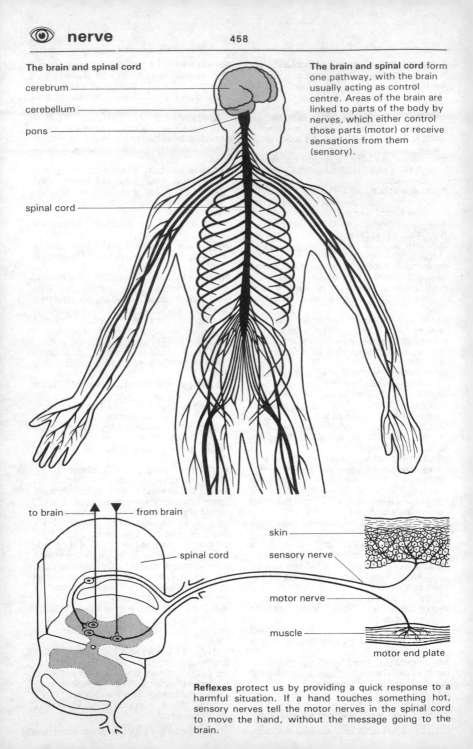

The brain and spinal cord

cerebrum

cerebellum

pons

spinal cord

The brain and spinal cord form one pathway, with the brain usually acting as control centre. Areas of the brain are linked to parts of the body by nerves, which either control those parts (motor) or receive sensations from them (sensory).

to brain — from brain

spinal cord

skin

sensory nerve

motor nerve

muscle

motor end plate

Reflexes protect us by providing a quick response to a harmful situation. If a hand touches something hot, sensory nerves tell the motor nerves in the spinal cord to move the hand, without the message going to the brain.

netball *n* a women's game in which teams make points by making a ball fall through one of the 2 high rings at the opposite ends of a court

nether *adj literature or humour* **1** in the lower place; lower **2 the nether regions/world** (esp. in ancient literature) the home of the dead down inside the earth

nethermost *adj literature* lowest

nets *n* (in cricket) one or more wickets surrounded by a net, in which people can practise batting

nett *adj* (of amounts and prices) net

netting *n* string, wire, etc., made into a net: *a fence of wire netting*

nettle¹ *n* any of various wild plants which may sting and make red marks on the skin

nettle² *v* **-tled, -tling** to annoy (someone); make (someone) angry or impatient

nettle rash *n* a rash on one's skin looking like the result of the stinging of a nettle

network *n* **1** a system of lines, tubes, wires, etc., that cross or meet one another: *Britain's railway network* **2** a group or system whose members are connected in some way **3** a group of radio or television stations in different places using many of the same broadcasts

neural *adj medical* of or related to the nervous system

neuralgia *n medical* sharp pain along the length of one or more nerves, usu. in the head — **-gic** *adj*

neurology *n* the scientific study of the nervous system, esp. of its diseases and their treatment — **-gist** *n*

neuron also **neurone**— *n* NERVE CELL — ~**al** *adj*

neurosis *n* **-ses** *medical* a disorder of the mind marked by strong unreasonable fears and ideas about the outside world, troubled relations with other people, and often by various feelings of illness in the body

neurotic¹ *adj* of or related to neurosis: *neurotic fears*

neurotic² *n* a person who is unbalanced in mind; someone with a neurosis

neuter¹ *adj* **1** (in grammar) in a class of words that are not masculine or feminine: *'It' is a neuter pronoun* **2** (of plants or animals) with no or undeveloped sexual organs: *Worker bees are neuter*

neuter² *n* the class of neuter words

neuter³ *v* to castrate —compare SPAY, ALTER

neutral¹ *adj* **1** in a position in between opposite or different choices; with no qualities of the stated kind, as of something **a** very weak or colourless: *trousers of a neutral colour that look good with any colour of socks* **b** (in chemistry) neither acid nor base **c** with no electrical charge ⊸ELECTRICITY **2** being or belonging to a country which is not fighting or helping either side in a war **3** without any feelings on either side of a question: *I'm neutral in this argument: I don't care who wins* **4** (in a car or other machine) of or concern-ing the position of the gears in which no power is carried from the engine to the wheels — ~**ity** *n* — ~**ly** *adv*

neutral² *n* the neutral position of the gears in a car or other machine

neutralize, -ise *v* **-ized, -izing** **1** to cause to have no effect; destroy the qualities, force, or activity of: *The airforce quickly neutralized the enemy's small navy* —compare NEGATE, COUNTERACT **2** to prevent (a country) by an international agreement from being used by or helping either side in a war — **-ization** *n*

neutralizer *n* a person, object, or chemical that neutralizes the effect of another

neutron *n* a very small piece of matter like a proton that is part of the centre of an atom and carries no electricity ⊸ATOM

neutron star *n* a star near the end of its life that is denser than a white dwarf and made of a compressed mass of neutrons

never *adv* **1** not ever; not at any time: *I've never met him and I hope I never will* **2** not: *Never fear!* | *This shirt will never do!* | *Never mind about the washing-up - I'll do it later* **3 Never mind** *esp. spoken* Don't worry, it does not matter

nevermore *adv poetic* never again

never-never *n* **on the never-never** *humour sl* by hire purchase

never-never land *n* an imaginary wonderful place: *to dream of a never-never land where everyone is rich*

nevertheless *adv* in spite of that; yet: *I can't take your advice. Nevertheless, thank you for giving it.* | *He's stupid, but I like him nevertheless*

new *adj* **1** having begun or been made only a short time ago or before: *a new government* | *new fashions* **2** not used by anyone before: *We sell new and used furniture* **3 a** being found or becoming known only now or recently: *a new star* **b** being in the stated position only a short time: *the new nations of Africa* **4** different from the earlier thing or things; fresh: *to learn a new language* | *a new day* **5** taken from the ground early in the season: *small new potatoes* — ~**ness** *n*

newborn *adj* (of a baby) recently or just born

newcomer *n* a person who has recently come

New Deal *n* a system of government laws and actions in the US in the 1930s to provide jobs and improve social and business conditions

newel also **newel post**— *n* **1** a post supporting the handrail at the top or bottom or at a turn in a set of stairs **2** the pillar at the centre of a spiral staircase

newfangled *adj offensive or humour* (of ideas, inventions, etc.) new and unnecessary or of no value — ~**ness** *n*

newly *adv* **1** recently; freshly: *a newly built house* **2** in a new way: *an old idea newly expressed*

newlywed *n esp. spoken* a man or woman recently married

new moon *n* **1** the time (about once a month)

when the moon's dark side is turned towards the earth **2** the bright thin edge of the moon seen in the sky a few days after this

news *n* **1** what is reported, esp. about a recent event or events; new information: *news of the election results* **2** any of the regular reports of recent events broadcast on radio and television

newsagent *n* a person in charge of a shop selling newspapers and magazines

newsboy also **paperboy**— *n* **-boys** a boy or man who sells or delivers newspapers

newscast *n* a radio or television broadcast of news

newscaster also **newsreader**— *n* a person who broadcasts news on radio or television

news conference *n* PRESS CONFERENCE

newsletter *n* a small sheet of news sent weekly or monthly to a particular group of people

newspaper *n* also (*esp. spoken*) **paper**— a paper printed and sold to the public usu. daily or weekly, with news, notices, etc.

newsprint *n technical* a cheap kind of paper used mostly for newspapers

newsreel *n* a short film of news

newsroom *n* the office in a newspaper or broadcasting station where news is received and rewritten for broadcasting to the public

newssheet *n* a small newspaper, usu. of one or 2 pages

newsstand *n* a stall from which newspapers and sometimes magazines and books are sold

newsvendor *n* a person who sells newspapers

newsworthy *adj* important and interesting enough to be reported as news

newt also **eft**— *n* a type of small 4-legged animal (SALAMANDER) living partly on land and partly in water

New Testament *n* the second half of the Bible, containing the Christian writings — compare OLD TESTAMENT

new town *n* any of several towns built in Britain since 1946, each planned and built as a whole with factories, houses, shops, etc.: *Harlow New Town* —compare GARDEN CITY

new wave *n* a group of ideas or ways of doing things in film, art, music, etc. which tries to be new, esp. a style of music like punk rock

New World *n* the Western Hemisphere; the Americas —compare OLD WORLD

new year *n* **1** the year which has just begun or will soon begin **2** the beginning of the year

New-Year *adj* of or related to the first day or beginning of the year

New Year's Day *n* **-days** the first day of the year; (in Western countries) January 1st

New Year's Eve *n* (the evening of) the last day of the year (in Western countries, December 31st)

next *adj, adv* **1** without anything coming between: *the next house* **2** following nearest in time: *next week* | *what happened next?*

next door *adv* in or being the next building: *the neighbours next door* — **next-door** *adj*

next of kin *n* next of kin the person most closely related to someone

next to[1] *prep* **1** also **next**— in the closest place to: *I don't like wool next to my skin* **2** closest in order, degree, etc. to: *Next to riding, I like swimming best*

next to[2] *adv esp. spoken* almost: *The speech said next to nothing*

nexus *n* a connection or network of connections between objects, ideas, etc.

NHS *abbrev. for:* National Health Service

niacin *n* a type of vitamin B found in foods like milk and eggs

nib *n* the pointed usu. metal piece fitting on the end of a pen, with a crack for ink to flow to the point

nibble[1] *v* **-bled, -bling** **1** to eat with small bites: *Aren't you hungry? You're only nibbling at your food* **2** to show interest; show signs of accepting something

nibble[2] *n esp. spoken* **1** an act of nibbling at something **2** a very small amount of food

nice *adj* **1** good, esp. **a** kind: *How nice of you to do that!* **b** well done or made: *a nice piece of work* **c** pleasant; pleasing: *How nice to see you!* **2** showing or needing careful understanding; delicate: *a nice point of law* **3** *offensive & esp. spoken* bad; wrong: *You're a nice friend: you won't even lend me $5!* — ~ly *adv* — ~ness *n* USAGE In writing it is better to avoid **nice**, and to use **amusing, beautiful, interesting**, etc., according to the meaning.

nicety *n* **-ties** **1** a pleasant or enjoyable thing: *the niceties of city life* **2** the quality of needing or showing exactness or delicateness: *a man with great nicety of judgment* **3** a fine or delicate point; detail

niche *n* **1** a recess in a wall, usu. for a bust or statue **2** a suitable place, job, position, etc.: *He's found a niche for himself doing the job he always wanted to do*

nick[1] *n* **1** a small cut, often made accidentally, in a surface or edge **2** *esp. spoken* prison **3** **in the nick of time** just in time; at the necessary moment

nick[2] *v* **1** to make or cut a nick in **2** *esp. spoken* to steal **3** *sl* to arrest

nick[3] *n sl* bodily condition; shape: *My heart is still in good nick*

nickel *n* **1** a hard silver-white metal that is an element and is used in the production of other metals **2** the coin of the US and Canada worth 5 cents

nicker *n* **nicker** *sl* a pound; £1

nickname[1] *n* a name used informally instead of one's own name, usu. given because of one's character or as a short form of the **real name**

nickname[2] *v* **-named, -naming** to give (someone) a nickname

nicotine *n* a chemical which is poisonous alone

and which provides the taste and effect of tobacco

niece n 1 the daughter of one's brother or sister ⏵FAMILY 2 the daughter of one's wife's or husband's brother or sister —compare NEPHEW

nifty adj **-tier, -tiest** esp. spoken very good, attractive, or effective, esp. well or cleverly done or made

niggard n offensive a person not willing to spend money; stingy person — ~ly adj — ~liness n

niggle v **-gled, -gling** to pay too much attention to small details, esp. to find fault — ~r n

niggling adj 1 slightly and continually annoying: a niggling doubt 2 (of a piece of work) needing too much attention to detail: the niggling job of mending all the small holes

nigh adv, prep poetic & old use near

night n 1 the dark part of each day 2 any of various parts of this period, such as a the evening: Saturday is our cinema night b the period after bedtime: sleep well all night 3 **have a good/bad night** to sleep well/badly 4 **make a night of it** esp. spoken to spend all or most of the night in enjoyment 5 **night and day** also **day and night**— esp. spoken all the time

night bird n esp. spoken a nighthawk

night blindness n inability to see things at night or in weak light

nightcap n 1 a soft cloth cap worn in bed esp. in former times 2 a usu. alcoholic drink taken before going to bed

nightclothes n garments worn in bed

nightclub n a restaurant open late at night where people may drink, dance, and see a show

nightdress also (esp. spoken) **nightie** — n a piece of women's clothing like a loose dress, made to be worn in bed

nightfall n the beginning of night; dusk

nighthawk also **night bird**— n esp. spoken a person with the habit of staying up and doing things at night

nightingale n any of several European birds related to the robin, known for their beautiful song

nightlight n a low light which is left on, or a small candle which is kept burning, through the night

nightly adj, adv (happening, done, used, etc.) every night

nightmare n 1 an unpleasant and terrible dream 2 a bad, fearful, or terrible experience or event: Driving on that ice was a nightmare — -marish adj — -marishly adv — -marishness n

night porter n a person who is on duty through the night at the front desk of a hotel

night safe n a safe in the outside wall of a bank, into which people may put money when the bank is closed

night school n a school or set of classes meeting in the evening, esp. for people who have jobs during the day

nightshade n any of a family of plants with flowers, related to the potato and including some poisonous plants such as deadly nightshade

nightshirt n a piece of men's clothing like a long loose shirt, made to be worn in bed

nihilism n 1 the belief that nothing has meaning or value 2 the belief that social and political organization should be destroyed, even if nothing better can take its place — -ist n — -istic adj

nil n 1 nothing; zero 2 (in a sport) a total of no points

nimble adj 1 quick, light, and neat in movement; agile: nimble fingers 2 quick in thinking or understanding: a nimble imagination — ~ness n — -bly adv

nimbus n **-buses** or **-bi** 1 a dark spreading cloud that may bring rain or snow ⏵CLOUD 2 a shining cloud or ring often shown in pictures around the heads of gods, angels, and holy people —compare HALO

nincompoop n esp. spoken a stupid person; fool

nine adj, n, pron 1 the number 9 2 (in the game of golf) the first or last half of a course of 18 holes 3 **nine times out of ten** esp. spoken almost always

nines n esp. spoken **dressed (up) to the nines** wearing one's best and most formal clothes

nineteen adj, n, pron the number 19 — ~th adj, adv, n, pron

ninety adj, n, pron **-ties** the number 90 — -tieth adj, n, adv, pron

ninny n **-nies** esp. spoken a silly foolish person

ninth adj, adv, n, pron 9th

nip¹ v **-pp-** 1 to catch (something or someone) in a tight sharp hold between 2 points or surfaces: The dog nipped the postman on the leg 2 to cut off by this means: to nip off the corner of the page with scissors 3 esp. spoken to go quickly; hurry: I'll nip out and buy a newspaper 4 **nip in the bud** to do harm to (something), esp. so as to keep from succeeding

nip² n 1 a coldness or cold wind: a nip in the air 2 the act or result of nipping

nip³ n esp. spoken a small amount of a strong alcoholic drink

nipper n esp. spoken a child, esp. a boy

nippers n any of various tools like pliers which are used for nipping

nipping adj sharp or cold; harsh: a nipping wind

nipple n one of the areas of darker skin which stand out from the breasts and through which a baby may suck milk from a woman —compare TEAT

nippy adj **-pier, -piest** 1 quick in movement 2 having a nip in the air — -piness n

Nirvana n 1 (in Buddhism and Hinduism) the state of rest and freedom from desire gained through self-control, and leading to union with the spirit of the universe 2 peace and happiness of mind

nisi SEE DECREE NISI

nit¹ n 1 an egg of an insect, usu. a louse, that is sometimes found in people's hair 2 a louse

nit² n offensive esp. spoken a nitwit

nitpicking adj, n offensive esp. spoken complaining, arguing, reasoning, etc., by noticing small and unimportant differences

nitrate n any of several chemicals containing nitrogen and oxygen in the group NO_3, used mainly as fertilizer ⊸ ECOLOGY

nitric adj technical (of a chemical compound) containing nitrogen: nitric oxide —see also NITROUS

nitric acid n a powerful corrosive acid (HNO_3) which is used in explosives and other chemical products

nitrogen n a gas that is an element without colour or smell, that forms most of the earth's air, and that is found in all living things ⊸ ECOLOGY

nitrogen fixation n the processes (often carried by bacteria in the soil) by which nitrogen from the air is changed into compounds of nitrogen that can be used by living things, such as plants

nitroglycerine, -rin n a type of powerful liquid explosive —see also DYNAMITE; compare TNT

nitrous adj (of a chemical compound) containing nitrogen (esp. with a lower valency than in nitric compounds): nitrous acid

nitwit n esp. spoken a silly foolish person

no¹ adv 1 (in an answer expressing refusal or disagreement): 'Will you come to the match?' 'No, thanks.' | 'Is it raining' 'No, it's snowing' 2 not any: I'm afraid he's no better today 3 (after or) not: You'll have to do it, whether or no

no² adj 1 not a; not one; not any: no flowers in the garden | no sugar | I have no umbrella 2 not any.... allowed: No smoking | No bicycles against this wall

no³ n noes an answer, decision, or vote —opposite aye

no. nos. abbrev. for: number

Noah's ark SEE ARK

nob n esp. spoken & offensive humour a person with money and a high social position

no ball n an act of bowling the ball in a way that is not allowed by the rules (in cricket)

nobble v -bled, -bling sl 1 to get the attention of (someone), esp. in order to persuade or gain a favour 2 to prevent (a racehorse) from winning, esp. by the unlawful use of drugs

Nobel prize n any of several prizes given in Sweden and Norway each year for important work in science, literature, and towards world peace

nobility n -ties 1 (in certain countries) the group of people of the highest social rank, who have titles 2 the quality or condition of being noble in rank 3 also nobleness — the quality or condition of being noble in character or appearance

noble¹ adj 1 of high quality, esp. morally; worthy; unselfish 2 admirable in appearance; grand: a noble-looking horse 3 of a high social rank with a title: a noble family 4 (of metals like gold and silver) not chemically changed by air —compare BASE METAL — nobly adv

noble² also nobleman (fem.noblewoman)— n a person belonging to the class of the nobility; peer

noblesse oblige French (a French sentence which means) 'People with high rank, money, good education, etc., must use these things for the good of everyone'

nobody¹ also no one— pron not anybody; no person: Nobody called while you were out. | She likes nobody and nobody likes her

nobody² n -ies a person of no importance: I want to be famous! I'm tired of being a nobody

nocturnal adj esp. written or technical of, done or happening, or active at night: a nocturnal bird —opposite diurnal — ~ly adv

nocturne n a work of art inspired by the night, esp. a piece of piano music in a quiet and thoughtful style : Chopin's nocturnes

nod¹ v -dd- 1 to bend (one's head) forwards and down, esp. to show agreement or give a greeting or sign 2 to let one's head drop in falling asleep while sitting down: I nodded off in the meeting and didn't hear what was said 3 to bend downwards or forwards: flowers nodding in the wind

nod² n an act of nodding

node n 1 a swelling or roundish lump, as on a tree trunk or a person's body 2 technical a point where half lines meet 3 a place where branches meet or join, as on a plant or in any treelike pattern or network 4 technical (in a system, body, etc., moving in waves) a point which remains still — -dal adj

no doubt adv almost certainly or very probably: No doubt you would like a drink. | No doubt he was just trying to help, but he's spoiled our work —see DOUBT (USAGE)

nodular adj of, related to, or marked by nodules

nodule n a small round mass or lump as of a mineral, or esp. a small round swelling on a plant or a person's body

Noel n poetic Christmas

noes pl. of NO

noggin n a small amount (usu. a gill) of an alcoholic drink

noise n 1 meaningless unwanted sound, esp. a the sound heard in any public place b unwanted sound which keeps wanted sounds on radio, telephones, etc., from being heard clearly 2 an unmusical sound that is difficult to describe or strange: What's wrong with my car? The engine makes funny noises — ~less adj — ~lessly adv — ~lessness n

noise about also noise abroad, noise around— v adv noised, noising about to make (a report, rumour, or news) public

noisome adj literature unpleasant; annoying: rude and noisome behaviour

noisy adj -ier, -iest making or full of noise: a

very noisy office — **noisily** *adv* — **noisiness** *n*

nom. *abbrev. for:* nominative

nomad *n* **1** a member of a tribe which travels about: *the nomads of the desert* **2** a person who travels with no fixed aim —compare VAGRANT — ~ic *adj* — ~ically *adv*

no-man's -land *n* the belt of land between 2 opposing armies

nom de plume *n* **noms de plume** *French* PEN NAME

nomenclature *n* a system of naming things, esp. in science: *medical nomenclature* —compare TERMINOLOGY

nominal *adj* **1** in name or form but usu. not in reality: *the nominal head of the government* **2** (of an amount of money) very small; negligible: *sold at a nominal price* **3** technical (of the price of something which is not often bought and sold) based on present opinion but not on what has been paid in the past — ~ly *adv*

nominate *v* **-nated, -nating** **1** to suggest (someone) for election to a position **2** to appoint (someone) to such a position — **-tion** *n*

nominative¹ *adj* showing esp. that a word is the subject of a verb, usu. by special endings or other forms

nominative² *n* (esp. in such languages as Latin, Greek, German, etc.) the set of forms (CASE) showing esp. that a word is the subject of a verb: *Put this noun into the nominative*

nominee *n* a person who has been nominated

nonagenarian *adj, n* (a person who is) 90 or more and less than 100 years old

nonaligned *adj* (of a country) not usually supporting the actions of any particular powerful country or group of countries —compare THIRD WORLD — **-lignment** *n*

nonce *n* **for the nonce** esp. spoken for the present time

nonchalant *adj* showing unforced calmness, and often lack of interest; cool — **-lance** *n* — ~ly *adv*

noncombatant *n* a person, esp. a member of the army or other military force (such as a chaplain, doctor, etc.), not part of or used in actual fighting

noncommissioned officer *n* a member of the army, navy, etc., (such as corporal, sergeant, or petty officer) who is lower in rank than a commissioned officer but has some responsibility to command others —compare COMMISSIONED OFFICER

noncommittal *adj* not expressing a clear opinion or a clear intention or promise to do something — ~ly *adv*

nonconductor *n* a material which allows little or no sound, heat, or esp. electricity to pass through it —compare INSULATOR

nonconformist *adj, n* (of, concerning, or being) a person who does not follow some customary way of living, acting, thinking, etc.: *nonconformist habits of dressing*

Nonconformist¹ *n* a member of a Nonconformist religious group

Nonconformist² *adj* of, being, or concerning any of several Christian religious groups which have separated from the Church of England

nonconformity also **nonconformism**— *n* the refusal to follow some customary practice

Nonconformity *n* the ideas and practices of Nonconformist groups

noncontributory *adj* (of a pension plan) paid for by the employer only and not by the employee

nondescript *adj* without any strong or interesting qualities; very ordinary-looking; dull

none¹ *pron* **1** no amount or part: *None of that money on the table is mine* **2** not one: *None of my friends ever come to see me* **3** **have none of** esp. written to take no part in, not allow, or not accept: *I'll have none of your stupid ideas!* **4** **none other** (*used for expressing surprise*) no one else: *It's none other than Tom! We thought you were in Africa!* —see EITHER (USAGE)

none² *adv* **1** **none the** in no way: *He spent 2 weeks in hospital but he's none the better for it* **2** **none the wiser** not knowing about or not discovering a fact, secret, trick, etc.; unaware: *If we take only one piece of cake, mother will be none the wiser* **3** **none too** not very or not at all: *The service in this restaurant is none too fast*

nonentity *n* **-ties** **1** a person without much ability, character, or importance **2** the condition of being unimportant

nonesuch *n* literature a person or thing without equal

nonetheless *adv* nevertheless

nonfiction *n* literature or writing that deals with facts or events —compare FICTION

nonflammable also **noninflammable**— *adj* difficult or impossible to set on fire —opposite **inflammable**

nonmetal *n* technical an element, such as silicon or oxygen, that is not a metal

nonpareil *adj, n* literature (a person or thing) so excellent as to have no equal

nonpayment *n* failure to pay (bills, tax, etc.): *in trouble for nonpayment of his last year's tax*

nonplus *v* **-ss-** to cause (someone) to be surprised and not know what to think or do

nonsense *n* **1** speech or writing with no meaning or that goes against good sense **2** foolish behaviour: *a strict teacher who would stand no nonsense* **3** humorous and fanciful poetry usu. telling a rather meaningless story: *Edward Lear's wonderful nonsense*

nonsensical *adj* being, showing, or full of nonsense; foolish or absurd — ~ly *adv*

non sequitur *n* **non sequiturs** esp. written & Latin a statement which does not follow from the facts or arguments which are given; an incorrect piece of reasoning

nonsmoker *n* **1** a person who does not smoke **2** a railway carriage where smoking is not allowed

non464

nonstandard *adj* (of words, expressions, pronunciations, etc.) not usually used by educated careful native speakers of a language
nonstarter *n esp. spoken* a person or idea without any chance of success
nonstick *adj* (as of a cooking pan) having a specially treated smooth inside surface that food will not stick to
nonstop *adv* without a pause or interruption: *Fly nonstop to New York!|music playing nonstop all night* — **nonstop** *adj*
non-U *adj humour* (esp. of words or behaviour) not of the upper class —opposite U
nonunion *n* not belonging to a trade union; not unionised: *nonunion workmen*
nonverbal *adj* not carried out or marked by the use of words: *Gestures are a nonverbal means of expression* — ~**ly** *adv*
nonviolence also **nonviolent resistance** (*now rare*) **passive resistance**— *n* opposition without using force or violence for fighting, shown esp. by not obeying laws or orders — **-nt** *adj*
nonwhite *adj, n* (a person) not of the division of mankind usu. described as white-skinned
noodle *n* a usu. long thin piece of a paste made from flour, water, and eggs. The pieces are boiled until soft and eaten in soups, with meat, etc.
nook *n* 1 a small space in a corner of a room 2 a sheltered and private place: *resting in a shady nook in the garden* 3 **nooks and crannies** hidden or little-known places: *search every nook and cranny* (=look everywhere)
noon *n* the middle of the day; 12 o'clock in the daytime
no one *pron* nobody
noose *n* 1 a ring formed by the end of a cord, rope, etc., which closes more tightly as it is pulled 2 a rope with such a ring in it, used to hang a person; death by hanging
nor *conj* 1 (used between the 2 or more choices after *neither*): *just warm, neither cold nor hot* —see NEITHER 2 (used before the 2nd, 3rd, etc., choices after *not*) and/or not: *The job cannot be done by you nor me nor anyone else* 3 and also not: *I don't want to go, nor will I* (=and I won't). | *We have many enemies; nor can we be sure of all our friends* see NEITHER (USAGE)
Nordic *adj* 1 of or related to the Germanic peoples of northern Europe 2 of or related to Scandinavia
Norfolk jacket *n* a man's short coat with a belt and with pleats down the right and left sides in front and at the back
norm *n* a standard of proper behaviour or principle of right and wrong; rule: *social norms*
normal *adj* 1 according to what is expected, usual, or average 2 (of a person) developing in the expected way; without any disorder in mind or body: *a normal child* 3 *technical* at right angles; perpendicular 4 *technical* (of a chemical solution) of the strength of 1 gram per litre — ~**ity** *n*
normal distribution *n technical* (in statis-

tics) a distribution such that the mean, median, and mode are equal, and there is symmetry in the frequency curve about the mean
normalize, -ise *v* **-ized, -izing** to make or become normal — **-ization** *n*
normally *adv* 1 in a normal way or to a normal degree 2 in the usual conditions; ordinarily
Norman *adj* 1 of or concerning the northern French people who conquered England in the 11th century ⌐⌐HISTORY 2 (of buildings in Britain) built in or related to a style of building (**Norman architecture**) in this period; in the romanesque style: *a Norman church*
north¹ *adv* towards the north: *Edinburgh is a long way north of London*
north² *n* 1 (the direction of) one of the 4 main points of the compass, which is on the left of a person facing the rising sun ⌐⌐GLOBE 2 (of a wind) (coming from) this direction: *a cold north wind*
North *n* the part of a country which is further north than the rest USAGE **North, South, East,** and **West** are clear divisions of the earth's surface. Uncertain divisions are usually **Northern, Southern, Eastern,** or **Western**: *South Africa* but *Southern England* | *the* **North** *Pole* but *Northern Europe*
northbound *adj* travelling or leading towards the north: *northbound traffic | the northbound carriageway*
northeast¹ *adv* towards the northeast
northeast² *n* 1 (the direction of) the point of the compass which is half-way between north and east ⌐⌐GLOBE 2 (of a wind) (coming from) this direction: *a northeast wind*
northeasterly *adj* 1 towards or in the northeast 2 (of a wind) coming from the northeast
northeastern *adj* of or belonging to the northeast part of anything
northeastward *adj* going towards the northeast
northeastwards *adv* towards the northeast
northerly *adj* 1 towards or in the north: *the northerly shore* 2 (of a wind) coming from the north: *a cold northerly wind*
northern *adj* of or belonging to the north part of anything: *The northern half of the Earth is called the Northern hemisphere* —see NORTH (USAGE)
Northerner *n* a person living in or coming from the northern part of a country
northern lights *n* see AURORA
northernmost *adj esp. written* furthest north: *the northernmost parts of Scotland*
north pole *n* 1 (the lands around) the most northerly point on the surface of the earth, or of another planet ⌐⌐GLOBE 2 the point in the sky to the north, around which stars seem to turn
northward *adj* going towards the north: *in a northward direction*
northwards *adv* towards the north: *They travelled northwards*

northwest¹ *adv* towards the northwest
northwest² *n* **1** (the direction of) the point of the compass which is half-way between north and west ⟶GLOBE **2** (of a wind) (coming from) this direction: *a northwest wind*
northwesterly *adj* **1** towards or in the northwest **2** (of a wind) coming from the northwest
northwestern *adj* of or belonging to the northwest part of anything
northwestward *adj* going towards the northwest: *in a northwestward direction*
northwestwards *adv* towards the northwest
Norwegian *adj* of or concerning the people, language, et   Norway ⟶LANGUAGE
nose¹ *n* **1** the part of the face above the mouth, which in human beings stands out from the face, through which air is breathed, and which is the organ of smell **2** *esp. spoken* this organ regarded as representing too great interest in things which do not concern one: *Keep your nose out of my affairs!* **3 a** the sense of smell: *a dog with a good nose* **b** the ability to find or recognize things: *Follow your nose and see what you can find out* **4** the front end of something, such as a car, plane, tool, or gun **5 lead (someone) by the nose** *esp. spoken* to control (someone) completely **6 pay through the nose** *esp. spoken* to pay a great deal too much money **7 turn up one's nose at** to consider (something) not good enough to eat, take part in, etc.
nose² *v*   **nosed, nosing** **1** to push with the nose **2** to move or push (oneself, a vehicle, etc.) ahead slowly or carefully
nosebag *n* a bag hung around a horse s head to hold its food
nosedive *v*   **-dived, -diving** (of an aircraft) to drop suddenly with the nose pointing straight down — **nosedive** *n*
nosegay *n*   **-gays** *literature* a small bunch of flowers, usu. to be worn on a dress
nose out *v adv esp. spoken* to discover by close searching
nosh¹ *v sl* to eat — **~er** *n*
nosh² *n sl* food
nosh-up *n sl* a usu. good or big meal
nostalgia *n* fondness for something formerly known or for some period in the past — **-gic** *adj* — **-gically** *adv*
nostril *n* either of the 2 openings at the end of the nose, through which air is drawn
nostrum *n offensive* a medicine of doubtful value and unknown contents —compare PANACEA
nosy, nosey *adj*   **-ier, -iest** *offensive & esp. spoken* interested in things that do not concern one — **nosiness** *n*
nosy parker *n esp. spoken* a nosy person
not *adv* **1** (used for changing a word or expression to one with the opposite meaning): *I will not pay that bill!* | *It's a cat, not a dog.* | *Not everyone likes that book.* | *(pompous) It's a not unwelcome piece of news* (= it is very welcome)

2 (used in place of a whole expression): *Are you coming or not?* | *Is she in? If not, could I speak to her sister?* —opposite **so** **3 not a** (used before a noun) no: *'How much did this cost?' 'Not a penny!'* **4 Not at all** (an answer to polite praise or thanks): *'Thanks for your trouble.' 'Not at all: I enjoyed it'* **5 not to say** *esp. spoken* and almost; or perhaps even: *He sounded impolite, not to say rude* USAGE **Not** can be shortened to **n't** when changing the following verbs to their opposite meaning: *is, are, was, were, has, have, had, do, does, did, can, could, would, should, must, ought, need, may, might, dare, used. Shall* **not** and *will* **not** can be shortened to *shan't, won't.* Otherwise **not** is not shortened. One cannot say *I hopen't.*
notable¹ *adj* worthy of notice; remarkable, important, or excellent — **-bility** *n*
notable² *n* a person of high rank, fame, or importance
notably *adv* noticeably, remarkably, or in a way which might attract attention; especially
notary also **notary public**— *n* **-ries** a person (in Britain usu. a solicitor) with the power in law to witness offically the signing of written statements
notation *n* (writing that uses) a set of written signs to describe the stated kinds of things: *musical notation* ⟶MUSIC
notch¹ *n* **1** a V-shaped cut in a surface or edge **2** a degree; step: *a good book, several notches above anything else by this writer*
notch² *v* **1** to make a notch in **2** *esp. spoken* to win or record (a victory or gain): *The team notched up their 3rd victory in a row*
note¹ *v* **noted, noting** **1** to pay attention to and remember. *Please note that this bill must be paid within 10 days* **2** to recognize; observe: *You may have noted that my address has changed* **3** to call attention to; show: *The newspaper does not note what happened next*
note² *n* **1 a** a musical sound, usu. of a particular length and pitch **b** a written sign for any of these sounds ⟶MUSIC **2 a** a quality of voice: *a note of anger in what he said* **b** any quality; element: *a note of carelessness in the way she acted* **3** a record or reminder in writing: *Make a note of how much money you spend* **4** a remark added to a piece of writing (as at the side or bottom of a page, or at the end) —compare FOOTNOTE **5** a short letter **6** a piece of paper money: *a pound note* —compare BANK NOTE **7 compare notes** to exchange one's experiences and opinions **8 mental note** something fixed in the mind or to be remembered **9 of note** of fame or importance: *a musician of note*
notebook *n* a book of plain paper in which notes may be written
noted *adj* well-known; famous: *a town noted for its cheeses*
notepaper *n* paper suitable for writing letters
noteworthy *adj* worthy of attention; notable
nothing¹ *pron* **1** no thing; not any thing: *There's nothing in the box.* | *Nothing's left.* | *I got it for nothing.* | *All that work was for nothing! He*

doesn't want it. | It's nothing serious **2 not... for nothing** esp. spoken not without some (stated or understood) reason: 'What delicious food!' 'I didn't go to cookery classes for nothing!' **3 to say nothing of** without even considering

nothing² n a thing or person with no value or importance

nothingness n **1** the state of being nothing; not being: Is there only nothingness after death? **2** emptiness or worthlessness: Her husband's death left a feeling of nothingness in her heart

notice¹ n **1 a** a warning or information about something to happen: Can you be ready at short notice? **b** formal instruction that a person will no longer live or work in a place **2** attention: Take particular notice of the road signs **3** a usu. short written statement of information or instruction **4** a review: The new play got mixed notices **5 until further notice** esp. written from now until another change is made: This office will close at 5 o'clock until further notice

notice² v **noticed, noticing** to pay attention (to) with the eyes, other senses, or mind: Did you notice whether I locked the door?

noticeable adj that can be noticed; worth noticing **— -ably** adv

notice board n a board on a wall for notices

notifiable adj technical (esp. of certain diseases) needing by law to be reported to an office of public health

notification n **1** the action or an act of notifying **2** something in writing which gives notice

notify v **-fied, -fying** to tell (someone), esp. formally

notion n an idea, belief, or opinion (in someone's mind): I haven't the faintest notion what you're talking about

notional adj abstract or imaginary

notoriety n the state or quality of being notorious

notorious adj widely and unfavourably known: a notorious thief — see FAMOUS (USAGE) **— ~ly** adv

notwithstanding¹ prep in spite of: Notwithstanding his objections the marriage took place

notwithstanding² adv however; nevertheless

nougat n sweet paste made of sugar, nuts, etc.

nought n (the figure) 0; zero

noughts and crosses a game played on a pattern of 9 squares, on which one tries to make 3 noughts or 3 crosses

noun n a word naming a person, thing, quality, action, etc., that can be used as the subject or object of a verb. Nouns are marked n in this dictionary —compare PRONOUN

nourish v **1** to give good health or growth: nourishing food **2** to keep alive: to nourish a dislike **— ~ment** n

nouveau riche n **nouveaux riches** French usu. offensive a person with new wealth

nova n ~s or **-vae** a star which suddenly becomes much brighter and then gradually becomes fainter —compare SUPERNOVA

novel¹ adj new, esp. clever or strange: a novel suggestion

novel² n a long written story, usu. in prose, about invented people: Dickens wrote many novels **— ~ist** n: the novelist Dickens ☞LITERATURE

novelette n a short usu. light novel

novelty n **-ties 1** the state or quality of being novel **2** something new and unusual: Hard work was no novelty to him **3** an unusual cheap small object: a novelty toy

November n the 11th month of the year

novice n **1** a person without experience; beginner: a novice at swimming **2** a member of a religious group training to become a monk or nun

novitiate, noviciate n **1** the period or state of training as a novice **2** the house of a religious group where novices are trained

now¹ adv **1** at this time; at present: We used to live in Bristol but now we live in Bath **2** (used to attract attention): Be careful, now! **3** calculating from or up to the present: He's been dead for years now

now² n the present moment: Now's the time for action

nowadays adv (esp. in comparisons with the past) in these modern times; now: We used to drive a lot, but nowadays petrol costs too much

no way adv sl (as an answer) no; certainly not

nowhere adv **1** not anywhere; (in/at/to) no place: nowhere to be found | The old lady went nowhere **2** (to/at) no purpose or result: That will get you nowhere

noxious adj harmful, unhealthy: noxious chemicals | a noxious book **— ~ly** adv **— ~ness** n

nozzle n a spout on a hose, pipe, etc.

nth adj **the nth degree/power** the highest, greatest, furthest, etc., degree or form: dull to the nth degree USAGE The letter n is usu. printed in italic.

nuance n a slight delicate quality or difference in colour, meaning, etc.

nub n **1** a stub or stump **2** a lump: a nub of coal **3** the point of real importance in an argument, story, etc.: the nub of the argument

nubile adj young and sexually attractive; marriageable

nuclear adj **1** of, concerning, or being a nucleus ☞ATOM **2** of, concerning, or using atomic energy, or the atom bomb: nuclear physics

nuclear disarmament n the giving up of atomic weapons

nuclear family n **-lies** a family containing only a father, mother, and children

nuclear reactor also **reactor, atomic pile**— n a large machine for the controlled production of atomic energy

nucleic acid n see DNA, RNA

nucleus *n* -**clei** **1** an original or central point, part, or group inside a larger thing, group, organization, etc.: *100 books as the nucleus of a new library* **2** the central part of an atom, made up of neutrons and protons ⊐ATOM **3** a part in or near the centre of many cells of living matter that acts as a control centre and contains the chromosomes

nude¹ *adj* not wearing clothes; naked: *nude swimming* — **nudity** *n*

nude² *n* **1** a usu. female nude person, esp. in a photograph or work of art **2** a work of art showing a nude person, often a woman **3** the state of being nude: *in the nude*

nudge¹ *v* **nudged, nudging** to touch or push gently: *nudged her to say it was time to go*

nudge² *n* a slight push

nudism *n* the practice of not wearing clothes — **-ist** *adj, n*

nugatory *adj* unimportant

nugget *n* a small rough lump of a precious metal

nuisance *n* a person, state of affairs, etc., that annoys: *Don't make a nuisance of yourself.* | *What a nuisance! I've forgotten my ticket*

null *adj technical* of, being, or concerning zero

null and void *adj* without force or effect in law

nullify *v* -**fied, -fying** to cause or declare to have no effect: *a claim nullified by the court* — **-ification** *n*

null set *n technical* EMPTY SET

numb¹ *adj* unable to feel anything: *numb with cold* — ~**ness** *n* — ~**ly** *adv*

numb² *v* to make numb: *fingers numbed with cold*

number¹ *n* **1** a member of the system used in counting and measuring; a written symbol for one of these, or a digit: *Let x be a number from 1 to 10.* | *page numbers in the right-hand corners* **2** (*before one of these, usu. written* No., *or* no.) (having) the stated size, place in order, etc.: *a number 9* (=size 9) (*shoe*) | *We live at no. 107 Church Street* —see also NUMBER ONE **3** (a) quantity or amount: *Members are few in number* **4** a group: *Their numbers were increased by new members* **5** a (copy of a) magazine printed at a particular time; issue **6** a piece of music: *She sang several numbers from the musical* **7** **opposite number** a person with the same position in another organization, team, etc. —see AMOUNT (USAGE)

number² *v* **1** to reach as a total; be . . . in number: *The books in the library number in the thousands* **2** to include or be included; count: *He numbers among the best writers* **3** to give a number to: *number the seats*

numberless *adj* too many to count

number one *n* **1** oneself and no one else: *Don't always think of number one* **2** the chief person in an organization **3** (the) highest in importance: *public enemy number one*

numberplate *n* a sign on a vehicle showing its official number

Numbers *n* the 4th book of the Bible

numeral *adj, n* (a sign) that represents a number —compare ROMAN NUMERAL, ARABIC NUMERAL

numerate *adj* having a general understanding of mathematics — **-racy** *n*

numerator *n* the number above the line in a fraction; : *5 is the numerator in* $\frac{5}{6}$ *and* $\frac{5}{x+y}$

numerical *adj* of, concerning, showing, or shown by a number or numbers: *numerical ability* — ~**ly** *adv*

numerology *n* the study of the magic meaning of numbers

numerous *adj* **1** many: *numerous books* **2** of large number: *Those birds have become more numerous lately* — ~**ly** *adv* — ~**ness** *n*

numismatics *n technical* the study or collection of coins and medals — **numismatic** *adj* — **-tist** *n*

numskull, numbskull *n sl* a stupid person

nun *n* a woman member of a religious order who swears to serve God by obedience, owning nothing, and not marrying —compare MONK, FRIAR

nunnery *n* -**ries** a building where nuns live; convent —compare MONASTERY

nuptial *adj* of or concerning marriage or the marriage ceremony

nurse¹ *n* **1** a person who cares for sick, hurt, or old people **2** also **nursemaid** — a woman employed to take care of a young child —compare NANNY **3** WET NURSE

nurse² *v* **nursed, nursing** **1** to give (a baby) milk from the breast **2** to act as or be a professional nurse **3** to take care of as or like a nurse: *He nursed her back to health* **4** to take care of someone suffering from: *This disease is very hard to nurse* **5** to use carefully so as to preserve: *nursed a drink all evening* **6** to hold (esp. a bad feeling) in the mind: *nursed a grudge*

nursery *n* -**ries** **1** a child's bedroom or playroom **2** a place where small children are looked after for a short time —compare PLAYGROUP, CRÈCHE, DAY NURSERY **3** a place where young plants and trees are grown for sale or replanting

nurseryman *n* -**men** a person who grows plants in a nursery

nursery rhyme *n* a short song or poem for children

nursery school also **kindergarten**— *n* a school for children below school age

nursing *n* the job of a nurse

nursing home *n* a place where people are cared for by nurses

nurture¹ *n* education, training, or development

nurture² *v* -**tured, -turing** **1** to give care and food to **2** to train, educate, or develop: *Nurture your mind*

nut *n* **1 a** a dry fruit with a kernel surrounded by a hard shell **b** this seed, which is eaten **2** a block, usu. of metal, with a threaded hole for screwing onto a bolt **3** *sl* a foolish or mad person:

He's crazy, he's a nut! **4** *sl* a person with a strong particular interest: *She's a Marlon Brando nut* —compare BUFF **5** *sl* one's head: *You must be off your nut* (=mad)! **6** a small lump of coal **7 a hard/tough nut to crack** a difficult question, person, etc. **8 do one's nut** *sl* to be very worried and/or angry

nutcase *n humour* a mad person

nutcracker *n* a tool for cracking the shell of a nut

nuthouse *n sl offensive* a psychiatric hospital

nutmeg *n* a small nut, used as a spice, from a tree grown on some South Pacific islands

nutria *n* the fur of the coypu

nutrient *adj, n* (a chemical or food) providing for life and growth

nutriment *n* nourishing food

nutrition *n* **1** providing or being provided with food; nourishment **2** the study of how the body uses food

nutritious *adj* valuable to the body as food; nourishing — ~ly *adv* — -tive *adj*

nuts *adj sl* **1** mad; foolish: *I'll go nuts if I have to wait much longer!* **2 nuts about/over** greatly interested in or attracted by: *nuts about flying | nuts over him*

nutshell *n* **1** the hard outer covering of a nut **2** a short description, explanation, etc. in a nutshell

nutty *adj* -tier, -tiest **1** tasting like, or filled with, nuts **2** *sl* mad; foolish — -tiness *n*

nuzzle *v* -zled, -zling **1** (esp. of an animal) to push with the nose: *The horse nuzzled up against me* **2** to press close: *She nuzzled up to him*

NW *abbrev. for:* northwest(ern)

nylon *n* a strong man-made elastic material, often made into cloth or thread ☞ REFINERY

nylons *n* women's nylon stockings

nymph *n* (in Greek and Roman literature) any of the less important goddesses of nature

O

O, o O's, o's *or* Os, os **1** the 15th letter of the English alphabet **2** (in speech) a zero

oaf *n* a stupid ungraceful person — ~ish *adj* — ~ishly *adv* — ~ishness *n*

oak *n* **1** any of several types of large tree with hard wood, common in northern countries **2** the wood of this

oak apple *n* a small round brown growth that forms on oak trees round the eggs of a type of wasp

oakum *n* small pieces taken from old rope and used for filling up small holes in the sides of wooden ships

OAP *abbrev. for:* OLD AGE PENSIONER

oar *n* a pole with a wide flat blade, used for rowing a boat —compare PADDLE

oarsman *fem.* **oarswoman**— *n* -men someone who rows a boat

oasis *n* -ses a place with trees and water in a desert

oast house *n* a building with a pointed top, for drying hops

oatcake *n* a flat bread or biscuit made of oatmeal

oath *n* **1** a solemn promise, or the form of words used in making this **2** an expression of strong feeling using religious or sexual words improperly **3 be on/under oath** *law* to have made a solemn promise to tell the truth

oatmeal *n* crushed grains of oats used for making cakes and breakfast food

oats *n* **1** a type of edible grain **2** oatmeal

obbligato *n* -tos *or* (*esp. technical*) -ti a musical accompaniment that forms an essential part of a work

obdurate *adj* stubborn — ~ly *adv* — -racy *n*

obedient *adj* doing what one is ordered to do; willing to obey — ~ly *adv* — -ence *n*

obeisance *n* a gesture to show respect or obedience

obelisk *n* **1** a tall pointed stone pillar **2** a dagger sign (†)

obese *adj* very fat — obesity *n*

obey *v* obeyed, obeying to fulfil the order of: *Obey your teachers*

obfuscate *v* -cated, -cating to confuse — -cation *n*

obituary *n* -ries a notice that someone has died

object¹ *n* **1** a thing **2** something or someone that attracts attention: *an object of interest/of fear* **3** purpose; aim **4** (in grammar) word(s) saying to whom or to what a preposition is most directly related (**object of a preposition**), who is concerned in the results of an action (**indirect object of a verb**), or to whom or to what something has been done (**direct object of a verb**), as shown, in that order, as follows: *In Rome John gave Mary a book* **5 no object** not a difficulty: *Money is no object*

object² *v* to be against something or someone: *Do you object to smoking?* — ~ion *n* — ~or *n*

objectionable *adj* unpleasant — -bly *adv*

objective¹ *adj* **1** existing outside the mind; real —compare SUBJECTIVE **2** not influenced by personal feelings; fair — ~ly *adv* — -tivity *n*

objective² *n* **1** the purpose of a plan **2** *technical* the lens of a microscope or telescope which is closest to the object being looked at ☞ TELESCOPE

objet d'art *n* objets d'art *French* an object, usu. small, of some artistic value

obligate *v* -gated, -gating **1** to have an obligation: *He felt obligated to visit his parents* **2** to place under an obligation: *He felt obligated to them for their kindness*

obligation n 1 a duty 2 **under an obligation** in moral debt

obligatory adj necessary; which mũst be done —opposites **voluntary, optional**

oblige v **obliged, obliging** 1 to make it necessary (to do something): *I feel obliged to say 'No'* 2 polite to do (someone) a favour: *Could you oblige me by opening the window?* 3 (I'm) much **obliged (to you)** polite (I'm) very grateful (to you)

obliging adj kind and eager to help — ~ly adv

oblique adj 1 indirect 2 in a sideways direction; sloping 3 (of an angle) more or less than 90°

obliterate v **-ated, -ating** to remove all signs of; destroy — **-ation** n

oblivion n the state of having forgotten or being forgotten

oblivious adj not noticing — ~ly adv — ~ness n

oblong adj, n (a figure) with 4 straight sides at right angles, longer than it is wide

obnoxious adj unpleasant; nasty — ~ly adv — ~ness n

oboe n a woodwind musical instrument, played by blowing through a double reed — **oboist** n

obscene adj indecent — ~ly adv — **-nity** n

obscure[1] adj 1 hard to understand 2 not well known — ~ly adv — **-rity** n

obscure[2] v **obscured, obscuring** to hide; make difficult to see

obsequious adj too eager to obey or serve

observance n 1 acting in accordance with a law, ceremony, or custom 2 an action performed as part of a religious ceremony

observatory n **-ries** a place from which scientists watch the stars

observe v **observed, observing** 1 to see and notice; watch carefully: *They were observed entering the bank* 2 to act in accordance with (law or custom, esp. religious) 3 to make a remark; say — **-vable** adj: *easily observable* — **-vably** adv — **-vant** adj: *an observant man* — **-vation** n *Keep him under observation | an observation post to watch the enemy | give me your observations on what's happened* — ~**r** n: *You can't speak at this meeting*-You're here as an observer

observing adj observant

obsess v to fill the mind continuously

obsession n a fixed idea from which the mind cannot be freed — **-ive** adj

obsessional adj 1 (of a person) having obsessions 2 (of an idea) causing obsessions 3 (of an illness) typically with obsessions

obsolescent adj becoming obsolete — **-cence** n

obsolete adj no longer used; out of date

obstacle n something which blocks the way

obstetrics n the branch of medicine concerned with the birth of children — **-ric(al)** adj — **-rician** n

obstinate adj 1 not easy to persuade or defeat 2 not willing to obey — ~ly adv — **-nacy** n

obstreperous adj noisy and uncontrolled — ~ly adv — ~ness n

obstruct v to block: *obstruct a road/a plan* — ~**ion** n : *an obstruction in the road*

obstructive adj intentionally obstructing — ~ly adv — ~ness n

obtain v to get — ~ **able** adj : *Is that record still obtainable?*

obtrude v **obtruded, obtruding** 1 to stick out, or cause to stick out 2 to be noticed or cause to be noticed, esp. when unwanted

obtrusive adj displeasingly obtruding — ~ly adv — ~ness n

obtuse adj 1 stupid 2 (of an angle) being between 90° and 180° ⊸MATHEMATICS 3 not pointed — ~ly adv — ~ness n

obverse n the front side of a coin or medal —opposite **reverse** — see also HEAD

obviate v **-ated, -ating** to clear away (a difficulty)

obvious adj easy to understand; clear — ~ly adv

ocarina n a type of small musical wind instrument

occasion[1] n 1 a particular time: *on that occasion* 2 a proper time for something: *A birthday is no occasion for tears* 3 a special event 4 the direct cause of other events 5 **have (no) occasion to** to have (no) reason to —see CHANCE (USAGE)

occasion[2] v to cause: *Your behaviour has occasioned (us) a lot of trouble*

occasional adj 1 not regular in time 2 written or intended for a special occasion — ~ly adv

Occident n esp. in literature *"the West"*, esp. *Europe and the Americas* —compare ORIENT — ~**al** n, adj

occult adj secret; magic and mysterious

occupation n 1 taking possession of; having in one's possession 2 a job; employment 3 a way of spending time — ~ **al** adj

occupational therapy n the treatment of illness of the body or mind through productive employment — **-pist** n

occupier n 1 a person who takes or has possession of 2 an occupant, esp. of a house

occupy v **-pied, -pying** 1 to take and hold possession of 2 to hold (an enemy's country, town, etc.) 3 to be in during a particular period of time: *occupy a bed/a taxi* 4 to fill: occupy space/a position/time — **-pant** n *occupant of the house* — **-pancy** n

occur v **-rr-** 1 to happen 2 to exist: *Such plants don't occur here*

occurrence n happening: *a rare occurrence*

occur to v prep to come to mind: *It's just occurred to me*

ocean n 1 the mass of water that covers most of the earth 2 a sea; part of this mass — ~**ic** adj

oceanography n the scientific study of the ocean — **-pher** n

ocelot n a type of large American wild cat

ochre n yellow earth used as a colouring matter, or its colour

o'clock adv (in telling time) exactly the hour stated: It's 9 o'clock

octagon n a flat figure (POLYGON) with 8 sides and 8 angles, or anything of this shape — ~**al** adj

octane n a number which shows the power and quality of petrol

octave n 1 a space of 8 degrees between musical notes 2 a musical note 8 degrees away from another, these played together, or played as a scale with the 6 notes in between 3 a group of 8 lines of poetry

octet n 1 a group of 8 people playing instruments or singing together, or a piece of music written for such a group 2 an octave in poetry

October n the 10th month of the year

octogenarian n a person aged between 80 and 89

octopus n **-puses** a deep-sea creature with 8 tentacles ☞EVOLUTION

ocular adj technical of the eyes

oculist n an optician

odd adj 1 strange; unusual 2 not part of a set: an odd shoe 3 occasional: odd job | odd moments 4 (after numbers) with rather more: 20-odd years 5 (of a whole number) not exactly divisible by 2: 1, 3, 5, etc., are odd —opposite even — ~ ly adv

oddball n esp. spoken a person who behaves strangely

oddity n **-ties** 1 strangeness 2 someone or something odd

odd-job man n **-men** a man who does odd jobs for pay

oddment n something left over or remaining

odds n 1 the probability of something happening: heavy odds against winning 2 at odds (with) in disagreement (with) 3 it/that makes no odds it/that makes no difference; has no importance 4 lay odds to offer odds 5 long odds odds that are strongly against (for example 100 to 1) 6 short odds odds that are not strongly against (for example, 2 to 1)

odds and ends also (sl) **odds and sods**— n small articles of different types without much value

odds-on adj very likely to win: odds-on favourite

ode n a type of usu. long poem

odious adj hateful; very unpleasant — ~**ly** adv

odium n widespread hatred

odour n a smell — ~**less** adj — **odorous** adj

odyssey n **-seys** esp. in literature a long adventurous journey

o'er adv, prep poetic over

oesophagus, esophagus n medical the food tube from the back of the mouth (PHARYNX) into the stomach ☞DIGESTION

oestrogen, estrogen n a substance produced esp. in the part of a female's body where eggs are formed (OVARY), which causes body changes in preparation for the production of young

oestrus cycle, estrus cycle n the set of changes which take place regularly over a fixed time in the parts of some female animals' bodies, but not those of women, concerned with sex and giving birth to young, in which the body gradually goes into, reaches, and then leaves the state in which it can produce young

of prep 1 (about qualities, possessions, etc.) belonging to: the roots of your hair 2 made from 3 containing: a bag of potatoes 4 (that is) one or some from the whole or all: several of my friends 5 made or done by: the shooting of the hunters | the plays of Shakespeare 6 that is/are: a friend of mine 7 done to: the shooting of the deer 8 connected or concerned with: the results of the experiment 9 that is: the city of New York 10 about: stories of adventure 11 that has: a woman of great charm 12 in relation to: east of Suez 13 (linking certain words in their own particular relationships with the words that complete the meaning of the phrase): a lover of good music (=one who loves) | He died of fever

off¹ adv 1 away; aside: drive off 2 in or into a state of being disconnected or removed: The handle came off. | with his shoes off 3 so as not to be in use: Turn the light/taps off 4 to or at a (stated) distance away: 2 miles off | several years off 5 so as to separate: cut off 6 to, into, or resulting in a state of nonexistence, completion, or discontinuance: kill off 7 away or free from regular work: have Monday off 8 better/worse off in a better/worse condition: You'd be better off with a bicycle 9 right/ straight off at once 10 well/badly off rich/poor —see BADLY-OFF, WELL-OFF

off² prep 1 not on; away from Keep off the grass 2 from (a support): Take the curtains off their hooks 3 away from, as when subtracting: cut a piece off 4 to or at a (stated) distance away from: The ship was blown off course. | We're going off the subject 5 (esp. of a road) leading from: a street off the High Street 6 in the sea near: an island off the coast 7 (of a person) no longer keen on or fond of; no longer taking (esp. medicine): He's off his food. | Bill's off drugs now —see also COME OFF it, off COLOUR, off the RECORD,

off³ adj 1 (of food) no longer good to eat or drink: That fish smells off 2 (of dishes in a restaurant) no longer being served 3 (of behaviour) not what one has a right to expect: I thought it was a bit off, not even answering my letter! 4 technical (of part of a horse or vehicle) being the right hand one of a pair of things —opposite near 5 not going to happen after having been arranged: The party's off 6 (of the runners in a race) started 7 (esp. of electrical apparatus) not in use 8 (of a time) unfortunate; quiet and dull:

one of his off days | *during the off season* **9** being the half of a cricket field to the right of a (right handed) batsman as he faces the bowler

offal *n* **1** parts of an animal which are not considered as good as the flesh for food (the heart, head, brains, etc.) **2** waste matter

offbeat *adj esp. spoken* unusual

off colour *adj* not well

offence *n* **1** a wrong; crime **2** something unpleasant **3** cause for hurt feelings: *give/cause offence to someone* | *take offence at something*

offend *v* **1** to do wrong **2** to cause displeasure to : *Her words offended me* — ~**er** *n*

offensive¹ *adj* **1** causing offence **2** attacking —opposite **defensive** — ~**ly** *adv* — ~**ness** *n*

offensive² *n* **1** a continued attack **2 take the offensive** to attack

offer¹ *v* **1** to hold out for acceptance or refusal: *She offered me £10, 000 for that book* **2** to express willingness: *offer to go*

offer² *n* **1** a statement offering (to do) something **2** that which is offered: *an offer of £5*

offering *n* something offered, esp. to God

offhand *adv, adj* **1** careless; disrespectful **2** at once, without time to consider: *I can't give an answer offhand* — ~**edly** *adv* — ~**edness** *n*

office *n* **1** a place where business, or written work connected with a business, is done **2** a place where a service is provided: *a ticket office* **3** a government department: *the Foreign Office* **4** employment and special duties: *the office of president* **5** a position of some importance, esp. in government: *in/out of office*

office boy (*fem.* **office girl**)— *n* **-boys** a boy employed to do some of the less important work in an office

officer *n* **1** a person in a position of command in the armed forces **2** a person who holds a position of some importance, esp. in government, a business, or a group **3** a policeman

offices *n* help (in the phrase **good offices**)

official¹ *n* a person who works in government — ~**dom** *n*

official² *adj* of or about a position of trust, power, and responsibility: *an official position* — opposite **unofficial** △ OFFICIOUS

officially *adv* **1** in an official manner **2** as (believed to have been) stated by officials: *Officially, he's on holiday*

officiate *v* **-ated, -ating** to act officially

officious *adj* too eager to give orders or to offer advice — ~**ly** *adv* — ~**ness** *n* △ OFFICIAL

offing *n* **in the offing** coming soon

off-licence *n* a shop where alcohol is sold to be taken away

off-load *v* to get rid of

off-peak *adj* less busy, or during less busy periods: *off-peak periods* | *off-peak prices*

offprint *n* a separately printed copy of a piece of writing that was originally part of a book, magazine, etc.

off-putting *adj* unpleasantly surprising and/or causing dislike —see PUT OFF

offset *v* **-tt-** to make up for

offside *adj, adv* **1** (in certain sports) in, of, or about a position in which play is not allowed —opposite **onside** **2** being on the right-hand side, esp. of an animal or of a car, road, etc. —opposite **nearside**

offspring *n* **offspring** the young of a human or animal

off-the-record *adj, adv* not to be written down in the notes of the meeting

off-white *n, adj* not (a) pure white

oft *adv poetic* often

often *adv* **1** (at) many times: *how often?* **2** usually: *Children often dislike homework*

ogle *v* **ogled, ogling** to look (at) with great, esp. sexual, interest

ogre *fem.* **ogress**— **1** (in stories) a large fierce man-like creature **2** a person who frightens others — **ogreish** *adj* — **ogreishly** *adv*

oh *interj* **1** (expressing surprise, fear, etc.) **2** (used before a name when calling someone)

ohm *n* (a standard measure of electrical resistance, equal to) the resistance which allows a current of a measured quantity (one AMPERE) to flow when a measured electrical force (one VOLT) is applied

oil¹ *n* any of several types of liquid used for burning, for making machines run easily, or for cooking ⌁REFINERY — **oily** *adj*

oil² *v* to put or rub oil on or into

oilcake *n* cattle food made from seeds after pressing out oil

oilcloth *n* cloth treated with oil to make it waterproof

oilfield *n* an area under which there is oil

oil-fired *adj* oil-burning

oil paint *n* oils

oil painting *n* the art of painting, or a picture painted, in oils

oilrig *n* machinery for getting oil from beneath the sea-bed ◉

oils *n* paints (esp. for pictures) containing oil —compare WATERCOLOUR

oilskin *n* cloth treated with oil to make it waterproof, or a garment made of this cloth

oil slick also **slick**— *n* a film of oil floating on water

ointment *n* a substance (often medicinal) containing oil or fat, to be rubbed on the skin

okapi *n* **-pis** *or* **pi** a type of rare African animal like a horse with a long neck, with black and white stripes on the legs

okay, OK¹ *adv, adi esp. spoken* **1** all right: *That car goes okay now* **2** (asking for, or expressing, agreement): *Let's go there, okay?*

okay, OK² *v, n* **okayed, OKed; okaying, OKing** *esp. spoken* (to give) approval or permission

old *adj* **1** advanced in age: *How old are you?* | *16 years old* **2** having lived, been in use, or continued for a longtime: *old people/shoes/friends* **3** former: *He got his old job back* **4** known for a long time: *the same old story* **5** (used for making a phrase stronger): *any old time* | *any old thing*

Oil production platform

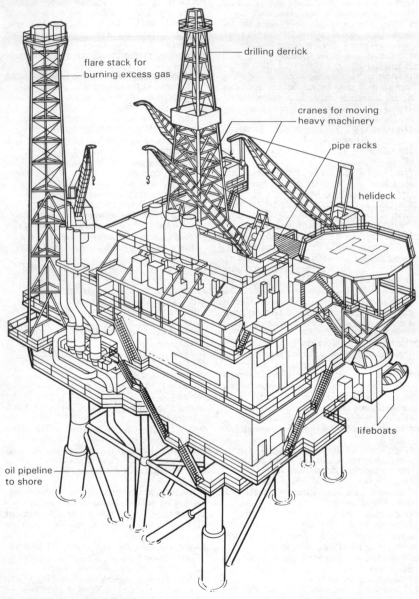

flare stack for
burning excess gas

drilling derrick

cranes for moving
heavy machinery

pipe racks

helideck

lifeboats

oil pipeline
to shore

An oil production platform like this one, in the North Sea, is built after oil has been discovered by test-drilling several boreholes in the area. The oil is either pumped ashore by pipeline, or is loaded into tankers. Pipelines require frequent maintenance, and divers often have to work at great depths and under hazardous conditions to build and repair them.

USAGE **Ancient** is used for very old things or civilizations, and sometimes of very old people. **Antique** means ' valuable ' as well as ' old '. **Venerable** means respected, honoured, and old. **Archaic,** and **antiquated,** and **old-fashioned** mean out-of-date (of ideas or people.) **Old fashioned** particularly applies to people. —compare ELDER
Old *adj* of an early period in the history of a language: *Old English* —compare MIDDLE
old age pension also **retirement pension**— *n* money paid regularly by the State to old people — ∼**er** *n* —compare SENIOR CITIZEN
old boy (*fem.* **old girl**)— *n* **-boys** **1** a former pupil of a school **2** a fellow; friend **3** *esp. spoken* an old person
old-boy network *n often offensive* **1** the tendency of former pupils of the same school to favour each other in later life **2** the former members of the public schools in England, esp. those in positions of importance
olden *adj literature & old use* long ago: *in olden days/times*
olde worlde *adj esp. spoken* of a too consciously old-fashioned style
old-fashioned *adj* (of a type that is) no longer common: *old-fashioned ideas* —compare FASHIONABLE; see OLD (USAGE)
old fogy, -gey *n* **-gies** someone whose ideas are too old-fashioned
old guard *n* the group of people who are against change
old hand *n* a very experienced person
old hat *adj* too old-fashioned
old lady *n* **-dies** *sl* one's wife or mother
old maid *n offensive* **1** an unmarried woman who is no longer young **2** a person (man or woman) who is very fussy
old man *n sl* one's husband or father
old master *n* an important painter of an earlier period, or a picture by such a painter
Old Nick also **Old Harry**— *n humour* the devil
old school *n* of the old school old-fashioned
old school tie *n* **1** a special tie worn to show that one has been a pupil at a certain school **2** the feeling that former pupils of the same school should help each other in later life
old-stager *n* an old hand
Old Testament *n* the first part of the Bible, containing ancient Hebrew writings about events before the birth of Christ —compare NEW TESTAMENT
old-timer *n* a person who has been somewhere or done something for a long time
old wives' tale *n* an ancient idea or belief
old woman *n* **-men** *sl* **1** one's wife or mother **2** *offensive* a person (usu. a man) who is difficult to please and often afraid
Old World *n* Europe, Asia, and Africa (the Eastern Hemisphere) —compare NEW WORLD
oleaginous *adj technical* oily; fatty
O level *n* ordinary level; the lower of the 2

standards of examination in the GCE —compare A LEVEL
olfactory *adj medical* of or about the sense of smell
oligarchy *n* **-chies** government or rule, or a state governed, by a group, or the ruling group
oligopoly *n* **-lies** something controlled or supplied by only a small number of people or groups: *The petrol market is an oligopoly* —compare MONOPOLY
olive *n* **1** a tree grown in the Mediterranean countries **2** the small egg-shaped fruit of this tree, used for food and for its oil (**olive oil**) **3** also **olive green**— a dull greyish-green
olive branch *n* a sign of peace
Olympiad *n* the modern Olympic Games
Olympian *n, adj* (like or connected with) any of the more important ancient Greek gods
Olympic *adj* of or connected with the Olympic Games
Olympic Games also **Olympics**— *n* Olympic Games **1** modern international sports events held once every 4 years **2** sports events held in ancient Greece once every 4 years
ombudsman *n* **-men** a person appointed by a government to receive and report on any complaints made by ordinary people against the government or the public service
omega *n* the 24th and last letter of the Greek alphabet (Ω ω)
omelet, -lette *n* eggs beaten together and fried
omen *n* a sign that something is going to happen in the future: *a good/bad omen* —compare PORTENT
ominous *adj* being a bad sign: *ominous black clouds* —compare PORTENTOUS — ∼**ly** *adv*
omit *v* **-tt-** to leave not included or not done — **omission** *n*
omnibus *n* **1** a book containing several works, esp. by one writer: *a Dickens omnibus* —compare ANTHOLOGY **2** old use a bus
omnipotent *adj* all-powerful — **-ence** *n*
omnipresent *adj* present everywhere — **-ence** *n*
omniscient *adj* all-knowing — **-ence** *n*
omnivore *n* an animal that eats all kinds of foods
omnivorous *adj* **1** eating both plant and animal food —compare HERBIVOROUS, CARNIVOROUS **2** interested in everything: *an omnivorous reader*
on¹ *prep* **1** also **upon**— (so as to be) touching; above and touching: *something on the table | a ring on my finger* **2** also **upon**— attached to **3** also **upon**— towards: *on my right | to march on Rome* **4** also **upon**— about: *a book on breeding rabbits* **5 a** during; at the time of: *on Tuesday | on June 1st* **b** also **upon**— at or directly after the event of: *on his appointment as manager* **6** also **upon**— by means of; using: *travel on the train | live on potatoes* **7** in a state of: *on purpose | on holiday* —see also **on one's** OWN, **on the other** HAND
on² *adv* **1** continuously: *He worked on right through lunchtime* **2** further; forward: *Shall we*

go on? **3** so as to be in use: *Switch the radio on* | *Put the alarm on for 7 o'clock* **4** so as to fasten to something: *sew the button on* **5** (of a clock) forward **6** **not on** *esp. spoken* impossible to do: *You can't refuse now - it's just not on!*

on³ *adj* **1** in use; working properly: *Is the gas on?* | *The radio's on but it isn't working* **2** happening or about to happen; performing or being performed: *There's a new play on tonight.* | *Is the match still on?* (= is it now taking place? *or* will it take place as arranged?) **3** being the half of a cricket field to the left of a (right-handed) batsman as he faces the bowler

once¹ *adj* **1** on one occasion: *I've done it once* **2** some time ago: *He once knew her* **3** **all at once** suddenly **4** **at once a** without delay: *Do it at once!* **b** at the same time: *Don't all speak at once!* **5** **once (and) for all** for the last time **6** **once or twice** several times; a few times **7** **once upon a time** some time ago

once² *n* on one occasion: *Do it just this once*

once³ *conj* from the moment that: *Once printed, this dictionary will be very popular!*

once-over *n* a quick examination

oncoming *adj* coming closer or towards one

one¹ *adj, n* **1 a** the number 1: *twenty-one* | *one o'clock* **b a:** *one/a thousand* (= 1, 000) | *one/a litre of wine* **c** (in the phrase **one of**): *one of your friends* **2** a certain: *one Sunday* **3** (esp. before past or future times) some: *one day soon* **4** the same: *of one mind* **5** (the) only necessary and desirable: *the one person for this job* **6** (as opposed to another, the other, *etc.*) a particular example or type (of): *He can't tell one tree from another* **7 a one** a bold amusing person: *Oh, you are a one!* **8 a right one** a fool **9 be one up (on someone)** to have the advantage (over someone) —see also ONE-UPMANSHIP **10** **one and the same** the very same

one² *pron* **1** (*used instead of a noun phrase that means a single thing or person*): *I haven't a pen; can you lend me one?* **2** any person: *One should do one's duty* USAGE 1 Do not use **ones** after **these** or **those**: *Do you want these* **ones** *or those* **ones?** Say: *Do you want these or those?* 2 **One** should be followed by **one's** and **oneself**: *One should wash oneself/one's hair regularly.* 3 It is now thought rather silly to use **one** too often instead of **I, me**, when talking about oneself.

one another *pron* each other

one-armed bandit *also* **fruit machine—** *n sl* a gambling machine with one long handle

one-horse *adj* small and uninteresting: *a one-horse town*

one-man band *n* someone who does an activity all on his own

one-piece *adj* (esp. of a bathing suit) made in one piece only

onerous troublesome: *an onerous duty* — ~ly *adv* — ~ness *n*

oneself *pron* **1** (*reflexive form of* ONE): *One can't enjoy oneself if one is too tired* **2** (*strong form of* ONE): *One can often make better cakes*

oneself than the kind the baker sells **3 to oneself** for one's own private use —see ONE (USAGE)

one-sided *adj* **1** seeing only one side (of a question); unfair **2** with one side much stronger than the other — ~ly *adv* — ~ness *n*

onetime *adj* former

one-track mind *n* a mind that thinks of only one thing at a time

one-upmanship *n humour* the art of getting an advantage over others by almost (but not quite) unlawful means

one-way *adj* moving or allowing movement in only one direction

onion *n* a round white vegetable, strong smelling, much used in cooking

onlooker *n* a person who watches something happening

only¹ *adj* having no others in the same group

only² *adv* **1** and nothing or no one else: *I had only 5 pence.* | *I only touched it!* | *Only the goalkeeper can handle the ball* USAGE In writing, put **only** directly before the part of the sentence that it concerns: *Only John saw the lion* (=no one else saw it). | *John only saw the lion* (=he didn't shoot it) etc.

only³ *conj* but: *You may go, only come back*

onomatopoeia *n* the formation of words by imitating natural sounds (as when cuckoo names the bird that makes that sound) — **-poeic** *adj*

onrush *n* a strong movement forward — ~ing *adj*

onset *n* the beginning (of something bad)

onside *adj, adv* not offside

onslaught *n* a fierce attack

onto *prep* to a position or point on: *He jumped onto/on the horse*

onus *n* duty; responsibility or blame

onward *adj* directed or moving forward

onwards *adv* forward in time or space: *from today onwards* | *moving onwards across the desert*

onyx *n* a precious stone having bands of various colours in it

oodles *n sl* lots: *oodles of cream*

oof *interj, n* often humour (a word like the sound that people make when hit in the stomach)

oomph *n sl* energy

oops *interj* (a word said when someone has made an ungraceful mistake)

oops-a-daisy *interj* **1** (an expression used when helping someone to climb over or onto something) **2** humour (an expression used when someone falls down)

ooze¹ *n* mud or thick liquid, as at the bottom of a river — **oozy** *adj*

ooze² *v* **oozed, oozing** to pass or flow slowly: *The meat oozed fat*

op *n* an operation

Op *abbrev for:* opus: *Beethoven's Op 106*

opal *n* a precious stone that looks like milky water with colours in it

opalescent *adj* like an opal — **-cence** *n*

opaque *adj* **1** not allowing light to pass

through **2** hard to understand — **-acity** *n* —
~**ly** *adv* — ~**ness** *n*
op art *n* a form of modern art (optical art) using
patterns that play tricks on the eyes ⇱PUZZLE
open¹ *adj* **1** not shut **2** not enclosed: *open
fields* **3** not blocked: *An open river is one without ice* **4** not covered: *an open boat* **5** not fastened: *an open shirt* **6** not finally decided or
answered: *an open question* **7** not closed to new
ideas or experiences: *an open mind* **8** not filled:
The job is still open **9** not hidden: *open hatred*
10 not hiding anything; honest: *Let's be open with
each other* **11** ready for business: *The bank isn't
open yet* **12** ready for use: *She kept her bank
account open* **13** that anyone can enter: *an open
competition* **14** spread out; unfolded: *The
flowers are open* **15** (of a cheque) not crossed
open² *v* **1** to make or become open **2** to spread
out or unfold: *to open a book* **3** to start or cause
to start **4** to start or cause to start the usual
activities: *to open a new hospital* **5** to make or
make usable (a passage) by unblocking it **6 open
fire** to start shooting —see also OPEN OUT
open³ *n* **1** the outdoors **2 in(to) the open** (of
opinions, secrets, etc.) in(to) general knowledge
opencast *adj* of mining from an open hole in the
ground
open-ended *adj* without any definite end, aim,
or time limit set in advance
opener *n* **1** a person or thing that opens something: *a bottle opener* **2** also **opening batsman**—
either of the two cricket batsmen who take the first
turn in their team's innings
open-eyed *adj, adv* **1** with one's eyes wide
open **2** with full knowledge
open-handed *adj* generous —opposite **closefisted** — ~**ly** *adv* — ~**ness** *n*
openhearted *adj* generous and freely given —
~**ly** *adv* — ~**ness** *n*
open-hearth *adj* of a way of making steel in an
open fireplace or one in which the heat comes from
a heated surface
opening¹ *n* **1** the act or an act of becoming or
causing to become open **2** a hole or clear space
3 a favourable set of conditions (for): *a business
opening* **4** an unfilled position in an organization
opening² *adj* first: *opening words*
opening time *n* the time an establishment, esp.
a pub, opens for business
openly *adv* **1** not secretly **2** in a way suggesting willingness to try new ideas — **openness** *n*
open out *v adv* to speak more freely
open sandwich *n* a single piece of bread with
food on top
open season *n* the period of each year when
certain animals or fish may lawfully be killed for
sport
open secret *n* something supposed to be a
secret but in fact known to everyone
open stage *n* *technical* a stage with no proscenium, with the audience seated on three or all
four sides

Open University *n* a British university that
teaches mainly by radio and television broadcasts
and by correspondence
open verdict *n* (in a coroner's court) a jury's
decision in which the fact and cause of a death are
stated, but not the reason behind it
opera *n* a musical play in which many or all of
the words are sung — ~**tic** *adj* — ~**tically**
adv
operable *adj* *medical* that is treatable by means
of an operation — **-bly** *adv*
opera glasses *n* small binoculars used in a
theatre
opera house *n* a theatre built especially for
operas
operate *v* **-rated, -rating** **1** to (cause to) work:
to operate a machine/a factory **2** to produce
effects: *The new law doesn't operate in our favour*
3 to be in action: *That business operates in several
countries* **4** *medical* to cut the body in order to
set right or remove a diseased part
operating theatre also **theatre**— *n* a special
room in a hospital, where operations are done
operation *n* **1** (a state of) working; the way a
thing works **2** a state in which effects can be
produced: *When does the law come into operation?* **3** an (esp. military) action or code name
for this: *the army's operations | Operation Sun-
shine* **4** a thing (to be) done **5** also **op**— *medical*
an act of operating **6** *technical* the use of a rule
to get one mathematical expression or figure from
others
operational *adj* **1** of or about operations:
operational costs **2** (of things) in operation;
ready for use —compare OPERATIVE — ~**ly**
adv
operational research also **operations
research**— *n* *technical* the study of how best to
build and use machines or plan organizations
operative¹ *adj* **1** (of plans, laws, etc.) in operation; producing effects **2** most important: *operative word*
operative² *n* a factory worker
operator *n* **1** a person who works a machine,
apparatus, etc. **2** a person who works a telephone
switchboard **3** *often offensive* a person whose
operations are successful but perhaps unfair: *a
clever/smooth operator*
operetta *n* a musical play in which many of the
words are spoken
opthalmic *adj* *medical* of the medical study
and treatment of the eyes
ophthalmology *n* *medical* the study of the
eyes and their diseases — **-ogist** *n*
opiate *n* a sleep-producing drug
opine *v* **opined, opining** *pompous* to express an
opinion
opinion *n* **1** that which a person thinks about
something **2** that which people in general think
about something **3** professional judgment or
advice
opinionated also **opinionative**— *adj* *offensive*
very sure of the rightness of one's opinions

opinion poll *n* a questioning of a number of people chosen by chance to find out the general opinion about something or someone

opium *n* a sleep-producing drug made from poppy juice

opossum *n* **-sums** *or* **-sum** a type of small American tree-climbing animal (MARSUPIAL) that pretends to be dead when caught

opponent *n* a person who takes the opposite side

opportune *adj* at the right time: *an opportune moment* — ~**ly** *adv*

opportunism *n* the taking advantage of every opportunity now — **-ist** *n*

opportunity *n* **-ties** a favourable moment or occasion (for doing something) —see CHANCE (USAGE)

oppose *v* **opposed, opposing** 1 to be, act, or set in action against 2 **be opposed to** to oppose —see also AS OPPOSED TO

opposite¹ *n* a person or thing that is as different as possible (from another): *Black and white are opposites*

opposite² *adj* 1 as different as possible from 2 facing: *the houses opposite*

opposite³ *also* **opposite to**— *prep* facing: *the houses opposite ours*

opposition *n* 1 the act or state of being opposed to or fighting against 2 the political parties, esp. the largest, opposed to the government 3 *technical* a situation when the sun, the earth, and one of the outer planets are in a straight line —compare CONJUNCTION

oppress *v* 1 to rule in a hard and cruel way 2 to cause to feel ill or sad: *oppressed by the heat* — ~**ion**, ~**iveness** *n* — ~**ive** *adj* — ~**ively** *adv* — ~**or** *n*

opt for *v prep* to choose —see also OPT OUT

optic *adj* of or belonging to the eyes or the sense of sight — ~**al** *adj* — ~**ally** *adv*

optical illusion *n* something that deceives the eye

optician *n* a person who makes and sells glasses (for the eyes)

optics *n* the scientific study of light ◎

optimism *n* the belief that things will end well; a hopeful feeling about life — **-mist** *n* — **-mistic** *adj* — **-mistically** *adv*

optimum *adj* best or most favourable

option *n* 1 the freedom to choose or something chosen or offered for choice: *You have no option* 2 the right to buy or sell something at a stated future time

optional *adj* which may be freely chosen—or not chosen —opposites **compulsory, obligatory** — ~**ly** *adv*

opt out *v adv* to choose not to take part —see also OPT FOR

opulent *adj* 1 very wealthy 2 in good supply 3 (too) richly ornamented with words, colours, etc. — **-ence** *n* — ~**ly** *adv*

opus *n* **opera** *or* **opuses** a work of music, esp. one numbered for identification: *Beethoven's Opus 106*

or *conj* 1 (*after a negative*) and not: *He never smokes or drinks* 2 (used in a list of possibilities): *Venice or Florence or Rome* —see EITHER (USAGE) 3 if not; otherwise: *Wear your coat or you'll be cold* 4 (*used when giving a preferred word*) that is : *This medicine, or rather drug, has a violent effect*

oracle *n* 1 (in ancient Greece) a place where, or a person through whom, a god was believed to answer human questions 2 a person who is thought to be, or believes himself to be, able to give the best advice — **-cular** *adj*

oral *adj* 1 spoken, not written 2 esp. *medical* of, about, or using the mouth — ~**ly** *adv*

orange¹ *n* a type of very common round bittersweet fruit from hot areas

orange² *adj* of a colour between red and yellow

orange³ *n* (an) orange colour

orangeade *n* a drink containing orange juice

Orangeman *n* **-men** a member of a Protestant political organization in Northern Ireland (Ulster)

orangutang *also* **-tan**— *n* a large ape with reddish hair, from Indonesia

oration *n* a formal and solemn public speech

orator *n* a public speaker

oratorio *n* **-ios** a long musical work with singing but without acting, usu. about a religious subject

oratory¹ *n* **-ries** a type of church

oratory² *n* 1 the art of making good speeches 2 highly ornamented language — **-orical** *adj* — **-orically** *adv*

orb *n* a ball standing for the sun or another heavenly body, esp. one carried by a king or queen on formal occasions

orbit¹ *n* 1 a the path of one heavenly body round another b the path of a man-made object round the earth or another heavenly body c the path of an electron around the central part of an atom 2 the area within which one person or thing can have an effect upon others — ~**al** *adj*

orbit² *v* to move in an orbit round

orchard *n* a place where fruit trees grow

orchestra *n* a large group of people who play music together on stringed, woodwind, brass, and percussion instruments —compare BAND — ~**l** *adj*

orchestrate *v* **-trated, -trating** to arrange (music) for an orchestra — **-tration** *n*

orchid *also* (*technical*) **orchis**— *n* any of a large number of related plants having often showy flowers of unusual shapes, or a flower of such a plant

ordain *v* 1 to make (someone) a priest or religious leader 2 (of God, the law, etc.) to order

ordeal *n* 1 a difficult or painful experience 2 **trial by ordeal** (in former times) judging a person by giving him a painful, frightening, and dangerous experience, and considering his behaviour

Binoculars

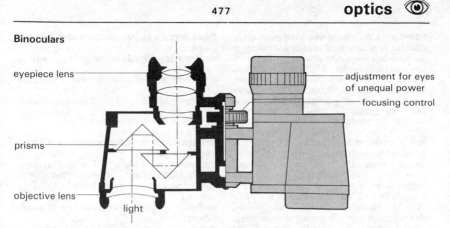

The prisms in a pair of binoculars compress the distance that light has to travel and also ensure that the image is the right way up. Since eyes are rarely of the same strength, an adjustment on the eyepiece allows both eyes to work equally.

Camera

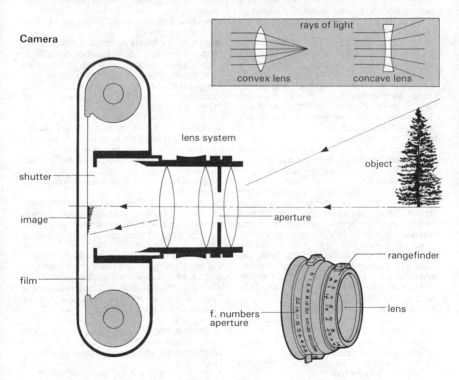

A camera is a light-proof box containing film opposite a lens. The shutter that closes the box off between the film and lens system can be briefly released to allow light to reach the film. The amount of light is controlled by the adjustable diaphragm. The lens can usually be focused on the object by means of the focusing ring. A view finder is often included to help the user see how much of the object he will be able to photograph.

order¹ *n* **1** the state in which things are neatly arranged in place: *I tried to bring some order to the bookshelf* —opposite **disorder 2** fitness for operation: *out of order* **3** the sequence in which a group of people, objects, etc., are arranged: *alphabetical order* **4** the condition in which laws and rules are obeyed —opposite **disorder**; see also LAW **5** a command or direction or something to be done **6** a request (as to a tradesman) to supply goods **7** the goods supplied in accordance with such a request: *collect an order* **8** a paper that allows the holder to be paid money, to see a house that is for sale, etc. —see also MONEY ORDER, POSTAL ORDER **9** the way things in general usually happen or are happening at a particular time in history **10** kind; sort: *something of that order* **11** (in biology) a division, used in putting animals, plants, etc., in groups according to relationship, which has a rank below the class and above the family **12** a group, social class, or rank in a society **13** a group of people who have all received any of several special honours given for service, bravery, etc., or the medal, ribbon, etc., worn as the sign of such an honour: *the Royal Victorian Order* | *wearing his orders* **14** a society of people who lead a holy life **15** *technical* (in mathematics) the number of columns or rows in a square arrangement (MATRIX) of these **16 in order that** so that **17 in order to** with the purpose or intention of: *He sent a telegram in order to warn them* **18 of/in the order of** about; about as much or as many as **19 Order!** (Order!)(spoken to call someone to order) —see also MARCHING ORDERS, POINT OF ORDER, TALL ORDER

order² *v* **1** to give an order; command: *They ordered him to stop* **2** to give an order that (something) should be done or made: *order an attack* **3** to command (someone or something) to go: *I shall order you out of the hall!* **4** (of a doctor) to advise (something) as necessary **5** to ask for (something) to be brought, made, etc., in return for payment **6** to arrange, direct: *We must order our affairs better* USAGE When one **charges** someone to do something, one gives an **order** which is also a moral duty: *She charged him not to forget the children.* **Enjoin**, **direct**, and **instruct** are not so strong as **command** or **order**.

ordered *adj* **1** arranged in good order; tidy; regular: *an ordered life* **2** arranged: *a well/badly ordered existence*

orderly¹ *adj* **1** well-arranged **2** of a tidy nature and habits **3** peace-loving and well-behaved — **-liness** *n*

orderly² *n* **-lies 1** a soldier who attends an officer **2** an attendant in a hospital

order paper *n* a list of what is to be talked about, esp. in Parliament

orders *n technical* the state of being a priest or other person permitted to perform Christian services and duties: *holy orders*

ordinal *n, adj* (a number) showing position or order in a set: *'1st' is an ordinal (number)* — compare CARDINAL NUMBER

ordinance *n* an order given by a ruler or governing body

ordinarily *adv* **1** in an ordinary way **2** usually

ordinary *adj* not unusual; common — **-iness** *n*

ordinary level *n, adj* (in British education) O level

ordinary seaman *n* **-men** (a sailor with) the lowest rank on a ship

ordination *n* the act or ceremony of ordaining a religious leader

ordnance *n* **1** artillery **2** military supplies

Ordnance Survey *n* (in Britain and Ireland) an organization that makes detailed maps of the country

ordure *n* **1** *polite* waste matter from the bowels **2** dirt

ore *n* rock, earth, etc., from which metal can be obtained

oread *n* (in ancient Greek literature) any of the young female spirits (NYMPHS) living in the mountains

oregano *n* a type of herb related to marjoram and used in cooking

organ *n* **1** a part of an animal or plant that has a special purpose **2** an organization, usu. official, that has a special purpose **3** newspapers, radio, etc., considered as able to have an effect on what people think **4** any of several musical instruments whose sound is like the largest and oldest of them, which sounds by forcing air through pipes, is played from a keyboard, and is often found in churches **5** any of certain other instruments using air to produce music, such as a mouth organ (HARMONICA) —see also BARREL ORGAN

organdie *n* very fine rather stiff cotton material

organ grinder *n* a street musician who plays a barrel organ

organic *adj* **1** of living things or the substances related to them —compare FUNCTIONAL **2** made of parts with specialized purposes: *an organic whole/system* **3** being one of those specialized parts: *an organic part* — ~**ally** *adv*

organism *n* **1** a living being **2** a whole made of specialized parts each of which is necessary

organist *n* a musician who plays an organ

organization, -sation *n* **1** the arrangement of parts to form an effective whole **2** a group of people with a special purpose — ~**al** *adj* — ~**ally** *adv*

organize, -ise *v* **-ized, -izing** to form (parts) into a whole — ~**r** *n* — ~**d** *adj*

orgasm *n* the highest point of sexual pleasure — ~**ic** *adj*

orgy *n* **orgies** a wild unrestrained party — **-giastic** *adj*

oriel window *n technical* a large upper window built out from the wall

orient *adj* eastern

Orient *n* Asia; the (Far) East —compare OCCIDENT, EAST — ~**al** *adj, n*

orientate also (*esp. US*) **orient**— *v* **-tated, -tating** to give direction or guidance to — **-ation** *n*

orifice *n* *esp. written* an opening; mouth

origin *n* **1** a starting point **2** parents and conditions of early life: *a woman of noble origin(s)*

original[1] *adj* **1** first; earliest **2** new; of a new type: *an original idea/invention* **3** able to be new or different from others: *an original thinker* **4** not copied: *an original painting* — ~**ity** *n*

original[2] *n* **1** (usu. of paintings) that from which copies can be made **2** the language in which something was originally written: *studying Greek to read Homer in the original*

originally *adv* **1** in the beginning **2** in a new or different way

original sin *n* man's first disobedience to God, which marks everyone from birth

originate *v* **-nated, -nating** to begin or cause to begin — **-nator** *n*

oriole *n* **1** also **golden oriole**— a type of European bird with black and yellow feathers **2** any of several North American birds with black and yellow feathers

Orion *n* a group of 7 bright stars thought to look like man a with a sword

Orlon *n* *trademark* a type of man-made material, from which cloth is made

ornament[1] *n* **1** that which is added to decorate something **2** an object possessed for its beauty **3** a grace note — ~**al** *adj* — ~**ally** *adv*

ornament[2] *v* to add ornament to —see DECORATE (USAGE) — ~**ation** *n*

ornate *adj* having a great deal of ornament; not simple — ~**ly** *adv* — ~**ness** *n*

ornithology *n* the scientific study of birds — **-gist** *n* — **-gical** *adj*

orotund *adj* **1** with a calm and grand manner **2** foolishly solemn

orphan[1] *n* a person (esp. a child) lacking one or both parents

orphan[2] *v* to cause to be an orphan

orphanage *n* a place where orphan children live

orris root *n* the sweet-smelling root of a type of plant, used for making perfume and in medicine

orthodox *adj* **1** generally or officially accepted **2** holding accepted opinions — ~**y** *n*

Orthodox Church *n* any of several Christian churches esp. in eastern Europe and the Near East ☞WORSHIP

orthography *n* spelling, esp. correct spelling — **-phic(al)** *adj* — **-phically** *adv*

orthopaedics, -pedics *n* *medical* the putting straight or prevention of unnaturally shaped bones, or the branch of medicine that deals with this — **-paedic** *adj*

Oscar *n* the most important American cinema award for the best actor, actress, director, etc., of the year

oscillate *v* **-lated, -lating** **1** to keep moving from side to side **2** to keep changing opinions — **-ation** *n*

oscillator *n* **1** a person or thing that oscillates **2** *technical* a machine that produces electrical oscillations

oscilloscope *n* *technical* a machine that shows electrical oscillations on a screen

osculation *n* *pompous & humorous* kissing

osier *n* a type of willow tree whose smaller branches are used for making baskets

osmosis *n* *technical* the passing of liquid through a membrane

osprey *n* **ospreys** a type of large fish-eating bird

ossify *v* **-fied, -fying** **1** to make or become hard and bonelike **2** to make or become unchanging in one's ideas

ostensible *adj* seeming or pretended — **-bly** *adv*

ostentation *n* unnecessary show of wealth, knowledge, etc. — **-tious** *adj* — **-tiously** *adv*

osteopathy *n* treatment of diseases by moving and pressing muscles and bones — **osteopath** *n*

ostler also **hostler**— *n* (in former times) a man who took care of guests' horses at an inn

ostracize, -cise *v* **-cized, -cizing** to refuse to have social dealings with — **-cism** *n*

ostrich *n* **1** a type of very large African bird with long legs and a long neck, which runs very quickly but cannot fly **2** a person who refuses to accept unpleasant reality

other *adj, pron* the remaining (one or ones) of a set; what is or are left as well as that or those mentioned; additional (ones); not the same (ones): *Where's my other glove?* | *John and the others are here.* | *I haven't brought many cakes. Could you get some others?* | *Think of others/other people as well as yourself*

other than *prep* **1** except **2** anything but: *She can hardly be other than grateful* **3** in any other way than: *You can't get there other than by swimming*

otherwise *adv* **1** differently **2** apart from that: *My mother still has a cold, but otherwise we're all well* **3** if not: *We'll go early, otherwise we may not get a seat*

otherworldly *adj* more concerned with spiritual than material things

otter *n* any of several types of fish-eating animal that can swim, or their fur

ottoman *n* **-mans** a long soft seat without back or arms

ouch *interj* (an expression of sudden pain)

ought *v* **1** should: *She ought to look after her children better* **2** will probably: *Prices ought to come down soon USAGE* Do NOT say: *He didn't ought to do it.* Say: *He oughtn't/ought not to do it.*

ouija board *n* a board with letters and other signs on it, which people try to use for receiving messages from the dead

ounce *abbrev.* **oz**— *n* **1** 1/16 of a pound avoir-

dupois 2 1/12 of a pound troy weight 3 (even) a small amount: *if you had an ounce of sense*
our *adj* (*possessive form of* WE) belonging to us: *She's our daughter, not yours*
ours *pron* (*possessive form of* WE) that/those belonging to us: *Ours are on the table*
ourselves *pron* 1 (*reflexive form of* WE): *We saved ourselves by jumping off* 2 (*strong form of* WE): *We built the house ourselves* 3 *esp. spoken* (in) our usual state of mind or body
oust *v* to force out (of): *to oust the president*
out¹ *adv* 1 in or to the open air, the outside, etc.: *He put his tongue out* 2 away from home, a building, etc. 3 away from a central point: *Spread out all over the room* 4 completely: *I'm tired out* 5 a (of one side or player in a game such as cricket) no longer allowed to bat b (of the ball in a game such as tennis) outside the line 6 no longer fashionable 7 (of a flower) fully open and ripe 8 no longer lit: *The fire's gone out* 9 on strike: *The railwaymen came out on Monday* 10 (of the tide) low 11 **out of** *technical* born to (the stated animal, esp. a horse) —compare BY
out² *v* to become known: *The truth will out*
out³ *adj* 1 used for sending something away: *the out tray* 2 impossible: *That's completely out* 3 incorrect: *He's badly out in his calculations* 4 no longer lit or burning
out⁴ *prep esp. spoken* out of: *He went out the door*
out⁵ *n* 1 an excuse for leaving an activity or for avoiding blame 2 **the ins and outs** see IN
outback *n* (esp. in Australia) the part of a country far away from cities
outbalance *v* to be of greater importance than
outbid *v* **-bid, -bidding** to offer more than
outboard motor *n* a motor fixed outside a small boat —compare INBOARD
outbound *adj* (going) away, esp. overseas
outbreak *n* a sudden appearance of something bad
outbuilding also **outhouse**— *n* a smaller building outside a main building
outburst *n* a sudden powerful expression of feeling or activity
outcast *n, adj* (a person) forced from home or without friends
outcaste *n, adj* (a person) not, or no longer, a member of a recognized social group (CASTE) in India
outclass *v* to be very much better than
outcome *n* a result
outcrop *n* an amount of rock that stands out of the ground
outcry *n* a public show of anger
outdated also **out-of-date**— *adj* no longer in general use
outdistance *v* **-tanced, -tancing** to go further or faster than
outdo *v* **-did, -done, -doing** to do better than
outdoor also **out-of-door**— *adj* existing, happening, done, or used not in a building

outdoors *adv, n* (in) the open air
outer *adj* on the outside further from the centre —opposite **inner**
outermost also **outmost**— *adj* furthest outside
outer space *n* the area where the stars and other distant heavenly bodies are
outface *v* **-faced, -facing** to meet and deal with bravely
outfield *n* the outer part of the playing field — ~**er** *n*
outfight *v* **-fought, -fighting** to fight better than
outfit *n* 1 everything, esp. clothes, needed for a particular purpose 2 a group of people, esp. if working together
outflank *v* to go round the side of (an enemy) and attack from behind; to take unawares
outfox *v* to outsmart
outgoing *adj* 1 going out or leaving 2 eager to mix socially —compare FORTHCOMING
outgoings *n* amounts of money spent
outgrow *v* **-grew, -grown, -growing** to grow more than, or too much for
outhouse *n* an outbuilding
outing *n* a short pleasure trip
outlandish *adj* strange and unpleasing — ~**ly** *adv* — ~**ness** *n*
outlast *v* to last longer than
outlaw¹ *n* a criminal
outlaw² *v* 1 to declare (someone) to have lost the protection given by law 2 to declare (something) unlawful
outlay *n* money spent for a purpose
outlet *n* 1 a way through which something may go out 2 a chance to use one's powers or express one's feelings
outline¹ *n* 1 the shape, or a line or flat figure showing the shape, of something 2 the main ideas
outline² *v* **-lined, -lining** to make an outline of
outlive *v* **-lived, -living** to live longer than
outlook *n* 1 a view on which one looks out 2 future probabilities —see VIEW (USAGE)
outlying *adj* far from the centre
outmanoeuvre *v* **-vred, -vring** to put in a position of disadvantage
outmatch *v* to be more than a match for
outmoded *adj* no longer in fashion
outpatient *n* a person who lives at home but goes to a hospital for treatment —compare IN-PATIENT
outplay *v* **-played, -playing** to play better than
outpoint *v* to defeat by gaining more points
outpost *n* a settlement at some distance from the base
output *n* production ☞COMPUTER
outrage¹ *n* an outrageous act
outrage² *v* **-raged, -raging** to offend greatly
outrageous *adj* 1 very offensive 2 unex-

pected and probably offensive: *her outrageous jokes* — ~ly *adv*

outré *adj French* very peculiar or unusual

outrider *n* a guard or attendant to a vehicle

outrigger *n* a piece of wood fixed to the side of a boat with 2 long poles, to prevent it from turning over, or a boat with such apparatus

outright¹ *adv* **1** solely; completely: *She won outright.* | *owning the car outright* **2** without delay: *be killed outright* **3** openly: *Tell him outright just what you think*

outright² *adj* **1** sole; complete: *the outright owner/winner* **2** open

outrun *v* **-ran, -run, -running** **1** to run better, faster, or further than **2** to go beyond

outsell *v* **-sold, -selling** to sell more, faster, or in larger quantities than

outset *n* the beginning: *at/from the outset*

outside¹ *n* **1** the outer part; the part furthest from the centre **2 at the (very) outside** at the most

outside² *adj* **1** facing the outside **2** in the open air **3** coming from or happening elsewhere: *outside help* **4** (of a possibility) unlikely **5** greatest acceptable (amount): *an outside figure of $100*

outside³ *adv* to or on the outside

outside⁴ *prep* **1** on or to the outside of **2** more than: *anything outside $100*

outsider *n* **1** a person not accepted as a member of a particular group **2** a person or animal thought unlikely to win

outsize *adj* (esp. of clothing) larger than average

outskirts *n* the outer areas

outsmart *v* to win by acting more cleverly than —compare OUTWIT

outspoken *adj* expressing openly what is thought or felt — ~ly *adv* — ~ness *n*

outstanding *adj* **1** better than others **2** important **3** not yet settled: *outstanding work/debts* — ~ly *adv*

outstay *v* **-stayed, -staying** to stay longer than: *Don't outstay your welcome*

outstrip *v* **-pp-** **1** to pass in running **2** to do better than

outward *adj* **1** outbound: *the outward voyage* **2** towards the outside **3** on the outside: *her outward calm* **4 outward bound** outbound

outwardly *adv* according to appearances

outwards also **outward**— *adv* **1** sideways (from the centre): *The branch is growing outwards* **2** away (from oneself): *Look outwards*

outweigh *v* **1** to be more important than **2** to weigh more than

outwit *v* **-tt-** to win by being cleverer

outwork *n* work for a business done outside the usual place of business — ~er *n*

ova *technical pl. of* OVUM

oval *n, adj* (anything which is) egg-shaped

ovary *n* **-ries** **1** the part of a female animal, bird, etc., that produces eggs ⸗ REPRODUCTION

2 the female part of a plant that produces seeds or fruit ⸗ FLOWER — **-arian** *adj*

ovation *n* an expression of public approval

oven *n* any of several types of heated boxlike spaces used for cooking, baking clay, etc.

ovenware *n* cooking pots, dishes, etc. that can be put in a hot oven without cracking

over¹ *adv* **1** downwards from an upright position **2** up, out, and downwards across an edge: *The milk's boiling over!* **3** so that another side is shown: *Turn the page over* **4** right through: *think it over* **5** across a distance: *We must ask our friends over* **6** (showing that something is repeated): *several times over* **7** remaining: *Was there any money over?* **8** so as to be exchanged: *Change these 2 over* **9** from one (person or group) to another: *sign over the money* **10** (before an adjective or adverb) too: *over anxious/not over keen* **11** so as to be covered: *Paint it over* **12 and/or over** and/or more: *children of 14 and over* —see also ONCE-OVER

over² *prep* **1** directly above: *The lamp hung over the table* **2** completely or partly covering: *hand over heart* **3** to the other side of, by going up and down: *to jump over the wall* **4** across: *a bridge over/across the river* **5** on the far side of: *over the street* **6** down across the edge of: *to fall over the cliff* **7** in, on, or through many or all parts of: *They travelled (all) over Europe* **8** (showing command or control): *rule over* **9** higher in rank than: *I don't want anyone over me* **10** more than: *over 30 books* **11** during: *over the years* **12** till the end of: *Are you staying over Christmas?* **13** by means of: *over the telephone* **14** on the subject of: *taking a long time over* **15 over and above** as well as

over³ *adj* finished: *get it over (with)*

over⁴ *n* (in cricket) a particular number of balls (usu. 6) thrown by the same bowler

overact *v* to overdo (a part)

overage *adj* too old for some purpose

overall¹ *adj, adv* **1** including everything: *overall measurements* **2** generally: *Overall, prices are still rising*

overall² *n* a coatlike garment worn over other clothes

overalls *n* loose trousers worn over other clothes

overarm *adj, adv* (in sport) with the arm moving above the shoulder

overawe *v* **-awed, -awing** to fill with respect and fear

overbalance *v* **-anced, -ancing** to make or become unbalanced

overbearing *adj* trying to make other people obey without regard for their feelings — ~ly *adv*

overblown *adj* using too many words and gestures

overboard *adv* **1** over the side of a ship or boat into the water **2 go overboard for/about** to become very attracted to **3 throw overboard** to get rid of

overcast adj 1 dark with clouds 2 covered with sadness

overcharge¹ v -charged, -charging 1 to charge too much 2 to fill or load too much

overcharge² n an act of overcharging

overcoat n a warm coat

overcome v -came, -come, -coming 1 to defeat 2 to take control of 3 to make (someone) weak or ill

overcrowd v to put or have too many people or things in

overdo v -did, -done, -doing 1 to do, ornament, perform, etc., too much 2 to use too much: *Don't overdo the salt in your cooking* 3 **overdo it** to work, practise a sport, etc., too much

overdone adj cooked too much —opposite **underdone**

overdose n too much of a drug

overdraft n a sum lent to a person by a bank

overdraw v -drew, -drawn, -drawing to get a bank to pay one more money than one has in (one's account) — ~n adj

overdrive n an apparatus that provides a higher gear when fixed to a normal gearbox

overdue adj 1 left unpaid too long 2 later than expected

overestimate v -mated, -mating to value too highly —see also ESTIMATE

overexpose v -posed, -posing to give too much light to (a film or photograph) —see also EXPOSE

overflow¹ v 1 to be so full that the contents flow over the edges: *The bath/river overflowed* 2 to be very full (of): *overflowing with kindness*

overflow² n 1 an act of overflowing, or that which overflows 2 a pipe or channel for carrying away extra water

overgrown adj 1 covered (esp. with plants growing uncontrolled) 2 that has grown too much or too fast — **-growth** n

overhang¹ v -hung, -hanging 1 to hang over or stand out over (something) 2 (of something bad) to threaten to happen to (someone)

overhang² n that which overhangs △ HANG-OVER

overhaul¹ v 1 to examine thoroughly and perhaps repair: *overhaul a car* 2 to come up to from behind and pass (something moving)

overhaul² n a thorough examination

overhead adj, adv 1 above one's head 2 of overheads: *overhead costs*

overheads n money spent regularly to keep a business running

overhear v -heard, -hearing to hear without the speakers' knowledge

overjoyed adj full of joy

overkill n 1 more than enough weapons (esp. atomic weapons) to kill everybody in an enemy country 2 something that causes harm by going beyond the desirable or safe limits

overland adv, adj by or on land

overlap¹ v -pp- to cover (something) partly and go beyond it

overlap² n the amount by which 2 or more things overlap each other

overleaf adv on the other side of the page

overload v -loaded or -laden, -loading 1 to load too heavily 2 to cause to produce too much electricity — **overload** n

overlook v 1 to have or give a view of from above 2 to look at but not see; not notice 3 to pretend not to see —compare LOOK OVER

overly adv too (much); very

overman v -nn- to provide too many workers for —compare UNDERMANNED — ~ning n

overmaster v esp. written to conquer by greater power: *an overmastering desire*

overmuch adv, adj, pron too much or very much

overnight adv, adj 1 for or during the night 2 suddenly: *Byron became famous overnight*

overpass n US a flyover

overpay v -paid, -paying to pay too much

overplay v -played, -playing 1 to make (something) appear larger or more important than it really is 2 **overplay one's hand** to try to do more than one really can do

overpopulated adj having too many people — **-ation** n

overpower v to overcome or conquer by greater power — ~ing adj — ~ingly adv

overrate v -rated, -rating to value too greatly

overreach also **overleap**— v to defeat (oneself) by trying to do too much

override v -rode, -ridden, -riding to take no notice of

overriding adj more important than anything else

overrule v -ruled, -ruling to reverse (someone else's decision)

overrun¹ v -ran, -run, -running 1 to spread over and usu. harm 2 to continue beyond

overrun² n 1 the fact of continuing beyond 2 the amount of this: *an overrun of 15 minutes/metres*

overseas adv, adj to, at, or in somewhere across the sea: *overseas news*

oversee v -saw, -seen, -seeing to watch to see that work is properly done — **-seer** n

oversell v -sold, -selling to praise too much

oversexed adj having too much sexual desire

overshadow v 1 to throw a shadow over 2 to make appear less important

overshoe also **galosh**— n a waterproof shoe worn over an ordinary shoe

overshoot v -shot, -shooting to go beyond and miss

oversight n (an) unintended failure to notice or do something

oversimplify v -fied, -fying to express so simply that the true meaning is changed or lost — **-fication** n

oversleep v -slept, -sleeping to sleep too long

overspill n people who leave a city because too many people live there

overstate v -stated, -stating to state too strongly: *overstate one's case* — ~ment n

oversteer v (of a car or other vehicle) to tend to turn too sharply when one turns the steering wheel

overstep v -pp- to go beyond (a limit of what is wise or proper)

overstock v to keep more than enough in

overstrung adj too sensitive and nervous

overt adj esp. written public — ~ly adv

overtake v -took, -taken, -taking 1 to come up level with from behind and usu. pass 2 (of something unpleasant) to catch unawares: *overtaken by events* —compare TAKE OVER

overtax v 1 to put too great a tax on 2 to force beyond a limit: *Don't overtax your strength!*

overthrow¹ v -threw, -thrown, -throwing to remove from power

overthrow² n 1 removal from power 2 (in cricket) a run made after a fielder has thrown the ball accidentally past the wicket

overtime n, adv 1 (time) beyond the usual working time 2 payment for working beyond the usual time

overtones n things that are suggested but not shown or stated clearly

overture n 1 a musical introduction to a large musical work, esp. an opera 2 a shortish musical piece meant to be played by itself esp. at the beginning of a concert

overtures n an approach to someone in the hope of reaching an agreement

overturn v 1 to turn or cause to turn over 2 to remove from power

overweening adj (of people who are) too proud and too sure of themselves — ~ly adv

overweight n, adj (of) too great weight, or weighing too much: *an overweight person*

overwhelm v 1 (of water) to cover, or (of feelings) to overcome, completely and usu. suddenly 2 to defeat or make powerless by much greater force of numbers — ~ing adi — ~ingly adv

overwork¹ v 1 to work or cause to work too much 2 to use too much

overwork² n too much work

overwrought adj too nervous and excited

oviduct n technical 1 also **Fallopian tube**— (in mammals) either one of the 2 tubes through which eggs pass into the womb 2 (in birds) the tube through which eggs pass to be laid

ovoid adj, n (an object that is) egg-shaped

ovulate v -lated, -lating to produce eggs from the ovary

ovule n the part inside a plant ovary that develops into a seed after fertilization

ovum n **ova** technical an egg, esp. one that develops inside the mother's body until ready for birth ⟶EMBRYO, REPRODUCTION

owe v **owed, owing** 1 to have to pay (a debt) (to) 2 to have an obligation or a moral debt (to): *We owe our parents a lot* — **owing** adi

owe to v prep to admit as the point of origin of: *She owes her wealth to hard work*

owing to prep because of —see DUE TO (USAGE)

owl n any of several types of flesh-eating night bird with large eyes ⟶BIRD — ~ish adj — ~ishly adv

own¹ adj, pron 1 that belongs to oneself and to nobody else: *I only borrowed it; it's not my own* 2 **come into one's own** to begin to be properly respected for one's qualities 3 **for one's very own** to have for oneself 4 **hold one's own (against)** to avoid defeat (by) 5 **on one's own** alone or without help

own² v 1 to possess, esp. by lawful right: *Who owns this house?* 2 to admit: *He owns he was wrong* — ~er n — ~ership n

own to v prep to admit: *I must own to feeling rather anxious*

own up v adv to admit a fault or crime

ox n **oxen** 1 a castrated male cow, used for pulling vehicles and for heavy work on farms —compare STEER, BULLOCK 2 any of several kinds of large animal of the cattle type, wild or used by man

Oxbridge n the universities of Oxford and Cambridge rather than the other British universities —compare REDBRICK

oxide n a chemical substance in which something else is combined with oxygen: *iron oxide*

oxidize, -dise v -dized, -dizing to combine or cause to combine with oxygen, esp. in such a way as to make or become rusty — **-dization** n

Oxon abbrev. (used esp. after the title of a degree) of Oxford University

Oxonian n, adj esp. written (of) a past or present member of Oxford University

oxtail n the tail of an ox, used as food

oxyacetylene n technical a mixture of oxygen and acetylene gas which produces a very hot white flame when burning

oxygen n a colourless tasteless gas that is an element and is necessary for all life forms on earth ⟶ECOLOGY

oxygen mask an apparatus placed over the nose and mouth to supply oxygen

oxygen tent n a tent-like apparatus within which oxygen can be supplied to people who are ill

oyez interj listen! (used in law courts, and, esp. in former times, by town criers)

oyster n a type of flat shellfish, eaten cooked or raw, which can produce a pearl

oystercatcher n a type of seabird that wades and catches shellfish for food

oz abbrev. for: ounce

ozone n 1 air that is pleasant to breathe 2 technical a type of oxygen

P

P, p P's, p's *or* Ps, ps **1** the 16th letter of the English alphabet **2 mind one's p's and q's** to be careful to speak politely

p¹ *abbrev for:* (new) penny/pence: *This newspaper costs 8p* —see PENNY (USAGE)

p² *abbrev for:* **1** page **2** piano —see also PP

P *abbrev for:* parking

pa *n becoming rare* a name for father

PA *n* **1** PERSONAL ASSISTANT **2** PUBLIC-ADDRESS SYSTEM

pace¹ *n* **1** rate or speed in activity or of development **2** a single step in running or walking, or the distance moved in one such step

pace² *v* **paced, pacing** **1** to walk with slow, regular steps: *They paced up and down* **2** to set the pace for: *Jones paced the runners at a moderate speed*

pace bowler also **pace man—** *n* (in cricket) a fast bowler

pacemaker *n* **1** a person or animal that sets the pace in a race **2** a machine used to improve weak or irregular heartbeats

pachyderm *n technical* any of several types of thick-skinned animal, such as the elephant and the rhinoceros

pacific *adj* helping to cause peace; peace-loving — ~**ally** *adv*

pacifism *n* the belief that all wars are wrong

pacifist *n* an active believer in pacifism; person who refuses to fight in a war because of such a belief

pacify *v* **-fied, -fying** **1** to make calm: *Try to pacify the baby* **2** to end war in — **-fication, -fier** *n*

pack¹ *n* **1** a number of things together, esp. for carrying on the back **2 a** a group of wild animals (esp. wolves) that hunt together, or a group of hunting dogs **b** (in rugby football) the forwards **c** a group of cubs of the boy scouts or brownies of the girl guides **3** a collection, group, etc.: *pack of thieves/lies* **4** a complete set of usu. 52 cards used in playing a game **5** *US* a packet: *a pack of cigarettes* **6** a compress, sometimes containing ice or medicine

pack² *v* **1** to put (things) into containers: *a packed meal* | *We leave tomorrow but I haven't begun to pack yet!* **2** to fit or crush into a space: *Pack those things down to make more room* **3** to cover, fill, or surround closely with a protective material **4** to choose members of (a committee or a jury) favourable to one's own purpose or ideas **5 send somebody packing** *esp. spoken* to cause somebody undesirable to leave quickly

package¹ *n* **1** an amount or a number of things packed together: *a large package of books* **2** the container of these things

package² *v* **-aged, -aging** **1** to make into or

tie up as a package **2** to place (food) in a special package before selling

package deal also **package offer—** *n* an offer or agreement that includes a number of things all of which must be accepted together

pack animal *n* an animal, such as a **packhorse**, used for carrying packs

packed *adj* full of people; crowded

packed-out *adj esp. spoken* completely full of people

packer *n* **a** a person or thing that packs **b** a person employed to pack for people moving house

packet *n* **1** a small package **2** also **packet boat —** a boat that carries mail, and usu. people also, at regular times **3** *sl* a large amount of money

pack ice *n* a large mass of ice floating on the sea

pack in *v adv esp. spoken* **1** to attract in large numbers: *The new music group is packing the crowds in* **2 pack it in** to cease an activity

packing case *n* a large strong box in which heavy articles are packed

pack up *v adv esp. spoken* **1** to finish work **2** (of a machine) to stop working

pact *n* a solemn agreement: *a peace pact*

pad¹ *n* **1** a soft material used to protect something or make it more comfortable, or to fill out a shape **2** also **inkpad, inking pad—** a piece of material which is made thoroughly wet with ink, and used to ink a stamp for printing **3** a number of sheets of paper fastened together along one edge **4** the usu. thick-skinned fleshy underpart of the foot of some 4-footed animals **5** LAUNCHING PAD **6** *sl* the room, house, etc., where one lives

pad² *v* **-dd-** **1** to protect, shape, or make more comfortable with a pad **2** to make (a speech, story, etc.) longer by adding unnecessary words

pad³ *v* **-dd-** to walk softly, with the feet flat on the ground

padding *n* **1** the act of padding **2** soft material used to pad something **3** unnecessary words or sentences used for padding

paddle¹ *n* **1** a short pole with a wide flat blade at one end or (if a **double paddle**) at both ends, used for pushing and guiding a small boat (esp. a canoe) —compare OAR **2** anything shaped like this, such as the foot of a duck

paddle² *v* **-dled, -dling** **1** to move (usu. a canoe) through water, using one or more paddles; row gently **2** to swim about in water as a dog or duck does

paddle³ *v* to walk about in water only a few inches deep —compare WADE

paddle wheel *n* a large wheel fixed to one of the sides or the back of a ship (**paddle steamer**), and turned by a steam engine to make the ship move

paddock *n* a grassy place where horses are kept or exercised, or (at a racecourse) paraded before a race

paddy[1] also **rice paddy, paddy field**— n -dies a muddy field where rice is grown

paddy[2] n esp. spoken a state of or show of bad temper

padlock[1] n a lock that can be put on and taken away

padlock[2] v to fasten or lock by means of a padlock

padre n esp. spoken a chaplain

paediatrics n the branch of medicine concerned with children and their diseases — -trician n

paella n cooked rice containing pieces of meat, fish, and vegetables

pagan n a person who is not a believer in any of the chief religions of the world, or who believes in many gods —compare HEATHEN — **pagan** adj — ~ism n

page[1] n 1 also **page boy** — a a boy servant, usu. uniformed b (at a wedding) a boy attendant on the bride 2 old use a boy of noble birth who was in training to be a knight

page[2] v **paged, paging** (in a hotel, club, etc.) to call aloud for (someone who is wanted)

page[3] n 1 one side of a sheet of paper in a book, newspaper, etc. 2 the whole sheet (both sides)

pageant n 1 a a splendid public show b a steady continuous movement of things developing or passing by: the pageant of history 2 a kind of play or show, usu. out of doors, in which scenes from the history of a town are acted

pageantry n -ries a splendid show of ceremonial grandness with people in fine dress

pagoda n a temple (esp. Buddhist or Hindu) built on several floors or levels, often with an ornamental roof at each level △ PERGOLA

paid past tense and past part. of PAY

paid-up adj having paid in full

pail n a bucket

pain[1] n 1 suffering; great discomfort of the body or mind 2 a feeling of suffering or discomfort in a particular part of the body —compare ACHE 3 also **pain in the neck** — sl a feeling of annoyance or displeasure, or a person, thing, or happening that causes this: She's / it's a real pain/pain in the neck —see also PAINS

pain[2] v 1 (of a part of the body) to cause pain; hurt 2 to cause to feel pain in the mind: It pains me to disobey you, but I must

pained adj hurt in one's feelings: She was pained when you refused her invitation

painful adj causing pain — ~ly adv — ~ness n

painkiller n a medicine which lessens or destroys pain

painless adj 1 causing no pain 2 needing no hard work: a painless way of learning a language — ~ly adv

pains n 1 effort: We must give him something for his pains 2 **be at pains to do something** to take great trouble or care in doing something

painstaking adj careful and thorough — ~ly adv

paint[1] v 1 to put paint on 2 to make (a picture or pictures of) using paint: I would very much like to paint him 3 (of a woman) to cover (the lips, face, or cheeks) with make-up 4 to describe in clear well-chosen words, with lifelike effect

paint[2] n 1 liquid colouring matter for putting or spreading on a surface —compare DYE 2 MAKE-UP

paintbrush n a brush for painting

painter[1] n 1 a person whose job is painting buildings, fences, etc. 2 a person who paints pictures; artist

painter[2] n technical a rope fastened to the front end of a small boat for tying it to a ship, a post on land, etc.

painting n 1 the act or action of painting 2 the art or practice of painting pictures, or a picture made in this way ◎

paintwork n the painted surfaces of an object

pair[1] n **pairs** or **pair** 1 something made up of 2 parts that are alike and which are joined and used together: a pair of trousers 2 a 2 things that are alike or of the same kind, and are usu. used together: a pair of shoes b 2 playing cards of the same value but of different suits: a pair of kings 3 2 people closely connected 4 2 animals (male and female) that stay together for a certain length of time or for life

pair[2] v to form or cause to form into one or more pairs

paisley n a soft woollen cloth with curved coloured patterns

Pakistani adj of Pakistan

pal n a close friend — ~ly adi

palace n a very large grand house △ PALAIS

palais also **palais de danse**— n **palais (de danse)** a large public hall usu. used for dancing △ PALACE

palanquin, -keen n a wheelless boxlike vehicle in which one person was carried, formerly used in the East —compare LITTER

palatable adj 1 pleasant to taste 2 acceptable to the mind — -bly adv

palate n 1 the roof of the inside of the mouth 2 a liking (for something) according to one's sense of taste, or one's feeling for beauty 3 the ability to judge good food or wine —see also CLEFT PALATE — **palatal** adj

palatial adj like a palace; grand and splendid — ~ly adv

palaver n esp. spoken 1 continuous meaningless talk about unimportant things 2 flattery 3 fuss

pale[1] adj rather white; not bright: a pale face | pale blue — ~ly adv — ~ness n

pale[2] v **paled, paling** 1 to make or become pale 2 to seem less important, beautiful, etc., when compared with

pale[3] n 1 a pointed piece of wood used with others in making a fence 2 **beyond/outside the pale** beyond the limit of what is considered proper behaviour in society

Development of painting, sculpture, and architecture

Historical period	Date	Development
Prehistoric period	30000BC	Paintings and engravings on walls of caves 1
	20000BC	Small stone sculptures
	10000BC	Amber carvings and figures moulded from clay
	7000BC	Earliest known pottery
3000–1500BC Ancient Egyptian civilization	5000BC	
	c2500BC	The Pyramids built; Egyptian sculpture and wall-painting 2
2000–1400BC Minoan civilization in Crete and Greece	2000BC	
	c2000BC	Stonehenge built 3
	c1500BC	Palace of Knossos in Crete built
900–500BC Archaic Greek period	1000BC	
	c700–500BC	Great age of Greek painted vases 4
500–146BC Classical Greek period	500BC	
	447–32	Parthenon at Athens built 5
146BC Rome conquers Greece	c150	'Venus de Milo' sculpted
43 Roman conquest of Britain	1AD	
	72–80	Colosseum at Rome built 6
117 Height of Roman Empire	100	
	125	Pantheon at Rome rebuilt
	200	
449 Anglo-Saxon invasion of England	300	
	400	
530 Rise of Byzantine civilization	500	
	532–7	Church of St Sophia in Istanbul built (Byzantine style)
	600	
789 First Viking attack on England	700	
	760	Book of Kells (Irish illuminated manuscript)
	800	
	900	
	c950	Beginning of Romanesque (Norman) style of architecture
	1000	
	1070	Building of Canterbury Cathedral begun
1066 Norman conquest of England	1080	Bayeux Tapestry 7
	1093	Building of Durham Cathedral begun
1096 First Crusade	1100	
	c1150	Beginning of Gothic style of architecture
	1200	
	1194–1240	Chartres Cathedral built
	1220–58	Salisbury Cathedral built
	1300	
	c1300	Rise of painting in Italy
	1309	Giotto's frescoes at Padua
	c1350	Development of method of oil-painting on wood or canvas
	1400	
	1410	Discovery of perspective in drawing
1430–1500 Early Renaissance period	1434	Jan van Eyck's painting Arnolfini Marriage Group
	1485	Botticelli's painting Birth of Venus 8
1492 Columbus discovers America	1500	
	1502	Leonardo da Vinci's painting Mona Lisa 9
	1508–12	Michelangelo paints the ceiling of the Sistine Chapel
1500–30 High Renaissance period	1509–12	Raphael's fresco School of Athens
1521 Protestant Reformation	1548	Tintoretto's painting St Mark Rescuing a Slave
1530–1600 Mannerist period	1580	El Greco's painting Dream of Philip
1588 Spanish Armada defeated	1600	
	1610	Ruben's painting Raising of the Cross
	1624	Hals' painting Laughing Cavalier
1600–80 Baroque period	1642	Rembrandt's painting Night Watch 10
1640–1700 Classical period		
1661–1715 Rule of Louis XIV in France	1650	Velazquez' painting Rokeby Venus 11
	1661–86	Palace of Versailles in France built
1666 Great Fire of London	1700	
	1675–1710	St Paul's Cathedral, London, built (by Wren) 12
1720–40 Rococo Period	1735	Hogarth's paintings The Rake's Progress
1750–1820 Neo-Classical period		
1789 French Revolution	1770	Gainsborough's painting Blue Boy
1803–15 Napoleonic Wars	1800	
	1810–13	Goya's etchings Disasters of War
1820–60 Romantic period	1821	Constable's painting Hay Wain
	1829	Delacroix's painting Sardanapalus
	1840–60	Houses of Parliament, London, built (Gothic revival) 13
1870 Modern period	1870	Impressionism (Manet, Monet)
	1880	Post-Impressionism (van Gogh, Gauguin)
	1900	
	1905	Cubism and abstract art (Picasso)
1914–18 World War I	1920	Surrealism (Magritte, Dali)
1939–45 World War II	1929–31	Empire State Building, New York, built 14
	1950	Pop Art (Warhol, Lichtenstein)
	1951	Henry Moore's sculpture Reclining Figure
	1951–62	Coventry Cathedral rebuilt

pale ale *n* a light-coloured beer usu. sold in bottles

paleface *n* *offensive & humour* (said to have been used by North American Indians for) a white person

paleography *n* the study of ancient writing — **-pher** *n* — **-phic** *adj* — **-phically** *adv*

paleolithic *adj* of the earliest known time (**Old Stone Age**) when man made and used weapons and tools of stone: *a paleolithic axe* —compare NEOLITHIC

palette *n* 1 a board on which an artist mixes his colours 2 the colours used by a particular artist or for a particular picture

palette knife *n* **-knives** a thin bendable knife with a rounded end

palindrome *n* a word, phrase, etc., that reads the same backwards as it does forwards: *The words 'deed' and 'level' are palindromes*

palings *n* a fence made out of pales

palisade *n* a fence made of strong pointed iron or wooden poles

pall¹ *n* 1 a large piece of ornamental cloth spread over a coffin 2 a heavy or dark covering: *a pall of darkness*

pall² *v* to become uninteresting or dull, esp. through being repeated too often

pallbearer *n* a person who walks beside or helps to carry a coffin at a funeral

pallet¹ *n* a cloth case filled usu. with straw for sleeping on

pallet² *n* 1 a large wooden or metal tray for lifting heavy goods, used with a forklift 2 a part of a machine that sticks out to connect with the teeth of a wheel

palliasse, paillasse *n* a straw pallet

palliate *v* **-ated, -ating** to lessen the unpleasant effects of (some kind of suffering) without removing the cause — **-ation** *n* — **-ative** *n, adj* : *Aspirin is a palliative for headaches*

pallid *adj* unusually pale; lacking colour — ~**ly** *adv* — ~**ness** *n*

pallor *n* unhealthy paleness of skin

palm¹ *n* 1 any of a large family of trees which grow mainly in the tropics, and which are usu. very tall with branchless stems and a mass of large leaves at the top 2 the leaf of this tree

palm² *n* 1 the inner surface of the hand between the base of the fingers and the wrist 2 **grease/oil somebody's palm (with)** to bribe somebody (with)

palm³ *v* to hide in one's palm, esp. when performing a trick

palmist *n* a person who claims to be able to tell someone's fortune by examining the lines on his palm —compare FORTUNE-TELLER — ~**ry** *n*

palm off *v adv* 1 to deceitfully gain acceptance for: *The greengrocer palmed off some bad oranges onto the old lady* 2 to deceive or cause to be satisfied by means of (lying or some other deception): *He palmed his brother off with some story or other*

Palm Sunday *n* **-days** the Sunday before Easter

palmy *adj* **-ier, -iest** (esp. of past events or periods) best

palomino *n* **-nos** a horse of a golden or cream colour, with a white mane and tail

palpable *adj* obvious — **-bly** *adv*

palpitate *v* **-tated, -tating** *medical* (of the heart) to beat fast and irregularly — **-tation** *n*

palsy *n* 1 *old use & medical* paralysis 2 a disease causing trembling of limbs

paltry *adj* **-trier, -triest** worthlessly small

pampas *n* the large wide treeless plains in parts of South America

pamper *v* to show too much attention to; treat too kindly

pamphlet *n* a small book with paper covers

pamphleteer *n* a person who writes (usu. political) pamphlets

pan¹ *n* 1 any of various kinds of metal container used esp. in cooking: *Usually cooking pots have 2 small handles but pans have one long handle* —see also BEDPAN, DUSTPAN, FRYING PAN, SAUCEPAN, WARMING PAN 2 the bowl of a WATER CLOSET 3 either of the 2 dishes on a small weighing machine 4 a container with holes or mesh in the bottom used for separating precious metals, such as gold, from other materials by washing them in water 5 a part of an old gun that held the explosive

pan² *v* **-nn-** 1 to wash (soil or gravel) in a pan looking for a precious metal, or to get (a precious metal) in this way 2 *esp. spoken* criticize very severely

pan³ *v* **-nn-** to move (a camera taking moving pictures) from side to side, following action

Pan *n* the Greek god of country things, who looks like a man with a goat's legs and feet, and plays music on a set of pipes (PANPIPES)

panacea *n* 1 something that will put right all troubles 2 a treatment that is supposed to cure any illness —compare NOSTRUM

panache *n* *French* a manner of doing things that is showy and splendid, and appears easy

panama also **panama hat** — *n* a lightweight hat for men made from dried palm leaves

panatela, -tella *n* a long thin cigar

pancake *n* 1 a thin soft flat cake made of batter, and cooked usu. in a pan 2 **as flat as a pancake** very flat

Pancake Day also **Pancake Tuesday** — *n* **-Days** Shrove Tuesday (on which, according to custom, pancakes are eaten)

pancake landing *n* a landing in which an aircraft drops flat to the ground, made usu. in emergency

panchromatic *adj* (of photographic film) equally sensitive to all colours

pancreas *n* *medical* a gland inside the body, near the stomach, which produces insulin and a liquid (**pancreatic juice**) that helps in digesting food ⏴DIGESTION —see also SWEETBREAD

panda *n* **-das** *or* **-da** 1 GIANT PANDA ⏴MAM-

MAL 2 a small bearlike animal with red-brown fur and a long tail, found chiefly in India ⟶MAMMAL

Panda car *n* a police patrol car

pandemic *adj, n medical* (of) a disease which is widespread over a large area or among a population —compare ENDEMIC, EPIDEMIC

pandemonium *n* wild and noisy disorder

pander to *v prep* to provide something that satisfies, often for one's own purposes: *The newspapers pander to people's liking for crime stories*

pandit *n* (in India) a wise man: *Pandit Nehru* △ PUNDIT

pane *n* a single sheet of glass for use in a frame, esp. of a window

panegyric *n* a speech or piece of writing giving praise

panel¹ *n* 1 a separate usu. 4-sided division of the surface of a door, wall, etc., which is different in some way to the surface round it 2 a piece of cloth of a different colour or material, set in a dress 3 a board on which controls or instruments of various kinds are fastened 4 a group of speakers who answer questions to inform or amuse the public, usu. on a radio or television show: *a panel game* —see also PANELLIST 5 a list of names of people chosen to form a jury, or the group of people on this list: *serve on a panel*

panel² *v* **-ll-** to divide into or ornament with panels

panelling *n* panels on a door, wall, etc.

panellist *n* a member of a panel (e.g. on television)

pang *n* a sudden sharp feeling of pain of the body or the mind

panic¹ *n* (a state of) sudden uncontrollable fear: *panic when the fire started* — ~ky *adj*

panic² *v* **-ck-** to feel or cause to feel panic: *The crowd panicked*

panic-stricken *adj* filled with panic

pannier *n* a basket, esp. either of a pair carried by a horse or donkey, on a bicycle, etc., or one used to carry a load on a person's back

panoply *n* **-plies** splendid ceremonial show or dress — **-plied** *adj*

panorama *n* 1 a wide or continuously changing view or scene 2 a thorough representation in words or pictures — **-mic** *adj* — **-mically** *adv*

panpipes *n* a simple musical instrument made of a number of shortish pipes and played by blowing across their open ends

pansy *n* **-sies** 1 a small plant with wide flat flowers 2 *esp. spoken* a girlish young man, or a male homosexual

pant¹ *v* 1 to breathe quickly, taking short breaths, esp. after great effort or in great heat 2 to desire strongly and eagerly — ~ingly *adv*

pant² *n* a short quick breath

Pantaloon *n* an old man in English pantomine, on whom others play tricks; father of Columbine —see also COMMEDIA DELL'ARTE

pantaloons *n* any of several different kinds of men's close-fitting trousers, worn esp. in former times

pantheism *n* the religious idea that God and the universe are the same thing — **-ist** *n* — **-istic** *adj*

pantheon *n* a temple built in honour of all gods, whether known or unknown ⟶GOD

panther *n* **-thers** or **-ther** a leopard, esp. a black one

panties *n* also **pants**— an undergarment worn below the waist and which does not cover the upper part of the leg, worn by women and girls

pantile *n* a tile shaped as a double curve, used in making roofs

pantomime *n* a family entertainment usu. produced at Christmas based on a fairy story

pantry *n* **-tries** 1 a small room where food is kept or prepared 2 a room in a big house, hotel, ship, where eating utensils are kept

pants *n* underpants, panties, or trousers

panty hose *n* tights

panzer *n German* a (usu. German) tank or other such armoured vehicle

pap *n* 1 soft or liquid-like food for babies or sick people 2 a wet mixture, more watery than a paste —compare MUSH

papa *n* (a name for father, used formerly)

papacy *n* **-cies** the power and office of the Pope

papal *adj* of the Pope or of the papacy

paper¹ *n* 1 material made in the form of sheets from very thin threads of wood or cloth, used for writing or printing on, covering parcels or walls, etc. 2 this material used for making things which are to be thrown away after use: *a paper plate* 3 a newspaper 4 a set of questions used as an examination, or the written answers to these 5 a piece of writing for specialists, or from an official group 6 **on paper** as written down or printed, but not yet tested: *These plans seem good on paper*

paper² *v* 1 to cover with wallpaper 2 to cover with paper in order to protect or hide

paperback *n* a book bound with a thin cardboard cover —compare HARDBACK

paperboy *n* **-boys** a boy who delivers newspapers

paper clip *n* a small piece of curved wire used for holding sheets of paper together

paper knife *n* a knife that is only slightly sharp, used usu. for opening envelopes

paper money *n* money in the form of notes

papers *n* documents

paper tape *n* a strip of paper that can instruct a computer in an understandable form

paperweight *n* a heavy object placed on top of loose papers to hold them down

paperwork *n* regular business writing work

papery *adj* thin or bendable like paper

papier-maché *n French* paper boiled into a soft mass, mixed with a stiffening material, and used for making boxes, ornamental figures, etc.

papist *n offensive* a member of the Roman Catholic Church

papoose *n* 1 a young child of North American Indian parents 2 a sort of bag used for carrying a baby on a person's back

paprika *n* a red powder made from a type of sweet pepper and used in cooking

papyrus *n* **-ruses** *or* **-ri** a grasslike water plant formerly common in Egypt, used in ancient times esp. for making paper; the paper thus made, or a piece of ancient writing on such paper

par¹ *n* 1 (in the game of golf) the number of strokes the average player should take to hit the ball into one or all of the holes 2 a level which is equal or almost the same: *These 2 things are on a par (with each other)* 3 **below par** also **under par**— not in the usual or average condition 4 **(not) up to par** (not) in the usual or average condition

par² also **para**— *abbrev. for:* paragraph

parable *n* a short simple story which teaches a moral or religious lesson — **-bolical** *adj* — **-bolically** *adv*

parabola *n* the curve formed when a cone is cut by a plane that is parallel to one of its sides: *The curve made by a ball when it is thrown in the air and falls to the ground is a parabola* ☞MATHEMATICS — **-lic** *adj* — **-lically** *adv*

parachute¹ *n* an apparatus which looks like a large umbrella, fastened to people or objects dropped from aircraft in order to make them fall slowly: *a parachute jump*

parachute² *v* **-chuted, -chuting** to drop or jump from an aircraft by means of a parachute — **-chutist** *n*

parade¹ *n* 1 (esp. of soldiers) a gathering together in ceremonial order, for the purpose of being officially looked at, or for a march: *on parade* 2 a number of people standing or walking together, for the purpose of being looked at or heard —see also IDENTIFICATION PARADE 3 an act of showing oneself with the intention of making others look and admire: *made a parade of* 4 also **parade ground**— a large flat area where soldiers parade 5 a wide public path or street, usu. beside the seashore

parade² *v* **paraded, parading** 1 (esp. of soldiers) to gather together in a parade 2 to walk showily about in order to gain admiration: *parading in her new dress* 3 to show in order to gain admiration: *parading his wealth*

paradise *n* 1 Heaven 2 (in the Bible) the Garden of Eden, home of Adam and Eve 3 a place of perfect happiness 4 a place with everything needed for a certain activity: *a hunter's paradise* 5 a state of perfect happiness

paradox *n* 1 a statement which seems to be foolish or impossible, but which has some truth in it: '*More haste, less speed' is a paradox* 2 an improbable combination of opposing qualities, ideas, etc.: *It is a paradox that in such a rich country there should be so many poor people* — ~**ical** *adj* — ~**ically** *adv*

paraffin *n* 1 also **paraffin oil**— an oil made from petroleum, coal, etc., burnt for heat and in

lamps for light ☞REFINERY 2 also **paraffin wax**— a waxy substance got from petroleum, coal, etc., used esp. in making candles

paragon *n* a person or thing that is or seems to be a perfect model: *a paragon of virtue*

paragraph *n* a division of a written or printed piece made up of 1 or more sentences, of which the first word begins a new line and is often set inwards a little from the margin 2 a short item in a newspaper

parakeet *n* any of several kinds of small parrot

parallel¹ *adj* 1 (of 2 or more lines or planes) running side by side but staying the same distance apart 2 comparable (to): *My feelings are parallel to yours*

parallel² *n* 1 a parallel line, or line of things or surfaces: *on a parallel with* ☞MATHEMATICS 2 a comparable person or thing: *without (a) parallel* 3 a comparison that shows likeness 4 an electrical arrangement in which a number of electrical apparatuses are connected in such a way that each may receive full electrical power whether or not the others are being used —compare SERIES ☞ELECTRICITY 5 also **parallel of latitude**— any of a number of lines on a map drawn parallel to the equator

parallel³ *v* **-l-** *or* **-ll-** 1 to equal: *No one has paralleled his success* 2 to compare

parallel bars *n* a pair of parallel bars on 4 posts, used for exercising the body

parallelogram *n* *technical* a flat 4-sided figure (QUADRILATERAL) with opposite sides equal and parallel ☞MATHEMATICS

paralyse *v* **-lysed, -lysing** 1 to cause (some or all of the body muscles) to become uncontrollable or stiff 2 to make ineffective: *The electricity failure paralysed the train service* — **-lysis** *n*

paralytic *n, adj* 1 (a person) suffering from paralysis 2 causing paralysis 3 *esp. spoken* (a person who is) very drunk — ~**ally** *adv*

paramilitary *adj* 1 connected with and helping a regular military force 2 being like a regular military force, or used as an irregular military force

paramount *adj* highest in power or importance — ~**cy** *n*

paramour *n* *old use* an unlawful lover of a married man or woman

paranoia *n* a lasting disease of the mind in which the sufferer believes that others are against him, or that he is a famous or important person

paranoid *adj, n* (of or like) one who suffers from paranoia

parapet *n* 1 a low wall at the edge of a roof, bridge, etc. ☞CASTLE 2 a wall of earth or stone built in front of the trenches used by soldiers in war

paraphernalia *n* a number of small articles of various kinds: *all my photographic paraphernalia*

paraphrase *n, v* **-phrased, -phrasing** (to make

or give) a re-expression of (something written or said) in different words

paraplegia n paralysis of the lower part of the body, including both legs — **-gic** adj, n — **-gically** adv

parasite n 1 a plant or animal that lives on or in another and gets food from it 2 a useless person who is supported by the wealth or efforts of others — **-sitic, -sitical** adj — **-sitically** adv

parasol n a sunshade

paratroops n a number of soldiers trained to parachute from aircraft, esp. as a fighting group — **-trooper** n

parboil v to boil until partly cooked

parcel n also **package**— a thing or things wrapped in paper and tied or fastened in some other way for easy carrying, posting, etc. — compare PACK

parcel out v adv **-ll-** to divide into parts or shares

parch v (of the sun or thirst) to make hot and dry

parchment n 1 a writing material used esp. in ancient times, made from the skin of a sheep or goat —compare VELLUM 2 any of various types of good quality paper that look like this 3 a piece of writing on parchment

pardon¹ n 1 forgiveness: *I beg your pardon* —compare EXCUSE **me** 2 *law* an action of a court or ruler forgiving a person for an unlawful act, forgiving the act itself, or giving freedom from punishment for such an act

pardon² v 1 to forgive 2 to give an official pardon to or for

pardonable adj that can be pardoned: *a pardonable mistake* — **-ably** adv

pare v **pared, paring** to cut away (the thin outer covering), usu. with a sharp knife — **parer** n

pare down v adv to reduce

parent n 1 the father or mother of a person —compare RELATION, RELATIVE ⇒FAMILY 2 any living thing that produces another: *the parent tree* 3 that which starts something else: *Our club is the parent association, and there are now 4 others* — **~al** adj — **~ally** adv — **~hood** n

parentage n 1 the state or fact of being a parent 2 origin: *of unknown parentage*

parent company n **-nies** a business company that controls one or more others

parenthesis n **-theses** 1 one or more words introduced as an added explanation or thought 2 also **round bracket**, *esp. spoken* **bracket**— either of a pair of small curved lines ( ), used together to enclose such added information

parent-teacher association n an organization of teachers and the parents of their pupils that works for the improvement of the school

par excellence adj *French* without equal, as the best and/or most typical of its kind

pariah n a person not accepted by society

parish n 1 an area in the care of a single priest

and served by one main church 2 a small area, esp. a village, having its own local government: *parish council* 3 a usu. small area which someone works in and knows very well

parishioner n a person living in a particular parish

parish-pump adj of local interest only

Parisian n, adj (a person) of or from Paris

parity n 1 the state or quality of being equal 2 the same or equal level, rate, etc.

park¹ n 1 a large usu. grassy enclosed place in a town, used by the public for pleasure 2 also **parkland**— a large enclosed stretch of land round a large country house —see also CAR PARK

park² v 1 to stop or leave (a vehicle) for a time: *Don't park here* 2 to leave (something) in a place for a time: *Don't park your books on my papers!* 3 to settle (oneself) with the intention of staying for some time

parka n a short coat with a hood for the head, usu. having a fur edging —compare ANORAK

parkin n esp. Scots & N. English a type of hard ginger cake

parking meter n an apparatus into which one puts a coin to pay for parking a car for a certain time

Parkinson's disease n a kind of paralysis, in which the muscles become stiff and the limbs continually shake

Parkinson's law n esp. humour the idea that work spreads to fill the time allowed for it

parky adj **-kier, -kiest** esp. spoken (of the air, weather, etc.) rather cold

parlance n a particular use of words: *In naval parlance, a floor is a "deck"*

parley v **-leyed, -leying** to talk in order to make peace — **parley** n

Parliament n 1 a body of people (**Members of Parliament**) wholly or partly elected by the people of a country to make laws 2 (in the United Kingdom) the main law-making body, made up of the King or Queen, the Lords, and the elected representatives of the people — **~ary** adj

parliamentarian n 1 a person who is a skilled and experienced member of a parliament 2 a Roundhead

parlour n esp. US a shop for selling a particular type of article or service: *an ice-cream parlour*

parlour game n a game which can be played indoors, usu. sitting down

parlous adj having or showing uncertainty and danger

Parmesan also **Parmesan cheese**— n a kind of hard strong-tasting cheese made in North Italy

parochial adj 1 (in religious matters) of a parish 2 (of one's interests, opinions, etc.) limited; narrow —compare INSULAR — **~ly** adv — **~ism** n

parody¹ n **-dies** 1 (a piece of) writing or music intended to amuse, which recognizably copies a known writer or musician 2 a weak and unsuccessful copy of somebody or something

parody² v **-died, -dying** to make a parody of — **-dist** n

parole¹ n 1 the letting out of a person from prison, conditional upon good behaviour: *on parole* 2 **break one's parole** to fail to follow the conditions of parole

parole² v **paroled, paroling** to set free on parole

paroxysm n 1 a sudden uncontrollable explosive expression: *paroxysms of anger* 2 a sudden but passing attack: *paroxysms of pain*

parquet n French small flat blocks of hard wood fitted together in a pattern: *a parquet floor*

parr n **parr** or **parrs** a young salmon

parricide n the murder of one's own parent (esp. father) or other near relative, or a person guilty of this

parrot¹ n 1 any of a large group of birds, usu. from tropical countries, having a curved beak and usu. brightly coloured feathers. Some can be taught to copy human speech 2 a person who repeats, often without understanding, the words or actions of another

parrot² v to repeat like a parrot

parry v **-ried, -rying** to turn aside (an attack or a weapon): *He parried the unwelcome question* — **parry** n

parse v **parsed, parsing** (in grammar) to give the part of speech, the inflection, and the use of (a word or all the words in a sentence)

parsec n a measurement of distance equal to 3·26 light years

Parsee, Parsi adj of an ancient Persian religious group in India

parsimonious adj too unwilling to spend money — **~ly** adv — **~ness** n

parsimony n too careful use of money

parsley n a small herb with curly strong-tasting leaves, used in cooking or on uncooked foods

parsnip n a plant with a thick white or yellowish root that is used as a vegetable

parson n a priest of the Church of England who is in charge of a parish

parsonage n the house where a parson lives

parson's nose n the piece of flesh at the tail end of a cooked bird such as a chicken

part¹ n 1 any of the pieces that make up a whole 2 any of the divisions into which something is or may be considered as being divided: *Parts of this town are beautiful* 3 any of several equal divisions which make up a whole: *3 parts wine and 2 parts water* 4 a necessary or important piece of a machine or other apparatus 5 a share or duty in some activity: *take part in* 6 a side or position: *Tom took my part in the disagreement* 7 a a character acted by an actor in a play b the words and actions of an actor in a play, or a written copy of these words 8 (in music) one of the tunes, esp. for a particular voice or instrument, which make up a piece of music, or a written copy of this 9 **in part** in some degree 10 **take in good part** not be offended by

part² v 1 to separate or no longer be together: *The war parted many men from their families* 2 to separate into parts or spread apart: *The clouds parted and the sun shone* 3 to separate or move apart: *He tried to part the 2 angry dogs* 4 to separate (hair on the head) along a line with a comb

part³ adv partly: *A centaur is part man, part horse*

part⁴ adj partial: *part payment*

partake v **-took, -taken, -taking** to eat or drink

parthenogenesis n technical the production of a new plant or animal from a female without sexual union with a male

partial adj 1 not complete: *a partial success* 2 favouring one side more than another, esp. in an unfair way —opposite **impartial** 3 having a liking for: *I'm partial to sweets*

partiality n **-ties** 1 the quality or fact of being partial; bias —opposite **impartiality** 2 a special liking

partially adv 1 partly 2 in a partial way

participate v **-pated, -pating** to take part or have a share in an activity or event — **-pant** n — **-pation** n

participle n (in grammar) a form of a verb which may be used as part of a verb (e.g. in compound tenses) or as an adjective. In English there are 2 sorts of participle —compare PAST PARTICIPLE, PRESENT PARTICIPLE

particle n 1 a a single very small piece: *dust/sand particles* b technical a piece of matter smaller than, and part of, an atom c a very small quantity: *particles of food* 2 (in grammar) a any of several usu. short words that are not as important in a sentence as the subject, verb, etc.: *Prepositions and conjunctions are particles* b an affix

particular¹ adj 1 worthy of notice; special: *of particular importance* 2 single and different from others; of a certain sort: *I don't like this particular hat* 3 hard to please 4 **in particular** especially — **~ity** n — **~ly** adv : *not particularly cold*

particular² n a detail: *correct in every particular/in all particulars | I want all the particulars*

particularize, -ise v **-ized, -izing** to give the details of (something) one by one — **-ization** n

parting¹ n 1 an example of, or the action of, parting 2 the line on the head where the hair is parted

parting² adj done or given at the time of parting: *a parting kiss*

parting shot n a last remark, special look, or action made at the moment of leaving

partisan, -zan n 1 a strong, esp. unreasoning, supporter of a party, group, plan, etc. 2 a member of an armed group that fights in secret against an enemy that has occupied its country — **~ship** n

partita n a piece of European instrumental music, esp. of former times, which is usu. either a suite or a set of variations

partition¹ n 1 division into 2 or more parts (esp. of a country) 2 a part formed by dividing 3 something that divides, esp. a thin inside wall

partition² v to divide into 2 or more parts

partly adv 1 not completely: *partly finished* 2 in some degree: *partly true*

partner¹ n 1 a person who shares (in the same activity): *dancing partner* 2 any of the owners of a business, who share the profits and losses —see also SLEEPING PARTNER 3 **be partners with** to be a partner of, esp. in a game — ~**ship** n

partner² v to act as partner to

part of speech n **parts of speech** (in grammar) any of the classes into which words are divided according to their use: *"Noun, " "verb, " and "adjective" are parts of speech*

partook past tense of PARTAKE

partridge n **-tridges** or **-tridge** any of various middle-size birds, with a round body and short tail, shot for sport and food

part-time adj, adv (working or giving work) during only a part of the regular working time —compare FULL-TIME

parturition n technical the act of giving birth

party n **-ties** 1 a group of people doing something together: *a party of schoolchildren* 2 a gathering of people, usu. by invitation, for food and amusement —see also HEN PARTY, HOUSE PARTY 3 an association of people having the same political aims 4 esp. law one of the people or sides in an agreement or argument: *the guilty party* 5 **be (a) party to** to be concerned in (some action or activity) 6 **the party line** the official opinion of a political party

party line n a telephone line connected to 2 or more telephones belonging to different people

paschal adj of the Jewish holiday of passover

pasha n (the title of) an army or government officer of high rank in Turkey or Egypt in former times

pass¹ v 1 to go forward: *Because of the crowd the carriage was unable to pass* 2 to reach and move beyond: *That car passed ours at 90mph* 3 to move through, across, over, or between: *No one may pass the gates* 4 to place or be placed (in or for a short space of time): *We can pass a rope round this dead tree* 5 to give or be given: *Please pass the bread* 6 (in various sports) to kick, throw, hit, etc. (esp. a ball) to a member of one's own side 7 to send out from the bowels or kidneys 8 a (of time) to go by b to cause (time) to go by: *She passed the time by picking flowers* 9 happen: *It came to pass that......* 10 to cause (money) to be accepted as lawful, esp. by dishonest means: *Somebody passed me a lead shilling!* 11 to say; speak: *pass a comment/a remark* 12 to give or be given official acceptance: *pass a law* 13 to succeed in (an examination) —opposite **fail** 14 to accept or be accepted as reaching a required standard: *I can't pass this bad piece of work!* 15 (of feelings, thoughts, etc.) to come to an end 16 (of actions, ideas, etc.) to go beyond the limits of:

It passes my understanding 17 to give (a judgment, opinion, etc.) 18 to go unnoticed, unchanged, unpunished, etc.: *let something pass* 19 to go from the control or possession of one to that of another 20 (in some games) to let one's turn go by without taking any action 21 **pass water** urinate —see also PASS AWAY, PASS BY, PASS DOWN, PASS FOR, PASSING, PASS OFF, PASS ON, PASS OUT, PASS OVER, PASS UP

pass² n a way by which one may pass, esp. over a range of mountains ☞GEOGRAPHY

pass³ n 1 an act of moving something (made esp. by the human hand or by an aircraft) over or in front of something else 2 (in various sports) an act of passing a ball 3 (in games) an act of passing 4 a printed piece of paper, which shows that one is permitted to do a certain thing 5 a successful result in an examination 6 a difficult state or condition 7 **make a pass at** sl to try to make (a member of the opposite sex) sexually interested in one

passable adj 1 (just) good enough to be accepted 2 a (of a road) fit to be used b (of a river) fit to be crossed —opposite **impassable**; compare IMPOSSIBLE

passage n 1 the action of going across, by, over, through, etc.: *the passage of heavy vehicles* 2 (of time) onward flow 3 a long journey by ship or aircraft or the cost of such a journey 4 a usu. narrow way through: *He forced a passage through the crowd* 5 the right or permission to go through or across something 6 a passageway 7 a usu. short part of a speech or a piece of writing or music, considered by itself 8 **bird of passage a** a bird that regularly migrates **b** a person who often moves from one place to another 9 **rough passage a** a stormy sea or air journey **b** a difficult time

pass away v adv also **pass on, pass over**— (esp. of a person) to die

pass by v adv 1 also **pass over**— to pay no attention to 2 to go past

pass down also **pass on**— v adv HAND DOWN

passé adj French old-fashioned

passenger n a traveller in a vehicle

passerby n **passersby** a person who happens to pass by

pass for v prep to gain (usu. false) recognition as: *She could pass for a boy*

passing¹ n 1 going by 2 ending; disappearance: *the passing of old customs* 3 death 4 **in passing** in the course of a statement about a different matter

passing² adj 1 going by 2 not lasting long: *a passing thought*

passion n 1 strong feeling, esp. of sexual love 2 a sudden show of anger 3 esp. spoken a strong liking — ~**less** adj — ~**lessly** adv

Passion n the suffering and death of Christ

passionate adj 1 able to feel strongly 2 showing passion : *a passionate speech* 3 very eager: *a passionate interest* — ~**ly** adv

passionflower n a usu. climbing plant with

large flowers and edible egg-shaped fruit (**passion-fruit**)

passion play n -**plays** a story of the Passion, often performed at Easter

passive¹ adj 1 not active 2 (esp. of animals) quiet; not dangerous 3 suffering but not opposing 4 technical expressing an action done to the subject of a sentence: ' Was thrown' is a passive verb phrase in ' The boy was thrown from his horse' —compare ACTIVE — ~ly adv

passive² n (in grammar) the passive forms of a verb

passive resistance n nonviolence

passivity also **passiveness**— n being passive

passkey n -**keys** 1 a private key to a particular door or gate 2 a key that will open several locks —compare MASTER KEY

pass off v adv 1 to stop: The storm passed off 2 to take place successfully: The meeting passed off well 3 to present falsely: She passed herself off as a boy 4 to direct attention away from: He passed off the question

pass on v adv 1 PASS AWAY 2 HAND DOWN 3 to move on: Let us pass on to the next subject

pass out v adv 1 to faint 2 (esp. at a military school) to graduate

pass over¹ v adv 1 to die 2 PASS BY

pass over² v prep to try not to mention: Let us pass over his rude remarks

Passover n a Jewish holiday in memory of the freeing of the Jews from Egypt

passport n 1 a citizen's official document of identification 2 something that permits a person easily to do or get something

pass up v adv to let slip: Never pass up a chance to learn

password n a secret word or phrase which one has to know in order to enter a building, camp, etc.

past¹ adj 1 (of time) earlier than the present: past years 2 ended: Winter is past 3 former: my past successes 4 (of a verb form) expressing something that happened before now: the past tense

past² prep 1 after: 10 past 7 2 up to and beyond: The boys rushed past us 3 put it past somebody esp. spoken to consider somebody very unlikely: I wouldn't put it past her to turn up without an invitation!

past³ n 1 the time before the present: If only one could change the past 2 a (of a country) history b (of a person) past life, actions, etc., esp. when these contain scandal: a woman with a past 3 the past tense

past⁴ adv to and beyond a point in time or space: The children hurried past. | The days flew past

pasta n food made from flour paste

paste¹ n 1 a thin mixture used for sticking paper 2 any soft wet mixture easily shaped or spread 3 a mixture of flour, fat, and liquid for pastry 4 a spread for bread made by crushing solid foods: fish paste —compare PATÉ 5 a shining

material made of lead and glass, used for imitation jewellery

paste² v pasted, pasting to stick with paste

pasteboard n stiff cardboard

pastel n 1 a solid chalklike colouring substance, often in a stick 2 a picture drawn using this substance 3 any soft light colour (often in the phrase **pastel shade**)

pastern n the narrow part of a horse's foot, above the hoof ☞ HORSE

pasteurize, -ise v -ized, -izing to heat (esp. milk) in a certain way to destroy bacteria — -**ization** n

pastiche n a work of art that imitates the style of a different artist

pastille n a small sweet, esp. one containing a medicine for the throat

pastime n something done to pass one's time pleasantly

past master n a person who is very clever or skilled at something

pastor n a Christian religious leader

pastoral¹ adj 1 esp. in literature concerning simple country life: a pastoral scene 2 (of land) grassy; suitable for feeding sheep and cattle 3 technical concerning a religious group, or its leader's duties: The rabbi makes pastoral visits every Tuesday

pastoral² n a pastoral poem, picture, etc.

pastoral care n nonmaterial help, esp. advice, offered esp. by a religious leader or by a teacher

pastorale n a piece of music in pastoral style

past participle also **perfect participle**— n (in grammar) a form of a verb used in compound forms to express actions in the past, or sometimes as an adjective: "Done" and "seen" are the past participles of "do" and "see"

past perfect n the pluperfect

pastry n -**tries** 1 baked paste made of flour, fat, and milk or water 2 an article of food (esp. a cake) made of this

pasturage n grass or grassland for feeding cattle, horses, etc.

pasture¹ n 1 grass as food for cattle —compare ARABLE 2 land where this is grown

pasture² v -tured, -turing to put (animals) in a pasture to feed

pasty¹ n -**ties** a small folded meat pie

pasty² adj -**ier, -iest** (of the face) white and unhealthy-looking

pat¹ n 1 a light friendly stroke 2 a small shaped mass esp. of butter

pat² v -**tt-** to touch or strike gently and repeatedly with a flat object, esp. the palm

pat³ adv 1 at once: The answer came pat 2 **have/know something (off) pat** to know something thoroughly

patch¹ n 1 a piece of material used to cover a hole or a damaged place 2 a part of a surface that is different from the space round it: wet patches on the wall 3 a protective piece of material worn over an eye that has been hurt 4 also **beauty patch, beauty spot**— (in the 17th and 18th century) a small round usu. black piece of material worn by woman on the face

patch² v to cover (a hole) with a patch

patchouli n a perfume made from a bushy Indian plant

patch pocket n a pocket made by sewing a square piece of material onto the outside of a garment

patch up v adv 1 MAKE UP 2 to mend with patches

patchwork n sewn work made by joining many pieces of cloth of different colours, patterns, and shapes

patchy adj -ier, -iest 1 having a number of, or made up of, patches 2 appearing in patches 3 only good in parts: *The concert was patchy* — -ily adv — -iness n

pate n old use or humour the top of the head (esp. in the phrase **bald pate**)

pâté n a food made by crushing solid foods into a paste —compare PASTE ; see also PÂTÉ DE FOIE GRAS

pâté de foie gras also (esp. spoken) **foie gras**— n French pâté made from the liver of a goose

patella n medical the kneecap

patent¹ adj 1 easy to see; obvious 2 protected, by a patent, from being copied 3 concerned with patents

patent² n 1 a document from a government office (**Patent Office**) giving someone the right to make or sell an invention 2 the right given in such a document

patent³ v to obtain a patent for

patent leather n thin shiny leather, usu. black

patently adv clearly and plainly: *He was patently lying*

patent medicine n medicine made of a secret mixture and claiming miraculous cures

pater n old public school sl father

paternal adj 1 of, like, or from a father — compare MATERNAL 2 fatherly; protecting; over-protective 3 related through the father's side — ~ly adv

paternalism n the paternal way of controlling an association or ruling a country — -ist n — -istic adj — -istically adv

paternity n 1 fatherhood 2 esp. law origin from the male parent 3 esp. written the beginnings from which something has developed

path n 1 a way made by people walking 2 a footpath 3 an open space made to allow forward movement 4 a line along which something moves: *the path of an arrow* 5 a way: *Hard work is the path to success* — ~less adj

pathetic adj 1 causing pity or sorrow 2 hopelessly unsuccessful — -ically adv

pathfinder n a person who goes on ahead of a group and finds the best way through unknown land —compare PIONEER

pathological adj 1 medical of or concerning pathology 2 medical caused by disease 3 esp.

spoken unreasonable; unnatural: *a pathological fear of the dark* — ~ly adv

pathology n medical the study of disease and diseased tissue — -gist n

pathos n esp. in literature the quality in speech, writing, etc., that causes pity and sorrow △ BATHOS

patience n 1 the ability **a** to wait calmly **b** to control oneself when angered **c** to suffer without complaining **d** to attend closely to difficult work 2 any of a number of card games, usu. for one player

patient¹ adj having patience — ~ly adv

patient² n a person receiving medical treatment

patina n 1 a usu. green surface formed on copper or bronze 2 a smooth shiny surface on wood, walls, etc.

patio n -os an open paved space outside a house

patisserie n French a shop that sells French-style cakes

patois n -tois French a regional dialect

patrial n a person who, because one of his parents or grandparents was born there, has a right to settle in the United Kingdom

patriarch n 1 **a** a bishop in the early Christian Church or Eastern Churches **b** a bishop of the Roman Catholic Church, in rank just below the pope 2 an old and respected man 3 esp. Bible the male head of a family

patriarchal adj 1 of or like a patriarch 2 ruled by the oldest men: *a patriarchal society*

patriarchy n -ies a social system ruled by men generally according to their seniority

patrician n 1 a member of the governing classes in ancient Rome —compare PLEBEIAN 2 a nobleman; aristocrat — **patrician** adj

patricide n 1 the murder of one's father 2 a person guilty of this

patrilineal adj of or being a system in which property passes through the male side of the family

patriot n a person who loves and will defend his country — ~ism n — ~ic adj — ~ically adv

patrol¹ n 1 the act or time of patrolling 2 a small group of people, vehicles, etc., sent out to search for the enemy 3 a small body of boy scouts or girl guides

patrol² v -ll- to go at regular times round (an area, building, etc.) to see that there is no trouble

patrol car n a car used by the police for patrolling roads

patrolman n esp. US a policeman who patrols a particular area

patron n 1 a person or group that gives money to a person, a group, or some worthy purpose 2 a person who allows his or her name to be used in connection with some group 3 a person who uses a particular shop, hotel, etc. —compare CUSTOMER

patronage n 1 the trade or support received from a patron 2 the right to appoint people to important positions 3 kind but patronizing treatment

patronize, -ise v -ized, -izing 1 to be a patron of 2 to act towards as if one is better or more important

patron saint n a saint, regarded as giving special protection to a place, activity, etc.: *Saint Christopher is the patron saint of travellers*

patter¹ v to say quickly and without thought

patter² n very fast continuous amusing talk

patter³ v 1 to make light quickly repeated noises 2 to run with short quick-sounding steps

patter⁴ n the sound of something striking a hard surface lightly, quickly, and repeatedly

pattern¹ n 1 a regularly repeated arrangement with ornamental effect 2 the way in which something develops 3 a sample of cloth 4 a shape used as a guide for making something 5 an excellent example to copy —compare MODEL

pattern² v 1 to copy exactly 2 to make an ornamental pattern on

paunch n a fat stomach —see also POT, POTBELLY — ~y adj — ~iness n

pauper n 1 esp. old use a person so poor he receives official help 2 a very poor person

pause¹ n 1 a short but noticeable break (in activity, or speech) 2 (in music) a mark (⌢) over a note, showing that the note is to be played or sung longer than usual

pause² v paused, pausing to make a pause

pave v paved, paving to cover with a hard level surface (esp. of paving stones)

pavement n a paved path at the side of a street

pavement artist n a person who chalks pictures on a pavement

pavilion n 1 a building beside a sports field, for the players and spectators 2 a large ornamental esp. temporary building for public amusements or exhibitions 3 a large tent, esp. for shows of flowers, farm goods, etc. —compare MARQUEE

paving n material used to pave a surface —see also CRAZY PAVING

paw¹ n an animal's foot with nails or claws —compare HOOF

paw² v 1 to touch or make a strike at with a paw 2 to strike at (the ground) with the hoof in anger, fear, etc. 3 esp. spoken to feel or touch with the hands

pawky adj -kier, -kiest amusing in an odd clever way, so that one cannot tell whether the thing said was meant to be funny — -kily adv — -kiness n

pawl n a piece of metal that fits between the teeth of a toothed wheel or bar (RATCHET) to allow movement one way only

pawn¹ n the state of being pawned (esp. in the phrase in pawn)

pawn² v to leave (something of value) with a pawnbroker as a promise that one will repay the money lent

pawn³ n 1 (in chess) one of the 8 least valuable pieces 2 an unimportant person used by somebody else for his own advantage

pawnbroker n a person to whom people bring valuables so that he will lend them money

pawnshop n a pawnbroker's place of business

pawpaw n a tall tropical tree, or its large yellow-green edible fruit

pay¹ v paid, paying 1 to give (money) for goods bought, work done, etc. 2 to settle (a bill, debt, etc.) 3 to be profitable: *We must make this farm pay* 4 to make or say (esp. in the phrases pay a visit, pay a call, pay a compliment, pay one's respects) 5 to give willingly (esp. in the phrases pay attention/heed) 6 to suffer for some bad action —see also PAY BACK, PAY OFF, PAY OUT, PAY UP — ~er n

pay² n 1 money received for work 2 in the pay of employed by: *This man is in the pay of the enemy* USAGE Remuneration and emoluments are sometimes used to mean pay. Emoluments may include expenses. A salary is usually paid monthly straight into a bank by one's employer. Wages are usually paid weekly in cash.

payable adj 1 (of a bill, debt, etc.) that must or may be paid 2 (on a cheque) to be paid to (a particular person)

pay back v adv 1 also (esp. spoken) pay off, pay out, serve out— to return punishment to 2 to return what is owing

payday n -days the day on which wages are paid

PAYE abbrev. for: pay as you earn; a system by which income tax is taken away before wages are paid

payee n technical a person to whom money is paid

payload n 1 (the weight of) the part of a load for which payment is received 2 the amount of explosive in a missile

paymaster n 1 an official who pays wages 2 a person who pays somebody and therefore controls his actions

paymaster general n paymasters general or paymaster generals a minister in the British government who may be given any duty (but usu. one connected with the Treasury)

payment n 1 paying 2 an amount of money paid 3 something done, said, or given in return —compare REWARD

payoff n esp. spoken 1 the act or time of paying 2 the end of a number of connected acts (esp. the end of a story when everything is explained) —compare PUNCH LINE 3 punishment; retribution

pay off v adv 1 to pay the whole of (a debt) 2 esp. spoken PAY BACK 3 to pay and dismiss (someone) 4 to be successful: *Did your plan pay off?*

pay out v adv 1 to pay (money) 2 to allow

(esp. a rope) to be pulled gradually longer   3 PAY BACK

pay packet n   1 an envelope containing an employee's weekly wages   2 the amount of wages a person earns

payroll n   1 a list of workers employed by a company and the amount each is to be paid   2 the total wages paid to all workers in a company

pay up v adv to pay a debt in full

PC abbrev. for: Police Constable

PE n esp. spoken physical education

pea n   1 a green edible seed   2 any of various climbing plants whose pods contain these seeds

peace n   1 a condition or period in which there is no war   2 freedom from disorder within a country (esp. in the phrases **keep the peace, a breach of the peace**)   3 a state of agreement among people living together   4 calmness; quietness   5 freedom from anxiety: peace of mind

peaceable adj   1 disliking argument or quarrelling   2 calm; free from disorder — **-bly** adv

Peace Corps n a body of trained people sent abroad from the US to help developing countries

peaceful adj   1 quiet; untroubled   2 loving peace — ~**ly** adv — ~**ness** n

peacemaker n a person who causes nations or people to stop fighting or quarrelling

peace pipe n an ornamental ceremonial tobacco pipe smoked by North American Indians

peacetime n a time when a nation is not at war —opposite **wartime**

peach¹ n   1 a small tree or its round fruit with soft yellowish-red skin, sweet juicy flesh, and a large rough seed   2 the colour of this fruit   3 esp. spoken a person (esp. a pretty young girl) or thing greatly admired

peach² v sl to give information about somebody who has done wrong

Peach Melba n **-bas** half a peach served with ice cream and raspberry juice

peacock n   1 (fem. **peahen**) —the male of a large ornamental bird (**peafowl**) whose long tail feathers can be spread out showing beautiful colours and patterns   2 a butterfly with large patterned wings

peacock blue n, adj bright shiny blue

peak n   1 a sharply pointed mountain ☞GEOGRAPHY   2 a part that curves to a point: The wind blew the waves into great peaks   3 the part of a cap which sticks out above the eyes   4 the highest point of a varying amount: Sales have reached a new peak

peaked adj (of a cap) having a peak

peaky adj **-kier, -kiest** also **peaked**— thin, weak, and sick-looking

peal¹ n   1 the loud ringing of bells   2 technical a musical pattern made by ringing several bells one after another   3 technical a set of bells on which these patterns can be played   4 a loud long sound: peals of laughter

peal² v to ring out or sound loudly

peanut n a groundnut

peanuts n sl esp. US a sum of money too small to be worth considering

pear n (a tree bearing) a sweet juicy fruit, tapering towards the stem

pear drop n a sweet shaped like a small pear

pearl n   1 a hard silvery-white ball formed inside shell fish, esp. oysters, very valuable as a jewel   2 something which has the shape or colour of this   3 mother-of-pearl   4 something or somebody very precious

pearl barley n the rolled grain of barley

pearl diver n a person who swims under the sea, looking for shells containing pearls

pearly adj **-ier, -iest** like or ornamented with pearls: pearly teeth — **-iness** n

peasant n   1 (now used esp. of developing countries or former times) a farm worker, esp. one who owns and lives on a small piece of land   2 a person without education or manners

peasantry n all the peasants   of a country

pease pudding n dried peas, boiled to a soft brown mass

peashooter n a small tube for blowing small objects (esp. dried peas) at people or things

pea souper n esp. spoken a thick yellow fog

peat n decayed vegetable matter used for fuel or for fertilizing plants — ~**y** adj

pebble n a small stone found esp. on the seashore

pebbledash n cement with lots of small pebbles in it used for covering outside walls

pebbly adj **-blier, -bliest** covered with pebbles

pecan n an edible nut

peccadillo n **-loes** or **-los** an unimportant fault

peck¹ v   1 to strike or eat with the beak   2 to make by striking with the beak: The bird pecked a hole in the tree   3 esp. spoken to kiss hurriedly

peck² n   1 a stroke or wound made by pecking   2 esp. spoken a hurried kiss

pecker n **keep one's pecker up** esp. spoken to remain cheerful

pecking order n the social order of a body of people, by means of which each knows who is more or less important than himself

peckish adj esp. spoken hungry

pectin n technical a sugar-like chemical compound found in certain fruits

pectoral adj technical of the chest: pectoral muscles

peculate v **-lated, -lating** esp. written to take and use for one's own purposes (money put into one's care) —compare EMBEZZLE — **-lation** n

peculiar adj   1 strange; unusual: This food has a peculiar taste   2 esp. spoken rather ill   3 special; particular

peculiarity n **-ties**   1 being peculiar   2 something peculiar, strange, or unusual

peculiarly adv   1 especially   2 strangely

pecuniary adj esp. written connected with or consisting of money — **-rily** adv

pedagogue *n old use or humour* a teacher
pedagogy also **pedagogics**— *n* the study of ways of teaching — **-gic** *adj* — **-gical** *adj* — **-gically** *adj*
pedal[1] *n* a barlike part of a machine which can be pressed with the foot to control or drive the machine
pedal[2] *adj technical* of the foot
pedal[3] *v* **-ll-** 1 to work the pedals of a machine 2 to work or move (a machine) by using pedals
pedant *n* a person whose attention to detail is too great — ~**ic** *adj* — ~**ically** *adv*
pedantry *n* **-ries** 1 being a pedant 2 a pedantic expression or action
peddle *v* **-dled, -dling** 1 to go from place to place trying to sell small goods 2 to try to make people accept (ideas, plans, etc.)
pedestal *n* the base on which a pillar or statue stands
pedestrian[1] *adj* 1 connected with walking 2 lacking in imagination; uninteresting
pedestrian[2] *n* a person walking
pedestrian crossing *n* a special place for pedestrians to cross the road
pedestrian precinct *n* an area of streets in the centre of a town where motor traffic is not allowed
pediatrics *n* see PAEDIATRICS — **-ician** *n*
pedicure *n* a treatment of the feet and toenails — **-curist** *n*
pedigree *n* 1 FAMILY TREE 2 people from whom or animals from which a person, family, or animal is descended; ancestry 3 a long and recorded (and usu. specially chosen) family of animals —compare THOROUGHBRED
pedlar *n* a person who travels trying to sell small articles
pee[1] *v* **peed, peeing** *sl* to urinate
pee[2] *n sl* 1 an act of urinating 2 urine
peek *v esp. spoken* to look (at something) quickly, esp. when one should not —compare PEEP, PEER — **peek** *n*
peel[1] *v* 1 to remove the outer covering from (a fruit, vegetable, etc.) 2 to lose an outer covering: *The walls were peeling* 3 (of an outer covering) to come off: *My skin always peels in the sun*
peel[2] *n* the outer covering, esp. of fruits and vegetables which one peels before eating — compare RIND
peeler[1] *n* a tool or machine for peeling fruit or vegetables
peeler[2] *n old sl* a policeman
peelings *n* parts peeled off (esp. from potatoes)
peel off *v adv* 1 to remove all one's clothes 2 (of an aircraft) to turn away from other aircraft in the air
peep[1] *n* a short weak high sound as made by a young bird
peep[2] *v* 1 to look (at something) quickly and secretly 2 to begin slowly to appear —compare PEEK, PEER
peep[3] *n* a short hurried look

peeper *n sl* an eye
peephole *n* a small hole through which one can peep
peeping Tom *n* a person who secretly looks at others esp. when they are undressing
peer[1] *n* 1 an equal in rank 2 a baron, viscount, earl, marquis, or duke 3 a person who has the right to sit in the House of Lords —see also PEERESS
peer[2] *v* to look very carefully or hard, esp. as if not able to see well —compare PEEK, PEEP
peerage *n* 1 a the whole body of peers b the rank of a peer 2 a book containing a list of peers and their families
peeress *n* 1 a female peer 2 the wife of a peer
peerless *adj* without an equal
peer of the realm *n* **peers of the realm** a person who has inherited the rank of peer and on whose death the rank will be passed on to his eldest son
peevish *adj* bad-tempered; easily annoyed — ~**ly** *adv* — ~**ness** *n*
peewit *n* a lapwing
peg[1] *n* 1 a short piece of wood, metal, etc., esp. a for holding esp. wooden surfaces together b fixed to a wall for hanging coats and hats on c hammered into the ground to hold the ropes supporting a tent 2 CLOTHES PEG 3 a wooden screw to tighten or loosen the strings of certain musical instruments 4 a base for a talk or argument: *a peg to hang an argument on* 5 **off the peg** (of clothes) not specially made to fit a particular person's measurements
peg[2] *v* **-gg-** to fasten with a peg
peg away *v adv esp. spoken* to work hard and steadily
peg leg *n esp. spoken* a wooden leg
peg out *v adv* 1 *esp. spoken* to die 2 to mark (a piece of ground) with sticks
pejorative *n, adj esp. written* (a word, phrase, etc.) that suggests that somebody or something is bad — ~**ly**
pekinese, pekingese also (*esp. spoken*) **peke** — *n* **-ese** *or* **-eses** a type of small dog
pekoe *n* a high quality black tea
pelagic *adj esp. written* in the deep sea far from the shore: *pelagic fishing*
pelf *n literature* money; wealth
pelican *n* **-cans** *or* **-can** a large water bird which eats fish, storing them in a pouch under its beak
pelican crossing *n* a road crossing where the walker can control the traffic lights —compare ZEBRA CROSSING
pellagra *n* a deficiency disease which produces great tiredness, and disorder of the skin and central nervous system
pellet *n* 1 a small ball of soft material made by or as if by rolling 2 a small ball to be fired from a gun 3 *technical* a small mass of feathers, bones, etc., thrown up from the stomach by certain meat-eating birds (e.g. owls)

pell-mell *adv* in disorderly haste — **pell-mell** *adj*

pellucid *adj* *literature* very clear: *a pellucid stream* — ~ly *adv*

pelmet also **valance**— *n* a narrow piece of wood or cloth above a window that hides the curtain rod

pelt¹ *n* 1 the skin of a dead animal with or without the fur or hair 2 the fur or hair of a living animal

pelt² *v* 1 to attack by throwing things at 2 (of rain) to fall heavily 3 to run very fast

pelvis *n* -**vises** *or* -**ves** the bowl-shaped frame of bones at the base of the backbone ⌐▀ANATOMY — **pelvic** *adj*

pemmican, pemican *n* dried meat beaten into small pieces used by travellers

pen¹ *n* a small piece of land enclosed by a fence, for keeping animals in

pen² *v* -**nn**- to shut in a pen or small place

pen³ *n* 1 an instrument for writing or drawing with ink, esp. a a piece of wood, with a nib which is dipped into the ink **b** FOUNTAIN PEN **c** a ballpoint **d** a quill —see also FELT-TIP PEN 2 the profession of writing: *He lives by his pen* 3 *literature* a writer: *a poem by an unknown pen*

pen⁴ *v* -**nn**- *pompous* to write

penal *adj* 1 of punishment: *penal laws* 2 punishable by law: *a penal offence* 3 very severe: *a penal tax* — **penally** *adv*

penalize, -ise *v* -**ized, -izing** 1 to put in a very unfavourable position 2 (in sports) to punish (a team, player, or action) by giving an advantage to the other team 3 to make punishable by law — -**ization** *n*

penalty *n* -**ties** 1 punishment for breaking a law, rule, or agreement 2 suffering or loss that is the result of one's action or state 3 (in sports) **a** a disadvantage given for breaking a rule **b** an advantage given because the other team have broken a rule (esp. a **penalty kick** in football) **c** also **penalty goal**— a goal scored by this means 4 (in sports) a handicap placed on a very good player or team to give the opponent a better chance of winning

penalty area *n* (in football) a space in front of the goal where the opposing team gets a penalty

penance *n* 1 self-punishment to show that one is sorry for having done wrong 2 something one must do which one greatly dislikes

pence *pl. of* PENNY —see also TWOPENCE, SIX-PENCE; see PENNY (USAGE)

penchant *n* *French* a strong liking

pencil¹ 1 a narrow pointed instrument containing a thin stick of graphite or coloured material, for writing or drawing 2 a stick of coloured material in a holder, for darkening the eyebrows 3 a narrow beam (of light) beginning or ending in a small point

pencil² *v* -**ll**- to draw, write, or mark with a pencil

pendant, -dent *n* a neck chain with a small ornament hanging from it

pendent *adj* 1 hanging from above 2 esp. *written* hanging over: *pendent rocks*—

pending¹ *prep* esp. *written* until: *This must wait pending his return*

pending² *adj* 1 happening soon 2 waiting to be decided

pendulous *adj* esp. *written* hanging so as to swing freely — ~ly *adv*

pendulum *n* 1 a weight hanging so as to swing freely 2 a weighted rod used to control the working of a clock

penetrate *v* -**trated, -trating** 1 to enter, pass, cut, or force a way into 2 to be easily heard at a distance 3 to see into or through 4 to understand 5 to fill: *The country is penetrated with fear* 6 to come to understand the truth behind (something false) — -**tration** *n* — -**trable, -trative** *adj* — -**trability** *n*

penetrating *adj* 1 (of the eye, sight, questions, etc.) sharp and searching 2 able to understand clearly 3 reaching everywhere: *penetrating cold* — ~ly *adv*

pen friend *n* a person whom one has come to know by the friendly exchange of letters

penguin *n* a large black and white flightless swimming seabird of esp. the Antarctic

penicillin *n* a medicine (an ANTIBIOTIC) used to destroy certain bacteria in people and animals

peninsula *n* a piece of land almost completely surrounded by water but joined to a larger mass ⌐▀GEOGRAPHY — ~r *adj*

penis *n* the outer sex organ of male animals ⌐▀REPRODUCTION

penitent¹ *adj* feeling or showing sorrow for having done wrong — ~ly *adv* — -**tence** *n*

penitent² *n* a penitent person

penitential *adj* of penitence or penance — ~ly *adv*

penitentiary *n* -**ries** a prison, esp. in the US

penknife *n* -**knives** a small knife with usu. 2 folding blades —compare JACK KNIFE

penmanship *n* skill in writing by hand

pen name *n* a name used instead of a writer's real name —see also PSEUDONYM

pennant *n* a long narrow pointed flag

penniless *adj* having no money

pennon *n* a long narrow pointed flag, esp. carried on the end of a lance

penny *n* -**nies** *or* **pence** *or* (*esp. spoken*) **p** 1 also (*esp. spoken*) **copper, p**— (in Britain after 1971) a small bronze coin ⌐▀MONEY 2 also **old penny,** (*esp. spoken*) **copper**— (in Britain before 1971) a bronze coin, 12 to a shilling; 1d 3 a small amount of money: *It won't cost a penny* 4 **spend a penny** to urinate USAGE **Pennies** is used when speaking of actual coins: *He had two* **pennies**. **Pence** or **p** is used for amounts of money: *It only costs a few* **pence.** Some people think it is bad English to say 5p as it is written, and would rather say 5 **pence.** Do NOT say: *I had one* **pence.**

penny-farthing *n* a 19th century bicycle with

a very large front wheel and a very small back wheel

penology n the study of the punishment of criminals and the operation of prisons

pen pusher n offensive a clerk

pension[1] n an amount of money paid regularly to someone who can no longer earn, esp. because of old age or illness —see also OLD AGE PENSION — ~**able** adj

pension[2] n French (not in English-speaking countries) a private boardinghouse

pensioner n a person receiving a pension

pension off v adv to dismiss from work with a pension

pensive adj deeply or sadly thoughtful — ~**ly** adv — ~**ness** n

pentagon n a polygon with 5 sides — ~**al** adj

Pentagon n 1 the building in Washington from which the U.S. armed forces are directed 2 the officers of high rank who work there

pentagram n a 5-pointed star —compare HEXA-GRAM ☞ MATHEMATICS

pentameter n a line of poetry with 5 beats

pentathlon n a sports event in which competitors compete in 5 different sports

Pentecost n a Jewish holiday 50 days after Passover

penthouse n a small house on top of a tall building

pent up adj shut up within narrow limits

penultimate adj next to the last

penumbra n a shaded area between full darkness and full light

penury n esp. written poverty — -**ious** adj

peony, paeony n -nies a garden plant with large round white, pink, or esp. dark red flowers

people[1] n 1 persons in general 2 the persons belonging to a particular place, trade, etc.: theatre people 3 persons without special rank or position: a man of the people 4 a race; nation 5 one's relatives: I'll take you home to meet my people 6 **go to the people** (of a political leader) to hold an election or referendum   USAGE The usual plural of **person** is **people; persons** is used sometimes in written English, when they are considered more as numbers than human beings: a **person** or **persons** unknown. An **individual** is one **person**, as opposed to a group: What is one **individual** against society? **Man** can be used for the whole human race, including women: **Man** is an inquisitive creature. A **people** is a national group —see FOLK (USAGE)

people[2] v -pled, -pling to fill (a place) with people

pep n esp. spoken vigour

pepper[1] n 1 a hot powder made from crushed peppercorns, used for flavouring —see also BLACK PEPPER, WHITE PEPPER, PAPRIKA 2 the capsicum plant, or its fruit (a RED PEPPER or GREEN PEPPER) used as a vegetable —compare CHILLI

pepper[2] v to hit repeatedly (esp. with shots)

pepper-and-salt adj having small spots of mixed black and white

peppercorn n 1 the seedlike fruit of certain plants, which is crushed to make pepper 2 also **peppercorn rent**— a very small rent

peppermint n 1 a type of mint plant used esp. in making sweets and medicine or its strong taste 2 also **mint**— a sweet with this taste

pepper pot n a container with small holes in the top, for shaking pepper onto food

peppery adj 1 tasting of pepper 2 having a quick temper

pep pill n esp. spoken a pill taken to make one quicker or happier, for a short time

pepsin n a chemical substance (ENZYME) that changes protein into a form the body can use

pep talk n esp. spoken a talk intended to encourage the listener to do well, to win, etc.

peptic adj of, relating to, or concerned with the digestive organs (esp. in the phrase **peptic ulcer**)

pep up v adv -pp- esp. spoken to make more active, or happier

per prep 1 for each: one apple per child 2 during each: 40 words per minute | 20 miles per gallon — see also M.P.G. 3 (esp. in business letters) according to: We have sent the parcel as per instructions

peradventure adv old use perhaps

perambulate v -lated, -lating esp. written to walk about or up and down without hurry — -**lation** n

perambulator n esp. written a pram

per annum adv esp. technical for or in each year

per capita adv esp. written or technical for or by each person — **per capita** adj

perceive v -ceived, -ceiving esp. written to have or come to have knowledge of; see — -**ceivable** adj

per cent[1] adv in each 100; %: I am 100 per cent in agreement

per cent[2] n **per cent** one part in each 100: This company can supply 30 per cent (= 30% = 30/100 = 3/10) of what we need

percentage n an amount stated as a part of 100; proportion ☞ MATHEMATICS

perceptible adj esp. written that can be perceived; noticeable — -**bly** adv — -**bility** n

perception n 1 keen natural understanding 2 something noticed and understood

perceptive adj quick to notice and understand —compare SENSITIVE — ~**ly** adv — ~**ness** n — -**tivity** n

perch[1] n 1 a branch, rod, etc., where a bird rests 2 a high position in which a person or building is placed 3 humour a seat 4 a rod; 5½ yards

perch[2] v 1 (of a bird) to come to rest from flying 2 to go or put into the stated position (esp. on something narrow or high): She perched on a tall chair

perch[3] n **perch** or **perches** an edible freshwater fish with prickly fins

per

500

perchance adv old use or literature perhaps

percipient adj esp. written quick to notice and understand — **-ence** n

percolate v **-lated, -lating** 1 to pass slowly (through small holes) 2 to make (coffee) in a special pot by passing hot water through crushed coffee beans 3 (of ideas, feelings, etc.) to become felt all through a group of people — **-lation** n

percolator n a pot in which coffee is percolated

percussion n 1 the forceful noisy striking together of 2 (usu. hard) objects 2 musical instruments that are played by being struck — **-sive** adj

percussionist n a person who plays percussion instruments

perdition n esp. written everlasting punishment after death

peregrination n literature or humour a long wandering journey

peregrine falcon n a large black and white hunting bird

peremptory adj 1 (of a person, his manner, etc.) a showing an expectation of being obeyed b impolitely quick 2 esp. written (of commands) that must be obeyed — **-rily** adv

perennial¹ adj 1 lasting through the whole year 2 lasting forever 3 (of a plant) that lives for more than 2 years — ~ly adv

perennial² n a perennial plant

perfect¹ adj 1 of the very best possible kind 2 absolutely correct: His English is almost perfect 3 satisfying in every way 4 complete: a perfect stranger 5 technical (of verb forms, tenses, etc.) referring to a time up to and including the present (**present perfect**), past (**past perfect**), or future (**future perfect**) (as in ' He has gone', ' He had gone', ' He will have gone'): the perfect tense

perfect² v to make perfect — ~ **ible** adj — ~ **ibility** n

perfect³ also (esp. written) **perfect tense** , **present perfect (tense)**— n technical the tense of a verb referring to a time up to and including the present —see also PAST PERFECT, PLUPERFECT

perfection n 1 being perfect 2 the act of making perfect 3 the perfect example

perfectionist n 1 a person who is not satisfied with anything other than perfection 2 a person who overvalues correctness — **-ism** n

perfective adj, n (an example) of a verb (esp. in Russian) which shows that the action referred to is completed (either in the past or the future)

perfectly adv 1 in a perfect way 2 completely

perfidy n **-dies** esp. written or literature also **perfidiousness**— disloyalty; treachery — **-dious** adj — **-diously** adv

perforate v **-rated, -rating** 1 to make a hole or holes through (something) 2 to make a line of small holes in (paper), so that a part may be torn off

perforation n 1 perforating or being perfor-

ated 2 a line of holes made by perforating something

perforce adv old use & literature because it is necessary

perform v 1 a to carry out (a piece of work) b to fulfil (a promise, order, etc.) 2 to give, act, or show (a play, a piece of music, etc.) 3 to go through the actions of (a ceremony) 4 to work or carry out an activity properly

performance n 1 the action of performing something 2 (of people or machines) the ability to do something 3 esp. spoken a (troublesome) set of preparations or activities

performer n 1 an actor, musician, etc. 2 a person or thing that performs: He is a good performer on the cricket field (=plays well)

perfume¹ also **scent**— n 1 a pleasant smell, as of flowers 2 sweet-smelling liquid for use on the body

perfume² v **-fumed, -fuming** 1 esp. written to fill with perfume 2 to put perfume on: a perfumed handkerchief

perfunctory adj hasty and without thought — **-rily** adv — **-riness** n

pergola n an arrangement of posts in a garden over which climbing plants can grow ⚠ PAGODA

perhaps adv 1 it may be: Perhaps he'll come by train 2 (in making polite requests): Perhaps you'll let me know

per head adv PER CAPITA; each

perigee n the point at which a body, such as the moon, a planet, or a spacecraft, is closest to the larger body round which it is revolving —compare APOGEE

perihelion n the point where the orbit of an object through space is closest to the sun

peril n 1 danger 2 something that causes danger

perilous adj dangerous; risky — ~ly adv — ~ness n

perimeter n 1 the border round any flat figure or area, esp. a camp or airfield: a perimeter fence 2 the length of this

period¹ n 1 a stretch of time with a beginning and an end ☞ERA 2 a division of a school day: a history period 3 a monthly flow of blood (the MENSES) from a woman's body —see also MENSTRUATE 4 esp. US FULL STOP

period² adj (of furniture, dress, etc.) belonging to or copying an earlier period in history

periodic also **periodical**— adj happening repeatedly, usu. at regular times — ~ally adv

periodical n a periodical magazine

periodic table n a list of elements arranged according to their atomic weights ☞ATOM

period piece n a fine piece of furniture, ornament, etc., of a certain period in history

peripatetic adj esp. written or technical travelling from place to place — ~ally adv

peripheral adj 1 of slight importance by comparison 2 of or connected with a periphery — ~ly adv

periphery n -ries 1 an outside edge: *the periphery of the town* 2 *medical* the places where the nerves end, as in fingers or toes

periphrasis n -ses the use of long words or phrases, or of unclear expressions — ~tic adj

periscope n a long tube containing mirrors so that people lower down (esp. in submarines) can see what is above them

perish v 1 (esp. in newspapers) to die, esp. suddenly; be completely destroyed 2 to decay or lose natural qualities: *Continuous washing has perished the rubber*

perishable adj (of food) that quickly decays — **perishables** n

perisher n sl a troublesome person

perishing[1] adj esp. spoken 1 very cold 2 cursed: *a perishing shame*

perishing[2] also **perishingly**— adv esp. spoken very

peritonitis n medical an inflammation of the inside wall of the abdomen

perjure v -jured, -juring perjure oneself to tell a lie on purpose after promising to tell the truth — ~r n

perjury n -ries 1 perjuring oneself 2 a lie told on purpose

perks also (esp. written) **perquisite**— n esp. spoken money, goods, or advantages that one gets from one's work apart from pay

perk up v adv to make or become more cheerful and confident

perky adj -ier, -iest boldly cheerful — -ily adv — -iness n

perm[1] n also (esp. written) **permanent wave** — the putting of lasting waves into straight hair by chemical treatment

perm[2] v esp. spoken to give a perm to

permafrost n a layer of permanently frozen soil below the earth's surface

permanent adj lasting for a long time or for ever —compare TEMPORARY — -ence, -ency n — ~ly adj

permanent way n -ways a railway track and the bed on which it is laid

permeate v -ated, -ating to pass into every part of — -ation, -ability n — -able adj

permissible adj allowed; permitted . — -bly adv

permission n an act of permitting; consent

permissive adj 1 allowing a great deal of, or too much, freedom 2 (esp. of laws) allowing something but not ordering it — ~ly adv — ~ness n

permit[1] v -tt- 1 to allow 2 to make possible: *weather permitting* 3 to admit: *The facts permit no other explanation*

permit[2] n an official written statement giving permission

permutation n an arrangement of the order of a set of objects: *There are 6 permutations of the letters ABC: ABC, ACB, BCA, BAC, CAB, and CBA*

permute v -muted, -muting technical to rearrange in a different order

pernicious adj very harmful; evil — ~ly adv — ~ness n

pernickety adj esp. spoken worrying about small things; fussy

Pernod n trademark a strong alcoholic French drink tasting of aniseed

peroration n the last part of a speech

peroxide also (esp. written) **hydrogen peroxide**— n esp. spoken a chemical liquid used to bleach and disinfect

perpendicular[1] adj 1 exactly upright 2 (of a line or surface) at an angle of 90° to a line or surface ⌐⃗MATHEMATICS 3 of the style of 14th and 15th century English buildings, esp. churches, ornamented with perpendicular lines — ~ly adv

perpendicular[2] n a perpendicular line or position

perpetrate v -trated, -trating esp. written c humour to do; commit (something criminal, foolish, or amusing) △ PERPETUATE — -tration n — -trator n

perpetual adj 1 lasting for ever or for a long time 2 a uninterrupted b happening often — ~ly adv

perpetuate v -a·ed, -ating to preserve; cause to be continued △ PERPETRATE — -ation n

perpetuity n -ties the state of being perpetual: *in perpetuity* (= for ever)

perplex v to confuse and puzzle

perplexed adj 1 confused and puzzled 2 difficult to understand — ~ly adv

perplexity n -ties 1 being perplexed 2 something that perplexes

perquisite n esp. written a perk △ PREREQUISITE

perry n an alcoholic drink from pears

per se adv Latin considered alone and not with other things

persecute v -cuted, -cuting 1 to treat cruelly (esp. for religious or political beliefs) 2 to annoy △ PROSECUTE — -cution n — -cutor n

persevere v -vered, -vering to continue firmly in spite of difficulties — -verance n

Persian adj 1 of the people, language, etc. of Persia (now Iran) 2 of a cat with long silky hair

persimmon n a tree with an orange-coloured soft edible fruit

persist v 1 to continue firmly in spite of opposition 2 to continue to exist

persistent adj 1 continuing in a habit or action 2 continuing to exist, happen, or appear: *a persistent cough* — ~ly adv — -tence n

person n 1 a human being —see PEOPLE (USAGE) 2 a living human body or its appearance: *She was small and neat of person* 3 (in grammar) any of the 3 forms of verbs or pronouns that show the speaker (**first person**), the one spoken to (**second person**), or the one spoken about (**third person**)

persona n (in psychology) the outward character a person shows to other people

personable adj attractive in appearance — -**bly** adv

personage n esp. written a famous or important person

personal adj 1 concerning, belonging to, or for a particular person; private 2 done directly by a particular person: a personal visit 3 of the body or appearance: personal cleanliness 4 (of things said) directed against a particular person; rude 5 see PERSONAL PRONOUN

personal assistant n a secretary employed to help one person

personal column n a part of a newspaper that gives or asks for personal messages, news, etc.

personality n -**ties** 1 the state of existing as a person 2 a person's character: He has a weak personality 3 unusual, strong, exciting character 4 a person well known to the public: a television personality

personalize, -ise v -**ized, -izing** to make personal, esp. by adding one's address or initials: personalized handkerchiefs — -**ization** n

personally adv 1 directly: He is personally in charge 2 speaking for oneself only 3 as a person

personal pronoun n a pronoun used for showing the speaker, the one spoken to, or the one spoken of: "I", "you", and "they" are personal pronouns

persona non grata n personae non gratae or persona non grata Latin an unacceptable or unwelcome person

personification n 1 a person or thing considered as a perfect example (of some quality): He's the personification of courage 2 the personifying of something

personify v -**fied, -fying** 1 to be a perfect example of 2 to think of (something without life) as human

personnel n 1 all the people employed somewhere 2 the department in a company that deals with (the complaints and difficulties of) these people

perspective n 1 the art of drawing solid objects on a flat surface so that they give an effect of depth, distance, and solidity —compare PLAN, ELEVATION 2 the way in which a matter is judged, so that consideration is given to each part 3 a view, esp. into the distance

perspex n trademark a strong transparent plastic material

perspicacious adj esp. written keen in judgment — ~**ly** adv — -**city** n

perspiration n 1 sweating 2 sweat

perspire v -**spired, -spiring** to sweat

persuade v -**suaded, -suading** 1 to cause to feel certain; convince 2 to cause to do something by reasoning, arguing, etc. —compare CONVINCE

persuasion n 1 persuading or being persuaded 2 the ability to influence others 3 a strongly held belief 4 a group holding a belief

persuasive adj having the power to influence others — ~**ly** adv — ~**ness** n

pert adj 1 amusingly disrespectful 2 gay; full of life — ~**ly** adv — ~**ness** n

pertain to v prep esp. written to belong to or have a connection with

pertinacious adj esp. written stubborn — ~**ly** adv — -**city** n

pertinent adj esp. written connected directly; relevant —opposite **irrelevant**, not **impertinent** — ~**ly** adv — -**nence** n

perturb v esp. written to cause to worry; put into disorder — ~**ation** n

peruse v perused, perusing 1 esp. written to read through carefully 2 esp. spoken to read — **perusal** n

pervade v -**vaded, -vading** (of smells and of ideas, feelings, etc.) to spread through every part of

pervasive adj widespread — ~**ly** adv — ~**ness** n

perverse adj 1 (of people, actions, etc.) annoyingly continuing in what is wrong or unreasonable 2 different from what is required or reasonable — ~**ly** adv — ~**ness** n — -**sity** n

perversion n 1 perverting or being perverted 2 unnatural sexual behaviour

pervert[1] v 1 to turn away from what is right and natural 2 to use for a bad purpose

pervert[2] n a person of unnatural sexual behaviour

peseta n the standard coin in the money system of Spain ⇒MONEY

pessary n -**ries** a solid medicine or instrument put into the vagina

pessimism n 1 the habit of thinking that whatever happens will be bad 2 the belief that evil is more powerful than good — -**mist** n — -**mistic** adj — -**mistically** adv

pest n 1 a destructive usu. small animal or insect 2 esp. spoken an annoying person or thing

pester v to annoy continually, esp. with demands

pesticide n a chemical used to kill pests

pestilence n esp. old use a plague (esp. bubonic plague)

pestilent also **pestilential**— adj 1 esp. old use concerning or causing pestilence 2 continually annoying and unpleasant

pestle n a rounded instrument for crushing substances in a mortar

pet[1] n 1 an animal kept as a companion 2 a specially favoured person or thing

pet[2] v -**tt**- 1 to touch kindly with the hands, showing love 2 to show special care for the comfort of 3 esp. spoken to kiss and touch in sexual play

pet[3] n a condition of sudden childish bad temper

petal n any of the (usu. coloured) leaflike divisions of a flower ⇒FLOWER

petard *n* **hoist with one's own petard** made to suffer by one's evil plan

peter out *v adv* to come gradually to an end

petiole *n* *technical* the stalk of a plant leaf

petit bourgeois also **petty bourgeois**— *n* petits bourgeois *French* a person, such as a small shopkeeper, of the lower middle class

petite *adj* (of a woman, her appearance, etc.) small and neat

petition¹ *n* 1 a request made to a government or other body, usu. signed by many people 2 an official letter to a court of law — ~er *n*

petition² *v* to make a petition to

pet name *n* an invented name given to someone whom one specially likes

petrel *n* a smallish black and white seabird —see also STORMY PETREL

petrify *v* -fied, -fying 1 to frighten so that the power of thought and action is lost 2 to turn into stone — -faction *n*

petrochemical *n* a chemical substance obtained from petroleum or natural gas

petrol *n* a liquid obtained esp. from petroleum, used esp. for producing power in engines ☞REFINERY

petroleum *n* a mineral oil from below the earth's surface, used to produce various chemical substances

petroleum jelly *n* a solid substance made from petroleum, used as a skin medicine and to lubricate machine parts

petrology *n* the scientific study of rocks — -gist *n*

petticoat *n* 1 a skirt worn as an undergarment 2 usu. offensive women: "Petticoat government" means control of men by women

pettifogging *adj* 1 needlessly concerned with small unimportant things 2 too small to be worth considering 3 (of lawyers) dishonest

petty *adj* -tier, -tiest 1 unimportant 2 having a limited ungenerous mind — -tily *adv* — -tiness *n*

petty cash *n* money kept ready in an office for small payments

petty larceny *n* -nies *law* the stealing of articles of little value

petty officer *n* a noncommissioned naval officer

petulant *adj* showing childish temper for no reason — ~ly *adv* — -lance *n*

petunia *n* a garden plant with esp. white or bluish-red trumpet-like flowers

pew *n* 1 a bench with a back, for sitting on in church 2 *humour* a seat (esp. in the phrase **take a pew**)

pewter *n* 1 a greyish metal made by mixing lead and tin 2 dishes and vessels made from this

peyote *n* a drug related to mescalin

pfennig *n* (a coin worth) 0.01 of a mark

phaeton *n* a light open 4-wheeled carriage, usu. pulled by 2 horses

phagocyte *n* *medical* a blood cell (such as a LEUCOCYTE) which protects the body by destroying ('eating') foreign bodies such as bacteria

phalanx *n* -lanxes *or* -langes 1 (esp. in ancient Greece) a group of soldiers packed together for protection 2 any group packed closely for attack or defence

phallus *n* an image of the penis, esp. as used in some religions as a sign of virility — **phallic** *adj*

phantasmagoria *n* a confused dreamlike scene of real or imagined things — -goric *adj* — -gorical *adj*

phantasy *n* -sies a fantasy

phantom *n* 1 a ghost 2 something imaginary

pharaoh *n* (the title of) the ruler of ancient Egypt

pharisaic also **pharisaical**— *adj* 1 making a show of being good and religious 2 of or like a pharisee — -ism *n*

pharisee *n* a person who values too highly the outward form of something (esp. a religion) compared with its true meaning

Pharisee *n* a member of an ancient group of Jews who were very careful in obeying religious laws, and considered themselves very holy

pharmaceutical *adj* connected with making medicine — ~ly *adv*

pharmacist *n* 1 a person skilled in making medicine 2 a person who sells medicine; chemist

pharmacology *n* the scientific study of medicines — -gist *n*

pharmacopoeia *n* an official book describing medicines

pharmacy *n* -cies 1 the making or giving out of medicine 2 a shop where medicines are sold

pharynx *n* *medical* the tube at the back of the mouth

phase¹ *n* 1 a stage of development 2 any of a fixed number of changes in the appearance of the moon or a planet at different times △ PHRASE phases

phase² *v* **phased, phasing** to plan in separate phases

PhD also **D Phil**— *abbrev. for:* Doctor of Philosophy

pheasant *n* -ant *or* -ants a large long-tailed game bird

phenol *n* *technical* a type of acid used in cleaning buildings for destroying bacteria and, in industry, for making plastics

phenomenal *adj* 1 very unusual 2 *esp. written* concerned with phenomena

phenomenally *adv* very; almost unbelievably

phenomenon *n* -na 1 a fact or event as it appears to the senses, esp. one that is unusual or of scientific interest 2 a very unusual person, thing, event, etc.

phi *n* the 21st letter of the Greek alphabet (Φ, φ)

phial *n* a small bottle, esp. for liquid medicines

philander *n* (of a man) to flirt — ~er *n*

philanthropist *n* a person who is kind and generous to those who are poor or in trouble —compare MISANTHROPE, MISOGYNIST

philanthropy *n* active kindness and love for all people — **-pic** *adj* — **-pically** *adv*

philately *n* *technical* stamp-collecting — **-list** *n* — **-lic** *adj*

philharmonic *adj* musical; of or for concerts

philistine *n* a person who does not understand and actively dislikes the arts — **-tinism** *n*

philology *n* the science of words and language — **-logical** *adj* — **-logist** *n*

philosopher *n* **1** a person who studies or has formed a philosphy **2 a** a person who is governed by reason and calmness **b** a person who thinks deeply

philosopher's stone *n* an imaginary substance once thought to have the power to change metal into gold

philosophical also **philosophic**— *adj* **1** accepting difficulty or unhappiness with quiet courage **2** of or concerning philosophy — ~**ly** *adv*

philosophize, -phise *v* **-phized, -phizing** to think, talk, or write like a philosopher

philosophy *n* **-phies** **1** the study or a theory of the nature and meaning of existence, reality, goodness, etc. **2** a set of rules for living one's life **3** quiet courage

philtre *n* a magic drink to make a person fall in love

phlegm *n* the thick jelly (MUCUS) produced in the nose and throat (esp. when one has a cold)

phlegmatic *adj* calm and unexcitable — ~**ally** *adv*

phloem *n* a plant tissue found in the roots, stems, and leaves that carries sugars, proteins, etc. to the plant cells —compare XYLEM

phlox *n* **phlox** *or* **phloxes** any of several types of tall garden plant with groups of bright flowers

phobia *n* a strong usu. unreasonable fear and dislike — **phobic** *n, adj*

phoenix *n* a legendary bird, believed to live for 500 years and then burn itself and be born again from the ashes

phone¹ *n* *esp. spoken* a telephone

phone² *v* **phoned, phoning** *esp. spoken* to telephone

phone-in *n* a radio or television programme during which telephoned questions, statements, etc., from the public are broadcast

phonetic *adj* (of a system of writing down speech sounds) using signs reflecting the actual quality of the sounds — ~**ally** *adv*

phonetics *n* the study and science of speech sounds

phoney, phony¹ *adj* **-ier, -iest** *sl* false; unreal — **-niness** *n*

phoney, phony² *n* **-neys** *or* **-nies** *sl* a phoney person

phonics *n* *technical* a way of teaching reading by the pronunciation of letters and groups of letters

phosphate *n* any of various forms of a salt of phosphoric acid, widely used in industry or in fertilizer

phosphorescence *n* **1** the giving out of light with little or no heat **2** the giving out of faint light, only noticeable in the dark — **-cent** *adj*

phosphorus *n* a poisonous yellowish waxlike element that shines faintly in the dark and burns in air

photo *n* *esp. spoken* a photograph

photocopy¹ *n* **-ies** a photographic copy — compare PHOTOSTAT, XEROX

photocopy² *v* **-ied, -ying** to make a photocopy of — **-ier** *n*

photoelectric *adj* of or using an electrical effect controlled by light

photoelectric cell *n* also (*esp. spoken*) **electric/magic eye**— an instrument by which light is made to work an electrical apparatus

photo finish *n* the end of a race in which the leaders finish so close together that a photograph has to be taken to show which is the winner

photogenic *adj* looking pleasing or effective when photographed

photograph¹ also (*esp. spoken*) **photo, picture**— *n* a picture obtained with a camera and film sensitive to light

photograph² *v* also (*esp. spoken*) **snap**— to take a photograph of — ~**er** *n* — ~**ic** *adj* — ~ **ically** *adv*

photography *n* th producing of photographs

photosensitize, -tise *v* **-tized, -tizing** to cause to change under the action of light — **-tive** *adj* — **-tization** *n*

photostat¹ *n* *trademark* **1** a type of photographic copy —compare PHOTOCOPY, XEROX **2** a machine for making this — ~**ic** *adj*

photostat² *v* **-tt-** *trademark* to make a photostat of

photosynthesis *n* the production of sugar-based substances that keep plants alive, caused by sunlight acting on the chlorophyll in leaves; the way green plants make their own food ⫸ FLOWER

phototropism *n* (a) movement of a plant part towards or away from light

phrasal verb also **phrasal**— *n* a group of words that consists of a verb with an adverb and/or a preposition: *"Get by"* and *"use up"* are phrasal verbs

phrase¹ *n* **1 a** a small group of words **b** (in grammar) a group of words without a finite verb: *"Walking along the road"* and *"a packet of cigarettes"* are phrases —compare CLAUSE, SENTENCE **2** a short passage of music that is part of a longer piece △ PHASE

phrase² *v* **phrased, phrasing** **1** to express in words: *a politely-phrased refusal* **2** to perform (music) so as to give full effect to separate phrases

phrenology *n* (formerly) the judging of a person's character by examining the natural bumps on the head

phylloxera *n* *technical* a small insect that destroys grape vines

phylum *n* **-la** a main division of animals or plants: *The molluscs form a phylum* —see also CLASS, ORDER, FAMILY, GENUS, SPECIES

physical *adj* **1** of or concerning matter or material things (as opposed to mind, spirit, etc.) **2** according to the laws of nature: *Is there a physical explanation for these happenings?* **3** of or concerning the body: *physical exercise* **4** connected with physics: *physical chemistry*

physical jerks *n* *humour* bodily exercises

physically *adv* **1** according to the laws of nature **2** with regard to the body: *physically fit*

physical training also (*esp. spoken*) PT, **physical education** , (*esp. spoken*) PE— *n* development of the body by games, exercises, etc.

physician *n* a doctor, esp. one who gives medicines (as opposed to a surgeon, who performs operations)

physicist *n* a person who studies physics

physics *n* the science of matter and natural forces (such as light, heat, movement, etc.) ◉

physiology *n* **-gies** **1** the science of how living bodies work **2** the system by which a living thing keeps alive — **-gist** *n* — **-gical** *adj*

physiotherapy *n* the treatment of disease by exercises, rubbing, heat, etc. — **-pist** *n*

physique *n* the form and character of a human body

pi *n* **1** the 16th letter of the Greek alphabet (Π, π) represented in English spelling by *p* **2** (in geometry) this letter representing the ratio of the circumference of a circle to its diameter: *Pi equals about 22/7 or 3.14159* ⸦MATHEMATICS

pianissimo *adv, adj, n* **-mos** *or* **-mi** (a piece of music) played very softly

pianist *n* a person who plays the piano

piano¹ *adv, adj, n* **-nos** (a piece of music) played softly —compare FORTE

piano² also (*esp. written)* **pianoforte**— *n* **-os** a large musical instrument, played by pressing keys which cause hammers to hit wires

Pianola *n* *trademark* a piano played by machinery, the music being controlled by a roll of paper with punched holes for the notes

picador *n* (in a bullfight) a rider who annoys the bull by sticking a lance into it

picaresque *adj* (of a story) dealing with the adventures and travels of an attractive rogue

piccalilli *n* hot-tasting chutney made with cut-up vegetables

piccolo *n* **-los** a small flute that plays high notes

pick¹ *v* **1** to choose **2** to pull or break off (part of a plant) by the stem **3** to remove pieces from **4** to steal or take from: *to have your pocket picked* **5** to unlock (a lock) with any instrument other than a key —see also PICK AT, PICK ON, PICK UP

pick² *n* **1** choice **2** the best (esp. in the phrase **the pick of)**

pick³ *n* **1** a sharp pointed instrument: *an ice pick | a toothpick* **2** *esp. spoken* a pickaxe

pick at *v prep* to eat with little interest

pickaxe *n* a large tool with a wooden handle fitted into a curved bar with 2 points, used for breaking up roads, rock, etc.

picker *n* a person or instrument that gathers

picket¹ *n* **1** somebody placed, esp. by a trade union, at the entrance to a factory, shop, etc., to prevent workers from going in until a strike is over **2** a strong pointed stick fixed into the ground, esp. to make a fence

picket² *v* **1** to surround with pickets: *The men picketed the factory* **2** to place (men) as guards — ~**er** *n*

pickle¹ *n* **1** liquid (esp. vinegar or salt water) used to preserve meat or vegetables **2** a vegetable preserved in this **3** *esp. spoken* a child who playfully does slightly harmful things

pickle² *v* **-led, -ling** to preserve in pickle

pick on *v prep* **1** to choose **2** to choose for punishment or blame: *Why pick on me?*

pickpocket *n* a person who steals from people's pockets, esp. in a crowd

pick up *v adv* **1** to take hold of and lift up **2** to improve **3** to gain (knowledge, information, etc.) **4** to cause to increase: *to pick up speed* **5** *esp. spoken* to become friendly with after a short meeting **6** to be able to hear or receive: *My radio can pick up France* **7** (in knitting) to form (a stitch) again

pick-up *n* **1** picking up **2** *esp. spoken* a person who is picked up **3** the part of a record-player which receives and plays the sound from a record (esp. the needle and arm) **4** a light open van with low sides

picnic¹ *n* **1** a pleasure trip in which food is taken to be eaten in the country **2** such a meal

picnic² *v* **-ck-** to have a picnic — **picnicker** *n*

pictorial *adj* having, or expressed in, pictures — ~**ly** *adv*

picture¹ *n* **1** a representation made by painting, drawing, photography, or television **2** a cinema film **3** an image in the mind produced by description: *This book gives a good picture of life 200 years ago*

picture² *v* **-tured, -turing** to imagine

picture book *n* a book made up mostly of pictures

picture card *n* a playing card with a king, queen, or jack on it

pictures *n* the cinema

picturesque *adj* **1** charming or interesting enough for a picture **2** (of language) unusually clear and descriptive — ~**ly** *adv* — ~**ness** *n*

piddle *v* **-dled, -dling** *esp. spoken* to urinate — **piddle** *n*

pidgin *n* a language which is a mixture of 2 or more languages, esp. as used between people who do not speak each other's language —compare CREOLE

SI units

unit	symbol	concept
Base SI units		
ampere	A	electric current
candela	cd	luminous intensity
kelvin	K	thermodynamic temperature
kilogram	kg	mass
metre	m	length
mole	mol	amount of substance
second	s	time
Supplementary SI units		
radian	rad	plane angle
steradian	sr	solid angle
Derived SI units with names		
coulomb	C	electric charge
farad	F	capacitance
henry	H	inductance
hertz	Hz	frequency
joule	J	work or energy
lumen	lm	luminous flux
lux	lx	illumination
newton	N	force
ohm	Ω	electric resistance
pascal	Pa	pressure
tesla	T	magnetic flux density
volt	V	electric potential (difference)
watt	W	power
weber	Wb	magnetic flux

Other units used with SI (in specialized fields)

unit	symbol	value	concept
ångstrom	Å	0.1 nm	length
astronomical unit	AU	$149,600 \times 10^6$ m	length
degree celcius	C	1 K	temperature
electron volt	eV	1.60219×10^{-19} J	energy
parsec	pc	30857×10^{12} m	length
Metric prefixes			
tera	T	10^{12}	1000 000 000 000
giga	G	10^9	1000 000 000
mega	M	10^6	1000 000
kilo	k	10^3	1000
hecto	h	10^2	100
deca	da	10^1	10
deci	d	10^{-1}	0.1
centi	c	10^{-2}	0.01
milli	m	10^{-3}	0.001
micro	μ	10^{-6}	0.000 001
nano	n	10^{-9}	0.000 000 001
pico	p	10^{-12}	0.000 000 000 001
femto	f	10^{-15}	0.000 000 000 000 001
atto	a	10^{-18}	0.000 000 000 000 000 001

Physics

When a substance is in a solid state, its atoms and molecules are held in fixed positions and it has a constant shape. In the liquid state a substance has weaker internal forces and it will flow to take the shape of a container but will not change its volume. A substance in the gaseous state will expand to fill any container and its atoms and molecules behave randomly. The three states have sharply defined changeover points.

At the boiling point, a liquid becomes a gas.
At the freezing point, a liquid becomes a solid.
At the melting point, a solid becomes a liquid.

substance	melting point °C	boiling point °C
aluminium	660	2350
chlorine	−101	−34
copper	1084	2580
ethanol	−117	78
iron	1540	2760
lead	327	1760
mercury	−39	357
nitrogen	−210	−196
oxygen	−219	−183
tin	232	2720
sodium	98	900
sodium chloride	801	1413

Important constant values

velocity of light	2.998×10^8 m s^{-1}
charge on electron	1.602×10^{-19} C
rest mass of electron	9.110×10^{-31} kg
rest mass of proton	1.673×10^{-27} kg
rest mass of neutron	1.675×10^{-27} kg
Avogadro constant	$6.022\ 52 \times 10^{23}$ mol^{-1}
standard atmospheric pressure	1.013 Pa
acceleration due to gravity	9.809 m s^{-2}
mean radius of Earth	6371 km
mean mass of Earth	5.976×10^{24} kg
surface area of Earth	5.101×10^{14} m^2

Roman numerals

I = 1	I = 1	XV	= 15
V = 5	II = 2	XX	= 20
X = 10	III = 3	XXV	= 25
L = 50	IV = 4	XL	= 40
C = 100	V = 5	XC	= 90
D = 500	VI = 6	CXVI	= 116
M = 1000	VII = 7	CM	= 900
	VIII = 8	ML	= 1050
	IX = 9	MCMLXXXI	= 1981
	X = 10	MMI	= 2001

In a Roman numeral if a letter is followed by one representing a greater number, then the earlier one is subtracted from the following number. If a letter is followed by one representing the same or a smaller number then the two are added together.

pie *n* a pastry case filled with meat or fruit, baked usu. in a deep dish USAGE In Britain a **pie** has a pastry lid. If the top is left open it is a **tart**, unless it contains meat or fish, when it is usually called a **flan**. In America, **tart** refers only to small, sweet **tarts** or **pies**.

piebald *adj, n* (a horse) with large black and white patches —compare SKEWBALD

piece *n* **1** a bit, such as: **a** a part which is separated or marked off from a whole: *a small piece of paper* **b** a single object that is an example of a kind: *a piece of furniture* **2 a** any of many parts to be fitted together **b** an object or person forming part of a set: *an 80-piece band* **3** one of a set of small objects or figures used in certain board games, esp. chess **4** a small amount **5** something made by an artist: *a piece of music* **6** a short written statement in a newspaper, magazine, etc. **7** a coin: *a 50-penny piece* —see also PIECE OF EIGHT

piecemeal *adj, adv* (done, made, etc.) bit by bit

piece of eight *n*   **pieces of eight** (esp. in stories) a silver coin formerly used in Spain

piece together *v adv* to make complete by adding part to part: *to piece together the facts*

piecework *n* work paid for by the amount done rather than by the hour

pie chart *n technical* (in statistics) a diagram in which the size of the sector of a circle corresponds to the frequency of the set represented

pied *adj* with 2 or more colours

pie-eyed *adj sl* drunk

pier *n* **1** a bridgelike framework of wood, metal, etc., built out into the sea, often with small buildings on it, at which boats can take in or land their passengers or goods **2** a pillar to support a bridge or roof ⌐⊐CATHEDRAL

pierce *v* **pierced, piercing 1** to make a hole in or through (something) with a point **2** (of light, sound, pain, etc.) to be suddenly seen, heard, or felt

piercing *adj* **1** (of wind) very strong and cold **2** (of sound) very sharp and clear **3** searching: *a piercing look* — ~ly *adv*

Pierrot *n* French a character in English pantomime with a whitened face and loose white clothes —see also COMMEDIA DELL'ARTE

piety *n* **-ties** deep respect for God and religion —see also FILIAL PIETY

piezoelectric *adj* worked by electricity produced by pressure on a piece of crystal

pig *n* **1** any of various fat short-legged animals with a usu. curly tail and thick skin with short stiff hairs, kept on farms for food **2** a person who eats too much, is dirty, or refuses to consider others — ~gish *adj* — ~gishly *adv* — ~gishness *n*

pigeon *n* **pigeons** or **pigeon** any of various quite large grey short-legged birds —compare CLAY PIGEON

pigeonhole[1] *n* one of a set of boxlike divisions (as on a wall or a desk) for putting esp. papers in

pigeonhole[2] *v* **-holed, -holing 1** to put into a pigeonhole **2** to put aside and intentionally do nothing about **3** to put into the proper group: *It's the sort of job you can't pigeonhole— he seems to do different things every week*

piggyback *adj, adv, n* (a ride given to a child) carried on the back

pigheaded *adj* determinedly holding to an opinion or action in spite of argument; stubborn — ~ly *adv* — ~ness *n*

pig iron *n* impure iron obtained directly from a blast furnace

piglet *n* a young pig

pigment *n* **1** dry coloured powder that is mixed with oil, water, etc., to make paint **2** natural colouring of plants and animals, as in leaves, skin, etc.

pigmentation *n* the colouring of living things

pigmy *n* **-mies** a pygmy

pignut *n* an earthnut

pigskin *n* leather made from pig's skin

pigsty *n* **-sties** an enclosure with a small building where pigs are kept

pigswill also **pigwash**— *n* waste food given to pigs

pigtail *n* a length of plaited hair that hangs from the back of the head —compare PONYTAIL — ~ed *adj*

pike[1] *n* **pike** or **pikes** a large fish-eating freshwater fish

pike[2] *n* a long-handled spear formerly used by foot soldiers

pilaster *n* a square esp. ornamental pillar partly sticking out beyond the wall of a building

pilau also **pilaf, pilaff**— *n* a hot-tasting dish made from rice and often meat

pilchard *n* any of various small sea fish like the herring

pile[1] *n* a heavy post hammered upright into the ground to support a building, a bridge, etc.

pile[2] *n* **1** a tidy heap **2** *esp. spoken* a lot: *piles of work* **3** *esp. spoken* a very large amount of money

pile[3] *v* **piled, piling 1** to make a pile of **2** to load; fill: *The cart was piled high with vegetables*

pile[4] *n* the soft surface of short threads on some cloths and carpets —compare NAP

pile driver *n* a machine for hammering piles into the ground

piles *n* haemorrhoids

pileup *n esp. spoken* a traffic accident involving several vehicles

pilfer *v* to steal (small things) — ~er *n* — ~age *n*

pilgrim *n* a person who travels to a holy place as a religious act

pilgrimage *n* **1** (a) journey by a pilgrim **2** a journey to a place in which one has a respectful interest

Pilgrim Fathers also **Pilgrims**— *n* the English

settlers who arrived on the ship 'Mayflower' at Plymouth, Massachusetts, in 1620

pill n 1 a small ball of solid medicine to be swallowed 2 a pill taken by women as a means of birth control

pillage v -laged, -laging to steal violently from (a place taken in war) — **pillage** n — ~r n

pillar n 1 a tall upright usu. round stone post 2 an active supporter: *She was a pillar of the church*

pillar-box also **postbox**— n a round pillar-shaped iron box in the street, with a hole to post letters in

pillbox n a hat like a large round box

pillion n a seat for a second person on a motorcycle, behind the driver

pillory[1] n -ries a wooden post with holes into which in former times the neck and wrists of wrongdoers were locked

pillory[2] v -ried, -rying 1 to put in a pillory 2 to attack with words, so as to cause ridicule

pillow[1] n 1 an oblong cloth bag filled with soft material, for supporting the head in bed 2 an object for supporting the head: *He used his boots for a pillow*

pillow[2] v to rest (esp. one's head) on a pillow

pillowcase also **pillow slip**— n a washable covering for a pillow

pilot[1] n 1 a person who flies an aircraft 2 a person who goes on board and guides ships that use a harbour 3 a person who guides through difficulties

pilot[2] v 1 to act as pilot of 2 to guide: *He piloted the old lady to her seat*

pilot[3] adj serving as a trial: *a pilot study to see if this product will sell*

pilot light n 1 a small electric light that shows when a piece of electrical apparatus is turned on 2 a small gas flame kept burning all the time, for lighting larger burners

pilot officer n an officer of the lowest officer rank in the Royal Air Force

pimento n -tos or -to the seeds of a West Indian tree, or a spice made from these

pimp[1] n a man who controls and makes a profit from the activities of prostitutes

pimp[2] v to act as a pimp

pimpernel n a small low-growing wild plant with white or esp. red flowers

pimple n a small raised diseased spot on the skin — -ply adj — ~d adj

pin[1] n 1 a short thin stiff piece of metal like a small nail, for fastening cloth, paper, etc. 2 an ornamented one of these used as jewellery 3 (in golf) a stick with a flag that is put into the hole

pin[2] v -nn- 1 to fasten with a pin 2 to keep in one position: *In the accident he was pinned under the car* —see also PIN DOWN

pinafore n 1 also (esp. spoken) **pinny**— a loose sleeveless and often backless garment worn over a dress to keep it clean 2 also **pinafore dress**— a sleeveless dress under which a blouse or sweater is worn

pinball n a game in which a ball is guided down a sloping board (PINTABLE)

pince-nez n -nez glasses held in position on the nose by a spring

pincer n either of the pair of claws of certain shellfish

pincers n a tool made of 2 crossed pieces of metal with curved ends for holding and pulling —compare PLIERS

pinch[1] v 1 to press (esp. a person's flesh) tightly between 2 hard surfaces, or between the thumb and a finger 2 to cause pain or distress to: *pinched with cold and hunger* 3 esp. spoken to steal — ~ed adj

pinch[2] n 1 an act of pinching 2 an amount that can be picked up between the thumb and a finger: *a pinch of salt* 3 suffering caused by poverty (esp. in the phrase **feel the pinch**) 4 **at a pinch** if necessary

pincushion n a small cushion into which pins are stuck until needed

pin down v adv 1 to prevent from moving 2 to make (someone) give details

pine[1] v **pined, pining** 1 to become thin and weak slowly, through disease or esp. grief 2 to have a strong but esp. unfulfillable desire

pine[2] n 1 also **pinetree**— any of several types of tall coniferous evergreen tree with thin sharp leaves (**pine needles**) 2 the white or yellowish soft wood of this tree

pineal adj of or concerning a small pinecone-shaped gland in the brain, whose purpose is not known but which may be sensitive to light

pineapple n 1 a large dark yellow tropical fruit with thin stiff leaves on top 2 its sweet juicy yellow flesh

pinecone n the woody fruit or seedcase of a pine

pine marten n tens or -ten a small European meat-eating forest animal

ping v, n (to make) a short sharp ringing sound, as made by tapping a glass

ping-pong n esp. spoken TABLE TENNIS

pinhead n 1 the head of a pin 2 a stupid person

pinion[1] n 1 the end of a bird's wing 2 poetic a wing

pinion[2] v 1 to tie up (the limbs) 2 technical to cut off the pinions from (a bird's wing) to prevent flight

pinion[3] n a small toothed wheel that turns or is turned by a larger gear wheel —compare COGWHEEL, RACK ⎯⎯MACHINERY

pink[1] v to cut with pinking shears

pink[2] n a plant related to the carnation with sweet-smelling pink, white, or red flowers

pink[3] n, adj pale red

pink[4] v (of a car engine) to make high knocking sounds

pink gin n gin with flavouring added to give a pink colour and a slightly bitter taste

pinking shears n scissors with blades that

have v-shaped teeth, used to cut cloth so that the threads along the edge will not fray

pin money *n esp. spoken* money earned by a woman esp. by doing small jobs, to spend on herself

pinnacle *n* 1 a pointed stone ornament like a small tower, on a church or castle roof ⤳CATHEDRAL 2 a tall pointed rock 3 the highest point

pinnate *adj technical* (of a leaf) made of little leaves arranged opposite each other in 2 rows along a stem

pinny *n* -nies *esp. spoken* a pinafore

pinpoint *v* to find the exact nature or position of

pins and needles *n esp. spoken* slight continuous pricking pains in a part of the body to which the blood is returning after having been stopped

pinstripe *n* 1 any of a number of thin lines on cloth 2 a suit made of cloth with these

pint *n* 1(a measure equal to) about 0·57 of a litre; half a quart 2 *esp. spoken* this amount of beer

pintable *n* a machine on which pinball is played

pinup *n* a picture of an admired person stuck up on a wall by the admirer

pioneer[1] *n* 1 one of the first settlers in a new land 2 a person who does something first: *a pioneer of operations on the heart* 3 a member of a group of soldiers who prepare the way for an army's advance

pioneer[2] *v* to begin the development of

pious *adj* respecting God and religion — ~ly *adv* — ~ness *n*

pip[1] *n esp. spoken* a star on the shoulder of an army officer's uniform

pip[2] *n* a small fruit seed

pip[3] *n* a short high-sounding note, as given on the radio to show the time

pip[4] *v* -pp- *esp. spoken* to defeat

pipe[1] *n* 1 a tube carrying liquids and gas: *a gas pipe* 2 a small tube with a bowl-like container at one end, for smoking tobacco 3 a a tubelike musical instrument, played by blowing b any of the tubelike parts through which air is forced in an organ

pipe[2] *v* **piped, piping** 1 to carry (esp. liquid or gas) through pipes 2 to play on a pipe or bagpipes 3 a (of a bird) to sing b (of a person) to speak or sing in a high childish voice 4 to ornament (a dress, cake, etc.) with piping

pipe cleaner *n* a length of thread-covered wire used to unblock a tobacco pipe

pipe dream *n* an impossible hope, plan, etc.

pipeline *n* 1 a long line of pipes connected end to end, for carrying liquids or gas ⤳OIL 2 **in the pipeline** on the way

piper *n* a musician who plays a pipe, or esp. bagpipes

pipes *n esp. spoken* bagpipes

pipette *n* a thin glass tube used in chemistry, into which small measured amounts of liquid can be sucked

piping[1] *n* 1 a number or system of pipes; pipes in general: *a length of piping* 2 a a narrow band of cloth, often enclosing thick string, for ornamenting the edges of garments, furniture, etc. b thin lines of icing on cakes 3 a the high song of a bird b the sound of high voices

piping[2] *adj* (esp. of a voice) high-sounding

piping[3] *adv* **piping hot** (esp. of liquids or food) very hot

pipit *n* any of several types of small bird like the lark

pipsqueak *n* a person not worth one's attention or respect

piquant *adj* 1 having a pleasant sharp taste 2 pleasantly interesting and exciting: *Her face had a piquant charm* — ~ly *adv* — -quancy *n*

pique[1] *n* displeasure, esp. caused by hurt pride

pique[2] *v* **piqued, piquing** 1 to make angry by hurting the pride 2 to excite (interest)

piranha *n* -nhas *or* -nha a fierce South American meat-eating river fish

pirate[1] *n* 1 (esp. formerly) a person who sails the seas robbing ships 2 a person who uses the work of other people without permission, such as one who prints a book when the copyright is held by someone else, or who works a private radio station and plays records without paying — -racy *n* — -ratical *adj* — -ratically *adv*

pirate[2] *v* **pirated, pirating** to make and sell (a book, newly invented article, etc.) without permission or payment

pirouette[1] *n* a very fast turn on one toe or one foot, as by a ballet dancer

pirouette[2] *v* -etted, -etting to dance pirouettes

piscatorial also **piscatory**— *adj* of or connected with fishing or fishermen

Pisces *n* -ces 1 a the 12th division of the zodiac belt of stars, represented by 2 fish b the constellation formerly in this division ⤳ZODIAC 2 a person born under this sign

pissed *adj vulgar* drunk

piss off *v adv vulgar* 1 to go away 2 to make (someone) lose interest

pistachio *n* -os a small pleasant-tasting green nut or the tree on which it grows: *pistachio ice cream*

pistil *n technical* the female organ (CARPEL) of a plant

pistol *n* a small gun held and fired in one hand ⤳WEAPON

piston *n* a round metal plate or a short solid pipe that fits tightly into a cylinder in which it is moved up and down by pressure or explosion, used in pumps and in engines to give movement to other parts of a machine by means of a connecting rod ⤳STEAM, CAR

pit[1] *n* 1 a hole in the ground 2 a coal mine 3 (in motor racing) a place beside a track where cars can come during a race for repair 4 a hole in the floor of a garage from which the underside of cars can be examined **5** an enclosed hole where fierce animals are kept in a zoo **6** a natural hollow in the surface of a living thing (esp. in the phrase **pit of the stomach**) —see also ARMPIT **7** a small hollow as left on the face after certain diseases, esp. smallpox **8** also **orchestra pit**— the space below and in front of a theatre stage where musicians sit

pit² *v* -tt- to mark with pits

pit against *v prep* to match against, in a fight, competition, etc.: *pitting his strength against that of a man twice his size*

pitch¹ *n* any of various black sticky substances used for making protective coverings or for putting between cracks to stop water coming through

pitch² *v* **1** to set up (a tent, camp, etc.) — opposite **strike** **2** (of a cricketer) to make (a ball) hit the ground when bowling **3** (of a ball in cricket or golf) to hit the ground **4** to throw with dislike or annoyance: *We pitched those noisy people out of our club* **5** to set the pitch of (a sound) **6** to fall or cause to fall heavily or suddenly **7** (of a ship or aircraft) to move backwards and forwards with the movement of the waves or air; move along with the back and front going up and down —compare ROLL **8** to slope downwards

pitch³ *n* **1** a place in some public area where somebody regularly tries to gain money from people who are passing, by performing, selling, etc. **2** a marked-out area of ground on which football, hockey, etc., are played **3** the place where the ball hits the ground after being bowled **4** a wicket **5** the degree of highness or lowness of a musical note or speaking voice **6** (esp. in building) the amount of slope **7** (of a ship or aircraft) a backward and forward movement; the action of pitching —compare ROLL

pitch-black also **pitch-dark**— *adj* very dark — ~**ness** *n*

pitchblende *n* a dark shiny ore from which uranium and radium are obtained

pitched battle *n* **1** a fierce and usu. long quarrel or argument **2** (in former times) a battle on a chosen ground with positions already prepared —compare SKIRMISH

pitcher¹ *n* a large container for liquids, usu. made of clay and having 2 ear-shaped handles

pitcher² (in baseball) a bowler

pitchfork¹ *n* a long-handled farm tool with 2 long curved metal points, used esp. in lifting hay

pitchfork² **1** to lift or throw with a pitchfork **2** to force without preparation

pitch into *v prep* **1** to make an eager start on (work or food) **2** to attack

piteous also **pitiful**— *adj* **1** causing pity: *The dog gave a piteous cry* **2** feeling or showing pity —see PITY (USAGE) — ~**ly** *adv* — ~**ness** *n*

pitfall *n* an unexpected danger or difficulty

pith *n* **1** a soft white springy substance in the stems of certain plants and trees **2** a white

material under the coloured outside skin of oranges, lemons, etc.

pithead *n* the entrance to a coal mine

pith helmet also **topee**— *n* a large light tropical hat of dried pith, worn to protect the head from the sun

pithy *adj* -ier, -iest **1** of, like, or having much pith **2** strongly stated without wasting any words — -ily *adv* — -iness *n*

pitiable *adj* **1** worthy of pity **2** worthless; weak —see PITY (USAGE) — -bly *adv*

pitiful *adj* **1** deserving pity **2** not deserving respect —see PITY (USAGE) — ~**ly** *adv* — ~**ness** *n*

pitiless *adj* merciless; showing no pity — ~**ly** *adv* — ~**ness** *n*

piton *French n* a short pointed metal rod that can be hammered into rock, with a hole to pass a rope through, used as a hold in mountain climbing

pit prop *n* a support for the roof of a coal mine

pittance *n* a very small ungenerous amount of money given regularly

pituitary also **pituitary gland**— *n* -ries a small roundish organ (ENDOCRINE GLAND) at the base of the brain which produces hormones which influence growth and development

pity¹ *n* -ies **1** sensitiveness to and sorrow for the suffering of others **2** a sad or inconvenient state of affairs   USAGE It is probably best to use **piteous** to mean "feeling **pity**", **pitiable** to mean "causing **pity**, " and **pitiful** to mean "shameful; causing a low opinion"; but they can each express more than one of these meanings: *She looked at the poor old man with a* **piteous/pitiful** *face.* | *The poor old man was a* **pitiable/pitiful** *sight.* | *Her performance on the piano was* **pitiful/pitiable.**

pity² *v* -ied, -ying to feel pity for

pivot¹ *n* **1** a central point or pin on which something turns **2** a person on whom or thing on which something depends: *The mother is often the pivot of family life* — ~**al** *adj*

pivot² *v* **1** to turn on or as if on a pivot **2** to provide with or fix by a pivot

pixie, pixy *n* a small fairy believed to like playing tricks

pizza *n* a plate-shaped piece of bread dough or pastry baked with a mixture of cheese, tomatoes, etc., on top

pizzicato *adj, adv, n* -tos (a piece of music) played by plucking strings with a finger instead of a bow

placard¹ *n* a large notice or advertisement, put up in a public place or carried about

placard² *v* **1** to stick placards on **2** to give public notice of, by placards

placate *v* -cated, -cating **1** to cause to stop feeling angry **2** to cause (anger) to stop — -catory *adj*

place¹ *n* **1** a particular part of space or position in space: *the place where the accident happened* **2** a position of importance: *Sports never had a place in his life* **3** a particular area on a surface:

a sore place on her hand **4** a (numbered) position in the result of a competition, race, etc.: *John took first place in the examination* **5** any of the first 3 positions in the result of a horse race **6** social rank: *one's place in society*

place^2 *v* **placed, placing** **1** to put in a certain position **2** to pass (an order) to a person, firm, etc. **3** to remember all the details of **4** to state the position of (a runner) at the end of a race **5** *US* to finish second in a race —compare PLACED

Place *n* **1** a large country house with land **2** a short street, square, etc., in a town

placebo *n* **-bos** *or* **-boes** a substance given instead of real medicine, as to a person who imagines he is ill

placed *adj* **be placed** (esp. of a horse) to be one of the first 3 to finish a race

placekick *n* (in rugby and American football) a kick at a ball that has first been placed in position —compare DROPKICK, PUNT

placement *n* (an act of finding) a suitable job for someone

placenta *n* **-tas** *or* **-tae** a thick mass inside the womb, which joins the unborn child to the mother ☞EMBRYO

place setting *n* a set of articles for one person to eat with

place value *n* *technical* the value of a digit as indicated by its position in a number: *In 29 the place value of 2 is 20, but in 2093 it is 2, 000*

placid *adj* **1** not easily angered or excited **2** (of things) calm; peaceful: *the placid surface of the lake* — **~ly** *adv* — **~ity** *n*

plagiarize, -rise *v* **-rized, -rizing** to use (words, ideas, etc.) from someone else's work without admitting one has done so — **-rism** *n* — **-rist** *n*

plague^1 *n* **1** any disease causing death and spreading quickly **2** a widespread harmful mass or number: *a plague of rats*

plague^2 *v* **plagued, plaguing** to cause continual discomfort or trouble to

plaice *n* **plaice** a European edible flatfish

plaid *n* **1** a long piece of woollen often tartan cloth, worn over the shoulder by Scotsmen **2** cloth having a pattern of squares formed by coloured crossing bands

plain^1 *n* a large stretch of flat land

plain^2 *adj* **1** easy to see, hear, or understand **2** simple; without ornament **3** (of paper) without lines **4** (esp. of a woman) rather ugly **5** showing honestly what is thought or felt, often in an impolite way **6** complete; undoubted: *plain foolishness*

plain^3 *n, adj technical* the base stitch in knitting —compare PURL; see also KNIT

plain chocolate *n* dark chocolate for eating, made without milk and with little sugar

plain-clothes *adj* (esp. of a policeman) wearing ordinary clothes rather than a uniform

plain flour *n* flour without baking powder

plainly *adv* **1** in a plain manner **2** it is clear that: *The door's locked, so plainly they must be out*

plainsong also **plainchant**— *n* a type of old Christian church music for voices, like sung speech

plaint *n poetic* an expression of sorrow

plaintiff *n law* a person who brings a charge against somebody in court —compare DEFENDANT

plaintive *adj* **1** expressing suffering and a desire for pity **2** expressing gentle sadness — **~ly** *adv* — **~ness** *n*

plait^1 also (*esp. US*) **braid**— *n* a length of something, esp. hair, made by plaiting

plait^2 also (*esp. US*) **braid**— *v* to twist 3 or more lengths of (hair, grass, etc.) over and under each other to form one ropelike length

plan^1 *n* **1** a considered arrangement for some future activity **2** a line drawing of a building or room as seen from above, showing the shape, measurements, etc. —compare ELEVATION, PERSPECTIVE ☞MATHEMATICS **3** a set of drawings showing the parts of a machine

plan^2 *v* **-nn-** to make a plan for: *planning this visit* — **~ner** *n*

plane^1 *v* **planed, planing** **1** to use a plane on (something) **2** to cut or make with a plane: *Plane the table smooth*

plane^2 *n* a tool that takes very thin pieces off wooden surfaces to make them smooth

plane^3 *n* **1 a** a completely flat surface **b** (in geometry) a surface such that a straight line joining any 2 points lies only on that surface **2** a level; standard: *Let's keep the conversation on a friendly plane* **3** *esp. spoken* an aeroplane

planet *n* a large body in space that moves round a star, esp. round the sun ☞SPACE — **~ary** *adj*

planetarium *n* **-riums** *or* **-ria** a building containing an apparatus that throws spots of light onto the inside of a curved roof to show the movements of planets and stars

plane tree also **plane**— *n* any of various broad-leaved wide-spreading trees common in towns

plank *n* **1** a long piece of board, esp. 2 to 6 inches thick and at least 8 inches wide **2** a main principle of a political party's stated aims

plank down *v adv sl* to put down heavily

planking *n* planks, esp. as a floor

plankton *n* the very small plant and animal forms that live in water ☞PLANT

plant^1 *v* **1** to put (plants or seeds) in the ground to grow **2** to supply (a place) with plants **3** to fix firmly **4** *esp. spoken* to hide (esp. stolen goods) on a person so that he will seem guilty **5** to put (a person) secretly in a group: *His supporters had been planted in the crowd, and began shouting*

plant^2 *n* **1** a living thing that has leaves and roots, and grows usu. in earth, esp. the kind smaller than trees 👁 ☞EVOLUTION **2 a** a

plant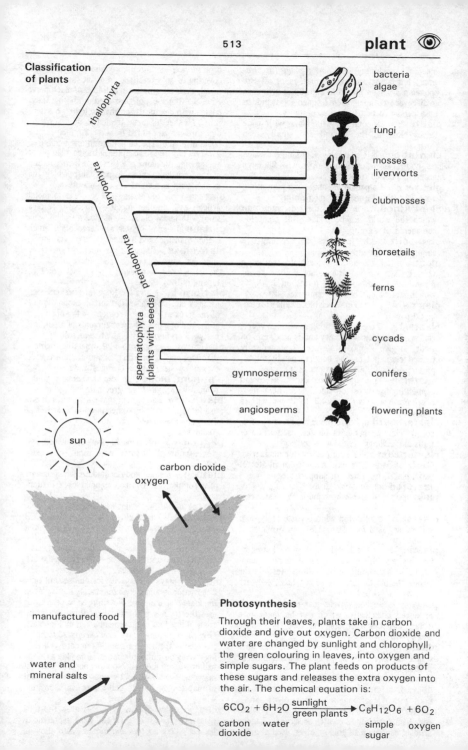

Classification of plants

thallophyta — bacteria algae

fungi

bryophyta — mosses liverworts

pteridophyta — clubmosses

horsetails

ferns

spermatophyta (plants with seeds) — cycads

gymnosperms — conifers

angiosperms — flowering plants

sun

carbon dioxide

oxygen

manufactured food

water and mineral salts

Photosynthesis

Through their leaves, plants take in carbon dioxide and give out oxygen. Carbon dioxide and water are changed by sunlight and chlorophyll, the green colouring in leaves, into oxygen and simple sugars. The plant feeds on products of these sugars and releases the extra oxygen into the air. The chemical equation is:

$$6CO_2 + 6H_2O \xrightarrow[\text{green plants}]{\text{sunlight}} C_6H_{12}O_6 + 6O_2$$

carbon dioxide   water   simple sugar   oxygen

machine; machinery: *our power plant for electricity* **b** a factory: *a new chemical plant* **3** *esp. spoken* **a** a person placed in a group of criminals to discover facts about them **b** stolen goods hidden on a person so that he will seem guilty

plantain *n* a common wild plant with wide leaves close to the ground and small green flowers

plantation *n* **1** a large piece of land on which tea, cotton, sugar, or rubber are grown **2** a large group of planted trees

planter *n* **1** a person in charge of a plantation: *a tea planter* **2** a machine for planting

plant kingdom *n* one of the 3 divisions into which the world can be divided; all plant life considered as a group

plant out *v adv* to place (esp. seedlings) in enough room for growth

plaque *n* **1** a metal or stone plate, usu. with writing, fixed to a wall as a memorial or ornament **2** *medical* a substance that forms on teeth, in which bacteria can breed —compare TARTAR

plasma *n* the liquid in which blood cells are held; liquid part of blood

plaster¹ *n* **1** a pastelike mixture of lime, water, etc., which hardens when dry and is used, esp. on walls, to give a smooth surface **2** a medically treated cloth put on the body to produce heat, protect a wound, etc. **3** STICKING PLASTER

plaster² *v* **1** to put plaster on **2** to spread (something) perhaps too thickly on: *They plastered the wall with signs* **3** to cover with a medical plaster

plasterboard *n* board made of sheets of cardboard held together with plaster, used to cover walls and ceilings

plaster cast *n* **1** a copy of a statue made from plaster of paris **2** a case made from plaster of paris, placed to protect or support a bone

plastered *adj humour* drunk

plasterer *n* a man whose job is to plaster esp. walls

plaster of paris *n* a whitish paste of gypsum and water, used for plaster casts, in ornamental building work, etc.

plastic¹ *adj* **1** easily formed into shapes by pressing, and able to keep the new shape **2** connected with modelling and sculpture (esp. in the phrase **the plastic arts**) — ~**ally** *adv* — ~**ity** *n*

plastic² *n* any of various man-made materials produced chemically, which can be made into different shapes when soft and keep their shape when hard ☞REFINERY

plasticine *n trademark* a soft claylike substance in many colours, for making small models, shapes, etc.

plastic surgery *n* the repairing of damaged, diseased, or unsatisfactorily shaped parts of the body with skin or bone taken from other parts

plate¹ *n* **1** a flat, usu. round dish with a raised edge from which food is eaten or served **2** metal articles, usu. made of gold or silver, used at meals or in services at church **3** common metal with a covering of gold or silver **4** a flat thin piece of metal, glass, etc., for use in building, in machinery, etc. **5** a thin sheet of glass used in photography, coated with chemicals sensitive to light **6** a denture **7** a sheet of metal treated so that words or a picture can be printed from it **8** a picture in a book, printed on special paper and often coloured **9** a sheet of metal fixed to the entrance of an office and bearing the name of a person or firm **10** any of the very large movable parts into which the earth's crust is divided ☞GEOGRAPHY

plate² *v* **plated, plating** **1** to cover (a metal article) with another metal **2** to cover (esp. a ship) with metal plates — **plating** *n*

plateau *n* **-eaus** *or* **-eaux** a large plain much higher than the land around it ☞GEOGRAPHY

plate glass *n* fine clear glass in large sheets for windows, mirrors, etc. — **plate-glass** *adj*

platelayer *n* a workman who puts down or repairs railway tracks

platform *n* **1** a raised floor for speakers, performers, etc. **2** a raised flat surface along the side of the track at a railway station **3** the open part at the end of a bus **4** the main aims of a political party **5** an unusually high shoe or sole

platinum *n* a greyish-white metallic element that does not become dirty or impure and is used esp. in jewellery and in chemical industries

platinum blonde *n esp. spoken* a young woman with light silver-grey hair

platitude *n* a statement that is true but not new or profound, made by someone who thinks it is all **3** —compare CLICHÉ, COMMONPLACE, TRUISM — **-tudinous** *adj*

platonic *adj* (of friendship between a man and woman) only of the mind; not sexual — ~**ally** *adv*

platoon *n* a small body of soldiers which is part of a company and is commanded by a lieutenant

platter *n old use* a flat usu. wooden dish

platypus also **duck-billed platypus**— *n* a small furry Australian mammal that lays eggs and has a beak like a duck's ☞MAMMAL

plausible *adj* (of a statement, argument, etc.) seeming true or reasonable —compare FEASIBLE — **-bly** *adv* — **-bility** *n*

play¹ *n* **plays** **1** activity for amusement only **2** the action in a game: *an interesting day's play in the match* **3 a** a piece of writing to be performed in a theatre **b** a performance of this ☞LITERATURE **4** freedom of movement given by looseness: *Give the rope some play—don't keep it so tight* **5** (somebody's) turn in a game, as in cards **6** risking money on games of chance **7 in play a** (of the ball in cricket, football, etc.) in a position where it may be played **b** without serious intention **8 out of play** (of the ball in ball games) in a position where it may not be played

play² *v* **played, playing** **1** to pass the time pleasantly; have fun **2** (of children) to pretend to be: *Let's play doctors and nurses* **3** to allow (a fish caught on a line) to become tired by pulling **4** (of an actor or theatre group) to perform: *Othello was played by Olivier* **5** (of a play or film) to be shown **6** (of a musical instrument or apparatus) to produce sounds **7** to perform on (a musical instrument) **8 a** to perform (a piece of music) **b** to perform the music of (a composer) **9** to reproduce (sounds) on an apparatus **10** to take part in (a sport or game) **11** to be set against in a match **12** to strike and send (a ball) **13** to place (a playing card) face upwards on the table **14** to risk (money) in a game of skill or chance —see also PLAY DOWN, PLAY OFF, PLAY ON, PLAY UP

playable *adj* (of ground for sports) fit to be played on

playback also **replay**— *n* a recording played at once after it is made, so that one can study it carefully

playboy *n* -**boys** a wealthy young man who lives mainly for pleasure

play down *v adv* to cause (something) to seem less important

player *n* **1** a person taking part in a game or sport **2** *esp. old use* an actor **3 a** a person playing a musical instrument **b** an apparatus for reproducing sounds: *a record player*

playful *adj* **1** gaily active **2** not intended seriously: *a playful kiss* — ~**fully** *adv* — ~**ness** *n*

playground *n* a piece of ground for children to play on

playgroup *n* a school where very young children (esp. of 3 to 5) learn to play with other children and learn other things mainly through play — compare CRÈCHE, NURSERY

playhouse *n* a theatre

playmate also **playfellow**— *n* a companion in children's games and play

play off *v adv* to set in opposition, esp. for one's advantage: *She played one friend off against the other*

play-off *n* a second match played to decide a winner

play on *v adv* *technical* (in cricket) to hit (the ball) accidentally on to the wicket and so be out

playpen *n* a frame enclosed by bars or a net for a small child to play safely in

plaything *n* **1** a toy **2** a person treated lightly and without consideration by another

play up *v adv* **1** to cause (something) to seem more important **2** to cause trouble or suffering to

playwright *n* a writer of plays ⟶LITERATURE

plaza *n* a public square or marketplace, esp. in Spanish-speaking areas

plea *n* **1** *esp. written* an eager request **2** an excuse **3** *law* a statement made by a person in court, saying whether he is guilty —see EXCUSE (USAGE)

plea bargaining *n law* the promising of a

light sentence to an accused person if he pleads guilty

plead *v* **pleaded** *or* **plead, pleading** **1** to make continual requests **2** to give as an excuse **3** to argue in support of: *pleading the rights of the unemployed* **4** *law* to answer a charge in court **5** *law* to declare that one is: *She pleaded guilty/not guilty* — ~**ing** *n*

pleasant *adj* **1** pleasing; enjoyable **2** (esp. of people) likeable; friendly **3** (of weather) fine — ~**ly** *adv*

pleasantry *n* -**ries** a light amusing remark

please[1] *v* **pleased, pleasing** **1** to make (someone) happy **2** to choose: *Come when you please*

please[2] *interj* (used to make a request or attract attention)**a** (more politely): *Please pass the sugar* **b** (with more force): *Please, John, do as I say | Please, Miss Jones, Andrew's kicking my chair!*

pleased *adj* satisfied; happy

pleasing *adj* likeable; giving satisfaction — ~**ly** *adv*

pleasure *n* happiness or satisfaction resulting from an experience that one likes — -**rable** *adj* — -**rably** *adv*

pleat[1] *v* to make pleats in

pleat[2] *n* a flattened narrow fold in cloth

plebeian *n, adj* **1** (in ancient Rome) (a member) of the common people —compare PATRICIAN **2** *offensive* (a member) of the lower social classes

plebiscite *n* a direct vote of a whole nation on a matter of national importance, esp. on a choice of government —compare REFERENDUM

plectrum *n* -**trums** *or* -**tra** a small thin piece of wood, metal, etc., used for playing certain stringed instruments by picking at the strings

pledge[1] *n* **1** a solemn promise **2** something given as a sign of faithful love or friendship **3 a** something valuable left with someone else as proof that one will fulfil an agreement **b** an object of value left, in return for money, with a pawnbroker until the money is repaid **4** the state of being kept for this purpose (esp. in the phrase **in pledge**) **5** **sign/take the pledge** *now humour* to promise no longer to drink alcohol

pledge[2] *v* **pledged, pledging** **1** to bind with a promise **2** to leave as a pledge **3** *esp. written* to drink to the health, success, etc., of

plenary *adj* **1** (of power of government) without limit **2** (of a meeting) attended by all who have the right (esp. in the phrase **plenary session**)

plenipotentiary *n, adj* -**ries** (of or as) a person having full power to represent his government

plenty[1] *n* the state of having a large supply: *years of plenty, when everyone has enough to eat* — -**tiful** *adj*

plenty[2] *pron* a large quantity or number; enough: *plenty of money | plenty to eat*

pleurisy *n* a serious disease of the lining of the

chest round the lungs, causing pain in the chest and sides

pliable *adj* 1 easily bent without breaking 2 willing to accept new ideas 3 easily influenced — **-bility** *n*

pliers *n* a tool made of 2 crossed pieces of metal with long often flat jaws, used to hold small things or to cut wire —compare PINCERS

plight *n* a (bad, serious, or sorrowful) state: *He was in a terrible plight, trapped at the back of the cave*

plimsoll *n* a light sports shoe with a heavy cloth top and a flat rubber bottom

Plimsoll line also **Plimsoll mark**— *n* a line on the outside of a ship showing the depth to which it may be allowed to settle in the water when loaded

plod *v* **-dd-** 1 to walk slowly, esp. with effort 2 to work steadily, esp. at something uninteresting

plodder *n* a slow, not very clever, but steady worker

plonk¹ also **plunk**— *n esp. spoken* a hollow sound as of something dropping onto or into a metal object

plonk² also **plunk**— *v esp. spoken* to fall with a plonk

plonk³ *n esp. spoken* cheap wine

plop¹ *n, adv esp. spoken* (with) a sound as of something dropping smoothly into liquid: *The soap fell plop into the bath*

plop² *v* **-pp-** *esp. spoken* to fall with a plop

plot¹ *n* 1 a small piece of ground for building or growing things 2 the connected events on which a story, film, etc., is based 3 a secret plan by several people to do harm

plot² *v* **-tt-** 1 to mark (the position of a moving aircraft or ship) on a map 2 to represent by pictures or a map 3 to make (a line or curve) on a graph 4 to plan together secretly 5 to make a plot for a story — ~**ter** *n*

plough¹ *n* 1 a farming tool with a heavy cutting blade drawn by a motor vehicle or animal(s). It breaks up and turns over the earth 2 any tool or machine that works like this —see also SNOW-PLOUGH 3 **under the plough** (of farmland) used for growing grain rather than feeding animals

plough² *v* 1 to break up or turn over (land) with a plough 2 to force a way: *The ship ploughed across the ocean*

Plough *n* a group of 7 bright stars in the northern sky

plough back *v adv* to put (profits) back into a business

ploughboy *n* **-boys** (esp. in former times) a boy who leads horses pulling a plough

ploughman's lunch *n* a simple lunch in a pub, usu. bread and cheese, with beer

ploughshare also **share**— *n* the broad metal blade of a plough

plough under *v adv* to cover and destroy (esp. a crop) by ploughing

plover *n* **-ers** *or* **-er** any of several types of land bird that live usu. near the sea, of which the lapwing is one

ploy *n* **ploys** a way of behaving to gain advantage—compare GAMBIT

pluck¹ *v* 1 to pull the feathers off (a bird being prepared for cooking) 2 to pull sharply; pick 3 to play a stringed musical instrument by pulling

pluck² *n* courage and will

pluck up also **muster up, summon up**— *v adv* **pluck up courage** to show bravery in spite of fears

plucky *adj* **-ier, -iest** brave and determined — **-ily** *adv* — **-iness** *n*

plug¹ *n* 1 something used for blocking a hole 2 an insulated electrical connector with projecting metal pins to push into a power socket 3 *esp. spoken* a publicly stated favourable opinion about a record, a book, etc. 4 *esp. spoken* SPARKING PLUG

plug² *v* **-gg-** 1 to block with a plug 2 *esp. spoken* to advertise by repeatedly mentioning: *plugging a new book on the radio*

plug in *v adv* to connect to a supply of electricity

plum *n* 1 (the tree which bears) a roundish sweet smooth-skinned fleshy fruit, usu. dark red, with a single stone 2 a dark reddish-blue colour

plumage *n* a bird's feathers

plumb¹ also **plummet**— *n* a mass of lead on the end of a string (**plumb line**), used to measure depth or to find whether something is upright

plumb² *adv esp. spoken* exactly

plumb³ *v* 1 to measure the depth of (water) with a plumb 2 to find whether (something) is upright by using a plumb

plumb⁴ *adj* upright

plumber *n* a man who fits and repairs water pipes, bathroom articles, etc.

plumbing *n* all the pipes, water tanks, etc., in a building

plum cake *n becoming rare* a large cake containing raisins and currants

plume¹ *n* 1 a feather, esp. a large showy one 2 something that rises in a shape like a feather: *a plume of smoke* — ~**d** *adj*

plume² *v* **plumed, pluming** (of a bird) to clean or smooth its feathers

plummet¹ *n* a plumb or plumbline

plummet² *v* to fall suddenly

plump *adj* 1 (or people) rather fat or nicely rounded 2 (of animals as food) well covered with flesh: *a nice plump chicken* — ~**ness** *n*

plump down *v adv esp. spoken* to fall or drop heavily

plump up *v adv* to make (esp. bed coverings) soft and rounded by shaking

plumule *n* the shoot of a young plant seed

plunder¹ *v* to seize (goods) unlawfully or by force from (people or a place) — **plunderer** *n*

plunder² *n* 1 goods seized by plundering or stolen 2 the act of plundering

plunge¹ *v* **plunged, plunging** 1 to move or be

thrown suddenly forwards and/or downwards 2 (of the neck of a woman's garment) to show a quite large area of the chest: *a plunging neckline*

plunge² *n* an act of plunging, esp. a dive

plunger *n* 1 a rubber cup on a handle, for unblocking pipes by suction 2 a part of a machine that moves up and down

pluperfect also **past perfect**— *adj, n* (a tense or word) that expresses an action completed before a time in the past, and is formed in English with *had* and a *past part*.

plural *adj, n* (a form or word) that expresses more than one: *"Dogs" is a plural noun* —opposite **singular** — ~**ly** *adv*

plus¹ *prep* with the addition of: *3 plus 6 is 9* (3+6=9)—opposite **minus**

plus² also **plus sign**— *n* a sign (+) showing that 2 or more numbers are to be added together, or that a number is greater than zero

plus³ *adj* 1 *esp. spoken* additional and welcome (often in the phrase **a plus factor**) 2 a (esp. of age) and above: *All the children are 12 plus* **b** (of a mark given for work) and slightly more: *B plus* (B+) *is better than B*

plus fours *n* trousers with loose wide legs drawn in closely below the knee, worn esp. in former times for golf —compare KNICKERBOCKERS

plush¹ *n* silk or cotton cloth with a furry surface —compare VELVET

plush² *adj esp. spoken* splendid and costly: *the plush new cinema*

Pluto *n* the planet 9th in order from the sun, the most distant of the group that includes the Earth

plutocracy *n* -cies 1 a ruling class of wealthy people 2 government by the rich

plutocrat *n* a very rich powerful person — ~**ic** *adj*

plutonium *n* a man-made element used esp. in the production of atomic power

ply¹ *v* plied, plying 1 (of a taxi driver, boatman, etc.) to wait or travel looking for passengers 2 (of taxis, buses, and esp. boats) to travel regularly (in or on): *boats plying the Thames* 3 *esp. in literature* to work at (a trade)

ply² *n* plies 1 a measure of the thickness of woollen thread, rope, etc., according to the number of single threads it is made from: *2-ply wool* 2 a measure of the thickness of plywood, according to the number of sheets of wood it is made from: *3-ply wood*

ply with *v prep* to keep supplying (someone) with (esp. food, drink, or questions)

plywood *n* a material made of several thin sheets of wood stuck together

p.m. *adv* post meridiem; after midday: *Today the sun sets at 5.49 p.m* —opposite **a.m.**

P M *abbrev. for: (esp. spoken)* prime minister

pneumatic *adj* 1 worked by air pressure: *a pneumatic drill* 2 containing air: *a pneumatic tyre* — ~**ally** *adv*

pneumoconiosis *n* a lung disease caused by dust, powder, etc., breathed in

pneumonia *n* a lung disease with inflammation and difficulty in breathing

P O *abbrev. for:* 1 postal order 2 post office

poach¹ *v* to cook (esp. eggs or fish) in gently boiling liquid

poach² *v* to catch or shoot (animals, birds, or fish) without permission

poacher *n* 1 a person who poaches animals, birds, etc. 2 a pan for poaching eggs

PO Box also (esp. written) **Post Office Box**— *n* a numbered box in a post office, to which a person's letters can be sent for collection

pock *n* 1 a diseased spot on the skin 2 a pockmark

pocket¹ *n* 1 a small flat cloth bag sewn into or onto a garment: *my coat pocket* 2 any of the 6 small bags round a billiard table, into which a ball may go 3 a region in the ground containing metal, oil, etc. 4 a small separate area or group: *pockets of mist down by the river* —see also AIRPOCKET 5 **out of pocket** having paid a certain amount

pocket² *v* 1 to put into one's pocket 2 to take for one's own use, esp. dishonestly

pocketknife *n* -knives a small knife with folding blades

pocket money *n* 1 money for small personal needs 2 money given weekly to a child — compare ALLOWANCE

pockmark also **pock**— *n* a hollow mark on a surface, or on the skin where a pock has been — ~**ed** *adj*

pod¹ *n* 1 a long narrow seed vessel of various plants, esp. beans and peas 2 a part of an aircraft or spacecraft that can be separated from the main part

pod² *v* -dd- to take (beans, peas, etc.) from the pod

podgy also **pudgy**— *adj* -ier, -iest *esp. spoken* short and fat — **-iness** *n*

poem *n* a piece of writing in patterns of lines and sounds, expressing something in imaginative language

poet *n* a person who writes poems ☞LITERATURE — ~**ical** *adj* — ~**ic** *adj* — ~**ically** *adv*

poetic justice *n* perfect justice, by which wrong-doers are punished in a way that seems particularly suitable

poetic licence *n* the freedom in writing poetry to change facts, not to obey the rules of grammar, etc.

poet laureate *n* poets laureate *or* poet laureates a poet appointed to the royal court, who writes poems on state occasions

poetry *n* poems: *a book of poetry* ☞LITERATURE

pogo stick *n* a pole with a spring and a bar for the feet, on which a child can stand and jump about

pogrom *n* a planned killing of helpless people (esp. Jews) for reasons of race or religion

poignant *adj* 1 producing a sharp feeling of sadness 2 (of sorrow) deeply felt △ PUNGENT — ~ly *adv* — **-nancy** *n*

point¹ *n* 1 a sharp end 2 a piece of land with a sharp end that stretches into the sea 3 a also **decimal point**— a sign(·) separating a whole number from decimals: *When we read out 4·23 we say '4 point 2 3'* b a full stop 4 (in geometry) an imaginary place that has position but no size 5 a place: *The bus stops at 4 or 5 points along this road* 6 an exact moment: *It was at that point that I left* 7 also **point of the compass**— a any of the 32 marks on a compass, showing direction b any of the equal divisions (each of 11° 15′) between any 2 of these 8 a degree of temperature: *the melting point of gold* 9 a measure of increase or decrease in cost, value, etc. 10 a single quantity used in deciding the winner in games: *We won by 12 points to 3* 11 the meaning of something said or done: *I didn't see the point of his remark* 12 a noticeable quality or ability: *Work isn't her strong point* 13 purpose; use: *There's no point in wasting time* 14 also **power point**— a fixed socket into which a plug can be fitted to connect an apparatus to the supply of electricity 15 (in cricket) (the fielder in) a position directly facing the batsman and about half way to the edge of the playing area

point² *v* 1 to hold out a finger, a stick, etc., in a direction 2 to aim, direct, or turn 3 to fill the spaces between the bricks of (a wall) with mortar or cement 4 (of a dog) to show where (a hunted animal or bird) is —see POINTER 5 to bring (the toes) to a point by bending the ankles forward

point-blank *adj, adv* 1 from a close position level with the object: *a point-blank shot* 2 forceful and direct: *a point-blank refusal*

point duty *n* the controlling of traffic by a policeman usu. at a point where 2 roads cross

pointed *adj* 1 shaped to a point: *pointed fingernails* 2 directed in a noticeable unfriendly way: *a pointed remark* 3 sharply expressed or shown (esp. in the phrase **pointed wit**) — ~ly *adv*

pointer *n* 1 a stick used to point at things on a map, board, etc. 2 the needle that points to the numbers on a measuring apparatus 3 a hunting dog that stops with its nose pointed towards a hunted animal or bird it has smelt 4 a useful suggestion

pointless *adj* 1 meaningless 2 useless; unnecessary — ~ly *adv* — ~ness *n*

point of order *n* **points of order** a matter connected with the organization of an official meeting

point of view also **viewpoint**— *n* **points of view** a way of considering or judging a thing, person, etc.: *From my point of view it would be better to come tomorrow*

point out *v adv* to draw attention to

points *n* 1 2 short rails moved to allow a train to change tracks 2 the ends of the toes, as danced on in ballet 3 a horse's feet, tail, and mane, or a cat's legs, tail, and face, where these differ from the

body colour 4 the bodily qualities considered in judging an animal in a show

pointsman *n* **-men** a railway worker in charge of the moving of points

point to also **point towards**— *v prep* to be a sign of

point-to-point *n* **-points** a cross-country horse-race, usu. with points marked along the way

poise¹ *v* **poised, poising** to balance in an unsteady position

poise² *n* 1 good judgment and quiet confidence: *He has a great deal of poise for a boy of only 14* 2 the way of holding oneself: *the dancer's graceful poise*

poised *adj* 1 in a condition of uncertainty: *poised between life and death* 2 having poise 3 still, as if hanging, in the air: *The bee hung poised above the flower* 4 lightly seated: *poised on the edge of a chair* 5 in a state of readiness to act or move: *poised for action*

poison¹ *n* 1 a substance that harms or kills if an animal or plant takes it in 2 an evil or unwanted influence

poison² *v* 1 to give poison to; harm or kill with poison 2 to put poison into or onto (something) 3 to infect: *a poisoned foot* 4 to make dangerously impure: *Chemicals are poisoning our rivers* 5 to influence in a harmful or evil way: *She poisoned her husband's mind against his sister* — ~er *n*

poisonous *adj* 1 containing poison: *poisonous snakes* 2 having the effects of poison: *This substance is poisonous* 3 harmful to the mind; evil: *poisonous ideas* 4 very unpleasant: *a poisonous green colour* — ~ly *adv*

poison-pen letter *n* a usu. unsigned letter making charges of misbehaviour, or saying bad things about someone

poke¹ *n* **(buy) a pig in a poke** *esp. spoken* (to buy) something which one has not seen, and which may prove worthless

poke² *v* **poked, poking** 1 to push sharply out of or through an opening: *His elbow was poking through his sleeve* 2 to push (a pointed thing) into (someone or something) 3 to move the wood or coal about in (a fire) with a poker or other such object 4 to make (a hole) by pushing, forcing, etc. 5 *esp. spoken* to hit with the hand closed 6 **poke fun at** to make jokes against 7 **poke one's nose into something** *esp. spoken* to enquire into something that does not concern one

poke³ *n* 1 an act of poking with something pointed 2 *esp. spoken* a blow with the closed hand: *He took a poke at his opponent*

poker¹ *n* a thin metal bar used to poke a fire to make it burn better

poker² *n* a card game usu. played for money

poker face *n* a face that shows nothing of a person's thoughts or feelings — **poker-faced** *adj*

pokerwork *n* ornamentation or the art of ornamenting wood or leather by burning the surface with hot instruments

poky *adj* **-ier, -iest** *esp. spoken* (of a place) uncomfortably small and unattractive — **pokiness** *n*

polar *adj* **1** of, near, like, or coming from lands near the North or South Poles **2** *esp. written* exactly opposite in kind, quality, etc.: *The two brothers were polar opposites*

polar bear *n* **-bears** *or* **-bear** a type of large white bear that lives near the North Pole

polarity *n* **-ties 1** the state of having or developing 2 opposite qualities: *a growing polarity between the 2 opinions* **2 a** the state of having 2 opposite poles **b** either of the 2 states of electricity possessed by poles: *negative/positive polarity*

polarize, -ise *v* **-ized, -izing 1** to gather about 2 opposite points: *Society has polarized into 2 classes* **2** to direct or cause to have a tendency: *a society polarized towards gaining money* **3** to give polarity to **4** to cause (light waves) to vibrate in a single particular pattern — **-ization** *n*

Polaroid *n* **trademark 1** a material with which glass is treated to make light shine less brightly through it, used for sunglasses, car windows, etc. **2** also **Polaroid camera**— a type of camera that produces a finished photograph almost immediately

polder *n* (esp. in the Netherlands) a piece of land, formerly covered by the sea, which has been made dry and can be used for farming

pole¹ *n* **1** a long, usu. thin rounded stick or post, used as a support, to guide a flat-bottomed boat, to join 2 animals to a cart, etc.: *a flagpole* **2 up the pole** *esp. spoken* **a** slightly mad **b** in difficulty

pole² *v* **poled, poling 1** to move (a boat) along by pushing a pole against the bed of the river, lake, etc. **2** to use ski poles or sticks to give oneself more speed

pole³ *n* **1** either end of an imaginary straight line (AXIS) round which a solid round mass turns, esp. **a** (the lands around) the most northern and southern points of the earth or another planet **b** the 2 points in the sky to the north and south round which stars seem to turn —see also MAGNETIC POLE, NORTH POLE, SOUTH POLE — GLOBE **2** either of the points at the ends of a magnet where its power is greatest **3** either of the points where wires may be fixed onto a battery to use its electricity: *negative/positive pole* **4** either of 2 completely different qualities, opinions, etc.: *Our opinions are at opposite poles* **5 poles apart** widely separated; having no shared quality, idea, etc.

Pole *n* a native of Poland

poleaxe *n* (in former times) a large axe used for fighting

polecat *n* a type of small fierce dark brown animal of northern Europe with a very unpleasant smell

polemics *n* the art or practice of arguing, attacking or defending opinions, ideas, etc.

pole star also **North Star**— *n* the bright star about which the sky appears to turn in the northern part of the world

pole vault *n, v* (to make) a jump over a high bar, the jumper using a long pole to lift himself

police¹ *n* an official body of men and women whose duty is to protect people and property, to make everyone obey the law, to catch criminals, etc.

police² *v* **policed, policing 1** to control (a place) by or as if using police **2** to keep a watch on: *a new body set up to police pay agreements*

policeman *fem.* **policewoman**— *n* **-men** a member of a police force

police state *n* *offensive* a country in which most activities of the citizens are controlled by political police

policy¹ *n* **-cies 1** a plan or course of action in directing affairs, chosen by a political party, government, company, etc. **2** sensible behaviour that is to one's own advantage: *It's bad policy to smoke too much*

policy² *n* a written statement of an agreement with an insurance company —see also INSURANCE POLICY

polio also (*technical*) **poliomyelitis**— *n* an infectious disease of the nerves in the spine, often resulting in a lasting inability to move certain muscles (PARALYSIS)

polish¹ *v* **1** to make or become smooth and shiny by continual rubbing **2** to make (a person, his behaviour, speech, etc.) less rough **3** to make (a speech, piece of writing, artistic performance, etc.) as perfect as possible: *The musicians gave a very polished performance* — **~er** *n*

polish² *n* **1** a liquid, paste, etc., used in polishing a surface **2** a smooth shiny surface produced by rubbing **3** an act of polishing **4** fine quality or perfection (of manners, education, writing, etc.)

Polish *adj* of Poland, its people, or their language

polish off *v adv* **1** to finish (something, such as food, work, etc.) **2** *sl* to kill (someone)

politburo *n* **-ros** the chief decision-making committee of a political party, esp. a Communist party

polite *adj* **1** having or showing good manners and consideration for others **2** having or showing (or pretending to have or show) fineness of feeling, high development in the arts, manners, etc.; refined: *polite society* — **~ly** *adv* — **~ness** *n*

politic *adj* *usu. in literature* **1** (of behaviour or actions) well-judged with regard to one's own advantage **2** (of a person) skilful in acting to obtain a desired result or one's own advantage —see also BODY POLITIC

political *adj* **1** of or concerning public affairs and/or the government of a country: *the loss of political freedoms* **2** of or concerned with (party) politics: *a political party* — **~ly** *adv*

political asylum *n* protection given by a government to someone who leaves his own country for political reasons

political economy *n* the scientific study of the way in which the political practices of a government direct the production and use of wealth by a nation — **-mist** *n*

political science *n* the study of politics and government — **political scientist** *n*

politician *n* **1** a person whose business is politics, esp. a member of a parliament **2** *offensive* a person concerned with party politics for his own selfish purpose or gain

politicking *n* *often offensive* an act or the action of taking part in political activity or talk, esp. for personal advantage

politics *n* **1** the art or science of government: *Tom is studying politics at university* **2** political affairs, esp. considered as a profession and/or as a means of winning and keeping governmental control: *local politics* **3** the political ideas or party that one favours: *What are your politics?* **4 play politics** *offensive* to speak or act in such a way as to make people argue amongst themselves, distrust each other, etc., in order to gain an advantage for oneself

polka *n* **1** a very quick dance for couples **2** a piece of music to which this is danced

polka dot *n* any of a number of large regularly-placed circular spots forming a pattern, used esp. on material

poll[1] *n* **1** the giving of votes in writing at an election: *The result of the poll won't be known until midnight* **2** the number of votes recorded at an election: *They expected a large poll* **3** an official list of electors

poll[2] *v* **1** to receive (a stated number of votes) at an election **2** to vote at an election **3** to question (people) in making a poll **4** to cut off or cut short the horns of (cattle)

pollard[1] *n* a tree of which the top has been cut off to make the branches below grow more strongly

pollard[2] *v* to cut the top off (a tree)

pollen *n* fine yellow dust on the male part of a flower that causes other flowers to produce seeds when it is carried to them ☞FLOWER

pollen count *n* a measure of the amount of pollen in the air, esp. as a guide for people made ill by hay fever

pollinate *v* **-nated, -nating** to enable (a flower or plant) to produce seeds by adding or bringing pollen — **-nation** *n*

polling *n* the giving of votes at an election; voting

polling booth *n* a partly enclosed place inside a polling station where a person records his vote secretly

polling station *n* a place where people go to vote at an election

pollutant *n* something that pollutes

pollute *v* **-luted, -luting** **1** to make (water, soil, etc.) dangerously impure **2** to destroy the purity of (the mind)

pollution *n* **1** the action of polluting **2** the state of being polluted **3** (an area or mass of) something that pollutes

polo *n* a team game played on horseback. The players try to get goals by hitting a ball with long-handled wooden hammers

polonaise *n* a piece of music of a grand slow kind, written esp. for the piano

polo neck *n* a round rolled collar, usu. woollen

polony *n* **-nies** partly-cooked pieces of pork made into a red sausage

poltergeist *n* a type of spirit that is said to make noises, throw objects etc.

poly *n* **-ys** *esp. spoken* a polytechnic

polyandry *n* the custom or practice of having more than one husband at the same time — **-rous** *adj*

polyester *n* a type of man-made material used esp. mixed with wool or cotton to make cloth for garments ☞REFINERY

polyethylene *n* *esp. US* polythene

polygamist *n* a man who has more than one wife

polygamy *n* the custom or practice of having more than one wife at the same time — **-ous** *adj*

polyglot *n, adj* (a person) speaking or knowing many languages

polygon *n* (in geometry) a figure on a flat surface bounded by straight sides

polyhedron *n* **-dra** *technical* a solid in which all the faces are polygons

polymer *n* a compound molecule built up from simple ones of the same kind

polynomial *n* *technical* a mathematical expression with several terms in it: $x^2 + 2xy + 5y$ *is a polynomial*

polyp *n* **1** a simple type of small water animal, having the form of a tubelike bag —compare CORAL **2** a type of small diseased growth in the body (esp. in the nose) — **~ous** *adj*

polyphony *n* a form of musical writing in which different patterns of notes are sung or played together and fit in with each other, according to certain rules; counterpoint — **-nic** *adj*

polystyrene *n* a type of light plastic material that prevents the escape of heat, used esp. for making containers ☞REFINERY

polysyllable *n* a word that must be pronounced in more than 3 separate parts (SYLLABLES): *'Unnecessary' is a polysyllable* — **-bic** *adj* — **-bically** *adv*

polytechnic also (*esp. spoken*) **poly**— *n* (esp. in Britain) a place of higher education providing training and often degrees in arts and esp. trades connected with skills and machines

polytheism *n* belief in the existence of more than one god —compare MONOTHEISM

polythene *n* a type of plastic not easily damaged by water or chemicals, used esp. as a protective covering, for making household articles, etc. ☞REFINERY

pomander n a small container holding sweet-smelling substances, herbs, etc., used for giving a room, cupboard, etc. a pleasant smell

pomegranate n (a type of tree with) round thick-skinned reddish fruit containing many small seeds in a red flesh

pommel[1] n **1** the rounded part of a horse's saddle that sticks up at the front **2** the ball-shaped end of a sword handle (HILT)

pommel[2] v -ll- to pummel

pommel horse n a vaulting horse with handles

pommy also **pom**— n -mies *Australian & New Zealand sl often offensive* an Englishman, esp. one who has recently come to live in Australia or New Zealand

pomp n **1** solemn ceremonial show, esp. on some public or official occasion **2** unnecessary show: *the empty pomp and show of the city*

pompom a small ball made of bits of wool worn as an ornament on garments, esp. hats

pompous adj foolishly solemn and self-important — ~ly adv — -posity, ~ness n

ponce n a man who lives on the money earned by a prostitute; pimp

poncho n -chos *Spanish* a garment for the top half of the body consisting of a single wide piece of woollen cloth with a hole in the middle for the head

pond n an area of still water smaller than a lake

ponder v to spend time in considering (a fact, difficulty, etc.)

ponderous adj **1** slow and awkward because of size and weight **2** *offensive* dull and solemn — ~ly adv — ~ness n

pong v, n sl (to have or make) an unpleasant smell — ~y adj

poniard n a type of small knife used in former times as a weapon

pontiff n (in former times) a Roman or Jewish chief priest

Pontiff n the Pope

pontifical adj **1** *offensive* **a** (of a person) making statements that one expects others to accept as the only truth or law **b** (of actions or statements) showing this quality **2** of or concerning a pope: *a pontifical letter* — ~ly adv

pontificate[1] n the position or period of office of a pontiff

pontificate[2] v -cated, -cating *usu. offensive* to speak or write as if one's own judgment is the only correct one

pontoon[1] n **1** any of a number of hollow metal containers or flat-bottomed boats fastened in a line to support a floating bridge (**pontoon bridge**) put quickly across a river **2** either of 2 boat-shaped supports put onto an aircraft to allow it to land on and take off from water

pontoon[2] n **1** a type of card game, usu. played for money **2** (in this game) a winning combination of cards

pony n ponies **1** a small horse **2** *esp. humour* a horse used for racing

ponytail n (worn esp. by young girls) a hair style in which the hair is tied high at the back of the head and falls like a horse's tail —compare PIG-TAIL

pony-trekking n a holiday sport in which people ride across the country on ponies

poodle n a type of dog with thick curling hair, sometimes cut in special shapes

pooh-pooh v *esp. spoken* to treat as not worthy of consideration

pool[1] n **1** a small area of still water in a hollow, usu. naturally formed: *The rain formed pools of water* **2** a small amount of any liquid poured or dropped on a surface: *The wounded man was lying in a pool of blood* **3** a large water-filled container built into the ground, used for swimming, keeping fish in, etc. **4** a deeper part of a stream where the water hardly moves

pool[2] n **1** a common supply of money, goods, workers, etc., which may be used by a number of people: *Our firm has a car pool* —see also TYPING POOL **2** the amount of money collected from and played for by all players in certain card games **3** any of various American billiard games played usu. with 15 numbered balls on a table with 6 pockets —compare SNOOKER

pool[3] v to combine; share

pools also **football pools**— an arrangement by which people bet small amounts of money on the results of certain football matches, and those who guess the results correctly (or nearly correctly) win large shares of the combined money

poop n *technical* the back end of a ship

poor adj **1** having very little money and therefore a low standard of living **2** less than is needed or expected; small: *a poor crop of beans* **3** much below the usual standard; low in quality: *The weather has been very poor this summer* **4** (of the bodily system) weak; not good: *in poor health* **5** *offensive* (of a person or his behaviour) not noble or respected: *He gets angry when he loses a game. He's a poor loser* **6** deserving pity; unlucky: *The poor old man had lost both his sons in the war* **7** *usu. polite or humour* of little worth; humble: *In my poor opinion you're wrong*

poorhouse n (in former times) a building provided by public money where poor people could live and be fed —compare WORKHOUSE

poor law n (in Britain in former times) a group of laws concerning help for poor people

poorly[1] adv **1** in a poor manner or condition; not well **2 think poorly of** to have a low opinion of

poorly[2] adj -lier, -liest ill

poorly off adj **1** having very little money **2** not well supplied: *We're poorly off for coal at the moment*

poorness n a low standard; lack of a desired quality: *the poorness of the materials* —compare POVERTY

poor relation n the lowest or least important

person or thing: *Theatre musicians often consider themselves the poor relations of the musical profession*

pop¹ *v* **-pp-** 1 to make or cause to make a short sharp explosive sound: *The cork popped when he pulled it out* 2 *esp. spoken* to spring: *The child's eyes almost popped out of her head with excitement* 3 *esp. spoken* to move, go, come, enter, etc., suddenly, lightly, or unexpectedly: *I've just popped in to see you* 4 *esp. spoken* to put quickly and lightly: *He popped his coat on* 5 *esp. spoken* to ask (a question) suddenly and directly 6 **pop the question** *esp. spoken* to make an offer of marriage; propose —see also POP OFF

pop² *n* 1 a sound like that of a slight explosion: *The lemonade bottle went pop* 2 a sweet fizzy drink

pop³ *n* 1 simple modern popular music with a strong beat and not usu. of lasting interest 2 **top of the pops** (being) the pop record selling the most copies at a particular time —compare ROCK

pop⁴ *abbrev. for:* 1 popularly 2 population

popadam, popadum *n* a type of flat Indian cake often eaten with curry

pop art *n* a type of modern painting or other art which uses the techniques of advertising, and often represents advertisements, strip-cartoons, and other objects from everyday life

popcorn *n* grains of maize that have been swollen and burst by heat

pope *n* the head of the Roman Catholic church

pop-eyed *adj esp. spoken* having wide open eyes, as with surprise, excitement, etc.

popgun *n* a toy gun that fires small objects (esp. corks) with a loud noise

poplar *n* any of several types of fast-growing tree, many of which are very tall with a straight thin trunk, or their soft wood

poplin *n* a type of strong shiny cotton cloth used esp. for making shirts

pop off *v adv esp. spoken* 1 to go away suddenly 2 to die

popper *n esp. spoken* a press-stud

poppet *n esp. spoken* a child or animal that one loves

popping crease also **batting crease**— *n* (in cricket) a line drawn on the ground, on which the batsman stands to hit the ball

poppy *n* **-pies** any of several types of plant that have a milky juice in the stems and bright, usu. red flowers

poppycock *n* foolish nonsense

populace *n esp. written* the common people of a country, esp. when seen as being without social position, wealth, political understanding, etc.

popular *adj* 1 favoured by many people: *a popular song* 2 well liked 3 *sometimes offensive* suited to the understanding, liking, or needs of the general public: *popular newspapers* 4 (of prices) cheap

popularity *n* the quality or state of being well liked, favoured, or admired

popularize, -ise *v* **-ized, -izing** 1 to make (something difficult) easily understandable to ordinary people 2 to make (something new) generally known and used: *The company are trying to popularize their new soap powder* 3 to cause to be well liked — **-ization** *n*

popularly *adv* 1 generally; by most people: *His name is Robert, but he's popularly known as Bob* 2 cheaply: *a popularly-priced car*

populate *v* **-lated, -lating** 1 to live in (a particular area): *a thickly-populated area* 2 to settle in and fill up (an area), esp. with people: *The new land was quickly populated*

population *n* 1 the number of people or animals living in an area 2 the people or animals living in an area: *The population in these villages still uses well water*

populist *n* a member of a political party that claims to represent ordinary people

populous *adj* (of a place) having a large population — **~ness** *n*

porcelain *n* 1 thin shiny material of fine quality, used to make cups, dishes, etc. and produced by baking a clay mixture 2 articles made of this —compare CHINA

porch *n* a built-out roofed entrance to a house or church ─☞CATHEDRAL

porcupine *n* a type of small short-legged animal that has long stiff prickles (QUILLS) on its back and sides, and is larger than a hedgehog ─☞MAMMAL

pore *n* a very small opening (esp. in the skin) through which liquids (esp. sweat) may pass ─☞SKIN

pore over *v prep* to study or give close attention to (usu. something written or printed)

pork *n* meat from pigs —compare BACON, HAM

porker *n* a young pig, fattened for food

porky *adj* **-ier, -iest** *esp. spoken* (esp. of a person) fat

porn *n esp. spoken* pornography

pornography *n* the treatment of sexual subjects in books, films, etc., in a way meant to cause sexual excitement — **-pher** *n* — **-phic** *adj* — **-phically** *adv*

porous *adj* 1 allowing liquid to pass slowly through: *porous soil* 2 *technical* having or full of pores: *porous skin* — **~ness** *n*

porpoise *n* a type of large fishlike sea animal that swims about in groups —compare DOLPHIN

porridge *n* a type of soft breakfast food made by boiling oatmeal in milk or water

porringer *n* a type of small wide bowl (esp. for a child) from which soft food is eaten

port¹ *n* 1 (a town with a) harbour 2 **Any port in a storm** Any means of escape from trouble must be accepted —see also AIRPORT, PORT OF CALL

port² *n* 1 an opening in the side of a ship for loading and unloading goods 2 a porthole

port³ *n* the left side of a ship or aircraft as one faces forward: *The damaged ship was leaning over to port* —compare STARBOARD ─☞SAIL

port⁴ *n* strong sweet often dark red Portuguese wine usu. drunk after a meal —compare SHERRY

portable *adj* that can be carried or moved easily: *a portable television* — **-bility** *n*

portage *n* 1 an act or the action of carrying goods, esp. across a stretch of land from one river or lake to another 2 a place where this is done

portal *n* *esp. written or literature* a very grand entrance to a building, esp. considered as representing the organization, company, etc., that uses that building

portcullis *n* (in old castles, forts, etc.) a strong gatelike framework of bars hung above an entrance and lowered as a protection against attack ⌐CASTLE

portend *v* *esp. written* to be a sign or warning of (a future undesirable event)

portent *n* a sign or warning, esp. of something strange or undesirable —compare OMEN

portentous *adj* 1 that warns or foretells (of evil happenings); threatening —compare OMINOUS 2 *offensive* solemnly self-important 3 most unusual; difficult to believe — ~ **ly** *adv*

porter¹ *n* a man in charge of the entrance to a hotel, school, hospital, etc.

porter² *n* 1 a person employed to carry luggage at railway stations, airports, etc. 2 a person employed to carry loads at markets

porter³ *n* (esp. in former times) a type of dark brown bitter beer

porterage *n* 1 the work of a porter 2 the charge made for this

porterhouse also **porterhouse steak—** *n* a large portion of best beef

porter's lodge *n* a small room for the porter at the entrance to a school, hospital, etc.

portfolio *n* **-os** 1 a large flat case like a large book cover, for carrying drawings, papers, etc. 2 a collection of drawings or other papers, such as would be contained in this 3 the office and duties of a minister of state: *the portfolio of foreign affairs*

porthole *n* 1 also **port—** a small usu. circular window or opening in a ship for light or air 2 any of the row of fixed windows along the side of an aircraft

portico *n* **-coes** *or* **-cos** a grand entrance to a building, consisting of a roof supported by pillars

portion *n* 1 a part separated or cut off: *the front portion of the train* 2 a share of something divided among 2 or more people: *A portion of the blame for the accident must be borne by the driver* 3 a quantity of food for one person as served in a restaurant 4 *esp. written & literature* a person's fate; lot

portly *adj* **-lier, -liest** *humour* (of a grown-up person, often rather old) round and fat — **-liness** *n*

portmanteau *n* **-teaus** *or* **-teaux** a type of large travelling case for clothes, esp. one that opens into 2 equal parts

portmanteau word *n* an invented word that combines the meaning and sound of 2 words: *'Motel' is a portmanteau word made up from 'motor' and 'hotel'*

port of call *n* **ports of call** *esp. spoken* a place where one stops or which one visits

portrait *n* 1 a painting, drawing, or photograph of a real person or animal 2 a lifelike description in words: *He called his book about modern Europe "A Portrait of Europe"*

portray *v* **-trayed, -traying** 1 to be or make a representation of (someone or something) in painting, drawing, etc. 2 to describe in words 3 to act the part of (a particular character) in a play — ~ **al** *n*

Portuguese *adj* 1 of Portugal or its people 2 of the language of Portugal, Brazil, etc. ⌐LANGUAGE

Portuguese man-of-war *n* **-men-of-war** a type of large poisonous jellyfish with long threadlike parts that hang beneath it

pose¹ *v* **posed, posing** 1 to sit or cause to sit or stand in a particular effective position, esp. for a photograph, painting, etc. 2 to state; offer for consideration: *You've posed us an awkward question* 3 to set; bring into being: *This rain poses a problem for the farmers* 4 *offensive* to behave or speak unnaturally in an effort to make people notice or admire one

pose² *n* 1 a position of the body, esp. as taken up to produce an effect in art 2 *offensive* a way of behaving which is pretended in order to produce an effect

pose as *v* *prep* to pretend to be

poser *n* *esp. spoken* a hard or awkward question or problem

posh *adj* *esp. spoken* 1 very fine; splendid 2 *sometimes offensive* fashionable; for people of high social rank: *a posh address*

position¹ *n* 1 the place where someone or something is or stands, esp. in relation to other objects, places, etc.: *Can you find our position on this map?* 2 the place where someone or something belongs; the proper place: *One of the chairs is out of position* 3 the place of advantage in a struggle: *The racing drivers manoeuvred for position* 4 the way or manner in which someone or something is placed or moves, stands, sits, etc.: *sitting in a most uncomfortable position* 5 a condition or state, esp. in relation to that of someone or something else: *I'd like to help, but I'm not in a position to do so* 6 a particular place or rank in a group 7 a job; employment —see JOB (USAGE) 8 an opinion or judgment on a matter: *He takes the position that what his sister does is no concern of his*

position² *v* to put in a position or in the proper position

positional *adj* dependent on position

positive¹ *adj* 1 (of a statement) direct: *a positive refusal* 2 certain; beyond any doubt 3 (of people) sure; having no doubt about something 4 thorough; real: *It was a positive delight to hear her sing* 5 (of people or their behaviour) boldly certain of oneself and one's opinions **6** actively noticeable: *In the night, the patient took a positive turn for the worse* **7** (of medical tests) showing signs of disease **8** effective; actually helpful: *positive thinking* **9** (in grammar) of the simple form of an adjective or adverb, which expresses no comparison: *'Good' is the positive form of the adjective;* *'better'* and *'best'* are not —compare COMPARATIVE, SUPERLATIVE **10** (in mathematics) a (of a number or quantity) greater than zero **b** concerning such a quantity: *The positive sign is* + **11** (of or in electricity) of the type that is based on protons and is produced by rubbing glass with silk **12** (of a photograph) having light and shadow as they are in nature, not the other way around; developed —compare NEGATIVE

positive² *n* **1** (in grammar) the positive degree or form of an adjective or adverb: *The positive of 'prettiest' is 'pretty'* **2** a positive photograph **3** (in mathematics) a quantity greater than zero **4** *esp. written* something that is clearly true or offers proof that something is true —compare NEGATIVE

positively *adv* **1** in a positive way, esp. with or as if with certainty **2** really; indeed: *This food is positively uneatable*

positiveness *n* certainty; confidence

positive pole *n* the end of a magnet which turns naturally towards the earth

positron *n* a very small particle of electricity that is like an electron but is positively charged

poss. *abbrev. for:* **1** *esp. spoken* possible: *Do it by Monday if poss.* **2** possessive

posse *n* **1** (in the US) a group of men gathered together by a local sheriff and given powers to hunt a criminal, keep order, etc. **2** *esp. spoken* a (large) group of people, often with a common purpose

possess *v* **1** to own; have as belonging to one, or as a quality **2** (of a feeling or idea) to influence (someone) so completely as to control one's actions: *Fear possessed him and prevented him from moving* **3** (of an evil spirit or the devil) to enter into and become master of (someone)

possessed *adj* **1** wildly mad, as if controlled by an evil spirit **2** *esp. written or literature* in a state of having: *The family is possessed of a large fortune* —see also SELF-POSSESSED

possession *n* **1** ownership **2** a piece of personal property **3** a country controlled or governed by another **4** the condition of being under or as if under the control of an evil spirit **5 in possession a** having or controlling a place or thing, esp. so that someone else is prevented from doing so: *Wales can't get any points while the England players are in possession* (=have the ball) **b** *often written* having, controlling, keeping, or living in: *He was found in possession of dangerous drugs* **6 Possession is nine tenths/ nine points of the law** A person who possesses a thing is in a better position to keep it than someone else who may have a more just claim to it

possessive¹ *adj* **1** *offensive* **a** unwilling to share one's own things with other people **b** showing a strong desire for the full attention of someone else **2** (in grammar) of or being a word or form that shows ownership or connection: *'My'* and *'its'* are possessive adjectives —compare GENITIVE — ~ly *adv* — ~ness *n*

possessive² *n* a possessive word, form, or case: *'Hers' is the possessive of 'she'*

possessor *n* an owner

possibility *n* -ties **1** the state or fact of being possible **2** a likelihood; chance: *Is there any possibility that you'll be able to come tomorrow?* **3** something that is possible: *The general would not accept that defeat was a possibility* **4** power of developing, or being used or useful in the future: *Although the house is old, it has possibilities if it's properly repaired* **5** *esp. spoken* a suitable person or thing: *Is Jane a possibility as a member of the team?*

possible¹ *adj* **1** that can exist, happen, or be done: *I'll do everything possible to help you* **2** that may or may not be, happen, or be expected: *It is possible that I shall go there next week* **3** acceptable; suitable: *one of many possible answers*

possible² *n* **1** that which can be or can be done: *Politics has been called the art of the possible* **2** a person or thing that might be suitable —compare PROBABLE

possibly *adv* **1** in accordance with what is possible: *I'll do all I possibly can* **2** perhaps

possum *n* -sums *or* -sum **1** *US* an opossum **2 play possum** to pretend to be asleep in order to deceive someone

post¹ *n* **1** a strong thick upright pole or bar made of wood, metal, etc., fixed into the ground or some other base esp. as a support: *a gatepost* **2** the starting or finishing place in a race, esp. a horse race: *My horse got beaten at the finishing post*

post² *v* **1** to make public or show by fixing to a wall, board, post, etc.: *The notice will be posted up today* **2** to make known by putting up a notice: *The ship was posted missing*

post³ *n* **1** the official system for carrying letters, parcels, etc., from the sender to the receiver **2** the official collection or delivery of letters, parcels, etc. —compare PILLAR-BOX, POSTBOX, POST OFFICE **3** (in former times) any of a number of stopping places on a road where travellers or messengers could rest, change horses, etc., and where letters could be passed to a fresh rider **4 by return of post** by the next post back

post⁴ *v* **1** to send by post, by taking to a post office or putting into a collection box for sending **2 keep someone posted** to continue to give someone all the latest news about something

post⁵ *n* **1** a small fort, camp, etc., esp. on a border or in a desert, at which a body of soldiers is kept **2** a special place of duty, esp. on guard or on watch: *All workers must be at their posts by half past 8* **3** a job —see JOB (USAGE) **4** either of 2 sets of notes played at sunset on a bugle, esp.

to call soldiers to their camp: *The soldier played the first post/last post*

post⁶ *v* **1** to place (soldiers or other men) on duty in a special place, esp. as a guard **2** to send or appoint (someone) to a particular army group, a place or duty with a firm, etc.

postage *n* the charge for carrying a letter, parcel, etc., by post

postage stamp *n* a stamp for sticking on things to be posted

postal *adj* **1** connected with the public letter service: *Postal charges have increased* **2** sent by post: *a postal vote*

postal order *n* a piece of paper bought from a post office, and sent to someone who can exchange it at a post office for a stated amount of money

postbag *n* **1** the letters received by someone at one particular time **2** a postman's bag for carrying letters

postbox *n* **1** an official metal box, often set into a wall, in which letters are posted **2** a pillar-box

postcard *n* **1** a usu. small card on which a message may be written and sent by post **2** also **picture postcard**— a card like this with a picture or photograph on one side

postcode *n* a group of letters and numbers that means a particular area and can be added to the address on letters or parcels to speed delivery

postdate *v* **-dated, -dating** **1** to write on (a letter, cheque, etc.) a date later than the date of writing **2** to give a later date to (an event) than the actual date of happening —opposite **ante-date**

poster *n* a large printed notice or drawing put up in a public place

poste restante *n* a post office department to which letters may be sent and kept until collected

posterior¹ *adj* **1** *esp. written* later in time or order; after —opposite **prior** **2** (in biology) placed behind or at the back —opposite **anterior**

posterior² *n humour* the part of the body a person sits on; bottom

posterity *n* **1** people who will be born and live after one's own time **2** *literature* a person's descendants

postern *n literature* a small or private gate or door

poster paint also **poster colour**— *n* a type of artist's paint, usu. very brightly coloured

postgraduate *n, adj* (a person doing studies that are) done at a university after completing one's first degree

posthaste *adv literature* at great speed

post horn *n* (in former times) a horn blown by a servant in a carriage as a signal or warning

posthumous *adj* **1** coming after one's death: *posthumous fame* **2** (of a book, musical work, etc.) printed and made public after the writer's death **3** (of a child) born after its father's death — ~**ly** *adv*

postilion, -till- *n* a servant who rides on one of the horses pulling a carriage when there is no driver

postman *n* **-men** a man employed to collect and deliver letters, parcels, etc.

postmark *v, n* (to make) an official mark on letters, parcels, etc., usu. over the stamp, showing when and where they are posted

postmaster (*fem.* **postmistress**)— *n* an official in charge of a post office

Postmaster General *n* **Postmasters General** an official in charge of a national postal system

post meridiem *adv esp. written & rare* p. m.

postmortem *n Latin* **1** an examination of a dead body to discover the cause of death; autopsy **2** an examination of a plan or event that failed in order to discover the cause of failure

post office *n* an office, shop, etc., which deals with the post and certain other government business for a particular area, such as telephone bills

postpone *v* **-poned, -poning** to delay; move to some later time — ~**ment** *n*

postscript *n* **1** also (*esp. spoken*) **P.S.**— a short addition to the end of a letter **2** a part added at the end of a book, statement, etc.

postulate¹ *v* **-lated, -lating** to accept (something that has not been proved) as true, as a base for reasoning

postulate² *n* something supposed or known (but not proved) to be true, on which a piece of reasoning is based

posture¹ *n* **1** the way of holding the body, esp. the back, shoulders, and head **2** a manner of behaving or thinking on some occasion; attitude

posture² *v* **-tured, -turing** **1** *often offensive* to place oneself in a bodily position or positions, esp. in order to be admired **2** *offensive* to pretend to be something that one is not: *posturing as a music lover*

posy *n* **posies** a small bunch of flowers

pot¹ *n* **1** any of several kinds of round vessel of baked clay, metal, etc., made to contain liquids or solids: *a pot of paint* | *a teapot* **2** a potty **3** *esp. spoken* an ornamental clay vessel made by hand **4** *esp. spoken* a large amount (of money): *They've got pots of money* **5** all the money risked on one card game and taken by the winner —compare KITTY **6** a stroke which sends the correct ball into a pocket in the game of billiards or snooker **7** *esp. spoken* an important person (esp. in the phrase **big pot**) **8** *sl* the drugs hashish or marijuana **9** *usu. offensive* a potbelly **10** *esp. spoken* a potshot **11** **go to pot** *esp. spoken* to pass into a state of worthlessness **12** **keep the pot boiling** to make the activity of a group continue **13** **the pot calling the kettle black** one person blaming another for having a fault which he himself has

pot² *v* **-tt-** **1** to shoot (esp. an animal or bird) **2** to set (a plant) in a pot filled with earth **3** *esp. spoken* to sit (a young child) on a potty **4** (in billiards) to hit (a ball) into one of the 6 bags at the edge of the table

potash *n* any of various salts of potassium, used esp. to feed the soil, and in making soap, strong glass, and various chemical compounds

potassium *n* a silver-white metal that is an element and is necessary to the existence of all living things

potation *n* *esp. written or humour* an (alcoholic) drink

potato *n* **-toes** **1** a type of roundish root vegetable with a thin, usu. brown skin, that is cooked and served in many ways —see also CHIP **2** a plant which has these growing on its roots

potato beetle also **Colorado beetle**— *n* **-beetle** *or* **-beetles** a type of small harmful insect that feeds on the leaves of potato plants

potbellied *adj* **1** *often offensive or humour* (of a person) having a potbelly **2** (of a stove) having a rounded middle part for burning coal or wood

potbelly *n* **-lies** *often offensive or humour* also **pot**— a large rounded stomach

potboiler *n* *offensive* a work of art or literature produced quickly in order to obtain money

potbound *adj* (of a plant growing in a pot) having roots that have grown to fill the pot, and therefore unable to grow further

poteen also **potheen**— *n* Irish whiskey, made secretly to avoid paying government tax

potent *adj* **1** (of medicines, drinks, etc.) having a strong or rapid effect **2** *esp. written* (of arguments, reasoning, etc.) strongly effective; causing one to agree **3** (of a male) able to have sexual relations —compare IMPOTENT **4** *literature or esp. written* having great power, esp. politically — **potency** *n* — **~ly** *adv*

potentate *n* **1** (esp. in former times) a ruler with direct power over his people **2** (esp. in newspaper style) a person possessing great power and influence

potential[1] *adj* existing in possibility but not at present active or developed: *Every seed is a potential plant* — **~ly** *adv*

potential[2] *n* **1** possibility for developing or being developed: *The boy has acting potential, but he needs training* **2** the degree of electricity or electrical force (usu. measured in volts)

potential energy *n* the amount of energy something has because of its position

potentiality *n* **-ties** **1** the quality or condition of being potential **2** a hidden unused power of mind or character

pothead *n* *sl* a person who habitually smokes pot

pother *n* *esp. spoken* **1** a state of worry arising from slight cause **2** noisy unnecessary activity

pothole *n* **1 a** a deep round hole in the surface of rock by which water enters and flows underground, often through a cave **b** the cave itself **2** a hole in a road surface caused by traffic or bad weather

potholing *n* the sport of exploring potholes — **potholer** *n*

potion *n* *esp. in literature* a drink intended as medicine, poison, or a magic charm: *a sleeping potion*

potluck *n* **take potluck a** to choose without enough information **b** (esp. of an unexpected guest) to have whatever food there is

potpourri *n* *French* **1** a mixture of dried petals and leaves, kept in a bowl to give a pleasant smell to a room **2** a mixed collection, esp. of pieces of popular music or writing

pot roast *n* a piece of meat cooked slowly with a little water, after light frying

potsherd *n* (in archaeology) a broken piece of a pot

potshot *n* *esp. spoken* a carelessly aimed shot

potted *adj* **1** (of meat, fish, or chicken) made into a paste and preserved in a pot, for eating spread on bread **2** *sometimes offensive* (of a book) produced in a shorter simpler form: *potted Shakespeare*

potter[1] *n* a person who makes pots, dishes, etc., out of baked clay

potter[2] *v* *esp. spoken* to move slowly or work at small unimportant jobs: *Grandmother just potters about the house* — **potter** *n*

potter's wheel *n* a round spinning plate fixed parallel to the ground, on which wet clay is shaped into a pot

pottery *n* **-ries** **1** the work of a potter **2** pots and other objects made out of baked clay **3** baked clay (EARTHENWARE), considered as the material of which pots are made: *a pottery dish* **4** a potter's workroom or factory

potting shed *n* a small building by a garden, allotment, etc., to hold tools, seeds, etc.

potty[1] *adj* **-tier, -tiest** **1** *esp.spoken* silly; slightly mad **2** *offensive* small and unimportant **3** *esp. spoken* having a strong interest in or admiration for (someone or something): *The girls are potty about the new singer* — **pottiness** *n*

potty[2] *n* **-ties** a chamber pot for children, now usu. made of plastic

pouch *n* **1** a small soft, often leather bag for tobacco, carried in the pocket **2** a baglike fold of skin inside each cheek, in which certain animals (such as hamsters) store food **3** a pocket of skin in the lower half of the body, in which certain animals (MARSUPIALS) carry their young **4** a baglike fold of skin that hangs down, esp. under the eye as a result of illness, old age, etc.

pouf, pouffe *n* a low drum-shaped seat or footrest

poulterer *n* a poultry-seller

poultice *n* a heated wet mass of any of various substances, spread on a cloth and laid against the skin to lessen pain, swelling, etc.

poultry *n* **1** farmyard birds, such as hens, ducks, etc., kept for supplying eggs and meat **2** chicken, duck, etc., considered as meat

pounce[1] *v* **pounced, pouncing** **1** to fly down or spring suddenly in order to seize something, esp. for food: *The bird pounced on the worm* **2**

to make a sudden attack, usu. from a hidden place: *Policemen pounced on the criminals*

pounce² *n* an attack made by pouncing

pounce on also **pounce upon**— *v prep* **1** to seize or accept eagerly **2** to notice at once and point sharply to (someone or something): *The teacher pounced on the pupil's mistake*

pound¹ *n* **1** a standard measure of weight equal to about 0.454 kilograms **2** a measure of weight for gold and silver, equal to about 0.373 kilograms **3 a** the standard of money in several countries: *the Egyptian pound* **b** also (*esp. written or technical*) **pound sterling**— the British standard of money, now divided into 100 pence ⌀MONEY **4** the British money system; value at any particular time of British money at international exchange rates: *The Bank of England had to support the pound*

pound² *v* **1** to crush into a soft mass or powder by striking repeatedly with a heavy object **2** to strike repeatedly, heavily, and noisily **3** to move with heavy quick steps that make a dull sound

pound³ *n* **1** a place where lost dogs and cats, and cars that have been unlawfully parked, are kept by the police until claimed **2** (in former times) an enclosure in which wandering animals were officially kept until claimed and paid for by the owner

pounding *n* **1** the act or sound of someone or something that pounds **2** *esp. spoken* a severe beating: *Our football team took a real pounding from Brazil last night*

pound note *n* a printed official piece of paper with which one can buy things to the value of a pound (or of a stated number of pounds): *a 10-pound note*

pour *v* **1** to flow steadily and rapidly: *Blood poured from the wound* **2** (of people) to rush together in large numbers: *At 5 o'clock workers poured out of the factories* **3** to cause to flow: *Pour away the dirty water* **4** to give or send as if in a flow: *She poured out her sorrows to me* **5 a** to rain hard and steadily: *It's pouring this morning* **b** (of rain) to fall hard and steadily: *The rain is really pouring down* **6** *esp. spoken* to fill cups of tea, coffee, etc., and serve them **7** to supply (someone) with a drink from a vessel: *Please pour me a cup of tea*

pour on *v prep* **1 pour cold water on** to discourage: *Don't pour cold water on the idea* **2 pour oil on the flames** to make matters worse **3 pour oil on troubled waters** to try to stop trouble by calming the people causing it

pout *v* to show childish bad temper and displeasure by pushing the lips or the lower lip forward — **pout** *n*

poverty *n* **1** the state of being very poor **2** *esp. written & offensive* low quality: *The book is boring because of the poverty of its ideas*

poverty-stricken *adj* very poor indeed

P O W *abbrev. for:* PRISONER OF WAR: *a POW camp*

powder¹ *n* **1** a substance in the form of very fine dry grains: *He crushed the chalk to powder*

2 a pleasant-smelling, often flesh-coloured substance in this form, for use on the skin: *face powder* **3** explosive material in this form, esp. gunpowder

powder² *v* **1** to put powder on **2** to break into powder

powdered *adj* **1** covered with powder **2** produced or dried in the form of powder: *powdered milk*

powder horn also **powder flask**— *n* a narrow-necked gunpowder container used in former times

powder keg *n* (in former times) a small barrel for holding gunpowder

powder magazine *n* a place for storing explosives, esp. on a warship

powder puff *n* a small thick piece, or ball, of soft material for spreading powder on the face or body

powder room *n polite* a women's public lavatory in a hotel, big shop, etc.

powdery *adj* **1** like powder **2** covered with powder

power¹ *n* **1** a sense or ability that forms part of the nature of body or mind: *Some animals have the power to see in the dark* **2** force; strength **3** control over others: *Power should be used wisely* **4** right to govern: *Which political party is in power now?* **5** right to act, given by law, rule, or official position: *The army has been given special powers to deal with this state of affairs* **6** a person, group, nation, etc., that has influence or control: *There is to be a meeting of the Great Powers* **7** an unearthly force or spirit believed to be able to influence men's fate: *the powers of evil* **8** force that may be used for doing work, driving a machine, or producing electricity: *Mills used to depend on wind or water power —see also* HORSE-POWER, MANPOWER **9** the degree of this force produced by something: *What is the power of this engine?* **10** (in mathematics) **a** the number of times that an amount is to be multiplied by itself: *The amount 2 to the power of 3 is written 2^3, and means $2 \times 2 \times 2$* **b** the result of this multiplying: *The 3rd power of 2 is 8 —see also* EXPONENT, INDEX **11** (of instruments containing a lens) a measure of the strength of the ability to make objects appear larger **12** *esp. spoken* a large amount: *Your visit did me a power of good* **13** **More power to your elbow!** *esp. spoken* May your efforts succeed! **14** **power behind the throne** a person who, though he has no official position, has great influence in private over a ruler or leader

power² *adj* (of an apparatus or vehicle usu. worked by hand) provided with or worked by a motor: *power steering*

power³ *v* to supply power to (esp. a moving machine) —see also HIGH-POWERED

powerboat *n* a motorboat, esp. one with a powerful engine

powerful *adj* **1** very strong; full of force: *a powerful swimmer* **2** of great ability; easily producing ideas: *a powerful imagination* **3** strong or great in effect: *Onions have a powerful smell* **4** having much control and influence **5** having or using great mechanical power — ~**ly** *adv*: *He's very powerfully built*

powerless *adj* lacking power or strength; unable: *The driver was powerless to stop the accident* — ~**ly** *adv* — ~**ness** *n*

power of attorney *n*   **powers of attorney** *law* the written right given to a person to act for someone else in business or law

power plant *n* an engine and other parts supplying power to a factory, an aircraft, etc.

power politics *n often offensive* the system of gaining an advantage for one's country in international politics by the use or show of armed force instead of by peaceful argument

power station *n* a large building in which electricity is generated

powwow *v, n* **1** (to hold) a meeting or council of North American Indians **2** *humour & becoming rare* (to hold) a long talk to decide some matter

pp *abbrev. for:* **1** pianissimo —see also P **2** pages: *see pp 15–37* —see also P

PPS *abbrev. for:* Parliamentary Private Secretary

PR *abbrev. for:* PUBLIC RELATIONS

practicable *adj* that can be successfully used or acted upon: *Is it practicable to try to grow crops in deserts?* — **-bly** *adv* — **-bility** *n* USAGE People are beginning to use **practical** with the same meaning as **practicable**: *a practical/practicable plan*. **Practicable** is not used of people.

practical¹ *adj* **1** concerned with action, practice, or actual conditions and results, rather than with ideas: *At scout camp he made practical use of his cookery lessons* **2** effective or convenient in actual use: *a very practical little table that folds up when not needed* **3 a** sensible; clever at doing things and concerned with facts rather than feelings: *We've got to be practical and buy only what we can afford* **b** offensive insensitive and lacking imagination **4** taught by actual experience or practice, not by studying books: *She's never been to cooking classes, but she's a good practical cook* **5 for all practical purposes** actually; in reality: *He does so little work in the office that for all practical purposes it would make no difference if he didn't come* —see PRACTICABLE (USAGE) — ~**ity** *n*

practical² *n esp. spoken* a practical lesson, test, or examination, as in science

practical joke *n* a trick played upon one person to give amusement to others

practically *adv* **1** usefully; suitably **2** very nearly: *She's practically always late*

practice *n* **1** actual use or performance as compared with the idea, rules, etc., on which the action is based: *We must put our plans into practice* **2** experience; knowledge of a skill as gained by this: *Have you had any practice in nursing?* **3** a repeated performance or exercise in order to gain

skill in some art, game, etc.: *We have 3 choir practices a week* **4** a standard course of action that is accepted as correct: *It is the practice in English law to consider a person innocent until he has been proved guilty* **5** *often written* a fixed custom or regular habit: *It's not the usual practice for shops to stay open after 6 o'clock* **6** *often offensive* an act that is often repeated, esp. secretly, in a fixed manner or with ceremony: *The Christian church had to stop magical practices among its people* **7 a** the business of a doctor or lawyer: *Is Doctor Jones still in practice?* **b** his place of business: *Doctor Smith's practice is in the High Street* **c** the kind or number of people using his services: *He has a small practice* **8 sharp practice** *offensive* behaviour or a trick in business or work that is dishonest but not quite unlawful

practise *v* **-tised, -tising 1** to act in accordance with (the ideas of one's religion or other firm belief): *a practising Jew* **2** *esp. written* to show or use (some necessary quality in behaviour): *In dealing with sick old people nurses must practise great patience* **3** *esp. written* to make a habit or practice of: *Our income has decreased and now we have to practise economy* **4** to do (an action) repeatedly or do exercises regularly (esp. on a musical instrument) in order to gain skill: *She's been practising the same tune on the piano for nearly an hour* **5** to do (something needing special knowledge) according to rule: *Some people practise magic* **6** to do (the work of a doctor, lawyer, etc.): *One practises medicine, the other practises law* **7** *esp. written* to make unfair use of (a trick) for one's own advantage **8 practise what one preaches** to do oneself what one is always telling others to do

practised *adj* **1** skilled through practice: *a practised cheat* **2** gained by practice: *The dancer moved with practised grace* **3** *offensive* gained only by practice; not natural: *My hostess welcomed me with a practised smile*

practitioner *n* **1** a person who works in a profession, esp. a doctor or lawyer: *medical practitioners* **2** a person who practises a skill or art —see also GENERAL PRACTITIONER

praetor *n* (in ancient Rome) a state officer of the rank below the heads of state, who held office for one year and had duties concerning the army and law

praetorian *adj* **1** of or concerning a praetor **2** of or like the guards of Roman rulers: *the praetorian guards*

pragmatic *adj* dealing with matters as seems best under the actual conditions, rather than following a general principle; practical — ~**ally** *adv*

pragmatism *n* pragmatic thinking or way of considering things — **-tist** *n*

prairie *n* (esp. in North America) a treeless grassy plain

prairie dog *n* a type of small furry North American animal that lives underground

praise[1] v praised, praising to speak favourably and with admiration of

praise[2] n 1 expression of admiration: *a book in praise of country life* 2 *esp. written or literature* glory; worship: *Let us give praise to God* 3 **praise be** thank God: *At last I've found you, praise be!*

praiseworthy adj deserving praise — **-thily** adv — **-thiness** n

praline n a type of sweet made of nuts cooked brown in boiling sugar

pram also (*esp. written*) **perambulator**— n a 4-wheeled carriage for a baby, which is pushed by hand

prance v pranced, prancing 1 (of a horse) to jump high or move quickly by raising the front legs and springing forwards on the back legs 2 to move quickly, gaily, or proudly, with a springing step — **prance** n

prank n a playful but foolish trick, not intended to harm

prankster n a person who plays pranks

prate v prated, prating to talk foolishly

prattle[1] v -tled, -tling 1 *esp. spoken* to talk lightly and continually in a simple way, or like a child 2 *offensive* to gossip — ~**r** n

prattle[2] n *esp. spoken often offensive* childish, unimportant, or careless talk

prawn n any of various types of small 10-legged sea animals, good for food, including esp. large shrimps

pray[1] v prayed, praying 1 to speak, often silently, to God (or the gods), privately or with others, showing love, giving thanks, or asking for something 2 *esp. spoken* to wish or hope very strongly: *We're praying for a fine day* 3 **past praying for** in a hopeless condition (of illness, wickedness, etc.)

pray[2] adv please: *Pray be quiet!*

prayer[1] n 1 the act or regular habit of praying to God or the gods 2 a fixed form of church service mainly concerned with praying: *Evening Prayer* 3 a quite informal daily religious service among a group of people: *school prayers* 4 a fixed form of words used in praying: *He said his prayers every night* 5 a solemn request made to God or the gods, or to someone in a position of power: *Her prayer was answered and her husband came home safely*

prayer[2] n a person who prays

praying mantis also **mantis**— n a type of large insect that presses its front legs together as if praying. It feeds on other insects

preach v 1 to make known (a particular religion or its teachings) by speaking in public: *Christ preached to large crowds* 2 to give a sermon as part of a church service 3 to advise or urge others to accept (a thing or course of behaviour): *She's always preaching the value of healthy eating* 4 to offer (unwanted advice on matters of right and wrong) in an irritating way: *Mum keeps preaching at me about my untidiness* — ~**er** n

preamble n a statement at the beginning of a speech or piece of writing, giving its reason and purpose

prearrange v -ranged, -ranging to arrange in advance — ~**ment** n

precarious adj 1 unsafe; unsteady 2 doubtful; not based firmly on facts: *precarious reasoning* — ~**ly** adv — ~**ness** n

precast adj (of concrete) formed into blocks ready for use in building

precaution n an action done or care taken in order to avoid danger, discomfort, etc.: *We have taken every precaution against disease* — ~**ary** adj

precede v -ceded, -ceding 1 to come or go in front of 2 to be higher in rank or importance than: *The king precedes all men* 3 to be earlier than: *The minister's statement preceded that of the president* 4 to introduce (an activity) in the stated way: *He preceded his speech with a warning against inattention* △ PROCEED

precedence n 1 the manner in which things happen one after another (esp. in the phrase **in order of precedence**) 2 greater importance: *Some say Shakespeare takes precedence over all other writers* 3 the right to a particular place before others, esp. on social or ceremonial occasions: *The ruler has precedence over all others in the country*

precedent n 1 the use of former customs or decisions as a guide to present actions: *The Queen has broken with precedent by sending her children to ordinary schools* 2 a former action or case that may be used as an example or rule for present or future action: *Failure to punish this crime will set a precedent for the future* 3 **without precedent** never known to have happened before

preceding adj that came just before in time or place: *preceding page*

precept n 1 a guiding rule on which behaviour, a way of thought, etc., is based 2 use of such rules for instruction

precession also **precession of the equinoxes**— n a slow westward change in the angle of the earth's axis, which causes the equinoxes to fall slightly earlier each year — ~**al** adj

precinct n 1 the space, often enclosed by walls, that surrounds an important building, group of buildings, or holy place 2 a part of a town planned for, or limited to, a special use: *a new shopping precinct* —see also PEDESTRIAN PRECINCT 3 a line that marks the limit of a place; boundary

precincts n 1 neighbourhood; area around (a town or other place) 2 the inside (of a building or place): *Women aren't allowed within the precincts of this men's club*

precious[1] adj 1 of great value and beauty: *a precious crystal vase* 2 that must not be wasted: *My time is precious; I can only give you a few minutes* 3 greatly loved or very dear 4 (of an art, use of words, manners, etc.) unnaturally fine; too concerned with unimportant details — ~**ly** adv — ~**ness** n

precious² *adv esp. spoken* very: *We have precious little time*

precious³ *n esp. spoken* dear one; a much loved person or animal

precious metal *n* a rare and valuable metal such as gold or silver, often used in ornaments —opposite **base metal**

precious stone also **stone**— *n* any kind of valuable rare mineral, such as diamond, emerald, etc., which can be used in jewellery —compare SEMIPRECIOUS

precipice *n* 1 a steep or almost upright side of a high rock, mountain, etc. 2 **on the edge of a precipice** in very great danger

precipitate¹ *v* -tated, -tating 1 to hasten the coming of (an event) 2 a *esp. written* to throw with great force forwards or downwards b to force (into a condition or state of affairs) 3 (in chemistry, of solid matter) to separate from a liquid because of chemical action

precipitate² *n* (in chemistry) a solid substance separated from a liquid by chemical action

precipitate³ *adj esp. written* acting or done hastily and without care or thought △ PRECIPITOUS — ~ly *adv*

precipitation *n* 1 *esp. written* unwise haste 2 *technical* (amount of) rain, snow, etc.

precipitous *adj* 1 dangerously steep 2 like the edge of a precipice; frighteningly high △ PRECIPITATE — ~ly *adv* — ~ness *n*

précis¹ *n* -cis *French* 1 a shortened form of a speech or piece of writing, giving only the main points 2 the writing of such shortened forms, esp. as a school exercise

précis² *v* to make a précis of

precise *adj* 1 exact in form, detail, measurements, time, etc. 2 particular; very: *At the precise moment that I put my foot on the step, the bus started* 3 sharply clear: *A lawyer needs a precise mind* 4 careful and correct in regard to the smallest details: *precise manners* — ~ness *n*

precisely *adv* 1 in a precise way 2 exactly: *at 10 o'clock precisely* 3 yes, you are right: *'So you think we ought to wait?' 'Precisely'*

precision *n* also **preciseness**— exactness: *She doesn't express her thoughts with precision, so people often misunderstand her*

preclude *v* -cluded, -cluding *esp. written* to prevent: *He repeated his words so as to preclude misunderstanding* — -clusion *n*

precocious *adj* 1 (of a young person) a showing unusually early development of mind or body b *offensive* having qualities that are more suited to an older person 2 (of knowledge or qualities of character) developing unusually early — ~ly *adv* — ~ness *n* — -city *n*

precognition *n esp. written* knowledge of something that will happen in the future, esp. as received in the form of an unexplainable message to the mind

preconceived *adj* (of an idea, opinion, etc.) formed in advance, without enough knowledge or experience — -conception *n*

precook *v* to cook (food) for eating later

precursor *n* a person or thing that comes before and is a sign or earlier type of one to follow: *The precursor of the modern car was a horseless carriage with a petrol engine in front*

predator *n* a predatory animal

predatory *adj* 1 (esp. of a wild animal) living by killing and eating other animals 2 concerned with or living by or as if by robbery and seizing the property of others: *predatory tribes | predatory hotel keepers who charge high prices*

predecessor *n* 1 a person who held a position before someone else: *Our new doctor is much younger than his predecessor* 2 something formerly used, which has now been changed: *This new plan is no better than its predecessors*

predestination *n* 1 the belief that God has decided everything that will happen, and that humans cannot change this —compare FREE WILL 2 the belief that by God's wish some souls will be saved and go to heaven, and others lost and go to hell

predestine *v* -tined, -tining to fix, as if by fate, the future of: *He felt that he was predestined to lead his country*

predetermine *v* -mined, -mining 1 to fix unchangeably from the beginning: *A person's eye colour is predetermined by that of his parents* 2 to predispose — -mination *n*

predicament *n* a difficult or unpleasant state of affairs in which one does not know what to do

predicate *n* the part of a sentence which makes a statement about the subject: *In 'She is an artist' 'is an artist' is a predicate*

predicative *adj* (of an adjective, noun, or phrase) coming after the noun being described or after the verb of which the noun is the subject: *In 'He is alive', 'alive' is a predicative adjective* —compare ATTRIBUTIVE — ~ly *adv*

predict *v* to see or describe (a future happening) in advance as a result of knowledge, experience, reason, etc.: *The weather scientists predicted a fine summer*

predictable *adj* 1 that can be predicted 2 *offensive* not doing anything unexpected or showing imagination: *I hate predictable men* — -bility *n* — -bly *adv*

prediction *n* 1 something that is predicted; prophecy 2 the act of predicting — -tive *adj* — -tively *adv*

predilection *n* a special liking that has become a habit: *Charles has a predilection for dangerous sports*

predispose *v* -posed, -posing 1 to influence (someone) in the stated way: *I have heard nothing that predisposes me to like her* 2 to cause (someone) to tend: *His weak chest predisposes him to colds* — -sition *n*

predominate *v* -nated, -nating 1 to have the main power or influence 2 to be greater or greatest in numbers, force, etc.; be most noticeable — -ance *n* — -ant *adj* — -antly *adv*

preeminent *adj* above all others in the possession of some (usu. good) quality, ability, or main activity — **-nence** *n*

preeminently *adv* above everything else; chiefly

preempt *v* 1 to buy or get by preemption 2 to act or seize upon beforehand — ~**or** *n*

preemption *n* the act or right of buying before others have a chance to buy

preemptive *adj* 1 of or concerning preemption: *preemptive buying* 2 done before others can act, and in order to prevent them from doing so: *preemptive attacks on the enemy's airforce bases*

preen *v* (of a bird) to clean or smooth (itself or its feathers) with the beak

prefab *n esp. spoken* a small house built from parts made in a factory (esp. of the type put up in Britain and elsewhere after World War 2)

prefabricate *v* **-cated, -cating** to make (the parts of a building, ship, etc.) in a factory in large numbers and to standard measurements for fitting together at a chosen building place — **-cation** *n* — ~**d** *adj*

preface[1] *n* 1 an introduction to a book or speech 2 an action that is intended to introduce something else more important USAGE A **preface**, an **introduction**, and a **foreword** all come in the first pages of a book before the main contents; an **introduction** is usually longer than a **preface**, and a **foreword** is less formal.

preface[2] *v* **-aced, -acing** 1 to serve as a preface to: *An introduction prefaces the novel* 2 to provide with a preface: *He prefaced his speech with an amusing story* — **-atory** *adj* : *few prefatory remarks*

prefect *n* 1 (in some schools) an older pupil given certain powers and duties with regard to keeping order over other pupils 2 (in ancient Rome and certain countries today) any of various public officers or judges with duties in government, the police, or the army: *the Prefect of Police of Paris*

prefecture *n* 1 a governmental division of certain countries, such as France and Japan 2 (in France) the home or place of work of a prefect 3 the office or period of time in office of a prefect — **-tural** *adj*

prefer *v* **-rr-** 1 to choose (one thing or action) rather than another; like better 2 *law* to put forward for official consideration or action according to law: *The police preferred charges on the drunken driver*

preferable *adj* better; to be preferred — **-bly** *adv*

preference *n* 1 desire or liking for one thing rather than another: *I'd choose the small car in preference to the larger one* 2 special favour or consideration shown to a person, group, etc. 3 an example of this: *special trade preferences*

preferential *adj* of, giving, receiving, or showing preference: *This garage gives preferential treatment to regular customers* — ~**ly** *adv*

prefix[1] *v* to add to the beginning: *We prefixed a few pages to the article*

prefix[2] *n* (in grammar) a group of letters or sounds (AFFIX) placed at the beginning of a word: *'Re-' (meaning 'again') is a prefix in 'refill'* —compare SUFFIX

pregnancy *n* **-cies** 1 the condition or time of being pregnant 2 an example of this: *her third pregnancy* 3 *literature* deep meaning; importance (for the future)

pregnancy test *n* a medical test made to discover whether a woman is pregnant

pregnant *adj* 1 (of a woman or female animal) having an unborn child or unborn young in the body 2 full of important but unexpressed or hidden meaning: *His words were followed by a pregnant pause* 3 *literature* clever; inventive: *the artist's pregnant imagination* — ~**ly** *adv*

preheat *v* to heat up (an oven) to a particular temperature before cooking

prehensile *adj* (of a part of the body) able to curl round, seize, and hold things: *The hand of humans is prehensile*

prehistoric also (*esp. written*) **prehistorical**— *adj* 1 of or belonging to a time before recorded history: *prehistoric man* ◉ 2 *offensive or humour* very old-fashioned — ~**ally** *adv*

prehistory *n* 1 the time in human history before there were written records 2 the study of this time, esp. by digging up ancient remains 3 the history of the earlier stages of some developing condition

prejudge *v* **-judged, -judging** to form an opinion about (someone or something) before knowing or examining all the facts — **-judgment, -judgement** *n*

prejudice[1] *n* 1 unfair and often unfavourable feeling or opinion not based on reason or knowledge, and sometimes resulting from distrust of ideas different from one's own: *A judge must be free from prejudice* 2 damage; harm: *He had to leave the university, to the prejudice of his own future as a scientist*

prejudice[2] *v* **-diced, -dicing** 1 to cause (someone or someone's mind) to have a prejudice; influence: *His pleasant voice prejudices me in his favour* 2 to weaken; harm (someone's case, expectations, etc.)

prejudiced *adj* feeling or showing unfair prejudice

prejudicial *adj esp. written* 1 harmful: *Too much smoking is prejudicial to health* 2 leading to judgment that is too quick or opinion that is without reason or proof — ~**ly** *adv*

prelate *n* a priest having the rank of bishop or above

prelim also (*esp. written*) **preliminary examination**— *n esp. spoken* (esp. in some British universities) an examination, the result of which decides whether one may continue one's studies

preliminary[1] *n* **-ries** a preparation; preliminary act or arrangement

preliminary[2] *adj* 1 coming before and intro-

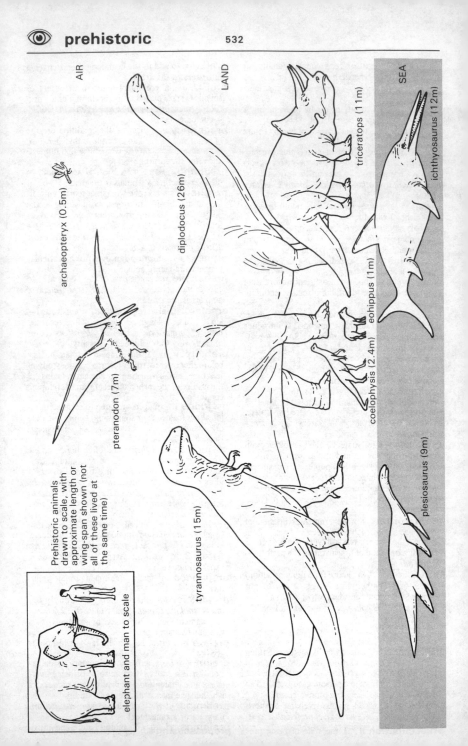

AIR

LAND

SEA

archaeopteryx (0.5m)

diplodocus (26m)

triceratops (11m)

ichthyosaurus (12m)

eohippus (1m)

coelophysis (2.4m)

pteranodon (7m)

tyrannosaurus (15m)

plesiosaurus (9m)

Prehistoric animals drawn to scale, with approximate length or wing-span shown (not all of these lived at the same time)

elephant and man to scale

ducing or preparing for something more important: *The chairman made a preliminary statement before beginning the main business* **2** (of a part of a sports competition) being the first part, in which the weaker people lose and the winners are left to compete in the main competition

preliterate *adj* not leaving or keeping written records: *preliterate societies whose past is hard to study* —compare ILLITERATE

prelude *n* **1** something that comes before and acts as an introduction to something more important: *I fear that the riots are a prelude to more serious trouble* **2 a** a short piece of music that introduces a large musical work **b** a short separate piece of piano or organ music: *Chopin's Preludes*

premarital *adj* happening or existing before marriage — ~ly *adv*

premature *adj* **1** developing, happening, or ripening before the natural or proper time: *his premature death at the age of 32* **2** (of a human or animal baby, or a birth) born, or happening, after less than the usual time inside the mother's body — ~ly *adv*

premeditate *v* -tated, -tating to plan (something) carefully in advance — -tation *n* — ~d *adj*

premier[1] *adj literature* first in position or importance

premier[2] *n* **1** the head of the government in certain countries: *Premier Mendès-France* **2** (esp. in newspaper style) PRIME MINISTER — ~ship *n*

premiere, -ère *n* the first public performance of a play or film

premise, -iss *n* a statement or idea on which reasoning is based

premises *n* a house or other building with any surrounding land, considered as a piece of property: *Food bought in this shop may not be eaten on the premises*

premium *n* **1** a sum of money paid regularly to an insurance company to protect oneself against some risk of loss or damage **2** an additional payment, esp. to a worker, made as a reward for special effort **3 at a premium a** (of a business share) at a rate above the usual value **b** difficult to obtain, and therefore worth more than usual: *During July and August hotel rooms are at a premium* **4 put a premium on** to cause (a quality or action) to be an advantage: *Work paid according to the amount done puts a premium on speed and not quality*

premium bond *n* a numbered piece of paper that can be bought from the government, and that gives the buyer the chance of a monthly prize of a small or large sum of money

premolar *n, adj* (any) of the 4 teeth in each jaw in front of the molars, used to crush and grind food

premonition *n* a feeling that something is going to happen; forewarning — -tory *adj*

preoccupation *n* **1** the state of being pre-

occupied **2** a matter which takes up all one's attention

preoccupy *v* -pied, -pying to fill the thoughts or hold the interest of (someone or someone's mind) almost completely, esp. so that not enough attention is given to other matters — -pied *adj*

preordain *v* (esp. of God or fate) to fix or decide before or from the beginning: *Some people believe that fate has preordained everything* — -dination *n* — ~ment *n*

prep *n esp. spoken* homework

prepack also **prepackage**— *v* to wrap up (food or other articles) in a factory or other place before sending to a shop

preparation *n* **1** the act of preparing for a future event: *He did too little preparation for his examination* **2** the state of being prepared: *Plans for selling the product are in preparation* **3** something that is made ready for use by mixing a number of substances: *a new preparation for cleaning metal* **4** *esp. written* prep

preparatory *adj* done in order to get ready for something

preparatory school also (*esp. spoken*) **prep school**— *n* a private school for pupils up to the age of 14, where they are made ready to attend a higher school (esp. a public school)

prepare *v* -pared, -paring **1** to put (something) in a condition ready for a purpose: *Please prepare the table for dinner* **2** to put together or make by treating in some special way (such as by mixing or heating substances): *Mother is preparing us a meal* **3** to get or make ready by collecting supplies, making arrangements, planning, studying, etc.: *They are busy preparing to go on holiday* **4** to accustom (someone or someone's mind) to some new idea, event, or condition: *Prepare yourself for a shock*

prepared *adj* **1** got ready in advance: *The chairman read out a prepared statement* **2** willing: *I'm not prepared to listen to your excuses*

preparedness *n* the state of being ready for something, esp. war

preponderant *adj* greater in amount, number, importance, influence, etc., than something else; main: *Yellow was the preponderant colour in the room* — -ance *n* — ~ly *adv*

preponderate *v* -rated, -rating *esp. written* to be greater in quantity, importance, influence, etc.

preposition *n* a word used with a noun, pronoun, or -ing form to show its connection with another word: *In 'a house made of wood' and 'a man like my brother', 'of' and 'like' are prepositions, and so is 'by' in 'she succeeded by working hard'* — ~al *adj* — ~ally *adv*

prepositional phrase *n technical* a phrase consisting of a preposition and the noun, pronoun, etc., following it: *"In bed" and 'on his bed' are prepositional phrases*

prepossessed *adj esp. written* **1** favourably influenced or impressed **2** preoccupied

prepossessing *adj* (of a person or a quality of

his character) very pleasing; producing a favourable effect at once

prepossession *n esp. written* **1** a liking or a dislike not based on personal experience **2** preoccupation

preposterous *adj* **1** completely unreasonable or improbable **2** laughably foolish: *She looked preposterous in that enormous hat* — ~**ly** *adv*

prep school *n esp. spoken* PREPARATORY SCHOOL

prepuce *n medical* a foreskin

Pre-Raphaelite *n, adj* (in England in the second half of the 19th century) (a person) belonging to the group of artists (**Pre-Raphaelite brotherhood**) who based their work on principles believed to have been those of Italian art before the painter Raphael

prerequisite *n, adj* (something) that is necessary before something else can happen or be done: *Her agreement is a prerequisite of my acceptance* ⚠ PERREQUISITE

prerogative *n* a special right belonging to someone by rank, position, or nature —see also ROYAL PREROGATIVE

presage[1] *n literature* a warning feeling or sign that something (esp. something bad) will happen

presage[2] *v* -**aged, -aging** *literature* to be a warning of; foretell

presbyter *n* **1** (in Presbyterian churches) an official person elected to the governing body of a church **2** (in Episcopal churches) a priest below a bishop in rank

Presbyterian *n, adj* (a member) of a Protestant church governed by a body of official people all of equal rank, as in Scotland — ~**ism** *n*

presbytery *n* -**ies** the eastern part of a church, behind the place where the choir sit

preschool *adj* of or concerning the time in a child's life before it goes to school

prescient *adj literature or esp. written* able to imagine or guess what will probably happen — -**ence** *n*

prescribe *v* -**scribed, -scribing** **1** to order (something) as a medicine or treatment for a sick person: *The doctor prescribed a cough medicine* **2** (of a person or body that has the right to do so) to fix (what must happen or be done): *What punishment does the law prescribe for this crime?*

prescription *n* **1** the act of prescribing **2 a** a particular medicine or treatment ordered by a doctor **b** a written order for this: *Take this prescription to the chemist's*

prescription charge *n* (in Britain) a sum of money that has to be paid when obtaining medicine under the National Health Service

presence *n* **1** the fact or state of being present: *She was so quiet that her presence was hardly noticed* **2** attendance: *Your presence is requested at the meeting* **3** personal appearance and manner, as having a strong effect on others **4** a spirit or an influence that cannot be seen but is felt to be

near **5 in the presence of someone** also **in someone's presence**— close enough to be seen or heard by someone

presence of mind *n* the ability to act calmly, quickly, and wisely in conditions of sudden danger or surprise: *When the fire started John had the presence of mind to turn off the gas*

present[1] *n* a gift

present[2] *v* **1** to give (something) away, esp. at a ceremonial occasion: *He presented her with a bunch of flowers* **2** to offer or bring (something) to someone's notice: *Can you present your report this afternoon?* **3** polite to offer: *He presented his apologies* **4** to introduce (someone) esp. to someone of higher rank **5** to give the public a chance to see and hear (a play or performer): *The theatre company is presenting Eric Williamson as Hamlet* **6** to show: *Although worried, he always presents a smiling face* **7** (of non-material things) to be the cause of: *He's clever at scientific studies; they present no difficulty to him* **8 present arms** to hold a weapon upright in front of the body as a ceremonial greeting **9 present itself a** (of a thought) to arrive in the mind **b** (of something possible) to happen: *If the chance to buy this farm presents itself, buy it* **10 present oneself** to attend; arrive

present[3] *adj* **1** (of a person) being in the place talked of or understood: *Who was present at the meeting?* **2** existing or happening now: *I'm not going to buy a house at the present high prices* **3** *esp. written or literature* felt or remembered as if actually there: *The terrible events of 5 years ago are still present to our minds* **4** *technical* (of a tense or a form of a verb) expressing state or action which is going on now: '*He wants*' *and* '*they are coming*' *are examples of verbs in present tenses* **5** '**present company excepted**' *polite* ' but the people here are not included in the unfavourable remarks I am making '

present[4] *n* **1** the present time **2** *technical* the present tense **3 at present** now; at this time **4 for the present** for now; for the time being **5 live in the present** to experience life as it comes, not thinking about the past or the future **6** (**there is**) **no time like the present** if you must do something, it is best to do it now

presentable *adj* fit to be seen, shown, heard, etc., in public — -**bly** *adv*

presentation *n* **1** the act or action of presenting something: *There are 2 presentations of the show each night* **2** the way in which something is said, offered, shown, explained, etc., to others: *The teacher praised the neat presentation of the homework*

present-day *adj* modern; existing now

presentiment *n* an unexplained uncomfortable feeling that something (esp. something bad) is going to happen; premonition

presently *adv* **1** soon: *The doctor will be here presently* **2** *esp. US and Scots* at present; now: *The doctor is presently writing a book* USAGE British speakers are beginning to use **presently** to mean "now", as the Americans do, rather than "soon".

present participle n (in grammar) a form of a verb which ends in -ing and may be used in compound forms of the verb to express continuing actions done or happening in the past, present, or future, or sometimes as an adjective

present perfect also **present perfect tense**— n esp. written & technical the grammatical perfect

preservation n 1 the act or action of preserving 2 the state of remaining in (a stated) condition after a long time: The old building is in good preservation

preservative n, adj (a usu. chemical substance) that can be used to preserve foods

preserve¹ v -served, -serving 1 esp. written or literature to keep (someone) safe or alive; protect 2 to keep (an article) carefully from destruction for a long time 3 to cause (a condition) to last: In times of danger he always preserves his calmness 4 to keep (a substance) in good condition or from decay by some means: Ancient Egyptians knew how to preserve dead bodies 5 to keep (a rare animal or plant) in existence — **-servable** adj

preserve² n 1 a substance made from fruit boiled in sugar, used esp. for spreading on bread; jam 2 a stretch of land or water kept for private hunting or fishing 3 something considered to belong to or be for the use of only a certain person or people: She considers the arranging of flowers in the church to be her own preserve

preserver n someone or something that preserves life

preset v -set, -setting to set in advance: He preset the cooker in the morning so that it would go on before he came home

preshrunk adj (of cloth used for making garments) shrunk before being offered for sale in order to prevent shrinking after use

preside v -sided, -siding to be in charge; lead: the presiding officer

presidency n -cies the office of president: Roosevelt was elected 4 times to the presidency of the US

president n 1 the head of government in many modern states that do not have a king or queen: the President of France 2 the head of some councils or government departments 3 the head of various societies concerned with art, science, sport, etc.: the president of the Yorkshire Cricket Club 4 the head of some British university colleges, and of some American universities 5 the head of a business company, bank, etc. — ~ **ial** adj

press¹ n 1 an act of pushing steadily against something 2 any of various apparatuses or machines used for pressing: a trouser press 3 esp. spoken an act of ironing a garment 4 newspapers and magazines in general (often including the news-gathering services of radio and television): the power of the press 5 newspaper writers in general: The minister invited the press to a meet-

ing 6 treatment given by newspapers in general when reporting a person or event: The play had a good press 7 a business for printing (and sometimes also for selling) books, magazines, etc.: the University Press 8 PRINTING PRESS 9 esp. written a crowd or close mass of moving people 10 continual hurry and effort 11 **freedom of the press** the freedom or right to print news or fair opinion on matters of public interest without fear of being stopped or harmed by a government or other official group 12 **go to press** (of a newspaper for any particular day) to start being printed

press² v 1 to push firmly and steadily 2 to iron 3 to direct force in order to crush, flatten, shape, pack tightly, or get liquid out 4 to push one's way, esp. in a mass: People pressed round the famous actress 5 to force an attack, a demand, etc. on: She pressed her guest to stay 6 **time presses** there is not much time —see also PRESS ON

press³ v 1 (in former times) to seize and force (a man) into the navy or army 2 **press into service** to use for some purpose in a time of need

press agent n a person who keeps an actor, musician, theatre, etc., in public notice by supplying photographs, facts, etc., to newspapers — **press agency** n

press box n a space at some outdoor events that is kept for the use of reporters

press conference also **news conference**— n a meeting arranged by an important person at which news reporters listen to a statement or ask questions

press cutting also **clipping**— n a short notice, picture, etc., cut out of a newspaper

pressed adj having hardly enough: pressed for time

pressgang n (esp. in the 18th century) a band of sailors employed to seize men for the navy

press home v adv 1 to push firmly into place 2 to get the greatest effect from (an attack)

pressing¹ n any of many copies of a gramophone record made from the same form (MATRIX)

pressing² adj 1 needing attention, action, etc., now 2 asking with strong urging: They were so pressing that I couldn't refuse — ~ **ly** adv

press on also **press forward**— v adv to continue bravely or without delay

press release n a prepared statement given out to news services

press-stud also esp. spoken **popper**— n a small round fastener for a garment, in which one part is pressed into another

press-up n an exercise in which a person lies face down and raises his body with his arms

pressure n 1 the action of pressing 2 the strength of this force: a pressure of 10 pounds to the square inch 3 discomfort caused by a sensation of pressing: a feeling of pressure in his chest 4 also **atmospheric pressure**— the force of the weight of the air 5 anxiety and difficulty 6 forcible influence: *We must bring pressure on him* **7 under pressure a** not of one's own free will **b** being forced or hurried: *He works best under pressure* —see also BLOOD PRESSURE, HIGH-PRESSURE

pressure cooker *n* a tightly covered pot in which food can be cooked very quickly by hot steam

pressure group *n* a group that tries to influence public opinion and government action

pressurize, -ise *v* **-ized, -izing 1** to make (someone) do something by forceful demands or influence **2** to control the air pressure inside (a high-flying aircraft): *a pressurized cabin* — **-ization** *n*

prestige *n* respect or admiration felt by reason of rank, proved quality, etc.: *the prestige of having such a famous brother*

prestigious *adj* bringing prestige

prestissimo *adj, adv* (in music) to be played as quickly as possible

presto *n, adj, adv* **-tos** (music) to be played very quickly

prestressed *adj* (of concrete) strengthened by stretched wires inside

presumable *adj* probable — **-bly** *adv* : *Presumably there's a good reason*

presume *v* **-sumed, -suming 1** to take as a fact without proof: *I presume he'll be back* **2** to accept as true until proved untrue: *If a person is missing for 7 years, he is presumed dead* **3** to dare: *He presumed to tell his employer how the work ought to be done*

presume upon *v prep esp. written* to take improper advantage of (someone's good nature or connection with oneself)

presumption *n* **1** an act of supposing **2** improper boldness

presumptuous *adj* too bold towards others — ~ly *adv*

presuppose *v* **-posed, -posing 1** to take to be true without trying to find out: *A scientist never presupposes the truth of an unproved fact* **2** to be necessary according to reason: *An honour given to a person presupposes that he has earned it* — **-position** *n*

pretence *n* **1** a false appearance, reason, or show: *She isn't really ill; it's only pretence* **2** a claim to possess (some desirable quality): *He has no pretence to education* **3 false pretences** *law* acts intended to deceive

pretend *v* **1** to give a deceiving appearance of: *He pretended to be reading* **2** (usu. of a child) to imagine as a game: *Let's pretend we're cats* **3** to attempt; dare: *I won't pretend to tell you how this machine works*

pretended *adj* unreal in spite of appearances

pretender *n* a person who makes a doubtful or unproved claim, such as to be the rightful king

pretension *n* **1** a claim to possess skill, qualities, etc.: *I make no pretensions to skill as an artist* **2** *esp. written* being pretentious

pretentious *adj* claiming importance that one does not possess — ~ness *n* — ~ly *adv*

preterite, -it *n, adj technical* (a tense or verb form) that expresses a past action or condition: *'Sang' is the preterite of 'sing'*

preternatural *adj* beyond what can be explained naturally — ~ly *adv*

pretext *n* an excuse: *He came under the pretext of seeing Mr Smith, but really to see Smith's daughter* —see EXCUSE (USAGE)

pretty[1] *adj* **-tier, -tiest 1** pleasing but not beautiful or grand —compare BEAUTIFUL, HANDSOME **2** (of a boy) charming and graceful but rather girlish **3** not nice; displeasing: *a pretty state of affairs* **4 sitting pretty** (of a person) in a favourable situation — **-tily** *adv* — **-tiness** *n*

pretty[2] *adv esp. spoken* rather; quite though not completely: *pretty sure | pretty good*

pretty-pretty *adj* (esp. of art) pretty in a silly weak way

pretzel *n* a hard salty biscuit in the shape of a stick or a loose knot

prevail *v esp. written* **1** to gain control or victory: *Justice has prevailed* **2** to continue to exist: *A belief in magic still prevails*

prevailing *adj* **1** (of a wind) that blows most of the time **2** most common or general: *the prevailing fashion* — ~ly *adv*

prevail upon also **prevail on**— *v prep esp. written* to persuade: *Can I prevail upon you to stay?*

prevalent *adj esp. written* existing commonly or widely: *Eye diseases are prevalent in some countries* — ~ly *adv* — **-lence** *n*

prevaricate *v* **-cated, -cating** *esp. written* to try to hide the truth by not answering plainly — **-cation** *n* — **-cator** *n*

prevent *v* **1** to keep from happening: *to prevent accidents* **2** to hold (someone) back: *You can't prevent me from going* — ~able *adj* — ~ion *n*

preventive also **preventative**— *n, adj* (something) serving to prevent something, esp. illness — ~ly *adv*

preview[1] *v* to give or see a preview of

preview[2] *n* **1** a private showing of paintings, a film, etc., before they are shown to the public **2** a foretaste

previous *adj* **1** earlier: *Have you had any previous experience?* **2** *esp. spoken* acting too soon: *You're a little previous in thanking me for something I haven't given you yet* — ~ly *adv*

prevision *n* *esp. written* knowledge of something before it happens △ PROVISION

prey *n* **1** an animal that is hunted and eaten by another **2** a way of life based on killing and eating other animals (in the phrases **beast/bird of prey**) **3 be/become/fall a prey to a** (of an animal) to be caught and eaten by (another animal) **b** (of a person) to be greatly troubled by: *Some people become a prey to fears of being murdered*

prey on also **prey upon**— *v prep* **1** to hunt and eat as prey: *Cats prey on birds and mice* **2** (of a person) to live by cheating (someone weak, helpless, etc.) **3** *esp. in literature* to attack suddenly and rob **4** (of sorrow, troubles, etc.) to trouble greatly

price¹ *n* **1** an amount of money for which a thing is offered or bought **2** that which one must suffer to get something one wants: *Loss of health is the price you pay for taking dangerous drugs* **3** (in betting) the difference between the money asked and the money one will get if one wins —see also STARTING PRICE **4 a price on one's head** a reward for one's capture **5 have one's price** to be willing to accept bribes —see also ASKING PRICE, CLOSING PRICE, COST PRICE, LIST PRICE

price² *v* **priced, pricing** **1** to fix the price of (goods for sale) **2** to ask the price of

priceless *adj* **1** of worth too great to be calculated —see WORTHLESS (USAGE) **2** very funny: *You look priceless in those trousers!*

pricey, pricy *adj* **-ier, -iest** *esp. spoken* dear; costly — **-cily** *adv* — **-ciness** *n*

prick¹ *n* **1** a small hole made by pricking **2** an act of pricking **3** a small sharp pain **4** a prickle **5 kick against the pricks** *esp. literature* to complain uselessly

prick² *v* **1** to make a very small hole in the skin or surface of, with a sharp-pointed object **2** to make (a small hole) in a surface with a pointed tool **3** to give a sensation of light sharp pain

prickle¹ *n* **1** any of a number of small sharp-pointed growths on the skin of some plants or animals **2** a pricking sensation

prickle² *v* **-led, -ling** to give a pricking sensation

prickly *adj* **-lier, -liest** **1** covered with prickles **2** that gives a pricking sensation: *prickly woollen underclothes* **3** *esp. spoken* (of a person) easily made angry — **-liness** *n*

prickly heat *n* an uncomfortable hot condition of the skin with painful red spots, common in tropical countries

prickly pear *n* a desert cactus with yellow flowers, prickles, and edible roundish fruit

prick out also **prick off**— *v adv* to place (a young plant) in a hole in the earth

prick up *v adv* **1 prick up its ears** (of an animal) to raise the ears to listen **2 prick up one's ears** (of a person) to listen carefully

pride *n* **1** too high an opinion of oneself **2** reasonable self-respect: *She wanted to beg him to stay but her pride wouldn't let her* **3** satisfaction in someone or something connected with oneself: *Why can't you take more pride in your appearance?* **4** one's most valuable person or thing **5** a group (of lions) **6 swallow one's pride** to make an effort to forget one's pride

pride on also **pride upon**— *v prep* **prided, priding on** to be pleased and satisfied with (oneself) about: *She prided herself on her painting*

priest *n* **1** (in the Christian church) a person, esp. a man, trained for various religious duties **2** (*fem.* **priestess**)— a person with related duties in certain non-Christian religions — ~**hood** *n* — ~**ly** *adj* — ~**liness** *n*

prig *n* a person who believes himself morally better than others and obeys rules eagerly — ~**gish** *adj* — ~**gishly** *adv* — ~**gishness** *n*

prim *adj* **-mm-** **1** easily shocked by anything improper **2** neat: *prim little dresses* — ~**ly** *adv* — ~**ness** *n*

prima ballerina *n* the leading woman dancer in a ballet

primacy *n* **1** *esp. written* being first in rank, importance, etc. **2** the position of a priest who is a primate

prima donna *n* **1** the leading woman singer in an opera **2** an excitable self-important person

primaeval *adj* primeval

prima facie *adj, adv Latin esp. law* based on what first seems to be true

primal *adj* *esp. written* **1** belonging to the earliest time in the world **2** first in importance: *a primal need* —compare PRIMORDIAL, PRISTINE

primarily *adv* mainly; chiefly

primary *adj* **1** earliest in time **2** main: *A primary cause of Tom's failure is his laziness* ⌐BIRD **3** (of education or a school) for children between 5 and 11 —compare SECONDARY, ELEMENTARY **4** *technical* which produces or passes on electricity: *a primary coil*

primary colour *n* any of 3 colours from which all others can be mixed

primate¹ *n* a priest of the highest rank; archbishop ◉

primate² *n* a member of the most highly developed group of mammals, which includes men, monkeys, and related animals ⌐MAMMAL

prime¹ *n* **1** the time of greatest perfection, strength, or activity: *in the prime of life* **2** *technical* PRIME NUMBER

prime² *adj* **1** first in importance: *a prime reason* **2** of the very best quality: *a prime joint of beef*

prime³ *v* **primed, priming** **1** to prepare (a machine) for working **2** to instruct (someone) in advance **3** to cover (a surface) with a base of paint, oil, etc.

prime meridian *n* the imaginary line drawn from north to south on the earth, which passes through Greenwich, and from which east and west are measured on a map in degrees ⌐GLOBE

prime minister also (*esp. spoken*) **P M**— *n* the chief government minister in Britain and many other countries — ~**ship** *n*

prime mover *n* **1** a natural force (such as wind or moving water) which can produce power **2** a person or thing that has great influence in starting something

prime number *n* *technical* a number that can be divided exactly only by itself and the number one: *23 is a prime number*

primer¹ *n* a simple beginner's book in any school subject

primer² *n* paint or other substance spread over bare wood before the main painting

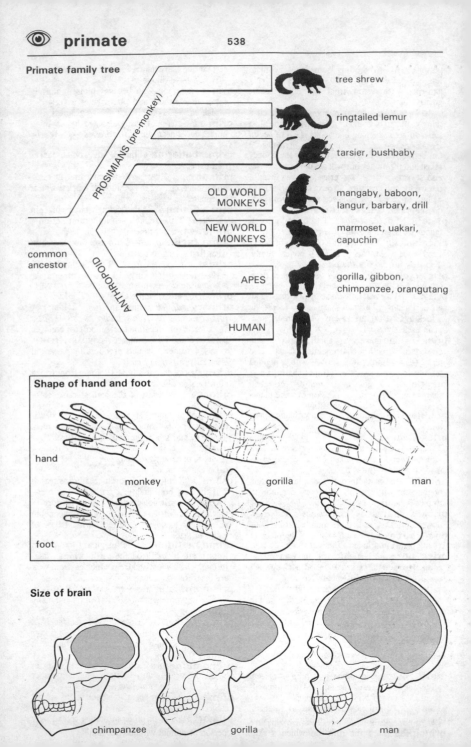

Primate family tree

PROSIMIANS (pre-monkey)

tree shrew

ringtailed lemur

tarsier, bushbaby

OLD WORLD MONKEYS — mangaby, baboon, langur, barbary, drill

NEW WORLD MONKEYS — marmoset, uakari, capuchin

APES — gorilla, gibbon, chimpanzee, orangutang

HUMAN

common ancestor

ANTHROPOID

Shape of hand and foot

hand

monkey   gorilla   man

foot

Size of brain

chimpanzee   gorilla   man

primeval, -mae- adj of the earliest period of the earth's existence

priming n gunpowder used to fire explosive

primitive¹ adj 1 of or belonging to the earliest stage of development: *primitive tools made from stones and bones* 2 old-fashioned and inconvenient: *Life in this village is too primitive for me* — ~ly adv — ~ness n

primitive² n 1 an artist who paints simple flat-looking pictures 2 a member of a primitive race or tribe

primordial adj existing from or at the beginning of time —compare PRIMAL, PRISTINE — ~ly adv

primrose n 1 a common wild plant with light yellow spring flowers 2 a light yellow colour 3 **the primrose path** the life of pleasure that may lead to ruin

primula n any of various types of plant (including the primrose), with bright flowers

primus n trademark a type of portable metal cooking stove

prince n 1 a son or near male relation of a king or queen 2 a ruler of a small country or protected state 3 esp. in literature a very great, successful, or powerful man: *Shakespeare, the prince of poets*

prince consort n princes consort a title sometimes given to the husband of a ruling queen

princely adj -lier, -liest 1 of a prince 2 splendid; generous: *a princely gift*

princess n 1 a daughter or near female relation of a king or queen 2 the wife of a prince

principal¹ adj chief; most important: *the principal rivers of Africa* ⚠ PRINCIPLE — ~ly adv

principal² n 1 the head of some universities, colleges, and schools 2 a sum of money on which interest is paid 3 a leading performer in a play, concert, etc. ⚠ PRINCIPLE

principal boy n -boys the hero in a pantomime, usu. played by an actress

principality n -ties a country that a prince rules

principal parts n technical the parts of a verb from which other parts are formed or can be guessed

principle n 1 a general truth or belief used as a base for reasoning or action: *the principle of freedom of speech* 2 a technical a scientific law of nature: *the principle of Archimedes* b such a law as governing the making or working of a machine, apparatus, etc. 3 a rule used as a guide for action 4 honourable behaviour: *a man of principle* 5 **in principle a** in regard to the main idea: *They agreed to the plan in principle* b according to what is supposed to be true : *There's no reason in principle why man shouldn't travel to the stars* 6 **on principle** because of settled fixed beliefs ⚠ PRINCIPAL

principled adj having or based upon principles: *a high-principled man* —see also UNPRINCIPLED

principles n 1 the rules on which a skill,

science, etc., is based: *the principles of cooking* 2 high personal standards of right and wrong

print¹ n 1 a mark on a surface showing the shape, pattern, etc., of the thing pressed into it: *footprints in the snow* 2 printed letters 3 a picture printed from metal: *a set of Chinese prints* 4 cloth on which a pattern has been printed: *print dresses* 5 a photograph printed from film 6 **in print** printed in a book, newspaper, etc.

print² v 1 to press (a mark) onto a surface 2 a to press using shapes covered with ink b to make (a book, magazine, etc.) in this way 3 to cause to appear in or as a book, newspaper, etc. 4 to ornament with a pattern pressed or rubbed on the surface: *printed wallpaper* 5 to make or copy (a photograph) on paper from film 6 to write without joining the letters —see also PRINT OUT

printable adj 1 fit for reading 2 that can be printed or printed from

printed circuit n a set of connections in an electrical apparatus in the form of a continuous line of a conductive substance

printer n 1 a person employed in printing 2 a machine for making copies, esp. photographs ⫘COMPUTER

printer's devil n a young boy who does small jobs in a printer's office

printing n 1 the act or art of printing 2 an act of printing copies: *the third printing of the book* 3 letters printed by hand

printing press also press, printing machine— n a machine that prints books, newspapers, etc.

printout n a printed record produced by a computer ⫘COMPUTER

print out v adv (of a computer) to produce (a printout)

prior¹ n 1 (fem. prioress)— the head of a priory 2 the priest next in rank below an abbot

prior² adj 1 earlier: *a prior engagement* 2 more important

priority n -ties 1 the state or right of being first: *The badly wounded take priority for medical attention* 2 something that needs attention before others: *The arranging of this agreement is* **a top priority**

prior to prep esp. written before

priory n -ries a monastery or convent which is smaller and less important than an abbey

prise v prised, prising to prize; pry

prism n 1 (in geometry) a solid with parallel upright edges and identical ends ⫘MATHEMATICS 2 a transparent 3-sided usu. glass block that breaks up white light into colours

prismatic adj 1 using a prism: *a prismatic compass* 2 of or a shape of a prism

prison n 1 a large building where criminals are kept locked up 2 a place or condition in which one feels a loss of freedom

prison-breaking n unlawful escaping from a prison

prisoner n 1 a person kept in a prison 2 a person or animal without freedom

prisoner of war also (*esp. spoken*) **POW**— *n* **prisoners of war** a member of the armed forces caught by the enemy during a war and kept prisoner

prison visitor *n* a person who visits prisoners to help them, keep their spirits up, etc.

prissy *adj* -sier, -siest annoyingly proper in behaviour — **prissily** *adv* — **prissiness** *n*

pristine *adj esp. written* 1 of the earliest time 2 undamaged; fresh and clean —compare PRIMAL, PRIMORDIAL

privacy *n* 1 the state of being away from the presence or notice of others: *Most people like privacy when they're undressing* 2 secrecy

private[1] *adj* 1 personal; not shared: *private letters* 2 not intended for everyone: *a private performance* 3 not connected with government: *a private hospital* 4 not connected with one's public life 5 without official position: *private citizens* 6 quiet; sheltered: *a private corner* 7 **in private** secretly —opposite **in public** —compare PUBLIC — ~**ly** *adv*

private[2] also **private soldier**— *n* a soldier of the lowest rank

private enterprise *n* capitalism

privateer *n* (in former times) a privately-owned ship that had government permission to attack and seize enemy ships

private eye *n esp. spoken* a person who does detective work but is not in the police service, esp. one who hires out his services to people

private member *n* a member of parliament who is not a minister

private parts *n polite* the outer sexual organs

private school *n* a school not supported by government money, where education must be paid for —compare PUBLIC SCHOOL

privation *n* a lack of the necessary things or the main comforts of life

privet *n* a bush with small white flowers and evergreen leaves, often grown to form a hedge

privilege *n* 1 a right or favour limited to one person or a few people 2 a right to do or say things without risk of punishment, esp. in parliament — ~**d** *adj*

privy *n* -ies *old use* a lavatory, esp. one without a water supply

Privy Council *n* (in Britain) a body of people of high rank who may advise the king or queen. Membership of this body is now chiefly a mark of honour — -**cillor** *n*

Privy Seal *n* (in Britain before 1885) a royal mark put on less important state papers — compare GREAT SEAL

prize[1] *n* 1 something of value given to someone who is successful 2 a reward given to a student for good work 3 something of value gained after a struggle: *To some men wealth is the greatest prize in life*

prize[2] *adj* 1 that has gained a prize: *a prize rose* 2 *esp. spoken* worthy of a prize: *That hen has produced a prize egg* 3 given as a prize: *prize money*

prize[3] *v* **prized, prizing** to value highly

prize, prise[4] *v* to pry: *We prized the top off the box*

prize day *n* -**days** (in school) a yearly awarding of prizes

prizefight *n* (in former times) a public boxing match for money, fought with bare hands — ~**er** *n* — ~**ing** *n*

pro[1] *n* **pros** 1 an argument in favour of something (esp. in the phrase **pros and cons**) 2 a person or vote in favour of a suggestion

pro[2] *n* **pros** *esp. spoken* 1 a professional: *a football pro* 2 a prostitute

PRO *n esp. spoken* public relations officer

pro-am *n, adj* (a golf competition) in which both professionals and amateurs take part

probability *n* -ties 1 being probable; likelihood 2 (the branch of mathematics concerned with) the chances of an event happening, expressed as a number between 0 and 1

probable *adj* likely: *a probable result* —compare POSSIBLE

probably *adv* almost but not quite certainly

probate *n law* the official proving that a dead person's will is legal

probation *n* 1 the testing of a person's character, behaviour, abilities, etc., esp. to decide whether he is fit to be accepted in some position, as a member, etc. 2 *law* the system of allowing a law-breaker to go unpunished if he will promise to behave well — ~**ary** *adj*

probationer *n* a person who is on probation, such as **a** a young hospital nurse **b** a law-breaker

probe[1] *n* 1 an apparatus (**space probe**) sent into the sky to examine conditions in outer space 2 an act of probing

probe[2] *v* **probed, probing** 1 to poke about in 2 to examine thoroughly: *She tried to probe my mind* — **probing** *adj* — **probingly** *adv*

probity *n esp. written* complete honesty

problem[1] *n* 1 a difficulty that needs attention 2 a question for which an answer is needed: *simple problems in subtraction*

problem[2] *adj* dealing with, or suffering from, social or moral difficulties: *problem plays* | *problem children*

problematic also **problematical**— *adj* doubtful; not settled — ~**ally** *adv*

proboscis *n* -**cises, cides** 1 the long movable nose of certain animals, esp. the elephant 2 a long tubelike part of the mouth of some insects (esp. the butterfly) and worms

procedural *adj* of procedure, esp. in a court of law

procedure *n* 1 the way or order of directing business in an official meeting, a law case, etc. 2 a set of actions necessary for doing something: *Writing a cheque is a simple procedure* —compare PROCESS

proceed *v* 1 to begin and continue: *Tell us*

your name and then proceed with your story **2** to continue after stopping **3** *esp. written* to advance; move forward △PRECEDE

proceed against *v prep esp. written* to take an action in law against

proceeding *n* a course of action or behaviour

proceedings *n* **1** happenings: *the evening's wild proceedings* **2** an action taken in law (esp. in the phrases **start/take proceedings**) **3** the records of the business, activities, etc., of a club

proceeds *n* money gained from sale or from some activity

process¹ *n* **1** any continued set of natural actions connected with the continuation, development, and change of life or matter: *Coal was formed by chemical processes* **2** a continued set of actions performed intentionally: *the process of learning to read* **3** course; time during which something is done: *in the process of moving to a new factory* **4** a system used in producing goods —compare PROCEDURE

process² *v* **1** to treat and preserve by a process: *processed cheese* **2** to develop or print (a film) **3** to put (facts, numbers, etc.) into a computer **4** to prepare and examine in detail: *The plans are now being processed*

procession *n* a line of people, vehicles, etc., moving forward in an orderly, often ceremonial, way

processional *adj* connected with or used in a procession: *a processional march*

processor *n* a usu. electronic device able to perform operations on computer data ⌐COMPUTER

proclaim *v* **1** *esp. written* to make known publicly: *The boy was proclaimed king* **2** *literature* to show clearly: *His pronunciation proclaimed that he was an American*

proclamation *n* **1** an official public statement **2** proclaiming

proclivity *n* -ties *esp. written* a strong natural tendency, esp. towards something bad

proconsul *n* **1** a governor of a part of the ancient Roman Empire **2** an early kind of African ape, perhaps an ancestor of man — ~ar *adj* — ~ate *n*

procrastinate *v* -nated, -nating *esp. written* to waste time — -nation *n*

procreate *v* -ated, -ating *esp. written or technical* to produce or give life to (the young of one's own type of animal) — -ation *n*

procurator fiscal also (*esp. spoken Scots*) **fiscal**— *n* (in Scotland) PUBLIC PROSECUTOR

procure *v* -cured, -curing **1** *esp. written* to obtain, esp. by effort **2** to provide (a woman) for sexual satisfaction — -curable *adj* — ~ment *n* — ~r *n*

prod *v* -dd- **1** to push or press with a finger or pointed object **2** to urge sharply into action or thought — **prod** *n*

prodigal *adj* **1** wasteful, esp. of money **2** *esp. written* giving or producing freely: *a mind prodigal of ideas* — ~ity *n* — ~ly *adv*

prodigious *adj* wonderful, esp. because of size, amount, or quality; very great — ~ly *adv: a prodigiously fat woman*

prodigy *n* -gies **1** a wonder in nature **2** an unusually clever child (often in the phrases **child prodigy, infant prodigy**) △PROGENY

produce¹ -duced, -ducing *v* **1** to show or offer for examination: *The magician produced a rabbit from a hat* **2** to bear (crops) or supply (substances): *Canada produces wheat and furs* **3** to give birth to **4** to lay (an egg) **5** to make from materials **6** to cause: *Gordon's jokes produced a great deal of laughter* **7** (in geometry) to lengthen (a line) to a point —see PRODUCTION (USAGE)

produce² *n* something produced, esp. by growing or farming: *The wine bottle was marked 'Produce of Spain '* —see PRODUCTION (USAGE) ⌐FOOD

producer *n* **1** a person or company that produces goods, foods, or materials **2** a person who has general control esp. of the money for a play, film, or broadcast, but who does not direct the actors —compare DIRECTOR; see PRODUCTION (USAGE)

product *n* **1** something produced: *Important products of South Africa are fruit and gold* **2** something produced as a result of planning, conditions, etc.: *Criminals are sometimes the product of bad homes* **3** (in mathematics) the number obtained by multiplying 2 or more numbers —see PRODUCTION (USAGE)

production *n* **1** producing or making products: *the production of cloth* **2** the amount produced: *Production has increased* **3** a play, film, or broadcast that is produced —see also MASS PRODUCTION USAGE Things **produced** on a farm, such as milk, potatoes, and wool, are **produce**. Things **produced** by industry are **products**.

production line *n* (esp. in a factory) an ordered arrangement of the stages in the production of an article —see also ASSEMBLY LINE

productive *adj* that produces well or much — ~ly *adv* — ~ness *n*

productivity *n* the measured ability to grow things or the rate of making goods

Prof. *abbrev. for:* professor

profane¹ *v* -faned, -faning to treat (something holy) disrespectfully — -fanation *n*

profane² *adj* **1** disrespectful to God or holy things: *To smoke in a mosque would be a profane act* —compare BLASPHEMOUS **2** (esp. of language) socially shocking, esp. because of improper use of religious words —compare OBSCENE **3** *esp. written* not holy; concerned with life in this world: *profane art* —opposite **sacred** — ~ly *adv* — -fanity *n*

profess *v* **1** *esp. written* to declare that one has (some personal feeling, belief, etc.) **2** to claim: *I don't profess to know about poetry*

professed *adj* **1** self-declared: *a professed Muslim* **2** pretended: *a professed sorrow*

profession *n* **1** a form of employment, obtained after education and training (such as law, medicine, and the Church): *He is a lawyer by profession* **2** *esp. written* a declaration of one's belief, opinion, or feeling

professional¹ *adj* **1** working in one of the professions **2** using the training of a member of a profession: *The magician performed with professional skill* **3** doing for money what others do for enjoyment: *a professional gardener* **4** done by people who are paid: *professional football* — ~**ly** *adv*

professional² *n* **1** a person who lives on the money he earns by a skill or sport —compare AMATEUR **2** a person employed by a club to play for it and to teach his sporting skills to its members **3** a person who has great experience and high professional standards

professionalism *n* the qualities shown by a professional person

professor *n* **1** (the title of) a university teacher of the highest rank **2** a title taken by those who teach various skills: *Madame Chores, professor of dancing* — ~**ial** *adj* — ~**ially** *adv* — ~**ship** *n*

proffer *v esp. written* to offer, esp. by holding out for acceptance: *He refused the proffered drink*

proficient *adj* thoroughly skilled — ~**ly** *adv* — **-ciency** *n*

profile *n* **1** a side view or edge of something against a background: *He drew her profile* **2** a short description, esp. of a person's life and character, on television or in a newspaper —see also LOW PROFILE

profit¹ *n* **1** money gain **2** *esp. written* advantage gained from some action: *Everyone gains profit from exercise* — ~**able** *adj* — ~**ably** *adv* —~**less** *adj* — ~**lessly** *adv*

profit² *v* **1** *esp. written* to be of service, use, or advantage to: *It will profit you nothing to do that* **2** to gain advantage: *You can profit by making mistakes*

profiteer *v* to make unfairly large profits, esp. by selling things at high prices in time of trouble or scarcity — **profiteer** *n*

profit margin *n* the difference between the cost of production and the selling price —compare MARGIN

profligate¹ *adj* **1** carelessly and boldly wasteful (esp. of money) **2** *esp. written* shamelessly immoral — **-gacy** *n*

profligate² *n esp. written* a profligate liver or spender

profound *adj* **1** deep; strongly felt: *profound silence* **2** *esp. written* far below the surface: *the profound depths of the ocean* **3** having or needing deep knowledge: *a profound thinker/subject* — ~**ly** *adv*: *profoundly grateful*

profundity *n* **-ties** depth or thoroughness, esp. of mind or feeling

profuse *adj* **1** in plenty: *profuse thanks* **2** eager or generous in giving — ~**ly** *adv* — ~**ness** *n*

profusion *n* great amount: *Flowers grow there in profusion*

progenitor *n* **1** *usu. technical* a person, animal, or plant of the distant past, from which a living being is descended **2** *esp. written* a person who starts a new idea : *Schoenberg was a progenitor of modern music*

progeny *n technical or literature* descendants or children — △ PRODIGY

progesterone *n* a substance produced in the egg-forming part of the female body (OVARY) that prepares the womb for pregnancy

prognosis *n* **-ses 1** *medical* a doctor's opinion of what course a disease will probably take — compare DIAGNOSIS **2** a judgment of the future

prognostic *n, adj esp. written* (a sign) that shows the future

prognosticate *v* **-cated, -cating** *esp. written* to forewarn of (an event or condition) — **-cation** *n* — **-cator** *n*

program¹ *n* a plan of the operations to be performed by a computer

program² *v* **-mm-** to supply (a computer) with a plan of operations

programme¹ *n* **1** a list of performers or things to be performed at a concert, a sports competition, etc. **2** a complete show or performance, esp. one made up of several acts **3** a fixed plan of a course of action: *The hospital building programme has been delayed*

programme² *v* **-grammed, -gramming** to plan or arrange: *The central heating is programmed to start working at 6*

programmed course *n* an educational course in which material is given in small amounts, each of which must be learnt before passing on to the next

programmed learning *n* an educational system where the learner teaches himself by a programmed course

programme music *n* descriptive music, suggesting a story, picture, etc.

programmer *n* a person who prepares a computer program

progress¹ *n* **1** forward movement in space **2** continual improvement: *Jane is still in hospital, but she's making progress* **3** the state of continuing or being done (often in the phrase **in progress**)

progress² *v* **1** to advance **2** to improve

progression *n* **1** progressing, esp. by stages **2** (in mathematics) the way in which each number in a set varies from the one before —see also ARITHMETICAL PROGRESSION, GEOMETRICAL PROGRESSION

progressive *adj* **1** moving forward continuously or by stages **2** (of a tax) higher on larger amounts of money **3** improving in accordance with new ideas: *a progressive firm* **4** modern (esp. in the phrase **progressive jazz**) — ~**ly** *adv* — ~**ness** *n*

prohibit *v esp. written* **1** to forbid by law or

rule **2** to prevent: *His small size prohibits his becoming a policeman*
prohibition *n* **1** prohibiting **2** the forbidding by law of the making or sale of alcoholic drinks **3** *esp. written* an order forbidding something
prohibitive *adj* **1** intended to prevent, or resulting in preventing, something: *a prohibitive tax on foreign goods* **2** (of price) so high that few people can pay it — ~ly *adv*
prohibitory *adj esp. written* intended to prohibit something: *a prohibitory rule*
project¹ *n* a plan for work or activity: *The government has begun a project to increase the size of the harbour*
project² *v* **1** to stick out: *His ears project noticeably* **2** to aim and throw **3** to direct (heat, sound, light, or shadow): *A singer must project his voice so as to be heard* **4 a** to make a picture of (a solid object) on a flat surface **b** to make (a map) by this means **5** to represent (oneself) favourably: *A politician must project himself if he wants to win an election* **6** to plan: *our projected visit to Australia*
projectile *n* an object or weapon shot forward, esp. from a gun
projection *n* **1** projecting **2** a forecast **3** an image, light, sound, etc., that has been projected **4** something that sticks out **5 a** a projected figure or map **b** a framework of squares upon which a map is drawn
projectionist *n* a person who works a projector
projector *n* an apparatus for projecting films or pictures onto a surface
proletarian *n, adj* (a member) of the proletariat
proletariat *n* **1** the class of esp. unskilled workers for wages —compare BOURGEOISIE **2** (in ancient Rome) the lowest class of society
proliferate *v* **-rated, -rating** **1** to increase rapidly in numbers **2** technical (of simple living forms, esp. cells) to grow or reproduce by producing new parts, separating into pieces, etc. — -ration *n*
prolific *adj* producing crops, babies, etc. in large numbers — ~ally *adv*
prologue *n* **1** an introduction to a play, long poem, etc. —opposite **epilogue** **2** an event that leads up to a more important one
prolong *v* to make longer — ~ation *n* — compare EXTENSION
prolonged *adj* continuing for a long time: *a prolonged absence*
prom *n* **1** *esp. spoken* PROMENADE CONCERT **2** *esp. spoken* a seaside promenade
promenade¹ *n* **1** *esp. written* an unhurried walk, ride, or drive **2** a wide path beside a coast road in a holiday town
promenade² *v* **-naded, -nading** *esp. written* to walk slowly to and fro
promenade concert *n* a concert at which parts of the hall without seats are used by standing listeners

prominence *n* **1** notice; importance: *This young artist is coming into prominence* **2** a thing or place that is prominent: *a low prominence in the middle of the desert*
prominent *adj* **1** sticking out: *prominent teeth* **2** noticeable **3** of great ability, fame, importance, etc. — ~ly *adv*
promiscuous *adj* **1** not limited to one sexual partner **2** showing a lack of consideration of the worth of one thing compared with another **3** *esp. written* mixed in a disorderly way — -cuity, ~ness *n* — ~ly *adv*
promise¹ *n* **1** a statement, which someone else has a right to believe, that one will or will not do something **2** expectation of something good: *The news brings little promise of peace* **3** reasons for such expectation: *The boy shows promise as a cricketer*
promise² *v* **-mised, -mising** **1** to make a promise **2** to cause one to hope for: *The clear sky promises fine weather*
Promised Land *n* **1** (in the Bible) the land of Canaan promised by God to Abraham and his people **2** a place or condition not yet experienced which one believes will bring happiness
promising *adj* showing signs of advance towards success — ~ly *adv*
promissory note *n* a written promise to pay money to a person when demanded, or at a particular time
promontory *n* **-ries** a high point of land stretching out into the sea
promote *v* **-moted, -moting** **1** to advance (someone) in rank **2** to help in forming or arranging (a business, concert, etc.): *Who is promoting this boxing match?* **3** to bring (goods) to public notice in order to increase sales **4** to help in the growth of: *Milk promotes health* **5** to bring forward (a bill) in parliament — ~r *n*
promotion *n* **1** advancement in rank **2** action to help something develop or succeed: *sales promotions* **3** a product being promoted — ~al *adj*
prompt¹ *v* **1** to cause: *Hunger prompted him to steal* **2** to help (a speaker who pauses) by suggesting how to continue: *The actor forgot his words and had to be prompted*
prompt² *adj* acting or done at once: *prompt payment of bills* — ~ly *adv* — ~ness *n*
prompter *n* a person who prompts actors
promulgate *v* **-gated, -gating** *esp. written* **1** to bring (a law or religious rule) into effect **2** to spread (a belief, idea, etc.) widely — -gation *n* — -gator *n*
prone *adj* **1** (of a person or position) stretched out face downwards —compare SUPINE, PROSTRATE **2** having the probability of (usu. something bad): *He is prone to colds* — ~ness *n*
prong¹ *n* any sharp-pointed thin part, such as one of the branched horns of a deer or points of a fork
prong² *v* to push a fork or other such tool into (and lift)

pronoun *n* (in grammar) a word used in place of a noun or a noun phrase: *Instead of saying 'the man came' you can use a pronoun and say 'he came'*

pronounce *v* **-nounced, -nouncing** 1 to make the sound of (a letter, a word, etc.): *In the word 'knew', the 'k' is not pronounced* 2 to declare officially: *The doctor pronounced the man dead* 3 *esp. law* to give judgement

pronounceable *adj* (of a sound, word, etc.) that can be pronounced

pronounced *adj* very strong or marked: *very pronounced ideas* — ~ly *adv*

pronouncement *n* a solemn declaration

pronto *adv esp. spoken* at once

pronunciation *n* 1 the way in which a word or language is pronounced 2 a particular person's way of pronouncing

proof¹ *n* 1 a way of showing that something is true: *Have you any proof that you weren't there?* 2 a test to find out whether someone or something has a quality, standard, etc. 3 (in mathematics) the reasoning that shows a statement to be true 4 a test copy made of a piece of printed matter so that mistakes can be put right before the proper printing is done 5 the standard of strength of some kinds of alcoholic drink —see PROVE

proof² *adj* 1 **a** giving protection: *This tent is proof against water* **b** unyielding; uninfluenced: *His courage is proof against the greatest pain* 2 (of spirits) of standard strength

proof³ *v* to treat in order to give protection, esp. against water

proofread *v* **-read, -reading** to read and correct the printer's proofs of (a book, magazine, etc.) — ~er *n*

proof spirit *n* a standard mixture of alcohol and water with which the strength of spirits is compared for purposes of taxation

prop¹ *n* 1 a support to hold up something heavy 2 a person on whom someone or something depends

prop² *v* **-pp-** 1 to support by placing something under or against 2 to put in a leaning position: *He propped his bicycle against the fence*

prop³ *n esp. spoken* an aircraft's propeller

prop⁴ *n* any small article (such as a weapon, telephone, etc.) used on the stage in a play

propaganda *n often offensive* action taken, esp. by a government, to influence public opinion by spreading ideas, news, etc.: *propaganda against smoking*

propagandist *n* a person who plans or spreads propaganda

propagate *v* **-gated, -gating** 1 to increase in number by producing young: *Most plants propagate by seed* 2 to cause (a quality) to pass to descendants 3 to spread among people: *The political party started the newspaper to propagate its ideas* 4 *technical* to cause or allow to pass through: *Water easily propagates sound* — -gation *n* — -gator *n*

propane *n* a colourless gas used for cooking and heating

propel *v* **-ll-** to push forward

propellant, -lent *n* 1 an explosive used for firing a bullet or rocket ⟹SPACE 2 a compressed gas in a bottle, which drives out the contents of the bottle

propeller *n* 2 or more blades fixed to a central bar turned at high speed by an engine, to drive a ship or aircraft ⟹AEROPLANE

propeller shaft *n* a shaft that transmits power from the engine to the driving device of a self-propelling vehicle ⟹CAR

propelling pencil *n* a pencil in which the lead is pushed forward by a screw inside

propensity *n* **-ties** *esp. written* a natural tendency: *a propensity to spend money*

proper *adj* 1 suitable; correct: *proper medical attention* 2 paying great attention to what is considered correct in society 3 complete: *a proper fool* 4 *esp. spoken* real: *a proper dog, not a toy dog* 5 itself; not including additional things: *areas that aren't part of the city proper*

proper fraction *n* a fraction in which the number above the line is smaller than the one below: *¼ and ⅛ are proper fractions*

properly *adv* 1 suitably; correctly; sensibly 2 really; actually; exactly

proper motion *n technical* the actual movement of a heavenly body through space, not as it appears from the earth

proper noun also **proper name**— *n* (in grammar) a name for a single particular thing or person, spelt with a capital letter: *'James' and 'China' are proper nouns* —opposite **common noun**

propertied *adj* owning a lot of property

property *n* **-ties** 1 that which is owned: *That car is my property* 2 land, buildings, or both together 3 ownership, with its rights and duties according to the law 4 a quality: *Many plants have medicinal properties* 5 *esp. written* a stage prop 6 **common property** something shared by all —see also LOST PROPERTY, REAL PROPERTY

prophecy *n* **-cies** 1 the power of foretelling future events 2 a statement telling something that is to happen in the future

prophesy *v* **-sied, -sying** 1 to give (a warning, statement about the future, etc.) as a result of a religious experience 2 to say in advance: *to prophesy who will win the election*

prophet (*fem.* **prophetess**)— *n* 1 (in the Christian, Jewish, and Muslim religions) a man directed by God to make known God's will or to teach a religion 2 a thinker, poet, etc., who teaches some new idea 3 a person who tells the future: *Farmers are usually good weather prophets* — ~ic, ~ical *adj* — ~ically *adv*

Prophet *n* Mohammed, who formed the Muslim religion —see also ISLAM, MUSLIM

Prophets *n* 1 the Jewish holy men whose writings form part of the Old Testament 2 the writings themselves

prophylactic *adj medical* intended to prevent disease — **prophylactic** *n* — ~**ally** *adv*
prophylaxis *n* -**laxes** *technical* (a) treatment for preventing disease
propinquity *n esp. written* nearness
propitiate *v* -**ated, -ating** to win the favour of (someone unfriendly) by some pleasing act — **-ation** *n* — **-atory** *adj*
propitious *adj* **1** lucky; giving a favourable chance of success **2** (of gods or fate) favourable; helpful — ~**ly** *adv*
propjet *n esp. spoken* (an aircraft driven by) a turboprop
proponent *n* a person in favour of something
proportion *n* **1** the correct relationship between the size, position, and shape of parts **2** compared relationship between the size, amount, etc. of 2 things: *the proportion of men to women in the population* **3** a part; share: *What proportion of your wages do you spend on rent?* **4** (in mathematics) a relation between quantities such that 2 ratios are equal: *2 sets are in proportion if their numbers are in the same ratio, such as {6, 4} and {24, 16}* —compare RATIO **5 in proportion to a** according to b as compared with **6 in/out of proportion** (not) according to real importance: *When one is angry one often does not see things in proportion* **7 in the proportion of** in the measure of: *The paint should be mixed in the proportion of one part of paint to 2 of water* **8 sense of proportion** ability to judge what matters and what does not
proportional *adj* **1** concerning proportion **2** in correct proportion: *The payment will be proportional to the damage* — ~**ly** *adv*
proportional representation *n* a voting system by which all political parties are represented in parliament in proportion to the number of votes they receive
proportionate *adj* in right proportion — ~**ly** *adv*
proportions *n* size and shape considered together: *a building of fine proportions*
proposal *n* **1** a suggestion **2** an offer of marriage —compare PROPOSITION
propose *v* -**posed, -posing** **1** to suggest **2** to intend: *I propose to go on Tuesday* **3** *esp. written* to put forward to be voted on (often in the phrase **propose a motion**) **4** to make an offer of (marriage) to someone **5** to ask a social gathering to offer (a wish for success, happiness, etc.) to someone, while drinking (usu. in the phrases **propose a toast/propose someone's health**) — ~**r** *n*
proposition *n* **1** an unproved statement **2** a suggestion **3** *esp. spoken* a person or thing that must be dealt with: *Be careful with Murray; he's a nasty proposition* **4** a suggested offer of sex (esp. in the phrase **make someone a proposition**) —compare PROPOSAL **5** (in geometry) a truth that must be proved, or a question to which the answer must be found — ~**al** *adj*
propound *v esp. written* to put forward as a question

proprietary *adj* **1** privately owned **2** like an owner: *Jane has rather a proprietary manner with John*
proprietor (*fem.* -**tress**) — *n esp. written* an owner
propriety *n esp. written* rightness of behaviour; suitability
propulsion *n technical* force that drives something forward: *jet propulsion* — -**sive** *adj*
pro rata *adv, adj technical Latin* according to the rate, fair share, etc., of each
prorogue *v* -**rogued, -roguing** *technical* to end a session of (a parliament) for a time — -**gation** *n*
prosaic *adj* **1** dull; uninteresting **2** lacking feeling and imagination — ~**ally** *adv*
proscenium *n* -**iums** or -**ia** the wall that separates a conventional stage from the audience, and provides the arch that frames it
proscribe *v* -**scribed, -scribing** **1** *esp. written* to forbid, esp. by law **2** *old use* to banish or outlaw — -**scription** *n*
prose *n* **1** written language in sentences and paragraphs as opposed to poetry **2** a student's exercise in translating into a foreign language: *2 French proses*
prosecute *v* -**cuted, -cuting** **1** to bring a criminal charge against (someone) **2** (of a lawyer) to represent in court the bringer of a criminal charge **3** *esp. written* to continue steadily (something that needs effort) △ PERSECUTE
prosecution *n* **1** prosecuting or being prosecuted by law **2** the people bringing a criminal charge in court —compare DEFENCE **3** *esp. written* continuation of something to be done: *to travel in the prosecution of his duties*
prosecutor *n* the person (often a lawyer) who prosecutes another —see also PUBLIC PROSECUTOR
proselyte *n* a person who has just joined a (religious) group; convert
proselytize, -ise *v* -**ized, -izing** to try to persuade people to become proselytes
prose poem *n* a work in prose that has some of the qualities of a poem
prosody *n* the science of writing poetry, and of the the ways in which its patterns of sounds and beats are arranged — -**dic** *adj* — -**dically** *adv*
prospect[1] *n* **1** reasonable hope (of something happening) **2** something considered probable: *the prospect of having to live alone* —see also PROSPECTS **3** a view: *a beautiful prospect over the valley* —see VIEW (USAGE) **4** a person who might be offered or might accept a position, office, etc.
prospect[2] *v* to explore an area for gold, oil, etc. — ~**or** *n*
prospective *adj* **1** not yet in effect **2** expected; intended: *her prospective husband*
prospects *n* **1** chances of success **2** *esp. written* expectations of future wealth, social position, etc.
prospectus *n* a printed statement of the advan-

tages of a private school, a business, etc., sent to people who might give their support

prosper v 1 to become successful and rich 2 to develop favourably

prosperous adj successful; wealthy — ~ly adv — -rity n

prostate n a gland in the male body that produces a liquid in which seeds (SPERMATOZOA) are carried out of the body ⫧REPRODUCTION

prosthesis n -ses an artificial limb or other man-made body part

prostitute (masc. **male prostitute**)— n a woman who earns money by having sex with anyone who will pay —compare COURTESAN

prostitution n being a prostitute

prostrate¹ adj 1 lying flat, with the face to the ground —compare PRONE, SUPINE 2 (of a nation, country, etc.) conquered and powerless 3 so weak that one can hardly move — -tration n

prostrate² v -trated, -trating 1 to put in a prostrate position: prostrated himself before the king 2 esp. written to conquer and destroy (a nation, country, etc.) 3 to make prostrate: a prostrating illness

prosy adj -ier, -iest saying too much in a dull manner — -ily adv — -iness n

protagonist n 1 a a noticeable supporter of some idea or purpose b technical a person or thing that opposes the action of an antagonist 2 the chief character in a play or story

protect v 1 to keep safe, esp. by covering: He raised his arm to protect his face. | electric wires protected by a rubber covering 2 to help (local industry or the sale of goods) by taxing foreign goods 3 to guard by means of insurance

protection n 1 protecting or being protected 2 a person or thing that protects 3 the condition of being protected by an insurance company 4 also **protection money** — sl money paid to people who run a protection racket

protectionism n the system of protecting one's own country's trade, esp. by tariffs — -ist n

protection racket n sl an organization by which criminals demand money for protection against damage that would be caused by the criminals themselves

protective adj 1 that gives protection: protective clothing 2 wishing to protect: She's too protective towards her daughter — ~ly adv — ~ness n

protective colouring n colours on an animal's or insect's body that make it difficult for enemies to see

protective custody n the state of being held, usu. in a prison, as a protection from other criminals

protector n 1 a person who protects 2 an article that protects: a chest protector 3 (in former times) a prince or nobleman appointed to rule during the childhood or illness of the king

Protector n the official title of Oliver and Richard Cromwell when they ruled Britain (1653–1659) —see PROTECTORATE

protectorate n a country controlled by a more powerful nation

Protectorate n the time (1653–1659) during which Oliver and Richard Cromwell ruled Britain

protégé (fem. **protégée**)— n French a person who is guided and helped by someone powerful

protein n any of many substances that are essential parts of all living things and are necessary in food for building up the body and keeping it healthy. They are found esp. in meat, eggs, and cheese

protest¹ n 1 a complaint or expression of dissatisfaction 2 opposition, dissatisfaction, etc.: went to bed without protest 3 under protest unwillingly

protest² v 1 to express annoyance or disagreement 2 to declare against disbelief: We urged her to come but she protested that she was too tired — ~er n

Protestant n, adj (a member) of the part of the Christian church that separated from the Roman Catholic church in the 16th century — ~ism n

protestation n esp. written 1 a declaration: protestations of friendship 2 the act of protesting

protocol n 1 the ceremonial system of rules and behaviour between rulers or representatives of governments, between people on official occasions, etc. 2 technical a first written signed form of an agreement being considered between nations

proton n a very small piece of matter that helps to form the central part of an atom and carries a standard amount of positive electricity ⫧ATOM

protoplasm n the colourless jellylike substance of living cells from which all plants and creatures are formed

prototype n the first form of anything, from which later forms develop

protozoan n, adj (a single member) of the protozoa —see PROTOZOON

protozoon n -zoa a microscopic living thing of the simplest kind that lives mainly in water and consists of a single cell

protract v to increase the time of; make longer: a protracted visit — ~ion n

protractor n a usu. semicircular instrument for measuring and drawing angles

protrude v -truded, -truding to stick out: protruding teeth — -trusion n

protuberance n 1 a swelling 2 being protuberant

protuberant adj swelling or bulging outwards — ~ly adv

proud¹ adj 1 having self-respect: too proud to beg 2 having too high an opinion of oneself 3 pleased with something connected with oneself: proud of his new car 4 noble; grand: this proud and great university —see PRIDE — ~ly adv

proud² adv **do someone proud** to treat someone splendidly

prove v proved , proved or proven, proving 1

to show to be true: *He has proved his courage* **2** to test the quality of **3** to be found to be: *My advice proved to be wrong* **4** technical (of a loaf or cake being baked) to rise properly —see PROOF — **-vable** adj — **-vably** adv

proven adj **1** also **proved**— tested and shown to be true: *a man of proven ability* **2** not proven (in Scots law) a decision that, as the facts neither prove nor disprove a prisoner's guilt, he must be set free

proverb n a short well-known saying: *"A cat has 9 lives" is a proverb*

proverbial adj **1** of, or like a proverb **2** spoken of in a proverb: *He seems to have 9 lives, like the proverbial cat* **3** very widely known: *His generosity is proverbial* — ~ly adv

Proverbs n a book in the Old Testament which contains wise thoughts

provide v **-vided, -viding** **1** to supply: *That hotel provides meals* **2** (of a law, agreement, etc.) to state a special arrangement: *The law provides that ancient buildings must be preserved* **3** to supply needs: *He has 5 children to provide for*

provide against v prep to take action against (a danger)

provided also **providing**— conj if and only if: *Provided it doesn't rain we'll walk there*

providence n a special act showing God's care: *It seemed like providence that the doctor came past just at the time of the accident*

Providence n God and fate as a kindly influence

provident adj careful in providing for future needs — ~ly adv

providential adj happening just when needed — ~ly adv

provider n a person who provides, esp. for a family

province n **1** one of the main divisions of some countries for purposes of government control **2** an area under an archbishop **3** a division of land in connection with its special plants and animals: *Australia is the province of the kangaroo* **4** a branch of knowledge or activity considered as having fixed limits: *Persian art is quite outside my province*

provinces n the parts of a country that are distant from the main city

provincial adj **1** of a province or the provinces **2** having the manners, speech, rather limited or old-fashioned customs, etc., regarded as typical of people of the provinces — ~ism n — ~ly adv

proving ground n a place where something new is tested

provision[1] n **1** providing **2** preparation for future needs: *to make provision for the future* **3** a supply **4** a condition in an agreement or law

provision[2] v to provide with food and supplies

provisional adj for the present time only — ~ly adv

provisions n food supplies

proviso n **-sos** something added that limits conditions: *I've agreed to do the work, with the proviso that I'm paid first*

provocation n **1** provoking or being provoked **2** a reason for being provoked

provocative adj causing interest, argument, etc.: *a provocative speech* — ~ly adv

provoke v **-voked, -voking** **1** to make angry or bad-tempered **2** to cause or force

provoking adj esp. *written* annoying — ~ly adv

Provost n **1** the head of certain colleges **2** (in Scotland) the head of a town council

prow n esp. *in literature* the pointed front part of a ship

prowess n esp. *written* **1** great personal bravery **2** unusual ability: *prowess as a footballer*

prowl v (esp. of an animal or thief) to move quietly about, trying not to be seen or heard — prowl n — ~er n

proximal adj *medical* nearest or next to the point of joining or origin; lying towards the centre of the body —opposite distal — ~ly adv

proximate adj esp. *written* **1** nearest; next **2** (of a cause) direct — ~ly adv

proximity n esp. *written* **1** nearness **2** in the proximity of pompous near

proxy n **-ies** **1** the right given to a person to let someone else act for him on a single occasion, esp. as a voter **2** a person whom one chooses to act for one

prude n a person who makes a show of being easily shocked at anything impure, esp. of a sexual nature — **-dish** adj — **-dishly** adv — **-dishness** n

prudent adj sensible and wise, esp. by avoiding risks: *It's prudent to wear a thick coat when it's cold* — **-dence** n — ~ly adv

prudential adj esp. *written* resulting from or showing prudence, esp. in business — ~ly adv

prudery n **-ies** **1** being a prude **2** a prudish act or remark

prune[1] n a dried plum, usu. boiled before eating

prune[2] v **pruned, pruning** **1** to cut off or shorten some branches of (a tree or bush) in order to improve the growth **2** to lessen in amount by careful choice: *You should prune the speech down; it's too long*

pruning adj made for pruning trees: *pruning scissors*

prurient adj unpleasantly interested in sex ⚠ PURULENT — **-ence** n — ~ly adv

Prussian blue n, adj a deep blue colour

prussic acid n a powerful poisonous acid that quickly causes death

pry[1] v **pried, prying** to look secretly at or find out about someone else's private affairs

pry[2] also **prize**— v to raise, move, lift, or break with a tool: *to pry the cover off a box*

P.S. n abbrev. for: postscript

psalm n a song or poem in praise of God

psalmist n a writer of psalms

Psalms *n* the collection of psalms in the Bible, forming part of some church services

psalter *n* a book of Psalms with music, for use in services

pseudonym *n* an invented name used in place of the real name — ~ous *adj*

psoriasis *n* a skin disease in which red sore marks appear and pieces of skin come off

psst *interj* (the sound of) a short spitting hiss, used for drawing attention secretly

psyche *n* 1 *technical* the human mind, as being a person's self 2 *esp. in literature* the human soul or spirit

psychedelic[1] *adj* 1 (of a drug) making the senses seem keener than in reality; causing strange excited sensations 2 (of art) affecting the brain by strong patterns of noise, colour, lines, moving lights, etc. — ~ally *adv*

psychedelic[2] *n* a psychedelic drug

psychiatrist *n* a doctor trained in psychiatry

psychiatry *n* the study and treatment of diseases of the mind —compare PSYCHOLOGY — -tric *adj* — -trically *adv*

psychic[1] also **psychical**— *adj* 1 concerning the soul or the spirits of the dead 2 (of a person) having unusual powers such as the ability to see the future 3 (of an illness) of the mind — ~ally *adv*

psychic[2] *n* a person who claims to receive messages from the dead; medium

psycho *n* -chos *sl* a person with a severe mental illness

psychoanalyse *v* -lysed, -lysing to treat by psychoanalysis

psychoanalysis *n* 1 a way of treating disorders of the mind by examination of all that the sufferer can remember of his past life 2 the scientific study of the hidden parts of the mind which influence one's behaviour. It was developed by Sigmund Freud — -lyst *n* — -lytic *adj* — -lytically *adv*

psychokinesis *n* the moving of solid objects by the power of the mind —compare TELEKINESIS — -netic *adj* — -netically *adv*

psychological *adj* 1 of the mind 2 using psychology: *psychological tests* — ~ly *adv*

psychology *n* -gies 1 the study of the mind and the way it works, and of behaviour as an expression of the mind 2 a branch of this study that deals with a particular division of human activity —compare PSYCHIATRY — -logist *n*

psychopath *n* a person who has a continual or incurable disorder of character that prevents him from fitting well into society — ~ic *adj* — ~ically *adv*

psychosis *n* -ses any of several serious disorders of the mind marked by a loss of touch with reality

psychosomatic *n* (of an illness) caused by fear or anxiety as well as, or rather than, by a bodily disorder — ~ally *adv*

psychotherapy *n* treatment of disorders of

the mind by action on the mind itself rather than by drugs, operations, etc. — -pist *n*

psychotic *n, adj* (of or being) a person suffering from a psychosis — ~ally *adv*

pt *abbrev. for:* 1 part 2 pint 3 port

P T *abbrev. for:* (*esp. spoken*) PHYSICAL TRAINING

PTA *abbrev. for:* Parent-Teacher Association

ptarmigan *n* -gans *or* -gan a bird of far northern lands, with grey or black feathers that turn white in winter

pterodactyl *n* a type of prehistoric flying animal

PTO *abbrev. for:* (written at the bottom of a page) please turn over

Ptolemaic system *n* the former system according to which the earth was believed to be at the centre of the universe, with the sun, stars, and planets travelling round it —compare COPERNICAN SYSTEM

pub also **public house**— *n* a building (not a club or hotel) where alcohol may be bought and drunk

puberty *n* the time of change in the human body to the state in which it is possible to produce children

pubic *adj* related to, or near, the sexual organs: *pubic hair*

public[1] *adj* 1 of, to, by, for, or concerning people in general: *a matter of public importance* 2 for the use of everyone: *public gardens* 3 not secret or private: *a public statement* 4 connected with government: *How long has he held public office?* —compare PRIVATE — ~ly *adv*

public[2] *n* 1 people in general: *The gardens are open to the public* 2 a group in society: *This singer has an admiring public* 3 **in public** in the presence of many people

public-address system *n* an apparatus for making a speaker clearly heard by crowds

publican *n* 1 a person who runs a pub 2 *esp. Bible* a tax collector

publication *n* 1 the making of something known to the public 2 the offering for sale of something printed 3 something published

public bar *n* a room in a pub where the cheapest prices are charged for drinks —compare SALOON BAR

public company *n* -nies a business company that offers shares for public sale

public convenience also **convenience**— *n* public toilets

public house *n* *esp. written* a pub

publicist *n* a person whose business is to bring something to public attention esp. products for sale

publicity *n* 1 public notice 2 the business of bringing someone or something to public notice, esp. for gain

publicize, -cise *v* -cized, -cizing to get publicity for

public nuisance *n* *law* an unlawful act or failure to act, which is harmful to everyone

public opinion *n* what most people think

public ownership *n* ownership of businesses, property, etc., by the state

public prosecutor *n* a government lawyer who brings charges for the state against criminals —compare ATTORNEY GENERAL

public relations *n* 1 the relations between an organization and the public 2 the work of keeping these relations friendly

public school *n* 1 any of a limited number of private secondary schools, usu. boarding schools 2 (esp. in Scotland and the US) a free local primary school

public servant *n* a government official or worker —compare CIVIL SERVANT

public spirit *n* willingness to help without personal advantage — **public-spirited** *adj*

publish *v* 1 to have printed for sale to the public (written work) 2 to make known generally

publisher *n* a person or firm whose business is to publish books, newspapers, etc., or (sometimes) to make and sell records

puce *n, adj* a brownish purple colour

puck *n* a hard flat circular piece of rubber used instead of a ball in ice hockey

Puck *n* (in old stories) a small male mischievous fairy

pucker *v* to tighten into folds — **pucker** *n*

puckish *adj literature* playful; full of tricks — ~ly *adv*

pud *n esp. spoken* a pudding

pudding *n* 1 a dessert 2 a usu. solid sweet dish based on pastry, rice, bread, etc., baked, boiled, or steamed, and served hot 3 a meat dish boiled with a pastry cover: *a steak and kidney pudding* 4 a sausage: *black pudding*

pudding stone *n* rock made of small rounded stones massed together; conglomerate

puddle *n* a small amount of rainwater in a hollow

pudendum *n* **-da** the outer sexual organs, esp. of a woman

puerile *adj esp. written* childish; silly — **-ility** *n*

puerperal *adj medical* of, after, or caused by childbirth

puff¹ *v* 1 to breathe rapidly and with effort 2 to breathe in and out while smoking (a cigarette, pipe, etc.) 3 a (of smoke or steam) to blow or come out repeatedly b to cause (esp. smoke or steam) to come out repeatedly

puff² *n* 1 an act of puffing 2 a sudden short rush of air, smoke, etc. 3 something light that is blown along 4 *esp. spoken humour* breath 5 *esp. spoken becoming rare* written praise of a new book, play, etc. 6 an ornamental part of a garment made by drawing the cloth together so that it swells out 7 a piece of light pastry with a sweet filling: *a cream puff* — see also POWDER PUFF

puff adder *n* a large poisonous African snake

puffball *n* a ball-shaped fungus, which when ripe bursts in a cloud of powder

puffin *n* a seabird of North Atlantic coasts with a large coloured beak

puff out *v adv* 1 to enlarge, esp. with air: *The bird puffed out its feathers* 2 to put out the flame of (something) by blowing

puff pastry *n* light pastry made from **puff paste** that rises and swells when cooked

puff up *v adv* 1 to swell 2 **be puffed up** *usu. Bible* to be too proud

puffy *adj* **-ier, -iest** 1 swollen 2 *esp. spoken* breathing with effort — **puffily** *adv* — **puffiness** *n*

pug also **pug dog**— *n* a small dog with a flat face and turned-up nose

pugilism *n pompous* boxing — **pugilist** *n* — **-istic** *adj*

pugnacious *adj esp. written* fond of quarrelling and fighting — **-ity,** ~**ness** *n* — ~ly *adv*

puissance¹ *n old use* power or strength, esp. of a king — **-ant** *adj*

puissance² *n* a competition in which riders jump their horses over high fences

puke *v, n* **puked, puking** *sl* vomit

pukka *adj Indian & Pakistani* of high quality; genuine

pulchritude *n esp. written* beauty — **-dinous** *adj*

pule *v* **puled, puling** *literature* to cry weakly

pull¹ *v* 1 to draw (something) along behind one 2 to move (someone or something) by holding and drawing: *to pull the door open* 3 to seize and draw roughly towards one 4 to draw or press (something) towards one to make an apparatus work 5 to stretch and damage: *He's pulled a muscle* 6 to remove by drawing out: *That tooth should be pulled out* 7 to hold back (a horse in a race, or a blow in boxing) so as to avoid victory 8 (esp. in golf) to strike (the ball) to the left of the intended direction (or right if one is left handed) 9 (in cricket and baseball) to hit (the ball) forward and across the body from right to left (or from left to right) 10 to draw (beer) out of a barrel 11 to draw out (a weapon) ready for use 12 to win, gain, or get (attention, votes, etc.): *The football match pulled in great crowds* 13 **pull a fast one** *esp. spoken* to get the advantage by a trick 14 **pull to pieces** to point out the faults of —see also PULL ABOUT, PULL AHEAD, PULL AWAY, PULL DOWN, PULL IN, PULL THROUGH, PULL TOGETHER, PULL UP, and compare PUSH

pull² *n* 1 an act of pulling 2 a difficult steep climb 3 a natural force that causes movement: *the moon's pull on the sea* 4 *esp. spoken* special influence; (unfair) personal advantage 5 an act of inhaling tobacco smoke from a pipe, cigarette, etc. 6 an act of taking a long drink 7 any article used for pulling something; *a bellpull*

pull about *v adv* to handle roughly

pull ahead *v adv* to get in front by moving faster

pull away *v adv* 1 to free oneself 2 (of a road vehicle) to start to move off

pul

pull down v adv to break in pieces and destroy (something built)

pullet n a young hen when first laying eggs

pulley n -leys an apparatus consisting of a wheel over which a rope or chain runs, for lifting heavy things

pull-in also **pull-up**— n esp. spoken a roadside café

pull in v adv 1 (of a train) to arrive at a station 2 esp. spoken to earn (money) 3 to draw in (the stomach muscles)

Pullman n -mans trademark 1 a specially comfortable railway carriage 2 a train with such carriages

pull off v adv esp. spoken to succeed in: She pulled off the trick

pull out v adv 1 (of a train) to leave a station 2 to leave a place or time of trouble —see also **pull one's** FINGER **out**, **pull all the** STOPS **out**

pullover n a woollen upper garment pulled on over the head —compare SWEATER, JUMPER

pull over v adv (of a vehicle) to move to one side of the road

pull through v adv 1 also **pull round**— to live or make live in spite of illness or wounds 2 to succeed or help to succeed in spite of difficulties

pull together v adv 1 (of a group) to work so as to help a common effort 2 to control(oneself): Pull yourself together!

pull-up n an arm-strengthening exercise in which a person holds onto a bar and pulls until his chin is level with it

pull up v adv 1 to bring or come to a stop 2 to come level (with another competitor in a race) 3 to scold

pulmonary adj medical of the lungs

pulp¹ n 1 soft plant or animal material, such as the inside of many fruits 2 the condition of being soft and liquid 3 vegetable materials softened for making paper 4 a cheap shocking book or magazine — ~y adj

pulp² v to make or become pulpy

pulpit n a raised structure in a church, from which the priest addresses the congregation

pulsar n a type of star that is known to exist because of its rhythmical radio signals

pulsate v -sated, -sating to shake or beat regularly — -sation n

pulse¹ n 1 the regular beating of blood in the arteries, esp. as felt at the wrist 2 a short sound as sent by radio or a small change in the quantity of electricity going through something

pulse² n the edible seeds of beans, peas, lentils, etc.

pulse³ v pulsed, pulsing to beat steadily as the heart does

pulverize, -ise v -ized, -izing 1 to make into or become powder by crushing 2 esp. spoken to defeat thoroughly — -ization n

puma n pumas or puma a cougar

pumice n a very light, silver-grey rock, used for cleaning and smoothing

pummel v -ll- to hit repeatedly, esp. with the fist

pump¹ n 1 a machine for forcing liquids or gas into or out of something: a petrol pump | a stomach pump 2 an act of pumping

pump² v 1 to move (liquids or gas) by using a pump 2 to empty or fill by means of a pump: He pumped up his tyres 3 to work a pump 4 to work like a pump: His heart was pumping fast 5 to move up and down like a pump handle 6 esp. spoken to ask (someone) questions in the hope of finding out something

pump³ n a light dancing shoe

pumpernickel n a heavy dark brown bread

pumpkin n a type of trailing plant, or its large yellow roundish fruit

pump room n a room in a building connected with a natural spring of medicinal waters

pun¹ also **play on words**— n an amusing use of words having the same sound but different meanings (as in ' 7 days without water make one weak ' (=week))

pun² v -nn- to make puns

punch¹ v 1 to strike hard with the fist 2 to make (a hole) using a punch 3 to drive (something) in or out using a punch — ~er n

punch² n 1 a quick strong blow with the fist 2 forcefulness: That statement lacks punch 3 **beat someone to the punch** to take action before someone else can do so

punch³ n 1 a steel tool for cutting holes or pressing a pattern: a ticket punch 2 a tool for hammering the heads of nails below a surface

punch⁴ n a usu. alcoholic drink made with fruit juice, sugar, water and spices

Punch-and-Judy show n a show for children in which the small puppet Punch fights humorously with his wife Judy

punch bowl n a large bowl in which punch is mixed

punch-drunk adj 1 (of a boxer) showing signs of brain damage from repeated head blows 2 esp. spoken confused because of continual misfortune

punched card also **punch card**— n a card with holes in it, each of which carries information to the computer into which the card is put

punch line n the last few words of a joke or story, that give meaning to the whole

punch-up n esp. spoken a fight

punctilious adj very particular about details — ~ly adv — ~ness n

punctual adj not late; prompt — ~ity n — ~ly adv

punctuate v -ated, -ating 1 to divide (written matter) into sentences, phrases, etc., by punctuation marks 2 to break repeatedly into: The game was punctuated by cheers

punctuation n 1 the punctuating of writing 2 the marks used in doing this

punctuation mark n any sign used in punctuating, such as a comma (,), a full stop (.), a question mark (?), etc.

puncture¹ *n* a small hole made with a sharp point through a soft surface, esp. in a tyre

puncture² *v* **-tured, -turing** 1 to burst as a result of a puncture 2 to make a small hole in: *a punctured lung*

pundit *n* *often humour* a person who knows a great deal about a subject and whose advice on it may be taken: *political pundits* △ PANDIT

pungent *adj* 1 having a strong, sharp, stinging taste or smell 2 (of speech or writing) sharp and direct △ POIGNANT — ~ly *adv* — -gency *n*

Punic *adj* of the ancient city of Carthage (in North Africa) or its people

punish *v* 1 to cause (someone) to suffer for a fault or crime 2 to deal roughly with (an opponent)

punishable *adj* that may be punished by law

punishing¹ *adj* *esp. spoken* very tiring: *a punishing climb* — ~ly *adv*

punishing² *n* *esp. spoken* a rough defeat; damage

punishment *n* 1 punishing or being punished 2 a way in which a person is punished 3 *esp. spoken* rough treatment; damage

punitive *adj* 1 intended as punishment 2 very severe: *punitive taxes* △ PUTATIVE — ~ly *adv*

punk¹ *n* *offensive sl* 1 *US* a rough unpleasant young man or boy 2 *rare* something worthless

punk² *adj* (in Britain in the 1970's) of a movement among certain young people opposed to the values of money-based society who express this esp. in loud violent music (**punk rock**)

punnet *n* a small square basket, for small soft fruits

punt¹ *n* a flat-bottomed river boat, propelled by a long pole

punt² *v* 1 to go by punt 2 to move (a boat, esp. a punt) by pushing a long pole against the river bed — ~er *n*

punt³ *v* *esp. spoken* to bet on a horse race — ~er *n*

punt⁴ *n* (esp. in rugby) an action of kicking a ball that has been dropped from the hands and has not yet hit the ground —compare PLACEKICK, DROPKICK

punt⁵ *v* to make a punt in rugby

puny *adj* **punier, puniest** small and weak — **-nily** *adv* — **-niness** *n*

pup *n* 1 a young seal or otter 2 a puppy

pupa *n* **pupas** *or* **pupae** an insect in the middle stage of its development to a full-grown form, protected by a hard or soft covering — ~l *adj*

pupate *v* **pupated, pupating** *technical* (of a young insect) to become or be a pupa — **-pation** *n*

pupil¹ *n* a person, esp. a child, who is being taught —see STUDENT (USAGE)

pupil² *n* the small transparent round opening in the middle of the coloured part of the eye (IRIS), that appears black, through which light passes, and which can grow larger or smaller

puppet *n* 1 a jointed figure moved by pulling

wires or strings —see also MARIONETTE 2 also **glove puppet**— a hollow cloth figure into which the hand is put to move the figure 3 a person or group controlled by the will of someone else: *a puppet government*

puppeteer *n* a person who performs with puppets

puppy also **pup**— *n* **-pies** a young dog

puppy fat *n* *esp. spoken* temporary fatness in boys and girls

puppy love also **calf love**— *n* a young boy's or girl's love for a (usu. older) member of the opposite sex, which does not last

purchase¹ *v* **-chased, -chasing** 1 to buy 2 *esp. written* to gain at the cost of loss — **-chasable** *adj* — ~r *n*

purchase² *n* 1 buying 2 an article just bought 3 a firm hold for pulling, raising, etc.: *The climber tried to gain a purchase on a ledge*

purchasing power *n* the value of goods that a standard amount of money can buy

pure *adj* 1 unmixed: *pure silver* 2 clean 3 of unmixed race: *a pure Arab horse* 4 free from sexual thoughts 5 (of colour or sound) clear 6 complete; thorough: *by pure chance* 7 (of an art or branch of study) considered only as a skill or exercise of the mind, separate from any use: *pure science* —compare APPLIED 8 *esp. written* clean according to religious rules

puree¹ *n* soft food boiled and sieved: *apple puree*

puree² *v* **pureed, pureeing** to make into a puree

purely *adv* completely; only: *purely out of friendship*

purgative *n, adj* (a medicine) that causes the bowels to empty

purgatory *n* **-ries** 1 (esp. according to the Roman Catholic religion) a place in which the soul of a dead person must suffer for wrong-doing on earth, until it is fit to enter Heaven 2 a place or time of great but temporary suffering — **-rial** *adj*

purge¹ *v* **purged, purging** 1 to make clean 2 to clear (the bowels) by medicine 3 to get rid of (an unwanted person) by removal from office, exile, killing, etc. — **-gation** *n*

purge² *n* 1 a medicine that purges the bowels 2 an act of getting rid of unwanted members of a group, suddenly, and often by force

purify *v* **-fied, -fying** to make pure — **-fication** *n*

purist *n* a person careful to be correct esp. in grammar, use of words, etc. — **-ism** *n*

puritan *adj, n* *usu. offensive* (of, like, or being) a person who has hard strict standards of behaviour and self-control — ~ism *n* — ~ical *adj* — ~ically *adv*

Puritan *n, adj* (in the 16th and 17th centuries) (a member) of a religious group that opposed the use of religious ceremonies not found in the Bible — ~ism *n*

purity also **pureness**— *n* being pure

purl¹ *n, adj technical* the second of the 2 main stitches in knitting in which the needle is put into the back of a stitch —compare KNIT, PLAIN

purl² *v technical* to use purl in knitting —see also KNIT, PLAIN

purlieus *n pompous* the area in and around; neighbourhood

purloin *v esp. written* to steal

purple¹ *adj* of a dark colour between red and blue — **purplish** *adj*

purple² *n* **1** (a) purple colour **2** (in former times) dark red or purple garments worn by people of very high rank

purple heart *n esp. spoken* a heart-shaped pill of a mind-exciting drug

purport¹ *n esp. written* general meaning or intention

purport² *v* to have an appearance of being: *His plans are not what they purport to be*

purpose¹ *n* **1** a reason for an action **2** use; effect: *Put your money to some good purpose* **3** willpower **4 on purpose** intentionally

purpose² *v* **-posed, -posing** *esp. written* to intend: *He purposes to visit America*

purpose-built *adj* specially made for a purpose

purposeful *adj* **1** full of will **2** directed towards a purpose — ~ly *adv*

purposeless *adj* aimless; meaningless — ~ly *adv* — ~ness *n*

purposely *adv* intentionally

purr¹ *n* **1** a low continuous sound produced by a pleased cat **2** a sound like this, made by a powerful machine working smoothly

purr² *v* **1** to make a purr **2** to express contentment in a pleasant low voice

purse¹ *n* **1** a small bag for carrying money **2** an amount of money collected for some good purpose or offered as a gift or prize

purse² *v* **pursed, pursing** to draw (esp. the lips) together in little folds

purser *n* an officer on a ship who keeps the accounts and is also in charge of the passengers' rooms, comfort, etc.

purse strings *n* **hold the purse strings** to control the money of a family, a firm, etc.

pursuance *n* **in pursuance of** *esp. written* continuing with: *He was wounded in the pursuance of his duty*

pursue *v* **-sued, -suing** **1** to chase **2** to follow closely **3** to follow and cause suffering to: *Bad luck pursued us* **4** to make continual efforts to gain: *to pursue fame* **5** to be busy with: *pursuing his studies* **6** *esp. written* to follow (a way, path, etc.) — ~r *n*

pursuit *n* **1** the act of pursuing **2** an activity to which one gives one's time: *His favourite pursuit is stamp collecting*

purulent *adj medical* full of pus ⚠ PRURIENT — **-lence** *n* — ~ly *adv*

purvey *v* **-veyed, -veying** *esp. written or technical* to supply (food or goods), esp. in large quantities — ~ance, ~or *n*

pus *n* a thick yellowish-white liquid produced in an infected or poisoned part of the body

push¹ *v* **1** to press (someone or something) forward, away, or to a different position **2** to urge: *My mother is pushing me to learn shorthand* **3** to force on the notice of others: *They aren't pushing their business enough* **4** to hurry or trouble (someone) by continual urging **5** *esp. spoken* to sell (unlawful drugs) —see also PUSH AROUND, PUSH IN, PUSH OFF, PUSH ON and compare PULL

push² *n* **1** an act of pushing **2** a planned advance by an army **3** active will to succeed **4** influence **5 at a push** if really necessary **6 get the push** *sl* to be dismissed from one's job

push around *v adv esp. spoken* to treat (someone) roughly and unfairly

pushbike *n esp. spoken* a pedal bicycle

push-button *adj* **1** operated by an object (**push button**) that one presses with the finger **2** using a lot of machinery: *a push-button age*

pushcart *n* a small handcart

pushchair *n* a folding chair on wheels for pushing a small child about

pushed *adj esp. spoken* having difficulty in finding enough: *pushed for money*

pusher *n* **1** *esp. spoken* a person who uses every means to gain success **2** *sl* a person who pushes drugs

push in *v adv esp. spoken* to interrupt rudely

push off *v adv sl* to go away

push on *v adv* to hurry: *We're late; we must push on*

pushover *n esp. spoken* **1** something very easy to do or win **2** someone easily influenced or deceived

pushy also **pushing**— *adj* too eager to make oneself noticed — **-ily** *adv* — **-iness** *n*

pusillanimous *adj esp. written* cowardly and weak — ~ly *adv* — **-mity** *n*

puss *n esp. spoken* **1** a pussy **2** a girl: *a clever little puss*

pussy *n* **-sies** *esp. spoken* also **puss, pussycat**— (a word used for calling a cat)

pussyfoot *v esp. spoken* to be too careful or afraid to act

pussy willow *n* a willow tree with small furry white or grey flowers spaced along the stems

pustule *n medical* a small raised or swollen spot on the skin

put¹ *v* **put, putting** **1** to move, place, or fix (someone or something) in, on, or to a stated place **2** *technical* to guide (a boat or horse) in a stated direction **3** to send: *He put a bullet through the animal's head* **4** to make, set, or fix (something or someone) as an act of the mind: *to put an end to the meeting* **5** to cause to be (in the stated condition): *He put his books in order* **6** to ask (a question) **7** to express in words: *I want to know how to put this in French* **8** to make (a written mark): *Put a cross opposite each mistake* **9** to cause to be busy: *Put the boys to work* **10** to throw (a heavy metal ball) as a sport: *putting* *the shot* **11 put paid to** to ruin —see also PUT ABOUT, PUT ACROSS, PUT ASIDE, PUT AWAY, PUT BACK, PUT BY, PUT DOWN, PUT DOWN AS, PUT DOWN FOR, PUT DOWN TO, PUT FORWARD, PUT IN, PUT IN FOR, PUT OFF, PUT ON, PUT ONTO, PUT OUT, PUT OVER, PUT THROUGH, PUT TO, PUT UP, PUT UP TO, PUT UP WITH

put² *n* an act of putting a heavy metal ball

put³ *adj* **stay put** to remain where placed

put about *v adv* to spread (news)

put across¹ also **put over**— *v adv* **1** to explain: *putting my meaning across* **2** to perform so as to cause admiration

put across² also **put over on**— *v prep esp. spoken* to deceive (someone) into believing: *She put it across me by selling me some bad eggs*

put aside *adv* **1** to save (money, time, etc.) **2** to pay no attention to

putative *adj esp. written* **1** generally supposed to be: *his putative parents* **2** supposed to exist or have existed: *a putative language* ⚠ PUNITIVE

put away *v adv* **1** also **put by**— to save (esp. money) **2** *esp. spoken* to eat **3** to place (someone) in prison or in a hospital for mad people

put back *v adv* **1** to cause to show an earlier time: *put the clocks back* **2** PUT OFF: *The meeting has been put back until next week*

put by *v adv* PUT AWAY

put-down *n esp. spoken & US* a rude shaming remark

put down *v adv* **1** to write (something) down **2** to defeat: *put down the opposition* **3** to pay (an amount) as part of the cost of something —see also DOWN PAYMENT **4** *sl* to make (someone) feel humble **5 a** to cause (an aircraft) to land **b** (of an aircraft) to land **6** to kill (an animal), esp. because of old age or illness —see also **put one's FOOT down**

put down as *v adv prep* to consider (someone) as: *I'd put him down as an uneducated man*

put down for *v adv prep* **1** to write the name of (someone) in a list of people willing to give money): *Put me down for $5* **2** to put on a waiting list for (a race, a school, etc.) **3** to consider (someone) as

put down to *v adv prep* **1** to state that (something) is caused by: *I put his bad temper down to his illness* **2** to charge (something) to

put forward *v adv* **1** to offer for consideration **2** to move (some event) to an earlier time **3** also **put on**— to cause to show a later time **4** to make (someone) noticed

put in *v adv* **1** to interrupt by saying: '*Don't forget us,*' *she put in* **2** to enter and make a short stop **3** *esp. spoken* to make (a request or claim) **4** to strike: *put in a blow* **5** to do or spend: *put in 3 years' work* —see also INPUT, **put one's FOOT in it**, **put someone in** MIND **of someone or something**

put in for *v adv prep* **1** to apply for **2 put in a good word for** to speak in favour of

put off *v adv* **1** to move to a later date **2** to make excuses for: *Don't be put off with a promise*

3 to discourage —see also OFF-PUTTING **4** turn off

put on *v adv* **1** to pretend to have (an opinion, quality, etc.) **2** to increase: *put on speed* **3** to perform (a play, show, etc.) **4** to cover (part of) the body with: *She put her coat on* **5** to put (a clock) forward **6** TURN ON: *Put on the radio* — see also **put on an** ACT

put onto *v prep esp. spoken* to give (someone) information about: *I can put you onto a good lawyer*

put out *v adv* **1** to make (something) stop burning **2** to trouble or annoy **3** to produce, broadcast, or print **4 put oneself out** to take trouble

put over *v adv* PUT ACROSS

putrefaction *n esp. written* the decomposition of dead plant or animal substance, causing bad smells

putrefy *v* **-fied, -fying** to decay

putrescent *adj esp. written* beginning to decay — **-cence** *n*

putrid *adj* very decayed and bad-smelling — **~ity** *n*

putsch *n* a sudden secretly planned attempt to overthrow a government

putt¹ *n* (in golf) an act or the result of putting the ball

putt² *v* (in golf) **1** to strike (the ball) gently along the ground towards or into the hole **2** to take a stated number of putts: *Nicklaus 2-putted at the 14th*

puttee *n* a strip of cloth wound round the leg from ankle to knee for support and protection

putter *n* (in golf) **1** a short golf club with a flat metal head used in putting **2** a person who putts

put through *v adv* **1** to connect by telephone **2** to make (a telephone call)

put to *v prep* **1** to ask (a question) of or make (an offer) to **2** to test by the stated means: *put the matter to a vote*

putty *n* a soft oily cement, used esp. in fixing glass to window frames

put up *v adv* **1** to raise: *put up a tent* **2** to put in a public place: *put up a notice* **3** to provide food and lodging for **4** to supply (money) **5** to offer in a struggle: *He didn't put up much of a fight!* **6** to offer for sale **7** to suggest

put-up job *n esp. spoken* something dishonestly arranged in advance

put-upon *adj* (of a person) taken advantage of

put up to *v adv prep* to give (someone) the idea of: *Who put you up to this trick?*

put up with *v adv prep esp. spoken* to suffer (someone or something) without complaining

puzzle¹ *v* **-zled, -zling** **1** to cause difficulty of thought to (someone) in the effort to understand **2** to think hard in order to understand something difficult — **puzzled** *adj* — **puzzler** *n*

puzzle² *n* **1** something that one cannot understand or explain **2** a game, toy, or apparatus in which parts must be fitted together correctly: *a*

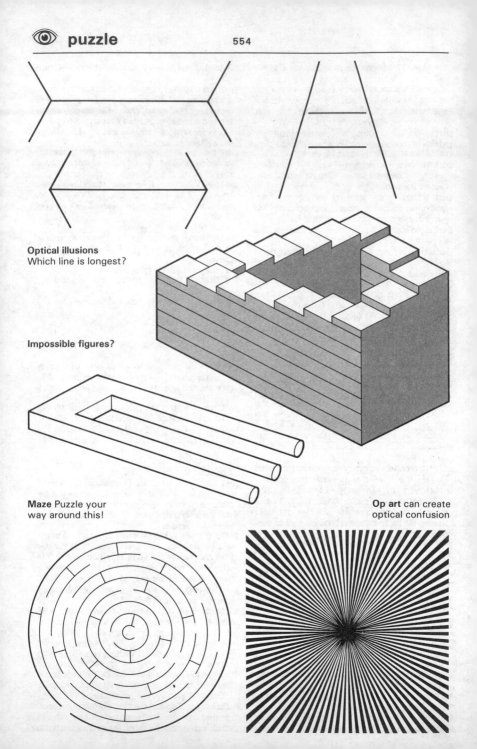

Optical illusions
Which line is longest?

Impossible figures?

Maze Puzzle your
way around this!

Op art can create
optical confusion

crossword puzzle | a jigsaw puzzle — ~ment n

puzzle out v adv to find the answer to (something) by thinking hard

PVC n a type of plastic ⟶REFINERY

pygmy, pigmy n -mies 1 a member of a race of very small people 2 any very small person or animal 3 a person of no importance

Pygmy n, adj (a member) of a tribal race of central Africa, whose average height is 1·4 metres or 4 feet 6 inches

pyjamas n soft loose-fitting trousers and a short coat to be worn in bed

pylon n a tall steel framework for supporting electricity wires

pyorrhoea, -rhea n a disease of the gums which may loosen the teeth

pyramid n 1 (in geometry) a solid figure with a base and straight flat triangular sides that slope upwards to meet at the vertex ⟶MATHEMATICS 2 a pile of objects in this shape 3 a very large ancient stone building in this shape , used formerly, esp. in Egypt, as the burial place of a king 4 any ancient stone building like this in shape, found esp. in Latin America

pyre n a high pile of wood for the ceremonial burning of a dead body

Pyrex n trademark special heat resistant glass used in making cooking containers

pyrites n a natural compound of sulphur with a metal, esp. iron or copper, found in the earth and looking like gold

pyromania n a disease of the mind causing desire to start fires — ~c n

pyrotechnics n 1 esp. technical a public show of fireworks 2 a splendid show of skill in words, music, etc. — -nic, -nical adj

Pyrrhic victory n -ries a victory in which the winner is left in a worse state than before

python n **pythons** or **python** a large non-poisonous tropical snake that kills small animals by crushing them

Q

Q, q Q's, q's or Qs, qs 1 the 17th letter of the English alphabet 2 mind one's p's and q's to be careful or polite

Q.C. also esp. written **Queen's Counsel**— n (the title given, while a queen is ruling, to) a British barrister of high rank —compare K.C.

QED abbrev. for: (Latin) **quod erat demonstrandum**; there is the answer to the question

qr abbrev. for: quarter

qt abbrev. for: quart

q.t. n **on the q.t.** on the quiet

qty abbrev. for: quantity

qua prep when thought of by itself: Money, qua money, cannot provide happiness

quack¹ v, n (to make) the sound that ducks make

quack² n a person dishonestly claiming to have special, esp. medical, knowledge —compare CHARLATAN — ~ery n

quad¹ also (esp. written) **quadrangle**— n esp. spoken a square open place with buildings around it, esp. in a college

quad² n esp. spoken a quadruplet

Quadragesima n the first Sunday in Lent

quadrant n 1 a quarter of a circle; a sector containing an angle of 90° 2 an instrument for measuring angles

quadratic equation n an equation of the form $ax^2 + bx + c = y$, where x is to be found and a, b, c, are given

quadrilateral adj, n (a flat figure) with 4 straight sides

quadrille n a dance in which the dancers form a square

quadruped n a mammal with 4 legs

quadruple¹ v -pled, -pling to multiply (a number) by 4

quadruple² adj, n, adv (an amount which is) 4 times as big as something mentioned or usual — -ply adv

quadruplet n one of 4 children born of the same mother at the same time

quadruple time n a musical time with 4 beats

quaff n literature to drink deeply

quagmire n a bog

quail¹ n quail or quails a kind of small edible bird like the partridge

quail² v to be afraid; tremble

quaint adj unusual and attractive, esp. because old — ~ly adv — ~ness n

quake v quaked, quaking to shake; tremble

Quaker n, adj (a member) of a Christian religious group which opposes violence

qualification n 1 qualifying 2 something which limits something said: I agree, with qualifications 3 a proof that one has passed examinations: a medical qualification

qualifications n the necessary ability or knowledge: the right qualifications for the job

qualified adj 1 limited: qualified agreement 2 having qualifications: a highly qualified man

qualify v 1 -fied, -fying to gain or give qualifications 2 to limit (meaning): Qualify that statement— it's too strong

qualitative adj of or about quality — ~ly adv

quality n -ties 1 a (high) degree of goodness 2 something typical of a person or material: moral qualities

qualm n an unpleasant nervous feeling

quandary n -ries a state of difficulty and inability to decide

quango n quasi-autonomous national governmental organization; any of various official bodies (such as the Hadrian's Wall Advisory Committee) that each have a particular task and are partly independent

quantify v -fied, -fying to measure (an amount or quantity) — -fiable adj — -fication n

quantitative adj of or about quantity — ~ly adv

quantity n -ties 1 a measurable property of something: *These goods are greater in quantity than in quality* 2 an amount or number

quantity surveyor n a person who gives the probable cost of materials for future building

quantum n -ta technical (esp. in physics) a fixed amount

quarantine[1] n a period when someone or something that may be carrying disease is kept separate from others so that the disease cannot spread

quarantine[2] v -tined, -tining to put in quarantine

quark n technical the smallest possible piece of the material of which atoms are made

quarrel[1] n 1 an argument 2 a point of disagreement: *I have no quarrel with his opinion*

quarrel[2] v -ll- to have an argument

quarrelsome adj likely to argue

quarrel with v prep to disagree with; complain about

quarry[1] n -ries a creature being hunted

quarry[2] n a place from which stone, sand, etc., are dug out —compare MINE

quarry[3] v -ried, -rying to dig out (stone, sand, etc.)

quart n ¼ of a gallon; 2 pints

quarter[1] n 1 a 4th part of a whole; ¼ 2 15 minutes before or after the hour: *a quarter past 10* (=10.15) 3 3 months of the year: *pay rent by the quarter* 4 ¼ of an animal including a leg: *hindquarters* 5 a place or person(s) supplying something: *Workers are arriving from all quarters* 6 a part of a town: *the student quarter* 7 the time twice a month when the moon shows ¼ of its surface: *At the end of the first week the moon is in its first quarter, at the end of the third it is in its last quarter* 8 mercy: *to give no quarter* 9 ¼ of a pound; 4 ounces 10 **at close quarters** near together —see also QUARTERS

quarter[2] v 1 to divide into 4 2 to provide lodgings for (esp. soldiers)

quarter day n -days a day which officially begins a 3-month period of the year, and on which payments are made

quarterdeck n technical part of the highest level of a ship, used only by officers

quarterfinal n any of 4 matches of which the winners will play in the 2 semifinal matches

quartering n 1 dividing into 4 2 the giving or finding of lodgings

quarterly[1] adj, adv (happening, appearing, etc.) every 3 months

quarterly[2] n -lies a magazine appearing every 3 months

quartermaster n 1 a military officer in charge of provisions 2 a seaman in charge of steering

quarters n lodgings

quarter sessions n a former law court held every 3 months

quarterstaff n -staves a long wooden pole formerly used as a weapon

quartet, -tette n (a piece of music for) 4 people playing or singing together

quartile n technical any of the 3 points of division when a range of numbers is divided into 4

quartz n a hard mineral substance

quasar n technical any of many mysterious objects outside our galaxy which produce intense radio waves rather like those of a star

quash v 1 to make nothing of or officially refuse to accept (esp. something which has been decided) 2 to suppress

quatrain n a poem or verse of 4 lines

quaver[1] v (of a voice, or music) to sing, speak, or be played in a shaky way — ~y adj

quaver[2] n 1 a shaking in the voice 2 a musical note which is half a crotchet ➜MUSIC

quay n -quays a man-made place where boats can load and unload

queasy adj -sier, -siest feeling sickness or dislike — -sily adv — -siness n

queen n 1 (the title of) a female ruler of a country or the wife of a king ➜KING 2 the leading female in a competition 3 the leading female insect of a group which lays eggs: *the queen ant* 4 any of the 4 playing cards with a picture of a queen and usu. a rank between the jack and the king: *the queen of hearts* 5 the most powerful piece in chess

queenly adj like, or suitable for, a queen

queen mother n the mother of a ruler

Queensberry rules n the rules of fair fighting in boxing

Queen's Counsel n esp. written a Q.C.

queer adj 1 strange: *a queer story* 2 esp. spoken not well: *I'm feeling queer* 3 esp. spoken mad (esp. in the phrase **queer in the head**) 4 in **queer street** sl in debt or money trouble — ~ly adv — ~ness n

quell v to put down; suppress

quench v to take away the heat of (flames, steel, desire, etc.) with water or by other methods: *to quench one's thirst*

querulous adj complaining — ~ly adv — ~ness n

query[1] n -ries a question or doubt

query[2] v -ried, -rying 1 to raise a doubt about: *to query a point* 2 to ask

quest[1] n literature a search; attempt to find

quest[2] v literature to search

question[1] n 1 a sentence or phrase which asks for information 2 a problem: *It's a question of finding time* 3 a doubt: *His honesty is beyond question* 4 **in question** being talked about 5 **out of the question** impossible 6 **there's no question of** there's no possibility of

question[2] v 1 to ask a question 2 to raise

doubts about — ~ing adj — ~ingly adv — ~er n

questionable adj 1 not certain: a questionable idea 2 of doubtful honesty: questionable friends — -bly adv

question mark n the mark (?)

question master n the chairman of a quiz game

questionnaire n a set of written questions to be answered for information

queue[1] n 1 a line of waiting people, cars, etc. 2 **jump the queue** to go ahead of people who have waited longer than you

queue[2] v **queued, queuing** to form or join a line while waiting

quibble[1] n 1 an argument about a small point 2 the small point argued about

quibble[2] v **-bled, -bling** to argue about small points — **quibbler** n — **quibbling** adj

quiche n French an open pastry case (FLAN) with a filling of eggs, cream, bacon, etc.

quick[1] adj 1 swift; soon finished 2 easily showing anger (in the phrases **a quick temper, quick tempered**) — ~ly adv — ~ness n

quick[2] n 1 living matter, usu. the flesh to which the fingernails and toenails are joined 2 **cut (a person) to the quick** to hurt a person's feelings deeply

quick[3] adv quickly

quick-change adj (of an actor) frequently changing clothes during a performance

quicken v to make or become quick

quickie n esp. spoken an act taking a very short time, or the story, film, etc. which results

quicklime n lime from limestone

quicksand n wet sand which pulls in any beings which try to cross it

quicksilver n mercury

quickstep n (the music of) a dance with swift steps

quick-witted adj swift to understand and act

quid n quid esp. spoken a pound (in money); £1

quid pro quo n quid pro quos Latin something given or received in exchange

quiescent adj still; at rest — **quiescence** n — **quiescently** adv

quiet[1] n 1 quietness 2 **on the quiet** secretly

quiet[2] adj 1 with little noise 2 calm: a quiet life 3 (of colours) not bright — ~ly adv — ~ness n

quieten v to make or become quiet

quietude n calmness; stillness

quietus n literature 1 death, or the act which brings it 2 inactivity

quiff n a man's tuft of hair standing up over the forehead

quill n 1 a bird's feather, esp. from the wing or tail 2 also **quill pen** — a pen made from this 3 a prickle on some animals, such as the porcupine

quilt n a padded cover for a bed

quilted adj padded and stitched across

quin n esp. spoken a quintuplet

quince n a hard fruit related to the apple, used in jelly

quinine n a drug used for treating fevers, esp. malaria

quintessence n **the quintessence of** the perfect type or example of — **-sential** adj — **-sentially** adv

quintet, -tette n (a piece of music for) 5 people playing or singing together

quintuplet n one of 5 children born of the same mother at the same time

quip[1] n a remark meant to sound clever

quip[2] v **-pp-** to make clever-sounding remarks

quire n 24 pieces of paper

quirk n 1 a strange happening or accident 2 a strange type of behaviour

quisling n someone who helps conquerors to run his country

quit[1] adj finished with; free of

quit[2] v **quitted** or **quit, quitting** 1 esp. spoken to stop (doing something): I've quit my job 2 old use to leave

quite adv 1 completely; perfectly: quite ready 2 rather: quite a good story

quits adj back on an even level after a fight, after repaying money, etc.

quitter n esp. spoken a person who doesn't have the courage to finish things once difficulties arise

quiver[1] n a container for arrows

quiver[2] v to tremble a little

quiver[3] n a trembling movement

quixotic adj trying to be generous to others while endangering oneself — ~**ally** adv

quiz[1] n **quizzes** a competition or game where questions are put

quiz[2] v **-zz-** to ask questions of

quizzical adj (of a smile or look) giving the idea that one knows something and is laughing at the other person — ~ly adv

quoits n a game using rings (**quoits**) to be thrown over a peg

quorum n a stated number of people, without whom a meeting cannot be held

quota n a stated number or amount, or a limit on numbers: The quota of foreigners allowed into the country has been reduced

quotable adj that can be, or is worthy of being, quoted — -**bility** n

quotation n 1 quoting 2 a sentence or piece taken from a work of art 3 the price of something as at present known: He gave me a quotation for a new house —compare ESTIMATE

quotation mark n either of a pair of marks (" ") or (' ') showing the beginning and end of words said or written by someone else

quote[1] v **quoted, quoting** 1 to repeat in speech or writing (the words of another person): He quotes the Bible 2 to mention (someone's actions) to add power to one's own point of view 3 to give a price —compare ESTIMATE

quote² *n esp. spoken* **1** a quotation **2 in quotes** in quotation marks

quoth *v* **quoth** I/he/she/it *old use* said I/he/she/it

quotient *n* the result obtained when one number is divided by another

q.v. *abbrev. for:* (*Latin*) **quod vide**; which see; (used for telling readers to look in another place)

R

R, r **R's, r's** *or* **Rs, rs** **1** the 18th letter of the English alphabet **2** the **3 R's** reading, (w)riting and (a)rithmetic, said to form the beginning of education

R *abbrev. for:* **1** royal, as in R.A.F. **2** Rex or Regina: *Elizabeth R*

rabbi *n* a trained Jewish religious leader and teacher — ~**nical** *adj*

rabbit¹ *n* **1** a small long-eared burrowing animal of the hare family MAMMAL **2 a** its fur **b** its meat —compare WELSH RAREBIT

rabbit² *v* **-tt-** **1** to hunt rabbits **2** *esp. spoken* to talk in a dull complaining way: *He keeps rabbitting on about his health*

rabble *n* **1** a disorderly crowd **2** *offensive* the common people

rabble-rousing *adj* (of a speaker or his words) exciting people to hatred and violence — **-ser** *n*

Rabelaisian *adj* (of stories, writings, etc.) full of harmless coarse jokes about sex and the body like the work of the French writer Rabelais (1490–1553): *Rabelaisian humour*

rabid *adj* **1** suffering from rabies **2** (of opinions) unreasonably violent: *a rabid hatrid*

rabies also (*esp. written*) **hydrophobia**— *n* a disease of the nervous system passed on by the bite of an infected animal, causing madness and death

RAC *abbrev. for:* Royal Automobile Club

raccoon, racoon *n* a small meat-eating North American animal, longtailed and thickly furred

race¹ *n* **1** a competition in speed **2** a strong flow of water: *A mill-race is the stream driving the wheel of a water-mill*

race² *v* **raced, racing** **1** to compete in a race (against) **2** to go or take very fast: *racing across the road* **3** to cause to run a race: *I can't race my horse* — ~**r** *n*

race³ *n* **1** one of a number of divisions of human beings, each of a different physical type: *the black/white/brown races* **2** a breed or type of animal or plant **3** a group of people with the same history, customs, etc.: *the German race* **4** a type of creature: *the human race* —see FOLK (USAGE) — **race, racial** *adj* — **racially** *adv*

racecourse *n* a track on which horses race

racehorse *n* a horse bred or kept for racing

racetrack *n esp. US* a course round which horses, cars, etc., race

racialism also **racism**— *n* political and social practices based largely on false differences between races of people, and on the belief that one's own race is best — **racialist, racist** *adj, n*

racing *adj* **1** used for racing: *a racing car* **2** concerned with racing: *a racing club*

rack¹ *n* **1** a framework with bars, hooks, etc., for holding things: *a plate rack* **2** a shelf for luggage in a plane, railway carriage, etc. **3** (in former times) an instrument of torture on which people were stretched by turning wheels **4** a bar with teeth on one edge, moved by or moving a toothed wheel (PINION) ⊃MACHINERY

rack² *v* **1** to cause great pain **2 rack one's brains** to think very deeply

rack, wrack³ *n* (usu. of buildings) the ruined state caused by lack of care (in the phrase **rack and ruin**)

racket, racquet¹ *n* a network usu. of nylon stretched in a frame with a handle, for hitting the ball in games such as tennis

racket² *n* **1** a loud noise **2** great social activity and hurry **3** *esp. spoken* a dishonest way of getting money **4** *humour* business or trade: *What racket are you in?*

racketeer *n offensive* someone who works a dishonest racket — ~**ing** *n*

rackets, racquets *n* a ball game for 2 or 4 players in an enclosed court, played with a hard ball

rack railway *n* **-ways** a mountain railway worked by a rack and pinion

raconteur *n French* someone good at telling stories

racoon *n* a raccoon

racy *adj* **-ier, -iest** (of speech or writing) amusing, full of life, and perhaps rather dirty — **racily** *adv* — **raciness** *n*

radar also **radiolocation**— *n* a method of finding the position of a solid object by sending out a pulse of high frequency radio waves, and measuring the time taken for that pulse to bounce off the object and return to the transmitter

radar dish *n* a dish-shaped aerial that receives and transmits radar signals

radial¹ *adj* arranged like a wheel — ~**ly** *adv*

radial² also **radial tyre**— *n* a car tyre with hollow radial lines in the rubber to give better control on slippery roads

radiant *adj* **1** sending out light or heat in all directions: *the radiant sun* **2** *technical* sent out by radiation: *radiant heat* **3** (of a person or his appearance) showing love and happiness: *radiant with joy* — **-ance** *n* — ~**ly** *adv*

radiate *v* **-ated, -ating** to send out (light or heat)

radiation *n* **1** radiating **2** something radiated: *harmful radiations* **3** radioactivity

radiation sickness *n* the illness caused by radioactivity

radiator *n* 1 an apparatus consisting of pipes with steam or hot water passing through them, for heating buildings 2 an electric heater for the same purpose 3 an apparatus for cooling a motor-engine

radical¹ *adj* 1 (of changes) thorough and complete: *radical improvements* 2 in favour of thorough and complete political change: *a radical politician* — ~ly *adv*

radical² *n* 1 a politically radical person 2 *technical* a group of atoms that is found unchanged in a number of compounds and acts like a single atom

radicalism *n* being politically radical

radicle *n* the root of a young plant, esp. before it comes out of the seed

radii *pl. of* RADIUS

radio¹ *n* 1 the sending or receiving of sounds through the air by electrical waves 2 also **radio set**— an apparatus to receive sounds broadcast in this way 3 the broadcasting industry

radio² *v* -oed, -oing 1 to send through the air by electrical waves: *The ship radioed for help* 2 to send a message to (a place or person) in this way

radioactivity *n* the quality that some elements have of giving out energy which can harm living things — -tive *adj*

radiogram *n* a piece of furniture combining a radio and a record player

radiograph *n* an X-ray photograph

radiography *n* the taking of radiographs — -pher *n*

radioisotope *n* *technical* any of the radioactive forms of an element —see also ISOTOPE

radiology *n* the use of X-rays and radioactivity in finding and treating illness — -gist *n*

radio telescope *n* a radio receiver used for following the movements of the stars and of spacecraft ⟶TELESCOPE

radiotherapist *n* a person who treats diseases by radioactive substances or X-rays — -py *n*

radish *n* a small vegetable or its red or white hot-tasting root, eaten raw

radium *n* a rare shining white metal that is an element, radioactive, and used in the treatment of certain diseases, esp. cancer

radius *n* -dii 1 (the line marking) the distance from the centre of a circle or sphere to its edge or surface ⟶MATHEMATICS 2 a circular area measured from its centre point 3 *medical* the long bone from the elbow to the thumb joint

R.A.F. *n* *abbrev. for:* Royal Air Force

raffia *n* soft string-like fibre from palm leaves, used for tying up plants and making hats, baskets, etc.

raffish *adj* happy, wild, and not very respectable — ~ly *adv* — ~ness *n*

raffle¹ *n* a sale of many low-priced numbered tickets of which one is chosen by chance to win an article of some value —compare LOTTERY

raffle² *v* -fled, -fling to sell in a raffle

raft¹ *n* 1 a flat wooden or rubber boat which

may be used for lifesaving or as a landing place for swimmers 2 a number of logs fastened together to be sent floating down the river

raft² *v* to carry or travel on a raft

rafter *n* one of the sloping beams that hold up a roof

raftered *adj* having rafters, esp. where these can be seen from below

rag¹ *n* 1 (a small piece of) old cloth 2 an old worn-out garment: *dressed in rags* 3 *esp. spoken* a badly-written newspaper

rag² *v* -gg- 1 to play about noisily and foolishly 2 to tease: *They ragged him about his big ears*

rag³ *n* 1 a rough noisy but harmless trick 2 an amusing procession of college students through the streets, collecting money for charity

rag⁴ *n* a piece of music written in ragtime

raga *n* (a piece of music based on) one of the many ancient patterns of notes in Indian music

ragamuffin *n* a dirty child, in torn clothes

ragbag *n* 1 a bag in which bits of old cloth are kept for mending clothes 2 a confused mixture: *a ragbag of disconnected facts*

rage¹ *n* 1 wild uncontrollable anger —see ANGRY (USAGE) 2 a fashion: *Long hair is all the rage now*

rage² *v* raged, raging 1 to be very angry 2 to be very violent: *a raging headache*

ragged *adj* 1 old and torn 2 dressed in rags 3 uneven: *a ragged beard* 4 unfinished and imperfect: *a ragged performance* — ~ly *adv* — ~ness *n*

raglan *adj* (of a sleeve) joined with 2 sideways seams from the arm to the neck of the garment

ragout *n* French meat and vegetable stew

ragtag *n* *offensive* the common people (in the phrase **ragtag and bobtail**)

ragtime *n* the form of syncopated music, song, and dance of black US origin, popular in the 1920's

rag trade *n* *esp. spoken* the garment industry

raid¹ *n* 1 a quick attack on an enemy position 2 a rapid visit to a place, to carry something away 3 an unexpected visit by the police, in search of criminals or forbidden goods

raid² *v* to visit or attack on a raid: *raid a bank*

raider *n* a person, ship, or plane that makes a raid

rail¹ *n* 1 a fixed bar, to hang things on or for protection 2 one of the pair of metal bars along which a train runs 3 **by rail** in a train

rail² *v* to enclose or separate with rails

rail³ *v* to curse or complain noisily

rail car *n* a single railway carriage that can be used alone, worked by oil or electricity

railhead *n* the end of a railway track

railing *n* one rail in a fence

raillery *n* -ries teasing

railroad *v* to hurry (someone) unfairly

rails *n* railway track

railway *n* -ways 1 a track for trains 2 a

system of these tracks, with its engines, stations, etc.

raiment *n literature* clothes

rain¹ *n* **1** water falling in drops from the clouds ⎯▷CLOUD **2** a thick fall of anything: *a rain of arrows* **3 as right as rain** *esp. spoken* in perfect health — ~**less** *adj*

rain² *v* **1** (of rain) to fall **2** to drop or fall like rain: *The bombs came raining down.* | *Tears rained down her cheeks* —see also RAIN OFF

rainbow *n* an arch of different colours that sometimes appears in the sky esp. after rain

rainbow trout *n* a freshwater food fish with black spots and pink or red lines on its body

raincoat *n* a waterproof coat

raindrop *n* a single drop of rain

rainfall *n* the amount of rain, hail, or snow that falls in an area in a certain time, as measured in depth per year

rain forest *n* a tropical forest, in an area of heavy rainfall, with tall trees growing thickly together

rain off *v adv esp. spoken* to prevent by rain: *The game was rained off*

rains *n* the rainy season in tropical countries; monsoon

rainwater *n* water fallen as rain

rainy *adj* **-ier, -iest** having a lot of rain

raise *v* **raised, raising** **1** to lift, push, or move upward **2** to make higher in amount, degree, etc.: *raise the rent* **3** to collect together: *raise an army* **4** *esp. US* to produce and look after (living things); bring up (children): *raise a family* **5** to bring up and talk about (a subject) **6** *esp. written* to build: *raise a monument* **7** to make or cause (a noise): *to raise a laugh* **8** to cause (feelings): *His absence raised fears about his safety* **9** to cause to end (an official rule forbidding something): *raise an embargo* **10** to bring back to life (a dead person) **11** to make a higher bid than (a card player) —see RISE (USAGE)

raisin *n* a dried grape

raison d'etre *n* **raisons d'etre** *French* a reason for existing

raj *n Indian & Pakistani* (a period of) rule, esp. British rule in India

rajah, raja *n* (the title of) an Indian ruler —see also RANEE

rake¹ *n* **1** a gardening tool consisting of a row of teeth at the end of a long handle, for levelling soil, gathering up leaves, etc. **2** the same kind of tool on wheels, pulled by a horse or tractor

rake² *v* **raked, raking** **1** to make level with a rake **2** to collect (as if) with a rake: *to rake in money* | *to rake out some facts* **3** to search by turning over and mixing up a pile **4** to examine or shoot in a sweeping movement along the whole length of: *He raked the hillside with powerful glasses*

rake³ *v* to slope

rake⁴ *n* the angle of a slope

rake⁵ *n old use* a rich man of good family who has led a wild life with regard to drink and women — **rakish** *adj* **rakishly** *adv*

rake-off *n* a share of usu. dishonest profits

rake up *v adv esp. spoken* **1** to produce with difficulty by searching **2** to remember and talk about (something that should be forgotten)

rallentando *n, adv, adi* **-dos** *Italian* (a part of a piece of music) becoming slower

rally¹ *v* **-lied, -lying** **1** to come or bring together for a purpose **2** to come or bring back into order, ready to make another effort: *The soldiers rallied and drove the enemy back* **3** to recover, as from illness or unhappiness

rally² *n* **-lies** **1** an act of rallying **2** a large public meeting **3** a motor race over public roads **4** (in tennis) a long struggle to gain a point

rally³ *v pompous* to tease

rally round *v adv esp. spoken* (esp. of a group) to come to someone's help

ram¹ *n* **1** a fully-grown male sheep that can father young —compare EWE **2** any machine that repeatedly drops or pushes a weight

ram² *v* **-mm-** **1** to run into (something) very hard **2** to force into place with heavy pressure

Ramadan *n* the 9th month of the Muslim year, during which there is strict daylight fasting

ramble¹ *v* **-bled, -bling** **1** to go on a ramble **2** to talk or write in a disordered wandering way **3** (of a plant) to grow loosely in all directions

ramble² *n* a walk for enjoyment — ~**r** *n* : *a keen rambler*

rambling *adj* **1** (of speech or writing) disordered and wandering **2** (of houses, streets, etc.) twisting and winding

rambunctious *adj humour* (of a person) noisy; full of life — ~**ly** *adv* — ~**ness** *n*

ramification *n* a branch of a system with many parts: *the ramifications of a railway system*

ramify *v* **-fied, -fying** to branch out in all directions

ramjet also **ramjet engine**— *n* a jet engine through which a flow of air is forced by forward movement

ramp¹ *n esp. spoken* a dishonest trick to make people pay a high price —compare RACKET

ramp² *n* a slope connecting 2 levels

rampage¹ *v* **-paged, -paging** to rush about wildly or angrily

rampage² *n* excited and violent behaviour: *be/go on the rampage* — ~**pageous** *adj*

rampant *adj* **1** (of crime, disease, etc.) widespread and impossible to control **2** (of an animal drawn on a shield or flag) standing on the back legs with the front legs raised as if to strike — ~**ly** *adv*

rampart *n* a wide bank protecting a fort or city

ramrod *n* **1** a stick for pushing the gunpowder into an old-fashioned gun **2** a stick for cleaning a small gun

ramshackle *adj* (of a building or vehicle) badly made or needing repair

ran *past tense of* RUN

ranch n a very large farm where sheep, cattle, or horses are produced — ~**er** n

rancid adj (of oily food or its taste or smell) not fresh — ~**ity** n

rancorous adj feeling or showing rancour — ~**ly** adv

rancour n the feeling of bitter, unforgiving hatred

rand n rand the standard coin in the money system of South Africa, divided into 100 cents ☞ MONEY

random[1] adj made or done aimlessly: a random shot — ~**ly** adv — ~**ness** n

random[2] n **at random** aimlessly

randy adj -ier, -iest esp. spoken (of a person or his feelings) full of sexual desire — **randiness** n

ranee, rani (the title of) a a female rajah b the wife of a rajah

rang past tense of RING

range[1] n **1** a connected line (of mountains, hills, etc.) **2** an area where shooting is practised, or where missiles are tested **3** (in North America) a wide stretch of grassy land where cattle feed **4** the distance that a gun can fire or a plane, missile, etc., travel **5** the distance at which one can see or hear **6** the limits between which something varies: a wide range of temperature **7** a set of different objects of the same kind: a range of tools **8** a cooking fireplace built in a kitchen **9** technical **a** (in statistics) the difference between the largest and smallest numbers of a set **b** (in set theory) a set of items to each of which a member of another set (the DOMAIN) is linked (MAPPED)

range[2] v ranged, ranging **1** (of a gun) to have a range of **2** to stretch or reach between limits: ranging between 5 and 15 **3** to wander freely over: The children ranged the hills **4** to arrange: range the goods neatly in the shop window

range finder n an instrument for finding the distance of an object **a** when shooting **b** when taking photographs ☞ OPTICS

ranger n **1** (in Britain) the keeper of a royal forest **2** (in N. America) **a** a forest guard **b** a policeman who rides through country areas to see that the law is kept **3** an older member of the Girl Guides

rank[1] adj **1** (of a plant) too thick and widespread **2** (of land) thickly covered (with useless plants) **3** (of smell or taste) very strong and unpleasant: rank tobacco **4** complete; utter: a rank beginner — ~**ly** adv — ~**ness** n

rank[2] n **1** a degree of value, importance, etc., in a group: the rank of general **2** social position: people of all ranks **3** a line (of policemen, soldiers, etc.) standing side by side **4** a line (of people or things): a taxi rank

rank[3] v **1** to be or put (in a certain class): This town ranks high among beauty spots **2** to arrange in regular order: cups ranked neatly on the shelf

rank and file n **1** the common soldiers **2** the people in an organization who are not the leaders

ranking adj esp. US (of an officer) of highest rank present

rankle v -kled, -kling to continue to be remembered with bitterness

ranks n **1** pompous the class or group (of): the ranks of the unemployed **2 reduce (someone) to the ranks** to reduce (a noncommissioned officer) to the rank of common soldier, as a punishment **3 rise from/through the ranks** to rise from the rank of a common soldier to that of an officer

ransack v **1** to search (a place) roughly **2** to search through and rob (a place)

ransom[1] n **1** a sum of money paid to free a prisoner **2 hold someone to ransom** to keep someone prisoner so as to demand payment **3 a king's ransom** pompous a great deal of money

ransom[2] v to set free by paying a ransom — ~**er** n

rant v to talk in a loud excited way — **rant** n — ~**er** n

rap[1] n **1** a quick light blow: a rap on the door **2 take the rap** esp. spoken to receive the punishment (for someone else's crime)

rap[2] v -pp- **1** to strike quickly and lightly **2** to speak severely to: The judge rapped the police

rap[3] n esp. spoken the least bit: I don't care a rap

rapacious adj taking everything one can, esp. by force: rapacious robbers — -**city** n — ~**ly** adv — ~**ness** n

rape[1] n a type of European plant grown as food for sheep and pigs and for oil from its seeds

rape[2] v raped, raping to have sex with, against the other's will — **rapist** n

rape[3] n **1** the act and crime of raping **2** spoiling: the rape of our forests

rapid[1] adj **1** fast **2** (of a slope) descending steeply — ~**ity** n — ~**ly** adv

rapid[2] n a part of a river where the water moves very fast over rocks

rapier n a long light thin 2-edged sword with a sharp point ☞ WEAPON

rapine n literature plunder

rap out v adv to say sharply and suddenly

rapport n French close agreement and understanding: be in rapport with someone

rapprochement n French a coming together again in friendship of former enemies

rapscallion n humour & old use rascal

rapt adj giving one's whole mind: rapt attention — ~**ly** adv — ~**ness** n

rapture n great joy and delight — -**rous** adj — -**rously** adv

rare[1] adj (of meat, esp. steak) lightly cooked —compare WELL-DONE

rare[2] adj unusual; uncommon — ~**ness** n

rarefied adj often humour grand

rarefy v -fied, -fying to make (a substance, esp. air) thinner, more widely spread, etc.

rarely adv not often

rarity *n* -ties **1** the quality of being rare **2** something uncommon

rascal *n* **1** a dishonest person **2** *humour* a person who plays tricks or misbehaves

rash[1] *adj* (of a person or his behaviour) not thinking enough of the results: *a rash decision* — ~ly *adv* — ~ness *n*

rash[2] *n* **1** a set of red spots on the skin, caused by illness **2** a sudden unpleasant appearance in large numbers: *a rash of complaints* **3 come out in a rash** to become covered with small red spots

rasher *n* a thin piece of ham or bacon

rasp[1] *v* **1** to rub with or as if with a rasp **2** to have an annoying effect like the sound made by a rasp: *her rasping voice* **3** to say in a rough voice: *'Leave!' he rasped* — ~ingly *adv*

rasp[2] *n* **1** a tool used for smoothing wood, metal, etc., with a long narrow metal blade covered with rough sharp points **2** a sound that might be made by this tool

raspberry *n* -ries **1** a type of bush or its a soft sweet usu. red berry **2** *sl* a rude sound made by putting one's tongue out and blowing

rat[1] *n* **1** any of several types of long-tailed rodent related to but larger than the mouse ⎯☞ MAMMAL **2** a low disloyal man **3 smell a rat** *esp. spoken* to guess that something wrong is happening

rat[2] *v* -tt- *esp. spoken* to break a promise: *They've ratted on us*

ratatouille *n* French a stew of mixed vegetables

ratchet *n* a toothed wheel (**ratchet wheel**) or bar, with a catch (PAWL) that can fit between the teeth so as to allow movement in one direction only

rate[1] *n* **1** a value, speed, etc., measured by its relation to some other amount: *The birth rate is the number of births compared to the number of the people* **2** a (stated) speed: *a steady rate* **3** a payment fixed according to a standard scale: *What rate are you getting?* **4** a local tax paid by owners and tenants of buildings **5** of the (numbered) quality: *first-rate* **6 at any rate** in any case **7 at this/that rate** if events continue in the same way as now/then **8 rate of exchange** the relationship between the money of 2 countries

rate[2] *v* to fix a value on: *I rate him high*

rateable, ratable *adj* (of a building or its value) on which rates are charged: *What's the rateable value of this shop?*

rather[1] *adv* **1** a little; quite; slightly: *rather cold weather* **2** more willingly: *I'd rather play tennis than swim* —compare SOONER **3** more; more exactly: *These shoes are comfortable rather than pretty*

rather[2] *interj* Yes, certainly!: *'Would you like a swim?' 'Rather!'*

ratify *v* -fied, -fying *esp. written* to approve and make official: *Parliament has ratified the treaty*

rating *n* **1** the value of a building for rates **2** the class in which a ship or machine is placed according to its size: *a rating of 500, 000 tons* **3** the position given to a radio or television pro-

gramme, or to a record, showing how popular it is: *good ratings* **4** (in the British navy) a sailor who is not an officer

ratio *n* -os the relation between 2 quantities as shown when one is divided by the other: *£0.14 and £1.00 are in the ratio 14: 100 or 7: 50* —compare PROPORTION

ration[1] *n* a share (of food, petrol, etc.) allowed to one person for a period

ration[2] *v* **1** to limit (someone) to a fixed ration **2** to limit and control (supplies)

rational *adj* **1** able to reason **2** (of ideas and behaviour) sensible: *a rational suggestion* — opposite **irrational** — ~ly *adv* — ~ity *n*

rationalist *adj, n* (typical of) a person who bases his opinions and actions on reason — ~ic *adj* — -lism *n*

rationalize, -ise *v* -ized, -izing **1** to find reasons (for one's own unreasonable behaviour or opinions) **2** to make (a method or system) more modern and sensible and less wasteful — -ization *n*

rational number *n* a number (e.g. -4, 3/2, 13/32) which when expressed as a decimal either stops after a certain number of places or recurs —compare IRRATIONAL NUMBER

ratline, -lin *n* one of a set of short ropes forming a rope ladder for sailors to climb the shrouds of a ship

rat race *n* *esp. spoken* the endless competition for success

rat-tat *n* a sound of knocking, esp. on a door

rattle[1] *v* -tled, -tling **1** to make or cause to make a lot of quick little noises as of objects hitting each other repeatedly **2** *esp. spoken* to make nervous or anxious **3** to say or talk quickly and easily: *He rattled off the poem*

rattle[2] *n* **1** a toy or instrument that rattles **2** a rattling noise

rattlebrained *adj* (of a person) foolish and always talking

rattlesnake *n* a poisonous American snake that makes a noise with its tail when angry

ratty *adj* -tier, -tiest **1** *esp. spoken* annoyed **2** full of rats

raucous *adj* (of voices) rough and unpleasant — ~ly *adv* — ~ness *n*

ravage *v* -aged, -aging **1** to ruin and destroy **2** (of an army or large crowd) to rob with violence (an area)

ravages *n* destroying effects: *the ravages of war*

rave[1] *v* raved, raving **1** to talk wildly as if mad **2** to speak with excited admiration: *They raved about the new singer*

rave[2] *n* **1** *esp. spoken* very eager praise (esp. of a work of art): *The play got rave reviews* **2** *sl* a wild exciting party

ravel *v* -ll- **1** to unravel **2** to make or become twisted and knotted

raven *n* **1** a very large shiny black bird of the crow family **2** *literature* the shiny black colour of this bird

ravenous adj very hungry △ RAVISH — ~**ly** adv

raver n esp. spoken an exciting person who leads an exciting modern life

rave-up n sl a very wild party

ravine n a deep narrow valley with steep sides —see VALLEY (USAGE)

raving adj, adv talking wildly

ravings n wild uncontrolled talk

ravioli n a food in the form of small cases of flour paste (PASTA) containing meat and other fillings —compare SPAGHETTI, MACARONI

ravish v 1 literature to rape 2 literature to seize or rob with violence 3 to fill with delight: ravished by her beauty △ RAVENOUS

ravishing adj very beautiful — ~**ly** adv

raw[1] adj 1 (of food) not cooked 2 in the natural state: raw silk 3 (of a person) not yet experienced: a raw recruit 4 (of a part of the body) without skin; painful: hands raw with cold 5 (of weather) cold and wet: a raw winter day — ~**ness** n

raw[2] n 1 **in the raw a** without civilization: life in the raw b nude 2 **touch (someone) on the raw** to hurt (someone's) feelings by mentioning a sensitive subject

rawhide n untreated cow's leather

raw material n a natural substance from which an article is made

ray[1] n **rays** any of various types of large flat sea fish, related to the shark

ray[2] n 1 a narrow beam (of light): the sun's rays 2 a very small bit: a ray of hope

rayon n a smooth silk-like material made from wool or cotton (CELLULOSE)

raze v **razed, razing** esp. written to flatten (buildings, towns, etc.) to the ground

razor n an instrument for shaving —see SAFETY RAZOR

razor edge also **razor's edge**— n a critical situation

razzle n a noisy pleasure party

R.C. n abbrev. for: Roman Catholic

Rd abbrev. for: Road

re[1] n the 2nd note in the (sol-fa) musical scale

re[2] prep (esp. in business letters) on the subject of; with regard to: re your enquiry of the 19th October

reach[1] v 1 to stretch out a hand or arm for some purpose 2 (of things or places) to be big enough to touch; stretch out as far as: The ladder won't reach the window 3 to get to: They reached London 4 to get a message to; get in touch with

reach[2] n 1 the distance that one can reach: within reach of the shops 2 a straight stretch of water between 2 bends in a river

react v 1 to act in reply 2 technical (of a substance) to change when mixed with another: An acid can react with a base to form a salt

reaction n 1 a case of reacting: What was your reaction to the news? 2 (in science) **a** a force exercised by a body in reply to another force **b** a change caused in a chemical substance by the action of another

reactionary adj, n **-ries** (a person) against or preventing changes in society

reactivate v **-ated, -ating** to make or become active again

reactive adj (of a chemical substance) that reacts — ~**ly** adv — ~**ness** n

reactor n 1 NUCLEAR REACTOR 2 a container for a chemical reaction

read[1] v **read, reading** 1 to understand (language in print or writing) **2** to understand (something printed or written): Can you read French? 3 to say (printed or written words): read aloud 4 to get information from print or writing: read about the murder 5 to study (a subject) at university level: John's reading history at Oxford 6 (of measuring instruments) to show 7 **read between the lines** to find a meaning that is not expressed

read[2] n esp. spoken 1 an act or period of reading: a read of the paper 2 something to be read: a good read

readable adj 1 interesting or easy to read 2 legible — **-bility** n

readdress also **redirect**— v to send, by writing a different address: readdress letters

reader n 1 a person who reads 2 (the job of) a university teacher above the rank of lecturer 3 a type of schoolbook for beginners

readership n 1 the number of readers of a newspaper 2 the position of a reader: a readership in history

readily adv 1 willingly 2 with no difficulty

readiness n 1 willingness: readiness to learn 2 quickness: readiness of tongue 3 the state of being ready: everything in readiness

reading n 1 the act or practice of reading 2 knowledge obtained through books: a man of little reading 3 a figure shown by a measuring instrument 4 matter to be read 5 (in Parliament) one of the 3 official occasions on which a suggested new bill is read aloud and considered

readjust v to get or put back into the proper position — ~**ment** n: a period of readjustment

readout n 1 the work of removing information from a computer and of showing it in an understandable form 2 the information produced in this way

ready[1] adj **-ier, -iest** 1 prepared and fit: The letters are ready 2 (of a person) willing and eager: ready to help 3 (of thoughts or their expression) quick: ready wit — **ready** adv : buy the meat ready cut

ready[2] n the state of being ready: at the ready

ready-made adj (of something bought) not made specially for the buyer

ready money also **ready cash**— n money that can be paid at once in coins and notes

reafforest v to plant again with trees — ~**ation** n

reagent n technical a substance that by causing

chemical reaction in a compound shows the presence of another substance

real *adj* 1 actually existing; true 2 *technical* (of a number) having a square greater than or equal to O: *Integers, rational numbers, and irrational numbers are all real*

real estate *n* also **real property**— *esp. written & law* property in land and houses

realign *v* to form into new groups, regular arrangements, etc: *to realign one's forces* — ~ment *n*

realism *n* 1 determination to face facts and deal with them practically, without being influenced by feelings or false ideas 2 (in art and literature) the showing of things as they really are —compare ROMANTICISM, CLASSICISM 3 (in philosophy) the belief that matter really exists outside our own minds —compare IDEALISM — **-list n**

realistic *adj* 1 showing realism 2 (of art or literature) life-like — ~**ally** *adv*

reality *n* **-ties** 1 the quality of being real 2 something real: *Her dream of marrying Frederick became a reality* 3 everything that is real: *to escape from reality by going to the cinema*

realize, -lise *v* **-lized, -lizing** 1 to understand and believe (a fact): *I didn't realize how late it was* 2 to make real (a hope): *She realized her intention of becoming an actress* — **-lization** *n*

really *adv* 1 in actual fact; truly 2 thoroughly: *I really hate him* 3 (used for showing interest or suprise): *'I collect rare coins.' 'Really?'*

realm *n* 1 *literature & law* a kingdom 2 a world; area: *the realm of science*

realpolitik *n* politics based on practical and material facts rather than on ideas or moral aims

real property *n esp. written, esp. law* REAL ESTATE

real tennis *n* an old form of tennis, played in a special indoor court

real time *n technical* the actual time in which an event takes place (used of events controlled by computers)

ream *n* 1 a measure for sheets of paper; (in Britain) 500 sheets 2 *esp. spoken* a lot (of writing): *reams of poetry*

reanimate *v* **-mated, -mating** to fill with new strength or courage; bring back to life

reap *v* to cut and gather (a crop of grain) — compare HARVEST — ~**er** *n*

reappear *v* to appear again after absence — ~**ance** *n*

reappraisal *n* 1 the act of examining something again to see whether one should change one's opinion 2 a new judgment formed in this way

rear[1] *v* 1 to care for until fully grown — compare RAISE 2 to lift up (a part of oneself): *reared his head* 3 (of a 4-legged animal) to rise upright on the back legs

rear[2] *n* 1 the back: *the rear wheel* 2 *polite* the buttocks 3 **bring up the rear** to come last

rear admiral *n* an officer of high rank in the navy

rearguard *n* 1 a formation of soldiers protecting the rear of an army —compare VANGUARD 2 **rearguard action** a fight by the rear of an army that is retreating

rearm *v* to provide (oneself or others) with new weapons — ~**ament** *n*

rearmost *adj* last; furthest back

rearrange *v* **-ranged, -ranging** to put into a different order — ~**ment** *n*

rearward also **rearwards**— *adj, adv, n* (at, in, or to) the rear

reason[1] *n* 1 the cause of an event; the explanation or excuse for an action 2 what makes one decide on an action: *What is your reason for leaving?* 3 the power to think, understand, and form opinions 4 good sense: *There's a great deal of reason in his advice* 5 **it stands to reason** it is clear to all sensible people 6 **listen to reason** to allow oneself to be persuaded by good advice 7 **with reason** (of something said or believed) rightly: *He thinks, with reason, that I don't like him* USAGE Some people think a sentence such as *The reason for my absence was because I was ill* is bad English. It may be better to say: *The reason for my absence was that I was ill.* —compare CAUSE; see EXCUSE (USAGE)

reason[2] *v* 1 to think: *to reason clearly* 2 to persuade (someone) by arguing: *Try to reason with him* — ~**er** *n*

reasonable *adj* 1 (of a person or his behaviour) sensible: *a reasonable thing to do* —opposite **unreasonable**; see LOGIC (USAGE) 2 (esp. of prices) fair; not too much — **-bleness** *n*

reasonably *adv* 1 sensibly 2 fairly; rather: *reasonably good*

reasoned *adj* (of a statement, argument, etc.) clearly thought out

reasoning *n* the use of one's reason

reassure *v* **-sured, -suring** to comfort and make free from fear (someone anxious) — **-surance** *n* — **-suringly** *adv*

rebate *n* an official return of part of a payment —compare DISCOUNT

rebel[1] *n* a person who rebels

rebel[2] *v* **-ll-** to fight, often with violence (against anyone in power, esp. the government)

rebellion *n* an act or the state of rebelling —compare REVOLUTION

rebellious *adj* disobedient and hard to control: *rebellious behaviour* — ~**ly** *adv* — ~**ness** *n*

rebirth *n* a renewal of life; return: *the rebirth of learning*

reborn *adj* as if born again: *hopes reborn*

rebound[1] *v* to fly back after hitting something: *The ball rebounded from the wall*

rebound[2] *n* **on the rebound a** while rebounding **b** as a quick action in reply to failure or unpleasantness: *marry a different girl on the rebound*

rebuff *v, n* (to give) a rough or cruel answer when someone is trying to be friendly or is asking for help

rebuild *v* **rebuilt, rebuilding** to build again or build new parts to

rebuke¹ _v_ rebuked, rebuking to give a rebuke to

rebuke² _n_ a short scolding esp. given officially

rebus _n_ any word game in which words are guessed from pictures or letters that suggest their sounds: _"R U 18" is a rebus for "Are you 18?"_

rebut _v_ -tt- to prove the falsity of (a statement or charge); refute — **rebuttal** _n_

recalcitrant _adj, n_ (a person) that is disobedient, refusing to obey or be controlled — -trance _n_

recall¹ _v_ 1 to remember 2 to call or take back: _The makers have recalled a lot of unsafe cars_ — ~able _adj_

recall² _n_ 1 a call to return: _the recall of the general from abroad_ 2 the power to remember something: _total recall_ 3 a signal to soldiers to come back

recant _v_ to say publicly that one no longer holds (a former political or religious opinion): _He recanted his faith_ — ~ation _n_

recap¹ _v_ -pp- esp. spoken to recapitulate

recap² _n_ esp. spoken a recapitulation: _a recap of what was said_

recapitulate _v_ -lated, -lating to repeat (the chief points of something that has been said) — -lation _n_

recapture _v_ -tured, -turing 1 to capture again 2 to bring back into the mind: _to recapture one's youth_

recd _abbrev. for:_ received

recede _v_ receded, receding (of things) to move or incline back or away

receipt _n_ 1 a written statement that one has received money 2 the event of receiving: _the receipt of the cheque_ 3 **be in receipt of** _pompous_ to have received

receipts _n_ the money received from a business: _higher receipts_

receivable _adj_ able or fit to be received

receive _v_ received, receiving 1 to get (something given or sent to one) —compare RECIPIENT 2 to suffer; be the subject of: _receive a blow on the head_

receiver _n_ 1 a person who deals in stolen property 2 the part of a telephone that is held to one's ear 3 an instrument for receiving radio, television, etc., signals 4 (in British law) the person officially appointed to take charge of affairs of a bankrupt 5 (in tennis, squash, and such games) a player who receives service from his opponent

receiving _n_ the crime of being a receiver of stolen property

recent _adj_ having happened only a short time ago — ~ly _adv_

receptacle _n_ technical a container for keeping things in

reception _n_ 1 an act of receiving: _a friendly reception_ 2 a large formal party: _a wedding reception_ 3 the office that receives visitors, guests, etc.: _Leave your key at reception_ 4 the receiving of radio or television signals: _good reception_

receptionist _n_ a person employed to receive people arriving in a hotel, visiting a doctor, etc.

reception room _n_ any room that is not a kitchen, bedroom, or bathroom

receptive _adj_ (of a person or his mind) willing to receive new ideas: _receptive to suggestions_ — ~ly _adv_ — ~ness _n_ — -tivity _n_

receptor _n_ technical a part of the body (such as an eye) that receives information from the outside world and passes it to the brain —compare EFFECTOR

recess¹ _n_ 1 a pause for rest during work 2 a space set back in a wall 3 literature a secret inner part of a place, that is hard to reach: _the recesses of his heart_

recess² _v_ to make or put into a recess: _a recessed bookshelf_

recession _n_ a period of reduced activity of trade

recessional _n_ a hymn sung at the end of a Christian church service

recessive _adj_ (of groups of qualities passed on from parent to child (GENES)) being the quality that is less likely to appear in the child: _Blue eyes are recessive and brown eyes are dominant_

recharge _v_ recharged, recharging to put a new charge of electricity into (a battery)

recherché _adj_ French (esp. of words, ideas, etc., or of food) carefully chosen and perhaps too rare and strange: _a recherché meal_

recidivist _n_ a person who keeps going back to a life of crime — -vism _n_

recipe _n_ a set of instructions for cooking a dish

recipient _n_ a person who receives something

reciprocal¹ _n_ technical the quantity which results when 1 is divided by a given quantity: _The reciprocal of 8 is_ $1/8 = 0.125$

reciprocal² _adj_ mutual — ~ly _adv_

reciprocate _v_ -cated, -cating 1 esp. written to give (something) in return: _He reciprocated my good wishes_ 2 (of a machine part) to move backwards and forwards in a straight line — -cation _n_

recital _n_ 1 a performance of poetry or music, given by one performer or a small group — compare CONCERT 2 a telling of a set of facts: _a recital of his experiences_

recitative _n_ a speech set to music but not to a tune, continuing the story of an opera between the songs

recite _v_ recited, reciting 1 to say (something learned) aloud from memory: _recite a poem_ 2 to give a list of: _recite his complaints_ — **recitation** _n_ — reciter _n_

reckless _adj_ (of a person or his behaviour) too hasty; not caring about danger: _reckless driving_ △ FECKLESS — ~ly _adv_ — ~ness _n_

reckon _v_ 1 to regard: _I reckon him as a friend_ 2 esp. spoken to suppose: _I reckon so_ 3 to add up — ~er _n_

reckoning *n* 1 the act of calculating 2 **day of reckoning** the time when one must suffer for a mistake

reckon on *v prep* to count or depend on

reckon with *v prep* to have to deal with: *We've got him to reckon with now*

reclaim *v* 1 to bring back from wrong behaviour 2 to claim the return of: *reclaim some tax* 3 to make (land) fit for use 4 to obtain from a waste product: *reclaim rubber from old tyres* — **reclamation** *n*

recline *v* **reclined, reclining** to lie back or down

recluse *n* a person who lives alone away from the world on purpose —compare HERMIT

recognition *n* 1 the power to recognize or state of being recognized 2 a reward given in order to recognize someone's behaviour 3 **change beyond/out of all recognition** to change so as to be impossible to recognize

recognize, -nise *v* **-nized, -nizing** 1 to know again (someone or something one has met before) 2 to admit (someone or something) as really being (something): *They refused to recognize him as king* 3 to show official gratefulness for: *The government recognized his services by making him a lord* — **-nizable** *adj* — **-nizably** *adv*

recoil[1] *v* 1 to draw back suddenly as in fear or dislike: *She recoiled at the sight of the snake* 2 (of a gun) to spring back when fired

recoil[2] *n* a sudden backward movement, esp. of a gun after firing

recollect *v* to remember

recollection *n* 1 the power or action of remembering 2 something in one's memory: *That evening is one of my happiest recollections*

recommend *v* 1 to praise as being good for a purpose: *Can you recommend a good dictionary?* 2 to advise: *I recommend you to wait* 3 (of a quality) to make attractive: *This hotel has nothing to recommend it*

recommendation *n* 1 advice; the act of recommending: *buy the car on Paul's recommendation* 2 a letter or statement that recommends (esp. someone for a job)

recommend to *v prep* to give in charge to: *The dying man recommended his soul to God*

recompense[1] *v* **-pensed, -pensing** to give a recompense to

recompense[2] *n* reward or payment for trouble or suffering: *receive £500 in recompense* —compare COMPENSATION, CONSOLATION

reconcile *v* **-ciled, -ciling** 1 to make peace between; make friendly again: *They quarrelled but now they're reconciled* 2 to find agreement between (2 conflicting actions or ideas): *I can't reconcile those 2 ideas* — **-cilable** *adj*

reconcile to *v prep* to cause to accept: *He became reconciled to the loss of his wife*

reconciliation also **reconcilement**— *n* a peace-making

recondition *v* to repair and bring back into working order: *a reconditioned engine*

reconnaissance *n* the act of reconnoitring

reconnoitre *v* **-tred, -tring** to go near (an enemy) in order to find out its position

reconsider *v* to think again and change one's mind about (a subject) — **~ation** *n*

reconstitute *v* **-tuted, -tuting** to form again: *reconstitute the committee/dried milk*

reconstruct *v* 1 to rebuild 2 to build up a description or picture of (something only partly known): *reconstruct a crime* — **~ion** *n*

record[1] *v* 1 to write down so that it will be known: *record past events* 2 to preserve (sound or vision) so that it can be heard or seen again: *a recorded broadcast* —*compare* LIVE 3 (of an instrument) to show by measuring

record[2] *n* 1 a written statement of facts, events, etc. 2 the known facts about someone's past 3 (often in sport) the best yet done 4 also **gramophone record, disc**— a circular piece of plastic on which sound is recorded 5 **for the record** to be reported as official 6 **off the record** unofficial(ly) 7 **on record** (of facts or events) ever recorded: *the coldest winter on record*

record[3] *adj* more, better, etc., than ever before: *a record crop*

recorded delivery *n* the method of sending 1st class mail with proof that it has been delivered

recorder *n* 1 a wooden musical instrument like a whistle, with 8 holes for the fingers 2 TAPE RECORDER

recording *n* a performance, speech, or piece of music that has been recorded

record player also **gramophone**— *n* an instrument which can reproduce the information stored in a record

recount[1] *v* to tell (a story); give an account of

recount[2] *v* to count again

recount[3] *n* another count, esp. of votes: *I demand a recount*

recoup *v* to regain: *I shall recoup my losses*

recourse *n* a means of help: *recourse to drugs to lessen pain* —compare RESORT

recover *v* 1 to get back (something lost or taken away) 2 to get well again: *to recover from a cold* 3 to get (oneself) back into a proper state: *She soon recovered herself and stopped crying* — **~able** *adj*

recovery *n* **-ies** 1 getting back or being got back 2 getting well

recreate *v* **-ated, -ating** to make again

recreation *n* a form of amusement, or way of spending free time

recreational *adj* providing recreation

recreation ground *n* a piece of public land set aside for games

recriminate *v* **-nated, -nating** to make a charge against a person who has made a charge against oneself — **-natory** *adj* : *recriminatory remarks*

recrimination *n* quarrelling and blaming one another

recruit[1] *n* 1 someone who has just joined one of

the armed forces **2** a new member of any organization

recruit² v **1** to find recruits **2** to get (someone) as a recruit: *recruit some new members* — ~**ment** n

rectangle n *technical* a 4-sided figure (PARALLELOGRAM) whose angles are right angles ☞ MATHEMATICS — **-gular** adj

rectification n rectifying or being rectified

rectifier n **1** someone or something that rectifies **2** *technical* a instrument that rectifies ☞ ELECTRICITY

rectify v **-fied, -fying** **1** to put right: *rectify the mistakes in my bill* **2** *technical* to change (the flow of electricity to and fro along a wire (ALTERNATING CURRENT)) so that it flows only one way (DIRECT CURRENT)

rectilinear adj *esp. written & technical* forming or moving in a straight line; having or made of straight lines

rectitude n *esp. written* honesty of character

rector n **1** (in the Church of England) the priest in charge of a parish from which he receives his income directly —compare VICAR **2** the head of certain colleges and schools

rectory n **-ries** the house where a rector lives

rectum n *medical* the lowest end of the large bowel, through which solid waste matter passes from the colon to the anus ☞ DIGESTION — **-tal** adj

recumbent adj *esp. written* lying down on the back or side

recuperate v **-rated, -rating** to recover from illness — **-ration** n

recuperative adj (of actions or events) helping one to recuperate

recur v **-rr-** **1** to happen again or often **2** (of a decimal) to be repeated for ever in the same order: *In 5.1515 . . . (also written 5.15) the figures 15 recur, and the number can be read "5.15 recurring"*

recurrence n the quality or an example of recurring

recurrent adj recurring: *recurrent pains* — ~**ly** adv

recusant adj, n *esp. written & old use* (someone) refusing to obey official rules: *People who refused to belong to the Church of England were once called 'recusants'*

recycle v **-cled, -cling** to treat (a used substance) so that it is can be used again: *recycle waste paper*

red¹ adj **-dd-** **1** of the colour of blood or of fire **2** (of hair) of a bright brownish orange colour **3** (of wine) of a dark purple colour —see also red HERRING — ~**ness** n — ~**dish** adj

red² n **1** (a) red colour: *mix red and yellow to make orange* **2** the state of owing money to the bank: *be in the red* —opposite **black** **3 paint the town red** *esp. spoken* to go out and be noisily merry **4 see red** to become angry suddenly

Red adj communist: *The Red Army is the army of the USSR*

red admiral n a kind of butterfly with bright red bands on its black wings

red blood cell also **red corpuscle**— n one of the cells in the blood which carry oxygen to every part of the body —compare WHITE BLOOD CELL; see also HAEMOGLOBIN

red-blooded adj (of a person, his behaviour, etc.) bold, strong, and forceful

redbrick n any English university started in the late 19th century in a city outside London — compare OXBRIDGE

Red Cross also (in some Muslim countries) **Red Crescent**— n an international charity that looks after sick and wounded people

redcurrant n a kind of bush or the small red edible berry that grows in bunches on it

red deer n **-deer** a type of large deer common in northern Europe and Asia, with a reddish brown coat

redden v to blush

redecorate v **-rated, -rating** to apply new paint, paper, etc.,

redeem v **1** to buy or gain the freedom of, esp. (in the Christian religion) the freedom from evil: *redeem us from sin* **2** to regain with money (what was pawned or mortgaged): *redeem my watch from the pawnshop* **3** to fulfil: *redeem one's promise* — ~**able** adj

Redeemer n Jesus Christ

redeeming feature n something good in an otherwise bad person or thing

redemption n redeeming or being redeemed

red ensign n the flag used by British non-naval ships —compare WHITE ENSIGN

redeploy v **-ployed, -ploying** to rearrange (soldiers, workers, etc.) in a more effective way — ~**ment** n

red flag n the flag or song of the political left

red giant n a coolish star, near to the middle of its life, larger and less solid than the sun — compare WHITE DWARF

red-handed adj in the act of doing something wrong: *They caught the thief red-handed*

redhead n a person with red hair

red-hot adj (of metal) so hot that it glows red

Red Indian n an American Indian

redistribute v **-buted, -buting** to share out again in a different way — **-ution** n

red-letter day n **-days** a specially good day

red-light district n the part of a town where one can hire women for sexual pleasure (PROSTITUTES)

red meat n mutton or beef

redo v **redid, redone, redoing** to do again: *redo a piece of work*

redolent adj *esp. written* smelling of; making one think of — **-lence** n

redouble v **-led, -ling** to double again; increase greatly

redoubtable adj *literature & humour* greatly respected and feared: *a redoubtable opponent*

redound to v prep *esp. written* to add to;

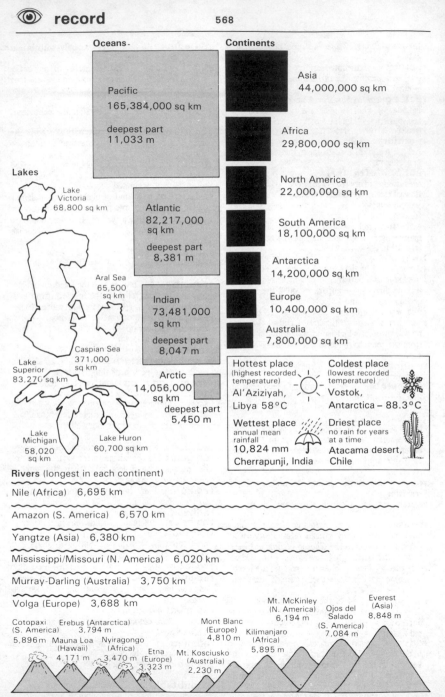

Oceans

Pacific
165,384,000 sq km
deepest part
11,033 m

Atlantic
82,217,000 sq km
deepest part
8,381 m

Indian
73,481,000 sq km
deepest part
8,047 m

Arctic
14,056,000 sq km
deepest part
5,450 m

Continents

Asia
44,000,000 sq km

Africa
29,800,000 sq km

North America
22,000,000 sq km

South America
18,100,000 sq km

Antarctica
14,200,000 sq km

Europe
10,400,000 sq km

Australia
7,800,000 sq km

Lakes

Lake Victoria
68,800 sq km

Aral Sea
65,500 sq km

Caspian Sea
371,000 sq km

Lake Superior
83,270 sq km

Lake Michigan
58,020 sq km

Lake Huron
60,700 sq km

Hottest place (highest recorded temperature)
Al'Aziziyah, Libya 58°C

Coldest place (lowest recorded temperature)
Vostok, Antarctica – 88.3°C

Wettest place annual mean rainfall
10,824 mm
Cherrapunji, India

Driest place
no rain for years at a time
Atacama desert, Chile

Rivers (longest in each continent)

Nile (Africa)   6,695 km

Amazon (S. America)   6,570 km

Yangtze (Asia)   6,380 km

Mississippi/Missouri (N. America)   6,020 km

Murray-Darling (Australia)   3,750 km

Volga (Europe)   3,688 km

Cotopaxi (S. America) 5,896 m
Erebus (Antarctica) 3,794 m
Mauna Loa (Hawaii) 4,171 m
Nyiragongo (Africa) 3,470 m
Etna (Europe) 3,323 m
Mt. Kosciusko (Australia) 2,230 m
Mont Blanc (Europe) 4,810 m
Kilimanjaro (Africa) 5,895 m
Mt. McKinley (N. America) 6,194 m
Ojos del Salado (S. America) 7,084 m
Everest (Asia) 8,848 m

Active volcanoes   **Mountains** (highest in each continent)

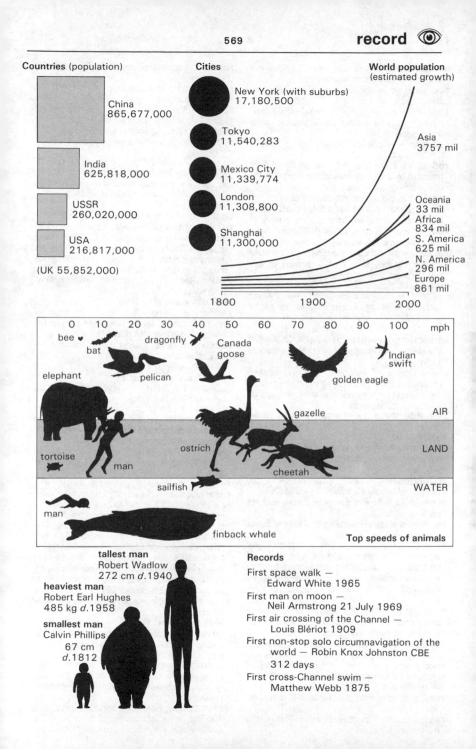

Countries (population)

China
865,677,000

India
625,818,000

USSR
260,020,000

USA
216,817,000

(UK 55,852,000)

Cities

New York (with suburbs)
17,180,500

Tokyo
11,540,283

Mexico City
11,339,774

London
11,308,800

Shanghai
11,300,000

World population
(estimated growth)

Asia
3757 mil

Oceania
33 mil
Africa
834 mil
S. America
625 mil
N. America
296 mil
Europe
861 mil

1800   1900   2000

0 10 20 30 40 50 60 70 80 90 100 mph

bee
bat
dragonfly
Canada goose
Indian swift
elephant
pelican
golden eagle

gazelle   AIR

ostrich
tortoise
man   cheetah   LAND

sailfish   WATER
man
finback whale   **Top speeds of animals**

tallest man
Robert Wadlow
272 cm d.1940

heaviest man
Robert Earl Hughes
485 kg d.1958

smallest man
Calvin Phillips
67 cm
d.1812

Records

First space walk —
Edward White 1965

First man on moon —
Neil Armstrong 21 July 1969

First air crossing of the Channel —
Louis Blériot 1909

First non-stop solo circumnavigation of the
world — Robin Knox Johnston CBE
312 days

First cross-Channel swim —
Matthew Webb 1875

increase (fame, honour, etc.): *Any help you can give us will redound to your credit*

red pepper *n* the red fruit of the capsicum plant, used as a vegetable

redress¹ *v esp. written* **1** to put right (a wrong, injustice, etc.) **2 redress the balance** to make things equal again

redress² *n esp. written* satisfaction for a wrong that has been done

red shift *n* the change in the quality of light produced by a tar, that tells astronomers that the star is moving away from us

redskin *n old use* an American Indian

red squirrel *n* a type of small animal with a long bushy tail and red fur that lives in trees

red tape *n* silly rules, full of details, that delay (esp. government) business

reduce *v* **reduced, reducing** **1** to make smaller, cheaper, etc. **2** (of a person) to lose weight on purpose — **reducible** *adj*

reduce to *v prep* **1** to bring down to: *The fire reduced the forest to a few trees.* | *reduced to the ranks* **2** to change (something) to (its parts): *reduce the rocks to dust* **3** to force (someone) into: *She was reduced to begging*

reductio ad absurdum *n Latin* the disproof of a piece of reasoning by showing that it leads to a silly result

reduction *n* **1** making or becoming smaller; the amount taken off in making something smaller **2** a smaller copy (of a picture, map, or photograph) —opposite **enlargement**

redundancy *n* **-cies** a case of being redundant

redundant *adj* **1** not needed; more than is necessary **2** (of a worker or group of workers) not needed because there is not enough work — **~ly** *adv*

reduplicate *v* **-cated, -cating** to make again; repeat: *reduplicate his efforts* — **-cation** *n*

redwing *n* a type of European thrush with red parts on its wings

redwood *n* any of several types of tall coniferous tree that grow in California

reed *n* **1** (the tall strong hollow stem of) any of various grasslike plants that grow in wet places **2** (in a musical instrument) a thin piece of wood or metal that produces sound by vibrating in an air stream **3 broken reed** *esp. spoken* a weak helper

reed instrument *n* a musical instrument such as the oboe, bassoon, or clarinet, in which sound is produced by the movement of a reed

reeducate *v* **-cated, -cating** to train (someone) again: *reeducate young criminals* — **-cation** *n*

reedy *adj* **-ier, -iest** **1** (of a place) full of reeds **2** (of a sound) thin and high: *a reedy voice* — **reediness** *n*

reef¹ *v* to tie up (part of a sail) so as to reduce the size

reef² *n* a line of rocks, coral, or sand, at or near the surface of the sea

reefer *n* a short thick close-fitting coat, as worn by sailors

reef knot *n* a kind of double knot that will not come undone easily

reek¹ *n* **1** a strong unpleasant smell: *a reek of fish* **2** *literature & Scots* a thick smoke

reek² *v* to give out smoke: *a reeking chimney*

reek of *v prep* to smell strongly and unpleasantly of

reel¹ *n* **1** a round object on which a length of wire, fishing line, recording tape, etc., can be wound **2** a usu. small wooden or plastic one of these on which sewing thread is sold —compare BOBBIN

reel² *v* to wind on a reel: *reel up the fish*

reel³ *v* **1** to walk unsteadily as if drunk **2** to step away suddenly and unsteadily, as after a blow or shock **3** to be confused in the mind: *Numbers make my head reel* **4** to seem to go round and round: *The room reeled*

reel⁴ *n* (the music for) a high-spirited Scottish or Irish dance

reel off *v adv* to rattle off

reentry *n* **-tries** **1** an act or the action of entering again **2** (of a spacecraft) an act or the action of returning into the earth's atmosphere

reeve *n* (in former times) the chief law officer of an English town or larger area

ref *n esp. spoken* a referee

ref. *abbrev. for:* reference

refectory *n* **-ries** (in schools, colleges, etc.) a large hall in which meals are served

referee¹ *n* **1** a judge in charge of a team game such as football —compare UMPIRE **2** a person who is asked to settle a disagreement **3** a person who is asked to supply a reference USAGE This word is used in connection with **basketball, billiards, boxing, football, hockey, rugby,** and **wrestling.**

referee² *v* **-eed, -eeing** to act as referee for

reference *n* **1** a case of mentioning: *a reference to Janet* **2** a case of looking at for information: *Keep this dictionary for reference* **3** a statement about someone's character, ability, etc., esp. when he is looked for employment **4 in/with reference to** in connection with USAGE A **testimonial** is shown to the person it describes and is therefore less frank than a **reference** which is not shown to him. The 2 words are now beginning to be used with the same meaning.

reference book *n* a book that is looked at for information

reference library *n* **-ries** **1** (the place containing) a collection of books that may be studied only in the place where they are kept **2** a collection of reference books

referendum *n* **-da** or **-dums** a direct vote by all the people of a nation or area on some particular question, such as a suggested law —compare PLEBISCITE

refer to *v prep* **-rr-** **1** to mention; speak about **2** to look at for information **3** to concern: *The new law does not refer to farm land* **4** to send back for decision or action: *The shop referred the complaint to the manufacturers* — ~**able to** *adj*

refill¹ *v* to fill again

refill² *n* a quantity of ink, petrol, etc., to refill something, often in a special container

refine *v* refined, refining to make pure

refined *adj* (of a person, his behaviour, etc.) having or showing education and manners

refinement *n* 1 the act of making pure 2 the quality of being refined 3 a clever addition or improvement

refiner *n* a machine that refines something

refinery *n* -ries a building and apparatus for refining metals, oil, or sugar: *a sugar refinery* ◉

refit¹ *v* -tt- (esp. of a ship) to be re-equipped and overhauled

refit² *n* a case of refitting

reflate *v* reflated, reflating to increase the supply of money in (a money system) to a desirable level

reflation *n* the official practice of increasing the amount of money to a desirable level in relation to the amount of goods —compare DEFLATION, INFLATION

reflect *v* 1 to throw back (heat, light, sound, or an image) 2 to give an idea of: *Does this letter reflect your opinion?* 3 to consider carefully

reflecting telescope *n* a telescope in which the image is enlarged by reflection in a mirror —compare REFRACTING TELESCOPE ⎯☞ TELESCOPE

reflection *n* 1 the reflecting of heat, light, sound, or an image 2 an image reflected in a mirror or polished surface 3 (a) deep and careful thought

reflective *adj* thoughtful

reflector *n* a surface that reflects light, heat, etc.

reflex also **reflex action**— *n* a movement that is made by instinct in reply to some outside influence, without power to prevent it —see also CONDITIONED REFLEX

reflex angle *n* technical an angle greater than 180°

reflex camera *n* a camera that shows the image on a small glass screen by means of a mirror

reflexes *n* actions done in reply to an outside influence, esp. considered for their speed: *The doctor hit my knee with a hammer to test my reflexes*

reflexive *n, adj* (in grammar) (a word) showing that the action in the sentence has its effect on the person or thing that does the action: *In 'I hurt myself'* myself *is a reflexive pronoun*

reform¹ *v* 1 to improve; make or become right: *We should try to reform criminals* 2 to cause reforms in: *try to reform society* —see REFORM (USAGE) — ~**er** *n*

reform² *n* social action to improve conditions, remove unfairness, etc.   USAGE The noun **reform** is used particularly of social and religious

improvement, while **reformation** is used also of improvement in a person's character and behaviour. The verb **reform** has both meanings.

re-form *v* to form again, esp. into ranks: *The soldiers re-formed*

reformation *n* improvement; reforming or being reformed —see REFORM (USAGE)

Reformation *n* the religious movement in Europe in the 16th century leading to the establishment of the reformed or Protestant churches

reformatory also **reformative**— *adj* of or leading to reform

refract *v* (of water, glass, etc.) to cause (light) to change direction when passing through at an angle — ~**ion** *n* *n*

refracting telescope *n* a telescope in which the image is refracted by passing through a lens —compare REFLECTING TELESCOPE ⎯☞ TELESCOPE

refractory *adj* 1 disobedient and troublesome: *a refractory horse* 2 technical (of materials, esp. metals) difficult to melt; able to bear high temperatures

refrain¹ *v* to hold oneself back (from); avoid: *to refrain from smoking*

refrain² *n* a part of a song that is repeated, esp. at the end of each verse

refresh *v* 1 to get rid of the tiredness of; make fresh again 2 **refresh one's memory** to cause oneself to remember again

refresher course *n* a training course to bring professional knowledge up to date: *refresher course on modern teaching methods*

refreshing *adj* producing a feeling of comfort and new strength — ~**ly** *adv*

refreshment *n* 1 the experience of being refreshed 2 food and drink

refreshments *n* (esp. light) food and drink

refrigerate *v* -rated, -rating to make cold; freeze (food, liquid, etc.) — ~**rant** *n* — -**ration** *n*

refrigerator also (*esp. spoken*) **fridge**— *n* a machine in which food or drink can be kept for a time at a low temperature —compare FREEZER

refuel *v* -ll- to fill up again with fuel

refuge *n* 1 a place that provides protection 2 also **traffic island** — technical a place in the middle of a street where people can wait until it is safe to cross the rest of the way

refugee *n* a person who has left his country for political reasons or during a war

refulgent *adj* literature (of light) very bright: *the refulgent glory of the midday sun* — -**gence** *n*

refund¹ *v* to give as a refund

refund² *n* a repayment

refurbish *v* to polish up or make bright again (something old)

refusal *n* 1 a case of refusing 2 **first refusal** the right to decide whether to buy something before it is offered to other people

refuse¹ *v* refused, refusing not to accept, do, or give: *She refused his offer*

refuse² *n* waste material: *kitchen refuse*

Refinery

Oil and gas, besides providing petrol for cars and heating for houses, can be refined into many other useful products. Plastics are the basis of fabrics like nylon, PVC, polyester, and acrylic, as well as polyurethane, polythene, and polystyrene.

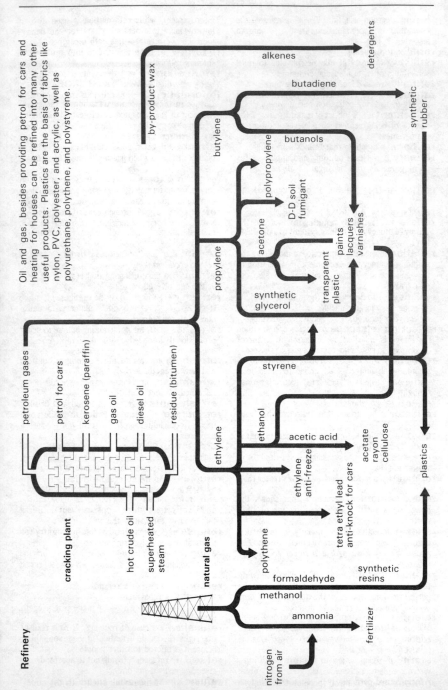

refutable adj that can be refuted —opposite irrefutable

refutation n a proof that something is untrue

refute v refuted, refuting to prove to be mistaken: *I refuted him easily* USAGE **Refute** does NOT mean **deny**. Do not say: *He refuted the newspaper's allegations* if you merely mean: *He denied the allegations*. To refute something one must use definite arguments.

regain v 1 to get or win back 2 to reach again: *to regain the shore* 3 **regain one's balance** to get back on one's feet after slipping

regal adj very splendid; of or suitable for a king — ~ly adv

regale with also regale on— v prep regaled, regaling with to give enjoyment to (oneself or another) with (something pleasant): *He regaled us with some jokes*

regalia n 1 the ornaments, crown, etc., worn or carried by a king or queen at royal ceremonies 2 the ceremonial clothes and ornaments that show one's official position: *a mayor's regalia*

regard¹ n 1 respect: *I hold her in high regard* 2 **in this regard** on this subject 3 **with regard to** regarding

regard² v 1 to look at 2 to consider: *I have always regarded him highly.* | *She regarded him as stupid*

regardful adj full of regard: *You should be regardful of your father's wishes*

regarding also as regards— prep esp. written on the subject of; in connection with

regardless adv whatever may happen: *Get the money, regardless!*

regards n 1 good wishes 2 **With kind regards** (a friendly but formal way of ending a letter)

regatta n a meeting for races between rowing or sailing boats

regelation n technical the freezing again of water that came from ice melting under temporary pressure, when the pressure is removed

regency n -cies government by a regent

Regency n 1 (in Britain) the period 1811–1820 2 the British style of the period 1810–1830: *a Regency chair*

regenerate v -rated, -rating 1 to improve morally 2 to grow again: *This creature's tail will regenerate if it's cut off* — -ration n

regent n a person who governs in place of a king or ruling queen

reggae n popular dance and music from the West Indies

regicide n (a person who commits) the crime of killing a king or queen

regime n French 1 a particular (type of) government 2 a regimen

regimen n a fixed plan of food, sleep, etc., in order to improve one's health

regiment¹ n 1 a large military group, commanded by a colonel 2 a very large number (of living creatures): *a regiment of ants* — ~al adj

regiment² v to control (people) too firmly:

Modern children don't like being regimented — ~ation n

regimentals n the uniform worn by the men of a particular regiment

Regina n Latin 1 (the title used after the name of a ruling queen): *Elizabeth Regina* 2 law (used, when a queen is ruling, in titles of lawsuits) the State; the crown: *Regina v Jones* (=the Crown against Jones) —compare REX

region n 1 a general area: *a tropical region* | *the region of the heart* 2 technical a flat space bounded by curved lines (ARCS) 3 **in the region of** about: *in the region of $3500* 4 **the lower regions** hell — ~al adj — ~ally adv

regions n the parts of a country away from the capital

register¹ n 1 a record or list: *a register of births and deaths* 2 a book containing such a record —see also CASH REGISTER 3 the range of a human voice or musical instrument

register² v 1 to put into an official list or record 2 (of machines or instruments) to show; record 3 (of a person or his face) to express: *Her face registered anxiety* 4 to send by registered post

registered post n a postal service that, for an additional charge, protects the sender of a valuable letter or parcel against loss

register office also registry office— n an office where marriages can lawfully take place and where births, marriages, and deaths are recorded

registrar n 1 a keeper of official records 2 an official in a British court of law, junior to a judge

registration n 1 the act of registering 2 a fact that has been registered

registration document n (in Britain) a document containing the details of a particular motor vehicle

registration number n the official set of figures and letters that must be shown on a motor vehicle

registry n -tries a place where records are kept

regnant adj esp. written reigning (esp. of a queen in her own right and not as the king's wife)

regress v to return to a worse or less developed earlier state — ~ion n — ~ive adj

regret¹ v -tt- to be sorry about

regret² n sadness — ~ful adj — ~fully adv — ~fulness n

regrets n 1 (used in polite expressions of refusal) a note or message refusing an invitation: *to send one's regrets* 2 **have no regrets** not to feel sorry about what has happened

regrettable adj that one should regret; worthy of blame: *Your choice of friends is regrettable* — -bly adv

regroup v to form into new groups or into groups again

regular¹ adj 1 happening often with the same

length of time between the occasions **2** frequent: *a regular customer* **3** happening every time: *regular attendance* **4** not varying: *a regular speed* **5** proper; according to rule or custom: *He knows a lot about the law but he's not a regular lawyer* **6** evenly shaped: *regular features* **7** *technical* (of a polygon) having all sides and angles equal: *A square is a regular quadrilateral* **8** professional: *the regular army* **9** living under a particular religious rule of life: *Ordinary Roman Catholic priests are not members of the regular clergy, but monks are* **10** (in grammar) following a common pattern: *The verb 'dance' is regular, but the verb 'be' is* **irregular 11 keep regular hours** to follow the same quiet sensible way of life all the time — ~**ity** *n*

regular² *n* **1** a soldier who is a member of a regular army **2** a regular visitor, customer, etc.

regularize, -ise *v* **-ized, -izing** to make lawful and official — **-ization** *n*

regularly *adv* **1** at regular times **2** in a regular way: *regularly shaped*

regulate *v* **-lated, -lating 1** to fix or control **2** to make (a machine, esp. a clock or watch) work correctly

regulation *n* **1** control **2** an official rule or order

regulator *n* a thing that regulates

regulo *n* **-los** a degree of heat in a gas oven: *regulo 4*

regurgitate *v* **-tated, -tating** *esp. written* to pour out again from the mouth (food already swallowed) — **-tation** *n*

rehabilitate *v* **-tated, -tating 1** to put back into good condition: *to rehabilitate old houses* **2** to make able to live an ordinary life again, as by training: *to rehabilitate criminals* **3** to put back to a former high rank, position, and fame — **-tation** *n*

rehash *v* *esp. spoken* to use (ideas) again in a new form but without real change

rehearsal *n* the act or an occasion of rehearsing —see also DRESS REHEARSAL

rehearse *v* **rehearsed, rehearsing** to learn and practise for later performance: *to rehearse a play*

rehouse *v* **rehoused, rehousing** to put into a new or better house

Reich *n* *German* the German state or kingdom

reign¹ *n* a period of reigning: *the reign of George VI*

reign² *v* **1** to be the king or queen: *Our Queen reigns but does not rule* **2** to exist noticeably: *After the storm, quietness reigned*

reimburse *v* **-bursed, -bursing** to pay back — ~**ment** *n*

rein¹ *n* **1** a long narrow band usu. of leather, by which a horse (or sometimes a small child) is controlled ⬅️ HORSE **2 give rein to** to give freedom to (feelings or desires) **3 take the reins** to become the leader and make the decisions

rein² *v* to stop or slow up (a horse) by pulling the reins

reincarnate *v* **-nated, -nating** to cause to become again a living body, after death

reincarnation *n* **1** the act of being reincarnated **2** the creature that results

reindeer *n* **-deer** a type of deer with long branching horns, native to the coldest parts of Europe

reinforce *v* **-forced, -forcing** to strengthen by adding **a** materials: *to reinforce a coat* **b** men, ships, etc.: *to reinforce an army*

reinforced concrete also **ferroconcrete**— *n* concrete strengthened by having metal bars placed in it before it hardens

reinforcement *n* the act of reinforcing: *This roof needs some reinforcement*

reinforcements *n* men sent to reinforce an army

reinstate *v* **-stated, -stating** to put back (into a position formerly held) — ~**ment** *n*

reiterate *v* **-rated, -rating** to repeat several times — **-ration** *n*

reject¹ *v* **1** to refuse to accept **2** to throw away as useless or imperfect — ~**ion** *n*

reject² *n* something rejected

rejection slip *n* a printed message rejecting something offered for publication

rejoice *v* **rejoiced, rejoicing** to feel or show great joy

rejoicings *n* feasting, dancing, etc., as signs of joy

rejoin *v* to answer: *'Not at all,' he rejoined rudely* —see ANSWER (USAGE)

rejoinder *n* an answer, esp. a rude one

rejuvenate *v* **-nated, -nating** to make or become young again — **-nation** *n*

relapse¹ *n* a return to a former and worse state, after an improvement

relapse² *v* **relapsed, relapsing** to fall back (into evil or illness) after an improvement

relate *v* **related, relating 1** to tell (a story) **2** to see a connection between: *to relate 2 ideas*

related *adj* connected; of the same family or kind: *She is related to me by marriage* —opposite **unrelated** — ~**ness** *n*

relation *n* **1** a member of one's family **2** connection: *the relation between wages and prices* USAGE Both **relation** and **relationship** (the more modern word) can mean 'connection'. To avoid confusion, it may be better to use **relative** rather than **relation** to mean 'a member of one's family'.

relations *n* **1** way of treating and thinking of each other: *friendly relations* **2** connections: *They have business relations with our firm*

relationship *n* **1** family connection **2** connection between things or ideas

relative¹ *n* a relation —see RELATION (USAGE)

relative² *adj* **1** compared to each other or to something else: *After his troubles, he's now in relative comfort* —opposite **absolute** **2** *esp. writ-*

ten connected (with): *the facts that are relative to this question*
relative clause *n* technical a clause that is joined to the rest of the sentence by a word such as 'who', 'which', 'that', 'where', or 'when', and that can play the part of an adjective or of a noun: *In ' The man who lives next door is a doctor ' the words ' who lives next door ' form a relative clause*
relatively *adv* quite; when compared to other people or things: *She walks relatively fast for a child of 3*
relativity *n* the relationship between time, size, and mass, which are said to change with increased speed: *Einstein's Theory of Relativity*
relax *v* 1 to make or become less active; stop worrying 2 to make or become less stiff or tight: *His muscles relaxed* 3 to make (effort or control) less severe: *Don't relax your efforts*
relaxation *n* 1 relaxing or being relaxed 2 something done for rest and amusement
relay¹ *n* **relays** 1 one part of a team that takes its turn in keeping an activity going continuously: *groups of men working in relays* 2 an electrical apparatus that receives messages by telephone, radio, etc., and passes them on over a further distance 3 *esp. spoken* also **relay race**— a race in which each member of 2 or more teams runs part of the distance
relay² *v* **relayed, relaying** to send out by relay: *to relay a broadcast*
release¹ *v* **released, releasing** 1 to set free; allow to come out 2 to allow **a** (a new film or record) to be shown or bought publicly **b** (a news story) to be printed 3 to press (a handle) so as to let something go: *to release the handbrake*
release² *n* 1 a setting free 2 a new film or record that has been released 3 **on general release** (of a film) able to be seen at all cinemas
relegate *v* **-gated, -gating** to put (someone or something) into a lower or worse position: *relegated to the second division* — **-gation** *n*
relent *v* to show pity; become less cruel
relentless *adj* without pity — ~ly *adv* — ~ness *n*
relevant *adj* connected with the subject — opposite **irrelevant** — ~ly *adv* — -vance, -vancy *n*
reliability *n* the quality of being reliable — opposite **unreliability**
reliable *adj* fit to be trusted; dependable — -bly *adv*
reliance *n* trust
reliant *adj* depending on; relying on —compare SELF-RELIANT
relic *n* 1 a part of the body or belongings of a holy person, which is kept and respected after his death 2 something old that reminds us of the past: *a relic of ancient times*
relics *n* literature the remains of a dead person
relict *n* old use someone's widow
relief *n* 1 a feeling of comfort at the ending of

anxiety or pain 2 a person or group taking over a duty for another: *a relief driver* 3 help for people in trouble: *send relief to flood victims* 4 the act of driving away an enemy: *the relief of the city* 5 (in art) a shape cut in wood or stone, or shaped in metal, so that it stands out above the surface 6 money that one is allowed not to pay in taxes, for some special reason 7 **in bold/sharp relief** (in art) painted so that it seems to stand out clearly from the rest of the picture 8 **in (high/low) relief** (in art) cut so that it stands out (a long way/a little) above the rest of the surface it is on —compare BAS-RELIEF 9 **light relief** pleasant and amusing change
relief map *n* a map with the high parts either cut in relief or painted to look like that
relieve *v* **relieved, relieving** 1 to lessen (pain or trouble): *a drug that relieves headaches* 2 to take over a duty from (someone) as a relief 3 to drive away the enemy from (a town, fort, etc.) 4 to give variety to; make more interesting: *to relieve a dull evening* 5 **relieve oneself** polite to urinate or empty the bowels 6 **relieve someone's mind** to free someone from anxiety
relieved *adj* (esp. of a person) given relief
relieve of *v prep* to take from (someone) (something heavy to carry or hard to do): *Let me relieve you of that heavy parcel*
religion *n* 1 belief in one or more gods 2 a particular system of belief and the worship, behaviour, etc., connected with it 3 something that one takes very seriously: *Cricket is a religion with John*
religious *adj* 1 of or concerning religion: *a religious service* 2 obeying the rules of a religion carefully —opposite **irreligious** 3 performing the stated duties very carefully: *She washes the floor with religious care* — ~ly *adv*
relinquish *v* to give up: *He relinquished his claim*
relish¹ *n* 1 enjoyment, esp. of food and drink 2 a substance eaten with a meal, such as pickles or sauce
relish² *v* to enjoy: *to relish a funny story*
relive *v* **relived, reliving** to experience again, as in the imagination
reload *v* to load (a gun) again
relocate *v* **-cated, -cating** to move to a new place: *to relocate the factory outside the city* — -cation *n*
reluctance *n* unwillingness
reluctant *adj* unwilling — ~ly *adv*
rely on also **rely upon**— *v prep* **relied, relying on** 1 to depend on (something, or something happening): *You can't rely on the weather* 2 to trust (someone, or someone to do something): *You may rely on me to help you* USAGE Some people think *rely on/count on my going* is better English than *rely on me going*; but in *rely on/count on me to go* one can only use *me*.
remain *v* 1 to stay or be left behind after others have gone 2 to continue to be (in an unchanged state): *Peter became a judge but John remained a*

fisherman **3 it remains to be seen** we shall know later on

remainder *n* what is left over; the rest

remains *n* **1** parts which are left **2** a dead body, usu. of a human being

remake *v* **remade, remaking** to make (esp. a film) again — **remake** *n*

remand *v* to send back to prison from a court of law, to be tried later after further enquiries: *remanded in custody* — **remand** *n*

remand home *n* (in Britain) a place where young people who have broken the law are sent for a while, till the court has decided what to do with them

remark¹ *v* to say: *He remarked that it was getting late*

remark² *n* a spoken or written opinion: *rude remarks*

remarkable *adj* worth speaking of; unusual: *a remarkable man* — **-bly** *adv* : *remarkably well*

remark on also **remark upon**— *v prep* to say or write something about: *Everyone remarked on his absence*

remediable *adj* that can be put right or cured —opposite **irremediable**

remedial *adj* curing or helping: *remedial exercises for a weak back* — **~ly** *adv*

remedy¹ *n* **-dies 1** a way of curing pain or disease: *Warmth is the best remedy for colds* **2** a way of setting right (anything bad): *evils that are past remedy*

remedy² *v* to put or make right: *to remedy a fault*

remember *v* **1** to keep in the memory; not forget **2** to give money or a present to: *Grandfather remembered me in his will*

remember to *v prep esp. spoken* to send (someone's) greetings to: *Please remember me to your mother*

remembrance *n* **1** a memory; remembering: *Christians eat bread and drink wine in remembrance of Jesus* **2** something kept or given to remind one

Remembrance Day also **Remembrance Sunday**— *n* **-days** the Sunday nearest to November 11th, when people remember those killed in the 2 world wars

remind *v* to cause (someone) to remember: *Remind me to write to Mother.* | *This reminds me of last year* — **~er** *n*

reminisce *v* **-nisced, -niscing** to talk pleasantly about the past

reminiscence *n* memory of past events

reminiscent *adj* **1** reminding one of **2** showing that one is remembering something: *a reminiscent smile*

remiss *adj* neglecting duty; careless — **~ness** *n*

remission *n* **1** remitting **2** a period when an illness is less severe **3** a lessening of time spent in prison

remit *v* **-tt- 1** to free from (a debt or punishment) **2** to send (money) by post

remittance *n* **1** the remitting of money **2** an amount of money remitted

remittent *adj* (of a disease) sometimes better and sometimes worse

remnant *n* **1** a part that remains: *the remnants of the feast* **2** a small piece of cloth left over from a larger piece

remodel *v* **-ll-** to change the shape of: *to remodel an old house*

remonstrate *v* **-strated, -strating** to complain — **-strance** *n*

remorse *n* sorrow for having done wrong — **~ful** *adj* — **~fully** *adv* — **~fulness** *n* — **~less** *adj* — **~lessly** *adv* — **~lessness** *n*

remote *adj* **1** distant: *remote stars* | *the remote future* **2** quiet and lonely: *a remote village* **3** not close: *a remote connection* **4** (of behaviour) not showing interest in others **5** slight: *Your chances are remote* — **~ly** *adv* — **~ness** *n*

remote control *n* the control of machinery from a distance by radio signals

remould *v* to retread

remount *n* a fresh horse

removal *n* an act of removing

removal van also **pantechnicon, moving van**— *n* a large covered van for taking furniture usu. from one house to another

remove¹ *v* **removed, removing 1** to take away; take off: *Remove your hat.* | *to remove a child from a class* **2** once/twice/etc., **removed** (of cousins) different by 1, 2, etc., generations: *a second cousin once removed* ☞ FAMILY — **removable** *adj*

remove² *n* **1** a stage or degree: *Great cleverness is only one remove from madness* **2** (in some schools) a class

remover *n* someone who moves furniture from one house to another

remunerate *v* **-rated, -rating** *esp. written* to reward; pay — **-ration** *n* —see PAY (USAGE)

remunerative *adj* (of work) well-paid — **~ly** *adv*

renaissance also **renascence**— *n* French a renewal of interest, esp. in a form of art

Renaissance *n* the period in Europe between the 14th and 16th centuries, when there was renewed interest in the art, literature, and ideas of ancient Greece —compare MIDDLE AGES

renal *adj medical* of the kidneys

rend *v* **rent, rending** *literature* **1** to divide by force; split **2** to pull violently

render *v esp. written* **1** to cause to be: *His fatness renders him lazy* **2** to perform **3** to give: *to render thanks/an account*

render down *v adv* to make (fat) pure by melting

rendering *n* a performance: *gave a splendid rendering of the song*

rendezvous¹ *n* **-vous 1** an arrangement to meet **2** the place chosen for meeting **3** a meeting place: *This club is a rendezvous for writers*

rendezvous² v to meet by arrangement
rendition n a performance
renegade n a traitor
renege, renegue v reneged or renegued, reneg-ing or reneguing esp. written to break a promise
renew v 1 to make as good as new 2 to replace: to renew one's library ticket 3 to repeat or take up again: The enemy renewed their attack — ~**able** adj — ~**al** n
rennet n a substance used for thickening milk for cheese, junket, etc.
renounce v renounced, renouncing 1 to give up formally: He renounced his claim to the prop-erty 2 to say formally that one has no more connection with: He renounced his religion — **renunciation** n
renovate v -vated, -vating to repair and do up (esp. old houses) — **-vation** n
renown n fame — ~**ed** adj
rent¹ n money paid regularly for the use of a property or object
rent² v 1 to pay rent for the use of 2 to allow to be used in return for rent: to rent a room to Mrs. Smith — ~**able** adj
rent³ n a large tear, in or as if in cloth
rent⁴ past tense & past part. of REND
rental n esp. written money to be paid as rent
rent-free adv, adj without payment of rent
rent strike n a refusal, by a group of people, to pay their rent, because they hope the law will decide that it is too high
reorganize, -ise v -ized, -izing to organize again, often in a new way — **-ization** n
rep¹ n sl a salesman
rep² adj, n esp. spoken repertory
repaid past tense & past part. of REPAY
repair¹ v 1 to mend: to repair a broken watch/a road 2 esp. written to put right (a wrong, mis-take, etc.) — ~**able** adj — ~**er** n
repair² n 1 an act or result of mending: the repairs to my car 2 in good/bad repair in good/bad condition
repair to v prep esp. written to go to (a place), often or in large numbers: We all repaired to a restaurant
reparable adj that can be repaired —opposite **irreparable**
reparation n esp. written repayment for loss or wrong
reparations n money paid by a defeated nation after a war
repartee n a quick amusing answer
repast n esp. written a meal
repatriate v -ated, -ating to return (someone) to his own country — compare EXPATRIATE — **-ation** n
repay v repaid, repaying 1 to pay (money) back 2 to pay (someone) back 3 to reward (an action): He repaid her kindness with blows — ~**able** adj — ~**ment** n
repeal v to do away with (a law) — **repeal** n
repeat¹ v 1 to say or do again: to repeat a word/a mistake 2 to say (something heard or

learnt): to repeat a poem 3 (of numbers, esp. decimals) to recur 4 (of a gun) to fire several times without reloading 5 **repeat oneself** to say or do the same thing again and again — ~**ed** adj — ~**edly** adv
repeat² n 1 a performance that is repeated 2 (in music) (a sign (:||)) showing) a passage to be played again
repeater n a repeating gun — **-ting** adj
repel v -ll- 1 to drive back by force: to repel an attack 2 to cause dislike in: That ugly man repels me —see REPULSE (USAGE) — ~**lent** adj
repellent n a substance that drives (esp. insects) away: a mosquito repellent
repent v esp. written to be sorry for (wrongdo-ing) — ~**ance** n — ~**ant** adj
repercussion n 1 a far-reaching unexpected effect 2 something springing or thrown back: heard the repercussions of the shot
repertoire n all the plays, music, etc., that a performer or theatre company has learned and can perform
repertory¹ also (esp. spoken) **rep**— adj giving several plays, with the same company of actors, one after the other on different days: a repertory theatre/company
repertory² n -ries 1 also (esp. spoken) **rep**— repertory theatre: a job in repertory 2 a reper-toire
repetition n 1 the act of repeating 2 the exercise of repeating words learned
repetitious also **repetitive**— adj containing parts said or done too many times: a repetitious speech — ~**ness** n
replace v replaced, replacing 1 to put back in the right place 2 to take the place of: George replaced Edward as captain — ~**able** adj — opposite **irreplaceable** —opposite **irreplaceable**
replacement n 1 the act of replacing: Your tyres need replacement 2 someone or something that replaces: We need a replacement for the dead officer
replay¹ v replayed, replaying to play (a match, music, etc.) again
replay² n replays 1 a match played again 2 a playback
replenish v to fill up again: to replenish the cupboard — ~**ment** n
replete adj esp. written quite full, esp. of food — **repletion** n
replica n a close copy, esp. of a work of art, often made by the same artist
replicate v -cated, -cating technical to repeat; duplicate
reply v replied, replying to answer: 'Of course not,' she replied —see ANSWER (USAGE) — **reply** n
report¹ n 1 an account of events, experiences, etc. 2 the noise of an explosion 3 a rumour 4 SCHOOL REPORT
report² v 1 to give an account of: They reported the disappearance of the ship 2 to arrive for work or duty: to report to the police 3 to complain

about to someone else: *He reported me to the head* **4** (of a reporter) to write an account of

reportedly *adv* according to what is said

reported speech *n* INDIRECT SPEECH — opposite **direct speech**

reporter *n* a person who collects and writes news for a newspaper, radio, etc. —compare JOURNALIST

repose[1] *v* **reposed, reposing** *esp. written* **1** to lie still and comfortably **2** to place for a rest: *She reposed her head on his shoulder* **3** to base or be supported: *to repose our trust in God*

repose[2] *n* **1** *esp. written* comfortable rest; sleep **2** calm; quiet: *the repose of a still afternoon* — ~**ful** *adj*

repository *n* **-ries** **1** a place where things are stored: *a furniture repository* **2** a person to whom secrets are told

repossess *v* to regain possession of (property) — ~**ion** *n*

repot *v* **-tt-** to put (a plant) into another (larger) pot

reprehend *v* *esp. written* to blame; scold

reprehensible *adj* deserving to be reprehended — **-bly** *adv*

represent *v* **1** to be a picture, sign, etc., of: *This painting represents a storm.* | *These stones represent armies* **2** to act officially for: *As a member of parliament, he represents Worcester* **3** to be present as an example of (a group): *a soup in which 20 kinds of vegetables were represented* **4** to declare or describe, perhaps falsely: *He represented himself as a friend*

re-present *v* to send in again: *to re-present a bill for payment*

representation *n* **1** representing or being represented **2** something that represents: *This painting is a representation of a storm*

representational *adj* (of art) showing things just as they look in real life — compare ABSTRACT

representations *n* polite official complaints (esp. in the phrase **make representations**)

representative[1] *adj* **1** typical; being an example: *a representative collection of ancient Greek art* —opposite **unrepresentative** **2** (of government) in which the people and their opinions are represented

representative[2] *n* a person acting in place of others —see also SALESMAN

repress *v* **1** to keep under strict and unnatural control **2** to put down by force: *to repress a rising of the people with the army* — ~**ive** *adj* — ~**ively** *adv*

repressed *adj* *technical* **1** suffering from repression: *a sad repressed little boy* **2** (of a feeling) in the state of repression: *a repressed desire to steal*

repression *n* **1** repressing or being repressed **2** *technical* (in psychology) **a** the forcing of feelings or desires of which one is ashamed out of the conscious mind into the unconscious mind with

odd effects upon one's behaviour **b** a feeling or desire in this state

reprieve *v* **reprieved, reprieving** to give an official order delaying a punishment to: *to reprieve the prisoner* — **reprieve** *n*

reprimand *v, n* (to give) a severe official scolding

reprint[1] *v* to print (a book) again

reprint[2] *n* a reprinted book —compare EDITION

reprisal *n* the punishment of others for harm done to oneself

reprise *n* a repeating of all or part of a piece of music

reproach[1] *n* **1** blame **2** words of blame: *loud reproaches* **3** something that brings shame: *This dirt is a reproach to the city* **4** above/beyond **reproach** perfect — ~**ful** *adj* — ~**fully** *adv*

reproach[2] *v* to blame, not angrily but sadly

reprobate *adj, n usu. humour* (typical of) a person of bad character

reproduce *v* **-duced, -ducing** **1** to produce young: *Birds reproduce by laying eggs* **2** to produce a copy of: *to reproduce a picture* — **-ducible** *adj*

reproduction *n* **1** the producing of young: *human reproduction* ⓖ **2** copying: *This recording has poor reproduction* **3** a copy, esp. of a work of art, less exact than a replica — **-tive** *adj*

reproof *n* *esp. written* blame; scolding

reprove *v* **reproved, reproving** *esp. written* to scold or blame

reptile *n* a scaly creature whose blood temperature depends on the temperature around it, such as a snake, turtle, or lizard ☞ EVOLUTION — **-tilian** *adj, n*

republic *n* **1** a state governed by elected representatives **2** a nation whose chief of state is not a king but a president — ~**an** *adj*

republican *n* a person who favours republics ~**ism** *n*

Republican *adj, n* (a member or supporter) of the **Republican party**, one of the 2 largest US political parties —compare DEMOCRAT — ~**ism** *n*

repudiate *v* **-ated, -ating** **1** to refuse to have anything to do with: *to repudiate offers of friendship* **2** to state that (something) is untrue or unjust: *to repudiate a charge of murder* **3** to refuse to pay (a debt) — **-ation** *n*

repugnance *n* strong dislike: *She turned away in repugnance* — **-nant** *adj*

repulse *v* **repulsed, repulsing** **1** to drive back (an enemy attack) **2** to refuse coldly; push away (a friendly person, or friendship) USAGE One can **repel** or **repulse** an enemy, but one can only **repulse** an offer of friendship. — **repulse** *n*

repulsion *n* **1** strong dislike and fear: *repulsion at the sight of a diseased animal* **2** (in science) the force by which bodies drive each other away —opposite **attraction** — **-sive** *adj* — **-sively** *adv* — **-siveness** *n*

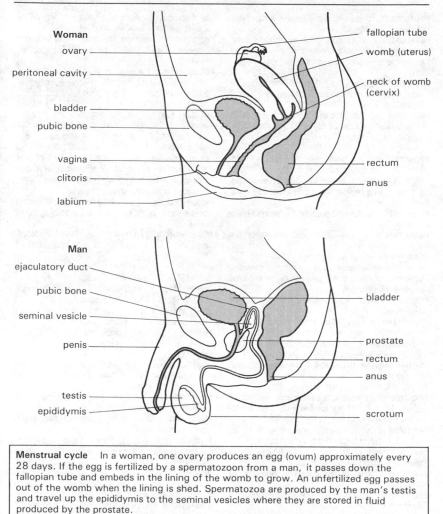

Woman
- fallopian tube
- ovary
- peritoneal cavity
- womb (uterus)
- neck of womb (cervix)
- bladder
- pubic bone
- vagina
- clitoris
- labium
- rectum
- anus

Man
- ejaculatory duct
- pubic bone
- seminal vesicle
- penis
- testis
- epididymis
- bladder
- prostate
- rectum
- anus
- scrotum

Menstrual cycle　In a woman, one ovary produces an egg (ovum) approximately every 28 days. If the egg is fertilized by a spermatozoon from a man, it passes down the fallopian tube and embeds in the lining of the womb to grow. An unfertilized egg passes out of the womb when the lining is shed. Spermatozoa are produced by the man's testis and travel up the epididymis to the seminal vesicles where they are stored in fluid produced by the prostate.

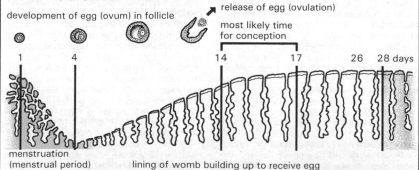

development of egg (ovum) in follicle

release of egg (ovulation)

most likely time for conception

1　　4　　14　　17　　26　　28 days

menstruation (menstrual period)

lining of womb building up to receive egg

reputable adj having a good name: a reputable company — **-bly** adv

reputation n opinion held by others about someone or something : to have a high reputation as a farmer —compare CHARACTER, CHARACTER-ISTIC

repute n esp. written 1 reputation (often in such phrases as **of good/bad/evil repute**) 2 good reputation: a hotel of repute

reputed adj 1 generally supposed, but with some doubt: his reputed father 2 reported; considered: She is reputed to be Europe's best singer — ~**ly** adv

request¹ n 1 a polite demand: a request for help 2 something asked for: Do they play requests on this radio show? 3 **in request** very popular 4 **on request** when asked for: The band will play on request

request² v to demand politely: I requested them to stop

requiem n a Mass for a dead person, or the music written for it

require v **required, requiring** 1 to need: The floor requires washing 2 esp. written to demand, expecting obedience: All passengers are required to show their tickets

requirement n something needed or demanded

requisite n, adj (something) needed: every requisite for camping

requisition¹ n formal demand, esp. by the army: made a requisition for horses

requisition² v to demand or take officially, esp. for the army

requital n esp. written a repayment

requite v **requited, requiting** esp. written to repay: He requited my kindess with cruel words —see also UNREQUITED

reredos n an ornamental wall or work of art behind a church altar

rerun v **reran, rerun, rerunning** to show (a film or television show) again — **rerun** n

rescind v law to repeal (a law, decision, or agreement)

rescue¹ v **-cued, -cuing** to save (from harm or danger); set free — **-cuer** n

rescue² n 1 an act of rescuing 2 **come/go to someone's rescue** to come/go and help someone

research¹ n 1 advanced study of a subject, so as to learn new facts: to do research on blood diseases 2 a piece of work of this kind

research² v to do research — ~**er** n

resemblance n likeness: a strong resemblance between the 2 brothers

resemble v **-bled, -bling** to be like

resent v to feel angry or bitter at — ~**ful** adj — ~**fully** adv — ~**fulness** n

resentment n the feeling of resenting bad treatment

reservation n 1 a limiting condition: I accept without reservations! 2 a private doubt: I have some reservations about his story 3 (in the US)

land set apart for American Indians to live on 4 a booking for a holiday, hotel, etc.

reserve¹ v **reserved, reserving** 1 to keep (for a special purpose) 2 to book (a holiday, hotel, etc.)

reserve² n 1 a quantity kept for future use: a reserve of food 2 the military force kept to support the regular army if needed 3 a price limit below which something is not to be sold 4 a piece of land reserved for a stated purpose: a nature reserve 5 the quality of being reserved in character: the well-known reserve of the Scots 6 a player whose job is to play in a team game instead of any member who cannot play 7 **in reserve** ready for use if needed 8 **without reserve** esp. written a freely and openly b without conditions: I believe your story without reserve

reserved adj 1 not liking to talk about oneself or to show one's feelings 2 booked: reserved seats

reservoir n 1 a place where liquid is stored, esp. water for a city 2 a large supply, often of facts or knowledge

resettle v **-tled, -tling** to settle in a new country: to resettle Vietnamese in Canada

reshuffle¹ v **-fled, -fling** 1 to shuffle (playing cards) again 2 to change around

reshuffle² n a changing around of jobs in an organization: a Government reshuffle

reside v **resided, residing** esp. written to have one's home (in a stated place) —see LIVE (USAGE)

residence n 1 esp. written the place where one lives; a house 2 the state of residing: took up residence in Jamaica

resident¹ adj living in a place: a resident doctor (=living in the hospital)

resident² n a person who lives in a place and is not just a visitor

Resident n (esp. in former times) a political representative of a country, living abroad as an adviser

residential adj (of an area) having private houses, without offices or factories

residual adj left over; remaining

residue n technical what is left over after part has been removed, after chemical treatment, etc.

resign v 1 to give up (a job or position) 2 **resign oneself** to become resigned

resignation n 1 being resigned: to accept one's fate with resignation 2 an act of resigning 3 a written statement that one resigns

resigned adj patiently prepared for, or suffering, something unpleasant — ~**ly** adv

resilient adj 1 (of a substance) able to spring back to the former shape or position when pressure is removed: Rubber is more resilient than wood 2 (of living things) able to recover from difficulty, disease, etc.: a resilient character — ~**ly** adv — **-ence, -ency** n

resin n 1 a sticky yellow substance obtained from certain trees such as the fir. It is used esp. for making paint and in medicine 2 any of various man-made plastic substances — ~ous *adj*

resist *v* 1 to oppose; fight against 2 to remain unharmed by: *a roof that resists the weather* 3 to refuse to yield to: *She could hardly resist laughing* 4 to force oneself to refuse: *I can't resist baked apples* — ~ant *adj* — ~er *n* — ~ible *adj* —opposite irresistible

resistance *n* 1 resisting 2 force opposed to anything; opposition: *wind resistance to an aircraft | resistance to the law* —see also SALES RESISTANCE, PASSIVE RESISTANCE 3 the ability to resist disease 4 (a measure of) the ability of a substance to resist the passing through of an electric current —see also VOLTAGE ⊒ ELECTRICITY 5 an organization that fights secretly against enemy armies that control its country 6 a resistor 7 the line of least resistance the easiest way

resistor *n* an electrical component providing resistance ⊒ ELECTRICITY

resolute *adj* firm; determined in purpose — compare IRRESOLUTE — ~ly *adv* — ~ness *n*

resolution *n* 1 also (*esp. written*) resolve— being resolute 2 the action of resolving: *the resolution of our difficulties* 3 a formal decision by vote: *a resolution against building a new library* 4 also (*esp. written*) resolve— a decision to do or stop doing something: *She's always making good resolutions*

resolvable *adj* 1 that can be resolved: *This difficulty should be easily resolvable* 2 that can be resolved into: *This mixture is resolvable into 2 simple substances*

resolve *v* resolved, resolving 1 to decide: *He resolved on going out* 2 to settle or clear up (a difficulty)

resolve into *v prep* to separate into (parts): *This mixture resolves into 2 substances*

resonant *adj* 1 (of a sound) deep, full, clear, and continuing 2 filled (with sound): *The air was resonant with shouts* — ~ly *adv* — -nance *n*

resonate *v* -nated, -nating (of a sound) to be resonant

resort *n* 1 a holiday place: *a health/mountain resort* 2 a place that one visits regularly: *This restaurant is my favourite resort* 3 resorting to: *to pass without resort to cheating* —compare RECOURSE 4 someone or something resorted to: *Her only resort is television* 5 in the last resort if everything else fails

resort to *v prep* to turn to (often something bad) for help: *When his wife left him he resorted to drink*

resound *v* 1 (of a musical instrument, sound, etc.) to be loudly and clearly heard: *The horn resounded through the forest* 2 (of a place) to be filled with sound: *The hall resounded with laughter*

resounding *adj* 1 loud and clear 2 very great: *a resounding success* — ~ly *adv*

resource *n* 1 a part of one's resources: *Oil is an important natural resource* 2 a means of comfort or help: *Religion is her only resource* 3 cleverness in finding a way round difficulties: *a man of great resource*

resourceful *adj* able to get round difficulties — ~ly *adv* — ~ness *n*

resources *n* 1 wealth, goods, and other possessions that help one to do things 2 leave someone to his own resources to leave someone to pass the time as he wishes

respect¹ *n* 1 admiration; feeling of honour: *to show respect for one's parents* 2 attention; care: *to have respect for the law* —compare SELF-RESPECT 3 a detail (in such phrases as in one/no respect, in several/many/all respects) 4 in respect of *esp. written* concerning; with regard to 5 without respect to without considering; without regard to 6 with respect to *esp. written* (introducing a new subject) with regard to: *With respect to the recent flood...*

respect² *v* to feel or show respect for: *I respect his courage. | I'll respect your wishes*

respectable *adj* 1 having character and standards acceptable to society 2 enough in amount or quality: *a respectable income* — -bly *adv* — ~ness *n* — -ability *n*

respectful *adj* feeling or showing respect: *respectful silence* — ~ly *adv* — ~ness *n*

respecting *prep* with respect to

respective *adj* particular; individual: *to visit our respective mothers*

respectively *adv* each separately in the order mentioned: *She gave beer to the man and a toy to the baby, respectively*

respects *n* 1 polite formal greetings: *Give my respects to your wife* 2 pay one's respects *esp. written* to pay a polite visit

respiration *n technical* 1 breathing ⊚ —see also ARTIFICIAL RESPIRATION 2 *technical* the chemical reactions by which living organisms obtain energy by combining foods with oxygen ⊒ ECOLOGY

respirator *n* an apparatus worn over the nose and mouth, to help breathing in spite of gas, smoke, etc.

respiratory *adj* connected with breathing

respire *v* respired, respiring *technical* to breathe

respite *n* a short pause, delay, or rest, esp. before punishment or during suffering: *a welcome respite from work*

resplendent *adj* gloriously bright and shining — ~ly *adv* — -dence, -dency *n*

respond *v* 1 to speak or act in answer: *I offered him a drink but he didn't respond. | The horse responded to his kick by jumping* —see ANSWER (USAGE) 2 (of people at a religious service) to make responses

respondent *n* one who answers a questionnaire or a charge in a law court —compare CORESPONDENT

response *n* 1 an answer 2 an action done in answer: *no response to our call for help* 3 one of the parts of a religious service said or sung by the people, in answer to the parts sung by the priest

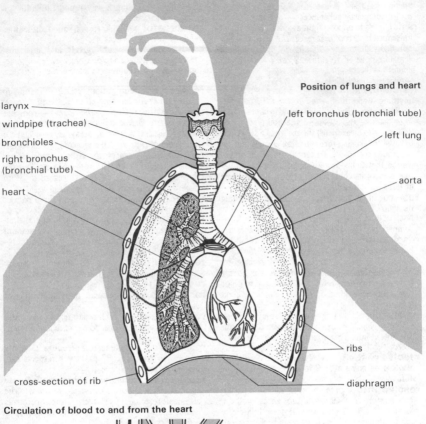

Position of lungs and heart

larynx
windpipe (trachea)
bronchioles
right bronchus (bronchial tube)
heart

left bronchus (bronchial tube)
left lung
aorta

ribs

cross-section of rib
diaphragm

Circulation of blood to and from the heart

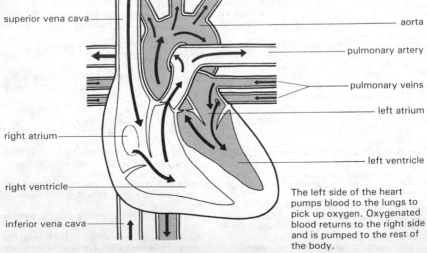

superior vena cava
aorta
pulmonary artery
pulmonary veins
left atrium
right atrium
left ventricle
right ventricle
inferior vena cava

The left side of the heart pumps blood to the lungs to pick up oxygen. Oxygenated blood returns to the right side and is pumped to the rest of the body.

responsibility *n* **-ties** 1 being responsible —opposite **irresponsibility** 2 something for which one is responsible: *A father has many responsibilities*

responsible *adj* 1 having the duty of looking after someone or something, so that one can be blamed if things go wrong: *You are responsible to your mother for keeping the house tidy* 2 trustworthy: *a responsible person* —opposite **irresponsible** 3 (of a job) needing a trustworthy person: *a responsible position* 4 **be responsible for** to be the cause of — **-ibly** *adv*

responsive *adj* answering readily with words or feelings: *She is responsive to kindness* — ~**ly** *adv* — ~**ness** *n*

rest¹ *n* 1 freedom from anything tiring; sleep: *to take a day's rest* 2 a support: *This wall will do as a rest for your camera* 3 (in music) a period of silence of fixed length ☞ MUSIC 4 **at rest** not moving 5 **come to rest** to stop moving

rest² *v* 1 to take a rest 2 to allow to rest: *rest your feet* 3 to lean or support 4 to lie buried 5 to stop: *Let the argument rest there* 6 (of farming land) to have nothing planted in it 7 **rest assured** to be certain: *You can rest assured that we will find him*

rest³ *n* what is left: *We'll eat some and keep the rest for breakfast*

restate *v* **restated, restating** to say again, perhaps in different words: *to restate one's opinions* — ~**ment** *n*

restaurant *n* French a place where food is sold and eaten —compare CAFé

restaurateur *n* a restaurant owner, esp. one who runs it himself

rest cure *n* a course of medical treatment, consisting of rest

restful *adj* peaceful: *a restful evening* — ~**ly** *adv* — ~**ness** *n*

rest home *n* a building where old or sick people are looked after

rest house *n* a house where travellers can stay, in a place where there are no hotels

restitution *n* esp. *written* the act of returning something lost or stolen, or paying for damage

restive *adj* restless; not still: *a restive horse* — ~**ly** *adv* — ~**ness** *n*

restless *adj* 1 never quiet or still: *the restless sea* 2 not giving rest: *a restless night* — ~**ly** *adv* — ~**ness** *n*

Restoration *n* (the period in England following) the return of Charles II in 1660

restorative *n, adj* (something) that restores health and strength

restore *v* **restored, restoring** 1 to give or put back: *to restore stolen property* 2 to introduce again: *to restore law and order* 3 to bring back to a proper state, esp. of health: *restored after one's holiday* 4 to put (old buildings, furniture, or works of art) back into the original state: *to restore an old painting* — **restoration** *n* : *the restoration of law and order* | *This castle is a fine restoration*

restorer *n* a person who restores things: *a picture restorer*

restrain *v* to control; hold back: *Restrain your dog from biting the milkman*

restrained *adj* 1 calm and controlled 2 not showy: *restrained colours*

restraint *n* 1 being restrained or restraining oneself: *You showed great restraint in not crying.* | *Dogs don't like restraint in cages* 2 something that restrains: *the restraints of a small town* 3 **without restraint** freely: *She talked to me without restraint*

restrict *v* to keep within limits, often by control or law: *to restrict oneself to 2 sweets a day* — ~**ed** *adj* : *a restricted demand for expensive cars* — ~**ion** *n* : *a restriction against smoking in schools*

restrictive *adj* that restricts (too much) — ~**ly** *adv* — ~**ness** *n*

restructure *v* **-tured, -turing** to arrange in a new way; give a new structure to

result¹ *v* to happen as an effect: *If the police leave, disorder will result*

result² *n* 1 what happens because of an action or event; effect: *His illness is the result of bad food* 2 a person's or team's success or failure in an examination, match, etc.: *the football results* 3 **with the result that** esp. *written* so that

resultant *adj* happening as an effect: *There was a fight, and the resultant damage was serious*

result in *v prep* to cause: *The accident resulted in his death*

resume *v* **resumed, resuming** esp. *written* 1 to begin again: *We resumed our journey after a rest* 2 to take again: *to resume one's seat* — **resumption** *n*

résumé *n* French a shortened form of a speech, book, etc.

resurgence *n* a rising up again: *a resurgence of hope* — **-gent** *adj*

resurrect *v* 1 to bring back into use, fashion, or attention: *to resurrect an old custom* 2 *rare* to bring back to life

resurrection *n* 1 renewal (of life, hope, etc.) 2 (in Christian belief) the rising from the grave of all dead people at the end of the world

Resurrection *n* the rising of Christ from his grave, remembered on Easter Sunday

resuscitate *v* **-tated, -tating** to bring back to life: *to resuscitate a drowned man* — **-tation** *n*

retail¹ *v* to sell by retail: *to retail tobacco in one's shop*

retail² *n* the sale of goods to customers for their own use and not for resale: *the retail of goods* | *a small retail business* —compare WHOLESALE — **retail** *adv* : *to buy retail*

retail³ *v* esp. *written* to pass on (news)

retail at *v prep* to be sold at (a retail price): *These shoes retail at $10*

retailer *n* a shopkeeper

retain *v* 1 to avoid losing: *to retain one's balance* 2 to hold in place: *a wall to retain the lake*

— **retention** n — **retentive** adj : a retentive memory — **retentively** adv

retainer n (in former times) a servant

retaliate v -ated, -ating to pay back evil with evil: Mary kicked Susan, and Susan retaliated by biting — -ation n — -atory, -ative adj

retard v esp. written to make slow; delay: Cold retards the growth of plants — ~ation n

retarded adj (of a child) slow in development

retch v to try to be sick without success

rethink v rethought, rethinking to reconsider: to rethink the plan

reticent adj not saying as much as is known or felt: reticent about the quarrel — ~ly adv — -cence n

reticulation n technical a netlike pattern: a snake covered with orange and black reticulations — -lated adj

reticule n old use or humour a small handbag

retina n -nas or -nae the light-sensitive area of nerves at the back of the eye

retinue n a group of servants and followers with an important person: the King's retinue of noble lords

retire v retired, retiring 1 to go away to a quiet place: to retire to one's room 2 (esp. of an army) to go back, but without being forced to —compare RETREAT 3 esp. written to go to bed 4 to stop working at one's job, usu. because of age

retired adj (of a person) having stopped working, usu. because of age: a retired general — -rement n : He was given a gold watch on his retirement

retiring adj 1 avoiding company: a retiring girl/nature 2 at which one retires (in the phrase **retiring age**)

retort[1] v to make a retort: 'Of course not,' she retorted —see ANSWER (USAGE)

retort[2] n a quick, rather angry, and often amusing answer

retort[3] n a bottle with a long narrow bent neck, for heating chemicals

retouch v to improve (a picture or photograph) slightly with brush or pencil

retrace v retraced, retracing to go over again: to retrace past events in one's mind

retract v 1 to draw back or in: A cat can retract its claws 2 to take back (a statement or offer made): to retract his remarks — ~ion n — ~able adj : a retractable offer | retractable wheels

retractile adj that can be retracted: retractile claws

retread also **remould**— v to renew the rubber tread on (a tyre)

retreat[1] n 1 an act of retreating: Napoleon's retreat from Moscow 2 a signal for retreating (often in the phrase **sound the retreat**) 3 a place of peace and safety 4 **beat a retreat** to retreat, esp. quickly to avoid something unpleasant

retreat[2] v 1 (esp. of an army) to move back,

esp. when forced to —compare RETIRE 2 to escape from something unpleasant

retrench v esp. written to reduce (one's spending) — ~ment n

retrial n a new trial

retribution n esp. written a deserved punishment — -tive adj : retributive acts against the killers

retrieval system n technical any of various methods of finding stored information when it is needed

retrieve v retrieved, retrieving 1 to find and bring back: to retrieve the lost bag 2 to put right (a mistake, loss, defeat, etc.) — **retrievable** adj — **retrieval** n

retriever n any of several types of middle-sized hunting dog, trained to bring back shot birds

retroactive adj affecting the past as well as the future: a retroactive pay increase — ~ly adv

retrogress v esp. technical to go back (to an earlier and worse state) — ~ion n — ~ive adj — ~ively adv

retrospect n the act of looking back towards the past (in the phrase **in retrospect**): One's school life seems happier in retrospect than in reality

retrospection n thought about the past

retrospective adj 1 concerned with the past: retrospective thoughts 2 (esp. of a law) retroactive — ~ly adv

retsina n a Greek wine that tastes of the juice (RESIN) of certain trees

return[1] v 1 to come or go back: to return to London | Spring will return 2 to give or send back: Please return my keys! 3 to answer: 'Yes!' she returned 4 to elect to a political position: We returned a Liberal as our Member of Parliament 5 to bring in as profit: These shares return interest 6 to state officially: He returned his earnings on the tax declaration. | The jury returned a verdict of 'Guilty' 7 **return a favour** to do a kind action in return for another

return[2] n 1 an act of returning: your return from China 2 a giving back: the return of the stolen books 3 a profit 4 an official statement: a tax return 5 a return ticket 6 **by return (of post)** by the next post 7 **in return** in exchange

return[3] adj (esp. of a ticket) for a trip from one place to another and back again

returnable adj that must or can be sent back: returnable bottles

returning officer n the official in each area who arranges an election and gives the result

returns n more birthdays (in the phrase **Many happy returns!** used as a birthday greeting)

reunion n a meeting of friends after a separation

reunite v -nited, -niting to come, bring, or join together again

reuse v reused, reusing to use again — **reusable** adj

rev v -vv- esp. spoken to increase the speed of (an engine)

Rev abbrev for: Reverend

revalue v -ued, -uing 1 to find again the value of: *to revalue our possessions for insurance* 2 to increase the value of: *to revalue the dollar* — compare DEVALUE — -uation n

revamp v esp. spoken to give a new or better form to: *to revamp an old play*

reveal v 1 to allow to be seen: *a dress that reveals all* 2 to make known: *to reveal a secret* — ~ing adj

reveille n the music played to waken soldiers in the morning

revel v -ll- old use to pass the time in dancing, feasting, etc. — ~ler n

revelation n 1 the making known of something secret 2 a surprising fact made known: *revelations about her past*

Revelation also **Revelations**— n the last book of the Bible

revel in v prep to enjoy greatly

revelry n -ries wild noisy dancing and feasting

revenge¹ v revenged, revenging 1 to do something in revenge for: *to revenge a defeat* 2 to punish someone for harm done to: *Hamlet revenged his dead father* USAGE **Avenge** has more the idea of a deserved though unofficial punishment than **revenge**, which just means paying back an injury.

revenge² n 1 a punishment given in return for harm done: *Hamlet wanted revenge for his father's murder* 2 **give someone his revenge** (in sport) to play another game against a defeated opponent — ~ful adj — ~fully adv — ~fulness n

revenue n income, esp. that of the government

reverberate v -rated, -rating (of sound) to be thrown back again and again: *Thunder reverberated across the valley* — -ration n — -rant adj

revere v revered, revering also reverence— to respect and admire greatly: *People revere the name of Mahatma Gandhi*

reverence n great respect and admiration mixed with love: *They hold him in great reverence* — -rent, -rential adj : *reverent behaviour* — -rently, -rentially adv

reverend adj esp. written 1 worthy of great respect: *a reverend old gentleman* 2 being a priest: *A reverend gentleman is here to see you*

Reverend n (a title of respect for a priest, minister, etc.): *Reverend Jones has moved to a new church.* | *Ask the Reverend about that*

reverie n pleasant thoughts and dreams while awake: *She fell into a reverie*

revers n -vers a part of a coat or dress turned back at the neck to show the inside —compare LAPEL

reverse¹ adj 1 opposite in position; back: *the reverse side of the cloth* 2 **in reverse order** from the end to the beginning

reverse² v reversed, reversing 1 to go or drive backwards or in the opposite direction: *He reversed the car.* | *The car reversed through the gate* 2 to turn (something) over, showing the back: *She reversed the paper* 3 to change (something) to the opposite: *He reversed the judgment and set the prisoner free after all* 4 **reverse arms** (of a soldier) to point one's gun downwards 5 **reverse the charges** to make a telephone call to be paid for by the person receiving it — **reversal** n : *By a reversal of fortune he lost his money* — **reversible** adj — **reversibility** n

reverse³ n 1 the opposite in position; the back: *the reverse of the cloth* 2 the opposite; the other way round: *Edwin is afraid of Angela, but the reverse is also true* 3 a defeat or change for the worse: *The failure of his business was a serious reverse* 4 the side (of a coin) that does not show the ruler's head —opposite **obverse** 5 the position of controls that causes backward movement: *Put the car into reverse*

reversion n a return or reverting to a former condition

revert to v prep 1 to go back to (a former condition, topic, owner, etc.) 2 **revert to type** to go back to an original state or pattern

review¹ n 1 an act of reviewing: *a careful review of political events* 2 a grand show of the armed forces 3 a a magazine containing articles giving judgments on new books, plays, and public events b an article of this kind 4 **under review** being considered and judged

review² v 1 to consider and judge; go over again in the mind: *to review the situation* 2 to hold a review of (armed forces) 3 to write a review of (a play, book, etc.)

reviewer n a person who writes reviews

revile v reviled, reviling esp. written to speak angrily to or of: *a speech reviling the Government* — **reviler** n

revise v revised, revising 1 to read (a piece of writing) carefully, making improvements 2 to change (opinions, intentions, etc.) because of more information or thought: *I'll have to revise my ideas about Tom* 3 to study again (lessons already learnt) — **reviser** n — **revision** n

revisionism n any political movement of the left that questions the main beliefs of an already existing Marxist political system — **-ist** adj, n

revitalize, -ise v -ized, -izing to put new strength or power into — **-lzation** n

revival n 1 a rebirth or renewal: *a revival of interest in ancient music* 2 a performance of an old play after many years

revive v revived, reviving 1 to make or become conscious or healthy again: *The fresh air soon revived him* 2 to bring or come back into use or existence: *to revive an old custom* 3 to perform (an old play) again after many years

revoke v revoked, revoking to end (a law, decision, etc.); cancel: *to revoke an order*

revolt¹ v 1 to act violently against those in power so as to win power: *The people revolted against their king* 2 to cause (someone) to feel violent dislike and sickness: *Such cruelty revolted him* —see also REVULSION

revolt² n the act of revolting: *The nation is in revolt*

revolting adj very nasty: *a revolting smell of bad eggs* — ~ly adv

revolution n 1 a great social change, esp. the changing of a political system by force 2 a complete change: *Air travel has caused a revolution in our way of living* 3 (one complete) circular movement round a fixed point: *the revolution of the moon round the earth* 4 (in a machine) one complete circular movement on a central point, as of a wheel: *a speed of 100 revolutions per minute* —see also REVOLVE

revolutionary¹ adj 1 connected with political revolution 2 completely new and different: *a revolutionary machine*

revolutionary² n -ries a person who favours or fights in a revolution

revolutionize, -ise v -ized, -izing to cause a complete change in

revolve v revolved, revolving 1 to spin round; make revolutions: *The wheels revolved slowly* 2 esp. written to consider carefully: *He revolved the main points in his mind*

revolver n a hand gun with several shots in a barrel that turns round after each one is fired, so that one need not reload every time ⊃ WEAPON

revue n a light theatrical show with songs and dances but no story, usu. centred on current events and fashions

revulsion n 1 a feeling of being shocked and sickened: *a revulsion against cruelty* 2 esp. written a sudden change of feeling: *a revulsion of public opinion*

reward¹ v 1 to give a reward to 2 to give a reward for: *How can I reward your kindness?*

reward² n something gained or given for work, service, finding something, etc.: *a reward of £900 for catching the criminal*

rewarding adj (of an experience or action) worth doing or having: *Nursing is a rewarding job*

rewire v rewired, rewiring to put new electric wires into (a building)

reword v to say or write again in different words

rewrite v rewrote, rewritten, rewriting to write again in a different way — **rewrite** n

Rex n Latin 1 (the title used after the name of a ruling king): *George Rex* 2 (used, when a king is ruling, in titles of lawsuits) the State: *the action Rex v Jones* (= the State against Jones) —compare REGINA

rhapsodize, -dise v -dized, -dizing to express great praise and excitement

rhapsody n -dies 1 an expression of great praise and excitement 2 a piece of music of irregular form

rhea n any of several kinds of large South American bird like the ostrich but smaller, with long legs and neck and 3 toes on each foot

rheostat n an instrument that controls the loud-

ness of radio sound or the brightness of electric light, by limiting the flow of electric current —see also RESISTANCE

rhesus n a small short-tailed pale brown North Indian monkey

Rhesus factor also **Rh factor**— n technical a substance whose presence (**Rhesus positive**) or absence (**Rhesus negative**) in the red blood cells may have dangerous effects on newborn babies

rhetoric n 1 the art of speaking or writing so as to persuade people 2 speech or writing that sounds fine, but is really without meaning — ~al adj — ~ally adv — ~ian n

rhetorical question n a question asked only for effect, not expecting any answer

rheumatic adj 1 connected with rheumatism: *a rheumatic condition* 2 having rheumatism: *a rheumatic old woman*

rheumatic fever n a serious infectious disease, esp. in children, with fever, swelling of the joints, and possible heart damage

rheumatics n esp. spoken rheumatism

rheumatism n any of various diseases causing pain and stiffness in the joints or muscles

rheumatoid adj technical of or concerning rheumatism or the disease (**rheumatoid arthritis**) causing pain and stiffness in the joints

rhinestone n 1 a piece of transparent quartz 2 a shining colourless jewel, often made from this

rhinoceros also (esp. spoken) **rhino**— n -ros or roses one of several kinds of large heavy thick-skinned animal of Africa or Asia, with 1 or 2 horns on its nose ⊃ MAMMAL

rhizome n technical the thick stem of some plants such as the iris, which lies flat just under the ground with roots and leaves growing from it

rho n the 17th letter of the Greek alphabet (P, ρ)

rhododendron n any of several types of evergreen bush, with large bright flowers

rhomboid also **rhomboidal**— adj technical in the shape of a rhombus

rhombus n -buses or -bi (in geometry) a quadrilateral with all sides equal and usu. unequal angles ⊃ MATHEMATICS

rhubarb n 1 a broad-leaved garden plant with thick juicy edible stems 2 esp. spoken the sound of many people talking

rhyme¹ n 1 a word that rhymes with another: *'Bold' and 'cold' are rhymes* 2 words that rhyme at the ends of lines in poetry: *Rhyme was not used in ancient poetry* 3 a short and not serious piece of writing, using words that rhyme 4 **rhyme or reason** sense; meaning

rhyme² v rhymed, rhyming 1 (of words) to end with the same sound: *'House' rhymes with 'mouse'* 2 to put together (2 words that end with the same sound): *You can rhyme 'duty' with 'beauty' but not 'box' and 'backs'*

rhymed adj written in lines that rhyme

rhyming couplet n 2 lines of poetry next to each other that rhyme

rhyming slang *n* a secret language using words that rhyme with those really meant: *'Plates of meat' is rhyming slang for 'feet'*

rhythm *n* **1** (in music or poetry) a regular pattern of beats: *the exciting rhythms of drum music* **2** the quality of happening at regular periods of time: *the rhythm of the seasons* — ~**ic**, ~**ical** *adj* — ~**ically** *adv*

rib¹ *n* **1** one of the many pairs of bones (12 in man) running from the backbone round to the front of the chest **2** a piece of meat that includes one of these bones **3** anything like a rib in shape or function: *the ribs of a boat/leaf* — ~**bed** *adj* : *ribbed socks*

rib² *v* **-bb-** *esp. spoken* to make fun of in a friendly way

ribald *adj* rudely humorous in a low disrespectful way: *ribald jokes / soldiers* — ~**ry** *n*

ribbing *n* a pattern of long thin raised lines in knitting

ribbon *n* **1** a long narrow band of cloth used for tying things, for ornament, etc. **2** such a band in a special colour or pattern, worn to show a title or honour: *the ribbon of the Victoria Cross* —see also MEDAL **3** a long irregular narrow band: *a ribbon of mist*

rib cage *n* the wall of ribs that protects the lungs

riboflavin *n* *technical* a substance (vitamin B₂) that exists naturally in meat, milk, and certain vegetables, and is important for human health

rice *n* **1** any of several kinds of food grain grown in hot wet places **2** the seed of this, which is cooked and eaten

rice paper *n* **1** a kind of thin paper **2** a special edible form of this, used in cooking

rice pudding *n* a sweet dish of rice baked in milk and sugar

rich *adj* **1** possessing a lot of money or property **2** containing a lot (of the stated thing): *fish rich in oil* **3** valuable and beautiful: *rich silk/furniture* **4** (of food) containing a lot of cream, sugar, eggs, etc. **5** (of land or soil) good for growing plants in **6** (of a sound or colour) deep, strong, and beautiful — ~**ly** *adv* — ~**ness** *n*

riches *n* wealth

rick¹ *n* a large pile of straw or hay, often shaped like a little house, that stands out in the open until needed

rick² *v* to twist (part of the body) slightly: *I've ricked my back*

rickets *n* a children's disease caused by lack of vitamin D, which makes the bones become soft and bent

rickety *adj* weak in the joints and likely to break: *a rickety cart*

rickshaw, -sha *n* a small 2-wheeled passenger vehicle pulled by a man on foot or cycling

ricochet¹ *n* **1** the skipping away in a new direction of a a bullet, stone, etc., when it hits a surface at an angle **2** a blow from an object to which this has happened: *wounded by a ricochet*

ricochet² *v* **-cheted** *or* **-chetted, -cheting** *or* **-chetting** to change direction in a ricochet: *The bullet ricocheted off the bridge*

riddance *n* *esp. spoken* a clearing away of something unwanted: *'They've gone at last.' 'Good riddance!'* (=I'm glad they've gone)

riddle¹ *n* **1** a difficult and amusing question to which one must guess the answer **2** something one cannot understand: *Robert's character is a complete riddle*

riddle² *n* a large sieve

riddle³ *v* **-dled, -dling 1** to pass (earth, corn, ashes, etc.) through a riddle **2** to shake (a grate) to make the ashes fall through

riddle with *v prep* to make many holes in: *I'll riddle you with bullets!*

ride¹ *v* **rode, ridden, riding 1** to travel along, controlling and sitting on (a horse, bicycle, etc.) —compare DRIVE **2** to travel on a horse: *teach the children to ride* —see also SIDESADDLE, ASTRIDE **3** to go along, across, or over (a place) on a horse: *He rides the borders*

ride² *n* **1** a journey (on an animal, in a vehicle, etc.) —compare DRIVE **2** a path made for horse riding **3 take someone for a ride** *esp. spoken* to deceive someone

rider *n* **1** a person who rides esp. a horse **2** *law* a statement or opinion added to an official judgment

ride up *v adv* (of clothing) to move upward into an uncomfortable position

ridge¹ *n* a long narrow raised part of any surface, such as the top of a mountain range or of a sloping roof

ridge² *v* **ridged, ridging** to make ridges in

ridicule¹ *n* unkind laughter; being made fun of

ridicule² *v* **-culed, -culing** to laugh unkindly at

ridiculous *adj offensive* silly; deserving ridicule — ~**ly** *adv* — ~**ness** *n*

Riding *n* (until 1974) any one of the 3 divisions of Yorkshire for local government purposes

riding breeches *n* trousers worn for riding

rid of *v prep* **rid** *or* **ridded, rid, ridding of 1** to make free of: *to rid the town of rats* **2 get rid of** to free oneself from; drive or give away

rife *adj* widespread; common

riff *n* a repeated phrase in popular music or jazz

riffle through *v prep* **-fled, -fling through** to turn over (papers, pages, etc.) quickly with one's finger

riffraff *n* badly-behaved people of the lowest class

rifle¹ *v* **rifled, rifling** to search and steal everything valuable out of: *The thieves rifled his pockets*

rifle² *v* to make grooves inside (a gun barrel) so as to make the bullets spin

rifle³ *n* a gun fired from the shoulder, with a long rifled barrel ☞ WEAPON

rifleman *n* **-men** a soldier armed with a rifle

rifle range *n* **1** a place where people practise

shooting with rifles   2 the distance that a rifle can shoot

rift *n esp. written* a break, separation, or crack: *a rift in the clouds* | *There's been a rift between my wife and me*

rift valley *n* -leys a valley with very steep sides, formed when part of the earth's surface sinks down

rig¹ *v* -gg- to fit out (a ship) with necessary ropes, sails, etc.

rig² *n*   1 the way a ship's sails and masts are arranged   2 a piece of apparatus: *an oilrig*

rig³ *v* -gg- to arrange (an event) dishonestly for one's own advantage: *The election was rigged* —see also RIG OUT, RIG UP

rigging *n* all the ropes, sails, etc., on a ship ☞ SAIL

right¹ *adj*   1 on the side of the body that does not contain the heart   2 in the direction of this side: *a right turn*   3 connected with the right in politics —opposite **left**

right² *n*   1 the right side or direction: *Keep to the right!*   2 political groups that favour fewer political changes and generally support the employers or those in official positions rather than the workers —opposite **left**

right³ *adj*   1 just; morally good   2 correct; true: *the right time* — ~ ness *n*

right⁴ *n*   1 what is just or good   2 a morally just or lawful claim: *She has a right to half your money*   3 **in one's own right** because of one's own just claim: *famous in one's own right*   4 **in the right** not deserving blame —see also RIGHTS

right⁵ *adv*   1 towards the right: *He turned right* —opposite **left**   2 directly; straight: *The marmalade's right in front of you*   3 properly; correctly: *to guess right*   4 all the way: *right back to the beginning*   5 all right: *Right! I'll do it*

right⁶ *v* to put right or upright: *The cat righted itself during the fall, and landed on its feet*

right-about turn also **right-about face**— *n* a complete turn that leaves one facing in the opposite direction

right angle *n* an angle of 90 degrees, as at any corner in a square ☞ TRIGONOMETRY, MATHEMATICS — **right-angled** *adj*

right away *adv* at once

righteous *adj literature*   1 lawful and morally good   2 (of feelings) having just cause: *righteous anger* — ~ly *adv* — ~ness *n*

rightful *adj* according to a just claim: *one's rightful share* — ~ly *adv* — ~ness *n*

right-hand *adj*   1 on or to the right side: *a right-hand turn*   2 of, for, with, or done by the right hand   3 turning the same way as the hands of a clock: *a right-hand screw*   4 **one's right-hand man** one's most valuable helper

right hand *n*   1 the hand on the right side of the body   2 one's most valuable helper

right-handed *adj*   1 using the right hand rather than the left   2 made for a person who does this: *right-handed scissors* — ~ly *adv* — ~ness *n*

rightist *adj, n* (a supporter) of the right in politics

rightly *adv*   1 correctly; truly   2 justly   3 *esp. spoken* for certain: *I can't rightly say what day it is*

right-minded *adj* having the right opinions, habits, etc. — ~ness *n*

right of common *n* **rights of common** *law* the right to use a particular area of land

right of way *n* **rights of way**   1 a a right to cross private land b a path over which someone holds this right: *a public right of way through the forest*   2 the right of traffic to drive, pass, etc., before other vehicles

rights *n*   1 the advantages to which someone has a moral or lawful claim: *women's rights*   2 **by rights** if things were done fairly   3 **set/put to rights** to make just, healthy, correct, etc.: *This medicine will soon put you to rights*   4 **the rights and wrongs** of the true facts of

right side *n*   1 the outer side of a garment or material   2 **get on the right side of someone** to win someone's favour   3 **keep on the right side of the law** not to break the law

rightward *adj* on or towards the right — **rightwards** *adv*

right wing *adj, n*   1 (of) a political group favouring fewer political changes   2 (in games like football) (of) the position or a player on the edge of the right of the field — ~ er *n*

rigid *adj*   1 stiff; not easy to bend   2 not easy to change: *rigid ideas* — ~ly *adv* — ~ity *n*

rigmarole *n*   1 a long confused story without much meaning   2 a long meaningless set of actions: *We had to go through a long rigmarole before we got our money*

rigor mortis *n Latin* the stiffening of the muscles after death

rigour *n*   1 hardness; lack of mercy: *the full rigour of the law*   2 severe conditions: *the rigours of winter*   3 (in a subject of study) care and exactness: *the rigour of a scientific proof* — **rigorous** *adj* ⚠ VIGOROUS

rig-out *n esp. spoken* a set of clothes

rig out *v adv* -gg- to give clothes to

rig up *v adv* -gg- *esp. spoken* to put together quickly for a short time: *to rig up a shelter*

rile *v* **riled, riling** *esp. spoken* to annoy; make angry —see ANGRY (USAGE)

rim¹ *n* the outside edge or border of esp. a circular object: *the rim of a wheel* — ~less *adj*

rim² *v* -mm- to surround (something circular)

rime *n literature* white frost

rind *n*   1 the thick outer covering of certain fruits: *lemon rind* —compare PEEL   2 the thick outer skin, which cannot be eaten, of certain foods: *cheese rind*

ring¹ *n*   1 a circular line or arrangement: *to dance in a ring*   2 a circular band: *the rings of Saturn* | *a key ring*   3 a metal band worn on the finger: *a wedding ring*   4 any closed-in space where things are shown or performed, as in a circus or for boxing   5 any group of people who work together, often dishonestly, to control some business: *a drug ring*

ring² *v* **1** to make a ring round: *Police ringed the building* **2** to put a ring in the nose of (an animal) or round the leg of (a bird)

ring³ *v* **rang, rung, ringing** **1** to cause (a bell) to sound **2** (of a bell, telephone, etc.) to sound: *The telephone's ringing* **3** (of the ears) to be filled with a continuous sound **4** to telephone **5** **ring a bell** *esp. spoken* to remind one of something **6** **ring true/false** to sound true/untrue

ring⁴ *n* **1** an act of sounding a bell **2** a loud clear sound like a bell: *the ring of laughter* **3** a quality: *Her story had a ring of truth* **4** **give someone a ring** to telephone someone

ring binder *n* a notebook whose loose pages are held by metal rings fastened to the back

ring finger *n* the third finger of the left hand

ringleader *n* a person who leads others to do wrong

ringlet *n* a long hanging curl of hair

ringmaster *n* a person who directs performances in the circus ring

ring off *v adv* **rang, rung, ringing off** to end a telephone conversation

ring road *n* a road round the edge of a large town

ring up *v adv* **rang, rung, ringing up** to record (money paid) on a machine which strikes a bell when the amount has been noted: *He sold me the shoes and rang up £10*

ringworm *n* a skin disease caused by a fungus and often passed on by touch, causing red rings often on the head

rink *n* a specially prepared surface of **a** ice, for skating **b** any hard material, for roller-skating

rinse¹ *v* **rinsed, rinsing** **1** to wash (esp. clothes) in clean water to take away soap, dirt, etc. **2** to wash (soap, dirt, etc.) out with clean water

rinse² *n* **1** an act of rinsing **2** liquid for colouring the hair

riot¹ *n* **1** a lot of violence, noise, etc., by many people together, esp. in a public place **2** *esp. spoken* a very funny and successful occasion or person: *The new show is a riot!* **3** **a riot of colour** a mass of disordered colours **4** **run riot** to become violent and uncontrollable

riot² *v* to take part in a riot — ~er *n*

riotous *adj* **1** wild and disorderly: *a riotous crowd* **2** noisy and exciting — ~ly *adv* — ~ness *n*

rip¹ *v* **-pp-** **1** to tear quickly and violently: *The wind ripped the sail* **2** **let rip** *esp. spoken* to let go at top seed or develop without control

rip² *n* a long tear

RIP *abbrev. for:* rest in peace (written on gravestones)

ripcord *n* the cord pulled to open a parachute when descending or to let gas out of a balloon

ripe *adj* **1** (of plants) fully grown and ready to be eaten —opposite **unripe** **2** fully developed: *ripe judgment* **3** ready; fit: *land ripe for develop-*

ment **4** *esp. spoken* concerned with sex, the lavatory, etc., in a shocking or amusing way: *a rather ripe joke* — ~ly *adv* — ~ness *n*

ripen *v* to make or become ripe

rip-off *n sl* an act of charging too much

rip off *v adv sl* to charge too much: *They ripped us off at that hotel!*

riposte¹ *n* **1** a quick return stroke with a sword **2** a quick clever reply, esp. in an argument

riposte² *v* **riposted, riposting** to make a riposte

ripple¹ *v* **-pled, -pling** **1** to move in or form ripples **2** to make a sound like gently running water: *a rippling stream*

ripple² *n* **1** a very small wave or wavelike mark: *ripples on a pool/on the sand* **2** a sound like gently running water

rip-roaring *adj esp. spoken* noisy and exciting

ripsaw *n* a coarse saw that cuts wood along the grain

riptide *n* a sea tide that makes rough water and currents

rise¹ *v* **rose , risen, rising** **1** (of the sun, moon, or stars) to appear above the horizon —opposite **set** **2** to go up; get higher; increase: *The river is rising after the rain.* | *The price of tea has risen* —opposite **fall** **3** *esp. written* to get out of bed: *She rises before it is light* **4** also (*esp. written*) **arise**— to stand up from lying, kneeling, or sitting **5** (of a river) to begin: *The river Rhine rises in Switzerland* **6** to move up in rank **7** (of uncooked bread) to swell as the yeast works **8** (of wind or storms) to get stronger **9** to show weakness or annoyance in reply to nasty words or behaviour: *He won't rise to your nasty jokes* **10** to come back to life after being dead **11** **rise to the occasion** to show that one can deal with a difficult matter   USAGE **Raise** is used when someone or something places a person or thing in a higher position. **Rise** is used when the person or thing moves to a higher position: *He raised the glass.* | *I rise at noon. BUT: He raised himself from the ground.*

rise² *n* **1** the act of growing greater or more powerful: *the rise of the Roman Empire* **2** an increase: *a rise in the cost of living* **3** a small hill **4** an increase in wages **5** **get/take a rise out of someone** intentionally to make someone show weakness or annoyance **6** **give rise to** to be the cause of

riser *n* **1** the upright part of a step, between 2 treads **2** **early/late riser** a person who gets out of bed early/late in the morning

risible *adj esp. written* causing or concerning laughter

rising¹ *n* a rising up against ruling powers, esp. the government

rising² *prep* nearly (the stated age): *She is rising 7*

rising damp *n* water that comes up from the ground into walls

risk¹ *n* **1** a danger; chance of loss: *a risk of*

ris

fire **2** a person who is a possible danger to a project: *a bad risk* **3 at one's own risk** agreeing to bear any loss or danger oneself **4 at risk** *esp. written* in danger: *children at risk* **5 run/take risks/a risk** to take chances — ~**y** *adj* : *a risky business* — ~**iness** *n*

risk² *v* **1** to place in danger: *to risk one's health* **2** to take the chance of: *to risk failure*

risotto *n* -**tos** rice cooked with cheese, onions, chicken, etc.

risqué *adj French* (of a joke, story, etc.) slightly rude

rissole *n* a small round flat mass of cut-up meat or fish, mixed with potato, egg, etc., and fried

rite *n* a fixed ceremony usu. religious: *funeral rites*

ritual *n* one or more ceremonies or acts usu. repeated in the same form — **ritual** *adj* — ~**ly** *adv*

rival¹ *n* a person with whom one competes — **rival** *adj* : *a rival team* — ~**ry** *n* : *rivalry between our teams*

rival² *v* -**ll**- to be as good as: *Ships can't rival planes for speed*

river *n* a wide natural stream of water

river basin *n* an area from which all the water flows into the same river

riverbed *n* the ground over which a river usu. flows

rivet¹ *n* a metal pin for fastening metal plates — ~**er** *n*

rivet² *v* **1** to fasten with rivets **2** to hold (someone's attention) strongly: *a riveting story*

rivet on *v prep* to fix (eyes or attention) firmly on

RN *abbrev. for*: Royal Navy

RNA *n technical* ribonucleic acid, an important chemical in all living cells; a form of nucleic acid

roach¹ *n* **roach** *or* **roaches** a European fresh-water fish related to the carp

roach² *n sl* the end of a marijuana cigarette

road *n* **1** a smooth broad prepared track for wheeled vehicles: *It's not really a road, only a path* —see STREET (USAGE) **2** also **roadstead**— an open stretch of deep water, as at the mouth of a river, where ships can float at anchor **3 on the road a** on a journey **b** (of esp. a theatrical company) giving performances at different places — ~**less** *adj*

roadbed *n* the base of hard materials on which a road surface is laid

roadblock *n* something used for closing a road to traffic, an enemy, etc.

road hog *n* a fast, selfish, and careless car driver

roadhouse *n* a large inn on a main road outside a city

roadman also **road mender**— *n* -**men** a man who mends roads

road manager also (*esp. spoken*) **roadie**— *n* a person whose job is making arrangements for a pop group when they are travelling

roadside *n, adj* (at or near) the edge of the road

roadway *n* -**ways** the part of a road where vehicles drive —compare FOOTPATH, PAVEMENT

road works *n* road repairs

roadworthy *adj* (of a vehicle) in fit condition to be driven — -**thiness** *n*

roam *v* to wander with no very clear aim — ~**er** *n*

roan¹ *adj, n* (of a horse or cow) (of) a mixed colour, esp. brown with white hairs in it

roan² *n* a roan horse

roar¹ *v* **1** to give a roar: *The lion/engine roared* **2** to go along making a roar **3** to say or express with a roar: *The crowd roared their approval* **4** *esp. spoken* to laugh long and loudly **5** (of a child) to weep or cry noisily **6 do a roaring trade** to sell one's goods very fast

roar² *n* a deep loud continuing sound: *the roar of an angry lion*

roaring¹ *n* an uninterrupted roar

roaring² *adj* great: *a roaring success* — **roaring** *adv*: *roaring drunk*

roaring forties *n* the part of the Atlantic Ocean about 40 degrees north of the equator where storms are very common

roast¹ *v* **1** to cook (esp. meat) by dry heat **2 fit to roast an ox** (of a fire) very hot **3 give someone a roasting** to scold someone severely

roast² *n* a large piece of roasted meat

roast³ *adj* roasted

roasting *adj, adv* very (hot): *a roasting hot summer day*

rob *v* -**bb**- to take the property of (a person or organization) unlawfully —see STEAL (USAGE) — ~**ber** *n*

robbery *n* -**ies** the crime of robbing

robe¹ *n* a long flowing garment **a** for informal occasions: *a bath robe* **b** for official occasions: *a judge's robes*

robe² *v* **robed, robing** to dress in robes: *robed in red*

robin also **robin redbreast**— *n* a common type of fat little European bird, with a brown back and a red breast

robot *n* **1** a machine that can do some human work, esp. an imaginary machine figure that acts as if alive **2** a person who acts without thought or feeling

robust *adj* **1** healthy and strong **2** (of jokes, conversation, etc.) not fit for polite society — ~**ly** *adv* — ~**ness** *n*

rock¹ *v* **1** to move backwards and forwards or from side to side **2** to cause great shock and surprise to: *The President's murder rocked the nation* **3** to dance to rock 'n' roll music **4 rock the boat** (of a member of a group) to do something that makes it hard for the group to work together

rock² *n* a kind of popular modern music played on electric instruments and with a strong beat —compare POP ☞ MUSIC

rock³ *n* **1** stone forming part of the earth's

surface **2** a large separate piece of stone **3** a hard sticky sweet made in long round bars **4 as firm/steady/solid as a rock** a perfectly firm and hard **b** (of people) trustworthy

rock and roll *n* rock 'n' roll

rock bottom *n* the lowest point: *Prices have reached rock bottom*

rock cake also **rock bun**— *n* a type of small hard cake with a rough surface

rock-climbing *n* the sport of climbing cliffs

rock crystal *n* a type of clear precious stone like glass; kind of quartz

rocker *n* **1** one of the curved pieces of wood on which a rocking chair, rocking horse, or cradle moves to and fro when pushed **2 off one's rocker** *sl* mad

rockery also **rock garden**— *n* -ries as a heap of rocks laid out with suitable low-growing plants

rocket¹ *n* **1** a kind of firework that shoots high into the air and lets out coloured flames **2** a machine of this kind driven by burning gases, used in powering aircraft and spacecraft ⌐☞ SPACE **3** a bomb or missile driven in this way **4 give someone/get a rocket** *sl* to scold someone/be scolded severely

rocket² *v* **1** to rise quickly and suddenly: *rocketing prices* **2** to move very fast: *The train rocketed downhill*

rocket base *n* a military base for rockets

rocketry *n* the science of using and making rockets

rocking chair *n* a chair fitted with rockers

rocking horse *n* a child's wooden horse fitted with rockers

rock 'n' roll also **rock and roll**— *n* an early form of rock music that was very popular in the late 1950s

rock plant *n* any of those kinds of plant that grow naturally among rocks

rocks *n* **1** a line of rock under or beside the sea **2 on the rocks** (of alcoholic drinks) with ice but no water

rock salt *n* common salt as found in mines, not in the sea

rocky *adj* -ier, -iest **1** full of rocks; made of rock **2** hard like rock — **rockiness** *n*

rococo *adj* (of buildings, art, etc.) of a style fashionable from the late 17th to the 18th century, with a great deal of curling ornament

rod *n* **1** a long thin stiff stick of wood, metal, etc. **2** a stick used for beating as a punishment **3** such as punishment **4** a type of cell in the light-sensitive area (RETINA) of the eye that is sensitive esp. to different amounts of light and allows one to see well in dim light —compare CONE **5 Spare the rod and spoil the child** A child who is never punished will grow up with bad habits

rode *past tense of* RIDE

rodent *n* any member of the family of small animals with strong sharp teeth that includes rats, mice, and rabbits ⌐☞ MAMMAL

rodeo *n* -os (in W North America) **1** a gather-

ing together of cattle **2** a show at which cowboys ride wild horses, catch cattle with ropes, etc.

roe *n* a mass of eggs or male seed in a fish

roe deer *n* -deer a small European and Asian forest deer

roentgen *n* *technical* the international measure for X-rays

roger *interj* (used in radio signalling) message received and understood

rogue¹ *n* a very dishonest person

rogue² *adj* (of a wild animal) living alone and having a bad temper: *a rogue elephant*

roguery *n* -ries behaviour typical of a rogue

roister *v* to behave in a rough and loud manner

role *n* **1** the behaviour or duties expected from one holding a particular position in a social group **2** the part taken by someone in a play or film —see also TITLE ROLE

roll¹ *n* **1** a flat piece of some material rolled into a tube shape: *a roll of film/cloth* **2** a small loaf of bread for one person **3** an official list of names: *the College Roll* **4 call the roll** to read aloud an official list of names to see who is there

roll² *v* **1** to move by or as if by turning over and over: *Tears rolled down her cheeks* **2** to turn over and over, round and round, or from side to side **3** to move steadily and smoothly along on or as if on wheels: *The years rolled by* **4** to form into a circular shape by curling round and round: *He rolled up the map* —opposite **unroll** **5** to make (a tubelike object) by curling round and round **6** (of a ship) to swing from side to side with the movement of the waves -compare PITCH **7 a** to make (a surface) flat by pressing with a roller: *roll the grass* **b** to be made flat in this way **8** to make a long deep sound: *The thunder/The drums rolled* **9** to cause (esp. film cameras) to begin working **10** to throw (dice) **11 keep the ball rolling** to keep things active **12 roll one's r's** to pronounce the sound with the tongue beating rapidly against the roof of the mouth, as is common in Scotland **13 set the ball rolling** to be the first to do something, hoping that others will follow —see also ROLL OUT, ROLL UP

roll³ *n* **1** a long deep sound: *a roll of thunder/of drums* **2 a** a rolling movement **b** an action which includes this movement: *a roll of the dice* —compare PITCH

roll call *n* the reading out of a list of names to see who is there

rolled gold *n* a thin covering of gold on top of another metal

roller *n* **1** a tube-shaped piece of wood, metal, etc., that rolls over and over **2** a rod round which something is rolled up: *a map on a roller* **3** a long heavy wave on the coast

roller blind *n* a kind of blind that is pulled down from a roller to cover a window

roller coaster *n* a kind of small railway with sharp slopes and curves, popular in amusement parks

roller-skate v -skated, -skating to go on roller skates — ~r n

roller skate n a frame with 4 wheels for fitting under a shoe, or a shoe with such wheels, for skating on a smooth hard surface

roller towel n a towel with the ends joined and hung on a roller

rollicking adj noisy and merry: a rollicking song

rolling adj 1 rising and falling in long gentle slopes: a rolling plain 2 sl very rich

rolling pin n a tube-shaped piece of wood, glass, etc., for making pastry flat and thin

rolling stock n everything on train wheels that belongs to a railway

rolling stone n a person who travels a lot and has no fixed address or responsibilities

roll of honour n   rolls of honour a list of people who have earned praise

roll out v adv to make (a piece of material) flat and thin by pressing with a roller or a rolling pin

rolltop desk n a desk with a cover that can be rolled out of the way

roll up v adv 1 to roll (something) up one's arms or legs: He rolled up his sleeves 2 esp. spoken to arrive (esp. late, drunk, etc.): He rolled up last 3 (used esp. when asking people to come inside and see a show at a circus, fair, etc.) to come in

roly-poly[1] also **roly-poly pudding**— n -lies a sweet food made of jam rolled up in pastry and then baked or boiled

roly-poly[2] adj (of a person) fat and round

roman n the ordinary style of printing with upright letters like the ones used up to here: printed in roman —compare ITALICS, CAPITALS

Roman[1] adj 1 connected with a the ancient empire of Rome b the city of Rome 2 (of a nose) curving out near the top

Roman[2] n a citizen of a the ancient Roman Empire b the city of Rome ◉ ᗦ HISTORY

Roman Catholic[1] adj connected with the branch of the Christian religion (the **Roman Catholic Church**) whose leader (POPE) rules from Rome ᗦ WORSHIP

Roman Catholic[2] n a member of the Roman Catholic Church

romance[1] n 1 a story of love, adventure, strange happenings, etc., more exciting than real life 2 the quality that such stories have: the romance of life in the Wild West 3 a love affair

romance[2] v romanced, romancing 1 to tell improbable stories: Is he romancing about this? 2 to carry on a love affair

Romance adj (of a language) having grown out of Latin: French and Portuguese are Romance languages ᗦ LANGUAGE

Romanesque adj of a style of building common in Western Europe in about the 11th century, with round arches and thick pillars

Roman numeral n a sign used, in ancient Rome and sometimes now, for numbers, such as I, II, III, IV... —compare ARABIC NUMERAL

romantic[1] adj 1 belonging to or suggesting romance: a romantic adventure 2 fanciful; not practical; dreamy 3 having the quality of romanticism: romantic poetry —compare CLASSICAL ᗦ LITERATURE — ~ally adv

romantic[2] n 1 a romantic dreamy impractical person 2 a writer, painter, etc., whose work shows romanticism

romanticism n (in art, literature, and music) the quality of admiring feeling rather than thought, and wild beauty rather than man-made things, and of valuing individual expression — compare REALISM, CLASSICISM — -cist n

romanticize, -cise v -cized, -cizing offensive to tell improbable and romantic stories; make (an event) sound more romantic by adding exciting detail

romantic movement n the period at the end of the 18th century and the beginning of the 19th century when Western European art and literature were marked by romanticism

Romany adj, n -nies (of) the gipsies or their language ᗦ LANGUAGE

romp v 1 to play noisily and roughly 2 **romp home** to win a race easily — romp n

rompers n a one-piece garment for babies combining a top and short trouser-like bottom

romp through v prep to succeed in, quickly and without effort

rondo n -dos a piece of music that repeats the main tune several times

roneo n -os a copy made on a **Roneo machine** (trademark), which presses ink through stencil

roodscreen n a partition in a church, dividing the part containing the choir from the part where other people sit, and often with a cross or crucifix (**rood**) on top

roof[1] n 1 the outside covering on top of a building 2 the top covering of a tent, closed vehicle, etc. 3 **a/no roof over one's head** somewhere/nowhere to live 4 **raise the roof** to make a loud angry noise 5 **the roof of the/one's mouth** the bony upper part of the inside of the mouth

roof[2] v to put a roof on; be a roof for

roofing n material for making roofs

roofless adj (of a person) with no home

rook[1] n a kind of large black European bird of the crow family ᗦ BIRD

rook[2] v to cheat (someone)

rook[3] n (in chess) a castle

rookery n -ries a group of rooks' nests

rookie n US sl a new soldier; recruit

room n 1 a division of a building, with its own walls, floor, and ceiling 2 space, esp. which could be filled or is enough for any purpose: room for 3 more books 3 the chance to do something: room to develop as a painter 4 a need for: room for improvement b reason for: no room for doubt — ~ful n

roommate n a person with whom one shares a rented room

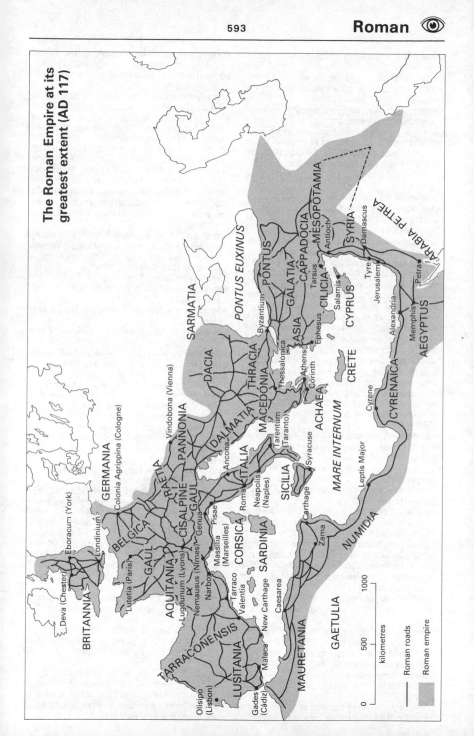

The Roman Empire at its greatest extent (AD 117)

BRITANNIA
Deva (Chester)
Eboracum (York)
Londinium

GERMANIA
Colonia Agrippina (Cologne)
Vindobona (Vienna)

BELGICA
GAUL
Lutetia (Paris)
Lugdunum (Lyons)
Nemausus (Nîmes)
Massilia (Marseilles)
Genua
Pisae
AQUITANIA
Narbo
Tarraco
Valentia

RAETIA
CISALPINE
GAUL
PANNONIA
DALMATIA

SARMATIA

DACIA

PONTUS EUXINUS

THRACIA
Byzantium
MACEDONIA
Thessalonica
Athens
ACHAEA
Corinth

ASIA
PONTUS
GALATIA
CAPPADOCIA
Ephesus
CILICIA
Tarsus
Antioch
SYRIA
Damascus
MESOPOTAMIA

ARABIA PETREA

CYPRUS
Salamis
Tyre
Jerusalem
Petra

ITALIA
Ancona
Roma
Neapolis (Naples)
Tarentum (Taranto)

CORSICA
SARDINIA
New Carthage
Caesarea
Malaca
Gades (Cádiz)
Olisipo (Lisbon)
LUSITANIA
TARRACONENSIS

SICILIA
Syracuse
Carthage
Zama

MARE INTERNUM
Leptis Major

CRETE

CYRENAICA
Cyrene

AEGYPTUS
Alexandria
Memphis

MAURETANIA
NUMIDIA
GAETULIA

kilometres
0   500   1000

—— Roman roads
▨ Roman empire

rooms n a rented set of rooms in a larger building

room service n a service provided by a hotel, by which food, drink, etc., are sent up to a person's room

roomy adj -ier, -iest with plenty of space: a roomy house — **roominess** n

roost¹ n 1 a bar, branch, etc., on which birds settle at night 2 **come home to roost** (of a bad action) to have a bad effect on the doer, esp. after a time 3 **rule the roost** to be the leader

roost² v (of a bird) to perch and sleep for the night

rooster n esp. US a cock

root¹ n 1 the part of a plant that grows down into the soil 2 the part of a tooth, hair, or organ that holds it to the body 3 origin; central part 4 technical (in mathematics) **a** a number that when multiplied by itself a stated number of times gives another stated number: 2 is the 4th root of 16 **b** a number that is a solution of a mathematical equation 5 technical (in grammar) the base part of a word to which other parts can be added: ' Music ' is the root of ' musician' and of ' unmusical ' 6 **root and branch** in all parts: destroy this system root and branch 7 **take/strike root** (of plants or ideas) to become established —see also ROOTS

root² v to form or cause to form roots

root³ also **rootle—** v 1 (esp. of pigs) to search for food by digging with the nose 2 to search for something by turning things over

root crop n a crop grown for its roots

rooted adj 1 fixed as if by roots 2 (of ideas, principles, etc.) fixed and unchangeable: a rooted belief

rootless adj without roots — ~ness n

root out v adv 1 to get rid of completely 2 to find (something) by searching

roots n 1 the feeling of belonging by origin to one particular place 2 **put down roots** to establish oneself in a place by joining in local activities, making friends, etc.

rope¹ n 1 strong thick cord made by twisting, or a piece of this 2 a fat twisted string (esp. of the stated objects): a rope of pearls/onions 3 hanging as a punishment 4 **give someone enough rope to hang himself** to allow freedom to a fool or evil person so he can show his true nature 5 **give someone rope** to allow someone freedom to act —see also ROPES

rope² v **roped, roping** 1 to tie up with a rope 2 esp. US to catch (an animal) with a rope

rope in v adv esp. spoken to make (someone) take part in an activity: I've been roped in

rope ladder n a ladder made of 2 ropes connected by cross pieces of wood, rope, etc.

ropes n **know the ropes** to know from experience the customs in some place or activity: He knows the ropes

ropeway n -ways a system of moving things around in buckets hanging from metal ropes

ropy, ropey adj -ier, -iest esp. spoken in bad condition; of bad quality — **ropiness** n

roquefort n a kind of strong French cheese with blue lines in it

rosary n -ries 1 a string of beads used esp. by Roman Catholics for counting prayers 2 **a** a Roman Catholic practice of saying the set of prayers that are counted in this way **b** a book containing this form of worship

rose¹ n 1 any of various bushes with strong prickly stems, divided leaves, and often sweet-smelling flowers 2 the flower of this bush 3 a circular piece of metal or plastic with holes in it fitted to the end of a pipe or watering can 4 **a bed of roses** a very pleasant state to be in 5 **be not all roses** (of a situation) to include some unpleasant things

rose² adj 1 (of a colour) from pink to a deep purplish red 2 **see (something) through rose-coloured spectacles** to think (something) is pleasanter than it really is

rose³ past tense of RISE

rosé n French any of several kinds of light pink wine

rosebud n a rose (the flower) that has not fully opened yet

rose hip n the red fruit of some kinds of rose bush

rosemary n a kind of low bush whose sweet-smelling leaves are used as a herb

rosette n 1 a bunch of ribbons in the form of a rose 2 a shape like this cut on a building

rose window n a circular window, usu. with small divisions spreading out from a centre and filled in with coloured glass

rosewood n any of several kinds of valuable hard dark red tropical wood. It does not come from the rose

roster n a rota

rostrum n -trums or -tra a raised place for a public speaker, conductor, etc.

rosy adj -ier, -iest 1 (esp. of the human skin) pink 2 (esp. of the future) giving hope: a rosy future — **rosiness** n

rot¹ v -tt- to decay or cause to decay —see also RTTEN

rot² n 1 decay or disease: a tree full of rot 2 sl foolish remarks or ideas: Don't talk rot! 3 **the rot sets in** things begin to go wrong

rota n a list of people's names that shows what jobs they are to do, and when

rotary adj 1 (of movement) turning round a fixed point 2 having a moving part that does this

rotate v **rotated, rotating** 1 to turn round a fixed point: The earth rotates once a day 2 to take turns or cause to take turns: rotate the crops

rotation n 1 the action of rotating 2 one complete turn round a fixed point 3 **in rotation** (of events) coming round one after the other in regular order 4 **rotation of crops** planting different crops in a field each year

rote n repeated study using memory rather than understanding

rotgut n sl strong cheap alcohol that is bad for the stomach

rotisserie n an apparatus for roasting meat by turning it round and round on a bar over heat

rotor n 1 a machine part that rotates 2 the blades that raise a helicopter by rotating

rotten adj 1 gone bad: *rotten eggs* 2 wicked; evil 3 sl bad: *What rotten weather!* 4 **rotten to the core** completely bad morally — ~ly adv — ~ness n

rotten borough n (before 1832) any of a number of places which elected a Member of Parliament although they had hardly any voters

rotter n old sl or humour a bad worthless person

rotund adj esp. written 1 (of a person) fat and round 2 (of the voice) sounding deep and full — ~ity n — ~ly adv

rotunda n a round building or hall

rouble, ruble n the standard coin or note in the money system of the USSR ☞ MONEY

rouge¹ n a red substance used to colour the cheeks

rouge² v **rouged, rouging** to put rouge on (one's face)

rough¹ adj 1 uneven; not smooth: *a rough road* 2 violent: *rough winds* 3 (of food and living conditions) simple: *a rough dinner* 4 (of plans, calculations, etc.) not yet in detail; not in finished form: *a rough drawing* 5 (of paper) for making the first attempts at drawing or writing something 6 (of sounds) not gentle or tuneful: *a rough voice* 7 sl unfortunate and hard to bear 8 **rough and ready** simple and without comfort —see also rough DIAMOND 9 **rough on (someone)** esp. spoken unfortunate for (someone)

rough² n 1 a violent noisy man 2 the uneven ground with long grass on a golf course 3 **in rough** unpolished: *Write it out in rough*

rough³ v **rough it** to live in a simple and not very comfortable way

rough⁴ adv 1 in rough conditions, esp. out of doors 2 using too much force 3 **cut up rough** esp. spoken to become angry 4 **sleep rough** (esp. of a homeless wanderer in a city) to sleep out of doors

roughage n coarse matter in food that helps the bowels to work

rough-and-tumble adj, n (an occasion of being) noisily violent

roughcast n a type of rough surface on the outside of a building

roughen v to make or become rough

rough-hewn adj (of wood or stone) roughly cut; not smoothed

roughhouse¹ n a noisy disorderly fight

roughhouse² v **-housed, -housing** to have a roughhouse

rough in v adv to put in (a few practice lines in a drawing): *I'll just rough it in*

roughly adv 1 in a rough manner 2 about: *roughly 200 people*

roughness n 1 the quality of being rough 2 a rough place: *a small roughness on my hand*

rough out v adv to make (a first practice drawing)

roughshod adv **ride roughshod over** to disregard (something or someone) in a way that hurts the feelings

rough stuff n esp. spoken violence

rouleau n **-eaux** or **-eaus** French a narrow tube of fabric fixed to the edge of a garment to neaten it

roulette n a game of chance in which a small ball is spun round a moving wheel and falls into a hole marked with a number —see also RUSSIAN ROULETTE

round¹ adj 1 circular 2 shaped like a ball 3 curved 4 (of numbers) full; complete: *a round dozen* 5 **in round figures** (of numbers) not exactly; about: *The car cost £9, 878—that's £10, 000 in round figures* — ~ness n

round² adv 1 with a circular movement or movements; spinning if in or as if in a circle 2 in a circular position; surrounding a central point 3 all over the place; in or into all parts: *Let's go into the palace and have a look round* 4 so as to face the other way: *Turn the picture round* 5 **all the year round** during the whole year 6 **round about** in the neighbourhood

round³ prep 1 with a circular movement about (a central point): *The earth goes round the sun* 2 in a circular position on all or some sides of (a central point): *to sit round the fire* 3 into all parts of; all over (a place): *to look round the shop* 4 to or at the other side of: *round the corner* 5 (with times, places, etc.) also **round about**— about: *They arrived round about 5 o'clock* 6 **round the clock** all the time

round⁴ n 1 something round like a plate or ball 2 a complete slice, esp. of bread 3 a regular journey to many houses, offices, etc.: *a paper round* 4 a number or set: *a round of wage claims* 5 a share given out to everyone present: *round of drinks* 6 (in sport) one stage, period, or game: *the first round of the FA Cup* 7 one single shot: *I've only 2 rounds left* 8 a song for 3 or 4 voices, in which each sings the same tune, one starting a line after another has just finished it 9 **in the round a** (of theatre) with people sitting on most or all 4 sides of the stage **b** (of a figure cut out of stone) not part of a wall but solid and separate 10 **one's daily round** one's duties to be done every day

round⁵ v 1 to make or become round: *The child's eyes rounded with excitement* 2 to travel round: *She rounded the corner* —see also ROUND OFF, ROUND ON, ROUND UP

roundabout¹ n 1 also **merry-go-round**— a circular machine on which children can ride, sitting on wooden animals 2 a circular area at a road junction

roundabout² adj (of the way to somewhere) indirect; *a roundabout route*

roundel n a coloured circle showing the nationality of a military aircraft

roundelay n -lays becoming rare a short simple song or poem with a refrain

rounders n a ball game usu. played by children, in which a player hits the ball and then runs round the sides of a square

round-eyed adj with the eyes wide open

Roundhead n a supporter of Parliament against the King in the Civil War in the 17th Century —compare CAVALIER

roundhouse n a round building where railway engines are kept and repaired

roundish adj fairly round in shape

roundly adv 1 strongly and forcefully 2 completely: roundly defeated)

round off v adv 1 to change (an exact figure) into the nearest whole number 2 to shorten (the decimal representation of a number): 3·14159 gives 3·14 when rounded off to 2 decimal places

round on also **round upon**— v prep 1 to turn and attack: The lion rounded on the hunters 2 to scold or blame suddenly

rounds n 1 one's rounds a customary tour: the watchman's nightly rounds 2 go the rounds (esp. of news) to be passed on

round-shouldered adj with bent shoulders

roundsman n -men a man employed to deliver goods to people's houses

round table n a table that makes everyone sitting round it of equal importance

round-the-clock adj done or happening all the time

roundup n a rounding up

round up v adv 1 to gather together or catch (scattered things, people, or animals, esp. cattle) 2 to change (an exact figure) to the next highest whole number

rouse v roused, rousing 1 to waken 2 to make (someone) more active, angry, or excited: The speaker tried to rouse the masses

rousing adj 1 that makes people excited 2 (esp. of a cheer) loud and eager

rout¹ n 1 a complete defeat and disorderly flight 2 **put someone to rout** to defeat completely and drive away someone

rout² v routed, routing to put to rout

route¹ n a way planned or followed from one place to another

route² v routed, routing to send by a particular route

route march n a long march by soldiers in training

routine¹ n 1 the regular ordinary way of doing things 2 a set of steps practised by a dancer

routine² adj 1 regular: a routine medical examination 2 not exciting: a routine job — ~ly adv

rout out v adv to get (someone) to appear: Rout him out of the bath!

roux n roux French a liquid mixture of fat and flour used to thicken soups and sauces

rove v roved, roving often in literature to wander — **rover** n

roving commission n 1 technical permission, given to a person inquiring into a matter, to travel when necessary 2 esp. spoken a job that takes one to many places

row¹ v 1 to move through the water with oars 2 to have (a race of this kind): row against Cambridge — ~er n — ~ing adj : a rowing club

row² n a trip in a rowing boat

row³ n a neat line of people or things side by side: a row of houses

row⁴ n esp. spoken 1 a noisy quarrel, sometimes with violence 2 a noise: Stop making such a row! 3 a scolding 4 **kick up/make a row** sl to cause trouble

row⁵ v esp. spoken to quarrel, often noisily or violently

rowan n also **mountain ash**— any of various small trees of the rose family that bear bright red berries in the autumn

rowdy adj -dier, -diest (of a person or his behaviour) noisy and rough — **rowdily** adv — **rowdiness, rowdyism** n — **rowdy** n : a group of rowdies

rowlock n a pin or U-shaped rest on the side of a boat, for holding an oar

royal¹ adj 1 for, belonging to, supported by, or connected with a king or queen 2 splendid: a right royal feast — ~ly adv

royal² n sl a member of the royal family

Royal Automobile Club n a British club for motorists, providing help on the road and other services

Royal Highness n (the words used when speaking to or of) a prince or princess: Your/His/Her Royal Highness

royalist adj, n (typical of) someone who supports a king or queen, or government by one

royal jelly n the food on which bees feed a young queen bee

royal prerogative n (one of) the special rights of a king or queen

royalty n -ties 1 royal power and rank 2 members of the royal family 3 a a percentage of a book's price, paid to the writer on each copy sold. It is also paid to the writer of a play or piece of music, when it is performed b a share of the profits, as of a mine or new machine, paid in this way to an owner or inventor

RPM abbrev. for: revolutions per minute

RSVP abbrev. for: répondez s'il vous plaît (French); (written on invitations) please reply

rub¹ v -bb- 1 to slide one surface with pressure, to and fro or round and round against (another) 2 to slide (2 surfaces against each other) in this way: He rubbed his hands 3 (of a surface) to slide in this way against/on another: My shoe's rubbing 4 to put (paste, liquid, etc.) on a surface in this way 5 to make (a hole) in this way 6 to bring (something) to a stated condition in this way: Rub *your hair dry* —see also RUB ALONG, RUB IN RUB UP, **rub** SHOULDERS **with**

rub² *n* 1 an act of rubbing: *Give the table a good rub* 2 the cause of trouble: *There's the rub*

rub along *v adv* 1 to continue to do what is necessary, but with difficulty: *He can only just rub along in class* 2 to succeed in living together: *My wife and I seem to rub along all right*

rubber¹ *n* 1 a substance, made chemically or from the juice of a tropical tree, which keeps out water and springs back into position after being stretched 2 a piece of this substance used for removing pencil marks; eraser

rubber² *n* 1 (when playing cards) a set of 3 games of whist or bridge 2 (in cricket) a set of international matches

rubber band *n* a thin circular piece of rubber used to fasten things together

rubber dinghy *n*   -ghies a small rubber boat blown up with air

rubberize, -ise *v* -ized, -izing to cover (cloth) with rubber

rubber plant *n* a type of ornamental house plant of the rubber tree family

rubber-stamp *v* to approve or support officially (a decision) without really thinking about it

rubber stamp *n* 1 a piece of rubber on a handle used for printing a name, date, etc., again and again 2 *usu. offensive* a person or body that acts only to make official the decisions already made by another

rubber tree *n* a type of tropical tree from which rubber is obtained

rubbery *adj* strong and springy like rubber

rubbing *n* a copy made from a raised shape or pattern, esp. in brass, by rubbing a piece of paper laid over it with wax, chalk, etc.

rubbish¹ *n* 1 waste material to be thrown away 2 silly remarks; nonsense — ~y *adj esp. spoken* : *a rubbishy story*

rubbish² *interj* How silly!

rubble *n* broken stones or bricks

rubella *n medical* GERMAN MEASLES

Rubicon *n* **cross/pass the Rubicon** to take an action that cannot later be changed

rubicund *adj esp. written or humour* (of a person, face, etc.) fat, red, and healthy-looking

rub in *v adv* 1 to make (liquid) go into a surface by rubbing: *Rub the polish in* 2 to say repeatedly: *'We'll be late.' 'I know; don't rub it in!'*

ruble *n* a rouble

rubric *n* a set of rules telling one what to do, as in a prayerbook or exam

rub up *v adv* 1 to polish by rubbing 2 BRUSH UP 3 **rub someone up the wrong way** to annoy someone — **rub-up** *n*

ruby¹ *n* **rubies** 1 a deep red precious stone 2 the colour of this

ruck¹ *n* an unwanted fold (in cloth)

ruck² *n* 1 the ordinary level of life: *to get out of the ruck* 2 (esp. in football) a disordered group

3 (in rugby) a group of players from both teams who compete to get possession of the ball

ruck³ *v* to take part in a ruck

rucksack *n* a bag fastened to both shoulders, in which climbers and walkers can carry their belongings —compare HAVERSACK

ruck up *v adv* (of cloth) to form rucks

ructions *n esp. spoken* noisy complaints and anger

rudder *n* 1 a blade at the back of a ship that is controls its direction ⊃̅ SAIL 2 an apparatus like this on an aircraft ⊃̅ AEROPLANE — ~less *adj*

healthy-looking 2 *esp. literature* red or reddish: *ruddy flames* — **ruddiness** *n*

ruddy² *adj, adv* (used, not in polite conversation, as an almost meaningless addition to speech): *that ruddy elephant*

rude *adj* 1 (of a person or his behaviour) not polite 2 simple and roughly made: *a rude hut* 3 (of people) wild and untaught: *a rude tribe* 4 in the natural state: *rude cotton* 5 sudden and violent (in the phrases **a rude shock, a rude awakening**) 6 connected with sexual jokes 7 **in rude health** very healthy — ~ly *adv* — ~ness *n*

rudimentary *adj* 1 (of facts, knowledge, etc.) simple; coming or learnt first 2 not developed: *a rudimentary tail*

rudiments *n* the rudimentary parts

rue¹ *v* rued, ruing *old use* 1 to regret 2 **rue the day when one did something** to be sorry that one did something — ~ful *adj* — ~fully *adv*

rue² *n* a type of small strong-smelling European bush with bitter-tasting leaves

ruff *n* 1 a kind of stiff wheel-shaped white collar worn in the 16th century 2 a ring of hair or feathers round an animal's or bird's neck

ruffian *n* a bad, perhaps violent, man — ~ly *adj*

ruffle¹ *v* -fled, -fling 1 to make uneven: *He ruffled the child's hair* 2 to make or become rather angry

ruffle² *n* a band of fine cloth sewn in folds round an edge, esp. at the neck or wrists of a garment

rug *n* 1 a thick usu. woollen floor mat 2 a large warm woollen covering to wrap round oneself when travelling or camping

rugby also (*esp. written*) **rugby football**, (*esp. spoken*) **rugger**— *n* a type of football played with an oval ball, by 2 teams of 13 (**rugby league**) or 15 (**rugby union**) men

rugged *adj* 1 large, rough, uneven, harsh, etc.: *a rugged face | a rugged shore* 2 (of a person or character) rough but strong and good — ~ly *adv* — ~ness *n*

ruin¹ *n* 1 the cause, state, or event of destruction and decay 2 a ruined building

ruin² *v* 1 to destroy and spoil completely 2 to cause total loss of money to: *I was ruined by that law case*

ruination *n* the cause or state of being ruined

ruinous *adj* 1 causing or being in a state of

ruin: *ruinous costs* **2** (of a building) partly or completely ruined — ~ly *adv*
ruins *n* remains: *the ruins of a castle*
rule¹ *n* **1** an order, law, etc., that guides action, describes events, etc.: *the rules of tennis* **2** power to rule: *under foreign rule* **3** a ruler: *a 2 foot rule* —see also SLIDE RULE **4 as a rule** usually; generally **5 bend/stretch the rules** to allow oneself to be influenced more by special conditions than by strict rules **6 rule of thumb** a quick and not exact way of doing something, based on experience USAGE When speaking of scientific facts it is usual to call them laws rather than rules: *the law that oil floats on water.*
rule² *v* **ruled, ruling** **1** to have and use the highest power over (a country, people, etc.), esp. as a government **2** (esp. in law) to decide officially: *The judge ruled that he must leave* **3 a** to draw (a line) as with the help of a ruler **b** to draw parallel lines on (paper) **4 be ruled by** to be guided or influenced by **5 rule (esp. a group) with a rod of iron** to govern (esp. a group) in a very severe way
rule off *v adv* to draw a line at the end of (something on a page)
rule out *v adv* to exclude
ruler *n* **1** a person who rules **2** a long narrow piece of hard material with straight edges
ruling¹ *n* an official decision —compare DICTUM
ruling² *adj* most powerful: *the ruling class*
rum¹ also **rummy**— *adj* **-mm-** *sl, becoming rare* unusual; strange
rum² *n* a strong alcoholic drink made from sugar cane
rumba *n* a popular dance from Cuba
rumble¹ *v* **-bled, -bling** **1** to make a deep continuous rolling sound **2** to go along making this sound: *The lorry rumbled down the street* **3** to say in a voice of this kind — **rumble** *n*
rumble² *v esp. spoken* to understand the secret or nature of: *I soon rumbled her disguise*
rumbling *n* **1** a rumbling sound **2** widespread unofficial complaint: *a lot of rumbling about* **3** a rumour: *I've heard rumblings that Tim may leave*
rumbustious *adj esp. spoken* (of a person or his behaviour) noisy and cheerful
ruminant *adj, n* (an animal) that ruminates
ruminate *v* **-nated, -nating** **1** (of cattle, deer, etc.) to bring back food from the stomach and chew it again **2** (of a person) to think deeply — **-nation** *n*
ruminative *adj* (of a person or his behaviour) seeming thoughtful — ~ly *adv*
rummage *v* **-maged, -maging** **1** to turn things over while trying to find something **2** to search (a place, esp. a ship) thoroughly — **rummage** *n*
rummy¹ *adj* **-mier, -miest** *sl, becoming rare* unusual; strange
rummy² *n* any of several card games played with either 1 or 2 packs of cards

rumour *n* **1** common talk, perhaps untrue **2** a story spread this way: *all kinds of strange rumours* —compare GOSSIP — ~ed *adj*
rumourmonger *n* a person who spreads rumours
rump *n* **1** the part of an animal at the back just above the legs **2** *humour* a (person's) bottom **3** the remaining part of something, esp. if worthless
rumple *v* **-pled, -pling** to disarrange (hair, clothes, etc.)
rumpus *n esp. spoken* a noisy quarrel or disagreement: *to kick up a rumpus*
run¹ *v* **ran, run, running** **1** to move on one's legs faster than walking **2** to travel (a distance) in this way **3 a** to take part in or hold (a race) **b** to cause (an animal) to race **4** to move quickly: *I'll run the car into town.* | *He ran his eyes down the list.* | *The car ran down the hill* **5 a** (of a machine) to work, often in a stated way: *The engine runs well* **b** to cause (a machine) to work, often in a stated way: *to run the trains on oil* **6 a** (of a public vehicle) to travel as arranged: *This bus runs between Manchester and Liverpool* **b** to cause (a public vehicle) to travel in this way: *They're running a special train* **7** (of liquids, sand, etc.) to flow, often in a stated way: *The water ran cold* **8** (of a container) to pour out liquid, often reaching a stated condition: *Your nose is running.* | *The well has run dry* **9 a** to cause (liquids, sand, etc.) to flow, esp. from a tap **b** to fill (a bath) for someone **10** to melt and spread by the action of heat or water: *The butter will run if you put it near the fire* **11** to stretch; continue: *The road runs beside the river* **12** to own and drive (a car) **13** to take (somebody or something, to somewhere) in a vehicle **14** to bring (something) into a country, unlawfully and secretly: *to run drugs/guns/arms* **15** to be in charge of and cause to work (an organization or system) **16** to continue in force, playing, being, etc.: *The insurance runs for another month* **17** (of a hole in a stocking) to become a ladder **18** (of words in fixed order, as in a poem or law) to be; consist of: *The line runs 'Time and the bell have buried the day'* **19 be run off one's feet** *esp. spoken* to be very busy, esp. working **20 run (a competitor) close/hard** to be nearly equal to (a competitor) **21 run for it** to escape by running **22 run foul of** to meet difficulty in **23 run (someone) off (someone's) feet** *esp. spoken* to keep someone very busy **24 run (oneself or another) into the ground** to tire (oneself or another) out with hard work **25 run the chance/danger of** to take the risk of —see also RUN ACROSS, **run** AMOK, **make someone's** BLOOD **run cold,** RUN DOWN, **run it** FINE, **run the** GAUNTLET, RUN IN, **run** LOW, RUN OFF, RUN OUT, RUN OUT ON, **run** RINGS **round, run** RIOT, **run** RISKS, **run to** SEED, **run SHORT, run a** TEMPERATURE, RUN THROUGH, RUN TO, RUN UP, **run to** WASTE
run² *n* **1** the action of running, often for a stated time or distance **2** a journey, often of a stated time or distance or to a stated place **3** a usu.

enclosed area where animals are kept: *a hen run* **4 a** an eager demand: *a run on beer in hot weather* **b** (in the money market) a general desire to sell **5** (in cricket) a point won by players running from one wicket to the other **6** (in card games) a set of cards with consecutive numbers **7** a continuous set or succession of performances, events, objects, etc.: *a run of 3 months* **8** a sloping course for a downhill sport: *a ski-run* **9** **a good run for one's money** satisfaction for money spent or effort made **10 a run on the bank** a sudden demand by many people to have money back from the bank **11 at a run** running **12 on the run a** trying to escape, or to hide, esp. from the police **b** busy **13 in the long run** after enough time: *It'll be cheaper in the long run to use real leather* **14 in the short run** for the near future **15 the common/ordinary run of** the usual sort of **16 the run of** the freedom to visit or use: *He gave them the run of his garden* —see also RUNS

run across *v prep* to find or meet by chance

run-around *n esp. spoken* delaying or keeping a person waiting and refusing to see him, answer his questions, etc.

runaway *adj* **1** out of control: *a runaway horse* **2** having run away: *a runaway child*

run-away *n* **-ways** a person who has run away

run-down[1] *n* **1** the running down of something: *the run-down of the old factory* **2** a detailed report of events

run-down[2] *adj* **1** (of a person) tired and in poor health **2** (of a thing) old and in bad condition

run down *v adv* **1** to knock down and hurt with one's vehicle **2 a** to chase and catch: *to run down a criminal* **b** to find by searching **3** to speak of as being less valuable, important, etc., than appears **4** (esp. of a clock or battery) to lose power and stop working **5** to stop working gradually: *The coal industry is being run down*

rune *n* **1** any letter of an ancient alphabet of N Europe, cut on stone, wood, etc. **2** a magic charm written or spoken mysteriously — **runic** *adj*

rung[1] *n* **1** one of the cross-bars that form the steps of a ladder **2 the highest/top/lowest/bottom rung of the ladder** the highest/lowest level in an organization or profession

rung[2] *past part. of* RING

run-in *n* a run-up

run in *v adv* **1** to bring (an engine) slowly into full use **2** *esp. spoken* (of the police) to arrest

runnel *n* an open drain beside the road

runner *n* **1** a person who runs, esp. in a race **2** one of the thin blades on which a sledge or skate slides over snow or ice **3** one of the stems with which a plant like the strawberry spreads itself along the ground **4** a long narrow piece of cloth

runner bean also **scarlet runner** — *n* a type of

climbing bean with long green pods used as food

runner-up *n* **runners-up** *or* **runner-ups** the person or team that comes second in a competition

running[1] *n* **1** the act or sport of running **2 in/out of the running** with some/no hope of winning **3 make the running** to set the speed at which a race is run, a relationship develops, etc.

running[2] *adj* **1** (of water) flowing, often from taps **2** done while running along **3** continuous: *a running battle* | *A* **running commentary** *is an account of an event given while it is actually happening* **4** (of money) spent or needed to keep something working: *the running costs of a car/factory* **5** giving out liquid: *a running nose/sore* **6 take a running jump** *sl, imperative* Go away! You annoy me

running[3] *adv* one after the other without a break: *3 times running*

runny *adj* **-nier, -niest** *esp. spoken* **1** more liquid than is usual or expected: *runny butter* **2** (of the nose or eyes) producing liquid, as when one has a cold

run off *v adv* **1** to allow (liquid) to flow out: *run off water from the barrel* **2** to print (copies)

run-of-the-mill *adj often offensive* ordinary; not special

run out *v adv* **1** to come to an end, so that there is no more **2** (in cricket) to end the innings of (a player in the middle of making a run) by hitting the wicket with the ball

run out on also **walk out on**— *v adv prep sl* to leave or desert (someone or something for whom/which one is responsible)

runs *n esp. spoken* diarrhoea: *to have the runs*

runt *n* a small badly-developed animal or person

run through *v adv* to stick one's sword right through (someone)

run to *v prep* **1 a** (of money) to be enough for **b** (of a person) to have enough money for **2** to have a tendency towards: *running to fat* **3** to add up to

run-up *n* **1** also **run-in**— the activities or time leading up to an event: *the run-up to the election* **2** (in sports) an act or distance of running in order to gain **3** enough speed for some activity: *a jumper's run-up*

run up *v adv* **1** to raise (a flag) **2** to make quickly, esp. by sewing **3** to cause oneself to have (bills or debts)

runway *n* **-ways** an area with a specially prepared hard surface, on which aircraft land and take off

rupee *n* the standard coin or note in the money system of India, Pakistan, Sri Lanka, etc. ☞ MONEY

rupture[1] *n* **1** sudden breaking apart or bursting **2** a hernia

rupture[2] *v* **-tured, -turing** **1 a** to cause (esp. a muscle) to break or burst **b** (esp. of a muscle) to break or burst **2** to give (oneself) a hernia

rural adj of or like the countryside or country life —compare URBAN, RUSTIC — ~ly adv

Ruritanian adj of or typical of Ruritania, an imaginary small European kingdom of former times, full of exciting adventure

ruse n a trick to deceive an opponent

rush¹ n any of several types of grasslike water plant whose long thin hollow stems are often dried and made into mats, baskets, and chair seats — **rushy** adj

rush² v 1 to hurry; act quickly 2 to move suddenly and hastily in the stated direction: *They rushed up the stairs* 3 to do (a job) hastily and usu. poorly 4 to force (someone) to act hastily: *Don't rush me* 5 to attack suddenly and all together 6 **rush someone off his feet** to make someone hurry too much or work too hard

rush³ n 1 a sudden rapid movement 2 too much haste 3 great activity and excitement: *the Christmas rush* 4 a sudden great demand: *a rush to see the new film* —see also GOLD RUSH

rushes n (in film-making) the first prints of a film before it has been cut

rush hour n one of the periods in the day when people are travelling to and from work and city streets are crowded

rushlight also **rush candle—** n a kind of candle made by dipping the inside of a rush into melted fat

rush out v adv to produce hastily and in large numbers: *They rushed out 1, 000 copies of the book*

rusk n a kind of hard dry biscuit, often made from hard bread and given to babies

russet n, adj esp. literature (of) a reddish brown or golden brown colour

Russian adj of or related to **a** the language and people of Russia **b** the chief language, people, and country of the USSR

Russian roulette n a dangerous game in which one fires at one's own head a revolver with a bullet in only one of the chambers

rust¹ n 1 the reddish brown surface that forms on iron and some other metals when attacked by water and air —compare RUSTY 2 the colour of this 3 any of various plant diseases (FUNGUS diseases) causing reddish-brown spots

rust² v to cover or become covered with rust

rustic¹ adj 1 connected with or suitable for the country 2 simple and rough compared to the town: *rustic voices* —compare URBAN, RURAL 3 roughly made out of wood with the bark left on — ~ity n

rustic² n often offensive a country person, esp. a farm worker

rusticate v -cated, -cating to send (a student) away from a university for a while as a punishment

rustle¹ v -tled, -tling 1 a (of paper, dry leaves, silk, etc.) to make slight sounds when moved or rubbed together **b** to cause (paper, dry leaves, silk, etc.) to make these sounds: *The wind rustled the dead leaves* 2 to move along making these

sounds: *The tiger rustled through the bushes* 3 esp. US to steal (cattle or horses left loose in open country)

rustle² n a sound of rustling

rustler n esp. US a person who rustles cattle

rustle up v adv to find a supply of (something): *to rustle up some food*

rusty adj -ier, -iest 1 covered with rust 2 **a** (of a person) having forgotten much of a subject: *a bit rusty on history* **b** (of one's knowledge of a subject) mostly forgotten — **rustiness** n

rut¹ n technical the season of sexual excitement for animals, esp. male deer

rut² n 1 a deep narrow track left by a wheel 2 **in a rut** in a fixed and dull way of life

rut³ v -tt- to form ruts in: *the rutted track*

ruthless adj 1 (of a person or his behaviour) very cruel; without pity 2 firm in taking unpleasant decisions — ~ly adv — ~ness n

rutting adj of or during sexual rut

rye n 1 a type of grass plant grown in cold countries 2 the grain of this plant, used for flour

rye whisky n whisky made from rye grain

S

S, s S's, s's or Ss, ss the 19th letter of the English alphabet

S abbrev. for: south or southern

Sabbath n 1 the 7th day of the week; Saturday, kept as a day of rest and worship by Jews and some Christians 2 Sunday, kept as such a day by most Christians 3 **keep/break the Sabbath** to keep/break the religious rules limiting activities on this day

sabbatical n a period, often 1 year in 7, allowed with pay esp. to a university teacher when he has no ordinary duties and may travel and study

sable¹ n 1 a type of small animal of northern Europe and Asia with dark fur 2 the fur of this animal

sable² adj black or very dark

sabot n a shoe cut from a wooden block — compare CLOG

sabotage¹ n 1 intentional damage to machines, buildings, etc., esp. to weaken a business or a country at war 2 indirect or secret action to prevent or ruin a plan

sabotage² v -taged, -taging to practise sabotage on — **-teur** n

sabre n 1 a heavy military sword with a curved blade ⟶WEAPON 2 a light sword for fencing, used to cut and stab —compare FOIL, EPEE.

sabre-toothed tiger n a type of large tiger that lived very long ago, and had 2 long curved teeth in the upper jaw

sac n technical a bag inside a plant or animal, usu. containing a particular liquid

saccharin *n* a sweet-tasting chemical used in place of sugar
saccharine *adj* **1** very sweet or unpleasantly sweet **2** unpleasantly or too friendly, nice, etc.
sachet *n* a small usu. plastic bag holding enough of a liquid to be used at one time
sack[1] *n* **1 a** large bag used for storing or moving goods **b** also **sackful**— the amount in one of these **2** *esp. spoken* the taking away of someone's job by an employer **3 hit the sack** *esp. spoken* to go to bed
sack[2] *v* to dismiss
sack[3] *n* any of various esp. Spanish white wines brought to England in the 16th and 17th centuries
sack[4] *n* the action of sacking a city
sack[5] *v* to destroy buildings, take valuables and usu. harm or kill people in (a conquered city)
sackbut *n* an early form of trombone
sackcloth and ashes *n* a spirit of sorrow or lack of pride
sacrament *n* any of several Christian ceremonies, including baptism, the Eucharist, and marriage — ~**al** *adj*
Sacrament also **Blessed Sacrament**— *n* the bread eaten at Mass or the Eucharist
sacred *adj* **1** religious, esp. in nature or use —opposite **secular, profane** **2** holy by connection with God **3** serious, solemn, and important: *a sacred promise* **4** for the honour of a stated person or god — ~**ly** *adv* — ~**ness** *n*
sacred cow *n* *offensive* a thing or idea so much accepted that it is beyond question
sacrifice[1] *n* **1** an offering to God or a god, esp. of an animal by killing **2** the loss of something of value, esp. for a particular purpose **3** something lost in this way: *His parents made many sacrifices for him* — -**ficial** *adj*
sacrifice[2] *v* -**ficed, -ficing** **1** to offer (something) as a sacrifice **2** to give up or lose, esp. for some good purpose
sacrilege *n* the act of treating a holy place or thing without respect — -**legious** *adj* — -**legiously** *adv*
sacristy *n* -**ties** a vestry
sacrosanct *adj* *often offensive or humour* too holy or important to be allowed any harm or disrespect: *His afternoon sleep is sacrosanct*
sad *adj* -**dd**- **1** feeling, showing, or causing grief or sorrow; unhappy **2 sadder but wiser** *esp. spoken* having learned from unpleasant experience **3 sad to say** (usu. at the beginning of a sentence) unfortunately — ~**ly** *adv* — ~**ness** *n*
sadden *v* to make or become sad
saddle[1] *n* **1** a usu. leather seat that fits on the back of an animal for a rider to sit on ☞ HORSE **2** the part of an animal's back where this is placed **3** a piece of meat from the back of a deer or sheep just in front of the back legs **4** a seat on a bicycle, motorcycle, etc. **5 in the saddle** a sitting on a saddle on an animal **b** *esp. spoken* in control
saddle[2] *v* -**dled, -dling** **1** to put a saddle on (an

animal) **2** to give (someone) an unpleasant duty, responsibility, etc.: *He's saddled with a large house which he can't sell*
saddlebag *n* **1** either of a joined pair of bags placed over an animal's back so that one hangs on each side **2** a bag fixed to a bicycle, motorcycle, etc.
saddler *n* a maker of saddles and other leather articles for horses
saddlery *n* goods made by a saddler
saddle-sore *adj* (of a person) sore and stiff from riding
sadism *n* **1** unnatural fondness for causing pain **2** *technical* the unnatural idea or action of getting sexual pleasure from causing pain — compare MASOCHISM — **sadist** *n* — **sadistic** *adj* — **sadistically** *adv*
s.a.e. *abbrev. for:* stamped addressed envelope
safari *n* a trip through wild country, esp. in Africa
safari park *n* a park in which wild animals are kept, so that one can drive round in a car and look at them
safe[1] *adj* **1** out of danger; not able to be hurt; protected **2** not hurt; unharmed: *came through the storm safe and sound* **3** not allowing danger or harm: *a safe place to swim* **4** not likely to cause risk or disagreement: *It's safe to say that the Queen is popular* **5** (of a seat in Parliament) certain to be won in an election by a particular party **6 as safe as houses** *esp. spoken* very safe from risk **7 on the safe side** taking no risks at all **8 play it safe** *esp. spoken* to take no risks — ~**ly** *adv* — ~**ness** *n*
safe[2] *n* a box or cupboard with thick metal sides and a lock, used to protect valuables
safebreaker *n* a thief who breaks into safes
safe-conduct *n* official protection given to a person passing through a particular area as in wartime
safe-deposit *n* safe storing of valuable objects, usu. in small boxes (**safe-deposit boxes**) in a bank
safeguard[1] *n* a protection against something unwanted
safeguard[2] *v* to protect
safekeeping *n* protection from harm or loss
safety *n* -**ties** **1** freedom from danger, harm, or risk **2** also **safety catch**— a lock on a weapon to keep it from firing accidentally
safety belt *n* **1** a belt for fastening to something solid, worn by someone working high up to keep him from falling **2** SEAT BELT
safety-first *adj* marked by a wish to take no risks
safety glass *n* strong (usu. LAMINATED) glass that breaks only into harmless small pieces which are not sharp
safety match *n* a match that lights only when rubbed along a special surface on its packet
safety pin *n* a wire pin with a cover at one end and bent round so that its point can be held inside the cover

safety razor n a razor with a cover over most of the blade

safety valve n a part of a machine, esp. of a steam engine, which allows gas, steam, etc., to escape when the pressure is too great

saffron n 1 powder of a deep orange colour used in cooking 2 orange-yellow colour

sag v -gg- to sink, settle, or bend downwards, esp. from the usual or correct position: *The branch sagged under his weight.* | *My spirits sagged when I heard the score* — **sag** n

saga n 1 any of the old Viking stories 2 any long story of exciting and brave action

sagacious adj *literature* having deep understanding and judgment; wise — **-city** n — ~**ly** adv

sage¹ adj esp. *in literature* wise, esp. as a result of thinking and experience — ~**ly** adv

sage² n a person known for his wisdom and experience

sage³ n a herb with grey-green leaves used in cooking

Sagittarius n 1 a the 9th division in the belt of stars (ZODIAC) represented by a half-horse half-human animal (CENTAUR) b the group of stars (CONSTELLATION) formerly in this division 2 a person born under this sign ⎯☞ ZODIAC

sago n a white starchy substance made from the stems of certain palm trees (esp. the **sago palm**) and used for making sweet dishes and for stiffening cloth

sahib n (in India in former times) a term of respect for a male European

said¹ adj esp. *written* aforesaid

said² past tense and past part. of SAY

sail¹ n 1 a a piece of cloth fixed on a ship to move it through the water by the force of the wind: *a ship in full sail* (=with all its sails spread) ◉ 2 a short trip in such a ship 3 any of the broad blades of a windmill 4 **set sail** to begin a trip or a new course at sea 5 **take the wind out of someone's sails** esp. *spoken* to take away someone's pride or advantage by actions of one's own

sail² v 1 a (of any ship) to travel on water b to direct (any ship) on water 2 to travel by water (across) 3 to make short trips as a sport in a sailing boat: *to go sailing* 4 to move proudly, smoothly, or easily: *sailed easily through the exam* —see also **sail close to the** WIND

sailing n 1 the skill of directing the course of a ship 2 the sport of riding in or directing a sailing boat 3 a voyage or departure by ship: *the times of sailing*

sailor n a person with a job on a ship

saint n 1 a person recognized after death by the Christian church as specially holy 2 a person with a holy or completely unselfish way of life — ~**ly** adj : *a saintly life* — ~**liness** n

Saint n (a title before a saint's name): *Saint Paul*

sainted adj (of one who has died) entered into heaven: *our sainted mother*

saint's day n -**days** the day each year on which the church honours a particular saint

saith old use or Bible says

sake¹ n 1 **for the sake of a** for the good or advantage of: *If you won't do it for your own sake* (=to help yourself), *then do it for my sake* (=to please me) b for the purpose of: *Art for art's sake* 2 **for God's/Christ's/goodness/pity's sake** esp.*spoken* (used for giving force to a request, or to express annoyance)

sake, saki² n a Japanese alcoholic drink made from rice and usu. served warm

salaam¹ n 1 (a greeting, meaning ' peace ' in Arabic, used in the East) 2 a low bow while putting the inside of the right hand on the forehead, used as a respectful greeting

salaam² v to make a salaam

salable, saleable adj that can be sold

salacious adj expressing, causing, etc., strong sexual feelings usu. in an improper or shocking way — ~**ly** adv — ~**ness** n

salad n 1 a mixture of foods, usu. mainly vegetables, served cold 2 a plant used for such a dish —see also FRUIT SALAD

salad days n esp. *spoken* one's time of youth and inexperience

salad dressing n also **salad cream**— a mixture for putting on a salad

salamander n a type of small 4-legged animal like a lizard but with soft skin

salami n a kind of large sausage with a strong salty taste

salaried adj having or receiving a salary, usu. as opposed to wages: *salaried workers*

salary n -**ries** fixed regular pay, usu. by the month or year, esp. as for workers of higher rank —compare WAGES; see PAY (USAGE)

sale n 1 an act of selling; agreement exchanging something for money 2 a special offering of goods at lower prices than usual —see also JUMBLE SALE 3 an auction 4 the total amount sold of something offered to be bought: *a large sale* 5 **for sale** offered to be bought 6 **on sale** available to be bought 7 **sale or return** supplied with agreement that what is used will be paid for, and the rest returned

saleable adj salable

sale of work n **sales of work** a sale in which small articles, food, etc., made at home are sold to make money for a particular purpose

saleroom n a place where auction sales are held

sales adj of or related to selling: *the sales department*

salesgirl n a usu. young female shop assistant

saleslady n -**dies** polite a female shop assistant

salesman fem. **saleswoman**— n -**men** 1 also (esp. *written*) **sales representative** — a man who sells a company's goods to businesses, homes, etc. 2 a usu. skilled shop assistant

sales resistance n unwillingness to buy something

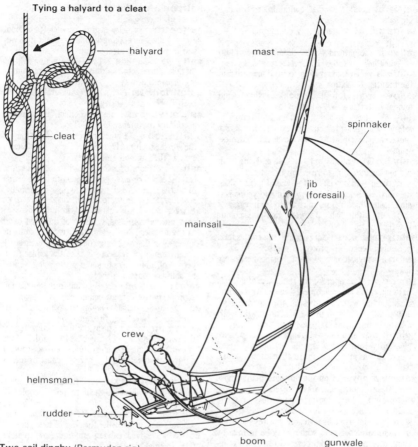

Tying a halyard to a cleat

halyard

cleat

mast

spinnaker

jib (foresail)

mainsail

crew

helmsman

rudder

boom

gunwale

Two-sail dinghy (Bermudan rig)
A dinghy consists of three main sections – the hull, the sails, and the rigging. 'Hull' refers to the main shell of the boat, the base of which is the keel. The term 'rigging' refers to the shrouds, sheets, and halyards used to raise and control the sails.

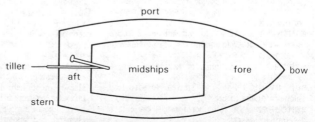

port

tiller

aft

midships

fore

bow

stern

starboard

Parts of a dinghy

salient *adj* standing out most noticeably or importantly

saliferous *adj technical* containing or producing salt

saline *adj* of, related to, or containing salt — **salinity** *n*

saliva *n* the natural watery liquid in the mouth — **-vary** *adj* : *salivary glands*

salivate *v* **-vated, -vating** to produce saliva in the mouth — **-vation** *n*

sallow *adj* (of the skin) yellow and unhealthy-looking — **~ness** *n*

sally *n* **-lies** 1 a quick attack and return to safety 2 a rush into action or expression 3 *esp. spoken* a little trip; jaunt 4 a clever usu. harmless remark

sally forth also **sally out**— *v* **-lied, -lying forth** *old use or humour* to rush out or set out

salmon *n* **-on** or **-ons** 1 a type of large fish of the northern seas with silvery skin and yellowish-pink flesh, which swims up rivers to lay its eggs 2 the flesh of this fish 3 a yellowish-pink colour like that of this flesh

salmonella *n* a type of bacteria that causes food poisoning because it grows on meat

salon *n* a stylish or fashionable business: *a beauty salon*

saloon *n* 1 a room for the social use of a ship's passengers 2 also **saloon car**— a car with a roof, closed sides, with windows, and a separate boot 3 (typically in a town in the American wild west) a large public drinking place

saloon bar also **saloon, lounge bar**— *n* a more pleasantly furnished room in an inn, pub, etc., where drinks usu. cost more than in the public bar

salsify *n* a type of purple-flowered plant whose long fleshy root is eaten as a vegetable

salt¹ *n* 1 a very common colourless or white solid substance (SODIUM CHLORIDE) used to preserve food, improve its taste, etc. 2 any of a class of chemical substances which may be formed by combining an acid and a base 3 pleasant excitement or interest: *Sports give salt to life* 4 *esp. spoken* experienced sailor: *He's* **an old salt** 5 **rub salt in someone's wounds** to make someone's sorrow, pain, etc., even worse 6 **take with a grain/pinch of salt** *esp. spoken* to be cautious in believing (wh at is said) 7 **the salt of the earth** *pompous* a person or people regarded as admirable 8 **worth one's salt** *esp. spoken* worthy of respect, or of one's pay

salt² *v* 1 to add salt to; put salt on 2 to preserve with salt 3 to add interest or excitement to: *a lecture salted with jokes*

salt³ *adj* of, containing, or tasting of salt — **~ness** *n*

salt away *v adv esp. spoken* to save (esp. money) for the future

saltcellar *n* a container for salt on a table —compare CASTER

saltlick *n* 1 a large salty block for animals to lick 2 a naturally salty place where animals lick salt

saltpan *n* a hollow place from which salt water dries up leaving salt

saltpetre *n* a salty-tasting powder (**potassium nitrate**) used in making gunpowder and matches and in preserving meat

salty *adj* **-ier, -iest** 1 of or containing salt 2 (of talk, stories, etc.) slightly improper in an amusing or exciting way — **saltiness** *n*

salubrious *adj esp. written* favourable to good health — **~ness, -brity** *n*

salutary *adj* having a good effect, as to health: *a salutary experience*

salutation *n* 1 greeting by words or action 2 the words, such as ' Dear Sir ', ' Dear Miss Jones ', etc., at the beginning of a letter

salute¹ *v* **saluted, saluting** 1 to make a salute (to) 2 *esp. written* to greet, esp. with polite words or with a sign 3 *esp. written* to honour formally: *a dinner to salute the president on his birthday*

salute² *n* 1 any of several military signs of recognition, such as **a** a raising of the right hand to the forehead **b** a ceremonial firing of guns or lowering of flags 2 a sign or ceremony expressing good feelings or respect 3 **take the salute** (of a person of high rank) to stand while being saluted by soldiers marching past

salvage¹ *n* 1 the act of saving from destruction 2 property saved from being destroyed

salvage² *v* **-vaged, -vaging** to save from loss or damage by wrecking, fire, etc.

salvation *n* 1 (esp. in the Christian religion) the saving or state of being saved from the power of evil 2 saving or preservation from loss, ruin, or failure 3 something that saves; a cause or means of saving

Salvation Army *n* a Christian organization that is known for its help to poor people — **salvationist** *n*

salve¹ *n* (an) oily paste for putting on a cut, wound, etc., to help the forming of new skin

salve² *v* **salved, salving** usu. *literature* to make (esp. feelings) less painful

salver *n* a usu. fine metal plate for serving food, drink, etc., formally

salvo *n* **-vos** or **-voes** a firing of several guns at once

Samaritan *n* 1 a member of the Samaritans 2 **good Samaritan** a person who gives kind and unselfish help to someone in need

Samaritans *n* an organization helping people who are troubled

samba *n* a lively Brazilian dance and its music

same¹ *adj* 1 being (always) only one single thing, person, etc.: *Father sits in the same chair every evening* 2 a being the particular one, or one already mentioned: *You've made the same mistakes as last time* **b** like something else in every way; alike in almost every way; not different or changed: 3 **amount/come to the same thing** to have the same result or meaning 4 **one and the**

same exactly the same —see also ALL **the same to, in the same** BOAT, **the same old** STORY   USAGE It is considered better English to use *as* after **same**, rather than *that: the* **same** *hat as/that you wore yesterday. As* must of course be used when no verb follows: *His car cost the* **same** *(amount) as mine.*

same² *pron* the same thing, person, etc.: *He ordered apple pie and I had the same*

same³ *adv* **the same** in the same way

sameness *n* the state of being the same

samovar *n* a container with a heating device used in Russia to boil water for making tea

sampan *n* a light flat-bottomed boat used along the coasts and rivers in China, Japan, etc.

sample¹ *n* **1** a small part representing the whole; typical small quantity, thing, event, etc. **2** a small trial amount of a product, often given away free

sample² *v* **-pled, -pling** **1** to examine a sample of: *sampled the wine* **2** to calculate by taking a sample from

sampler *n* a piece of cloth embroidered with the alphabet, a picture, etc., to show skill in sewing

samurai *n* **-rai** *or* **-rais** a Japanese military nobleman in former times

sanatorium *n* **-ums** *or* **-a** an establishment for sick people who need long periods of treatment or rest

sanctify *v* **-fied, -fying** to make holy — **-fication** *n*

sanctimonious *adj* making a show of being religious — ~**ly** *adv* — ~**ness** *n*

sanction¹ *n* **1** permission, approval, or acceptance **2** an action, such as the stopping of trade, taken by one or more countries against another country **3** a formal action or punishment which is ordered when a law or rule is broken **4** something that forces the keeping of a rule or standard: *societies where shame is the only sanction against wrongdoing*

sanction² *v* to accept, approve, or permit

sanctity *n* holiness

sanctuary *n* **-ries** **1** the part of a religious building considered most holy, as in a Christian church the area in front of the altar **2** a protection from harm **b** a place of safety **3** an area where birds or animals are protected from hunters and animal enemies

sanctum *n* **-tums** *or* **-ta** **1** a holy place **2** a quiet private place

sand¹ *n* loose material of very small fine grains, found along seacoasts and in deserts

sand² *v* **1** to make smoother by rubbing with a rough surface, esp. sandpaper **2** to put sand on, esp. to prevent slipping

sandal *n* a light shoe made of a usu. flat bottom and bands to hold it on the foot

sandalwood *n* a type of hard yellowish sweet-smelling south Asian wood

sandbag *n* a bag filled with sand or earth

sandbank *n* a high underwater bank of sand in a river, harbour, etc.

sandbar *n* a stretch of sand formed by moving currents esp. across the mouth of a river

sandblast *v* to clean or cut metal, glass, etc., with a machine sending out a stream of sand

sandcastle *n* a small model, esp. of a castle, built in sand by children

sander also **sanding machine**— *n* a machine with a fast moving rough surface for makng surfaces smoother

sandglass *n* a glass for measuring time

sandpaper¹ *n* paper with a covering of sand on one side, used for rubbing over surfaces to make them smoother —see also GLASSPAPER

sandpaper² *v* to rub with sandpaper

sandpiper *n* any of various types of small long-legged bird found esp. around muddy and sandy shores

sandpit *n* a box, hollow place in the ground, etc., with sand for children to play in

sandstone *n* rock of a kind formed by sand fixed in a natural cement

sandstorm *n* a desert windstorm in which sand is blown about

sandwich¹ *n* **1** 2 slices of bread with some other food between them —compare OPEN SANDWICH **2** also **sandwich cake**— a cake of 2 flat parts with jam and cream between them

sandwich² *v* to put tightly in between 2 things of a different kind

sandwich board *n* a pair of large advertising signs for hanging at the front and back of a **sandwich man** who walks about

sandwich course *n* a course of study including periods spent in working for a company

sandy *adj* **-ier, -iest** **1** containing or full of sand **2** (esp. of hair) yellowish-brown in colour, like sand — **sandiness** *n*

sane *adj* **1** not mad **2** produced by good reasonable thinking — ~**ly** *adv* — **-ity** *n*

sang *past tense of* SING

sangfroid *n* French calm courage

sanguine *adj* eagerly hopeful — **-guinity** *n*

sanitary *adj* **1** of or concerning health, esp. the treatment of human waste substances, dirt, or infection **2** free from danger to health

sanitary towel *n* a small pad of soft paper worn by a woman during menstruation

sanitation *n* the protecting of public health

sank *past tense of* SINK

sans *prep* French without

Sanskrit *adj, n* (of or in) the ancient holy language of India ☞ LANGUAGE

Santa Claus *n* FATHER CHRISTMAS

sap¹ *n* the watery juice carrying food, chemical products, etc., through a plant

sap² *v* **-pp-** to weaken or destroy, esp. during a long time

sapling *n* a young tree

sapper *n* a member, esp. of the lowest rank, of the branch of the Army (the engineers) doing digging and building

sapphire *n* a kind of precious stone of a transparent bright blue colour

sap

saprophyte *n* a living organism that gets its food from dead and decaying matter — **-phytic** *adj*

sapwood *n* the younger outer wood in a tree —compare HEARTWOOD

saraband, -bande *n* a Spanish court dance of the 17th-18th centuries, or its music

sarcasm *n* speaking or writing which tries to hurt someone's feelings, csp. by expressions which clearly mean the opposite to what is felt ⚠ SAR-DONIC — **-castic** *adj* — **-castically** *adv*

sarcophagus *n* **-gi** or **-guses** a usu. ornamented stone coffin

sardine *n* **1** any of various young small edible fish **2 like sardines** packed tightly together

sardonic *adj* marked by a feeling of being too good or important to consider a matter, person, etc., seriously ⚠ SARCASTIC — **~ally** *adv*

sarge *n* *esp. spoken* a sergeant

sari *n* a length of light cloth wrapped around the body, worn esp. by Hindu women

sarong *n* a length of cloth wrapped around the waist to form a loose skirt, as worn by Malayan women and men

sartorial *adj* *literature* of or concerning the making or esp. wearing of men's formal clothes — **~ly** *adv*

sash¹ *n* a beltlike length of cloth worn around the waist, or (in ceremonial dress and usu. as a mark of some honour) over one shoulder

sash² *n* a frame holding the glass of a window, door, etc.

sash window *n* a window which opens by sliding one of 2 sashes up or down behind or in front of the other —compare CASEMENT WINDOW

sat *past tense and past part. of* SIT

Satan *n* the Devil

satanic *adj* evil, wicked — **~ically** *adv*

Satanism *n* the worship of the Devil — **-ist** *adj, n*

satchel *n* a small bag of strong cloth or leather

sate *v* **sated, sating** to satisfy with more than enough, or unpleasantly much, of something

satellite *n* **1** a heavenly body moving around a planet **2** a man-made object intended to move around the earth, moon, etc. ☞ SPACE **3** something, esp. a country, that is in, and depends on, the power or influence of another

satiate *v* **-ated, -ating** to satisfy fully or sometimes too fully ⚠ SATURATE — **-iety** *n* — **-iable** *adj*

satin *n, adj* (made of) a kind of fine smooth cloth mainly of silk, shiny on one side

satinwood *n* the very hard smooth wood of a kind of East Indian tree

satiny also **satin**— *adj* smooth, shiny, and soft

satire *n* (a work of) literature, theatre, speaking, etc., intended to show the foolishness or evil of some establishment or practice in an amusing way ⚠ SATYR

satirical also **satiric**— *adj* fond of, being, using, etc., satire — **~ly** *adv*

satirize, -ise *v* **-ized, -izing** to write or speak using satire against

satisfaction *n* **1** contentment **2** something that pleases **3** *esp. written* fulfilment of a need, desire, etc. **4** *esp. written* condition of being fully persuaded; certainty

satisfactory *adj* good enough to be pleasing, or for a purpose, rule, standard, etc. — **-rily** *adv*

satisfy *v* **-fied, -fying** **1** to make happy; please **2** to be or give enough for; fulfil **3** to persuade fully: *Are you satisfied that I am telling the truth?* — **~ing** *adj* : *a satisfying meal*

satsuma *n* a type of small seedless orange

saturate *v* **-rated, -rating** **1** to put as much liquid as possible into **2** to fill completely so that no more can be held **3** *technical* to put into (a chemical solution) as much of the solid substance as possible ⚠ SATIATE

saturation *n* **1** the act or result of saturating **2** *technical* (of a colour) freedom from mixture with white; vividness

Saturday *n* **-days** the 7th day of the week

Saturn *n* the planet which is 6th in order from the sun and is surrounded by large rings

saturnine *adj* *esp. literature* sad and solemn by nature

satyr *n* (in ancient literature) a god usu. represented as half human and half goat ⚠ SATIRE

sauce *n* **1** any of various kinds of usu. cooked liquids put on or eaten with food **2** cheeky disrespectful talk

saucepan *n* a deep usu. round metal cooking pot with a handle and usu. a lid

saucer *n* a small plate made for setting a cup on

saucy *adj* **-ier, -iest** **1** rude or disrespectful **2** sexy in an amusing way — **saucily** *adv* — **sauciness** *n*

sauerkraut *n* *German* a dish made from chopped cabbage kept in salt

sauna also **sauna bath**— *n* **1** a Finnish type of steam bath **2** a room or building for this

saunter¹ *v* to walk in an unhurried way — **~er** *n*

saunter² *n* an unhurried walk

saurian *n, adj* *technical* (of or like) a lizard or other animal of its family

sausage *n* **1** a thin eatable tube of animal skin filled with a mixture of meat, cereal, spices, etc. **2** this meat mixture

sausage roll *n* a small piece of sausage in a covering pastry

sauté *v* **-téed** or **téd, -téeing** or **-téing** to fry quickly in a little hot oil or fat — **sauté** *adj: sauté potatoes*

Sauternes, -terne *n* a sweet gold-coloured French wine

savage¹ *adj* **1** forcefully cruel or violent; uncontrollable; fierce **2** (typical) of an uncivilized place or people **3** *esp. spoken* very angry — **~ly** *adv* — **~ness, ~ry** *n*

savage² *n* **1** a member of an uncivilized tribe or group **2** a cruel, violent, or wild person

savage³ v -aged, -aging (esp. of an animal) to attack and bite fiercely

savanna, -nah n an open flat stretch of grassy land in a warm part of the world

savant n French a person having great knowledge of some subject

save¹ v saved, saving 1 to make safe from danger 2 to keep and add to an amount of money for later use 3 to keep and not spend or use 4 to make unnecessary 5 (in Christianity and some other religions) to free (a person) from the power and effect of evil —see also save FACE — ~r n

save² n (in football) an action by the goalkeeper which prevents a goal

save³ also saving— prep literature except: answered all the questions save one —compare BUT FOR, EXCEPT FOR

saveloy n -loys a kind of dry cooked sausage

saving adj that makes good or acceptable in spite of weakness, faults, etc.

savings n money saved

savings account n any of various kinds of building society or bank account earning higher interest than a deposit account —compare CURRENT ACCOUNT, DEPOSIT ACCOUNT

savings bank n a bank which has only interest-earning kinds of accounts

saviour n a person or thing that saves from danger or loss

Saviour n (in the Christian religion) Jesus Christ

savoir-faire n French the ability to do and say the right thing on every social occasion

savory n a type of herb used in cooking to add taste to meat, beans, etc.

savour¹ n 1 a taste or smell 2 interest

savour² v to enjoy, as by tasting, slowly and purposefully

savoury¹ adj -ier, -iest 1 pleasant or attractive in taste 2 morally attractive or good — opposite unsavoury 3 (of a dish) having the taste of meat, cheese, vegetables, etc. —opposite sweet

savoury² n a small salty dish, sometimes served at the end of a formal meal

savvy¹ v -vied, -vying sl to understand

savvy² n esp. spoken practical knowledge and ability; know-how

saw¹ n a tool for cutting materials, having a thin flat blade with a row of V-shaped teeth on the edge

saw² v sawed, sawn or sawed, sawing 1 to cut with or as if with a saw 2 (of a material) to be able to be cut by a saw

saw³ past tense of SEE

sawdust n very small pieces (as of wood) made by a saw in cutting

sawmill n a factory where logs are cut into boards by a saw

saxifrage n any of various types of small plant with bright flowers, growing esp. in rocky places

Saxon adj of or concerning a people of north Germany who settled in England in the 5th century

saxophone also (esp. spoken) sax— n a metal musical instrument with a curved shape, played with a reed and most usu. used in jazz, military, and dance music — -ist n

say¹ v said, saying 1 to pronounce (a sound, word, etc.) 2 to express (a thought, intention, opinion, question, etc.) in words 3 to show: What time does your watch say? 4 to suppose: Let's say your plan fails: then what? 5 to direct or instruct someone: She says to meet her at 10 6 it goes without saying of course; clearly 7 say for oneself/something to offer as an excuse or as something in favour or defence: You're late again! What have you got to say for yourself? 8 that is to say also (abbrev.) i.e.— in other words: working as hard as before, that is to say not very hard 9 they say people say 10 what do you say? you'll agree, won't you? —see also NOT to say, to say NOTHING of, say the WORD

say² n 1 a power or right of acting or deciding: I've got no say in where we go 2 have/say one's say to have/use the chance to express one's opinion

say³ interj US (used for expressing surprise or a sudden idea): Say, haven't I seen you before?

saying n a well-known wise statement

say-so n 1 a personal statement without proof: Why should I believe that just on your say-so? 2 permission: allowed to come home on the doctor's say-so

scab n a hard mass of dried blood which forms over a wound while it is healing — ~by adj

scabbard n a sheath for a sword, knife, etc.

scabies n a skin disease caused by a mite living under the skin and marked by intense itching

scabious n any of various types of tall European plant with usu. light purple flowers

scabrous adj literature having a rough or scab-covered surface

scaffold n 1 a framework built up from poles and boards, as for workmen to stand on 2 a board for a workman to stand on when working high up 3 a raised stage for the execution of criminals

scaffolding n poles and boards used for building scaffolds

scalar adj, n technical (of or concerning) a number without an associated direction (as opposed to a vector)

scald¹ v 1 to burn with hot liquid 2 to clean or treat with boiling water or steam

scald² n a skin burn from hot liquid or steam

scalding adj (seeming to be) boiling or as hot as boiling

scale¹ n 1 a pair of pans for weighing an object by comparing it with a known weight 2 any weighing machine 3 turn/tip the scales to be the fact, action, etc., that decides a result in favour of one thing or the other 4 tip the scales at to weigh

scale² n 1 one of the small nearly flat stiff pieces forming the outer body covering (or part of it) of some animals, esp. fish and reptiles 2 material like this covering a surface, as greyish material forming around the inside of a kettle, water pipes, etc. —see also FUR 3 (a small piece of) dry skin which comes away from the healthy skin below, as in some diseases 4 **the scales fell from my eyes** esp. literature I was suddenly able to see what had always been clear

scale³ v **scaled, scaling** 1 to remove from or come off a surface in thin small pieces 2 to cover with scale

scale⁴ n 1 a set of numbers or standards for measuring or comparing: wind forces measured on a standard scale of 0–12 2 **a** a set of marks, esp. numbers, on an instrument at exactly fixed distances apart **b** a piece of wood, plastic, etc., with such marks on the edge 3 a rule or set of numbers comparing measurements on a map or model with actual measurements 4 size, esp. in relation to other things or to what is usual: on a large/grand scale 5 a set of musical notes in upward and downward order at fixed separations 6 **to scale** according to a fixed rule for reducing the size of something in a drawing, model, etc.

scale⁵ v 1 to climb up 2 to increase or reduce, esp. by a fixed rate: **scale up/down taxes**

scale diagram n technical a drawing in which the actual dimensions of the figure represented are all reduced by the same scale factor

scale factor n technical 1 (in geometry) the ratio of corresponding lengths of similar figures 2 (in algebra) the ratio between corresponding members of proportional sets

scalene adj technical (of a triangle) having no 2 equal sides ☞ MATHEMATICS

scallion n US & old use an onion whose round white part is small △ SCULLION

scallop, scol-¹ n 1 a kind of shellfish good for food and having a pair of rounded shells marked with raised lines 2 one of a row of small curves forming an edge or pattern

scallop, scol-² v to cut or make scallops in

scallywag n usu. humour a trouble-making or dishonest person

scalp¹ n the skin on the top of the human head

scalp² v to cut off the scalp of (a dead enemy) as a mark of victory as done in former times by American Indians

scalpel n a small delicate very sharp knife used by doctors in operations

scaly adj -ier, -iest covered with scales or scale — **scaliness** n

scamp n a trouble-making but usu. playful person

scamper v to run quickly

scampi n (a dish made from) large prawns

scan v -nn- 1 to examine closely 2 to look at quickly without careful reading 3 **a** to examine (a poem) to show the pattern of music-like beats in each line **b** (of a poem) to have a regular pattern

of this kind 4 (of a beam of electrons) to be directed to (a surface) so as to cover with lines which are close together (as in the making of a television picture) — **scan** n

scandal n 1 a state or action which offends people's ideas of what is right and proper 2 a public feeling or action caused by such behaviour 3 true or false talk which brings harm, shame, or disrespect to another

scandalize, -ise v **-ized, -izing** to offend (someone's) feelings of what is right or proper

scandalous adj offensive to feelings of what is right or proper — **~ly** adv

Scandinavian adj of or concerning the countries Denmark, Norway, Sweden, and Iceland, or their people or language

scanner n an instrument for scanning

scansion n 1 the way a line of a poem scans 2 the act of showing this

scant adj hardly enough

scanty adj -ier, -iest hardly enough; almost too small, few, etc. — **-tily** adv — **-tiness** n

scapegoat n a person or thing taking the blame for others —see also WHIPPING BOY

scapula n medical SHOULDER BLADE

scar¹ n 1 a mark remaining on the skin or an organ from a wound, cut, etc. 2 a mark of damage like this on objects

scar² v -rr- to mark or be marked with a scar

scarab n 1 also **scarab beetle** — a type of large black beetle 2 a representation of this, used in ancient Egypt as an ornament and sign of life after death

scarce adj 1 not much or many compared with what is wanted; hard to find 2 **make oneself scarce** esp. spoken to go away

scarcely adv 1 hardly; almost not; barely 2 (almost) certainly not: You could scarcely have found a better person —see HARDLY (USAGE)

scarcity n -ties a state of being scarce

scare¹ v **scared, scaring** 1 **a** to cause sudden fear to **b** to become fearful 2 to drive, cause to go or become, etc., by fear: His gun scared off the thief — **~d** adj

scare² n a sudden feeling of fear

scarecrow n an object in the shape of a man, set up in a field to keep birds away from crops

scarf n **scarfs** or **scarves** a piece of cloth for wearing around the neck, head, or shoulders

scarify v **-fied, -fying** to break up and loosen the surface of (a road or field) with a pointed tool

scarlet adj, n (of) a very bright red colour

scarlet fever also **scarlatina**— n a serious and easily-spread disease, marked by red spots on the skin

scarlet woman n **-en** usu. humour a woman who does not have proper morals

scarp n a natural steep slope; escarpment

scarper v sl to run away

scat v -tt- sl to go away fast

scathing adj (of speech or writing) bitterly cruel in judgment — **~ly** adv

scatter v 1 **a** to cause (a group) to separate

widely **b** (of a group) to do this **2** to spread widely in all directions by or as if by throwing: *scatter seed*

scatterbrain *n* a likeable but careless, forgetful, or unthinking person — ~**ed** *adj*

scattered *adj* small and far apart

scatty *adj* -**tier, -tiest** *esp. spoken* slightly mad or scatterbrained — -**tiness** *n*

scavenge *v* -**enged, -enging 1** to search for or find (usable objects) at no cost, esp. among waste or unwanted things —compare SCROUNGE **2** (of animals) to feed (on waste or decaying flesh) — ~**r** *n*

scenario *n* -**rios 1** a written description of the action to take place in a film, play, etc. **2** a description of a possible course of action or events

scene *n* **1 a** (in a play) any of the divisions during which there is no change of place **b** (in a film, broadcast, etc.) a single piece of action in one place **2** the background for the action of a play **3** a view of a place: *a beautiful scene* **4** a place where an event happens: *the scene of the crime* **5** an event or course of action regarded as like something in a play or film: *angry scenes in Parliament* **6** a show of anger or feelings, esp. between 2 people in public **7** *esp. spoken* an area of activity: *What's new on the film scene?* **8 behind the scenes** out of sight; secretly **9 on the scene** present; appearing: *came on the scene just when we needed him* **10 set the scene** to prepare; make ready **11 steal the scene** to take attention away from who or what ought to be most important

scenery *n* **1** the set of painted backgrounds and other articles used on a theatre stage **2** natural surroundings, esp. in the country

scenic *adj* of, concerning, or showing natural scenery: *a scenic road* — ~**ally** *adv*

scent¹ *v* **1** (esp. of animals) to smell, esp. to tell the presence of by smelling **2** to get a feeling or belief of the presence or fact of: *She scented that all was not well* **3** to fill with a scent

scent² *n* **1** a smell, esp. **a** as left by an animal and followed by hunting dogs **b** a particular usu. pleasant smell: *the scent of roses* **2** a way to the discovering: *a scientist on the scent of a discovery* **3** (of animals) a power of smelling **4** a feeling of the presence (of something): *a scent of danger* **5** a perfume — ~**less** *adj*

sceptic *n* a sceptical person, esp. about the claims of a religion △ SEPTIC

sceptical *adj* unwilling to believe a claim or promise — ~**ly** *adv*

scepticism *n* a doubting state or habit of mind

sceptre *n* a short rod carried by a ruler on ceremonial occasions

schedule¹ *n* **1** a timetable of things to be done **2** a formal list: *a schedule of postal charges* **3 ahead of/on/behind schedule** before/at/after the planned or expected time

schedule² *v* -**uled, -uling 1** to plan for a

certain future time **2** to put (a flight, train, etc.) into a timetable; make a regular service

schema *n* -**mata** *esp. written* a diagram of an arrangement or plan

schematic *adj* of or like a scheme or schema — ~**ally** *adv*

schematize *v* -**tized, -tizing** to express or show in a very simple, formal way

scheme¹ *n* **1** a clever dishonest plan **2** an official or business plan **3** a general arrangement —see also COLOUR SCHEME

scheme² *v* **schemed, scheming** to make clever dishonest plans — **schemer** *n*

scherzo *n* -**zos** a quick playful piece of instrumental music

schism *n* **1** a separation between parts originally of the same group, esp. the Christian church **2** the action of causing this

schismatic *adj* typical of, fond of, or taking part in a schism — **schismatic** *n*

schist *n* *technical* rock formed from clay by heat or pressure, naturally splitting into thin flat pieces

schizoid *adj* *technical* (typical) of or like schizophrenia or a split personality

schizophrenia *n* *technical* a disorder of the mind marked by a separation of a person's mind and feelings, causing a withdrawal into a life in the imagination only — -**nic** *n, adj* — -**nically** *adv*

schmaltz, schmalz *n* *German* art or esp. music which brings out feelings in a too easy way — ~**y** *adj*

schnapps *n* a kind of strong alcoholic drink rather like gin

schnitzel *n* a piece of veal covered with breadcrumbs and fried

scholar *n* **1** a person with great knowledge of a subject **2** the holder of a scholarship **3** *old use* a child at school —see STUDENT (USAGE)

scholarly *adj* **1** concerned with serious detailed study **2** of or like a scholar

scholarship *n* **1** a sum of money or other prize given to a student, esp. to pay or help to pay for a course of study **2** exact and serious study —see STUDENT (USAGE)

scholastic *adj* of or concerning schools and teaching

school¹ *n* **1** a place of education for children **2 a** attendance or study at such a place **b** one session at such a place: *School begins at 8: 30* **3** a university department concerned with a particular subject **4** a group of people with the same methods, opinions, (of artists) style, etc.: *Rembrandt and his school* —see also OLD SCHOOL

school² *v* to train

school³ *n* a large group of one kind of fish, whale, etc.

schoolboy *(fem.* **schoolgirl)**— *n* -**boys** a boy attending school

schoolhouse *n* a school building, esp. for a small village school

schooling n education or attendance at school

schoolmarm n esp. written & humour 1 a woman school teacher 2 a woman thought to be like this, esp. in being commanding, old-fashioned, exact, and easily shocked

schoolmaster (fem. schoolmistress)— n a male teacher at a school

school report also report— n a written statement by teachers about a child's work at school

schoolwork n study for or during school classes

schooner n 1 a fast sailing ship with 2 or sometimes more masts 2 a large drinking glass

sciatic adj medical of or concerning the hips

sciatica n pain in the area of the lower back, hips, and legs

science n 1 (the study of) knowledge which can be made into a system and which usu. depends on seeing and testing facts and stating general natural laws ⊚ 2 a branch of such knowledge, esp. a anything which may be studied exactly: the science of cooking | military science —see also SOCIAL SCIENCE b any of the branches usu. studied at universities, such as physics, biology, chemistry, engineering (the sciences) —compare ARTS —see also NATURAL SCIENCE — scientist n

science fiction also (esp. spoken) sci-fi— n literature which deals with imaginary future developments in science and their effect ☞ LITERATURE

scientific adj 1 of, being, or concerning science or its principles or rules 2 needing or showing exact knowledge, skill, or use of a system — ~ally adv

scimitar n a sword with a curved blade formerly used in Turkey, Persia, etc. ☞ WEAPON

scintillate v -lated, -lating to sparkle — -lation n

scion n 1 a living part of a plant that is cut off, esp. for grafting onto another plant 2 literature a young or most recent member (of a usu. noble or famous family)

scissors n 2 sharp blades having handles at one end with holes for the fingers, fastened at the centre so that they open in the shape of the letter X and cut when they close: a pair of scissors —compare SHEARS

sclerosis n -ses medical a hardening of some usu. soft part of the body —see also ARTERIOSCLEROSIS, MULTIPLE SCLEROSIS

scoff[1] v to speak or act disrespectfully; laugh at — ~er n

scoff[2] v esp. spoken to eat eagerly and fast

scold[1] n a person, typically a woman, who scolds

scold[2] v to speak angrily, esp. to blame — ~ing n

scollop n, v scallop

scone n a small soft usu. round breadlike cake

scoop[1] n 1 a a small deep shovel-shaped or spoonlike tool held in the hand for digging out corn, flour, soft food, etc. b a container for loose things weighed on scales c the bucket on an earth-moving machine d also scoopful — the amount held by any of these 2 an action of taking with or as if with one of these 3 a usu. exciting news report made by a newspaper before any other newspapers

scoop[2] v to take up or out, with or as if with a scoop: scoop up a handful of sand

scoot v esp. spoken to move quickly and suddenly

scooter n 1 a child's vehicle, pushed by one foot touching the ground 2 MOTOR SCOOTER

scope n 1 the area within the limits of a question, subject, action, etc. 2 space or chance for action or thought

scorbutic adj technical of, concerning, or having scurvy

scorch[1] v 1 a to burn a surface or part of it so as to change its colour, taste, or feeling but not completely destroy it b (of such a surface) to burn in this way 2 to dry up (plants): fields scorched by the sun

scorch[2] n a scorched place; mark made by burning on a surface

scorched earth n the destruction by an army of all useful things, esp. crops, in an area before leaving it to an advancing enemy: a scorched earth policy

scorcher n 1 esp. spoken a very hot day 2 sl something which seems to scorch in being very exciting, angry, fast, powerful, etc.

score[1] n 1 the number of points, runs, goals, etc., made by opponents in a game, sport, etc. 2 one of these points 3 a total of points won esp. in an examination 4 also score mark — a line made or cut on a surface with a sharp instrument 5 a reason; account (esp. in the phrases on this/that score, on the score of): It's not the colour I wanted but it's no less pretty on that score 6 an old disagreement or hurt kept in mind: a score to settle 7 a written copy of a piece of music, esp. for a large group of performers b music for a film or play 8 know the score esp. spoken to understand the true and usu. unfavourable facts of a matter

score[2] v scored, scoring 1 to gain (one or more points, goals, etc.) in a sport, game, or competition 2 to give (a certain number of points) to in a sport, game, or competition 3 to keep an official record of the score of a sports match as it is played 4 to win (a total of points) in an examination 5 to gain or win (a success, victory, prize, etc.) 6 to make (a clever and successful point), esp. in an argument against someone 7 to mark or cut 1 or more lines with something sharp

score[3] adj, n score or scores 1 20 2 scores (of) large numbers (of)

scoreboard n a sign on which the score of a game is recorded as it is played

score for v prep to write a piece of music to be performed by (particular kinds of performers)

score out also score through— v adv esp. writ-

Development of science and technology

World events	Date	Science and technology
	4000BC	c4000BC First use of copper
		c3500BC Invention of wheel, plough, sail 1
2500BC Pyramids built	3000BC	c3000BC bronze in use
2000BC Stonehenge built	2000BC	c2000BC First use of iron
		c1500BC First use of glass
		c1400BC First use of steel
500–146BC Height of	1000BC	c580–500BC Pythagoras, Greek mathematician 2
Greek civilization		c300BC Foundations of geometry laid by Euclid
		c220BC Archimedean screw invented
Birth of Christ	1AD	
476 Fall of Roman Empire	100	c100 Invention of paper in China
711 Muslim army invades	500	c700 Invention of gunpowder in China
Spain	1000	c750–1200 Great age of Arabic science
	1100	c1100–1150 Introduction of arabic numerals to Europe
	1200	c1270 Mechanical clock invented
	1300	c1300 Gunpowder first used in Europe
		c1330 Spinning wheel introduced to Europe 3
	1400	1455 First printed book 4
1492 Columbus sails to	1500	1543 Copernicus suggests the earth revolves round the sun
America		1585 Decimals first used in maths
1588 Spanish Armada	1600	c1600 Invention of compound microscope
		1600 First modern treatise on magnetism
		1608 Telescope developed by Galileo
		1609–19 Kepler's laws of planetary motion published 5
		1614 Logarithms invented
		1628 Circulation of blood discovered by Harvey
1633 Galileo forced to recant		1632 Slide rule invented 6
1662 Royal Society		1662 Boyle's Law formulated
founded in London		1684 Newton's Law of Gravity published
	1700	1712 Thomas Newcomen's steam engine invented
Beginning of Industrial		1770 Spinning jenny invented
Revolution		1774 Discovery of oxygen
1789 French Revolution		1775 James Watt perfects the steam engine 7
1803–15 Napoleonic Wars	1800	1821 Principle of electric motor established by Faraday 8
		1842 First use of ether as anaesthetic
1854–6 Crimean War	1850	1859 First oil-well drilled 9
		1864 Pasteurization invented
		1867 Internal combustion engine first demonstrated
1871 Unification of		1873 First commercial electric motor produced
Germany		1874 Typewriter invented 10
		1876 Telephone invented
		1877 Edison's phonograph (forerunner of gramophone)
		1878 Electric light developed
		1884 Steam turbine engine invented
1892 Keir Hardie–first		1888 Camera perfected
Labour MP		1896 Diesel engine designed
		1897 Discovery of the electron 11
	1900	1900 First successful radio experiments
		1901 First automatic assembly line established
		1903 First powered aircraft flight 12
1914–18 World War I		1916 Einstein's theory of relativity
		1919 First splitting of the atom
		1920 First plastic developed
		1924 First use of insecticides
		1925 J. L. Baird's experiments with television 13
1929 World economic		1928 Discovery of penicillin
depression begins		1937 First jet engine built
1939–45 World War II		1942 First electronic computer developed
		1945 First atomic bomb exploded 14
		1946 First fast-breeder nuclear reactor built
The 'Cold War'		1948 Transistors invented
	1950	1953 Structure of DNA (deoxyribonucleic acid) determined
		1957 First artificial satellite launched 15
		1967 First heart transplant operation
		c1972 Development of microprocessor (silicon chip)

ten to draw a line through (one or more written words) to show that they should not be read; cross out

scorer *n* **1** a person who keeps the official record of a sports match and its score as it is played **2** a player who scores points, goals, etc.

scorn¹ *n* **1** strong, usu. angry feeling of disrespect; contempt **2** an object of such a feeling **3** **laugh someone/something to scorn** also **pour scorn on—** to express scorn for; treat with scorn — compare DISDAIN, CONTEMPT — ~**ful** *adj* — ~**fully** *adv*

scorn² *v usu. literature* **1** to refuse because of pride **2** to feel scorn for

Scorpio *n* -os **1 a** the 8th division of the belt of stars (ZODIAC), represented by a scorpion **b** the group of stars (CONSTELLATION) formerly in this division ⟶ ZODIAC **2** a person born under this sign

scorpion *n* any of several types of tropical insect having a long body and curving tail which stings poisonously ⟶ EVOLUTION

scotch *v* to put an end to: *scotch a false story*

Scotch *n* also **Scotch whisky** — a type of whisky made in Scotland

Scotch broth *n* thick soup made from vegetables and meat

Scotch egg *n* a boiled egg cooked inside a covering of sausage meat

Scotch mist *n* a type of thick mist with light rain

scot-free *adj esp. spoken* without harm or esp. punishment: *to get off/escape/go scot-free*

Scotland Yard *n* (the main office of) the London police and esp. the division dealing with serious or difficult cases of crime

Scottish also **Scots, Scotch—** *adj* of, being, concerning, or typical of Scotland or its people USAGE **Scotch** is sometimes thought rather insulting, but it is often used without any such idea, esp. in connection with Scottish products: **Scotch** *wool* | **Scotch** *whisky*. **Scottish** and **Scots** are, perhaps, more polite. *Scots* is used only of people.

Scottish terrier *n* a type of small terrier with short legs and tail and wirelike hair

scoundrel *n* a wicked man

scour¹ *v* to go through (an area) thoroughly in search of something

scour² *v* **1** to clean (a surface) by hard rubbing with a rough material **2** (of a stream of water) to form by wearing or washing away: *Water had scoured out a passage in the soft sand*

scourer *n* a tool, esp. a small ball of plastic wire or net, for cleaning cooking pots and pans

scourge¹ *n* a cause of great punishment, harm, or suffering: *the scourge of war*

scourge² *v* scourged, scourging **1** to beat with a whip **2** to cause great harm or suffering to

scout¹ *v* **1** to go looking for something: *Scout around for a meal* **2** to go through or look carefully at (a place) to get information about it

scout² *n* **1** a soldier sent out to search the land ahead of an army, esp. for information about the enemy **2** a person who gets information for a sports team about players who should be hired **3** BOY SCOUT **4** a servant at Oxford University who looks after students living in college rooms **5** an act of scouting: *took a scout round*

scoutmaster *n* a grown-up leader of a group of boy scouts

scout out *v adv* to find by scouting

scowl *v* to make an angry threatening frown — scowl *n*

scrabble *v* -bled, -bling to move wildly and quickly (as if) looking for something

Scrabble *n trademark* a game in which players make points by forming words from separate letters on a board

scrag also **scrag end—** *n* the bony part of a sheep's neck, used usu. for stew or soup

scraggy *adj* -gier, -giest thin and bony

scram *v* -mm- *sl* to get away fast

scramble¹ *v* -bled, -bling **1** to move or climb quickly, esp. over a rough or steep surface **2** to struggle or compete with others or against difficulty: *scrambling out of the way* **3** to mix together without order **4** to mix the white and yellow parts of (1 or more eggs) together while cooking them **5** to change the signals in (a radio or telephone message) with a machine (a **scrambler**) so that it can be understood only on a special receiver

scramble² *n* **1** an act of moving or climbing, esp. over a rough surface **2** an eager and disorderly struggle **3** a motorcycle race over rough ground

scrap¹ *n* **1** a small piece: *a scrap of paper* **2** material which cannot be used for its original purpose but which may have some value —see also SCRAPS, SCRAP PAPER

scrap² *v* -pp- **1** to get rid of as no longer useful or wanted **2** to make into scrap

scrap³ *v* -pp- *esp. spoken* to quarrel or fight — scrap *n*

scrapbook *n* a book of empty pages on which photographs, newspaper articles, etc., are/may be fastened

scrape¹ *v* scraped, scraping **1** to remove (material) from a surface by moving an edge firmly across it repeatedly **2** to clean or make smooth in this way **3** to rub roughly **4** to hurt or damage in this way: *He scraped his knee when he fell* **5** to make in this way: *She scraped a hollow in the ground* **6 a** to live with no more than the necessary money **b** to succeed by doing work of the lowest acceptable quality **7 scrape the bottom of the barrel** *esp. spoken* to take, use, suggest, etc., something of the lowest quality

scrape² *n* **1** an act or sound of scraping **2** a hurt made by scraping **3** *esp. spoken* an unpleasant position or affair, esp. caused by one's breaking a rule

scraper *n* a tool for scraping such as: **a** a fixed metal edge near the front door of a house for removing mud, snow, etc., from shoes **b** a kitchen tool for removing food from the sides of a bowl **c** a tool with a sharp metal blade for removing paint

scrapings *n* things scraped from a surface

scrap paper *n* paper, esp. in sheets already used on one side, which may be used for notes

scrappy *adj* **-pier,** **-piest** made or appearing to be made of small pieces; not well arranged or planned

scraps *n* pieces of food not eaten at a meal, and thrown away

scratch¹ *v* **1** to rub and tear or mark with something pointed or rough **2** to make a sound or movement as if doing this **3** to remove in this way: *scratched the paint off the wall* **4** to hurt in this way: *scratched her elbow on a nail* **6** to rub lightly, as to stop itching **7** to remove (oneself, a horse, etc.) from a race or competition before it starts **8 scratch the surface** to deal with only the beginning of a matter or only a few of many cases

scratch² *n* **1** a mark or injury made by scratching **2** a sound made by or as if made by scratching **3** an act of scratching **4** a golf handicap of 0 **5** something put together in a hurry: *a scratch cricket team* **6 from scratch** *esp. spoken* starting from zero or with nothing **7 up to scratch** *esp. spoken* up to an acceptable standard **8 without a scratch** *esp. spoken* completely unhurt

scratch out *v adv* to make marks over (something written) to show that it should not be read

scratchy *adj* **-ier, -iest** **1** (of writing) as if made by scratching **2** (of a recording or its sound) marked by scratches **3** (of clothes) rough and pricking — **scratchiness** *n*

scrawl *v* to write in a careless, irregular, or unskilful way — **scrawl** *n*

scrawny *adj* **-ier, -iest** *offensive* without much flesh on the bones

scream¹ *v* **1** to cry out loudly on a high note **2** to say or express in this way: *He screamed out a warning*

scream² *n* **1** a sudden loud cry on a high note **2** *sl* a very funny person, thing, joke, etc.: *It was a scream!*

screamingly *adv* **screamingly funny** very funny

scree *n* a mass of small loose rocks on the side of a mountain ☞ GEOGRAPHY

screech *v* **1** to cry out on a very high sharp note **2** (of machines, esp. of tyres and brakes) to make a noise like this — **screech** *n*

screed *n* a long and usu. dull speech or piece of writing

screen¹ *n* **1** any of various kinds of upright covered frames, used for protecting people from cold or heat, or for hiding something from view **2** something that protects, shelters, or hides **3** a large flat surface on which films or slides are shown **4** *esp. pompous* the cinema industry **5** the front surface of an electrical instrument show-

ing information, esp. the surface of a television set on which the picture appears **6** a frame holding a thin wire net, put in a window to keep out insects **7** a frame holding a net or surface with holes, used for separating large things from smaller ones —see also WINDSCREEN, SMOKESCREEN

screen² *v* **1** to shelter or protect, as from light, wind, etc. or from view **2** to protect or try to protect from harm or punishment **3** to examine or prove the ability or suitability of (people for a job, requests to be allowed to do something, etc.) **4** to show (a film)

screenplay *n* **-plays** a story written in a form for production as a film

screw¹ *n* **1** a device like a nail having a thread winding round it which helps to hold it in place —see also THUMBSCREW, CORKSCREW **2** an act of turning one of these **3** a propeller **4** *sl* (used by prisoners) a prison guard **5 a** a small twisted piece (of paper) **b** the amount contained by one of these **6 a screw loose** *humour* something wrong or not working properly (esp. in one's mind) **7 put the screws on/to someone** *sl* to force someone to do as one wishes, esp. by threatening

screw² *v* **1** to fasten with 1 or more screws **2 a** to turn or tighten (a screw or something that moves in the same way) **b** (of such a thing) to turn or tighten: *The 2 pieces screw together* **3** to twist **a** (a part of the face) **b** (paper or cloth) carelessly or to make a ball **4** to get by forcing or twisting or by great effort or threats **5** *sl* to cheat **6 have one's head screwed on (right)** to be sensible

screwdriver *n* a tool with a narrow blade to fit into the heads of screws for turning them

screw top *n* **1** a cover which is made to be twisted tightly onto the top of a container **2** an opening of a container made for such a cover to twist onto

screw up *v adv* **1** *sl* to mess up **2 screw up one's courage** to stop oneself from being afraid

screwy *adj* **-ier, iest** *sl* (esp. of ideas and people) seeming unusual, and often funny or annoying

scribble *v* **-bled, -bling** **1** to write (meaningless marks) **2** to write carelessly or in a hurry — **scribble** *n*

scribbler *n* *offensive & humour* a writer

scribe *n* a person employed to copy things in writing, esp. in times before the invention of printing

Scribe *n* a Jewish teacher expert in the laws of religion before and during the time of Jesus

scrimmage *n* a disorderly fight between 2 or usu. more people

scrimp *v* to save (money) slowly and with difficulty, esp. by living poorly

script *n* **1** writing done by hand, esp. with the letters of words joined **2** the set of letters used in writing a language: *Arabic script* **3** a written form of a speech, play, or broadcast to be spoken **4** a piece of writing done by a student in an examination, to be read and given a mark by a teacher

scripted *adj* having, or read from, a script

scripture *n* 1 the Bible 2 a statement in the Bible 3 the holy books of a religion — **-ral** *adj*

scroll *n* 1 a long straight piece of animal skin, papyrus or paper, often rolled around handles and used for writing on esp. in ancient times 2 an ornament or shape with a curve like this

scrollwork *n* ornament marked by patterns with fancy curves

scrooge *n* esp. *spoken & offensive* a miser

scrotum *n* **-ta** or **-tums** *technical* the bag of flesh holding the testicles of some male mammals ➜ REPRODUCTION

scrounge *v* **scrounged, scrounging** 1 to get without spending money 2 to go looking for things — **scrounger** *n*

scrub¹ *n* low-growing plants including bushes and short trees growing in poor soil

scrub² *v* **-bb-** 1 to clean by hard rubbing, as with a stiff brush 2 to remove in this way: *scrubbed the spot out* 3 to remove from consideration or from a list

scrub³ *n* an act of scrubbing

scrubber *n* *sl* 1 a woman who does not have proper morals 2 a prostitute

scrubbing brush *n* a stiff brush for heavy cleaning jobs

scrubby *adj* **-bier, -biest** 1 covered by, or like scrub 2 esp. *spoken & offensive* of small size or importance

scruff¹ *n* **the scruff of the neck** the flesh at the back of the neck

scruff² *n* esp. *spoken* a dirty and untidy person

scruffy *adj* **-fier, -fiest** dirty and untidy

scrum also (esp. *written*) **scrummage**— *n* 1 (in rugby) a group formed by the forward players of both teams pushing against each other with heads down to try to get the ball which is thrown onto the ground between them 2 esp. *spoken* a disorderly struggling crowd

scrumhalf *n* **-halves** a player whose job is to put the ball into the scrum, and to pass it out quickly to other players

scrummage *v* **-maged, -maging** to take part in a scrum

scrumptious *adj* esp. *spoken* (esp. of food) delicious

scrumpy *n* a strong kind of cider of South West England

scrunch *v* 1 to crush; crunch 2 to make a sound/an action like this 3 to press into a ball in the hand — **scrunch** *n*

scruple¹ *n* 1 a moral principle which keeps one from doing something; a doubt about the rightness of an action 2 the desire to do what is right

scruple² *v* **-pled, -pling** to raise a moral argument against doing something; be unwilling because of scruples

scrupulous *adj* 1 carefully doing only what is

right 2 carefully correct in the smallest detail: *scrupulous care* — **~ly** *adv* — **~ness** *n*

scrutineer *n* an official examiner in an election

scrutinize, -nise *v* **-nized, -nizing** to examine closely

scrutiny *n* **-nies** a close study; careful and thorough examination

scuba *n* an instrument used for breathing while swimming under water, made of 1 or more containers of air fastened to the back and connected by a rubber pipe to the mouth

scud¹ *v* **-dd-** (esp. of clouds and ships) to move along quickly

scud² *n* rain or light cloud driven by the wind

scuff¹ *v* to make a rough mark or marks on a surface or to be marked in this way: *badly scuffed shoes*

scuff² also **scuffmark**— *n* a mark made by scuffing

scuffle¹ *v* **-fled, -fling** to be in a scuffle

scuffle² *n* a disorderly fight

scull¹ *n* 1 a type of short oar 2 a small light racing boat for 1 person rowing with a pair of these

scull² *v* to row with sculls — **~er** *n*

scullery *n* **-ries** a room next to the kitchen, for cleaning and keeping dishes and cooking pots

scullion *n* (in former times) a boy doing cleaning work in a kitchen △ SCALLION

sculptor (*fem.* **sculptress**)— *n* an artist who makes works of sculpture

sculpture¹ *n* 1 the art of shaping solid figures (as people or things) out of stone, wood, clay, metal, etc. 2 (a piece of) work produced by this art ➜ PAINTING — **-ral** *adj*

sculpture² also **sculpt**— *v* **-tured, -turing** 1 to make by shaping 2 to make a figure of (a person or thing) in sculpture

scum *n* 1 a filmy covering that typically forms over a pool of still water 2 impure material in a liquid which rises and floats on the surface 3 *offensive* worthless evil people — **~my** *adj*

scupper *v* 1 to sink (one's ship) intentionally 2 esp. *spoken* to wreck or ruin (a plan)

scurf *n* dead skin in small dry bits — **~y** *adj*

scurrility *n* **-ties** scurrilousness

scurrilous *adj* making or containing very rude, improper, or evil statements — **~ly** *adv* — **~ness, -ility** *n*

scurry¹ *v* **-ried, -rying** to move in haste, esp. with short quick steps

scurry² *n* a movement or esp. sound of scurrying

scurvy¹ *adj* **-vier, -viest** dishonourable: *a scurvy trick* — **scurvily** *adv*

scurvy² *n* a disease caused by not eating fruit and vegetables

scut *n* the short upright tail of some animals, like the rabbit and deer

scuttle¹ *n* a coalscuttle

scuttle² *v* **-tled, -tling** to sink (a ship) by making holes in the bottom

scuttle³ *v* to rush in short quick movements, esp. to escape

Scylla *n* **Scylla and Charybdis** *literature* a pair of dangers, of which a person may run into one by trying to avoid the other

scythe¹ *n* a tool having a long curving blade fixed to a long pole to cut grain or long grass —compare SICKLE

scythe² *v* **scythed, scything** to cut with a scythe

SE *abbrev. for:* southeast(ern)

sea *n* **1** the great body of salty water that covers much of the earth's surface —see also HIGH SEAS **2** a large body of water smaller than an ocean, as a part of the ocean: *the North Sea* **b** a body of water almost or wholly enclosed by land: *the Dead Sea* **3** a large mass or quantity regarded as being like one of these: *a sea of faces* **4** the seaside (often in names of towns in the phrase **-on-sea**) **5** movement of waves: *heavy seas* **6** any of a number of broad plains on the moon: *the Sea of Tranquillity* **7 at sea a** during a ship's voyage on the sea **b** *esp. spoken* bewildered: *I'm all at sea when people talk about the government* **8 by sea** on a ship or using ships

sea anemone *n* a type of simple sea animal with a jelly-like body (POLYP) and brightly-coloured flower-like parts that can often sting

seabed *n* the floor of the sea

seaboard *n* the part of a country along a seacoast

seaborne *n* carried or brought in ships

sea breeze *n* a light wind blowing off the sea

sea captain *n* a captain of a merchant ship

sea change *n* *esp. literature* a complete and usu. sudden change

sea cow *n* any of various mammals, such as the manatee, living in the sea

seafaring *adj* *esp. literature* **1** of, about, or doing the job of a sailor **2** also **seagoing**— having strong connections with the sea and sailing

sea fog *n* (a) fog on land coming from the sea or caused by a warm wind from the sea

seafood *n* fish and fishlike animals (esp. shellfish) as food

seafront *n* the part of a coastal town that is on the edge of the sea

seagirt *n* *poetic* surrounded by the sea

seagull *n* a gull

seahorse *n* a type of very small fish with a neck and head that look like those of a horse

seal¹ *n* **seals** *or* **seal** any of several types of large fish-eating animals having broad flat flippers for swimming ☞ MAMMAL

seal² *n* **1 a** an official often round pattern (EMBLEM) as of a government, university, company, or (esp. in former times) a powerful person **b** a piece of wax or soft metal into which such a pattern is pressed and which is fixed to some official writings **c** such a pattern pressed into a piece of writing on paper **2** a metal tool with such a pattern for pressing it into paper or hot

metal or wax —compare SIGNET **3** a small piece of paper, wax, etc. which is fixed across an opening, and which must be broken in order to open it **4 a** a part of a machine for keeping a gas or liquid in or out **b** a tight connection allowing no liquid or gas to escape **5** a mark or sign **6 set the seal on** *literature* to bring to an end in a suitable way

seal³ *v* **1** to make or fix a seal onto **2** to fasten or close with or as if with a seal or a tight cover or band **3** to settle; make certain, formal, or solemn: *sealed their agreement*

sea legs *n* *esp. spoken* the ability to feel comfortable and not be seasick on a ship

sealer *n* a thing or material which seals, esp. (a covering of) paint, paste, etc.

sea level *n* the average height of the sea, used as a standard for measuring heights on land

sealing wax *n* a solid substance which melts and then hardens quickly, used to make seals

sea lion *n* **-lions** *or* **-lion** a type of large seal of the Pacific Ocean

seal off *v adv* to close tightly so as not to allow entrance or escape

seam¹ *n* **1** a line of stitches joining 2 pieces of cloth, leather, etc., at or near their edges **2** the crack, line, or raised mark where 2 edges meet **3** a narrow band of one kind of mineral, esp. coal, between masses of other rocks — ~less *adj*

seam² *v* **1** to mark with lines like seams **2** to sew 1 or more seams in

seaman *n* **-men** **1** a member of the navy with any of the lowest group of ranks (below Petty Officer) **2** a man skilled in handling ships at sea

seam bowler also **seamer**— *n* (in cricket) a person who bowls the ball in such a way that when it hits the ground its hard seam makes it change direction

seamstress also **sempstress**— *n* a woman whose job is sewing

seamy *adj* **-ier, -iest** unpleasant; rough: *the seamy side of city life* — **seaminess** *n*

séance *n* *French* a meeting where people try to talk to or receive messages from the dead

sear *v* to burn with a sudden powerful heat, as **a** to hurt or damage in this way **b** to cook the outside of (a piece of meat) quickly

search¹ *v* **1** to look at, through, into, etc., or examine carefully and thoroughly to try to find something **2 search me!** *esp. spoken* I don't know! — ~er *n*

search² *n* an act of searching

searching *adj* sharp and thorough: *a searching look* — ~ly *adv*

searchlight *n* a large adjustable light with a powerful beam

search warrant *n* a written order given by a court to police to allow them to search a place

searing *adj* burning; very hot

seashell *n* a shell of a small sea animal

seashore *n* land along the edge of the sea

seasick adj feeling sick because of the movement of a ship on water — ~**ness** n

seaside n the edge of the sea, esp. as a holiday place

season[1] n 1 a period of time each year, as a spring, summer, autumn, or winter b marked by weather: *the cold season* c for a particular activity: *the planting season* 2 **for a season** *literature* for a short time 3 **in season a** (of fresh foods) at the time of usual fitness for eating b (esp. of holiday business) at the busiest time of year: c (of certain female animals) on heat d (of animals) permitted to be hunted at the time

season[2] v 1 to give special taste to (a food) by adding salt, pepper, a spice, etc. 2 **a** to make (wood) fit for use by gradual drying b (of wood) to become fit for use 3 to give long experience to: *a seasoned traveller*

seasonable adj 1 suitable or useful for the time of year 2 coming at a good or proper time: *seasonable advice* △ SEASONAL — **-bly** adv

seasonal adj depending on the seasons, esp. happening or active at a particular season △ SEASONABLE

seasoning n something that seasons food

season ticket also (esp. spoken) **season**— n a ticket usable any number of times during a fixed period of time

seat[1] n 1 a place for sitting 2 the part on which one sits 3 a place of a particular power or activity; centre 4 a place as a member of an official body: *a seat in Parliament* 5 *technical* a way of sitting on a horse 6 **take/have a seat** please sit down 7 **in the driver's seat** *esp. spoken* in charge 8 **take a back seat** *esp. spoken* to allow someone else to take control or have the more important job —see also COUNTRY SEAT

seat[2] v 1 to cause or help to sit 2 (of a room, table, etc.) to have room for seats for (a certain number of people)

seat belt also **safety belt**— n a belt fastened around a person sitting in a seat (as in a car or plane) for safety

seating n provision or arranging of seats

sea urchin n any of several types of small ball-shaped sea animals having a hard shell with many sharp points

seaward adj going towards the sea — ~**s** adv

seaway n **-ways** a course followed by ship traffic on the sea

seaweed n any of various plants growing in the sea

seaworthy adj (of a ship) fit for a sea voyage

sebaceous adj of, relating to, producing, or containing a fatty substance released from the skin

sec[1] n esp. spoken a second

sec[2] abbrev. for: a secretary

secateurs n strong scissors for cutting plants

secede v **seceded, seceding** to leave a group or organization — **secession, secessionist** n

seclude v **secluded, secluding** to keep from association with others

secluded adj very quiet and private: *a secluded house* — **-usion** n

seclusive adj esp. written fond of seclusion; liking to be away from others — ~**ly** adv — ~**ness** n

second[1] adj, adv, n, pron 1 2nd 2 a person who helps another, esp. someone who is fighting in a match 3 an article of imperfect quality for sale at a lower price 4 a formal act of seconding a motion 5 a British university examination result of middle quality 6 **second to none** esp. spoken the best

second[2] n 1 a length of time equal to 1/60 of a minute 2 a measure of an angle equal to 1/3600 of a degree 3 a moment

second[3] v 1 to make a second person's statement in favour of (a motion at a meeting) 2 to support in an argument, decision, or effort — ~**er** n

second[4] v to move (someone) from usual duties to a special duty — ~**ment** n

secondary adj 1 of 2nd, or less than 1st, rank, value, importance, etc. ⫣ BIRD 2 later than, developing from, taken from, etc., something earlier or original 3 (of education or a school) for children over 11 years old —compare PRIMARY 4 *technical* carrying or being an electric current caused by another electric current by induction — **-arily** adv

secondary modern also (esp. spoken) **secondary mod**— n a secondary school which does not prepare students for university or further study

secondary picketing n the picketing of a business that uses the goods or services of a firm involved in a labour dispute

second best adj 2nd in value, importance, etc.

second childhood n the period when an old person's mind becomes weak and childish

second-class adj inferior

second class n 1 a class of mail for letters delivered slower than first class 2 the ordinary type of seating, furnishing, etc. (cheaper than first class), esp. on a train 3 (of a university examination result) second

Second Coming n a future glorious coming of Christ from heaven

second cousin n see COUSIN ⫣ FAMILY

second-degree adj of the next to the most serious kind: *second-degree burns*

second-hand adj, adv 1 used or worn by an earlier owner; not new 2 from somewhere other than the original place or person

second lieutenant n an army officer of the lowest rank

second nature n a very firmly fixed habit

second person n a form of verb or pronoun showing the person or thing spoken to: '*You*' *is a second person pronoun*

second-rate adj of less than the best quality

seconds n esp. spoken 2nd servings of food

second sight n the supposed ability to see future or far-away things

second thought n a thought that a past opinion may not be right (esp. in the phrases **to have second thoughts** and **on second thoughts**)

secrecy n 1 the practice of keeping secrets 2 the state of being secret

secret¹ adj 1 kept from the knowledge of others, or of all except a few 2 (of a person) undeclared; unadmitted: *a secret admirer* 3 secretive — ~**ly** adv

secret² n 1 something known to only a few 2 something (so far) unexplained: *the secret of life* 3 a single or most important means of gaining a good result: *the secret of success*

secret agent n a spy

secretariat n an official office or department with a secretary or esp. secretary-general as its head

secretary n -ries 1 a person with the job of preparing letters, keeping records, arranging meetings, etc., for another 2 any of various government officers, as a minister, or the highest non-elected officer in a department 3 an officer of an organization who keeps records, writes official letters, etc. — **-rial** adj

secretary bird n a large long-legged African bird with a crest of feathers on its head

secretary-general n secretaries-general the chief officer of a large organization (esp. an international organization)

secrete¹ v secreted, secreting (esp. of an animal or plant organ) to produce (a usu. liquid substance) —compare EXCRETE

secrete² v to hide

secretion n 1 a the production of some usu. liquid material by part of a plant or animal b such a product 2 the act of hiding something

secretive adj hiding one's intentions or plans — ~**ly** adv — ~**ness** n

secret service n a government department dealing with intelligence work

sect n a group of people having particular beliefs, usu. within or separated from a larger group — ~**arian** adj

sectarian also **sectary**— n a member of a sect, esp. a person with fixed opinions — ~**ism** n

section¹ n 1 a part of a larger object, place, etc., that is, or is regarded as, more or less separate 2 any of the equal parts of some fruits, such as an orange 3 a representation of something as if it were cut from top to bottom and looked at from the side 4 (in mathematics) the figure formed by the points where a solid body is cut by a plane 5 a very thin flat piece cut from skin, plant growth, etc., to be looked at under a microscope

section² v 1 to cut or divide into sections 2 to cut or show a section from

sectional adj 1 made up of sections 2 of or connected with 1 or more sections, esp. areas of a country 3 of or based on a section: *a sectional view*

sectionalism n (too) great loyalty or shared interest within only 1 section of a group

sector n 1 a part of a field of activity 2 a region in a circle enclosed by 2 straight lines drawn from the centre to the edge; a region bounded by part of a circle and 2 radii —compare SEGMENT ⊸ MATHEMATICS

secular adj 1 not connected with or controlled by a church; not religious 2 of matters to do with the nonreligious affairs or government of a society

secularism n a system of social teaching or organization which allows no part for religion or the church — **-ist** n, adj

secure¹ adj 1 safe; protected against danger or risk 2 sure; certain: *a secure job* — ~**ly** adv

secure² v secured, securing 1 esp. *written* to get, esp. as the result of effort: *to secure a place in the team* 2 to make safe 3 to hold or close tightly: *They secured the windows when the storm began*

security n -ties 1 the state of being secure 2 something which protects or makes secure 3 property of value promised to a lender in case repayment is not made or other conditions are not met —compare COLLATERAL 4 protection against lawbreaking, violence, enemy acts, etc. 5 a writing giving the owner the right to some property: *government securities*

Security Council n a body within the United Nations concerned with peacekeeping

security risk n a person whose loyalty is doubtful and who cannot be given certain government jobs

sedan chair also **sedan**— n an vehicle for one person carried on poles by 2 men, 1 in front and 1 behind

sedate¹ adj not easily troubled; calm — ~**ly** adv — ~**ness** n

sedate² v sedated, sedating to give a sedative to — **-ion** n : *He's under sedation and resting in bed*

sedative adj, n (a drug) acting against nervousness, excitement, or pain and usu. causing sleep

sedentary adj used to, or needing, much sitting ⚠ SEDIMENTARY

sedge n any of various grasslike plants growing on low-lying wet ground — **sedgy** adj

sediment n 1 solid material that settles to the bottom of a liquid 2 material carried along and then left in a place by water or ice

sedimentary adj of, concerning, or made of sediment ⚠ SEDENTARY

sedimentation n the forming or coming down of sediment

sedition n speaking, writing, or action intended to cause disobedience or violence against a government — **-ious** adj — **-iously** adv — **-iousness** n

seduce v seduced, seducing 1 to persuade (esp. someone inexperienced) to have sex 2 to cause or persuade (someone) to do something more or less wrong by making it seem attractive — **seducer** n

seduction n 1 the action or an act of seducing 2 a thing or quality that attracts

seductive adj having qualities likely to seduce; attractive: a seductive voice — ~**ly** adv — ~**ness** n

sedulous adj esp. written marked by steady attention and care — ~**ly** adv

see[1] v saw, seen, seeing 1 to use the eyes; have or use the power of sight 2 to look at; get sight of; notice, examine, or recognize by looking: Can you see that? | Let me see your ticket 3 to understand or recognize: Do you see what I mean? 4 to find out or try to find out or determine: I'll see what I can do 5 to make sure; take care: See that you're ready 6 to form a picture in the mind of: I can't see myself lending her money 7 literature to be an occasion of (an event or course in history): The 19th century saw many changes 8 to have experience of: This old house has seen better days 9 to visit, call upon, or meet: The doctor can't see you yet 10 to go with: to see her home 11 (in the game of poker) to answer (an opponent) by risking an equal amount of money 12 **see the back/last of** esp. spoken to be through with; have no more to do with 13 **see things** to think that one sees something that is not there —see also SEE ABOUT, SEE OFF, SEE OUT, SEE OVER, SEE THROUGH, SEE TO, **see** FIT, **see one's** WAY, **see** RED

see[2] n the office of, area governed by, or centre of government of a bishop —compare DIOCESE

see about v prep 1 to attend to; make arrangements for: to see about dinner 2 **We'll see about that!** esp. spoken I will put a stop to that!

seed[1] n 1 the part of a plant from which a new plant can grow 2 something that starts growth or development: seeds of trouble 3 a seeded player 4 kept for planting or producing seeds 5 **go/run to seed a** (of a plant) to produce seed **b** (of a person) to lose one's power of freshness 6 in seed (of a plant) in the condition of bearing seeds — ~**less** adj USAGE When speaking of a large quantity one says **seed**: a sack of grass seed Seeds is a small amount: a packet of seeds

seed[2] v 1 to grow and produce seed 2 to plant seeds in (a piece of ground) 3 to place (a sports, esp. tennis, player at the start of a competition) in order of likelihood to win

seedbed n 1 a place specially prepared for sowing seeds 2 a favourable place or condition for development

seedling n a young plant grown from a seed

seedy adj -ier, -iest 1 having a poor uncared-for appearance 2 full of seeds 3 esp. spoken slightly unwell — **seedily** adv — **seediness** n

seek v sought, seeking 1 usu. written or literature to make a search for; look for; try to find or get 2 to ask for: to seek advice 3 esp. literature to try: They sought to punish him 4 to move naturally to: Water seeks its own level 5 not far

to **seek** easily seen or understood —see also HIDE-AND-SEEK, SOUGHT AFTER — ~**er** n

seem v 1 to give the idea or effect of being; be in appearance; appear 2 to appear to be true

seeming adj that seems to be so, usu. as opposed to what is: a seeming piece of good luck

seemingly adv 1 as far as one can tell: Seemingly there is nothing we can do 2 according to what appears, usu. opposed to what actually is so

seemly adj -lier, -liest (esp. of behaviour) pleasing by being suitable to an occasion — **seemliness** n

seen past part. of SEE

see off v adv to go to the airport, station, etc., with (someone who is beginning a trip)

see out v adv 1 to last until the end of 2 to go to the door with (someone who is leaving)

see over v adv 1 to examine: to see over a report 2 also **see round**— to visit and examine: to see over the house

seep v (of a liquid) to flow slowly through small openings in a material — ~**age** n

seer n literature & old use one who is thought to know about the future

seersucker n a kind of light cloth with flat bands between bands with small folds

seesaw[1] n (play on) a board for children to sit on at opposite ends, balanced so that when one end goes up the other goes down

seesaw[2] v 1 to move backwards and forwards, up and down, or between opponents or opposite sides 2 to play on a seesaw

seethe v seethed, seething 1 (of a liquid) to move about as if boiling: the sea seethed around the rocks 2 to be very excited or angry

see-through adj esp. spoken allowing what is inside to be (partly) seen

see through v prep 1 to recognize the truth about (an excuse, false statement, etc.) 2 to provide for or support throughout (a time or difficulty)

see to v prep to attend to

segment n 1 any of the parts into which something may be cut or divided 2 the region inside a circle between its edge and a straight line across it; a region bounded by part of a circle and a chord —compare SECTOR ☞ MATHEMATICS 3 LINE SEGMENT

segregate v -gated, -gating to separate; keep or be set apart, esp. from the rest of a group — ~**d** adj : In the U.S.A., blacks and whites used to go to segregated schools

segregation n 1 the act or state of separation 2 the separation of a social or esp. racial group from others, as by laws —opposite **integration** —compare APARTHEID

seigneur n (in a feudal system) a nobleman or landowner; lord

seismic adj technical of, concerning, or caused by earthquakes

seismograph n an instrument for recording and measuring shaking of the ground

seismology *n technical* the scientific study of shaking movements in the surface of the earth — **-gist** *n*

seize *v* **seized, seizing** 1 to take possession of a by official order b by force: *The army seized the fort* 2 to take hold of eagerly, quickly, or forcefully; grab 3 to attack or take control of (someone's body or mind): *He was seized with pain*

seize up *v adv* (as of a machine or part) to become stuck and fail to move; jam

seizure *n* 1 the act or result of seizing 2 a sudden attack of an illness

seldom *adv* not often; rarely

select[1] *adj* 1 chosen, or choosing, from a larger group 2 carefully chosen by quality; limited and exclusive: *a select group*

select[2] *v* to choose as best, most suitable, etc., from a group — ~**or** *n*

select committee *n* a committee of Parliament that considers a particular matter

selection *n* 1 the act of selecting 2 one that is selected 3 a collection of things of a kind: *a selection of cheeses* —see also NATURAL SELECTION

selective *adj* 1 acting with, or concerning, only certain articles; not general: *selective controls on goods* 2 careful in choosing — ~**ly** *adv* — ~**ness** *n* — **-tivity** *n*

self *n* **selves** 1 a person with his whole nature, character, etc.: *He put his whole self into the job* 2 a particular part of one's nature 3 one's own advantage or profit 4 (written; esp. in business matters) the person concerned; the signer

self-absorption *n* attention to oneself and to nothing else — **self-absorbed** *adj*

self-acting *n* working by itself; automatic

self-addressed *adj* addressed for return to the sender

self-assertion *n* the action of pushing forward one's own claims or abilities over those of others — **-tive** *adj* — **-tiveness** *n*

self-assurance *n* sure belief in one's own abilities; self-confidence — **-red** *adj*

self-centred *adj* interested only in oneself; selfish — ~**ness** *n*

self-coloured *adj* of a single colour

self-complacent *adj* too pleased and satisfied by one's own position or success

self-confessed *adj* admitted by oneself to be the stated kind

self-confidence *n* a feeling of power to do things successfully — **-dent** *adj*

self-conscious *adj* 1 aware of or knowing about oneself or itself; conscious 2 nervous and uncomfortable about oneself as seen by others — ~**ly** *adv* — ~**ness** *n*

self-contained *adj* 1 complete in itself; sharing no part with another: *a self-contained flat* 2 not showing feelings or depending on others

self-contradictory *adj* containing 2 opposite parts or statements which cannot both be true

self-control *n* control over one's feelings — **-trolled** *adj*

self-defence *n* the act or skill of defending oneself

self-denial *n* the act or habit of not allowing oneself pleasures — **self-denying** *adj*

self-determination *n* the right or action of a people or nation to decid e freely on the form of their government

self-discipline *n* the training of oneself to control one's habits and actions

self-drive *adj* for hire to be driven by oneself, not by a chauffeur

self-educated *adj* educated by one's own efforts and not formally in school

self-effacing *adj* avoiding the attention of others

self-employed *adj* running one's own business; not working for another

self-esteem *n* one's good opinion of one's own worth

self-evident *adj* plainly true without need of proof

self-examination *n* consideration of one's own actions, state, etc., esp. according to some standards

self-explanatory *adj* (esp. of speaking or writing) needing no further explanation

self-government also **self-rule**— *n* government free from outside control; independence — **self-governing** *adj*

self-help *n* the action of helping oneself without depending on others

self-importance *n* too high an opinion of one's own importance — **-ant** *adj* — **-antly** *adv*

self-imposed *adj* that one has forced oneself to accept

self-indulgence *n* the too easy allowance of pleasure or comfort to oneself — **-ent** *adj* — **-ently** *adv*

self-interest *n* concern for the advantage of oneself; selfishness — ~**ed** *adj*

selfish *adj* concerned with or directed towards one's own advantage without care for others — ~**ly** *adv* — ~**ness** *n*

selfless *adj* caring only for others; completely unselfish — ~**ly** *adv* — ~**ness** *n*

self-locking *adj* locking by its own action when closed

self-made *adj* raised to success or wealth by one's own efforts starting without advantages (esp. in the phrase **a self-made man**)

self-opinionated *adj* holding firmly on to one's own opinions even when wrong

self-pity *n* too strongly felt or expressed pity for one's own sorrows or troubles

self-possession *n* calm control over one's own feelings and actions, even in difficult conditions — **-sed** *adj*

self-preservation *n* the keeping of oneself from death or harm, esp. done naturally by living things

self-raising flour n flour that contains baking powder

self-reliance n the use of one's own abilities, judgment, etc., without depending on others — **-ant** adj

self-respect n proper respect for, or pride in, oneself

self-respecting adj keeping up proper standards; not feeling shame

self-righteous adj offensive sure of one's own rightness or goodness, esp. in opposition to the beliefs of others — ~**ly** adv — ~**ness** n

self-sacrifice n the giving up of one's pleasure or interests in favour of a worthier purpose — **-icing** adj

selfsame adj literature exactly same; very same

self-satisfaction n a too satisfied opinion about one's own success — **-fied** adj

self-seeking n, adj (action) that works only for one's own advantage: a self-seeking politician — **-seeker** n

self-service adj, n (working by) the system in many restaurants, shops, petrol stations, etc., in which buyers collect what they want and then pay at special desks

self-starter n a usu. electric apparatus for starting a car engine without turning it by hand

self-styled adj given the stated title by oneself, usu. without any right

self-sufficient also **self-sufficing**— adj able to provide for one's needs without outside help, esp. (of a country) without buying goods and services from abroad — **-ency** n

self-supporting adj earning enough money to pay all its/one's costs

self-will n strong unreasonable determination to follow one's own wishes — ~**ed** adj

self-winding adj (of a wristwatch) winding itself as a result of being in movement on the arm

sell v **sold, selling** 1 to give to another for money or other value 2 to cause to be bought: Bad news sells newspapers 3 to offer (goods) for sale 4 to be bought; get a buyer or buyers 5 sl to persuade (someone) to like, believe, or agree to something 6 sl trick; cheat: The things we bought are no good: we've been sold! 7 **sell oneself a** to make oneself or one's ideas attractive to others **b** to give up one's principles for gain 8 **sell short** to sell something, esp. shares in a company, not yet owned but expected to be bought later at a lower price 9 **sell something/someone short** to value something or someone too low

seller n 1 a person who sells 2 a product that sells well

seller's market n a situation in which goods are scarce, buyers have little choice, and prices are high —compare BUYER'S MARKET

selling point n something that helps a product to be sold

sell off v adv to get rid of (goods) by selling, usu. cheaply

sellotape[1] n trademark sticky thin clear celluloid in long narrow lengths sold in rolls, for sticking paper, mending light objects, etc.

sellotape[2] v **-taped, -taping** trademark to put together or mend with sellotape

sell-out n 1 a performance, sports match, etc., for which all tickets are sold 2 an act of disloyalty to one's purposes or friends

sell out v adv 1 **a** to sell all of (what was for sale) **b** (of things for sale) to be all bought 2 to sell one's share in a business: At 65 he sold out and retired 3 to be disloyal to (one's purposes or friends, esp. for money

sell up v adv to sell (something, esp. a business) completely

selvage, -vedge n a cloth edge strengthened and finished to prevent threads from coming out

selves pl. of SELF

semantics n 1 the study of the meanings of words and other parts of language 2 the general study of signs and what they stand for — **semantic** adj

semaphore[1] n 1 a tall post with coloured lights and a movable arm, used as a signal on railways 2 a system of sending messages, using 2 flags in various positions to represent letters and numbers ⟹ CODE

semaphore[2] v **-phored, -phoring** to send (a message) by semaphore

semblance n an appearance or seeming likeness

semen n the liquid produced by male sex organs that carries sperm and is passed into the female during sexual intercourse

semester n either of the 2 periods into which a year at universities, esp. in the US, is divided —compare TERM

semibreve n a musical note with a time value equal to 2 minims ⟹ MUSIC

semicircle n 1 half a circle ⟹ MATHEMATICS 2 a group arranged in this shape: to sit in a semicircle — **-cular** adj

semicolon n a mark (;) used in writing to separate different members of lists and sometimes independent parts of a sentence

semiconductor n a substance which allows the passing of an electric current more easily at high temperatures

semidetached also (esp. spoken) **semi**— n a house joined to another house by one shared wall — **semidetached** adj

semifinal n either of a pair of matches whose winners will compete in the final

semifinalist n a player who reaches the semifinals in a competition

seminal adj 1 containing the seeds of later development; influencing others in a new way 2 of or containing semen

seminar n a small class of usu. advanced students studying some subject with a teacher

seminary n **-ries** a college for training priests, esp. in the Roman Catholic Church — **-rist** n

semiprecious *adj* of lower value than a precious stone

semiquaver *n* a musical note ♪, with a time value half as long as a quaver ☞ MUSIC

Semitic *adj* **1** of or concerning the languages or peoples of a race including Jews, Arabs, and in ancient times others including Babylonians and Assyrians **2** Jewish —compare ANTI-SEMITISM

semitone *n* a difference in pitch equal to that between 2 neighbouring notes on a piano

semiweekly *adv, adj* appearing or happening twice a week

semolina *n* hard grains of crushed wheat used in making pasta and smooth milky dishes

SEN *abbrev. for*: State Enrolled Nurse

Senate *n* **1** the smaller of the 2 law-making bodies in Australia, Canada, France, the US, and other countries —compare HOUSE OF REPRESENTATIVES **2** the ruling council in ancient Rome **3** the governing council at some universities — **-torial** *adj*

senator *n* a member of a Senate

send *v* **sent, sending** **1** to cause or order to go or be taken to a place, in a direction, etc. **2** to put or bring into a particular state: *The news sent us into great excitement* **3** to cause a message, request, or order to go out **4** (of a natural object) to produce from itself: *branches sending forth their fruit* **5** *literature* (esp. of God) to give or provide: *Heaven send us a safe journey!* **6** (of a radio or radio operator) to transmit — ~**er** *n*

send away for also **send off for**— *v adv* to order (goods) to be sent by post

send down *v adv* **1** to cause to go down **2** to send a message, order, etc., to some lower place: *I'll send down to the kitchen for coffee* **3** to dismiss (a student) from university for bad behaviour **4** *sl* to send to prison

sender *n* *esp. written* a person who sends esp. a letter, parcel, message, etc.

send-off *n* a usu. planned show of good wishes at the start of a trip, new business, etc.

send off *v adv* (esp. in football) to cause (a player) to leave the field because of a serious breaking of the rules

send-up *n* *esp. spoken* something which sends up a subject, person, etc.; parody

send up *v adv* **1** to cause to go up **2** to copy the funny or silly qualities, actions, etc. of (a subject, person, etc.); make fun of

senescent *adj* *esp. written* growing old; showing signs of old age — **-cence** *n*

seneschal *n* an important servant and official of a nobleman in the Middle Ages

senile *adj* weak in body or esp. mind because of old age — **-lity** *n*

senior *adj* **1** older **2** of higher rank or position — **senior** *n* — ~**ity** *n*

Senior *n* the older: *John Smith Senior*

senior citizen *n* *polite* an old person

Señor *n* **Señores** *or* **Señors** the title of a Spanish(-speaking) man

Señora *n* the title of a (married) Spanish(-speaking) woman

Señorita *n* the title of an unmarried Spanish(-speaking) girl

sensation *n* **1** a direct feeling, as of heat or pain, from the senses ☞ NERVE **2** a general feeling in the mind or body **3** a state of excited interest or the cause of it: *The new discovery caused a great sensation*

sensational *adj* **1** *often offensive* causing excited interest or attention **2** (esp. of writing or news reports) intended to cause quick excitement or shock **3** *sl* wonderful; very good — ~**ly** *adv*

sensationalism *n* *offensive* the intentional producing of excitement or shock, as by books, magazines, etc. — **-ist** *n*

sense[1] *n* **1** a meaning **2** any of the 5 senses —see also SIXTH SENSE **3** power to understand and make judgments about something: *a good business sense* **4** a feeling, esp. one hard to describe exactly **5** good and esp. practical understanding and judgment —see also COMMON SENSE, HORSE SENSE **6 in a sense** in one way; partly **7 make sense a** to have a clear meaning **b** to be a wise course of action **8 make sense of** to understand **9 no sense in** *esp. spoken* no good reason for **10 talk sense** *esp. spoken* to speak reasonably

sense[2] *v* **sensed, sensing** to feel; perceive; detect: *The horse sensed danger and stopped*

senseless *adj* **1** in a sleeplike state, as after a blow on the head; unconscious **2** marked by a lack of meaning or thinking; foolish; purposeless —compare INSENSIBLE — ~**ly** *adv* — ~**ness** *n*

sense organ *n* a part of the body, such as the eye, from which the brain receives messages from the outside world

senses *n* **1** the 5 natural powers (sight, hearing, feeling, tasting, and smelling) which give a living thing information about the outside world **2** one's powers of thinking: *Have you taken leave of/lost your senses?*

sensibility *n* **-ties** **1** a tender or delicate feeling about what is correct, as in art or behaviour **2** sensitiveness **3** *esp. written* awareness: *our sensibility to your trouble* —see SENSIBLE (USAGE)

sensible *adj* **1** reasonable; having good sense **2** *esp. written* recognizing; aware: *sensible of the trouble he caused* **3** noticeable; that can be sensed **4** sensitive — **-bly** *adv* USAGE **Sensibility** is not connected with the meaning of **sensible** as 'reasonable and practical'. It is closer to **sensible of**, meaning 'conscious of'. A **sensitive** person has great **sensibility**; he has delicate feelings and is quick to enjoy or suffer. **Sensual** means 'of the body rather than of the mind or spirit', and is often used in a bad sense. **Sensuous** is used about the beauties of colour, sound, etc., and is not used critically.

sensitive *adj* **1** quick to show or feel the effect of a force **2** (of an apparatus) measuring accurately **3** showing delicate feelings or judgment

4 *sometimes offensive* easily hurt in the feelings, esp. of self-respect; easily offended —compare HYPERSENSITIVE — ~ly *adv* — -tivity *n* —see SENSIBLE (USAGE)

sensitize, -tise *v* **-tized, -tizing** to make sensitive

sensor *n technical* any apparatus used to discover the presence of light, heat, sound, pressure, electricty, etc.

sensory *adj* of or concerning the bodily senses

sensual *adj* **1** *literature & usu. offensive* interested in, related to, etc., giving pleasure to one's own body, as by sex, food, and drink ⚠ SENSUOUS **2** of, or seen, felt, etc. by the senses —see SENSIBLE (USAGE)

sensuality *n* the state of being sensual; fondness for sensual pleasure

sensuous *adj literature* of, concerning, interested in, etc., feelings esp. of pleasure by the senses —see SENSIBLE (USAGE) ⚠ SENSUAL — ~ly *adv* — ~ness *n*

sent *past tense and past part. of* SEND

sentence¹ *n* **1** a punishment for a criminal found guilty: *a heavy/light* (=long/short) *sentence* **2** a group of words that forms a statement, command, exclamation, or question, contains a verb and usu. a subject, and (in writing) begins with a capital letter and ends with one of the marks '.!?' —compare CLAUSE, PHRASE **3 a life sentence** an order to spend an unlimited amount of time in prison

sentence² *v* **-tenced, -tencing** (of a judge or court) to give a punishment to

sententious *adj* showing too great care about what is supposed to be right and wrong — ~ly *adv*

sentient *adj* having feelings and consciousness

sentiment *n* **1** a feeling, usu. of a stated kind **2** a tender or fine feeling, as of pity, love, etc: *There's no place for sentiment in business* **3** an expression of a wish or feeling

sentimental *adj* marked by, arising from, or appealing to tender feelings, esp. rather than reasonable or practical ones — ~ly *adv* — ~ism, ~ity, ~ist *n*

sentimentalize, -ise *v* **-ized, -izing** *offensive* **1** to think or behave sentimentally **2** to treat or consider in a sentimental way

sentry *n* **-tries** **1** also (*literature*) **sentinel**— a soldier standing guard, outside a building, entrance, etc. **2 on sentry-go** on duty as a guard

sepal *n technical* any of the leaves forming a calyx

separable *adj* that can be made or considered separate — -bly *adv* — -bility *n*

separate¹ *v* **-rated, -rating** **1** to set or move apart; make or become disconnected **2** to keep apart; mark a division between: *a wall separating the rooms* **3** to divide up into parts forming the whole **4 a** to cause (a part of a mixture) to leave a mixture and form a mass by itself **b** (of a part of a mixture) to do this **5 a** (of a husband and wife)

to live apart, esp. by formal agreement **b** to cause (a husband and wife) to do this

separate² *adj* **1** not the same; different **2** not shared with another; individual: *everyone thinking of his own separate interests* **3** apart; not joined — ~ness *n* — ~ly *adv*

separation *n* **1** a breaking or coming apart **2** a distance apart **3** esp. a person's being or living apart: *his separation from his mother* **4** *law* a formal agreement by a husband and wife to live apart —compare DIVORCE

separatism *n* the belief of a group that wants to separate from a political or religious body — -ist *n*

sepia *n* a brown paint or ink made from liquid produced by cuttlefish

sepoy *n* **sepoys** an Indian soldier, esp. in the British army in India before 1947

sepsis *n* **-ses** *medical* a poisoning of part of the body by bacteria, often producing pus there

September *n* the 9th month of the year

septet *n* a piece of music written for 7 people, or such a group playing or singing together

septic *adj* **1** infected; marked by sepsis **2** causing, or related to decomposition caused by bacteria ⚠ SCEPTIC

septic tank *n* a large underground container, esp. near country buildings, where body waste matter carried by pipes is broken up and changed by the action of bacteria

septuagenarian *adj, n* (a person who is) between 70 and 79 years old

septum *n* **-ta** a dividing wall between parts of a plant or animal

sepulchral *adj* **1** of or related to the dead **2** like, suitable for, etc., a grave

sepulchre *n old use & Bible* a burial place; tomb

sequel *n* **1** a book, film, etc., which continues the story, or has the same characters, as an earlier one **2** something that follows on, esp. as a result

sequence *n* **1** a group of things arranged in an order, esp. following one another in time **2** the order in which things or esp. events follow one another **3** a part of a story, esp. in a film, about a single subject or action; scene **4** (in mathematics) a set of terms derived according to a rule: *A common number pattern is the fibonacci sequence: 1, 1, 2, 3, 5, 8, 13, -----, where each number is the sum of the two before it* — -ntial *adj* -ntially *adv*

sequencing *n* arrangement in an order, esp. in time

sequin *n* a very small flat round shiny ornament of metal or plastic, sewn onto clothing — ~ed *adj*

sequoia *n* any of several types of very large long-living tree of the western US, including the redwood

seraglio *n* **-glios** a harem

serenade¹ *n* **1** a song or other music for the open air at night, esp. sung to a woman by a lover **2** a piece of music, usu. in several parts, played by a small group of instruments

serenade² v -naded, -nading to sing or play a serenade to

serendipity n the natural ability to find interesting or valuable things which one is not looking for

serene adj completely calm and peaceful without trouble, sudden activity, etc. — ~ly adv — **serenity** n

serf n a person, not quite a slave, forced to stay and work on his master's land, esp. in a feudal system — ~dom n

serge n a type of strong cloth, usu. woollen, used esp. for suits, coats, and dresses

sergeant n **1** a noncommissioned officer of upper rank in the army, airforce, or marines, usu. having 3 v-shaped marks on the upper arm of the uniform **2** a police officer with next to the lowest rank, usu. also with such uniform marks

sergeant major n a warrant officer in the British army or marines

serial¹ adj **1** of, happening, or arranged in, or concerning a series **2** of, being, or concerning a serial — ~ly adv

serial² n **1** a story appearing in parts at fixed times **2** technical (a book, magazine, etc. printed as one of) a continuing set with a single name and numbered 1, 2, 3, etc.

serial rights n the lawful right to print (a long piece of writing) as a serial

series n series **1** a group of related objects, events, etc., coming one after another or in order **2** (in mathematics) the sum of the members of a sequence: The series $1 + x + x^2 + x^3 + \ldots$ **3** an electrical arrangement connected without branches, so that the same current passes through each part: lamps in series —compare PARALLEL ☞ ELECTRICITY

serious adj **1** solemn; not gay or cheerful; grave **2** not joking or funny; to be considered as sincere **3** not easily or lightly dealt with: serious damage **4** of an important kind; needing or having great skill or thought: a serious artist — ~ly adv — ~ness n

serjeant-at-arms, sergeant- n serjeants-at-arms an officer of a law court, parliament, etc., who keeps order

sermon n **1** a talk usu. based on a sentence from the Bible, given in a church service **2** esp. spoken a long and solemn warning or piece of advice

sermonize, -ise v -ized, -izing to try to teach moral lessons, esp. in a long and solemn way; preach

serpent n **1** a snake, esp. a large one **2** a wicked person who leads people to do wrong or harms those who are kind to him

serpentine adj literature twisting like a snake; turning one way and another

serrated adj having a row of connected V-shapes like teeth

serried adj literature **1** pressed closely together; crowded **2** **serried ranks** rows (as of people) close together

serum n -rums or -ra **1** the watery part of an animal or plant liquid (as of blood) **2** such liquid from animal blood containing disease-fighting substances and prepared for putting into a person's or other animal's blood —compare VACCINE

servant n **1** a person who works for another, esp. in the other's house, as a cook, gardener, maid, etc. **2** a person or thing willing to be used for the service of another: Politicians are the servants of the people —see also CIVIL SERVANT, PUBLIC SERVANT

serve¹ v served, serving **1** to work or do a useful job for: Serve your country **2** to have an office or job, often for a stated period: served in the army **3** to provide with something: a pipeline serving the houses with water **4** to be good enough for (a purpose or need): This stone should serve my purpose **5** to give food to or be food for (people) **6** to attend to (someone buying something) **7** to spend (time) in prison: served 10 years **8** (in tennis, volleyball, etc.) to begin play by striking (the ball) to the opponent **9** law to deliver (an order to appear in court) to (someone) **10** technical (of a male animal) to mate with (a female) **11** **serve someone right** esp. spoken a fair punishment for someone

serve² n an act or manner of serving, as in tennis

server n **1** a person who serves food **2** a person who serves, as in tennis **3** a person who helps a priest during the Eucharist **4** something used in serving food, esp. a specially-shaped tool for putting a particular kind of food onto a plate

service¹ n **1** work or duty done for someone **2** esp. written an act or job done for someone: the services of a lawyer **3** now rare employment as a servant in someone's home **4** any of the armed services **5** duty in the army, navy, etc.: He saw active service in the war **6** any of several government departments **7** attention to buyers in a shop or esp. to guests in a hotel, restaurant, etc. **8** the dishes, tools, etc., needed to serve a stated food, meal, or number of people **9** a fixed form of public worship; a religious ceremony **10** a useful business or job that usu. does not produce goods: a good postal service **11** a/the repair of a machine: Take your car for regular services **12** an act or manner of serving, as in tennis: a fast service **13** technical the act of serving a female animal **14** **at your service** polite yours to command or use **15** **do someone a service** to do something which helps someone **16** **of service** of use; helpful

service² v -viced, -vicing to repair or put in good condition

serviceable adj **1** fit for esp. long or hard use **2** useful; helpful: a serviceable tool — -bility n — ~ness n — -bly adv

service charge n an amount of money

charged for a particular service, sometimes in addition to other charges

service flat *n* a flat of which the rent includes a charge for certain services, such as cleaning, providing food, etc.

serviceman *n* **-men** a male member of the army, navy, etc.

service road *n* a small road beside a main road, for the use of local traffic

service station *n* **1** FILLING STATION **2** a region near a motorway where petrol, car parks, and restaurants are available

serviette *n* a table napkin

servile *adj* **1** behaving like a slave: *servile praise* **2** of or concerning slaves or slavery **3** (esp. in art, writing etc.) following others without showing anything new; slavish — **-vility** *n* — **~ly** *adv*

serving *n* an amount of food for 1 person; helping

servitude *n* *literature* the condition of a slave

servomechanism *n* an apparatus that supplies power to a machine and controls its operation

servomotor also **servo—** *n* a machine which allows a heavy operation to be done with only a slight effort by the user

sesame *n* a type of tropical plant grown for its seeds and their oil, used esp. in cooking

session *n* **1 a** a formal meeting of an organization, esp. an official body **b** a time during which such meetings take place: *Parliament will be in session for 3 months* **2** *US & Scots* one of the parts of the year when teaching is given at a university **3** a meeting or period used esp. by a group for a particular purpose: *a dancing session*

sessions *n* *law* any of certain meetings of English law courts

sestet *n* a group of 6 lines of poetry, esp. the last 6 of a sonnet

set¹ *v* **set, setting** **1** to put in a place **2** to put in a stated condition: *Set the bird free* **3** to fix or determine (a rule, time, standard, etc.) **4** to give (a piece of work) for (someone) to do: *He set them to write reports* **5** to put into a position, arrange: *set the clock* | *He set his jaw and refused* **6 a** to put (a broken bone) into position for proper joining **b** (of a broken bone) to become joined in a fixed position **7** to put into action: *He set the machine going* **8 a** to cause (a liquid, paste, etc.) to become solid **b** (of such materials) to become solid **9 a** to fix (a colour) against being changed as by water **b** (of a colour) to become fixed **10** *technical* to put (a bird) onto eggs to hatch them **11** (of a heavenly body) to pass downwards out of sight: *The sun is setting* —opposite **rise** **12** to arrange type for printing **13 a** to arrange (hair) when wet to give the desired style when dry **b** (of hair) to dry after being arranged in this way **14** (of a plant) to form and develop seed or fruit **15** to give a particular setting to (a story, play, etc.)

—see also set FOOT **on**, **set something/someone to** RIGHTS, **set** SAIL, SET ABOUT, SET ASIDE, SET DOWN, SET IN, SET OFF, SET ON, SET TO, SET UP, SET UP AS, **set** STORE **by**, **set someone** STRAIGHT, **set someone's** TEETH **on edge**

set² *adj* **1** placed; located **2** determined: *He's set on going* **3** fixed; prescribed **4** given or fixed for study: *set books* **5** (of part of the body, manner, etc.) fixed in position; unmoving: *a set smile* —see also **set in one's** WAYS **6** ready; prepared: *Are you set?* **7** (of a restaurant meal) complete and at a fixed price

set³ *n* **1** a group of naturally connected things: *a set of tools* **2** (in mathematics) a formal object which is a collection of members clearly defined either by a rule or by listing the members: *the set of all numbers greater than 3* ☞ MATHEMATICS **3** a group of people of a similar social type or age group **4** a position of part of the body, a garment, etc.: *the set of a collar* **5** a direction, as of movement, opinion, etc.: *The wind had a western set* **6** an electrical apparatus, esp. a radio or television **9** a place, usu. built and provided with furniture, scenery, etc., where a play or film is acted **10** a part of a tennis match including at least 6 games **11** a young plant to be set out **12** an act or result of setting hair **13 make a dead set at a** to combine to attack (someone) **b** to try to gain the favour of (someone of the opposite sex)

set about *v prep* to begin to do or deal with

set aside *v adv* *law* to declare to be of no effect: *to set aside the decision of a lower court*

setback *n* **1** a going or return to a less good position than before: *She seemed better until her setback* **2** a defeat; reverse

set down *v adv* **1** to put down **2** to make a record of: *I have set down the whole story*

set in *v adv* (of a disease, unfavourable weather, or other natural condition) to begin and (probably) continue

set off *v adv* **1** also **set out,** (*esp. literature*) **set forth—** to begin a journey **2** to cause to explode **3** to cause (sudden activity): *The news set off a rush of activity* **4** to make (something) more noticeable or beautiful by putting it near something different: *Black sets off the jewels*

set on *v prep* **1** to attack: *He was set on by robbers* **2** to cause to attack or chase

set piece *n* **1** a work of art, literature, etc., with a well-known formal pattern or style **2** any of certain football plays which take place when the ordinary action of the game is stopped, such as a corner or free kick

setscrew *n* a screw for holding 2 machine parts against one another or at a distance apart, or for controlling a spring's tightness

setsquare *n* a flat 3-sided plate with one right angle, used for drawing straight lines and angles exactly

settee *n* a long seat with a back and usu. arms for more than 1 person

setter *n* any of 3 types of long-haired dogs often

trained to point out the positions of animals for shooting

set theory n the branch of mathematics that deals with sets

setting n 1 the action of a person or thing that sets: *the setting of the sun* 2 the way or position in which something is set 3 a a set of surroundings b the time and place where the action of a book, film, etc., happens 4 a set of articles (dishes, knives, forks, spoons, etc.) arranged on a table or at one place on a table

settle¹ n a long wooden seat with a high solid back, and a bottom part which is a chest

settle² v -tled, -tling 1 to live or cause to live in a place 2 to provide people to live in (a place): *We settled the desert* 3 to bring or place down, often in a comfortable position: *settled himself in his chair* 4 to sink or come down, usu. to a position of rest 5 to make or become quiet, calm, still, etc.: *to settle one's nerves* 6 a to separate (solid material or a liquid containing it) each from the other, usu. by causing the solid to fall slowly to the bottom: *to settle the wine/dregs* b (of the solid or liquid) to separate like this 7 (of a building, the ground etc.) to sink slowly to a lower level; subside 8 to decide on; fix; arrange 9 to end (an argument, esp. in law); bring (a matter) to an agreement 10 to pay (a bill or money claimed) 11 **settle one's affairs** to put all one's business into order, esp. for the last time

settled adj 1 unlikely to change: *settled habits* 2 not moving about: *a desert with no settled population* 3 (of a place) having people living in homes 4 established; fixed: *settled principles*

settle down v adv 1 to sit or cause to sit comfortably 2 to establish a home and live quietly 3 to become used to a way of life, job, etc. 4 to give one's attention to a job, working, etc. —see also SETTLE

settlement n 1 the movement of new people into a place to live there 2 a usu. recently-built small village in an area with few people 3 an agreement or decision ending an argument, question, etc. 4 a payment of money claimed 5 a formal gift of money or property: *made a settlement on his daughter* 6 a usu. private organisation in an inner city area providing social services

settle on also settle upon— v prep to give (money, property etc.) formally in law

settler n a person who settles, esp. in an area with few people

settle up v adv 1 to pay what is owed: *settle up after a meal* 2 (of a group) to pay and receive what is owed

set-to n a usu. short fight or quarrel

set to v adv 1 to begin with energy 2 to begin a quarrel or fight

set-up n an arrangement or organization: *the office set-up*

set up v adv 1 to establish (an organization, business, etc.) 2 to provide (someone) with what is necessary or useful

set up as v adv prep 1 to establish (oneself) in business as 2 to show (oneself), often falsely as: *He set himself up as an art expert*

seven adj n, pron the number 7 — ~th adj, n, pron, adv

seventeen adj n, pron the number 17 — ~th adj, n, pron, adv

seventh heaven n sl the place of highest happiness

seventy adj, n, pron -ties the number 70 — -tieth adj, n, pron, adv

seven-year itch n the dissatisfaction with one's marriage said to develop after 7 years

sever v 1 to break or be cut up, esp. into 2 parts 2 to go or cause to go apart; separate: *The handle of the cup severed when it hit the floor*

several¹ adj esp. written (with pl. nouns) 1 of the stated people or things; separate: *busy with their several jobs* 2 various; different

several² adj, pron more than 2 but fewer than many; some but not man y

severally adv esp. written separately; each by itself: *Shall we consider these questions severally?*

severance n 1 the act or result of severing 2 esp. written the ending of a contract, esp. for employment

severe adj 1 not kind or gentle; not allowing failure or change in rules, standards, etc.; strict: *a severe look* 2 very harmful or painful; serious or uncomfortable: *a severe winter* 3 needing effort; difficult: *a severe test of ability* 4 plain; without ornament: *the severe beauty of the building* — compare STRICT — ~ly adv — -rity n

sew v sewed, sewn, sewing 1 to join or fasten (cloth, leather, paper, etc.) by stitching with thread; make or mend with needle and thread 2 to enclose in this way: *sewed a £5 note into his pocket* — ~er n

sewage n the waste material and water carried in sewers

sewer n a man-made passage or large pipe under the ground for carrying away water and waste material, esp. in a city, to a body of water or for chemical treatment (**sewage disposal**)

sewerage n the system of removing and dealing with waste matter through sewers

sewing n 1 the act or way of making, mending, etc., with thread, by hand or machine 2 work made in this way

sewing machine n a machine for stitching material

sew up v adv 1 to close or enclose by sewing 2 sl to put into one's control; determine or settle: *I want to sew up 1, 000 votes*

sex¹ n 1 the condition of being either male or female 2 the set of all male or female people: *a member of the opposite sex* 3 the act of sexual intercourse between people, or related activity — sex adj

sex² v esp. technical to find out the sex of (esp. an animal)

sexagenarian *adj, n* (a person who is) between 60 and 69 years old

sex appeal *n* attractiveness to one of the opposite sex

sexism *n* the opinion that one sex is not as good as the other, esp. that women are less able than men — **-ist** *adj, n*

sexless *adj* **1** sexually uninteresting **2** not male or female; neuter

sextant *n* an instrument for measuring angles between stars, used on a ship or aircraft to calculate its position —compare ASTROLABE

sextet *n* a piece of music written for 6 people, or such a group playing or singing together

sexton *n* a person who takes care of a church building and sometimes digs graves

sextuplet *n* one of 6 people or animals born at one birth

sexual *adj* of, related to, or concerning sex — **~ly** *adv*

sexual intercourse also **intercourse**— *n* the bodily act between 2 animals or people in which the male sex organ (PENIS) enters the female (VAGINA)

sexuality *n* fondness or readiness for, or interest in, sexual activity

sexy *adj* **-ier, -iest** exciting in a sexual way — **sexily** *adv* — **sexiness** *n*

SF *abbrev. for:* SCIENCE FICTION

sforzando *n, adj, adv* **-dos** *or* **-di** ((a musical note) played) with additional force

sh, shh, ssh *interj* (used for asking for silence or less noise)

shabby *adj* **-bier, -biest** **1** appearing poor because of wear **2** (of a person) wearing such clothes **3** ungenerous or not worthy; unfair; mean: *a shabby trick* — **-bily** *adv* — **-biness** *n*

shack *n* a small roughly built house; hut

shackle[1] *n* **1** a metal band for fastening round a wrist or ankle (as of an animal, prisoner, etc.) to something else by a chain, to prevent movement **2** a U-shaped fastener, such as the movable part of a padlock **3** *literature* something that prevents freedom of action or expression

shackle[2] *v* **-led, -ling** to bind as with shackles

shack up *v adv sl* (of a man and/or woman) to live together while unmarried

shade[1] *n* **1** slight darkness, shelter from direct light, or somthing that provides this **2** something that keeps out light or its full brightness: *a lampshade* **3** representation of shadow or darkness in a picture, painting, etc. **4** a slightly different colour: *light blue and a deeper shade* **5** a slight difference of meaning or varying: *a word with several shades of meaning* **6** *esp. before adjectives or adverbs*) a little bit: *a shade too loud* **8 put someone/something in the shade** *esp. spoken* to make someone/something seem less important by comparison

shade[2] *v* **shaded, shading** **1** to shelter from direct light or heat **2** to represent the effect of

shade or shadow on (an object in a picture) **3** to change slowly or by slight degrees: *blue shading off into grey*

shading *n* the representation of darkness in a picture by filling in of an area

shadow[1] *n* **1** greater darkness where direct light is blocked **2** a dark shape made on a surface by something between it and direct light: *The tree cast its shadow on the wall* **3** a dark place like this: *shadows under the eyes* **4** a form without real substance: *He is but a shadow of his former self* **5** a person or thing who follows another closely: *The dog is your shadow* **6** a slightest bit: *no shadow of an excuse* **7** the very strong power or influence of someone or something: *He lived in the shadow of his famous father* **8** an unhappy or threatened feeling **9 be afraid of one's own shadow** to be fearful or nervous

shadow[2] *v* **1** to darken as with a shadow **2** to follow and watch closely, esp. secretly

shadow[3] *adj* **1** belonging to a group of politicians (the **shadow cabinet**) in the opposition party in Parliament who each study the work of a particular minister and are themselves ready to form a government **2** able to be active or become the stated thing when the proper or expected occasion comes

shadowbox *v* to fight with an imaginary opponent — **~ing** *n*

shadowy *adj* **-ier, -iest** **1** hard to see or know about clearly: *a shadowy figure* **2** full of shade

shady *adj* **-ier, -iest** **1** in or producing shade **2** of very doubtful honesty or character

shaft[1] *n* **1** a long or thin pole, such as the body of a spear or arrow **2** the long handle of a hammer, axe, golf club, etc. **3** one of the pair of poles that an animal is fastened between to pull a vehicle **4** a bar which turns, or around which a belt or wheel turns, to pass power through a machine **5** a beam of light **6** *literature* something shot like an arrow: *well-aimed shafts of wit* **7** a long passage, usu. in an up and down or sloping direction: *a mine shaft*

shagged also **shagged out**— *adj sl* very tired

shaggy *adj* **-gier, -giest** being or covered with long, uneven, and untidy hair — **-gily** *adv* — **-giness** *n*

shaggy-dog story *n* **-ries** a long joke a which is not so funny as the teller thinks b which has an ending that is purposely without point

shagreen *n* a type of leather with a rough surface, often coloured green

shah *n* (the title of) the former ruler of Iran

shake[1] *v* **shook , shaken, shaking** **1** to move quickly up and down and to and fro: *The explosion shook the house* **2** to put or remove by such action: *He shook salt on his food* **3** to take (someone's right hand) in one's own for a moment, moving it up and down, as a sign of greeting, goodbye, agreement, etc. (esp. in the phrase **shake hands (with someone)**) **4** to trouble the feelings of; upset **5** to make less certain **6** *sl* to escape from; get rid of: *Try to shake him off* **7 shake**

one's head to move one's head from side to side to show ' no ' or disapproval

shake² *n* **1** an action of shaking **2** *sl* a moment: *I'll be ready in 2 shakes*

shakedown¹ *n* a place prepared as a bed

shakedown² *adj* being the last test operation of a new ship or aircraft

shake down *v adv* **1** to use something prepared quickly as a bed: *shake down on the floor* **2** to become used to new surroundings

shaker *n* a container or instrument used in shaking

shakes *n sl* **1** nervous shaking of the body from disease, fear, strong drink, etc. **2** no great shakes not very good, skilful, etc.

shake up *v adv* **1** to rearrange (an organization) **2** to mix by shaking **3 shake it up** *sl* hurry up — **shake-up** *n*

shaky *adj* -ier, -iest **1** shaking or unsteady **2** not firm; easily shaken; undependable — **shakily** *adv* — **shakiness** *n*

shale *n* soft rock made of hardened mud or clay which divides into thin sheets

shale oil *n* impure oil produced from shale by heating

shall *v* **should,** *negative short form* **shan't** **1** (used with *I* and *we* to express) **a** (the simple future tense): *I shall have finished my work by next Friday* **b** (a question or offer): *Shall I get you a chair?* **2** (used to express a promise, command, or strong intention): *The enemy shall not enter* —see also SHALT, SHOULD **USAGE** In writing it is best to use **shall** only with *I* or *we* unless it is meant to express a strong intention or promise, when *will* is used with *I/we*: *I shall go tomorrow.* | *We will not let them pass!* The first is a statement of what I expect to do. The second implies determination. With *you, he, she, it,* or *they,* use **will** for the ordinary future of a verb, and **shall** to express intention, promise, etc.: *They will bring Auntie.* | *You shall go to the ball*

shallot *n* a kind of small onion-like vegetable containing small bulbs used for their taste in cooking

shallow¹ *adj* **1** not deep; not far from top to bottom **2** lacking deep or serious thinking: *shallow arguments* **3** (of breathing) not taking in much air — **~ly** *adv* — **~ness** *n*

shallow² *v* to become shallow

shallows *n* a shallow area in a body of water

shalom *interj* (a Jewish greeting or goodbye meaning ' peace ' in Hebrew)

shalt **thou shalt** *old use* (when talking to one person) you shall

sham¹ *n* **1** something false pretending to be the real thing: *The agreement is just a sham* **2** falseness; pretence

sham² *adj* not real; imitation

sham³ *v* -mm- to pretend to be or have (some disease, condition, etc.)

shamble *v* -bled, -bling to walk awkwardly, dragging the feet

shambles *n* a place or scene of great disorder;

wreck: *After the party the house was a shambles*

shame¹ *n* **1** painful feeling of guilt, wrongness, inability, or failure **2** the condition in which this should be felt; disgrace: *behaviour which brings shame on us all* **3** something that deserves blame; something that ought not to be: *What a shame that it rained today* **4** put someone/something to shame **a** to cause shame to someone/something **b** to show someone/something to be lacking in ability, quality, etc., by comparison **5 Shame!** (called out against a speaker) You ought to be ashamed to say that!

shame² *v* **shamed, shaming** **1** to bring dishonour to **2** to appear very much better than: *a record which shames other companies* **3** to cause to feel shame **4** to force or urge by causing shame: *I shamed her into voting in the election*

shamefaced *n* showing shame or unsureness about oneself — **~ly** *adv*

shameful *adj* deserving blame; causing shame — **~ly** *adv* — **~ness** *n*

shameless *adj* **1** (of a person) unable to feel shame **2** done without shame — **~ly** *adv* — **~ness** *n*

shampoo¹ *v* -pooed, -pooing **1** to wash (the head and hair) **2** to clean (heavy woven material) with shampoo

shampoo² *n* -poos **1** an act of shampooing **2** a usu. liquid soaplike product used for shampooing

shamrock *n* any of various plants, esp. a type of clover, with 3 leaves on each stem, taken for the national sign of Ireland

shandy *n* -dies a mixture of beer and ginger ale or lemonade

shanghai *v* -haied, -haiing **1** (esp. in former times) to make senseless by a blow or by drink and then put on a ship to serve as a sailor **2** *sl* to trick or force into doing something

Shangri-La *n* a distant beautiful imaginary place where everything is pleasant

shank *n* *esp. technical* a straight long or narrow usu. central or connecting part of something, such as the straight part of a nail, the smooth part of a screw, or the smooth end of a drill where it is to be turned

shanks's pony *n* usu. humour one's own legs as a method of travelling

shantung *n* a type of silk cloth with a slightly rough surface

shanty¹ *n* -ties a small badly built usu. wooden house; shack

shanty² *n* -ties a song formerly sung by sailors in time to their work

shantytown *n* a town or area of badly built houses of thin metal, wood, etc., where poor people live

shape¹ *v* **shaped, shaping** **1** to make in a particular usu. finished form **2** to influence and determine: *a powerful person who can shape events* **3** to develop well or in the stated way: *Our plans are shaping up well*

shape² n 1 the appearance or form of something seen: *Houses come in all shapes and sizes* 2 the organization or form in which something is expressed, arranged, etc. 3 condition: *Our garden is in good shape* 4 a way of appearing; form 5 **get/put something into shape** to arrange or plan something properly 6 **in/out of** shape in/out of good condition of the body 7 **take shape** to begin to have a shape, esp. like the finished form — ~**less** *adj* — ~**lessly** *adv* — ~**lessness** n

shaped *adj* having the stated shape

shapely *adj* **-lier, -liest** (esp. of a woman's body or legs) having a good-looking shape — **shapeliness** n

shard also **sherd, potsherd**— n a broken piece of a vessel of glass or pottery

share¹ n 1 the part belonging to or done by a person: *Do your fair share of the work* 2 any of the equal parts into which the ownership of a company may be divided 3 **go shares** to divide the cost, profit, etc., among 2 or more people

share² *adj* of or concerning company shares

share³ v **shared, sharing** 1 to use, pay, have, take part in, etc., with others or among a group: *Everyone shares the bathroom* 2 to divide and give out in shares 3 to tell others about: *He shared the story with us* 4 to join with others esp. in (an opinion or idea) 5 **share and share alike** esp. spoken to have an equal share in everything — **sharer** n

sharecropper n a farmer, esp. in the southern US, who farms the land of another, is given tools and supplies by him, and is paid a share of the crop

shareholder n an owner of 1 or more shares in a business

share-out n an act of giving out shares of something

shares n ownership rights in companies, bought and sold in the form of printed statements (**share certificates**)

shark¹ n any of several kinds of large fierce flesh-eating fish which have several rows of sharp teeth, and can be dangerous to people

shark² n *sl* a person who cleverly and mercilessly gets money from others as by lending money at high rates

sharp¹ *adj* 1 a having or being a thin cutting edge b having or being a fine point 2 quick and sensitive in thinking, seeing, hearing, etc.: *a sharp mind* 3 causing a sensation like that of cutting, biting, stinging: *a sharp wind* 4 not rounded; marked by angles: *a sharp nose* 5 sudden and steep; strong, etc.: *a sharp rise/fall in prices* 6 clear in shape or detail; distinct: *a sharp image* 7 (of a pain) severe and sudden —opposite **dull** 8 (as of words) intended to hurt; harsh 9 clever and usu. dishonest: *This sale sounds like sharp practice* 10 (of a note in music) raised by ½ tone (in the phrases **F sharp, C sharp,** etc.) —compare FLAT, ♪ MUSIC — ~**ly** *adv* — ~**ness** n

sharp² *adv* 1 exactly at the stated time 2 sharply (esp. in such phrases as **turn sharp left/right**) 3 higher than the correct note: *She sang sharp* —compare FLAT 4 **look sharp** *sl* a to watch out; be careful b to hurry up

sharp³ n (in music) 1 a note higher by ½ tone than a named note 2 a sign, (♯), used before a note to raise it by this amount —compare FLAT

sharpen v to make or become sharp or sharper — ~**er** n

sharpshooter n a person skilful in shooting; good marksman

shatter v 1 to break suddenly into small pieces 2 to damage badly; wreck: *Illness shattered his health* 3 to shock the feelings of: *a shattered look* 4 esp. spoken to cause to be very tired and weak

shave¹ v **shaved, shaving** 1 to cut off (hair) close to the skin with a razor 2 to cut off in very thin pieces 3 esp. spoken to come close to or touch in passing: *The car just shaved the wall*

shave² n 1 an act or result of shaving 2 a **close/narrow shave** esp. spoken an almost unsuccessful avoiding of something bad; narrow escape

shaver n a tool for shaving, esp. an electric hand tool for shaving hair

shaving n 1 the act of closely cutting off hair 2 a very thin piece cut from a surface: *wood shavings*

shaving cream n soapy cream or foam for putting on the face to keep the hair soft and wet during shaving with a razor blade

shawl n a piece of usu. soft heavy cloth for wearing over a woman's head or shoulders or wrapping round a baby

she¹ *pron* 1 that female person or animal: *She's a pretty girl* 2 (used esp. of vehicles and countries) that thing regarded as female: *What's wrong with the car? She won't start*

she² n esp. spoken a female: *Is the cat a he or a she?*

sheaf n **sheaves** 1 a bunch of grain plants tied together, esp. to stand in a field to dry after gathering 2 a handful of long or thin things laid together: *a sheaf of notes*

shear¹ n *technical* a transformation in which the points of a certain line are invariant, and all points not on the invariant line move parallel to it, the distance that they move being proportional to their distance from the invariant line

shear² v **sheared, sheared** or **shorn, shearing** 1 to cut off wool from (sheep) 2 *technical* (esp. of thin rods, pins, etc.) to break in 2 under a sideways or twisting force 3 **be shorn of** to lose by the action of another

shears n large scissors or any similar but heavier cutting tool

sheath n 1 a closefitting case for a knife, blade, etc. 2 a usu. rubber covering worn over a man's sex organ when having sex to keep the woman from having a child and to prevent infection —see also CONDOM

sheathe *v* **sheathed, sheathing** to put into or cover with a sheath

sheath knife *n* **-knives** a knife with a fixed blade for carrying in a sheath

shed¹ *v* **shed, shedding** **1** *literature* to cause to flow out: *She shed tears.* | *to shed new light on a question* **2** (of a surface) to keep (a liquid) from entering: *A duck's back sheds water* **3** (as of a plant or animal) to throw off or get rid of naturally (outer skin, leaves, hair, etc.) **4** (of a vehicle) to drop (a load of goods) by acccident **5 shed blood** to cause wounding or esp. killing —see also BLOODSHED

shed² *n* a lightly built, often partly enclosed, building, usu. for storing things

she'd *short form of* **1** she would **2** she had

sheen *n* bright or shiny condition on a surface

sheep *n* **sheep** **1** a type of grass-eating animal farmed for its wool and meat (mutton, lamb) —compare RAM, EWE **2 a black sheep** an unsatisfactory or shameful member of a group **3 make/cast sheep's eyes at someone** *sl* to behave fondly towards someone, esp. in a foolish way

sheepdip *n* a chemical bath for sheep to kill insects in their wool

sheepdog *n* a dog trained to drive sheep and keep them together

sheepish *adj* slightly ashamed or fearful of others — ~**ly** *adv* — ~**ness** *n*

sheepskin *n* the skin of a sheep, made into leather, esp. with the wool left on —compare FLEECE

sheer¹ *adj* **1** very thin, fine, light, and almost transparent: *sheer stockings* **2** pure; unmixed with anything else: *sheer luck* **3** very steep; straight up and down: *a sheer cliff*

sheer² *adv* straight up or down

sheer³ *v* to turn as if to avoid hitting something; change direction quickly: *The boat sheered away*

sheet¹ *n* **1** a large 4-sided piece of cloth used usu. in a pair on a bed **2** a piece of paper **3** a broad stretch, piece, mass of something thin: *a sheet of ice* **4 white as a sheet** *esp. spoken* very pale in the face, as because of fear or a shock

sheet² *n* *technical* a rope or chain controlling the angle between a sail and the wind

sheet anchor *n* a ship's largest anchor, used only in time of danger

sheeting *n* material for making sheets

sheet lightning *n* lightning that brightens the whole sky —compare FORKED LIGHTNING

sheikh, sheik *n* **1** an Arab chief or prince **2** a Muslim religious teacher

sheila *n* *sl, esp. Australian* a girl

shekel *n* The standard coin of Israel ☞ MONEY

shelduck (*masc.* **sheldrake**)— *n* **-ducks** *or* **duck** a type of large often brightly-coloured European duck

shelf *n* **shelves** **1** a flat usu. long and narrow board fixed against a wall or in a frame, for placing things on **2** a group of things filling one of these:

a shelf of books **3** something shaped like this, such as a narrow surface of rock —compare CONTINENTAL SHELF **4 on the shelf** *sl* (esp. of a person) not active, esp. put aside by others as of no use

shell¹ *n* **1** a hard covering, as of an animal, egg, nut, etc. —see also SEASHELL **2** the outer surface of something, not the contents or substance **3** the outside frame of a building **4** an explosive for firing from a large gun —compare BULLET, SHOT **5 come out of one's shell** *sl* to begin to be friendly or interested in others

shell² *v* **1** to remove a natural covering from: *to shell peas/oysters* **2** to fire shells at

shellac *n* a kind of thick orange or clear alcohol-based liquid used as a shiny protective covering

shellfish *n* **-fish** **1** any animal without a backbone that lives in water in a shell (a mollusc or crustacean) **2** such animals as food

shell out *v adv sl* to pay (money)

shellshock *n* illness of the mind, esp. in soldiers, caused by war

shelter¹ *n* **1** anything that protects, esp. a building **2** protection or the state of being protected: *the shelter of a tree*

shelter² *v* **1** to protect from harm; give shelter to **2** to take shelter; find protection: *We sheltered in the doorway*

sheltered *adj* kept from harm, risk, or unpleasantness

shelve *v* **shelved, shelving** **1** to put aside, esp. as not to be used or considered: *We've shelved our holiday plans* **2** (of land) to slope gradually

shelves *pl. of* SHELF

shelving *n* (material for) shelves

shenanigan *n* *esp. spoken* **1** a funny and attention-getting act **2** a dishonest practice or trick

shepherd¹ *n fem.* ~**ess**— a man or boy who takes care of sheep in the field

shepherd² *v* to lead, guide, or take care of like sheep: *The teacher shepherded the children into the bus*

shepherd's pie also **cottage pie**— *n* a baked dish of finely cut-up meat covered with a thick paste of potato

Sheraton *adj* (of, being, or related to) an English furniture style made first around 1800 and known for its straight lines and graceful proportions

sherbet *n* sweet powder for adding to water to make a cool drink, esp. for children

sherd *n* (esp. in archaeology) a shard

sheriff *n* **1** (in Britain) HIGH SHERIFF **2** (in the US) county officer who carries out court orders and preserves public order

Sherpa *n* a member of a Himalayan tribe often employed to guide mountain climbers

sherry *n* **-ries** a pale or dark brown strong wine, often drunk before a meal —compare PORT

she's *short form of* **1** she is **2** she has: *She's got a new job*

Shetland pony n **-ponies** a type of rough-haired strong very small horse

shibboleth n a once-important old phrase or custom which no longer has much meaning

shield¹ n **1** a broad piece of metal, wood, or leather once carried by soldiers to protect them from arrows, blows, etc. **2** a representation of this used for a coat of arms, badge, etc.

shield² v to protect or hide from harm or danger

shift¹ v **1** to change in position or direction: *The wind shifted and blew the mist away* **2** to take care of oneself; manage (esp. in the phrase **shift for oneself**)

shift² n **1** a change in position or direction **2 a** a group of workers which takes turns with other groups: *the day/night shift* **b** the period worked by such a group **3** a loosefitting straight simple woman's dress **4** a means or trick used in a difficulty **5 make shift** to use what can be found; make do —compare MAKESHIFT

shift key n **-keys** the part of a typewriter which is pressed to print a capital letter

shiftless adj lacking in purpose, ability, or effort — ~ly adv — ~ness n

shifty adj **-ier, -iest** tricky and deceitful — **shiftily** adv — **shiftiness** n

shilling n **1** an amount of money in use in Britain until 1971, equal to 12 old pence and 1/20 of £1 **2** a coin worth this amount, now 5 new pence ☞ MONEY

shilly-shally v **shilly-shallied, shilly-shallying** esp. spoken to waste time without taking action

shimmer v to shine with a soft trembling light — **shimmer** n

shin¹ n the bony front part of the leg below the knee

shin² v **-nn-** to climb (a tree, pole, etc.), esp. quickly and easily, using the hands and legs

shinbone also (medical) **tibia**— n the front bone in the leg below the knee ☞ ANATOMY

shindy n **-dies** sl a noisy quarrel or disagreement

shine¹ v **shone, shining 1** to give off light; look bright **2** to direct (a lamp, beam of light, etc.) **3** to appear clearly as excellent: *He really shines at sports* — **-ning** adj

shine² v **shined, shining** to polish; make bright by rubbing

shine³ n **1** brightness; shining quality **2** an act of polishing, esp. of shoes **3 rain or shine** in good or bad weather; whatever happens

shingle¹ n a small thin piece of wood, asbestos, etc., laid in rows on a roof or wall

shingle² v **-gled, -gling** to cover (esp. a roof) with shingles

shingle³ n small rounded pieces of stone lying in masses on a beach or river bank — **-gly** adj

shingles n a painful disease caused by an infection of certain nerves and producing red spots often in a band around the waist —compare HERPES

Shinto also **Shintoism**— the ancient religion of Japan, including spirit worship

shiny adj **-ier, -iest** (esp. of a smooth surface) looking polished; bright — **shininess** n

ship¹ n **1** a large boat **2** esp. spoken a large aircraft or spacecraft **3 when one's ship comes in/home** esp. spoken when one becomes rich —see VESSEL (USAGE)

ship² v **-pp-** **1** to send by ship **2** to send (esp. a large article) over some distance by post or other means: *We ship our products everywhere in Britain* **3** (of a boat) to take (water) over the side **4** to take a job on a ship **5** to hold one's oars to the side of the boat without rowing

shipboard n **on shipboard** on a ship

shipment n **1** the action of sending, carrying, and delivering goods **2** a load of goods sent together

shipper n a dealer who ships goods

shipping n **1** ship traffic; ships as a group **2** the business of making shipments **3** the sending and delivery of something

ship's biscuit also **hard tack**— n a kind of hard-baked bread eaten esp. formerly by sailors at sea

ship's chandler also **ship chandler**— n a dealer in ship supplies

shipshape adj clean, neat, and orderly

shipwreck¹ n a/the destruction of a ship, as by hitting rocks or sinking

shipwreck² v **1** to cause to suffer shipwreck **2** to wreck; ruin

shipwright n a person who builds and repairs ships

shipyard n a place where ships are built or repaired

shire n old use a county

shire horse n a large powerful kind of English horse used for pulling loads

shirk v to avoid (unpleasant work) — ~er n

shirring n the gathering of cloth into small folds made by drawing it along rows of threads pulled tight or by stitching in rows of tight rubber thread

shirt n **1** a piece of clothing for the upper body, usu. of light cloth with a collar and sleeves — compare SWEATSHIRT, NIGHTSHIRT **2 lose one's shirt** sl to lose all one has; lose a lot of money **3 stuffed shirt** sl a person who acts grand and important; pompous person

shirtsleeve n esp. spoken **1** the sleeve of a shirt **2 in one's shirtsleeves** not wearing a coat over one's shirt

shirttail n the front or back part of a shirt below the wearer's waist

shirtwaister n a woman's dress in the style of a man's shirt

shirty adj **-ier, -iest** sl bad-tempered; angry and rude

shish kebab n a kebab

shiver¹ v to shake, esp. from cold or fear

shiver² n a feeling of fear or cold: *a shiver up my spine*

shivers *n esp. spoken* feelings of strong dislike or fear

shivery *adj* **-ier, -iest** **1** (of weather) cold **2** (of a person) trembling as if feverish

shoal¹ *n* a sand bank not far below the surface of the water, making it dangerous to boats

shoal² *n* **1** a large group of fish swimming together **2** a large number

shock¹ *n* **1** violent force, as from a hard blow, crash, explosion, etc. **2** the strong feeling caused by something unexpected and usu. very unpleasant **3** something causing this; an unpleasant piece of news: *His death was a shock* **4** the sudden violent effect of electricity passing through the body **5** *medical* the weakened state of the body with less activity of the heart, lungs, etc., usu. following damage to the body

shock² *v* **1** to cause usu. unpleasant or angry surprise to (someone) **2** to give an electric shock to

shock³ *n* a thick bushy mass of hair

shock absorber *n* an apparatus fixed near each wheel of a vehicle to lessen the effect of rough roads or on an aircraft to make a smoother landing

shockheaded *n* having a shock of hair on the head

shocking *adj* **1** causing shock; very improper, or sad **2** very bad (though not evil): *What a shocking waste of time!* — **~ly** *adv*

shockproof *adj* (esp. of a watch) not easily damaged by being dropped, hit, etc.

shock troops *n* soldiers used in sudden forceful attacking

shod *adj usu. literature* wearing or provided with shoes

shoddy¹ *n* **1** cloth made using wool from old used cloth **2** poor cheap material

shoddy² *adj* **-dier, -diest** **1** made or done cheaply and badly: *shoddy workmanship* **2** ungenerous or not worthy; dishonourable: *a shoddy trick* — **-dily** *adv* — **-diness** *n*

shoe¹ *n* **1** an outer covering for the human foot, usu. of leather and having a hard base (SOLE) and a support (HEEL) under the heel of the foot — compare BOOT, SANDAL, SLIPPER **2** either of a pair of curved plates around a vehicle wheel which may press against it to stop it or slow it down: *Your car has worn brake shoes* **3** a horseshoe **4 to fill someone's shoes** to take the place or job of someone **5 in someone's shoes** in someone's position

shoe² *v* **shod** *or* **shoed, shoeing** to fix a shoe on (an animal)

shoehorn *n* a curved piece of metal or plastic for putting inside the back of a shoe when slipping it on, to help the heel go in easily

shoelace *n* a thin cord passed through holes on both sides of the front opening of a shoe and tied to fasten the shoe on

shoemaker *n* a person who makes shoes and boots

shoeshine *n* an act of polishing shoes

shoestring *n* a very small amount of money: *He started his business on a shoestring*

shone *past tense. and past part. of* SHINE

shoo¹ *interj* (said, usu. not angrily, to animals or small children) go away!

shoo² *v* **shooed, shooing** to drive away as if by saying ' shoo '

shook *past tense of* SHAKE

shoot¹ *v* **shot, shooting** **1** to let fly with force (a bullet, arrow, etc.) **2** to fire (a weapon) **3** to hit or kill with something as from a gun: *He was shot in the arm* **4** to make (one's way) by firing a gun at anyone in the way: *He shot his way out of prison* **5** to cause to go or become by hitting with something from a gun: *His foot was shot away* **6** to send out as from a gun: *Everyone shot questions at the chairman* **7** to go fast or suddenly: *Pain shot through his arm* **8** to kick, throw, etc., a ball in order to score in a game **9** to make a photograph or film (of): *This story was shot quickly* **10** *US* to play (a game of billiards, pool, marbles, etc.) **11** to pass quickly by or along: *a boat shooting the rapids* **12** (esp. in cricket) (of a ball) to keep very low after bouncing **13 a** to move (a bolt) across **b** (of a bolt) to move across **14** *drug-users' sl* to take (a drug) directly with a needle —see also SHOOT OUT, SHOT

shoot² *n* **1** a new growth from a plant, esp. a young stem and leaves **2** an occasion for shooting guns

shooting match *n* **the whole shooting match** *sl* the whole thing or affair

shooting star *also* **falling star**— *n* a small meteor from space which burns brigh tly as it passes through the earth's air

shooting stick *n* a pointed walking-stick with a top which opens out to form a seat

shoot-out *n* a battle between gunfighters

shoot out *v adv* to decide (a quarrel) by shooting

shop¹ *n* **1** (*US* **store**)— a room or building where goods are regularly kept and sold **2** such a place, esp. small or selling special kinds of goods **3** a place where things are made or repaired; workshop **4** business; activity (esp. in the phrases **set up shop, close/shut up shop**) **5 (talk) shop** (to talk about) one's work

shop² *v* **-pp-** **1** to visit 1 or more shops in order to buy; buy goods (often in the phrase **go shopping**) **2** *sl* to tell the police about (a criminal) — **~per** *n*

shop around *v adv* to compare prices or values in different shops before buying

shop assistant *n* a person who serves buyers in a shop

shop floor *n* the place where ordinary workers do their work: *What's the feeling on the shop floor?*

shopkeeper *n* a person, usu. the owner, in charge of a small shop

shoplift *v* to steal from a shop — **~er** *n*

shopping centre *n* a group of shops of different kinds, planned and built as a whole

shopsoiled *adj* slightly damaged or dirty from being handled or kept on view in a shop for a long time

shop steward *n* a trade union officer elected by union members in a particular place of work

shopworn *adj* (as of ideas) no longer fresh, interesting, or valuable

shore[1] *n* 1 the land along the edge of a large stretch of water 2 **on shore** on land; away from one's ship —see also ASHORE

shore[2] *v* **shored, shoring** 1 to support, esp. with timbers: *shored up the wall* 2 to strengthen or give support to (something weak); keep from failing or falling: *to shore up farm prices*

shore[3] *n* a length of usu. wood placed under or against something to prevent its falling down; support

shorn *past part. of* SHEAR

short[1] *adj* 1 not far from one end to the other; little in distance of length (opposite **long**) or height (opposite **tall**) 2 lasting only a little time; brief: *a short visit* —opposite **long** 3 lacking enough; insufficient or scarce: *short weights/measures* —see LACK (USAGE) 4 rudely impatient; curt: *I'm sorry I was short with you* 5 (of pastry) falling easily into pieces; crumbly 6 (of a drink) of a kind (such as spirits) usu. served in a small glass 7 (in cricket) **a** (of a fielder) in a position close to the batsman **b** (of a bowled ball) hitting the ground quite far from the batsman 8 **for short** as a shorter way of saying something 9 **in short** to put it into a few words; all I mean is 10 **little/nothing short of** *pompous* little/nothing less than; almost/completely 11 **short and sweet** not wasting time; short and direct 12 **short for** a shorter way of saying — ~**ness** *n*

short[2] *adv* 1 suddenly; abruptly: *The driver stopped short* 2 **be taken/caught short** *esp. spoken* to have a sudden need to empty the bowels or esp. pass water from the body 3 **cut short** to stop suddenly before the end: *They cut their holiday short* 4 **fall short (of)** to be less than good enough (for) 5 **go short** to be without enough 6 **run short a** to use almost all one has and not have enough left **b** to become less than enough —see also SELL **short**

short[3] *n* 1 a drink of strong alcohol, such as whisky or rum 2 SHORT CIRCUIT

shortage *n* a condition of having less than needed; an amount lacking: *a food shortages*

shortbread also **shortcake**— *n* a thin hard kind of sweet biscuit made with a lot of butter

short-change *v* **-changed, -changing** to give back too little money to (a buyer who pays with a large note or coin)

short-circuit *v* 1 to have or cause to have a short circuit 2 to do something without going through: *to short-circuit all the formality by a telephone call*

short circuit *n* a faulty electrical connection that makes too short a path for a current and so usu. puts the power supply out of operation

shortcoming *n* a failing to reach what is expected or right: *his shortcomings as a sailor*

short cut *n* a quicker more direct way

shorten *v* to make or become short or shorter

shortening *n* *esp. US* fat for combining with flour in pastry

shortfall *n* an amount lacking to reach the needed or expected amount

shorthand *n* rapid writing in a system using signs for letters, words, phrases, etc. —compare LONGHAND

shorthanded *adj* lacking the needed number of workers

shorthand typist also (*esp. US*) **stenographer**— *n* a person who records speech in shorthand and then types it out in full

short-list *v* to put on a short list

short list *n* a list of the most suitable people for an appointment, chosen from all those first considered and from whom 1 or more successful ones are chosen

short-lived *adj* lasting only a short time

shortly *adv* 1 soon 2 at a short distance 3 in a few words 4 impatiently; not politely: *He answered shortly*

short of *prep* 1 not quite reaching to: *to stop short of war* 2 except for; without: *short of calling a meeting*

short-range *adj* of, concerning, or covering a short distance or time

shorts *n* trousers ending above the knees

short shrift *n* unfairly quick treatment; little attention (esp. in the phrases **get/give short shrift**)

shortsighted *adj* 1 unable to see things clearly if they are not close to the eyes —opposite **longsighted** 2 not considering the likely future effects of present action — ~**ly** *adv* — ~**ness** *n*

short story *n* **-ries** a short invented story usu. containing only a few characters and dealing with description rather than plot

short-term *adj* (esp. in money matters) happening in or concerning a short period; in or for the near future: *short-term planning*

short wave *n* radio broadcasting or receiving on waves of less than 60 metres in length

short-winded *adj* quickly becoming tired and out of breath after a little running

shot[1] *n* 1 an action of shooting a weapon 2 a person who shoots with the stated degree of skill —see also DEAD SHOT 3 a kick, throw, etc., of a ball intended to score a point: *His shot went wide* 4 a sending up of a space vehicle or rocket 5 a chance or effort to do something; try: *I'd like a shot at cooking* 6 nonexplosive metal balls for shooting from some kinds of guns, such as shotguns —see also BUCKSHOT; compare BULLET, SHELL 7 the heavy metal ball used in the shot put 8 a photograph 9 a single part of a cinema film made by one camera without interruption: *an action shot* 10 a taking of a drug through a needle; injection 11 *esp. spoken* a bill for drinks (esp. in the phrase **pay one's shot**) **12** a chance at the stated degree of risk: *The horse is an 8 to 5 shot* —see also LONG SHOT **13** a small drink, esp. of whisky, for swallowing at once **14 a shot in the arm** something to bring back a happy active condition **15 a shot in the dark** a wild guess **16 big shot** *offensive* an important person **17 like a shot** quickly or without delay

shot² *adj* **1** woven in 2 different colours, one along and one across the material **2** *esp. spoken* rid of; finished with

shot³ *past tense and past part. of* SHOOT

shotgun *n* a gun fired from the shoulder, which is smooth inside its 1 or usu. 2 barrels and fires a quantity of small metal balls (SHOT) for a short distance

shot put *n* a competition to throw (PUT) a heavy metal ball the furthest distance

should *v* *negative short form* **shouldn't** **1** (used in indirect speech) shall: *We said we shoul dn't arrive till 6* **2** (used usu. with *that*, after certain verbs and adjectives esp. expressing an intention or wish): *He was keen that she should go to college* **3** (used with *I* and *we* in conditional sentences): *I should have been very lonely without my dog* **4** (expressing duty or what is necessary) ought to: *The lid should go on like this* **5** (expressing what is likely): *It should be fine tomorrow* **6** (expressing what is possible but not likely): *If I should see him, I'll tell him*

shoulder¹ *n* **1 a** the part of the body at each side of the neck where the arms are connected **b** the part of a garment that covers this part **2** the upper part of the back including these, esp. considered as where loads are carried **3** something like these in shape, such as an outward curve on a bottle or a slope on a mountain near the top ☞ GEOGRAPHY **4** either edge of a road outside the travelled part **5** the upper part of the front leg of an animal as meat **6 head and shoulders above** very much better than **7 rub shoulders with** to meet socially **8 shoulder to shoulder** a side by side **b** together; with the same intentions **9 straight from the shoulder** expressed plainly and directly —see also COLD SHOULDER, **put one's shoulder to the** WHEEL

shoulder² *v* **1** to place (as a load) on the shoulder(s) **2** to push with the shoulders: *He shouldered his way to the front*

shoulder blade also (*medical*) **scapula—** *n* either of the 2 flat bones on each side of the upper back ☞ ANATOMY

shouldst **thou shouldst** *old use or Bible* (when talking to one person) you should

shout¹ *v* to speak or say very loudly

shout² *n* **1** a loud cry or call **2** *sl* a particular person's turn to buy alcoholic drinks for others

shouting *n* shouts

shove¹ *v* **shoved, shoving** **1** to push, esp. in a rough or careless way: *Shove this furniture aside* **2** *esp. spoken* to move oneself: *Shove over, friend, and make room for me*

shove² *n* a strong push

shove around *v adv* *sl* PUSH AROUND

shove-ha'penny *n* the original form of shuffleboard, played with coins on a table esp. in inns

shovel¹ *n* **1** a long-handled tool with a broad blade for lifting and moving loose material — compare SPADE **2** also **shovelful** — the amount of material carried in any of these

shovel² -ll- **1** to take up, move, make, or work with a shovel **2** to move roughly as if with a shovel: *He shovelled the papers into his desk*

shove off *v adv* *esp. spoken* to go away; leave

show¹ *v* **showed, shown, showing** **1** to offer for seeing; allow or cause to be seen: *He showed his ticket* **2** to appear; be in or come into view; be visible: *His happiness showed in his smile* **3** to point to as a mark or number; indicate: *The clock showed 20 past 2* **4** to go with and guide or direct: *May I show you to your seat?* **5** to state or prove: *His speech showed no understanding of the subject* **6** to explain; make clear to by words or esp. actions; demonstrate **7 a** to offer as a performance **b** (esp. of a cinema film) to be offered at present **8** to allow to be easily seen: *A white dress will show dirt* **9** to prove (oneself) to be: *He showed himself a brave soldier* **10** *literature* to make to be felt in one's actions: *They showed their enemies kindness* **11** *sl* to arrive; show up: *My friend never showed* **12 show one's face** to be present in a company —see also SHOW OFF, SHOW UP

show² *n* **1** a showing of some quality; display: *a show of strength* **2** an outward appearance, esp. as opposed to what is really true, happening, etc.: *a show of interest* **3** grandness; splendid appearance or ceremony **4** a public showing; collection of things for looking at; exhibition **5** a performance, esp. in a theatre or nightclub or on radio or television **6** *esp. spoken* an organization or activity: *He's in charge of the whole show* **7** *esp. spoken* an effort; act of trying (often in such phrases as **put up a good show**) **8 get this show on the road** *esp. spoken* to start to work; get going **9 Good show!** *esp. spoken* Very good! Well done! **10 steal the show** to get all the attention and praise expected by someone else

show business also (*esp. spoken*) **show biz—** *n* the business of performing; the job of people who work in television, films, the theatre, etc.

showcase *n* a set of one or more shelves enclosed with glass in which objects are placed for looking at in a shop or museum

showdown *n* an open direct settlement of a quarrel or disagreement

shower¹ *n* **1** a short-lasting fall of rain or snow **2** a fall of many small things or drops of liquid: *A shower of paint fell on the men below* **3** a quantity or rush of things coming at the same time: *a shower of cards* **4 a** a washing of the body by standing under an opening from which water comes out in many small streams **b** an apparatus for this, with controls for water and usu. built as an enclosure in a bathroom **5** *esp. spoken offensive* a group of unpleasant, lazy, etc., people

shower² *v* **1** to rain or pour down in showers **2 a** to pour (on), scatter heavily (on) **b** to give in large quantity: *They showered her with gifts* **3** to take a shower

showery *adj* **-ier, -iest** bringing rain from time to time but not for long

showgirl *n* a girl in a group of singers or dancers, usu. in very fancy dress, in a musical show

showing *n* **1** an act of putting on view **2** a record of success or quality; performance: *a good showing by the local team*

show jumping *n* a form of horseriding competition judged on ability and often speed in jumping a course of fences — **-per** *n*

showman *n* **-men 1** a person whose business is producing plays, musical shows, etc. **2** a person who behaves always as if performing for others

showmanship *n* skill in drawing public attention

shown *past part. of* SHOW

show off *v adv* **1** to behave so as to try to get admiration for oneself, one's abilities, etc. **2** to show, esp. as something fine, beautiful, etc. — **show-off** *n*

show of hands *n* **shows of hands** a vote taken by counting the raised hands of voters

showpiece *n* a fine example fit to be admired by everyone

showplace *n* a place to be admired for its beauty or for some quality

showroom *n* a room where examples of goods for sale may be looked at

show up *v adv* **1** to be or cause to be easily seen **2** to make clear the (esp. unpleasant) truth about: *to show up a liar* **3** *esp. spoken* to arrive; be present **4** to make (someone) feel shame

showy *adj* **-ier, -iest** too colourful, attention-getting, etc., usu. without much real beauty — **showily** *adv* — **showiness** *n*

shrank *past tense of* SHRINK

shrapnel *n* metal scattered in small pieces from an exploding bomb or esp. shell fired from a large gun

shred¹ *n* **1** a small narrow piece torn or roughly cut off **2** a smallest piece; bit: *a shred of truth*

shred² *v* **-dd-** to cut or tear into shreds — ~**der** *n*

shrew *n* **1** any of several types of very small mouselike animal with a long pointed nose ☞ MAMMAL **2** a bad-tempered scolding woman

shrewd *adj* **1** clever in judgment, esp. of what is to one's own advantage: *a shrewd lawyer* **2** well-reasoned and likely to be right — ~**ly** *adv* — ~**ness** *n*

shrewish *adj* typical of a bad-tempered woman — ~**ly** *adv* — ~**ness** *n*

shriek *v* to cry out with a high sound; screech — **shriek** *n*

shrift *n* see SHORT SHRIFT

shrike *n* any of several kinds of mostly greyish birds with hooked strong beaks

shrill *adj* **1** high and sounding sharp or even painful to the ear; piercing **2** marked by continuous complaining — ~**y** *adv* — ~**ness** *n*

shrimp *n* **shrimp** *or* **shrimps 1** any of many types of small sea creature with long legs and a fanlike tail —compare PRAWN, SCAMPI **2** *usu. offensive* a small person

shrine *n* **1** a chest containing the remains of a holy person's body **2** a place for worship; place held in respect for its religious or other connections

shrink *v* **shrank, shrunk** *or* **shrunken, shrinking 1** to make or become smaller, as from the effect of heat or water **2** to move back and away; retire: *The dog shrank into a corner*

shrinkage *n* the/an act or amount of shrinking; loss in size

shrivel *v* **-ll-** to dry out and make or become smaller by twisting into small folds: *plants shrivelling in the heat*

shroud¹ *n* **1** also **winding sheet**— the cloth for covering a dead body at burial **2** something that covers and hides: *a shroud of secrecy* **3** any of the supporting ropes in pairs connecting a ship's central masts to its sides

shroud² *v* to cover and hide

Shrove Tuesday *n* **-days** the day before Ash Wednesday; the last day before the solemn period of Lent

shrub *n* a low bush with several woody stems

shrubbery *n* **-ries** (part of a garden planted with) shrubs forming a mass or group

shrug *v* **-gg-** to raise (one's shoulders), esp. as an expression of doubt or lack of interest — **shrug** *n*

shrug off *v adv* to treat as easy or not important: *to shrug off troubles*

shuck *v, n esp. US* (to remove) an outer shell, pod, or husk (from)

shudder *v* to shake uncontrollably for a moment, as from fear, cold, or strong dislike; tremble — **shudder** *n*

shuffle¹ *v* **-fled, -fling 1** to mix up the order of (playing cards) so as to produce a chance order ready for a game to begin **2** to move or push to and fro or to different positions: *to shuffle papers around* **3** to walk by dragging (one's feet) slowly along — ~**r** *n*

shuffle² *n* **1** a slow dragging walk **2** an act of shuffling cards

shuffleboard also **shovelboard**— *n* a game, played esp. on ships, in which round flat wooden pieces are driven by means of a long-handled pusher, along a smooth surface to try to make them come to rest on numbered areas

shufty *n sl* a quick view or look

shun *v* **-nn-** to avoid with determination; keep away from

shunt¹ *v* **1** to turn (a railway train or carriage) from one track to another, esp. to a siding **2** (of a train) to be turned in this way

shunt² *n* an apparatus that can reduce the amount of current in an electrical circuit

shunter *n* a railway shunting engine or its driver

shush *v* 1 to become quiet; hush 2 to tell to be quiet, as by saying ' sh '

shut *v* **shut, shutting** 1 to move into a covered, blocked, or folded-together position; close 2 to keep or hold by closing: *He shut himself in his room* 3 to stop in operation; close

shutdown *n* a stopping of work, as in a factory because of a labour quarrel, holiday, repairs, lack of demand, etc.

shut-eye *n esp. spoken* sleep

shutter¹ *n* 1 a wood or metal cover that can be placed, usu. by unfolding in pairs, in front of a window to block the view or keep out the light 2 a part of a camera which opens for an exact usu. very short time in taking a picture to let light fall on the film

shutter² *v* to close as with shutters

shuttle¹ *n* 1 a pointed instrument used in weaving to pass the thread across and between the threads that form the length of the cloth 2 a sliding thread carrier on a sewing machine for the lower of the 2 threads which lock to make a stitch 3 a regular going to and fro by air, railway, bus, etc., along a way between 2 points 4 a shuttlecock

shuttle² *v* **-tled, -tling** 1 to move to and fro often or regularly 2 to move by a shuttle

shuttlecock *n* a small light feathered object with a round base, for hitting across a net in a game of badminton

shut up *v adv sl* to stop talking

shy¹ *adj* **shyer** *or* **shier, shyest** *or* **shiest** 1 nervous in the company of others; not putting oneself forward; bashful 2 having doubts or distrust: *I'm shy of acting in this case* 3 (of animals) unwilling to come near people 4 **fight shy of** to try to avoid — ~**ly** *adv* — ~**ness** *n*

shy² *v* **shied, shying** 1 (esp. of a horse) to make a sudden movement, as from fear 2 to avoid something unpleasant, as by moving aside

shy³ *v* **shied, shying** *esp. spoken* to throw with a quick movement — **shy** *n*

shyster *n US esp. spoken* a dishonest person, esp. a lawyer

S I *abbrev. for:* International System of Units

Siamese cat also **Siamese**— *n* a type of blue-eyed short-haired cat, pale grey or light brown

Siamese twin *n* either of a pair of twins joined together from birth at some part of their bodies

sibilant *adj, n* (making or being) a sound like that of *s* or *sh*

sibling *n esp. written* a brother or sister

sibyl *n* any of several women in the ancient world who were thought to know the future — ~**line** *adj*

sic *adv Latin* (usu. in brackets) written in this wrong or strange way intentionally

sick *adj* 1 ill; having a disease 2 upset in the stomach so as to want to throw up what is in it 3 causing or typical of this feeling 4 feeling something so unpleasant as (almost) to cause this feeling 5 having a dislike from too much of something: *I'm sick of winter* 6 unhealthy; unnaturally cruel in likings, humour, etc.; morbid: *a sick joke* 7 for or related to illness: *sick pay* 8 **go/report sick** to excuse oneself from work because of illness USAGE In British English to feel or be sick is to vomit, or feel that one is about to vomit. It is therefore confusing to say *I was sick yesterday* meaning "I was ill", but it is all right to use **sick** to mean ill before a noun: *a sick child.* One may be on **sick leave**, or receive **sick pay**, because one is ill with a disease, or has had an accident involving broken bones, etc. One can speak of *the* **sick**, meaning sick people, but not of *the* **ill.**

sickbay *n* **-bays** a room, as on a ship, with beds for ill people

sickbed *n* the bed where a person lies ill

sicken *v* 1 to cause strong (almost) sick feelings of dislike in 2 to become ill; show signs of a disease

sickening *adj* which sickens a person; very displeasing or unpleasant: *sickening cruelty* — ~**ly** *adv*

sicken of *v prep* to become tired of

sickle *n* a hand tool with a hook-shaped blade, used for cutting grain or long grass —compare SCYTHE

sick leave *n* (permitted amount of) time spent away from a job during illness

sickly *adj* **-lier, -liest** 1 habitually ill; weak and unhealthy 2 unpleasantly weak, pale, or silly: *a sickly yellow* 3 causing a sick feeling

sickness *n* 1 a/the condition of being ill; illness or disease 2 the condition of feeling sick

sickness benefit *n* money paid, esp. by the government, to someone who is too ill to work

sickroom *n* a room where someone lies ill in bed

side¹ *n* 1 a more or less upright surface of something, not the top, bottom, front, or back 2 any of the flat surfaces of something: *Which side of the box is up?* 3 a part, place, or division according to a real or imaginary central line: *the other side of town* 4 the right or left part of the body, esp. from the shoulder to the top of the leg 5 the place next to someone, often regarded as the place of a helper, friend, tool, etc. 6 an edge or border: *A square has 4 equal sides* 7 either of the 2 surfaces of a thin flat object 8 a part to be considered, usu. in opposition to another; aspect: *Try to look at all sides of the question* 9 (a group which holds) a position in a quarrel, disagreement, war, etc. 10 a sports team: *cricket side* 11 the part of a line of a family that is related to a particular person: *He's Welsh on his mother's side* 12 either half of an animal body cut along the backbone 13 **hold/split one's sides** to be weak with uncontrollable laughter 14 **on the side** as a usu. cheating or dishonest additional activity **15 put on/to one side** to take out of consideration, for the present; keep for possible use later **16 this side of** *esp. spoken* without going as far as —see also ALONGSIDE, ASIDE, BACK-SIDE, BESIDE, COUNTRYSIDE, INSIDE, OUTSIDE

side² *adj* **1** at, from, towards, etc., the side **2** beside or in addition to the main or regular thing: *the drug had serious side effects*

side³ *v* **sided, siding** to be a party in a quarrel, disagreement, etc.; take a side

sidearm *n* a weapon carried or worn at one's side, such as a sword or pistol

sideboard *n* a piece of dining room furniture like a long table with a cupboard below to hold dishes, glasses, etc.

sideboards *n* growths of hair on the sides of a man's face in front of the ears, esp. worn long

sidecar *n* a usu. one-wheeled enclosed seat fastened to the side of a motorcycle to hold a passenger

side issue *n* a question or subject apart from the main one; something of not much importance

sidelight *n* **1** (a piece of) interesting though not very important information **2** either of a pair of lamps at the sides of a vehicle —compare HEADLIGHT

sideline *n* **1** a line marking the limit of play at the side of a football field, tennis court, etc. **2** the area just outside this and out of play: *to stand on the sidelines* **3** an activity in addition to one's regular job

sidelong *adv, adj* directed sideways

sidereal *adj technical* related to or calculated by the stars. Sidereal measurements of time are based on the **sidereal day**, equal to 23 hours 56 minutes 4.09 seconds

sidesaddle *adv, n* (on, or as if on) a woman's saddle on which both legs are placed on the same side of the horse's back

sideshow *n* **1** a separate small show at a fair or circus usu. with strange people (a sword swallower, bearded lady, etc.) on view **2** a usu. amusing activity beside a more serious main one

sideslip *v* **-pp-** to slip or skid sideways — **sideslip** *n*

sidesman *n* **-men** (in the Church of England) a man who collects offerings of money in church

sidesplitting *adj* causing uncontrollable laughter; very funny

sidestep *v* **-pp-** **1** to take a step to the side, (as) to avoid (a blow) **2** to avoid (an unwelcome question, duty, etc.) as if by moving aside; evade

side street *n* a narrow less-travelled street, esp. one that meets a main street

sidetrack *v* to cause to leave a more important or purposeful line of thought and follow some unimportant one — **sidetrack** *n*

sideward *adj* directed or moving to one side

sidewards *adv* to one side

sideways *adv, adj* **1** with one side (and not the front or back) forward or up: *The fat lady could*

only *get through the door sideways* **2** to or towards one side

siding *n* a short railway track connected to a main track, used for loading and unloading, for carriages not in use, etc.

sidle *v* **sidled, sidling** to walk as if ready to turn and go the other way, esp. secretively or nervously: *He sidled up to the stranger*

siege *n* an operation by an army surrounding a defended place to force it to yield, by repeated attacks, blocking of its supplies, etc.: *to lay siege to a fort*

sienna *n* brownish yellow earthy material which turns reddish brown when burned (**burnt sienna**), used as colouring matter for paint

sierra *n Spanish* a row, range, or area of sharply-pointed mountains

siesta *n Spanish* a short sleep after the midday meal, as is the custom in hot countries

sieve¹ *n* **1** a tool of wire or plastic net on a frame, or of a solid sheet with holes, used for separating large and small solid bits, or solid things from liquid **2 a head/memory like a sieve** *esp. spoken* a mind that forgets quickly

sieve² *v* **sieved, sieving** to put through or separate by means of a sieve

sift *v* **1** to put through a sieve, sifter, or net **2** to make a close examination of (things in a mass or group): *He sifted through his papers* **3** to separate or get rid of in either of these ways **4** (of a fine-grained material) to pass (as) through a sieve: *Snow sifted through the crack*

sifter *n* a container with many small holes in the top, for scattering powdery foods

sigh¹ *v* **1** to let out a deep breath slowly and with a sound, usu. expressing tiredness, sadness, or satisfaction **2** (as of the wind) to make a sound like this **3** *literature* to feel fondly sorry, esp. about something past, far away, etc.

sigh² *n* an act or sound of sighing

sight¹ *n* **1** something that is seen **2** the seeing of something **3** the sense of seeing; the power of the eye; eyesight; vision —see also SECOND SIGHT **4** presence in one's view; the range of what can be seen: *within sight of land* **5** something worth seeing, esp. a place visited by tourists: *the sights of London* **6** something which looks very bad or laughable: *What a sight you are!* **7** a part of an instrument or weapon which guides the eye in aiming **8** a lot; a great deal: *It cost me a sight more than expected* **9 in sight a** in view; visible **b** within a little of being reached; near: *Peace was in sight* **10 lose sight of a** to cease to see **b** to cease to have news about; lose touch with **c** to forget; fail to consider **11 out of sight a** out of the range of being seen **b** *esp. spoken* very high, great, etc.: *Costs have gone out of sight*

sight² *v* **1** to get a view of, esp. after a time of looking; see for the first time: *to sight land* **2** to aim or look in a certain direction — ~**ing** *n*

sighted *adj* (of a person) able to see

sightless *adj literature* unable to see; blind

sightly *adj* -lier, -liest pleasant-looking; good in appearance —opposite **unsightly** — -liness *n*

sight-read *v* -read, -reading to play or sing (written music) at first sight without practice — ~er *n* — ~ing *n*

sightscreen also screen— *n* (in cricket) either of 2 large movable white walls placed at the ends of the field to make it easier for players to see the ball

sightseeing *n* the activity of visiting places of interest, esp. while on holiday — -seer *n*

sigma *n* the 18th letter of the Greek alphabet (Σ, σ)

sign[1] *n* 1 a standard mark; something which is seen and represents a known meaning; symbol 2 a movement of the body intended to express a meaning; signal 3 a board or other notice giving information, warning, directions, etc. 4 something that shows a quality, or the presence or coming of something else: *Swollen ankles can be a sign of heart disease* 5 also **sign of the zodiac**— any of the 12 divisions of the year represented by groups of stars ☞ ZODIAC 6 **a sign of the times** something that is typical of the way things are just now

sign[2] *v* 1 to write (one's name) on (a written paper), esp. for official purposes, to show one's agreement, show that one is the writer, etc. 2 to make a movement as a sign to (someone): signal: *The policeman signed me to stop* 3 SIGN UP; SIGN ON —see also SIGN AWAY, SIGN OFF, SIGN OVER

signal[1] *n* 1 a sound or action intended to warn, command, or give a message 2 an action which causes something else to happen 3 a railway apparatus (usu. with coloured lights) near the track to direct train drivers 4 TRAFFIC LIGHT 5 a sound, image, or message sent by waves, as in radio or television

signal[2] *v* -ll- 1 to give a signal 2 to express, warn, or tell by a signal or signals 3 to be a sign of; mark: *The defeat of 1066 signalled the end of Saxon rule in England*

signal[3] *adj* literature noticeable, important, and usu. excellent; outstanding: *signal courage*

signal box *n* a small raised building near a railway from which traffic on the line is controlled

signalize, -ise *v* -ized, -izing to make known; draw attention to; show as important

signaller *n* a member of the army or navy trained in signalling

signally *adv* literature very noticeably; unmistakably

signalman *n* -men a man who controls railway traffic and signals

signatory *n* -ries any of the signers of an agreement, esp. among nations

signature *n* 1 a person's name written by his own hand, as at the end of a written statement, letter, cheque, etc. 2 the act of signing one's name: *to witness a signature* ~ see also KEY SIGNATURE, TIME SIGNATURE

signature tune *n* a short piece of music used

regularly in broadcasting to begin and end a particular show or as the special mark of a radio station

sign away *v adv* to give up formally (ownership, a claim, right, etc.), esp. by signing a paper

signet *n* an object used for printing a small pattern in wax as an official or private seal, and often fixed to or part of a ring

significance *n* importance; meaning; value

significant *adj* 1 of noticeable importance or effect 2 having a special meaning: *a significant smile* — ~ly *adv*

significant figures *n* technical the figures of a number, which are considered to give correct or sufficient information on its accuracy, that are read from the first non-zero digit on the left to the last non-zero digit on the right, unless a final zero expresses greater accuracy

signify *v* -fied, -fying 1 esp. written to be a sign of; represent; mean; denote 2 esp. written to make known (esp. an opinion) by an action: *to signify (agreement) by raising hands* 3 esp. spoken to matter; have importance (for)

sign language *n* any of various systems of hand movements for expressing meanings, as used by the deaf and dumb, by some American Indians, etc.

sign off *v adv* to end a letter, as with a signature: *'I'd better sign off now. Love, John'*

sign on *v adv* to join or cause to join (a working force), by signing a paper; enlist

Signor *n* Signori or Signors the title of an Italian (-speaking) man

Signora *n* Signore or Signoras the title of a (married) Italian (-speaking) woman

Signorina *n* -ne or -nas the title of an unmarried Italian (-speaking) girl

sign over *v adv* to give formally (one's rights, ownership, etc.) to another, esp. by signing a paper

signpost *n* a sign showing directions and distances, as at a meeting of roads — ~ed *adj*

sign up *v adv* to sign or cause to sign an agreement to take part in something, or to take a job; enlist

Sikh *n* a member of a religion founded in India about 1500 that holds beliefs similar to Hinduism, but believes in one God and rejects the caste system and worship of idols — Sikh *adj*

silage *n* grass or other plants (FODDER) cut and stored in a silo away from air for preservation as winter food for cattle

silence[1] *n* 1 absence of sound; stillness 2 the state of not speaking or making a noise 3 failure to write a letter or letters 4 failure to mention or say a particular thing: *Why silence on this matter?* 5 a moment or period of any of these conditions

silence[2] *v* silenced, silencing 1 to cause or force to stop making a noise 2 to force to stop expressing opinions, making opposing statements, etc.: *They were silenced by imprisonment*

silencer *n* an apparatus for reducing noise, such

as **a** a part for fitting around the end of the barrel of a small gun **b** a part of a petrol engine which fits onto the pipe where burnt gases come out ☞ CAR

silent adj **1** not speaking; not using spoken expression **2** free from noise; quiet **3** making no statement; expressing no opinion, decision, etc.: *The law is silent on this point* **4** (of a letter in a word) not pronounced: *silent ' w ' in ' wreck '* **5** being or concerning films with no sound — ~ly adv

silhouette¹ n **1** a shadow-like representation of the shape of something, filled in with a solid colour, usu. black **2** a shape or figure; profile

silhouette² v **-etted, -etting** to cause to appear as a silhouette

silica also (*technical*) **silicon dioxide—** n the substance found naturally as sand, quartz, and flint

silicate n technical any of a large group of solid substances making up most of the earth and most building materials

silicon n a nonmetallic element found naturally in combined forms in great quantities ☞ CHIP

silicosis n a lung disease (esp. among miners, stonecutters, etc.) caused by long breathing of silica dust

silk n **1 a** a fine thread which is produced by a silkworm and made into thread for sewing and into cloth **b** smooth soft cloth made from this **2 silk and satins** literature fine rich clo thes

silken adj literature **1** soft, smooth, or shiny like silk; silky **2** made of silk

silk screen n a way of printing on a surface by forcing paint or ink through a specially prepared stretched piece of cloth onto it

silkworm n a type of caterpillar bred originally in China which produces a cocoon of silk

silky adj **-ier, -iest** like silk; soft, smooth, or shiny — **silkiness** n

sill n the flat piece at the base of an opening or frame, esp. a windowsill

silly¹ adj **-lier, -liest** **1** having or showing little judgment; foolish; stupid; not serious; ridiculous **2** esp. spoken senseless; stunned: *That speaker bores me silly* **3** (of a player or his position in cricket) very close to the batsman (in the phrases **silly point, silly mid-on, silly mid-off**)

silly² n **-lies** a silly person

- **silo** n **silos** **1** a usu. round tower-like enclosure on a farm for storing green winter food for cattle (SILAGE) or farm produce **2** an underground base from which a guided missile may be fired

silt n loose sand, mud, soil, etc., carried in running water and then dropped (as at the entrance to a harbour, bend in a river, etc.)

silt up v adv to fill or become filled with silt

silver¹ n **1** a soft whitish precious metal that is an element, carries electricity very well, can be brightly polished, and is used esp. in ornaments and coins **2** silver money; coins made of this, or of some white metal like it, and not of copper **3** spoons, forks, dishes, etc., for the table, made of this or a metal like it

silver² adj **1** made of silver **2** like silver in colour **3** literature pleasantly musical

silver³ v **1** to cover with a thin shiny silver-coloured surface: *to silver the back of a mirror* **2** literature to make or become silver-coloured

silver birch n the common white birch tree, which has a silvery-white trunk and branches

silverfish n **-fish** or **~ fishes** a type of small silver-coloured wingless insect found about houses and sometimes harmful to paper and cloth

silver jubilee n the return after 25 years of the date of some important personal event, esp. of becoming a king or queen

silver paper also **silver foil—** n paper with one bright metallic surface, as used in packets for cigarettes, food, etc.

silverside n the top side of beef cut from the leg of the cattle

silversmith n a maker of silver vessels, jewellery, etc.

silver wedding also **silver wedding anniversary —** n the 25th yearly return of the date of a wedding

silvery adj **1** having a pleasant musical sound **2** like silver in shine and colour

similar adj **1** like or alike; of the same kind; partly or almost the same **2** technical exactly the same in shape but not size: *similar triangles* — ~ly adv

similarity n **-ties** **1** the quality of being alike or like something else; resemblance **2** a point of likeness

simile n an expression making a comparison in the imagination between 2 things, using the words *like* or *as*: *'As white as snow' is a simile —* compare METAPHOR

simmer v **1** to cook gently in liquid at or just below boiling heat **2** to be filled (with hardly controlled excitement, anger, etc.) — **simmer** n

simper v to smile in a silly unnatural way — **simper** n — ~**ingly** adv

simple adj **1** not ornamented; plain **2** easy to understand or do; not difficult **3** of the ordinary kind, without special qualities, rules, difficulties, etc.; not complicated; basic **4** not (able to be) divided; of only one thing or part: *A simple sentence has only 1 verb* —compare COMPOUND, COMPLEX **5** not mixed with anything else; with nothing added; pure: *a simple statement* **6** sincere; natural and honest: *a woman of simple goodness* **7** easily tricked; foolish; gullible **8** literature of low rank or unimportant position: *a simple farm worker* **9** old use weak-minded **10 the simple life** esp. spoken life considered as better without the difficulties of having many possessions, using machines, etc.

simple interest n interest calculated on an original sum of money without first adding in the interest already earned . —compare COMPOUND INTEREST

simple-minded adj 1 foolish; feebleminded 2 not wise; simple and trusting in mind

simplicity n 1 the state of being simple 2 **simplicity itself** esp. spoken very easy

simplify v -fied, -fying to make plainer, easier, or less full of detail: *to simplify an explanation* —see also OVERSIMPLIFY — **-fication** n

simply adv 1 in a simple way; easily, plainly, clearly, or naturally 2 just; only: *I drive simply to get to work each day* 3 really; very (much): *It's simply wonderful to see you!*

simulate v -lated, -lating to give the effect or appearance of; imitate — ~d adj

simulation n (a) representation; pretending; imitation

simulator n an apparatus which allows a trainee to feel what real conditions are like (in traffic, in an aircraft, space vehicle, etc.)

simultaneous adj happening or done at the same moment: *they made a simultaneous appearance* — ~ly adv — -neity, ~ness n

sin¹ n 1 disobedience to God; the breaking of law regarded as holy 2 an example of this — compare CRIME 3 esp. humour something that should not be done; a serious offence 4 **live in sin** usu. polite or humour (of 2 unmarried people) to live together as if married

sin² v -nn- to break God's laws; do wrong according to some standard — ~ner n

since¹ adv 1 at a time between then and now; subsequently; from then until now: *He came to England 3 years ago and has lived here ever since* 2 ago: *I've long since forgotten our quarrel*

since² prep from (a point in past time) until now; during the period after: *I haven't seen her since her illness*

since³ conj 1 a after the past time when b continuously from the time when: *We've been friends since we met* 2 as; as it is a fact that: *Since you can't answer, I'll ask someone else*

sincere adj free from deceit or falseness; real, true, or honest; genuine — ~ly adv — -rity n

sine n technical a measure of the size of an angle calculated by dividing the length of the side opposite it in a right-angled triangle by the length of the side opposite the right angle (HYPOTENUSE) ☞ TRIGONOMETRY

sinecure n a position usu. giving an income but with few or no duties; easy, well-paid job △ CYNOSURE

sinew n a strong cord in the body connecting a muscle to a bone; tendon

sinewy adj strong; (as if) having strong muscles

sinful adj 1 guilty of, or being, sin 2 esp. spoken shameful; seriously wrong or bad — ~ly adv — ~ness n

sing v sang, sung, singing 1 to produce (music, musical sounds, songs, etc.) with the voice 2 to make or be filled with a ringing sound: *My ears sang after the crash* 3 literature to speak, tell about, or praise in poetry — ~able adj — ~er n

singe v singed, singeing 1 to burn off the ends from (hair, threads, etc.) by passing near a flame 2 to burn lightly on the surface; scorch: *singed the shirt with a hot iron* — **singe** n

singing n 1 the art of the singer 2 the act or sound of voices in song

single¹ adj 1 being (the) only one 2 having only one part, quality, etc.; not double or multiple 3 separate; considered by itself: *Food is our most important single need* 4 unmarried 5 for the use of only one person 6 (of a ticket or its cost) for a trip from one place to another but not back again

single² n 1 a single ticket 2 (in cricket) a single run 3 a record with only one short song on each side —opposite LP 4 esp. spoken a single room

single-breasted adj (of a coat) closing in the centre at the front with only one row of buttons

single-decker n a bus with one floor

single file also **Indian file**— n, adv (moving or standing in) a line of people, vehicles, etc., one behind another

single-handed adj, adv done by one person; working alone, without help

single-minded adj having or showing one clear purpose and effort to serve it — ~ly adv — ~ness n

singleness n the directing of thoughts, efforts etc., together; concentration

single out v adv -gled, -gling out to separate or choose from a group, esp. for special treatment or notice

singles n -gles a match or competition made up of matches, esp. of tennis, with one player against one

singlet n a man's vest sometimes worn as an outer shirt when playing some sports

singly adv separately; by itself or themselves; one by one

singsong n 1 a dull repeated rising and falling of the voice in speaking 2 an informal gathering or party for singing songs

singular adj 1 of or being a word or form representing exactly one: *'Mouse ' is the singular form of 'mice '* —opposite **plural** 2 of unusual quality; extraordinary 3 becoming rare very unusual or strange; peculiar — ~ity n

singularly adv 1 particularly; very (much): *singularly wet weather for June* 2 strangely; in an unusual way

Sinhalese adj of or concerning the language, people, etc. of Sri Lanka

sinister adj threatening, intending, or leading to evil: *a sinister look*

sink¹ v sank, sunk, sinking 1 to go or cause to go down below a surface, out of sight, or to the bottom (of water) 2 to fall to a lower level or position: *The flames sank* 3 to get smaller; go down in number, value, strength, etc.: *His voice sank to a whisper* 4 to fall (as) from lack of strength: *She sank to the ground* **5** to become weaker; fail: *He's sinking fast* **6** to dig out or force into the earth: *to sink fence posts/a well* **7** to stop considering; forget: *to sink a disagreement* **8** to put (money, labour, etc.) into; invest **9** (in games like golf and billiards) to cause (a ball) to go into a hole **10 sink or swim** to fail or succeed without help from others —see also SUNKEN — ~**able** *adj*

sink² *n* a large basin in a kitchen, for washing pots, vegetables, etc., fixed to a wall and usu. with pipes to supply and carry away water

sink in *v adv* **1** to enter a solid through the surface **2** to become well understood: *I think the lesson has sunk in*

sinless *adj* free from sin; pure and holy — ~**ness** *n*

Sinn Fein *n* an Irish nationalist organization

sinuous *adj* twisting like a snake; full of curves; winding — ~**ity** *n*

sinus *n* a hollow place inside a bone, esp. any of the air-filled spaces in the facial bones that have an opening into the nose

sip *v* -**pp**- to drink, taking only a little at a time into the front of the mouth — **sip** *n*

siphon, syphon¹ *n* **1** a tube bent so that a liquid is drawn upwards and then downwards through it to a lower level **2** a kind of bottle for holding soda-water and forcing it out by gas pressure **3** any of various tube-like organs, esp. in water animals such as squids, for taking in and squirting out liquids

siphon, syphon² *v* to draw off or take away by a siphon

sir *n* **1** (a respectful address to an older man or one of higher rank; to an officer by a soldier; to a male teacher by a British school child; to a male customer in a shop; etc.) **2** *pompous* (an angry scolding form of address): *Come here at once, sir!*

Sir *n* **1** (a title used before the name of a knight or baronet) **2** (used at the beginning of a formal letter): *Dear Sir*

sire¹ *n* **1** the father of an animal, esp. of a horse —compare DAM **2** *old use* (a form of address to a king)

sire² *v* **sired, siring** (esp. of a horse) to be the father of

siren *n* **1** an apparatus for making a loud long warning sound, as used on ships, police cars, fire engines, and for air-attack warnings **2** (in ancient Greek literature) any of a group of woman-like creatures whose sweet singing charmed sailors and caused the wreck of their ships **3** a dangerous beautiful woman; FEMME FATALE

sirloin also **sirloin steak**— *n* (a piece of) beef cut from the best part of the lower back

sirocco *n* -**cos** a hot wind blowing from the desert of North Africa across to S Europe

sis *n* *esp. spoken* sister

sisal *n* (a West Indian plant whose leaves produce) a strong white thread-like substance used in making cord, rope, and mats

sissy, cissy *n* -**sies** *offensive* a person (often a boy) who seems silly and weak or cowardly — **sissy** *adj*

sister¹ *n* **1** a female relative with the same parents ☞ FAMILY **2** a woman in close association with the speaker **3** (a title for) a nurse in charge of a ward of a hospital **4** (a title for) a woman member of a religious group, esp. a nun — ~**hood** *n*

sister² *adj* (of women or things considered female) with the same purpose; in the same group; fellow: *a sister ship*

sister-in-law *n* -**s-in-law** **1** the sister of one's husband or wife **2** the wife of one's brother **3** the wife of the brother of one's husband or wife ☞ FAMILY

sisterly *adj* of or like a sister; typical of a loving sister

sit *v* **sat, sitting** **1** to rest in a position with the upper body upright and supported at the bottom of the back, as on a chair or other seat **2** to go or cause to go into this position; take or cause to take a seat: *She sat the baby on the grass* **3** (of an animal or bird) to be in or go into a position with the tail end of the body resting on a surface **4** to have a position in an official body —see also SIT FOR **5** (of an official body) to have 1 or more meetings: *The court sat longer than expected* **6** to lie; rest; have a place (and not move): *books sitting unread on the shelf* **7** to have one's picture painted or photographed; pose **8** to take (a written examination) **9** (of a hen) to cover eggs to bring young birds to life **10 sit on one's hands** *esp. spoken* to take no action **11 sit pretty** to be in a very good position —see also SIT FOR, SIT IN, SIT IN ON, SIT OUT, SIT WITH

sitar *n* a N Indian metal-stringed instrument with a long neck

sit-down *adj* (of a meal) at which people are served while seated at a table —compare BUFFET

site¹ *n* **1** a place where something was or happened **2** a piece of ground for building on

site² *v* **sited, siting** to provide with a site; locate

sit for *v prep* to be a Member of Parliament for (a place)

sit-in *n* an act of social dissatisfaction and anger by a group of people who enter a public place, stop its usual business, and refuse to leave

sit in *v adv* **1** to take another's regular place, as in a meeting or office job **2** to take part in a sit-in

sit in on *v adv prep* to attend (as a meeting) without taking an active part

sit on *v prep* **1** to delay taking action on: *He's been sitting on my letter for months* **2** *esp. spoken* to force rudely into silence or inactivity

sit out *v adv* **1** to remain seated during (a dance); not take part in **2** also **sit through**— to stay until the end of (a performance), esp. without enjoyment

sitter *n* a person whose picture is taken or

painted; one who sits for an artist or photographer

sitting[1] *n* 1 a period of time spent seated in a chair 2 a serving of a meal for a number of people at one time 3 a meeting of an official body; session

sitting[2] *adj* 1 that now has a seat on an official body (such as Parliament): *The sitting member for Oxford* 2 that now lives in a place: *sitting tenants*

sitting duck *n* someone or something easy to attack or cheat

sitting room *n* LIVING ROOM

situated *adj* 1 in a particular place; located 2 *esp. spoken* placed among possibilities; in a condition

situation *n* 1 a position or condition at the moment; state of affairs 2 *esp. written* a job; position in work 3 a position with regard to surroundings: *an island situation*

sit-up *n* a muscle-training movement in which a person sits up from a lying position keeping his legs straight and on the floor

sit with *v prep* to help to nurse (a sick person)

six[1] *adj, n, pron* 1 the number 6 2 a cricket hit worth 6 runs 3 **at sixes and sevens** in disorder, esp. of mind; confused or undecided — ~th *adj, n, pron, adv*

sixpence *n* (in Britain until 1971) (a coin worth) the sum of 6 (old) pennies; 6d

six-shooter also **sixgun**— *n* a type of small revolver holding 6 bullets

sixteen *adj, n, pron* the number 16 — ~th *adj, n, pron, adv*

sixth form *n* the highest form in a British school; the group of students usu. aged 16 or older who have taken O Levels

sixth sense *n* an ability to see or know that does not come from the 5 senses; intuition

sixty *adj, n, pron* -ties the number 60 — -tieth *adj, n, pron, adv*

sixty-four *adj* **the sixty-four-thousand-dollar question** *esp. spoken* the most important question; question on whose answer a very great deal depends

sizable, sizeable *adj* rather large

size[1] *n* 1 (a degree of) bigness or smallness 2 bigness: *not of any size* 3 any of a set of measures in which objects are made (such as clothes, for fitting people) 4 **cut someone down to size** to show someone to be really less good, important, etc. 5 **That's about the size of it** *esp. spoken* That's a fair statement of the matter

size[2] also **sizing**— *n* pastelike material used for giving stiffness and a hard shiny surface to paper, cloth, etc.

size[3] *v* **sized, sizing** to cover or treat with size

size up *v adv* to form an opinion or judgment about; get an idea of

sizzle *v* -zled, -zling to make a hissing sound, as of food cooking in hot fat

skate[1] *n* **skate** or **skates** any of a large family of edible large flat sea fish

skate[2] *n* 1 also **ice skate**— either of a pair of metal blades fitted to the bottom of boots to allow the wearer to go swiftly on ice 2 ROLLER SKATE 3 **get/put one's skates on** *esp. spoken* to hurry

skate[3] *v* **skated, skating** to move on skates — ~r *n*

skateboard *n* a short board with 2 small wheels at each end for standing on and riding

skate over also **skate round**— *v prep* to avoid treating seriously; make to seem unimportant; GLOSS OVER

skedaddle *v* -dled, -dling *esp. spoken* to run away; hurry off

skein *n* 1 a loosely wound length (of thread or yarn) 2 a large group (of wild geese) flying in the sky

skeleton[1] *n* 1 the framework of all the bones in a human or animal body ⇨ ANATOMY 2 a set of these bones (or models of them) held in their positions, as for use by medical students 3 an unnaturally very thin person 4 something forming a framework 5 *esp. spoken* a secret of which a person or family is ashamed

skeleton[2] *adj* enough to keep an operation or organization going, and no more: *a skeleton rail service*

skeleton key *n* -keys a key made to open a number of different locks

sketch[1] *n* 1 a rough not detailed drawing 2 a short description in words 3 a short informal piece of literature or stage acting

sketch[2] *v* 1 to draw sketches 2 to make a sketch of 3 to describe roughly with few details: *to sketch in/out the main points* — ~er *n*

sketchy *adj* -ier, -iest not thorough or complete; lacking details; rough — **sketchily** *adv* — **sketchiness** *n*

skew *adj* 1 not straight; sloping or twisted; oblique 2 *technical* (of lines in space) not parallel and not intersecting

skewbald *adj, n* (a horse) coloured with large white and esp. brown patches —compare PIEBALD

skewer[1] *n* a long wooden or metal pin for holding meat together while cooking or for putting through small pieces of meat and vegetables (such as shish kebab) for cooking

skewer[2] *v* to fasten or make a hole through (as) with a skewer

ski[1] *n* **skis** either of a pair of long thin narrow pieces of wood, plastic, or metal curving up in front, for fastening to a boot for travelling (often in sports) on snow

ski[2] *v* **skied, skiing** to go on skis for travel or sport —see also WATER SKIING — ~er *n*

skid[1] *n* 1 a piece of usu. wood placed under a heavy object to raise it off the floor or move it 2 an act or path of skidding: *The car went into a skid* 3 **put the skids on/under** *esp. spoken* **a** to stop or defeat; frustrate **b** to forc e to hurry

skid[2] *v* -dd- (of a vehicle or a wheel) to fail to stay in control on a road; slip sideways out of control

skidpan *n* a prepared slippery surface where drivers practise controlling skidding vehicles

skid row *n US* a poor dirty part of town where unemployed and alcoholic people gather

skiff *n* a small light one-man boat for rowing or sailing

skiffle *n* music popular in the late 1950's, based on American folk music and played partly on instruments made by the performers

ski jump *n* 1 competition in jumping on skis at high speed from a steep downward slope ending in a cliff 2 the slope and cliff set up for this event

skilful *adj* having or showing skill — ~ly *adv*

ski lift *n* a power-driven endless wire rope with seats for carrying skiers to the top of a slope

skill *n* (a use of) practical knowledge and power; ability to do something (well): *a writer of great skill* —see GENIUS (USAGE) — ~ed *adj*

skillet *n* a type of frying pan

skim *v* **-mm-** 1 to remove (floating fat or solids) from the surface of a liquid: *skim cream from milk* 2 to remove unwanted floating material from (liquid) 3 to read quickly to get the main ideas; scan 4 to move swiftly in a path near or touching (a surface): *to skim stones over a lake*

skimp *v* to spend, provide, or use less (of) than is really needed — ~y *adj* — ~ily *adv* — ~iness *n*

skin¹ *n* 1 the natural outer covering of an animal or human body, from which hair may grow ⊚ 2 this part of an animal body for use as leather, fur, etc. 3 a natural outer covering of some fruits and vegetables; peel 4 an outer surface built over a framework or solid inside 5 the more solid surface that forms over a liquid, as when it gets cool 6 a case for a sausage 7 **by the skin of one's teeth** *esp. spoken* narrowly; only just 8 **get under someone's skin** *esp. spoken* to annoy or excite someone deeply 9 **save one's skin** *esp. spoken* to save oneself, esp. in a cowardly way, from death, ruin, punishment, etc. — ~less *adj*

skin² *v* **-nn-** 1 to remove the skin from 2 to hurt by rubbing off some skin: *He skinned his knee*

skin-deep *adj* on the surface only; superficial

skin-dive *v* **-dived, -diving** to go deep under water without heavy breathing apparatus and not wearing a protective suit — **skin diver** *n* — *compare* FROGMAN — **skin diving** *n*

skinflint *n offensive* a person who is not generous; one who will not spend money; miser

skin graft *n* an operation to repair a burn, wound, etc., by replacing the damaged skin with a piece of healthy skin

skinny *adj* **-nier, -niest** *offensive* thin; without much flesh

skint *adj sl* completely without money; broke

skin-tight *adj* (of clothes) fitting tightly against the body

skip¹ *v* **-pp-** 1 to move in a light dancing way, as with quick steps and jumps 2 to move in no fixed order: *to skip from one subject to another* 3 to pass over or leave out (something in order); not do or deal with (the next thing) 4 to fail to attend or to take part in (an activity); miss: *to skip school* 5 to jump over a rope passed repeatedly beneath one's feet 6 *esp. spoken* to leave hastily and secretly, esp. to avoid being punished or paying money: *She skipped off without paying*

skip² *n* a light quick stepping and jumping movement

skip³ *n* a builder's large metal container for carrying away heavy materials, esp. old bricks, wood, etc.

skipper *v, n esp. spoken* 1 (to be) a ship's captain 2 (to be) a captain of a sports team

skirmish¹ *n* 1 a fight between small groups of soldiers, ships, etc., at a distance from the main forces and not part of a large battle 2 a slight or unplanned exchange of arguments between opponents

skirmish² *v* to fight in a skirmish — ~er *n*

skirt¹ *n* 1 a woman's outer garment that fits around the waist and hangs down with one lower edge all round 2 a part of a coat or dress that hangs below the waist 3 *sl* girls or women considered as sexual objects: *a nice bit of skirt*

skirt² *v* 1 to be or go around the outside of; go around: *a road skirting the town* 2 to avoid (a question, subject, difficulty, etc.)

skirting board *n* (a) board fixed along the base of a wall where it meets the floor of a room

ski stick *n* either of a pair of pointed short poles held by a skier for balance and for pushing against the snow

skit *n* a short usu. humorous acted-out scene, often copying and ridiculing something

skitter *v* (of a small creature) to run quickly and lightly

skittish *adj* 1 not serious or responsible; silly and changeable in mind 2 (esp. of a horse) easily excited and made afraid — ~ly *adv* — ~ness *n*

skittle also **skittle pin**— *n* a bottle-shaped object used in skittles

skittles *n* an English usu. informal game in which a player tries to knock down 9 skittles by throwing a ball or other object at them

skive *v* **skived, skiving** *esp. spoken* to avoid work, often by staying out of the way — **skiver** *n*

skivvy *n* **-vies** *esp. spoken offensive* a house servant, esp. a girl, who does the dirty unpleasant jobs

skua *n* any of several kinds of large N Atlantic seabird

skulduggery, skullduggery *n esp. humour* secretly dishonest or unfair action

skulk *v* to move about secretly or hide, through fear or for some evil purpose — ~er *n*

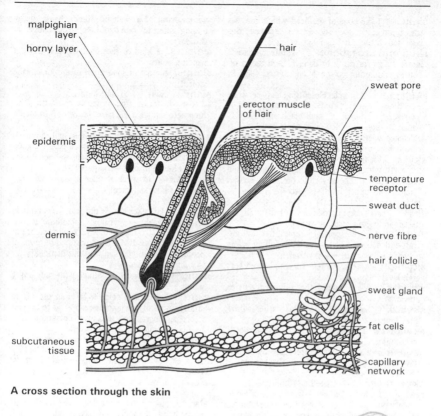

A cross section through the skin

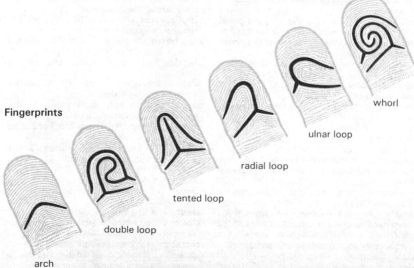

Fingerprints

arch

double loop

tented loop

radial loop

ulnar loop

whorl

skull *n* 1 the bone of the head which encloses the brain ☞ ANATOMY 2 *esp. spoken* this regarded as the mind or its covering

skull and crossbones *n*   **skulls and crossbones** a sign for death or danger, used esp. **a** on bottles containing poison **b** on pirates' flags in former times

skullcap *n* a simple closefitting cap as worn sometimes by some priests, Jewish men, etc.

skunk *n* 1 a type of small black and white N American animal which gives out a bad smell as a defence when attacked 2 *usu. humour* a person who is bad, unfair, unkind, etc.

sky¹ *n* **skies** 1 the upper air; the space above the earth where clouds and the sun, moon, and stars appear 2 **The sky's the limit** *esp. spoken* There is no upper limit (esp. to the amount of money that may be spent)

sky² *v* **skied, skying** to knock (a ball) high into the air in a game, esp. by mistake

skydiving *n* the sport of jumping from an aircraft and making movements while falling before opening a parachute — **skydiver** *n*

sky-high *adv esp. spoken* very high; to a very high level

skylark¹ *n* a kind of lark that sings while flying upwards

skylark² *v esp. spoken* to play rather wildly; have fun; lark about

skylight *n* a glass-covered opening in a roof to let in light

skyline *n* a shape or picture made by scenery (esp. tall city buildings) against the background of the sky

skyscraper *n* a very tall city building

slab *n* 1 a thick flat usu. 4-sided piece of metal, stone, wood, food, etc. 2 the often stone table top on which a dead body is laid in a hospital or mortuary

slack¹ *adj* 1 (of a rope, wire, etc.) not pulled tight 2 not firm; weak; loose 3 not busy or active: *Business is slack* 4 not properly careful or quick — ~ly *adv* — ~ness *n*

slack² *v* 1 to be lazy; not work well or quickly enough: *scolded for slacking* 2 to reduce (in) speed, effort, or tightness; slacken: *to slack off towards the end of the day*

slack³ *n* the part of a rope, wire, etc., that hangs loose

slack⁴ *n* coal dust

slacken *v* to make or become slack; reduce in activity, force, etc., or in tightness

slacker *n* a person who is lazy or avoids work

slacks *n* trousers, esp. of a loosefitting informal kind

slack water *n* the time of still water when the tide is turning

slag *n* 1 lighter glasslike waste material left when metal is separated from its natural rock 2 *offensive sl* an unpleasant ugly woman, esp. one with socially unacceptable sexual morals

slain *past part. of* SLAY

slake *v* **slaked, slaking** 1 to satisfy (thirst) with a drink 2 **a** to change (lime) chemically by adding water; hydrate **b** (of lime) to be changed in this way

slalom *n* a kind of race (e.g. on skis) down a winding course

slam¹ *n* the act or loud noise of a door closing violently

slam² *v* **-mm-** 1 to shut loudly and with force 2 to push, move, etc., hurriedly and with great force: *He slammed the papers down* 3 to attack with words

slander¹ *n* 1 an intentional false spoken report, story, etc., that unfairly damages a person's good reputation 2 the making of such a statement, esp. as an offence in law —compare LIBEL

slander² *v* to speak slander against; harm by making a false statement — ~er *n* — ~ous *adj* — ~ously *adv*

slang¹ *n* language that is not usu. acceptable in serious speech or writing, including words, expressions, etc., regarded as very informal or not polite, and those used among particular groups of people. These are marked *sl* in this dictionary — ~y *adj* — ~iness *n*

slang² *v esp. spoken* to attack with rude angry words

slant¹ *v* 1 to be or cause to be at an angle from straight up and down across; slope 2 to express (facts, a report, etc.) in a way favourable to a particular opinion — ~ingly *adv*

slant² *n* 1 a slanting direction or position: *a steep upward slant* 2 a particular way of looking at or expressing: *an interesting new slant on the news*

slap¹ *n* a quick blow with the flat part of the hand

slap² *v* **-pp-** 1 to strike quickly with the flat part of the hand 2 to place quickly, roughly, or carelessly: *to slap paint on a wall*

slap³ *adv esp. spoken* directly; right; smack: *to run slap up against a wall*

slap-bang *adv esp. spoken* suddenly and violently

slapdash *adj* done, made, etc., hastily and carelessly

slaphappy *adj esp. spoken* 1 wildly and carelessly happy 2 slapdash

slapstick *n* comedy that depends on rather violent fast action and simple jokes

slap-up *adj esp. spoken* excellent; fine and esp. fancy

slash¹ *v* 1 to cut with long sweeping forceful strokes, as with a knife or sword 2 to move or force with this kind of cutting movement: *He slashed his way through the bush* 3 to attack fiercely in words 4 to reduce (an amount, price, etc.) steeply

slash² *n* a long sweeping cut or blow

slat *n* a thin narrow flat piece of usu. wood, esp. in furniture or venetian blinds — ~ted *adj*

slate¹ *n* 1 fine smooth rock formed from mud by heat or pressure, easily splitting into thin flat pieces 2 a small piece of this or other material used for laying in rows to cover a roof **3** a small board made of this or of wood, used for writing on with chalk **4** an imaginary record of the past, esp. of mistakes, faults, disagreements, etc.: *Let's wipe the slate clean and forget our past quarrels*

slate² *v* **slated, slating** to blame severely or attack in words; berate

slattern *n literature* a dirty untidy woman — ~**ly** *adj*

slaty *adj* **-ier, -iest** containing or like slate

slaughter *n* **1** (a) killing of many people or animals, esp. cruelly, wrongly, or as in a battle; massacre **2** the killing of animals for meat

slaughter² *v* **1** to kill (animals) for food; butcher **2** to kill (esp. many people) cruelly or wrongly; massacre

slaughterhouse *also* **abattoir**— *n* a building where animals are killed for meat

slave¹ *n* **1** a person owned in law by another; servant without personal freedom **2** a person completely in the control of another person or thing; one who must obey: *a slave to duty* **3** *usu. humour* a person who works hard at uninteresting work for another

slave² *v* **slaved, slaving** to work like a slave; work hard with little rest

slave driver *n esp. spoken* a person who demands hard work from those in his employment or under him

slave labour *n* **1** work by slaves **2** *humour* hard work done for little or no pay, or forced to be done

slaver¹ *v* **1** to let saliva come out of the mouth; drool **2** *usu. offensive* to be eager or excited

slaver² *n* saliva running down from the mouth

slaver³ *n* a person or esp. a ship in the business of carrying or selling slaves

slavery *n* **1** the system of having slaves **2** the condition of being a slave

slave trade *also* **slave traffic**— *n* the buying and selling of slaves, esp. the forced carrying away of Africans as slaves in the 17th–19th centuries

Slavic *also* **Slavonic**— *adj* of or concerning the E European people (**Slavs**) including Russians, Czechs, Poles, Yugoslavs, etc., or their languages

slavish *adj* **1** slavelike; needing or showing hard work, complete dependence on others, etc. **2** copying or copied very closely or exactly from something else; not fresh or changed — ~**ly** *adv*

slay *v* **slew , slain, slaying** *literature* to kill, esp. violently; put to death — ~**er** *n*

sleazy *adj* **-ier, -iest** cheap and poor-looking; disreputable; shabby — **-ziness** *n*

sledge¹ *also*(*esp.*US)**sled**— *n* **1** a vehicle made for sliding along snow or ice on 2 metal blades. Small light kinds are used in play and sport for going fast down slopes **2** one of these made for carrying heavy loads across snow

sledge² *v* **sledged, sledging** to go or race down slopes on a sledge

sledgehammer *n* a large heavy hammer for swinging with both hands to drive in posts, break stones, etc.

sleek¹ *v* to cause (hair or fur) to be smooth and shining

sleek² *adj* **1** (esp. of hair or fur) smooth and shining, as from good health and care **2** (too) neat, fashionable, or stylish in appearance — ~**ly** *adv* — ~**ness** *n*

sleep¹ *n* **1** the natural resting state of unconsciousness of the body **2** a period of time of this **3** the substance that sometimes gathers in the corners of the eyes when one is tired or asleep **4** **go to sleep a** to begin to sleep; fall asleep **b** (of an arm, leg, etc.) to become unable to feel, or to feel pins and needles **5** **put to sleep a** to kill (a suffering animal) mercifully **b** to make (a person) unconscious, as for an operation —see also ASLEEP

sleep² *v* **slept, sleeping** **1** to rest in sleep; be naturally unconscious, as at night **2** to provide beds or places for sleep for (a number of people) —see also SLEEP IN, SLEEP ON, SLEEP WITH

sleeper *n* **1** a person sleeping **2** a person who sleeps in the stated way: *a heavy sleeper* **3** any of the row of heavy pieces of wood, metal, etc., supporting a railway track **4** a train with beds for sleeping through the night **5** a small ring worn in the ear, so as to keep open a hole for an earring

sleep in *v adv* **1** to sleep at one's place of work **2** to sleep late in the morning; lie in

sleeping bag *n* a large thick bag of warm material for sleeping in when camping

sleeping car *n* a railway carriage with beds for passengers

sleeping partner *n* a partner in a business who takes no active part in its operation

sleeping pill *also* **sleeping tablet**— *n* a pill which helps a person to sleep

sleeping sickness *n* any of various serious diseases, esp. one in Africa carried by the tsetse fly, causing loss of weight, fever, and esp. great tiredness

sleepless *adj* **1** not providing sleep: *a sleepless night* **2** *literature* unable to sleep — ~**ly** *adv* — ~**ness** *n*

sleep on *v prep* to delay deciding on (a question) until the next day

sleepwalker *n* a person who gets up and walks about while asleep — -**king** *n*

sleep with *v prep* to have sex with (another person)

sleepy *adj* **-ier, -iest** **1** tired and ready for sleep **2** quiet; inactive or slow-moving: *a sleepy country town* — **sleepily** *adv* — **sleepiness** *n*

sleepyhead *n* a sleepy person, esp. a child

sleet¹ *n* partly frozen rain; ice falling in fine bits mixed with water — **sleety** *adj*

sleet² *v* (of sleet) to fall

sleeve *n* **1** a part of a garment for covering (part of) an arm **2** a stiff envelope for keeping a gramophone record in usu. with information about the contents **3** a tube with 2 open ends for enclosing something, esp. a machine part **4**

sle

646

have/keep something up one's sleeve to keep a secret for use in the future **5 roll up one's sleeves** to get to work — ~**less** *adj*

sleigh *v, n* (to go in) a vehicle which slides along snow on 2 metal blades, esp. for carrying people and for pulling by a horse —compare SLEDGE

sleight of hand *n* **1** skill and quickness of the hands in doing tricks, as with cards **2** clever deception

slender *n* **1** delicately or gracefully thin in the body; not fat; slim —see THIN (USAGE) **2** pleasingly thin compared to length or height; not wide or thick **3** slight; small and hardly enough: *a slender chance of success* — ~**ly** *adv* — ~**ness** *n*

slept *past tense and part. of* SLEEP

sleuth *n humour* a detective

slew[1] *v* to turn or swing violently: *The car slewed out of control*

slew[2] *past tense of* SLAY

slice[1] *n* **1** a thin flat piece cut from something **2** a kitchen tool with a broad blade for lifting and serving pieces of food —see also FISH SLICE **3** (in sports like golf and tennis) a flight of a ball away from a course straight ahead and towards the side of the player's stronger hand

slice[2] *v* **sliced, slicing** **1** to cut into slices **2** to cut off as a slice **3** to cut with a knife: *He sliced his fingers* **4** to hit (a ball) in a slice

slick[1] *adj* **1** smooth and slippery **2** good-looking on the surface but without much depth; glib **3** clever or effective (but often not honest): *a slick salesman* — ~**ly** *adv* — ~**ness** *n*

slick[2] *n* OIL SLICK

slick down *v adv* to make (esp. hair) shiny with water, oil, etc.

slicker *n esp. spoken* a well-dressed fast-talking person who should not be trusted

slide[1] *v* **slid, sliding** **1** to go or cause to go smoothly over a surface **2** to pass smoothly or continuously; go slowly and unnoticed; slip **3 let something slide** *esp. spoken* to pay no attention; do nothing

slide[2] *n* **1** a slipping movement over a surface: *The car went into a slide on the ice* **2** a sliding machine part, such as the U-shaped tube on a trombone **3** a track or apparatus for sliding down: *a children's slide* **4** a usu. square piece of framed film for passing strong light through to show a picture on a surface **5** a small piece of thin glass to put an object on for seeing under a microscope ⟶ MICROSCOPE **6** HAIR SLIDE

slide rule *n* an instrument for calculating numbers, usu. made of a ruler (marked with logarithms) with a middle part that slides along its length

sliding scale *n* a system of pay, taxes, etc., calculated by rates which may vary or depend on outside facts

slight[1] *adj* **1** not strong-looking; thin; frail **2** not great; not considerable; small or weak — ~**ly** *adv* — ~**ness** *n*

slight[2] *v* to treat rudely, without respect, or as if unimportant — **slight** *n* — ~**ingly** *adv*

slim[1] *adj* **-mm-** **1** (esp. of people) attractively thin; not fat —see THIN (USAGE) **2** (of hope, probability, etc.) poor; slight; not considerable — ~**ly** *adv* — ~**ness** *n*

slim[2] *v* **-mm-** to make or try to make oneself slim; lose weight — ~**mer** *n* — ~**ming** *n*

slime *n* **1** partly liquid mud, esp. regarded as ugly, bad-smelling, etc. **2** thick sticky liquid produced by the skin of various fish and snails

slimy *adj* **-ier, -iest** **1** like, being, or covered with slime; unpleasantly slippery **2** very unpleasant and offensive; disgusting — **sliminess** *n*

sling[1] *v* **slung, slinging** **1** to throw, esp. roughly or with effort: *He slung his coat over his shoulder* **2** to throw (a stone) in a sling — ~**er** *n*

sling[2] *n* **1** a piece of material for hanging from the neck to support a damaged arm or hand **2** an apparatus of ropes, bands, etc., for lifting or carrying heavy objects **3** a length of cord with a piece of leather in the middle, held at the ends and swung, for throwing stones with force

sling[3] *v* **slung, slinging** to move or hold in a sling

slink *v* **slunk, slinking** to move quietly and secretly, as if fearful or ashamed; steal — ~**iness** *n*

slip[1] *v* **-pp-** **1** to slide out of place or fall by sliding **2** to move slidingly, smoothly, secretly, or unnoticed: *She slipped into/out of the room* **3** to put on or take off (a garment) **4** to fall from a standard; get worse or lower: *He has slipped in my opinion* **5** to make a slight mistake **6** to give secretly **7** to get free from (a fastening): *The dog slipped his collar* **8** to escape from (one's attention, memory, etc.); be forgotten or unnoticed by **9 let slip a** to fail to follow (a chance, offer, etc.) **b** to say without intending **10 slip a disc** to get a slipped disc

slip[2] *n* **1** an act of slipping or sliding **2** a usu. slight mistake **3** a woman's dresslike undergarment not covering the arms or neck **4** a long surface sloping down into water, for moving ships into or out of water, or for ships to land at **5** (the position of) a cricket fielder who stands close behind and to the right of a (right handed) batsman, to catch balls that come off the edge of the bat **6 give someone the slip** *esp. spoken* to escape from someone —see also PILLOWCASE, GYMSLIP

slip[3] *n* **1** a usu. small or narrow piece of paper **2** a small branch cut for planting; cutting **3** *becoming rare* a small thin one: *a slip of a boy*

slip[4] *n* a mixture of clay and water used in pottery-making for ornamenting a surface and as cement

slipknot *n* a knot that can be tightened round something by pulling one of its ends

slipped disc *n* a painful displacement of one of the discs in the back

slipper also (*esp. written*) **carpet slipper**— *n* a light indoor shoe with the top made from soft material

slippery adj -ier, -iest **1** difficult to hold or to stand, drive, etc., on without slipping **2** difficult to understand exactly; elusive **3** esp. spoken not to be trusted; shifty — **-iness** n

slip road n a road for driving onto or off a motorway

slipshod adj careless; not exact or thorough

slipstream n **1** the area just behind a fast-moving vehicle where a following driver may keep up his speed easily **2** a stream of air driven backwards by an aircraft engine

slip-up n a usu. slight mistake

slipway n -ways a track sloping down into the water for moving ships into or out of water

slit v slit to make a narrow cut or opening in — slit n

slither v **1** to move in a slipping or twisting way like a snake **2** to slide unsteadily △ SLIVER — ~y adj

sliver n a small thin sharp piece cut or torn off △ SLITHER

slob n esp. spoken a man who is rude, lazy, dirty, or carelessly-dressed

slobber[1] v **1** to let (liquid) fall from the lips **2** to make wet in this way **3** to express fond feelings too openly and indelicately

slobber[2] n liquid that runs down from the mouth; slaver

sloe n a small bitter plumlike fruit of the blackthorn with dark purple skin

sloe gin n a sweet reddish alcoholic drink made from gin and sloes

slog v -gg- **1** to do hard dull work without stopping; make one's way by continuous effort **2** (esp. in cricket) to hit (the ball) hard and wildly — slog, ~ger n

slogan n a short phrase expressing a usu. political or advertising message —compare MOTTO

sloop n a small kind of sailing ship with one central mast and sails along its length

slop[1] n **1 a** food waste, esp. for feeding to animals **b** liquid food for sick people **2** human solid and liquid waste

slop[2] v -pp- **1** to cause some of (a liquid) to go over the side of a container; spill; splash **2** (of a liquid) to do this **3** to make wet in this way **4** to go in mud or wetness; slosh

slop basin also **slop bowl** — n a bowl used for holding tea or coffee dregs poured back from the bottom of cups

slope[1] v sloped, sloping to lie or move in a sloping direction; be or go at an angle

slope[2] n **1** a surface that slopes; a piece of ground going up or down **2** a degree of sloping; a measure of an angle from a level direction

slope off v adv esp. spoken to go away secretly, as to escape or avoid work

slop out v adv (of a prisoner) to remove slops from (a room)

sloppy adj -pier, -piest **1** (as of clothes) loose, informal, and careless- or dirty-looking **2** not careful or thorough enough **3** wet and dirty **4** silly in showing feelings — **-pily** adv — **-piness** n

slosh v **1** to go through water or mud **2 a** (of liquid) to move about as against the sides of a container **b** to cause (a liquid) to do this **3** sl to hit; punch; bash

sloshed adj esp. spoken drunk

slot[1] n **1** a long straight narrow opening or hollow place, esp. in a machine or tool **2** esp. spoken a place or position in a list, system, organization, etc.

slot[2] v -tt- **1** to cut a slot in **2** to put into a slot **3** to find a place for

sloth n **1** esp. in literature unwillingness to work; dislike of doing things actively; laziness **2** any of several types of slow-moving tree animal of central and S America that hang by all 4 legs from branches ⟶ MAMMAL

slothful adj esp. in literature unwilling to work or be active; lazy — ~ly adv — ~ness n

slot machine n a machine, esp. for selling drinks, cigarettes, etc., which is made to work by putting a coin into it; vending machine

slouch[1] n **1** a tired-looking round-shouldered way of standing or walking **2** esp. spoken a lazy, untidy, or useless person

slouch[2] v to carry the body at a slouch — ~ingly adv

slough n a bad condition from which one cannot easily get free

slough off v adv to throw off (dead outer skin)

sloven n literature a person of untidy habits; one who is careless in dress or appearance — ~ly adj — ~liness n

slow[1] adj **1** not moving or going on quickly; having less than a usual or standard speed **2** taking a long time or too long: slow to act **3** not good or quick in understanding **4** not very active; dull; not brisk **5** (of a clock) showing a time that is earlier than the true time **6** (of a surface) not allowing quick movement: a slow wicket **7** slow off the mark slow to understand (esp. the point of a joke) — ~ly adv — ~ness n

slow[2] adv slowly —see also GO SLOW, GO-SLOW

slow[3] v to make or become slower

slowcoach n esp. spoken a person who seems to be moving too slowly

slow motion n action which takes place at a much slower speed than in real life, esp. as shown for special effect in films

slowworm n a type of small harmless European lizard with very small eyes and no legs, that moves like a snake

sludge n **1** thick mud **2** the product of sewage treatment

slug[1] n any of several types of small limbless plant-eating creature, related to the snail but with no shell, that often do damage to gardens

slug[2] n a lump or piece of metal, esp. a bullet

slug[3] v -gg- US esp. spoken to strike with a heavy

blow, esp. with the closed hand and so as to make unconscious

sluggish adj slow-moving; not very active or quick — ~ly adv — ~ness n

sluice[1] n a passage for water with an opening (a **sluice gate** or **sluice valve**) through which the flow can be controlled or stopped

sluice[2] v **sluiced, sluicing** 1 to wash with floods or streams of water, as from a sluice 2 (of water) to come (as if) from a sluice; come in streams

slum[1] n 1 a city area of poor living conditions and dirty unrepaired buildings 2 esp. spoken a very untidy place — ~my adj

slum[2] v -mm- esp. spoken 1 to amuse oneself by visiting a place on a much lower social level 2 **slum it** to live very cheaply, not having things that others find necessary

slumber v literature to lie asleep; sleep peacefully — slumber, ~er n — ~ous, -brous adj

slump[1] v 1 to sink down; fall heavily or in a heap; collapse 2 to go down in number or strength; fall off; decline

slump[2] n a time of seriously bad business conditions and unemployment; depression

slung past tense and past part. of SLING

slunk past tense and past part. of SLINK

slur[1] v -rr- 1 to write a slur over (musical notes) 2 to sing or play (notes) connectedly 3 to pronounce unclearly or not at all

slur[2] a curved line,⁀ or ⁀ written over or under musical notes directing them to be played smoothly —compare TIE

slur[3] v -rr- to say unfair bad things about — **slur** n

slurp v to eat (soft food) or drink noisily

slurry n a watery mixture, esp. of clay, mud, lime, or plaster

slush n 1 partly melted snow; watery snow 2 literature, films, etc., concerned with silly love stories; mush — **slushy** adj

slut n 1 a woman who acts immodestly or immorally 2 an untidy lazy woman — ~tish adj

sly adj **slyer** or **slier, slyest** or **sliest** 1 clever in deceiving; dishonestly tricky; crafty 2 playfully unkind 3 **on the sly** secretly (as of something done dishonestly or unlawfully) — ~ly adv — ~ness n

smack[1] n a particular taste; flavour

smack[2] v 1 to open and close (one's lips) noisily 2 to strike loudly, as with the flat part of the hand 3 to put so as to make a short loud sound

smack[3] n 1 a quick loud noise; sound of smacking 2 a loud kiss 3 a quick loud forceful blow

smack[4] adv esp. spoken with force: run smack into a wall

smack[5] n a small sailing boat used for fishing

smacker n sl a loud kiss

smack of v prep to have a taste or suggestion of

small[1] adj 1 little in size, weight, force, importance, etc. 2 doing only a limited amount of a business or activity: a small farmer 3 very little; slight 4 (of letters) LOWER CASE 5 **feel small** to feel ashamed or humble —see also SMALLS — ~ness n

small[2] adv in a small manner: to write small

small[3] n the small narrow part of something, esp. the middle part of the back where it curves in

small ad n an advertisement placed in a newspaper offering goods for sale, employment, etc.

small arms n guns made to be held in one or both hands for firing

small change n money in coins of small value

small fry n -fry esp. spoken a young or unimportant person

smallholding n a piece of farmland smaller than an ordinary farm (usu. less than 50 acres) — **smallholder** n

small intestine n the long narrow twisting tube in the body, into which food first passes from the stomach and where most of its chemical change takes place —compare LARGE INTESTINE

small-minded adj having narrow selfish interests; unwilling to change one's mind or listen to others —compare BROADMINDED — ~ness n

smallpox n a serious infectious disease (esp. in former times), causing spots which leave marks on the skin

smalls n esp. spoken small pieces of underclothing, handkerchiefs, etc., esp. for washing

small talk n light conversation on unimportant or nonserious subjects

small-time adj limited in activity, profits, wealth, ability, etc.; unimportant — -timer n

smarmy adj -ier, -iest sl unpleasantly and falsely polite

smart[1] v 1 to cause or feel a painful stinging sensation, usu. in one part of the body and not lasting long 2 to be hurt in one's feelings

smart[2] adj 1 quick or forceful; lively; vigorous: a smart blow 2 good or quick in thinking 3 neat and stylish in appearance; spruce 4 used by, concerning, etc., very fashionable people — ~ly adv — ~ness n

smart[3] n 1 a smarting pain 2 something that hurts the feelings or pride

smarten up v adv to make or become good looking, neat, or stylish

smash[1] v 1 to break into pieces violently 2 to go, drive, throw, or hit forcefully, as against something solid; crash 3 to be or cause to be destroyed or ruined 4 (in games like tennis) to hit (the ball) with a smash

smash[2] n 1 a powerful blow 2 a breaking into pieces 3 also **smash hit**— a great success, as of a new play, book, film, etc. 4 a hard downward attacking shot, as in tennis

smash-and-grab adj (of a robbery) done by quickly breaking a shop window, taking the valuable things inside it, and running away

smashed adj esp. spoken drunk

smashing adj esp. spoken very fine; wonderful

smash-up n a road or railway accident

smattering n a small amount (esp. of knowledge)

smear[1] n 1 a spot made by an oily or sticky material; mark made by smearing 2 esp. medical a small bit of some material prepared for examining under a microscope 3 an unproved charge made intentionally to try to turn public feelings against someone

smear[2] v 1 a to cause (a sticky or oily material) to spread on or go across (a surface) b (of such material) to do this 2 to lose or cause to lose clearness in this way or by rubbing 3 to charge unfairly

smell[1] v smelled or smelt, smelling 1 to use the nose; have or use the sense of the nose 2 to notice, examine, discover, or recognize by this sense 3 to notice, come to know of, recognize, etc., by some natural unexplained ability: I smelt trouble —see also smell a RAT 4 to have an effect on the nose; have a particular smell, often unpleasant

smell[2] n 1 the power of using the nose; the sense that can discover the presence of gases in the air 2 a quality that has an effect on the nose; something that excites this sense 3 an act of smelling something

smelling salts n a strong-smelling chemical (esp. AMMONIA), formerly often carried in a small bottle, for curing fainting

smelly adj -ier, -iest unpleasant-smelling — smelliness n

smelt v to melt ore for separating and removing the metal, as is done in smelters

smile[1] v smiled, smiling 1 to have or make (a smile): —compare GRIN 2 to act or look favourably: The weather smiled on us — smilingly adv

smile[2] n an expression of the face with the mouth turned up at the ends and the eyes bright, that usu. expresses amusement, happiness, approval, or sometimes bitter feelings

smirch v to bring dishonour on; discredit — smirch n

smirk v to smile in a false or too satisfied way — smirk n

smite v smote, smitten, smiting 1 old use & literature to strike hard: smote his enemy with the sword 2 esp. Bible & literature to destroy, attack, or punish as if by a blow 3 to have a powerful sudden effect on: smitten by/with desire

smith n a worker in metal

smithereens n (in)to smithereens esp. spoken into small bits; to complete destruction

smithy n -ies a blacksmith's place of work

smock n 1 a light loose coatlike garment for putting on over one's other clothing while working 2 a woman's loose shirtlike garment, often worn by future mothers to hide their shape

smocking n ornamentation, esp. on dresses,

made by gathering cloth into small regular folds held tightly with fancy stitching

smog n the unhealthy dark mixture of gases (esp. fog, smoke, and vehicle exhaust) in the air in some large cities

smoke[1] n 1 gas mixed with very small bits of solid material (esp. carbon) that can be seen in the air and is usu. given off by burning 2 a esp. spoken something (esp. a cigarette) for smoking b an act of smoking — ~less adj

smoke[2] v smoked, smoking 1 to suck or breathe in smoke from (esp. tobacco, as in cigarettes, a pipe, etc.) —see also SMOKING 2 to give off smoke 3 to darken (a surface with smoke) 4 to preserve and give a special taste to (meat, fish, cheese, etc.) by hanging in smoke

smoker n 1 a person who smokes 2 a railway carriage where smoking is allowed

smokescreen n 1 a cloud of smoke produced for hiding a place or activity from enemy sight 2 something for others to see, hear, etc., which hides one's real intentions

smokestack n 1 a tall chimney for taking off smoke, esp. from a factory or ship 2 US the funnel of a railway steam engine

smoking[1] n the practice or habit of sucking in tobacco smoke from cigarettes, a pipe, etc.

smoking[2] adj where one may smoke

smoking jacket n a man's short usu. fancy coat for wearing (esp. formerly) at home indoors

smoky adj -ier, -iest 1 filled with or producing (too much) smoke 2 with the taste or appearance of smoke — smokiness n

smooch v esp. spoken to kiss and hold someone lovingly — smooch n — ~er n

smooth[1] adj 1 having an even surface without sharply raised or lowered places, points, lumps, etc.; not rough 2 even in movement without sudden changes or breaks: bring to a smooth stop 3 (of a liquid mixture) without lumps; evenly thick 4 not bitter or sour 5 very or too pleasant, polite, or untroubled in manner; avoiding or not showing difficulties — ~ly adv — ~ness n

smooth[2] v to make smooth

smorgasbord n (a restaurant meal in which people serve themselves from) a large number of different Scandinavian dishes

smote past tense of SMITE

smother v 1 to cover thickly or heavily: cake smothered with cream 2 to die or kill from lack of air; suffocate 3 to put out or keep down (a fire) by keeping out air

smoulder v 1 to burn slowly without a flame 2 to have, be, or show violent feelings that are kept from being expressed

smudge v smudged, smudging 1 to make or become dirty with a mark of rubbing 2 to make or cause to make such a mark — smudge n — smudgy adj

smug adj -gg- too pleased with oneself; showing

too much satisfaction with one's own qualities, position, etc. — ~**ly** *adv* — ~**ness** *n*

smuggle *v* **-gled, -gling** to take from one country to another unlawfully (esp. goods without paying the necessary duty) — **-gler** *n* — **-gling** *n*

smut *n* **1** (a small piece of) material like dirt or soot that blackens or makes dark marks **2** material for reading, hearing, or seeing that is morally improper and offensive

smutty *adj* **-tier, -tiest** morally improper; obscene — **-tily** *adv* — **-tiness** *n*

snack *n* an amount of food smaller than a meal; something eaten informally between meals

snack bar *n* an informal public eating place that serves snacks; place for buying and eating sandwiches, drinks, etc.

snaffle also **snaffle bit**— *n* a kind of bit made of 2 short joined bars, for putting in a horse's mouth

snag¹ *n* **1** a dangerous, rough, sharp part of something that may catch and hold or cut things passing against it **2** a pulled thread in a cloth, esp. a stocking **3** a hidden or unexpected difficulty

snag² *v* **-gg-** to catch on a snag

snail *n* any of several kinds of mollusc with a soft body, no limbs, and usu. a hard spiral-shaped shell on its back

snake¹ *n* **1** any of many kinds of reptile with a long limbless body, large mouth, and fork-shaped tongue, usu. feeding on other animals and often with a poisonous bite **2** a system in which the values of certain countries' money are allowed to vary against each other within narrow limits **3** a **snake in the grass** usu. humour a false friend

snake² *v* **snaked, snaking** to move in a twisting way; wind (one's way or body) in moving — **snaky** *adj*

snakebite *n* the result or condition of being bitten by a poisonous snake

snake charmer *n* a person who controls snakes, usu. by playing music

snakes and ladders *n* a board game in which players may move pieces upwards and forward along pictures of ladders and be forced downwards and backwards along pictures of snakes

snap¹ *v* **-pp-** **1** to close the jaws quickly (on) **2** to break suddenly off or in 2: *The branch snapped under all that snow* **3** to make or cause to make a sound as of either of these actions **4** to move so as to cause such a short sound: *The lid snapped shut* **5** to say quickly, usu. in an annoyed or angry way **6** *esp. spoken* to photograph; take a snapshot of **7 snap out of it** *esp. spoken* to make oneself quickly get free from a bad state of mind —see also SNAP UP

snap² *n* **1** an act or sound of snapping **2** a type of card game in which players lay down cards one after the other and try to be the first to notice and call out 'Snap!' when 2 like cards are laid down together **3** *esp. spoken* a snapshot —see also COLD SNAP

snap³ *adj* done, made, arrived at, etc., in haste or without (long) warning

snap⁴ *interj* **1** (said in the game of snap when one notices that 2 like cards have been laid down) **2** *esp. spoken* (said when one notices 2 like things together)

snapdragon *n* also **antirrhinum** a kind of garden plant with white, red, or yellow flowers suggesting the face of a dragon

snappish *adj* speaking habitually in a rude annoyed way; bad-tempered; testy — ~**ly** *adv* — ~**ness** *n*

snappy *adj* **-pier, -piest** **1** full of snap; lively **2** stylish; fashionable **3 Make it snappy!** (also **Look snappy!**)— *esp. spoken* Hurry up! — **-pily** *adv* — **-piness** *n*

snapshot *n* an informal picture taken with a hand-held camera

snap up *v adv* to take or buy quickly and eagerly

snare¹ *n* **1** a trap for catching an animal, esp. one with a rope which catches the animal's foot **2** something in which one may be caught; a course which leads to being trapped **3** any of the metal strings on the bottom of a snare drum

snare² *v* **snared, snaring** **1** to catch (as if) in a snare **2** to get by skilful action: *snare a good job*

snare drum *n* a small flat military kind of drum used also in bands, having metal strings stretched across the bottom to allow a continuous sound

snarl¹ *n* a knotty twisted confused mass or state; tangle

snarl² *v* to put into a snarl; make confused or difficult; tangle: *Traffic was snarled (up) near the accident*

snarl³ *v* **1** (of an animal) to make a low angry sound while showing the teeth **2** (of a person) to speak or say in an angry bad-tempered way — **snarl** *n*

snarl-up *n* a confused state, esp. of traffic

snatch¹ *v* to get hold of (something) hastily: make every effort to get: *snatch at a chance* — ~**er** *n*

snatch² *n* **1** an act of snatching (at) something **2** a short period of time or activity: *to sleep in snatches* **3** a short and incomplete part of something that is seen or heard

snazzy *adj* **-zier, -ziest** *esp. spoken* good-looking in a neat, stylish, or showy way

sneak¹ *v* **1** to go or cause to go, quietly and secretly; go or take so as not to be seen: *sneak past a guard* **2** *sl* to steal secretly **3** *school sl* to give information, esp. to a teacher, about the wrongdoings (of another pupil)

sneak² *n* **1** a sneaky person; one who acts secretly and should not be trusted **2** unexpected; secret until the last moment; surprise **3** *school sl* a person who sneaks

sneaker *n* *esp. US* a plimsoll

sneaking *adj* **1** secret; not expressed, as if shameful **2** (of a feeling or suspicion) not proved but probably right

sneak thief n -thieves a thief who takes things within reach without using force

sneak up v adv to come near (to someone), keeping out of sight until the last moment

sneer[1] v to express proud dislike ; treat something as if not worthy of serious notice — ~er n — ~ingly adv

sneer[2] n a sneering expression of the face, way of speaking, or remark

sneeze[1] v sneezed, sneezing 1 to have a sudden uncontrolled burst of air out of the nose and mouth, usu. caused by discomfort in the nose 2 not to be sneezed at esp. spoken, often humour worthy of consideration

sneeze[2] n an act, sound, etc., of sneezing

snick v (in cricket) to hit (the ball) off the edge of the bat — snick n

snide adj intending or intended to hurt the feelings in a pretendedly funny way; mean; insinuating — ~ly adv — ~ness n

sniff[1] v 1 to draw air into the nose with a sound, esp. in short repeated actions 2 to do this to discover a smell in or on 3 to say in a proud complaining way — ~er n

sniff[2] n an act or sound of sniffing

sniffle[1] also snuffle— v -fled, -fling to sniff repeatedly in order to keep liquid from running out of the nose, as when one is crying or has a cold — ~r n

sniffle[2] also snuffle— n an act or sound of sniffling

sniffles also snuffles —— n the signs of a cold in the nose; liquid blocking or running from the nose

snifter n a small amount of an alcoholic drink

snigger also (esp. US) snicker— v to laugh in a disrespectful more or less secret way — snigger n

snip[1] n 1 a short quick cut with scissors 2 a small piece (cut off); bit 3 esp. spoken an attractive and surprisingly cheap article for sale; bargain

snip[2] v -pp- to cut (as if) with scissors, esp. in short quick strokes

snipe[1] n snipe or snipes any of several birds with very long thin beaks, living in wet places and often shot for sport

snipe[2] v sniped, sniping 1 to shoot from a hidden position at unprotected people (such as an enemy not in battle) 2 to attack a person or thing in an indirect way; make repeated small attacks — sniper n

snippet n a small bit of something, esp. a short piece from something spoken or written

snips n heavy scissors for cutting metal sheet

snitch v esp. spoken 1 to tell about the wrong-doings of a friend 2 to steal (esp. something of no great value)

snivel v -ll- 1 to have liquid blocking or coming from the nose; sniffle 2 to act or speak in a weak complaining crying way — ~ler n

snob n 1 a person who dislikes or keeps away from those he feels to be of lower social class 2 a person who is too proud of having special knowledge or judgment in a subject — ~bish adj — ~bishly adv — ~bishness n

snobbery n the practice or talk of snobs

snog v -gg- esp. spoken to kiss — snog n

snood n an ornamental thick net used (esp. formerly) for holding in a woman's hair at the back; type of hairnet

snooker n a billiards game played on a table with 6 pockets, with 15 red balls and 6 balls of other colours

snoop v to search, look into, or concern oneself with others' property without permission, or something not one's concern — ~er n

snooty adj -ier, -iest esp. spoken proudly rude; supercilious — snootily adv — snootiness n

snooze v snoozed, snoozing esp. spoken to have a short sleep; doze — snooze n

snore[1] v snored, snoring to breathe heavily and noisily through the nose and mouth while asleep — snorer n

snore[2] n a noisy way of breathing when asleep; a noise of snoring

snorkel n an air tube that can rise above the surface of water, as for allowing a swimmer under water to breathe or for carrying air to a submarine

snort[1] v 1 to make a rough noise by blowing air down the nose 2 to express (esp. impatience or anger, or sometimes amusement) (as) by this sound

snort[2] n an act or sound of snorting

snot n vulgar the mucus produced in the nose

snotty adj -tier, -tiest sl 1 also snotty-nosed — trying to act as if one is important; rude 2 wet with snot

snout n the long nose of any of various animals (such as pigs)

snow[1] n 1 water frozen into small flat 6-sided flakes that fall like rain in cold weather and may cover the ground thickly 2 a fall of this 3 sl cocaine in powder form

snow[2] v (of snow) to fall —see also SNOW UNDER

snowball[1] n a ball pressed or rolled together from snow, as thrown at each other by children

snowball[2] v to increase in size faster and faster or uncontrolledly: Prices are snowballing

snow blindness n pain and (near) blindness for a time, caused by long looking at snow in bright sunlight — snow-blind adj

snowbound adj blocked or kept indoors by heavy snow

snow-capped adj literature (of a mountain) covered in snow at the top

snowdrift n a deep bank or mass of snow formed by the wind

snowdrop n a type of European small white flower which appears in the early spring, often when snow is still on the ground

snowfall n a fall of snow

snowfield n a wide stretch of ground always covered in snow

snowflake n one of, or a small mass of, the small flat 6-sided bits of frozen water which fall as snow

snowline n the height above sea level above which snow never melts

snowman n -men a figure of a man made out of snow, esp. by children

snowplough n an apparatus or vehicle for pushing snow off roads or railways

snowshoe n a light flat frame around a strong net, for fastening in pairs under the shoes, to allow a person to walk on snow without sinking in

snow under v adv to load too heavily (as with work or things to do); overwhelm

snowy adj -ier, -iest 1 full of snow or snowing 2 pure (white) — **snowiness** n

Snr abbrev. for: Senior

snub¹ v -bb- to treat rudely as by paying no attention to — **snub** n

snub² adj (of a nose) flat and short; stubby

snuff¹ v **snuff it** sl to die

snuff² v (esp. of animals) to draw (air or a smell) into the nose with a sound; sniff — **snuff** n

snuff³ n tobacco made into powder for breathing into the nose, esp. used in former times

snuffer n a tool with a small bell-shaped end on a handle, for putting out candles

snuffle v, n -fled, -fling sniffle

snug adj -gg- giving or enjoying warmth, comfort, peace, protection, etc.; cosy — ~ly adv — ~ness n

snuggle v -gled, -gling to move or lie close for warmth and comfort; nestle

so¹ adv 1 in the way I show: Push the needle so 2 in that way; in the way stated 3 a to such a degree: You mustn't worry so b in such a way: The book is so written in order to offend 4 (used in place of an idea, expression, etc., stated already): He hopes he'll win and I hope so too 5 in the same way; also: You have pride and so have I 6 indeed; certainly: 'Father, you promised!' 'So I did.' 7 up to a limit; to a certain degree: I can hold so much and no more 8 in that same way/time: As the wind blew harder, so the sea grew rougher —see also so FAR as

so² conj 1 with the result that: I broke my glasses, so I couldn't see 2 with the purpose (that) 3 therefore: I had a headache, so I went to bed

so³ adj 1 in agreement with the facts; true: It just isn't so 2 (used in place of an adjective already stated): He's clever—probably too much so for his own good

soak¹ v 1 to remain or leave in a liquid, esp. to become soft or completely wet 2 (of a liquid) to enter (a solid) through the material of a surface — ~ed adj — ~ing adj, adv

soak² n 1 an act or state of soaking 2 sl a person who is often or usually drunk

so-and-so n so-and-sos 1 someone or something; a certain one (not to be named) 2 (used instead of a stronger word) a rude, wicked, etc., person

soap¹ n a product made from fat and alkali, for use with water to clean the body or other things —compare DETERGENT — **soapy** adj

soap² v to rub soap on or over

soapbox n a real or imaginary box for someone to stand on to give a speech to a crowd outdoors

soap opera n a daily or weekly television or radio serial which is usu. about the characters' private troubles

soapstone n a kind of soft stone which feels like soap

soapsuds n suds

soar v esp. in literature 1 to fly; go fast or high (as) on wings; sail in the air 2 to go upwards, esp. far or fast: The temperature soared to 80° 3 to go beyond what is ordinary or limiting: a soaring imagination 4 (of a glider or people in it) to go through the air

sob v -bb- to breathe while weeping, in sudden short bursts making a sound in the throat — **sob** n — **sobbingly** adv

sober¹ adj 1 in control of oneself; not drunk 2 thoughtful, serious, or solemn; not silly; grave 3 not ornamental or brightly-coloured; restrained — ~ly adv

sober² v to make or become serious or thoughtful

sober up v adv to make or become sober; get or be rid of the effect of alcohol

sobriety n usu. literature the quality or state of being sober

sob story n -ries a story intended to make the hearer or reader cry, feel pity, or feel sorry

so-called adj 1 called or named the stated thing 2 improperly or falsely named so

soccer also football, Association Football— n a football game between 2 teams of 11 players who kick or head a round ball without using the arms or hands

sociable adj fond of being with others; enjoying social life; friendly — -bility n — -bly adv
USAGE It is better to use **sociable**, rather than **social**, to mean 'cheerful and friendly'. Social is never used of people: We're a sociable lot. Use social to mean 'connected with society': social history; or 'connected with community life': living in a social whirl

social¹ adj 1 of or concerning human society, its organization, or quality of life 2 of, concerning, or spent in time or activities with friends 3 forming groups or living together by nature: social insects like ants — ~ly adv

social² n a planned informal friendly gathering of members of a group or esp. church

social climber n offensive a person who spends money or tries to make friends in order to be accepted in society of a higher class

social democracy n the aim of politicians (**social democrats**), esp. in W Europe, who support many of the aims of socialism

socialism n any of various beliefs or systems (sometimes considered to include communism) aiming at public ownership of the means of production and the establishment of a society in which every person is equal —compare COMMUNISM

socialist *n, adj* (a follower) of socialism, or of any of various esp. W European parties who support more equality of wealth and government ownership of business

socialite *n* a person well known for going to many fashionable parties

socialize, -ise *v* -ized, -izing **1** to spend time with others in a friendly way **2** *technical* to cause to fit into a society — **-ization** *n*

social science *n* **1** also **social studies**— the study of people in society, usu. including history, politics, economics, sociology, and anthropology **2** any of these

social security *n* government money paid to people without jobs, old, ill, etc.

social service *n* any of the services provided by a government, esp. those paid for (partly) by taxes, such as roads, medical care, police, and sometimes house-building, railways, etc.

social work *n* work done by government or private organizations to improve bad social conditions and help people in need — ~**er** *n*

society *n* -ties **1** a large group of people with a particular organization and shared customs, laws, etc. **2** people living and working together considered as a whole **3** an organization of people with like aims, interests, etc. **4** the companionship or presence of others **5** the fashionable group of people of a high class in a place: *a society occasion*

sociology *n* the scientific study of societies and human behaviour in groups — **-gical** *adj* — **-gically** *adv* — **-gist** *n*

sock¹ *n* a covering of soft material for the foot and usu. part of the lower leg, usu. worn inside a shoe

sock² *v esp. spoken* to strike hard — **sock** *n*

socket *n* an opening, hollow place, or machine part that forms a holder or into which something fits: *an electric light socket*

sod¹ *n* **1** earth with grass and roots growing in it **2** a piece of this; turf

sod² *n sl* a man thought to be foolish and/or annoying

soda *n* **1** SODA WATER **2** ICE-CREAM SODA **3** sodium (in such phrases as **bicarbonate of soda**) —see also WASHING SODA

soda water *n* water filled under pressure with gas (CARBON DIOXIDE) which gives it a pleasant pricking taste

sodden *adj* heavy with wetness; soaked

sodium *n* a silver-white metal that is an element, found in nature only in combination with other substances

sodium chloride *n technical* salt

sofa *n* a comfortable seat with raised arms and a back and wide enough for usu. 2 or 3 people

soft *adj* **1** not firm against pressure; giving in to the touch; changeable in shape; not hard or stiff **2** less hard than average: *Lead is one of the softer metals* **3** smooth and delicate to the touch **4** restful and pleasant to the senses, esp. the eyes: *soft lights* **5** quiet; not making much noise; not loud **6** not violent; gentle **7** easily persuaded; easy to make agree or do what one wishes; weak **8** (of a drink) containing no alcohol and usu. sweet **9 a** (of *c*) having the sound of c in 'acid' **b** (of *g*) having the sound of g in 'age' **10** (of water) free from certain minerals; allowing soap to act easily **11** not of the worst, most harmful, etc., kind: *soft drugs* **12** *esp. spoken* foolish or mad — ~**ly** *adv* — ~**ness** *n*

softball *n* a game like baseball, but played on a smaller field with a slightly larger and softer ball

soft-boiled *adj* (of an egg) boiled not long enough for the inside to become solid

soften *v* to make or become soft, gentle, less stiff, or less severe

soften up *v adv* to prepare (someone) for persuasion; break down the opposition of (someone)

soft furnishings *n* the curtains, mats, seat covers, etc., in a room

softhearted *adj* having tender feelings; easily moved to pity; merciful — ~**ness** *n*

soft-pedal *v* -ll- *esp. spoken* to play down

soft-soap *v esp. spoken* to persuade by saying nice things — **soft soap** *n*

soft spot *n esp. spoken* a feeling of special kindness or liking; fondness

software *n technical* the set of systems (in the form of programs rather than machine parts) which control the operation of a computer — opposite **hardware**

softwood *n* wood from evergreen trees (such as pine and fir) that is cheap and easy to cut — opposite **hardwood**

soggy *adj* -gier, -giest completely wet; heavy and usu. unpleasant with wetness — **-gily** *adv* — **-giness** *n*

soil¹ *v* to make or become dirty, esp. slightly or on the surface

soil² *n* material that soils; dirt

soil³ *n* the top covering of the earth in which plants grow; ground ⟳ ECOLOGY

sojourn¹ *n esp. in literature* a stay in a place other than one's home for a time

sojourn² *v literature* to live for a time in a place — ~**er** *n*

sol also **soh**— *n* the 5th note in the sol-fa musical scale

solace¹ *n* **1** comfort in grief or anxiety; lessening of trouble in the mind **2** something that provides this

solace² *v* -aced, -acing to give comfort in mind to or for

solar *adj* **1** of, from, or concerning the sun **2** using the power of the sun's light and heat

solar cell *n* an apparatus for producing electric power from sunlight

solarium *n* -ia or -iums a usu. glass-enclosed

room in a house or esp. a hospital, where one can sit in bright sunlight

solar plexus n 1 the system of nerves between the stomach and the backbone 2 *esp. spoken* the abdomen

solar system n the sun together with all the bodies going around it

sold *past tense and past part. of* SELL

solder¹ n soft metal, usu. a mixture of lead and tin, used when melted for joining other metal surfaces

solder² v to join or repair with solder

soldering iron n a hand tool with a copper end which is heated in a flame or by electricity for melting and putting on solder

soldier n a member of an army, esp. a man and esp. one of low rank (not an officer) — ~ly adj

soldier of fortune n soldiers of fortune a person who travels in search of military action, for adventure or pay

soldier on v adv to continue working; work steadily, esp. in spite of difficulties

sole¹ n 1 the bottom surface of the foot, esp. the part on which one walks or stands 2 the part of a piece of footwear covering this, esp. the flat bottom part of a shoe not including the heel

sole² v soled, soling to put a sole on (a shoe)

sole³ n sole *or* soles any of various kinds of flat fishes with small mouths, eyes, and fins, of which large types make fine food

sole⁴ adj 1 having no sharer; being the only one 2 belonging or allowed to one and no other; unshared — ~ly adv

solecism n a breaking of rules about what is proper, as in grammar or social politeness

solemn adj 1 done, made, etc., seriously, having a sense of religious-like importance 2 too serious for humour; grave — ~ly adv — ~ness n

solemnity n -ties 1 the quality of being solemn; formality or seriousness 2 a formal act or quality proper for a grand or solemn event

solemnize, -nise v -nized, -nizing *literature & esp. written* to perform a formal religious ceremony of (esp. marriage) — -nization n

solenoid n a coil of wire that, when an electrical current passes through it, behaves like a magnet

sol-fa n the system which represents each note of the musical scale by one of 7 short words, esp. for singing

solicit v 1 to ask for (money, help, a favour, etc.) from (a person) 2 (esp. of a woman) to offer oneself for sex for pay — ~ation n

solicitor n (esp. in England) a kind of lawyer who gives advice, appears in lower courts, and prepares cases for a barrister to argue in a high court —compare BARRISTER

solicitor general n solicitors general the chief law officer next below the Attorney General of a country

solicitous adj 1 taking eager, kind, or helpful care 2 anxious; carefully interested — ~ly adv — ~ness n

solicitude n anxious, kind, or eager care

solid¹ adj 1 not needing a container to hold its shape; not liquid or gas 2 having an inside filled up; not hollow 3 made of material tight together; dense; compact: *They hit solid rock* 4 that may be depended on; reputable: *solid citizens* 5 completely of the stated material without mixture of others 6 in or showing complete agreement 7 being or concerning space with length, width, and height; 3-dimensional: **Solid geometry** *is the study of lines, figures, angles, measurements, etc., in space* —compare PLANE **geometry** 8 written or printed as 1 word without a hyphen — ~ly adv — ~ness n △ STOLID

solid² n 1 a solid object; something that does not flow ☞ PHYSICS 2 any of the solid material in a liquid 3 (esp. in geometry) an object that takes up space; object with length, width, and height 4 an article of non-liquid food: *He's still too ill to take solids*

solidarity n agreement of interests, aims, or standards

solidify v -fied, -fying to make or become solid, hard, or firm — -fication n

solidity n the quality or state of being firm, not hollow, well made, dependable, or in agreement

solid-state adj of, being, or having electrical parts (esp. transistors) that run without heated or moving parts

soliloquize, -quise v -quized, -quizing to speak or say in soliloquy

soliloquy n -quies an act or the action of talking to oneself alone, esp. a speech in a play in which a character's thoughts are spoken to those watching the play

solitaire n 1 (a piece of jewellery having) a single jewel, esp. a diamond 2 *US* a card game for one; patience

solitary adj 1 alone without companions 2 fond of, or habitually, being alone 3 in a lonely place 4 single; sole —seeALONE (USAGE) — -tarily adv

solitary confinement also (sl) solitary— n the keeping of a person in a closed place without any chance of seeing or talking to others

solitude n the quality or state of being alone away from companionship

solo¹ n solos a piece of music played or sung by one person

solo² adj, adv 1 without a companion 2 of, for, or played or heard as, a musical solo

solo³ n a card game like whist but in which each player plays on his own and states how many tricks he hopes to make

soloist n a performer of a musical solo

solstice n either of the 2 times each year (June 21 and December 21) when the sun is farthest from the equator, causing the longest day and longest night

soluble adj 1 that can be dissolved 2 solvable — -bility n

solution n 1 an answer to a difficulty or problem 2 (a) liquid containing a solid or gas mixed into it, usu. without chemical change 3 the state or action of being mixed into liquid like this

solve v solved, solving to find a solution to; come to an answer, explanation, or way of dealing with (something) — **solvable** adj — **solver** n

solvent[1] adj having enough to pay all money owed; not in debt — **-vency** n

solvent[2] n (a) liquid able to break down and bring a solid substance into solution

sombre adj 1 sadly serious; grave; gloomy 2 like or full of shadows; dark — ~ly adv — ~ness n

sombrero n -ros a man's high usu. cloth hat with a very wide brim around it, rolled up at the edges, worn esp. in Mexico

some[1] adj, pron 1 a little, few, or certain or small number or amount (of): I saw some people I knew 2 an unknown one; a certain: Come back some other time

some[2] adv (used usu. before a number) about: There were some 40 or 50 people there

somebody also **someone**— pron a person; some but no particular or known person —see EVERY-BODY (USAGE)

someday adv at some future time

somehow adv by some means; in some way not yet known or stated: We must reach an agreement somehow

somersault n, v (to make) a jump or rolling backward or forward movement in which the feet go over the head before the body returns upright — compare CARTWHEEL

something pron some unstated or unknown thing: Something must be done!

sometime[1] adv at some uncertain or unstated time: We'll take our holiday sometime in August

sometime[2] adj having been once but now no longer; former: Sir Richard Marsh, sometime chairman of British Rail

sometimes adv at times; now and then; occasionally: Sometimes he comes by train, and sometimes by car

somewhat adv by some degree or amount; a little; rather: a price somewhat higher than expected

somewhere adv (in/at/to) some place

somnambulism n sleepwalking — -list n

somnolent adj literature 1 nearly falling asleep; drowsy 2 causing or suggesting sleep — ~ly adv

son n 1 someone's male child ☞ FAMILY 2 (used by an older man in speaking to a much younger man or boy)

Son n (in the Christian religion) the 2nd person of the Trinity; Christ

sonar n an apparatus using sound waves for finding the position of underwater objects like mines or submarines

sonata n a piece of music for 1 or 2 instruments, one of which is usu a piano, made up of usu. 3 or 4 short parts of varying speeds played in order

son et lumiere n French a performance which uses lights and recorded sounds to tell the stories of historical events

song n 1 a usu. short piece of music with words for singing 2 the act or art of singing 3 the music-like sound of a bird or birds 4 **for a song** esp. spoken for a very small price; very cheaply

songbird n any of the many kinds of birds that can produce musical sounds

songster fem. **songstress**— n literature 1 a singer or writer of songs 2 a songbird

sonic adj of or concerning sound waves

sonic boom also **sonic bang**— n an explosive sound produced by the shock wave from an aircraft beginning to go faster than the speed of sound

son-in-law n sons-in-law the husband of one's daughter ☞ FAMILY

sonnet n a 14-line poem with any of several fixed formal patterns of rhymes

sonny n -nies (used in speaking to a young boy)

son of a bitch n sons of bitches very rude a wicked person; bastard

sonorous adj having a pleasantly full loud sound — ~ly adv — -rity n

soon adv 1 within a short time 2 (making comparisons) readily; willingly: He'd just as soon have water as coffee 3 **no sooner...than** when...at once: No sooner had we sat down, than we found it was time to go —see HARDLY (USAGE)

soot n black powder produced by burning, and carried into the air and left on surfaces by smoke — ~y adj

soothe v soothed, soothing 1 to make less angry, excited, or anxious; comfort or calm 2 to make less painful — **soothingly** adv

soothsayer n old use a person believed to be able to tell the future

sop[1] n something offered to a displeased person to win his favour

sop[2] v -pp- to dip and fill with a liquid: sop bread in gravy

sophisticated adj 1 having or showing a knowledge of social life and behaviour; worldly-wise; urbane 2 having many parts; complicated; complex — **-cation** n

sophistry n -ries 1 the use of false deceptive arguments 2 also **sophism**— an argument which looks correct but is false, esp. one intended to deceive — **sophist** n

soporific adj causing or tending to sleep — ~ally adv

sopping adv, adj esp. spoken very (wet)

soppy adj -pier, -piest esp. spoken 1 foolish 2 (as of a story) too full of expressions of tender feelings like sorrow, love, etc.

soprano[1] n -nos 1 (a woman or child with, or a musical part for) a singing voice in the highest usual range, above alto 2 (of a family of instruments) the instrument which plays notes in the highest range

soprano² adj of, for, concerning, or having the range or part of a soprano

sorbet n a dish usu. with the taste of a fruit, made like ice cream using mostly water instead of cream

sorcerer fem. **sorceress**— n a person believed to do magic by using the power of evil spirits

sorcery n -ies the practice of a sorcerer; magic done by evil spirits

sordid adj 1 unpleasant and esp. shameful; base; vile 2 very dirty or poor: sordid living conditions — ~ly adv — ~ness n

sore¹ adj 1 painful or aching from a wound, infection, or (of muscles) hard use 2 likely to cause pain of mind or offence: It's a sore subject with him — ~ness n

sore² n a painful usu. infected place on the body

sorely adv severely or painfully; very

sorrel¹ adj, n (a horse whose colour is) bright reddish-brown, often with a white tail

sorrel² n any of various plants with sour-tasting leaves used in cooking

sorrow¹ n (a cause of) unhappiness over loss or wrongdoing; sadness; grief — ~ful adj — ~fully adv — ~fulness n

sorrow² v esp. in literature to feel or express sorrow; grieve

sorry¹ adj -rier, -riest 1 grieved; sad 2 having a sincere feeling of shame or unhappiness at one's past actions, and expressing a wish that one had not done them 3 (used for expressing polite refusal, disagreement, excusing of oneself, etc.) (esp. in the phrase I'm sorry) 4 causing pity mixed with disapproval: a sorry sight

sorry² interj 1 (used for expressing polite refusal, disagreement, excusing of oneself, etc.) 2 (used for asking someone to repeat something one has not heard properly)

sort¹ n 1 a group of people, things, etc., all having certain qualities; type; kind —see KIND (USAGE) 2 a sort of a weak, unexplained, or unusual kind of 3 out of sorts in a bad temper; feeling unwell or annoyed

sort² v to put (things) in order; place according to kind, rank, etc.; arrange — ~er n

sortie n 1 a short trip into an unfamiliar or unfriendly place 2 a flight to bomb an enemy centre 3 a short attack made by an army from a position of defence

sort of adv esp. spoken in some way or degree; rather; kind of

SOS n 1 the letters SOS as an international signal calling for help, used esp. by ships in trouble 2 an urgent message from someone in trouble

so-so adj, adv esp. spoken not very bad(ly) but also not very good/well

sou n esp. spoken the smallest amount of money

soufflé n 1 a light airy dish made from eggs, flour, milk, and usu. cheese or some other food to

give taste, baked and eaten at once while hot 2 a mousse

sought past tense and past part. of SEEK

sought after adj highly regarded, wanted, or popular because of rarity or high quality — **sought-after** adj

soul¹ n 1 the part of a person that is not the body and is thought not to die 2 a person: She's a dear old soul 3 a fine example; embodiment 4 SOUL MUSIC

soul² adj US esp. spoken of or concerning black people

soul-destroying adj giving no chance for the mind to work; very uninteresting

soulful adj full of feeling; expressing deep feeling — ~ly adv — ~ness n

soulless adj having or showing no attractive or tender human qualities — ~ly adv — ~ness n

soul music n a type of popular music usu. performed by black singers and supposed to show feelings strongly and directly

soul-searching adj, n (making a) deep examination of one's mind and conscience

sound¹ adj 1 in good condition; without disease or damage 2 solid; firm; strong: a sound basis for study 3 based on truth or good judgment; not wrong 4 (of sleep) deep and untroubled 5 severe; hard: a sound slap — ~ly adv — ~ness n

sound² n 1 what is or may be heard; (something that causes) a sensation in the ear 2 a quality of something read or heard — ~less adj — ~lessly adv

sound³ v 1 to have the effect of being; seem when heard: Your idea sounds a good one 2 to make or cause to make a sound; produce an effect that can be heard 3 to express as a sound; pronounce

sound⁴ n 1 a fairly broad stretch of sea water mostly surrounded by coast 2 a water passage connecting 2 larger bodies of water and wider than a strait

sound⁵ v to measure the depth of (esp. the bottom of a body of water), as by using a weighted line

sound barrier n the sudden increase in the force opposing an object in flight as it gets near the speed of sound

sound effects n sounds produced by people or machines to give the effect of natural sounds needed in a radio or television broadcast or a film

sounding board n a means used for spreading news or opinions

soundings n measurements made by using a sounding line

sound out v adv to try to find out the opinion or intention of

soundproof¹ adj keeping sound from getting in or out

soundproof² v to make soundproof

soundtrack n 1 the band near the edge of a

film where sound is recorded **2** the recorded music from a film

soup *n* **1** liquid cooked food often containing small pieces of meat, fish, or vegetables **2 in the soup** *esp. spoken* in trouble

soup kitchen *n* a place where people with no money may get free food

soup up *v adv* to increase the power of (an engine), as with a supercharger

sour¹ *adj* **1** having the taste that is not bitter, salty, or sweet, and is produced esp. by acids **2** having or expressing a bad temper; unsmiling — ~ly *adv* — ~ness *n*

sour² *v* to make or become sour

source *n* **1** a place from which something comes; producing place or force **2** the place where a stream of water starts —compare SPRING **3** a person or thing that supplies information

sour cream *n* a cream made sour by adding a kind of bacteria, and used in various foods

sourpuss *n humour* a person with no sense of humour, who always complains and is never satisfied

sousaphone *n* a type of very large brass musical instrument, played by blowing, used esp. in bands, and usu. fitted round the player's left shoulder

souse *v* **soused, sousing 1** to dip in water or pour water over; make completely wet **2** to preserve (esp. fish) by placing in salted water, vinegar, etc.

soused *adj sl* drunk

south¹ *adv* towards the south

south² *n* **1** (the direction of) one of the 4 main points of the compass, on the right of a person facing the rising sun ◁ GLOBE **2** (of a wind) (coming from) this direction —compare SOUTHERLY

southbound *adj* travelling towards the south

southeast¹ *adv* towards the southeast ◁ GLOBE

southeast² *n* **1** (the direction of) the point of the compass that is halfway between south and east **2** (of a wind) (coming from) this direction —compare SOUTHEASTERLY

southeasterly *adj* **1** towards or in the southeast **2** (of a wind) coming from the southeast

southeastern *adj* of or belonging to the southeast part, esp. of a country

southeastward *adj* going towards the south east —compare SOUTHEASTERLY

southeastwards *adv* (towards the) southeast

southerly *adj* **1** towards or in the south **2** (of a wind) coming from the south

southern *adj* of or belonging to the south part, esp. of the world or a country —see NORTH (USAGE)

Southerner *n* a person who lives in or comes from the southern part of a country

southern lights *n* see AURORA

southernmost *adj esp. written* furthest south

southpaw *n* a left-handed fighter, esp. a boxer

South pole *n* **1** (the lands around) the most southern point on the surface of the earth, or of another planet ◁ GLOBE **2** the point in the sky to the south around which stars seem to turn

southward *adj* going towards the south — compare SOUTHERLY

southwards *adv* towards the south

southwest¹ *adv* towards the southwest

southwest² *n* **1** (the direction of) the point of the compass which is halfway between south and west ◁ GLOBE **2** (of a wind) (coming from) this direction —compare SOUTHWESTERLY

southwesterly *adj* **1** towards or in the southwest **2** (of a wind) coming from the southwest

southwestern *adj* of or belonging to the southwest part, esp. of a country

southwestward *adj* going towards the southwest —compare SOUTHWESTERLY

southwestwards *adv* (towards the) southwest

souvenir *n* an object (to be) kept as a reminder of an event, trip, place, etc.

sou'wester *n* a hat of oilskin with a wide band coming far down over the neck and worn esp. by sailors in storms

sovereign¹ *n* **1** the person with the highest political power in a country; a ruler such as a king or queen; monarch **2** a former British gold coin worth £1

sovereign² *adj* **1** in control of a country; ruling: *Sovereign power must lie with the people* **2** (of a country) independent and self-governing

sovereignty *n* complete freedom and power to act or govern

soviet *n* an elected council at any of various levels in Communist countries

Soviet *adj* of or concerning the USSR (the **Soviet Union**) or its people

sow¹ *n* a fully grown female pig —compare BOAR, HOG

sow² *v* **sowed, sown** *or* **sowed, sowing** to plant or scatter (seeds) on (a piece of ground) — ~er *n*

soya bean also **soybean**— *n* (the bean of) a plant native to Asia grown for food from its seeds which produce oil and are rich in protein

soy sauce *n* dark brown liquid made from soya beans allowed to become sour-tasting in salt water, and eaten esp. with E Asian food

sozzled *adj sl* drunk

spa also **watering place**— *n* a usu. fashionable place with a spring of mineral water where people come for cures of various diseases

space¹ *n* **1** something limited and measurable in length, width, or depth and regarded as not filled up; distance, area, or volume; room **2** a quantity or bit of this for a particular purpose **3** that which surrounds all objects and continues outward in all directions **4** what is outside the earth's air; where other heavenly bodies move

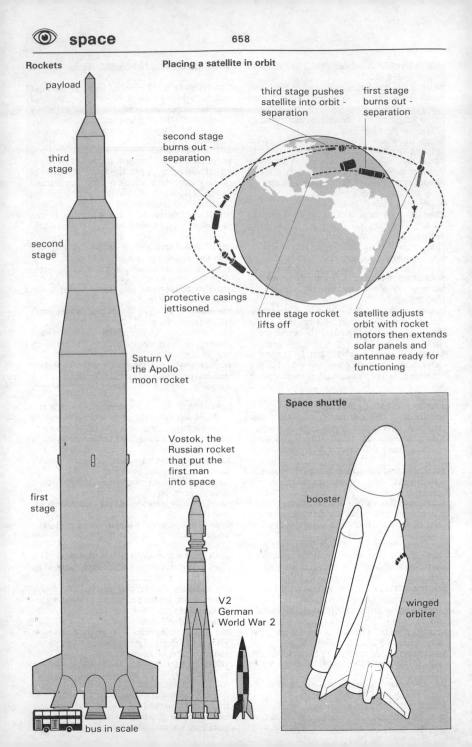

Rockets

payload

third stage

second stage

first stage

Saturn V
the Apollo
moon rocket

Vostok, the
Russian rocket
that put the
first man
into space

V2
German
World War 2

bus in scale

Placing a satellite in orbit

third stage pushes satellite into orbit - separation

first stage burns out - separation

second stage burns out - separation

protective casings jettisoned

three stage rocket lifts off

satellite adjusts orbit with rocket motors then extends solar panels and antennae ready for functioning

Space shuttle

booster

winged orbiter

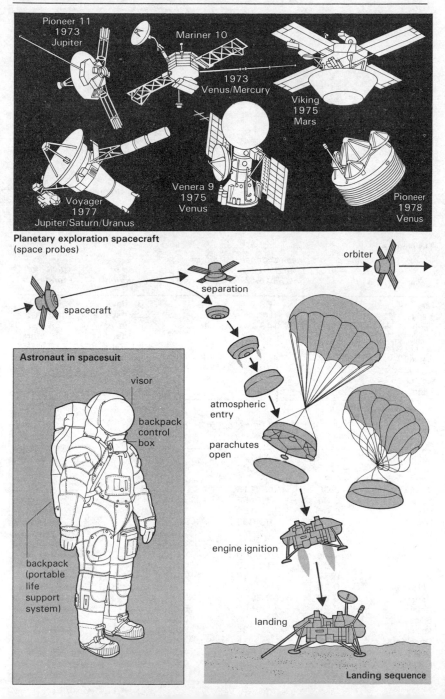

Planetary exploration spacecraft
(space probes)

Pioneer 11
1973
Jupiter

Mariner 10

1973
Venus/Mercury

Viking
1975
Mars

Voyager
1977
Jupiter/Saturn/Uranus

Venera 9
1975
Venus

Pioneer
1978
Venus

orbiter

spacecraft

separation

atmospheric
entry

parachutes
open

engine ignition

landing

Landing sequence

Astronaut in spacesuit

visor

backpack
control
box

backpack
(portable
life
support
system)

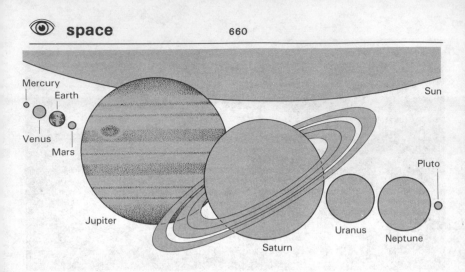

Mercury
Earth
Venus
Mars
Jupiter
Sun
Pluto
Uranus
Neptune
Saturn

The planets

planet	diameter relative to earth	mean distance from Sun (million km)	no. of satellites (moons)	period of revolution	period of rotation
Mercury	0.4	58		88 days	59 days
Venus	0.96	108		225 days	243 days
Earth	1	149	1	365 days	24 hrs
Mars	0.5	228	2	687 days	24½ hrs
Jupiter	11.2	778	14	11.9 yrs	10 hrs
Saturn	9.5	1430	11	29.5 yrs	10¼ hrs
Uranus	3.9	2870	5	84 yrs	11 hrs
Neptune	3.5	4500	2	164.8 yrs	16 hrs
Pluto	0.5	5910	1	247.7 yrs	6¼ days

Brightest stars

star	apparent magnitude	no. of times brighter than the Sun	distance in light years
Sirius	− 1.42	26	8.7
Canopus	− 0.72	80,000	650
Alpha Centauri	− 0.27	1.5	4.3
Arcturus	− 0.06	115	36
Vega	0.04	55	27
Capella	0.05	150	45
Rigel	0.08	60,000	900
Procyon	0.37	7	11
Achernar	0.51	720	118
Betelgeuse	variable	15,000	520
Agena	0.63	10,500	490
Altair	0.77	10	16
Aldebaran	0.78	165	68
Acrux	0.83	3200,2000	370
Antares	0.86	9600	520
Spica	0.91	1800	220
Pollux	1.16	34	35
Fomalhaut	1.19	15	23
Deneb	1.26	60,000	1600
Beta Crucis	1.28	6000	490
Regulus	1.36	170	84

☞ **5** (an area of) land not built on (esp. in the phrase **open space**) **6** a period of time **7** an area or distance left between written or printed words, lines, etc.

space² v **spaced, spacing** to place apart; arrange with spaces between

spacecraft n spacecraft a vehicle able to travel in space

spaced out adj sl, esp. US in a state of mind like that caused by taking mind-influencing drugs; high

spaceship n (esp. in stories) a space vehicle for carrying people

space shuttle n a rocket that travels to and fro between the earth and a space station

spacesuit n a suit for wearing in space, covering the whole body and provided with an air supply ☞ SPACE

spacing n placement or arrangement apart, esp. of written or typed lines

spacious adj having a lot of room; not narrow; roomy — ~**ly** adv — ~**ness** n

spade¹ n a tool like a shovel for digging earth, with a broad metal blade for pushing with the foot into the ground

spade² n a playing card with 1 or more figures shaped like a pointed leaf printed on it in black —compare CLUB, DIAMOND, HEART

spadework n hard work done in preparation for an event or course of action

spaghetti n an Italian food made of pasta in long strings, usu. sold in dry form for making soft again in boiling water —compare MACARONI, RAVIOLI, CANNELLONI

spake old use or poetic past tense of SPEAK

spam n trademark a kind of tinned meat usu. eaten cold

span¹ n **1** a stretch between 2 limits, esp. in time —compare WINGSPAN **2** a length of time over which something continues or works well **3** (the length of) a bridge, arch, etc., between supports **4** the distance from the end of the thumb to the end of the little finger in a spread hand; about 9 inches or 0.23 metres

span² v **-nn- 1** to form an arch or bridge over **2** to enclose in space or time; reach over: His interest spans many subjects

spangle¹ n a small piece of shiny metal or plastic sewn in large numbers esp. on dresses to give a shining effect; sequin

spangle² v **-gled, -gling** to give a shining effect to, with or as if with spangles; ornament with shining objects

spaniel n any of various breeds of small short-legged dogs with long ears and long wavy hair

Spanish adj of or belonging to Spain or its language ☞ LANGUAGE

spank¹ v to strike with quick force (as if) with the open hand, esp. on the buttocks — **spank** n — ~**ing** n

spank² v to go or esp. sail quickly

spanner n a metal hand tool with jaws

(**open-ended spanner**) or a hollow end (**ring spanner**), for fitting over and twisting nuts

spar¹ n a thick pole, esp. one used on a ship to support sails or ropes —compare MAST

spar² v **-rr- 1** to box without hitting hard, as in practice (between **sparring partners**) or in testing an opponent's defence **2** to fight with words; wrangle

spar³ n any of various nonmetallic rather shiny minerals, esp. found naturally along with metal

spare¹ v **spared, sparing 1** to keep from punishing, harming, or attacking: Spare my life! **2** to save (someone) (need or trouble) **3** to give up as not completely needed; afford to give: Can you spare me 5 minutes? **4 to spare** left over; extra

spare² adj **1** not in use but kept for use **2** not needed for use; free: spare time **3 go spare** sl to become very anxious and/or angry

spare³ n a second object of the same kind that is kept for possible use

spareribs n (some of) a pig's ribs with the meat which sticks to them

spare tyre n **1** an extra tyre carried in a vehicle for use if a tyre is damaged on the road **2** humour a noticeably fat waist

sparing adj using or giving little; frugal — ~**ly** adv

spark¹ n **1** a small bit of burning material thrown out by a fire or by the striking together of 2 hard objects **2** a light-producing passage of electricity across a space **3** a very small but important bit, esp. of a quality **4 bright spark** esp. spoken a clever or cheerful person

spark² v **1** to throw out sparks **2** to produce a spark

sparking plug n a part which screws into a petrol engine and makes an electric spark to explode the petrol mixture ☞ CAR

sparkle¹ v **-kled, -kling 1** to shine in small flashes **2** (of a drink) to give off gas in small bubbles —compare STILL **3** to show spirit and excitement; be bright

sparkle² n an act, or the quality, of sparkling

sparkler n a kind of stick made to give off harmless bright sparks as it burns down

sparks n an electrician or radio operator

sparrow n any of various kinds of small brownish birds very common in many parts of the world

sparse adj scattered; with few members; thin; scanty — ~**ly** adv — ~**ness, sparsity** n

spartan adj simple and without attention to comfort; severe

spasm n **1** a sudden uncontrolled tightening of muscles **2** a sudden violent effort, feeling, or act; fit: spasms of laughter

spasmodic adj **1** of or like a spasm: spasmodic pain **2** not continuous; irregular; intermittent; fitful — ~**ally** adv

spastic n, adj (a person) suffering from a disease (**spastic paralysis**) in which some parts of the body will not move because the muscles stay tightened

spat[1] *n* a cloth covering for the ankle, worn esp. formerly by men above a shoe, fastened by side buttons and a band under the shoe

spat[2] *past tense and past part. of* SPIT

spate *n* 1 a large number or amount, esp. coming together in time 2 **in spate** flooding; full of rushing water

spatial *adj esp. written* of, concerning, or being in space — ~ly *adv*

spatter[1] *v* 1 to scatter (drops of a liquid) on (a surface) 2 (of a liquid) to fall or be thrown off in drops onto a surface

spatula *n* any of various tools with a dull-edged flat blade, for spreading, mixing, or lifting soft or powdery substances

spawn *n* 1 the eggs of water animals like fishes and frogs, laid together in a soft mass 2 rootlike parts of mushrooms, esp. prepared for growing

spay *v* **spayed, spaying** to remove (part of) the sex organs of (a female animal) — compare NEUTER

speak *v* **spoke , spoken, speaking** 1 to say things; express thoughts aloud; use the voice; talk 2 to express thoughts, ideas, etc., in some other way than this: *Actions speak louder than words* 3 to be able to talk in (a language) 4 to express or say

speakeasy *n* **-ies** (esp. in the US in the 1920's and 1930's) an unlawful place for going to buy and drink alcohol

speaker *n* 1 a person making a speech, or who makes speeches in a stated way 2 a person who speaks a language 3 the person who controls the course of business in a lawmaking body (note the phrase **Mr Speaker**) 4 a loudspeaker

speak out *v adv* to speak boldly, freely, and plainly

speak up *v adv* 1 to speak more loudly 2 SPEAK OUT

spear[1] *n* a pole with a sharp point at one end used esp. formerly for throwing as a weapon

spear[2] *v* to make a hole in or catch (as) with the point of a spear; impale

spearhead[1] *n* something that begins an attack or course of action forcefully; a leading force

spearhead[2] *v* to act as a spearhead for; lead forcefully

spearmint *n* a common mint plant widely grown and used for its fresh taste, as in some chewing gum

spec *n* **on spec** *esp. spoken* as a risk or spec ulation

special[1] *adj* of a particular kind; not ordinary or usual

special[2] *n* 1 something not ordinary or usual 2 *esp. spoken* an advertised reduced price in a shop

specialist *n* 1 a person who has special interests or skills in a limited field of work or study; expert 2 a doctor who gives treatment in a particular way or to certain kinds of people or diseases

speciality *n* **-ties** 1 a special field of work or study 2 a particularly fine or best product: *Fish is a speciality of this restaurant*

specialize, -ise *v* **-ized, -izing** to limit all or most of one's study, business, etc., to particular things or subjects — **-ization** *n*

specialized, -ised *adj* fit or developed for one particular use

special licence *n law* an official permission given by the Church of England for a marriage at a time or place not usu. allowed

specially *adv* 1 for one particular purpose 2 in a special way 3 especially

species *n* **-cies** 1 a group of plants or animals that are of the same kind, which are alike in all important ways, and which can breed together to produce young of the same kind —compare GENUS 2 a type; sort

specific *adj* 1 detailed and exact; clear in meaning; careful in explanation; not vague 2 particular; certain; fixed, determined, or named — ~ity *n*

specifically *adv* 1 exactly and clearly 2 of the stated kind and no other; particularly

specification *n* 1 the action of specifying 2 any of the parts of a detailed plan or set of descriptions or directions

specific gravity *n* **-ties** *technical* the weight of a material divided by the weight of the amount of water which would fill the same space; density compared with water

specifics *n* matters to be decided exactly; details

specify *v* **-fied, -fying** to mention exactly; describe fully so as to choose or name

specimen *n* 1 a single typical thing or example 2 one or a piece or amount of something for being shown, tested, etc.

specious *adj esp. written* seeming right or correct but not so in fact; plausible — ~ly *adv* — ~ness *n*

speck *n* a small spot, coloured mark, or dot

speckle *n* a small irregular mark; coloured speck, esp. in a large number covering a surface — **-led** *adj*

spectacle *n* 1 a grand public show or scene 2 a silly sight; object of laughing or disrespect: *to make a spectacle of oneself*

spectacled *adj* wearing spectacles

spectacles also (*esp. spoken*) **specs**— *n* glasses, esp. of the usual kind with side parts fitting on top of the ears

spectacular[1] *adj* grandly out of the ordinary; attracting excited notice — ~ly *adv*

spectacular[2] *n* a spectacular entertainment

spectator *n* a person who watches (esp. an event or sport) without taking part

spectre *n* 1 a spirit without a body; ghost 2 something that is seen in the mind and causes fear — **-tral** *adj*

spectrum *n* **-tra** 1 a set of bands of coloured light in the order of their wavelengths, into which a beam of light may be separated (as by a prism) 2 a range of any of various kinds of waves

speculate v -lated, -lating 1 to think (about a matter) in a light way or without facts that would lead to a firm result 2 to buy or deal in goods, shares etc., whose future price is still very uncertain, in the hope of a large profit — **-lation** n — **-lator** n

speculative adj 1 of or being speculation 2 based on reason alone and not facts about the world — ~**ly** adv

speech n 1 the act or power of speaking; spoken language 2 a an act of speaking formally to a group of listeners b the words so spoken 3 a usu. long set of lines for an actor to say in a play

speechless adj unable for the moment to speak because of strong feeling, shock, etc. — ~**ly** adv — ~**ness** n

speech therapy n treatment for people with various kinds of difficulties in speaking plainly — **-pist** n

speed[1] n 1 rate of movement; distance divided by time of travel: a speed of 55 miles per hour 2 the action, ability, or state of moving swiftly 3 drug-users' sl amphetamine

speed[2] v speeded or sped, speeding 1 to go or send quickly 2 to go or drive too fast; break the speed limit

speeding n the offence of driving faster than the lawful limit

speed limit n the fastest speed allowed by law on a particular stretch of road

speedometer esp. spoken also speedo— n an instrument in a vehicle for telling its speed

speed trap n a stretch of road watched by hidden policemen to catch drivers going too fast

speedway n -ways 1 a track for racing motor vehicles, esp. motorcycles 2 the sport of racing motorcycles on such a track

speedwell n any of several types of small European wild plant with light bluish flowers

speedy adj -ier, -iest going, working, or passing fast; quick; swift — **speedily** adv — **speediness** n

speleology, spelæ- n the sport of walking and climbing in caves — **-logical** adj — **-ogist** n

spell[1] n 1 a a condition caused by magical power: enchantment b the magic words producing this condition 2 a strong attractive power

spell[2] v spelt or spelled, spelling 1 to name in order the letters of (a word) 2 (of letters in order) to form (a word) 3 to form words correctly from letters — ~**er** n

spell[3] v spelled, spelling to take the turn of; allow (another) to rest by taking over work; relieve

spell[4] n an unbroken period of time of usu. unstated length: a spell of work abroad

spellbind v -bound, -binding to hold the complete attention of; fascinate — ~**er** n

spelling n 1 the action or proper way of forming words from letters 2 an ordered set of letters forming a word

spell out v adv 1 to explain in the plainest or

most detailed way 2 to write or say (a word) letter by letter

spend v spent, spending 1 to give out (esp. money) in payment 2 to pass or use (time) 3 esp. written or literature to wear out or use completely: The storm soon spent itself

spendthrift n a person who spends money wastefully

spent adj 1 worn out; exhausted 2 already used; no longer for use: spent bullets

sperm n sperm or sperms 1 a cell produced by the sex organs of a male animal, which usu. swims in a liquid and is able to unite with the female egg to produce new life 2 the liquid (SEMEN) from the male sex organs in which these swim

spermatozoa n sing. -zoon technical sperms ☞ EMBRYO, REPRODUCTION

sperm whale n a kind of large whale up to 18 metres or 60 feet long which is hunted for the oil in its head, for fat, and for ambergris

spew v 1 to come or send out in a rush or flood; gush 2 sl to vomit

sphagnum n any of a large group of mosses growing in wet areas which can go to make up peat and which are used by gardeners for packing plants

sphere n 1 a round figure in space; ball-shaped mass; solid figure all points of which are equally distant from a centre ☞ MATHEMATICS 2 an area or range of existence, force, meaning, action, etc.: famous in many spheres 3 (in ancient science) any of the transparent shells which were thought to turn around the earth with the heavenly bodies fixed in them

spherical adj having the form of a sphere

spheroid n a figure which is not quite a sphere, esp. one that is longer in one direction and has 2 end points

sphinx n an ancient Egyptian image of a lion, lying down, with a human head

spice[1] n 1 any of various vegetable products used esp. in powder form for flavouring foods 2 interest or excitement, esp. as added to something else

spice[2] v spiced, spicing to add spice to

spick-and-span adj clean and bright; like new

spicy adj -ier, -iest 1 containing or tasting like spice 2 exciting, esp. from being slightly improper or rude; racy — **spicily** adv — **spiciness** n

spider n any of many kinds of small 8-legged creatures which make silk threads, sometimes into nets for catching insects to eat ☞ EVOLUTION

spidery adj long and thin like a spider's legs or suggesting a pattern like its web

spiel n sl a fast-flowing line of talk, esp. intended to persuade

spigot n an apparatus for turning on and off a flow of liquid, esp. from a container such as a barrel; tap

spike n 1 a long pointed piece of esp. metal with an outward or upward point 2 any of several pieces of metal fixed in the bottom of shoes for holding the ground, esp. in sports — **spiky** *adj*

spill¹ *v* spilt *or* spilled, spilling **1** to pour out accidentally, as over the edge of a container **2** to spread or rush beyond limits **3** *esp. literature* to cause (blood) to flow by wounding

spill² *n* **1** an act or amount of spilling **2** a fall from a horse, bicycle, etc.

spill³ *n* a thin piece of wood or twisted paper for lighting lamps, pipes, etc.

spillway *n* **-ways** a passage for water over or round a dam

spin¹ *v* spun, spinning **1** to make (thread) by twisting (cotton, wool, etc.) **2** (of a spider or silkworm) to produce (thread, esp. in a mass or net) **3** to turn round and round fast; whirl **4** to move fast on wheels **5** to produce in a threadlike form

spin² *n* **1** an act of spinning **2** fast turning movement **3** a short trip for pleasure

spina bifida *n medical* a serious condition in which the backbone is split down the middle from birth, leaving the spinal cord unprotected

spinach *n* a type of widely-grown vegetable whose broad green leaves are eaten cooked

spinal *adj* of, for, or concerning the spine

spinal cord *n* the thick cord of nerves enclosed in the spine and attached to the brain, by which nervous messages are carried to the body

spindle *n* **1** a round rod used for twisting the thread in spinning **2** a machine part around which something turns **3** a thin rod that forms part of a machine

spindly *adj* **-dlier, -dliest** long, thin, and weak-looking

spin-dry *v* **-dried, -drying** to remove water from (clothes) after washing, esp. in a washing machine with a special part (**spin dryer**), that spins round and round fast

spine *n* **1** also **spinal column**— the row of bones in the centre of the back of higher animals that supports the body and protects the spinal cord **2** the end of a book where the pages are fastened and the title is usu. printed **3** any of various stiff sharp-pointed plant or animal parts; prickle

spineless *adj* without moral strength or courage — ~**ly** *adv* — ~**ness** *n*

spinet *n* a small harpsichord

spinnaker *n* a large 3-sided sail that has a rounded shape when blown out by the wind, carried on some racing boats for going with the force of the wind ➥ SAIL

spinner *n* **1** a cricket ball bowled with a spinning action **2** a bowler of such balls —see also MONEY-SPINNER

spinney *n* **-neys** a small area full of trees and low plants

spinning jenny *n* **-nies** an early machine allowing one person to spin a number of threads at once

spinning wheel *n* a small machine used esp. formerly at home for spinning thread, in which a foot-driven wheel moves a spindle

spin-off *n* a usu. useful product or result other than the main one; by-product

spinster *n* **1** an unmarried woman —compare BACHELOR GIRL **2** *sometimes offensive* old maid — ~**hood** *n*

spiny *adj* **-ier, -iest** like or full of spines

spiral¹ *n* **1** a curve on a plane formed by a point winding round a centre and getting always closer to or further from it ➥ MATHEMATICS **2** a curve in space winding round a central line **3** a continuous upward or downward change: *the inflationary spiral*

spiral² *v* **-ll-** **1** to move in a spiral; rise or fall esp. in a winding way **2** to fall or esp. rise continuously

spire *n* a roof rising steeply to a point on top of a tower, as on a church; (the top of a) steeple ➥ CATHEDRAL

spirit¹ *n* **1** *literature* a person apart from the body; one's mind or soul **2** a being without a body, such as a ghost **3** a power regarded as able to take control of a person **4** life or thought regarded as independently existing **5** a person of the stated kind or temper **6** an intention or feeling in the mind; attitude: *to take a remark in the right spirit* **7** excitement, force, or effort shown; energy; liveliness **8** the central quality or force of something **9** an alcoholic drink (such as whisky or brandy) produced by distillation from a weaker alcohol-containing drink or mixture **10** any of various liquids such as alcohol used esp. for breaking down solids or as fuels —see also METHYLATED SPIRITS, WHITE SPIRIT

spirit² *v* to carry away; take, esp. in a secret or mysterious way; make off with

Spirit *n* see HOLY SPIRIT

spirited *adj* full of spirit; forceful; animated

spiritless *adj* **1** weak or lazy; without spirit **2** sad; in low spirits — ~**ly** *adv* — ~**ness** *n*

spirit level *n* a tool for testing whether a surface is level, made of a bar containing a short glass tube of liquid with a bubble which will be in the centre if the surface is level

spirits *n* **1** the cheerful or sad state of one's mind **2** spirit

spiritual¹ *adj* **1** nonmaterial; of the nature of spirit —compare INTELLECTUAL **2** religious; sacred — ~**ly** *adv*

spiritual² *n* a religious song of the type sung originally by the black peoples of the US

spiritualism *n* the belief that the dead may send messages to living people usu. through a person (MEDIUM) with special powers — ~**ist** *n* — **-istic** *adj*

spirituality *n* fondness for religious things, worship, prayer, etc.; devotion

spiritualize, -ise *v* **-ized, -izing** to give a purer, more religious, less material meaning to — **-ization** *n*

spit¹ *n* **1** a thin pointed rod for sticking meat onto and turning, for cooking over a fire **2** a small usu. sandy point of land running out into a stretch of water

spit² v spat or spit, spitting 1 to force (liquid) from the mouth 2 spit it out esp. spoken Go ahead and say what is on your mind

spit³ n 1 the liquid in the mouth; saliva 2 esp. spoken the exact likeness (esp in the phrases the spit and image of, the dead spit of) —see also SPITTING IMAGE

spit and polish n esp. spoken (too) great attention to a clean and shiny appearance, as esp. in the army, navy, etc.

spite¹ n 1 unreasonable dislike for and desire to annoy another person, esp. in some small way 2 in spite of in opposition to the presence or efforts of; despite — ~ful adj — ~fully adv — ~fulness n

spite² v spited, spiting to treat with spite; annoy intentionally

spitting image n an exact likeness

spittle n spit; saliva

spittoon n a vessel for spitting into

splash¹ v 1 to move or hit usu. noisily in a liquid 2 a (of a liquid) to fall, strike, or move noisily, in drops, waves, etc. b to cause (a liquid) to do this 3 esp. spoken to give a lot of space to (esp. a news story); report as if very important 4 to spend (money) on unnecessary but fine things

splash² n 1 a splashing act, movement, or noise 2 a mark made by splashing

splash³ adv with a splash

splash down v adv (esp. of a spacecraft) to land in the sea — splashdown n

splatter v to spatter; splash

splay v splayed, splaying to spread out or make or become larger at one end

spleen n a small organ near the upper end of the stomach that controls the quality of the blood supply and produces certain blood cells

splendid adj 1 grand in appearance; glorious; sumptuous 2 very fine; excellent — ~ly adv

splendour n excellent or grand beauty; magnificence

splice v spliced, splicing 1 to fasten end to end to make one continuous length, as by weaving (ropes), sticking (pieces of film), nailing (beams), etc. 2 esp. spoken to join in marriage — splice n

splint n a flat piece of wood, metal, etc., used for protecting and keeping a damaged part of the body, esp. a broken bone, in position

splinter¹ n a small needle-like piece broken off something; sliver

splinter² v 1 to break into small needle-like pieces 2 to separate from a larger organization

splinter³ adj (of a group) that has separated from a larger body

split¹ v split, splitting 1 to divide along a length, esp. with force or by a blow or tear 2 to divide into separate parts 3 to end a friendship, marriage, etc. 4 sl to tell secret information (about someone) 5 sl to leave quickly 6 split an infinitive to put a word such as an adverb between ' to ' and its following verb (as in 'I want to quietly

go') —see TO (USAGE) —see also split the DIFFERENCE, split HAIRS, split one's SIDES

split² n 1 a cut or break made by splitting 2 a division or separation 3 a dish made from fruit (esp. a banana) cut into 2 pieces with ice cream on top

split-level adj (of a building) having floors at different heights in different parts

split pea n a dried pea separated into its 2 natural halves

split personality n -ties a set of 2 very different ways of behaving present in one person at different times

splits n a movement in which a person's legs are spread wide and touch the floor along their whole length

split second n a small part of a second; flash; instant — split-second adj

splitting adj (esp. of a headache) giving the feeling of a sharp blow; very painful

splutter¹ n a spitting noise; sputter

splutter² v 1 to say or talk quickly and as if confused 2 to make a light explosive noise; sputter

spoil¹ n things taken without payment, as a by an army from a defeated enemy or place b by thieves

spoil² v spoiled or spoilt, spoiling 1 to make or become of no use or value; ruin 2 to make (esp. a child) selfish from having too much attention or praise — ~er n

spoil for v prep 1 to be very eager for (esp. in the phrase be spoiling for a fight) 2 to cause to be unsatisfied with

spoils n the rewards of getting political power, esp. public offices for one's friends, party workers, etc.

spoilsport n a person who puts an end to another's jokes or fun

spoke¹ n any of the bars which connect the outer ring of a wheel to the centre, as on a bicycle

spoke² past tense of SPEAK

spoken past part. of SPEAK

spokeshave n a tool with a blade between 2 handles, used for making curved surfaces smooth

spokesman (fem. spokeswoman)— n -men a person who speaks as a representative of others

spoliation n esp. written the action of violent spoiling or destruction

spondee n a measure of poetry consisting of 2 strong (or long) beats — -daic adj

sponge¹ n 1 any of a group of sea creatures which grow a spreading rubber-like skeleton full of small holes ⟹EVOLUTION 2 a piece of this animal's frame or of rubber or plastic like it, which is used in washing surfaces 3 esp. spoken a person who sponges on other people 4 SPONGE CAKE

sponge² v sponged, sponging 1 to clean (as if) with a wet cloth or sponge 2 to remove (liquid) with a cloth, sponge, etc. 3 to get (money, meals, etc.) free by taking advantage of another's good nature — **sponger** n

sponge bag n a small usu. plastic bag for carrying one's soap, toothbrush, etc.

sponge cake n (a) soft light sweet cake

spongy adj -ier, -iest like a sponge; soft and full of holes — **sponginess** n

sponsor[1] n 1 a person who takes responsibility for a person or thing 2 a business which pays for a show, broadcast, sports event, etc., usu. in return for advertising — ~**ship** n

sponsor[2] v to act as sponsor for

spontaneous adj produced from natural feelings or causes without outside force; unplanned: a spontaneous cheer — ~**ly** adv — ~**ness**, **-neity** n

spoof v to make fun of — **spoof** n

spook n esp. spoken a ghost

spooky adj -ier, -iest esp. spoken causing fear; suggesting ghosts; eerie

spool n 1 a round object usu. with a hole through the centre for winding a length of electric wire, recording tape, camera film, etc. 2 an amount held by any of these

spoon[1] n 1 a tool for mixing, serving, and eating food, consisting of a small bowl with a handle 2 a spoonful

spoon[2] v to take up or move with a spoon

spoonerism n an expression in which the first sounds of 2 words have changed places usu. with a funny result (as in sew you to a sheet for show you to a seat)

spoon-feed v -fed, -feeding 1 to feed (esp. a baby) with a spoon 2 to offer (a subject) to (students) in very easy lessons that need no thinking

spoonful n -s or **spoonsful** the amount that a spoon will hold

spoor n a mark or waste droppings (as left by a wild animal) which can be followed

sporadic adj happening irregularly — ~**ally** adv

spore n a very small seedlike cell produced by some plants and animals and able to develop into a new plant or animal

sporran n a fur-covered bag worn as a purse in front of a kilt

sport[1] v to wear or show publicly; show off

sport[2] n 1 an outdoor or indoor game, competition, or activity carried on by rules and needing bodily effort 2 active amusement; play: It's great sport, swimming in the sea 3 a generous-minded person of a kind who accepts defeat or a joke good-temperedly 4 technical a plant or animal that is different in some way from its usual type

sporting adj 1 offering the kind of fair risk that is usual in a game: a sporting chance 2 of or fond of field sports like hunting or horse racing — ~**ly** adv

sportive adj being or fond of sport; playful — ~**ly** adv — ~**ness** n

sports adj 1 of or connected with sports 2 informal in style: a sports jacket

sports car n a low usu. open fast car

sportsman (fem. **sportswoman**)— n -men 1 a good sport; one who plays sports in a fair spirit 2 a person who plays or enjoys sports — ~**like** adj

sportsmanship n a spirit of graceful winning and losing

sporty adj -ier, -iest good-looking in a bright informal way — **sportiness** n

spot[1] n 1 a part or area different from the main surface, as in colour, usu. of a round shape 2 a particular place: the spot where it happened 3 a small part of something: a bright spot in the news 4 a dirty mark 5 a pimple 6 an area of mind or feelings: I have a soft spot for my old school 7 a usu. difficult state of affairs; fix: We're really in a spot! 8 a little bit; small amount 9 a place in a broadcast 10 **on the spot a** at once **b** at the place of the action **c** in a position of having to make the right action or answer: The question put me on the spot

spot[2] v -tt- 1 to pick out, esp. with the eye; see; recognize 2 to mark with coloured or dirty spots 3 to place in position: Guards were spotted around the building

spot[3] adv esp. spoken exactly (in the phrase **spot on**): spot on time

spot[4] adj limited to a few times or places as representing all: to make spot checks

spot-check v to give a spot check to; test as a typical case

spotless adj completely clean — ~**ly** adv — ~**ness** n

spotlight[1] n 1 (a bright round area of light made by) a lamp with a directable narrow beam 2 public attention

spotlight[2] v -lighted, -lighting to direct attention to, with, or as if with a spotlight

spot-on adj, adv esp. spoken exactly (right)

spotted adj marked with coloured or dirty spots

spotted dick also **spotted dog**— n a kind of boiled heavy sweet pudding with currants

spotter n 1 a person who keeps watch for the stated thing 2 used for keeping watch on an enemy's actions: a spotter plane

spotty adj -tier, -tiest esp. spoken having, or being still of the age to have, acne

spouse n usu. written or law a husband or wife

spout[1] v 1 to throw or come out in a forceful stream 2 to pour out in a stream of words: to spout Shakespeare — ~**er** n

spout[2] n 1 an opening from which liquid comes out from a container 2 a forceful esp. rising stream of liquid 3 **up the spout** esp. spoken ruined; in a hopeless condition

sprain[1] n an act or result of spraining a joint —compare STRAIN

sprain[2] v to damage (a joint in the body) by sudden twisting

sprang past tense of SPRING

sprat *n* a small kind of European herring (a food fish)

sprawl¹ *v* **1** to stretch out (oneself or one's limbs) awkwardly : *sprawled out in a chair* **2** to spread ungracefully: *The city sprawls for miles*

sprawl² *n* **1** a sprawling position **2** an irregular spreading mass or group

spray¹ *n* **sprays** (an arrangement of flowers, jewels, etc. in the shape of) a small branch with leaves and flowers

spray² *n* **1** water in very small drops blown from the sea, a waterfall, etc. **2** (a can or other container holding) liquid to be sprayed out under pressure

spray³ *v* **sprayed, spraying 1 a** to scatter (liquid) in small drops under pressure **b** (of liquid) to be scattered in this way **2** to throw or force out liquid in small drops upon (a surface, field of crops etc.) — ~**er** *n*

spray gun *n* an apparatus like a gun for pumping to spray out liquid

spread¹ *v* **spread, spreading 1** to open, reach, or stretch out; be or make longer, broader, wider, etc.: *a ship with sails spread* **2** to put (a covering) on: *spread butter on bread* **3** to share or divide over an area, period of time, etc.: *spread the cost over 3 years* **4** to make or become (more) widely known **5** to have or give a wider effect: *The fire soon spread* **6** to prepare (a table or meal) for eating — ~**able** *adj*

spread² *n* **1** the act or action of spreading **2** a distance, area, or time of spreading: *a tree with a spread of 100 feet* **3** a newspaper or magazine article or advertisement running across one or more pages **4** a large or grand meal **5** a soft food for spreading on bread

spread-eagle *v* **-gled, -gling** to put (someone, esp. oneself) or go into a position with arms and legs spread out

spree *n* a time of free and wild fun, spending, drinking, etc.

sprig *n* a small end of a stem or branch with leaves

sprigged *adj* (esp. of fine cloth) having an ornamented pattern of plant sprigs

sprightly *adj* **-lier, -liest** gay and light; lively — **-liness** *n*

spring¹ *v* **sprang, sprung, springing 1** to move quickly as if by jumping; bound **2** to come into being or action quickly; arise: *A wind suddenly sprang up* **3** to come out (as if) in a spring of water; issue **4** to crack or split: *The weight sprang the beam* **5** to open or close (as if) by the force of a spring: *The box sprang open* **6** *sl* to cause to leave prison, lawfully or by escaping **7** to produce as a surprise **8 spring a leak** to begin to let liquid through a crack, hole, etc.

spring² *n* **1** a place where water comes up naturally from the ground **2** the season between winter and summer **3** a metal spiral, which tends to push, pull, or twist and return to its original shape **4** the quality of this object; elasticity **5** an act of springing — ~**less** *adj*

springboard *n* a strong bendable board for jumping off to give height to a dive or jump

springbok *n* **-boks** *or* **-bok** a kind of S African gazelle

spring-clean *v* to clean (a place) thoroughly, esp. in the spring — **spring-clean, spring-cleaning** *n*

spring onion *n* a kind of onion with a small white bulb and green stem, usu. eaten raw

spring roll *n* a Chinese dish made of a thin case of egg pastry filled with bits of vegetable and often meat and usu. cooked in oil

spring tide *n* a large tide occurring after the new and full moon —compare NEAP TIDE

springy *adj* **-ier, -iest** having spring; elastic

sprinkle *v* **-kled, -kling 1** to scatter in drops or small grains **2** to scatter liquid, small bits, etc., on or among: *a book sprinkled with humour* — **sprinkle** *n*

sprinkler *n* any of various apparatuses for scattering drops of water

sprinkling *n* a small scattered group or amount

sprint¹ *v* to run at one's fastest speed — ~**er** *n*

sprint² *n* **1** an act of sprinting **2** a short race; dash

sprite *n* a fairy, esp. a playful graceful one

sprocket *n* **1** also **sprocket wheel**— a wheel with 1 or more rows of teeth for fitting into and turning a chain **2** a single one of these teeth

sprout¹ *v* **1** to grow or send out **2** to send up new growth, as from a seed; bud: *The potatoes have sprouted*

sprout² *n* **1** a new growth on a plant; shoot **2** BRUSSELS SPROUT

spruce¹ *n* any of several kinds of ornamental evergreen coniferous tree found in colder northern parts of the world, or their light soft wood

spruce² *adj* tidy and trim, esp. in appearance; smart — ~**ly** *adv* — ~**ness** *n*

spruce³ *v* **spruced, sprucing** to make (something or oneself) spruce; smarten (something or oneself) up

sprung¹ *past part. of* SPRING

sprung² *adj* supported by springs

spry *adj* **spryer** *or* **sprier, spryest** *or* **spriest** active; quick in movement — ~**ly** *adv* — ~**ness** *n*

spud *n* *esp. spoken* a potato

spume *n* *esp. in literature* white air-filled matter on the top of a liquid; foam; froth .

spun *past tense and past part. of* SPIN

spunk *n* *esp. spoken* courage; pluck — **spunky** *adj*

spur¹ *n* **1** a U-shaped object worn on a rider's boot to direct a horse **2** a force leading to action; incentive **3** a railway track that goes away from a main line **4** a length of high ground coming out from a range of mountains **5 on the spur of the moment** without preparation

spur² *v* **-rr- 1** to prick (a horse) with spurs **2** to urge to (faster) action or effort

spurious *adj* **1** not genuine; not what it claims to be **2** bad in reasoning; wrong — ~**ly** *adv* — ~**ness** *n*

spurn *v* to treat or refuse with angry pride

spurt[1] *n* a short sudden increase of activity; burst

spurt[2] *v* to make a spurt

spurt, spirt[3] *v* to flow or send out suddenly or violently; gush; spout

spurt, spirt[4] *n* a sudden usu. short coming out, as of liquid; surge: *a spurt of steam from the teapot*

sputter *v* **1** to say or speak in confusion; splutter **2** to make repeated spitting sounds: *The engine sputtered and died* — **sputter** *n*

sputum *n* liquid (MUCUS) from the mouth and lungs, esp. coughed up in some diseases

spy[1] *v* **spied, spying** **1** to watch secretly: *spy on one's neighbours* **2** to try to get information secretly **3** to catch sight of

spy[2] *n* **spies** **1** a person employed to find out secret information, usu. from an enemy **2** a person who keeps watch secretly

spyglass *n* a small telescope

sq *abbrev. for:* square

squabble[1] *n* a petty quarrel

squabble[2] *v* **-bled, -bling** to quarrel, esp. noisily

squad *n* **1** a group of soldiers smaller than a platoon **2** a group of people working as a team

squadron *n* **1** a body of soldiers with tanks or (formerly) horses of the same size as a battalion **2** a large group of warships; any of the largest parts of a fleet **3** the main size of a fighting organization in an airforce; any of the parts of a wing

squadron leader *n* an officer of middle rank in the Royal Air Force

squalid *adj* **1** very dirty and uncared-for; filthy **2** having, expressing, or about low moral standards — ~**ly** *adv*

squall[1] *v* to cry noisily — **squall**, ~**er** *n*

squall[2] *n* a sudden violent gust of wind — **squally** *adj*

squalor *n* the condition of being squalid

squander *v* to spend foolishly; waste — ~**er** *n*

square[1] *n* **1** a figure with 4 straight equal sides forming 4 right angles ☞MATHEMATICS **2** a piece of material in this shape **3** a straight-edged often L-shaped tool for testing right angles —see also SETSQUARE, T-SQUARE **4** an open space surrounded by buildings **5** a number equal to another number multiplied by itself: *16 is the square of 4* —see also SQUARE ROOT **6** *esp. spoken* a person who does not know or follow the latest ideas, styles, etc. **7 square one** the very beginning

square[2] *adj* **1** having 4 equal sides and 4 right angles **2** forming a (nearly) right angle: *a square jaw* **3** being a measurement of area equal to that of a square with sides of the stated length **4** being the stated length from a corner in both directions: *The room is 10 feet square* **5** fair; honest: *a square deal* **6** paid and settled: *Our account is all*

square **7** *esp. spoken* old fashioned **8** (in cricket) in a position at (about) right angles to the batsman **9 a square meal** a good satisfying meal — ~**ly** *adv* — ~**ness** *n*

square[3] *v* **squared, squaring** **1** to put into a shape with straight lines and right angles: *square up a wall* **2** to mark squares on; divide into squares **3** to multiply (a number) by itself once **4** to fit to a particular explanation or standard **5** to pay or pay for; settle: *square an account* **6** to cause (totals of points or games won) to be equal —see also SQUARE UP TO

square[4] *also* **squarely**— *adv esp. spoken* **1** fairly; honestly —see also FAIR **and square 2** directly: *He looked her square in the eye*

square dance *n* a dance in which 4 pairs of dancers face each other to form a square

square root *n* the number which when multiplied by itself equals a particular number: *3 is the square root of 9*

square up to *v adv prep* to face with determination

squash[1] *v* **1** to force or be forced into a flat shape; crush **2** to push or fit into a small space; squeeze: *May I squash in next to you?* **3** to force into silence; put down

squash[2] *n* **1** an act or sound of squashing **2** a crowd of people in a small space **3** a game played in a 4-walled court by 2 or 4 people with rackets and a small rubber ball **4** a sweet fruit drink without alcohol

squashy *adj* **-ier, -iest** **1** soft and easy to press or crush **2** (of ground) wet and soft — **squashiness** *n*

squat[1] *v* **-tt-** **1** to sit on a surface with legs drawn fully up or under the body **2** to live in a place without owning it or paying rent; be a squatter

squat[2] *n* **1** a squatting position **2** *sl* an empty building for squatting

squat[3] *adj* ungracefully short or low and thick

squatter *n* **1** a person who lives in an empty building without payment of rent **2** a settler on unowned land who does not pay rent but has rights over it in law (**squatter's rights**) and may sometimes become its owner

squaw *n* an American Indian woman

squawk *v* **1** (esp. of some birds) to make a loud rough-sounding cry **2** *esp. spoken* to complain loudly — **squawk**, ~**er** *n*

squeak[1] *v* **1** to make a high but not loud sound **2** *sl* to tell a secret to avoid punishment; squeal — ~**er** *n*

squeak[2] *n* **1** a short high soft noise: *the squeak of a mouse* **2 a narrow squeak** a narrow escape; near thing —see also BUBBLE AND SQUEAK

squeaky *adj* **-ier, -iest** tending to squeak

squeal[1] *v* **1** to make a long very high sound or cry **2** *sl* to tell criminal secrets; squeak; inform — ~**er** *n*

squeal[2] *n* a high cry or noise: *squeals of delight*

squeamish adj easily shocked; unable to stand unpleasantness — ~ly adv — ~ness n

squeegee a tool for removing or spreading liquid on a surface (as in window washing) with a straight-edged rubber blade and short handle

squeeze¹ v **squeezed, squeezing** 1 to press together, esp. from opposite sides; compress: *squeeze out a wet cloth* 2 to fit by forcing, crowding, or pressing 3 to get or force out (as if) by pressure: *squeeze the juice from an orange* 4 to cause money difficulties to

squeeze² n 1 an act of pressing in from opposite sides or around 2 a small amount squeezed out 3 a condition of crowding or pressing; squash: *There's room for one more, but it'll be a squeeze* 4 a difficult state of affairs caused by short supplies or high costs: *a credit squeeze*

squelch v 1 to force into silence; crush 2 to make a sound of partly liquid material being pressed down (as when stepping through mud) — **squelch** n

squib n a small banger (=toy explosive)

squid n **squid** or **squids** a sea creature with 10 arms at one end of a long body ⊏⫧EVOLUTION

squidgy adj **-ier, -iest** esp. spoken pastelike; soft and wet

squiffy adj **-fier, -fiest** esp. spoken slightly drunk

squiggle n esp. spoken a short wavy line, esp. written or printed — **-gly** adj

squint¹ v 1 to look with almost closed eyes, as at a bright light 2 to have a squint

squint² n 1 a disorder of the eye muscles causing the eyes to look in 2 different directions 2 an act of looking hard, usu. through nearly closed eyes

squire n 1 (esp. formerly) the main landowner in a village or country place 2 (in former times) a knight's armour-bearer 3 esp. spoken (used esp. by market shopkeepers, salesmen, etc., in addressing a man, sometimes not very respectfully)

squirearchy n **-chies** the class of country landowners holding political power, esp. in England until 1832

squirm v to twist the body about, as from discomfort or nervousness; writhe — **squirm** n

squirrel n a small 4-legged animal with a long furry tail that climbs trees and eat nuts —compare RED SQUIRREL

squirt¹ v 1 to force or be forced out in a thin stream 2 to hit or cover with such a stream of liquid: *I was squirted with water*

squirt² n 1 a quick thin stream; jet 2 esp. spoken a silly person, who makes big claims

squirter n a machine or container for squirting out liquid

Sr abbrev. for: Senior

Sri n Indian & Pakistani Mr

SRN abbrev. for: State Registered Nurse

SS abbrev. for: steamship

Ssh interj sh

St abbrev. for: 1 Street 2 Saint

stab¹ n 1 a wound made by a pointed weapon 2 an act of stabbing 3 a sudden painful feeling; pang: *a stab of guilt* 4 an act of trying; go: *have a stab at the job* 5 **a stab in the back** an attack from someone supposed to be a friend; betrayal

stab² v **-bb-** to strike forcefully into with something pointed, esp. with a weapon — ~**ber** n

stabbing adj (esp. of pain) as if made by a knife; sharp and sudden

stability n the quality or state of being stable

stabilize, -ise v **-ized, -izing** to make or become steady, or unchanging; keep in balance — **-ization** n

stabilizer -iser n an apparatus or chemical that stabilizes something

stable¹ n 1 a building for keeping and feeding animals, esp. horses, in 2 a group of racing horses with one owner or trainer

stable² v **-bled, -bling** to put or keep (animals) in a stable

stable³ adj 1 not easily moved or changed; steady 2 purposeful in mind; dependable 3 (of a substance) tending to keep the same chemical or atomic state; not breaking down naturally — opposite **unstable** — **-bly** adv

stable boy also **stable lad**— n **-boys** a man who works in a stable, looks after horses, etc.

stabling n space in stables

staccato adj, adv (of music) (having notes) cut short in playing; disconnected(ly) —compare LEGATO

stack¹ n 1 a usu. orderly pile or heap of things one above another: *a stack of papers* 2 a large pile of grain, grass, etc., for storing outdoors 3 esp. spoken a large amount or number 4 a pipe, or group of pipes in a chimney, for carrying away smoke

stack² v 1 to form a neat pile or put piles of things on or in: *stack (up) books* 2 esp. US spoken to arrange unfairly and dishonestly 3 **a** (of an aircraft) to fly in a pattern with others waiting for a turn to land **b** to make (an aircraft) wait like this

stack up v adv to form into a usu. waiting crowd or line: *Traffic stacked up for miles*

stadium n **-diums** or **-dia** a large usu. unroofed building with rows of seats surrounding a sports field

staff¹ n **staves** or **staffs** 1 a thick stick of the kind carried in the hand when walking, or used as a mark of office 2 a pole for flying a flag on 3 also **stave**— a set of one or more groups of the 5 lines on which music is written ⊏⫧MUSIC 4 **the staff of life** pompous bread

staff² n 1 the group of workers who do the work of an organization 2 members of such a group

staff³ v to supply with staff; provide the workers for

staff sergeant n a sergeant of the highest rank in the British army

stag¹ n **stags** or **stag** a fully grown male deer

stag² *adj* for men only: *a stag party* —compare HEN PARTY

stage¹ *n* 1 a period in a course of events; state reached at a particular time: *a plan in its early stages* 2 the raised floor on which plays are performed in a theatre 3 *usu. literature* the art or life of an actor; work in the theatre 4 a part of a trip: *We travelled by easy stages* 5 a self-contained driving part of a rocket —☞SPACE 6 **set the stage for** to prepare for; make possible

stage² *v* **staged, staging** 1 to perform or arrange for public show; put on 2 to cause to happen, esp. for show or public effect

stagecoach *n* (in former times) a horse-drawn closed vehicle carrying passengers on regular services between fixed places

stage direction *n* a description of scene and characters, with instructions for movements, entrances, exits, etc., in the text of a play

stage-manage *v* **-aged,** to direct, or show for public effect, esp. without taking part

stage manager *n* the person in charge of a theatre stage during a performance

stagestruck *adj* in love with the theatre and esp. with the idea of being an actor

stage whisper *n* 1 an actor's loud whisper supposedly not heard by others on stage 2 a loud whisper intended to be heard by everyone

stagger¹ *v* 1 to have trouble standing or walking; move unsteadily on one's feet 2 to seem almost unbelievable to; shock 3 to arrange not to come at the same place or time: *Working hours are staggered*

stagger² *n* an unsteady movement of a person having trouble walking or standing

staggering *adj* almost unbelievable; astonishing — ~ly *adv*

staging post *n* a place at which regular stops are made on long journeys, esp. by aircraft

stagnant *adj* 1 (as of water) not flowing or moving 2 not developing or growing; inactive — ~ly *adv*

stagnate *v* **-nated, -nating** to become stagnant; stop moving or developing — **-nation** *n*

stagy *adj* **-ier, -iest** as if acted on stage; not natural; theatrical — **stagily** *adv* — **staginess** *n*

staid *adj* settled and unexciting; dull — ~ly *adv* — ~ness *n*

stain¹ *v* to discolour or darken in a way that is lasting

stain² *n* 1 a stained place or spot 2 a chemical for darkening or colouring (esp. wood) 3 *literature* a mark of guilt or shame; taint

stained glass *n* glass coloured in its production and used esp. in church windows

stainless *adj* 1 of a kind not easily broken down chemically (esp. rusted) by air and water: *stainless steel* 2 *literature* without a stain; spotless

stair *n* any of the steps in a set of stairs

staircase also **stairway**— *n* a length of stairs —see also MOVING STAIRCASE

stairs *n* a fixed length of steps connecting floors in a building (often in the phrase **a flight of stairs**) —see also DOWNSTAIRS, UPSTAIRS

stairwell *n* the space going up through the floors of a building where the stairs are

stake¹ *n* 1 a pointed piece of wood, metal, etc., for driving into the ground 2 (in former times) a post to which a person was bound for being killed, esp. by burning 3 something that may be gained or lost; interest 4 **at stake** at risk; dependent on what happens

stake² *v* **staked, staking** 1 to risk (money, one's life, etc.) on a result; bet: *I've staked all my hopes on you* 2 to fasten or strengthen with stakes 3 to mark (an area of ground) with stakes 4 **stake (out) a claim** to make a claim

stakeholder *n* a person chosen to hold the money given by opponents in a race, bet, etc., and give it all to the winner

stakes *n* 1 the amounts risked in a game 2 a horse race in which the prize money is made up equally by the owners of the horses 3 the prize in this or any race, competition, etc.

stalactite *n* a sharp downward-pointing part of a cave roof (like an icicle), formed by water dropping from the roof

stalagmite *n* an upward-pointing part of a cave floor formed by drops from a stalactite and often joining it to form a solid pillar

stale *adj* 1 no longer fresh 2 no longer interesting: *stale jokes* 3 (of a person) worn out; without new ideas — ~ness *n*

stalemate *n* 1 (in the game of chess) a position from which a player can only move into check and back again 2 a condition in which neither side in a quarrel, argument, etc., can get an advantage; deadlock

stalk¹ *v* 1 to hunt (esp. an animal) by following quietly and staying hidden 2 to walk stiffly, proudly, or with long steps — ~er *n*

stalk² *n* 1 the main upright part of a plant 2 a long narrow part of a plant supporting one or more leaves, fruits, or flowers; stem —☞FLOWER

stall¹ *n* 1 an indoor enclosure (as in a barn or stable or inside a room) for one animal or person 2 a table or open-fronted shop in a public place 3 any in a row of seats along the sides in the central part of some churches, esp. the seats for the use of canons

stall² *v* 1 a (of an engine) to stop for lack of power b to cause or force (an engine) to do this 2 to go or put into a stall when flying

stall³ *n* a loss of control in an aircraft caused by trying to climb too steeply too slowly

stall⁴ *v* esp. spoken to delay; intentionally take little or no action

stallholder *n* a person who rents and keeps a market stall

stallion *n* a fully-grown male horse kept for breeding

stalls *n* the seats in the front part of the main level of a theatre

stalwart¹ *adj* strong and unmoving in body,

mind, etc.: *a stalwart supporter* — ~**ly** *adv* — ~**ness** *n*
stalwart² *n* a firm dependable follower, esp. of a political party
stamen *n technical* the male pollen-producing part of a flower ⟹FLOWER
stamina *n* the strength of body or mind to fight tiredness, discouragement, or illness
stammer¹ *v* to speak with pauses and repeated sounds, because of excitement, fear, etc. — compare STUTTER — ~**er** *n* — ~**ingly** *adv*
stammer² *n* the fault of stammering in speech
stamp¹ *v* 1 to strike (esp. a surface) downwards with (the foot) 2 to mark (a pattern, letters, etc.) on (a surface) by pressing 3 to stick a stamp onto 4 to put into a class; categorize; distinguish: *His manners stamped him a military man* 5 to produce by a forceful blow (as by factory machinery): *stamp out a car body*
stamp² *n* 1 also **postage stamp**— a small usu. 4-sided piece of paper sold by post offices for sticking on a piece of mail to be sent 2 a piece of paper like this for sticking to certain official papers to show that tax (**stamp duty**) has been paid 3 an instrument or tool for pressing or printing onto a surface —see also RUBBER STAMP 4 a mark or pattern made by this 5 an act of stamping, as with the foot 6 a lasting result; effect: *The events left their stamp on his mind*
stampede¹ *n* 1 a sudden rush of frightened animals 2 a sudden mad rush
stampede² *v* -**peded**, -**peding** to go or drive in a stampede
stamping ground *n esp. spoken* a favourite very familiar place
stamp out *v adv* to put an end to completely; do away with
stance *n* 1 a way of standing, esp. in various sports 2 a way of thinking; standpoint; attitude
stanchion *n* a strong upright bar used as a support
stand¹ *v* **stood, standing** 1 to support oneself on the feet upright 2 to rise or raise to a position of doing this 3 to be in or take a stated position (of doing this): *Stand clear of the doors, please* 4 to be in height: *He stands 5 feet 10 inches* 5 to be in a particular state of affairs or condition: *How do things stand?* 6 to have a position in a range of values 7 to be in a position to gain or lose 8 to rest in a position, esp. upright 9 to remain unmoving: *machinery standing idle* (unused) 10 to accept; bear; tolerate —see BEAR (USAGE) 11 to be found in a particular form in writing: *Copy it as it stands* 12 to remain true or in force: *My offer still stands* 13 to pay the cost of (something) for (someone else); give as a treat: *Let me stand you a dinner* 14 to make oneself a choice in an election; be a candidate 15 **know how/where one stands (with someone)** to know how someone feels about one 16 **stand a chance** to have a chance 17 **stand on one's own (two) feet** to be able to do without help from others 18

stand something on its head to change or upset violently —see also STAND BY, STAND DOWN, STAND FOR, STAND IN, STAND OUT, STAND UP, STAND UP FOR, **stand EASY** — ~**er** *n*
stand² *n* 1 a strong effort or position of defence: *the army made a stand* 2 a fixed public decision or opinion (often in the phrase **take a stand**) 3 a place or act of standing 4 a raised stage, esp. at a public place 5 a small often outdoor shop or place for showing things; stall 6 a frame, desk, or other piece of furniture for putting something on 7 a place where taxis wait to be hired 8 an open-fronted building at a sports ground with rows of seats or standing space rising behind each other
standard¹ *n* 1 a level of quality that is considered proper or acceptable: *He sets high standards for his pupils* 2 something fixed as a rule for measuring weight, purity, etc. 3 any of various ceremonial flags 4 a pole with an image or shape at the top formerly carried by armies 5 the system of using one particular material (esp. gold) for fixing the value of a country's money
standard² *adj* 1 ordinary; of the usual kind: *standard sizes* 2 generally recognized as correct or acceptable: *It's one of the standard books on the subject* —compare NONSTANDARD
standard form also **scientific notation**— *n technical* a number that is expressed as a number equal to or greater than 1 and less than 10, multiplied by a power of 10. It is a convenient way of representing very large or very small numbers: *0.00001715 is expressed in standard form as 1.7 x 10^{-5}*
standardize, -**ise** *v* -**ized**, -**izing** to cause to fit a single standard; make to be alike in every case — -**ization** *n*
standard lamp *n* a lamp on a tall base which stands on the floor of a room
standard of living also **living standard**— *n* **standards of living** the degree of wealth and comfort in everyday life enjoyed by a person, group, country, etc.
standard time *n* the time calculated as the average according to the sun in a particular area of the world, and to which all clocks in the area are set —compare SUMMER TIME
standby¹ *n* -**bys** 1 a person or thing that is kept ready and can always be called on and used 2 **on standby** ready to be called on at any time
standby² *adj* (of a seat on a passenger aircraft) unbooked, and given out after all reservations have been filled
stand by¹ *v adv* 1 to be present or near 2 to remain inactive when action is needed 3 (esp. in radio and military use) to wait; stay ready
stand by² *v prep* 1 to try to help and support 2 to be faithful or loyal to: *I'll stand by my promise*
stand down *v adv* 1 to yield one's position or chance of election 2 to leave the witness box in court

stand for v prep 1 to be a sign of; represent; mean 2 to allow to go on; accept; put up with
stand-in n 1 a person who takes the part of an actor at certain unimportant or dangerous moments in a film 2 a person who takes the place or job of another for a time
stand in v adv to act as a stand-in
standing¹ adj 1 remaining; kept in use: a standing invitation 2 done from a standing position: a standing start
standing² n 1 rank; position in a system, organization, or list: a student of first-year standing in the university 2 continuance; time during which something has kept on; duration (esp. in such phrases as of long standing) 3 in good standing having kept all the rules
standing order n 1 a rule or order that stays in force and is not repeated for each case 2 an order to pay a fixed amount from a bank account each month, year, etc.
standoff half n FLY HALF
standoffish adj esp. spoken rather unfriendly; coldly formal; aloof — ~ly adv — ~ness n
stand out v adv 1 to have an easily-seen shape, colour, etc. 2 to be much better or the best 3 to be firm in opposition; not yield: I'm standing out against him
standpipe n a pipe connected directly to a water supply and providing water to a central or public place
standpoint n a position from which things are seen and opinions formed; point of view
standstill n a condition of no movement; stop: bring the car to a standstill
stand-up adj 1 (of comedy) depending on telling jokes rather than on acting 2 face-to-face and not yielding: a stand-up fight
stand up v adv 1 to stay in good condition after hard use 2 to be accepted as true: Will the charge stand up in court? 3 esp. spoken to fail to meet (someone) as arranged
stand up for v adv prep to defend against attack; stick up for
stank past tense of STINK
stanza n a group of 4 or more lines in a poem
staple¹ n 1 a small bit of thin wire, usu. bent over to hold sheets of light material (esp. paper) 2 a small U-shaped piece of strong wire for holding other wire in place
staple² v -pled, -pling to fasten with one or more staples
staple³ n 1 a main product that is produced or sold 2 a food that is used and needed in the kitchen all the time 3 something that forms the main or most important part: a staple diet of rice and vegetable 4 the length of one fibre of a kind of thread
stapler n a usu. small hand instrument for driving staples into paper
star¹ n 1 a very hot heavenly body of great size, such as the sun 2 esp. spoken any heavenly body (such as a planet) that appears as a bright point in the sky —see also SHOOTING STAR 3 a 5- or more

pointed figure 4 a piece of metal in this shape for wearing as a mark of office, honour, etc. 5 a heavenly body regarded as determining one's fate 6 a sign used with numbers from usu. 1 to 5 in various systems, to judge quality: a 3 star hotel 7 a famous or very skilful performer 8 an asterisk — ~ry, — ~less adj
star² v -rr- 1 to mark with one or more stars; asterisk 2 to have or appear as a main performer
starboard n the right side of a ship or aircraft as one faces forward —compare PORT ⟷SAIL
starch¹ v to stiffen with starch
starch² n 1 a white tasteless substance (a CARBOHYDRATE) forming an important part of foods such as grain, rice, beans, and potatoes 2 a product made from this, usu. in powder form, for stiffening cloth
star chamber n a court or like body that acts in secret and gives severe judgments
starchy adj -ier, -iest 1 full of, or like, starch 2 esp. spoken stiff and formal; stuffy
star-crossed adj literature unlucky; ill-fated
stardom n the position of a famous performer
stardust n something that is light and fine; a dreamlike magic quality or feeling
stare¹ v stared, staring 1 to look fixedly with wide-open eyes 2 stare one in the face to be so near or so obvious as to be very easily seen
stare² n an act or way of staring; long fixed look: admiring stares
starfish n -fish or fishes a type of flat sea animal with 5 arms forming a star shape ⟷EVOLUTION
stargazer n humour an astrologer
stargazing n (the habit or practice of) thinking about impractical ideas
staring adj noticeable to the eye
stark¹ adj 1 bare or severe in appearance; not made pleasant 2 complete; utter: stark terror — ~ly adv
stark² adv 1 stark naked esp. spoken without any clothes; completely naked 2 stark staring mad humour completely mad
starkers adj humour sl naked
starlet n a young actress who plays small parts in films
starlight n the light given by the stars
starling n a common kind of greenish-black speckled bird that eats harmful insects but damages crops
starlit adj literature bright with many stars
starry-eyed adj full of unreasonable hopes
Stars and Stripes n the flag of the US
start¹ v 1 to begin (a course, journey, etc.); set out (on) 2 to come or bring into being; begin 3 to go or cause to go into (movement or activity); begin: Give it a push to start it 4 to begin doing a job or a piece of work 5 to go from a particular point: Prices start at $5 6 to begin using: Start each page on the 2nd line 7 to make a quick uncontrolled movement, as from sudden surprise;

be startled **8 to start with** also **for a start**— (used before the first in a list of facts, reasons, etc.)

start² n **1** a beginning of activity; condition or place of starting —see also FALSE START **2** a sudden uncontrolled movement, as of surprise: *to wake with a start* **3** an advantage, esp. in a race

starter n **1** a person, horse, car, etc., in a race or match at the start **2** a person who gives the signal for a race to begin **3** a person who begins doing something **4** an instrument for starting a machine, esp. an electric motor for starting a petrol engine **5** esp. spoken something (e.g. the first part of a meal) that is just a beginning or a first step **6** a possibility with any chance of success: *I'm afraid your idea isn't a starter* —compare BEGINNER

starters n esp. spoken the first part of a 3-course meal

starting block n one of a pair of blocks fixed to the ground against which a runner's feet push off at the start of a race

starting gate n a set of gates which open at the same moment to start a horse or dog race

starting price n the odds that are in effect just as a horse or dog race begins

startle v **-led, -ling** to cause to jump; give an unexpected slight shock to — **-lingly** adv

starvation n suffering or death from lack of food

starve v **starved, starving** **1** to die or kill by lack of food **2** to suffer or cause to suffer from great hunger **3** to suffer or cause to suffer from not having some stated thing: *starved for companionship*

starveling n literature a person or animal that is thin and unhealthy from lack of food

stash v to store secretly; hide

state¹ n **1** a condition in which a person or thing is: *the state of one's health* **2** a very anxious or excited condition (esp. in the phrases **in/into a state**) **3** the government of a country **4** the ceremony connected with high-level government: *The Queen drove to the palace in state* **5** any of the smaller parts making up certain nations —see FOLK (USAGE)

state² v **stated, stating** **1** to say or put into words, esp. formally **2** to set in advance; specify: *only to be used on the stated date*

State n the branch of the US government dealing with foreign affairs

stateless adj having no citizenship; not belonging to any country — ~ness n

stately adj **-lier, -liest** formal; grand; dignified — **-liness** n

statement n **1** something that is stated, esp. of a formal kind **2** a list showing amounts of money paid, received, etc., and their total: *a bank statement*

stateroom n a passenger's private room on a ship; cabin

statesman n **-men** a political or government leader — ~ship n

static¹ adj **1** not moving or changing; stationary **2** lacking the effect of action, and usu. uninteresting —opposite **dynamic** **3** of or being electricity not flowing in a current: *static electricity* **4** technical of or concerning objects at rest

static² n radio noise caused by electricity in the air

statics n the branch of mechanics dealing with the forces that produce balance in objects at rest

station¹ n **1** a building on a railway (or bus) line where passengers or goods arrive or leave **2** a building that is a centre for the stated kind of service: *a police station* **3** a company or apparatus that broadcasts on television or radio **4** a place or building for some special scientific work: *a research station* **5** a usu. small military establishment **6** literature one's position in life; social rank: *She married beneath her station*

station² v to put into a certain place; post: *Guards were stationed around the prison*

stationary adj standing still; not moving

stationer n a person or shop that sells stationery

stationery n materials for writing; paper, ink, pencils, etc.

stationmaster n the person in charge of a railway (or bus) station

statistic n a single number in a collection of statistics

statistics n **1** collected numbers which represent facts or measurements —see also VITAL STATISTICS **2** a branch of mathematics dealing with the collection, representation, and analysis of numerical data which may be drawn from many sources — **-tical** adj — **-tically** adv — **-tician** n

statuary n statues as a group — **statuary** adj

statue n a human or animal figure, made in some solid material (such as stone, metal, or plastic)

statuesque adj like a statue in grace, beauty, etc.

statuette n a small statue

stature n **1** a person's natural height **2** quality or position gained by development or proved worth: *a man of stature*

status n **1** a condition that determines one's formal position : *What's your status in this country? Are you a citizen?* **2** high social position; prestige **3** a state of affairs

status quo n Latin the state of things as they are

statute n esp. written a law passed by a law-making body and formally written down

statute book n a real or imaginary written collection of the statutes in force

statutory adj fixed or controlled by statute

staunch¹ v to stop the flow of (esp. blood)

staunch² adj dependably loyal; firm — ~ly adv — ~ness n

stave n **1** any of the pieces of wood fitted edge

to edge to form the sides of a barrel 2 a musical staff

stave in v adv **staved** or **stove, staving in** to break or be broken inwards

stave off v adv **staved, staving off** to keep away; hold at a distance; fend off: *to stave off hunger pains*

staves pl. of STAFF

stay¹ n **stays** a strong rope used for supporting a mast on a ship

stay² v **stayed, staying** 1 to stop and remain 2 to continue to be; remain 3 to live in a place for a while; be a visitor or guest 4 to last out; continue for the whole length of: *stay the course in a mile race* 5 to stop from going on, moving, or having effect; hold back 6 **be here/come to stay** less to become generally accepted 7 **stay put** to remain in one place; not move

stay³ n **stays** 1 a usu. limited time of living in a place 2 a stopping or delay by order of a judge: *The prisoner was given (a) stay of execution*

stay⁴ n **stays** *literature* a person or thing that acts as a support

stay-at-home n esp. spoken a person in the habit of staying at home and not liking to travel

stayer n a horse or person who can keep going to the end of a long race, course, etc.

staying power n the power to keep going to the end; endurance; stamina

stays n a lady's old-fashioned undergarment stiffened by pieces of bone

St Bernard n a Swiss breed of large strong dog used esp. formerly for helping lost mountain travellers

std abbrev. for: standard

STD n subscriber trunk dialling; the telephone system allowing people to dial their own long-distance calls

stead n 1 **in someone's stead** in someone's place 2 **stand one in good stead** to be of good use when needed —see also INSTEAD

steadfast adj 1 faithful; steadily loyal 2 fixed; not moving or movable — ~**ly** adv — ~**ness** n

steady¹ adj **-ier, -iest** 1 firm; not shaking: *a steady hand* 2 moving or developing evenly; regular: *a steady speed* 3 not changing; stable: *a steady job* 4 dependable; serious — **steadily** adv — **steadiness** n

steady² v **-ied, -ying** to make or become steady or settled

steady³ also **steady on**— interj esp. spoken be careful; watch what you're doing

steady state theory n the idea that things in space have always existed and always been moving further apart as new atoms come into being — compare BIG BANG THEORY

steak n 1 a flat piece of beef, or meat from a stated animal or fish, cut from the fleshy part and in a direction across the animal 2 beef of a less good quality, usu. used in small pieces in pies or stews

steal v **stole, stolen, stealing** 1 to take (what

belongs to another) without any right 2 to take quickly, without permission: *steal a kiss* 3 to move secretly or quietly —see also **steal a** MARCH, **steal the** SCENE, **steal the** SHOW   USAGE One steals things. One robs people (of things): *I've been robbed! He robbed me of my watch! He stole my watch!*

stealth n the action of going or acting secretly or unseen (esp. in the phrase **by stealth**) — ~**y** adj — ~**ily** adv

steam¹ n 1 water in the state of a gas produced by boiling 2 the mist formed by water becoming cool 3 feelings and power considered as trapped by self-control (esp. in the phrases **let off/work off steam**) 4 **get up steam** to begin to move with power and speed 5 **under one's/its own steam** by one's/its own power or effort

steam² v 1 to give off steam, esp. when very hot 2 to travel by steam power: *The ship steamed into the harbour* 3 to cook by allowing steam to heat 4 to use steam on, esp. for unsticking or softening —see also STEAM UP

steam³ adj using steam under pressure to produce power or heat ⊚

steamer n 1 a vessel for holding food for cooking with steam 2 a large non-naval ship driven by steam power

steam iron n an electric iron that holds water and makes steam which goes into the clothes for easier pressing

steamroller¹ n a heavy usu. steam-powered machine for driving over and flattening road surfaces

steamroller² v esp. spoken to crush or force using very great power or pressure

steam up v adv 1 to cover or be covered with steam 2 to make angry or excited: *He got very steamed up about it*

steed n usu. poetic a horse, esp. for riding

steel¹ n 1 iron in a hard strong form containing some carbon and sometimes other metals 2 great strength

steel² v to make hard or determined: *He steeled himself to say he was sorry*

steel band n a band playing drums cut from metal oil barrels to sound particular notes

steel wool n WIRE WOOL

steelworks n steelworks a factory where steel is made

steely adj **-ier, -iest** like steel, esp. in colour or hardness

steep¹ adj 1 rising or falling quickly; precipitous: *steep rise in prices* 2 esp. spoken (of a demand or esp. a price) unreasonable; too much — ~**ly** adv — ~**ness** n

steep² v 1 to stay, or leave, in a liquid, for softening, cleaning, bringing out a taste, etc.; soak 2 **steeped in** thoroughly filled or familiar with

steepen v to make or become steeper

steeple n a church tower with a top part rising to a usu. high sharp point ⌐CATHEDRAL

steeplechase n 1 a 3000-metre footrace with 35 high and long jumps to be made during the

The steam engine

arch head

beam

water supply to top of piston

piston

cylinder

injection watercock

mine pump rod

steam valve

boiler

fire

injection water pump

ash

In a steam engine, steam produced by the boiler expands, so pushing the piston. The early Newcomen engine (above) condensed the steam in the cylinder and obtained a vacuum, causing the piston to return. In the later double-acting engine (below), the steam is applied alternately to either side of a piston, driving it back and forth.

Double-acting steam engine

steam from boiler

crankshaft valve

flywheel

piston

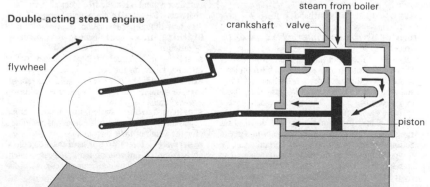

run 2 a horserace over a course of more than 2 miles with about 15 various jumps to be made —compare FLAT RACING

steeplejack *n* a person whose work is building or repairing towers, tall chimneys, steeples, etc.

steer¹ *n* a male animal of the cattle family with its sexual organs removed —compare OX, BULLOCK

steer² *v* 1 to direct the course of (as a ship or vehicle) 2 to go in or hold to (a course); follow (a way) 3 to allow being directed: *Does your car steer well?* 4 **steer clear (of)** to keep away from; avoid

steerage *n* (esp. in former times) the part of a passenger ship for those with the cheapest tickets

steering wheel *n* the wheel which controls a car or ship's movement

steersman *n* -men a person who steers, esp. a helmsman

stegosaurus *n* a kind of large dinosaur with heavy armour

stein *n* a tall thick mug for beer

stele *n* -lae a stone standing up straight, with writing or pictures cut into it, esp. an ancient Greek gravestone

stellar *adj technical* of or concerning the stars

stem¹ *n* 1 the central part of a plant above the ground, or the smaller part which supports leaf or flower 2 any narrow upright part which supports another: *the stem of a wine glass* 3 the narrow part of a tobacco pipe, through which smoke is drawn 4 the part of a word which remains the same, even when combining with different endings 5 a large block of wood set upright in the bow of a ship

stem² *v* -mm- 1 to stop (the flow of): *to stem the blood* 2 to prevent; stand against: *to stem the tide of public opinion*

stem from *v prep* to have as origin

stench *n esp. written* a (strong) bad smell

stencil¹ *n* 1 a piece of material, esp. waxed paper or metal, in which patterns or letters have been cut 2 the pattern or letters made by putting paint or ink through the spaces in this

stencil² *v* -ll- to make (a copy of) by using a stencil

stenography *n* shorthand writing — -pher *n*

stentorian *adj esp. written or literature* (of the voice) very loud; powerful

step¹ *n* 1 the act of putting one foot in front of the other to move along 2 the sound this makes 3 a the distance between the feet when stepping b a short distance: *It's just a step from here* —compare PACE 4 a flat edge, esp. in a set of surfaces each higher than the other, on which the foot is placed for climbing up and down; stair, rung of a ladder, etc. 5 an act, esp. in a set of actions, which should produce a certain result 6 a type of movement of the feet in dancing 7 in **step a** (esp. of soldiers) stepping with the left and right leg at the same time as one or more others

b (of a person or behaviour) in accordance or agreement with others 8 **keep step** to march together in step 9 **take steps (to do something)** to take action 10 **watch one's step** to behave or act carefully

step² *v* -pp- 1 to put one foot down usu. in front of the other, in order to move along 2 to walk 3 to bring the foot down (on); less tread 4 **step on it** *esp. spoken* to go faster 5 **step out of line** to act differently from others or from what is expected

stepbrother *n* a male whose father or mother has married one's mother or father ☞FAMILY

stepchild *n* -children the child of one's husband/wife by an earlier marriage; a **stepson** or **stepdaughter** ☞FAMILY

step down *also* **step aside**— *v adv* to give one's place to another person

stepladder *n* a short ladder with flat steps, which can be folded together for storing

stepparent *n* the person to whom one's father or mother has been remarried; one's **stepmother** or **stepfather** ☞FAMILY

steppe *n* a large area of land without trees, esp. that belonging to Russia and covering parts of Europe and Asia

stepping-stone *n* 1 one of a row of large stones with a level top, which one walks on to cross a river or stream 2 a way of improvement or getting ahead

steps *n* 1 a number of steps, usu. outside and made of stone (often in the phrase **a flight of steps**) —compare STAIR, STAIRCASE 2 a stepladder

stepsister *n* a female whose father or mother has married one's mother or father ☞FAMILY

stereo *also* **stereo set**— *n* -os a record player or radio which gives out sound by means of 2 loudspeakers — **stereo(phonic)** *adj*

stereoscope *n* an apparatus which shows a scene as if real, with distance, depth, etc., by showing a separate picture to each eye — -pic *adj*

stereotype¹ *n* a fixed pattern which is believed to represent a type of person or event

stereotype² *v* -typed, -typing to fix in one form or type

sterile *adj* 1 (of living things) which cannot produce young 2 made free from all germs and bacteria 3 (of land) not producing crops 4 lacking new thought, imagination, etc. — -ility *n*

sterilize, -ise *v* -ized, -izing to make sterile — -ization *n*

sterling¹ *n technical* the type of money used in Britain, based on the pound (£) ☞MONEY

sterling² *adj* 1 *technical* (of gold and esp. silver) of standard value 2 of good true qualities: *a sterling helper*

sterling area *n* (esp. in former times) a group of countries who used British money as a standard for the value of their own money

stern¹ *adj* 1 very firm or hard towards others' behaviour 2 difficult or hard to bear: *a stern punishment* 3 showing firmness, esp. with disapproval — ~ly *adv* — ~ness *n*

stern² *n* the back end of a ship —compare BOW ⟜⎺SAIL

sternum *n* -nums *or* -na *medical* the breast-bone

steroid *n, adj* (of) a type of substance (HORMONE) produced in the body, related to fats, and controlling many important processes (such as REPRODUCTION and INFLAMMATION)

stertorous *adj literature or humour* making a noisy sound while breathing —compare SNORE — ~ly *adv*

stet *interj* (used as a note for asking a printer not to remove or change writing which has been crossed out) let it stay or remain

stethoscope *n* a medical instrument with 2 pipelike parts to be fitted into the doctor's ears and another to be placed on someone's chest, so that the doctor may hear the sounds of the heartbeat and lungs

stetson *n* a type of hat, with a wide brim, worn esp. by cowboys

stevedore *n* a person whose job is loading and unloading ships

stew¹ *n* **1** a meal with meat, vegetables, etc., cooked together in liquid **2** *esp. spoken* a confused anxious state of mind (in the phrase **in a stew**)

stew² *v* to cook (something) slowly and gently in liquid in a closed vessel

steward¹ *n* **1** a man who controls supplies of food in a place such as a club or college **2** one of a number of men who serve passengers on a ship or plane **3** one of a number of men who arrange a public amusement, such as a horse race, a meeting, etc. **4** a man who is employed to look after a house and lands, such as a farm

steward² *v* to act as a steward

stewardess *n* a woman who serves passengers on a plane

stewed *adj* **1** (of tea) kept too long before pouring, thus being strong-tasting **2** *esp. spoken* drunk

stick¹ *n* **1** a small thin piece of wood **2** a thin rod of wood used for supporting the body when walking; walking stick **3** a thin rod of any material: *a stick of rock* (=a hard kind of sweet) **4** an uninteresting person (in the phrases **dull/dry old stick**) **5** **get the wrong end of the stick** to misunderstand

stick² *v* **stuck, sticking 1** to push (in) (esp. a pointed object): *to stick pins into the material* **2** to fix or be fixed with a sticky substance **3** to remain or become fixed **4** *esp. spoken* to put: *Stick it on the table* **5** *esp. spoken* to bear (a person or activity) **6 stick in one's throat a** to be hard to accept **b** to be hard to say —see also STICK AROUND, STICK AT, STICK BY, STICK OUT, STICK OUT FOR, STICK TOGETHER, STICK UP, STICK UP FOR, STICK WITH, STUCK

stick around *v adv esp. spoken* to stay or wait in a place

stick at *v prep* to continue to work hard at

stick by *v prep esp. spoken* to continue to support: *to stick by a friend*

sticker *n* **1** a person or thing which sticks **2** a small label with sticky material on the back and a picture or message on the front

sticking plaster also **plaster**— *n* (a thin band of) material that can be stuck to the skin to protect small wounds

stick-in-the-mud *n esp. spoken* a person who will not change or accept new things

stickleback *n* any of several types of small fierce fish with a number of prickles on their backs

stickler *n* a person who has a strong determination to get a particular quality from others

stick-on *adj* with a sticky substance on the back by which to be fixed

stick out *v adv* **1** to position or be positioned beyond the rest; reach or cause to reach further than usual **2** *esp. spoken* to be clearly seen **3** to continue to the end (of something difficult)

stick out for *v adv prep* to continue action to get (what one asked for)

sticks *n* a country area far from the modern life

stick together *v adv esp. spoken* to stay loyal to each other

stick up *v adv* **1** to rob or threaten with a gun **2** to raise (the hands) when threatened with a gun (esp. in the phrase **stick 'em up**) — **stick-up** *n*

stick up for *v adv prep* to defend by words or actions

stick with *v prep* to stay loyal to

sticky *adj* -ier, -iest **1** made of or containing material which can stick to or around anything else **2** *esp. spoken* difficult: awkward **3 (come to/meet) a sticky end** *esp. spoken* at last to suffer ruin, dishonour, death, etc. — **stickily** *adv* — **stickiness** *n*

sticky wicket *n* **1** (in cricket) a wicket that has been made wet, and is then being quickly dried by the hot sun, and is therefore very difficult to play on **2 be/bat on a sticky wicket** *esp. spoken* to be in a state of affairs that is or may become difficult

stiff¹ *adj* **1** not easily bent **2** painful when moving or moved: *stiff muscles* **3** firm: *Beat the eggs until stiff* **4** formal; not friendly **5** (of a drink of strong alcohol) large and without water or other liquid added **6** difficult to do: *a stiff job* **7** *esp. spoken* too much to accept; unusual in degree —see also THICK, STEEP — ~ly *adv* — ~ness *n*

stiff² *adv* **1 bore someone stiff** to make someone very tired with dull talk **2 scare someone stiff** to make someone very afraid

stiff³ *n sl* a dead body

stiffen *v* **1** to make or become hard or firm **2** to make or become stiff and painful **3** to become anxious or less friendly: *He stiffened at her rude remarks*

stiffener *n* a thing which stiffens

stiffening _n_ material which stiffens esp. clothing

stiff-necked _adj_ proudly obstinate

stifle _v_ **-fled, -fling** 1 to stop or cause to stop breathing properly 2 to prevent from happening or continuing: _Their ideas were stifled_

stigma _n_ 1 a sign of shame; feeling of being ashamed 2 the top of the centre part of a flower which receives pollen ⎯◢FLOWER

stigmatize, -tise _v_ **-tized, -tizing** to mark out by a sign of shame

stile _n_ an arrangement of (usu. 2) high steps which must be climbed to cross a fence or wall outdoors

stiletto _n_ **-tos** a knife used as a weapon, with a long thin sharp point; small dagger

stiletto heel _n_ a high thin heel of a shoe for women

still¹ _adj_ 1 **a** not moving **b** without wind 2 quiet or silent 3 (of drinks) not containing gas —compare SPARKLE — ~ness _n_

still² _v_ 1 to make quiet or calm: _The food stilled the baby's cries_ 2 to prevent from moving

still³ _adv_ 1 (even) up to and at the present time/the time referred to: _Does this dress still fit you?_ 2 even so; nevertheless 3 even; yet: _He gave still another reason_

still⁴ _n_ 1 quietness or calm: _the still of the evening_ 2 a photograph printed from one frame of a cinema film

still⁵ _n_ an apparatus for making alcohol

still birth _n_ a child born dead —compare ABORTION, MISCARRIAGE

stillborn _adj_ born dead

still life _n_ **-lifes** a (type of) painting, esp. of flowers and fruit

stilt _n_ one of a pair of poles, with foot-rests for walking raised above the ground

stilted _adj_ (of a style of writing or speaking) very formal and unnatural — ~ly _adv_

Stilton _n_ a type of thick white cheese with greenish marks in it

stimulant _n_ 1 a drug which gives the body more power to be active for a time 2 anything which encourages further or greater activity

stimulate _v_ **-lated, -lating** 1 to increase in activity: _Exercise is stimulating_ 2 to encourage or excite — **-lation** _n_

stimulus _n_ **-li** something which is the cause of activity

sting¹ _v_ **stung, stinging** 1 to cause sharp pain to, or to feel such a pain 2 (of an insect) to prick with a sting 3 _sl_ to take too much money from: _They stung him for 1000 dollars_

sting² _n_ 1 a sharp organ used as a weapon by some animals, often poisonous 2 a pain-producing substance contained in hairs on a plant's surface 3 a sharp pain, wound, or mark caused by a plant or animal 4 a strong burning pain, usu. on the outer skin 5 an ability to cause pain or hurt feelings: _the sting of her tongue_

stingray _n_ **-rays** a type of large seafish with a tail which can be used as a weapon

stingy _adj_ **-gier, -giest** _esp. spoken_ unwilling to give — **-gily** _adv_ — **-giness** _n_

stink¹ _v_ **stank, stunk, stinking** 1 to give a strong bad smell 2 _sl_ to be very unpleasant or disliked: _Your plan stinks_

stink² _n_ 1 a strong unpleasant smell 2 **raise a stink** _esp. spoken_ to make trouble by complaining

stinking¹ _adj_ 1 having a very bad smell 2 _sl_ very unpleasant

stinking² _adv_ very (in the phrase **stinking rich**)

stint¹ _v_ to give too small an amount (of): _Don't stint yourself; take all you want_

stint² _n_ 1 a limit (in the phrase **without stint**) 2 a fixed amount, esp. of work

stipend _n_ money paid for professional work, esp. to a priest — ~**iary** _adj_

stipple _v_ **-pled, -pling** to draw or paint (a picture, pattern, etc.) on by using dots to make areas of colour, darkness, etc., instead of lines

stipulate _v_ **-lated, -lating** to demand as a condition — **-ation** _n_

stir¹ _v_ **-rr-** 1 to move around and mix (esp. something mainly liquid) by means of an object such as a spoon 2 to put in by such a movement 3 to move from a position: _She stirred in her sleep_ 4 _esp. spoken_ to cause oneself to move or wake 5 to excite (the feelings) (of): _He was stirred by stories of battle_ 6 _sl_ to cause trouble between others, esp. by telling stories —see also STIRRER

stir² _n_ 1 an act of stirring 2 a movement

stir³ _n_ **in stir** _sl_ in prison

stirrer _n_ _sl_ a person who causes trouble between others

stirring _adj_ which excites the feelings — ~ly _adv_

stirrup _n_ 1 a metal piece for the rider's foot to go in, hanging from the sides of a horse's saddle ⎯◢HORSE 2 a small bone inside the ear

stirrup cup _n_ a cupful of strong drink, usu. wine, given to someone setting out on a journey, esp. (originally) a rider

stitch¹ _n_ 1 a movement of a needle and thread into cloth at one point and out at another in sewing 2 a turn of the wool round the needle in knitting: _to drop a stitch_ 3 the piece of thread or wool seen in place after the completion of such a movement 4 a particular style of sewing or knitting and the effect which it gives 5 _technical_ a piece of thread which sews the edges of a wound together 6 a sharp pain in the side, esp. caused by running 7 _esp. spoken_ clothes (esp. in the phrases **haven't got a stitch, not a stitch on**) 8 **in stitches** laughing helplessly

stitch² _v_ to sew; put stitches on to fasten together or for ornament

stoat _n_ a type of small brown furry animal that eats other animals —compare ERMINE

stock¹ _n_ 1 a supply (of something) for use 2 goods for sale 3 a piece of wood used as a support or handle, as for a gun or tool 4 **a** a plant from which cuttings are grown **b** a stem onto which another plant is grafted **5** a group of animals used for breeding **6** farm animals, usu. cattle; livestock **7** a family line, esp. of the stated character **8** money lent to a government at a fixed rate of interest **9** the money (CAPITAL) owned by a company, divided into shares **10** a type of garden flower with a sweet smell **11** a liquid made from the juices of meat, bones, etc., used in cooking **12** (in former times) a stiff cloth worn by men round the neck of a shirt **13 take stock (of)** to consider the state of things so as to take a decision —compare STOCKTAKING; see also LAUGH-INGSTOCK, LOCK, **stock, and barrel**

stock² v **1** to keep supplies of **2** to supply

stock³ adj **1** commonly used, esp. without much meaning **2** kept in stock, esp. because of a standard or average type: *stock sizes*

stockade n a wall or fence of stakes for defence

stockbreeder n a farmer who breeds cattle

stockbroker n a man whose job is buying and selling stocks and shares

stockcar n a car that has had changes made to it in order to take part in rough car races — compare HOT ROD

stock cube n a solid lump of dried material which when mixed with water forms a stock for cooking

Stock Exchange also **stock market—** n **1** the place where stocks and shares are bought and sold **2** the business of doing this

stockholder n US a shareholder

stocking n a garment for a woman's foot and leg which is shaped to fit closely

stock-in-trade n **1** things used in carrying on a business **2** ways or actions habitually used: *Silly jokes are his stock-in-trade*

stockist n a person or firm that keeps certain goods for sale

stockman n -men a man employed to look after farm animals

stockpile v, n -piled, -piling (to keep adding to) a store of (materials), esp. in case of future need

stockroom n a store room, esp. for goods in a shop

stocks n **1** a wooden frame in which criminals were in former times imprisoned by the feet **2** a framework in which a ship is held while being built (esp. in the phrase **on the stocks**)

stock-still adv without the slightest movement

stocktaking n **1** the making of a list of goods held in a business **2** the act of considering the state of one's affairs

stocky adj -ier, -iest thick, short, and strong (in body) — **stockily** adv — **stockiness** n

stockyard n a place where cattle or sheep are kept before being taken away

stodge n esp. spoken **1** food that is heavy and uninteresting **2** something difficult to learn, read, etc.

stodgy adj -ier, -iest esp. spoken **1** (of food)

heavy and uninteresting **2** dull; lacking excitement — **stodginess** n

stoic n a person who remains calm when faced with something unpleasant —compare EPICUREAN, HEDONIST — **~al**, **stoic** adj — **~ally** adv — **~ism** n

stoke v stoked, stoking to fill (an enclosed fire) with fuel: *stoke up the fire*

stoker a person or machine that puts fuel into a furnace

STOL n short take-off and landing

stole¹ n a long straight piece of material worn on the shoulders by women

stole² past tense of STEAL

stolen past part. of STEAL

stolid adj showing no excitement when strong feelings might be expected ⚠ SOLID — **~ly** adv — **~ness**, **~ity** n

stomach¹ n **1** a baglike organ in the body where food is digested after being eaten ☞DIGESTION **2** esp. spoken the front part of the body below the chest; abdomen **3 a** a desire to eat **b** liking; acceptance

stomach² v to accept without displeasure: *I can't stomach his jokes*

stomachache n (a) pain in the abdomen

stomach pump n an apparatus with a tube for drawing out the contents of the stomach, as after taking poison

stomp v esp. spoken to walk or dance with a heavy step

stone¹ n **1** a piece of rock, either of natural shape or cut out specially for building **2** solid mineral material; (a type of) rock **3** a single hard seed inside some fruits, such as the cherry, plum, and peach **4** a piece of hard material formed in an organ of the body, esp. the bladder or kidney —see also GALLSTONE **5** a gravestone —see also HAILSTONE, MILLSTONE, STEPPING-STONE

stone² v stoned, stoning **1** to throw stones at **2** to take the seeds or stones out of (usu. dried fruit)

stone³ n stone or stones (a measure of weight equal to) 14 pounds (lbs)

Stone Age n the earliest known time in the history of man, when only stone was used for making tools, weapons, etc. —compare IRON AGE

stoned adj sl **1** very drunk **2** excited by the use of drugs

stonemason also **mason—** n a person whose job is cutting stone into shape for building

stone's throw n a short distance

stoneware n heavy pottery made from clay that contains flint

stonework n the parts of a building made of stone

stony adj -ier, -iest **1** containing or covered with stones **2** cruel; hard: *a stony stare* — **stonily** adv

stony broke adj sl having no money at all

stood past tense and past part. of STAND

stooge¹ n **1** a person who acts as partner in a

of a race
ng/home
7 sl a
n which
n 2 an
one of a
her

comedy act and is made to seem silly **2** a person who does what another person wants

stooge² v **stooged, stooging** to be a stooge on stage

stool n **1** a seat without a supporting part for the back or arms **2** esp. written & technical a piece of solid waste matter passed from the body

stoolpigeon n sl a person, such as a criminal, who helps the police to trap another

stoop¹ v **1** to bend (the head and shoulders) forwards and down **2** to stand habitually with the head and shoulders bent over **3** to allow oneself (to do something), so falling to a low standard of behaviour

stoop² n a habitual position with the shoulders bent or rounded

stop¹ v **-pp- 1** to cease or cause to cease moving or continuing an activity **2** to prevent: You can't stop me **3** to end **4** to pause **5** to remain: Stop here a moment **6** to block **7** to prevent from being given or paid: to stop a cheque **8** (in music) to use the fingers on (holes or strings) in order to change the note played by an instrument — ~**pable** adj

stop² n **1** the act of stopping or state of being stopped **2** a place on a road where buses or other public vehicles stop for passengers **3** a dot as a mark of punctuation, esp. a full stop **4** a movable part of a musical instrument used for changing the pitch **5** a set of pipes on an organ **6** the part of a camera which moves to control the amount of light entering —compare APERTURE **7 pull all the stops out** to do everything possible to complete an action

stopcock also **turncock**— n a valve or tap which controls the flow of water in a pipe

stopgap n something or someone that fills a need for a time

stop-go adj, n (of or being) a time in which periods of a large supply of money and rising prices (INFLATION) and of a smaller supply of money and steady prices (DEFLATION) quickly follow each other

stop off v adv to make a short visit to a place while making a journey somewhere else

stopover n a short stay between parts of a journey, as on a long plane journey

stoppage n **1** a blocked state which stops movement, as in a waste pipe or a pipe in the body **2** the state of being held back **3** the act of stopping work, as in a strike

stopper n an object which fits in and closes the opening to esp. a bottle or jar

stop press n the last news added to a newspaper after the main part has been printed

stopwatch n a watch which can be stopped and started at any time, so that the time taken by an event or action can be measured exactly

storage n **1** the act of storing **2** a place for storing goods (esp. in the phrase **in storage**) —see also COLD STORAGE

store¹ v **stored, storing 1** to make up and keep a supply of **2** to keep in a warehouse **3** to put away for future use: to store one's winter clothes

store² n **1** a supply for future use **2** a place for keeping things **3** a warehouse **4** a large shop —see also CHAIN STORE, STORES **5** a large number or amount: a store of jokes **6 in store a** kept ready (for future use) **b** about to happen **7 set store by** to feel to be of importance

storehouse n **1** a place or person full of information **2** a warehouse

storeroom n a room where goods are kept till needed

stores n **1** military or naval apparatus, goods, and food **2** the building, room, etc., (in an army camp, ship, etc.) where these are kept **3** a shop in which many different types of goods are sold

storey n **-reys** a floor or level in a building

stork n a type of large white bird, with a long beak, neck, and legs

storm¹ n **1** a rough weather condition with wind, rain, and often lightning **2** a sudden violent show of feeling: a storm of tears **3** a loud noise **4 take by storm a** to conquer by a sudden violent attack **b** to win success from (those who watch a performance) —see also **storm in a** TEACUP

storm² v **1** to attack with sudden violence: to storm the city **2** to blow violently **3** to show or express violent anger

stormbound adj prevented from travelling by stormy weather

storm cloud n a sign of something dangerous: the storm clouds of war

storm lantern n a lamp for carrying in the hand, in which the light is covered with glass so that wind cannot blow it out

storm trooper n (in Germany before and during World War 2) a soldier in a private political army, known for cruelty and violence

stormy adj **-ier, -iest 1** having one or more storms: stormy weather **2** showing noisy expressions of feeling — **stormily** adv

stormy petrel also **storm petrel**— n a type of small black and white seabird of the north Atlantic Ocean and the Mediterranean Sea

story n **-ries 1** an account of events, real or imagined ⬦LITERATURE **2** esp. spoken (used by and to children) a lie (esp. in the phrase **to tell stories**) —see also TALL STORY **3** the plot of a book, film, play, etc. —see also STORY LINE **4** (material for) an article in a newspaper, magazine, etc. **5 the same old story** the usual excuse or difficulty

storybook adj as perfectly happy as in a fairy story for children: a storybook romance

story line n the type of plot in a film, book, or play

storyteller n **1** a person who is or was telling a story, esp. to children **2** a person, esp. a child, who tells lies

stout¹ adj **1** rather fat and heavy **2** strong; thick; too solid to break **3** brave; determined: a

musi
letters
or type
to dev
strain
the wh
efforts
body)
hold c

stout supporter of the team — ~**ly** *adv* —
~**ness** *n*

stout² *n* a kind of strong dark beer

stouthearted *adj* *esp. in literature* brave; of a firm character

stove¹ *n* an enclosed apparatus for cooking or heating which works by burning coal, oil, gas, etc., or by electricity —see also COOKER, HEATER, FIRE

stove² *past tense and past part. of* STAVE

stow *v* to put away or pack, esp. for some time

stowage *n* 1 the act of stowing goods 2 the space allowed for keeping goods, as on a ship

stow away *v adv* to hide oneself on a ship or plane in order to make a free journey — **stowaway** *n*

straddle *v* -dled, -dling 1 to sit, stand, or move with the legs out at the sides (of): *to straddle a horse* 2 to be, land, etc., on either side of (something), rather than the middle: *The shots straddled the target*

strafe *v* **strafed, strafing** to attack with heavy gunfire from a low-flying aircraft

straggle *v* -gled, -gling 1 to move or spread untidily, without ordered shape 2 to fall (back) away from the main group while walking or marching — **-gler** *n*

straggly *adj* -glier, -gliest growing or lying out in an untidy shape: *straggly hair*

straight¹ *adj* 1 not bent or curved: *A straight line is the shortest distance between 2 points* 2 level or upright 3 tidy; neat 4 honest; truthful — opposite **bent** 5 correct (esp. in the phrases **set/put someone/the record straight**) 6 (of alcohol) without added water —compare NEAT 7 (in the theatre) serious; of the established kind 8 (of the face) not laughing; with a serious expression △ STRAIT — ~**ness** *n*

straight² *adv* 1 in a straight line 2 directly: *go straight home* 3 **go straight** to leave a life of crime

straight³ *n* a straight part or place, esp. on a racetrack

straightaway also (*esp. spoken*) **straight off**—*adv* at once

straighten *v* to make or become straight, level, or tidy

straightforward *adj* 1 honest, without hidden meanings 2 expressed or understood in a direct way, without difficulties — ~**ly** *adv*

straight up *adv* *sl* (used esp. in asking or replying to a question) honestly; truly

strain¹ *n* 1 esp. in literature a tune; notes of __ 2 a manner or style of using words: *Her _ written in a happy strain* 3 a breed _nt or animal 4 a quality which tends _. one passed down a family __ _tretch or pull tightly 2 to use __ *one's ears* 3 to make great __ weaken (a part of the __ to press against or __ *child to her* 6 to

separate (a liquid and solid) by pouring through a narrow space, esp. the fine holes in a strainer

strain³ *n* 1 a the condition of being strained b the force causing this 2 a state of tension: *She's under a lot of strain* 3 damage to a part of the body caused by too great effort and often stretching of muscles —compare SPRAIN

strained *adj* 1 not natural in behaviour; unfriendly 2 forced beyond acceptable limits 3 nervous or tired

strainer *n* an instrument for separating solids from liquids, with small spaces in the material it is made of, such as a sieve made of fine wire, a colander, or a filter

strait¹ *adj* *esp. Bible* narrow or difficult △ STRAIGHT

strait² *n* a narrow passage of water between land and (esp.) connecting 2 seas —see also STRAITS

straitened *adj* lacking money (usu. in the phrase **in straitened circumstances**)

straitjacket *n* 1 a garment which holds the arms down, preventing the wearer, esp. a madman, from violent movement 2 something which prevents free development: *the straitjacket of poverty*

straitlaced *adj* *offensive* having very firm ideas about morals, esp. the belief that many things must not be done

straits *n* a difficult position in life such as illness or lack of money

strand¹ *v* *technical* to cause (a ship) to run onto the shore

strand² *n* a single piece or thread (of a material made up of many threads, wires, etc.)

stranded *adj* in a helpless position; unable to get away

strange *adj* 1 hard to accept or understand; surprising 2 not known or experienced before; unfamiliar 3 *old use* foreign: *a traveller in a strange country* — ~**ly** *adv* — ~**ness** *n*

stranger *n* 1 a person who is unfamiliar 2 a person in a new or unfamiliar place

strangle *v* -gled, -gling to kill by pressing on the throat

stranglehold *n* 1 a strong hold round the neck 2 a strong control which prevents action

strangulation *n* strangling or being strangled

strap¹ *n* 1 a strong narrow band of material, such as leather, used as a fastening 2 the giving of punishment by beating with a thick narrow piece of leather

strap² *v* -pp- 1 to fasten in place with one or more straps 2 to beat with a strap 3 to bind (a part of the body that has been hurt, esp. a limb) with bandages

straphanging *n* the position in travelling on public vehicles in which one stands and holds a strap which hangs from the roof — **straphanger** *n*

strapping *adj* big and strong

stratagem *n* a trick or plan to deceive an enemy or to gain an advantage

strategy *n* -gies **1** the art of planning movements of armies or forces in war —compare TACTICS **2** a particular plan for winning success in a particular activity, as in war, a game, a competition, or for personal advantage — **-gic** *adj* — **-gically** *adv* — **-gist** *n*

stratify *v* -fied, -fying to arrange or become arranged in separate levels or strata — **-fication** *n*

stratosphere *n* the outer part of the air which surrounds the earth, starting at about 6 miles (10 kilometres) above the earth —compare ATMOSPHERE

stratum *n* -ta **1** a band of rock of a certain kind, esp. with other types above and below it in the ground **2** a level of earth, such as one where remains of an ancient civilization are found by digging **3** a level of people in society; social class

straw *n* **1** dried stems of grain plants, such as wheat, used for animals to sleep on, for making baskets, mats, etc. **2 a** one stem of wheat, rice, etc. **b** a thin tube of paper or plastic for sucking up liquid **3 clutch at straws** to attempt to save oneself from trouble by means which cannot succeed

strawberry *n* -ries **1** a type of plant which grows near the ground, or its juicy fruit, eaten fresh and in jam **2** the colour of this fruit, dark pink to red

strawberry mark *n* a reddish area of skin, present from birth

straw-coloured *adj* light yellow

straw poll also **straw vote**— *n* an unofficial examination of opinions before any votes, esp. before an election, to see what the result is likely to be

stray¹ *v* strayed, straying **1** to wander away **2** (of thoughts or conversation) to move away from the subject

stray² *n* strays **1** an animal lost from its home **2** a child without a home (in the phrase **waifs and strays**)

stray³ *adj* **1** lost; separated from home or others of the kind **2** met by chance; scattered: *hit by a stray shot*

streak¹ *n* **1** a thin line or band, different from what surrounds it **2** a quality which sometimes appears among different qualities of character

streak² *v* **1** to move very fast **2** to cover with streaks

streaker *n* (in the 1970's) a person who runs swiftly across a public place with no clothes on, except possibly on the feet or head

streaky *adj* -ier, -iest marked with streaks

stream¹ *n* **1** a natural flow of water, usu. smaller than a river **2** anything flowing or moving on continuously: *a stream of people* **3** (the direction of) a current of water: *float with the stream* —see also DOWNSTREAM, UPSTREAM **4** (in schools) a level of ability within a group of pupils of the same age, esp. of a class

stream² *v* **1** to flow fast and strong; pour out **2** to move in a continuous flowing mass **3** to float in the air: *The wind caught her hair, and it streamed out* **4** to group (pupils) in streams

streamer *n* a long narrow piece of coloured paper or material; narrow flag or banner, used for ornament on buildings at a time of public enjoyment

streamline *v* -lined, -lining **1** to form into a smooth shape which moves easily through water or air **2** to make (a business, organization, etc.) more simple but more effective in working — **~d** *adj*

street *n* **1** a road with houses or other town buildings on one or both sides **2 up one's street** in one's area of interest or activity **USAGE A street** is usually in the middle of a town. A **road** is often in the country or in the suburbs. British people say: *in the road/Oxford* **Street. Americans** say: *on the road | on Main* **Street.**

strength *n* **1** the quality or degree of being strong or something that provides this **2** force, esp. measured in numbers: *They came in strength to see the fight* **3 on the strength of** because of

strengthen *v* **1** to make strong or stronger **2** to gain strength: *The wind strengthened*

strenuous *adj* **1** taking great effort **2** showing great activity: *a strenuous supporter of women's rights* — **~ly** *adv* — **~ness** *n*

streptomycin *n* a drug (ANTIBIOTIC) used for killing harmful bacteria

stress¹ *n* **1** force or pressure caused by difficulties in life **2** force of weight caused by something heavy **3** a sense of special importance: *not enough stress on the need for exactness* **4** the degree of force put on a part of a word, making it seem stronger than other parts: *In 'under', the main stress is on 'un'*

stress² *v* **1** to give a sense of importance to (a certain matter) **2** to give force to (a word or part of a word)

stretch¹ *v* **1** to make or become wider or longer **2** to cause to reach full length or width: *to stretch a rope between 2 poles* **3** to spread out **4** to be elastic **5** to straighten (the limbs or body) to full length **6** to cause to go beyond a limit (of rule, or time) **7** to last — **~able** *adj*

stretch² *n* **1** an act of stretching, esp. the body **2** the (degree of) ability to increase in length or width: *There's not much stretch in this collar* **3** a level area (of land or water) **4** technical a mathematical transformation in which all lengths are increased by a constant amount (the SCALE FACTOR) **5** a part, esp. one of 2 straight sides, of a race track, considered as a pa̶r̶t̶ (esp. in the phrases the **final/**̶ **stretch**) **6** a continuous period ̶o̶̶ period of time in prison

stretcher *n* **1** a covered ̶ a sick person can be c̶̶ apparatus for stretch̶̶

stretcher-bear̶̶ team of 2) whos̶̶

stretchy adj -ier, -iest (of a material) elastic — -iness n

strew v strewed, strewn or strewed, strewing 1 to scatter 2 esp. in literature or poetic to lie scattered on or over

strewth interj sl (an expression of surprise, annoyance, etc.)

striated adj technical having narrow lines, bands of colour, etc.; striped

stricken adj 1 showing the effect of trouble, anxiety, etc. 2 experiencing the effects of trouble, illness, etc.

strict adj 1 severe, esp. in rules of behaviour —compare SEVERE 2 a exact: a strict analysis b complete; not to be broken: strict secrecy — ~ly adv — ~ness n

stricture n 1 (an expression of) blame or judgment 2 technical a place where a tube in the body becomes narrower

stride v strode, stridden, striding to walk with long steps or cross with one long step — stride n

strident adj with a hard sharp sound or voice, esp. containing a high unpleasant note — ~ly adv — -dency n

stridulate v -lated, -lating technical (of certain insects, esp. grasshoppers and crickets) to make a rough high sound by rubbing parts of the body together — -lation n

strife n trouble between people

strike[1] v struck, striking 1 to hit 2 to give (a blow) 3 to make suddenly or unexpectedly: They were struck silent 4 to light by hitting against a hard surface: strike a match 5 (of a person or machine) to make (a sound), by a finger or moving part which hits an object 6 to have a (strong) effect on: How does the room strike you? 7 to come suddenly to the mind of: An idea struck me 8 to find (a material or place) 9 technical to produce (a coin or like object) 10 to stop working because of disagreement 11 to produce or reach (agreement) (esp. in the phrases strike a bargain, strike a balance) 12 to take up and hold (a bodily position) for effect: to strike a pose 13 strike camp to take down tents when leaving a camping place —see also STRICKEN, STRIKE OUT, STRIKE UP

strike[2] n 1 a time when no work is done because of disagreement, as over pay or working conditions 2 an attack, esp. by aircraft whose bombs hit the place attacked 3 success in finding esp. a mineral in the earth: an oil strike

strikebreaker n a person who works when most others are on strike —see also BLACKLEG — strikebreaking n

strike out v adv 1 to swim hard in a certain direction 2 also strike through— esp. written to cross out (a mistake in writing, an unwanted piece of writing, etc.) —see also SCORE OUT

strike pay n money paid to workmen on strike ...m their trade union's strike fund(s)

...r n 1 a person on strike 2 a forward in

strike up v adv to start to make (a friendship)

striking adj which draws the attention, esp. because of being attractive or unusual — ~ly adv

string[1] n 1 thin cord 2 anything like this, esp. used for tying things up 3 a thin piece of material, often one of several, stretched across a musical instrument, to give sound —see also STRINGS 4 a set (of things) connected together on a thread: a string of onions 5 a set (of words, actions, etc.) following each other closely 6 no strings attached (esp. of an agreement) with no limiting conditions

string[2] v strung, stringing 1 to put one or more strings on (a musical instrument) 2 to thread (beads) on a string 3 highly strung very sensitive and easily excited, hurt in feelings, etc. 4 strung up very excited, nervous, or worried —see also STRING ALONG, STRING OUT, STRING UP

string along v adv esp. spoken to encourage (someone's) hopes deceitfully

stringed instrument n a musical instrument with one or more strings —see also STRINGS

stringent adj (of rules) severe; which must be obeyed — ~ly adv — -gency n

string out v adv to spread (something) out in a line: She strung out 12 pairs of socks on the line

strings n the set of (players with) stringed instruments in an orchestra

string up v adv 1 to hang (something) high 2 esp. spoken to put to death by hanging, as a punishment

stringy adj -ier, -iest having threadlike flesh or muscle — stringiness n

strip[1] v -pp- 1 to remove (the covering or parts of) 2 to undress or be undressed 3 to tear the twisting thread from (a gear or screw)

strip[2] n 1 a narrow piece 2 an occasion or performance of taking the clothes off, esp. as in striptease 3 the clothes of a particular colour worn by a team in football

strip cartoon n COMIC STRIP

stripe n 1 a band of colour, among one or more other colours 2 a band of colour worn on a uniform as a sign of rank

striped adj having stripes of colour

strip lighting n a method of lighting a room by long, esp. fluorescent, tubes

stripling n a young man or youth

stripper also strip artist— n esp. spoken a striptease performer

striptease also strip show— n (a) removal of clothes by a person, esp. a woman, performed as a show

stripy adj -ier, -iest covered in stripes of colour

strive v strove, striven, striving to struggle hard (to get or conquer) — striver n

strode past tense of STRIDE

stroke[1] v stroked, stroking to pass the hand over gently, esp. for pleasure

stroke² n 1 a blow, esp. with (the edge of) a weapon 2 a sudden illness in part of the brain which damages it and can cause loss of the ability to move some part of the body 3 an unexpected piece (of luck) 4 a single movement, esp. in a sport or game 5 a line made by a single movement of a pen or brush in writing or painting 6 a rower who sets the speed for others rowing with him 7 the sound made by a clock on the hour
stroke³ v to hit (a ball)
stroll v to walk, esp. slowly, for pleasure — **stroll** n — ~**er** n
strong adj 1 having (a degree of) power 2 powerful against harm; not easily broken, spoilt, moved, or changed: strong beliefs 3 of a certain number: Our club is 50 strong 4 (esp. of drinks) having a lot of the material which gives taste —compare WEAK 5 (of a verb) which does not add a regular ending in the past tense, but may change a vowel: "Speak" is a strong verb; its past tense is "spoke" —compare WEAK 6 technical of worth: Is the pound stronger today? — ~**ly** adv
strongarm adj using (unnecessary) force
strongbox n a usu. metal box or safe for keeping valuable things, such as jewels
stronghold n 1 a fort 2 a place where an activity is common or general
strong language n swearing; curses
strong-minded adj firm in beliefs, wishes, etc. — ~**ly** adv — ~**ness** n
strong point n a skill, quality, etc., which one possesses to a high degree
strong room n a room, as in a bank, with a special thick door and walls, where valuable objects can be kept
strontium n a type of soft metal that is an element
strontium 90 n the form of strontium which is given off by atomic explosions and is thought to have harmful effects on people and animals
strop v **-pp-** to sharpen (a razor) on a narrow piece of leather
stroppy adj **-pier, -piest** esp. spoken rather forceful in behaviour, esp. going against others
strove past tense of STRIVE
struck past tense and past part. of STRIKE
structure¹ n 1 the way in which parts are formed into a whole 2 anything formed of many parts, esp. a building — **-ral** adj — **-rally** adv
structure² v **-tured, -turing** to form (esp. ideas) into a whole form, in which each part is related to others
strudel n a sweet food, with fruit inside a light kind of pastry, particularly **apple strudel** as made in Austria
struggle¹ v **-gled, -gling** to make violent movements, esp. when fighting against a person or thing
struggle² n a hard fight or effort
strum v **-mm-** to play (a stringed instrument) carelessly or informally, esp. without skill
strumpet n old use a prostitute

strung past tense and past part. of STRING
strut¹ v **-tt-** to walk in a proud strong way, esp. with the chest out and trying to look important
strut² n 1 a piece of wood or metal holding the weight of another in a part of a building, an aircraft, etc. 2 a strutting way of walking
strychnine n a type of poisonous drug used as a medicine in very small amounts
stub¹ n 1 a short end left when something has been used, esp. of a cigarette or pencil 2 the piece of a cheque or ticket left in a book of these as a record after use
stub² v **-bb-** to hurt (one's toe) by hitting against something
stubble n short stiff pieces of something which grows, esp. a short beard or the remains of wheat after being cut — **-bly** adv
stubborn adj determined; with a strong will — ~**ly** adv — ~**ness** n
stubby adj **-bier, -biest** short and thick
stub out v adv to stop (a cigarette) burning by pressing down the end
stucco n plaster used on buildings to cover walls and form ornamental shapes
stuck¹ adj 1 fixed in place, not moving 2 unable to go or do anything further, esp. because of difficulties 3 esp. spoken having to do or have, esp. unwillingly: We were stuck with unexpected visitors 4 **get stuck in(to)** esp. spoken to start work or action (on) forcefully
stuck² past tense and past part. of STICK
stuck-up adj esp. spoken proud in manner, as though thinking others of less worth
stud¹ n 1 a number of horses or other animals kept for breeding 2 esp. US a male horse kept for breeding
stud² n 1 a type of fastener used instead of a button and button hole, esp. one of 2 flat pieces joined by a narrow part (**collarstud**) or one of 2 separate parts which are pressed together (**press stud**) 2 a nail or flat-topped object, esp. those used for marking off parts of a road, or anything like this used as an ornament
stud³ v **-dd-** to cover with (something like) studs
student n 1 a person who is studying at a place of education or training 2 a person with a stated interest: a student of human nature USAGE Anyone studying at a college or university is a **student**. In the US, this word is also used for children who are too young for college, but in Britain these are **pupils**. Grown-up people studying under a famous musician may also be called **pupils**. A **scholar** is either someone whose education is being paid for because he has won a scholarship or someone who studies professionally and knows a great deal about his subject. This person may be quite old.
students' union n 1 the association of students, esp. in a college or university or combi those in many places of education 2 a (par building where students have a so together

stud farm n a place where horses are bred

studied adj carefully thought or considered, esp. before being expressed

studio n -os 1 a workroom for a painter, photographer, etc. 2 a room from which broadcasts are made 3 a specially equipped room or place where cinema films are made

studio couch n a piece of furniture for sitting on, which can be made into a bed

studious adj 1 eager to study and habitually doing so 2 esp. written careful — ~ly adv — ~ness n

study[1] n -ies 1 the act of studying one or more subjects 2 a subject studied 3 a room used for studying and work 4 a drawing or painting of a detail, esp. for combining later into a larger picture

study[2] v -ied, -ying 1 to spend time in learning (one or more subjects) 2 to examine carefully

stuff[1] n 1 esp. spoken things in a mass; matter: I can't carry all my stuff alone 2 material of any sort, of which something is made

stuff[2] v 1 to fill with a substance 2 to fill the skin of (a dead animal), to make it look real 3 to put stuffing inside: to stuff a chicken 4 esp. spoken to cause (oneself) to eat as much as possible

stuffed shirt n a dull person, esp. a man, who thinks himself important

stuffing n 1 material used as a filling for something 2 finely cut-up food with a special taste placed inside a bird or piece of meat before cooking

stuffy adj -ier, -iest 1 (having air) which is not fresh 2 (having a way of thought) which is dull, old-fashioned, etc. — **stuffily** adv — **stuffiness** n

stultify v -fied, -fying to make stupid or dull in mind — **-fication** n

stumble v -bled, -bling 1 to catch the foot on the ground while moving along and start to fall 2 to stop and/or make mistakes in speaking or reading aloud — ~r n

stumble across also **stumble upon, stumble on—** v prep to meet or discover by chance

stumbling block n something which prevents action

stump[1] n 1 the base of a tree left after the rest has been cut down 2 the remaining part of a limb which has been cut off 3 the stub of a pencil or the useless end of something long which has been worn down, such as a tooth 4 (in cricket) one of the 3 upright pieces of wood at which the ball is thrown

stump[2] v 1 to move, esp. heavily 2 (in cricket) to end the innings of (a batsman) who has moved outside the hitting area, by touching the stumps with the ball 3 esp. spoken to put an unanswerable question or point to

stumpy adj -ier, -iest short and thick in body

stun v -nn- 1 to make unconscious by hitting the head 2 to cause to lose the senses or sense of balance 3 to shock into helplessness: He was stunned by their unfairness 4 to delight

stung past tense and past part. of STING

stunk past part. of STINK

stunner n esp. spoken a very attractive person, esp. a woman, or thing

stunning adj very attractive; delightful; beautiful — ~ly adv

stunt[1] v to prevent (full growth) (of)

stunt[2] n 1 an act of bodily skill, often dangerous 2 an action which gains attention, as in advertising 3 any trick movement, as of a plane

stunt man (fem. **stunt woman**)— n -men a person who does dangerous acts in a film so that the actor does not have to take risks

stupefy v -fied, -fying 1 to make unable to think: stupefied with tiredness 2 to surprise very much — **-faction** n

stupendous adj surprisingly great — ~ly adv

stupid adj silly or foolish, either generally or in a certain action — ~ity n — ~ly adv

stupor n a state in which one cannot think or use the senses

sturdy adj -dier, -diest 1 strong and firm, esp. in body 2 determined in action: a sturdy opposition — **sturdily** adv — **sturdiness** n

sturgeon n a type of large fish which can be eaten, from which caviar and isinglass are obtained

stutter v to speak with difficulty in producing sounds, esp. habitually holding back the first consonant —compare STAMMER — **stutter,** — ~er n — ~ingly adv

sty[1] n sties a pigsty

sty, stye[2] n sties, styes an infected place on the edge of the eyelid, usu. red and swollen

Stygian adj literature unpleasantly dark

style[1] n 1 a type of choice of words, esp. which marks out the speaker or writer as different from others 2 a general manner or way of doing anything which is typical or representative of a person or group, time in history, etc.: the modern style of building 3 high quality of social behaviour, appearance, or manners 4 fashion, esp. in clothes 5 a type or sort, esp. of goods 6 the rodlike part inside a flower which supports the stigma at the top FLOWER — ~less adj

style[2] v styled, styling 1 to form in a certain (good) pattern, shape, etc. 2 to give (a title) to

stylish adj fashionable — ~ly adv — ~ness n

stylistic adj of or concerning style, esp. in writing or art

stylize, -ise v -ized, -izing (in art or description) to treat or present in a fixed style, not in a natural representation

stylus n 1 a pointed instrument used in ancient times for writing on wax 2 the needle-like instrument, with a hard jewel, such as a diamond, on the end, that is the part of a record player that picks up the sound signals from a record

stymie v **-mied, -mieing** to prevent from taking or being put into action; stop

styptic adj, n (a substance) which stops bleeding

suave adj having or showing very good smooth manners which please people, sometimes in spite of bad character — **suavity** n — ~**ly** adv

sub n esp. spoken **1** an amount of money paid to a worker from his wages before the usual day of payment —compare SUBSIDY **2** a subscription **3** a submarine

subatomic adj technical (of very small parts of matter) smaller than an atom

subcommittee n a smaller group formed from a larger committee to deal with a certain matter in more detail

subconscious[1] adj (of thoughts, feelings, etc.) not fully known or understood by the mind in its conscious workings; present at a hidden level of the mind —see CONSCIOUS (USAGE) — ~**ly** adv

subconscious[2] also **unconscious**— n the hidden level of the mind and the thoughts that go on there, beyond conscious knowledge

subcontinent n a large mass of land not quite large enough to be called a continent

subcontract v to hire another contractor (a **subcontractor**) to fulfil (a contract or part of it)

subcutaneous adj technical beneath the skin ⫍SKIN — ~**ly** adv

subdivide v **-vided, -viding** to divide (something that is already divided) into smaller parts — **-vision** n

subdue v **-dued, -duing** **1** to conquer or control the actions of **2** to make gentler or less rough in effect

subdued adj **1** gentle; reduced in strength of light, sound, movement, etc. **2** quiet in behaviour, not forceful, esp. unnaturally or not habitually so

subeditor n a person who looks at and puts right others' work, such as newspaper articles, esp. one who helps a main editor

subheading n a usu. smaller written title phrase lower down in the body of a piece of writing that has a main title phrase at the beginning

subhuman adj **1** of less than human qualities **2** at a point of development between man and animal

subject[1] n **1** a person owing loyalty to a certain state or royal ruler —compare CITIZEN **2** something being considered, as in conversation **3** a branch of knowledge studied, as in a system of education **4** a cause: *His clothes were the subject of amusement* **5** a certain occasion, object, etc., represented in art **6** a person or animal chosen to experience something or to be studied in an experiment **7** (in music) a group of notes forming the tune on which a longer piece is based **8** (in grammar) the noun, pronoun, etc., about which a statement is made or a question asked

subject[2] adj **1** governed by someone else; not independent **2** tending or likely (to have): *subject to ill health*

subject[3] v to cause to be controlled or ruled — ~**ion** n

subjective adj **1** existing only in the mind; imaginary **2** influenced by personal feelings: *a subjective judgment* —compare OBJECTIVE — ~**ly** adv — **-tivity** n

subject to[1] prep depending on; on condition that (there is)

subject to[2] v prep to cause to experience: *They were subjected to great suffering*

sub judice adj law, Latin (of a case in court) now being considered in law, and therefore not allowed to be mentioned (as in a newspaper)

subjugate v **-gated, -gating** to conquer or take power over — **-gation** n

subjunctive[1] adj being or concerning a mood of the verb used in certain languages, often to express doubt, wishes, a dependent verb, etc.

subjunctive[2] n **1** the special form of the verb used in certain languages to express a subjunctive mood **2** a verb which is in the subjunctive mood: *In the sentence 'I wish I were a bird', 'were' is a subjunctive*

sublet v **-let, -letting** (of a person who rents property from its owner) to rent (a property or part of it) to someone else —see also LET

sublieutenant n an officer of the lowest rank in the British navy

sublimate[1] v **-mated, -mating** **1** (in chemistry) to change (a solid substance) to a gas by heating and back to a solid, without its passing through the liquid state, in order to make pure **2** to make pure — **-mation** n

sublimate[2] n a solid after being sublimated

sublime adj very noble or wonderful; of the highest quality; which causes pride, joy, etc. — ~**ly** adv — ~**ness** n — **-limity** n

subliminal adj (shown) at a level of the mind which the senses are not conscious of

submachine gun n a type of light machinegun

submarine[1] adj technical growing or used under or in the sea

submarine[2] also (esp. spoken) **sub**— n a ship, esp. a warship, which can stay under water

submariner n a sailor working and living in a submarine

submerge v **-merged, -merging** to go or cause to go under the surface of water — ~**nce** n

submersible n, adj (a boat or diving bell) which can go under water

submission n **1** submitting or being submitted **2** obedience **3** esp. written a suggestion

submissive adj gentle, willing to take orders from others, etc. — ~**ly** adv — ~**ness** n

submit v **-tt-** **1** to cause (oneself) to yield or agree to obey **2** to offer for consideration **3** law to suggest or say

subnormal adj less than is usual, average, etc., esp. in power of the mind

subordinate¹ *adj* of a lower rank or position — ~ly *adv*

subordinate² *n* a person who is of lower rank in a job, and takes orders from his superior

subordinate³ *v* -nated, -nating to put in a position of less importance — -ation *n* — -ative *adj*

subordinate clause *n* DEPENDENT CLAUSE

suborn *v* *esp. written* to persuade (another person) to do wrong, esp. to tell lies in a court of law, usu. for payment

subplot *n* a plot that is of less importance than and separate from the main plot of a play, story, etc.

subpoena¹ *n* (in law) a written order to attend a court of law

subpoena² *v* -naed, -naing to order to court by a subpoena

subscribe *v* -scribed, -scribing **1** to give (money) **2** to pay regularly in order to receive a magazine, newspaper, etc.

subscriber *n* **1** a person who subscribes or has subscribed **2** a person who receives the use of a service over a period of time, for which he pays: *a telephone subscriber*

subscribe to *v prep* to agree with; approve of

subscription *n* **1** the act of subscribing **2** also (*esp. spoken*) **sub—** an amount of money given, esp. regularly to a society

subsequent *adj* coming after something else, sometimes as a result of it — ~ly *adv*

subservient *adj* habitually willing to do what others want; tending to obey others' wishes — ~ly *adv* — -ience *n*

subside *v* -sided, -siding **1** (of land) to fall away suddenly, because of lack of support **2** (of bad weather or other violent conditions) to go back to the usual level **3** to sink down; settle

subsidence *n* **1** subsiding or the state which results; collapse of land or buildings **2** an example of this

subsidiary *adj* connected but of second importance to the main company, plan, work, etc. — **subsidiary** *n*

subsidize, -dise *v* -dized, -dizing (of someone other than the buyer) to pay part of the costs of (something) for (someone) — -dization *n* — -dizer *n*

subsidy *n* -dies money paid, esp. by the government or an organization, to make prices lower, make it cheaper to produce goods, etc.

subsist *v* to keep alive, esp. when having small amounts of money or food — ~ence *n*

subsistence crop *n* a crop grown for use by the grower rather than for sale —compare CASH CROP

subsoil *n* the lower level of soil, coarser than that on the surface, but above the hard rock

subsonic *adj* (flying at a speed) below the speed of sound

substance *n* **1** a material; type of matter **2** the important part or quality; strength: *no sub-stance in the speech* **3** the real meaning, without the unimportant details: *Tell me the substance of what he said* **4** solidity **5** *esp. old use* wealth: *a man of substance*

substandard *adj* **1** not as good as the average **2** not of an acceptable sort

substantial *adj* **1** solid; strongly made **2** big or important enough to be satisfactory **3** concerning the important part or meaning: *in substantial agreement* **4** wealthy

substantially *adv* **1** mainly; in the important part **2** quite a lot

substantiate *v* -ated, -ating to prove the truth of (something said, claimed, etc.) — -ation *n*

substation *n* a place where electricity is passed on from a generating station into the general system

substitute¹ *n* a person or thing acting in place of another

substitute² *v* -tuted, -tuting **1** to put (something or someone) in place of another **2** to act as a substitute; be used instead of — -tution *n*

substructure *n* a solid base underground which supports something above ground

subtenant *n* a person to whom a place is sublet by the tenant; person who pays rent to the original renter

subtend *v* *technical* (in geometry) to have (the stated angle or arc) opposite to it

subterfuge *n* **1** a trick or dishonest way of succeeding in something **2** the attempt to gain one's aims secretly

subterranean *adj* underground

subtitle *n* *rare* a title printed beneath the main title of a book

subtitles *n* words printed over a film in a foreign language to translate what is being said

subtle *adj* **1** delicate, hardly noticeable, and esp. pleasant: *a subtle taste* **2** very clever in noticing and understanding **3** clever in arrangement — -tly *adv*

subtlety *n* -ties **1** the quality of being subtle **2** a subtle idea, thought, or detail

subtopia *n* a modern area of houses, esp. which has been planned for many people to live in but which is not very interesting to see —compare SUBURB, UTOPIA

subtract *v* to take (a part or amount) from something larger —compare DEDUCT — ~ion *n*

subtropical also **semitropical—** *adj* of or suited to an area near the tropics

suburb *n* an outer area of a town or city, where people live

suburban *adj* of or in the suburbs, esp. when considered uninteresting and full of dull ideas, lack of change, etc.

suburbia *n* *often offensive* the suburbs

suburbs *n* the area generally where most people live, on the edge of any city, as opposed to the shopping and business centre

subversive *adj* which may cause, or attempts to

cause, the destruction of those in power or of established ideas — ~ly *adv* — ~ness *n*

subvert *v esp. written* **1** to try to destroy the power and influence of (esp. a governing body) **2** *rare* to make less loyal, esp. to a person in power — **-version** *n*

subway *n* **-ways** **1** a path under a road or railway by which it can be safely crossed **2** *US* an underground railway

succeed *v* **1** to gain a purpose or reach an aim **2** to do well, esp. in gaining position or popularity in life **3** to follow after **4** to be the next heir after, or the next to take a position or rank

success *n* **1** the act of succeeding in something **2** a good result **3** a person or thing that succeeds or has succeeded — ~ful *adj* — ~fully *adv*

succession *n* **1** the act of following one after the other: *His words came out in quick succession* **2** a number (of people or things) following on one after the other **3** the act of succeeding to an office or position

successive *adj* following one after the other —compare CONSECUTIVE — ~ly *adv*

successor *n* **1** a person or thing that comes after another **2** a person who takes an office or position formerly held by another

succinct *adj* clearly expressed in few words — ~ly *adv* — ~ness *n*

succour *v literature* to give help to (someone in difficulty) — **succour** *n*

succubus *n* **-bi** a female devil supposed to have sex with a sleeping man —compare INCUBUS

succulent[1] *adj* **1** juicy **2** *technical* (of a plant) thick and fleshy — **-lence** *n*

succulent[2] *n technical* a succulent plant, such as a cactus

succumb *v* **1** to yield **2** to die (because of)

such *adj, pron* **1** so great: *Don't be such a fool!* — compare so **2** of the same kind; like: *flowers such as roses, sunflowers, etc.* **3 and such** and suchlike **4 any/no/some** any/no/some (person or thing) like that **5 as such** in that form or kind **6 such as** esp. *written* any that **7 such as it is/they are** although it/they may not be of much worth

suchlike *adj, pron esp. spoken* (things) of that kind

suck *v* **1** to draw (liquid) into the mouth by using the tongue, lips, and muscles at the side of the mouth, with the lips tightened into a small hole **2** to eat (something) by holding in the mouth and melting by movements of the tongue — **suck** *n*

sucker *n* **1** a person or thing that sucks **2** an organ by which some animals can hold on to a surface **3** a flat piece which sticks to a surface by suction **4** a shoot growing out through the ground from the root or lower stem of a plant **5** *esp. spoken* a foolish person who is or has been easily cheated

sucking pig *n* (a) young pig still taking food

from its mother, esp. used as special food, as at *christmas according to custom*

suckle *v* **-led, -ling** to give milk to (the young) from the mother's breast or milk-producing organ —see also NURSE; compare BREAST-FEED

suckling *n* a young human or animal still taking milk from the mother

suck up *v adv esp. spoken* to try to make oneself liked, esp. by unnaturally nice behaviour to someone

sucrose *n* the common form of sugar

suction *n* the act of drawing air or liquid away so that another gas or liquid enters or a solid sticks to another surface, because of the pressure of the air outside

sudden *adj* happening, done, etc., unexpectedly — ~ly *adv* — ~ness *n*

suds also **soapsuds**— *n* the form taken by soap when mixed with water, esp. the part on top containing bubbles — **sudsy** *adj*

sue *v* **sued, suing** to bring a claim in law against, esp. for an amount of money

suede, suède *n* soft leather with a rough surface

suet *n* a kind of hard fat used in cooking, from round the kidneys of an animal — **suety** *adj*

suffer *v* **1** to experience pain or difficulty **2** to experience (something painful): *She suffered the loss of her pupils' respect* **3** to grow worse; lessen in quality **4** *Bible* to allow **5** to accept without dislike (esp. in the phrase **to suffer fools gladly**)

sufferable *adj* which can be borne —see also INSUFFERABLE

sufferance *n* **on sufferance** with permission, though not welcomed

sufferer *n* a person who is suffering, or often suffers, as from an illness

suffering *n* pain and difficulty generally

suffice *v* **-ficed, -ficing** *esp. written* **1** to be enough **2 suffice it to say that...** I will say only that...

sufficiency *n* **1** the state of being or having enough **2** a supply which satisfies

sufficient *adj* enough

suffix *n* a group of letters or sounds (AFFIX) that is placed at the end of a word —compare PREFIX

suffocate *v* **-cated, -cating** to kill or die by lack of air — **-cation** *n*

suffrage *n* the right to vote in national elections

suffragette *n* (in Britain in the early 20th century) a woman who was a member of a group which tried to gain the right to vote, esp. by acts bringing them to public notice

suffuse *v* **-fused, -fusing** to cover or spread over, esp. with a colour or liquid — **-fusion** *n*

sugar[1] *n* **1** a sweet usu. white substance used in food; sucrose, as obtained from sugarcane and sugar beet **2** *technical* any of several types of sweet substance formed in plants —compare GLUCOSE — ~less *adj*

sugar² v **1** to put sugar in **2** to make less unpleasant (esp. in the phrase **to sugar the pill**)

sugar beet n a type of plant which grows under the ground and from which beet sugar is obtained

sugarcane n a type of tall upright tropical grass plant from whose stems cane sugar is obtained

sugar daddy n **-dies** esp. spoken an older man who has a relationship, esp. sexual, with a younger woman, providing her with money and presents

sugary adj **1** (as if) containing sugar **2** too sweet, nice, kind, etc., in manner to be acceptable

suggest v **1** to cause to come to the mind **2** to say or write (an idea to be considered) **3** to give signs (of)

suggestible adj who can be influenced easily

suggestion n **1** something suggested **2** a slight sign; trace **3** (in psychology) a way of causing an idea to be accepted by the mind by indirect connection with other ideas

suggestive adj **1** which brings new ideas to the mind, in addition to what is expressed **2** which suggests immorality or (unacceptable) thoughts of sex — ~ly adv

suicidal adj **1** of or with a tendency to suicide **2** wishing to kill oneself **3** which leads or will lead to death or destruction — ~ly adv

suicide n **1** the act of killing oneself **2** an example of this **3** law a person who does this **4** an act which destroys the position of the person concerned

suit¹ n **1 a** a set of outer clothes which match, usu. including a jacket with trousers or skirt **b** a garment or set of garments for a special purpose **2** one of the 4 sets of cards used in games **3** a lawsuit

suit² v **1** to satisfy or please; be convenient for **2** to match or look right with **3** to be good for (the health of)

suitable adj fit (for a purpose); right; convenient — -bility n — ~ness n — -bly adv

suitcase n a flat bag for carrying clothes and possessions when travelling —see also CASE

suite n **1** a set (of furniture) for a room, esp. a settee and 2 chairs (**3-piece suite**) **2** a set (of rooms), esp. in a hotel **3** (in music) a piece of music for instruments that has several loosely connected parts

suitor n esp. old use a man wishing to marry a woman

sulk v to show lasting annoyance against others, esp. silently and for slight cause — **sulks, sulki**ness n — ~y adj — ~ily adv

sullen adj **1** silently showing dislike, lack of cheerfulness and interest, etc., esp. over a period of time **2** dark and unpleasant — ~ly adv — ~ness n

sully v **-lied, -lying** esp. in literature to spoil or reduce the (high) value of

sulphate n a salt formed from sulphuric acid

sulphide n a mixture of sulphur with another substance

sulphur n an element that is found in different forms (esp. a light yellow powder) and is used in the chemical and paper industries and in medicines — ~ous adj

sulphuric acid n a type of powerful acid

sultan n a Muslim ruler, as formerly in Turkey

sultana n **1** the wife, mother, or daughter of a sultan **2** a small seedless kind of raisin used in baking

sultanate n **1** the position of or rule by a sultan **2** a country ruled by a sultan

sultry adj **-trier, -triest** **1** (of weather) hot, with a lack of air or air which is hard to breathe **2** causing strong sexual attraction or desire — -trily adv — -triness n

sum n **1** the total produced when numbers, amounts, etc., are added together **2** an amount: a large sum of money **3** a usu. simple calculation, adding, multiplying, dividing, etc. **4** the whole; a complete summary (esp. in the phrase **sum total**) —see also SUM UP

summarize, -ise v **-ized, -izing** to be or make a short general account out of (something longer or more detailed) —see also SUM UP

summary¹ adj esp. written **1** short; expressed as a summary **2** done at once without attention to formalities or details, esp. (of punishments) without considering mercy — -rily adv

summary² n **-ries** a short account giving the main points

summation n esp. written a summary of a speech, usu. by the speaker; summing-up

summer¹ n the season between spring and autumn when the sun is hot and there are many flowers

summer² v to cause (animals) to live and feed during the summer

summerhouse n a small building in a garden, with seats in the shade

summer school n a course of lessons, lectures, etc., arranged in addition to the year's work in a university or college during the summer vacation

summer time n the system of having the time on the clocks usu. one hour later than natural time according to the sun, so as to make use of daylight hours in the summer

summery adj like or suitable for summer

summing-up n **summings-up** a summary spoken at the end of a speech or (esp.) by the judge at the end of a court case

summit n **1** the top, esp. the highest part on the top of a mountain —☞GEOGRAPHY **2** the highest point, degree, etc. **3** a meeting between heads of state

summon v esp. written to give an official order (to come, do, etc.)

summons¹ n **-monses** an order to appear, esp. in court, often written

summons² v to give a summons to; order to appear in court

summon up v adv to draw (a quality) out of oneself, esp. with an effort

sump n 1 a place at the bottom, as of a mine, where water collects 2 a part of an engine, at the bottom, which holds the supply of oil ☞CAR

sumptuous adj costly and great in amount; showing great value, generosity, etc.; grand — ~ly adv — ~ness n

sum up v adv -mm- 1 to give the main points of (something); summarize, esp. as a judge at the end of a court case —see also SUMMING-UP 2 to consider and judge quickly

sun¹ n 1 the very hot bright body in the sky, which the earth goes round and from which it receives light and heat 2 a light and heat from the sun b a place with sunlight: *Let's lie over there in the sun* 3 a star round which planets may turn

sun² v -nn- to place (oneself) or stay in sunlight; allow sunlight to fall on (oneself)

sunbaked adj 1 hardened by strong sunlight 2 also **sundrenched**— esp. spoken having much hot sunshine

sunbathe v -bathed, -bathing to spend time in strong sunlight, usu. sitting or lying, in order to make the body brown — ~r n

sunbeam n a beam of light from the sun

sunblind n a piece of material which can be pulled over a window or door to keep out sunlight

sunburn n the condition of having sore skin after experiencing the effects of strong sunlight

sunburnt also **sunburned**— adj having a brown skin; suntanned

sundae n a dish made from ice cream with fruit, sweet-tasting juice, nuts, etc.

Sunday n -days the first day of the week; day before Monday, on which Christians worship

Sunday best also **Sunday clothes**— n **in one's Sunday best** wearing very good clothes which are only worn on special occasions, esp. (originally) for church

Sunday school n (a) place or occasion for giving children religious teaching on a Sunday

sundeck n a flat roof where one may lie in the sun

sunder v esp. written & literature to separate or break into 2 parts —see also ASUNDER

sundew n a type of plant that catches insects in its sticky leaves

sundial n an apparatus used esp. in former times which shows the time according to where the shadow of a pointer falls when the sun shines on it

sundown n sunset

sundrenched adj esp. spoken sunbaked

sundries n 1 small articles of any type, esp. for sale or as bought but not named separately in an account 2 various small matters that do not need special mention

sundry¹ adj 1 various 2 **all and sundry** all types of people; everybody

sundry² n -dries *Australian* an extra in cricket

sunflower n a type of garden plant which grows very tall, with a large yellow flower which turns towards the sun

sung past part. of SING

sunglasses n glasses with dark glass in them to protect the eyes from sunlight

sunk past part. of SINK

sunken adj 1 which has (been) sunk 2 hollow; having fallen inwards or lower than the surface: *sunken eyes* 3 built below the surrounding level

sunlamp also **sunray lamp**— n a lamp which gives out ultraviolet light which browns and gives health to the skin like that of the sun itself

sunlight n the light from the sun

sun lounge n a room with large windows which let in a lot of bright sunlight

sunny adj -nier, -niest 1 having bright sunlight 2 cloudless 3 cheerful — -nily adv — -niness n

sunrise also (esp. spoken) **sun-up**— n the time when the sun is seen to appear after the night

sunroof n 1 a flat roof of a building where one may enjoy the sun 2 also **sunshine roof**— a part in the top of a car which can be moved back to let in air and light

sunset n the time when the sun is seen to disappear as night begins

sunshade n 1 a light folding circular frame covered with usu. ornamental cloth and held over the head to protect a person from the sun — compare PARASOL, UMBRELLA 2 a sunblind over a shop

sunshine n 1 strong sunlight, as when there are no clouds 2 a place where there is bright light and heat from the sun

sunspot n 1 one of the small dark areas on the sun's surface 2 esp. spoken a place with much sunshine and heat, where people like to go on holiday

sunstroke also **heatstroke**— n an illness with fever, weakness, headache, etc., caused by the effects of too much strong sunlight, esp. on the head

suntan n the brownness of the skin after the effects of sunshine — **suntanned** adj

suntrap n a place which is unusually sunny

sun worship n esp. spoken love of sunbathing — ~per n

sup¹ v -pp- *Scots & N English* to drink — **sup** n

sup² v -pp- old use to eat (as) supper

super adj esp. spoken wonderful

superabundance n esp. written a very large amount, even more than necessary — -dant adj

superannuation n 1 the giving up of, or dismissing from, work in old age 2 money paid as a pension, esp. from one's place of work, when one leaves work in old age

superb *adj* perfect in form, quality, etc.; wonderful — ~ly *adv*

supercharged *adj* unusually full of power, as of an engine with additional fuel, or a person who is very full of life, acts quickly, etc.

supercharger *n* an apparatus for producing more power from an engine by forcing air into the place where the fuel, such as petrol, burns

supercilious *adj* (as if) thinking others of little importance; scornful; haughty — ~ly *adv* — ~ness *n*

superconductivity *n* the ability of certain metals to allow electricity to pass without resistance when at the lowest temperatures possible (near absolute zero)

superficial *adj* 1 on the surface; not deep 2 not serious, complete, or searching in thought, ideas, etc. — ~ity *n* — ~ly *adv*

superfluous *adj* more than is necessary; not needed or wanted — ~ly *adv* — ~ness, -fluity *n*

superhuman *adj* (as if) beyond or better than human powers

superimpose *v* -posed, -posing to put over something else or over each other, esp. so as to show the form of both: *to superimpose one film image on another*

superintend *v* to be in charge of and direct (work or people working)

superintendent *n* 1 a person in charge of some work, building, hospital, home for criminal children, etc. 2 a British police officer of middle rank

superior[1] *adj* 1 *esp. written & technical* higher in position; upper 2 good or better in quality or value 3 of higher rank or class 4 (as if) thinking oneself better than others — ~ity *n*

superior[2] *n* 1 a person of higher rank, esp. in a job —compare INFERIOR 2 (a title for) the head of a religious group: *Mother Superior*

superlative[1] *adj* 1 best; most good 2 (in grammar) of the superlative —compare POSITIVE, COMPARATIVE

superlative[2] *n* 1 the highest degree of comparison of an adjective or adverb: *"Good" becomes "best" in the superlative* 2 an example of this; word in this form

superlatively *adv* (esp. of something good) to a very high degree

superman *n* -men 1 (in stories) a man with powers of mind and body much greater than others' 2 *esp. spoken* a man of great ability

supermarket *n* a large shop where one serves oneself with food and goods

supernatural *adj* 1 not explained by natural laws but (esp.) by the powers of spirits, gods, and magic 2 connected with unknown forces and spirits — see NATURAL (USAGE) — ~ly *adv*

supernova *n* -vas *or* -vae a very large exploding star seen in the sky as a bright mass for a while —compare NOVA

superscription *n* words written on top of or on the outside of something

supersede *v* -seded, -seding to replace, esp. as an improvement on — -session *n*

supersonic *adj* faster than the speed of sound

superstar *n* an unusually famous and popular performer

superstition *n* (a) belief which is not based on reason or fact but on association of ideas, as in magic — -tious *adj* — -tiously *adv*

superstructure *n* 1 an arrangement of parts built up on top of another, such as the upper parts of a ship 2 the part of a building above the ground

supertax *n* (in Britain in former times) additional income tax only on very high incomes —compare SURTAX

supervene *v* -vened, -vening *esp. written* (of an event) to come into a state of affairs causing a change to it: *The meeting went on until lack of time supervened*

supervise *v* -vised, -vising to keep watch over (work and workers) as the person in charge — -vision *n* — -visor *n* — -visory *adj*

supine *adj* 1 lying on the back looking upwards —compare PRONE, PROSTRATE 2 lacking in action, strength, etc.; lazy — ~ly *adv*

supper *n* the last meal of the day, taken in the evening — ~less *adj*

supplant *v* to take the place of, often by tricks or deceit — ~er *n*

supple *adj* 1 bending or moving easily, esp. in the joints of the body 2 quick in thinking, changing one's ideas, values, etc. — ~ness *n*

supplement[1] *n* 1 an additional amount of something 2 an additional written part, at the end of a book, or as a separate part of a newspaper, magazine, etc.

supplement[2] *v* to make additions to

supplementary *adj* 1 additional 2 (of angles or an angle) making up 180° together, or with the other angle

supplementary benefit *n* (in Britain) additional money given by the state to someone who already receives money from it, but not enough to live on

supplicant *n* a person begging for something, esp. from a person in power or God

supplies *n* food and/or necessary materials for daily life, esp. for a group of people over a period of time

supply[1] *v* -plied, -plying to provide (something) — -ier *n*

supply[2] -plies *n* 1 a store which can be used 2 an amount: *a large supply of food* 3 the rate at which an amount is provided —see also SUPPLIES; compare DEMAND 4 **in short supply** scarce

supply and demand *n* the balance between the amount of goods and how much is needed, esp. as shown in price changes

supply teacher *n* a teacher who takes the

support¹ *v* 1 to bear the weight of, esp. preventing from falling 2 **a** to provide money for (a person) to live on **b** to help, with sympathy, or practical advice, money, food, etc. 3 to approve of and encourage 4 to be in favour of — ~ive *adj*

support² *n* 1 the act or means of supporting 2 a piece of material which bears the weight of something 3 an apparatus which holds a weak or displaced part of the body 4 a person who provides money to live, esp. for his family 5 the amount of attendance or number of people who are loyal attenders: *The theatre gets a lot of support*

supportable *adj esp. written* bearable — compare INSUPPORTABLE

supporter *n* a person who gives loyalty and attendance to (an activity), defends (a principle), etc.

supporting part also **supporting role**— *n* a small part in a play, usu. for a less important actor

supporting programme *n* a short film or less important part of a performance, as opposed to the main film or part

suppose¹ *v.* -posed, -posing 1 to take as likely; consider as true 2 **a** to expect, because of duty, responsibility, law, or other conditions: *Everyone is supposed to wear a seat belt in the car* **b** to allow: *not supposed to smoke*

suppose² also **supposing**— *conj* 1 why not?; I suggest 2 if: *Suppose it rains, what shall we do?*

supposed *adj* believed to be (so), though without much proof — ~ly *adv*

supposition *n* 1 the act of supposing or guessing 2 an idea which is a result of this

suppository *n* -ries a form of medicine shaped into a small piece to be placed inside a lower opening of the body, usu. the rectum

suppress *v* 1 to crush (esp. an action or state) by force 2 to prevent from appearing: *to suppress the truth* 3 to prevent from being printed and made public — ~ion *n*

suppressor *n* 1 a person or thing that suppresses 2 a small apparatus which prevents an electrical machine from causing interference on a television or radio set

suppurate *v* -rated, -rating (of a wound) to give out pus — -ration *n*

supremacy *n* 1 the state of being supreme 2 the highest level of power; highest position

supreme *adj* 1 highest in position, esp. of power 2 highest in degree — ~ly *adv*

Supreme Court *n* the highest court of law in a state of the US or in the US as a whole

surcharge *v* -charged, -charging to make an additional charge to or for — **surcharge** *n*

surd *n technical* an irrational number in the form of or involving a root

sure¹ *adj* 1 having no doubt 2 certain: *It's sure to rain* — ~ness *n*

sure² *adv esp. spoken esp. US* certainly: '*Are you all right?*' '*Sure*'

surefire *adj esp. spoken* certain to happen or succeed

surefooted *adj* footsure — ~ly *adv* — ~ness *n*

surely *adv* 1 safely: *slowly but surely* 2 certainly 3 I believe or hope (something must be or become so)

sure thing *n esp. spoken* a certainty

surety *n* -ties 1 a person who takes responsibility for another's behaviour 2 money given to make sure that a person will appear in court —see also BAIL

surf¹ *n* the white foam formed by waves when they break on rocks, a shore, etc.

surf² also **surf ride**— *v* to ride as a sport with breaking waves near the shore, on a surfboard — ~er *n*

surface¹ *n* 1 the outer part: *the earth's surface* 2 the top of a body of liquid —see also SUPERFICIAL

surface² *v* -faced, -facing 1 to come to the surface of water 2 to cover (esp. a road) with hard material

surface³ *adj* (of post) travelling by land and sea

surfboard *n* a narrow piece of wood, plastic, etc., for riding with the waves as they break on the shore

surfeit *v* to fill with too much of something, esp. food — **surfeit** *n*

surge *v* surged, surging 1 to move, esp. forward, in or like powerful waves: *The crowd surged past him* 2 (of a feeling) to arise powerfully — **surge** *n* compare TIDE

surgeon *n* a doctor whose job is to perform medical operations —see also **dental surgeon** (DENTIST)

surgery *n* -ries 1 a place where one or a group of doctors or dentists receives people to give them advice on their health and medicines to treat illnesses 2 the time during which this takes place 3 the skill and practice of performing medical operations 4 the performing of such an operation, usu. including the cutting open of the skin

surgical *adj* 1 of, by, or for surgery 2 (of a garment) made and worn as a treatment for a particular bodily condition —compare MEDICAL — ~ly *adv*

surly *adj* -lier, -liest angry, bad-mannered, etc., esp. habitually

surmise *v* -mised, -mising *esp. written* to suppose as a reasonable guess — **surmise** *n*

surmount *v* 1 to conquer (esp. difficulties) 2 to get over or above: *The horse surmounted the fence* 3 to be over or on top of — ~able *adj*

surname *n* the name one shares with the other members of one's family, often the last name —compare FIRST NAME

surpass v to go beyond, in amount or degree — ~ing adj — ~ingly adv

surplice n a garment made of white material worn over a darker garment during religious services by some priests and choirboys —see also VESTMENT — ~d adj

surplus n, adj (an amount) additional to what is needed or used, as of money

surprise¹ n 1 (the feeling caused by) an unexpected event 2 the act of coming on (someone, often an enemy) unprepared (esp. in the phrase **take by surprise**)

surprise² v -prised, -prising 1 to cause surprise to 2 to shock or cause to disbelieve 3 to come on or attack when unprepared

surprising adj unusual; causing surprise — ~ly adv

surrealism n a modern type of art and literature in which the artist represents, in a dreamlike way, unrelated images and objects in the mind — -ist adj, n — -istic adj

surrender¹ v 1 to yield to the power of esp. an enemy, as a sign of defeat 2 esp. written to give up possession of (esp. a paper, in return for money or services)

surrender² n the act of surrendering

surreptitious adj done, gained, etc., secretly, esp. for dishonest reasons — ~ly adv — ~ness n

surrogate n, adj 1 (a person) acting for another, such as a priest or judge 2 substitute

surround¹ v 1 to be all around on every side 2 to go around on every side — ~ing adj

surround² n an edge, esp. ornamental as part of the furnishing in a house, or an open space around a carpet

surroundings n the place and conditions of life

surtax n an additional tax on high incomes —compare SUPERTAX

surveillance n a close watch kept on someone, esp. a prisoner (esp. in the phrase **under surveillance**)

survey¹ v -veyed, -veying 1 to look at (a person, group, place, or condition) as a whole 2 to examine the condition of and give a value for (a building) 3 to measure, judge, and record on a map the details of (an area of land)

survey² n -veys 1 a general view or considering (of a place or condition) 2 (an) examination of a house, esp. for someone who may buy it 3 (an) act of surveying land 4 a map showing the details and nature of such land —see also ORDNANCE SURVEY

surveyor n 1 a person whose job is to examine buildings, esp. houses for sale 2 a person whose job is to measure land, record details in maps, etc.

survival n 1 the fact or likelihood of surviving 2 something which has continued to exist from an earlier time, (esp.) which is not useful now

survive v -vived, -viving 1 to continue to live,

esp. after coming close to death 2 to continue to live after: *She survived her sons*

survivor n a person who has continued to live, esp. in spite of coming close to death

susceptible adj 1 easily influenced 2 likely to experience strong feelings, esp. to fall in love easily 3 sensitive; likely to feel a strong effect (from) — -bility n

suspect¹ adj of uncertain truth, rightness, quality, etc.

suspect² n a person who is suspected of guilt, esp. in a crime

suspect³ v 1 to believe to exist or be true; think likely 2 to believe to be guilty 3 to be doubtful about the truth or value of

suspend v 1 to hang from above ⟳BRIDGE 2 to hold still in liquid or air: *Dust could be seen suspended in the beam of light* 3 to put off or stop (esp. the fulfilment of a decision) for a period of time 4 to prevent from taking part in a team, belonging to a group, etc., for a time, usu. because of misbehaviour or breaking rules

suspender n 1 a garter with a fastener hanging down, formerly used by men to hold a sock up 2 a fastener hanging down from an undergarment to hold a woman's stockings up

suspender belt n a light undergarment for women with suspenders fixed to it

suspense n a state of uncertain expectation

suspension n 1 the act of suspending or state of being suspended ⟳BRIDGE 2 a liquid mixture with very small pieces of solid material contained but not combined in the liquid —see SUSPEND 3 the pieces of apparatus fixed to the wheels of a car, motorcycle, etc., to lessen the effects of rough road surfaces ⟳ CAR

suspicion n 1 the act or feeling of suspecting or state of being suspected 2 a slight amount (of something seen, heard, tasted, etc.)

suspicious adj 1 likely to suspect (guilt) 2 causing to suspect guilt, wrongness, etc.; suspect — ~ly adv

sustain v 1 a to bear (difficulty) b to do this without loss of strength 2 to keep in continuance: *to sustain a note in music* 3 to keep strong; strengthen 4 esp. written to hold up (the weight of)

sustenance n 1 the ability (of food) to keep strong or strengthen 2 food which does this

suttee n a former Hindu custom in which a wife was burnt with her dead husband

suture n 1 a (type of) thread used for stitching a wound together —see also GUT, CATGUT 2 the stitch(es) made with this

suzerain n 1 a state which controls the foreign affairs of another state 2 (in former times) a ruling lord — ~ty n

svelte adj (esp. of a woman) thin, graceful, and well-shaped

SW abbrev. for: southwest(ern)

swab¹ n 1 medical a piece of material which will hold liquid to be tested for infection 2 medical the liquid taken on this material 3 a cleaning cloth which will hold water, as for use on the decks of a ship

swab² v **-bb-** 1 to take liquid on a swab from (a part of the body) 2 to clean (esp. the decks of a ship) 3 to remove by cleaning in this way

swaddle v **-dled, -dling** to wrap (a person) in many coverings, esp. (in former times) to wind (a baby) in narrow pieces of cloth

swaddling clothes also **swaddling bands—** n esp. *Bible* the cloth(s) wound round swaddled babies

swag n *Australian* a set of clothes and belongings in a bundle, as carried by travellers and wanderers

swagger¹ v 1 to walk with a swinging movement, as if proud 2 to talk in a boasting way — ~er n — ~ingly adv

swagger² n a proud manner of walking

swain n esp. *in literature or poetic* a young man in a country village, esp. a lover or admirer of a girl

swallow¹ n a type of small insect-eating bird with pointed wings and a tail that comes to 2 points, which comes to the northern countries in summer ⟶BIRD

swallow² v 1 to move (food or drink) down the throat from the mouth 2 to make the same movement of the throat, esp. as a sign of nervousness 3 a to accept patiently b esp. *spoken* to believe, in spite of doubt — ~er n

swallow³ n an act of swallowing

swam *past tense of* SWIM

swamp¹ n (an area of) soft wet land; (a) bog — ~y adj

swamp² v 1 to fill with water, esp. causing to sink 2 to crush with a large amount, as of work or difficulties

swan¹ n a type of large white bird with a long neck, which lives on rivers and lakes

swan² v **-nn-** esp. *spoken* to go or travel, esp. where and when one likes

swank¹ v esp. *spoken* to act or speak in an unpleasantly proud way

swank² n esp. *spoken* 1 (the attempt to make people think well of one by) proud and showy behaviour, speech, etc. 2 a person who boasts — ~y adj — ~iness n

swansdown n soft small feathers which grow underneath the larger feathers of a swan, near its skin

swansong n 1 the last piece of work or performance, of an artist, poet, etc. 2 a song supposed to be sung by a swan just before its death

swap, swop v **-pp-** esp. *spoken* to exchange — **swap, swop** n

swarf n small bits of metal, plastic, etc., produced by a cutting tool in operation

swarm¹ n 1 a large group (of insects) moving in a mass, esp. bees with a queen 2 a crowd (of people) or moving mass (of animals)

swarm² v 1 (of bees) to leave the hive or other living place in a mass to find another 2 to move in a crowd or mass

swarm³ v *becoming rare* to climb using the hands and feet

swarm with v prep to be full of: *The place swarmed with tourists*

swarthy adj **-thier, -thiest** (of the skin or face) dark-coloured

swashbuckler n (esp. in films and stories) a daring fellow who is fond of showy adventures, sword fighting, etc. — **-ling** adj

swastika n a pattern in the form of a cross with each arm bent back at a right angle, used as a sign for the sun in ancient times and for the Nazi Party in modern times

swat¹ v **-tt-** to hit (an insect) with a flat object or hand, esp. so as to cause death

swat² n 1 an act of swatting 2 a flat object with a wire handle, for killing flies

swatch n a piece of cloth as an example of a type or quality of material; sample

swath also **swathe—** n 1 an amount of grass or crops cut with one movement of the hand, by scythe 2 a line of grass or crops that has been cut by a machine 3 **cut a swath through** to cause the main part of (something) to be destroyed

swathe v **swathed, swathing** esp. *in literature or written* to wrap round in cloth, esp. a bandage —compare SWADDLE

sway¹ v **swayed, swaying** 1 to swing from side to side or to one side 2 to influence

sway² n 1 swaying movement 2 influence 3 *old use & literature* power to rule

swear v **swore, sworn, swearing** 1 to promise formally or by an oath 2 esp. *spoken* to state firmly 3 to take or cause to take an oath, as in court: *They swore him to silence* 4 a to take (an oath) b to declare the truth of by oath: *a sworn statement* 5 to curse —see also SWEAR BY, SWEAR IN — ~er n

swear by v prep esp. *spoken* to trust in and encourage the use of: *She swears by hand washing*

swear in v adv to cause to make a promise of responsible action, or to take the oath in court

swearword n a word used as a curse

sweat¹ v 1 to have sweat coming out on the skin 2 to cause to do this: *to sweat a horse* 3 to show liquid on the surface, from inside: *The cheese is sweating* 4 to work or force to work very hard for little money —see also SWEATSHOP 5 **sweat blood** esp. *spoken* to work unusually hard —see also SWEAT OUT

sweat² n 1 also **perspiration—** liquid which comes out from the body through the skin to cool it 2 the action of sweating 3 fever with sweating 4 esp. *spoken* hard work — ~y adj

sweatband n a narrow piece of a leather around the inside of a hat b cloth worn round the wrist or forehead to soak up sweat

sweater n 1 a heavy woollen garment for the top of the body 2 a knitted top garment; jumper

sweat gland n any of the many small organs

under the skin from which sweat is lost ⟱ SKIN

sweat out *v adv* **1** to get rid of (an illness) by causing oneself to sweat **2 sweat it out a** to take hard exercise **b** to suffer unpleasantness until it ends

sweatshirt *n* a sort of T-shirt

sweatshop *n* a place where workers produce goods by sweated labour

swede *n* a type of round yellow vegetable like a turnip

Swedish *adj* of or concerning the people, language, etc. of Sweden ⟱ LANGUAGE

sweep[1] *v* swept, sweeping **1** to clean by brushing **2** to move or touch with a brushing movement: *The wind swept the leaves away* **3** to move in, or extend in, a curve: *The hills sweep round the valley* **4** to cover quickly: *A storm swept over the country* **5** to spread throughout: *The new fashion swept the country* **6** to move in a grand manner: *She swept from the room* **7 sweep the board** to win easily and completely **8 sweep someone off his feet** to cause someone to fall suddenly in love with one

sweep[2] *n* **1** an act of sweeping **2** a swinging movement, or the distance covered by this: *the sweep of his sword* **3** a long curved line or area: *the sweep of the hills* **4** a strong forward movement **5** an act of moving out over a broad area to search, attack, etc. **6** *technical* one of the large broad arms of a windmill **7** a sweepstake **8** a chimneysweep **9 clean sweep** a complete removal

sweeper *n* **1** a person or thing that sweeps **2** (in football) a player who defends from behind other defenders

sweeping *adj* **1** covering many things: *sweeping plans* **2** too general: *a sweeping statement* — ~ly *adv*

sweepstake *n* a form of betting in which the winners gain all the money paid in

sweet[1] *adj* **1** tasting like or containing sugar **2** having a pleasant taste, smell, or sound: *sweet music* **3** gentle or attractive in manner **4** small and charming: *a sweet little kitten* **5** (of wine) not dry **6** pleasant: *the sweet smell of success* **7** sweet on *esp. spoken* in love with —see also SHORT and sweet — ~ly *adv* — ~ness *n* — ~ish *adj*

sweet[2] *n* **1** a small sweet thing, mainly sugar or chocolate, eaten for pleasure —see also CANDY **2** a dessert

sweet-and-sour *adj* having both sweet and sharp tastes together

sweetbread *n* the pancreas of a sheep or calf, used as food

sweet corn *n* a type of maize used as a vegetable

sweeten 1 to make or become sweet **2** to make pleasanter: *Holidays sweeten life* — ~er *n*

sweetening *n* any substance which makes food sweeter

sweetheart *n* a person whom another loves

sweetie *n esp. spoken* a lovable person or thing

sweetmeat *n old use* a sweet

sweet pea *n* a type of climbing plant with sweet smelling flowers

sweet pepper *n* GREEN PEPPER —see also PEPPER

sweet tooth *n* a liking for sweet things

swell[1] *v* swelled, swollen *or* swelled, swelling **1** to increase in fullness and roundness —see also SWOLLEN **2** to increase the amount of **3** to fill with strong feeling: *Her heart swelled*

swell[2] *n* **1** the movement of large stretches of the sea **2** an increase of sound: *the great swell of the organ* **3** roundness and fullness

swell[3] *adj US esp. spoken* very good: *a swell teacher*

swelling *n* **1** swelling or being swollen **2** a swollen place on the body

swelter *v* to feel the effects of great heat

sweltering *adj* unpleasantly hot

swept *past tense and past part. of* SWEEP

swerve[1] *v* swerved, swerving **1** to turn suddenly to one side, when moving **2** to change from a course or purpose

swerve[2] *n* a swerving movement

swift[1] *adj* rapid, fast, short, or sudden — ~ly *adv* — ~ness *n*

swift[2] *n* a type of small bird with long wings

swig *v* -gg- *sl* to drink, esp. in large mouthfuls — swig *n* : *a swig of beer*

swill[1] *v* **1** to wash by pouring water on **2** *sl* to drink, esp. in large amounts

swill[2] *n* **1** also swill down , swill out— an act of swilling **2** pig food in partly liquid form

swim[1] *v* swam, swum, swimming **1** to move through water by moving limbs or tail **2** to cross or complete (a distance) by doing this: *to swim a river* **3** to be full of or covered with liquid: *swimming in fat* **4** to feel dizzy: *His head swam* **5 swim with the tide** to follow the behaviour of others — ~mer *n*

swim[2] *n* **1** an act of swimming **2 in the swim** knowing about and concerned in what is going on

swimming *n* the act or sport of those who swim

swimming bath also swimming baths— *n* a public swimming pool —see also BATHS

swimming costume also swimsuit— *n* a type of clothing worn by women for bathing or swimming

swimmingly *adv* easily and well

swimming pool *n* a special pool for swimming in

swindle[1] *v* -dled, -dling to cheat (someone) — -dler *n*

swindle[2] *n* **1** an example of swindling **2** something which is not of the value paid for —compare FRAUD

swine *n* swine **1** *old use or technical* a pig **2** *sl* a disliked unpleasant person — -nish *adj*

swineherd n (in former times) a man or boy who looks after pigs

swing[1] v **swung, swinging** 1 to move backwards and forwards, round and round, or in a curve from a fixed point 2 to move (oneself) in this way: *swinging on the gate* 3 to wave (something) around in the air: *He swung his sword* 4 *esp. spoken* to be hanged to death, as a punishment 5 to turn quickly: *He swung round* 6 to change by a large degree: *She swung from happiness to tears* 7 to move or start to move smoothly and rapidly: *swing into action* 8 **no/not enough room to swing a cat** very little space

swing[2] n 1 the/an act or method of swinging: *the swing of his arms* 2 the distance covered by a swinging movement: *a wide swing* 3 a strong regular beat: *walk with a swing* 4 a type of jazz music of the 1930's and 40's with a strong regular beat 5 a seat on which one can swing 6 a large change: *a swing in public opinion* 7 **go with a swing** to happen successfully 8 **in full swing** fully active

swingeing adj very great in force, degree, etc.

swinger n a person who is gay and active, or who lives a free modern life

swinging adj 1 gay and full of life: *a swinging party* 2 fashionably free and modern — ~ly adv

swipe[1] n a sweeping stroke

swipe[2] v **swiped, swiping** 1 to hit violently, esp. with a swing of the arm 2 *esp. spoken* to steal by seizing

swirl[1] n 1 a swirling movement 2 a twisting mass of water, dust, etc.

swirl[2] v to move with twisting turns: *The water swirled*

swish[1] v 1 to cut through the air making a sharp noise: *to swish past* 2 (esp. of clothes) to make a soft sound in movement — **swish** n

swish[2] adj esp. spoken fashionable or costly-seeming

Swiss adj of or from Switzerland

swiss roll n a type of cake baked as a thin piece and then rolled with a filling of jam or cream

switch[1] n 1 an apparatus for interrupting an electric current ☞ ELECTRICITY 2 a change: *a switch of plan* 3 a small thin stick, esp. taken from a tree

switch[2] v 1 to change or exchange: *He switched positions* 2 to change by a switch 3 **a** to hit with a switch **b** to move quickly; twitch: *He switched his hand away* —see also SWITCH OFF, SWITCH ON, SWITCH OVER — ~able adj

switchback n 1 a railway going up and down steep slopes, esp. for amusement at fairs 2 anything changing direction steeply

switchboard n the arrangement of telephone lines, or the people who work it, on a central board for connections

switched-on adj aware and alert 2 modern and fashionable

switchgear n machinery for making electrical connections in a system

switch off v adv 1 to turn off by means of a switch 2 to stop concentrating

switch on v adv to turn on by means of a switch —see also SWITCHED-ON

switch over v adv to change completely — **switchover** n

swivel[1] n an apparatus joining 2 parts in such a way that they can turn independently

swivel[2] v -ll- to pivot

swiz n esp. spoken something which cheats one's expectations

swizzle stick n a rod for mixing drinks

swollen[1] adj 1 of an increased size, often because of the presence of surplus water or air within 2 too great: *a swollen opinion of oneself* — ~ness n

swollen[2] past part. of SWELL

swoon[1] v literature or humour to faint or nearly faint from the effects of joy, desire, etc. — **swoon** n : *The traveller was not dead but in a swoon*

swoop[1] v to descend sharply or rush on someone, esp. in attack — ~er n

swoop[2] n 1 a swooping action 2 **at one fell swoop** all at once

swop v, n swap

sword n a weapon with a long blade and a handle ☞ ARMOUR, WEAPON

sword dance n an esp. Scottish type of dance including jumping over swords laid on the ground — **sword dancer** n

swordfish n **-fish** or **-fishes** a sort of large fish with a long sharp upper jaw

swordplay n the movement and skill used in fighting with swords

swordsman n **-men** a fighter with a sword — ~ship n

swordstick n a sword enclosed in a walking stick

swore past tense of SWEAR

sworn[1] adj complete; totally so: *sworn enemies*

sworn[2] past part. of SWEAR

swot[1] n esp. spoken a person who studies too hard

swot[2] v -tt- esp. spoken to study hard — ~ter n

swum past part. of SWIM

swung past tense and past part. of SWING

sybarite n a person who lives in great comfort — -itic adj

sycamore n a type of maple tree, or its wood

sycophant n a person who flatters those more powerful, so as to gain advantage — ~ic adj

syllable n a word or part of a word which contains a vowel sound or consonant acting as a vowel: *There are 2 syllables in "button"* — -abic adj

syllabub n a dish made of sweetened cream or milk mixed with wine and usu. egg whites

syllabus n **-buses** or **-bi** an arrangement or

written account of subjects for study —see also TIMETABLE

sylph n 1 (in ancient beliefs) a female spirit of the air 2 a slim and graceful woman — ~ **like** adj

sylvan, sil- adj esp. in literature of or in woods

symbiosis n -ses the state of life of 2 different living things which depend on each other, often with one living on the other's body

symbol n 1 a sign, shape, or object which represents a person, idea, value, etc. —compare EMBLEM 2 a letter or figure which expresses a sound, number, or chemical substance: 'H_2O' is the symbol for water — ~ **ic**, ~ **ical** adj — ~ **ically** adv

symbolism n 1 the use of symbols 2 a system of literature and art, esp. in 19th century France, in which reality is suggested by symbols — -**list** n

symbolize, -ise v -ized, -izing 1 to represent by symbols 2 to be a symbol of — -**ization** n

symmetry n -tries exact likeness between the opposite sides of something ⟋MATHEMATICS — -**trical** adj — -**trically** adv —compare ASYMMETRIC

sympathetic adj 1 of, feeling, or showing sympathy 2 connecting ideas or events as cause and result, because one follows the other: sympathetic magic — ~ **ally** adv

sympathies n 1 feelings of support 2 a message of comfort in grief: send one's sympathies

sympathize, -ise v -thized, -thizing to feel or show sympathy or approval — -**thizer** n — -**thizingly** adv

sympathy n 1 the ability to share or understand the feelings of another —compare EMPATHY 2 pity 3 agreement: sympathy for his opinions 4 come out in sympathy to stop work in support of workers who have gone on strike

symphony n -nies a musical work for an orchestra — -**onic** adj

symposium n -siums or -sia a meeting between experts to talk about a certain area of interest

symptom n 1 an outward sign of inner change 2 a change in body or mind which shows disease or disorder — ~ **atic** adj — ~ **atically** adv

synagogue n a place where Jews worship according to their religion

sync, synch n technical synchronization: to be in/out of sync

synchromesh n a part of the gears in a car that allows them to change smoothly

synchronize, -nise v -nized, -nizing 1 to happen or cause to happen at the same speed: They synchronized their steps 2 to set (clocks and watches) to the same time 3 to match (recorded sound) correctly to a piece of film — -**nization** n

syncopate v -pated, -pating to change the rhythm of (music), by giving force to the usu. less forceful beats — -**pation** n

syndic n technical a person chosen to represent a firm's or group's business interests

syndicalism n a type of trade unionism whose aim is control of industry by the workers — -**list** adj, n

syndicate¹ n 1 a group of businesses or people combined for a particular purpose 2 an organization that sells articles to several newspapers

syndicate² v -cated, -cating to produce (newspaper articles) through a syndicate — -**cation** n

syndrome n 1 a collection of symptoms which represent a disorder of the body or the mind 2 any pattern of qualities, happenings, etc., typical of a general condition

synod n a meeting to decide important matters for a group of churches

synonym n a word with the same or nearly the same meaning as another —opposite **antonym** — ~ **ous** adj : 'Sad' and 'unhappy' are synonymous — ~ **ously** adv

synopsis n -ses a short account of something longer

syntax n the rules of grammar which describe the way in which the words in a sentence are ordered and connected

synthesize, -sise v -sized, -sizing 1 to make up or produce by combining parts —compare ANALYSE 2 to make by combining chemicals: to synthesize a drug — -**sis** n : a synthesis of ideas —compare ANALYSIS

synthesizer, -siser n a person or machine that synthesizes parts into a whole, esp. an electronic musical instrument that can make many different types of sound

synthetic adj 1 of or concerning synthesis 2 produced by synthesizing; artificial — ~ **ally** adv

syphilis n a serious venereal disease which can be passed on during sexual activity and also from parent to child by inheritance —compare GONORRHEA — -**itic** adj

syphon n, v siphon

syringe¹ n a sort of pipe used in science and medicine, into which liquid can be drawn and from which it can be pushed out —see also HYPODERMIC

syringe² v syringed, syringing to treat with liquid from a syringe

syrup n 1 sweet liquid, esp. sugar and water 2 treacle or sugarcane juice — ~ **y** adj

system n 1 a group of related parts working together 2 an ordered set of ideas, methods, or ways of working 3 a plan

systematic adj based on a regular plan or fixed method; thorough: a systematic search — ~ **ally** adv

systematize, -tise v -tized, -tizing to arrange in a system or by a set method — -**tization** n

systems analyst n a person who works out the best way an activity or organisation can be run, usu. using a computer

T, t T's, t's *or* Ts, ts   **1** the 20th letter of the English alphabet **2 to a T** exactly; perfectly: *That dress fits Jean to a T* —see also CROSS **one's 't's and dot one's 'i's,** T-BONE, T-SHIRT

tab *n* **1** a piece of cloth, paper, etc., fixed to something to help in opening or handling, or as a sign of what it is, who owns it, etc. **2** *esp. spoken* a bill; statement of money owed **3 keep tabs/a tab on** *esp. spoken* to watch closely

tabard *n* a short sleeveless outer garment, esp. one worn by knights over armour or by heralds

tabasco also **tabasco sauce**— *n trademark* a very hot-tasting pepper sauce

tabby *n* -bies a cat whose fur has dark stripes

tabernacle *n* **1** a movable framework of wood hung with curtains, used in worship by the Jews before they settled in Palestine **2** the name used by several Christian churches for a building of worship **3** a small box in which the holy bread and wine are kept in certain Christian churches

table¹ *n* **1** a piece of furniture with a flat top supported by legs **2** such a piece of furniture made for a specific activity: *a card table* **3** the people sitting at a table **4** a collection of information arranged in an orderly way: *a bus timetable* **5** also **multiplication table** — a list which young children repeat to learn what number results when a number from 1 to 12 is multiplied by any of the numbers from 1 to 12 **6 under the table** *esp. spoken* (of money) given in order to influence somebody dishonestly

table² *adj* made to be placed and used on a table: *a table lamp*

table³ *v* tabled, tabling **1** to suggest; bring forward (a matter, report, etc.) for consideration **2** to put (facts, information, etc.) into the form of a table

tableau *n* -leaux *or* -leaus a representation, on a stage, of a scene or event by a group of people who do not move or speak

tablecloth *n* a cloth for covering a table

table d'hôte *n French* a complete meal of several dishes served at a fixed price —compare À LA CARTE

tableland *n* a large area of high flat land; plateau

table manners *n* behaviour at meals

tablemat *n* a small mat used for protecting a table's surface

tablespoon *n* a large spoon used for serving food from a bowl or dish — ~ful *n*

tablet 1 a hard flat block of some substance, esp. a small round one of medicine **2** a small slab of stone or metal with words cut into it **3** a thin sheet of clay or wax used as a writing surface in ancient times

table tennis *n* a game played on a table with bats, a net, and a small ball

tableware *n* the plates, cutlery, etc., used for a meal

tabloid *n* a newspaper with a small page size

taboo *n* taboos **1** a strong social custom forbidding an act or the naming of certain things **2** religious, social, or magical rules forbidding the naming, use, or touching of a person or object considered too holy or evil — **taboo** *adj* : *a taboo act*

tabor *n* a small drum beaten with the hand, usu. played together with a pipe

tabulate *v* -lated, -lating to arrange (facts, figures, information, etc.) in the form of a table — **-lar** *adj*: *information in tabular form* — **-lation** *n*

tabulator *n* an apparatus on a typewriter used for typing information in columns

tacit *adj* understood without being put into words: *a tacit agreement* — ~ly *adv*

taciturn *adj* speaking little — ~ity *n* — ~ly *adv*

tack¹ *n* **1** a small nail with a broad flat head **2** the course of a sailing ship in relation to the position of its sails **3** a course of action: *to try a new tack* **4** a long loose stitch —see also **get down to** BRASS TACKS

tack² *v* **1** to fasten with a tack **2** to change tack **3** to sew with long loose straight stitches

tackle¹ *n* **1** the apparatus used in a sport, such as the rod, line, hooks, etc., used in fishing **2** a system of pulleys for working a ship's sails, raising heavy weights, etc. **3** (in games such as football) an act of trying to take the ball from an opponent

tackle² *v* -led, -ling **1** to try to take the ball away from (an opponent) **2** *esp. spoken* **a** to deal with: *The children didn't know how to tackle the question* **b** to deal with by speaking forcefully: *If Bill's late again I'll have to tackle him about it*

tack on *v adv esp. spoken* to add (something) to the end of a speech, book, etc.

tacky *adj* -ier, -iest sticky — **-iness** *adj*

tact *n* skill in handling people without causing offence — ~ful *adj* — ~fully *adv* — ~less *adj* — ~lessly *adv* — ~lessness *n*

tactic *n* a means of getting a desired result

tactician *n* a person skilled in tactics

tactics *n* **1** the art of arranging military forces and moving them during battle **2** the art of using existing means to get a desired result —compare STRATEGY — **-tical** *adj* — **-tically** *adv*

tactile *adj* technical **1** that can be felt by touch **2** of or related to the sense of touch: *tactile organs*

tadpole *n* the young of a frog or toad

taffeta *n* a thin shiny smooth cloth made from silk, nylon, etc.

taffrail *n* technical the rail around the stern of a ship or boat

tag¹ *n* **1** a small narrow length of paper, material, etc., fixed to something to show what it

699   **tak**

is, details about it, etc. **2** a metal or plastic point at the end of a cord, shoelace, etc. **3** a phrase or sentence spoken (too) often, esp. one in Latin

tag² v **-gg- 1** to fasten a tag to (something) **2** to put (someone) into a kind or class **3** to follow closely: *tagging along behind*

tag³ also **tick, tig, he—** n a children's chasing game

tail¹ n **1** the movable part growing at the back of a creature's body ⨾BIRD **2** anything like this in appearance, shape, or position **3** the back, last, or lowest part of various things **4** the side of a coin which does not bear the head of a ruler (esp. in the phrase **heads or tails**) —compare HEAD, REVERSE **5** sl a person employed to watch and follow someone **6 turn tail** to run away —see also **not be able to make** HEAD **or tail of** — ~**less** adj

tail² v esp. spoken **1** to follow closely behind (someone): *The police have been tailing me* **2** to cut the stems off the bottom of (berries)

tailback n a queue of traffic caused because the road ahead is blocked

tailcoat also **tails—** n a man's formal evening coat with a long shaped back

tail end n the last part

tailgate² n **1** a door which opens upwards at the back of a car **2** also **tailboard** —the board at the back of a vehicle that can be let down or removed for loading and unloading

taillight n a red light at the back of a vehicle

tail off also **tail away—** v adv to lessen in quantity, strength, or quality

tailor¹ n a person who makes outer garments to order, esp. for men

tailor² v to make an outer garment by cutting and sewing cloth

tailor-made adj **1** (of clothes) made specially for the buyer —compare READY-MADE **2** exactly suited to a special need: *John's tailor-made for this job*

tailwind n a wind coming from behind

taint¹ v **1** to touch or infect as with something undesirable **2** to make unfit for use: *The warm weather's tainted this meat*

taint² n a touch of decay, infection, or bad or immoral influence

take¹ v **took, taken, taking 1** to get possession of; gain; seize; win **2** to hold with the hands **3** to borrow or use without asking permission or by mistake **4** to hold: *This bottle takes a litre* **5** to carry from one place to another **6** to carry (to a person): *Take him a cup of tea* **7** to use in getting from one place to another: *take the bus* **8** to gain: *If he wins he will take the title* **9** to buy: *We take 2 newspapers a day* **10** to eat, drink, breathe in, etc.: *Take your medicine* **11** to have: *taking a walk* **12** to test, measure, etc.: *Take your temperature* **13** to subtract: *Take 5 from 12* **14** to follow: *a difficult course to take* **15** to swear (an oath) **16** to understand: *The girl took his smile to mean yes* **17** to attract; delight: *really taken by the little dog* **18** to study as a course: *take history*

19 to last: *How long does the flight take?* **22** to need: *It takes a thief to know a thief* **21** to cost: *Keeping a horse takes a lot of money* **22** to accept: *This machine only takes 5-pence coins* **23** to make by photography: *I had my picture taken* **24** to have an intended effect: *The colour took and her white dress is now red* **25** to become or cause to become: *John was taken ill* **26** to write down: *He took my name and address* **27** to jump over: *The horse took that fence well* **28** to accept: *I won't take less than $500* **29 take to one's heels/legs** to run away —see also TAKE ABACK, TAKE AFTER, TAKE BACK, TAKE FOR, TAKE IN, TAKE OFF, TAKE ON, TAKE OUT, TAKE OUT ON, TAKE OVER, TAKE TO, TAKE UP, TAKE UP WITH — **taker** n

take² n **1** a scene that has been or is to be photographed for a film: *6 takes before the director was satisfied* **2** the amount of money taken by a business, thief, etc. **3** a share of this

take aback v adv to surprise and confuse (someone)

take after v prep to look or behave like: *Mary takes after her mother*

takeaway (US & Scots **carryout**)— adj, n **-ways** (from) a shop where cooked meals are bought and taken away to be eaten

take back v adv to agree to receive back

take for v prep to believe to be, esp. by mistake

take-home pay n pay left after all taxes, union payments, etc., have been paid

take in v adv **1** to provide lodgings for **2** to include: *The British Empire once took in a quarter of the world* **3** to reduce the size of (a garment) —compare LET OUT **4** to understand: *It took me a long time to take it all in* **5** to deceive; cheat

takeoff n **1** the beginning of a flight, when a plane, spacecraft, etc., rises from the ground **2** esp. spoken a copy of someone's typical behaviour, usu. done to amuse others: *a takeoff of the head-master*

take off v adv **1** to remove (a garment) **2** esp. spoken to copy (someone, esp. his speech or manners) —compare IMPERSONATE, MIMIC **3** (of a plane, spacecraft, etc.) to rise into the air at the beginning of a flight —see also **take the** EDGE **off**

take on v adv **1** to employ **2** to begin to have (a quality or appearance) **3** to start a quarrel or fight with: *Why don't you take on someone your own size?* **4** to accept (work, responsibility, etc.)

take out v adv **1** to remove from inside **2** to go somewhere with (a person): *He's taking me out* **3** to obtain officially: *Have you taken out insurance?* **4 take someone out of himself** to amuse or interest someone so that worries are forgotten **5 take it out of someone** esp. spoken to use all the strength of someone: *The long journey seems to have taken it out of mother* —see also **take the wind out of someone's** SAILS

take out on v adv prep to express (one's feelings) by making (someone else) suffer

takeover *n* an act of gaining control, esp. over a business company by buying most of the shares

take over *v adv* to gain control over and responsibility for —compare OVERTAKE

take to *v prep* 1 to like 2 to begin as a practice, habit, etc.: *John's taken to riding a motorcycle* 3 to go to: *The criminal took to the woods* —see also **take someone to** TASK

take up *v adv* 1 to begin to spend time doing: *took up art* 2 to continue: *take up the story* 3 to raise consideration of

take up with *v adv prep* to become friendly with

taking *adj esp. spoken* attractive

takings *n* receipts of money, esp. by a shop

talc *n* 1 a soft smooth mineral, used in making paints, plastics, and various body powders 2 talcum powder

talcum powder also **talc powder**— *n* a very fine powder of crushed talc, spread over the body esp. after a bath

tale *n* 1 a story of real or imaginary events 2 a piece of news, esp. when false or intended to hurt: *to tell tales*

talebearer also **taleteller**— *n* a person who nastily spreads false or unkind pieces of news around

talent *n* 1 (a) special natural or learnt ability or skill, esp. of a high quality —see GENIUS (USAGE) 2 people of such ability: *The school has plenty of talent* — ~ed *adj*

talisman *n* -s an object believed to give power or protection

talk¹ *v* 1 to use words; have the power of speech; speak 2 to make thoughts, ideas, etc., known by means of speech 3 to express thoughts as if by speech: *People who cannot speak or hear can talk by using signs* 4 to speak about: *We talked music all night* 5 **talk big** to boast —see also TALK DOWN, TALK DOWN TO, TALK OUT, TALK OVER, TALK ROUND, **talk** SHOP

talk² *n* 1 a particular way of speech or conversation: *baby talk* 2 a conversation 3 an informal speech 4 a subject of conversation: *She's the talk of the street* 5 empty speech: *His threats were just talk* see also TALKS

talkative *adj* liking to talk a lot — ~ness *n*

talk down *v adv* to guide (a plane) safely to the ground by giving instructions by radio

talk down to *v adv prep* to speak to (someone) as if one believes oneself to be more important or clever

talkie *n* old use esp.spoken a film with sounds

talking point *n* a subject of argument or conversation

talk out *v adv* to settle by talking: *talk out our differences*

talk over *v adv* to consider (something) thoroughly; speak about

talk round¹ *v adv* to persuade (someone)

talk round² *v prep* to avoid speaking directly about (a matter)

talks *n* a formal exchange of views

tall *adj* 1 having a greater than average height 2 having the stated height: *4 feet tall* — ~ish *adj* — ~ness *n*

tallboy *n* -boys a tall chest of drawers

tall order *n* a request that is unreasonably difficult

tallow *n* hard animal fat used for making candles

tall story also **tall tale**— *n* -ries a story that is difficult to believe

tally¹ *n* -lies an account, record of points, or score, or anything on which this is kept

tally² *v* -lied, -lying 1 to agree or cause to agree or equal exactly: *Our stories must tally if we want the police to believe us* 2 to calculate

tallyho *interj* (an expression shouted by a fox-hunter when he sees the fox)

tallyman *n* -men a person who sells cheap goods and collects weekly or monthly payments for them

Talmud *n* the body of Jewish law

talon *n* the powerful claw of a bird of prey

tamarisk *n* a type of bush or small tree with pink flowers

tambourine *n* a small hand-held drum, with jingling metal discs around the edge

tame¹ *adj* 1 gentle and unafraid; not fierce; trained to live with man 2 unexciting; uninteresting — ~ly *adv* — ~ness *n*

tame² *v* **tamed, taming** 1 to train (a wild or fierce animal) to be gentle and unafraid in man's presence — compare DOMESTICATE 2 to make (something dangerous) useful and safe — **tamable** or **tameable** *adj* — **tamer** *n*

tam-o'-shanter also **tammy**— *n* a flat-topped soft hat of Scottish origin

tamp *v* to pack tightly or force down by repeated blows

tamper with *v prep* to make changes in (something) without permission

tampon *n* a small pad of soft material which fits inside a woman's sex organ (VAGINA) to absorb the monthly flow from the womb

tan¹ *v* -nn- 1 to make (animal skin) into leather by treating with tannin 2 to make or become brown, esp. by sunlight 3 esp. spoken to beat (someone) severely: *I'll tan your hide!*

tan² *n* 1 a yellowish brown colour 2 the brown colour given to the skin by sunlight

tan³ *adj* -nn- having a yellowish brown colour

tan⁴ *abbrev. for:* tangent

tandem¹ *n* a bicycle built for 2 riders sitting one behind the other

tandem² *adv* arranged one behind the other

tang *n* a strong taste or smell special to something — ~y *adj*

tangent *n* 1 a straight line touching the edge of a curve but not cutting across it ⟋MATHEMATICS 2 *technical* a measure of the size of an angle calculated by dividing the length of the side opposite it in a right-angled triangle by the length of the side next to it: $\tan \theta = opposite/adjacent$

⊏⃔TRIGONOMETRY **3 go/fly off at a tangent** *esp. spoken* to change suddenly from one course of action, thought, etc., to another

tangential *adj* **1** *technical* related to or having the nature of a tangent: *After you've drawn the circle, draw a line tangential to it* **2** incidental

tangerine *n* **1** a small sweet edible orange **2** a dark orange colour

tangible *adj* **1** that can be felt by touch **2** real; not imaginary — **-bility** *n* — **-bly** *adv*

tangle[1] *v* **-gled, -gling** to make or become a confused mass of disordered and twisted threads

tangle[2] *n* **1** a confused mass of hair, thread, string, etc. **2** a confused disordered state

tangle with *v prep esp.spoken* to quarrel, argue, or fight with (someone)

tango *n, v* **-gos; -goed, -going** (to perform) a spirited dance of Spanish American origin

tank *n* **1** a large container for storing liquid or gas **2** an enclosed heavily armed armoured vehicle that moves on 2 metal belts

tankard *n* a large mug

tanker *n* a ship, plane, or railway or road vehicle built to carry large quantities of gas or liquid ⊏⃔OIL

tanner *n* a person who tans animal skin to make leather

tannery *n* **-ries** a place where animal skin is made into leather

tannin also **tannic acid**— *n* a reddish acid made from the bark of certain trees, used in preparing leather, and also found naturally in tea leaves, grape skins, etc.

tannoy *n* **-noys** a system of giving out information by means of loudspeakers

tansy *n* **-sies** a wild plant with yellow flowers and bitter tasting leaves

tantalize, -lise *v* to worry or annoy (a person or animal) by keeping something strongly desired just out of reach; cause anger by raising hopes that cannot be satisfied

tantamount *adj* equal in value, force, or effect

tantrum *n* a sudden uncontrolled attack of bad temper

Taoism *n* a religion developed from a mixture of ancient Chinese philosophy, popular Chinese beliefs, and Buddhism — **-ist** *adj, n*

tap[1] *n* **1** any apparatus for controlling the flow of liquid or gas from a pipe, barrel, etc. **2 on tap** *esp.spoken* ready for use when needed

tap[2] *v* **-pp-** **1** to use or draw from: *to tap the nation's natural mineral wealth* **2** to make a connection to (a telephone) in order to listen to conversations

tap[3] *v* **-pp-** to strike lightly against something

tap[4] *n* a short light blow

tap dancing *n* stage dancing in which musical time is beaten by the feet of the dancer, who wears special shoes — **-cer** *n*

tape[1] *n* **1** narrow material in the form of a band **2** a string stretched across the winning line in a race and broken by the winner **3** (a length

of) narrow material covered with a magnetic substance on which sound can be recorded **4** also **tape recording**— a length of this on which a recording has been made —see also RED TAPE

tape[2] *v* **taped, taping** **1** also **tape-record**— to record on tape **2** to fasten or tie (a parcel, packet, etc.) with tape **3 have someone taped** *sl* to understand a person, esp. their weakness, thoroughly

tape deck *n* the apparatus in a tape recorder that is in contact with the tape

tape measure *n* a band of narrow cloth or bendable steel marked with divisions of length

taper[1] *n* **1** a gradual decrease in the width of a long object **2** a length of string covered in wax, used for lighting candles, pipes, etc. **3** a very thin candle

taper[2] *v* to make or become gradually narrower towards one end

tape recorder *n* an instrument which can record and play back sound using tape

tapestry *n* **-tries** **1** a heavy cloth into which a picture or pattern is woven **2** a wall-hanging made of this — **-tried** *adj*

tapeworm *n* a long flat worm that lives in the bowels of man and other animals

tapioca *n* grains made from the crushed dried roots of cassava

tapir *n* **tapir** or **tapirs** a type of long-nosed piglike animal of tropical America ⊏⃔MAMMAL

tappet *n* a part that rests on a cam in a machine ⊏⃔CAR

taproot *n* the main root of a plant, which grows straight down

tar[1] *n* a black substance used for making roads, preserving wood, etc.

tar[2] *v* **-rr-** **1** to cover with tar **2 tar and feather** to put tar on (someone) and then cover with feathers as a punishment

tarantella also **tarantelle**— *n* a rapid Italian dance for two people, or music for this △ TARANTULA

tarantula *n* a type of large hairy poisonous spider △ TARANTELLA

tardy *adj* **-dier, -diest** slow or late in acting — **tardily** *adv* — **tardiness** *n*

tare[1] *n* *Bible* a type of weed which grows among corn

tare[2] *n* *technical* **1** the weight of an unloaded goods vehicle **2** an amount subtracted for this when weighing a loaded goods vehicle

target *n* **1** anything at which shots, missiles, etc. are aimed **2** a person or thing that is made the object of unfavourable remarks, jokes, etc. **3** a total or object which one desires to reach

tariff *n* **1** a tax collected by a government on goods coming into or sometimes going out of a country **2** a list of fixed prices

tarmac[1] also **tarmacadam**— *adj, n* (made of) a mixture of tar and very small stones used for making road surfaces

tarmac[2] *n* an area covered with tarmac, esp. a runway

tarmac³ also **tarmacadam**— v -ck- to cover (a road's surface) with tarmac

tarn n a small mountain lake or pool

tarnish¹ v to make or become dull or discoloured

tarnish² n dullness; loss of polish

tarot n a pack of special cards used for fortune-telling

tarpaulin n (a sheet or cover of) heavy water-proof cloth

tarragon n a plant with strong smelling leaves used in cookery

tarry v -ried, -rying to delay

tarsus n -si medical a collection of 7 small bones in the ankle — -sal adj

tart¹ adj 1 sharp to the taste 2 spoken sharply and unkindly — ~ly adv — ~ness n

tart² n 1 fruit or jam cooked on a pastry base —see PIE (USAGE) 2 sl a girl or woman who is regarded as having a sexually immoral character

tartan n 1 woollen cloth with checks of various colours 2 a special pattern on this cloth worn by a Scottish clan

tartar¹ n 1 a hard substance that forms on the teeth 2 also **cream of tartar**— a white powder used in cookery and in medicine

tartar² n a fierce person with a violent temper

tartaric acid n a strong acid of plant origin used in preparing certain foods and medicines

tartar sauce, tartare sauce n a kind of cold sauce

task n 1 a piece of work (that must be) done, esp. if hard or unpleasant 2 **take someone to task** to scold someone

task force n a military force sent to a place for a special purpose

taskmaster fem. **taskmistress**— n a person who gives jobs, esp. hard and unpleasant ones, to other people: a hard taskmaster

tassel n a bunch of threads tied together into a round ball at one end and hung as an ornament — ~led adj

taste¹ v **tasted, tasting** 1 to test the taste of (food or drink) by taking a little into the mouth 2 to experience the taste of 3 to eat or drink: He had not tasted food in 3 days 4 to have a particular taste: This soup tastes of chicken 5 to experience: to taste freedom

taste² n 1 the sense by which one knows one food from another by its sweetness, bitterness, etc. 2 the quality special to any food or drink which makes one able to recognize it by taste 3 a small quantity of food or drink: a taste of soup 4 the judgement of beauty, art, music, etc.; choice and use of manners, fashions, etc.: good/bad/poor taste 5 a personal liking for something: a taste for adventure 6 an experience: a taste of success

taste bud n a group of cells on the tongue which can tell the difference between foods according to their taste

tasteful adj having or showing good taste — ~ly adv — ~ness n

tasteless adj 1 having no taste 2 having or showing poor taste — ~ly adv — ~ness n
USAGE Tasteless is used of food, meaning that it has no taste. When tasteless is used of anything else (furniture, people, etc.) it means ' having or showing bad taste ': The potatoes were tasteless. | His remarks were tasteless. Distasteful is not used in either of these meanings. It refers only to unpleasant things that must be done: The task was distasteful but necessary.

taster n a person whose job is testing the quality of foods, teas, wines, etc., by tasting them

tasty adj -ier, -iest pleasing to the taste — tastily adv

tatter n a ragged shred of cloth, paper, etc.

tattered adj torn; ragged

tatters n old worn-out clothing

tatting n 1 a kind of lace made by hand 2 the art of making this

tattle v -tled, -tling to talk about unimportant things — ~r n

tattoo¹ n -toos 1 a rapid beating of drums played late at night to signal that soldiers should go to their rooms 2 a rapid continuous beating of drums 3 an outdoor military show with music, usu. at night

tattoo² n -toos a pattern, picture, or message put on the skin by tattooing

tattoo³ v -tooed, -tooing to mark (a pattern, message, etc.) on the skin by pricking it and putting in coloured dyes — ~ist n

tatty adj -tier, -tiest esp. spoken untidy — -tily adv — -tiness n

taught past tense & past part. of TEACH

taunt¹ v to try to make (someone) angry or upset by making unkind remarks, laughing at faults or failures, etc. — ~ingly adv

taunt² n a remark or joke intended to hurt someone's feelings or make him angry

Taurus n 1 a the 2nd division in the zodiac belt of stars, represented by a bull b the group of stars (CONSTELLATION) formerly in this division ⊸ZODIAC 2 a person born under this sign

taut adj 1 stretched tight 2 showing signs of anxiety: a taut expression — ~ly adv — ~ness n

tautology n -gies an unnecessary repeating of the same idea in different words (as in He sat alone by himself) — -gical adj

tavern n old use an inn

tawdry adj -drier, -driest cheaply showy — -drily adv — -driness n

tawny adj -nier, -niest having a brownish yellow colour

tax¹ v 1 to charge a tax on 2 to make heavy demands (on); tire — ~ability n — ~able adj

tax² n 1 (a sum of) money paid to the government according to income, property, goods bought, etc. 2 a heavy demand: a tax on your strength

taxation n 1 the act of taxing 2 money raised from taxes

tax collector *n* an official who collects taxes

tax haven *n* a place where people live because there is little or no taxation

taxi also *esp. written* **taxicab** — *n* a car which may be hired by the public with its driver

taxi² *v* **-ied, -iing** *or* - **ying** (of a plane) to move along the ground,

taxidermy *n* the art of stuffing the skins of animals so that they look like living creatures — **-mist** *n*

taxi rank *n* a place where taxis wait to be hired

taxonomy *n* the branch of science dealing with putting plants and animals into various classes according to their natural relationships

tax with *v prep* to accuse (someone) of

TB *abbrev. for:* tuberculosis

T-bone also **T-bone steak**— *n* a piece of beef with a T-shaped bone in it

tea *n* **1** a type of bush mainly grown in South and East Asia for its leaves **2** (a drink made by pouring boiling water onto) the dried and cut leaves of this bush **3** a cup of this: *3 teas please!* **4** a small meal, served in the afternoon **5** a medicinal drink made by putting roots or leaves in hot water: *herb tea* **7 one's cup of tea** the sort of thing one likes

teabag *n* a small bag with tea leaves inside, put into boiling water to make tea

tea break also **coffee break**— *n* a short pause from work for a drink, a rest, etc.

tea caddy *n* **-dies** a small box in which tea is kept

teacake *n* a type of bun, eaten with butter

teach *v* **taught, teaching** to give knowledge or skill of, or training or lessons to

teacher *n* a person who teaches, esp. as a profession

teach-in *n spoken* an exchange of opinions about a subject of interest, as held in a college by students, teachers, guest speakers, etc.

teaching *n* **1** the work of a teacher **2** that which is taught

teaching hospital *n* a hospital where medical students can practise medicine under guidance

tea cloth *n* TEA TOWEL

tea cosy *n* **-cosies** a thick covering put over a teapot to keep the contents hot

teacup *n* **1** a cup in which tea is served **2 storm in a teacup** a lot of worry over something unimportant

teahouse *n* a restaurant in China or Japan where tea is served

teak *n* a large South Asian tree or its very hard yellow wood

teal *n* teal a type of small wild duck

tealeaf *n* **-leaves** one of the pieces of leaf used for making tea

team *n* **1** 2 or more animals pulling the same vehicle: *a team of horses* **2** a group of people who work, play, or act together

team up *v adv* to work together; combine

teamwork *n* the ability of a group of people to work effectively; combined effort

tea party *n* **-ties** a social gathering in the afternoon, at which tea is drunk

teapot *n* a vessel in which tea is made and served

tear¹ *n* **1** a drop of liquid from the eye **2 in tears** crying

tear² *v* **tore, torn, tearing** **1** to pull apart or into pieces by force **2** to make by doing this: *tear a hole* **3** to remove by force: *Our roof was torn off* **4** to become torn: *This material tears easily* **5** to divide by the pull of opposing forces: *torn apart by war* **6** to move excitedly with great speed: *They tore down the street* —see also TEAR APART, TEAR INTO, TEAR OFF, TEAR UP

tear³ *n* a torn place in cloth, paper, etc.

tear apart *v adv esp. spoken* to express a very poor opinion of (someone or his work)

tearaway *n sl* a noisy and violent youth

teardrop *n* a single tear

tearful *adj* **1** crying; wet with tears **2** likely to weep — ~**ly** *adv* — ~**ness** *n*

teargas *n* a stinging chemical gas that causes blindness for a short time by making the eyes water

tear into *v prep* to attack (someone) violently with blows or words

tear off *v adv esp. spoken* **1** to do (a job) rapidly **2 tear someone off a strip** to scold someone severely

tearoom *n* a restaurant where tea and light meals are served

tear up *v adv* to destroy completely by tearing

tease *v* **teased, teasing** **1** to make fun of playfully or unkindly **2** to separate and straighten threads

teasel, -zel, -zle *n* **1** a type of plant with prickly leaves and flowers **2** a dried flower from this plant, used in former times for teasing threads

teaser *n* **1** *sl* a difficult question **2** also **tease**— a person who teases a lot

teaspoon *n* a small spoon used for stirring tea — ~**ful** *n*

tea strainer *n* a small bowl-shaped object with holes in it through which tea is poured to keep leaves out of the cup

teat *n* **1** a shaped rubber object fixed to the end of a baby's feeding bottle **2** a nipple, or the part which serves the same purpose on an animal

tea towel *n* a cloth for drying cups, plates, etc.

tech *n esp. spoken* a college (**technical college**) providing courses in sciences, practical skills, art, social studies, etc. —compare POLYTECHNIC

technical *adj* **1** having special knowledge, esp. of an industrial or scientific subject **2** of or related to a particular and esp. a practical or scientific subject —compare ACADEMIC **3** belonging to a particular art, science, profession, etc. — ~**ly** *adv*

technicality *n* **-ties** a technical point, detail, or expression

technical knockout *n* the ending of a boxing match because one of the fighters cannot continue

technician *n* a highly skilled scientific or industrial worker; specialist in practical details

technique *n* 1 the method or manner in which a skilled activity is carried out 2 skill in art or some specialist activity

technocracy *n* -cies (organization and control of industry by) a group of skilled specialists

technocrat *n* a member or supporter of (a) technocracy

technology *n* -gies the branch of knowledge dealing with scientific and industrial methods and their practical use in industry; practical science ⌐ SCIENCE — -gical *adj* — -gically *adv* — -gist *n*

tectonics *n* geology dealing with the earth's structure and its folding and faults ⌐ GEOGRAPHY

teddy bear also **teddy**— *n* a toy bear

Te Deum *n* -ums *Latin* 1 an ancient Christian song of praise 2 a piece of music written specially for this

tedious *adj* long and boring — ~ly *adv* — ~ness *n*

tedium *n* tediousness

tee *n* (in golf) (the area surrounding) a heap of sand or a shaped object from which the ball is first driven at each hole

teem¹ *v esp. in literature* to be present in large numbers

teem² *v esp. spoken* to rain very heavily

teeming *adj esp. in literature* full of a type of creature

teem with *v prep esp. in literature* to have (a type of creature) present in great numbers

teenage also **teenaged**— *adj* of, for, or being a teenager

teenager *n* a person aged between 13 and 19

teens *n* the period of life between the ages of 13 and 19

tee off *v adv* **teed, teeing off** (in golf) to drive the ball from a tee

tee shirt *n* a T-shirt

teeter *v* to stand or move unsteadily

teeth¹ *n* 1 *esp. spoken* effective force or power: *When will the police be given the necessary teeth to deal with young criminals?* 2 armed to the teeth very heavily armed 3 escape by the skin of one's teeth to have a narrow escape 4 get one's teeth into to do (a job) very actively and purposefully 5 in the teeth of against the strength of 6 set someone's teeth on edge to give someone the unpleasant sensation caused by certain acid tastes or high sounds 7 show one's teeth to act threateningly

teeth² *pl. of* TOOTH

teethe *v* **teethed, teething** (esp. of babies) to grow teeth

teething troubles *n* troubles and difficulties happening during the early stages of an activity or operation

teetotal *adj* never drinking, or opposed to the drinking of, alcohol — ~ler *n*

Teflon *n trademark* a man-made substance used for moulding things and to which food will not stick

telecommunications *n* the various methods of receiving or sending messages by telephone or telegraph

telegram *n* 1 a message sent by telegraph 2 a piece of paper on which this message is delivered

telegraph¹ *n* 1 a method of sending messages along wire by electric signals 2 the apparatus that receives or sends messages in this way

telegraph² *v* to send by telegraph

telegraphese *n* a manner of writing in which unnecessary words are not used (as in *Arriving Wednesday* for *I am arriving on Wednesday*)

telegraphic *adj* of, for, like, or sent by a telegram — ~ally *adv*

telekinesis *n* the moving of solid objects by the power of the mind —compare PSYCHOKINESIS

telemeter *n technical* an instrument that measures quantities and sends the results by radio to a home station

telemetry *n technical* the collection of information by telemeter

telepathist *n* a person able to communicate by telepathy

telepathy *n* the sending of thoughts from one person's mind to another's — -thic *adj* : *telepathic messages/people* — -thically *adv*

telephone¹ also *(esp. spoken)* **phone**— *n* 1 a method of talking over distances by electrical means: *radio telephone* 2 the apparatus that receives or sends sounds in this way

telephone² also *(esp. spoken)* **phone**— *v* -phoned, -phoning 1 to speak (a message) to (someone) by telephone: *I telephoned your aunt the news* 2 to send (something) to (someone) by telephone: *We telephoned Jean a greetings telegram* 3 to reach or try to reach by telephone

telephone directory also **telephone book**— *n* -ries a book containing a list of all the people in an area who have a telephone, with their telephone numbers and addresses

telephone exchange *n* a place where telephone connections are made

telephonist *n* a person who works at a telephone exchange

telephony *n* the practice of using telephones

telephotography *n* the photography of objects too distant for ordinary cameras by cameras made for the purpose — -phic *adj*

telephoto lens *n* a lens that allows a camera to take enlarged pictures of distant objects

teleprinter *n* a machine used for sending and receiving written messages by telegraphic methods

Teleprompter *n trademark* a machine that unrolls lines of enlarged writing, placed in front of a person appearing on television so that he can read it

telescope¹ n an instrument used for seeing distant objects —compare RADIO TELESCOPE ◉

telescope² v **-scoped, -scoping** to make or become shorter by crushing, as in a violent accident

telescopic adj 1 of, like, or related to a telescope 2 made of parts that slide one over another so that the whole can be made shorter

televise v **-vised, -vising** to broadcast or be broadcast by television

television also (esp. spoken) **telly**— n 1 the method of transmitting pictures and usu. sound by means of electrical waves 2 the news, plays, etc., broadcast in this way: the television news 3 also **television set**— a boxlike apparatus for receiving television pictures and sound 4 the industry of making and broadcasting plays, films, etc., on television 5 **on (the) television** a broadcast by television: What's on television? b broadcasting by television: The President spoke on television

telex¹ n 1 an international service provided by post offices whereby written messages are passed by teleprinter 2 a message sent in this way

telex² v to send (a message, news, etc.) to (a person, place, etc.) by telex

tell v **told, telling** 1 to make (something) known in words to (someone) 2 to warn; advise: I told you so 3 to show; make known: This light tells you if the machine is on 4 to find out; know: It's impossible to tell who'll win 5 to order; direct: I told you to get here early 6 to recognize; know: I can't tell if it's him or not 7 to be noticeable; have an effect: Her nervousness began to tell —see also TELL ON 8 to speak someone's secret to someone else —see also TELL ON 9 **all told** altogether 10 **tell me another** esp. spoken I don't believe you 11 **tell the time** to read the time from a clock or watch 12 **there is/was/will be no telling** it is/was/will be impossible to know: There's no telling what will happen 13 **you're telling me** esp. spoken (a strong way of saying) I know this already

teller n a person who counts votes, as at an election

telling adj 1 very effective: a telling blow 2 that shows, perhaps unintentionally, one's feelings — ~ly adv

tell off v adv 1 esp. spoken to scold 2 to separate (a group) from the whole body (for special work or to do something)

tell on v prep 1 also **tell upon**— to have a bad effect on: Late nights are telling on your work 2 esp. spoken (used esp. by children) to inform against (someone)

telltale¹ n esp. spoken a person who informs on other people

telltale² adj revealing: a telltale look

telly n **-lies** esp. spoken television

temerity n esp. written foolish boldness; rashness △ TIMOROUS

temp n a person, esp. a secretary, employed to work in an office for a short time

temper¹ n 1 a particular state of mind with

regard to anger: in a good temper 2 an angry or impatient state of mind: John's in a temper today 3 **fly/get into a temper** to become angry suddenly 4 **keep one's temper** to stay calm 5 **lose one's temper** to become angry 6 **out of temper** esp. written angry

temper² v 1 to bring (metal, clay, etc.) to the desired degree of toughness or firmness by treatment 2 to make less severe: justice tempered with mercy

tempera n technical 1 thick paint that can be thinned with egg, water, etc. 2 painting done with this, esp. on wet plaster

temperament n a person's nature, esp. as it influences his thinking or behaviour

temperamental adj 1 caused by one's nature 2 having frequent changes of temper — ~ly adv

temperance n never drinking alcohol

temperate adj 1 practising self-control 2 (of places, climate, etc.) free from very high or very low temperatures

temperature n 1 the degree of heat of a place, object, etc. 2 **have/run a temperature** to have a bodily temperature higher than normal 3 **take someone's temperature** to measure the temperature of someone's body

tempest n literature a violent storm

tempestuous adj stormy; violent — ~ly adv

template, templet n a thin board or plate cut into a pattern, used as a guide for cutting metal, wood, etc.

temple¹ n a place for worship in various religions

temple² n one of the flattish places on each side of the forehead

tempo n **-pos** or **-pi** 1 the rate of movement, work, or activity 2 the speed at which music is played

temporal adj 1 of or limited by time: "When" and "while" are temporal conjunctions 2 of or related to practical material affairs as opposed to religious affairs —opposite **spiritual** △ TEMPORARY

temporary n lasting for a limited time — compare PERMANENT — **-rarily** adv — **-rariness** n

tempt v 1 to persuade or try to persuade (someone) to do something unwise or wrong 2 **tempt Providence** to take an unnecessary risk — ~er (fem. ~ress) n — ~ingly adv

temptation n 1 the act of tempting or the state of being tempted 2 something very attractive: the temptations of a city

ten adj, n, pron 1 the number 10 2 **ten a penny** esp. spoken very common 3 **ten to one** very likely: Ten to one he will be late — **tenth** adj, n, pron, adv

tenacious adj 1 unyielding; firm 2 (of memory) able to keep information well 3 esp. written holding firmly — ~ly adv — ~ness n — **-city** n

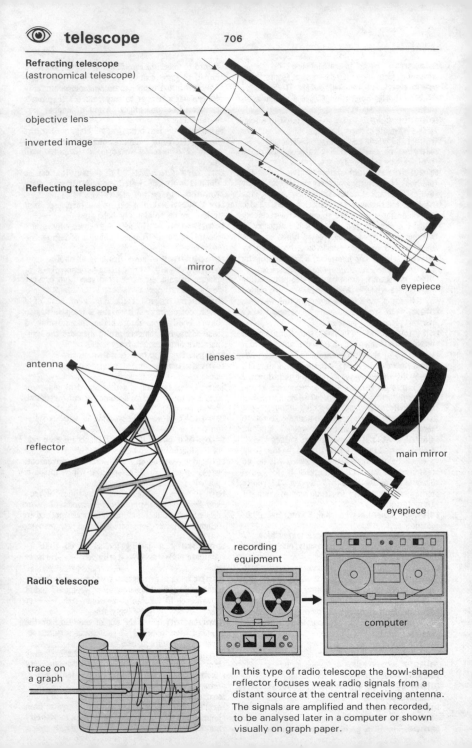

Refracting telescope
(astronomical telescope)

objective lens

inverted image

Reflecting telescope

mirror

eyepiece

antenna

lenses

reflector

main mirror

eyepiece

recording
equipment

computer

Radio telescope

trace on
a graph

In this type of radio telescope the bowl-shaped
reflector focuses weak radio signals from a
distant source at the central receiving antenna.
The signals are amplified and then recorded,
to be analysed later in a computer or shown
visually on graph paper.

tenancy *n* **-cies** **1** the possession and use of a building, land, etc., for which rent is paid **2** the period of a person's tenancy

tenant[1] *n* a person who pays rent for a building, land, etc.

tenant[2] *v* to pay rent for the use of (a building, land, etc.)

tenant farmer *n* a farmer who rents his land

tend[1] *v* to take care of; look after

tend[2] *v* **1** to move in a certain direction: *Interest rates are tending upwards* **2** to have a tendency: *Janet tends to get angry if you annoy her*

tendency *n* **-cies** **1** a likelihood of developing or acting in a particular way **2** a natural skill

tender[1] *adj* **1** not hard; soft **2** delicate: *tender flowers* **3** painful; sore **4** gentle; kind: *a tender heart* — ~ly *adv* — ~ness *n*

tender[2] *n* **1** a wagon carrying coal and/or water behind a railway engine **2** a small boat for travelling between the shore and a larger boat

tender[3] *n* a statement of the price one would charge for goods or services

tenderfoot *n* **-foots** *or* **-feet** an inexperienced beginner

tender for *v prep* to offer formally to do (something) at a certain price

tenderhearted *adj* easily moved to love or pity — ~ly *adv* — ~ness *n*

tenderize, -ise *v* **-ized, -izing** to make (meat) tender by special preparation

tenderloin *n* meat from each side of the backbone of cows or pigs

tendon *n* a strong cord connecting a muscle to a bone ☞ ANATOMY

tendril *n* a stem by which a climbing plant attaches itself to a support

tend to *v prep* tend; attend to

tenement *n* a large building divided into flats, esp. in a poor town area

tenet *n esp. written* a belief held by a person or group

tenner *n sl* £10 or a 10 pound note

tennis *n* a game for 2 (**singles**) or 2 pairs (**doubles**) who use rackets to hit a ball across a net dividing a court —compare REAL TENNIS

tennis elbow *n* an uncomfortable medical condition of the elbow caused by too much effort

tenon *n* an end of a piece of wood cut to fit exactly into a shaped opening (MORTISE) in another

tenon saw *n* a short saw for wood

tenor *n* **1** (a man with) the highest male singing voice in general use **2** an instrument with the same range of notes **3** *esp. written* (esp. of a person's life) the general direction or style **4** *esp. written* (of speech or writing) the general meaning: *the tenor of his speech*

tenpin bowling (*US* **tenpin**)— *n* bowling

tense[1] *n* any of the forms of a verb that show the time of the action or state expressed by the verb

tense[2] *adj* **1** stretched tight **2** nervous or anxious — ~ly *adv* — ~ness *n*

tense[3] *v* **tensed, tensing** to make or become tense

tensile *adj technical* **1** of or related to tension: *tensile strength* **2** that can be stretched: *tensile rubber*

tension *n* **1** the degree of tightness of a wire, rope, etc. **2** the amount of a force stretching something **3** nervous anxiety, worry, or pressure **4** an anxious, untrusting relationship between people, countries, etc. **5** electric power: *high tension*

tent *n* a movable shelter made of cloth supported by a framework of poles and ropes —see also OXYGEN TENT

tentacle *n* a long snakelike limb on certain creatures, used for moving, feeling, seizing, touching, etc.

tentative *adj* made or done only as a suggestion — ~ly *adv* — ~ness *n*

tenterhooks *n* **on tenterhooks** in a worried or nervous state of mind

tenth *n, pron, adv, adj* 10th

tenuous *adj* **1** very thin **2** (of ideas, opinions, etc.) having little meaning — ~ly *adv* — ~ness *n*

tenure *n* the act or right of holding land or office

tepee *n* a round tent of the type used by North American Indians

tepid *adj* only slightly warm — ~ity *n* — ~ly *adv* — ~ness *n*

tequila *n* a strong alcoholic drink made in Mexico

term[1] *n* **1** one of the periods of time into which the school, university, legal, etc., year is divided **2** a fixed period of time: *a 4-year term* **3** a period of time after which something is to end: *Our agreement is getting near its term* **4** a word or expression with a special meaning or used in a technical sense: *a medical term* **5** each of the quantities in a ratio, a sum, or an algebraic expression: *The expression $X^2 + 3XY$ contains the terms X^2 and $3XY$* **6** **in the long/short term** over a long/short period of time

term[2] *v* to call: *You wouldn't term this house beautiful*

termagant *n esp. in literature* a noisy quarrelsome woman

terminal[1] *adj* **1** *technical* of or happening at the end of a term **2** related to an illness that will cause death **3** of or at the end or limit — ~ly *adv*

terminal[2] *n* **1** a place in the centre of a town for passengers travelling to or from an airport **2** a point at which connections can be made to an electric circuit **3** an apparatus by which a user can give instructions to and get information from a computer

terminate *v* **-nated, -nating** to come to or bring to an end — **-ation** *n*

terminology *n* **-gies** specialized words and expressions: *scientific terminology* —compare NOMENCLATURE — **-ogical** *adj* — **-ogically** *adv*

terminus *n* -ni *or* -nuses the last stop on a railway or bus route

termite *n* a type of tropical antlike insect that lives in very large groups ☞ INSECT

terms *n* **1** the conditions of an agreement, contract, etc. **2** conditions with regard to payment, prices, etc. **3 come to terms with** to accept (something one does not want to accept) **4 in no uncertain terms** clearly and usu. angrily **5 in terms of** with regard to: *In terms of money we're quite rich, but not in terms of happiness* **6 on equal terms** as equals **7 on good/bad/speaking/friendly terms** having a stated relationship

tern *n* any of several types of smallish long-winged black and white fork-tailed seabird

terrace¹ *n* **1** a flat level area cut from a slope **2** a flat outdoor living area next to a house or on its roof **3** a row of houses joined to each other

terrace² *v* -raced, -racing to form into terraces

terracotta *n* hard reddish brown baked clay

terra firma *n* *Latin* dry land

terrain *n* a stretch of land, esp. in relation to its nature: *rocky terrain*

terrapin *n* -pin *or* -pins a type of small turtle that lives in warm areas

terrestrial *adj* **1** of or related to the earth rather than to the moon, space, etc. **2** of, being, related to, or living on land rather than in water — ~ly *adv*

terrible *adj* very bad indeed

terribly *adv* **1** very badly, severely, etc. **2** *esp. spoken* very: *terribly lucky*

terrier *n* any of several types of small active dogs

terrific *adj* *esp. spoken* **1** very good: *a terrific party* **2** very great: *terrific speed*

terrifically *adv* *esp. spoken* very

terrify *v* -fied, -fying to fill with terror or fear

territorial¹ *adj* of, related to, or limited to a territory

territorial² *n* a member of the Territorial Army

Territorial Army *n* (in Britain) an army of people who are trained in their free time — compare HOME GUARD

territorial waters *n* the sea near a country's coast, over which its laws apply

territory *n* -ries **1** an area of land, esp. ruled by one government **2** an area regarded by a person, animal, group, etc., as belonging to it alone **3** an area for which one person or branch of an organization is responsible

terror *n* **1** very great fear **2** someone or something that causes such fear **3** *esp. spoken* an annoying person

terrorism *n* the use of violence to obtain political demands — -ist *adj, n*

terrorize, -ise *v* -ized, -izing to fill with terror by violence

terror-stricken also **terror-struck**— *adj* filled with terror

terrycloth also **terry**— *n* towelling

terse *adj* using few words — ~ly *adv* — ~ness *n*

tertiary *adj* *esp. written* being at a third level or stage

Terylene *adj, n* *trademark* a type of man-made cloth

tessellated *adj* made of small coloured tiles forming a pattern

test¹ *n* **1** a number of questions, tasks, etc., set to measure someone's ability or knowledge **2** a short medical examination **3** a practical examination or trial: *a test drive* **4** something used as a standard: *a test case* **5** TEST MATCH

test² *v* **1** to study or examine by means of a test **2** to be a severe or difficult test of or for: *These roads test a car's tyres* **3** to search by means of tests: *testing for oil* — ~er *n*

testa *n* -tae the skin of a plant seed

testament *n* *law* a will (esp. in the phrase **last will and testament**)—see also OLD TESTAMENT, NEW TESTAMENT — ~ary *adj*

testate *adj* *technical* having made a will which leaves one's property to named people — opposite **intestate**

testator (*fem.* **testatrix**)— *n* *technical* the maker of a will

test ban *n* an agreement to stop testing atomic bombs

test case *n* a case in a court of law which is used as a future standard

testicle *n* one of the 2 round sperm-producing organs in the male ☞ REPRODUCTION

testify *v* -fied, -fying **1** to bear witness **2** to serve as proof: *Her red face testified to her guilt*

testimonial *n* **1** a formal written statement of a person's character —see REFERENCE (USAGE) **2** something given or done as an expression of respect, thanks, etc.

testimony *n* -nies **1** a formal statement that something is true **2** any information in support of a fact or statement

testis *n* -tes *technical* a testicle

test match also **test**— *n* an international cricket or rugby match

test pilot *n* a pilot who tests new aircraft

test tube *n* a small glass tube, closed at one end, used in scientific tests

test-tube baby *n* -babies **1** a baby born as the result of artificial insemination **2** a baby started outside the body and then planted inside

testy *adj* -tier, -tiest easily annoyed — -tily *adv* — -tiness *n*

tetanus also **lockjaw**— *n* a serious disease which stiffens the muscles, esp. of the jaw

tête-à-tête *n* a private conversation or state of privacy between 2 people — **tête-à-tête** *adv* : *had dinner tête-à-tête*

tether¹ *n* **1** a rope or chain to which an animal is tied so as to limit movement **2 at the end of one's tether** unable to suffer any more

tether² v to fasten (an animal) with a tether

tetrahedron n technical a solid figure with 4 faces, esp. 4 triangular faces

Teutonic adj of or related to the peoples who lived in northwestern Europe in former times

text n 1 the main body of writing in a book 2 the original words of a speech, article, etc. 3 any of the various forms in which a book, article, etc., exists: the original text 4 a textbook

textbook n a book for the study of a particular subject

textile n material made by weaving

texture n the degree of roughness or smoothness, coarseness or fineness, of a substance

thalidomide n a tranquillizing drug which was found to cause unborn babies to develop wrongly

than conj, prep (used for introducing the second part of a comparison of inequality): I know him better than you —see ME (USAGE), HARDLY (USAGE), DIFFERENT (USAGE)

thane n (in early English history) a member of a class of a rank between nobles and ordinary men, who held land from the king in return for military service

thank v 1 to express gratefulness to —see also THANK YOU 2 have (oneself) to thank to be responsible 3 thank God/goodness/heaven (an expression of great thankfulness)

thankful adj showing, feeling, or expressing thanks — ~ly adv — ~ness n

thankless adj 1 ungrateful 2 not likely to be rewarded with thanks — ~ly adv — ~ness n

thanks n 1 words expressing gratefulness 2 **thanks to** on account of; because of

thanksgiving n an expression of gratefulness, esp. to God

thankyou adj, n an act of expressing thanks: a special thankyou

thank you also (esp. spoken) **thanks**— interj I am grateful to you

that¹ adj, pron those 1 (being) the one or amount stated, shown, or understood: Those sweets tasted very nice. | Who told you that? 2 (being) the one of 2 or more people or things that is further away: This is my glass and that is yours

that² adv esp. spoken so; to such a degree: I like him but not all that much! —see THIS (USAGE)

that³ conj 1 (used for introducing various kinds of clause): It's true that he's French. | He was so rude that she refused to speak to him 2 who, whom, or which: It's Jean that makes the decisions here. | Did you see the letter that I sent him? 3 in, on, for, or at which: the day that he arrived

thatch¹ v to cover with thatch

thatch² n 1 roof covering of straw, reeds, etc. 2 humour a mass of thick or untidy hair on the head

thaw¹ v 1 to warm to above freezing point and so make or become liquid, soft, or bendable 2 (of the weather) to become warm enough for snow

and ice to melt 3 (of a person) to become friendlier, less formal, etc.

thaw² n a period of warm weather during which snow and ice melt

the¹ definite article 1 (used when it is clearly understood who or what is meant): We have a cat and a dog. The cat is black and the dog white. | This is the book you wanted 2 a (used with a person, thing, or group that is the only one of its kind): the sun | the year 2000 | sitting on the ground b (used to suggest that a person, thing, or group is the only or best or most important one of its kind): Her wedding was the event of the year. | You didn't meet the Charlie Chaplin! 3 (used with or as part of a title or proper name): Peter the Great | the Rhine 4 (used with an adjective or participle to make it into a noun): the impossible | the dead | the English 5 (used with a singular noun to make it general): The lion is a wild animal

the² adv 1 (used before each of a pair of comparative adjectives or adverbs, to show that 2 things increase or decrease together): The more he has the more he wants 2 (used before a comparative adjective or adverb, to mean) in or by that; on that account; in or by so much; in some degree: He's had a holiday and looks the better for it 3 above all others; very much: He likes you the best. | He has the greatest difficulty

theatre n 1 a special building or place for the performance of plays 2 the work or activity of people who write or act in plays: the modern theatre 3 OPERATING THEATRE

theatrical adj 1 of, related to, or for the theatre 2 (of behaviour, manner, a person, etc.) showy; not natural — ~ly adv

theatricals n stage performances, esp. as done by amateurs

thee pron old use (object form of THOU) you: "Shall I compare thee to a summer's day?" (Shakespeare)

theft n the crime of stealing

their adj (possessive form of THEY) belonging to them: They cooked their own breakfast

theirs pron (possessive form of THEY) that/those belonging to them: They used our phone while theirs was out of order

theism n the belief that a personal God exists — -ist n — -istic adj — -istically adv

them pron (object form of THEY): He bought them drinks. | Where are my shoes? I can't find them —see ME, HIM (USAGE)

theme n 1 the subject of a talk or piece of writing 2 a short simple tune on which a piece of music is based

themselves pron 1 (reflexive form of THEY): The children seem to be enjoying themselves 2 (strong form of THEY): They built the house themselves 3 esp. spoken (in) their usual state of mind or body: When they came to themselves they found their money had been stolen 4 **in themselves** without considering the rest: These little things aren't important in themselves

then adv 1 at that time: We lived in the country

then. | When you see her, then you'll understand **2** next in time, space, or order: *The elephants were followed by the camels and then came the horses* **3** in that case: *If you want to go home, then go* **4** as a result: *Go into the cave, then they won't see you* **5 but then (again)** however: *I like watching television but then (again) I wouldn't miss it if I didn't have one*

thence *adv* **1** from that place on: *We can drive to London and thence to Paris by air* **2** for that reason: *He was recently in Africa; thence we may argue that it was there he caught this tropical disease*

thenceforth *adv* from that time on

theocracy *n* **-cies** **1** government by priests **2** a state governed in this way — **-cratic** *adj*

theodolite *n* an instrument used by surveyors for measuring angles

theology *n* **-gies** **1** the study of religion and religious ideas and beliefs **2** a particular body of opinion about religion: *Muslim theology* — **-ogical** *adj* — **-ogically** *adv* — **-ogian** *n*

theorem *n technical* (in mathematics) a statement that can be proved by reasoning

theoretical also **theoretic**— *adj* **1** based on theory, not on experience **2** existing only in theory; hypothetical — **~ly** *adv*

theorist *n* a person who forms or deals with the theory of a subject

theorize, -rise *v* **-rized, -rizing** to form a theory or theories

theory *n* **-ries** **1** an explanation of a particular fact or event for which certain proof is still needed but which appears to be reasonable **2** the part of a science or art that deals with general principles, rules and methods **3** an opinion based on limited information or knowledge **4** (in mathematics) a body of principles, theorems, etc., belonging to one part of the subject: *set theory*

therapeutic *adj* of or related to the treating or curing of disease — **~ally** *adv*

therapeutics *n* the branch of medicine concerned with the treatment and cure of disease

therapist *n* a specialist in a particular branch of therapy

therapy *n* **-pies** the treatment of illnesses or disorders of the mind or body, esp. without drugs or operations —see also OCCUPATIONAL THERAPY, RADIO THERAPY

there¹ *adv* **1** to, at, or in that place: *Paul's hiding there, under the trees.* | *There goes John!* **2** at that point of time: *I washed the car and decided to stop there* **3 all there** *esp. spoken* healthy in the mind

there² *adv* (*used as the first word in a sentence or clause or as the second word in a question, as the subject of the verb when the real subject follows later*): *There's a man at the door.* | *Is there something wrong?*

there³ *interj* (used for comforting someone or for expressing various feelings, the meaning changing according to the setting and the way it is expressed

): *There! Do you feel better now?* | *There, there. Stop crying.* | *There. I told you I was right!*

thereabouts *adv* near that place, time, number, degree, etc.: *at 9 o'clock or thereabouts* | *The people who lived thereabouts were very worried*

thereafter *adv* after that in time or order: *Thereafter we heard no more of this suggestion* —compare HEREAFTER

thereby *adv* **1** *esp. written* by that means; by doing or saying that: *He treated everyone fairly, and thereby gained the trust of the school* — compare HEREBY **2 (and) thereby hangs a tale** There is an interesting story connected with what I have just said

therefore *adv* **1** as a result; for that reason; so: *I've never been to China and therefore I don't know much about it* **2** (used in reasoning) as this proves; it follows that: *I think. Therefore, I exist*

therein *adv esp. written* in that particular matter: *He knew how to flatter the king and therein lay the cause of his rise to power*

therm *n* (a measurement of heat equal to) 100,000 British Thermal Units, used in Britain in measuring the amount of gas used

thermal¹ *adj* of, using, producing, or caused by heat; of or related to heat or temperature

thermal² *n* a rising current of warm air

thermionic valve— *n technical* a system of electrodes arranged in a vacuum tube, esp. used in radios and televisions —compare TRANSISTOR

thermodynamics *n* the branch of science that deals with the relationship between heat and mechanics

thermometer *n* an instrument for measuring and showing temperature —see also CLINICAL THERMOMETER

thermonuclear *adj* of, using, or caused by the very high temperatures that result from atomic fusion

thermos also **thermos flask**— *n trademark* a vacuum flask

thermostat *n* an apparatus that can control temperature

thesaurus *n* a collection of words put in groups together according to likenesses in their meaning

these *pl. of* THIS

thesis *n* **-ses** **1** an opinion or statement put forward and supported by reasoned argument **2** a long article written on a particular subject for a higher university degree

theta *n* the 8th letter of the Greek alphabet (Θ, θ)

they *pron* **1** those people, animals, or things: *They arrive on Monday* **2** people in general: *They say prices are going to increase again*

they'd *short form of* **1** they had: *If only they'd been there* **2** they would: *They'd never believe you*

thick¹ *adj* **1 a** having a large distance between opposite surfaces; not thin **b** (of a round solid object) wide: *thick wire* **2** measuring in depth, width, or from side to side: *ice 5 centimetres thick* **3** (of liquid) not watery: *thick soup* **4** difficult to see through: *thick mist* **5** (esp. of an accent) very noticeable **6** full of; covered with: *thick with smoke/dust* **7** (of a voice) not clear in sound **8** made of many objects set close together: *a thick forest* **9** *sl* (of a person) stupid: *as thick as two short planks* **10** *sl* beyond what is reasonable or satisfactory: *It's a bit thick* **11** *esp. spoken* very friendly: *Jean and John seem very thick* **12** **lay it on thick** *esp. spoken* to praise, thank, etc., someone too much — ~**ly** *adv*

thick² *adv* so as to be thick; thickly: *The flowers grew thickest near the wall*

thick³ *n* **1** the most packed part; place or time of greatest activity **2** the thick part of anything **3 through thick and thin** through both good and bad times

thick ear *n* *sl* a swollen ear caused by a blow

thicken *v* **1** to make or become thick **2** to make or become more involved or confused: *The plot thickened*

thicket *n* a thick growth of bushes and small trees

thickheaded also **thickwitted**— *adj* stupid

thickness *n* **1** the state, degree, or quality of being thick **2** a layer: *3 thicknesses of newspaper*

thickset *adj* **1** having a short broad body **2** set thickly: *thickset rose bushes*

thick-skinned *adj* insensitive

thief *n* **thieves** a person who steals

thieve *v* **thieved, thieving** to act as a thief — -**ving** *n, adj* — -**vish** *adj* — -**vishly** *adv* — -**vishness** *n*

thigh *n* **1** the top part of the leg between the knee and the hip **2** a part like this on the back legs of certain animals

thimble *n* a protective cap put over the finger that pushes the needle during sewing

thin¹ *adj* -**nn**- **1 a** having a small distance between opposite surfaces; not thick **b** (of a round solid object) narrow: *thin string* **2** having little fat on the body; not fat —see USAGE **3** (of a liquid) watery: *This soup's too thin* **4** not closely packed: *Your hair's getting thin* **5** easy to see through: *thin mist* **6** (esp. of a sound) lacking in strength: *thin high notes* **7** lacking force: *a thin excuse* **8 a thin time** an unpleasant, uncomfortable, or esp. unsuccessful time **9 thin on the ground** scarce — ~**ly** *adv* : *Spread the butter thinly* — ~**ness** *n* USAGE **Thin** is the opposite of both **fat** and **thick**. One can use **slim** or **slender** for someone who is **thin** in a beautiful way. **Delicate** also has this meaning, but suggests softness and weakness as well. **Delicate** and **fine** are used of things that are small and fragile and that have been worked on carefully or are used for careful work: *fine silk thread* | *a delicate line drawing* | *a fine mapping pen*

thin² *adv* so as to be thin; thinly: *Don't cut the bread so thin*

thin³ *v* -**nn**- **1** to make or become thin **2** to pull up the weaker of (a mass of young plants) so that the stronger ones have room to grow

thine¹ *pron* old use (*possessive form of* THOU) that/those belonging to thee; yours: *'For thine is the kingdom, the power, and the glory'* (prayer)

thine² *adj* old use (*before a vowel or* h) thy: *'Drink to me only with thine eyes'* (Ben Jonson)

thing *n* **1** any material object; an object that need not or cannot be named **2** that which is not material; subject; matter: *What a nasty thing to say!* **3** a creature **4** an act: *the next thing to do* **5** an event: *The murder was a terrible thing wasn't it?* **6** *sl* an activity satisfying to one personally: *to do one's thing* **7 first thing** early; before anything else **8 for one thing** (used for introducing a reason): *For one thing I think you're stupid, for another I don't like you* **9 have a thing about** to have a strong like or dislike for

thingamajig, thingumajig also **thingamabob, thingummy**— *n* *esp. spoken* a person or thing, esp. one whose name one has forgotten or does not know

things *n* **1** personal belongings **2** the general state of affairs **3 be seeing things** to see things which do not exist

think¹ *v* **thought, thinking** **1** to use one's reason; make judgments; use the mind to form opinions; have (a thought) **2** to imagine; understand; believe; consider carefully **3** to remember: *I can't think what his name is* **4** to expect: *We didn't think we'd be this late* **5** to think aloud to speak one's thoughts as they come **6 think twice** to think very carefully — ~**er** *n*

think² *n* *esp. spoken* an act of thinking

thinkable *adj* conceivable

thinking¹ *n* **1** the act of using one's mind to produce thoughts and ideas **2** opinion; judgment; thought **3 put on one's thinking cap** *esp. spoken* to think seriously about something

thinking² *adj* thoughtful; reasoning; that can think clearly and seriously

think of *v prep* **1** also **think about**— to consider before making a decision: *We're thinking of going to France* **2 not think much of** to have a low opinion of **3 think better of someone** to have a higher opinion of someone **4 think better of something** to change one's opinion about something **5 think highly/well/little/poorly/etc. of** to have a good/bad/etc. opinion of **6 think nothing of** to regard as usual or easy

think out also **think over**— *v adv* to consider (something) carefully

think tank *n* a committee of people experienced in a particular subject, which considers matters related to it

thinner *n* a liquid added to paint to make it spread more easily

thin-skinned *adj* sensitive; easily offended

third *adj, adv, n, pron* **1** 3rd **2** the lowest

passing degree standard at many British universities

third degree *n esp. spoken* rough treatment of a prisoner in order to obtain a confession

third party *n* **-ties** *technical* a person not named in an insurance agreement but who will be protected by the insurance in the event of an accident

third person *n technical* a form of verb, or pronoun, used for showing the person or thing spoken of (not the one who is spoken to or speaking): *'He is' is the third person present singular of 'to be'*

third rail *n* (in some railway systems) an additional rail for carrying electric current

third-rate *adj* of very poor quality

Third World *n* the industrially less developed countries that do not actively support either the communist or capitalist groups of countries — compare NONALIGNED

thirst *n* **1** a sensation of dryness in the mouth caused by the need to drink; desire for drink **2** a strong desire: *the thirst for excitement*

thirst for also (*literature*) **thirst after—** *v prep* to have a strong desire for

thirsty *adj* **-ier, -iest** **1** feeling thirst **2** causing thirst — **thirstily** *adv*

thirteen *adj, n, pron* the number 13 — **~th** *adj, pron, adv*

thirty *adj, n, pron* **-ties** the number 30 — **-tieth** *adj, n, pron, adv*

this¹ *adj, pron* **these** **1** (being) the one or amount stated, going to be stated, shown, or understood: *I saw Mrs Jones this morning. | Wait until you've heard this story! | Who's this? | Would you like this?* **2** (being) the one of 2 or more people or things that is nearer: *You look in this box here. | This is my sister*

this² *adv esp. spoken* so; this degree: *I've never been out this late before* USAGE Some people think it is not very good English to use **this** and **that** as adverbs; instead of **this** *late* they say *as late as* **this**

thistle *n* any of several types of wild plant with prickly leaves and yellow, white, or purple flowers. The thistle is the national sign of Scotland

thistledown *n* the soft substance fastened to the seeds of the thistle, by which they float through the air

thither *adv old use* to that place; in that direction

thong *n* a narrow length of leather

thorax *n* **-races** *or* **-raxes** *technical* **1** the part of the human body between the neck and abdomen; chest **2** a part like this in other animals **3** the middle part of an insect's body ☞ INSECT

thorn *n* **1** a prickle growing on a plant **2** any of various types of bush, plant, or tree having such prickles **3 a thorn in one's flesh/side** a continual cause of annoyance

thorny *adj* **-ier, -iest** **1** prickly; having thorns **2** troublesome: *a thorny matter* — **thorniness** *n*

thorough *adj* **1** complete in every way **2** careful with regard to detail — **~ly** *adv* — **~ness** *n*

thoroughbred *adj, n* (an animal, esp. a horse) descended from parents of one particular type

thoroughfare *n* **1** a road for public traffic **2 No thoroughfare** (as written on signs) not open to the public; no way through

thoroughgoing *adj* very thorough; complete in every way

those *pl. of* THAT

thou *pron old use* (used as the subject of a sentence with special old forms of verbs such as art, canst, didst, *etc.*) the person to whom one is speaking, now usu. God; you: *'Thou shalt not kill'* (The Bible)

though¹ *adv* in spite of the fact; nevertheless: *It's hard work. I enjoy it though*

though² *conj* **1** in spite of the fact that; even if: *Even though it's hard work, I enjoy it. | He spoke firmly though pleasantly* **2 as though** as if

thought¹ *n* **1** the act of thinking **2** serious consideration **3** (a) product of thinking; idea, opinion, etc. **4** the particular way of thinking of a period, country, etc: *Ancient Greek thought* **5** regard: *with no thought for her own safety* —see also SECOND THOUGHT

thought² *past tense and past part. of* THINK

thoughtful *adj* **1** given to or expressing thought **2** paying attention to the feelings of other people; considerate — **~ly** *adv* — **~ness** *n*

thoughtless *adj* not thinking; selfish — **~ly** *adv* — **~ness** *n*

thousand *adj, n, pron* **-sand** *or* **-sands** **1** the number 1, 000 **2 one in a thousand** very good indeed — **~th** *adj, n, pron, adv*

thrall *n* **1** a slave; serf **2** slavery (esp. in the phrase **in thrall (to)**) — **thralldom** *n*

thrash *v* **1** to beat with a whip or stick **2** to defeat thoroughly **3** to move wildly: *The fish thrashed about in the net*

thrashing *n* **1** a severe beating **2** a severe defeat

thrash out *v adv* **1** to discuss (something) thoroughly to find an answer **2** to produce by much talk and consideration

thread¹ *n* **1** (a length of) very fine cord **2** a logical connection: *to lose the thread* **3** a raised line that winds around the outside of a screw; a bolt, or the inside of a nut

thread² *v* **1** to pass one end of a thread through the eye of (a needle) **2** to put a film in place on a projector **3 thread one's way through** to make one's way carefully through

threadbare *adj* **1** (of cloth, clothes, etc.) worn thin **2** having been so much used as to be no longer interesting

threat *n* **1** an expression of an intention to hurt, punish, cause pain, etc. **2** a person, thing, or idea regarded as a possible danger

threaten *v* **1** to express a threat against (someone) **2** to give warning of (something bad) — ~**ingly** *adv*

three *adj, n, pron* the number 3

three-cornered *adj* **1** having 3 corners **2** having 3 competitors

three-dimensional *adj* having or seeming to have length, depth, and height

three-line whip *n* an order given by party leaders to their Members of Parliament, telling them that they must vote in a certain way on a particular matter

threepenny bit *n* a coin formerly used in Britain with a value of 3 (old) pence

three-quarter¹ *adj* consisting of 3 fourths (¾) of the whole: *a three-quarter length coat*

three-quarter² *n* (in rugby) one of a group of fast-running players whose main job is to score a try

three R's *n* reading, writing, and arithmetic considered as the base for children's education

threnody *n* -**dies** *literature* a funeral song for the dead

thresh *v* to separate the grain from corn, wheat, etc., by beating

thresher *n* a machine or person that threshes

threshold *n* **1** a piece of wood or stone forming the bottom of a doorway **2** the point of beginning **3** *technical* (in psychology) the lowest level at which an influence becomes perceptible: *on the threshold of pain*

threw *past tense of* THROW

thrice *adj, adv* 3 times

thrift *n* **1** wise use of money and goods **2** a type of plant that grows by the sea with small pink or white flowers

thrifty *adj* -**ier**, -**iest** avoiding waste in the use of money — **thriftily** *adv* — **thriftiness** *n*

thrill¹ *v* to feel or cause to feel a thrill — ~**ingly** *adv*

thrill² *n* a wave of joy, fear, etc.

thriller *n* a book, play, or film that tells an exciting story

thrive *v* **thrived** *or* **throve, thrived** *or* **thriven, thriving** to develop well and be healthy; be successful

throat *n* **1** the passage inside the neck, that divides into 2, one taking air to the lungs, the other food to the stomach **2** the front of the neck: *The murderer cut the old man's throat*

throaty *adj* -**ier**, -**iest** *esp. spoken* having a low rough voice — **throatily** *adv* — **throatiness** *n*

throb¹ *v* -**bb**- to beat strongly and rapidly

throb² *n* a strong low continuous beat —see also HEARTTHROB

throes *n* **1** severe pains **2 in the throes of** struggling with (some difficulty)

thrombosis *n* -**ses** *medical* a blood clot in a blood vessel —compare CORONARY THROMBOSIS

throne *n* **1** the ceremonial chair of a king, bishop, etc. **2** the rank or office of a king or queen

throng *v* to move (as if) in a crowd in — **throng** *n*

throttle¹ *v* -**tled**, -**tling** **1** to seize (someone) tightly by the throat **2** to reduce the flow of fuel (e.g. petrol) to (an engine) so lessening speed

throttle² *n* a valve that opens and closes to control the flow of fuel into an engine

through¹ *prep* **1** in at one side, end, or surface of (something) and out at the other **2** by means of: *I got this book through the library* **3** as a result of: *The war was lost through bad organization* **4** from the beginning to the end of **5** over the surface of or within the limits of: *through France and Belgium* **6** among or between the parts or single members of: *through the trees* **7** having finished, or so as to finish, successfully: *Did you get through your examinations?* —see also THRU

through² *adv* **1** in at one side, end, or surface, and out at the other **2** all the way; along the whole distance: *right through to London* **3** from the beginning to the end: *Have you read the letter through?* **4** to a favourable or successful state: *I got through with good marks* **5** (when telephoning) in a state of being connected to a person or place: *Can you put me through to Mr Jones?* **6** in every part; thoroughly: *I got wet through in the rain* USAGE When one is telephoning in Britain, *Are you* **through**? means "Are you connected to the other speaker?" In the US, it means "Have you finished?".

through³ *adj* **1** passing from one end or side to another: *a through beam* **2** allowing a free or continuous journey: *a through road* **3** finished: *I'm not through just yet*

throughout *adv, prep* in, to, through, or during every part (of)

throughput *n* *technical* the work dealt with by a computer in a given time

throw¹ *v* **threw, thrown, throwing** **1** to send (something) through the air by a sudden movement of the arm **2** to move (oneself or part of one's body) suddenly and with force **3** to cause to go or come into some place, condition, etc., as if by throwing **4** to put on or take off (a garment) hastily **5** *technical* (of an animal) to give birth to (a young one) **6** to move (a switch, handle, etc.) in order to connect or disconnect parts of a machine, apparatus, etc. **7** to shape (an object) on a potter's wheel **8** to cause to fall to the ground **9** to roll (a dice) **10** to get (a particular number) by rolling a dice **11** *esp. spoken* to give (a party) **12 throw a fit** to have a sudden attack of uncontrolled temper **13 throw oneself into** to work very busily at —see also THROW AWAY, THROW OVER, THROW TOGETHER, THROW UP — ~**er** *n*

throw² *n* **1** an act of throwing **2** the distance to which something is thrown: *a throw of 100 metres*

throwaway *adj* **1** (of a remark) said with false carelessness **2** to be thrown away after use

throw away *v adv* to waste; lose by foolishness; fail to use

throwback *n* (an example of) one or more of the typical qualities of a person from whom one is descended

throw-in *n* (in football) an act of throwing the ball from the side of the field after it has gone out of play

throw out *v adv* to refuse to accept

throw over also **throw overboard**— *v adv* to end a relationship with (somebody)

throw together *v adv* **1** to build or make hastily **2** to bring together: *Chance threw us together*

throw up *v adv* **1** to produce (a famous person) **2** *sl* to vomit

thru *adv, adj, prep* through

thrum *v* -mm- to make a low heavy continuous sound

thrush¹ *n* any of several types of singing birds with a brownish back and spotted breast

thrush² *n* an infectious disease of the mouth, throat, or vagina

thrust¹ *v* thrust, thrusting **1** to push forcefully and suddenly as with a sword, knife, etc. **2** to make a sudden forward stroke with a sword, knife, etc. **3 thrust oneself forward** to draw attention to oneself

thrust² *n* **1** an act of thrusting; forceful forward push **2** a swift forward stroke with a knife, sword, etc.

thud *v, n* -dd- (to make) a dull sound as caused by a heavy object striking something soft

thug *n* a violent criminal — **thuggery** *n*

thumb¹ *n* **1** a short movable part of the human hand set apart from the fingers **2** the part of a glove that fits over this **3 stick out like a sore thumb** *esp. spoken* to seem very out of place **4 under somebody's thumb** *esp. spoken* under the control of someone

thumb² *v esp. spoken* to ask for or get a lift by holding out one's hand with the thumb raised

thumbscrew *n* an instrument used in former times to torture by crushing the thumbs

thump¹ *v* to strike with a heavy blow; produce a knocking sound

thump² *n* **1** a heavy blow **2** the dull sound produced by this

thumping *adj esp. spoken* very: *a thumping great house*

thunder¹ *n* **1** the noise that follows a flash of lightning **2** any loud noise like this

thunder² *v* **1** to produce thunder **2** to produce loud sounds like this — ~**er** *n*

thunderbolt *n* **1** a flash of lightning from which thunder is heard **2** a sudden event which causes great shock, anxiety, etc.

thunderclap *n* a single loud crash of thunder

thundercloud *n* a large dark cloud producing thunder and lightning

thundering *adj, adv esp. spoken* very: *a thundering big house*

thunderous *adj* producing thunder or a loud noise like thunder — ~**ly** *adv*

thunderstorm *n* a storm of very heavy rain and thunder and lightning

thunderstruck *adj* very surprised indeed

thundery *adj* giving signs that thunder is likely

Thursday *n* -days the 5th day of the week

thus *adv* **1** in this manner; in the way or by the means stated **2** with this result; hence **3 thus far** until now; to this point

thwart¹ *v* to oppose successfully

thwart² *n technical* a seat across a rowing boat

thy *adj old use possessive form of* THOU belonging to thee; your: *Death, where is thy sting?*

thyme *n* a type of small plant with fragrant leaves used in cooking

thyroid also **thyroid gland**— *n* an endocrine gland in the neck that produces a hormone important in the development of the mind and body

thyself *pron old use* **1** *reflexive form of* THOU **2** (*strong form of* THOU)

ti also **si**— *n* the 7th note in the sol-fa musical scale

tiara *n* **1** a jewelled coronet worn by women **2** the crown worn by the Pope

tibia *n* -iae *or* -ias a shinbone

tic *n* a sudden involuntary movement in the face or limbs

tick¹ *n* any of various types of small blood-sucking animals

tick² *n* **1** a short sudden regularly repeated sound made by a clock or watch **2** a mark (usu. √) put against something to show that it is correct

tick³ *v* **1** (of a clock, watch, etc.) to make a regularly repeated tick **2** to show that (an item) is correct by marking with a tick **3 make someone or something tick** to make a person or thing act, behave, etc., in a particular way —see also TICK OFF, TICK OVER

tick⁴ *n esp. spoken* credit

ticker *n* **1** a telegraphic machine that prints information on long narrow lengths of paper **2** *sl* a watch

tickertape *n* very long narrow lengths of paper used in a ticker

ticket¹ *n* **1** a printed piece of paper or card entitling a person to a service such as a journey on a bus, entrance into a cinema, etc. **2** a piece of card or paper fastened to an object giving its price, size, quality, etc. **3** a printed notice of an offence against the driving laws

ticket² *v* to put a ticket, tag, or label on (something)

ticking also **tick**— *n* the thick strong cloth used for making mattress and pillow covers

tickle¹ *v* -led, -ling **1** to touch lightly to produce laughter, nervous excitement, etc. **2** to (cause (someone) to) feel nervous excitement **3** to delight or amuse **4 tickled pink** *sl* very pleased or amused

tickle² *n* the act or sensation of tickling

ticklish *adj esp. spoken* **1** (of a person) sensi-

til

tive to tickling; easily tickled **2** (of a problem) difficult; needing special attention — ~**ly** adv — ~**ness** n

tick off v adv esp. spoken to scold

tick over v adv **1** (of an engine) to work normally at the slowest possible speed **2** to be quiet or inactive

tidal adj of, having, or related to the tide

tidal wave n a very large dangerous ocean wave

tiddler n **1** a very small fish **2** esp. spoken a small child

tiddly, -dley adj -**dlier, -dliest** esp. spoken slightly drunk

tiddlywinks, -dley- n a game in which the players try to make small discs jump into a cup by pressing their edges down hard with a larger disc

tide n **1** the regular rise and fall of the seas —see also HIGH TIDE, LOW TIDE **2** a current of water caused by this **3 swim/go with/against the tide** to act in accordance with/opposition to what most other people are doing or thinking

tidemark n **1** the highest point reached by a tide **2** humour a dirty mark left by incomplete washing

tide over v prep **tided, tiding over** to help (someone) through (a difficult period)

tidings n old use news

tidy¹ adj **tidier, tidiest 1** neatly arranged or liking things to be so **2** esp. spoken fairly large: a tidy income — -**dily** adv — -**diness** n

tidy² v **tidied, tidying** to make (something or someone) neat

tie¹ n **1** a band of cloth worn round the neck and tied in a knot **2** a cord, string, etc., used for fastening something **3** something that unites; bond **4** something that limits one's freedom: Young children can be a tie **5** an equality of results, score, etc. **6** a length of wood, metal, etc., that joins parts of a framework and gives support **7** a curved line connecting 2 printed musical notes of the same level showing that they are to be played or sung as one unbroken note —compare SLUR **8** a railway sleeper

tie² v **tied, tying 1** to fasten with a cord, rope, etc. **2** to fasten or be fastened by drawing together and knotting string, laces, etc.: tie your shoes **3** to be fastened by string, laces, etc., that are drawn together and knotted **4** to make (a knot or bow) **5** to finish (a match, competition) with equal points **6** to connect (musical notes of the same level) so that there is no interruption in playing or singing —see also TIE DOWN, TIE UP

tiebreaker also **tiebreak**— n a number of quickly-played points at the end of a set in tennis, to decide the winner of that set

tied cottage n a house owned by a farmer and rented to one of his workers

tied house n an inn that is controlled by a particular beer-making firm

tie down v adv to limit the freedom of (someone)

tie-dye v -**dyed, -dyeing** to tie (a garment) in knots and dye

tier n any of a number of rows rising one behind or above another

tie-up n a connection; link

tie up v adv **1** to use (money) so that its free use is limited **2** to connect **3** to stop: The traffic was tied up by the accident

tiff n a slight quarrel

tiffin n Indian & Pakistani a midday meal

tiger (fem. **tigress**)— n **tigers** or **tiger** a large fierce Asian cat that is yellowish with black stripes

tigerish adj cruel; fierce; of or like a tiger

tight¹ adj **1** closely fastened, held, knotted, etc.; fitting too closely **2** drawn out as far as possible; fully stretched **3** leaving no free room or time; fully packed **4** closely or firmly put together **5** esp. spoken (of money) in short supply **6** sl drunk — ~**ly** adv — ~**ness** n

tight² adv closely; firmly; tightly USAGE Some people think **tight** should not be used as an adverb. They say fasten it tightly/more tightly | the most tightly shut, and not fasten it tight/tighter | the tightest shut.

tighten v to make or become tight or tighter

tighten up v adv to make or become firmer or more severe

tightfisted also **tight**— adj esp. spoken very ungenerous, esp. with money — ~**ness** n

tight-lipped adj **1** having the lips pressed together **2** not wanting to talk; silent; not saying much

tightrope n a tightly stretched rope or wire, high above the ground, used by **tightrope walkers** (people skilled in walking on this)

tights n a very close fitting garment covering the legs and lower part of the body

tightwad n sl a very ungenerous person

tigress n a female tiger

tike n a tyke

tile¹ n a thin shaped piece of baked clay, plastic, etc., used for covering roofs, floors, etc.

tile² v **tiled, tiling** to cover (a roof, floor, etc.) with tiles — **tiler** n

till¹ v to cultivate (the ground) — ~**er** n

till² n **1** a drawer in a shop where money is kept **2 have one's fingers in the till** esp. spoken to steal money from the shop where one works

till³ prep, conj until —see INCLUSIVE (USAGE)

tillage n **1** the act or practice of cultivating land **2** cultivated land

tiller n a long handle fastened to the top of a boat's rudder so that it can be turned ☞ SAIL

tilt¹ v to slope or cause to slope as by raising one end

tilt² n **1** a slope **2** an act of tilting; tilting movement **3 (at) full tilt** at full speed; with full force

tilt at v prep **1** to attack (someone) in speech or writing **2** (in former times) to charge at (someone) with a lance

timber¹ n 1 wood for building 2 trees suitable for building 3 a wooden beam

timber² interj (a warning shouted when a cut tree is about to fall down)

timbered adj 1 made partly of wood: half-timbered 2 covered with growing trees

timberline n 1 the height above sea level beyond which trees will not grow 2 the northern or southern limit beyond which trees will not grow

timbre n technical, French the different quality of sounds of the same level and loudness when made by different instruments or voices

time¹ n 1 a continuous measurable quantity from the past, through the present, and into the future 2 the passing of the days, months, and years, taken as a whole 3 a system of measuring this 4 a limited period 5 a period in history: in ancient times 6 a period or occasion and the particular experience connected with it: a good time 7 the rate of pay received for an hour's work: double time for Sundays 8 sl a period of imprisonment: to do/serve time 9 free or unfilled time: No time to watch television 10 a particular point in the day stated in hours, minutes, seconds, etc.: What's the time? 11 a particular point in the year, day, etc.; moment for a particular activity or event: summertime | bedtime 12 an unlimited period in the future: In time you'll forget him 13 technical the rate of speed of a piece of music 14 **ahead of one's time** having ideas too modern or original for the period in which one is living 15 **all the time** continuously 16 **at one time** formerly 17 **bide one's time** to wait for a suitable chance 18 **from time to time** sometimes 19 **have no time for** esp. spoken to dislike 20 **in no time (at all)** very quickly 21 **keep time** (of a clock, watch, etc.) to work correctly 22 **kill time** to make time pass by doing something 23 **many a time** frequently 24 **on time** at the right time 25 **once upon a time** (often used at the beginning of children's stories, to mean) at a time in the past 26 **pass the time of day** to have a short conversation

time² v **timed, timing** 1 to arrange or set the time at which (something) happens or is to happen 2 to record the time taken by/for (something or someone) 3 to choose the right moment to hit (a ball) or make (a shot)

time bomb n a bomb that can be set to explode at a particular time

time-honoured adj respected because of age or long use

timeless adj 1 lasting for ever; independent of time; unending 2 not changed by time — ~ly adv — ~ness n

time limit n a period of time within which something must be done

timely adj **-lier, -liest** happening at just the right time — **-liness** n

timepiece n technical or old use a clock or watch

timer n a person or machine that measures or records time —see also EGG TIMER

times¹ prep multiplied by: 3 times (usu. written x) $3 = 9$

times² n 1 the present: a sign of the times 2 occasions 3 **behind the times** old-fashioned 4 **for old times' sake** because of or as a reminder of happy times in the past

timesaving n quicker

time-sharing n the handling by a computer of more than one program at the same time

time signal n a signal showing an exact moment in time

time signature n technical a mark that usu. looks like a fraction, used when writing music to indicate the number and value of beats in a bar ☞ MUSIC

time switch n a switch that can be set to start a machine, activity, etc., at a particular time

timetable¹ n 1 a table of the times at which buses, planes, etc., arrive and leave 2 a table of the times of classes in a school, college, etc.

timetable² v **-bled, -bling** 1 to plan for a future time 2 to arrange according to a timetable

time zone n any of the 24 parts, each about 15° wide, into which the earth is divided for the purpose of time

timid adj fearful; lacking courage — ~ity n — ~ly adv — ~ness n

timing n the arrangement and control of events, actions, etc., to get the desired results; control over the rate of an activity

timorous adj (of a person) fearful; timid; lacking courage △ TEMERITY — ~ly adv — ~ness n

timpani n a set of 2, 3, or 4 kettledrums played by one musician in an orchestra or a band — ~st n

tin¹ n 1 a soft metal that is an element, used to plate metal objects with a protective surface 2 a small metal box or container

tin² v **-nn-** to preserve (esp. food) by packing in tins

tin³ adj made of tin

tincture n 1 a medical substance mixed with alcohol 2 literature a slight suggestion (of a colour, taste, etc.)

tinder n any material that catches fire easily

tinderbox n a box containing tinder, a flint, and steel, used for providing a flame

tine n a point or narrow pointed part, as of a fork or a deer's antlers

tinfoil n a very thin bendable sheet of shiny metal, used as a protective wrapping

tingaling n a high clear ringing sound

tinge¹ v **tinged, tingeing** or **tinging** 1 to give a slight degree of a colour to (an object or colour) 2 to show signs of

tinge² n a slight degree (of colour or some quality)

tingle v **-gled, -gling** to feel a slight prickly sensation — **tingle** n

tin god n esp. spoken a person of limited import-

ance who acts as though he were more important

tinker¹ n   1 a travelling mender of metal pots,
pans, etc.   2 an act of tinkering   3 *esp. spoken* a
disobedient or annoying young child

tinker² v   to try to repair without useful results:
Don't tinker with my television

tinkle v   -kled, -kling to make or cause to make
light metallic sounds   — **tinkle** n

tinny adj   -nier, -niest   1 of, like, or containing
tin   2 having a thin metallic sound   3 *sl* worthless; of very poor quality   — **-niness** n

tinplate n   thin sheets of iron or steel covered
with tin

tinsel n   1 thin lengths of shiny material used
for ornaments   2 anything showy that is really
worthless   — ~ly adj

tint¹ n   1 a pale or delicate shade of a colour   2
any of various dyes for the hair   3 an act of tinting
the hair

tint² v   to give a slight colour to (e.g. the hair) —
~er n

tiny adj   tinier, tiniest very small

tip¹ n   1 the end of something   2 a small piece or
part serving as an end, cap, or point   3 **have
(something) on the tip of one's tongue** to be about
to remember (a name, word, etc.)

tip² v   -pp-   1 to lean or cause to lean at an
angle   2 to upset or cause to upset; fall or cause
to fall over   3 to throw or leave (unwanted
articles) somewhere   4 to pour (a substance) from
one container into another, onto a surface, etc.

tip³ n   a place where unwanted waste is left

tip⁴ v   -pp- to give (a tip) to (a waiter, waitress, etc.)
    — ~per n

tip⁵ n   a small amount of money given for a small
service

tip⁶ n   a helpful piece of advice

tip-off n   a piece of helpful information; warning

tip off v adv   to give (someone) a warning

tipple v   -pled, -pling *esp. spoken* to drink
alcohol habitually   — ~r n

tipstaff n   -staves *or* staffs an attendant with
special duties in a court of law

tipster n   a person who gives advice about horse
and dog races

tipsy adj   -sier, -siest slightly drunk   — **-sily** adv
    — **-siness** n

tiptoe v   -toed, -toeing to walk on one's toes

tip-top adj *esp. spoken* of the highest quality —
tip-top adv

tirade n   a long angry speech

tire v   tired, tiring to make or become tired

tired adj   1 having or showing a lack of power in
the mind or body, esp. after activity; having or
showing a need for rest or sleep   2 no longer
interested: *I'm tired of your conversation*   — ~ly
adv   — ~ness n

tireless adj   never or rarely getting tired   — ~ly
adv

tiresome adj   1 annoying   2 tiring or uninteresting, esp. because of dullness   — ~ly adv

tissue n   1 animal or plant cells of the same type
that make up a particular organ   2 also **tissue
paper**— light thin paper used for wrapping, packing, etc.   3 a piece of soft paper

tit also **titmouse**— n   any of several types of small
European birds

titan n   a person of great strength, size, etc.   —
~ic adj

titanium n   a silvery grey light strong metal that
is an element used esp. for making compounds
with other metals

titbit n   1 a small piece of particularly nice
food   2 an interesting piece of news

tithe n   1 1/10 of one's yearly produce or
income paid for the support of the local priest   2
a 1/10 part (of anything)

titillate v   -lated, -lating to excite pleasantly △
TITIVATE   — **-lation** n

titivate, titti- v   -vated, -vating *esp. spoken* to
make (esp. oneself) pretty or tidy △ TITILLATE

title n   1 a name given to a book, painting, play,
etc.   2 a word or name, such as ' Mr ', ' Lord ',
' Doctor ', etc., given to a person to be used before
his name as a sign of rank, profession, etc.   3
technical the lawful right to ownership or possession   4 the position of unbeaten winner in
certain competitions

titled adj   having a noble title

title deed n   a paper giving proof of a person's
ownership of property

title page n   the page at the front of a book
giving the title, writer's name, etc.

title role n   the part in a play after which the play
is named

titrate v   -rated, -rating to determine the
amount of a substance in (a solution) by reaction
with another solution of known composition   —
-tion n

titter v   to laugh very quietly   — **titter** n

tittle-tattle n, v   -tattled, -tattling *esp. spoken*
gossip

titular adj   1 holding a title but not having the
duties, responsibilities, or power of that office   2
of, belonging to, or related to a title

tizzy n   -zies *sl* a state of excited confusion

T-junction n   a place where 2 roads, pipes, etc.,
join in the shape of T

TNT n   trinitrotoluene, a type of powerful explosive —compare NITROGLYCERINE

to¹ prep   1 in a direction towards   2 in the direction of; so as to have reached: *sent to prison*   3 as
far as   4 reaching the state of: *She sang the baby
to sleep*   5 as far as the state of: *until the lights
change to green*   6 in a touching position with:
cheek to cheek   7 facing or in front of: *face to
face*   8 until and including: *Count (from 10) to 20*
—see INCLUSIVE (USAGE)   9 for the attention or
possession of: *to Mildred from George*   10 for; of:
the key to the lock   11 in relation with; in comparison with: *5 goals to 3*   12 forming; making up:
100 pence to every pound   13 in honour of: *a
temple to Mars*   14 (of time) before: *5 (minutes)
to 4*   15 in the position of: *to the north of England*

16 in connection with: *What's your answer to that?* | *kind to animals* **17 (a number) to (a number) a** between (a number) and (a number): *in 10 to 12 feet of water* **b** compared with: *100 to 1 he'll lose* (=100 times as likely) —see also TO AND FRO

to² *adv* **1** into consciousness: *John didn't come to for half an hour after he'd hit his head* **2** into a shut position: *The wind blew the door to*

to³ (*used before a verb to show it is the infinitive*) USAGE Many people think it bad English to put another word, such as an adverb, between to and the verb that follows it. This is called a **split infinitive**: *to boldly go where no man has gone before.* Sometimes it is necessary to put the adverb between to and the verb: *Your job is to really understand these children.* | *He likes to half close his eyes.*

toad *n* an animal like a large frog, that usu. lives on land, but goes into water for breeding

toad-in-the-hole *n* sausages baked in batter

toadstool *n* any of several types of fleshy fungus, often poisonous

toady *v* **-ied, -ying** *offensive* to be too nice to someone of higher rank, esp. for personal advantage — **toady** *n*

to and fro *adv* (of repeated movements or journeys) backwards and forwards; from side to side

toast¹ *v* **1** to make (bread, cheese, etc.) brown by holding close to heat **2** to warm thoroughly

toast² *n* bread made brown by being held in front of heat

toast³ *v* to drink or suggest a drink to the success, happiness, etc., of (someone) — **toast** *n*

toaster *n* an apparatus for toasting bread electrically

toasting fork *n* a long-handled fork for toasting bread in front of the fire

toastmaster *n* a person who speaks the toasts and introduces speakers at a formal dinner

tobacco *n* **-cos** a type of leafy plant , specially prepared for use in cigarettes, pipes, etc.

tobacconist *n* a person who sells tobacco, cigarettes, etc.

toboggan¹ *n* *esp. US* a long light board curved up at the front, for carrying people over snow, esp. down slopes for sport

toboggan² *v* to go or race down slopes on a sledge, as done by children or in the sport of **tobogganing**

toby jug *n* a small drinking vessel, in the form of a fat old man wearing a 3-cornered hat

toccata *n* a special piece of music, in a free style with difficult passages that show the player's skill

today *adv, n* **1** (during or on) this present day **2** (during or at) this present time: *young people of today*

toddle *v* **-dled, -dling** to walk with short unsteady steps, as a small child does

toddler *n* a child who has just learnt to walk

toddy *n* a sweetened mixture of whisky and hot water

to-do *n* **to-dos** *sl* a state of excited confusion

toe¹ *n* **1** one of the 5 movable parts on each foot **2** the part of a sock, shoe, etc., that fits over these **3 on one's toes** ready for action —see also TREAD **on someone's toes**

toe² *v* **toed, toeing toe the line** to obey orders

toe cap *n* a leather covering over the toe of a shoe to strengthen it

toenail *n* the nail on a toe

toffee, **toffy** *n* (a piece of) a hard sticky sweet brown substance made by boiling sugar and butter with water

toffee apple *n* an apple covered with toffee

toga *n* a long loose flowing outer garment worn by the citizens of ancient Rome

together *adv* **1** in or into one group, body, or place; in or into a relationship **2** in or into union **3** at the same time **4** without interruption: *for 4 days together* —see also GET TOGETHER, PULL TOGETHER

togetherness *n* a feeling of being united with other people

toggle *n* a short shaped bar of wood used in place of a button

togs *n* *sl* clothes

toil¹ *n* *esp. written* hard or continuous work —see WORK (USAGE)

toil² *v* *esp. written* **1** to work hard and untiringly **2** to move with difficulty or pain

toilet *n* see LAVATORY

toilet paper *n* thin paper for cleaning oneself after using the toilet

toiletries *n* articles or substances used in dressing, washing, etc.

toilet roll *n* a rolled-up length of toilet paper

toilet train *v* to teach (a child) to pass waste matter from the body only when using the toilet

toilet water *n* a sweet-smelling liquid used as a light perfume

token *n* **1** an outward sign; small part representing something greater **2** keepsake; souvenir **3** a piece of metal used instead of coins for a particular purpose **4** a receipt, usu. fixed to a greetings card, which one can exchange for the stated thing in a shop

told *past tense & past part. of* TELL

tolerable *adj* fairly good; that can be tolerated

tolerably *adv* to a limited degree; fairly: *tolerably well*

tolerance *n* **1** the quality of being able to suffer pain, hardship, etc., without being damaged **2** the quality of allowing people to behave in a way that may not please one, without becoming annoyed **3** *technical* (in engineering) the amount by which a value can vary from the amount intended without causing difficulties **4** *technical* the degree to which a cell, animal, plant, etc., can successfully oppose the effect of a poison, drug, etc.

tolerant *adj* showing or practising toleration — ~**ly** *adv*

tolerate *v* **-rated, -rating** **1** to allow (something one does not agree with) to be practised or done freely without opposition **2** to suffer (someone or something) without complaining —see BEAR (USAGE)

toleration *n* the quality or practice of allowing opinions, beliefs, customs, behaviour, etc., different from one's own, to be held and practised freely

toll¹ *n* **1** a tax paid for the right to use a road, harbour, etc. **2** the cost in health, life, etc., from illness, an accident, etc.

toll² *v* (of a bell) to ring or cause to ring slowly and repeatedly

toll³ *n* the sound of a tolling bell

tollgate *n* a gate across a road at which a toll must be paid

tollhouse *n* a house by a tollgate where the toll collector lives

tomahawk *n* a light axe used by North American Indians in war and hunting

tomato *n* **-toes** a type of yellow-flowered plant, or its red fruit used as a vegetable

tomb *n* a grave

tombola *n* any of various games in which tickets are drawn by chance to win prizes

tomboy *n* **-boys** a spirited girl who likes boyish games — ~**ish** *adj*

tombstone *n* a gravestone

tomcat also (*esp.spoken*) **tom**— *n* a male cat

tome *n* *esp. literature or humour* a large book

tomfoolery *n* foolish behaviour

tommy gun *n* *sl* a light machinegun

tomorrow *adv* **1** (during or on) the day following today **2** (in) the future: *tomorrow's world*

tom-tom *n* **1** a long narrow African or Asian drum played with the hands **2** a large modern drum played with a stick

ton *n* **tons** *or* **ton** **1** a measurement of weight equal in Britain to 2, 240 pounds (**long ton**) and in the United States to 2, 000 pounds (**short ton**) **2** also **tonne, metric ton**— a measurement of weight equal to 1, 000 kilos **3** a measurement of **a** the size of a ship equal to 100 cubic feet **b** the amount of goods a ship can carry equal to 40 cubic feet **4** *sl* a very large quantity or weight: *tons of fruit* **5** *sl* 100 miles per hour **6** *sl* (in cricket) a century —see also TON-UP

tonal *adj* of or related to tone

tonality *n* **-ties** *technical* **1** the character of a tune depending on the musical key in which it is played **2** a musical key

tone *n* **1** any sound considered with regard to its quality, highness or lowness, strength, etc. **2** the quality or character of a particular instrument or singing voice as regards the sound it produces **3** *technical* a difference in the pitch of a musical note equal to 2 semitones **4** a manner of expression **5** a particular (change of) pitch of a speech sound **6** a variety of a colour, different from the ordinary

colour because of more light or darkness **7** *technical* the effect in painting of light and shade together with colour **8** the general quality or nature: *the tone of the neighbourhood*

tone-deaf *adj* unable to tell the difference between musical notes

tone down *v adv* **toned, toning down** to reduce the violence, excitement, or force of (something)

tone in *v adv* **toned, toning in** to match: *I think black shoes would tone in better with your coat*

tone language *n* any of those languages, such as Chinese or Yoruba, in which the pitch of the voice is used to distinguish between different words with the same vowels and consonants

toneless *adj* lacking colour, spirit, etc.; dull — ~**ly** *adv*

tone poem *n* a piece of music written to represent musically a poetic idea, scene, etc.

tongs *n* an instrument consisting of 2 movable arms joined at one end, used for holding or lifting various objects

tongue *n* **1** the large movable fleshy organ in the mouth **2** this organ taken from an animal, cooked as food **3** any of various objects like this in shape or purpose **4** a language **5** **get one's tongue around** to pronounce (a difficult word, name, etc.) correctly —see also **have (something) on the** TIP **of one's tongue**

tongue-tied *adj* unable to speak easily

tongue twister *n* a word or phrase difficult to speak quickly

tonic¹ *adj* **1** *esp. written* strengthening: *the tonic quality of sea air* **2** (in music) of or based on the tonic

tonic² *n* **1** anything which increases health or strength **2** a medicine intended to give the body more strength, esp. when tired **3** the first note of a musical scale of 8 notes —compare DOMINANT

tonic sol-fa *n* a method of showing musical notes by the first letters of the words in the sol-fa system

tonic water also **tonic**— *n* gassy water made bitter by the addition of quinine, often added to drinks: *a gin and tonic*

tonight *adv, n* (on or during) the night of today

tonnage *n* **1 a** the amount of goods a ship can carry **b** a charge made for the goods carried **2** the size of a ship or of the total shipping of a navy, port, or country, expressed in 100s of cubic feet

tonne *n* **tonnes** *or* **tonne** a metric ton

tonsil *n* either of 2 small roundish organs at the sides of the throat near the top —compare ADENOIDS

tonsillitis, tonsilitis *n* a painful soreness of the tonsils

tontine *n* a form of interest paid to those who have combined to lend a sum of money, arranged so that it increases for those remaining as each lender dies

ton-up *adj* liking to drive at high speeds, esp. over 100 miles per hour

too *adv* **1** (*before adjectives and adverbs*) more

too

than enough; to a higher degree than is necessary or good; excessively **2** also; in addition; as well **3** only too very: *only too pleased*

took *past tense of* TAKE

tool¹ *n* **1** any instrument or apparatus for doing special jobs **2** anything necessary for doing one's job: *Words are his tools* **3** a person unfairly or dishonestly used by another for his own purposes **4 down tools** to stop working

tool² *v* to shape or make (something) with a tool

tool up *v adv* to prepare (a factory) for production by providing the necessary machinery

toot *v* **1** to make a short sound on a horn, whistle, etc. **2** (of a horn, whistle, etc.) to produce a short sound — **toot** *n*

tooth *n* **teeth 1** one of the small hard bony objects growing in the upper and lower mouth of most animals **2** any of the narrow pointed parts that stand out from a comb, saw, cog, etc. **3 long in the tooth** *esp. spoken* old **4 tooth and nail** very violently: *They fought tooth and nail* —see also TEETH — **~less** *adj*

toothache *n* (a) pain in a tooth

toothbrush *n* a brush used for cleaning the teeth

toothpaste *n* a substance used for cleaning the teeth

toothpick *n* a pointed piece of wood used for removing food between the teeth

toothy *adj* **-ier, -iest** *esp. spoken* having or showing teeth that stick out

tootle *v* **-led, -ling** *esp. spoken* to toot continuously — **tootle** *n*

top¹ *n* **1** the highest part or point **2** the upper surface **3** the most important part of anything **4** the highest leaves of a plant: *turnip tops* **5** the lid **6** a garment worn on the upper part of the body **7 in top (gear)** in the highest gear

top² *v* **-pp- 1** to reach the top of **2** to provide or form a top for: *topped with cream* **3** to be higher, better, or more than: *Our profits have topped $1, 000* **4** to remove the top from (a vegetable, fruit, etc.) **5** (esp. in golf) to hit (a ball) above the centre **6 top the bill** to be the chief performer in an entertainment —see also TOP UP

top³ *adj* of, related to, or being at the top

top⁴ *n* **1** a toy that is made to balance on its point by spinning **2 sleep like a top** to sleep deeply

topaz *n* (a cut and polished piece of) a transparent yellow or blue mineral, regarded as a precious stone

topcoat *n* an overcoat

top dog *n sl* the person in the highest or most important position

top-dress *v* to spread a covering of lime, sand, manure, etc. over the surface of (a field) — **~ing** *n*

top-flight *adj* of highest rank or quality

top hat *n* a man's tall silk hat

top-heavy *adj* too heavy at the top in relation to the bottom; not properly balanced for this reason

topiary *adj, n* (of, related to, shaped by, or being) the art of cutting trees and bushes into ornamental shapes

topic *n* a subject for conversation, talk, writing, etc.

topical *adj* of, related to, dealing with, or being a subject of present interest — **~ly** *adv* — **~ity** *n*

topknot *n* a knot or bunch of hair, feathers, ribbons, etc., on the top of the head

topless *adj* having or leaving the upper part of the body bare

topmast *n technical* the second part of the mast above the deck on a sailing ship

topmost *adj* highest

top-notch *adj esp. spoken* first rate; being one of the best possible

topographer *n* a person skilled in topography

topography *n* **1** the character of a particular place in terms of shape, height, etc., of the land **2** the science of describing or representing the topography of a place in detail, as on a map — **-phical** *adj* — **-phically** *adv*

topology *n technical* the study of the properties of a geometrical figure that are unaffected when it is subjected to any continuous bending or twisting

topper *n esp. spoken* a top hat

topping *n* something put on top of food to make it look nicer, taste better, etc.

topple *v* **-pled, -pling** to fall down

tops *n sl* the very best

top-secret *adj* to be kept very secret

topside *n* high quality beef cut from the upper leg

topsoil *n* the upper level of soil

topspin *n* turning movement given to a ball so that it spins in the air

topsy-turvy *adv, adj* (being) in a state of complete disorder and confusion

top up *v adv* to fill (a partly full container) with liquid

tor *n* a small rocky hill

torch *n* **1** a small electric light carried in the hand **2** a mass of burning material used for giving light

torchlight *n* light produced by torches

tore *past tense of* TEAR

toreador *n* a man who takes part in a Spanish bullfight riding on a horse

torment¹ *n* **1** (a) very great pain or suffering in mind or body **2** something or someone that causes this

torment² *v* **1** to cause to suffer great pain in mind or body **2** to annoy — **~or** *n*

torn *past part. of* TEAR

tornado *n* **-does** *or* **-dos** a violent storm in the form of a very tall wide pipe of air that spins at speeds of over 300 miles per hour —see TYPHOON (USAGE)

torpedo¹ *n* **-does** a self-propelled explosive shell that travels underwater torpedo² v -doed, -doing to attack or destroy (a ship) with a torpedo

torpedo boat n a small fast warship used mainly for torpedo attacks

torpid adj 1 inactive; slow; lazy 2 (esp. of animals that sleep through the winter) having lost the power of feeling or moving — ~ity, ~ness n — ~ly adv

torpor n the state of being torpid; condition of lazy inactivity

torque n 1 an ornamental band of twisted metal worn round the neck or arms by ancient Britons or Gauls 2 the force that causes a shaft to spin in an engine; twisting force

torrent n a violently rushing stream, esp. of water — ~ial adj

torrid adj 1 very hot 2 concerning or describing strong feelings and uncontrolled activity, esp. sexual — ~ly adv

torsion n technical 1 the act of twisting or turning 2 the state of being twisted or turned

torso n -sos the human trunk

tortilla n (a) thin round flat cake made by baking a mixture of crushed corn and eggs

tortoise n a slow-moving land reptile that has a body covered by a hard shell into which the legs, tail, and head can be pulled for protection

tortoiseshell n 1 the hard shell of the tortoise or turtle, sometimes used for ornament 2 a cat with brown, black, and yellowish fur 3 a type of butterfly with brownish markings

tortuous adj 1 twisted; winding; full of bends 2 not direct in speech, thought, or action — ~ly adv — ~ness n

torture¹ n 1 the act of causing someone severe pain, done out of cruelty, as a punishment, etc. 2 severe pain or suffering caused in the mind or body 3 a method of causing such pain or suffering

torture² v -tured, -turing to cause great pain or suffering to (a person or animal) out of cruelty, as a punishment, etc. — ~r n

Tory n, adj Tories (a member or supporter) of the British Conservative party — ~ism n

toss¹ v 1 to throw 2 to move about rapidly and pointlessly: tossed about in the sea 3 to mix lightly: Toss the vegetables in butter 4 to throw (a coin) to decide something according to which side lands face upwards

toss² n 1 an act of tossing: a toss of the head 2 a tossing movement

toss off v adv to produce (something) quickly with little effort

toss-up n 1 sl an even chance 2 an act of tossing for something

tot n 1 a very small child 2 a small amount of a strong alcoholic drink —see also TOT UP

total¹ adj complete; whole — ~ly adv : I totally agree

total² n the sum obtained as the result of addition; complete amount

total³ v -ll- 1 to equal a total of; add up to 2 to find the total of

totalitarian adj of, being, or related to a political system in which a single person or political party controls all actions and does not allow opposition parties to exist — ~ism n

totality n -ties 1 the state of being whole; completeness 2 esp. written a total amount

totalizator, -isator n the tote

tote¹ v toted, toting esp. spoken to carry: to tote a gun

tote² n a machine that shows the number of bets placed on each horse or dog in a race and the amount to be paid to the people who betted on the winners

totem n 1 an animal, plant, or object thought by certain tribes, esp. North American Indians, to have a close relationship with the family group 2 a representation of this, esp. on wood

totter v to move in an unsteady way as if about to fall — ~y adj

tot up v adv -tt- to add up

toucan n a type of tropical American bird with a very large beak

touch¹ v 1 to be separated from (something) by no space 2 to feel with a part of the body, esp. the hands or fingers 3 to eat or drink a little of 4 to compare with; be equal to: Your work will never touch the standard set by Robert 5 to deal with; concern: a serious matter that touches your future 6 to cause (someone) to feel pity, sympathy, etc. 7 to mark with light strokes; put in with a pencil or brush —see also TOUCH DOWN, TOUCH FOR, TOUCH OFF, TOUCH ON, TOUCH UP — ~able adj — ~er n

touch² n 1 that sense by which a material object is felt and by which it is known to be hard, smooth, rough, etc. 2 the effect caused by touching something; way something feels 3 an act of touching 4 a slight amount: a touch of fever 5 an addition or detail that improves or completes something: the finishing touches 6 a special ability to do, or a particular way of doing, something needing skill: I hope you're not losing your touch 7 (in soccer or rugby) the area of the pitch outside the field of play 8 in/out of touch a regularly/not regularly exchanging news and information b having/not having information about something

touch-and-go adj risky; of uncertain result

touch down v adv 1 (in rugby) to win a try 2 (of a plane) to land — touchdown n

touché interj That is a good point against me

touched adj sl 1 slightly mad 2 feeling grateful: very touched

touch for v prep esp. spoken to persuade (someone) to give one (a sum of money)

touchline n a line along each of the 2 longer sides of a sports field, esp. in football

touch off v adv 1 to cause to explode 2 to start; cause

touch on v prep to mention briefly

touchstone n anything used as a test or standard

touch-type v -typed, -typing to type without having to look at the letters on the typewriter

touch up *v adv* to improve by making small changes or additions

touchy *adj* **-ier, -iest** easily offended or annoyed; too sensitive — **touchily** *adv* — **touchiness** *n*

tough[1] *adj* **1** strong; able to suffer uncomfortable conditions **2** not easily cut, worn, or broken: *as tough as leather* **3** difficult **4** unyielding; hard: *The government will get tough with tax evaders* **5** rough; violent **6** *esp. spoken* too bad; unfortunate — ~**ly** *adv* — ~**ness** *n*

tough[2] also **toughie**— *n esp. spoken* a rough violent person

toughen *v* to make or become tough

toupee *n* a small wig or hairpiece specially shaped to fit exactly over a bald place on the head

tour[1] *n* **1** a journey during which several places of interest are visited **2** a short trip to or through a place in order to see it **3** a period of duty at a single place or job, *esp. abroad* **4** a journey from place to place as made by a company of actors in order to perform, by an important person to make official visits, by a sports team, etc.

tour[2] *v* to visit as a tourist

tour de force *n French* a show of strength or great skill

tourism *n* **1** the practice of travelling for pleasure, esp. on holiday **2** the business of providing holidays, tours, hotels, etc., for tourists

tourist *n* **1** a person travelling for pleasure **2** a sportsman on tour

tourist class *n* travelling conditions that are fairly cheap

tournament *n* **1** a series of competitions of skill between players, the winner of one match playing the winner of another, until the most skilful is found **2** also **tourney**— (in former times) a competition of courage and skill between knights

tourniquet *n* anything, esp. a band of cloth with a small pad of cloth underneath, twisted tightly round a limb to stop bleeding

tousle *v* **-sled, -sling** to disarrange (esp. the hair)

tout[1] *v* **1** to try repeatedly to persuade people to buy one's goods, use one's services, etc. **2** to sell (tickets in short supply) at a price higher than usual

tout[2] *n* a person who touts

tow[1] *v* to pull (a vehicle) along by a rope or chain

tow[2] *n* **1** an act of towing **2** the state of being towed **3 in tow** *esp. spoken* following closely behind

towards also **toward**— *prep* **1** in the direction of, without necessarily reaching **2** in a position facing: *with his back towards me*

towel[1] *n* **1** a piece of cloth or paper used for rubbing or drying wet skin, dishes, etc. **2 throw in the towel/sponge** *esp. spoken* to admit defeat

towel[2] *v* **-ll-** to rub or dry with a towel

towelling *n* thickish cloth suitable for making towels

tower[1] *n* **1** a tall building standing alone or forming part of a castle, church, etc. ⟹ CASTLE, CACATHEDRAL **2** a tall metal framework

tower[2] *v* to be very tall in relation to the height of the surroundings

tower block *n* a tall block of flats or offices

towering *adj* **1** very tall **2** very great: *a towering temper*

town *n* **1** a large group of houses and other buildings where people live and work **2** the business or shopping centre of such a place: *We went to town* **3** the people who live in a town: *The whole town is angry* **4** towns and cities in general, as opposed to the country

town clerk *n* an official who keeps the records, advises on matters regarding the law, and acts as secretary of a town

town council *n* an elected governing body of a town

town crier *n* a person employed to walk about the streets shouting out news, warnings, etc.

town hall *n* a building used for a town's local government offices and public meetings

township *n* **1** (in Canada and the US) a town, or town and the area around it, that has certain powers of local government **2** (in South Africa) an urban area where nonwhite citizens live

townspeople also **townsfolk**— *n* **1** the people who live in a particular town **2** people who live in towns as opposed to the country

towpath *n* a path along the bank of a canal or river, used by horses pulling boats

toxic *adj* **1** of, related to, or caused by poisonous substances **2** poisonous: *a toxic drug* — ~**ity** *n*

toxin *n* a poisonous substance

toy *n* **toys 1** an object for children to play with **2** a small breed of dog

toy with *v prep* **toyed, toying with** to consider or play with, not very seriously

trace[1] *v* **traced, tracing 1** to follow the course or line of (something or someone) **2** to find the origins of **3** to find or discover: *I can't trace the letter you sent* **4** to copy by drawing on transparent paper (a drawing, map, etc.) placed underneath **5** to draw the course or shape of — ~**able** *adj*

trace[2] *n* **1** a mark or sign showing the former presence or passing of some person, vehicle, or event **2** a very small amount of something

trace[3] *n* either of the ropes, chains, or lengths of leather by which a cart, carriage, etc., is fastened to an animal that is pulling it

trace element *n* a simple chemical substance that is necessary for healthy growth and development

tracery *n* **-ries** ornamental work done with branching and crossing lines

trachea *n medical* the windpipe

tracing *n* a copy of a map, drawing, etc., made by tracing

tracing paper n strong transparent paper used for tracing

track¹ n 1 a line or number of marks left by a person, animal, vehicle, etc., that has passed before 2 a rough path or road 3 the metal lines of a railway 4 the course taken by something 5 an endless belt used over the wheels of some very heavy farm, building, or military vehicles 6 a course prepared for racing 7 one of the pieces of music on a long-playing record or tape 8 one of the bands on which material can be recorded on a tape 9 **on the right/wrong track** thinking or working correctly/incorrectly

track² v 1 to follow the track of 2 (of a television or film camera or the person working it) to move round while taking a picture — ~**er** n

trackless adj 1 without paths, roads, etc. 2 not running on a railway

tracksuit n a loose-fitting suit of warm material worn by sportsmen when training but not when playing, racing, etc. — ~**ed** adj

tract¹ n a short article on a religious or moral subject

tract² n a wide stretch of land

tractable adj esp. written easily controlled — -**ability** n

traction n 1 the act of drawing or pulling a heavy load over a surface 2 the form or type of power used for this 3 the force that prevents a wheel from slipping over the surface on which it runs

traction engine n a large vehicle used for pulling heavy loads

tractor n a powerful motor vehicle used for pulling farm machinery or other heavy objects

trad n a style of jazz originally played in New Orleans about 1920, marked by free expression within a set instrumental framework

trade¹ n 1 the business of buying, selling, or exchanging goods 2 a particular business or industry 3 the people who work in a particular business or industry 4 a job, esp. one needing special skill with the hands: *a printer by trade* 5 amount of business: *a good trade in flowers*

trade² v **traded, trading** 1 to carry on trade 2 to buy, sell, or exchange (a product, goods, etc.) — ~**r** n

trade gap n the difference between the value of a country's imports and exports

trade in v adv to give (something) in part payment when buying something new — **trade-in** n

trademark n 1 a particular producer's own mark on a product 2 a distinctive mannerism or characteristic by which a person may be recognized

trade name also **brand name**— n the name of a particular product, by which it may be recognized from similar products made by other producers

trade price n the price at which goods are sold by producers to shops

tradesman n -**men** a person who buys and sells goods, esp. a shopkeeper

Trades Union Congress n the association of British trade unions

trade union also **trades union**— n an organization of workers to represent their interests and deal as a group with employers — ~**ism** n — ~**ist** n

trade wind n a tropical wind that blows almost continually towards the equator from the northeast or southeast

trading estate n an industrial area containing factories that are usu. rented

trading post n a small place for buying and selling things, started by settlers in a lonely part of a country

tradition n 1 the passing down of beliefs, customs, etc., from the past to the present 2 belief, custom, etc., passed down in this way 3 the body of beliefs, practices, etc., passed down — ~**al** adj — ~**ally** adv

traduce v -**duced, -ducing** esp. written to speak falsely of (someone, his character, etc.) — -**ducer** n

traffic n 1 the movement of people or vehicles along roads or streets, of ships in the seas, planes in the sky, etc. —compare CIRCULATION 2 the people, vehicles, etc., in this movement 3 trade; buying and selling 4 business done by a railway, ship or air travel company, etc., in carrying goods or passengers

traffic in v prep -**ck**- to carry on trade, esp. of an unlawful or improper kind: *trafficking in stolen goods* — ~**ker** n

traffic lights also **traffic signals**— n a set of coloured lights used for controlling and directing traffic

traffic warden n an official responsible for controlling traffic and parking

tragedy n -**dies** 1 a serious play that ends sadly, esp. with the main character's death 2 this type of play, film, etc. 3 a terrible, unhappy, or unfortunate event

tragic adj of or related to tragedy — ~**ally** adv

tragicomedy n -**dies** 1 a play or story with both sad and funny parts 2 such plays and stories considered as a group

trail¹ v 1 to drag or allow to drag behind 2 to be dragged along behind 3 to follow the tracks of 4 to walk tiredly 5 (of a plant) to grow over or along the ground

trail² n 1 the track or smell of a person or animal 2 a path across rough country made by the passing of people or animals 3 a stream of dust, smoke, people, vehicles, etc., behind something moving 4 **blaze a/the trail** to be the very first in doing something

trailer n 1 short pieces from a new film or television programme, shown in advance to advertise it 2 a vehicle pulled by another vehicle

trail off v adv to become gradually weaker and fade away

train[1] *n* **1** a line of connected railway carriages drawn by an engine **2** a series or line of people, things, events, etc. **3** a part of a long dress that spreads behind the wearer **4** a group of servants or officers attending a person of high rank

train[2] *v* **1** to direct the growth of (a plant) by bending, cutting, tying, etc. **2** to give teaching or practice, esp. in an act, profession, or skill **3** to be taught or given practice, esp. in an art, profession, or skill: *I trained to be a doctor* **4** to make ready for a test of skill: *training for the race* **5** to aim (a gun) at something or someone — ~**able** *adj* — ~**er** *n*

trainee *n* a person who is being trained

training *n* **1** the act of training or being trained **2** a course of special exercises, practice, food, etc., to keep sportsmen or animals healthy and fit

training college *n* a college for training teachers

traipse, trapes *v* **traipsed, traipsing** *esp. spoken* to walk tiredly

trait *n* a particular characteristic

traitor *n* a person who is disloyal, esp. to his country

trajectory *n* **-ries** the curved path of an object fired or thrown through the air

tram also **tramcar**— *n* a public vehicle that runs along rails set in or by a road

tramline *n* one of the rails, set in the road, along which a tram runs

trammel *v* **-ll-** *esp. written* to prevent the free movement, action, or development of (someone or something) — ~**s** *n*

tramp[1] *v* **1** to walk with firm heavy steps **2** to walk steadily through or over

tramp[2] *n* **1** the sound of heavy walking **2** a long walk **3** also **tramp steamer** — a ship that takes goods to any port **4** a person with no home or job, who wanders from place to place

trample *v* **-pled, -pling** to step heavily with the feet; crush under the feet

trampoline *n* an apparatus consisting of a sheet of material tightly stretched and held to a metal frame by strong springs, on which acrobats and gymnasts jump up and down to perform exercises

trance *n* a sleeplike condition of the mind in which one does not notice the things around one

tranny *n* **-nies** *esp. spoken* a transistor radio

tranquil *adj* calm; quiet; peaceful; free from anxiety, worry, etc. — ~**lity** *n* — ~**ly** *adv*

tranquillize, -lise *v* **-lized, -lizing** to cause to become calm or peaceful

tranquillizer, -liser *n* a drug used for reducing anxiety

transact *v* to carry (a piece of business, matter, etc.) through to an agreement — ~**ion** *n*

transatlantic *adj* **1** on the other side of the Atlantic ocean **2** crossing the Atlantic ocean **3** concerning countries on both sides of the Atlantic ocean

transcend *v* to go or be above or beyond (a limit, some specified quality, etc.)

transcendent *adj* **1** going beyond ordinary limits **2** (of God) existing beyond the limits of the universe — ~**ly** *adv* — **-ence, -ency** *n*

transcendental *adj* going beyond human knowledge, thought, belief, and experience — ~**ly** *adv*

transcontinental *adj* crossing a continent

transcribe *v* **-scribed, -scribing** **1** to write or make a full copy of **2** to write in the alphabet of another language or in phonetic symbols **3** to arrange (a piece of music) for some instrument or voice other than the original — **-scription** *n*

transcript *n* a written or printed copy; something transcribed

transept *n* the part of a cross-shaped church that crosses the main body of the church at right angles ⏞CATHEDRAL

transfer[1] *v* **-rr-** **1** to move officially from one place, job, etc., to another **2** to move or change from one vehicle to another **3** to move (a pattern, set of marks, etc.) from one surface to another **4** to give the ownership of (property) to another person — ~**ability** *n* — ~**able** *adj* — ~**ence** *n*

transfer[2] *n* **1** the act of transferring **2** someone or something that has transferred **3** a drawing, pattern, etc., for sticking or printing onto a surface

Transfiguration *n* **1** the glorious change in the appearance of Christ as described in the Bible **2** the day on which this event is commemorated

transfigure *v* **-ured, -uring** to change in outward form or appearance — **-uration** *n*

transfix *v* **1** to pierce through **2** to paralyse with terror, shock, etc.

transform *v* to change completely in appearance or nature — ~**able** *adj*

transformation *n* **1** (an example of) the act of transforming; complete change **2** *technical* (in mathematics) a process by which one shape or configuration is made into another one **3** a stage effect, esp. in pantomime, in which one scene is apparently transformed into another by magic

transformer *n* an apparatus for changing electrical voltage ⏞ ELECTRICITY

transfuse *v* **-fused, -fusing** to put (the blood of one person) into the body of another — **-fusion** *n*

transgress *v* *esp. written* **1** to go beyond (a proper limit) **2** to break (a law, agreement, etc.) — ~**ion** *n* — ~**or** *n*

tranship, transship *v* **-pp-** to transfer from one ship to another — ~**ment** *n*

transient also **transitory**— *adj* lasting or staying for only a short time — ~**ence, -ency** *n*

transistor *n* **1** a small solid electrical apparatus for controlling the flow of an electrical current —compare VALVE **2** also **transistor radio**— a radio that uses these instead of valves

transistorize, -ise *v* **-ized, -izing** to provide with transistors

transit *n* **1** the passing of people or goods from one place to another **2** *technical* the movement of a planet or moon across the face of a larger heavenly body

transition *n* the act of changing or passing from one form, state, subject, or place to another — ~al *adj* — ~ally *adv*

transitive *adj, n* (a verb) describing an action which directly affects some person or thing other than the doer of the action: *'Play games' is a transitive use of 'play' whereas 'play all the time' is intransitive*

translate *v* -lated, -lating to express in another language — compare INTERPRET, TRANSLITERATE — -latable *adj* — -lator *n*

translation *n* **1** the act of translating or being translated **2** something that has been translated **3** *technical* (in mathematics) the process of moving from one position to another so that each point of the object moves the same distance in the same direction as every other point; movement without turning

transliterate *v* -rated, -rating to write (a word, name, etc.) in the alphabet of a different language or system — -ation *n*

translucent *adj* allowing some light to pass through — -cence, -cency *n*

transmigration *n* the passing of the soul at death into another body

transmission *n* **1** transmitting or being transmitted **2** something broadcast **3** the parts in a vehicle which carry power from an engine to the road wheels

transmit *v* -tt- **1** to send or pass from one person, place, or thing to another **2** to broadcast **3** to allow to travel through or along itself **4** to carry (force, power, etc.) from one part of a machine to another

transmitter *n* **1** someone or something that transmits **2** an instrument in a telegraphic system that sends out messages **3** an apparatus that sends out radio or television signals

transmogrify *v* -fied, -fying to change completely, as if by magic — -fication *n*

transmute *v* -muted, -muting to change from one form into another — -mutable *adj* — -mutation *n*

transom *n* **1** a bar separating a door from a window above **2** a bar of wood or stone fitted across a window to divide it in 2 **3** a window divided in this way

transparency *n* -cies **1** the state of being transparent **2** a photographic slide

transparent *adj* **1** allowing light to pass through so that objects behind can be clearly seen **2** clear; easily seen or understood — ~ly *adv*

transpire *v* -spired, -spiring **1** *technical* (of the body, plants, etc.) to give off through the surface of the body, leaves, etc. **2** (of an event, secret, etc.) to become gradually known **3** *esp. spoken* to happen — -piration *n* USAGE Everyone agrees that it is bad English to use

transpire when one means "happen", but the word is often used in this way.

transplant[1] *v* **1** to move (a plant) from one place and plant in another **2** to move (an organ, piece of skin, hair, etc.) from one part of the body to another or from one person or animal to another — ~ation *n*

transplant[2] *n* **1** something transplanted **2** an act of transplanting

transport[1] *v* **1** to carry (goods, people, etc.) from one place to another **2** (in former times) to send (a criminal) to a distant land as a punishment — ~able *adj*

transport[2] *n* **1** transporting or of being transported **2** a means or system of transporting ☉ **3** a ship or aircraft for carrying soldiers or supplies

transportation *n* (in former times) the act or a period of transporting someone as a punishment

transport cafe *n* a cheap cafe , used esp. by long-distance lorry drivers

transporter *n* a long vehicle for carrying cars

transpose *v* -posed, -posing **1** to change the order or position of **2** to write or perform (a piece of music) in a key other than the original — -position *n*

transship *v* -pp- to tranship — ~ment *n*

transubstantiation *n* *technical* the belief that the bread and wine offered at the Mass become the body and blood of Christ —compare CONSUBSTANTIATION

transverse *adj* lying or placed across — ~ly *adv*

transvestite *adj, n* (of or related to) a person who likes to wear the clothing of the opposite sex — -tism *n*

trap[1] *n* **1** an apparatus for catching and holding animals **2** a position in which one is caught; plan for catching a person **3** a U or S shaped part of a pipe, which holds water and so prevents gas from waste escaping **4** a light 2-wheeled vehicle pulled by a horse **5** *sl* a mouth: *Keep your trap shut* **6** an apparatus from which a dog is set free at the beginning of a race

trap[2] *v* -pp- **1** to catch by a trick or deception **2** to block: *to trap water* **3** to catch (an animal) in a trap

trapdoor *n* a door covering an opening in the roof or floor

trapes *v* to traipse

trapeze *n* a short bar hung from 2 ropes, used by acrobats and gymnasts

trapezium -iums *or* -ia *technical* a 4-sided figure in which only one pair of sides is parallel ⟿ MATHEMATICS

trapezoid *n* *technical* a 4-sided figure in which no sides are parallel

trapper *n* a person who traps wild animals, esp. for their fur

trappings *n* articles of dress or ornamentation: *the trappings of office*

Development of transport

Historical events	Date	Date	Development
Stone Age	20000BC	c20000BC	Use of rafts and dugout canoes
	5000BC		
		c3500BC	Invention of wheel and sail **1**
		c3000BC	Horse-drawn chariots in use
Pyramids built		c2500BC	Egyptian ships developed **2**
	1000BC	c1100BC	Bireme, ship with double banks of oars, invented
		c300BC–	Road-building in the Roman Empire
Birth of Christ	1AD	200AD	
476 Fall of Western Roman Empire	500		
789 First Viking attack on England	800	c800	Viking ships **3**
	900	c900	First use of horseshoes
	1000		
1096 First Crusade	1100		
	1200	c1230	Rudder first used in European ships
		c1250	Navigational charts first used by sailors
1271 Marco Polo travels to China	1300		
Age of Exploration	1400	1456	Quadrants in use **4**
		1466	The carrack, multi-masted trading vessel
		1492	Columbus sails to America **5**
		1498	Vasco da Gama sails to India
	1500	1521	Magellan sails across the Pacific and round the world
		1545	Introduction of the galleon **6**
		1564	Horse-drawn coach introduced to England
1588 Spanish Armada		1595	Mercator's *Atlas* published
	1600	1606	Proportional compass invented
	1700	1731	Sextant invented **7**
		1765	H.M.S. Victory launched
		1768	Cook sails to Australia
		1769	First steam-propelled road vehicle
c1770 start of Industrial Revolution		1770–1850	Great age of canals
		1775	Watt perfects the steam engine
1789 French Revolution		1783	First hot-air and hydrogen balloon flights **8**
1805 Battle of Trafalgar	1800	1804	First steam locomotive
		c1815	Macadamized roads built
		1825	First passenger steam railway service
1837 Reign of Queen Victoria begins		1839	First pedal-driven bicycle
		1843	First iron screw steamship **9**
	1850	1852	Wells Fargo & Co. founded
		1863	London underground railway opened
		1867	Internal combustion engine first demonstrated
		1869	Suez Canal completed
1873 Jules Verne's *Around the World in 80 Days*		1871	Penny-farthing bicycle invented **10**
		1881	Electric trams introduced
		1885	First cars built
		1888	Pneumatic tyre invented **11**
		1894	First standard production car
		c1896	Diesel engine designed
	1900	c1900	Development of modern submarine
		1903	First powered aircraft flight **12**
		1905	First motorbuses in London
		1906	First hydrofoil built
		1911	First English trolleybus
1914–18 World War I		1914	Panama Canal opened
		1919	First nonstop plane flight across the Atlantic
		1926	First liquid-fuelled rockets launched **13**
1935 First experiments with radar		1937	First jet engine built
1939–45 World War II		1939	First practical helicopter built
		1947	First supersonic flight
	1950	1954	First nuclear-powered submarine **14**
		1957	First artificial satellite launched
		1959	First commercial hovercraft; first British motorway
		1961	First manned space flight
		1969	First man on moon; test flight of Concorde **15**

Trappist *n* a member of a Roman Catholic religious order whose members never speak

trash *n* anything of low quality; rubbish

trashy *adj* **-ier, -iest** worthless — **-iness** *n*

trauma *n* **-mas** *or* **-mata** **1** damage to the mind caused by a sudden shock or terrible experience **2** a wound

traumatic *adj* deeply shocking — ~**ally** *adv*

travel[1] *v* **-ll-** **1** to go from place to place; make a journey **2** *sl* to go very quickly: *We were really travelling when the police caught us*

travel[2] *n* the act of travelling   USAGE When a person **journeys** *about the world* we speak of his **travels**. A **journey** is the time spent and the distance covered in going from one place to another. A **voyage** is a sea **journey**.

travel agency *n* **-cies** a business that arranges people's journeys

travel agent *n* a person who owns or works in a travel agency

travelled *adj* **1** (of a person) experienced in travel: *widely travelled* **2** (of a road, area, etc.) used or visited by travellers: *well travelled*

traveller *n* **1** a person on a journey **2** also **travelling salesman**— a person who goes from place to place trying to sell goods

traveller's cheque *n* a cheque sold by a bank or travel agent that can be cashed anywhere

travelogue *n* a talk or film describing travel

travels *n* travelling; journeys —see TRAVEL (USAGE)

traverse[1] *v* **-versed, -versing** **1** to pass across, over, or through **2** *technical* to make a traverse in climbing

traverse[2] *n* *technical* a movement to the side across a steep slope of rock or ice

travesty *n* **-ties** a copy, account, or example of something that misrepresents the real thing

trawl[1] *v* to fish with a trawl

trawl[2] *n* a fishing net with a wide mouth, drawn along the sea bottom

trawler *n* a fishing vessel that uses a trawl

tray *n* **trays** a flat piece of material with raised edges, used for carrying small articles or holding papers

treacherous *adj* **1** disloyal; deceitful **2** dangerous — ~**ly** *adv*

treachery *n* **-ries** **1** disloyalty; deceit; unfaithfulness; falseness —compare TREASON **2** a treacherous action

treacle *n* a thick dark sticky liquid produced when sugar is being refined

treacly *adj* **-clier, -cliest** too thick and sweet

tread[1] *v* **trod, trodden, treading** **1** to walk on, over, or along **2** to press or crush with the feet **3 tread on air** *sl* to be very happy **4 tread on somebody's toes** to offend somebody **5 tread water** keep oneself upright in deep water

tread[2] *n* **1** the act, manner, or sound of walking **2** the part of a step or stair on which the foot is placed **3** the raised lines on a tyre

treadle[1] *n* an apparatus worked by the feet to drive a machine

treadle[2] *v* **-dled, -dling** to work a treadle with the feet

treadmill *n* **1** a mill worked by people or animals endlessly walking **2** uninteresting work

treason *n* disloyalty to one's country —compare TREACHERY — ~**able** *adj* : *a treasonable crime* — ~**ably** *adv*

treasure[1] *n* **1** wealth in the form of gold, silver, etc. **2** a very valuable object **3** *esp. spoken* a person considered precious

treasure[2] *v* **-sured, -suring** to keep as precious; regard as valuable

treasurer *n* a person in charge of the money belonging to a club, organization, etc.

treasure trove *n* treasure found in the ground

treasury *n* **-ries** a collection of valuable things

Treasury *n* the government department that controls and spends public money —compare EXCHEQUER

treat[1] *v* **1** to act or behave towards **2** to deal with; handle **3** to regard; consider: *My employer treated our request as a joke* **4** to try to cure by medical means **5** to buy or give (someone) something special **6** to put (a substance) through a chemical or industrial action in order to change it in some way — ~**able** *adj* — ~**er** *n*

treat[2] *n* **1** something that gives pleasure **2** **one's treat** one's act of treating

treatise *n* a book or article that examines a subject and gives the writer's opinions on it

treatment *n* **1** the act or manner of treating someone or something **2** a substance or method used in treating someone medically

treaty *n* **-ies** an agreement made between countries and formally signed by their representatives, or between people

treble[1] *n* **1** (a person with or a musical part for) a high singing voice **2** (of a family of instruments) the instrument with this range of notes **3** the upper half of the whole range of musical notes ☞ MUSIC —compare BASS

treble[2] *adv, adj* high in sound

treble[3] *adj* 3 times as big, as much, or as many as

treble[4] *v* **-led, -ling** to make or become 3 times as great

treble clef *n* a clef 𝄞 showing that the following notes are higher than middle C —compare BASS CLEF

tree *n* **1** a type of tall plant with a wooden trunk and branches **2** a bush or other plant with a treelike form **3** a wooden object with a special purpose, such as a shoe tree, clothes tree, etc. **4** a diagram with a branching form, esp. as used for showing family relationships —see also FAMILY TREE — ~**less** *adj*

trefoil *n* any of various types of plant, such as clover, that have leaves divided into 3 little leaves

trek v -kk- to make a long journey — **trek** n

trellis n a light upright framework

tremble¹ v **-bled, -bling** to shake uncontrollably — **-blingly** adv

tremble² n an act of trembling; shudder

tremendous adj 1 very great in size, amount, or degree 2 wonderful: a tremendous party — ~ly adv

tremolo n **-los** technical a slightly shaking effect produced by rapidly varying the pitch of a musical note, or by playing notes very fast

tremor n 1 a shaking movement of the earth 2 a shaking movement caused by fear, weakness, etc.

tremulous adj slightly shaking; nervous — ~ly adv — ~ness n

trench¹ n a deep ditch dug in the ground (e.g. as a protection for soldiers) —compare DUGOUT

trench² v to dig trenches in

trenchant adj (of language) forceful; effective — ~ly adv — **-ancy** n

trench coat n a loose-fitting military-style coat

trend¹ v to have a certain tendency, course, or direction of development

trend² n a general direction or course of development; tendency

trendy¹ adj **-ier, -iest** esp. spoken very fashionable — **trendiness** n

trendy² n **-ies** esp. spoken a trendy person

trepidation n a state of anxiety or fear

trespass v 1 to go onto private land without permission 2 old use & Bible to sin — **trespass** n — ~er n

trespass upon also **trespass on**— v prep to take more of (something) than one ought: trespassing upon your time

tresses n literature long hair

trestle n a wooden beam on legs, used in pairs to support a flat surface

trestle table n a table supported by trestles

trews n close fitting tartan trousers

trial n 1 the act of hearing and judging a person, case, or point of law in a court 2 the act of testing: horse trials 3 an attempt; effort; try: trial and error 4 an annoying thing or person: That child is a trial 5 **on trial a** for the purpose of testing: He took the car on trial **b** being tried in a court of law

triangle n 1 a flat figure with 3 straight sides and 3 angles; a 3-sided polygon ☞ MATHEMATICS 2 an object or piece of that shape 3 a 3-sided musical percussion instrument 4 a group of 3

triangular adj 1 of or shaped like a triangle 2 having 3 people or groups

tribalism n the organization of a social group into a tribe

tribe n 1 a social group made up of people of the same race, language, etc. —see FOLK (USAGE) 2 a group of related plants or animals — **tribal** adj

tribesman n **-men** a male member of a tribe

tribulation n (a cause of) trouble, grief, suffering, etc.

tribunal n a court of people appointed officially, with powers to deal with special matters

tribune n 1 an official of Ancient Rome 2 a popular leader

tributary n **-ries** a stream or river that flows into a larger one

tribute n 1 (a) payment made by one ruler, government, or country to another as the price of peace, protection, etc. 2 something done, said, or given to show respect or admiration

trice n **in a trice** in the shortest possible time

trick¹ n 1 an act needing special skill, esp. done to confuse or amuse 2 a special skill: the trick of adding up quickly 3 something done to deceive or cheat someone 4 something done to someone to make him look stupid 5 a strange or typical habit 6 the cards (one from each player) played or won in one round of some card games 7 **not/never miss a trick** esp. spoken to know everything that is going on — ~ery n

trick² adj 1 made for playing tricks: a trick spoon 2 full of hidden and unexpected difficulties 3 of, concerned with, or related to a special skill

trick³ v to cheat (someone)

trickle¹ v **-led, -ling** to flow or cause to flow in drops or in a thin stream

trickle² n a small thin flow

trickster n a person who deceives or cheats people

tricky adj **-ier, -iest** 1 difficult to handle or deal with 2 deceitful; sly — **trickiness** n

tricolour n a flag with 3 equal bands of different colours

tricycle n a bicycle with 3 wheels

trident n a forklike instrument or weapon with 3 points

tried¹ adj found to be good by experience: a tried method

tried² past tense and past part. of TRY

triennial adj done or happening every 3 years or lasting for 3 years

trier n a person who tries hard

trifle n 1 an article or thing of little importance 2 a dish of plain cakes set in fruit and jelly and covered with cream or custard 3 **a trifle** rather

trifler n a person who trifles with someone or something

trifle with v prep to deal lightly with, without the necessary respect

trifling adj of little importance

trigger¹ n the tongue of metal pressed by the finger to fire a gun

trigger² v to start; set off

trigger-happy adj too ready to shoot for the slightest reason; too dependent on violent methods

trigonometry n the branch of mathematics that deals with the relationship between the sides and angles of triangles ◎

trike n esp. spoken a tricycle

Trigonometry

The trigonomical ratios

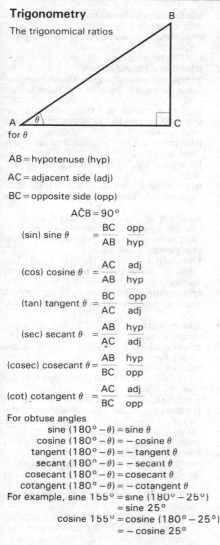

for θ

AB = hypotenuse (hyp)

AC = adjacent side (adj)

BC = opposite side (opp)

$$A\hat{C}B = 90°$$

(sin) sine $\theta \quad = \dfrac{BC}{AB} \quad \dfrac{opp}{hyp}$

(cos) cosine $\theta \quad = \dfrac{AC}{AB} \quad \dfrac{adj}{hyp}$

(tan) tangent $\theta \quad = \dfrac{BC}{AC} \quad \dfrac{opp}{adj}$

(sec) secant $\theta \quad = \dfrac{AB}{AC} \quad \dfrac{hyp}{adj}$

(cosec) cosecant $\theta = \dfrac{AB}{BC} \quad \dfrac{hyp}{opp}$

(cot) cotangent $\theta \quad = \dfrac{AC}{BC} \quad \dfrac{adj}{opp}$

For obtuse angles

$$\text{sine } (180° - \theta) = \text{sine } \theta$$
$$\text{cosine } (180° - \theta) = -\text{cosine } \theta$$
$$\text{tangent } (180° - \theta) = -\text{tangent } \theta$$
$$\text{secant } (180° - \theta) = -\text{secant } \theta$$
$$\text{cosecant } (180° - \theta) = \text{cosecant } \theta$$
$$\text{cotangent } (180° - \theta) = -\text{cotangent } \theta$$

For example, sine $155° = \text{sine } (180° - 25°)$
$$= \text{sine } 25°$$
$$\text{cosine } 155° = \text{cosine } (180° - 25°)$$
$$= -\text{cosine } 25°$$

Relations between the trigonometrical ratios:

$$\text{tangent } \theta = \frac{\text{sine } \theta}{\text{cosine } \theta}$$

$$\text{sine}^2 \theta + \text{cosine}^2 \theta = 1$$

$$\text{secant } \theta = \frac{1}{\text{cosine } \theta}$$

$$\text{cosecant } \theta = \frac{1}{\text{sine } \theta}$$

$$\text{cotangent } \theta = \frac{1}{\text{tangent } \theta}$$

Trigonometrical formulae

Sine formula In triangle ABC,

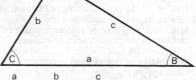

$$\frac{a}{\text{sine A}} = \frac{b}{\text{sine B}} = \frac{c}{\text{sine C}}$$

Cosine formula In triangle ABC,

$$a^2 = b^2 + c^2 - 2bc \text{ cosine A}$$
$$b^2 = c^2 + a^2 - 2ca \text{ cosine B}$$
$$c^2 = a^2 + b^2 - 2ab \text{ cosine C}$$

Pythagoras' theorem

In the right-angled triangle PQR, $PQ^2 = PR^2 + QR^2$, or: the square of the hypotenuse equals the sum of the squares of the two smaller sides.

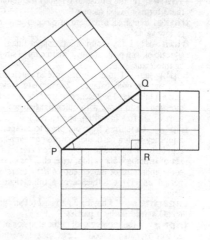

Thus the area of the square formed with PQ as one side is the sum of the areas of the two squares formed with PR and QR as sides.

trilateral adj having 3 sides — ~ly adv
trilby also **trilby hat**— n -bies a man's soft hat
trilingual adj of, using, or able to speak, 3 languages — ~ly adv
trill¹ n 1 the rapid repeating of 2 musical notes 2 a sound like this made by a bird
trill² v to sing, play, or pronounce with a trill
trillion adj, n, pron -trillion or -trillions 1, 000, 000, 000, 000, 000, 000; 10¹⁸
trilobite n a type of small sea creature of very long ago
trilogy n -gies a group of 3 related books, plays, etc.
trim¹ v -mm- 1 to make neat, even, or tidy by cutting 2 to ornament: *trimmed with fur* 3 to move or be moved into the desired position: *Trim the sail* 4 to adjust the load of (a ship or aircraft) for balance 5 to reduce: *trim one's costs*
trim² adj -mm- tidy — ~ly adv
trim³ n 1 an act of cutting 2 proper shape, order, or condition
trimaran n a type of sailing boat with 3 hulls
trimming n 1 an ornament or pleasant addition 2 a piece cut off from a larger piece
Trinity n (in the Christian religion) the union of the 3 forms of God as one
trinket n a small ornament or piece of jewellery of low value
trio n -os 1 any group of 3 people or things 2 a group of, or a piece of music written for, 3 singers or musicians
trip¹ v -pp- 1 to catch or cause to catch one's foot and lose one's balance 2 to make or cause to make a mistake: *The teacher tripped me with that question* 3 to move with quick light steps 4 to start or set free (a switch, spring, etc.)
trip² n 1 a journey from one place to another 2 a journey with a particular purpose or happening regularly 3 a mistake: *a trip of the tongue* 4 an act of tripping 5 a switch, wire, etc., for starting some apparatus or movement 6 *drug users' sl* a period under the influence of a mind-changing drug
tripartite adj 1 having 3 parts 2 (of an agreement) agreed on by 3 parties
tripe n 1 the rubbery wall of the stomach of the cow or ox, eaten as food 2 *esp. spoken* worthless or stupid talk, ideas, etc.
triple¹ v -led, -ling to multiply by 3
triple² adj 1 having 3 parts or members 2 3 times repeated
triple jump n an athletics event in which one has to make in a continuous movement first a hop, then a step, then a jump
triplet n 1 any one of 3 children born of the same mother at the same time 2 a group of 3 musical notes to be played in the time of 2 ordinary notes of the same kind 3 a group or set of 3 (as of lines in a poem)
triple time n a musical time with 3 beats
triplex n *trademark* a safety glass esp. used in car windows

triplicate¹ adj consisting of or existing in 3 parts that are exactly alike
triplicate² v -cated, -cating to make triplicate
triplicate³ n one of 3 like things
tripod n a 3-legged support
tripos n (a course of study for) the set of examinations for the BA degree at Cambridge University
tripper n a person on a short pleasure trip
tripping adj (of a step, movement, etc.) light and easy — ~ly adv
triptych n a picture or carving done on 3 boards fixed side by side
trireme n a galley with 3 rows of oars on each side
trite adj (of remarks, ideas, etc.) too often repeated to be effective — ~ly adv — ~ness n
triumph¹ n 1 a complete victory or success 2 the joy or satisfaction caused by this 3 (in Ancient Rome) a procession in honour of a victorious general — ~al adj
triumph² v 1 to be victorious (over) 2 to show joy and satisfaction because of success or victory
triumphant adj 1 victorious; successful 2 rejoicing in one's success or victory — ~ly adv
triumvirate n a group of 3 men together governing a country
trivet n a 3-legged stand for holding a vessel, usu. over a fire
trivia n unimportant or useless things
trivial adj of little worth or importance — ~ly adv — ~ity n
trivialize, -ise v -ized, -izing to make trivial
trochee n *technical* a measure of poetry consisting of one strong beat followed by one weak beat, as in 'father' — **trochaic** adj
trod *past tense of* TREAD
trodden *past part. of* TREAD
troglodyte n a prehistoric cave-dweller
Trojan n **work like a Trojan** to work very hard
troll n a man-like monster from Scandinavian legends
trolley n -leys 1 any of various low carts, esp. one pushed by hand 2 a small table on small wheels from which food and drinks are served
trollop n a very untidy, often sexually immoral, woman
trombone n a brass musical instrument with a sliding tube that is pushed out or in to vary the note — -nist n
troop¹ n 1 a band of people or wild animals 2 a body of soldiers, esp. a group of cavalry 3 a group of about 32 boy scouts ⚠ TROUPE
troop² v 1 to move together in a band 2 to carry (the regimental flag (colour)) in a ceremonial way
troop carrier n a ship or aircraft used for carrying soldiers

trooper *n* (the title of) a soldier of the lowest rank in the cavalry or the armoured regiments

troops *n* soldiers

troopship *n* a ship for carrying soldiers

trophy *n* -phies **1** a prize given for winning at sport **2** something taken after much effort, esp. in war or hunting

tropic *n* one of the 2 lines of latitude drawn around the world at about 23½° north (the **tropic of Cancer**) and south (the **tropic of Capricorn**) of the equator ⇨ GLOBE

tropical *adj* **1** of, related to, concerning, or living in the tropics **2** very hot: *tropical weather* — ~ly *adv*

tropics *n* the area between the tropics

tropism *n* (a) response of a plant part that involves movement or growth towards or away from a stimulus —compare GEOTROPISM, PHOTOTROPISM

trot¹ *n* **1** (of a horse) a way of moving at a speed between a walk and a gallop **2** a ride on a horse moving at this speed **3** a human speed between a walk and a run **4** a journey at this speed **5 have the trots** also **be on the trot**— *sl* to have diarrhoea **6 on the trot a** in a state of continuous activity **b** one after another

trot² *v* -tt- to move or cause to move at a trot; to hurry

troth *n old use* faithfulness; loyalty; truth

Trotskyism *n* the political principles of Leon Trotsky — -ist, -ite *n, adj*

trotter *n* **1** a horse specially bred and trained for trotting **2** a pig's foot

troubadour *n* a travelling singer of Southern France in the 12th and 13th centuries

trouble¹ *v* -bled, -bling **1** to cause worry, anxiety, etc. to (someone) **2** to cause inconvenience to (someone or oneself) **3** to cause (someone) pain as a disease does: *troubled with a bad back* **4 fish in troubled waters** to try to win some advantage from a confused state of affairs

trouble² *n* **1** (a) difficulty, worry, annoyance, dangerous state of affairs, etc.; an inconvenience **2** the position where one is blamed for doing wrong or thought to have done wrong: *in trouble* **3** a fault **4** a medical condition; illness **5 ask/look for trouble** to behave so as to cause difficulty or danger for oneself **6 get (a girl) into trouble** *esp. spoken* to make (a girl) pregnant

troubleshooter *n* a person employed to discover and remove causes of trouble in machines, organizations, etc.

troublesome *adj* causing trouble, anxiety, or difficulty

trough *n* **1** a long narrow boxlike object, esp. for holding water or food for animals **2** a long narrow hollow area; depression **3** *technical* (in meteorology) a long area of (fairly low pressure) between 2 areas of high pressure

trounce *v* trounced, trouncing to beat or punish severely; defeat completely

troupe *n* a company (of singers, actors, dancers, etc.) △ TROOP

trouper *n* a member of a troupe

trousers *n* an outer garment divided into 2 parts each fitting a leg, worn from the waist down — **trouser** *adj* : *a trouser factory*

trousseau *n* -seaux *or* -seaus the personal possessions that a woman brings with her when she marries

trout *n* trout any of various types of esp. river fish, highly regarded for sport and food

trove *n* —see TREASURE TROVE

trowel *n* **1** a tool for spreading cement, plaster, etc. **2** a garden tool for digging small holes, lifting up plants, etc.

troy weight *n* a system of measuring the weight of gold, silver, and jewels —compare AVOIRDUPOIS

truant *n* **1** a pupil who purposely stays away from school without permission **2 play truant**— to stay away from school in this way — **-ancy** *n*

truce *n* (an agreement between 2 enemies for) the stopping of fighting for a period

truck¹ *n* **have no truck with** to have nothing to do with

truck² *n* **1** an open railway goods vehicle **2** a simple goods vehicle, pulled or pushed by hand **3** a fairly large motor vehicle for carrying goods **4** *esp. US* a lorry

trucking *n US* the business of carrying goods on motor vehicles

truckle bed *n* a low bed on wheels, pushed under another bed when not in use

truculent *adj* **1** cruel; fierce; violent **2** bitterly cruel in judgment **3** always willing to quarrel or attack — ~ly *adv* — **-ence, -ency** *n*

trudge¹ *v* trudged, trudging to walk with heavy steps, slowly and with effort

trudge² *n* a long tiring walk

true¹ *adj* **1** in accordance with fact or reality; actual; not false **2** faithful; loyal; sincere **3** exact; proper; correct; sure **4** correctly fitted, placed, or formed: *The door's not exactly true* **5 true to type** behaving or acting just as one would expect from a person or thing of that type

true² *n* **1** that which is true: *the good, the beautiful, the true* **2 out of true** not having the exact position or correct shape or balance

true³ *adv* in a true manner

true blue *n* a completely loyal Conservative

true-blue *adj* **1** completely honest or faithful **2** of, being, or related to a Conservative

trueborn *adj* actually so by birth; legitimate

true up *v adv* trued, truing up to change (something) slightly in order to give a perfect shape or fit

truffle *n* **1** a type of fleshy fungus that grows underground and is highly regarded as a food **2** a type of soft sweet, usu. made with rum

trug *n* a broad flattish basket used in gardens

truism *n* a statement of something that is clearly true —compare CLICHÉ, COMMONPLACE, PLATITUDE

truly *adv* **1** exactly; in accordance with the truth; sincerely; certainly; really **2 yours truly**

(used at the end of a formal letter before the signature)

trump¹ *n* **1** any card of a suit chosen to be of higher rank than the other 3 suits **2 turn/come up trumps** to behave in a helpful way, esp. unexpectedly

trump² *v* to beat (a card that is not a trump) or win (a trick) by playing a trump

trumpery *n, adj esp. written* (objects, ideas, opinions, etc., that are) showy but of very little value

trumpet¹ *n* **1** a brass wind instrument consisting of a long metal tube curved round once or twice, controlled by 3 valves on top **2** something shaped like the bell-shaped end of this **3** the loud cry of an elephant **4 blow one's own trumpet** to praise oneself

trumpet² *v* **1** to play a trumpet **2** (of an elephant) to make a loud sound **3** to declare or shout loudly — ~er *n*

trump up *v adv* to invent (a reason, charge, etc.) falsely or dishonestly

truncate *v* **-cated, -cating** to cut short

truncheon *n* a stick carried as a weapon by policemen

trundle *v* **-dled, -dling** to move or roll (something heavy or awkward on wheels)

trunk *n* **1** the main stem of a tree **2** the human body without the head and limbs **3** a large case or box **4** the long muscular nose of an elephant

trunk call *n* a telephone call made over a long distance

trunk road *n* a main road for long-distance travel

trunks *n* a short trouser-like garment worn by men

truss¹ *v* **1** to tie up firmly with cord, rope, etc. **2** to support (a roof, bridge, etc.) with a truss

truss² *n* **1** a framework built to support a roof, bridge, etc. **2** a special belt worn to support muscles **3** a tied bundle of hay or straw

trust¹ *n* **1** firm belief in the honesty, worth, power, etc., of someone or something **2** solemn responsibility **3** care; keeping **4** the act of holding and controlling property or money for the advantage of someone else: *in trust* | *a trust fund* **5** a group of people doing this **6** a property or sum of money so held and controlled **7** belief in the intention of a person to pay in the future for goods received now: *supplied on trust* **8** a group of firms that have combined to reduce competition and control prices to their own advantage **9 take on trust** to accept without proof or close examination

trust² *v* **1** to believe in the honesty and worth of (someone or something); have faith in; depend on **2** to hope: *I trust you enjoyed yourself*

trustee *n* **1** a person or firm that holds and controls property in trust; person to whom property or money is given in trust **2** a member of a group appointed to control the affairs of a company, firm, college, etc.

trusteeship *n* **1** the position of trustee **2** government of an area by a country or countries appointed by the United Nations **3** also **trust territory**— an area under such government

trustful also **trusting**— *adj* ready to trust others — ~ly *adv* — ~ness *n*

trust fund *n* money belonging to one person held and controlled by a trustee

trustworthy worthy of trust; dependable — **-thiness** *n*

trusty¹ *adj* **-ier, -iest** *esp. old use* that may be trusted; dependable; faithful

trusty² *n* **-ies** a trusty prisoner given special rights

truth *n* the true facts; the state or quality of being true

truthful *adj* telling the truth — ~ly *adv* — ~ness *n*

try¹ *v* **tried, trying** **1** to test by use and experience, in order to find the quality, worth, effect, etc. **2** to attempt **3** to attempt to open (a door, window, etc.): *Try the door* **4** to examine (a person thought guilty or a case) in a court of law **5** to cause to suffer; annoy

try² *n* **tries** **1** an attempt **2** (in rugby) points won by placing the ball on the ground behind the opposing team's try line

try on *v adv* **1** to put on (a garment, shoes, etc.) to test the fit, appearance, etc. **2 try it on** *sl* to see if one can get away with bad behaviour

tsar, czar, tzar *n* the male ruler of Russia until 1917

tsarina, czarina, tzarina *n* the female ruler of Russia, or the wife of the tsar, until 1917

tsetse fly, tzetze fly *n* **-flies** a type of blood-sucking African fly

T-shirt, tee shirt *n* a close-fitting collarless shirt

tsp *abbrev. for*: a teaspoon

T-square *n* a large ruler shaped like a letter T, used in drawing

tub *n* **1** a large round vessel for packing, storing, washing, etc. **2** a bath

tuba *n* a large brass wind instrument that produces low notes

tubby *adj* **-bier, -biest** *esp. spoken* shortish and fattish

tube *n* **1** a hollow round pipe of metal, glass, rubber, etc. **2** a small soft container of this shape for holding toothpaste, paint, etc. **3** any hollow pipe or organ in the body **4** an underground railway: *travel by tube* **5** CATHODE RAY TUBE — **-bular** *adj*

tubeless *adj.* having no inner tube: *tubeless tyres*

tuber *n* a fleshy underground stem, such as the potato

tuberculosis *n* a serious infectious disease that attacks esp. the lungs — **-lar** *adj*

tubing *n* metal, plastic, etc., in the form of a tube

tub-thumper *n* a public speaker who tries to stir up his listeners

TUC *abbrev. for:* TRADES UNION CONGRESS

tuck¹ *v* to put into a convenient narrow space for protection, safety, etc.

tuck² *n* **1** a flat fold of material sewn into a garment **2** cakes, sweets, etc., esp. as eaten by people at school

tuck in *v adv esp. spoken* to eat eagerly

tuck into *v prep* to eat eagerly

tuck up *v adv* to make (someone) comfortable in bed

Tues. *abbrev. for:* Tuesday

Tuesday *n* **-days** the third day of the week

tuft *n* a bunch (of hair, grass, etc.) growing or held closely together at a base — ~ed *adj*

tug¹ *v* **-gg-** to pull hard with force or much effort

tug² *n* a sudden strong pull

tugboat also **tug**— *n* a small powerful boat used for guiding large vessels

tug-of-war *n* **tugs-of-war** a test of strength in which 2 teams pull against each other on a rope

tuition *n* instruction, teaching, or the charge made for this

tulip *n* a type of garden plant that grows from a bulb, or its flowers

tulle *n* a thin soft silk or nylon netlike material

tumble¹ *v* **-bled, -bling 1** to fall suddenly or helplessly; roll over or down quickly or violently **2** to fall to pieces; fall down; collapse

tumble² *n* **1** a fall **2** a state of disorder and confusion

tumbledown *adj* in a condition of near ruin

tumbler *n* **1** a flat-bottomed drinking glass with no handle or stem **2** the part in a lock that must be turned by a key before the lock will open **3** an acrobat; gymnast

tumbleweed *n* a type of North American desert plant

tumescent *adj technical* swollen — **-cence** *n*

tummy *n* **-mies** *esp. spoken* stomach

tumour *n* a mass of diseased cells, often a cancer, in the body

tumult *n* the confused noise and excitement of a big crowd; state of confusion and excitement

tumultuous *adj* disorderly; noisy — ~ly *adv*

tumulus also **barrow**— *n* **-luses** or **-li** a large pile of earth heaped over a grave in prehistoric times

tun *n* a large barrel for holding 250 gallons of liquids

tuna *n* **tuna** or **tunas 1** also **tunny**— a type of large edible sea fish **2** its flesh

tundra *n* a cold treeless plain in the far north of Europe, Asia, and North America

tune¹ *n* **1** a number of musical notes, one after the other, that produce a pleasing pattern of sound **2 call the tune** to be in a position to give orders, command, etc. **3 change one's tune** to change one's opinion, decision, behaviour, etc. **4 in/out**

of tune a at/not at the correct pitch **b** in/not in agreement or sympathy

tune² *v* **tuned, tuning 1** to set (a musical instrument) at the proper pitch **2** to put an engine in good working order

tune in *v adv* **1** to set a radio to a particular radio station **2 tuned in (to)** in touch with

tuner *n* a person who tunes musical instruments

tungsten also **wolfram**— *n* a hard metal that is an element, used esp. in the production of steel

tunic *n* **1** a loose-fitting short-armed or armless knee length outer garment **2** a specially-shaped short coat worn by policemen, soldiers, etc., as part of a uniform

tuning fork *n* a fork-shaped steel instrument producing a pure musical note when struck

tunnel¹ *n* an underground or underwater passage; passage for a road, railway, etc., through or under a hill, river, etc.

tunnel² *v* **-ll-** to make or make like a tunnel — ~ler *n*

tunny *n* **-ny** or **nies** a tuna

tuppence *n sl* twopence

turban *n* a head-covering worn by men in parts of North Africa and southern Asia — ~ed *adj*

turbid *adj* **1** not clear; dark; thick **2** confused — ~ness, ~ity *n*

turbine *n* an engine or motor in which the pressure of a liquid or gas drives a wheel and thus changes into circular movement

turbojet *n* an aircraft or its engine that produces movement by forcing out a stream of hot air and gases behind itself

turboprop *n* an aircraft or its turbine engine that drives a propeller

turbot *n* **-bot** or **-bots** a type of large European edible fish with a diamond-shaped body

turbulence also **turbulency**— *n* **1** the state of being turbulent **2** irregular and violent movement of the air

turbulent *adj* violent; disorderly; uncontrolled; stormy

turd *n vulgar* a piece of solid waste material passed from the body

tureen *n* a deep dish from which food is served at a table

turf¹ *n* **-s** or **turves 1** (a piece of) soil with grass and roots growing in it **2** a block or piece of peat dug to be burnt **3 a** horse racing **b** the grassy course over which horses race

turf² *v* to cover land with turf

turf accountant *n* a bookmaker

turf out *v adv esp. spoken* to throw out; get rid of

turgid *adj* **1** swollen, as by a liquid or inner pressure **2** (of language or style) too solemn and self-important — ~ity *n* — ~ly *adv*

turkey *n* **-keys** a type of large bird bred for its meat

Turkish *adj* of Turkey, its people, or their language

Turkish bath *n* a type of bath in very hot steam

Turkish delight *n* a sweet jelly-like substance eaten in lumps as a sweet

turmeric *n* a type of Asian plant whose yellowish root is used for giving a special taste and colour to food

turmoil *n* a state of confusion, excitement, and trouble

turn¹ *v* 1 to move round a fixed point 2 to change direction 3 to aim in a particular direction 4 to make or become: *to turn brown* 5 to make or become sour: *The heat's turned the milk* 6 to shape wood or metal: *to turn wood* 7 to feel or cause to feel uncomfortable, sick, etc.: *Fat turns my stomach* 8 to change the form or nature of: *She turned her old dress into a skirt* 9 to cause to go; send; drive: *My father would turn me out if he knew I played truant* 10 to throw into disorder or confusion: *The robbers had turned the room upside down* 11 to change position so that the bottom becomes the top, the hidden side uncovered, etc. —see also TURN AGAINST, TURN DOWN, TURN IN, TURN OUT, TURN OVER, TURN TO, TURN UP

turn² *n* 1 a single movement completely round a fixed point 2 a change of direction 3 a point of change in time: *the turn of the century* 4 a movement or development: *a turn for the worse* 5 a place or appointed time in a particular order: *You've missed your turn* 6 a deed or action with the stated effect: *a good turn* 7 *esp. spoken* a shock: *You gave me quite a turn* 8 *esp. spoken* an attack of illness: *She's had one of her turns* 9 **at every turn** at every moment

turnabout *n* an act of turning in a different or opposite direction

turn against *v prep* to make or become opposed to

turncoat *n offensive* a person who changes his principles or loyalty

turncock *n* a stopcock

turn down *v adv* 1 to lessen the force, strength, loudness, etc., of (something) by using controls: *Turn that radio down* 2 to refuse

turner *n* a person who shapes wood or metal on a lathe

turn in *v adv* 1 *esp. spoken* to go to bed 2 to deliver (a person or thing) to the police 3 to give back; return

turning *n* a place where one road branches off from another

turning point *n* a point in time at which a very important change takes place

turnip *n* a type of plant grown for its large round edible root

turnkey *n* **-keys** *now rare* a jailer

turn-off *n* a smaller road branching off from a main road

turn on *v adv* 1 to cause something to start by unscrewing a tap or moving a switch 2 also **turn upon**— to attack (someone) suddenly and without warning 3 *sl* to have or cause to have a very

strong and unusual experience, esp. by taking a drug for the first time

turnout *n* 1 the number of people who attend a meeting 2 the manner or style in which a person is dressed 3 the amount of goods produced by a worker or factory

turn out *v adv* 1 to stop (a gas, oil, or electric light, heating apparatus, etc.) 2 to come out or gather as for a meeting, public event, etc. 3 to produce 4 to clear or empty a cupboard, drawer, etc. 5 to be in the end: *His statement turned out to be false*

turnover *n* 1 an act of turning over 2 the number of times a particular article is sold during a particular period 3 the amount of business done in a particular period 4 the number of workers that are hired by a firm to fill the places of workers who have left 5 a small fruit pie

turn over *v adv* 1 to think about; consider 2 to cause (an engine) to run at lowest speed 3 to deliver (someone or something) to the police 4 to do business or sell goods worth (the stated amount)

turnstile *n* a small gate with arms turning on a central post, set in an entrance to admit people one at a time

turntable *n* 1 a flat round apparatus, sunk into the ground to be level with the surface, on which railway engines can be turned round or matched to different tracks 2 the round spinning part or the whole machine on which a record is placed to be played

turn to *v prep* to go to for help, comfort, etc.

turn-up *n* 1 a narrow band of cloth turned upwards at the bottom of a trouser leg 2 also **turn-up for the book**— *esp. spoken* an unexpected and surprising event

turn up *v adv* 1 to find 2 to be found 3 to shorten (a garment) by folding up the bottom 4 to arrive; make one's appearance 5 to increase the force, strength, loudness, etc., of (something) by using controls 6 to happen, esp. unexpectedly

turpentine also (*esp. spoken*) **turps**— *n* a thin oil used for removing unwanted paint from clothes, brushes, etc., and for thinning paint

turquoise¹ *n* (a shaped piece of) bluish-green precious mineral

turquoise² *adj, n* (of) the colour of turquoise

turret *n* 1 a small tower, usu. at an angle of a larger building ☞ CASTLE 2 (on a tank, plane, warship, etc.) a heavily-armoured dome that spins round to allow its guns to be aimed

turtle *n* **-tles** or **-tle** 1 a cold-blooded animal living esp. in water and having a hard shell into which the soft head, legs, and tail can be pulled 2 **turn turtle** (of a ship) to capsize

turtledove *n* a type of bird with a pleasing soft cry

turtleneck *n* POLO NECK

tusk *n* a long pointed tooth that comes out beyond the mouth in certain animals such as the elephant

tussle v -sled, -sling *esp. spoken* to fight roughly without weapons — **tussle** n

tussock n a small thick mass of grass

tut *interj* the sound of 't' made by sucking , used for expressing disapproval or annoyance

tutelage n 1 responsibility for someone, his education, property, actions, etc. 2 the state or period of being under someone's care and protection

tutor[1] n 1 a teacher who gives private instruction to a single pupil or a very small class 2 (in British universities and colleges) a teacher who directs the studies of students whom he also meets separately — ~**ial** *adj*

tutor[2] v to act as a tutor to

tutorial n (esp. in British universities and colleges) a period of instruction given by a tutor

tutti frutti n ice cream with pieces of mixed fruit and sometimes nuts

tutu n a short skirt made of many folds of stiffened material

tuxedo also (*esp. spoken*) **tux**— n -dos *US* DINNER JACKET

TV *abbrev. for:* television

twaddle n foolish talk or writing

twain n *old use & poetic* a pair; set of 2

twang n a sound such as that made by pulling then suddenly freeing a tight wire

tweak v to seize, pull, and twist (the ear, nose, etc.) — **tweak** n

twee *adj esp. spoken* unpleasantly dainty

tweed n a coarse woollen cloth woven from threads of several different colours

tweeds n (a suit of) tweed clothes

'tween *prep poetic* between

tweet v, n (to make) the short weak high noise of a small bird

tweeter n a loudspeaker that reproduces high sounds

tweezers n a v-shaped tool used for picking up, pulling out, and handling small objects

twelfth *adj, adv, n, pron* 12th

twelve *adj, n, pron* the number 12

twenty *adj, n, pron* -ties the number 20 — -tieth *adj, n, pron, adv*

twenty-one *adj, n, pron* the number 21

twerp, twirp n *sl* an annoying unpleasant person

twice *adj, adv* 2 times —see also THINK **twice**

twiddle v -dled, -dling to play with (something) purposelessly with the hands

twig[1] n a thin stem going off from a branch — **twiggy** *adj*

twig[2] v -gg- *sl* to understand

twilight n 1 the time when night is about to become day or (more usually) day night — compare DAWN, DUSK 2 a period or condition of decay, failure, etc., before or following one of growth, glory, success, etc.

twill n strong cloth woven to have parallel sloping lines across its surface

twin[1] n 1 either of 2 children born of the same mother at the same time 2 either of 2 people or things closely related or connected

twin[2] v -nn- to join (a town) closely with another town in another country

twin bed n either of a pair of single beds in a room for 2 people

twine[1] n strong cord or string made by twisting together 2 or more threads or strings

twine[2] v **twined, twining** 1 to twist 2 to make by twisting

twinge n a sudden sharp pain

twinkle[1] v -kled, -kling 1 to shine with an unsteady light that rapidly changes from bright to faint 2 (of the eyes) to be bright with cheerfulness, amusement, etc. 3 (of the eyelids, feet in dancing, etc.) to move rapidly up and down

twinkle[2] n 1 a repeated momentary bright shining of light 2 a brightness in the eyes as from cheerfulness, amusement, etc. 3 a twinkling

twinkling n a moment

twin set n a woman's jumper and cardigan of the same colour and style

twirl[1] v 1 to spin 2 to curl — ~**er** n

twirl[2] n a sudden quick spin — ~**y** *adj*

twirp n *sl* a twerp

twist[1] v 1 to wind strands together or round something else 2 to make (something) by doing this 3 to move in a winding course 4 to turn: *Twist the handle* 5 to hurt (a joint or limb) by pulling and turning sharply 6 to pull or break off by turning and bending forcefully 7 to change the true or intended meaning of (a statement, words, etc.)

twist[2] n 1 something made by twisting 2 or more lengths together 2 a particular tendency of mind or character 3 a bend 4 an unexpected change or development: *a twist of fate* — **twisty** *adj*

twister n 1 a dishonest person who cheats other people 2 a difficult job —see also TONGUE TWISTER

twit[1] v -tt- *esp. spoken* to make fun of (someone)

twit[2] n *sl* a fool

twitch[1] v to move suddenly and quickly, usu. without control — ~**er** n

twitch[2] n 1 a repeated short sudden movement of a muscle, done without control —compare TIC 2 a sudden quick pull

twitter[1] v 1 (of a bird) to make a number of short rapid sounds 2 (of a person) to talk rapidly, as from nervous excitement — ~**er** n

twitter[2] n 1 short high rapid sounds made by birds 2 a state of nervous excitement — ~**y** *adj*

twixt *prep old use & poetic* between

two *adj, n, pron* **twos** 1 the number 2 2 **put two and two together** to calculate the meaning of what one sees or hears

two-edged *adj* 1 having 2 cutting edges 2 having 2 possible meanings or results, one favourable and one unfavourable

twofaced *adj* deceitful

two-handed *adj* **1** used with both hands **2** (esp. of a tool) needing or worked by 2 people **3** having, or able to work effectively with, 2 hands

twopence also **tuppence** *n* **1** 2 pence (old or new) **2** also **twopenny piece**— a British coin worth 2 new pence

two-piece¹ *adj* consisting of 2 matching parts

two-piece² *n* a matching pair of outer garments to be worn together

twosome *n* esp. spoken a group of 2 people or things

two-step *n* (a piece of music for) a dance with long sliding steps

two-time *v* **-timed, -timing** esp. spoken to be unfaithful to (a girlfriend or boyfriend) by having a relationship with somebody else — **two-timer** *n*

two-tone *adj* coloured in 2 colours or in 2 varieties of one colour

two-way *adj* **1** moving or allowing movement in both directions **2** (of radio apparatus) for sending and receiving signals

tycoon *n* a businessman or industrialist with great wealth and power

tying *pres. part. of* TIE

tyke, tike *n* esp. N English a badly-behaved or worthless person

tympanum *n* **-na** or **-nums** medical an eardrum

type¹ *n* **1** a particular kind, class, or group **2** a person or thing considered an example of such a group or class **3** one or many small block(s) of metal or wood with the shape of a letter on the upper end, dipped in ink and pressed on paper to print the letter(s) **4** printed words

type² *v* **typed, typing** to write (something) with a typewriter

typecast *v* **-cast, -casting** to repeatedly give (an actor) the same kind of part

typeface *n* the size and style of letters used in printing

typescript *n* a typewritten copy of something

typesetter *n* a person who types for printing

typewriter *n* a machine that prints letters by means of keys which press onto paper through an inked ribbon

typewritten *adj* typed

typhoid also **typhoid fever**— *n* an infectious disease that attacks the bowel causing fever and often death

typhoon *n* a violent tropical storm in the western Pacific   USAGE A **whirlwind** is a small tropical circular wind. A **cyclone** may be very large and destructive. A **whirlwind** in the western Atlantic is called a **hurricane**, and the same thing in the China Sea is a **typhoon**. When funnel-shaped and moving over land, it is a **tornado**, over water it is a **waterspout**.

typhus *n* an infectious disease, carried by lice and fleas, that causes severe fever and nervous sickness

typical *adj* combining and showing the main signs of a particular kind, group, or class — compare FORMAL, CONVENTIONAL — ~**ly** *adv*

typify *v* **-fied, -fying** to serve as a typical example of

typing pool *n* a group of typists in a large office

typist *n* a secretary employed mainly for typing letters

typography *n* **1** the work of preparing and setting matter for printing **2** (the study of) the arrangement, style, and appearance of printed matter — **-pher** *n* — **-phic** *adj* — **-phically** *adv*

tyrannize, -nise *v* **-nized, -nizing** to use power over (a person, country, etc.) with unjust cruelty

tyrannosaurus also **tyrannosaurus rex**— *n* a type of large flesh-eating dinosaur

tyranny *n* **-nies** the use of cruel or unjust power to rule a person or country — **-nical** *adj* — **-nically** *adv*

tyrant *n* a person with complete power who rules cruelly and unjustly

tyre *n* **1** a thick rubber band, solid or filled with air, that fits round the outside edge of a wheel **2** a protective metal band fitted round a wooden wheel

U

U, u **U's, u's** or **Us, us** the 21st letter of the alphabet

U *n, adj* **1** (in Britain) (a film) that anyone of any age may see in a cinema **2** UPPER CLASS — opposite **non-U**

ubiquitous *adj* esp. written appearing, happening, done, etc., everywhere

U-boat *n* a German submarine

UCCA *n* the Universities Central Council on Admissions; a body that deals with applications to do degree courses at British universities

udder *n* a baglike organ of a cow, female goat, etc., from which milk is produced

UFO *n* UFO's unidentified flying object; the name for a flying object thought to come from another planet

ugh *interj* (a shout of dislike)

ugly *adj* **uglier, ugliest** **1** unpleasant to see **2** threatening; bad-tempered — **-liness** *n*

ugly duckling *n* a person less attractive, skilful, etc., than others in early life but developing beyond them later

UHF also (esp. written) **ultrahigh frequency**— *n* (the sending out of radio waves at) the rate of 300, 000, 000 to 3, 000, 000, 000 hertz —compare *VHF*

UK *abbrev. for:* United Kingdom

ukulele *n* a small guitar-like musical instrument with 4 strings

ulcer *n* a rough place on the skin inside or outside the body which may bleed or produce poisonous matter — ~**ous** *adj*

ulcerate *v* **-rated, -rating** to make or become covered by one or more ulcers — **-ation** *n*

ulna *n medical* the inner bone of the arm, in man, or front leg, in animals

ulterior *adj esp. spoken* hidden or kept secret, esp. because bad

ultimate *adj* **1** (the) last or farthest distant; being at the end or happening in the end **2** considered as an origin or base: *The ultimate responsibility lies with the president*

ultimately *adv* in the end; after all else or all others

ultimatum *n* **-tums** or **-ta** a statement of conditions to be met

ultrahigh frequency *n* **-cies** *esp. written* UHF

ultramarine *adj, n* (of) a very bright blue colour

ultrasonic *adj* (of sound waves) beyond the range of human hearing

ultraviolet *adj* (of light that is) beyond the purple end of the spectrum —compare INFRA-RED

umber *n, adj* (of) a brown earthlike colour

umbilical cord *n* **1** the tube of flesh which joins the young of a mammal to the mother before birth ⟆ EMBRYO **2** also **umbilical line**— a cable or supply line for an astronaut outside a spacecraft or a diver under water

umbra *n* **-ae** or **-as** an area of dull shadow or darkness

umbrage *n* offence (in the phrase **take umbrage** (at))

umbrella *n* **1** an arrangement of cloth over a frame, used for keeping rain off the head **2** a protecting power or influence

umlaut *n* **1** (a) change of quality in a vowel sound **2** a written sign representing such a change

umpire¹ *n* a judge in charge of a game such as cricket or of a swimming competition   USAGE This word is used in connection with **badminton, baseball, cricket, table tennis, tennis,** and **volleyball.** —compare REFEREE

umpire² *v* **umpired, umpiring** to act as umpire for (a game or competition)

umpteen *adj esp. spoken* a large number of — ~**th** *n, adj*

UN *abbrev. for:* United Nations

unabashed *adj* fearless, not discouraged or ashamed, etc. —see also ABASH

unabated *adj* (of a wind, a person's strength, etc.) without losing force —see also ABATE

unable *adj* not able —compare INABILITY

unabridged *adj* (esp. of something written, a speech, etc.) given in full form, not shortened —see also ABRIDGE

unaccompanied *adj* alone —see also ACCOMPANY

unaccountable *adj* surprising; not easily explained — **-bly** *adv*

unaccustomed *adj* unusual; not accustomed

unadulterated *adj* **1** not mixed with impure or less pure substances **2** complete; utter

unaffected *adj* **1** natural in behaviour or character **2** not affected — ~**ly** *adv*

unalloyed *adj esp. literature* not mixed, esp. with unpleasant feelings —compare ALLOY

unanimous *adj* **1** (of people) all agreeing **2** (of agreements, statements, etc.) supported by everyone in the same way — ~**ly** *adv* — **-mity** *n*

unannounced *adj* appearing unexpectedly

unarmed *adj* **1** not carrying a weapon **2** using no weapons

unassuming *adj* not showing a wish to be noticed; quiet in manner — ~**ly** *adv*

unattended *adj* alone, unguarded

unawares *adv* **1** unintentionally or without noticing **2** **take someone unawares** to surprise someone by one's presence

unbalance *v* **-anced, -ancing** to cause to have a lack of normal values (in the mind), esp. shown by sudden changes in behaviour

unbearable *adj* which cannot be borne — **-ly** *adv*

unbeknown also **unbeknownst**— *adj, adv* without the knowledge of the person stated

unbelievable *adj* very surprising — **-bly** *adv*

unbeliever *n* a person who has no faith (in something, esp. religion)

unbend *v* **unbent, unbending** to behave in an informal manner; relax

unbending *adj* unable to change opinions, decisions, etc., esp. refusing to do so

unblushing *adj* without showing any sense of shame — ~**ly** *adv*

unborn *adj* not yet born

unbosom *v* to tell the secret feelings, esp. troubles and worries, of (oneself)

unbounded *adj* limitless; far-reaching — compare BOUND

unbowed *adj esp. literature* not conquered or defeated —see also BOW

unbridled *adj* not controlled, and (esp.) too active or violent —compare BRIDLE

unbuckle *v* **-kled, -kling** to undo by loosening one or more buckles

unburden *v* **1** to take away a load or worry from **2** to free one's mind by talking about a secret trouble

uncalled-for *adj* not deserved or right

uncanny *adj* **-nier, -niest** mysterious; not natural or usual — **-nily** *adv*

unceremonious *adj* **1** informal **2** not done politely; rudely quick — ~**ly** *adv* — ~**ness** *n*

uncertain *adj* **1** not certain; doubtful **2** changeable: *uncertain weather* — ~**ly** *adv* — ~**ness** *n* — ~**ty** *n*

uncharitable adj not kind, helpful, fair in judging others, etc. — -**bly** adv

unchecked adj 1 not prevented from moving, developing, etc. —see also CHECK 2 not tested for quality, correctness, etc. —see also CHECK

unchristian adj not kind, helpful, generous, etc. —compare CHRISTIAN

uncle n 1 the brother of one's father or mother, the husband of one's aunt, or a man whose brother or sister has a child ☞ FAMILY 2 a man who is a friend of a small child or its parents

unclean adj 1 Bible (esp. in the Jewish religion) (of animals) that cannot be eaten 2 (of people) not considered pure, esp. in a religious way — ~**ness** n

Uncle Sam n the US

unclouded adj clear or untroubled

uncomfortable adj 1 not comfortable 2 shy — -**bly** adv

uncommitted adj not having given loyalty or promises to any one thing, group, political belief, etc.

uncommonly adv esp. written very; unusually: uncommonly kind

uncompromising adj firm in beliefs, ways, etc. — ~**ly** adv

unconcerned adj 1 not worried, anxious, or interested 2 not about: unconcerned with details — ~**ly** adv

unconditional adj not limited by any conditions — ~**ly** adv

unconscionable adj esp. written unreasonable in degree or amount — -**bly** adv

unconscious¹ adj 1 having lost consciousness 2 not intentional —see CONSCIOUS (USAGE) — ~**ly** adv — ~**ness** n

unconscious² n subconscious

unconsidered adj 1 not carefully thought out 2 disregarded; unnoticed

uncork v to open (esp. a bottle or barrel) by removing the cork

uncouple v -**led**, -**ling** to separate

uncouth adj not having good manners — ~**ly** adv — ~**ness** n

uncover v 1 to remove a covering from 2 to find out (something unknown or kept secret)

uncritical adj accepting, without critical thought

uncrowned adj 1 not crowned as king, but with the power of a ruler or leader 2 **the uncrowned king/queen (of)** the person generally considered to be the best in a particular activity

uncrushable adj (of materials and cloth) which does not form unwanted folds

unctuous adj 1 not sincere but showing interest, etc., for effect: unctuous praise 2 technical oily — ~**ly** adv — ~**ness** n

uncut adj 1 (of a film or story) not made shorter 2 (of a diamond or precious stone) not shaped and polished

undaunted adj bold —see also DAUNT

undecided adj in doubt, or with no definite result — ~**ly** adv — ~**ness** n

undeclared adj (of goods) which have not been made known when entering a country so that tax (CUSTOMS DUTY) could be paid on them

undeniable adj not disputed: His skill is undeniable, but he works too slowly — -**bly** adv

under¹ adv in or to a lower place —see also DOWN under, GO UNDER

under² prep 1 in or to a lower place than; directly below 2 less than: under $5 3 lower in rank than; serving or obeying: They work under a kind leader 4 beneath the surface, covering, or concealment of 5 during; in the state or act of: under discussion 6 in; during: under difficulties 7 technical (of land) bearing (a crop) 8 **under age** legally too young

underact v to act on stage with a small amount of force

underarm also **underhand**— adj, adv (esp. in sports) with the hand not moving above the shoulder

underbrush n thick undergrowth in a forest

undercarriage n the wheels and lower part of an aircraft, which support it on the ground ☞ AEROPLANE

undercharge v -**charged**, -**charging** to charge too little

underclothes also **underclothing**— n underwear

undercoat n a covering of paint as a base for a top covering

undercover adj acting or done secretly

undercurrent n 1 a hidden current of water beneath the surface 2 a hidden tendency in general feelings, opinions, etc.

undercut v -**cut**, -**cutting** to sell goods more cheaply or to work for smaller wages than (someone doing the same)

underdeveloped country also **underdeveloped nation**— n -**tries** DEVELOPING COUNTRY

underdog n a person, country, etc., which is treated badly by or gets the worst deal in any activity —compare top DOG

underdone adj not completely cooked

underestimate¹ v -**mated**, -**mating** 1 to have too low an opinion of the degree or number of 2 to give too low a value for (an amount) —see also ESTIMATE

underestimate² n an estimate which is too small

underfelt n soft rough material placed between a carpet and the floor

underfloor adj (esp. of heating systems) laid beneath the surface of the floor —see also CENTRAL HEATING

underfoot adv 1 under the foot 2 below one's feet 3 in the way: The children are always getting underfoot

undergarment n an article of underwear

undergo v -**went**, -**gone**, -**going** to experience (esp. suffering or difficulty)

undergraduate also (esp. spoken) **under-**

grad— n a university student who has not yet taken his first degree

underground¹ adv **1** under the earth's surface **2** secretly

underground² adj **1** below the surface of the earth **2** representing a political view which is not publicly accepted

underground³ also **tube—** n a railway system in which the trains run under the earth —compare METRO

undergrowth n bushes, tall plants, etc., smaller than the trees around them

underhand adj, adv underarm

underhanded also **underhand—** adj dishonest, esp. secretly — ~**ly** adv — ~**ness** n

underlay n -lays material placed between a carpet and the floor

underlie v -lay, -lain, -lying (of feelings and qualities) to be present as an explanation or real meaning of

underline also **underscore—** v -lined, -lining **1** to emphasise (one or more words) by drawing a line underneath **2** to give force to (an idea, feeling, etc., which has been expressed or shown)

underling n offensive a servant

undermanned adj having too few workers; understaffed —see also MAN

undermentioned adj which is mentioned later in the same piece of writing

undermine v -mined, -mining to wear away or destroy gradually

underneath prep, adv (so as to go) under (something)

undernourish v to give too little and/or bad quality food, causing lack of growth and development — ~**ment** n

underpants n short underclothes for men, covering the lower part of the body

underpass n a way under a road

underpin v -nn- **1** to use a solid piece of material to support (esp. a wall) **2** to give strength or support to (an argument)

underplay v -played, -playing to give less force in expressing than one could

underprivileged adj lacking in good chances for education, social life, etc.

underrate v -rated, -rating to give too low a value to

underscore v -scored, -scoring to underline

undersecretary n -ries a person who is in charge of the daily work of a government department (either a member of parliament of the government party (**parliamentary undersecretary**) or a civil servant (**permanent undersecretary**)) and helps and advises a minister

undersell v -sold, -selling to sell goods at a lower price than (a business competitor)

undersigned adj who has signed the paper

undersized also **undersize—** adj too small or smaller than usual

understaffed adj having too few workers, or fewer than usual

understand v -stood, -standing **1** to know or

get the meaning of (something) **2** to know or feel closely the nature of (a person, feelings, etc.) **3** often written or polite to have been informed **4** to take or judge (as the meaning): 'Children' is understood to mean those under 14 **5** to add (esp. a word) in the mind for completion: When I say 'Come and help', the object 'me' is understood — ~**able** adj — ~**ably** adv

understanding n **1** the act of understanding; power to judge sympathetically **2** power of the brain; intelligence **3** a private agreement

understate v -stated, -stating to cause to seem of less importance or strength than is so

understatement n (a) statement which is not strong enough to express facts or feelings with full force (such as not bad meaning rather good)

understudy¹ v -ied, -ying to act as an understudy to (an actor or actress) in a play

understudy² n -ies an actor or actress learning an important part in a play so as to be able if necessary to take the place of the actor who plays that part

undertake v -took, -taken, -taking **1** to take up (a position); start on (work) **2** to promise or agree

undertaker n a person whose job it is to arrange funerals

undertaking n **1** a task, or piece of work needing effort **2** a promise

undertone n **1** a low voice **2** a hidden feeling or meaning —compare OVERTONES

undertow n the current beneath the surface which pulls back towards the sea as a wave breaks on the shore

underwater adj, adv (used, done, etc.) below the surface of a stretch of water

underwear also **underclothes, underclothing—** n the clothes worn next to the body under other clothes —see also UNDIES

underweight adj weighing too little or less than is usual

underwent past tense of UNDERGO

underworld n **1** (in ancient Greek stories) the place where the spirits of the dead live **2** the criminal world

underwrite v -wrote, -written, -writing **1** to agree to buy from a company (all new shares not bought by the public) **2** to take responsibility for fulfilling (an insurance agreement)

underwriter n **1** a person who buys new shares from a company when not sold to the public **2** an insurance agent, esp. one who underwrites agreements

undesirable¹ adj unpleasant; not wanted — -**bility** n — -**bly** adv

undesirable² n a person not thought good or useful

undeveloped adj (usu. of a place) in its natural state, esp. not having industry, modern farming, etc.

undies n esp. spoken (esp. women's) underwear

undischarged adj **1** (esp. of goods on a ship)

not unloaded 2 (of an account or debt) not paid 3 (of a person who owes money) still in debt by law: *an undischarged bankrupt*

undistinguished *adj* not marked by remarkable ability, character, etc.

undivided *adj* complete

undo *v* undid, undone, undoing 1 to unfasten or untie —see also UNDONE, DO UP 2 to remove the effects of: *In 10 minutes he undid my whole day's work*

undoing *n* the cause of ruin, shame, failure, etc.

undomesticated *adj* 1 (of an animal) not serving man; not tame 2 (of a person) not interested in cooking, housework, etc.

undone *adj* 1 unfastened or loose 2 not done

undoubted *adj* known for certain to be so — ~ly *adv*: *that is undoubtedly true*

undreamed-of also **undreamt-of**— *adj* which is beyond, and esp. better or more than, what might be imagined

undress[1] *v* 1 to take one's clothes off 2 to take the clothes off (someone)

undress[2] *n* lack of clothes

undressed *adj* 1 not wearing clothes, esp. ordinary day clothes 2 (of animal skins) not yet fully treated or preserved as leather 3 (of wounds) not treated and covered

undue *adj* too much: *undue haste*

undulate *v* -lated, -lating to move or lie like waves

undulation *n* 1 a rising and falling movement or shape, like waves 2 a smooth curve among a number of others

unduly *adv* too much; very

undying *adj* which will never end

unearth *v* 1 to dig up 2 to discover

unearthly *adj* not natural; ghostly — -liness *n*

uneasy *adj* -ier, -iest 1 not comfortable or at rest 2 worried; anxious — -ily *adv* — -iness *n*

uneconomic also **uneconomical**— *adj* 1 resulting in loss of money or not profitable 2 wasteful — ~ally *adv*

uneducated *adj* showing a lack of good education; not socially well trained

unemployed *adj* not having a job

unemployment *n* the condition of lacking a job or jobs

unenlightened *adj* not having been informed; lacking knowledge; ignorant

unenviable *adj* unpleasant; not to be wished for

unequal *adj* 1 not of equal size, value, etc. 2 not having enough strength, ability, etc. 3 uneven — ~ly *adv* — ~ness *n*

unequalled *adj* too good, clever, etc., for anything to be found of equal quality —see also EQUAL

unequivocal *adj* plain in meaning —opposite EQUIVOCAL — ~ly *adv*

unerring *adj* without making a mistake — ~ly *adv*

UNESCO *n* United Nations Educational, Scientific, and Cultural Organization

uneven *adj* 1 not smooth or even; irregular 2 (of numbers) odd — ~ly *adv* — ~ness *n*

uneventful *adj* dull or calm — ~ly *adv* — ~ness *n*

unexceptionable *adj* quite satisfactory — -bly *adv*

unfailing *adj* (esp. of something good) never ceasing — ~ly *adv*

unfaithful *adj* 1 disloyal to one's marriage partner by having a sexual relationship with another person 2 not faithful or loyal —compare FAITHFUL — ~ly *adv* — ~ness *n*

unfaltering *adj* unhesitating —see also FALTER — ~ly *adv*

unfathomable *adj* which cannot be understood — -bly *adv*

unfathomed *adj* the nature of which or reason for which has not been understood

unfavourable *adj* not favourable — -bly *adv*

unfeeling *adj* cruel; hard; not sympathetic towards others — ~ly *adv*

unfettered *adj* free from responsibility

unflagging *adj* without tiring — ~ly *adv*

unflappable *adj* always calm mannered — -bly *adv*

unflinching *adj* fearless — ~ly *adv*

unfold *v* 1 to open from a folded position 2 to make or become clear, more fully known, etc. 3 (of a bud) to open into a flower

unforeseen *adj* unexpected

unforgettable *adj* too good or bad, to be forgotten — -bly *adv*

unfortunate *adj* 1 unlucky 2 deserving of pity 3 unsuitable: *an unfortunate remark* 4 unsuccessful: *an unfortunate business venture*

unfortunately *adv* 1 by bad luck 2 it is/was a bad thing that . . .: *Unfortunately, we crashed*

unfounded *adj* not supported by facts

unfrequented *adj* not often visited by many people —see also FREQUENT

ungainly *adj* -lier, -liest clumsy — -liness *n*

ungenerous *adj* 1 not generous 2 unfair — ~ly *adv*

ungodly *adj* -lier, -liest 1 showing lack of respect for God and religion; wicked 2 *esp. spoken* unpleasant: *What an ungodly noise!*

ungovernable *adj* uncontrollable —see also GOVERN

ungracious *adj* not polite — ~ly *adv*

ungrateful *adj* not grateful — ~ly *adv* — ~ness *n*

unguarded *adj* careless over what is made known

unguent *n* an ointment —see also UNCTUOUS

unhappy *adj* -pier, -piest 1 not happy 2 unfortunate — -piness *n* — -pily *adv*

unhealthy *adj* -ier, -iest **1** not generally in good health; showing illness **2** not good for the mind or body **3** unnatural: *an unhealthy interest in cruelty* — **unhealthily** *adv* — **unhealthiness** *n*

unheard *adj* **1** not heard, esp. in court —see also HEAR **2** not listened to

unheard-of *adj* very strange and unusual

unhinge *v* **unhinged, unhinging** to unbalance (someone's mind)

unholy *adj* -lier, -liest **1** wicked **2** *esp. spoken* ungodly: *an unholy noise* — **-liness** *n*

unhoped-for *adj* too good to be expected

unhorse *v* **unhorsed, unhorsing** to cause to fall from a horse

UNICEF *n* United Nations International Children's Emergency Fund

unicorn *n* an imaginary horselike animal with one horn

unidentified *adj* of which the name, nature, or origin has not been found or given —see also UFO

uniform[1] *adj* the same; even; regular — ~ity *n* — ~ly *adv*

uniform[2] *n* clothing which all members of a group wear — ~ed *adj* : *uniformed soldiers*

unify *v* -fied, -fying **1** to make all the same **2** to make into one — -fication *n* : *the unification of Italy*

unilateral *adj* done by or having an effect on only one of the groups in an agreement — ~ly *adv*

unimpeachable *adj* blameless; that cannot be doubted —compare IMPEACH — -bly *adv*

uninformed *adj* **1** without enough knowledge **2** ignorant

uninhabitable *adj* unfit to be lived in — compare INHABIT, HABITABLE

uninhibited *adj* free in action and behaviour; not worrying about what other people think — ~ly *adv*

uninterested *adj* not interested —see DISINTERESTED

union *n* **1** the act of joining or state of being joined into one **2** a group of countries or states joined together **3** a state of agreement and unity, esp. in marriage **4** a club, society, or trade union **5** *technical* a connecting part for pipes **6** *technical* (in mathematics) the set of members that occur in either or both of two sets —compare INTERSECTION

unionism *n* **1** a former political movement giving support for the continued union of Great Britain and Ireland **2** TRADE UNIONISM — -ist *n*, *adj*

Union Jack also (*technical*) **Union Flag**— *n* the national flag of the United Kingdom

unique *adj* **1** being the only one of its type **2** *often considered bad usage* unusual: *a rather unique position* — ~ly *adv* — ~ness *n*

unisex *adj* which can be used by both male and female

unison *n* **1** the singing of the same note by everybody at the same time —compare HARMONY **2** perfect agreement

unit *n* **1** one complete thing **2** a group of things or people forming a complete whole but usu. part of a larger group: *an army unit* **3 a** the number 1 **b** any whole number less than 10 **4** an amount or quantity taken as a standard of measurement: *The pound is the standard unit of money in Britain* **5** an article, esp. of furniture, which can be fitted with others of the same type: *a kitchen unit*

unite *v* **united, uniting** **1** to join together into one **2** to act together for a purpose **3** to join in marriage

united *adj* **1** in agreement **2** with everyone concerned having the same aim: *a united effort* — ~ly *adv*

unit trust *n* a company formed to control investments of many different types

unity *n* -ties ⟨ **1** the state of being united: *church unity* **2** agreement of aims and interests **3** *technical* the number one: *greater than unity*

universal *adj* **1** concerning all members of a group **2** for all people or every purpose; widespread **3** in all parts of the world: *universal travel* — ~ity *n* — ~ly *adv*

universal joint *n* a joint that can turn in all directions while transmitting a rotational motion

universe *n* all space and the matter which exists in it

university *n* -ties a place of education at the highest level, or the members of this place

unkempt *adj* untidy

unkind *adj* not kind; cruel or thoughtless — ~ly *adv*

unknowing *adj* not knowing of something — ~ly *adv* : *unknowingly deceived*

unknown *n, adj* (something or someone) whose name, value, or origin is not known

unlawful *adj* against the law — ~ly *adv*

unleash *v* **1** to remove (a dog) from a lead **2** to release (feelings, forces, etc.)

unleavened *adj* (of bread) made without yeast, and therefore flat and unrisen —see also LEAVEN

unless *conj* if ... not; except in the case that: *I will leave at 9, unless you want to go earlier*

unlike *adj, prep* not like; different (from)

unlikely *adj* -lier, -liest **1** not expected; improbable **2** not likely to happen or be true — -liness, -lihood *n*

unload *v* **1** to remove (a load) from; get rid of (a load) **2** to get rid of (something unwanted) **3** to remove the charge from (a gun) or film from (a camera) — ~er *n*

unlock *v* to unfasten the lock of

unloosen *v* to loosen

unmannerly *adj* impolite

unmask *v* **1** to remove a mask from **2** to show the hidden truth about

unmatched *adj* with no equal —compare MATCH, MATCHLESS

unmeasured adj beyond measure —compare MEASURELESS

unmentionable adj not fit to be spoken of

unmistakable adj clearly recognizable — -bly adv

unmitigated adj not lessened or excused in any way —compare MITIGATE — ~ly adv

unmoved adj 1 not having feelings of pity 2 not worried

unnatural adj not natural; abnormal —see NATURAL (USAGE) — ~ly adv

unnecessary adj not necessary or wanted — -rily adv : unnecessarily rude

unnerve v unnerved, unnerving to take away the courage of

unnumbered adj 1 too many to be counted 2 not having a number marked

unobtrusive adj not too easily seen or noticed; discreet — ~ly adv — ~ness n

unofficial adj 1 not official; informal 2 not yet said to be true by those in charge — ~ly adv

unorthodox adj not according to usual beliefs, methods, etc.

unpack v to remove (possessions) from (a container)

unparalleled adj too great to be equalled

unparliamentary adj (of something said or done in Parliament) not suitable; showing bad behaviour

unpick v to take out (stitches)

unplaced adj not one of the first usu. 3 in a race or competition

unpleasant adj causing dislike; not enjoyable; displeasing or unkind — ~ly adv — ~ness n

unpractised adj not skilful because of lack of experience

unprecedented adj never having happened before —see also PRECEDENT — ~ly adv

unprejudiced adj fair in judgement; not prejudiced

unpretentious adj not showing signs of wealth, size, importance, etc., or not wishing to do so — ~ly adv — ~ness n

unprincipled adj without regard to moral values, honourable behaviour, etc. —see also PRINCIPLE

unprintable adj (of words) unacceptable for printing

unprofessional adj (of behaviour) unsuitable in a certain profession — ~ly adv

unprompted adj produced without being asked for, suggested, etc.

unprovoked adj (esp. of a bad action) not caused or forced

unqualified adj 1 not limited: unqualified agreement 2 not having suitable knowledge or qualifications

unquestionable adj which cannot be doubted — -bly adv

unquestioning adj without doubt or worry: unquestioning trust

unquote adv (a word used in speech for showing that one has come to the end of a quotation)

unravel v -ll- 1 also ravel— to make or become separated or unwoven 2 to make clear (a mystery)

unreadable adj 1 too dull to be read 2 illegible — -bly adv

unreal adj (of an experience) unlike reality

unreasonable adj 1 unfair in demands; not sensible 2 (of prices, costs, etc.) too great — -bly adv — ~ness n

unreasoning adj thoughtless

unrelenting adj continuous; without decreasing in power —compare RELENT, RELENTLESS — ~ly adv

unrelieved adj not varied in any way; continuous —see also RELIEVE — ~ly adv

unremitting adj never stopping —see also REMIT — ~ly adv

unrequited adj not given in return —see also REQUITE

unreserved adj without limits or reservations; frank — ~ly adv

unrest n 1 lack of calmness 2 dissatisfaction, esp. socially

unrestrained adj not held back or reduced

unrip v -pp- to tear open

unrivalled adj unequalled; very good —see also RIVAL

unroll v to open from a rolled position

unruffled adj calm; not worried —see also RUFFLE

unruly adj -lier, -liest 1 wild in behaviour 2 not easily kept in place — -liness n

unsaid adj (thought of but) not spoken about

unsavoury adj morally unpleasant or unacceptable

unscathed adj not harmed

unschooled adj untrained; not experienced

unscramble v -bled, -bling to put (a message in code) back into order so as to be understood —see also SCRAMBLE

unscrew v 1 to remove screws from 2 to undo by twisting

unscripted adj (of a broadcast, talk, or conversation) not written or planned before; spoken naturally —opposite scripted

unscrupulous adj not careful in details, esp. not caring about honesty and fairness —opposite scrupulous — ~ly adv — ~ness n

unseat v also unsaddle— (of a horse) to throw off (a rider)

unseeing adj not noticing; as if blind — ~ly adv

unseemly adj -lier, -liest not suitable in behaviour —opposite seemly — -liness n

unseen n a piece of writing to be translated into one's own language without having been seen before

unserviceable adj not usable because broken, worn out, etc.

unsettle v -tled, -tling 1 to make less calm,

more dissatisfied, etc. **2** to make (esp. the stomach) ill

unsettled *adj* (of weather) changeable

unsex *v literature* to take away the typical qualities of one's sex

unsexed *adj* (of very young chickens) not separated by sex

unshakeable, -kable *adj* firm (in belief)

unshod *adj* **1** wearing no shoes **2** (of a horse) not having had shoes fitted

unsightly *adj* **-lier, -liest** not pleasant to look at — **-liness** *n*

unskilled *adj* **1** not trained for a particular type of job **2** not needing special skill

unsociable *adj* not friendly; not fond of being with people —see SOCIABLE (USAGE)

unsocial *adj* not suitable for combining with family and social life

unsophisticated *adj* simple in ways, tastes, etc.

unsound *adj* **1** not strong **2** (of ideas) not having a firm base in fact **3 of unsound mind** *law* mad, and therefore not responsible for one's actions

unsparing *adj* **1** giving no mercy —see also SPARE **2** holding nothing back, esp. money or help — ~**ly** *adv*

unspeakable *adj* terrible — **-bly** *adv*

unstable *adj* (in psychology) not stable in mind; not having good control over emotions and behaviour

unstop *v* **-pp-** **1** to open (something closed by a stopper) **2** to remove something that stops a flow in

unstrung *adj* having lost control over the nerves and feelings

unstuck *adj* **1** not fastened or stuck on —see also STICK **2 come unstuck** to go wrong; be unsuccessful

unstudied *adj* natural —compare STUDIED

unsung *adj* not praised formally; undeservedly not famous

unswerving *adj* firm in purpose, esp. loyal —see also SWERVE

untangle *v* **-gled, -gling** to remove tangles from

untapped *adj* not used or drawn from —see also TAP

untenable *adj* which cannot be defended

unthinkable *adj* not acceptable; which one cannot believe

unthinking *adj* careless; thoughtless — ~**ly** *adv*

unthought-of *adj* quite unexpected; not imagined

untie *v* **untied, untying** to undo

until also **till**— *prep, conj* up to (the time that)

untimely *adj* **1** not suitable for the time or occasion **2** happening too soon — **-liness** *n*

untiring *adj* not showing or experiencing tiredness

unto *prep old use* to: *She spoke unto him*

untold *adj* **1** not told or expressed **2** too great to be counted: *untold wealth*

untouchable *adj, n* (a person) of the lowest social group, esp. in the Hindu caste system

untoward *adj* unfortunate; not wanted — ~**ly** *adv* — ~**ness** *n*

untruth *n* a lie

untruthful *adj* **1** lying, esp. habitually **2** not true — ~**ly** *adv*

unused *adj* **1** not having been used **2** not accustomed

unusual *adj* **1** rare **2** interesting because different from others — ~**ly** *adv*

unutterable *adj* **1** terrible **2** complete: *an unutterable fool* — **-bly** *adv*

unvarnished *adj* plain: *the unvarnished truth*

unveil *v* **1** to take off one's veil **2** to remove a covering from

unversed *adj* not experienced or informed

unwarranted *adj* done without good reason

unwell *adj* ill, esp. for a short time

unwieldy *adj* awkward to move or use — **-diness** *n*

unwind *v* **unwound, unwinding** **1** to undo (something that has been wound round) **2** to become clear, esp. if twisting or detailed: *The story unwound* **3** to relax

unwitting *adj* not knowing or intended — ~**ly** *adv*

unzip *v* **-pp-** to open by undoing a zip

up[1] *adv* **1** towards or into a higher position; from below to a higher place **2** above; at or in a higher position **3** to, into, or in a sitting or standing position **4** from or off a surface: *The dog jumped up* **5** to the surface from below it: *to come up for air* **6** so as to be completely finished: *The money's all used up* **7** so as to be all in small pieces: *to tear up the newspaper* **8** out of the stomach through the mouth, when vomiting **9** in or towards (the north) **10** to or in a city or place of importance: *up to London* **11** to or towards a point away from the speaker: *up to the shop* **12** towards and as far as the speaker: *up to me* **13** firmly; tightly; so as to be closed, covered, or joined: *to tie up* **14** (showing or making an increase or higher level of price, quantity, or quality): *The price is going up* **15** to a state of greater activity, force, strength, power, etc.: *Please turn the radio up* **16** so as to be together: *Add up the figures* **17** to or in a higher or better condition: *come up in the world* **18** (so as to be) in a raised position or on top: *He turned up his collar* **19 Up (with)** We want or approve of: *Up the workers!* —see also UP TO

up[2] *adj* **1** in a raised position; so as to be in place or be seen: *high up in the mountains* **2** out of bed: *to get up* **3** directed or going up: *the up train* **4** at a higher level: *The temperature is up today* **5** finished; ended: *Time's up!* **6** (of a road) being repaired; with a broken surface **7** charged with an offence: *had up for stealing* **8 be up** to be happening; be the matter **9 be well up in/on** to know a lot about **10 not up** (in tennis and like games) (of a ball) having bounced more than once before being hit **11 up for** intended or being considered for: *The house is up for sale*

up³ *v* **-pp-** *esp. spoken* **1** to raise; increase: *to up the price of petrol* **2** to get or jump up (and): *He upped and left*

up⁴ *prep* **1** to or in a higher or rising position; along; to the far end of: *He climbed up the hill* **2** against the direction of the current: *to go up river* **3** **up and down** away and back along: *His eyes moved up and down the rows* **4** **up yours** *vulgar sl* (used for expressing great dislike for or annoyance at a person)

up-and-coming *adj* showing signs of being about to succeed

up-and-up *n* **on the up-and-up** *esp. spoken* improving; succeeding

upbeat *n* the beat in music which does not have the force —compare DOWNBEAT

upbraid *v* to scold

upbringing *n* training and caring for a child

upcoming *adj* about to happen

up-country *adj, adv* in or from the inner parts of the country

update *v* **updated, updating** to make more modern or up to date

upend *v* **1** to cause to stand on end **2** to knock down: *He upended his opponent*

upgrade *v* **upgraded, upgrading** to give a higher position to

upheaval *n* a great change and movement

uphill *adj* **1** on an upward slope **2** difficult (esp. in the phrase **an uphill task**) — **uphill** *adv*

uphold *v* **upheld, upholding** **1** to support: *to uphold a right* **2** to declare to be right: *The judge upheld the court's decision* — **~er** *n*

upholster *v* to fit (furniture for sitting on) with soft coverings over padding — **~er** *n*

upholstery *n* the trade of or materials used by an upholsterer

upkeep *n* the act or cost of keeping something repaired and in order

uplift *v* **1** to raise high; support upward **2** to encourage cheerful or holy feelings in — **uplift** *n*

upon *prep* *esp. written* on

upper¹ *adj* **1** in a higher position **2** farther from the sea: *the upper reaches of the Nile* **3** of greater importance or higher rank

upper² *n* the top part of a shoe or boot above the heel and sole

upper case *n* (writing in) capital letters — compare LOWER CASE

upper class *adj, n* (of) a social class whose members belong to a few old families

upper crust *adj, n* *esp. spoken & often humour* (of or belonging to) the higher classes of society

uppercut *n* (in boxing) a blow with the hand moving upwards to the chin

upper hand *n* control (esp. in the phrases **have/get the upper hand**)

Upper House also **Upper Chamber**— *n* one of the 2 branches of a parliament: *The House of Lords is the British Upper House*

uppermost also **upmost**— *adv, adj* in the highest or strongest position

uppish *adj* **1** *esp. spoken* too proud **2** (in cricket) (of a stroke) hit in the air, and in danger of being caught — **~ly** *adv* — **~ness** *n*

upright¹ *adj* **1** standing straight up; vertical **2** honest, fair, responsible, etc. — **~ly** *adv* — **~ness** *n*

upright² *adv* straight up; not bent

upright³ *n* a supporting beam which stands straight up

upright piano *n* **-os** a piano with strings that are set vertically —compare GRAND PIANO

uprising *n* a rising; insurrection

uproar *n* confused noisy activity

uproarious *adj* **1** noisy **2** causing loud laughter — **~ly** *adv*

uproot *v* **1** also **root up**— to tear up by the roots **2** to remove from one's home, settled habits, etc.

upset *v* **upset, upsetting** **1 a** to turn over, causing confusion **b** to overflow or cause to overflow or scatter by a knock **2** to cause to worry, not be calm, etc. **3** to make ill, usu. in the stomach —compare UNSETTLE — **upset** *n, adj*

upshot *n* the outcome

upside down *adv* **1** in a position with the top turned to the bottom **2** in disorder

upstage¹ *adv* towards the back of the stage in the theatre

upstage² *v* **upstaged, upstaging** to take attention away from (someone else) for oneself

upstairs *adv, adj* at, on, or to the upper floor or floors of a building — **upstairs** *n*

upstanding *adj* **1** tall and strong **2** honest and responsible —compare UPRIGHT

upstart *n* *offensive* a person who has risen suddenly or unexpectedly to a high position

upstream *adv, adj* (moving) against the current

upsurge *n* an act of rising suddenly to the surface, esp. of the mind

upswing *n* a change to a higher stronger degree or greater number

uptake *n* ability to understand esp. something new (in the phrases **quick/slow on the uptake**)

uptight *adj* *esp. spoken* very nervous, anxious, etc.

up to *prep* **1** as far as; to and including **a** a number: *up to 10 men* **b** a higher degree or position in a set: *Everyone works, from the lift boy up to the President* **2** also **up till**— until **3** equal to; good, well, clever enough for: *Michael's not really up to that job* **4** the duty or responsibility of: *It's up to you* **5** **be/get up to** to do (something bad): *The children are always getting up to mischief*

up to date *adj* **1** modern **2** having the latest information

upturn *n* a favourable change

upturned adj   **1** turning upwards at the end   **2** having been turned over

upward also **upwards**— adj increasing, getting higher, etc.; going up: an upward movement

upwards also **upward**— adv towards a higher level, position, or price: A tree grows upwards

upwards of— prep upward or more than, esp. in number or price: upwards of £50 | upwards of 50 years old

uranium n a heavy white metallic radioactive element used in the production of atomic power

Uranus n the planet 7th in order from the sun

urban adj of a town or city —compare RURAL, RUSTIC

urbane adj having very good social manners — ~ly adv — -banity n

urchin n a small boy, esp. a dirty untidy one —see also SEA URCHIN

urge¹ v   **urged, urging**   **1** to drive or force (forward)   **2** to beg or persuade with force   **3** to tell of with force: She urged its importance

urge² n a strong wish or need

urgent adj   **1** very important, esp. which must be dealt with quickly   **2** showing that something must be done quickly: He was urgent in his demands — ~ly adv — -gency n

urinal n a building or vessel for use by men for passing urine

urinary adj concerning the organs and passages of the body used for collecting and passing out urine

urinate v -nated, -nating to pass urine from the body — -nation n

urine n waste liquid passed out of the body

urn n   **1** any large metal container in which large quantities of tea or coffee may be heated and kept   **2** a large vase in which the ashes of a burnt dead body are kept

us pron   **1** (object form of WE): They helped us. | The waiter brought us the drinks we had ordered   **2** bad usage me: ' Lend us your pen a minute —see ME, HIM (USAGE)

US also **USA**— abbrev. for: the United States (of America)

usage n   **1** the way of using something; the type or degree of use   **2** one or more standards practised by users, esp. in using a language: modern English usage

use¹ n   **1** the act of using or state of being used   **2** the ability or right to use something   **3** the purpose or reason for using something: What use does this tool have?   **4** the usefulness or advantage given by something: Is this book any use?   **5** custom; habit; practice   **6 make use of** to use well; take advantage of   **7 of use** useful   **8 out of use** no longer used

use² v   **used, using**   **1** to employ; put to use   **2** esp. written to treat in the stated manner: to use someone ill (=badly)   **3** to finish: All the paper has been used —see also USE UP   **4** to treat (someone) with consideration only for one's own advantage — **user** n — **usable** adj

use³ v used, negative short form **usedn't**

to have done regularly or habitually: We used to go there every year. | Usen't you to keep a dog? | This used to be a shabby house   USAGE Some people think that He used not to is better than He didn't used/use to, but both are possible.

used adj   **1** (usu. of goods) which has already had an owner; second-hand   **2** accustomed: to get used to Indian food

useful adj   **1** effective in use   **2** helpful — ~ly adv   — ~ness n

useless adj   **1** not of any use   **2** not giving hope of success   **3** esp. spoken not able to do anything properly — ~ly adv   — ~ness n

use up v adv to finish completely

usher¹ n   **1** a man who shows people to their seats on an important occasion   **2** a person who keeps order in a law court

usher² v esp. written to bring; come, bringing or causing to enter

usherette n a woman who shows people to their seats, sells icecream, etc., in a cinema

USSR abbrev. for: Union of Soviet Socialist Republics (Soviet Union)

usual adj   **1** customary   **2 as usual** as is common — ~ly adv

usurer n a person who lends money at an unfairly high rate of interest

usurp v to seize (power or position) for oneself unlawfully — ~ation n — ~er n

usury n the practice of lending money at an unfairly high rate of interest — -rious adj — -riously adv — -riousness n

utensil n a tool

uterus n -ri or -ruses technical the womb ☞ EMBRYO, REPRODUCTION — -rine adj

utilitarian adj   **1** concerned with practical use   **2** believing in utilitarianism —compare MATERIAL-ISTIC

utilitarianism n a belief that an act is better according to the number of people it helps

utility n -ties   **1** usefulness   **2** any useful service for the public

utilize, -ise v -ized, -izing to make use of; use — -izable adj   — -ization n

utmost¹ adj of the greatest degree

utmost² n the most that can be done (esp. in the phrase **to do one's utmost**)

utopia n a perfect society

utopian adj concerning ideas of perfection, esp. socially, which are not practical —compare IDEAL-ISTIC

utter¹ adj complete — ~ly adv

utter² v to pronounce; express — ~ance n

U-turn n a turning movement in a car on a road taking one back in the direction one came from

V

V, v V's, v's *or* Vs, vs   **1** the 22nd letter of the English alphabet   **2** the Roman numeral for 5

v *abbrev. for:*   **1** velocity   **2** verb   **3** very   **4** volume

V *abbrev for:* volt

v. *abbrev for:* (esp. in sport) versus (against): *Arsenal v. Everton*

vac *n esp. spoken* a university vacation

vacancy *n* **-cies**   **1** the state of being vacant   **2** an unfilled place or job   **3** emptiness of mind

vacant *adj*   **1** empty; not filled with anything   **2** (of a house, room, or seat) not being used or lived in   **3** (of a job) not at present filled   **4** (of the mind) not thinking; foolishly empty; senseless — ~ly *adv*

vacate *v* **vacated, vacating** to cease to occupy or live in

vacation¹ *n*   **1 a** one of the periods of holiday when universities, law courts, etc., are closed   **b** *US* a holiday   **2** an act or the action of vacating —see HOLIDAY (USAGE)

vaccinate *v* **-ated, -ating** to introduce vaccine into the body of (someone) —compare INOCULATE, INJECT — **-ation** *n*

vaccine *n* a substance used for protecting people against diseases, esp. smallpox

vacillate *v* **-lated, -lating** to be continually changing one's mind — **-lation** *n*

vacuole *n* a fluid-containing bag inside a plant or animal cell

vacuous *adj esp. written* foolish, esp. in showing no ideas or feeling — ~ly *adv* — ~ness *n*

vacuum¹ *n* **-uums** *or (technical)* **-ua**   **1** a space that is completely, or almost completely, empty of all gas   **2** emptiness: *Her death left a vacuum in his life*

vacuum² *v esp. spoken* to clean (a room, floor, etc.) using a vacuum cleaner

vacuum cleaner *also (esp. spoken, trademark)* **hoover**— *n* an apparatus which cleans floors and floor coverings by sucking up the dirt

vacuum-packed *adj* (esp. of food offered for sale in shops) packed in a wrapping from which most of the air has been removed

vacuum pump *n* a pump for removing air or gas from an enclosed space

vagabond *n* a person who wanders from place to place, esp. one thought to be lazy or worthless —compare VAGRANT

vagina *n* the passage which leads from the outer sex organs of female mammals to the womb ☞ EMBRYO, REPRODUCTION — ~l *adj*

vagrancy *n* the state or offence of being a vagrant

vagrant *n*   **1** a person who lives a wandering life with no steady home or work, esp. one who is poor and begs —compare VAGABOND   **2** *law* any-

one who is found by the police wandering about without any lawful means of support

vague *adj* not clear — ~ly *adv* — ~ness *n*

vain *adj*   **1** too admiring of one's appearance, abilities, etc.   **2** without result; useless: *vain attempt*   **3 in vain** uselessly; without a successful result — ~ly *adv*

valance *n* a narrow length of cloth hanging as a border from the edge of a shelf, or from the frame of a bed to the floor

vale *n* (as part of a place name or in poetry) a broad low valley

valediction *n esp. written* a speech or remark used when saying goodbye — **-tory** *n*

valency valence— *n* **-cies** the measure of the power of atoms to combine together to form compounds ☞ ATOM

valentine *n*   **1** a lover chosen on **Saint Valentine's Day** (February 14th)   **2** a greeting card sent (often unsigned) to arrive on February 14th, declaring one's love

valerian *n* any of several types of plant with strong-smelling red or white flowers

valet *n*   **1** a gentleman's personal male servant   **2** a male hotel worker who cleans and presses the clothes of people staying there

valiant *also* **valorous**— *adj esp. written or literature* (of a person or act) very brave — ~ly *adv*

valid *adj*   **1** (of a reason, argument, etc.) having a strong firm base; that can be defended   **2** *law* written or done in a proper manner so that a court of law would agree with it   **3** having value; that can be used lawfully for a stated period or in certain conditions — ~ity *n: the validity of a statement* — ~ly *adv*

valley *n* **-leys**   **1** the land lying between 2 lines of hills or mountains ☞ GEOGRAPHY   **2** the land through which a stated river or great river system flows: *the Thames Valley* USAGE A deep narrow mountain **valley**, with steep sides, is a **ravine** or **gorge**. If it is very small and steep it is a **gully**; if it is very large it is a **canyon**. **Cwm** is a Welsh word for **valley**.

valour *n esp. written or literature* great bravery

valse *n French* a type of waltz

valuable¹ *adj*   **1** worth a lot of money   **2** having great usefulness or value —see WORTHLESS (USAGE)

valuable² *n* something (esp. something small) that is worth a lot of money

value¹ *n*   **1** the (degree of) usefulness or desirability of something, esp. in comparison with other things   **2** the worth of something in money or as compared with other goods for which it might be changed   **3** a standard or idea which most people have about the worth of good qualities: *One way of judging a society is to consider its values*   **4** (in the science of numbers) the quantity expressed by a letter of the alphabet or other sign: *Let ' x ' have the value 25* —see WORTHLESS (USAGE) — ~less *adj*

value² v -ued, -uing 1 to calculate the value, price, or worth of (something) 2 to consider (someone or something) to be of great worth — ~ation n

value-added tax also **VAT**— n (in Britain and some other European countries) a tax paid to the government by those who make, sell, and buy an article or service

valuer n a person whose work is to decide how much money things are worth —compare ESTIMATOR

valve n 1 a doorlike part of a pipe (or of a pipelike part inside the body), which opens and shuts so as to control the flow of liquid, air, gas, etc., through the pipe ☞ CAR. STEAM 2 THERMIONIC VALVE 3 a hard shell protecting the soft body of certain sea creatures, esp. one of 2 enclosing the animal —see also BIVALVE

valvular adj connected with a valve or valves, esp. of the heart

vamoose v **vamoosed, vamoosing** US sl to go away hastily

vamp v esp. spoken to play a (a tune) on a musical instrument esp. a piano, in simple sets of notes invented by the player b a short, informal piece of music introducing a song — **vamp** n

vampire n 1 an evil spirit which is believed to live in the bodies of dead people and suck the blood of people who are asleep at night 2 an evil person who lives by forcing others to give him money, or takes from them time or strength which they cannot afford

vampire bat also **vampire**— n any of various South American bats which suck the blood of other animals

van¹ n esp. written or literature a vanguard

van² n a covered vehicle for carrying goods and sometimes people

vanadium n a type of hard silvery metal that is an element, used in making certain types of steel and dyes

vandal n a person who intentionally damages or destroys beautiful or useful things

vandalism n intentional needless damage

vandalize, -ise v **-ized, -izing** to damage or destroy (esp. a piece of public property) intentionally

vane n 1 a bladelike part of certain machines 2 also **weather vane**— a movable metal apparatus which shows the wind direction

vanguard n 1 the soldiers sent on ahead of an army to protect it against surprise attack — compare REARGUARD 2 the leading part of any marching body of people, or of ships in battle 3 the leading part of any kind of advancement in human affairs

vanilla n, adj (tasting of) a substance made from the beans of a tropical climbing plant (ORCHID), used for flavouring certain foods

vanish v 1 to disappear; go out of sight 2 to cease to exist; come to an end

vanishing cream n a creamy substance used to make the skin soft

vanishing point n (in the drawing of solid objects) the distant point at which parallel lines appear to meet

vanity n -ties the quality or state of being too proud of oneself or one's appearance, abilities, etc.

vanquish v esp. literature to conquer; defeat completely

vapid adj (of speech or writing, or of a person) lacking force, interest, or ideas — ~ly adv — ~ness n — ~ity n

vaporize, -ise v **-ized, -izing** to change into vapour — **-ization** n

vapour n 1 a gaslike form of a liquid (such as mist or steam) 2 technical the gas to which the stated liquid or solid can be changed by the action of heat: water vapour — **vaporous** adj

variability n the quality or condition of being variable; probability that something will vary

variable¹ adj 1 changeable; not staying the same; not steady 2 that can be intentionally varied — **-bly** adv — ~ness n

variable² n usu. technical 1 something which represents something (such as temperature) which can vary in quantity or size 2 a letter representing this

variant n a (slightly) different form, as of a word or part of a story — **variant** adj

variation n 1 the action of varying 2 an example or degree of this 3 one of a set of repeated parts of a piece of music each with certain different developments made to it 4 (an example of) change from what is usual in the form of a group or kind of living things, such as animals

varicoloured adj of many different colours

varicose adj (of a blood vessel, esp. in the leg) that has become greatly and incurably swollen

varied adj 1 of different kinds 2 not staying the same

variegated adj (esp. of a flower or leaf) marked irregularly in spots, lines, etc., of different colours — **-gation** n

variety n -ties 1 the state of varying; difference of condition or quality 2 a group or collection containing different sorts of the same thing or people 3 a type which is different from others in a group to which it belongs: new varieties of wheat 4 a show in which a number of short performances are given (such as singing, dancing, acts of skill, etc.)

variform adj technical or esp. written having various forms

various adj 1 different from each other; of (many) different kinds 2 several; a number of: various people

variously adv 1 in various ways or at various times; differently 2 by various names: Queen Elizabeth I, known variously as 'The Virgin Queen' and 'Good Queen Bess'

varnish¹ n 1 (any of several types of) liquid based on oil, which, when brushed onto articles and allowed to dry, gives a clear hard bright surface —see also NAIL VARNISH 2 the shiny appearance produced by using this substance

varnish² v 1 to cover with varnish or with nail varnish 2 to cover (something unpleasant) over with a smooth appearance —see also UNVARNISHED

varsity n -ties esp. spoken or pompous a university (esp. Oxford or Cambridge)

vary v -ied, -ying to be or cause to be different

vascular adj technical concerning or containing vessels through which liquids move in the bodies of animals or plants

vascular bundle n the fluid-carrying part of a plant made up of the tissue (PHLOEM) that carries sugars and proteins and the tissue (XYLEM) that carries water and salts

vase n a container used either for flowers or as an ornament

vasectomy n -mies (an operation for) removing a male's ability to become a father

Vaseline n trademark a jelly, obtained from petroleum, used for medical and other purposes

vassal n 1 (during the Middle Ages) (a person) who promised to serve a lord and was given land in return 2 a person who serves another in a slavelike way

vassalage n the state of being a vassal

vast adj great in size or amount

vastly adv very greatly

vat n a very large container for holding liquids (such as beer, whisky, dye, etc.), esp. when they are being made

VAT n VALUE-ADDED TAX

Vatican n 1 the place in Rome where the Pope lives 2 the Pope's government or office

vaudeville n US a variety show —compare MUSIC HALL

vault¹ n 1 a number of arches that form a roof or ceiling ☞ CATHEDRAL 2 a burial room beneath the floor of a church or in a churchyard 3 an underground room in which things are stored 4 a room at a bank used to store money, important papers, etc. 5 poetic a covering like a large curved roof

vault² v to jump over (something) in one movement using the hands or a pole to gain more height — ~er n

vault³ n a jump made by vaulting —see also POLE VAULT

vaulted adj covered with a curved roof

vaulting horse also **horse**— n a wooden apparatus over which people can vault for exercise

VC n VICTORIA CROSS

VD n VENEREAL DISEASE

veal n meat from a calf

vector n 1 (in science) a quantity which has direction as well as size and which can be represented by an arrow the length of which has a direct relationship with the size ☞ MATHEMATICS 2 an insect (such as a fly or mosquito) which can

carry a disease from one living thing to another 3 the course of an aircraft

veer v 1 to turn or change direction 2 technical (of the wind) to change direction clockwise

veg n veg esp. spoken (a type of) vegetable, usu. when cooked: meat and 2 veg

vegan n a person who believes in and practises vegetarianism but who also does not eat eggs or cheese or drink milk —compare VEGETARIAN

vegetable¹ n 1 a (part of a) plant that is grown for food 2 plant life 3 a human being who exists but has little or no power of thought (or sometimes also movement)

vegetable² adj of, related to, growing like, or made or obtained from plants

vegetable marrow n esp. written or technical a marrow

vegetarian n a person who believes in and practises vegetarianism —compare VEGAN — **vegetarian** adj

vegetarianism n the belief in and practice of eating only fruit, vegetables, nuts, etc., or of avoiding eating meat and fish

vegetate v -tated, -tating to live without activity of mind or body; have a dull life

vegetation n plant life

vehement adj fiercely strong or eager in support of or esp. in opposition to someone or something — ~ly adv — -mence n

vehicle n 1 something in or on which people or goods can be carried from one place to another 2 a means by which something can be passed on or a person's abilities shown off

vehicular adj concerning or connected with vehicles on roads

veil¹ n 1 a covering of fine cloth or net for all or part of the head or face 2 something which covers or hides something else — ~ed adj

veil² v to cover (as if) with a veil

vein n 1 a tube that carries blood from any part of the body to the heart —compare ARTERY ☞ RESPIRATION 2 one of a system of thin lines which run in a forked pattern through leaves and wings 3 a thin coloured line found in some kinds of stone and certain other substances 4 a crack in rock, filled with useful material: a vein of silver 5 a small but noticeable amount (of some quality): a vein of cruelty — ~ed adj

veld, veldt n (a stretch of) the high, flat, mostly treeless grassland of South Africa

vellum n 1 a material made from the skins of calves, kids, or lambs, used for book covers, lampshades, etc. 2 thick smooth paper of fine quality —compare PARCHMENT

velocipede n an early type of bicycle, often pushed by the rider's feet against the ground

velocity n -ties 1 technical speed in a certain direction; rate of movement 2 high speed —see also ESCAPE VELOCITY

velour, velours n a heavy cloth made from silk, cotton, etc., having a soft slightly raised surface

velvet n a fine closely-woven cloth made of silk, nylon, cotton, etc., having a short soft thick raised surface of cut threads on one side only —compare PLUSH — ~y adj

velveteen n a cheap cloth made of cotton, having the appearance of velvet

venal adj esp. written 1 (of an action, practice, or behaviour) done in order to gain money 2 (of a person) acting or ready to act unfairly or wrongly, esp. in return for money or other reward △ VENIAL — ~ity n — ~ly adv

vend v to offer (small articles) for sale, usu. in public places

vendetta n 1 a long-lasting quarrel between two families (esp. in Italy) whose members believe it their duty to kill each other in turn 2 a long-lasting state of affairs in which two people always try to harm one another

vending machine n a machine from which goods can be bought

vendor, -er n 1 a seller of small articles —see also NEWSVENDOR 2 law a seller of anything

veneer¹ n 1 a thin covering of good quality wood on some cheaper material 2 an outer appearance which hides the unpleasant reality

veneer² v 1 to cover with a veneer 2 to hide (an unpleasant quality) under a pleasing appearance

venerable adj considered to deserve great respect or honour —see OLD (USAGE)

venerate v -rated, -rating to treat with great respect and honour — -ration n

venereal adj medical resulting from or passed on by sexual activity

venereal disease also VD— n a disease passed from one person to another during sexual activity

venetian blind n a window covering made of slats that can be raised or lowered, or turned, to let in or shut out light and air

vengeance n 1 a punishment for harm done to oneself, one's family, etc. 2 with a vengeance esp. spoken to a high degree; with greater force than is usual —see REVENGE

venial adj (of a mistake, wrongdoing, etc.) of only slight importance and therefore forgivable —compare DEADLY SIN △ VENAL

venison n the flesh of a deer as food

Venn Diagram n technical a diagram showing the relations between sets

venom n 1 liquid poison 2 great hatred

venomous adj 1 (of a creature) having an organ that produces poison 2 (of speech, behaviour, etc.) showing a strong desire to hurt — ~ly adv

venous adj 1 medical concerning or connected with veins —see also INTRAVENOUS 2 (of blood that is) returning to the heart —compare ARTERIAL

vent¹ v 1 to give expression to (one's feelings) 2 technical to make a vent in

vent² n 1 an opening by which matter can enter or leave an enclosed space 2 technical the opening through which small animals, birds, fishes, and snakes get rid of waste matter from their bodies 3

give vent to to express freely (a strong feeling or natural desire for activity)

vent³ n technical a long narrow straight opening at the bottom of a coat

ventilate v -lated, -lating 1 to allow or cause fresh air to enter and move around inside (a room, building, etc.) 2 to permit or cause full public examination of (a subject or question) — -lation n

ventilator n any apparatus for ventilating a room, building, etc.

vent on v prep to express (a feeling) at the cost of (someone or something)

ventral adj of, on, or near the front, esp. of an animal — ~ly adv

ventricle n 1 either of the 2 spaces in the bottom of the heart that receive blood from the atria and then push it out into the main blood vessels of the body ☞ RESPIRATION 2 any of various small hollow places in an animal body or organ, esp. in the brain

ventriloquism n the art of speaking or singing with little or no movement of the lips or jaws, in such a way that the sound seems to come from someone else or from some distance away — -ist n

venture¹ v -tured, -turing 1 to risk going somewhere or doing something (dangerous) 2 to take the risk of saying (something that may be opposed or considered foolish)

venture² n a course of action of which the result is uncertain — ~r n

venturesome also venturous— adj esp. literature 1 (of an action) risky 2 (of a person) daring — ~ness n

venue n a meeting place arranged for some activity

Venus n the planet 2nd in order from the sun, and next to the earth

veracious adj esp. written truthful △ VORACIOUS — -city n

veranda, -dah n an outside part of a house with its own floor and roof

verb n a word or phrase that tells what someone or something is, does, or experiences: In "She is tired" and "He wrote a letter", "is" and "wrote" are verbs

verbal adj 1 spoken, not written: a verbal description 2 connected with words and their use 3 of, coming from, or connected with a verb △ VERBOSE — ~ly adv

verbalize, -ise v -ized, -izing to express (something) in words

verbal noun also gerund— n a noun which describes an action or experience having in English the form of a present participle and in some other languages the form of the infinitive: 'Building' is a verbal noun in 'the building of the bridge'

verbatim adj, adv repeating the actual words exactly

verbiage n too many unnecessary words

verbose adj using or containing too many words △ VERBAL — ~ly adv — -sity, ~ness n

verdant adj literature or poetic **1** (of land) covered with green plants **2** of a fresh leafy green — **-dancy** n

verdict n **1** the official decision in a court of law at the end of a trial —see also OPEN VERDICT **2** esp. spoken a judgment or decision given on any matter

verdigris n a greenish substance which forms on unprotected copper or brass

verge n an edge or border

verge on also **verge upon**— v prep **verged**, **verging on** to be near to (the stated quality or condition)

verger n a person paid to look after the inside of a church

verify v **-fied**, **-fying** to make sure that (a fact, statement, etc.) is correct or true — **-fiable** adj — **-fication** n

verily adv Bible or old use truly

veritable adj that may be described as true or real — **-bly** adv

verity n **-ties 2** literature or esp. written truth

vermiform adj shaped like a worm

vermilion adj, n bright reddish-orange (colour)

vermin n **1** any kind of insect that lives on the body of man or animals **2** any kind of animal or bird that destroys crops, spoils food, or does other damage, and is difficult to control — ~**ous** adj

vermouth n a type of pale yellow or dark red drink, made from wine with the addition of bitter tasting substances and herbs

vernacular adj, n (using) the native spoken language of a country or area

vernal adj literature or technical of, like, or appearing in the spring

verruca n **-cas** or **-cae** a small hard often infectious growth on the skin

versatile adj **1** having many different kinds of skill or ability; easily able to change from one kind of activity to another **2** having many different uses: Nylon is a versatile material — **-tility** n

verse n **1** writing arranged in regular lines, with a pattern of repeated beats as in music —see also BLANK VERSE, FREE VERSE **2** a set of lines that forms one part of a poem or song, and usu. has a pattern that is repeated in the other parts **3** one of the numbered parts of a chapter in the Bible

versed adj possessing a thorough knowledge or skill

versify v **-fied**, **-fying** to turn into the form of poetry — **-fier** n — **-fication** n

version n **1** one person's account of an event, as compared with that of another person **2** a translation **3** a form of a written or musical work that exists in more than one form **4** a slightly different form, copy, or style of something

versus prep esp. written against

vertebra n **-brae** one of the small hollow bones down the centre of the back which form the spine — **-bral** adj

vertebrate adj, n technical (a mammal, bird, fish, etc.) which has a backbone —compare INVERTEBRATE

vertex n **-texes** or **-tices 1** technical **a** the angle opposite the base (of any figure, such as a pyramid, cone, triangle, etc.) **b** the meeting point of the 2 lines (of an angle) **c** the point where 2 edges meet on a polyhedron **2** technical or esp. written the highest point: the vertex of an arch | the vertex of a hill

vertical adj **1** upright; forming an angle of 90 degrees with the level ground, or with a straight line in a figure —compare HORIZONTAL **2** pointing or moving directly upwards or downwards — ~**ly** adv

vertigo n a feeling of great unsteadiness, caused usu. by looking down from a great height — **-ginous** adj

verve n a strong feeling of life, force, and eager enjoyment

very¹ adj **verier**, **veriest** (used for giving force to an expression): He wrote his novels with this very pen. | the very top of her profession

very² adv **1** especially; in a high degree: a very good cake | very quickly | How very annoying! **2** in the greatest possible degree: the very best butter | the very same house

very high frequency n **-cies** esp. written VHF

vesicle n medical a small hollow part in an organ or other bodily part, or a small swelling on the skin, usu. filled with liquid — **-cular** adj

vespers n (in some divisions of the Christian church) the evening service

vessel n esp. written **1** a container used esp. for holding liquids **2** a ship or large boat **3** a tube (such as a vein) that carries blood or other liquid through the body, or sap through a plant —see also BLOOD VESSEL USAGE It is better to use **ship** or **boat** unless writing formally. **Ship** is usually used for a large vessel, **boat** for a small one, although this is not always the case.

vest n **1** a short undergarment worn on the upper part of the body **2** US a waistcoat

vestal virgin also **vestal**— n one of the young women who promised to remain unmarried, and whose duty was to tend the holy fire in the temple of Vesta, the Roman goddess of the house

vested interest n often offensive (a person having) a share or right in something that is of advantage

vestibule n a passage or room just inside the outer door of a public building through which all other rooms are reached; entrance hall

vestige n **1** a sign, track, or other proof that someone or something formerly existed or was present **2** the very small slight remains (of something) **3** the smallest possible amount: not a vestige of truth **4** the remains or imperfectly developed form of some limb or organ that was formerly important but is not now used — **-gial** adj

vest in also **vest with**— v prep esp. written **1**

to give (someone) the official and lawful right to possess or use (power, property, etc.): *In Britain, the right to make new laws is vested in the representatives of the people* **2** (of power, property, etc.) to belong by right to (someone): *this power vested in the church*

vestment *n esp. written* a ceremonial garment

vestry *n* **-tries** also **sacristy**— a small room in a church where holy vessels, official records, etc., are stored, and where the priest and choir put on their ceremonial garments ☞ CATHEDRAL

vet[1] also (*esp. written*) **veterinary surgeon**— *n* an animal doctor

vet[2] *v* **-tt-** *esp. spoken* to examine (something or someone) carefully for correctness, past record, etc.

vetch *n* a plant of the pea family, often found growing wild

veteran *n, adj* **1** a person who in the past has had experience in the stated form of activity — compare EX-SERVICEMAN **2** old: *Every year a race is held in England for veteran cars* (= those made before 1916) —compare VINTAGE

veterinary *adj* connected with the medical care and treatment of domestic animals —see also VET

veto[1] *n* **-toes** a refusal to give permission for something, or to allow something to be done; act of forbidding something completely

veto[2] *v* **vetoed, vetoing** to prevent or forbid (some action); refuse to allow (something) — **vetoer** *n*

vex *v* to displease (someone) —see ANGRY (USAGE) — ~**ation** *n* — ~**atious** *adj* — ~**atiously** *adv*

vexed question *n* something that has caused much fierce argument

VHF also (*esp. written*) **very high frequency**— *n* (the sending out of radio waves at) the rate of 30, 000, 000 to 300, 000, 000 hertz —compare UHF

via *prep* **1** travelling or sent through (a place) on the way **2** by means of: *I sent a message to Mary via her sister*

viable *adj* able to succeed in operation — **-bility** *n* — **-bly** *adv*

viaduct *n* a bridge that carries a road or railway across a valley

vibrant *adj* **1** *literature* strongly vibrating **2** (of colour or light) bright and strong, esp. pleasantly so **3** alive; powerful and exciting — ~**ly** *adv* — **-ancy** *n*

vibraphone also (*esp. spoken*) **vibes**— *n* a type of musical instrument consisting of a set of metal bars in a frame, which are struck to produce notes that are made to vibrate by a special apparatus

vibrate *v* **vibrated, vibrating** to shake continuously and very rapidly with a fine slight movement

vibration *n* **1** a slight continuous shaky movement **2** a regular to and fro movement of a stretched or touched wire **3** *esp. spoken* an influ-

ence, favourable or unfavourable, felt by a sensitive person as coming from someone or something else

vibrato *n* **-tos** *technical* (in music) a slightly shaking effect given to the sound of the voice, or of stringed or wind instruments, for added expressiveness

vicar *n* **1** (in the Church of England) a priest in charge of a church and its parish who receives a yearly payment for his duties —compare RECTOR **2** (in the Roman Catholic Church) a representative: *The Pope is known as the vicar of Christ*

vicarage *n* a vicar's house

vicarious *adj* experienced through watching or reading about other people — ~**ly** *adv* — ~**ness** *n*

vice[1] *n* **1** evil living **2** a serious fault of character —opposite **virtue**

vice[2] *n* a tool with jaws that can be tightened, used for holding material so that it can be worked on

vice-chancellor *n* the officer who controls the affairs of a university

vicelike *adj* very firm; giving no chance of movement or escape

viceroy *n* **-roys** a king's representative ruling for him in another country — **viceregal** *adj*

vice versa *adv Latin* in the opposite way from that just stated

vicinity *n* **-ties** **1** the neighbourhood **2** *esp. written* nearness

vicious *adj* **1** having or showing hate and the desire to hurt **2** able or likely to cause severe hurt — ~**ly** *adv* — ~**ness** *n*

vicious circle *n* a set of events in which cause and effect follow each other until this results in a return to the first position and the whole matter begins again

vicissitudes *n* changes from good to bad and bad to good in one's condition of life

victim *n* a person, animal, or thing that suffers pain, death, etc., as a result of other people's actions, or bad luck, etc.

victimize, -ise *v* **-ized, -izing** to cause (someone) to suffer unfairly or receive punishment or blame which should really be shared by others — **-ization** *n*

victor *n esp. written, literature, or pompous* **1** a conqueror in battle **2** a winner in a race, competition, or other struggle

Victoria Cross also **VC**— *n* a medal given to members of the British armed forces who have done acts of great bravery in battle

Victorian *adj, n* (any English person) of or living in the time when Queen Victoria ruled (1837–1901)

victorious *adj* **1** having won or conquered —opposite **vanquished** **2** of, related to, or showing victory — ~**ly** *adv*

victory *n* **-ries** the act of winning or state of having won —opposite **defeat**

victualler *n technical* a person who deals in or supplies victuals —see also LICENSED VICTUALLER

victuals *n old use or dialect* food and drink

vide *v Latin* (used for telling a reader where to find more about the subject) see; look at: *Vide page 32*

video *adj* **1** *technical* connected with or used in the showing of pictures by television —compare AUDIO **2** using videotape: *a video recording*

videotape[1] *n* a long band of magnetic tape on which television pictures and sound are recorded

videotape[2] *v* **-taped, -taping** to make a recording of (a television show) on videotape

vie *v* **vied, vying** to compete (against someone) (for something)

view[1] *n* **1** ability to see or be seen from a particular place **2** something seen, esp. a stretch of pleasant country **3** a picture or photograph of a piece of scenery, a building, etc. **4** a general consideration of a matter in all its details **5** a personal opinion, belief, idea, etc., about something USAGE The **aspect** or **outlook** of a house is the way it faces: *a room with a southern* **aspect**. What one sees from the windows is a **view**. These words can also be used more generally: *What are your* **views** *on football?* | *Look at it from every* **aspect** . What is likely to happen in the future is the **outlook** or the **prospect**.

view[2] *v* **1** *esp. technical* to examine; look at thoroughly: *to view the house* **2** to consider; regard; think about: *He viewed his son's lawless behaviour as an attack on himself*

viewer *n* an apparatus for looking at transparent colour photographs

viewfinder *n* a piece of apparatus on a camera, which shows what is to be photographed ☞ OPTICS

viewpoint *n* POINT OF VIEW

vigil *n* (an act of) remaining watchful for some purpose, esp. while staying awake during the night

vigilant *adj* continually watchful or on guard — ~ly *adv* — **-ance** *n*

vigilante *n* a member of a group of people who form themselves into an unofficial organization to keep order and punish crime

vigorous *adj* **1** forceful; strong; healthy **2** (of a plant) healthy; growing strongly △ RIGOROUS — ~ly *adv*

vigour *n* forcefulness; strength

Viking *n* a Scandinavian sea-faring adventurer active in the 8th-10th centuries ☞ HISTORY

vile *adj* **1** hateful; shameful; low **2** *esp. spoken* very bad: nasty: *a vile temper* — ~ly *adv* — ~ness *n*

vilify *v* **-fied, -fying** *esp. written* to speak evil of (someone or something) without cause — **-fication** *n*

villa *n* **1** a house in its own garden, often used for holidays **2** a house on the edge of a town **3** a large ancient Roman country house

village *n* **1** a small collection of houses and other buildings, smaller than a town **2** the people in this place as forming a society

villain *n* **1** (in a story or a play) the bad man —opposite **hero** **2** *esp. spoken* a criminal — ~ous *adj*

villainy *n* **-ies** *esp. literature* evil or wicked behaviour

villein *n* a land worker in the Middle Ages who paid rent for his small plot by working for his landlord

vim *n* *esp. spoken* active bodily force; healthy good spirits (often in the phrase **vim and vigour**)

vinaigrette *n* a mixture of oil, vinegar, salt, pepper, etc.

vindicate *v* **-cated, -cating** to show that charges made against (someone or something) are untrue — **-cation** *n*

vindictive *adj* unwilling to forgive; having the desire to harm someone from whom harm has been received — ~ly *adv* — ~ness *n*

vine *n* **1** also **grapevine**— a type of climbing plant that produces grapes **2 a** any creeping or climbing plant **b** the main stem of this: *a hop vine*

vinegar *n* an acid liquid made usu. from malt or sour wine — ~y *adj*

vineyard *n* a piece of land planted with vines

vino *n* **-noes** *esp. spoken* a cheap ordinary wine —see also PLONK

vinous *adj* *esp. written, technical or humour* like, caused by, connected with, or coloured like wine

vintage[1] *n* (a fine wine made in) a particular year, and named by the date of the year

vintage[2] *adj* **1** *esp. spoken* (of wines) of a type that is of a high enough quality to be given a named vintage **2** high quality, esp. from the past **3** (of a car) made between 1916 and 1930 —compare VETERAN

vintner *n* a person whose business is buying and selling wines

vinyl *n* a firm bendable plastic

viol *n* a type of stringed musical instrument of the 16th and 17th centuries

viola *n* a type of stringed musical instrument, like the violin but a little larger

violate *v* **-lated, -lating** **1** to disregard or act against something solemnly promised **2** *esp. written* to break, spoil, or destroy what should be respected or left untouched **3** to rape (a person) — **-lation** *n*

violence *n* **1** very great force in action or feeling **2** rough treatment; use of bodily force on others, esp. to hurt or harm

violent *adj* **1** fierce and dangerous in action **2** forceful beyond what is usual or necessary **3** produced by or being the effect of damaging force — ~ly *adv*

violet *n, adj* **1** a small plant with purplish-blue flowers **2** (having) a purplish-blue colour **3** *humour* a modest person (esp. in the phrase **shrinking violet**)

violin *n* **1** a type of 4-stringed wooden musical instrument, supported between the left shoulder and the chin and played by drawing a bow across the strings ☞ MUSIC **2** *esp. spoken* a person who plays this instrument in a band — ~**ist** *n*

violoncello *n* **-los** *esp. written* a cello — **violoncellist** *n*

VIP *n* *esp. spoken* a very important person

viper *n* any of several types of small poisonous snake

virago *n* **-goes** or **-gos** a fierce-tempered woman with a loud voice

virgin[1] *n* a person (esp. a woman or girl) who has not had sexual relations with a member of the opposite sex — ~**ity** *n*

virgin[2] *adj* **1** without sexual experience **2** fresh; unspoiled; unchanged by human activity

virginal[1] *adj* of, concerning, or suitable to a virgin

virginal[2] also **virginals**— *n* a small legless piano-like musical instrument popular in the 16th and 17th centuries

Virgin Mary also **Blessed Virgin Mary**— *n* (in the Christian religion) Mary, the mother of Christ

Virgo *n* **-gos 1 a** the 6th division in the zodiac belt of stars, represented by a virgin **b** the group of stars (CONSTELLATION) formerly in this division ☞ ZODIAC **2** a person born under this sign

virile *adj* (of a man) having the full amount of strong qualities expected of a man — **virility** *n*

virology *n* the scientific study of viruses, and of diseases caused by them — **-gist**

virtual *adj* almost what is stated; in fact though not in name: *the virtual ruler of the country*

virtually *adv* almost; very nearly: *My book's virtually finished; I've only a few changes to make*

virtue *n* **1** goodness; nobleness —opposite **vice 2** any good quality of character or behaviour **3** an advantage: *Plastic has many virtues* **4 by virtue of** also (*esp. written*) **in virtue of**— as a result of; by means of **5 woman of easy virtue** a woman who has sex with many men

virtuoso *n* **-sos** or **-si** a person who has a high degree of skill in one of the arts, esp. music — **-sity** *n*

virtuous *adj* possessing, showing, or practising virtue or virtues — ~**ly** *adv*

virulent *adj* **1** (of a poison, a disease caused by bacteria, etc.) very powerful and dangerous **2** (of a feeling) very bitter; full of hatred — ~**ly** *adv* — **-ence, -ency** *n*

virus *n* a living thing smaller than bacteria which causes infectious disease in the body, in plants, etc. —compare GERM

visa *n* an official mark put onto a passport by a representative of a country, giving a foreigner permission to enter, pass through, or leave that country

visage *n* *literature* the human face

vis-à-vis *prep esp. written or pompous* with regard to; when compared to: *This year's crop shows an improvement vis-à-vis last year's*

viscera *n* the large inside organs of the body — ~**l** *adj*

viscosity *n* **-ties** (a measure of) the unwillingness of a thick liquid or a gas to obey forces that try to make it flow

viscount *n* (the title of) a British nobleman next in rank below an earl — ~**cy** *n*

viscountess *n* (the title of) **a** the wife of a viscount **b** a woman of the rank of viscount in her own right

viscous also (*technical*) **viscid**— *adj* (of a liquid) that does not flow easily

visibility *n* **-ties 1** ability to give a clear view **2** the degree of clearness with which objects can be seen according to the condition of the air and the weather: *poor visibility*

visible *adj* **1** that can be seen **2** noticeable to the mind: *This object serves no visible purpose*

visibly *adv* noticeably: *visibly anxious*

vision *n* **1** the ability to see **2** wisdom and power of imagination esp. with regard to the future **3** something seen in or as if in a dream **4** a picture seen in the mind, as a fulfilment of a desire **5** a rare or beautiful sight: *a brief vision of the mountain top* —see also FIELD OF VISION

visionary[1] *adj* **1** having or showing vision **2** fanciful; existing in the mind only

visionary[2] *n* **-ries** a person whose aims for the future are noble but not easy to put into practice

visit[1] *v* **1** to go and spend some time in (a place or someone's house) **2** to go to (a place) in order to make an official examination

visit[2] *n* **1** an act or time of visiting **2 pay a visit** to visit someone or something usu. for a short time

visitant *n* *literature* a person who, or thing that, visits, esp. one thought to be a spirit from the world of the dead

visitation *n* **1** a formal visit by someone in charge or by a priest **2** an event believed to be an act of punishment or sometimes of favour from heaven

visiting *n* the act of making visits: *In her free time Mrs Evans does hospital visiting*

visiting card *n* a small card with one's name (and address) on it

visitor *n* **1** a person who visits or is visiting **2** a bird which spends only part of the year in a country

visor *n* **1** (in a suit of armour) the part of the helmet which can be raised or lowered over the face ☞ ARMOUR **2** also **sun visor**— a shield fitted to protect the eyes from bright sunshine **3** the front part of a cap; peak

vista *n* **1** a view into the distance **2** a set of events stretching far into the future or back into the past, as seen in the imagination

visual *adj* **1** gained by seeing: *visual knowledge of a place* **2** having an effect on the sense of sight: *The visual arts are painting, dancing, etc., as opposed to music and literature* **3** *technical* concerned with the power of sight

visual aid *n* any object that can be looked at, used for helping people to learn

visual display unit *n* a device like a television set, on which the results of computer operations can be displayed ☞ COMPUTER

visualize, -ise *v* **-ized, -izing** to form a picture of (something or someone) in the mind — **-ization** *n*

visually *adv* **1** in appearance: *Visually the chair is very pleasing* **2** using visual aids: *He explained the journey visually*

vital *adj* **1** very necessary; of the greatest importance **2** full of life and force: *a vital and cheerful manner* **3** necessary in order to stay alive: *a vital organ* (=any organ without which life cannot continue, such as the heart, brain, etc.)

vitality *n* **1** liveliness of character or manner- **2** ability to stay alive or working in an effective way

vitalize, -ise *v* **-ized, -izing** to give force to; bring (something or someone) to life —see also REVITALIZE

vitally *adv* in the highest possible degree: *vitally important*

vitals *n* the vital organs without which a person cannot continue to live

vital statistics *n* **1** *esp. spoken* the measurements of a woman's body round the chest, waist, and hips **2** certain facts about people's lives, esp. their births, marriages, deaths, and length of life

vitamin *n* **1** any one of several chemical substances which are found in small quantities in certain foods, and lack of which causes weaknesses and diseases **2** any particular type of this, named by a letter of the alphabet (A, B, C, etc.): *Oranges contain vitamin C*

vitiate *v* **-ated, -ating** *esp. spoken* to weaken; spoil; harm the quality of — **-ation** *n*

vitreous *adj* *technical* of, made of, or like glass

vitriolic *adj* (of a feeling or its expression) bitter and harmful

vituperate *v* **-rated, -rating** *esp. written* to scold or blame (someone or something) fiercely

vituperation *n* angry speech and cursing — **-tive** *adj*

vivace *adv, adj* (in music) (that is to be played) quickly and with spirit

vivacious *adj* (esp. of a woman) full of life and high spirits — ~**ly** *adv* — **vivacity** *n* — ~**ness** *n*

vivarium *n* **-ums** or **-a** *technical* an enclosed place where animals are kept indoors in conditions as like as possible to their natural surroundings

viva voce[1] *adv, adj* *Latin* orally; (carried out) by means of speaking: *a viva voce examination*

viva voce[2] *n* *Latin* a spoken examination

vivid *adj* **1** (of light or colour) bright and strong **2** that produces sharp clear pictures in the mind **3** (of a person's power of expression) full of life and force — ~**ly** *adv* — ~**ness** *n*

viviparous *adj* *technical* (of an animal) giving birth to living young ones (not by means of eggs)

vivisect *v* to perform an operation on (a living

animal) as a scientific test, esp. in order to increase knowledge of diseases — ~**ion** *n* — ~**ionist** *n*

vixen *n* **1** a female fox **2** a nasty bad-tempered woman

vixenish *adj* (of a woman) fierce and bad-tempered

viz. *adv* in other words; that is to say: *On most English farms you'll find only 4 kinds of animal, viz. horses, sheep, cattle, and pigs* —compare I.E., NAMELY **USAGE** Usually read aloud as ' namely '.

vizier *n* (in former times) a minister in some Muslim countries

V-neck *n* a neck opening of a dress, shirt, etc., with the front cut in the shape of a V — **V-necked** *adj* : *a V-necked sweater*

vocabulary *n* **-ries** **1** all the words known to a particular person **2** the special set of words used in a particular kind of work: *the vocabulary of the lawcourts* **3** also (*esp. spoken*) **vocab** – a list of words much shorter than a dictionary

vocal[1] *adj* **1** connected with the voice; used in speaking **2** produced by or for the voice; spoken or sung: *vocal music* — ~**ly** *adv*

vocal[2] *n* a performance of a popular song by a singer

vocal cords, vocal chords *n* thin bands of muscle at the upper end of a person's windpipe that can be made to move rapidly in the air stream and thus produce sound

vocalist *n* a singer of popular songs, esp. one who sings with a band —compare INSTRUMENTAL-IST

vocation *n* **1** a job which one does because one believes one has a special ability to give service to other people **2** a special call from God for the religious life **3** a person's work or employment

vocational *adj* preparing for or connected with a vocation

vocative *adj, n* (a noun, or the special form of a noun) used in some languages, such as Latin, when addressing someone or something

vociferate *v* **-ated, -ating** to shout or speak (words) in a loud way — **-ation** *n*

vociferous *adj* **1** noisy in the expression of one's feelings **2** expressed noisily by shouting — ~**ly** *adv* — ~**ness** *n*

vodka *n* a type of strong colourless alcoholic drink, first made in Russia and Poland

vogue *n* **1** the generally accepted fashion or custom at a certain time **2** the state of being in popular favour **3** **in vogue** fashionable

voice[1] *n* **1** the sound or sounds produced by man in speaking and singing or his ability to produce them **2** the quality of such sound as particular to a certain person: *The boy's voice is breaking* (=becoming lower like a man's) **3** the expressing of an opinion; the right to influence other opinions, decisions, etc. **4** ability as a singer: *a good voice* **5** an expression of ideas: *the voice of reason* **6** the form of the verb which shows whether the subject of a sentence acts (**active voice**) or is acted on (**passive voice**) **7 at the top of one's voice** very loudly **8 raise one's voice a** to speak louder **b** to speak loudly and angrily (to someone) **c** to express one's displeasure, disagreement, etc. **9 with one voice** with everyone expressing the same opinion

voice² v **voiced, voicing** **1** to express in words, esp. forcefully **2** to produce (a sound, esp. a consonant) with vibration of the vocal cords: '*D*' *and* '*g*' *are voiced consonants, but* '*t*' *and* '*k*' *aren't*

voice box n esp. spoken the larynx

voiceless adj **1** making no sound **2** (of a speech sound, esp. a consonant) produced without vibrating the vocal cords

void¹ adj **1** empty; without; lacking **2** esp. law (of any kind of official agreement) having no value or effect from the beginning —see also NULL AND VOID

void² n **1** an empty space **2** a feeling of emptiness or loss

void³ v esp. written or technical to get rid of (the usu. unwanted contents of something) by emptying

voile n a very fine thin almost transparent material of cotton, silk, or wool

volatile adj **1** (of a person or his character) of a quickly-changing nature **2** (of a liquid or oil) easily changing into a gas — **-tility** n

vol-au-vent n French a light small puff pastry case filled with chicken, mushrooms, etc.

volcanic adj of, from, or produced by a volcano

volcano n **-noes** or **-nos** a mountain with a large opening (CRATER) at the top through which melted rock (LAVA), steam, etc., escape from time to time: *An* **active volcano** *may explode at any time.* | *A* **dormant volcano** *is quiet at present.* | *An* **extinct volcano** *has ceased to be able to explode* ☞ GEOGRAPHY

vole n any of several types of small thick-bodied short-tailed animal of the rat and mouse family

volition n the act of using one's will; one's power to decide or choose (a course of action) — ~**al** adj

volley¹ n **-leys** **1** a number of shots fired at the same time by soldiers, police, etc. **2 a** an attack with stones, arrows, etc. **b** a number of blows given, words spoken, etc., with speed and force **3** (of a ball) the condition of not having hit the ground after being thrown, kicked, or hit **4** a kicking or hitting of a ball in this condition, esp., in tennis, a stroke by which the player returns the ball to his opponent without allowing it to touch the ground first —see also HALF VOLLEY

volley² v **-leyed, -leying** **1** (of shots fired or objects thrown) to come flying together through the air **2** to hit or kick (a ball) on the volley **3** (in tennis) to make a volley against (one's opponent)

volleyball n a game in which a large ball is struck by hand backwards and forwards across a net without being allowed to touch the ground

volt n the amount of electrical force needed to produce one standard measure (AMPERE) of electrical current where the resistance of the conductor is another standard measure (OHM) —COMPARE AMPERE

voltage n electrical force measured in volts

volte-face n French a change to a completely opposite opinion

voltmeter n an instrument for measuring volts ☞ ELECTRICITY

voluble adj often offensive having, always ready to produce, or expressed in a great flow of words — **-bility** n — **-bly** adv

volume n **1** one of a set of books of the same kind **2** a book, esp. a large one **3** size or quantity thought of as measurement of the space inside or filled by something: *The volume of this container is 100, 000 cubic metres* **4** esp. technical amount produced by some kind of (industrial) activity: *the volume of passenger travel* **5** loudness of sound

volumes n **1** a large quantity or mass (esp. of something that pours or flows) **2 speak volumes (for something)** to show or express (something) very clearly or fully

voluminous adj **1** (of a garment) very loose and full **2** (of a container) very large **3** producing or containing too much writing: *a voluminous report* — ~**ly** adv — ~**ness** n

voluntary¹ adj **1** (of a person or an action) acting or done willingly, without payment — opposite **compulsory, obligatory** **2** supported by people who give their money, services, etc., of their own free will **3** technical under the control of the will: *voluntary movements* —opposite **involuntary** — **-tarily** adv : *He made the promise quite voluntarily*

voluntary² n **-ries** a piece of music played in church before or after the service

volunteer¹ n a person who volunteers

volunteer² v **1** to offer one's services or help without payment **2** to offer to join the army, navy, or airforce of one's own free will **3** to tell (something) without being asked

voluptuary n **-ries** literature, usu. offensive a person who gets great enjoyment from comfort and costly living and delights in the pleasures of the senses

voluptuous adj **1** of a kind that suggests sexual pleasure **2** too much concerned with the enjoyment of bodily pleasures **3** giving delight to the senses — ~**ly** adv — ~**ness** n

vomit¹ n **1** food or other matter that has been vomited **2** an act of vomiting

vomit² v **1** to throw up (the contents of the stomach) through the mouth; be sick **2** to pour out suddenly with force and in great quantity (usu. something unpleasant or unwanted)

voodoo n a set of magical beliefs and practices, used as a form of religion, found particularly in parts of the West Indies — ~**ism** n

voracious adj **1** eating or desiring large quantities of food **2** having or showing eagerness, like

a hunger, for something △ VERACIOUS — ~**ly**
adv

voracity *n* the state of being voracious

vortex *n* **-texes** *or* **-tices** a mass of water or wind, making forceful circular movement

vote[1] *n* **1** an act of making a choice or decision on a matter by means of voting —see also CARD VOTE **2** a (person's) choice or decision, as expressed by voting **3** the piece of paper on which a choice is expressed **4** the whole number of such choices made either for or against someone or something **5 put something to the vote** to try to obtain a decision about something by asking everyone to vote on it

vote[2] *v* **voted,-voting 1** to express one's choice officially (usu. done by marking a piece of paper secretly, or by calling out or raising one's hand at a meeting) **2** to elect **3** to agree, as the result of a vote, to provide (something)

vote of confidence *n* **votes of confidence** a declaration of support for someone's actions, usu. expressed by voting

vote of thanks *n* **votes of thanks** a public expression of thanks passed by voting

voter *n* **1** a person who is voting **2** a person who has the right to vote

voucher *n* **1** a kind of ticket that may be used instead of money for a particular purpose: *a travel voucher* **2** a kind of ticket that gives the right to receive certain goods free or at a lower price

vouch for *v prep* **1** to declare one's belief in (someone or something) **2** to take the responsibility for (someone's future behaviour)

vouchsafe *v* **-safed, -safing** *literature or esp. written* to offer, give, say, or do (something) as an act of favour or kindness

vow[1] *n* **1** a solemn promise or declaration of intention **2 take vows** to begin to live in a religious house (as a monk or nun)

vow[2] *v* **1** to declare or swear solemnly **2** to promise (something) by swearing solemnly, esp. to God: *Priests vow their lives to the service of the church*

vowel *n* **1** any one of the more open sounds uttered when speaking **2** a letter used for representing any of these: *The vowels in the English alphabet are a, e, i, o, u, and, sometimes, y* — compare CONSONANT, DIPHTHONG

vox populi *n Latin* the voice of the people; public opinion

voyage[1] *n* a journey, usu. long, made by boat or ship

voyage[2] *v* **-aged, -aging** *literature or esp. written* to make a long journey by sea —see TRAVEL (USAGE) — ~**r** *n*

V-sign *n* a sign made by holding the hand up with the first 2 fingers in the shape of a V and the palm of the hand facing forwards, used for expressing victory or the hope of it

VTOL *n, adj* vertical takeoff and landing

vulcanite *n* a type of rubber which has been vulcanized

vulcanize, -ise *v* **-ized, -izing** to treat (rubber)

at high temperature, with sulphur, so as to give strength for industrial use — **-ization** *n*

vulgar *adj* **1** (of a person or behaviour) very rude, low, or having bad manners **2** showing a lack of feeling or judgment in the choice of what is suitable or beautiful, esp. in matters of art: *vulgar furniture* — ~**ly** *adv*

vulgar fraction *n* a fraction expressed by a number above and a number below a line (rather than as a decimal): *¾ is a vulgar fraction*

vulgarian *n* a rich person whose behaviour is considered vulgar

vulgarism *n* **1** a word or expression not usu. used by educated people **2** vulgarity

vulgarity *n* **-ties 1** the state or quality of being vulgar **2** vulgar speech or action

vulgarize, -ise *v* **-ized, -izing** to spoil the quality of: *This music has been vulgarized by being made into a dance tune* — **-ization** *n*

Vulgar Latin *n* the form of Latin spoken in ancient Rome, esp. by the common people, as opposed to the written language, and from which many modern languages have developed

vulnerable *adj* **1** (of a place, thing, or person) not well protected **2** (of a person or his feelings) easily harmed or wounded — **-bility** *n* — **-bly** *adv*

vulture *n* **1** a large bird with almost featherless head and neck, which feeds on dead animals **2** a person who has no mercy and who uses people for his own advantage

vulva *n* **-vae** *or* **-vas** the place where the passage leading to the female sex organs has its opening on the body

vying *pres. part. of* VIE

W, w W's, w's *or* Ws, ws the 23rd letter of the alphabet

W *abbrev. for:* **a** west; western **b** watt

wacky *adj* **-ier, -iest** *esp. spoken, esp. US* (of people, ideas, behaviour, etc.) silly or strange — **wackiness** *n*

wad[1] *n* **1** a thick mass of material pressed into a hole used for filling space, etc. **2** a thick piece of cloth, or pieces of paper folded or fastened together: *a wad of letters* **3** a large amount of paper money rolled up —see also WADGE

wad[2] *v* **-dd- 1** to make a wad of: *Wad the newspaper and hit the flies with it* **2** to fill with a wad

wadding *n* material used for wads, esp. for packing or in medicine

waddle[1] *v* **-dled, -dling** to walk with short steps, bending from one side to the other, as if having short legs and a heavy body: *Ducks waddle*

waddle[2] *n* a way of walking like that of a duck

wade *v* **waded, wading** to walk through water —compare PADDLE

wade in *v adv esp. spoken* to begin something difficult or heavy in a determined manner

wader *n* **1** a person who wades **2** a high waterproof boot **3** WADING BIRD

wadge *n esp. spoken* a mass of things rolled tightly together: *a wadge of papers*

wadi, wady *n* **-ies** a usu. dry river bed of the sort common in desert countries

wading bird *n* any of various long-legged water birds that wade into water to find their food

wafer *n* a thin crisp biscuit

waffle¹ *n* a large light often sweet cake, usu. marked with raised squares

waffle² *v* **-fled, -fling** *sl* to talk nonsense

waffle iron *n* a cooking apparatus with 2 joined metal parts, for making waffles

waft¹ *v literature* to move lightly on or as if on wind or waves: *Cooking smells wafted along the hall*

waft² *n* **1** a sudden smell, carried by moving air: *wafts of cigarette smoke* **2** a short light current of air

wag¹ *v* **-gg-** **1** to shake to and fro: *The dog wagged its tail* **2 a case of the tail wagging the dog** *esp. spoken* a state of affairs in which the followers control the leader **3 Their tongues wagged** *esp. spoken* They talked a lot

wag² *n* an act of wagging; shake

wag³ *n* a clever and amusing talker

wage¹ *v* **waged, waging** to begin and continue (a struggle) (esp. in the phrase **wage war**)

wage² *n* **1** wages: *a high wage level* **2 a living wage** an amount of pay large enough to buy food, clothing, etc.

wage earner *n* a person who works for wages or a salary

wage freeze — *n* an attempt, esp. by government, to keep pay from rising

wager¹ *n* a bet

wager² *v* to bet

wages *n* a payment for labour or services usu. received daily or weekly —compare SALARY; see PAY (USAGE)

waggish *adj* of, like, or typical of a wag: *waggish remarks* — ~**ly** *adv* — ~**ness** *n*

waggle *v* **-gled, -gling** to move frequently from side to side: *The dog waggled its tail* — **waggle** *n*

waggon, wagon *n* **1** a 4-wheeled vehicle, mainly for heavy loads, drawn by horses, oxen, railway engines, or road vehicles **2 on the waggon** *sl* unwilling to drink alcohol

waggoner, wagoner *n* the driver of a waggon

wagtail *n* a small black and white or black, grey, and yellow European bird with a long tail constantly moving up and down as it walks

waif *n esp. in literature* **1** a child without a home: *a pitiful little waif* **2 waifs and strays** neglected children or animals

wail *v* **1** to make a long cry suggesting grief or pain **2** to cry out in grief or pain: *"You've taken my apple, " he wailed* **3** to complain — **wail** *n*

wainscot *n* panelling on the lower part of the walls of a room — ~**ed** *adj*

waist *n* **1** the narrow part of the human body just above the hips **2** the part of a garment that goes round this: *the waist of a dress* **3** the narrow middle part of any apparatus, such as a musical instrument

waistband *n* the strengthened part of a garment that fastens round the waist

waistcoat *n* a close-fitting armless garment that reaches to the waist

waistline *n* a line surrounding the waist at its narrowest part

wait¹ *v* **1** to stay somewhere without doing anything until somebody comes or something happens: *Don't keep her waiting* **2** to be ready: *Your tea is waiting for you* **3** to remain not dealt with: *This news can't wait* **4** to hold back until (the stated occasion): *just waiting his chance to strike* **5 wait at table** to serve meals

wait² *n* **1** an act or period of waiting: *a long wait* **2 lie in wait** to hide, waiting to attack: *robbers lying in wait for the traveller*

waiter (*fem.* **waitress**)— *n* a person who serves food at the tables in a restaurant

waiting list *n* a list of those who want theatre tickets, a house, etc. often giving first the names of those who asked first

waiting room *n* a room for those who are waiting

wait on *v prep* to serve: *They wait on you very well in this shop*

waits *n* carol singers who go round to people's houses

wait up *v adv* to delay going to bed

waive *v* **waived, waiving** to give up willingly (a right, a rule, etc.)

waiver *n law* the official waiving of a right, claim, etc.

wake¹ *v* **woke** *or* **waked, woken, waking** **1** to cease to sleep or stop someone sleeping: *She usually wakes early* **2** to make or become active: *The lonely child woke our pity* **3** *literature* to begin moving: *A light wind woke among the trees*

wake² *n* a gathering to watch and grieve over a dead person on the night before the burial

wake³ *n* **1** a track or path, esp. that left by a moving body in water: *the broad white wake of the great ship* **2 in the wake of** following as a result of: *hunger and disease in the wake of the war*

wakeful *adj* sleepless — ~**ly** *adv* — ~**ness** *n*

waken *v* to wake

wakey wakey *interj humour* Wake up!

waking *adj* of the time when one is awake: *his waking hours*

walk¹ *v* **1** to move at a walk: *to walk to town* **2** to pass over, through, or along on foot: *to walk a tightrope* **3** to take for a walk: *walking the dog* | *I walked her home* **4** to cause to move in a manner suggesting a walk: *Let's walk the heavy ladder to the other end of the room* **5** (of a spirit) to move about visibly: *Spirits walk at night* **6 walk (someone) off (their) feet/legs** *esp. spoken* to tire (someone) by making (them) move about on foot too much —see also WALK INTO, WALK OFF WITH, WALK OUT, WALK OUT ON, WALK OVER — ~ *n*

walk² *n* **1** (of people and creatures with legs) a natural and unhurried way of moving on foot **2** a journey on foot: *Let's go for a short walk* **3** a place for walking: *a beautiful walk along the river* **4** a distance to be walked: *a 10-minute walk from here* **5** the style of walking: *His walk is like his father's*

walkabout *n* a walk through crowds by an important person, mixing and talking informally with the people

walkie-talkie *n esp. spoken* a 2-way portable radio, allowing one to talk as well as listen

walk-in *adj* large enough to be walked into: *a walk-in cupboard*

walking *adj* **1** human: *She knows so many words that she's a walking dictionary!* **2** for going on foot: *walking shoes* **3** done on foot: *a walking holiday*

walking stick *n* a stick used for supporting someone while walking

walk into *v prep* **1** to obtain (a job) very easily **2** to meet through carelessness: *He walked into the trap*

walk off with also **walk away with**— *v adv prep esp . spoken* **1** to steal and take away **2** to win easily

walk-on *n* (a person who has) a small, usu. non-speaking, part in a play

walkout *n* **1** a strike **2** the action of leaving as an expression of disapproval

walk out *v adv* to go on strike

walk out on *v adv prep sl* to desert: *He walked out on his wife and family*

walkover *n sl* an easy or unopposed victory

walk over *v prep sl* to treat badly

wall¹ *n* **1** an upright dividing surface (esp. of stone or brick) enclosing something: *fields surrounded by stone walls* | *the city wall of London* **2** the side of a room: *Hang that picture on the wall* **3** an upright mass: *a wall of water* **4** something that separates; barrier: *a wall of silence* **5** the covering of something hollow: *the walls of a blood vessel* **6 bang one's head against a wall** *esp. spoken* to try to do the impossible **7 to the wall** into a hopeless position **8 up the wall** into a state of or near madness

wall² *v* **1** to provide with a wall: *an old walled town* **2** to close or enclose with a wall: *to wall up a door/a prisoner* **3** to separate with walls

wallaby *n* any of various types of kangaroos of small to middle size

wallet *n* a small flat leather case for papers and paper money

wallflower *n* **1** a sweet-smelling European yellow or red flower that grows best near walls **2** a person who sits by the wall at a dance because no one has asked them to dance

wallop¹ *n sl* a powerful blow

wallop² *v sl* to hit forcefully

wallow¹ *v* **1** (of a ship) to roll and struggle in a rough sea **2** to move about with pleasure in deep mud, water, etc.

wallow² *n* **1** an act of wallowing **2** a place to wallow

wallow in *v prep humour esp. spoken* to enjoy too greatly: *wallowing in praise*

wall painting *n* a picture painted on a wall, esp. a fresco

wallpaper¹ *n* ornamental paper to cover the walls of a room

wallpaper² *v* to cover with wallpaper

Wall Street *n* the US centre for money matters, in New York —compare the CITY

wall-to-wall *adj, adv* over the whole floor: *wall-to-wall carpets*

walnut *n* a brain-shaped eatable nut which grows on a **walnut tree**, and has a rough shell easily divided into 2 parts

walrus *n* **-ruses** or **-rus** either of 2 types of large seal-like sea-animals with 2 long downward-pointing tusks ☞ MAMMAL

waltz¹ *n* (music for) a social dance for a couple, made up of 6 steps in 3/4 time

waltz² *v* **1** to dance a waltz **2** *esp. spoken* to move easily or showily: *We can't just waltz up to a complete stranger*

wampum *n* shells put into strings, belts, etc., used as money or ornaments by North American Indians

wan *adj esp. in literature* ill, weak, and tired: *a wan smile* — ~**ly** *adv* — ~**ness** *n*

wand *n* a thin stick carried in the hand, esp. by a person who does magic tricks

wander *v* **1** to move about aimlessly **2** to follow a winding course: *The river wanders through beautiful country* **3** (of people or thoughts) to become confused: *His mind is wandering*

wanderer *n* a person who wanders

wandering *adj* **1** aimless, slow, and irregular: *the wandering course of a stream* **2** moving from place to place: *wandering tribes*

wanderings *n* wandering movements

wanderlust *n* a strong desire to wander

wane *v* **waned, waning** to grow gradually smaller or less powerful

wangle¹ *v* **-gled, -gling** *sl* **1** to get cleverly or by a trick: *I wangled an invitation.* | *I wangled George into a good job* **2** to get cleverly out of a difficulty: *Let's see you wangle your way out of this one!*

wangle² *n sl* an act of wangling

want¹ *v* **1** to have a desire for **2** to need: *The house wants painting* **3** ought: *You don't want to work so hard* **4** to lack; be without: *His answer wants politeness* **5** to look for in order to catch: *He is wanted for murder*

want² *n* **1** lack, absence, or need: *The plants*

died from want of water **2** severe lack of the things necessary to life: *How terrible to live in want!* —see LACK (USAGE)

wanting[1] *adj* lacking

wanting[2] *prep* without: *a letter wanting a stamp*

wanton[1] *adj* **1** *literature* wild and full of fun: *a wanton mind* **2** uncontrolled: *wanton growth of plant life* **3** sexually improper: *She gave him a wanton look* **4** having no good reason: *wanton waste* — ~ly *adv* — ~ness *n*

wanton[2] *n* a woman of improper sexual behaviour

wants *n* needs

war[1] *n* **1** armed fighting between nations **2** a period of this **3** a struggle: *a war against disease* **4** (having) been in the wars *esp. spoken* (having) been hurt or damaged

war[2] *v* **-rr-** **1** *literature* to take part in a war **2** to struggle: *warring beliefs*

warble[1] *n* a bird's or birdlike song

warble[2] *v* **-bled, -bling** **1** (esp. of birds) to sing with a clear, continuous, yet varied note **2** to sing in an untrained, uncontrolled way —compare TRILL

warbler *n* any of several types of small song bird

war cry also **battle cry**— *n* **cries** **1** a cry used in battle to show courage and frighten the enemy **2** a political slogan

ward *n* **1** a separate room or division of a hospital: *the heart ward* **2** a political division of a city **3** a person who is under the protection of another, or of a law court

warden *n* a person who looks after a place and people: *the warden of an old people's home*

warder (*fem.* **wardress**)— *n* a prison guard

ward off *v adv* to prevent (something bad)

wardrobe *n* **1** a room or cupboard in which one hangs up clothes **2** a collection of clothes: *a new summer wardrobe* **3** a collection of theatre costumes and ornaments

warehouse *n* a building for storing things

wares *n* articles for sale

warfare *n* **1** war **2** struggle

warhead *n* the explosive front end of a bomb or esp. a missile

warily *adv* see WARY — **-iness** *n*

warlike *adj* **1** threatening war: *a warlike appearance* **2** liking war: *a warlike nation*

warlock *n* (esp. in stories) a male witch

warlord *n* *usu. offensive* **1** a high military leader **2** (esp. in China in the 1920s and '30s) a military commander who gets political power by force

warm[1] *adj* **1** having or producing enough heat: *a warm fire* **2** able to keep in heat: *warm clothes* **3** feeling hot: *We were warm from exercise* **4** showing good feeling: *a warm welcome* **5** marked by excitement or anger: *a warm argument* **6** recently made; fresh (esp. in the phrases **warm scent/smell/trail**) **7** (esp. in children's games) near a hidden object, the right answer to a ques-

tion, etc. **8** giving a cheerful feeling: *warm colours* — ~ish *adj* — ~ly *adv* — ~ness *n*

warm[2] *v* to make or become warm

warm[3] *n* **1** a warm place: *Come into the warm* **2** the act of making oneself warm

warm-blooded *adj technical* (of birds, mammals, etc.) able to keep the body temperature rather high whether the outside temperature is high or low — ~ly *adv* — ~ness *n*

warming pan *n* a round covered long-handled metal vessel to contain hot coals formerly used to warm a bed

warmonger *n* a person who tries to start a war

warmth *n* the quality of being warm

warm up *v adv* to make or become ready for action by exercise before the real test comes: *singers warming up for a concert*

warn *v* **1** to tell of something bad that may happen, or of how to prevent something bad **2** to tell of some future need or action: *You should warn the police when you go away on holiday*

warning *n* **1** of warning or being warned **2** something that warns: *Let that be a warning to you* **3** an example of what *not* to do: *He is a warning to us all of what happens to people who drink too much*

war of nerves *n* **wars of nerves** an attempt to worry the enemy by threats, propaganda, etc.

warp[1] *n* **1** the downward threads running along the length of cloth —compare WEFT **2** a twist out of a straight line: *a warp in a board* **3** a rope or wire for pulling a net along behind a fishing boat

warp[2] *v* to turn or twist out of shape

war paint *n* paint that members of some tribes put, esp. formerly, on their bodies before going to war

warpath *n* the behaviour of a person ready to fight (esp. in the phrase **on the warpath**)

warrant[1] *n* **1** proper reason for action **2** a written order signed by an official of the law

warrant[2] *v* **1** to cause to appear reasonable **2** to guarantee **3** *esp. spoken* to declare as if certain: *I'll warrant he's there*

warrant officer *n* a member of the British army, airforce, or Royal Marines with a rank between noncommissioned officer and commissioned officer

warranty *n* **-ties** *technical* a written guarantee

warren *n* an area in which small animals live, esp. rabbits

warrior *n* **1** *literature* a soldier **2** a man who fights for his tribe: *The Indian warriors charged bravely*

warship *n* a naval ship used for war

wart *n* a small hard ugly swelling on the skin — ~y *adj*

warthog *n* **-hogs** *or*-hog a type of African wild pig with long front teeth that stick out and lumps on its face

wartime n a period during which a war is going on —opposite **peacetime**

wary adj **-ier, -iest** careful; looking out for danger — **warily** adv — **wariness** n

was 1st and 3rd person sing. past tense of BE: I/He was happy

wash¹ v 1 to clean or clean oneself with liquid: to wash clothes | to wash before dinner 2 esp. spoken to be easy to believe: His story just won't wash 3 to flow over or against continually: The waves washed against the shore 4 to cause to be carried with liquid: I washed the dirt off. | The waves washed the swimmer away 5 **wash one's hands of** esp. spoken to refuse to accept any more responsibility for

wash² n 1 washing or being washed: to have a wash 2 things to be washed; laundry 3 the flow, sound, or action of a mass of water: the wash of the waves 4 water thrown back by a boat 5 a movement of air caused by an aircraft passing through it 6 the liquid with which something is washed or coloured: mouthwash | a copper-coloured hairwash 7 **come out in the wash** esp. spoken to turn out all right in the end

washable adj that can be washed without damage

washbasin n a fixed basin for washing hands and face

washboard n a movable board with a wavy surface against which clothes may be rubbed when washing

washday n **-days** the day when clothes are washed

wash down v adv 1 to clean with a lot of water: to wash down the car 2 to swallow with the help of liquid: Wash the dry cake down with tea

wash drawing n a drawing made in water paint of one colour

washed-out adj very tired

washed-up adj sl finished; with no further possibilities of success

washer n 1 a person who washes 2 a ring put over a bolt or a screw to give a softer or larger pressing surface, or between 2 pipes to make a better joint 3 a washing machine

washerwoman n **-women** (in former times) a woman whose job it was to wash clothes

washing n clothes washed or to be washed

washing machine n a machine for washing clothes

washing soda n a rough chemical powder (**sodium carbonate**) used esp. in washing very dirty things

washing-up n the washing of dishes, plates, etc. after a meal

wash-leather n yellow, soft, oiled, esp. sheepskin leather used for polishing metal

washout n sl a failure

washroom n US polite a room containing a lavatory

washstand n a table in a bedroom, holding things for washing face and hands

wash up v adv esp. spoken 1 to do the washing-up 2 US to wash one's face and hands

wasp n any of many types of flying stinging insect related to the bee, usu. yellow and black ➣ INSECT

waspish adj quarrelsome: a nasty waspish remark — ~ly adv — ~ness n

wassail n 1 noisy merry feasting and drinking at Christmas time in England in former times 2 **go wassailing** to go from house to house at Christmas, esp. in former times, singing carols

wast v thou wast old use (when talking to one person) you were

wastage n wasting or that which is wasted: a wastage of 25% of all the goods produced

waste¹ n 1 often literature a wide empty lonely stretch of water or land: stony wastes 2 loss, wrong use, or lack of full use: Waste of food is wicked while people are hungry 3 used, damaged, or unwanted matter: poisonous waste from the chemical works 4 **go/run to waste** to be wasted —compare REFUSE

waste² v **wasted, wasting** 1 to use wrongly, not use, or use too much of 2 (esp. of a disease) to cause to lose flesh, muscle, strength, etc., slowly 3 to make useless by damage: Long dry periods wasted the land 4 **waste one's breath** esp. spoken to speak without persuading anyone

waste³ adj 1 (esp. of land) not productive; ruined or destroyed 2 got rid of as worthless: waste material 3 used for holding or carrying away what is worthless: waste pipes

waste away v adv to weaken or lose flesh, muscle, etc.

wasteful adj tending to waste: wasteful habits — ~ly adv — ~ness n

wastepaper basket n a container for unnecessary material, esp. waste paper

waste product n something useless produced by the same action that produces something useful

waster n a person or thing that uses wastefully, or causes waste: a time-waster

wastrel n literature a person who uses foolishly or too quickly the things that belong to him

watch¹ v 1 to look at (some activity or event): Do you often watch television? | Watch how to do this 2 to look for; expect and wait: She watched to see what I would do 3 to take care of: I'll watch the baby while you are away 4 literature to stay awake at night: She watched beside her sick mother's bed 5 **watch it!** esp. spoken Be careful! 6 **watch one's step** esp. spoken to act with great care 7 **watch the clock** esp. spoken to be waiting for one's working day to end instead of thinking about one's work — ~er n

watch² n 1 a small clock to be worn or carried 2 one or more people ordered to watch: In spite of the watch set on the house, the thief escaped 3 any of the periods into which the night was once divided for policing duty: the watches of the night 4 (sailors who have to be on duty during) a period of 2 or 4 hours at sea 5 **keep a close/careful**

watch on to fix one's attention on, carefully **6 on the watch for** waiting for

watchdog *n* **1** a fierce dog kept to guard property **2** a person or group that tries to guard against undesirable practices: *a watchdog of public morals*

watchful *adj* careful to notice things — ~**ly** *adv* — ~**ness** *n*

watchman *n* **-men** a guard, esp. of a building

watchtower *n* a high tower from the top of which people can see what is coming a long way off

watchword *n* **1** a word or phrase used as a sign of recognition; a password **2** a word or phrase that expresses a principle; a slogan

water¹ *n* **1** the most common liquid, without colour, taste, or smell, which falls from the sky as rain, forms rivers, lakes, and seas, and is drunk by people and animals **2** a liquid like or containing this liquid, produced by some part of the body **3** the tide: *high/low water* **4 above water** *esp. spoken* out of difficulty (esp. in the phrase **keep one's head above water** (=keep out of difficulty)) **5 in/into deep water(s)** *esp. spoken* in/into trouble **6 in/into hot water** *esp. spoken* in/into trouble related to anger or punishment **7 like water** *esp. spoken* in great quantity and without considering the cost: *The wine flowed like water* **8 make/pass water** *polite* to urinate **9 hold water** to be true or reasonable: *Your story just doesn't hold water* **10 throw cold water on** *esp. spoken* to speak against; point out difficulties in **11 water on the brain/knee/etc.** liquid on the brain, knee, etc. as the result of disease —see also WATERS, TREAD **water**

water² *v* **1** to pour water on **2** to supply with water: *to water the horses* **3** (esp. of the eyes or mouth) to form or let out water **4** (esp. of rivers) to flow through and provide with water: *Colombia is watered by many rivers* —see also WATER DOWN

waterborne *adj* supported or carried by water: *waterborne trade/diseases*

water butt *n* a barrel for collecting rainwater from the roof

water cannon *n* an apparatus for forcing out a stream of water under high pressure

water closet *n* esp. written a WC

watercolour *n* **1** paint to be mixed with water, not oil —compare OILS **2** a picture painted in this way

watercourse *n* **1** a passage through which water flows **2** a stream of water

watercress *n* any of several kinds of hot-tasting plant grown in water and eaten raw

water down *v adv* **1** to weaken (a liquid) by adding water **2** to weaken the effect of: *His political statement has been watered down so as not to offend anyone*

watered silk *n* moiré

waterfall *n* water falling straight down over rocks

waterfront *n* land or a part of a town near a stretch of water, esp. when used as a port

water hen *n* a moorhen

waterhole *n* a small area of water in dry country, where animals drink

water ice *n* a frozen sweet made of fruit juice or flavoured and coloured water

watering can *n* a container from which water can be poured through a long spout

watering place *n* **1** a spa **2** a waterhole

water lily *n* **-ies** any of several types of flat-leaved water plant with large flowers, often seen floating on the surface of an ornamental pool

waterline *n* technical the position which the water reaches along a ship's side

waterlogged *adj* full of water, as of wet earth

waterloo *n* **-loos** an experience which crushes one after unusual success

water main *n* a large underground water pipe

waterman *n* **-men** a man who lives and works by water, esp. one who rows people in a boat

watermark *n* **1** a faint mark made on paper by the maker **2 high/low watermark** a mark showing the highest/lowest level reached by a river or the sea

water meadow *n* a field often flooded

watermelon *n* a large round melon with juicy red flesh and black seeds

watermill *n* a mill powered by moving water

water polo *n* a ball game played by 2 teams of swimmers

waterpower *n* the power from moving water used for electricity and/or to work machines

waterproof¹ *adj, n* (an outer garment) which does not allow water to go through

waterproof² *v* to make waterproof

water rate *n* (in Britain) the charge made to each house-owner for public water

waters *n* **1** sea near or belonging to the stated country: *Icelandic waters* **2** the water of the stated river, lake, etc.: *the waters of the Amazon* **3** spring water containing minerals supposed to be good for the health

watershed *n* the high land separating 2 river systems, from which each has its origin in many little streams

water skiing *n* the sport in which one travels over water on skis, pulled by a boat

water softener *n* a machine or chemical used for taking unwanted minerals out of water

water table *n* the level at and below which water can be found in the ground

watertight *adj* **1** through which no water can go **2** allowing of no mistakes: *a watertight argument*

water tower *n* a tower which gives height to a supply of water so that it can flow in pipes to all places lower than that

water vole also (esp. spoken) **water rat**— *n* a

small swimming animal which lives in holes near a river

waterwheel *n* a wheel turned by moving water, esp. to power machines

waterwings *n* a joined pair of winglike air-filled bags, worn under the arms to support a swimmer

waterworks *n* buildings, pipes, and supplies of water forming a public water system

watery *adj* 1 containing too much water 2 full of water 3 very pale: *a watery sun*

watt *n* (a standard measure of electrical power equal to) the amount produced when a voltage of one volt causes a current of one ampere to flow: *A kilowatt is 1000 watts*

wattage *n* power in watts of an electrical apparatus

wattle *n* 1 a mixture of thin sticks woven over thicker poles to form a fence or wall 2 the red flesh on the head or throat of some birds

wave¹ *v* **waved, waving** 1 to move in the air, backwards and forwards, up and down 2 to move one's hand as a signal, esp. in greeting 3 to lie, or cause to lie, in regular curves: *Her hair waves naturally*

wave² *n* 1 a raised curving line of water on the surface, esp. of the sea 2 the movement of the hand in waving 3 an evenly curved part of the hair 4 a suddenly rising and increasing feeling, way of behaviour, etc., passed on from person to person: *a wave of fear* —see also HEAT WAVE 5 a form in which some forms of energy move: *radio waves*

wave band *n* a set of waves of like lengths, esp. of radio waves

wavelength *n* 1 the distance between one energy wave and another 2 a radio signal sent out on radio waves a particular distance apart

waver *v* to be unsteady or uncertain — **waverer** *n* — **waveringly** *adv*

wavy *adj* **-ier, -iest** in the shape of waves; having regular curves — **waviness** *n*

wax¹ *n* a solid material made of fats or oils and changing to a thick liquid when melted —see also BEESWAX, REFINERY

wax² *v* to put wax on, esp. as a polish

wax³ *v* (esp. of the moon) to grow —see also WANE

waxen *adj* 1 made of wax 2 very pale

waxworks *n* **waxworks** wax models of human beings

waxy *adj* **-ier, -iest** like wax —see also WAXEN — **waxiness** *n*

way¹ *n* **ways** 1 a road or path: *a cycle way* 2 the right direction to follow: *Is this the way out?* 3 the distance to be travelled to reach a place: *a long way from home* 4 a method: *the right way of addressing the Queen* 5 **by way of a** by going through: *by way of London* **b** as a sort of: *by way of help* 6 **go out of one's way** to take the trouble 7 **have it both ways** to gain advantage from opposing opinions or actions 8 **mend one's ways** to improve one's behaviour 9 **out of the**

way unusual or not commonly known 10 **pay one's way** never to owe money 11 **set in one's ways** having very fixed habits 12 **to my way of thinking** in my opinion

waylay *v* **-laid, -laying** to stop (a person moving somewhere) for a purpose

way-out *adj sl* unusually good, strange, modern, etc.

ways *n* customs; habits

ways and means *n* methods of doing or obtaining something: *ways and means of getting money*

wayside *n* 1 the side of the road 2 **fall by the wayside** to fail and give up

wayward *adj* changeable in character and not easy to guide

WC also (*esp. written*) **water closet**— *n* a lavatory which is emptied by a flow of water from the pipes

we *pron* 1 (*pl. of* I) the people speaking: *We came together* 2 (used by a king or queen) I: *We are grateful to our people for their greetings*

weak *adj* 1 not strong enough to work or last properly: *a weak wall/ heart* 2 not strong in character 3 not well: *His legs felt weak* 4 containing mainly water: *weak soup* 5 (of a verb) forming the past in a regular way, with the usual endings: *Stepped is a weak form; swam and swum are strong* — ~**ly** *adv*

weaken *v* 1 to make or become weak 2 to become less determined: *She asked so many times that in the end we weakened and let her go*

weak-kneed *adj* habitually nervous; cowardly

weakling *n* a person lacking strength in body or character

weakness *n* 1 the state of being weak 2 a weak part or fault: *Drinking is his weakness* 3 a strong liking: *a weakness for chocolate*

weal *n* a welt on the skin

wealth *n* 1 a large amount of money and possessions 2 a large number: *a wealth of examples*

wealthy *adj* **-ier, -iest** rich — **wealthily** *adv*

wean *v* to accustom (a baby or young animal) to food instead of mother's milk

wean from *v prep* to cause (someone) to leave (an interest, habit, companion, etc.): *She tried to wean him away from football*

weapon *n* a tool for harming or killing ⊚ — ~**less** *adj* — ~**ry** *n*

wear¹ *v* **wore, worn, wearing** 1 to have (esp. clothes) on the body 2 to have (a look): *She wore an angry expression* 3 to reduce by continued use: *The noise wore her nerves to shreds* 4 to last: *Considering her age, she has worn well* 5 *esp. spoken* to find acceptable: *Fiji would be lovely for our holiday, but I don't think father will wear it* — ~**able** *adj*

wear² *n* 1 clothes of the stated type: *evening wear* 2 use or damage which reduces the material: *This mat has had a lot of wear* 3 the

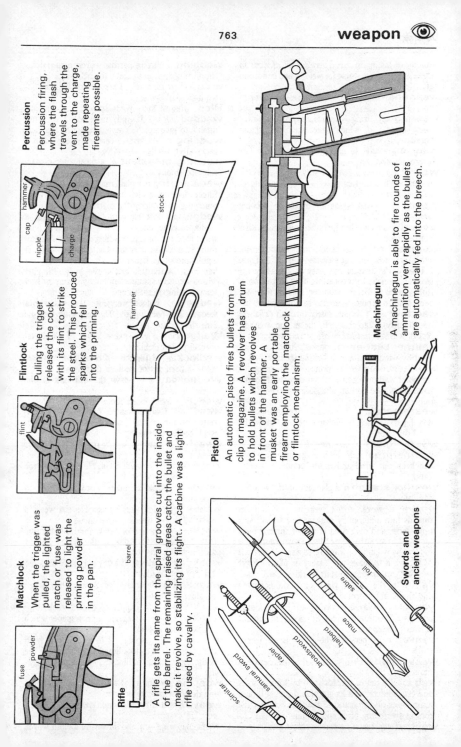

Matchlock

When the trigger was pulled, the lighted match or fuse was released to light the priming powder in the pan.

Flintlock

Pulling the trigger released the cock with its flint to strike the steel. This produced sparks which fell into the priming.

Percussion

Percussion firing, where the flash travels through the vent to the charge, made repeating firearms possible.

Rifle

A rifle gets its name from the spiral grooves cut into the inside of the barrel. The remaining raised areas catch the bullet and make it revolve, so stabilizing its flight. A carbine was a light rifle used by cavalry.

Pistol

An automatic pistol fires bullets from a clip or magazine. A revolver has a drum to hold bullets which revolves in front of the hammer. A musket was an early portable firearm employing the matchlock or flintlock mechanism.

Machinegun

A machinegun is able to fire rounds of ammunition very rapidly as the bullets are automatically fed into the breech.

Swords and ancient weapons

scimitar, samurai sword, rapier, broadsword, halberd, mace, sabre, foil

quality of lasting in use: *There's a lot of wear in these shoes* **4 the worse for wear** in bad condition after use

wear and tear *n* the damaging effects of ordinary use

wearing *adj* tiring —see also HARDWEARING

wearisome *adj* which makes one feel tired and bored

wear on *v adv* to pass slowly (in time): *The afternoon wore on*

weary¹ *adj* **-ier, -iest** **1** very tired **2** which makes one tired: *a weary day* — **wearily** *adv* — **weariness** *n*

weary² *v* **-ied, -ying** to make or become weary

weasel *n* a small thin furry fierce animal with a pointed face

weather¹ *n* **1** the condition of wind, rain, sunshine, snow, etc., at a certain time ☞ CLOUD **2 keep one's weather eye open** to be ready for trouble **3 make heavy weather of** to make (something) seem difficult **4 under the weather** not very well or happy —see also FAIR-WEATHER

weather² *v* **1** to pass safely through (a storm or difficulty) **2** to change by the air and weather: *Rocks weather until they are worn away*

weather-beaten *adj* marked, lined, or damaged by wind, sun, etc.: *a weather-beaten face*

weatherboard *n* **1** protective covering for the outer walls of a house **2** one or several boards fixed across the bottom of a door, to keep floods out

weathercock *n* a movable arrangement of metal parts which is blown round to show the wind direction

weatherglass *n* *now rare* a barometer

weatherproof *adj* (esp. of garments) which can keep out wind and rain —compare WATER-PROOF

weather station *n* a place for noting weather conditions

weave¹ *v* **wove, woven, weaving** **1** to form threads into material by drawing one thread at a time under and over a set of longer threads on a loom **2** to make by doing this: *to weave a mat* **3** to form by twisting or winding: *to weave a nest out of sticks* **4** to make up (a story or plan) **5 get weaving** *esp. spoken* to start working hard

weave² *n* the way in which a material is woven and the pattern formed by this

weave³ *v* **weaved, weaving** to move along, changing direction frequently: *weaving in and out between the cars*

weaver *n* a person whose job is to weave cloth

weaver bird *n* a tropical bird that makes woven nests

web *n* **1** a net of threads spun by some insects and esp. spiders **2** a length of material still on a loom —see also WEBBING **3** the skin between the toes of swimming birds and animals

webbed *adj* having a web: *webbed toes*

webbing *n* strong narrow woven material for supporting springs in seats, for belts, etc.

we'd *short form of* **1** we would: *We'd go* **2** we had: *We'd gone*

Wed *abbrev. for:* Wednesday

wedded *adj* **1** lawfully married **2** keen on; unable to give up: *He's very wedded to the idea*

wedding *n* a marriage ceremony, esp. with a party after a religious service

wedding breakfast *n* a meal after a marriage ceremony

wedding ring *n* a plain ring placed on the third finger of a person's left hand by the person who is marrying one, during the marriage ceremony

wedge¹ *n* **1** a piece of (esp.) wood with a V-shaped edge, one end thin and the other quite wide, used for making or filling a space **2** something shaped like this: *shoes with wedge heels* **3** a golf club with a heavy metal head for driving the ball high **4 the thin end of the wedge** the part which seems least important but will open the way for more important things

wedge² *v* **wedged, wedging** **1** to fix with a wedge **2** to pack tightly: *The people wedged me into the corner*

Wedgwood *n* *trademark* a type of usu. ornamental plate or china

wedlock *n* **1** the state of being lawfully married **2 born out of wedlock** illegitimate

Wednesday *n* **-days** the 4th day of the week

wee *adj* **weer, weest** *Scots* very small

weed¹ *n* **1** an unwanted wild plant **2** cigarettes or tobacco **3** *usu. offensive* a tall thin weak-bodied person

weed² *v* to remove weeds from: *to weed the garden*

weed out *v adv* to get rid of: *He weeded out the books he didn't want*

weeds *n* black garments worn as a sign of mourning

weedy *adj* **-ier, -iest** *esp. spoken* **1** weak in body **2** full of weeds — **weediness** *n*

week *n* **1** a period of 7 days (and nights), esp. from Sunday to Saturday **2** the period of time during which one works

weekday *n* **-days** **1** a day not at the weekend **2** a day not Sunday

weekend *n* Saturday and Sunday, esp. when considered a holiday

weekly¹ *adj, adv* happening once a week

weekly² *n* **-lies** a magazine or newspaper which appears once a week

weep *v* **wept, weeping** **1** to let fall tears from the eyes; cry **2** to lose liquid from a part of the body, esp. because of illness: *The wound is weeping*

weeping *adj* (of trees) with the branches hanging down: *a weeping willow*

weevil *n* a small beetle which spoils grain, seeds, etc. ☞ INSECT

weft also **woof**— *n* the threads of a cloth woven

across the downward set of threads —compare WARP

weigh v 1 to find the weight of, esp. by a machine 2 to have a certain weight: *I weigh less than I used to* 3 to consider carefully: *He weighed the ideas in his mind* 4 to be important: *Your suggestion does not weigh with me* 5 to raise (an anchor)

weighbridge n a machine onto which vehicles and their loads are driven to be weighed

weigh down v adv to make heavy: *weighed down with grief*

weigh in v adv 1 to test one's weight before a fight or race 2 to join in a fight or argument: *He weighed in with his own views*

weigh on v prep to cause worry to: *The lack of money weighed on his mind*

weigh out v adv to measure in amounts by weight

weight¹ n 1 heaviness: *She is losing weight* 2 technical the force with which a body is drawn towards the centre of the earth: *The weight of an object is related to the force of gravity, which is fixed, and to its mass* 3 a piece of metal of a standard heaviness: *a one-pound weight* 4 a heavy object for holding something down: *a paperweight* 5 a system of measures of weight: *metric weight* 6 value or importance: *a man of political weight* 7 a worry: *The loss of the money is a weight on my mind* 8 **pull one's weight** to join in work equally with others 9 **throw one's weight about** to give orders because one thinks oneself important

weight² v to add something heavy to: *Fishing nets are weighted*

weighted adj giving advantage: *tests weighted in favour of girls*

weighting adj something additional, esp. additional pay given because of the high cost of living

weightless adj having no weight, as when in space, when free from gravity: *a weightless flight* — **~ly** adv — **~ness** n

weight lifting n lifting weights for sports or exercise — **weight lifter** n

weighty adj -ier, -iest important: *weighty problems* — **weightily** adv — **weightiness** n

weir n 1 a wall across a river, stopping or controlling its flow 2 a wooden fence across a stream for catching fish

weird adj 1 strange; unnatural 2 esp. spoken not sensible or acceptable: *weird ideas* — **~ly** adv — **~ness** n

welch v to welsh

welcome¹ v -comed, -coming 1 to greet with pleasure (a person) when arriving in a new place 2 to receive (an idea): *They welcomed the idea with little interest*

welcome² adj 1 acceptable and wanted: *a welcome suggestion* 2 allowed freely: *You're welcome to try, but you won't succeed* 3 **You're welcome** (a polite expression when thanked for

something) 4 **make (someone) welcome** to receive (a guest) with friendliness

welcome³ n, interj a greeting to someone on arrival: *The crowd gave a joyful welcome to the home team.* | *'Welcome home!' said my father*

weld¹ v to join (usu. metals) by pressure or melting together when hot — **~er** n

weld² n the part joined in welding

welfare¹ n 1 well-being; comfort and happiness 2 government help for those in special need: *on welfare* —compare SUPPLEMENTARY BENEFIT

welfare² adj helping with living conditions, social difficulties, etc.: *the welfare officer*

welfare state n a country, or system, based on the principle that the economic welfare of every citizen is the collective responsibility of the community

welkin n poetic the sky

well¹ n 1 a place where water comes from underground 2 a such a place with walls leading down to the water b a hole through which oil is drawn from underground

well² v (of liquid) to flow: *Blood welled from the cut*

well³ adv better, best 1 in the right manner; satisfactorily: *well clothed* 2 to a high standard: *She paints very well* 3 thoroughly: *Wash it well* 4 much; quite: *He was well within the time* 5 with kindness or favour: *They speak well of him* 6 **as well** in addition; also 7 **do well out of** to gain profit from 8 **just as well** There's no harm done; There's no loss 9 **may well** could suitably: *You may well ask!* 10 **may as well** could with the same result: *You might as well ask for the moon as for a bicycle* 11 **pretty well** almost 12 **well out of** lucky enough to be free from: *It's lucky you left before the trouble; you were well out of it* 13 **well up in** well informed about

well⁴ interj 1 (an expression of surprise, doubt, acceptance, etc.): *She's got a new job. Well, well!* 2 (used when continuing a story): *Well, then she said...*

well⁵ adj better, best 1 in good health 2 right; acceptable: *All is well* 3 most suitable: *It would be just as well to let them know* 4 **It's all very well** (an expression of dissatisfaction): *It's all very well to say that, but what can I do?*

well-advised adj (of behaviour) sensible

well-appointed adj having all the necessary apparatus or furniture: *a well-appointed hotel*

well-balanced adj 1 (of people and characters) strong in the mind; sensible 2 (of meals) containing the right amounts of what is good for the body

wellbeing n personal and bodily comfort, esp. good health

well-bred adj well-behaved and polite

well-connected adj knowing people of power and importance socially, esp. being related to them

well-disposed adj favouring; showing kindness

well-done adj (of food, esp. meat) cooked for a

longer rather than shorter period —compare
RARE

well-favoured *adj old use* good-looking

well-founded *adj* based on facts: *well-founded suspicions*

well-groomed *adj* having a very neat clean appearance, as if special care has been taken

well-grounded *adj* **1** instructed fully **2** well-founded

well-informed *adj* knowing a lot about several subjects

wellington *n* a waterproof, usu. rubber, boot

well-intentioned *adj* acting in the hope of good results, though often failing: *a well-intentioned effort to help*

well-knit also **well-set**— *adj* strong and with good muscles

well-known *adj* known by many people —see FAMOUS (USAGE)

well-meaning *adj* well-intentioned

well-meant *adj* said or done for a good purpose, though not with a good result

well-nigh *adv* almost: *well-nigh impossible*

well-off *adj* **1** rich **2** lucky (esp. in the phrase **you don't know when you're well off**)

well-read *adj* well-informed through having read a lot

well-spoken *adj* using a socially acceptable variety of pronunciation, grammar, and vocabulary

well-timed *adj* said or done at the most suitable time

well-to-do *adj* rich

well-wisher *n* a person giving good wishes to another

well-worn *adj* (of phrases) with little meaning, because over-used

welsh, welch *v* **1** to avoid payment: *He welshed on his debts* **2** to break one's promise — ~**er** *n*

Welsh *adj* of Wales, its people, or their Celtic language ⫝̸ LANGUAGE

Welsh rarebit also **Welsh rabbit**— *n* melted cheese on toast often flavoured with beer, mustard, etc.

welt *n* **1** also **weal**— a raised mark on the skin as from a stroke of a whip **2** a piece of leather round the edge of a shoe to which the top and bottom are stitched

welter *n* a disordered mixture: *a welter of words*

welterweight *n, adj* (in boxing) a man weighing between 135 and 147 pounds

wench *n old use & dialect* a girl

wend *v* **wend one's way** *esp. in literature* to travel over a distance, esp. slowly

Wensleydale *n* a type of cheese made from cow's milk and originally from Yorkshire

went *past tense of* GO

wept *past tense and past part. of* WEEP

were *pl. and 2nd person sing. past tense of* BE: *You/We/They were happy*

werewolf *n* **-wolves** (in stories) a man who sometimes turns into a wolf

wert **thou wert** *old use*   (when talking to one person) you were

Wesleyan *n, adj* (a member) of the branch of the Protestant church established by John Wesley; Methodist

west¹ *adv* **1** towards the west **2 go west** to die or be damaged or broken

west² *n, adj* **1** (in the direction of) one of the 4 main points of the compass, which is on the left of a person facing north: *The sun sets in the west* ⫝̸ GLOBE **2** (of a wind) coming from this direction —compare WESTERLY

West *n* **1** the western part of the world, esp. western Europe and the United States —compare OCCIDENT **2** the part of a country which is further west than the rest **3** (in the US) the part of the country west of the Mississippi —see NORTH (USAGE)

westbound *adj* travelling or leading west: *a westbound ship* | *the westbound carriageway of the M4*

West End *n* the western part of central London, where the shops, theatres, etc., are

westerly *adj* **1** towards or in the west: *in a westerly direction* **2** (of a wind) coming from the west

western¹ *adj* of or belonging to the west: *the Western nations* —see NORTH (USAGE)

western² *n* a story, usu. on a film, about life in the US West in the past, esp. about cowboys, gunfights, etc.

westernize, -ise *v* **-ized, -izing** to cause (esp. African or Asian people) to copy the customs of America and Europe — **-ization** *n*

westernmost *adj* farthest west

West Indian *adj* of the West Indies: *West Indian cooking*

westward *adj* going towards the west: *in a westward direction* —compare WESTERLY

westwards *adv* towards the west: *They travelled westwards*

wet¹ *adj* **-tt-** **1** covered in liquid or not dry: *wet ground* | *wet paint* | *to get wet* **2** rainy: *wet weather* **3** *esp. spoken* lacking in strength of mind; weak: *Don't be so wet! Of course you can do it* — ~**ly** *adv* — ~**ness** *n*

wet² *n* rainy weather: *to go out in the wet*

wet³ *v* **wet** *or* **wetted, wetting** **1** to make wet **2 wet the bed** to pass water from the body in bed, because of a loss of control while asleep

wet blanket *n* a person who prevents others enjoying what they do

wet dream *n* an occasion during sleep when the penis pours out semen as in the sexual act, though the sleeper knows nothing of it at the time

wet nurse *n* a woman employed to give breast milk to another woman's baby

wet suit *n* a close-fitting suit which keeps underwater swimmers warm, though it lets some water through —compare CAT SUIT, LEOTARD

wetting agent *n* a chemical substance which makes a solid surface hold liquid

whack¹ also **thwack**— *v* to hit with a blow making a loud noise

whack² *n* **1** also **thwack**— (the noise made by) a hard blow **2** *esp. spoken* a fair share: *Have you all had your whack?* **3** *esp. spoken* a try; attempt

whacked *adj esp. spoken* very tired

whacker *n* a whopper

whacking¹ *adj esp. spoken* whopping

whacking² *n* a beating

whale *n* **1** any of several types of very large animals which live in the sea and look like fish, but are mammals, and therefore warm-blooded ☞ MAMMAL **2 a whale of a time** *esp. spoken* a very enjoyable experience

whalebone *n* a material taken from the upper jaw of whales, used esp. formerly for stiffening things

whaler *n* a man or ship that hunts whales

whaling *n* the hunting of whales and the treatment of them at sea to produce oil and other materials

wham *n esp. spoken* (the sound made by) a hard blow

wharf *n* **wharfs** or **wharves** a platform built along the edge of or out into the sea or river, where ships load and unload goods

what¹ *adj, pron* **1 a** which (thing or person)?: *What time will you come? | What are you doing?* **b** (used for having words repeated): '*I got up at half past 4.' 'What?'* **2** that which; a/the thing that: *I believed what he told me* **3 and what not** and other things: *sugar, tea, and what not* **4 give someone what for** *esp. spoken* to punish and/or scold someone **5 what have you** *esp. spoken* anything (else) like that: *In his pocket I found a handkerchief, string, and what have you* **6 what's what** the important things (in the phrase **know what's what**) **7 what it takes** *esp. spoken* the qualities necessary for success **8 what though** *literature* even if (used in comparing something bad with something better): *What though the battle be lost? We can fight again!*

what² *adj* (an exclamation showing surprise): *What a big house! | What pretty flowers!*

what³ *adv* **1** in what way?; to what degree?: *What do you care about it?* **2 what with** (used for introducing the causes of something): *What with the bad weather and the bad news, no wonder we're miserable!*

whatever¹ also (*literature*) **what·so·ev·er** — *adj, pron* **1** anything at all that: *They eat whatever they can find* **2** no matter what: *Whatever I said, he'd disagree*

whatever² *pron* **1** anything else like that: *bags, boxes, or whatever* —see also WHATNOT, WHAT **have you** **2** (showing surprise) what?: *Look at that strange animal! Whatever is it?* — see EVER (USAGE)

whatever³ also **whatsoever**— *adj* at all: *Have you any interest whatever?*

whatnot *n* **1** *esp. spoken* anything else: *carrying his bags and whatnot* **2** a piece of furniture with open shelves for showing ornaments

wheat *n* **1** a plant from whose grain flour is made **2** the grain from this plant

wheaten *adj* made from wheat

wheat germ *n* the centre of the wheat grain, containing much of the goodness and vitamins

wheedle *v* **-dled, -dling** to persuade by pleasant but insincere behaviour and words: *She wheedled him into going*

wheedle out *v adv* to obtain by wheedling: *I wheedled a promise out of her*

wheel¹ *v* **1** to push (a wheeled object or something on one): *He wheeled his bicycle into the street. | The mother wheeled the baby round the park* **2** to turn suddenly: *I called him and he wheeled to face me* **3** to fly round and round in circles: *gulls wheeling over the sea*

wheel² *n* **1** a circular object with an outer frame which turns around an inner part (HUB) to which it is joined, used for turning machinery, making vehicles move, etc. **2** the steering wheel of a car or ship **3 at the wheel** driving or steering —see also STEERING WHEEL **4 oil the wheels** to make matters go more smoothly **5 on wheels** by car: *meals on wheels* (= delivered to the homes of old people) **6 put one's shoulder to the wheel** to start work **7 wheels within wheels** hidden influences

wheelbarrow also **barrow**— *n* a movable container with one wheel at the front, 2 handles at the back, 2 legs, and a part in which things can be carried

wheelbase *n* the distance between the front and back axle on a vehicle

wheelchair *n* a wheeled chair in which a person who cannot walk can move himself or be pushed

wheeling *n* **wheeling and dealing** *esp. spoken* getting   what one wants by any methods, including unfair ones

wheelwright *n* (esp. in former times) a person who makes and repairs wheels

wheeze¹ *v* **wheezed, wheezing 1** (of people) to make a noisy whistling sound when breathing **2** (of objects) to make any sound like this — **-zy** *adj* : *a wheezy old man* — **-zily** *adv* — **-ziness** *n*

wheeze² *n* **1** the act or sound of wheezing **2** *sl* a joke, trick, or idea

whelk *n* a type of edible shellfish

whelp *n*, *v* (to give birth to) a young animal, esp. a dog or a doglike or catlike animal

when¹ *adv* **1** at what time?: *When will they come?* **2** (of time) at or on which: *the day when we met*

when² *conj* **1** at the time at which: *When I came home she was cooking dinner* **2** if: *No one can make a dress when they haven't learnt how* **3** although: *She stopped trying, when she might have succeeded next time* **4 hardly/scarcely**

when only just... when: *Hardly had I opened the door when he hit me*

when³ *pron* **1** what time?: *Since when has that been so?* **2** which time: *She wrote a month ago, since when we've heard nothing*

whence *adv* **1** old use from where?: *Whence come you?* **2** from which: *the bridge over the river Cam, whence came the name of the town of Cambridge* —compare WHITHER

whenever¹ *conj* **1** at any time at all that: *Come whenever you like* **2** every time: *Whenever we see him we speak to him*

whenever² *adv* **1** at any such time: *tonight, tomorrow, or whenever* **2** (showing surprise) when?: *Whenever did you find time to do it?* —see EVER (USAGE)

where¹ *adv* **1** at/to what place?: *Where will you go?* **2** (of place) at or to which: *the office where I work*

where² *conj* **1** at, to the place (at) which: *Keep him where you can see him* **2** whereas **3 where it's at** *sl* very good, esp. as being fashionable: *This party's really where it's at, man!*

whereabouts¹ *adv* (used when an exact answer is not expected) where?: *Whereabouts did I leave my bag?*

whereabouts² *n* the place a person or thing is in: *The escaped prisoner's whereabouts is/are still unknown*

whereas *conj* **1** (*used for introducing an opposite*) but: *They want a house, whereas we would rather live in a flat* **2** law (at the beginning of a sentence) since; because of the fact that

whereby *adv* esp. written **1** by means of which: *a system whereby a new discovery may arise* **2** according to which: *a law whereby all children are to receive cheap milk*

wherefore *adv, conj* old use **1** why? **2** for which reason

wherefores *n* see WHYS

wherein *adv, conj* **1** in what?: *Wherein lies the difficulty?* **2** in which: *the part wherein lies the fault*

whereupon *conj* at once after that: *He saw me coming, whereupon he offered me his seat*

wherever¹ *adv* **1** (showing surprise) where?: *Wherever did you get that idea?* **2** at any such place: *at home, at school, or wherever* —see EVER (USAGE)

wherever² *conj* at/to all places or any place: *Wherever you go, I go too*

wherewithal *n* the necessary means (to do something), esp. money: *I'd like a new car but I lack the wherewithal to pay for it*

wherry *n* -ries a small rowing boat

whet *v* -tt- **1** to sharpen: *He whetted his knife* **2 whet someone's appetite** (of a short experience) to make someone wish for more: *That first visit to Switzerland just whetted her appetite*

whether *conj* **1** if... or not: *He asked whether she was coming* **2** no matter if...: *I shall go, whether you come with me or stay at home*

whetstone *n* a stone for sharpening cutting tools

whey *n* the watery part of sour milk after the solid part has been removed —compare CURD

which *adj, pron* **1** (used when a choice is to be made) what (thing or person)?: *Which shoes shall I wear?* **2** being the one or ones that: *the book which I like best* **3** (used esp. in written language, with commas) and/because it/they, them: *Books, which you can change at the shop, make good presents* **4** (and) this: *He changed his mind, which made me very angry* **5 which is which?** what is the difference between the 2?

whichever *adj, pron* **1** any one that: *I'll give it to whichever of you wants it* **2** no matter which: *It has the same result, whichever way you do it* **3** (showing surprise) which: *Whichever did you choose?* —see EVER (USAGE)

whiff¹ *n* **1** a short-lasting smell **2** a breath in: *A few whiffs of this gas and she'll fall asleep*

whiff² *v* esp. spoken to smell bad — ~y *adj*

Whig *n, adj* (a member) of the Liberal party, a name used esp. in the last century but not in modern use

while¹ *n* **1** a space of time: *a long while* **2 once in a while** sometimes, but not often **3 worth one's while** worthwhile to one

while² also whilst— *conj* **1** during the time that: *While I was out he started to misbehave* **2** although; whereas: *You like sports, while I'd rather read*

while away, wile away *v adv* whiled, whiling away to pass (time) lazily: *to while away the hours*

whim *n* a sudden often unreasonable idea or wish

whimper *n, v* **1** (to make) a small weak cry: *The little dog whimpered when I tried to bath it* **2** (to make) a weak complaint

whimsical *adj* fanciful; with strange ideas — ~ly *adv*

whimsy, whimsey *n* -sies **1** strangeness in thought and behaviour, esp. making odd things seem humorous **2** a strange act or idea

whine¹ *v* whined, whining **1** to make a high sad sound: *The dog whined at the door* **2** to complain unnecessarily: *Stop whining, child!*

whine² *n* the sound of whining

whinny *v* -nied, -nying to make a gentle sound which horses make — **whinny** *n*

whip¹ *n* **1** a long piece of rope or leather fastened to a handle used for hitting animals or people **2** a Member of Parliament responsible for making other members attend **3** an order given to Members of Parliament to attend and vote **4** a sweet food made of beaten eggs and other foods whipped together

whip² *v* -pp- **1** to beat with a whip **2** to conquer; beat: *Ali really whipped Frazier* **3** to move quickly: *He whipped it into his pocket* **4** to beat until stiff (esp. cream or white of egg): *whipped cream* **6 a** to sew over (the edge of material) with a close stitch **b** to cover (the end of a stick or rope) closely with thread, string, etc. **7** to spin (a top) by means of a whip

whipcord *n* a strong type of cord

whip hand *n* control; power: *The new captain soon got the whip hand over the crew*

whiplash *n* **1** the blow from a whip **2** also **whiplash injury**— harm done to the body by the sudden violent movement of the head and neck, as in an accident

whippersnapper *n* a young important person who says and does too much

whippet *n* a small thin racing dog like a greyhound

whipping boy *n* **-boys 1** a child who, in former times, was educated with and punished instead of a noble's son **2** anyone who gets the blame —see also SCAPEGOAT

whippy *adj* **-pier, -piest** (of a rod, stem, etc.) which bends or springs back easily

whip-round *n* a quickly arranged collection of money among a group of people

whip up *v adv* **1** to cause (feelings) to rise: *to whip up interest* **2** to make quickly: *to whip up a meal*

whirl¹ *v* **1** to move round and round very fast **2** to move away in a hurry: *The car whirled them off to the wedding*

whirl² *n* **1** the act or sensation of whirling: *My head's in a whirl* **2** very fast confused movement: *a whirl of activity* **3** give something a whirl *esp. spoken* to try something

whirlpool *n* a circular current of water in a sea or river, which can draw objects into it

whirlwind *n* a tall pipe-shaped body of air moving rapidly in a circle —see TYPHOON (USAGE)

whirr *n*, *v* (to make) a regular sound of something beating against the air: *the whirring of the machinery*

whisk¹ *n* **1** a quick movement, esp. to brush something off: *with a whisk of his hand* **2** a small brush consisting of a bunch of feathers, hair, etc., tied to a handle: *a flywhisk* **3** a small hand-held apparatus for beating eggs, whipping cream, etc.

whisk² *v* **1** to move (something) quickly, esp. so as to brush something off: *The horse was whisking its tail* **2** to remove suddenly: *She whisked the cups away* **3** to beat (esp. eggs), esp. with a whisk

whisker *n* one of the long stiff hairs near the mouth of a cat, rat, etc.

whiskers *n* hair allowed to grow on the sides of a man's face, not meeting at the chin

whisky *n* **-kies** strong alcoholic drink made from grain, produced esp. in Scotland

whisper¹ *v* **1** to speak with noisy breath, but not much of the voice: *'Listen!' she whispered* **2** to make a soft sound: *the wind whispering in the roof* **3** to tell (a secret) widely: *His adventures have been whispered everywhere* — ~er *n*

whisper² *n* **1** whispered words: *She said it in a whisper* **2** a soft windy sound **3** a rumour

whist *n* any of several card games in which one suit is made trumps

whist drive *n* a meeting to play whist between several pairs of partners who change opponents

whistle¹ *n* **1** a simple musical instrument for making a high sound by passing air or steam through **2** the high sound made by passing air or steam through an instrument, a mouth, or a beak: *gave a loud whistle of surprise* **3 wet one's whistle** *humour* to drink (esp. alcohol)

whistle² *v* **-tled, -tling 1** to make the sound of a whistle **2** to produce (music) by doing this: *He whistled 'God save the Queen'*

whistle up *v adv* to make from poor or scarce material: *whistle up some new ideas*

whit *n esp. written* a small amount: *not a whit of sense*

Whit *n* Whitsun

white¹ *adj* **1 a** of the colour of snow or milk: *white hair* —opposite **black b** pale: *white wine* **2** (of a person) of a pale-skinned race **3** (of coffee) with milk or cream —opposite **black** — ~ness *n*

white² *n* **1** the colour that is white: *dressed in white* **2** a person of a pale-skinned race **3** the white part of the eye **4** the part of an egg which is white after cooking

whitebait *n* very small young edible fish of several types

white blood cell also **white corpuscle**— *n* one of the cells in the blood which fight infection (not the ones which carry oxygen) —compare RED BLOOD CELL

white-collar *adj* of office workers: *a white-collar job*

white dwarf *n technical* a hot star, near the end of its life, more solid but less bright than the sun —compare RED GIANT

white elephant *n* a usu. big object not useful to its owner, which he wants to get rid of

white ensign *n* the flag used by the British navy —compare RED ENSIGN

white feather *n* (a sign of) unwillingness to fight

white flag *n* a sign that one accepts defeat

Whitehall *n* **1** the London street (near) where British government offices stand **2** the British government departments: *What action have Whitehall taken on this matter?*

white heat *n* the temperature at which a metal turns white (when it becomes **white-hot** instead of **red-hot**)

white hope *n* the person who will bring great success: *our great white hope for the future*

White House *n* the official home in Washington of the President of the United States

white lead *n* a poisonous compound of lead with carbon and oxygen, formerly used in paint

white lie *n* a lie told so as not to hurt someone, and therefore not thought of as bad

white magic *n* magic used for good purposes

white man *n* **-men** a member of the European race which has a pale skin

white meat *n* pale meat such as chicken breast, veal, and pork

whiten *v* to make or become white

whitening also **whiting**— *n* white material used for giving a clean white colour: *to put whitening on tennis shoes*

white paper *n* an official report from the British government on a subject

white pepper *n* pepper made from seeds from which the dark outer covering has been removed

white sauce *n* a thick white liquid cooked with flour, used on or in certain types of food

white slavery *n* the business of taking girls abroad and forcing them to be prostitutes (**white slaves**) there

white spirit *n* a strong liquid made from petrol, used for thinning paint and cleaning clothes

white tie *n* **1** a small bow tie worn as part of men's formal clothing for social occasions **2** the set of such formal clothing: *a white-tie affair*

whitewash¹ *n, v* **1** (to cover with) a white liquid mixture made from lime, used for covering walls: *whitewashing farm buildings* **2** (to make) an attempt to hide something wrong: *What he said was just to whitewash the politician's actions*

whither *adv poetic* **1** to what place?: *Whither are you going?* — compare WHENCE **2** (esp. in newspapers, political language, etc.) What is the likely future of?: *Whither France?*

whiting¹ *n* **-ting** or **-tings** a type of edible sea fish

whiting² *n* whitening

Whitsun also **Whit**— *n* **1** also **Whit Sunday**— the 7th Sunday after Easter **2** also **Whitsuntide**— the public holiday including this Sunday

whittle *v* **-tled, -tling** to cut (wood) to a smaller size by taking off small thin pieces — ~**r** *n*

whiz, whizz *v* **-zz-** *esp. spoken* to move very fast, often with a noisy sound: *Cars were whizzing past*

whiz kid *n sl* a clever person who moves ahead in life and business very fast

who *pron* **1** what person or people?: *Who's at the door?* **2** that one person/those ones: *a man who wants to see you* **3** (*used esp. in written language, with commas*) and/but he, she, etc.: *George, who lives in Scotland, came late* —see also WHOM USAGE **Who** is used as an object pronoun in *spoken* English, except directly after a preposition: **Who** *did you see?* | *I wonder* **who** *he met?* ; but NOT *I wonder to* **who** *he's talkng.*

WHO *abbrev. for:* the World Health Organization

whoa *interj* (a call to a horse to) stop

who'd *short form of* **1** who had **2** who would

whodunit *n esp. spoken* a detective story

whoever *pron* **1** anybody that: *I'll take whoever wants to go* **2** no matter who: *The business would be a success, whoever owned it* **3** (*showing surprise*) who?: *Whoever can that be?* —see EVER (USAGE)

whole¹ *adj* **1** not spoilt or divided: *a whole cake* **2** all (the): *the whole truth* **3** **swallow something whole** to accept something without thinking

whole² *n* **1** the complete amount, thing, etc.: *the whole of that area* **2** the sum of the parts: *2 halves make a whole* **3** **on the whole** generally; mostly

whole-hearted also **full-hearted**— *adj* with all one's ability, interest, sincerity, etc. —compare HALF-HEARTED — ~**ly** *adv*

wholemeal also **whole wheat**— *adj* containing all the grain, from which flour is made: *wholemeal bread*

whole number *n* an integer

wholesale¹ *n* the business of selling goods in large quantities, esp. to shopkeepers —compare RETAIL — ~**r** *n*

wholesale² *adj, adv* **1** of or concerned in selling in large quantities or at the lower prices fixed for such sales: *They sell machines wholesale* **2** in unlimited numbers: *a wholesale rush from the burning cinema*

wholesome *adj* good for people; with no bad effects: *wholesome food* — ~**ness** *n*

wholly *adv* completely

whom *pron* (*object form of* WHO): *the man with whom he talked* —see THAT, WHO (USAGE)

whoop *v, n* **1** (to make) a loud shout (of joy) **2** (to give) a noisy breathless cough typical of whooping cough

whoopee¹ *interj* a cry of joy

whoopee² *n* **make whoopee** *esp. spoken* to go out enjoying oneself

whooping cough *n* a disease in which each attack of coughing is followed by a long noisy drawing in of the breath

whoosh *n* a soft sound, as of air rushing out

whop *v* **-pp-** *sl* to beat or defeat

whopper also **whacker**— *n esp. spoken* **1** a big thing **2** a big lie: *told a real whopper*

whopping also **whacking**— *adj esp. spoken* very big

whore *n* a prostitute

whorl *n* **1** a ring, esp. of leaves on a stem **2** the shape a line makes when going round in a circle and continuing outward from the centre esp. in some fingerprints or in the growth of some seashells ⟶ MATHEMATICS

who's *short form of* **1** who is **2** who has

whose *adj, pron* **1** of whom?: *Whose house is this?* **2 a** of whom: *the man whose house was burned down* **b** of which: *a factory whose workers are all women* USAGE Some people think it is bad English to use **whose** to mean 'of which'.

whosoever also **whoso**— *pron* whoever

why¹ *adv* for what reason?: *Why did you do it?*

why² *conj* the reason for which: *I don't see why it shouldn't work*

whys n the whys and wherefores (of) the reasons and explanation (for)

wick n 1 a piece of twisted thread in a candle, which burns as the wax melts 2 a tubelike piece of material in an oil lamp which draws up oil while burning

wicked adj very bad; evil: *wicked cruelty* | *a wicked man* — ~ly adv — ~ness n   USAGE This is a very strong word, for real moral evil. Noisy disobedient children are usually called not **wicked**, but **naughty**.

wicker n wickerwork: *a wicker basket*

wickerwork n, adj (objects) produced by weaving twigs, reeds, etc.: *wickerwork furniture*

wicket n 1 (in cricket) a either of 2 sets of 3 stumps, with 2 small pieces of wood (BAILS) on top, at which the ball is bowled b also **pitch**— the stretch of grass between these 2 sets 2 (in cricket) one turn of a player to bat: *England have lost 3 wickets* (= 3 of their players are out) 3 also **wicket gate** — a small gate or door which is part of a larger one

wicket keeper n (in cricket) a player who stands behind the wicket to catch the ball

wide¹ adj 1 large from side to side: *The skirt's too wide.* | *4 inches wide* 2 covering a large range: *wide interests* 3 sl clever in cheating: *a wide boy* 4 **wide of the mark** not suitable, correct, etc., at all: *What he told me was quite wide of the mark* — ~ly adv

wide² adv completely (open): *wide-eyed with amazement*

wide³ n (in cricket) a ball bowled too far to the right or left of the wicket

wide-angle adj (of the lens in a camera) able to give a view of a wider angle than the ordinary lens

wide-awake adj 1 fully awake 2 having fully active senses; alert

widen v to make wider

widespread adj found in many places: *a widespread disease*

widgeon n -geon or -geons a kind of duck which lives on freshwater lakes and pools

widow n a woman whose husband has died, and who has not married again — ~hood n

widowed adj left alone after the death of one's husband/wife

widower n a man whose wife has died, and who has not married again

width n 1 size from side to side 2 a piece of material of the full width, as it was woven

wield v to control the action of: *to wield power* | *(old use) to wield a weapon* — ~er n

wife n **wives** the woman to whom a man is married ☞ FAMILY

wig n an arrangement of false hair to cover the head —see also BIGWIG

wigging n sl a severe scolding

wiggle v, n -gled, -gling (to repeatedly move in) a small side to side, up and down, or turning movement: *to wiggle one's toes* — -gler n

wigwam n a tent of the type used by some North American Indians

wilco interj (used esp. on a 2-way radio, to say that a message has been understood and will be acted upon)

wild¹ adj 1 usu. living in natural conditions and having natural qualities not produced by man, esp. (in animals) violence; not tame or cultivated: *a wild elephant* | *wild flowers* 2 a not civilized; savage: *wild tribes* b disordered in appearance or behaviour: *a wild party* 3 (of places) natural; without the presence of man 4 (of natural forces) violent; strong: *a wild wind* 5 having strong feelings: *I felt so wild when she hit the baby.* | *He was wild about racing cars* 6 without (much) thought or control: *a wild idea* | *a wild guess* 7 (of a playing card in certain games) able to be used, to represent any card in the pack — ~ly adv — ~ness n

wild² n natural areas full of animals and plants, with few people: *lost in the wilds of an unknown country*

wild³ adv 1 wildly 2 **run wild** to behave without control 3 **go wild** to be filled with anger or joy: *They went wild over his good looks*

wild boar n a type of large fierce hairy European wild pig

wildcat¹ n a very fierce naturally wild type of cat

wildcat² adj 1 (in business) unlikely to succeed; risky: *wildcat schemes* 2 (in industry) happening unofficially and unexpectedly: *wildcat strikes*

wildebeest n -beest or -beests a gnu

wilderness n an area of land with little life and no sign of human presence

wildfire n **like wildfire** very fast

wildfowl n birds shot for sport, esp. ones that live near water such as ducks

wild-goose chase n a useless search

wildlife n animals and plants which live and grow wild

wild oats n **sow one's wild oats** to behave wildly while young

wile away v adv **wiled, wiling away** WHILE AWAY

wiles n tricks; deceitful persuasion

wilful adj 1 doing what one likes, in spite of other people: *a wilful child* 2 done on purpose: *wilful misbehaviour* — ~ly adv — ~ness n

will¹ v **would**, present short form **-'ll**, negative short form **won't** 1 (expressing the simple future tense): *They say that it will rain* 2 a to be willing to: *Will you come now?* b (expressing a polite request or question): *Will you have some tea?* 3 a is/are/proved or expected to: *These things will happen.* | *Oil will float on water* b is/are able to: *This car will hold 6 people* 4 may likely (be): *That's your knife, so this will be mine* —see also WOULD —see SHALL (USAGE)

will² n 1 the power in the mind to choose one's actions: *Free will makes us able to choose our way of life* 2 intention to make things happen: *the will* *to live* **3** what is wished: *to do God's will* **4** the wishes of a person in regard to sharing his property among other people after his death, esp. in an official written form: *Have you made your will yet?*

will³ *v* **1** *old use* to wish **2** to try to make happen by power of the mind: *We willed him to stop, but he went past* **3** to leave (possessions) in a will: *Grandfather willed me his watch*

willies *n* esp. *spoken* nervous fear: *The way he speaks gives me the willies*

willing *adj* eager; ready: *willing to help* — ~ **ly** *adv* — ~ **ness** *n*

will-o'-the-wisp *n* **1** a bluish moving light produced by burning gases from decayed plants **2** an undependable person or aim: *chasing the will-o'-the-wisp of perfection*

willow *n* a tree which often grows near water, or its wood

willow pattern *n* a set of pictures painted in blue on china

willowy *adj* pleasantly thin and graceful: *a willowy figure*

willpower *n* strength of will

willy-nilly *adv* regardless of whether wanted or not

wilt¹ *v* **1** (of a plant) to become less fresh and start to die: *The flowers are wilting for lack of water* **2** (of a person) to become tired and weaker: *I'm wilting in this heat*

wilt² thou wilt *old use* (when talking to one person) you will

wily *adj* -ier, -iest clever in tricks: *a wily fox* —see also WILES

wimple *n* a covering of cloth over the head and round the neck, formerly worn by women in the Middle Ages, and now by some nuns

win¹ *v* won, winning **1** to be the best or first in (a struggle, competition, or race) **2** to get as the result of success in a competition, race, or game of chance: *He won a prize* **3** to guess successfully (the result of a race or game of chance): *to win at cards* **4** win the day to succeed —see also WIN THROUGH

win² *n* (esp. in sport) a victory or success

wince¹ *v* winced, wincing to move suddenly, as if drawing away from something unpleasant: *She winced as she touched the cold body*

wince² *n* a wincing movement

winceyette *n* a fairly light soft material, used esp. for night clothes —compare FLANNELETTE

winch¹ *n* a machine for pulling up objects by means of a turning part —compare CAPSTAN

winch² *v* to pull by a winch: *winched the car out of the ditch*

wind¹ *n* **1** moving air: *heavy winds* —compare BREEZE **2** breath or breathing: *He couldn't get his wind* **3** air or gas in the stomach **4** wind instrument players: *The wind are playing too loud* **5** break wind *polite* to pass air or gas from the bowel **6** put/get the wind up esp. *spoken* to make/become afraid or anxious **7** (sail) close to the wind to be near to dishonesty or improper

behaviour **8** second wind steady breathing regained during hard exercise —see also take the wind out of someone's SAILS

wind² *v* winded, winding to make breathless: *He hit him in the stomach and winded him*

wind³ *v* wound, winding **1** to turn round and round: *to wind the handle* **2** to follow a twisting direction: *The path winds through the woods* **3** to tighten the working parts of by turning: *to wind a clock* **4** wound up very excited —see also WIND UP

wind⁴ *n* a bend or turn

windbag *n* esp. *spoken* a person who talks too much

windbreak *n* a wall, line of trees, etc., to prevent the wind coming through

windcheater *n* a short coat, tight at the wrists and neck, to keep out the wind —see also ANORAK, PARKA

windfall *n* **1** a fruit fallen from a tree **2** an unexpected lucky gift: *a windfall of $100*

windily *adv* see WINDY

winding sheet *n* a shroud

wind instrument *n* any musical instrument played by blowing air through it

windjammer *n* **1** a large sailing ship **2** a windcheater

windlass *n* a machine that moves objects by means of a turning part, often with a handle —compare WINCH

windmill *n* **1** a building containing a machine that crushes corn into flour and is driven by large sails turned round by the wind **2** a toy consisting of a stick with usu. 4 small curved pieces at the end which turn round when blown

window *n* a space in a wall to let in light and air, esp. of glass which can be opened

window box *n* a box of earth in which plants can be grown outside a window

window dressing *n* **1** the arranging of goods in a shop window **2** something intended to give an effect or to disguise a lack

windowsill *n* the flat shelf below a window, inside or outside

windpipe *n* the air passage from the throat to the top of the lungs ☞ RESPIRATION

windscreen *n* the front window of a car

windscreen wiper *n* a movable arm which clears rain from a windscreen

windshield *n* the piece of transparent material at the front of a motorcycle

windsock also **windsleeve**— *n* a piece of tube-shaped material, closed at one end, fastened to a pole at airports to show wind direction

windswept *adj* **1** (of country) open to the wind **2** blown into an untidy state: *a windswept appearance*

wind tunnel *n* a manmade tunnel through which air is forced to test aircraft

wind up *v adv* wound, winding up **1** to bring to an end: *to wind up a company* **2** esp. *spoken* to put oneself in a certain state or place, accidentally: *He wound up drunk* —see also WIND

windward¹ *adv, adj* into the direction of the wind —compare LEEWARD

windward² *n* the direction from which the wind blows

windy *adj* **-ier, -iest** **1** with a lot of wind: *windy weather* **2** *sl* afraid — **windily** *adv* — **windiness** *n*

wine *n* alcoholic drink made from grapes or other fruit, plants, etc.

wine and dine *v* to have or give a meal and wine

wineglass *n* a glass, usu. rounded with a stem and base, to hold wine

winepress *n* a vat in which the juice is pressed out of grapes, to make wine

wing¹ *n* **1** one of the 2 feathered limbs by which a bird flies, or a limb of flight on an insect ☞ BIRD **2** one of the parts of a plane which support it in flight **3** any part which stands out from the side: *the west wing of the house* **4** a group of 3 squadrons in an airforce **5** (in sport) the position or player on the far right or left of the field **6** an extreme group in a political party: *the right wing of the Labour party* **7 under someone's wing** being protected, helped, etc., by someone — **~less** *adj*

wing² *v* **1** to fly **2** to wound in the arm or wing

wing commander *n* an officer of middle rank in the Royal Air Force

winger *n* (in games like football) a player on the far left or right of the field

wing nut also **butterfly nut**— *n* a nut with sides which one can hold while turning it

wings *n* **1** a pilot's badge, to show he can fly an aircraft **2** the sides of a stage, where an actor is hidden from view

wingspan also **wingspread**— *n* the distance from the end of one outstretched wing to the end of the other

wink¹ *v* to close and open (one eye) rapidly, usu. as a signal

wink² *n* **1** a winking movement **2** (used of sleep) a short time: *I didn't sleep a wink*

winker *n* a car indicator

winkle also **periwinkle**— *n* a type of small edible shellfish

winkle out *v adv* **-kled, -kling out** *esp. spoken* to get by force or hard work: *At last I winkled the truth out of him*

winner *n* a person, animal, or idea that has won or is thought likely to win : *That idea's a real winner*

winnings *n* money which has been won

winnow *v* **1** to blow the husks from (grain) **2** *Bible* to separate the (good from the bad)

win over also **win round**— *v adv* to gain the support of (someone), often by persuading

winsome *adj* nice-looking; attractive; bright — **~ly** *adv* — **~ness** *n*

winter¹ *n* the cold season between autumn and spring — **-try, ~y** *adj*

winter² *v* to spend the winter: *to winter in a warm country*

winter garden *n* an enclosed glass place where plants are grown in winter, and where people may sit, esp. a large hotel room or public hall used for concerts and other amusements

winter sports *n* sports on snow or ice

win through also **win out**— *v adv* to succeed, esp. after some time or difficulties

wipe¹ *v* **wiped, wiping** to pass something against (something) to remove dirt, liquid, etc.: *Wipe your feet*

wipe² *n* a wiping movement: *Give your nose a wipe*

wipe out *v adv* to destroy all of: *The enemy wiped out the whole nation*

wire¹ *n* **1** a thin metal thread **2** *esp. spoken* a telegram

wire² *v* **wired, wiring** **1** to connect up wires in (something), esp. in an electrical system: *to wire a house* **2** to fasten with wire **3** to send a telegram to

wireless¹ *n* **1** radio **2** a radio set **3** radio broadcasts

wire netting *n* wires woven into a network, with quite large spaces between them

wire wool *n* material made of a mass of fine sharp-edged steel threads, used for smoothing or cleaning metal surfaces

wireworm *n* any of several types of wormlike insect larvae which destroy plants by eating them

wiring *n* the wired electrical system in a building

wiry *adj* **-ier, -iest** rather thin, with strong muscles — **wiriness** *n*

wisdom *n* being wise

wisdom tooth *n* **-teeth** one of the 4 large back teeth in man, which appear in adulthood

wise *adj* **1** sensible, clever, and able to understand **2 get wise to** *sl* to learn to understand the tricks of — **~ly** *adv*

wisecrack *v, n* *esp. spoken* (to make) a joking remark

wise guy also **wiseacre**— *n* **-guys** *esp. spoken* a person who thinks he knows more than others

wish¹ *v* **1** to want (what is at present impossible): *I wish we had a cat* **2** to try to cause a particular thing by magic: *Go to the well and wish* **3** to want (something or someone) to be or to have: *We wish you a merry Christmas* **4** *polite* to want: *Do you wish to eat alone?* USAGE It is better to use *were* after **wish** when writing sentences like *I wish I were a cat*, although this is becoming unusual in speech. Americans always use *were* in these sentences.

wish² *n* **1** a feeling of wanting: *a wish to see the world* **2** an attempt to make a particular thing happen by magic **3** what is wished for

wishbone *n* a V-shaped bone in a cooked chicken or other poultry

wishful thinking *n* making oneself believe that something longed for is true or will happen

wishy-washy *adj* **-washier, -washiest** weak: *wishy-washy tea*

wisp *n* a small twisted piece of hay, hair, smoke, etc. — ~**y** *adj*

wisteria *n* any of several kinds of climbing plant with purple or white flowers

wistful *adj* having thoughts of past happiness or impossible wishes — ~**ly** *adv* — ~**ness** *n*

wit¹ *v* to wit *esp. law* that is (to say)

wit² *n* **1** power of thought; intelligence : *He had the wit to say no* **2** (a person who has) the ability to say clever amusing things — ~**ty** *adj* — ~**tily** *adv* — ~**tiness** *n*

witch *n* a woman who has magic powers, esp. who can cast spells on people —compare WARLOCK, WIZARD — ~**ery** *n*

witchcraft *n* the practice of magic

witchdoctor *n* a man in an undeveloped society who is believed to have magical powers; medicine man

witch-hunt *n* **1** (in former times) an act of finding and killing witches **2** a search for people with disliked political views, so that they may be removed from their jobs — **witch-hunting** *n*

with *prep* **1** in the presence of; beside, near, among, or including: *staying with a friend | with his dog* **2** having: *a book with a green cover* **3** by means of; using: *to eat with a spoon* **4** in the same direction as: *to sail with the wind* **5** against: *Don't fight with your brother* **6** concerning; in the case of: *Be careful with the baby* **7** because of: *wild with excitement*

withdraw *v* **-drew, -drawn, -drawing** **1** to take away or out: *to withdraw $5 from a bank account | He withdrew his horse from the race* **2** to move away or back: *The army withdrew* **3** to take back (a remark): *I withdraw that point* — ~**al** *n*

withdrawal symptom *n* a painful feeling of lacking something (esp. drugs) which one has become used to

withdrawn *adj* habitually quiet; concerned with one's own thoughts

wither *v* **1** to become reduced in size, colour, etc.: *The flowers withered in the cold* —compare WILT **2** to crush or humiliate by a look or remark: *One look withered her opponent* — ~**ing** *adj* — ~**ingly** *adv*

withers *n* the high part above a horse's shoulders ☞ HORSE

withhold *v* **-held, -holding** to keep back on purpose: *to withhold the money*

within *adv, prep* inside; not beyond or more than

without *adv, prep* **1 a** not having; lacking: *to go out without a coat* **b** not: *He left without telling me* **2** *old use* outside: *The King waits without* —opposite **within**

withstand *v* **-stood, -standing** to oppose or resist without yielding: *to withstand an attack | Children's furniture must withstand kicks and blows*

witless *adj* lacking in ability to think — ~**ly** *adv* — ~**ness** *n*

witness¹ *n* **1** also **eyewitness**— a person who is present when something happens: *a witness of the accident* **2** a person who tells in a court of law what he saw or knows **3** a person who is present at the writing of an official paper, and who signs it **4** what is said about an event, person, etc., esp. in court

witness² *v* **1** to be present and notice: *We witnessed a strange change in her* **2** to be a witness of (an official paper) **3** to be a sign of: *His tears witnessed the shame he felt*

witness box *n* the raised area where witnesses stand in court

witticism *n* a witty remark

wives *pl. of* WIFE

wizard *n* **1** (esp. in stories) a man who has magic powers, esp. to cast spells —compare WITCH **2** a person with unusual abilities: *He's a wizard at playing the piano* — ~**ry** *n*

wizened *adj* dried up and wrinkled

wk *abbrev. for:* week

woad *n* a blue dye, esp. used in former times for colouring the body

wobble¹ *v* **-bled, -bling** to move unsteadily from one direction to another

wobble² *n* a wobbling movement — **wobbly** *adj*

woe *n* **1** great sorrow **2** a trouble: *all her woe*

woebegone *adj* very sad in appearance

woeful *adj* **1** very unhappy **2** regrettable: *a woeful lack of understanding* — ~**ly** *adv*

woke *past tense of* WAKE

woken *past part. of* WAKE

wold *n* an area of hilly open country

wolf¹ *n* **wolves** **1** a wild animal of the dog family which hunts in a pack **2** a man who charms women to seduce them **3** **cry wolf** to call for help unnecessarily **4** **keep the wolf from the door** to earn enough to eat and live — ~**ish** *adj*

wolf² *v* to eat quickly, in large amounts: *wolfed his meal*

wolf whistle *n* a double-note whistle to show admiration of a woman

woman *n* **women** **1** a fully grown human female **2** women in general: *Woman lives longer than man in most countries* **3** a man's wife or lover — ~**ly** *adj* —see PEOPLE (USAGE)

womanhood *n* the condition or time of being a woman

womanish *adj usu. offensive* (of a man) like a woman in character, behaviour, appearance, etc. —compare MANNISH, EFFEMINATE

womanize, -ise *v* **-ized, -izing** to spend a lot of time trying to seduce women — ~**r** *n*

womankind *n* women considered together —compare MANKIND

womb *n* the female sex organ of a mammal where her young develop ☞ EMBRYO, REPRODUCTION

wombat *n* a type of smallish bearlike Australian animal (MARSUPIAL) with soft hair ☞ MAMMAL

won *past tense and past part. of* WIN

wonder¹ *n* **1** a feeling of strangeness usu. combined with admiration and curiosity: *filled with wonder at the sight of the great new aircraft* **2** a wonderful act, object, or person **3 It's a wonder** It's surprising: *It's a wonder you recognized me* **4 (It's) no wonder** naturally; of course

wonder² *v* **1** to be surprised: *I wonder at his rudeness* **2** to wish to know: *wondering how to do it* — ~**ingly** *adv*

wonderful *adj* unusually good: *wonderful news* — ~**ly** *adv*

wonderland *n* **1** fairyland **2** a place which is unusually beautiful, rich, etc.

wonderment *n* surprise

wondrous *adj poetic* wonderful

wonky *adj* -**kier, -kiest** *esp. spoken* not steady: *a wonky table*

wont *n esp. written* one's habit or custom: *He spoke for too long, as is his wont*

woo *v* **wooed, wooing** **1** *esp. old use* to try to persuade into love and marriage **2** to make efforts to gain the support of: *to woo the voters before an election* — ~**er** *n*

wood¹ *n* **1** the material of which trunks and branches of trees are made **2** a place where trees grow, smaller than a forest: *We went for a ride in the wood* **3** one of the set of 4 golf clubs with wooden heads used for driving a ball long distances —compare IRON

wood² *adj* wooden

woodblock *n* a piece of wood with a shape cut on it for printing

woodcock *n* -**cock** *or* -**cocks** a brown woodland game bird with a long thin beak

woodcraft *n* the skill of finding one's way in wooded country

woodcut *n* a picture or print, made by pressing down a piece of carved wood on dye or paint and then onto material or paper

wooded *adj* covered with trees: *wooded hills*

wooden *adj* **1** made of wood **2** stiff; unbending: *wooden movements* — ~**ly** *adv* — ~**ness** *n*

woodland *n* wooded country

woodlouse *n* -**lice** a very small insect-like animal with 14 legs which lives under wood, stones, etc.

woodpecker *n* any of several types of bird with a long beak, which make holes in trees and pull out insects

woodshed *n* a place for storing firewood

woodsman *n* -**men** a man who works with trees, protecting or felling them

woodwind *n* (the players of) the set of instruments in an orchestra, usu. wooden, which are played by blowing

woodwork *n* **1** the skill of making wooden objects **2** the objects produced **3** the parts of a house that are made of wood

woodworm *n* -**worm** *or* -**worms** the larva of certain beetles, which makes holes in wood

woody *adj* -**ier, -iest** **1** with woods: *a woody valley* **2** of wood: *plants with woody stems*

woof¹ *n technical* weft

woof² *n, interj esp. spoken* (a word describing the bark of a dog)

woofer *n* a loudspeaker giving out deep sounds

wool *n* **1** the soft thick hair of sheep and some goats **2** thread or cloth made from this —see also WORSTED **3** soft material from plants, such as cotton before it is spun: *cotton wool* — ~**len** *adj*

woolgather *v* **be woolgathering** to be absent-minded — ~**ing** *n*

woollens *n* garments made of wool, esp. knitted —see also WOOLLY

woolly¹ *adj* -**lier, -liest** **1** of or like wool: *woolly socks* **2** not clear in the mind: *woolly ideas* — -**liness** *n*

woolly² *n* -**lies** *esp. spoken* a garment made of wool, esp. knitted: *winter woollies*

woolsack *n* the seat on which the Lord Chancellor sits in the House of Lords

woozy *adj* -**zier, -ziest** *esp. spoken* dizzy

Worcester sauce *n* a dark strong-tasting sauce made from vinegar, spices, and soy

word¹ *n* **1** a sound or sounds which form a unit of meaning and can be used to express an idea: *Tell me in your own words* **2** the written representation of this **3** a short speech or conversation: *Can I have a word with you?* **4** news: *Word came of his success* **5** a number of units of information (e.g. 12, 32, or 64 bits) treated as a unit in a computer **6** a promise: *I give you my word I'll go* **7 eat one's words** to admit to having said something wrong —see also MAN **of his word**, WORDS — ~**less** *adj* — ~**lessly** *adv* — ~**lessness** *n*

word² *v* to express in words: *He worded the explanation well*

word blindness *n* dyslexia

word for word *adv* in the same words: *Tell me what she said, word for word* — **word-for-word** *adj*

wording *n* the words chosen to express something: *The wording of a business agreement should be exact*

word-perfect *adj* correct in repeating every word: *Her speech was word-perfect*

words *n* **have words** to argue angrily

wordy *adj* -**ier, -iest** using too many words: *a wordy explanation* — **wordily** *adv* — **wordiness** *n*

wore *past tense of* WEAR

work¹ *n* **1** activity which uses effort, esp. with a special purpose, not for amusement **2** a job or business: *My work is in medicine* **3** what is produced by work: *This mat is my own work* **4** *technical* force multiplied by distance **5** an object produced by writing, painting, etc.: *Shakespeare's works* —see also WORKS USAGE This is a general word that can be used of activities of the mind and of the body. Both **labour** and **toil** can be used instead, but both express the idea of tiring and unpleasant effort. —see JOB (USAGE)

work² v 1 to do an activity which uses effort, esp. as employment: *working in a factory* 2 (of a plan, machine, etc.) to be active in the proper way, without failing: *Your idea won't work* 3 to make (a person) work: *They work us too hard* 4 to make (a machine) work 5 to get through by effort: *He worked his way to the front* 6 to produce (an effect): *to work a change* 7 to shape with the hands: *to work clay* 8 to stitch: *a baby's dress worked by hand* 9 technical to ferment 10 **work to rule** to obey the rules of one's work exactly in such a way as to cause inconvenience —see also WORK OFF, WORK OUT, WORK OVER

workable adj 1 which can work or be worked 2 (of substances) which can be shaped with the hands: *workable clay* — ~**ness** n

workaday adj ordinary and dull

workbasket also **workbox**— n a small stiff container for small sewing objects

workbench n a hard surface for working on with tools

workbook n 1 a book which tells how something works —compare HANDBOOK, MANUAL 2 a book which gives information about a subject or guidance to the student

worked up adj very excited, esp. when worried

worker n 1 a person or animal which works 2 a person who works with his hands rather than his mind: *a factory worker*

work force n the people who work in factories and industry generally

workhorse n a very useful person or machine, esp. performing ordinary continuous jobs

workhouse n (in former times) a place for the old or unemployed poor to live

work-in n the taking-over of a place of work by workers

working adj 1 concerning or including work: *a working breakfast* 2 who works with the hands: *a working man* —see also WORKMAN 3 (of ideas) useful as a base for planning: *a working theory*

working class n, adj (of) the social class to which people belong who work with their hands

working party n -ties a committee which examines a particular point and reports what it finds

workings n 1 the way in which something works: *the workings of an engine* 2 the parts of a mine which have been dug out

workman n -men a man who works with his hands

workmanlike adj showing the qualities of a good workman: *workmanlike methods*

workmanship n 1 skill in making things: *good workmanship* 2 something produced by work

work off v adv to remove, by activity: *to work off one's anger*

workout n esp. spoken a period of bodily exercise and training

work out v adv 1 to calculate the answer to: *to work out a sum* 2 to have a good result: *I wonder how their ideas worked out in practice?* 3 esp. spoken to exercise: *to work out in the gymnasium* 4 to complete the use of (esp. a mine)

work over v adv US sl to attack violently

works¹ n the moving parts (of a machine)

works² n **works** a factory: *a gas works*

workshop n a place where heavy work on machines is done

work-shy adj not liking work and trying to avoid it

work-study n the practice of increasing production by making improvements in work-processes

worktop n a flat surface on top of a piece of kitchen furniture, for doing work on

work-to-rule n an action of working to rule —see WORK

world n 1 a the earth b a particular part of it: *the Third World* 2 a planet or star system: *Is there life on other worlds?* 3 people generally: *The whole world knows about it* 4 a particular group or area of common interest: *the cricket world* 5 esp. written material standards (not spiritual): *to give up the world and serve God* 6 a large amount: *The fire makes a world of difference* 7 a group of living things: *the animal world* 8 **world without end** (in prayers) for ever —see also MAN **of the world**

World Bank n an international bank formed in 1944 to give help to poorer nations

worldly adj -lier, -liest 1 of the material world: *all my worldly goods* 2 concerned with the ways of society, esp. social advantage; not spiritual —opposite **unworldly** — **-liness** n

worldly-wise adj experienced in the ways of society

world power n an important nation whose trade, politics, etc., have an effect on many other parts of the world

world war n a war in which many nations join

world-weary adj tired of life — **-iness** n

worldwide adj, adv in or over all the world

worm¹ n 1 a small thin tubular fleshy creature with no backbone or limbs, esp. the one which lives in earth ☞ EVOLUTION 2 a person who is thought worthless, cowardly, etc. 3 the curving line round a screw

worm² v 1 to remove living worms from the body of, esp. by chemical means: *to worm the dog* 2 to move by twisting or effort: *He wormed himself out of the way*

worm-eaten adj 1 full of holes, esp. (of furniture) from woodworm 2 sl old

worm gear also **worm wheel**— n a gear with an arrangement inside curving round and round

worm out v adv to obtain (information) by questioning: *He wormed the secret out of her*

worn *past part. of* WEAR

worn-out *adj* **1** completely finished by continued use: *worn-out shoes* **2** very tired

worrisome *adj* which makes anxious

worry[1] *v* **-ried, -rying** **1** to make or be anxious: *a worrying state of affairs | worrying about your health* **2** (esp. of a dog) to chase and bite: *The dog was worrying sheep* **3** to keep trying to persuade: *She worried him for a present* — ~**ingly** *adv*

worry[2] *n* **-ries** **1** a feeling of anxiety **2** a person or thing which makes one worried: *Money is just one of our worries* — **-ried** *adj* — **-riedly** *adv*

worse[1] *adj* **1** (*comparative of* BAD) more bad or less good: *I'm worse at sums than Jean* **2** (*comparative of* ILL) more ill: *At least, he's no worse* —see also **worse** LUCK

worse[2] *adv* (*comparative of* BADLY) in a worse way: *people who behave worse than animals* USAGE Some people think that this word should not be used as an adverb, in expressions like *to behave worse*, and that it is better to say *to behave in a worse way*.

worsen *v* to make or become worse

worship[1] *n* **1** great respect to God or a god **2** a religious service

worship[2] *v* **-pp-** **1** to show great respect, admiration, etc. **2** to attend a church service — ~**per** *n*

Worship *n* **your/his Worship** (a title of respect used to/of certain officials such as a magistrate or a mayor) — ~**ful** *adj*

worst[1] *adj* (*superlative of* BAD) most bad: *the worst accident for years*

worst[2] *n* **1** the most bad thing or part: *The worst of it is I could have prevented the accident* **2** **at (the) worst** if one thinks of it in the worst way **3** **do one's worst** to do as much harm as one can **4** **if the worst comes to the worst** if the worst happens

worst[3] *adv* (*superlative of* BADLY) most badly: *the worst-dressed woman*

worsted *n* wool cloth

worth[1] *prep* **1** of the value of: *a piece of land worth £4, 500* **2** deserving: *You're not worth helping* **3** **for all one is worth** with all possible effort **4** **for what it's worth** though I'm not sure it's of value **5** **worth it** useful; worth the trouble —see also **worth one's/someone's** WHILE

worth[2] *n* value: *I know the true worth of his friendship* — ~**less** *adj* — ~**lessly** *adv* — ~**lessness** *n* USAGE Things of great value are **priceless**, **valuable**, or **invaluable** (=very useful). Things of little or no value are **valueless** or **worthless**.

worthwhile *adj* worth doing: *a worthwhile job* —see also **worth one's** WHILE

worthy[1] *adj* **-thier, -thiest** deserving: *worthy of help* — **-thily** *adv* — **-thiness** *n*

worthy[2] *n* **-thies** *sometimes humour* a person of importance

would *v* *short form* '**d**, *negative short form*

wouldn't **1** *past tense of* WILL: *They said it would be fine* **2** (used to show that one is annoyed at something that always happens): *That's exactly like Jocelyn—she would lose the key!* **3** **would rather** (expressing a choice): *Which would you rather do, go to the cinema or stay at home?* USAGE **Would've** is short for **would have**. Do NOT write **would of**.

would-be *adj* which one wishes to be, but is not: *a would-be musician*

wound[1] *n* an injury to the body caused by violent means, or an injury to one's feelings: *a gun wound | a wound to her pride* —see also **rub** SALT **in someone's wounds** USAGE To be **wounded** suggests being hurt, on purpose, by sword, knife, or bullet. One is **injured**, or receives an **injury**, accidentally, and this often involves broken bones. Both words are more serious than **hurt**.

wound[2] *v* to cause a wound to

wound[3] *past tense and past part. of* WIND

wove *past tense of* WEAVE

woven *past part. of* WEAVE

wow[1] *interj* *esp. spoken* an expression of surprise and admiration

wow[2] *n* *esp. spoken* a great success

wow[3] *n* faulty rising and falling sounds in a machine for playing recorded sound, caused by a variance in the speed of the motor —compare FLUTTER

WRAC *n* a member of the Women's Royal Army Corps

wrack[1] *n* rack (in the phrase **rack and ruin**)

wrack[2] *n* a type of seaweed

wraith *n* **1** a shape like a person's body, esp. seen just before his death **2** a very thin person

wrangle[1] *v* **-gled, -gling** to argue

wrangle[2] *n* an angry or noisy argument

wrangler *n* *US* a cowboy, esp. one who looks after horses

wrap[1] *v* **-pp-** to cover; fold round: *I wrapped the present in paper*

wrap[2] *n* an outer garment or covering, such as a scarf, shawl, or rug

wrapper *n* **1** a loose paper cover on a book **2** a piece of paper used as a covering when a book, newspaper, etc., is posted

wrapping *n* material for wrapping

wrap up *v adv* **1** to wear warm clothes **2** to hide (an idea) in words **3** to end (a business arrangement, a meeting, etc.) **4** *sl* to shut up

wrath *n* *literature* great anger — ~**ful** *adj* — ~**fully** *adv*

wreak *v* to do (violence) or express (strong feelings) in violence: *to wreak vengeance*

wreath *n* **1** a circle of flowers and/or leaves **2** a curl of smoke, mist, etc.

wreathe *v* **wreathed, wreathing** *esp. literature* **1** to encircle completely: *Mist wreathed the hilltops* **2** (of a snake) to wind round (itself) **3** (of smoke, mist, etc.) to move gently in circles

wreck[1] *n* **1** a ship lost at sea or destroyed on rocks —see also SHIPWRECK **2** the state of being

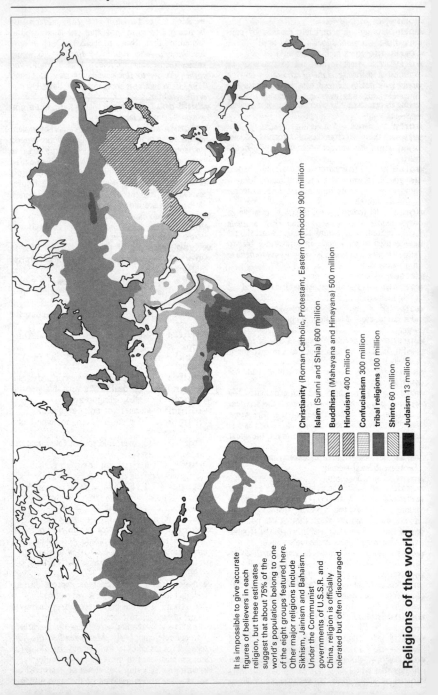

It is impossible to give accurate figures of believers in each religion, but these estimates suggest that about 75% of the world's population belong to one of the eight groups featured here. Other major religions include Sikhism, Jainism and Bahaism. Under the Communist governments of U.S.S.R. and China, religion is officially tolerated but often discouraged.

Christianity (Roman Catholic, Protestant, Eastern Orthodox) 900 million

Islam (Sunni and Shia) 600 million

Buddhism (Mahayana and Hinayana) 500 million

Hinduism 400 million

Confucianism 300 million

tribal religions 100 million

Shinto 60 million

Judaism 13 million

Religions of the world

ruined: *the wreck of her hopes* **3** a person whose health is destroyed

wreck² *v* **1** to destroy (a ship) **2** to destroy: *The weather has wrecked our plans*

wreckage *n* the broken parts of a destroyed thing: *the wreckage of the cars*

wrecker *n* **1** a person who destroys, esp. (in former times) one who caused a shipwreck in order to steal from the ship **2** a person who salvages cargo from shipwrecks

wren *n* a very small song bird

wrench¹ *v* **1** to pull violently with a twisting or turning movement **2** to twist and damage (a joint of the body): *to wrench one's ankle*

wrench² *n* **1** an act of twisting and pulling **2** twisting to a joint of the body **3** painful grief at a separation: *the wrench of leaving home* **4** a spanner with adjustable jaws

wrest *v* **1** to pull (away) violently **2** to obtain with difficulty: *to wrest the truth out of someone*

wrestle *v* **-tled, -tling** **1** to fight by holding and throwing one's opponent to the ground **2** to fight (someone) in this way as a sport (**wrestling**) — **wrestler** *n*

wretch *n* a poor unhappy person — ~ed *adj* — ~edly *adv* — ~edness *n*

wriggle¹ *v* **-gled, -gling** **1** to twist from side to side **2** to move (a part of the body) in this way; wiggle

wriggle² *n* a wriggling movement

wriggle out of *v adv prep esp. spoken* to escape (a difficulty) by tricks: *to wriggle out of trouble*

wring¹ *v* **wrung, wringing** **1 a** to twist (esp. the neck, causing death) **b** to press hard on; squeeze: *He wrung my hand* **2** to remove water from, by twisting and pressing: *Wring those wet things out* **3** to force: *They wrung the truth out of her*

wring² *n* **1** an act of wringing **2** a machine which presses cheese into shape or presses the juice out of apples

wringer *n* a machine to press water out of wet washing —compare MANGLE

wrinkle¹ *n* **1** a line in something which is folded or crushed, esp. on the skin **2** *esp. spoken* a clever piece of advice — **-kly** *adj*

wrinkle² *v* **-kled, -kling** to form into wrinkles: *She wrinkled her nose at the bad smell*

wrist *n* the joint between the hand and the lower arm

wristband *n* **1** a cuff **2** a band for fastening something to the wrist

wristlet *n* a metal band for fastening a watch to the wrist

wristwatch *n* a watch made to be fastened on the wrist

writ *n* a written command issued by a law court

write *v* **wrote**, **written, writing** **1** to make (marks that represent letters or words), esp. with a pen or pencil on paper **2** to express and record

in this way, or by means of a typewriter: *to write a letter* **3 writ large** *esp. pompous* made larger or grander

write-off *n* anything which is completely ruined

write off *v adv* to accept the loss or failure of: *to write off a debt*

writer *n* a person who writes

writer's cramp *n* stiffness of the hand after writing for too long

write-up *n esp. spoken* a written report, as of goods or a play: *The concert got a good write-up in the newspaper*

writhe *v* **writhed, writhing** to twist the body, as when in great pain

writing *n* **1** the activity of writing, esp. books **2** handwriting: *I can't read the doctor's writing* **3** anything written —see also WRITINGS

writing paper also **note paper**— *n* paper for writing letters on, usu. cut into various standard sizes

writings *n* written material: *Darwin's scientific writings*

written *past part. of* WRITE

wrong¹ *n* **1** standards according to which some things are bad: *to know right from wrong* **2** any bad action **3 in the wrong** mistaken or deserving blame

wrong² *adj* **1** not correct: *the wrong answer* **2** evil: *Telling lies is wrong* **3** not suitable: *the wrong time to make a visit* — ~ly *adv*

wrong³ *adv* **1** wrongly **2 get it wrong** to misunderstand **3 go wrong a** to make a mistake **b** to end badly: *The day went wrong* **c** to act badly, immorally, etc.: *His so-called friends helped him go wrong*

wrong⁴ *v* to be unfair to or cause difficulty, pain, etc., to

wrongdoing *n* bad, evil, or unlawful behaviour — **-doer** *n*

wrongful *adj* unjust; unlawful — ~ly *adv*

wrongheaded *adj* obstinately mistaken: *a wrongheaded idea* — ~ly *adv* — ~ness *n*

wrong side *n* **1** the inner side of a garment or material **2 get on the wrong side of someone** to lose someone's favour

wrote *past tense of* WRITE

wrought *adj old use* made or done: *wrought of stone*

wrought iron *n* iron shaped into a pattern

wrought-up *adj* very nervous and excited — compare OVERWROUGHT, WORKED UP

wrung *past tense and past part. of* WRING

wry *adj* **wryer, wryest** showing dislike, lack of pleasure, etc.: *a wry face/ smile* — ~ly *adv*

wt *abbrev. for:* weight

X

X, x X's, x's *or* Xs, xs **1** the 24th letter of the English alphabet **2** the Roman numeral for 10 **3** (a mark on a letter meaning) a kiss

x *n* (in mathematics) a quantity that is unknown until a calculation has been made: *If 3x=6, x=2*

X¹ *n* a person whose name is not made known: *At the trial, Mrs X kept her face covered*

X² *n, adj* (a film) that children under 18 may not see in a cinema —compare A, AA, U

X chromosome *n* a type of chromosome which exists in pairs in female cells and singly in male cells, and will produce a female when combined with another of its own type, and a male when combined with a Y chromosome

xerox *v, n* *trademark* (to make) a photographic copy of (printed or written matter) from a special electric copying machine —compare PHOTOSTAT, PHOTOCOPY

Xmas *n* Christmas

x-ray *v* **x-rayed, x-raying** to photograph, examine, or treat by X-rays

X-ray *n* **x-rays** **1** a powerful unseen beam of light which can pass through substances that are not transparent, and which is used for photographing conditions inside the body, for treating certain diseases, and for various purposes in industry **2** a photograph taken using this

xylem *n* a plant tissue that is found in the roots, stems, and leaves, carries water and salts, and gives support to the plant —compare PHLOEM

xylophone *n* a type of musical instrument made of flat wooden bars which produce musical notes when struck with small wooden hammers

Y, y Y's, y's *or* Ys, ys the 25th letter of the English alphabet

yacht *n* **1** a light sailing boat, esp. one used for racing **2** a pleasure cruiser, often large and luxurious — ~**ing** *n* : *They went yachting* — ~**sman** *n*

yak¹ *n* a long-haired ox of central Asia

yak² *v* -**kk**- *esp. spoken* to chatter

yam *n* a root of a tropical climbing plant, eaten as a vegetable

yank *v, n* *esp. spoken* (to make) a sudden sharp pull

Yankee *n* *esp. spoken* **1** also **Yank**— a citizen of the United States of America **2** *US* a person born or living in the northern United States

yap¹ *v* -**pp**- **1** (esp. of dogs) to make short sharp excited barks **2** *sl* to chatter

yap² *n* **1** a short sharp bark **2** *sl* noisy empty talk

yard¹ *n* **1** a measure of length that is a little less than a metre; 3 feet **2** a long pole that supports a square sail

yard² *n* **1** an enclosed area next to a building **2** an area enclosed for a special purpose: *shipyard | coalyard*

yardarm *n* either end of a ship's yard

yardstick *n* **1** a measuring stick one yard long **2** any standard of measurement: *Is profit the only yardstick of success?*

yarn¹ *n* **1** spun thread **2** an adventure story

yarn² *v* *esp. spoken* to tell yarns

yarrow *n* a plant with flat-topped groups of flowers, used in medicine

yashmak *n* a veil worn by some Muslim women

yaw¹ *v* *technical* (of a ship, aircraft, etc.) to make a yaw —compare PITCH, ROLL

yaw² *n* *technical* a turn to the side, esp. out of the proper course

yawl *n* a 2-masted sailing boat with the smaller mast in the stern

yawn¹ *v* **1** to open the mouth wide involuntarily as when tired or bored **2** to become wide open: *The hole yawned before him*

yawn² *n* an act of yawning

Y chromosome *n* a type of chromosome which exists singly in male cells, and will produce a male when combined with an X chromosome

yd *abbrev. for:* yard(s)

ye¹ *pron* *old use* (used esp. when addressing more than one person, usu. only as the subject of a sentence) you

ye² *adj* (a word used esp. in names, to make them seem historical, meaning) the: *Ye Old Tea Shop*

yea¹ *adv* *old use* yes

yea² *n* *technical* a vote, voter, or reply in favour of an idea, plan, law, etc. —opposite **nay**

year *n* **1** the time (365¼ days) it takes the earth to travel round the sun **2** also **calendar year**— a period of 365 or 366 days beginning on January 1st and ending on December 31st **3** a period of 365 days measured from any point: *2 years ago today* **4** a period of about a year in the life of an organization: *the school year* —see also LEAP YEAR

yearbook *n* a reference book published yearly

yearling *n* an animal between 1 and 2 years old

yearly *adj, adv* happening once a year

yearn *v* to have a strong, loving, or sad desire: *She yearned for his return* — ~**ing** *n*

years *n* age, esp. old age: *He is very healthy for a man of his years*

yeast *n* a form of very small plant life used to ferment alcohol and for making bread rise

yeasty *adj* -**ier, -iest** frothy; bubbly

yell *v* to shout loudly; cry out — **yell** *n*

yellow¹ *adj* **1** of the colour of butter, gold, or the yolk of an egg **2** having a light brown or yellowish skin

yellow² n (a) yellow colour — ~**ish** adj
yellow fever n a dangerous tropical disease
yellow peril n the supposed danger of East Asia's population overrunning western civilizations
yelp v, n (to make) a short sharp high cry, as of pain or excitement
yen¹ n yen the standard unit in the money system of Japan ⏤☞ MONEY
yen² n a strong desire
yeoman n **-men** a farmer who owns and works his own land
yeomanry n the body of country landowners
yes¹ adv (in an answer expressing willingness or agreement): '*Is this a dictionary?*' '*Yes.*' | '*Michael?*' '*Yes, Mum?*'
yes² n a vote, voter, or reply in favour of an idea, plan, law, etc.
yes-man n **-men** a person who always agrees with his superior
yesterday adv, n **-days** 1 (on) the day before this one 2 only a short time ago: *the fashions of yesterday* — **yesterday** adj : *yesterday morning*
yet¹ adv 1 at this moment; then; so far; still; at a future time; even; in addition; again 2 **as yet** up to this moment —see JUST (USAGE)
yet² conj but even so; but: *strange yet true*
yeti also **abominable snowman**— n a large hairy manlike animal supposed to live in the Himalayas
yew n a type of evergreen tree with small dark green leaves and small red berries
Yiddish n a language spoken by Jews, esp. in eastern Europe ⏤☞ LANGUAGE
yield¹ v 1 to give, produce, bear, etc.: *That tree yields fruit* 2 to give up control (of); surrender 3 to bend, break, etc., because of force: *The shelf is beginning to yield under that heavy weight*
yield² n the amount produced: *The trees gave a high yield*
yielding adj 1 able to bend 2 likely to agree with others: *a yielding character*
yobbo also **yob**— n **-bos** an idle badly-behaved youth
yodel v **-ll-** to sing with many rapid changes between low and very high notes
yoga n a Hindu system of exercises to free the self from the body, will, and mind
yoghurt, yogurt, yoghourt n fermented milk
yogi n one who practises yoga
yoke¹ n 1 a wooden bar used for joining 2 animals together to pull heavy loads 2 a frame fitted across a person's shoulders for carrying 2 equal loads 3 that piece of a garment from which the rest hangs, such as the part of a shirt around the shoulders 4 power, control, etc.: *under the yoke of the king* 5 something that binds people or things together: *the yoke of marriage*
yoke² v **yoked, yoking** to join with a yoke
yokel n a foolish country man
yolk n the yellow central part of an egg

yonder also **yon**— adj, adv *becoming rare* over there
yore n *esp. written* time long past: *in days of yore*
york v to bowl out with a yorker
yorker n (in cricket) a ball bowled in such a way that it passes underneath the bat
Yorkshire pudding n baked batter, usu. eaten with beef and gravy
you pron 1 the person or people being spoken to: *You are kind* 2 one; anyone: *You have to be careful with people you don't know* —see HIM (USAGE)
you'd *short form of* 1 you would: *You'd go* 2 you had: *You'd gone*
young¹ adj 1 in an early stage of life 2 fresh and good: *young vegetables* 3 inexperienced — ~**ish** adj
young² n 1 young people or animals as a group 2 **with young** (esp. of animals) pregnant
youngster n a child
your adj (*possessive form of* YOU) belonging to you: *your book*
yours pron 1 (*possessive form of* YOU) that/those belonging to you: *a friend of yours* 2 (written at the end of a letter): *yours faithfully*
yourself pron **-selves** 1 (*reflexive form of* YOU): *You'll hurt yourself* 2 (*strong form of* YOU): *You yourself know it* 3 *esp. spoken* (in) your usual state of mind or body: *You don't seem yourself today*
youth n 1 the period of being young; early life 2 the appearance, health, etc., of someone young 3 a young male person 4 young people as a group: *the youth of the country* — ~**ful** adj — ~**fully** adv — ~**fulness** n
Youth Hostel n a hostel for usu. young holidaymakers who subscribe to the Youth Hostels Association (YHA)
yowl v, n (esp. of an animal)(to make) a long loud mournful howl
yoyo n **-yos** a toy made of a spool of wood, plastic, etc., that can be made to run up and down a string tied to it
yuletide also **yule**— n *esp. pompous* Christmastime: *Yuletide greetings*

#

Z, z Z's, z's or Zs, zs the 26th and last letter of the English alphabet
zany adj **zanier, zaniest** foolish; amusing
zeal n eagerness; keenness
zealot n usu. offensive a fanatic
zealous adj eager; keen — ~**ly** adv — ~**ness** n
zebra n **zebras** or **zebra** an African wild animal, horselike with dark brown and white stripes
zebra crossing n a street crossing marked by

alternate black and white lines —compare PELICAN CROSSING

zed *n* the name of the letter Z, z

Zen *n* a Japanese form of the Buddhist religion, stating that one must look inside oneself for understanding, rather than depend on holy writings ☞ WORSHIP

zenith *n* **1** the point in the heavens directly overhead —opposite **nadir** **2** the highest point of success, hope, or fortune —compare MERIDIAN

zephyr *n poetic* a soft gentle west wind

zeppelin *n* a cigar-shaped German airship used in World War I

zero *n* **zeros** *or* **zeroes** **1** the figure 0; a nought; nothing **2** the point between + and - on a scale; on the centigrade scale, the temperature at which water freezes —compare ABSOLUTE ZERO USAGE In saying a number, **zero** is generally used for 0 in scientific matters.

zero hour *n* the hour at which an action (usu. military) is planned to begin

zero in on *v adv prep* **zeroed, zeroing in on** to aim (gunfire, a camera, etc.) directly at

zest *n* **1** enthusiasm; pleasant excitement **2** the outer skin of an orange or lemon used for flavouring

ziggurat *n* a Mesopotamian pyramidlike temple

zigzag *v, n* **-gg-** (to go in) a line shaped like a row of Z's — **zigzag** *adv*

zinc *n* a bluish-white metallic element, used in alloys and for plating metal surfaces

Zionism *n* the political movement to establish an independent state of Israel in Palestine for the Jews — **-ist** *adj, n*

zip¹ *v* **-pp-** **1** to open or fasten with a zip **2** to make the sound of something moving quickly through the air

zip² *n* **1** also **zip fastener**— a fastening device with interlocking teeth, opened and shut with a sliding tab **2** a zipping sound **3** *esp. spoken* energy: *full of zip*

zippy *adj* **-pier, -piest** *esp. spoken* lively

zither *n* a flat musical instrument with 30–40 strings, played with the fingers or with a plectrum

zodiac *n* **1** an imaginary belt in space along which the sun and planets appear to travel, divided into 12 signs each named after constellations **2** a circular representation of this used by astrologers ◉ — ~**al** *adj*

zombie, -bi *n* **1** (according to certain African and Caribbean religions) a corpse made to move by magic **2** someone who moves very slowly and behaves as if he were not really alive

zone¹ *n* **1** a division or area marked off from others : *a war/danger zone* **2** one of the 5 divisions of the earth's surface according to temperature, marked by latitude: *the torrid zone, the 2 temperate zones and the 2 frigid zones* — **-nal** *adj*

zone² *v* **zoned, zoning** to divide into zones

zonked *adj sl* under the influence of alcohol or a drug; high

zoo also **zoological gardens**— *n* **zoos** a park where animals are kept for show

zoology *n* the scientific study of animals — **-gical** *adj* — **-gist** *n*

zoom¹ *v* **1** *esp. spoken* to go or rise quickly **2** (of a cinema camera) to move quickly between a distant and a close-up view

zoom² *n* (the deep low sound of) the upward flight of an aircraft

zoom lens *n* a photographic lens that can zoom while keeping in focus

Zulu *adj* of or related to the language or people of Zululand in South Africa

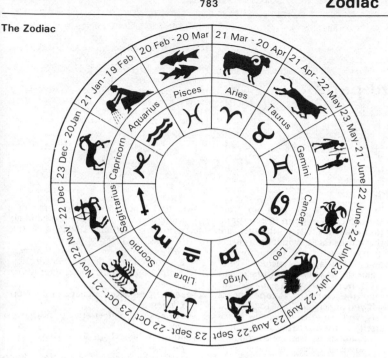

The Zodiac

Arians are typically red-headed or blond. They are active, enthusiastic, always in a hurry and looking for new excitement. They like to have things their own way.

Taureans are often thick-set and muscular. They are cautious and stubborn; steady workers who are practical and determined but not great thinkers or innovators.

Geminians are tall and slim and have many-sided personalities. They are alert, curious, quick to learn, having a good memory and a love of words.

Cancerians are usually pale with long limbs. They are shy and quiet in company, and are emotional and easily hurt.

Leos are sturdy and energetic people with tremendous self-confidence. They are good actors and like to be the centre of attention.

Virgoans enjoy their work — they are quick and aim at perfection. However they may be rather cold-hearted and too critical of other people.

Librans are frequently good-looking and graceful. They are charming, polite, and diplomatic but are sometimes too aware of their own attractiveness.

Scorpios may be stocky and large-nosed. They are practical, passionate, cunning, and hungry for power. Business and politics are suitable professions.

Sagittarians are attractive, tall, and well-shaped. They are imaginative, impulsive, romantic, wanting to enjoy life and be liked.

Capricornians tend to have small heads and be narrow-bodied. This can make them appear serious, sober, and dignified but inwardly they are highly-strung and very ambitious.

Aquarians are frequently tall. They love to attract attention in public and try to live life to the full; fame is their goal, and it is not always easy to make friends with them.

Pisceans are often tall, with pale hair and skin. They are imaginative rather than practical; often they live in a world of fantasy, dreaming up great plans which cannot possibly come true.

Word parts

Many English words are built up from other words, such as **eggcup** (a cup for an egg) or **teatime** (time for tea). But there are many other words that are built up by using word parts, such as **unhappy** or **landscape**. **Unhappy** means "not happy", and the beginning part **un-** means "not". A **landscape** is "a view of the land", and the end part **-scape** means "view". If you understand how to use these word parts, you can often make new words for yourself: a **moonscape** would be a view of the moon, as seen by astronauts. Here are some of the commoner word parts.

Endings

-able, -ible 1 that can have something done to it: *eatable* **2** having a particular quality: *fashionable*

-ade a drink: *lemonade*

-age (makes a noun): *drainage|postage*

-al 1 (makes an adjective): *musical* **2** an action: *dismissal*

-an see -IAN

-ance, -ence (makes a noun): *assistance| existence*

-ant, -ent (a person or thing) that does something: *inhabitant|disinfectant*

-ation (makes a noun): *exploration*

-cide killing: *insecticide*

-cy a state or condition: *tenancy*

-dom 1 a condition: *freedom* **2** an area ruled: *kingdom*

-ed 1 (makes parts of verbs): *laughed* **2** possessing something: *kind-hearted*

-ee 1 a person to whom something is done: *trainee* **2** something small: *bootee*

-eer a person concerned with something: *mountaineer|auctioneer*

-en 1 made of something: *wooden* **2** to make or become something: *deafen*

-ence see -ANCE

-ent see -ANT

-er, -or 1 a person who does something: *waiter* **2** a thing that does something: *screwdriver* **3** (makes the comparative of adjectives): *faster*

-ery 1 behaviour or condition: *bravery* **2** a collection of things: *crockery* **3** a place for doing something: *refinery*

-es see -S

-ese the people or language of a country: *Chinese*

-est (makes the superlative of adjectives): *fastest*

-esque in the style of something: *picturesque*

-ess female: *lioness* (Some women do not like to be called by words ending in *-ess*, *-ette*.)

-ette 1 small: *kitchenette* **2** female: *usherette* (see -ESS) **3** not real: *leatherette*

-fold a number of times: *fourfold*

-ful 1 having or causing something: *painful* (Some people dislike new adjectives like *meaningful*.) **2** the amount needed to fill something: *spoonful*

-gram something written or drawn: *telegram*

-graph something written or reproduced: *autograph|photograph*

-hood the time of being something: *childhood*

-ian, -an 1 (a person) coming from somewhere or believing in something: *American|Christian* **2** a person skilled in a subject: *mathematician*

-ible see -ABLE

-ic, -ical connected with something: *atomic|poetical*

-ics a science or activity: *physics| acrobatics*

-ie see -Y

-ify to cause to be something: *terrify|beautify*

-ing 1 (makes parts of verbs): *dancing* **2** (makes nouns): *earnings*

-**ise** see -IZE

-**ish 1** coming from somewhere: *Turkish*
  2 like; resembling: *foolish* (This is often
  used in a bad sense; it is unkind to call
  someone *childish* but all right to call
  them *childlike*.) **3** near to; rather:
  youngish|sixish

-**ism** the beliefs or qualities of something:
  socialism|heroism

-**ist 1** (a person) believing in something:
  socialist **2** a person who does
  something: *pianist*

-**ite 1** (a person) believing in something:
  Labourite **2** (forming the name of a
  chemical substance): *bauxite*

-**itis** disease; infection: *appendicitis*

-**ity** the quality of something: *stupidity*

-**ive** (makes adjectives): *explosive|*
  productive

-**ize, -ise** to put into a condition; change
  into: *modernize* (New verbs like
  hospitalize, finalize are being formed all
  the time. Many of them are disliked
  by old-fashioned people.)

-**less** without: *rainless|harmless*

-**let** something small: *booklet*

-**like** like; resembling: *cowlike*

-**ling** something or someone small or
  unimportant: *duckling|hireling*

-**logy** a science: *geology*

-**logist** a person skilled in a science:
  geologist

-**ly 1** (makes adverbs): *quickly* **2** having
  the qualities of something: *friendly|*
  queenly **3** happening at regular times:
  hourly

-**man** (fem.-**woman**) a person who lives
  in a place or works at something:
  Frenchman|postman

-**ment** the cause or result of doing
  something: *entertainment*

-**meter** an instrument for measuring:
  speedometer

-**monger** a person who sells or deals in
  something: *fishmonger|warmonger*

-**ness** (makes nouns): *sadness*

-**ocracy** a system of government:
  democracy

-**ocrat** a person who believes in or
  belongs to a system of government:
  democrat

-**oid** looking like or shaped like
  something: *asteroid*

-**or** see -ER

-**ory** a place for doing something:
  observatory

-**osis 1** a process: *hypnosis* **2** a disease:
  silicosis

-**ous** (makes adjectives): *dangerous*

-**phile** (a person) liking something:
  anglophile

-**philia** a liking for something: *anglophilia*

-**phone** sound; hearing: *earphone*

-**proof** protecting against something;
  resisting: *bulletproof*

-**s, -es 1** (makes plurals): *cats|glasses*
  2 (makes 3rd person sing. of present
  tense): *sits|washes*

-'**s** (makes possessives): *woman's*

-**scape** a view: *landscape*

-**scope** sight; seeing: *microscope*

-**ship 1** a state or position: *friendship|*
  dictatorship **2** skill: *seamanship*

-**sphere** of a sphere; spherical:
  atmosphere

-**wards, -ward** in a direction: *skywards*

-**wise 1** in the manner of something:
  crabwise **2** with regard to something:
  taxwise (New adverbs like *saleswise,*
  moneywise are being formed all the
  time. They are often disliked by old-
  fashioned people.)

-**y 1** like; covered with: *sandy* **2** also
  -**ie** — (makes a pet name):
  Daddy|doggie

Beginnings

a- 1 without, not: *amoral* **2** in;
  on; at: *abed|afire*

aero- aircraft: *aeroengine*

ambi- both; double: *ambidextrous*

ante- before: *antenatal*

anthropo- human: *anthropology*

anti- against: *antifreeze*

arch- highest; chief: *archbishop*

astro- stars: *astronomy*

audio- hearing: *audio-visual*

auto- self; oneself: *autobiography*

be- (makes verbs): *bedevil|becalm*

bi- two; twice: *bicycle*

biblio- book: *bibliography*

bio- life: *biology*

by- of less importance: *by-election*

chrom-, chromo- colour: *chromatic*

chron-, chrono- time: *chronology*

co- with, together: *coeducation*

con-, col, com-, cor- with; together:
  conduct|collaborate|combine|
  correlate

contra- against: *contradict*

counter- 1 opposite; opposing:
  counterattack **2** matching:
  counterpart

crypto- hidden; secret:
  crypto-communist

de- 1 to do the opposite: *decentralize*
  2 to remove something: *debone*

demi- half: *demigod*

derm- skin: *dermatitis*

di- two: *dioxide*

dis- not: *disagree*

electro- electricity: *electrocute*

en-, em- 1 to put into a place or condition: *endanger* **2** to cause to be something: *enrich*

equi- equal: *equidistant*

ex- former: *ex-wife*

extra- outside: *extraterrestrial*

fore- 1 before: *foretell* **2** front: *forepaw*

geo- earth: *geography*

great- one generation further away: *great-grandmother*

haemo-, hemo- blood: *haemorrhage*

hemi- half: *hemisphere*

hetero- opposite; different: *heterosexual*

homo- same; like: *homogeneous*

hydro- water: *hydroelectric*

hyper- very much; too: *hypersensitive*

in-, il-, im-, ir- not: *infinite|illogical| impossible|irregular*

inter- between: *intercity*

intra- inside: *intravenous*

mal- bad; badly: *maltreat*

matri- mother: *matricide*

mega- 1 large: *megaphone* **2** million: *megahertz*

micro- small: *microfilm*

mini- small: *minicab*

mis- bad; badly: *misunderstand*

mono- one; single: *monorail*

multi- many: *multinational*

neo- new: *neoclassical*

neuro- nerves: *neurologist*

non- not: *nonfiction*

omni- all: *omnivorous*

ortho- correct; right: *orthopaedics*

out- 1 outside: *outhouse* **2** better; longer; faster: *outlive|outrun*

over- 1 above: *overhang* **2** too much: *overcook*

palaeo-, paleo- old: *palaeolithic*

pan- all: *panchromatic*

patri- father: *patricide*

photo- 1 light: *photoelectric* **2** photography: *photocopy*

physi-, physio- nature; the body: *physiology*

poly- many: *polygamy*

post- after: *postwar*

pre- before: *prefabricate*

pro- in favour of: *pro-American*

proto- first: *prototype*

pseudo- not real: *pseudonym*

psycho-, psych- the mind: *psychoanalyse*

quasi- seeming; not really: *quasi-scientific*

re- again: *rebroadcast*

retro- back; backwards: *retrospect*

self- oneself or itself: *self-locking| self-taught*

semi- half: *semiquaver*

socio- society: *sociology*

sub- under: *subsoil|subeditor*

super- more; greater: *superhuman*

sym-, syn- together; sharing: *sympathy| synchronize*

techn-, techno- skill; practical science: *technology*

tele- over a distance: *television*

theo- God; gods: *theology*

therm-, thermo- heat: *thermometer*

trans- across: *transatlantic*

tri- three: *triangle*

ultra- beyond: *ultraviolet*

un- 1 not: *unfair* **2** to do the opposite: *unwind*

under- 1 below: *underpass* **2** too little: *underdone*

uni- one: *unicorn*

vice- the person next below: *vice-captain*

Spelling table

To find a word that you have heard but
not seen

Sound	Some other spellings
bad	plaid, meringue
father	heart, bazaar, clerk, Shah, laugh, half
ball	caught, board, draw, four, floor, port, George, extraordinary
make	pay, steak, vein, weigh, reign, straight, prey, gauge, gaol, train, café, matinée, Gaelic, eh
about	fountain, clarity, parliament, purpose, luncheon, dangerous, tortoise, nation, restaurant, autumn, the, sergeant, cupboard, actor, theatre, bigger, surprise, furniture, beggar, soldier, colour, chauffeur, guerilla
back	rubber
cheer	match, nature, question, cello, Czech
day	ladder, called, could
bed	any, said, bread, says, guest, bury, leopard, leisure, friend
sheep	field, ceiling, police, team, key, people, scene, quay, amoeba, Caesar
here	appear, idea, fierce, beer, souvenir, weir, sphere, theory
there	hair, bare, bear, their, prayer, scarce, aeroplane, mayor, heir
few	coffee, cough, physics, half, often
gay	bigger, ghost, vague, guard
hot	who
ship	savage, women, carriage, valley, mountain, foreign, always, coffee, lynch, guilt, sieve, busy
bite	eye, pie, buy, aye, try, dye, guide, sigh, height, aisle
tire	buyer, dyer, higher, quiet, lion, giant, fiery, tyrant, Isaiah
bird	burn, fern, worm, earn, journal, err, myrtle, myrrh, Guernsey, connoisseur
jump	edge, age, soldier, exaggerate, gradual, adjust, sandwich
key	cool, school, biscuit, lock, tobacco, saccharine, cheque, walk, lacquer, khaki, queen (= kw)
led	ball, battle, pedal, tunnel
sum	bomb, hammer, autumn, calm, phlegm, government
sun	know, gnaw, funny, pneumonia, mnemonic, kitten, certain, cotton
sung	sink, tongue, handkerchief
pot	watch, John, cough, laurel
note	sew, soap, soul, grow, toe, oh, brooch, beau, yeoman, mauve, owe, though, folk
boot	move, shoe, group, flew, blue, fruit, rude, through, rheumatism, manoeuvre
poor	sure, tour, cruel, amateur
now	ounce, plough, sauerkraut
tower	our, hour, Howard, sauerkraut
boy	poison, lawyer, buoy
pen	happen, shepherd
red	marry, wriggle, rhubarb, diarrhoea
soon	city, nice, psychology, scene, mess, fasten, sword
fish	ocean, sure, machine, station, tissue, fascism, fuchsia, conscious, passion, tension, politician, schedule, luxury, (= ksh)
pleasure	rouge, vision, usual, seizure
tea	butter, Thomas, walked, yacht, doubt, fright, pterodactyl
then	bathe
cut	some, does, blood, young

put	wood, wolf, could	yet	onion, **Eu**rope, b**eau**ty, **u**se,
view	of, Step**h**en, nav**v**y		new, halleluja, strenu**ou**s,
wet	**o**ne, ch**oi**r (= kw), q**u**een		q**ueue** (= ky)
	(= kw), **wh**en	zero	wa**s**, sci**ss**ors, **x**ylophone,
box	a**cc**ident, ex**c**ept, sti**ck**s, for**k**s		da**zz**le, e**x**ample (= gz)

Foreign alphabets

Gaelic

ᴀ	bad
b	back
c	cool
ċ	city
ᴅ	day
e	bed
ꜰ	few
ᵹ	gay
ᵹ̇	jump
h	hat
ı	ship
l	led
m	sum
ṁ	wet
n	now
o	pot
p	pen
ṗ	few
ʀ	red
s	soon
ś	shave
ᴄ	tea
ċ	thumb
u	you
ú	cut

Hebrew

א	aleph	father
ב	beth	back
ג	gimel	gay doghouse
ד	daleth	day, Roundhead
ה	he	hat
ו	waw	view
ז	zayin	zero
ח	heth	loch
ט	teth	get there
י	yodh	yet
כ ך	kaph	ugh
ל	lamedh	led
מ ם	mem	sum
נ ן	nun	now
ס	samekh	see
ע	ayin	hat
פ ף	pe	pen, clap hands
צ ץ	sadhe	yes, Robin
ק	qoph	calm
ר	resh	red
ש	sin	last
ש	shin	shave
ת	taw	peat

Russian

А а	**f**ather	
Б б	**b**ack	
В в	**v**iew	
Г г	**g**ay	
Д д	**d**ay	
Е е	**y**e**t**	
Ё ё	**yo**ghourt	
Ж ж	ple**a**sure	
З з	**z**ero	
И и	sh**ee**p	
Й й	shi**p**	
К к	**k**ey	
Л л	**l**ed	
М м	su**m**	
Н н	**n**ow	
О о	p**o**t	
П п	**p**en	
Р р	**r**ed	
С с	**s**oon	
Т т	**t**ea	
У у	b**oo**t	
Ф ф	**f**ew	
Х х	lo**ch**	
Ц ц	lo**ts**	
Ч ч	**ch**eer	
Ш ш	**sh**ave	
Щ щ	fre**sh ch**eese	
Ъ ъ	(hard sign, used after consonant)	
Ы ы	Fr. faut**eui**l	
Ь ь	(soft sign, used after consonant)	
Э э	b**e**d	
Ю ю	**you**	
Я я	**ya**rd	

Greek

Α	α	alpha	**f**ather
Β	β	beta	**b**ack
Γ	γ	gamma	**g**ay
Δ	δ	delta	**d**ay
Ε	ε	epsilon	b**e**d
Ζ	ζ	zeta	**z**ero
Η	η	eta	sh**ee**p
Θ	θ	theta	**th**umb
Ι	ι	iota	shi**p**
Κ	κ	kappa	**k**ey
Λ	λ	lambda	**l**ed
Μ	μ	mu	su**m**
Ν	ν	nu	**n**ow
Ξ	ξ	xi	bo**x**
Ο	ο	omicron	p**o**t
Π	π	pi	**p**en
Ρ	ρ	rho	**r**ed
Σ ς	σ ς	sigma	**s**oon
Τ	τ	tau	**t**ea
Υ	υ	upsilon	**c**ut
Φ	φ	phi	**ph**ysics
Χ	χ	chi	**ch**eer
Ψ	ψ	psi	ma**ps**
Ω	ω	omega	n**o**te

Arabic

ا	alif	b**a**d f**a**ther
ب	bā	**b**ack
ت	tā	**t**ea
ث	thā	**th**umb
ج	jîm	**j**ump
ح	hā	**h**a ha
خ	khā	lo**ch**
د	dāl	**d**ay
ذ	dhāl	(stressed **th**)
ر	rā	Ger. **r**ichtig
ز	zāy	**z**ero
س	sīn	**s**ee
ش	shīn	**sh**ave
ص	sād	(emphatic 's')
ض	dād	(stressed **th**)
ط	tā	**t**ea
ظ	zā	(stressed **th**)
ع	'ayn	(guttural stop)
غ	ghayn	Fr. th**éo**rie
ف	fā	**f**ew
ق	qāf	su**q**
ك	kāf	**c**alm
ل	lām	**l**ed
م	mīm	su**m**
ن	nūn	**n**ow
ه	hā	**h**at
و	wāw	**w**et
ي	yā	**y**ard
ء	hamza	(glottal stop)

Bengali and Devanagari

Bengali	Devanagari	
ক	क	**k**ey
খ	ख	bla**ck h**at
গ	ग	**g**ay
ঘ	घ	e**gg h**ead
ঙ	ङ	fa**ng**
চ	च	**ch**eer
ছ	छ	bea**ch h**ut
জ	ज	**j**ump
ঝ	झ (or झ)	lar**ge h**at
ঞ	ञ	A**nn** writes
ট	ट	**t**ea
ঠ	ठ	ba**t h**andle
ড	ड	**d**ay
ঢ	ढ	be**d h**ead
ণ (or ण)	ण	**n**ow
ত	त	ge**t** that
থ	थ	chea**t h**im
দ	द	rea**d** that
ধ	ध	dea**d h**eat
ন	न	dar**n** this
প	प	**p**et
ফ	फ	**gr**ip hold
ব	ब	**b**ack
ভ	भ	da**b h**and
ম	म	su**m**
য	य	**y**et
র	र	**r**ed
ল	ल	**l**ed
ব	व	**v**iew
শ	श	**sh**ave
ষ	ष	ye**s**, Sheila
স	स	ble**ss** them
হ	ह	**h**at
ক্ষ (or द्व)	क्ष (or द्व)	**r**i**cksh**aw
অ	अ (or ऋ)	**cu**t
আ	आ	f**a**ther
ই	इ	sh**i**p
ঈ	ई	sh**ee**p
উ	उ	p**u**t
ঊ	ऊ	b**oo**t
এ	ए	m**a**ke
ঐ	ऐ	b**i**te
ও	ओ (or ओ)	n**o**te
ঔ	औ (or औ)	n**ow**
ঋ	ऋ	**r**ight

Weights and measures
Imperial

Linear measure

		1 inch	=	25.4	mm
12 inches	=	1 foot	=	0.305	m
3 feet	=	1 yard	=	0.914	m
1760 yards	=	1 mile	=	1.61	km

Square measure

		1 square inch	=	6.452	cm^2
144 sq in	=	1 square foot	=	9.29	dm^2
9 sq ft	=	1 square yard	=	0.836	m^2
4840 sq yd	=	1 acre	=	4047	m^2
640 acres	=	1 square mile	=	259	ha

Cubic measure

		1 cubic inch	=	16.4	cm^3
1728 cu in	=	1 cubic foot	=	0.0283	m^3
27 cu ft	=	1 cubic yard	=	0.765	m^3

Capacity measure

		1 fluid ounce	=	28.4	cm^3
20 fl oz	=	1 pint	=	0.568	l
2 pt	=	1 quart	=	1.136	l
4 qt	=	1 gallon	=	4.546	l

Avoirdupois weight

		1 grain	=	64.8	mg
		1 dram	=	1.772	g
16 drams	=	1 ounce	=	28.35	g
16 oz	=	1 pound	=	0.4536	kg
14 pounds	=	1 stone	=	6.35	kg
2 stones	=	1 quarter	=	12.7	kg
4 quarters	=	1 hundredweight	=	50.8	kg
20 cwt	=	1 ton	=	1.016	tonnes
2000 lb	=	1 short ton	=	0.907	tonnes

US measure

1 (liquid) pint	=	0.83 UK pint	=	0.47	l
8 pints	=	0.83 UK gallon	=	3.78	l

Temperature

$$°\text{Fahrenheit} = \left(\frac{9}{5} \times x°C\right) + 32$$

$$°\text{Centigrade} = \frac{5}{9} \times \left(x°F - 32\right)$$

where x is the temperature needing converting

Metric

Linear measure

		1 millimetre	=	0.039	in
10 mm	=	1 centimetre	=	0.394	in
10 cm	=	1 decimetre	=	3.94	in
10 dm	=	1 metre	=	39.37	in
1000 m	=	1 kilometre	=	0.6214	mile

Square measure

		1 sq centimetre	=	0.155	sq in
100 cm^2	=	1 sq metre	=	1.196	sq yd
100 m^2	=	1 are	=	119.6	sq yd
100 ares	=	1 hectare	=	2.471	acres
100 ha	=	1 sq kilometre	=	0.386	sq miles

Cubic measure

		1 cu centimetre	=	0.061	in^3
1000 cu cm	=	1 cu decimetre	=	0.035	ft^3
1000 cu dm	=	1 cu metre	=	1.308	yd^3

Capacity measure

		1 millilitre	=	0.002	pt
10 ml	=	1 centilitre	=	0.018	pint
10 cl	=	1 decilitre	=	0.176	pt
10 dl	=	1 litre	=	1.76	pt
1000 l	=	1 kilolitre	=	220.0	gall

Weight

		1 milligram	=	0.015	grain
10 mg	=	1 centigram	=	0.154	grain
10 cg	=	1 decigram •	=	1.543	grain
10 dg	=	1 gram	=	15.43	grain
					= 0.035 oz
1000 g	=	1 kilogram	=	2.205	lb
1000 kg	=	1 t o n n e			
		(metric ton)	=	0.984	(long)ton

Metric prefixes

	Symbol	Value
tera-	T	10^{12}
giga-	G	10^{9}
mega-	M	10^{6}
kilo-	k	10^{3}
hecto-	h	10^{2}
deca-	da	10
deci-	d	10^{-1}
centi-	c	10^{-2}
milli-	m	10^{-3}
micro-	μ	10^{-6}
nano-	n	10^{-9}
pico-	p	10^{-12}
femto-	f	10^{-15}
atto-	a	10^{-18}

Signs and symbols

Money

%	per cent
$	dollar
£	pound
@	1) at: *eggs @ 40p a dozen*
	2) to: *linen per metre*
	£2.50@£3.75

Miscellaneous

♂	, xy	male
♀	, xx	female
*		birth, born
†		death, died
®		registered trademark
©		copyright
☠		poison
'		foot/feet
"		inch/inches
,,		ditto, same as above
∞		infinity
∴		therefore
☮		peace

Cards

♣	clubs
♦	diamonds
♥	hearts
♠	spades

Language

´	acute
`	grave
^	circumflex
¸	cedilla
~	tilde
··	1) dieresis
	2) umlaut
᾿	smooth breathing
῾	rough breathing

Chess

K	♔	king
Q	♕	queen
R	♖	rook
B	♗	bishop
N or Kt	♘	knight
P	♙	pawn
x		captures
–		moves to
ch		check
e.p.		en passant
mate		checkmate

Religion

† cross, crucifix. Christian symbol

✟ Celtic cross

☦ Russian cross. Symbol of Russian Orthodox Church

☩ Greek cross. Symbol of Greek Orthodox Church

🕎 menorah. Ancient symbol of Judaism

✡ star of David. Recent symbol of Judaism and the Jewish people

☥ ankh. Ancient Egyptian symbol of fertility or enduring life

☯ yin yang. Ancient Chinese symbol of the balance between female (yin) and male (yang) principles of the universe

⛩ torii. Emblem of Shinto

卐 swastika. Form of cross used by early Christians. Also a sacred sign among Indian Buddhists

Memory aids

The months

Thirty days hath September,
April, June, and November,
All the rest have thirty-one
Excepting February alone
Which has but twenty-eight days clear
And twenty-nine in each Leap Year.

i before e

To spell ie, ei words with the sound "ee":
I before E, except after C
(Examples: *field*, *ceiling*. Exception: *seize*)

The colours of the rainbow

Richard (red) Of (orange) York (yellow) Gave (green) Battle (blue) In (indigo) Vain (violet).
Or, going the other way: Violets (violet) In (indigo) Bunches (blue) Give (green) You
(yellow) Odours (orange) Rare (red).

Wiring up a plug

– the bLue wire goes on the Left, the bRown one on the Right.

Crossing the International Date Line

When going west –
ward in a ship,
It's always best
A day to skip
When going east
It's very nice,
For then you have
Your birthday twice.

The order of the planets

MEn (Mercury) VEry (Venus) EAsily (Earth) MAke (Mars) JUgs (Jupiter) Serve
(Saturn) Useful (Uranus) NEeds (Neptune).
(This leaves out Pluto!)

The notes on the lines of the treble clef

Every (E) Green (G) Bus (B) Drives (D) Fast (F).
And the notes on the spaces: Face (F-A-C-E).

The notes on the lines of the bass clef

Great (G) Big (B) Dogs (D) Frighten (F) Amy (A).
And the notes on the spaces: All (A) Cows (C) Eat (E) Grass (G).

The musical sharps

Fat (F) Cats (C) Go (G) Down (D) And (A) Eat (E) Bread (B).
And the flats: Baby (B) Elephants (E) And (A) Dragons (D) Get (G) Completely (C)
Foxed (F).

The words used in trigonometry

Some People Have (sine = perpendicular-over-hypotenuse)
Curly Brown Hair (cosine = base-over-hypotenuse)
Till Painted Black (tangent = perpendicular-over-base).

The Kings and Queens of England

Willy, Willy, Harry, Ste
Harry, Dick, John, Harry three
One, two, three Ned, Richard II
Henry four, five, six, then who?
Edward four, five, Dick the bad
Harrys twain and Ned the lad
Mary, Bessy, James the vain
Charlie, Charlie, James again
William and Mary, Anna Gloria
Four Georges, William and Victoria
Ned, George, Ned, and George again,
Now Elizabeth, till when?

Short forms used in the Dictionary

abbrev.	abbreviation
adj	adjective
adv	adverb
&	and
conj	conjunction
E	East
esp.	especially
etc.	et cetera; and so on
fem.	feminine
interj	interjection
masc.	masculine
n	noun
N	North
part.	participle
pl.	plural
prep	preposition
pres.	present
pron	pronoun
S	South
sing.	singular
sl	slang
US	America; American English
usu.	usually
v	verb
W	West

Signs used in the Dictionary

( )	see page 12a
/	see page 13a
|	
~	see page 13a
☞	
◉	
⚠	see page 15a